Bill James presents. .

STATS™
Minor League Handbook
1997

STATS, Inc.
and
Howe Sportsdata International

STATS PUBLISHING

Published by STATS Publishing
A Division of Sports Team Analysis & Tracking Systems, Inc.
Dr. Richard Cramer, Chairman • John Dewan, President

Cover by Ron Freer and the Big Blue Image

Photo by Steve Eddy/ Team Photographer for the Harrisburg Senators

First Edition: November, 1996

Printed in the United States of America

ISBN 1-884064-31-0

Acknowledgments

Putting together a book as comprehensive as this one requires a real team effort. We'd like to let you know who it was that worked so hard to bring you this book.

The STATS name continues to spread into more and more homes and offices thanks to the vision and dedication of John Dewan, STATS President and CEO. He is assisted by Heather Schwarze, who has the *second*-busiest job in the company.

Our Systems Department, headed by Sue Dewan, Mike Canter and Art Ashley, takes an *ordinary* statistic and makes it extraordinary with just a few keystrokes. You can thank Dave Carlson, Marty Couvillon, Mike Hammer, Stefan Kretschmann, Steve Moyer, Brent Osland, Dave Pinto, Pat Quinn and Jeff Schinski for all the superb figures you find within these pages. Special thanks go to Stefan Kretschmann, who served as chief programmer for both of our Handbooks.

Of course, someone has to collect the data before we can start having fun with it. Jeff Chernow, Jason Kinsey, Jim Osborne, Allan Spear and Peter Woelflein head up a reporter network which leaves no stone unturned.

Don Zminda and the STATS Publications Department takes all those final numbers and presents them in the "user-friendly" fashion you've come to expect from our books. Chuck Miller is the guy with an eye for a pretty page, and Ethan Cooperson, Jim Henzler and Tony Nistler all got their two cents in by writing the prose for this book.

Our Marketing Department does yeoman's work making sure the world knows about STATS, Inc. Jim Capuano is Director of National Sales, and he is assisted by Kristen Beauregard. Ron Freer is our advertising guru, and Jim Musso and Oscar Palacios make our fantasy games the best in the business.

The Departments responsible for Publications Sales, Finances and Administration, headed by Bob Meyerhoff, keep the ship afloat on a daily basis. The group includes Marc Elman, Drew Faust, Mark Hong, Betty Moy, and Mike Wenz. Stephanie Seburn manages the complex and vast Administrative group's responsibilities, getting plenty of help from Ken Gilbert, Virginia Hamill, Tiffany Heingarten, Antoinette Kelly and Leena Sheth.

Howe Sportsdata International is responsible for the collection of our minor league statistics. We'd like to offer our thanks to President Jay Virshbo, and the following people: Tom Graham, Jim Keller, Mike Walczak, John Foley, Vin Vitro, Paul La Rocca, Brian Joura, Bob Chaban, Dan Landesman, Walter Kent, Marshall Wright and William Weiss. Special thanks go to Chris Pollari, who, as usual, was particularly helpful in the production of this book.

But a book without a reader is just a waste of paper. Your enjoyment is what makes our efforts so satisfying!

—Mat Olkin

This book is dedicated to
STATS' 1996 Rookies of the Year:

Alison Rose Capuano
Harmony Riley Moyer

Table of Contents

Introduction

This is the sixth edition of the *STATS Minor League Handbook,* and we believe it's the best yet. As usual, we begin with the career register, listing every player who played in Double-A or Triple-A in 1996 (unless they spent time in the majors last year; in that event, you can find their records in our sister publication, the *STATS Major League Handbook*). We're always striving to give you more information, and this year, for the first time, the Career Register lists the major league organization for all the player's minor league teams.

The *Minor League Handbook* also includes the complete 1996 statistical lines for each players who played in Class A or the Rookie leagues last year. Once again, we now list the appropriate major league organizations, and even mark the Class A and Rookie Leagues with pluses and minuses (like A+) to indicate the caliber of play within the classification. After that, you'll find the team totals for each minor league club, as well as individual leader boards for Triple-A and Double-A.

But wait, it gets better. Let's say you're flipping through the career register section, and you spot some young kid who hit 25 home runs in Double-A. How can you tell if this guy is a diamond in the rough, or just a dead-red pull hitter who played in a bandbox last year? Check out our park data section. We've got complete home/road park splits for every single park in the minors, and this year we even list the playing surface for the Double- and Triple-A teams (another innovation for 1997!). Next, we show you platoon splits for last year's Triple-A players. It's more complete than ever this year, and now includes home run and RBI splits for hitters (HR and SO for pitchers).

We wrap it all up with a list of "major league equivalencies" for the primary Double-A and Triple-A hitters in each teams' system. The MLEs, first developed by Bill James, show you how a hitter's numbers would have looked in a major league environment, after adjusting for the home park and the level of competition. We've improved the look of MLE section for this edition to make it even easier for you to locate the potential Alex Rodriguezes in your organization.

We're proud to present you with the our best *Minor League Handbook* yet, and we hope you'll enjoy it. If you think of a way we can improve it, let us know!

—Mat Olkin

Career Stats

As in previous editions of the *STATS Minor League Handbook,* any player who spent time at Double-A and/or Triple-A in 1996 gets a complete profile in this section—unless the player appeared in the major leagues as well, in which case you'll find him in our *STATS Major League Handbook.*

For the players on the following pages, we present their career minor league stats (with a few exceptions. . . minor league statistics prior to 1984 are unavailable for a small group of players, but as you can imagine, that group is small and getting smaller each year). When we list a player's age, we show his age as of July 1, 1997. In other words, it's the age at which he'll play the majority of the 1997 season.

TBB and **IBB** are Total Bases on Balls and Intentional Bases on Balls.

SB% is Stolen Base Percentage (stolen bases divided by attempts).

OBP and **SLG** are On-Base Percentage and Slugging Percentage.

BFP, Bk and **ShO** are Batters Facing Pitcher, Balks and Shutouts. Barring some unforeseen statistical catastrophe, we expect them to remain as such in the future.

Minor league A and Rookie leagues are now classified as A+, A, A-, R+ and R to denote the caliber of competition at each level—for instance, the California League is rated "A+," the Midwest League is an "A," and the New York-Penn League an "A-."

Andy Abad

Bats: Left **Throws:** Left **Pos:** 1B-OF **Ht:** 6'1" **Wt:** 185 **Born:** 8/25/72 **Age:** 24

				BATTING														BASERUNNING				PERCENTAGES		
Year	Team	Lg	Org	G	AB	H	2B	3B	HR	TB	R	RBI	TBB	IBB	SO	HBP	SH	SF	SB	CS	SB%	GDP	Avg	OBP	SLG
1993	Red Sox	R	Bos	59	230	57	9	2	1	73	24	28	25	0	27	2	2	4	2	2	.50	2	.248	.322	.317
1994	Sarasota	A+	Bos	111	354	102	20	0	2	128	39	35	42	4	58	5	5	5	2	12	.14	9	.288	.367	.362
1995	Trenton	AA	Bos	89	287	69	14	3	4	101	29	32	36	2	58	3	6	3	5	7	.42	6	.240	.328	.352
	Sarasota	A+	Bos	18	59	17	3	0	0	20	5	10	6	0	13	0	0	0	4	3	.57	0	.288	.354	.339
1996	Sarasota	A+	Bos	58	202	58	15	1	2	81	28	41	37	1	28	3	2	2	10	3	.77	6	.287	.402	.401
	Trenton	AA	Bos	65	213	59	22	1	4	95	33	39	33	2	41	0	0	3	5	3	.63	4	.277	.369	.446
4 Min. YEARS				400	1345	362	83	7	13	498	158	185	179	9	225	13	15	17	28	30	.48	27	.269	.356	.370

Jeff Abbott

Bats: Right **Throws:** Left **Pos:** OF **Ht:** 6'2" **Wt:** 190 **Born:** 8/17/72 **Age:** 24

				BATTING														BASERUNNING				PERCENTAGES		
Year	Team	Lg	Org	G	AB	H	2B	3B	HR	TB	R	RBI	TBB	IBB	SO	HBP	SH	SF	SB	CS	SB%	GDP	Avg	OBP	SLG
1994	White Sox	R	ChA	4	15	7	1	0	1	11	4	3	4	0	0	0	0	0	2	1	.67	1	.467	.579	.733
	Hickory	A	ChA	63	224	88	16	6	6	134	47	48	38	1	33	1	1	1	2	1	.67	4	.393	.481	.598
1995	Pr. William	A+	ChA	70	264	92	16	0	4	120	41	47	26	0	25	2	1	5	7	1	.88	8	.348	.404	.455
	Birmingham	AA	ChA	55	197	63	11	1	3	85	25	28	19	2	20	2	3	2	1	3	.25	3	.320	.382	.431
1996	Nashville	AAA	ChA	113	440	143	27	1	14	214	64	60	32	1	50	2	1	0	12	4	.75	12	.325	.373	.486
3 Min. YEARS				305	1140	393	71	8	28	564	181	186	119	4	128	7	6	8	24	10	.71	28	.345	.407	.495

Paul Abbott

Pitches: Right **Bats:** Right **Pos:** P **Ht:** 6' 3" **Wt:** 194 **Born:** 9/15/67 **Age:** 29

				HOW MUCH HE PITCHED						WHAT HE GAVE UP												THE RESULTS					
Year	Team	Lg	Org	G	GS	CG	GF	IP	BFP	H	R	ER	HR	SH	SF	HB	TBB	IBB	SO	WP	Bk	W	L	Pct.	ShO	Sv	ERA
1985	Elizabethtn	R+	Min	10	10	1	0	35	172	33	32	27	3	1	0	0	32	0	34	7	1	1	5	.167	0	0	6.94
1986	Kenosha	A	Min	25	15	1	7	98	462	102	62	49	13	3	2	2	73	3	73	7	0	6	10	.375	0	0	4.50
1987	Kenosha	A	Min	26	25	1	0	145.1	620	102	76	59	11	5	6	3	103	0	138	11	2	13	6	.684	0	0	3.65
1988	Visalia	A+	Min	28	28	4	0	172.1	799	141	95	80	9	8	6	4	143	5	205	12	9	11	9	.550	2	0	4.18
1989	Orlando	AA	Min	17	17	1	0	90.2	389	71	48	44	6	2	1	0	48	0	102	7	7	9	3	.750	0	0	4.37
1990	Portland	AAA	Min	23	23	4	0	128.1	568	110	75	65	9	3	3	1	82	0	129	8	5	5	14	.263	1	0	4.56
1991	Portland	AAA	Min	8	8	1	0	44	193	36	19	19	2	0	1	3	28	0	40	1	0	2	3	.400	1	0	3.89
1992	Portland	AAA	Min	7	7	0	0	46.1	191	30	13	12	2	0	0	0	31	0	46	0	0	4	1	.800	0	0	2.33
1993	Charlotte	AAA	Cle	4	4	0	0	19	91	25	16	14	4	3	1	0	7	0	12	3	0	0	1	.000	0	0	6.63
	Canton-Akrn	AA	Cle	13	12	1	0	75.1	315	71	34	34	4	1	0	1	28	2	86	6	0	4	5	.444	0	0	4.06
1994	Omaha	AAA	KC	15	10	0	4	57.1	262	57	32	31	8	1	0	2	45	0	48	3	0	4	1	.800	0	0	4.87
1995	Iowa	AAA	ChN	46	11	0	7	115.1	498	104	50	47	12	4	1	0	64	4	127	12	0	7	7	.500	0	0	3.67
1996	Las Vegas	AAA	SD	28	0	0	14	28	124	27	14	13	4	3	1	1	12	4	37	4	0	4	2	.667	0	7	4.18
1990	Minnesota	AL		7	7	0	0	34.2	162	37	24	23	0	1	1	1	28	0	25	1	0	0	5	.000	0	0	5.97
1991	Minnesota	AL		15	3	0	1	47.1	210	38	27	25	5	7	3	0	36	1	43	5	0	3	1	.750	0	0	4.75
1992	Minnesota	AL		6	0	0	5	11	50	12	4	4	1	0	1	1	5	0	13	1	0	0	0	.000	0	0	3.27
1993	Cleveland	AL		5	5	0	0	18.1	84	19	15	13	5	0	0	0	11	1	7	1	0	0	1	.000	0	0	6.38
12 Min. YEARS				250	170	14	32	1055	4684	909	566	494	87	34	22	17	696	18	1077	81	24	70	67	.511	4	7	4.21
4 Maj. YEARS				33	15	0	6	111.1	506	106	70	65	11	8	5	2	80	2	88	8	0	3	7	.300	0	0	5.25

Juan Acevedo

Pitches: Right **Bats:** Right **Pos:** P **Ht:** 6' 2" **Wt:** 218 **Born:** 5/5/70 **Age:** 27

				HOW MUCH HE PITCHED						WHAT HE GAVE UP												THE RESULTS					
Year	Team	Lg	Org	G	GS	CG	GF	IP	BFP	H	R	ER	HR	SH	SF	HB	TBB	IBB	SO	WP	Bk	W	L	Pct.	ShO	Sv	ERA
1992	Bend	A-	Col	1	0	0	0	2	13	4	3	3	0	1	0	1	1	0	3	0	0	0	0	.000	0	0	13.50
	Visalia	A+	Col	12	12	1	0	64.2	289	75	46	39	2	2	2	3	33	0	37	1	2	3	4	.429	0	0	5.43
1993	Central Val	A+	Col	27	20	1	3	118.2	529	119	68	58	8	5	4	9	58	0	107	12	4	9	8	.529	0	0	4.40
1994	New Haven	AA	Col	26	26	5	0	174.2	697	142	56	46	16	4	3	5	38	0	161	4	5	17	6	.739	2	0	2.37
1995	Norfolk	AAA	NYN	2	2	0	0	3	9	0	0	0	0	0	0	1	1	0	2	0	0	0	0	.000	0	0	0.00
	Colo. Sprng	AAA	Col	5	5	0	0	17.2	77	18	11	10	0	1	1	3	8	0	9	2	1	1	1	.500	0	0	5.09
1996	Norfolk	AAA	NYN	19	19	2	0	102.2	472	116	70	68	15	3	7	8	53	0	83	11	1	4	8	.333	1	0	5.96
1995	Colorado	NL		17	11	0	0	65.2	291	82	53	47	15	4	2	6	20	2	40	2	1	4	6	.400	0	0	6.44
5 Min. YEARS				92	84	9	3	483.1	2086	474	254	224	41	16	17	30	192	0	402	30	13	34	27	.557	3	0	4.17

Sharnol Adriana

Bats: Right **Throws:** Right **Pos:** 3B **Ht:** 6'1" **Wt:** 185 **Born:** 11/13/70 **Age:** 26

				BATTING														BASERUNNING				PERCENTAGES		
Year	Team	Lg	Org	G	AB	H	2B	3B	HR	TB	R	RBI	TBB	IBB	SO	HBP	SH	SF	SB	CS	SB%	GDP	Avg	OBP	SLG
1991	St. Cathrns	A-	Tor	51	170	35	8	0	5	58	27	20	26	0	33	5	1	4	9	4	.69	6	.206	.322	.341
1992	Dunedin	A+	Tor	69	210	58	6	3	0	70	25	18	31	1	43	0	4	0	9	4	.69	5	.276	.369	.333
1993	Knoxville	AA	Tor	64	177	38	3	1	0	43	19	18	24	2	59	2	2	2	9	8	.53	4	.215	.312	.243
1994	Syracuse	AAA	Tor	17	30	4	2	0	0	6	2	0	6	0	8	0	1	0	1	0	1.00	1	.133	.278	.200
	Knoxville	AA	Tor	69	189	47	7	1	3	65	28	21	31	1	39	2	3	1	7	7	.50	5	.249	.359	.344
1995	Knoxville	AA	Tor	75	261	74	17	1	3	102	33	33	32	1	64	4	2	2	12	13	.48	6	.284	.368	.391
1996	Syracuse	AAA	Tor	90	292	82	12	5	10	134	48	37	24	1	72	8	2	0	18	7	.72	5	.281	.352	.459
6 Min. YEARS				435	1329	338	55	11	21	478	182	147	174	6	318	21	15	9	65	43	.60	32	.254	.348	.360

Benny Agbayani

Bats: Right **Throws:** Right **Pos:** OF **Ht:** 5'11" **Wt:** 175 **Born:** 12/28/71 **Age:** 25

				BATTING														BASERUNNING				PERCENTAGES		
Year	Team	Lg	Org	G	AB	H	2B	3B	HR	TB	R	RBI	TBB	IBB	SO	HBP	SH	SF	SB	CS	SB%	GDP	Avg	OBP	SLG
1993	Pittsfield	A-	NYN	51	167	42	6	3	2	60	26	22	20	0	43	0	0	0	7	2	.78	4	.251	.332	.359
1994	St. Lucie	A+	NYN	119	411	115	13	5	5	153	72	63	58	2	67	10	1	5	8	6	.57	9	.280	.378	.372
1995	St. Lucie	A+	NYN	44	155	48	9	3	2	69	24	29	26	1	27	5	1	4	8	3	.73	4	.310	.416	.445
	Binghamton	AA	NYN	88	295	81	11	2	1	99	38	26	39	0	51	5	1	1	12	3	.80	6	.275	.368	.336
1996	Binghamton	AA	NYN	21	53	9	1	0	2	16	7	8	11	0	13	1	1	1	1	0	1.00	2	.170	.318	.302
	Norfolk	AAA	NYN	99	331	92	13	9	7	144	43	56	30	3	57	3	3	5	14	5	.74	5	.278	.339	.435
4 Min. YEARS				422	1412	387	53	22	19	541	210	204	184	6	258	24	7	16	50	19	.72	30	.274	.364	.383

Juan Agosto

Pitches: Left **Bats:** Left **Pos:** P **Ht:** 6' 2" **Wt:** 190 **Born:** 2/23/58 **Age:** 39

				HOW MUCH HE PITCHED						WHAT HE GAVE UP												THE RESULTS					
Year	Team	Lg	Org	G	GS	CG	GF	IP	BFP	H	R	ER	HR	SH	SF	HB	TBB	IBB	SO	WP	Bk	W	L	Pct.	ShO	Sv	ERA
1985	Buffalo	AAA	ChA	6	0	0	5	12.2	52	13	3	3	0	1	0	0	2	0	11	0	0	0	0	.000	0	2	2.13
1986	Toledo	AAA	Min	21	0	0	18	35	149	33	11	9	0	1	0	1	14	0	29	4	0	4	3	.571	0	6	2.31
1987	Tucson	AAA	Hou	44	0	0	24	50	214	48	16	11	1	4	0	2	19	2	31	4	1	4	2	.667	0	7	1.98
1992	Calgary	AAA	Sea	10	0	0	4	21.2	92	20	12	12	2	0	1	2	13	0	12	1	0	1	0	1.000	0	1	4.98
1993	Las Vegas	AAA	SD	19	0	0	5	18	78	21	8	8	2	0	0	1	5	2	15	1	0	2	0	1.000	0	0	4.00
	Tucson	AAA	Hou	32	0	0	13	33	168	45	24	22	2	3	5	2	24	3	18	5	0	5	3	.625	0	3	6.00
1996	Calgary	AAA	Pit	24	0	0	7	27	123	28	16	11	4	1	1	1	12	3	10	1	0	2	3	.400	0	0	3.67
1981	Chicago	AL		2	0	0	1	6	22	5	3	3	1	0	0	1	0	0	3	0	0	0	0	.000	0	0	4.50
1982	Chicago	AL		1	0	0	1	2	13	7	4	4	0	0	0	0	0	0	1	0	0	0	0	.000	0	0	18.00
1983	Chicago	AL		39	0	0	13	41.2	166	41	20	19	2	5	4	1	11	1	29	2	0	2	2	.500	0	7	4.10
1984	Chicago	AL		49	0	0	18	55.1	243	54	20	19	2	5	1	3	34	7	26	1	0	2	1	.667	0	7	3.09
1985	Chicago	AL		54	0	0	21	60.1	246	45	27	24	3	3	3	3	23	1	39	0	0	4	3	.571	0	1	3.58
1986	Chicago	AL		9	0	0	1	4.2	24	6	5	4	0	0	0	0	4	0	3	0	0	0	2	.000	0	0	7.71
	Minnesota	AL		17	1	0	3	20.1	115	43	25	20	1	2	0	2	14	0	9	1	0	1	2	.333	0	1	8.85
1987	Houston	NL		27	0	0	13	27.1	118	26	12	8	1	3	0	0	10	1	6	1	0	1	1	.500	0	2	2.63
1988	Houston	NL		75	0	0	33	91.2	371	74	27	23	6	9	5	0	30	13	33	3	5	10	2	.833	0	4	2.26
1989	Houston	NL		71	0	0	28	83	361	81	32	27	3	5	6	2	32	10	46	4	1	4	5	.444	0	1	2.93
1990	Houston	NL		82	0	0	29	92.1	404	91	46	44	4	7	2	7	39	8	50	1	0	9	8	.529	0	4	4.29
1991	St. Louis	NL		72	0	0	22	86	377	92	52	46	4	11	3	8	39	4	34	6	0	5	3	.625	0	2	4.81
1992	St. Louis	NL		22	0	0	10	31.2	143	39	24	22	2	3	3	3	9	2	13	2	0	2	4	.333	0	0	6.25
	Seattle	AL		17	1	0	2	18.1	84	27	12	12	0	2	1	0	3	0	12	0	0	0	0	.000	0	0	5.89
1993	Houston	NL		6	0	0	3	6	26	8	4	4	1	0	0	0	0	0	3	0	1	0	0	.000	0	0	6.00
6 Min. YEARS				156	0	0	76	197.1	876	208	90	76	11	10	7	9	89	10	126	16	1	18	11	.621	0	19	3.47
13 Maj. YEARS				543	2	0	198	626.2	2713	639	313	279	30	55	28	30	248	47	307	21	7	40	33	.548	0	29	4.01

Pat Ahearne

Pitches: Right **Bats:** Right **Pos:** P **Ht:** 6' 3" **Wt:** 195 **Born:** 12/10/69 **Age:** 27

				HOW MUCH HE PITCHED						WHAT HE GAVE UP												THE RESULTS					
Year	Team	Lg	Org	G	GS	CG	GF	IP	BFP	H	R	ER	HR	SH	SF	HB	TBB	IBB	SO	WP	Bk	W	L	Pct.	ShO	Sv	ERA
1992	Lakeland	A+	Det	1	1	0	0	4.2	17	4	2	1	0	0	0	0	0	0	4	0	0	0	0	.000	0	0	1.93
1993	Lakeland	A+	Det	25	24	2	0	147.1	650	160	87	73	8	7	4	6	48	0	51	3	1	6	15	.286	0	0	4.46
1994	Trenton	AA	Det	30	13	2	3	108.2	467	126	55	48	8	1	6	5	25	1	57	5	0	7	5	.583	0	0	3.98
1995	Toledo	AAA	Det	25	23	1	0	139.2	599	165	83	73	11	2	5	5	37	3	54	2	0	7	9	.438	1	0	4.70
1996	Norfolk	AAA	NYN	5	4	0	0	25.1	108	26	14	13	1	3	0	1	9	1	14	0	1	1	2	.333	0	0	4.62
	Duluth-Sup.	IND	—	1	1	0	0	4.1	24	10	6	6	3	0	0	0	1	0	1	1	0	0	0	.000	0	0	12.46
	San Antonio	AA	LA	8	8	0	0	45.1	208	59	34	29	3	2	2	1	18	0	21	4	0	2	4	.333	0	0	5.76
	Vero Beach	A+	LA	6	6	1	0	47	179	38	16	11	1	2	1	1	5	0	26	2	0	3	2	.600	1	0	2.11
1995	Detroit	AL		4	3	0	0	10	55	20	13	13	2	0	0	0	5	1	4	1	0	0	2	.000	0	0	11.70
5 Min. YEARS				101	80	6	3	522.1	2252	588	297	254	35	17	18	19	143	5	228	17	2	26	37	.413	2	0	4.38

Israel Alcantara

Bats: Right **Throws:** Right **Pos:** 3B **Ht:** 6'2" **Wt:** 165 **Born:** 5/6/73 **Age:** 24

				BATTING														BASERUNNING				PERCENTAGES		
Year	Team	Lg	Org	G	AB	H	2B	3B	HR	TB	R	RBI	TBB	IBB	SO	HBP	SH	SF	SB	CS	SB%	GDP	Avg	OBP	SLG
1992	Expos	R	Mon	59	224	62	14	2	3	89	29	37	17	4	35	1	0	2	6	5	.55	8	.277	.328	.397
1993	Burlington	A	Mon	126	470	115	26	3	18	201	65	73	20	2	125	7	1	5	6	7	.46	5	.245	.283	.428
1994	W. Palm Bch	A+	Mon	125	471	134	26	4	15	213	65	69	26	0	130	3	1	3	9	3	.75	6	.285	.324	.452
1995	Harrisburg	AA	Mon	71	237	50	12	2	10	96	25	29	21	1	81	2	1	1	1	1	.50	5	.211	.280	.405
	W. Palm Bch	A+	Mon	39	134	37	7	2	3	57	16	22	9	0	35	2	2	1	3	0	1.00	0	.276	.329	.425
1996	Harrisburg	AA	Mon	62	218	46	5	0	8	75	26	19	14	0	62	1	0	1	1	1	.50	5	.211	.261	.344
	Expos	R	Mon	7	30	9	2	0	2	17	4	10	3	2	6	0	0	0	0	1	.00	1	.300	.364	.567
	W. Palm Bch	A+	Mon	15	61	19	2	0	4	33	11	14	3	0	13	1	0	1	0	0	.00	1	.311	.348	.541
5 Min. YEARS				504	1845	472	94	13	63	781	241	273	113	9	487	17	5	14	26	18	.59	31	.256	.303	.423

Antonio Alfonseca

Pitches: Right **Bats:** Right **Pos:** P **Ht:** 6'4" **Wt:** 160 **Born:** 4/16/72 **Age:** 25

				HOW MUCH HE PITCHED						WHAT HE GAVE UP												THE RESULTS					
Year	Team	Lg	Org	G	GS	CG	GF	IP	BFP	H	R	ER	HR	SH	SF	HB	TBB	IBB	SO	WP	Bk	W	L	Pct.	ShO	Sv	ERA
1991	Expos	R	Mon	11	10	0	0	51	225	46	33	22	2	1	4	3	25	0	38	1	0	3	3	.500	0	0	3.88

Year Team	Lg Org	HOW MUCH HE PITCHED						WHAT HE GAVE UP												THE RESULTS					
Year Team	Lg Org	G	GS	CG	GF	IP	BFP	H	R	ER	HR	SH	SF	HB	TBB	IBB	SO	WP	Bk	W	L	Pct.	ShO	Sv	ERA
1992 Expos	R Mon	12	10	1	0	66	282	55	31	27	0	2	6	3	35	0	62	8	2	3	4	.429	1	0	3.68
1993 Jamestown	A- Mon	15	4	0	3	33.2	151	31	26	23	3	0	2	3	22	1	29	4	1	2	2	.500	0	1	6.15
1994 Kane County	A Fla	32	9	0	7	86.1	361	78	41	39	5	2	3	2	21	1	74	14	0	6	5	.545	0	0	4.07
1995 Portland	AA Fla	19	17	1	0	96.1	405	81	43	39	6	3	3	4	42	1	75	5	4	9	3	.750	0	0	3.64
1996 Charlotte	AAA Fla	14	13	0	1	71.2	321	86	47	44	6	1	4	3	22	0	51	2	0	4	4	.500	0	1	5.53
6 Min. YEARS		103	63	2	11	405	1745	377	221	194	22	9	22	18	167	3	329	34	7	27	21	.563	1	2	4.31

Edgar Alfonzo

Bats: Right **Throws:** Right **Pos:** 3B-SS **Ht:** 6'0" **Wt:** 167 **Born:** 6/10/67 **Age:** 30

Year Team	Lg Org	BATTING															BASERUNNING				PERCENTAGES		
Year Team	Lg Org	G	AB	H	2B	3B	HR	TB	R	RBI	TBB	IBB	SO	HBP	SH	SF	SB	CS	SB%	GDP	Avg	OBP	SLG
1985 Quad City	A Cal	8	21	6	0	0	0	6	3	0	2	0	2	1	0	0	0	2	.00	0	.286	.375	.286
Salem	A- Cal	56	209	57	10	2	4	83	29	25	17	0	28	2	2	2	0	3	.00	3	.273	.330	.397
1986 Quad City	A Cal	67	219	47	8	1	1	60	21	12	22	0	42	2	6	0	1	1	.50	9	.215	.292	.274
1987 Palm Spring	A+ Cal	36	92	28	4	0	1	35	13	15	13	0	21	0	3	1	1	1	.50	1	.304	.387	.380
Quad City	A Cal	51	198	50	9	3	4	77	25	25	12	0	35	2	3	3	3	7	.30	3	.253	.298	.389
1988 Palm Spring	A+ Cal	5	9	1	0	0	0	1	0	2	1	0	3	0	0	0	0	0	.00	0	.111	.200	.111
Quad City	A Cal	102	406	83	12	2	2	105	36	36	23	1	58	6	8	6	5	5	.50	4	.204	.254	.259
1989 Palm Spring	A+ Cal	77	242	58	10	2	3	81	31	27	40	0	37	3	3	3	8	3	.73	4	.240	.351	.335
1990 Edmonton	AAA Cal	4	11	2	0	0	0	2	1	1	0	0	0	0	1	0	0	0	.00	1	.182	.182	.182
Midland	AA Cal	37	121	36	4	1	1	45	20	9	8	0	18	2	1	1	1	0	1.00	4	.298	.348	.372
Palm Spring	A+ Cal	57	203	56	4	2	2	70	44	12	30	0	37	0	5	2	5	4	.56	2	.276	.366	.345
1991 Palm Spring	A+ Cal	81	292	81	11	4	4	112	43	38	38	3	32	1	10	2	5	7	.42	8	.277	.360	.384
Midland	AA Cal	26	83	23	1	1	4	38	13	13	2	0	7	1	2	0	0	0	.00	2	.277	.302	.458
1992 Palm Spring	A+ Cal	65	257	92	18	2	3	123	52	42	31	3	25	2	0	3	1	4	.20	8	.358	.427	.479
Midland	AA Cal	61	220	65	9	1	4	88	39	30	26	0	30	5	1	0	2	2	.50	8	.295	.382	.400
1993 Bowie	AA Bal	130	459	121	22	3	5	164	45	49	37	1	49	4	5	11	14	4	.78	15	.264	.317	.357
1994 Bowie	AA Bal	124	463	143	35	1	11	213	75	73	40	2	63	4	3	6	13	8	.62	13	.309	.365	.460
1995 Orioles	R Bal	6	18	3	0	0	0	3	1	1	0	0	0	1	0	0	0	0	.00	0	.167	.211	.167
Bowie	AA Bal	28	112	34	6	0	1	43	14	19	10	1	16	0	0	1	1	2	.33	2	.304	.358	.384
Rochester	AAA Bal	18	54	10	3	0	1	16	5	6	2	0	10	0	3	1	0	0	.00	3	.185	.211	.296
1996 Midland	AA Cal	83	310	85	22	1	4	121	37	40	24	2	45	3	1	4	1	2	.33	10	.274	.328	.390
12 Min. YEARS		1122	3999	1081	188	26	55	1486	547	475	378	13	558	39	57	46	61	55	.53	100	.270	.336	.372

Jose Alguacil

Bats: Left **Throws:** Right **Pos:** 2B **Ht:** 6'2" **Wt:** 175 **Born:** 8/9/72 **Age:** 24

Year Team	Lg Org	BATTING															BASERUNNING				PERCENTAGES		
Year Team	Lg Org	G	AB	H	2B	3B	HR	TB	R	RBI	TBB	IBB	SO	HBP	SH	SF	SB	CS	SB%	GDP	Avg	OBP	SLG
1993 Giants	R SF	42	145	35	6	1	1	46	28	13	6	0	23	1	3	1	8	1	.89	3	.241	.275	.317
1994 Clinton	A SF	74	245	71	13	0	1	87	40	25	13	0	42	5	11	1	6	6	.50	2	.290	.337	.355
Everett	A- SF	45	169	36	7	0	0	43	24	7	10	1	41	8	3	0	18	4	.82	4	.213	.289	.254
1995 Burlington	A SF	38	136	30	2	0	0	32	15	5	7	0	27	2	3	0	13	1	.93	2	.221	.269	.235
Shreveport	AA SF	1	4	1	0	0	0	1	1	1	0	0	1	0	0	0	1	0	1.00	0	.250	.250	.250
San Jose	A+ SF	58	225	53	10	3	0	69	30	17	14	0	44	4	8	2	11	6	.65	2	.236	.290	.307
1996 Shreveport	AA SF	13	24	5	0	0	0	5	2	0	3	0	9	1	0	0	0	0	.00	0	.208	.321	.208
San Jose	A+ SF	79	272	72	11	3	1	92	53	31	24	1	53	7	10	2	18	7	.72	8	.265	.338	.338
4 Min. YEARS		350	1220	303	49	7	3	375	193	99	77	2	240	28	38	6	75	25	.75	21	.248	.307	.307

Jeff Alkire

Pitches: Left **Bats:** Right **Pos:** P **Ht:** 6'1" **Wt:** 200 **Born:** 11/15/69 **Age:** 27

Year Team	Lg Org	HOW MUCH HE PITCHED						WHAT HE GAVE UP												THE RESULTS					
Year Team	Lg Org	G	GS	CG	GF	IP	BFP	H	R	ER	HR	SH	SF	HB	TBB	IBB	SO	WP	Bk	W	L	Pct.	ShO	Sv	ERA
1993 Savannah	A StL	28	28	0	0	171.2	711	143	56	47	10	5	3	11	68	0	175	8	0	15	6	.714	0	0	2.46
1994 Arkansas	AA StL	8	8	0	0	37.1	171	50	27	25	0	2	0	0	17	0	31	3	0	4	3	.571	0	0	6.03
St. Pete	A+ StL	12	12	2	0	70	289	61	32	22	2	3	5	3	22	0	56	4	1	4	5	.444	0	0	2.83
1995 Arkansas	AA StL	2	0	0	0	3	13	4	1	1	0	1	0	0	0	0	2	1	0	0	0	.000	0	0	3.00
St. Paul	IND —	21	18	2	0	117.1	503	127	59	55	13	3	2	7	40	1	83	9	0	8	3	.727	0	0	4.22
1996 Portland	AA Fla	11	0	0	4	19.2	93	26	15	14	4	1	0	1	7	1	24	1	0	0	2	.000	0	0	6.41
St. Paul	IND —	18	18	0	0	120	518	121	49	45	5	2	3	5	50	0	87	7	0	6	2	.750	0	0	3.38
4 Min. YEARS		100	84	4	4	539	2298	532	239	209	34	17	13	27	204	2	458	33	1	37	21	.638	0	0	3.49

Cedric Allen

Pitches: Left **Bats:** Left **Pos:** P **Ht:** 5'10" **Wt:** 183 **Born:** 1/13/72 **Age:** 25

Year Team	Lg Org	HOW MUCH HE PITCHED						WHAT HE GAVE UP												THE RESULTS					
Year Team	Lg Org	G	GS	CG	GF	IP	BFP	H	R	ER	HR	SH	SF	HB	TBB	IBB	SO	WP	Bk	W	L	Pct.	ShO	Sv	ERA
1994 Princeton	R+ Cin	13	10	1	2	73	284	48	18	11	2	3	2	4	17	0	62	1	2	6	1	.857	1	1	1.36
1995 Charlstn-WV	A Cin	27	27	5	0	170.1	690	143	64	54	8	6	4	14	46	4	108	6	4	13	7	.650	2	0	2.85
1996 Winston-Sal	A+ Cin	12	12	1	0	68.1	293	73	37	29	10	4	3	0	28	0	40	4	0	7	3	.700	1	0	3.82
Chattanooga	AA Cin	12	3	1	1	27.2	126	31	23	20	4	0	0	4	11	0	12	2	0	1	2	.333	1	0	6.51
3 Min. YEARS		64	52	8	3	339.1	1393	295	142	114	24	13	9	22	102	4	222	13	6	27	13	.675	5	1	3.02

Chris Allison

Bats: Right **Throws:** Right **Pos:** 2B **Ht:** 5'10" **Wt:** 165 **Born:** 10/22/71 **Age:** 25

			BATTING															BASERUNNING				PERCENTAGES		
Year Team	Lg	Org	G	AB	H	2B	3B	HR	TB	R	RBI	TBB	IBB	SO	HBP	SH	SF	SB	CS	SB%	GDP	Avg	OBP	SLG
1994 Utica	A-	Bos	39	144	48	4	3	0	58	19	16	10	0	16	1	4	2	11	3	.79	3	.333	.376	.403
1995 Michigan	A	Bos	87	298	94	8	4	0	110	46	22	52	1	39	7	4	0	36	4	.90	5	.315	.429	.369
1996 Trenton	AA	Bos	109	357	82	7	1	0	91	49	22	28	0	61	3	4	0	14	11	.56	7	.230	.291	.255
3 Min. YEARS			235	799	224	19	8	0	259	114	60	90	1	116	11	12	2	61	18	.77	15	.280	.360	.324

Carlos Almanzar

Pitches: Right **Bats:** Right **Pos:** P **Ht:** 6'2" **Wt:** 166 **Born:** 11/6/73 **Age:** 23

			HOW MUCH HE PITCHED						WHAT HE GAVE UP												THE RESULTS					
Year Team	Lg	Org	G	GS	CG	GF	IP	BFP	H	R	ER	HR	SH	SF	HB	TBB	IBB	SO	WP	Bk	W	L	Pct.	ShO	Sv	ERA
1994 Medicne Hat	R+	Tor	14	14	0	0	84.2	351	82	38	27	2	7	1	1	19	0	77	3	2	7	4	.636	0	0	2.87
1995 Knoxville	AA	Tor	35	19	0	7	126.1	546	144	77	56	10	3	6	3	32	1	93	4	1	3	12	.200	0	2	3.99
1996 Knoxville	AA	Tor	54	0	0	29	94.2	418	106	58	51	13	1	2	3	33	6	105	3	0	7	8	.467	0	9	4.85
3 Min. YEARS			103	33	0	36	305.2	1315	332	173	134	25	11	9	7	84	7	275	10	3	17	24	.415	0	11	3.95

Gabe Alvarez

Bats: Right **Throws:** Right **Pos:** 3B **Ht:** 6'1" **Wt:** 185 **Born:** 3/6/74 **Age:** 23

			BATTING															BASERUNNING				PERCENTAGES		
Year Team	Lg	Org	G	AB	H	2B	3B	HR	TB	R	RBI	TBB	IBB	SO	HBP	SH	SF	SB	CS	SB%	GDP	Avg	OBP	SLG
1995 Rancho Cuca	A+	SD	59	212	73	17	2	6	112	41	36	29	0	30	5	0	2	1	0	1.00	3	.344	.431	.528
Memphis	AA	SD	2	9	5	1	0	0	6	0	4	1	0	1	0	0	0	0	0	.00	0	.556	.600	.667
1996 Memphis	AA	SD	104	368	91	23	1	8	140	58	40	64	1	87	3	0	3	2	3	.40	10	.247	.361	.380
2 Min. YEARS			165	589	169	41	3	14	258	99	80	94	1	118	8	0	5	3	3	.50	13	.287	.389	.438

Manuel Amador

Bats: Both **Throws:** Right **Pos:** 3B **Ht:** 6'0" **Wt:** 165 **Born:** 11/21/75 **Age:** 21

			BATTING															BASERUNNING				PERCENTAGES		
Year Team	Lg	Org	G	AB	H	2B	3B	HR	TB	R	RBI	TBB	IBB	SO	HBP	SH	SF	SB	CS	SB%	GDP	Avg	OBP	SLG
1993 Martinsvlle	R+	Phi	61	234	55	7	1	9	91	38	35	26	0	49	1	1	1	5	1	.83	4	.235	.313	.389
1994 Spartanburg	A	Phi	91	341	85	14	3	6	123	54	42	30	2	65	8	3	2	5	3	.63	4	.249	.323	.361
1995 Piedmont	A	Phi	1	4	0	0	0	0	0	0	0	0	0	0	1	0	0	0	1	.00	0	.000	.200	.000
Clearwater	A+	Phi	96	330	92	19	4	6	137	45	47	22	0	38	6	1	0	5	2	.71	6	.279	.335	.415
1996 Reading	AA	Phi	10	18	5	2	0	1	10	5	3	5	0	4	0	0	0	0	0	.00	1	.278	.435	.556
Clearwater	A+	Phi	52	172	47	10	0	5	72	24	21	19	0	46	2	2	1	1	1	.50	5	.273	.351	.419
4 Min. YEARS			311	1099	284	52	8	27	433	166	148	102	2	202	18	7	4	16	8	.67	20	.258	.330	.394

Charlie Anderson

Bats: Right **Throws:** Right **Pos:** DH **Ht:** 6'0" **Wt:** 190 **Born:** 3/18/70 **Age:** 27

			BATTING															BASERUNNING				PERCENTAGES		
Year Team	Lg	Org	G	AB	H	2B	3B	HR	TB	R	RBI	TBB	IBB	SO	HBP	SH	SF	SB	CS	SB%	GDP	Avg	OBP	SLG
1992 Johnson Cty	R+	StL	45	154	30	2	1	3	43	17	15	14	1	32	1	2	6	4	3	.57	2	.195	.257	.279
1993 Savannah	A	StL	46	146	36	7	2	4	59	17	20	10	1	37	0	1	2	3	1	.75	5	.247	.291	.404
1994 Madison	A	StL	127	437	113	26	5	10	179	61	45	31	4	119	5	3	2	9	8	.53	9	.259	.314	.410
1995 Louisville	AAA	StL	1	0	0	0	0	0	0	0	0	0	0	0	0	0	0	0	0	.00	0	.000	.000	.000
Arkansas	AA	StL	77	240	68	15	2	4	99	31	29	21	1	55	0	0	1	1	2	.33	10	.283	.340	.413
1996 Arkansas	AA	StL	2	1	0	0	0	0	0	0	0	1	0	0	0	0	0	0	0	.00	0	.000	.500	.000
5 Min. YEARS			298	978	247	50	10	21	380	126	109	77	7	243	6	6	11	17	14	.55	26	.253	.308	.389

Cliff Anderson

Bats: Left **Throws:** Right **Pos:** SS **Ht:** 5'8" **Wt:** 165 **Born:** 7/4/70 **Age:** 26

			BATTING															BASERUNNING				PERCENTAGES		
Year Team	Lg	Org	G	AB	H	2B	3B	HR	TB	R	RBI	TBB	IBB	SO	HBP	SH	SF	SB	CS	SB%	GDP	Avg	OBP	SLG
1992 Yakima	A-	LA	51	142	31	11	2	3	55	24	18	24	2	29	4	2	4	2	4	.33	2	.218	.339	.387
1993 Yakima	A-	LA	23	81	18	4	0	1	25	7	7	7	2	19	2	0	1	1	0	1.00	2	.222	.297	.309
Bakersfield	A+	LA	12	36	5	3	0	0	8	4	3	1	0	13	0	3	0	0	1	.00	2	.139	.162	.222
Great Falls	R+	LA	37	141	42	9	2	1	58	19	22	5	1	27	1	3	1	1	3	.25	3	.298	.324	.411
1994 Vero Beach	A+	LA	23	72	24	4	0	0	28	7	9	3	0	12	1	1	1	0	0	.00	2	.333	.364	.389
San Antonio	AA	LA	41	99	24	9	0	1	36	8	15	4	1	25	2	1	1	0	0	.00	0	.242	.283	.364
1995 Vero Beach	A+	LA	113	365	99	20	2	6	141	48	44	10	1	58	8	6	2	1	4	.20	4	.271	.304	.386
1996 San Antonio	AA	LA	7	26	6	0	1	0	8	2	2	1	0	7	1	2	0	0	1	.00	0	.231	.286	.308
Albuquerque	AAA	LA	64	186	50	9	2	4	75	19	17	21	2	53	4	2	1	3	3	.50	3	.269	.354	.403
San Bernrdo	A+	LA	55	230	68	16	2	11	121	43	44	15	0	50	6	4	2	7	5	.58	2	.296	.352	.526
5 Min. YEARS			426	1378	367	85	11	27	555	181	181	91	9	293	29	24	13	15	21	.42	20	.266	.322	.403

Jimmy Anderson

Pitches: Left **Bats:** Left **Pos:** P **Ht:** 6'1" **Wt:** 180 **Born:** 1/22/76 **Age:** 21

			HOW MUCH HE PITCHED						WHAT HE GAVE UP												THE RESULTS					
Year Team	Lg	Org	G	GS	CG	GF	IP	BFP	H	R	ER	HR	SH	SF	HB	TBB	IBB	SO	WP	Bk	W	L	Pct.	ShO	Sv	ERA
1994 Pirates	R	Pit	10	10	0	0	56.1	230	35	21	10	1	2	1	2	27	0	66	5	1	5	1	.833	0	0	1.60
1995 Lynchburg	A+	Pit	10	9	0	1	52.1	231	56	29	24	1	4	1	5	21	1	32	7	3	1	5	.167	0	0	4.13

Year Team	Lg Org	G	GS	CG	GF	IP	BFP	H	R	ER	HR	SH	SF	HB	TBB	IBB	SO	WP	Bk	W	L	Pct.	ShO	Sv	ERA
		HOW MUCH HE PITCHED						WHAT HE GAVE UP												THE RESULTS					
Augusta	A Pit	24	23	0	1	129	536	107	44	37	2	5	1	9	52	1	107	16	4	5	7	.417	0	0	2.58
1996 Lynchburg	A+ Pit	11	11	1	0	65.1	267	51	25	14	2	2	0	2	21	0	56	1	0	5	3	.625	1	0	1.93
Carolina	AA Pit	17	16	0	0	97	411	92	40	36	3	1	0	3	44	3	79	13	5	8	3	.727	0	0	3.34
3 Min. YEARS		72	69	1	2	400	1675	341	159	121	9	14	3	21	165	5	340	42	13	24	19	.558	1	0	2.72

Marlon Anderson

Bats: Left **Throws:** Right **Pos:** 2B **Ht:** 5'10" **Wt:** 190 **Born:** 1/3/74 **Age:** 23

Year Team	Lg Org	G	AB	H	2B	3B	HR	TB	R	RBI	TBB	IBB	SO	HBP	SH	SF	SB	CS	SB%	GDP	Avg	OBP	SLG
		BATTING															BASERUNNING				PERCENTAGES		
1995 Batavia	A- Phi	74	312	92	13	4	3	122	52	40	15	2	20	4	2	4	22	8	.73	2	.295	.331	.391
1996 Clearwater	A+ Phi	60	257	70	10	3	2	92	37	22	14	1	18	2	4	0	26	1	.96	4	.272	.315	.358
Reading	AA Phi	75	314	86	14	3	3	115	38	28	26	2	44	1	3	1	17	9	.65	5	.274	.330	.366
2 Min. YEARS		209	883	248	37	10	8	329	127	90	55	5	82	7	9	5	65	18	.78	11	.281	.326	.373

Mike Anderson

Pitches: Right **Bats:** Right **Pos:** P **Ht:** 6' 3" **Wt:** 200 **Born:** 7/30/66 **Age:** 30

Year Team	Lg Org	G	GS	CG	GF	IP	BFP	H	R	ER	HR	SH	SF	HB	TBB	IBB	SO	WP	Bk	W	L	Pct.	ShO	Sv	ERA
		HOW MUCH HE PITCHED						WHAT HE GAVE UP												THE RESULTS					
1988 Reds	R Cin	2	2	0	0	7.1	34	6	7	4	0	0	0	0	5	0	11	3	4	0	1	.000	0	0	4.91
Billings	R+ Cin	17	4	0	12	44.1	192	36	17	16	1	0	4	2	21	1	52	4	0	3	1	.750	0	2	3.25
1989 Greensboro	A Cin	25	25	4	0	154.1	647	117	64	49	7	2	3	8	72	0	154	9	2	11	6	.647	2	0	2.86
1990 Cedar Rapds	A Cin	23	23	2	0	138.1	613	134	67	52	6	8	7	5	62	0	101	10	0	10	5	.667	0	0	3.38
1991 Chattanooga	AA Cin	28	26	3	1	155.1	698	142	94	76	8	4	4	8	93	2	115	17	1	10	9	.526	3	0	4.40
1992 Chattanooga	AA Cin	28	26	4	1	171.2	716	155	59	48	4	0	3	7	61	1	149	15	3	13	7	.650	4	0	2.52
1993 Chattanooga	AA Cin	2	2	1	0	15	54	10	3	2	0	1	1	0	1	0	14	0	0	1	1	.500	0	0	1.20
Indianapols	AAA Cin	23	23	2	0	151	647	150	73	63	10	7	7	4	56	5	111	8	0	10	6	.625	1	0	3.75
1994 Iowa	AAA ChN	40	14	0	9	110	510	132	90	75	6	6	7	5	57	6	78	12	0	4	8	.333	0	0	6.14
1995 Iowa	AAA ChN	27	27	3	0	171.2	715	156	71	66	23	3	3	12	69	3	123	7	1	7	9	.438	1	0	3.46
1996 Okla. City	AAA Tex	11	4	0	3	32.2	154	45	32	23	7	1	1	0	11	1	21	2	0	3	4	.429	0	0	6.34
1993 Cincinnati	NL	3	0	0	0	5.1	30	12	11	11	3	0	0	0	3	0	4	0	0	0	0	.000	0	0	18.56
9 Min. YEARS		226	176	19	26	1151.2	4980	1083	577	474	72	32	40	51	508	19	929	87	11	72	57	.558	11	2	3.70

Doug Angeli

Bats: Right **Throws:** Right **Pos:** SS **Ht:** 5'11" **Wt:** 183 **Born:** 1/7/71 **Age:** 26

Year Team	Lg Org	G	AB	H	2B	3B	HR	TB	R	RBI	TBB	IBB	SO	HBP	SH	SF	SB	CS	SB%	GDP	Avg	OBP	SLG
		BATTING															BASERUNNING				PERCENTAGES		
1993 Batavia	A- Phi	75	252	55	7	3	0	68	20	15	18	0	33	1	7	1	5	6	.45	5	.218	.272	.270
1994 Spartanburg	A Phi	43	165	40	8	0	0	48	16	14	15	0	29	0	0	1	5	3	.63	5	.242	.304	.291
Clearwater	A+ Phi	77	265	69	14	2	1	90	25	26	23	0	39	0	5	0	2	2	.50	6	.260	.319	.340
1995 Clearwater	A+ Phi	16	47	9	3	0	0	12	4	3	3	0	13	1	2	1	0	1	.00	0	.191	.250	.255
1996 Reading	AA Phi	56	187	44	9	0	8	77	24	29	20	3	43	2	6	2	3	2	.60	1	.235	.313	.412
4 Min. YEARS		267	916	217	41	5	9	295	89	87	79	3	157	4	20	5	15	14	.52	17	.237	.299	.322

Matt Apana

Pitches: Right **Bats:** Right **Pos:** P **Ht:** 6'0" **Wt:** 195 **Born:** 1/16/71 **Age:** 26

Year Team	Lg Org	G	GS	CG	GF	IP	BFP	H	R	ER	HR	SH	SF	HB	TBB	IBB	SO	WP	Bk	W	L	Pct.	ShO	Sv	ERA
		HOW MUCH HE PITCHED						WHAT HE GAVE UP												THE RESULTS					
1993 Bellingham	A- Sea	14	14	0	0	61	282	50	38	30	7	5	1	4	43	0	59	7	2	5	3	.625	0	0	4.43
1994 Riverside	A+ Sea	26	26	3	0	165.1	694	142	63	52	8	5	3	4	70	0	137	5	0	14	4	.778	3	0	2.83
1995 Port City	AA Sea	6	6	0	0	33.1	154	34	24	16	4	1	0	2	24	1	28	2	0	1	3	.250	0	0	4.32
Tacoma	AAA Sea	27	26	0	0	137	635	155	96	73	13	4	6	7	85	1	86	8	0	9	11	.450	0	0	4.80
1996 Port City	AA Sea	18	18	0	0	96.1	431	86	58	57	8	2	6	4	69	0	55	13	0	3	8	.273	0	0	5.33
4 Min. YEARS		91	90	3	0	493	2196	467	279	228	40	17	16	21	291	2	365	35	2	32	29	.525	3	0	4.16

Kurt Archer

Pitches: Right **Bats:** Right **Pos:** P **Ht:** 6'4" **Wt:** 230 **Born:** 4/27/69 **Age:** 28

Year Team	Lg Org	G	GS	CG	GF	IP	BFP	H	R	ER	HR	SH	SF	HB	TBB	IBB	SO	WP	Bk	W	L	Pct.	ShO	Sv	ERA
		HOW MUCH HE PITCHED						WHAT HE GAVE UP												THE RESULTS					
1990 Helena	R+ Mil	10	0	0	9	19.2	83	19	9	8	0	0	0	2	3	2	23	0	1	0	2	.000	0	3	3.66
Beloit	A Mil	11	0	0	3	29.1	122	24	11	5	1	1	3	1	9	1	27	2	1	5	0	1.000	0	0	1.53
1991 Stockton	A+ Mil	27	6	0	9	46.1	219	45	36	22	1	3	4	7	29	3	26	5	0	2	4	.333	0	1	4.27
1992 Stockton	A+ Mil	55	0	0	42	76.2	317	60	19	16	2	5	3	5	32	8	49	2	0	11	3	.786	0	15	1.88
1993 El Paso	AA Mil	54	5	0	28	104.2	457	129	63	57	10	6	6	8	38	8	50	6	0	9	8	.529	0	11	4.90
1994 Stockton	A+ Mil	5	0	0	4	5	22	6	2	2	0	0	0	0	1	1	5	0	0	0	1	.000	0	2	3.60
El Paso	AA Mil	44	1	0	16	77	327	87	40	35	6	4	4	2	17	2	58	2	0	5	3	.625	0	9	4.09
1995 El Paso	AA Mil	4	0	0	2	6	24	4	2	2	0	0	0	0	1	0	5	0	0	0	0	.000	0	1	3.00
New Orleans	AAA Mil	42	0	0	13	67	280	61	25	24	5	6	3	5	18	2	46	5	0	2	6	.250	0	3	3.22
1996 New Orleans	AAA Mil	23	0	0	11	31.1	133	39	20	19	5	1	3	0	9	3	15	1	0	1	3	.250	0	0	5.46
7 Min. YEARS		275	12	0	137	463	1984	474	227	190	30	26	26	30	157	30	304	23	2	35	30	.538	0	45	3.69

Amador Arias

Bats: Both **Throws:** Right **Pos:** 2B **Ht:** 5'10" **Wt:** 160 **Born:** 5/28/72 **Age:** 25

				BATTING															BASERUNNING				PERCENTAGES		
Year	Team	Lg	Org	G	AB	H	2B	3B	HR	TB	R	RBI	TBB	IBB	SO	HBP	SH	SF	SB	CS	SB%	GDP	Avg	OBP	SLG
1990	Reds	R	Cin	61	248	63	8	3	1	80	46	27	21	0	37	0	7	0	23	6	.79	4	.254	.312	.323
1991	Cedar Rapds	A	Cin	21	59	11	0	1	0	13	5	4	4	0	14	1	0	0	7	3	.70	0	.186	.250	.220
	Erie	A-	Cin	52	200	46	14	2	2	70	24	17	18	1	42	0	1	2	13	5	.72	3	.230	.291	.350
1992	Charlstn-WV	A	Cin	58	149	36	4	0	0	40	17	7	9	0	37	1	2	2	7	6	.54	3	.242	.286	.268
1993	Winston-Sal	A+	Cin	58	179	47	3	0	0	50	25	12	7	0	28	0	4	1	5	6	.45	5	.263	.289	.279
	Chattanooga	AA	Cin	18	65	14	1	1	0	17	6	2	4	0	23	0	1	0	1	1	.50	0	.215	.261	.262
1994	Winston-Sal	A+	Cin	75	193	46	7	0	2	59	25	15	11	0	33	1	3	1	7	6	.54	5	.238	.282	.306
1995	Indianapols	AAA	Cin	5	15	6	0	0	0	6	2	1	2	0	1	0	0	0	1	0	1.00	0	.400	.471	.400
	Chattanooga	AA	Cin	71	108	24	3	1	0	29	17	4	6	0	15	0	1	0	3	2	.60	4	.222	.263	.269
1996	Indianapols	AAA	Cin	1	3	0	0	0	0	0	0	0	0	0	1	0	0	0	0	0	.00	0	.000	.000	.000
	Winston-Sal	A+	Cin	116	378	109	17	1	10	158	53	56	40	1	72	2	5	3	30	10	.75	6	.288	.357	.418
	Chattanooga	AA	Cin	1	1	0	0	0	0	0	0	0	0	0	0	0	0	0	0	0	.00	0	.000	.000	.000
7 Min. YEARS				537	1598	402	57	9	15	522	220	145	122	2	303	5	24	9	97	45	.68	30	.252	.305	.327

Jamie Arnold

Pitches: Right **Bats:** Right **Pos:** P **Ht:** 6'2" **Wt:** 188 **Born:** 3/24/74 **Age:** 23

				HOW MUCH HE PITCHED						WHAT HE GAVE UP												THE RESULTS					
Year	Team	Lg	Org	G	GS	CG	GF	IP	BFP	H	R	ER	HR	SH	SF	HB	TBB	IBB	SO	WP	Bk	W	L	Pct.	ShO	Sv	ERA
1992	Braves	R	Atl	7	5	0	2	20	85	16	12	9	0	0	2	4	6	0	22	0	2	0	1	.000	0	0	4.05
1993	Macon	A	Atl	27	27	1	0	164.1	692	142	67	57	5	3	4	16	56	0	124	13	2	8	9	.471	0	0	3.12
1994	Durham	A+	Atl	25	25	0	0	145	656	144	96	75	26	3	1	14	79	4	91	8	4	7	7	.500	0	0	4.66
1995	Greenville	AA	Atl	10	10	0	0	56.2	266	76	42	40	8	0	2	7	25	1	19	6	0	1	5	.167	0	0	6.35
	Durham	A+	Atl	25	24	1	0	136.2	613	162	84	75	13	4	3	16	46	1	63	10	0	5	13	.278	0	0	4.94
1996	Greenville	AA	Atl	23	23	2	0	128	573	149	79	70	17	0	5	10	44	1	64	6	1	7	7	.500	0	0	4.92
5 Min. YEARS				117	114	4	2	650.2	2885	689	380	326	69	10	17	67	256	7	383	43	9	28	42	.400	0	0	4.51

Ken Arnold

Bats: Right **Throws:** Right **Pos:** SS **Ht:** 6'1" **Wt:** 180 **Born:** 5/10/69 **Age:** 28

				BATTING															BASERUNNING				PERCENTAGES		
Year	Team	Lg	Org	G	AB	H	2B	3B	HR	TB	R	RBI	TBB	IBB	SO	HBP	SH	SF	SB	CS	SB%	GDP	Avg	OBP	SLG
1992	Peoria	A	ChN	91	271	57	4	3	1	70	41	22	42	0	65	3	4	1	11	4	.73	11	.210	.322	.258
1993	Thunder Bay	IND	—	55	183	54	7	0	0	61	22	19	11	1	36	1	2	1	12	6	.67	4	.295	.337	.333
1994	Bowie	AA	Bal	86	228	61	8	1	5	86	29	27	23	0	48	1	9	1	4	5	.44	3	.268	.336	.377
1995	Bowie	AA	Bal	10	22	0	0	0	0	0	3	0	6	0	8	0	0	0	0	0	.00	1	.000	.214	.000
	Winnipeg	IND	—	85	322	74	12	1	1	91	43	32	20	1	73	2	5	2	6	3	.67	4	.230	.277	.283
1996	Charlotte	A+	Tex	52	144	35	4	1	0	41	23	12	16	0	42	2	3	0	2	3	.40	1	.243	.327	.285
	Tulsa	AA	Tex	28	58	8	1	0	0	9	9	7	5	0	24	0	0	1	0	0	.00	2	.138	.203	.155
5 Min. YEARS				407	1228	289	36	6	7	358	170	119	123	2	296	9	23	6	35	21	.63	26	.235	.308	.292

Matt Arrandale

Pitches: Right **Bats:** Right **Pos:** P **Ht:** 6'0" **Wt:** 170 **Born:** 12/14/70 **Age:** 26

				HOW MUCH HE PITCHED						WHAT HE GAVE UP												THE RESULTS					
Year	Team	Lg	Org	G	GS	CG	GF	IP	BFP	H	R	ER	HR	SH	SF	HB	TBB	IBB	SO	WP	Bk	W	L	Pct.	ShO	Sv	ERA
1993	Glens Falls	A-	StL	12	12	0	0	68.2	298	77	42	35	6	1	1	2	14	0	53	4	2	3	4	.429	0	0	4.59
	St. Pete	A+	StL	2	2	0	0	14	49	8	2	2	1	0	0	0	3	0	11	1	0	1	0	1.000	0	0	1.29
1994	Savannah	A	StL	19	19	5	0	133.1	519	112	36	26	2	1	2	4	21	1	121	3	0	15	3	.833	0	0	1.76
	St. Pete	A+	StL	9	9	0	0	59	244	65	26	22	0	2	1	2	11	0	29	2	1	3	4	.429	0	0	3.36
1995	Arkansas	AA	StL	47	3	0	23	68.2	296	72	28	25	1	2	2	1	22	4	28	1	0	3	5	.375	0	2	3.28
1996	Louisville	AAA	StL	63	0	0	22	79	351	83	51	42	6	0	2	4	33	9	38	4	0	5	4	.556	0	3	4.78
4 Min. YEARS				152	45	5	45	422.2	1757	417	185	152	16	6	8	13	104	14	280	15	3	30	20	.600	0	5	3.24

Joe Ausanio

Pitches: Right **Bats:** Right **Pos:** P **Ht:** 6' 1" **Wt:** 205 **Born:** 12/9/65 **Age:** 31

				HOW MUCH HE PITCHED						WHAT HE GAVE UP												THE RESULTS					
Year	Team	Lg	Org	G	GS	CG	GF	IP	BFP	H	R	ER	HR	SH	SF	HB	TBB	IBB	SO	WP	Bk	W	L	Pct.	ShO	Sv	ERA
1988	Watertown	A-	Pit	28	0	0	23	47.2	200	29	10	7	1	6	1	3	27	5	56	3	0	2	4	.333	0	13	1.32
1989	Salem	A+	Pit	54	0	0	51	89	368	51	29	21	9	7	2	3	44	6	97	5	0	5	4	.556	0	20	2.12
1990	Harrisburg	AA	Pit	43	0	0	38	54	211	36	15	11	2	6	1	2	16	4	49	4	0	3	2	.600	0	15	1.83
1991	Carolina	AA	Pit	3	0	0	3	3	9	0	0	0	0	0	0	0	0	0	2	0	0	0	0	.000	0	2	0.00
	Buffalo	AAA	Pit	22	0	0	14	30.1	144	33	17	13	5	1	3	0	19	3	26	2	1	2	2	.500	0	3	3.86
1992	Buffalo	AAA	Pit	53	0	0	39	83.2	352	64	35	27	5	6	2	1	40	6	66	4	0	6	4	.600	0	15	2.90
1993	Expos	R	Mon	5	0	0	0	5	18	3	1	0	0	1	0	0	1	0	6	0	0	0	0	.000	0	0	0.00
	Harrisburg	AA	Mon	19	0	0	15	22.1	86	16	3	3	1	0	0	0	4	1	30	0	0	2	0	1.000	0	6	1.21
1994	Columbus	AAA	NYA	44	0	0	29	60.1	243	45	21	16	5	2	6	1	16	1	69	3	0	3	3	.500	0	13	2.39
1995	Columbus	AAA	NYA	11	0	0	9	12	53	12	10	10	1	1	2	1	5	0	20	1	0	1	0	1.000	0	3	7.50
1996	Norfolk	AAA	NYN	35	0	0	17	43	197	38	31	28	8	2	4	2	29	1	40	2	0	3	3	.500	0	4	5.86
	Colo. Sprng	AAA	Col	13	1	0	6	18.2	84	18	10	9	2	0	2	0	10	2	18	2	0	1	1	.500	0	0	4.34
1994	New York	AL		13	0	0	5	15.2	69	16	9	9	3	0	0	0	6	0	15	0	0	2	1	.667	0	0	5.17
1995	New York	AL		28	0	0	10	37.2	173	42	24	24	9	1	2	0	23	0	36	3	0	2	0	1.000	0	1	5.73
9 Min. YEARS				330	1	0	244	469	1965	345	182	145	39	32	23	13	211	29	479	26	1	28	23	.549	0	94	2.78
2 Maj. YEARS				41	0	0	15	53.1	242	58	33	33	12	1	2	0	29	0	51	3	0	4	1	.800	0	1	5.57

James Austin

Pitches: Right **Bats:** Right **Pos:** P **Ht:** 6' 2" **Wt:** 200 **Born:** 12/7/63 **Age:** 33

		HOW MUCH HE PITCHED						WHAT HE GAVE UP												THE RESULTS					
Year Team	Lg Org	G	GS	CG	GF	IP	BFP	H	R	ER	HR	SH	SF	HB	TBB	IBB	SO	WP	Bk	W	L	Pct.	ShO	Sv	ERA
1986 Spokane	A- SD	28	0	0	19	59.2	0	53	24	15	1	0	0	1	22	2	74	7	0	5	4	.556	0	5	2.26
1987 Charlstn-SC	A SD	31	21	2	3	152	642	138	89	71	10	4	1	1	56	2	123	20	1	7	10	.412	1	0	4.20
1988 Riverside	A+ SD	12	12	2	0	80	333	65	31	24	5	2	3	0	35	0	73	2	0	6	2	.750	1	0	2.70
Wichita	AA SD	12	12	4	0	73	313	76	46	39	9	2	3	0	23	0	52	10	0	5	6	.455	1	0	4.81
1989 Stockton	A+ Mil	7	7	0	0	48.1	204	51	19	14	3	2	1	0	14	0	44	2	0	3	3	.500	0	0	2.61
El Paso	AA Mil	22	13	2	5	85	406	121	60	55	6	2	3	4	34	1	69	4	0	3	10	.231	0	1	5.82
1990 El Paso	AA Mil	38	3	0	24	92.1	384	91	36	25	5	2	3	1	26	4	77	8	0	11	3	.786	0	6	2.44
1991 Denver	AAA Mil	20	3	0	10	44	184	35	12	12	4	2	0	2	24	3	37	1	0	6	3	.667	0	3	2.45
1993 New Orleans	AAA Mil	8	3	0	0	16	72	17	11	9	3	0	1	0	7	0	7	4	1	1	2	.333	0	0	5.06
1995 Buffalo	AAA Cle	2	1	0	0	3	19	7	6	4	1	0	0	0	2	0	1	1	0	1	1	.500	0	0	12.00
1996 Pawtucket	AAA Bos	10	0	0	6	14	64	15	14	14	6	1	1	0	9	2	7	2	1	0	1	.000	0	0	9.00
1991 Milwaukee	AL	5	0	0	1	8.2	46	8	8	8	1	2	1	3	11	1	3	1	0	0	0	.000	0	0	8.31
1992 Milwaukee	AL	47	0	0	12	58.1	235	38	13	12	2	1	1	2	32	6	30	1	0	5	2	.714	0	0	1.85
1993 Milwaukee	AL	31	0	0	8	33	137	28	15	14	3	1	0	1	13	1	15	4	0	1	2	.333	0	0	3.82
9 Min. YEARS		190	75	10	67	667.1	2621	669	348	282	53	17	16	9	252	14	564	61	3	48	45	.516	3	15	3.80
3 Maj. YEARS		83	0	0	21	100	418	74	36	34	6	4	2	6	56	8	48	6	0	6	4	.600	0	0	3.06

Bruce Aven

Bats: Right **Throws:** Right **Pos:** OF **Ht:** 5'9" **Wt:** 180 **Born:** 3/4/72 **Age:** 25

		BATTING															BASERUNNING				PERCENTAGES		
Year Team	Lg Org	G	AB	H	2B	3B	HR	TB	R	RBI	TBB	IBB	SO	HBP	SH	SF	SB	CS	SB%	GDP	Avg	OBP	SLG
1994 Watertown	A- Cle	61	220	73	14	5	5	112	49	33	20	0	45	12	2	5	12	3	.80	1	.332	.409	.509
1995 Kinston	A+ Cle	130	479	125	23	5	23	227	70	69	41	3	109	13	0	1	15	9	.63	7	.261	.335	.474
1996 Canton-Akrn	AA Cle	131	481	143	31	4	23	251	91	79	43	0	101	17	0	3	22	6	.79	9	.297	.373	.522
Buffalo	AAA Cle	3	9	6	0	0	1	9	5	2	1	0	1	1	0	0	0	1	.00	0	.667	.727	1.000
3 Min. YEARS		325	1189	347	68	14	52	599	215	183	105	3	256	43	2	9	49	19	.72	17	.292	.368	.504

Joe Aversa

Bats: Both **Throws:** Right **Pos:** 3B-SS **Ht:** 5'10" **Wt:** 155 **Born:** 5/20/68 **Age:** 29

		BATTING															BASERUNNING				PERCENTAGES		
Year Team	Lg Org	G	AB	H	2B	3B	HR	TB	R	RBI	TBB	IBB	SO	HBP	SH	SF	SB	CS	SB%	GDP	Avg	OBP	SLG
1990 Cardinals	R StL	9	34	8	1	0	0	9	5	4	8	0	8	1	0	0	2	3	.40	1	.235	.395	.265
Johnson Cty	R+ StL	41	93	15	1	0	0	16	10	8	10	0	18	1	0	0	2	1	.67	2	.161	.250	.172
1991 Springfield	A StL	78	184	43	2	0	1	48	19	14	43	0	37	0	5	0	5	6	.45	2	.234	.379	.261
1992 St. Pete	A+ StL	25	44	7	1	0	0	8	4	3	8	0	8	0	0	1	0	1	.00	3	.159	.283	.182
Arkansas	AA StL	49	106	25	4	1	0	31	16	3	21	0	20	0	2	0	3	2	.60	1	.236	.362	.292
1993 Arkansas	AA StL	95	199	36	4	2	0	44	23	5	17	0	34	1	2	1	3	1	.75	3	.181	.248	.221
1994 St. Pete	A+ StL	15	31	5	2	0	0	7	6	3	8	0	2	0	0	0	0	0	.00	0	.161	.333	.226
Arkansas	AA StL	52	99	20	5	2	0	29	10	6	7	1	25	1	1	0	0	1	.00	2	.202	.262	.293
1995 Louisville	AAA StL	85	141	31	6	0	0	37	23	9	26	2	29	0	3	2	7	3	.70	1	.220	.337	.262
1996 Binghamton	AA NYN	13	32	6	0	0	0	6	3	1	7	0	8	1	2	0	0	0	.00	1	.188	.350	.188
Portland	AA Fla	54	135	33	8	0	0	41	22	21	23	0	22	0	3	1	2	3	.40	3	.244	.352	.304
7 Min. YEARS		516	1098	229	34	5	1	276	141	77	178	3	211	5	18	5	24	21	.53	19	.209	.320	.251

Rolo Avila

Bats: Right **Throws:** Right **Pos:** OF **Ht:** 5'8" **Wt:** 170 **Born:** 8/10/73 **Age:** 23

		BATTING															BASERUNNING				PERCENTAGES		
Year Team	Lg Org	G	AB	H	2B	3B	HR	TB	R	RBI	TBB	IBB	SO	HBP	SH	SF	SB	CS	SB%	GDP	Avg	OBP	SLG
1994 Bluefield	R+ Bal	56	200	55	14	1	1	74	41	17	28	0	30	8	3	3	28	7	.80	0	.275	.381	.370
1995 High Desert	A+ Bal	52	180	43	10	1	2	61	26	10	29	0	26	4	5	0	19	8	.70	0	.239	.357	.339
Frederick	A+ Bal	52	175	46	8	1	1	59	26	13	14	0	27	3	5	0	15	5	.75	2	.263	.328	.337
Bowie	AA Bal	16	43	10	2	0	0	12	8	4	6	0	8	0	1	1	2	2	.50	0	.233	.320	.279
1996 High Desert	A+ Bal	68	296	98	17	2	4	131	54	33	22	0	32	3	4	2	15	7	.68	5	.331	.381	.443
Bowie	AA Bal	60	233	62	12	1	2	82	31	17	19	0	34	8	1	2	8	5	.62	4	.266	.340	.352
Rochester	AAA Bal	12	47	14	2	1	0	18	7	6	3	0	4	1	0	0	2	0	1.00	0	.298	.353	.383
3 Min. YEARS		316	1174	328	65	7	10	437	193	100	121	0	161	27	19	8	89	34	.72	11	.279	.358	.372

Manuel Aybar

Pitches: Right **Bats:** Right **Pos:** P **Ht:** 6'1" **Wt:** 165 **Born:** 10/5/74 **Age:** 22

		HOW MUCH HE PITCHED						WHAT HE GAVE UP												THE RESULTS					
Year Team	Lg Org	G	GS	CG	GF	IP	BFP	H	R	ER	HR	SH	SF	HB	TBB	IBB	SO	WP	Bk	W	L	Pct.	ShO	Sv	ERA
1994 Cardinals	R StL	13	13	1	0	72.1	295	69	25	17	0	2	4	4	9	0	79	4	3	6	1	.857	0	0	2.12
1995 St. Pete	A+ StL	9	9	0	0	48.1	202	42	27	18	4	0	1	1	16	0	43	7	1	2	5	.286	0	0	3.35
Savannah	A StL	27	27	2	0	161	663	124	73	56	12	7	5	3	52	0	142	15	2	5	13	.278	1	0	3.13
1996 Arkansas	AA StL	20	20	0	0	121	507	120	53	41	10	6	3	0	34	0	83	3	3	8	6	.571	0	0	3.05
Louisville	AAA StL	5	5	0	0	30.2	123	26	12	11	1	0	1	0	7	0	25	3	2	2	2	.500	0	0	3.23
3 Min. YEARS		74	74	3	0	433.1	1790	381	190	143	27	15	14	8	118	0	372	32	11	23	27	.460	1	0	2.97

Jesus Azuaje

Bats: Right **Throws:** Right **Pos:** 2B **Ht:** 5'10" **Wt:** 170 **Born:** 1/16/73 **Age:** 24

		BATTING															BASERUNNING				PERCENTAGES		
Year Team	Lg Org	G	AB	H	2B	3B	HR	TB	R	RBI	TBB	IBB	SO	HBP	SH	SF	SB	CS	SB%	GDP	Avg	OBP	SLG
1993 Burlington	R+ Cle	62	254	71	10	1	7	104	46	41	22	0	53	0	1	3	19	2	.90	4	.280	.333	.409
Kinston	A+ Cle	3	11	5	2	0	0	7	1	0	2	0	1	0	0	0	0	2	.00	0	.455	.538	.636
1994 Columbus	A Cle	118	450	127	20	1	7	170	77	57	69	0	72	5	6	0	21	7	.75	6	.282	.384	.378
1995 Norfolk	AAA NYN	5	14	6	1	0	0	7	1	0	2	0	2	0	0	0	1	1	.50	0	.429	.500	.500
Binghamton	AA NYN	24	86	17	5	0	0	22	10	8	11	0	25	2	3	0	1	1	.50	1	.198	.303	.256
St. Lucie	A+ NYN	91	306	73	5	1	2	86	35	20	36	1	55	7	11	0	14	9	.61	5	.239	.332	.281
1996 Columbia	A NYN	1	3	2	1	0	0	3	1	1	0	0	0	0	1	1	0	0	.00	0	.667	.500	1.000
Binghamton	AA NYN	86	249	59	16	0	2	81	36	26	45	1	33	1	3	1	5	6	.45	5	.237	.355	.325
4 Min. YEARS		390	1373	360	60	3	18	480	207	153	187	2	241	15	25	5	61	28	.69	21	.262	.356	.350

Brett Backlund

Pitches: Right **Bats:** Right **Pos:** P **Ht:** 6'0" **Wt:** 195 **Born:** 12/16/69 **Age:** 27

		HOW MUCH HE PITCHED						WHAT HE GAVE UP												THE RESULTS					
Year Team	Lg Org	G	GS	CG	GF	IP	BFP	H	R	ER	HR	SH	SF	HB	TBB	IBB	SO	WP	Bk	W	L	Pct.	ShO	Sv	ERA
1992 Augusta	A Pit	5	4	0	1	25	91	10	3	1	1	1	0	0	4	0	31	1	1	3	0	1.000	0	0	0.36
Carolina	AA Pit	3	3	0	0	19	71	11	6	4	0	1	1	0	3	0	17	0	1	1	1	.500	0	0	1.89
Buffalo	AAA Pit	4	4	2	0	25	101	15	8	6	2	0	0	0	11	0	9	0	0	3	0	1.000	0	0	2.16
1993 Buffalo	AAA Pit	5	5	0	0	21.1	109	30	25	25	5	3	1	2	14	0	10	0	0	0	4	.000	0	0	10.55
Carolina	AA Pit	20	20	0	0	106	457	115	66	54	22	1	4	2	28	3	94	7	2	7	5	.583	0	0	4.58
1994 Carolina	AA Pit	25	25	4	0	147	627	147	81	59	14	5	7	7	47	0	86	7	0	5	13	.278	0	0	3.61
1995 Calgary	AAA Pit	12	8	0	3	50	213	59	29	29	6	1	2	0	9	0	29	0	0	2	3	.400	0	0	5.22
Carolina	AA Pit	34	22	0	4	143	601	140	75	66	16	5	5	5	44	2	109	2	0	7	9	.438	0	0	4.15
1996 Calgary	AAA Pit	7	7	0	0	39	179	47	26	26	4	0	3	1	16	1	16	7	0	3	2	.600	0	0	6.00
Carolina	AA Pit	26	9	0	3	80.2	342	77	47	46	14	1	2	5	28	2	84	3	2	4	6	.400	0	0	5.13
5 Min. YEARS		141	107	6	11	656	2791	651	366	316	84	18	25	22	204	8	485	27	6	35	43	.449	0	0	4.34

Mike Badorek

Pitches: Right **Bats:** Right **Pos:** P **Ht:** 6'5" **Wt:** 230 **Born:** 5/15/69 **Age:** 28

		HOW MUCH HE PITCHED						WHAT HE GAVE UP												THE RESULTS					
Year Team	Lg Org	G	GS	CG	GF	IP	BFP	H	R	ER	HR	SH	SF	HB	TBB	IBB	SO	WP	Bk	W	L	Pct.	ShO	Sv	ERA
1991 Hamilton	A- StL	13	11	1	1	63.1	282	56	33	19	2	1	1	3	30	0	48	9	0	2	5	.286	0	0	2.70
1992 Springfield	A StL	29	28	1	0	187.1	780	175	74	61	6	3	4	9	39	1	119	10	0	17	8	.680	0	0	2.93
1993 St. Pete	A+ StL	29	28	2	1	170	712	170	76	65	6	4	5	4	53	1	60	3	0	15	7	.682	0	0	3.44
1994 Arkansas	AA StL	40	15	2	4	123.1	528	119	61	43	8	5	2	3	36	4	95	4	0	8	8	.500	0	0	3.14
1995 Arkansas	AA StL	18	17	4	1	101.1	446	119	61	49	4	4	5	3	30	0	50	2	0	7	5	.583	2	1	4.35
1996 Louisville	AAA StL	20	6	0	6	49.1	216	52	34	29	3	4	2	4	18	2	22	1	0	0	4	.000	0	0	5.29
6 Min. YEARS		149	105	10	13	694.2	2964	691	339	266	29	21	19	26	206	8	394	29	0	49	37	.570	2	1	3.45

Kevin Baez

Bats: Right **Throws:** Right **Pos:** SS-2B **Ht:** 5'11" **Wt:** 175 **Born:** 1/10/67 **Age:** 30

		BATTING															BASERUNNING				PERCENTAGES		
Year Team	Lg Org	G	AB	H	2B	3B	HR	TB	R	RBI	TBB	IBB	SO	HBP	SH	SF	SB	CS	SB%	GDP	Avg	OBP	SLG
1988 Little Fall	A- NYN	70	218	58	7	1	1	70	23	19	32	1	30	2	2	3	7	3	.70	3	.266	.361	.321
1989 Columbia	A NYN	123	426	108	25	1	5	150	59	44	58	3	53	6	9	3	11	9	.55	5	.254	.349	.352
1990 Jackson	AA NYN	106	327	76	11	0	2	93	29	29	37	4	44	2	11	2	3	4	.43	7	.232	.313	.284
1991 Tidewater	AAA NYN	65	210	36	8	0	0	44	18	13	12	1	32	4	5	4	0	1	.00	5	.171	.226	.210
1992 Tidewater	AAA NYN	109	352	83	16	1	2	107	30	33	13	1	57	4	5	5	1	1	.50	9	.236	.267	.304
1993 Norfolk	AAA NYN	63	209	54	11	1	2	73	23	21	20	1	29	1	2	1	0	2	.00	3	.258	.325	.349
1994 Rochester	AAA Bal	110	359	85	17	1	2	110	50	42	40	0	52	2	5	5	2	7	.22	13	.237	.313	.306
1995 Toledo	AAA Det	116	376	87	13	2	4	116	30	37	22	1	57	1	10	2	1	6	.14	13	.231	.274	.309
1996 Toledo	AAA Det	98	302	74	12	3	11	125	34	44	24	0	53	2	5	4	3	0	1.00	6	.245	.301	.414
1990 New York	NL	5	12	2	1	0	0	3	0	0	0	0	0	0	0	0	0	0	.00	2	.167	.167	.250
1992 New York	NL	6	13	2	0	0	0	2	0	0	0	0	0	0	0	0	0	0	.00	1	.154	.154	.154
1993 New York	NL	52	126	23	9	0	0	32	10	7	13	1	17	0	4	0	0	0	.00	1	.183	.259	.254
9 Min. YEARS		860	2779	661	120	10	29	888	296	282	258	12	407	24	54	29	28	33	.46	64	.238	.305	.320
3 Maj. YEARS		63	151	27	10	0	0	37	10	7	13	1	17	0	4	0	0	0	.00	4	.179	.244	.245

Scott Bakkum

Pitches: Right **Bats:** Right **Pos:** P **Ht:** 6'4" **Wt:** 205 **Born:** 11/20/69 **Age:** 27

		HOW MUCH HE PITCHED						WHAT HE GAVE UP												THE RESULTS					
Year Team	Lg Org	G	GS	CG	GF	IP	BFP	H	R	ER	HR	SH	SF	HB	TBB	IBB	SO	WP	Bk	W	L	Pct.	ShO	Sv	ERA
1992 Red Sox	R Bos	4	1	0	2	11	52	19	11	11	0	1	1	0	5	0	8	0	1	0	1	.000	0	0	9.00
Winter Havn	A+ Bos	5	4	2	0	27.2	109	19	9	9	1	3	1	1	10	0	10	0	0	1	3	.250	0	0	2.93
1993 Lynchburg	A+ Bos	26	26	6	0	169.2	717	201	87	71	23	1	3	2	31	0	98	7	2	12	11	.522	4	0	3.77
1994 Sarasota	A+ Bos	12	12	1	0	69	311	86	50	40	8	2	2	2	26	0	43	3	0	3	6	.333	0	0	5.22
New Britain	AA Bos	3	3	0	0	15	68	20	8	8	1	1	1	0	9	0	7	0	0	0	2	.000	0	0	4.80
Lynchburg	A+ Bos	11	8	0	1	44.2	206	58	39	35	3	1	1	0	18	0	37	1	0	1	6	.143	0	0	7.05
1995 Pawtucket	AAA Bos	15	0	0	4	26.1	114	21	13	5	3	0	1	2	7	0	15	4	0	1	0	1.000	0	2	1.71
Trenton	AA Bos	43	0	0	14	73.1	295	52	25	12	7	1	2	4	16	2	39	5	0	7	4	.636	0	2	1.47
1996 Pawtucket	AAA Bos	14	2	0	4	44.1	192	51	33	30	8	0	1	3	8	0	25	0	0	4	2	.667	0	0	6.09
Scranton-WB	AAA Phi	30	2	0	15	49	237	68	44	33	8	1	1	0	20	6	25	1	0	1	5	.167	0	6	6.06

		HOW MUCH HE PITCHED						WHAT HE GAVE UP												THE RESULTS					
Year Team	Lg Org	G	GS	CG	GF	IP	BFP	H	R	ER	HR	SH	SF	HB	TBB	IBB	SO	WP	Bk	W	L	Pct.	ShO	Sv	ERA
5 Min. YEARS		163	58	9	40	530	2301	595	319	254	62	11	14	14	150	8	307	21	3	30	40	.429	4	10	4.31

Paul Bako

Bats: Left **Throws:** Right **Pos:** C **Ht:** 6'2" **Wt:** 205 **Born:** 6/20/72 **Age:** 25

		BATTING															BASERUNNING				PERCENTAGES		
Year Team	Lg Org	G	AB	H	2B	3B	HR	TB	R	RBI	TBB	IBB	SO	HBP	SH	SF	SB	CS	SB%	GDP	Avg	OBP	SLG
1993 Billings	R+ Cin	57	194	61	11	0	4	84	34	30	22	0	37	1	1	3	5	1	.83	5	.314	.382	.433
1994 Winston-Sal	A+ Cin	90	289	59	9	1	3	79	29	26	35	0	81	4	8	0	2	2	.50	6	.204	.299	.273
1995 Winston-Sal	A+ Cin	82	249	71	11	2	7	107	29	27	42	6	66	1	6	1	3	1	.75	6	.285	.389	.430
1996 Chattanooga	AA Cin	110	360	106	27	0	8	157	53	48	48	5	93	5	2	4	1	0	1.00	5	.294	.381	.436
4 Min. YEARS		339	1092	297	58	3	22	427	145	131	147	11	277	11	17	8	11	4	.73	22	.272	.362	.391

Jeff Ball

Bats: Right **Throws:** Right **Pos:** 1B **Ht:** 5'10" **Wt:** 185 **Born:** 4/17/69 **Age:** 28

		BATTING															BASERUNNING				PERCENTAGES		
Year Team	Lg Org	G	AB	H	2B	3B	HR	TB	R	RBI	TBB	IBB	SO	HBP	SH	SF	SB	CS	SB%	GDP	Avg	OBP	SLG
1990 Auburn	A- Hou	70	263	76	18	1	5	111	40	38	22	1	35	4	3	5	20	5	.80	4	.289	.347	.422
1991 Osceola	A+ Hou	118	392	96	15	3	5	132	53	51	49	4	74	10	3	4	20	8	.71	9	.245	.341	.337
1992 Jackson	AA Hou	93	278	53	14	1	5	84	27	24	20	1	58	10	2	1	5	3	.63	9	.191	.269	.302
1993 Quad City	A Hou	112	389	114	28	2	14	188	68	76	58	3	63	7	1	5	40	19	.68	11	.293	.390	.483
1994 Jackson	AA Hou	111	358	113	30	3	13	188	65	57	34	3	74	5	5	3	9	8	.53	9	.316	.380	.525
1995 Tucson	AAA Hou	110	362	106	25	2	4	147	58	56	25	3	66	7	4	5	11	5	.69	13	.293	.346	.406
1996 Tucson	AAA Hou	116	429	139	31	2	19	231	64	73	34	1	83	1	0	1	10	8	.56	12	.324	.374	.538
7 Min. YEARS		730	2471	697	161	14	65	1081	375	375	242	16	453	44	18	24	115	56	.67	67	.282	.353	.437

Travis Baptist

Pitches: Left **Bats:** Both **Pos:** P **Ht:** 6'0" **Wt:** 190 **Born:** 12/30/71 **Age:** 25

		HOW MUCH HE PITCHED						WHAT HE GAVE UP												THE RESULTS					
Year Team	Lg Org	G	GS	CG	GF	IP	BFP	H	R	ER	HR	SH	SF	HB	TBB	IBB	SO	WP	Bk	W	L	Pct.	ShO	Sv	ERA
1991 Medicne Hat	R+ Tor	14	14	1	0	85.1	379	100	52	39	5	2	2	1	21	0	48	4	1	4	4	.500	1	0	4.11
1992 Myrtle Bch	A Tor	19	19	2	0	118	455	81	24	19	2	6	2	4	22	0	97	5	4	11	2	.846	1	0	1.45
1993 Knoxville	AA Tor	7	7	0	0	33	139	37	17	15	2	2	3	2	7	0	24	3	0	1	3	.250	0	0	4.09
1994 Syracuse	AAA Tor	24	22	1	0	122.2	539	145	80	62	20	3	4	0	33	2	42	6	2	8	8	.500	0	0	4.55
1995 Syracuse	AAA Tor	15	13	0	0	79	356	83	56	38	12	2	3	2	32	2	52	4	1	3	4	.429	0	0	4.33
1996 Syracuse	AAA Tor	30	21	2	1	141	633	187	91	85	15	5	10	2	48	2	77	7	2	7	6	.538	0	0	5.43
6 Min. YEARS		109	96	6	1	579	2501	633	320	258	56	20	24	11	163	6	340	29	10	34	27	.557	2	0	4.01

Marc Barcelo

Pitches: Right **Bats:** Right **Pos:** P **Ht:** 6'3" **Wt:** 210 **Born:** 1/10/72 **Age:** 25

		HOW MUCH HE PITCHED						WHAT HE GAVE UP												THE RESULTS					
Year Team	Lg Org	G	GS	CG	GF	IP	BFP	H	R	ER	HR	SH	SF	HB	TBB	IBB	SO	WP	Bk	W	L	Pct.	ShO	Sv	ERA
1993 Fort Myers	A+ Min	7	3	0	3	23	89	18	10	7	1	0	1	1	4	0	24	1	0	1	1	.500	0	0	2.74
Nashville	AA Min	2	2	0	0	9.1	42	9	5	4	2	1	1	1	5	0	5	1	1	1	0	1.000	0	0	3.86
1994 Nashville	AA Min	29	28	4	0	183.1	760	167	74	54	11	5	2	9	45	0	153	8	0	11	6	.647	0	0	2.65
1995 Salt Lake	AAA Min	28	28	2	0	143	684	214	131	112	19	5	5	6	59	2	63	4	2	8	13	.381	0	0	7.05
1996 Salt Lake	AAA Min	12	9	0	1	59.1	267	82	45	43	8	4	3	3	17	1	34	4	0	2	2	.500	0	0	6.52
New Britain	AA Min	14	13	3	1	80	377	98	53	45	7	2	5	4	38	0	59	5	0	3	8	.273	1	0	5.06
4 Min. YEARS		92	83	9	5	498	2219	588	318	265	48	17	17	24	168	3	338	23	3	26	30	.464	1	0	4.79

Mike Barger

Bats: Right **Throws:** Right **Pos:** OF **Ht:** 6'0" **Wt:** 165 **Born:** 4/6/71 **Age:** 26

		BATTING															BASERUNNING				PERCENTAGES		
Year Team	Lg Org	G	AB	H	2B	3B	HR	TB	R	RBI	TBB	IBB	SO	HBP	SH	SF	SB	CS	SB%	GDP	Avg	OBP	SLG
1993 Bellingham	A- Sea	68	203	53	7	3	0	66	30	21	26	1	26	5	3	1	14	6	.70	7	.261	.357	.325
1994 Appleton	A Sea	136	541	160	22	6	0	194	90	34	42	1	48	8	6	2	40	18	.69	9	.296	.354	.359
1995 Riverside	A+ Sea	82	344	109	10	1	2	127	77	41	38	1	45	2	5	1	33	14	.70	3	.317	.387	.369
1996 Port City	AA Sea	108	366	75	17	4	0	100	45	26	26	0	47	6	7	0	19	4	.83	9	.205	.269	.273
4 Min. YEARS		394	1454	397	56	14	2	487	242	122	132	3	166	21	21	4	106	42	.72	28	.273	.341	.335

Brian Bark

Pitches: Left **Bats:** Left **Pos:** P **Ht:** 5' 9" **Wt:** 170 **Born:** 8/26/68 **Age:** 28

		HOW MUCH HE PITCHED						WHAT HE GAVE UP												THE RESULTS					
Year Team	Lg Org	G	GS	CG	GF	IP	BFP	H	R	ER	HR	SH	SF	HB	TBB	IBB	SO	WP	Bk	W	L	Pct.	ShO	Sv	ERA
1990 Pulaski	R+ Atl	5	5	0	0	23.2	100	17	19	7	3	1	0	1	13	0	33	2	0	2	2	.500	0	0	2.66
1991 Durham	A+ Atl	13	13	0	0	82.1	330	66	23	23	0	3	2	6	24	0	76	4	3	4	3	.571	0	0	2.51
Greenville	AA Atl	9	3	1	2	17.2	79	19	10	7	0	0	0	2	8	1	15	3	1	2	1	.667	0	1	3.57
1992 Greenville	AA Atl	11	11	2	0	55	215	36	11	7	1	0	1	3	13	0	49	3	0	5	0	1.000	1	0	1.15
Richmond	AAA Atl	22	4	0	4	42	197	63	32	28	3	1	2	1	15	1	50	1	1	1	2	.333	0	2	6.00
1993 Richmond	AAA Atl	29	28	1	0	162	705	153	81	66	13	6	7	9	72	4	110	9	0	12	9	.571	1	0	3.67
1994 Richmond	AAA Atl	37	16	0	8	126.2	543	128	76	67	15	8	4	3	51	5	87	8	0	4	9	.308	0	0	4.76
1995 Richmond	AAA Atl	13	5	0	0	40.2	168	42	16	16	2	1	1	0	17	0	22	1	0	2	2	.500	0	0	3.54
Pawtucket	AAA Bos	43	5	0	15	72.1	291	63	24	24	3	2	2	1	31	0	43	4	0	5	3	.625	0	7	2.99

Year	Team	Lg	Org	G	GS	CG	GF	IP	BFP	H	R	ER	HR	SH	SF	HB	TBB	IBB	SO	WP	Bk	W	L	Pct.	ShO	Sv	ERA
	HOW MUCH HE PITCHED									WHAT HE GAVE UP												THE RESULTS					
1996	Norfolk	AAA	NYN	12	0	0	2	11.2	51	9	6	6	2	1	0	1	6	0	13	0	1	1	0	1.000	0	0	4.63
1995	Boston	AL		3	0	0	2	2.1	8	2	0	0	0	0	0	0	1	0	0	0	0	0	0	.000	0	0	0.00
7 Min. YEARS				194	90	4	31	634	2679	596	298	251	42	23	19	27	250	11	498	35	6	38	31	.551	2	10	3.56

Glen Barker

Bats: Right **Throws:** Right **Pos:** OF **Ht:** 5'10" **Wt:** 180 **Born:** 5/10/71 **Age:** 26

Year	Team	Lg	Org	G	AB	H	2B	3B	HR	TB	R	RBI	TBB	IBB	SO	HBP	SH	SF	SB	CS	SB%	GDP	Avg	OBP	SLG
	BATTING																		BASERUNNING				PERCENTAGES		
1993	Niagara Fal	A-	Det	72	253	55	11	4	5	89	49	23	24	0	71	4	2	3	37	12	.76	1	.217	.292	.352
1994	Fayettevlle	A	Det	74	267	61	13	5	1	87	38	30	33	0	79	9	2	1	41	13	.76	5	.228	.332	.326
	Lakeland	A+	Det	28	104	19	5	1	2	32	10	6	4	0	34	2	0	0	5	3	.63	2	.183	.227	.308
1995	Jacksonvlle	AA	Det	133	507	121	26	4	10	185	74	49	33	0	143	9	12	1	39	16	.71	1	.239	.296	.365
1996	Fayettevlle	A	Det	37	132	38	1	0	1	42	23	9	16	1	34	3	3	0	20	6	.77	2	.288	.377	.318
	Toledo	AAA	Det	24	80	20	2	1	0	24	13	2	9	0	25	0	2	0	6	6	.50	1	.250	.326	.300
	Jacksonvlle	AA	Det	43	120	19	2	1	0	23	9	8	8	0	36	0	2	0	6	4	.60	2	.158	.211	.192
4 Min. YEARS				411	1463	333	60	16	19	482	216	127	127	1	422	27	23	5	154	60	.72	14	.228	.300	.329

Tim Barker

Bats: Right **Throws:** Right **Pos:** 2B-SS **Ht:** 6'0" **Wt:** 175 **Born:** 6/30/68 **Age:** 29

Year	Team	Lg	Org	G	AB	H	2B	3B	HR	TB	R	RBI	TBB	IBB	SO	HBP	SH	SF	SB	CS	SB%	GDP	Avg	OBP	SLG
	BATTING																		BASERUNNING				PERCENTAGES		
1989	Great Falls	R+	LA	59	201	63	9	6	5	99	54	36	37	0	55	2	1	1	25	9	.74	2	.313	.423	.493
1990	Bakersfield	A+	LA	125	443	120	22	6	8	178	83	62	71	1	116	5	4	4	33	14	.70	7	.271	.375	.402
1991	San Antonio	AA	LA	119	401	117	20	4	2	151	70	46	80	2	61	6	8	5	32	13	.71	6	.292	.413	.377
1992	San Antonio	AA	LA	97	350	95	17	3	1	121	47	26	33	2	91	5	6	1	25	9	.74	2	.271	.342	.346
1993	Harrisburg	AA	Mon	49	185	57	10	1	4	81	40	16	30	0	32	2	6	2	7	4	.64	1	.308	.406	.438
	Ottawa	AAA	Mon	51	167	38	5	1	2	51	25	14	26	0	42	3	7	1	5	3	.63	3	.228	.340	.305
1994	New Orleans	AAA	Mil	128	436	115	25	7	5	169	71	44	76	2	97	6	10	1	41	17	.71	6	.264	.380	.388
1995	New Orleans	AAA	Mil	80	264	68	9	5	1	90	44	24	29	0	39	4	8	1	10	8	.56	2	.258	.339	.341
1996	Columbus	AAA	NYA	116	402	107	27	8	2	156	71	45	56	1	57	2	2	4	24	8	.75	3	.266	.356	.388
8 Min. YEARS				824	2849	780	144	41	30	1096	505	313	438	8	590	35	52	20	202	85	.70	32	.274	.375	.385

Brian Barkley

Pitches: Left **Bats:** Left **Pos:** P **Ht:** 6'2" **Wt:** 170 **Born:** 12/8/75 **Age:** 21

Year	Team	Lg	Org	G	GS	CG	GF	IP	BFP	H	R	ER	HR	SH	SF	HB	TBB	IBB	SO	WP	Bk	W	L	Pct.	ShO	Sv	ERA
	HOW MUCH HE PITCHED									WHAT HE GAVE UP												THE RESULTS					
1994	Red Sox	R	Bos	4	3	0	0	18.2	71	11	7	2	1	1	0	0	4	0	14	2	1	0	1	.000	0	0	0.96
1995	Sarasota	A+	Bos	24	24	2	0	146.2	611	147	66	53	5	2	3	5	37	3	70	4	1	8	10	.444	2	0	3.25
1996	Trenton	AA	Bos	22	21	0	0	119.2	535	126	79	76	17	6	5	5	56	4	89	7	2	8	8	.500	0	0	5.72
3 Min. YEARS				50	48	2	0	285	1217	284	152	131	23	9	8	10	97	7	173	13	4	16	19	.457	2	0	4.14

Brian Barnes

Pitches: Left **Bats:** Left **Pos:** P **Ht:** 5' 9" **Wt:** 170 **Born:** 3/25/67 **Age:** 30

Year	Team	Lg	Org	G	GS	CG	GF	IP	BFP	H	R	ER	HR	SH	SF	HB	TBB	IBB	SO	WP	Bk	W	L	Pct.	ShO	Sv	ERA
	HOW MUCH HE PITCHED									WHAT HE GAVE UP												THE RESULTS					
1989	Jamestown	A-	Mon	2	2	0	0	9	33	4	1	1	0	0	0	0	3	0	15	1	1	1	0	1.000	0	0	1.00
	W. Palm Bch	A+	Mon	7	7	4	0	50	187	25	9	4	0	3	1	0	16	0	67	4	0	4	3	.571	3	0	0.72
	Indianapols	AAA	Mon	1	1	0	0	6	24	5	1	1	0	0	0	0	2	0	5	0	0	1	0	1.000	0	0	1.50
1990	Jacksonvlle	AA	Mon	29	28	3	0	201.1	828	144	78	62	12	7	5	9	87	2	213	8	1	13	7	.650	1	0	2.77
1991	W. Palm Bch	A+	Mon	2	2	0	0	7	27	3	0	0	0	0	0	0	4	0	6	3	0	0	0	.000	0	0	0.00
	Indianapols	AAA	Mon	2	2	0	0	11	44	6	2	2	0	1	0	1	8	0	10	0	0	2	0	1.000	0	0	1.64
1992	Indianapols	AAA	Mon	13	13	2	0	83	338	69	35	34	8	1	2	1	30	1	77	2	2	4	4	.500	1	0	3.69
1994	Charlotte	AAA	Cle	13	0	0	2	18.1	80	17	10	8	2	0	0	1	8	2	23	1	0	0	1	.000	0	1	3.93
	Albuquerque	AAA	LA	9	9	0	0	47	221	57	38	33	9	0	1	1	23	2	44	1	0	5	1	.833	0	0	6.32
1995	Pawtucket	AAA	Bos	21	18	2	0	106.1	454	107	62	50	12	0	2	4	30	0	90	5	1	7	5	.583	0	0	4.23
1996	Jacksonvlle	AA	Det	13	12	1	0	74.2	320	74	37	31	8	6	1	4	25	1	74	3	0	4	6	.400	1	0	3.74
	Toledo	AAA	Det	14	13	2	0	88	373	85	49	39	8	0	1	4	29	0	70	6	1	6	6	.500	0	0	3.99
1990	Montreal	NL		4	4	1	0	28	115	25	10	9	2	2	0	0	7	0	23	2	0	1	1	.500	0	0	2.89
1991	Montreal	NL		28	27	1	0	160	684	135	82	75	16	9	5	6	84	2	117	5	1	5	8	.385	0	0	4.22
1992	Montreal	NL		21	17	0	2	100	417	77	34	33	9	5	1	3	46	1	65	1	2	6	6	.500	0	0	2.97
1993	Montreal	NL		52	8	0	8	100	442	105	53	49	9	8	3	0	48	2	60	5	1	2	6	.250	0	3	4.41
1994	Cleveland	AL		6	0	0	2	13.1	67	12	10	8	2	0	1	0	15	2	5	0	0	0	1	.000	0	0	5.40
	Los Angeles	NL		5	0	0	1	5	29	10	4	4	1	0	0	0	4	1	5	2	0	0	0	.000	0	0	7.20
7 Min. YEARS				126	107	14	2	701.2	2929	596	322	265	59	18	13	25	265	8	694	34	6	47	33	.588	6	1	3.40
5 Maj. YEARS				116	56	2	13	406.1	1754	364	193	178	39	24	10	9	204	8	275	15	4	14	22	.389	0	3	3.94

Manuel Barrios

Pitches: Right **Bats:** Right **Pos:** P **Ht:** 6'0" **Wt:** 145 **Born:** 9/21/74 **Age:** 22

Year	Team	Lg	Org	G	GS	CG	GF	IP	BFP	H	R	ER	HR	SH	SF	HB	TBB	IBB	SO	WP	Bk	W	L	Pct.	ShO	Sv	ERA
	HOW MUCH HE PITCHED									WHAT HE GAVE UP												THE RESULTS					
1994	Quad City	A	Hou	43	0	0	11	65	295	73	44	43	4	5	2	7	23	4	63	8	2	0	6	.000	0	4	5.95
1995	Quad City	A	Hou	50	0	0	48	52	219	44	16	13	1	2	1	4	17	1	55	1	0	1	5	.167	0	23	2.25

		HOW MUCH HE PITCHED						WHAT HE GAVE UP												THE RESULTS					
Year Team	Lg Org	G	GS	CG	GF	IP	BFP	H	R	ER	HR	SH	SF	HB	TBB	IBB	SO	WP	Bk	W	L	Pct.	ShO	Sv	ERA
1996 Jackson	AA Hou	60	0	0	53	68.1	298	60	29	18	4	4	2	3	29	5	69	3	0	6	4	.600	0	23	2.37
3 Min. YEARS		153	0	0	112	185.1	812	177	89	74	9	11	5	14	69	10	187	12	2	7	15	.318	0	50	3.59

Jeff Barry

Bats: Both **Throws:** Right **Pos:** 3B-OF **Ht:** 6' 0" **Wt:** 200 **Born:** 9/22/68 **Age:** 28

		BATTING															BASERUNNING				PERCENTAGES		
Year Team	Lg Org	G	AB	H	2B	3B	HR	TB	R	RBI	TBB	IBB	SO	HBP	SH	SF	SB	CS	SB%	GDP	Avg	OBP	SLG
1990 Jamestown	A- Mon	51	197	62	6	1	4	82	30	23	17	2	25	0	2	0	25	5	.83	1	.315	.369	.416
1991 W. Palm Bch	A+ Mon	116	437	92	16	3	4	126	47	31	34	4	67	4	2	2	20	14	.59	7	.211	.273	.288
1992 St. Lucie	A+ NYN	3	9	3	2	0	0	5	0	1	0	0	0	0	0	0	0	0	.00	0	.333	.333	.556
Mets	R NYN	8	23	4	1	0	0	5	5	2	6	1	2	0	0	0	2	0	1.00	1	.174	.345	.217
1993 St. Lucie	A+ NYN	114	420	108	17	5	4	147	68	50	49	4	37	5	2	6	17	14	.55	7	.257	.338	.350
1994 Binghamton	AA NYN	110	388	118	24	3	9	175	48	69	35	4	62	6	1	8	10	11	.48	10	.304	.364	.451
1995 Norfolk	AAA NYN	12	41	9	2	0	0	11	3	6	3	0	6	1	0	2	0	0	.00	2	.220	.277	.268
Binghamton	AA NYN	80	290	78	17	6	11	140	49	53	31	6	61	9	0	9	4	1	.80	4	.269	.348	.483
1996 Las Vegas	AAA SD	4	12	1	0	0	0	1	1	0	3	0	0	0	0	0	0	0	.00	0	.083	.267	.083
Memphis	AA SD	91	226	55	7	0	3	71	29	25	29	5	48	1	1	6	3	7	.30	6	.243	.324	.314
1995 New York	NL	15	15	2	1	0	0	3	2	0	1	0	8	0	0	0	0	0	.00	0	.133	.188	.200
7 Min. YEARS		589	2043	530	92	18	35	763	280	260	207	26	308	26	8	33	81	52	.61	38	.259	.330	.373

Juan Bautista

Bats: Right **Throws:** Right **Pos:** SS **Ht:** 6'0" **Wt:** 163 **Born:** 6/24/75 **Age:** 22

		BATTING															BASERUNNING				PERCENTAGES		
Year Team	Lg Org	G	AB	H	2B	3B	HR	TB	R	RBI	TBB	IBB	SO	HBP	SH	SF	SB	CS	SB%	GDP	Avg	OBP	SLG
1993 Albany	A Bal	98	295	70	17	2	0	91	24	28	14	0	72	7	3	4	11	3	.79	11	.237	.284	.308
1994 Orioles	R Bal	21	65	10	2	2	0	16	4	3	2	0	19	1	1	0	3	1	.75	3	.154	.191	.246
1995 Bowie	AA Bal	13	38	4	2	0	0	6	3	0	3	0	5	2	1	0	1	0	1.00	3	.105	.209	.158
High Desert	A+ Bal	99	374	98	13	4	11	152	54	51	18	0	74	7	6	3	22	9	.71	8	.262	.306	.406
1996 Bowie	AA Bal	129	441	103	18	3	3	136	35	33	21	1	102	5	8	2	15	12	.56	6	.234	.275	.308
4 Min. YEARS		360	1213	285	52	11	14	401	120	115	58	1	272	22	19	9	52	25	.68	31	.235	.280	.331

Bob Baxter

Pitches: Left **Bats:** Left **Pos:** P **Ht:** 6'1" **Wt:** 180 **Born:** 2/17/69 **Age:** 28

		HOW MUCH HE PITCHED						WHAT HE GAVE UP												THE RESULTS					
Year Team	Lg Org	G	GS	CG	GF	IP	BFP	H	R	ER	HR	SH	SF	HB	TBB	IBB	SO	WP	Bk	W	L	Pct.	ShO	Sv	ERA
1990 Jamestown	A- Mon	13	13	2	0	74.1	321	85	44	32	4	2	1	0	25	1	67	4	0	5	4	.556	0	0	3.87
1991 Rockford	A Mon	45	0	0	39	65	262	56	20	18	1	4	1	1	16	6	52	2	0	6	5	.545	0	19	2.49
W. Palm Bch	A+ Mon	1	0	0	0	1.1	8	4	3	3	0	0	0	0	0	0	1	0	0	0	0	.000	0	0	20.25
1992 W. Palm Bch	A+ Mon	42	0	0	27	63.2	231	46	12	10	1	2	1	0	9	1	54	2	0	6	2	.750	0	7	1.41
1993 W. Palm Bch	A+ Mon	33	0	0	18	59.1	232	55	20	15	1	4	4	0	5	1	29	2	1	2	2	.500	0	6	2.28
1994 Harrisburg	AA Mon	40	11	0	6	105	451	107	61	49	10	3	3	0	32	0	56	4	0	11	3	.786	0	0	4.20
1995 Ottawa	AAA Mon	39	13	0	10	101	426	125	51	44	6	4	5	0	25	1	39	3	0	5	5	.500	0	0	3.92
1996 Ottawa	AAA Mon	54	2	0	23	81.2	362	104	55	50	8	1	3	3	23	2	60	5	0	3	3	.500	0	3	5.51
7 Min. YEARS		267	39	2	123	551.1	2293	582	266	221	31	20	18	4	135	12	358	22	1	38	24	.613	0	35	3.61

Tony Beasley

Bats: Right **Throws:** Right **Pos:** OF **Ht:** 5'8" **Wt:** 165 **Born:** 12/5/66 **Age:** 30

		BATTING															BASERUNNING				PERCENTAGES		
Year Team	Lg Org	G	AB	H	2B	3B	HR	TB	R	RBI	TBB	IBB	SO	HBP	SH	SF	SB	CS	SB%	GDP	Avg	OBP	SLG
1989 Erie	A- Bal	65	247	69	12	2	1	88	39	14	25	0	31	4	5	0	19	4	.83	4	.279	.355	.356
1990 Frederick	A+ Bal	124	399	100	14	6	1	129	57	31	30	1	68	7	12	2	10	9	.53	6	.251	.313	.323
1991 Frederick	A+ Bal	124	387	96	11	10	1	130	50	34	27	0	74	6	6	3	29	8	.78	6	.248	.305	.336
1992 Salem	A+ Pit	72	237	62	10	2	7	97	34	25	16	0	44	3	2	1	12	4	.75	5	.262	.315	.409
Carolina	AA Pit	49	158	41	5	3	1	55	12	13	8	0	33	0	1	1	13	8	.62	0	.259	.293	.348
1993 Buffalo	AAA Pit	30	95	18	3	0	0	21	9	8	4	0	17	2	4	1	1	0	1.00	0	.189	.235	.221
Carolina	AA Pit	82	252	51	7	3	4	76	39	13	23	2	52	0	3	1	11	6	.65	10	.202	.268	.302
1995 Carolina	AA Pit	105	335	94	16	4	2	124	59	34	31	2	44	4	4	6	20	4	.83	6	.281	.343	.370
1996 Carolina	AA Pit	96	269	84	17	5	4	123	40	30	30	4	33	2	2	4	10	9	.53	5	.312	.380	.457
7 Min. YEARS		747	2379	615	95	35	21	843	339	202	194	9	396	28	39	19	125	52	.71	42	.259	.319	.354

Blaine Beatty

Pitches: Left **Bats:** Left **Pos:** P **Ht:** 6' 2" **Wt:** 185 **Born:** 4/25/64 **Age:** 33

		HOW MUCH HE PITCHED						WHAT HE GAVE UP												THE RESULTS					
Year Team	Lg Org	G	GS	CG	GF	IP	BFP	H	R	ER	HR	SH	SF	HB	TBB	IBB	SO	WP	Bk	W	L	Pct.	ShO	Sv	ERA
1986 Newark	A- Bal	15	15	8	0	119.1	475	98	37	28	6	5	2	1	30	3	93	6	0	11	3	.786	3	0	2.11
1987 Hagerstown	A+ Bal	13	13	4	0	100	389	81	32	28	7	3	1	1	11	0	65	5	0	11	1	.917	1	0	2.52
Charlotte	AA Bal	15	15	3	0	105.2	438	110	38	36	2	1	4	1	20	2	57	4	0	6	5	.545	1	0	3.07
1988 Jackson	AA NYN	30	28	12	1	208.2	824	191	64	57	13	12	6	0	34	3	103	3	7	16	8	.667	5	0	2.46
1989 Tidewater	AAA NYN	27	27	6	0	185	764	173	86	68	14	4	8	1	43	0	90	3	2	12	10	.545	3	0	3.31
1991 Tidewater	AAA NYN	28	28	3	0	175.1	750	192	86	80	18	7	4	5	43	6	74	0	1	12	9	.571	1	0	4.11
1992 Indianapolis	AAA Mon	26	12	2	3	94	412	109	52	45	8	4	4	1	24	3	54	4	1	7	5	.583	0	0	4.31
1993 Carolina	AA Pit	17	13	2	1	94.1	378	67	42	30	8	3	0	2	35	0	67	4	0	7	3	.700	0	0	2.86

				HOW MUCH HE PITCHED						WHAT HE GAVE UP												THE RESULTS					
Year	Team	Lg	Org	G	GS	CG	GF	IP	BFP	H	R	ER	HR	SH	SF	HB	TBB	IBB	SO	WP	Bk	W	L	Pct.	ShO	Sv	ERA
	Buffalo	AAA	Pit	20	4	0	5	36	168	51	25	22	2	2	2	2	8	0	14	3	0	2	3	.400	0	1	5.50
1994	Chattanooga	AA	Cin	27	26	6	1	196.1	770	146	66	52	15	6	3	8	43	0	162	4	0	14	7	.667	4	0	2.38
1995	Chattanooga	AA	Cin	8	8	1	0	52	225	60	22	20	2	3	3	1	17	2	34	2	1	3	2	.600	0	0	3.46
	Indianapols	AAA	Cin	28	16	1	1	119.1	518	140	55	47	9	7	4	3	33	2	71	5	3	10	3	.769	0	0	3.54
1996	Carolina	AA	Pit	23	22	1	0	145	594	135	58	53	15	3	3	4	34	6	117	3	2	11	5	.688	1	0	3.29
1989	New York	NL		2	1	0	0	6	25	5	1	1	1	0	0	0	2	0	3	0	0	0	0	.000	0	0	1.50
1991	New York	NL		5	0	0	1	9.2	42	9	3	3	0	1	1	0	4	1	7	1	0	0	0	.000	0	0	2.79
10 Min. YEARS				277	227	49	12	1631	6705	1553	663	566	119	60	44	30	375	27	1001	46	17	122	64	.656	19	1	3.12
2 Maj. YEARS				7	1	0	1	15.2	67	14	4	4	1	1	1	0	6	1	10	1	0	0	0	.000	0	0	2.30

Matt Beaumont

Pitches: Left **Bats:** Left **Pos:** P **Ht:** 6'3" **Wt:** 210 **Born:** 4/22/73 **Age:** 24

				HOW MUCH HE PITCHED						WHAT HE GAVE UP												THE RESULTS					
Year	Team	Lg	Org	G	GS	CG	GF	IP	BFP	H	R	ER	HR	SH	SF	HB	TBB	IBB	SO	WP	Bk	W	L	Pct.	ShO	Sv	ERA
1994	Boise	A-	Cal	12	10	0	0	64	268	52	27	25	2	4	2	7	22	1	77	3	0	3	3	.500	0	0	3.52
1995	Lk Elsinore	A+	Cal	27	26	0	0	175.1	724	162	80	64	15	1	6	7	57	1	149	1	1	16	9	.640	0	0	3.29
1996	Midland	AA	Cal	28	28	2	0	161.2	746	198	124	105	20	4	6	12	71	0	132	5	0	7	16	.304	0	0	5.85
3 Min. YEARS				67	64	2	0	401	1738	412	231	194	37	9	14	26	150	2	358	9	1	26	28	.481	0	0	4.35

Eric Bell

Pitches: Left **Bats:** Left **Pos:** P **Ht:** 6' 0" **Wt:** 165 **Born:** 10/27/63 **Age:** 33

				HOW MUCH HE PITCHED						WHAT HE GAVE UP												THE RESULTS					
Year	Team	Lg	Org	G	GS	CG	GF	IP	BFP	H	R	ER	HR	SH	SF	HB	TBB	IBB	SO	WP	Bk	W	L	Pct.	ShO	Sv	ERA
1984	Hagerstown	A+	Bal	3	1	0	0	3.2	23	6	4	4	0	0	1	1	5	0	6	0	0	0	0	.000	0	0	9.82
	Newark	A-	Bal	15	15	4	0	102.1	424	82	40	28	6	2	2	2	26	0	114	8	1	8	3	.727	1	0	2.46
1985	Hagerstown	A+	Bal	26	26	5	0	158.1	664	141	73	55	7	3	3	1	63	0	162	4	0	11	6	.647	2	0	3.13
1986	Charlotte	AA	Bal	18	18	6	0	129.2	539	109	49	44	7	3	1	1	66	0	104	5	0	9	6	.600	1	0	3.05
	Rochester	AAA	Bal	11	11	4	0	76.2	323	68	26	26	3	0	1	0	35	1	59	7	0	7	3	.700	0	0	3.05
1988	Rochester	AAA	Bal	7	7	0	0	36.1	148	28	10	8	0	3	1	0	13	0	33	1	2	3	1	.750	0	0	1.98
1989	Hagerstown	AA	Bal	9	7	0	1	43	170	32	11	9	3	1	0	1	11	1	35	0	1	4	2	.667	0	1	1.88
	Rochester	AAA	Bal	7	7	0	0	39.2	172	40	24	22	5	1	2	0	15	0	27	4	2	1	2	.333	0	0	4.99
1990	Rochester	AAA	Bal	27	27	3	0	148	667	168	90	80	16	4	8	9	65	0	90	11	1	9	6	.600	0	0	4.86
1991	Canton-Akrn	AA	Cle	18	16	1	0	93.1	402	82	47	30	1	3	5	2	37	1	84	6	0	9	5	.643	0	0	2.89
	Colo. Sprng	AAA	Cle	4	4	1	0	25.1	108	23	6	6	1	1	0	0	11	1	16	1	0	2	1	.667	1	0	2.13
1992	Colo. Sprng	AAA	Cle	26	18	5	8	137.2	575	161	64	57	10	5	4	0	30	1	56	6	2	10	7	.588	0	1	3.73
1993	Tucson	AAA	Hou	22	16	3	1	106.2	474	131	59	48	8	7	4	1	39	0	53	5	0	4	6	.400	1	0	4.05
1994	Tucson	AAA	Hou	30	29	0	1	171.1	769	209	112	85	12	7	11	6	60	1	82	4	2	8	8	.500	0	0	4.46
1995	Buffalo	AAA	Cle	28	24	3	1	161.1	687	177	76	70	18	1	4	7	47	0	86	3	0	13	9	.591	1	0	3.90
1996	Tucson	AAA	Hou	30	21	1	4	127.1	599	177	114	80	7	6	9	1	48	4	58	4	0	4	14	.222	0	0	5.65
1985	Baltimore	AL		4	0	0	3	5.2	24	4	3	3	1	0	0	0	4	0	4	0	0	0	0	.000	0	0	4.76
1986	Baltimore	AL		4	4	0	0	23.1	105	23	14	13	4	1	1	0	14	0	18	0	0	1	2	.333	0	0	5.01
1987	Baltimore	AL		33	29	2	1	165	729	174	113	100	32	4	2	2	78	0	111	11	1	10	13	.435	0	0	5.45
1991	Cleveland	AL		10	0	0	3	18	61	5	2	1	0	0	0	1	5	0	7	0	0	4	0	1.000	0	0	0.50
1992	Cleveland	AL		7	1	0	2	15.1	75	22	13	13	1	1	1	1	9	0	10	1	0	0	2	.000	0	0	7.63
1993	Houston	NL		10	0	0	2	7.1	34	10	5	5	0	0	0	0	2	0	2	0	0	0	1	.000	0	0	6.14
12 Min. YEARS				281	247	36	16	1560.2	6744	1634	805	652	104	47	56	32	571	10	1065	69	11	102	79	.564	7	2	3.76
6 Maj. YEARS				68	34	2	11	234.2	1028	238	150	135	38	6	4	4	112	0	152	12	1	15	18	.455	0	0	5.18

Jason Bell

Pitches: Right **Bats:** Right **Pos:** P **Ht:** 6'3" **Wt:** 205 **Born:** 9/30/74 **Age:** 22

				HOW MUCH HE PITCHED						WHAT HE GAVE UP												THE RESULTS					
Year	Team	Lg	Org	G	GS	CG	GF	IP	BFP	H	R	ER	HR	SH	SF	HB	TBB	IBB	SO	WP	Bk	W	L	Pct.	ShO	Sv	ERA
1995	Fort Wayne	A	Min	9	6	0	2	34.1	139	26	11	5	0	3	0	1	6	0	40	6	2	3	1	.750	0	0	1.31
1996	Fort Myers	A+	Min	13	13	0	0	90.1	350	61	20	17	1	4	2	6	22	0	83	3	0	6	3	.667	0	0	1.69
	New Britain	AA	Min	16	16	2	0	94	410	93	54	46	13	5	2	5	38	1	94	6	1	2	6	.250	1	0	4.40
2 Min. YEARS				38	35	2	2	218.2	899	180	85	68	14	12	4	12	66	1	217	15	3	11	10	.524	1	0	2.80

Juan Bell

Bats: Both **Throws:** Right **Pos:** 2B **Ht:** 5'11" **Wt:** 170 **Born:** 3/29/68 **Age:** 29

				BATTING															BASERUNNING				PERCENTAGES		
Year	Team	Lg	Org	G	AB	H	2B	3B	HR	TB	R	RBI	TBB	IBB	SO	HBP	SH	SF	SB	CS	SB%	GDP	Avg	OBP	SLG
1985	Dodgers	R	LA	42	106	17	0	0	0	17	11	8	12	0	20	1	2	0	2	1	.67	1	.160	.252	.160
1986	Dodgers	R	LA	59	217	52	6	2	0	62	38	26	29	1	28	1	0	3	12	2	.86	2	.240	.328	.286
1987	Bakersfield	A+	LA	134	473	116	15	3	4	149	54	58	43	3	91	3	7	5	21	7	.75	4	.245	.309	.315
1988	San Antonio	AA	LA	61	215	60	4	2	5	83	37	21	16	2	37	2	3	1	11	3	.79	3	.279	.333	.386
	Albuquerque	AAA	LA	73	257	77	9	3	8	116	42	45	16	1	70	1	6	3	7	10	.41	3	.300	.339	.451
1989	Rochester	AAA	Bal	116	408	107	15	6	2	140	50	32	39	0	92	1	2	4	17	10	.63	8	.262	.325	.343
1990	Rochester	AAA	Bal	82	326	93	12	5	6	133	59	35	36	1	59	3	0	2	16	12	.57	9	.285	.360	.408
1992	Rochester	AAA	Bal	39	138	27	6	3	2	45	21	14	14	0	40	0	2	3	2	4	.33	3	.196	.265	.326
	Okla. City	AAA	Bal	24	82	21	4	1	1	30	12	9	4	0	19	0	0	0	2	0	1.00	0	.256	.291	.366
1994	W. Palm Bch	A+	Mon	5	20	4	1	0	1	8	1	3	3	0	2	0	0	0	0	0	.00	0	.200	.304	.400
	Harrisburg	AA	Mon	11	45	13	4	2	0	21	7	6	9	0	6	0	1	0	1	1	.50	0	.289	.407	.467
	Ottawa	AAA	Mon	7	24	6	1	0	0	7	5	1	4	0	6	0	0	0	1	2	.33	0	.250	.357	.292

Year Team	Lg Org	G	AB	H	2B	3B	HR	TB	R	RBI	TBB	IBB	SO	HBP	SH	SF	SB	CS	SB%	GDP	Avg	OBP	SLG
		BATTING															BASERUNNING				PERCENTAGES		
1995 Pawtucket	AAA Bos	68	262	69	18	1	6	107	42	23	21	0	46	0	1	0	4	5	.44	7	.263	.318	.408
1996 Pawtucket	AAA Bos	68	210	52	13	2	5	84	28	23	22	0	43	0	5	2	2	2	.50	5	.248	.316	.400
1989 Baltimore	AL	8	4	0	0	0	0	0	2	0	0	0	1	0	0	0	1	0	1.00	0	.000	.000	.000
1990 Baltimore	AL	5	2	0	0	0	0	0	1	0	0	0	1	0	0	0	0	0	.00	0	.000	.000	.000
1991 Baltimore	AL	100	209	36	9	2	1	52	26	15	8	0	51	0	4	2	0	0	.00	1	.172	.201	.249
1992 Philadelphia	NL	46	147	30	3	1	1	38	12	8	18	5	29	1	0	2	5	0	1.00	1	.204	.292	.259
1993 Philadelphia	NL	24	65	13	6	1	0	21	5	7	5	0	12	1	2	0	0	1	.00	0	.200	.268	.323
Milwaukee	AL	91	286	67	6	2	5	92	42	29	36	0	64	1	3	1	6	6	.50	4	.234	.321	.322
1994 Montreal	NL	38	97	27	4	0	2	37	12	10	15	0	21	0	1	1	4	0	1.00	1	.278	.372	.381
1995 Boston	AL	17	26	4	2	0	1	9	7	2	2	0	10	0	0	1	0	0	.00	0	.154	.207	.346
10 Min. YEARS		789	2783	714	108	30	40	1002	407	304	268	8	559	12	29	23	98	59	.62	45	.257	.322	.360
7 Maj. YEARS		329	836	177	30	6	10	249	107	71	84	5	189	3	10	7	16	7	.70	7	.212	.284	.298

Mike Bell

Bats: Right **Throws:** Right **Pos:** 3B **Ht:** 6'2" **Wt:** 185 **Born:** 12/7/74 **Age:** 22

Year Team	Lg Org	G	AB	H	2B	3B	HR	TB	R	RBI	TBB	IBB	SO	HBP	SH	SF	SB	CS	SB%	GDP	Avg	OBP	SLG
		BATTING															BASERUNNING				PERCENTAGES		
1993 Rangers	R Tex	60	230	73	13	6	3	107	48	34	27	0	23	4	1	2	9	2	.82	2	.317	.395	.465
1994 Charlstn-SC	A Tex	120	475	125	22	6	6	177	58	58	47	1	76	3	1	6	16	12	.57	14	.263	.330	.373
1995 Charlotte	A+ Tex	129	470	122	20	1	5	159	49	52	48	0	72	0	3	2	9	8	.53	11	.260	.327	.338
1996 Tulsa	AA Tex	128	484	129	31	3	16	214	62	59	42	1	75	3	4	0	3	1	.75	13	.267	.329	.442
4 Min. YEARS		437	1659	449	86	16	30	657	217	203	164	2	246	10	9	10	37	23	.62	40	.271	.338	.396

Mark Bellhorn

Bats: Both **Throws:** Right **Pos:** 2B-SS **Ht:** 6'1" **Wt:** 195 **Born:** 8/23/74 **Age:** 22

Year Team	Lg Org	G	AB	H	2B	3B	HR	TB	R	RBI	TBB	IBB	SO	HBP	SH	SF	SB	CS	SB%	GDP	Avg	OBP	SLG
		BATTING															BASERUNNING				PERCENTAGES		
1995 Modesto	A+ Oak	56	229	59	12	0	6	89	35	31	27	0	52	4	2	0	5	2	.71	9	.258	.346	.389
1996 Huntsville	AA Oak	131	468	117	24	5	10	181	84	71	73	7	124	4	7	4	19	2	.90	7	.250	.353	.387
2 Min. YEARS		187	697	176	36	5	16	270	119	102	100	7	176	8	9	4	24	4	.86	16	.253	.351	.387

Ronnie Belliard

Bats: Right **Throws:** Right **Pos:** 2B **Ht:** 5'9" **Wt:** 176 **Born:** 7/4/76 **Age:** 20

Year Team	Lg Org	G	AB	H	2B	3B	HR	TB	R	RBI	TBB	IBB	SO	HBP	SH	SF	SB	CS	SB%	GDP	Avg	OBP	SLG
		BATTING															BASERUNNING				PERCENTAGES		
1994 Brewers	R Mil	39	143	42	7	3	0	55	32	27	14	1	25	3	2	1	7	0	1.00	3	.294	.366	.385
1995 Beloit	A Mil	130	461	137	28	5	13	214	76	76	36	2	67	7	2	1	16	12	.57	10	.297	.356	.464
1996 El Paso	AA Mil	109	416	116	20	8	3	161	73	57	60	1	51	4	4	3	26	10	.72	11	.279	.373	.387
3 Min. YEARS		278	1020	295	55	16	16	430	181	160	110	4	143	14	8	5	49	22	.69	24	.289	.365	.422

Clay Bellinger

Bats: Right **Throws:** Right **Pos:** SS **Ht:** 6'3" **Wt:** 195 **Born:** 11/18/68 **Age:** 28

Year Team	Lg Org	G	AB	H	2B	3B	HR	TB	R	RBI	TBB	IBB	SO	HBP	SH	SF	SB	CS	SB%	GDP	Avg	OBP	SLG
		BATTING															BASERUNNING				PERCENTAGES		
1989 Everett	A- SF	51	185	37	8	1	4	59	29	16	19	0	47	1	1	0	3	2	.60	4	.200	.278	.319
1990 Clinton	A SF	109	382	83	17	4	10	138	52	48	28	0	102	7	5	3	13	6	.68	5	.217	.281	.361
1991 San Jose	A+ SF	105	368	95	29	2	8	152	65	62	53	3	88	11	7	6	13	4	.76	3	.258	.363	.413
1992 Shreveport	AA SF	126	433	90	18	3	13	153	45	50	36	1	82	3	4	4	7	8	.47	15	.208	.271	.353
1993 Phoenix	AAA SF	122	407	104	20	3	6	148	50	49	38	4	81	4	7	5	7	7	.50	8	.256	.322	.364
1994 Phoenix	AAA SF	106	337	90	15	1	7	128	48	50	18	0	56	7	2	3	6	1	.86	8	.267	.315	.380
1995 Phoenix	AAA SF	97	277	76	16	1	2	100	34	32	27	1	52	2	2	3	3	2	.60	5	.274	.340	.361
1996 Rochester	AAA Bal	125	459	138	34	4	15	225	68	78	33	0	90	6	1	11	8	4	.67	6	.301	.348	.490
8 Min. YEARS		841	2848	713	157	19	65	1103	391	385	252	9	598	41	29	35	60	34	.64	54	.250	.317	.387

Alonso Beltran

Pitches: Right **Bats:** Right **Pos:** P **Ht:** 6'3" **Wt:** 180 **Born:** 3/4/72 **Age:** 25

Year Team	Lg Org	G	GS	CG	GF	IP	BFP	H	R	ER	HR	SH	SF	HB	TBB	IBB	SO	WP	Bk	W	L	Pct.	ShO	Sv	ERA
		HOW MUCH HE PITCHED						WHAT HE GAVE UP												THE RESULTS					
1991 Blue Jays	R Tor	14	3	0	7	33	126	26	9	7	0	1	3	1	7	0	30	1	1	2	0	1.000	0	3	1.91
1992 Medicne Hat	R+ Tor	15	15	1	0	91.2	378	78	46	32	7	4	3	7	25	0	66	4	2	4	5	.444	0	0	3.14
1993 St. Cathrns	A- Tor	15	15	1	0	99	392	63	36	26	4	1	3	6	28	0	101	2	0	11	2	.846	1	0	2.36
1994 Dunedin	A+ Tor	7	5	0	0	25.1	109	22	13	13	4	0	2	1	10	0	10	1	0	2	1	.667	0	0	4.62
1995 Knoxville	AA Tor	28	6	0	7	87	399	111	60	55	8	3	4	5	32	0	54	6	2	3	6	.333	0	1	5.69
1996 Winston-Sal	A+ Cin	14	1	0	4	38.1	148	26	9	8	2	2	0	1	10	1	26	1	2	2	1	.667	0	0	1.88
Chattanooga	AA Cin	3	3	0	0	13.1	62	18	13	12	2	0	0	1	6	0	10	0	0	0	1	.000	0	0	8.10
6 Min. YEARS		96	48	2	18	387.2	1614	344	186	153	27	11	15	22	118	1	297	15	7	24	16	.600	1	4	3.55

Rigo Beltran

Pitches: Left **Bats:** Left **Pos:** P **Ht:** 5'11" **Wt:** 185 **Born:** 11/13/69 **Age:** 27

Year Team	Lg Org	G	GS	CG	GF	IP	BFP	H	R	ER	HR	SH	SF	HB	TBB	IBB	SO	WP	Bk	W	L	Pct.	ShO	Sv	ERA
		HOW MUCH HE PITCHED						WHAT HE GAVE UP												THE RESULTS					
1991 Hamilton	A- StL	21	4	0	4	48	206	41	17	14	4	4	2	2	19	0	69	3	12	5	2	.714	0	0	2.63

Year	Team	Lg	Org	G	GS	CG	GF	IP	BFP	H	R	ER	HR	SH	SF	HB	TBB	IBB	SO	WP	Bk	W	L	Pct.	ShO	Sv	ERA
				HOW MUCH HE PITCHED						WHAT HE GAVE UP												THE RESULTS					
1992	Savannah	A	StL	13	13	2	0	83	316	38	20	20	4	1	0	4	40	0	106	8	6	6	1	.857	1	0	2.17
	St. Pete	A+	StL	2	2	0	0	8	30	6	0	0	0	1	0	0	2	0	3	0	0	0	0	.000	0	0	0.00
1993	Arkansas	AA	StL	18	16	0	1	88.2	376	74	39	32	8	5	0	6	38	1	82	11	4	5	5	.500	0	0	3.25
1994	Arkansas	AA	StL	4	4	1	0	28	95	12	3	2	2	1	0	0	3	0	21	0	0	4	0	1.000	1	0	0.64
	Louisville	AAA	StL	23	23	1	0	138.1	624	147	82	78	15	7	7	5	68	2	87	18	5	11	11	.500	0	0	5.07
1995	Louisville	AAA	StL	24	24	0	0	129.2	575	156	81	75	12	2	8	5	34	0	92	4	2	8	9	.471	0	0	5.21
1996	Louisville	AAA	StL	38	16	3	5	130.1	548	132	67	63	17	2	4	5	24	1	132	8	1	8	6	.571	1	0	4.35
6	Min. YEARS			143	102	7	10	654	2770	606	309	284	62	23	21	27	228	4	592	52	30	47	34	.580	3	0	3.91

Freddie Benavides

Bats: Right **Throws:** Right **Pos:** SS **Ht:** 6' 2" **Wt:** 185 **Born:** 4/7/66 **Age:** 31

Year	Team	Lg	Org	G	AB	H	2B	3B	HR	TB	R	RBI	TBB	IBB	SO	HBP	SH	SF	SB	CS	SB%	GDP	Avg	OBP	SLG
				BATTING															BASERUNNING				PERCENTAGES		
1987	Cedar Rapds	A	Cin	5	15	2	1	0	0	3	2	0	0	0	7	0	0	0	0	1	.00	1	.133	.133	.200
1988	Cedar Rapds	A	Cin	88	314	70	9	2	1	86	38	32	35	3	75	2	4	4	18	7	.72	7	.223	.301	.274
1989	Chattanooga	AA	Cin	88	284	71	14	3	0	91	25	27	22	0	46	2	2	3	1	4	.20	2	.250	.305	.320
	Nashville	AAA	Cin	31	94	16	4	0	1	23	9	12	6	0	24	0	1	0	0	0	.00	1	.170	.220	.245
1990	Chattanooga	AA	Cin	55	197	51	10	1	1	66	20	28	11	0	25	2	3	2	4	2	.67	4	.259	.302	.335
	Nashville	AAA	Cin	77	266	56	7	3	2	75	30	20	12	3	50	3	4	1	3	1	.75	4	.211	.252	.282
1991	Nashville	AAA	Cin	94	331	80	8	0	0	88	24	21	16	3	55	0	3	0	7	7	.50	10	.242	.277	.266
1993	Colo. Sprng	AAA	Col	5	16	7	1	0	0	8	3	2	1	0	0	0	0	0	0	0	.00	0	.438	.471	.500
1995	Iowa	AAA	ChN	106	315	76	14	4	4	110	30	26	25	0	47	5	1	1	2	3	.40	12	.241	.306	.349
1996	Columbus	AAA	NYA	1	4	0	0	0	0	0	0	1	0	0	0	0	0	0	0	0	.00	0	.000	.000	.000
1991	Cincinnati	NL		24	63	18	1	0	0	19	11	3	1	1	15	1	1	1	1	0	1.00	1	.286	.303	.302
1992	Cincinnati	NL		74	173	40	10	1	1	55	14	17	10	4	34	1	2	0	0	1	.00	3	.231	.277	.318
1993	Colorado	NL		74	213	61	10	3	3	86	20	26	6	1	27	0	3	1	3	2	.60	4	.286	.305	.404
1994	Montreal	NL		47	85	16	5	1	0	23	8	6	3	1	15	1	0	1	0	0	.00	2	.188	.222	.271
8	Min. YEARS			550	1836	429	68	13	9	550	181	169	128	9	329	14	18	11	35	25	.58	41	.234	.287	.300
4	Maj. YEARS			219	534	135	26	5	4	183	53	52	20	7	91	3	6	3	4	3	.57	10	.253	.282	.343

Lou Benbow

Bats: Right **Throws:** Right **Pos:** 3B **Ht:** 6'0" **Wt:** 167 **Born:** 1/12/71 **Age:** 26

Year	Team	Lg	Org	G	AB	H	2B	3B	HR	TB	R	RBI	TBB	IBB	SO	HBP	SH	SF	SB	CS	SB%	GDP	Avg	OBP	SLG
				BATTING															BASERUNNING				PERCENTAGES		
1991	St. Cathrns	A-	Tor	54	147	26	0	0	0	26	13	4	18	0	40	6	9	0	6	7	.46	1	.177	.292	.177
1992	St. Cathrns	A-	Tor	50	171	29	10	0	0	39	8	5	11	0	43	1	2	1	1	0	1.00	4	.170	.223	.228
1993	Hagerstown	A	Tor	71	193	32	5	2	1	44	22	12	13	0	47	2	2	2	2	1	.67	4	.166	.224	.228
1994	Dunedin	A+	Tor	28	69	8	3	0	0	11	7	5	6	0	17	2	1	0	1	2	.33	4	.116	.208	.159
	St. Lucie	A+	NYN	15	34	9	1	0	0	10	2	3	10	0	10	1	2	0	1	2	.33	0	.265	.444	.294
1995	Binghamton	AA	NYN	3	1	1	0	0	0	1	0	0	1	0	0	0	0	0	0	0	.00	0	1.000	1.000	1.000
	St. Lucie	A+	NYN	12	33	12	2	0	0	14	4	2	1	0	7	1	1	0	0	1	.00	0	.364	.400	.424
	Durham	A+	Atl	82	245	54	7	0	4	73	20	17	11	0	53	3	3	0	2	3	.40	8	.220	.263	.298
1996	Richmond	AAA	Atl	91	250	58	8	0	1	69	21	23	16	1	65	0	1	3	3	4	.43	6	.232	.275	.276
6	Min. YEARS			406	1143	229	36	2	6	287	97	71	87	1	282	16	21	6	16	20	.44	27	.200	.265	.251

Bob Bennett

Pitches: Right **Bats:** Right **Pos:** P **Ht:** 6'4" **Wt:** 205 **Born:** 12/30/70 **Age:** 26

Year	Team	Lg	Org	G	GS	CG	GF	IP	BFP	H	R	ER	HR	SH	SF	HB	TBB	IBB	SO	WP	Bk	W	L	Pct.	ShO	Sv	ERA
				HOW MUCH HE PITCHED						WHAT HE GAVE UP												THE RESULTS					
1992	Sou. Oregon	A-	Oak	17	6	0	3	48	222	60	41	31	4	1	0	2	20	0	41	4	1	2	6	.250	0	2	5.81
1993	Madison	A	Oak	26	17	0	3	107	435	103	45	39	7	0	1	1	23	3	102	4	1	7	8	.467	0	1	3.28
1994	W. Michigan	A	Oak	6	4	0	1	24.2	103	23	8	6	1	2	0	2	6	0	23	0	0	0	2	.000	0	1	2.19
	Modesto	A+	Oak	20	10	0	4	80.2	332	75	31	27	2	1	0	1	25	0	71	5	1	8	2	.800	0	0	3.01
1995	Huntsville	AA	Oak	23	21	0	0	117.1	482	119	62	55	13	4	3	3	28	0	70	3	1	10	7	.588	0	0	4.22
1996	Huntsville	AA	Oak	38	2	0	12	83.2	380	92	55	49	10	6	1	4	36	7	83	4	0	5	3	.625	0	0	5.27
5	Min. YEARS			130	60	0	23	461.1	1954	472	242	207	37	14	5	13	138	10	390	20	4	32	28	.533	0	4	4.04

Joel Bennett

Pitches: Right **Bats:** Right **Pos:** P **Ht:** 6' 1" **Wt:** 160 **Born:** 1/31/70 **Age:** 27

Year	Team	Lg	Org	G	GS	CG	GF	IP	BFP	H	R	ER	HR	SH	SF	HB	TBB	IBB	SO	WP	Bk	W	L	Pct.	ShO	Sv	ERA
				HOW MUCH HE PITCHED						WHAT HE GAVE UP												THE RESULTS					
1991	Red Sox	R	Bos	2	2	0	0	10	38	6	2	2	0	0	1	1	4	0	8	2	1	0	0	.000	0	0	1.80
	Elmira	A-	Bos	13	12	1	0	81	325	60	29	22	3	3	1	6	30	0	75	7	0	5	3	.625	1	0	2.44
1992	Winter Havn	A+	Bos	26	26	4	0	161.2	690	161	86	76	7	7	5	7	55	2	154	7	3	7	11	.389	0	0	4.23
1993	Lynchburg	A+	Bos	29	29	3	0	181	754	151	93	77	17	7	9	4	67	6	221	18	0	7	12	.368	1	0	3.83
1994	New Britain	AA	Bos	23	23	1	0	130.2	560	119	65	59	9	2	2	4	56	0	130	10	0	11	7	.611	1	0	4.06
	Pawtucket	AAA	Bos	4	4	0	0	21	91	19	16	16	8	0	0	1	12	0	24	1	0	1	3	.250	0	0	6.86
1995	Pawtucket	AAA	Bos	20	13	0	2	77	357	91	57	50	6	0	4	3	45	3	50	6	0	2	4	.333	0	0	5.84
1996	Trenton	AA	Bos	3	0	0	1	4.1	18	3	4	4	2	0	0	0	2	0	8	0	0	1	0	1.000	0	0	8.31
	Newburgh	IND	—	9	9	2	0	57	211	18	8	5	2	0	1	2	16	0	82	3	0	6	0	1.000	2	0	0.79
	Bowie	AA	Bal	10	8	0	0	54.2	211	36	21	20	5	0	0	1	17	0	48	0	0	2	3	.400	0	0	3.29
6	Min. YEARS			139	126	11	3	778.1	3255	664	381	331	59	19	23	29	304	11	800	54	4	42	43	.494	5	0	3.83

Pitches: Right **Bats:** Right **Pos:** P

Shayne Bennett

Ht: 6'5" **Wt:** 200 **Born:** 4/10/72 **Age:** 25

				HOW MUCH HE PITCHED						WHAT HE GAVE UP												THE RESULTS					
Year	Team	Lg	Org	G	GS	CG	GF	IP	BFP	H	R	ER	HR	SH	SF	HB	TBB	IBB	SO	WP	Bk	W	L	Pct.	ShO	Sv	ERA
1993	Red Sox	R	Bos	2	1	0	1	7	25	2	1	1	1	0	0	0	1	0	4	1	0	0	0	.000	0	1	1.29
	Ft. Laud	A+	Bos	23	0	0	18	31.1	128	26	8	6	1	4	1	0	11	1	23	2	2	1	2	.333	0	6	1.72
1994	Sarasota	A+	Bos	15	8	0	4	48.1	216	46	31	24	1	2	1	3	27	0	28	1	1	1	6	.143	0	3	4.47
1995	Trenton	AA	Bos	10	0	0	6	10.2	48	16	6	6	0	3	1	0	3	0	6	1	0	0	1	.000	0	3	5.06
	Sarasota	A+	Bos	62	0	0	49	70.1	303	66	29	23	3	7	3	4	24	4	75	6	1	2	6	.250	0	27	2.94
1996	Harrisburg	AA	Mon	53	0	0	27	92.2	393	83	32	26	6	3	3	5	35	2	89	2	2	8	8	.500	0	12	2.53
4 Min. YEARS				165	9	0	105	260.1	1113	239	107	86	12	19	9	12	101	7	225	13	6	12	23	.343	0	52	2.97

Pitches: Left **Bats:** Left **Pos:** P

Jacob Benz

Ht: 5'9" **Wt:** 162 **Born:** 2/27/72 **Age:** 25

				HOW MUCH HE PITCHED						WHAT HE GAVE UP												THE RESULTS					
Year	Team	Lg	Org	G	GS	CG	GF	IP	BFP	H	R	ER	HR	SH	SF	HB	TBB	IBB	SO	WP	Bk	W	L	Pct.	ShO	Sv	ERA
1994	Vermont	A-	Mon	28	0	0	12	46	188	24	11	8	1	1	2	4	19	3	36	1	0	4	1	.800	0	3	1.57
1995	W. Palm Bch	A+	Mon	44	0	0	38	54	220	44	13	7	0	3	2	3	18	3	48	4	1	0	2	.000	0	22	1.17
1996	Harrisburg	AA	Mon	34	0	0	20	37.2	181	42	30	25	7	3	2	2	27	3	25	4	0	1	4	.200	0	4	5.97
	W. Palm Bch	A+	Mon	17	0	0	9	20.1	93	19	10	5	0	4	0	0	11	1	14	7	0	2	4	.333	0	2	2.21
3 Min. YEARS				123	0	0	79	158	682	129	64	45	8	11	6	9	75	10	123	16	1	7	11	.389	0	31	2.56

Bats: Right **Throws:** Right **Pos:** 2B

Jeff Berblinger

Ht: 6'0" **Wt:** 190 **Born:** 11/19/70 **Age:** 26

				BATTING															BASERUNNING				PERCENTAGES		
Year	Team	Lg	Org	G	AB	H	2B	3B	HR	TB	R	RBI	TBB	IBB	SO	HBP	SH	SF	SB	CS	SB%	GDP	Avg	OBP	SLG
1993	Glens Falls	A-	StL	38	138	43	9	0	2	58	26	21	11	0	14	3	1	3	9	4	.69	2	.312	.368	.420
	St. Pete	A+	StL	19	70	13	1	0	0	14	7	5	5	0	10	1	2	0	3	1	.75	1	.186	.250	.200
1994	Savannah	A	StL	132	479	142	27	7	8	207	86	67	52	0	85	25	6	5	24	5	.83	8	.296	.390	.432
1995	Arkansas	AA	StL	87	332	106	15	4	5	144	66	29	48	1	40	9	1	2	16	16	.50	2	.319	.417	.434
1996	Arkansas	AA	StL	134	500	144	32	7	11	223	78	53	52	0	66	8	3	7	23	10	.70	9	.288	.360	.446
4 Min. YEARS				410	1519	448	84	18	26	646	263	175	168	1	215	46	13	17	75	36	.68	22	.295	.378	.425

Bats: Right **Throws:** Right **Pos:** SS

Dave Berg

Ht: 5'11" **Wt:** 185 **Born:** 9/3/70 **Age:** 26

				BATTING															BASERUNNING				PERCENTAGES		
Year	Team	Lg	Org	G	AB	H	2B	3B	HR	TB	R	RBI	TBB	IBB	SO	HBP	SH	SF	SB	CS	SB%	GDP	Avg	OBP	SLG
1993	Elmira	A-	Fla	75	281	74	13	1	4	101	37	28	35	1	37	8	4	3	6	4	.60	8	.263	.358	.359
1994	Kane County	A	Fla	121	437	117	27	8	9	187	80	53	54	0	80	8	15	6	8	6	.57	10	.268	.354	.428
1995	Brevard Cty	A+	Fla	114	382	114	18	1	3	143	71	39	68	1	61	8	7	9	9	4	.69	5	.298	.407	.374
1996	Portland	AA	Fla	109	414	125	28	5	9	190	64	73	42	1	60	5	8	6	17	7	.71	10	.302	.368	.459
4 Min. YEARS				419	1514	430	86	15	25	621	252	193	199	3	238	29	34	24	40	21	.66	33	.284	.373	.410

Bats: Right **Throws:** Right **Pos:** 3B

Steve Bernhardt

Ht: 6'0" **Wt:** 180 **Born:** 10/9/70 **Age:** 26

				BATTING															BASERUNNING				PERCENTAGES		
Year	Team	Lg	Org	G	AB	H	2B	3B	HR	TB	R	RBI	TBB	IBB	SO	HBP	SH	SF	SB	CS	SB%	GDP	Avg	OBP	SLG
1993	Bend	A-	Col	54	162	31	7	0	1	41	16	9	19	1	24	2	3	2	5	3	.63	1	.191	.281	.253
1994	Central Val	A+	Col	68	204	52	9	0	0	61	23	14	23	0	21	0	3	1	1	3	.25	3	.255	.329	.299
1995	Salem	A+	Col	59	180	39	3	2	4	58	18	16	8	0	38	5	5	2	2	3	.40	5	.217	.267	.322
1996	Salem	A+	Col	63	203	61	12	2	1	80	17	19	12	0	23	2	5	1	4	4	.50	4	.300	.344	.394
	New Haven	AA	Col	32	84	24	3	0	0	27	5	10	4	1	14	2	1	2	0	2	.00	1	.286	.326	.321
4 Min. YEARS				276	833	207	34	4	6	267	79	68	66	2	120	11	17	8	12	15	.44	14	.248	.309	.321

Bats: Right **Throws:** Right **Pos:** OF

Harry Berrios

Ht: 5'11" **Wt:** 205 **Born:** 12/2/71 **Age:** 25

				BATTING															BASERUNNING				PERCENTAGES		
Year	Team	Lg	Org	G	AB	H	2B	3B	HR	TB	R	RBI	TBB	IBB	SO	HBP	SH	SF	SB	CS	SB%	GDP	Avg	OBP	SLG
1993	Albany	A	Bal	46	145	30	5	1	3	46	16	16	18	1	20	5	0	2	2	0	1.00	3	.207	.312	.317
1994	Albany	A	Bal	42	162	54	12	2	6	88	42	35	18	1	23	9	0	1	14	0	1.00	4	.333	.426	.543
	Frederick	A+	Bal	86	325	113	13	0	13	165	70	71	32	2	47	18	2	2	42	14	.75	6	.348	.432	.508
	Bowie	AA	Bal	1	4	1	1	0	0	2	1	0	0	0	1	0	0	0	0	0	.00	0	.250	.250	.500
1995	Frederick	A+	Bal	71	240	50	5	2	10	89	33	28	32	3	66	4	0	2	10	6	.63	3	.208	.309	.371
	Bowie	AA	Bal	56	208	51	13	0	5	79	32	21	26	1	44	1	1	0	12	2	.86	6	.245	.332	.380
1996	Bowie	AA	Bal	37	123	23	4	0	6	45	19	17	16	1	24	6	1	1	7	2	.78	3	.187	.308	.366
	Frederick	A+	Bal	43	161	37	9	1	4	60	25	20	12	0	21	3	1	2	8	3	.73	5	.230	.292	.373
	Kinston	A+	Cle	24	73	14	5	0	2	25	7	11	9	0	16	0	1	1	2	0	1.00	2	.192	.277	.342
4 Min. YEARS				406	1441	373	67	6	49	599	245	219	163	9	262	46	6	11	97	27	.78	32	.259	.350	.416

Mike Berry

Bats: Right **Throws:** Right **Pos:** 3B **Ht:** 5'10" **Wt:** 185 **Born:** 8/12/70 **Age:** 26

		BATTING															BASERUNNING				PERCENTAGES		
Year Team	Lg Org	G	AB	H	2B	3B	HR	TB	R	RBI	TBB	IBB	SO	HBP	SH	SF	SB	CS	SB%	GDP	Avg	OBP	SLG
1993 Burlington	A Mon	31	92	22	2	0	1	27	15	6	20	0	22	0	3	0	0	1	.00	4	.239	.375	.293
1994 Burlington	A Mon	94	334	105	18	1	10	155	67	45	53	0	59	1	1	1	7	3	.70	7	.314	.409	.464
1995 W. Palm Bch	A+ Mon	24	79	13	3	1	1	21	16	2	13	0	16	0	0	0	0	1	.00	1	.165	.283	.266
Visalia	A+ Mon	98	368	113	28	4	9	176	69	61	57	1	70	5	1	3	12	6	.67	9	.307	.404	.478
1996 Frederick	A+ Bal	3	8	1	0	0	1	4	2	1	4	0	2	0	0	0	0	0	.00	1	.125	.417	.500
Bowie	AA Bal	2	7	1	0	0	0	1	1	2	0	0	4	0	0	1	0	0	.00	0	.143	.125	.143
High Desert	A+ Bal	121	463	167	44	5	13	260	109	113	99	3	67	7	0	3	7	4	.64	9	.361	.477	.562
4 Min. YEARS		373	1351	422	95	11	35	644	279	230	246	4	240	13	5	8	26	15	.63	31	.312	.421	.477

Johnny Bess

Bats: Both **Throws:** Right **Pos:** DH-C **Ht:** 6'1" **Wt:** 190 **Born:** 4/6/70 **Age:** 27

		BATTING															BASERUNNING				PERCENTAGES		
Year Team	Lg Org	G	AB	H	2B	3B	HR	TB	R	RBI	TBB	IBB	SO	HBP	SH	SF	SB	CS	SB%	GDP	Avg	OBP	SLG
1992 Princeton	R+ Cin	48	173	36	9	1	2	53	22	21	15	2	55	4	1	0	3	2	.60	0	.208	.286	.306
1993 Winston-Sal	A+ Cin	11	33	8	0	0	2	14	4	7	6	1	7	0	0	0	2	1	.67	0	.242	.359	.424
Charlstn-WV	A Cin	106	358	82	16	7	5	127	35	67	47	2	107	6	2	2	10	5	.67	4	.229	.327	.355
1994 Winston-Sal	A+ Cin	58	186	56	7	0	8	87	41	29	34	1	51	2	3	2	8	6	.57	1	.301	.411	.468
Chattanooga	AA Cin	37	103	21	5	1	0	28	9	9	13	0	34	2	2	2	1	1	.50	1	.204	.300	.272
1995 Winston-Sal	A+ Cin	88	246	46	10	2	4	72	35	21	30	4	83	8	2	0	12	4	.75	4	.187	.296	.293
Indianapols	AAA Cin	2	5	0	0	0	0	0	0	0	0	0	2	0	0	0	0	0	.00	0	.000	.000	.000
1996 Burlington	A SF	15	43	6	1	0	3	16	5	11	10	0	12	2	0	0	0	1	.00	0	.140	.327	.372
Shreveport	AA SF	57	175	43	10	3	7	80	25	30	19	1	63	2	1	3	1	1	.50	1	.246	.322	.457
5 Min. YEARS		422	1322	298	58	14	31	477	176	195	174	11	414	26	11	9	37	21	.64	11	.225	.325	.361

Randy Betten

Bats: Right **Throws:** Right **Pos:** 3B **Ht:** 5'11" **Wt:** 170 **Born:** 7/28/71 **Age:** 25

		BATTING															BASERUNNING				PERCENTAGES		
Year Team	Lg Org	G	AB	H	2B	3B	HR	TB	R	RBI	TBB	IBB	SO	HBP	SH	SF	SB	CS	SB%	GDP	Avg	OBP	SLG
1995 Boise	A- Cal	2	8	3	0	0	0	3	2	2	1	0	2	0	0	0	0	0	.00	0	.375	.444	.375
Cedar Rapds	A Cal	36	60	14	2	0	0	16	8	4	13	0	8	0	0	1	6	2	.75	0	.233	.365	.267
1996 Lk Elsinore	A+ Cal	74	274	71	15	3	3	101	32	34	22	1	49	3	3	1	11	3	.79	6	.259	.320	.369
Midland	AA Cal	28	82	14	2	0	0	16	5	5	5	0	19	0	1	0	3	1	.75	2	.171	.218	.195
2 Min. YEARS		140	424	102	19	3	3	136	47	45	41	1	78	3	4	2	20	6	.77	8	.241	.311	.321

Rick Betti

Pitches: Left **Bats:** Right **Pos:** P **Ht:** 5'11" **Wt:** 170 **Born:** 9/16/73 **Age:** 23

		HOW MUCH HE PITCHED						WHAT HE GAVE UP												THE RESULTS					
Year Team	Lg Org	G	GS	CG	GF	IP	BFP	H	R	ER	HR	SH	SF	HB	TBB	IBB	SO	WP	Bk	W	L	Pct.	ShO	Sv	ERA
1993 Braves	R Atl	9	2	0	5	20.1	78	10	5	2	1	0	0	1	8	0	27	1	0	1	0	1.000	0	2	0.89
Danville	R+ Atl	11	5	0	1	34.1	140	20	13	8	0	0	1	2	19	0	28	1	0	2	1	.667	0	0	2.10
1995 Red Sox	R Bos	3	1	0	2	7.1	30	7	3	2	0	0	0	1	3	0	13	1	0	1	0	1.000	0	1	2.45
Utica	A- Bos	12	0	0	5	17.2	65	9	2	2	1	0	0	0	2	0	25	1	0	2	1	.667	0	2	1.02
Michigan	A Bos	1	0	0	0	2	7	0	0	0	0	0	0	0	1	0	1	0	0	0	0	.000	0	0	0.00
1996 Sarasota	A+ Bos	13	0	0	13	15.2	70	13	6	5	0	0	1	3	7	2	21	0	0	0	2	.000	0	7	2.87
Trenton	AA Bos	31	8	0	10	81	361	70	39	33	7	2	1	3	44	5	65	5	0	9	1	.900	0	1	3.67
3 Min. YEARS		80	16	0	36	178.1	751	129	68	52	9	2	3	10	84	7	180	9	0	15	5	.750	0	13	2.62

Todd Betts

Bats: Left **Throws:** Right **Pos:** 3B **Ht:** 6'0" **Wt:** 190 **Born:** 6/24/73 **Age:** 24

		BATTING															BASERUNNING				PERCENTAGES		
Year Team	Lg Org	G	AB	H	2B	3B	HR	TB	R	RBI	TBB	IBB	SO	HBP	SH	SF	SB	CS	SB%	GDP	Avg	OBP	SLG
1993 Burlington	R+ Cle	56	168	39	9	0	7	69	40	27	32	2	26	3	0	1	6	1	.86	4	.232	.363	.411
1994 Watertown	A- Cle	65	227	74	18	2	10	126	49	53	54	2	29	4	1	2	3	2	.60	1	.326	.460	.555
1995 Kinston	A+ Cle	109	331	90	15	3	9	138	52	44	88	2	56	6	1	4	2	3	.40	5	.272	.429	.417
1996 Canton-Akrn	AA Cle	77	238	60	13	0	1	76	35	26	38	2	51	5	0	4	0	1	.00	6	.252	.361	.319
4 Min. YEARS		307	964	263	55	5	27	409	176	150	212	8	162	18	2	11	11	7	.61	16	.273	.409	.424

Jim Betzsold

Bats: Right **Throws:** Right **Pos:** OF **Ht:** 6'3" **Wt:** 210 **Born:** 8/7/72 **Age:** 24

		BATTING															BASERUNNING				PERCENTAGES		
Year Team	Lg Org	G	AB	H	2B	3B	HR	TB	R	RBI	TBB	IBB	SO	HBP	SH	SF	SB	CS	SB%	GDP	Avg	OBP	SLG
1994 Watertown	A- Cle	66	212	61	18	0	12	115	48	46	53	1	68	15	1	2	3	3	.50	2	.288	.457	.542
1995 Kinston	A+ Cle	126	455	122	22	2	25	223	77	71	55	3	137	10	0	4	3	5	.38	4	.268	.357	.490
1996 Canton-Akrn	AA Cle	84	268	64	11	5	3	94	35	35	30	1	74	6	1	1	4	1	.80	3	.239	.328	.351
3 Min. YEARS		276	935	247	51	7	40	432	160	152	138	5	279	31	2	7	10	9	.53	9	.264	.374	.462

Jay Beverlin

Pitches: Right **Bats:** Left **Pos:** P **Ht:** 6'5" **Wt:** 230 **Born:** 11/27/73 **Age:** 23

			HOW MUCH HE PITCHED						WHAT HE GAVE UP												THE RESULTS					
Year	Team	Lg Org	G	GS	CG	GF	IP	BFP	H	R	ER	HR	SH	SF	HB	TBB	IBB	SO	WP	Bk	W	L	Pct.	ShO	Sv	ERA
1994	W. Michigan	A Oak	17	1	0	5	41	168	32	12	8	0	1	0	2	14	0	48	3	4	3	2	.600	0	1	1.76
1995	Greensboro	A NYA	7	7	1	0	51	198	49	15	15	1	0	0	0	6	0	31	4	0	2	4	.333	1	0	2.65
	W. Michigan	A Oak	29	21	1	1	140	590	125	66	55	5	3	3	8	46	0	115	9	5	5	13	.278	1	0	3.54
1996	Norwich	AA NYA	8	4	0	1	16	81	25	21	15	2	0	2	0	6	1	17	0	0	0	3	.000	0	0	8.44
	Tampa	A+ NYA	25	1	0	6	46.1	194	43	22	18	5	1	1	1	17	2	38	4	1	2	0	1.000	0	1	3.50
3 Min. YEARS			86	34	2	13	294.1	1231	274	136	111	13	5	6	11	89	3	249	20	10	12	22	.353	2	2	3.39

Steve Bieser

Bats: Both **Throws:** Right **Pos:** OF **Ht:** 5'10" **Wt:** 170 **Born:** 8/4/67 **Age:** 29

			BATTING															BASERUNNING				PERCENTAGES		
Year	Team	Lg Org	G	AB	H	2B	3B	HR	TB	R	RBI	TBB	IBB	SO	HBP	SH	SF	SB	CS	SB%	GDP	Avg	OBP	SLG
1989	Batavia	A- Phi	25	75	18	3	1	1	26	13	13	12	0	20	2	2	2	2	1	.67	1	.240	.352	.347
1990	Batavia	A- Phi	54	160	37	11	1	0	50	36	12	26	1	27	1	2	2	13	2	.87	3	.231	.339	.313
1991	Spartanburg	A Phi	60	168	41	6	0	0	47	25	13	31	0	35	3	4	3	17	4	.81	4	.244	.366	.280
1992	Clearwater	A+ Phi	73	203	58	6	5	0	74	33	10	39	3	28	9	8	0	8	8	.50	2	.286	.422	.365
	Reading	AA Phi	33	139	38	5	4	0	51	20	8	6	0	25	4	4	0	8	3	.73	3	.273	.322	.367
1993	Reading	AA Phi	53	170	53	6	3	1	68	21	19	15	1	24	2	1	0	9	5	.64	2	.312	.374	.400
	Scranton-WB	AAA Phi	26	83	21	4	0	0	25	3	4	2	0	14	1	1	0	3	0	1.00	0	.253	.279	.301
1994	Scranton-WB	AAA Phi	93	228	61	13	1	0	76	42	15	17	1	40	5	4	2	12	8	.60	2	.268	.329	.333
1995	Scranton-WB	AAA Phi	95	245	66	12	6	1	93	37	33	22	1	56	10	6	2	14	5	.74	5	.269	.351	.380
1996	Ottawa	AAA Mon	123	382	123	24	4	1	158	63	32	35	4	55	6	23	2	27	7	.79	6	.322	.386	.414
8 Min. YEARS			635	1853	516	90	25	4	668	293	159	205	11	324	43	55	13	113	43	.72	28	.278	.361	.360

Brian Blair

Bats: Left **Throws:** Left **Pos:** OF **Ht:** 6'0" **Wt:** 180 **Born:** 4/9/72 **Age:** 25

			BATTING															BASERUNNING				PERCENTAGES		
Year	Team	Lg Org	G	AB	H	2B	3B	HR	TB	R	RBI	TBB	IBB	SO	HBP	SH	SF	SB	CS	SB%	GDP	Avg	OBP	SLG
1993	Erie	A- Tex	65	233	58	11	2	5	88	33	26	24	0	47	5	2	3	11	4	.73	4	.249	.328	.378
1994	Charlstn-SC	A Tex	121	411	102	21	0	7	144	65	38	53	1	90	3	2	4	30	8	.79	7	.248	.335	.350
1995	Charlotte	A+ Tex	69	264	59	5	3	0	70	34	9	34	3	42	1	2	1	14	6	.70	4	.223	.313	.265
1996	Tulsa	AA Tex	113	379	93	28	3	3	136	47	29	45	2	86	2	6	1	7	8	.47	6	.245	.328	.359
4 Min. YEARS			368	1287	312	65	8	15	438	179	102	156	6	265	11	12	9	62	26	.70	21	.242	.327	.340

Mike Blais

Pitches: Right **Bats:** Right **Pos:** P **Ht:** 6'5" **Wt:** 226 **Born:** 10/2/71 **Age:** 25

			HOW MUCH HE PITCHED						WHAT HE GAVE UP												THE RESULTS					
Year	Team	Lg Org	G	GS	CG	GF	IP	BFP	H	R	ER	HR	SH	SF	HB	TBB	IBB	SO	WP	Bk	W	L	Pct.	ShO	Sv	ERA
1993	Red Sox	R Bos	22	0	0	17	26	99	15	6	4	0	1	2	2	8	0	22	2	0	3	1	.750	0	4	1.38
	Ft. Laud	A+ Bos	3	0	0	3	6	26	4	1	1	0	1	0	0	3	1	7	0	0	1	1	.500	0	0	1.50
1994	Lynchburg	A+ Bos	25	10	0	6	77.1	354	99	66	57	12	2	2	1	18	0	46	3	1	1	6	.143	0	1	6.63
1995	Trenton	AA Bos	13	0	0	7	25	96	19	8	7	1	1	2	1	7	0	20	0	0	2	0	1.000	0	0	2.52
	Michigan	A Bos	45	0	0	33	71	280	53	20	17	1	4	6	2	18	3	55	4	0	4	1	.800	0	10	2.15
1996	Trenton	AA Bos	53	0	0	27	77.2	323	74	37	34	10	5	1	2	23	4	52	3	0	10	3	.769	0	5	3.94
4 Min. YEARS			161	10	0	93	283	1178	264	138	120	24	14	13	8	77	8	202	12	1	21	12	.636	0	20	3.82

Henry Blanco

Bats: Right **Throws:** Right **Pos:** C **Ht:** 5'11" **Wt:** 168 **Born:** 8/29/71 **Age:** 25

			BATTING															BASERUNNING				PERCENTAGES		
Year	Team	Lg Org	G	AB	H	2B	3B	HR	TB	R	RBI	TBB	IBB	SO	HBP	SH	SF	SB	CS	SB%	GDP	Avg	OBP	SLG
1990	Dodgers	R LA	60	178	39	8	0	1	50	23	19	26	0	43	1	0	4	7	2	.78	6	.219	.316	.281
1991	Vero Beach	A+ LA	5	7	1	0	0	0	1	0	0	2	0	0	0	0	0	0	0	.00	0	.143	.333	.143
	Great Falls	R+ LA	62	216	55	7	1	5	79	35	28	27	0	39	1	2	3	3	6	.33	5	.255	.336	.366
1992	Bakersfield	A+ LA	124	401	94	21	2	5	134	42	52	51	3	91	9	10	9	10	6	.63	10	.234	.328	.334
1993	San Antonio	AA LA	117	374	73	19	1	10	124	33	42	29	0	80	4	2	1	3	3	.50	7	.195	.260	.332
1994	San Antonio	AA LA	132	405	93	23	2	6	138	36	38	53	2	67	2	5	3	6	6	.50	12	.230	.320	.341
1995	San Antonio	AA LA	88	302	77	18	4	12	139	37	48	29	2	52	4	0	0	1	1	.50	4	.255	.328	.460
	Albuquerque	AAA LA	29	97	22	4	1	2	34	11	13	10	1	23	0	1	2	0	0	.00	3	.227	.294	.351
1996	San Antonio	AA LA	92	307	82	14	1	5	113	39	40	28	2	38	0	3	5	2	3	.40	8	.267	.324	.368
	Albuquerque	AAA LA	2	6	1	0	0	0	1	1	0	0	0	3	0	0	0	0	0	.00	0	.167	.167	.167
7 Min. YEARS			711	2293	537	114	12	46	813	257	280	255	10	436	21	23	27	32	27	.54	55	.234	.313	.355

Ben Blomdahl

Pitches: Right **Bats:** Right **Pos:** P **Ht:** 6' 2" **Wt:** 185 **Born:** 12/30/70 **Age:** 26

			HOW MUCH HE PITCHED						WHAT HE GAVE UP												THE RESULTS					
Year	Team	Lg Org	G	GS	CG	GF	IP	BFP	H	R	ER	HR	SH	SF	HB	TBB	IBB	SO	WP	Bk	W	L	Pct.	ShO	Sv	ERA
1991	Niagara Fal	A- Det	16	13	0	2	78.2	344	72	43	39	2	1	3	2	50	0	30	7	6	6	6	.500	0	0	4.46
1992	Fayettevlle	A Det	17	17	2	0	103.1	423	94	46	31	5	2	0	4	26	0	65	6	3	10	4	.714	2	0	2.70
	Lakeland	A+ Det	10	10	2	0	62	264	77	35	32	3	2	1	3	5	0	41	2	0	5	3	.625	0	0	4.65
1993	London	AA Det	17	17	3	0	119	498	108	58	49	7	4	6	7	42	1	72	4	3	6	6	.500	0	0	3.71
	Toledo	AAA Det	11	10	0	0	62.2	264	67	34	34	8	1	4	2	19	0	27	4	0	3	4	.429	0	0	4.88

Year	Team	Lg	Org	G	GS	CG	GF	IP	BFP	H	R	ER	HR	SH	SF	HB	TBB	IBB	SO	WP	Bk	W	L	Pct.	ShO	Sv	ERA
	HOW MUCH HE PITCHED									WHAT HE GAVE UP												THE RESULTS					
1994	Toledo	AAA	Det	28	28	0	0	165.1	729	192	92	82	18	6	10	7	47	3	83	5	0	11	11	.500	0	0	4.46
1995	Toledo	AAA	Det	41	0	0	23	56	232	55	24	22	6	1	1	2	13	4	39	3	0	5	4	.556	0	3	3.54
1996	Toledo	AAA	Det	53	0	0	27	59.1	271	77	42	41	9	1	1	1	18	1	34	9	0	2	6	.250	0	2	6.22
1995	Detroit	AL		14	0	0	5	24.1	115	36	21	21	5	1	0	0	13	0	15	2	0	0	0	.000	0	1	7.77
	6 Min. YEARS			193	95	7	52	706.1	3025	742	374	330	58	18	26	28	220	9	391	40	12	48	44	.522	2	5	4.20

Greg Blosser

Bats: Left **Throws:** Left **Pos:** OF-DH **Ht:** 6' 3" **Wt:** 215 **Born:** 6/26/71 **Age:** 26

Year	Team	Lg	Org	G	AB	H	2B	3B	HR	TB	R	RBI	TBB	IBB	SO	HBP	SH	SF	SB	CS	SB%	GDP	Avg	OBP	SLG
	BATTING																		BASERUNNING				PERCENTAGES		
1989	Red Sox	R	Bos	40	146	42	7	3	2	61	17	20	25	1	19	1	0	2	3	0	1.00	7	.288	.391	.418
	Winter Havn	A+	Bos	28	94	24	1	1	2	33	6	14	8	0	14	1	0	1	1	0	1.00	1	.255	.317	.351
1990	Lynchburg	A+	Bos	119	447	126	23	1	18	205	63	62	55	3	99	1	0	1	5	4	.56	13	.282	.361	.459
1991	New Britain	AA	Bos	134	452	98	21	3	8	149	48	46	63	0	114	1	0	4	9	4	.69	16	.217	.312	.330
1992	New Britain	AA	Bos	129	434	105	23	4	22	202	59	71	64	9	122	1	0	3	0	2	.00	7	.242	.339	.465
	Pawtucket	AAA	Bos	1	0	0	0	0	0	0	1	0	1	0	0	0	0	0	0	0	.00	0	.000	1.000	.000
1993	Pawtucket	AAA	Bos	130	478	109	22	2	23	204	66	66	58	5	139	2	1	4	3	3	.50	4	.228	.312	.427
1994	Pawtucket	AAA	Bos	97	350	91	21	1	17	165	52	54	44	5	97	0	0	1	11	3	.79	9	.260	.342	.471
1995	Pawtucket	AAA	Bos	17	50	10	0	0	1	13	5	4	5	0	13	0	0	1	0	0	.00	0	.200	.268	.260
	Trenton	AA	Bos	49	179	44	13	0	11	90	25	34	13	0	42	0	1	3	3	2	.60	4	.246	.292	.503
1996	Rochester	AAA	Bal	38	115	27	6	1	2	41	11	12	12	0	29	0	0	0	2	1	.67	3	.235	.307	.357
1993	Boston	AL		17	28	2	1	0	0	3	1	1	2	0	7	0	0	0	1	0	1.00	0	.071	.133	.107
1994	Boston	AL		5	11	1	0	0	0	1	2	1	4	0	4	0	0	0	0	0	.00	0	.091	.333	.091
	8 Min. YEARS			782	2745	676	137	16	106	1163	353	383	348	23	688	7	2	20	37	19	.66	64	.246	.330	.424
	2 Maj. YEARS			22	39	3	1	0	0	4	3	2	6	0	11	0	0	0	1	0	1.00	0	.077	.200	.103

Geoff Blum

Bats: Both **Throws:** Right **Pos:** 2B **Ht:** 6'3" **Wt:** 193 **Born:** 4/26/73 **Age:** 24

Year	Team	Lg	Org	G	AB	H	2B	3B	HR	TB	R	RBI	TBB	IBB	SO	HBP	SH	SF	SB	CS	SB%	GDP	Avg	OBP	SLG
	BATTING																		BASERUNNING				PERCENTAGES		
1994	Vermont	A-	Mon	63	241	83	15	1	3	109	48	38	33	0	21	3	1	1	5	5	.50	4	.344	.428	.452
1995	W. Palm Bch	A+	Mon	125	457	120	20	2	1	147	54	62	34	1	61	3	1	7	6	5	.55	12	.263	.313	.322
1996	Harrisburg	AA	Mon	120	396	95	22	2	1	124	47	41	59	2	51	3	11	3	6	7	.46	11	.240	.341	.313
	3 Min. YEARS			308	1094	298	57	5	5	380	149	141	126	3	133	9	13	11	17	17	.50	27	.272	.349	.347

Jeff Bock

Pitches: Right **Bats:** Right **Pos:** P **Ht:** 6'5" **Wt:** 200 **Born:** 4/26/71 **Age:** 26

Year	Team	Lg	Org	G	GS	CG	GF	IP	BFP	H	R	ER	HR	SH	SF	HB	TBB	IBB	SO	WP	Bk	W	L	Pct.	ShO	Sv	ERA
	HOW MUCH HE PITCHED									WHAT HE GAVE UP												THE RESULTS					
1993	Danville	R+	Atl	5	0	0	1	6.1	28	6	5	5	0	0	1	0	3	0	2	1	0	0	0	.000	0	0	7.11
	Idaho Falls	R+	Atl	15	1	0	8	31.2	129	31	16	10	2	1	0	0	12	1	21	1	0	3	2	.600	0	1	2.84
	Macon	A	Atl	3	3	1	0	16.2	72	12	9	4	0	0	3	0	8	0	11	2	1	2	1	.667	0	0	2.16
1994	Durham	A+	Atl	39	11	1	7	101.2	461	123	83	66	21	3	4	5	34	4	68	7	1	4	8	.333	1	1	5.84
1995	Durham	A+	Atl	32	4	0	11	67	282	58	31	25	9	4	3	1	31	8	45	3	0	5	1	.833	0	2	3.36
1996	Greenville	AA	Atl	20	19	0	0	106	474	136	67	63	10	5	4	0	41	0	51	4	0	6	5	.545	0	0	5.35
	4 Min. YEARS			114	38	2	27	329.1	1446	366	211	173	42	13	15	6	129	13	198	18	2	20	17	.541	1	4	4.73

Sean Bogle

Pitches: Right **Bats:** Right **Pos:** P **Ht:** 6'2" **Wt:** 195 **Born:** 10/3/73 **Age:** 23

Year	Team	Lg	Org	G	GS	CG	GF	IP	BFP	H	R	ER	HR	SH	SF	HB	TBB	IBB	SO	WP	Bk	W	L	Pct.	ShO	Sv	ERA
	HOW MUCH HE PITCHED									WHAT HE GAVE UP												THE RESULTS					
1994	Williamsprt	A-	ChN	15	6	0	1	33.2	165	34	31	28	1	0	1	3	33	0	23	4	2	1	1	.500	0	0	7.49
1995	Williamsprt	A-	ChN	12	0	0	5	22	99	22	12	5	0	2	1	1	8	0	15	2	1	1	0	1.000	0	1	2.05
	Rockford	A	ChN	25	0	0	8	44.1	183	39	15	8	0	4	2	1	17	0	30	3	1	2	0	1.000	0	1	1.62
1996	Rockford	A	ChN	16	0	0	5	23.1	125	26	23	11	1	0	1	4	24	0	15	6	0	0	0	.000	0	0	4.24
	Daytona	A+	ChN	13	0	0	5	17.2	92	28	17	14	0	1	2	0	13	1	18	3	0	3	1	.750	0	0	7.13
	Orlando	AA	ChN	4	0	0	1	5.2	24	2	0	0	0	0	0	0	6	1	6	1	0	0	0	.000	0	0	0.00
	3 Min. YEARS			85	6	0	25	146.2	688	151	98	66	2	7	7	9	101	2	107	19	4	7	2	.778	0	2	4.05

Kurtiss Bogott

Pitches: Left **Bats:** Left **Pos:** P **Ht:** 6'4" **Wt:** 195 **Born:** 9/30/72 **Age:** 24

Year	Team	Lg	Org	G	GS	CG	GF	IP	BFP	H	R	ER	HR	SH	SF	HB	TBB	IBB	SO	WP	Bk	W	L	Pct.	ShO	Sv	ERA
	HOW MUCH HE PITCHED									WHAT HE GAVE UP												THE RESULTS					
1993	Red Sox	R	Bos	3	2	0	0	15	57	10	3	3	1	0	0	2	4	0	20	3	0	0	1	.000	0	0	1.80
	Utica	A-	Bos	13	10	0	0	56.2	260	64	37	28	4	2	1	3	23	0	53	8	3	1	7	.125	0	0	4.45
1994	Red Sox	R	Bos	3	2	0	0	13.2	49	7	1	1	0	0	0	1	3	0	12	2	0	1	0	1.000	0	0	0.66
	Lynchburg	A+	Bos	6	6	0	0	26.1	127	32	23	18	1	1	1	1	14	0	14	2	0	2	3	.400	0	0	6.15
1995	Trenton	AA	Bos	2	0	0	2	3.1	13	3	1	1	1	0	0	0	1	0	2	0	0	0	1	.000	0	0	2.70
	Sarasota	A+	Bos	43	9	0	17	92	401	92	45	31	4	4	1	4	42	0	64	8	3	6	5	.545	0	0	3.03
1996	Knoxville	AA	Tor	33	0	0	9	54	256	64	34	32	2	0	2	5	29	2	56	12	1	2	2	.500	0	3	5.33
	Dunedin	A+	Tor	19	0	0	8	30.1	133	22	16	6	2	0	0	3	20	1	41	8	0	1	1	.500	0	4	1.78
	4 Min. YEARS			122	29	0	36	291.1	1296	294	160	120	15	7	5	19	136	3	262	43	7	13	20	.394	0	7	3.71

Tom Bolton

Pitches: Left **Bats:** Left **Pos:** P **Ht:** 6' 2" **Wt:** 185 **Born:** 5/6/62 **Age:** 35

			HOW MUCH HE PITCHED						WHAT HE GAVE UP												THE RESULTS					
Year	Team	Lg Org	G	GS	CG	GF	IP	BFP	H	R	ER	HR	SH	SF	HB	TBB	IBB	SO	WP	Bk	W	L	Pct.	ShO	Sv	ERA
1980	Elmira	A- Bos	23	1	1	15	56	237	43	26	15	4	1	1	0	22	0	43	0	0	6	2	.750	1	5	2.41
1981	Wintr Haven	A+ Bos	24	0	0	3	92	420	125	62	46	5	2	3	3	41	0	47	7	1	2	3	.400	0	0	4.50
1982	Wintr Haven	A+ Bos	28	25	4	1	163	682	161	67	54	3	6	4	2	63	0	77	7	4	9	8	.529	0	0	2.98
1983	New Britain	AA Bos	16	16	2	0	99.2	416	93	36	32	7	1	0	1	41	0	62	5	0	7	3	.700	1	0	2.89
	Pawtucket	AAA Bos	6	6	0	0	29	144	33	26	21	4	1	0	1	25	0	20	1	1	0	5	.000	0	0	6.52
1984	New Britain	AA Bos	33	9	0	11	87	380	87	54	40	5	2	3	4	34	3	66	6	2	4	5	.444	0	1	4.14
1985	New Britain	AA Bos	34	10	1	14	101	437	106	53	48	3	5	3	2	40	1	74	3	2	5	6	.455	0	1	4.28
1986	Pawtucket	AAA Bos	29	7	1	11	86	356	80	30	26	6	9	2	0	25	2	58	1	1	3	4	.429	0	2	2.72
1987	Pawtucket	AAA Bos	5	4	0	1	21.2	93	25	14	13	0	0	1	0	12	1	8	1	0	2	1	.667	0	0	5.40
1988	Pawtucket	AAA Bos	18	1	0	8	19.1	81	17	7	6	0	0	0	0	10	0	15	2	0	3	0	1.000	0	0	2.79
1989	Pawtucket	AAA Bos	25	22	5	2	143.1	606	140	57	46	13	6	1	4	47	2	99	0	1	12	5	.706	2	1	2.89
1990	Pawtucket	AAA Bos	4	2	0	1	11.2	50	9	6	5	2	0	1	0	7	0	8	2	0	1	0	1.000	0	0	3.86
1994	Rochester	AAA Bal	16	0	0	7	20	76	13	5	5	1	0	0	0	8	0	16	2	1	2	0	1.000	0	2	2.25
1995	Nashville	AAA ChA	19	17	1	1	101.2	433	106	52	50	10	0	1	3	31	0	82	3	2	5	7	.417	1	0	4.43
1996	Calgary	AAA Pit	40	14	0	11	116.1	517	121	64	52	7	4	2	7	47	5	92	6	0	12	5	.706	0	2	4.02
1987	Boston	AL	29	0	0	5	61.2	287	83	33	30	5	3	3	2	27	2	49	3	0	1	0	1.000	0	0	4.38
1988	Boston	AL	28	0	0	8	30.1	140	35	17	16	1	2	1	0	14	1	21	2	1	1	3	.250	0	1	4.75
1989	Boston	AL	4	4	0	0	17.1	83	21	18	16	1	0	1	0	10	1	9	1	0	0	4	.000	0	0	8.31
1990	Boston	AL	21	16	3	2	119.2	501	111	46	45	6	3	5	3	47	3	65	1	1	10	5	.667	0	0	3.38
1991	Boston	AL	25	19	0	4	110	499	136	72	64	16	2	4	1	51	2	64	3	0	8	9	.471	0	0	5.24
1992	Boston	AL	21	1	0	6	29	135	34	11	11	0	0	0	2	14	1	23	2	1	1	2	.333	0	0	3.41
	Cincinnati	NL	16	8	0	3	46.1	210	52	28	27	9	1	1	2	23	2	27	3	1	3	3	.500	0	0	5.24
1993	Detroit	AL	43	8	0	9	102.2	462	113	57	51	5	7	2	7	45	10	66	5	1	6	6	.500	0	0	4.47
1994	Baltimore	AL	22	0	0	3	23.1	109	29	15	14	3	1	1	0	13	1	12	1	0	1	2	.333	0	0	5.40
14 Min. YEARS			320	134	15	86	1147.2	4928	1159	559	459	70	37	22	27	453	14	767	46	15	73	54	.575	5	14	3.60
8 Maj. YEARS			209	56	3	40	540.1	2426	614	297	274	46	19	18	17	244	23	336	21	5	31	34	.477	0	1	4.56

Rob Bonanno

Pitches: Right **Bats:** Right **Pos:** P **Ht:** 6'0" **Wt:** 178 **Born:** 1/5/71 **Age:** 26

			HOW MUCH HE PITCHED						WHAT HE GAVE UP												THE RESULTS					
Year	Team	Lg Org	G	GS	CG	GF	IP	BFP	H	R	ER	HR	SH	SF	HB	TBB	IBB	SO	WP	Bk	W	L	Pct.	ShO	Sv	ERA
1994	Boise	A- Cal	6	6	0	0	39.2	155	23	11	6	1	0	0	2	10	0	41	2	0	5	0	1.000	0	0	1.36
	Cedar Rapds	A Cal	9	9	0	0	51	219	56	25	25	4	1	2	4	16	1	40	6	1	3	2	.600	0	0	4.41
1995	Midland	AA Cal	3	3	0	0	13.1	68	24	16	14	5	0	1	0	6	0	6	0	0	1	1	.500	0	0	9.45
	Lk Elsinore	A+ Cal	20	20	4	0	125.1	523	136	65	52	15	2	5	3	22	0	78	0	0	9	5	.643	2	0	3.73
1996	Midland	AA Cal	23	6	1	7	64.1	289	79	44	38	8	1	1	3	23	1	52	5	0	1	2	.333	0	2	5.32
	Lk Elsinore	A+ Cal	13	2	0	9	32.2	131	34	11	8	0	1	1	1	10	1	34	1	0	3	2	.600	0	1	2.20
3 Min. YEARS			74	46	5	16	326.1	1385	352	172	143	33	5	10	13	87	3	251	14	1	22	12	.647	2	3	3.94

Ken Bonifay

Bats: Left **Throws:** Right **Pos:** 3B **Ht:** 6'1" **Wt:** 185 **Born:** 9/1/70 **Age:** 26

			BATTING														BASERUNNING				PERCENTAGES		
Year	Team	Lg Org	G	AB	H	2B	3B	HR	TB	R	RBI	TBB	IBB	SO	HBP	SH	SF	SB	CS	SB%	GDP	Avg	OBP	SLG
1991	Pirates	R Pit	20	64	22	1	0	1	26	13	9	14	0	8	1	0	1	4	1	.80	3	.344	.463	.406
	Welland	A- Pit	37	140	33	5	3	2	50	17	13	11	1	38	0	0	0	2	1	.67	2	.236	.291	.357
1992	Augusta	A Pit	15	47	12	2	0	2	20	8	9	11	2	10	2	0	2	2	0	1.00	1	.255	.403	.426
	Salem	A+ Pit	71	209	42	6	0	1	51	20	20	28	0	36	3	1	2	1	2	.33	4	.201	.302	.244
1993	Salem	A+ Pit	100	361	100	19	1	18	175	59	60	42	1	63	4	0	6	12	2	.86	3	.277	.354	.485
1994	Carolina	AA Pit	95	290	64	21	2	6	107	36	28	32	3	58	4	2	2	3	1	.75	4	.221	.305	.369
1995	Lynchburg	A+ Pit	116	375	92	22	2	10	148	57	54	63	4	88	11	0	4	3	5	.38	6	.245	.366	.395
1996	Carolina	AA Pit	95	272	66	18	2	6	106	33	42	41	2	68	4	2	0	4	3	.57	4	.243	.350	.390
6 Min. YEARS			549	1758	431	94	10	46	683	243	235	242	13	369	29	5	17	31	15	.67	27	.245	.343	.389

James Bonnici

Bats: Right **Throws:** Right **Pos:** 1B **Ht:** 6'4" **Wt:** 230 **Born:** 1/21/72 **Age:** 25

			BATTING														BASERUNNING				PERCENTAGES		
Year	Team	Lg Org	G	AB	H	2B	3B	HR	TB	R	RBI	TBB	IBB	SO	HBP	SH	SF	SB	CS	SB%	GDP	Avg	OBP	SLG
1991	Mariners	R Sea	51	178	59	2	4	0	69	36	38	44	0	31	6	0	5	8	2	.80	1	.331	.468	.388
1992	Bellingham	A- Sea	53	168	44	6	1	4	64	13	20	22	2	54	2	1	0	5	2	.71	3	.262	.354	.381
1993	Riverside	A+ Sea	104	375	115	21	1	9	165	69	58	58	2	72	9	3	1	0	0	.00	7	.307	.411	.440
1994	Riverside	A+ Sea	113	397	111	23	3	10	170	71	71	58	0	81	18	0	3	1	2	.33	14	.280	.393	.428
1995	Port City	AA Sea	138	508	144	36	3	20	246	75	91	76	15	97	9	0	3	2	2	.50	14	.283	.384	.484
1996	Tacoma	AAA Sea	139	497	145	25	0	26	248	76	74	59	4	100	2	1	3	1	3	.25	13	.292	.367	.499
6 Min. YEARS			598	2123	618	113	12	69	962	340	352	317	23	435	46	5	15	17	11	.61	52	.291	.392	.453

Aaron Boone

Bats: Right **Throws:** Right **Pos:** 3B **Ht:** 6'2" **Wt:** 190 **Born:** 3/9/73 **Age:** 24

			BATTING														BASERUNNING				PERCENTAGES		
Year	Team	Lg Org	G	AB	H	2B	3B	HR	TB	R	RBI	TBB	IBB	SO	HBP	SH	SF	SB	CS	SB%	GDP	Avg	OBP	SLG
1994	Billings	R+ Cin	67	256	70	15	5	7	116	48	55	36	3	35	3	0	6	6	3	.67	7	.273	.362	.453
1995	Chattanooga	AA Cin	23	66	15	3	0	0	18	6	3	5	0	12	0	1	2	2	0	1.00	5	.227	.274	.273

Year	Team	Lg	Org	G	AB	H	2B	3B	HR	TB	R	RBI	TBB	IBB	SO	HBP	SH	SF	SB	CS	SB%	GDP	Avg	OBP	SLG
BATTING																			BASERUNNING				PERCENTAGES		
	Winston-Sal	A+	Cin	108	395	103	19	1	14	166	61	50	43	7	77	9	4	2	11	7	.61	4	.261	.345	.420
1996	Chattanooga	AA	Cin	136	548	158	44	7	17	267	86	95	38	4	77	5	1	4	21	10	.68	5	.288	.338	.487
3 Min. YEARS				334	1265	346	81	13	38	567	201	203	122	14	201	17	6	14	40	20	.67	21	.274	.342	.448

Richie Borrero

Bats: Right **Throws:** Right **Pos:** C **Ht:** 6'1" **Wt:** 195 **Born:** 1/5/73 **Age:** 24

Year	Team	Lg	Org	G	AB	H	2B	3B	HR	TB	R	RBI	TBB	IBB	SO	HBP	SH	SF	SB	CS	SB%	GDP	Avg	OBP	SLG
BATTING																			BASERUNNING				PERCENTAGES		
1990	Red Sox	R	Bos	34	109	23	6	0	1	32	13	10	16	1	28	0	0	1	0	2	.00	5	.211	.310	.294
1991	Red Sox	R	Bos	35	118	26	3	1	1	34	11	16	2	1	23	1	0	2	4	2	.67	1	.220	.236	.288
1992	Red Sox	R	Bos	34	99	18	5	2	1	30	9	12	14	0	24	1	1	1	2	1	.67	1	.182	.287	.303
1993	Utica	A-	Bos	44	120	19	2	0	2	27	10	14	11	0	39	1	1	3	3	1	.75	2	.158	.230	.225
1994	Sarasota	A+	Bos	44	145	28	8	0	3	45	15	14	9	0	50	4	1	0	0	1	.00	2	.193	.259	.310
1995	Sarasota	A+	Bos	34	98	20	5	0	0	25	9	4	5	0	22	2	1	2	0	1	.00	1	.204	.252	.255
	Michigan	A	Bos	23	70	16	4	1	2	28	8	6	6	0	17	4	0	0	0	1	.00	2	.229	.325	.400
1996	Michigan	A	Bos	11	30	5	1	0	0	6	3	1	2	0	5	0	0	0	0	1	.00	1	.167	.219	.200
	Sarasota	A+	Bos	27	92	23	5	0	3	37	15	13	6	0	17	1	1	0	1	1	.50	3	.250	.303	.402
	Trenton	AA	Bos	26	71	22	5	2	3	40	12	26	8	0	16	0	1	0	2	1	.67	2	.310	.380	.563
7 Min. YEARS				312	952	200	44	6	16	304	105	116	79	2	241	14	6	9	12	12	.50	20	.210	.278	.319

Heath Bost

Pitches: Right **Bats:** Right **Pos:** P **Ht:** 6'4" **Wt:** 200 **Born:** 10/13/74 **Age:** 22

Year	Team	Lg	Org	G	GS	CG	GF	IP	BFP	H	R	ER	HR	SH	SF	HB	TBB	IBB	SO	WP	Bk	W	L	Pct.	ShO	Sv	ERA
HOW MUCH HE PITCHED										WHAT HE GAVE UP												THE RESULTS					
1995	Asheville	A	Col	9	2	0	4	23.2	90	20	6	4	1	0	0	1	3	0	17	1	2	4	1	.800	0	0	1.52
	Portland	A-	Col	19	2	0	5	39.2	153	35	12	10	2	0	0	1	3	0	42	2	2	5	1	.833	0	0	2.27
1996	New Haven	AA	Col	4	0	0	2	6	24	5	1	1	0	0	0	0	2	0	7	0	0	1	0	1.000	0	0	1.50
	Asheville	A	Col	41	0	0	29	76	293	45	13	11	3	6	0	1	19	5	102	2	0	5	2	.714	0	15	1.30
2 Min. YEARS				73	4	0	40	145.1	560	105	32	26	6	6	0	3	27	5	168	5	4	15	4	.789	0	15	1.61

D.J. Boston

Bats: Left **Throws:** Left **Pos:** 1B **Ht:** 6'7" **Wt:** 230 **Born:** 9/6/71 **Age:** 25

Year	Team	Lg	Org	G	AB	H	2B	3B	HR	TB	R	RBI	TBB	IBB	SO	HBP	SH	SF	SB	CS	SB%	GDP	Avg	OBP	SLG
BATTING																			BASERUNNING				PERCENTAGES		
1991	Medicne Hat	R+	Tor	59	207	58	12	0	1	73	34	25	33	0	33	2	1	1	4	8	.33	5	.280	.383	.353
1992	St. Cathrns	A-	Tor	72	256	60	7	1	5	84	25	36	36	4	41	2	0	3	20	3	.87	2	.234	.330	.328
1993	Hagerstown	A	Tor	127	464	146	35	4	13	228	76	92	54	6	77	4	0	3	31	11	.74	10	.315	.389	.491
1994	Dunedin	A+	Tor	119	433	125	20	1	7	168	59	52	55	2	65	0	2	5	19	9	.68	8	.289	.365	.388
1995	Knoxville	AA	Tor	132	479	117	27	1	11	179	51	71	47	1	100	2	2	3	12	8	.60	12	.244	.313	.374
1996	Syracuse	AAA	Tor	26	85	21	7	0	4	40	12	12	14	0	23	0	0	1	0	1	.00	3	.247	.350	.471
	Carolina	AA	Pit	93	321	90	16	4	8	138	47	48	49	3	61	3	0	4	5	3	.63	7	.280	.377	.430
6 Min. YEARS				628	2245	617	124	11	49	910	304	336	288	16	400	13	5	20	91	43	.68	47	.275	.358	.405

Denis Boucher

Pitches: Left **Bats:** Right **Pos:** P **Ht:** 6' 1" **Wt:** 195 **Born:** 3/7/68 **Age:** 29

Year	Team	Lg	Org	G	GS	CG	GF	IP	BFP	H	R	ER	HR	SH	SF	HB	TBB	IBB	SO	WP	Bk	W	L	Pct.	ShO	Sv	ERA
HOW MUCH HE PITCHED										WHAT HE GAVE UP												THE RESULTS					
1988	Myrtle Bch	A	Tor	33	32	1	0	196.2	809	161	81	62	11	7	6	8	63	1	169	15	21	13	12	.520	0	0	2.84
1989	Dunedin	A+	Tor	33	28	1	1	164.2	675	142	80	56	6	3	8	6	58	2	117	13	8	10	10	.500	1	0	3.06
1990	Dunedin	A+	Tor	9	9	2	0	60	226	45	8	5	1	0	0	2	8	0	62	4	0	7	0	1.000	2	0	0.75
	Syracuse	AAA	Tor	17	17	2	0	107.2	449	100	51	46	7	4	4	2	37	2	80	6	0	8	5	.615	1	0	3.85
1991	Syracuse	AAA	Tor	8	8	1	0	56.2	241	57	24	20	5	4	1	3	19	1	28	2	0	2	1	.667	0	0	3.18
	Colo. Sprng	AAA	Cle	3	3	0	0	14.1	59	14	8	8	1	0	1	0	2	0	9	0	0	1	0	1.000	0	0	5.02
1992	Colo. Sprng	AAA	Cle	20	18	6	1	124	497	119	50	48	4	3	4	2	30	1	40	7	2	11	4	.733	0	0	3.48
1993	Las Vegas	AAA	SD	24	7	1	2	70	331	101	59	50	12	4	1	6	27	3	46	4	1	4	7	.364	0	1	6.43
	Ottawa	AAA	Mon	11	6	0	1	43	169	36	13	13	0	2	0	1	11	0	22	3	0	6	0	1.000	0	0	2.72
1994	Ottawa	AAA	Mon	18	18	0	0	114	480	110	52	47	10	3	3	2	37	1	49	1	1	7	6	.538	0	0	3.71
1995	Ottawa	AAA	Mon	14	11	0	1	55.1	254	65	39	35	1	3	3	0	31	0	22	4	0	2	3	.400	0	0	5.69
1996	W. Palm Bch	A+	Mon	2	2	0	0	12.2	50	12	4	4	1	0	0	1	2	0	5	1	0	1	0	1.000	0	0	2.84
	Harrisburg	AA	Mon	1	1	0	0	6	22	2	1	1	0	1	0	0	2	0	6	0	0	1	0	1.000	0	0	1.50
	Ottawa	AAA	Mon	17	11	0	4	61	306	90	63	63	17	2	3	1	40	0	24	1	0	3	7	.300	0	0	9.30
1991	Toronto	AL		7	7	0	0	35.1	162	39	20	18	6	3	1	2	16	1	16	0	4	0	3	.000	0	0	4.58
	Cleveland	AL		5	5	0	0	22.2	108	35	21	21	6	0	0	0	8	0	13	1	0	1	4	.200	0	0	8.34
1992	Cleveland	AL		8	7	0	0	41	184	48	29	29	9	1	3	1	20	0	17	1	0	2	2	.500	0	0	6.37
1993	Montreal	NL		5	5	0	0	28.1	111	24	7	6	1	0	3	0	3	1	14	0	2	3	1	.750	0	0	1.91
1994	Montreal	NL		10	2	0	3	18.2	84	24	16	14	6	2	1	0	7	0	17	1	0	0	1	.000	0	0	6.75
9 Min. YEARS				210	171	14	10	1086	4568	1054	533	458	76	36	34	34	367	11	679	61	33	76	55	.580	4	1	3.80
4 Maj. YEARS				35	26	0	3	146	649	170	93	88	28	6	8	3	54	2	77	3	6	6	11	.353	0	0	5.42

Mike Bovee

Pitches: Right **Bats:** Right **Pos:** P **Ht:** 5'10" **Wt:** 200 **Born:** 8/21/73 **Age:** 23

				HOW MUCH HE PITCHED						WHAT HE GAVE UP												THE RESULTS					
Year	Team	Lg	Org	G	GS	CG	GF	IP	BFP	H	R	ER	HR	SH	SF	HB	TBB	IBB	SO	WP	Bk	W	L	Pct.	ShO	Sv	ERA
1991	Royals	R	KC	11	11	0	0	61.2	251	52	19	14	1	0	1	1	12	0	76	4	0	3	1	.750	0	0	2.04
1992	Appleton	A	KC	28	24	1	0	149.1	618	143	85	59	8	4	9	3	41	1	120	13	3	9	10	.474	0	0	3.56
1993	Rockford	A	KC	20	20	2	0	109	469	118	58	51	1	4	4	6	30	0	111	15	0	5	9	.357	0	0	4.21
1994	Wilmington	A+	KC	28	26	0	1	169.2	675	149	58	50	10	4	3	4	32	0	154	8	1	13	4	.765	0	0	2.65
1995	Wichita	AA	KC	20	20	1	0	114	486	118	60	53	12	2	4	2	43	0	72	4	0	8	6	.571	0	0	4.18
1996	Wichita	AA	KC	27	27	3	0	176.2	783	223	113	95	21	9	8	6	40	1	102	10	0	10	11	.476	2	0	4.84
6 Min. YEARS				134	128	7	1	780.1	3282	803	393	322	53	23	29	22	198	2	635	54	4	48	41	.539	2	0	3.71

Ryan Bowen

Pitches: Right **Bats:** Right **Pos:** P **Ht:** 6' 0" **Wt:** 185 **Born:** 2/10/68 **Age:** 29

				HOW MUCH HE PITCHED						WHAT HE GAVE UP												THE RESULTS					
Year	Team	Lg	Org	G	GS	CG	GF	IP	BFP	H	R	ER	HR	SH	SF	HB	TBB	IBB	SO	WP	Bk	W	L	Pct.	ShO	Sv	ERA
1987	Asheville	A	Hou	26	26	6	0	160.1	704	143	86	72	12	7	4	5	78	1	126	8	2	12	5	.706	2	0	4.04
1988	Osceola	A+	Hou	4	4	0	0	13.2	65	12	8	6	0	1	0	1	10	0	12	2	0	1	0	1.000	0	0	3.95
1989	Columbus	AA	Hou	27	27	1	0	139.2	655	123	83	66	11	7	4	8	116	0	136	12	0	8	6	.571	1	0	4.25
1990	Tucson	AAA	Hou	10	7	0	0	34.2	177	41	36	36	5	2	0	0	38	1	29	0	0	1	3	.250	0	0	9.35
	Columbus	AA	Hou	18	18	2	0	113	491	103	59	47	7	4	6	0	49	0	109	5	1	8	4	.667	2	0	3.74
1991	Tucson	AAA	Hou	18	18	2	0	98.2	450	114	56	48	3	3	0	3	56	2	78	9	0	5	5	.500	2	0	4.38
1992	Tucson	AAA	Hou	21	20	1	0	122.1	555	128	68	56	7	6	2	5	64	1	94	8	0	7	6	.538	1	0	4.12
1994	Edmonton	AAA	Fla	5	5	0	0	19	85	22	13	13	3	0	1	0	11	0	13	1	0	1	0	1.000	0	0	6.16
	Brevard Cty	A+	Fla	2	1	0	0	6.2	28	4	3	3	0	0	0	2	3	0	5	0	0	0	1	.000	0	0	4.05
1995	Charlotte	AAA	Fla	1	1	0	0	4.2	22	5	5	5	1	0	0	0	4	0	3	0	0	0	1	.000	0	0	9.64
	Brevard Cty	A+	Fla	4	4	0	0	15.2	65	11	8	8	2	0	0	0	10	0	13	0	0	0	3	.000	0	0	4.60
1996	New Orleans	AAA	Mil	6	6	0	0	27.1	125	27	18	15	4	0	1	1	19	0	23	3	0	2	2	.500	0	0	4.94
1991	Houston	NL		14	13	0	0	71.2	319	73	43	41	4	2	6	3	36	1	49	8	1	6	4	.600	0	0	5.15
1992	Houston	NL		11	9	0	2	33.2	179	48	43	41	8	3	0	2	30	3	22	5	0	0	7	.000	0	0	10.96
1993	Florida	NL		27	27	2	0	156.2	693	156	83	77	11	5	4	3	87	7	98	10	4	8	12	.400	1	0	4.42
1994	Florida	NL		8	8	1	0	47.1	208	50	28	26	9	2	2	2	19	0	32	2	0	1	5	.167	0	0	4.94
1995	Florida	NL		4	3	0	0	16.2	85	23	11	7	3	1	2	0	12	2	15	0	0	2	0	1.000	0	0	3.78
9 Min. YEARS				142	137	12	0	755.2	3422	733	443	375	55	30	18	25	458	5	641	48	3	45	36	.556	8	0	4.47
5 Maj. YEARS				64	60	3	2	326	1484	350	208	192	35	13	14	10	184	13	216	25	5	17	28	.378	1	0	5.30

Shane Bowers

Pitches: Right **Bats:** Right **Pos:** P **Ht:** 6'6" **Wt:** 215 **Born:** 7/27/71 **Age:** 25

				HOW MUCH HE PITCHED						WHAT HE GAVE UP												THE RESULTS					
Year	Team	Lg	Org	G	GS	CG	GF	IP	BFP	H	R	ER	HR	SH	SF	HB	TBB	IBB	SO	WP	Bk	W	L	Pct.	ShO	Sv	ERA
1993	Elizabethtn	R+	Min	7	1	0	4	11.1	48	13	7	6	0	1	1	0	1	0	13	3	0	2	0	1.000	0	0	4.76
1994	Fort Wayne	A	Min	27	11	1	9	81.2	333	76	32	30	3	5	1	6	18	1	72	8	0	6	4	.600	0	5	3.31
	Fort Myers	A+	Min	13	0	0	5	17.2	85	28	7	7	1	0	0	0	4	0	19	2	0	0	0	.000	0	0	3.57
1995	Fort Myers	A+	Min	23	23	1	0	145.2	580	119	43	35	6	2	4	12	32	1	103	6	1	13	5	.722	0	0	2.16
1996	New Britain	AA	Min	27	22	1	1	131	569	134	71	61	15	2	3	6	42	1	96	11	0	6	8	.429	0	0	4.19
4 Min. YEARS				97	57	3	19	387.1	1615	370	160	139	25	10	9	24	97	3	303	30	1	27	17	.614	0	5	3.23

Justin Bowles

Bats: Left **Throws:** Left **Pos:** OF **Ht:** 6'0" **Wt:** 185 **Born:** 8/20/73 **Age:** 23

				BATTING															BASERUNNING				PERCENTAGES		
Year	Team	Lg	Org	G	AB	H	2B	3B	HR	TB	R	RBI	TBB	IBB	SO	HBP	SH	SF	SB	CS	SB%	GDP	Avg	OBP	SLG
1996	Sou. Oregon	A-	Oak	56	214	61	20	1	11	116	41	45	31	2	53	1	0	0	8	3	.73	1	.285	.378	.542
	Huntsville	AA	Oak	3	12	4	0	0	0	4	1	2	0	0	5	1	0	0	0	0	.00	0	.333	.385	.333
1 Min. YEARS				59	226	65	20	1	11	120	42	47	31	2	58	2	0	0	8	3	.73	1	.288	.378	.531

Tyrone Boykin

Bats: Right **Throws:** Right **Pos:** 1B **Ht:** 6'0" **Wt:** 195 **Born:** 4/25/68 **Age:** 29

				BATTING															BASERUNNING				PERCENTAGES		
Year	Team	Lg	Org	G	AB	H	2B	3B	HR	TB	R	RBI	TBB	IBB	SO	HBP	SH	SF	SB	CS	SB%	GDP	Avg	OBP	SLG
1991	Boise	A-	Cal	52	162	34	8	2	4	58	26	22	33	0	54	0	1	2	4	1	.80	4	.210	.340	.358
1992	Quad City	A	Cal	119	383	87	18	1	7	128	77	43	93	1	108	4	2	6	20	12	.63	5	.227	.379	.334
1993	Palm Spring	A+	Cal	77	286	93	13	1	3	117	48	40	51	0	52	0	2	3	22	8	.73	13	.325	.424	.409
	Midland	AA	Cal	35	132	37	3	3	2	52	29	17	17	0	17	2	0	2	1	0	1.00	8	.280	.366	.394
1994	Midland	AA	Cal	119	426	100	21	3	5	142	67	63	73	1	78	1	5	8	9	10	.47	9	.235	.343	.333
1995	Midland	AA	Cal	62	210	57	11	3	7	95	34	25	21	1	36	0	1	3	2	1	.67	3	.271	.333	.452
1996	Midland	AA	Cal	49	127	32	10	1	6	62	27	30	36	0	28	0	4	1	0	2	.00	2	.252	.415	.488
6 Min. YEARS				513	1726	440	84	14	34	654	308	240	324	3	373	7	15	25	58	34	.63	44	.255	.370	.379

Doug Brady

Bats: Both **Throws:** Right **Pos:** 2B **Ht:** 5'11" **Wt:** 165 **Born:** 11/23/69 **Age:** 27

				BATTING															BASERUNNING				PERCENTAGES		
Year	Team	Lg	Org	G	AB	H	2B	3B	HR	TB	R	RBI	TBB	IBB	SO	HBP	SH	SF	SB	CS	SB%	GDP	Avg	OBP	SLG
1991	Utica	A-	ChA	65	226	53	6	3	2	71	37	31	31	0	31	1	3	4	21	6	.78	5	.235	.324	.314
1992	South Bend	A	ChA	24	92	27	5	1	0	34	12	7	17	1	13	0	2	1	16	3	.84	0	.293	.400	.370

BATTING																			BASERUNNING				PERCENTAGES		
Year	Team	Lg	Org	G	AB	H	2B	3B	HR	TB	R	RBI	TBB	IBB	SO	HBP	SH	SF	SB	CS	SB%	GDP	Avg	OBP	SLG
	White Sox	R	ChA	3	8	1	0	0	0	1	1	2	1	0	1	0	0	2	0	0	.00	0	.125	.182	.125
	Sarasota	A+	ChA	56	184	50	6	0	2	62	21	27	25	1	33	3	6	2	5	7	.42	4	.272	.364	.337
1993	Sarasota	A+	ChA	115	449	113	16	6	5	156	75	44	55	2	54	6	4	5	26	9	.74	4	.252	.338	.347
	Nashville	AAA	ChA	2	3	0	0	0	0	0	0	0	0	0	0	0	0	0	0	0	.00	0	.000	.000	.000
1994	Birmingham	AA	ChA	127	516	128	18	8	4	174	59	47	38	1	59	1	6	5	34	12	.74	4	.248	.298	.337
1995	Nashville	AAA	ChA	125	450	134	15	6	5	176	71	27	31	3	76	0	4	3	32	6	.84	4	.298	.341	.391
1996	Nashville	AAA	ChA	115	427	103	18	7	6	153	59	42	31	1	61	2	6	2	20	6	.77	4	.241	.294	.358
1995	Chicago	AL		12	21	4	1	0	0	5	4	3	2	0	4	0	0	0	0	1	.00	1	.190	.261	.238
6	Min. YEARS			632	2355	609	84	31	24	827	335	227	229	9	328	13	31	24	154	49	.76	25	.259	.325	.351

Derek Brandow

Pitches: Right **Bats:** Right **Pos:** P **Ht:** 6'1" **Wt:** 200 **Born:** 1/25/70 **Age:** 27

HOW MUCH HE PITCHED										WHAT HE GAVE UP												THE RESULTS					
Year	Team	Lg	Org	G	GS	CG	GF	IP	BFP	H	R	ER	HR	SH	SF	HB	TBB	IBB	SO	WP	Bk	W	L	Pct.	ShO	Sv	ERA
1992	St. Cathrns	A-	Tor	22	2	0	9	58.1	249	51	23	16	6	3	3	2	26	0	74	5	1	5	2	.714	0	3	2.47
1993	Hagerstown	A	Tor	40	1	0	27	76.1	340	76	38	31	5	2	2	4	34	1	62	6	0	4	5	.444	0	6	3.66
1994	Dunedin	A+	Tor	29	21	0	3	140.1	593	122	59	50	6	4	5	2	58	0	123	11	1	7	6	.538	0	1	3.21
1995	Knoxville	AA	Tor	25	21	1	1	107	466	95	60	51	13	1	8	6	50	1	106	9	0	5	6	.455	0	1	4.29
1996	Knoxville	AA	Tor	5	1	0	3	11.2	50	11	10	10	3	2	2	0	5	0	6	2	1	1	2	.333	0	2	7.71
	Syracuse	AAA	Tor	24	20	2	0	124	539	118	64	59	14	4	5	3	57	0	103	8	0	8	7	.533	0	0	4.28
5	Min. YEARS			145	66	3	43	517.2	2237	473	254	217	47	16	25	17	230	2	474	41	3	30	28	.517	0	13	3.77

Scott Bream

Bats: Both **Throws:** Right **Pos:** OF **Ht:** 6'1" **Wt:** 170 **Born:** 11/4/70 **Age:** 26

BATTING																			BASERUNNING				PERCENTAGES		
Year	Team	Lg	Org	G	AB	H	2B	3B	HR	TB	R	RBI	TBB	IBB	SO	HBP	SH	SF	SB	CS	SB%	GDP	Avg	OBP	SLG
1989	Padres	R	SD	28	97	17	3	1	0	22	15	8	18	0	22	1	0	0	9	5	.64	2	.175	.310	.227
1990	Charlstn-SC	A	SD	4	14	1	0	0	0	1	2	0	4	0	7	0	1	0	1	0	1.00	0	.071	.278	.071
1991	Charlstn-SC	A	SD	52	174	24	2	1	0	28	17	7	20	0	61	1	1	1	10	6	.63	1	.138	.230	.161
	Spokane	A-	SD	68	262	56	4	5	0	70	37	26	25	1	57	5	3	3	16	7	.70	5	.214	.292	.267
1992	Waterloo	A	SD	124	392	90	9	6	1	114	50	29	33	0	126	2	4	0	17	9	.65	4	.230	.293	.291
1993	Rancho Cuca	A+	SD	113	405	114	15	6	4	153	70	52	74	3	85	2	4	3	30	14	.68	10	.281	.393	.378
1994	Wichita	AA	SD	109	333	100	8	3	5	129	40	35	42	4	81	3	3	2	18	8	.69	4	.300	.382	.387
1995	Las Vegas	AAA	SD	87	303	73	7	1	0	82	33	15	35	1	59	3	2	0	7	5	.58	7	.241	.326	.271
	Iowa	AAA	ChN	29	82	13	1	0	2	20	10	9	11	0	20	0	3	0	1	0	1.00	1	.159	.258	.244
1996	Jacksonvlle	AA	Det	36	108	26	3	1	3	40	18	12	10	0	31	1	3	0	2	1	.67	0	.241	.311	.370
8	Min. YEARS			650	2170	514	52	24	15	659	292	193	272	9	549	18	24	9	111	55	.67	34	.237	.326	.304

Brian Brewer

Pitches: Left **Bats:** Left **Pos:** P **Ht:** 5'11" **Wt:** 210 **Born:** 12/10/71 **Age:** 25

HOW MUCH HE PITCHED										WHAT HE GAVE UP												THE RESULTS					
Year	Team	Lg	Org	G	GS	CG	GF	IP	BFP	H	R	ER	HR	SH	SF	HB	TBB	IBB	SO	WP	Bk	W	L	Pct.	ShO	Sv	ERA
1993	Bluefield	R+	Bal	6	3	1	2	26	112	18	8	4	1	0	0	2	10	0	18	2	0	3	0	1.000	0	0	1.38
	Albany	A	Bal	6	3	0	0	21	104	19	14	6	1	1	3	1	21	0	19	3	0	0	3	.000	0	0	2.57
1994	Albany	A	Bal	26	16	2	6	123.1	529	127	65	54	5	3	4	2	42	0	92	9	2	6	8	.429	0	2	3.94
1995	Frederick	A+	Bal	14	8	0	3	67.2	263	49	22	19	2	3	2	3	19	1	48	5	2	2	4	.333	0	1	2.53
	High Desert	A+	Bal	31	23	1	3	148.1	639	145	88	68	4	7	2	8	61	2	113	10	4	3	13	.188	0	1	4.13
1996	Bowie	AA	Bal	11	11	0	0	57	253	61	40	31	10	1	0	2	27	0	35	2	2	2	4	.333	0	0	4.89
	High Desert	A+	Bal	18	13	0	1	75	345	77	53	43	8	4	4	4	48	0	57	11	2	5	4	.556	0	0	5.16
4	Min. YEARS			112	77	4	15	518.1	2245	496	290	225	31	19	15	22	228	3	382	42	12	21	36	.368	0	4	3.91

Jamie Brewington

Pitches: Right **Bats:** Right **Pos:** P **Ht:** 6' 4" **Wt:** 190 **Born:** 9/28/71 **Age:** 25

HOW MUCH HE PITCHED										WHAT HE GAVE UP												THE RESULTS					
Year	Team	Lg	Org	G	GS	CG	GF	IP	BFP	H	R	ER	HR	SH	SF	HB	TBB	IBB	SO	WP	Bk	W	L	Pct.	ShO	Sv	ERA
1992	Everett	A-	SF	15	11	1	1	68.2	317	65	40	33	2	0	3	5	47	2	63	9	1	5	2	.714	1	0	4.33
1993	Clinton	A	SF	26	25	1	0	133.2	580	126	78	71	20	1	3	5	61	1	111	19	2	13	5	.722	0	0	4.78
1994	Clinton	A	SF	10	10	0	0	53	226	46	29	29	5	1	3	2	24	0	62	7	1	2	4	.333	0	0	4.92
	San Jose	A+	SF	13	13	0	0	76	310	61	38	27	3	2	2	2	25	0	65	7	1	7	3	.700	0	0	3.20
1995	Shreveport	AA	SF	16	16	1	0	88.1	376	72	39	30	8	2	7	0	55	0	74	4	0	8	3	.727	1	0	3.06
1996	Phoenix	AAA	SF	35	17	0	7	110.1	526	130	93	86	14	5	3	6	72	1	75	15	0	6	9	.400	0	1	7.02
1995	San Francisco	NL		13	13	0	0	75.1	334	68	38	38	8	4	4	4	45	6	45	3	0	6	4	.600	0	0	4.54
5	Min. YEARS			115	92	3	8	530	2335	500	317	276	52	11	21	20	284	4	450	61	5	41	26	.612	2	1	4.69

Kary Bridges

Bats: Left **Throws:** Right **Pos:** 2B **Ht:** 5'10" **Wt:** 165 **Born:** 10/27/71 **Age:** 25

BATTING																			BASERUNNING				PERCENTAGES		
Year	Team	Lg	Org	G	AB	H	2B	3B	HR	TB	R	RBI	TBB	IBB	SO	HBP	SH	SF	SB	CS	SB%	GDP	Avg	OBP	SLG
1993	Quad City	A	Hou	65	263	74	9	0	3	92	37	24	31	1	18	2	1	3	15	10	.60	7	.281	.358	.350
1994	Quad City	A	Hou	117	447	135	20	4	1	166	66	53	38	3	29	3	8	4	14	11	.56	9	.302	.358	.371
1995	Jackson	AA	Hou	118	418	126	22	4	3	165	56	43	48	3	18	0	6	4	10	12	.45	12	.301	.370	.395
1996	Jackson	AA	Hou	87	338	110	12	2	4	138	51	33	32	1	14	1	7	3	4	5	.44	11	.325	.382	.408

BATTING																	BASERUNNING				PERCENTAGES		
Year Team	Lg Org	G	AB	H	2B	3B	HR	TB	R	RBI	TBB	IBB	SO	HBP	SH	SF	SB	CS	SB%	GDP	Avg	OBP	SLG
Tucson	AAA Hou	42	140	44	9	1	1	58	24	21	9	1	8	1	0	2	1	3	.25	3	.314	.355	.414
4 Min. YEARS		429	1606	489	72	11	12	619	234	174	158	9	87	7	22	16	44	41	.52	42	.304	.366	.385

Stoney Briggs

Bats: Right **Throws:** Right **Pos:** OF **Ht:** 6'2" **Wt:** 215 **Born:** 12/26/71 **Age:** 25

BATTING																	BASERUNNING				PERCENTAGES		
Year Team	Lg Org	G	AB	H	2B	3B	HR	TB	R	RBI	TBB	IBB	SO	HBP	SH	SF	SB	CS	SB%	GDP	Avg	OBP	SLG
1991 Medicne Hat	R+ Tor	64	236	70	8	0	8	102	45	29	18	0	62	2	0	2	9	5	.64	2	.297	.349	.432
1992 Myrtle Bch	A Tor	136	514	123	18	5	11	184	75	41	43	0	156	8	6	2	33	14	.70	6	.239	.307	.358
1993 Waterloo	A SD	125	421	108	15	5	9	160	57	55	30	1	103	12	4	5	21	8	.72	3	.257	.321	.380
1994 Rancho Cuca	A+ SD	121	417	112	22	2	17	189	63	76	54	1	124	9	2	7	14	13	.52	7	.269	.359	.453
1995 Memphis	AA SD	118	385	95	14	7	8	147	60	46	40	5	133	10	1	3	17	8	.68	13	.247	.331	.382
1996 Memphis	AA SD	133	452	124	24	6	12	196	72	80	62	4	123	4	4	3	28	11	.72	18	.274	.365	.434
6 Min. YEARS		697	2425	632	101	25	65	978	372	327	247	11	701	45	17	22	122	59	.67	49	.261	.337	.403

Darryl Brinkley

Bats: Right **Throws:** Right **Pos:** OF **Ht:** 5'11" **Wt:** 205 **Born:** 12/23/68 **Age:** 28

BATTING																	BASERUNNING				PERCENTAGES		
Year Team	Lg Org	G	AB	H	2B	3B	HR	TB	R	RBI	TBB	IBB	SO	HBP	SH	SF	SB	CS	SB%	GDP	Avg	OBP	SLG
1994 Winnipeg	IND —	72	294	86	18	3	8	134	48	44	21	0	31	6	3	1	32	13	.71	5	.293	.351	.456
1995 Winnipeg	IND —	30	131	44	2	1	4	60	22	19	8	1	13	3	1	2	6	4	.60	4	.336	.382	.458
1996 Rancho Cuca	A+ SD	65	259	94	28	2	9	153	52	59	23	2	37	2	0	6	18	10	.64	13	.363	.410	.591
Memphis	AA SD	60	203	60	9	0	9	96	36	29	22	2	33	3	1	1	13	5	.72	2	.296	.371	.473
3 Min. YEARS		227	887	284	57	6	30	443	158	151	74	5	114	14	5	10	69	32	.68	24	.320	.378	.499

Luis Brito

Bats: Both **Throws:** Right **Pos:** SS **Ht:** 6'0" **Wt:** 155 **Born:** 4/12/71 **Age:** 26

BATTING																	BASERUNNING				PERCENTAGES		
Year Team	Lg Org	G	AB	H	2B	3B	HR	TB	R	RBI	TBB	IBB	SO	HBP	SH	SF	SB	CS	SB%	GDP	Avg	OBP	SLG
1989 Martinsvlle	R+ Phi	9	16	5	0	0	0	5	1	1	0	0	3	0	0	0	0	0	.00	0	.313	.313	.313
1990 Princeton	R+ Phi	27	95	23	2	0	0	25	15	4	2	0	11	2	1	0	4	2	.67	1	.242	.273	.263
1991 Martinsvlle	R+ Phi	31	123	33	5	0	0	38	17	9	5	0	21	2	1	2	5	2	.71	3	.268	.303	.309
Batavia	A- Phi	22	76	24	2	1	0	28	13	10	6	0	8	0	2	0	9	3	.75	1	.316	.366	.368
1992 Spartanburg	A Phi	34	105	23	1	1	0	26	11	9	4	0	17	0	1	0	7	8	.47	1	.219	.248	.248
Clearwater	A+ Phi	65	188	41	4	0	0	45	18	11	5	0	21	1	6	1	4	7	.36	0	.218	.241	.239
1993 Spartanburg	A Phi	127	467	146	16	4	0	170	56	33	11	0	47	1	8	3	9	12	.43	12	.313	.328	.364
1994 Clearwater	A+ Phi	31	108	35	4	3	1	48	18	13	2	0	3	0	1	1	2	1	.67	4	.324	.333	.444
Reading	AA Phi	86	284	63	6	2	3	82	33	21	13	0	38	2	4	2	4	4	.50	4	.222	.259	.289
1995 Reading	AA Phi	2	3	1	0	0	0	1	1	1	0	0	0	0	0	0	1	0	1.00	0	.333	.333	.333
Clearwater	A+ Phi	109	383	105	14	3	3	134	42	41	17	0	35	1	5	3	12	5	.71	14	.274	.304	.350
1996 Greenville	AA Atl	19	43	5	0	0	0	5	4	4	1	0	6	0	2	0	1	1	.50	2	.116	.136	.116
Durham	A+ Atl	81	315	90	16	1	3	117	35	34	10	0	33	3	6	1	6	3	.67	5	.286	.313	.371
8 Min. YEARS		643	2206	594	70	15	10	724	264	191	76	0	243	12	37	13	64	48	.57	47	.269	.296	.328

Mario Brito

Pitches: Right **Bats:** Right **Pos:** P **Ht:** 6'3" **Wt:** 179 **Born:** 4/9/66 **Age:** 31

HOW MUCH HE PITCHED								WHAT HE GAVE UP												THE RESULTS					
Year Team	Lg Org	G	GS	CG	GF	IP	BFP	H	R	ER	HR	SH	SF	HB	TBB	IBB	SO	WP	Bk	W	L	Pct.	ShO	Sv	ERA
1986 Expos	R Mon	11	11	1	0	59.1	254	58	29	27	4	3	4	4	24	0	40	4	1	5	3	.625	0	0	4.10
1987 Jamestown	A- Mon	15	15	3	0	95.1	414	83	50	32	6	5	3	2	40	0	89	3	0	6	5	.545	0	0	3.02
1988 Rockford	A Mon	27	27	7	0	186	775	161	83	62	11	2	2	5	52	1	144	4	7	13	8	.619	2	0	3.00
1989 W. Palm Bch	A+ Mon	23	23	4	0	149.1	624	134	64	48	2	3	3	4	49	2	90	5	2	11	8	.579	1	0	2.89
1990 Jacksonvlle	AA Mon	18	18	1	0	115.2	488	100	57	41	6	4	3	3	34	1	49	4	0	9	7	.563	0	0	3.19
1991 Vancouver	AAA ChA	19	13	1	2	78.1	366	106	69	62	8	2	6	3	25	2	41	0	0	0	10	.000	0	0	7.12
Birmingham	AA ChA	10	10	4	0	71	284	53	31	26	4	2	0	2	16	0	37	5	0	2	4	.333	1	0	3.30
1992 Indianapols	AAA Mon	2	0	0	0	5.1	23	5	2	2	1	0	0	0	3	0	1	0	0	2	0	1.000	0	0	3.38
Harrisburg	AA Mon	46	0	0	15	77.1	317	65	25	19	3	3	0	3	24	4	66	4	0	6	4	.600	0	3	2.21
1993 Harrisburg	AA Mon	36	0	0	22	50.1	207	41	17	15	5	3	0	3	11	3	51	0	0	4	3	.571	0	10	2.68
Ottawa	AAA Mon	23	0	0	9	34	139	25	6	5	0	2	0	1	17	0	29	3	0	2	0	1.000	0	2	1.32
1994 New Orleans	AAA Mil	40	0	0	32	57.2	225	39	18	16	3	3	0	1	20	0	74	5	0	6	2	.750	0	11	2.50
1996 Charlotte	AAA Fla	6	0	0	6	5	21	3	1	1	1	0	0	0	2	0	10	0	0	1	0	1.000	0	4	1.80
10 Min. YEARS		276	117	21	86	984.2	4137	873	452	356	54	32	21	31	317	13	721	37	10	67	54	.554	4	30	3.25

Donald Broach

Bats: Right **Throws:** Right **Pos:** OF **Ht:** 6'0" **Wt:** 185 **Born:** 7/18/71 **Age:** 25

BATTING																	BASERUNNING				PERCENTAGES		
Year Team	Lg Org	G	AB	H	2B	3B	HR	TB	R	RBI	TBB	IBB	SO	HBP	SH	SF	SB	CS	SB%	GDP	Avg	OBP	SLG
1993 Princeton	R+ Cin	55	181	42	5	1	1	52	29	19	15	0	31	4	2	1	8	3	.73	0	.232	.303	.287
1994 Billings	R+ Cin	63	270	84	11	1	3	106	55	38	24	0	40	7	3	1	17	12	.59	7	.311	.381	.393
1995 Winston-Sal	A+ Cin	117	460	120	23	4	8	175	74	34	50	2	73	5	5	2	16	14	.53	9	.261	.338	.380
1996 Chattanooga	AA Cin	110	349	91	10	2	6	123	58	37	39	2	51	11	5	1	20	9	.69	7	.261	.353	.352
4 Min. YEARS		345	1260	337	49	8	18	456	216	128	128	4	195	27	15	5	61	38	.62	23	.267	.346	.362

Chris Brock

Pitches: Right **Bats:** Right **Pos:** P **Ht:** 6'0" **Wt:** 175 **Born:** 2/5/70 **Age:** 27

				HOW MUCH HE PITCHED						WHAT HE GAVE UP												THE RESULTS					
Year	Team	Lg	Org	G	GS	CG	GF	IP	BFP	H	R	ER	HR	SH	SF	HB	TBB	IBB	SO	WP	Bk	W	L	Pct.	ShO	Sv	ERA
1992	Idaho Falls	R+	Atl	15	15	1	0	78	333	61	27	20	3	3	2	3	48	0	72	12	8	6	4	.600	0	0	2.31
1993	Macon	A	Atl	14	14	1	0	80	333	61	37	24	3	1	0	2	33	0	92	8	1	7	5	.583	0	0	2.70
	Durham	A+	Atl	12	12	1	0	79	335	63	28	22	7	1	2	5	35	0	67	6	0	5	2	.714	0	0	2.51
1994	Greenville	AA	Atl	25	23	2	0	137.1	576	128	68	57	9	4	4	5	47	0	94	8	3	7	6	.538	2	0	3.74
1995	Richmond	AAA	Atl	22	9	0	5	60	270	68	37	36	2	3	3	1	27	2	43	1	2	2	8	.200	0	0	5.40
1996	Richmond	AAA	Atl	26	25	3	0	150.1	652	137	95	78	20	3	8	6	61	0	112	9	0	10	11	.476	0	0	4.67
5 Min. YEARS				114	98	8	5	584.2	2499	518	292	237	44	15	19	22	251	2	480	44	14	37	36	.507	2	0	3.65

Russ Brock

Pitches: Right **Bats:** Right **Pos:** P **Ht:** 6'5" **Wt:** 210 **Born:** 10/13/69 **Age:** 27

				HOW MUCH HE PITCHED						WHAT HE GAVE UP												THE RESULTS					
Year	Team	Lg	Org	G	GS	CG	GF	IP	BFP	H	R	ER	HR	SH	SF	HB	TBB	IBB	SO	WP	Bk	W	L	Pct.	ShO	Sv	ERA
1991	Sou. Oregon	A-	Oak	8	8	1	0	43.1	180	37	19	15	2	1	0	1	12	1	48	4	1	4	0	1.000	1	0	3.12
	Modesto	A+	Oak	4	4	0	0	27	111	25	15	12	3	1	0	1	6	0	12	1	0	1	2	.333	0	0	4.00
1992	Reno	A+	Oak	25	23	0	0	90	414	109	61	44	10	1	3	5	34	3	72	3	0	3	10	.231	0	0	4.40
1993	Modesto	A+	Oak	27	26	1	0	139.1	586	137	69	59	12	2	3	5	44	0	121	4	1	12	4	.750	0	0	3.81
1994	Huntsville	AA	Oak	10	9	1	0	64.2	269	58	27	21	4	3	2	2	23	3	49	1	1	2	3	.400	1	0	2.92
	Tacoma	AAA	Oak	19	18	1	0	119.2	514	115	61	50	13	2	1	3	54	0	85	0	0	6	8	.429	0	0	3.76
1995	Edmonton	AAA	Oak	18	8	0	2	55	266	75	44	42	6	0	3	3	31	4	44	2	1	1	8	.111	0	1	6.87
1996	Columbus	AAA	NYA	1	0	0	0	1	5	2	1	1	0	0	0	0	0	0	2	0	0	0	0	.000	0	0	9.00
	Norwich	AA	NYA	4	0	0	0	11	48	14	10	10	1	1	0	0	5	0	14	0	0	0	1	.000	0	0	8.18
6 Min. YEARS				116	96	4	2	551	2393	572	307	254	51	11	12	20	209	11	447	15	4	29	36	.446	2	1	4.15

Tarrik Brock

Bats: Left **Throws:** Left **Pos:** OF **Ht:** 6'3" **Wt:** 170 **Born:** 12/25/73 **Age:** 23

				BATTING															BASERUNNING				PERCENTAGES		
Year	Team	Lg	Org	G	AB	H	2B	3B	HR	TB	R	RBI	TBB	IBB	SO	HBP	SH	SF	SB	CS	SB%	GDP	Avg	OBP	SLG
1991	Bristol	R+	Det	55	177	47	7	3	1	63	26	13	22	0	42	3	1	1	14	6	.70	3	.266	.355	.356
1992	Fayettevlle	A	Det	100	271	59	5	4	0	72	35	17	31	1	69	4	5	1	15	10	.60	2	.218	.306	.266
1993	Fayettevlle	A	Det	116	427	92	8	4	3	117	60	47	54	2	108	5	5	4	25	16	.61	5	.215	.308	.274
1994	Lakeland	A+	Det	86	331	77	17	14	2	128	43	32	38	2	89	2	2	2	15	6	.71	5	.233	.314	.387
	Trenton	AA	Det	34	115	16	1	4	2	31	12	11	13	0	43	2	1	0	3	3	.50	2	.139	.238	.270
1995	Toledo	AAA	Det	9	31	6	1	0	0	7	4	0	2	0	17	0	0	0	2	2	.50	0	.194	.242	.226
	Jacksonvlle	AA	Det	9	26	3	0	0	0	3	4	2	3	0	14	1	1	0	2	0	1.00	0	.115	.233	.115
	Lakeland	A+	Det	28	91	19	3	0	0	22	12	5	12	0	32	0	1	0	5	3	.63	2	.209	.301	.242
	Visalia	A+	Det	45	138	31	5	2	1	43	21	15	17	0	52	4	2	0	11	1	.92	2	.225	.327	.312
1996	Lakeland	A+	Det	53	212	59	11	4	5	93	42	27	17	0	61	5	0	3	9	2	.82	4	.278	.342	.439
	Jacksonvlle	AA	Det	37	102	13	2	0	0	15	14	6	10	0	36	1	0	0	3	3	.50	0	.127	.212	.147
	Fayettevlle	A	Det	32	119	35	5	2	1	47	21	11	14	1	31	4	0	1	4	5	.44	3	.294	.384	.395
6 Min. YEARS				604	2040	457	65	37	15	641	294	186	233	6	594	31	18	12	108	57	.65	28	.224	.311	.314

Troy Brohawn

Pitches: Left **Bats:** Left **Pos:** P **Ht:** 6'1" **Wt:** 190 **Born:** 1/14/73 **Age:** 24

				HOW MUCH HE PITCHED						WHAT HE GAVE UP												THE RESULTS					
Year	Team	Lg	Org	G	GS	CG	GF	IP	BFP	H	R	ER	HR	SH	SF	HB	TBB	IBB	SO	WP	Bk	W	L	Pct.	ShO	Sv	ERA
1994	San Jose	A+	SF	4	4	0	0	16.2	80	27	15	13	2	1	0	2	5	0	13	1	0	0	2	.000	0	0	7.02
1995	San Jose	A+	SF	11	10	0	1	65.1	246	45	14	12	4	1	1	1	20	0	57	5	1	7	3	.700	0	0	1.65
1996	Shreveport	AA	SF	28	28	0	0	156.2	668	163	99	80	30	7	3	6	49	0	82	8	3	9	10	.474	0	0	4.60
3 Min. YEARS				43	42	0	1	238.2	994	235	128	105	36	9	4	9	74	0	152	14	4	16	15	.516	0	0	3.96

Jason Brosnan

Pitches: Left **Bats:** Left **Pos:** P **Ht:** 6'1" **Wt:** 190 **Born:** 1/26/68 **Age:** 29

				HOW MUCH HE PITCHED						WHAT HE GAVE UP												THE RESULTS					
Year	Team	Lg	Org	G	GS	CG	GF	IP	BFP	H	R	ER	HR	SH	SF	HB	TBB	IBB	SO	WP	Bk	W	L	Pct.	ShO	Sv	ERA
1989	Great Falls	R+	LA	13	13	0	0	67	294	41	24	19	1	1	1	3	55	0	89	10	4	6	2	.750	0	0	2.55
1990	Bakersfield	A+	LA	26	25	0	0	136	607	113	63	47	4	3	4	7	91	1	157	7	2	12	4	.750	0	0	3.11
1991	San Antonio	AA	LA	2	2	0	0	7.2	49	15	15	15	2	0	0	0	11	0	8	0	0	0	1	.000	0	0	17.61
	Vero Beach	A+	LA	11	9	0	0	36.1	164	34	27	23	2	1	2	2	21	0	25	5	0	1	2	.333	0	0	5.70
1992	Albuquerque	AAA	LA	8	0	0	3	8.2	44	13	9	8	2	1	0	1	4	0	12	2	0	0	0	.000	0	1	8.31
	San Antonio	AA	LA	8	8	0	0	32.1	163	44	33	28	9	2	2	1	21	1	27	4	0	1	7	.125	0	0	7.79
	Vero Beach	A+	LA	18	8	2	3	58	255	69	32	30	2	2	1	2	26	2	51	11	1	3	4	.429	0	0	4.66
1993	Vero Beach	A+	LA	23	0	0	9	25.2	127	30	22	13	1	1	1	1	19	2	32	4	0	0	2	.000	0	1	4.56
	Bakersfield	A+	LA	9	6	0	1	36.1	161	36	20	14	2	1	1	2	15	0	34	4	0	4	1	.800	0	0	3.47
	San Antonio	AA	LA	3	3	0	0	20.1	83	21	11	10	1	0	0	0	7	0	10	1	0	0	2	.000	0	0	4.43
1994	San Antonio	AA	LA	17	1	0	8	30.2	141	34	16	12	3	0	1	2	12	1	29	3	0	2	3	.400	0	1	3.52
	Albuquerque	AAA	LA	24	7	0	5	61.2	275	75	36	36	4	2	1	0	30	0	43	3	2	2	4	.333	0	1	5.25
1995	San Antonio	AA	LA	19	0	0	7	22.2	94	24	9	9	1	1	0	0	4	0	21	1	0	1	0	1.000	0	2	3.57
	Albuquerque	AAA	LA	42	1	0	18	53.2	222	54	25	24	4	1	2	0	13	1	39	1	1	3	0	1.000	0	4	4.02
1996	Tacoma	AAA	Sea	12	2	0	3	31.2	125	19	14	10	2	1	1	3	15	1	26	2	0	3	1	.750	0	1	2.84
	Port City	AA	Sea	30	9	1	7	77	327	71	33	31	8	2	2	1	32	1	76	2	0	5	6	.455	1	1	3.62
8 Min. YEARS				265	94	3	64	705.2	3131	693	389	329	48	19	19	25	376	10	679	60	10	43	39	.524	1	12	4.20

Jim Brower

Pitches: Right **Bats:** Right **Pos:** P **Ht:** 6'2" **Wt:** 205 **Born:** 12/29/72 **Age:** 24

				HOW MUCH HE PITCHED						WHAT HE GAVE UP												THE RESULTS					
Year	Team	Lg	Org	G	GS	CG	GF	IP	BFP	H	R	ER	HR	SH	SF	HB	TBB	IBB	SO	WP	Bk	W	L	Pct.	ShO	Sv	ERA
1994	Hudson Vall	A-	Tex	4	4	1	0	19.2	83	14	10	7	0	0	2	1	6	0	15	0	1	2	1	.667	0	0	3.20
	Charlstn-SC	A	Tex	12	12	3	0	78.2	312	52	18	15	2	1	1	5	26	1	84	6	0	7	3	.700	2	0	1.72
1995	Charlotte	A+	Tex	27	27	2	0	173.2	740	170	93	75	16	3	3	8	62	1	110	11	0	7	10	.412	1	0	3.89
1996	Charlotte	A+	Tex	23	21	2	2	145	607	148	67	61	11	5	4	4	40	0	86	7	2	9	8	.529	0	0	3.79
	Tulsa	AA	Tex	5	5	1	0	33.1	140	35	16	14	4	0	1	1	10	0	16	1	0	3	2	.600	1	0	3.78
	3 Min. YEARS			71	69	9	2	450.1	1882	419	204	172	33	9	11	19	144	2	311	25	3	28	24	.538	4	0	3.44

Adrian Brown

Bats: Right **Throws:** Right **Pos:** OF **Ht:** 6'0" **Wt:** 185 **Born:** 2/7/74 **Age:** 23

				BATTING															BASERUNNING				PERCENTAGES		
Year	Team	Lg	Org	G	AB	H	2B	3B	HR	TB	R	RBI	TBB	IBB	SO	HBP	SH	SF	SB	CS	SB%	GDP	Avg	OBP	SLG
1992	Pirates	R	Pit	39	121	31	2	2	0	37	11	12	0	0	12	2	0	0	8	4	.67	3	.256	.268	.306
1993	Lethbridge	R+	Pit	69	282	75	12	9	3	114	47	27	17	1	34	5	3	0	22	7	.76	8	.266	.319	.404
1994	Augusta	A	Pit	79	308	80	17	1	1	102	41	18	14	0	38	0	6	0	19	12	.61	2	.260	.292	.331
1995	Augusta	A	Pit	76	287	86	15	4	4	121	64	31	33	0	23	1	3	2	25	14	.64	2	.300	.372	.422
	Lynchburg	A+	Pit	54	215	52	5	2	1	64	30	14	12	0	20	1	4	1	11	6	.65	3	.242	.284	.298
1996	Lynchburg	A+	Pit	52	215	69	9	3	4	96	39	25	14	1	24	2	1	0	18	9	.67	1	.321	.368	.447
	Carolina	AA	Pit	84	341	101	11	3	3	127	48	25	25	3	40	1	5	1	27	11	.71	4	.296	.345	.372
	5 Min. YEARS			453	1769	494	71	24	16	661	280	152	115	5	191	12	22	4	130	63	.67	23	.279	.327	.374

Chad Brown

Pitches: Left **Bats:** Left **Pos:** P **Ht:** 6'0" **Wt:** 185 **Born:** 12/9/71 **Age:** 25

				HOW MUCH HE PITCHED						WHAT HE GAVE UP												THE RESULTS					
Year	Team	Lg	Org	G	GS	CG	GF	IP	BFP	H	R	ER	HR	SH	SF	HB	TBB	IBB	SO	WP	Bk	W	L	Pct.	ShO	Sv	ERA
1992	Medicne Hat	R+	Tor	21	0	0	9	37	180	46	28	18	4	0	0	1	21	1	28	7	1	3	3	.500	0	1	4.38
1993	St. Cathrns	A-	Tor	18	0	0	18	20.2	71	7	4	4	2	0	0	0	5	0	23	0	0	2	0	1.000	0	10	1.74
1994	Dunedin	A+	Tor	52	0	0	20	78	326	59	29	28	1	4	3	0	41	1	56	3	2	6	7	.462	0	4	3.23
1995	Syracuse	AAA	Tor	11	0	0	5	22	106	21	11	8	1	2	2	0	20	3	14	4	0	1	1	.500	0	0	3.27
	Knoxville	AA	Tor	51	0	0	19	63.1	287	59	34	29	3	3	3	1	42	4	49	9	0	2	4	.333	0	1	4.12
1996	Knoxville	AA	Tor	46	0	0	23	64.1	285	72	33	29	2	1	1	1	23	1	63	6	1	2	4	.333	0	7	4.06
	5 Min. YEARS			199	0	0	94	285.1	1255	264	139	116	13	10	9	3	152	10	233	29	4	16	19	.457	0	23	3.66

Charlie Brown

Pitches: Right **Bats:** Right **Pos:** P **Ht:** 6'3" **Wt:** 178 **Born:** 9/13/73 **Age:** 23

				HOW MUCH HE PITCHED						WHAT HE GAVE UP												THE RESULTS					
Year	Team	Lg	Org	G	GS	CG	GF	IP	BFP	H	R	ER	HR	SH	SF	HB	TBB	IBB	SO	WP	Bk	W	L	Pct.	ShO	Sv	ERA
1992	Yankees	R	NYA	12	7	0	0	45	197	45	20	16	1	0	0	2	14	0	34	3	2	2	1	.667	0	0	3.20
1993	Yankees	R	NYA	16	6	0	5	52.2	223	51	28	21	2	3	0	1	13	0	54	2	1	3	3	.500	0	1	3.59
	Pr. William	A+	NYA	2	1	0	0	6.2	30	5	4	4	1	0	0	2	6	0	4	2	0	0	0	.000	0	0	5.40
1994	Tampa	A+	NYA	1	0	0	0	2.1	13	5	3	3	0	0	0	0	2	0	2	0	0	0	0	.000	0	0	11.57
	Oneonta	A-	NYA	17	0	0	11	21	95	20	14	12	0	1	0	0	12	1	22	3	0	2	1	.667	0	2	5.14
1995	Greensboro	A	NYA	45	2	0	22	57	252	57	31	28	6	3	3	2	23	5	69	11	1	4	4	.500	0	4	4.42
1996	Norwich	AA	NYA	1	0	0	0	2.1	9	1	0	0	0	0	0	0	1	0	1	0	0	0	0	.000	0	0	0.00
	Tampa	A+	NYA	12	0	0	8	15.2	69	16	9	6	2	0	1	1	5	0	16	0	0	0	0	.000	0	0	3.45
	Greensboro	A	NYA	23	0	0	21	28.1	114	13	6	5	1	2	0	2	13	2	33	1	0	2	2	.500	0	8	1.59
	5 Min. YEARS			129	16	0	67	231	1002	213	115	95	13	9	4	10	89	8	235	22	4	13	11	.542	0	15	3.70

Dickie Brown

Pitches: Right **Bats:** Right **Pos:** P **Ht:** 5'9" **Wt:** 170 **Born:** 8/13/70 **Age:** 26

				HOW MUCH HE PITCHED						WHAT HE GAVE UP												THE RESULTS					
Year	Team	Lg	Org	G	GS	CG	GF	IP	BFP	H	R	ER	HR	SH	SF	HB	TBB	IBB	SO	WP	Bk	W	L	Pct.	ShO	Sv	ERA
1990	Burlington	R+	Cle	13	12	0	0	67.1	307	76	45	43	6	2	2	4	30	0	53	10	2	3	4	.429	0	0	5.75
1991	Columbus	A	Cle	27	26	1	1	152.1	678	167	111	92	11	4	4	10	61	2	109	6	1	8	11	.421	1	0	5.44
1992	Kinston	A+	Cle	4	1	0	1	13.2	63	16	15	13	2	0	1	0	7	0	7	0	1	0	0	.000	0	0	8.56
	Columbus	A	Cle	29	3	0	5	80	344	60	25	21	3	2	2	3	49	4	65	7	0	8	3	.727	0	0	2.36
1993	Kinston	A+	Cle	31	8	0	7	82	366	77	40	30	6	4	2	7	42	0	62	5	0	4	3	.571	0	2	3.29
1994	High Desert	A+	Cle	18	18	4	0	114.2	487	114	57	49	10	3	4	8	37	1	100	5	0	6	6	.500	1	0	3.85
	Kinston	A+	Cle	7	7	1	0	41	171	33	21	18	5	1	0	2	14	0	40	0	0	4	2	.667	0	0	3.95
1995	Canton-Akrn	AA	Cle	37	9	0	11	98.1	449	88	56	51	9	7	3	4	67	7	51	9	0	8	5	.615	0	3	4.67
1996	Canton-Akrn	AA	Cle	6	0	0	1	12.1	62	13	12	11	3	0	0	1	9	1	11	0	0	0	2	.000	0	0	8.03
	Newburgh	IND	—	2	2	0	0	11	42	7	1	1	0	0	0	1	2	0	8	0	0	1	0	1.000	0	0	0.82
	Stockton	A+	Mil	5	0	0	0	6.1	31	9	5	4	1	0	0	1	4	0	7	0	0	0	0	.000	0	0	5.68
	7 Min. YEARS			179	86	6	26	679	3000	660	388	333	56	23	18	41	322	15	513	42	4	42	36	.538	2	5	4.41

Jarvis Brown

Bats: Right **Throws:** Right **Pos:** OF **Ht:** 5' 7" **Wt:** 170 **Born:** 9/26/67 **Age:** 29

				BATTING															BASERUNNING				PERCENTAGES		
Year	Team	Lg	Org	G	AB	H	2B	3B	HR	TB	R	RBI	TBB	IBB	SO	HBP	SH	SF	SB	CS	SB%	GDP	Avg	OBP	SLG
1986	Elizabethtn	R+	Min	40	100	41	4	0	3	54	28	23	18	0	41	4	5	1	15	3	.83	3	.228	.310	.300
1987	Elizabethtn	R+	Min	67	258	63	9	1	1	77	52	15	48	1	50	5	3	0	30	2	.94	3	.244	.373	.298

Year	Team	Lg	Org	G	AB	H	2B	3B	HR	TB	R	RBI	TBB	IBB	SO	HBP	SH	SF	SB	CS	SB%	GDP	Avg	OBP	SLG
	Kenosha	A	Min	43	117	22	4	1	3	37	17	16	19	0	24	2	1	2	6	2	.75	2	.188	.307	.316
1988	Kenosha	A	Min	138	531	156	25	7	7	216	108	45	71	0	89	10	7	5	72	15	.83	10	.294	.384	.407
1989	Visalia	A+	Min	141	545	131	21	6	4	176	95	46	73	0	112	13	4	4	49	13	.79	12	.240	.342	.323
1990	Orlando	AA	Min	135	527	137	22	7	14	215	104	57	80	1	79	9	5	2	33	19	.63	13	.260	.366	.408
1991	Portland	AAA	Min	108	436	126	5	8	3	156	62	37	36	1	66	6	3	1	26	12	.68	6	.289	.351	.358
1992	Portland	AAA	Min	62	224	56	8	2	2	74	25	16	20	0	37	5	1	1	17	1	.94	2	.250	.324	.330
1993	Las Vegas	AAA	SD	100	402	124	27	9	3	178	74	47	41	1	55	5	5	2	22	5	.81	10	.308	.378	.443
1994	Richmond	AAA	Atl	71	270	72	11	5	4	105	41	30	36	1	35	4	2	3	8	3	.73	4	.267	.358	.389
1995	Norfolk	AAA	NYN	45	148	42	12	3	0	60	29	17	18	0	29	1	2	0	6	3	.67	3	.284	.365	.405
	Bowie	AA	Bal	58	219	61	12	1	6	93	50	23	33	0	49	4	2	1	12	3	.80	5	.279	.381	.425
	Rochester	AAA	Bal	17	70	22	4	2	0	30	12	4	10	0	20	0	2	0	1	1	.50	2	.314	.400	.429
1996	Rochester	AAA	Bal	57	204	43	6	6	4	73	28	19	19	0	36	2	0	3	9	1	.90	5	.211	.281	.358
	Thunder Bay	IND	—	43	160	48	7	1	4	69	27	20	19	0	20	2	0	2	9	3	.75	4	.300	.377	.431
1991	Minnesota	AL		38	37	8	0	0	0	8	10	0	2	0	8	0	1	0	7	1	.88	0	.216	.256	.216
1992	Minnesota	AL		35	15	1	0	0	0	1	8	0	2	0	4	1	0	0	2	2	.50	0	.067	.222	.067
1993	San Diego	NL		47	133	31	9	2	0	44	21	8	15	0	26	6	2	1	3	3	.50	4	.233	.335	.331
1994	Atlanta	NL		17	15	2	1	0	1	6	3	1	0	0	2	0	1	0	0	0	.00	1	.133	.133	.400
1995	Baltimore	AL		18	27	4	1	0	0	5	2	1	7	0	9	0	3	0	1	1	.50	0	.148	.324	.185
11 Min. YEARS				1134	4291	1144	177	59	58	1613	752	415	541	5	742	72	42	27	315	86	.79	84	.267	.356	.376
5 Maj. YEARS				155	227	46	11	2	1	64	44	10	26	0	49	7	7	1	13	7	.65	5	.203	.303	.282

Randy Brown

Bats: Right **Throws:** Right **Pos:** SS **Ht:** 5'11" **Wt:** 160 **Born:** 5/1/70 **Age:** 27

		BATTING																	BASERUNNING				PERCENTAGES		
Year	Team	Lg	Org	G	AB	H	2B	3B	HR	TB	R	RBI	TBB	IBB	SO	HBP	SH	SF	SB	CS	SB%	GDP	Avg	OBP	SLG
1990	Elmira	A-	Bos	74	212	50	4	0	1	57	27	8	17	0	47	4	9	0	17	4	.81	1	.236	.305	.269
1991	Red Sox	R	Bos	44	143	27	7	0	0	34	25	10	23	0	31	2	3	1	19	0	1.00	4	.189	.308	.238
	Winter Havn	A+	Bos	63	135	21	3	0	0	24	14	5	16	0	42	1	4	0	10	3	.77	2	.156	.250	.178
1992	Winter Havn	A+	Bos	121	430	101	18	2	2	129	39	24	28	0	115	6	8	4	8	9	.47	1	.235	.288	.300
1993	Lynchburg	A+	Bos	128	483	114	25	7	2	159	57	45	25	0	127	13	2	4	10	8	.56	6	.236	.290	.329
1994	New Britain	AA	Bos	114	389	87	14	2	8	129	51	30	30	0	102	5	7	4	9	5	.64	1	.224	.285	.332
1995	Pawtucket	AAA	Bos	74	212	53	6	1	2	67	27	12	10	0	53	4	4	2	5	1	.83	4	.250	.294	.316
1996	Pawtucket	AAA	Bos	3	6	1	0	0	0	1	0	1	1	0	1	0	0	0	0	0	.00	1	.167	.286	.167
	Trenton	AA	Bos	72	245	73	15	2	11	125	46	38	27	2	56	5	1	0	9	4	.69	3	.298	.379	.510
7 Min. YEARS				693	2255	527	92	14	26	725	286	173	177	2	574	40	38	15	87	34	.72	23	.234	.299	.322

Ray Brown

Bats: Left **Throws:** Right **Pos:** 1B **Ht:** 6'2" **Wt:** 205 **Born:** 7/30/72 **Age:** 24

		BATTING																	BASERUNNING				PERCENTAGES		
Year	Team	Lg	Org	G	AB	H	2B	3B	HR	TB	R	RBI	TBB	IBB	SO	HBP	SH	SF	SB	CS	SB%	GDP	Avg	OBP	SLG
1994	Billings	R+	Cin	60	218	80	19	3	9	132	50	49	27	1	32	10	0	5	3	5	.38	5	.367	.450	.606
1995	Winston-Sal	A+	Cin	122	445	118	26	0	19	201	63	77	52	12	85	11	0	4	3	2	.60	8	.265	.354	.452
	Charlstn-WV	A	Cin	6	17	2	1	0	0	3	3	0	4	0	3	0	0	0	0	0	.00	0	.118	.286	.176
1996	Chattanooga	AA	Cin	115	364	119	26	5	13	194	68	52	52	7	62	3	0	3	2	1	.67	11	.327	.412	.533
3 Min. YEARS				303	1044	319	72	8	41	530	184	178	135	20	182	24	0	12	8	8	.50	24	.306	.393	.508

Ron Brown

Bats: Right **Throws:** Right **Pos:** OF **Ht:** 6'3" **Wt:** 185 **Born:** 1/17/70 **Age:** 27

		BATTING																	BASERUNNING				PERCENTAGES		
Year	Team	Lg	Org	G	AB	H	2B	3B	HR	TB	R	RBI	TBB	IBB	SO	HBP	SH	SF	SB	CS	SB%	GDP	Avg	OBP	SLG
1993	Elmira	A-	Fla	75	285	82	22	1	9	133	53	55	37	2	59	2	1	3	4	2	.67	2	.288	.370	.467
1994	Kane County	A	Fla	109	411	109	22	3	9	164	51	75	26	1	75	4	0	5	4	2	.67	14	.265	.312	.399
1995	Brevard Cty	A+	Fla	121	404	105	22	2	3	140	48	51	31	0	79	3	1	9	6	12	.33	14	.260	.311	.347
1996	Portland	AA	Fla	4	10	1	0	1	0	3	1	1	1	0	1	0	0	0	0	0	.00	0	.100	.182	.300
	Duluth-Sup.	IND	—	61	231	61	16	0	7	98	36	35	22	1	38	1	1	4	4	2	.67	4	.264	.326	.424
4 Min. YEARS				370	1341	358	82	7	28	538	189	217	117	4	252	10	3	21	18	18	.50	34	.267	.326	.401

Willie Brown

Pitches: Right **Bats:** Right **Pos:** P **Ht:** 6'4" **Wt:** 215 **Born:** 4/14/72 **Age:** 25

		HOW MUCH HE PITCHED								WHAT HE GAVE UP												THE RESULTS					
Year	Team	Lg	Org	G	GS	CG	GF	IP	BFP	H	R	ER	HR	SH	SF	HB	TBB	IBB	SO	WP	Bk	W	L	Pct.	ShO	Sv	ERA
1993	Boise	A-	Cal	15	15	0	0	83.2	356	64	41	36	4	2	1	7	42	1	68	6	1	5	4	.556	0	0	3.87
1994	Cedar Rapds	A	Cal	27	27	5	0	176	728	158	89	74	6	6	4	12	45	2	129	4	6	6	9	.400	2	0	3.78
1995	Midland	AA	Cal	27	27	2	0	147.2	651	188	92	85	17	9	3	9	47	1	81	9	0	9	10	.474	0	0	5.18
1996	Midland	AA	Cal	9	8	0	1	33.1	170	58	45	43	8	2	1	4	9	0	16	1	0	0	6	.000	0	0	11.61
4 Min. YEARS				78	77	7	1	440.2	1905	468	267	238	35	19	9	32	143	4	294	20	7	20	29	.408	2	0	4.86

Byron Browne

Pitches: Right **Bats:** Right **Pos:** P **Ht:** 6'7" **Wt:** 200 **Born:** 8/8/70 **Age:** 26

		HOW MUCH HE PITCHED								WHAT HE GAVE UP												THE RESULTS					
Year	Team	Lg	Org	G	GS	CG	GF	IP	BFP	H	R	ER	HR	SH	SF	HB	TBB	IBB	SO	WP	Bk	W	L	Pct.	ShO	Sv	ERA
1991	Brewers	R	Mil	13	11	0	0	58	312	68	65	52	2	0	4	5	67	1	68	14	2	1	6	.143	0	0	8.07

			HOW MUCH HE PITCHED						WHAT HE GAVE UP												THE RESULTS					
Year	Team	Lg Org	G	GS	CG	GF	IP	BFP	H	R	ER	HR	SH	SF	HB	TBB	IBB	SO	WP	Bk	W	L	Pct.	ShO	Sv	ERA
1992	Beloit	A Mil	25	25	2	0	134.2	621	109	84	76	8	8	4	11	114	0	111	24	6	9	8	.529	0	0	5.08
1993	Stockton	A+ Mil	27	27	0	0	143.2	661	117	73	65	9	7	6	11	117	1	110	13	0	10	5	.667	0	0	4.07
1994	Stockton	A+ Mil	11	11	1	0	62	260	46	30	19	4	4	1	3	30	0	67	3	0	2	6	.250	0	0	2.76
	El Paso	AA Mil	5	5	0	0	29	124	26	11	8	3	0	1	0	13	0	33	1	0	2	1	.667	0	0	2.48
1995	El Paso	AA Mil	25	20	2	3	126	540	106	55	48	7	3	9	6	78	2	110	7	0	10	4	.714	1	0	3.43
1996	New Orleans	AAA Mil	23	21	1	0	107.1	489	104	79	74	18	3	5	7	73	1	80	7	1	3	9	.250	0	0	6.20
6 Min. YEARS			129	120	6	3	660.2	3007	576	397	342	51	25	30	43	492	5	579	69	9	37	39	.487	1	0	4.66

Mark Brownson

Pitches: Right **Bats:** Right **Pos:** P **Ht:** 6'2" **Wt:** 175 **Born:** 6/17/75 **Age:** 22

			HOW MUCH HE PITCHED						WHAT HE GAVE UP												THE RESULTS					
Year	Team	Lg Org	G	GS	CG	GF	IP	BFP	H	R	ER	HR	SH	SF	HB	TBB	IBB	SO	WP	Bk	W	L	Pct.	ShO	Sv	ERA
1994	Rockies	R Col	19	4	0	6	54.1	224	48	18	10	2	2	2	3	6	0	72	2	2	4	1	.800	0	3	1.66
1995	New Haven	AA Col	1	1	0	0	6	24	4	2	1	1	0	0	0	1	0	4	0	0	0	0	.000	0	0	1.50
	Salem	A+ Col	9	1	0	5	15.2	71	16	8	7	0	0	1	1	10	4	9	4	0	2	1	.667	0	1	4.02
	Asheville	A Col	33	14	0	9	120.1	517	126	62	52	13	2	3	5	40	4	107	8	2	8	8	.500	0	2	3.89
1996	New Haven	AA Col	37	19	1	10	144	619	141	73	56	10	6	3	6	43	5	155	7	2	8	13	.381	0	3	3.50
3 Min. YEARS			99	39	1	30	340.1	1455	335	163	126	26	10	9	15	100	13	347	21	6	22	23	.489	0	9	3.33

Duff Brumley

Pitches: Right **Bats:** Right **Pos:** P **Ht:** 6' 4" **Wt:** 220 **Born:** 8/25/70 **Age:** 26

			HOW MUCH HE PITCHED						WHAT HE GAVE UP												THE RESULTS					
Year	Team	Lg Org	G	GS	CG	GF	IP	BFP	H	R	ER	HR	SH	SF	HB	TBB	IBB	SO	WP	Bk	W	L	Pct.	ShO	Sv	ERA
1990	Johnson Cty	R+ StL	12	11	0	0	55.2	263	61	48	40	4	0	3	3	29	0	43	2	1	2	6	.250	0	0	6.47
1991	Hamilton	A- StL	15	15	0	0	89	384	90	49	36	7	1	4	5	24	0	80	5	2	2	6	.250	0	0	3.64
1992	Hamilton	A- StL	9	9	2	0	59.2	234	38	19	18	3	1	3	2	21	0	83	0	1	6	0	1.000	0	0	2.72
	Savannah	A StL	5	5	0	0	31	128	17	9	6	1	1	2	0	14	0	46	2	2	2	1	.667	0	0	1.74
1993	St. Pete	A+ StL	8	8	0	0	56	203	26	5	4	2	2	0	2	13	0	67	1	0	5	1	.833	0	0	0.64
	Arkansas	AA StL	12	12	2	0	69.1	292	57	30	27	9	3	1	1	26	5	79	2	1	4	5	.444	1	0	3.50
	Tulsa	AA Tex	6	6	0	0	41.1	165	30	13	9	4	1	1	2	9	1	42	2	0	3	2	.600	0	0	1.96
1994	Okla. City	AAA Tex	29	15	0	11	101.1	470	107	71	62	9	5	12	8	64	0	100	8	1	3	6	.333	0	2	5.51
1995	Okla. City	AAA Tex	3	0	0	1	5	24	6	4	3	0	1	0	0	2	0	3	0	0	1	1	.500	0	1	5.40
	Chattanooga	AA Cin	28	0	0	10	53.1	217	37	15	12	0	4	2	2	18	2	63	3	2	6	2	.750	0	2	2.03
1996	Scranton-WB	AAA Phi	20	0	0	7	20	104	19	18	13	1	0	1	0	22	1	15	6	2	2	1	.667	0	0	5.85
	Port City	AA Sea	6	5	0	0	28	127	27	13	12	1	0	2	0	21	0	17	6	3	0	1	.000	0	0	3.86
1994	Texas	AL	2	0	0	1	3.1	22	6	6	6	1	0	2	0	5	0	4	0	0	0	0	.000	0	0	16.20
7 Min. YEARS			153	86	4	29	609.2	2611	515	294	242	41	19	31	25	263	9	638	37	15	36	32	.529	1	5	3.57

Mike Brumley

Bats: Both **Throws:** Right **Pos:** SS **Ht:** 5'10" **Wt:** 175 **Born:** 4/9/63 **Age:** 34

			BATTING															BASERUNNING				PERCENTAGES		
Year	Team	Lg Org	G	AB	H	2B	3B	HR	TB	R	RBI	TBB	IBB	SO	HBP	SH	SF	SB	CS	SB%	GDP	Avg	OBP	SLG
1984	New Britain	AA Bos	34	121	28	6	2	0	38	14	9	18	0	33	0	2	1	3	0	1.00	5	.231	.329	.314
	Midland	AA ChN	73	255	55	11	3	6	90	37	21	48	3	49	0	1	1	5	2	.71	2	.216	.339	.353
1985	Pittsfield	AA ChN	131	460	127	23	14	3	187	66	58	74	5	95	0	2	9	29	7	.81	8	.276	.370	.407
1986	Iowa	AAA ChN	139	458	103	21	5	10	164	74	44	63	3	102	0	5	4	35	14	.71	5	.225	.316	.358
1987	Iowa	AAA ChN	92	319	81	20	5	6	129	44	42	35	1	61	1	3	2	27	10	.73	4	.254	.328	.404
1988	Las Vegas	AAA SD	113	425	134	16	7	3	173	77	41	56	2	84	0	3	2	41	14	.75	6	.315	.393	.407
1989	Toledo	AAA Det	8	26	6	2	2	0	12	4	1	3	1	11	1	0	0	1	0	1.00	0	.231	.333	.462
1990	Calgary	AAA Sea	8	28	9	1	0	0	10	4	1	1	1	3	0	0	0	3	0	1.00	1	.321	.345	.357
1991	Pawtucket	AAA Bos	32	108	29	2	2	4	47	25	16	24	1	21	1	1	0	8	4	.67	2	.269	.406	.435
1992	Pawtucket	AAA Bos	101	365	96	16	5	4	134	50	41	37	0	76	1	3	6	14	6	.70	12	.263	.328	.367
1993	Tucson	AAA Hou	93	346	122	25	8	0	163	65	46	44	6	71	0	0	6	24	11	.69	4	.353	.419	.471
1994	Tacoma	AAA Oak	13	49	13	4	1	1	22	11	5	7	0	9	0	0	0	3	1	.75	3	.265	.357	.449
	Edmonton	AAA Fla	72	263	76	20	3	11	135	43	36	29	0	58	0	1	2	5	2	.71	3	.289	.357	.513
1995	Tucson	AAA Hou	94	330	86	20	10	4	138	56	33	41	5	67	3	1	3	17	6	.74	8	.261	.345	.418
1996	Tucson	AAA Hou	88	278	65	11	7	4	102	40	28	40	4	79	2	1	2	9	3	.75	5	.234	.332	.367
1987	Chicago	NL	39	104	21	2	2	1	30	8	9	10	1	30	1	1	1	7	1	.88	2	.202	.276	.288
1989	Detroit	AL	92	212	42	5	2	1	54	33	11	14	0	45	1	3	0	8	4	.67	4	.198	.251	.255
1990	Seattle	AL	62	147	33	5	4	0	46	19	7	10	0	22	0	4	1	2	0	1.00	5	.224	.272	.313
1991	Boston	AL	63	118	25	5	0	0	30	16	5	10	0	22	0	4	0	2	0	1.00	0	.212	.273	.254
1992	Boston	AL	2	1	0	0	0	0	0	0	0	0	0	0	0	0	0	0	0	.00	0	.000	.000	.000
1993	Houston	NL	8	10	3	0	0	0	3	1	2	1	0	3	0	0	0	0	1	.00	0	.300	.364	.300
1994	Oakland	AL	11	25	6	0	0	0	6	0	2	1	0	8	0	0	0	0	0	.00	0	.240	.269	.240
1995	Houston	NL	18	18	1	0	0	1	4	1	2	0	0	6	0	0	0	1	0	1.00	0	.056	.056	.222
13 Min. YEARS			1091	3831	1030	198	74	56	1544	610	422	520	32	819	9	23	38	224	80	.74	68	.269	.354	.403
8 Maj. YEARS			295	635	131	17	8	3	173	78	38	46	1	136	2	12	2	20	6	.77	11	.206	.261	.272

Julio Bruno

Bats: Right **Throws:** Right **Pos:** 2B **Ht:** 5'11" **Wt:** 190 **Born:** 10/15/72 **Age:** 24

			BATTING															BASERUNNING				PERCENTAGES		
Year	Team	Lg Org	G	AB	H	2B	3B	HR	TB	R	RBI	TBB	IBB	SO	HBP	SH	SF	SB	CS	SB%	GDP	Avg	OBP	SLG
1990	Charlstn-SC	A SD	19	75	17	1	1	0	20	11	5	1	0	21	0	1	1	0	0	.00	0	.227	.234	.267

Year	Team	Lg	Org	G	AB	H	2B	3B	HR	TB	R	RBI	TBB	IBB	SO	HBP	SH	SF	SB	CS	SB%	GDP	Avg	OBP	SLG
	Spokane	A-	SD	68	251	63	7	2	2	80	36	22	25	1	78	2	0	0	7	5	.58	10	.251	.324	.319
1991	Waterloo	A	SD	86	277	64	10	3	1	83	34	25	29	0	78	4	4	1	11	6	.65	8	.231	.312	.300
1992	High Desert	A+	SD	118	418	116	22	5	3	157	57	62	33	4	92	1	5	3	2	3	.40	8	.278	.330	.376
1993	Rancho Cuca	A+	SD	54	201	62	11	2	3	86	37	16	19	2	56	1	1	2	15	6	.71	7	.308	.368	.428
	Wichita	AA	SD	70	246	70	17	1	3	98	34	24	11	3	46	2	1	1	3	5	.38	9	.285	.319	.398
1994	Rancho Cuca	A+	SD	6	25	14	2	1	2	24	11	7	4	0	4	1	0	0	2	0	1.00	0	.560	.633	.960
	Las Vegas	AAA	SD	123	450	117	25	4	6	168	48	52	24	3	83	4	5	5	4	5	.44	15	.260	.300	.373
1995	Las Vegas	AAA	SD	38	139	34	6	1	0	42	13	6	8	0	24	0	0	1	1	3	.25	6	.245	.284	.302
	Memphis	AA	SD	59	196	53	6	3	2	71	16	25	8	0	35	2	3	2	3	2	.60	9	.270	.303	.362
1996	Memphis	AA	SD	27	84	20	8	1	0	30	11	9	6	1	18	0	1	1	1	2	.33	2	.238	.286	.357
	Las Vegas	AAA	SD	80	297	81	16	1	2	105	36	30	17	3	33	2	5	1	6	5	.55	3	.273	.315	.354
7 Min. YEARS				748	2659	711	131	25	24	964	344	283	185	17	568	19	26	18	55	42	.57	77	.267	.318	.363

William Brunson

Pitches: Left **Bats:** Left **Pos:** P **Ht:** 6'4" **Wt:** 185 **Born:** 3/20/70 **Age:** 27

				HOW MUCH HE PITCHED						WHAT HE GAVE UP												THE RESULTS					
Year	Team	Lg	Org	G	GS	CG	GF	IP	BFP	H	R	ER	HR	SH	SF	HB	TBB	IBB	SO	WP	Bk	W	L	Pct.	ShO	Sv	ERA
1992	Princeton	R+	Cin	13	13	0	0	72.2	313	68	34	29	6	4	2	3	28	0	48	2	0	5	5	.500	0	0	3.59
1993	Charlstn-WV	A	Cin	37	15	0	4	123.2	545	119	68	54	10	4	4	11	50	1	103	7	2	5	6	.455	0	0	3.93
1994	Winston-Sal	A+	Cin	30	22	3	3	165	711	161	83	73	22	5	7	12	58	2	129	6	4	12	7	.632	0	0	3.98
1995	San Bernrdo	A+	LA	13	13	0	0	83.1	334	68	24	19	4	3	5	5	21	0	70	3	0	10	0	1.000	0	0	2.05
	San Antonio	AA	LA	27	27	0	0	163.1	690	173	70	63	8	6	6	9	43	0	114	8	1	14	5	.737	0	0	3.47
1996	San Antonio	AA	LA	11	5	0	1	42	166	32	13	10	2	2	0	1	15	0	38	2	1	3	1	.750	0	0	2.14
	Albuquerque	AAA	LA	9	9	1	0	54.1	239	53	29	27	7	2	1	2	23	1	47	2	0	3	4	.429	0	0	4.47
5 Min. YEARS				140	104	4	8	704.1	2998	674	321	275	59	26	25	43	238	4	549	30	8	52	28	.650	0	0	3.51

Adam Bryant

Pitches: Right **Bats:** Right **Pos:** P **Ht:** 6'6" **Wt:** 225 **Born:** 12/27/71 **Age:** 25

				HOW MUCH HE PITCHED						WHAT HE GAVE UP												THE RESULTS					
Year	Team	Lg	Org	G	GS	CG	GF	IP	BFP	H	R	ER	HR	SH	SF	HB	TBB	IBB	SO	WP	Bk	W	L	Pct.	ShO	Sv	ERA
1994	Billings	R+	Cin	23	0	0	16	41.1	164	32	15	13	0	2	1	3	11	0	49	4	2	3	1	.750	0	4	2.83
1995	Billings	R+	Cin	29	0	0	26	37.1	157	39	13	13	3	0	1	2	5	1	30	4	4	4	2	.667	0	11	3.13
1996	Charlstn-WV	A	Cin	22	0	0	20	29.2	114	22	7	7	2	0	1	2	2	0	25	1	0	1	1	.500	0	7	2.12
	Winston-Sal	A+	Cin	28	0	0	23	34	149	39	13	9	1	0	3	2	10	0	16	0	1	4	3	.571	0	8	2.38
	Chattanooga	AA	Cin	1	0	0	0	1	3	0	0	0	0	0	0	0	0	0	1	0	0	0	0	.000	0	0	0.00
3 Min. YEARS				103	0	0	85	143.1	587	132	48	42	6	2	6	9	28	1	121	9	7	12	7	.632	0	30	2.64

Pat Bryant

Bats: Right **Throws:** Right **Pos:** OF **Ht:** 5'11" **Wt:** 182 **Born:** 10/27/72 **Age:** 24

				BATTING															BASERUNNING				PERCENTAGES		
Year	Team	Lg	Org	G	AB	H	2B	3B	HR	TB	R	RBI	TBB	IBB	SO	HBP	SH	SF	SB	CS	SB%	GDP	Avg	OBP	SLG
1990	Indians	R	Cle	17	51	10	2	0	0	12	3	3	8	0	18	4	0	1	2	0	1.00	0	.196	.344	.235
	Burlington	R+	Cle	17	50	5	0	0	1	8	3	2	7	0	23	0	0	0	7	1	.88	0	.100	.211	.160
1991	Columbus	A	Cle	100	326	68	11	0	7	100	51	27	49	0	108	7	2	2	30	6	.83	2	.209	.323	.307
1992	Columbus	A	Cle	49	151	33	14	2	2	57	36	19	30	2	52	7	2	0	10	2	.83	1	.219	.372	.377
	Watertown	A-	Cle	63	220	58	13	1	7	94	41	30	33	1	61	5	1	1	35	8	.81	0	.264	.371	.427
1993	Columbus	A	Cle	121	483	127	26	2	16	205	82	61	43	1	117	13	0	2	43	11	.80	6	.263	.338	.424
1994	Canton-Akrn	AA	Cle	124	377	89	14	2	12	143	61	53	48	0	87	5	5	3	23	14	.62	4	.236	.328	.379
1995	Canton-Akrn	AA	Cle	127	421	109	22	3	17	188	60	59	52	0	116	4	5	3	16	8	.67	5	.259	.344	.447
1996	Canton-Akrn	AA	Cle	34	109	21	2	1	3	34	13	17	17	1	24	4	1	2	8	2	.80	1	.193	.318	.312
	Buffalo	AAA	Cle	27	64	11	1	0	0	12	6	0	5	0	20	1	1	0	0	2	.00	2	.172	.243	.188
7 Min. YEARS				679	2252	531	105	11	65	853	356	271	292	5	626	50	17	14	174	54	.76	21	.236	.335	.379

Ralph Bryant

Bats: Left **Throws:** Right **Pos:** DH **Ht:** 6' 2" **Wt:** 200 **Born:** 5/20/61 **Age:** 36

				BATTING															BASERUNNING				PERCENTAGES		
Year	Team	Lg	Org	G	AB	H	2B	3B	HR	TB	R	RBI	TBB	IBB	SO	HBP	SH	SF	SB	CS	SB%	GDP	Avg	OBP	SLG
1996	Midland	AA	Cal	60	216	45	16	0	9	88	33	26	19	1	75	0	0	2	1	1	.50	7	.208	.270	.407
1985	Los Angeles	NL		6	6	2	0	0	0	2	0	1	0	0	2	0	0	0	0	0	.00	0	.333	.333	.333
1986	Los Angeles	NL		27	75	19	4	2	6	45	15	13	5	0	25	1	0	1	0	1	.00	1	.253	.305	.600
1987	Los Angeles	NL		46	69	17	2	1	2	27	7	10	10	2	24	1	0	1	2	1	.67	0	.246	.346	.391
3 Maj. YEARS				79	150	38	6	3	8	74	22	24	15	2	51	2	0	2	2	2	.50	1	.253	.325	.493

Scott Bryant

Bats: Right **Throws:** Right **Pos:** OF **Ht:** 6'2" **Wt:** 215 **Born:** 10/31/67 **Age:** 29

				BATTING															BASERUNNING				PERCENTAGES		
Year	Team	Lg	Org	G	AB	H	2B	3B	HR	TB	R	RBI	TBB	IBB	SO	HBP	SH	SF	SB	CS	SB%	GDP	Avg	OBP	SLG
1989	Cedar Rapds	A	Cin	49	186	47	7	0	9	81	26	39	30	0	46	0	1	1	2	4	.33	7	.253	.355	.435
1990	Cedar Rapds	A	Cin	67	212	56	10	3	14	114	40	48	50	5	47	1	0	3	6	4	.60	7	.264	.402	.538
	Chattanooga	AA	Cin	44	131	41	10	3	6	75	23	30	22	0	28	2	0	0	1	1	.50	5	.313	.419	.573
1991	Chattanooga	AA	Cin	91	306	93	14	6	8	143	42	43	34	1	77	3	0	2	2	3	.40	8	.304	.377	.467
1992	Charlotte	AA	ChN	6	20	3	1	1	1	9	3	2	1	0	9	0	0	0	0	0	.00	0	.150	.190	.450

Year Team	Lg Org	G	AB	H	2B	3B	HR	TB	R	RBI	TBB	IBB	SO	HBP	SH	SF	SB	CS	SB%	GDP	Avg	OBP	SLG
		BATTING															BASERUNNING				PERCENTAGES		
Iowa	AAA ChN	98	315	79	22	3	18	161	35	49	25	2	73	3	2	2	0	2	.00	8	.251	.310	.511
1993 Ottawa	AAA Mon	112	364	103	19	1	12	160	48	65	53	3	90	2	0	6	1	2	.33	11	.283	.372	.440
1994 Calgary	AAA Sea	105	416	133	32	3	20	231	69	87	39	2	66	1	0	5	1	2	.33	12	.320	.375	.555
1995 Edmonton	AAA Oak	119	406	117	33	3	10	186	58	69	49	3	87	6	0	5	1	3	.25	7	.288	.369	.458
1996 Okla. City	AAA Tex	12	41	11	3	0	0	14	4	3	4	0	10	0	0	1	0	0	.00	0	.268	.326	.341
Tacoma	AAA Sea	58	214	57	10	3	2	79	21	19	13	1	41	0	1	1	0	3	.00	5	.266	.307	.369
8 Min. YEARS		761	2611	740	161	26	100	1253	369	454	320	17	574	18	4	26	14	24	.37	70	.283	.362	.480

Jim Buccheri

Bats: Right **Throws:** Right **Pos:** OF **Ht:** 5'11" **Wt:** 165 **Born:** 11/12/68 **Age:** 28

Year Team	Lg Org	G	AB	H	2B	3B	HR	TB	R	RBI	TBB	IBB	SO	HBP	SH	SF	SB	CS	SB%	GDP	Avg	OBP	SLG
		BATTING															BASERUNNING				PERCENTAGES		
1988 Sou. Oregon	A- Oak	58	232	67	8	1	0	77	42	17	20	0	35	4	0	3	25	7	.78	7	.289	.351	.332
1989 Madison	A Oak	115	433	101	9	0	2	116	56	28	26	1	61	5	3	3	43	12	.78	5	.233	.283	.268
1990 Modesto	A+ Oak	36	125	35	4	1	0	41	27	7	25	0	16	2	2	0	15	9	.63	2	.280	.408	.328
Huntsville	AA Oak	84	278	58	2	1	0	62	39	22	40	0	38	3	7	1	14	6	.70	5	.209	.314	.223
1991 Huntsville	AA Oak	100	340	72	15	0	0	87	48	22	71	0	60	7	5	4	35	7	.83	5	.212	.355	.256
1992 Huntsville	AA Oak	20	60	9	2	1	1	16	8	5	9	0	18	0	1	1	5	3	.63	2	.150	.257	.267
Reno	A+ Oak	63	259	95	14	2	4	125	65	38	56	3	40	2	2	2	33	13	.72	5	.367	.480	.483
Tacoma	AAA Oak	46	127	38	6	3	0	50	24	13	27	1	25	2	0	0	10	5	.67	2	.299	.429	.394
1993 Modesto	A+ Oak	2	7	2	0	0	0	2	3	1	2	0	2	1	0	0	0	0	.00	1	.286	.500	.286
Tacoma	AAA Oak	90	293	81	9	3	2	102	45	40	39	1	46	2	10	1	12	9	.57	6	.276	.364	.348
1994 Tacoma	AAA Oak	121	448	136	8	3	3	159	59	39	42	1	45	4	7	2	32	14	.70	8	.304	.367	.355
1995 Ottawa	AAA Mon	133	470	126	16	4	0	150	64	30	49	5	58	3	11	2	44	11	.80	7	.268	.340	.319
1996 Ottawa	AAA Mon	65	206	53	3	4	1	67	40	12	33	0	28	2	1	2	33	6	.85	1	.257	.362	.325
9 Min. YEARS		933	3278	873	96	23	13	1054	520	274	439	12	472	37	49	21	301	102	.75	56	.266	.357	.322

Travis Buckley

Pitches: Right **Bats:** Right **Pos:** P **Ht:** 6' 4" **Wt:** 208 **Born:** 6/15/70 **Age:** 27

Year Team	Lg Org	G	GS	CG	GF	IP	BFP	H	R	ER	HR	SH	SF	HB	TBB	IBB	SO	WP	Bk	W	L	Pct.	ShO	Sv	ERA
		HOW MUCH HE PITCHED						WHAT HE GAVE UP												THE RESULTS					
1989 Rangers	R Tex	16	4	0	2	50.1	211	41	28	19	1	1	2	0	24	1	34	3	5	3	3	.500	0	0	3.40
1990 Gastonia	A Tex	27	26	3	0	161.2	684	149	66	51	10	3	5	4	61	0	149	7	0	12	6	.667	0	0	2.84
1991 Charlotte	A+ Tex	28	21	3	3	128	553	115	58	46	7	8	5	6	67	4	131	8	1	8	9	.471	3	1	3.23
1992 Harrisburg	AA Mon	26	26	0	0	160	676	146	58	51	8	2	4	12	64	2	123	4	1	7	7	.500	0	0	2.87
1993 Colo. Sprng	AAA Col	6	1	0	1	9	48	12	13	6	0	1	1	3	7	0	5	2	0	1	2	.333	0	0	6.00
Chattanooga	AA Cin	2	2	0	0	8	37	7	6	3	1	0	1	1	4	0	6	2	0	0	1	.000	0	0	3.38
Jacksonvlle	AA Sea	10	9	0	0	48.1	216	57	35	33	7	0	5	3	18	0	38	1	1	2	3	.400	0	0	6.14
1994 Jacksonvlle	AA Sea	14	11	0	2	71.1	308	70	41	38	3	2	6	3	30	2	31	8	0	2	6	.250	0	0	4.79
Chattanooga	AA Cin	27	24	2	2	156.1	659	145	73	64	9	4	9	7	56	3	96	14	0	9	8	.529	0	0	3.68
1995 Chattanooga	AA Cin	3	3	0	0	14.1	69	21	12	12	4	0	1	1	5	0	10	1	0	1	2	.333	0	0	7.53
Indianapols	AAA Cin	26	21	3	0	146.1	630	162	92	81	12	3	5	4	38	3	95	5	0	11	11	.500	2	0	4.98
1996 Chattanooga	AA Cin	8	8	2	0	53.2	234	57	40	29	6	3	2	2	13	1	41	3	0	3	4	.429	1	0	4.86
Indianapols	AAA Cin	22	20	1	0	122	518	126	68	61	23	2	3	4	32	0	58	2	0	11	7	.611	0	0	4.50
8 Min. YEARS		215	176	14	10	1129.1	4843	1108	590	494	91	29	49	50	419	16	817	60	8	70	69	.504	6	1	3.94

Mike Buddie

Pitches: Right **Bats:** Right **Pos:** P **Ht:** 6'3" **Wt:** 210 **Born:** 12/12/70 **Age:** 26

Year Team	Lg Org	G	GS	CG	GF	IP	BFP	H	R	ER	HR	SH	SF	HB	TBB	IBB	SO	WP	Bk	W	L	Pct.	ShO	Sv	ERA
		HOW MUCH HE PITCHED						WHAT HE GAVE UP												THE RESULTS					
1992 Oneonta	A- NYA	13	13	1	0	67.1	301	69	36	29	3	0	1	3	34	0	87	7	5	1	4	.200	0	0	3.88
1993 Greensboro	A NYA	27	26	0	0	155.1	686	138	104	84	19	2	4	8	89	0	143	22	2	13	10	.565	0	0	4.87
1994 Tampa	A+ NYA	25	24	2	0	150.1	643	143	75	67	7	5	8	5	66	2	113	9	4	12	5	.706	0	0	4.01
1995 Norwich	AA NYA	29	27	2	1	149.2	689	155	102	80	4	6	8	15	81	2	106	13	1	10	12	.455	0	1	4.81
1996 Norwich	AA NYA	29	26	4	0	159.2	708	176	101	79	10	8	5	8	71	5	103	16	0	7	12	.368	0	0	4.45
5 Min. YEARS		123	116	9	1	682.1	3027	681	418	339	43	21	26	39	341	9	552	67	12	43	43	.500	0	1	4.47

Jason Bullard

Pitches: Right **Bats:** Right **Pos:** P **Ht:** 6'2" **Wt:** 185 **Born:** 10/23/68 **Age:** 28

Year Team	Lg Org	G	GS	CG	GF	IP	BFP	H	R	ER	HR	SH	SF	HB	TBB	IBB	SO	WP	Bk	W	L	Pct.	ShO	Sv	ERA
		HOW MUCH HE PITCHED						WHAT HE GAVE UP												THE RESULTS					
1991 Welland	A- Pit	6	0	0	6	7	28	4	0	0	0	0	0	0	4	0	8	0	0	0	0	.000	0	4	0.00
Augusta	A Pit	21	0	0	17	25.2	116	21	13	10	1	1	0	1	15	1	29	2	1	2	2	.500	0	7	3.51
1992 Carolina	AA Pit	19	0	0	10	24.1	121	37	25	20	3	2	2	2	11	1	23	3	0	0	2	.000	0	3	7.40
1993 Pirates	R Pit	4	0	0	1	7	33	11	3	3	0	1	0	1	2	0	8	1	0	0	1	.000	0	0	3.86
1994 St. Paul	IND —	33	4	0	23	59.1	248	53	31	25	2	5	2	4	25	1	47	10	0	6	5	.545	0	10	3.79
1995 Colo. Sprng	AAA Col	4	0	0	1	8.2	48	18	13	7	1	0	0	1	5	1	5	0	1	0	0	.000	0	0	7.27
St. Paul	IND —	21	17	0	1	97	454	131	71	58	10	0	5	8	38	2	52	8	1	3	3	.500	0	0	5.38
1996 Norfolk	AAA NYN	24	0	0	7	38.2	178	45	23	21	2	2	2	6	16	1	24	6	0	0	3	.000	0	0	4.89
Binghamton	AA NYN	8	0	0	3	10	46	11	4	3	0	1	0	0	5	2	10	0	0	0	0	.000	0	0	2.70
Canton-Akrn	AA Cle	9	0	0	5	11	45	7	3	3	1	2	0	1	6	1	12	0	0	1	1	.500	0	0	2.45
6 Min. YEARS		149	21	0	74	288.2	1317	338	186	150	20	14	11	24	127	10	218	30	3	12	17	.414	0	24	4.68

Kirk Bullinger

Pitches: Right **Bats:** Right **Pos:** P **Ht:** 6'2" **Wt:** 170 **Born:** 10/28/69 **Age:** 27

		HOW MUCH HE PITCHED						WHAT HE GAVE UP												THE RESULTS					
Year Team	Lg Org	G	GS	CG	GF	IP	BFP	H	R	ER	HR	SH	SF	HB	TBB	IBB	SO	WP	Bk	W	L	Pct.	ShO	Sv	ERA
1992 Hamilton	A- StL	35	0	0	7	48.2	191	24	7	6	0	1	1	2	15	4	61	3	1	2	2	.500	0	2	1.11
1993 Springfield	A StL	50	0	0	46	51.1	208	26	19	13	5	3	2	2	21	1	72	6	0	1	3	.250	0	33	2.28
1994 St. Pete	A+ StL	39	0	0	18	53.2	220	37	16	7	0	4	0	1	20	5	50	4	3	2	0	1.000	0	6	1.17
1995 Harrisburg	AA Mon	56	0	0	39	67	282	61	22	18	4	4	1	0	25	5	42	2	2	5	3	.625	0	7	2.42
1996 Ottawa	AAA Mon	10	0	0	4	15.1	62	10	6	6	3	0	0	0	9	1	9	1	0	2	1	.667	0	0	3.52
Harrisburg	AA Mon	47	0	0	40	45.2	193	46	16	10	5	3	1	1	18	3	29	3	0	3	4	.429	0	22	1.97
5 Min. YEARS		237	0	0	154	281.2	1156	204	86	60	17	15	5	6	108	19	263	19	6	15	13	.536	0	70	1.92

Mel Bunch

Pitches: Right **Bats:** Right **Pos:** P **Ht:** 6' 1" **Wt:** 170 **Born:** 11/4/71 **Age:** 25

		HOW MUCH HE PITCHED						WHAT HE GAVE UP												THE RESULTS					
Year Team	Lg Org	G	GS	CG	GF	IP	BFP	H	R	ER	HR	SH	SF	HB	TBB	IBB	SO	WP	Bk	W	L	Pct.	ShO	Sv	ERA
1992 Royals	R KC	5	4	0	1	24	87	11	6	4	2	0	0	1	3	0	26	0	0	2	1	.667	0	0	1.50
Eugene	A- KC	10	10	0	0	64.2	265	62	23	20	5	2	2	1	13	0	69	2	1	5	3	.625	0	0	2.78
1993 Rockford	A KC	19	11	1	8	85	337	79	24	20	4	7	3	2	18	0	71	6	1	6	4	.600	0	4	2.12
Wilmington	A+ KC	10	10	1	0	65.2	256	52	22	17	3	1	2	1	14	0	54	2	0	5	3	.625	0	0	2.33
1994 Wilmington	A+ KC	15	12	0	0	61	252	52	30	23	8	1	1	0	15	0	62	2	0	5	3	.625	0	0	3.39
1995 Omaha	AAA KC	12	11	1	0	65	272	63	37	33	10	3	4	0	20	2	50	8	1	1	7	.125	0	0	4.57
1996 Omaha	AAA KC	33	27	0	2	146.2	663	181	106	99	32	1	4	7	59	1	94	8	1	8	9	.471	0	0	6.08
1995 Kansas City	AL	13	5	0	3	40	175	42	25	25	11	0	0	0	14	1	19	6	0	1	3	.250	0	0	5.63
5 Min. YEARS		104	85	3	11	512	2132	500	248	216	64	15	16	12	142	3	426	28	4	32	30	.516	0	4	3.80

Jamie Burke

Bats: Right **Throws:** Right **Pos:** 3B **Ht:** 6'0" **Wt:** 195 **Born:** 9/24/71 **Age:** 25

		BATTING															BASERUNNING				PERCENTAGES		
Year Team	Lg Org	G	AB	H	2B	3B	HR	TB	R	RBI	TBB	IBB	SO	HBP	SH	SF	SB	CS	SB%	GDP	Avg	OBP	SLG
1993 Boise	A- Cal	66	226	68	11	1	1	84	32	30	39	3	28	5	2	2	2	3	.40	4	.301	.412	.372
1994 Cedar Rapds	A Cal	127	469	124	24	1	1	153	57	47	40	3	64	12	4	8	6	8	.43	15	.264	.333	.326
1995 Lk Elsinore	A+ Cal	106	365	100	15	6	2	133	47	56	32	1	53	9	11	4	6	4	.60	12	.274	.344	.364
1996 Midland	AA Cal	45	144	46	8	2	2	64	24	16	20	1	22	2	1	0	1	1	.50	1	.319	.410	.444
Vancouver	AAA Cal	41	156	39	5	0	1	47	12	14	7	0	18	1	1	2	2	1	.67	5	.250	.283	.301
4 Min. YEARS		385	1360	377	63	10	7	481	172	163	138	8	185	29	19	16	17	17	.50	37	.277	.353	.354

Ben Burlingame

Pitches: Right **Bats:** Right **Pos:** P **Ht:** 6'5" **Wt:** 210 **Born:** 1/31/70 **Age:** 27

		HOW MUCH HE PITCHED						WHAT HE GAVE UP												THE RESULTS					
Year Team	Lg Org	G	GS	CG	GF	IP	BFP	H	R	ER	HR	SH	SF	HB	TBB	IBB	SO	WP	Bk	W	L	Pct.	ShO	Sv	ERA
1991 Geneva	A- ChN	14	5	0	4	50.2	207	49	22	16	2	1	0	1	12	0	38	1	1	5	2	.714	0	1	2.84
1992 Winston-Sal	A+ ChN	31	25	3	2	160.2	666	164	79	65	13	5	8	3	44	1	82	3	0	8	12	.400	0	0	3.64
1993 Daytona	A+ ChN	8	1	0	2	17.1	85	27	16	15	4	0	2	2	9	0	10	0	0	0	1	.000	0	0	7.79
Peoria	A ChN	20	20	4	0	126.1	537	122	59	50	9	0	4	15	32	0	102	3	3	9	7	.563	1	0	3.56
1994 Orlando	AA ChN	25	22	0	0	139	586	132	75	60	14	7	4	10	41	1	84	7	0	4	11	.267	0	0	3.88
1995 Orlando	AA ChN	37	10	0	10	97	415	93	39	38	7	3	6	4	38	8	73	4	0	9	2	.818	0	1	3.53
1996 Orlando	AA ChN	11	0	0	5	17	82	21	7	7	1	2	2	0	10	2	16	2	0	1	1	.500	0	0	3.71
Iowa	AAA ChN	27	11	0	5	98.1	410	104	49	47	13	0	4	3	20	3	66	1	0	5	6	.455	0	0	4.30
6 Min. YEARS		173	94	7	28	706.1	2988	712	346	298	63	18	30	38	206	15	471	21	4	41	42	.494	1	2	3.80

Darren Burton

Bats: Both **Throws:** Right **Pos:** OF **Ht:** 6'1" **Wt:** 185 **Born:** 9/16/72 **Age:** 24

		BATTING															BASERUNNING				PERCENTAGES		
Year Team	Lg Org	G	AB	H	2B	3B	HR	TB	R	RBI	TBB	IBB	SO	HBP	SH	SF	SB	CS	SB%	GDP	Avg	OBP	SLG
1990 Royals	R KC	15	58	12	0	1	0	14	10	2	4	0	17	0	1	2	6	0	1.00	0	.207	.250	.241
1991 Appleton	A KC	134	532	143	32	6	2	193	78	51	45	4	122	1	3	6	37	12	.76	18	.269	.324	.363
1992 Baseball Cy	A+ KC	123	431	106	15	6	4	145	54	36	49	7	93	6	4	3	16	14	.53	7	.246	.329	.336
1993 Wilmington	A+ KC	134	549	152	23	5	10	215	82	45	48	1	111	1	13	4	30	10	.75	7	.277	.334	.392
1994 Memphis	AA KC	97	373	95	12	3	3	122	55	37	35	4	53	1	4	5	10	6	.63	5	.255	.316	.327
1995 Omaha	AAA KC	2	5	0	0	0	0	0	0	0	0	0	1	0	0	0	0	0	.00	0	.000	.000	.000
Wichita	AA KC	41	163	39	9	1	1	53	13	20	12	0	27	1	9	0	6	6	.50	2	.239	.295	.325
Orlando	AA ChN	62	222	68	16	2	4	100	40	21	27	2	42	0	0	0	7	4	.64	5	.306	.382	.450
1996 Omaha	AAA KC	129	463	125	28	5	15	208	75	67	59	6	82	6	9	4	7	7	.50	10	.270	.357	.449
7 Min. YEARS		737	2796	740	135	29	39	1050	407	279	279	24	548	16	43	24	119	59	.67	54	.265	.332	.376

Essex Burton

Bats: Right **Throws:** Right **Pos:** 2B **Ht:** 5'9" **Wt:** 155 **Born:** 5/16/69 **Age:** 28

		BATTING															BASERUNNING				PERCENTAGES		
Year Team	Lg Org	G	AB	H	2B	3B	HR	TB	R	RBI	TBB	IBB	SO	HBP	SH	SF	SB	CS	SB%	GDP	Avg	OBP	SLG
1991 White Sox	R ChA	50	194	54	5	2	0	63	37	17	26	0	27	1	3	0	21	7	.75	2	.278	.367	.325
Utica	A- ChA	15	58	16	0	0	0	16	11	4	8	0	12	1	2	0	6	2	.75	1	.276	.373	.276
1992 South Bend	A ChA	122	459	116	6	3	0	128	78	29	67	0	109	3	9	1	65	23	.74	1	.253	.351	.279
1993 South Bend	A ChA	134	501	128	6	8	1	153	95	36	85	0	94	4	8	2	74	24	.76	3	.255	.367	.305

BATTING																	BASERUNNING				PERCENTAGES		
Year Team	Lg Org	G	AB	H	2B	3B	HR	TB	R	RBI	TBB	IBB	SO	HBP	SH	SF	SB	CS	SB%	GDP	Avg	OBP	SLG
1994 Pr. William	A+ ChA	131	503	143	22	10	3	194	94	50	67	1	88	5	6	6	66	19	.78	5	.284	.370	.386
1995 Birmingham	AA ChA	142	554	141	15	2	1	163	95	43	80	4	79	5	15	2	60	22	.73	9	.255	.353	.294
1996 Scranton-WB	AAA Phi	16	58	10	3	0	0	13	4	1	7	0	16	1	0	0	5	3	.63	1	.172	.273	.224
Reading	AA Phi	102	381	116	19	5	1	148	66	30	37	0	56	2	16	2	40	12	.77	4	.304	.367	.388
6 Min. YEARS		712	2708	724	76	30	6	878	480	210	377	5	481	22	59	13	337	112	.75	26	.267	.360	.324

Homer Bush

Bats: Right **Throws:** Right **Pos:** 2B **Ht:** 5'11" **Wt:** 180 **Born:** 11/12/72 **Age:** 24

BATTING																	BASERUNNING				PERCENTAGES		
Year Team	Lg Org	G	AB	H	2B	3B	HR	TB	R	RBI	TBB	IBB	SO	HBP	SH	SF	SB	CS	SB%	GDP	Avg	OBP	SLG
1991 Padres	R SD	32	127	41	3	2	0	48	16	16	4	1	33	1	0	0	11	7	.61	2	.323	.348	.378
1992 Charlstn-SC	A SD	108	367	86	10	5	0	106	37	18	13	0	85	3	0	2	14	11	.56	3	.234	.265	.289
1993 Waterloo	A SD	130	472	152	19	3	5	192	63	51	19	0	87	1	1	1	39	14	.74	10	.322	.349	.407
1994 Rancho Cuca	A+ SD	39	161	54	10	3	0	70	37	16	9	0	29	4	1	1	9	2	.82	2	.335	.383	.435
Wichita	AA SD	59	245	73	11	4	3	101	35	14	10	0	39	3	1	0	20	7	.74	6	.298	.333	.412
1995 Memphis	AA SD	108	432	121	12	5	5	158	53	37	15	0	83	2	4	0	34	12	.74	6	.280	.307	.366
1996 Las Vegas	AAA SD	32	116	42	11	1	2	61	24	3	3	1	33	2	5	0	3	5	.38	2	.362	.388	.526
6 Min. YEARS		508	1920	569	76	23	15	736	265	155	73	2	389	16	12	4	130	58	.69	31	.296	.327	.383

Albert Bustillos

Pitches: Right **Bats:** Right **Pos:** P **Ht:** 6'1" **Wt:** 230 **Born:** 4/8/68 **Age:** 29

HOW MUCH HE PITCHED								WHAT HE GAVE UP												THE RESULTS					
Year Team	Lg Org	G	GS	CG	GF	IP	BFP	H	R	ER	HR	SH	SF	HB	TBB	IBB	SO	WP	Bk	W	L	Pct.	ShO	Sv	ERA
1988 Dodgers	R LA	17	6	1	7	68	261	46	13	11	2	3	1	1	12	1	65	2	1	6	3	.667	0	2	1.46
1989 Vero Beach	A+ LA	7	7	1	0	43	183	42	19	14	4	2	0	1	11	0	30	4	1	2	4	.333	0	0	2.93
Bakersfield	A+ LA	19	19	2	0	125	521	115	53	44	7	2	5	1	42	0	80	3	1	8	4	.667	1	0	3.17
1990 San Antonio	AA LA	5	0	0	1	8.1	38	8	6	6	0	1	1	0	5	0	6	1	1	0	1	.000	0	1	6.48
Vero Beach	A+ LA	22	20	2	0	136	563	131	50	46	3	3	2	0	45	5	89	6	0	11	5	.688	1	0	3.04
1991 Bakersfield	A+ LA	11	5	1	4	42.2	176	31	15	7	2	2	1	1	16	0	37	5	0	2	3	.400	0	1	1.48
San Antonio	AA LA	16	14	1	1	93	402	113	51	48	6	1	3	1	23	0	47	1	1	5	5	.500	0	0	4.65
1992 San Antonio	AA LA	6	0	0	2	13	52	8	3	1	0	1	0	0	3	0	10	0	0	1	0	1.000	0	2	0.69
Albuquerque	AAA LA	26	0	0	13	37.2	164	41	20	20	4	4	1	0	16	5	23	2	0	1	2	.333	0	3	4.78
1993 Albuquerque	AAA LA	20	0	0	4	30.1	139	37	15	15	4	5	2	0	13	4	17	2	0	2	1	.667	0	2	4.45
1994 San Antonio	AA LA	16	8	0	3	65.2	272	75	28	23	3	2	2	0	16	2	34	0	2	5	2	.714	0	1	3.15
Albuquerque	AAA LA	15	4	0	2	42.2	194	57	37	29	5	1	1	0	14	1	25	2	0	2	2	.500	0	1	6.12
1995 Colo. Sprng	AAA Col	34	19	0	5	132.2	572	151	82	68	15	4	2	4	33	0	77	8	0	8	4	.667	0	3	4.61
1996 Colo. Sprng	AAA Col	33	22	1	2	144.2	629	167	91	84	26	5	2	6	44	2	95	1	2	6	10	.375	1	1	5.23
9 Min. YEARS		247	124	9	44	982.2	4166	1022	483	416	81	36	23	15	293	20	635	37	9	59	46	.562	3	17	3.81

Mike Butcher

Pitches: Right **Bats:** Right **Pos:** P **Ht:** 6' 1" **Wt:** 200 **Born:** 5/10/66 **Age:** 31

HOW MUCH HE PITCHED								WHAT HE GAVE UP												THE RESULTS					
Year Team	Lg Org	G	GS	CG	GF	IP	BFP	H	R	ER	HR	SH	SF	HB	TBB	IBB	SO	WP	Bk	W	L	Pct.	ShO	Sv	ERA
1986 Eugene	A- KC	14	14	1	0	72.1	0	51	39	31	2	0	0	7	49	0	68	5	1	5	4	.556	0	0	3.86
1987 Fort Myers	A+ KC	5	5	1	0	31.1	133	33	20	19	3	0	0	1	8	0	17	0	0	2	2	.500	0	0	5.46
Appleton	A KC	20	19	3	0	121.1	525	101	50	36	4	5	5	5	56	5	89	9	2	10	4	.714	1	0	2.67
1988 Baseball Cy	A+ KC	6	6	0	0	32.2	143	32	19	14	2	1	4	2	10	1	20	1	0	1	4	.200	0	0	3.86
Appleton	A KC	4	4	0	0	18	73	17	7	6	0	1	1	2	5	0	7	3	0	0	1	.000	0	0	3.00
Quad City	A Cal	3	0	0	0	6	28	6	3	3	0	1	0	2	4	0	7	1	0	0	0	.000	0	0	4.50
Palm Spring	A+ Cal	7	7	0	0	42.2	199	57	33	27	3	0	1	4	19	0	37	6	0	3	2	.600	0	0	5.70
1989 Midland	AA Cal	15	15	0	0	68.2	331	92	54	50	6	2	4	3	41	1	49	7	2	2	6	.250	0	0	6.55
1990 Midland	AA Cal	35	8	0	6	87	413	109	68	60	8	6	9	3	55	2	84	3	1	3	7	.300	0	0	6.21
1991 Midland	AA Cal	41	6	0	13	88	394	93	54	51	6	2	7	8	46	0	70	3	0	9	6	.600	0	3	5.22
1992 Edmonton	AAA Cal	26	0	0	16	29.1	130	24	12	10	2	5	1	2	18	2	32	1	0	5	2	.714	0	4	3.07
1993 Vancouver	AAA Cal	14	1	0	5	24.1	108	21	16	12	3	2	1	1	12	0	12	3	2	2	3	.400	0	3	4.44
1994 Vancouver	AAA Cal	19	0	0	13	28.2	125	29	14	12	2	1	0	2	11	0	30	3	1	5	1	.833	0	5	3.77
1996 Tacoma	AAA Sea	14	8	0	3	42	223	70	59	55	14	0	3	7	27	0	42	3	0	1	4	.200	0	0	11.79
Buffalo	AAA Cle	12	2	0	5	22	115	31	24	20	4	0	0	4	13	0	21	2	0	1	2	.333	0	0	8.18
1992 California	AL	19	0	0	6	27.2	125	29	11	10	3	0	0	2	13	1	24	0	0	2	2	.500	0	0	3.25
1993 California	AL	23	0	0	11	28.1	124	21	12	9	2	1	3	2	15	1	24	0	0	1	0	1.000	0	8	2.86
1994 California	AL	33	0	0	12	29.2	140	31	24	22	2	2	0	2	23	5	19	2	0	2	1	.667	0	1	6.67
1995 California	AL	40	0	0	13	51.1	227	49	28	27	7	1	3	1	31	2	29	3	0	6	1	.857	0	0	4.73
10 Min. YEARS		235	95	5	61	714.1	2940	766	472	406	59	26	36	53	374	11	585	50	9	49	48	.505	1	15	5.12
4 Maj. YEARS		115	0	0	42	137	616	130	75	68	14	4	6	7	82	9	96	5	0	11	4	.733	0	9	4.47

Adam Butler

Pitches: Left **Bats:** Left **Pos:** P **Ht:** 6'2" **Wt:** 225 **Born:** 8/17/73 **Age:** 23

HOW MUCH HE PITCHED								WHAT HE GAVE UP												THE RESULTS					
Year Team	Lg Org	G	GS	CG	GF	IP	BFP	H	R	ER	HR	SH	SF	HB	TBB	IBB	SO	WP	Bk	W	L	Pct.	ShO	Sv	ERA
1995 Eugene	A- Atl	23	0	0	18	25.1	109	15	0	7	0	1	0	3	12	5	50	1	0	4	1	.800	0	8	2.49
1996 Macon	A Atl	12	0	0	12	14.2	53	5	3	2	1	0	0	1	3	0	23	1	0	0	1	.000	0	8	1.23
Durham	A+ Atl	9	0	0	9	11	41	2	0	0	0	0	0	1	7	0	14	0	0	0	0	.000	0	5	0.00
Greenville	AA Atl	38	0	0	31	35.1	161	36	22	20	6	5	3	2	16	3	31	3	0	1	4	.200	0	17	5.09

Year Team	Lg Org	G	GS	CG	GF	IP	BFP	H	R	ER	HR	SH	SF	HB	TBB	IBB	SO	WP	Bk	W	L	Pct.	ShO	Sv	ERA
		HOW MUCH HE PITCHED						WHAT HE GAVE UP												THE RESULTS					
2 Min. YEARS		82	0	0	70	86.1	364	58	34	29	7	6	3	7	38	8	118	5	0	5	6	.455	0	38	3.02

Rob Butler

Bats: Left **Throws:** Left **Pos:** OF **Ht:** 5'11" **Wt:** 185 **Born:** 4/10/70 **Age:** 27

Year Team	Lg Org	G	AB	H	2B	3B	HR	TB	R	RBI	TBB	IBB	SO	HBP	SH	SF	SB	CS	SB%	GDP	Avg	OBP	SLG
		BATTING															BASERUNNING				PERCENTAGES		
1991 St. Cathrns	A- Tor	76	311	105	16	5	7	152	71	45	20	5	21	2	6	3	31	15	.67	2	.338	.378	.489
1992 Dunedin	A+ Tor	92	391	140	13	7	4	179	67	41	22	2	36	2	2	1	19	14	.58	7	.358	.394	.458
1993 Syracuse	AAA Tor	55	208	59	11	2	1	77	30	14	15	2	29	3	3	2	7	5	.58	6	.284	.338	.370
1994 Syracuse	AAA Tor	25	95	25	6	1	1	36	16	11	8	1	12	1	0	2	2	0	1.00	1	.263	.321	.379
1995 Scranton-WB	AAA Phi	92	327	98	16	4	3	131	46	35	24	2	39	6	4	4	5	8	.38	14	.300	.355	.401
1996 Scranton-WB	AAA Phi	91	298	76	15	8	4	119	39	34	20	1	45	1	2	0	3	5	.38	6	.255	.304	.399
1993 Toronto	AL	17	48	13	4	0	0	17	8	2	7	0	12	1	0	0	2	2	.50	0	.271	.375	.354
1994 Toronto	AL	41	74	13	0	1	0	15	13	5	7	0	8	1	4	2	0	1	.00	3	.176	.250	.203
6 Min. YEARS		431	1630	503	77	27	20	694	269	180	109	13	182	15	17	12	67	47	.59	36	.309	.355	.426
2 Maj. YEARS		58	122	26	4	1	0	32	21	7	14	0	20	2	4	2	2	3	.40	3	.213	.300	.262

Matt Byrd

Pitches: Right **Bats:** Both **Pos:** P **Ht:** 6'2" **Wt:** 200 **Born:** 5/17/71 **Age:** 26

Year Team	Lg Org	G	GS	CG	GF	IP	BFP	H	R	ER	HR	SH	SF	HB	TBB	IBB	SO	WP	Bk	W	L	Pct.	ShO	Sv	ERA
		HOW MUCH HE PITCHED						WHAT HE GAVE UP												THE RESULTS					
1993 Danville	R+ Atl	25	0	0	15	41.1	169	23	10	9	2	4	1	2	17	2	57	5	0	5	2	.714	0	7	1.96
1994 Durham	A+ Atl	29	0	0	20	37.1	156	22	20	19	7	0	0	2	19	2	39	5	0	2	4	.333	0	3	4.58
1995 Durham	A+ Atl	60	0	0	53	69.2	296	52	24	23	8	0	3	3	32	4	79	9	0	5	4	.556	0	27	2.97
1996 Greenville	AA Atl	51	4	0	29	90.1	421	108	77	70	12	8	5	2	40	4	66	11	0	4	9	.308	0	2	6.97
4 Min. YEARS		165	4	0	117	238.2	1042	205	131	121	29	12	9	9	108	12	241	30	0	16	19	.457	0	39	4.56

Tony Byrd

Bats: Both **Throws:** Right **Pos:** OF **Ht:** 5'11" **Wt:** 190 **Born:** 11/13/70 **Age:** 26

Year Team	Lg Org	G	AB	H	2B	3B	HR	TB	R	RBI	TBB	IBB	SO	HBP	SH	SF	SB	CS	SB%	GDP	Avg	OBP	SLG
		BATTING															BASERUNNING				PERCENTAGES		
1992 Kenosha	A Min	46	150	35	5	3	0	46	15	10	12	0	35	0	3	0	7	1	.88	2	.233	.290	.307
1993 Fort Wayne	A Min	123	479	140	19	10	16	227	84	79	58	4	78	3	0	3	24	11	.69	6	.292	.370	.474
1994 Nashville	AA Min	132	512	121	25	6	7	179	62	38	37	0	114	3	4	3	28	10	.74	10	.236	.290	.350
1995 New Britain	AA Min	123	442	109	20	8	3	154	54	51	28	2	85	3	5	5	21	10	.68	13	.247	.293	.348
1996 New Britain	AA Min	59	194	48	8	1	1	61	23	10	18	1	35	1	3	1	11	9	.55	3	.247	.313	.314
5 Min. YEARS		483	1777	453	77	28	27	667	238	188	153	7	347	10	15	12	91	41	.69	34	.255	.316	.375

Timothy Byrdak

Pitches: Left **Bats:** Left **Pos:** P **Ht:** 5'11" **Wt:** 170 **Born:** 10/31/73 **Age:** 23

Year Team	Lg Org	G	GS	CG	GF	IP	BFP	H	R	ER	HR	SH	SF	HB	TBB	IBB	SO	WP	Bk	W	L	Pct.	ShO	Sv	ERA
		HOW MUCH HE PITCHED						WHAT HE GAVE UP												THE RESULTS					
1994 Eugene	A- KC	15	15	0	0	73.1	302	60	33	25	6	2	2	4	20	0	77	1	1	4	5	.444	0	0	3.07
1995 Wilmington	A+ KC	27	26	0	0	166.1	657	118	46	40	7	3	3	10	45	2	127	1	0	11	5	.688	0	0	2.16
1996 Wichita	AA KC	15	15	0	0	84.2	388	112	73	65	15	5	1	0	44	0	47	8	0	5	7	.417	0	0	6.91
3 Min. YEARS		57	56	0	0	324.1	1347	290	152	130	28	10	6	14	109	2	251	10	1	20	17	.541	0	0	3.61

Earl Byrne

Pitches: Left **Bats:** Left **Pos:** P **Ht:** 6'1" **Wt:** 165 **Born:** 7/2/72 **Age:** 24

Year Team	Lg Org	G	GS	CG	GF	IP	BFP	H	R	ER	HR	SH	SF	HB	TBB	IBB	SO	WP	Bk	W	L	Pct.	ShO	Sv	ERA
		HOW MUCH HE PITCHED						WHAT HE GAVE UP												THE RESULTS					
1994 Cubs	R ChN	4	1	0	1	11	41	5	3	2	0	1	1	0	6	0	11	0	1	1	1	.500	0	0	1.64
1995 Rockford	A ChN	13	11	0	0	60	269	54	36	31	2	3	6	3	38	0	51	8	1	4	3	.571	0	0	4.65
1996 Orlando	AA ChN	11	6	1	2	37	170	36	28	23	5	1	1	0	26	1	30	1	2	1	2	.333	0	0	5.59
Daytona	A+ ChN	18	3	1	6	45.1	201	44	22	17	5	2	0	1	21	2	47	4	2	1	4	.200	0	1	3.38
3 Min. YEARS		46	21	2	9	153.1	681	139	89	73	12	7	8	4	91	3	139	13	6	7	10	.412	0	1	4.28

Jolbert Cabrera

Bats: Right **Throws:** Right **Pos:** SS **Ht:** 6'0" **Wt:** 177 **Born:** 12/8/72 **Age:** 24

Year Team	Lg Org	G	AB	H	2B	3B	HR	TB	R	RBI	TBB	IBB	SO	HBP	SH	SF	SB	CS	SB%	GDP	Avg	OBP	SLG
		BATTING															BASERUNNING				PERCENTAGES		
1991 Sumter	A Mon	101	324	66	4	0	1	73	33	20	19	0	62	4	4	2	10	11	.48	5	.204	.255	.225
1992 Albany	A Mon	118	377	86	9	2	0	99	44	23	34	0	77	1	6	0	22	11	.67	8	.228	.294	.263
1993 Burlington	A Mon	128	507	129	24	2	0	157	62	38	39	0	93	7	11	4	31	11	.74	13	.254	.314	.310
1994 W. Palm Bch	A+ Mon	83	266	54	4	0	0	58	32	13	14	0	48	8	4	0	7	10	.41	4	.203	.264	.218
San Bernrdo	A+ Mon	30	109	27	5	1	0	34	14	11	14	0	24	0	4	2	2	2	.50	1	.248	.328	.312
Harrisburg	AA Mon	3	2	0	0	0	0	0	0	0	0	0	1	0	0	0	0	0	.00	0	.000	.000	.000
1995 W. Palm Bch	A+ Mon	103	357	102	23	2	1	132	62	25	38	0	61	8	6	4	19	12	.61	3	.286	.364	.370
Harrisburg	AA Mon	9	35	10	2	0	0	12	4	1	1	0	3	0	2	0	3	1	.75	1	.286	.306	.343
1996 Harrisburg	AA Mon	107	354	85	18	2	3	116	40	29	23	3	63	1	5	4	10	5	.67	9	.240	.285	.328
6 Min. YEARS		682	2331	559	89	9	5	681	291	160	182	3	432	29	42	16	104	63	.62	44	.240	.301	.292

Jose Cabrera

Pitches: Right **Bats:** Right **Pos:** P **Ht:** 6'0" **Wt:** 160 **Born:** 3/24/72 **Age:** 25

				HOW MUCH HE PITCHED						WHAT HE GAVE UP												THE RESULTS					
Year	Team	Lg	Org	G	GS	CG	GF	IP	BFP	H	R	ER	HR	SH	SF	HB	TBB	IBB	SO	WP	Bk	W	L	Pct.	ShO	Sv	ERA
1992	Burlington	R+	Cle	13	13	1	0	92.1	367	74	27	18	6	2	0	2	18	0	79	3	1	8	3	.727	0	0	1.75
1993	Columbus	A	Cle	26	26	1	0	155.1	624	122	54	46	8	2	4	1	53	2	105	8	4	11	6	.647	0	0	2.67
1994	Kinston	A+	Cle	24	24	0	0	133.2	575	134	84	66	15	6	3	5	43	0	110	5	5	4	13	.235	0	0	4.44
1995	Canton-Akrn	AA	Cle	24	11	1	4	85	350	83	32	31	7	1	6	1	21	1	61	0	2	5	3	.625	1	0	3.28
1996	Bakersfield	A+	Cle	7	7	0	0	41.1	183	40	25	18	7	2	2	1	21	0	52	5	0	2	2	.500	0	0	3.92
	Kinston	A+	Cle	4	3	0	0	17.2	68	7	2	2	0	1	1	1	8	0	19	3	0	1	1	.500	0	0	1.02
	Canton-Akrn	AA	Cle	15	9	1	4	62.1	278	78	45	39	10	2	3	1	17	2	40	4	0	4	3	.571	0	0	5.63
5 Min. YEARS				113	93	4	8	587.2	2445	538	269	220	53	16	19	12	181	5	466	28	12	35	31	.530	1	0	3.37

Edgar Caceres

Bats: Both **Throws:** Right **Pos:** SS **Ht:** 6' 1" **Wt:** 170 **Born:** 6/6/64 **Age:** 33

				BATTING															BASERUNNING				PERCENTAGES		
Year	Team	Lg	Org	G	AB	H	2B	3B	HR	TB	R	RBI	TBB	IBB	SO	HBP	SH	SF	SB	CS	SB%	GDP	Avg	OBP	SLG
1984	Dodgers	R	LA	20	77	23	3	1	0	28	11	11	10	0	6	0	1	0	5	2	.71	0	.299	.379	.364
1985	Dodgers	R	LA	53	176	53	6	0	0	59	37	22	18	1	11	2	2	0	5	2	.71	4	.301	.372	.335
1986	W. Palm Bch	A+	Mon	111	382	106	9	5	0	125	52	37	24	2	28	2	4	4	25	6	.81	4	.277	.320	.327
1987	Jacksonvlle	AA	Mon	18	62	8	0	1	0	10	7	3	3	0	7	0	0	0	2	0	1.00	2	.129	.169	.161
	W. Palm Bch	A+	Mon	105	390	105	14	1	2	127	55	37	27	0	30	5	7	1	30	5	.86	4	.269	.324	.326
1988	Rockford	A	Mon	36	117	31	2	0	0	33	25	8	12	0	12	0	5	1	13	3	.81	2	.265	.331	.282
	Tampa	A+	ChA	32	74	15	2	0	1	20	5	8	10	2	8	1	2	3	3	0	1.00	2	.203	.295	.270
1989	Sarasota	A+	ChA	106	373	110	16	4	0	134	45	50	24	4	38	2	9	2	8	3	.73	12	.295	.339	.359
1990	Birmingham	AA	ChA	62	213	56	5	1	0	63	31	17	16	0	26	1	3	1	7	4	.64	7	.263	.316	.296
1992	El Paso	AA	Mil	114	378	118	14	6	2	150	50	52	23	4	41	2	5	1	9	2	.82	8	.312	.354	.397
1993	New Orleans	AAA	Mil	114	420	133	20	2	5	172	73	45	35	5	39	1	3	3	7	4	.64	14	.317	.368	.410
1994	Omaha	AAA	KC	67	236	64	7	3	2	83	39	18	16	1	23	0	6	3	5	3	.63	7	.271	.314	.352
1995	Omaha	AAA	KC	37	107	22	3	1	0	27	13	12	8	3	10	0	1	1	3	1	.75	2	.206	.259	.252
1996	New Orleans	AAA	Mil	115	397	107	10	2	4	133	40	29	23	3	32	2	5	2	8	5	.62	9	.270	.311	.335
1995	Kansas City	AL		55	117	28	6	2	1	41	13	17	8	0	15	1	3	1	2	2	.50	3	.239	.291	.350
12 Min. YEARS				990	3402	951	111	27	16	1164	483	349	249	25	311	18	53	22	130	40	.76	77	.280	.330	.342

Greg Cadaret

Pitches: Left **Bats:** Left **Pos:** P **Ht:** 6' 3" **Wt:** 215 **Born:** 2/27/62 **Age:** 35

				HOW MUCH HE PITCHED						WHAT HE GAVE UP												THE RESULTS					
Year	Team	Lg	Org	G	GS	CG	GF	IP	BFP	H	R	ER	HR	SH	SF	HB	TBB	IBB	SO	WP	Bk	W	L	Pct.	ShO	Sv	ERA
1984	Modesto	A+	Oak	26	26	6	0	171.1	0	162	79	58	7	0	0	1	82	0	138	14	2	13	8	.619	2	0	3.05
1985	Huntsville	AA	Oak	17	17	0	0	82.1	387	96	61	56	9	2	4	3	57	0	60	9	0	3	7	.300	0	0	6.12
	Modesto	A+	Oak	12	12	1	0	61.1	0	59	50	40	4	0	0	1	54	0	43	10	0	3	9	.250	1	0	5.87
1986	Huntsville	AA	Oak	28	28	1	0	141.1	666	166	106	85	6	1	4	1	98	0	113	15	0	12	5	.706	0	0	5.41
1987	Huntsville	AA	Oak	24	0	0	21	40.1	172	31	16	13	1	1	0	0	20	3	48	6	1	5	2	.714	0	9	2.90
	Tacoma	AAA	Oak	7	0	0	4	13	57	5	6	5	1	2	0	0	13	1	12	0	0	1	2	.333	0	1	3.46
1995	Louisville	AAA	StL	12	0	0	2	11.2	50	14	4	4	0	1	0	0	1	0	7	0	0	1	0	1.000	0	0	3.09
	Las Vegas	AAA	SD	40	4	0	8	63.2	284	70	44	38	6	3	3	0	23	0	59	10	0	4	5	.444	0	0	5.37
1996	Calgary	AAA	Pit	9	0	0	3	12.1	69	20	18	10	2	2	0	1	12	2	10	4	0	0	3	.000	0	0	7.30
	Buffalo	AAA	Cle	32	3	0	9	64	274	59	28	26	3	3	2	2	29	2	44	4	0	1	5	.167	0	2	3.66
1987	Oakland	AL		29	0	0	7	39.2	176	37	22	20	6	2	2	1	24	1	30	1	0	6	2	.750	0	0	4.54
1988	Oakland	AL		58	0	0	16	71.2	311	60	26	23	2	5	3	1	36	1	64	5	3	5	2	.714	0	3	2.89
1989	Oakland	AL		26	0	0	6	27.2	119	21	9	7	0	0	2	0	19	3	14	0	0	0	0	.000	0	0	2.28
	New York	AL		20	13	3	1	92.1	412	109	53	47	7	3	3	2	38	1	66	6	2	5	5	.500	1	0	4.58
1990	New York	AL		54	6	0	9	121.1	525	120	62	56	8	9	4	1	64	5	80	14	0	5	4	.556	0	3	4.15
1991	New York	AL		68	5	0	17	121.2	517	110	52	49	8	6	3	2	59	6	105	3	1	8	6	.571	0	3	3.62
1992	New York	AL		46	11	1	9	103.2	471	104	53	49	12	3	3	2	74	7	73	5	1	4	8	.333	1	1	4.25
1993	Cincinnati	NL		34	0	0	15	32.2	158	40	19	18	3	3	0	1	23	5	23	2	0	2	1	.667	0	1	4.96
	Kansas City	AL		13	0	0	3	15.1	62	14	5	5	0	1	0	1	7	0	2	0	0	1	1	.500	0	0	2.93
1994	Toronto	AL		21	0	0	8	20	100	24	15	13	4	0	0	0	17	2	15	6	0	0	1	.000	0	0	5.85
	Detroit	AL		17	0	0	9	20	91	17	9	8	0	0	0	0	16	3	14	3	0	1	0	1.000	0	2	3.60
6 Min. YEARS				207	90	8	47	661.1	1959	682	412	335	39	15	13	9	389	8	534	72	3	43	46	.483	3	12	4.56
8 Maj. YEARS				386	35	4	100	666	2942	656	325	295	50	32	20	11	377	34	486	45	7	37	30	.552	2	13	3.99

Rocco Cafaro

Pitches: Right **Bats:** Right **Pos:** P **Ht:** 6'0" **Wt:** 163 **Born:** 12/12/72 **Age:** 24

				HOW MUCH HE PITCHED						WHAT HE GAVE UP												THE RESULTS					
Year	Team	Lg	Org	G	GS	CG	GF	IP	BFP	H	R	ER	HR	SH	SF	HB	TBB	IBB	SO	WP	Bk	W	L	Pct.	ShO	Sv	ERA
1993	Orioles	R	Bal	14	8	1	2	80.2	312	58	21	16	1	1	3	3	12	0	57	2	2	2	2	.500	0	1	1.79
1994	Albany	A	Bal	30	1	0	15	68.1	304	73	41	37	3	3	4	8	27	4	53	7	4	3	5	.375	0	3	4.87
1995	High Desert	A+	Bal	44	1	0	39	66.2	290	69	42	33	10	2	4	2	25	0	52	6	1	4	5	.444	0	8	4.46
1996	Bowie	AA	Bal	27	15	1	1	103.1	467	130	67	57	14	3	5	5	36	0	55	5	2	4	8	.333	0	0	4.96
	Frederick	A+	Bal	8	0	0	7	20	85	19	10	10	2	0	0	1	6	0	16	0	0	1	3	.250	0	2	4.50
4 Min. YEARS				123	25	2	64	339	1458	349	181	153	30	9	16	19	106	4	233	20	9	14	23	.378	0	14	4.06

Tim Cain

Pitches: Right **Bats:** Both **Pos:** P — **Ht:** 6'1" **Wt:** 180 **Born:** 10/9/69 **Age:** 27

		HOW MUCH HE PITCHED						WHAT HE GAVE UP												THE RESULTS					
Year Team	Lg Org	G	GS	CG	GF	IP	BFP	H	R	ER	HR	SH	SF	HB	TBB	IBB	SO	WP	Bk	W	L	Pct.	ShO	Sv	ERA
1990 Rangers	R Tex	16	1	0	4	36	146	27	22	15	1	0	0	5	6	0	38	2	2	0	3	.000	0	1	3.75
1991 Bend	A- Tex	17	6	0	4	58.1	267	65	49	37	2	0	1	4	25	0	59	8	0	1	3	.250	0	2	5.71
1993 Rochester	IND —	20	12	2	1	102.1	428	76	37	27	4	7	1	13	28	0	73	3	1	4	4	.500	1	1	2.37
1994 Winnipeg	IND —	6	6	1	0	43	167	30	11	11	2	1	0	1	6	0	50	1	0	5	1	.833	0	0	2.30
New Britain	AA Bos	10	10	0	0	50.2	226	65	39	32	8	2	0	3	18	0	37	1	1	2	4	.333	0	0	5.68
1995 Pawtucket	AAA Bos	14	0	0	5	27.2	111	24	7	7	0	1	1	1	8	1	19	1	0	4	0	1.000	0	4	2.28
Trenton	AA Bos	43	1	0	13	78.1	326	70	32	28	1	5	1	7	25	4	64	4	0	8	3	.727	0	8	3.22
1996 Pawtucket	AAA Bos	11	0	0	1	19.1	80	15	4	4	1	0	0	2	6	1	10	0	0	1	0	1.000	0	0	1.86
6 Min. YEARS		137	36	3	28	415.2	1751	372	201	161	19	16	4	36	122	6	350	20	4	25	18	.581	1	16	3.49

Daniel Camacho

Pitches: Right **Bats:** Right **Pos:** P — **Ht:** 5'11" **Wt:** 190 **Born:** 11/11/73 **Age:** 23

		HOW MUCH HE PITCHED						WHAT HE GAVE UP												THE RESULTS					
Year Team	Lg Org	G	GS	CG	GF	IP	BFP	H	R	ER	HR	SH	SF	HB	TBB	IBB	SO	WP	Bk	W	L	Pct.	ShO	Sv	ERA
1993 Great Falls	R+ LA	28	0	0	13	65.1	253	38	14	10	6	1	2	6	18	1	79	9	0	5	2	.714	0	5	1.38
1994 Bakersfield	A+ LA	10	0	0	4	22.1	86	9	3	3	0	0	1	0	15	1	25	5	0	0	0	.000	0	0	1.21
1995 San Antonio	AA LA	11	0	0	10	11.1	47	9	2	2	0	0	0	0	8	0	8	2	0	1	1	.500	0	2	1.59
San Bernrdo	A+ LA	54	1	0	37	79.2	342	75	34	32	7	5	1	1	38	3	87	7	1	7	3	.700	0	11	3.62
1996 Vero Beach	A+ LA	10	10	0	0	54.1	227	38	16	15	4	3	1	5	29	0	50	4	2	5	1	.833	0	0	2.48
San Antonio	AA LA	4	2	0	0	16.2	73	11	5	5	0	1	1	0	17	0	11	1	0	1	1	.500	0	0	2.70
San Bernrdo	A+ LA	14	13	0	1	74	343	81	56	55	12	0	3	3	52	1	72	11	2	4	5	.444	0	1	6.69
4 Min. YEARS		131	26	0	65	323.2	1371	261	130	122	29	10	9	15	177	6	332	39	5	23	13	.639	0	19	3.39

Stanton Cameron

Bats: Right **Throws:** Right **Pos:** OF — **Ht:** 6'5" **Wt:** 195 **Born:** 7/5/69 **Age:** 27

		BATTING															BASERUNNING				PERCENTAGES		
Year Team	Lg Org	G	AB	H	2B	3B	HR	TB	R	RBI	TBB	IBB	SO	HBP	SH	SF	SB	CS	SB%	GDP	Avg	OBP	SLG
1987 Kingsport	R+ NYN	26	53	7	1	0	1	11	6	5	10	0	24	0	1	1	1	1	.50	1	.132	.266	.208
1988 Mets	R NYN	51	171	40	10	1	1	55	24	15	25	0	33	3	1	0	10	5	.67	7	.234	.342	.322
1989 Pittsfield	A- NYN	71	253	65	13	1	10	110	35	50	41	2	71	4	1	1	7	2	.78	3	.257	.368	.435
1990 Columbia	A NYN	87	302	90	19	1	15	156	57	57	52	1	68	4	0	7	3	2	.60	7	.298	.400	.517
1991 St. Lucie	A+ NYN	83	232	43	7	0	2	56	25	26	46	0	82	4	3	1	1	1	.50	2	.185	.329	.241
1992 Frederick	A+ Bal	127	409	101	16	1	29	206	76	92	90	3	121	11	2	5	2	3	.40	7	.247	.392	.504
1993 Bowie	AA Bal	118	384	106	27	1	21	198	65	64	84	2	103	6	0	6	6	7	.46	11	.276	.408	.516
1994 Buffalo	AAA Pit	38	139	24	4	0	4	40	10	14	8	1	29	2	0	0	3	0	1.00	5	.173	.228	.288
Carolina	AA Pit	88	327	102	28	3	11	169	58	56	34	2	74	2	0	4	10	2	.83	7	.312	.376	.517
1995 Calgary	AAA Pit	7	24	5	4	0	0	9	8	4	4	0	4	0	0	0	0	0	.00	0	.208	.321	.375
Okla. City	AAA Tex	5	12	2	1	0	0	3	2	0	4	0	3	0	0	0	0	0	.00	0	.167	.375	.250
Canton-Akrn	AA Cle	35	82	21	8	0	1	32	11	12	10	0	18	4	2	2	1	0	1.00	1	.256	.357	.390
1996 Wichita	AA KC	2	7	1	0	0	0	1	0	2	0	0	4	0	0	0	0	0	.00	0	.143	.143	.143
Meridian	IND —	61	214	73	17	2	19	151	56	72	46	4	31	2	0	8	10	3	.77	3	.341	.448	.706
Columbia	IND —	8	29	8	0	1	2	16	6	6	5	0	5	1	0	0	1	0	1.00	0	.276	.400	.552
10 Min. YEARS		807	2638	688	155	11	116	1213	439	475	459	15	670	43	10	35	55	26	.68	54	.261	.375	.460

Jesus Campos

Bats: Right **Throws:** Right **Pos:** OF — **Ht:** 5'9" **Wt:** 145 **Born:** 10/12/73 **Age:** 23

		BATTING															BASERUNNING				PERCENTAGES		
Year Team	Lg Org	G	AB	H	2B	3B	HR	TB	R	RBI	TBB	IBB	SO	HBP	SH	SF	SB	CS	SB%	GDP	Avg	OBP	SLG
1993 Expos	R Mon	2	8	1	0	0	0	1	1	1	2	0	1	0	0	0	0	0	.00	0	.125	.300	.125
Jamestown	A- Mon	70	285	69	6	6	1	90	43	22	18	0	39	2	0	2	9	9	.50	12	.242	.290	.316
1994 Burlington	A Mon	12	44	6	0	0	0	6	1	1	1	0	7	0	0	0	0	1	.00	2	.136	.156	.136
Expos	R Mon	3	11	4	0	0	0	4	0	3	1	0	0	0	0	1	0	0	.00	1	.364	.385	.364
W. Palm Bch	A+ Mon	62	240	66	11	2	0	81	37	16	17	1	23	0	1	1	13	2	.87	5	.275	.322	.338
1995 W. Palm Bch	A+ Mon	107	326	72	6	2	0	82	32	21	25	0	40	2	6	2	18	7	.72	5	.221	.279	.252
1996 W. Palm Bch	A+ Mon	44	148	37	6	1	0	45	24	20	12	0	24	2	1	2	8	3	.73	1	.250	.311	.304
Harrisburg	AA Mon	73	208	54	4	0	0	58	15	17	9	2	17	2	1	0	5	9	.36	5	.260	.297	.279
4 Min. YEARS		373	1270	309	33	11	1	367	153	101	85	3	151	8	9	8	53	31	.63	31	.243	.293	.289

Miguel Campos

Bats: Right **Throws:** Right **Pos:** C — **Ht:** 6'1" **Wt:** 185 **Born:** 3/28/76 **Age:** 21

		BATTING															BASERUNNING				PERCENTAGES		
Year Team	Lg Org	G	AB	H	2B	3B	HR	TB	R	RBI	TBB	IBB	SO	HBP	SH	SF	SB	CS	SB%	GDP	Avg	OBP	SLG
1994 Cubs	R ChN	19	42	11	4	0	1	18	3	8	2	0	15	1	1	1	0	0	.00	1	.262	.304	.429
Orlando	AA ChN	4	8	1	0	0	0	1	0	0	1	0	4	0	0	0	0	0	.00	0	.125	.222	.125
1995 Cubs	R ChN	36	115	24	6	0	3	39	21	13	8	0	37	3	2	0	5	1	.83	2	.209	.278	.339
1996 Daytona	A+ ChN	8	12	5	0	0	0	5	1	1	1	0	1	1	0	0	0	0	.00	0	.417	.500	.417
Iowa	AAA ChN	2	4	1	0	0	0	1	0	0	0	0	2	0	0	0	0	0	.00	0	.250	.250	.250
Williamsprt	A- ChN	6	20	3	1	0	0	4	1	1	0	0	11	0	0	0	0	0	.00	0	.150	.150	.200
3 Min. YEARS		75	201	45	11	0	4	68	26	23	12	0	70	5	3	1	5	1	.83	3	.224	.283	.338

Benjamin Candelaria

Bats: Left **Throws:** Right **Pos:** OF **Ht:** 5'11" **Wt:** 167 **Born:** 1/29/75 **Age:** 22

		BATTING															BASERUNNING				PERCENTAGES		
Year Team	Lg Org	G	AB	H	2B	3B	HR	TB	R	RBI	TBB	IBB	SO	HBP	SH	SF	SB	CS	SB%	GDP	Avg	OBP	SLG
1992 Blue Jays	R Tor	29	77	12	2	1	0	16	10	3	6	0	16	0	1	1	4	3	.57	0	.156	.214	.208
1993 Medicne Hat	R+ Tor	62	208	55	7	1	5	79	24	34	27	1	49	3	5	4	3	3	.50	3	.264	.351	.380
1994 Hagerstown	A Tor	3	13	3	0	0	1	6	2	3	0	0	4	0	0	0	0	0	.00	0	.231	.231	.462
St. Cathrns	A- Tor	71	250	66	15	1	2	89	36	37	35	1	55	1	3	1	8	4	.67	6	.264	.355	.356
1995 Dunedin	A+ Tor	125	471	122	21	5	5	168	66	49	53	1	98	0	3	5	11	4	.73	11	.259	.331	.357
1996 Knoxville	AA Tor	55	162	45	11	2	3	69	16	14	18	0	40	2	2	0	3	3	.50	7	.278	.357	.426
Dunedin	A+ Tor	39	125	25	5	0	1	33	13	6	12	0	25	0	1	0	1	4	.20	1	.200	.270	.264
5 Min. YEARS		384	1306	328	61	10	17	460	167	146	151	3	287	6	15	11	30	21	.59	28	.251	.329	.352

Carmine Cappuccio

Bats: Left **Throws:** Right **Pos:** OF **Ht:** 6'3" **Wt:** 185 **Born:** 2/1/70 **Age:** 27

		BATTING															BASERUNNING				PERCENTAGES		
Year Team	Lg Org	G	AB	H	2B	3B	HR	TB	R	RBI	TBB	IBB	SO	HBP	SH	SF	SB	CS	SB%	GDP	Avg	OBP	SLG
1992 Utica	A- ChA	22	87	24	4	2	0	32	15	13	6	0	10	1	0	1	5	0	1.00	3	.276	.326	.368
South Bend	A ChA	49	182	53	9	2	0	66	23	19	21	1	21	1	1	1	2	3	.40	4	.291	.366	.363
1993 Sarasota	A+ ChA	24	90	17	2	2	1	26	9	12	4	1	10	0	0	0	3	0	1.00	1	.189	.223	.289
South Bend	A ChA	101	383	117	26	5	4	165	59	52	42	6	56	6	0	1	2	6	.25	11	.305	.382	.431
1994 Pr. William	A+ ChA	101	401	117	30	1	12	185	71	60	25	1	53	9	2	4	8	4	.67	7	.292	.344	.461
1995 Birmingham	AA ChA	65	248	69	13	3	4	100	34	38	22	4	21	2	3	2	2	2	.50	10	.278	.339	.403
Nashville	AAA ChA	66	216	59	14	0	5	88	30	24	29	4	26	1	1	1	0	2	.00	6	.273	.360	.407
1996 Nashville	AAA ChA	120	407	111	22	3	10	169	55	61	25	7	48	6	3	2	1	3	.25	15	.273	.323	.415
5 Min. YEARS		548	2014	567	120	18	36	831	296	279	174	24	245	26	10	12	23	20	.53	57	.282	.345	.413

Gary Caraballo

Bats: Right **Throws:** Right **Pos:** 3B **Ht:** 5'11" **Wt:** 205 **Born:** 7/11/71 **Age:** 25

		BATTING															BASERUNNING				PERCENTAGES		
Year Team	Lg Org	G	AB	H	2B	3B	HR	TB	R	RBI	TBB	IBB	SO	HBP	SH	SF	SB	CS	SB%	GDP	Avg	OBP	SLG
1989 Royals	R KC	46	160	38	6	0	1	47	18	25	16	0	18	6	0	4	4	4	.50	2	.238	.323	.294
Baseball Cy	A+ KC	3	9	3	0	0	0	3	0	0	0	0	2	0	0	0	0	0	.00	0	.333	.333	.333
1990 Appleton	A KC	123	406	87	14	3	6	125	37	50	39	1	62	12	0	7	6	5	.55	8	.214	.297	.308
1991 Appleton	A KC	79	275	69	16	1	2	93	39	44	34	0	33	7	0	7	13	1	.93	7	.251	.341	.338
Baseball Cy	A+ KC	50	179	40	9	3	3	64	28	24	22	0	32	3	0	2	3	2	.60	5	.223	.316	.358
1992 Baseball Cy	A+ KC	67	239	69	9	4	4	98	30	40	24	1	43	6	3	4	6	3	.67	3	.289	.363	.410
Memphis	AA KC	58	195	41	6	2	3	60	17	17	7	0	37	5	3	1	1	3	.25	2	.210	.255	.308
1993 Wilmington	A+ KC	39	145	44	8	3	2	64	20	26	20	1	25	5	0	0	3	0	1.00	5	.303	.406	.441
1994 Memphis	AA KC	127	429	106	21	1	10	159	45	59	32	0	69	7	3	3	6	3	.67	16	.247	.308	.371
1995 Fort Myers	A+ Min	85	309	95	24	2	7	144	51	55	34	3	44	5	0	3	5	6	.45	10	.307	.382	.466
1996 New Britain	AA Min	85	292	70	16	0	7	107	32	32	27	0	62	2	1	5	1	3	.25	7	.240	.304	.366
8 Min. YEARS		762	2638	662	129	19	45	964	317	372	255	6	427	58	10	36	48	30	.62	65	.251	.326	.365

Johnny Cardenas

Bats: Right **Throws:** Right **Pos:** C **Ht:** 6'3" **Wt:** 210 **Born:** 7/23/70 **Age:** 26

		BATTING															BASERUNNING				PERCENTAGES		
Year Team	Lg Org	G	AB	H	2B	3B	HR	TB	R	RBI	TBB	IBB	SO	HBP	SH	SF	SB	CS	SB%	GDP	Avg	OBP	SLG
1993 Bellingham	A- Sea	47	157	32	5	1	2	45	17	24	17	0	34	7	2	1	1	0	1.00	4	.204	.308	.287
1994 Riverside	A+ Sea	58	178	37	3	0	1	43	16	13	14	1	36	3	3	1	0	1	.00	6	.208	.276	.242
1995 Port City	AA Sea	57	195	44	9	0	0	53	17	17	9	1	45	0	1	1	1	3	.25	9	.226	.259	.272
1996 Port City	AA Sea	27	74	14	0	0	1	17	4	6	1	0	16	0	2	0	1	0	1.00	5	.189	.200	.230
Okla. City	AAA Tex	30	77	13	5	0	0	18	8	2	1	0	23	0	0	0	0	0	.00	2	.169	.179	.234
4 Min. YEARS		219	681	140	22	1	4	176	62	62	42	2	154	10	8	3	3	4	.43	26	.206	.261	.258

Todd Carey

Bats: Left **Throws:** Right **Pos:** 3B **Ht:** 6'1" **Wt:** 180 **Born:** 8/14/71 **Age:** 25

		BATTING															BASERUNNING				PERCENTAGES		
Year Team	Lg Org	G	AB	H	2B	3B	HR	TB	R	RBI	TBB	IBB	SO	HBP	SH	SF	SB	CS	SB%	GDP	Avg	OBP	SLG
1992 Elmira	A- Bos	54	197	40	7	2	0	51	18	19	9	1	40	0	1	3	0	4	.00	2	.203	.234	.259
1993 Ft. Laud	A+ Bos	118	444	109	14	5	3	142	41	31	24	1	44	0	5	3	2	6	.25	10	.245	.282	.320
1994 Lynchburg	A+ Bos	105	363	85	14	2	13	142	42	42	49	0	77	3	1	2	1	4	.20	5	.234	.329	.391
1995 Sarasota	A+ Bos	25	85	26	6	0	4	44	15	19	9	0	17	0	0	0	2	1	.67	3	.306	.372	.518
Trenton	AA Bos	76	228	62	11	1	8	99	30	36	28	0	44	4	1	2	3	4	.43	2	.272	.359	.434
1996 Trenton	AA Bos	125	440	110	34	3	20	210	78	78	48	9	123	3	3	3	4	4	.50	3	.250	.326	.477
5 Min. YEARS		503	1757	432	86	13	48	688	224	225	167	11	345	10	11	13	12	23	.34	25	.246	.313	.392

Ron Caridad

Pitches: Right **Bats:** Right **Pos:** P **Ht:** 5'10" **Wt:** 180 **Born:** 3/22/72 **Age:** 25

		HOW MUCH HE PITCHED						WHAT HE GAVE UP												THE RESULTS					
Year Team	Lg Org	G	GS	CG	GF	IP	BFP	H	R	ER	HR	SH	SF	HB	TBB	IBB	SO	WP	Bk	W	L	Pct.	ShO	Sv	ERA
1990 Twins	R Min	5	1	0	1	7	33	5	6	6	0	0	0	1	8	0	2	1	0	0	0	.000	0	0	7.71
1991 Elizabethtn	R+ Min	6	6	0	0	20.1	101	24	19	11	0	1	0	0	13	0	17	4	1	0	4	.000	0	0	4.87
1992 Elizabethtn	R+ Min	12	11	0	1	64	277	56	35	29	0	2	3	7	35	0	53	13	1	5	3	.625	0	0	4.08

				HOW MUCH HE PITCHED						WHAT HE GAVE UP												THE RESULTS					
Year	Team	Lg	Org	G	GS	CG	GF	IP	BFP	H	R	ER	HR	SH	SF	HB	TBB	IBB	SO	WP	Bk	W	L	Pct.	ShO	Sv	ERA
1993	Fort Wayne	A	Min	27	27	0	0	143.2	653	138	68	56	7	12	3	11	91	0	124	19	5	6	8	.429	0	0	3.51
1995	Fort Myers	A+	Min	17	0	0	9	41.1	171	27	15	11	1	1	2	3	18	0	38	4	0	2	3	.400	0	3	2.40
1996	New Britain	AA	Min	20	0	0	5	32.1	148	29	21	18	3	1	2	2	24	0	21	7	1	0	2	.000	0	0	5.01
	Stockton	A+	Mil	18	0	0	5	30	130	29	9	5	2	1	1	2	13	0	19	1	0	1	0	1.000	0	1	1.50
6 Min. YEARS				105	45	0	21	338.2	1513	308	173	136	13	18	11	26	202	0	274	49	8	14	20	.412	0	4	3.61

Ken Carlyle

Pitches: Right **Bats:** Right **Pos:** P **Ht:** 6'1" **Wt:** 185 **Born:** 9/16/69 **Age:** 27

				HOW MUCH HE PITCHED						WHAT HE GAVE UP												THE RESULTS					
Year	Team	Lg	Org	G	GS	CG	GF	IP	BFP	H	R	ER	HR	SH	SF	HB	TBB	IBB	SO	WP	Bk	W	L	Pct.	ShO	Sv	ERA
1992	Niagara Fal	A-	Det	1	1	0	0	6	26	6	1	1	0	0	0	0	1	0	9	1	1	1	0	1.000	0	0	1.50
	Fayettevlle	A	Det	14	14	1	0	79.2	319	64	21	17	3	0	1	4	24	0	59	6	1	8	4	.667	1	0	1.92
1993	Toledo	AAA	Det	15	14	1	0	75.2	339	88	59	54	13	2	2	1	36	1	43	4	2	2	10	.167	0	0	6.42
	London	AA	Det	12	12	1	0	78	341	72	40	32	8	1	3	5	35	1	50	0	2	4	6	.400	0	0	3.69
1994	Trenton	AA	Det	19	19	5	0	116.1	519	125	75	53	6	4	3	3	47	3	69	5	2	3	9	.250	1	0	4.10
	Toledo	AAA	Det	12	1	0	3	24.1	104	23	13	11	2	1	2	2	8	0	12	1	0	1	0	1.000	0	1	4.07
1995	Toledo	AAA	Det	32	20	0	0	124.2	541	139	65	60	10	2	5	4	44	2	63	7	0	8	8	.500	0	0	4.33
1996	Jacksonvlle	AA	Det	27	26	1	0	155.2	671	167	92	70	8	7	6	9	51	2	89	6	0	8	5	.615	1	0	4.05
5 Min. YEARS				132	107	9	3	660.1	2860	684	366	298	50	17	22	28	246	9	394	30	8	35	42	.455	3	1	4.06

Brian Carpenter

Pitches: Right **Bats:** Right **Pos:** P **Ht:** 6'0" **Wt:** 220 **Born:** 3/3/71 **Age:** 26

				HOW MUCH HE PITCHED						WHAT HE GAVE UP												THE RESULTS					
Year	Team	Lg	Org	G	GS	CG	GF	IP	BFP	H	R	ER	HR	SH	SF	HB	TBB	IBB	SO	WP	Bk	W	L	Pct.	ShO	Sv	ERA
1993	Savannah	A	StL	28	28	0	0	154.1	629	145	55	49	8	2	5	2	41	0	147	2	1	10	8	.556	0	0	2.86
1994	St. Pete	A+	StL	26	20	0	3	131.2	572	152	76	70	16	2	5	7	38	1	76	2	1	12	7	.632	0	1	4.78
1995	St. Pete	A+	StL	16	7	0	2	59	226	40	17	14	4	1	1	0	11	0	51	4	0	5	3	.625	0	0	2.14
	Arkansas	AA	StL	33	11	0	3	111.2	458	97	49	43	10	7	3	3	32	1	86	5	1	7	4	.636	0	0	3.47
1996	Arkansas	AA	StL	37	6	0	3	74	305	63	26	26	6	2	7	1	26	3	53	2	0	1	2	.333	0	0	3.16
4 Min. YEARS				140	72	0	11	530.2	2190	497	223	202	44	14	21	13	148	5	413	15	3	35	24	.593	0	1	3.43

Bubba Carpenter

Bats: Left **Throws:** Left **Pos:** OF **Ht:** 6'1" **Wt:** 185 **Born:** 7/23/68 **Age:** 28

				BATTING															BASERUNNING				PERCENTAGES		
Year	Team	Lg	Org	G	AB	H	2B	3B	HR	TB	R	RBI	TBB	IBB	SO	HBP	SH	SF	SB	CS	SB%	GDP	Avg	OBP	SLG
1991	Pr. William	A+	NYA	69	236	66	10	3	6	100	33	34	40	3	50	2	1	3	4	1	.80	7	.280	.384	.424
1992	Albany-Colo	AA	NYA	60	221	51	11	5	4	84	24	31	25	0	41	2	0	1	2	3	.40	8	.231	.313	.380
	Pr. William	A+	NYA	68	240	76	15	2	5	110	41	41	35	2	44	1	1	6	4	4	.50	4	.317	.397	.458
1993	Albany-Colo	AA	NYA	14	53	17	4	0	2	27	8	14	7	0	4	0	0	1	2	2	.50	2	.321	.393	.509
	Columbus	AAA	NYA	70	199	53	9	0	5	77	29	17	29	3	35	3	0	1	2	2	.50	4	.266	.366	.387
1994	Albany-Colo	AA	NYA	116	378	109	14	1	13	164	47	51	58	5	65	3	3	3	9	5	.64	3	.288	.385	.434
	Columbus	AAA	NYA	7	15	4	0	0	0	4	0	2	0	0	7	0	0	0	0	0	.00	1	.267	.267	.267
1995	Columbus	AAA	NYA	116	374	92	12	3	11	143	57	49	40	2	70	1	2	3	13	6	.68	2	.246	.318	.382
1996	Columbus	AAA	NYA	132	466	114	23	3	7	164	55	48	48	1	80	0	2	1	10	7	.59	7	.245	.315	.352
6 Min. YEARS				652	2182	582	98	17	53	873	294	287	282	16	396	12	9	19	46	30	.61	38	.267	.351	.400

Chris Carpenter

Pitches: Right **Bats:** Right **Pos:** P **Ht:** 6'6" **Wt:** 220 **Born:** 4/27/75 **Age:** 22

				HOW MUCH HE PITCHED						WHAT HE GAVE UP												THE RESULTS					
Year	Team	Lg	Org	G	GS	CG	GF	IP	BFP	H	R	ER	HR	SH	SF	HB	TBB	IBB	SO	WP	Bk	W	L	Pct.	ShO	Sv	ERA
1994	Medicne Hat	R+	Tor	15	15	0	0	84.2	366	76	40	26	3	2	3	8	39	0	80	9	2	6	3	.667	0	0	2.76
1995	Knoxville	AA	Tor	12	12	0	0	64.1	287	71	47	37	3	1	4	1	31	1	53	9	0	3	7	.300	0	0	5.18
	Dunedin	A+	Tor	27	27	0	0	163.2	707	154	76	61	6	3	4	5	81	1	109	18	3	6	12	.333	0	0	3.35
1996	Knoxville	AA	Tor	28	28	1	0	171.1	755	161	94	75	13	9	3	8	91	4	150	8	2	7	9	.438	0	0	3.94
3 Min. YEARS				82	82	1	0	484	2115	462	257	199	25	15	14	22	242	6	392	44	7	22	31	.415	0	0	3.70

Mark Carper

Pitches: Right **Bats:** Right **Pos:** P **Ht:** 6'2" **Wt:** 200 **Born:** 9/29/68 **Age:** 28

				HOW MUCH HE PITCHED						WHAT HE GAVE UP												THE RESULTS					
Year	Team	Lg	Org	G	GS	CG	GF	IP	BFP	H	R	ER	HR	SH	SF	HB	TBB	IBB	SO	WP	Bk	W	L	Pct.	ShO	Sv	ERA
1991	Frederick	A+	Bal	26	9	1	5	87.2	401	92	59	42	5	3	3	2	51	1	49	3	2	3	8	.273	0	0	4.31
1992	Hagerstown	AA	Bal	11	9	0	1	59	258	59	23	22	2	2	2	1	37	0	38	4	1	4	3	.571	0	0	3.36
	Albany-Colo	AA	NYA	20	10	1	3	74.1	309	62	22	20	4	0	1	2	30	1	36	8	0	5	4	.556	0	0	2.42
1993	Albany-Colo	AA	NYA	25	25	0	0	155.1	667	148	96	78	9	5	6	4	70	3	98	17	4	7	10	.412	0	0	4.52
1994	Columbus	AAA	NYA	26	18	2	4	117.2	520	128	68	57	9	3	3	10	48	1	58	6	0	8	6	.571	1	1	4.36
1995	Norwich	AA	NYA	1	1	0	0	5	26	9	6	6	2	0	1	2	1	0	3	2	0	0	0	.000	0	0	10.80
	Columbus	AAA	NYA	34	15	0	3	111.1	504	123	67	63	12	2	3	9	56	0	64	12	0	8	9	.471	0	1	5.09
1996	Columbus	AAA	NYA	15	4	0	2	35.1	163	43	30	26	7	0	0	3	16	0	16	4	0	1	2	.333	0	0	6.62
	Greenville	AA	Atl	4	0	0	2	6.1	27	4	1	0	0	0	0	0	5	0	1	0	0	0	0	.000	0	0	0.00
6 Min. YEARS				162	91	4	20	652	2875	668	372	314	50	15	19	33	314	6	363	56	7	36	42	.462	1	2	4.33

Jeremy Carr

Bats: Right **Throws:** Right **Pos:** OF — **Ht:** 5'10" **Wt:** 170 **Born:** 3/30/71 **Age:** 26

		BATTING																BASERUNNING				PERCENTAGES		
Year	Team	Lg Org	G	AB	H	2B	3B	HR	TB	R	RBI	TBB	IBB	SO	HBP	SH	SF	SB	CS	SB%	GDP	Avg	OBP	SLG
1993	Eugene	A- KC	42	136	31	2	5	0	43	33	12	20	1	18	6	2	2	30	3	.91	4	.228	.348	.316
1994	Rockford	A KC	121	437	112	9	5	1	134	85	32	60	1	59	16	2	4	52	22	.70	8	.256	.364	.307
1995	Wilmington	A+ KC	5	13	3	1	0	0	4	1	0	1	0	3	0	0	0	0	1	.00	0	.231	.286	.308
	Bakersfield	A+ KC	128	499	128	22	2	1	157	92	38	79	0	73	11	6	0	52	21	.71	9	.257	.370	.315
1996	Wichita	AA KC	129	453	118	23	2	6	163	68	40	47	1	64	12	3	3	41	9	.82	15	.260	.344	.360
4 Min. YEARS			425	1538	392	57	14	8	501	279	122	207	3	217	45	13	9	175	56	.76	36	.255	.358	.326

Troy Carrasco

Pitches: Left **Bats:** Both **Pos:** P — **Ht:** 5'11" **Wt:** 172 **Born:** 1/27/75 **Age:** 22

		HOW MUCH HE PITCHED						WHAT HE GAVE UP												THE RESULTS					
Year	Team	Lg Org	G	GS	CG	GF	IP	BFP	H	R	ER	HR	SH	SF	HB	TBB	IBB	SO	WP	Bk	W	L	Pct.	ShO	Sv	ERA
1993	Elizabethtn	R+ Min	14	10	0	3	70.1	292	46	32	25	2	5	1	3	39	3	75	6	2	2	4	.333	0	2	3.20
1994	Fort Wayne	A Min	28	28	2	0	160.2	685	159	88	73	14	5	1	4	60	0	146	9	0	10	10	.500	1	0	4.09
1995	Fort Myers	A+ Min	25	25	2	0	138	596	131	62	48	6	4	7	8	63	0	96	11	2	12	4	.750	0	0	3.13
1996	New Britain	AA Min	34	17	1	8	110	504	113	74	62	9	5	2	9	66	1	69	15	1	6	9	.400	1	0	5.07
4 Min. YEARS			101	80	5	11	479	2077	449	256	208	31	19	11	24	228	4	386	41	5	30	27	.526	2	2	3.91

Andy Carter

Pitches: Left **Bats:** Left **Pos:** P — **Ht:** 6' 5" **Wt:** 220 **Born:** 11/9/68 **Age:** 28

		HOW MUCH HE PITCHED						WHAT HE GAVE UP												THE RESULTS					
Year	Team	Lg Org	G	GS	CG	GF	IP	BFP	H	R	ER	HR	SH	SF	HB	TBB	IBB	SO	WP	Bk	W	L	Pct.	ShO	Sv	ERA
1987	Utica	A- Phi	12	1	0	1	28.2	140	27	25	18	1	1	2	4	19	0	19	2	1	0	1	.000	0	0	5.65
1988	Spartanburg	A Phi	25	25	4	0	156.2	657	110	55	40	7	5	1	6	75	0	99	5	3	11	6	.647	1	0	2.30
1989	Clearwater	A+ Phi	12	12	2	0	68.2	310	73	46	37	3	4	7	6	32	0	31	5	2	1	5	.167	1	0	4.85
	Spartanburg	A Phi	15	15	1	0	90.2	393	73	38	33	5	2	2	3	51	0	72	7	1	6	5	.545	1	0	3.28
1990	Clearwater	A+ Phi	26	26	2	0	131	582	121	82	71	8	3	7	9	69	2	90	10	1	4	14	.222	0	0	4.88
1991	Reading	AA Phi	20	20	1	0	102.1	452	86	57	55	10	1	3	8	57	0	64	5	1	11	5	.688	0	0	4.84
1992	Reading	AA Phi	7	6	0	0	25.1	127	37	28	26	3	2	0	1	15	0	17	3	0	0	4	.000	0	0	9.24
	Clearwater	A+ Phi	16	13	1	1	87	340	60	30	18	2	3	2	4	13	1	68	9	0	3	4	.429	1	0	1.86
1993	Reading	AA Phi	4	4	0	0	22.1	90	15	8	7	1	1	1	1	12	0	16	0	0	1	1	.500	0	0	2.82
	Scranton-WB	AAA Phi	30	13	0	6	109	462	104	59	55	7	2	4	8	35	0	68	10	1	7	7	.500	0	1	4.54
1994	Scranton-WB	AAA Phi	25	0	0	14	31	125	22	10	9	1	2	0	1	13	1	27	5	0	1	0	1.000	0	2	2.61
1995	Scranton-WB	AAA Phi	14	1	0	5	20.2	91	17	10	10	2	0	1	3	13	2	18	1	1	1	2	.333	0	0	4.35
1996	Phoenix	AAA SF	37	8	0	8	79.2	373	98	61	49	5	2	4	5	36	2	50	7	0	1	5	.167	0	0	5.54
1994	Philadelphia	NL	20	0	0	7	34.1	149	34	18	17	5	1	3	6	12	2	18	0	0	0	2	.000	0	0	4.46
1995	Philadelphia	NL	4	0	0	1	7.1	28	4	5	5	3	0	1	1	2	1	6	0	0	0	0	.000	0	0	6.14
10 Min. YEARS			243	144	11	35	953	4142	843	509	428	55	28	34	59	440	8	639	69	11	47	59	.443	4	3	4.04
2 Maj. YEARS			24	0	0	8	41.2	177	38	23	22	8	1	4	7	14	3	24	0	0	0	2	.000	0	0	4.75

Jeff Carter

Bats: Both **Throws:** Right **Pos:** 2B — **Ht:** 5'10" **Wt:** 160 **Born:** 10/20/63 **Age:** 33

		BATTING																BASERUNNING				PERCENTAGES		
Year	Team	Lg Org	G	AB	H	2B	3B	HR	TB	R	RBI	TBB	IBB	SO	HBP	SH	SF	SB	CS	SB%	GDP	Avg	OBP	SLG
1985	Everett	A- SF	54	207	63	9	4	4	92	45	22	36	0	33	2	1	1	28	8	.78	2	.304	.411	.444
1986	Clinton	A SF	128	472	107	13	3	3	135	62	47	58	0	76	3	3	2	60	20	.75	2	.227	.314	.286
1987	Fresno	A+ SF	135	510	140	14	11	6	194	109	50	94	4	75	5	4	7	49	25	.66	6	.275	.388	.380
1988	Shreveport	AA SF	124	409	101	9	8	3	135	50	41	51	0	52	6	6	2	15	10	.60	6	.247	.338	.330
1989	Shreveport	AA SF	127	445	129	16	4	3	162	77	52	63	2	47	4	8	5	33	16	.67	4	.290	.379	.364
1990	Phoenix	AAA SF	121	435	127	21	9	2	172	80	63	63	1	81	5	2	2	28	11	.72	4	.292	.386	.395
1991	Phoenix	AAA SF	92	246	67	5	2	2	82	47	24	34	1	51	0	2	1	11	7	.61	2	.272	.359	.333
1992	Tacoma	AAA Oak	123	379	102	14	5	1	129	60	36	70	0	63	5	9	5	22	9	.71	6	.269	.386	.340
1993	Portland	AAA Min	101	381	124	21	7	0	159	73	48	63	1	53	3	1	3	17	12	.59	7	.325	.422	.417
1994	Salt Lake	AAA Min	122	460	149	18	6	5	194	105	70	89	2	78	7	0	3	26	12	.68	14	.324	.438	.422
1995	Charlotte	AAA Fla	124	428	115	20	6	0	141	78	22	62	0	86	5	9	1	22	10	.69	5	.269	.367	.329
1996	Colo. Sprng	AAA Col	50	161	41	9	0	1	53	19	12	23	0	33	1	1	0	3	6	.33	3	.255	.351	.329
12 Min. YEARS			1301	4533	1265	169	62	30	1648	805	487	706	11	728	46	46	32	314	146	.68	61	.279	.379	.364

John Carter

Pitches: Right **Bats:** Right **Pos:** P — **Ht:** 6'1" **Wt:** 195 **Born:** 2/16/72 **Age:** 25

		HOW MUCH HE PITCHED						WHAT HE GAVE UP												THE RESULTS					
Year	Team	Lg Org	G	GS	CG	GF	IP	BFP	H	R	ER	HR	SH	SF	HB	TBB	IBB	SO	WP	Bk	W	L	Pct.	ShO	Sv	ERA
1991	Pirates	R Pit	10	9	0	0	41	179	42	20	15	0	0	0	5	13	0	28	5	2	5	4	.556	0	0	3.29
1992	Augusta	A Pit	1	1	0	0	5	19	3	0	0	0	1	0	2	1	0	4	0	1	0	0	.000	0	0	0.00
	Welland	A- Pit	3	3	0	0	15.2	68	12	11	6	2	0	1	1	7	0	15	1	1	0	3	.000	0	0	3.45
	Watertown	A Cle	13	11	3	0	63	269	55	36	29	2	0	3	2	32	0	39	4	4	4	4	.500	0	0	4.14
1993	Columbus	A Cle	29	29	1	0	180.1	731	147	72	56	7	4	2	7	48	0	134	8	2	17	7	.708	0	0	2.79
1994	Canton-Akrn	AA Cle	22	22	3	0	131	564	134	68	63	15	4	2	6	53	1	73	7	1	9	6	.600	1	0	4.33
1995	Canton-Akrn	AA Cle	5	5	0	0	27.1	118	27	13	12	0	0	0	3	13	2	14	1	0	1	2	.333	0	0	3.95
1996	St. Lucie	A+ NYN	4	4	0	0	20	93	26	18	16	2	1	0	1	11	1	6	3	1	1	2	.333	0	0	7.20
	Binghamton	AA NYN	19	19	3	0	110.2	485	120	60	52	10	6	3	6	54	1	48	6	0	9	3	.750	1	0	4.23
6 Min. YEARS			106	103	10	0	594	2526	566	298	249	38	16	11	33	232	5	361	35	12	46	31	.597	2	0	3.77

Mike Carter

Bats: Right **Throws:** Right **Pos:** OF **Ht:** 5'9" **Wt:** 170 **Born:** 5/5/69 **Age:** 28

				BATTING													BASERUNNING				PERCENTAGES		
Year Team	Lg Org	G	AB	H	2B	3B	HR	TB	R	RBI	TBB	IBB	SO	HBP	SH	SF	SB	CS	SB%	GDP	Avg	OBP	SLG
1990 Helena	R+ Mil	61	241	74	11	3	0	91	45	30	16	0	20	6	2	5	22	7	.76	0	.307	.358	.378
1991 Beloit	A Mil	123	452	126	24	4	2	164	62	40	26	5	42	4	2	3	46	13	.78	5	.279	.322	.363
1992 Stockton	A+ Mil	67	252	66	9	1	3	86	38	26	17	1	26	2	3	5	31	8	.79	4	.262	.308	.341
El Paso	AA Mil	50	165	42	4	4	1	57	20	15	16	2	31	0	3	1	10	8	.56	3	.255	.319	.345
1993 El Paso	AA Mil	17	73	27	4	1	2	39	16	16	3	0	7	0	0	0	6	4	.60	1	.370	.395	.534
New Orleans	AAA Mil	104	369	102	18	5	3	139	49	31	17	0	52	4	11	4	20	11	.65	6	.276	.312	.377
1994 Iowa	AAA ChN	122	421	122	24	3	6	170	56	30	14	1	43	4	12	4	16	14	.53	7	.290	.316	.404
1995 Iowa	AAA ChN	107	421	137	16	3	8	183	57	40	14	3	46	6	3	3	12	12	.50	5	.325	.354	.435
1996 Iowa	AAA ChN	113	384	102	13	1	2	123	41	18	10	0	42	1	5	1	4	6	.40	5	.266	.285	.320
7 Min. YEARS		764	2778	798	123	25	27	1052	384	246	133	12	309	27	41	26	167	83	.67	36	.287	.323	.379

Jhonny Carvajal

Bats: Right **Throws:** Right **Pos:** SS-2B **Ht:** 5'10" **Wt:** 165 **Born:** 7/24/74 **Age:** 22

				BATTING													BASERUNNING				PERCENTAGES		
Year Team	Lg Org	G	AB	H	2B	3B	HR	TB	R	RBI	TBB	IBB	SO	HBP	SH	SF	SB	CS	SB%	GDP	Avg	OBP	SLG
1993 Princeton	R+ Cin	67	253	74	10	5	0	94	41	16	29	1	31	4	8	0	7	11	.39	3	.292	.374	.372
1994 Charlstn-WV	A Cin	67	198	45	6	0	0	51	27	13	19	0	25	2	2	3	12	3	.80	3	.227	.297	.258
Princeton	R+ Cin	53	218	59	10	4	2	83	35	29	14	2	38	5	5	3	31	11	.74	0	.271	.325	.381
1995 Charlstn-WV	A Cin	135	486	128	18	5	0	156	78	42	58	0	77	6	4	4	44	19	.70	4	.263	.347	.321
1996 W. Palm Bch	A+ Mon	114	426	101	18	0	2	125	50	38	44	0	73	6	7	4	14	16	.47	9	.237	.315	.293
Harrisburg	AA Mon	16	60	18	3	2	0	25	7	4	5	0	10	1	1	0	1	1	.50	1	.300	.364	.417
4 Min. YEARS		452	1641	425	65	16	4	534	238	142	169	3	254	24	27	14	109	61	.64	20	.259	.334	.325

Jovino Carvajal

Bats: Both **Throws:** Right **Pos:** OF **Ht:** 6'1" **Wt:** 160 **Born:** 9/2/68 **Age:** 28

				BATTING													BASERUNNING				PERCENTAGES		
Year Team	Lg Org	G	AB	H	2B	3B	HR	TB	R	RBI	TBB	IBB	SO	HBP	SH	SF	SB	CS	SB%	GDP	Avg	OBP	SLG
1990 Oneonta	A- NYA	52	171	49	3	1	0	54	19	18	7	0	37	0	3	0	15	11	.58	1	.287	.315	.316
1991 Ft. Laud	A+ NYA	117	416	96	6	9	1	123	49	29	28	5	84	0	3	1	33	17	.66	7	.231	.279	.296
1992 Ft. Laud	A+ NYA	113	435	100	7	1	1	112	53	29	30	0	63	1	3	4	40	14	.74	6	.230	.279	.257
1993 Pr. William	A+ NYA	120	445	118	20	9	1	159	52	42	21	1	69	1	8	3	17	13	.57	8	.265	.298	.357
1994 Cedar Rapds	A Cal	121	503	147	23	8	6	204	82	54	40	3	76	1	3	1	68	25	.73	5	.292	.345	.406
1995 Midland	AA Cal	79	348	109	13	5	2	138	58	23	18	2	42	1	5	2	39	21	.65	3	.313	.347	.397
Vancouver	AAA Cal	41	163	53	3	3	1	65	25	10	3	0	18	1	1	0	10	7	.59	6	.325	.341	.399
1996 Vancouver	AAA Cal	77	272	65	6	2	4	87	29	31	14	2	38	1	6	3	17	7	.71	8	.239	.276	.320
Midland	AA Cal	41	160	43	5	2	2	58	20	22	10	1	24	0	1	0	7	7	.50	4	.269	.312	.363
7 Min. YEARS		761	2913	780	86	40	18	1000	387	258	171	14	451	6	33	14	246	122	.67	48	.268	.308	.343

Hector Castaneda

Bats: Left **Throws:** Right **Pos:** C-DH **Ht:** 6'2" **Wt:** 190 **Born:** 11/1/71 **Age:** 25

				BATTING													BASERUNNING				PERCENTAGES		
Year Team	Lg Org	G	AB	H	2B	3B	HR	TB	R	RBI	TBB	IBB	SO	HBP	SH	SF	SB	CS	SB%	GDP	Avg	OBP	SLG
1992 Orioles	R Bal	42	122	35	9	0	0	44	18	14	27	1	23	3	0	0	2	1	.67	3	.287	.428	.361
Kane County	A Bal	5	13	2	1	0	0	3	1	0	0	0	4	0	0	0	0	0	.00	1	.154	.154	.231
1993 Bluefield	R+ Bal	22	56	10	4	0	0	14	8	8	9	0	12	0	1	1	0	0	.00	1	.179	.288	.250
1994 Albany	A Bal	54	150	50	6	0	2	62	22	17	24	1	20	0	4	0	5	0	1.00	6	.333	.425	.413
1995 Frederick	A+ Bal	17	47	10	1	1	0	13	6	4	6	0	9	0	2	1	0	0	.00	2	.213	.296	.277
Bowie	AA Bal	34	65	10	2	0	0	12	3	6	10	0	10	0	0	1	0	0	.00	1	.154	.263	.185
1996 Bowie	AA Bal	14	51	11	1	0	1	15	6	5	3	0	12	1	0	0	2	0	1.00	0	.216	.273	.294
5 Min. YEARS		188	504	128	24	1	3	163	64	54	79	2	90	4	7	3	9	1	.90	14	.254	.358	.323

Carlos Castillo

Pitches: Right **Bats:** Right **Pos:** P **Ht:** 6'2" **Wt:** 225 **Born:** 5/9/71 **Age:** 26

		HOW MUCH HE PITCHED						WHAT HE GAVE UP												THE RESULTS					
Year Team	Lg Org	G	GS	CG	GF	IP	BFP	H	R	ER	HR	SH	SF	HB	TBB	IBB	SO	WP	Bk	W	L	Pct.	ShO	Sv	ERA
1991 Yakima	A- LA	22	3	0	7	51	229	49	25	22	2	1	1	1	30	4	59	4	5	5	3	.625	0	2	3.88
1992 Bakersfield	A+ LA	9	1	0	4	14	71	18	15	14	1	1	0	0	10	1	12	0	1	0	0	.000	0	0	9.00
Visalia	A+ Min	27	0	0	13	45.1	199	47	22	17	2	2	4	2	24	3	40	4	2	1	1	.500	0	2	3.38
1995 Lk Elsinore	A+ Cal	52	0	0	52	52.1	223	55	18	14	2	1	0	5	15	0	40	2	1	2	1	.667	0	32	2.41
1996 Lk Elsinore	A+ Cal	27	0	0	26	29.1	122	26	16	12	2	1	0	0	8	0	27	6	0	2	3	.400	0	13	3.68
Midland	AA Cal	25	0	0	8	38	169	37	19	18	4	2	0	2	21	2	15	6	1	2	3	.400	0	1	4.26
4 Min. YEARS		162	4	0	110	230	1013	232	115	97	13	8	5	10	108	10	193	22	10	12	11	.522	0	50	3.80

Juan Castillo

Pitches: Right **Bats:** Right **Pos:** P **Ht:** 6' 5" **Wt:** 205 **Born:** 6/23/70 **Age:** 27

		HOW MUCH HE PITCHED						WHAT HE GAVE UP												THE RESULTS					
Year Team	Lg Org	G	GS	CG	GF	IP	BFP	H	R	ER	HR	SH	SF	HB	TBB	IBB	SO	WP	Bk	W	L	Pct.	ShO	Sv	ERA
1988 Mets	R NYN	9	3	0	3	19.2	97	28	19	14	2	0	1	1	9	0	16	1	3	0	2	.000	0	0	6.41
1989 Mets	R NYN	14	13	2	0	84.1	370	84	41	27	1	3	5	7	29	0	59	13	3	4	7	.364	1	0	2.88
1990 Pittsfield	A- NYN	16	14	0	1	70.1	333	64	52	37	0	0	1	2	58	2	65	13	2	5	8	.385	0	0	4.73

			HOW MUCH HE PITCHED						WHAT HE GAVE UP												THE RESULTS					
Year Team	Lg	Org	G	GS	CG	GF	IP	BFP	H	R	ER	HR	SH	SF	HB	TBB	IBB	SO	WP	Bk	W	L	Pct.	ShO	Sv	ERA
1991 Columbia	A	NYN	28	27	3	1	157.2	698	148	82	67	6	3	10	9	89	0	144	15	6	12	9	.571	1	0	3.82
1992 St. Lucie	A+	NYN	24	24	7	0	153.2	617	135	53	44	9	2	2	10	27	1	80	9	7	11	8	.579	3	0	2.58
1993 Binghamton	AA	NYN	26	26	2	0	165.2	716	167	93	84	27	6	2	13	55	1	118	6	1	7	11	.389	0	0	4.56
1994 Binghamton	AA	NYN	18	18	3	0	111.1	463	98	40	32	6	3	2	6	44	2	80	4	2	11	2	.846	0	0	2.59
Norfolk	AAA	NYN	6	6	1	0	28.2	131	35	24	23	6	1	2	3	15	0	9	3	0	1	5	.167	0	0	7.22
1995 Tucson	AAA	Hou	11	10	0	1	40.1	206	66	51	49	4	1	3	5	27	0	21	5	0	0	4	.000	0	0	10.93
Jackson	AA	Hou	23	22	0	1	107.2	507	134	90	79	9	3	4	12	54	0	59	9	0	4	8	.333	0	0	6.60
1996 Tulsa	AA	Tex	19	17	0	0	89.1	408	94	64	50	11	2	3	10	49	0	37	6	0	6	6	.500	0	0	5.04
1994 New York	NL		2	2	0	0	11.2	54	17	9	9	2	2	0	0	5	0	1	0	0	0	0	.000	0	0	6.94
9 Min. YEARS			194	180	18	7	1028.2	4546	1053	609	506	81	24	35	78	456	6	688	84	24	61	70	.466	5	0	4.43

Marino Castillo

Pitches: Right **Bats:** Right **Pos:** P **Ht:** 6'0" **Wt:** 168 **Born:** 3/17/71 **Age:** 26

			HOW MUCH HE PITCHED						WHAT HE GAVE UP												THE RESULTS					
Year Team	Lg	Org	G	GS	CG	GF	IP	BFP	H	R	ER	HR	SH	SF	HB	TBB	IBB	SO	WP	Bk	W	L	Pct.	ShO	Sv	ERA
1992 San Jose	A+	SF	10	1	0	2	21	92	19	15	10	1	2	2	0	10	0	10	2	2	0	3	.000	0	0	4.29
Clinton	A	SF	13	0	0	5	19.1	88	23	15	13	1	1	0	2	5	1	15	1	0	1	3	.250	0	1	6.05
1993 Clinton	A	SF	40	0	0	19	69	291	64	31	26	3	4	6	1	19	1	59	1	0	4	2	.667	0	6	3.39
1994 San Jose	A+	SF	45	0	0	15	106.2	448	106	49	41	10	9	2	2	27	2	81	5	0	10	7	.588	0	5	3.46
1995 San Jose	A+	SF	21	0	0	8	56.2	226	49	14	10	1	2	0	2	13	0	51	1	0	4	4	.500	0	3	1.59
Shreveport	AA	SF	43	0	0	12	94	387	87	31	23	5	6	0	2	26	3	82	1	0	7	5	.583	0	3	2.20
1996 Shreveport	AA	SF	38	0	0	26	50.1	208	48	21	20	7	3	0	3	14	2	53	2	0	5	5	.500	0	3	3.58
San Jose	A+	SF	10	0	0	8	11.1	42	8	1	1	1	0	0	0	0	0	19	0	0	3	0	1.000	0	1	0.79
5 Min. YEARS			220	1	0	95	428.1	1782	404	177	144	29	27	10	12	114	9	370	13	2	34	29	.540	0	22	3.03

Kevin Castleberry

Bats: Left **Throws:** Right **Pos:** 2B **Ht:** 5'10" **Wt:** 170 **Born:** 4/22/68 **Age:** 29

			BATTING															BASERUNNING				PERCENTAGES		
Year Team	Lg	Org	G	AB	H	2B	3B	HR	TB	R	RBI	TBB	IBB	SO	HBP	SH	SF	SB	CS	SB%	GDP	Avg	OBP	SLG
1989 Burlington	A	Atl	64	224	55	8	0	1	66	27	20	20	1	32	0	2	2	14	8	.64	5	.246	.305	.295
1990 Durham	A+	Atl	119	372	90	18	4	7	137	59	27	23	1	64	2	3	2	15	4	.79	3	.242	.288	.368
1991 Miami	A+	Atl	20	64	14	4	2	0	22	12	4	9	0	9	0	2	0	8	1	.89	1	.219	.315	.344
Birmingham	AA	ChA	1	1	0	0	0	0	0	0	0	0	0	0	0	0	0	0	0	.00	0	.000	.000	.000
Sarasota	A+	ChA	94	346	94	14	3	4	126	70	39	54	3	54	4	6	7	23	9	.72	2	.272	.370	.364
1992 Sarasota	A+	ChA	24	98	28	4	0	0	32	16	10	14	0	12	2	1	1	8	3	.73	2	.286	.383	.327
Birmingham	AA	ChA	104	382	98	9	5	2	123	57	26	48	1	59	3	0	1	13	10	.57	3	.257	.343	.322
1993 El Paso	AA	Mil	98	327	98	9	5	2	123	46	49	26	3	38	2	0	3	13	3	.81	9	.300	.352	.376
1994 El Paso	AA	Mil	74	251	69	6	8	1	94	44	35	26	1	50	3	2	0	12	7	.63	4	.275	.350	.375
1995 Ottawa	AAA	Mon	118	428	126	18	4	7	173	65	56	52	3	59	0	5	4	9	7	.56	5	.294	.368	.404
1996 Ottawa	AAA	Mon	66	193	54	8	3	3	77	27	22	21	4	27	0	6	2	9	5	.64	2	.280	.347	.399
8 Min. YEARS			782	2686	726	98	34	27	973	423	288	293	17	404	16	27	22	124	57	.69	36	.270	.343	.362

Frank Catalanotto

Bats: Left **Throws:** Right **Pos:** 2B **Ht:** 6'0" **Wt:** 170 **Born:** 4/27/74 **Age:** 23

			BATTING															BASERUNNING				PERCENTAGES		
Year Team	Lg	Org	G	AB	H	2B	3B	HR	TB	R	RBI	TBB	IBB	SO	HBP	SH	SF	SB	CS	SB%	GDP	Avg	OBP	SLG
1992 Bristol	R+	Det	21	50	10	2	0	0	12	6	4	8	0	8	0	0	0	0	1	.00	0	.200	.310	.240
1993 Bristol	R+	Det	55	199	61	9	5	3	89	37	22	15	1	19	3	3	0	3	6	.33	3	.307	.364	.447
1994 Fayettevlle	A	Det	119	458	149	24	8	3	198	72	56	37	1	54	3	5	1	4	5	.44	4	.325	.379	.432
1995 Jacksonvlle	AA	Det	134	491	111	19	5	8	164	66	48	49	4	56	9	6	4	13	8	.62	9	.226	.306	.334
1996 Jacksonvlle	AA	Det	132	497	148	34	6	17	245	105	67	74	8	69	11	3	3	15	14	.52	8	.298	.398	.493
5 Min. YEARS			461	1695	479	88	24	31	708	286	197	183	14	206	26	17	8	35	34	.51	24	.283	.360	.418

Mike Cather

Pitches: Right **Bats:** Right **Pos:** P **Ht:** 6'2" **Wt:** 180 **Born:** 12/17/70 **Age:** 26

			HOW MUCH HE PITCHED						WHAT HE GAVE UP												THE RESULTS					
Year Team	Lg	Org	G	GS	CG	GF	IP	BFP	H	R	ER	HR	SH	SF	HB	TBB	IBB	SO	WP	Bk	W	L	Pct.	ShO	Sv	ERA
1993 Rangers	R	Tex	25	0	0	17	30.2	124	20	7	6	0	0	0	3	9	0	30	2	1	1	1	.500	0	4	1.76
1994 Charlotte	A+	Tex	44	0	0	37	60.1	270	56	33	26	2	3	2	3	40	3	53	1	0	8	6	.571	0	6	3.88
1995 Tulsa	AA	Tex	18	0	0	12	21.2	90	20	11	8	0	4	1	1	7	5	15	0	0	0	2	.000	0	0	3.32
Winnipeg	IND	—	45	0	0	36	52.2	213	38	17	13	1	6	1	1	19	8	50	2	0	4	4	.500	0	8	2.22
1996 Greenville	AA	Atl	53	0	0	18	87.2	384	89	42	36	2	6	2	8	29	5	61	2	1	3	4	.429	0	5	3.70
4 Min. YEARS			185	0	0	120	253	1081	223	110	89	5	19	6	16	104	21	209	7	2	16	17	.485	0	23	3.17

Blas Cedeno

Pitches: Right **Bats:** Right **Pos:** P **Ht:** 6'0" **Wt:** 165 **Born:** 11/15/72 **Age:** 24

			HOW MUCH HE PITCHED						WHAT HE GAVE UP												THE RESULTS					
Year Team	Lg	Org	G	GS	CG	GF	IP	BFP	H	R	ER	HR	SH	SF	HB	TBB	IBB	SO	WP	Bk	W	L	Pct.	ShO	Sv	ERA
1991 Bristol	R+	Det	14	2	0	6	45	202	47	36	19	7	0	3	2	18	1	37	3	4	1	4	.200	0	0	3.80
1992 Bristol	R+	Det	13	13	3	0	80.2	335	64	21	18	2	3	1	5	41	0	77	6	0	8	2	.800	2	0	2.01
Fayettevlle	A	Det	2	1	1	1	9	32	3	3	3	0	0	0	0	4	0	12	0	0	0	1	.000	0	1	3.00
1993 Fayettevlle	A	Det	28	22	1	3	148.2	621	145	64	52	11	5	3	11	55	0	103	6	0	6	6	.500	1	0	3.15

Year	Team	Lg	Org	G	GS	CG	GF	IP	BFP	H	R	ER	HR	SH	SF	HB	TBB	IBB	SO	WP	Bk	W	L	Pct.	ShO	Sv	ERA
				HOW MUCH HE PITCHED						WHAT HE GAVE UP												THE RESULTS					
1994	Lakeland	A+	Det	5	0	0	3	14	52	9	3	2	1	1	1	0	4	0	16	1	0	1	0	1.000	0	0	1.29
	Trenton	AA	Det	34	0	0	18	52.1	228	50	18	15	5	4	0	2	27	2	40	4	0	1	3	.250	0	3	2.58
1995	Jacksonvlle	AA	Det	48	5	0	13	80.2	329	71	34	31	7	1	1	1	36	1	53	2	1	3	2	.600	0	0	3.46
1996	Lakeland	A+	Det	10	0	0	5	16.1	72	17	10	10	3	0	0	1	7	0	11	2	0	1	1	.500	0	0	5.51
	Jacksonvlle	AA	Det	26	2	0	8	46.2	219	63	34	28	7	2	3	3	26	0	30	3	0	0	0	.000	0	0	5.40
6 Min. YEARS				180	45	5	57	493.1	2090	469	223	178	43	16	12	25	218	4	379	27	5	21	19	.525	3	4	3.25

Brett Cederblad

Pitches: Right **Bats:** Both **Pos:** P **Ht:** 6'5" **Wt:** 195 **Born:** 3/6/73 **Age:** 24

Year	Team	Lg	Org	G	GS	CG	GF	IP	BFP	H	R	ER	HR	SH	SF	HB	TBB	IBB	SO	WP	Bk	W	L	Pct.	ShO	Sv	ERA
				HOW MUCH HE PITCHED						WHAT HE GAVE UP												THE RESULTS					
1995	Trenton	AA	Bos	8	5	2	1	44.2	182	43	19	18	4	2	2	0	11	1	36	2	0	3	2	.600	1	0	3.63
	Sarasota	A+	Bos	32	17	2	3	137	566	141	69	60	8	2	6	6	32	1	107	9	2	10	8	.556	1	0	3.94
1996	Trenton	AA	Bos	27	3	0	9	58	245	59	27	24	8	1	3	3	16	3	49	5	1	1	3	.250	0	2	3.72
	Pawtucket	AAA	Bos	10	0	0	2	20	90	26	10	8	4	0	0	1	4	0	19	3	0	0	0	.000	0	0	3.60
2 Min. YEARS				77	25	4	15	259.2	1083	269	125	110	24	5	11	10	63	5	211	19	3	14	13	.519	2	2	3.81

Wes Chamberlain

Bats: Right **Throws:** Right **Pos:** DH-OF **Ht:** 6' 2" **Wt:** 230 **Born:** 4/13/66 **Age:** 31

Year	Team	Lg	Org	G	AB	H	2B	3B	HR	TB	R	RBI	TBB	IBB	SO	HBP	SH	SF	SB	CS	SB%	GDP	Avg	OBP	SLG
				BATTING															BASERUNNING				PERCENTAGES		
1987	Watertown	A-	Pit	66	258	67	13	4	5	103	50	35	25	2	48	1	0	3	22	7	.76	6	.260	.324	.399
1988	Augusta	A	Pit	27	107	36	7	2	1	50	22	17	11	0	11	1	2	0	1	3	.25	4	.336	.403	.467
	Salem	A+	Pit	92	365	100	15	1	11	150	66	50	38	2	59	0	0	2	14	4	.78	7	.274	.341	.411
1989	Harrisburg	AA	Pit	129	471	144	26	3	21	239	65	87	32	4	82	2	0	7	11	10	.52	14	.306	.348	.507
1990	Buffalo	AAA	Pit	123	416	104	24	2	6	150	43	52	34	0	58	8	2	5	14	19	.42	19	.250	.315	.361
1991	Scranton-WB	AAA	Phi	39	144	37	7	2	2	54	12	20	8	1	13	0	0	4	7	4	.64	6	.257	.288	.375
1992	Scranton-WB	AAA	Phi	34	127	42	6	2	4	64	16	26	11	0	13	2	1	2	6	2	.75	2	.331	.387	.504
1994	Clearwater	A+	Phi	6	25	9	1	0	3	19	5	6	1	1	1	1	0	0	0	1	.00	0	.360	.407	.760
1995	Pawtucket	AAA	Bos	48	183	64	17	1	12	119	28	40	3	0	45	3	0	1	5	3	.63	3	.350	.368	.650
	Omaha	AAA	KC	16	64	14	3	0	1	20	2	6	2	0	15	2	0	1	0	0	.00	4	.219	.261	.313
1996	Syracuse	AAA	Tor	37	131	45	5	0	10	80	20	37	19	2	19	0	0	1	2	1	.67	5	.344	.424	.611
1990	Philadelphia	NL		18	46	13	3	0	2	22	9	4	1	0	9	0	0	0	4	0	1.00	0	.283	.298	.478
1991	Philadelphia	NL		101	383	92	16	3	13	153	51	50	31	0	73	2	1	0	9	4	.69	8	.240	.300	.399
1992	Philadelphia	NL		76	275	71	18	0	9	116	26	41	10	2	55	1	1	2	4	0	1.00	7	.258	.285	.422
1993	Philadelphia	NL		96	284	80	20	2	12	140	34	45	17	3	51	1	0	4	2	1	.67	8	.282	.320	.493
1994	Philadelphia	NL		24	69	19	5	0	2	30	7	6	3	0	12	0	0	0	0	0	.00	3	.275	.306	.435
	Boston	AL		51	164	42	9	1	4	65	13	20	12	2	38	0	0	0	0	2	.00	6	.256	.307	.396
1995	Boston	AL		19	42	5	1	0	1	9	4	1	3	0	11	0	0	0	1	0	1.00	2	.119	.178	.214
9 Min. YEARS				617	2291	662	124	17	76	1048	329	376	184	12	364	20	5	26	82	54	.60	70	.289	.344	.457
6 Maj. YEARS				385	1263	322	72	6	43	535	144	167	77	7	249	4	2	6	20	7	.74	34	.255	.299	.424

Frank Charles

Bats: Right **Throws:** Right **Pos:** C-DH **Ht:** 6'4" **Wt:** 210 **Born:** 2/23/69 **Age:** 28

Year	Team	Lg	Org	G	AB	H	2B	3B	HR	TB	R	RBI	TBB	IBB	SO	HBP	SH	SF	SB	CS	SB%	GDP	Avg	OBP	SLG
				BATTING															BASERUNNING				PERCENTAGES		
1991	Everett	A-	SF	62	239	76	17	1	9	122	31	49	21	0	55	1	0	1	1	2	.33	5	.318	.374	.510
1992	Clinton	A	SF	2	5	0	0	0	0	0	1	0	0	0	3	0	0	0	0	0	.00	0	.000	.000	.000
	San Jose	A+	SF	87	286	83	16	1	0	101	27	34	11	2	61	4	1	0	4	4	.50	12	.290	.326	.353
1993	St. Paul	IND	—	58	216	59	13	0	2	78	27	37	11	0	33	3	5	1	5	3	.63	9	.273	.316	.361
1994	Charlotte	A+	Tex	79	254	67	17	1	2	92	23	33	16	1	52	3	5	2	2	3	.40	2	.264	.313	.362
1995	Tulsa	AA	Tex	126	479	121	24	3	13	190	51	72	22	0	93	4	1	4	1	0	1.00	19	.253	.289	.397
1996	Okla. City	AAA	Tex	35	113	21	7	2	1	35	10	8	4	0	29	1	0	2	0	3	.00	3	.186	.217	.310
	Tulsa	AA	Tex	41	147	39	6	0	5	60	18	15	10	0	28	0	0	0	2	0	1.00	1	.265	.312	.408
6 Min. YEARS				490	1739	466	100	8	32	678	188	248	95	3	354	16	12	10	15	15	.50	51	.268	.310	.390

Rafael Chaves

Pitches: Right **Bats:** Right **Pos:** P **Ht:** 6'0" **Wt:** 195 **Born:** 11/1/68 **Age:** 28

Year	Team	Lg	Org	G	GS	CG	GF	IP	BFP	H	R	ER	HR	SH	SF	HB	TBB	IBB	SO	WP	Bk	W	L	Pct.	ShO	Sv	ERA
				HOW MUCH HE PITCHED						WHAT HE GAVE UP												THE RESULTS					
1986	Charleston	A	SD	39	2	0	8	81	354	77	46	30	6	2	2	2	37	2	43	1	3	5	3	.625	0	1	3.33
1987	Charlstn-SC	A	SD	53	0	0	32	87.1	371	86	36	29	2	2	1	3	21	6	59	3	0	8	5	.615	0	11	2.99
1988	Riverside	A+	SD	46	0	0	34	64.2	273	58	20	17	1	1	3	2	28	1	49	2	4	2	3	.400	0	19	2.37
1989	Wichita	AA	SD	37	2	0	12	76	338	84	51	45	4	4	2	2	32	9	43	9	3	1	5	.167	0	3	5.33
1990	Wichita	AA	SD	46	1	0	36	84	354	85	46	39	4	3	4	3	16	1	46	8	1	6	5	.545	0	9	4.18
1991	Wichita	AA	SD	38	0	0	11	71	338	80	54	41	6	3	2	6	41	3	49	7	0	3	0	1.000	0	3	5.20
1992	High Desert	A+	SD	68	0	0	53	88.1	356	64	28	18	5	5	4	3	36	3	67	2	0	4	5	.444	0	34	1.83
1993	Bowie	AA	Bal	45	0	0	40	48	210	56	23	21	4	1	1	1	16	2	39	4	0	2	5	.286	0	20	3.94
1994	Portland	AA	Fla	12	0	0	6	16	82	17	14	12	0	0	3	1	13	1	10	3	1	0	0	.000	0	1	6.75
1995	Augusta	A	Pit	7	0	0	2	8.2	36	2	3	2	0	2	0	0	6	0	9	0	0	1	0	1.000	0	2	2.08
	Lynchburg	A+	Pit	49	0	0	43	56	227	37	20	16	3	6	0	1	19	3	54	5	1	2	3	.400	0	24	2.57
1996	Lynchburg	A+	Pit	30	0	0	28	32	139	35	18	9	3	3	0	3	8	6	20	1	1	1	3	.250	0	5	2.53
	Carolina	AA	Pit	19	0	0	9	26.1	109	21	5	4	1	1	0	0	8	3	15	2	0	1	2	.333	0	0	1.37

		HOW MUCH HE PITCHED						WHAT HE GAVE UP												THE RESULTS					
Year Team	Lg Org	G	GS	CG	GF	IP	BFP	H	R	ER	HR	SH	SF	HB	TBB	IBB	SO	WP	Bk	W	L	Pct.	ShO	Sv	ERA
11 Min. YEARS		489	5	0	314	739.1	3187	702	364	283	39	33	22	27	281	40	503	47	14	36	39	.480	0	132	3.44

Carlos Chavez

Pitches: Right **Bats:** Right **Pos:** P **Ht:** 6'1" **Wt:** 200 **Born:** 8/25/72 **Age:** 24

		HOW MUCH HE PITCHED						WHAT HE GAVE UP												THE RESULTS					
Year Team	Lg Org	G	GS	CG	GF	IP	BFP	H	R	ER	HR	SH	SF	HB	TBB	IBB	SO	WP	Bk	W	L	Pct.	ShO	Sv	ERA
1992 Bluefield	R+ Bal	15	7	0	3	45.2	219	49	42	35	5	1	4	1	34	0	44	10	6	1	2	.333	0	1	6.90
1993 Albany	A Bal	20	0	0	13	34	155	33	20	20	3	3	0	3	18	0	28	6	2	1	3	.250	0	3	5.29
Bluefield	R+ Bal	14	13	0	0	82	356	80	43	34	15	1	2	3	37	1	71	14	1	6	3	.667	0	0	3.73
1994 Albany	A Bal	5	0	0	3	9.1	41	9	3	3	0	0	0	0	7	0	4	0	0	1	0	1.000	0	0	2.89
Bluefield	R+ Bal	13	13	2	0	85.2	346	58	38	28	11	2	5	6	32	0	92	12	1	7	5	.583	1	0	2.94
1995 Rochester	AAA Bal	1	0	0	0	1.2	11	3	2	2	0	0	1	0	3	0	1	2	0	0	0	.000	0	0	10.80
Bowie	AA Bal	1	0	0	0	2	6	0	0	0	0	0	0	0	1	0	2	0	0	0	0	.000	0	0	0.00
Frederick	A+ Bal	45	1	0	16	85	359	65	40	25	4	1	1	2	44	2	110	18	1	5	5	.500	0	6	2.65
1996 Bowie	AA Bal	56	1	0	27	83	369	69	44	40	8	1	3	6	52	0	80	19	0	4	6	.400	0	7	4.34
5 Min. YEARS		170	35	2	62	428.1	1862	366	232	187	46	9	16	21	228	3	432	81	11	25	24	.510	1	17	3.93

Tony Chavez

Pitches: Right **Bats:** Right **Pos:** P **Ht:** 5'10" **Wt:** 175 **Born:** 10/22/70 **Age:** 26

		HOW MUCH HE PITCHED						WHAT HE GAVE UP												THE RESULTS					
Year Team	Lg Org	G	GS	CG	GF	IP	BFP	H	R	ER	HR	SH	SF	HB	TBB	IBB	SO	WP	Bk	W	L	Pct.	ShO	Sv	ERA
1992 Boise	A- Cal	14	0	0	2	16	75	22	13	7	0	0	0	0	4	2	21	3	0	1	1	.500	0	0	3.94
1993 Cedar Rapds	A Cal	41	0	0	35	59.1	252	44	17	10	1	6	2	2	24	2	87	3	1	4	5	.444	0	16	1.52
Midland	AA Cal	5	0	0	3	8.2	41	11	5	4	1	0	1	0	4	1	9	3	0	0	0	.000	0	1	4.15
1994 Lk Elsinore	A+ Cal	12	0	0	7	13.1	75	21	19	15	0	2	1	2	11	2	12	2	0	0	5	.000	0	1	10.13
Cedar Rapds	A Cal	39	1	0	34	50	227	48	33	24	0	3	2	2	28	4	52	7	0	4	3	.571	0	16	4.32
1995 Vancouver	AAA Cal	8	0	0	5	12	46	7	4	2	0	1	0	0	4	0	8	0	0	2	0	1.000	0	1	1.50
Midland	AA Cal	7	0	0	6	9	42	13	9	8	1	0	0	1	1	0	4	1	0	0	1	.000	0	2	8.00
Lk Elsinore	A+ Cal	48	0	0	25	65.2	294	71	41	31	3	3	3	5	24	2	61	6	0	6	3	.667	0	3	4.25
1996 Lk Elsinore	A+ Cal	10	0	0	8	13.2	53	8	4	3	0	0	0	3	3	0	16	0	0	3	0	1.000	0	4	1.98
Midland	AA Cal	31	0	0	16	72.2	322	81	40	34	4	6	7	2	24	2	55	3	1	2	4	.333	0	1	4.21
5 Min. YEARS		215	1	0	141	320.1	1427	326	185	138	10	21	16	17	127	15	325	28	2	22	22	.500	0	45	3.88

Dan Chergey

Pitches: Right **Bats:** Right **Pos:** P **Ht:** 6'2" **Wt:** 195 **Born:** 1/29/71 **Age:** 26

		HOW MUCH HE PITCHED						WHAT HE GAVE UP												THE RESULTS					
Year Team	Lg Org	G	GS	CG	GF	IP	BFP	H	R	ER	HR	SH	SF	HB	TBB	IBB	SO	WP	Bk	W	L	Pct.	ShO	Sv	ERA
1993 Elmira	A- Fla	15	10	1	1	79.2	329	85	34	31	5	3	3	8	14	0	53	3	1	3	5	.375	0	0	3.50
1994 Edmonton	AAA Fla	13	0	0	6	19.2	88	22	13	13	2	0	1	2	5	0	17	0	0	2	1	.667	0	0	5.95
Brevard Cty	A+ Fla	32	0	0	21	42	160	29	12	8	1	1	0	1	11	1	41	0	0	1	3	.250	0	9	1.71
1995 Portland	AA Fla	55	0	0	27	80.1	331	62	35	31	7	7	2	3	26	6	75	2	0	6	7	.462	0	5	3.47
1996 Portland	AA Fla	13	0	0	8	18	80	18	9	8	1	1	0	0	6	2	16	0	0	0	2	.000	0	2	4.00
Charlotte	AAA Fla	45	1	0	11	75.1	333	86	55	52	16	0	6	1	28	0	43	2	0	0	1	.000	0	1	6.21
4 Min. YEARS		173	11	1	74	315	1321	302	158	143	32	12	12	15	90	9	245	7	1	12	19	.387	0	17	4.09

Joel Chimelis

Bats: Right **Throws:** Right **Pos:** SS **Ht:** 6' 0" **Wt:** 175 **Born:** 7/27/67 **Age:** 29

		BATTING														BASERUNNING				PERCENTAGES		
Year Team	Lg Org	G	AB	H	2B	3B	HR	TB	R	RBI	TBB	IBB	SO	HBP	SH	SF	SB	CS	SB%	GDP	Avg	OBP	SLG
1988 Sou. Oregon	A- Oak	61	225	62	8	0	1	73	40	28	31	1	35	1	1	2	14	7	.67	4	.276	.363	.324
1989 Modesto	A+ Oak	69	211	40	1	0	1	44	18	14	33	0	41	3	3	1	2	3	.40	8	.190	.306	.209
1990 Reno	A+ Oak	85	343	96	12	9	2	132	58	47	31	4	36	3	3	2	20	10	.67	17	.280	.343	.385
Modesto	A+ Oak	46	188	65	14	1	2	87	29	23	18	0	20	0	3	1	10	5	.67	4	.346	.401	.463
1991 Huntsville	AA Oak	68	238	51	10	2	1	68	26	16	18	0	30	0	7	3	4	3	.57	4	.214	.266	.286
San Jose	A+ SF	42	126	31	5	1	0	38	19	14	16	0	22	1	1	4	9	4	.69	3	.246	.327	.302
1992 Shreveport	AA SF	75	279	89	13	1	9	131	47	32	18	3	34	1	4	1	6	6	.50	4	.319	.361	.470
Phoenix	AAA SF	49	185	56	9	3	1	74	26	23	5	1	24	1	5	2	1	4	.20	3	.303	.321	.400
1993 Shreveport	AA SF	36	114	23	5	0	6	46	10	18	8	0	14	2	0	2	3	0	1.00	2	.202	.262	.404
Phoenix	AAA SF	80	262	81	14	3	13	140	40	46	22	1	41	3	1	2	4	3	.57	3	.309	.367	.534
1994 Shreveport	AA SF	127	478	141	43	1	10	216	74	72	41	2	58	13	1	5	8	6	.57	10	.295	.363	.452
1995 Phoenix	AAA SF	118	398	103	32	1	7	158	48	66	28	4	53	5	3	8	1	2	.33	7	.259	.310	.397
1996 Norfolk	AAA NYN	25	76	29	6	0	0	35	9	4	5	1	12	0	2	0	1	0	1.00	4	.382	.420	.461
9 Min. YEARS		881	3123	867	172	22	53	1242	444	403	274	17	420	33	34	33	83	53	.61	73	.278	.339	.398

Dan Cholowsky

Bats: Right **Throws:** Right **Pos:** 3B **Ht:** 6'0" **Wt:** 195 **Born:** 10/30/70 **Age:** 26

		BATTING														BASERUNNING				PERCENTAGES		
Year Team	Lg Org	G	AB	H	2B	3B	HR	TB	R	RBI	TBB	IBB	SO	HBP	SH	SF	SB	CS	SB%	GDP	Avg	OBP	SLG
1991 Hamilton	A- StL	20	69	16	1	1	1	22	9	6	0	0	17	1	0	0	6	3	.67	0	.232	.329	.319
1992 Savannah	A StL	69	232	76	6	4	8	114	44	34	51	2	48	3	0	2	34	16	.68	1	.328	.451	.491
St. Pete	A+ StL	59	201	57	8	0	1	68	19	17	33	0	31	2	1	4	14	10	.58	8	.284	.383	.338
1993 St. Pete	A+ StL	54	208	60	12	0	2	78	30	22	20	2	54	2	0	0	6	8	.43	5	.288	.357	.375

BATTING																			BASERUNNING				PERCENTAGES		
Year	Team	Lg	Org	G	AB	H	2B	3B	HR	TB	R	RBI	TBB	IBB	SO	HBP	SH	SF	SB	CS	SB%	GDP	Avg	OBP	SLG
	Arkansas	AA	StL	68	212	46	10	2	3	69	31	16	38	3	54	2	1	1	10	2	.83	7	.217	.340	.325
1994	Arkansas	AA	StL	131	454	101	18	4	14	169	57	51	65	2	114	4	1	1	20	9	.69	9	.222	.324	.372
1995	Arkansas	AA	StL	54	190	59	12	0	7	92	41	35	24	2	41	5	0	2	7	6	.54	2	.311	.398	.484
	Louisville	AAA	StL	76	238	52	9	1	7	84	27	25	36	0	64	5	0	6	10	4	.71	5	.218	.326	.353
1996	Louisville	AAA	StL	17	56	10	2	0	1	15	3	6	4	0	16	1	0	0	1	2	.33	1	.179	.246	.268
	Iowa	AAA	ChN	26	52	9	5	0	2	20	10	5	11	0	18	0	1	0	0	0	.00	0	.173	.317	.385
	Orlando	AA	ChN	45	143	34	4	0	4	50	21	14	23	0	38	3	0	1	2	4	.33	3	.238	.353	.350
6 Min. YEARS				619	2055	520	87	12	50	781	292	231	314	11	495	28	4	17	110	64	.63	41	.253	.357	.380

Eddie Christian

Bats: Both **Throws:** Left **Pos:** OF **Ht:** 5'11" **Wt:** 180 **Born:** 8/26/71 **Age:** 25

BATTING																			BASERUNNING				PERCENTAGES		
Year	Team	Lg	Org	G	AB	H	2B	3B	HR	TB	R	RBI	TBB	IBB	SO	HBP	SH	SF	SB	CS	SB%	GDP	Avg	OBP	SLG
1992	Marlins	R	Fla	59	219	61	10	3	0	77	33	29	31	2	35	1	0	3	14	5	.74	6	.279	.366	.352
1993	Kane County	A	Fla	112	366	98	21	5	3	138	49	46	58	6	77	0	3	10	9	11	.45	7	.268	.359	.377
1994	Portland	AA	Fla	65	228	53	11	0	1	67	27	21	19	0	52	1	3	2	1	4	.20	7	.232	.292	.294
	Brevard Cty	A+	Fla	54	192	50	11	0	2	67	20	22	18	0	35	1	4	3	3	2	.60	5	.260	.322	.349
1995	Long Beach	IND	—	83	333	113	27	2	1	147	66	50	48	1	39	0	9	1	27	11	.71	9	.339	.421	.441
1996	Lk Elsinore	A+	Cal	16	58	23	5	0	2	34	10	9	12	0	10	2	1	0	1	2	.33	0	.397	.514	.586
	Midland	AA	Cal	107	426	130	30	5	5	185	59	46	36	0	72	0	4	3	7	9	.44	8	.305	.357	.434
5 Min. YEARS				496	1822	528	115	15	14	715	264	223	222	9	320	5	24	22	62	44	.58	42	.290	.365	.392

Eric Christopherson

Bats: Right **Throws:** Right **Pos:** C **Ht:** 6'1" **Wt:** 190 **Born:** 4/25/69 **Age:** 28

BATTING																			BASERUNNING				PERCENTAGES		
Year	Team	Lg	Org	G	AB	H	2B	3B	HR	TB	R	RBI	TBB	IBB	SO	HBP	SH	SF	SB	CS	SB%	GDP	Avg	OBP	SLG
1990	San Jose	A+	SF	7	23	4	0	0	0	4	4	1	3	0	6	0	0	0	0	0	.00	0	.174	.269	.174
	Everett	A-	SF	48	162	43	8	1	1	56	20	22	31	1	28	0	1	2	7	2	.78	2	.265	.379	.346
1991	Clinton	A	SF	110	345	93	18	0	5	126	45	58	68	1	54	1	1	6	10	7	.59	10	.270	.386	.365
1992	Shreveport	AA	SF	80	270	68	10	1	6	98	36	34	37	0	44	1	0	2	1	6	.14	5	.252	.342	.363
1993	Giants	R	SF	8	22	9	1	1	0	12	7	4	9	0	1	0	0	0	0	0	.00	0	.409	.581	.545
	Shreveport	AA	SF	15	46	7	2	0	0	9	5	2	9	0	10	0	0	0	1	1	.50	1	.152	.291	.196
1994	Shreveport	AA	SF	88	267	67	22	0	6	107	30	39	42	4	55	0	1	2	5	1	.83	2	.251	.350	.401
1995	Phoenix	AAA	SF	94	282	62	9	1	1	76	21	25	35	1	54	3	5	5	1	1	.50	12	.220	.308	.270
1996	Tucson	AAA	Hou	67	223	64	15	3	6	103	31	36	21	2	47	1	1	4	2	0	1.00	1	.287	.345	.462
7 Min. YEARS				517	1640	417	85	7	25	591	199	221	255	9	299	6	9	21	27	18	.60	33	.254	.353	.360

Joe Ciccarella

Pitches: Left **Bats:** Left **Pos:** P **Ht:** 6' 3" **Wt:** 200 **Born:** 12/29/69 **Age:** 27

HOW MUCH HE PITCHED										WHAT HE GAVE UP												THE RESULTS					
Year	Team	Lg	Org	G	GS	CG	GF	IP	BFP	H	R	ER	HR	SH	SF	HB	TBB	IBB	SO	WP	Bk	W	L	Pct.	ShO	Sv	ERA
1992	Winter Havn	A+	Bos	38	0	0	30	40.2	177	35	13	12	2	4	3	0	26	1	45	0	0	2	1	.667	0	12	2.66
1993	Pawtucket	AAA	Bos	12	0	0	2	17.2	89	27	13	11	2	0	0	2	12	0	8	0	0	0	1	.000	0	0	5.60
	New Britain	AA	Bos	30	0	0	30	32	151	31	19	15	1	1	1	1	23	4	34	5	0	0	4	.000	0	15	4.22
1994	New Britain	AA	Bos	31	18	0	1	113.2	524	134	68	53	11	5	3	7	54	0	95	5	2	6	6	.500	0	0	4.20
1995	Pawtucket	AAA	Bos	11	5	0	2	25.2	112	22	15	11	2	3	0	4	10	1	13	4	0	0	1	.000	0	0	3.86
	Trenton	AA	Bos	33	7	0	8	58.2	250	53	28	21	5	4	3	4	22	1	46	4	0	2	2	.500	0	0	3.22
1996	Orlando	AA	ChN	1	0	0	0	1.1	7	1	0	0	0	0	0	0	2	0	0	0	0	0	0	.000	0	0	0.00
5 Min. YEARS				156	30	0	73	289.2	1310	303	156	123	23	17	10	18	149	7	241	18	2	10	15	.400	0	27	3.82

Frank Cimorelli

Pitches: Right **Bats:** Right **Pos:** P **Ht:** 6' 0" **Wt:** 175 **Born:** 8/2/68 **Age:** 28

HOW MUCH HE PITCHED										WHAT HE GAVE UP												THE RESULTS					
Year	Team	Lg	Org	G	GS	CG	GF	IP	BFP	H	R	ER	HR	SH	SF	HB	TBB	IBB	SO	WP	Bk	W	L	Pct.	ShO	Sv	ERA
1989	Johnson Cty	R+	StL	12	12	1	0	65	286	78	40	33	2	1	1	3	17	1	36	3	3	2	4	.333	0	0	4.57
1990	Springfield	A	StL	41	15	1	6	120.1	535	125	80	61	9	2	1	7	41	7	86	8	0	4	8	.333	0	0	4.56
1991	Springfield	A	StL	29	29	3	0	191.2	825	203	94	73	12	4	8	9	51	1	98	10	1	8	14	.364	0	0	3.43
1992	Springfield	A	StL	65	0	0	25	72.2	289	48	22	14	2	3	0	2	22	1	66	1	0	4	2	.667	0	9	1.73
1993	Arkansas	AA	StL	37	0	0	9	56.2	232	44	20	16	3	4	1	3	23	5	36	2	0	1	1	.500	0	1	2.54
	Louisville	AAA	StL	27	0	0	13	43	181	34	16	14	1	4	1	3	25	5	24	7	0	2	1	.667	0	2	2.93
1994	Louisville	AAA	StL	48	0	0	17	60.2	267	64	30	27	6	4	3	5	20	1	46	7	0	5	3	.625	0	4	4.01
1995	El Paso	AA	Mil	2	0	0	0	2	11	1	1	1	0	0	1	2	2	0	0	0	0	0	0	.000	0	0	4.50
	Louisville	AAA	StL	8	0	0	2	7	37	13	8	6	2	0	1	2	2	0	3	0	0	1	1	.500	0	0	7.71
1996	New Haven	AA	Col	5	0	0	3	9	39	10	6	5	1	1	0	1	1	1	8	0	0	0	1	.000	0	0	5.00
1994	St. Louis	NL		11	0	0	2	13.1	73	20	14	13	0	1	2	2	10	2	1	2	0	0	0	.000	0	1	8.78
8 Min. YEARS				274	56	5	75	628	2702	620	317	250	38	23	17	37	204	22	403	38	4	27	35	.435	0	16	3.58

Chris Clapinski

Bats: Both **Throws:** Right **Pos:** SS **Ht:** 6'0" **Wt:** 165 **Born:** 8/20/71 **Age:** 25

BATTING																			BASERUNNING				PERCENTAGES		
Year	Team	Lg	Org	G	AB	H	2B	3B	HR	TB	R	RBI	TBB	IBB	SO	HBP	SH	SF	SB	CS	SB%	GDP	Avg	OBP	SLG
1992	Marlins	R	Fla	59	212	51	8	1	1	64	36	15	49	2	42	4	3	2	5	6	.45	4	.241	.390	.302

Batting																			Baserunning				Percentages		
Year	Team	Lg	Org	G	AB	H	2B	3B	HR	TB	R	RBI	TBB	IBB	SO	HBP	SH	SF	SB	CS	SB%	GDP	Avg	OBP	SLG
1993	Kane County	A	Fla	82	214	45	12	1	0	59	22	27	31	0	55	1	8	4	3	8	.27	3	.210	.308	.276
1994	Brevard Cty	A+	Fla	65	157	45	12	3	1	66	33	13	23	2	28	3	7	1	3	2	.60	2	.287	.386	.420
1995	Portland	AA	Fla	87	208	49	9	3	4	76	32	30	28	2	44	2	5	5	5	2	.71	4	.236	.325	.365
1996	Portland	AA	Fla	23	73	19	7	0	3	35	15	11	13	1	13	2	1	1	3	1	.75	2	.260	.382	.479
	Charlotte	AAA	Fla	105	362	103	20	1	10	155	74	39	47	0	54	3	8	5	13	6	.68	7	.285	.367	.428
5 Min. YEARS				421	1226	312	68	9	19	455	212	135	191	7	236	15	32	18	32	25	.56	22	.254	.357	.371

Dera Clark

Pitches: Right **Bats:** Right **Pos:** P **Ht:** 6'1" **Wt:** 204 **Born:** 4/14/65 **Age:** 32

How Much He Pitched										What He Gave Up												The Results					
Year	Team	Lg	Org	G	GS	CG	GF	IP	BFP	H	R	ER	HR	SH	SF	HB	TBB	IBB	SO	WP	Bk	W	L	Pct.	ShO	Sv	ERA
1987	Royals	R	KC	21	0	0	8	56.1	230	42	20	14	1	3	1	1	17	5	51	3	0	3	4	.429	0	4	2.24
1988	Baseball Cy	A+	KC	34	0	0	13	79.2	335	73	28	24	2	3	4	1	31	6	46	9	2	5	2	.714	0	4	2.71
1989	Memphis	AA	KC	30	13	1	5	106.1	459	103	63	52	11	2	5	8	29	0	93	15	2	5	5	.500	1	1	4.40
1990	Omaha	AAA	KC	17	17	0	0	91.2	396	82	40	38	14	1	5	3	44	0	66	6	1	8	3	.727	0	0	3.73
1991	Omaha	AAA	KC	25	23	0	1	129.2	577	126	76	65	10	5	6	4	74	0	108	17	0	6	9	.400	0	0	4.51
1992	Royals	R	KC	2	1	0	0	8.2	40	7	4	2	0	0	1	0	2	0	13	2	0	0	0	.000	0	0	2.08
	Baseball Cy	A+	KC	3	3	0	0	16	63	15	3	3	0	0	0	0	3	0	7	0	0	2	0	1.000	0	0	1.69
	Omaha	AAA	KC	9	9	0	0	43	197	57	39	38	9	1	3	1	16	0	32	3	0	1	6	.143	0	0	7.95
1993	Omaha	AAA	KC	51	0	0	19	82.1	355	86	43	40	16	1	6	0	30	2	53	4	1	4	4	.500	0	5	4.37
1994	Richmond	AAA	Atl	8	0	0	1	10.1	48	9	8	7	1	0	2	0	7	0	11	0	1	0	0	.000	0	0	6.10
1995	Memphis	AA	SD	23	0	0	13	26.1	111	18	7	7	1	0	0	0	14	3	29	5	0	2	2	.500	0	5	2.39
1996	Memphis	AA	SD	9	9	0	0	46	199	47	24	16	6	2	2	2	13	0	42	3	0	4	3	.571	0	0	3.13
10 Min. YEARS				232	75	1	60	696.1	3010	665	355	306	71	18	35	20	280	16	551	67	7	40	38	.513	1	19	3.96

Howie Clark

Bats: Left **Throws:** Right **Pos:** 2B **Ht:** 5'10" **Wt:** 171 **Born:** 2/13/74 **Age:** 23

Batting																			Baserunning				Percentages		
Year	Team	Lg	Org	G	AB	H	2B	3B	HR	TB	R	RBI	TBB	IBB	SO	HBP	SH	SF	SB	CS	SB%	GDP	Avg	OBP	SLG
1992	Orioles	R	Bal	43	138	33	7	1	0	42	12	6	12	2	21	2	1	0	1	2	.33	2	.239	.309	.304
1993	Albany	A	Bal	7	17	4	0	0	0	4	2	1	0	0	3	0	0	0	1	0	1.00	1	.235	.235	.235
	Bluefield	R+	Bal	58	180	53	10	1	3	74	29	30	26	2	34	4	1	4	2	2	.50	4	.294	.388	.411
1994	Frederick	A+	Bal	2	7	1	1	0	0	2	1	0	0	0	2	0	0	0	0	0	.00	1	.143	.143	.286
	Albany	A	Bal	108	353	95	22	7	2	137	56	47	51	3	58	7	4	1	5	4	.56	7	.269	.371	.388
1995	High Desert	A+	Bal	100	329	85	20	2	5	124	50	40	32	0	51	4	3	3	12	6	.67	4	.258	.329	.377
1996	Bowie	AA	Bal	127	449	122	29	3	4	169	55	52	59	1	54	2	10	7	2	8	.20	8	.272	.354	.376
5 Min. YEARS				445	1473	393	89	14	14	552	205	176	180	8	223	19	19	15	23	22	.51	27	.267	.351	.375

Jerald Clark

Bats: Right **Throws:** Right **Pos:** OF **Ht:** 6' 4" **Wt:** 205 **Born:** 8/10/63 **Age:** 33

Batting																			Baserunning				Percentages		
Year	Team	Lg	Org	G	AB	H	2B	3B	HR	TB	R	RBI	TBB	IBB	SO	HBP	SH	SF	SB	CS	SB%	GDP	Avg	OBP	SLG
1985	Spokane	A-	SD	73	283	92	24	3	2	128	45	50	34	0	38	4	1	6	9	4	.69	7	.325	.398	.452
1986	Reno	A+	SD	95	389	118	34	3	7	179	76	58	29	3	46	9	0	7	5	4	.56	8	.303	.359	.460
	Beaumont	AA	SD	16	56	18	4	1	0	24	9	6	5	0	9	3	1	0	1	2	.33	2	.321	.406	.429
1987	Wichita	AA	SD	132	531	165	36	8	18	271	86	95	40	6	82	7	0	6	6	5	.55	11	.311	.363	.510
1988	Las Vegas	AAA	SD	107	408	123	27	7	9	191	65	67	17	2	66	9	2	2	6	2	.75	7	.301	.342	.468
1989	Las Vegas	AAA	SD	107	419	131	27	4	22	232	84	83	38	3	81	5	0	5	5	2	.71	11	.313	.373	.554
1990	Las Vegas	AAA	SD	40	161	49	7	4	12	100	30	32	5	0	35	0	0	2	2	0	1.00	1	.304	.321	.621
1996	Calgary	AAA	Pit	75	248	66	20	1	8	112	33	45	12	0	43	4	0	2	0	1	.00	10	.266	.308	.452
1988	San Diego	NL		6	15	3	1	0	0	4	0	3	0	0	4	0	0	0	0	0	.00	0	.200	.200	.267
1989	San Diego	NL		17	41	8	2	0	1	13	5	7	3	0	9	0	0	0	0	1	.00	0	.195	.250	.317
1990	San Diego	NL		52	101	27	4	1	5	48	12	11	5	0	24	0	0	1	0	0	.00	3	.267	.299	.475
1991	San Diego	NL		118	369	84	16	0	10	130	26	47	31	2	90	6	1	4	2	1	.67	10	.228	.295	.352
1992	San Diego	NL		146	496	120	22	6	12	190	45	58	22	3	97	4	1	3	3	0	1.00	7	.242	.278	.383
1993	Colorado	NL		140	478	135	26	6	13	212	65	67	20	2	60	10	3	1	9	6	.60	12	.282	.324	.444
1995	Minnesota	AL		36	109	37	8	3	3	60	17	15	2	0	11	1	0	1	3	0	1.00	5	.339	.354	.550
7 Min. YEARS				645	2495	762	179	31	78	1237	428	436	180	14	400	41	4	30	34	20	.63	57	.305	.358	.496
7 Maj. YEARS				515	1609	414	79	16	44	657	170	208	83	7	295	21	5	10	17	8	.68	37	.257	.301	.408

Craig Clayton

Pitches: Right **Bats:** Right **Pos:** P **Ht:** 6'0" **Wt:** 185 **Born:** 11/29/70 **Age:** 26

How Much He Pitched										What He Gave Up												The Results					
Year	Team	Lg	Org	G	GS	CG	GF	IP	BFP	H	R	ER	HR	SH	SF	HB	TBB	IBB	SO	WP	Bk	W	L	Pct.	ShO	Sv	ERA
1991	Bellingham	A-	Sea	1	0	0	1	0.2	3	1	0	0	0	0	0	0	0	0	0	0	0	0	0	.000	0	0	0.00
1993	Jacksonvlle	AA	Sea	3	0	0	3	4	17	3	0	0	0	0	0	1	1	0	1	0	0	0	0	.000	0	0	0.00
1994	Jacksonvlle	AA	Sea	10	0	0	6	12.1	52	8	6	5	1	0	0	1	6	0	13	3	4	0	0	.000	0	1	3.65
	Riverside	A+	Sea	20	1	0	4	26.1	135	29	24	23	7	2	1	1	26	0	35	1	0	1	1	.500	0	0	7.86
1995	Riverside	A+	Sea	28	28	0	0	160.1	738	171	102	89	16	11	6	7	83	3	156	7	1	9	8	.529	0	0	5.00
1996	Rancho Cuca	A+	SD	11	3	0	2	28.1	127	34	18	15	4	0	0	2	8	0	29	5	0	2	3	.400	0	0	4.76
	Memphis	AA	SD	5	0	0	0	9.2	52	14	12	6	3	0	1	1	5	0	9	3	0	0	0	.000	0	0	5.59
	Clinton	A	SD	27	0	0	18	37.1	154	27	10	6	1	0	1	3	8	0	29	3	0	2	1	.667	0	9	1.45
5 Min. YEARS				105	32	0	34	279	1278	287	172	144	32	13	9	16	137	3	272	22	5	14	13	.519	0	10	4.65

Royal Clayton

Pitches: Right **Bats:** Right **Pos:** P **Ht:** 6'2" **Wt:** 210 **Born:** 11/25/65 **Age:** 31

				HOW MUCH HE PITCHED						WHAT HE GAVE UP												THE RESULTS					
Year	Team	Lg	Org	G	GS	CG	GF	IP	BFP	H	R	ER	HR	SH	SF	HB	TBB	IBB	SO	WP	Bk	W	L	Pct.	ShO	Sv	ERA
1987	Oneonta	A-	NYA	2	0	0	1	4	16	4	1	1	0	0	0	0	2	0	3	0	0	0	1	.000	0	0	2.25
	Yankees	R	NYA	3	1	0	2	10.1	44	12	5	4	0	0	1	0	2	1	5	0	0	0	2	.000	0	1	3.48
	Pr. William	A+	NYA	9	4	0	4	37.1	181	49	25	19	4	0	0	0	17	0	20	1	2	2	1	.667	0	0	4.58
1988	Pr. William	A+	NYA	22	11	3	8	91.1	372	81	31	24	2	3	1	2	25	1	44	1	2	5	5	.500	1	0	2.36
	Ft. Laud	A+	NYA	6	6	5	0	43.2	166	38	10	7	2	0	0	0	3	0	16	1	0	4	2	.667	2	0	1.44
1989	Albany-Colo	AA	NYA	25	25	6	0	175	715	166	72	58	8	1	3	4	48	2	74	5	3	16	4	.800	0	0	2.98
1990	Columbus	AAA	NYA	4	4	0	0	26	111	33	12	11	1	0	0	0	7	0	15	1	0	1	2	.333	0	0	3.81
	Albany-Colo	AA	NYA	21	21	6	0	141.2	590	148	58	50	13	8	3	1	43	4	68	2	3	10	9	.526	2	0	3.18
1991	Columbus	AAA	NYA	32	19	1	2	150	650	152	76	64	15	2	4	2	53	1	100	2	1	11	7	.611	0	0	3.84
1992	Columbus	AAA	NYA	36	15	1	10	130.2	557	132	62	52	5	2	6	3	45	2	72	6	3	10	5	.667	1	1	3.58
1993	Columbus	AAA	NYA	47	11	0	21	117	489	119	56	46	12	5	3	2	31	3	66	3	0	7	6	.538	0	8	3.54
1994	Columbus	AAA	NYA	58	3	0	21	90	394	103	47	42	2	3	2	0	30	4	54	7	0	12	7	.632	0	5	4.20
1995	Phoenix	AAA	SF	5	5	0	0	23	108	35	18	15	1	2	0	0	6	2	13	0	0	0	2	.000	0	0	5.87
1996	Bowie	AA	Bal	3	2	0	0	8.1	38	12	10	10	3	0	0	0	4	0	5	0	0	0	1	.000	0	0	10.80
10 Min. YEARS				273	127	22	69	1048.1	4431	1084	483	403	68	26	23	14	316	20	555	29	14	78	54	.591	6	15	3.46

Chris Clemons

Pitches: Right **Bats:** Right **Pos:** P **Ht:** 6'4" **Wt:** 220 **Born:** 10/31/72 **Age:** 24

				HOW MUCH HE PITCHED						WHAT HE GAVE UP												THE RESULTS					
Year	Team	Lg	Org	G	GS	CG	GF	IP	BFP	H	R	ER	HR	SH	SF	HB	TBB	IBB	SO	WP	Bk	W	L	Pct.	ShO	Sv	ERA
1994	White Sox	R	ChA	2	2	0	0	7	27	5	3	3	0	0	0	0	1	0	5	0	0	0	1	.000	0	0	3.86
	Hickory	A	ChA	12	12	0	0	69.1	290	74	37	34	5	4	2	5	18	0	42	6	0	4	2	.667	0	0	4.41
1995	Pr. William	A+	ChA	27	27	1	0	137	606	136	78	72	18	4	4	11	64	2	92	2	0	7	12	.368	0	0	4.73
1996	Pr. William	A+	ChA	6	6	0	0	36	150	36	16	9	6	0	2	4	8	0	26	1	0	1	4	.200	0	0	2.25
	Birmingham	AA	ChA	19	16	1	2	94.1	400	91	39	33	7	0	1	6	40	2	69	1	1	5	2	.714	0	0	3.15
3 Min. YEARS				66	63	2	2	343.2	1473	342	173	151	36	8	9	26	131	4	234	10	1	17	21	.447	0	0	3.95

Danny Clyburn

Bats: Right **Throws:** Right **Pos:** OF-DH **Ht:** 6'3" **Wt:** 217 **Born:** 4/6/74 **Age:** 23

				BATTING														BASERUNNING				PERCENTAGES		
Year	Team	Lg	Org	G	AB	H	2B	3B	HR	TB	R	RBI	TBB	IBB	SO	HBP	SH	SF	SB	CS	SB%	GDP	Avg	OBP	SLG
1992	Pirates	R	Pit	39	149	51	9	0	4	72	26	25	5	0	20	1	0	2	7	3	.70	4	.342	.363	.483
1993	Augusta	A	Pit	127	457	121	21	4	9	177	55	66	37	1	97	5	0	0	5	5	.50	7	.265	.327	.387
1994	Salem	A+	Pit	118	461	126	19	0	22	211	57	90	20	2	96	0	0	5	4	5	.44	7	.273	.300	.458
1995	Winston-Sal	A+	Cin	59	227	59	10	2	11	106	27	41	13	1	59	4	0	2	2	4	.33	5	.260	.309	.467
	Frederick	A+	Bal	15	45	9	4	0	0	13	4	4	4	0	18	2	0	0	1	1	.50	0	.200	.294	.289
	High Desert	A+	Bal	45	160	45	3	1	12	86	20	37	17	1	41	4	0	3	2	1	.67	3	.281	.359	.538
1996	Bowie	AA	Bal	95	365	92	14	5	18	170	51	55	17	1	88	4	0	4	4	3	.57	5	.252	.290	.466
5 Min. YEARS				498	1864	503	80	12	76	835	240	318	113	6	419	20	0	16	25	22	.53	31	.270	.316	.448

Craig Colbert

Bats: Right **Throws:** Right **Pos:** C **Ht:** 6' 0" **Wt:** 214 **Born:** 2/13/65 **Age:** 32

				BATTING														BASERUNNING				PERCENTAGES		
Year	Team	Lg	Org	G	AB	H	2B	3B	HR	TB	R	RBI	TBB	IBB	SO	HBP	SH	SF	SB	CS	SB%	GDP	Avg	OBP	SLG
1986	Clinton	A	SF	72	263	60	12	0	1	75	26	17	23	1	53	3	0	1	4	1	.80	7	.228	.297	.285
1987	Fresno	A+	SF	115	388	95	12	4	6	133	41	51	22	2	89	4	3	5	5	5	.50	11	.245	.289	.343
1988	Clinton	A	SF	124	455	106	19	2	11	162	56	64	41	0	100	1	2	2	8	9	.47	4	.233	.297	.356
1989	Shreveport	AA	SF	106	363	94	19	3	7	140	47	34	23	5	67	0	2	2	3	7	.30	11	.259	.302	.386
1990	Phoenix	AAA	SF	111	400	112	22	2	8	162	41	47	31	3	80	3	1	2	4	5	.44	8	.280	.335	.405
1991	Phoenix	AAA	SF	42	142	35	6	2	2	51	9	13	11	2	38	0	0	1	0	1	.00	7	.246	.299	.359
1992	Phoenix	AAA	SF	36	140	45	8	1	1	58	16	12	3	0	16	1	2	2	0	1	.00	4	.321	.336	.414
1993	Phoenix	AAA	SF	13	45	10	2	1	1	17	5	7	0	0	11	1	0	1	0	0	.00	1	.222	.234	.378
1994	Charlotte	AAA	Cle	69	182	47	7	1	4	68	19	25	19	1	40	0	1	1	1	1	.50	9	.258	.327	.374
1995	Las Vegas	AAA	SD	74	241	60	8	1	1	73	30	24	21	0	44	0	1	1	1	0	1.00	14	.249	.308	.303
1996	Las Vegas	AAA	SD	65	200	50	8	0	5	73	18	19	8	0	48	0	0	4	3	1	.75	4	.250	.274	.365
1992	San Francisco	NL		49	126	29	5	2	1	41	10	16	9	0	22	0	2	2	1	0	1.00	8	.230	.277	.325
1993	San Francisco	NL		23	37	6	2	0	1	11	2	5	3	1	13	0	0	0	0	0	.00	0	.162	.225	.297
11 Min. YEARS				827	2819	714	123	17	47	1012	308	313	202	14	586	13	12	22	29	31	.48	80	.253	.304	.359
2 Maj. YEARS				72	163	35	7	2	2	52	12	21	12	1	35	0	2	2	1	0	1.00	8	.215	.266	.319

Victor Cole

Pitches: Right **Bats:** Both **Pos:** P **Ht:** 5'10" **Wt:** 160 **Born:** 1/23/68 **Age:** 29

				HOW MUCH HE PITCHED						WHAT HE GAVE UP												THE RESULTS					
Year	Team	Lg	Org	G	GS	CG	GF	IP	BFP	H	R	ER	HR	SH	SF	HB	TBB	IBB	SO	WP	Bk	W	L	Pct.	ShO	Sv	ERA
1988	Eugene	A-	KC	15	0	0	13	23.2	94	16	6	4	0	0	0	2	8	0	39	3	0	1	0	1.000	0	9	1.52
	Baseball Cy	A+	KC	10	5	0	2	35	149	27	9	8	0	1	1	1	21	0	29	2	0	5	0	1.000	0	1	2.06
1989	Memphis	AA	KC	13	13	0	0	63.2	303	67	53	45	4	4	1	5	51	1	52	4	1	1	9	.100	0	0	6.36
	Baseball Cy	A+	KC	9	9	0	0	42	186	43	23	18	2	1	1	1	22	0	30	2	1	3	1	.750	0	0	3.86
1990	Memphis	AA	KC	46	6	0	15	107.2	479	91	61	52	6	4	1	3	70	2	102	2	2	3	8	.273	0	4	4.35
1991	Omaha	AAA	KC	6	0	0	1	13	54	9	6	6	1	0	0	0	9	1	12	0	0	1	1	.500	0	0	4.15
	Carolina	AA	Pit	20	0	0	17	28.1	116	13	8	6	1	0	1	2	19	1	32	3	2	0	2	.000	0	12	1.91

Year	Team	Lg	Org	G	GS	CG	GF	IP	BFP	H	R	ER	HR	SH	SF	HB	TBB	IBB	SO	WP	Bk	W	L	Pct.	ShO	Sv	ERA
	HOW MUCH HE PITCHED									WHAT HE GAVE UP												THE RESULTS					
	Buffalo	AAA	Pit	19	1	0	9	24	115	23	11	10	2	0	1	1	20	0	23	3	0	1	2	.333	0	0	3.75
1992	Buffalo	AAA	Pit	19	19	3	0	115.2	498	102	46	40	8	3	3	4	61	0	69	8	0	11	6	.647	1	0	3.11
1993	Buffalo	AAA	Pit	6	6	0	0	26.1	134	35	25	25	5	2	1	0	24	0	14	1	0	1	3	.250	0	0	8.54
	Carolina	AA	Pit	27	0	0	13	41	189	39	30	27	5	1	0	2	31	2	35	6	0	0	4	.000	0	8	5.93
	New Orleans	AAA	Mil	6	1	0	0	6	34	9	7	7	0	0	1	1	7	0	5	0	0	0	2	.000	0	0	10.50
1994	El Paso	AA	Mil	8	0	0	2	8	50	18	17	16	4	0	0	1	9	1	3	0	1	0	1	.000	0	0	18.00
	Memphis	AA	KC	6	6	0	0	35.2	162	32	22	19	3	0	4	0	23	0	22	2	0	2	1	.667	0	0	4.79
1995	Las Vegas	AAA	SD	4	4	0	0	19.2	86	19	17	14	4	1	1	0	10	0	12	1	1	0	2	.000	0	0	6.41
	Salinas	IND	—	4	4	0	0	22.2	104	25	16	9	0	2	2	0	13	0	22	2	0	1	1	.500	0	0	3.57
	Memphis	AA	SD	16	10	0	3	62.1	271	59	38	26	4	3	3	0	31	1	51	3	1	2	3	.400	0	0	3.75
1996	Pine Bluff	IND	—	8	0	0	2	23.1	89	16	2	2	0	1	0	2	4	0	27	2	0	3	0	1.000	0	0	0.77
	Memphis	AA	SD	8	1	0	4	15	65	11	3	2	0	0	0	1	8	0	13	0	0	1	0	1.000	0	1	1.20
1992	Pittsburgh	NL		8	4	0	2	23	104	23	14	14	1	1	1	0	14	0	12	1	0	0	2	.000	0	0	5.48
9 Min. YEARS				250	85	3	81	713	3178	654	400	336	49	23	21	26	441	9	592	44	9	36	46	.439	1	35	4.24

Dan Collier

Bats: Right **Throws:** Right **Pos:** OF **Ht:** 6'3" **Wt:** 205 **Born:** 8/13/70 **Age:** 26

Year	Team	Lg	Org	G	AB	H	2B	3B	HR	TB	R	RBI	TBB	IBB	SO	HBP	SH	SF	SB	CS	SB%	GDP	Avg	OBP	SLG
	BATTING																		BASERUNNING				PERCENTAGES		
1991	Red Sox	R	Bos	42	131	33	4	2	6	59	27	25	27	1	42	14	0	0	1	1	.50	1	.252	.430	.450
1992	Elmira	A-	Bos	59	193	34	8	0	9	69	26	24	9	0	86	10	2	1	2	2	.50	0	.176	.249	.358
1993	Utica	A-	Bos	67	226	49	11	1	15	107	39	48	29	1	95	7	0	2	4	0	1.00	5	.217	.322	.473
1994	Lynchburg	A+	Bos	84	299	67	16	0	11	116	39	40	16	1	134	8	1	1	5	2	.71	6	.224	.281	.388
1995	Sarasota	A+	Bos	67	242	62	12	1	12	112	30	44	20	0	83	5	0	3	5	9	.36	3	.256	.322	.463
1996	Trenton	AA	Bos	28	94	20	3	0	4	35	12	9	9	1	36	0	1	0	2	1	.67	4	.213	.282	.372
	Bakersfield	A+	Bos	56	212	58	15	1	5	90	22	40	6	0	63	7	2	2	9	3	.75	2	.274	.313	.425
6 Min. YEARS				403	1397	323	69	5	62	588	195	230	116	4	539	51	6	9	28	18	.61	21	.231	.312	.421

Lou Collier

Bats: Right **Throws:** Right **Pos:** SS **Ht:** 5'10" **Wt:** 170 **Born:** 8/21/73 **Age:** 23

Year	Team	Lg	Org	G	AB	H	2B	3B	HR	TB	R	RBI	TBB	IBB	SO	HBP	SH	SF	SB	CS	SB%	GDP	Avg	OBP	SLG
	BATTING																		BASERUNNING				PERCENTAGES		
1993	Welland	A-	Pit	50	201	61	6	2	1	74	35	19	12	0	31	5	1	1	8	7	.53	2	.303	.356	.368
1994	Augusta	A	Pit	85	318	89	17	4	7	135	48	40	25	0	53	8	0	3	32	10	.76	4	.280	.345	.425
	Salem	A+	Pit	43	158	42	4	1	6	66	25	16	15	0	29	6	2	2	5	8	.38	4	.266	.348	.418
1995	Lynchburg	A+	Pit	114	399	110	19	3	4	147	68	38	51	4	60	7	3	3	31	11	.74	13	.276	.365	.368
1996	Carolina	AA	Pit	119	443	124	20	3	3	159	76	49	48	4	73	7	2	6	29	9	.76	11	.280	.355	.359
4 Min. YEARS				411	1519	426	66	13	21	581	252	162	151	8	246	33	8	15	105	45	.70	34	.280	.355	.382

Bartolo Colon

Pitches: Right **Bats:** Right **Pos:** P **Ht:** 6'0" **Wt:** 185 **Born:** 5/24/75 **Age:** 22

Year	Team	Lg	Org	G	GS	CG	GF	IP	BFP	H	R	ER	HR	SH	SF	HB	TBB	IBB	SO	WP	Bk	W	L	Pct.	ShO	Sv	ERA
	HOW MUCH HE PITCHED									WHAT HE GAVE UP												THE RESULTS					
1994	Burlington	R+	Cle	12	12	0	0	66	291	46	32	23	3	2	1	4	44	0	84	6	2	7	4	.636	0	0	3.14
1995	Kinston	A+	Cle	21	21	0	0	128.2	493	91	31	28	8	1	2	0	39	0	152	4	3	13	3	.813	0	0	1.96
1996	Canton-Akrn	AA	Cle	13	12	0	0	62	253	44	17	12	2	0	1	2	25	0	56	3	1	2	2	.500	0	0	1.74
	Buffalo	AAA	Cle	8	0	0	1	15	69	16	10	10	2	1	1	0	8	0	19	2	0	0	0	.000	0	0	6.00
3 Min. YEARS				54	45	0	1	271.2	1106	197	90	73	15	4	5	6	116	0	311	15	6	22	9	.710	0	0	2.42

Dennis Colon

Bats: Left **Throws:** Right **Pos:** 1B **Ht:** 5'10" **Wt:** 165 **Born:** 8/4/73 **Age:** 23

Year	Team	Lg	Org	G	AB	H	2B	3B	HR	TB	R	RBI	TBB	IBB	SO	HBP	SH	SF	SB	CS	SB%	GDP	Avg	OBP	SLG
	BATTING																		BASERUNNING				PERCENTAGES		
1991	Astros	R	Hou	54	193	46	5	2	2	61	20	28	10	2	28	1	1	1	4	7	.36	4	.238	.278	.316
1992	Burlington	A	Hou	123	458	116	27	7	6	175	54	63	32	1	50	2	2	6	4	7	.36	9	.253	.301	.382
1993	Osceola	A+	Hou	118	469	148	20	6	2	186	51	59	17	1	41	0	0	3	10	4	.71	12	.316	.337	.397
1994	Jackson	AA	Hou	118	380	105	17	6	5	149	37	52	18	5	43	0	4	5	8	5	.62	12	.276	.305	.392
1995	Jackson	AA	Hou	106	378	85	10	0	5	110	33	31	24	2	38	5	2	6	3	6	.33	8	.225	.276	.291
1996	Jackson	AA	Hou	127	432	121	23	1	12	182	49	58	21	6	49	0	0	0	0	3	.00	19	.280	.313	.421
6 Min. YEARS				646	2310	621	102	22	32	863	244	291	122	17	249	8	9	21	29	32	.48	64	.269	.305	.374

Julio Colon

Pitches: Right **Bats:** Right **Pos:** P **Ht:** 6'2" **Wt:** 210 **Born:** 10/30/72 **Age:** 24

Year	Team	Lg	Org	G	GS	CG	GF	IP	BFP	H	R	ER	HR	SH	SF	HB	TBB	IBB	SO	WP	Bk	W	L	Pct.	ShO	Sv	ERA
	HOW MUCH HE PITCHED									WHAT HE GAVE UP												THE RESULTS					
1994	Bakersfield	A+	LA	8	8	0	0	44.2	196	47	30	28	8	0	0	3	23	0	36	4	1	1	5	.167	0	0	5.64
	Great Falls	R+	LA	9	6	0	0	41.2	170	29	17	10	1	0	0	0	18	0	45	7	0	6	2	.750	0	0	2.16
	Vero Beach	A+	LA	4	3	0	0	16.2	67	14	7	7	1	0	0	0	7	0	11	1	0	1	1	.500	0	0	3.78
1995	San Bernrdo	A+	LA	49	0	0	30	79	343	68	47	38	7	1	1	2	37	2	76	12	0	6	3	.667	0	12	4.33
1996	Vero Beach	A+	LA	8	8	0	0	41.1	182	44	21	12	2	0	2	1	19	0	49	2	0	3	2	.600	0	0	2.61
	San Antonio	AA	LA	6	6	0	0	36.1	159	35	20	18	2	1	2	3	17	0	14	6	0	2	3	.400	0	0	4.46
3 Min. YEARS				84	31	0	30	259.2	1117	237	142	113	21	2	5	9	121	2	230	32	1	19	16	.543	0	12	3.92

Jeff Conger

Bats: Left **Throws:** Left **Pos:** OF **Ht:** 6'0" **Wt:** 185 **Born:** 8/6/71 **Age:** 25

				BATTING															BASERUNNING				PERCENTAGES		
Year	Team	Lg	Org	G	AB	H	2B	3B	HR	TB	R	RBI	TBB	IBB	SO	HBP	SH	SF	SB	CS	SB%	GDP	Avg	OBP	SLG
1990	Pirates	R	Pit	46	120	22	3	1	0	27	19	6	18	0	52	1	1	0	3	1	.75	0	.183	.295	.225
1991	Pirates	R	Pit	15	37	12	0	0	0	12	5	4	4	0	8	0	0	0	7	2	.78	0	.324	.390	.324
	Welland	A-	Pit	32	81	22	2	2	1	31	15	7	7	0	31	1	0	0	5	2	.71	0	.272	.337	.383
1992	Augusta	A	Pit	98	303	74	12	6	6	116	56	36	44	2	93	3	2	1	36	13	.73	1	.244	.345	.383
1993	Salem	A+	Pit	110	391	90	12	1	4	116	40	31	31	2	125	1	7	1	24	10	.71	7	.230	.288	.297
1994	Salem	A+	Pit	111	362	83	8	3	9	124	65	37	53	0	105	9	6	4	13	8	.62	5	.229	.339	.343
1995	Lynchburg	A+	Pit	90	318	84	13	5	3	116	44	23	35	1	74	6	7	3	26	16	.62	1	.264	.345	.365
	Carolina	AA	Pit	39	128	37	6	1	1	48	15	17	18	2	31	1	2	1	8	2	.80	0	.289	.378	.375
1996	Carolina	AA	Pit	66	177	41	7	1	3	59	19	17	17	1	51	3	4	0	12	4	.75	3	.232	.310	.333
7 Min. YEARS				607	1917	465	63	20	27	649	278	178	227	8	570	25	29	10	134	58	.70	17	.243	.329	.339

Scott Conner

Pitches: Right **Bats:** Right **Pos:** P **Ht:** 6'2" **Wt:** 192 **Born:** 3/22/72 **Age:** 25

				HOW MUCH HE PITCHED						WHAT HE GAVE UP												THE RESULTS					
Year	Team	Lg	Org	G	GS	CG	GF	IP	BFP	H	R	ER	HR	SH	SF	HB	TBB	IBB	SO	WP	Bk	W	L	Pct.	ShO	Sv	ERA
1991	Orioles	R	Bal	12	7	0	4	48.2	210	49	33	29	0	2	2	3	18	0	35	6	0	1	4	.200	0	1	5.36
1992	Orioles	R	Bal	12	11	3	0	70	294	56	29	15	2	1	4	5	31	0	39	4	0	4	5	.444	1	0	1.93
1993	Albany	A	Bal	37	13	0	8	115.2	546	133	92	66	8	3	3	2	71	2	90	12	1	6	6	.500	0	0	5.14
1994	Frederick	A+	Bal	53	0	0	22	73.1	325	65	34	29	5	4	1	5	49	2	61	8	0	2	1	.667	0	8	3.56
1995	Bowie	AA	Bal	44	0	0	9	82	378	57	43	38	7	4	7	10	74	2	82	13	2	5	1	.833	0	0	4.17
1996	Frederick	A+	Bal	12	10	0	0	61.2	260	52	29	25	7	0	0	2	27	0	47	5	0	1	2	.333	0	0	3.65
	Bowie	AA	Bal	21	11	0	1	82	362	86	54	46	12	2	3	3	36	0	59	3	3	1	5	.167	0	0	5.05
6 Min. YEARS				191	52	3	44	533.1	2375	498	314	248	41	16	20	30	306	6	413	51	6	20	24	.455	1	9	4.19

Matt Connolly

Pitches: Right **Bats:** Right **Pos:** P **Ht:** 6'8" **Wt:** 230 **Born:** 10/1/68 **Age:** 28

				HOW MUCH HE PITCHED						WHAT HE GAVE UP												THE RESULTS					
Year	Team	Lg	Org	G	GS	CG	GF	IP	BFP	H	R	ER	HR	SH	SF	HB	TBB	IBB	SO	WP	Bk	W	L	Pct.	ShO	Sv	ERA
1991	Erie	A-	—	19	0	0	9	41.2	188	39	23	20	1	1	2	2	25	1	43	5	1	2	1	.667	0	1	4.32
1992	Visalia	A+	Col	30	2	0	12	67.2	293	70	35	25	3	4	1	5	26	1	42	3	1	5	1	.833	0	1	3.33
1993	W. Palm Bch	A+	Mon	6	0	0	0	14.2	67	14	9	8	0	2	0	1	9	0	8	0	0	1	1	.500	0	0	4.91
	Sioux City	IND	—	17	17	2	0	100.2	439	111	61	53	6	2	8	5	32	2	71	4	0	5	8	.385	0	0	4.74
1994	Sioux City	IND	—	16	16	2	0	108	468	117	51	43	9	1	4	1	34	0	107	6	1	7	1	.875	1	0	3.58
1995	Daytona	A+	ChN	18	2	0	7	55.1	216	37	14	6	0	3	0	2	9	2	77	6	0	7	1	.875	0	2	0.98
	Orlando	AA	ChN	39	6	0	18	95	381	71	32	24	5	3	0	4	20	5	120	7	0	10	5	.667	0	4	2.27
1996	Orlando	AA	ChN	31	10	1	9	87	374	79	45	32	8	2	4	6	35	1	80	3	0	7	3	.700	0	2	3.31
6 Min. YEARS				176	53	5	55	570	2426	538	270	211	32	18	19	26	190	12	548	34	3	44	21	.677	1	10	3.33

Hayward Cook

Bats: Right **Throws:** Right **Pos:** OF **Ht:** 5'10" **Wt:** 195 **Born:** 6/24/72 **Age:** 25

				BATTING															BASERUNNING				PERCENTAGES		
Year	Team	Lg	Org	G	AB	H	2B	3B	HR	TB	R	RBI	TBB	IBB	SO	HBP	SH	SF	SB	CS	SB%	GDP	Avg	OBP	SLG
1994	Elmira	A-	Fla	63	227	62	10	8	5	103	36	29	20	0	45	2	1	1	7	6	.54	1	.273	.336	.454
1995	Kane County	A	Fla	78	261	73	5	1	8	104	50	23	12	0	61	1	2	1	23	4	.85	4	.280	.313	.398
1996	Brevard Cty	A+	Fla	80	284	83	11	9	7	133	45	47	29	1	87	6	1	1	14	7	.67	5	.292	.369	.468
	Portland	AA	Fla	14	46	14	3	0	0	17	7	2	4	0	11	0	0	0	2	1	.67	1	.304	.360	.370
3 Min. YEARS				235	818	232	29	18	20	357	138	101	65	1	204	9	4	3	46	18	.72	11	.284	.342	.436

Brent Cookson

Bats: Right **Throws:** Right **Pos:** OF **Ht:** 6' 0" **Wt:** 195 **Born:** 9/7/69 **Age:** 27

				BATTING															BASERUNNING				PERCENTAGES		
Year	Team	Lg	Org	G	AB	H	2B	3B	HR	TB	R	RBI	TBB	IBB	SO	HBP	SH	SF	SB	CS	SB%	GDP	Avg	OBP	SLG
1991	Sou. Oregon	A-	Oak	6	9	0	0	0	0	0	0	0	0	0	7	0	0	0	0	0	.00	1	.000	.000	.000
	Athletics	R	Oak	1	1	0	0	0	0	0	0	0	0	0	1	0	0	0	0	0	.00	0	.000	.000	.000
1992	Clinton	A	SF	46	145	31	5	1	8	62	30	20	22	0	48	3	1	1	9	3	.75	4	.214	.327	.428
	San Jose	A+	SF	68	255	74	8	4	12	126	44	49	25	0	69	3	0	2	9	5	.64	8	.290	.358	.494
1993	San Jose	A+	SF	67	234	60	10	1	17	123	43	50	43	1	73	3	2	5	14	6	.70	5	.256	.372	.526
1994	Shreveport	AA	SF	62	207	67	21	3	11	127	32	41	18	2	57	1	2	2	4	1	.80	4	.324	.377	.614
	Phoenix	AAA	SF	14	43	12	0	1	1	17	7	6	5	0	14	1	0	0	0	1	.00	1	.279	.367	.395
1995	Phoenix	AAA	SF	68	210	63	9	3	15	123	38	46	25	2	36	1	1	2	3	3	.50	4	.300	.374	.586
	Omaha	AAA	KC	40	137	55	13	0	4	80	28	20	17	0	24	4	0	2	0	0	.00	3	.401	.475	.584
1996	Pawtucket	AAA	Bos	73	255	69	13	1	19	141	51	50	24	1	72	5	0	2	2	4	.33	9	.271	.343	.553
	Rochester	AAA	Bal	30	113	30	7	0	6	55	22	21	9	0	20	2	0	1	2	1	.67	5	.265	.328	.487
1995	Kansas City	AL		22	35	5	1	0	0	6	2	5	2	0	7	0	1	0	1	0	1.00	0	.143	.189	.171
6 Min. YEARS				475	1609	461	86	14	93	854	295	303	188	6	421	23	6	17	43	24	.64	44	.287	.366	.531

Mike Coolbaugh

Bats: Right **Throws:** Right **Pos:** 1B **Ht:** 6'1" **Wt:** 190 **Born:** 6/5/72 **Age:** 25

			BATTING															BASERUNNING				PERCENTAGES		
Year	Team	Lg Org	G	AB	H	2B	3B	HR	TB	R	RBI	TBB	IBB	SO	HBP	SH	SF	SB	CS	SB%	GDP	Avg	OBP	SLG
1990	Medicne Hat	R+ Tor	58	211	40	9	0	2	55	21	16	13	0	47	1	1	2	3	2	.60	8	.190	.238	.261
1991	St. Cathrns	A- Tor	71	255	58	13	2	3	84	28	26	17	0	40	3	4	4	4	5	.44	1	.227	.280	.329
1992	St. Cathrns	A- Tor	15	49	14	1	1	0	17	3	2	3	0	12	0	2	0	0	2	.00	1	.286	.327	.347
1993	Hagerstown	A Tor	112	389	94	23	1	16	167	58	62	32	5	94	3	4	4	4	3	.57	9	.242	.301	.429
1994	Dunedin	A+ Tor	122	456	120	33	3	16	207	53	66	28	3	94	7	3	4	3	4	.43	14	.263	.313	.454
1995	Knoxville	AA Tor	142	500	120	32	2	9	183	71	56	37	3	110	11	4	3	7	11	.39	13	.240	.305	.366
1996	Charlotte	A+ Tex	124	449	129	33	4	15	215	76	75	42	4	80	8	0	3	8	10	.44	10	.287	.357	.479
	Tulsa	AA Tex	7	23	8	3	0	2	17	6	9	2	0	3	2	0	0	1	0	1.00	0	.348	.444	.739
7 Min. YEARS			651	2332	583	147	13	63	945	316	312	174	15	480	35	18	20	30	37	.45	56	.250	.309	.405

Scott Coolbaugh

Bats: Right **Throws:** Right **Pos:** 3B **Ht:** 5'11" **Wt:** 195 **Born:** 6/13/66 **Age:** 31

			BATTING															BASERUNNING				PERCENTAGES		
Year	Team	Lg Org	G	AB	H	2B	3B	HR	TB	R	RBI	TBB	IBB	SO	HBP	SH	SF	SB	CS	SB%	GDP	Avg	OBP	SLG
1987	Charlotte	A+ Tex	66	233	64	21	0	2	91	27	20	24	1	56	0	1	2	0	1	.00	5	.275	.340	.391
1988	Tulsa	AA Tex	136	470	127	15	4	13	189	52	75	76	4	79	1	2	8	2	4	.33	14	.270	.368	.402
1989	Okla. City	AAA Tex	144	527	137	28	0	18	219	66	74	57	5	93	2	2	3	1	2	.33	13	.260	.333	.416
1990	Okla. City	AAA Tex	76	293	66	17	2	6	105	39	30	27	2	62	1	0	3	0	1	.00	6	.225	.290	.358
1991	Las Vegas	AAA SD	60	209	60	9	2	7	94	29	29	34	2	53	0	0	2	2	2	.50	9	.287	.384	.450
1992	Las Vegas	AAA SD	65	199	48	13	2	8	89	30	39	19	1	52	3	1	1	0	0	.00	8	.241	.315	.447
	Nashville	AAA Cin	59	188	48	8	3	5	77	25	23	32	0	50	0	2	5	3	2	.60	5	.255	.356	.410
1993	Rochester	AAA Bal	118	421	103	26	4	18	191	52	67	27	2	110	2	1	2	0	0	.00	9	.245	.292	.454
1994	Louisville	AAA StL	94	333	101	25	6	19	195	60	75	39	10	69	10	0	4	3	5	.38	10	.303	.389	.586
1996	Ottawa	AAA Mon	58	173	36	12	1	3	59	20	22	23	1	37	0	1	4	2	2	.50	7	.208	.295	.341
1989	Texas	AL	25	51	14	1	0	2	21	7	7	4	0	12	0	1	1	0	0	.00	2	.275	.321	.412
1990	Texas	AL	67	180	36	6	0	2	48	21	13	15	0	47	1	4	1	1	0	1.00	2	.200	.264	.267
1991	San Diego	NL	60	180	39	8	1	2	55	12	15	19	2	45	1	4	1	0	3	.00	8	.217	.294	.306
1994	St. Louis	NL	15	21	4	0	0	2	10	4	6	1	0	4	0	0	1	0	0	.00	3	.190	.217	.476
9 Min. YEARS			876	3046	790	174	24	99	1309	400	454	358	28	661	19	10	34	13	19	.41	86	.259	.338	.430
4 Maj. YEARS			167	432	93	15	1	8	134	44	41	39	2	108	2	9	4	1	3	.25	15	.215	.281	.310

Reid Cornelius

Pitches: Right **Bats:** Right **Pos:** P **Ht:** 6' 0" **Wt:** 200 **Born:** 6/2/70 **Age:** 27

			HOW MUCH HE PITCHED						WHAT HE GAVE UP												THE RESULTS					
Year	Team	Lg Org	G	GS	CG	GF	IP	BFP	H	R	ER	HR	SH	SF	HB	TBB	IBB	SO	WP	Bk	W	L	Pct.	ShO	Sv	ERA
1989	Rockford	A Mon	17	17	0	0	84.1	391	71	58	40	6	3	3	11	63	0	66	13	3	5	6	.455	0	0	4.27
1990	W. Palm Bch	A+ Mon	11	11	0	0	56	245	54	25	21	1	0	4	5	25	0	47	3	3	2	3	.400	0	0	3.38
1991	W. Palm Bch	A+ Mon	17	17	0	0	109.1	449	79	31	29	3	9	4	7	43	1	81	3	6	8	3	.727	0	0	2.39
	Harrisburg	AA Mon	3	3	1	0	18.2	76	15	6	6	3	0	0	2	7	0	12	0	0	2	1	.667	1	0	2.89
1992	Harrisburg	AA Mon	4	4	0	0	23	92	11	8	8	0	2	0	6	8	0	17	1	0	1	0	1.000	0	0	3.13
1993	Harrisburg	AA Mon	27	27	1	0	157.2	698	146	95	73	10	3	5	13	82	1	119	8	0	10	7	.588	0	0	4.17
1994	Ottawa	AAA Mon	25	24	1	1	148	661	149	89	72	18	1	4	8	75	2	87	10	0	9	8	.529	0	0	4.38
1995	Ottawa	AAA Mon	4	3	0	0	10.2	54	16	12	8	1	0	1	2	5	0	7	2	0	1	1	.500	0	0	6.75
	Norfolk	AAA NYN	14	13	1	0	81	341	73	22	15	3	3	2	8	24	0	50	3	0	8	1	.889	0	0	1.67
1996	Buffalo	AAA Cle	20	18	0	2	90	422	101	64	56	6	4	2	5	49	1	62	3	0	5	7	.417	0	0	5.60
1995	Montreal	NL	8	0	0	1	9	43	11	8	8	3	0	0	2	5	0	4	1	0	0	0	.000	0	0	8.00
	New York	NL	10	10	0	0	57.2	258	64	36	33	8	4	3	1	25	5	35	1	1	3	7	.300	0	0	5.15
8 Min. YEARS			142	137	4	3	778.2	3429	715	410	328	51	25	25	67	381	5	548	46	12	51	37	.580	1	0	3.79

Edwin Corps

Pitches: Right **Bats:** Right **Pos:** P **Ht:** 5'11" **Wt:** 180 **Born:** 11/3/72 **Age:** 24

			HOW MUCH HE PITCHED						WHAT HE GAVE UP												THE RESULTS					
Year	Team	Lg Org	G	GS	CG	GF	IP	BFP	H	R	ER	HR	SH	SF	HB	TBB	IBB	SO	WP	Bk	W	L	Pct.	ShO	Sv	ERA
1994	San Jose	A+ SF	29	29	0	0	168.1	731	180	95	74	6	5	6	20	43	1	91	4	1	10	6	.625	0	0	3.96
1995	Shreveport	AA SF	27	27	2	0	165.2	712	195	80	71	16	2	6	8	41	2	53	4	2	13	6	.684	0	0	3.86
1996	Shreveport	AA SF	38	3	0	6	70.1	305	74	46	35	6	1	1	3	26	2	39	2	0	2	3	.400	0	1	4.48
3 Min. YEARS			94	59	2	6	404.1	1748	449	221	180	28	8	13	31	110	5	183	10	3	25	15	.625	0	1	4.01

Miguel Correa

Bats: Both **Throws:** Right **Pos:** OF **Ht:** 6'2" **Wt:** 165 **Born:** 9/10/71 **Age:** 25

			BATTING															BASERUNNING				PERCENTAGES		
Year	Team	Lg Org	G	AB	H	2B	3B	HR	TB	R	RBI	TBB	IBB	SO	HBP	SH	SF	SB	CS	SB%	GDP	Avg	OBP	SLG
1990	Braves	R Atl	33	109	26	6	0	0	32	19	10	6	1	20	0	3	2	10	4	.71	1	.239	.274	.294
1991	Braves	R Atl	47	171	43	8	2	0	55	21	6	7	0	29	1	2	0	10	6	.63	2	.251	.285	.322
1992	Idaho Falls	R+ Atl	66	266	79	7	5	3	105	43	28	14	0	49	4	0	2	14	10	.58	2	.297	.342	.395
1993	Macon	A Atl	131	495	131	26	8	10	203	58	61	30	5	84	4	2	5	18	17	.51	6	.265	.309	.410
1994	Greenville	AA Atl	38	124	25	2	0	0	27	11	6	6	2	22	1	6	0	4	4	.50	0	.202	.244	.218
	Durham	A+ Atl	83	290	64	12	4	8	108	43	19	18	0	53	2	2	0	12	7	.63	3	.221	.271	.372
1995	Durham	A+ Atl	118	398	94	19	1	19	172	43	70	19	2	95	3	2	3	9	13	.41	6	.236	.274	.432
1996	Greenville	AA Atl	64	225	50	13	2	5	82	20	25	11	2	65	1	5	0	2	2	.50	3	.222	.262	.364
	Durham	A+ Atl	65	248	64	17	2	7	106	39	27	14	2	46	2	2	1	15	6	.71	2	.258	.302	.427

Year	Team	Lg	Org	G	AB	H	2B	3B	HR	TB	R	RBI	TBB	IBB	SO	HBP	SH	SF	SB	CS	SB%	GDP	Avg	OBP	SLG
7 Min. YEARS				645	2326	576	110	24	52	890	297	252	125	14	463	18	24	11	94	69	.58	25	.248	.290	.383

Ramser Correa

Pitches: Right **Bats:** Right **Pos:** P **Ht:** 6'5" **Wt:** 225 **Born:** 11/13/70 **Age:** 26

				HOW MUCH HE PITCHED						WHAT HE GAVE UP												THE RESULTS					
Year	Team	Lg	Org	G	GS	CG	GF	IP	BFP	H	R	ER	HR	SH	SF	HB	TBB	IBB	SO	WP	Bk	W	L	Pct.	ShO	Sv	ERA
1987	Helena	R+	Mil	3	2	0	0	6	38	10	12	11	1	1	1	0	8	0	0	1	0	0	1	.000	0	0	16.50
1988	Helena	R+	Mil	13	7	0	2	43.1	187	38	22	19	2	0	2	0	24	0	34	4	4	2	2	.500	0	0	3.95
1989	Helena	R+	Mil	2	1	0	1	3	14	3	0	0	0	0	0	0	2	0	2	1	0	0	0	.000	0	0	0.00
1990	Beloit	A	Mil	4	4	0	0	24.2	105	24	8	6	1	0	0	0	9	0	30	1	0	3	0	1.000	0	0	2.19
1991	Stockton	A+	Mil	10	8	0	0	33.2	147	31	14	11	1	1	1	2	20	0	21	2	0	2	1	.667	0	0	2.94
1992	Stockton	A+	Mil	35	4	0	9	70.1	309	71	31	28	2	3	3	2	38	2	55	5	1	3	2	.600	0	1	3.58
1993	Stockton	A+	Mil	21	10	0	6	67.2	304	78	38	34	2	1	5	1	30	1	32	2	1	4	3	.571	0	3	4.52
	El Paso	AA	Mil	5	1	0	2	10.2	57	15	15	6	2	1	5	0	7	1	5	2	0	1	0	1.000	0	0	5.06
1994	Kinston	A+	Cle	4	4	0	0	18.1	87	14	11	9	3	0	0	0	19	0	17	1	1	2	1	.667	0	0	4.42
	Canton-Akrn	AA	Cle	19	8	0	5	67.1	310	72	41	32	6	0	2	0	51	3	41	6	0	2	4	.333	0	0	4.28
1995	Albuquerque	AAA	LA	2	0	0	0	4	16	5	0	0	0	0	0	0	1	1	3	0	0	0	0	.000	0	0	0.00
	San Antonio	AA	LA	44	0	0	32	53.2	237	59	29	25	5	0	2	0	22	1	37	4	0	1	4	.200	0	17	4.19
1996	Albuquerque	AAA	LA	23	0	0	15	36	170	44	29	23	3	1	2	0	22	4	30	3	1	0	3	.000	0	1	5.75
	San Antonio	AA	LA	31	0	0	27	34.1	140	26	12	11	2	1	0	0	16	0	29	3	0	4	1	.800	0	9	2.88
10 Min. YEARS				216	49	0	99	473	2121	490	262	215	30	9	23	5	269	13	336	35	8	24	22	.522	0	31	4.09

Rod Correia

Bats: Right **Throws:** Right **Pos:** SS **Ht:** 5'11" **Wt:** 185 **Born:** 9/13/67 **Age:** 29

				BATTING															BASERUNNING				PERCENTAGES		
Year	Team	Lg	Org	G	AB	H	2B	3B	HR	TB	R	RBI	TBB	IBB	SO	HBP	SH	SF	SB	CS	SB%	GDP	Avg	OBP	SLG
1988	Sou. Oregon	A-	Oak	56	207	52	7	3	1	68	23	19	18	0	42	3	1	1	6	1	.86	9	.251	.319	.329
1989	Modesto	A+	Oak	107	339	71	9	3	0	86	31	26	34	0	64	12	4	1	7	7	.50	10	.209	.303	.254
1990	Modesto	A+	Oak	87	246	60	6	3	0	72	27	16	22	0	41	4	5	1	4	6	.40	6	.244	.315	.293
1991	Modesto	A+	Oak	5	19	5	0	0	0	5	8	3	2	0	1	0	1	0	1	0	1.00	1	.263	.333	.263
	Tacoma	AAA	Oak	17	56	14	0	0	1	17	9	7	4	0	6	1	3	0	0	0	.00	1	.250	.311	.304
	Huntsville	AA	Oak	87	290	64	10	1	1	79	25	22	31	0	50	6	8	1	2	4	.33	11	.221	.308	.272
1992	Midland	AA	Cal	123	482	140	23	1	6	183	73	56	28	2	72	8	5	6	20	11	.65	14	.290	.336	.380
1993	Vancouver	AAA	Cal	60	207	56	10	4	4	86	43	28	15	1	25	1	3	5	11	4	.73	5	.271	.316	.415
1994	Vancouver	AAA	Cal	106	376	103	12	3	6	139	54	49	25	0	54	6	8	7	8	7	.53	11	.274	.324	.370
1995	Vancouver	AAA	Cal	73	264	80	6	5	1	99	42	39	26	3	33	0	4	4	8	4	.67	7	.303	.361	.375
1996	Louisville	AAA	StL	35	113	18	3	0	2	27	7	8	3	0	22	0	1	0	1	2	.33	3	.159	.181	.239
	Edmonton	AAA	Oak	8	23	2	0	0	0	2	1	0	0	0	2	0	0	0	1	0	1.00	1	.087	.087	.087
	Huntsville	AA	Oak	66	241	61	9	1	2	78	38	30	28	1	24	7	3	4	11	1	.92	8	.253	.343	.324
1993	California	AL		64	128	34	5	0	0	39	12	9	6	0	20	4	5	0	2	4	.33	1	.266	.319	.305
1994	California	AL		6	17	4	1	0	0	5	4	0	0	0	0	2	0	0	0	0	.00	0	.235	.316	.294
1995	California	AL		14	21	5	1	1	0	8	3	3	0	0	5	0	1	0	0	0	.00	1	.238	.238	.381
9 Min. YEARS				830	2863	726	95	24	24	941	381	303	236	7	436	48	46	30	80	47	.63	87	.254	.318	.329
3 Maj. YEARS				84	166	43	7	1	0	52	19	12	6	0	25	6	6	0	2	4	.33	2	.259	.309	.313

Tim Cossins

Bats: Right **Throws:** Right **Pos:** C **Ht:** 6'1" **Wt:** 192 **Born:** 3/31/70 **Age:** 27

				BATTING															BASERUNNING				PERCENTAGES		
Year	Team	Lg	Org	G	AB	H	2B	3B	HR	TB	R	RBI	TBB	IBB	SO	HBP	SH	SF	SB	CS	SB%	GDP	Avg	OBP	SLG
1993	Erie	A-	Tex	4	10	4	1	0	0	5	1	3	2	0	0	0	0	0	0	1	.00	0	.400	.500	.500
	Charlstn-SC	A	Tex	27	89	13	2	0	0	15	8	10	7	0	21	3	0	1	0	1	.00	3	.146	.230	.169
1994	Hudson Vall	A-	Tex	6	17	2	1	0	1	6	1	2	0	0	4	0	0	0	0	0	.00	0	.118	.118	.353
	Charlotte	A+	Tex	10	28	3	0	0	0	3	2	2	4	0	6	0	1	0	1	0	1.00	1	.107	.219	.107
1995	Rangers	R	Tex	2	4	0	0	0	0	0	0	0	0	0	1	0	0	0	0	0	.00	0	.000	.000	.000
	Charlstn-SC	A	Tex	22	59	12	5	0	1	20	8	8	9	0	13	1	0	0	2	0	1.00	2	.203	.319	.339
	Charlotte	A+	Tex	7	17	1	0	0	0	1	1	0	4	1	5	0	0	0	0	1	.00	0	.059	.238	.059
1996	Tulsa	AA	Tex	3	4	2	0	0	0	2	0	1	3	0	0	0	0	0	0	0	.00	0	.500	.714	.500
	Charlotte	A+	Tex	67	233	56	16	0	3	81	34	32	13	0	44	2	3	2	1	1	.50	11	.240	.284	.348
4 Min. YEARS				148	461	93	25	0	5	133	55	58	42	1	94	6	4	3	4	4	.50	17	.202	.275	.289

Tony Costa

Pitches: Right **Bats:** Right **Pos:** P **Ht:** 6'4" **Wt:** 210 **Born:** 12/19/70 **Age:** 26

				HOW MUCH HE PITCHED						WHAT HE GAVE UP												THE RESULTS					
Year	Team	Lg	Org	G	GS	CG	GF	IP	BFP	H	R	ER	HR	SH	SF	HB	TBB	IBB	SO	WP	Bk	W	L	Pct.	ShO	Sv	ERA
1992	Martinsvlle	R+	Phi	12	4	0	6	24.2	133	44	40	25	3	0	0	2	13	0	21	5	3	0	4	.000	0	1	9.12
1993	Batavia	A-	Phi	10	9	0	0	51	228	56	32	28	1	3	3	2	19	0	37	5	0	3	4	.429	0	0	4.94
1994	Spartanburg	A	Phi	17	17	2	0	116.1	487	109	60	46	11	5	0	13	31	0	106	4	2	6	9	.400	0	0	3.56
	Clearwater	A+	Phi	8	8	1	0	47	204	44	25	22	3	0	1	0	31	0	27	1	0	3	5	.375	1	0	4.21
1995	Clearwater	A+	Phi	25	25	2	0	145	631	155	75	62	5	6	5	10	39	0	71	11	4	9	10	.474	1	0	3.85
1996	Reading	AA	Phi	27	26	1	0	153.1	702	150	107	82	20	5	4	14	92	2	112	16	3	5	13	.278	0	0	4.81
5 Min. YEARS				99	89	6	6	537.1	2385	558	339	265	43	19	13	41	225	2	374	42	12	26	45	.366	2	1	4.44

Tim Costo

Bats: Right **Throws:** Right **Pos:** 1B **Ht:** 6' 5" **Wt:** 230 **Born:** 2/16/69 **Age:** 28

		BATTING															BASERUNNING				PERCENTAGES		
Year Team	Lg Org	G	AB	H	2B	3B	HR	TB	R	RBI	TBB	IBB	SO	HBP	SH	SF	SB	CS	SB%	GDP	Avg	OBP	SLG
1990 Kinston	A+ Cle	56	206	65	13	1	4	92	34	42	23	0	47	6	0	8	4	0	1.00	3	.316	.387	.447
1991 Canton-Akrn	AA Cle	52	192	52	10	3	1	71	28	24	15	0	44	0	0	6	2	1	.67	10	.271	.315	.370
Chattanooga	AA Cin	85	293	82	19	3	5	122	31	29	20	0	65	4	0	2	11	4	.73	5	.280	.332	.416
1992 Chattanooga	AA Cin	121	424	102	18	2	28	208	63	71	48	1	128	11	1	2	4	5	.44	10	.241	.332	.491
1993 Indianapolis	AAA Cin	106	362	118	30	2	11	185	49	57	22	1	60	5	1	1	3	2	.60	5	.326	.372	.511
1994 Indianapolis	AAA Cin	19	36	7	3	0	0	10	6	5	6	0	4	1	1	0	0	0	.00	0	.194	.326	.278
1995 Buffalo	AAA Cle	105	324	80	11	2	11	128	41	60	27	0	65	8	3	7	2	0	1.00	7	.247	.314	.395
1996 Buffalo	AAA Cle	83	252	54	12	0	8	90	25	28	19	4	59	0	4	1	1	2	.33	7	.214	.268	.357
1992 Cincinnati	NL	12	36	8	2	0	0	10	3	2	5	0	6	0	0	1	0	0	.00	4	.222	.310	.278
1993 Cincinnati	NL	31	98	22	5	0	3	36	13	12	4	0	17	0	0	2	0	0	.00	1	.224	.250	.367
7 Min. YEARS		627	2089	560	116	13	68	906	277	316	180	6	472	35	10	27	27	14	.66	47	.268	.332	.434
2 Maj. YEARS		43	134	30	7	0	3	46	16	14	9	0	23	0	0	3	0	0	.00	5	.224	.267	.343

John Cotton

Bats: Left **Throws:** Right **Pos:** OF **Ht:** 6'0" **Wt:** 170 **Born:** 10/30/70 **Age:** 26

		BATTING															BASERUNNING				PERCENTAGES		
Year Team	Lg Org	G	AB	H	2B	3B	HR	TB	R	RBI	TBB	IBB	SO	HBP	SH	SF	SB	CS	SB%	GDP	Avg	OBP	SLG
1989 Burlington	R+ Cle	64	227	47	5	1	2	60	36	22	22	0	56	3	4	1	20	3	.87	5	.207	.285	.264
1990 Watertown	A- Cle	73	286	60	9	4	2	83	53	27	40	3	71	2	2	1	24	7	.77	4	.210	.310	.290
1991 Columbus	A Cle	122	405	92	11	9	13	160	88	42	93	1	135	3	3	3	56	15	.79	6	.227	.373	.395
1992 Kinston	A+ Cle	103	360	72	7	3	11	118	67	39	48	1	106	2	1	2	23	7	.77	3	.200	.296	.328
1993 Kinston	A+ Cle	127	454	120	16	3	13	181	81	51	59	1	130	11	5	2	28	24	.54	3	.264	.361	.399
1994 Springfield	A SD	24	82	19	5	3	1	33	14	8	12	0	19	0	0	0	7	1	.88	0	.232	.330	.402
Wichita	AA SD	34	85	16	4	0	3	29	9	14	13	3	20	1	0	2	2	0	1.00	3	.188	.297	.341
Rancho Cuca	A+ SD	48	171	35	3	2	4	54	35	19	22	0	48	2	0	0	9	3	.75	3	.205	.303	.316
1995 Memphis	AA SD	121	407	103	19	8	12	174	60	47	38	0	101	4	6	4	15	6	.71	2	.253	.320	.428
1996 Toledo	AAA Det	50	171	32	7	1	4	53	14	19	7	0	64	2	2	0	4	4	.50	1	.187	.228	.310
Jacksonvlle	AA Det	63	217	52	7	4	13	106	34	39	19	2	66	2	0	1	15	3	.83	2	.240	.305	.488
8 Min. YEARS		829	2865	648	93	38	78	1051	491	327	373	11	816	32	23	16	203	73	.74	32	.226	.320	.367

Kevin Coughlin

Bats: Left **Throws:** Left **Pos:** 1B-OF **Ht:** 6'0" **Wt:** 175 **Born:** 9/7/70 **Age:** 26

		BATTING															BASERUNNING				PERCENTAGES		
Year Team	Lg Org	G	AB	H	2B	3B	HR	TB	R	RBI	TBB	IBB	SO	HBP	SH	SF	SB	CS	SB%	GDP	Avg	OBP	SLG
1989 White Sox	R ChA	24	74	19	2	0	0	21	11	13	12	0	8	0	0	0	9	2	.82	1	.257	.360	.284
1990 Utica	A- ChA	68	215	59	6	3	0	71	37	16	27	2	41	0	3	2	17	8	.68	4	.274	.352	.330
1991 South Bend	A ChA	131	431	131	12	2	0	147	60	38	62	3	67	2	19	3	19	17	.53	6	.304	.392	.341
1992 White Sox	R ChA	4	15	5	0	0	0	5	1	2	2	0	1	0	0	0	0	0	.00	0	.333	.412	.333
Sarasota	A+ ChA	81	291	79	7	1	1	91	39	28	22	1	51	2	8	1	14	4	.78	3	.271	.326	.313
1993 Sarasota	A+ ChA	112	415	128	19	2	2	157	53	32	42	5	51	0	4	2	4	4	.50	9	.308	.370	.378
Nashville	AAA ChA	2	7	4	1	0	0	5	0	3	0	0	1	0	0	0	0	0	.00	0	.571	.571	.714
1994 Birmingham	AA ChA	112	369	95	10	0	0	105	51	26	40	3	42	3	4	4	5	8	.38	9	.257	.332	.285
1995 Nashville	AAA ChA	10	22	4	1	0	0	5	0	0	4	0	3	0	0	0	0	1	.00	1	.182	.308	.227
Birmingham	AA ChA	96	327	126	29	2	3	168	56	49	34	7	43	5	8	2	5	2	.71	3	.385	.448	.514
1996 Trenton	AA Bos	52	170	46	2	1	0	50	24	18	22	4	24	3	4	3	5	4	.56	2	.271	.359	.294
8 Min. YEARS		692	2336	696	89	11	6	825	332	225	267	25	332	15	50	17	78	50	.61	38	.298	.371	.353

Craig Counsell

Bats: Left **Throws:** Right **Pos:** 2B **Ht:** 6' 0" **Wt:** 170 **Born:** 8/21/70 **Age:** 26

		BATTING															BASERUNNING				PERCENTAGES		
Year Team	Lg Org	G	AB	H	2B	3B	HR	TB	R	RBI	TBB	IBB	SO	HBP	SH	SF	SB	CS	SB%	GDP	Avg	OBP	SLG
1992 Bend	A- Col	18	61	15	6	1	0	23	11	8	9	1	10	1	1	0	1	2	.33	2	.246	.352	.377
1993 Central Val	A+ Col	131	471	132	26	3	5	179	79	59	95	1	68	3	5	4	14	8	.64	8	.280	.401	.380
1994 New Haven	AA Col	83	300	84	20	1	5	121	47	37	37	4	32	5	1	2	4	1	.80	6	.280	.366	.403
1995 Colo. Sprng	AAA Col	118	399	112	22	6	5	161	60	53	34	7	47	2	3	6	10	2	.83	11	.281	.336	.404
1996 Colo. Sprng	AAA Col	25	75	18	3	0	2	27	17	10	24	1	7	0	0	0	4	3	.57	2	.240	.424	.360
1995 Colorado	NL	3	1	0	0	0	0	0	0	0	1	0	0	0	0	0	0	0	.00	0	.000	.500	.000
5 Min. YEARS		375	1306	361	77	11	17	511	214	167	199	14	164	11	10	12	33	16	.67	29	.276	.374	.391

John Courtright

Pitches: Left **Bats:** Left **Pos:** P **Ht:** 6' 2" **Wt:** 185 **Born:** 5/30/70 **Age:** 27

		HOW MUCH HE PITCHED						WHAT HE GAVE UP												THE RESULTS					
Year Team	Lg Org	G	GS	CG	GF	IP	BFP	H	R	ER	HR	SH	SF	HB	TBB	IBB	SO	WP	Bk	W	L	Pct.	ShO	Sv	ERA
1991 Billings	R+ Cin	1	1	0	0	6	21	2	0	0	0	0	0	0	1	0	4	0	1	1	0	1.000	0	0	0.00
1992 Charlstn-WV	A Cin	27	26	1	0	173	688	147	64	48	5	5	4	7	55	2	147	9	5	10	5	.667	1	0	2.50
1993 Chattanooga	AA Cin	27	27	1	0	175	752	179	81	68	5	8	11	8	70	6	96	5	2	5	11	.313	0	0	3.50
1994 Chattanooga	AA Cin	4	4	0	0	21.2	95	19	16	13	2	2	1	1	14	0	12	1	0	1	2	.333	0	0	5.40
Indianapolis	AAA Cin	24	23	2	0	142	595	144	61	56	9	8	1	4	46	3	73	2	1	9	10	.474	2	0	3.55
1995 Indianapolis	AAA Cin	13	2	0	1	33.2	147	29	18	16	2	2	1	2	15	1	13	4	1	2	1	.667	0	0	4.28
Salt Lake	AAA Min	31	19	1	1	118.1	531	137	88	80	8	7	8	2	51	8	55	8	3	5	8	.385	0	0	6.08
1996 New Britain	AA Min	14	3	0	3	32.2	154	42	25	24	2	3	1	1	16	0	12	1	2	1	1	.500	0	0	6.61

		HOW MUCH HE PITCHED						WHAT HE GAVE UP												THE RESULTS					
Year Team	Lg Org	G	GS	CG	GF	IP	BFP	H	R	ER	HR	SH	SF	HB	TBB	IBB	SO	WP	Bk	W	L	Pct.	ShO	Sv	ERA
Bowie	AA Bal	9	0	0	3	15.1	75	19	15	11	2	1	0	1	8	1	10	0	0	0	0	.000	0	0	6.46
Chattanooga	AA Cin	9	9	0	0	60.1	236	52	18	16	3	1	3	2	11	0	36	2	1	8	0	1.000	0	0	2.39
1995 Cincinnati	NL	1	0	0	0	1	5	2	1	1	0	1	0	0	0	0	0	0	0	0	0	.000	0	0	9.00
6 Min. YEARS		159	114	5	8	778	3294	770	386	332	38	37	30	28	287	21	458	32	16	42	38	.525	3	0	3.84

Darron Cox

Bats: Right **Throws:** Right **Pos:** C **Ht:** 6'1" **Wt:** 205 **Born:** 11/21/67 **Age:** 29

		BATTING															BASERUNNING				PERCENTAGES		
Year Team	Lg Org	G	AB	H	2B	3B	HR	TB	R	RBI	TBB	IBB	SO	HBP	SH	SF	SB	CS	SB%	GDP	Avg	OBP	SLG
1989 Billings	R+ Cin	49	157	43	6	0	0	49	20	18	21	0	34	5	2	0	11	3	.79	1	.274	.377	.312
1990 Charlstn-WV	A Cin	103	367	93	11	3	1	113	53	44	40	2	75	7	4	3	14	3	.82	12	.253	.336	.308
1991 Cedar Rapds	A Cin	21	60	16	4	0	0	20	12	4	8	0	11	4	1	0	7	1	.88	2	.267	.389	.333
Chattanooga	AA Cin	13	38	7	1	0	0	8	2	3	2	0	9	0	1	1	0	0	.00	1	.184	.220	.211
Charlstn-WV	A Cin	79	294	71	14	1	2	93	37	28	24	0	40	2	1	7	8	4	.67	7	.241	.297	.316
1992 Chattanooga	AA Cin	98	331	84	19	1	1	108	29	38	15	0	63	5	1	6	8	3	.73	7	.254	.291	.326
1993 Chattanooga	AA Cin	89	300	65	9	5	3	93	35	26	38	2	63	3	7	1	7	4	.64	7	.217	.310	.310
1994 Iowa	AAA ChN	99	301	80	15	1	3	106	35	26	28	4	47	4	3	0	5	2	.71	12	.266	.336	.352
1995 Orlando	AA ChN	33	102	29	5	0	4	46	8	15	8	0	16	1	2	2	3	3	.50	3	.284	.336	.451
Iowa	AAA ChN	33	94	22	6	0	1	31	7	14	8	0	21	2	2	4	0	0	.00	0	.234	.296	.330
1996 Richmond	AAA Atl	55	168	40	9	0	3	58	19	20	5	0	22	3	2	2	1	0	1.00	5	.238	.270	.345
8 Min. YEARS		672	2212	550	99	11	18	725	257	236	197	8	401	36	26	26	64	23	.74	57	.249	.317	.328

Steven Cox

Bats: Left **Throws:** Left **Pos:** 1B **Ht:** 6'4" **Wt:** 200 **Born:** 10/31/74 **Age:** 22

		BATTING															BASERUNNING				PERCENTAGES		
Year Team	Lg Org	G	AB	H	2B	3B	HR	TB	R	RBI	TBB	IBB	SO	HBP	SH	SF	SB	CS	SB%	GDP	Avg	OBP	SLG
1992 Athletics	R Oak	52	184	43	4	1	1	52	30	35	27	1	51	3	0	2	2	1	.67	2	.234	.338	.283
1993 Sou. Oregon	A- Oak	15	57	18	4	1	2	30	10	16	5	0	15	0	0	2	0	0	.00	0	.316	.359	.526
1994 W. Michigan	A Oak	99	311	75	19	2	6	116	37	32	41	3	95	4	1	3	2	6	.25	5	.241	.334	.373
1995 Modesto	A+ Oak	132	483	144	29	3	30	269	95	110	84	6	88	14	0	10	5	4	.56	12	.298	.409	.557
1996 Huntsville	AA Oak	104	381	107	21	1	12	166	59	61	51	6	65	6	2	3	2	2	.50	10	.281	.372	.436
5 Min. YEARS		402	1416	387	77	8	51	633	231	254	208	16	314	27	3	20	11	13	.46	29	.273	.372	.447

Rickey Cradle

Bats: Right **Throws:** Right **Pos:** OF **Ht:** 6'2" **Wt:** 180 **Born:** 6/20/73 **Age:** 24

		BATTING															BASERUNNING				PERCENTAGES		
Year Team	Lg Org	G	AB	H	2B	3B	HR	TB	R	RBI	TBB	IBB	SO	HBP	SH	SF	SB	CS	SB%	GDP	Avg	OBP	SLG
1991 Blue Jays	R Tor	44	132	28	4	3	1	41	16	6	24	1	37	3	1	1	4	5	.44	0	.212	.344	.311
1992 Medicne Hat	R+ Tor	65	217	49	8	0	9	84	38	36	42	0	69	6	1	2	16	2	.89	5	.226	.363	.387
1993 Hagerstown	A Tor	129	441	112	26	4	13	185	72	62	68	2	125	11	1	4	19	14	.58	5	.254	.365	.420
1994 Dunedin	A+ Tor	114	344	88	14	3	10	138	65	39	59	0	87	9	0	1	20	10	.67	5	.256	.378	.401
1995 Knoxville	AA Tor	41	117	21	5	1	4	40	17	13	17	0	29	3	1	1	3	3	.50	3	.179	.297	.342
Dunedin	A+ Tor	50	178	49	10	3	7	86	33	27	28	0	49	2	1	2	6	2	.75	2	.275	.376	.483
1996 Knoxville	AA Tor	92	333	94	23	2	12	157	59	47	55	1	65	10	7	7	15	11	.58	2	.282	.393	.471
Syracuse	AAA Tor	40	130	26	5	3	8	61	22	22	14	1	39	1	0	2	1	0	1.00	2	.200	.279	.469
6 Min. YEARS		575	1892	467	95	19	64	792	322	252	307	5	500	45	12	20	84	47	.64	24	.247	.362	.419

Jay Cranford

Bats: Right **Throws:** Right **Pos:** 3B **Ht:** 6'3" **Wt:** 175 **Born:** 4/7/71 **Age:** 26

		BATTING															BASERUNNING				PERCENTAGES		
Year Team	Lg Org	G	AB	H	2B	3B	HR	TB	R	RBI	TBB	IBB	SO	HBP	SH	SF	SB	CS	SB%	GDP	Avg	OBP	SLG
1992 Welland	A- Pit	60	223	57	9	6	0	78	22	27	14	1	58	0	0	2	7	7	.50	0	.256	.297	.350
1993 Augusta	A Pit	128	469	125	31	0	6	174	55	72	32	0	101	6	3	9	17	2	.89	6	.267	.316	.371
1994 Salem	A+ Pit	110	417	110	27	4	13	184	66	53	23	0	97	6	0	3	6	6	.50	8	.264	.310	.441
Carolina	AA Pit	17	59	11	3	0	0	14	9	5	6	1	15	1	1	2	0	0	.00	1	.186	.265	.237
1995 Carolina	AA Pit	93	288	66	12	1	5	95	30	42	52	1	67	4	2	7	3	4	.43	6	.229	.348	.330
1996 Carolina	AA Pit	90	268	72	15	2	2	97	34	37	47	4	68	3	0	3	6	4	.60	3	.269	.380	.362
5 Min. YEARS		498	1724	441	97	13	26	642	216	236	174	7	406	20	6	26	39	23	.63	24	.256	.327	.372

Joe Crawford

Pitches: Left **Bats:** Left **Pos:** P **Ht:** 6'3" **Wt:** 225 **Born:** 5/2/70 **Age:** 27

		HOW MUCH HE PITCHED						WHAT HE GAVE UP												THE RESULTS					
Year Team	Lg Org	G	GS	CG	GF	IP	BFP	H	R	ER	HR	SH	SF	HB	TBB	IBB	SO	WP	Bk	W	L	Pct.	ShO	Sv	ERA
1991 Kingsport	R+ NYN	19	0	0	16	32.1	118	16	5	4	0	0	0	1	8	0	43	3	1	0	0	.000	0	11	1.11
Columbia	A NYN	3	0	0	2	3	9	0	0	0	0	0	0	0	0	0	6	0	0	0	0	.000	0	0	0.00
1992 St. Lucie	A+ NYN	25	1	0	16	43.2	174	29	18	10	1	1	3	0	15	3	32	1	3	3	3	.500	0	3	2.06
1993 St. Lucie	A+ NYN	34	0	0	19	37	156	38	15	15	0	2	0	2	14	5	24	0	0	3	3	.500	0	5	3.65
1994 St. Lucie	A+ NYN	33	0	0	15	42.2	155	22	8	7	1	1	2	2	9	2	31	1	0	1	1	.500	0	5	1.48
Binghamton	AA NYN	13	0	0	6	14.2	70	20	10	9	2	0	2	0	8	0	9	0	0	1	0	1.000	0	0	5.52
1995 Norfolk	AAA NYN	8	0	0	1	18.2	70	9	5	4	0	1	0	0	4	0	13	0	0	1	1	.500	0	0	1.93
Binghamton	AA NYN	50	1	0	16	79.1	309	57	22	19	4	4	7	5	21	4	56	3	1	8	3	.727	0	0	2.16
1996 Binghamton	AA NYN	7	7	1	0	49.2	190	34	10	8	4	2	0	0	9	1	34	1	2	5	1	.833	1	0	1.45

		HOW MUCH HE PITCHED						WHAT HE GAVE UP												THE RESULTS					
Year Team	Lg Org	G	GS	CG	GF	IP	BFP	H	R	ER	HR	SH	SF	HB	TBB	IBB	SO	WP	Bk	W	L	Pct.	ShO	Sv	ERA
Norfolk	AAA NYN	20	16	2	2	96.2	403	98	45	37	10	3	1	4	20	1	68	0	1	6	5	.545	1	0	3.44
6 Min. YEARS		212	25	3	93	417.2	1654	323	138	113	22	14	15	14	108	16	316	9	8	28	17	.622	2	24	2.43

Pitches: Right **Bats:** Right **Pos:** P

Ryan Creek

Ht: 6'1" **Wt:** 180 **Born:** 9/24/72 **Age:** 24

		HOW MUCH HE PITCHED						WHAT HE GAVE UP												THE RESULTS					
Year Team	Lg Org	G	GS	CG	GF	IP	BFP	H	R	ER	HR	SH	SF	HB	TBB	IBB	SO	WP	Bk	W	L	Pct.	ShO	Sv	ERA
1993 Astros	R Hou	12	11	2	1	69.1	291	53	22	18	0	1	5	4	30	0	62	6	0	7	3	.700	1	1	2.34
1994 Quad City	A Hou	21	15	0	3	74	356	86	62	41	6	3	5	14	41	2	66	9	3	3	5	.375	0	0	4.99
1995 Jackson	AA Hou	26	24	1	1	143.2	622	137	74	58	11	6	8	6	64	0	120	12	2	9	7	.563	1	0	3.63
1996 Jackson	AA Hou	27	26	1	1	142	674	139	95	83	9	3	7	11	121	0	119	14	1	7	15	.318	0	0	5.26
4 Min. YEARS		86	76	4	6	429	1943	415	253	200	26	13	25	35	256	2	367	41	6	26	30	.464	2	1	4.20

Pitches: Right **Bats:** Right **Pos:** P

Andy Croghan

Ht: 6'5" **Wt:** 205 **Born:** 10/26/69 **Age:** 27

		HOW MUCH HE PITCHED						WHAT HE GAVE UP												THE RESULTS					
Year Team	Lg Org	G	GS	CG	GF	IP	BFP	H	R	ER	HR	SH	SF	HB	TBB	IBB	SO	WP	Bk	W	L	Pct.	ShO	Sv	ERA
1991 Oneonta	A- NYA	14	14	0	0	78.1	352	92	59	49	6	1	1	2	28	0	54	5	0	5	4	.556	0	0	5.63
1992 Greensboro	A NYA	33	19	1	3	122.1	544	128	78	61	11	2	9	3	57	0	98	9	0	10	8	.556	0	0	4.49
1993 Pr. William	A+ NYA	39	14	1	19	105	455	117	66	56	9	4	4	3	27	0	80	6	0	5	11	.313	0	11	4.80
1994 Albany-Colo	AA NYA	36	0	0	33	36.2	153	33	7	7	1	2	1	0	14	0	38	1	0	0	1	.000	0	16	1.72
Columbus	AAA NYA	21	0	0	17	24	110	25	11	11	6	5	0	0	13	1	28	3	0	2	2	.500	0	8	4.13
1995 Columbus	AAA NYA	20	0	0	13	25	113	21	10	10	1	0	0	1	22	0	22	1	2	1	1	.500	0	4	3.60
1996 Columbus	AAA NYA	14	0	0	3	22.1	108	27	24	21	6	3	1	2	13	0	21	3	0	2	0	1.000	0	0	8.46
Norwich	AA NYA	35	0	0	19	41	181	41	23	14	4	2	0	1	16	3	49	5	0	9	5	.643	0	4	3.07
6 Min. YEARS		212	47	2	107	454.2	2016	484	278	229	44	19	16	12	190	4	390	33	2	34	32	.515	0	43	4.53

Bats: Left **Throws:** Right **Pos:** SS

Brandon Cromer

Ht: 6'2" **Wt:** 175 **Born:** 1/25/74 **Age:** 23

		BATTING															BASERUNNING				PERCENTAGES		
Year Team	Lg Org	G	AB	H	2B	3B	HR	TB	R	RBI	TBB	IBB	SO	HBP	SH	SF	SB	CS	SB%	GDP	Avg	OBP	SLG
1992 Blue Jays	R Tor	49	180	51	12	3	1	72	26	21	14	0	26	5	2	2	7	8	.47	2	.283	.348	.400
1993 St. Cathrns	A- Tor	75	278	64	9	2	5	92	29	20	21	2	64	1	3	1	2	4	.33	1	.230	.286	.331
1994 Hagerstown	A Tor	80	259	35	8	5	6	71	25	26	25	0	98	0	2	3	0	2	.00	4	.135	.209	.274
1995 Dunedin	A+ Tor	106	329	78	11	3	6	113	40	43	43	3	84	5	5	3	0	5	.00	6	.237	.332	.343
1996 Knoxville	AA Tor	98	318	88	15	8	7	140	56	32	60	3	84	2	2	3	3	6	.33	2	.277	.392	.440
5 Min. YEARS		408	1364	316	55	21	25	488	176	142	163	8	356	13	14	12	12	25	.32	15	.232	.317	.358

Bats: Right **Throws:** Right **Pos:** SS

Tripp Cromer

Ht: 6' 2" **Wt:** 170 **Born:** 11/21/67 **Age:** 29

		BATTING															BASERUNNING				PERCENTAGES		
Year Team	Lg Org	G	AB	H	2B	3B	HR	TB	R	RBI	TBB	IBB	SO	HBP	SH	SF	SB	CS	SB%	GDP	Avg	OBP	SLG
1989 Hamilton	A- StL	35	137	36	6	3	0	48	18	6	17	0	30	1	2	1	4	4	.50	5	.263	.346	.350
1990 St. Pete	A+ StL	121	408	88	12	5	5	125	53	38	46	0	79	5	3	5	7	12	.37	11	.216	.300	.306
1991 St. Pete	A+ StL	43	137	28	3	1	0	33	11	10	9	0	17	1	3	1	0	0	.00	8	.204	.257	.241
Arkansas	AA StL	73	227	52	12	1	1	69	28	18	15	1	37	3	2	3	0	1	.00	7	.229	.282	.304
1992 Arkansas	AA StL	110	339	81	16	6	7	130	30	29	22	1	82	4	4	2	4	6	.40	9	.239	.292	.383
Louisville	AAA StL	6	25	5	1	1	1	11	5	7	1	0	6	0	0	1	0	0	.00	0	.200	.222	.440
1993 Louisville	AAA StL	86	309	85	8	4	11	134	39	33	15	3	60	2	2	0	1	3	.25	10	.275	.313	.434
1994 Louisville	AAA StL	124	419	115	23	9	9	183	53	50	33	1	85	3	6	2	5	6	.45	12	.274	.330	.437
1996 Louisville	AAA StL	80	244	55	4	4	4	79	28	25	22	2	47	2	3	1	3	1	.75	12	.225	.294	.324
1993 St. Louis	NL	10	23	2	0	0	0	2	1	0	1	0	6	0	0	0	0	0	.00	0	.087	.125	.087
1994 St. Louis	NL	2	0	0	0	0	0	0	1	0	0	0	0	0	0	0	0	0	.00	0	.000	.000	.000
1995 St. Louis	NL	105	345	78	19	0	5	112	36	18	14	2	66	4	1	5	0	0	.00	14	.226	.261	.325
7 Min. YEARS		678	2245	545	85	34	38	812	265	216	180	8	443	21	25	16	24	33	.42	74	.243	.303	.362
3 Maj. YEARS		117	368	80	19	0	5	114	38	18	15	2	72	4	1	5	0	0	.00	14	.217	.253	.310

Bats: Left **Throws:** Right **Pos:** C

Mike Crosby

Ht: 6'1" **Wt:** 200 **Born:** 2/24/69 **Age:** 28

		BATTING															BASERUNNING				PERCENTAGES		
Year Team	Lg Org	G	AB	H	2B	3B	HR	TB	R	RBI	TBB	IBB	SO	HBP	SH	SF	SB	CS	SB%	GDP	Avg	OBP	SLG
1992 Columbus	A Cle	53	149	25	3	0	0	28	14	13	6	0	32	4	2	2	0	1	.00	3	.168	.217	.188
1993 Kinston	A+ Cle	72	203	44	9	0	3	62	20	17	7	0	45	3	4	2	1	2	.33	6	.217	.251	.305
1994 Canton-Akrn	AA Cle	55	162	36	7	1	2	51	12	10	4	0	44	2	4	0	1	1	.50	3	.222	.250	.315
1995 Canton-Akrn	AA Cle	75	224	37	5	1	5	59	18	20	10	0	60	3	7	1	1	1	.50	4	.165	.210	.263
1996 Fargo-Mh	IND —	3	9	1	0	0	0	1	0	0	0	0	0	0	1	0	0	0	.00	0	.111	.111	.111
Harrisburg	AA Mon	31	99	20	4	0	1	27	3	6	3	1	25	0	2	3	0	0	.00	3	.202	.219	.273
5 Min. YEARS		289	846	163	28	2	11	228	67	66	30	1	206	12	20	8	3	5	.38	19	.193	.229	.270

Rich Croushore

Pitches: Right **Bats:** Right **Pos:** P **Ht:** 6'4" **Wt:** 210 **Born:** 8/7/70 **Age:** 26

		HOW MUCH HE PITCHED						WHAT HE GAVE UP												THE RESULTS					
Year Team	Lg Org	G	GS	CG	GF	IP	BFP	H	R	ER	HR	SH	SF	HB	TBB	IBB	SO	WP	Bk	W	L	Pct.	ShO	Sv	ERA
1993 Glens Falls	A- StL	31	0	0	11	41.1	184	38	16	14	1	4	1	2	22	4	36	6	0	4	1	.800	0	1	3.05
1994 Madison	A StL	62	0	0	14	94.1	410	90	49	43	5	4	2	5	46	2	103	10	4	6	6	.500	0	0	4.10
1995 St. Pete	A+ StL	12	11	0	0	59	251	44	25	23	2	3	1	4	32	0	57	5	0	6	4	.600	0	0	3.51
1996 Arkansas	AA StL	34	17	2	11	108	486	113	75	59	18	4	1	2	51	1	85	7	0	5	10	.333	0	3	4.92
4 Min. YEARS		139	28	2	36	302.2	1331	285	165	139	26	15	5	13	151	7	281	28	4	21	21	.500	0	4	4.13

Dean Crow

Pitches: Right **Bats:** Left **Pos:** P **Ht:** 6'5" **Wt:** 212 **Born:** 8/21/72 **Age:** 24

		HOW MUCH HE PITCHED						WHAT HE GAVE UP												THE RESULTS					
Year Team	Lg Org	G	GS	CG	GF	IP	BFP	H	R	ER	HR	SH	SF	HB	TBB	IBB	SO	WP	Bk	W	L	Pct.	ShO	Sv	ERA
1993 Bellingham	A- Sea	25	0	0	12	47.2	190	31	14	10	1	1	2	0	21	1	38	0	0	5	3	.625	0	4	1.89
1994 Appleton	A Sea	16	0	0	8	15.1	80	25	15	12	4	2	3	1	7	4	11	1	0	2	4	.333	0	2	7.04
1995 Riverside	A+ Sea	51	0	0	47	61.2	249	54	21	18	1	3	2	3	13	0	46	2	0	3	4	.429	0	22	2.63
1996 Port City	AA Sea	60	0	0	49	68	285	64	35	23	4	5	1	1	20	1	43	6	0	2	3	.400	0	26	3.04
4 Min. YEARS		152	0	0	116	192.2	804	174	85	63	10	11	8	5	61	6	138	9	0	12	14	.462	0	54	2.94

Brent Crowther

Pitches: Right **Bats:** Right **Pos:** P **Ht:** 6'4" **Wt:** 220 **Born:** 5/15/72 **Age:** 25

		HOW MUCH HE PITCHED						WHAT HE GAVE UP												THE RESULTS					
Year Team	Lg Org	G	GS	CG	GF	IP	BFP	H	R	ER	HR	SH	SF	HB	TBB	IBB	SO	WP	Bk	W	L	Pct.	ShO	Sv	ERA
1994 Bend	A- Col	13	9	0	1	56	271	68	41	29	2	0	4	9	24	0	44	8	3	3	5	.375	0	0	4.66
1995 Salem	A+ Col	12	12	3	0	78.1	322	70	31	24	4	5	0	2	25	5	60	7	2	3	6	.333	1	0	2.76
Colo. Sprng	AAA Col	1	1	0	0	6	30	11	6	5	1	0	1	0	2	0	1	0	0	0	1	.000	0	0	7.50
Asheville	A Col	28	28	6	0	183	745	160	68	54	9	5	2	5	52	5	133	18	3	15	10	.600	4	0	2.66
1996 Salem	A+ Col	8	8	1	0	51.1	210	52	23	23	2	4	0	3	14	0	28	2	0	3	3	.500	1	0	4.03
New Haven	AA Col	25	12	0	2	85.2	385	109	64	59	10	8	1	1	30	5	54	2	2	3	7	.300	0	1	6.20
3 Min. YEARS		87	70	10	3	460.1	1963	470	233	194	28	22	8	20	147	15	320	37	10	27	32	.458	6	1	3.79

Ivan Cruz

Bats: Left **Throws:** Left **Pos:** 1B **Ht:** 6'3" **Wt:** 210 **Born:** 5/3/68 **Age:** 29

		BATTING															BASERUNNING				PERCENTAGES		
Year Team	Lg Org	G	AB	H	2B	3B	HR	TB	R	RBI	TBB	IBB	SO	HBP	SH	SF	SB	CS	SB%	GDP	Avg	OBP	SLG
1989 Niagara Fal	A- Det	64	226	62	11	2	7	98	43	40	27	4	29	3	0	1	2	0	1.00	2	.274	.358	.434
1990 Lakeland	A+ Det	118	414	118	23	2	11	178	61	73	49	3	71	5	2	4	8	1	.89	8	.285	.364	.430
1991 Toledo	AAA Det	8	29	4	0	0	1	7	2	4	2	0	12	1	0	0	0	0	.00	0	.138	.219	.241
London	AA Det	121	443	110	21	0	9	158	45	47	36	5	74	4	1	2	3	3	.50	12	.248	.309	.357
1992 London	AA Det	134	524	143	25	1	14	212	71	104	37	1	102	4	0	6	1	1	.50	16	.273	.322	.405
1993 Toledo	AAA Det	115	402	91	18	4	13	156	44	50	30	2	85	3	0	2	1	1	.50	5	.226	.284	.388
1994 Toledo	AAA Det	97	303	75	11	2	15	135	36	43	28	0	83	2	0	3	1	0	1.00	7	.248	.313	.446
1995 Toledo	AAA Det	11	36	7	2	0	0	9	5	3	6	0	9	0	0	1	0	0	.00	1	.194	.302	.250
Jacksonvlle	AA Det	108	397	112	17	1	31	224	65	93	60	15	94	0	0	3	0	0	.00	7	.282	.374	.564
1996 Columbus	AAA NYA	130	446	115	26	0	28	225	84	96	48	3	99	8	2	9	2	4	.33	9	.258	.335	.504
8 Min. YEARS		906	3220	837	154	12	129	1402	456	553	323	33	658	30	5	31	18	10	.64	67	.260	.330	.435

Jose Cruz

Bats: Both **Throws:** Right **Pos:** OF **Ht:** 6'0" **Wt:** 190 **Born:** 4/19/74 **Age:** 23

		BATTING															BASERUNNING				PERCENTAGES		
Year Team	Lg Org	G	AB	H	2B	3B	HR	TB	R	RBI	TBB	IBB	SO	HBP	SH	SF	SB	CS	SB%	GDP	Avg	OBP	SLG
1995 Everett	A- Sea	3	11	5	0	0	0	5	6	2	3	0	3	0	0	0	1	0	1.00	0	.455	.571	.455
Riverside	A+ Sea	35	144	37	7	1	7	67	34	29	24	1	50	0	0	2	3	1	.75	1	.257	.359	.465
1996 Lancaster	A+ Sea	53	203	66	17	1	6	103	38	43	39	1	33	0	0	6	7	1	.88	4	.325	.423	.507
Port City	AA Sea	47	181	51	10	2	3	74	39	31	27	4	38	0	0	1	5	0	1.00	8	.282	.373	.409
Tacoma	AAA Sea	22	76	18	1	2	6	41	15	15	18	1	12	0	1	0	1	1	.50	2	.237	.383	.539
2 Min. YEARS		160	615	177	35	6	22	290	132	120	111	7	136	0	1	9	17	3	.85	15	.288	.392	.472

Nelson Cruz

Pitches: Right **Bats:** Right **Pos:** P **Ht:** 6'1" **Wt:** 160 **Born:** 9/13/72 **Age:** 24

		HOW MUCH HE PITCHED						WHAT HE GAVE UP												THE RESULTS					
Year Team	Lg Org	G	GS	CG	GF	IP	BFP	H	R	ER	HR	SH	SF	HB	TBB	IBB	SO	WP	Bk	W	L	Pct.	ShO	Sv	ERA
1991 Expos	R Mon	12	8	1	0	48.1	207	40	18	13	1	3	1	2	19	0	34	2	3	2	4	.333	1	0	2.42
1995 Bristol	R+ ChA	1	0	0	1	1	6	2	1	1	0	0	1	1	0	0	0	0	0	0	0	.000	0	0	9.00
Pr. William	A+ ChA	9	0	0	7	19.1	75	12	1	1	1	0	0	2	6	0	18	0	0	2	1	.667	0	1	0.47
Hickory	A ChA	54	0	0	37	87	366	79	33	22	7	3	2	7	21	2	86	5	0	4	8	.333	0	10	2.28
1996 Birmingham	AA ChA	37	18	2	8	149	627	150	65	53	10	7	6	8	41	2	142	3	1	6	6	.500	1	1	3.20
3 Min. YEARS		113	26	3	53	304.2	1281	283	118	90	19	13	10	20	87	4	280	10	4	14	19	.424	2	12	2.66

Chris Cumberland

Pitches: Left **Bats:** Right **Pos:** P **Ht:** 6'1" **Wt:** 185 **Born:** 1/15/73 **Age:** 24

Year Team	Lg	Org	G	GS	CG	GF	IP	BFP	H	R	ER	HR	SH	SF	HB	TBB	IBB	SO	WP	Bk	W	L	Pct.	ShO	Sv	ERA
			HOW MUCH HE PITCHED						WHAT HE GAVE UP												THE RESULTS					
1993 Oneonta	A-	NYA	15	15	0	0	89	393	109	43	33	2	1	5	0	28	0	62	6	2	4	4	.500	0	0	3.34
1994 Greensboro	A	NYA	22	22	1	0	137.2	559	123	55	45	9	4	2	4	41	0	95	11	2	14	5	.737	1	0	2.94
1995 Yankees	R	NYA	4	4	0	0	7	26	3	1	1	0	0	0	0	1	0	7	0	0	0	1	.000	0	0	1.29
Tampa	A+	NYA	9	9	0	0	31.2	130	31	11	6	1	1	0	1	6	0	17	1	0	1	3	.250	0	0	1.71
1996 Columbus	AAA	NYA	12	12	1	0	58	272	86	45	42	9	4	1	4	23	0	35	3	0	2	7	.222	0	0	6.52
Norwich	AA	NYA	16	16	2	0	95.2	427	112	73	56	13	2	5	4	37	2	44	4	0	5	7	.417	1	0	5.27
4 Min. YEARS			78	78	4	0	419	1807	464	228	183	34	12	13	13	136	2	260	25	4	26	27	.491	2	0	3.93

Will Cunnane

Pitches: Right **Bats:** Right **Pos:** P **Ht:** 6'2" **Wt:** 165 **Born:** 4/24/74 **Age:** 23

Year Team	Lg	Org	G	GS	CG	GF	IP	BFP	H	R	ER	HR	SH	SF	HB	TBB	IBB	SO	WP	Bk	W	L	Pct.	ShO	Sv	ERA
			HOW MUCH HE PITCHED						WHAT HE GAVE UP												THE RESULTS					
1993 Marlins	R	Fla	16	9	0	4	66.2	290	75	32	20	1	3	0	0	8	0	64	2	1	3	3	.500	0	2	2.70
1994 Kane County	A	Fla	32	16	5	6	138.2	540	110	27	22	2	4	1	6	23	4	106	5	1	11	3	.786	4	1	1.43
1995 Portland	AA	Fla	21	21	1	0	117.2	497	120	48	48	10	3	0	5	34	1	83	2	0	9	2	.818	1	0	3.67
1996 Portland	AA	Fla	25	25	4	0	151.2	631	156	73	63	15	5	2	1	30	6	101	4	0	10	12	.455	0	0	3.74
4 Min. YEARS			94	71	10	10	474.2	1958	461	180	153	28	15	3	12	95	11	354	13	2	33	20	.623	5	3	2.90

Chris Curtis

Pitches: Right **Bats:** Right **Pos:** P **Ht:** 6'2" **Wt:** 185 **Born:** 5/8/71 **Age:** 26

Year Team	Lg	Org	G	GS	CG	GF	IP	BFP	H	R	ER	HR	SH	SF	HB	TBB	IBB	SO	WP	Bk	W	L	Pct.	ShO	Sv	ERA
			HOW MUCH HE PITCHED						WHAT HE GAVE UP												THE RESULTS					
1991 Butte	R+	Tex	6	3	0	2	12.2	69	27	23	14	1	0	0	1	4	0	7	0	3	0	2	.000	0	0	9.95
Rangers	R	Tex	7	7	0	0	35	134	27	9	8	1	0	4	2	9	0	23	0	2	4	0	1.000	0	0	2.06
1992 Gastonia	A	Tex	24	24	1	0	147	590	117	60	43	3	1	5	6	54	0	107	6	7	8	11	.421	1	0	2.63
1993 Charlotte	A+	Tex	27	26	1	0	151	637	159	76	67	6	4	2	8	51	0	55	4	5	8	8	.500	0	0	3.99
1994 Tulsa	AA	Tex	25	23	3	1	142.2	639	173	102	85	17	4	7	7	57	5	62	9	7	3	13	.188	1	0	5.36
1995 Okla. City	AAA	Tex	51	0	0	22	77.1	358	81	53	43	5	6	3	5	39	3	40	2	0	3	5	.375	0	5	5.00
1996 Okla. City	AAA	Tex	41	2	0	13	75.2	344	91	50	43	6	4	2	3	34	3	38	10	1	2	5	.286	0	1	5.11
6 Min. YEARS			181	85	5	38	641.1	2771	675	373	303	39	19	23	32	248	11	332	31	25	28	44	.389	2	6	4.25

Kevin Curtis

Bats: Right **Throws:** Right **Pos:** OF **Ht:** 6'2" **Wt:** 210 **Born:** 8/19/72 **Age:** 24

Year Team	Lg	Org	G	AB	H	2B	3B	HR	TB	R	RBI	TBB	IBB	SO	HBP	SH	SF	SB	CS	SB%	GDP	Avg	OBP	SLG
			BATTING															BASERUNNING				PERCENTAGES		
1993 Albany	A	Bal	59	180	36	7	0	7	64	26	27	38	0	36	3	1	1	4	3	.57	6	.200	.347	.356
1994 Orioles	R	Bal	12	38	15	5	0	1	23	3	4	6	0	4	0	0	0	1	0	1.00	1	.395	.477	.605
Albany	A	Bal	20	67	15	3	0	1	21	5	7	8	0	14	2	0	0	0	2	.00	1	.224	.325	.313
1995 High Desert	A+	Bal	112	399	117	26	1	21	208	70	70	54	1	83	12	0	5	8	6	.57	7	.293	.389	.521
1996 Bowie	AA	Bal	129	460	113	21	2	18	192	69	58	54	4	95	3	0	1	2	1	.67	10	.246	.328	.417
4 Min. YEARS			332	1144	296	62	3	48	508	173	166	160	5	232	20	1	7	15	12	.56	25	.259	.358	.444

Jim Czajkowski

Pitches: Right **Bats:** Both **Pos:** P **Ht:** 6' 4" **Wt:** 215 **Born:** 12/18/63 **Age:** 33

Year Team	Lg	Org	G	GS	CG	GF	IP	BFP	H	R	ER	HR	SH	SF	HB	TBB	IBB	SO	WP	Bk	W	L	Pct.	ShO	Sv	ERA
			HOW MUCH HE PITCHED						WHAT HE GAVE UP												THE RESULTS					
1986 Idaho Falls	R+	Atl	16	13	3	1	88.2	0	90	44	36	5	0	0	3	16	0	46	3	0	7	5	.583	0	0	3.65
1987 Sumter	A	Atl	50	0	0	40	68.2	288	63	26	17	2	2	1	2	17	3	59	4	0	4	6	.400	0	20	2.23
1988 Durham	A+	Atl	48	0	0	39	58.1	263	65	26	22	4	5	3	0	24	5	26	5	2	8	5	.615	0	17	3.39
1989 Durham	A+	Atl	32	0	0	23	45.1	178	33	8	5	2	2	4	2	10	2	34	2	0	2	3	.400	0	14	0.99
Greenville	AA	Atl	17	4	0	3	34	161	39	31	21	4	1	2	1	16	0	18	0	0	1	6	.143	0	0	5.56
1990 Harrisburg	AA	Pit	9	0	0	4	14.2	67	17	7	7	1	0	1	1	6	0	6	1	0	0	0	.000	0	0	4.30
Salem	A+	Pit	18	0	0	17	28	113	17	10	8	3	3	2	3	11	3	26	1	0	1	1	.500	0	6	2.57
Beloit	A	Mil	21	0	0	21	27.1	110	16	7	5	1	1	2	3	8	4	37	0	0	2	0	1.000	0	11	1.65
Stockton	A+	Mil	2	0	0	1	2.2	10	1	0	0	0	1	0	0	2	0	2	0	0	0	0	.000	0	1	0.00
1991 El Paso	AA	Mil	43	0	0	32	78.1	366	100	54	43	5	4	2	3	29	4	69	5	1	5	2	.714	0	11	4.94
1992 El Paso	AA	Mil	57	2	0	28	79.1	351	92	44	43	8	4	1	7	26	4	62	1	0	5	7	.417	0	10	4.88
1993 Orlando	AA	ChN	10	0	0	4	19	76	15	7	6	0	0	1	1	3	1	16	0	1	1	2	.333	0	1	2.84
Iowa	AAA	ChN	42	0	0	18	70.1	304	64	31	30	3	4	3	3	32	2	43	4	0	7	5	.583	0	0	3.84
1994 Colo. Sprng	AAA	Col	44	1	0	21	63	254	53	24	19	4	3	5	5	16	1	36	3	1	5	4	.556	0	8	2.71
1995 Colo. Sprng	AAA	Col	60	0	0	44	83.2	382	90	54	47	8	6	8	2	52	7	56	4	0	3	10	.231	0	17	5.06
1996 Syracuse	AAA	Tor	48	2	0	20	89.1	395	85	52	38	4	6	9	3	37	6	71	3	0	6	4	.600	0	1	3.83
1994 Colorado	NL		5	0	0	2	8.2	42	9	4	4	2	1	0	3	6	1	2	1	0	0	0	.000	0	0	4.15
11 Min. YEARS			517	22	3	316	850.2	3318	840	425	347	54	42	44	39	305	42	607	36	5	57	60	.487	0	117	3.67

Fred Dabney

Pitches: Left **Bats:** Right **Pos:** P **Ht:** 6'3" **Wt:** 190 **Born:** 11/20/67 **Age:** 29

Year Team	Lg	Org	G	GS	CG	GF	IP	BFP	H	R	ER	HR	SH	SF	HB	TBB	IBB	SO	WP	Bk	W	L	Pct.	ShO	Sv	ERA
			HOW MUCH HE PITCHED						WHAT HE GAVE UP												THE RESULTS					
1988 Utica	A-	ChA	19	13	1	3	87.2	382	83	40	26	1	2	0	1	41	1	69	2	5	9	4	.692	0	0	2.67

Year	Team	Lg	Org	G	GS	CG	GF	IP	BFP	H	R	ER	HR	SH	SF	HB	TBB	IBB	SO	WP	Bk	W	L	Pct.	ShO	Sv	ERA
				HOW MUCH HE PITCHED						WHAT HE GAVE UP												THE RESULTS					
1989	South Bend	A	ChA	26	26	3	0	163.1	676	128	50	38	2	4	2	11	65	1	150	7	6	11	7	.611	0	0	2.09
1990	Sarasota	A+	ChA	24	21	1	1	126.1	569	146	82	73	3	4	4	6	57	1	77	6	6	6	7	.462	0	0	5.20
1991	Sarasota	A+	ChA	26	8	1	5	96.1	414	88	45	32	6	3	4	4	44	1	72	2	4	11	3	.786	1	1	2.99
1992	Birmingham	AA	ChA	25	14	0	5	105.1	460	116	57	45	9	5	7	1	41	1	86	6	1	2	8	.200	0	0	3.84
1993	Nashville	AAA	ChA	51	0	0	15	63	280	65	43	34	7	1	3	9	21	0	44	3	1	2	5	.286	0	3	4.86
1994	Canton-Akrn	AA	Cle	39	0	0	17	58	243	50	20	18	4	4	2	5	19	2	44	2	0	4	3	.571	0	2	2.79
1995	Orlando	AA	ChN	13	0	0	4	17.1	78	13	9	4	0	2	0	2	10	4	9	1	1	2	1	.667	0	1	2.08
	Iowa	AAA	ChN	46	1	0	8	73.1	340	81	51	41	8	7	3	5	39	7	42	6	1	6	7	.462	0	1	5.03
1996	Orlando	AA	ChN	12	0	0	2	14	62	15	5	4	1	2	0	0	5	1	16	0	0	0	0	.000	0	0	2.57
	Iowa	AAA	ChN	33	3	1	5	64.1	287	76	38	31	9	2	0	3	24	1	33	2	1	2	3	.400	0	0	4.34
9 Min. YEARS				314	86	7	65	869	3791	861	440	346	50	36	25	47	366	20	642	37	26	55	48	.534	1	8	3.58

Derek Dace

Pitches: Left **Bats:** Left **Pos:** P **Ht:** 6'7" **Wt:** 200 **Born:** 4/9/75 **Age:** 22

Year	Team	Lg	Org	G	GS	CG	GF	IP	BFP	H	R	ER	HR	SH	SF	HB	TBB	IBB	SO	WP	Bk	W	L	Pct.	ShO	Sv	ERA
				HOW MUCH HE PITCHED						WHAT HE GAVE UP												THE RESULTS					
1994	Astros	R	Hou	11	11	1	0	59	245	55	26	22	2	5	2	1	21	0	52	2	3	2	3	.400	0	0	3.36
1995	Kissimmee	A+	Hou	1	1	0	0	2.2	17	4	5	5	0	0	1	0	5	0	1	0	0	0	1	.000	0	0	16.88
	Astros	R	Hou	12	11	2	1	72	291	64	25	20	2	3	2	1	11	0	78	5	2	3	5	.375	1	0	2.50
1996	Kissimmee	A+	Hou	12	0	0	3	18.1	73	19	6	6	0	0	0	0	7	0	11	1	0	0	0	.000	0	1	2.95
	Jackson	AA	Hou	1	1	0	0	4	21	5	1	1	1	0	0	0	5	0	0	0	0	0	0	.000	0	0	2.25
	Auburn	A-	Hou	15	15	0	0	97	400	89	41	35	7	2	1	2	35	2	87	1	0	9	4	.692	0	0	3.25
3 Min. YEARS				52	39	3	4	253	1047	236	104	89	12	10	6	4	84	2	229	9	5	14	13	.519	1	1	3.17

Mark Dalesandro

Bats: Right **Throws:** Right **Pos:** DH **Ht:** 6' 0" **Wt:** 185 **Born:** 5/14/68 **Age:** 29

Year	Team	Lg	Org	G	AB	H	2B	3B	HR	TB	R	RBI	TBB	IBB	SO	HBP	SH	SF	SB	CS	SB%	GDP	Avg	OBP	SLG
				BATTING															BASERUNNING				PERCENTAGES		
1990	Boise	A-	Cal	55	223	75	10	2	6	107	35	44	19	2	42	1	0	1	6	1	.86	6	.336	.389	.480
1991	Quad City	A	Cal	125	487	133	17	8	5	181	63	69	34	1	58	6	0	4	1	2	.33	10	.273	.326	.372
1992	Palm Spring	A+	Cal	126	492	146	30	3	7	203	72	92	33	6	50	5	0	6	6	2	.75	20	.297	.343	.413
1993	Palm Spring	A+	Cal	46	176	43	5	3	1	57	22	25	15	1	20	0	0	7	3	2	.60	9	.244	.293	.324
	Midland	AA	Cal	57	235	69	9	0	2	84	33	36	8	2	30	4	0	5	1	1	.50	9	.294	.321	.357
	Vancouver	AAA	Cal	26	107	32	8	1	2	48	16	15	6	1	13	1	0	1	1	0	1.00	4	.299	.339	.449
1994	Vancouver	AAA	Cal	51	199	63	9	1	1	77	29	31	7	0	19	1	0	2	1	0	1.00	6	.317	.340	.387
1995	Vancouver	AAA	Cal	34	123	41	13	1	1	59	16	18	6	0	12	1	0	1	2	0	1.00	2	.333	.366	.480
1996	Columbus	AAA	NYA	78	255	72	29	4	2	115	34	38	17	0	31	5	0	2	2	0	1.00	9	.282	.337	.451
1994	California	AL		19	25	5	1	0	1	9	5	2	2	0	4	0	0	0	0	0	.00	2	.200	.259	.360
1995	California	AL		11	10	1	1	0	0	2	1	0	0	0	2	0	0	0	0	0	.00	0	.100	.100	.200
7 Min. YEARS				598	2297	674	130	23	27	931	320	368	145	13	275	24	0	29	23	8	.74	75	.293	.338	.405
2 Maj. YEARS				30	35	6	2	0	1	11	6	2	2	0	6	0	0	0	0	0	.00	2	.171	.216	.314

Dee Dalton

Bats: Right **Throws:** Right **Pos:** 3B **Ht:** 5'11" **Wt:** 170 **Born:** 6/17/72 **Age:** 25

Year	Team	Lg	Org	G	AB	H	2B	3B	HR	TB	R	RBI	TBB	IBB	SO	HBP	SH	SF	SB	CS	SB%	GDP	Avg	OBP	SLG
				BATTING															BASERUNNING				PERCENTAGES		
1993	Johnson Cty	R+	StL	68	240	65	13	2	11	115	36	46	30	0	56	2	4	4	5	3	.63	4	.271	.351	.479
1994	Madison	A	StL	129	466	112	33	5	12	191	69	77	53	2	104	4	2	6	11	6	.65	11	.240	.319	.410
1995	St. Pete	A+	StL	118	385	79	16	1	2	103	36	30	45	0	81	3	2	3	10	4	.71	7	.205	.291	.268
1996	Arkansas	AA	StL	113	345	82	17	2	6	121	38	42	38	2	61	2	6	3	4	4	.50	10	.238	.314	.351
4 Min. YEARS				428	1436	338	79	10	31	530	179	195	166	4	302	11	14	16	30	17	.64	32	.235	.316	.369

Brad Dandridge

Bats: Right **Throws:** Right **Pos:** OF **Ht:** 6'0" **Wt:** 190 **Born:** 11/29/71 **Age:** 25

Year	Team	Lg	Org	G	AB	H	2B	3B	HR	TB	R	RBI	TBB	IBB	SO	HBP	SH	SF	SB	CS	SB%	GDP	Avg	OBP	SLG
				BATTING															BASERUNNING				PERCENTAGES		
1993	Spokane	A-	SD	64	248	59	8	2	4	83	26	41	16	1	38	5	1	4	2	0	1.00	5	.238	.293	.335
1994	Ogden	R+	—	43	171	63	11	1	2	82	41	45	17	2	15	3	1	5	6	2	.75	5	.368	.423	.480
	St. Paul	IND	—	19	67	14	4	0	0	18	4	6	8	0	22	0	2	0	0	1	.00	1	.209	.293	.269
1995	San Antonio	AA	LA	3	12	5	0	0	0	5	1	1	0	0	1	0	0	0	0	1	.00	0	.417	.417	.417
	San Bernrdo	A+	LA	82	322	103	14	2	11	154	56	61	14	0	34	3	1	2	16	5	.76	11	.320	.352	.478
1996	Albuquerque	AAA	LA	30	80	21	4	0	2	31	14	7	3	0	7	1	0	0	0	0	.00	4	.263	.298	.388
	San Antonio	AA	LA	47	177	50	7	0	3	66	22	25	12	1	19	1	0	3	4	3	.57	3	.282	.326	.373
4 Min. YEARS				288	1077	315	48	5	22	439	164	186	70	4	136	13	5	14	28	12	.70	29	.292	.339	.408

Lee Daniels

Pitches: Right **Bats:** Right **Pos:** P **Ht:** 6'4" **Wt:** 180 **Born:** 3/31/71 **Age:** 26

Year	Team	Lg	Org	G	GS	CG	GF	IP	BFP	H	R	ER	HR	SH	SF	HB	TBB	IBB	SO	WP	Bk	W	L	Pct.	ShO	Sv	ERA
				HOW MUCH HE PITCHED						WHAT HE GAVE UP												THE RESULTS					
1991	Medicne Hat	R+	Tor	1	0	0	1	1.1	5	1	0	0	0	0	0	0	0	0	2	0	0	0	0	.000	0	0	0.00
1992	St. Cathrns	A-	Tor	17	4	0	5	58	242	61	34	28	4	3	2	2	20	0	37	6	4	3	6	.333	0	0	4.34
1993	Dunedin	A+	Tor	2	1	0	1	4.1	22	6	4	3	0	0	0	0	2	0	5	1	0	0	1	.000	0	0	6.23

Year	Team	Lg	Org	G	GS	CG	GF	IP	BFP	H	R	ER	HR	SH	SF	HB	TBB	IBB	SO	WP	Bk	W	L	Pct.	ShO	Sv	ERA
	Hagerstown	A	Tor	33	0	0	28	39.1	179	31	20	15	2	6	1	2	26	1	38	5	0	2	4	.333	0	12	3.43
1994	Dunedin	A+	Tor	49	0	0	41	60	258	55	30	25	3	3	1	3	26	0	48	5	2	3	6	.333	0	15	3.75
1995	Durham	A+	Atl	21	0	0	7	23.1	113	26	13	11	1	3	0	1	14	1	24	4	2	1	4	.200	0	4	4.24
1996	Greenville	AA	Atl	16	0	0	15	17	73	10	5	5	1	0	0	0	14	0	23	4	0	2	0	1.000	0	9	2.65
6	Min. YEARS			139	5	0	98	203.1	892	190	106	87	11	15	4	8	102	2	177	25	8	11	21	.344	0	40	3.85

Vic Darensbourg

Pitches: Left **Bats:** Left **Pos:** P **Ht:** 5'10" **Wt:** 165 **Born:** 11/13/70 **Age:** 26

Year	Team	Lg	Org	G	GS	CG	GF	IP	BFP	H	R	ER	HR	SH	SF	HB	TBB	IBB	SO	WP	Bk	W	L	Pct.	ShO	Sv	ERA
1992	Marlins	R	Fla	8	4	0	2	42	161	28	5	3	1	0	0	3	11	2	37	0	0	2	1	.667	0	2	0.64
1993	Kane County	A	Fla	46	0	0	31	71.1	300	58	17	17	3	3	3	4	28	3	89	2	0	9	1	.900	0	16	2.14
	High Desert	A+	Fla	1	0	0	0	1	4	1	0	0	0	0	0	0	0	0	1	0	0	0	0	.000	0	0	0.00
1994	Portland	AA	Fla	34	21	1	9	149	631	146	76	63	18	7	4	6	60	3	103	4	2	10	7	.588	1	4	3.81
1996	Brevard Cty	A+	Fla	2	0	0	1	3	10	1	0	0	0	0	0	0	1	0	5	0	0	0	0	.000	0	0	0.00
	Charlotte	AAA	Fla	47	0	0	25	63.1	280	61	30	26	7	3	2	2	32	3	66	3	1	1	5	.167	0	7	3.69
4	Min. YEARS			138	25	1	68	329.2	1386	295	128	109	29	13	9	15	132	11	301	9	3	22	14	.611	1	29	2.98

Jamie Daspit

Pitches: Right **Bats:** Right **Pos:** P **Ht:** 6'7" **Wt:** 210 **Born:** 8/10/69 **Age:** 27

Year	Team	Lg	Org	G	GS	CG	GF	IP	BFP	H	R	ER	HR	SH	SF	HB	TBB	IBB	SO	WP	Bk	W	L	Pct.	ShO	Sv	ERA
1990	Great Falls	R+	LA	14	9	0	1	51	222	45	26	23	0	3	2	5	30	0	40	1	0	5	2	.714	0	0	4.06
1991	Bakersfield	A+	LA	22	9	0	6	64.2	276	58	29	23	1	4	2	1	36	2	47	6	1	3	2	.600	0	2	3.20
1992	Vero Beach	A+	LA	26	25	0	0	149.1	625	135	67	57	10	6	3	7	57	1	109	7	1	6	12	.333	0	0	3.44
1993	Vero Beach	A+	LA	1	1	0	0	3	15	4	0	0	0	0	0	0	2	0	2	0	0	0	0	.000	0	0	0.00
	San Antonio	AA	LA	15	15	0	0	81.1	363	92	48	40	5	4	4	8	33	0	58	5	0	3	8	.273	0	0	4.43
1994	Jackson	AA	Hou	28	10	1	7	71	274	48	22	18	1	2	0	2	23	0	74	3	0	5	1	.833	1	1	2.28
1995	Edmonton	AAA	Oak	38	0	0	11	68	294	69	36	31	5	2	5	2	24	1	54	7	0	5	2	.714	0	1	4.10
	Tucson	AAA	Hou	38	0	0	11	68	294	69	36	31	5	2	5	2	24	1	54	7	0	5	2	.714	0	1	4.10
1996	Edmonton	AAA	Oak	33	9	0	5	89.2	394	96	50	41	5	1	4	4	29	9	76	6	0	4	5	.444	0	0	4.12
7	Min. YEARS			215	78	1	41	646	2757	616	314	264	32	24	25	31	258	14	514	42	2	36	34	.514	1	5	3.68

Brian Daubach

Bats: Left **Throws:** Right **Pos:** 1B **Ht:** 6'1" **Wt:** 201 **Born:** 2/11/72 **Age:** 25

Year	Team	Lg	Org	G	AB	H	2B	3B	HR	TB	R	RBI	TBB	IBB	SO	HBP	SH	SF	SB	CS	SB%	GDP	Avg	OBP	SLG
1990	Mets	R	NYN	45	152	41	8	4	1	60	26	19	22	0	41	2	0	3	2	1	.67	2	.270	.363	.395
1991	Kingsport	R+	NYN	65	217	52	9	1	7	84	30	42	33	5	64	6	1	2	1	3	.25	1	.240	.353	.387
1992	Pittsfield	A-	NYN	72	260	63	15	2	2	88	26	40	30	2	61	3	1	4	4	0	1.00	5	.242	.323	.338
1993	Capital Cty	A	NYN	102	379	106	19	3	7	152	50	72	52	5	84	5	1	7	6	1	.86	14	.280	.368	.401
1994	St. Lucie	A+	NYN	129	450	123	30	2	6	175	52	74	58	5	120	5	3	4	14	9	.61	3	.273	.360	.389
1995	Binghamton	AA	NYN	135	469	115	25	2	10	174	61	72	51	5	104	7	1	7	6	2	.75	5	.245	.324	.371
	Norfolk	AAA	NYN	2	7	0	0	0	0	0	0	0	2	1	0	0	0	0	0	0	.00	0	.000	.222	.000
1996	Norfolk	AAA	NYN	17	54	11	2	0	0	13	7	6	6	0	14	0	0	1	1	1	.50	1	.204	.279	.241
	Binghamton	AA	NYN	122	436	129	24	1	22	221	80	76	74	9	103	7	0	4	7	9	.44	8	.296	.403	.507
7	Min. YEARS			689	2424	640	132	15	55	967	332	401	328	32	591	35	7	32	41	26	.61	39	.264	.356	.399

Donnie Dault

Pitches: Right **Bats:** Right **Pos:** P **Ht:** 6'6" **Wt:** 185 **Born:** 4/15/72 **Age:** 25

Year	Team	Lg	Org	G	GS	CG	GF	IP	BFP	H	R	ER	HR	SH	SF	HB	TBB	IBB	SO	WP	Bk	W	L	Pct.	ShO	Sv	ERA
1991	Astros	R	Hou	3	0	0	0	3.2	14	0	0	0	0	1	1	1	2	0	3	1	0	0	0	.000	0	0	0.00
1992	Astros	R	Hou	8	4	0	1	25	109	20	13	10	1	0	0	2	10	0	25	3	2	0	1	.000	0	1	3.60
1993	Auburn	A-	Hou	20	0	0	5	36	180	38	32	16	2	3	3	4	21	3	51	4	1	0	3	.000	0	0	4.00
1995	Kissimmee	A+	Hou	41	5	0	16	108	445	95	52	37	2	4	0	5	36	0	95	8	5	4	7	.364	0	6	3.08
1996	Kissimmee	A+	Hou	29	0	0	14	39	166	33	24	22	4	2	0	2	20	2	42	1	1	2	2	.500	0	3	5.08
	Tucson	AAA	Hou	1	0	0	1	2	10	4	2	2	1	0	0	0	0	0	2	0	0	0	0	.000	0	0	9.00
	Jackson	AA	Hou	1	0	0	1	2	9	2	0	0	0	0	0	0	2	0	1	0	0	0	0	.000	0	0	0.00
5	Min. YEARS			103	9	0	38	215.2	933	192	123	87	10	10	4	14	91	5	219	17	9	6	13	.316	0	10	3.63

David Davalillo

Bats: Right **Throws:** Right **Pos:** 2B **Ht:** 5'11" **Wt:** 165 **Born:** 12/27/74 **Age:** 22

Year	Team	Lg	Org	G	AB	H	2B	3B	HR	TB	R	RBI	TBB	IBB	SO	HBP	SH	SF	SB	CS	SB%	GDP	Avg	OBP	SLG
1994	Angels	R	Cal	54	231	58	8	3	3	81	28	31	12	0	39	0	4	1	1	1	.50	4	.251	.287	.351
1995	Cedar Rapds	A	Cal	44	141	38	7	1	0	47	17	16	7	0	32	0	4	1	1	0	1.00	3	.270	.302	.333
	Boise	A-	Cal	36	112	25	9	1	1	39	17	12	6	0	21	1	1	0	1	0	1.00	4	.223	.269	.348
1996	Cedar Rapds	A	Cal	98	378	104	22	0	3	135	63	34	28	0	51	3	3	3	4	6	.40	4	.275	.328	.357
	Midland	AA	Cal	25	82	14	1	0	0	15	6	5	4	0	16	1	3	0	2	0	1.00	2	.171	.218	.183
3	Min. YEARS			257	944	239	47	5	7	317	131	98	57	0	159	5	15	5	9	7	.56	17	.253	.298	.336

Clint Davis

Pitches: Right **Bats:** Right **Pos:** P **Ht:** 6'3" **Wt:** 205 **Born:** 9/26/69 **Age:** 27

		HOW MUCH HE PITCHED						WHAT HE GAVE UP												THE RESULTS					
Year Team	Lg Org	G	GS	CG	GF	IP	BFP	H	R	ER	HR	SH	SF	HB	TBB	IBB	SO	WP	Bk	W	L	Pct.	ShO	Sv	ERA
1991 Cardinals	R StL	21	0	0	9	26.2	130	35	23	17	0	2	3	3	12	0	25	1	2	3	3	.500	0	0	5.74
1992 Savannah	A StL	51	0	0	23	65	272	49	24	16	0	4	3	4	21	6	61	3	0	4	2	.667	0	1	2.22
1993 St. Pete	A+ StL	29	0	0	26	28	118	26	8	6	0	1	0	0	10	0	44	0	0	1	0	1.000	0	19	1.93
Arkansas	AA StL	28	0	0	10	37	143	22	10	8	1	2	1	3	10	3	37	0	0	2	0	1.000	0	1	1.95
1995 Louisville	AAA StL	4	0	0	0	3.2	19	6	5	5	1	0	0	0	2	1	4	0	1	0	0	.000	0	0	12.27
Rio Grande	IND —	42	0	0	36	43.2	181	35	22	17	5	2	0	1	11	3	63	0	2	3	2	.600	0	21	3.50
1996 Okla. City	AAA Tex	8	0	0	1	13	60	14	5	5	1	1	0	3	6	0	16	0	0	0	0	.000	0	0	3.46
Tulsa	AA Tex	32	0	0	24	48	186	31	11	10	3	4	1	3	12	1	40	1	0	3	3	.500	0	10	1.88
5 Min. YEARS		215	0	0	129	265	1109	218	108	84	11	16	8	17	84	14	290	5	5	16	10	.615	0	52	2.85

Jay Davis

Bats: Left **Throws:** Left **Pos:** OF **Ht:** 5'11" **Wt:** 172 **Born:** 10/3/70 **Age:** 26

		BATTING															BASERUNNING				PERCENTAGES		
Year Team	Lg Org	G	AB	H	2B	3B	HR	TB	R	RBI	TBB	IBB	SO	HBP	SH	SF	SB	CS	SB%	GDP	Avg	OBP	SLG
1989 Mets	R NYN	52	195	48	6	5	0	64	26	18	12	0	33	2	0	2	7	11	.39	3	.246	.294	.328
1990 Kingsport	R+ NYN	68	261	60	6	0	5	81	39	28	8	1	37	1	1	4	19	9	.68	8	.230	.252	.310
1991 Columbia	A NYN	132	511	152	29	8	0	197	79	63	30	2	72	7	2	5	25	18	.58	14	.297	.342	.386
1992 St. Lucie	A+ NYN	134	524	147	15	7	1	179	56	36	7	0	70	6	2	3	21	17	.55	15	.281	.296	.342
1993 Binghamton	AA NYN	119	409	114	15	4	1	140	52	35	21	2	71	1	2	3	5	8	.38	8	.279	.313	.342
1994 Norfolk	AAA NYN	6	14	3	1	0	0	4	3	0	1	0	1	0	0	0	0	0	.00	0	.214	.267	.286
Binghamton	AA NYN	105	325	107	15	3	5	143	51	42	14	4	39	3	3	2	9	3	.75	4	.329	.360	.440
1995 Norfolk	AAA NYN	10	26	5	1	1	0	8	1	3	0	0	2	0	0	0	0	1	.00	1	.192	.192	.308
Binghamton	AA NYN	116	443	113	17	6	3	151	64	50	26	1	68	8	1	6	11	5	.69	7	.255	.304	.341
1996 Tucson	AAA Hou	33	101	34	7	1	1	46	18	17	5	0	16	1	0	2	4	1	.80	0	.337	.367	.455
8 Min. YEARS		775	2809	783	112	35	16	1013	389	292	124	10	409	29	11	27	101	73	.58	60	.279	.313	.361

Jeff Davis

Pitches: Right **Bats:** Right **Pos:** P **Ht:** 6'0" **Wt:** 170 **Born:** 8/20/72 **Age:** 24

		HOW MUCH HE PITCHED						WHAT HE GAVE UP												THE RESULTS					
Year Team	Lg Org	G	GS	CG	GF	IP	BFP	H	R	ER	HR	SH	SF	HB	TBB	IBB	SO	WP	Bk	W	L	Pct.	ShO	Sv	ERA
1993 Erie	A- Tex	27	0	0	24	37	155	32	18	15	3	2	2	4	10	2	41	2	0	0	5	.000	0	13	3.65
1994 Charlstn-SC	A Tex	45	0	0	43	49.2	214	53	25	22	3	0	1	2	11	0	72	2	1	2	3	.400	0	19	3.99
1995 Tulsa	AA Tex	1	1	0	0	7	24	2	0	0	0	0	0	0	1	0	4	1	0	1	0	1.000	0	0	0.00
Charlotte	A+ Tex	27	27	0	0	172.1	715	161	74	53	10	6	2	11	38	0	109	7	2	13	7	.650	0	0	2.77
1996 Tulsa	AA Tex	16	15	3	0	98	420	110	57	50	10	2	6	2	20	1	51	1	0	7	2	.778	0	0	4.59
4 Min. YEARS		116	43	3	67	364	1528	358	174	140	26	10	11	19	80	3	277	13	3	23	17	.575	0	32	3.46

Ray Davis

Pitches: Right **Bats:** Right **Pos:** P **Ht:** 6'1" **Wt:** 225 **Born:** 2/6/73 **Age:** 24

		HOW MUCH HE PITCHED						WHAT HE GAVE UP												THE RESULTS					
Year Team	Lg Org	G	GS	CG	GF	IP	BFP	H	R	ER	HR	SH	SF	HB	TBB	IBB	SO	WP	Bk	W	L	Pct.	ShO	Sv	ERA
1991 Cardinals	R StL	11	10	0	0	54.2	254	72	47	41	2	0	3	1	24	0	31	3	1	2	3	.400	0	0	6.75
1992 Cardinals	R StL	11	11	4	0	76	296	57	30	21	1	5	2	1	22	0	74	3	1	5	4	.556	4	0	2.49
1993 Savannah	A StL	26	26	1	0	131.1	569	141	73	53	10	4	4	3	53	0	120	7	1	9	7	.563	1	0	3.63
1994 Madison	A StL	27	27	1	0	167	691	149	68	55	9	5	5	7	58	2	127	2	3	12	10	.545	1	0	2.96
1995 Arkansas	AA StL	21	18	0	1	110	467	112	67	55	14	5	5	4	30	0	70	6	1	7	6	.538	0	0	4.50
1996 Arkansas	AA StL	12	3	0	4	22.2	105	25	15	13	2	1	0	0	10	0	15	0	0	0	1	.000	0	0	5.16
Winnipeg	IND —	8	8	0	0	45	206	52	33	25	7	2	0	2	19	2	29	1	0	4	3	.571	0	0	5.00
6 Min. YEARS		116	103	6	5	606.2	2588	608	333	263	45	22	19	18	216	4	466	22	7	39	34	.534	6	0	3.90

Tommy Davis

Bats: Right **Throws:** Right **Pos:** 1B **Ht:** 6'1" **Wt:** 195 **Born:** 5/21/73 **Age:** 24

		BATTING															BASERUNNING				PERCENTAGES		
Year Team	Lg Org	G	AB	H	2B	3B	HR	TB	R	RBI	TBB	IBB	SO	HBP	SH	SF	SB	CS	SB%	GDP	Avg	OBP	SLG
1994 Albany	A Bal	61	216	59	10	1	5	86	35	35	18	0	52	2	0	3	2	4	.33	6	.273	.331	.398
1995 Frederick	A+ Bal	130	496	133	26	3	15	210	62	57	41	7	105	4	1	3	7	1	.88	14	.268	.327	.423
Bowie	AA Bal	9	32	10	3	0	3	22	5	10	1	0	9	1	0	0	0	0	.00	1	.313	.353	.688
1996 Bowie	AA Bal	137	524	137	32	2	14	215	75	54	41	4	113	10	3	3	5	8	.38	16	.261	.325	.410
3 Min. YEARS		337	1268	339	71	6	37	533	177	156	101	11	279	17	4	9	14	13	.52	37	.267	.328	.420

Walt Dawkins

Bats: Right **Throws:** Right **Pos:** OF **Ht:** 5'10" **Wt:** 190 **Born:** 8/6/72 **Age:** 24

		BATTING															BASERUNNING				PERCENTAGES		
Year Team	Lg Org	G	AB	H	2B	3B	HR	TB	R	RBI	TBB	IBB	SO	HBP	SH	SF	SB	CS	SB%	GDP	Avg	OBP	SLG
1995 Batavia	A- Phi	58	203	64	11	4	1	86	46	31	27	0	36	4	2	3	15	6	.71	6	.315	.401	.424
1996 Clearwater	A+ Phi	47	174	51	13	2	2	74	22	23	20	0	38	3	1	1	4	5	.44	3	.293	.374	.425
Reading	AA Phi	77	254	68	16	3	4	102	40	28	37	0	48	0	1	0	4	4	.50	3	.268	.361	.402
2 Min. YEARS		182	631	183	40	9	7	262	108	82	84	0	122	7	4	4	23	15	.61	12	.290	.377	.415

Lorenzo de la Cruz

Bats: Right **Throws:** Right **Pos:** OF **Ht:** 6'1" **Wt:** 199 **Born:** 9/5/71 **Age:** 25

		BATTING															BASERUNNING				PERCENTAGES		
Year Team	Lg Org	G	AB	H	2B	3B	HR	TB	R	RBI	TBB	IBB	SO	HBP	SH	SF	SB	CS	SB%	GDP	Avg	OBP	SLG
1993 Medicne Hat	R+ Tor	62	208	62	11	6	11	118	44	43	23	0	59	7	3	2	5	1	.83	2	.298	.383	.567
St. Cathrns	A- Tor	6	16	0	0	0	0	0	2	0	3	0	5	0	1	0	0	0	.00	0	.000	.158	.000
1994 Hagerstown	A Tor	125	457	111	20	4	19	196	72	62	30	1	152	6	1	0	12	8	.60	13	.243	.298	.429
1995 Knoxville	AA Tor	140	508	139	20	12	8	207	63	61	36	3	129	15	1	0	11	11	.50	14	.274	.340	.407
1996 Knoxville	AA Tor	122	441	109	24	4	18	195	60	79	36	1	123	7	0	4	8	4	.67	11	.247	.311	.442
4 Min. YEARS		455	1630	421	75	26	56	716	241	245	128	5	468	35	6	6	36	24	.60	40	.258	.325	.439

Maximo de la Rosa

Pitches: Right **Bats:** Right **Pos:** P **Ht:** 5'11" **Wt:** 170 **Born:** 7/12/71 **Age:** 25

		HOW MUCH HE PITCHED						WHAT HE GAVE UP												THE RESULTS					
Year Team	Lg Org	G	GS	CG	GF	IP	BFP	H	R	ER	HR	SH	SF	HB	TBB	IBB	SO	WP	Bk	W	L	Pct.	ShO	Sv	ERA
1993 Burlington	R+ Cle	14	14	2	0	76.1	319	53	38	32	3	3	2	5	37	2	69	3	2	7	2	.778	1	0	3.77
1994 Columbus	A Cle	14	14	0	0	75.1	310	49	33	28	2	1	1	10	38	0	71	5	2	4	2	.667	0	0	3.35
Kinston	A+ Cle	13	13	0	0	69.2	324	82	56	39	7	2	4	4	38	0	53	3	2	0	11	.000	0	0	5.04
1995 Canton-Akrn	AA Cle	1	0	0	0	0.1	3	1	2	2	1	0	0	0	1	0	0	0	0	0	0	.000	0	0	54.00
Kinston	A+ Cle	44	0	0	21	62	269	47	25	17	1	5	2	4	38	3	61	7	1	5	2	.714	0	8	2.47
1996 Canton-Akrn	AA Cle	40	15	0	17	119.2	530	104	60	52	7	2	4	3	81	3	109	12	2	11	5	.688	0	3	3.91
4 Min. YEARS		126	56	2	38	403.1	1755	336	214	170	21	13	13	26	233	8	363	30	9	27	22	.551	1	11	3.79

Mariano De Los Santos

Pitches: Right **Bats:** Right **Pos:** P **Ht:** 5'10" **Wt:** 200 **Born:** 7/13/70 **Age:** 26

		HOW MUCH HE PITCHED						WHAT HE GAVE UP												THE RESULTS					
Year Team	Lg Org	G	GS	CG	GF	IP	BFP	H	R	ER	HR	SH	SF	HB	TBB	IBB	SO	WP	Bk	W	L	Pct.	ShO	Sv	ERA
1989 Pirates	R Pit	13	4	0	6	37.1	172	41	27	24	2	1	5	2	19	0	24	5	0	2	2	.500	0	2	5.79
1991 Pirates	R Pit	9	5	0	3	33.1	127	23	5	5	1	1	1	0	5	0	50	0	2	3	2	.600	0	1	1.35
Welland	A- Pit	8	6	0	0	32.2	156	41	24	20	6	1	1	3	21	0	22	7	0	1	3	.250	0	0	5.51
1992 Augusta	A Pit	52	1	0	28	96	390	75	33	24	2	4	4	6	38	2	103	4	3	7	8	.467	0	12	2.25
1993 Salem	A+ Pit	18	18	2	0	99	429	90	46	37	8	5	0	5	41	0	80	8	5	9	5	.643	1	0	3.36
Carolina	AA Pit	8	8	0	0	40	181	49	24	21	1	1	3	4	15	1	34	2	0	1	2	.333	0	0	4.73
1994 Carolina	AA Pit	14	14	1	0	76.1	322	77	34	31	7	3	3	8	24	0	57	2	0	7	2	.778	1	0	3.66
Buffalo	AAA Pit	9	9	0	0	48.2	208	46	27	26	5	2	2	4	17	0	26	0	0	2	6	.250	0	0	4.81
1995 Calgary	AAA Pit	14	14	0	0	71.2	321	85	57	49	4	4	4	3	22	0	36	2	1	3	6	.333	0	0	6.15
Carolina	AA Pit	35	14	0	3	99	443	113	73	60	9	5	4	5	36	3	56	3	1	4	6	.400	0	0	5.45
1996 Carolina	AA Pit	52	0	0	15	66.1	288	67	28	26	1	3	4	10	23	4	79	3	0	3	5	.375	0	1	3.53
7 Min. YEARS		232	93	3	55	700.1	3037	707	378	323	46	30	31	50	261	10	567	36	12	42	47	.472	2	16	4.15

Darrell Deak

Bats: Both **Throws:** Right **Pos:** DH **Ht:** 6'0" **Wt:** 180 **Born:** 7/5/69 **Age:** 27

		BATTING															BASERUNNING				PERCENTAGES		
Year Team	Lg Org	G	AB	H	2B	3B	HR	TB	R	RBI	TBB	IBB	SO	HBP	SH	SF	SB	CS	SB%	GDP	Avg	OBP	SLG
1991 Johnson Cty	R+ StL	66	215	65	23	2	9	119	43	34	43	1	44	5	0	4	1	6	.14	2	.302	.423	.553
1992 Springfield	A StL	126	428	122	28	7	16	212	84	79	65	2	71	7	1	5	12	2	.86	9	.285	.384	.495
1993 Arkansas	AA StL	121	414	100	22	1	19	181	63	73	58	6	103	10	1	5	4	8	.33	8	.242	.345	.437
1994 Louisville	AAA StL	133	486	132	23	2	18	213	65	73	50	5	107	4	1	3	1	2	.33	15	.272	.343	.438
1995 Louisville	AAA StL	106	336	81	21	2	7	127	42	34	53	6	90	5	0	6	2	2	.50	5	.241	.348	.378
1996 Louisville	AAA StL	70	164	38	4	0	8	66	19	18	24	4	47	1	0	1	2	1	.67	3	.232	.332	.402
6 Min. YEARS		622	2043	538	121	14	77	918	316	311	293	24	462	32	3	24	22	21	.51	42	.263	.361	.449

Greg Dean

Pitches: Right **Bats:** Right **Pos:** P **Ht:** 6'1" **Wt:** 220 **Born:** 4/16/74 **Age:** 23

		HOW MUCH HE PITCHED						WHAT HE GAVE UP												THE RESULTS					
Year Team	Lg Org	G	GS	CG	GF	IP	BFP	H	R	ER	HR	SH	SF	HB	TBB	IBB	SO	WP	Bk	W	L	Pct.	ShO	Sv	ERA
1995 Bluefield	R+ Bal	10	6	0	3	37	159	34	22	16	3	1	1	2	17	0	33	4	1	6	2	.750	0	1	3.89
1996 Bowie	AA Bal	3	3	0	0	12.2	70	21	15	12	2	0	1	0	13	0	4	1	0	0	3	.000	0	0	8.53
High Desert	A+ Bal	37	12	0	10	105.1	493	110	68	51	5	4	1	8	71	2	76	23	1	10	7	.588	0	3	4.36
2 Min. YEARS		50	21	0	13	155	722	165	105	79	10	5	3	10	101	2	113	28	2	16	12	.571	0	4	4.59

Joe DeBerry

Bats: Left **Throws:** Left **Pos:** 1B-DH **Ht:** 6'2" **Wt:** 195 **Born:** 6/30/70 **Age:** 27

		BATTING															BASERUNNING				PERCENTAGES		
Year Team	Lg Org	G	AB	H	2B	3B	HR	TB	R	RBI	TBB	IBB	SO	HBP	SH	SF	SB	CS	SB%	GDP	Avg	OBP	SLG
1991 Billings	R+ Cin	65	236	62	13	0	10	105	41	47	36	1	46	3	0	1	5	4	.56	4	.263	.366	.445
1992 Cedar Rapds	A Cin	127	455	109	22	4	15	184	58	68	43	1	102	2	0	3	3	3	.50	5	.240	.306	.404
1993 Albany-Colo	AA NYA	125	446	114	19	7	12	183	58	63	24	1	111	3	2	5	3	7	.30	6	.256	.295	.410
1994 Albany-Colo	AA NYA	15	53	15	4	1	0	21	3	3	5	0	11	0	0	0	0	1	.00	2	.283	.345	.396
1995 Columbus	AAA NYA	10	24	7	2	2	0	13	3	4	1	0	6	0	0	0	0	0	.00	1	.292	.320	.542
Norwich	AA NYA	2	4	0	0	0	0	0	0	0	0	0	2	0	0	0	0	0	.00	0	.000	.000	.000
Greensboro	A NYA	12	45	18	3	0	5	36	14	11	9	3	6	0	0	0	0	0	.00	1	.400	.500	.800
Tampa	A+ NYA	58	196	44	9	3	1	62	16	18	19	3	45	0	0	1	1	0	1.00	3	.224	.292	.316
1996 Norwich	AA NYA	9	26	4	0	0	0	4	1	6	0	0	7	0	0	0	0	0	.00	1	.154	.154	.154

		BATTING															BASERUNNING				PERCENTAGES		
Year Team	Lg Org	G	AB	H	2B	3B	HR	TB	R	RBI	TBB	IBB	SO	HBP	SH	SF	SB	CS	SB%	GDP	Avg	OBP	SLG
Stockton	A+ Mil	54	190	51	7	2	7	83	33	25	23	0	55	1	0	3	3	0	1.00	0	.268	.346	.437
6 Min. YEARS		477	1675	424	79	19	50	691	227	245	160	9	391	9	2	13	15	15	.50	23	.253	.319	.413

Rob Deboer

Bats: Right **Throws:** Right **Pos:** C **Ht:** 5'10" **Wt:** 205 **Born:** 2/4/71 **Age:** 26

		BATTING															BASERUNNING				PERCENTAGES		
Year Team	Lg Org	G	AB	H	2B	3B	HR	TB	R	RBI	TBB	IBB	SO	HBP	SH	SF	SB	CS	SB%	GDP	Avg	OBP	SLG
1994 Sou. Oregon	A- Oak	45	129	33	4	0	4	49	23	21	18	0	43	2	0	1	7	0	1.00	4	.256	.353	.380
1995 W. Michigan	A Oak	104	339	82	25	2	6	129	57	50	58	1	110	4	1	4	11	6	.65	6	.242	.356	.381
1996 Modesto	A+ Oak	73	249	71	8	6	12	127	68	52	74	0	75	4	0	2	12	5	.71	5	.285	.453	.510
Huntsville	AA Oak	44	122	34	6	0	5	55	24	21	25	0	45	1	1	1	1	3	.25	3	.279	.403	.451
3 Min. YEARS		266	839	220	43	8	27	360	172	144	175	1	273	11	2	8	31	14	.69	18	.262	.393	.429

Jon Declue

Pitches: Left **Bats:** Right **Pos:** P **Ht:** 6'2" **Wt:** 198 **Born:** 9/17/70 **Age:** 26

		HOW MUCH HE PITCHED						WHAT HE GAVE UP												THE RESULTS					
Year Team	Lg Org	G	GS	CG	GF	IP	BFP	H	R	ER	HR	SH	SF	HB	TBB	IBB	SO	WP	Bk	W	L	Pct.	ShO	Sv	ERA
1994 Cedar Rapds	A Cal	22	3	0	9	62.1	271	67	28	26	4	1	1	4	13	2	56	6	2	6	1	.857	0	0	3.75
1995 Lk Elsinore	A+ Cal	30	18	0	3	143.1	590	145	64	56	16	4	3	5	32	0	112	4	1	11	6	.647	0	0	3.52
Visalia	A+ Cal	30	18	0	3	143.1	590	145	64	56	16	4	3	5	32	0	112	4	1	11	6	.647	0	0	3.52
1996 Midland	AA Cal	32	15	2	5	111.2	512	137	83	66	11	4	2	2	51	1	76	6	1	6	9	.400	0	0	5.32
3 Min. YEARS		114	54	2	20	460.2	1963	494	239	204	47	13	9	16	128	3	356	20	5	34	22	.607	0	0	3.99

Jim Dedrick

Pitches: Right **Bats:** Both **Pos:** P **Ht:** 6' 0" **Wt:** 185 **Born:** 4/4/68 **Age:** 29

		HOW MUCH HE PITCHED						WHAT HE GAVE UP												THE RESULTS					
Year Team	Lg Org	G	GS	CG	GF	IP	BFP	H	R	ER	HR	SH	SF	HB	TBB	IBB	SO	WP	Bk	W	L	Pct.	ShO	Sv	ERA
1990 Wausau	A Bal	3	1	0	1	10	41	6	4	3	0	0	0	0	4	0	8	0	3	0	1	.000	0	0	2.70
1991 Kane County	A Bal	16	15	0	0	88.1	380	84	38	29	2	1	2	5	38	1	71	5	2	4	5	.444	0	0	2.95
1992 Frederick	A+ Bal	38	5	1	19	108.2	454	94	41	37	5	5	0	5	42	4	86	4	3	8	4	.667	0	3	3.06
1993 Bowie	AA Bal	38	6	1	14	106.1	426	84	36	30	4	5	0	3	32	1	78	1	0	8	3	.727	1	3	2.54
Rochester	AAA Bal	1	1	1	0	7	27	6	2	2	2	0	0	0	0	0	3	0	0	1	0	1.000	0	0	2.57
1994 Rochester	AAA Bal	44	1	0	18	99	421	98	56	42	7	3	1	3	35	7	70	4	1	3	6	.333	0	1	3.82
1995 Bowie	AA Bal	10	10	0	0	60.1	267	59	24	20	7	2	2	5	25	2	48	5	1	4	2	.667	0	0	2.98
Rochester	AAA Bal	34	12	0	4	106	457	104	33	29	7	4	6	6	39	3	79	9	1	8	2	.800	0	1	2.46
1996 Rochester	AAA Bal	39	3	0	20	66.1	316	88	59	48	14	2	4	1	41	0	37	5	1	6	3	.667	0	4	6.51
Bowie	AA Bal	13	0	0	4	26.2	116	28	10	10	3	1	0	0	14	1	21	1	0	1	1	.500	0	0	3.38
1995 Baltimore	AL	6	0	0	1	7.2	35	8	2	2	1	0	2	1	6	0	3	0	0	0	0	.000	0	0	2.35
7 Min. YEARS		236	54	3	80	678.2	2905	651	303	250	51	23	15	28	270	19	501	34	12	43	27	.614	1	12	3.32

Rick DeHart

Pitches: Left **Bats:** Left **Pos:** P **Ht:** 6'1" **Wt:** 180 **Born:** 3/21/70 **Age:** 27

		HOW MUCH HE PITCHED						WHAT HE GAVE UP												THE RESULTS					
Year Team	Lg Org	G	GS	CG	GF	IP	BFP	H	R	ER	HR	SH	SF	HB	TBB	IBB	SO	WP	Bk	W	L	Pct.	ShO	Sv	ERA
1992 Albany	A Mon	38	10	1	15	117	476	91	42	32	11	5	5	4	40	1	133	5	6	9	6	.600	1	3	2.46
1993 San Bernrdo	A+ Mon	9	9	0	0	53.1	237	56	28	18	4	3	1	0	25	0	44	0	0	4	3	.571	0	0	3.04
Harrisburg	AA Mon	12	7	0	1	34	163	45	31	29	5	1	2	2	19	0	18	2	0	2	4	.333	0	0	7.68
W. Palm Bch	A+ Mon	7	7	1	0	42	175	42	14	14	0	1	1	1	17	0	33	2	0	1	3	.250	1	0	3.00
1994 W. Palm Bch	A+ Mon	30	20	3	5	136.1	566	132	61	51	12	7	2	3	34	0	88	7	1	9	7	.563	2	0	3.37
1995 Harrisburg	AA Mon	35	12	0	4	93	417	94	62	50	13	4	6	5	39	3	64	4	4	6	7	.462	0	0	4.84
1996 Harrisburg	AA Mon	30	2	0	14	43.2	196	46	19	13	4	1	2	3	19	0	30	1	0	1	2	.333	0	1	2.68
5 Min. YEARS		161	67	5	39	519.1	2230	506	257	207	49	22	19	18	193	4	410	21	11	32	32	.500	4	4	3.59

Mike DeJean

Pitches: Right **Bats:** Right **Pos:** P **Ht:** 6'2" **Wt:** 205 **Born:** 9/28/70 **Age:** 26

		HOW MUCH HE PITCHED						WHAT HE GAVE UP												THE RESULTS					
Year Team	Lg Org	G	GS	CG	GF	IP	BFP	H	R	ER	HR	SH	SF	HB	TBB	IBB	SO	WP	Bk	W	L	Pct.	ShO	Sv	ERA
1992 Oneonta	A- NYA	20	0	0	19	20.2	78	12	3	1	1	0	0	0	3	0	20	0	0	0	0	.000	0	16	0.44
1993 Greensboro	A NYA	20	0	0	18	18	87	22	12	10	1	1	1	0	8	2	16	1	0	2	3	.400	0	9	5.00
1994 Tampa	A+ NYA	34	0	0	33	34	156	39	15	9	1	1	2	2	13	0	22	2	0	0	2	.000	0	16	2.38
Albany-Colo	AA NYA	16	0	0	10	24.2	110	22	14	12	1	4	1	2	15	3	13	6	0	0	2	.000	0	4	4.38
1995 Norwich	AA NYA	59	0	0	40	78.1	323	58	29	26	5	2	3	5	34	2	57	4	1	5	5	.500	0	20	2.99
1996 New Haven	AA Col	16	0	0	15	22.1	90	20	9	8	2	0	1	0	8	0	12	2	0	0	0	.000	0	11	3.22
Colo. Sprng	AAA Col	30	0	0	17	40.1	186	52	24	23	3	0	0	2	21	3	31	2	0	0	2	.000	0	1	5.13
5 Min. YEARS		195	0	0	152	238.1	1030	225	106	89	14	8	8	11	102	10	171	17	1	7	14	.333	0	77	3.36

Jose DeJesus

Pitches: Right **Bats:** Right **Pos:** P **Ht:** 6' 5" **Wt:** 225 **Born:** 1/6/65 **Age:** 32

		HOW MUCH HE PITCHED						WHAT HE GAVE UP												THE RESULTS					
Year Team	Lg Org	G	GS	CG	GF	IP	BFP	H	R	ER	HR	SH	SF	HB	TBB	IBB	SO	WP	Bk	W	L	Pct.	ShO	Sv	ERA
1985 Fort Myers	A+ KC	27	26	3	0	129.2	563	119	70	62	9	1	4	7	59	0	94	4	3	8	10	.444	1	0	4.30
1986 Fort Myers	A+ KC	22	22	1	0	110	500	87	64	42	4	3	2	4	82	1	97	8	3	4	9	.308	0	0	3.44

		HOW MUCH HE PITCHED						WHAT HE GAVE UP												THE RESULTS					
Year Team	Lg Org	G	GS	CG	GF	IP	BFP	H	R	ER	HR	SH	SF	HB	TBB	IBB	SO	WP	Bk	W	L	Pct.	ShO	Sv	ERA
1987 Memphis	AA KC	25	24	2	0	130.1	589	106	78	65	8	3	7	4	99	0	79	11	2	4	11	.267	0	0	4.49
1988 Memphis	AA KC	20	20	4	0	116	502	88	56	50	5	3	2	5	70	0	149	9	2	9	9	.500	1	0	3.88
Omaha	AAA KC	7	7	3	0	49.2	208	44	22	19	1	3	3	2	14	0	57	3	1	2	3	.400	0	0	3.44
1989 Omaha	AAA KC	31	21	2	7	145.1	638	112	78	61	9	4	6	6	98	1	158	11	2	8	11	.421	0	1	3.78
1990 Scranton-WB	AAA Phi	10	10	1	0	56	249	41	30	21	2	2	3	2	39	0	45	6	4	1	4	.200	0	0	3.38
1993 Clearwater	A+ Phi	11	10	1	0	55.1	244	65	32	25	5	1	1	0	19	0	33	2	1	3	6	.333	0	0	4.07
1994 Omaha	AAA KC	30	2	0	10	58	254	51	29	26	6	4	1	4	37	1	54	3	1	4	4	.500	0	4	4.03
1995 Omaha	AAA KC	36	6	0	19	61.2	288	56	45	42	10	2	5	2	52	3	49	7	0	3	6	.333	0	10	6.13
1996 Columbus	AAA NYA	3	0	0	0	5	26	9	8	8	1	0	0	0	1	0	6	1	0	0	0	.000	0	0	14.40
1988 Kansas City	AL	2	1	0	0	2.2	19	6	10	8	0	0	0	0	5	1	2	0	0	0	1	.000	0	0	27.00
1989 Kansas City	AL	3	1	0	1	8	37	7	4	4	1	0	0	0	8	0	2	0	0	0	0	.000	0	0	4.50
1990 Philadelphia	NL	22	22	3	0	130	544	97	63	54	10	8	0	2	73	3	87	4	0	7	8	.467	1	0	3.74
1991 Philadelphia	NL	31	29	3	1	181.2	801	147	74	69	7	11	3	4	128	4	118	10	0	10	9	.526	0	1	3.42
1994 Kansas City	AL	5	4	0	0	26.2	112	27	14	14	2	1	0	0	13	0	12	3	0	3	1	.750	0	0	4.73
10 Min. YEARS		222	148	17	36	917	4061	778	512	421	60	26	34	36	570	6	821	65	19	46	73	.387	2	15	4.13
5 Maj. YEARS		63	57	6	2	349	1513	284	165	149	20	20	3	6	227	8	221	17	0	20	19	.513	1	1	3.84

Roland Dela Maza

Pitches: Right **Bats:** Right **Pos:** P **Ht:** 6'2" **Wt:** 195 **Born:** 11/11/71 **Age:** 25

		HOW MUCH HE PITCHED						WHAT HE GAVE UP												THE RESULTS					
Year Team	Lg Org	G	GS	CG	GF	IP	BFP	H	R	ER	HR	SH	SF	HB	TBB	IBB	SO	WP	Bk	W	L	Pct.	ShO	Sv	ERA
1993 Watertown	A- Cle	15	15	1	0	100	402	90	39	28	8	2	1	3	14	0	81	0	1	10	3	.769	0	0	2.52
1994 Columbus	A Cle	21	21	1	0	112.2	473	102	59	37	13	5	4	6	25	0	97	3	2	13	2	.867	0	0	2.96
1995 Canton-Akrn	AA Cle	7	7	0	0	37.1	162	35	19	17	5	0	0	2	18	0	27	1	0	2	1	.667	0	0	4.10
Kinston	A+ Cle	33	19	0	5	147.2	607	134	50	46	18	7	0	5	46	3	127	4	0	8	1	.889	0	1	2.80
1996 Canton-Akrn	AA Cle	40	14	0	9	139.2	587	122	75	68	15	6	1	1	49	3	132	3	2	9	7	.563	0	1	4.38
4 Min. YEARS		116	76	2	14	537.1	2231	483	242	196	59	20	6	17	152	6	464	11	5	42	14	.750	0	2	3.28

Glenn Delafield

Bats: Right **Throws:** Right **Pos:** OF **Ht:** 6'2" **Wt:** 185 **Born:** 2/15/72 **Age:** 25

		BATTING															BASERUNNING				PERCENTAGES		
Year Team	Lg Org	G	AB	H	2B	3B	HR	TB	R	RBI	TBB	IBB	SO	HBP	SH	SF	SB	CS	SB%	GDP	Avg	OBP	SLG
1992 Yankees	R NYA	51	182	46	7	0	1	56	28	23	26	0	38	1	0	2	6	4	.60	3	.253	.346	.308
Oneonta	A- NYA	7	24	7	0	1	0	9	2	2	2	0	4	0	1	0	1	2	.33	1	.292	.346	.375
1994 Greensboro	A NYA	88	305	70	5	2	4	91	41	23	40	0	90	4	2	0	11	12	.48	11	.230	.327	.298
1995 Tampa	A+ NYA	7	26	7	1	0	1	11	4	6	2	0	11	1	0	0	1	0	1.00	0	.269	.345	.423
Greensboro	A NYA	107	384	80	14	0	4	106	37	29	16	0	107	1	5	1	3	7	.30	12	.208	.241	.276
1996 Norwich	AA NYA	22	46	9	1	0	0	10	3	3	2	0	15	0	0	0	1	1	.50	1	.196	.229	.217
Greensboro	A NYA	30	98	25	4	1	2	37	16	11	6	0	30	3	1	2	1	0	1.00	0	.255	.312	.378
4 Min. YEARS		312	1065	244	32	4	12	320	131	97	94	0	295	10	9	5	24	26	.48	28	.229	.296	.300

Sean Delaney

Bats: Right **Throws:** Right **Pos:** C **Ht:** 5'11" **Wt:** 190 **Born:** 5/22/70 **Age:** 27

		BATTING															BASERUNNING				PERCENTAGES		
Year Team	Lg Org	G	AB	H	2B	3B	HR	TB	R	RBI	TBB	IBB	SO	HBP	SH	SF	SB	CS	SB%	GDP	Avg	OBP	SLG
1992 Appleton	A KC	22	56	12	3	0	0	15	2	4	5	0	13	1	0	1	0	1	.00	4	.214	.286	.268
1993 Rockford	A KC	20	45	8	0	0	0	8	7	2	2	0	15	0	0	0	1	0	1.00	1	.178	.213	.178
1995 Springfield	A KC	62	188	56	8	2	5	83	24	22	19	1	27	5	1	1	5	1	.83	5	.298	.376	.441
1996 Wichita	AA KC	23	48	10	3	0	2	19	5	5	5	0	15	0	1	0	2	0	1.00	1	.208	.283	.396
4 Min. YEARS		127	337	86	14	2	7	125	38	33	31	1	70	6	2	2	8	2	.80	11	.255	.327	.371

Roberto DeLeon

Bats: Right **Throws:** Right **Pos:** 2B **Ht:** 5'10" **Wt:** 188 **Born:** 3/29/71 **Age:** 26

		BATTING															BASERUNNING				PERCENTAGES		
Year Team	Lg Org	G	AB	H	2B	3B	HR	TB	R	RBI	TBB	IBB	SO	HBP	SH	SF	SB	CS	SB%	GDP	Avg	OBP	SLG
1992 Spokane	A- SD	42	119	25	4	1	1	34	10	7	9	0	25	1	2	1	7	4	.64	3	.210	.269	.286
1993 Waterloo	A SD	118	391	104	20	5	11	167	51	59	19	0	67	3	9	4	6	2	.75	10	.266	.302	.427
1994 Rancho Cuca	A+ SD	123	435	110	21	3	7	158	53	74	22	1	64	6	1	11	3	3	.50	8	.253	.291	.363
1995 Memphis	AA SD	73	236	63	10	0	7	94	24	34	12	0	32	2	1	1	2	2	.50	1	.267	.307	.398
1996 San Jose	A+ SF	3	11	1	0	0	0	1	0	0	0	0	2	0	0	0	0	1	.00	0	.091	.091	.091
Shreveport	AA SF	85	263	62	11	4	4	93	30	34	23	3	43	1	1	3	0	2	.00	5	.236	.297	.354
Phoenix	AAA SF	19	36	7	2	0	0	9	1	2	0	0	7	0	0	0	0	0	.00	1	.194	.194	.250
5 Min. YEARS		463	1491	372	68	13	30	556	169	210	85	4	240	13	14	20	18	14	.56	28	.249	.292	.373

David Dellucci

Bats: Left **Throws:** Left **Pos:** OF **Ht:** 5'10" **Wt:** 180 **Born:** 10/31/73 **Age:** 23

		BATTING															BASERUNNING				PERCENTAGES		
Year Team	Lg Org	G	AB	H	2B	3B	HR	TB	R	RBI	TBB	IBB	SO	HBP	SH	SF	SB	CS	SB%	GDP	Avg	OBP	SLG
1995 Bluefield	R+ Bal	20	69	23	5	1	2	30	11	12	6	1	7	1	0	1	3	1	.75	1	.333	.390	.522
Frederick	A+ Bal	28	96	27	3	0	1	33	16	10	12	1	10	3	0	0	1	2	.33	3	.281	.378	.344
1996 Frederick	A+ Bal	59	185	60	11	1	4	85	33	28	38	3	34	0	0	1	5	6	.45	2	.324	.438	.459
Bowie	AA Bal	66	251	73	14	1	2	95	27	33	28	1	56	1	2	1	2	7	.22	4	.291	.363	.378

		BATTING															BASERUNNING				PERCENTAGES		
Year Team	Lg Org	G	AB	H	2B	3B	HR	TB	R	RBI	TBB	IBB	SO	HBP	SH	SF	SB	CS	SB%	GDP	Avg	OBP	SLG
2 Min. YEARS		173	601	183	33	3	9	249	87	83	84	6	107	5	2	3	11	16	.41	10	.304	.392	.414

Nick Delvecchio

Bats: Left **Throws:** Right **Pos:** DH **Ht:** 6'5" **Wt:** 203 **Born:** 1/23/70 **Age:** 27

		BATTING															BASERUNNING				PERCENTAGES		
Year Team	Lg Org	G	AB	H	2B	3B	HR	TB	R	RBI	TBB	IBB	SO	HBP	SH	SF	SB	CS	SB%	GDP	Avg	OBP	SLG
1992 Oneonta	A- NYA	68	241	66	12	1	12	116	43	35	35	3	76	8	1	0	0	1	.00	3	.274	.384	.481
1993 Greensboro	A NYA	137	485	131	30	3	21	230	90	80	80	9	156	23	0	2	4	3	.57	9	.270	.397	.474
1994 Yankees	R NYA	4	13	5	0	0	0	5	1	0	2	0	3	0	0	0	0	0	.00	0	.385	.467	.385
Tampa	A+ NYA	27	95	27	3	0	7	51	17	18	11	0	20	1	0	1	0	0	.00	0	.284	.361	.537
1995 Norwich	AA NYA	125	430	112	23	4	19	200	66	74	72	8	133	23	0	6	2	1	.67	6	.260	.390	.465
1996 Columbus	AAA NYA	2	1	1	0	0	0	1	0	0	3	0	0	0	0	0	0	0	.00	0	1.000	1.000	1.000
Yankees	R NYA	5	18	11	4	0	2	21	4	8	6	0	1	1	0	0	1	0	1.00	1	.611	.720	1.167
Tampa	A+ NYA	17	52	14	2	0	2	22	9	4	17	1	15	3	0	0	2	1	.67	2	.269	.472	.423
Norwich	AA NYA	12	36	10	3	0	2	19	7	7	6	0	9	5	0	0	1	0	1.00	2	.278	.447	.528
5 Min. YEARS		397	1371	377	77	8	65	665	237	226	232	21	413	64	1	9	10	6	.63	23	.275	.402	.485

Chris Demetral

Bats: Left **Throws:** Right **Pos:** 2B **Ht:** 5'11" **Wt:** 175 **Born:** 12/8/69 **Age:** 27

		BATTING															BASERUNNING				PERCENTAGES		
Year Team	Lg Org	G	AB	H	2B	3B	HR	TB	R	RBI	TBB	IBB	SO	HBP	SH	SF	SB	CS	SB%	GDP	Avg	OBP	SLG
1991 Yakima	A- LA	65	226	64	11	0	2	81	43	41	34	2	32	1	6	0	4	3	.57	2	.283	.379	.358
1992 Bakersfield	A+ LA	90	306	84	14	1	4	112	38	36	33	7	45	1	4	3	7	8	.47	3	.275	.344	.366
1993 Vero Beach	A+ LA	122	437	142	22	3	5	185	63	48	69	2	47	2	6	3	6	6	.50	9	.325	.417	.423
1994 San Antonio	AA LA	108	368	96	26	3	6	146	44	39	34	5	44	1	11	2	5	2	.71	8	.261	.323	.397
1995 Albuquerque	AAA LA	87	187	52	7	1	3	70	34	19	24	2	28	0	3	0	1	6	.14	7	.278	.360	.374
1996 San Bernrdo	A+ LA	11	32	9	3	0	1	15	5	4	6	1	5	0	0	0	0	3	.00	0	.281	.395	.469
Albuquerque	AAA LA	99	209	55	8	0	4	75	30	26	40	5	35	0	5	5	4	3	.57	6	.263	.374	.359
6 Min. YEARS		582	1765	502	91	8	25	684	257	213	240	24	236	5	35	13	27	31	.47	35	.284	.369	.388

Shane Dennis

Pitches: Left **Bats:** Right **Pos:** P **Ht:** 6'3" **Wt:** 200 **Born:** 7/3/71 **Age:** 25

		HOW MUCH HE PITCHED						WHAT HE GAVE UP												THE RESULTS					
Year Team	Lg Org	G	GS	CG	GF	IP	BFP	H	R	ER	HR	SH	SF	HB	TBB	IBB	SO	WP	Bk	W	L	Pct.	ShO	Sv	ERA
1994 Spokane	A- SD	12	12	1	0	77.1	322	76	38	35	5	4	3	3	25	0	80	2	2	1	7	.125	1	0	4.07
Springfield	A SD	3	3	0	0	17	61	5	2	2	1	0	0	0	8	0	10	0	0	1	0	1.000	0	0	1.06
1995 Rancho Cuca	A+ SD	11	11	2	0	79	316	63	27	22	8	3	2	0	22	1	77	1	0	8	2	.800	1	0	2.51
Clinton	A SD	25	25	5	0	165	680	131	78	59	13	7	2	2	57	4	157	6	0	11	11	.500	1	0	3.22
1996 Rancho Cuca	A+ SD	9	9	1	0	59	247	57	22	21	6	1	1	1	19	0	54	2	0	4	2	.667	0	0	3.20
Memphis	AA SD	19	19	1	0	115	471	83	35	29	11	4	2	5	45	0	131	8	1	9	1	.900	0	0	2.27
3 Min. YEARS		79	79	10	0	512.1	2097	415	202	168	44	19	10	11	176	5	509	19	3	34	23	.596	3	0	2.95

Drew Denson

Bats: Right **Throws:** Right **Pos:** DH **Ht:** 6' 5" **Wt:** 220 **Born:** 11/16/65 **Age:** 31

		BATTING															BASERUNNING				PERCENTAGES		
Year Team	Lg Org	G	AB	H	2B	3B	HR	TB	R	RBI	TBB	IBB	SO	HBP	SH	SF	SB	CS	SB%	GDP	Avg	OBP	SLG
1984 Braves	R Atl	62	239	77	20	3	10	133	43	45	17	0	41	3	0	1	5	2	.71	8	.322	.373	.556
1985 Sumter	A Atl	111	383	115	18	4	14	183	59	74	53	3	76	4	0	4	5	3	.63	16	.300	.387	.478
1986 Durham	A+ Atl	72	231	54	6	3	4	78	31	23	25	0	46	2	1	0	6	1	.86	10	.234	.314	.338
1987 Greenville	AA Atl	128	447	98	23	1	14	165	54	55	33	1	95	11	1	2	1	2	.33	15	.219	.288	.369
1988 Greenville	AA Atl	140	507	136	26	4	13	209	85	78	44	1	116	14	3	4	11	9	.55	11	.268	.341	.412
1989 Richmond	AAA Atl	138	463	118	32	0	9	177	50	59	42	2	116	12	1	5	0	1	.00	4	.255	.330	.382
1990 Richmond	AAA Atl	90	295	68	4	1	7	95	25	29	26	2	57	9	0	3	0	0	.00	9	.231	.309	.322
1992 Vancouver	AAA ChA	105	340	94	7	3	13	146	43	70	36	3	58	7	0	0	1	0	1.00	12	.276	.358	.429
1993 Nashville	AAA ChA	136	513	144	36	0	24	252	82	103	46	7	98	23	0	8	0	0	.00	22	.281	.361	.491
1994 Nashville	AAA ChA	138	505	133	31	2	30	258	94	103	56	7	74	35	0	7	3	2	.60	13	.263	.371	.511
1995 Indianapols	AAA Cin	107	357	99	21	0	18	174	59	69	34	5	68	18	0	3	1	0	1.00	10	.277	.367	.487
1996 Rochester	AAA Bal	16	60	21	7	1	2	36	14	10	7	0	12	0	0	0	0	0	.00	1	.350	.418	.600
1989 Atlanta	NL	12	36	9	1	0	0	10	1	5	3	0	9	0	0	0	1	0	1.00	0	.250	.308	.278
1993 Chicago	AL	4	5	1	0	0	0	1	0	0	0	0	2	0	0	0	0	0	.00	0	.200	.200	.200
12 Min. YEARS		1243	4340	1157	231	22	158	1906	639	718	419	31	857	138	6	37	33	20	.62	131	.267	.347	.439
2 Maj. YEARS		16	41	10	1	0	0	11	1	5	3	0	11	0	0	0	1	0	1.00	0	.244	.295	.268

John DeSilva

Pitches: Right **Bats:** Right **Pos:** P **Ht:** 6' 0" **Wt:** 195 **Born:** 9/30/67 **Age:** 29

		HOW MUCH HE PITCHED						WHAT HE GAVE UP												THE RESULTS					
Year Team	Lg Org	G	GS	CG	GF	IP	BFP	H	R	ER	HR	SH	SF	HB	TBB	IBB	SO	WP	Bk	W	L	Pct.	ShO	Sv	ERA
1989 Niagara Fal	A- Det	4	4	0	0	24	95	15	5	5	0	1	0	2	8	0	24	3	1	3	0	1.000	0	0	1.88
Fayetteville	A Det	9	9	1	0	52.2	215	40	23	16	4	1	2	0	21	0	54	2	3	2	2	.500	0	0	2.73
1990 Lakeland	A+ Det	14	14	0	0	91	349	54	18	15	4	1	2	4	25	0	113	3	1	8	1	.889	0	0	1.48
London	AA Det	14	14	1	0	89	372	87	47	37	4	1	4	2	27	0	76	3	0	5	6	.455	1	0	3.74
1991 London	AA Det	11	11	2	0	73.2	294	51	24	23	4	2	2	0	24	0	80	1	0	5	4	.556	1	0	2.81

Year	Team	Lg	Org	HOW MUCH HE PITCHED						WHAT HE GAVE UP												THE RESULTS					
				G	GS	CG	GF	IP	BFP	H	R	ER	HR	SH	SF	HB	TBB	IBB	SO	WP	Bk	W	L	Pct.	ShO	Sv	ERA
	Toledo	AAA	Det	11	11	1	0	58.2	254	62	33	30	10	0	1	1	21	0	56	1	0	5	4	.556	0	0	4.60
1992	Toledo	AAA	Det	7	2	0	3	19	89	26	18	18	5	1	0	0	8	0	21	0	0	0	3	.000	0	0	8.53
	London	AA	Det	9	9	1	0	52.1	216	51	24	24	4	1	2	1	13	0	53	2	1	2	4	.333	1	0	4.13
1993	Toledo	AAA	Det	25	24	1	0	161	675	145	73	66	13	2	5	0	60	2	136	3	1	7	10	.412	0	0	3.69
1994	Albuquerque	AAA	LA	25	6	0	4	66.2	317	90	62	58	7	1	3	4	27	0	39	3	0	3	5	.375	0	1	7.83
	San Antonio	AA	LA	25	2	0	7	46	202	46	29	26	3	2	1	1	18	2	46	2	1	1	3	.250	0	2	5.09
1995	Rochester	AAA	Bal	26	25	2	1	150.2	644	156	78	70	19	3	3	6	51	0	82	2	1	11	9	.550	0	0	4.18
1996	Palm Spring	IND	—	1	1	0	0	5	18	1	2	2	1	0	0	0	2	0	7	0	0	1	0	1.000	0	0	3.60
	Pawtucket	AAA	Bos	16	16	0	0	84.2	373	99	55	49	12	2	1	0	27	0	68	1	0	4	3	.571	0	0	5.21
1993	Detroit	AL		1	0	0	1	1	4	2	1	1	0	0	1	0	0	0	0	0	0	0	0	.000	0	0	9.00
	Los Angeles	NL		3	0	0	2	5.1	23	6	4	4	0	0	0	0	1	0	6	0	0	0	0	.000	0	0	6.75
1995	Baltimore	AL		2	2	0	0	8.2	41	8	7	7	3	1	1	1	7	0	1	0	0	1	0	1.000	0	0	7.27
8 Min. YEARS				197	148	9	15	974.1	4113	923	491	439	90	18	26	21	332	4	855	26	9	57	54	.514	3	3	4.06
2 Maj. YEARS				6	2	0	3	15	68	16	12	12	3	1	2	1	8	0	7	0	0	1	0	1.000	0	0	7.20

Kris Detmers

Pitches: Left **Bats:** Both **Pos:** P **Ht:** 6'5" **Wt:** 215 **Born:** 6/22/74 **Age:** 23

Year	Team	Lg	Org	HOW MUCH HE PITCHED						WHAT HE GAVE UP												THE RESULTS					
				G	GS	CG	GF	IP	BFP	H	R	ER	HR	SH	SF	HB	TBB	IBB	SO	WP	Bk	W	L	Pct.	ShO	Sv	ERA
1994	Madison	A	StL	16	16	0	0	90.1	380	88	45	34	4	1	1	4	31	0	74	0	1	5	7	.417	0	0	3.39
1995	St. Pete	A+	StL	25	25	1	0	146.2	606	120	64	53	12	3	7	2	57	0	150	3	2	10	9	.526	0	0	3.25
1996	Arkansas	AA	StL	27	27	0	0	163.2	698	154	72	61	15	6	3	4	70	0	97	8	0	12	8	.600	0	0	3.35
3 Min. YEARS				68	68	1	0	400.2	1684	362	181	148	31	10	11	10	158	0	321	11	3	27	24	.529	0	0	3.32

John Dettmer

Pitches: Right **Bats:** Right **Pos:** P **Ht:** 6' 0" **Wt:** 185 **Born:** 3/4/70 **Age:** 27

Year	Team	Lg	Org	HOW MUCH HE PITCHED						WHAT HE GAVE UP												THE RESULTS					
				G	GS	CG	GF	IP	BFP	H	R	ER	HR	SH	SF	HB	TBB	IBB	SO	WP	Bk	W	L	Pct.	ShO	Sv	ERA
1992	Gastonia	A	Tex	15	15	3	0	98	374	74	25	22	1	0	4	2	17	0	102	2	2	10	1	.909	1	0	2.02
1993	Charlotte	A+	Tex	27	27	5	0	163	648	132	44	39	6	4	1	7	33	0	128	2	5	16	3	.842	2	0	2.15
1994	Tulsa	AA	Tex	10	10	2	0	74.2	288	57	23	20	3	1	2	1	12	1	65	1	0	6	1	.857	0	0	2.41
	Okla. City	AAA	Tex	8	8	1	0	46.1	209	59	33	29	7	1	4	2	11	0	26	1	0	3	2	.600	1	0	5.63
1995	Okla. City	AAA	Tex	5	0	0	3	8.2	37	10	3	2	1	1	0	0	4	0	10	1	1	0	0	.000	0	0	2.08
	Rochester	AAA	Bal	26	11	1	6	91.1	396	108	55	45	10	3	3	2	20	0	56	3	2	4	7	.364	1	1	4.43
1996	Greenville	AA	Atl	26	0	0	4	40.2	173	43	19	13	3	0	1	3	6	1	28	1	0	3	3	.500	0	0	2.88
	Richmond	AAA	Atl	19	6	0	3	59.2	249	69	27	26	8	4	2	1	9	1	26	2	0	3	5	.375	0	0	3.92
1994	Texas	AL		11	9	0	0	54	250	63	42	26	10	2	5	3	20	3	27	1	0	0	6	.000	0	0	4.33
1995	Texas	AL		1	0	0	0	0.1	4	2	1	1	0	0	1	0	0	0	0	0	0	0	0	.000	0	0	27.00
5 Min. YEARS				136	77	12	16	582.1	2374	552	229	196	39	14	17	18	112	3	441	13	10	45	22	.672	5	1	3.03
2 Maj. YEARS				12	9	0	0	54.1	254	65	43	27	10	2	6	3	20	3	27	1	0	0	6	.000	0	0	4.47

Eddy Diaz

Bats: Right **Throws:** Right **Pos:** SS **Ht:** 5'10" **Wt:** 160 **Born:** 9/29/71 **Age:** 25

Year	Team	Lg	Org	BATTING															BASERUNNING				PERCENTAGES		
				G	AB	H	2B	3B	HR	TB	R	RBI	TBB	IBB	SO	HBP	SH	SF	SB	CS	SB%	GDP	Avg	OBP	SLG
1991	Bellingham	A-	Sea	61	246	68	14	1	3	93	48	23	24	1	33	1	3	2	9	2	.82	4	.276	.341	.378
1992	San Bernrdo	A+	Sea	114	436	119	15	2	9	165	80	39	38	0	46	6	12	2	33	16	.67	11	.273	.338	.378
1993	Appleton	A	Sea	46	189	63	14	2	3	90	28	33	15	2	13	0	0	0	13	9	.59	7	.333	.382	.476
	Jacksonvlle	AA	Sea	77	259	65	16	0	6	99	36	26	17	1	31	2	7	4	6	3	.67	5	.251	.298	.382
1994	Jacksonvlle	AA	Sea	104	340	84	20	0	8	128	43	42	21	1	23	2	9	3	13	5	.72	8	.247	.292	.376
1995	Tacoma	AAA	Sea	11	36	12	2	0	0	14	5	5	4	0	2	0	0	0	0	0	.00	0	.333	.400	.389
	Port City	AA	Sea	110	421	110	22	0	16	180	66	47	40	3	39	8	1	4	9	7	.56	9	.261	.334	.428
1996	Tacoma	AAA	Sea	107	422	118	28	4	13	193	63	58	15	1	38	10	5	2	3	4	.43	9	.280	.318	.457
6 Min. YEARS				630	2349	639	131	9	58	962	369	273	174	9	225	29	37	17	86	46	.65	53	.272	.328	.410

Edwin Diaz

Bats: Right **Throws:** Right **Pos:** 2B **Ht:** 5'11" **Wt:** 170 **Born:** 1/15/75 **Age:** 22

Year	Team	Lg	Org	BATTING															BASERUNNING				PERCENTAGES		
				G	AB	H	2B	3B	HR	TB	R	RBI	TBB	IBB	SO	HBP	SH	SF	SB	CS	SB%	GDP	Avg	OBP	SLG
1993	Rangers	R	Tex	43	154	47	10	5	1	70	27	23	19	1	21	4	0	2	12	5	.71	4	.305	.391	.455
1994	Charlstn-SC	A	Tex	122	413	109	22	7	11	178	52	60	22	0	107	8	8	9	11	14	.44	7	.264	.308	.431
1995	Charlotte	A+	Tex	115	450	128	26	5	8	188	48	56	33	0	94	7	3	2	8	13	.38	10	.284	.341	.418
1996	Tulsa	AA	Tex	121	499	132	33	6	16	225	70	65	25	4	122	9	8	4	8	9	.47	9	.265	.309	.451
4 Min. YEARS				401	1516	416	91	23	36	661	197	204	99	5	344	28	19	17	39	41	.49	30	.274	.327	.436

Freddy Diaz

Bats: Both **Throws:** Right **Pos:** SS **Ht:** 5'11" **Wt:** 175 **Born:** 9/10/72 **Age:** 24

Year	Team	Lg	Org	BATTING															BASERUNNING				PERCENTAGES		
				G	AB	H	2B	3B	HR	TB	R	RBI	TBB	IBB	SO	HBP	SH	SF	SB	CS	SB%	GDP	Avg	OBP	SLG
1992	Angels	R	Cal	14	37	10	3	0	0	13	6	4	5	0	7	0	2	1	3	1	.75	0	.270	.340	.351
1993	Boise	A-	Cal	26	75	22	4	1	2	34	13	14	9	0	11	0	3	0	1	3	.25	0	.293	.369	.453
1994	Lk Elsinore	A+	Cal	110	350	100	29	1	5	146	48	64	35	0	71	4	7	6	4	4	.50	5	.286	.352	.417

BATTING																			BASERUNNING				PERCENTAGES		
Year	Team	Lg	Org	G	AB	H	2B	3B	HR	TB	R	RBI	TBB	IBB	SO	HBP	SH	SF	SB	CS	SB%	GDP	Avg	OBP	SLG
1995	Midland	AA	Cal	8	25	6	3	0	0	9	3	4	0	0	12	0	2	0	0	0	.00	1	.240	.240	.360
	Lk Elsinore	A+	Cal	49	149	35	12	2	1	54	25	25	11	0	54	0	3	6	1	1	.50	6	.235	.277	.362
1996	Midland	AA	Cal	54	156	31	7	2	3	51	23	18	13	1	43	0	4	3	1	1	.50	3	.199	.256	.327
	Vancouver	AAA	Cal	34	123	32	9	2	3	54	19	23	14	0	25	0	3	3	0	0	.00	1	.260	.329	.439
5 Min. YEARS				295	915	236	67	8	14	361	137	152	87	1	223	4	24	19	10	10	.50	16	.258	.319	.395

Lino Diaz

Bats: Right **Throws:** Right **Pos:** 3B **Ht:** 5'11" **Wt:** 182 **Born:** 7/22/70 **Age:** 26

BATTING																			BASERUNNING				PERCENTAGES		
Year	Team	Lg	Org	G	AB	H	2B	3B	HR	TB	R	RBI	TBB	IBB	SO	HBP	SH	SF	SB	CS	SB%	GDP	Avg	OBP	SLG
1993	Eugene	A-	KC	53	183	46	7	1	1	58	19	23	13	0	25	3	2	4	6	2	.75	2	.251	.305	.317
1994	Rockford	A	KC	127	414	131	23	1	4	168	57	44	32	4	33	14	2	5	11	6	.65	14	.316	.381	.406
1995	Wilmington	A+	KC	51	173	52	6	2	2	68	20	23	11	0	9	4	2	0	0	5	.00	2	.301	.356	.393
	Wichita	AA	KC	62	226	79	15	3	6	118	40	43	14	0	21	6	0	1	0	3	.00	5	.350	.401	.522
1996	Omaha	AAA	KC	75	266	72	13	2	3	98	32	28	17	0	29	6	1	1	0	3	.00	9	.271	.328	.368
	Wichita	AA	KC	44	159	40	8	1	3	59	18	19	9	0	11	2	0	0	2	1	.67	7	.252	.300	.371
4 Min. YEARS				412	1421	420	72	10	19	569	186	180	96	4	128	35	7	11	19	20	.49	39	.296	.353	.400

Mario Diaz

Bats: Right **Throws:** Right **Pos:** 2B **Ht:** 5'10" **Wt:** 160 **Born:** 1/10/62 **Age:** 35

BATTING																			BASERUNNING				PERCENTAGES		
Year	Team	Lg	Org	G	AB	H	2B	3B	HR	TB	R	RBI	TBB	IBB	SO	HBP	SH	SF	SB	CS	SB%	GDP	Avg	OBP	SLG
1984	Chattanooga	AA	Sea	108	322	67	7	1	1	79	23	19	21	0	18	0	13	5	6	5	.55	14	.208	.253	.245
1985	Chattanooga	AA	Sea	115	400	101	6	7	0	121	38	38	21	2	20	0	14	7	3	4	.43	15	.253	.285	.303
1986	Calgary	AAA	Sea	109	379	107	17	6	1	139	40	41	13	2	29	0	5	4	1	3	.25	13	.282	.303	.367
1987	Calgary	AAA	Sea	108	376	106	17	3	4	141	52	52	19	2	25	1	10	1	1	5	.17	13	.282	.317	.375
1988	Calgary	AAA	Sea	46	164	54	18	0	1	75	16	30	9	0	10	3	1	3	1	2	.33	5	.329	.369	.457
1989	Calgary	AAA	Sea	37	127	43	8	1	2	59	22	9	8	0	7	1	0	1	1	4	.20	2	.339	.380	.465
1990	Calgary	AAA	Sea	32	105	35	5	1	1	45	10	19	1	0	8	1	0	1	0	1	.00	4	.333	.343	.429
	Tidewater	AAA	NYN	29	104	33	8	0	1	44	15	9	6	0	6	1	0	0	1	2	.33	3	.317	.360	.423
1992	Calgary	AAA	Sea	18	52	14	4	0	0	18	8	11	0	0	6	0	1	1	1	1	.50	3	.269	.264	.346
	Okla. City	AAA	Tex	43	167	56	11	0	3	76	24	20	2	1	12	0	0	2	1	0	1.00	7	.335	.339	.455
1993	Okla. City	AAA	Tex	48	177	58	12	2	3	83	24	20	7	0	15	1	1	2	3	1	.75	7	.328	.353	.469
1994	Pawtucket	AAA	Bos	30	120	40	6	1	3	57	14	19	4	1	7	0	0	3	0	1	.00	2	.333	.346	.475
1996	Columbus	AAA	NYA	16	61	16	3	0	2	25	9	11	1	0	6	0	1	0	0	2	.00	3	.262	.274	.410
	Scranton-WB	AAA	Phi	46	180	50	6	0	3	65	20	22	11	0	9	1	0	1	0	0	.00	5	.278	.321	.361
1987	Seattle	AL		11	23	7	0	1	0	9	4	3	0	0	4	0	0	0	0	0	.00	0	.304	.304	.391
1988	Seattle	AL		28	72	22	5	0	0	27	6	9	3	0	5	0	0	1	0	0	.00	3	.306	.329	.375
1989	Seattle	AL		52	74	10	0	0	1	13	9	7	7	0	7	0	5	0	0	0	.00	2	.135	.210	.176
1990	New York	NL		16	22	3	1	0	0	4	0	1	0	0	3	0	0	1	0	0	.00	0	.136	.130	.182
1991	Texas	AL		96	182	48	7	0	1	58	24	22	15	0	18	0	4	1	0	1	.00	5	.264	.318	.319
1992	Texas	AL		19	31	7	1	0	0	8	2	1	1	1	2	0	1	0	0	1	.00	2	.226	.250	.258
1993	Texas	AL		71	205	56	10	1	2	74	24	24	8	0	13	1	7	5	1	0	1.00	6	.273	.297	.361
1994	Florida	NL		32	77	25	4	2	0	33	10	11	6	0	6	1	0	1	0	0	.00	1	.325	.376	.429
1995	Florida	NL		49	87	20	3	0	1	26	5	6	1	0	12	0	1	0	0	0	.00	4	.230	.239	.299
11 Min. YEARS				785	2734	780	128	22	25	1027	315	320	123	8	178	9	46	31	19	31	.38	96	.285	.315	.376
9 Maj. YEARS				374	773	198	31	4	5	252	84	84	41	1	70	2	18	9	1	2	.33	23	.256	.292	.326

Tony Diggs

Bats: Both **Throws:** Right **Pos:** OF **Ht:** 6'0" **Wt:** 175 **Born:** 4/20/67 **Age:** 30

BATTING																			BASERUNNING				PERCENTAGES		
Year	Team	Lg	Org	G	AB	H	2B	3B	HR	TB	R	RBI	TBB	IBB	SO	HBP	SH	SF	SB	CS	SB%	GDP	Avg	OBP	SLG
1989	Helena	R+	Mil	51	148	36	1	1	0	39	24	20	14	0	29	1	5	1	5	3	.63	0	.243	.311	.264
1990	Beloit	A	Mil	2	4	0	0	0	0	0	0	0	0	0	0	0	0	0	0	0	.00	0	.000	.000	.000
	Helena	R+	Mil	42	129	33	5	0	0	38	18	13	11	0	19	2	1	2	10	5	.67	1	.256	.319	.295
1991	Beloit	A	Mil	124	448	121	9	8	3	155	70	34	65	2	76	3	5	1	52	19	.73	6	.270	.366	.346
1992	El Paso	AA	Mil	107	281	61	6	3	0	73	47	20	29	2	48	3	7	3	31	8	.79	6	.217	.294	.260
1993	New Orleans	AAA	Mil	11	27	7	3	0	0	10	4	1	3	0	6	0	1	0	4	2	.67	0	.259	.333	.370
	El Paso	AA	Mil	18	63	9	1	0	1	13	5	3	1	0	14	1	3	0	3	0	1.00	0	.143	.169	.206
	Stockton	A+	Mil	81	285	84	14	3	1	107	48	31	43	2	34	3	1	3	31	11	.74	2	.295	.389	.375
1994	Arkansas	AA	StL	105	288	62	13	4	0	83	33	13	20	4	36	3	4	0	7	6	.54	4	.215	.273	.288
1995	Arkansas	AA	StL	78	235	63	9	8	2	94	33	21	35	5	41	2	2	1	7	6	.54	3	.268	.366	.400
	Louisville	AAA	StL	23	36	9	3	0	0	12	4	0	5	1	4	0	0	0	2	1	.67	1	.250	.341	.333
1996	Arkansas	AA	StL	35	138	42	7	3	3	64	23	22	12	0	16	1	1	3	7	4	.64	0	.304	.357	.464
	Louisville	AAA	StL	92	308	63	14	2	7	102	35	23	33	1	49	2	11	0	5	5	.50	6	.205	.286	.331
8 Min. YEARS				769	2390	590	85	32	17	790	344	201	271	17	372	21	41	14	164	70	.70	29	.247	.327	.331

Glenn Disarcina

Bats: Left **Throws:** Right **Pos:** SS-3B **Ht:** 6'1" **Wt:** 180 **Born:** 4/29/70 **Age:** 27

BATTING																			BASERUNNING				PERCENTAGES		
Year	Team	Lg	Org	G	AB	H	2B	3B	HR	TB	R	RBI	TBB	IBB	SO	HBP	SH	SF	SB	CS	SB%	GDP	Avg	OBP	SLG
1991	Utica	A-	ChA	56	202	51	9	1	0	62	27	27	22	0	30	0	2	0	11	2	.85	5	.252	.326	.307
1992	South Bend	A	ChA	126	467	123	29	6	1	167	60	50	44	4	105	0	3	6	12	5	.71	11	.263	.323	.358

Year	Team	Lg	Org	G	AB	H	2B	3B	HR	TB	R	RBI	TBB	IBB	SO	HBP	SH	SF	SB	CS	SB%	GDP	Avg	OBP	SLG
	BATTING																		BASERUNNING				PERCENTAGES		
	Sarasota	A+	ChA	1	4	0	0	0	0	0	0	0	0	0	1	0	0	0	0	0	.00	0	.000	.000	.000
1993	Sarasota	A+	ChA	120	477	135	29	5	4	186	73	47	33	4	77	2	0	6	11	5	.69	7	.283	.328	.390
	Birmingham	AA	ChA	3	5	2	0	0	0	2	1	1	2	0	2	0	0	1	1	0	1.00	0	.400	.500	.400
1994	Birmingham	AA	ChA	118	452	116	26	2	7	167	50	57	25	3	74	3	4	4	10	5	.67	12	.257	.298	.369
1995	White Sox	R	ChA	9	36	7	3	1	0	12	6	3	0	0	4	1	0	0	1	0	1.00	3	.194	.216	.333
	Birmingham	AA	ChA	9	26	7	1	0	0	8	4	2	2	0	3	0	0	0	0	0	.00	0	.269	.321	.308
1996	Birmingham	AA	ChA	43	175	64	10	3	7	101	25	36	7	1	45	1	0	2	4	0	1.00	3	.366	.389	.577
	Nashville	AAA	ChA	38	97	23	9	0	0	32	8	11	5	0	20	0	1	0	1	1	.50	2	.237	.275	.330
6 Min. YEARS				523	1941	528	116	18	19	737	254	234	140	12	361	7	10	19	51	18	.74	43	.272	.320	.380

Jamie Dismuke

Bats: Left **Throws:** Right **Pos:** 1B **Ht:** 6'1" **Wt:** 210 **Born:** 10/17/69 **Age:** 27

Year	Team	Lg	Org	G	AB	H	2B	3B	HR	TB	R	RBI	TBB	IBB	SO	HBP	SH	SF	SB	CS	SB%	GDP	Avg	OBP	SLG
	BATTING																		BASERUNNING				PERCENTAGES		
1989	Reds	R	Cin	34	98	18	1	0	1	22	6	5	8	2	19	3	0	0	0	1	.00	0	.184	.266	.224
1990	Reds	R	Cin	39	124	44	8	4	7	81	22	28	28	5	8	5	0	2	3	3	.50	4	.355	.484	.653
1991	Cedar Rapds	A	Cin	133	492	125	35	1	8	186	56	72	50	3	80	4	2	9	4	2	.67	10	.254	.323	.378
1992	Charlstn-WV	A	Cin	134	475	135	22	0	17	208	77	71	67	5	71	15	3	5	3	4	.43	15	.284	.386	.438
1993	Chattanooga	AA	Cin	136	497	152	22	1	20	236	69	91	48	6	60	14	0	4	4	2	.67	10	.306	.380	.475
1994	Indianapols	AAA	Cin	121	391	104	22	0	13	165	51	49	47	6	52	7	2	2	1	0	1.00	13	.266	.353	.422
1995	Indianapols	AAA	Cin	13	36	9	1	0	0	10	6	2	3	1	3	0	0	0	0	0	.00	1	.250	.308	.278
	Chattanooga	AA	Cin	99	347	99	11	0	20	170	56	69	44	10	45	10	0	1	0	0	.00	11	.285	.381	.490
1996	Syracuse	AAA	Tor	19	42	7	1	0	0	8	3	5	5	0	5	0	0	1	1	0	1.00	1	.167	.250	.190
	Jacksonvlle	AA	Det	29	79	21	4	1	4	39	7	12	14	2	14	2	0	0	0	0	.00	3	.266	.389	.494
8 Min. YEARS				757	2581	714	127	7	90	1125	353	404	314	40	357	60	7	24	16	12	.57	68	.277	.365	.436

Bubba Dixon

Pitches: Left **Bats:** Left **Pos:** P **Ht:** 5'10" **Wt:** 165 **Born:** 1/7/72 **Age:** 25

Year	Team	Lg	Org	G	GS	CG	GF	IP	BFP	H	R	ER	HR	SH	SF	HB	TBB	IBB	SO	WP	Bk	W	L	Pct.	ShO	Sv	ERA
	HOW MUCH HE PITCHED									WHAT HE GAVE UP												THE RESULTS					
1994	Spokane	A-	SD	32	0	0	26	45.1	189	31	8	6	0	1	3	1	24	5	81	2	0	2	1	.667	0	11	1.19
1995	Rancho Cuca	A+	SD	47	12	2	15	141.2	572	118	61	51	14	5	1	8	46	0	133	6	2	10	7	.588	0	5	3.24
1996	Memphis	AA	SD	42	0	0	12	63.1	267	53	32	29	6	2	1	2	28	2	77	4	1	2	3	.400	0	3	4.12
	Rancho Cuca	A+	SD	11	0	0	3	16.1	73	20	16	13	3	0	1	0	4	0	20	1	0	0	3	.000	0	0	7.16
3 Min. YEARS				132	12	2	56	266.2	1101	222	117	99	23	8	6	11	102	7	311	13	3	14	14	.500	0	19	3.34

Steve Dixon

Pitches: Left **Bats:** Left **Pos:** P **Ht:** 6' 0" **Wt:** 190 **Born:** 8/3/69 **Age:** 27

Year	Team	Lg	Org	G	GS	CG	GF	IP	BFP	H	R	ER	HR	SH	SF	HB	TBB	IBB	SO	WP	Bk	W	L	Pct.	ShO	Sv	ERA
	HOW MUCH HE PITCHED									WHAT HE GAVE UP												THE RESULTS					
1989	Johnson Cty	R+	StL	18	3	0	5	43.1	200	50	34	29	1	4	3	2	23	2	29	4	2	1	3	.250	0	0	6.02
1990	Savannah	A	StL	64	0	0	21	83.2	355	59	34	18	1	8	0	4	38	5	92	4	0	7	3	.700	0	8	1.94
1991	St. Pete	A+	StL	53	0	0	23	64.1	269	54	32	27	3	7	4	0	24	1	54	2	2	5	4	.556	0	1	3.78
1992	Arkansas	AA	StL	40	0	0	20	49	192	34	11	10	2	3	2	0	15	4	65	2	0	2	1	.667	0	2	1.84
	Louisville	AAA	StL	18	0	0	8	19.2	94	20	12	11	0	0	0	1	19	2	16	0	1	1	2	.333	0	2	5.03
1993	Louisville	AAA	StL	57	0	0	41	67.2	292	57	38	37	8	4	2	4	33	7	61	2	0	5	7	.417	0	20	4.92
1994	Louisville	AAA	StL	59	0	0	29	60.2	270	51	25	17	4	1	1	8	30	2	62	3	0	3	2	.600	0	11	2.52
1995	Iowa	AAA	ChN	53	0	0	19	41	176	34	16	13	4	0	2	5	19	4	38	2	0	6	3	.667	0	0	2.85
1996	Binghamton	AA	NYN	5	0	0	1	8.1	41	10	5	5	0	1	0	1	8	1	11	0	1	0	1	.000	0	0	5.40
	Rochester	AAA	Bal	32	0	0	9	34.1	147	27	15	13	1	1	3	3	23	0	32	2	0	0	2	.000	0	2	3.41
	Louisville	AAA	StL	5	0	0	4	4.1	20	4	5	5	2	1	1	1	3	1	2	0	0	0	0	.000	0	0	10.38
1993	St. Louis	NL		4	0	0	0	2.2	20	7	10	10	1	2	0	0	5	0	2	0	0	0	0	.000	0	0	33.75
1994	St. Louis	NL		2	0	0	0	2.1	18	3	6	6	0	0	1	0	8	0	1	0	0	0	0	.000	0	0	23.14
8 Min. YEARS				404	3	0	180	476.1	2056	400	227	185	26	30	18	29	235	29	462	21	6	30	28	.517	0	46	3.50
2 Maj. YEARS				6	0	0	0	5	38	10	16	16	1	2	1	0	13	0	3	0	0	0	0	.000	0	0	28.80

Bill Dobrolsky

Bats: Right **Throws:** Right **Pos:** C **Ht:** 6'2" **Wt:** 205 **Born:** 3/16/70 **Age:** 27

Year	Team	Lg	Org	G	AB	H	2B	3B	HR	TB	R	RBI	TBB	IBB	SO	HBP	SH	SF	SB	CS	SB%	GDP	Avg	OBP	SLG
	BATTING																		BASERUNNING				PERCENTAGES		
1991	Brewers	R	Mil	5	23	7	4	0	0	11	3	5	0	0	3	1	0	0	0	0	.00	0	.304	.333	.478
	Helena	R+	Mil	9	31	5	2	0	0	7	2	2	3	0	7	0	0	0	0	0	.00	0	.161	.235	.226
1992	Denver	AAA	Mil	1	1	0	0	0	0	0	0	0	0	0	0	0	0	0	0	0	.00	0	.000	.000	.000
	Helena	R+	Mil	11	29	7	3	0	0	10	4	4	5	0	8	0	0	0	0	1	.00	1	.241	.353	.345
	Beloit	A	Mil	48	133	38	5	0	3	52	13	19	14	0	28	1	1	1	3	2	.60	4	.286	.356	.391
1993	Stockton	A+	Mil	67	190	40	2	0	1	45	18	21	16	0	43	5	2	1	2	1	.67	4	.211	.288	.237
1994	Beloit	A	Mil	72	197	52	12	0	3	73	29	25	35	0	55	3	5	0	1	1	.50	4	.264	.383	.371
1995	Stockton	A+	Mil	88	252	68	14	3	2	94	28	30	25	0	37	6	2	5	3	4	.43	4	.270	.344	.373
1996	El Paso	AA	Mil	68	202	57	11	1	2	76	20	21	17	0	37	5	3	3	1	4	.20	5	.282	.348	.376
6 Min. YEARS				369	1058	274	53	4	11	368	123	127	115	0	218	21	13	10	10	13	.43	22	.259	.341	.348

Robert Dodd

Pitches: Left **Bats:** Left **Pos:** P **Ht:** 6'3" **Wt:** 195 **Born:** 3/14/73 **Age:** 24

		HOW MUCH HE PITCHED						WHAT HE GAVE UP												THE RESULTS					
Year Team	Lg Org	G	GS	CG	GF	IP	BFP	H	R	ER	HR	SH	SF	HB	TBB	IBB	SO	WP	Bk	W	L	Pct.	ShO	Sv	ERA
1994 Batavia	A- Phi	14	7	0	2	52	209	42	16	13	0	2	1	2	14	1	44	4	0	2	4	.333	0	1	2.25
1995 Reading	AA Phi	1	0	0	0	1.1	5	0	0	0	0	0	0	0	2	0	0	0	0	0	0	.000	0	0	0.00
Clearwater	A+ Phi	27	26	0	0	152.1	641	144	64	53	4	3	6	1	60	0	110	3	7	8	7	.533	0	0	3.13
1996 Reading	AA Phi	18	5	0	4	43	185	41	21	17	4	4	3	3	24	2	35	0	1	2	3	.400	0	0	3.56
Scranton-WB	AAA Phi	8	2	0	2	20	101	32	21	18	4	0	0	1	9	0	12	1	0	0	0	.000	0	0	8.10
3 Min. YEARS		68	40	0	8	268.2	1141	259	122	101	12	9	10	7	109	3	201	8	8	12	14	.462	0	1	3.38

Bo Dodson

Bats: Left **Throws:** Left **Pos:** 1B **Ht:** 6'2" **Wt:** 195 **Born:** 12/7/70 **Age:** 26

		BATTING															BASERUNNING				PERCENTAGES		
Year Team	Lg Org	G	AB	H	2B	3B	HR	TB	R	RBI	TBB	IBB	SO	HBP	SH	SF	SB	CS	SB%	GDP	Avg	OBP	SLG
1989 Helena	R+ Mil	65	216	67	13	1	6	100	38	42	52	2	52	4	1	3	5	1	.83	4	.310	.447	.463
1990 Stockton	A+ Mil	120	363	99	16	4	6	141	70	46	73	2	103	3	1	1	1	1	.50	3	.273	.398	.388
1991 Stockton	A+ Mil	88	298	78	13	3	9	124	51	42	66	7	63	4	0	2	4	2	.67	1	.262	.400	.416
1992 El Paso	AA Mil	109	335	83	19	6	4	126	47	46	72	6	81	0	0	1	3	7	.30	7	.248	.380	.376
1993 El Paso	AA Mil	101	330	103	27	4	9	165	58	59	42	4	69	6	0	2	1	6	.14	3	.312	.397	.500
1994 El Paso	AA Mil	26	68	10	3	0	0	13	6	7	12	0	18	1	0	0	0	1	.00	2	.147	.284	.191
New Orleans	AAA Mil	79	257	67	13	0	2	86	41	29	42	2	44	2	3	1	2	3	.40	8	.261	.368	.335
1995 El Paso	AA Mil	63	223	80	20	4	7	129	46	43	37	2	42	7	0	0	1	1	.50	6	.359	.464	.578
New Orleans	AAA Mil	62	203	57	5	1	9	91	29	34	36	6	27	0	0	5	0	0	.00	4	.281	.381	.448
1996 Pawtucket	AAA Bos	82	276	95	20	0	11	148	37	43	32	1	50	1	1	3	4	0	1.00	7	.344	.410	.536
8 Min. YEARS		795	2569	739	149	23	63	1123	423	391	464	32	549	28	6	18	21	22	.49	45	.288	.400	.437

Roger Doman

Pitches: Right **Bats:** Right **Pos:** P **Ht:** 6'5" **Wt:** 185 **Born:** 1/26/73 **Age:** 24

		HOW MUCH HE PITCHED						WHAT HE GAVE UP												THE RESULTS					
Year Team	Lg Org	G	GS	CG	GF	IP	BFP	H	R	ER	HR	SH	SF	HB	TBB	IBB	SO	WP	Bk	W	L	Pct.	ShO	Sv	ERA
1991 Blue Jays	R Tor	13	10	0	0	50.1	214	54	29	27	2	0	1	2	17	0	28	9	1	2	2	.500	0	0	4.83
1992 St. Cathrns	A- Tor	15	14	0	1	68.2	316	70	47	35	3	3	2	2	47	0	53	12	1	2	7	.222	0	0	4.59
1993 Hagerstown	A Tor	26	26	0	0	146.2	650	153	78	67	11	3	4	6	73	0	102	15	2	8	6	.571	0	0	4.11
1994 Dunedin	A+ Tor	32	12	0	11	103.1	460	119	72	60	10	2	7	3	40	0	64	12	0	3	9	.250	0	2	5.23
1995 Hagerstown	A Tor	14	6	0	3	51	233	65	32	25	0	0	1	3	13	0	24	4	0	2	2	.500	0	1	4.41
Knoxville	AA Tor	28	6	0	9	81.2	373	107	57	45	2	1	2	4	24	0	40	7	0	2	5	.286	0	1	4.96
1996 Dunedin	A+ Tor	18	0	0	9	30	148	36	22	11	2	1	2	1	14	2	19	0	0	0	1	.000	0	0	3.30
Hagerstown	A Tor	2	1	0	0	4	19	4	3	3	0	0	0	1	4	0	4	3	0	0	0	.000	0	0	6.75
Knoxville	AA Tor	17	1	0	6	39.1	177	51	30	24	2	0	0	0	14	0	30	5	1	1	1	.500	0	0	5.49
6 Min. YEARS		165	76	0	39	575	2590	659	370	297	32	10	19	22	246	2	364	67	5	20	33	.377	0	4	4.65

Dan Donato

Bats: Left **Throws:** Right **Pos:** 3B **Ht:** 6'1" **Wt:** 205 **Born:** 11/15/72 **Age:** 24

		BATTING															BASERUNNING				PERCENTAGES		
Year Team	Lg Org	G	AB	H	2B	3B	HR	TB	R	RBI	TBB	IBB	SO	HBP	SH	SF	SB	CS	SB%	GDP	Avg	OBP	SLG
1995 Greensboro	A NYA	108	387	123	30	1	7	176	55	69	37	5	46	4	0	3	7	6	.54	12	.318	.381	.455
Tampa	A+ NYA	3	8	2	0	0	1	5	1	1	0	0	2	1	0	0	0	0	.00	0	.250	.333	.625
1996 Norwich	AA NYA	134	459	131	27	1	2	166	47	48	34	2	51	7	5	1	5	6	.45	19	.285	.343	.362
2 Min. YEARS		245	854	256	57	2	10	347	103	118	71	7	99	12	5	4	12	12	.50	31	.300	.360	.406

Brendan Donnelly

Pitches: Right **Bats:** Right **Pos:** P **Ht:** 6'3" **Wt:** 200 **Born:** 7/4/71 **Age:** 25

		HOW MUCH HE PITCHED						WHAT HE GAVE UP												THE RESULTS					
Year Team	Lg Org	G	GS	CG	GF	IP	BFP	H	R	ER	HR	SH	SF	HB	TBB	IBB	SO	WP	Bk	W	L	Pct.	ShO	Sv	ERA
1992 White Sox	R ChA	9	7	0	1	41.2	191	41	25	17	0	0	2	8	21	0	31	6	0	0	3	.000	0	1	3.67
1993 Geneva	A- ChN	21	3	0	7	43	198	39	34	30	4	1	1	6	29	0	29	7	3	4	0	1.000	0	1	6.28
1994 Ohio Valley	IND —	10	0	0	1	13.2	59	13	5	4	1	0	0	3	4	0	20	1	0	1	1	.500	0	0	2.63
1995 Winston-Sal	A+ Cin	23	0	0	14	35.1	138	20	6	4	1	2	0	2	14	2	32	0	1	1	2	.333	0	2	1.02
Indianapolis	AAA Cin	3	0	0	0	2.2	18	7	8	7	2	0	1	1	2	0	1	2	0	1	1	.500	0	0	23.63
Charlstn-WV	A Cin	50	0	0	36	68.1	268	41	18	15	3	3	3	4	23	3	66	3	1	3	4	.429	0	14	1.98
1996 Chattanooga	AA Cin	22	0	0	10	29.1	133	27	21	18	4	0	1	1	17	2	22	1	0	1	2	.333	0	0	5.52
5 Min. YEARS		138	10	0	69	234	1005	188	117	95	15	6	8	25	110	7	201	20	5	11	13	.458	0	18	3.65

Blake Doolan

Pitches: Right **Bats:** Right **Pos:** P **Ht:** 6'0" **Wt:** 178 **Born:** 2/11/69 **Age:** 28

		HOW MUCH HE PITCHED						WHAT HE GAVE UP												THE RESULTS					
Year Team	Lg Org	G	GS	CG	GF	IP	BFP	H	R	ER	HR	SH	SF	HB	TBB	IBB	SO	WP	Bk	W	L	Pct.	ShO	Sv	ERA
1992 Batavia	A- Phi	19	9	3	3	85.1	354	78	33	27	8	5	1	3	25	0	62	6	3	6	2	.750	2	1	2.85
1993 Spartanburg	A Phi	8	8	1	0	58.1	228	50	16	11	2	1	1	0	9	1	34	2	0	2	2	.500	0	0	1.70
Reading	AA Phi	27	15	1	3	109.2	491	135	70	62	13	0	3	5	36	0	61	3	2	7	8	.467	0	0	5.09
1994 Clearwater	A+ Phi	9	0	0	9	10.1	35	3	0	0	0	0	0	0	0	0	12	0	0	0	0	.000	0	5	0.00
Reading	AA Phi	50	0	0	22	67.1	297	70	45	40	5	5	3	3	28	3	42	8	1	3	2	.600	0	6	5.35
1995 Reading	AA Phi	60	0	0	45	73	300	63	22	18	3	3	5	0	27	4	50	4	1	11	5	.688	0	16	2.22

		HOW MUCH HE PITCHED						WHAT HE GAVE UP												THE RESULTS					
Year Team	Lg Org	G	GS	CG	GF	IP	BFP	H	R	ER	HR	SH	SF	HB	TBB	IBB	SO	WP	Bk	W	L	Pct.	ShO	Sv	ERA
1996 Scranton-WB	AAA Phi	18	0	0	3	18	87	26	15	13	1	3	1	2	7	1	8	2	0	1	1	.500	0	1	6.50
5 Min. YEARS		191	32	5	85	422	1792	425	201	171	32	17	14	13	132	9	269	25	7	30	20	.600	2	29	3.65

Dave Doorneweerd

Pitches: Right **Bats:** Right **Pos:** P **Ht:** 6'1" **Wt:** 185 **Born:** 9/29/72 **Age:** 24

		HOW MUCH HE PITCHED						WHAT HE GAVE UP												THE RESULTS					
Year Team	Lg Org	G	GS	CG	GF	IP	BFP	H	R	ER	HR	SH	SF	HB	TBB	IBB	SO	WP	Bk	W	L	Pct.	ShO	Sv	ERA
1991 Pirates	R Pit	10	10	0	0	44.2	175	34	12	9	1	0	1	1	7	0	55	2	1	3	1	.750	0	0	1.81
1992 Augusta	A Pit	25	24	1	0	148	631	129	66	50	13	4	2	6	58	0	152	15	1	9	13	.409	0	0	3.04
1993 Salem	A+ Pit	15	15	1	0	70.2	324	70	54	43	12	5	4	3	44	0	47	12	1	2	8	.200	0	0	5.48
Augusta	A Pit	13	13	0	0	77.1	325	60	30	17	3	5	3	4	30	0	70	2	0	1	5	.167	0	0	1.98
1994 Salem	A+ Pit	25	15	2	3	103.2	444	95	53	42	13	1	2	7	36	2	91	0	0	6	9	.400	0	0	3.65
1995 Lynchburg	A+ Pit	5	0	0	2	8	38	8	6	6	0	0	0	1	5	0	9	1	0	0	1	.000	0	0	6.75
St. Paul	IND —	23	18	1	2	122	505	103	56	54	10	1	3	4	41	0	113	6	1	10	5	.667	0	0	3.98
1996 Midland	AA Cal	9	1	0	3	18.2	94	25	15	12	2	1	0	1	12	0	20	5	0	1	2	.333	0	0	5.79
Lk Elsinore	A+ Cal	11	2	0	3	21	105	23	17	14	3	1	1	2	18	0	24	2	0	1	0	1.000	0	0	6.00
6 Min. YEARS		136	98	5	13	614	2641	547	309	247	57	18	16	29	251	2	581	45	4	33	44	.429	0	0	3.62

Aaron Dorlarque

Pitches: Right **Bats:** Right **Pos:** P **Ht:** 6'3" **Wt:** 180 **Born:** 2/16/70 **Age:** 27

		HOW MUCH HE PITCHED						WHAT HE GAVE UP												THE RESULTS					
Year Team	Lg Org	G	GS	CG	GF	IP	BFP	H	R	ER	HR	SH	SF	HB	TBB	IBB	SO	WP	Bk	W	L	Pct.	ShO	Sv	ERA
1992 Eugene	A- KC	32	0	0	31	40.1	162	30	12	8	0	1	0	1	10	2	46	2	1	1	2	.333	0	13	1.79
1993 Rockford	A KC	28	0	0	26	49.1	198	37	12	8	3	3	3	3	12	0	51	4	0	2	3	.400	0	16	1.46
1994 Memphis	AA KC	50	0	0	33	75	336	88	41	33	5	5	6	2	26	6	51	4	0	7	4	.636	0	14	3.96
1995 Wichita	AA KC	20	1	0	4	47	179	37	8	6	2	2	0	3	10	4	32	2	0	1	1	.500	0	0	1.15
Omaha	AAA KC	44	2	0	17	87.1	345	75	27	25	9	3	3	6	25	5	56	3	0	3	3	.500	0	4	2.58
1996 Harrisburg	AA Mon	13	0	0	3	24	111	32	17	16	4	2	1	2	7	1	14	0	0	1	0	1.000	0	0	6.00
Ottawa	AAA Mon	14	0	0	1	19.2	108	39	30	29	6	0	1	2	11	1	13	0	0	1	1	.500	0	0	13.27
5 Min. YEARS		201	3	0	115	342.2	1439	338	147	125	29	16	14	19	101	19	263	15	1	16	14	.533	0	47	3.28

Derrin Doty

Bats: Right **Throws:** Right **Pos:** OF **Ht:** 6'2" **Wt:** 220 **Born:** 6/3/70 **Age:** 27

		BATTING														BASERUNNING				PERCENTAGES		
Year Team	Lg Org	G	AB	H	2B	3B	HR	TB	R	RBI	TBB	IBB	SO	HBP	SH	SF	SB	CS	SB%	GDP	Avg	OBP	SLG
1993 Boise	A- Cal	64	211	55	13	2	3	81	50	33	46	0	45	6	2	1	11	3	.79	6	.261	.405	.384
1994 Cedar Rapds	A Cal	60	229	74	12	0	5	101	43	34	25	1	52	4	0	1	20	4	.83	5	.323	.398	.441
Lk Elsinore	A+ Cal	64	238	65	12	0	7	98	41	24	21	1	46	5	5	0	12	5	.71	7	.273	.345	.412
1995 Lk Elsinore	A+ Cal	94	324	80	12	0	8	116	46	35	37	0	54	3	2	2	16	6	.73	4	.247	.328	.358
1996 Midland	AA Cal	50	158	43	10	3	5	74	32	25	25	1	29	3	1	3	3	5	.38	2	.272	.376	.468
Fargo-Mh	IND —	18	58	11	1	0	3	21	11	4	6	0	10	0	0	0	1	0	1.00	2	.190	.266	.362
4 Min. YEARS		350	1218	328	60	5	31	491	223	155	160	3	236	21	10	7	63	23	.73	26	.269	.362	.403

Anthony Dougherty

Pitches: Right **Bats:** Right **Pos:** P **Ht:** 6'2" **Wt:** 205 **Born:** 4/12/73 **Age:** 24

		HOW MUCH HE PITCHED						WHAT HE GAVE UP												THE RESULTS					
Year Team	Lg Org	G	GS	CG	GF	IP	BFP	H	R	ER	HR	SH	SF	HB	TBB	IBB	SO	WP	Bk	W	L	Pct.	ShO	Sv	ERA
1994 Watertown	A- Cle	26	0	0	13	40.2	178	33	20	13	0	3	0	4	19	2	37	3	2	6	1	.857	0	2	2.88
1995 Columbus	A Cle	27	10	0	3	87.2	405	85	61	46	5	2	4	8	50	4	78	4	1	4	4	.500	0	0	4.72
1996 Columbus	A Cle	19	1	0	8	49	202	30	16	16	3	2	2	4	22	0	44	4	1	3	1	.750	0	2	2.94
Canton-Akrn	AA Cle	3	0	0	0	5	26	3	5	5	1	0	0	0	8	1	6	0	0	0	0	.000	0	0	9.00
Kinston	A+ Cle	18	0	0	15	33.1	135	29	6	6	2	3	0	1	11	2	32	3	1	3	1	.750	0	8	1.62
3 Min. YEARS		93	11	0	39	215.2	946	180	108	86	11	10	6	17	110	9	197	14	5	16	7	.696	0	12	3.59

Dee Dowler

Bats: Right **Throws:** Right **Pos:** OF **Ht:** 5'9" **Wt:** 175 **Born:** 7/23/71 **Age:** 25

		BATTING														BASERUNNING				PERCENTAGES		
Year Team	Lg Org	G	AB	H	2B	3B	HR	TB	R	RBI	TBB	IBB	SO	HBP	SH	SF	SB	CS	SB%	GDP	Avg	OBP	SLG
1993 Geneva	A- ChN	75	291	79	26	2	5	124	49	38	24	0	54	8	2	2	21	11	.66	3	.271	.342	.426
1994 Daytona	A+ ChN	126	481	136	17	3	9	186	80	62	36	2	83	6	10	3	15	7	.68	6	.283	.338	.387
1995 Orlando	AA ChN	9	31	7	2	0	0	9	6	1	2	0	5	0	0	0	1	0	1.00	0	.226	.273	.290
Daytona	A+ ChN	112	415	104	12	2	3	129	70	59	45	0	51	8	7	4	26	15	.63	11	.251	.333	.311
1996 Daytona	A+ ChN	12	47	19	3	0	0	22	5	8	5	0	5	1	2	1	4	1	.80	1	.404	.463	.468
Orlando	AA ChN	113	352	98	15	6	6	143	59	47	47	2	42	3	6	2	25	5	.83	10	.278	.366	.406
4 Min. YEARS		447	1617	443	75	13	23	613	269	215	159	4	240	26	27	12	92	39	.70	31	.274	.346	.379

Tom Doyle

Pitches: Left **Bats:** Left **Pos:** P **Ht:** 6'3" **Wt:** 205 **Born:** 1/20/70 **Age:** 27

		HOW MUCH HE PITCHED						WHAT HE GAVE UP												THE RESULTS					
Year Team	Lg Org	G	GS	CG	GF	IP	BFP	H	R	ER	HR	SH	SF	HB	TBB	IBB	SO	WP	Bk	W	L	Pct.	ShO	Sv	ERA
1993 Spokane	A- SD	6	0	0	2	6	37	12	9	9	0	1	0	3	6	0	5	2	0	0	0	.000	0	0	13.50
Waterloo	A SD	4	0	0	1	6.2	34	7	6	5	2	0	1	2	6	0	7	2	0	0	0	.000	0	0	6.75

				HOW MUCH HE PITCHED						WHAT HE GAVE UP												THE RESULTS					
Year	Team	Lg	Org	G	GS	CG	GF	IP	BFP	H	R	ER	HR	SH	SF	HB	TBB	IBB	SO	WP	Bk	W	L	Pct.	ShO	Sv	ERA
1994	Riverside	A+	Sea	9	0	0	5	11	68	21	20	19	0	0	0	3	11	0	12	1	2	0	0	.000	0	0	15.55
	Regina	IND	—	19	10	1	5	74	343	74	57	43	6	2	0	7	49	0	76	8	2	3	7	.300	0	1	5.23
1995	Charlstn-WV	A	Cin	14	12	1	0	62	272	57	34	30	3	2	1	7	30	3	66	9	0	6	4	.600	0	0	4.35
	Winston-Sal	A+	Cin	35	15	1	3	93.1	412	89	52	42	5	3	1	10	42	3	88	14	0	9	5	.643	0	1	4.05
1996	Chattanooga	AA	Cin	53	0	0	14	54.1	246	54	34	29	1	2	4	3	39	3	32	8	2	4	2	.667	0	0	4.80
	Indianapols	AAA	Cin	1	0	0	1	2.1	10	2	1	1	0	1	0	0	1	1	1	0	0	0	1	.000	0	0	3.86
4 Min. YEARS				141	37	3	31	309.2	1422	316	213	178	17	11	7	35	184	10	287	44	6	22	19	.537	0	2	5.17

Brian Drahman

Pitches: Right **Bats:** Right **Pos:** P **Ht:** 6' 3" **Wt:** 231 **Born:** 11/7/66 **Age:** 30

				HOW MUCH HE PITCHED						WHAT HE GAVE UP												THE RESULTS					
Year	Team	Lg	Org	G	GS	CG	GF	IP	BFP	H	R	ER	HR	SH	SF	HB	TBB	IBB	SO	WP	Bk	W	L	Pct.	ShO	Sv	ERA
1986	Helena	R+	Mil	18	10	0	5	65.1	0	79	49	43	4	0	0	0	33	1	40	4	0	4	6	.400	0	2	5.92
1987	Beloit	A	Mil	46	0	0	41	79	318	63	28	19	2	4	2	3	22	3	60	5	1	6	5	.545	0	18	2.16
1988	Stockton	A+	Mil	44	0	0	40	62.1	266	57	17	14	2	1	0	1	27	3	50	3	0	4	5	.444	0	14	2.02
1989	El Paso	AA	Mil	19	0	0	8	31	151	52	31	25	3	3	0	1	11	1	23	3	0	3	4	.429	0	2	7.26
	Stockton	A+	Mil	12	0	0	10	27.2	112	22	11	10	0	1	0	2	9	0	30	2	0	3	2	.600	0	4	3.25
	Sarasota	A+	ChA	7	2	0	3	16.2	73	18	9	6	1	1	0	1	5	1	9	1	0	0	1	.000	0	1	3.24
1990	Birmingham	AA	ChA	50	1	0	31	90.1	383	90	50	41	6	9	4	3	24	2	72	12	1	6	4	.600	0	17	4.08
1991	Vancouver	AAA	ChA	22	0	0	21	24.1	106	21	12	12	2	4	0	0	13	1	17	1	1	2	3	.400	0	12	4.44
1992	Vancouver	AAA	ChA	48	0	0	44	58.1	242	44	16	13	5	3	2	0	31	1	34	2	0	2	4	.333	0	30	2.01
1993	Nashville	AAA	ChA	54	0	0	50	55.2	249	59	29	18	3	3	4	2	19	8	49	6	0	9	4	.692	0	20	2.91
1994	Edmonton	AAA	Fla	45	0	0	35	60.1	261	60	38	32	9	2	2	1	25	0	62	4	0	3	2	.600	0	13	4.77
1995	Charlotte	AAA	Fla	21	0	0	15	20	99	28	14	14	1	2	1	0	11	1	17	3	0	2	1	.667	0	4	6.30
	Indianapols	AAA	Cin	24	0	0	15	35	157	39	11	11	3	1	1	2	15	3	22	0	0	2	2	.500	0	4	2.83
	Okla. City	AAA	Tex	45	0	0	30	55	256	67	25	25	4	3	2	2	26	4	39	3	0	4	3	.571	0	8	4.09
1996	Indianapols	AAA	Cin	3	0	0	0	5	27	7	6	4	0	0	0	0	4	0	1	1	0	0	0	.000	0	0	7.20
	Las Vegas	AAA	SD	9	0	0	4	9	33	4	1	1	0	1	0	0	4	0	10	0	0	1	0	1.000	0	0	1.00
1991	Chicago	AL		28	0	0	8	30.2	125	21	12	11	4	2	1	0	13	1	18	0	0	3	2	.600	0	0	3.23
1992	Chicago	AL		5	0	0	2	7	29	6	3	2	0	0	0	0	2	0	1	1	0	0	0	.000	0	0	2.57
1993	Chicago	AL		5	0	0	4	5.1	23	7	0	0	0	0	0	0	2	0	3	0	0	0	0	.000	0	1	0.00
1994	Florida	NL		9	0	0	3	13	59	15	9	9	2	1	2	0	6	1	7	2	0	0	0	.000	0	0	6.23
11 Min. YEARS				467	13	0	352	695	2733	710	347	288	45	38	18	18	279	29	535	50	3	51	46	.526	0	149	3.73
4 Maj. YEARS				47	0	0	17	56	236	49	24	22	6	3	3	0	23	2	29	3	0	3	2	.600	0	1	3.54

Kirk Dressendorfer

Pitches: Right **Bats:** Right **Pos:** P **Ht:** 5'11" **Wt:** 190 **Born:** 4/8/69 **Age:** 28

				HOW MUCH HE PITCHED						WHAT HE GAVE UP												THE RESULTS					
Year	Team	Lg	Org	G	GS	CG	GF	IP	BFP	H	R	ER	HR	SH	SF	HB	TBB	IBB	SO	WP	Bk	W	L	Pct.	ShO	Sv	ERA
1990	Sou. Oregon	A-	Oak	7	4	0	0	19.1	78	18	7	5	0	1	1	1	2	0	22	1	0	0	1	.000	0	0	2.33
1991	Tacoma	AAA	Oak	8	7	0	0	24	120	31	29	29	4	1	2	1	20	0	19	2	0	1	3	.250	0	0	10.88
1992	Modesto	A+	Oak	3	3	0	0	13	56	8	7	7	1	0	0	1	6	0	18	1	0	0	2	.000	0	0	4.85
1993	Modesto	A+	Oak	5	5	0	0	11.1	51	14	5	5	2	0	0	0	5	0	15	0	0	0	0	.000	0	0	3.97
1994	Athletics	R	Oak	6	6	0	0	12.1	45	3	1	0	0	0	0	1	4	0	17	0	0	0	1	.000	0	0	0.00
1995	Huntsville	AA	Oak	9	4	0	1	20	79	13	7	7	1	0	0	2	5	0	18	1	0	0	1	.000	0	0	3.15
	Modesto	A+	Oak	36	20	0	3	57	250	52	31	26	6	2	2	4	23	0	68	7	0	0	7	.000	0	0	4.11
1996	Edmonton	AAA	Oak	10	0	0	2	13	66	23	11	8	1	0	0	0	3	1	10	3	0	0	1	.000	0	0	5.54
	Huntsville	AA	Oak	30	1	0	14	52.1	233	54	38	29	3	1	1	4	21	1	43	6	0	4	4	.500	0	2	4.99
1991	Oakland	AL		7	7	0	0	34.2	159	33	28	21	5	2	1	0	21	0	17	3	0	3	3	.500	0	0	5.45
7 Min. YEARS				114	50	0	20	222.1	978	216	136	116	18	5	6	14	89	2	230	21	0	5	20	.200	0	2	4.70

Matt Drews

Pitches: Right **Bats:** Right **Pos:** P **Ht:** 6'8" **Wt:** 205 **Born:** 8/29/74 **Age:** 22

				HOW MUCH HE PITCHED						WHAT HE GAVE UP												THE RESULTS					
Year	Team	Lg	Org	G	GS	CG	GF	IP	BFP	H	R	ER	HR	SH	SF	HB	TBB	IBB	SO	WP	Bk	W	L	Pct.	ShO	Sv	ERA
1994	Oneonta	A-	NYA	14	14	1	0	90	369	76	31	21	1	1	2	8	19	0	69	3	0	7	6	.538	1	0	2.10
1995	Tampa	A+	NYA	28	28	3	0	182	748	142	73	46	5	5	5	17	58	0	140	8	2	15	7	.682	0	0	2.27
1996	Columbus	AAA	NYA	7	7	0	0	20.1	113	18	27	19	4	1	5	7	27	0	7	8	0	0	4	.000	0	0	8.41
	Tampa	A+	NYA	4	4	0	0	17.2	93	26	20	14	0	2	1	3	12	2	12	1	0	0	3	.000	0	0	7.13
	Norwich	AA	NYA	9	9	0	0	46	210	40	26	23	4	1	0	5	33	1	37	1	0	1	3	.250	0	0	4.50
	Jacksonvlle	AA	Det	6	6	1	0	31	138	26	18	15	3	0	0	4	19	0	40	2	1	0	4	.000	0	0	4.35
3 Min. YEARS				68	68	5	0	387	1671	328	195	138	17	10	13	44	168	3	305	23	3	23	27	.460	1	0	3.21

Steve Dreyer

Pitches: Right **Bats:** Right **Pos:** P **Ht:** 6' 3" **Wt:** 188 **Born:** 11/19/69 **Age:** 27

				HOW MUCH HE PITCHED						WHAT HE GAVE UP												THE RESULTS					
Year	Team	Lg	Org	G	GS	CG	GF	IP	BFP	H	R	ER	HR	SH	SF	HB	TBB	IBB	SO	WP	Bk	W	L	Pct.	ShO	Sv	ERA
1990	Butte	R+	Tex	8	8	0	0	35.2	146	32	21	18	2	0	0	0	10	0	29	1	0	1	1	.500	0	0	4.54
1991	Gastonia	A	Tex	25	25	3	0	162	661	137	51	43	5	5	4	5	62	1	122	4	0	7	10	.412	1	0	2.39
1992	Charlotte	A+	Tex	26	26	4	0	168.2	675	164	54	45	8	10	0	6	37	2	111	4	0	11	7	.611	3	0	2.40
1993	Tulsa	AA	Tex	5	5	1	0	31.1	128	26	13	13	4	0	1	0	8	1	27	0	0	2	2	.500	1	0	3.73
	Okla. City	AAA	Tex	16	16	1	0	107	445	108	39	36	5	4	3	2	31	1	59	4	0	4	6	.400	0	0	3.03
1994	Okla. City	AAA	Tex	4	4	0	0	23	103	26	14	9	2	0	0	0	9	0	16	1	0	0	1	.000	0	0	3.52

Year Team	Lg Org	G	GS	CG	GF	IP	BFP	H	R	ER	HR	SH	SF	HB	TBB	IBB	SO	WP	Bk	W	L	Pct.	ShO	Sv	ERA
		HOW MUCH HE PITCHED						WHAT HE GAVE UP												THE RESULTS					
1995 Rangers	R Tex	2	2	0	0	9	34	6	1	1	0	0	1	0	2	0	7	0	0	0	1	.000	0	0	1.00
Tulsa	AA Tex	12	12	1	0	71.1	286	62	23	21	6	2	2	2	21	1	55	4	0	2	5	.286	0	0	2.65
1996 Okla. City	AAA Tex	29	14	0	9	118	500	130	55	51	6	1	3	4	31	1	79	2	0	6	8	.429	0	2	3.89
1993 Texas	AL	10	6	0	1	41	186	48	26	26	7	0	0	1	20	1	23	0	0	3	3	.500	0	0	5.71
1994 Texas	AL	5	3	0	0	17.1	80	19	15	11	1	0	1	1	8	0	11	1	0	1	1	.500	0	0	5.71
7 Min. YEARS		127	112	10	9	726	2978	691	271	237	38	22	14	19	211	7	505	20	0	33	41	.446	5	2	2.94
2 Maj. YEARS		15	9	0	1	58.1	266	67	41	37	8	0	1	2	28	1	34	1	0	4	4	.500	0	0	5.71

Sean Drinkwater

Bats: Right **Throws:** Right **Pos:** 3B **Ht:** 6'3" **Wt:** 195 **Born:** 6/22/71 **Age:** 26

Year Team	Lg Org	G	AB	H	2B	3B	HR	TB	R	RBI	TBB	IBB	SO	HBP	SH	SF	SB	CS	SB%	GDP	Avg	OBP	SLG
		BATTING															BASERUNNING				PERCENTAGES		
1992 Huntington	R+ ChN	19	44	6	2	0	2	14	14	6	11	0	16	2	0	0	0	0	.00	0	.136	.333	.318
Spokane	A- SD	66	256	77	12	2	4	105	35	41	25	0	27	0	1	6	7	4	.64	8	.301	.355	.410
1993 Rancho Cuca	A+ SD	121	486	131	29	1	10	192	69	84	35	1	78	2	1	12	2	0	1.00	6	.270	.314	.395
1994 Wichita	AA SD	91	299	71	17	3	5	109	34	39	21	1	40	1	1	6	4	0	1.00	11	.237	.284	.365
Rancho Cuca	A+ SD	28	96	22	6	0	1	31	15	12	10	0	29	1	1	2	1	0	1.00	2	.229	.303	.323
1995 Memphis	AA SD	102	287	69	12	1	6	101	29	26	26	1	49	1	2	3	3	4	.43	6	.240	.303	.352
1996 Tacoma	AAA Sea	9	31	8	1	0	0	9	2	1	1	0	5	0	0	0	0	0	.00	0	.258	.281	.290
Port City	AA Sea	32	101	27	9	0	1	39	10	13	13	0	18	0	0	1	1	3	.25	0	.267	.348	.386
5 Min. YEARS		468	1600	411	88	7	29	600	208	222	142	3	262	7	6	30	18	11	.62	33	.257	.315	.375

Travis Driskill

Pitches: Right **Bats:** Right **Pos:** P **Ht:** 6'0" **Wt:** 185 **Born:** 8/1/71 **Age:** 25

Year Team	Lg Org	G	GS	CG	GF	IP	BFP	H	R	ER	HR	SH	SF	HB	TBB	IBB	SO	WP	Bk	W	L	Pct.	ShO	Sv	ERA
		HOW MUCH HE PITCHED						WHAT HE GAVE UP												THE RESULTS					
1993 Watertown	A- Cle	21	8	0	7	63	276	62	38	29	4	3	6	5	21	0	53	6	0	5	4	.556	0	3	4.14
1994 Columbus	A Cle	62	0	0	59	64.1	267	51	25	18	2	5	2	1	30	4	88	6	0	5	5	.500	0	35	2.52
1995 Kinston	A+ Cle	15	0	0	9	23	90	17	7	7	2	0	3	1	5	1	24	1	0	0	2	.000	0	0	2.74
Canton-Akrn	AA Cle	48	0	0	31	69.1	290	63	31	31	5	1	4	2	24	2	63	1	1	3	6	.333	0	4	4.02
1996 Canton-Akrn	AA Cle	29	24	4	0	172	732	169	89	69	8	6	6	3	63	0	148	10	2	13	7	.650	2	0	3.61
4 Min. YEARS		175	32	4	106	391.2	1655	362	190	154	21	15	21	12	143	7	376	24	3	26	24	.520	2	42	3.54

Mike Drumright

Pitches: Right **Bats:** Left **Pos:** P **Ht:** 6'4" **Wt:** 210 **Born:** 4/19/74 **Age:** 23

Year Team	Lg Org	G	GS	CG	GF	IP	BFP	H	R	ER	HR	SH	SF	HB	TBB	IBB	SO	WP	Bk	W	L	Pct.	ShO	Sv	ERA
		HOW MUCH HE PITCHED						WHAT HE GAVE UP												THE RESULTS					
1995 Lakeland	A+ Det	5	5	0	0	21	87	19	11	10	2	1	0	0	9	0	19	1	2	1	1	.500	0	0	4.29
Jacksonvlle	AA Det	10	10	0	0	52.2	224	49	24	23	6	1	0	2	24	1	53	2	7	1	2	.333	0	0	3.93
1996 Jacksonvlle	AA Det	18	18	1	0	99.2	418	80	51	44	11	1	3	3	48	0	109	10	6	6	4	.600	1	0	3.97
2 Min. YEARS		33	33	1	0	173.1	729	148	86	77	19	3	3	5	81	1	181	13	15	8	7	.533	1	0	4.00

Matt Dunbar

Pitches: Left **Bats:** Left **Pos:** P **Ht:** 6' 0" **Wt:** 160 **Born:** 10/15/68 **Age:** 28

Year Team	Lg Org	G	GS	CG	GF	IP	BFP	H	R	ER	HR	SH	SF	HB	TBB	IBB	SO	WP	Bk	W	L	Pct.	ShO	Sv	ERA
		HOW MUCH HE PITCHED						WHAT HE GAVE UP												THE RESULTS					
1990 Yankees	R NYA	3	0	0	2	6	24	4	2	2	0	1	0	2	3	0	7	0	1	0	0	.000	0	1	3.00
Oneonta	A- NYA	19	2	0	8	30.1	145	32	23	14	1	2	2	1	24	2	24	5	1	1	4	.200	0	0	4.15
1991 Greensboro	A NYA	24	2	1	14	44.2	184	36	14	11	1	0	1	3	15	0	40	2	0	2	2	.500	0	1	2.22
1992 Pr. William	A+ NYA	44	0	0	21	81.2	350	68	37	26	5	7	4	6	33	2	68	7	1	5	4	.556	0	2	2.87
1993 Pr. William	A+ NYA	49	0	0	20	73	292	50	21	14	0	6	0	3	30	1	66	6	0	6	2	.750	0	4	1.73
Albany-Colo	AA NYA	15	0	0	6	23.2	91	23	8	7	0	0	0	0	6	0	18	0	0	1	0	1.000	0	0	2.66
1994 Albany-Colo	AA NYA	34	0	0	12	39.2	163	30	10	9	1	2	2	4	14	0	41	1	0	2	1	.667	0	4	2.04
Columbus	AAA NYA	19	0	0	6	26	104	20	5	5	1	0	1	1	10	1	21	2	1	0	1	.000	0	2	1.73
1995 Columbus	AAA NYA	36	0	0	9	44.1	201	50	22	20	1	0	1	3	19	2	33	5	1	2	3	.400	0	0	4.06
1996 Greensboro	A NYA	2	2	0	0	14	56	6	3	3	1	0	0	1	4	0	19	1	0	1	1	.500	0	0	1.93
Norwich	AA NYA	33	6	0	11	70.2	306	59	33	14	3	6	4	5	28	3	59	2	0	4	2	.667	0	1	1.78
Columbus	AAA NYA	14	0	0	1	20.2	84	12	6	4	0	0	1	2	13	0	16	0	0	2	0	1.000	0	0	1.74
1995 Florida	NL	8	0	0	1	7	45	12	9	9	0	2	0	1	11	3	5	1	0	0	1	.000	0	0	11.57
7 Min. YEARS		292	12	1	110	474.2	2000	390	184	129	14	24	16	31	199	11	412	31	5	26	20	.565	0	15	2.45

Andres Duncan

Bats: Both **Throws:** Right **Pos:** SS **Ht:** 5'11" **Wt:** 155 **Born:** 11/30/71 **Age:** 25

Year Team	Lg Org	G	AB	H	2B	3B	HR	TB	R	RBI	TBB	IBB	SO	HBP	SH	SF	SB	CS	SB%	GDP	Avg	OBP	SLG
		BATTING															BASERUNNING				PERCENTAGES		
1991 Clinton	A SF	109	347	77	6	5	1	96	49	24	31	1	106	3	8	2	36	8	.82	2	.222	.290	.277
1992 San Jose	A+ SF	109	308	71	7	3	1	87	46	32	35	2	76	9	13	4	19	9	.68	8	.231	.323	.282
1993 Shreveport	AA SF	35	75	11	2	1	1	18	4	9	5	1	25	1	1	1	2	0	1.00	2	.147	.207	.240
Phoenix	AAA SF	5	4	2	0	0	0	2	1	0	1	0	0	0	0	0	0	0	.00	1	.500	.600	.500
San Jose	A+ SF	36	111	25	1	2	1	33	17	12	12	0	28	2	2	2	14	3	.82	3	.225	.307	.297
Fort Myers	A+ Min	5	22	8	0	0	1	11	3	1	3	0	6	0	0	0	4	2	.67	0	.364	.440	.500
1994 Nashville	AA Min	122	397	101	15	0	9	143	50	46	28	1	98	5	7	3	20	8	.71	5	.254	.309	.360

BATTING																			BASERUNNING				PERCENTAGES		
Year	Team	Lg	Org	G	AB	H	2B	3B	HR	TB	R	RBI	TBB	IBB	SO	HBP	SH	SF	SB	CS	SB%	GDP	Avg	OBP	SLG
1995	Salt Lake	AAA	Min	12	36	10	2	1	0	14	2	6	4	0	5	1	2	1	2	0	1.00	0	.278	.357	.389
	New Britain	AA	Min	83	230	52	5	2	0	61	28	10	14	1	51	3	2	3	10	5	.67	2	.226	.276	.265
1996	Phoenix	AAA	SF	42	106	24	7	2	1	38	11	12	8	0	22	2	0	0	2	0	1.00	1	.226	.293	.358
	Shreveport	AA	SF	68	193	51	6	2	2	67	33	10	20	0	38	0	2	0	8	3	.73	6	.264	.333	.347
6 Min. YEARS				626	1829	432	51	18	17	570	244	162	161	6	455	26	37	16	117	38	.75	30	.236	.305	.312

Chip Duncan

Pitches: Right **Bats:** Right **Pos:** P **Ht:** 5'11" **Wt:** 185 **Born:** 6/27/65 **Age:** 32

HOW MUCH HE PITCHED										WHAT HE GAVE UP												THE RESULTS					
Year	Team	Lg	Org	G	GS	CG	GF	IP	BFP	H	R	ER	HR	SH	SF	HB	TBB	IBB	SO	WP	Bk	W	L	Pct.	ShO	Sv	ERA
1987	Watertown	A-	Pit	24	0	0	16	49.2	222	45	20	13	1	5	2	3	22	3	57	4	0	4	2	.667	0	4	2.36
1988	Salem	A+	Pit	28	28	0	0	156.2	713	168	103	79	18	5	4	5	70	2	102	17	8	8	10	.444	0	0	4.54
1989	Salem	A+	Pit	26	4	0	10	68.2	305	64	49	39	4	3	8	6	33	1	55	5	4	2	4	.333	0	2	5.11
1990	Salem	A+	Pit	37	3	2	17	84.2	406	105	61	49	5	4	3	4	48	3	95	9	1	6	4	.600	0	1	5.21
1991	Carolina	AA	Pit	6	0	0	6	8	45	17	8	7	1	0	0	1	4	0	9	1	0	0	0	.000	0	1	7.88
	Memphis	AA	KC	22	9	2	5	80.1	342	82	42	40	11	2	1	3	28	0	58	5	1	6	3	.667	1	0	4.48
1992	Memphis	AA	KC	33	2	1	12	73.1	316	72	49	38	7	6	4	2	24	1	51	3	1	0	3	.000	0	3	4.66
1994	Reading	AA	Phi	17	11	0	2	77.2	339	79	40	36	9	1	3	4	34	2	62	3	4	4	2	.667	0	0	4.17
1995	Okla. City	AAA	Tex	3	0	0	1	5.1	22	6	2	2	0	1	1	0	1	0	3	0	0	0	0	.000	0	0	3.38
	New Orleans	AAA	Mil	17	5	0	6	39.2	183	50	28	26	7	2	3	2	19	2	26	5	1	1	4	.200	0	0	5.90
	Tulsa	AA	Tex	34	6	0	17	75.2	336	84	40	38	9	3	3	3	36	8	57	9	1	3	5	.375	0	1	4.52
1996	Greenville	AA	Atl	8	1	0	2	13.1	69	23	17	17	2	1	1	0	11	1	10	0	0	0	2	.000	0	0	11.48
9 Min. YEARS				255	69	5	94	733	3298	795	459	384	74	33	33	33	330	23	585	61	21	34	39	.466	1	12	4.71

Steve Dunn

Bats: Left **Throws:** Left **Pos:** 1B-DH **Ht:** 6' 4" **Wt:** 225 **Born:** 4/18/70 **Age:** 27

BATTING																			BASERUNNING				PERCENTAGES		
Year	Team	Lg	Org	G	AB	H	2B	3B	HR	TB	R	RBI	TBB	IBB	SO	HBP	SH	SF	SB	CS	SB%	GDP	Avg	OBP	SLG
1988	Elizabethtn	R+	Min	26	95	27	4	0	2	37	9	14	8	0	22	0	0	0	0	0	.00	0	.284	.340	.389
1989	Kenosha	A	Min	63	219	48	8	0	0	56	17	23	18	4	55	1	1	2	2	1	.67	2	.219	.279	.256
	Elizabethtn	R+	Min	57	210	64	12	3	6	100	34	42	22	2	41	0	1	4	0	2	.00	1	.305	.364	.476
1990	Kenosha	A	Min	130	478	142	29	1	10	203	48	72	49	8	104	6	1	6	13	6	.68	4	.297	.365	.425
1991	Visalia	A+	Min	125	458	105	16	1	13	162	64	59	58	6	103	6	0	6	9	6	.60	12	.229	.320	.354
1992	Visalia	A+	Min	125	492	150	36	3	26	270	93	113	41	6	103	7	0	4	8	3	.73	13	.305	.364	.549
1993	Nashville	AA	Min	97	366	96	20	2	14	162	48	60	35	3	88	1	0	4	1	2	.33	4	.262	.325	.443
1994	Salt Lake	AAA	Min	90	330	102	21	2	15	172	61	73	24	6	75	2	0	8	0	0	.00	5	.309	.352	.521
1995	Salt Lake	AAA	Min	109	402	127	31	1	12	196	57	83	30	4	63	1	0	6	3	2	.60	6	.316	.360	.488
1996	Buffalo	AAA	Cle	92	300	87	20	1	12	145	35	48	30	7	74	2	0	3	2	1	.67	3	.290	.355	.483
1994	Minnesota	AL		14	35	8	5	0	0	13	2	4	1	0	12	0	0	0	0	0	.00	1	.229	.250	.371
1995	Minnesota	AL		5	6	0	0	0	0	0	0	0	1	0	3	0	0	0	0	0	.00	0	.000	.143	.000
9 Min. YEARS				914	3350	948	197	14	110	1503	466	587	315	46	728	26	3	43	38	23	.62	50	.283	.345	.449
2 Maj. YEARS				19	41	8	5	0	0	13	2	4	2	0	15	0	0	0	0	0	.00	1	.195	.233	.317

Todd Dunwoody

Bats: Left **Throws:** Left **Pos:** OF **Ht:** 6'2" **Wt:** 185 **Born:** 4/11/75 **Age:** 22

BATTING																			BASERUNNING				PERCENTAGES		
Year	Team	Lg	Org	G	AB	H	2B	3B	HR	TB	R	RBI	TBB	IBB	SO	HBP	SH	SF	SB	CS	SB%	GDP	Avg	OBP	SLG
1993	Marlins	R	Fla	31	109	21	2	2	0	27	13	7	7	0	28	2	1	1	5	0	1.00	2	.193	.252	.248
1994	Kane County	A	Fla	15	45	5	0	0	1	8	7	1	5	0	17	0	1	0	1	0	1.00	1	.111	.200	.178
	Marlins	R	Fla	46	169	44	6	6	1	65	32	25	21	1	28	4	1	1	11	3	.79	1	.260	.354	.385
1995	Kane County	A	Fla	132	494	140	20	8	14	218	89	89	52	7	105	8	2	9	39	11	.78	7	.283	.355	.441
1996	Portland	AA	Fla	138	552	153	30	6	24	267	88	93	45	6	149	7	0	5	24	19	.56	10	.277	.337	.484
4 Min. YEARS				362	1369	363	58	22	40	585	229	215	130	14	327	21	5	16	80	33	.71	21	.265	.335	.427

Roberto Duran

Pitches: Left **Bats:** Left **Pos:** P **Ht:** 6'0" **Wt:** 190 **Born:** 3/6/73 **Age:** 24

HOW MUCH HE PITCHED										WHAT HE GAVE UP												THE RESULTS					
Year	Team	Lg	Org	G	GS	CG	GF	IP	BFP	H	R	ER	HR	SH	SF	HB	TBB	IBB	SO	WP	Bk	W	L	Pct.	ShO	Sv	ERA
1992	Dodgers	R	LA	9	8	0	0	38.2	166	22	17	12	1	1	1	2	31	0	57	8	0	4	3	.571	0	0	2.79
	Vero Beach	A+	LA	2	1	0	0	5	24	6	5	5	1	0	0	1	4	0	5	1	0	0	0	.000	0	0	9.00
1993	Vero Beach	A+	LA	8	0	0	2	9.2	43	10	4	4	0	0	0	0	8	1	9	0	0	1	1	.500	0	0	3.72
	Yakima	A-	LA	20	3	0	6	40	201	37	34	31	3	1	2	6	42	0	50	10	0	2	2	.500	0	0	6.98
1994	Bakersfield	A+	LA	42	4	0	29	65.1	300	61	43	35	5	3	4	5	48	0	86	6	0	6	5	.545	0	10	4.82
1995	Vero Beach	A+	LA	23	22	0	0	101.1	446	82	42	38	8	3	1	1	70	0	114	12	2	7	4	.636	0	0	3.38
1996	Dunedin	A+	Tor	8	8	1	0	48.1	188	31	9	6	1	1	1	2	19	0	54	5	0	3	1	.750	1	0	1.12
	Knoxville	AA	Tor	19	16	0	1	80.2	366	72	52	46	8	1	1	3	61	1	74	13	2	4	6	.400	0	0	5.13
5 Min. YEARS				131	62	1	38	389	1734	321	206	177	27	10	10	20	283	2	449	55	4	27	22	.551	1	10	4.10

Chris Durkin

Bats: Left **Throws:** Left **Pos:** DH-OF **Ht:** 6'5" **Wt:** 210 **Born:** 8/12/70 **Age:** 26

Year	Team	Lg	Org	BATTING G	AB	H	2B	3B	HR	TB	R	RBI	TBB	IBB	SO	HBP	SH	SF	BASERUNNING SB	CS	SB%	GDP	PERCENTAGES Avg	OBP	SLG
1991	Auburn	A-	Hou	69	246	63	10	3	5	94	31	35	30	1	64	2	0	2	20	7	.74	3	.256	.339	.382
1992	Asheville	A	Hou	100	314	80	21	2	8	129	59	55	67	5	89	3	0	2	27	17	.61	6	.255	.389	.411
1993	Quad City	A	Hou	25	77	21	6	1	1	32	14	6	15	3	13	0	0	0	6	4	.60	0	.273	.391	.416
1994	Osceola	A+	Hou	103	329	77	21	1	4	112	46	31	53	3	86	3	0	5	20	9	.69	5	.234	.341	.340
1995	San Bernrdo	A+	LA	57	164	44	10	1	8	80	24	31	28	0	48	1	1	3	9	6	.60	3	.268	.372	.488
1996	Vero Beach	A+	LA	56	202	54	11	0	16	113	49	34	28	3	54	1	0	1	4	0	1.00	3	.267	.358	.559
	San Antonio	AA	LA	8	30	9	2	0	1	14	6	3	4	0	9	0	0	0	0	0	.00	0	.300	.382	.467
6 Min. YEARS				418	1362	348	81	8	43	574	229	195	225	15	363	10	1	13	86	43	.67	20	.256	.362	.421

Gabe Duross

Bats: Left **Throws:** Left **Pos:** 1B **Ht:** 6'1" **Wt:** 195 **Born:** 4/6/72 **Age:** 25

Year	Team	Lg	Org	BATTING G	AB	H	2B	3B	HR	TB	R	RBI	TBB	IBB	SO	HBP	SH	SF	BASERUNNING SB	CS	SB%	GDP	PERCENTAGES Avg	OBP	SLG
1993	Geneva	A-	ChN	62	225	61	15	2	6	98	35	41	6	1	16	3	2	0	9	4	.69	3	.271	.299	.436
1994	Peoria	A	ChN	119	465	136	27	2	6	185	48	95	13	4	26	5	1	4	3	4	.43	16	.292	.316	.398
1995	Orlando	AA	ChN	68	244	64	10	1	3	85	23	40	10	3	20	1	0	2	3	2	.60	12	.262	.292	.348
	Daytona	A+	ChN	60	224	54	9	0	3	72	20	34	11	2	12	2	0	3	4	4	.50	6	.241	.279	.321
1996	Orlando	AA	ChN	17	58	9	0	1	0	11	2	6	2	2	3	1	0	1	0	0	.00	2	.155	.194	.190
	Birmingham	AA	ChA	37	140	31	3	0	0	34	14	15	7	1	17	2	0	0	1	1	.50	4	.221	.268	.243
	Newburgh	IND	—	48	193	62	14	2	3	89	27	38	5	1	7	3	0	2	3	3	.50	3	.321	.345	.461
4 Min. YEARS				411	1549	417	78	8	21	574	169	269	54	14	101	17	3	12	23	18	.56	46	.269	.299	.371

Chris Eddy

Pitches: Left **Bats:** Left **Pos:** P **Ht:** 6' 3" **Wt:** 200 **Born:** 11/27/69 **Age:** 27

Year	Team	Lg	Org	HOW MUCH HE PITCHED G	GS	CG	GF	IP	BFP	WHAT HE GAVE UP H	R	ER	HR	SH	SF	HB	TBB	IBB	SO	WP	Bk	THE RESULTS W	L	Pct.	ShO	Sv	ERA
1992	Eugene	A-	KC	23	0	0	11	45.1	191	25	13	8	1	2	2	6	23	1	63	3	3	4	2	.667	0	5	1.59
1993	Wilmington	A+	KC	55	0	0	38	54	237	39	23	18	4	4	6	3	37	1	67	8	1	2	2	.500	0	14	3.00
1994	Memphis	AA	KC	43	0	0	19	78.1	336	74	37	34	3	4	2	1	32	3	86	5	0	9	2	.818	0	1	3.91
1995	Wichita	AA	KC	9	0	0	5	9	38	8	4	4	1	0	0	1	3	0	10	0	0	1	0	1.000	0	1	4.00
	Omaha	AAA	KC	23	0	0	11	26.1	122	28	19	18	2	1	2	3	15	2	22	0	0	2	1	.667	0	1	6.15
1996	Wichita	AA	KC	30	0	0	16	30.1	138	33	16	10	6	1	0	1	18	1	22	3	0	0	0	.000	0	0	2.97
	New Orleans	AAA	Mil	12	0	0	4	8.1	49	13	9	9	3	0	0	0	11	0	11	1	0	0	0	.000	0	0	9.72
1995	Oakland	AL		6	0	0	0	3.2	22	7	3	3	0	2	0	2	2	0	2	1	0	0	0	.000	0	0	7.36
5 Min. YEARS				195	0	0	104	251.2	1111	220	121	101	20	12	12	15	139	8	281	20	4	18	7	.720	0	22	3.61

Bill Eden

Pitches: Left **Bats:** Left **Pos:** P **Ht:** 6'2" **Wt:** 205 **Born:** 4/4/73 **Age:** 24

Year	Team	Lg	Org	HOW MUCH HE PITCHED G	GS	CG	GF	IP	BFP	WHAT HE GAVE UP H	R	ER	HR	SH	SF	HB	TBB	IBB	SO	WP	Bk	THE RESULTS W	L	Pct.	ShO	Sv	ERA
1994	Rockies	R	Col	1	0	0	0	2	6	0	0	0	0	0	0	0	0	0	2	0	0	1	0	1.000	0	0	0.00
	Bend	A-	Col	16	0	0	5	30.1	140	39	26	23	1	2	1	0	14	0	31	6	1	2	3	.400	0	2	6.82
1995	Asheville	A	Col	33	0	0	17	67.1	269	55	22	16	4	1	0	1	14	0	80	7	2	5	3	.625	0	9	2.14
1996	Salem	A+	Col	11	0	0	7	13.1	56	8	4	4	0	0	0	1	7	1	15	2	0	0	1	.000	0	1	2.70
	New Haven	AA	Col	29	0	0	10	41.1	197	48	26	24	6	2	4	2	24	2	41	6	0	1	1	.500	0	0	5.23
3 Min. YEARS				90	0	0	39	154.1	668	150	78	67	11	5	5	4	59	3	169	21	3	9	8	.529	0	12	3.91

Tom Edens

Pitches: Right **Bats:** Left **Pos:** P **Ht:** 6' 2" **Wt:** 190 **Born:** 6/9/61 **Age:** 36

Year	Team	Lg	Org	HOW MUCH HE PITCHED G	GS	CG	GF	IP	BFP	WHAT HE GAVE UP H	R	ER	HR	SH	SF	HB	TBB	IBB	SO	WP	Bk	THE RESULTS W	L	Pct.	ShO	Sv	ERA
1984	Columbia	A	NYN	16	15	4	1	95.1	409	65	44	33	1	2	4	1	58	1	60	10	1	7	4	.636	1	0	3.12
	Lynchburg	A+	NYN	3	2	0	0	14.1	65	11	6	4	1	1	0	0	8	0	15	1	0	1	1	.500	0	0	2.51
1985	Lynchburg	A+	NYN	16	16	0	0	82	353	86	40	35	4	2	5	2	34	0	48	3	2	6	4	.600	0	0	3.84
1986	Jackson	AA	NYN	16	16	4	0	106	431	76	36	30	4	5	2	1	41	1	72	10	0	9	4	.692	0	0	2.55
	Tidewater	AAA	NYN	11	11	2	0	61.1	280	71	33	31	5	1	1	1	28	1	31	4	0	5	3	.625	1	0	4.55
1987	Tidewater	AAA	NYN	25	22	0	1	138	605	140	69	55	10	6	6	7	55	0	61	2	1	9	7	.563	0	1	3.59
1988	Tidewater	AAA	NYN	24	21	3	0	135.1	582	128	67	52	7	1	0	5	53	1	89	3	1	7	6	.538	0	0	3.46
1989	Tidewater	AAA	NYN	18	8	0	3	65	295	76	43	38	3	0	2	4	28	2	31	2	0	1	5	.167	0	1	5.26
	Scranton-WB	AAA	Phi	7	6	0	0	42.1	177	45	16	15	2	1	2	1	11	2	16	2	0	1	1	.500	0	0	3.19
1990	Denver	AAA	Mil	19	0	0	9	36.2	154	32	23	22	3	1	1	0	22	0	26	3	0	1	1	.500	0	4	5.40
1991	Portland	AAA	Min	25	24	3	0	161.1	668	145	67	54	6	5	5	7	62	3	100	4	0	10	7	.588	1	0	3.01
1993	Osceola	A+	Hou	3	1	0	0	4	17	5	0	0	0	0	0	1	1	0	4	0	0	1	0	1.000	0	0	0.00
	Tucson	AAA	Hou	5	0	0	1	7.1	34	9	5	5	0	0	0	1	3	0	6	0	0	1	0	1.000	0	0	6.14
1995	Iowa	AAA	ChN	20	3	0	5	41.2	175	36	17	16	3	1	0	3	17	1	28	2	0	2	0	1.000	0	1	3.46
1996	Rochester	AAA	Bal	20	10	0	4	67.2	300	73	43	39	9	2	4	4	23	1	36	2	0	4	6	.400	0	0	5.19
1987	New York	NL		2	2	0	0	8	42	15	6	6	2	2	0	0	4	0	4	2	0	0	0	.000	0	0	6.75
1990	Milwaukee	AL		35	6	0	9	89	387	89	52	44	8	6	4	4	33	3	40	1	0	4	5	.444	0	2	4.45
1991	Minnesota	AL		8	6	0	0	33	143	34	15	15	2	0	0	0	10	1	19	1	0	2	2	.500	0	0	4.09
1992	Minnesota	AL		52	0	0	14	76.1	317	65	26	24	1	4	0	2	36	3	57	5	0	6	3	.667	0	3	2.83
1993	Houston	NL		38	0	0	20	49	203	47	17	17	4	4	1	0	19	7	21	3	0	1	1	.500	0	0	3.12

Year	Team	Lg	Org	G	GS	CG	GF	IP	BFP	H	R	ER	HR	SH	SF	HB	TBB	IBB	SO	WP	Bk	W	L	Pct.	ShO	Sv	ERA
				HOW MUCH HE PITCHED						WHAT HE GAVE UP												THE RESULTS					
1994	Houston	NL		39	0	0	13	50	214	55	25	25	3	2	3	2	17	4	38	5	1	4	1	.800	0	1	4.50
	Philadelphia	NL		3	0	0	2	4	17	4	1	1	0	1	0	0	1	0	1	0	0	1	0	1.000	0	0	2.25
1995	Chicago	NL		5	0	0	1	3	18	6	3	2	0	0	0	0	3	0	2	0	0	1	0	1.000	0	0	6.00
11	Min. YEARS			228	155	16	24	1058.1	4545	998	509	429	58	28	32	38	444	13	623	48	5	65	49	.570	3	7	3.65
7	Maj. YEARS			182	14	0	59	312.1	1341	315	145	134	20	19	8	8	123	18	182	17	1	19	12	.613	0	6	3.86

Tim Edge

Bats: Right **Throws:** Right **Pos:** C **Ht:** 6'0" **Wt:** 210 **Born:** 10/26/68 **Age:** 28

Year	Team	Lg	Org	G	AB	H	2B	3B	HR	TB	R	RBI	TBB	IBB	SO	HBP	SH	SF	SB	CS	SB%	GDP	Avg	OBP	SLG
				BATTING															BASERUNNING				PERCENTAGES		
1990	Welland	A-	Pit	63	149	32	5	0	1	40	6	12	19	1	27	2	0	1	4	3	.57	1	.215	.310	.268
1991	Salem	A+	Pit	96	298	67	16	2	6	105	36	30	44	1	67	5	5	0	4	2	.67	7	.225	.334	.352
1992	Carolina	AA	Pit	4	9	1	0	0	0	1	1	0	2	1	5	0	0	0	0	0	.00	0	.111	.273	.111
	Salem	A+	Pit	68	216	39	5	1	6	64	18	26	21	0	55	5	0	1	3	2	.60	3	.181	.267	.296
1993	Buffalo	AAA	Pit	1	2	0	0	0	0	0	0	0	0	0	0	0	0	0	0	0	.00	0	.000	.000	.000
	Carolina	AA	Pit	46	160	35	8	0	3	52	12	16	11	0	41	1	2	0	1	2	.33	5	.219	.273	.325
1994	Augusta	A	Pit	11	29	9	3	0	0	12	2	4	3	0	5	0	0	0	0	0	.00	0	.310	.375	.414
	Carolina	AA	Pit	6	20	3	1	0	0	4	1	2	1	0	9	0	0	0	0	0	.00	0	.150	.190	.200
	Buffalo	AAA	Pit	8	18	4	2	0	0	6	0	0	1	0	4	0	0	0	0	0	.00	0	.222	.263	.333
1995	Carolina	AA	Pit	45	126	27	5	0	4	44	15	19	10	0	33	0	0	1	0	0	.00	4	.214	.270	.349
1996	Calgary	AAA	Pit	12	36	12	3	0	2	21	6	11	2	0	9	0	1	0	0	0	.00	2	.333	.368	.583
	Carolina	AA	Pit	53	153	37	10	0	4	59	18	21	16	1	44	2	1	1	1	0	1.00	4	.242	.320	.386
7	Min. YEARS			413	1216	266	58	3	26	408	115	141	130	4	299	15	9	4	13	9	.59	26	.219	.301	.336

Brian Edmondson

Pitches: Right **Bats:** Right **Pos:** P **Ht:** 6'2" **Wt:** 165 **Born:** 1/29/73 **Age:** 24

Year	Team	Lg	Org	G	GS	CG	GF	IP	BFP	H	R	ER	HR	SH	SF	HB	TBB	IBB	SO	WP	Bk	W	L	Pct.	ShO	Sv	ERA
				HOW MUCH HE PITCHED						WHAT HE GAVE UP												THE RESULTS					
1991	Bristol	R+	Det	12	12	1	0	69	289	72	38	35	7	1	2	3	23	1	42	5	2	4	4	.500	0	0	4.57
1992	Fayettevlle	A	Det	28	27	3	0	155.1	665	145	69	58	10	5	3	6	67	0	125	6	2	10	6	.625	1	0	3.36
1993	Lakeland	A+	Det	19	19	1	0	114.1	483	115	44	38	6	1	0	3	43	0	64	7	0	8	5	.615	0	0	2.99
	London	AA	Det	5	5	1	0	23	109	30	23	16	2	1	0	0	13	0	17	1	0	0	4	.000	0	0	6.26
1994	Trenton	AA	Det	26	26	2	0	162	703	171	89	82	12	2	6	6	61	1	90	11	2	11	9	.550	0	0	4.56
1995	Binghamton	AA	NYN	23	22	2	0	134.1	601	150	82	71	17	5	5	6	59	2	69	7	0	7	11	.389	1	0	4.76
1996	Binghamton	AA	NYN	39	13	1	9	114.1	502	130	69	54	16	7	7	4	38	5	83	3	1	6	6	.500	0	0	4.25
6	Min. YEARS			152	124	11	9	772.1	3352	813	414	354	70	22	23	28	304	9	490	40	7	46	45	.505	2	0	4.13

Geoff Edsell

Pitches: Right **Bats:** Right **Pos:** P **Ht:** 6'2" **Wt:** 195 **Born:** 12/12/71 **Age:** 25

Year	Team	Lg	Org	G	GS	CG	GF	IP	BFP	H	R	ER	HR	SH	SF	HB	TBB	IBB	SO	WP	Bk	W	L	Pct.	ShO	Sv	ERA
				HOW MUCH HE PITCHED						WHAT HE GAVE UP												THE RESULTS					
1993	Boise	A-	Cal	13	13	1	0	64	296	64	52	49	10	1	5	3	40	0	63	6	3	4	3	.571	0	0	6.89
1994	Cedar Rapds	A	Cal	17	17	4	0	125.1	538	109	54	42	10	5	0	6	65	1	84	10	4	11	5	.688	1	0	3.02
	Lk Elsinore	A+	Cal	9	7	0	1	40	174	38	21	18	3	0	0	2	24	1	26	3	2	2	2	.500	0	0	4.05
1995	Midland	AA	Cal	5	5	1	0	32	140	39	26	21	5	1	2	0	16	0	19	5	0	2	3	.400	0	0	5.91
	Lk Elsinore	A+	Cal	28	27	2	0	171.2	740	166	107	78	16	8	5	7	83	0	153	11	1	10	15	.400	1	0	4.09
1996	Midland	AA	Cal	14	14	0	0	88	382	84	53	46	10	3	5	6	47	0	60	5	1	5	5	.500	0	0	4.70
	Vancouver	AAA	Cal	15	15	3	0	105	437	93	45	40	7	5	4	3	45	1	48	2	2	4	6	.400	2	0	3.43
4	Min. YEARS			101	98	11	1	626	2707	593	358	294	61	23	21	27	320	3	453	42	13	38	39	.494	4	0	4.23

Kurt Ehmann

Bats: Right **Throws:** Right **Pos:** SS **Ht:** 6'1" **Wt:** 185 **Born:** 8/18/70 **Age:** 26

Year	Team	Lg	Org	G	AB	H	2B	3B	HR	TB	R	RBI	TBB	IBB	SO	HBP	SH	SF	SB	CS	SB%	GDP	Avg	OBP	SLG
				BATTING															BASERUNNING				PERCENTAGES		
1992	Everett	A-	SF	64	215	57	9	0	2	72	25	20	31	0	51	4	4	0	6	3	.67	1	.265	.368	.335
1993	San Jose	A+	SF	123	439	115	20	1	5	152	81	57	75	2	69	11	3	4	12	9	.57	4	.262	.380	.346
1994	Shreveport	AA	SF	124	426	104	20	0	1	127	46	40	27	1	85	11	13	6	9	3	.75	5	.244	.302	.298
1995	Phoenix	AAA	SF	67	216	58	5	2	0	67	21	7	24	1	41	3	4	4	8	3	.73	1	.269	.344	.310
	Shreveport	AA	SF	38	130	30	5	0	1	38	24	17	22	1	15	5	4	2	1	2	.33	5	.231	.358	.292
1996	Phoenix	AAA	SF	50	134	27	6	2	0	37	14	12	12	1	35	3	2	0	0	2	.00	0	.201	.282	.276
5	Min. YEARS			466	1560	391	65	5	9	493	211	153	191	6	296	37	30	16	36	22	.62	16	.251	.343	.316

Dave Eiland

Pitches: Right **Bats:** Right **Pos:** P **Ht:** 6' 3" **Wt:** 210 **Born:** 7/5/66 **Age:** 30

Year	Team	Lg	Org	G	GS	CG	GF	IP	BFP	H	R	ER	HR	SH	SF	HB	TBB	IBB	SO	WP	Bk	W	L	Pct.	ShO	Sv	ERA
				HOW MUCH HE PITCHED						WHAT HE GAVE UP												THE RESULTS					
1987	Oneonta	A-	NYA	5	5	0	0	29.1	109	20	6	6	1	0	0	0	3	0	16	2	0	4	0	1.000	0	0	1.84
	Ft. Laud	A+	NYA	8	8	4	0	62.1	248	57	17	13	0	2	0	0	8	0	28	1	1	5	3	.625	1	0	1.88
1988	Albany-Colo	AA	NYA	18	18	7	0	119.1	472	95	39	34	8	4	5	1	22	3	66	2	0	9	5	.643	2	0	2.56
	Columbus	AAA	NYA	4	4	0	0	24.1	106	25	8	7	4	0	1	1	6	0	13	1	0	1	1	.500	0	0	2.59
1989	Columbus	AAA	NYA	18	18	2	0	103	427	107	47	43	10	1	3	1	21	0	45	1	1	9	4	.692	0	0	3.76
1990	Columbus	AAA	NYA	27	26	11	0	175.1	707	155	63	56	8	3	1	1	32	0	96	2	2	16	5	.762	3	0	2.87

				HOW MUCH HE PITCHED						WHAT HE GAVE UP												THE RESULTS					
Year	Team	Lg	Org	G	GS	CG	GF	IP	BFP	H	R	ER	HR	SH	SF	HB	TBB	IBB	SO	WP	Bk	W	L	Pct.	ShO	Sv	ERA
1991	Columbus	AAA	NYA	9	9	2	0	60	244	54	22	16	5	1	1	2	7	0	18	1	0	6	1	.857	0	0	2.40
1992	Las Vegas	AAA	SD	14	14	0	0	63.2	276	78	43	37	4	7	6	0	11	2	31	0	0	4	5	.444	0	0	5.23
1993	Charlotte	AAA	Cle	8	8	0	0	35.2	154	42	22	21	8	1	0	1	12	0	13	0	0	1	3	.250	0	0	5.30
	Okla. City	AAA	Tex	7	7	1	0	35.2	155	39	18	17	1	1	1	1	9	0	15	0	0	3	1	.750	0	0	4.29
1994	Columbus	AAA	NYA	26	26	0	0	140.2	597	141	72	56	12	6	7	1	33	0	84	2	0	9	6	.600	0	0	3.58
1995	Columbus	AAA	NYA	19	18	1	0	109	444	109	44	38	0	2	1	3	22	2	62	1	0	8	7	.533	1	0	3.14
1996	Louisville	AAA	StL	8	6	0	0	24.1	110	27	17	15	2	2	1	2	8	0	17	0	0	0	1	.000	0	0	5.55
	Columbus	AAA	NYA	15	15	3	0	92.1	360	77	37	30	9	3	3	2	13	0	76	2	0	8	4	.667	0	0	2.92
1988	New York	AL		3	3	0	0	12.2	57	15	9	9	6	0	0	2	4	0	7	0	0	0	0	.000	0	0	6.39
1989	New York	AL		6	6	0	0	34.1	152	44	25	22	5	1	2	2	13	3	11	0	0	1	3	.250	0	0	5.77
1990	New York	AL		5	5	0	0	30.1	127	31	14	12	2	0	0	0	5	0	16	0	0	2	1	.667	0	0	3.56
1991	New York	AL		18	13	0	4	72.2	317	87	51	43	10	0	3	3	23	1	18	0	0	2	5	.286	0	0	5.33
1992	San Diego	NL		7	7	0	0	27	120	33	21	17	1	0	0	0	5	0	10	0	1	0	2	.000	0	0	5.67
1993	San Diego	NL		10	9	0	0	48.1	217	58	33	28	5	2	2	1	17	1	14	1	0	0	3	.000	0	0	5.21
1995	New York	AL		4	1	0	1	10	51	16	10	7	1	0	1	1	3	1	6	1	0	1	1	.500	0	0	6.30
10	Min. YEARS			186	182	31	0	1075	4409	1026	455	389	72	33	30	16	207	7	580	15	4	83	46	.643	7	0	3.26
7	Maj. YEARS			53	44	0	5	235.1	1041	284	163	138	30	3	8	9	70	6	82	2	1	6	15	.286	0	0	5.28

Donnie Elliott

Pitches: Right **Bats:** Right **Pos:** P **Ht:** 6' 5" **Wt:** 225 **Born:** 9/20/68 **Age:** 28

				HOW MUCH HE PITCHED						WHAT HE GAVE UP												THE RESULTS					
Year	Team	Lg	Org	G	GS	CG	GF	IP	BFP	H	R	ER	HR	SH	SF	HB	TBB	IBB	SO	WP	Bk	W	L	Pct.	ShO	Sv	ERA
1988	Martinsvlle	R+	Phi	15	10	0	2	59	257	47	37	24	4	0	0	3	31	0	77	4	9	4	2	.667	0	1	3.66
1989	Batavia	A-	Phi	8	8	0	0	57	231	45	21	9	2	1	0	0	14	1	48	4	0	4	1	.800	0	0	1.42
	Spartanburg	A	Phi	7	7	1	0	43.2	183	46	19	12	1	1	1	0	14	0	36	4	0	2	3	.400	1	0	2.47
1990	Spartanburg	A	Phi	20	20	0	0	105.1	450	101	52	41	6	3	5	2	46	0	109	7	1	4	8	.333	0	0	3.50
1991	Spartanburg	A	Phi	10	10	0	0	51	235	42	37	24	1	1	0	3	36	0	81	8	0	3	4	.429	0	0	4.24
	Clearwater	A+	Phi	18	18	1	0	107	435	78	34	33	1	4	4	1	51	0	103	10	1	8	5	.615	1	0	2.78
1992	Clearwater	A+	Phi	3	3	0	0	18	71	12	6	6	1	0	0	0	8	0	12	2	0	1	1	.500	0	0	3.00
	Reading	AA	Phi	6	6	0	0	35.2	153	37	10	10	2	2	1	0	11	1	23	0	0	3	3	.500	0	0	2.52
	Greenville	AA	Atl	19	17	0	0	103.2	416	76	28	24	8	1	3	5	35	1	100	4	0	7	2	.778	0	0	2.08
1993	Richmond	AAA	Atl	18	18	1	0	103	449	108	65	54	16	3	2	0	39	0	99	5	0	8	5	.615	0	0	4.72
	Las Vegas	AAA	SD	8	7	0	0	41	198	48	32	29	6	1	2	1	24	0	44	3	0	2	5	.286	0	0	6.37
1994	Las Vegas	AAA	SD	6	0	0	1	13.1	65	13	11	8	3	0	1	0	11	2	12	5	0	2	0	1.000	0	0	5.40
1995	Las Vegas	AAA	SD	7	0	0	3	8	35	8	4	4	1	1	1	0	4	1	2	0	0	1	0	1.000	0	1	4.50
1996	Scranton-WB	AAA	Phi	21	19	1	1	103.1	466	105	62	55	12	7	5	5	59	3	93	9	0	5	11	.313	0	0	4.79
1994	San Diego	NL		30	1	0	10	33	148	31	12	12	3	2	0	1	21	2	24	2	0	0	1	.000	0	0	3.27
1995	San Diego	NL		1	0	0	1	2	9	2	0	0	0	0	0	0	1	0	3	0	0	0	0	.000	0	0	0.00
9	Min. YEARS			166	143	4	7	849	3644	766	418	333	64	25	25	20	383	9	839	65	11	54	50	.519	2	2	3.53
2	Maj. YEARS			31	1	0	11	35	157	33	12	12	3	2	0	1	22	2	27	2	0	0	1	.000	0	0	3.09

Paul Ellis

Bats: Left **Throws:** Right **Pos:** C **Ht:** 6'1" **Wt:** 205 **Born:** 11/28/68 **Age:** 28

				BATTING														BASERUNNING				PERCENTAGES		
Year	Team	Lg	Org	G	AB	H	2B	3B	HR	TB	R	RBI	TBB	IBB	SO	HBP	SH	SF	SB	CS	SB%	GDP	Avg	OBP	SLG
1990	Hamilton	A-	StL	15	58	18	4	0	3	31	8	18	6	3	13	0	0	2	0	0	.00	1	.310	.364	.534
	Springfield	A	StL	50	183	43	5	0	5	63	18	25	26	1	34	2	0	0	0	1	.00	2	.235	.336	.344
1991	St. Pete	A+	StL	119	402	82	11	0	6	111	26	42	52	1	35	6	0	4	0	0	.00	8	.204	.302	.276
1992	St. Pete	A+	StL	84	308	67	17	0	2	90	22	29	26	1	22	3	0	4	0	1	.00	4	.218	.282	.292
	Arkansas	AA	StL	25	79	18	2	0	2	26	9	8	13	2	14	1	0	1	0	1	.00	0	.228	.340	.329
1993	Arkansas	AA	StL	24	78	26	3	0	1	32	5	11	16	0	2	3	0	0	0	2	.00	1	.333	.464	.410
	Louisville	AAA	StL	50	125	25	6	0	0	31	12	8	13	2	16	1	0	1	0	0	.00	3	.200	.279	.248
1994	Arkansas	AA	StL	102	281	65	9	0	6	92	28	39	35	4	34	0	6	2	0	0	.00	11	.231	.314	.327
1995	Arkansas	AA	StL	78	229	52	6	0	2	64	17	25	49	4	18	4	4	1	0	1	.00	9	.227	.371	.279
1996	Arkansas	AA	StL	65	157	40	5	0	3	54	16	26	22	0	20	3	0	0	0	0	.00	3	.255	.357	.344
7	Min. YEARS			612	1900	436	68	0	30	594	161	231	258	18	208	23	10	15	0	6	.00	42	.229	.327	.313

Narciso Elvira

Pitches: Left **Bats:** Left **Pos:** P **Ht:** 5'10" **Wt:** 160 **Born:** 10/29/67 **Age:** 29

				HOW MUCH HE PITCHED						WHAT HE GAVE UP												THE RESULTS					
Year	Team	Lg	Org	G	GS	CG	GF	IP	BFP	H	R	ER	HR	SH	SF	HB	TBB	IBB	SO	WP	Bk	W	L	Pct.	ShO	Sv	ERA
1987	Beloit	A	Mil	4	4	1	0	27	102	15	5	4	1	1	0	0	12	0	29	3	0	3	0	1.000	1	0	1.33
1988	Stockton	A+	Mil	25	23	0	1	135.1	563	87	49	44	6	6	7	7	79	1	161	10	4	7	6	.538	0	0	2.93
1989	El Paso	AA	Mil	7	7	0	0	33	157	48	34	28	4	0	1	1	23	0	18	4	3	2	2	.500	0	0	7.64
	Stockton	A+	Mil	17	17	6	0	115.1	470	92	45	39	5	3	1	5	43	0	135	11	1	8	5	.615	2	0	3.04
1990	Beloit	A	Mil	8	7	0	1	38.1	160	37	16	10	1	1	2	0	9	0	45	2	0	3	2	.600	0	1	2.35
	El Paso	AA	Mil	4	4	0	0	18	77	17	11	9	4	0	0	0	6	0	12	0	0	0	2	.000	0	0	4.50
1991	Denver	AAA	Mil	18	13	1	1	80	374	100	62	53	8	6	3	4	40	1	52	3	1	0	4	.000	0	0	5.96
1992	Okla. City	AAA	Tex	19	16	0	2	88.2	370	87	54	49	9	5	3	3	28	0	45	2	1	4	5	.444	0	0	4.97
1996	Albuquerque	AAA	LA	3	3	0	0	17	76	19	12	9	1	0	1	0	9	0	14	0	0	1	1	.500	0	0	4.76
1990	Milwaukee	AL		4	0	0	2	5	25	6	3	3	0	0	0	0	5	0	6	0	0	0	0	.000	0	0	5.40
7	Min. YEARS			105	94	8	5	552.2	2349	502	288	245	39	22	18	20	249	2	511	35	10	28	27	.509	3	1	3.99

Scott Emerson

Pitches: Left **Bats:** Both **Pos:** P **Ht:** 6'5" **Wt:** 175 **Born:** 12/22/71 **Age:** 25

				HOW MUCH HE PITCHED						WHAT HE GAVE UP												THE RESULTS					
Year	Team	Lg	Org	G	GS	CG	GF	IP	BFP	H	R	ER	HR	SH	SF	HB	TBB	IBB	SO	WP	Bk	W	L	Pct.	ShO	Sv	ERA
1992	Bluefield	R+	Bal	14	11	0	0	69	301	72	31	22	5	0	3	3	35	0	41	6	0	4	3	.571	0	0	2.87
1993	Albany	A	Bal	27	27	1	0	147.1	633	143	72	58	6	4	5	7	62	1	115	10	2	10	9	.526	0	0	3.54
1994	Frederick	A+	Bal	28	22	2	0	129.2	573	141	78	61	6	5	5	4	62	1	87	4	1	8	8	.500	0	0	4.23
1995	Bowie	AA	Bal	4	4	0	0	16	82	19	18	9	3	0	1	0	14	0	13	3	0	0	2	.000	0	0	5.06
	Trenton	AA	Bos	8	4	0	0	21.2	111	28	21	12	3	0	1	0	16	0	18	4	0	0	2	.000	0	0	4.98
	Sarasota	A+	Bos	24	15	1	1	82	384	94	59	44	5	2	3	6	45	2	65	10	0	2	7	.222	0	0	4.83
1996	Sarasota	A+	Bos	4	0	0	0	6.2	37	11	4	4	0	1	0	1	6	1	7	1	0	0	0	.000	0	0	5.40
	Trenton	AA	Bos	19	0	0	6	32.1	154	34	24	21	4	0	1	1	26	0	23	7	0	1	0	1.000	0	0	5.85
5 Min. YEARS				128	83	4	7	504.2	2275	542	307	231	32	12	19	22	266	5	369	45	3	25	31	.446	0	0	4.12

Brad Erdman

Bats: Right **Throws:** Right **Pos:** C **Ht:** 6'3" **Wt:** 190 **Born:** 2/23/70 **Age:** 27

				BATTING															BASERUNNING				PERCENTAGES		
Year	Team	Lg	Org	G	AB	H	2B	3B	HR	TB	R	RBI	TBB	IBB	SO	HBP	SH	SF	SB	CS	SB%	GDP	Avg	OBP	SLG
1989	Geneva	A-	ChN	26	85	15	2	0	0	17	6	3	6	1	26	0	0	1	1	1	.50	2	.176	.228	.200
1990	Peoria	A	ChN	37	119	23	3	0	0	26	9	4	12	0	42	1	1	0	0	0	.00	2	.193	.273	.218
	Geneva	A-	ChN	34	111	25	4	0	0	29	12	15	11	0	31	1	3	0	2	0	1.00	0	.225	.301	.261
1991	Peoria	A	ChN	83	280	71	19	1	4	104	33	26	32	1	59	3	8	1	5	0	1.00	6	.254	.335	.371
1992	Winston-Sal	A+	ChN	65	219	42	4	0	3	55	29	14	12	0	53	4	4	1	1	5	.17	5	.192	.246	.251
1993	Peoria	A	ChN	20	57	14	1	0	1	18	7	10	6	0	12	2	3	1	2	0	1.00	0	.246	.333	.316
	Orlando	AA	ChN	69	171	31	5	0	1	39	12	17	18	5	42	6	9	3	2	2	.50	2	.181	.278	.228
1994	Daytona	A+	ChN	76	236	60	12	1	2	80	26	24	21	0	47	9	3	0	2	2	.50	8	.254	.338	.339
	Orlando	AA	ChN	1	0	0	0	0	0	0	0	0	0	0	0	0	0	0	0	0	.00	0	.000	.000	.000
1995	Daytona	A+	ChN	8	26	4	1	0	0	5	6	3	4	0	6	0	1	0	0	0	.00	0	.154	.267	.192
	Orlando	AA	ChN	14	36	4	0	0	0	4	4	0	1	0	6	2	0	0	0	0	.00	4	.111	.179	.111
1996	Iowa	AAA	ChN	57	171	30	6	0	2	42	18	16	16	0	38	1	3	2	1	0	1.00	8	.175	.247	.246
8 Min. YEARS				490	1511	319	57	2	13	419	162	132	139	7	362	29	35	9	16	10	.62	37	.211	.289	.277

Kelvim Escobar

Pitches: Right **Bats:** Right **Pos:** P **Ht:** 6'1" **Wt:** 195 **Born:** 4/11/76 **Age:** 21

				HOW MUCH HE PITCHED						WHAT HE GAVE UP												THE RESULTS					
Year	Team	Lg	Org	G	GS	CG	GF	IP	BFP	H	R	ER	HR	SH	SF	HB	TBB	IBB	SO	WP	Bk	W	L	Pct.	ShO	Sv	ERA
1994	Blue Jays	R	Tor	11	10	1	0	65	257	56	23	17	0	0	1	2	18	0	64	5	3	4	4	.500	0	0	2.35
1995	Medicne Hat	R+	Tor	14	14	1	0	69.1	307	66	47	44	6	2	5	6	33	0	75	4	4	3	3	.500	1	0	5.71
1996	Dunedin	A+	Tor	18	18	1	0	110.1	460	101	44	33	5	2	1	3	33	0	113	7	2	9	5	.643	0	0	2.69
	Knoxville	AA	Tor	10	10	0	0	54	238	61	36	32	7	0	1	1	24	0	44	6	1	3	4	.429	0	0	5.33
3 Min. YEARS				53	52	3	0	298.2	1262	284	150	126	18	4	8	12	108	0	296	22	10	19	16	.543	1	0	3.80

Ramon Espinosa

Bats: Right **Throws:** Right **Pos:** OF **Ht:** 6'0" **Wt:** 175 **Born:** 2/7/72 **Age:** 25

				BATTING															BASERUNNING				PERCENTAGES		
Year	Team	Lg	Org	G	AB	H	2B	3B	HR	TB	R	RBI	TBB	IBB	SO	HBP	SH	SF	SB	CS	SB%	GDP	Avg	OBP	SLG
1991	Pirates	R	Pit	19	63	15	2	0	0	17	7	5	2	0	7	0	0	0	3	0	1.00	2	.238	.262	.270
1992	Welland	A-	Pit	60	208	56	12	5	4	90	27	22	9	0	23	0	0	2	10	5	.67	9	.269	.297	.433
1993	Augusta	A	Pit	70	266	79	9	3	2	100	32	27	12	2	51	2	1	3	17	5	.77	12	.297	.329	.376
	Salem	A+	Pit	54	208	56	8	2	8	92	30	25	6	0	36	1	2	0	11	6	.65	6	.269	.293	.442
1994	Carolina	AA	Pit	82	291	78	16	3	2	106	44	40	11	1	38	1	2	4	12	10	.55	4	.268	.293	.364
1995	Carolina	AA	Pit	134	489	140	28	2	3	181	69	48	17	3	64	5	8	1	14	6	.70	15	.286	.316	.370
1996	Calgary	AAA	Pit	78	245	69	8	8	0	93	37	25	6	3	28	2	3	0	2	3	.40	6	.282	.304	.380
6 Min. YEARS				497	1770	493	83	23	19	679	246	192	63	9	247	11	16	10	69	35	.66	54	.279	.306	.384

Mauricio Estavil

Pitches: Left **Bats:** Left **Pos:** P **Ht:** 6'0" **Wt:** 185 **Born:** 6/27/72 **Age:** 25

				HOW MUCH HE PITCHED						WHAT HE GAVE UP												THE RESULTS					
Year	Team	Lg	Org	G	GS	CG	GF	IP	BFP	H	R	ER	HR	SH	SF	HB	TBB	IBB	SO	WP	Bk	W	L	Pct.	ShO	Sv	ERA
1994	Batavia	A-	Phi	14	5	0	5	39.1	184	43	23	17	1	1	4	5	17	0	31	7	2	3	2	.600	0	1	3.89
1995	Piedmont	A	Phi	42	0	0	18	44	202	33	20	18	0	0	0	2	37	1	58	6	0	3	5	.375	0	1	3.68
1996	Reading	AA	Phi	20	0	0	6	18.2	110	30	28	24	3	0	0	1	22	1	19	4	0	0	3	.000	0	0	11.57
	Clearwater	A+	Phi	29	0	0	12	34	140	20	15	13	0	0	2	1	20	0	25	1	0	5	3	.625	0	2	3.44
3 Min. YEARS				105	5	0	41	136	636	126	86	72	4	1	6	9	96	2	133	18	2	11	13	.458	0	4	4.76

Osmani Estrada

Bats: Right **Throws:** Right **Pos:** 3B **Ht:** 5'8" **Wt:** 180 **Born:** 1/23/69 **Age:** 28

				BATTING															BASERUNNING				PERCENTAGES		
Year	Team	Lg	Org	G	AB	H	2B	3B	HR	TB	R	RBI	TBB	IBB	SO	HBP	SH	SF	SB	CS	SB%	GDP	Avg	OBP	SLG
1993	Erie	A-	Tex	60	225	60	11	0	4	83	24	22	17	1	26	6	1	2	1	7	.13	4	.267	.332	.369
1994	Charlotte	A+	Tex	131	501	128	29	4	4	177	64	30	57	0	60	11	7	5	8	10	.44	10	.255	.341	.353
1995	Tulsa	AA	Tex	120	410	109	23	3	3	147	44	43	35	2	49	9	5	4	0	2	.00	9	.266	.334	.359
1996	Tulsa	AA	Tex	27	85	22	4	0	2	32	12	16	9	0	13	1	0	1	1	1	.50	2	.259	.333	.376
	Okla. City	AAA	Tex	50	130	34	6	1	1	45	15	13	14	0	26	1	1	1	3	1	.75	3	.262	.336	.346

		BATTING															BASERUNNING				PERCENTAGES		
Year Team	Lg Org	G	AB	H	2B	3B	HR	TB	R	RBI	TBB	IBB	SO	HBP	SH	SF	SB	CS	SB%	GDP	Avg	OBP	SLG
4 Min. YEARS		388	1351	353	73	8	14	484	159	124	132	3	174	28	14	13	13	21	.38	28	.261	.337	.358

Roger Etheridge

Pitches: Left **Bats:** Left **Pos:** P **Ht:** 6'5" **Wt:** 215 **Born:** 5/31/72 **Age:** 25

			HOW MUCH HE PITCHED						WHAT HE GAVE UP												THE RESULTS					
Year	Team	Lg Org	G	GS	CG	GF	IP	BFP	H	R	ER	HR	SH	SF	HB	TBB	IBB	SO	WP	Bk	W	L	Pct.	ShO	Sv	ERA
1992	Princeton	R+ Cin	17	5	0	5	35.1	165	37	33	27	3	0	0	1	25	1	35	5	1	1	1	.500	0	1	6.88
1993	Princeton	R+ Cin	9	9	1	0	54.1	227	40	14	9	2	2	1	2	28	1	60	3	1	3	2	.600	0	0	1.49
	Charlstn-WV	A Cin	13	8	0	0	43.2	208	43	41	35	2	2	2	4	35	0	28	1	1	3	3	.500	0	0	7.21
1994	Charlstn-WV	A Cin	10	10	0	0	58.1	258	64	35	29	6	4	1	4	27	0	42	2	0	2	2	.500	0	0	4.47
	Macon	A Atl	17	14	0	1	91.1	408	103	52	42	9	4	2	6	35	0	61	3	0	5	3	.625	0	0	4.14
	Durham	A+ Atl	9	9	1	0	64.1	245	41	12	10	2	2	1	0	16	0	36	3	0	6	2	.750	1	0	1.40
1995	Greenville	AA Atl	32	16	1	6	101.2	462	120	73	64	10	4	5	3	52	1	47	8	1	2	10	.167	0	0	5.67
1996	Greenville	AA Atl	49	1	0	16	66.2	324	71	55	51	8	3	4	3	55	2	43	8	0	4	2	.667	0	2	6.89
5 Min. YEARS			156	72	3	28	515.2	2297	519	315	267	42	21	16	23	273	5	352	33	4	26	25	.510	1	3	4.66

Bart Evans

Pitches: Right **Bats:** Right **Pos:** P **Ht:** 6'1" **Wt:** 190 **Born:** 12/30/70 **Age:** 26

			HOW MUCH HE PITCHED						WHAT HE GAVE UP												THE RESULTS					
Year	Team	Lg Org	G	GS	CG	GF	IP	BFP	H	R	ER	HR	SH	SF	HB	TBB	IBB	SO	WP	Bk	W	L	Pct.	ShO	Sv	ERA
1992	Eugene	A- KC	13	1	0	4	26	126	17	20	18	1	1	2	4	31	0	39	14	0	1	1	.500	0	0	6.23
1993	Rockford	A KC	27	16	0	4	99	439	95	52	48	5	1	2	4	60	0	120	10	1	10	4	.714	0	0	4.36
1994	Wilmington	A+ KC	26	26	0	0	145	587	107	53	48	7	1	0	4	61	0	145	10	0	10	3	.769	0	0	2.98
1995	Wichita	AA KC	7	7	0	0	22.1	123	22	28	26	3	1	0	1	45	0	13	7	1	0	4	.000	0	0	10.48
	Wilmington	A+ KC	23	13	0	4	69	338	52	49	41	3	1	1	6	89	0	60	14	1	4	5	.444	0	2	5.35
1996	Wichita	AA KC	9	7	0	0	24.1	146	31	38	32	7	3	2	6	36	0	16	12	0	1	2	.333	0	0	11.84
5 Min. YEARS			105	70	0	12	385.2	1759	324	240	213	26	8	7	25	322	0	393	67	3	26	19	.578	0	2	4.97

Dave Evans

Pitches: Right **Bats:** Right **Pos:** P **Ht:** 6'3" **Wt:** 185 **Born:** 1/1/68 **Age:** 29

			HOW MUCH HE PITCHED						WHAT HE GAVE UP												THE RESULTS					
Year	Team	Lg Org	G	GS	CG	GF	IP	BFP	H	R	ER	HR	SH	SF	HB	TBB	IBB	SO	WP	Bk	W	L	Pct.	ShO	Sv	ERA
1990	San Bernrdo	A+ Sea	26	26	4	0	155	673	135	83	72	9	4	7	7	74	0	143	10	0	14	9	.609	0	0	4.18
1991	Jacksonvlle	AA Sea	21	20	1	0	115.2	507	118	74	67	15	2	7	9	49	0	76	12	0	5	9	.357	0	0	5.21
1993	Appleton	A Sea	5	5	0	0	27.2	117	21	9	7	0	0	0	2	15	0	23	5	2	2	1	.667	0	0	2.28
	Riverside	A+ Sea	8	8	1	0	41.2	187	41	22	21	5	1	1	5	23	0	42	2	0	3	2	.600	1	0	4.54
1994	Jacksonvlle	AA Sea	31	6	0	8	81.1	354	86	59	50	11	3	4	5	31	2	62	4	0	3	5	.375	0	2	5.53
1995	Tucson	AAA Hou	2	0	0	0	3	12	2	0	0	0	0	0	0	1	0	4	0	0	0	0	.000	0	0	0.00
	Jackson	AA Hou	51	0	0	37	70.2	290	52	29	25	2	5	3	4	29	6	58	0	1	2	9	.182	0	18	3.18
1996	Tucson	AAA Hou	43	15	0	12	111.2	511	120	77	65	8	8	3	12	47	3	80	11	0	6	12	.333	0	1	5.24
6 Min. YEARS			187	80	6	57	606.2	2651	575	353	307	50	23	25	44	269	11	488	44	3	35	47	.427	1	21	4.55

Tom Evans

Bats: Right **Throws:** Right **Pos:** 3B-DH **Ht:** 6'1" **Wt:** 180 **Born:** 7/9/74 **Age:** 22

			BATTING															BASERUNNING				PERCENTAGES		
Year	Team	Lg Org	G	AB	H	2B	3B	HR	TB	R	RBI	TBB	IBB	SO	HBP	SH	SF	SB	CS	SB%	GDP	Avg	OBP	SLG
1992	Medicne Hat	R+ Tor	52	166	36	3	0	1	42	17	21	33	0	29	1	1	1	4	3	.57	4	.217	.348	.253
1993	Hagerstown	A Tor	119	389	100	25	1	7	148	47	54	53	2	61	3	0	4	9	2	.82	7	.257	.347	.380
1994	Hagerstown	A Tor	95	322	88	16	2	13	147	52	48	51	1	80	1	1	1	2	1	.67	3	.273	.373	.457
1995	Dunedin	A+ Tor	130	444	124	29	3	9	186	63	66	51	0	80	8	3	7	7	2	.78	10	.279	.359	.419
1996	Knoxville	AA Tor	120	394	111	27	1	17	191	87	65	115	0	113	9	0	2	4	0	1.00	7	.282	.452	.485
5 Min. YEARS			516	1715	459	100	7	47	714	266	254	303	3	363	22	5	15	26	8	.76	31	.268	.382	.416

Bryan Eversgerd

Pitches: Left **Bats:** Right **Pos:** P **Ht:** 6' 1" **Wt:** 190 **Born:** 2/11/69 **Age:** 28

			HOW MUCH HE PITCHED						WHAT HE GAVE UP												THE RESULTS					
Year	Team	Lg Org	G	GS	CG	GF	IP	BFP	H	R	ER	HR	SH	SF	HB	TBB	IBB	SO	WP	Bk	W	L	Pct.	ShO	Sv	ERA
1989	Johnson Cty	R+ StL	16	1	0	5	29.2	127	30	16	12	1	2	6	0	12	1	19	2	0	2	3	.400	0	0	3.64
1990	Springfield	A StL	20	15	2	2	104.1	457	123	60	48	6	5	4	4	26	1	55	2	0	6	8	.429	0	0	4.14
1991	Savannah	A StL	72	0	0	22	93.1	390	71	43	36	7	2	0	3	34	4	98	11	0	1	5	.167	0	1	3.47
1992	St. Pete	A+ StL	57	1	0	13	74	305	65	25	22	0	9	4	2	25	4	57	1	1	3	2	.600	0	0	2.68
	Arkansas	AA StL	6	0	0	2	5.1	25	7	4	4	0	1	0	0	2	1	4	0	0	0	1	.000	0	0	6.75
1993	Arkansas	AA StL	62	0	0	32	66	269	60	24	16	3	2	1	1	19	4	68	7	1	4	4	.500	0	0	2.18
1994	Louisville	AAA StL	9	0	0	2	12	54	11	7	6	0	1	1	0	8	0	8	1	0	1	1	.500	0	0	4.50
1995	Ottawa	AAA Mon	38	0	0	9	53	232	49	21	14	1	2	3	1	26	1	45	2	0	6	2	.750	0	2	2.38
1996	Trenton	AA Bos	4	0	0	2	7	31	6	2	2	0	1	0	1	4	1	2	0	1	1	0	1.000	0	0	2.57
	Okla. City	AAA Tex	38	5	0	14	65.2	266	57	21	20	3	2	1	4	14	0	60	3	0	3	3	.500	0	4	2.74
1994	St. Louis	NL	40	1	0	8	67.2	283	75	36	34	8	5	2	2	20	1	47	3	1	2	3	.400	0	0	4.52
1995	Montreal	NL	25	0	0	5	21	95	22	13	12	2	1	2	1	9	2	8	1	0	0	0	.000	0	0	5.14
8 Min. YEARS			322	22	2	103	510.1	2156	479	223	180	21	27	20	16	170	17	416	29	3	27	29	.482	0	7	3.17
2 Maj. YEARS			65	1	0	13	88.2	378	97	49	46	10	6	4	3	29	3	55	4	1	2	3	.400	0	0	4.67

Scott Eyre

Pitches: Left **Bats:** Left **Pos:** P **Ht:** 6'1" **Wt:** 160 **Born:** 5/30/72 **Age:** 25

		HOW MUCH HE PITCHED						WHAT HE GAVE UP												THE RESULTS					
Year Team	Lg Org	G	GS	CG	GF	IP	BFP	H	R	ER	HR	SH	SF	HB	TBB	IBB	SO	WP	Bk	W	L	Pct.	ShO	Sv	ERA
1992 Butte	R+ Tex	15	14	2	0	80.2	339	71	30	26	6	1	0	4	39	0	94	6	1	7	3	.700	1	0	2.90
1993 Charlstn-SC	A Tex	26	26	0	0	143.2	597	115	74	55	6	3	6	6	59	1	154	2	1	11	7	.611	0	0	3.45
1994 South Bend	A ChA	19	18	2	1	111.2	481	108	56	43	7	2	4	3	37	0	111	8	3	8	4	.667	0	0	3.47
1995 White Sox	R ChA	9	9	0	0	27.1	106	16	7	7	0	0	1	1	12	0	40	2	0	0	2	.000	0	0	2.30
1996 Birmingham	AA ChA	27	27	0	0	158.1	709	170	90	77	12	3	6	8	79	3	137	12	0	12	7	.632	0	0	4.38
5 Min. YEARS		96	94	4	1	521.2	2232	480	257	208	31	9	17	22	226	4	536	30	5	38	23	.623	1	0	3.59

Dan Fagley

Bats: Right **Throws:** Right **Pos:** C **Ht:** 5'10" **Wt:** 185 **Born:** 12/18/74 **Age:** 22

		BATTING														BASERUNNING				PERCENTAGES		
Year Team	Lg Org	G	AB	H	2B	3B	HR	TB	R	RBI	TBB	IBB	SO	HBP	SH	SF	SB	CS	SB%	GDP	Avg	OBP	SLG
1994 Marlins	R Fla	14	41	6	1	0	0	7	4	2	7	0	15	1	0	0	0	1	.00	1	.146	.286	.171
1995 Marlins	R Fla	16	33	6	0	0	0	6	4	4	4	0	8	1	0	0	0	0	.00	0	.182	.289	.182
1996 Utica	A- Fla	1	3	0	0	0	0	0	0	0	1	0	2	0	0	0	0	0	.00	0	.000	.250	.000
Brevard Cty	A+ Fla	20	53	5	2	0	0	7	1	2	5	0	19	2	1	0	0	0	.00	3	.094	.200	.132
Charlotte	AAA Fla	2	1	0	0	0	0	0	1	0	0	0	0	0	0	0	0	0	.00	0	.000	.000	.000
3 Min. YEARS		53	131	17	3	0	0	20	10	8	17	0	44	4	1	0	0	1	.00	4	.130	.250	.153

Steve Falteisek

Pitches: Right **Bats:** Right **Pos:** P **Ht:** 6'2" **Wt:** 200 **Born:** 1/28/72 **Age:** 25

		HOW MUCH HE PITCHED						WHAT HE GAVE UP												THE RESULTS					
Year Team	Lg Org	G	GS	CG	GF	IP	BFP	H	R	ER	HR	SH	SF	HB	TBB	IBB	SO	WP	Bk	W	L	Pct.	ShO	Sv	ERA
1992 Jamestown	A- Mon	15	15	2	0	96	407	84	47	38	3	4	1	5	31	2	82	9	10	3	8	.273	0	0	3.56
1993 Burlington	A Mon	14	14	0	0	76.1	345	86	59	50	4	4	1	2	35	0	63	4	1	3	5	.375	0	0	5.90
1994 W. Palm Bch	A+ Mon	27	24	1	0	159.2	658	144	72	45	3	0	6	3	49	0	91	11	4	9	4	.692	0	0	2.54
1995 Ottawa	AAA Mon	3	3	1	0	23	86	17	4	3	0	0	0	1	5	0	18	0	1	2	0	1.000	1	0	1.17
Harrisburg	AA Mon	28	28	6	0	191	793	169	78	58	3	7	5	12	69	4	130	6	2	11	6	.647	1	0	2.73
1996 Ottawa	AAA Mon	12	12	0	0	58	272	75	45	41	10	1	0	5	25	0	26	3	0	2	5	.286	0	0	6.36
Harrisburg	AA Mon	17	17	1	0	115.2	492	111	60	49	9	7	0	5	48	1	62	5	3	6	5	.545	0	0	3.81
5 Min. YEARS		116	113	11	0	719.2	3053	686	365	284	32	23	13	33	262	7	472	38	21	36	33	.522	2	0	3.55

Paul Faries

Bats: Right **Throws:** Right **Pos:** 2B **Ht:** 5'10" **Wt:** 165 **Born:** 2/20/65 **Age:** 32

		BATTING														BASERUNNING				PERCENTAGES		
Year Team	Lg Org	G	AB	H	2B	3B	HR	TB	R	RBI	TBB	IBB	SO	HBP	SH	SF	SB	CS	SB%	GDP	Avg	OBP	SLG
1987 Spokane	A- SD	74	280	86	9	3	0	101	67	27	36	0	25	5	4	5	30	9	.77	7	.307	.390	.361
1988 Riverside	A+ SD	141	579	183	39	4	2	236	108	77	72	1	79	8	7	7	65	30	.68	14	.316	.395	.408
1989 Wichita	AA SD	130	513	136	25	8	6	195	79	52	47	0	52	2	2	1	41	13	.76	13	.265	.329	.380
1990 Las Vegas	AAA SD	137	552	172	29	3	5	222	109	64	75	1	60	6	7	1	48	15	.76	16	.312	.399	.402
1991 High Desert	A+ SD	10	42	13	2	2	0	19	6	5	2	1	3	0	1	1	1	0	1.00	2	.310	.333	.452
Las Vegas	AAA SD	20	75	23	2	1	1	30	16	12	12	0	5	0	2	1	7	3	.70	2	.307	.398	.400
1992 Las Vegas	AAA SD	125	457	134	15	6	1	164	77	40	40	1	53	3	4	2	28	9	.76	13	.293	.353	.359
1993 Phoenix	AAA SF	78	327	99	14	5	2	129	56	32	22	1	30	1	3	1	18	11	.62	8	.303	.348	.394
1994 Phoenix	AAA SF	124	503	141	21	4	2	176	77	50	28	0	53	6	7	3	31	10	.76	19	.280	.324	.350
1995 Edmonton	AAA Oak	117	424	127	15	2	0	146	67	46	34	1	47	2	7	5	14	8	.64	12	.300	.351	.344
1996 Iowa	AAA ChN	37	115	30	4	2	0	38	14	8	14	2	12	2	2	1	6	1	.86	2	.261	.348	.330
New Orleans	AAA Mil	35	110	25	1	1	1	31	7	8	11	0	13	1	3	0	1	1	.50	2	.227	.303	.282
Buffalo	AAA Cle	49	172	43	9	1	2	60	24	15	12	0	24	1	4	2	3	1	.75	2	.250	.299	.349
1990 San Diego	NL	14	37	7	1	0	0	8	4	2	4	0	7	1	2	1	0	1	.00	0	.189	.279	.216
1991 San Diego	NL	57	130	23	3	1	0	28	13	7	14	0	21	1	4	0	3	1	.75	5	.177	.262	.215
1992 San Diego	NL	10	11	5	1	0	0	6	3	1	1	0	2	0	0	0	0	0	.00	0	.455	.500	.545
1993 San Francisco	NL	15	36	8	2	1	0	12	6	4	1	0	4	0	1	1	2	0	1.00	1	.222	.237	.333
10 Min. YEARS		1077	4149	1212	185	42	22	1547	707	436	405	8	456	37	53	30	293	111	.73	112	.292	.358	.373
4 Maj. YEARS		96	214	43	7	2	0	54	26	14	20	0	34	2	7	2	5	2	.71	6	.201	.273	.252

Jon Farrell

Bats: Right **Throws:** Right **Pos:** OF **Ht:** 6'2" **Wt:** 185 **Born:** 7/30/71 **Age:** 25

		BATTING														BASERUNNING				PERCENTAGES		
Year Team	Lg Org	G	AB	H	2B	3B	HR	TB	R	RBI	TBB	IBB	SO	HBP	SH	SF	SB	CS	SB%	GDP	Avg	OBP	SLG
1991 Welland	A- Pit	69	241	61	20	3	8	111	37	35	31	1	71	4	0	2	9	6	.60	1	.253	.345	.461
1992 Augusta	A Pit	92	320	71	11	5	8	116	44	48	39	2	93	4	1	6	8	7	.53	5	.222	.309	.363
1993 Salem	A+ Pit	105	386	92	9	1	20	163	58	51	40	0	103	8	1	0	5	6	.45	5	.238	.323	.422
1994 Salem	A+ Pit	123	445	120	21	4	11	182	67	42	41	1	91	4	0	1	11	2	.85	8	.270	.336	.409
1995 Carolina	AA Pit	94	314	69	13	0	10	112	34	47	15	0	82	4	3	3	3	4	.43	9	.220	.262	.357
1996 Lynchburg	A+ Pit	24	78	28	3	0	1	34	8	11	19	1	16	3	0	1	0	0	.00	1	.359	.495	.436
Carolina	AA Pit	22	51	11	3	0	0	14	6	3	6	2	22	2	0	1	0	0	.00	0	.216	.317	.275
St. Lucie	A+ NYN	1	1	0	0	0	0	0	0	0	1	0	0	0	0	0	0	0	.00	0	.000	.500	.000
6 Min. YEARS		530	1836	452	80	13	58	732	254	237	192	7	478	29	5	14	36	25	.59	29	.246	.325	.399

Mike Farrell

Pitches: Left **Bats:** Left **Pos:** P **Ht:** 6'2" **Wt:** 184 **Born:** 1/28/69 **Age:** 28

		HOW MUCH HE PITCHED						WHAT HE GAVE UP												THE RESULTS					
Year Team	Lg Org	G	GS	CG	GF	IP	BFP	H	R	ER	HR	SH	SF	HB	TBB	IBB	SO	WP	Bk	W	L	Pct.	ShO	Sv	ERA
1991 Brewers	R Mil	6	2	0	1	21.1	100	25	15	11	1	0	1	0	3	0	17	0	1	2	1	.667	0	0	4.64
Helena	R+ Mil	5	3	2	1	32	119	17	5	3	2	1	0	0	8	1	22	0	3	4	0	1.000	0	0	0.84
Beloit	A Mil	6	5	0	1	36.1	148	33	13	8	2	0	1	2	8	0	38	1	1	2	3	.400	0	0	1.98
1992 Stockton	A+ Mil	13	13	3	0	92.2	371	82	28	24	6	5	3	5	21	0	67	1	3	8	4	.667	1	0	2.33
El Paso	AA Mil	14	14	5	0	106.1	435	95	42	31	5	7	0	7	25	4	66	0	1	7	6	.538	0	0	2.62
1993 New Orleans	AAA Mil	26	26	3	0	152	637	164	92	82	22	2	2	6	32	1	63	2	2	9	9	.500	1	0	4.86
1994 El Paso	AA Mil	5	5	0	0	29	127	39	18	18	5	1	1	1	5	0	16	1	2	3	0	1.000	0	0	5.59
New Orleans	AAA Mil	30	11	0	7	89	401	110	67	57	8	8	4	8	27	3	51	6	3	6	4	.600	0	0	5.76
1995 New Orleans	AAA Mil	25	24	0	0	141.2	619	173	84	72	19	2	5	4	38	3	74	2	1	8	10	.444	0	0	4.57
1996 New Orleans	AAA Mil	29	4	0	6	64.1	276	72	31	30	7	5	0	0	13	3	39	0	2	5	3	.625	0	2	4.20
El Paso	AA Mil	11	0	0	3	13.2	51	6	3	1	1	1	0	0	2	0	13	0	0	1	0	1.000	0	1	0.66
6 Min. YEARS		170	107	13	19	778.1	3284	816	398	337	78	32	17	33	182	15	466	13	19	55	40	.579	2	3	3.90

Bryan Farson

Pitches: Left **Bats:** Left **Pos:** P **Ht:** 6'2" **Wt:** 198 **Born:** 7/22/72 **Age:** 24

		HOW MUCH HE PITCHED						WHAT HE GAVE UP												THE RESULTS					
Year Team	Lg Org	G	GS	CG	GF	IP	BFP	H	R	ER	HR	SH	SF	HB	TBB	IBB	SO	WP	Bk	W	L	Pct.	ShO	Sv	ERA
1994 Augusta	A Pit	30	0	0	9	38.2	166	35	19	15	1	4	2	1	11	1	49	5	0	2	5	.286	0	0	3.49
1995 Lynchburg	A+ Pit	27	6	0	7	51	228	51	41	33	13	1	2	2	19	4	35	3	0	7	3	.700	0	0	5.82
1996 Carolina	AA Pit	4	0	0	1	5	29	9	10	9	3	0	0	0	4	0	3	0	0	0	0	.000	0	0	16.20
3 Min. YEARS		61	6	0	17	94.2	423	95	70	57	17	5	4	3	34	5	87	8	0	9	8	.529	0	0	5.42

Ken Felder

Bats: Right **Throws:** Right **Pos:** OF **Ht:** 6'3" **Wt:** 220 **Born:** 2/9/71 **Age:** 26

		BATTING														BASERUNNING				PERCENTAGES		
Year Team	Lg Org	G	AB	H	2B	3B	HR	TB	R	RBI	TBB	IBB	SO	HBP	SH	SF	SB	CS	SB%	GDP	Avg	OBP	SLG
1992 Helena	R+ Mil	74	276	60	8	1	15	115	58	48	35	0	102	16	0	4	11	2	.85	3	.217	.335	.417
1993 Beloit	A Mil	32	99	18	4	2	3	35	12	8	10	0	40	2	0	0	1	1	.50	5	.182	.270	.354
1994 Stockton	A+ Mil	121	435	119	21	2	10	174	56	60	32	1	112	11	5	4	4	4	.50	6	.274	.336	.400
1995 El Paso	AA Mil	114	367	100	24	4	12	168	51	55	48	3	94	6	0	4	2	6	.25	10	.272	.362	.458
1996 New Orleans	AAA Mil	122	430	93	20	1	17	166	55	45	28	3	129	7	0	1	2	4	.33	12	.216	.275	.386
5 Min. YEARS		463	1607	390	77	10	57	658	232	216	153	7	477	42	5	13	20	17	.54	36	.243	.322	.409

Mike Felder

Bats: Both **Throws:** Right **Pos:** OF **Ht:** 5' 9" **Wt:** 175 **Born:** 11/18/62 **Age:** 34

		BATTING														BASERUNNING				PERCENTAGES		
Year Team	Lg Org	G	AB	H	2B	3B	HR	TB	R	RBI	TBB	IBB	SO	HBP	SH	SF	SB	CS	SB%	GDP	Avg	OBP	SLG
1984 El Paso	AA Mil	122	496	144	19	2	9	194	98	72	63	2	57	1	2	9	58	16	.78	4	.290	.366	.391
1985 Vancouver	AAA Mil	137	563	177	16	11	2	221	91	43	55	1	70	2	3	5	61	12	.84	14	.314	.374	.393
1986 El Paso	AA Mil	8	31	14	3	0	0	17	10	2	5	1	3	0	1	1	7	0	1.00	1	.452	.514	.548
Vancouver	AAA Mil	39	153	40	3	4	1	54	21	15	17	2	15	0	0	3	4	3	.57	2	.261	.329	.353
1987 Denver	AAA Mil	27	113	41	6	2	2	57	26	20	14	1	6	1	1	1	17	1	.94	0	.363	.434	.504
1988 Denver	AAA Mil	20	78	21	4	1	0	27	10	5	5	0	10	0	0	1	8	1	.89	2	.269	.310	.346
1995 Corp.Chrsti	IND —	79	307	108	15	6	4	147	68	37	33	1	27	0	3	6	11	3	.79	5	.352	.408	.479
1996 Tennessee	IND —	49	198	67	14	0	7	102	41	30	23	5	5	2	0	5	9	3	.75	3	.338	.404	.515
Calgary	AAA Pit	21	81	23	3	0	1	29	14	5	3	1	8	0	1	1	0	0	.00	1	.284	.306	.358
1985 Milwaukee	AL	15	56	11	1	0	0	12	8	0	5	0	6	0	1	0	4	1	.80	2	.196	.262	.214
1986 Milwaukee	AL	44	155	37	2	4	1	50	24	13	13	1	16	0	1	5	16	2	.89	2	.239	.289	.323
1987 Milwaukee	AL	108	289	77	5	7	2	102	48	31	28	0	23	0	9	2	34	8	.81	3	.266	.329	.353
1988 Milwaukee	AL	50	81	14	1	0	0	15	14	5	0	0	11	1	3	0	8	2	.80	1	.173	.183	.185
1989 Milwaukee	AL	117	315	76	11	3	3	102	50	23	23	2	38	0	7	0	26	5	.84	4	.241	.293	.324
1990 Milwaukee	AL	121	237	65	7	2	3	85	38	27	22	0	17	0	8	5	20	9	.69	0	.274	.330	.359
1991 San Francisco	NL	132	348	92	10	6	0	114	51	18	30	2	31	1	4	0	21	6	.78	1	.264	.325	.328
1992 San Francisco	NL	145	322	92	13	3	4	123	44	23	21	1	29	2	3	3	14	4	.78	3	.286	.330	.382
1993 Seattle	AL	109	342	72	7	5	1	92	31	20	22	2	34	2	7	1	15	9	.63	2	.211	.262	.269
1994 Houston	NL	58	117	28	2	2	0	34	10	13	4	0	12	0	2	0	3	0	1.00	1	.239	.264	.291
7 Min. YEARS		502	2020	635	83	26	26	848	379	229	218	14	201	6	11	32	175	39	.82	32	.314	.377	.420
10 Maj. YEARS		899	2262	564	59	32	14	729	318	173	168	8	217	6	45	16	161	46	.78	19	.249	.301	.322

Lauro Felix

Bats: Right **Throws:** Right **Pos:** SS **Ht:** 5'9" **Wt:** 160 **Born:** 6/24/70 **Age:** 27

		BATTING														BASERUNNING				PERCENTAGES		
Year Team	Lg Org	G	AB	H	2B	3B	HR	TB	R	RBI	TBB	IBB	SO	HBP	SH	SF	SB	CS	SB%	GDP	Avg	OBP	SLG
1992 Sou. Oregon	A- Oak	11	24	10	1	0	1	14	5	3	8	0	5	0	0	1	2	1	.67	0	.417	.545	.583
Madison	A Oak	53	199	42	4	0	0	46	29	13	29	0	41	3	8	0	7	6	.54	2	.211	.320	.231
1993 Modesto	A+ Oak	102	302	62	6	2	2	78	55	35	69	0	70	1	8	2	7	4	.64	10	.205	.353	.258
1994 Modesto	A+ Oak	49	141	34	12	1	3	57	17	16	15	0	40	3	3	0	4	1	.80	0	.241	.327	.404
Tacoma	AAA Oak	43	131	23	5	0	0	28	13	5	17	0	34	2	4	1	0	4	.00	5	.176	.278	.214
1995 Huntsville	AA Oak	10	27	3	0	0	1	6	3	1	2	0	8	0	0	0	0	0	.00	1	.111	.172	.222
El Paso	AA Mil	81	220	61	13	1	3	85	51	25	45	0	44	4	5	2	6	1	.86	4	.277	.406	.386
1996 New Orleans	AAA Mil	2	4	0	0	0	0	0	0	0	0	0	2	0	0	0	0	0	.00	0	.000	.000	.000

Year Team	Lg Org	G	AB	H	2B	3B	HR	TB	R	RBI	TBB	IBB	SO	HBP	SH	SF	SB	CS	SB%	GDP	Avg	OBP	SLG
BATTING																	BASERUNNING				PERCENTAGES		
Stockton	A+ Mil	12	33	6	0	0	2	12	5	5	18	0	9	1	1	0	1	2	.33	0	.182	.481	.364
El Paso	AA Mil	101	301	81	15	2	10	130	71	59	74	1	69	6	12	6	11	5	.69	4	.269	.416	.432
5 Min. YEARS		464	1382	322	56	6	22	456	249	162	277	1	322	20	41	12	38	24	.61	26	.233	.366	.330

Jeff Ferguson

Bats: Right **Throws:** Right **Pos:** 2B **Ht:** 5'10" **Wt:** 175 **Born:** 6/18/73 **Age:** 24

Year Team	Lg Org	G	AB	H	2B	3B	HR	TB	R	RBI	TBB	IBB	SO	HBP	SH	SF	SB	CS	SB%	GDP	Avg	OBP	SLG
BATTING																	BASERUNNING				PERCENTAGES		
1994 Fort Wayne	A Min	22	89	23	7	1	1	35	15	6	11	0	18	1	0	0	4	1	.80	1	.258	.347	.393
1996 New Britain	AA Min	89	284	81	16	2	5	116	46	20	37	2	67	3	0	1	5	4	.56	2	.285	.372	.408
2 Min. YEARS		111	373	104	23	3	6	151	61	26	48	2	85	4	0	1	9	5	.64	3	.279	.366	.405

Ramon Fermin

Pitches: Right **Bats:** Right **Pos:** P **Ht:** 6' 3" **Wt:** 180 **Born:** 11/25/72 **Age:** 24

Year Team	Lg Org	G	GS	CG	GF	IP	BFP	H	R	ER	HR	SH	SF	HB	TBB	IBB	SO	WP	Bk	W	L	Pct.	ShO	Sv	ERA
HOW MUCH HE PITCHED								WHAT HE GAVE UP												THE RESULTS					
1991 Athletics	R Oak	7	3	1	1	25.1	102	20	6	6	2	1	0	4	4	0	11	0	1	3	0	1.000	0	0	2.13
Modesto	A+ Oak	3	2	0	0	12.1	52	16	7	6	1	1	0	1	3	0	5	0	0	1	0	1.000	0	0	4.38
1992 Madison	A Oak	14	14	1	0	77.2	330	66	33	21	2	2	4	1	35	0	37	6	2	5	5	.500	0	0	2.43
Modesto	A+ Oak	14	5	0	4	42.2	196	50	31	27	5	1	0	2	19	1	18	3	1	2	3	.400	0	1	5.70
1993 Modesto	A+ Oak	31	5	0	8	67.1	321	78	56	46	7	3	2	5	37	5	47	10	0	4	6	.400	0	1	6.15
1994 Modesto	A+ Oak	29	18	0	8	133	565	129	71	53	12	3	3	9	42	1	120	16	1	9	6	.600	0	5	3.59
1995 Huntsville	AA Oak	32	13	0	16	100.1	435	105	53	43	5	6	1	6	45	5	58	6	1	6	7	.462	0	7	3.86
1996 Jacksonvlle	AA Det	46	6	0	13	84	378	82	56	42	5	2	3	5	46	2	48	11	0	6	6	.500	0	3	4.50
1995 Oakland	AL	1	0	0	1	1.1	9	4	2	2	0	0	0	0	1	0	0	1	0	0	0	.000	0	0	13.50
6 Min. YEARS		176	66	2	50	542.2	2379	546	313	244	39	19	13	33	231	14	344	52	6	36	33	.522	0	17	4.05

Jared Fernandez

Pitches: Right **Bats:** Right **Pos:** P **Ht:** 6'2" **Wt:** 225 **Born:** 2/2/72 **Age:** 25

Year Team	Lg Org	G	GS	CG	GF	IP	BFP	H	R	ER	HR	SH	SF	HB	TBB	IBB	SO	WP	Bk	W	L	Pct.	ShO	Sv	ERA
HOW MUCH HE PITCHED								WHAT HE GAVE UP												THE RESULTS					
1994 Utica	A- Bos	21	1	0	15	30	144	43	18	12	4	0	0	0	8	2	24	0	1	1	1	.500	0	4	3.60
1995 Utica	A- Bos	5	5	1	0	38	148	30	11	8	2	0	1	1	9	1	23	1	0	3	2	.600	0	0	1.89
Trenton	AA Bos	16	15	2	0	105	438	94	43	37	6	3	2	6	37	2	63	3	0	8	6	.571	0	0	3.17
1996 Trenton	AA Bos	30	29	3	0	179	798	185	115	101	19	5	9	10	83	5	94	10	0	9	9	.500	0	0	5.08
3 Min. YEARS		72	50	6	15	352	1528	352	187	158	31	8	12	17	137	10	204	14	1	21	18	.538	0	4	4.04

Osvaldo Fernandez

Pitches: Left **Bats:** Left **Pos:** P **Ht:** 6'2" **Wt:** 193 **Born:** 4/15/70 **Age:** 27

Year Team	Lg Org	G	GS	CG	GF	IP	BFP	H	R	ER	HR	SH	SF	HB	TBB	IBB	SO	WP	Bk	W	L	Pct.	ShO	Sv	ERA
HOW MUCH HE PITCHED								WHAT HE GAVE UP												THE RESULTS					
1994 Riverside	A+ Sea	14	13	1	0	84.2	353	67	33	27	8	1	2	3	37	0	80	3	4	8	2	.800	1	0	2.87
1995 Port City	AA Sea	27	26	0	0	156.1	654	139	78	62	6	4	1	5	60	1	160	12	1	12	7	.632	0	0	3.57
1996 Tacoma	AAA Sea	1	1	0	0	3.1	15	4	2	2	0	0	0	0	0	0	4	0	0	0	0	.000	0	0	5.40
3 Min. YEARS		42	40	1	0	244.1	1022	210	113	91	14	5	3	8	97	1	244	15	5	20	9	.690	1	0	3.35

Sean Fesh

Pitches: Left **Bats:** Left **Pos:** P **Ht:** 6'2" **Wt:** 165 **Born:** 11/3/72 **Age:** 24

Year Team	Lg Org	G	GS	CG	GF	IP	BFP	H	R	ER	HR	SH	SF	HB	TBB	IBB	SO	WP	Bk	W	L	Pct.	ShO	Sv	ERA
HOW MUCH HE PITCHED								WHAT HE GAVE UP												THE RESULTS					
1991 Astros	R Hou	6	0	0	2	12.1	53	5	4	3	0	0	0	0	11	0	7	4	0	0	0	.000	0	0	2.19
1992 Osceola	A+ Hou	3	0	0	2	5.1	24	5	3	1	0	0	0	0	1	0	5	3	0	0	1	.000	0	0	1.69
Astros	R Hou	18	0	0	12	36.1	142	25	7	7	0	3	0	4	8	0	35	4	0	1	0	1.000	0	6	1.73
1993 Asheville	A Hou	65	0	0	58	82.1	353	75	39	33	4	11	6	5	37	8	49	4	1	10	6	.625	0	20	3.61
1994 Osceola	A+ Hou	43	0	0	29	49.2	222	50	27	14	2	5	0	6	24	6	32	2	0	2	4	.333	0	11	2.54
Jackson	AA Hou	20	1	0	5	25.2	122	34	17	12	2	2	1	0	11	0	19	2	0	1	2	.333	0	0	4.21
1995 Tucson	AAA Hou	10	0	0	1	13.1	52	11	2	2	0	0	0	0	3	0	7	0	0	1	0	1.000	0	0	1.35
Las Vegas	AAA SD	40	0	0	12	51.1	237	64	23	16	2	4	0	3	19	5	25	1	1	3	1	.750	0	1	2.81
1996 Memphis	AA SD	7	0	0	2	8	36	7	5	5	2	0	0	0	7	1	5	0	0	1	1	.500	0	0	5.63
6 Min. YEARS		212	1	0	123	284.1	1241	276	127	93	12	25	7	18	121	20	184	20	2	19	15	.559	0	38	2.94

Chris Fick

Bats: Left **Throws:** Right **Pos:** OF **Ht:** 6'2" **Wt:** 190 **Born:** 10/4/69 **Age:** 27

Year Team	Lg Org	G	AB	H	2B	3B	HR	TB	R	RBI	TBB	IBB	SO	HBP	SH	SF	SB	CS	SB%	GDP	Avg	OBP	SLG
BATTING																	BASERUNNING				PERCENTAGES		
1994 San Bernrdo	A+ —	44	144	32	10	1	7	65	20	28	15	0	47	3	1	0	2	3	.40	2	.222	.309	.451
1995 St. Pete	A+ StL	113	348	102	25	3	13	172	56	52	38	2	79	10	0	3	1	2	.33	9	.293	.376	.494
1996 Arkansas	AA StL	134	448	115	25	2	19	201	64	74	67	8	93	4	0	5	2	5	.29	16	.257	.355	.449
3 Min. YEARS		291	940	249	60	6	39	438	140	154	120	10	219	17	1	8	5	10	.33	27	.265	.356	.466

Mike Figga

Bats: Right **Throws:** Right **Pos:** C **Ht:** 6'0" **Wt:** 200 **Born:** 7/31/70 **Age:** 26

			BATTING															BASERUNNING				PERCENTAGES		
Year Team	Lg	Org	G	AB	H	2B	3B	HR	TB	R	RBI	TBB	IBB	SO	HBP	SH	SF	SB	CS	SB%	GDP	Avg	OBP	SLG
1990 Yankees	R	NYA	40	123	35	1	1	2	44	19	18	17	2	33	1	0	1	4	2	.67	2	.285	.373	.358
1991 Pr. William	A+	NYA	55	174	34	6	0	3	49	15	17	19	0	51	0	2	1	2	1	.67	9	.195	.273	.282
1992 Pr. William	A+	NYA	3	10	2	1	0	0	3	0	0	2	0	3	0	0	0	1	0	1.00	0	.200	.333	.300
Ft. Laud	A+	NYA	80	249	44	13	0	1	60	12	15	13	1	78	2	3	0	3	1	.75	7	.177	.223	.241
1993 San Bernrdo	A+	NYA	83	308	82	17	1	25	176	48	71	17	0	84	2	2	3	2	3	.40	7	.266	.306	.571
Albany-Colo	AA	NYA	6	22	5	0	0	0	5	3	2	2	0	9	0	0	0	1	0	1.00	0	.227	.292	.227
1994 Albany-Colo	AA	NYA	1	2	1	1	0	0	2	1	0	0	0	1	0	0	0	0	0	.00	0	.500	.500	1.000
Tampa	A+	NYA	111	420	116	17	5	15	188	48	75	22	1	94	2	1	5	3	0	1.00	12	.276	.312	.448
1995 Norwich	AA	NYA	109	399	108	22	4	13	177	59	61	43	3	90	1	2	6	1	0	1.00	10	.271	.339	.444
Columbus	AAA	NYA	8	25	7	1	0	1	11	2	3	3	0	5	0	1	0	0	0	.00	0	.280	.357	.440
1996 Columbus	AAA	NYA	4	11	3	1	0	0	4	3	0	1	0	3	0	0	0	0	0	.00	0	.273	.333	.364
7 Min. YEARS			500	1743	437	80	11	60	719	210	262	139	7	451	8	11	16	17	7	.71	47	.251	.306	.413

Bien Figueroa

Bats: Right **Throws:** Right **Pos:** 2B **Ht:** 5'10" **Wt:** 170 **Born:** 2/7/64 **Age:** 33

			BATTING															BASERUNNING				PERCENTAGES		
Year Team	Lg	Org	G	AB	H	2B	3B	HR	TB	R	RBI	TBB	IBB	SO	HBP	SH	SF	SB	CS	SB%	GDP	Avg	OBP	SLG
1986 Erie	A-	StL	73	249	59	4	0	0	63	31	30	32	1	26	1	1	3	13	4	.76	9	.237	.323	.253
1987 Springfield	A	StL	134	489	136	13	3	2	161	52	83	34	2	46	4	12	7	7	7	.50	16	.278	.326	.329
1988 Arkansas	AA	StL	126	407	113	17	2	0	134	48	32	22	1	49	3	7	1	2	6	.25	16	.278	.319	.329
1989 Louisville	AAA	StL	74	221	48	3	0	0	51	18	14	12	0	22	0	5	1	0	1	.00	7	.217	.256	.231
1990 Louisville	AAA	StL	128	396	95	19	2	0	118	41	39	24	2	37	3	7	2	5	1	.83	15	.240	.287	.298
1991 Louisville	AAA	StL	97	269	55	8	2	0	67	18	14	20	2	27	2	5	0	1	4	.20	10	.204	.265	.249
1992 Louisville	AAA	StL	94	319	91	11	1	1	107	44	23	33	0	32	2	6	3	2	0	1.00	8	.285	.353	.335
1993 Louisville	AAA	StL	93	272	65	17	1	0	84	44	15	16	1	27	3	1	1	1	1	.50	6	.239	.288	.309
1994 Harrisburg	AA	Mon	13	40	10	1	0	0	11	6	4	6	0	3	2	1	0	0	0	.00	2	.250	.375	.275
Ottawa	AAA	Mon	72	223	54	13	1	1	72	22	26	14	0	28	0	0	3	2	0	1.00	9	.242	.283	.323
1995 Okla. City	AAA	Tex	9	20	2	0	0	0	2	1	2	0	0	2	0	1	1	1	0	1.00	0	.100	.095	.100
1996 Colo. Sprng	AAA	Col	10	29	6	2	0	0	8	2	6	1	0	3	0	0	1	0	0	.00	2	.207	.226	.276
Rochester	AAA	Bal	50	154	48	7	0	1	58	25	16	14	0	11	0	1	0	3	1	.75	5	.312	.369	.377
1992 St. Louis	NL		12	11	2	1	0	0	3	1	4	1	0	2	0	0	0	0	0	.00	0	.182	.250	.273
11 Min. YEARS			973	3088	782	115	12	5	936	352	304	228	9	313	20	47	23	37	25	.60	105	.253	.307	.303

John Finn

Bats: Right **Throws:** Right **Pos:** 2B **Ht:** 5'8" **Wt:** 168 **Born:** 10/18/67 **Age:** 29

			BATTING															BASERUNNING				PERCENTAGES		
Year Team	Lg	Org	G	AB	H	2B	3B	HR	TB	R	RBI	TBB	IBB	SO	HBP	SH	SF	SB	CS	SB%	GDP	Avg	OBP	SLG
1989 Beloit	A	Mil	73	274	82	8	7	1	107	49	20	38	0	27	4	5	2	29	11	.73	3	.299	.390	.391
1990 Stockton	A+	Mil	95	290	60	4	0	1	67	48	23	52	0	50	1	6	6	29	15	.66	1	.207	.324	.231
1991 Stockton	A+	Mil	65	223	57	12	1	0	71	45	25	44	1	28	9	6	3	19	9	.68	5	.256	.394	.318
El Paso	AA	Mil	63	230	69	12	2	2	91	48	24	16	0	27	2	5	2	8	4	.67	0	.300	.348	.396
1992 El Paso	AA	Mil	124	439	121	12	6	1	148	83	47	71	3	44	11	9	7	30	12	.71	7	.276	.384	.337
1993 New Orleans	AAA	Mil	117	335	94	13	2	1	114	47	37	33	1	36	6	9	0	27	9	.75	8	.281	.356	.340
1994 New Orleans	AAA	Mil	76	229	66	12	0	2	84	36	24	35	1	21	7	6	4	15	10	.60	3	.288	.393	.367
1995 New Orleans	AAA	Mil	35	117	38	4	1	3	53	20	19	13	2	7	2	4	0	9	2	.82	1	.325	.402	.453
1996 Calgary	AAA	Pit	69	193	49	13	1	0	64	24	32	25	4	28	3	2	5	2	5	.29	4	.254	.341	.332
Iowa	AAA	ChN	17	55	15	1	0	1	19	10	5	4	0	7	2	2	1	1	1	.50	2	.273	.339	.345
8 Min. YEARS			734	2385	651	91	20	12	818	410	256	331	12	275	47	54	30	169	78	.68	34	.273	.368	.343

Gar Finnvold

Pitches: Right **Bats:** Right **Pos:** P **Ht:** 6' 5" **Wt:** 200 **Born:** 3/11/68 **Age:** 29

			HOW MUCH HE PITCHED						WHAT HE GAVE UP												THE RESULTS					
Year Team	Lg	Org	G	GS	CG	GF	IP	BFP	H	R	ER	HR	SH	SF	HB	TBB	IBB	SO	WP	Bk	W	L	Pct.	ShO	Sv	ERA
1990 Elmira	A-	Bos	15	15	5	0	95	400	91	43	33	2	3	5	5	22	0	89	6	5	5	5	.500	1	0	3.13
1991 Lynchburg	A+	Bos	6	6	0	0	38	157	30	16	14	3	2	1	1	7	1	29	2	0	2	3	.400	0	0	3.32
Pawtucket	AAA	Bos	3	3	0	0	15	71	19	13	11	4	0	0	0	7	0	12	0	0	1	2	.333	0	0	6.60
New Britain	AA	Bos	16	16	0	0	101.1	426	97	46	43	7	1	3	3	36	2	80	8	1	5	8	.385	0	0	3.82
1992 New Britain	AA	Bos	25	25	3	0	165	695	156	69	64	6	6	2	6	52	4	135	6	4	7	13	.350	0	0	3.49
1993 Pawtucket	AAA	Bos	24	24	0	0	136	581	128	68	57	21	2	2	4	51	0	123	3	0	5	9	.357	0	0	3.77
1994 Pawtucket	AAA	Bos	7	7	0	0	42.1	173	32	19	17	5	0	1	2	15	0	32	1	0	5	1	.833	0	0	3.61
1995 Pawtucket	AAA	Bos	1	1	0	0	3.2	15	1	1	0	0	0	0	0	1	0	3	0	0	0	0	.000	0	0	0.00
1996 Pawtucket	AAA	Bos	8	8	0	0	35.1	167	50	29	26	7	0	4	3	11	0	35	5	1	3	2	.600	0	0	6.62
1994 Boston	AL		8	8	0	0	36.1	167	45	27	24	4	0	1	3	15	0	17	0	0	0	4	.000	0	0	5.94
7 Min. YEARS			105	105	8	0	631.2	2685	604	304	265	55	14	18	24	202	7	538	31	11	33	43	.434	1	0	3.78

Tony Fiore

Pitches: Right **Bats:** Right **Pos:** P **Ht:** 6'4" **Wt:** 200 **Born:** 10/12/71 **Age:** 25

			HOW MUCH HE PITCHED						WHAT HE GAVE UP												THE RESULTS					
Year Team	Lg	Org	G	GS	CG	GF	IP	BFP	H	R	ER	HR	SH	SF	HB	TBB	IBB	SO	WP	Bk	W	L	Pct.	ShO	Sv	ERA
1992 Martinsvlle	R+	Phi	17	2	0	9	32.1	161	32	20	15	0	2	1	3	31	1	30	11	0	2	3	.400	0	0	4.18
1993 Batavia	A-	Phi	16	16	1	0	97.1	411	82	51	33	1	3	4	4	40	0	55	15	0	2	8	.200	0	0	3.05

Year	Team	Lg	Org	G	GS	CG	GF	IP	BFP	H	R	ER	HR	SH	SF	HB	TBB	IBB	SO	WP	Bk	W	L	Pct.	ShO	Sv	ERA
				HOW MUCH HE PITCHED						**WHAT HE GAVE UP**												**THE RESULTS**					
1994	Spartanburg	A	Phi	28	28	9	0	166.2	719	162	94	76	10	2	5	4	77	1	113	19	1	12	13	.480	1	0	4.10
1995	Clearwater	A+	Phi	24	10	0	3	70.1	323	70	41	29	4	3	5	2	44	2	45	9	3	6	2	.750	0	0	3.71
1996	Clearwater	A+	Phi	22	22	3	0	128	533	102	61	45	4	1	1	5	56	1	80	13	1	8	4	.667	1	0	3.16
	Reading	AA	Phi	5	5	0	0	31	146	32	21	15	2	0	1	1	18	0	19	6	0	1	2	.333	0	0	4.35
5	Min. YEARS			112	83	13	12	525.2	2293	480	288	213	21	11	17	19	266	5	342	73	5	31	32	.492	2	0	3.65

David Fisher

Bats: Right **Throws:** Right **Pos:** 3B **Ht:** 6'0" **Wt:** 160 **Born:** 2/26/70 **Age:** 27

Year	Team	Lg	Org	G	AB	H	2B	3B	HR	TB	R	RBI	TBB	IBB	SO	HBP	SH	SF	SB	CS	SB%	GDP	Avg	OBP	SLG
				BATTING															**BASERUNNING**				**PERCENTAGES**		
1992	Martinsvlle	R+	Phi	50	188	57	14	1	3	82	31	42	30	2	27	0	1	1	6	1	.86	2	.303	.397	.436
	Batavia	A-	Phi	21	80	27	4	1	1	36	10	14	6	0	5	4	2	0	3	2	.60	2	.338	.411	.450
1993	Clearwater	A+	Phi	126	430	103	25	2	6	150	54	54	52	1	42	8	8	10	11	16	.41	7	.240	.326	.349
1994	Reading	AA	Phi	118	412	103	24	3	7	154	57	42	57	0	65	7	8	4	5	6	.45	6	.250	.348	.374
1995	Reading	AA	Phi	79	204	47	18	1	1	70	18	20	14	0	29	3	2	4	4	4	.50	0	.230	.284	.343
1996	Scranton-WB	AAA	Phi	26	64	10	1	0	1	14	6	3	7	0	15	1	0	0	1	1	.50	0	.156	.250	.219
	Reading	AA	Phi	57	171	46	9	0	4	67	21	24	12	1	18	0	4	2	5	3	.63	7	.269	.314	.392
5	Min. YEARS			477	1549	393	95	8	23	573	197	199	178	4	201	23	25	21	35	33	.51	24	.254	.335	.370

Grant Fithian

Bats: Right **Throws:** Right **Pos:** C **Ht:** 6'0" **Wt:** 192 **Born:** 11/20/71 **Age:** 25

Year	Team	Lg	Org	G	AB	H	2B	3B	HR	TB	R	RBI	TBB	IBB	SO	HBP	SH	SF	SB	CS	SB%	GDP	Avg	OBP	SLG
				BATTING															**BASERUNNING**				**PERCENTAGES**		
1994	Tampa	A+	NYA	5	11	2	1	0	0	3	1	0	1	0	3	0	0	0	0	0	.00	1	.182	.250	.273
1995	Tampa	A+	NYA	3	4	1	0	0	0	1	0	1	0	0	2	0	0	0	0	0	.00	0	.250	.250	.250
	Greensboro	A	NYA	51	151	34	8	1	2	50	16	12	19	0	45	1	3	3	5	4	.56	5	.225	.310	.331
1996	Norwich	AA	NYA	63	178	35	7	1	5	59	19	26	11	1	46	1	4	1	1	0	1.00	4	.197	.246	.331
3	Min. YEARS			122	344	72	16	2	7	113	36	39	31	1	96	2	7	4	6	4	.60	10	.209	.276	.328

Benjamin Fleetham

Pitches: Right **Bats:** Right **Pos:** P **Ht:** 6'1" **Wt:** 205 **Born:** 8/3/72 **Age:** 24

Year	Team	Lg	Org	G	GS	CG	GF	IP	BFP	H	R	ER	HR	SH	SF	HB	TBB	IBB	SO	WP	Bk	W	L	Pct.	ShO	Sv	ERA
				HOW MUCH HE PITCHED						**WHAT HE GAVE UP**												**THE RESULTS**					
1994	Vermont	A-	Mon	17	0	0	2	28.2	125	23	13	8	0	2	2	1	16	1	29	2	2	0	0	.000	0	2	2.51
	Burlington	A	Mon	6	0	0	2	13.1	51	5	4	3	1	0	0	0	4	0	27	2	3	1	0	1.000	0	0	2.03
	Harrisburg	AA	Mon	2	0	0	2	3	14	2	0	0	0	0	0	1	2	0	0	1	1	0	0	.000	0	0	0.00
1995	Pueblo	IND	—	2	0	0	2	2	8	1	0	0	0	0	0	0	0	0	2	0	0	0	0	.000	0	1	0.00
1996	Delmarva	A	Mon	16	0	0	15	19.2	74	9	4	3	2	2	0	0	7	0	34	3	0	1	0	1.000	0	13	1.37
	W. Palm Bch	A+	Mon	31	0	0	29	30.2	122	15	8	7	0	0	1	0	15	0	48	9	2	0	1	.000	0	17	2.05
	Harrisburg	AA	Mon	4	0	0	3	6	23	2	0	0	0	0	0	0	5	0	6	0	0	0	0	.000	0	1	0.00
3	Min. YEARS			78	0	0	55	103.1	417	57	29	21	3	4	3	2	49	1	146	17	8	2	1	.667	0	34	1.83

Carlton Fleming

Bats: Both **Throws:** Right **Pos:** 2B **Ht:** 5'11" **Wt:** 175 **Born:** 8/25/71 **Age:** 25

Year	Team	Lg	Org	G	AB	H	2B	3B	HR	TB	R	RBI	TBB	IBB	SO	HBP	SH	SF	SB	CS	SB%	GDP	Avg	OBP	SLG
				BATTING															**BASERUNNING**				**PERCENTAGES**		
1992	Oneonta	A-	NYA	3	11	2	0	0	0	2	2	2	1	0	2	1	0	0	1	0	1.00	0	.182	.308	.182
	Greensboro	A	NYA	68	236	78	1	1	0	81	35	24	31	0	20	0	1	0	9	7	.56	2	.331	.408	.343
1993	Pr. William	A+	NYA	120	442	132	14	2	0	150	72	25	80	2	23	0	6	1	21	10	.68	14	.299	.405	.339
1994	Albany-Colo	AA	NYA	117	378	92	12	1	0	106	39	37	52	0	37	3	10	4	20	10	.67	8	.243	.336	.280
1995	Columbus	AAA	NYA	32	86	19	6	0	0	25	9	5	8	0	6	0	1	0	0	2	.00	3	.221	.287	.291
	Norwich	AA	NYA	40	125	38	3	1	0	43	15	16	12	0	10	0	2	1	5	3	.63	4	.304	.362	.344
1996	Norwich	AA	NYA	15	28	9	0	0	0	9	4	1	5	0	1	0	0	0	0	1	.00	1	.321	.424	.321
	St. Paul	IND	—	80	319	96	9	2	0	109	54	27	41	3	14	1	0	3	14	4	.78	8	.301	.379	.342
5	Min. YEARS			475	1625	466	45	7	0	525	230	137	230	5	113	5	20	9	70	37	.65	40	.287	.375	.323

Kevin Flora

Bats: Right **Throws:** Right **Pos:** OF **Ht:** 6' 0" **Wt:** 185 **Born:** 6/10/69 **Age:** 28

Year	Team	Lg	Org	G	AB	H	2B	3B	HR	TB	R	RBI	TBB	IBB	SO	HBP	SH	SF	SB	CS	SB%	GDP	Avg	OBP	SLG
				BATTING															**BASERUNNING**				**PERCENTAGES**		
1987	Salem	A-	Cal	35	88	24	5	1	0	31	17	12	21	0	14	0	3	0	8	4	.67	2	.273	.413	.352
1988	Quad City	A	Cal	48	152	33	3	4	0	44	19	15	18	4	33	0	1	0	5	3	.63	4	.217	.300	.289
1989	Quad City	A	Cal	120	372	81	8	4	1	100	46	21	57	2	107	6	5	3	30	10	.75	3	.218	.329	.269
1990	Midland	AA	Cal	71	232	53	16	5	5	94	35	32	23	0	53	0	3	1	11	5	.69	6	.228	.297	.405
1991	Midland	AA	Cal	124	484	138	14	15	12	218	97	67	37	0	92	3	3	3	40	8	.83	2	.285	.338	.450
1992	Edmonton	AAA	Cal	52	170	55	8	4	3	80	35	19	29	0	25	1	4	2	9	8	.53	6	.324	.421	.471
1993	Vancouver	AAA	Cal	30	94	31	2	0	1	36	17	12	10	0	20	1	2	1	6	2	.75	2	.330	.396	.383
1994	Vancouver	AAA	Cal	6	12	2	1	0	0	3	5	1	4	0	4	0	1	0	1	0	1.00	1	.167	.375	.250
	Lk Elsinore	A+	Cal	19	72	13	3	2	0	20	13	6	12	0	17	0	1	1	7	1	.88	2	.181	.294	.278
1995	Vancouver	AAA	Cal	38	124	37	7	0	3	53	22	14	16	0	33	0	1	1	7	4	.64	2	.298	.376	.427
1996	St. Lucie	A+	NYN	11	39	6	0	2	0	10	8	3	9	1	14	0	0	0	2	0	1.00	0	.154	.313	.256
	Norfolk	AAA	NYN	46	135	30	8	1	3	49	20	15	11	2	40	4	0	0	9	2	.82	5	.222	.300	.363

Year	Team	Lg	Org	G	AB	H	2B	3B	HR	TB	R	RBI	TBB	IBB	SO	HBP	SH	SF	SB	CS	SB%	GDP	Avg	OBP	SLG
				BATTING															BASERUNNING				PERCENTAGES		
1991	California	AL		3	8	1	0	0	0	1	1	0	1	0	5	0	1	0	1	0	1.00	1	.125	.222	.125
1995	California	AL			2	1	0	0	0	0	0	1	0	0	0	1	0	0	0	0	0	.00	0	.000	.000
	Philadelphia	NL			24	75	16	3	0	2	25	12	7	4	0	22	0	2	0	1	0	1.00	0	.213	.253
10 Min. YEARS				600	1974	503	75	38	28	738	334	217	247	9	452	15	24	12	135	47	.74	35	.255	.340	.374
2 Maj. YEARS				29	84	17	3	0	2	26	14	7	5	0	28	0	3	0	2	0	1.00	1	.202	.247	.310

Don Florence

Pitches: Left **Bats:** Right **Pos:** P **Ht:** 6' 0" **Wt:** 195 **Born:** 3/16/67 **Age:** 30

Year	Team	Lg	Org	G	GS	CG	GF	IP	BFP	H	R	ER	HR	SH	SF	HB	TBB	IBB	SO	WP	Bk	W	L	Pct.	ShO	Sv	ERA
				HOW MUCH HE PITCHED						WHAT HE GAVE UP												THE RESULTS					
1988	Winter Havn	A+	Bos	27	16	4	7	120.2	542	136	68	53	4	3	4	4	50	1	56	13	2	6	8	.429	0	0	3.95
1989	Winter Havn	A+	Bos	51	2	0	31	93.2	395	81	46	30	1	7	2	2	34	3	71	7	1	2	7	.222	0	15	2.88
1990	New Britain	AA	Bos	34	4	0	12	79.2	341	85	37	31	3	2	3	1	26	3	39	4	0	6	4	.600	0	1	3.50
1991	New Britain	AA	Bos	55	2	0	28	84.1	382	85	59	52	7	6	5	7	43	4	73	4	1	3	8	.273	0	2	5.55
1992	New Britain	AA	Bos	58	0	0	30	74.2	311	65	23	20	0	8	0	3	27	3	51	4	0	3	1	.750	0	6	2.41
1993	Pawtucket	AAA	Bos	57	0	0	18	59	246	56	24	22	6	6	1	0	18	5	46	8	0	7	8	.467	0	2	3.36
1994	Pawtucket	AAA	Bos	61	0	0	24	59	259	66	24	24	2	3	1	1	24	4	43	1	0	1	4	.200	0	7	3.66
1995	Norfolk	AAA	NYN	41	0	0	16	47	191	37	6	5	0	5	1	1	17	3	29	2	0	0	1	.000	0	4	0.96
1996	Rochester	AAA	Bal	36	8	0	10	85	388	111	62	58	11	2	7	0	30	1	53	3	1	4	4	.500	0	0	6.14
1995	New York	NL		14	0	0	3	12	57	17	3	2	0	1	0	0	6	0	5	0	0	3	0	1.000	0	0	1.50
9 Min. YEARS				420	32	4	176	703	3055	722	349	295	34	42	24	19	269	27	461	46	5	32	45	.416	0	37	3.78

Jose Flores

Bats: Right **Throws:** Right **Pos:** SS-2B **Ht:** 5'11" **Wt:** 160 **Born:** 6/26/73 **Age:** 24

Year	Team	Lg	Org	G	AB	H	2B	3B	HR	TB	R	RBI	TBB	IBB	SO	HBP	SH	SF	SB	CS	SB%	GDP	Avg	OBP	SLG
				BATTING															BASERUNNING				PERCENTAGES		
1994	Batavia	A-	Phi	68	229	58	7	3	0	71	41	16	41	0	31	6	2	2	23	8	.74	3	.253	.378	.310
1995	Clearwater	A+	Phi	49	185	41	4	3	1	54	25	19	15	0	27	4	7	1	12	5	.71	4	.222	.293	.292
	Piedmont	A	Phi	61	186	49	7	0	0	56	22	19	24	0	29	3	5	4	11	8	.58	6	.263	.350	.301
1996	Scranton-WB	AAA	Phi	26	70	18	1	0	0	19	10	3	12	0	10	2	1	1	0	1	.00	2	.257	.376	.271
	Clearwater	A+	Phi	84	281	64	6	5	1	83	39	39	34	0	42	3	5	1	15	2	.88	6	.228	.317	.295
3 Min. YEARS				288	951	230	25	11	2	283	137	96	126	0	139	18	20	9	61	24	.72	21	.242	.339	.298

Tim Florez

Bats: Right **Throws:** Right **Pos:** 2B **Ht:** 5'10" **Wt:** 170 **Born:** 7/23/69 **Age:** 27

Year	Team	Lg	Org	G	AB	H	2B	3B	HR	TB	R	RBI	TBB	IBB	SO	HBP	SH	SF	SB	CS	SB%	GDP	Avg	OBP	SLG
				BATTING															BASERUNNING				PERCENTAGES		
1991	Everett	A-	SF	59	193	48	8	4	0	64	33	25	12	1	33	1	2	1	7	1	.88	4	.249	.295	.332
1992	Clinton	A	SF	81	292	68	12	2	2	90	39	25	30	2	53	3	0	2	20	5	.80	6	.233	.309	.308
	San Jose	A+	SF	38	131	32	6	1	1	43	15	17	4	0	21	0	4	4	3	3	.50	2	.244	.259	.328
1993	Shreveport	AA	SF	106	318	81	17	2	1	105	33	26	16	4	43	2	3	2	3	5	.38	9	.255	.293	.330
1994	Phoenix	AAA	SF	13	24	6	1	0	1	10	5	2	1	0	4	0	0	0	0	0	.00	1	.250	.280	.417
	Shreveport	AA	SF	61	158	34	10	0	1	47	21	13	21	3	34	1	2	1	0	3	.00	4	.215	.309	.297
1995	Shreveport	AA	SF	100	295	79	11	2	9	121	37	46	26	1	49	4	3	3	4	3	.57	7	.268	.332	.410
1996	Shreveport	AA	SF	18	66	18	1	0	2	25	9	8	7	1	11	1	0	0	2	0	1.00	0	.273	.351	.379
	Phoenix	AAA	SF	113	366	106	31	3	4	155	42	39	34	4	56	10	0	3	0	5	.00	12	.290	.363	.423
6 Min. YEARS				589	1843	472	97	14	21	660	234	201	151	16	304	22	14	16	39	25	.61	45	.256	.317	.358

Bill Flynt

Pitches: Left **Bats:** Left **Pos:** P **Ht:** 6'5" **Wt:** 215 **Born:** 11/23/67 **Age:** 29

Year	Team	Lg	Org	G	GS	CG	GF	IP	BFP	H	R	ER	HR	SH	SF	HB	TBB	IBB	SO	WP	Bk	W	L	Pct.	ShO	Sv	ERA
				HOW MUCH HE PITCHED						WHAT HE GAVE UP												THE RESULTS					
1991	San Bernrdo	A+	Sea	22	0	0	7	38	186	46	27	19	1	2	2	4	25	0	40	5	1	1	0	1.000	0	0	4.50
1995	Carolina	AA	Pit	4	0	0	1	3.2	16	3	0	0	0	1	0	0	2	0	6	0	0	0	0	.000	0	0	0.00
	Calgary	AAA	Pit	16	1	0	4	25.1	119	30	15	13	4	2	1	0	14	0	18	1	0	1	0	1.000	0	0	4.62
1996	Rochester	AAA	Bal	4	4	0	0	16.1	86	26	15	15	2	1	1	0	13	0	9	1	0	1	1	.500	0	0	8.27
3 Min. YEARS				46	5	0	12	83.1	407	105	57	47	7	6	4	4	54	0	73	7	1	3	1	.750	0	0	5.08

P.J. Forbes

Bats: Right **Throws:** Right **Pos:** 2B **Ht:** 5'10" **Wt:** 160 **Born:** 9/22/67 **Age:** 29

Year	Team	Lg	Org	G	AB	H	2B	3B	HR	TB	R	RBI	TBB	IBB	SO	HBP	SH	SF	SB	CS	SB%	GDP	Avg	OBP	SLG
				BATTING															BASERUNNING				PERCENTAGES		
1990	Boise	A-	Cal	43	170	42	9	1	0	53	29	19	23	1	21	0	7	1	11	4	.73	5	.247	.335	.312
1991	Palm Spring	A+	Cal	94	349	93	14	2	2	117	45	26	36	1	44	4	12	0	18	8	.69	7	.266	.342	.335
1992	Quad City	A	Cal	105	376	106	16	5	2	138	53	46	44	1	51	2	24	5	15	6	.71	4	.282	.356	.367
1993	Midland	AA	Cal	126	498	159	23	2	15	231	90	64	26	1	50	4	14	2	6	8	.43	13	.319	.357	.464
	Vancouver	AAA	Cal	5	16	4	2	0	0	6	1	3	0	0	3	0	1	0	0	0	.00	1	.250	.250	.375
1994	Angels	R	Cal	2	6	0	0	0	0	0	1	0	0	0	1	0	0	0	0	0	.00	0	.000	.000	.000
	Vancouver	AAA	Cal	90	318	91	21	2	1	119	39	40	22	0	42	2	7	5	4	2	.67	6	.286	.331	.374
1995	Vancouver	AAA	Cal	109	369	101	22	3	1	132	47	52	21	0	46	2	7	10	4	6	.40	4	.274	.308	.358
1996	Vancouver	AAA	Cal	117	409	112	24	2	0	140	58	46	42	3	44	5	10	4	4	3	.57	13	.274	.346	.342
7 Min. YEARS				691	2511	708	131	17	21	936	363	296	214	7	302	19	82	27	62	37	.63	53	.282	.340	.373

Tom Fordham

Pitches: Left **Bats:** Left **Pos:** P **Ht:** 6'2" **Wt:** 210 **Born:** 2/20/74 **Age:** 23

		HOW MUCH HE PITCHED						WHAT HE GAVE UP												THE RESULTS					
Year Team	Lg Org	G	GS	CG	GF	IP	BFP	H	R	ER	HR	SH	SF	HB	TBB	IBB	SO	WP	Bk	W	L	Pct.	ShO	Sv	ERA
1993 White Sox	R ChA	3	0	0	1	10	41	9	2	2	0	0	0	0	3	0	12	1	0	1	1	.500	0	0	1.80
Sarasota	A+ ChA	2	0	0	1	5	21	3	1	0	0	0	0	0	3	2	5	1	1	0	0	.000	0	0	0.00
Hickory	A ChA	8	8	1	0	48.2	194	36	21	21	3	1	6	0	21	0	27	3	2	4	3	.571	0	0	3.88
1994 Hickory	A ChA	17	17	1	0	109	452	101	47	38	10	1	1	3	30	1	121	5	4	10	5	.667	1	0	3.14
South Bend	A ChA	11	11	1	0	74.2	315	82	46	36	4	4	3	0	14	0	48	4	0	4	4	.500	1	0	4.34
1995 Pr. William	A+ ChA	13	13	1	0	84	340	66	20	19	7	2	1	2	35	2	78	1	0	9	0	1.000	1	0	2.04
Birmingham	AA ChA	27	27	3	0	166.2	688	145	55	50	16	4	3	2	63	4	139	4	0	15	3	.833	2	0	2.70
1996 Birmingham	AA ChA	6	6	0	0	37.1	147	26	13	11	4	0	2	0	14	1	37	2	0	2	1	.667	0	0	2.65
Nashville	AAA ChA	22	22	3	0	140.2	589	117	60	54	15	4	2	4	69	1	118	7	1	10	8	.556	2	0	3.45
4 Min. YEARS		109	104	10	2	676	2787	585	265	231	59	16	18	11	252	11	585	28	8	55	25	.688	7	0	3.08

Troy Forkerway

Bats: Right **Throws:** Right **Pos:** SS **Ht:** 5'11" **Wt:** 175 **Born:** 5/17/71 **Age:** 26

		BATTING															BASERUNNING				PERCENTAGES		
Year Team	Lg Org	G	AB	H	2B	3B	HR	TB	R	RBI	TBB	IBB	SO	HBP	SH	SF	SB	CS	SB%	GDP	Avg	OBP	SLG
1994 Thunder Bay	IND —	78	269	72	9	0	1	84	35	28	31	0	29	3	9	3	10	7	.59	5	.268	.346	.312
1995 Daytona	A+ ChN	75	188	38	4	0	1	45	22	11	20	0	29	1	4	1	10	1	.91	5	.202	.281	.239
1996 Daytona	A+ ChN	49	143	40	6	1	0	48	27	13	17	0	17	3	1	1	7	6	.54	0	.280	.366	.336
Orlando	AA ChN	59	161	39	9	1	3	59	22	20	11	0	24	4	1	3	0	2	.00	8	.242	.302	.366
3 Min. YEARS		261	761	189	28	2	5	236	106	72	79	0	99	11	15	8	27	16	.63	18	.248	.325	.310

Tim Forkner

Bats: Left **Throws:** Right **Pos:** 3B **Ht:** 5'11" **Wt:** 180 **Born:** 3/28/73 **Age:** 24

		BATTING															BASERUNNING				PERCENTAGES		
Year Team	Lg Org	G	AB	H	2B	3B	HR	TB	R	RBI	TBB	IBB	SO	HBP	SH	SF	SB	CS	SB%	GDP	Avg	OBP	SLG
1993 Auburn	A- Hou	72	267	76	14	9	0	108	32	39	38	0	29	3	1	1	3	3	.50	8	.285	.379	.404
1994 Quad City	A Hou	124	429	128	23	4	6	177	57	57	57	3	72	7	10	8	6	8	.43	10	.298	.383	.413
1995 Kissimmee	A+ Hou	89	296	84	20	4	1	115	42	34	60	2	40	5	2	4	4	2	.67	11	.284	.408	.389
Jackson	AA Hou	35	119	32	11	0	3	52	19	23	19	0	14	2	0	0	1	3	.25	3	.269	.379	.437
1996 Jackson	AA Hou	114	379	111	20	3	7	158	55	46	55	1	47	4	4	2	0	4	.00	10	.293	.386	.417
4 Min. YEARS		434	1490	431	88	20	17	610	205	199	229	6	202	21	17	15	14	20	.41	42	.289	.388	.409

Scott Forster

Pitches: Left **Bats:** Right **Pos:** P **Ht:** 6'1" **Wt:** 194 **Born:** 10/27/71 **Age:** 25

		HOW MUCH HE PITCHED						WHAT HE GAVE UP												THE RESULTS					
Year Team	Lg Org	G	GS	CG	GF	IP	BFP	H	R	ER	HR	SH	SF	HB	TBB	IBB	SO	WP	Bk	W	L	Pct.	ShO	Sv	ERA
1994 Vermont	A- Mon	12	9	0	0	52.2	236	38	32	19	0	0	1	4	34	0	39	6	2	1	6	.143	0	0	3.25
1995 W. Palm Bch	A+ Mon	26	26	1	0	146.2	643	129	78	66	6	5	4	7	80	1	92	16	0	6	11	.353	0	0	4.05
1996 Harrisburg	AA Mon	28	28	0	0	176.1	755	164	92	74	15	3	4	7	67	2	97	5	0	10	7	.588	0	0	3.78
3 Min. YEARS		66	63	1	0	375.2	1634	331	202	159	21	8	9	18	181	3	228	27	2	17	24	.415	0	0	3.81

Tim Fortugno

Pitches: Left **Bats:** Left **Pos:** P **Ht:** 6' 0" **Wt:** 185 **Born:** 4/11/62 **Age:** 35

		HOW MUCH HE PITCHED						WHAT HE GAVE UP												THE RESULTS					
Year Team	Lg Org	G	GS	CG	GF	IP	BFP	H	R	ER	HR	SH	SF	HB	TBB	IBB	SO	WP	Bk	W	L	Pct.	ShO	Sv	ERA
1986 Bellingham	A- Sea	6	0	0	4	8	0	2	2	1	0	0	0	1	12	1	11	1	0	0	0	.000	0	1	1.13
Wausau	A Sea	19	0	0	13	31	139	18	17	9	0	2	2	0	26	0	38	6	1	1	1	.500	0	3	2.61
1987 Salinas	A+ Sea	46	4	1	17	93.1	409	43	36	29	1	3	3	3	84	1	141	19	3	8	2	.800	1	6	2.80
1988 Reading	AA Phi	29	4	0	11	50.2	229	42	29	25	5	1	4	1	36	0	48	5	6	1	5	.167	0	0	4.44
Clearwater	A+ Phi	9	3	0	2	26	109	17	10	7	1	1	1	0	15	0	28	2	3	1	3	.250	0	0	2.42
1989 Reno	A+ —	5	5	1	0	35.2	161	28	20	10	2	2	0	3	20	2	38	2	2	2	3	.400	0	0	2.52
El Paso	AA Mil	10	4	0	2	26	126	29	24	23	3	1	1	1	21	2	22	4	0	0	3	.000	0	0	7.96
Stockton	A+ Mil	13	2	0	3	33	134	9	6	5	0	1	0	4	20	1	52	2	1	2	1	.667	0	1	1.36
1990 Beloit	A Mil	31	0	0	29	63.1	263	38	16	11	1	3	0	0	38	3	106	4	0	8	4	.667	0	7	1.56
El Paso	AA Mil	12	2	0	4	28.2	133	23	12	10	0	2	3	1	22	2	24	4	0	2	3	.400	0	2	3.14
1991 El Paso	AA Mil	20	3	0	13	54.1	227	40	15	12	1	0	2	0	25	1	73	3	1	5	1	.833	0	1	1.99
Denver	AAA Mil	26	0	0	10	35.1	152	30	15	14	1	3	2	3	20	2	39	4	0	0	1	.000	0	2	3.57
1992 Edmonton	AAA Cal	26	7	0	4	73.1	318	69	36	29	5	0	1	2	33	0	82	3	1	6	4	.600	0	1	3.56
1993 Ottawa	AAA Mon	28	4	0	7	40	175	28	17	16	4	0	1	4	31	4	42	7	1	2	1	.667	0	1	3.60
1994 Chattanooga	AA Cin	22	0	0	17	26.2	115	19	15	8	0	2	1	1	16	1	36	4	1	0	1	.000	0	8	2.70
1995 Vancouver	AAA Cal	10	0	0	7	11.2	45	8	2	2	1	0	0	0	4	1	7	0	0	1	1	.500	0	1	1.54
1996 Chattanooga	AA Cin	11	0	0	9	11.1	38	4	0	0	0	1	0	0	4	0	10	0	0	2	0	1.000	0	6	0.00
Indianapolis	AAA Cin	41	5	0	19	58	253	55	27	22	6	7	3	2	25	3	46	3	1	5	5	.500	0	2	3.41
1992 California	AL	14	5	1	5	41.2	177	37	24	24	5	0	1	0	19	0	31	2	1	1	1	.500	1	1	5.18
1994 Cincinnati	NL	25	0	0	9	30	132	32	14	14	2	3	1	3	14	0	29	4	2	1	0	1.000	0	0	4.20
1995 Chicago	AL	37	0	0	11	38.2	163	30	24	24	7	1	2	0	19	2	24	5	3	1	3	.250	0	0	5.59
11 Min. YEARS		364	43	2	171	706.1	3026	502	299	233	31	29	24	26	452	24	843	73	21	46	39	.541	1	42	2.97
3 Maj. YEARS		76	5	1	25	110.1	472	99	62	62	14	4	4	3	52	2	84	11	6	3	4	.429	1	1	5.06

Jim Foster

Bats: Right **Throws:** Right **Pos:** C **Ht:** 6'4" **Wt:** 220 **Born:** 8/18/71 **Age:** 25

		BATTING															BASERUNNING				PERCENTAGES		
Year Team	Lg Org	G	AB	H	2B	3B	HR	TB	R	RBI	TBB	IBB	SO	HBP	SH	SF	SB	CS	SB%	GDP	Avg	OBP	SLG
1993 Bluefield	R+ Bal	61	218	71	21	1	10	124	59	45	42	1	34	3	0	3	3	1	.75	4	.326	.436	.569
1994 Albany	A Bal	121	421	112	29	3	8	171	61	56	54	0	59	11	0	6	5	3	.63	13	.266	.360	.406
1995 Frederick	A+ Bal	128	429	112	27	3	6	163	44	56	51	5	63	8	0	5	2	3	.40	10	.261	.347	.380
1996 Frederick	A+ Bal	82	278	70	20	2	7	115	35	42	39	1	32	4	0	3	6	3	.67	7	.252	.349	.414
Bowie	AA Bal	9	33	10	0	1	2	18	7	9	7	0	6	0	0	1	0	0	.00	0	.303	.415	.545
4 Min. YEARS		401	1379	375	97	10	33	591	206	208	193	7	194	26	0	18	16	10	.62	34	.272	.368	.429

Mark Foster

Pitches: Left **Bats:** Left **Pos:** P **Ht:** 6'1" **Wt:** 200 **Born:** 12/24/71 **Age:** 25

		HOW MUCH HE PITCHED						WHAT HE GAVE UP												THE RESULTS					
Year Team	Lg Org	G	GS	CG	GF	IP	BFP	H	R	ER	HR	SH	SF	HB	TBB	IBB	SO	WP	Bk	W	L	Pct.	ShO	Sv	ERA
1993 Martinsvlle	R+ Phi	13	13	0	0	69.1	330	77	55	38	3	1	4	6	42	1	50	6	4	1	9	.100	0	0	4.93
1994 Spartanburg	A Phi	32	0	0	25	42.1	192	41	23	21	0	5	1	4	24	0	40	10	3	4	2	.667	0	11	4.46
Clearwater	A+ Phi	16	1	0	5	26.2	118	28	13	10	0	0	0	0	14	0	22	0	1	2	2	.500	0	1	3.38
1995 Clearwater	A+ Phi	24	0	0	6	23.1	108	30	17	14	1	1	0	4	10	0	13	1	1	0	1	.000	0	1	5.40
Reading	AA Phi	49	0	0	10	44	214	55	32	27	2	3	1	5	27	3	28	3	5	1	2	.333	0	2	5.52
1996 Reading	AA Phi	50	8	0	12	76	349	84	54	49	6	4	4	4	45	6	56	4	1	4	5	.444	0	0	5.80
4 Min. YEARS		184	22	0	58	281.2	1311	315	194	159	12	14	10	23	162	10	209	24	15	12	21	.364	0	15	5.08

Keith Foulke

Pitches: Right **Bats:** Right **Pos:** P **Ht:** 6'1" **Wt:** 195 **Born:** 10/19/72 **Age:** 24

		HOW MUCH HE PITCHED						WHAT HE GAVE UP												THE RESULTS					
Year Team	Lg Org	G	GS	CG	GF	IP	BFP	H	R	ER	HR	SH	SF	HB	TBB	IBB	SO	WP	Bk	W	L	Pct.	ShO	Sv	ERA
1994 Everett	A- SF	4	4	0	0	19.1	79	17	4	2	0	1	0	2	3	0	22	0	0	2	0	1.000	0	0	0.93
1995 San Jose	A+ SF	28	26	2	0	177.1	723	166	85	69	16	10	3	7	32	0	168	6	2	13	6	.684	1	0	3.50
1996 Shreveport	AA SF	27	27	4	0	182.2	712	149	61	56	16	6	7	3	35	0	129	6	1	12	7	.632	2	0	2.76
3 Min. YEARS		59	57	6	0	379.1	1514	332	150	127	32	17	10	12	70	0	319	12	3	27	13	.675	3	0	3.01

Chad Fox

Pitches: Right **Bats:** Right **Pos:** P **Ht:** 6'2" **Wt:** 180 **Born:** 9/3/70 **Age:** 26

		HOW MUCH HE PITCHED						WHAT HE GAVE UP												THE RESULTS					
Year Team	Lg Org	G	GS	CG	GF	IP	BFP	H	R	ER	HR	SH	SF	HB	TBB	IBB	SO	WP	Bk	W	L	Pct.	ShO	Sv	ERA
1992 Princeton	R+ Cin	15	8	0	4	49.1	238	55	43	26	2	1	1	2	34	1	37	6	2	4	2	.667	0	0	4.74
1993 Charlstn-WV	A Cin	27	26	0	0	135.2	638	138	100	81	7	6	8	13	97	0	81	15	1	9	12	.429	0	0	5.37
1994 Winston-Sal	A+ Cin	25	25	1	0	156.1	674	121	77	67	18	5	5	9	94	0	137	20	1	12	5	.706	0	0	3.86
1995 Chattanooga	AA Cin	20	17	0	1	80	363	76	49	45	2	2	2	3	52	1	56	14	0	4	5	.444	0	0	5.06
1996 Richmond	AAA Atl	18	18	1	0	93.1	415	91	57	49	9	8	6	3	49	1	87	8	1	3	10	.231	0	0	4.73
5 Min. YEARS		105	94	2	5	514.2	2328	481	326	268	38	22	22	30	326	3	398	63	5	32	34	.485	0	0	4.69

Eric Fox

Bats: Both **Throws:** Left **Pos:** OF **Ht:** 5'10" **Wt:** 180 **Born:** 8/15/63 **Age:** 33

		BATTING															BASERUNNING				PERCENTAGES		
Year Team	Lg Org	G	AB	H	2B	3B	HR	TB	R	RBI	TBB	IBB	SO	HBP	SH	SF	SB	CS	SB%	GDP	Avg	OBP	SLG
1986 Salinas	A+ Sea	133	526	137	17	3	5	175	80	42	69	7	78	1	9	4	41	27	.60	1	.260	.345	.333
1987 Chattanooga	AA Sea	134	523	139	28	10	8	211	76	54	40	5	93	2	4	5	22	10	.69	2	.266	.318	.403
1988 Vermont	AA Sea	129	478	120	20	6	3	161	55	39	39	3	69	2	7	4	33	12	.73	1	.251	.308	.337
1989 Huntsville	AA Oak	139	498	125	10	5	15	190	84	51	72	1	85	0	11	2	49	15	.77	3	.251	.344	.382
1990 Tacoma	AAA Oak	62	221	61	9	2	4	86	37	34	20	0	34	0	5	2	8	8	.50	2	.276	.333	.389
1991 Tacoma	AAA Oak	127	522	141	24	8	4	193	85	52	57	4	82	2	9	4	17	11	.61	6	.270	.342	.370
1992 Huntsville	AA Oak	59	240	65	16	2	5	100	42	14	27	4	43	0	0	3	16	5	.76	2	.271	.341	.417
Tacoma	AAA Oak	37	121	24	3	1	1	32	16	7	16	1	25	0	2	2	5	0	1.00	2	.198	.288	.264
1993 Tacoma	AAA Oak	92	317	99	14	5	11	156	49	52	41	3	48	1	7	3	18	8	.69	4	.312	.390	.492
1994 Tacoma	AAA Oak	52	191	60	15	2	3	88	30	19	20	2	28	2	4	1	7	2	.78	4	.314	.383	.461
1995 Okla. City	AAA Tex	92	349	97	22	5	6	147	52	50	30	7	68	2	4	3	5	5	.50	7	.278	.336	.421
1996 Albuquerque	AAA LA	30	91	30	6	1	0	38	8	2	4	1	20	0	0	0	1	2	.33	2	.330	.358	.418
1992 Oakland	AL	51	143	34	5	2	3	52	24	13	13	0	29	0	6	1	3	4	.43	1	.238	.299	.364
1993 Oakland	AL	29	56	8	1	0	1	12	5	5	2	0	7	0	3	0	0	2	.00	0	.143	.172	.214
1994 Oakland	AL	26	44	9	2	0	1	14	7	1	3	0	8	0	0	0	2	0	1.00	0	.205	.255	.318
1995 Texas	AL	10	15	0	0	0	0	0	2	0	3	0	4	0	1	0	0	0	.00	0	.000	.167	.000
11 Min. YEARS		1086	4077	1098	184	50	65	1577	614	416	435	38	673	12	62	33	222	105	.68	36	.269	.339	.387
4 Maj. YEARS		116	258	51	8	2	5	78	38	19	21	0	48	0	10	1	5	6	.45	1	.198	.257	.302

David Francisco

Bats: Right **Throws:** Right **Pos:** OF **Ht:** 6'0" **Wt:** 165 **Born:** 2/27/72 **Age:** 25

		BATTING															BASERUNNING				PERCENTAGES		
Year Team	Lg Org	G	AB	H	2B	3B	HR	TB	R	RBI	TBB	IBB	SO	HBP	SH	SF	SB	CS	SB%	GDP	Avg	OBP	SLG
1991 Athletics	R Oak	56	208	50	7	4	1	68	34	34	24	0	30	2	2	1	14	5	.74	6	.240	.323	.327
1992 Athletics	R Oak	10	37	14	1	1	1	20	12	8	5	0	6	4	0	0	6	2	.75	0	.378	.500	.541
Reno	A+ Oak	7	15	3	0	0	0	3	5	0	3	0	5	0	1	0	1	0	1.00	0	.200	.333	.200
Madison	A Oak	43	133	26	5	1	0	33	9	11	16	0	32	2	7	0	3	1	.75	1	.195	.291	.248

BATTING																BASERUNNING				PERCENTAGES		
Year Team	Lg Org	G	AB	H	2B	3B	HR	TB	R	RBI	TBB	IBB	SO	HBP	SH	SF	SB	CS	SB%	GDP	Avg	OBP	SLG
1993 Madison	A Oak	129	484	134	24	8	2	180	87	50	50	1	108	12	9	4	27	16	.63	7	.277	.356	.372
1994 Modesto	A+ Oak	130	499	138	18	5	9	193	86	48	61	0	110	9	11	2	29	18	.62	1	.277	.364	.387
1995 Huntsville	AA Oak	129	477	133	17	1	5	167	75	48	38	0	92	11	5	3	30	8	.79	10	.279	.344	.350
1996 Huntsville	AA Oak	114	386	100	12	1	3	123	59	28	28	0	72	9	12	2	13	4	.76	6	.259	.322	.319
6 Min. YEARS		618	2239	598	84	21	21	787	367	227	225	1	455	49	47	12	123	54	.69	31	.267	.345	.351

Micah Franklin

Bats: Both **Throws:** Right **Pos:** OF **Ht:** 6'0" **Wt:** 195 **Born:** 4/25/72 **Age:** 25

BATTING																BASERUNNING				PERCENTAGES		
Year Team	Lg Org	G	AB	H	2B	3B	HR	TB	R	RBI	TBB	IBB	SO	HBP	SH	SF	SB	CS	SB%	GDP	Avg	OBP	SLG
1990 Kingsport	R+ NYN	39	158	41	9	2	7	75	29	25	8	0	44	1	0	2	4	1	.80	2	.259	.296	.475
1991 Pittsfield	A- NYN	26	94	27	4	2	0	35	17	14	21	0	20	1	2	1	12	3	.80	3	.287	.419	.372
Erie	A- NYN	39	153	37	4	0	2	47	28	8	25	0	35	2	0	1	4	5	.44	3	.242	.354	.307
1992 Billings	R+ Cin	75	251	84	13	2	11	134	58	60	53	3	65	15	0	3	18	17	.51	3	.335	.472	.534
1993 Winston-Sal	A+ Cin	20	69	16	1	1	3	28	10	6	10	1	19	2	1	0	0	1	.00	0	.232	.346	.406
Charlstn-WV	A Cin	102	343	90	14	4	17	163	56	68	47	4	109	18	3	6	6	1	.86	4	.262	.374	.475
1994 Winston-Sal	A+ Cin	42	150	45	7	0	21	115	44	44	27	5	48	6	0	1	7	0	1.00	1	.300	.424	.767
Chattanooga	AA Cin	79	279	77	17	0	10	124	46	40	33	3	79	13	0	3	2	2	.50	3	.276	.375	.444
1995 Calgary	AAA Pit	110	358	105	28	0	21	196	64	71	47	8	95	1	0	5	3	3	.50	7	.293	.372	.547
1996 Toledo	AAA Det	53	179	44	10	1	7	77	32	21	27	0	60	3	0	0	3	2	.60	1	.246	.354	.430
Louisville	AAA StL	86	289	67	18	3	15	136	43	53	40	2	71	8	1	3	2	3	.40	4	.232	.338	.471
7 Min. YEARS		671	2323	633	125	15	114	1130	427	410	338	26	645	70	7	25	61	38	.62	31	.272	.378	.486

Ryan Franklin

Pitches: Right **Bats:** Right **Pos:** P **Ht:** 6'3" **Wt:** 160 **Born:** 3/5/73 **Age:** 24

HOW MUCH HE PITCHED								WHAT HE GAVE UP												THE RESULTS					
Year Team	Lg Org	G	GS	CG	GF	IP	BFP	H	R	ER	HR	SH	SF	HB	TBB	IBB	SO	WP	Bk	W	L	Pct.	ShO	Sv	ERA
1993 Bellingham	A- Sea	15	14	1	0	74	321	72	38	24	2	2	1	3	27	0	55	7	3	5	3	.625	1	0	2.92
1994 Appleton	A Sea	18	18	5	0	118	493	105	60	41	6	3	1	17	23	0	102	6	3	9	6	.600	1	0	3.13
Calgary	AAA Sea	1	1	0	0	5.2	28	9	6	5	2	0	0	0	1	0	2	0	0	0	0	.000	0	0	7.94
Riverside	A+ Sea	8	8	1	0	61.2	261	61	26	21	5	1	3	4	8	0	35	0	1	4	2	.667	1	0	3.06
1995 Port City	AA Sea	31	20	1	2	146	627	153	84	70	13	11	3	12	43	4	102	6	2	6	10	.375	1	0	4.32
1996 Port City	AA Sea	28	27	2	0	182	764	186	99	81	23	6	3	16	37	0	127	4	2	6	12	.333	0	0	4.01
4 Min. YEARS		101	88	10	2	587.1	2494	586	313	242	51	23	11	52	139	4	423	23	11	30	33	.476	4	0	3.71

John Frascatore

Pitches: Right **Bats:** Right **Pos:** P **Ht:** 6' 1" **Wt:** 210 **Born:** 2/4/70 **Age:** 27

HOW MUCH HE PITCHED								WHAT HE GAVE UP												THE RESULTS					
Year Team	Lg Org	G	GS	CG	GF	IP	BFP	H	R	ER	HR	SH	SF	HB	TBB	IBB	SO	WP	Bk	W	L	Pct.	ShO	Sv	ERA
1991 Hamilton	A- StL	30	1	0	7	30.1	162	44	38	31	3	3	1	2	22	1	18	1	2	2	7	.222	0	1	9.20
1992 Savannah	A StL	50	0	0	44	58.2	266	49	32	25	4	8	1	3	29	2	56	4	5	5	7	.417	0	23	3.84
1993 Springfield	A StL	27	26	2	1	157.1	654	157	84	66	6	7	5	3	33	0	126	2	3	7	12	.368	1	0	3.78
1994 Arkansas	AA StL	12	12	4	0	78.1	324	76	37	27	3	1	2	3	15	0	63	3	0	7	3	.700	1	0	3.10
Louisville	AAA StL	13	12	2	0	85	366	82	34	32	3	6	4	2	33	2	58	2	0	8	3	.727	1	0	3.39
1995 Louisville	AAA StL	28	10	1	15	82	370	89	54	36	5	5	2	3	34	3	55	5	0	2	8	.200	0	5	3.95
1996 Louisville	AAA StL	36	21	3	5	156.1	692	180	106	90	22	7	6	7	42	2	95	5	0	6	13	.316	0	0	5.18
1994 St. Louis	NL	1	1	0	0	3.1	18	7	6	6	2	0	0	0	2	0	2	1	0	0	1	.000	0	0	16.20
1995 St. Louis	NL	14	4	0	3	32.2	151	39	19	16	3	1	1	2	16	1	21	0	0	1	1	.500	0	0	4.41
6 Min. YEARS		196	82	12	72	648	2834	677	385	307	46	37	21	23	208	10	471	22	10	37	53	.411	3	29	4.26
2 Maj. YEARS		15	5	0	3	36	169	46	25	22	5	1	1	2	18	1	23	1	0	1	2	.333	0	0	5.50

Ron Frazier

Pitches: Right **Bats:** Right **Pos:** P **Ht:** 6'2" **Wt:** 185 **Born:** 6/13/69 **Age:** 28

HOW MUCH HE PITCHED								WHAT HE GAVE UP												THE RESULTS					
Year Team	Lg Org	G	GS	CG	GF	IP	BFP	H	R	ER	HR	SH	SF	HB	TBB	IBB	SO	WP	Bk	W	L	Pct.	ShO	Sv	ERA
1990 Oneonta	A- NYA	13	13	0	0	80.1	328	67	32	22	5	2	7	2	33	0	67	4	5	6	2	.750	0	0	2.46
1991 Greensboro	A NYA	25	25	3	0	169	692	140	65	45	10	3	6	9	42	0	127	8	4	12	6	.667	1	0	2.40
1992 Pr. William	A+ NYA	16	7	0	4	56.1	236	51	27	20	10	2	0	5	11	0	52	2	1	4	3	.571	0	0	3.20
1993 Pr. William	A+ NYA	15	15	1	0	101	403	79	34	24	5	2	1	1	23	0	108	4	1	8	3	.727	0	0	2.14
Albany-Colo	AA NYA	12	12	0	0	79.2	341	93	43	34	5	1	6	1	16	0	65	3	1	4	3	.571	0	0	3.84
1994 Columbus	AAA NYA	20	17	1	1	104	454	108	59	54	9	5	2	5	43	0	62	3	2	6	6	.500	1	0	4.67
Albany-Colo	AA NYA	10	10	1	0	60.1	257	53	30	21	5	3	1	3	21	3	29	2	0	3	4	.429	0	0	3.13
1995 Columbus	AAA NYA	24	5	0	9	54	240	54	33	27	4	4	2	4	23	2	31	7	1	1	2	.333	0	0	4.50
1996 Indianapols	AAA Cin	2	2	0	0	7.1	34	8	11	9	2	1	0	0	3	0	4	0	0	0	1	.000	0	0	11.05
Chattanooga	AA Cin	31	4	0	10	71	333	91	51	46	11	0	6	3	25	1	54	1	0	2	5	.286	0	0	5.83
7 Min. YEARS		168	110	6	24	783	3318	744	385	302	66	23	31	33	240	6	599	34	15	46	35	.568	2	0	3.47

Scott Fredrickson

Pitches: Right **Bats:** Right **Pos:** P **Ht:** 6' 3" **Wt:** 215 **Born:** 8/19/67 **Age:** 29

HOW MUCH HE PITCHED								WHAT HE GAVE UP												THE RESULTS					
Year Team	Lg Org	G	GS	CG	GF	IP	BFP	H	R	ER	HR	SH	SF	HB	TBB	IBB	SO	WP	Bk	W	L	Pct.	ShO	Sv	ERA
1990 Spokane	A- SD	26	1	0	15	46.2	197	35	22	17	3	4	1	2	17	1	61	6	4	3	3	.500	0	8	3.28

		HOW MUCH HE PITCHED						WHAT HE GAVE UP												THE RESULTS					
Year Team	Lg Org	G	GS	CG	GF	IP	BFP	H	R	ER	HR	SH	SF	HB	TBB	IBB	SO	WP	Bk	W	L	Pct.	ShO	Sv	ERA
1991 Waterloo	A SD	26	0	0	22	38.1	153	24	9	5	1	1	2	1	15	3	40	3	2	3	5	.375	0	6	1.17
High Desert	A+ SD	23	0	0	19	35	154	31	15	9	2	2	1	1	18	2	26	6	0	4	1	.800	0	7	2.31
1992 Wichita	AA SD	56	0	0	22	73.1	303	50	29	26	9	2	5	2	38	3	66	11	0	4	7	.364	0	5	3.19
1993 Colo. Sprng	AAA Col	23	0	0	18	26.1	119	25	16	16	3	2	1	0	19	3	20	2	0	1	3	.250	0	7	5.47
1995 Colo. Sprng	AAA Col	58	1	0	20	75.2	348	70	40	29	2	8	3	5	47	5	70	15	2	11	3	.786	0	4	3.45
1996 Colo. Sprng	AAA Col	55	0	0	17	63.2	303	71	56	47	9	3	6	3	40	6	66	8	0	2	2	.500	0	2	6.64
1993 Colorado	NL	25	0	0	4	29	137	33	25	20	3	2	2	1	17	2	20	4	1	0	1	.000	0	0	6.21
6 Min. YEARS		267	2	0	133	359	1577	306	187	149	29	22	19	14	194	23	349	51	8	28	24	.538	0	39	3.74

Mike Freehill

Pitches: Right **Bats:** Right **Pos:** P **Ht:** 6'3" **Wt:** 177 **Born:** 6/2/71 **Age:** 26

		HOW MUCH HE PITCHED						WHAT HE GAVE UP												THE RESULTS					
Year Team	Lg Org	G	GS	CG	GF	IP	BFP	H	R	ER	HR	SH	SF	HB	TBB	IBB	SO	WP	Bk	W	L	Pct.	ShO	Sv	ERA
1994 Boise	A- Cal	28	0	0	19	45	179	37	20	16	2	4	0	1	10	5	38	2	1	3	6	.333	0	8	3.20
1995 Cedar Rapds	A Cal	54	0	0	49	55	234	54	25	16	4	3	0	7	12	5	47	10	1	4	5	.444	0	28	2.62
1996 Vancouver	AAA Cal	7	0	0	3	10	53	16	11	11	1	0	1	1	8	1	5	4	0	1	1	.500	0	0	9.90
Midland	AA Cal	47	0	0	45	50	224	49	25	19	4	3	1	1	21	1	48	10	2	7	6	.538	0	17	3.42
3 Min. YEARS		136	0	0	116	160	690	156	81	62	11	10	2	10	51	12	138	26	4	15	18	.455	0	53	3.49

Chris Freeman

Pitches: Right **Bats:** Right **Pos:** P **Ht:** 6'4" **Wt:** 205 **Born:** 8/27/72 **Age:** 24

		HOW MUCH HE PITCHED						WHAT HE GAVE UP												THE RESULTS					
Year Team	Lg Org	G	GS	CG	GF	IP	BFP	H	R	ER	HR	SH	SF	HB	TBB	IBB	SO	WP	Bk	W	L	Pct.	ShO	Sv	ERA
1994 Dunedin	A+ Tor	17	3	0	5	50.2	205	44	16	14	1	2	2	0	21	1	45	5	2	3	2	.600	0	1	2.49
1995 Knoxville	AA Tor	39	5	0	16	81.1	354	78	53	49	12	5	5	1	38	0	80	1	0	2	3	.400	0	8	5.42
1996 Knoxville	AA Tor	26	0	0	8	45.2	200	45	23	17	3	0	3	1	23	3	54	1	0	6	1	.857	0	0	3.35
3 Min. YEARS		82	8	0	29	177.2	759	167	92	80	16	7	10	2	82	4	179	7	2	11	6	.647	0	9	4.05

Sean Freeman

Bats: Left **Throws:** Left **Pos:** 1B **Ht:** 6'3" **Wt:** 205 **Born:** 9/10/71 **Age:** 25

		BATTING															BASERUNNING				PERCENTAGES		
Year Team	Lg Org	G	AB	H	2B	3B	HR	TB	R	RBI	TBB	IBB	SO	HBP	SH	SF	SB	CS	SB%	GDP	Avg	OBP	SLG
1994 Jamestown	A- Det	67	222	65	14	1	2	87	22	31	19	3	46	4	0	4	2	2	.50	3	.293	.353	.392
1995 Lakeland	A+ Det	119	414	120	21	2	6	163	42	65	49	3	98	2	0	7	3	4	.43	3	.290	.362	.394
1996 Jacksonvlle	AA Det	124	412	110	18	1	25	205	72	74	66	2	117	6	1	4	3	4	.43	8	.267	.373	.498
3 Min. YEARS		310	1048	295	53	4	33	455	136	170	134	8	261	12	1	15	8	10	.44	14	.281	.365	.434

Mike Freitas

Pitches: Right **Bats:** Right **Pos:** P **Ht:** 6'1" **Wt:** 160 **Born:** 9/22/69 **Age:** 27

		HOW MUCH HE PITCHED						WHAT HE GAVE UP												THE RESULTS					
Year Team	Lg Org	G	GS	CG	GF	IP	BFP	H	R	ER	HR	SH	SF	HB	TBB	IBB	SO	WP	Bk	W	L	Pct.	ShO	Sv	ERA
1989 Pittsfield	A- NYN	13	2	0	8	33.1	137	37	19	15	2	4	1	0	5	1	16	2	4	3	0	1.000	0	0	4.05
1990 Pittsfield	A- NYN	5	0	0	1	9.1	37	7	4	4	0	1	1	0	4	0	8	0	2	1	0	1.000	0	0	3.86
Columbia	A NYN	13	9	0	2	70	285	60	27	19	5	1	1	2	14	0	47	5	0	5	2	.714	0	0	2.44
1991 Columbia	A NYN	25	12	4	11	114.1	475	115	48	42	4	2	3	6	31	0	111	4	1	5	8	.385	2	2	3.31
St. Lucie	A+ NYN	5	0	0	4	10.2	45	11	4	3	1	2	0	1	1	0	6	0	0	0	1	.000	0	0	2.53
1992 St. Lucie	A+ NYN	45	0	0	39	57.2	231	51	17	8	2	1	6	4	9	1	30	0	2	6	3	.667	0	24	1.25
1993 Wichita	AA SD	8	0	0	7	7.2	43	13	14	9	1	0	1	0	2	0	4	2	0	0	2	.000	0	0	10.57
1994 Padres	R SD	4	0	0	2	6	23	2	1	1	0	0	0	0	3	0	7	1	0	1	0	1.000	0	1	1.50
1995 Memphis	AA SD	54	0	0	16	59	246	55	26	24	3	2	3	2	26	8	36	3	1	0	6	.000	0	2	3.66
1996 Las Vegas	AAA SD	3	0	0	2	5.2	25	8	2	2	1	0	0	0	1	1	1	0	0	0	1	.000	0	0	3.18
Memphis	AA SD	44	0	0	6	68.2	307	78	41	39	8	3	0	3	26	2	36	6	0	3	0	1.000	0	0	5.11
8 Min. YEARS		219	23	4	98	442.1	1854	437	203	166	27	16	16	18	122	13	302	23	10	24	23	.511	2	29	3.38

Hanley Frias

Bats: Both **Throws:** Right **Pos:** SS **Ht:** 6'0" **Wt:** 160 **Born:** 12/5/73 **Age:** 23

		BATTING															BASERUNNING				PERCENTAGES		
Year Team	Lg Org	G	AB	H	2B	3B	HR	TB	R	RBI	TBB	IBB	SO	HBP	SH	SF	SB	CS	SB%	GDP	Avg	OBP	SLG
1992 Rangers	R Tex	58	205	50	9	2	0	63	37	28	27	0	30	2	2	2	28	6	.82	1	.244	.335	.307
1993 Charlstn-SC	A Tex	132	473	109	20	4	4	149	61	37	40	0	108	3	4	4	27	14	.66	8	.230	.292	.315
1994 High Desert	A+ Mon	124	452	115	17	6	3	153	70	59	41	1	74	2	5	3	37	12	.76	9	.254	.317	.338
1995 Charlotte	A+ Tex	33	120	40	6	3	0	52	23	14	15	0	11	1	3	1	8	6	.57	0	.333	.409	.433
Tulsa	AA Tex	93	360	101	18	4	0	127	44	27	45	0	53	1	8	2	14	12	.54	6	.281	.360	.353
1996 Tulsa	AA Tex	134	505	145	24	12	2	199	73	41	30	2	73	0	5	3	9	9	.50	19	.287	.325	.394
5 Min. YEARS		574	2115	560	94	31	9	743	308	206	198	3	349	9	27	15	123	59	.68	43	.265	.328	.351

Jason Friedman

Bats: Left **Throws:** Left **Pos:** DH **Ht:** 6'1" **Wt:** 200 **Born:** 8/8/69 **Age:** 27

		BATTING															BASERUNNING				PERCENTAGES		
Year Team	Lg Org	G	AB	H	2B	3B	HR	TB	R	RBI	TBB	IBB	SO	HBP	SH	SF	SB	CS	SB%	GDP	Avg	OBP	SLG
1989 Red Sox	R Bos	32	116	29	4	2	0	37	8	9	5	1	13	2	1	0	0	2	.00	4	.250	.293	.319
Winter Havn	A+ Bos	21	62	12	0	2	0	16	5	5	2	0	12	0	0	0	0	0	.00	0	.194	.219	.258

							BATTING										BASERUNNING				PERCENTAGES		
Year	Team	Lg Org	G	AB	H	2B	3B	HR	TB	R	RBI	TBB	IBB	SO	HBP	SH	SF	SB	CS	SB%	GDP	Avg	OBP	SLG
1990	Winter Havn	A+ Bos	50	163	26	5	0	1	34	12	11	16	1	26	0	1	2	1	0	1.00	3	.160	.232	.209
	Elmira	A- Bos	67	213	51	16	0	0	67	25	23	26	1	27	2	0	2	3	4	.43	3	.239	.325	.315
1991	Elmira	A- Bos	70	253	68	13	2	8	109	36	36	35	5	43	3	1	2	2	0	1.00	4	.269	.362	.431
1992	Lynchburg	A+ Bos	135	495	132	26	1	14	202	68	68	46	5	61	4	1	2	5	4	.56	9	.267	.333	.408
1993	New Britain	AA Bos	81	294	73	15	1	1	93	22	24	20	4	50	3	1	4	2	0	1.00	7	.248	.299	.316
1994	Sarasota	A+ Bos	124	469	154	35	11	7	232	60	87	22	9	74	1	1	12	2	3	.40	3	.328	.351	.495
1995	Pawtucket	AAA Bos	14	51	15	3	0	2	24	6	9	2	1	3	0	1	1	0	0	.00	1	.294	.315	.471
	Bowie	AA Bal	63	228	53	11	0	3	73	22	27	16	2	23	2	1	1	1	1	.50	7	.232	.287	.320
	Rochester	AAA Bal	25	61	23	4	0	4	39	9	9	6	0	8	1	0	0	0	0	.00	2	.377	.441	.639
1996	Port City	AA Sea	45	133	25	5	3	1	39	7	11	8	1	16	1	0	0	0	0	.00	2	.188	.239	.293
	Tacoma	AAA Sea	20	73	12	6	1	1	23	9	4	2	0	14	1	0	2	0	1	.00	0	.164	.192	.315
8 Min. YEARS			747	2611	673	143	23	42	988	289	323	206	30	370	20	8	28	16	15	.52	45	.258	.314	.378

Troy Fryman

Bats: Left **Throws:** Right **Pos:** OF **Ht:** 6'4" **Wt:** 195 **Born:** 10/2/71 **Age:** 25

							BATTING										BASERUNNING				PERCENTAGES		
Year	Team	Lg Org	G	AB	H	2B	3B	HR	TB	R	RBI	TBB	IBB	SO	HBP	SH	SF	SB	CS	SB%	GDP	Avg	OBP	SLG
1991	White Sox	R ChA	7	26	6	3	0	0	9	2	3	4	0	7	0	0	1	1	0	1.00	1	.231	.323	.346
	Utica	A- ChA	52	178	43	15	1	2	66	23	16	14	1	45	1	1	2	1	0	1.00	2	.242	.297	.371
1992	South Bend	A ChA	129	432	75	26	2	8	129	45	34	60	5	130	5	3	2	7	2	.78	3	.174	.281	.299
1993	South Bend	A ChA	51	173	55	7	6	7	95	34	41	33	5	45	3	0	4	2	0	1.00	1	.318	.427	.549
	Sarasota	A+ ChA	78	285	68	16	3	5	105	42	46	31	3	55	3	0	1	0	0	.00	0	.239	.319	.368
1994	Birmingham	AA ChA	123	445	100	22	4	6	148	55	43	31	3	88	3	2	0	2	5	.29	11	.225	.280	.333
1995	Birmingham	AA ChA	112	356	79	13	3	8	122	48	41	49	6	97	6	2	3	9	1	.90	4	.222	.324	.343
1996	Birmingham	AA ChA	14	49	10	2	0	1	15	8	3	5	0	11	1	1	0	0	0	.00	0	.204	.291	.306
	Orlando	AA ChN	54	200	46	16	1	1	67	27	25	20	1	50	2	1	3	2	2	.50	1	.230	.302	.335
6 Min. YEARS			620	2144	482	120	20	38	756	284	252	247	24	528	24	10	16	24	10	.71	23	.225	.310	.353

Aaron Fuller

Bats: Both **Throws:** Right **Pos:** OF **Ht:** 5'10" **Wt:** 170 **Born:** 9/7/71 **Age:** 25

							BATTING										BASERUNNING				PERCENTAGES		
Year	Team	Lg Org	G	AB	H	2B	3B	HR	TB	R	RBI	TBB	IBB	SO	HBP	SH	SF	SB	CS	SB%	GDP	Avg	OBP	SLG
1993	Red Sox	R Bos	6	11	6	0	1	0	8	5	2	3	0	0	0	0	0	3	0	1.00	1	.545	.643	.727
	Utica	A- Bos	53	176	44	3	0	1	50	31	17	20	0	26	4	5	3	24	4	.86	0	.250	.335	.284
1994	Sarasota	A+ Bos	118	414	108	17	2	2	135	89	28	82	1	90	5	14	2	45	13	.78	7	.261	.388	.326
1995	Trenton	AA Bos	58	204	40	7	4	0	55	27	10	15	0	45	2	3	1	16	4	.80	2	.196	.257	.270
	Visalia	A+ Bos	49	186	47	7	3	1	63	27	19	19	0	32	1	3	2	11	10	.52	0	.253	.322	.339
1996	Sarasota	A+ Bos	115	434	130	20	5	5	175	74	49	63	0	60	4	4	5	33	12	.73	4	.300	.389	.403
	Pawtucket	AAA Bos	1	2	1	0	0	0	1	0	0	0	0	0	0	0	0	0	0	.00	0	.500	.500	.500
4 Min. YEARS			400	1427	376	54	15	9	487	253	125	202	1	253	16	29	13	132	43	.75	14	.263	.358	.341

Mark Fuller

Pitches: Right **Bats:** Left **Pos:** P **Ht:** 6'6" **Wt:** 216 **Born:** 8/5/70 **Age:** 26

			HOW MUCH HE PITCHED						WHAT HE GAVE UP												THE RESULTS				
Year	Team	Lg Org	G	GS	CG	GF	IP	BFP	H	R	ER	HR	SH	SF	HB	TBB	IBB	SO	WP	Bk	W	L	Pct.	ShO	Sv	ERA
1992	Pittsfield	A- NYN	26	0	0	18	50	207	39	15	9	0	2	0	3	10	0	44	4	2	2	1	.667	0	6	1.62
1993	St. Lucie	A+ NYN	40	0	0	18	47.1	201	53	13	10	0	4	1	3	12	2	31	0	1	4	3	.571	0	2	1.90
1994	Binghamton	AA NYN	19	0	0	2	30.1	140	35	23	20	2	1	3	7	9	0	24	0	0	0	2	.000	0	0	5.93
	St. Lucie	A+ NYN	27	0	0	16	41.2	165	31	9	8	2	1	0	1	15	3	31	1	0	5	4	.556	0	3	1.73
1995	Norfolk	AAA NYN	4	0	0	4	4.1	18	7	2	1	0	0	0	0	0	0	2	0	0	0	0	.000	0	1	2.08
	Binghamton	AA NYN	51	1	0	16	83.2	348	90	35	27	7	2	3	5	22	5	36	0	4	4	3	.571	0	2	2.90
1996	Binghamton	AA NYN	51	0	0	17	75.1	332	86	41	35	7	5	2	3	22	3	43	2	0	5	4	.556	0	1	4.18
5 Min. YEARS			218	1	0	91	332.2	1411	341	138	110	18	15	9	22	90	13	211	7	7	20	17	.541	0	15	2.98

Brad Fullmer

Bats: Left **Throws:** Right **Pos:** OF **Ht:** 6'1" **Wt:** 185 **Born:** 1/17/75 **Age:** 22

							BATTING										BASERUNNING				PERCENTAGES		
Year	Team	Lg Org	G	AB	H	2B	3B	HR	TB	R	RBI	TBB	IBB	SO	HBP	SH	SF	SB	CS	SB%	GDP	Avg	OBP	SLG
1995	Albany	A Mon	123	468	151	38	4	8	221	69	67	36	4	33	17	0	6	10	10	.50	9	.323	.387	.472
1996	W. Palm Bch	A+ Mon	102	380	115	29	1	5	161	52	63	32	2	43	11	0	8	4	6	.40	9	.303	.367	.424
	Harrisburg	AA Mon	24	98	27	4	1	4	45	11	14	3	0	8	2	0	0	0	0	.00	3	.276	.311	.459
2 Min. YEARS			249	946	293	71	6	17	427	132	144	71	6	84	30	0	14	14	16	.47	21	.310	.371	.451

Eddy Gaillard

Pitches: Right **Bats:** Right **Pos:** P **Ht:** 6'1" **Wt:** 180 **Born:** 8/13/70 **Age:** 26

			HOW MUCH HE PITCHED						WHAT HE GAVE UP												THE RESULTS				
Year	Team	Lg Org	G	GS	CG	GF	IP	BFP	H	R	ER	HR	SH	SF	HB	TBB	IBB	SO	WP	Bk	W	L	Pct.	ShO	Sv	ERA
1993	Niagara Fal	A- Det	3	3	0	0	14.2	63	15	6	6	0	0	0	0	4	0	12	0	0	1	2	.333	0	0	3.68
	Fayettevlle	A Det	11	11	0	0	61.2	261	64	30	28	8	2	0	4	20	0	41	1	1	5	2	.714	0	0	4.09
1994	Lakeland	A+ Det	30	9	0	8	92	389	82	37	29	3	1	2	10	29	0	51	3	1	6	1	.857	0	2	2.84
1995	Jacksonvlle	AA Det	8	0	0	2	8	42	11	5	5	0	2	1	0	5	1	4	0	0	0	1	.000	0	0	5.63
	Lakeland	A+ Det	51	0	0	40	63	269	59	18	13	1	3	4	0	23	3	55	2	1	2	5	.286	0	25	1.86

				HOW MUCH HE PITCHED						WHAT HE GAVE UP												THE RESULTS					
Year	Team	Lg	Org	G	GS	CG	GF	IP	BFP	H	R	ER	HR	SH	SF	HB	TBB	IBB	SO	WP	Bk	W	L	Pct.	ShO	Sv	ERA
1996	Jacksonville	AA	Det	56	0	0	24	88	389	82	40	33	8	4	3	5	50	7	76	10	0	9	6	.600	0	1	3.38
4 Min. YEARS				159	23	0	74	327.1	1413	313	136	114	20	12	10	19	131	11	239	16	3	23	17	.575	0	28	3.13

Jay Gainer

Bats: Left **Throws:** Left **Pos:** 1B **Ht:** 6' 0" **Wt:** 188 **Born:** 10/8/66 **Age:** 30

				BATTING															BASERUNNING				PERCENTAGES		
Year	Team	Lg	Org	G	AB	H	2B	3B	HR	TB	R	RBI	TBB	IBB	SO	HBP	SH	SF	SB	CS	SB%	GDP	Avg	OBP	SLG
1990	Spokane	A-	SD	74	281	100	21	0	10	151	41	54	31	3	49	5	1	4	4	3	.57	4	.356	.424	.537
1991	High Desert	A+	SD	127	499	131	17	0	32	244	83	120	52	3	105	3	0	16	4	3	.57	8	.263	.326	.489
1992	Wichita	AA	SD	105	376	98	12	1	23	181	57	67	46	6	101	0	1	6	4	2	.67	5	.261	.336	.481
1993	Colo. Sprng	AAA	Col	86	293	86	11	3	10	133	51	74	22	2	70	1	1	4	4	2	.67	6	.294	.341	.454
1994	Colo. Sprng	AAA	Col	94	283	70	13	2	9	114	38	34	25	2	62	0	1	1	2	3	.40	6	.247	.307	.403
1995	Colo. Sprng	AAA	Col	112	358	104	19	1	23	194	57	86	42	9	64	0	0	6	2	3	.40	7	.291	.360	.542
1996	Colo. Sprng	AAA	Col	108	333	78	16	0	14	136	51	49	36	4	71	0	0	3	6	2	.75	9	.234	.306	.408
1993	Colorado	NL		23	41	7	0	0	3	16	4	6	4	0	12	0	0	0	1	1	.50	0	.171	.244	.390
7 Min. YEARS				706	2423	667	109	7	121	1153	378	484	254	29	522	9	4	40	26	18	.59	45	.275	.341	.476

Steve Gajkowski

Pitches: Right **Bats:** Right **Pos:** P **Ht:** 6'2" **Wt:** 200 **Born:** 12/30/69 **Age:** 27

				HOW MUCH HE PITCHED						WHAT HE GAVE UP												THE RESULTS					
Year	Team	Lg	Org	G	GS	CG	GF	IP	BFP	H	R	ER	HR	SH	SF	HB	TBB	IBB	SO	WP	Bk	W	L	Pct.	ShO	Sv	ERA
1990	Burlington	R+	Cle	14	10	1	1	63.2	287	74	34	29	0	0	3	3	23	0	44	0	1	2	6	.250	0	0	4.10
1991	Columbus	A	Cle	3	0	0	2	6	24	3	2	2	0	0	0	0	5	0	5	0	0	0	0	.000	0	0	3.00
	Watertown	A-	Cle	20	4	0	7	48	221	41	36	28	0	1	2	6	32	1	34	7	2	3	3	.500	0	0	5.25
1992	Utica	A-	ChA	29	0	0	26	47	184	33	14	7	1	0	2	1	10	1	38	6	0	3	2	.600	0	14	1.34
1993	Sarasota	A+	ChA	43	0	0	38	69.2	273	52	21	16	1	3	3	4	17	5	45	5	1	3	3	.500	0	15	2.07
	Birmingham	AA	ChA	1	0	0	0	2.1	8	0	0	0	0	0	0	0	0	0	2	0	0	0	0	.000	0	0	0.00
1994	Birmingham	AA	ChA	58	0	0	32	82.1	355	78	35	28	6	6	3	5	26	1	44	2	0	11	5	.688	0	8	3.06
1995	Nashville	AAA	ChA	15	0	0	5	24.2	103	26	15	7	2	0	1	1	8	1	12	1	0	0	1	.000	0	0	2.55
	Birmingham	AA	ChA	50	0	0	19	76.1	333	90	42	31	6	2	1	3	24	2	41	2	0	4	5	.444	0	2	3.66
1996	Nashville	AAA	ChA	49	8	0	17	107.1	472	113	61	47	11	4	5	5	41	5	47	6	0	5	6	.455	0	2	3.94
7 Min. YEARS				282	22	1	147	527.1	2260	510	260	195	27	16	20	28	186	16	312	29	4	31	31	.500	0	41	3.33

Kevin Gallaher

Pitches: Right **Bats:** Right **Pos:** P **Ht:** 6'3" **Wt:** 190 **Born:** 8/1/68 **Age:** 28

				HOW MUCH HE PITCHED						WHAT HE GAVE UP												THE RESULTS					
Year	Team	Lg	Org	G	GS	CG	GF	IP	BFP	H	R	ER	HR	SH	SF	HB	TBB	IBB	SO	WP	Bk	W	L	Pct.	ShO	Sv	ERA
1991	Auburn	A-	Hou	16	8	0	3	48	243	59	48	37	2	3	9	9	37	0	25	6	1	2	5	.286	0	0	6.94
1992	Osceola	A+	Hou	1	1	0	0	6.1	26	2	2	2	1	0	0	0	3	0	5	1	0	0	1	.000	0	0	2.84
	Burlington	A	Hou	20	20	1	0	117	529	108	70	50	5	7	4	9	80	0	89	9	1	6	10	.375	0	0	3.85
1993	Osceola	A+	Hou	21	21	1	0	135	586	132	68	57	7	3	3	4	57	1	93	8	3	7	7	.500	1	0	3.80
	Jackson	AA	Hou	4	4	0	0	24	95	14	7	7	3	1	2	2	10	0	30	6	0	0	2	.000	0	0	2.63
1994	Jackson	AA	Hou	18	18	0	0	106	468	88	57	46	5	1	2	8	67	1	112	13	0	6	6	.500	0	0	3.91
	Tucson	AAA	Hou	9	9	2	0	53.2	240	55	35	32	5	3	2	3	25	0	58	3	0	3	4	.429	0	0	5.37
1995	Jackson	AA	Hou	6	6	1	0	42.1	179	31	18	16	1	3	1	0	23	1	28	4	0	2	2	.500	0	0	3.40
	Tucson	AAA	Hou	3	3	0	0	14	70	19	11	10	1	0	2	2	9	0	11	2	0	1	1	.500	0	0	6.43
	Kissimmee	A+	Hou	16	16	1	0	73.2	335	58	40	37	2	3	3	5	56	1	60	8	0	4	4	.500	0	0	4.52
1996	Tucson	AAA	Hou	35	3	0	6	87	392	88	50	45	5	5	6	3	45	3	81	11	1	4	2	.667	0	1	4.66
	Toledo	AAA	Det	2	0	0	0	3	22	9	7	7	0	0	0	0	4	1	4	1	0	0	0	.000	0	0	21.00
6 Min. YEARS				151	109	6	9	710	3185	663	413	346	37	29	34	45	416	8	596	72	6	35	44	.443	1	1	4.39

Javier Gamboa

Pitches: Right **Bats:** Right **Pos:** P **Ht:** 6'1" **Wt:** 185 **Born:** 3/17/74 **Age:** 23

				HOW MUCH HE PITCHED						WHAT HE GAVE UP												THE RESULTS					
Year	Team	Lg	Org	G	GS	CG	GF	IP	BFP	H	R	ER	HR	SH	SF	HB	TBB	IBB	SO	WP	Bk	W	L	Pct.	ShO	Sv	ERA
1994	Eugene	A-	KC	16	14	0	1	62	277	58	45	40	8	1	2	7	29	0	62	6	2	0	5	.000	0	0	5.81
1995	Wilmington	A+	KC	8	8	0	0	49	202	42	23	22	6	3	0	1	13	0	33	2	0	3	4	.429	0	0	4.04
	Springfield	A	KC	27	27	1	0	154.2	631	125	68	59	16	6	2	1	45	0	99	6	0	9	10	.474	0	0	3.43
1996	Wilmington	A+	KC	6	6	0	0	34.1	138	36	12	12	3	1	0	1	2	0	24	1	0	3	1	.750	0	0	3.15
	Wichita	AA	KC	15	15	0	0	91	414	118	68	60	19	3	5	2	33	0	39	2	0	5	5	.500	0	0	5.93
3 Min. YEARS				72	70	1	1	391	1662	379	216	193	52	14	9	12	122	0	257	17	2	20	25	.444	0	0	4.44

Chris Gambs

Pitches: Right **Bats:** Right **Pos:** P **Ht:** 6'2" **Wt:** 210 **Born:** 10/26/73 **Age:** 23

				HOW MUCH HE PITCHED						WHAT HE GAVE UP												THE RESULTS					
Year	Team	Lg	Org	G	GS	CG	GF	IP	BFP	H	R	ER	HR	SH	SF	HB	TBB	IBB	SO	WP	Bk	W	L	Pct.	ShO	Sv	ERA
1991	Giants	R	SF	13	8	0	0	47.1	241	65	51	44	1	2	3	2	34	1	36	4	3	1	5	.167	0	0	8.37
1992	Clinton	A	SF	26	26	0	0	134.1	623	119	101	84	7	4	6	8	101	1	98	18	0	5	10	.333	0	0	5.63
1993	Clinton	A	SF	21	21	0	0	112	493	100	56	50	12	2	1	2	76	2	82	8	1	9	5	.643	0	0	4.02
1994	Clinton	A	SF	13	4	0	1	33.1	157	37	27	22	3	1	3	0	29	1	21	3	0	0	2	.000	0	0	5.94
	San Jose	A+	SF	4	0	0	2	5	26	6	9	8	1	1	0	0	6	0	4	0	0	0	0	.000	0	0	14.40
1995	Batavia	A-	Phi	7	7	0	0	34.1	148	31	21	21	0	1	1	0	22	0	21	4	0	3	2	.600	0	0	5.50

				HOW MUCH HE PITCHED						WHAT HE GAVE UP												THE RESULTS					
Year	Team	Lg	Org	G	GS	CG	GF	IP	BFP	H	R	ER	HR	SH	SF	HB	TBB	IBB	SO	WP	Bk	W	L	Pct.	ShO	Sv	ERA
	High Desert	A+	Bal	3	0	0	2	3	16	4	4	4	0	0	0	0	4	0	1	0	0	0	0	.000	0	0	12.00
	Piedmont	A	Phi	19	7	0	4	57	259	59	42	40	2	1	3	1	40	0	37	7	0	3	2	.600	0	0	6.32
1996	Orlando	AA	ChN	2	0	0	1	5	23	3	3	3	0	0	1	0	5	0	3	1	0	0	0	.000	0	0	5.40
	Daytona	A+	ChN	13	0	0	5	23	115	28	22	16	2	0	1	1	21	1	17	1	0	0	2	.000	0	0	6.26
6 Min. YEARS				121	73	0	15	454.1	2101	452	336	292	28	12	19	14	338	6	320	46	4	21	28	.429	0	0	5.78

Joe Ganote

Pitches: Right **Bats:** Right **Pos:** P **Ht:** 6'1" **Wt:** 185 **Born:** 1/22/68 **Age:** 29

				HOW MUCH HE PITCHED						WHAT HE GAVE UP												THE RESULTS					
Year	Team	Lg	Org	G	GS	CG	GF	IP	BFP	H	R	ER	HR	SH	SF	HB	TBB	IBB	SO	WP	Bk	W	L	Pct.	ShO	Sv	ERA
1990	St. Cathrns	A-	Tor	18	0	0	12	29.2	120	26	9	9	0	1	1	3	7	0	33	2	2	3	0	1.000	0	4	2.73
1991	Myrtle Bch	A	Tor	20	20	3	0	118.1	491	104	61	45	9	1	3	2	46	0	127	10	2	8	6	.571	1	0	3.42
	Dunedin	A+	Tor	4	4	1	0	26.1	110	26	10	9	1	3	2	1	9	0	13	0	0	2	1	.667	1	0	3.08
1992	Dunedin	A+	Tor	23	21	4	0	140.2	604	148	72	62	10	6	9	10	40	1	101	9	1	6	10	.375	1	0	3.97
1993	Knoxville	AA	Tor	33	19	1	6	138.2	589	150	70	64	11	3	10	5	52	0	88	13	0	8	6	.571	0	1	4.15
1994	Knoxville	AA	Tor	11	11	3	0	66	273	53	29	20	4	4	2	6	24	0	43	7	0	4	6	.400	1	0	2.73
	Syracuse	AAA	Tor	18	14	1	1	79	351	79	41	36	6	2	1	2	41	0	55	9	0	3	7	.300	0	0	4.10
1995	Syracuse	AAA	Tor	3	3	0	0	10.2	51	16	15	12	3	0	1	0	4	0	3	0	0	0	2	.000	0	0	10.13
	El Paso	AA	Mil	12	7	0	1	50.1	207	40	18	9	3	2	1	3	16	0	39	4	0	5	1	.833	0	1	1.61
	New Orleans	AAA	Mil	29	23	2	2	142.2	606	144	68	52	12	7	4	9	41	2	98	10	0	12	7	.632	1	1	3.28
1996	El Paso	AA	Mil	1	1	0	0	4.2	23	9	3	3	0	0	0	0	1	0	5	0	0	0	0	.000	0	0	5.79
	New Orleans	AAA	Mil	41	12	0	9	109.1	484	121	77	63	17	7	4	6	44	8	65	6	1	6	11	.353	0	0	5.19
7 Min. YEARS				213	135	15	31	916.1	3909	916	473	384	76	36	38	47	325	11	670	70	6	57	57	.500	5	7	3.77

Al Garcia

Pitches: Right **Bats:** Both **Pos:** P **Ht:** 6'2" **Wt:** 175 **Born:** 6/11/74 **Age:** 23

				HOW MUCH HE PITCHED						WHAT HE GAVE UP												THE RESULTS					
Year	Team	Lg	Org	G	GS	CG	GF	IP	BFP	H	R	ER	HR	SH	SF	HB	TBB	IBB	SO	WP	Bk	W	L	Pct.	ShO	Sv	ERA
1993	Cubs	R	ChN	9	7	0	2	49.2	210	47	26	18	0	5	3	4	7	0	33	3	5	2	5	.286	0	0	3.26
	Huntington	R+	ChN	3	3	0	0	20	86	23	11	11	2	0	2	2	1	0	11	0	0	1	2	.333	0	0	4.95
1994	Huntington	R+	ChN	8	4	0	3	30	129	35	23	15	3	0	0	1	6	0	28	0	0	1	4	.200	0	1	4.50
	Williamsprt	A-	ChN	8	7	3	1	45.1	190	41	16	15	1	1	3	1	17	1	39	4	1	3	3	.500	1	1	2.98
1995	Rockford	A	ChN	27	27	1	0	177	755	176	94	74	13	4	4	15	43	0	120	10	0	14	9	.609	1	0	3.76
1996	Daytona	A+	ChN	7	7	0	0	47	187	48	20	15	1	3	1	2	5	0	28	2	0	4	1	.800	0	0	2.87
	Orlando	AA	ChN	23	16	1	3	118.2	528	149	71	64	17	6	5	7	32	1	66	4	0	6	7	.462	0	0	4.85
4 Min. YEARS				85	71	5	9	487.2	2085	519	261	212	37	19	18	32	111	2	325	23	6	31	31	.500	2	2	3.91

Frank Garcia

Pitches: Right **Bats:** Right **Pos:** P **Ht:** 5'11" **Wt:** 170 **Born:** 3/5/74 **Age:** 23

				HOW MUCH HE PITCHED						WHAT HE GAVE UP												THE RESULTS					
Year	Team	Lg	Org	G	GS	CG	GF	IP	BFP	H	R	ER	HR	SH	SF	HB	TBB	IBB	SO	WP	Bk	W	L	Pct.	ShO	Sv	ERA
1994	Cardinals	R	StL	27	0	0	25	29.2	116	16	7	4	0	1	0	3	7	0	39	0	0	1	1	.500	0	18	1.21
1995	St. Pete	A+	StL	16	0	0	8	16.2	98	27	22	19	1	0	1	1	18	0	8	3	0	0	1	.000	0	1	10.26
	Savannah	A	StL	50	0	0	40	53.2	254	53	39	32	4	0	2	3	33	0	49	11	0	0	4	.000	0	25	5.37
1996	St. Pete	A+	StL	28	0	0	5	32	147	35	11	9	1	1	0	1	18	2	24	2	0	2	0	1.000	0	0	2.53
	Arkansas	AA	StL	11	0	0	2	19.1	84	20	11	8	1	1	1	1	7	0	12	1	0	0	0	.000	0	0	3.72
3 Min. YEARS				132	0	0	80	151.1	699	151	90	72	7	3	4	9	83	2	132	17	0	3	6	.333	0	44	4.28

Guillermo Garcia

Bats: Right **Throws:** Right **Pos:** C **Ht:** 6'3" **Wt:** 190 **Born:** 4/4/72 **Age:** 25

				BATTING														BASERUNNING				PERCENTAGES		
Year	Team	Lg	Org	G	AB	H	2B	3B	HR	TB	R	RBI	TBB	IBB	SO	HBP	SH	SF	SB	CS	SB%	GDP	Avg	OBP	SLG
1990	Mets	R	NYN	42	136	25	1	2	0	30	9	6	7	1	34	1	2	1	1	1	.50	2	.184	.228	.221
1991	Kingsport	R+	NYN	15	33	8	1	1	0	11	9	2	4	0	4	0	0	0	0	0	.00	1	.242	.324	.333
	Pittsfield	A-	NYN	45	157	43	13	2	0	60	22	24	15	0	38	1	3	3	4	1	.80	5	.274	.335	.382
1992	Pittsfield	A-	NYN	73	272	54	11	1	2	73	36	26	20	0	52	2	0	3	3	4	.43	5	.199	.256	.268
1993	Capital Cty	A	NYN	119	429	124	28	2	3	165	64	72	49	1	60	10	1	3	10	8	.56	11	.289	.373	.385
1994	St. Lucie	A+	NYN	55	203	48	9	1	1	62	22	23	13	1	24	3	2	0	0	2	.00	6	.236	.292	.305
1995	Winston-Sal	A+	Cin	78	245	58	10	2	3	81	26	29	28	0	32	1	2	2	2	2	.50	7	.237	.315	.331
1996	Indianapols	AAA	Cin	16	47	12	2	0	0	14	4	0	2	2	6	0	0	0	0	0	.00	5	.255	.286	.298
	Chattanooga	AA	Cin	60	203	64	12	0	6	94	25	36	12	2	32	1	2	1	3	3	.50	3	.315	.355	.463
7 Min. YEARS				503	1725	436	87	11	15	590	217	218	150	7	282	19	12	13	23	21	.52	45	.253	.317	.342

Jose Garcia

Pitches: Right **Bats:** Right **Pos:** P **Ht:** 6'3" **Wt:** 146 **Born:** 6/12/72 **Age:** 25

				HOW MUCH HE PITCHED						WHAT HE GAVE UP												THE RESULTS					
Year	Team	Lg	Org	G	GS	CG	GF	IP	BFP	H	R	ER	HR	SH	SF	HB	TBB	IBB	SO	WP	Bk	W	L	Pct.	ShO	Sv	ERA
1993	Bakersfield	A+	LA	27	0	0	22	29	142	47	23	22	6	1	4	0	12	1	25	3	2	0	3	.000	0	4	6.83
	Yakima	A-	LA	36	0	0	30	44.2	188	40	14	12	1	0	2	3	19	2	19	2	0	2	2	.500	0	5	2.42
1994	Vero Beach	A+	LA	20	0	0	13	32.2	129	32	7	5	0	1	0	0	2	0	24	2	1	3	1	.750	0	4	1.38
	San Antonio	AA	LA	7	0	0	7	11	40	7	2	2	0	1	1	0	6	2	8	0	1	2	0	1.000	0	3	1.64
	Albuquerque	AAA	LA	37	0	0	7	57.2	258	66	39	33	6	2	3	3	26	5	38	2	0	4	1	.800	0	0	5.15

		HOW MUCH HE PITCHED						WHAT HE GAVE UP												THE RESULTS					
Year Team	Lg Org	G	GS	CG	GF	IP	BFP	H	R	ER	HR	SH	SF	HB	TBB	IBB	SO	WP	Bk	W	L	Pct.	ShO	Sv	ERA
1995 Albuquerque	AAA LA	11	0	0	4	15.2	73	19	11	11	3	2	4	0	7	1	10	0	0	1	3	.250	0	0	6.32
San Antonio	AA LA	49	0	0	19	73.2	315	69	43	37	7	6	8	6	31	1	46	6	2	3	9	.250	0	2	4.52
1996 San Antonio	AA LA	8	0	0	5	11.1	38	4	0	0	0	1	0	0	0	0	8	1	0	2	0	1.000	0	2	0.00
Albuquerque	AAA LA	44	0	0	10	78.1	361	97	49	41	10	4	1	2	40	10	34	2	0	6	1	.857	0	0	4.71
4 Min. YEARS		239	0	0	117	354	1544	381	188	163	33	18	23	14	143	22	212	18	6	23	20	.535	0	20	4.14

Luis Garcia

Bats: Right **Throws:** Right **Pos:** SS **Ht:** 6'0" **Wt:** 174 **Born:** 5/20/75 **Age:** 22

		BATTING															BASERUNNING				PERCENTAGES		
Year Team	Lg Org	G	AB	H	2B	3B	HR	TB	R	RBI	TBB	IBB	SO	HBP	SH	SF	SB	CS	SB%	GDP	Avg	OBP	SLG
1993 Bristol	R+ Det	24	57	12	1	0	1	16	7	7	3	0	11	0	1	0	3	1	.75	1	.211	.250	.281
1994 Jamestown	A- Det	67	239	47	8	2	1	62	21	19	8	0	48	1	6	3	6	9	.40	4	.197	.223	.259
1995 Lakeland	A+ Det	102	361	101	10	4	2	125	39	35	8	0	42	1	4	4	9	10	.47	6	.280	.294	.346
Jacksonvlle	AA Det	17	47	13	0	0	0	13	6	5	1	0	8	1	0	0	2	1	.67	0	.277	.306	.277
1996 Jacksonvlle	AA Det	131	522	128	22	4	9	185	68	46	12	1	90	2	7	2	15	12	.56	9	.245	.264	.354
4 Min. YEARS		341	1226	301	41	10	13	401	141	112	32	1	199	5	18	9	35	33	.51	20	.246	.266	.327

Omar Garcia

Bats: Right **Throws:** Right **Pos:** 1B **Ht:** 6'0" **Wt:** 192 **Born:** 11/16/71 **Age:** 25

		BATTING															BASERUNNING				PERCENTAGES		
Year Team	Lg Org	G	AB	H	2B	3B	HR	TB	R	RBI	TBB	IBB	SO	HBP	SH	SF	SB	CS	SB%	GDP	Avg	OBP	SLG
1989 Mets	R NYN	32	98	25	3	1	0	30	15	8	10	0	22	1	0	1	6	2	.75	1	.255	.327	.306
1990 Kingsport	R+ NYN	67	246	82	15	2	6	119	42	36	24	1	24	0	0	2	10	5	.67	3	.333	.390	.484
1991 Columbia	A NYN	108	394	99	11	4	4	130	63	50	31	0	55	0	1	3	12	5	.71	9	.251	.304	.330
1992 Columbia	A NYN	126	469	136	18	5	3	173	66	70	55	1	37	1	0	11	35	11	.76	11	.290	.358	.369
1993 St. Lucie	A+ NYN	129	485	156	17	7	3	196	73	76	57	2	47	2	2	5	25	8	.76	14	.322	.392	.404
1994 Binghamton	AA NYN	64	246	88	14	4	5	125	38	42	22	1	31	1	0	4	3	5	.38	3	.358	.407	.508
Norfolk	AAA NYN	67	227	55	9	2	0	68	28	28	19	1	35	0	1	5	7	4	.64	6	.242	.295	.300
1995 Norfolk	AAA NYN	115	430	133	21	7	3	177	55	64	21	3	58	0	1	7	3	4	.43	13	.309	.336	.412
Binghamton	AA NYN	5	19	10	1	1	0	13	4	1	4	1	0	0	0	0	0	0	.00	1	.526	.609	.684
1996 Richmond	AAA Atl	93	311	82	15	1	4	111	36	35	9	1	32	1	2	2	4	4	.50	6	.264	.285	.357
8 Min. YEARS		806	2925	866	124	34	28	1142	420	410	252	11	341	6	7	40	105	48	.69	67	.296	.349	.390

Vicente Garcia

Bats: Right **Throws:** Right **Pos:** 2B **Ht:** 6'0" **Wt:** 170 **Born:** 2/14/75 **Age:** 22

		BATTING															BASERUNNING				PERCENTAGES		
Year Team	Lg Org	G	AB	H	2B	3B	HR	TB	R	RBI	TBB	IBB	SO	HBP	SH	SF	SB	CS	SB%	GDP	Avg	OBP	SLG
1993 Rockies	R Col	38	137	41	10	0	0	51	13	13	18	0	27	1	0	0	12	2	.86	2	.299	.385	.372
1994 Asheville	A Col	123	397	87	22	1	4	123	41	44	35	0	56	5	6	3	5	10	.33	9	.219	.289	.310
1995 Salem	A+ Col	119	457	111	26	1	10	169	62	41	53	3	73	1	5	2	5	0	1.00	10	.243	.322	.370
1996 New Haven	AA Col	87	295	63	10	1	3	84	32	18	28	1	43	5	6	2	1	2	.33	7	.214	.291	.285
4 Min. YEARS		367	1286	302	68	3	17	427	148	116	134	4	199	12	17	7	23	14	.62	28	.235	.311	.332

Mike Gardiner

Pitches: Right **Bats:** Both **Pos:** P **Ht:** 6' 0" **Wt:** 200 **Born:** 10/19/65 **Age:** 31

		HOW MUCH HE PITCHED						WHAT HE GAVE UP												THE RESULTS					
Year Team	Lg Org	G	GS	CG	GF	IP	BFP	H	R	ER	HR	SH	SF	HB	TBB	IBB	SO	WP	Bk	W	L	Pct.	ShO	Sv	ERA
1987 Bellingham	A- Sea	2	1	0	0	10	35	6	0	0	0	0	0	0	1	0	11	0	0	2	0	1.000	0	0	0.00
Wausau	A Sea	13	13	2	0	81	368	91	54	47	9	2	5	3	33	2	80	3	1	3	5	.375	1	0	5.22
1988 Wausau	A Sea	11	6	0	4	31.1	132	31	16	11	1	0	0	1	13	0	24	1	1	2	1	.667	0	1	3.16
1989 Wausau	A Sea	15	1	0	11	30.1	120	21	5	2	0	2	0	1	11	0	48	0	0	4	0	1.000	0	7	0.59
Williamsprt	AA Sea	30	3	1	14	63.1	274	54	25	20	6	1	3	1	32	6	60	4	1	4	6	.400	0	2	2.84
1990 Williamsprt	AA Sea	26	26	5	0	179.2	697	136	47	38	8	4	3	1	29	1	149	4	1	12	8	.600	1	0	1.90
1991 Pawtucket	AAA Bos	8	8	2	0	57.2	220	39	16	15	2	3	2	1	11	0	42	0	0	7	1	.875	1	0	2.34
1992 Pawtucket	AAA Bos	5	5	2	0	32.2	138	32	14	12	3	0	0	0	9	0	37	0	0	1	3	.250	0	0	3.31
1993 Ottawa	AAA Mon	5	5	0	0	25	101	17	8	6	2	1	2	0	9	0	25	1	0	1	1	.500	0	0	2.16
Toledo	AAA Det	4	0	0	2	5	22	6	3	3	0	0	0	0	2	0	10	2	0	0	1	.000	0	1	5.40
1995 Toledo	AAA Det	11	1	0	4	16.1	77	19	8	8	2	1	1	0	13	0	10	1	0	0	1	.000	0	0	4.41
1996 Norfolk	AAA NYN	24	24	2	0	146	590	125	58	52	18	3	5	2	38	3	125	3	0	13	3	.813	2	0	3.21
1990 Seattle	AL	5	3	0	1	12.2	66	22	17	15	1	0	1	2	5	0	6	0	0	0	2	.000	0	0	10.66
1991 Boston	AL	22	22	0	0	130	562	140	79	70	18	1	3	0	47	2	91	1	0	9	10	.474	0	0	4.85
1992 Boston	AL	28	18	0	3	130.2	566	126	78	69	12	3	5	2	58	2	79	8	0	4	10	.286	0	0	4.75
1993 Montreal	NL	24	2	0	3	38	173	40	28	22	3	1	3	1	19	2	21	0	0	2	3	.400	0	0	5.21
Detroit	AL	10	0	0	1	11.1	51	12	5	5	0	1	0	0	7	1	4	2	0	0	0	.000	0	0	3.97
1994 Detroit	AL	38	1	0	14	58.2	254	53	35	27	10	2	2	0	23	5	31	1	0	2	2	.500	0	5	4.14
1995 Detroit	AL	9	0	0	1	12.1	66	27	20	20	5	3	2	0	2	1	7	1	0	0	0	.000	0	0	14.59
9 Min. YEARS		154	93	14	35	678.1	2774	577	254	214	51	17	21	10	201	12	621	19	4	49	30	.620	5	11	2.84
6 Maj. YEARS		136	46	0	23	393.2	1738	420	262	228	49	11	16	5	161	13	239	13	0	17	27	.386	0	5	5.21

Sean Gavaghan

Pitches: Right **Bats:** Right **Pos:** P **Ht:** 6'1" **Wt:** 194 **Born:** 12/19/69 **Age:** 27

				HOW MUCH HE PITCHED						WHAT HE GAVE UP												THE RESULTS					
Year	Team	Lg	Org	G	GS	CG	GF	IP	BFP	H	R	ER	HR	SH	SF	HB	TBB	IBB	SO	WP	Bk	W	L	Pct.	ShO	Sv	ERA
1992	Kenosha	A	Min	20	6	0	8	57	243	63	22	13	2	5	4	2	18	1	39	3	3	2	3	.400	0	1	2.05
1993	Fort Wayne	A	Min	11	0	0	5	22	89	14	5	3	0	2	0	0	7	0	25	2	1	3	1	.750	0	1	1.23
	Fort Myers	A+	Min	19	0	0	13	31	134	37	10	9	1	1	0	0	8	1	24	2	0	1	3	.250	0	4	2.61
	Nashville	AA	Min	20	1	0	5	36.2	143	21	3	2	0	0	1	4	12	1	30	3	2	4	0	1.000	0	1	0.49
1994	Nashville	AA	Min	56	0	0	35	85	366	59	35	22	5	6	4	1	56	1	63	3	0	5	5	.500	0	13	2.33
1995	New Britain	AA	Min	21	0	0	21	28.2	119	18	10	7	0	2	2	2	10	2	30	0	1	2	1	.667	0	5	2.20
	Salt Lake	AAA	Min	56	0	0	36	76	340	71	42	36	3	8	3	5	41	5	58	3	1	3	5	.375	0	10	4.26
1996	New Britain	AA	Min	28	0	0	16	39	187	42	28	28	5	1	3	4	29	1	44	3	2	2	2	.500	0	6	6.46
	El Paso	AA	Mil	24	0	0	9	37	175	48	27	21	3	3	2	2	15	1	24	0	0	4	1	.800	0	0	5.11
5 Min. YEARS				255	7	0	148	412.1	1796	373	182	141	19	28	19	20	196	13	337	19	10	26	21	.553	0	41	3.08

Dave Geeve

Pitches: Right **Bats:** Right **Pos:** P **Ht:** 6'3" **Wt:** 190 **Born:** 10/19/69 **Age:** 27

				HOW MUCH HE PITCHED						WHAT HE GAVE UP												THE RESULTS					
Year	Team	Lg	Org	G	GS	CG	GF	IP	BFP	H	R	ER	HR	SH	SF	HB	TBB	IBB	SO	WP	Bk	W	L	Pct.	ShO	Sv	ERA
1991	Gastonia	A	Tex	14	14	1	0	79.1	323	74	40	38	7	2	2	1	20	1	69	0	1	6	4	.600	1	0	4.31
1992	Charlotte	A+	Tex	25	24	0	1	139.1	572	138	61	52	8	4	3	6	22	1	97	6	0	8	8	.500	0	0	3.36
1993	Charlotte	A+	Tex	24	23	1	1	132.2	539	141	52	42	7	3	2	3	19	0	80	8	1	11	8	.579	1	0	2.85
1994	Tulsa	AA	Tex	9	8	0	0	53	203	43	14	14	7	0	0	3	10	0	53	0	0	4	2	.667	0	0	2.38
1995	Okla. City	AAA	Tex	10	10	2	0	55.2	249	72	36	35	7	3	5	4	13	1	30	0	2	2	5	.286	0	0	5.66
	Tulsa	AA	Tex	25	24	5	0	149.2	649	180	97	89	23	4	7	6	33	1	68	1	2	5	13	.278	1	0	5.35
1996	Tulsa	AA	Tex	18	17	0	0	82.2	364	105	53	51	12	2	3	2	23	0	60	7	0	7	6	.538	0	0	5.55
6 Min. YEARS				125	120	9	2	692.1	2899	753	353	321	71	18	22	25	140	4	457	22	6	43	46	.483	3	0	4.17

Phil Geisler

Bats: Left **Throws:** Left **Pos:** OF **Ht:** 6'3" **Wt:** 200 **Born:** 10/23/69 **Age:** 27

				BATTING															BASERUNNING				PERCENTAGES		
Year	Team	Lg	Org	G	AB	H	2B	3B	HR	TB	R	RBI	TBB	IBB	SO	HBP	SH	SF	SB	CS	SB%	GDP	Avg	OBP	SLG
1991	Martinsvlle	R+	Phi	32	114	37	5	0	1	45	22	18	23	1	25	1	0	0	1	0	1.00	1	.325	.442	.395
	Spartanburg	A	Phi	36	129	21	3	0	1	27	19	8	14	0	36	0	1	0	0	0	.00	2	.163	.245	.209
1992	Clearwater	A+	Phi	120	400	87	10	3	6	121	39	33	41	1	88	4	1	2	4	9	.31	8	.218	.295	.303
1993	Clearwater	A+	Phi	87	344	105	23	4	15	181	72	62	29	3	70	6	2	1	4	5	.44	5	.305	.368	.526
	Reading	AA	Phi	48	178	48	14	1	3	73	25	14	17	2	50	3	1	0	4	2	.67	3	.270	.343	.410
1994	Scranton-WB	AAA	Phi	54	183	36	5	1	0	43	14	11	18	3	48	1	1	2	2	2	.50	3	.197	.270	.235
	Reading	AA	Phi	74	254	70	12	1	7	105	32	40	24	5	55	2	0	2	4	7	.36	5	.276	.340	.413
1995	Reading	AA	Phi	76	272	63	10	3	2	85	27	35	21	3	65	4	0	2	4	2	.67	5	.232	.294	.313
	Scranton-WB	AAA	Phi	20	43	8	5	0	1	16	2	7	2	0	13	0	1	0	0	0	.00	2	.186	.222	.372
1996	Binghamton	AA	NYN	107	355	89	17	2	11	143	47	59	33	6	96	3	1	5	5	4	.56	7	.251	.316	.403
6 Min. YEARS				654	2272	564	104	15	47	839	299	287	222	24	546	24	8	14	28	31	.47	41	.248	.320	.369

Scott Gentile

Pitches: Right **Bats:** Right **Pos:** P **Ht:** 5'11" **Wt:** 210 **Born:** 12/21/70 **Age:** 26

				HOW MUCH HE PITCHED						WHAT HE GAVE UP												THE RESULTS					
Year	Team	Lg	Org	G	GS	CG	GF	IP	BFP	H	R	ER	HR	SH	SF	HB	TBB	IBB	SO	WP	Bk	W	L	Pct.	ShO	Sv	ERA
1992	Jamestown	A-	Mon	13	13	0	0	62.2	282	59	32	27	3	0	0	6	34	0	44	5	0	4	4	.500	0	0	3.88
1993	W. Palm Bch	A+	Mon	25	25	0	0	138.1	592	132	72	62	8	4	5	7	54	0	108	6	0	8	9	.471	0	0	4.03
1994	Harrisburg	AA	Mon	6	2	0	1	10.1	72	16	21	20	1	1	0	0	25	0	14	6	0	0	1	.000	0	0	17.42
	W. Palm Bch	A+	Mon	53	1	0	40	65.1	255	44	16	14	0	3	0	1	19	0	90	4	2	5	2	.714	0	26	1.93
1995	Harrisburg	AA	Mon	37	0	0	26	49.2	202	36	19	19	3	2	1	4	15	2	48	1	0	2	2	.500	0	11	3.44
1996	Expos	R	Mon	5	1	0	2	7.1	30	5	4	4	0	0	0	0	4	0	5	0	1	1	1	.500	0	1	4.91
	W. Palm Bch	A+	Mon	7	0	0	5	10	39	8	0	0	0	1	0	0	2	0	5	1	0	0	0	.000	0	1	0.00
	Harrisburg	AA	Mon	15	0	0	6	24	100	14	8	7	2	2	0	3	14	1	23	0	0	2	2	.500	0	1	2.63
5 Min. YEARS				161	42	0	80	367.2	1572	314	172	153	17	13	6	21	167	3	337	23	3	22	21	.512	0	40	3.75

Ray Giannelli

Bats: Left **Throws:** Right **Pos:** 3B **Ht:** 6' 0" **Wt:** 195 **Born:** 2/5/66 **Age:** 31

				BATTING															BASERUNNING				PERCENTAGES		
Year	Team	Lg	Org	G	AB	H	2B	3B	HR	TB	R	RBI	TBB	IBB	SO	HBP	SH	SF	SB	CS	SB%	GDP	Avg	OBP	SLG
1988	Medicne Hat	R+	Tor	47	123	30	8	3	4	56	17	28	19	2	22	0	1	3	0	0	.00	6	.244	.338	.455
1989	Myrtle Bch	A	Tor	127	458	138	17	1	18	211	76	84	78	4	53	5	1	8	2	6	.25	10	.301	.403	.461
1990	Dunedin	A+	Tor	118	416	120	18	1	18	194	64	57	66	7	56	1	1	3	4	8	.33	12	.288	.385	.466
1991	Knoxville	AA	Tor	112	362	100	14	3	7	141	53	37	64	6	66	2	5	2	8	5	.62	6	.276	.386	.390
1992	Syracuse	AAA	Tor	84	249	57	9	2	5	85	23	22	48	2	44	0	0	2	2	2	.50	4	.229	.351	.341
1993	Syracuse	AAA	Tor	127	411	104	18	4	11	163	51	42	38	1	79	2	2	5	1	6	.14	8	.253	.316	.397
1994	Syracuse	AAA	Tor	114	327	94	19	1	10	145	43	51	48	2	77	2	0	3	0	1	.00	5	.287	.379	.443
1995	Louisville	AAA	StL	119	390	115	19	1	16	184	56	70	44	5	85	3	0	4	3	7	.30	6	.295	.367	.472
1996	Salt Lake	AAA	Min	10	31	8	1	0	0	9	2	4	2	0	8	1	0	1	0	0	.00	0	.258	.314	.290
	Colo. Sprng	AAA	Col	44	117	26	8	0	2	40	14	13	23	1	19	1	0	0	1	2	.33	3	.222	.355	.342
1991	Toronto	AL		9	24	4	1	0	0	5	2	0	5	0	9	0	0	0	1	0	1.00	0	.167	.310	.208
1995	St. Louis	NL		9	11	1	0	0	0	1	0	0	3	0	4	0	0	0	0	0	.00	0	.091	.286	.091
9 Min. YEARS				902	2884	792	131	16	91	1228	399	408	430	30	509	17	10	31	21	37	.36	60	.275	.369	.426

Year Team	Lg Org	G	AB	H	2B	3B	HR	TB	R	RBI	TBB	IBB	SO	HBP	SH	SF	SB	CS	SB%	GDP	Avg	OBP	SLG
		BATTING															BASERUNNING				PERCENTAGES		
2 Maj. YEARS		18	35	5	1	0	0	6	2	0	8	0	13	0	0	0	1	0	1.00	0	.143	.302	.171

Derrick Gibson

Bats: Right **Throws:** Right **Pos:** OF **Ht:** 6'2" **Wt:** 227 **Born:** 2/5/75 **Age:** 22

Year Team	Lg Org	G	AB	H	2B	3B	HR	TB	R	RBI	TBB	IBB	SO	HBP	SH	SF	SB	CS	SB%	GDP	Avg	OBP	SLG
		BATTING															BASERUNNING				PERCENTAGES		
1993 Rockies	R Col	34	119	18	2	2	0	24	13	10	5	0	55	3	0	1	3	0	1.00	1	.151	.203	.202
1994 Bend	A- Col	73	284	75	19	5	12	140	47	57	29	5	102	9	0	1	14	4	.78	4	.264	.350	.493
1995 Asheville	A Col	135	506	148	16	10	32	280	91	115	29	5	136	19	1	6	31	13	.70	10	.292	.350	.553
1996 New Haven	AA Col	122	449	115	21	4	15	189	58	62	31	1	125	8	1	4	3	12	.20	15	.256	.313	.421
4 Min. YEARS		364	1358	356	58	21	59	633	209	244	94	11	418	39	2	12	51	29	.64	30	.262	.325	.466

Shawn Gilbert

Bats: Right **Throws:** Right **Pos:** 3B-2B **Ht:** 5'9" **Wt:** 170 **Born:** 3/12/65 **Age:** 32

Year Team	Lg Org	G	AB	H	2B	3B	HR	TB	R	RBI	TBB	IBB	SO	HBP	SH	SF	SB	CS	SB%	GDP	Avg	OBP	SLG
		BATTING															BASERUNNING				PERCENTAGES		
1987 Visalia	A+ Min	82	272	61	5	0	5	81	39	27	34	0	59	7	4	4	6	4	.60	8	.224	.322	.298
1988 Visalia	A+ Min	14	43	16	3	2	0	23	10	8	10	0	7	1	0	0	1	1	.50	0	.372	.500	.535
Kenosha	A Min	108	402	112	21	2	3	146	80	44	63	2	61	2	0	5	49	10	.83	6	.279	.375	.363
1989 Visalia	A+ Min	125	453	113	17	1	2	138	52	43	54	1	70	3	6	3	42	16	.72	11	.249	.331	.305
1990 Orlando	AA Min	123	433	110	18	2	4	144	68	44	61	0	69	5	4	3	31	9	.78	10	.254	.351	.333
1991 Orlando	AA Min	138	529	135	12	5	3	166	69	38	53	1	70	11	6	6	43	19	.69	18	.255	.332	.314
1992 Portland	AAA Min	138	444	109	17	2	3	139	60	52	36	2	55	4	5	2	31	8	.79	10	.245	.307	.313
1993 Nashville	AAA ChA	104	278	63	17	2	0	84	28	17	12	0	41	2	2	1	6	2	.75	4	.227	.263	.302
1994 Scranton-WB	AAA Phi	141	547	139	33	4	7	201	81	52	66	3	86	7	3	3	20	15	.57	9	.254	.340	.367
1995 Scranton-WB	AAA Phi	136	536	141	26	2	2	177	84	42	64	0	102	6	4	4	16	11	.59	8	.263	.346	.330
1996 Norfolk	AAA NYN	131	493	126	28	1	9	183	76	50	46	0	97	5	14	4	17	9	.65	5	.256	.323	.371
10 Min. YEARS		1240	4430	1125	197	23	38	1482	647	417	499	9	717	53	48	35	262	104	.72	89	.254	.334	.335

Charles Gipson

Bats: Right **Throws:** Right **Pos:** OF-SS **Ht:** 6'2" **Wt:** 180 **Born:** 12/16/72 **Age:** 24

Year Team	Lg Org	G	AB	H	2B	3B	HR	TB	R	RBI	TBB	IBB	SO	HBP	SH	SF	SB	CS	SB%	GDP	Avg	OBP	SLG
		BATTING															BASERUNNING				PERCENTAGES		
1992 Mariners	R Sea	39	124	39	2	0	0	41	30	14	13	1	19	6	2	1	11	5	.69	0	.315	.403	.331
1993 Appleton	A Sea	109	348	89	13	1	0	104	63	20	61	0	76	27	9	1	21	15	.58	3	.256	.405	.299
1994 Riverside	A+ Sea	128	481	141	12	3	1	162	102	41	76	4	67	12	7	2	34	15	.69	8	.293	.401	.337
1995 Port City	AA Sea	112	391	87	11	2	0	102	36	29	30	0	66	8	7	1	10	12	.45	13	.223	.291	.261
1996 Port City	AA Sea	119	407	109	12	3	1	130	54	30	41	1	62	7	6	0	26	15	.63	9	.268	.345	.319
5 Min. YEARS		507	1751	465	50	9	2	539	285	134	221	6	290	60	31	5	102	62	.62	33	.266	.366	.308

Emiliano Giron

Pitches: Right **Bats:** Right **Pos:** P **Ht:** 6'2" **Wt:** 170 **Born:** 1/5/72 **Age:** 25

Year Team	Lg Org	G	GS	CG	GF	IP	BFP	H	R	ER	HR	SH	SF	HB	TBB	IBB	SO	WP	Bk	W	L	Pct.	ShO	Sv	ERA
		HOW MUCH HE PITCHED						WHAT HE GAVE UP												THE RESULTS					
1994 Princeton	R+ Cin	21	0	0	14	56.2	235	31	20	14	4	6	4	5	26	2	77	7	1	4	3	.571	0	5	2.22
1995 Winston-Sal	A+ Cin	17	0	0	11	27.1	121	23	15	7	1	0	0	3	10	0	29	2	2	2	0	1.000	0	0	2.30
Charlstn-WV	A Cin	47	0	0	39	56	229	35	18	10	1	1	0	4	18	0	68	3	4	2	0	1.000	0	20	1.61
1996 Winston-Sal	A+ Cin	12	0	0	3	17	80	21	14	14	7	0	0	2	11	0	17	0	0	0	0	.000	0	0	7.41
Charlstn-WV	A Cin	32	1	0	17	45.2	191	33	17	14	2	1	2	3	23	1	63	9	2	1	2	.333	0	5	2.76
Chattanooga	AA Cin	4	0	0	1	8	33	5	3	2	1	0	1	1	5	1	8	0	0	0	0	.000	0	0	2.25
3 Min. YEARS		133	1	0	85	210.2	889	148	87	61	16	8	7	18	93	4	262	21	9	9	5	.643	0	30	2.61

John Giudice

Bats: Right **Throws:** Right **Pos:** OF **Ht:** 6'1" **Wt:** 205 **Born:** 6/19/71 **Age:** 26

Year Team	Lg Org	G	AB	H	2B	3B	HR	TB	R	RBI	TBB	IBB	SO	HBP	SH	SF	SB	CS	SB%	GDP	Avg	OBP	SLG
		BATTING															BASERUNNING				PERCENTAGES		
1993 Bend	A- Col	57	184	43	8	0	5	66	28	17	36	0	57	6	2	0	5	2	.71	5	.234	.376	.359
1994 Asheville	A Col	66	252	73	12	1	9	114	36	22	17	1	56	5	0	0	6	5	.55	2	.290	.347	.452
Central Val	A+ Col	53	195	55	13	2	4	84	30	33	18	1	55	6	2	2	6	2	.75	3	.282	.357	.431
1995 Salem	A+ Col	99	356	92	21	4	7	142	49	48	24	2	81	4	0	3	7	4	.64	7	.258	.310	.399
1996 Salem	A+ Col	101	373	109	30	1	16	189	58	67	45	6	66	7	3	3	11	8	.58	11	.292	.376	.507
New Haven	AA Col	32	118	30	4	1	4	48	13	13	10	2	25	0	0	2	2	4	.33	2	.254	.308	.407
4 Min. YEARS		408	1478	402	88	9	45	643	214	200	150	12	340	28	7	10	37	25	.60	30	.272	.348	.435

Darrin Glenn

Bats: Right **Throws:** Right **Pos:** C **Ht:** 6'0" **Wt:** 195 **Born:** 1/4/71 **Age:** 26

Year Team	Lg Org	G	AB	H	2B	3B	HR	TB	R	RBI	TBB	IBB	SO	HBP	SH	SF	SB	CS	SB%	GDP	Avg	OBP	SLG
		BATTING															BASERUNNING				PERCENTAGES		
1994 Sioux Falls	IND —	76	268	75	19	3	9	127	47	48	37	1	73	1	3	3	0	2	.00	2	.280	.366	.474
1995 Burlington	A SF	62	182	39	4	1	9	72	35	27	23	0	59	5	0	1	4	3	.57	8	.214	.318	.396
1996 San Jose	A+ SF	3	9	2	0	0	1	5	2	1	2	0	4	0	0	0	0	0	.00	0	.222	.364	.556
Phoenix	AAA SF	12	18	1	0	0	0	1	3	1	1	0	8	1	0	0	0	0	.00	1	.056	.150	.056

				BATTING															BASERUNNING				PERCENTAGES		
Year	Team	Lg	Org	G	AB	H	2B	3B	HR	TB	R	RBI	TBB	IBB	SO	HBP	SH	SF	SB	CS	SB%	GDP	Avg	OBP	SLG
	Shreveport	AA	SF	7	11	2	0	0	1	5	1	4	1	0	3	0	0	1	0	0	.00	0	.182	.231	.455
3 Min. YEARS				160	488	119	23	4	20	210	88	81	64	1	147	7	3	5	12	5	.71	11	.244	.337	.430

Leon Glenn

Bats: Left **Throws:** Right **Pos:** 1B **Ht:** 6'2" **Wt:** 200 **Born:** 9/16/69 **Age:** 27

				BATTING															BASERUNNING				PERCENTAGES		
Year	Team	Lg	Org	G	AB	H	2B	3B	HR	TB	R	RBI	TBB	IBB	SO	HBP	SH	SF	SB	CS	SB%	GDP	Avg	OBP	SLG
1988	Brewers	R	Mil	55	212	72	13	10	8	129	54	53	24	2	29	2	2	3	5	4	.56	2	.340	.407	.608
1989	Helena	R+	Mil	6	15	0	0	0	0	0	0	0	0	0	6	0	0	0	0	0	.00	0	.000	.000	.000
	Brewers	R	Mil	51	212	81	10	7	7	126	42	50	14	5	46	2	0	2	21	9	.70	2	.382	.422	.594
1990	Beloit	A	Mil	65	202	39	4	3	5	64	19	29	20	1	93	0	2	0	10	6	.63	1	.193	.266	.317
	Helena	R+	Mil	42	153	36	6	2	4	58	19	26	29	1	41	1	1	1	12	3	.80	1	.235	.359	.379
1991	Beloit	A	Mil	51	161	28	2	2	6	52	23	27	13	0	60	0	3	2	18	3	.86	2	.174	.233	.323
	Bend	A-	Mil	73	262	59	9	3	15	119	46	55	36	2	96	0	0	4	16	3	.84	3	.225	.315	.454
1992	Stockton	A+	Mil	88	275	57	12	2	10	103	36	36	40	0	86	0	1	2	17	8	.68	0	.207	.306	.375
1993	Stockton	A+	Mil	114	431	119	27	3	15	197	77	76	49	4	110	4	1	6	35	15	.70	9	.276	.351	.457
1994	El Paso	AA	Mil	67	219	56	12	3	8	98	40	32	20	2	67	1	1	0	8	7	.53	4	.256	.321	.447
	New Orleans	AAA	Mil	48	155	37	9	2	4	62	22	22	15	0	56	0	1	4	7	0	1.00	4	.239	.299	.400
1995	Midland	AA	Cal	120	433	110	19	11	17	202	68	65	34	1	126	2	3	3	16	11	.59	9	.254	.309	.467
1996	Midland	AA	Cal	94	319	68	14	2	10	116	30	53	23	2	86	2	0	2	8	9	.47	8	.213	.269	.364
9 Min. YEARS				874	3049	762	137	50	109	1326	476	524	317	20	902	14	15	29	173	78	.69	45	.250	.321	.435

Darrell Goedhart

Pitches: Right **Bats:** Right **Pos:** P **Ht:** 6'3" **Wt:** 210 **Born:** 7/18/70 **Age:** 26

				HOW MUCH HE PITCHED						WHAT HE GAVE UP												THE RESULTS					
Year	Team	Lg	Org	G	GS	CG	GF	IP	BFP	H	R	ER	HR	SH	SF	HB	TBB	IBB	SO	WP	Bk	W	L	Pct.	ShO	Sv	ERA
1989	Martinsvlle	R+	Phi	15	12	0	1	72	313	67	43	24	7	1	3	4	31	0	50	4	8	5	5	.500	0	0	3.00
1990	Spartanburg	A	Phi	29	28	1	0	150.1	669	162	96	74	7	4	5	5	62	0	92	13	3	8	10	.444	0	0	4.43
1991	Clearwater	A+	Phi	25	23	1	0	117.2	529	136	65	55	5	4	8	4	44	2	86	4	5	10	8	.556	1	0	4.21
1992	Clearwater	A+	Phi	8	8	0	0	40.2	165	39	15	14	2	0	1	1	10	0	32	1	0	4	3	.571	0	0	3.10
	Reading	AA	Phi	16	16	0	0	86.1	372	95	48	41	5	3	0	2	24	2	56	3	0	4	8	.333	0	0	4.27
1993	Reading	AA	Phi	27	26	1	0	152.1	654	160	94	88	17	1	6	2	54	0	110	10	1	9	12	.429	0	0	5.20
1994	Clearwater	A+	Phi	21	1	0	4	38	161	34	23	15	1	2	0	1	17	4	33	6	0	2	3	.400	0	0	3.55
1995	Palm Spring	IND	—	25	11	1	2	83.1	396	112	65	44	7	5	5	4	30	5	49	15	1	6	5	.545	0	0	4.75
1996	Palm Spring	IND	—	7	4	0	1	29	132	29	13	11	1	1	2	4	11	0	26	1	0	4	1	.800	0	0	3.41
	Grays Harbr	IND	—	8	8	1	0	55.2	250	69	35	26	8	0	0	0	16	0	53	7	0	4	2	.667	0	0	4.20
	Lk Elsinore	A+	Cal	4	2	0	2	13.1	59	17	6	2	0	0	0	0	4	0	12	0	0	2	1	.667	0	0	1.35
	Midland	AA	Cal	3	2	0	1	14	57	15	9	6	0	1	1	0	4	0	5	3	0	0	1	.000	0	0	3.86
8 Min. YEARS				188	141	5	11	852.2	3757	935	512	400	60	22	31	27	307	13	604	67	18	58	59	.496	1	0	4.22

Al Gogolin

Pitches: Right **Bats:** Right **Pos:** P **Ht:** 6'5" **Wt:** 215 **Born:** 1/14/72 **Age:** 25

				HOW MUCH HE PITCHED						WHAT HE GAVE UP												THE RESULTS					
Year	Team	Lg	Org	G	GS	CG	GF	IP	BFP	H	R	ER	HR	SH	SF	HB	TBB	IBB	SO	WP	Bk	W	L	Pct.	ShO	Sv	ERA
1994	W. Michigan	A	Oak	11	0	0	3	18.1	83	13	6	3	0	1	1	0	14	0	23	0	2	0	0	.000	0	1	1.47
1996	Athletics	R	Oak	6	2	0	1	15	79	24	14	13	0	2	1	2	10	0	20	2	0	0	2	.000	0	0	7.80
	Sou. Oregon	A-	Oak	6	0	0	2	9.1	49	10	9	9	1	0	1	2	14	1	3	1	1	1	1	.500	0	0	8.68
	Huntsville	AA	Oak	5	0	0	3	6	23	3	0	0	0	1	0	0	2	1	4	1	0	0	0	.000	0	0	0.00
2 Min. YEARS				28	2	0	9	48.2	234	50	29	25	1	4	3	4	40	2	50	4	3	1	3	.250	0	1	4.62

Matt Golden

Pitches: Right **Bats:** Right **Pos:** P **Ht:** 6'3" **Wt:** 190 **Born:** 1/23/72 **Age:** 25

				HOW MUCH HE PITCHED						WHAT HE GAVE UP												THE RESULTS					
Year	Team	Lg	Org	G	GS	CG	GF	IP	BFP	H	R	ER	HR	SH	SF	HB	TBB	IBB	SO	WP	Bk	W	L	Pct.	ShO	Sv	ERA
1994	New Jersey	A-	StL	13	11	0	2	60	263	70	34	33	4	3	2	4	12	0	45	6	0	5	3	.625	0	0	4.95
1995	Savannah	A	StL	64	0	0	24	90	355	71	22	20	2	2	2	0	21	4	94	4	2	7	3	.700	0	1	2.00
1996	St. Pete	A+	StL	8	0	0	7	10	36	5	1	1	0	1	0	1	1	0	7	1	0	0	0	.000	0	7	0.90
	Arkansas	AA	StL	52	0	0	41	63	285	74	40	29	1	2	1	0	26	3	43	10	0	3	4	.429	0	18	4.14
3 Min. YEARS				137	11	0	74	223	939	220	97	83	7	8	5	5	60	7	189	21	2	15	10	.600	0	26	3.35

Jason Goligoski

Bats: Left **Throws:** Right **Pos:** SS **Ht:** 6'1" **Wt:** 180 **Born:** 10/2/71 **Age:** 25

				BATTING															BASERUNNING				PERCENTAGES		
Year	Team	Lg	Org	G	AB	H	2B	3B	HR	TB	R	RBI	TBB	IBB	SO	HBP	SH	SF	SB	CS	SB%	GDP	Avg	OBP	SLG
1993	White Sox	R	ChA	54	163	42	12	2	2	64	30	27	34	0	18	1	3	3	16	9	.64	5	.258	.383	.393
1994	Hickory	A	ChA	135	499	135	18	7	1	170	98	67	99	0	82	9	5	9	17	5	.77	7	.271	.394	.341
1995	Pr. William	A+	ChA	95	300	65	7	2	0	76	42	24	52	0	47	3	2	3	16	5	.76	4	.217	.335	.253
1996	New Haven	AA	Col	30	64	11	0	1	0	13	6	3	8	2	12	1	3	0	0	2	.00	2	.172	.274	.203
	Red Sox	R	Bos	3	8	0	0	0	0	0	0	1	1	0	2	0	0	0	0	0	.00	0	.000	.111	.000
	Sarasota	A+	Bos	4	13	5	0	0	0	5	1	3	2	0	2	0	1	0	0	1	.00	0	.385	.467	.385
4 Min. YEARS				321	1047	258	37	12	3	328	177	125	196	2	163	14	14	15	49	22	.69	18	.246	.368	.313

Wayne Gomes

Pitches: Right **Bats:** Right **Pos:** P **Ht:** 6'0" **Wt:** 215 **Born:** 1/15/73 **Age:** 24

			HOW MUCH HE PITCHED						WHAT HE GAVE UP													THE RESULTS					
Year	Team	Lg Org	G	GS	CG	GF	IP	BFP	H	R	ER	HR	SH	SF	HB	TBB	IBB	SO	WP	Bk	W	L	Pct.	ShO	Sv	ERA
1993	Batavia	A- Phi	5	0	0	3	7.1	32	1	1	1	0	0	0	0	8	0	11	0	1	1	0	1.000	0	0	1.23
	Clearwater	A+ Phi	9	0	0	8	7.2	37	4	1	1	0	0	0	0	9	0	13	2	0	0	0	.000	0	4	1.17
1994	Clearwater	A+ Phi	23	21	1	0	104.1	474	85	63	55	5	2	4	3	82	2	102	27	4	6	8	.429	1	0	4.74
1995	Reading	AA Phi	22	22	1	0	104.2	462	89	54	46	8	3	1	1	70	0	102	6	6	7	4	.636	1	0	3.96
1996	Reading	AA Phi	67	0	0	55	64.1	291	53	35	32	7	1	3	1	48	3	79	14	0	0	4	.000	0	24	4.48
4 Min. YEARS			126	43	2	66	288.1	1296	232	154	135	20	6	8	5	217	5	307	49	11	14	16	.467	2	28	4.21

Alex Gonzalez

Bats: Right **Throws:** Right **Pos:** SS **Ht:** 6'0" **Wt:** 150 **Born:** 2/15/77 **Age:** 20

			BATTING														BASERUNNING				PERCENTAGES		
Year	Team	Lg Org	G	AB	H	2B	3B	HR	TB	R	RBI	TBB	IBB	SO	HBP	SH	SF	SB	CS	SB%	GDP	Avg	OBP	SLG
1995	Brevard Cty	A+ Fla	17	59	12	2	1	0	16	6	8	1	0	14	1	0	0	1	1	.50	2	.203	.230	.271
	Marlins	R Fla	53	187	55	7	4	2	76	30	30	19	0	27	2	1	4	11	2	.85	2	.294	.358	.406
1996	Marlins	R Fla	10	41	16	3	0	0	19	6	6	2	0	4	0	0	0	1	0	1.00	1	.390	.419	.463
	Kane County	A Fla	4	10	2	0	0	0	2	2	0	2	0	4	1	1	0	0	0	.00	1	.200	.385	.200
	Portland	AA Fla	11	34	8	0	1	0	10	4	1	2	2	10	1	0	0	0	0	.00	2	.235	.297	.294
2 Min. YEARS			95	331	93	12	6	2	123	48	45	26	2	59	5	2	4	13	3	.81	8	.281	.339	.372

Gabe Gonzalez

Pitches: Left **Bats:** Both **Pos:** P **Ht:** 6'1" **Wt:** 160 **Born:** 5/24/72 **Age:** 25

			HOW MUCH HE PITCHED						WHAT HE GAVE UP													THE RESULTS					
Year	Team	Lg Org	G	GS	CG	GF	IP	BFP	H	R	ER	HR	SH	SF	HB	TBB	IBB	SO	WP	Bk	W	L	Pct.	ShO	Sv	ERA
1995	Kane County	A Fla	32	0	0	10	43.1	181	32	18	11	0	2	1	2	14	2	41	1	0	4	4	.500	0	1	2.28
1996	Charlotte	AAA Fla	2	0	0	1	3	15	4	1	1	0	0	0	0	2	0	3	0	0	0	0	.000	0	0	3.00
	Brevard Cty	A+ Fla	47	0	0	32	76.1	308	56	20	15	2	9	1	3	23	7	62	2	0	2	7	.222	0	9	1.77
2 Min. YEARS			81	0	0	43	122.2	504	92	39	27	2	11	2	5	39	9	106	3	0	6	11	.353	0	10	1.98

Geremis Gonzalez

Pitches: Right **Bats:** Right **Pos:** P **Ht:** 6'1" **Wt:** 180 **Born:** 1/8/75 **Age:** 22

			HOW MUCH HE PITCHED						WHAT HE GAVE UP													THE RESULTS					
Year	Team	Lg Org	G	GS	CG	GF	IP	BFP	H	R	ER	HR	SH	SF	HB	TBB	IBB	SO	WP	Bk	W	L	Pct.	ShO	Sv	ERA
1992	Rockies/Cub	R ChN	14	7	0	1	45	238	65	59	39	0	0	6	10	22	0	39	11	1	0	5	.000	0	0	7.80
1993	Huntington	R+ ChN	12	12	1	0	67.2	319	82	59	47	6	1	2	5	38	0	42	5	2	3	9	.250	0	0	6.25
1994	Peoria	A ChN	13	13	1	0	71.1	325	86	53	44	4	2	3	7	32	0	39	5	2	1	7	.125	0	0	5.55
	Williamsprt	A- ChN	16	12	1	2	80.2	357	83	46	38	6	3	3	10	29	0	64	4	1	4	6	.400	1	1	4.24
1995	Rockford	A ChN	12	12	1	0	65.1	297	63	43	37	4	1	4	8	28	0	36	8	1	4	4	.500	0	0	5.10
	Daytona	A+ ChN	31	14	1	7	109.2	475	97	58	43	4	2	6	9	41	1	66	12	3	9	5	.643	0	4	3.53
1996	Orlando	AA ChN	17	14	0	2	97	415	95	39	36	6	1	2	4	28	1	85	2	0	6	3	.667	0	0	3.34
5 Min. YEARS			115	84	5	12	536.2	2426	571	357	284	30	10	26	53	218	2	371	47	10	27	39	.409	1	5	4.76

Jimmy Gonzalez

Bats: Right **Throws:** Right **Pos:** C **Ht:** 6'3" **Wt:** 210 **Born:** 3/8/73 **Age:** 24

			BATTING														BASERUNNING				PERCENTAGES		
Year	Team	Lg Org	G	AB	H	2B	3B	HR	TB	R	RBI	TBB	IBB	SO	HBP	SH	SF	SB	CS	SB%	GDP	Avg	OBP	SLG
1991	Astros	R Hou	34	103	21	3	0	0	24	7	3	7	0	33	0	1	0	3	5	.38	1	.204	.255	.233
1992	Burlington	A Hou	91	301	53	13	0	4	78	32	21	34	0	119	1	0	0	0	3	.00	6	.176	.262	.259
1993	Quad City	A Hou	47	154	35	9	1	0	46	20	15	14	1	36	4	1	1	2	2	.50	4	.227	.306	.299
	Asheville	A Hou	43	149	33	5	0	4	50	16	15	7	0	37	0	2	1	3	1	.75	3	.221	.255	.336
1994	Jackson	AA Hou	4	6	0	0	0	0	0	0	0	0	0	0	0	0	0	0	0	.00	0	.000	.000	.000
	Osceola	A+ Hou	99	321	74	18	0	5	107	33	38	20	0	80	4	2	2	2	0	1.00	10	.231	.282	.333
1995	Quad City	A Hou	35	78	19	3	1	1	27	4	14	9	0	13	1	0	1	1	2	.33	2	.244	.326	.346
1996	Jackson	AA Hou	2	5	1	0	0	0	1	1	0	1	0	1	0	0	0	0	0	.00	0	.200	.333	.200
	Kissimmee	A+ Hou	73	208	35	4	1	6	59	19	17	25	0	59	3	2	3	1	0	1.00	8	.168	.264	.284
6 Min. YEARS			428	1325	271	55	3	20	392	132	123	117	1	378	13	8	8	12	13	.48	34	.205	.274	.296

Pete Gonzalez

Bats: Right **Throws:** Right **Pos:** C **Ht:** 6'0" **Wt:** 190 **Born:** 11/24/69 **Age:** 27

			BATTING														BASERUNNING				PERCENTAGES		
Year	Team	Lg Org	G	AB	H	2B	3B	HR	TB	R	RBI	TBB	IBB	SO	HBP	SH	SF	SB	CS	SB%	GDP	Avg	OBP	SLG
1989	Dodgers	R LA	34	94	23	5	0	0	28	16	13	14	0	16	0	0	0	3	1	.75	2	.245	.343	.298
1990	Vero Beach	A+ LA	90	198	43	12	0	2	61	31	21	42	2	40	11	5	3	2	2	.50	5	.217	.378	.308
1991	Vero Beach	A+ LA	74	207	45	12	0	1	60	26	14	31	0	32	6	5	1	1	0	1.00	4	.217	.335	.290
1992	Fayetteville	A Det	42	110	25	5	0	0	30	17	19	38	0	23	6	1	3	5	2	.71	2	.227	.439	.273
	Toledo	AAA Det	9	17	2	2	0	0	4	1	0	1	0	3	0	1	0	0	0	.00	0	.118	.167	.235
	Lakeland	A+ Det	32	81	24	7	0	1	34	15	13	19	0	9	2	1	0	1	0	1.00	0	.296	.441	.420
1993	Lakeland	A+ Det	63	200	50	4	1	2	62	20	25	31	4	28	2	2	3	7	2	.78	8	.250	.352	.310
	London	AA Det	25	64	10	3	0	0	13	5	6	14	0	12	2	0	1	0	0	.00	0	.156	.321	.203
1994	Trenton	AA Det	16	55	15	3	0	0	18	3	8	4	0	7	1	0	0	2	1	.67	0	.273	.333	.327
	Toledo	AAA Det	60	151	41	9	0	3	59	24	18	26	1	35	1	1	1	2	6	.25	1	.272	.380	.391
1995	Toledo	AAA Det	6	19	4	1	0	0	5	0	2	3	0	6	1	0	0	0	0	.00	0	.211	.348	.263

Year	Team	Lg	Org	G	AB	H	2B	3B	HR	TB	R	RBI	TBB	IBB	SO	HBP	SH	SF	SB	CS	SB%	GDP	Avg	OBP	SLG
	BATTING																		BASERUNNING				PERCENTAGES		
1996	Colo. Sprng	AAA	Col	36	86	15	7	0	2	28	10	13	17	0	20	2	0	1	1	1	.50	1	.174	.321	.326
	New Haven	AA	Col	42	119	22	1	0	2	29	9	8	14	1	19	2	2	0	1	2	.33	8	.185	.281	.244
8 Min. YEARS				529	1401	319	71	1	13	431	177	160	254	8	250	36	18	13	25	17	.60	31	.228	.357	.308

Raul Gonzalez

Bats: Right **Throws:** Right **Pos:** OF **Ht:** 5'8" **Wt:** 175 **Born:** 12/27/73 **Age:** 23

Year	Team	Lg	Org	G	AB	H	2B	3B	HR	TB	R	RBI	TBB	IBB	SO	HBP	SH	SF	SB	CS	SB%	GDP	Avg	OBP	SLG
	BATTING																		BASERUNNING				PERCENTAGES		
1991	Royals	R	KC	47	160	47	5	3	0	58	24	17	19	0	21	0	1	2	3	4	.43	4	.294	.365	.363
1992	Appleton	A	KC	119	449	115	32	1	9	176	82	51	57	1	58	2	4	6	13	5	.72	4	.256	.339	.392
1993	Wilmington	A+	KC	127	461	124	30	3	11	193	59	55	54	1	58	4	1	4	13	5	.72	8	.269	.348	.419
1994	Wilmington	A+	KC	115	414	108	19	8	9	170	60	51	45	2	50	2	2	4	0	4	.00	8	.261	.333	.411
1995	Wichita	AA	KC	22	79	23	3	2	2	36	14	11	8	0	13	0	0	0	4	0	1.00	1	.291	.356	.456
	Wilmington	A+	KC	86	308	90	19	3	11	148	36	49	14	3	34	2	3	7	6	4	.60	3	.292	.320	.481
1996	Wichita	AA	KC	23	84	24	5	1	1	34	17	9	5	0	12	1	0	0	1	2	.33	3	.286	.333	.405
6 Min. YEARS				539	1955	531	113	21	43	815	292	243	202	7	246	11	11	23	40	24	.63	31	.272	.340	.417

Keith Gordon

Bats: Right **Throws:** Right **Pos:** OF **Ht:** 6' 2" **Wt:** 200 **Born:** 1/22/69 **Age:** 28

Year	Team	Lg	Org	G	AB	H	2B	3B	HR	TB	R	RBI	TBB	IBB	SO	HBP	SH	SF	SB	CS	SB%	GDP	Avg	OBP	SLG
	BATTING																		BASERUNNING				PERCENTAGES		
1990	Billings	R+	Cin	49	154	36	5	1	1	46	21	14	24	1	49	3	2	1	6	4	.60	2	.234	.346	.299
1991	Charlstn-WV	A	Cin	123	388	104	14	10	8	162	63	46	50	2	134	5	7	1	25	9	.74	5	.268	.358	.418
1992	Cedar Rapds	A	Cin	114	375	94	19	3	12	155	59	63	43	2	135	3	1	4	21	10	.68	5	.251	.329	.413
1993	Chattanooga	AA	Cin	116	419	122	26	3	14	196	69	59	19	0	132	4	0	2	13	17	.43	15	.291	.327	.468
1994	Indianapols	AAA	Cin	18	58	12	1	0	1	16	3	4	4	0	25	0	1	0	0	0	.00	1	.207	.258	.276
	Chattanooga	AA	Cin	82	254	71	16	2	8	115	46	38	21	0	74	1	0	2	11	7	.61	6	.280	.335	.453
1995	Indianapols	AAA	Cin	89	265	70	14	1	6	104	36	38	15	0	94	0	1	0	3	4	.43	3	.264	.304	.392
1996	Rochester	AAA	Bal	33	104	26	4	1	5	47	15	19	9	0	27	0	0	0	0	3	.00	3	.250	.310	.452
	Bowie	AA	Bal	82	306	80	13	2	5	112	38	28	22	0	80	1	1	0	13	11	.54	5	.261	.313	.366
1993	Cincinnati	NL		3	6	1	0	0	0	1	0	0	0	0	2	0	0	0	0	0	.00	0	.167	.167	.167
7 Min. YEARS				706	2323	615	112	23	60	953	350	309	207	5	750	17	13	10	92	65	.59	45	.265	.328	.410

Clint Gould

Pitches: Right **Bats:** Right **Pos:** P **Ht:** 6'1" **Wt:** 230 **Born:** 8/18/71 **Age:** 25

Year	Team	Lg	Org	G	GS	CG	GF	IP	BFP	H	R	ER	HR	SH	SF	HB	TBB	IBB	SO	WP	Bk	W	L	Pct.	ShO	Sv	ERA
				HOW MUCH HE PITCHED						WHAT HE GAVE UP												THE RESULTS					
1994	Thunder Bay	IND	—	1	0	0	1	1	6	2	0	0	0	0	0	0	2	0	0	0	0	0	0	.000	0	0	0.00
1995	Tacoma	AAA	Sea	1	0	0	1	0.1	1	0	0	0	0	0	0	0	0	0	0	0	0	0	0	.000	0	0	0.00
	Wisconsin	A	Sea	26	0	0	16	34.2	165	34	24	22	4	1	0	2	28	1	20	1	0	0	0	.000	0	0	5.71
1996	Bakersfield	A+	Sea	2	0	0	1	1	6	1	1	1	0	0	0	0	2	0	1	1	0	0	0	.000	0	0	9.00
	Wisconsin	A	Sea	6	0	0	3	10.1	44	8	4	4	0	1	1	0	5	0	10	3	1	1	0	1.000	0	1	3.48
	Tacoma	AAA	Sea	1	1	0	0	4	20	4	3	2	0	0	1	2	2	0	2	0	0	0	1	.000	0	0	4.50
	Lancaster	A+	Sea	24	0	0	14	33.2	159	35	22	12	0	1	0	2	17	1	17	3	0	3	2	.600	0	2	3.21
	Port City	AA	Sea	11	0	0	4	21.1	89	17	11	8	2	0	1	0	6	0	9	1	0	0	1	.000	0	0	3.38
3 Min. YEARS				72	1	0	40	106.1	490	101	65	49	6	3	3	6	62	2	59	9	1	4	4	.500	0	3	4.15

Ryan Graves

Pitches: Left **Bats:** Left **Pos:** P **Ht:** 6'2" **Wt:** 185 **Born:** 2/15/74 **Age:** 23

Year	Team	Lg	Org	G	GS	CG	GF	IP	BFP	H	R	ER	HR	SH	SF	HB	TBB	IBB	SO	WP	Bk	W	L	Pct.	ShO	Sv	ERA
				HOW MUCH HE PITCHED						WHAT HE GAVE UP												THE RESULTS					
1996	Williamsprt	A-	ChN	4	0	0	2	5	20	4	0	0	0	0	0	0	2	0	3	0	1	0	0	.000	0	0	0.00
	Daytona	A+	ChN	6	0	0	6	12	56	16	8	7	2	0	1	0	5	0	9	2	0	0	0	.000	0	0	5.25
	Orlando	AA	ChN	4	1	0	3	9	52	16	15	12	0	2	0	1	9	0	3	2	0	0	2	.000	0	1	12.00
1 Min. YEARS				14	1	0	11	26	128	36	23	19	2	2	1	1	16	0	15	4	1	0	2	.000	0	1	6.58

Dennis Gray

Pitches: Left **Bats:** Left **Pos:** P **Ht:** 6'6" **Wt:** 225 **Born:** 12/24/69 **Age:** 27

Year	Team	Lg	Org	G	GS	CG	GF	IP	BFP	H	R	ER	HR	SH	SF	HB	TBB	IBB	SO	WP	Bk	W	L	Pct.	ShO	Sv	ERA
				HOW MUCH HE PITCHED						WHAT HE GAVE UP												THE RESULTS					
1991	St. Cathrns	A-	Tor	15	14	0	0	77	341	63	42	32	1	3	1	1	54	0	78	4	4	4	4	.500	0	0	3.74
1992	Myrtle Bch	A	Tor	28	28	0	0	155.1	659	122	82	66	8	2	5	6	93	0	141	13	4	11	12	.478	0	0	3.82
1993	Dunedin	A+	Tor	26	26	0	0	141.1	607	115	71	56	7	7	6	7	97	1	108	6	0	8	10	.444	0	0	3.57
1994	Knoxville	AA	Tor	30	16	0	6	100.2	488	118	83	59	5	12	8	11	65	0	77	13	1	5	11	.313	0	0	5.27
1995	Syracuse	AAA	Tor	15	0	0	3	24.1	106	27	16	12	3	0	0	2	10	0	15	3	0	2	2	.500	0	0	4.44
	Knoxville	AA	Tor	39	0	0	13	57	249	56	41	35	5	2	0	3	30	0	37	8	0	2	5	.286	0	0	5.53
1996	Harrisburg	AA	Mon	9	0	0	1	10.2	54	12	9	9	1	0	0	0	14	0	10	0	1	0	0	.000	0	0	7.59
	Ottawa	AAA	Mon	3	0	0	2	5.1	32	9	4	4	1	0	0	2	5	0	3	1	0	0	1	.000	0	0	6.75
	Port City	AA	Sea	21	1	0	6	33.1	168	34	32	29	1	3	1	1	42	2	24	4	0	2	0	1.000	0	0	7.83
	Greenville	AA	Atl	7	0	0	3	13	58	11	8	7	1	1	0	0	9	2	13	1	0	1	2	.333	0	0	4.85
6 Min. YEARS				193	85	0	34	618	2762	567	388	309	33	30	21	33	419	5	506	53	10	35	47	.427	0	0	4.50

Brian Grebeck

Bats: Right **Throws:** Right **Pos:** 3B **Ht:** 5'7" **Wt:** 160 **Born:** 8/31/67 **Age:** 29

		BATTING															BASERUNNING				PERCENTAGES		
Year Team	Lg Org	G	AB	H	2B	3B	HR	TB	R	RBI	TBB	IBB	SO	HBP	SH	SF	SB	CS	SB%	GDP	Avg	OBP	SLG
1990 Boise	A- Cal	58	202	57	10	2	1	74	45	33	64	1	57	1	5	2	1	3	.25	3	.282	.454	.366
1991 Quad City	A Cal	121	408	100	20	3	0	126	80	34	103	0	76	10	15	4	19	10	.66	8	.245	.406	.309
1992 Palm Spring	A+ Cal	91	289	97	14	2	0	115	71	39	83	2	55	0	8	3	6	5	.55	10	.336	.480	.398
1993 Midland	AA Cal	118	405	119	20	4	5	162	65	54	64	1	81	8	6	7	6	1	.86	8	.294	.395	.400
1994 Midland	AA Cal	55	184	58	18	2	1	83	27	17	27	1	33	5	1	1	1	1	.50	7	.315	.415	.451
Vancouver	AAA Cal	38	127	38	7	0	2	51	23	18	16	0	14	3	2	3	1	2	.33	5	.299	.383	.402
1995 Vancouver	AAA Cal	81	241	59	11	2	5	89	41	30	38	1	38	5	5	3	4	0	1.00	6	.245	.355	.369
1996 Vancouver	AAA Cal	78	237	55	10	3	1	74	25	27	34	0	27	1	4	4	1	1	.50	2	.232	.326	.312
7 Min. YEARS		640	2093	583	110	18	15	774	377	252	429	6	381	33	46	27	39	23	.63	49	.279	.405	.370

Bert Green

Bats: Right **Throws:** Right **Pos:** OF **Ht:** 5'10" **Wt:** 170 **Born:** 6/9/74 **Age:** 23

		BATTING															BASERUNNING				PERCENTAGES		
Year Team	Lg Org	G	AB	H	2B	3B	HR	TB	R	RBI	TBB	IBB	SO	HBP	SH	SF	SB	CS	SB%	GDP	Avg	OBP	SLG
1993 Cardinals	R StL	33	95	21	3	1	0	26	16	11	7	0	17	3	1	0	3	2	.60	1	.221	.295	.274
1994 Johnson Cty	R+ StL	54	199	48	5	0	0	53	32	11	25	1	61	0	4	2	22	7	.76	0	.241	.323	.266
1995 Savannah	A StL	132	429	98	7	6	1	120	48	25	55	0	101	3	9	1	26	9	.74	6	.228	.320	.280
1996 St. Pete	A+ StL	36	140	41	4	1	1	50	26	11	21	1	22	2	2	0	13	9	.59	1	.293	.393	.357
Arkansas	AA StL	92	300	60	6	3	3	81	45	24	38	1	58	3	3	1	21	8	.72	3	.200	.295	.270
4 Min. YEARS		347	1163	268	25	11	5	330	167	82	146	3	259	11	19	4	85	35	.71	11	.230	.321	.284

Rick Greene

Pitches: Right **Bats:** Right **Pos:** P **Ht:** 6'5" **Wt:** 200 **Born:** 1/2/71 **Age:** 26

		HOW MUCH HE PITCHED						WHAT HE GAVE UP												THE RESULTS					
Year Team	Lg Org	G	GS	CG	GF	IP	BFP	H	R	ER	HR	SH	SF	HB	TBB	IBB	SO	WP	Bk	W	L	Pct.	ShO	Sv	ERA
1993 Lakeland	A+ Det	26	0	0	11	40.2	184	57	28	28	1	6	0	1	16	1	32	5	2	2	3	.400	0	2	6.20
London	AA Det	23	0	0	11	29	135	31	22	21	1	3	3	1	20	3	19	3	2	2	2	.500	0	0	6.52
1994 Trenton	AA Det	20	0	0	14	19.1	92	17	17	17	0	3	2	0	21	2	5	2	0	1	1	.500	0	3	7.91
Lakeland	A+ Det	19	2	0	11	33.1	158	50	23	16	0	1	1	0	10	1	28	6	0	0	4	.000	0	4	4.32
1995 Jacksonvlle	AA Det	32	0	0	6	38.2	177	45	19	15	3	1	0	3	15	2	29	0	0	6	2	.750	0	0	3.49
1996 Jacksonvlle	AA Det	57	0	0	48	56	275	67	44	31	8	6	0	2	39	4	42	2	0	2	7	.222	0	30	4.98
4 Min. YEARS		177	2	0	101	217	1021	267	153	128	13	20	6	7	121	13	155	18	4	13	19	.406	0	39	5.31

Tommy Greene

Pitches: Right **Bats:** Right **Pos:** P **Ht:** 6' 5" **Wt:** 222 **Born:** 4/6/67 **Age:** 30

		HOW MUCH HE PITCHED						WHAT HE GAVE UP												THE RESULTS					
Year Team	Lg Org	G	GS	CG	GF	IP	BFP	H	R	ER	HR	SH	SF	HB	TBB	IBB	SO	WP	Bk	W	L	Pct.	ShO	Sv	ERA
1985 Pulaski	R+ Atl	12	12	1	0	50.2	226	49	45	43	7	1	1	2	27	0	32	4	0	2	5	.286	1	0	7.64
1986 Sumter	A Atl	28	28	5	0	174.2	758	162	95	91	17	4	3	8	82	3	169	15	7	11	7	.611	3	0	4.69
1987 Greenville	AA Atl	23	23	4	0	142.1	590	103	60	52	13	4	2	4	66	1	101	7	2	11	8	.579	2	0	3.29
1988 Richmond	AAA Atl	29	29	4	0	177.1	765	169	98	94	10	7	8	3	70	1	130	5	8	7	17	.292	3	0	4.77
1989 Richmond	AAA Atl	26	26	2	0	152	638	136	74	61	9	9	5	2	50	0	125	10	0	9	12	.429	1	0	3.61
1990 Richmond	AAA Atl	19	18	2	0	109	459	88	49	45	5	5	3	0	65	3	65	8	3	5	8	.385	0	0	3.72
Scranton-WB	AAA Phi	1	1	0	0	7	27	5	0	0	0	0	0	0	2	0	4	0	0	0	0	.000	0	0	0.00
1992 Reading	AA Phi	1	1	0	0	2	10	3	2	2	1	0	0	0	2	0	2	0	0	0	0	.000	0	0	9.00
Scranton-WB	AAA Phi	5	5	1	0	21.2	86	15	7	6	3	0	0	1	4	0	21	0	0	2	1	.667	1	0	2.49
1994 Clearwater	A+ Phi	1	1	0	0	5	17	2	0	0	0	0	0	0	1	0	4	0	0	0	0	.000	0	0	0.00
Scranton-WB	AAA Phi	1	1	0	0	4	15	3	1	0	0	0	0	0	1	0	6	0	0	0	0	.000	0	0	0.00
Reading	AA Phi	2	2	0	0	10.1	46	12	5	5	1	0	0	1	3	0	12	2	0	1	0	1.000	0	0	4.35
1995 Clearwater	A+ Phi	3	3	0	0	20	77	12	7	7	2	0	0	2	7	0	20	1	0	0	3	.000	0	0	3.15
Scranton-WB	AAA Phi	7	7	0	0	48.1	182	30	15	14	3	1	1	2	13	0	39	6	0	3	3	.500	0	0	2.61
1996 Clearwater	A+ Phi	7	4	0	1	27	108	25	8	6	2	3	2	1	4	0	23	0	0	1	1	.500	0	0	2.00
Scranton-WB	AAA Phi	5	5	0	0	31	129	31	13	13	3	0	2	0	7	0	26	0	0	2	0	1.000	0	0	3.77
1989 Atlanta	NL	4	4	1	0	26.1	103	22	12	12	5	1	2	0	6	1	17	1	0	1	2	.333	1	0	4.10
1990 Atlanta	NL	5	2	0	0	12.1	61	14	11	11	3	2	0	1	9	0	4	0	0	1	0	1.000	0	0	8.03
Philadelphia	NL	10	7	0	1	39	166	36	20	18	5	3	0	0	17	1	17	1	0	2	3	.400	0	0	4.15
1991 Philadelphia	NL	36	27	3	3	207.2	857	177	85	78	19	9	11	3	66	4	154	9	1	13	7	.650	2	0	3.38
1992 Philadelphia	NL	13	12	0	0	64.1	298	75	39	38	5	4	2	0	34	2	39	1	0	3	3	.500	0	0	5.32
1993 Philadelphia	NL	31	30	7	0	200	834	175	84	76	12	9	9	3	62	3	167	15	0	16	4	.800	2	0	3.42
1994 Philadelphia	NL	7	7	0	0	35.2	164	37	20	18	5	5	1	0	22	0	28	2	0	2	0	1.000	0	0	4.54
1995 Philadelphia	NL	11	6	0	3	33.2	167	45	32	31	6	2	1	3	20	0	24	3	1	0	5	.000	0	0	8.29
10 Min. YEARS		170	166	19	1	982.1	4133	845	479	439	76	34	27	26	404	8	779	58	20	54	65	.454	11	0	4.02
7 Maj. YEARS		117	95	11	7	619	2650	581	303	282	60	35	26	10	236	11	450	32	2	38	24	.613	5	0	4.10

Kenny Greer

Pitches: Right **Bats:** Right **Pos:** P **Ht:** 6' 2" **Wt:** 215 **Born:** 5/12/67 **Age:** 30

		HOW MUCH HE PITCHED						WHAT HE GAVE UP												THE RESULTS					
Year Team	Lg Org	G	GS	CG	GF	IP	BFP	H	R	ER	HR	SH	SF	HB	TBB	IBB	SO	WP	Bk	W	L	Pct.	ShO	Sv	ERA
1988 Oneonta	A- NYA	15	15	4	0	112.1	470	109	40	30	0	5	4	7	18	2	60	6	6	5	5	.500	0	0	2.40
1989 Pr. William	A+ NYA	29	13	3	7	111.2	461	101	56	52	3	2	2	7	22	0	44	4	1	7	3	.700	1	2	4.19
1990 Ft. Laud	A+ NYA	38	5	0	11	89.1	417	115	64	54	5	9	5	7	33	2	55	3	3	4	9	.308	0	1	5.44

		HOW MUCH HE PITCHED						WHAT HE GAVE UP												THE RESULTS					
Year Team	Lg Org	G	GS	CG	GF	IP	BFP	H	R	ER	HR	SH	SF	HB	TBB	IBB	SO	WP	Bk	W	L	Pct.	ShO	Sv	ERA
Pr. William	A+ NYA	1	1	0	0	7.2	32	7	2	2	0	0	1	0	2	0	7	0	0	1	0	1.000	0	0	2.35
1991 Ft. Laud	A+ NYA	31	1	0	12	57.1	245	49	31	27	3	1	1	7	22	2	46	5	0	4	3	.571	0	0	4.24
1992 Pr. William	A+ NYA	13	0	0	6	27	112	25	11	11	1	0	0	1	9	0	30	1	0	1	2	.333	0	1	3.67
Albany-Colo	AA NYA	40	1	0	18	68.2	280	48	19	14	1	2	1	0	30	4	53	6	0	4	1	.800	0	4	1.83
Columbus	AAA NYA	1	0	0	1	1	7	3	2	1	0	0	0	0	1	0	1	0	0	0	0	.000	0	0	9.00
1993 Columbus	AAA NYA	46	0	0	21	79.1	347	78	41	39	5	4	4	2	36	6	50	2	0	9	4	.692	0	6	4.42
1994 Mets	R NYN	4	2	0	0	6	24	7	2	2	0	0	0	0	0	0	3	1	0	0	0	.000	0	0	3.00
Norfolk	AAA NYN	25	0	0	12	31	138	35	14	13	2	0	1	3	11	2	8	3	0	1	1	.500	0	1	3.77
1995 Phoenix	AAA SF	38	0	0	13	63.1	270	65	29	28	1	3	2	2	19	1	41	5	0	5	2	.714	0	1	3.98
1996 Calgary	AAA Pit	46	1	0	19	68	294	74	34	30	9	5	2	3	17	5	36	2	0	5	4	.556	0	3	3.97
1993 New York	NL	1	0	0	1	1	3	0	0	0	0	0	0	0	0	0	2	0	0	1	0	1.000	0	0	0.00
1995 San Francisco	NL	8	0	0	1	12	61	15	12	7	3	2	1	1	5	2	7	0	0	0	2	.000	0	0	5.25
9 Min. YEARS		327	39	7	120	722.2	3097	716	351	303	30	31	23	39	220	24	434	38	10	46	34	.575	1	19	3.77
2 Maj. YEARS		9	0	0	2	13	64	15	12	7	3	2	1	1	5	2	9	0	0	1	2	.333	0	0	4.85

Tommy Gregg

Bats: Left **Throws:** Left **Pos:** 1B **Ht:** 6' 1" **Wt:** 190 **Born:** 7/29/63 **Age:** 33

		BATTING															BASERUNNING				PERCENTAGES		
Year Team	Lg Org	G	AB	H	2B	3B	HR	TB	R	RBI	TBB	IBB	SO	HBP	SH	SF	SB	CS	SB%	GDP	Avg	OBP	SLG
1985 Macon	A Pit	72	259	81	14	2	1	102	43	18	49	3	38	0	1	0	16	7	.70	6	.313	.422	.394
1986 Nashua	AA Pit	126	421	113	13	4	1	137	55	29	66	3	48	3	6	1	11	8	.58	12	.268	.371	.325
1987 Harrisburg	AA Pit	133	461	171	22	9	10	241	99	82	84	14	47	1	0	4	35	10	.78	9	.371	.465	.523
1988 Buffalo	AAA Pit	72	252	74	12	0	6	104	34	27	25	4	26	1	0	4	7	9	.44	3	.294	.355	.413
1991 Richmond	AAA Atl	3	13	6	0	0	1	9	3	4	1	0	2	0	0	0	1	1	.50	0	.462	.500	.692
1992 Richmond	AAA Atl	39	125	36	9	2	0	49	17	12	19	1	27	1	0	0	3	1	.75	2	.288	.386	.392
1993 Indianapols	AAA Cin	71	198	63	12	5	7	106	34	30	26	0	28	1	1	1	3	5	.38	3	.318	.398	.535
1995 Charlotte	AAA Fla	34	124	48	10	1	9	87	30	32	21	2	13	1	0	1	7	0	1.00	3	.387	.476	.702
1996 Charlotte	AAA Fla	119	405	116	24	0	22	206	69	80	49	3	62	3	0	4	10	1	.91	8	.286	.364	.509
1987 Pittsburgh	NL	10	8	2	1	0	0	3	3	0	0	0	2	0	0	0	0	0	.00	2	.250	.250	.375
1988 Pittsburgh	NL	14	15	3	1	0	1	7	4	3	1	0	4	0	0	1	0	1	.00	0	.200	.235	.467
Atlanta	NL	11	29	10	3	0	0	13	1	4	2	1	2	0	0	0	0	0	.00	1	.345	.387	.448
1989 Atlanta	NL	102	276	67	8	0	6	93	24	23	18	2	45	0	3	1	3	4	.43	4	.243	.288	.337
1990 Atlanta	NL	124	239	63	13	1	5	93	18	32	20	4	39	1	0	1	4	3	.57	1	.264	.322	.389
1991 Atlanta	NL	72	107	20	8	1	1	33	13	4	12	2	24	1	0	0	2	2	.50	1	.187	.275	.308
1992 Atlanta	NL	18	19	5	0	0	1	8	1	1	1	0	7	0	0	0	1	0	1.00	1	.263	.300	.421
1993 Cincinnati	NL	10	12	2	0	0	0	2	1	1	0	0	0	0	0	1	0	0	.00	0	.167	.154	.167
1995 Florida	NL	72	156	37	5	0	6	60	20	20	16	1	33	2	0	2	3	1	.75	3	.237	.313	.385
9 Min. YEARS		669	2258	708	116	23	57	1041	384	314	340	30	291	11	8	15	93	42	.69	46	.314	.404	.461
8 Maj. YEARS		433	861	209	39	2	20	312	85	88	70	10	156	4	3	6	13	11	.54	13	.243	.301	.362

Kris Gresham

Bats: Right **Throws:** Right **Pos:** C **Ht:** 6'2" **Wt:** 206 **Born:** 8/30/70 **Age:** 26

		BATTING															BASERUNNING				PERCENTAGES		
Year Team	Lg Org	G	AB	H	2B	3B	HR	TB	R	RBI	TBB	IBB	SO	HBP	SH	SF	SB	CS	SB%	GDP	Avg	OBP	SLG
1991 Bluefield	R+ Bal	34	116	28	5	2	0	37	16	16	6	0	19	4	1	3	6	3	.67	6	.241	.295	.319
1992 Kane County	A Bal	38	113	22	4	0	2	32	10	17	4	0	21	0	2	0	0	0	.00	1	.195	.222	.283
1993 Frederick	A+ Bal	66	188	41	13	1	4	68	22	17	13	0	41	7	3	0	1	0	1.00	2	.218	.293	.362
1994 Bowie	AA Bal	69	204	40	8	2	3	61	27	20	10	0	57	6	1	3	1	0	1.00	6	.196	.251	.299
1995 Bowie	AA Bal	5	13	1	0	0	0	1	1	0	3	0	5	0	0	0	1	0	1.00	0	.077	.250	.077
Rochester	AAA Bal	21	64	16	2	1	0	20	5	4	4	0	15	2	0	0	0	0	.00	2	.250	.314	.313
High Desert	A+ Bal	47	140	36	8	0	5	59	25	15	12	1	31	4	2	2	1	3	.25	6	.257	.329	.421
1996 Bowie	AA Bal	42	129	26	7	0	0	33	12	6	10	1	28	5	1	1	1	2	.33	2	.202	.283	.256
High Desert	A+ Bal	2	8	3	0	0	2	9	2	4	0	0	1	0	0	0	0	0	.00	0	.375	.375	1.125
6 Min. YEARS		324	975	213	47	6	16	320	120	99	62	2	218	28	10	9	11	8	.58	25	.218	.282	.328

Ben Grieve

Bats: Left **Throws:** Right **Pos:** OF **Ht:** 6'4" **Wt:** 200 **Born:** 5/4/76 **Age:** 21

		BATTING															BASERUNNING				PERCENTAGES		
Year Team	Lg Org	G	AB	H	2B	3B	HR	TB	R	RBI	TBB	IBB	SO	HBP	SH	SF	SB	CS	SB%	GDP	Avg	OBP	SLG
1994 Sou. Oregon	A- Oak	72	252	83	13	0	7	117	44	50	51	7	48	10	0	3	2	2	.50	6	.329	.456	.464
1995 W. Michigan	A Oak	102	371	97	16	1	4	127	53	62	60	6	75	8	0	6	11	3	.79	10	.261	.371	.342
Modesto	A+ Oak	28	107	28	5	0	2	39	17	14	15	1	22	0	0	2	2	0	1.00	3	.262	.347	.364
1996 Modesto	A+ Oak	72	281	100	20	1	11	155	61	51	38	2	52	1	1	3	8	7	.53	5	.356	.430	.552
Huntsville	AA Oak	63	232	55	8	1	8	89	34	32	35	5	53	2	0	3	0	3	.00	3	.237	.338	.384
3 Min. YEARS		337	1243	363	62	3	32	527	209	209	199	21	250	21	1	17	23	15	.61	27	.292	.394	.424

Craig Griffey

Bats: Right **Throws:** Right **Pos:** OF **Ht:** 5'11" **Wt:** 175 **Born:** 6/3/71 **Age:** 26

		BATTING															BASERUNNING				PERCENTAGES		
Year Team	Lg Org	G	AB	H	2B	3B	HR	TB	R	RBI	TBB	IBB	SO	HBP	SH	SF	SB	CS	SB%	GDP	Avg	OBP	SLG
1991 Mariners	R Sea	45	150	38	1	1	0	41	36	20	28	0	35	1	2	2	11	6	.65	0	.253	.370	.273
1992 Bellingham	A- Sea	63	220	55	6	1	1	66	30	21	22	0	35	3	2	2	15	8	.65	1	.250	.324	.300
1993 Appleton	A Sea	37	102	26	7	0	2	39	14	20	12	0	18	1	1	3	9	3	.75	1	.255	.331	.382

Year	Team	Lg	Org	G	AB	H	2B	3B	HR	TB	R	RBI	TBB	IBB	SO	HBP	SH	SF	SB	CS	SB%	GDP	Avg	OBP	SLG
				BATTING															**BASERUNNING**				**PERCENTAGES**		
	Riverside	A+	Sea	58	191	46	4	4	3	67	30	25	17	3	25	2	3	7	10	2	.83	3	.241	.300	.351
1994	Jacksonvlle	AA	Sea	106	327	72	13	1	3	96	37	29	33	0	68	3	10	5	20	10	.67	3	.220	.293	.294
1995	Port City	AA	Sea	96	299	53	11	1	0	66	43	24	46	0	77	9	3	3	13	3	.81	5	.177	.303	.221
1996	Port City	AA	Sea	120	396	88	14	7	2	122	43	35	46	0	88	6	2	6	20	7	.74	6	.222	.308	.308
6 Min. YEARS				525	1685	378	56	15	11	497	233	174	204	3	346	25	23	28	98	39	.72	19	.224	.313	.295

Pedro Grifol

Bats: Right **Throws:** Right **Pos:** C **Ht:** 6'1" **Wt:** 205 **Born:** 11/28/69 **Age:** 27

Year	Team	Lg	Org	G	AB	H	2B	3B	HR	TB	R	RBI	TBB	IBB	SO	HBP	SH	SF	SB	CS	SB%	GDP	Avg	OBP	SLG
				BATTING															**BASERUNNING**				**PERCENTAGES**		
1991	Elizabethtn	R+	Min	55	202	53	12	0	7	86	24	36	16	0	33	2	0	4	0	1	.00	6	.262	.317	.426
	Orlando	AA	Min	6	20	3	0	0	0	3	0	2	0	0	6	0	0	0	0	0	.00	0	.150	.150	.150
1992	Miracle	A+	Min	94	333	76	13	1	4	103	24	32	17	1	38	2	3	1	1	0	1.00	19	.228	.269	.309
	Orlando	AA	Min	14	40	11	2	0	0	13	2	5	2	0	9	0	0	1	0	0	.00	2	.275	.302	.325
1993	Nashville	AA	Min	58	197	40	13	0	5	68	22	29	11	0	38	2	5	3	0	1	.00	6	.203	.249	.345
	Portland	AAA	Min	28	94	31	4	2	2	45	14	17	4	0	14	0	2	2	0	0	.00	5	.330	.350	.479
1994	Nashville	AA	Min	20	55	7	0	0	1	10	4	4	10	0	7	1	0	1	0	0	.00	1	.127	.269	.182
1995	New Britain	AA	Min	77	226	40	9	0	3	58	23	21	23	1	33	1	1	1	1	0	1.00	8	.177	.255	.257
1996	Binghamton	AA	NYN	64	202	48	3	0	7	72	22	28	13	2	29	0	8	0	0	0	.00	6	.238	.284	.356
6 Min. YEARS				416	1369	309	56	3	29	458	135	174	96	4	207	8	19	13	2	2	.50	53	.226	.278	.335

Benji Grigsby

Pitches: Right **Bats:** Right **Pos:** P **Ht:** 6'1" **Wt:** 200 **Born:** 12/2/70 **Age:** 26

Year	Team	Lg	Org	G	GS	CG	GF	IP	BFP	H	R	ER	HR	SH	SF	HB	TBB	IBB	SO	WP	Bk	W	L	Pct.	ShO	Sv	ERA
				HOW MUCH HE PITCHED						**WHAT HE GAVE UP**												**THE RESULTS**					
1992	Athletics	R	Oak	3	3	0	0	11	35	4	2	2	2	0	0	0	1	0	7	0	0	1	1	.500	0	0	1.64
1993	Modesto	A+	Oak	39	10	0	10	90.1	396	90	49	48	12	2	1	3	42	2	72	9	1	5	6	.455	0	6	4.78
1994	Modesto	A+	Oak	16	8	0	5	65.1	272	59	28	24	4	1	3	1	18	0	49	6	2	4	1	.800	0	4	3.31
	Huntsville	AA	Oak	17	7	0	5	47	205	43	17	15	2	1	1	2	23	2	30	1	0	3	2	.600	0	1	2.87
1995	Huntsville	AA	Oak	30	6	0	8	76.1	306	66	40	34	7	0	3	1	20	1	55	6	0	3	5	.375	0	3	4.01
1996	Edmonton	AAA	Oak	11	3	0	5	22.1	104	29	20	18	2	0	1	0	7	2	15	4	0	0	3	.000	0	0	7.25
	Canton-Akrn	AA	Cle	16	0	0	8	28.2	120	22	11	4	0	4	2	3	11	1	21	1	0	1	2	.333	0	2	1.26
	Buffalo	AAA	Cle	8	0	0	4	13.1	63	18	13	8	6	0	0	0	4	0	3	0	0	0	0	.000	0	0	5.40
5 Min. YEARS				140	37	0	45	354.1	1501	331	180	153	35	8	11	10	126	8	252	27	3	17	20	.459	0	16	3.89

Kevin Grijak

Bats: Left **Throws:** Right **Pos:** 1B **Ht:** 6'2" **Wt:** 195 **Born:** 8/6/70 **Age:** 26

Year	Team	Lg	Org	G	AB	H	2B	3B	HR	TB	R	RBI	TBB	IBB	SO	HBP	SH	SF	SB	CS	SB%	GDP	Avg	OBP	SLG
				BATTING															**BASERUNNING**				**PERCENTAGES**		
1991	Idaho Falls	R+	Atl	52	202	68	9	1	10	109	33	58	16	1	15	1	2	4	4	1	.80	5	.337	.381	.540
1992	Pulaski	R+	Atl	10	31	11	3	0	0	14	1	6	6	0	0	0	0	0	2	2	.50	1	.355	.459	.452
	Macon	A	Atl	47	157	41	13	0	5	69	20	21	15	2	16	3	0	2	3	0	1.00	3	.261	.333	.439
1993	Macon	A	Atl	120	389	115	26	5	7	172	50	58	37	4	37	6	2	12	9	5	.64	9	.296	.356	.442
1994	Durham	A+	Atl	22	68	25	3	0	11	61	18	22	12	4	6	3	0	1	1	1	.50	1	.368	.476	.897
	Greenville	AA	Atl	100	348	94	19	1	11	148	40	58	20	1	40	6	0	7	2	3	.40	11	.270	.315	.425
1995	Greenville	AA	Atl	21	74	32	5	0	2	43	14	11	7	0	9	2	0	2	0	1	.00	0	.432	.482	.581
	Richmond	AAA	Atl	106	309	92	16	5	12	154	35	56	25	4	47	4	0	4	1	3	.25	10	.298	.354	.498
1996	Richmond	AAA	Atl	13	30	11	3	0	1	17	3	8	5	0	7	1	0	0	0	1	.00	1	.367	.472	.567
6 Min. YEARS				491	1608	489	97	12	59	787	214	298	143	16	177	26	4	32	22	17	.56	41	.304	.364	.489

Mike Groppuso

Bats: Right **Throws:** Right **Pos:** 3B **Ht:** 6'3" **Wt:** 195 **Born:** 3/9/70 **Age:** 27

Year	Team	Lg	Org	G	AB	H	2B	3B	HR	TB	R	RBI	TBB	IBB	SO	HBP	SH	SF	SB	CS	SB%	GDP	Avg	OBP	SLG
				BATTING															**BASERUNNING**				**PERCENTAGES**		
1991	Asheville	A	Hou	63	197	36	12	1	4	62	31	25	34	2	60	3	0	0	3	1	.75	3	.183	.312	.315
1992	Osceola	A+	Hou	115	369	80	19	1	4	113	53	37	43	2	98	9	3	3	6	3	.67	4	.217	.311	.306
1993	Jackson	AA	Hou	114	370	89	18	0	10	137	41	49	35	4	121	5	0	1	3	3	.50	8	.241	.314	.370
1994	Jackson	AA	Hou	118	352	93	16	2	12	149	49	47	35	2	97	5	1	4	6	7	.46	10	.264	.336	.423
1995	Jackson	AA	Hou	24	79	17	3	1	1	25	5	5	16	3	17	1	0	1	2	1	.67	1	.215	.351	.316
1996	Tucson	AAA	Hou	50	145	37	3	1	5	57	15	18	8	0	45	2	0	2	2	0	1.00	3	.255	.299	.393
	Jackson	AA	Hou	33	111	28	0	2	3	41	17	12	11	1	35	3	0	0	1	1	.50	6	.252	.336	.369
6 Min. YEARS				517	1623	380	71	8	39	584	211	193	182	14	473	28	4	11	23	16	.59	35	.234	.320	.360

Jeff Grotewold

Bats: Left **Throws:** Right **Pos:** DH **Ht:** 6' 0" **Wt:** 215 **Born:** 12/8/65 **Age:** 31

Year	Team	Lg	Org	G	AB	H	2B	3B	HR	TB	R	RBI	TBB	IBB	SO	HBP	SH	SF	SB	CS	SB%	GDP	Avg	OBP	SLG
				BATTING															**BASERUNNING**				**PERCENTAGES**		
1987	Spartanburg	A	Phi	113	381	96	22	2	15	167	56	70	47	10	114	4	0	3	4	6	.40	5	.252	.338	.438
1988	Clearwater	A+	Phi	125	442	97	23	2	6	142	35	39	42	9	103	1	1	1	2	1	.67	16	.219	.288	.321
1989	Clearwater	A+	Phi	91	301	84	17	2	6	123	32	55	32	4	43	1	0	4	8	2	.80	12	.279	.346	.409
	Reading	AA	Phi	25	80	16	2	0	0	18	9	11	8	0	14	0	0	2	0	0	.00	2	.200	.267	.225
1990	Reading	AA	Phi	127	412	111	33	1	15	191	56	72	62	5	83	1	2	4	2	2	.50	11	.269	.363	.464

Year	Team	Lg	Org	G	AB	H	2B	3B	HR	TB	R	RBI	TBB	IBB	SO	HBP	SH	SF	SB	CS	SB%	GDP	Avg	OBP	SLG
	BATTING																		BASERUNNING				PERCENTAGES		
1991	Scranton-WB	AAA	Phi	87	276	71	13	5	5	109	33	38	25	1	61	1	2	0	0	2	.00	6	.257	.321	.395
1992	Scranton-WB	AAA	Phi	17	51	15	1	1	1	21	8	8	7	1	10	2	0	0	0	0	.00	1	.294	.400	.412
1993	Portland	AAA	Min	52	151	38	6	3	6	68	27	30	27	0	41	2	1	1	2	1	.67	7	.252	.370	.450
1994	San Bernrdo	A+	—	32	117	36	10	0	6	64	19	25	15	0	29	2	0	2	0	3	.00	2	.308	.390	.547
	Duluth-Sup.	IND	—	35	141	39	7	1	6	66	15	24	7	1	41	0	0	0	1	1	.50	1	.277	.311	.468
1995	Omaha	AAA	KC	105	350	103	19	0	17	173	70	60	82	5	88	5	3	1	0	2	.00	14	.294	.434	.494
1996	Omaha	AAA	KC	98	338	94	20	0	10	144	63	51	58	3	84	8	1	2	1	3	.25	11	.278	.394	.426
1992	Philadelphia	NL		72	65	13	2	0	3	24	7	5	9	0	16	1	0	0	0	0	.00	4	.200	.307	.369
1995	Kansas City	AL		15	36	10	1	0	1	14	4	6	9	0	7	0	0	0	0	0	.00	2	.278	.422	.389
10	Min. YEARS			907	3040	800	173	17	93	1286	423	483	412	39	711	27	10	20	20	23	.47	88	.263	.354	.423
2	Maj. YEARS			87	101	23	3	0	4	38	11	11	18	0	23	1	0	0	0	0	.00	6	.228	.350	.376

Matt Grott

Pitches: Left **Bats:** Left **Pos:** P **Ht:** 6' 1" **Wt:** 205 **Born:** 12/5/67 **Age:** 29

Year	Team	Lg	Org	G	GS	CG	GF	IP	BFP	H	R	ER	HR	SH	SF	HB	TBB	IBB	SO	WP	Bk	W	L	Pct.	ShO	Sv	ERA
	HOW MUCH HE PITCHED									WHAT HE GAVE UP												THE RESULTS					
1989	Athletics	R	Oak	9	5	0	0	35	139	29	10	9	0	0	0	2	9	0	44	1	2	3	1	.750	0	0	2.31
1990	Madison	A	Oak	22	0	0	19	25	102	15	5	1	0	0	0	0	14	1	36	1	1	2	0	1.000	0	12	0.36
	Modesto	A+	Oak	12	0	0	8	17.2	78	10	7	4	0	1	0	0	14	1	28	4	0	2	0	1.000	0	4	2.04
	Huntsville	AA	Oak	10	0	0	6	15.2	62	8	5	5	1	1	3	0	10	0	12	0	0	0	0	.000	0	1	2.87
1991	Huntsville	AA	Oak	42	0	0	23	57.2	276	65	40	33	6	8	3	0	37	7	65	6	0	2	9	.182	0	3	5.15
	Harrisburg	AA	Mon	10	1	0	2	15.1	69	14	8	8	4	0	0	0	8	0	16	0	0	2	1	.667	0	1	4.70
1992	Chattanooga	AA	Cin	32	0	0	20	40.1	180	39	16	12	4	4	1	0	25	4	44	5	2	1	2	.333	0	6	2.68
1993	Indianapols	AAA	Cin	33	9	0	10	100.1	423	88	45	40	8	3	4	1	40	2	73	7	1	7	5	.583	0	1	3.59
1994	Indianapols	AAA	Cin	26	16	2	2	116.1	468	106	44	33	10	5	1	0	32	0	64	7	1	10	3	.769	1	1	2.55
1995	Indianapols	AAA	Cin	25	18	2	2	114.2	468	99	61	54	10	2	5	3	24	2	74	11	0	7	3	.700	1	2	4.24
1996	Scranton-WB	AAA	Phi	27	12	0	4	86.2	365	92	48	47	18	2	4	1	22	2	63	4	1	1	3	.250	0	0	4.88
	Rochester	AAA	Bal	5	1	0	1	9.1	46	13	10	4	3	2	0	0	7	0	5	0	0	0	0	.000	0	0	3.86
	Bowie	AA	Bal	9	0	0	3	21.2	93	26	15	12	3	0	2	0	5	0	15	2	0	2	1	.667	0	0	4.98
1995	Cincinnati	NL		2	0	0	0	1.2	11	6	4	4	1	0	0	0	0	0	2	0	0	0	0	.000	0	0	21.60
8	Min. YEARS			262	62	4	100	655.2	2769	604	314	262	67	28	23	7	247	19	539	48	8	39	28	.582	2	31	3.60

Phillip Grundy

Pitches: Right **Bats:** Right **Pos:** P **Ht:** 6'2" **Wt:** 195 **Born:** 9/8/72 **Age:** 24

Year	Team	Lg	Org	G	GS	CG	GF	IP	BFP	H	R	ER	HR	SH	SF	HB	TBB	IBB	SO	WP	Bk	W	L	Pct.	ShO	Sv	ERA
	HOW MUCH HE PITCHED									WHAT HE GAVE UP												THE RESULTS					
1993	Eugene	A-	KC	15	13	0	0	69	301	68	31	25	7	2	1	5	37	1	61	5	1	3	5	.375	0	0	3.26
1994	Rockford	A	KC	27	26	2	0	151.1	622	135	65	54	6	1	4	1	51	3	116	14	0	15	8	.652	0	0	3.21
1995	Wichita	AA	KC	6	2	0	1	17.1	75	16	17	16	6	1	1	1	7	0	11	3	0	1	1	.500	0	0	8.31
	Wilmington	A+	KC	26	18	0	4	123.1	520	122	63	55	13	5	2	6	39	2	101	10	0	7	7	.500	0	1	4.01
1996	Wichita	AA	KC	1	1	0	0	7	26	4	1	1	0	0	0	0	2	0	0	1	0	1	0	1.000	0	0	1.29
	Wilmington	A+	KC	27	26	3	0	164.2	679	155	87	65	17	8	4	6	49	3	117	5	2	7	11	.389	2	0	3.55
4	Min. YEARS			102	86	5	5	532.2	2223	500	264	216	49	17	12	19	185	9	406	38	3	34	32	.515	2	1	3.65

Keith Grunewald

Bats: Both **Throws:** Right **Pos:** 2B **Ht:** 6'1" **Wt:** 185 **Born:** 10/15/71 **Age:** 25

Year	Team	Lg	Org	G	AB	H	2B	3B	HR	TB	R	RBI	TBB	IBB	SO	HBP	SH	SF	SB	CS	SB%	GDP	Avg	OBP	SLG
	BATTING																		BASERUNNING				PERCENTAGES		
1993	Bend	A-	Col	56	183	50	4	2	3	67	29	21	30	1	44	0	1	0	7	2	.78	2	.273	.376	.366
1994	New Haven	AA	Col	8	18	8	0	0	0	8	2	0	0	0	5	0	0	0	0	0	.00	1	.444	.444	.444
	Asheville	A	Col	111	406	109	11	0	10	150	47	37	36	2	98	0	4	1	4	5	.44	5	.268	.327	.369
1995	Salem	A+	Col	118	412	109	22	1	6	151	48	45	46	8	84	10	2	3	8	4	.67	8	.265	.350	.367
1996	Salem	A+	Col	10	37	9	1	0	0	10	1	4	2	0	12	1	1	1	0	3	.00	0	.243	.293	.270
	New Haven	AA	Col	111	352	80	13	2	3	106	27	28	25	3	98	5	7	3	2	1	.67	3	.227	.286	.301
4	Min. YEARS			414	1408	365	51	5	22	492	154	135	139	14	341	16	15	8	21	15	.58	19	.259	.331	.349

Mike Grzanich

Pitches: Right **Bats:** Right **Pos:** P **Ht:** 6'1" **Wt:** 180 **Born:** 8/24/72 **Age:** 24

Year	Team	Lg	Org	G	GS	CG	GF	IP	BFP	H	R	ER	HR	SH	SF	HB	TBB	IBB	SO	WP	Bk	W	L	Pct.	ShO	Sv	ERA
	HOW MUCH HE PITCHED									WHAT HE GAVE UP												THE RESULTS					
1992	Astros	R	Hou	17	3	0	9	33.2	159	38	21	17	0	2	3	6	14	0	29	1	0	2	5	.286	0	3	4.54
1993	Auburn	A-	Hou	16	14	4	1	93.1	409	106	63	50	11	3	3	3	27	0	71	7	1	5	8	.385	1	0	4.82
1994	Quad City	A	Hou	23	22	3	1	142.2	598	145	55	49	5	2	1	11	43	2	101	5	0	11	7	.611	0	0	3.09
1995	Jackson	AA	Hou	50	0	0	23	65.2	276	55	22	20	0	5	3	6	38	5	44	4	0	5	3	.625	0	8	2.74
1996	Jackson	AA	Hou	57	0	0	19	72.1	316	60	47	32	10	4	2	8	43	2	80	6	0	5	4	.556	0	6	3.98
5	Min. YEARS			163	39	7	53	407.2	1758	404	208	168	26	16	12	34	165	9	325	23	1	28	27	.509	1	17	3.71

Creighton Gubanich

Bats: Right **Throws:** Right **Pos:** C **Ht:** 6'4" **Wt:** 220 **Born:** 3/27/72 **Age:** 25

Year	Team	Lg	Org	G	AB	H	2B	3B	HR	TB	R	RBI	TBB	IBB	SO	HBP	SH	SF	SB	CS	SB%	GDP	Avg	OBP	SLG
	BATTING																		BASERUNNING				PERCENTAGES		
1991	Sou. Oregon	A-	Oak	43	132	30	7	2	4	53	23	18	19	0	35	6	0	0	0	4	.00	2	.227	.350	.402

		BATTING															BASERUNNING				PERCENTAGES		
Year Team	Lg Org	G	AB	H	2B	3B	HR	TB	R	RBI	TBB	IBB	SO	HBP	SH	SF	SB	CS	SB%	GDP	Avg	OBP	SLG
1992 Madison	A Oak	121	404	100	19	3	9	152	46	55	41	1	102	16	8	1	0	7	.00	8	.248	.340	.376
1993 Madison	A Oak	119	373	100	19	2	19	180	65	78	63	2	105	11	2	12	3	3	.50	7	.268	.379	.483
1994 Modesto	A+ Oak	108	375	88	20	3	15	159	53	55	54	0	102	7	5	2	5	4	.56	9	.235	.340	.424
1995 Huntsville	AA Oak	94	274	60	7	1	13	108	37	43	48	0	82	7	2	5	1	0	1.00	2	.219	.344	.394
1996 Huntsville	AA Oak	62	217	60	19	0	9	106	40	43	31	1	71	4	3	2	1	0	1.00	5	.276	.374	.488
Edmonton	AAA Oak	34	117	29	7	1	4	50	14	19	6	0	33	1	0	1	3	0	1.00	5	.248	.288	.427
6 Min. YEARS		581	1892	467	98	12	73	808	278	311	262	4	530	52	20	23	13	18	.42	38	.247	.350	.427

Mark Guerra

Pitches: Right **Bats:** Right **Pos:** P **Ht:** 6'2" **Wt:** 185 **Born:** 11/4/71 **Age:** 25

		HOW MUCH HE PITCHED						WHAT HE GAVE UP												THE RESULTS					
Year Team	Lg Org	G	GS	CG	GF	IP	BFP	H	R	ER	HR	SH	SF	HB	TBB	IBB	SO	WP	Bk	W	L	Pct.	ShO	Sv	ERA
1994 Pittsfield	A- NYN	14	14	2	0	94	392	105	47	36	4	4	5	4	21	1	62	2	2	7	6	.538	0	0	3.45
1995 Binghamton	AA NYN	6	5	1	0	32.2	139	35	24	21	6	1	0	0	9	1	24	0	0	2	1	.667	0	0	5.79
St. Lucie	A+ NYN	29	28	5	0	192.2	783	183	79	68	11	5	4	4	42	2	134	2	3	11	10	.524	3	0	3.18
1996 Binghamton	AA NYN	27	20	1	3	140.1	577	143	60	55	23	5	2	2	34	3	84	1	1	7	6	.538	0	0	3.53
3 Min. YEARS		76	67	9	3	459.2	1891	466	210	180	44	15	11	10	106	7	304	5	6	27	23	.540	3	0	3.52

Vladimir Guerrero

Bats: Right **Throws:** Right **Pos:** OF **Ht:** 6' 2" **Wt:** 195 **Born:** 2/9/76 **Age:** 21

		BATTING															BASERUNNING				PERCENTAGES		
Year Team	Lg Org	G	AB	H	2B	3B	HR	TB	R	RBI	TBB	IBB	SO	HBP	SH	SF	SB	CS	SB%	GDP	Avg	OBP	SLG
1994 Expos	R Mon	37	137	43	13	3	5	77	24	25	11	0	18	2	0	3	0	7	.00	0	.314	.366	.562
1995 Albany	A Mon	110	421	140	21	10	16	229	77	63	30	3	45	7	0	4	12	7	.63	8	.333	.383	.544
1996 W. Palm Bch	A+ Mon	20	80	29	8	0	5	52	16	18	3	0	10	1	0	1	2	2	.50	1	.363	.388	.650
Harrisburg	AA Mon	118	417	150	32	8	19	255	84	78	51	13	42	9	0	2	17	10	.63	8	.360	.438	.612
1996 Montreal	NL	9	27	5	0	0	1	8	2	1	0	0	3	0	0	0	0	0	.00	1	.185	.185	.296
3 Min. YEARS		285	1055	362	74	21	45	613	201	184	95	16	115	19	0	10	31	26	.54	17	.343	.404	.581

Giomar Guevara

Bats: Both **Throws:** Right **Pos:** SS **Ht:** 5'8" **Wt:** 150 **Born:** 10/23/72 **Age:** 24

		BATTING															BASERUNNING				PERCENTAGES		
Year Team	Lg Org	G	AB	H	2B	3B	HR	TB	R	RBI	TBB	IBB	SO	HBP	SH	SF	SB	CS	SB%	GDP	Avg	OBP	SLG
1993 Bellingham	A- Sea	62	211	48	8	3	1	65	31	23	34	2	46	2	4	0	4	7	.36	3	.227	.340	.308
1994 Appleton	A Sea	110	385	116	23	3	8	169	57	46	42	1	77	2	5	1	9	16	.36	6	.301	.372	.439
Jacksonvlle	AA Sea	7	20	4	2	0	1	9	2	3	2	0	9	0	1	0	0	0	.00	0	.200	.273	.450
1995 Riverside	A+ Sea	83	292	71	12	3	2	95	53	34	30	1	71	1	6	6	7	4	.64	4	.243	.310	.325
1996 Port City	AA Sea	119	414	110	18	2	2	138	60	41	54	1	102	4	9	4	21	7	.75	12	.266	.353	.333
4 Min. YEARS		381	1322	349	63	11	14	476	203	147	162	5	305	9	25	11	41	34	.55	25	.264	.346	.360

Aaron Guiel

Bats: Left **Throws:** Right **Pos:** 3B **Ht:** 5'10" **Wt:** 190 **Born:** 10/5/72 **Age:** 24

		BATTING															BASERUNNING				PERCENTAGES		
Year Team	Lg Org	G	AB	H	2B	3B	HR	TB	R	RBI	TBB	IBB	SO	HBP	SH	SF	SB	CS	SB%	GDP	Avg	OBP	SLG
1993 Boise	A- Cal	35	104	31	6	4	2	51	24	12	26	1	21	4	2	0	3	0	1.00	1	.298	.455	.490
1994 Cedar Rapds	A Cal	127	454	122	30	1	18	208	84	82	64	2	93	6	5	3	21	7	.75	7	.269	.364	.458
1995 Lk Elsinore	A+ Cal	113	409	110	25	7	7	170	73	58	69	0	96	7	4	4	7	6	.54	7	.269	.380	.416
1996 Midland	AA Cal	129	439	118	29	7	10	191	72	48	56	0	71	10	2	1	11	7	.61	6	.269	.364	.435
4 Min. YEARS		404	1406	381	90	19	37	620	253	200	215	3	281	27	13	8	42	20	.68	21	.271	.376	.441

Michael Guilfoyle

Pitches: Left **Bats:** Left **Pos:** P **Ht:** 5'11" **Wt:** 187 **Born:** 4/29/68 **Age:** 29

		HOW MUCH HE PITCHED						WHAT HE GAVE UP												THE RESULTS					
Year Team	Lg Org	G	GS	CG	GF	IP	BFP	H	R	ER	HR	SH	SF	HB	TBB	IBB	SO	WP	Bk	W	L	Pct.	ShO	Sv	ERA
1990 Bristol	R+ Det	16	7	0	3	64.2	278	54	35	22	6	3	1	1	25	0	80	4	3	4	6	.400	0	1	3.06
1991 Fayettevlle	A Det	40	0	0	34	47.1	213	41	22	13	3	4	4	5	26	1	44	2	1	1	4	.200	0	8	2.47
1992 Lakeland	A+ Det	45	0	0	31	51	214	48	23	18	1	1	1	1	16	1	32	2	1	4	1	.800	0	11	3.18
1993 Lakeland	A+ Det	9	0	0	9	9.1	37	5	1	1	0	1	0	0	3	0	10	0	0	0	0	.000	0	5	0.96
London	AA Det	49	0	0	18	41	181	43	19	17	2	5	2	2	16	0	35	0	1	1	2	.333	0	3	3.73
1994 Trenton	AA Det	42	0	0	32	50.1	227	60	27	25	4	4	2	1	25	0	36	1	1	7	8	.467	0	5	4.47
1995 Jacksonvlle	AA Det	56	0	0	14	59.1	256	55	23	19	2	2	2	0	31	3	50	1	0	5	1	.833	0	3	2.88
1996 Toledo	AAA Det	54	0	0	12	49	230	59	35	28	7	4	1	0	31	4	42	6	0	5	5	.500	0	1	5.14
7 Min. YEARS		311	7	0	153	372	1636	365	185	143	25	24	13	10	173	9	329	16	7	27	27	.500	0	37	3.46

Matthew Guiliano

Bats: Right **Throws:** Right **Pos:** SS **Ht:** 5'7" **Wt:** 175 **Born:** 6/7/72 **Age:** 25

		BATTING															BASERUNNING				PERCENTAGES		
Year Team	Lg Org	G	AB	H	2B	3B	HR	TB	R	RBI	TBB	IBB	SO	HBP	SH	SF	SB	CS	SB%	GDP	Avg	OBP	SLG
1994 Martinsvlle	R+ Phi	58	190	42	5	0	5	62	33	16	24	0	57	7	3	2	16	3	.84	4	.221	.327	.326
1995 Piedmont	A Phi	129	451	102	22	12	4	160	67	59	51	1	114	7	9	6	6	8	.43	7	.226	.311	.355
1996 Reading	AA Phi	74	220	44	9	3	0	59	19	19	25	1	59	3	3	1	0	0	.00	4	.200	.289	.268
Clearwater	A+ Phi	55	166	37	8	2	1	52	12	14	6	0	46	6	6	3	2	3	.40	3	.223	.271	.313

		BATTING															BASERUNNING				PERCENTAGES		
Year Team	Lg Org	G	AB	H	2B	3B	HR	TB	R	RBI	TBB	IBB	SO	HBP	SH	SF	SB	CS	SB%	GDP	Avg	OBP	SLG
3 Min. YEARS		316	1027	225	44	17	10	333	131	108	106	2	276	23	21	12	24	14	.63	18	.219	.303	.324

Mike Gulan

Bats: Right **Throws:** Right **Pos:** 3B **Ht:** 6'1" **Wt:** 190 **Born:** 12/18/70 **Age:** 26

		BATTING															BASERUNNING				PERCENTAGES		
Year Team	Lg Org	G	AB	H	2B	3B	HR	TB	R	RBI	TBB	IBB	SO	HBP	SH	SF	SB	CS	SB%	GDP	Avg	OBP	SLG
1992 Hamilton	A- StL	62	242	66	8	4	7	103	33	36	23	0	53	1	0	4	12	4	.75	7	.273	.333	.426
1993 Springfield	A StL	132	455	118	28	4	23	223	81	76	34	0	135	9	3	3	8	4	.67	4	.259	.321	.490
1994 St. Pete	A+ StL	120	466	113	30	2	8	171	39	56	26	2	108	2	0	6	2	8	.20	8	.242	.282	.367
1995 Arkansas	AA StL	64	242	76	16	3	12	134	47	48	11	1	52	6	0	1	4	2	.67	4	.314	.358	.554
Louisville	AAA StL	58	195	46	10	4	5	79	21	27	10	1	53	3	0	2	2	2	.50	6	.236	.281	.405
1996 Louisville	AAA StL	123	419	107	27	4	17	193	47	55	26	1	119	7	1	2	7	2	.78	10	.255	.308	.461
5 Min. YEARS		559	2019	526	119	21	72	903	268	298	130	5	520	28	4	18	35	22	.61	39	.261	.312	.447

Jim Gutierrez

Pitches: Right **Bats:** Right **Pos:** P **Ht:** 6'2" **Wt:** 190 **Born:** 11/28/70 **Age:** 26

		HOW MUCH HE PITCHED						WHAT HE GAVE UP												THE RESULTS					
Year Team	Lg Org	G	GS	CG	GF	IP	BFP	H	R	ER	HR	SH	SF	HB	TBB	IBB	SO	WP	Bk	W	L	Pct.	ShO	Sv	ERA
1989 Bellingham	A- Sea	13	11	0	1	57.2	268	68	44	25	4	0	1	1	24	0	33	1	0	1	5	.167	0	0	3.90
1990 Peninsula	A+ Sea	28	28	4	0	186	758	171	82	71	9	6	11	6	41	0	95	6	1	11	13	.458	2	0	3.44
1991 San Bernrdo	A+ Sea	17	14	1	0	82.2	377	100	65	60	11	0	3	2	37	0	66	4	0	4	4	.500	0	0	6.53
1992 Jacksonvlle	AA Sea	15	11	0	1	54	234	58	34	30	7	1	2	3	17	0	44	0	0	1	5	.167	0	0	5.00
1993 Riverside	A+ Sea	27	27	2	0	171.1	742	182	95	72	15	11	6	4	53	2	84	5	1	12	9	.571	0	0	3.78
1994 Jacksonvlle	AA Sea	28	21	6	4	151.2	655	175	76	72	16	4	3	4	42	4	89	1	0	8	11	.421	1	0	4.27
1995 Jacksonvlle	AA Det	45	1	0	14	58.2	243	60	22	18	2	3	2	0	25	4	36	3	0	8	4	.667	0	4	2.76
1996 Jacksonvlle	AA Det	51	10	0	10	105.1	452	98	55	44	6	3	5	1	54	5	71	6	0	8	6	.571	0	1	3.76
8 Min. YEARS		224	123	13	30	867.1	3729	912	473	392	70	28	33	21	293	15	518	26	2	53	57	.482	3	5	4.07

Rick Gutierrez

Bats: Right **Throws:** Right **Pos:** 2B **Ht:** 6'0" **Wt:** 170 **Born:** 3/23/70 **Age:** 27

		BATTING															BASERUNNING				PERCENTAGES		
Year Team	Lg Org	G	AB	H	2B	3B	HR	TB	R	RBI	TBB	IBB	SO	HBP	SH	SF	SB	CS	SB%	GDP	Avg	OBP	SLG
1994 Watertown	A- Cle	65	249	65	7	1	2	80	48	21	39	1	40	0	3	1	25	5	.83	4	.261	.360	.321
1995 Kinston	A+ Cle	117	439	115	21	7	4	162	63	46	67	3	62	4	7	4	43	16	.73	3	.262	.362	.369
1996 Canton-Akrn	AA Cle	119	484	122	11	3	7	160	69	55	37	0	56	2	4	5	18	9	.67	8	.252	.305	.331
3 Min. YEARS		301	1172	302	39	11	13	402	180	122	143	4	158	6	14	10	86	30	.74	15	.258	.339	.343

Jose Guzman

Pitches: Right **Bats:** Right **Pos:** P **Ht:** 6' 3" **Wt:** 195 **Born:** 4/9/63 **Age:** 34

		HOW MUCH HE PITCHED						WHAT HE GAVE UP												THE RESULTS					
Year Team	Lg Org	G	GS	CG	GF	IP	BFP	H	R	ER	HR	SH	SF	HB	TBB	IBB	SO	WP	Bk	W	L	Pct.	ShO	Sv	ERA
1984 Tulsa	AA Tex	25	25	7	0	140.1	597	137	75	65	6	1	8	0	55	1	82	8	0	7	9	.438	1	0	4.17
1985 Okla. City	AAA Tex	25	23	4	2	149.2	606	131	60	52	11	5	6	2	40	0	76	2	2	10	5	.667	1	1	3.13
1990 Charlotte	A+ Tex	2	2	0	0	8.1	37	10	3	2	0	1	1	0	4	0	7	0	0	0	1	.000	0	0	2.16
Tulsa	AA Tex	1	1	0	0	3	12	3	2	2	0	0	0	0	0	0	2	0	0	0	0	.000	0	0	6.00
Okla. City	AAA Tex	7	7	0	0	28.2	126	35	20	18	2	2	3	2	9	0	26	1	1	0	3	.000	0	0	5.65
1991 Okla. City	AAA Tex	3	3	0	0	20.2	84	18	9	9	1	1	0	0	4	0	18	2	1	1	1	.500	0	0	3.92
1994 Orlando	AA ChN	1	1	0	0	5	19	3	1	1	0	0	0	0	3	0	4	0	0	0	0	.000	0	0	1.80
1995 Cubs	R ChN	2	2	0	0	6	24	5	1	1	1	0	0	0	0	0	3	0	0	0	0	.000	0	0	1.50
1996 Daytona	A+ ChN	2	2	0	0	11	44	8	3	3	0	0	0	0	7	0	14	1	0	1	0	1.000	0	0	2.45
Iowa	AAA ChN	8	8	0	0	38.1	185	51	39	36	9	3	0	1	19	1	24	5	0	1	6	.143	0	0	8.45
Tacoma	AAA Sea	5	2	0	0	15.1	64	14	7	6	0	0	1	1	6	0	11	0	0	0	1	.000	0	0	3.52
1985 Texas	AL	5	5	0	0	32.2	140	27	13	10	3	0	0	0	14	1	24	1	0	3	2	.600	0	0	2.76
1986 Texas	AL	29	29	2	0	172.1	757	199	101	87	23	7	4	6	60	2	87	3	0	9	15	.375	0	0	4.54
1987 Texas	AL	37	30	6	1	208.1	880	196	115	108	30	6	8	3	82	0	143	6	5	14	14	.500	0	0	4.67
1988 Texas	AL	30	30	6	0	206.2	876	180	99	85	20	4	6	5	82	3	157	10	12	11	13	.458	2	0	3.70
1991 Texas	AL	25	25	5	0	169.2	730	152	67	58	10	2	3	4	84	1	125	8	1	13	7	.650	1	0	3.08
1992 Texas	AL	33	33	5	0	224	947	229	103	91	17	9	7	4	73	0	179	6	0	16	11	.593	0	0	3.66
1993 Chicago	NL	30	30	2	0	191	819	188	98	92	25	8	5	3	74	6	163	6	5	12	10	.545	1	0	4.34
1994 Chicago	NL	4	4	0	0	19.2	93	22	20	20	1	2	1	1	13	0	11	1	0	2	2	.500	0	0	9.15
7 Min. YEARS		81	76	11	2	426.1	1798	415	220	195	30	13	19	6	147	2	267	19	4	20	26	.435	2	1	4.12
8 Maj. YEARS		193	186	26	1	1224.1	5242	1193	616	551	129	38	34	26	482	13	889	41	23	80	74	.519	4	0	4.05

Jeff Gyselman

Bats: Right **Throws:** Right **Pos:** C **Ht:** 6'3" **Wt:** 193 **Born:** 7/10/70 **Age:** 26

		BATTING															BASERUNNING				PERCENTAGES		
Year Team	Lg Org	G	AB	H	2B	3B	HR	TB	R	RBI	TBB	IBB	SO	HBP	SH	SF	SB	CS	SB%	GDP	Avg	OBP	SLG
1993 Batavia	A- Phi	36	120	23	5	2	0	32	7	8	8	0	33	2	3	1	1	1	.50	1	.192	.252	.267
1994 Batavia	A- Phi	2	7	2	0	0	1	5	2	1	0	0	2	0	0	0	0	0	.00	0	.286	.286	.714
Spartanburg	A Phi	12	28	2	0	0	0	2	4	2	3	0	8	0	0	0	0	0	.00	0	.071	.161	.071
1995 Clearwater	A+ Phi	26	64	11	0	0	0	11	8	3	6	0	14	0	0	0	0	0	.00	4	.172	.243	.172
1996 Reading	AA Phi	49	128	22	2	0	0	24	9	12	14	0	36	1	5	1	0	2	.00	3	.172	.257	.188

Year Team	Lg Org	BATTING															BASERUNNING				PERCENTAGES		
		G	AB	H	2B	3B	HR	TB	R	RBI	TBB	IBB	SO	HBP	SH	SF	SB	CS	SB%	GDP	Avg	OBP	SLG
4 Min. YEARS		125	347	60	7	2	1	74	30	26	31	0	93	3	8	2	1	3	.25	8	.173	.245	.213

John Halama

Pitches: Left **Bats:** Left **Pos:** P **Ht:** 6'5" **Wt:** 195 **Born:** 2/22/72 **Age:** 25

Year Team	Lg Org	HOW MUCH HE PITCHED						WHAT HE GAVE UP												THE RESULTS					
		G	GS	CG	GF	IP	BFP	H	R	ER	HR	SH	SF	HB	TBB	IBB	SO	WP	Bk	W	L	Pct.	ShO	Sv	ERA
1994 Auburn	A- Hou	6	3	0	3	28	107	18	5	4	1	2	0	0	5	0	27	1	1	4	1	.800	0	1	1.29
Quad City	A Hou	9	9	1	0	51.1	222	63	31	26	2	3	0	2	18	1	37	3	0	3	4	.429	1	0	4.56
1995 Quad City	A Hou	55	0	0	26	62.1	241	48	16	14	7	2	1	3	22	1	56	1	0	1	2	.333	0	2	2.02
1996 Jackson	AA Hou	27	27	0	0	162.2	691	151	77	58	10	7	7	8	59	0	110	7	0	9	10	.474	0	0	3.21
3 Min. YEARS		97	39	1	29	304.1	1261	280	129	102	20	14	8	13	104	2	230	12	1	17	17	.500	1	3	3.02

Shane Hale

Pitches: Left **Bats:** Right **Pos:** P **Ht:** 6'1" **Wt:** 180 **Born:** 12/30/68 **Age:** 28

Year Team	Lg Org	HOW MUCH HE PITCHED						WHAT HE GAVE UP												THE RESULTS					
		G	GS	CG	GF	IP	BFP	H	R	ER	HR	SH	SF	HB	TBB	IBB	SO	WP	Bk	W	L	Pct.	ShO	Sv	ERA
1990 Wausau	A Bal	12	9	1	0	56.1	250	47	34	30	5	2	2	3	39	0	57	8	5	3	4	.429	1	0	4.79
1991 Frederick	A+ Bal	16	9	0	3	71	311	61	45	27	5	5	1	6	34	0	72	5	3	0	6	.000	0	1	3.42
1992 Orioles	R Bal	2	0	0	0	2	12	2	2	2	0	0	0	1	3	0	4	0	0	0	1	.000	0	0	9.00
1993 Orioles	R Bal	3	3	0	0	4	13	2	0	0	0	0	0	0	0	0	2	0	0	0	0	.000	0	0	0.00
1994 Albany	A Bal	11	10	0	0	55.1	239	54	31	25	3	2	2	5	22	0	52	2	5	2	3	.400	0	0	4.07
Frederick	A+ Bal	11	11	0	0	62	277	68	38	34	10	4	3	3	30	0	49	5	3	4	3	.571	0	0	4.94
1995 Orioles	R Bal	2	2	0	0	7	32	6	2	1	0	0	0	0	4	0	6	0	0	0	0	.000	0	0	1.29
Frederick	A+ Bal	8	4	0	0	21	101	27	20	18	1	1	3	1	10	2	12	1	0	0	2	.000	0	0	7.71
1996 Bowie	AA Bal	24	24	0	0	135	591	146	81	75	18	6	3	6	51	2	86	4	3	5	13	.278	0	0	5.00
7 Min. YEARS		89	72	1	3	413.2	1826	413	253	212	42	20	14	25	193	4	340	25	19	14	32	.304	1	1	4.61

Billy Hall

Bats: Both **Throws:** Right **Pos:** 2B **Ht:** 5'9" **Wt:** 180 **Born:** 6/17/69 **Age:** 28

Year Team	Lg Org	BATTING															BASERUNNING				PERCENTAGES		
		G	AB	H	2B	3B	HR	TB	R	RBI	TBB	IBB	SO	HBP	SH	SF	SB	CS	SB%	GDP	Avg	OBP	SLG
1991 Charlstn-SC	A SD	72	279	84	6	5	2	106	41	28	34	1	54	0	0	2	25	9	.74	2	.301	.375	.380
1992 High Desert	A+ SD	119	495	176	22	5	2	214	92	39	54	2	77	1	1	3	49	27	.64	2	.356	.418	.432
1993 Wichita	AA SD	124	486	131	27	7	4	184	80	46	37	1	88	3	4	4	29	19	.60	6	.270	.323	.379
1994 Wichita	AA SD	29	111	40	5	1	1	50	14	12	11	1	19	1	0	0	10	5	.67	5	.360	.423	.450
Las Vegas	AAA SD	70	280	74	11	3	3	100	43	21	32	0	61	1	5	1	24	6	.80	2	.264	.341	.357
1995 Las Vegas	AAA SD	86	249	56	3	1	1	64	42	22	20	1	47	1	1	3	22	5	.81	3	.225	.282	.257
1996 Chattanooga	AA Cin	117	461	136	24	3	2	172	80	43	57	5	72	0	4	2	34	11	.76	9	.295	.371	.373
6 Min. YEARS		617	2361	697	98	25	15	890	392	211	245	11	418	7	15	15	193	82	.70	29	.295	.361	.377

Joe Hall

Bats: Right **Throws:** Right **Pos:** OF **Ht:** 6' 0" **Wt:** 180 **Born:** 3/6/66 **Age:** 31

Year Team	Lg Org	BATTING															BASERUNNING				PERCENTAGES		
		G	AB	H	2B	3B	HR	TB	R	RBI	TBB	IBB	SO	HBP	SH	SF	SB	CS	SB%	GDP	Avg	OBP	SLG
1988 Hamilton	A- StL	70	274	78	9	1	2	95	46	37	30	1	37	5	1	2	30	8	.79	6	.285	.363	.347
Springfield	A StL	1	1	0	0	0	0	0	0	0	0	0	1	0	0	0	0	0	.00	0	.000	.000	.000
1989 St. Pete	A+ StL	134	504	147	9	3	0	162	72	54	60	2	57	8	3	9	45	28	.62	11	.292	.370	.321
1990 Arkansas	AA StL	115	399	108	14	4	4	142	44	44	35	4	41	3	2	6	21	14	.60	7	.271	.330	.356
1991 Vancouver	AAA ChA	118	427	106	16	1	4	136	41	39	23	2	45	4	3	4	11	11	.50	18	.248	.290	.319
1992 Vancouver	AAA ChA	112	367	104	19	7	6	155	46	56	60	1	44	4	10	3	11	5	.69	15	.283	.387	.422
1993 Nashville	AAA ChA	116	424	123	33	5	10	196	66	58	52	3	56	4	1	2	10	9	.53	14	.290	.371	.462
1994 Birmingham	AA ChA	19	67	14	6	0	0	20	9	6	15	0	11	1	0	1	0	0	.00	4	.209	.357	.299
Nashville	AAA ChA	22	72	21	7	0	4	40	14	21	16	1	10	2	0	2	0	0	.00	1	.292	.424	.556
1995 Toledo	AAA Det	91	319	102	19	2	11	158	52	47	36	1	50	2	1	2	4	1	.80	7	.320	.390	.495
1996 Rochester	AAA Bal	131	479	138	26	10	19	241	96	95	67	3	69	2	0	6	15	9	.63	8	.288	.374	.503
1994 Chicago	AL	17	28	11	3	0	1	17	6	5	2	0	4	1	0	0	0	0	.00	2	.393	.452	.607
1995 Detroit	AL	7	15	2	0	0	0	2	2	0	2	0	3	0	0	0	0	0	.00	1	.133	.235	.133
9 Min. YEARS		929	3333	941	158	33	60	1345	486	457	394	18	421	35	21	37	147	85	.63	91	.282	.361	.404
2 Maj. YEARS		24	43	13	3	0	1	19	8	5	4	0	7	1	0	0	0	0	.00	3	.302	.375	.442

Mike Halperin

Pitches: Left **Bats:** Left **Pos:** P **Ht:** 5'10" **Wt:** 170 **Born:** 9/8/73 **Age:** 23

Year Team	Lg Org	HOW MUCH HE PITCHED						WHAT HE GAVE UP												THE RESULTS					
		G	GS	CG	GF	IP	BFP	H	R	ER	HR	SH	SF	HB	TBB	IBB	SO	WP	Bk	W	L	Pct.	ShO	Sv	ERA
1994 St. Cathrns	A- Tor	9	1	0	5	24	86	11	5	3	0	0	1	0	5	0	19	2	0	2	1	.667	0	1	1.13
Hagerstown	A Tor	6	6	0	0	30	116	25	4	4	1	1	0	0	7	0	27	3	1	2	1	.667	0	0	1.20
1995 Dunedin	A+ Tor	14	12	0	0	69.2	298	70	36	28	4	1	0	3	29	1	63	2	0	3	5	.375	0	0	3.62
1996 Knoxville	AA Tor	28	28	0	0	155	658	156	67	60	6	8	2	6	71	3	112	11	4	13	7	.650	0	0	3.48
3 Min. YEARS		57	17	0	5	278.2	1158	262	112	95	11	10	3	9	112	4	221	18	5	20	14	.588	0	1	3.07

Shane Halter

Bats: Right **Throws:** Right **Pos:** OF **Ht:** 5'10" **Wt:** 160 **Born:** 11/8/69 **Age:** 27

			BATTING															BASERUNNING				PERCENTAGES		
Year Team	Lg	Org	G	AB	H	2B	3B	HR	TB	R	RBI	TBB	IBB	SO	HBP	SH	SF	SB	CS	SB%	GDP	Avg	OBP	SLG
1991 Eugene	A-	KC	64	236	55	9	1	1	69	41	18	49	0	59	3	2	1	12	6	.67	3	.233	.370	.292
1992 Appleton	A	KC	80	313	83	22	3	3	120	50	33	41	1	54	1	5	3	21	6	.78	4	.265	.349	.383
Baseball Cy	A+	KC	44	117	28	1	0	1	32	11	14	24	0	31	0	5	4	5	5	.50	4	.239	.359	.274
1993 Wilmington	A+	KC	54	211	63	8	5	5	96	44	32	27	2	55	2	12	4	5	4	.56	3	.299	.377	.455
Memphis	AA	KC	81	306	79	7	0	4	98	50	20	30	1	74	2	10	3	4	7	.36	3	.258	.326	.320
1994 Memphis	AA	KC	129	494	111	23	1	6	154	61	35	39	0	102	3	15	6	10	14	.42	10	.225	.282	.312
1995 Omaha	AAA	KC	124	392	90	19	3	8	139	42	39	40	0	97	0	19	1	2	3	.40	6	.230	.300	.355
1996 Charlotte	AAA	Fla	16	41	12	1	0	0	13	3	4	2	0	8	0	0	2	0	0	.00	0	.293	.311	.317
Omaha	AAA	KC	93	299	77	24	0	3	110	43	33	31	0	49	2	8	1	7	2	.78	6	.258	.330	.368
6 Min. YEARS			685	2409	598	114	13	31	831	345	228	283	4	529	13	76	25	66	47	.58	39	.248	.327	.345

Jonas Hamlin

Bats: Right **Throws:** Right **Pos:** 1B **Ht:** 6'4" **Wt:** 200 **Born:** 4/18/70 **Age:** 27

			BATTING															BASERUNNING				PERCENTAGES		
Year Team	Lg	Org	G	AB	H	2B	3B	HR	TB	R	RBI	TBB	IBB	SO	HBP	SH	SF	SB	CS	SB%	GDP	Avg	OBP	SLG
1990 Cardinals	R	StL	52	216	75	11	4	8	118	45	39	13	2	27	1	0	1	0	2	.00	5	.347	.385	.546
1991 St. Pete	A+	StL	121	442	93	23	4	4	136	36	45	24	1	107	0	0	4	1	0	1.00	14	.210	.249	.308
1992 Savannah	A	StL	128	455	108	19	3	13	172	48	71	46	1	105	3	0	6	5	6	.45	8	.237	.308	.378
1993 Springfield	A	StL	121	428	93	19	2	17	167	57	62	40	2	119	3	2	2	3	2	.60	6	.217	.288	.390
1994 Beloit	A	Mil	133	495	124	29	1	14	197	63	88	39	2	124	6	1	9	14	9	.61	10	.251	.308	.398
1995 Stockton	A+	Mil	99	388	129	32	5	16	219	65	69	17	2	86	4	1	6	5	4	.56	7	.332	.361	.564
1996 El Paso	AA	Mil	131	515	146	35	8	21	260	81	94	37	0	101	5	1	10	9	7	.56	14	.283	.332	.505
7 Min. YEARS			785	2939	768	168	27	93	1269	395	468	216	10	669	22	5	38	37	30	.55	64	.261	.313	.432

Marcus Hanel

Bats: Right **Throws:** Right **Pos:** C **Ht:** 6'4" **Wt:** 205 **Born:** 10/19/71 **Age:** 25

			BATTING															BASERUNNING				PERCENTAGES		
Year Team	Lg	Org	G	AB	H	2B	3B	HR	TB	R	RBI	TBB	IBB	SO	HBP	SH	SF	SB	CS	SB%	GDP	Avg	OBP	SLG
1989 Pirates	R	Pit	28	78	18	3	1	0	23	11	8	6	0	18	0	4	0	2	1	.67	2	.231	.286	.295
1990 Welland	A-	Pit	40	98	15	2	0	0	17	5	8	5	2	26	1	0	0	1	2	.33	2	.153	.202	.173
1991 Augusta	A	Pit	104	364	60	10	1	1	75	33	29	17	1	88	9	2	5	9	3	.75	8	.165	.218	.206
1992 Salem	A+	Pit	75	231	43	8	0	3	60	12	17	11	0	53	2	6	1	4	0	1.00	6	.186	.229	.260
1993 Salem	A+	Pit	69	195	36	6	2	2	52	18	16	18	2	65	4	9	2	5	3	.63	2	.185	.265	.267
1994 Salem	A+	Pit	87	286	70	9	1	5	96	36	27	14	0	54	6	5	3	3	2	.60	5	.245	.291	.336
1995 Carolina	AA	Pit	21	60	11	1	0	0	12	1	3	4	0	18	1	1	1	0	1	.00	2	.183	.242	.200
Lynchburg	A+	Pit	40	135	25	4	1	3	40	14	8	4	0	33	1	2	0	0	1	.00	1	.185	.214	.296
Calgary	AAA	Pit	2	8	1	0	0	0	1	1	0	0	0	1	0	0	0	0	0	.00	0	.125	.125	.125
1996 Carolina	AA	Pit	101	332	59	19	1	5	95	22	36	16	4	57	7	3	4	2	2	.50	9	.178	.228	.286
8 Min. YEARS			567	1787	338	62	7	19	471	153	152	95	9	413	31	32	16	26	15	.63	37	.189	.241	.264

Brent Hansen

Pitches: Right **Bats:** Right **Pos:** P **Ht:** 6'2" **Wt:** 195 **Born:** 8/4/70 **Age:** 26

			HOW MUCH HE PITCHED						WHAT HE GAVE UP												THE RESULTS					
Year Team	Lg	Org	G	GS	CG	GF	IP	BFP	H	R	ER	HR	SH	SF	HB	TBB	IBB	SO	WP	Bk	W	L	Pct.	ShO	Sv	ERA
1992 Red Sox	R	Bos	3	2	0	1	10	38	4	1	1	0	0	0	1	4	0	5	0	0	0	0	.000	0	0	0.90
Elmira	A-	Bos	13	11	1	1	59	255	59	33	28	3	2	4	3	21	0	65	4	2	3	5	.375	1	0	4.27
1993 Ft. Laud	A+	Bos	14	14	4	0	102.2	432	94	37	30	6	2	2	4	37	2	59	1	1	4	6	.400	2	0	2.63
New Britain	AA	Bos	15	15	1	0	93.1	398	99	55	51	9	1	5	4	30	2	56	2	0	2	11	.154	0	0	4.92
1994 Sarasota	A+	Bos	8	7	0	1	40.1	167	37	15	13	0	0	1	0	15	0	27	3	0	2	2	.500	0	0	2.90
1995 Trenton	AA	Bos	11	11	3	0	77.1	327	70	32	28	5	3	2	12	17	1	52	1	2	4	5	.444	1	0	3.26
Pawtucket	AAA	Bos	25	25	5	0	169.2	712	160	80	72	17	3	5	17	40	1	102	2	2	11	10	.524	1	0	3.82
1996 Sarasota	A+	Bos	8	8	1	0	47.1	220	54	36	29	1	4	1	4	21	0	25	3	0	2	4	.333	1	0	5.51
Pawtucket	AAA	Bos	2	2	0	0	8.2	41	8	6	6	1	0	0	0	8	0	3	0	0	1	0	1.000	0	0	6.23
5 Min. YEARS			99	95	15	3	608.1	2590	585	295	258	42	15	20	45	193	6	394	16	7	29	43	.403	6	0	3.82

Jed Hansen

Bats: Right **Throws:** Right **Pos:** 2B **Ht:** 6'1" **Wt:** 195 **Born:** 8/19/72 **Age:** 24

			BATTING															BASERUNNING				PERCENTAGES		
Year Team	Lg	Org	G	AB	H	2B	3B	HR	TB	R	RBI	TBB	IBB	SO	HBP	SH	SF	SB	CS	SB%	GDP	Avg	OBP	SLG
1994 Eugene	A-	KC	66	235	57	8	2	3	78	26	17	24	2	56	8	2	1	6	4	.60	1	.243	.332	.332
1995 Springfield	A	KC	122	414	107	27	7	9	175	86	50	78	0	73	7	6	1	44	10	.81	8	.258	.384	.423
1996 Wichita	AA	KC	99	405	116	27	4	12	187	60	50	29	0	72	4	4	2	14	8	.64	6	.286	.339	.462
Omaha	AAA	KC	29	99	23	4	0	3	36	14	9	12	0	22	3	1	1	2	0	1.00	1	.232	.330	.364
3 Min. YEARS			316	1153	303	66	13	27	476	186	126	143	2	223	22	13	5	66	22	.75	16	.263	.354	.413

Terrel Hansen

Bats: Right **Throws:** Right **Pos:** OF **Ht:** 6' 3" **Wt:** 210 **Born:** 9/25/66 **Age:** 30

			BATTING															BASERUNNING				PERCENTAGES		
Year Team	Lg	Org	G	AB	H	2B	3B	HR	TB	R	RBI	TBB	IBB	SO	HBP	SH	SF	SB	CS	SB%	GDP	Avg	OBP	SLG
1987 Jamestown	A-	Mon	29	67	16	3	0	1	22	8	14	10	1	20	0	0	2	1	2	.33	3	.239	.329	.328

Year	Team	Lg	Org	G	AB	H	2B	3B	HR	TB	R	RBI	TBB	IBB	SO	HBP	SH	SF	SB	CS	SB%	GDP	Avg	OBP	SLG
				BATTING															BASERUNNING				PERCENTAGES		
1988	W. Palm Bch	A+	Mon	58	190	49	9	0	4	70	17	28	10	1	38	6	0	2	2	2	.50	5	.258	.313	.368
1989	Rockford	A	Mon	125	468	126	24	3	16	204	60	81	25	4	120	23	1	7	5	2	.71	8	.269	.333	.436
1990	Jacksonvlle	AA	Mon	123	420	109	26	2	24	211	72	83	43	2	88	24	1	3	3	4	.43	14	.260	.359	.502
1991	Tidewater	AAA	NYN	107	368	100	19	2	12	159	54	62	40	2	82	20	0	3	0	0	.00	20	.272	.371	.432
1992	Tidewater	AAA	NYN	115	395	98	18	0	12	152	43	47	24	1	96	7	1	4	4	2	.67	13	.248	.300	.385
1993	Ottawa	AAA	Mon	108	352	81	19	0	10	130	45	39	18	0	103	27	2	4	1	1	.50	7	.230	.314	.369
1994	Jacksonvlle	AA	Sea	110	404	128	21	1	22	217	57	78	18	0	88	16	0	2	2	4	.33	9	.317	.368	.537
	Calgary	AAA	Sea	2	8	4	1	0	0	5	0	3	0	0	0	0	0	0	0	0	.00	0	.500	.500	.625
1995	Tacoma	AAA	Sea	20	50	11	1	0	3	21	5	10	2	0	12	1	0	1	0	0	.00	5	.220	.259	.420
	Jacksonvlle	AA	Det	55	179	40	8	0	9	75	22	22	10	1	40	8	0	2	0	1	.00	2	.223	.291	.419
1996	Toledo	AAA	Det	5	16	2	0	0	1	5	2	1	1	0	8	3	0	0	1	0	1.00	0	.125	.300	.313
	Jacksonvlle	AA	Det	104	367	97	18	2	25	194	49	66	19	4	107	24	0	5	5	2	.71	8	.264	.337	.529
10 Min. YEARS				961	3284	861	167	10	139	1465	434	534	220	16	802	159	5	35	24	20	.55	94	.262	.335	.446

Craig Hanson

Pitches: Right **Bats:** Right **Pos:** P **Ht:** 6'3" **Wt:** 190 **Born:** 9/30/70 **Age:** 26

Year	Team	Lg	Org	G	GS	CG	GF	IP	BFP	H	R	ER	HR	SH	SF	HB	TBB	IBB	SO	WP	Bk	W	L	Pct.	ShO	Sv	ERA
				HOW MUCH HE PITCHED						WHAT HE GAVE UP												THE RESULTS					
1991	Spokane	A-	SD	13	10	1	2	61	284	76	56	44	3	2	5	0	24	0	39	11	2	1	3	.250	0	0	6.49
1992	Charlstn-SC	A	SD	28	17	0	4	118	509	115	60	43	7	3	8	5	49	4	75	7	0	2	10	.167	0	0	3.28
1993	Waterloo	A	SD	28	16	1	3	112	511	120	78	61	10	7	5	6	62	2	90	8	1	7	14	.333	0	0	4.90
1994	Rancho Cuca	A+	SD	49	2	0	13	83	374	78	37	29	9	2	2	1	47	4	83	9	0	7	5	.583	0	3	3.14
1995	Rancho Cuca	A+	SD	9	9	0	0	36.2	175	43	29	25	6	1	2	6	19	1	31	3	1	3	4	.429	0	0	6.14
	Memphis	AA	SD	34	12	0	8	85.2	422	107	65	60	14	1	5	8	58	5	64	8	1	3	7	.300	0	1	6.30
1996	Port City	AA	Sea	5	0	0	2	9.1	38	5	4	4	1	0	0	0	6	0	9	1	0	0	0	.000	0	0	3.86
6 Min. YEARS				166	66	2	32	505.2	2313	544	329	266	50	16	27	26	265	16	391	47	5	23	43	.348	0	4	4.73

Shawn Hare

Bats: Left **Throws:** Left **Pos:** OF **Ht:** 6' 1" **Wt:** 200 **Born:** 3/26/67 **Age:** 30

Year	Team	Lg	Org	G	AB	H	2B	3B	HR	TB	R	RBI	TBB	IBB	SO	HBP	SH	SF	SB	CS	SB%	GDP	Avg	OBP	SLG
				BATTING															BASERUNNING				PERCENTAGES		
1989	Lakeland	A+	Det	93	290	94	16	4	2	124	32	36	41	4	32	2	2	1	11	5	.69	7	.324	.410	.428
1990	Toledo	AAA	Det	127	429	109	25	4	9	169	53	55	49	9	77	4	0	3	9	6	.60	10	.254	.334	.394
1991	London	AA	Det	31	125	34	12	0	4	58	20	28	12	1	23	1	0	0	2	2	.50	5	.272	.341	.464
	Toledo	AAA	Det	80	252	78	18	2	9	127	44	42	30	1	53	2	1	5	1	2	.33	6	.310	.381	.504
1992	Toledo	AAA	Det	57	203	67	12	2	5	98	31	34	31	2	28	0	0	4	6	1	.86	8	.330	.412	.483
1993	Toledo	AAA	Det	130	470	124	29	3	20	219	81	76	34	5	90	2	0	5	8	4	.67	7	.264	.313	.466
1994	Toledo	AAA	Det	29	99	30	6	0	5	51	19	9	17	0	28	2	0	0	5	2	.71	0	.303	.415	.515
	Norfolk	AAA	NYN	64	209	58	15	1	6	93	26	28	33	5	42	1	0	3	4	4	.50	2	.278	.374	.445
1995	Okla. City	AAA	Tex	68	238	63	13	3	4	94	27	30	23	2	47	4	1	1	3	1	.75	9	.265	.338	.395
1996	Louisville	AAA	StL	15	49	8	1	0	1	12	3	1	3	0	11	0	0	0	1	0	1.00	2	.163	.212	.245
1991	Detroit	AL		9	19	1	1	0	0	2	0	0	2	0	1	0	0	0	0	0	.00	3	.053	.143	.105
1992	Detroit	AL		15	26	3	1	0	0	4	0	5	2	0	4	0	0	1	0	0	.00	0	.115	.172	.154
1994	New York	NL		22	40	9	1	1	0	12	7	2	4	0	11	0	0	0	0	0	.00	4	.225	.295	.300
1995	Texas	AL		18	24	6	1	0	0	7	2	2	4	0	6	0	0	0	0	0	.00	1	.250	.357	.292
8 Min. YEARS				694	2364	665	147	19	65	1045	336	339	273	29	431	18	4	22	50	27	.65	56	.281	.357	.442
4 Maj. YEARS				64	109	19	4	1	0	25	9	9	12	0	22	0	0	1	0	0	.00	8	.174	.254	.229

Mike Harkey

Pitches: Right **Bats:** Right **Pos:** P **Ht:** 6' 5" **Wt:** 235 **Born:** 10/25/66 **Age:** 30

Year	Team	Lg	Org	G	GS	CG	GF	IP	BFP	H	R	ER	HR	SH	SF	HB	TBB	IBB	SO	WP	Bk	W	L	Pct.	ShO	Sv	ERA
				HOW MUCH HE PITCHED						WHAT HE GAVE UP												THE RESULTS					
1987	Peoria	A	ChN	12	12	3	0	76	343	81	45	30	3	6	2	6	28	2	48	2	3	2	3	.400	0	0	3.55
	Pittsfield	AA	ChN	1	0	0	0	2	6	1	0	0	0	0	0	0	0	0	2	0	0	0	0	.000	0	0	0.00
1988	Pittsfield	AA	ChN	13	13	3	0	85.2	358	66	29	13	1	3	0	3	35	1	73	5	5	9	2	.818	1	0	1.37
	Iowa	AAA	ChN	12	12	3	0	78.2	317	55	36	31	6	3	3	1	33	0	62	3	1	7	2	.778	1	0	3.55
1989	Iowa	AAA	ChN	12	12	0	0	63	277	67	37	31	7	1	3	3	25	0	37	3	1	2	7	.222	0	0	4.43
1992	Peoria	A	ChN	2	2	0	0	12	54	15	6	4	2	0	0	1	3	0	17	1	0	1	0	1.000	0	0	3.00
	Iowa	AAA	ChN	4	4	0	0	22.2	101	21	15	14	3	1	3	4	13	0	16	3	0	0	1	.000	0	0	5.56
	Charlotte	AA	ChN	1	1	0	0	8	33	9	5	5	2	0	0	0	0	0	5	0	0	0	1	.000	0	0	5.63
1993	Orlando	AA	ChN	1	1	0	0	5.1	21	4	1	1	0	0	0	0	2	0	5	0	0	0	0	.000	0	0	1.69
1994	Colo. Sprng	AAA	Col	2	2	0	0	10	53	19	14	14	2	0	1	2	3	0	4	1	0	1	1	.500	0	0	12.60
1996	Albuquerque	AAA	LA	49	13	0	28	118.2	530	146	79	71	11	3	2	1	39	4	90	3	0	7	11	.389	0	13	5.38
1988	Chicago	NL		5	5	0	0	34.2	155	33	14	10	0	5	0	2	15	3	18	2	1	0	3	.000	0	0	2.60
1990	Chicago	NL		27	27	2	0	173.2	728	153	71	63	14	5	4	7	59	8	94	8	1	12	6	.667	1	0	3.26
1991	Chicago	NL		4	4	0	0	18.2	84	21	11	11	3	0	1	0	6	1	15	1	0	0	2	.000	0	0	5.30
1992	Chicago	NL		7	7	0	0	38	159	34	13	8	4	1	2	1	15	0	21	3	1	4	0	1.000	0	0	1.89
1993	Chicago	NL		28	28	1	0	157.1	676	187	100	92	17	8	8	3	43	4	67	1	3	10	10	.500	0	0	5.26
1994	Colorado	NL		24	13	0	3	91.2	415	125	61	59	10	5	2	1	35	4	39	0	2	1	6	.143	0	0	5.79
1995	Oakland	AL		14	12	0	1	66	296	75	46	46	12	3	2	3	31	0	28	2	0	4	6	.400	0	0	6.27
	California	AL		12	8	1	0	61.1	277	80	32	31	12	1	2	1	16	2	28	0	0	4	3	.571	0	0	4.55
7 Min. YEARS				109	72	9	28	482	2093	484	267	214	37	17	14	21	181	7	359	21	10	29	28	.509	2	13	4.00
7 Maj. YEARS				121	104	4	4	641.1	2790	708	348	320	72	28	21	18	220	22	310	17	8	35	36	.493	1	0	4.49

Kris Harmes

Bats: Left **Throws:** Right **Pos:** C **Ht:** 6'2" **Wt:** 190 **Born:** 6/13/71 **Age:** 26

				BATTING															BASERUNNING				PERCENTAGES		
Year	Team	Lg	Org	G	AB	H	2B	3B	HR	TB	R	RBI	TBB	IBB	SO	HBP	SH	SF	SB	CS	SB%	GDP	Avg	OBP	SLG
1990	Medicne Hat	R+	Tor	50	165	43	8	1	1	56	18	18	24	1	21	1	0	0	2	4	.33	7	.261	.358	.339
	St. Cathrns	A-	Tor	3	10	5	0	0	0	5	1	1	0	0	2	0	0	1	0	1	.00	0	.500	.455	.500
1991	Dunedin	A+	Tor	16	44	11	3	0	0	14	4	3	9	1	7	0	3	0	2	0	1.00	0	.250	.377	.318
	St. Cathrns	A-	Tor	68	230	45	16	0	6	79	31	31	37	2	38	1	7	1	6	6	.50	1	.196	.309	.343
1992	Dunedin	A+	Tor	21	51	14	2	0	1	19	7	6	7	0	13	3	2	0	0	0	.00	2	.275	.393	.373
	St. Cathrns	A-	Tor	66	229	56	7	0	5	78	20	25	23	2	41	0	1	3	0	4	.00	2	.245	.310	.341
	Knoxville	AA	Tor	7	23	7	1	0	0	8	2	4	1	0	1	0	0	0	0	0	.00	0	.304	.333	.348
1993	Hagerstown	A	Tor	130	482	133	29	1	14	206	68	73	69	0	86	4	2	2	3	4	.43	9	.276	.370	.427
1994	Dunedin	A+	Tor	105	403	116	34	4	11	191	56	71	36	7	59	5	1	5	2	6	.25	4	.288	.350	.474
1995	Knoxville	AA	Tor	86	259	59	14	2	4	89	28	29	36	5	47	0	1	3	0	1	.00	8	.228	.319	.344
1996	Knoxville	AA	Tor	44	122	26	8	1	2	42	16	8	13	1	17	1	0	0	1	0	1.00	4	.213	.294	.344
7 Min. YEARS				596	2018	515	122	9	44	787	251	269	255	19	332	15	17	15	16	26	.38	37	.255	.341	.390

Denny Harriger

Pitches: Right **Bats:** Right **Pos:** P **Ht:** 5'11" **Wt:** 185 **Born:** 7/21/69 **Age:** 27

				HOW MUCH HE PITCHED						WHAT HE GAVE UP												THE RESULTS					
Year	Team	Lg	Org	G	GS	CG	GF	IP	BFP	H	R	ER	HR	SH	SF	HB	TBB	IBB	SO	WP	Bk	W	L	Pct.	ShO	Sv	ERA
1987	Kingsport	R+	NYN	12	7	0	2	43.2	198	43	31	21	3	4	1	4	22	0	24	1	0	2	5	.286	0	0	4.33
1988	Kingsport	R+	NYN	13	13	2	0	92.1	375	83	35	22	3	1	1	0	24	1	59	2	1	7	2	.778	1	0	2.14
1989	Pittsfield	A-	NYN	3	3	1	0	21	84	20	4	4	0	2	0	1	0	0	17	0	0	2	0	1.000	1	0	1.71
	St. Lucie	A+	NYN	11	11	0	0	67.2	284	72	33	24	6	0	0	2	17	0	17	1	0	5	3	.625	0	0	3.19
1990	St. Lucie	A+	NYN	27	7	1	9	71.2	293	73	36	28	0	0	0	1	20	0	47	2	1	5	3	.625	0	2	3.52
1991	Columbia	A	NYN	2	2	1	0	11	37	5	0	0	0	1	0	0	2	0	13	0	0	2	0	1.000	1	0	0.00
	St. Lucie	A+	NYN	14	11	2	1	71.1	286	67	20	18	2	4	2	1	12	0	37	1	0	6	1	.857	2	0	2.27
1992	Binghamton	AA	NYN	11	0	0	5	21.1	88	22	11	9	2	2	0	1	7	0	8	0	0	2	2	.500	0	0	3.80
	St. Lucie	A+	NYN	27	10	0	9	88.1	372	89	30	22	1	6	0	3	14	1	65	5	1	7	3	.700	0	3	2.24
1993	Binghamton	AA	NYN	35	24	4	4	170.2	716	174	69	56	8	6	2	7	40	0	89	9	1	13	10	.565	3	1	2.95
1994	Las Vegas	AAA	SD	30	25	3	0	157.1	720	216	122	104	16	6	5	4	44	0	87	3	1	6	11	.353	0	0	5.95
1995	Las Vegas	AAA	SD	29	28	7	0	177	776	187	94	80	12	6	5	4	60	2	97	4	1	9	9	.500	2	0	4.07
1996	Las Vegas	AAA	SD	26	25	1	0	164.1	711	183	91	77	12	3	8	7	51	1	102	4	1	10	7	.588	0	0	4.22
10 Min. YEARS				240	166	22	30	1157.2	4940	1234	576	465	65	41	24	35	313	5	662	32	7	76	56	.576	10	6	3.62

Doug Harris

Pitches: Right **Bats:** Right **Pos:** P **Ht:** 6'4" **Wt:** 205 **Born:** 9/27/69 **Age:** 27

				HOW MUCH HE PITCHED						WHAT HE GAVE UP												THE RESULTS					
Year	Team	Lg	Org	G	GS	CG	GF	IP	BFP	H	R	ER	HR	SH	SF	HB	TBB	IBB	SO	WP	Bk	W	L	Pct.	ShO	Sv	ERA
1990	Eugene	A-	KC	15	15	0	0	69.1	309	74	46	34	5	3	2	4	28	0	46	6	2	4	5	.444	0	0	4.41
1991	Appleton	A	KC	7	7	1	0	45	181	41	14	11	1	2	1	1	10	1	39	2	0	2	2	.500	1	0	2.20
	Baseball Cy	A+	KC	19	18	3	0	116.2	466	92	38	32	3	4	3	3	27	4	84	4	1	10	6	.625	1	0	2.47
1992	Baseball Cy	A+	KC	7	7	0	0	29.1	122	25	11	7	3	0	0	2	6	0	22	2	0	0	2	.000	0	0	2.15
1993	Memphis	AA	KC	22	12	1	4	86.2	367	99	52	45	6	3	2	3	13	0	38	3	0	3	6	.333	0	0	4.67
1994	Memphis	AA	KC	30	13	0	9	100	449	122	70	53	8	4	10	9	28	2	43	6	0	3	9	.250	0	2	4.77
1995	Orioles	R	Bal	1	0	0	1	1	4	2	0	0	0	0	0	0	0	0	0	0	0	1	0	1.000	0	0	0.00
	Bowie	AA	Bal	12	11	2	1	61.2	263	68	30	27	6	1	1	0	15	1	32	2	2	4	5	.444	0	0	3.94
1996	Rochester	AAA	Bal	7	3	0	1	17.2	86	22	19	8	3	0	0	5	6	0	4	1	0	2	3	.400	0	0	4.08
	Bowie	AA	Bal	3	3	0	0	13	67	17	16	16	2	2	1	3	7	0	5	1	0	0	2	.000	0	0	11.08
	Portland	AA	Fla	20	0	0	10	35.1	152	33	15	14	4	1	1	0	14	3	26	1	0	6	3	.667	0	1	3.57
	Charlotte	AAA	Fla	3	0	0	1	3	12	3	1	1	0	0	1	0	0	0	1	0	0	0	0	.000	0	0	3.00
7 Min. YEARS				146	89	7	27	578.2	2478	598	312	248	41	20	22	30	154	11	340	28	5	35	43	.449	2	3	3.86

Gene Harris

Pitches: Right **Bats:** Right **Pos:** P **Ht:** 5'11" **Wt:** 195 **Born:** 12/5/64 **Age:** 32

				HOW MUCH HE PITCHED						WHAT HE GAVE UP												THE RESULTS					
Year	Team	Lg	Org	G	GS	CG	GF	IP	BFP	H	R	ER	HR	SH	SF	HB	TBB	IBB	SO	WP	Bk	W	L	Pct.	ShO	Sv	ERA
1986	Jamestown	A-	Mon	4	4	0	0	20.1	86	15	8	5	0	0	2	0	11	0	16	0	1	0	2	.000	0	0	2.21
	Burlington	A	Mon	7	6	4	0	53.1	210	37	12	8	1	0	3	1	15	0	32	2	2	4	2	.667	3	0	1.35
	W. Palm Bch	A+	Mon	2	2	0	0	11	52	14	7	5	0	2	1	0	7	0	5	0	0	0	0	.000	0	0	4.09
1987	W. Palm Bch	A+	Mon	26	26	7	0	179	773	178	101	87	7	5	4	2	77	1	121	11	3	9	7	.563	1	0	4.37
1988	Jacksonvlle	AA	Mon	18	18	7	0	126.2	500	95	43	37	4	2	2	2	45	0	103	7	4	9	5	.643	0	0	2.63
1989	Indianapols	AAA	Mon	6	0	0	4	11	46	4	0	0	0	4	0	0	10	1	9	0	0	2	0	1.000	0	2	0.00
	Calgary	AAA	Sea	5	0	0	4	6	20	4	0	0	0	0	0	0	1	0	4	0	0	0	0	.000	0	2	0.00
1990	Calgary	AAA	Sea	6	0	0	6	7.2	30	7	2	2	0	0	0	0	4	0	9	2	0	3	0	1.000	0	2	2.35
1991	Calgary	AAA	Sea	25	0	0	18	35	152	37	16	13	2	1	3	1	11	1	23	2	1	4	0	1.000	0	4	3.34
1992	Las Vegas	AAA	SD	18	0	0	9	34.1	153	36	15	14	4	4	1	1	16	5	35	4	1	0	2	.000	0	4	3.67
1994	Toledo	AAA	Det	7	1	0	2	8.2	36	11	6	5	0	0	0	0	1	0	6	2	0	0	1	.000	0	1	5.19
1996	Pirates	R	Pit	9	1	0	2	14	61	16	7	5	0	0	0	1	4	0	14	0	0	0	2	.000	0	1	3.21
	Carolina	AA	Pit	4	0	0	2	3.1	19	6	6	6	2	0	0	0	3	1	7	0	0	0	2	.000	0	0	16.20
1989	Montreal	NL		11	0	0	7	20	84	16	11	11	1	7	1	0	10	0	11	3	0	1	1	.500	0	0	4.95
	Seattle	AL		10	6	0	2	33.1	152	47	27	24	3	0	3	1	15	1	14	0	0	1	4	.200	0	1	6.48
1990	Seattle	AL		25	0	0	12	38	176	31	25	20	5	0	2	1	30	5	43	2	0	1	2	.333	0	0	4.74
1991	Seattle	AL		8	0	0	3	13.1	66	15	8	6	1	1	0	0	10	3	6	1	0	0	0	.000	0	1	4.05
1992	Seattle	AL		8	0	0	2	9	40	8	7	7	3	0	0	0	6	0	6	0	1	0	0	.000	0	0	7.00

		HOW MUCH HE PITCHED						WHAT HE GAVE UP												THE RESULTS					
Year Team	Lg Org	G	GS	CG	GF	IP	BFP	H	R	ER	HR	SH	SF	HB	TBB	IBB	SO	WP	Bk	W	L	Pct.	ShO	Sv	ERA
San Diego	NL	14	1	0	2	21.1	90	15	8	7	0	3	0	1	9	0	19	1	1	0	2	.000	0	0	2.95
1993 San Diego	NL	59	0	0	48	59.1	269	57	27	20	3	5	2	1	37	8	39	7	0	6	6	.500	0	23	3.03
1994 San Diego	NL	13	0	0	3	12.1	64	21	11	11	2	2	0	0	8	2	9	3	0	1	1	.500	0	0	8.03
Detroit	AL	11	0	0	3	11.1	53	13	10	9	1	0	0	1	4	1	10	1	0	0	0	.000	0	1	7.15
1995 Philadelphia	NL	21	0	0	5	19	82	19	9	9	2	1	0	0	8	0	9	0	0	2	2	.500	0	0	4.26
Baltimore	AL	3	0	0	0	4	17	4	2	2	0	1	0	0	1	0	4	2	0	0	0	.000	0	0	4.50
9 Min. YEARS		137	58	18	47	510.1	2138	460	223	187	20	18	16	8	205	9	384	30	12	31	23	.574	4	16	3.30
7 Maj. YEARS		183	7	0	87	241	1093	246	145	126	21	20	8	5	138	20	170	20	2	12	18	.400	0	26	4.71

Greg W. Harris

Pitches: Right **Bats:** Right **Pos:** P **Ht:** 6' 2" **Wt:** 191 **Born:** 12/1/63 **Age:** 33

		HOW MUCH HE PITCHED						WHAT HE GAVE UP												THE RESULTS					
Year Team	Lg Org	G	GS	CG	GF	IP	BFP	H	R	ER	HR	SH	SF	HB	TBB	IBB	SO	WP	Bk	W	L	Pct.	ShO	Sv	ERA
1985 Spokane	A- SD	13	13	1	0	87.1	0	80	36	33	5	0	0	3	36	0	90	6	0	5	4	.556	0	0	3.40
1986 Charleston	A SD	27	27	8	0	191.1	803	176	69	56	13	10	5	3	54	2	176	6	0	13	7	.650	2	0	2.63
1987 Wichita	AA SD	27	27	7	0	174.1	780	205	103	83	32	4	2	3	49	3	170	7	6	12	11	.522	2	0	4.28
1988 Las Vegas	AAA SD	26	25	5	0	159.2	692	160	84	73	15	4	4	1	65	2	147	8	5	9	5	.643	2	0	4.11
1991 Las Vegas	AAA SD	4	4	0	0	20.2	92	24	20	17	1	0	2	0	8	2	16	0	1	1	2	.333	0	0	7.40
1992 High Desert	A+ SD	1	1	0	0	5.1	19	2	0	0	0	0	0	0	1	0	5	2	0	0	0	.000	0	0	0.00
Las Vegas	AAA SD	2	2	0	0	16	56	8	1	1	0	0	0	0	1	0	15	0	0	2	0	1.000	0	0	0.56
1995 Fort Myers	A+ Min	3	3	1	0	19	69	12	3	2	1	1	0	0	4	0	11	1	1	1	1	.500	0	0	0.95
1996 Rancho Cuca	A+ SD	13	4	0	3	33.1	158	44	28	22	5	0	2	4	11	0	34	2	1	1	3	.250	0	0	5.94
Las Vegas	AAA SD	1	1	0	0	4	26	11	9	8	3	0	0	0	3	0	2	0	0	0	1	.000	0	0	18.00
1988 San Diego	NL	3	1	1	2	18	68	13	3	3	0	0	0	0	3	0	15	0	0	2	0	1.000	0	0	1.50
1989 San Diego	NL	56	8	0	25	135	554	106	43	39	8	5	2	2	52	9	106	3	3	8	9	.471	0	6	2.60
1990 San Diego	NL	73	0	0	33	117.1	488	92	35	30	6	9	7	4	49	13	97	2	3	8	8	.500	0	9	2.30
1991 San Diego	NL	20	20	3	0	133	537	116	42	33	16	9	2	1	27	6	95	2	0	9	5	.643	2	0	2.23
1992 San Diego	NL	20	20	1	0	118	496	113	62	54	13	8	3	2	35	2	66	2	1	4	8	.333	0	0	4.12
1993 San Diego	NL	22	22	4	0	152	639	151	65	62	18	8	2	3	39	6	83	2	3	10	9	.526	0	0	3.67
Colorado	NL	13	13	0	0	73.1	336	88	62	53	15	6	2	4	30	3	40	4	3	1	8	.111	0	0	6.50
1994 Colorado	NL	29	19	1	2	130	588	154	99	96	22	12	6	5	52	4	82	5	1	3	12	.200	0	1	6.65
1995 Minnesota	AL	7	6	0	0	32.2	160	50	35	32	5	1	2	0	16	0	21	3	0	0	5	.000	0	0	8.82
8 Min. YEARS		117	107	22	3	711	2695	722	353	295	75	19	15	14	232	9	666	32	14	44	34	.564	6	0	3.73
8 Maj. YEARS		243	109	10	62	909.1	3866	883	446	402	103	58	26	21	303	43	605	23	14	45	64	.413	2	16	3.98

Mike Harris

Bats: Left **Throws:** Left **Pos:** OF **Ht:** 5'11" **Wt:** 195 **Born:** 4/30/70 **Age:** 27

		BATTING														BASERUNNING				PERCENTAGES		
Year Team	Lg Org	G	AB	H	2B	3B	HR	TB	R	RBI	TBB	IBB	SO	HBP	SH	SF	SB	CS	SB%	GDP	Avg	OBP	SLG
1991 Beloit	A Mil	50	145	31	4	2	1	42	27	12	27	1	30	1	5	0	16	3	.84	4	.214	.341	.290
1992 Stockton	A+ Mil	40	101	27	6	4	1	44	15	16	11	0	21	0	0	0	6	0	1.00	1	.267	.339	.436
1993 Stockton	A+ Mil	104	363	112	17	3	9	162	64	65	63	4	56	6	8	4	19	7	.73	5	.309	.415	.446
1994 El Paso	AA Mil	105	372	102	22	12	5	163	76	61	55	4	68	5	1	4	12	6	.67	8	.274	.372	.438
1995 New Orleans	AAA Mil	21	56	13	3	0	0	16	3	5	4	1	9	0	0	0	1	1	.50	1	.232	.283	.286
Beloit	A Mil	12	41	14	1	1	0	17	8	5	4	0	5	0	0	0	7	1	.88	0	.341	.400	.415
Brewers	R Mil	6	23	7	2	1	0	11	5	4	2	0	7	0	0	0	0	1	.00	0	.304	.360	.478
El Paso	AA Mil	8	24	8	2	0	1	13	4	5	2	0	3	0	0	1	0	0	.00	0	.333	.370	.542
1996 El Paso	AA Mil	76	260	80	15	5	7	126	47	35	29	3	29	2	2	3	5	2	.71	5	.308	.378	.485
New Orleans	AAA Mil	40	150	29	2	1	2	39	17	11	6	0	30	2	1	2	1	2	.33	4	.193	.231	.260
6 Min. YEARS		462	1535	423	74	29	26	633	266	219	203	13	258	16	17	14	67	23	.74	28	.276	.363	.412

Brian Harrison

Pitches: Right **Bats:** Right **Pos:** P **Ht:** 6'1" **Wt:** 175 **Born:** 12/18/68 **Age:** 28

		HOW MUCH HE PITCHED						WHAT HE GAVE UP												THE RESULTS					
Year Team	Lg Org	G	GS	CG	GF	IP	BFP	H	R	ER	HR	SH	SF	HB	TBB	IBB	SO	WP	Bk	W	L	Pct.	ShO	Sv	ERA
1992 Appleton	A KC	16	15	1	0	98.2	419	114	47	40	5	1	5	1	16	0	54	2	1	5	6	.455	0	0	3.65
1993 Wilmington	A+ KC	26	26	1	0	173	707	168	76	63	16	7	6	2	38	0	98	6	1	13	6	.684	1	0	3.28
1994 Memphis	AA KC	28	28	1	0	172	717	180	87	69	11	5	9	5	31	0	94	2	0	9	10	.474	0	0	3.61
1995 Wichita	AA KC	15	0	0	5	26.2	120	35	18	14	1	1	1	1	7	1	11	0	0	1	1	.500	0	2	4.73
Omaha	AAA KC	31	8	1	6	81	368	111	57	51	8	4	4	2	17	1	23	1	0	5	3	.625	0	2	5.67
1996 Wichita	AA KC	49	7	0	17	118	472	118	54	48	11	1	5	2	14	3	80	0	0	9	2	.818	0	6	3.66
5 Min. YEARS		165	84	4	28	669.1	2803	726	339	285	52	19	30	13	123	5	360	11	2	42	28	.600	1	10	3.83

Tommy Harrison

Pitches: Right **Bats:** Right **Pos:** P **Ht:** 6'2" **Wt:** 180 **Born:** 9/30/71 **Age:** 25

		HOW MUCH HE PITCHED						WHAT HE GAVE UP												THE RESULTS					
Year Team	Lg Org	G	GS	CG	GF	IP	BFP	H	R	ER	HR	SH	SF	HB	TBB	IBB	SO	WP	Bk	W	L	Pct.	ShO	Sv	ERA
1995 Durham	A+ Atl	7	6	0	0	37.2	145	22	5	4	1	0	0	1	13	1	25	0	0	3	1	.750	0	0	0.96
Richmond	AAA Atl	9	6	0	1	42	182	34	17	15	2	4	3	2	20	1	16	0	1	2	1	.667	0	1	3.21
Greenville	AA Atl	30	26	1	1	168	697	143	72	62	12	11	4	5	60	5	98	5	1	11	6	.647	0	1	3.32
1996 Richmond	AAA Atl	10	0	0	3	19	87	16	12	11	5	0	2	2	12	0	12	3	0	0	0	.000	0	0	5.21
Greenville	AA Atl	20	16	0	3	99.1	421	88	55	52	11	2	6	3	34	0	82	7	1	8	4	.667	0	0	4.71
2 Min. YEARS		76	54	1	8	366	1532	303	161	144	31	17	15	13	139	7	233	15	3	24	12	.667	0	2	3.54

Jason Hart

Pitches: Right **Bats:** Right **Pos:** P — **Ht:** 6'0" **Wt:** 195 **Born:** 11/14/71 **Age:** 25

				HOW MUCH HE PITCHED						WHAT HE GAVE UP												THE RESULTS					
Year	Team	Lg	Org	G	GS	CG	GF	IP	BFP	H	R	ER	HR	SH	SF	HB	TBB	IBB	SO	WP	Bk	W	L	Pct.	ShO	Sv	ERA
1994	Peoria	A	ChN	20	0	0	10	37.1	149	29	17	15	4	1	1	0	7	0	33	3	0	4	2	.667	0	3	3.62
	Daytona	A+	ChN	26	0	0	23	37.1	150	26	11	7	1	0	2	2	6	0	39	3	0	3	3	.500	0	12	1.69
1995	Orlando	AA	ChN	14	0	0	10	17	69	14	5	4	0	1	3	1	4	0	20	1	0	0	1	.000	0	3	2.12
	Daytona	A+	ChN	51	0	0	44	57.2	241	43	20	14	2	3	3	2	22	2	70	1	0	0	4	.000	0	27	2.18
1996	Orlando	AA	ChN	51	0	0	22	73	300	59	29	26	11	2	0	1	28	4	78	5	0	3	5	.375	0	4	3.21
3 Min. YEARS				162	0	0	109	222.1	909	171	82	66	18	7	9	6	67	6	240	13	0	10	15	.400	0	49	2.67

Raymond Harvey

Bats: Left **Throws:** Left **Pos:** OF — **Ht:** 6'1" **Wt:** 185 **Born:** 1/1/69 **Age:** 28

				BATTING														BASERUNNING				PERCENTAGES		
Year	Team	Lg	Org	G	AB	H	2B	3B	HR	TB	R	RBI	TBB	IBB	SO	HBP	SH	SF	SB	CS	SB%	GDP	Avg	OBP	SLG
1991	Columbus	A	Cle	129	443	124	22	7	10	190	75	80	71	6	66	10	2	9	7	4	.64	12	.280	.385	.429
1992	Kinston	A+	Cle	97	331	94	18	0	2	118	35	45	36	4	43	4	1	2	2	1	.67	6	.284	.359	.356
1993	Canton-Akrn	AA	Cle	14	41	10	1	0	0	11	5	4	7	0	5	1	3	1	0	1	.00	1	.244	.360	.268
	Kinston	A+	Cle	88	335	95	19	2	3	127	36	39	28	1	43	3	3	1	3	6	.33	8	.284	.343	.379
1994	Canton-Akrn	AA	Cle	137	508	149	24	5	6	201	66	72	61	6	88	5	2	3	1	5	.17	14	.293	.373	.396
1995	Canton-Akrn	AA	Cle	122	444	115	20	1	3	146	52	32	43	1	75	3	7	2	1	4	.20	6	.259	.327	.329
1996	Canton-Akrn	AA	Cle	5	17	6	3	0	0	9	3	0	2	1	2	0	0	0	0	0	.00	1	.353	.421	.529
	Grays Harbr	IND	—	68	273	99	22	3	11	160	62	55	36	0	27	3	1	1	5	2	.71	8	.363	.441	.586
	Kinston	A+	Cle	32	114	32	7	0	2	45	14	16	12	1	26	1	0	1	0	0	.00	2	.281	.352	.395
6 Min. YEARS				692	2506	724	136	18	37	1007	348	343	296	20	375	30	19	20	19	23	.45	58	.289	.368	.402

Lionel Hastings

Bats: Right **Throws:** Right **Pos:** 3B — **Ht:** 5'9" **Wt:** 175 **Born:** 1/26/73 **Age:** 24

				BATTING														BASERUNNING				PERCENTAGES		
Year	Team	Lg	Org	G	AB	H	2B	3B	HR	TB	R	RBI	TBB	IBB	SO	HBP	SH	SF	SB	CS	SB%	GDP	Avg	OBP	SLG
1994	Elmira	A-	Fla	73	282	77	17	0	5	109	39	43	28	0	48	4	3	4	4	5	.44	3	.273	.343	.387
1995	Brevard Cty	A+	Fla	120	469	128	20	0	7	169	60	45	44	0	64	3	5	2	3	3	.50	14	.273	.338	.360
1996	Portland	AA	Fla	97	293	68	12	1	6	100	30	44	15	2	50	8	10	1	5	2	.71	8	.232	.287	.341
3 Min. YEARS				290	1044	273	49	1	18	378	129	132	87	2	162	15	18	7	12	10	.55	25	.261	.325	.362

Chris Hatcher

Bats: Right **Throws:** Right **Pos:** OF — **Ht:** 6'3" **Wt:** 220 **Born:** 1/7/69 **Age:** 28

				BATTING														BASERUNNING				PERCENTAGES		
Year	Team	Lg	Org	G	AB	H	2B	3B	HR	TB	R	RBI	TBB	IBB	SO	HBP	SH	SF	SB	CS	SB%	GDP	Avg	OBP	SLG
1990	Auburn	A-	Hou	72	259	64	10	0	9	101	37	45	27	3	86	5	0	5	8	2	.80	4	.247	.324	.390
1991	Burlington	A	Hou	129	497	117	23	6	13	191	69	65	46	4	180	9	0	4	10	5	.67	6	.235	.309	.384
1992	Osceola	A+	Hou	97	367	103	19	6	17	185	49	68	20	1	97	5	0	5	11	0	1.00	5	.281	.322	.504
1993	Jackson	AA	Hou	101	367	95	15	3	15	161	45	64	11	0	104	11	0	3	5	8	.38	8	.259	.298	.439
1994	Tucson	AAA	Hou	108	349	104	28	4	12	176	55	73	19	0	90	4	0	6	5	1	.83	6	.298	.336	.504
1995	Jackson	AA	Hou	11	39	12	1	0	1	16	5	3	4	0	6	1	0	1	0	2	.00	1	.308	.378	.410
	Tucson	AAA	Hou	94	290	83	19	2	14	148	59	50	42	2	107	4	1	2	7	3	.70	9	.286	.382	.510
1996	Jackson	AA	Hou	41	156	48	9	1	13	98	29	36	9	2	39	4	0	1	2	1	.67	5	.308	.359	.628
	Tucson	AAA	Hou	95	348	105	21	4	18	188	53	61	14	1	87	5	0	5	10	8	.56	9	.302	.333	.540
7 Min. YEARS				748	2672	731	145	26	112	1264	401	465	192	13	796	48	1	32	58	30	.66	53	.274	.330	.473

Gary Haught

Pitches: Right **Bats:** Both **Pos:** P — **Ht:** 6'1" **Wt:** 180 **Born:** 9/29/70 **Age:** 26

				HOW MUCH HE PITCHED						WHAT HE GAVE UP												THE RESULTS					
Year	Team	Lg	Org	G	GS	CG	GF	IP	BFP	H	R	ER	HR	SH	SF	HB	TBB	IBB	SO	WP	Bk	W	L	Pct.	ShO	Sv	ERA
1992	Sou. Oregon	A-	Oak	19	4	0	9	68.1	266	58	18	15	3	1	1	2	14	0	69	1	2	8	2	.800	0	2	1.98
1993	Madison	A	Oak	17	12	2	1	83.2	333	62	27	24	8	3	1	2	29	2	75	1	2	7	1	.875	0	0	2.58
	Modesto	A+	Oak	12	0	0	4	23	106	25	14	13	3	0	2	1	17	2	15	0	0	0	1	.000	0	0	5.09
1994	Modesto	A+	Oak	39	1	0	13	70.2	292	66	35	34	8	6	1	2	26	0	52	2	0	4	3	.571	0	2	4.33
1995	Huntsville	AA	Oak	9	3	0	3	23	97	23	14	11	4	1	0	1	8	1	20	0	0	1	1	.500	0	0	4.30
	Modesto	A+	Oak	43	7	0	9	109.2	452	99	43	36	14	11	0	7	32	2	101	0	0	10	6	.625	0	4	2.95
1996	Huntsville	AA	Oak	45	0	0	18	67	295	67	33	29	4	2	1	7	24	4	52	2	0	3	2	.600	0	4	3.90
5 Min. YEARS				184	27	2	57	445.1	1841	400	184	162	44	24	6	22	150	11	384	6	4	33	16	.673	0	12	3.27

Scott Haws

Bats: Left **Throws:** Right **Pos:** C — **Ht:** 6'0" **Wt:** 190 **Born:** 1/11/72 **Age:** 25

				BATTING														BASERUNNING				PERCENTAGES		
Year	Team	Lg	Org	G	AB	H	2B	3B	HR	TB	R	RBI	TBB	IBB	SO	HBP	SH	SF	SB	CS	SB%	GDP	Avg	OBP	SLG
1992	Martinsvlle	R+	Phi	36	128	27	3	0	0	30	20	9	18	2	12	0	0	0	0	0	.00	3	.211	.308	.234
1993	Spartanburg	A	Phi	73	234	57	7	0	1	67	23	21	37	0	44	0	1	1	2	3	.40	5	.244	.346	.286
1994	Clearwater	A+	Phi	64	181	42	8	1	1	55	18	14	27	3	19	0	2	0	0	1	.00	4	.232	.332	.304
	Reading	AA	Phi	10	26	6	0	0	0	6	3	1	4	0	4	0	0	0	0	1	.00	3	.231	.333	.231
1995	Clearwater	A+	Phi	2	1	0	0	0	0	0	0	0	1	0	0	0	0	0	0	0	.00	0	.000	.500	.000
1996	Reading	AA	Phi	1	1	1	0	0	0	1	0	0	2	0	0	0	0	0	0	0	.00	0	1.000	1.000	1.000
	Clearwater	A+	Phi	37	114	21	1	0	1	25	15	11	22	2	21	1	1	1	0	0	.00	7	.184	.319	.219

BATTING																	BASERUNNING				PERCENTAGES		
Year Team	Lg Org	G	AB	H	2B	3B	HR	TB	R	RBI	TBB	IBB	SO	HBP	SH	SF	SB	CS	SB%	GDP	Avg	OBP	SLG
5 Min. YEARS		223	685	154	19	1	3	184	79	56	111	7	100	1	4	2	2	5	.29	22	.225	.333	.269

Steve Hazlett

Bats: Right **Throws:** Right **Pos:** OF **Ht:** 5'11" **Wt:** 170 **Born:** 3/30/70 **Age:** 27

BATTING																	BASERUNNING				PERCENTAGES		
Year Team	Lg Org	G	AB	H	2B	3B	HR	TB	R	RBI	TBB	IBB	SO	HBP	SH	SF	SB	CS	SB%	GDP	Avg	OBP	SLG
1991 Elizabethtn	R+ Min	64	210	42	11	0	4	65	50	24	63	0	53	6	1	1	13	7	.65	0	.200	.396	.310
1992 Kenosha	A Min	107	362	96	23	4	6	145	68	32	52	0	77	7	2	4	20	9	.69	5	.265	.365	.401
1993 Fort Myers	A+ Min	29	115	39	5	2	0	48	19	6	15	1	21	1	2	0	12	5	.71	0	.339	.420	.417
1994 Nashville	AA Min	123	457	134	31	1	14	209	63	54	37	1	99	8	6	3	9	3	.75	3	.293	.354	.457
1995 Salt Lake	AAA Min	127	427	128	25	6	4	177	71	49	41	1	65	4	2	3	8	10	.44	9	.300	.364	.415
1996 Salt Lake	AAA Min	101	301	61	14	4	10	113	44	41	33	1	85	5	2	5	7	2	.78	6	.203	.288	.375
6 Min. YEARS		551	1872	500	109	17	38	757	315	206	241	4	400	31	15	16	69	36	.66	23	.267	.357	.404

Mike Heathcott

Pitches: Right **Bats:** Right **Pos:** P **Ht:** 6'3" **Wt:** 180 **Born:** 5/16/69 **Age:** 28

HOW MUCH HE PITCHED								WHAT HE GAVE UP												THE RESULTS					
Year Team	Lg Org	G	GS	CG	GF	IP	BFP	H	R	ER	HR	SH	SF	HB	TBB	IBB	SO	WP	Bk	W	L	Pct.	ShO	Sv	ERA
1991 Utica	A- ChA	6	6	0	0	33	138	26	19	13	4	1	1	1	14	0	14	1	0	3	1	.750	0	0	3.55
1992 South Bend	A ChA	15	14	0	1	82	340	67	28	14	3	5	2	0	32	0	49	8	0	9	5	.643	0	0	1.54
1993 Sarasota	A+ ChA	26	26	6	0	179.1	739	174	90	72	5	12	10	4	62	7	83	16	1	11	10	.524	1	0	3.61
1994 Birmingham	AA ChA	17	17	0	0	98	449	126	71	63	11	1	6	2	44	4	44	9	0	3	7	.300	0	0	5.79
Pr. William	A+ ChA	9	8	1	1	43	193	51	28	19	7	1	0	1	23	0	27	6	0	1	2	.333	0	0	3.98
1995 Pr. William	A+ ChA	27	14	1	4	88.2	387	96	56	46	8	2	7	2	36	3	68	18	0	4	9	.308	0	3	4.67
1996 Birmingham	AA ChA	23	23	1	0	147.2	625	138	72	66	9	5	5	4	55	3	108	5	0	11	8	.579	0	0	4.02
6 Min. YEARS		123	108	9	6	671.2	2871	678	364	293	47	27	31	14	266	17	393	63	1	42	42	.500	1	3	3.93

Doug Hecker

Pitches: Right **Bats:** Right **Pos:** P **Ht:** 6'4" **Wt:** 210 **Born:** 1/21/71 **Age:** 26

HOW MUCH HE PITCHED								WHAT HE GAVE UP												THE RESULTS					
Year Team	Lg Org	G	GS	CG	GF	IP	BFP	H	R	ER	HR	SH	SF	HB	TBB	IBB	SO	WP	Bk	W	L	Pct.	ShO	Sv	ERA
1995 Visalia	A+ Bos	2	0	0	2	2	9	1	1	0	0	0	1	1	1	0	2	1	0	0	0	.000	0	0	0.00
Red Sox	R Bos	2	0	0	1	1.2	11	4	2	1	0	0	0	0	0	0	4	0	0	0	0	.000	0	0	5.40
Sarasota	A+ Bos	10	1	0	2	21	96	24	9	8	0	1	1	1	7	0	16	4	1	1	2	.333	0	1	3.43
Trenton	AA Bos	14	1	0	5	24.2	116	29	12	9	0	1	2	2	8	0	22	5	1	1	2	.333	0	1	3.28
1996 Sarasota	A+ Bos	26	3	0	15	41.2	180	46	25	23	0	3	1	1	12	0	39	3	3	2	2	.500	0	6	4.97
Trenton	AA Bos	13	0	0	7	20	82	18	5	5	1	2	2	1	5	2	12	2	0	0	1	.000	0	2	2.25
2 Min. YEARS		67	5	0	32	111	494	122	54	46	1	7	7	6	33	2	95	15	5	4	7	.364	0	10	3.73

Bert Heffernan

Bats: Left **Throws:** Right **Pos:** C **Ht:** 5'10" **Wt:** 185 **Born:** 3/3/65 **Age:** 32

BATTING																	BASERUNNING				PERCENTAGES		
Year Team	Lg Org	G	AB	H	2B	3B	HR	TB	R	RBI	TBB	IBB	SO	HBP	SH	SF	SB	CS	SB%	GDP	Avg	OBP	SLG
1988 Beloit	A Mil	5	14	3	0	0	0	3	1	0	5	0	0	0	0	0	0	0	.00	1	.214	.421	.214
Helena	R+ Mil	65	196	55	13	0	4	80	47	31	61	1	40	0	2	4	14	5	.74	2	.281	.444	.408
1989 Beloit	A Mil	127	425	126	20	1	4	160	53	59	70	4	57	4	3	4	9	8	.53	7	.296	.398	.376
1990 El Paso	AA Mil	110	390	109	18	2	1	134	49	42	60	4	68	1	7	3	6	3	.67	16	.279	.374	.344
1991 Albuquerque	AAA LA	67	161	39	10	1	0	51	17	13	22	1	19	0	3	2	1	3	.25	7	.242	.330	.317
1992 Calgary	AAA Sea	15	46	14	2	0	1	19	8	4	7	0	7	0	0	0	1	1	.50	1	.304	.396	.413
Jacksonvlle	AA Sea	58	196	56	9	0	2	71	16	23	29	0	28	2	2	2	4	7	.36	5	.286	.380	.362
1993 Shreveport	AA SF	33	98	23	2	0	0	25	8	7	10	1	14	3	0	1	1	1	.50	4	.235	.321	.255
Phoenix	AAA SF	16	49	14	1	1	0	17	7	6	9	1	11	0	1	0	2	2	.50	0	.286	.397	.347
Giants	R SF	7	25	8	0	0	0	8	3	4	6	1	2	0	0	0	2	1	.67	0	.320	.452	.320
1995 Ottawa	AAA Mon	36	102	22	5	0	1	30	13	12	7	0	13	2	3	1	1	0	1.00	3	.216	.277	.294
1996 Ottawa	AAA Mon	64	198	60	8	1	1	73	20	27	14	0	15	1	0	2	1	4	.20	5	.303	.349	.369
1992 Seattle	AL	8	11	1	1	0	0	2	0	1	0	0	1	0	0	0	0	0	.00	1	.091	.091	.182
8 Min. YEARS		603	1900	529	88	6	14	671	242	228	300	13	274	13	21	19	42	35	.55	51	.278	.377	.353

Dan Held

Bats: Right **Throws:** Right **Pos:** 1B **Ht:** 6'0" **Wt:** 200 **Born:** 10/7/70 **Age:** 26

BATTING																	BASERUNNING				PERCENTAGES		
Year Team	Lg Org	G	AB	H	2B	3B	HR	TB	R	RBI	TBB	IBB	SO	HBP	SH	SF	SB	CS	SB%	GDP	Avg	OBP	SLG
1993 Batavia	A- Phi	45	151	31	8	1	3	50	18	16	16	0	40	6	1	2	2	3	.40	3	.205	.303	.331
1994 Spartanburg	A Phi	130	484	123	32	1	18	211	69	69	52	2	119	9	1	11	2	0	1.00	11	.254	.331	.436
1995 Clearwater	A+ Phi	134	489	133	35	1	21	233	82	82	56	1	127	19	1	4	2	1	.67	13	.272	.366	.476
Reading	AA Phi	2	4	2	1	0	1	6	2	3	2	0	1	0	0	0	1	0	1.00	0	.500	.667	1.500
1996 Reading	AA Phi	136	497	121	17	5	26	226	77	92	60	4	141	22	0	6	3	8	.27	10	.243	.347	.455
Scranton-WB	AAA Phi	4	14	0	0	0	0	0	1	0	1	0	6	1	0	0	0	0	.00	0	.000	.125	.000
4 Min. YEARS		451	1639	410	93	8	69	726	249	262	187	7	434	57	3	23	10	12	.45	37	.250	.343	.443

Eric Helfand

Bats: Left **Throws:** Right **Pos:** C **Ht:** 6' 0" **Wt:** 195 **Born:** 3/25/69 **Age:** 28

				BATTING														BASERUNNING				PERCENTAGES		
Year Team	Lg	Org	G	AB	H	2B	3B	HR	TB	R	RBI	TBB	IBB	SO	HBP	SH	SF	SB	CS	SB%	GDP	Avg	OBP	SLG
1990 Sou. Oregon	A-	Oak	57	207	59	12	0	2	77	29	39	20	1	49	7	0	1	4	0	1.00	3	.285	.366	.372
1991 Modesto	A+	Oak	67	242	62	15	1	7	100	35	38	37	2	56	2	2	2	0	1	.00	6	.256	.357	.413
1992 Modesto	A+	Oak	72	249	72	15	0	10	117	40	44	47	4	46	6	1	3	0	1	.00	5	.289	.410	.470
Huntsville	AA	Oak	37	114	26	7	0	2	39	13	9	5	0	32	1	0	0	0	0	.00	4	.228	.267	.342
1993 Huntsville	AA	Oak	100	302	69	15	2	10	118	38	48	43	2	78	8	3	7	1	1	.50	5	.228	.333	.391
1994 Tacoma	AAA	Oak	57	178	36	10	0	2	52	22	25	23	2	37	2	1	3	0	0	.00	3	.202	.296	.292
1995 Edmonton	AAA	Oak	19	56	12	4	2	1	23	5	12	9	1	10	0	5	1	0	1	.00	3	.214	.318	.411
1996 Buffalo	AAA	Cle	90	258	54	10	0	5	79	31	22	46	8	51	11	3	2	0	3	.00	2	.209	.350	.306
1993 Oakland	AL		8	13	3	0	0	0	3	1	1	0	0	1	0	0	0	0	0	.00	0	.231	.231	.231
1994 Oakland	AL		7	6	1	0	0	0	1	1	1	0	0	1	0	0	0	0	0	.00	0	.167	.167	.167
1995 Oakland	AL		38	86	14	2	1	0	18	9	7	11	0	25	1	3	0	0	0	.00	2	.163	.265	.209
7 Min. YEARS			499	1606	390	88	5	39	605	213	237	230	20	359	37	15	19	5	7	.42	31	.243	.347	.377
3 Maj. YEARS			53	105	18	2	1	0	22	11	9	11	0	27	1	3	0	0	0	.00	2	.171	.256	.210

Wesley Helms

Bats: Right **Throws:** Right **Pos:** 3B **Ht:** 6'4" **Wt:** 210 **Born:** 5/12/76 **Age:** 21

				BATTING														BASERUNNING				PERCENTAGES		
Year Team	Lg	Org	G	AB	H	2B	3B	HR	TB	R	RBI	TBB	IBB	SO	HBP	SH	SF	SB	CS	SB%	GDP	Avg	OBP	SLG
1994 Braves	R	Atl	56	184	49	15	1	4	78	22	29	22	0	36	4	0	1	6	1	.86	3	.266	.355	.424
1995 Macon	A	Atl	136	539	149	32	1	11	216	89	85	50	0	107	10	0	3	2	2	.50	8	.276	.347	.401
1996 Durham	A+	Atl	67	258	83	19	2	13	145	40	54	12	0	51	7	0	1	1	1	.50	7	.322	.367	.562
Greenville	AA	Atl	64	231	59	13	2	4	88	24	22	13	2	48	4	1	0	2	1	.67	6	.255	.306	.381
3 Min. YEARS			323	1212	340	79	6	32	527	175	190	97	2	242	25	1	5	11	5	.69	24	.281	.345	.435

Todd Helton

Bats: Left **Throws:** Left **Pos:** 1B **Ht:** 6'2" **Wt:** 195 **Born:** 8/20/73 **Age:** 23

				BATTING														BASERUNNING				PERCENTAGES		
Year Team	Lg	Org	G	AB	H	2B	3B	HR	TB	R	RBI	TBB	IBB	SO	HBP	SH	SF	SB	CS	SB%	GDP	Avg	OBP	SLG
1995 Asheville	A	Col	54	201	51	11	1	1	67	24	15	25	1	32	1	0	0	1	1	.50	7	.254	.339	.333
1996 New Haven	AA	Col	93	319	106	24	2	7	155	46	51	51	5	37	1	3	1	2	5	.29	8	.332	.425	.486
Colo. Sprng	AAA	Col	21	71	25	4	1	2	37	13	13	11	0	12	0	0	0	0	0	.00	3	.352	.439	.521
2 Min. YEARS			168	591	182	39	4	10	259	83	79	87	6	81	2	3	1	3	6	.33	18	.308	.398	.438

Scott Hemond

Bats: Right **Throws:** Right **Pos:** C **Ht:** 6' 0" **Wt:** 215 **Born:** 11/18/65 **Age:** 31

				BATTING														BASERUNNING				PERCENTAGES		
Year Team	Lg	Org	G	AB	H	2B	3B	HR	TB	R	RBI	TBB	IBB	SO	HBP	SH	SF	SB	CS	SB%	GDP	Avg	OBP	SLG
1986 Madison	A	Oak	22	85	26	2	0	2	34	9	13	5	0	19	0	0	1	2	1	.67	0	.306	.341	.400
1987 Madison	A	Oak	90	343	99	21	4	8	152	60	52	40	1	79	1	0	2	27	12	.69	10	.289	.363	.443
Huntsville	AA	Oak	33	110	20	3	1	1	28	10	8	4	0	30	0	1	0	5	1	.83	3	.182	.211	.255
1988 Huntsville	AA	Oak	133	482	106	22	4	9	163	51	53	48	1	114	3	1	7	29	8	.78	7	.220	.291	.338
1989 Huntsville	AA	Oak	132	490	130	26	6	5	183	89	62	62	0	77	7	13	6	45	17	.73	11	.265	.352	.373
1990 Tacoma	AAA	Oak	72	218	53	11	0	8	88	32	35	24	3	52	1	3	3	10	5	.67	7	.243	.317	.404
1991 Tacoma	AAA	Oak	92	327	89	19	5	3	127	50	31	39	1	69	7	5	1	11	8	.58	11	.272	.361	.388
1992 Huntsville	AA	Oak	9	27	9	0	0	0	9	3	2	4	0	8	0	0	0	2	0	1.00	0	.333	.419	.333
Tacoma	AAA	Oak	8	33	8	3	0	0	11	6	3	5	0	6	0	0	0	1	0	1.00	1	.242	.342	.333
1995 Louisville	AAA	StL	1	3	0	0	0	0	0	1	0	0	0	0	0	0	0	0	0	.00	0	.000	.000	.000
1996 Louisville	AAA	StL	50	150	39	10	1	3	60	15	15	13	0	35	0	1	1	1	2	.33	2	.260	.317	.400
1989 Oakland	AL		4	0	0	0	0	0	0	2	0	0	0	0	0	0	0	0	0	.00	0	.000	.000	.000
1990 Oakland	AL		7	13	2	0	0	0	2	0	1	0	0	5	0	0	0	0	0	.00	0	.154	.154	.154
1991 Oakland	AL		23	23	5	0	0	0	5	4	0	1	0	7	0	0	0	1	2	.33	0	.217	.250	.217
1992 Oakland	AL		17	27	6	1	0	0	7	7	1	3	0	7	0	0	0	1	0	1.00	2	.222	.300	.259
Chicago	AL		8	13	3	1	0	0	4	1	1	1	0	6	0	0	1	0	0	.00	0	.231	.267	.308
1993 Oakland	AL		91	215	55	16	0	6	89	31	26	32	0	55	1	6	1	14	5	.74	2	.256	.353	.414
1994 Oakland	AL		91	198	44	11	0	3	64	23	20	16	0	51	0	2	0	7	6	.54	5	.222	.280	.323
1995 St. Louis	NL		57	118	17	1	0	3	27	11	9	12	0	31	2	1	1	0	0	.00	8	.144	.233	.229
9 Min. YEARS			642	2268	579	117	21	39	855	326	274	244	6	489	19	24	21	133	54	.71	52	.255	.330	.377
7 Maj. YEARS			298	607	132	30	0	12	198	79	58	65	0	162	3	9	3	23	13	.64	17	.217	.295	.326

Rodney Henderson

Pitches: Right **Bats:** Right **Pos:** P **Ht:** 6' 4" **Wt:** 193 **Born:** 3/11/71 **Age:** 26

			HOW MUCH HE PITCHED						WHAT HE GAVE UP												THE RESULTS					
Year Team	Lg	Org	G	GS	CG	GF	IP	BFP	H	R	ER	HR	SH	SF	HB	TBB	IBB	SO	WP	Bk	W	L	Pct.	ShO	Sv	ERA
1992 Jamestown	A-	Mon	1	1	0	0	3	13	2	3	2	0	0	0	0	5	0	2	0	0	0	0	.000	0	0	6.00
1993 W. Palm Bch	A+	Mon	22	22	1	0	143	580	110	50	46	3	4	5	6	44	0	127	8	6	12	7	.632	1	0	2.90
Harrisburg	AA	Mon	5	5	0	0	29.2	125	20	10	6	0	1	0	0	15	0	25	2	1	5	0	1.000	0	0	1.82
1994 Harrisburg	AA	Mon	2	2	0	0	12	44	5	2	2	1	0	0	0	4	0	16	0	0	2	0	1.000	0	0	1.50
Ottawa	AAA	Mon	23	21	0	1	122.2	545	123	67	63	16	2	5	2	67	3	100	1	0	6	9	.400	0	1	4.62
1995 Harrisburg	AA	Mon	12	12	0	0	56.1	240	51	28	27	4	0	1	5	18	0	53	1	0	3	6	.333	0	0	4.31
1996 Ottawa	AAA	Mon	25	23	3	0	121.1	528	117	75	70	12	1	4	4	52	1	83	2	0	4	11	.267	1	0	5.19
1994 Montreal	NL		3	2	0	0	6.2	37	9	9	7	1	3	0	0	7	0	3	0	0	0	1	.000	0	0	9.45

Year Team	Lg Org	G	GS	CG	GF	IP	BFP	H	R	ER	HR	SH	SF	HB	TBB	IBB	SO	WP	Bk	W	L	Pct.	ShO	Sv	ERA
		HOW MUCH HE PITCHED						WHAT HE GAVE UP												THE RESULTS					
5 Min. YEARS		90	86	4	1	488	2075	428	235	216	36	8	15	17	205	4	406	14	7	32	33	.492	2	1	3.98

Ryan Henderson

Pitches: Right **Bats:** Right **Pos:** P **Ht:** 6'1" **Wt:** 190 **Born:** 9/30/69 **Age:** 27

Year Team	Lg Org	G	GS	CG	GF	IP	BFP	H	R	ER	HR	SH	SF	HB	TBB	IBB	SO	WP	Bk	W	L	Pct.	ShO	Sv	ERA
		HOW MUCH HE PITCHED						WHAT HE GAVE UP												THE RESULTS					
1992 Great Falls	R+ LA	11	11	1	0	55	228	37	22	13	0	3	0	2	25	0	54	5	6	5	1	.833	1	0	2.13
Bakersfield	A+ LA	3	3	0	0	16	72	17	10	9	1	0	0	0	9	1	15	0	3	0	2	.000	0	0	5.06
1993 Vero Beach	A+ LA	30	0	0	25	34	158	29	24	15	2	4	1	0	28	4	34	4	1	0	3	.000	0	10	3.97
San Antonio	AA LA	23	0	0	20	25	110	19	10	7	0	3	1	0	16	2	22	1	1	0	0	.000	0	5	2.52
1994 Bakersfield	A+ LA	29	0	0	27	31.1	145	26	14	10	1	2	0	1	26	0	38	8	1	0	1	.000	0	14	2.87
San Antonio	AA LA	11	1	0	0	21.2	105	25	18	17	2	0	1	1	18	1	15	3	1	1	2	.333	0	0	7.06
1995 Vero Beach	A+ LA	39	6	0	10	104.1	453	98	53	45	1	6	1	5	58	3	86	9	2	11	5	.688	0	2	3.88
1996 Albuquerque	AAA LA	3	0	0	1	5.2	31	5	9	5	0	0	1	0	6	0	7	1	2	0	0	.000	0	0	7.94
San Antonio	AA LA	39	0	0	19	63.2	275	59	29	27	2	2	4	5	29	0	46	4	0	3	3	.500	0	6	3.82
5 Min. YEARS		188	21	1	102	356.2	1577	315	189	148	9	20	9	14	215	11	317	35	17	20	17	.541	1	37	3.73

Bob Henley

Bats: Right **Throws:** Right **Pos:** C **Ht:** 6'2" **Wt:** 190 **Born:** 1/30/73 **Age:** 24

Year Team	Lg Org	G	AB	H	2B	3B	HR	TB	R	RBI	TBB	IBB	SO	HBP	SH	SF	SB	CS	SB%	GDP	Avg	OBP	SLG
		BATTING															BASERUNNING				PERCENTAGES		
1993 Jamestown	A- Mon	60	206	53	10	4	7	92	25	29	20	1	60	1	1	1	0	1	.00	5	.257	.325	.447
1994 Burlington	A Mon	98	346	104	20	1	20	186	72	67	49	1	91	10	1	3	1	2	.33	8	.301	.400	.538
1995 Albany	A Mon	102	335	94	20	1	3	125	45	46	83	3	57	11	1	2	1	2	.33	11	.281	.436	.373
1996 Harrisburg	AA Mon	103	289	66	12	1	3	89	33	27	70	1	78	3	9	2	1	2	.33	14	.228	.382	.308
4 Min. YEARS		363	1176	317	62	7	33	492	175	169	222	6	286	25	12	8	3	7	.30	38	.270	.394	.418

Dwayne Henry

Pitches: Right **Bats:** Right **Pos:** P **Ht:** 6' 3" **Wt:** 230 **Born:** 2/16/62 **Age:** 35

Year Team	Lg Org	G	GS	CG	GF	IP	BFP	H	R	ER	HR	SH	SF	HB	TBB	IBB	SO	WP	Bk	W	L	Pct.	ShO	Sv	ERA
		HOW MUCH HE PITCHED						WHAT HE GAVE UP												THE RESULTS					
1984 Tulsa	AA Tex	33	12	1	15	85	373	65	42	32	1	1	4	1	60	2	79	6	1	5	8	.385	1	8	3.39
1985 Tulsa	AA Tex	34	11	0	19	81.1	339	51	32	24	1	3	2	1	44	3	97	8	1	7	6	.538	0	9	2.66
1986 Okla. City	AAA Tex	28	1	0	16	44.1	204	51	30	29	3	2	3	0	27	0	41	7	1	2	1	.667	0	3	5.89
1987 Okla. City	AAA Tex	30	8	0	15	69	317	66	39	38	11	1	3	0	50	3	55	3	0	4	4	.500	0	3	4.96
1988 Okla. City	AAA Tex	46	3	0	24	75.2	336	57	51	47	3	3	6	4	54	0	98	11	1	5	5	.500	0	7	5.59
1989 Richmond	AAA Atl	41	6	0	20	84.2	359	43	28	23	4	3	3	3	61	3	101	7	0	11	5	.688	0	1	2.44
1990 Richmond	AAA Atl	13	0	0	6	27	109	12	7	7	1	2	0	1	16	1	36	0	0	1	1	.500	0	2	2.33
1995 Toledo	AAA Det	41	0	0	28	48.1	212	43	21	18	3	1	3	3	24	0	52	5	0	1	1	.500	0	11	3.35
1996 Colo. Sprng	AAA Col	28	0	0	10	39.2	188	43	38	34	6	2	2	3	30	0	33	5	1	1	4	.200	0	0	7.71
Toledo	AAA Det	18	0	0	5	18.2	92	21	19	15	3	0	0	1	12	0	23	0	0	1	0	1.000	0	1	7.23
1984 Texas	AL	3	0	0	1	4.1	25	5	4	4	0	1	0	0	7	0	2	0	0	0	1	.000	0	0	8.31
1985 Texas	AL	16	0	0	10	21	86	16	7	6	0	2	1	0	7	0	20	1	0	2	2	.500	0	3	2.57
1986 Texas	AL	19	0	0	4	19.1	93	14	11	10	1	1	2	1	22	0	17	7	1	1	0	1.000	0	0	4.66
1987 Texas	AL	5	0	0	1	10	50	12	10	10	2	0	0	0	9	0	7	1	0	0	0	.000	0	0	9.00
1988 Texas	AL	11	0	0	5	10.1	59	15	10	10	1	0	1	3	9	1	10	3	1	0	1	.000	0	1	8.71
1989 Atlanta	NL	12	0	0	6	12.2	55	12	6	6	2	2	0	0	5	1	16	1	0	0	2	.000	0	1	4.26
1990 Atlanta	NL	34	0	0	14	38.1	176	41	26	24	3	0	1	0	25	0	34	2	1	2	2	.500	0	0	5.63
1991 Houston	NL	52	0	0	25	67.2	282	51	25	24	7	6	2	2	39	7	51	5	0	3	2	.600	0	2	3.19
1992 Cincinnati	NL	60	0	0	11	83.2	352	59	31	31	4	7	3	1	44	6	72	12	0	3	3	.500	0	0	3.33
1993 Cincinnati	NL	3	0	0	1	4.2	26	6	8	2	0	0	0	0	4	1	2	1	0	0	1	.000	0	0	3.86
Seattle	AL	31	1	0	15	54	249	56	40	40	6	3	4	2	35	4	35	7	0	2	1	.667	0	2	6.67
1995 Detroit	AL	10	0	0	6	8.2	47	11	6	6	0	1	0	0	10	2	9	1	0	1	0	1.000	0	5	6.23
9 Min. YEARS		312	41	1	158	573.2	2529	452	307	267	36	18	26	17	378	12	615	52	5	38	35	.521	1	45	4.19
11 Maj. YEARS		256	1	0	99	334.2	1500	298	184	173	26	23	14	9	216	22	275	41	3	14	15	.483	0	14	4.65

Santiago Henry

Bats: Right **Throws:** Right **Pos:** SS **Ht:** 5'11" **Wt:** 156 **Born:** 7/27/72 **Age:** 24

Year Team	Lg Org	G	AB	H	2B	3B	HR	TB	R	RBI	TBB	IBB	SO	HBP	SH	SF	SB	CS	SB%	GDP	Avg	OBP	SLG
		BATTING															BASERUNNING				PERCENTAGES		
1991 Blue Jays	R Tor	59	220	44	10	3	0	60	23	14	11	0	44	0	1	2	7	5	.58	2	.200	.236	.273
1992 St. Cathrns	A- Tor	70	232	44	4	3	0	54	23	12	7	0	54	2	7	1	7	4	.64	1	.190	.219	.233
1993 Hagerstown	A Tor	115	404	111	30	12	8	189	65	54	20	0	110	2	3	1	13	4	.76	7	.275	.311	.468
1994 Dunedin	A+ Tor	109	408	103	22	6	6	155	56	46	19	2	99	7	2	4	9	4	.69	7	.252	.295	.380
1995 Knoxville	AA Tor	138	454	100	25	4	2	139	47	30	10	0	91	5	7	5	16	6	.73	7	.220	.243	.306
1996 Knoxville	AA Tor	110	371	100	15	7	3	138	37	32	19	1	66	3	4	2	11	7	.61	5	.270	.309	.372
6 Min. YEARS		601	2089	502	106	35	19	735	251	188	86	3	464	19	24	15	63	30	.68	29	.240	.275	.352

Kevin Henthorne

Pitches: Right **Bats:** Both **Pos:** P **Ht:** 6'2" **Wt:** 182 **Born:** 12/9/69 **Age:** 27

				HOW MUCH HE PITCHED						WHAT HE GAVE UP												THE RESULTS					
Year	Team	Lg	Org	G	GS	CG	GF	IP	BFP	H	R	ER	HR	SH	SF	HB	TBB	IBB	SO	WP	Bk	W	L	Pct.	ShO	Sv	ERA
1994	Winnipeg	IND	—	7	0	0	4	5.1	26	7	3	1	1	1	0	0	3	0	5	0	1	0	0	.000	0	0	1.69
1996	Norwich	AA	NYA	12	8	0	2	59.2	252	50	25	15	3	1	2	2	22	2	47	3	1	5	3	.625	0	0	2.26
	Tampa	A+	NYA	19	13	0	0	93.1	360	88	31	27	4	3	2	2	12	0	82	1	2	7	4	.636	0	0	2.60
2 Min. YEARS				38	21	0	6	158.1	638	145	59	43	8	5	4	4	37	2	134	4	4	12	7	.632	0	0	2.44

Julian Heredia

Pitches: Right **Bats:** Right **Pos:** P **Ht:** 6'1" **Wt:** 160 **Born:** 9/22/69 **Age:** 27

				HOW MUCH HE PITCHED						WHAT HE GAVE UP												THE RESULTS					
Year	Team	Lg	Org	G	GS	CG	GF	IP	BFP	H	R	ER	HR	SH	SF	HB	TBB	IBB	SO	WP	Bk	W	L	Pct.	ShO	Sv	ERA
1989	Angels	R	Cal	14	13	3	1	92.1	402	109	55	44	5	2	2	1	21	0	74	2	11	3	4	.429	0	0	4.29
1990	Angels	R	Cal	5	5	0	0	26	114	26	14	11	1	0	1	0	10	0	18	0	1	2	2	.500	0	0	3.81
	Quad City	A	Cal	5	0	0	3	7	34	6	6	3	0	0	1	0	6	0	10	0	2	0	0	.000	0	0	3.86
1991	Boise	A-	Cal	25	0	0	10	77	290	42	17	9	1	3	1	1	16	1	99	4	3	8	1	.889	0	5	1.05
1992	Quad City	A	Cal	29	0	0	25	43.1	162	27	8	8	0	2	1	0	11	1	45	3	1	6	1	.857	0	10	1.66
	Palm Spring	A+	Cal	30	0	0	27	28.1	121	28	16	15	2	2	3	1	9	3	36	3	1	3	1	.750	0	10	4.76
1993	Midland	AA	Cal	46	1	0	19	89.1	361	77	42	31	10	0	1	8	19	0	89	3	2	5	3	.625	0	0	3.12
1994	Midland	AA	Cal	45	2	0	10	97.2	414	87	47	35	10	5	4	6	37	5	109	11	3	5	3	.625	0	1	3.23
1995	Vancouver	AAA	Cal	51	0	0	37	74.1	319	69	34	30	8	5	1	5	23	3	65	9	0	5	3	.625	0	10	3.63
1996	Phoenix	AAA	SF	52	2	1	27	69.2	299	71	40	38	12	3	7	6	23	1	59	3	0	0	5	.000	0	4	4.91
8 Min. YEARS				302	23	4	159	605	2516	542	279	224	49	22	22	28	175	14	604	38	24	37	23	.617	0	40	3.33

Matt Herges

Pitches: Right **Bats:** Right **Pos:** P **Ht:** 6'0" **Wt:** 200 **Born:** 4/1/70 **Age:** 27

				HOW MUCH HE PITCHED						WHAT HE GAVE UP												THE RESULTS					
Year	Team	Lg	Org	G	GS	CG	GF	IP	BFP	H	R	ER	HR	SH	SF	HB	TBB	IBB	SO	WP	Bk	W	L	Pct.	ShO	Sv	ERA
1992	Yakima	A-	LA	27	0	0	23	44.2	194	33	21	16	2	1	0	3	24	1	57	2	3	2	3	.400	0	9	3.22
1993	Bakersfield	A+	LA	51	0	0	17	90.1	403	70	49	37	6	6	4	10	56	6	84	4	3	2	6	.250	0	2	3.69
1994	Vero Beach	A+	LA	48	3	1	12	111	476	115	45	41	8	8	2	4	33	3	61	3	3	8	9	.471	0	3	3.32
1995	San Antonio	AA	LA	19	0	0	13	27.2	130	34	16	15	2	3	0	0	16	1	18	3	0	0	3	.000	0	8	4.88
	San Bernrdo	A+	LA	41	2	0	17	79.1	361	92	45	36	5	5	1	2	31	1	53	3	0	5	5	.500	0	9	4.08
1996	San Antonio	AA	LA	30	6	0	10	83	355	83	38	25	3	2	5	2	28	0	45	5	1	3	2	.600	0	3	2.71
	Albuquerque	AAA	LA	10	4	2	1	34.2	140	33	11	10	2	2	2	0	14	0	15	1	0	4	1	.800	1	0	2.60
5 Min. YEARS				226	15	3	93	470.2	2059	460	225	180	28	27	14	21	202	12	333	21	10	24	29	.453	1	34	3.44

Fernando Hernandez

Pitches: Right **Bats:** Right **Pos:** P **Ht:** 6'2" **Wt:** 185 **Born:** 6/16/71 **Age:** 26

				HOW MUCH HE PITCHED						WHAT HE GAVE UP												THE RESULTS					
Year	Team	Lg	Org	G	GS	CG	GF	IP	BFP	H	R	ER	HR	SH	SF	HB	TBB	IBB	SO	WP	Bk	W	L	Pct.	ShO	Sv	ERA
1990	Indians	R	Cle	11	11	2	0	69.2	289	61	36	31	3	2	2	1	30	0	43	2	7	4	4	.500	0	0	4.00
1991	Burlington	R+	Cle	14	13	0	1	77	326	74	33	25	4	2	0	7	19	0	86	12	1	4	4	.500	0	0	2.92
1992	Columbus	A	Cle	11	11	1	0	68.2	268	42	16	12	4	1	0	6	33	1	70	4	1	4	5	.444	1	0	1.57
	Kinston	A+	Cle	8	8	1	0	41.2	177	36	23	21	2	3	3	1	22	0	32	3	0	1	3	.250	0	0	4.54
1993	Kinston	A+	Cle	8	8	0	0	51	200	34	15	10	1	2	1	2	18	0	53	1	0	2	3	.400	0	0	1.76
	Canton-Akrn	AA	Cle	2	2	0	0	7.2	40	14	11	10	1	0	1	1	5	0	8	0	0	0	1	.000	0	0	11.74
	Rancho Cuca	A+	SD	17	17	1	0	99.2	441	90	54	46	8	3	4	2	67	0	121	4	1	7	5	.583	0	0	4.15
1994	Wichita	AA	SD	23	23	1	0	131.1	595	124	82	70	12	8	9	10	77	6	95	8	0	7	9	.438	1	0	4.80
1995	Las Vegas	AAA	SD	8	8	0	0	37.2	186	43	32	32	3	0	2	3	31	3	40	4	0	1	6	.143	0	0	7.65
	Memphis	AA	SD	20	20	0	0	104	489	115	78	70	7	0	2	6	73	4	114	12	1	5	12	.294	0	0	6.06
1996	Memphis	AA	SD	27	27	0	0	147.1	655	128	83	76	8	3	8	8	85	4	161	11	1	11	10	.524	0	0	4.64
7 Min. YEARS				149	148	6	1	835.2	3666	761	463	403	53	24	32	47	460	18	823	61	12	46	62	.426	2	0	4.34

Gary Herrmann

Pitches: Left **Bats:** Right **Pos:** P **Ht:** 6'4" **Wt:** 205 **Born:** 10/15/69 **Age:** 27

				HOW MUCH HE PITCHED						WHAT HE GAVE UP												THE RESULTS					
Year	Team	Lg	Org	G	GS	CG	GF	IP	BFP	H	R	ER	HR	SH	SF	HB	TBB	IBB	SO	WP	Bk	W	L	Pct.	ShO	Sv	ERA
1992	Batavia	A-	Phi	11	6	0	1	38.2	173	41	30	21	2	0	2	3	16	0	35	3	1	1	3	.250	0	0	4.89
1993	Spartanburg	A	Phi	13	13	0	0	83.1	352	74	40	29	6	4	2	3	31	0	76	6	1	7	3	.700	0	0	3.13
1994	Clearwater	A+	Phi	1	1	0	0	1.2	6	1	0	0	0	0	0	0	0	0	1	0	0	0	0	.000	0	0	0.00
1995	Clearwater	A+	Phi	42	3	0	10	70	295	64	31	28	3	3	3	0	28	1	56	1	0	7	2	.778	0	3	3.60
1996	Reading	AA	Phi	23	5	0	7	39.2	185	43	25	22	7	1	3	3	27	2	31	1	1	1	5	.167	0	0	4.99
5 Min. YEARS				90	28	0	18	233.1	1011	223	126	100	18	8	10	9	102	3	199	11	3	16	13	.552	0	3	3.86

Mike Hickey

Bats: Both **Throws:** Right **Pos:** 3B-2B **Ht:** 6'2" **Wt:** 180 **Born:** 6/22/70 **Age:** 27

				BATTING															BASERUNNING				PERCENTAGES		
Year	Team	Lg	Org	G	AB	H	2B	3B	HR	TB	R	RBI	TBB	IBB	SO	HBP	SH	SF	SB	CS	SB%	GDP	Avg	OBP	SLG
1992	Bellingham	A-	Sea	15	57	14	2	0	0	16	8	11	4	0	14	0	0	0	3	0	1.00	1	.246	.295	.281
1993	Appleton	A	Sea	69	255	73	14	3	2	99	35	41	38	1	49	1	1	3	14	7	.67	6	.286	.377	.388
1994	Riverside	A+	Sea	130	487	137	23	7	10	204	75	90	68	5	94	6	5	5	15	8	.65	12	.281	.373	.419
1995	Port City	AA	Sea	120	447	117	24	1	6	161	59	59	60	2	83	5	4	4	6	3	.67	9	.262	.353	.360

Year	Team	Lg	Org	G	AB	H	2B	3B	HR	TB	R	RBI	TBB	IBB	SO	HBP	SH	SF	SB	CS	SB%	GDP	Avg	OBP	SLG
				BATTING															BASERUNNING				PERCENTAGES		
1996	Port City	AA	Sea	75	247	63	14	3	1	86	35	23	58	3	51	1	5	2	9	6	.60	4	.255	.396	.348
	Wisconsin	A	Sea	26	85	28	7	0	0	35	15	11	23	0	20	0	1	1	0	1	.00	1	.329	.468	.412
5 Min. YEARS				435	1578	432	84	14	19	601	227	235	251	11	311	13	16	15	47	25	.65	33	.274	.375	.381

Jamie Hicks

Bats: Right **Throws:** Right **Pos:** 1B **Ht:** 6'2" **Wt:** 200 **Born:** 11/15/71 **Age:** 25

Year	Team	Lg	Org	G	AB	H	2B	3B	HR	TB	R	RBI	TBB	IBB	SO	HBP	SH	SF	SB	CS	SB%	GDP	Avg	OBP	SLG
				BATTING															BASERUNNING				PERCENTAGES		
1994	Idaho Falls	R+	Atl	5	21	8	1	0	0	9	0	4	0	0	1	0	0	0	0	0	.00	0	.381	.381	.429
	Macon	A	Atl	31	95	23	4	1	0	29	8	7	3	0	15	2	1	1	0	0	.00	2	.242	.277	.305
1995	Durham	A+	Atl	41	105	23	6	0	0	29	9	14	5	2	18	0	0	1	0	2	.00	5	.219	.252	.276
1996	Greenville	AA	Atl	3	6	1	0	0	0	1	0	0	0	0	0	0	0	0	0	0	.00	0	.167	.167	.167
	Macon	A	Atl	68	186	41	7	0	3	57	17	17	9	1	33	1	0	2	3	1	.75	4	.220	.258	.306
3 Min. YEARS				148	413	96	18	1	3	125	34	42	17	3	67	3	1	4	3	3	.50	11	.232	.265	.303

Richard Hidalgo

Bats: Right **Throws:** Right **Pos:** OF **Ht:** 6'2" **Wt:** 175 **Born:** 7/2/75 **Age:** 21

Year	Team	Lg	Org	G	AB	H	2B	3B	HR	TB	R	RBI	TBB	IBB	SO	HBP	SH	SF	SB	CS	SB%	GDP	Avg	OBP	SLG
				BATTING															BASERUNNING				PERCENTAGES		
1992	Astros	R	Hou	51	184	57	7	3	1	73	20	27	13	0	27	3	1	3	14	5	.74	1	.310	.360	.397
1993	Asheville	A	Hou	111	403	109	23	3	10	168	49	55	30	0	76	4	2	5	21	13	.62	3	.270	.324	.417
1994	Quad City	A	Hou	124	476	139	47	6	12	234	68	76	23	1	80	7	1	4	12	12	.50	6	.292	.331	.492
1995	Jackson	AA	Hou	133	489	130	28	6	14	212	59	59	32	1	76	2	0	7	8	9	.47	11	.266	.309	.434
1996	Jackson	AA	Hou	130	513	151	34	2	14	231	66	78	29	2	55	11	1	7	11	7	.61	24	.294	.341	.450
5 Min. YEARS				549	2065	586	139	20	51	918	262	295	127	4	314	27	5	26	66	46	.59	45	.284	.330	.445

Mike Higgins

Bats: Right **Throws:** Right **Pos:** C **Ht:** 6'0" **Wt:** 205 **Born:** 6/3/71 **Age:** 26

Year	Team	Lg	Org	G	AB	H	2B	3B	HR	TB	R	RBI	TBB	IBB	SO	HBP	SH	SF	SB	CS	SB%	GDP	Avg	OBP	SLG
				BATTING															BASERUNNING				PERCENTAGES		
1993	Bend	A-	Col	51	167	45	10	1	7	78	23	19	20	1	47	1	0	1	3	4	.43	1	.269	.349	.467
1994	New Haven	AA	Col	1	1	0	0	0	0	0	0	0	0	0	0	0	0	0	0	0	.00	0	.000	.000	.000
	Asheville	A	Col	56	205	55	14	0	3	78	29	15	18	0	35	2	0	1	1	2	.33	5	.268	.332	.380
	Central Val	A+	Col	45	157	34	4	0	0	38	15	16	15	0	37	1	1	1	2	1	.67	8	.217	.287	.242
1995	Salem	A+	Col	53	158	38	9	0	0	47	9	18	17	1	30	1	2	4	1	3	.25	0	.241	.311	.297
	New Haven	AA	Col	17	49	12	0	0	0	12	4	6	3	0	10	0	3	1	0	0	.00	1	.245	.283	.245
1996	New Haven	AA	Col	22	72	13	2	1	0	17	6	5	2	0	14	0	0	0	1	1	.50	1	.181	.203	.236
	Salem	A+	Col	66	219	52	11	0	5	78	24	18	24	2	50	2	3	1	1	4	.20	6	.237	.317	.356
4 Min. YEARS				311	1028	249	50	2	15	348	110	97	99	4	223	7	9	9	9	15	.38	22	.242	.311	.339

Vee Hightower

Bats: Both **Throws:** Right **Pos:** OF **Ht:** 6'5" **Wt:** 205 **Born:** 4/26/72 **Age:** 25

Year	Team	Lg	Org	G	AB	H	2B	3B	HR	TB	R	RBI	TBB	IBB	SO	HBP	SH	SF	SB	CS	SB%	GDP	Avg	OBP	SLG
				BATTING															BASERUNNING				PERCENTAGES		
1993	Peoria	A	ChN	2	10	2	0	0	0	2	0	0	0	0	1	0	0	0	1	0	1.00	1	.200	.200	.200
1994	Peoria	A	ChN	46	147	35	6	4	1	52	28	10	28	1	30	2	1	1	6	3	.67	5	.238	.365	.354
1995	Rockford	A	ChN	64	238	63	11	1	7	97	51	36	39	1	52	6	0	1	23	6	.79	6	.265	.380	.408
1996	Orlando	AA	ChN	19	75	5	0	0	0	5	2	4	4	0	24	0	0	0	3	0	1.00	1	.067	.114	.067
	Daytona	A+	ChN	87	293	95	13	5	6	136	59	27	52	1	44	8	0	1	25	7	.78	3	.324	.438	.464
4 Min. YEARS				218	763	200	30	10	14	292	140	77	123	3	151	16	1	3	58	16	.78	16	.262	.375	.383

Erik Hiljus

Pitches: Right **Bats:** Right **Pos:** P **Ht:** 6'5" **Wt:** 230 **Born:** 12/25/72 **Age:** 24

Year	Team	Lg	Org	G	GS	CG	GF	IP	BFP	H	R	ER	HR	SH	SF	HB	TBB	IBB	SO	WP	Bk	W	L	Pct.	ShO	Sv	ERA
				HOW MUCH HE PITCHED						WHAT HE GAVE UP												THE RESULTS					
1991	Mets	R	NYN	9	9	1	0	38	183	31	27	18	1	0	1	1	37	0	38	5	1	2	3	.400	1	0	4.26
1992	Kingsport	R+	NYN	12	11	0	1	70.2	317	66	49	40	5	2	2	2	40	0	63	7	2	3	6	.333	0	0	5.09
1993	Capital Cty	A	NYN	27	27	1	0	145.2	640	114	76	70	8	2	7	4	111	1	157	17	4	7	10	.412	0	0	4.32
1994	St. Lucie	A+	NYN	26	26	3	0	160.2	709	159	85	71	8	6	10	5	90	3	140	10	8	11	10	.524	1	0	3.98
1995	Binghamton	AA	NYN	10	10	0	0	55.1	252	60	38	36	8	2	1	1	32	1	40	4	2	2	4	.333	0	0	5.86
	St. Lucie	A+	NYN	27	27	0	0	166.2	705	145	84	73	12	8	6	4	82	3	138	14	8	10	8	.556	0	0	3.94
1996	Arkansas	AA	StL	10	10	0	0	45.2	221	62	37	31	6	3	2	0	30	1	21	4	0	3	5	.375	0	0	6.11
6 Min. YEARS				121	120	5	1	682.2	3027	637	396	339	48	23	29	17	422	9	597	61	25	38	46	.452	2	0	4.47

Milt Hill

Pitches: Right **Bats:** Right **Pos:** P **Ht:** 6' 0" **Wt:** 180 **Born:** 8/22/65 **Age:** 31

Year	Team	Lg	Org	G	GS	CG	GF	IP	BFP	H	R	ER	HR	SH	SF	HB	TBB	IBB	SO	WP	Bk	W	L	Pct.	ShO	Sv	ERA
				HOW MUCH HE PITCHED						WHAT HE GAVE UP												THE RESULTS					
1987	Billings	R+	Cin	21	0	0	10	32.2	125	25	10	6	1	1	0	0	4	2	40	5	0	3	1	.750	0	7	1.65
1988	Cedar Rapds	A	Cin	44	0	0	38	78.1	300	52	21	18	3	3	1	1	17	7	69	4	8	9	4	.692	0	13	2.07
1989	Chattanooga	AA	Cin	51	0	0	42	70	281	49	19	16	4	1	5	0	28	6	63	1	4	6	5	.545	0	13	2.06
1990	Nashville	AAA	Cin	48	0	0	11	71.1	276	51	20	18	4	1	5	2	18	1	58	4	2	4	4	.500	0	3	2.27

Year	Team	Lg	Org	G	GS	CG	GF	IP	BFP	H	R	ER	HR	SH	SF	HB	TBB	IBB	SO	WP	Bk	W	L	Pct.	ShO	Sv	ERA
				HOW MUCH HE PITCHED						WHAT HE GAVE UP												THE RESULTS					
1991	Nashville	AAA	Cin	37	0	0	16	67.1	269	59	26	22	3	3	3	0	15	1	62	3	3	3	3	.500	0	3	2.94
1992	Nashville	AAA	Cin	53	0	0	39	74.1	292	56	30	22	7	3	1	1	17	4	70	4	1	0	5	.000	0	18	2.66
1993	Indianapols	AAA	Cin	20	5	0	9	53	227	53	27	24	1	5	0	3	17	4	45	3	0	3	5	.375	0	2	4.08
1994	Jacksonvlle	AA	Sea	7	7	1	0	39.1	166	37	27	20	6	2	1	1	12	1	26	1	0	4	2	.667	0	0	4.58
1995	Carolina	AA	Pit	10	10	0	0	56	226	53	27	25	6	4	1	2	6	0	46	0	0	2	2	.500	0	0	4.02
	Calgary	AAA	Pit	34	15	0	5	116.2	486	122	65	58	14	7	4	3	20	2	77	2	1	3	5	.375	0	0	4.47
1996	Bowie	AA	Bal	25	16	2	4	87.2	400	126	73	65	15	1	3	3	18	0	66	2	1	5	7	.417	0	1	6.67
1991	Cincinnati	NL		22	0	0	8	33.1	137	36	14	14	1	4	3	0	8	2	20	1	0	1	1	.500	0	0	3.78
1992	Cincinnati	NL		14	0	0	5	20	80	15	9	7	1	2	1	1	5	2	10	0	0	0	0	.000	0	1	3.15
1993	Cincinnati	NL		19	0	0	2	28.2	125	34	18	18	5	0	3	0	9	1	23	1	0	3	0	1.000	0	0	5.65
1994	Atlanta	NL		10	0	0	5	11.1	56	18	10	10	3	1	0	0	6	1	10	1	1	0	0	.000	0	0	7.94
	Seattle	AL		13	0	0	2	23.2	111	30	19	17	4	1	1	0	11	3	16	0	0	1	0	1.000	0	0	6.46
10	Min. YEARS			350	53	3	183	746.2	3048	683	345	294	64	31	24	16	172	28	622	29	20	42	43	.494	0	60	3.54
4	Maj. YEARS			78	0	0	22	117	509	133	70	66	14	8	8	1	39	9	79	3	1	5	1	.833	0	1	5.08

Scott Hilt

Bats: Left **Throws:** Right **Pos:** C **Ht:** 6'2" **Wt:** 215 **Born:** 12/9/72 **Age:** 24

Year	Team	Lg	Org	G	AB	H	2B	3B	HR	TB	R	RBI	TBB	IBB	SO	HBP	SH	SF	SB	CS	SB%	GDP	Avg	OBP	SLG
				BATTING															BASERUNNING				PERCENTAGES		
1994	Fort Wayne	A	Min	43	125	35	6	0	2	47	13	11	16	1	40	3	0	1	0	1	.00	2	.280	.372	.376
1995	Fort Myers	A+	Min	19	42	7	0	0	1	10	3	3	3	0	12	1	0	0	0	0	.00	4	.167	.239	.238
	Fort Wayne	A	Min	30	92	17	5	1	1	27	13	15	11	0	28	2	0	0	0	0	.00	3	.185	.286	.293
1996	New Britain	AA	Min	70	180	35	5	1	2	48	19	19	34	1	53	1	2	1	3	2	.60	7	.194	.324	.267
3	Min. YEARS			162	439	94	16	2	6	132	48	48	64	2	133	7	2	2	3	3	.50	16	.214	.322	.301

Rob Hinds

Bats: Right **Throws:** Right **Pos:** 2B **Ht:** 6'1" **Wt:** 180 **Born:** 4/26/71 **Age:** 26

Year	Team	Lg	Org	G	AB	H	2B	3B	HR	TB	R	RBI	TBB	IBB	SO	HBP	SH	SF	SB	CS	SB%	GDP	Avg	OBP	SLG
				BATTING															BASERUNNING				PERCENTAGES		
1992	Oneonta	A-	NYA	69	264	76	8	2	0	88	40	11	34	0	51	7	0	0	21	9	.70	3	.288	.384	.333
1993	Greensboro	A	NYA	126	503	114	14	3	0	134	80	50	72	0	101	13	1	2	51	22	.70	12	.227	.337	.266
1994	Tampa	A+	NYA	110	405	118	10	3	1	137	63	32	31	0	76	4	7	3	24	11	.69	8	.291	.345	.338
1995	Norwich	AA	NYA	132	445	112	8	1	1	125	71	37	50	0	102	12	6	3	27	10	.73	4	.252	.341	.281
1996	Columbus	AAA	NYA	11	23	2	0	0	0	2	4	1	4	0	3	1	3	1	1	0	1.00	0	.087	.241	.087
	Norwich	AA	NYA	85	180	41	3	1	2	52	25	15	20	0	48	0	10	2	9	5	.64	1	.228	.302	.289
5	Min. YEARS			533	1820	463	43	10	4	538	283	146	211	0	381	37	27	11	133	57	.70	28	.254	.342	.296

Rich Hines

Pitches: Left **Bats:** Left **Pos:** P **Ht:** 6'1" **Wt:** 185 **Born:** 5/20/69 **Age:** 28

Year	Team	Lg	Org	G	GS	CG	GF	IP	BFP	H	R	ER	HR	SH	SF	HB	TBB	IBB	SO	WP	Bk	W	L	Pct.	ShO	Sv	ERA
				HOW MUCH HE PITCHED						WHAT HE GAVE UP												THE RESULTS					
1990	Yankees	R	NYA	11	9	0	0	61	242	44	18	12	0	0	3	2	19	0	73	9	1	5	2	.714	0	0	1.77
1991	Greensboro	A	NYA	26	26	6	0	155.1	667	147	76	55	8	5	2	2	68	1	126	7	3	8	9	.471	2	0	3.19
1992	Pr. William	A+	NYA	25	24	0	1	140	610	131	75	56	12	3	3	7	61	3	84	10	0	11	7	.611	0	0	3.60
1993	Albany-Colo	AA	NYA	14	0	0	3	26	102	17	9	6	1	1	1	0	11	2	27	0	0	0	1	.000	0	0	2.08
	Columbus	AAA	NYA	43	0	0	17	56	248	50	28	25	3	1	1	1	34	6	40	2	1	2	5	.286	0	4	4.02
1994	Columbus	AAA	NYA	49	2	0	12	84.1	367	87	48	43	11	1	2	0	41	4	54	6	0	3	2	.600	0	2	4.59
1995	Norwich	AA	NYA	54	0	0	28	62	283	58	38	25	2	1	4	5	34	7	50	7	2	3	5	.375	0	7	3.63
1996	Columbus	AAA	NYA	32	5	0	7	66.1	303	70	42	38	7	4	0	5	37	0	48	8	2	6	3	.667	0	0	5.16
7	Min. YEARS			254	66	6	68	651	2822	604	334	260	44	16	16	22	305	23	502	49	9	38	34	.528	2	13	3.59

Chris Hmielewski

Pitches: Left **Bats:** Left **Pos:** P **Ht:** 6'4" **Wt:** 210 **Born:** 7/18/70 **Age:** 26

Year	Team	Lg	Org	G	GS	CG	GF	IP	BFP	H	R	ER	HR	SH	SF	HB	TBB	IBB	SO	WP	Bk	W	L	Pct.	ShO	Sv	ERA
				HOW MUCH HE PITCHED						WHAT HE GAVE UP												THE RESULTS					
1993	Burlington	A	Mon	5	0	0	5	4.2	28	7	8	2	0	0	1	2	3	0	5	0	0	0	0	.000	0	0	3.86
1994	W. Palm Bch	A+	Mon	41	1	0	10	78.2	327	75	41	37	7	0	6	0	32	0	54	9	1	3	2	.600	0	1	4.23
1995	W. Palm Bch	A+	Mon	36	2	0	15	57.2	259	57	31	23	4	3	2	2	28	4	41	6	0	1	3	.250	0	0	3.59
1996	Harrisburg	AA	Mon	3	0	0	1	3	17	4	4	4	0	1	0	2	3	1	2	1	0	1	2	.333	0	0	12.00
	Duluth-Sup.	IND	—	9	9	0	0	49.2	241	60	41	36	4	3	3	3	37	2	19	3	1	1	7	.125	0	0	6.52
4	Min. YEARS			94	12	0	31	193.2	872	203	125	102	15	7	12	9	103	7	121	19	2	6	14	.300	0	1	4.74

Ray Holbert

Bats: Right **Throws:** Right **Pos:** SS **Ht:** 6' 0" **Wt:** 175 **Born:** 9/25/70 **Age:** 26

Year	Team	Lg	Org	G	AB	H	2B	3B	HR	TB	R	RBI	TBB	IBB	SO	HBP	SH	SF	SB	CS	SB%	GDP	Avg	OBP	SLG
				BATTING															BASERUNNING				PERCENTAGES		
1988	Padres	R	SD	49	170	44	1	0	3	54	38	19	37	0	32	2	1	0	20	7	.74	4	.259	.397	.318
1989	Waterloo	A	SD	117	354	55	7	1	0	64	37	20	41	0	99	2	7	1	13	13	.50	9	.155	.246	.181
1990	Waterloo	A	SD	133	411	84	10	1	3	105	51	37	51	0	117	4	9	1	16	16	.50	10	.204	.298	.255
1991	High Desert	A+	SD	122	386	102	14	2	4	132	76	51	56	1	83	6	9	3	19	6	.76	10	.264	.364	.342
1992	Wichita	AA	SD	95	304	86	7	3	2	105	46	23	42	2	68	1	3	1	26	8	.76	7	.283	.371	.345
1993	Wichita	AA	SD	112	388	101	13	5	5	139	56	48	54	0	87	2	3	9	30	17	.64	6	.260	.347	.358

Year	Team	Lg	Org	G	AB	H	2B	3B	HR	TB	R	RBI	TBB	IBB	SO	HBP	SH	SF	SB	CS	SB%	GDP	Avg	OBP	SLG
				BATTING															BASERUNNING				PERCENTAGES		
1994	Las Vegas	AAA	SD	118	426	128	21	5	8	183	68	52	50	2	99	2	10	4	27	11	.71	8	.300	.373	.430
1995	Las Vegas	AAA	SD	9	26	3	1	0	0	4	3	3	5	0	10	0	0	0	1	1	.50	1	.115	.258	.154
1996	Tucson	AAA	Hou	28	97	24	3	2	0	31	13	10	7	0	19	2	0	1	4	1	.80	3	.247	.308	.320
1994	San Diego	NL		5	5	1	0	0	0	1	1	0	0	0	4	0	0	0	0	0	.00	0	.200	.200	.200
1995	San Diego	NL		63	73	13	2	1	2	23	11	5	8	1	20	2	3	0	4	0	1.00	3	.178	.277	.315
9 Min. YEARS				783	2562	627	77	19	25	817	388	263	343	5	614	21	42	20	156	80	.66	58	.245	.336	.319
2 Maj. YEARS				68	78	14	2	1	2	24	12	5	8	1	24	2	3	0	4	0	1.00	3	.179	.273	.308

Nate Holdren

Bats: Right **Throws:** Right **Pos:** 1B **Ht:** 6'5" **Wt:** 245 **Born:** 12/8/71 **Age:** 25

Year	Team	Lg	Org	G	AB	H	2B	3B	HR	TB	R	RBI	TBB	IBB	SO	HBP	SH	SF	SB	CS	SB%	GDP	Avg	OBP	SLG
				BATTING															BASERUNNING				PERCENTAGES		
1993	Bend	A-	Col	62	203	46	10	2	12	96	30	43	24	5	78	4	0	1	8	0	1.00	4	.227	.319	.473
1994	Asheville	A	Col	111	377	89	19	0	28	192	56	74	28	1	129	10	0	0	3	4	.43	5	.236	.306	.509
1995	Salem	A+	Col	119	420	103	16	2	15	168	48	69	34	0	126	6	2	2	6	3	.67	7	.245	.310	.400
1996	Salem	A+	Col	114	426	118	24	0	16	190	53	64	29	3	109	5	1	5	15	5	.75	6	.277	.327	.446
	New Haven	AA	Col	10	36	6	1	0	1	10	3	6	2	0	11	0	0	0	1	1	.50	0	.167	.211	.278
4 Min. YEARS				416	1462	362	70	4	72	656	190	256	117	9	453	25	3	8	33	13	.72	22	.248	.313	.449

David Holdridge

Pitches: Right **Bats:** Right **Pos:** P **Ht:** 6'3" **Wt:** 195 **Born:** 2/5/69 **Age:** 28

Year	Team	Lg	Org	G	GS	CG	GF	IP	BFP	H	R	ER	HR	SH	SF	HB	TBB	IBB	SO	WP	Bk	W	L	Pct.	ShO	Sv	ERA
				HOW MUCH HE PITCHED						WHAT HE GAVE UP												THE RESULTS					
1988	Quad City	A	Cal	28	28	0	0	153.2	686	151	92	66	4	5	4	13	79	1	110	8	4	6	12	.333	0	0	3.87
1989	Clearwater	A+	Phi	24	24	3	0	132.1	610	147	100	84	11	2	6	8	77	0	77	16	1	7	10	.412	0	0	5.71
1990	Reading	AA	Phi	24	24	1	0	127.2	571	114	74	64	13	3	5	6	79	0	78	8	0	8	12	.400	0	0	4.51
1991	Reading	AA	Phi	7	7	0	0	26.1	135	26	24	16	3	2	3	1	34	0	19	3	0	0	2	.000	0	0	5.47
	Clearwater	A+	Phi	15	0	0	4	25	126	34	23	21	2	0	2	1	21	0	23	4	0	0	0	.000	0	1	7.56
1992	Palm Spring	A+	Cal	28	27	3	0	159	726	169	99	75	5	5	3	5	87	4	135	21	0	12	12	.500	2	0	4.25
1993	Midland	AA	Cal	27	27	1	0	151	700	202	117	102	13	4	2	11	55	0	123	13	1	8	10	.444	1	0	6.08
1994	Vancouver	AAA	Cal	4	0	0	1	7	36	12	7	4	1	0	1	1	4	0	4	0	0	0	0	.000	0	0	5.14
	Midland	AA	Cal	38	2	0	17	66.1	286	66	33	29	4	1	3	5	23	0	59	2	0	7	4	.636	0	2	3.93
1995	Lk Elsinore	A+	Cal	12	0	0	8	18.1	74	13	3	2	0	1	1	2	5	1	24	3	0	3	0	1.000	0	0	0.98
	Vancouver	AAA	Cal	11	0	0	6	13.2	68	18	10	7	0	2	0	1	7	1	13	3	0	0	2	.000	0	1	4.61
	Midland	AA	Cal	37	0	0	25	57.1	242	51	21	14	1	4	1	4	20	2	60	8	0	4	2	.667	0	2	2.20
1996	Vancouver	AAA	Cal	29	0	0	17	35	163	39	19	18	4	0	2	2	23	2	26	3	0	2	1	.667	0	1	4.63
	Lk Elsinore	A+	Cal	12	0	0	12	13	53	11	3	3	1	0	0	1	2	0	21	0	0	0	0	.000	0	6	2.08
9 Min. YEARS				296	139	8	90	985.2	4476	1053	625	505	62	29	33	61	516	11	772	92	6	57	67	.460	3	13	4.61

Rick Holifield

Bats: Left **Throws:** Left **Pos:** OF **Ht:** 6'2" **Wt:** 165 **Born:** 3/25/70 **Age:** 27

Year	Team	Lg	Org	G	AB	H	2B	3B	HR	TB	R	RBI	TBB	IBB	SO	HBP	SH	SF	SB	CS	SB%	GDP	Avg	OBP	SLG
				BATTING															BASERUNNING				PERCENTAGES		
1988	Medicne Hat	R+	Tor	31	96	26	4	1	1	35	16	6	9	0	27	4	0	0	6	0	1.00	2	.271	.358	.365
1989	St. Cathrns	A-	Tor	60	209	46	7	1	4	67	22	21	15	1	74	1	0	2	4	7	.36	2	.220	.273	.321
1990	Myrtle Bch	A	Tor	99	279	56	9	2	3	78	37	18	28	0	88	6	1	0	13	8	.62	7	.201	.288	.280
1991	Myrtle Bch	A	Tor	114	324	71	15	5	1	99	37	25	34	1	94	7	1	1	14	15	.48	0	.219	.306	.306
1992	Myrtle Bch	A	Tor	93	281	56	15	2	8	99	32	27	23	1	81	5	3	3	6	5	.55	2	.199	.269	.352
1993	Dunedin	A+	Tor	127	407	112	18	12	20	214	84	68	56	6	129	16	6	4	30	13	.70	2	.275	.381	.526
1994	Knoxville	AA	Tor	71	238	59	10	9	4	99	31	31	24	2	64	3	1	1	23	5	.82	2	.248	.323	.416
	Scranton-WB	AAA	Phi	18	55	7	1	0	0	8	5	0	3	0	19	2	0	0	0	1	.00	0	.127	.200	.145
	Reading	AA	Phi	42	155	44	8	3	7	79	29	19	18	0	34	3	1	0	21	7	.75	1	.284	.369	.510
1995	Scranton-WB	AAA	Phi	76	223	46	6	3	3	67	32	24	24	0	52	6	1	3	21	5	.81	1	.206	.297	.300
	Reading	AA	Phi	30	93	23	3	1	1	31	18	5	22	3	18	1	2	0	5	2	.71	0	.247	.397	.333
1996	Pawtucket	AAA	Bos	9	29	2	1	0	0	3	1	1	1	0	12	0	0	0	1	1	.50	0	.069	.100	.103
	Trenton	AA	Bos	109	375	100	20	4	10	158	73	38	53	3	98	9	9	3	35	18	.66	2	.267	.368	.421
9 Min. YEARS				879	2764	648	117	43	62	1037	417	283	310	17	790	63	25	17	179	87	.67	21	.234	.324	.375

Adrian Hollinger

Pitches: Right **Bats:** Left **Pos:** P **Ht:** 6'0" **Wt:** 180 **Born:** 9/23/70 **Age:** 26

Year	Team	Lg	Org	G	GS	CG	GF	IP	BFP	H	R	ER	HR	SH	SF	HB	TBB	IBB	SO	WP	Bk	W	L	Pct.	ShO	Sv	ERA
				HOW MUCH HE PITCHED						WHAT HE GAVE UP												THE RESULTS					
1991	Padres	R	SD	8	0	0	3	12	76	21	20	17	1	1	1	0	16	2	14	1	2	1	1	.500	0	0	12.75
1992	Spokane	A-	SD	21	2	0	4	53.2	254	61	43	37	4	3	1	4	29	1	39	8	1	0	6	.000	0	1	6.20
1993	Waterloo	A	SD	44	0	0	18	60.1	254	44	23	17	3	3	2	3	40	4	67	7	1	8	3	.727	0	5	2.54
1994	Rancho Cuca	A+	SD	19	0	0	9	23.2	111	20	17	15	3	1	0	3	19	0	32	3	2	0	1	.000	0	1	5.70
	Wichita	AA	SD	25	0	0	10	46.2	218	47	32	25	4	0	2	3	33	2	42	7	0	1	3	.250	0	0	4.82
1995	Sonoma Cty	IND	—	8	8	3	0	60	241	44	25	19	4	4	3	5	18	1	46	2	0	3	4	.429	0	0	2.85
	Greenville	AA	Atl	7	6	1	0	44.2	196	43	26	23	2	0	4	1	20	1	28	2	1	1	4	.200	0	0	4.63
	Brevard Cty	A+	Fla	26	18	4	4	129.2	555	113	68	57	7	4	8	7	56	2	92	5	2	4	10	.286	0	2	3.96
1996	Greenville	AA	Atl	20	0	0	3	29.2	136	30	19	18	6	2	0	5	17	0	24	2	0	2	1	.667	0	0	5.46
	Midland	AA	Cal	13	0	0	10	16.2	80	18	11	8	0	2	1	3	11	1	8	6	0	1	1	.500	0	2	4.32
	Lk Elsinore	A+	Cal	12	0	0	4	17.1	77	15	6	3	1	1	1	1	11	0	15	1	1	1	0	1.000	0	0	1.56

			HOW MUCH HE PITCHED						WHAT HE GAVE UP												THE RESULTS					
Year	Team	Lg Org	G	GS	CG	GF	IP	BFP	H	R	ER	HR	SH	SF	HB	TBB	IBB	SO	WP	Bk	W	L	Pct.	ShO	Sv	ERA
6 Min. YEARS			203	34	8	65	494.1	2198	456	290	239	35	21	23	35	270	14	407	44	10	22	34	.393	0	11	4.35

Damon Hollins

Bats: Right **Throws:** Left **Pos:** OF **Ht:** 5'11" **Wt:** 180 **Born:** 6/12/74 **Age:** 23

				BATTING													BASERUNNING				PERCENTAGES		
Year	Team	Lg	Org	G	AB	H	2B	3B	HR	TB	R	RBI	TBB	IBB	SO	HBP	SH	SF	SB	CS	SB%	GDP	Avg	OBP	SLG
1992	Braves	R	Atl	49	179	41	12	1	1	58	35	15	30	0	22	2	2	0	15	2	.88	3	.229	.346	.324
1993	Danville	R+	Atl	62	240	77	15	2	7	117	37	51	19	0	30	1	0	3	10	2	.83	5	.321	.369	.488
1994	Durham	A+	Atl	131	485	131	28	0	23	228	76	88	45	0	115	4	2	3	12	7	.63	9	.270	.335	.470
1995	Greenville	AA	Atl	129	466	115	26	2	18	199	64	77	44	6	120	4	0	6	6	6	.50	7	.247	.313	.427
1996	Richmond	AAA	Atl	42	146	29	9	0	0	38	16	8	16	1	37	0	1	0	2	3	.40	2	.199	.278	.260
5 Min. YEARS				413	1516	393	90	5	49	640	228	239	154	7	324	11	5	12	45	20	.69	26	.259	.330	.422

Stacy Hollins

Pitches: Right **Bats:** Right **Pos:** P **Ht:** 6'3" **Wt:** 175 **Born:** 7/31/72 **Age:** 24

				HOW MUCH HE PITCHED						WHAT HE GAVE UP												THE RESULTS					
Year	Team	Lg	Org	G	GS	CG	GF	IP	BFP	H	R	ER	HR	SH	SF	HB	TBB	IBB	SO	WP	Bk	W	L	Pct.	ShO	Sv	ERA
1992	Athletics	R	Oak	15	14	3	0	93	392	89	47	35	0	2	2	4	19	0	93	5	3	6	3	.667	2	0	3.39
1993	Madison	A	Oak	26	26	2	0	150.2	653	145	100	86	21	4	4	8	52	6	105	4	1	10	11	.476	1	0	5.14
1994	Modesto	A+	Oak	29	22	0	3	143.1	610	133	57	54	10	4	2	8	55	1	131	7	1	13	6	.684	0	0	3.39
1995	Edmonton	AAA	Oak	7	7	0	0	29.2	156	47	43	34	4	0	1	1	21	3	25	6	0	0	7	.000	0	0	10.31
	Huntsville	AA	Oak	22	22	0	0	112.1	520	127	95	83	14	4	3	5	63	9	87	14	2	3	15	.167	0	0	6.65
1996	Huntsville	AA	Oak	28	26	3	0	141	623	149	100	80	18	3	2	6	56	6	102	13	1	9	9	.500	2	0	5.11
5 Min. YEARS				127	117	8	3	670	2954	690	442	372	67	17	14	32	266	25	543	49	8	41	51	.446	5	0	5.00

Ron Hollis

Pitches: Right **Bats:** Left **Pos:** P **Ht:** 6'3" **Wt:** 205 **Born:** 8/13/73 **Age:** 23

				HOW MUCH HE PITCHED						WHAT HE GAVE UP												THE RESULTS					
Year	Team	Lg	Org	G	GS	CG	GF	IP	BFP	H	R	ER	HR	SH	SF	HB	TBB	IBB	SO	WP	Bk	W	L	Pct.	ShO	Sv	ERA
1994	Yakima	A-	LA	15	9	0	3	61.1	275	63	34	27	5	2	0	4	23	2	52	5	1	4	2	.667	0	1	3.96
1995	Vero Beach	A+	LA	43	0	0	13	73	306	55	22	20	1	3	2	2	38	6	56	1	0	2	5	.286	0	0	2.47
1996	Vero Beach	A+	LA	19	0	0	17	21.1	89	20	10	7	1	0	0	0	7	0	27	0	0	0	1	.000	0	11	2.95
	San Antonio	AA	LA	25	0	0	13	39.1	175	38	21	15	2	1	1	0	19	0	36	1	0	0	3	.000	0	1	3.43
3 Min. YEARS				102	9	0	46	195	845	176	87	69	9	6	3	6	87	8	171	7	1	6	11	.353	0	13	3.18

Craig Holman

Pitches: Right **Bats:** Both **Pos:** P **Ht:** 6'2" **Wt:** 200 **Born:** 3/13/69 **Age:** 28

				HOW MUCH HE PITCHED						WHAT HE GAVE UP												THE RESULTS					
Year	Team	Lg	Org	G	GS	CG	GF	IP	BFP	H	R	ER	HR	SH	SF	HB	TBB	IBB	SO	WP	Bk	W	L	Pct.	ShO	Sv	ERA
1991	Batavia	A-	Phi	15	12	0	1	79.1	327	67	27	17	2	2	1	2	22	1	53	7	1	6	2	.750	0	0	1.93
1992	Spartanburg	A	Phi	25	24	3	1	143.1	611	153	72	59	9	4	4	4	39	0	129	10	2	9	6	.600	1	0	3.70
1993	Clearwater	A+	Phi	7	1	0	2	18	71	17	7	5	1	0	0	0	1	0	7	1	0	0	0	.000	0	0	2.50
	Reading	AA	Phi	24	24	4	0	139	586	134	73	64	5	3	2	12	43	1	86	6	1	8	13	.381	1	0	4.14
1994	Reading	AA	Phi	7	4	0	1	27.2	126	33	22	19	3	0	0	1	13	1	18	1	0	2	5	.286	0	0	6.18
1995	Reading	AA	Phi	32	1	0	13	56.2	235	55	27	22	10	2	2	2	16	2	40	2	1	1	1	.500	0	1	3.49
1996	Scranton-WB	AAA	Phi	36	3	0	9	62.2	291	77	44	41	10	6	5	4	34	5	36	6	1	3	2	.600	0	0	5.89
	Reading	AA	Phi	8	8	0	0	46.1	186	42	21	18	6	4	0	2	13	0	34	3	0	6	1	.857	0	0	3.50
6 Min. YEARS				154	77	7	27	573	2433	578	293	245	46	21	14	27	181	10	403	36	6	35	30	.538	2	1	3.85

Shawn Holman

Pitches: Right **Bats:** Right **Pos:** P **Ht:** 6' 2" **Wt:** 185 **Born:** 11/10/64 **Age:** 32

				HOW MUCH HE PITCHED						WHAT HE GAVE UP												THE RESULTS					
Year	Team	Lg	Org	G	GS	CG	GF	IP	BFP	H	R	ER	HR	SH	SF	HB	TBB	IBB	SO	WP	Bk	W	L	Pct.	ShO	Sv	ERA
1984	Macon	A	Pit	9	6	1	2	46.2	210	48	19	10	1	3	1	1	25	0	32	3	0	3	2	.600	1	0	1.93
	Pr. William	A+	Pit	15	14	1	0	77.2	345	74	46	35	4	1	2	2	49	0	47	9	0	7	4	.636	0	0	4.06
1985	Pr. William	A+	Pit	24	23	4	0	142.1	596	123	69	56	11	3	8	6	53	2	65	11	2	10	11	.476	2	0	3.54
	Nashua	AA	Pit	2	2	0	0	8	38	10	6	4	0	1	1	0	7	0	2	0	0	0	1	.000	0	0	4.50
1986	Nashua	AA	Pit	25	17	1	3	109.1	484	108	61	58	9	5	2	4	67	3	39	8	0	4	13	.235	1	0	4.77
1987	Harrisburg	AA	Pit	27	0	0	11	62	277	67	32	25	6	4	2	4	35	2	27	0	0	4	3	.571	0	2	3.63
	Glens Falls	AA	Det	18	5	0	5	42.1	201	49	33	29	4	0	1	4	25	2	22	6	0	1	3	.250	0	1	6.17
1988	Glens Falls	AA	Det	52	0	0	26	91.2	377	82	36	19	3	7	2	7	26	1	44	7	2	8	3	.727	0	10	1.87
1989	Toledo	AAA	Det	51	0	0	31	89.2	372	74	21	19	2	5	1	10	36	2	38	3	0	3	1	.750	0	11	1.91
1990	Toledo	AAA	Det	17	0	0	3	20.1	110	27	22	17	3	0	1	3	14	0	10	0	0	2	1	.667	0	0	7.52
	London	AA	Det	28	0	0	14	31	147	35	26	21	2	1	0	5	15	0	26	1	0	0	3	.000	0	8	6.10
1993	Richmond	AAA	Atl	37	22	0	3	155	661	174	88	72	12	5	4	5	46	3	101	8	0	12	7	.632	0	0	4.18
1994	Ottawa	AAA	Mon	59	0	0	52	69.1	301	65	28	23	1	2	2	3	35	4	44	4	1	2	4	.333	0	31	2.99
1995	Albuquerque	AAA	LA	49	1	0	22	79	386	107	58	45	3	5	5	5	39	7	60	7	0	5	6	.455	0	5	5.13
1996	Carolina	AA	Pit	5	1	0	1	8.2	43	11	4	3	0	0	0	1	6	1	6	0	0	1	0	1.000	0	0	3.12
1989	Detroit	AL		5	0	0	3	10	50	8	2	2	0	0	1	0	11	1	9	0	0	0	0	.000	0	0	1.80
11 Min. YEARS				418	91	7	173	1033	4548	1054	549	436	61	42	32	60	478	27	563	67	5	62	62	.500	4	68	3.80

Jeff Horn

Bats: Right **Throws:** Right **Pos:** C **Ht:** 6'1" **Wt:** 197 **Born:** 8/23/70 **Age:** 26

			BATTING															BASERUNNING				PERCENTAGES		
Year Team	Lg	Org	G	AB	H	2B	3B	HR	TB	R	RBI	TBB	IBB	SO	HBP	SH	SF	SB	CS	SB%	GDP	Avg	OBP	SLG
1992 Elizabethtn	R+	Min	41	144	35	6	0	1	44	20	26	25	1	25	4	0	2	2	0	1.00	5	.243	.366	.306
1993 Fort Wayne	A	Min	66	200	39	7	0	5	61	19	23	18	0	51	4	1	4	1	2	.33	3	.195	.270	.305
1994 Fort Myers	A+	Min	34	100	28	3	0	0	31	10	9	8	1	11	3	0	1	0	2	.00	6	.280	.348	.310
1995 Salt Lake	AAA	Min	3	10	5	1	0	0	6	0	2	0	0	1	0	0	0	0	0	.00	0	.500	.500	.600
Fort Myers	A+	Min	66	199	53	5	1	0	60	25	20	38	1	30	4	1	3	2	3	.40	4	.266	.389	.302
1996 Salt Lake	AAA	Min	25	83	28	5	0	3	42	14	13	12	1	5	2	2	2	0	1	.00	4	.337	.424	.506
New Britain	AA	Min	12	45	12	2	0	0	14	4	3	6	1	7	0	0	0	0	1	.00	0	.267	.353	.311
5 Min. YEARS			247	781	200	29	1	9	258	92	96	107	5	130	17	4	12	5	9	.36	22	.256	.353	.330

Tyrone Horne

Bats: Left **Throws:** Right **Pos:** OF **Ht:** 5'10" **Wt:** 185 **Born:** 11/2/70 **Age:** 26

			BATTING															BASERUNNING				PERCENTAGES		
Year Team	Lg	Org	G	AB	H	2B	3B	HR	TB	R	RBI	TBB	IBB	SO	HBP	SH	SF	SB	CS	SB%	GDP	Avg	OBP	SLG
1989 Expos	R	Mon	24	68	14	3	2	0	21	7	13	11	0	29	0	0	0	4	4	.50	0	.206	.316	.309
1990 Gate City	R+	Mon	56	202	57	11	2	1	75	26	13	24	1	62	2	2	2	23	8	.74	1	.282	.361	.371
Jamestown	A-	Mon	7	23	7	2	1	0	11	1	5	4	0	5	0	0	0	3	0	1.00	1	.304	.407	.478
1991 Sumter	A	Mon	118	428	114	20	3	10	170	69	49	42	1	133	2	1	4	23	12	.66	4	.266	.332	.397
1992 Rockford	A	Mon	129	480	134	27	4	12	205	71	48	62	5	141	1	2	2	23	13	.64	1	.279	.361	.427
Harrisburg	AA	Mon	1	1	1	0	0	0	1	0	0	0	0	0	0	0	0	0	0	.00	0	1.000	1.000	1.000
1993 W. Palm Bch	A+	Mon	82	288	85	19	2	10	138	43	44	40	1	72	0	1	3	11	10	.52	1	.295	.378	.479
Harrisburg	AA	Mon	35	128	46	8	1	4	68	22	22	22	0	37	1	1	0	3	2	.60	3	.359	.457	.531
1994 Expos	R	Mon	7	29	7	1	0	1	11	3	7	4	0	9	0	0	0	1	0	1.00	0	.241	.333	.379
Harrisburg	AA	Mon	90	311	89	15	0	9	131	56	48	50	1	92	1	1	2	11	13	.46	7	.286	.385	.421
1995 Harrisburg	AA	Mon	87	294	87	17	4	14	154	59	47	58	2	65	1	3	3	14	8	.64	3	.296	.410	.524
Norwich	AA	NYA	46	166	47	16	1	2	71	23	22	26	1	36	0	0	3	4	2	.67	4	.283	.374	.428
1996 Edmonton	AAA	Oak	67	204	47	7	2	4	70	28	16	32	1	53	1	0	2	5	3	.63	6	.230	.335	.343
Binghamton	AA	NYN	43	125	34	10	0	3	53	17	19	15	4	39	1	0	0	3	0	1.00	4	.272	.355	.424
8 Min. YEARS			792	2747	769	156	22	70	1179	425	353	390	17	773	10	11	21	128	75	.63	35	.280	.369	.429

Vince Horsman

Pitches: Left **Bats:** Right **Pos:** P **Ht:** 6' 2" **Wt:** 180 **Born:** 3/9/67 **Age:** 30

			HOW MUCH HE PITCHED						WHAT HE GAVE UP												THE RESULTS					
Year Team	Lg	Org	G	GS	CG	GF	IP	BFP	H	R	ER	HR	SH	SF	HB	TBB	IBB	SO	WP	Bk	W	L	Pct.	ShO	Sv	ERA
1985 Medicne Hat	R+	Tor	18	1	0	2	40.1	0	56	31	28	1	0	0	0	23	3	30	1	0	0	3	.000	0	1	6.25
1986 Florence	A	Tor	29	9	1	10	90.2	419	93	56	41	8	1	6	1	49	0	64	5	4	4	3	.571	1	1	4.07
1987 Myrtle Bch	A	Tor	30	28	0	1	149	621	144	74	55	20	6	5	2	37	2	109	5	2	7	7	.500	0	0	3.32
1988 Knoxville	AA	Tor	20	6	1	6	58.1	260	57	34	30	5	4	4	3	28	3	40	4	1	3	2	.600	0	0	4.63
Dunedin	A+	Tor	14	2	0	3	39.2	159	28	7	6	1	1	1	1	13	2	34	4	1	3	1	.750	0	1	1.36
1989 Dunedin	A+	Tor	35	1	0	23	79	330	72	24	22	3	5	1	1	27	3	60	3	4	5	6	.455	0	8	2.51
Knoxville	AA	Tor	4	0	0	3	5	19	3	1	1	0	0	0	0	2	1	3	0	0	0	0	.000	0	1	1.80
1990 Dunedin	A+	Tor	28	0	0	14	50	209	53	21	18	0	2	2	1	15	2	41	2	0	4	7	.364	0	1	3.24
Knoxville	AA	Tor	8	0	0	2	11.2	51	11	7	6	1	1	0	0	5	2	10	1	0	2	1	.667	0	0	4.63
1991 Knoxville	AA	Tor	42	2	0	17	80.2	335	80	23	21	2	3	1	0	19	5	80	3	1	4	1	.800	0	3	2.34
1993 Tacoma	AAA	Oak	26	0	0	10	33.2	149	37	25	16	11	1	2	0	9	2	23	1	1	1	2	.333	0	3	4.28
1994 Tacoma	AAA	Oak	7	0	0	2	7	26	5	2	2	1	1	0	0	1	0	6	0	0	1	0	1.000	0	0	2.57
1995 Salt Lake	AAA	Min	16	0	0	7	13	64	23	15	15	3	0	0	0	4	2	10	1	0	1	0	1.000	0	0	10.38
1996 Syracuse	AAA	Tor	29	0	0	15	35	150	37	22	21	7	1	0	1	11	0	21	3	0	0	3	.000	0	0	5.40
1991 Toronto	AL		4	0	0	2	4	16	2	0	0	0	1	0	0	3	1	2	0	0	0	0	.000	0	0	0.00
1992 Oakland	AL		58	0	0	9	43.1	180	39	13	12	3	3	1	0	21	4	18	1	0	2	1	.667	0	1	2.49
1993 Oakland	AL		40	0	0	5	25	116	25	15	15	2	0	0	3	15	1	17	1	0	2	0	1.000	0	0	5.40
1994 Oakland	AL		33	0	0	6	29.1	127	29	17	16	2	3	3	1	11	2	20	1	1	0	1	.000	0	0	4.91
1995 Minnesota	AL		6	0	0	3	9	43	12	8	7	2	2	1	0	4	1	4	0	0	0	0	.000	0	0	7.00
11 Min. YEARS			306	49	2	115	693	2792	699	342	282	63	26	22	10	243	27	531	33	14	35	36	.493	1	19	3.66
5 Maj. YEARS			141	0	0	25	110.2	482	107	53	50	9	9	5	4	54	9	61	3	1	4	2	.667	0	1	4.07

Marcus Hostetler

Pitches: Right **Bats:** Right **Pos:** P **Ht:** 6'3" **Wt:** 210 **Born:** 7/4/69 **Age:** 27

			HOW MUCH HE PITCHED						WHAT HE GAVE UP												THE RESULTS					
Year Team	Lg	Org	G	GS	CG	GF	IP	BFP	H	R	ER	HR	SH	SF	HB	TBB	IBB	SO	WP	Bk	W	L	Pct.	ShO	Sv	ERA
1993 Braves	R	Atl	3	0	0	3	9	32	2	1	1	0	0	0	1	2	1	12	0	4	2	0	1.000	0	0	1.00
Danville	R+	Atl	20	0	0	12	31.2	121	18	8	7	0	1	0	3	5	0	37	1	1	0	1	.000	0	5	1.99
1994 Macon	A	Atl	46	0	0	34	73.1	311	57	19	13	2	3	0	5	30	6	84	5	0	5	4	.556	0	9	1.60
1995 Durham	A+	Atl	12	0	0	3	16.1	80	23	13	12	3	1	2	1	7	0	6	0	0	1	1	.500	0	0	6.61
Greenville	AA	Atl	45	0	0	22	60	279	70	43	32	9	5	5	3	28	2	30	3	0	6	3	.667	0	2	4.80
1996 Bowie	AA	Bal	32	0	0	9	57	243	51	29	21	4	4	1	3	22	0	44	5	1	3	0	1.000	0	1	3.32
4 Min. YEARS			158	0	0	83	247.1	1066	221	113	86	18	14	8	16	94	9	213	14	6	17	9	.654	0	17	3.13

Mike Hostetler

Pitches: Right **Bats:** Right **Pos:** P **Ht:** 6'2" **Wt:** 195 **Born:** 6/5/70 **Age:** 27

				HOW MUCH HE PITCHED						WHAT HE GAVE UP												THE RESULTS					
Year	Team	Lg	Org	G	GS	CG	GF	IP	BFP	H	R	ER	HR	SH	SF	HB	TBB	IBB	SO	WP	Bk	W	L	Pct.	ShO	Sv	ERA
1991	Pulaski	R+	Atl	9	9	0	0	47	184	35	12	10	4	1	1	2	9	2	61	4	1	3	2	.600	0	0	1.91
1992	Durham	A+	Atl	13	13	3	0	88	354	75	25	21	2	0	1	2	19	3	88	2	3	9	3	.750	2	0	2.15
	Greenville	AA	Atl	16	13	1	0	80.2	339	78	37	35	11	3	2	4	23	1	57	3	0	6	2	.750	0	0	3.90
1993	Richmond	AAA	Atl	9	9	0	0	48	212	50	29	27	5	1	0	4	18	2	36	0	0	1	3	.250	0	0	5.06
	Greenville	AA	Atl	19	19	2	0	135.2	559	122	48	41	9	6	2	7	36	3	105	6	0	8	5	.615	0	0	2.72
1994	Richmond	AAA	Atl	6	6	0	0	23.1	105	27	16	16	3	0	1	1	10	1	13	0	2	0	2	.000	0	0	6.17
1995	Greenville	AA	Atl	28	28	0	0	162.2	711	182	102	95	24	8	4	6	46	4	93	6	1	10	10	.500	0	0	5.26
1996	Richmond	AAA	Atl	27	24	2	1	148	632	168	80	72	8	7	9	5	41	1	81	8	0	11	9	.550	0	0	4.38
6 Min. YEARS				127	121	8	1	733.1	3096	737	349	317	66	26	20	31	202	17	534	29	7	48	36	.571	2	0	3.89

Chris Howard

Bats: Right **Throws:** Right **Pos:** C **Ht:** 6' 2" **Wt:** 220 **Born:** 2/27/66 **Age:** 31

				BATTING															BASERUNNING				PERCENTAGES		
Year	Team	Lg	Org	G	AB	H	2B	3B	HR	TB	R	RBI	TBB	IBB	SO	HBP	SH	SF	SB	CS	SB%	GDP	Avg	OBP	SLG
1988	Bellingham	A-	Sea	2	9	3	0	0	1	6	3	3	1	0	2	0	0	0	0	0	.00	0	.333	.400	.667
	Wausau	A	Sea	61	187	45	10	1	7	78	20	20	18	0	60	3	0	1	1	3	.25	4	.241	.316	.417
1989	Wausau	A	Sea	36	125	30	8	0	4	50	13	32	13	1	35	1	0	1	0	0	.00	2	.240	.314	.400
	Williamsprt	AA	Sea	86	296	75	13	0	9	115	30	36	28	0	79	5	2	0	0	1	.00	10	.253	.328	.389
1990	Williamsprt	AA	Sea	118	401	95	19	1	5	131	48	49	37	1	91	3	4	4	3	1	.75	16	.237	.303	.327
1991	Calgary	AAA	Sea	82	293	72	12	1	8	110	32	36	16	1	56	2	3	1	1	1	.50	10	.246	.288	.375
1992	Calgary	AAA	Sea	97	319	76	16	0	8	116	29	45	14	0	73	5	3	2	3	7	.30	9	.238	.279	.364
1993	Calgary	AAA	Sea	94	331	106	23	0	6	147	40	55	23	1	62	5	5	2	1	5	.17	4	.320	.371	.444
1994	Calgary	AAA	Sea	75	266	67	10	0	11	110	41	44	27	2	66	1	2	3	1	0	1.00	11	.252	.320	.414
1995	Tacoma	AAA	Sea	83	268	65	14	0	4	91	33	31	18	2	70	2	4	2	0	1	.00	9	.243	.293	.340
1996	Norfolk	AAA	NYN	56	119	19	6	0	2	31	8	15	5	1	30	0	5	1	0	0	.00	2	.160	.192	.261
1991	Seattle	AL		9	6	1	1	0	0	2	1	0	1	0	2	0	0	0	0	0	.00	0	.167	.286	.333
1993	Seattle	AL		4	1	0	0	0	0	0	0	0	0	0	0	0	0	0	0	0	.00	0	.000	.000	.000
1994	Seattle	AL		9	25	5	1	0	0	6	2	2	1	0	6	1	1	1	0	0	.00	0	.200	.250	.240
9 Min. YEARS				790	2614	653	131	3	65	985	297	366	200	9	624	27	28	17	10	19	.34	77	.250	.308	.377
3 Maj. YEARS				22	32	6	2	0	0	8	3	2	2	0	8	1	1	1	0	0	.00	0	.188	.250	.250

Dann Howitt

Bats: Left **Throws:** Right **Pos:** OF **Ht:** 6' 5" **Wt:** 205 **Born:** 2/13/64 **Age:** 33

				BATTING															BASERUNNING				PERCENTAGES		
Year	Team	Lg	Org	G	AB	H	2B	3B	HR	TB	R	RBI	TBB	IBB	SO	HBP	SH	SF	SB	CS	SB%	GDP	Avg	OBP	SLG
1986	Medford	A-	Oak	66	208	66	9	2	6	97	36	37	49	3	37	1	1	1	5	1	.83	7	.317	.448	.466
1987	Modesto	A+	Oak	109	336	70	11	2	8	109	44	42	59	1	110	4	3	3	7	9	.44	8	.208	.331	.324
1988	Modesto	A+	Oak	132	480	121	20	2	18	199	75	86	81	3	106	2	0	2	11	5	.69	9	.252	.361	.415
	Tacoma	AAA	Oak	4	15	2	1	0	0	3	1	0	0	0	4	0	0	0	0	0	.00	0	.133	.133	.200
1989	Huntsville	AA	Oak	138	509	143	28	2	26	253	78	111	68	7	107	3	2	6	2	1	.67	6	.281	.365	.497
1990	Tacoma	AAA	Oak	118	437	116	30	1	11	181	58	69	38	3	95	2	0	4	4	4	.50	16	.265	.324	.414
1991	Tacoma	AAA	Oak	122	449	120	28	6	14	202	58	73	49	2	92	2	1	5	5	2	.71	14	.267	.339	.450
1992	Tacoma	AAA	Oak	43	140	41	13	1	1	59	25	27	23	0	20	2	0	5	5	3	.63	3	.293	.388	.421
	Calgary	AAA	Sea	50	178	54	9	5	6	91	29	33	12	1	38	1	2	1	4	0	1.00	7	.303	.349	.511
1993	Calgary	AAA	Sea	95	333	93	20	1	21	178	57	77	39	2	67	1	1	7	7	5	.58	4	.279	.350	.535
1994	Nashville	AAA	ChA	66	231	59	15	1	8	100	30	36	19	1	48	2	0	1	4	0	1.00	4	.255	.316	.433
1995	Nashville	AAA	ChA	45	133	30	6	1	3	47	16	15	16	4	32	0	0	2	0	3	.00	5	.226	.305	.353
	Buffalo	AAA	Cle	41	119	36	8	3	4	62	19	18	14	2	30	0	0	0	0	0	.00	2	.303	.376	.521
1996	Louisville	AAA	StL	46	141	36	6	1	4	56	19	18	16	2	31	1	2	1	4	1	.80	2	.255	.333	.397
	Indianapols	AAA	Cin	50	156	43	6	1	4	63	19	22	14	2	35	1	0	1	0	3	.00	4	.276	.337	.404
1989	Oakland	AL		3	3	0	0	0	0	0	0	0	0	0	2	0	0	0	0	0	.00	0	.000	.000	.000
1990	Oakland	AL		14	22	3	0	1	0	5	3	1	3	0	12	0	0	0	0	0	.00	0	.136	.240	.227
1991	Oakland	AL		21	42	7	1	0	1	11	5	3	1	0	12	0	0	1	0	0	.00	1	.167	.182	.262
1992	Oakland	AL		22	48	6	0	0	1	9	1	2	5	1	4	0	1	0	0	0	.00	4	.125	.208	.188
	Seattle	AL		13	37	10	4	1	1	19	6	8	3	0	5	0	0	3	1	1	.50	2	.270	.302	.514
1993	Seattle	AL		32	76	16	3	1	2	27	6	8	4	0	18	0	0	0	0	0	.00	0	.211	.250	.355
1994	Chicago	AL		10	14	5	3	0	0	8	4	0	1	0	7	0	0	0	0	0	.00	1	.357	.400	.571
11 Min. YEARS				1125	3865	1030	210	29	134	1700	564	664	497	33	852	22	12	39	58	37	.61	91	.266	.350	.440
6 Maj. YEARS				115	242	47	11	3	5	79	25	22	17	1	60	0	1	4	1	1	.50	8	.194	.243	.326

Bob Howry

Pitches: Right **Bats:** Left **Pos:** P **Ht:** 6'5" **Wt:** 215 **Born:** 8/4/73 **Age:** 23

				HOW MUCH HE PITCHED						WHAT HE GAVE UP												THE RESULTS					
Year	Team	Lg	Org	G	GS	CG	GF	IP	BFP	H	R	ER	HR	SH	SF	HB	TBB	IBB	SO	WP	Bk	W	L	Pct.	ShO	Sv	ERA
1994	Everett	A-	SF	5	5	0	0	19	97	29	19	15	3	0	1	1	10	2	16	5	0	0	4	.000	0	0	7.11
	Clinton	A	SF	9	8	0	0	49.1	219	61	29	23	1	3	4	3	16	0	22	4	2	1	3	.250	0	0	4.20
1995	San Jose	A+	SF	27	25	1	1	165.1	695	171	79	65	6	12	4	8	54	0	107	7	3	12	10	.545	0	0	3.54
1996	Shreveport	AA	SF	27	27	0	0	156.2	682	163	90	81	17	6	4	9	56	3	57	3	1	10	8	.556	0	0	4.65
3 Min. YEARS				68	65	1	1	390.1	1693	424	217	184	27	21	13	21	136	5	202	19	6	23	25	.479	0	0	4.24

Mark Hubbard

Pitches: Left **Bats:** Left **Pos:** P **Ht:** 6'2" **Wt:** 190 **Born:** 2/2/70 **Age:** 27

				HOW MUCH HE PITCHED						WHAT HE GAVE UP												THE RESULTS					
Year	Team	Lg	Org	G	GS	CG	GF	IP	BFP	H	R	ER	HR	SH	SF	HB	TBB	IBB	SO	WP	Bk	W	L	Pct.	ShO	Sv	ERA
1994	Greensboro	A	NYA	26	26	2	0	149.1	642	162	69	59	11	1	5	7	46	0	139	4	3	13	7	.650	1	0	3.56
	Tampa	A+	NYA	2	1	0	1	6.2	33	9	6	3	2	0	0	1	2	0	5	0	0	0	1	.000	0	0	4.05
1995	Tampa	A+	NYA	13	11	1	0	68.1	269	52	22	14	2	1	2	4	21	0	40	2	0	4	3	.571	0	0	1.84
	Norwich	AA	NYA	26	23	1	1	141	579	133	60	48	4	3	4	10	46	1	79	3	1	8	7	.533	0	1	3.06
1996	Tampa	A+	NYA	4	4	0	0	22	96	27	17	14	1	0	0	3	6	0	12	0	0	1	2	.333	0	0	5.73
	Norwich	AA	NYA	4	4	0	0	19.2	89	19	13	12	2	1	0	1	10	1	14	0	0	2	0	1.000	0	0	5.49
3 Min. YEARS				75	69	4	2	407	1708	402	187	150	22	6	11	26	131	2	289	9	4	28	20	.583	1	1	3.32

Dan Hubbs

Pitches: Right **Bats:** Right **Pos:** P **Ht:** 6'2" **Wt:** 200 **Born:** 1/23/71 **Age:** 26

				HOW MUCH HE PITCHED						WHAT HE GAVE UP												THE RESULTS					
Year	Team	Lg	Org	G	GS	CG	GF	IP	BFP	H	R	ER	HR	SH	SF	HB	TBB	IBB	SO	WP	Bk	W	L	Pct.	ShO	Sv	ERA
1993	Great Falls	R+	LA	3	0	0	1	7.2	29	3	1	1	0	0	0	2	2	0	12	0	1	1	1	.500	0	0	1.17
	Bakersfield	A+	LA	19	1	0	8	44.2	181	36	12	9	4	1	2	0	15	1	44	3	1	2	1	.667	0	1	1.81
1994	Bakersfield	A+	LA	13	0	0	6	35.1	145	29	17	15	3	3	0	1	10	0	51	0	0	3	1	.750	0	2	3.82
	San Antonio	AA	LA	38	1	0	13	80	340	82	34	28	3	1	6	4	27	7	75	5	0	5	5	.500	0	1	3.15
1995	San Antonio	AA	LA	31	0	0	6	61	248	58	25	24	3	3	1	1	16	0	52	0	1	2	1	.667	0	0	3.54
1996	Albuquerque	AAA	LA	49	0	0	15	75.2	356	89	51	40	4	0	3	3	47	12	82	2	0	7	1	.875	0	2	4.76
4 Min. YEARS				153	2	0	49	304.1	1299	297	140	117	17	8	12	11	117	20	316	10	3	20	10	.667	0	6	3.46

Ken Huckaby

Bats: Right **Throws:** Right **Pos:** C **Ht:** 6' 1" **Wt:** 205 **Born:** 1/27/71 **Age:** 26

				BATTING															BASERUNNING				PERCENTAGES		
Year	Team	Lg	Org	G	AB	H	2B	3B	HR	TB	R	RBI	TBB	IBB	SO	HBP	SH	SF	SB	CS	SB%	GDP	Avg	OBP	SLG
1991	Great Falls	R+	LA	57	213	55	16	0	3	80	39	37	17	0	38	4	1	3	3	2	.60	4	.258	.321	.376
1992	Vero Beach	A+	LA	73	261	63	9	0	0	72	14	21	7	0	42	1	2	2	1	1	.50	5	.241	.262	.276
1993	Vero Beach	A+	LA	79	281	75	14	1	4	103	22	41	11	1	35	2	3	2	2	1	.67	3	.267	.297	.367
	San Antonio	AA	LA	28	82	18	1	0	0	19	4	5	2	1	7	2	0	1	0	0	.00	0	.220	.253	.232
1994	San Antonio	AA	LA	11	41	11	1	0	1	15	3	9	1	1	1	0	0	0	1	0	1.00	1	.268	.286	.366
	Bakersfield	A+	LA	77	270	81	18	1	2	107	29	30	10	0	37	2	0	1	2	3	.40	7	.300	.329	.396
1995	Albuquerque	AAA	LA	89	278	90	16	2	1	113	30	40	12	1	26	4	3	1	3	1	.75	16	.324	.359	.406
1996	Albuquerque	AAA	LA	103	286	79	16	2	3	108	37	41	17	1	35	2	3	1	0	0	.00	10	.276	.320	.378
6 Min. YEARS				517	1712	472	91	6	14	617	178	224	77	5	221	17	12	11	12	8	.60	46	.276	.312	.360

Bobby Hughes

Bats: Right **Throws:** Right **Pos:** C **Ht:** 6'4" **Wt:** 220 **Born:** 3/10/71 **Age:** 26

				BATTING															BASERUNNING				PERCENTAGES		
Year	Team	Lg	Org	G	AB	H	2B	3B	HR	TB	R	RBI	TBB	IBB	SO	HBP	SH	SF	SB	CS	SB%	GDP	Avg	OBP	SLG
1992	Helena	R+	Mil	11	40	7	1	1	0	10	5	6	4	0	14	2	0	0	0	0	.00	0	.175	.283	.250
1993	Beloit	A	Mil	98	321	89	11	3	17	157	42	56	23	0	77	6	5	0	1	3	.25	2	.277	.337	.489
1994	El Paso	AA	Mil	12	36	10	4	1	0	16	3	12	5	0	7	1	0	2	0	1	.00	1	.278	.364	.444
	Stockton	A+	Mil	95	322	81	24	3	11	144	54	53	33	0	83	9	1	2	2	1	.67	8	.252	.336	.447
1995	Stockton	A+	Mil	52	179	42	9	2	8	79	22	31	17	1	41	1	0	3	2	2	.50	10	.235	.300	.441
	El Paso	AA	Mil	51	173	46	12	0	7	79	11	27	12	1	30	2	0	2	0	2	.00	4	.266	.317	.457
1996	New Orleans	AAA	Mil	37	125	25	5	0	4	42	11	15	4	0	31	3	0	0	1	1	.50	2	.200	.242	.336
	El Paso	AA	Mil	67	237	72	18	1	15	137	43	39	30	1	40	2	0	3	3	3	.50	5	.304	.382	.578
5 Min. YEARS				423	1433	372	84	11	62	664	191	239	128	3	323	26	6	12	9	13	.41	32	.260	.329	.463

Troy Hughes

Bats: Right **Throws:** Right **Pos:** OF **Ht:** 6'4" **Wt:** 212 **Born:** 1/3/71 **Age:** 26

				BATTING															BASERUNNING				PERCENTAGES		
Year	Team	Lg	Org	G	AB	H	2B	3B	HR	TB	R	RBI	TBB	IBB	SO	HBP	SH	SF	SB	CS	SB%	GDP	Avg	OBP	SLG
1989	Braves	R	Atl	36	110	24	5	0	0	29	17	10	11	0	29	1	1	1	8	4	.67	0	.218	.293	.264
1990	Pulaski	R+	Atl	46	145	39	7	1	1	51	22	17	16	0	39	0	2	1	5	1	.83	3	.269	.340	.352
1991	Macon	A	Atl	112	404	121	33	2	9	185	69	80	36	1	76	3	1	5	22	13	.63	6	.300	.357	.458
1992	Durham	A+	Atl	128	449	110	21	4	16	187	64	53	49	3	97	1	2	6	12	7	.63	7	.245	.317	.416
1993	Greenville	AA	Atl	109	383	102	20	4	14	172	49	58	44	1	67	5	0	3	7	3	.70	10	.266	.347	.449
1994	Richmond	AAA	Atl	81	228	49	9	1	1	63	24	18	29	3	48	5	0	6	6	2	.75	7	.215	.310	.276
	Greenville	AA	Atl	27	89	27	7	0	3	43	14	12	11	0	11	0	0	1	4	0	1.00	2	.303	.376	.483
1995	Greenville	AA	Atl	73	200	51	7	1	6	78	24	25	17	0	52	2	0	2	3	6	.33	1	.255	.317	.390
	Norwich	AA	NYA	15	55	18	2	1	1	25	7	8	4	0	11	1	0	1	0	2	.00	3	.327	.377	.455
1996	Orlando	AA	ChN	123	450	123	26	3	18	209	75	93	50	4	86	1	0	2	3	4	.43	8	.273	.346	.464
8 Min. YEARS				750	2513	664	137	17	69	1042	365	374	267	12	516	19	6	28	70	42	.63	47	.264	.336	.415

Rich Humphrey

Pitches: Right **Bats:** Right **Pos:** P **Ht:** 6'1" **Wt:** 185 **Born:** 6/24/71 **Age:** 26

				HOW MUCH HE PITCHED						WHAT HE GAVE UP												THE RESULTS					
Year	Team	Lg	Org	G	GS	CG	GF	IP	BFP	H	R	ER	HR	SH	SF	HB	TBB	IBB	SO	WP	Bk	W	L	Pct.	ShO	Sv	ERA
1993	Auburn	A-	Hou	29	0	0	26	39.2	168	34	18	11	2	1	1	3	10	2	49	2	1	4	3	.571	0	9	2.50
1994	Astros	R	Hou	4	0	0	0	7	30	7	3	1	0	1	0	1	1	1	8	0	0	1	0	1.000	0	0	1.29

Year	Team	Lg	Org	G	GS	CG	GF	IP	BFP	H	R	ER	HR	SH	SF	HB	TBB	IBB	SO	WP	Bk	W	L	Pct.	ShO	Sv	ERA
				HOW MUCH HE PITCHED						WHAT HE GAVE UP												THE RESULTS					
	Osceola	A+	Hou	3	0	0	0	6	32	8	8	7	0	1	0	2	3	0	5	0	0	0	0	.000	0	0	10.50
1995	Jackson	AA	Hou	9	0	0	1	16	66	11	5	3	0	2	1	0	9	2	9	1	0	1	1	.500	0	0	1.69
	Kissimmee	A+	Hou	55	0	0	40	71	299	56	21	15	1	7	3	3	29	2	42	3	1	4	2	.667	0	14	1.90
1996	Tucson	AAA	Hou	10	0	0	7	13.1	71	23	20	16	3	0	2	1	7	0	8	4	0	1	1	.500	0	0	10.80
	Kissimmee	A+	Hou	5	0	0	5	8.2	34	6	3	2	0	2	0	2	1	0	5	1	0	0	1	.000	0	2	2.08
	Jackson	AA	Hou	43	0	0	22	64.2	257	53	21	18	6	3	1	3	15	0	37	2	0	4	2	.667	0	1	2.51
4 Min. YEARS				158	0	0	101	226.1	957	198	99	73	12	17	8	15	75	7	163	13	2	15	10	.600	0	26	2.90

Torii Hunter

Bats: Right **Throws:** Right **Pos:** OF **Ht:** 6'2" **Wt:** 205 **Born:** 7/18/75 **Age:** 21

Year	Team	Lg	Org	G	AB	H	2B	3B	HR	TB	R	RBI	TBB	IBB	SO	HBP	SH	SF	SB	CS	SB%	GDP	Avg	OBP	SLG
				BATTING															BASERUNNING				PERCENTAGES		
1993	Twins	R	Min	28	100	19	3	0	0	22	6	8	4	0	23	9	1	0	4	2	.67	1	.190	.283	.220
1994	Fort Wayne	A	Min	91	335	98	17	1	10	147	57	50	25	1	80	10	0	2	8	10	.44	5	.293	.358	.439
1995	Fort Myers	A+	Min	113	391	96	15	2	7	136	64	36	38	1	77	12	5	1	7	4	.64	8	.246	.330	.348
1996	Fort Myers	A+	Min	4	16	3	0	0	0	3	1	1	2	0	5	0	0	0	1	1	.50	0	.188	.278	.188
	New Britain	AA	Min	99	342	90	20	3	7	137	49	33	28	1	60	7	9	1	7	7	.50	7	.263	.331	.401
4 Min. YEARS				335	1184	306	55	6	24	445	177	128	97	3	245	38	15	4	27	24	.53	21	.258	.333	.376

Jimmy Hurst

Bats: Right **Throws:** Right **Pos:** OF **Ht:** 6'6" **Wt:** 225 **Born:** 3/1/72 **Age:** 25

Year	Team	Lg	Org	G	AB	H	2B	3B	HR	TB	R	RBI	TBB	IBB	SO	HBP	SH	SF	SB	CS	SB%	GDP	Avg	OBP	SLG
				BATTING															BASERUNNING				PERCENTAGES		
1991	White Sox	R	ChA	36	121	31	4	0	0	35	14	12	13	0	32	1	0	0	6	1	.86	3	.256	.333	.289
1992	Utica	A-	ChA	68	220	50	8	5	6	86	31	35	27	1	78	4	2	5	11	3	.79	4	.227	.316	.391
1993	South Bend	A	ChA	123	464	113	26	0	20	199	79	79	37	3	141	8	0	5	15	2	.88	9	.244	.307	.429
1994	Pr. William	A+	ChA	127	455	126	31	6	25	244	90	91	72	4	128	4	0	5	15	8	.65	9	.277	.377	.536
1995	Birmingham	AA	ChA	91	301	57	11	0	12	104	47	34	33	0	95	1	0	2	12	5	.71	5	.189	.270	.346
1996	Birmingham	AA	ChA	126	472	125	23	1	18	204	62	88	53	2	128	3	0	8	19	11	.63	10	.265	.338	.432
	Nashville	AAA	ChA	3	6	2	1	0	1	6	2	2	1	0	3	0	0	0	0	0	.00	0	.333	.429	1.000
6 Min. YEARS				574	2039	504	104	12	82	878	325	341	236	10	605	21	2	25	78	30	.72	40	.247	.328	.431

Gary Hust

Bats: Right **Throws:** Right **Pos:** OF **Ht:** 6'4" **Wt:** 215 **Born:** 3/15/72 **Age:** 25

Year	Team	Lg	Org	G	AB	H	2B	3B	HR	TB	R	RBI	TBB	IBB	SO	HBP	SH	SF	SB	CS	SB%	GDP	Avg	OBP	SLG
				BATTING															BASERUNNING				PERCENTAGES		
1990	Athletics	R	Oak	43	147	28	1	2	1	36	12	9	11	0	60	2	0	0	2	2	.50	2	.190	.256	.245
1991	Sou. Oregon	A-	Oak	64	246	68	5	5	10	113	42	49	24	0	94	8	3	0	8	5	.62	5	.276	.360	.459
1992	Madison	A	Oak	114	387	75	13	3	10	124	41	45	36	1	163	6	1	4	5	2	.71	7	.194	.270	.320
1993	Madison	A	Oak	118	364	81	20	2	14	147	52	54	51	1	141	0	4	1	7	4	.64	3	.223	.317	.404
1994	Modesto	A+	Oak	72	236	50	10	2	8	88	36	44	29	1	99	6	0	5	4	5	.44	4	.212	.308	.373
1995	Modesto	A+	Oak	128	467	111	20	2	27	216	85	87	61	3	169	4	4	3	10	4	.71	4	.238	.329	.463
1996	Huntsville	AA	Oak	60	197	44	11	0	3	64	22	26	18	0	64	1	4	0	3	0	1.00	6	.223	.292	.325
	Modesto	A+	Oak	12	42	10	2	0	2	18	6	10	10	0	14	1	0	0	0	2	.00	2	.238	.396	.429
7 Min. YEARS				611	2086	467	82	16	75	806	296	324	240	6	804	28	16	13	39	24	.62	33	.224	.311	.386

David Hutcheson

Pitches: Right **Bats:** Right **Pos:** P **Ht:** 6'2" **Wt:** 185 **Born:** 8/29/71 **Age:** 25

Year	Team	Lg	Org	G	GS	CG	GF	IP	BFP	H	R	ER	HR	SH	SF	HB	TBB	IBB	SO	WP	Bk	W	L	Pct.	ShO	Sv	ERA
				HOW MUCH HE PITCHED						WHAT HE GAVE UP												THE RESULTS					
1993	Peoria	A	ChN	15	12	1	1	89	357	71	26	23	2	5	2	5	29	0	82	9	1	4	3	.571	1	0	2.33
1994	Daytona	A+	ChN	25	24	4	0	162	663	139	57	46	6	4	6	8	35	0	102	3	3	13	5	.722	3	0	2.56
	Orlando	AA	ChN	3	3	1	0	19	80	12	10	7	2	0	0	1	7	0	12	0	0	1	2	.333	0	0	3.32
1995	Orlando	AA	ChN	28	27	1	1	168.1	708	178	84	75	23	5	3	8	45	3	103	6	0	8	10	.444	1	0	4.01
1996	Orlando	AA	ChN	19	13	0	2	84.2	363	82	43	33	8	2	5	5	28	2	60	3	0	4	3	.571	0	0	3.51
4 Min. YEARS				90	79	7	4	523	2171	482	220	184	41	16	16	27	144	5	359	21	4	30	23	.566	5	0	3.17

Rich Hyde

Pitches: Right **Bats:** Right **Pos:** P **Ht:** 6'0" **Wt:** 185 **Born:** 12/24/68 **Age:** 28

Year	Team	Lg	Org	G	GS	CG	GF	IP	BFP	H	R	ER	HR	SH	SF	HB	TBB	IBB	SO	WP	Bk	W	L	Pct.	ShO	Sv	ERA
				HOW MUCH HE PITCHED						WHAT HE GAVE UP												THE RESULTS					
1991	Everett	A-	SF	26	0	0	24	36.2	156	37	20	18	3	0	1	4	8	0	25	1	1	3	3	.500	0	7	4.42
1992	Clinton	A	SF	8	0	0	7	7	24	3	0	0	0	0	0	0	1	0	1	0	0	0	0	.000	0	3	0.00
	San Jose	A+	SF	37	4	0	12	82.2	352	81	42	37	4	2	6	3	33	2	43	2	1	6	2	.750	0	1	4.03
1993	Shreveport	AA	SF	6	3	0	1	19.2	92	33	17	17	1	0	2	2	2	1	14	1	0	1	1	.500	0	0	7.78
	San Jose	A+	SF	23	1	0	11	47	209	59	31	25	4	1	1	1	14	2	34	3	1	2	0	1.000	0	2	4.79
1994	Sioux Falls	IND	—	18	17	4	0	114.2	492	134	54	48	6	3	3	3	21	3	60	4	0	8	7	.533	1	0	3.77
1995	San Jose	A+	SF	16	0	0	15	18	77	19	6	4	1	2	0	0	5	1	13	3	0	0	2	.000	0	7	2.00
	Shreveport	AA	SF	49	0	0	31	62	265	67	27	23	3	3	1	4	15	4	37	4	0	5	3	.625	0	14	3.34
1996	Shreveport	AA	SF	19	0	0	5	33.1	150	36	26	22	4	6	1	0	12	4	25	2	1	1	2	.333	0	1	5.94
	Sioux Falls	IND	—	13	13	2	0	96	397	93	37	29	3	5	2	1	21	0	68	7	0	9	3	.750	0	0	2.72
6 Min. YEARS				215	38	6	106	517	2214	562	260	223	29	22	17	18	132	17	320	27	4	35	23	.603	1	35	3.88

Adam Hyzdu

Bats: Right **Throws:** Right **Pos:** OF **Ht:** 6'2" **Wt:** 210 **Born:** 12/6/71 **Age:** 25

		BATTING															BASERUNNING				PERCENTAGES		
Year Team	Lg Org	G	AB	H	2B	3B	HR	TB	R	RBI	TBB	IBB	SO	HBP	SH	SF	SB	CS	SB%	GDP	Avg	OBP	SLG
1990 Everett	A- SF	69	253	62	16	1	6	98	31	34	28	1	78	2	0	5	2	4	.33	4	.245	.319	.387
1991 Clinton	A SF	124	410	96	14	5	5	135	47	50	64	1	131	3	7	2	4	5	.44	10	.234	.340	.329
1992 San Jose	A+ SF	128	457	127	25	5	9	189	60	60	55	4	134	1	1	8	10	5	.67	6	.278	.351	.414
1993 San Jose	A+ SF	44	165	48	11	3	13	104	35	38	29	0	53	0	1	2	1	1	.50	3	.291	.393	.630
Shreveport	AA SF	86	302	61	17	0	6	96	30	25	20	2	82	1	1	1	0	5	.00	5	.202	.253	.318
1994 Winston-Sal	A+ Cin	55	210	58	11	1	15	116	30	39	18	0	33	2	0	2	1	5	.17	3	.276	.336	.552
Chattanooga	AA Cin	38	133	35	10	0	3	54	17	9	8	0	21	1	1	0	0	2	.00	1	.263	.310	.406
Indianapols	AAA Cin	12	25	3	2	0	0	5	3	3	1	0	5	0	0	2	0	0	.00	0	.120	.143	.200
1995 Chattanooga	AA Cin	102	312	82	14	1	13	137	55	48	45	2	56	4	2	1	3	2	.60	4	.263	.362	.439
1996 Trenton	AA Bos	109	374	126	24	3	25	231	71	80	56	6	75	2	0	2	1	8	.11	7	.337	.424	.618
7 Min. YEARS		767	2641	698	144	19	95	1165	379	386	324	16	668	16	13	25	22	37	.37	43	.264	.345	.441

Blaise Ilsley

Pitches: Left **Bats:** Left **Pos:** P **Ht:** 6' 1" **Wt:** 195 **Born:** 4/9/64 **Age:** 33

		HOW MUCH HE PITCHED						WHAT HE GAVE UP												THE RESULTS					
Year Team	Lg Org	G	GS	CG	GF	IP	BFP	H	R	ER	HR	SH	SF	HB	TBB	IBB	SO	WP	Bk	W	L	Pct.	ShO	Sv	ERA
1985 Auburn	A- Hou	13	12	2	1	90	354	55	18	14	1	5	0	3	32	0	116	0	0	9	1	.900	0	0	1.40
1986 Asheville	A Hou	15	15	9	0	120	453	74	27	26	11	2	2	2	23	0	146	2	2	12	2	.857	3	0	1.95
Osceola	A+ Hou	14	13	6	1	86.2	337	67	24	17	1	3	4	0	19	0	74	6	1	8	4	.667	2	0	1.77
1987 Columbus	AA Hou	26	26	3	0	167.2	712	162	84	72	13	8	7	4	63	1	130	6	2	10	11	.476	0	0	3.86
1988 Columbus	AA Hou	8	8	0	0	39.1	187	49	28	26	4	0	0	0	21	0	38	2	0	3	1	.750	0	0	5.95
1989 Osceola	A+ Hou	2	2	0	0	7	28	8	5	5	2	0	0	0	0	0	6	0	0	0	0	.000	0	0	6.43
Columbus	AA Hou	4	4	0	0	20.2	87	19	10	3	2	1	0	0	5	0	11	2	1	1	1	.500	0	0	1.31
Tucson	AAA Hou	20	17	1	0	103	443	120	68	67	12	2	3	6	23	2	49	2	0	4	9	.308	0	0	5.85
1990 Columbus	AA Hou	12	12	3	0	83.2	324	70	26	18	5	4	0	3	13	1	70	1	0	6	4	.600	3	0	1.94
Tucson	AAA Hou	20	6	1	4	62.2	295	87	50	45	4	1	2	3	24	0	39	8	0	2	1	.667	0	2	6.46
1991 Tucson	AAA Hou	46	4	0	17	86.1	383	105	51	41	7	9	6	3	27	1	52	2	0	8	6	.571	0	0	4.27
1992 Louisville	AAA StL	33	10	1	10	98.1	429	114	56	47	15	7	4	4	23	2	56	3	0	5	4	.556	0	1	4.30
1993 Iowa	AAA ChN	48	16	0	13	134.2	565	147	61	59	10	5	3	4	32	2	78	7	0	12	7	.632	0	4	3.94
1994 Iowa	AAA ChN	22	16	2	0	116	487	120	68	57	11	1	7	3	21	0	51	2	1	10	4	.714	0	0	4.42
1995 Scranton-WB	AAA Phi	29	29	2	0	185.1	786	210	96	80	17	8	4	5	34	2	102	6	0	8	10	.444	1	0	3.88
1996 Ottawa	AAA Mon	20	4	0	1	45.1	198	49	27	26	9	2	1	1	15	0	22	2	0	5	2	.714	0	0	5.16
Scranton-WB	AAA Phi	5	3	0	1	16	75	24	12	11	2	0	0	0	4	0	9	1	0	1	2	.333	0	0	6.19
1994 Chicago	NL	10	0	0	1	15	74	25	13	13	2	0	0	0	9	2	9	1	0	0	0	.000	0	0	7.80
12 Min. YEARS		337	197	30	48	1462.2	6143	1480	711	614	126	58	43	41	379	11	1049	52	7	104	69	.601	9	7	3.78

Jason Imrisek

Bats: Right **Throws:** Right **Pos:** C **Ht:** 5'11" **Wt:** 185 **Born:** 6/10/74 **Age:** 23

		BATTING															BASERUNNING				PERCENTAGES		
Year Team	Lg Org	G	AB	H	2B	3B	HR	TB	R	RBI	TBB	IBB	SO	HBP	SH	SF	SB	CS	SB%	GDP	Avg	OBP	SLG
1995 Yankees	R NYA	15	53	15	3	0	1	21	5	8	2	0	12	2	0	0	2	2	.50	1	.283	.333	.396
Oneonta	A- NYA	6	13	1	0	0	0	1	1	1	1	0	2	0	0	0	0	0	.00	0	.077	.143	.077
1996 Tampa	A+ NYA	4	3	0	0	0	0	0	0	0	0	0	1	0	0	0	0	0	.00	0	.000	.000	.000
Norwich	AA NYA	2	6	2	1	0	0	3	2	2	0	0	1	0	1	0	0	0	.00	0	.333	.333	.500
Will County	IND —	7	25	2	1	0	0	3	3	3	2	0	5	0	0	0	1	0	1.00	0	.080	.148	.120
Evansville	IND —	13	32	7	1	0	0	8	4	2	3	0	6	3	0	0	0	1	.00	1	.219	.342	.250
2 Min. YEARS		47	132	27	6	0	1	36	15	16	8	0	27	5	1	0	3	3	.50	2	.205	.276	.273

Garey Ingram

Bats: Right **Throws:** Right **Pos:** 2B **Ht:** 5'11" **Wt:** 185 **Born:** 7/25/70 **Age:** 26

		BATTING															BASERUNNING				PERCENTAGES		
Year Team	Lg Org	G	AB	H	2B	3B	HR	TB	R	RBI	TBB	IBB	SO	HBP	SH	SF	SB	CS	SB%	GDP	Avg	OBP	SLG
1990 Great Falls	R+ LA	56	198	68	12	8	2	102	43	21	22	0	37	3	0	1	10	6	.63	3	.343	.415	.515
1991 Bakersfield	A+ LA	118	445	132	16	4	9	183	75	61	52	4	70	14	5	6	30	13	.70	5	.297	.383	.411
San Antonio	AA LA	1	1	0	0	0	0	0	0	1	0	0	1	0	0	1	0	0	.00	0	.000	.000	.000
1992 San Antonio	AA LA	65	198	57	9	5	2	82	34	17	28	2	43	12	2	1	11	6	.65	4	.288	.406	.414
1993 San Antonio	AA LA	84	305	82	14	5	6	124	43	33	31	0	50	5	2	2	19	6	.76	3	.269	.344	.407
1994 San Antonio	AA LA	99	345	89	24	3	8	143	68	28	43	3	61	9	2	0	19	5	.79	5	.258	.355	.414
Albuquerque	AAA LA	2	8	2	0	0	0	2	2	0	0	0	1	0	0	0	1	0	1.00	1	.250	.250	.250
1995 Albuquerque	AAA LA	63	232	57	11	4	1	79	28	30	21	1	40	3	0	3	10	4	.71	4	.246	.313	.341
1996 Albuquerque	AAA LA	6	10	1	0	0	0	1	1	0	1	0	2	0	0	0	0	0	.00	1	.100	.182	.100
1994 Los Angeles	NL	26	78	22	1	0	3	32	10	8	7	3	22	0	1	0	0	0	.00	3	.282	.341	.410
1995 Los Angeles	NL	44	55	11	2	0	0	13	5	3	9	0	8	0	2	0	3	0	1.00	0	.200	.313	.236
7 Min. YEARS		494	1742	488	86	29	28	716	294	191	198	10	305	46	11	14	100	40	.71	26	.280	.366	.411
2 Maj. YEARS		70	133	33	3	0	3	45	15	11	16	3	30	0	3	0	3	0	1.00	3	.248	.329	.338

Riccardo Ingram

Bats: Right **Throws:** Right **Pos:** OF **Ht:** 6' 0" **Wt:** 205 **Born:** 9/10/66 **Age:** 30

		BATTING															BASERUNNING				PERCENTAGES		
Year Team	Lg Org	G	AB	H	2B	3B	HR	TB	R	RBI	TBB	IBB	SO	HBP	SH	SF	SB	CS	SB%	GDP	Avg	OBP	SLG
1988 Lakeland	A+ Det	37	117	24	3	1	0	29	10	10	10	0	30	0	1	0	2	0	1.00	1	.205	.268	.248

				BATTING															BASERUNNING				PERCENTAGES		
Year	Team	Lg	Org	G	AB	H	2B	3B	HR	TB	R	RBI	TBB	IBB	SO	HBP	SH	SF	SB	CS	SB%	GDP	Avg	OBP	SLG
1989	Lakeland	A+	Det	109	365	88	13	3	6	125	40	30	29	1	56	1	0	3	5	2	.71	13	.241	.296	.342
1990	London	AA	Det	92	271	69	10	2	0	83	27	26	27	1	49	4	1	0	3	1	.75	8	.255	.331	.306
1991	London	AA	Det	118	421	114	14	1	18	184	57	64	40	0	77	4	5	3	6	5	.55	15	.271	.338	.437
1992	Toledo	AAA	Det	121	410	103	15	6	8	154	45	41	31	4	52	5	4	5	8	6	.57	11	.251	.308	.376
1993	Toledo	AAA	Det	123	415	112	20	4	13	179	41	62	32	5	66	5	0	5	9	7	.56	6	.270	.326	.431
1994	Toledo	AAA	Det	90	314	90	16	4	9	141	39	56	24	3	45	5	0	3	11	6	.65	9	.287	.344	.449
1995	Salt Lake	AAA	Min	122	477	166	43	2	12	249	80	85	41	3	60	3	0	5	4	5	.44	22	.348	.399	.522
1996	Las Vegas	AAA	SD	124	409	102	21	1	8	149	54	51	49	7	64	3	0	2	6	6	.50	11	.249	.333	.364
1994	Detroit	AL		12	23	5	0	0	0	5	3	2	1	0	2	0	0	1	0	1	.00	0	.217	.240	.217
1995	Minnesota	AL		4	8	1	0	0	0	1	0	1	2	0	1	0	0	0	0	0	.00	1	.125	.300	.125
9 Min. YEARS				936	3199	868	155	24	74	1293	393	425	283	24	499	30	11	26	54	38	.59	96	.271	.334	.404
2 Maj. YEARS				16	31	6	0	0	0	6	3	3	3	0	3	0	0	1	0	1	.00	1	.194	.257	.194

Todd Ingram

Pitches: Right **Bats:** Right **Pos:** P **Ht:** 6'4" **Wt:** 200 **Born:** 4/1/68 **Age:** 29

				HOW MUCH HE PITCHED						WHAT HE GAVE UP												THE RESULTS					
Year	Team	Lg	Org	G	GS	CG	GF	IP	BFP	H	R	ER	HR	SH	SF	HB	TBB	IBB	SO	WP	Bk	W	L	Pct.	ShO	Sv	ERA
1991	Sou. Oregon	A-	Oak	17	12	1	1	81.1	355	72	39	31	4	2	2	6	39	0	64	5	3	6	5	.545	0	1	3.43
1992	Reno	A+	Oak	41	9	0	23	67.1	332	91	69	54	8	0	3	3	40	4	44	12	2	1	7	.125	0	9	7.22
1993	Modesto	A+	Oak	32	0	0	24	42.2	196	49	30	26	4	1	2	2	18	3	39	11	1	5	7	.417	0	9	5.48
1994	Huntsville	AA	Oak	48	0	0	28	59.1	278	63	40	36	4	5	0	1	37	4	55	7	0	3	8	.273	0	11	5.46
1995	Trenton	AA	Bos	18	0	0	7	24.2	125	27	19	16	2	2	2	1	21	4	16	1	1	1	1	.500	0	0	5.84
	Knoxville	AA	Tor	38	0	0	16	58.2	268	53	36	30	5	3	4	1	37	4	35	2	1	2	2	.500	0	3	4.60
1996	Tyler	IND	—	5	5	0	0	32.1	154	43	28	24	2	0	2	2	15	0	26	6	0	1	3	.250	0	0	6.68
	Midland	AA	Cal	15	0	0	6	22.2	114	25	22	20	1	1	1	3	21	0	11	7	0	0	1	.000	0	0	7.94
6 Min. YEARS				214	26	1	105	389	1822	423	283	237	30	14	16	19	228	19	290	51	8	19	34	.358	0	33	5.48

Gavin Jackson

Bats: Right **Throws:** Right **Pos:** SS **Ht:** 5'10" **Wt:** 170 **Born:** 7/19/73 **Age:** 23

				BATTING															BASERUNNING				PERCENTAGES		
Year	Team	Lg	Org	G	AB	H	2B	3B	HR	TB	R	RBI	TBB	IBB	SO	HBP	SH	SF	SB	CS	SB%	GDP	Avg	OBP	SLG
1993	Red Sox	R	Bos	42	160	50	7	2	0	61	29	11	14	0	18	11	2	0	11	5	.69	2	.313	.405	.381
1994	Sarasota	A+	Bos	108	321	77	6	1	0	85	46	27	33	0	40	7	12	0	9	10	.47	1	.240	.324	.265
1995	Sarasota	A+	Bos	100	342	91	19	1	0	112	61	36	40	3	43	6	8	4	11	12	.48	8	.266	.349	.327
1996	Trenton	AA	Bos	6	20	5	2	0	0	7	2	3	2	0	3	0	0	0	0	1	.00	0	.250	.318	.350
	Pawtucket	AAA	Bos	15	44	11	2	0	0	13	5	1	3	0	8	0	1	0	0	1	.00	0	.250	.298	.295
	Sarasota	A+	Bos	87	276	66	13	2	0	83	26	24	33	0	47	7	8	3	4	6	.40	6	.239	.332	.301
4 Min. YEARS				358	1163	300	49	6	0	361	169	102	125	3	159	31	31	7	35	35	.50	17	.258	.344	.310

Ryan Jacobs

Pitches: Left **Bats:** Right **Pos:** P **Ht:** 6'2" **Wt:** 175 **Born:** 2/3/74 **Age:** 23

				HOW MUCH HE PITCHED						WHAT HE GAVE UP												THE RESULTS					
Year	Team	Lg	Org	G	GS	CG	GF	IP	BFP	H	R	ER	HR	SH	SF	HB	TBB	IBB	SO	WP	Bk	W	L	Pct.	ShO	Sv	ERA
1992	Braves	R	Atl	12	2	0	6	35	148	30	18	10	1	3	2	1	8	2	40	2	0	1	3	.250	0	1	2.57
1993	Danville	R+	Atl	10	10	0	0	42.2	188	35	24	19	5	1	2	1	25	0	32	6	0	4	3	.571	0	0	4.01
1994	Macon	A	Atl	27	18	1	2	121.2	532	105	54	39	9	4	2	3	62	2	81	6	1	8	7	.533	1	1	2.88
1995	Durham	A+	Atl	29	25	1	3	148.2	640	145	72	58	12	6	5	3	57	3	99	10	0	11	6	.647	0	0	3.51
1996	Greenville	AA	Atl	21	21	0	0	99.2	468	127	83	74	19	3	4	4	57	1	64	8	0	3	9	.250	0	0	6.68
5 Min. YEARS				99	76	2	11	447.2	1976	442	251	200	46	17	15	12	209	8	316	32	1	27	28	.491	1	2	4.02

Joe Jacobsen

Pitches: Right **Bats:** Right **Pos:** P **Ht:** 6'3" **Wt:** 225 **Born:** 12/26/71 **Age:** 25

				HOW MUCH HE PITCHED						WHAT HE GAVE UP												THE RESULTS					
Year	Team	Lg	Org	G	GS	CG	GF	IP	BFP	H	R	ER	HR	SH	SF	HB	TBB	IBB	SO	WP	Bk	W	L	Pct.	ShO	Sv	ERA
1992	Dodgers	R	LA	6	3	0	2	26	100	17	7	5	0	0	0	0	6	0	25	2	2	1	1	.500	0	0	1.73
	Great Falls	R+	LA	6	6	1	0	32.1	143	37	22	19	2	0	1	1	9	0	24	3	0	2	2	.500	0	0	5.29
1993	Yakima	A-	LA	25	0	0	7	37.2	174	27	16	10	0	2	3	1	28	2	55	1	0	1	0	1.000	0	3	2.39
	Bakersfield	A+	LA	6	0	0	3	19.2	88	22	16	10	1	1	0	0	8	0	23	3	0	1	0	1.000	0	2	4.58
1994	Bakersfield	A+	LA	3	0	0	1	7.1	26	2	1	1	1	1	0	0	1	0	5	0	0	1	0	1.000	0	0	1.23
	San Antonio	AA	LA	18	0	0	12	25	108	21	9	7	0	2	2	2	12	2	15	2	1	2	1	.667	0	1	2.52
	Vero Beach	A+	LA	37	0	0	34	43	193	40	15	13	1	3	0	2	23	2	44	3	0	0	5	.000	0	15	2.72
1995	San Bernrdo	A+	LA	4	0	0	3	3.2	17	4	2	0	0	0	0	0	2	0	5	1	0	0	0	.000	0	2	0.00
	Vero Beach	A+	LA	51	0	0	47	52.2	232	46	24	20	2	5	2	2	25	2	59	11	1	1	3	.250	0	34	3.42
1996	San Antonio	AA	LA	38	0	0	23	58	256	62	33	27	4	4	3	1	24	2	39	7	0	1	4	.200	0	5	4.19
5 Min. YEARS				194	9	1	132	305.1	1337	278	145	112	11	18	11	9	138	10	294	33	4	10	16	.385	0	62	3.30

Pete Janicki

Pitches: Right **Bats:** Right **Pos:** P **Ht:** 6'4" **Wt:** 190 **Born:** 1/26/71 **Age:** 26

				HOW MUCH HE PITCHED						WHAT HE GAVE UP												THE RESULTS					
Year	Team	Lg	Org	G	GS	CG	GF	IP	BFP	H	R	ER	HR	SH	SF	HB	TBB	IBB	SO	WP	Bk	W	L	Pct.	ShO	Sv	ERA
1993	Palm Spring	A+	Cal	1	1	0	0	1.2	10	3	2	2	0	0	0	0	2	0	2	0	1	0	0	.000	0	0	10.80
1994	Midland	AA	Cal	14	14	1	0	70	327	86	68	54	4	3	1	6	33	1	54	15	3	2	6	.250	0	0	6.94

Year	Team	Lg	Org	G	GS	CG	GF	IP	BFP	H	R	ER	HR	SH	SF	HB	TBB	IBB	SO	WP	Bk	W	L	Pct.	ShO	Sv	ERA
				HOW MUCH HE PITCHED						WHAT HE GAVE UP												THE RESULTS					
	Lk Elsinore	A+	Cal	3	3	0	0	12	61	17	12	9	2	1	1	4	4	0	12	0	0	1	2	.333	0	0	6.75
1995	Vancouver	AAA	Cal	9	9	0	0	48.2	227	64	38	38	8	1	4	1	23	0	34	0	0	1	4	.200	0	0	7.03
	Lk Elsinore	A+	Cal	29	29	0	0	172	759	194	104	80	15	4	10	6	51	0	140	6	1	10	8	.556	0	0	4.19
1996	Midland	AA	Cal	5	5	0	0	31	136	37	28	22	4	0	0	2	10	0	17	4	0	1	3	.250	0	0	6.39
	Vancouver	AAA	Cal	31	14	0	10	104	485	135	82	78	15	5	4	13	37	1	86	4	0	2	9	.182	0	1	6.75
	4 Min. YEARS			92	75	1	10	439.1	2005	536	334	283	48	14	20	32	160	2	345	29	5	17	32	.347	0	1	5.80

Link Jarrett

Bats: Both **Throws:** Right **Pos:** 2B **Ht:** 5'10" **Wt:** 165 **Born:** 1/26/72 **Age:** 25

Year	Team	Lg	Org	G	AB	H	2B	3B	HR	TB	R	RBI	TBB	IBB	SO	HBP	SH	SF	SB	CS	SB%	GDP	Avg	OBP	SLG
				BATTING															BASERUNNING				PERCENTAGES		
1994	Bend	A-	Col	74	279	67	13	0	0	80	31	15	24	0	45	2	4	2	4	4	.50	6	.240	.303	.287
1995	Asheville	A	Col	116	404	95	11	0	0	106	46	20	62	1	60	2	10	2	12	10	.55	5	.235	.338	.262
1996	New Haven	AA	Col	56	164	32	6	0	1	41	18	9	14	0	23	0	3	1	1	1	.50	5	.195	.257	.250
	Salem	A+	Col	38	98	22	3	1	0	27	9	8	8	0	14	1	3	0	1	2	.33	3	.224	.290	.276
	3 Min. YEARS			284	945	216	33	1	1	254	104	52	108	1	142	5	20	5	18	17	.51	19	.229	.310	.269

Matt Jarvis

Pitches: Left **Bats:** Right **Pos:** P **Ht:** 6'4" **Wt:** 185 **Born:** 2/22/72 **Age:** 25

Year	Team	Lg	Org	G	GS	CG	GF	IP	BFP	H	R	ER	HR	SH	SF	HB	TBB	IBB	SO	WP	Bk	W	L	Pct.	ShO	Sv	ERA
				HOW MUCH HE PITCHED						WHAT HE GAVE UP												THE RESULTS					
1991	Orioles	R	Bal	11	5	0	2	37.1	163	44	22	18	2	1	2	0	17	0	30	2	1	3	1	.750	0	1	4.34
1992	Kane County	A	Bal	34	7	0	8	71.1	327	84	53	36	3	2	1	1	35	2	43	7	3	4	4	.500	0	0	4.54
1993	Albany	A	Bal	29	29	8	0	185.1	797	173	82	63	7	5	2	5	82	4	118	10	1	11	13	.458	1	0	3.06
1994	Frederick	A+	Bal	31	14	0	3	103.2	459	92	58	48	7	5	2	9	48	0	67	3	0	10	4	.714	0	1	4.17
1995	Bowie	AA	Bal	26	21	0	1	118	531	154	71	67	11	4	4	4	42	1	60	5	3	9	8	.529	0	0	5.11
1996	Bowie	AA	Bal	6	4	0	0	19.1	91	31	17	16	2	0	2	1	7	0	13	4	1	1	3	.250	0	0	7.45
	Winnipeg	IND	—	17	15	2	1	103	454	99	46	41	11	3	2	6	55	1	63	3	3	11	3	.786	0	0	3.58
	6 Min. YEARS			154	95	10	15	638	2822	677	349	289	43	20	15	26	286	8	394	34	12	49	36	.576	1	2	4.08

Domingo Jean

Pitches: Right **Bats:** Right **Pos:** P **Ht:** 6' 2" **Wt:** 175 **Born:** 1/9/69 **Age:** 28

Year	Team	Lg	Org	G	GS	CG	GF	IP	BFP	H	R	ER	HR	SH	SF	HB	TBB	IBB	SO	WP	Bk	W	L	Pct.	ShO	Sv	ERA
				HOW MUCH HE PITCHED						WHAT HE GAVE UP												THE RESULTS					
1990	White Sox	R	ChA	13	13	1	0	78.2	312	55	32	20	1	0	1	6	16	0	65	10	2	2	5	.286	0	0	2.29
1991	South Bend	A	ChA	25	25	2	0	158	680	121	75	58	7	3	7	10	65	0	141	17	5	12	8	.600	0	0	3.30
1992	Ft. Laud	A+	NYA	23	23	5	0	158.2	637	118	57	46	3	7	6	6	49	1	172	4	1	6	11	.353	1	0	2.61
	Albany-Colo	AA	NYA	1	1	0	0	4	17	3	2	1	0	0	0	0	3	0	6	1	0	0	0	.000	0	0	2.25
1993	Albany-Colo	AA	NYA	11	11	1	0	61	257	42	24	17	1	1	1	5	33	0	41	4	0	5	3	.625	0	0	2.51
	Columbus	AAA	NYA	7	7	1	0	44.2	180	40	15	14	2	0	2	2	13	0	39	3	0	2	2	.500	0	0	2.82
	Pr. William	A+	NYA	1	0	0	0	1.2	6	1	0	0	0	0	0	0	0	0	1	0	0	0	0	.000	0	0	0.00
1994	Tucson	AAA	Hou	6	3	0	1	19	88	20	13	12	3	0	1	2	11	1	16	0	0	0	0	.000	0	0	5.68
1995	Tucson	AAA	Hou	3	3	0	0	13.2	62	15	10	10	1	0	0	0	7	0	14	3	0	2	1	.667	0	0	6.59
	Indianapols	AAA	Cin	26	13	1	9	90	425	103	70	60	12	5	2	1	61	1	73	14	3	4	8	.333	0	1	6.00
	Okla. City	AAA	Tex	29	16	1	9	103.2	487	118	80	70	13	5	2	1	68	1	87	17	3	6	9	.400	0	1	6.08
1996	Indianapols	AAA	Cin	7	0	0	2	9.1	49	13	11	9	2	0	0	0	8	1	5	0	0	1	1	.500	0	0	8.68
	Chattanooga	AA	Cin	39	0	0	37	39.2	169	34	19	18	1	3	0	0	17	2	33	5	0	2	3	.400	0	31	4.08
1993	New York	AL		10	6	0	1	40.1	176	37	20	20	7	0	1	0	19	1	20	1	0	1	1	.500	0	0	4.46
	7 Min. YEARS			191	115	12	58	782	3369	683	408	335	46	24	22	33	351	8	693	78	14	42	51	.452	1	33	3.86

Brett Jenkins

Bats: Right **Throws:** Right **Pos:** DH **Ht:** 6'1" **Wt:** 195 **Born:** 4/5/70 **Age:** 27

Year	Team	Lg	Org	G	AB	H	2B	3B	HR	TB	R	RBI	TBB	IBB	SO	HBP	SH	SF	SB	CS	SB%	GDP	Avg	OBP	SLG
				BATTING															BASERUNNING				PERCENTAGES		
1991	Jamestown	A-	Mon	31	106	29	3	1	4	46	16	17	9	0	12	4	0	2	1	2	.33	9	.274	.347	.434
1992	W. Palm Bch	A+	Mon	99	362	95	21	2	4	132	39	45	22	3	45	6	1	5	8	5	.62	12	.262	.311	.365
	San Jose	A+	SF	8	26	3	1	0	0	4	1	2	3	0	5	1	0	1	0	0	.00	1	.115	.226	.154
1993	San Jose	A+	SF	52	189	44	11	0	7	76	25	25	16	1	25	7	0	2	1	0	1.00	5	.233	.313	.402
1994	Clinton	A	SF	12	42	8	1	0	1	12	5	10	10	0	13	1	0	0	2	0	1.00	2	.190	.358	.286
	San Jose	A+	SF	48	175	47	10	1	5	74	21	23	15	1	41	3	2	3	2	0	1.00	4	.269	.332	.423
	San Bernrdo	A+	SF	4	16	4	2	0	1	9	3	2	1	0	2	0	0	0	0	0	.00	0	.250	.294	.563
1996	New Orleans	AAA	Mil	26	71	16	3	0	6	37	9	11	3	0	17	1	0	2	0	1	.00	2	.225	.260	.521
	5 Min. YEARS			280	987	246	52	4	28	390	119	135	79	5	160	23	3	15	14	8	.64	35	.249	.315	.395

Geoff Jenkins

Bats: Left **Throws:** Left **Pos:** DH **Ht:** 6'1" **Wt:** 195 **Born:** 7/21/74 **Age:** 22

Year	Team	Lg	Org	G	AB	H	2B	3B	HR	TB	R	RBI	TBB	IBB	SO	HBP	SH	SF	SB	CS	SB%	GDP	Avg	OBP	SLG
				BATTING															BASERUNNING				PERCENTAGES		
1995	Helena	R+	Mil	7	28	9	0	1	0	11	2	9	3	0	11	0	0	1	0	2	.00	0	.321	.375	.393
	Stockton	A+	Mil	13	47	12	2	0	3	23	13	12	10	0	12	0	0	2	2	0	1.00	0	.255	.370	.409
	El Paso	AA	Mil	21	79	22	4	2	1	33	12	13	8	0	23	0	0	1	3	1	.75	1	.278	.341	.418
1996	El Paso	AA	Mil	22	77	22	5	4	1	38	17	11	12	1	21	2	0	1	1	2	.33	2	.286	.391	.494

BATTING																		BASERUNNING				PERCENTAGES		
Year Team	Lg Org	G	AB	H	2B	3B	HR	TB	R	RBI	TBB	IBB	SO	HBP	SH	SF	SB	CS	SB%	GDP	Avg	OBP	SLG	
Stockton	A+ Mil	37	138	48	8	4	3	73	27	25	20	1	32	3	1	3	3	3	.50	3	.348	.433	.529	
2 Min. YEARS		100	369	113	19	11	8	178	71	70	53	2	99	5	1	8	9	8	.53	6	.306	.393	.482	

Mike Jerzembeck

Pitches: Right **Bats:** Right **Pos:** P **Ht:** 6'1" **Wt:** 185 **Born:** 5/18/72 **Age:** 25

HOW MUCH HE PITCHED								WHAT HE GAVE UP												THE RESULTS					
Year Team	Lg Org	G	GS	CG	GF	IP	BFP	H	R	ER	HR	SH	SF	HB	TBB	IBB	SO	WP	Bk	W	L	Pct.	ShO	Sv	ERA
1993 Oneonta	A- NYA	14	14	0	0	77.1	327	70	25	23	1	3	1	3	26	0	76	2	2	8	4	.667	0	0	2.68
1994 Tampa	A+ NYA	16	16	0	0	68.2	274	59	27	24	6	1	2	2	22	0	45	2	1	4	3	.571	0	0	3.15
1995 Tampa	A+ NYA	2	0	0	0	3	17	5	4	3	1	0	0	0	2	0	1	1	0	0	1	.000	0	0	9.00
1996 Columbus	AAA NYA	1	0	0	0	1.2	7	1	1	1	0	0	0	0	1	0	0	0	0	0	0	.000	0	0	5.40
Norwich	AA NYA	14	13	1	0	69.2	303	74	38	35	9	4	2	3	26	0	65	2	4	3	6	.333	1	0	4.52
Tampa	A+ NYA	12	12	0	0	73.1	297	67	26	24	4	1	1	0	13	0	60	3	0	4	2	.667	0	0	2.95
4 Min. YEARS		59	55	1	0	293.2	1225	276	121	110	21	9	6	8	90	0	247	10	7	19	16	.543	1	0	3.37

Manny Jimenez

Bats: Right **Throws:** Right **Pos:** SS **Ht:** 5'11" **Wt:** 160 **Born:** 7/4/71 **Age:** 25

BATTING																	BASERUNNING				PERCENTAGES		
Year Team	Lg Org	G	AB	H	2B	3B	HR	TB	R	RBI	TBB	IBB	SO	HBP	SH	SF	SB	CS	SB%	GDP	Avg	OBP	SLG
1991 Pulaski	R+ Atl	57	234	66	10	7	1	93	37	29	12	2	48	1	2	0	19	8	.70	4	.282	.320	.397
1992 Macon	A Atl	117	401	88	9	3	1	106	25	32	16	1	106	8	4	2	13	15	.46	7	.219	.262	.264
1993 Durham	A+ Atl	127	427	96	16	4	6	138	55	29	21	0	93	7	10	1	7	9	.44	12	.225	.272	.323
1994 Greenville	AA Atl	64	195	39	6	1	1	50	13	14	5	0	38	1	1	1	3	4	.43	6	.200	.223	.256
Durham	A+ Atl	31	104	20	6	0	0	26	6	9	2	0	18	2	0	0	1	1	.50	2	.192	.222	.250
1995 Durham	A+ Atl	121	375	92	16	2	2	118	40	23	17	1	71	5	3	0	8	6	.57	11	.245	.287	.315
1996 Greenville	AA Atl	131	474	130	21	2	3	164	68	57	28	3	67	6	4	3	12	7	.63	18	.274	.321	.346
6 Min. YEARS		648	2210	531	84	19	14	695	244	193	101	7	441	30	24	7	63	50	.56	60	.240	.282	.314

Miguel Jimenez

Pitches: Right **Bats:** Right **Pos:** P **Ht:** 6' 2" **Wt:** 205 **Born:** 8/19/69 **Age:** 27

HOW MUCH HE PITCHED								WHAT HE GAVE UP												THE RESULTS					
Year Team	Lg Org	G	GS	CG	GF	IP	BFP	H	R	ER	HR	SH	SF	HB	TBB	IBB	SO	WP	Bk	W	L	Pct.	ShO	Sv	ERA
1991 Sou. Oregon	A- Oak	10	9	0	0	34.2	159	22	21	12	0	0	0	2	34	0	39	6	6	0	2	.000	0	0	3.12
1992 Madison	A Oak	26	19	2	0	120.1	514	78	48	39	3	2	2	8	78	1	135	12	14	7	7	.500	1	0	2.92
Huntsville	AA Oak	1	1	0	0	5	19	3	1	1	1	0	0	0	3	0	8	0	0	1	0	1.000	0	0	1.80
1993 Huntsville	AA Oak	20	19	0	0	107	476	92	49	35	10	2	1	4	64	0	105	6	2	10	6	.625	0	0	2.94
Tacoma	AAA Oak	8	8	0	0	37.2	164	32	23	20	4	2	1	0	24	0	34	3	0	2	3	.400	0	0	4.78
1994 Tacoma	AAA Oak	23	15	0	2	74	372	82	83	75	9	1	4	4	79	0	64	12	2	3	9	.250	0	0	9.12
1995 Modesto	A+ Oak	4	4	0	0	18	83	14	13	12	5	0	1	2	14	0	11	4	0	1	2	.333	0	0	6.00
Huntsville	AA Oak	6	6	0	0	30	124	25	12	12	3	1	0	0	11	0	28	1	0	3	2	.600	0	0	3.60
Edmonton	AAA Oak	16	13	0	2	55.1	250	51	35	34	8	1	2	2	35	0	43	5	0	4	4	.500	0	0	5.53
1996 Huntsville	AA Oak	19	2	0	5	37.2	180	43	37	37	7	0	4	2	27	2	28	5	0	0	4	.000	0	0	8.84
Modesto	A+ Oak	13	12	0	0	70.2	320	87	40	36	6	0	2	1	28	0	75	10	0	7	1	.875	0	0	4.58
1993 Oakland	AL	5	4	0	0	27	120	27	12	12	5	0	0	1	16	0	13	0	0	1	0	1.000	0	0	4.00
1994 Oakland	AL	8	7	0	0	34	173	38	33	28	9	1	1	1	32	2	22	3	3	1	4	.200	0	0	7.41
6 Min. YEARS		146	108	2	9	590.1	2661	529	362	313	56	9	17	25	397	3	570	64	24	38	40	.487	1	0	4.77
2 Maj. YEARS		13	11	0	0	61	293	65	45	40	14	1	1	2	48	2	35	3	3	2	4	.333	0	0	5.90

Keith Johns

Bats: Right **Throws:** Right **Pos:** SS **Ht:** 6'1" **Wt:** 175 **Born:** 7/19/71 **Age:** 25

BATTING																	BASERUNNING				PERCENTAGES		
Year Team	Lg Org	G	AB	H	2B	3B	HR	TB	R	RBI	TBB	IBB	SO	HBP	SH	SF	SB	CS	SB%	GDP	Avg	OBP	SLG
1992 Hamilton	A- StL	70	275	78	11	1	1	94	36	28	27	0	42	1	1	3	15	10	.60	5	.284	.346	.342
1993 Springfield	A StL	132	467	121	24	1	2	153	74	40	70	0	68	4	9	5	40	20	.67	8	.259	.357	.328
1994 St. Pete	A+ StL	122	464	106	20	0	3	135	52	47	37	1	49	2	12	4	18	9	.67	7	.228	.286	.291
1995 Arkansas	AA StL	111	396	111	13	2	2	134	69	28	55	0	53	2	11	2	14	7	.67	11	.280	.369	.338
Louisville	AAA StL	5	10	0	0	0	0	0	0	0	0	0	2	0	0	0	0	0	.00	0	.000	.000	.000
1996 Arkansas	AA StL	127	447	110	17	1	1	132	52	40	47	0	61	4	7	1	8	9	.47	17	.246	.323	.295
5 Min. YEARS		567	2059	526	85	5	9	648	283	183	236	1	275	13	40	15	95	55	.63	48	.255	.334	.315

Barry Johnson

Pitches: Right **Bats:** Right **Pos:** P **Ht:** 6'4" **Wt:** 200 **Born:** 8/21/69 **Age:** 27

HOW MUCH HE PITCHED								WHAT HE GAVE UP												THE RESULTS					
Year Team	Lg Org	G	GS	CG	GF	IP	BFP	H	R	ER	HR	SH	SF	HB	TBB	IBB	SO	WP	Bk	W	L	Pct.	ShO	Sv	ERA
1991 Expos	R Mon	7	1	0	3	12.2	55	10	9	5	0	0	0	4	6	0	10	2	0	0	2	.000	0	0	3.55
1992 South Bend	A ChA	16	16	5	0	109.1	463	111	56	46	5	1	5	6	23	0	74	8	1	7	5	.583	1	0	3.79
1993 Sarasota	A+ ChA	18	1	0	7	54.1	205	33	5	4	1	5	2	2	8	0	40	1	1	5	0	1.000	0	1	0.66
Birmingham	AA ChA	13	1	0	8	21.2	97	27	11	8	2	1	1	0	6	0	16	2	1	2	0	1.000	0	1	3.32
1994 Birmingham	AA ChA	51	4	0	12	97.2	427	100	51	35	7	8	3	2	30	3	67	2	0	6	2	.750	0	1	3.23
1995 Birmingham	AA ChA	47	0	0	10	78	308	64	21	16	1	2	1	2	15	1	53	2	1	7	4	.636	0	0	1.85
1996 Birmingham	AA ChA	9	0	0	7	10.2	35	2	0	0	0	1	0	0	1	0	15	0	0	0	0	.000	0	4	0.00
Nashville	AAA ChA	38	8	0	8	103	430	93	38	32	11	2	3	1	39	3	68	4	0	7	2	.778	0	0	2.80

		HOW MUCH HE PITCHED						WHAT HE GAVE UP												THE RESULTS					
Year Team	Lg Org	G	GS	CG	GF	IP	BFP	H	R	ER	HR	SH	SF	HB	TBB	IBB	SO	WP	Bk	W	L	Pct.	ShO	Sv	ERA
6 Min. YEARS		199	31	5	55	487.1	2020	440	191	146	27	20	15	17	128	7	343	21	4	34	15	.694	1	7	2.70

Earl Johnson

Bats: Both **Throws:** Right **Pos:** OF **Ht:** 5'9" **Wt:** 163 **Born:** 10/3/71 **Age:** 25

		BATTING															BASERUNNING				PERCENTAGES		
Year Team	Lg Org	G	AB	H	2B	3B	HR	TB	R	RBI	TBB	IBB	SO	HBP	SH	SF	SB	CS	SB%	GDP	Avg	OBP	SLG
1992 Padres	R SD	35	101	17	1	0	0	18	20	1	10	0	28	1	0	0	19	5	.79	0	.168	.250	.178
1993 Spokane	A- SD	63	199	49	3	1	0	54	33	14	16	0	49	1	5	1	19	3	.86	2	.246	.304	.271
1994 Springfield	A SD	136	533	149	11	3	1	169	80	43	37	0	94	3	13	4	80	25	.76	2	.280	.328	.317
1995 Rancho Cuca	A+ SD	81	341	100	11	3	0	117	51	25	25	0	51	1	5	0	34	12	.74	5	.293	.343	.343
Memphis	AA SD	2	10	2	0	0	0	2	0	0	1	0	0	0	0	0	0	1	.00	0	.200	.273	.200
1996 Memphis	AA SD	82	337	85	10	6	2	113	50	33	18	1	59	1	5	3	15	13	.54	5	.252	.290	.335
5 Min. YEARS		399	1521	402	36	13	3	473	234	116	107	1	281	7	28	8	167	59	.74	14	.264	.314	.311

Erik Johnson

Bats: Right **Throws:** Right **Pos:** 2B **Ht:** 5'11" **Wt:** 175 **Born:** 10/11/65 **Age:** 31

		BATTING															BASERUNNING				PERCENTAGES		
Year Team	Lg Org	G	AB	H	2B	3B	HR	TB	R	RBI	TBB	IBB	SO	HBP	SH	SF	SB	CS	SB%	GDP	Avg	OBP	SLG
1987 Pocatello	R+ SF	43	129	34	7	0	4	53	19	12	13	0	21	0	3	0	6	2	.75	1	.264	.331	.411
Shreveport	AA SF	9	21	2	1	0	0	3	1	3	0	0	5	0	0	0	0	1	.00	0	.095	.095	.143
1988 Clinton	A SF	90	322	72	12	3	5	105	29	38	28	3	39	3	4	2	4	7	.36	6	.224	.290	.326
San Jose	A+ SF	44	160	40	3	1	1	48	25	16	18	0	29	2	1	0	4	2	.67	5	.250	.333	.300
1989 Shreveport	AA SF	87	246	56	5	4	3	78	28	29	23	3	37	1	4	4	3	2	.60	10	.228	.292	.317
1990 Phoenix	AAA SF	2	3	0	0	0	0	0	0	0	1	0	1	0	0	0	0	0	.00	1	.000	.250	.000
Shreveport	AA SF	91	270	60	6	0	1	69	35	15	22	3	38	3	3	0	6	6	.50	8	.222	.288	.256
1991 Phoenix	AAA SF	16	34	11	1	1	0	14	6	4	3	1	5	0	0	1	0	0	.00	0	.324	.368	.412
Shreveport	AA SF	58	146	32	7	0	2	45	27	20	16	4	20	1	4	0	6	2	.75	3	.219	.301	.308
1992 Phoenix	AAA SF	90	229	55	5	1	0	62	24	19	20	2	38	2	5	1	8	10	.44	9	.240	.306	.271
1993 Phoenix	AAA SF	101	363	90	8	5	0	108	33	33	29	2	51	1	2	3	3	9	.25	13	.248	.303	.298
1994 Phoenix	AAA SF	106	384	112	19	3	1	140	43	45	35	3	57	3	1	5	2	6	.25	16	.292	.351	.365
1995 Calgary	AAA Pit	123	455	135	35	6	3	191	64	58	39	6	40	0	3	6	5	4	.56	12	.297	.348	.420
1996 Charlotte	AAA Fla	67	185	33	6	0	0	39	19	10	8	0	35	1	1	1	0	2	.00	7	.178	.215	.211
1993 San Francisco	NL	4	5	2	2	0	0	4	1	0	0	0	1	0	0	0	0	0	.00	0	.400	.400	.800
1994 San Francisco	NL	5	13	2	0	0	0	2	0	0	0	0	4	0	0	0	0	0	.00	0	.154	.154	.154
10 Min. YEARS		927	2947	732	115	24	20	955	353	302	255	27	416	17	31	23	47	53	.47	91	.248	.310	.324
2 Maj. YEARS		9	18	4	2	0	0	6	1	0	0	0	5	0	0	0	0	0	.00	0	.222	.222	.333

J.J. Johnson

Bats: Right **Throws:** Right **Pos:** OF **Ht:** 6'0" **Wt:** 195 **Born:** 8/31/73 **Age:** 23

		BATTING															BASERUNNING				PERCENTAGES		
Year Team	Lg Org	G	AB	H	2B	3B	HR	TB	R	RBI	TBB	IBB	SO	HBP	SH	SF	SB	CS	SB%	GDP	Avg	OBP	SLG
1991 Red Sox	R Bos	31	110	19	1	0	0	20	14	9	10	0	15	2	0	2	3	1	.75	2	.173	.250	.182
1992 Elmira	A- Bos	30	114	26	3	1	1	34	8	12	4	0	32	1	4	1	8	0	1.00	2	.228	.258	.298
1993 Utica	A- Bos	43	170	49	17	4	2	80	33	27	9	1	34	7	2	3	5	3	.63	2	.288	.344	.471
Lynchburg	A+ Bos	25	94	24	3	0	4	39	10	17	7	0	20	2	2	2	1	2	.33	3	.255	.314	.415
1994 Lynchburg	A+ Bos	131	515	120	28	4	14	198	66	51	36	3	132	4	1	1	4	7	.36	9	.233	.288	.384
1995 Sarasota	A+ Bos	107	391	108	16	4	10	162	49	43	26	0	74	6	2	2	7	8	.47	9	.276	.329	.414
Trenton	AA Bos	2	6	3	0	0	0	3	1	1	0	0	0	0	0	0	0	0	.00	0	.500	.500	.500
1996 New Britain	AA Min	119	440	120	23	3	16	197	62	59	40	3	90	7	2	3	10	11	.48	4	.273	.341	.448
Salt Lake	AAA Min	13	56	19	3	1	1	27	8	13	1	0	11	1	1	0	0	1	.00	1	.339	.362	.482
6 Min. YEARS		501	1896	488	94	17	48	760	251	232	133	7	408	30	14	14	38	33	.54	32	.257	.314	.401

Jonathan Johnson

Pitches: Right **Bats:** Right **Pos:** P **Ht:** 6'0" **Wt:** 180 **Born:** 7/16/74 **Age:** 22

		HOW MUCH HE PITCHED						WHAT HE GAVE UP												THE RESULTS					
Year Team	Lg Org	G	GS	CG	GF	IP	BFP	H	R	ER	HR	SH	SF	HB	TBB	IBB	SO	WP	Bk	W	L	Pct.	ShO	Sv	ERA
1995 Charlotte	A+ Tex	8	7	1	1	43.1	178	34	14	13	2	2	0	1	16	0	25	3	3	1	5	.167	0	0	2.70
1996 Okla. City	AAA Tex	1	1	1	0	9	29	2	0	0	0	0	0	0	1	0	6	0	0	1	0	1.000	1	0	0.00
Tulsa	AA Tex	26	25	6	1	174.1	728	176	86	69	15	3	5	6	41	1	97	2	3	13	10	.565	0	0	3.56
2 Min. YEARS		35	33	8	2	226.2	935	212	100	82	17	5	5	7	58	1	128	5	6	15	15	.500	1	0	3.26

Keith Johnson

Bats: Right **Throws:** Right **Pos:** SS **Ht:** 5'11" **Wt:** 190 **Born:** 4/17/71 **Age:** 26

		BATTING															BASERUNNING				PERCENTAGES		
Year Team	Lg Org	G	AB	H	2B	3B	HR	TB	R	RBI	TBB	IBB	SO	HBP	SH	SF	SB	CS	SB%	GDP	Avg	OBP	SLG
1992 Yakima	A- LA	57	197	40	6	0	1	49	27	17	16	0	37	10	1	1	5	1	.83	4	.203	.295	.249
1993 Vero Beach	A+ LA	111	404	96	22	0	4	130	37	48	18	0	71	4	6	5	13	13	.50	8	.238	.274	.322
1994 Bakersfield	A+ LA	64	210	42	12	1	2	62	19	19	16	0	49	5	3	2	13	7	.65	3	.200	.270	.295
1995 San Bernrdo	A+ LA	111	417	101	26	1	17	180	64	68	17	0	83	4	11	2	20	12	.63	4	.242	.277	.432
1996 San Antonio	AA LA	127	521	143	28	6	10	213	74	57	17	1	82	4	9	3	15	8	.65	15	.274	.301	.409
Albuquerque	AAA LA	4	16	4	1	0	0	5	2	2	1	0	1	0	0	0	0	0	.00	0	.250	.294	.313
5 Min. YEARS		474	1765	426	95	8	34	639	223	211	85	1	323	27	30	13	66	41	.62	34	.241	.285	.362

Russ Johnson

Bats: Right **Throws:** Right **Pos:** SS **Ht:** 5'10" **Wt:** 185 **Born:** 2/22/73 **Age:** 24

BATTING																		BASERUNNING				PERCENTAGES		
Year Team	Lg	Org	G	AB	H	2B	3B	HR	TB	R	RBI	TBB	IBB	SO	HBP	SH	SF	SB	CS	SB%	GDP	Avg	OBP	SLG
1995 Jackson	AA	Hou	132	476	118	16	2	9	165	65	53	50	1	61	7	2	5	10	5	.67	11	.248	.325	.347
1996 Jackson	AA	Hou	132	496	154	24	5	15	233	86	74	56	1	50	3	5	3	9	4	.69	16	.310	.382	.470
2 Min. YEARS			264	972	272	40	7	24	398	151	127	106	2	111	10	7	8	19	9	.68	27	.280	.354	.409

Bobby Jones

Pitches: Left **Bats:** Right **Pos:** P **Ht:** 6'0" **Wt:** 175 **Born:** 4/11/72 **Age:** 25

HOW MUCH HE PITCHED								WHAT HE GAVE UP												THE RESULTS					
Year Team	Lg	Org	G	GS	CG	GF	IP	BFP	H	R	ER	HR	SH	SF	HB	TBB	IBB	SO	WP	Bk	W	L	Pct.	ShO	Sv	ERA
1992 Helena	R+	Mil	14	13	1	0	76.1	341	93	51	37	7	4	2	1	23	0	53	6	5	5	4	.556	0	0	4.36
1993 Beloit	A	Mil	25	25	4	0	144.2	661	159	82	66	9	1	6	9	65	1	115	4	4	10	10	.500	0	0	4.11
1994 Stockton	A+	Mil	26	26	2	0	147.2	638	131	90	69	12	4	4	4	64	0	147	5	2	6	12	.333	0	0	4.21
1995 Colo. Sprng	AAA	Col	11	8	0	0	40.2	204	50	38	33	5	4	1	2	33	1	48	4	1	1	2	.333	0	0	7.30
New Haven	AA	Col	38	16	0	9	114	519	111	65	54	9	7	4	10	69	3	118	11	1	6	4	.600	0	3	4.26
1996 Colo. Sprng	AAA	Col	57	0	0	17	88.2	410	88	54	49	8	5	2	4	63	4	78	7	2	2	8	.200	0	3	4.97
5 Min. YEARS			171	88	7	26	612	2773	632	380	308	50	25	19	30	317	9	559	37	15	30	40	.429	0	6	4.53

Calvin Jones

Pitches: Right **Bats:** Right **Pos:** P **Ht:** 6' 3" **Wt:** 185 **Born:** 9/26/63 **Age:** 33

HOW MUCH HE PITCHED								WHAT HE GAVE UP												THE RESULTS					
Year Team	Lg	Org	G	GS	CG	GF	IP	BFP	H	R	ER	HR	SH	SF	HB	TBB	IBB	SO	WP	Bk	W	L	Pct.	ShO	Sv	ERA
1984 Bellingham	A-	Sea	10	9	0	0	59.2	0	29	23	16	0	0	0	7	36	0	59	8	1	5	0	1.000	0	0	2.41
1985 Wausau	A	Sea	20	19	1	0	106	473	96	59	46	10	0	2	5	65	1	71	9	2	4	11	.267	0	0	3.91
1986 Salinas	A+	Sea	26	25	2	0	157.1	680	141	76	63	9	4	4	4	90	2	137	15	2	11	8	.579	0	0	3.60
1987 Chattanooga	AA	Sea	26	10	0	12	81.1	372	90	58	45	5	5	1	2	38	0	77	4	0	2	9	.182	0	2	4.98
1988 Vermont	AA	Sea	24	4	0	6	74.2	312	52	26	22	1	0	2	0	47	2	58	4	3	7	5	.583	0	0	2.65
1989 San Bernrdo	A+	Sea	5	0	0	4	12.1	49	8	1	1	0	0	1	0	7	0	15	0	2	2	0	1.000	0	1	0.73
Williamsprt	AA	Sea	5	0	0	3	6.2	34	13	9	9	1	0	0	0	4	0	5	1	0	0	0	.000	0	0	12.15
1990 San Bernrdo	A+	Sea	53	0	0	27	67	298	43	32	22	4	1	3	4	54	2	94	6	0	5	3	.625	0	8	2.96
1991 Calgary	AAA	Sea	20	0	0	15	23	109	19	12	10	1	0	0	2	19	1	25	6	2	1	1	.500	0	7	3.91
1992 Calgary	AAA	Sea	21	1	0	13	32.2	145	23	15	14	3	1	3	0	22	0	32	4	0	2	0	1.000	0	3	3.86
1993 Canton-Akrn	AA	Cle	43	0	0	36	62.2	253	40	25	23	1	3	1	1	26	2	73	9	1	5	5	.500	0	22	3.30
1994 Charlotte	AAA	Cle	55	0	0	35	62.2	275	64	30	27	7	1	3	1	27	2	47	10	0	3	3	.500	0	14	3.88
1995 Nashville	AAA	ChA	5	0	0	0	6.2	38	13	8	5	3	0	0	0	3	1	5	0	0	0	0	.000	0	0	6.75
Pawtucket	AAA	Bos	38	0	0	27	44.2	203	50	31	22	8	3	2	0	18	2	41	6	0	5	2	.714	0	8	4.43
1996 Albuquerque	AAA	LA	10	0	0	5	12	58	11	6	6	0	0	0	1	12	1	15	1	0	0	0	.000	0	0	4.50
1991 Seattle	AL		27	0	0	6	46.1	194	33	14	13	0	6	0	1	29	5	42	6	0	2	2	.500	0	2	2.53
1992 Seattle	AL		38	1	0	14	61.2	275	50	39	39	8	1	4	2	47	1	49	10	0	3	5	.375	0	0	5.69
13 Min. YEARS			361	68	3	183	809.1	3299	692	411	331	53	18	22	27	468	16	754	83	13	52	47	.525	0	65	3.68
2 Maj. YEARS			65	1	0	20	108	469	83	53	52	8	7	4	3	76	6	91	16	0	5	7	.417	0	2	4.33

Ryan Jones

Bats: Right **Throws:** Right **Pos:** 1B **Ht:** 6'3" **Wt:** 220 **Born:** 11/5/74 **Age:** 22

BATTING																		BASERUNNING				PERCENTAGES		
Year Team	Lg	Org	G	AB	H	2B	3B	HR	TB	R	RBI	TBB	IBB	SO	HBP	SH	SF	SB	CS	SB%	GDP	Avg	OBP	SLG
1993 Medicne Hat	R+	Tor	47	171	42	5	0	3	56	20	27	12	0	46	3	0	1	1	1	.50	9	.246	.305	.327
1994 Hagerstown	A	Tor	115	402	96	29	0	18	179	60	72	45	0	124	6	0	5	1	0	1.00	6	.239	.321	.445
1995 Dunedin	A+	Tor	127	478	119	28	0	18	201	65	78	41	3	92	7	0	5	1	1	.50	7	.249	.315	.421
1996 Knoxville	AA	Tor	134	506	137	26	3	20	229	70	97	60	6	88	6	0	6	2	2	.50	6	.271	.351	.453
4 Min. YEARS			423	1557	394	88	3	59	665	215	274	158	9	350	22	0	17	5	4	.56	28	.253	.327	.427

Randy Jorgensen

Bats: Left **Throws:** Left **Pos:** 1B **Ht:** 6'2" **Wt:** 200 **Born:** 4/3/72 **Age:** 25

BATTING																		BASERUNNING				PERCENTAGES		
Year Team	Lg	Org	G	AB	H	2B	3B	HR	TB	R	RBI	TBB	IBB	SO	HBP	SH	SF	SB	CS	SB%	GDP	Avg	OBP	SLG
1993 Bellingham	A-	Sea	67	228	60	13	0	5	88	42	22	37	2	33	3	2	4	7	4	.64	6	.263	.368	.386
1994 Riverside	A+	Sea	110	368	97	13	1	3	121	45	42	39	2	63	5	5	2	1	2	.33	19	.264	.341	.329
1995 Riverside	A+	Sea	133	495	148	32	2	12	220	78	97	46	1	74	15	0	8	4	2	.67	13	.299	.371	.444
1996 Port City	AA	Sea	137	460	129	32	1	8	187	61	81	58	10	75	7	5	5	2	1	.67	15	.280	.366	.407
4 Min. YEARS			447	1551	434	90	4	28	616	226	242	180	15	245	30	12	19	14	9	.61	53	.280	.362	.397

Felix Jose

Bats: Both **Throws:** Right **Pos:** DH **Ht:** 6' 1" **Wt:** 220 **Born:** 5/8/65 **Age:** 32

BATTING																		BASERUNNING				PERCENTAGES		
Year Team	Lg	Org	G	AB	H	2B	3B	HR	TB	R	RBI	TBB	IBB	SO	HBP	SH	SF	SB	CS	SB%	GDP	Avg	OBP	SLG
1984 Idaho Falls	R+	Oak	45	152	33	6	0	1	42	16	18	18	1	37	1	0	2	5	1	.83	4	.217	.301	.276
1985 Madison	A	Oak	117	409	89	13	3	3	117	46	33	33	2	82	5	1	2	6	6	.50	8	.218	.283	.286
1986 Modesto	A+	Oak	127	516	147	22	8	14	227	77	77	36	5	89	2	3	2	14	9	.61	5	.285	.333	.440
1987 Huntsville	AA	Oak	91	296	67	11	1	5	95	29	42	28	1	61	2	1	3	3	3	.50	11	.226	.295	.321
1988 Tacoma	AAA	Oak	134	508	161	29	5	12	236	72	83	53	9	77	1	2	4	16	8	.67	10	.317	.380	.465
1989 Tacoma	AAA	Oak	104	387	111	26	0	14	179	59	63	41	8	82	3	1	2	11	7	.61	14	.287	.358	.463

Year	Team	Lg	Org	G	AB	H	2B	3B	HR	TB	R	RBI	TBB	IBB	SO	HBP	SH	SF	SB	CS	SB%	GDP	Avg	OBP	SLG
				BATTING															BASERUNNING				PERCENTAGES		
1992	Louisville	AAA	StL	2	7	1	0	0	0	1	0	0	1	0	0	0	0	0	0	0	.00	0	.143	.250	.143
	St. Pete	A+	StL	6	18	8	1	1	0	11	2	2	1	0	2	0	0	0	1	0	1.00	0	.444	.474	.611
1994	Memphis	AA	KC	6	21	7	2	0	0	9	3	6	5	2	6	0	0	0	1	1	.50	0	.333	.462	.429
1995	Iowa	AAA	ChN	10	37	5	3	0	0	8	2	1	1	0	6	1	0	0	0	0	.00	1	.135	.179	.216
1996	Pawtucket	AAA	Bos	11	32	7	3	0	2	16	3	5	3	0	10	0	0	0	0	0	.00	0	.219	.286	.500
	Syracuse	AAA	Tor	88	327	84	14	2	16	150	47	61	32	4	63	0	0	2	3	0	1.00	9	.257	.321	.459
1988	Oakland	AL		8	6	2	1	0	0	3	2	1	0	0	1	0	0	0	1	0	1.00	0	.333	.333	.500
1989	Oakland	AL		20	57	11	2	0	0	13	3	5	4	0	13	0	0	0	0	1	.00	2	.193	.246	.228
1990	Oakland	AL		101	341	90	12	0	8	126	42	39	16	0	65	5	2	1	8	2	.80	8	.264	.306	.370
	St. Louis	NL		25	85	23	4	1	3	38	12	13	8	0	16	0	0	0	4	4	.50	1	.271	.333	.447
1991	St. Louis	NL		154	568	173	40	6	8	249	69	77	50	8	113	2	0	5	20	12	.63	12	.305	.360	.438
1992	St. Louis	NL		131	509	150	22	3	14	220	62	75	40	8	100	1	0	1	28	12	.70	9	.295	.347	.432
1993	Kansas City	AL		149	499	126	24	3	6	174	64	43	36	5	95	1	1	2	31	13	.70	5	.253	.303	.349
1994	Kansas City	AL		99	366	111	28	1	11	174	56	55	35	6	75	0	0	2	10	12	.45	9	.303	.362	.475
1995	Kansas City	AL		9	30	4	1	0	0	5	2	1	2	0	9	0	0	0	0	0	.00	1	.133	.188	.167
10 Min. YEARS				741	2710	720	130	20	67	1091	356	391	252	32	515	15	8	17	60	35	.63	62	.266	.330	.403
8 Maj. YEARS				696	2461	690	134	14	50	1002	312	309	191	27	487	9	3	11	102	56	.65	47	.280	.333	.407

Jarod Juelsgaard

Pitches: Right **Bats:** Right **Pos:** P **Ht:** 6'3" **Wt:** 190 **Born:** 6/27/68 **Age:** 29

Year	Team	Lg	Org	G	GS	CG	GF	IP	BFP	H	R	ER	HR	SH	SF	HB	TBB	IBB	SO	WP	Bk	W	L	Pct.	ShO	Sv	ERA
				HOW MUCH HE PITCHED						WHAT HE GAVE UP												THE RESULTS					
1991	Everett	A-	SF	20	6	0	8	62	270	62	36	30	3	1	1	2	27	2	46	16	4	3	5	.375	0	3	4.35
1992	Clinton	A	SF	35	9	1	11	76.2	368	86	58	45	2	4	4	3	52	6	60	12	1	6	9	.400	0	2	5.28
1993	Kane County	A	Fla	11	2	1	3	26	101	21	11	11	0	0	0	1	7	0	18	2	2	3	0	1.000	0	0	3.81
	High Desert	A+	Fla	17	16	0	1	79.1	359	81	57	49	8	1	1	1	58	0	58	4	1	6	5	.545	0	0	5.56
1994	Portland	AA	Fla	36	12	0	13	92.2	443	115	74	68	9	4	5	4	55	4	55	7	2	4	9	.308	0	0	6.60
1995	Portland	AA	Fla	48	0	0	13	71.2	313	65	35	31	3	1	2	2	44	2	44	5	0	3	1	.750	0	2	3.89
1996	Charlotte	AAA	Fla	26	5	0	9	44	192	43	23	17	1	1	2	0	21	0	29	3	0	4	2	.667	0	1	3.48
6 Min. YEARS				193	50	2	58	452.1	2046	473	294	251	26	12	15	13	264	14	310	49	10	29	31	.483	0	8	4.99

Mike Juhl

Pitches: Left **Bats:** Left **Pos:** P **Ht:** 5'9" **Wt:** 180 **Born:** 8/10/69 **Age:** 27

Year	Team	Lg	Org	G	GS	CG	GF	IP	BFP	H	R	ER	HR	SH	SF	HB	TBB	IBB	SO	WP	Bk	W	L	Pct.	ShO	Sv	ERA
				HOW MUCH HE PITCHED						WHAT HE GAVE UP												THE RESULTS					
1991	Spartanburg	A	Phi	25	0	0	13	49.1	197	43	23	16	5	1	0	1	7	0	45	0	0	3	2	.600	0	1	2.92
1992	Spartanburg	A	Phi	41	0	0	18	64	255	54	28	25	3	2	2	1	15	0	83	6	0	5	5	.500	0	1	3.52
1993	Clearwater	A+	Phi	21	0	0	13	28	107	23	6	3	0	2	0	0	3	0	24	1	0	2	1	.667	0	4	0.96
1994	Clearwater	A+	Phi	18	0	0	11	22.2	110	30	18	14	0	2	4	0	13	4	14	1	1	0	4	.000	0	0	5.56
1995	Scranton-WB	AAA	Phi	1	0	0	1	0.1	1	0	0	0	0	0	0	0	0	0	1	0	0	0	0	.000	0	0	0.00
	Reading	AA	Phi	50	0	0	17	46.2	209	43	32	22	4	4	1	1	28	1	40	2	1	1	8	.111	0	6	4.24
1996	Reading	AA	Phi	9	0	0	1	9.2	40	8	3	3	0	0	0	1	5	0	4	0	0	1	1	.500	0	0	2.79
	Newburgh	IND	—	3	0	0	2	2.2	18	9	6	6	0	0	1	1	0	0	0	1	0	0	1	.000	0	0	20.25
6 Min. YEARS				168	0	0	76	223.1	937	210	116	89	12	11	8	5	71	5	211	11	2	12	22	.353	0	12	3.59

Ryan Karp

Pitches: Left **Bats:** Left **Pos:** P **Ht:** 6' 4" **Wt:** 214 **Born:** 4/5/70 **Age:** 27

Year	Team	Lg	Org	G	GS	CG	GF	IP	BFP	H	R	ER	HR	SH	SF	HB	TBB	IBB	SO	WP	Bk	W	L	Pct.	ShO	Sv	ERA
				HOW MUCH HE PITCHED						WHAT HE GAVE UP												THE RESULTS					
1992	Oneonta	A-	NYA	14	13	1	0	70.1	300	66	38	32	2	1	1	3	30	0	58	2	0	6	4	.600	1	0	4.09
1993	Greensboro	A	NYA	17	17	0	0	109.1	436	73	26	22	2	0	2	2	40	0	132	6	1	13	1	.929	0	0	1.81
	Pr. William	A+	NYA	8	8	1	0	49	189	35	17	12	4	2	2	2	12	0	34	5	1	3	2	.600	1	0	2.20
	Albany-Colo	AA	NYA	3	3	0	0	13	60	13	7	6	1	0	1	0	9	0	10	1	0	0	0	.000	0	0	4.15
1994	Reading	AA	Phi	21	21	0	0	121.1	528	123	67	60	12	0	4	3	54	3	96	4	0	4	11	.267	0	0	4.45
1995	Reading	AA	Phi	7	7	0	0	47	190	44	18	16	4	3	0	0	15	0	37	1	2	1	2	.333	0	0	3.06
	Scranton-WB	AAA	Phi	20	20	0	0	128.1	547	125	61	54	10	5	2	4	46	0	110	3	2	8	3	.727	0	0	3.79
1996	Scranton-WB	AAA	Phi	7	7	0	0	41	168	35	14	14	1	1	0	0	14	1	30	3	0	1	1	.500	0	0	3.07
1995	Philadelphia	NL		1	0	0	0	2	10	1	1	1	0	0	0	0	3	0	2	1	0	0	0	.000	0	0	4.50
5 Min. YEARS				97	96	2	0	579.1	2418	514	248	216	36	12	12	14	220	4	507	25	6	36	24	.600	2	0	3.36

Robbie Katzaroff

Bats: Right **Throws:** Right **Pos:** OF **Ht:** 5'8" **Wt:** 170 **Born:** 7/29/68 **Age:** 28

Year	Team	Lg	Org	G	AB	H	2B	3B	HR	TB	R	RBI	TBB	IBB	SO	HBP	SH	SF	SB	CS	SB%	GDP	Avg	OBP	SLG
				BATTING															BASERUNNING				PERCENTAGES		
1990	Jamestown	A-	Mon	74	294	107	15	7	1	139	57	20	29	4	18	5	1	0	34	13	.72	3	.364	.430	.473
1991	Harrisburg	AA	Mon	137	558	162	21	2	3	196	94	50	54	3	61	5	9	1	33	18	.65	5	.290	.358	.351
1992	Binghamton	AA	NYN	119	450	127	18	7	0	159	65	29	40	1	45	5	6	4	24	18	.57	8	.282	.345	.353
1993	Phoenix	AAA	SF	9	26	4	0	0	0	4	2	3	1	0	4	0	0	1	0	0	.00	0	.154	.179	.154
	Shreveport	AA	SF	104	406	122	22	4	0	152	52	30	35	3	33	8	5	4	15	13	.54	3	.300	.364	.374
1994	Midland	AA	Cal	32	105	29	3	2	0	36	22	11	15	0	10	1	5	1	10	4	.71	2	.276	.369	.343
	Lk Elsinore	A+	Cal	70	281	79	12	4	1	102	54	33	38	1	10	0	2	4	25	7	.78	1	.281	.374	.363
1995	Portland	AA	Fla	116	441	134	16	4	10	188	87	49	49	3	33	7	4	4	18	10	.64	4	.304	.379	.426
1996	Yankees	R	NYA	7	27	11	2	0	0	13	9	3	6	0	0	1	0	0	3	1	.75	1	.407	.529	.481

BATTING																		BASERUNNING				PERCENTAGES		
Year	Team	Lg	Org	G	AB	H	2B	3B	HR	TB	R	RBI	TBB	IBB	SO	HBP	SH	SF	SB	CS	SB%	GDP	Avg	OBP	SLG
	Norwich	AA	NYA	23	84	23	4	0	0	27	11	5	7	0	9	0	0	0	0	2	.00	1	.274	.330	.321
	Columbus	AAA	NYA	2	9	4	0	0	0	4	0	0	0	0	0	0	0	0	0	1	.00	0	.444	.444	.444
7	Min. YEARS			693	2681	802	113	30	15	1020	453	233	274	15	229	38	32	19	162	87	.65	31	.299	.370	.380

Brad Kaufman

Pitches: Right **Bats:** Right **Pos:** P **Ht:** 6'2" **Wt:** 210 **Born:** 4/26/72 **Age:** 25

HOW MUCH HE PITCHED										WHAT HE GAVE UP												THE RESULTS					
Year	Team	Lg	Org	G	GS	CG	GF	IP	BFP	H	R	ER	HR	SH	SF	HB	TBB	IBB	SO	WP	Bk	W	L	Pct.	ShO	Sv	ERA
1993	Spokane	A-	SD	25	8	1	11	53.2	264	56	56	41	8	0	3	3	41	2	48	4	2	5	4	.556	0	4	6.88
1994	Springfield	A	SD	31	20	3	4	145.1	602	124	62	54	9	5	3	4	63	6	122	14	1	10	9	.526	0	0	3.34
1995	Memphis	AA	SD	27	27	0	0	148.1	676	142	112	95	17	6	5	14	90	4	119	10	0	11	10	.524	0	0	5.76
1996	Memphis	AA	SD	29	29	3	0	178.1	768	161	84	72	18	8	4	4	83	4	163	8	0	12	10	.545	1	0	3.63
4	Min. YEARS			112	84	7	15	525.2	2310	483	314	262	52	19	15	25	277	16	452	36	3	38	33	.535	1	4	4.49

Jamie Keefe

Bats: Right **Throws:** Right **Pos:** 2B **Ht:** 5'11" **Wt:** 180 **Born:** 8/29/73 **Age:** 23

BATTING																		BASERUNNING				PERCENTAGES		
Year	Team	Lg	Org	G	AB	H	2B	3B	HR	TB	R	RBI	TBB	IBB	SO	HBP	SH	SF	SB	CS	SB%	GDP	Avg	OBP	SLG
1992	Pirates	R	Pit	33	100	19	0	1	0	21	12	8	11	0	23	1	0	0	5	3	.63	2	.190	.277	.210
1993	Pirates	R	Pit	5	14	7	0	0	0	7	3	2	2	0	2	0	1	0	3	1	.75	0	.500	.563	.500
	Lethbridge	R+	Pit	46	137	28	2	1	0	32	27	9	26	1	27	1	4	2	11	5	.69	3	.204	.331	.234
1994	Augusta	A	Pit	50	124	33	3	0	0	36	16	7	13	1	27	3	5	0	11	7	.61	5	.266	.350	.290
	Welland	A-	Pit	27	87	20	4	0	0	24	6	9	4	0	17	0	3	0	2	5	.29	0	.230	.264	.276
1995	Clinton	A	SD	67	175	42	3	1	1	50	28	10	23	0	42	2	3	0	12	3	.80	2	.240	.335	.286
1996	Clinton	A	SD	32	106	32	5	0	3	46	25	15	34	0	18	1	0	0	8	1	.89	1	.302	.475	.434
	Memphis	AA	SD	12	17	3	0	0	0	3	2	0	3	0	5	1	1	0	0	0	.00	0	.176	.333	.176
	Rancho Cuca	A+	SD	24	64	15	5	1	2	28	12	10	11	0	26	2	0	2	1	0	1.00	3	.234	.354	.438
5	Min. YEARS			296	824	199	22	4	6	247	131	70	127	2	187	11	17	4	53	25	.68	16	.242	.349	.300

Korey Keling

Pitches: Right **Bats:** Right **Pos:** P **Ht:** 6'5" **Wt:** 210 **Born:** 11/24/68 **Age:** 28

HOW MUCH HE PITCHED										WHAT HE GAVE UP												THE RESULTS					
Year	Team	Lg	Org	G	GS	CG	GF	IP	BFP	H	R	ER	HR	SH	SF	HB	TBB	IBB	SO	WP	Bk	W	L	Pct.	ShO	Sv	ERA
1991	Boise	A-	Cal	15	14	0	1	83	340	71	31	28	3	5	1	3	30	0	96	5	4	6	2	.750	0	1	3.04
1992	Palm Spring	A+	Cal	30	18	0	2	124	536	138	72	66	4	4	8	4	53	0	107	15	3	7	6	.538	0	0	4.79
1993	Palm Spring	A+	Cal	31	21	2	1	158.2	667	152	69	58	9	3	7	3	62	1	131	7	2	8	8	.500	0	0	3.29
1994	Midland	AA	Cal	27	27	1	0	155	720	207	108	89	16	5	8	7	60	1	133	8	0	10	11	.476	0	0	5.17
1995	Vancouver	AAA	Cal	3	3	0	0	17.2	75	18	9	8	1	0	0	0	6	0	16	0	0	0	2	.000	0	0	4.08
	Midland	AA	Cal	32	15	1	7	140	593	131	62	55	8	0	1	1	58	3	117	9	2	8	7	.533	1	1	3.54
1996	Midland	AA	Cal	17	1	0	4	30	140	42	29	23	4	0	3	0	14	0	13	1	0	0	1	.000	0	1	6.90
	Lk Elsinore	A+	Cal	10	2	0	2	15	77	21	15	11	2	1	3	0	14	0	10	0	0	0	1	.000	0	0	6.60
6	Min. YEARS			165	101	4	17	723.1	3148	780	395	338	47	18	31	18	297	5	623	45	11	39	38	.506	1	3	4.21

Rob Kell

Pitches: Left **Bats:** Right **Pos:** P **Ht:** 6'1" **Wt:** 200 **Born:** 9/21/70 **Age:** 26

HOW MUCH HE PITCHED										WHAT HE GAVE UP												THE RESULTS					
Year	Team	Lg	Org	G	GS	CG	GF	IP	BFP	H	R	ER	HR	SH	SF	HB	TBB	IBB	SO	WP	Bk	W	L	Pct.	ShO	Sv	ERA
1993	Erie	A-	Tex	18	1	0	10	33.2	135	16	8	7	2	1	0	3	18	0	44	1	0	2	0	1.000	0	1	1.87
1994	Charlstn-SC	A	Tex	38	0	0	17	54.2	228	43	27	24	6	4	2	3	21	0	57	7	0	0	2	.000	0	1	3.95
1995	Charlstn-SC	A	Tex	7	7	0	0	44	184	38	20	17	2	3	1	2	9	0	47	3	0	1	4	.200	0	0	3.48
	Charlotte	A+	Tex	18	7	0	5	64.2	277	54	29	24	3	3	1	4	24	0	68	5	0	2	4	.333	0	1	3.34
1996	Bakersfield	A+	Tex	13	13	1	0	88	376	94	43	37	6	2	0	3	22	0	103	3	1	5	3	.625	1	0	3.78
	Charlotte	A+	Tex	11	11	3	0	78	317	71	39	33	4	2	5	3	17	0	61	3	2	6	4	.600	2	0	3.81
	Tulsa	AA	Tex	2	0	0	1	0.2	3	1	0	0	0	0	1	0	0	0	0	0	0	0	0	.000	0	0	0.00
4	Min. YEARS			107	39	4	33	363.2	1520	317	166	142	23	15	10	18	111	0	380	22	3	16	17	.485	3	3	3.51

Frank Kellner

Bats: Both **Throws:** Right **Pos:** SS **Ht:** 5'11" **Wt:** 175 **Born:** 1/5/67 **Age:** 30

BATTING																		BASERUNNING				PERCENTAGES		
Year	Team	Lg	Org	G	AB	H	2B	3B	HR	TB	R	RBI	TBB	IBB	SO	HBP	SH	SF	SB	CS	SB%	GDP	Avg	OBP	SLG
1990	Osceola	A+	Hou	109	369	91	9	7	0	114	43	34	65	2	65	1	9	3	14	7	.67	11	.247	.358	.309
	Tucson	AAA	Hou	19	60	18	1	0	0	19	13	7	15	0	6	0	2	0	1	0	1.00	0	.300	.440	.317
1991	Osceola	A+	Hou	53	204	44	8	1	1	57	27	15	20	2	24	0	4	0	8	1	.89	6	.216	.286	.279
	Jackson	AA	Hou	83	311	84	7	4	2	105	47	25	29	2	37	0	2	2	6	5	.55	8	.270	.330	.338
1992	Jackson	AA	Hou	125	474	113	18	5	3	150	45	48	42	5	89	3	4	2	8	7	.53	9	.238	.303	.316
1993	Jackson	AA	Hou	121	355	107	27	2	4	150	51	36	38	5	51	2	2	6	11	12	.48	10	.301	.367	.423
1994	Tucson	AAA	Hou	106	296	88	13	5	1	114	32	35	46	3	40	0	3	2	5	4	.56	4	.297	.390	.385
1995	Jackson	AA	Hou	75	269	85	15	1	0	102	31	29	35	2	52	2	4	5	1	7	.13	2	.316	.392	.379
	Tucson	AAA	Hou	28	89	16	3	1	0	21	11	7	15	0	12	0	1	1	1	0	1.00	2	.180	.295	.236
1996	Tucson	AAA	Hou	96	254	69	12	5	1	94	37	31	22	1	43	0	7	6	3	6	.33	7	.272	.323	.370
7	Min. YEARS			815	2681	715	113	31	12	926	337	267	327	22	419	8	38	27	58	49	.54	59	.267	.345	.345

John Kelly

Pitches: Right **Bats:** Right **Pos:** P **Ht:** 6'4" **Wt:** 185 **Born:** 7/3/67 **Age:** 29

		HOW MUCH HE PITCHED						WHAT HE GAVE UP												THE RESULTS					
Year Team	Lg Org	G	GS	CG	GF	IP	BFP	H	R	ER	HR	SH	SF	HB	TBB	IBB	SO	WP	Bk	W	L	Pct.	ShO	Sv	ERA
1990 Johnson Cty	R+ StL	25	0	0	22	34.1	144	22	7	3	1	1	1	2	12	3	41	1	3	1	2	.333	0	13	0.79
1991 Savannah	A StL	56	0	0	50	58.2	230	43	14	9	5	3	0	0	16	6	62	2	0	6	5	.545	0	30	1.38
1992 St. Pete	A+ StL	56	0	0	52	62	243	47	15	14	1	3	3	1	13	2	59	3	1	4	4	.500	0	38	2.03
1993 Arkansas	AA StL	51	0	0	45	58.1	245	53	28	23	4	8	0	1	12	5	40	1	0	2	4	.333	0	27	3.55
1994 Arkansas	AA StL	27	0	0	24	30.2	134	37	23	18	2	3	3	1	5	1	29	0	0	1	2	.333	0	16	5.28
Louisville	AAA StL	9	0	0	4	20.2	91	23	12	12	2	0	1	3	5	1	14	0	0	0	0	.000	0	0	5.23
1995 Jacksonvlle	AA Det	66	0	0	58	77.1	322	76	24	18	4	6	2	0	21	5	47	3	1	7	7	.500	0	29	2.09
1996 Visalia	A+ Det	19	18	1	1	96	475	115	100	76	10	5	11	13	63	1	89	16	2	2	10	.167	0	1	7.13
Jacksonvlle	AA Det	9	9	1	0	55	243	54	38	28	2	1	1	1	35	1	29	5	0	2	2	.500	1	0	4.58
7 Min. YEARS		318	27	2	256	493	2127	470	261	201	31	30	22	22	182	25	410	31	7	25	36	.410	1	154	3.67

Jeremey Kendall

Bats: Right **Throws:** Right **Pos:** OF **Ht:** 5'9" **Wt:** 170 **Born:** 9/3/71 **Age:** 25

		BATTING															BASERUNNING				PERCENTAGES		
Year Team	Lg Org	G	AB	H	2B	3B	HR	TB	R	RBI	TBB	IBB	SO	HBP	SH	SF	SB	CS	SB%	GDP	Avg	OBP	SLG
1992 Martinsvlle	R+ Phi	49	204	56	8	2	3	77	37	23	13	0	42	5	0	3	14	5	.74	1	.275	.329	.377
1993 Batavia	A- Phi	73	275	77	17	4	1	105	48	23	27	1	60	16	3	2	31	13	.70	2	.280	.375	.382
1994 Spartanburg	A Phi	133	515	148	32	7	8	218	98	60	57	1	128	23	4	6	62	27	.70	3	.287	.379	.423
1995 Clearwater	A+ Phi	36	135	29	1	2	3	43	18	10	14	0	40	6	1	2	15	5	.75	2	.215	.312	.319
1996 Reading	AA Phi	35	131	22	5	1	1	32	23	10	12	0	35	11	3	0	5	5	.50	4	.168	.292	.244
Clearwater	A+ Phi	81	291	71	15	1	4	100	42	40	34	0	86	19	2	2	22	5	.81	2	.244	.358	.344
5 Min. YEARS		407	1551	403	78	17	20	575	266	166	157	2	391	80	13	15	149	60	.71	14	.260	.355	.371

Kenny Kendrena

Pitches: Right **Bats:** Right **Pos:** P **Ht:** 5'11" **Wt:** 170 **Born:** 10/29/70 **Age:** 26

		HOW MUCH HE PITCHED						WHAT HE GAVE UP												THE RESULTS					
Year Team	Lg Org	G	GS	CG	GF	IP	BFP	H	R	ER	HR	SH	SF	HB	TBB	IBB	SO	WP	Bk	W	L	Pct.	ShO	Sv	ERA
1992 Erie	A- Fla	22	0	0	10	54.2	229	47	33	23	5	5	3	5	12	2	61	2	1	5	4	.556	0	3	3.79
1993 High Desert	A+ Fla	40	0	0	25	66.2	307	78	50	49	16	2	4	4	26	1	63	7	0	6	0	1.000	0	2	6.62
1994 Brevard Cty	A+ Fla	21	1	0	7	38	141	19	5	5	0	3	1	0	10	0	32	1	0	5	1	.833	0	0	1.18
Portland	AA Fla	13	0	0	3	24.2	118	28	22	15	0	1	1	2	15	2	21	2	0	0	1	.000	0	0	5.47
1995 W. Palm Bch	A+ Mon	16	0	0	5	23.2	102	23	9	8	2	1	1	0	11	2	19	3	0	3	3	.500	0	2	3.04
Harrisburg	AA Mon	46	0	0	13	88.1	379	81	36	26	7	3	2	4	36	4	65	6	0	6	5	.545	0	3	2.65
1996 Harrisburg	AA Mon	7	0	0	3	11.2	46	10	6	6	3	0	0	1	2	0	4	0	0	1	0	1.000	0	0	4.63
5 Min. YEARS		165	1	0	66	307.2	1322	286	161	132	33	15	12	16	112	11	265	21	1	26	14	.650	0	10	3.86

Darryl Kennedy

Bats: Right **Throws:** Right **Pos:** C **Ht:** 5'10" **Wt:** 170 **Born:** 1/23/69 **Age:** 28

		BATTING															BASERUNNING				PERCENTAGES		
Year Team	Lg Org	G	AB	H	2B	3B	HR	TB	R	RBI	TBB	IBB	SO	HBP	SH	SF	SB	CS	SB%	GDP	Avg	OBP	SLG
1991 Rangers	R Tex	5	18	2	1	0	0	3	4	1	1	0	1	0	0	0	0	0	.00	0	.111	.158	.167
Charlotte	A+ Tex	23	68	7	3	0	0	10	5	4	5	0	11	2	1	2	0	0	.00	2	.103	.182	.147
1992 Gastonia	A Tex	13	33	3	1	0	0	4	2	2	6	1	6	1	0	1	0	2	.00	1	.091	.244	.121
Charlotte	A+ Tex	13	28	13	4	0	0	17	3	6	3	0	3	0	0	0	0	1	.00	0	.464	.516	.607
Tulsa	AA Tex	30	98	22	2	0	0	24	6	9	8	0	18	2	2	1	0	0	.00	4	.224	.294	.245
1993 Okla. City	AAA Tex	6	16	1	0	0	0	1	2	0	3	0	4	0	1	0	0	0	.00	0	.063	.211	.063
Charlotte	A+ Tex	106	347	97	23	0	1	123	47	30	47	0	38	1	5	2	5	7	.42	7	.280	.365	.354
1994 Charlotte	A+ Tex	53	177	47	5	2	1	59	24	22	25	1	20	1	2	0	1	2	.33	7	.266	.360	.333
Tulsa	AA Tex	23	70	16	3	0	1	22	5	5	8	0	10	0	2	0	1	1	.50	1	.229	.308	.314
1995 Tulsa	AA Tex	61	195	49	9	1	3	69	26	26	17	0	22	3	3	4	0	0	.00	5	.251	.315	.354
Okla. City	AAA Tex	3	11	2	0	0	1	5	1	3	0	0	2	0	0	0	0	0	.00	0	.182	.182	.455
1996 Okla. City	AAA Tex	2	7	2	0	0	0	2	0	0	0	0	2	0	0	0	0	0	.00	0	.286	.286	.286
Tulsa	AA Tex	15	43	13	3	1	1	21	11	10	4	0	5	1	1	0	0	1	.00	2	.302	.375	.488
Phoenix	AAA SF	64	192	59	11	3	2	82	27	24	12	3	25	3	4	4	2	2	.50	5	.307	.351	.427
6 Min. YEARS		417	1303	333	65	7	10	442	163	142	139	5	167	14	21	14	9	16	.36	34	.256	.331	.339

Dave Kennedy

Bats: Right **Throws:** Right **Pos:** 1B **Ht:** 6'4" **Wt:** 215 **Born:** 9/3/70 **Age:** 26

		BATTING															BASERUNNING				PERCENTAGES		
Year Team	Lg Org	G	AB	H	2B	3B	HR	TB	R	RBI	TBB	IBB	SO	HBP	SH	SF	SB	CS	SB%	GDP	Avg	OBP	SLG
1993 Boise	A- Cal	74	248	59	14	2	10	107	53	49	65	7	63	0	0	2	2	0	1.00	1	.238	.394	.431
1994 St. Paul	IND —	25	72	21	6	1	4	41	13	15	8	0	17	1	1	0	2	2	.50	4	.292	.370	.569
1995 New Haven	AA Col	128	484	148	22	2	22	240	75	96	48	1	131	5	0	4	4	1	.80	12	.306	.372	.496
1996 Colo. Sprng	AAA Col	117	333	85	27	0	11	145	46	50	36	1	82	2	0	0	1	2	.33	16	.255	.332	.435
4 Min. YEARS		344	1137	313	69	5	47	533	187	210	157	9	293	8	1	6	9	5	.64	33	.275	.365	.469

Keith Kessinger

Bats: Both **Throws:** Right **Pos:** SS **Ht:** 6' 2" **Wt:** 185 **Born:** 2/19/67 **Age:** 30

		BATTING																BASERUNNING				PERCENTAGES		
Year	Team	Lg Org	G	AB	H	2B	3B	HR	TB	R	RBI	TBB	IBB	SO	HBP	SH	SF	SB	CS	SB%	GDP	Avg	OBP	SLG
1989	Bluefield	R+ Bal	28	99	27	4	0	2	37	17	9	8	0	12	1	2	0	1	0	1.00	1	.273	.333	.374
1990	Wausau	A Bal	37	134	29	8	0	0	37	17	9	6	0	23	3	0	0	1	1	.50	2	.216	.266	.276
	Frederick	A+ Bal	64	145	22	4	0	0	26	18	8	20	0	36	3	5	0	0	0	.00	2	.152	.268	.179
1991	Frederick	A+ Bal	26	56	10	3	0	0	13	5	4	8	0	12	0	1	0	2	1	.67	3	.179	.281	.232
	Cedar Rapds	A Cin	59	206	42	5	0	1	50	15	15	23	1	46	3	5	1	0	1	.00	4	.204	.292	.243
1992	Cedar Rapds	A Cin	95	308	73	15	1	4	102	41	38	36	2	57	1	5	1	2	0	1.00	7	.237	.318	.331
1993	Chattanooga	AA Cin	56	161	50	9	0	3	68	24	28	24	2	18	0	5	0	0	3	.00	4	.311	.400	.422
	Indianapolis	AAA Cin	35	120	34	9	0	2	49	17	15	14	4	14	1	1	0	0	1	.00	0	.283	.363	.408
1994	Indianapolis	AAA Cin	115	393	98	19	3	3	132	37	48	36	4	60	0	4	1	3	1	.75	11	.249	.312	.336
1995	Orlando	AA ChN	18	62	16	5	0	0	21	8	5	6	0	3	1	2	0	0	0	.00	1	.258	.333	.339
	Iowa	AAA ChN	68	210	48	11	0	2	65	21	20	25	2	23	1	7	2	1	1	.50	6	.229	.311	.310
1996	Iowa	AAA ChN	55	184	44	8	0	4	64	19	26	22	3	30	0	5	3	0	1	.00	6	.239	.316	.348
1993	Cincinnati	NL	11	27	7	1	0	1	11	4	3	4	0	4	0	0	1	0	0	.00	1	.259	.344	.407
	8 Min. YEARS		656	2078	493	100	4	21	664	239	225	228	18	334	14	42	8	10	10	.50	47	.237	.316	.320

Tim Kester

Pitches: Right **Bats:** Right **Pos:** P **Ht:** 6'4" **Wt:** 185 **Born:** 12/1/71 **Age:** 25

		HOW MUCH HE PITCHED						WHAT HE GAVE UP												THE RESULTS					
Year	Team	Lg Org	G	GS	CG	GF	IP	BFP	H	R	ER	HR	SH	SF	HB	TBB	IBB	SO	WP	Bk	W	L	Pct.	ShO	Sv	ERA
1993	Auburn	A- Hou	15	13	4	1	96.1	398	78	40	22	2	2	0	10	19	1	83	5	2	4	6	.400	1	0	2.06
1994	Osceola	A+ Hou	24	22	2	0	134	580	159	85	73	7	8	5	8	30	5	71	3	0	5	12	.294	0	0	4.90
1995	Quad City	A Hou	28	23	2	3	160.2	665	158	80	53	8	5	6	10	20	1	111	4	0	12	5	.706	0	0	2.97
1996	Tucson	AAA Hou	1	1	0	0	1.2	15	8	8	8	1	1	1	0	1	0	1	0	0	0	1	.000	0	0	43.20
	Jackson	AA Hou	48	4	0	7	103.2	435	105	52	43	8	4	4	6	16	0	55	8	0	2	4	.333	0	1	3.73
	4 Min. YEARS		116	63	8	11	496.1	2093	508	265	199	26	20	16	34	86	7	321	20	2	23	28	.451	1	1	3.61

Joe Keusch

Pitches: Right **Bats:** Left **Pos:** P **Ht:** 6'1" **Wt:** 175 **Born:** 1/20/72 **Age:** 25

		HOW MUCH HE PITCHED						WHAT HE GAVE UP												THE RESULTS					
Year	Team	Lg Org	G	GS	CG	GF	IP	BFP	H	R	ER	HR	SH	SF	HB	TBB	IBB	SO	WP	Bk	W	L	Pct.	ShO	Sv	ERA
1994	Hudson Vall	A- Tex	14	0	0	6	24	104	28	20	18	0	1	4	3	3	0	25	2	0	0	1	.000	0	0	6.75
1995	Tulsa	AA Tex	2	0	0	2	2.2	10	1	0	0	0	0	0	0	0	0	0	0	0	0	0	.000	0	0	0.00
	Charlotte	A+ Tex	42	0	0	29	67	267	57	19	13	3	2	3	2	14	2	36	3	1	9	4	.692	0	8	1.75
1996	Tulsa	AA Tex	8	0	0	4	11	64	25	21	21	5	0	0	2	5	1	8	0	0	0	0	.000	0	0	17.18
	Rangers	R Tex	2	0	0	2	3	10	1	1	1	0	0	0	0	0	0	3	0	0	0	0	.000	0	0	3.00
	3 Min. YEARS		68	0	0	43	107.2	455	112	61	53	8	3	7	7	22	3	72	5	1	9	5	.643	0	8	4.43

Rusty Kilgo

Pitches: Left **Bats:** Left **Pos:** P **Ht:** 6'0" **Wt:** 175 **Born:** 8/9/66 **Age:** 30

		HOW MUCH HE PITCHED						WHAT HE GAVE UP												THE RESULTS					
Year	Team	Lg Org	G	GS	CG	GF	IP	BFP	H	R	ER	HR	SH	SF	HB	TBB	IBB	SO	WP	Bk	W	L	Pct.	ShO	Sv	ERA
1989	Jamestown	A- Mon	30	3	0	21	64.2	259	46	16	10	3	4	0	0	20	1	74	4	1	6	3	.667	0	8	1.39
1990	Rockford	A Mon	45	0	0	31	88.2	347	62	26	22	1	2	1	3	20	1	85	6	2	4	4	.500	0	9	2.23
1991	W. Palm Bch	A+ Mon	33	1	0	10	74	286	56	14	13	1	3	0	2	24	1	48	1	0	6	3	.667	0	5	1.58
	Harrisburg	AA Mon	14	0	0	10	25.2	105	24	11	10	1	3	1	1	4	1	20	3	0	1	0	1.000	0	1	3.51
1992	Rockford	A Mon	4	0	0	2	8.2	28	3	0	0	0	0	0	0	0	0	8	0	0	0	0	.000	0	1	0.00
	Cedar Rapds	A Cin	25	0	0	21	33.2	125	18	4	3	0	3	1	1	6	0	34	2	0	3	0	1.000	0	10	0.80
	Chattanooga	AA Cin	24	0	0	10	31.2	123	22	16	11	3	1	3	0	11	1	11	2	0	1	3	.250	0	0	3.13
1993	Chattanooga	AA Cin	53	1	0	20	80.1	360	92	30	25	2	5	0	5	31	6	61	4	1	11	7	.611	0	6	2.80
1994	Indianapolis	AAA Cin	50	0	0	11	62.1	274	75	32	28	6	4	2	0	17	5	30	2	0	5	6	.455	0	1	4.04
1995	Indianapolis	AAA Cin	2	0	0	0	2	10	4	2	1	0	0	0	0	1	0	1	0	0	0	0	.000	0	0	4.50
	Chattanooga	AA Cin	56	0	0	47	68	283	71	23	18	0	2	0	0	14	5	62	4	0	8	2	.800	0	29	2.38
1996	Memphis	AA SD	48	0	0	24	74	314	80	35	30	6	1	2	5	18	0	58	2	0	1	4	.200	0	2	3.65
	8 Min. YEARS		384	5	0	207	613.2	2514	553	209	171	23	28	10	17	166	21	492	30	4	46	32	.590	0	72	2.51

Tim Killeen

Bats: Left **Throws:** Right **Pos:** C **Ht:** 6'0" **Wt:** 195 **Born:** 7/26/70 **Age:** 26

		BATTING																BASERUNNING				PERCENTAGES		
Year	Team	Lg Org	G	AB	H	2B	3B	HR	TB	R	RBI	TBB	IBB	SO	HBP	SH	SF	SB	CS	SB%	GDP	Avg	OBP	SLG
1992	Sou. Oregon	A- Oak	39	119	28	7	0	3	44	20	12	17	1	30	2	0	0	5	3	.63	2	.235	.341	.370
1993	Madison	A Oak	76	243	49	15	0	10	94	33	36	39	1	70	3	0	1	0	0	.00	11	.202	.318	.387
	Tacoma	AAA Oak	3	9	4	0	0	0	4	4	0	1	0	4	0	0	0	0	1	.00	0	.444	.500	.444
1994	Modesto	A+ Oak	101	365	87	18	3	16	159	53	75	49	2	107	2	2	5	5	2	.71	5	.238	.328	.436
1995	Memphis	AA SD	77	230	54	14	0	9	95	27	40	27	6	71	0	0	1	2	0	1.00	5	.235	.314	.413
1996	Memphis	AA SD	83	224	58	10	6	11	113	44	51	27	1	57	1	1	6	0	2	.00	4	.259	.333	.504
	5 Min. YEARS		379	1190	280	64	9	49	509	181	214	160	11	339	8	3	13	12	8	.60	27	.235	.327	.428

Keith Kimsey

Bats: Right **Throws:** Right **Pos:** OF **Ht:** 6'7" **Wt:** 200 **Born:** 8/15/72 **Age:** 24

				BATTING														BASERUNNING				PERCENTAGES		
Year	Team	Lg	Org	G	AB	H	2B	3B	HR	TB	R	RBI	TBB	IBB	SO	HBP	SH	SF	SB	CS	SB%	GDP	Avg	OBP	SLG
1991	Bristol	R+	Det	53	164	26	3	0	3	38	10	17	14	0	60	1	1	1	2	3	.40	5	.159	.228	.232
1992	Niagara Fal	A-	Det	73	281	63	7	6	12	118	35	46	9	0	106	3	0	1	14	6	.70	4	.224	.255	.420
1993	Fayettevlle	A	Det	120	469	115	19	6	19	203	79	85	50	2	168	2	0	3	2	0	1.00	16	.245	.319	.433
1994	Lakeland	A+	Det	121	448	100	19	3	12	161	47	58	29	0	136	3	0	3	4	3	.57	17	.223	.273	.359
1995	Jacksonvlle	AA	Det	34	118	19	4	1	1	28	8	10	7	0	39	2	0	1	1	1	.50	6	.161	.219	.237
	Lakeland	A+	Det	54	175	38	8	2	6	68	30	16	22	0	58	0	0	0	1	1	.50	4	.217	.305	.389
1996	Visalia	A+	Det	99	394	108	17	3	21	194	64	72	43	2	140	2	0	3	13	4	.76	7	.274	.346	.492
	Jacksonvlle	AA	Det	31	106	19	0	1	2	27	8	6	13	0	50	0	0	0	2	4	.33	2	.179	.269	.255
6 Min. YEARS				585	2155	488	77	22	76	837	281	310	187	4	757	13	1	12	39	22	.64	61	.226	.291	.388

Andre King

Bats: Right **Throws:** Right **Pos:** OF **Ht:** 6'1" **Wt:** 190 **Born:** 11/26/73 **Age:** 23

				BATTING														BASERUNNING				PERCENTAGES		
Year	Team	Lg	Org	G	AB	H	2B	3B	HR	TB	R	RBI	TBB	IBB	SO	HBP	SH	SF	SB	CS	SB%	GDP	Avg	OBP	SLG
1993	Danville	R+	Atl	60	223	69	10	6	0	91	41	18	36	2	40	5	0	1	15	5	.75	4	.309	.415	.408
1994	Macon	A	Atl	129	496	122	22	6	4	168	80	38	34	1	139	15	12	2	31	10	.76	3	.246	.313	.339
1995	Durham	A+	Atl	111	421	106	22	3	9	161	59	33	39	1	126	10	5	4	15	13	.54	5	.252	.327	.382
	Pr. William	A+	ChA	9	32	5	1	1	0	8	4	3	6	0	9	0	1	0	1	0	1.00	2	.156	.289	.250
1996	Chattanooga	AA	Cin	13	43	3	0	1	0	5	1	3	1	0	21	1	0	0	0	1	.00	1	.070	.111	.116
	Winston-Sal	A+	Cin	82	261	50	9	3	8	89	43	28	34	0	88	10	4	2	16	7	.70	2	.192	.306	.341
4 Min. YEARS				404	1476	355	64	20	21	522	228	123	150	4	423	41	22	9	78	36	.68	17	.241	.326	.354

Brett King

Bats: Right **Throws:** Right **Pos:** SS **Ht:** 6'1" **Wt:** 180 **Born:** 7/20/72 **Age:** 24

				BATTING														BASERUNNING				PERCENTAGES		
Year	Team	Lg	Org	G	AB	H	2B	3B	HR	TB	R	RBI	TBB	IBB	SO	HBP	SH	SF	SB	CS	SB%	GDP	Avg	OBP	SLG
1993	Everett	A-	SF	69	243	55	10	0	2	71	43	24	40	2	63	5	9	0	26	11	.70	2	.226	.347	.292
1994	San Jose	A+	SF	48	188	47	8	2	1	62	24	11	19	1	62	4	1	0	6	8	.43	0	.250	.332	.330
	Clinton	A	SF	68	261	57	13	2	5	89	45	30	23	1	86	2	3	2	12	3	.80	2	.218	.285	.341
1995	San Jose	A+	SF	107	394	108	29	4	3	154	61	41	41	1	86	5	5	6	28	8	.78	8	.274	.345	.391
1996	Shreveport	AA	SF	127	459	107	23	4	7	159	61	48	49	0	116	6	17	1	19	9	.68	5	.233	.315	.346
4 Min. YEARS				419	1545	374	83	12	18	535	234	154	172	5	413	22	35	9	91	39	.70	17	.242	.325	.346

Curt King

Pitches: Right **Bats:** Right **Pos:** P **Ht:** 6'5" **Wt:** 205 **Born:** 10/25/70 **Age:** 26

				HOW MUCH HE PITCHED						WHAT HE GAVE UP												THE RESULTS					
Year	Team	Lg	Org	G	GS	CG	GF	IP	BFP	H	R	ER	HR	SH	SF	HB	TBB	IBB	SO	WP	Bk	W	L	Pct.	ShO	Sv	ERA
1994	New Jersey	A-	StL	5	4	0	0	20.2	92	19	7	6	0	0	1	0	11	0	14	2	1	1	0	1.000	0	0	2.61
	Savannah	A	StL	8	8	2	0	53	202	37	14	11	4	2	1	4	9	0	40	1	0	4	1	.800	2	0	1.87
1995	St. Pete	A+	StL	28	21	3	1	136	567	117	49	39	3	4	2	11	49	2	65	6	0	7	8	.467	0	0	2.58
1996	Arkansas	AA	StL	5	0	0	3	5	37	15	12	11	1	0	0	0	6	1	5	0	0	0	1	.000	0	1	19.80
	St. Pete	A+	StL	48	0	0	46	55.2	232	41	20	17	0	5	2	5	24	4	27	2	0	3	3	.500	0	30	2.75
3 Min. YEARS				94	33	5	50	270.1	1130	229	102	84	8	11	6	20	99	7	151	11	1	15	13	.536	2	31	2.80

Mark Kingston

Bats: Both **Throws:** Right **Pos:** 3B **Ht:** 6'4" **Wt:** 210 **Born:** 5/16/70 **Age:** 27

				BATTING														BASERUNNING				PERCENTAGES		
Year	Team	Lg	Org	G	AB	H	2B	3B	HR	TB	R	RBI	TBB	IBB	SO	HBP	SH	SF	SB	CS	SB%	GDP	Avg	OBP	SLG
1992	Helena	R+	Mil	39	122	32	7	1	1	44	21	14	12	0	32	1	1	1	0	0	.00	3	.262	.331	.361
1993	Geneva	A-	ChN	3	9	2	0	0	0	2	0	0	0	0	3	1	0	0	0	0	.00	0	.222	.300	.222
	Peoria	A	ChN	64	224	57	14	1	4	85	25	24	28	0	44	5	3	3	3	0	1.00	2	.254	.346	.379
1994	Daytona	A+	ChN	109	370	83	14	1	4	111	42	35	34	1	79	6	1	4	1	2	.33	12	.224	.297	.300
1995	Daytona	A+	ChN	49	170	40	8	0	2	54	23	23	14	2	33	1	0	3	1	1	.50	5	.235	.293	.318
	Orlando	AA	ChN	66	199	53	13	0	5	81	17	24	22	5	41	1	2	2	0	1	.00	4	.266	.339	.407
1996	Orlando	AA	ChN	60	122	25	9	0	3	43	21	17	22	0	39	2	2	1	1	1	.50	0	.205	.333	.352
5 Min. YEARS				390	1216	292	65	3	19	420	149	137	132	8	271	17	9	14	6	5	.55	26	.240	.320	.345

Jay Kirkpatrick

Bats: Left **Throws:** Right **Pos:** 1B-DH **Ht:** 6'4" **Wt:** 210 **Born:** 7/10/69 **Age:** 27

				BATTING														BASERUNNING				PERCENTAGES		
Year	Team	Lg	Org	G	AB	H	2B	3B	HR	TB	R	RBI	TBB	IBB	SO	HBP	SH	SF	SB	CS	SB%	GDP	Avg	OBP	SLG
1991	Great Falls	R+	LA	50	168	54	11	1	2	73	25	26	13	0	23	3	0	0	1	2	.33	3	.321	.380	.435
1992	Vero Beach	A+	LA	114	385	108	22	2	6	152	32	50	31	4	82	4	1	6	2	2	.50	9	.281	.336	.395
1993	Bakersfield	A+	LA	103	375	108	21	0	8	153	42	63	35	2	78	4	1	3	1	4	.20	7	.288	.353	.408
	San Antonio	AA	LA	27	97	31	6	1	6	57	17	17	14	4	15	0	0	0	0	1	.00	4	.320	.405	.588
1994	San Antonio	AA	LA	123	449	133	40	1	18	229	61	75	45	7	91	3	0	6	2	2	.50	12	.296	.360	.510
	Albuquerque	AAA	LA	3	5	1	1	0	0	2	0	1	1	0	1	0	0	0	0	0	.00	0	.200	.333	.400
1995	Albuquerque	AAA	LA	13	40	10	1	1	1	16	4	6	2	1	6	0	0	0	0	0	.00	0	.250	.286	.400
	San Bernrdo	A+	LA	71	267	72	19	0	15	136	38	50	40	3	75	0	0	2	3	0	1.00	3	.270	.362	.509
1996	San Antonio	AA	LA	30	91	22	4	0	3	35	6	10	11	3	26	0	0	0	1	0	1.00	5	.242	.324	.385

Year	Team	Lg	Org	G	AB	H	2B	3B	HR	TB	R	RBI	TBB	IBB	SO	HBP	SH	SF	SB	CS	SB%	GDP	Avg	OBP	SLG
	BATTING																		BASERUNNING				PERCENTAGES		
	Albuquerque	AAA	LA	51	107	26	5	0	0	31	12	9	10	2	35	0	0	2	0	0	.00	4	.243	.303	.290
6 Min. YEARS				585	1984	565	130	6	59	884	237	307	202	26	432	14	2	19	10	11	.48	47	.285	.352	.446

Steven Kline

Pitches: Left **Bats:** Both **Pos:** P **Ht:** 6'2" **Wt:** 200 **Born:** 8/22/72 **Age:** 24

HOW MUCH HE PITCHED										WHAT HE GAVE UP												THE RESULTS					
Year	Team	Lg	Org	G	GS	CG	GF	IP	BFP	H	R	ER	HR	SH	SF	HB	TBB	IBB	SO	WP	Bk	W	L	Pct.	ShO	Sv	ERA
1993	Burlington	R+	Cle	2	1	0	0	7.1	34	11	4	4	0	1	0	0	2	1	4	0	0	1	1	.500	0	0	4.91
	Watertown	A-	Cle	13	13	2	0	79	332	77	36	28	3	3	2	4	12	0	45	5	0	5	4	.556	1	0	3.19
1994	Columbus	A	Cle	28	28	2	0	185.2	744	175	67	62	14	1	2	7	36	0	174	6	2	18	5	.783	1	0	3.01
1995	Canton-Akrn	AA	Cle	14	14	0	0	89.1	377	86	34	24	6	4	1	1	30	3	45	1	1	2	3	.400	0	0	2.42
1996	Canton-Akrn	AA	Cle	25	24	0	0	146.2	658	168	98	89	16	10	4	6	55	2	107	5	1	8	12	.400	0	0	5.46
4 Min. YEARS				82	80	4	0	508	2145	517	239	207	39	19	9	18	135	6	375	17	4	34	25	.576	2	0	3.67

Kevin Kloek

Pitches: Right **Bats:** Right **Pos:** P **Ht:** 6'3" **Wt:** 175 **Born:** 8/15/70 **Age:** 26

HOW MUCH HE PITCHED										WHAT HE GAVE UP												THE RESULTS					
Year	Team	Lg	Org	G	GS	CG	GF	IP	BFP	H	R	ER	HR	SH	SF	HB	TBB	IBB	SO	WP	Bk	W	L	Pct.	ShO	Sv	ERA
1992	Beloit	A	Mil	15	14	2	0	94	386	79	32	22	7	4	2	4	27	1	76	5	7	10	1	.909	1	0	2.11
1993	El Paso	AA	Mil	23	23	1	0	135.2	587	148	75	62	11	7	5	7	53	4	97	5	0	9	6	.600	1	0	4.11
1994	Brewers	R	Mil	3	3	0	0	19	71	9	3	3	0	0	0	0	3	0	19	1	0	2	0	1.000	0	0	1.42
	El Paso	AA	Mil	9	9	0	0	55.1	223	46	26	24	3	0	4	1	18	0	37	0	0	5	1	.833	0	0	3.90
1995	El Paso	AA	Mil	28	27	3	0	157	699	196	103	86	6	2	5	10	48	0	121	12	0	7	11	.389	1	0	4.93
1996	El Paso	AA	Mil	9	9	0	0	53.2	230	58	29	24	7	2	1	2	18	2	46	3	0	3	1	.750	0	0	4.02
	New Orleans	AAA	Mil	1	0	0	0	1	6	3	1	1	1	0	0	0	1	0	0	0	0	0	0	.000	0	0	9.00
5 Min. YEARS				88	85	6	0	515.2	2202	539	269	222	35	15	17	24	168	7	396	26	7	36	20	.643	3	0	3.87

Joe Kmak

Bats: Right **Throws:** Right **Pos:** C **Ht:** 6' 0" **Wt:** 185 **Born:** 5/3/63 **Age:** 34

BATTING																			BASERUNNING				PERCENTAGES		
Year	Team	Lg	Org	G	AB	H	2B	3B	HR	TB	R	RBI	TBB	IBB	SO	HBP	SH	SF	SB	CS	SB%	GDP	Avg	OBP	SLG
1985	Everett	A-	SF	40	129	40	10	1	1	55	21	14	20	0	23	3	0	2	0	1	.00	3	.310	.409	.426
1986	Fresno	A+	SF	60	163	44	5	0	1	52	23	9	15	0	38	3	0	1	3	2	.60	6	.270	.341	.319
1987	Fresno	A+	SF	48	154	34	8	0	0	42	18	12	15	0	32	3	3	0	1	2	.33	3	.221	.302	.273
	Shreveport	AA	SF	15	41	8	0	1	0	10	5	3	3	0	4	1	0	0	0	0	.00	1	.195	.267	.244
1988	Shreveport	AA	SF	71	178	40	5	2	1	52	16	14	11	2	19	4	1	1	0	0	.00	3	.225	.284	.292
1989	Reno	A+	—	78	248	68	10	5	4	100	39	34	40	1	41	5	0	1	8	4	.67	9	.274	.384	.403
1990	El Paso	AA	Mil	35	109	31	3	2	2	44	8	11	7	0	22	2	3	2	0	0	.00	2	.284	.333	.404
	Denver	AAA	Mil	28	95	22	3	0	1	28	12	10	4	0	16	3	5	0	1	1	.50	3	.232	.284	.295
1991	Denver	AAA	Mil	100	294	70	17	2	1	94	34	33	28	0	44	5	8	1	7	3	.70	5	.238	.314	.320
1992	Denver	AAA	Mil	67	225	70	11	4	3	98	27	31	19	0	39	3	5	2	6	3	.67	5	.311	.369	.436
1993	New Orleans	AAA	Mil	24	76	23	3	2	1	33	9	13	8	0	14	0	0	0	1	0	1.00	1	.303	.369	.434
1994	Norfolk	AAA	NYN	86	264	66	5	0	5	86	28	31	31	1	51	5	1	1	2	3	.40	6	.250	.339	.326
1995	Iowa	AAA	ChN	34	98	17	3	0	2	26	6	7	6	0	24	0	3	2	0	0	.00	4	.173	.217	.265
1996	Indianapols	AAA	Cin	48	143	40	3	0	2	49	20	19	26	1	35	1	1	0	3	0	1.00	4	.280	.394	.343
1993	Milwaukee	AL		51	110	24	5	0	0	29	9	7	14	0	13	2	1	0	6	2	.75	2	.218	.317	.264
1995	Chicago	NL		19	53	13	3	0	1	19	7	6	6	0	12	1	0	1	0	0	.00	2	.245	.328	.358
12 Min. YEARS				734	2217	573	86	19	24	769	266	241	233	5	402	38	30	13	32	19	.63	55	.258	.337	.347
2 Maj. YEARS				70	163	37	8	0	1	48	16	13	20	0	25	3	1	1	6	2	.75	4	.227	.321	.294

Mike Knapp

Bats: Right **Throws:** Right **Pos:** C **Ht:** 6'0" **Wt:** 195 **Born:** 10/6/64 **Age:** 32

BATTING																			BASERUNNING				PERCENTAGES		
Year	Team	Lg	Org	G	AB	H	2B	3B	HR	TB	R	RBI	TBB	IBB	SO	HBP	SH	SF	SB	CS	SB%	GDP	Avg	OBP	SLG
1986	Salem	A-	Cal	64	224	66	12	1	3	89	31	39	31	1	37	3	1	3	4	4	.50	2	.295	.383	.397
1987	Quad City	A	Cal	91	327	84	14	3	1	107	34	31	27	0	48	4	0	7	1	6	.14	7	.257	.315	.327
1988	Midland	AA	Cal	100	327	86	12	1	3	109	34	33	35	0	64	2	6	5	1	3	.25	5	.263	.333	.333
1989	Midland	AA	Cal	20	64	21	2	0	2	29	7	6	3	0	8	2	1	0	0	0	.00	2	.328	.377	.453
	Edmonton	AAA	Cal	51	144	38	8	0	1	49	15	22	15	0	27	4	3	1	0	4	.00	2	.264	.348	.340
1990	Midland	AA	Cal	57	193	50	8	0	2	64	16	21	16	0	29	0	0	1	1	1	.50	3	.259	.314	.332
	Edmonton	AAA	Cal	12	39	8	0	1	0	10	3	4	4	0	6	0	0	0	0	0	.00	0	.205	.279	.256
1991	Charlotte	AA	ChN	92	266	68	12	0	1	83	19	33	19	3	53	1	7	1	4	0	1.00	8	.256	.307	.312
1992	Iowa	AAA	ChN	54	138	34	5	0	3	48	16	15	10	0	28	3	0	0	2	2	.50	1	.246	.311	.348
1993	Omaha	AAA	KC	70	200	58	7	0	2	71	22	19	34	0	32	3	3	1	2	4	.33	6	.290	.399	.355
1994	Omaha	AAA	KC	52	151	34	5	1	5	56	19	19	14	0	27	2	2	2	2	2	.50	1	.225	.296	.371
1995	Indianapols	AAA	Cin	14	39	10	2	0	1	15	8	6	3	0	7	1	0	0	1	0	1.00	0	.256	.326	.385
	High Desert	A+	Bal	5	15	4	1	0	0	5	1	1	2	0	6	0	0	1	0	1	.00	0	.267	.333	.333
	Rochester	AAA	Bal	40	126	23	1	1	1	29	10	12	12	0	26	1	0	1	1	1	.50	3	.183	.257	.230
1996	Tacoma	AAA	Sea	59	184	35	10	1	3	56	12	18	21	0	51	0	3	1	1	2	.33	3	.190	.272	.304
11 Min. YEARS				781	2437	619	99	9	28	820	247	279	246	4	449	26	26	24	20	30	.40	43	.254	.326	.336

Eric Knowles

Bats: Right **Throws:** Right **Pos:** SS **Ht:** 5'11" **Wt:** 157 **Born:** 10/21/73 **Age:** 23

			BATTING															BASERUNNING				PERCENTAGES		
Year	Team	Lg	Org	G	AB	H	2B	3B	HR	TB	R	RBI	TBB	IBB	SO	HBP	SH	SF	SB	CS	SB%	GDP	Avg	OBP	SLG
1991	Yankees	R	NYA	49	186	36	1	0	0	37	26	10	20	0	54	2	0	0	11	1	.92	1	.194	.279	.199
1992	Oneonta	A-	NYA	58	196	35	6	2	1	48	22	22	29	0	66	2	3	6	2	1	.67	4	.179	.283	.245
1993	Pr. William	A+	NYA	105	353	68	16	0	4	96	33	37	30	0	96	4	2	2	2	5	.29	7	.193	.262	.272
1994	Greensboro	A	NYA	125	439	114	31	3	2	157	68	42	62	1	104	3	4	7	11	5	.69	10	.260	.350	.358
1995	Tampa	A+	NYA	115	391	106	24	4	1	141	45	33	45	0	58	3	3	2	7	3	.70	8	.271	.349	.361
1996	Norwich	AA	NYA	126	396	97	23	1	7	143	56	42	32	1	92	4	8	5	9	6	.60	8	.245	.304	.361
6 Min. YEARS				578	1961	456	101	10	15	622	250	186	218	2	470	18	20	22	42	21	.67	38	.233	.312	.317

Ramsey Koeyers

Bats: Right **Throws:** Right **Pos:** C **Ht:** 6'1" **Wt:** 187 **Born:** 8/7/74 **Age:** 22

			BATTING															BASERUNNING				PERCENTAGES		
Year	Team	Lg	Org	G	AB	H	2B	3B	HR	TB	R	RBI	TBB	IBB	SO	HBP	SH	SF	SB	CS	SB%	GDP	Avg	OBP	SLG
1992	Expos	R	Mon	42	125	21	2	0	0	23	7	16	8	1	28	0	0	6	1	0	1.00	1	.168	.209	.184
1993	W. Palm Bch	A+	Mon	4	12	2	0	0	0	2	0	3	0	0	3	0	1	0	0	0	.00	0	.167	.167	.167
	Jamestown	A-	Mon	65	233	52	9	2	4	77	25	29	10	0	69	2	0	2	1	1	.50	5	.223	.259	.330
1994	W. Palm Bch	A+	Mon	79	241	62	11	1	3	84	27	31	21	0	61	1	3	0	3	3	.50	9	.257	.319	.349
1995	W. Palm Bch	A+	Mon	77	244	46	6	1	0	54	19	18	9	0	64	0	5	3	2	1	.67	10	.189	.215	.221
1996	Harrisburg	AA	Mon	25	77	16	3	0	1	22	6	9	2	0	27	1	3	1	0	1	.00	1	.208	.235	.286
	Expos	R	Mon	7	19	3	1	0	0	4	2	0	3	0	6	0	0	0	0	0	.00	0	.158	.273	.211
	W. Palm Bch	A+	Mon	10	33	4	2	0	0	6	2	2	0	0	8	0	0	0	0	0	.00	4	.121	.121	.182
5 Min. YEARS				309	984	206	34	4	8	272	88	108	53	1	266	4	12	12	7	6	.54	30	.209	.250	.276

Danny Kolb

Pitches: Right **Bats:** Right **Pos:** P **Ht:** 6'4" **Wt:** 190 **Born:** 3/29/75 **Age:** 22

			HOW MUCH HE PITCHED						WHAT HE GAVE UP												THE RESULTS					
Year	Team	Lg	Org	G	GS	CG	GF	IP	BFP	H	R	ER	HR	SH	SF	HB	TBB	IBB	SO	WP	Bk	W	L	Pct.	ShO	Sv	ERA
1995	Rangers	R	Tex	12	11	0	0	53	219	38	22	13	0	0	2	3	28	0	46	8	2	1	7	.125	0	0	2.21
1996	Charlstn-SC	A	Tex	20	20	4	0	126	514	80	50	36	5	6	0	6	60	2	127	22	4	8	6	.571	2	0	2.57
	Charlotte	A+	Tex	6	6	0	0	38	162	38	18	18	1	1	0	1	14	0	28	2	0	2	2	.500	0	0	4.26
	Tulsa	AA	Tex	2	2	0	0	11.2	45	5	1	1	0	0	0	1	8	0	7	0	0	1	0	1.000	0	0	0.77
2 Min. YEARS				40	39	4	0	228.2	940	161	91	68	6	7	2	11	110	2	208	32	6	12	15	.444	2	0	2.68

Jerry Koller

Pitches: Right **Bats:** Right **Pos:** P **Ht:** 6'3" **Wt:** 190 **Born:** 6/30/72 **Age:** 25

			HOW MUCH HE PITCHED						WHAT HE GAVE UP												THE RESULTS					
Year	Team	Lg	Org	G	GS	CG	GF	IP	BFP	H	R	ER	HR	SH	SF	HB	TBB	IBB	SO	WP	Bk	W	L	Pct.	ShO	Sv	ERA
1990	Braves	R	Atl	13	8	1	1	51	210	45	24	12	0	0	1	4	13	2	45	4	8	4	3	.571	1	0	2.12
1991	Braves	R	Atl	2	2	0	0	8	40	9	6	3	0	0	0	0	3	0	10	1	0	0	0	.000	0	0	3.38
	Idaho Falls	R+	Atl	9	9	0	0	36	171	49	29	25	1	0	2	1	14	0	29	7	2	2	2	.500	0	0	6.25
1992	Macon	A	Atl	21	21	2	0	133	526	104	41	35	8	2	4	5	31	0	114	8	2	10	5	.667	0	0	2.37
1993	Durham	A+	Atl	27	26	1	0	157.2	666	168	91	80	20	7	6	8	47	1	102	7	2	8	10	.444	0	0	4.57
1994	Greenville	AA	Atl	22	22	0	0	119.2	498	110	60	56	8	4	5	3	42	0	56	7	4	7	5	.583	0	0	4.21
1995	Greenville	AA	Atl	25	25	3	0	147.2	629	163	86	81	16	5	7	2	37	4	84	5	1	9	12	.429	0	0	4.94
1996	Greenville	AA	Atl	14	13	0	0	73.2	321	83	50	45	7	5	2	1	27	1	45	5	0	2	10	.167	0	0	5.50
7 Min. YEARS				133	126	7	1	726.2	3061	731	387	337	60	23	27	24	214	8	485	44	19	42	47	.472	1	0	4.17

Paul Konerko

Bats: Right **Throws:** Right **Pos:** 1B **Ht:** 6'2" **Wt:** 205 **Born:** 3/5/76 **Age:** 21

			BATTING															BASERUNNING				PERCENTAGES		
Year	Team	Lg	Org	G	AB	H	2B	3B	HR	TB	R	RBI	TBB	IBB	SO	HBP	SH	SF	SB	CS	SB%	GDP	Avg	OBP	SLG
1994	Yakima	A-	LA	67	257	74	15	2	6	111	25	58	36	4	52	6	0	7	1	0	1.00	6	.288	.379	.432
1995	San Bernrdo	A+	LA	118	448	124	21	1	19	204	77	77	59	2	88	4	2	6	3	1	.75	12	.277	.362	.455
1996	San Antonio	AA	LA	133	470	141	23	2	29	255	78	86	72	6	85	8	0	7	1	3	.25	7	.300	.397	.543
	Albuquerque	AAA	LA	4	14	6	0	0	1	9	2	2	1	0	2	0	0	0	0	1	.00	0	.429	.467	.643
3 Min. YEARS				322	1189	345	59	5	55	579	182	223	168	12	227	18	2	20	5	5	.50	25	.290	.381	.487

Dom Konieczki

Pitches: Left **Bats:** Right **Pos:** P **Ht:** 6'1" **Wt:** 170 **Born:** 6/16/69 **Age:** 28

			HOW MUCH HE PITCHED						WHAT HE GAVE UP												THE RESULTS					
Year	Team	Lg	Org	G	GS	CG	GF	IP	BFP	H	R	ER	HR	SH	SF	HB	TBB	IBB	SO	WP	Bk	W	L	Pct.	ShO	Sv	ERA
1991	Erie	A-	—	24	0	0	19	31.2	139	25	15	11	1	3	0	3	16	1	46	5	0	2	5	.286	0	10	3.13
1992	Kenosha	A	Min	49	0	0	31	56.1	230	44	14	11	2	6	0	0	19	2	79	3	0	5	3	.625	0	13	1.76
1993	Nashville	AA	Min	42	0	0	23	48.2	221	65	47	36	4	3	2	1	16	1	39	5	0	2	6	.250	0	4	6.66
	Fort Myers	A+	Min	12	0	0	9	16.2	83	18	7	7	0	1	0	1	16	0	15	1	0	0	2	.000	0	2	3.78
1994	Fort Myers	A+	Min	47	0	0	15	74	336	74	44	29	1	3	2	3	36	5	74	10	1	3	5	.375	0	4	3.53
1995	New Britain	AA	Min	39	0	0	15	32.1	146	28	10	7	1	2	1	1	19	2	35	3	0	0	1	.000	0	1	1.95
1996	Fort Myers	A+	Min	14	0	0	8	14	54	7	1	1	0	0	0	0	6	0	22	2	0	0	0	.000	0	1	0.64
	Salt Lake	AAA	Min	4	0	0	2	3	23	8	7	6	0	0	0	0	5	0	2	2	0	0	0	.000	0	0	18.00
	New Britain	AA	Min	28	0	0	11	34.1	159	32	19	19	2	1	2	4	23	2	23	3	0	1	3	.250	0	2	4.98
6 Min. YEARS				259	0	0	133	311	1391	301	164	127	11	19	7	13	156	13	335	34	1	13	25	.342	0	37	3.68

Dennis Konuszewski

Pitches: Right **Bats:** Right **Pos:** P **Ht:** 6' 3" **Wt:** 210 **Born:** 2/4/71 **Age:** 26

			HOW MUCH HE PITCHED						WHAT HE GAVE UP												THE RESULTS					
Year Team	Lg	Org	G	GS	CG	GF	IP	BFP	H	R	ER	HR	SH	SF	HB	TBB	IBB	SO	WP	Bk	W	L	Pct.	ShO	Sv	ERA
1992 Welland	A-	Pit	2	2	0	0	7	30	6	1	1	0	1	0	0	4	0	4	1	1	0	0	.000	0	0	1.29
Augusta	A	Pit	17	8	0	4	62.1	258	50	19	16	1	4	0	5	19	0	45	2	7	3	3	.500	0	1	2.31
1993 Salem	A+	Pit	39	13	0	7	103	463	121	66	53	14	3	7	5	43	3	81	6	4	4	10	.286	0	1	4.63
1994 Carolina	AA	Pit	51	0	0	19	77.2	346	81	39	31	5	2	2	2	31	5	53	6	1	6	5	.545	0	1	3.59
1995 Carolina	AA	Pit	48	0	0	18	61.2	278	63	33	25	3	3	1	1	26	5	48	5	1	7	7	.500	0	2	3.65
1996 Carolina	AA	Pit	32	10	0	8	80	362	103	61	56	12	3	4	6	36	0	59	3	0	2	8	.200	0	0	6.30
Calgary	AAA	Pit	3	0	0	2	3.1	28	13	11	9	0	0	0	0	5	0	0	0	0	0	0	.000	0	0	24.30
1995 Pittsburgh	NL		1	0	0	0	0.1	5	3	2	2	0	1	0	0	1	0	0	0	0	0	0	.000	0	0	54.00
5 Min. YEARS			192	33	0	58	395	1765	437	230	191	35	16	14	19	164	13	290	23	14	22	33	.400	0	5	4.35

Clint Koppe

Pitches: Right **Bats:** Right **Pos:** P **Ht:** 6'4" **Wt:** 220 **Born:** 8/14/73 **Age:** 23

			HOW MUCH HE PITCHED						WHAT HE GAVE UP												THE RESULTS					
Year Team	Lg	Org	G	GS	CG	GF	IP	BFP	H	R	ER	HR	SH	SF	HB	TBB	IBB	SO	WP	Bk	W	L	Pct.	ShO	Sv	ERA
1994 Billings	R+	Cin	14	14	1	0	89.1	360	85	48	42	4	3	3	2	23	3	61	4	2	9	2	.818	0	0	4.23
1995 Charlstn-WV	A	Cin	30	22	2	1	157.2	653	144	66	59	10	4	5	6	47	5	119	8	1	7	13	.350	0	0	3.37
1996 Winston-Sal	A+	Cin	16	15	3	0	95.1	388	87	41	35	10	3	3	4	25	0	46	7	1	8	2	.800	1	0	3.30
Chattanooga	AA	Cin	10	9	1	1	56.2	232	54	27	22	3	1	3	0	18	0	30	4	1	4	2	.667	0	1	3.49
3 Min. YEARS			70	60	7	2	399	1633	370	182	158	27	11	14	12	113	8	256	23	5	28	19	.596	1	1	3.56

Bryn Kosco

Bats: Left **Throws:** Right **Pos:** 3B **Ht:** 6'1" **Wt:** 185 **Born:** 3/9/67 **Age:** 30

			BATTING															BASERUNNING				PERCENTAGES		
Year Team	Lg	Org	G	AB	H	2B	3B	HR	TB	R	RBI	TBB	IBB	SO	HBP	SH	SF	SB	CS	SB%	GDP	Avg	OBP	SLG
1988 Jamestown	A-	Mon	63	229	65	19	2	8	112	26	42	18	4	48	1	0	3	1	0	1.00	7	.284	.335	.489
1989 Rockford	A	Mon	77	292	78	16	0	11	127	47	44	39	6	61	2	0	2	2	0	1.00	5	.267	.355	.435
W. Palm Bch	A+	Mon	60	203	46	10	1	1	61	16	22	21	5	42	0	0	4	2	2	.50	4	.227	.294	.300
1990 Jacksonvlle	AA	Mon	33	113	28	8	0	0	36	7	15	11	2	23	0	2	1	0	0	.00	4	.248	.312	.319
1991 Harrisburg	AA	Mon	113	381	92	23	5	10	155	50	58	48	4	79	2	0	3	4	1	.80	9	.241	.327	.407
1992 Harrisburg	AA	Mon	106	341	78	17	0	5	110	35	41	31	2	75	1	1	5	2	0	1.00	6	.229	.291	.323
1993 High Desert	A+	Fla	121	450	138	25	3	27	250	96	121	62	3	97	5	0	8	1	6	.14	13	.307	.390	.556
1994 New Haven	AA	Col	132	479	116	24	3	22	212	64	90	59	6	124	4	1	6	2	2	.50	17	.242	.327	.443
1995 Iowa	AAA	ChN	119	363	91	24	3	15	166	50	52	30	5	85	1	2	3	2	2	.50	18	.251	.307	.457
1996 Iowa	AAA	ChN	29	79	20	2	0	2	28	8	7	5	1	22	0	0	1	0	0	.00	1	.253	.294	.354
9 Min. YEARS			853	2930	752	168	17	101	1257	399	492	324	38	656	16	6	36	16	13	.55	84	.257	.330	.429

Mike Kotarski

Pitches: Left **Bats:** Left **Pos:** P **Ht:** 6'1" **Wt:** 195 **Born:** 9/18/70 **Age:** 26

			HOW MUCH HE PITCHED						WHAT HE GAVE UP												THE RESULTS					
Year Team	Lg	Org	G	GS	CG	GF	IP	BFP	H	R	ER	HR	SH	SF	HB	TBB	IBB	SO	WP	Bk	W	L	Pct.	ShO	Sv	ERA
1992 Bend	A-	Col	25	3	0	9	55.2	247	48	30	23	1	1	1	6	36	2	65	1	0	3	1	.750	0	0	3.72
1993 Central Val	A+	Col	52	0	0	32	88.1	396	87	44	38	9	11	2	3	37	3	81	3	1	6	2	.750	0	11	3.87
1994 New Haven	AA	Col	18	0	0	12	21	109	29	29	23	7	0	3	0	13	0	14	3	0	0	1	.000	0	3	9.86
Central Val	A+	Col	41	1	0	11	62.1	278	69	39	27	8	1	3	3	29	3	58	7	4	1	3	.250	0	2	3.90
1995 Colo. Sprng	AAA	Col	22	0	0	11	30	162	48	37	36	5	1	2	2	20	1	21	4	0	2	2	.500	0	0	10.80
New Haven	AA	Col	53	0	0	21	80	396	91	62	54	9	5	4	3	56	5	75	7	5	4	5	.444	0	2	6.08
1996 Columbus	AAA	NYA	1	1	0	0	4	18	3	4	3	0	0	1	0	2	0	5	1	0	0	0	.000	0	0	6.75
Norwich	AA	NYA	42	1	0	14	72.1	320	73	40	35	3	2	4	4	29	4	66	8	0	1	2	.333	0	3	4.35
5 Min. YEARS			254	6	0	110	413.2	1926	448	285	239	42	21	20	21	222	18	385	34	10	17	16	.515	0	21	5.20

Brian Kowitz

Bats: Left **Throws:** Left **Pos:** OF **Ht:** 5'10" **Wt:** 182 **Born:** 8/7/69 **Age:** 27

			BATTING															BASERUNNING				PERCENTAGES		
Year Team	Lg	Org	G	AB	H	2B	3B	HR	TB	R	RBI	TBB	IBB	SO	HBP	SH	SF	SB	CS	SB%	GDP	Avg	OBP	SLG
1990 Pulaski	R+	Atl	43	182	59	13	1	8	98	40	19	16	2	16	1	2	2	12	6	.67	4	.324	.378	.538
Greenville	AA	Atl	20	68	9	0	0	0	9	4	4	8	1	10	0	1	0	1	0	1.00	2	.132	.224	.132
1991 Durham	A+	Atl	86	323	82	13	5	3	114	41	21	23	0	56	3	4	1	18	8	.69	3	.254	.309	.353
Greenville	AA	Atl	35	112	26	5	0	3	40	15	17	10	0	7	2	2	2	1	4	.20	3	.232	.302	.357
1992 Durham	A+	Atl	105	382	115	14	7	7	164	53	64	44	4	53	2	6	7	22	11	.67	3	.301	.370	.429
Greenville	AA	Atl	21	56	16	4	0	0	20	9	6	6	0	10	0	0	0	1	4	.20	0	.286	.355	.357
1993 Greenville	AA	Atl	122	450	125	20	5	5	170	63	48	60	0	56	2	1	1	13	10	.57	7	.278	.365	.378
Richmond	AAA	Atl	12	45	12	1	3	0	19	10	8	5	0	8	1	2	1	1	0	1.00	0	.267	.346	.422
1994 Richmond	AAA	Atl	124	466	140	29	7	8	207	68	57	43	2	53	2	1	7	22	8	.73	8	.300	.357	.444
1995 Richmond	AAA	Atl	100	353	99	14	5	2	129	53	34	41	1	43	3	3	0	11	8	.58	4	.280	.360	.365
1996 Toledo	AAA	Det	24	68	13	5	0	0	18	9	3	9	0	12	0	1	0	2	2	.50	3	.191	.286	.265
Syracuse	AAA	Tor	34	108	26	6	3	1	41	14	19	9	0	20	0	3	2	2	2	.50	1	.241	.294	.380
1995 Atlanta	NL		10	24	4	1	0	0	5	3	3	2	0	5	1	1	0	0	1	.00	0	.167	.259	.208
7 Min. YEARS			726	2613	722	124	36	37	1029	379	300	274	10	344	16	26	23	106	63	.63	38	.276	.346	.394

Jeff Kramer

Pitches: Right **Bats:** Right **Pos:** P **Ht:** 5'11" **Wt:** 180 **Born:** 10/6/73 **Age:** 23

		HOW MUCH HE PITCHED						WHAT HE GAVE UP												THE RESULTS					
Year Team	Lg Org	G	GS	CG	GF	IP	BFP	H	R	ER	HR	SH	SF	HB	TBB	IBB	SO	WP	Bk	W	L	Pct.	ShO	Sv	ERA
1994 Helena	R+ Mil	16	10	0	6	70.1	309	62	23	16	0	4	1	6	28	2	82	11	4	5	2	.714	0	2	2.05
1995 Stockton	A+ Mil	32	24	0	2	149	662	174	87	74	9	8	4	12	58	0	108	9	6	12	7	.632	0	1	4.47
1996 El Paso	AA Mil	21	5	0	6	59.2	280	76	57	42	5	2	6	3	29	1	36	5	0	3	4	.429	0	1	6.34
Stockton	A+ Mil	15	7	0	2	59	272	62	43	29	4	2	1	4	31	0	46	6	0	6	4	.600	0	0	4.42
3 Min. YEARS		84	46	0	16	338	1523	374	210	161	18	16	12	25	146	3	272	31	10	26	17	.605	0	4	4.29

Tom Kramer

Pitches: Right **Bats:** Both **Pos:** P **Ht:** 6' 0" **Wt:** 220 **Born:** 1/9/68 **Age:** 29

		HOW MUCH HE PITCHED						WHAT HE GAVE UP												THE RESULTS					
Year Team	Lg Org	G	GS	CG	GF	IP	BFP	H	R	ER	HR	SH	SF	HB	TBB	IBB	SO	WP	Bk	W	L	Pct.	ShO	Sv	ERA
1987 Burlington	R+ Cle	12	11	2	1	71.2	292	57	31	24	2	0	1	1	26	0	71	0	0	7	3	.700	1	1	3.01
1988 Waterloo	A Cle	27	27	10	0	198.2	814	173	70	56	9	10	3	3	60	3	152	5	3	14	7	.667	2	0	2.54
1989 Kinston	A+ Cle	18	17	5	1	131.2	527	97	44	38	7	5	3	4	42	3	89	4	1	9	5	.643	1	0	2.60
Canton-Akrn	AA Cle	10	8	1	0	43.1	202	58	34	30	6	3	4	0	20	0	26	3	0	1	6	.143	0	0	6.23
1990 Kinston	A+ Cle	16	16	2	0	98	402	82	34	31	5	1	2	2	29	0	96	2	1	7	4	.636	1	0	2.85
Canton-Akrn	AA Cle	12	10	2	0	72	287	67	25	24	3	2	1	0	14	1	46	1	0	6	3	.667	0	0	3.00
1991 Canton-Akrn	AA Cle	35	5	0	13	79.1	320	61	23	21	5	6	1	1	34	3	61	3	0	7	3	.700	0	6	2.38
Colo. Sprng	AAA Cle	10	1	0	6	11.1	43	5	1	1	1	0	0	0	5	0	18	1	0	1	0	1.000	0	4	0.79
1992 Colo. Sprng	AAA Cle	38	3	0	11	75.2	344	88	43	41	2	4	3	1	43	2	72	0	0	8	3	.727	0	3	4.88
1994 Charlotte	AAA Cle	13	0	0	6	19	85	15	11	10	2	2	1	0	11	1	20	2	0	1	3	.250	0	0	4.74
Indianapols	AAA Cin	23	13	0	3	102.2	431	109	55	51	12	5	3	2	32	2	54	6	0	5	4	.556	0	0	4.47
1995 Toledo	AAA Det	6	5	0	0	27.1	116	23	15	14	6	0	2	0	16	0	15	0	0	3	1	.750	0	0	4.61
Chattanooga	AA Cin	27	23	2	1	154.1	629	140	69	61	14	5	7	2	44	4	141	4	0	15	2	.882	0	0	3.56
1996 Colo. Sprng	AAA Col	41	10	0	17	112.1	512	129	74	67	16	5	5	0	47	3	79	4	2	8	4	.667	0	4	5.37
1991 Cleveland	AL	4	0	0	1	4.2	30	10	9	9	1	0	3	0	6	0	4	0	0	0	0	.000	0	0	17.36
1993 Cleveland	AL	39	16	1	6	121	535	126	60	54	19	3	2	2	59	7	71	1	0	7	3	.700	0	0	4.02
9 Min. YEARS		288	149	24	59	1197.1	5004	1104	529	469	90	48	36	16	423	22	940	35	7	92	48	.657	5	18	3.53
2 Maj. YEARS		43	16	1	7	125.2	565	136	69	63	20	3	5	2	65	7	75	1	0	7	3	.700	0	0	4.51

Scott Krause

Bats: Right **Throws:** Right **Pos:** OF **Ht:** 6'1" **Wt:** 187 **Born:** 8/16/73 **Age:** 23

		BATTING														BASERUNNING				PERCENTAGES		
Year Team	Lg Org	G	AB	H	2B	3B	HR	TB	R	RBI	TBB	IBB	SO	HBP	SH	SF	SB	CS	SB%	GDP	Avg	OBP	SLG
1994 Helena	R+ Mil	63	252	90	18	3	4	126	51	52	18	2	49	9	1	2	13	6	.68	2	.357	.416	.500
1995 Beloit	A Mil	134	481	119	30	4	13	196	83	76	50	5	126	12	3	7	24	10	.71	7	.247	.329	.407
1996 El Paso	AA Mil	24	85	27	5	2	3	45	16	11	2	0	19	1	1	0	2	0	1.00	1	.318	.341	.529
Stockton	A+ Mil	108	427	128	22	4	19	215	82	83	32	0	101	16	1	3	25	6	.81	9	.300	.368	.504
3 Min. YEARS		329	1245	364	75	13	39	582	232	222	102	7	295	38	6	12	64	22	.74	19	.292	.361	.467

Frank Kremblas

Bats: Right **Throws:** Right **Pos:** 3B-2B **Ht:** 5'11" **Wt:** 180 **Born:** 10/25/66 **Age:** 30

		BATTING														BASERUNNING				PERCENTAGES		
Year Team	Lg Org	G	AB	H	2B	3B	HR	TB	R	RBI	TBB	IBB	SO	HBP	SH	SF	SB	CS	SB%	GDP	Avg	OBP	SLG
1989 Reds	R Cin	60	213	49	10	1	1	64	32	18	28	1	44	1	1	2	8	4	.67	5	.230	.320	.300
1990 Cedar Rapds	A Cin	92	266	67	13	0	5	95	18	26	23	0	54	1	4	3	2	7	.22	7	.252	.311	.357
1991 Chattanooga	AA Cin	102	320	77	17	0	3	103	35	41	29	1	61	2	4	2	3	4	.43	9	.241	.306	.322
1992 Chattanooga	AA Cin	100	282	65	16	1	0	83	29	28	18	1	58	1	5	2	4	5	.44	2	.230	.277	.294
1993 Indianapols	AAA Cin	108	341	83	15	4	8	130	38	46	42	2	78	0	3	0	7	4	.64	4	.243	.326	.381
1994 Chattanooga	AA Cin	47	144	37	3	2	1	47	11	14	8	0	31	1	1	0	8	4	.67	3	.257	.301	.326
Indianapols	AAA Cin	43	150	36	9	2	1	52	21	11	10	0	42	0	2	1	2	3	.40	1	.240	.286	.347
1995 Indianapols	AAA Cin	27	75	12	2	0	0	14	7	3	12	1	25	0	2	0	4	2	.67	2	.160	.276	.187
Chattanooga	AA Cin	19	67	10	2	0	1	15	8	6	7	0	10	1	0	2	1	1	.50	2	.149	.234	.224
1996 Columbia	IND —	50	188	48	9	1	3	68	31	19	26	1	28	1	0	2	9	4	.69	3	.255	.346	.362
Indianapols	AAA Cin	23	91	18	5	0	0	23	14	8	7	0	30	0	1	0	3	1	.75	1	.198	.255	.253
8 Min. YEARS		671	2137	502	101	11	23	694	244	220	210	7	461	8	23	14	51	39	.57	39	.235	.304	.325

Marc Kroon

Pitches: Right **Bats:** Right **Pos:** P **Ht:** 6' 2" **Wt:** 195 **Born:** 4/2/73 **Age:** 24

		HOW MUCH HE PITCHED						WHAT HE GAVE UP												THE RESULTS					
Year Team	Lg Org	G	GS	CG	GF	IP	BFP	H	R	ER	HR	SH	SF	HB	TBB	IBB	SO	WP	Bk	W	L	Pct.	ShO	Sv	ERA
1991 Mets	R NYN	12	10	1	2	47.2	208	39	33	24	1	0	1	4	22	0	39	10	5	2	3	.400	0	0	4.53
1992 Kingsport	R+ NYN	12	12	0	0	68	307	52	41	31	3	0	3	1	57	0	60	13	2	3	5	.375	0	0	4.10
1993 Capital Cty	A NYN	29	19	0	8	124.1	542	123	65	48	6	1	8	5	70	0	122	10	2	2	11	.154	0	2	3.47
1994 Rancho Cuca	A+ SD	26	26	0	0	143.1	655	143	86	77	14	4	9	11	81	1	153	9	3	11	6	.647	0	0	4.83
1995 Memphis	AA SD	22	19	0	2	115.1	497	90	49	45	12	2	2	6	61	1	123	16	1	7	5	.583	0	2	3.51
1996 Memphis	AA SD	44	0	0	43	46.2	208	33	19	15	4	1	4	3	28	1	56	6	1	2	4	.333	0	22	2.89
1995 San Diego	NL	2	0	0	1	1.2	7	1	2	2	0	0	0	0	2	0	2	0	0	0	1	.000	0	0	10.80
6 Min. YEARS		145	86	1	55	545.1	2417	480	293	240	40	8	27	30	319	3	553	64	14	27	34	.443	0	26	3.96

Tim Kubinski

Pitches: Left **Bats:** Left **Pos:** P **Ht:** 6'4" **Wt:** 205 **Born:** 1/20/72 **Age:** 25

				HOW MUCH HE PITCHED						WHAT HE GAVE UP												THE RESULTS					
Year	Team	Lg	Org	G	GS	CG	GF	IP	BFP	H	R	ER	HR	SH	SF	HB	TBB	IBB	SO	WP	Bk	W	L	Pct.	ShO	Sv	ERA
1993	Athletics	R	Oak	1	1	0	0	3	13	5	2	2	1	0	0	0	0	0	3	0	0	0	1	.000	0	0	6.00
	Sou. Oregon	A-	Oak	12	12	1	0	70	294	67	36	22	4	2	2	6	18	0	51	2	2	5	5	.500	0	0	2.83
1994	W. Michigan	A	Oak	30	23	1	4	158.2	677	168	82	64	8	13	4	7	36	0	126	8	10	14	6	.700	0	0	3.63
1995	Edmonton	AAA	Oak	6	5	0	0	32	136	34	18	17	4	0	0	4	10	0	12	0	4	1	2	.333	0	0	4.78
	Modesto	A+	Oak	31	22	0	4	141	621	160	91	77	16	6	5	12	34	0	95	10	5	7	12	.368	0	2	4.91
1996	Huntsville	AA	Oak	43	3	0	15	102	418	84	41	27	7	4	3	3	36	6	78	8	3	8	7	.533	0	3	2.38
	Edmonton	AAA	Oak	1	0	0	1	1	4	1	0	0	0	0	0	0	1	0	0	0	0	0	0	.000	0	0	0.00
4 Min. YEARS				124	66	2	24	507.2	2163	519	270	209	40	25	14	32	135	6	365	28	24	35	33	.515	0	5	3.71

Mike Kusiewicz

Pitches: Left **Bats:** Right **Pos:** P **Ht:** 6'2" **Wt:** 185 **Born:** 11/1/76 **Age:** 20

				HOW MUCH HE PITCHED						WHAT HE GAVE UP												THE RESULTS					
Year	Team	Lg	Org	G	GS	CG	GF	IP	BFP	H	R	ER	HR	SH	SF	HB	TBB	IBB	SO	WP	Bk	W	L	Pct.	ShO	Sv	ERA
1995	Salem	A+	Col	1	1	0	0	6	26	7	1	1	0	0	0	2	0	0	7	0	1	0	0	.000	0	0	1.50
	Asheville	A	Col	22	22	0	0	128.1	510	99	41	29	6	2	0	8	34	0	110	9	2	8	4	.667	0	0	2.03
1996	Salem	A+	Col	5	3	0	2	23	100	19	15	13	2	1	1	1	12	0	18	2	0	0	1	.000	0	1	5.09
	New Haven	AA	Col	14	14	0	0	76.1	326	83	38	28	4	2	3	2	27	2	64	0	1	2	4	.333	0	0	3.30
2 Min. YEARS				42	40	0	2	233.2	962	208	95	71	12	5	4	13	73	2	199	11	4	10	9	.526	0	1	2.73

Cleveland Ladell

Bats: Right **Throws:** Right **Pos:** OF **Ht:** 5'11" **Wt:** 170 **Born:** 9/19/70 **Age:** 26

				BATTING															BASERUNNING				PERCENTAGES		
Year	Team	Lg	Org	G	AB	H	2B	3B	HR	TB	R	RBI	TBB	IBB	SO	HBP	SH	SF	SB	CS	SB%	GDP	Avg	OBP	SLG
1992	Princeton	R+	Cin	64	241	64	6	4	4	90	37	32	13	0	45	1	2	2	24	3	.89	1	.266	.304	.373
	Charlstn-WV	A	Cin	8	30	6	0	0	0	6	3	0	3	0	14	0	0	0	3	1	.75	0	.200	.273	.200
1993	Winston-Sal	A+	Cin	132	531	151	15	7	20	240	90	66	16	0	95	3	4	5	24	7	.77	13	.284	.306	.452
1994	Chattanooga	AA	Cin	33	99	16	4	1	1	25	9	9	4	0	26	0	0	1	4	1	.80	2	.162	.192	.253
	Winston-Sal	A+	Cin	75	283	71	11	3	12	124	46	40	26	0	63	2	2	3	17	7	.71	3	.251	.315	.438
1995	Chattanooga	AA	Cin	135	517	151	28	7	5	208	76	43	39	1	88	2	4	2	28	15	.65	12	.292	.343	.402
1996	Indianapolis	AAA	Cin	8	7	0	0	0	0	0	0	0	1	0	1	0	0	0	0	0	.00	1	.000	.125	.000
	Chattanooga	AA	Cin	121	405	102	15	7	4	143	59	41	31	5	88	5	4	1	31	14	.69	11	.252	.312	.353
5 Min. YEARS				576	2113	561	79	29	46	836	320	231	133	6	420	13	16	14	131	48	.73	43	.265	.311	.396

Rick Ladjevich

Bats: Right **Throws:** Right **Pos:** 3B **Ht:** 6'3" **Wt:** 220 **Born:** 2/17/72 **Age:** 25

				BATTING															BASERUNNING				PERCENTAGES		
Year	Team	Lg	Org	G	AB	H	2B	3B	HR	TB	R	RBI	TBB	IBB	SO	HBP	SH	SF	SB	CS	SB%	GDP	Avg	OBP	SLG
1994	Bellingham	A-	Sea	68	235	73	12	0	1	88	36	31	22	1	39	22	1	1	3	4	.43	5	.311	.418	.374
1995	Riverside	A+	Sea	122	470	145	26	0	7	192	74	71	26	2	65	22	3	4	3	2	.60	8	.309	.370	.409
1996	Port City	AA	Sea	115	414	117	23	1	7	163	44	48	35	1	58	15	1	1	1	4	.20	14	.283	.359	.394
3 Min. YEARS				305	1119	335	61	1	15	443	154	150	83	4	162	59	5	6	7	10	.41	27	.299	.376	.396

Joseph LaGarde

Pitches: Right **Bats:** Right **Pos:** P **Ht:** 5'9" **Wt:** 180 **Born:** 1/17/75 **Age:** 22

				HOW MUCH HE PITCHED						WHAT HE GAVE UP												THE RESULTS					
Year	Team	Lg	Org	G	GS	CG	GF	IP	BFP	H	R	ER	HR	SH	SF	HB	TBB	IBB	SO	WP	Bk	W	L	Pct.	ShO	Sv	ERA
1993	Yakima	A-	LA	15	12	0	2	70.2	303	69	28	26	4	2	1	0	28	0	45	7	1	5	4	.556	0	2	3.31
1994	Vero Beach	A+	LA	25	15	0	3	105.2	446	101	57	49	5	2	3	7	41	0	66	8	1	6	8	.429	0	0	4.17
1995	Bakersfield	A+	LA	28	28	0	0	145	655	154	91	70	10	4	7	9	81	0	127	15	1	6	11	.353	0	0	4.34
	San Bernrdo	A+	LA	28	28	0	0	145	655	154	91	70	10	4	7	9	81	0	127	15	1	6	11	.353	0	0	4.34
1996	Vero Beach	A+	LA	14	4	0	5	44.1	194	41	17	12	0	2	1	4	22	1	46	1	1	4	3	.571	0	1	2.44
	San Antonio	AA	LA	24	0	0	21	31	129	28	7	6	0	1	0	0	10	0	22	4	0	3	1	.750	0	9	1.74
	Albuquerque	AAA	LA	10	0	0	4	12	59	14	7	7	2	1	0	2	9	2	11	4	0	0	0	.000	0	0	5.25
4 Min. YEARS				144	87	0	35	553.2	2441	561	298	240	31	16	19	31	272	3	444	54	5	30	38	.441	0	12	3.90

Todd Landry

Bats: Right **Throws:** Left **Pos:** 1B **Ht:** 6'4" **Wt:** 215 **Born:** 8/21/72 **Age:** 24

				BATTING															BASERUNNING				PERCENTAGES		
Year	Team	Lg	Org	G	AB	H	2B	3B	HR	TB	R	RBI	TBB	IBB	SO	HBP	SH	SF	SB	CS	SB%	GDP	Avg	OBP	SLG
1993	Helena	R+	Mil	29	124	39	10	1	5	66	27	24	8	1	20	2	0	1	5	0	1.00	2	.315	.363	.532
	Beloit	A	Mil	38	149	45	6	0	4	63	26	24	4	0	36	0	0	2	4	4	.50	6	.302	.316	.423
1994	Stockton	A+	Mil	105	356	95	12	6	8	143	55	49	28	0	53	5	4	4	4	1	.80	10	.267	.326	.402
1995	El Paso	AA	Mil	132	511	149	33	4	16	238	76	79	33	1	100	7	2	4	9	7	.56	21	.292	.341	.466
1996	New Orleans	AAA	Mil	113	391	94	19	2	5	132	41	44	32	0	61	3	2	3	14	4	.78	15	.240	.301	.338
4 Min. YEARS				417	1531	422	80	13	38	642	225	220	105	2	270	17	8	14	36	16	.69	54	.276	.326	.419

Aaron Lane

Pitches: Left **Bats:** Left **Pos:** P **Ht:** 6'1" **Wt:** 180 **Born:** 6/2/71 **Age:** 26

			HOW MUCH HE PITCHED						WHAT HE GAVE UP												THE RESULTS					
Year	Team	Lg Org	G	GS	CG	GF	IP	BFP	H	R	ER	HR	SH	SF	HB	TBB	IBB	SO	WP	Bk	W	L	Pct.	ShO	Sv	ERA
1992	Bluefield	R+ Bal	14	7	0	1	45	195	36	24	15	7	2	0	0	24	0	39	3	1	5	1	.833	0	0	3.00
1993	Albany	A Bal	29	11	0	8	76	359	92	62	42	6	6	1	6	42	2	48	6	5	2	10	.167	0	0	4.97
1994	Albany	A Bal	35	0	0	30	54.2	232	42	20	14	0	1	3	2	24	0	56	4	3	3	2	.600	0	11	2.30
	Frederick	A+ Bal	5	0	0	5	7.1	32	10	3	3	1	0	0	0	3	0	6	1	0	1	1	.500	0	2	3.68
1995	Rochester	AAA Bal	9	0	0	2	10	47	11	11	7	2	0	0	2	5	0	9	2	0	0	0	.000	0	0	6.30
	Bowie	AA Bal	49	0	0	20	55.1	247	56	34	28	4	5	0	3	26	3	40	5	1	5	3	.625	0	2	4.55
1996	Rochester	AAA Bal	9	0	0	2	22.1	104	31	16	14	0	0	1	2	8	0	13	1	0	1	0	1.000	0	1	5.64
	Bowie	AA Bal	13	8	1	2	51	224	44	37	26	7	6	3	0	24	4	35	1	0	3	5	.375	1	2	4.59
5 Min. YEARS			163	26	1	70	321.2	1440	322	207	149	27	20	8	15	156	9	246	23	10	20	22	.476	1	18	4.17

Ryan Lane

Bats: Right **Throws:** Right **Pos:** 2B **Ht:** 6'1" **Wt:** 175 **Born:** 7/6/74 **Age:** 22

			BATTING															BASERUNNING				PERCENTAGES		
Year	Team	Lg Org	G	AB	H	2B	3B	HR	TB	R	RBI	TBB	IBB	SO	HBP	SH	SF	SB	CS	SB%	GDP	Avg	OBP	SLG
1993	Twins	R Min	43	138	20	3	2	0	27	15	5	15	0	38	2	3	1	3	1	.75	2	.145	.237	.196
1994	Elizabethtn	R+ Min	59	202	48	13	0	3	70	32	18	26	0	47	2	3	2	4	3	.57	4	.238	.328	.347
1995	Fort Wayne	A Min	115	432	115	37	1	6	172	69	56	65	0	92	7	6	4	17	9	.65	9	.266	.368	.398
1996	Fort Myers	A+ Min	106	404	110	20	7	9	171	74	62	60	0	96	6	6	9	21	9	.70	2	.272	.367	.423
	New Britain	AA Min	33	117	26	5	1	2	39	13	12	8	0	29	0	2	1	3	4	.43	1	.222	.270	.333
4 Min. YEARS			356	1293	319	78	11	20	479	203	153	174	0	302	17	20	17	48	26	.65	18	.247	.340	.370

Frank Lankford

Pitches: Right **Bats:** Right **Pos:** P **Ht:** 6'2" **Wt:** 190 **Born:** 3/26/71 **Age:** 26

			HOW MUCH HE PITCHED						WHAT HE GAVE UP												THE RESULTS					
Year	Team	Lg Org	G	GS	CG	GF	IP	BFP	H	R	ER	HR	SH	SF	HB	TBB	IBB	SO	WP	Bk	W	L	Pct.	ShO	Sv	ERA
1993	Oneonta	A- NYA	16	7	0	1	64.2	276	60	41	24	3	3	2	1	22	0	61	5	0	4	5	.444	0	0	3.34
1994	Greensboro	A NYA	54	0	0	27	82.1	352	79	37	27	3	6	1	1	18	3	74	7	1	7	6	.538	0	7	2.95
1995	Tampa	A+ NYA	55	0	0	36	73	305	64	29	21	0	7	0	2	22	6	58	1	0	4	6	.400	0	15	2.59
1996	Norwich	AA NYA	61	0	0	25	88	392	82	42	26	4	9	1	2	40	6	61	3	0	7	8	.467	0	4	2.66
4 Min. YEARS			186	7	0	89	308	1325	285	149	98	10	25	4	6	102	15	254	16	1	22	25	.468	0	26	2.86

Greg Larocca

Bats: Right **Throws:** Right **Pos:** 2B **Ht:** 5'11" **Wt:** 185 **Born:** 11/10/72 **Age:** 24

			BATTING															BASERUNNING				PERCENTAGES		
Year	Team	Lg Org	G	AB	H	2B	3B	HR	TB	R	RBI	TBB	IBB	SO	HBP	SH	SF	SB	CS	SB%	GDP	Avg	OBP	SLG
1994	Spokane	A- SD	42	158	46	9	2	0	59	20	14	14	0	18	2	2	0	7	2	.78	4	.291	.356	.373
	Rancho Cuca	A+ SD	28	85	14	5	1	1	24	7	8	7	0	11	2	1	1	3	1	.75	2	.165	.242	.282
1995	Rancho Cuca	A+ SD	125	466	150	36	5	8	220	77	74	44	0	77	12	0	2	15	4	.79	13	.322	.393	.472
	Memphis	AA SD	2	7	1	0	0	0	1	0	0	0	0	1	0	0	0	0	1	.00	1	.143	.143	.143
1996	Memphis	AA SD	128	445	122	22	5	6	172	66	42	51	4	58	10	5	5	5	9	.36	9	.274	.358	.387
3 Min. YEARS			325	1161	333	72	13	15	476	170	138	116	4	165	26	8	8	30	17	.64	29	.287	.362	.410

Edgardo Larregui

Bats: Right **Throws:** Right **Pos:** OF **Ht:** 6'0" **Wt:** 185 **Born:** 12/1/72 **Age:** 24

			BATTING															BASERUNNING				PERCENTAGES		
Year	Team	Lg Org	G	AB	H	2B	3B	HR	TB	R	RBI	TBB	IBB	SO	HBP	SH	SF	SB	CS	SB%	GDP	Avg	OBP	SLG
1990	Huntington	R+ ChN	34	102	19	3	0	2	28	13	16	7	0	12	0	2	3	3	0	1.00	1	.186	.232	.275
1991	Geneva	A- ChN	71	269	67	12	2	1	86	34	28	16	0	29	5	2	2	13	3	.81	10	.249	.301	.320
1992	Peoria	A ChN	129	478	137	24	2	5	180	62	71	30	1	68	4	9	4	15	6	.71	12	.287	.331	.377
1993	Daytona	A+ ChN	95	329	78	10	5	2	104	26	34	15	0	24	2	5	2	1	11	.08	13	.237	.273	.316
1994	Daytona	A+ ChN	74	283	82	12	2	6	116	40	51	21	0	32	1	0	2	6	9	.40	10	.290	.339	.410
	Orlando	AA ChN	35	111	32	2	1	0	36	14	7	5	0	13	1	2	1	3	6	.33	0	.288	.322	.324
1995	Orlando	AA ChN	122	423	127	18	1	11	180	55	60	32	2	39	1	0	4	3	10	.23	15	.300	.348	.426
1996	Orlando	AA ChN	17	69	18	5	0	1	26	12	5	6	1	9	0	0	0	0	2	.00	3	.261	.320	.377
	Birmingham	AA ChA	65	213	51	9	1	0	62	26	14	16	1	31	0	3	1	1	1	.50	4	.239	.291	.291
7 Min. YEARS			642	2277	611	95	14	28	818	282	286	148	5	257	14	23	19	45	48	.48	68	.268	.314	.359

Toby Larson

Pitches: Right **Bats:** Right **Pos:** P **Ht:** 6'3" **Wt:** 210 **Born:** 2/22/73 **Age:** 24

			HOW MUCH HE PITCHED						WHAT HE GAVE UP												THE RESULTS					
Year	Team	Lg Org	G	GS	CG	GF	IP	BFP	H	R	ER	HR	SH	SF	HB	TBB	IBB	SO	WP	Bk	W	L	Pct.	ShO	Sv	ERA
1994	Pittsfield	A- NYN	21	1	0	9	46.1	187	34	18	15	1	1	2	1	13	0	40	2	1	4	2	.667	0	4	2.91
1995	Columbia	A NYN	8	8	0	0	51.1	224	43	24	15	2	1	2	1	19	0	53	5	1	3	3	.500	0	0	2.63
	St. Lucie	A+ NYN	27	26	3	0	173	732	165	68	49	7	5	2	8	49	2	135	12	2	9	10	.474	1	0	2.55
1996	Norfolk	AAA NYN	1	1	0	0	5.2	23	6	3	3	1	0	0	0	1	0	1	0	0	1	0	1.000	0	0	4.76
	Binghamton	AA NYN	11	8	1	1	48	209	57	36	32	5	6	3	1	14	0	25	2	0	2	4	.333	0	0	6.00
	Columbia	A NYN	1	1	1	0	7	31	6	1	1	0	0	0	0	4	0	4	0	0	1	0	1.000	0	0	1.29
	St. Lucie	A+ NYN	9	9	1	0	48	210	60	28	25	4	0	1	3	10	0	36	1	0	4	3	.571	0	0	4.69
3 Min. YEARS			78	54	6	10	379.1	1616	371	178	140	20	13	10	14	110	2	294	22	4	24	22	.522	1	4	3.32

Chris Latham

Bats: Both **Throws:** Right **Pos:** OF **Ht:** 6'0" **Wt:** 188 **Born:** 5/26/73 **Age:** 24

				BATTING															BASERUNNING				PERCENTAGES		
Year	Team	Lg	Org	G	AB	H	2B	3B	HR	TB	R	RBI	TBB	IBB	SO	HBP	SH	SF	SB	CS	SB%	GDP	Avg	OBP	SLG
1991	Dodgers	R	LA	43	109	26	2	1	0	30	17	11	16	0	45	0	0	1	14	4	.78	0	.239	.333	.275
1992	Great Falls	R+	LA	17	37	12	2	0	0	14	8	3	8	0	8	0	0	0	1	1	.50	0	.324	.444	.378
	Dodgers	R	LA	14	48	11	2	0	0	13	4	2	5	1	17	0	1	1	2	3	.40	0	.229	.296	.271
1993	Yakima	A-	LA	54	192	50	2	6	4	76	46	17	39	0	53	1	0	0	24	9	.73	2	.260	.388	.396
	Bakersfield	A+	LA	6	27	5	1	0	0	6	1	3	4	0	5	0	0	0	2	2	.50	2	.185	.290	.222
1994	Bakersfield	A+	LA	52	191	41	5	2	2	56	29	15	28	1	49	2	4	0	28	7	.80	2	.215	.321	.293
	Yakima	A-	LA	71	288	98	19	8	5	148	69	32	55	7	66	2	3	0	33	20	.62	1	.340	.449	.514
1995	Vero Beach	A+	LA	71	259	74	13	4	6	113	53	39	56	4	54	2	2	3	42	11	.79	2	.286	.413	.436
	San Antonio	AA	LA	58	214	64	14	5	9	115	38	37	33	0	59	2	1	1	11	11	.50	2	.299	.396	.537
	Albuquerque	AAA	LA	5	18	3	0	1	0	5	2	3	1	0	4	0	0	1	1	0	1.00	0	.167	.200	.278
1996	Salt Lake	AAA	Min	115	376	103	16	6	9	158	59	50	36	1	91	2	4	3	26	9	.74	5	.274	.338	.420
6	Min. YEARS			506	1759	487	76	33	35	734	326	212	281	14	451	11	15	10	184	77	.70	16	.277	.378	.417

Sean Lawrence

Pitches: Left **Bats:** Left **Pos:** P **Ht:** 6'4" **Wt:** 215 **Born:** 9/2/70 **Age:** 26

				HOW MUCH HE PITCHED						WHAT HE GAVE UP												THE RESULTS					
Year	Team	Lg	Org	G	GS	CG	GF	IP	BFP	H	R	ER	HR	SH	SF	HB	TBB	IBB	SO	WP	Bk	W	L	Pct.	ShO	Sv	ERA
1992	Welland	A-	Pit	15	15	0	0	74	330	75	55	43	10	2	2	2	34	1	71	6	3	3	6	.333	0	0	5.23
1993	Augusta	A	Pit	22	22	0	0	121	516	108	59	42	9	7	4	4	50	1	96	6	0	6	8	.429	0	0	3.12
	Salem	A+	Pit	4	4	0	0	15	77	25	19	17	1	2	1	0	9	0	14	2	0	1	3	.250	0	0	10.20
1994	Salem	A+	Pit	12	12	0	0	72	312	76	38	21	8	1	2	3	18	0	66	2	0	4	2	.667	0	0	2.63
1995	Carolina	AA	Pit	12	3	0	3	21.1	96	27	13	13	2	0	0	1	8	1	19	0	0	0	2	.000	0	0	5.48
	Lynchburg	A+	Pit	32	22	0	3	132.1	561	142	69	65	18	3	3	2	33	1	101	3	0	5	10	.333	0	0	4.42
1996	Carolina	AA	Pit	37	9	0	13	82	362	80	40	36	11	2	1	3	36	1	81	0	1	3	5	.375	0	2	3.95
5	Min. YEARS			134	87	0	19	517.2	2254	533	293	237	59	17	13	15	188	5	448	19	4	22	36	.379	0	2	4.12

Jalal Leach

Bats: Left **Throws:** Left **Pos:** OF **Ht:** 6'2" **Wt:** 200 **Born:** 3/14/69 **Age:** 28

				BATTING															BASERUNNING				PERCENTAGES		
Year	Team	Lg	Org	G	AB	H	2B	3B	HR	TB	R	RBI	TBB	IBB	SO	HBP	SH	SF	SB	CS	SB%	GDP	Avg	OBP	SLG
1990	Oneonta	A-	NYA	69	257	74	7	1	2	89	41	18	37	3	52	0	4	0	33	13	.72	1	.288	.378	.346
1991	Ft. Laud	A+	NYA	122	468	119	13	9	2	156	48	42	44	3	122	0	3	3	28	12	.70	5	.254	.317	.333
1992	Pr. William	A+	NYA	128	462	122	22	7	5	173	61	65	47	2	114	0	3	5	18	9	.67	8	.264	.329	.374
1993	Albany-Colo	AA	NYA	125	457	129	19	9	14	208	64	79	47	3	113	1	0	4	16	12	.57	5	.282	.348	.455
1994	Columbus	AAA	NYA	132	444	116	18	9	6	170	56	56	39	3	106	1	3	4	14	12	.54	8	.261	.320	.383
1995	Columbus	AAA	NYA	88	272	66	12	5	6	106	37	31	22	1	60	2	1	4	11	4	.73	5	.243	.300	.390
1996	Harrisburg	AA	Mon	83	268	88	22	3	6	134	38	48	21	4	55	0	2	4	3	7	.30	6	.328	.372	.500
	Ottawa	AAA	Mon	37	101	32	4	0	3	45	12	9	8	1	17	0	0	0	0	0	.00	1	.317	.367	.446
7	Min. YEARS			784	2729	746	117	43	44	1081	357	348	265	20	639	4	16	24	123	69	.64	39	.273	.336	.396

Bob Leary

Bats: Left **Throws:** Left **Pos:** 1B **Ht:** 6'3" **Wt:** 195 **Born:** 7/9/71 **Age:** 25

				BATTING															BASERUNNING				PERCENTAGES		
Year	Team	Lg	Org	G	AB	H	2B	3B	HR	TB	R	RBI	TBB	IBB	SO	HBP	SH	SF	SB	CS	SB%	GDP	Avg	OBP	SLG
1991	Athletics	R	Oak	59	213	69	11	1	2	88	42	44	51	1	21	3	1	4	2	2	.50	4	.324	.454	.413
1992	Madison	A	Oak	116	365	93	18	3	4	129	47	48	66	4	64	4	3	3	3	3	.50	10	.255	.372	.353
1993	Madison	A	Oak	8	28	4	0	0	0	4	2	0	2	0	10	0	0	0	0	0	.00	0	.143	.200	.143
1994	Sioux City	IND	—	77	289	89	24	3	12	155	42	61	43	4	61	1	2	5	10	4	.71	3	.308	.393	.536
1995	Lynchburg	A+	Pit	63	208	54	9	0	8	87	42	31	44	4	43	5	0	2	9	4	.69	3	.260	.398	.418
	Carolina	AA	Pit	67	243	74	14	3	6	112	38	42	40	2	38	3	0	3	3	3	.50	7	.305	.405	.461
1996	Sioux City	IND	—	42	160	49	12	0	6	79	29	23	28	1	19	1	1	0	2	3	.40	4	.306	.413	.494
	Carolina	AA	Pit	32	109	20	4	1	4	38	13	12	22	3	31	2	0	0	2	2	.50	2	.183	.331	.349
	St. Paul	IND	—	42	147	42	6	0	9	75	35	30	43	2	18	4	0	4	0	2	.00	5	.286	.449	.510
6	Min. YEARS			506	1762	494	98	11	51	767	290	291	339	21	305	23	7	21	31	23	.57	38	.280	.399	.435

Ricky Ledee

Bats: Left **Throws:** Left **Pos:** OF **Ht:** 6'2" **Wt:** 160 **Born:** 11/22/73 **Age:** 23

				BATTING															BASERUNNING				PERCENTAGES		
Year	Team	Lg	Org	G	AB	H	2B	3B	HR	TB	R	RBI	TBB	IBB	SO	HBP	SH	SF	SB	CS	SB%	GDP	Avg	OBP	SLG
1990	Yankees	R	NYA	19	37	4	2	0	0	6	5	1	6	0	18	0	0	0	2	0	1.00	1	.108	.233	.162
1991	Yankees	R	NYA	47	165	44	6	2	0	54	22	18	22	0	41	0	0	1	3	1	.75	3	.267	.351	.327
1992	Yankees	R	NYA	52	179	41	9	2	2	60	25	23	24	1	47	1	0	1	1	4	.20	2	.229	.322	.335
1993	Oneonta	A-	NYA	52	192	49	7	6	8	92	32	20	25	0	46	2	1	0	7	5	.58	2	.255	.347	.479
1994	Greensboro	A	NYA	134	484	121	23	9	22	228	87	71	91	4	126	4	3	6	10	11	.48	7	.250	.369	.471
1995	Greensboro	A	NYA	89	335	90	16	6	14	160	65	49	51	6	66	2	0	1	10	4	.71	3	.269	.368	.478
1996	Norwich	AA	NYA	39	137	50	11	1	8	87	27	37	16	0	25	1	1	5	2	2	.50	4	.365	.421	.635
	Columbus	AAA	NYA	96	358	101	22	6	21	198	79	64	44	2	95	1	0	2	6	3	.67	4	.282	.360	.553
7	Min. YEARS			528	1887	500	96	32	75	885	342	283	279	13	464	11	5	16	41	30	.58	26	.265	.360	.469

Aaron Ledesma

Bats: Right **Throws:** Right **Pos:** SS **Ht:** 6' 2" **Wt:** 200 **Born:** 6/3/71 **Age:** 26

		BATTING															BASERUNNING				PERCENTAGES		
Year Team	Lg Org	G	AB	H	2B	3B	HR	TB	R	RBI	TBB	IBB	SO	HBP	SH	SF	SB	CS	SB%	GDP	Avg	OBP	SLG
1990 Kingsport	R+ NYN	66	243	81	11	1	5	109	50	38	30	2	28	8	0	4	23	6	.79	4	.333	.418	.449
1991 Columbia	A NYN	33	115	39	8	0	1	50	19	14	8	0	16	4	3	3	3	2	.60	1	.339	.392	.435
1992 St. Lucie	A+ NYN	134	456	120	17	2	2	147	51	50	46	1	66	11	2	7	20	12	.63	13	.263	.340	.322
1993 Binghamton	AA NYN	66	206	55	12	0	5	82	23	22	14	0	43	2	4	1	2	1	.67	6	.267	.318	.398
1994 Norfolk	AAA NYN	119	431	118	20	1	3	149	49	56	28	0	41	6	9	6	18	8	.69	16	.274	.323	.346
1995 Norfolk	AAA NYN	56	201	60	12	1	0	74	26	28	10	1	22	1	1	0	6	3	.67	5	.299	.335	.368
1996 Vancouver	AAA Cal	109	440	134	27	4	1	172	60	51	32	2	59	7	2	1	2	3	.40	18	.305	.360	.391
1995 New York	NL	21	33	8	0	0	0	8	4	3	6	1	7	0	0	0	0	0	.00	2	.242	.359	.242
7 Min. YEARS		583	2092	607	107	9	17	783	278	259	168	6	275	39	21	22	74	35	.68	63	.290	.351	.374

Derek Lee

Bats: Left **Throws:** Right **Pos:** OF **Ht:** 6' 1" **Wt:** 200 **Born:** 7/28/66 **Age:** 30

		BATTING															BASERUNNING				PERCENTAGES		
Year Team	Lg Org	G	AB	H	2B	3B	HR	TB	R	RBI	TBB	IBB	SO	HBP	SH	SF	SB	CS	SB%	GDP	Avg	OBP	SLG
1988 Utica	A- ChA	76	252	86	7	5	2	109	51	47	50	5	48	3	3	4	54	15	.78	2	.341	.450	.433
1989 South Bend	A ChA	125	448	128	24	7	11	199	89	48	87	4	83	9	4	2	45	26	.63	5	.286	.410	.444
1990 Birmingham	AA ChA	126	411	105	21	3	7	153	68	75	71	5	93	6	3	5	14	10	.58	8	.255	.369	.372
1991 Birmingham	AA ChA	45	154	50	10	2	5	79	36	16	46	5	23	6	0	1	9	7	.56	1	.325	.493	.513
Vancouver	AAA ChA	87	319	94	28	5	6	150	54	44	35	2	62	2	3	1	4	2	.67	1	.295	.367	.470
1992 Vancouver	AAA ChA	115	381	104	20	6	7	157	58	50	56	7	65	6	4	2	17	7	.71	11	.273	.373	.412
1993 Portland	AAA Min	106	381	120	30	7	10	194	79	80	60	2	51	4	4	4	16	5	.76	10	.315	.410	.509
1994 Ottawa	AAA Mon	131	463	139	35	9	13	231	62	75	66	9	81	2	0	6	12	6	.67	7	.300	.385	.499
1995 Norfolk	AAA NYN	112	351	89	17	0	18	160	56	60	48	4	62	7	2	5	11	6	.65	11	.254	.350	.456
1996 Edmonton	AAA Oak	9	25	5	1	0	0	6	3	1	6	1	2	0	0	0	0	1	.00	2	.200	.355	.240
Okla. City	AAA Tex	120	409	123	32	2	13	198	59	62	50	7	69	2	0	6	6	9	.40	13	.301	.375	.484
1993 Minnesota	AL	15	33	5	1	0	0	6	3	4	1	0	4	0	0	0	0	0	.00	0	.152	.176	.182
9 Min. YEARS		1052	3594	1043	225	46	92	1636	615	558	575	51	639	47	23	36	188	94	.67	71	.290	.392	.455

Derrek Lee

Bats: Right **Throws:** Right **Pos:** 1B **Ht:** 6'5" **Wt:** 220 **Born:** 9/6/75 **Age:** 21

		BATTING															BASERUNNING				PERCENTAGES		
Year Team	Lg Org	G	AB	H	2B	3B	HR	TB	R	RBI	TBB	IBB	SO	HBP	SH	SF	SB	CS	SB%	GDP	Avg	OBP	SLG
1993 Padres	R SD	15	52	17	1	1	2	26	11	5	6	1	7	0	0	0	4	0	1.00	1	.327	.397	.500
Rancho Cuca	A+ SD	20	73	20	5	1	1	30	13	10	10	0	20	1	0	0	0	2	.00	0	.274	.369	.411
1994 Rancho Cuca	A+ SD	126	442	118	19	2	8	165	66	53	42	2	95	7	0	6	18	14	.56	11	.267	.336	.373
1995 Rancho Cuca	A+ SD	128	502	151	25	2	23	249	82	95	49	2	130	7	0	7	14	7	.67	8	.301	.366	.496
Memphis	AA SD	2	9	1	0	0	0	1	0	1	0	0	2	0	0	0	0	0	.00	0	.111	.111	.111
1996 Memphis	AA SD	134	500	140	39	2	34	285	98	104	65	3	170	2	0	8	13	6	.68	8	.280	.360	.570
4 Min. YEARS		425	1578	447	89	8	68	756	270	268	172	8	424	17	0	21	49	29	.63	28	.283	.356	.479

Mark Lee

Pitches: Left **Bats:** Left **Pos:** P **Ht:** 6' 3" **Wt:** 200 **Born:** 7/20/64 **Age:** 32

		HOW MUCH HE PITCHED						WHAT HE GAVE UP												THE RESULTS					
Year Team	Lg Org	G	GS	CG	GF	IP	BFP	H	R	ER	HR	SH	SF	HB	TBB	IBB	SO	WP	Bk	W	L	Pct.	ShO	Sv	ERA
1985 Bristol	R+ Det	15	1	0	11	33	127	18	5	4	1	1	0	0	12	0	40	2	0	3	0	1.000	0	5	1.09
1986 Lakeland	A+ Det	41	0	0	31	62.2	281	73	44	36	4	4	1	2	21	8	39	5	0	2	5	.286	0	10	5.17
1987 Glens Falls	AA Det	7	0	0	4	8.1	38	13	9	8	1	1	1	0	1	0	3	0	0	0	0	.000	0	0	8.64
Lakeland	A+ Det	30	0	0	15	53	223	48	17	15	1	0	1	1	18	3	42	1	0	3	2	.600	0	4	2.55
1988 Lakeland	A+ Det	10	0	0	2	19	73	16	7	3	0	2	3	0	4	1	15	0	1	1	0	1.000	0	1	1.42
Glens Falls	AA Det	14	0	0	6	26	106	27	10	7	0	2	1	0	4	2	25	0	0	3	0	1.000	0	1	2.42
Toledo	AAA Det	22	0	0	6	19.1	79	18	7	6	0	0	2	0	7	2	13	0	0	0	1	.000	0	0	2.79
1989 Memphis	AA KC	25	24	0	1	122.2	558	149	84	71	13	4	4	3	44	2	79	6	8	5	11	.313	0	0	5.21
1990 Stockton	A+ Mil	5	0	0	2	7.2	32	5	2	2	0	1	0	0	3	0	7	0	0	1	0	1.000	0	1	2.35
Denver	AAA Mil	20	0	0	6	28	110	25	7	7	2	1	0	0	6	1	35	1	1	3	1	.750	0	4	2.25
1992 Denver	AAA Mil	48	0	0	14	68.2	309	78	45	32	5	3	0	0	26	4	57	1	1	2	4	.333	0	1	4.19
1993 Okla. City	AAA Tex	52	1	0	21	101.2	454	112	61	49	4	3	7	0	43	5	65	4	1	5	3	.625	0	4	4.34
1994 Iowa	AAA ChN	54	0	0	29	61.1	265	69	27	23	3	0	2	1	21	8	42	4	0	1	3	.250	0	10	3.38
1995 Rochester	AAA Bal	25	0	0	8	28.2	108	18	6	5	0	1	0	0	5	0	35	1	0	4	2	.667	0	3	1.57
1996 Norfolk	AAA NYN	33	0	0	9	32	136	39	11	9	3	3	2	1	6	1	35	2	0	2	1	.667	0	1	2.53
Richmond	AAA Atl	20	0	0	9	35	141	30	12	11	3	0	1	1	11	1	36	0	0	2	4	.333	0	0	2.83
1988 Kansas City	AL	4	0	0	4	5	21	6	2	2	0	0	0	0	1	0	0	0	0	0	0	.000	0	0	3.60
1990 Milwaukee	AL	11	0	0	1	21.1	85	20	5	5	1	1	2	0	4	0	14	0	0	1	0	1.000	0	0	2.11
1991 Milwaukee	AL	62	0	0	9	67.2	291	72	33	29	10	4	1	1	31	7	43	0	0	2	5	.286	0	1	3.86
1995 Baltimore	AL	39	0	0	7	33.1	148	31	18	18	5	1	2	1	18	3	27	0	0	2	0	1.000	0	1	4.86
11 Min. YEARS		421	26	0	174	707	3040	738	354	288	40	26	25	9	232	38	568	27	12	37	37	.500	0	45	3.67
4 Maj. YEARS		116	0	0	21	127.1	545	129	58	54	16	6	5	2	54	10	84	0	0	5	5	.500	0	2	3.82

Kevin Legault

Pitches: Right **Bats:** Right **Pos:** P **Ht:** 6'1" **Wt:** 200 **Born:** 3/5/71 **Age:** 26

HOW MUCH HE PITCHED										WHAT HE GAVE UP												THE RESULTS					
Year	Team	Lg	Org	G	GS	CG	GF	IP	BFP	H	R	ER	HR	SH	SF	HB	TBB	IBB	SO	WP	Bk	W	L	Pct.	ShO	Sv	ERA
1992	Elizabethtn	R+	Min	17	2	0	6	55.2	221	38	20	13	0	4	2	2	11	0	53	1	0	7	0	1.000	0	2	2.10
1993	Fort Wayne	A	Min	12	0	0	3	26.2	120	28	13	10	1	0	0	2	12	1	28	4	3	1	1	.500	0	2	3.38
	Fort Myers	A+	Min	18	18	3	0	110.1	493	142	80	70	4	1	4	4	32	1	60	4	0	3	9	.250	0	0	5.71
1994	Fort Myers	A+	Min	26	26	1	0	154.2	693	196	87	73	8	6	4	5	52	5	68	9	0	7	11	.389	0	0	4.25
1995	New Britain	AA	Min	47	1	0	17	87	367	79	31	31	3	6	5	4	28	4	52	5	0	6	1	.857	0	3	3.21
1996	Salt Lake	AAA	Min	50	0	0	13	80.2	353	100	51	48	10	3	3	0	24	2	57	4	1	5	4	.556	0	0	5.36
5 Min. YEARS				170	47	4	39	515	2247	583	282	245	26	20	18	17	159	13	318	27	4	29	26	.527	0	7	4.28

Tim Leiper

Bats: Left **Throws:** Right **Pos:** 2B **Ht:** 5'11" **Wt:** 175 **Born:** 7/19/66 **Age:** 30

BATTING																			BASERUNNING				PERCENTAGES		
Year	Team	Lg	Org	G	AB	H	2B	3B	HR	TB	R	RBI	TBB	IBB	SO	HBP	SH	SF	SB	CS	SB%	GDP	Avg	OBP	SLG
1985	Gastonia	A	Det	31	106	30	4	2	1	41	16	14	9	0	17	0	2	1	4	3	.57	1	.283	.336	.387
	Lakeland	A+	Det	25	77	17	2	1	0	21	13	5	10	0	11	0	0	1	1	0	1.00	2	.221	.307	.273
	Bristol	R+	Det	61	211	65	16	0	3	90	37	47	15	1	18	1	0	2	7	4	.64	3	.308	.354	.427
1986	Lakeland	A+	Det	107	407	108	17	4	3	142	46	49	33	5	21	1	1	5	4	8	.33	23	.265	.318	.349
1987	Glens Falls	AA	Det	46	176	56	12	0	4	80	31	26	12	2	12	0	1	4	4	1	.80	5	.318	.354	.455
1988	Toledo	AAA	Det	22	48	8	1	0	0	9	6	4	6	0	7	0	1	0	0	1	.00	2	.167	.259	.188
	Glens Falls	AA	Det	91	329	95	23	0	2	124	63	36	37	1	33	3	7	5	10	3	.77	10	.289	.361	.377
1989	London	AA	Det	27	101	37	6	0	1	46	13	9	13	1	10	1	0	0	0	2	.00	0	.366	.443	.455
	Toledo	AAA	Det	101	376	90	13	2	3	116	43	30	28	0	33	3	7	1	3	6	.33	1	.239	.297	.309
1990	London	AA	Det	48	166	50	7	0	2	63	30	20	26	1	14	1	3	2	8	2	.80	3	.301	.395	.380
	Toledo	AAA	Det	74	249	73	14	1	2	95	26	34	27	1	21	0	1	2	2	1	.67	2	.293	.360	.382
1991	Tidewater	AAA	NYN	93	282	71	11	1	2	90	33	30	35	5	32	1	4	4	0	3	.00	12	.252	.332	.319
1992	Memphis	AA	KC	73	246	63	10	2	2	83	37	21	31	0	29	1	4	4	4	1	.80	6	.256	.337	.337
1993	Carolina	AA	Pit	44	132	34	4	0	1	41	11	11	10	0	6	2	1	0	0	1	.00	2	.258	.319	.311
	Buffalo	AAA	Pit	75	208	68	15	5	2	99	21	33	11	2	18	2	0	6	1	3	.25	3	.327	.357	.476
1994	Buffalo	AAA	Pit	114	349	92	20	2	4	128	36	39	21	5	39	1	7	1	3	3	.50	5	.264	.306	.367
1995	Toledo	AAA	Det	18	66	14	1	0	0	15	3	6	4	0	8	0	0	1	0	0	.00	3	.212	.254	.227
	Jacksonvlle	AA	Det	110	375	97	19	1	8	142	60	46	48	6	30	3	3	6	3	3	.50	11	.259	.343	.379
1996	Binghamton	AA	NYN	6	6	1	0	0	0	1	0	0	1	0	0	0	0	0	0	0	.00	0	.167	.286	.167
12 Min. YEARS				1166	3910	1069	195	21	40	1426	525	460	377	30	359	20	42	45	54	45	.55	94	.273	.337	.365

Chris Lemp

Pitches: Right **Bats:** Right **Pos:** P **Ht:** 6'0" **Wt:** 175 **Born:** 7/23/71 **Age:** 25

HOW MUCH HE PITCHED										WHAT HE GAVE UP												THE RESULTS					
Year	Team	Lg	Org	G	GS	CG	GF	IP	BFP	H	R	ER	HR	SH	SF	HB	TBB	IBB	SO	WP	Bk	W	L	Pct.	ShO	Sv	ERA
1991	Bluefield	R+	Bal	25	0	0	23	39.1	161	22	14	9	0	0	4	2	24	0	43	6	1	0	1	.000	0	12	2.06
1992	Kane County	A	Bal	58	1	0	46	65	275	41	27	25	6	0	2	0	49	5	74	10	0	2	3	.400	0	26	3.46
1993	Frederick	A+	Bal	52	0	0	33	60.2	278	51	32	24	5	3	1	4	35	1	51	5	2	4	1	.800	0	8	3.56
1994	Frederick	A+	Bal	52	0	0	47	66.1	284	53	28	20	6	6	2	4	29	1	60	6	0	5	5	.500	0	21	2.71
1995	Rochester	AAA	Bal	3	0	0	1	4	21	7	5	5	1	0	1	0	3	0	4	1	0	0	1	.000	0	0	11.25
	Bowie	AA	Bal	18	0	0	16	20	94	28	13	12	0	1	2	2	7	3	14	3	0	2	4	.333	0	4	5.40
	Frederick	A+	Bal	62	0	0	53	69.1	309	79	34	29	5	4	5	2	27	5	68	12	0	4	8	.333	0	23	3.76
1996	Bowie	AA	Bal	27	1	0	12	47.2	219	53	27	25	4	1	6	4	24	0	35	3	3	1	3	.250	0	1	4.72
	Winnipeg	IND	—	18	0	0	9	27.2	119	23	14	13	5	1	0	0	12	1	34	4	1	0	3	.000	0	1	4.23
6 Min. YEARS				315	2	0	240	400	1760	357	194	162	32	16	23	18	210	16	383	50	7	18	29	.383	0	96	3.65

Mark Leonard

Bats: Left **Throws:** Right **Pos:** DH-OF **Ht:** 6' 1" **Wt:** 195 **Born:** 8/14/64 **Age:** 32

BATTING																			BASERUNNING				PERCENTAGES		
Year	Team	Lg	Org	G	AB	H	2B	3B	HR	TB	R	RBI	TBB	IBB	SO	HBP	SH	SF	SB	CS	SB%	GDP	Avg	OBP	SLG
1986	Everett	A-	SF	2	8	1	0	0	0	1	0	2	2	0	2	0	0	1	0	0	.00	0	.125	.273	.125
	Tri-City	A-	SF	36	120	32	6	0	4	50	21	15	25	0	19	1	0	0	4	2	.67	7	.267	.397	.417
1987	Clinton	A	SF	128	413	132	31	2	15	212	57	80	71	3	61	5	0	3	5	8	.38	7	.320	.423	.513
1988	San Jose	A+	SF	142	510	176	50	6	15	283	102	118	118	13	82	5	0	11	11	6	.65	10	.345	.464	.555
1989	Shreveport	AA	SF	63	219	68	15	3	10	119	29	52	33	8	40	3	0	3	1	5	.17	7	.311	.403	.543
	Phoenix	AAA	SF	27	78	21	4	0	0	25	7	6	9	1	15	0	0	1	1	1	.50	3	.269	.341	.321
1990	Phoenix	AAA	SF	109	390	130	22	2	19	213	76	82	76	1	81	4	0	4	6	3	.67	7	.333	.443	.546
1991	Phoenix	AAA	SF	41	146	37	7	0	8	68	27	25	21	1	29	0	0	2	1	0	1.00	5	.253	.343	.466
1992	Phoenix	AAA	SF	39	139	47	4	1	5	68	17	25	21	1	29	3	0	2	1	2	.33	1	.338	.430	.489
1993	Rochester	AAA	Bal	97	330	91	23	1	17	167	57	58	60	4	81	10	0	6	0	1	.00	4	.276	.397	.506
1994	Phoenix	AAA	SF	89	314	93	19	2	11	149	51	49	50	2	53	0	0	3	2	2	.50	13	.296	.390	.475
1995	Phoenix	AAA	SF	112	392	116	25	3	14	189	73	79	81	8	63	0	1	10	3	2	.60	19	.296	.408	.482
1996	Salt Lake	AAA	Min	59	192	48	6	2	5	73	25	27	41	4	39	2	0	3	0	2	.00	6	.250	.382	.380
1990	San Francisco	NL		11	17	3	1	0	1	7	3	2	3	0	8	0	0	0	0	0	.00	0	.176	.300	.412
1991	San Francisco	NL		64	129	31	7	1	2	46	14	14	12	1	25	1	1	2	0	1	.00	3	.240	.306	.357
1992	San Francisco	NL		55	128	30	7	0	4	49	13	16	16	0	31	3	0	1	0	1	.00	3	.234	.331	.383
1993	Baltimore	AL		10	15	1	1	0	0	2	1	3	3	0	7	0	0	3	0	0	.00	0	.067	.190	.133
1994	San Francisco	NL		14	11	4	1	1	0	7	2	2	3	0	2	0	0	0	0	0	.00	0	.364	.500	.636
1995	San Francisco	NL		14	21	4	1	0	1	8	4	4	5	1	2	0	0	0	0	0	.00	0	.190	.346	.381
11 Min. YEARS				944	3251	992	212	22	123	1617	542	618	608	46	594	33	1	49	35	34	.51	89	.305	.414	.497

Year Team	Lg Org	BATTING															BASERUNNING				PERCENTAGES		
		G	AB	H	2B	3B	HR	TB	R	RBI	TBB	IBB	SO	HBP	SH	SF	SB	CS	SB%	GDP	Avg	OBP	SLG
6 Maj. YEARS		168	321	73	18	2	8	119	37	41	42	2	75	4	1	6	0	2	.00	6	.227	.319	.371

John Leroy

Pitches: Right **Bats:** Right **Pos:** P **Ht:** 6'3" **Wt:** 175 **Born:** 4/19/75 **Age:** 22

Year Team	Lg Org	HOW MUCH HE PITCHED						WHAT HE GAVE UP												THE RESULTS					
		G	GS	CG	GF	IP	BFP	H	R	ER	HR	SH	SF	HB	TBB	IBB	SO	WP	Bk	W	L	Pct.	ShO	Sv	ERA
1993 Braves	R Atl	10	2	0	4	26.1	107	21	9	6	1	1	1	0	8	1	32	2	0	2	2	.500	0	1	2.05
1994 Macon	A Atl	10	9	0	0	40.1	173	36	21	20	4	2	1	0	20	0	44	1	5	3	3	.500	0	0	4.46
1995 Durham	A+ Atl	24	22	1	0	125.2	545	128	82	76	17	2	5	5	57	1	77	5	1	6	9	.400	0	0	5.44
1996 Durham	A+ Atl	19	19	0	0	110.2	463	91	47	43	6	4	5	2	52	0	94	10	2	7	4	.636	0	0	3.50
Greenville	AA Atl	8	8	0	0	45.1	193	43	18	15	5	2	2	2	18	1	38	4	1	1	1	.500	0	0	2.98
4 Min. YEARS		71	60	1	4	348.1	1481	319	177	160	33	11	14	9	155	3	285	22	9	19	19	.500	0	1	4.13

Dana Levangie

Bats: Right **Throws:** Right **Pos:** C **Ht:** 5'10" **Wt:** 185 **Born:** 8/11/69 **Age:** 27

Year Team	Lg Org	BATTING															BASERUNNING				PERCENTAGES		
		G	AB	H	2B	3B	HR	TB	R	RBI	TBB	IBB	SO	HBP	SH	SF	SB	CS	SB%	GDP	Avg	OBP	SLG
1991 Elmira	A- Bos	35	94	14	3	0	0	17	6	4	10	1	18	0	0	0	0	1	.00	1	.149	.231	.181
1992 Winter Havn	A+ Bos	76	245	47	5	0	1	55	21	22	20	0	49	2	1	3	1	2	.33	6	.192	.256	.224
1993 Ft. Laud	A+ Bos	80	250	47	5	0	0	52	17	11	26	0	46	0	2	0	0	2	.00	5	.188	.264	.208
1994 Lynchburg	A+ Bos	79	239	56	8	2	3	77	19	21	25	2	36	3	6	0	1	2	.33	5	.234	.315	.322
New Britain	AA Bos	8	21	3	1	0	1	7	2	5	1	0	6	1	0	0	0	0	.00	0	.143	.217	.333
1995 Pawtucket	AAA Bos	6	17	4	0	0	0	4	1	0	2	0	3	0	1	0	0	0	.00	0	.235	.316	.235
Trenton	AA Bos	42	129	23	3	1	0	28	10	7	11	0	30	1	0	1	1	3	.25	3	.178	.246	.217
1996 Trenton	AA Bos	23	55	12	3	0	2	21	5	7	12	0	11	0	2	0	2	2	.50	0	.218	.358	.382
Pawtucket	AAA Bos	2	4	1	0	0	0	1	1	1	0	0	1	0	1	1	0	0	.00	0	.250	.200	.250
6 Min. YEARS		351	1054	207	28	3	7	262	82	78	107	3	200	7	13	5	5	12	.29	20	.196	.274	.249

Anthony Lewis

Bats: Left **Throws:** Left **Pos:** DH **Ht:** 5'11" **Wt:** 185 **Born:** 2/2/71 **Age:** 26

Year Team	Lg Org	BATTING															BASERUNNING				PERCENTAGES		
		G	AB	H	2B	3B	HR	TB	R	RBI	TBB	IBB	SO	HBP	SH	SF	SB	CS	SB%	GDP	Avg	OBP	SLG
1989 Cardinals	R StL	51	187	46	10	0	2	62	32	27	11	1	45	0	0	4	11	3	.79	1	.246	.282	.332
1990 Savannah	A StL	128	465	118	22	4	8	172	55	49	24	6	79	1	2	1	10	13	.43	13	.254	.291	.370
1991 St. Pete	A+ StL	124	435	100	17	7	6	149	40	43	50	7	100	2	0	2	5	5	.50	7	.230	.311	.343
1992 St. Pete	A+ StL	128	454	101	18	2	15	168	50	55	46	6	105	5	1	4	2	4	.33	7	.222	.299	.370
1993 Arkansas	AA StL	112	326	86	28	2	13	157	48	50	25	3	98	0	1	3	3	4	.43	5	.264	.314	.482
1994 Arkansas	AA StL	88	335	85	18	1	17	156	58	50	27	0	69	0	0	2	2	1	.67	9	.254	.308	.466
Louisville	AAA StL	21	74	9	0	1	0	11	3	6	0	0	27	0	0	0	0	0	.00	1	.122	.122	.149
1995 Arkansas	AA StL	115	407	102	21	3	24	201	55	85	44	5	117	2	0	1	0	2	.00	7	.251	.326	.494
1996 New Britain	AA Min	134	458	116	15	2	24	207	58	95	47	4	99	1	0	6	6	9	.40	9	.253	.320	.452
8 Min. YEARS		901	3141	763	149	22	109	1283	399	460	274	32	739	11	4	23	39	41	.49	59	.243	.304	.408

Jim Lewis

Pitches: Right **Bats:** Right **Pos:** P **Ht:** 6'4" **Wt:** 190 **Born:** 1/31/70 **Age:** 27

Year Team	Lg Org	HOW MUCH HE PITCHED						WHAT HE GAVE UP												THE RESULTS					
		G	GS	CG	GF	IP	BFP	H	R	ER	HR	SH	SF	HB	TBB	IBB	SO	WP	Bk	W	L	Pct.	ShO	Sv	ERA
1991 Auburn	A- Hou	7	7	0	0	38.1	157	30	20	16	3	1	1	3	14	0	26	2	1	3	2	.600	0	0	3.76
1992 Tucson	AAA Hou	1	1	0	0	1	4	0	0	0	0	0	0	0	2	0	0	0	0	0	0	.000	0	0	0.00
Osceola	A+ Hou	13	13	1	0	80.1	324	54	18	10	0	6	1	2	32	0	65	5	0	5	1	.833	0	0	1.12
Jackson	AA Hou	12	12	2	0	70	291	64	33	32	4	5	6	2	30	0	43	4	0	3	5	.375	1	0	4.11
1993 Osceola	A+ Hou	4	4	0	0	7.2	34	8	4	2	1	0	0	0	2	0	3	0	0	0	0	.000	0	0	2.35
1994 Osceola	A+ Hou	16	16	0	0	63	265	64	37	22	3	1	0	1	16	0	33	3	0	1	8	.111	0	0	3.14
Jackson	AA Hou	8	8	0	0	48	191	41	13	13	2	2	1	1	10	2	39	4	0	2	1	.667	0	0	2.44
1995 Buffalo	AAA Cle	18	16	1	2	94	405	101	42	38	7	1	3	9	25	0	50	4	0	6	4	.600	0	1	3.64
1996 Buffalo	AAA Cle	21	21	2	0	120.1	530	134	79	67	10	5	5	7	49	0	71	10	1	9	6	.600	2	0	5.01
6 Min. YEARS		100	98	6	2	522.2	2201	496	246	200	30	21	17	25	180	2	330	32	2	29	27	.518	3	1	3.44

Scott Lewis

Pitches: Right **Bats:** Right **Pos:** P **Ht:** 6' 3" **Wt:** 178 **Born:** 12/5/65 **Age:** 31

Year Team	Lg Org	HOW MUCH HE PITCHED						WHAT HE GAVE UP												THE RESULTS					
		G	GS	CG	GF	IP	BFP	H	R	ER	HR	SH	SF	HB	TBB	IBB	SO	WP	Bk	W	L	Pct.	ShO	Sv	ERA
1988 Bend	A- Cal	9	9	2	0	61.2	262	63	33	24	3	1	3	5	12	0	53	3	2	5	3	.625	0	0	3.50
Quad City	A Cal	3	3	1	0	21.1	85	19	12	11	0	1	0	0	5	0	20	1	2	1	2	.333	0	0	4.64
Palm Spring	A+ Cal	2	1	0	0	8	37	12	5	5	3	0	0	0	2	0	7	0	0	0	1	.000	0	0	5.63
1989 Midland	AA Cal	25	25	4	0	162.1	729	195	121	89	15	2	3	8	55	9	104	12	9	11	12	.478	1	0	4.93
1990 Edmonton	AAA Cal	27	27	6	0	177.2	749	198	90	77	16	4	3	7	35	1	124	2	0	13	11	.542	0	0	3.90
1991 Edmonton	AAA Cal	17	17	4	0	110	489	132	71	55	7	4	4	8	26	2	87	5	3	3	9	.250	0	0	4.50
1992 Edmonton	AAA Cal	22	22	5	0	146.2	630	159	74	68	9	5	3	7	40	2	88	7	2	10	6	.625	0	0	4.17
1993 Midland	AA Cal	1	1	0	0	6	25	6	1	1	0	0	1	0	0	0	2	0	0	1	0	1.000	0	0	1.50
Vancouver	AAA Cal	24	0	0	18	39.1	156	31	7	6	1	2	1	2	9	2	38	1	0	3	1	.750	0	9	1.37
1994 Lk Elsinore	A+ Cal	2	0	0	1	4	19	5	3	2	0	0	0	0	1	0	5	0	0	0	0	.000	0	0	4.50

Year	Team	Lg	Org	G	GS	CG	GF	IP	BFP	H	R	ER	HR	SH	SF	HB	TBB	IBB	SO	WP	Bk	W	L	Pct.	ShO	Sv	ERA
				HOW MUCH HE PITCHED						WHAT HE GAVE UP												THE RESULTS					
	Vancouver	AAA	Cal	4	0	0	1	6.2	23	2	2	2	1	1	0	0	1	0	4	1	0	2	0	1.000	0	1	2.70
	Tucson	AAA	Hou	12	0	0	5	15	64	13	9	8	1	1	1	0	6	2	12	2	0	3	1	.750	0	1	4.80
1995	Tacoma	AAA	Sea	3	2	0	0	9.1	47	13	10	10	1	1	1	3	4	0	11	0	1	1	1	.500	0	0	9.64
	Pawtucket	AAA	Bos	6	2	0	1	14	66	20	12	12	3	1	1	3	4	0	12	1	1	1	1	.500	0	0	7.71
1996	Las Vegas	AAA	SD	29	21	2	2	150	645	174	96	89	22	6	4	6	36	3	109	3	0	3	9	.250	1	0	5.34
1990	California	AL		2	2	1	0	16.1	60	10	4	4	2	0	0	0	2	0	9	0	0	1	1	.500	0	0	2.20
1991	California	AL		16	11	0	0	60.1	281	81	43	42	9	2	0	2	21	0	37	3	0	3	5	.375	0	0	6.27
1992	California	AL		21	2	0	7	38.1	160	36	18	17	3	0	3	2	14	1	18	1	1	4	0	1.000	0	0	3.99
1993	California	AL		15	4	0	2	32	142	37	16	15	3	2	7	2	12	1	10	1	0	1	2	.333	0	0	4.22
1994	California	AL		20	0	0	6	31	143	46	23	21	5	3	0	2	10	2	10	0	0	0	1	.000	0	0	6.10
9 Min. YEARS				186	130	24	28	932	4026	1042	546	459	82	29	25	49	236	21	676	38	20	57	57	.500	2	11	4.43
5 Maj. YEARS				74	19	1	15	178	786	210	104	99	22	7	10	8	59	4	84	5	1	9	9	.500	0	0	5.01

T.R. Lewis

Bats: Right **Throws:** Right **Pos:** OF **Ht:** 6'0" **Wt:** 180 **Born:** 4/17/71 **Age:** 26

Year	Team	Lg	Org	G	AB	H	2B	3B	HR	TB	R	RBI	TBB	IBB	SO	HBP	SH	SF	SB	CS	SB%	GDP	Avg	OBP	SLG
				BATTING															BASERUNNING				PERCENTAGES		
1989	Bluefield	R+	Bal	40	151	50	11	1	10	93	31	32	9	0	21	0	0	2	0	2	.00	2	.331	.364	.616
1990	Wausau	A	Bal	115	404	115	24	2	8	167	60	45	46	0	64	5	1	1	10	5	.67	14	.285	.364	.413
	Frederick	A+	Bal	22	80	26	4	3	1	39	12	11	11	1	11	2	0	0	5	0	1.00	1	.325	.419	.488
1991	Frederick	A+	Bal	49	159	33	7	2	0	44	18	7	19	2	25	1	2	1	1	1	.50	4	.208	.294	.277
1992	Kane County	A	Bal	45	134	40	10	0	2	56	26	22	13	0	22	3	1	4	5	4	.56	3	.299	.364	.418
	Frederick	A+	Bal	84	313	96	27	6	7	156	58	54	36	0	46	2	0	5	5	2	.71	5	.307	.376	.498
1993	Bowie	AA	Bal	127	480	146	26	2	5	191	73	64	36	4	80	3	0	7	22	8	.73	12	.304	.352	.398
1994	Orioles	R	Bal	5	20	6	1	0	1	10	2	5	2	0	3	0	0	0	1	1	.50	0	.300	.364	.500
	Bowie	AA	Bal	17	72	18	5	0	3	32	13	8	6	0	15	0	0	1	1	0	1.00	1	.250	.304	.444
	Rochester	AAA	Bal	55	174	53	10	0	6	81	25	31	16	2	33	3	0	2	6	1	.86	1	.305	.369	.466
1995	Bowie	AA	Bal	86	309	91	19	1	5	127	57	44	40	2	43	1	1	6	12	3	.80	8	.294	.371	.411
	Rochester	AAA	Bal	22	78	23	7	0	4	42	12	19	7	0	14	1	0	1	1	1	.50	2	.295	.356	.538
1996	Pawtucket	AAA	Bos	79	274	86	23	1	14	153	55	52	34	1	50	2	1	2	2	2	.50	8	.314	.391	.558
8 Min. YEARS				746	2648	783	174	18	66	1191	442	394	275	12	427	23	6	32	71	30	.70	61	.296	.363	.450

Cory Lidle

Pitches: Right **Bats:** Right **Pos:** P **Ht:** 6'0" **Wt:** 175 **Born:** 3/22/72 **Age:** 25

Year	Team	Lg	Org	G	GS	CG	GF	IP	BFP	H	R	ER	HR	SH	SF	HB	TBB	IBB	SO	WP	Bk	W	L	Pct.	ShO	Sv	ERA
				HOW MUCH HE PITCHED						WHAT HE GAVE UP												THE RESULTS					
1991	Twins	R	Min	4	0	0	1	4.2	19	5	3	3	0	0	0	0	0	0	5	1	2	1	1	.500	0	0	5.79
1992	Elizabethtn	R+	Min	19	2	0	11	43.2	190	40	29	18	2	0	2	0	21	0	32	3	1	2	1	.667	0	6	3.71
1993	Pocatello	R+	—	17	16	3	1	106.2	463	104	59	49	6	1	4	5	54	0	91	14	1	8	4	.667	0	1	4.13
1994	Stockton	A+	Mil	25	1	0	12	42.2	200	60	32	21	2	0	0	1	13	1	38	1	0	1	2	.333	0	4	4.43
	Beloit	A	Mil	13	9	1	0	69	279	65	24	20	4	1	0	2	11	0	62	6	0	3	4	.429	1	0	2.61
1995	El Paso	AA	Mil	45	9	0	12	109.2	480	126	52	41	6	6	1	6	36	3	78	6	0	5	4	.556	0	2	3.36
1996	Binghamton	AA	NYN	27	27	6	0	190.1	779	186	78	70	13	6	2	3	49	4	141	14	3	14	10	.583	1	0	3.31
6 Min. YEARS				150	64	10	37	566.2	2410	586	277	222	33	14	9	17	184	8	447	45	7	34	26	.567	2	13	3.53

Kevin Lidle

Bats: Right **Throws:** Right **Pos:** C **Ht:** 5'11" **Wt:** 170 **Born:** 3/22/72 **Age:** 25

Year	Team	Lg	Org	G	AB	H	2B	3B	HR	TB	R	RBI	TBB	IBB	SO	HBP	SH	SF	SB	CS	SB%	GDP	Avg	OBP	SLG
				BATTING															BASERUNNING				PERCENTAGES		
1992	Niagara Fal	A-	Det	58	140	34	6	2	1	47	21	18	8	0	42	1	6	3	3	2	.60	1	.243	.283	.336
1993	Fayettevlle	A	Det	58	197	42	14	1	5	73	29	25	34	0	42	1	0	1	2	0	1.00	0	.213	.330	.371
1994	Lakeland	A+	Det	56	187	49	13	2	6	84	26	30	19	0	46	4	1	1	1	1	.50	2	.262	.341	.449
1995	Jacksonvlle	AA	Det	36	80	13	7	0	1	23	12	5	1	0	31	0	1	0	1	0	1.00	1	.163	.173	.288
	Fayettevlle	A	Det	36	113	16	4	1	4	34	15	13	16	0	44	1	3	2	0	1	.00	1	.142	.250	.301
1996	Lakeland	A+	Det	97	320	69	18	1	8	113	37	41	30	0	90	3	0	1	1	1	.50	4	.216	.288	.353
	Jacksonvlle	AA	Det	4	8	2	0	0	1	5	2	2	1	0	2	0	0	0	1	0	1.00	0	.250	.333	.625
5 Min. YEARS				345	1045	225	62	7	26	379	142	134	109	0	297	10	11	8	9	5	.64	9	.215	.294	.363

Keith Linebarger

Pitches: Right **Bats:** Right **Pos:** P **Ht:** 6'6" **Wt:** 220 **Born:** 5/11/71 **Age:** 26

Year	Team	Lg	Org	G	GS	CG	GF	IP	BFP	H	R	ER	HR	SH	SF	HB	TBB	IBB	SO	WP	Bk	W	L	Pct.	ShO	Sv	ERA
				HOW MUCH HE PITCHED						WHAT HE GAVE UP												THE RESULTS					
1992	Elizabethtn	R+	Min	11	8	1	0	52.1	227	47	25	17	3	1	1	4	26	0	41	6	0	4	2	.667	0	0	2.92
1993	Fort Wayne	A	Min	35	11	1	12	97.1	445	113	60	46	3	8	2	5	43	2	76	6	2	5	7	.417	1	0	4.25
1994	Fort Wayne	A	Min	23	0	0	10	45.1	177	24	11	10	1	2	0	2	21	0	41	4	0	3	0	1.000	0	4	1.99
	Fort Myers	A+	Min	16	0	0	10	27	138	39	22	18	0	1	2	1	14	0	21	2	0	2	2	.500	0	1	6.00
1995	Fort Myers	A+	Min	29	10	1	12	103	418	74	30	24	6	3	2	9	35	1	73	4	0	7	4	.636	1	4	2.10
1996	New Britain	AA	Min	42	4	1	19	99	428	98	53	36	9	7	4	7	32	6	69	2	0	7	5	.583	0	4	3.27
5 Min. YEARS				156	33	4	63	424	1833	395	201	151	22	22	11	28	171	9	321	24	2	28	20	.583	2	13	3.21

Joe Lis

Bats: Right **Throws:** Right **Pos:** 2B **Ht:** 5'10" **Wt:** 170 **Born:** 11/3/68 **Age:** 28

			BATTING															BASERUNNING				PERCENTAGES		
Year	Team	Lg Org	G	AB	H	2B	3B	HR	TB	R	RBI	TBB	IBB	SO	HBP	SH	SF	SB	CS	SB%	GDP	Avg	OBP	SLG
1991	St. Cathrns	A- Tor	66	206	60	12	1	5	89	36	27	41	0	19	4	9	4	3	3	.50	5	.291	.412	.432
1992	Myrtle Bch	A Tor	125	434	130	25	0	13	194	70	79	68	5	54	7	2	7	5	11	.31	11	.300	.397	.447
1993	Knoxville	AA Tor	129	448	130	29	3	8	189	66	64	42	1	58	16	2	5	6	9	.40	12	.290	.368	.422
1994	Syracuse	AAA Tor	89	319	93	20	0	11	146	53	49	25	2	39	2	4	3	3	1	.75	14	.292	.344	.458
1995	Syracuse	AAA Tor	130	485	127	33	4	17	219	68	56	46	1	54	2	0	5	6	2	.75	8	.262	.325	.452
1996	Buffalo	AAA Cle	51	146	34	8	0	6	60	21	22	18	0	19	1	1	1	0	0	.00	5	.233	.319	.411
6 Min. YEARS			590	2038	574	127	8	60	897	314	297	240	9	243	32	18	25	23	26	.47	55	.282	.362	.440

Lew List

Bats: Right **Throws:** Right **Pos:** DH-OF **Ht:** 6'3" **Wt:** 200 **Born:** 11/17/65 **Age:** 31

			BATTING															BASERUNNING				PERCENTAGES		
Year	Team	Lg Org	G	AB	H	2B	3B	HR	TB	R	RBI	TBB	IBB	SO	HBP	SH	SF	SB	CS	SB%	GDP	Avg	OBP	SLG
1987	Salem	A- Cal	13	18	0	0	0	0	0	2	0	4	0	7	0	0	0	0	0	.00	0	.000	.182	.000
1990	Mariners	R Sea	14	44	11	1	3	1	21	7	8	12	1	5	1	0	0	1	2	.33	0	.250	.421	.477
1991	Augusta	A Pit	12	33	9	3	0	1	15	7	10	7	1	10	0	0	2	1	0	1.00	0	.273	.381	.455
	Carolina	AA Pit	7	20	3	0	1	0	5	1	2	0	0	6	0	0	0	0	0	.00	2	.150	.150	.250
	Salem	A+ Pit	94	336	107	22	5	10	169	60	46	39	1	74	1	0	2	12	3	.80	6	.318	.389	.503
1992	Carolina	AA Pit	9	24	5	1	0	0	6	3	1	3	1	3	0	0	0	0	0	.00	0	.208	.296	.250
	Gastonia	A Tex	51	182	64	11	3	8	105	32	40	23	0	26	4	0	1	5	9	.36	2	.352	.433	.577
	Tulsa	AA Tex	34	130	38	7	1	1	50	17	14	13	0	30	0	0	0	1	1	.50	1	.292	.357	.385
1993	Tulsa	AA Tex	40	125	25	3	1	0	30	8	6	10	0	30	3	0	2	2	6	.25	6	.200	.271	.240
	Colo. Sprng	AAA Col	18	50	15	7	1	0	24	9	5	3	0	8	0	0	0	0	0	.00	2	.300	.340	.480
	Central Val	A+ Col	33	120	35	6	2	8	69	21	27	17	0	19	2	0	1	0	3	.00	5	.292	.386	.575
1994	New Haven	AA Col	81	271	68	13	1	8	107	45	40	32	5	69	5	1	0	1	2	.33	9	.251	.341	.395
1995	New Haven	AA Col	82	212	59	10	4	6	95	26	44	20	0	43	1	0	1	2	2	.50	4	.278	.342	.448
1996	Colo. Sprng	AAA Col	7	12	1	0	0	0	1	1	1	0	0	6	0	0	0	0	0	.00	0	.083	.083	.083
	Minot	IND —	73	301	103	20	2	24	199	64	75	17	1	47	2	0	5	10	2	.83	9	.342	.375	.661
8 Min. YEARS			568	1878	543	104	24	67	896	303	319	200	10	383	19	1	14	35	30	.54	46	.289	.361	.477

Martin Lister

Pitches: Left **Bats:** Left **Pos:** P **Ht:** 6'2" **Wt:** 210 **Born:** 6/12/72 **Age:** 25

			HOW MUCH HE PITCHED						WHAT HE GAVE UP												THE RESULTS					
Year	Team	Lg Org	G	GS	CG	GF	IP	BFP	H	R	ER	HR	SH	SF	HB	TBB	IBB	SO	WP	Bk	W	L	Pct.	ShO	Sv	ERA
1992	Billings	R+ Cin	26	2	0	3	34.1	174	36	33	30	2	0	0	3	37	1	39	11	3	3	1	.750	0	1	7.86
1993	Charlstn-WV	A Cin	51	0	0	46	52	228	38	16	12	0	3	0	2	31	0	57	6	0	1	2	.333	0	32	2.08
1994	Winston-Sal	A+ Cin	6	0	0	4	5	33	7	7	3	0	0	1	0	11	1	4	1	0	0	2	.000	0	2	5.40
	Quad City	A Hou	46	0	0	32	47	207	31	18	15	0	1	1	0	37	1	54	2	1	2	4	.333	0	13	2.87
1995	Jackson	AA Hou	15	13	1	1	69.2	299	80	35	31	2	3	2	1	24	0	27	6	0	4	3	.571	1	0	4.00
1996	Winston-Sal	A+ Cin	7	0	0	3	10	47	9	7	6	1	2	1	0	9	0	9	0	0	0	0	.000	0	0	5.40
	Chattanooga	AA Cin	19	0	0	9	20.1	94	25	13	12	2	1	1	1	11	1	10	3	0	0	1	.000	0	0	5.31
5 Min. YEARS			170	15	1	98	238.1	1082	226	129	109	7	10	6	7	160	4	200	29	4	10	13	.435	1	48	4.12

Mark Little

Bats: Right **Throws:** Right **Pos:** OF **Ht:** 6'0" **Wt:** 200 **Born:** 7/11/72 **Age:** 24

			BATTING															BASERUNNING				PERCENTAGES		
Year	Team	Lg Org	G	AB	H	2B	3B	HR	TB	R	RBI	TBB	IBB	SO	HBP	SH	SF	SB	CS	SB%	GDP	Avg	OBP	SLG
1994	Hudson Vall	A- Tex	54	208	61	15	5	3	95	33	27	22	1	38	1	0	4	14	5	.74	4	.293	.357	.457
1995	Charlotte	A+ Tex	115	438	112	31	8	9	186	75	50	51	1	108	14	2	2	20	14	.59	4	.256	.350	.425
1996	Tulsa	AA Tex	101	409	119	24	2	13	186	69	50	48	0	88	10	5	3	22	10	.69	5	.291	.377	.455
3 Min. YEARS			270	1055	292	70	15	25	467	177	127	121	2	234	25	7	9	56	29	.66	13	.277	.362	.443

Shane Livsey

Bats: Both **Throws:** Right **Pos:** 2B **Ht:** 5'11" **Wt:** 180 **Born:** 7/21/73 **Age:** 23

			BATTING															BASERUNNING				PERCENTAGES		
Year	Team	Lg Org	G	AB	H	2B	3B	HR	TB	R	RBI	TBB	IBB	SO	HBP	SH	SF	SB	CS	SB%	GDP	Avg	OBP	SLG
1991	Astros	R Hou	46	151	37	2	2	0	43	20	14	20	0	23	2	1	0	13	9	.59	2	.245	.341	.285
1992	Astros	R Hou	38	117	32	3	2	1	42	20	14	29	0	12	4	0	3	10	5	.67	2	.274	.425	.359
1993	Asheville	A Hou	124	453	119	26	1	2	153	50	60	62	0	92	9	1	6	26	15	.63	7	.263	.358	.338
1994	Osceola	A+ Hou	108	373	84	15	3	1	108	36	43	34	2	46	2	0	4	10	5	.67	7	.225	.291	.290
1995	Rockford	A ChN	57	226	64	10	1	2	82	39	27	22	3	30	2	0	0	21	7	.75	0	.283	.352	.363
1996	Daytona	A+ ChN	50	194	63	14	3	2	89	39	28	24	2	32	2	1	3	17	6	.74	1	.325	.399	.459
	Orlando	AA ChN	75	257	66	15	2	2	91	36	33	27	0	39	5	3	5	13	8	.62	9	.257	.333	.354
6 Min. YEARS			498	1771	465	85	14	10	608	240	219	218	7	274	26	6	21	110	55	.67	28	.263	.348	.343

Carlton Loewer

Pitches: Right **Bats:** Both **Pos:** P **Ht:** 6'6" **Wt:** 220 **Born:** 9/24/73 **Age:** 23

				HOW MUCH HE PITCHED						WHAT HE GAVE UP												THE RESULTS					
Year	Team	Lg	Org	G	GS	CG	GF	IP	BFP	H	R	ER	HR	SH	SF	HB	TBB	IBB	SO	WP	Bk	W	L	Pct.	ShO	Sv	ERA
1995	Reading	AA	Phi	8	8	0	0	50	212	42	17	12	3	1	0	1	31	0	35	4	0	4	1	.800	0	0	2.16
	Clearwater	A+	Phi	28	28	1	0	164.2	714	166	76	54	9	4	5	6	67	0	118	11	3	11	6	.647	0	0	2.95
1996	Reading	AA	Phi	27	27	3	0	171	753	191	115	100	24	7	3	8	57	3	119	9	1	7	10	.412	1	0	5.26
2 Min. YEARS				63	63	4	0	385.2	1679	399	208	166	36	12	8	15	155	3	272	24	4	22	17	.564	1	0	3.87

Joey Long

Pitches: Left **Bats:** Right **Pos:** P **Ht:** 6'2" **Wt:** 195 **Born:** 7/15/70 **Age:** 26

				HOW MUCH HE PITCHED						WHAT HE GAVE UP												THE RESULTS					
Year	Team	Lg	Org	G	GS	CG	GF	IP	BFP	H	R	ER	HR	SH	SF	HB	TBB	IBB	SO	WP	Bk	W	L	Pct.	ShO	Sv	ERA
1991	Spokane	A-	SD	13	11	0	0	56.2	282	78	57	44	2	1	3	2	39	0	40	8	4	1	9	.100	0	0	6.99
1993	Waterloo	A	SD	33	7	0	7	96.1	415	96	56	52	7	3	1	3	36	2	90	8	3	4	3	.571	0	0	4.86
1994	Rancho Cuca	A+	SD	46	0	0	17	52	248	69	36	27	3	6	2	1	22	1	52	8	0	2	4	.333	0	3	4.67
1995	Memphis	AA	SD	25	0	0	3	21.2	104	28	15	8	0	1	1	1	10	2	18	0	0	0	2	.000	0	0	3.32
	Las Vegas	AAA	SD	50	0	0	12	53	247	66	37	24	1	1	5	1	26	4	31	0	0	1	5	.167	0	0	4.08
1996	Memphis	AA	SD	10	0	0	1	18	79	16	4	4	0	1	0	0	11	1	14	3	0	2	0	1.000	0	0	2.00
	Las Vegas	AAA	SD	32	0	0	13	34	156	39	21	16	2	2	3	0	23	3	23	5	0	3	3	.500	0	1	4.24
5 Min. YEARS				209	18	0	53	331.2	1531	392	226	175	15	15	15	8	167	13	268	32	7	13	26	.333	0	4	4.75

Kevin Long

Bats: Left **Throws:** Left **Pos:** OF **Ht:** 5'9" **Wt:** 165 **Born:** 12/30/66 **Age:** 30

				BATTING															BASERUNNING				PERCENTAGES		
Year	Team	Lg	Org	G	AB	H	2B	3B	HR	TB	R	RBI	TBB	IBB	SO	HBP	SH	SF	SB	CS	SB%	GDP	Avg	OBP	SLG
1989	Eugene	A-	KC	69	260	81	19	1	3	111	54	45	36	6	40	1	1	6	15	3	.83	7	.312	.389	.427
1990	Baseball Cy	A+	KC	85	308	87	17	5	2	120	53	33	32	0	28	0	7	2	22	6	.79	4	.282	.348	.390
1991	Memphis	AA	KC	106	407	112	18	2	3	143	60	35	45	1	63	2	6	3	27	10	.73	8	.275	.348	.351
1992	Omaha	AAA	KC	88	312	71	16	3	1	96	28	29	29	2	41	0	2	3	9	5	.64	4	.228	.291	.308
1993	Omaha	AAA	KC	17	51	13	2	0	0	15	7	4	2	0	13	0	1	1	3	0	1.00	0	.255	.278	.294
	Memphis	AA	KC	79	301	82	14	6	1	111	47	20	37	2	56	5	2	2	7	12	.37	4	.272	.359	.369
1994	Memphis	AA	KC	10	24	5	3	0	0	8	5	1	5	0	2	0	0	0	2	0	1.00	2	.208	.345	.333
1995	Omaha	AAA	KC	22	64	16	3	0	0	19	7	0	5	0	8	0	1	0	1	2	.33	3	.250	.304	.297
	Wichita	AA	KC	67	250	73	14	1	1	92	38	26	41	2	29	2	0	0	9	6	.60	3	.292	.396	.368
1996	Wichita	AA	KC	128	436	119	31	3	3	165	62	48	56	1	36	0	3	5	9	14	.39	11	.273	.352	.378
8 Min. YEARS				671	2413	659	137	21	14	880	361	241	288	14	316	10	23	22	104	58	.64	46	.273	.350	.365

R.D. Long

Bats: Both **Throws:** Right **Pos:** 2B **Ht:** 6'1" **Wt:** 183 **Born:** 4/2/71 **Age:** 26

				BATTING															BASERUNNING				PERCENTAGES		
Year	Team	Lg	Org	G	AB	H	2B	3B	HR	TB	R	RBI	TBB	IBB	SO	HBP	SH	SF	SB	CS	SB%	GDP	Avg	OBP	SLG
1992	Oneonta	A-	NYA	42	153	39	9	1	0	50	26	15	24	0	31	0	2	2	13	3	.81	2	.255	.352	.327
1993	Greensboro	A	NYA	58	170	41	4	4	3	62	21	20	33	0	45	0	4	1	6	4	.60	1	.241	.363	.365
1994	Tampa	A+	NYA	94	257	61	9	2	6	92	44	33	43	1	66	2	0	2	37	9	.80	3	.237	.349	.358
1995	Norwich	AA	NYA	9	33	7	3	0	0	10	4	5	7	0	11	0	0	0	2	1	.67	1	.212	.350	.303
	Tampa	A+	NYA	110	384	96	15	10	4	143	70	36	72	1	100	2	9	2	28	13	.68	4	.250	.370	.372
1996	Norwich	AA	NYA	6	10	3	0	0	0	3	4	3	4	0	2	0	0	0	0	0	.00	0	.300	.500	.300
	Columbus	AAA	NYA	61	124	28	3	2	0	35	18	9	15	0	36	1	1	0	5	2	.71	4	.226	.314	.282
5 Min. YEARS				380	1131	275	43	19	13	395	187	121	198	2	291	5	16	7	91	32	.74	15	.243	.356	.349

Ryan Long

Bats: Right **Throws:** Right **Pos:** OF-DH **Ht:** 6'2" **Wt:** 185 **Born:** 2/3/73 **Age:** 24

				BATTING															BASERUNNING				PERCENTAGES		
Year	Team	Lg	Org	G	AB	H	2B	3B	HR	TB	R	RBI	TBB	IBB	SO	HBP	SH	SF	SB	CS	SB%	GDP	Avg	OBP	SLG
1991	Royals	R	KC	48	177	54	2	2	0	60	17	20	10	0	20	2	0	1	5	4	.56	3	.305	.347	.339
1992	Eugene	A-	KC	54	183	42	5	2	0	51	19	18	3	0	33	4	2	1	7	5	.58	4	.230	.257	.279
1993	Rockford	A	KC	107	396	115	27	6	8	178	46	68	16	3	76	18	2	5	16	6	.73	6	.290	.343	.449
1994	Wilmington	A+	KC	123	494	130	25	5	11	198	69	68	16	0	72	8	3	3	7	3	.70	4	.263	.296	.401
1995	Wichita	AA	KC	102	342	79	26	0	5	120	36	34	10	1	48	5	1	0	4	4	.50	9	.231	.263	.351
1996	Wichita	AA	KC	122	442	125	29	1	20	216	64	78	17	0	71	5	1	2	6	5	.55	9	.283	.315	.489
6 Min. YEARS				556	2034	545	114	16	44	823	251	286	72	4	320	42	9	12	45	27	.63	35	.268	.305	.405

Brian Looney

Pitches: Left **Bats:** Left **Pos:** P **Ht:** 5'10" **Wt:** 185 **Born:** 9/26/69 **Age:** 27

				HOW MUCH HE PITCHED						WHAT HE GAVE UP												THE RESULTS					
Year	Team	Lg	Org	G	GS	CG	GF	IP	BFP	H	R	ER	HR	SH	SF	HB	TBB	IBB	SO	WP	Bk	W	L	Pct.	ShO	Sv	ERA
1991	Jamestown	A-	Mon	11	11	2	0	62.1	246	42	12	8	0	2	2	0	28	0	64	6	0	7	1	.875	1	0	1.16
1992	Rockford	A	Mon	17	0	0	5	31.1	141	28	13	11	0	2	0	1	23	0	34	1	0	3	1	.750	0	0	3.16
	Albany	A	Mon	11	11	1	0	67.1	265	51	22	16	1	1	3	0	30	0	56	4	0	3	2	.600	1	0	2.14
1993	W. Palm Bch	A+	Mon	18	16	0	1	106	451	108	48	37	2	7	3	5	29	0	109	2	1	4	6	.400	0	0	3.14
	Harrisburg	AA	Mon	8	8	1	0	56.2	221	36	15	15	2	1	1	1	17	1	76	0	0	3	2	.600	1	0	2.38
1994	Ottawa	AAA	Mon	27	16	0	2	124.2	565	134	71	60	10	3	6	3	67	4	90	2	0	7	7	.500	0	0	4.33
1995	Pawtucket	AAA	Bos	18	18	1	0	100.2	438	106	44	39	9	2	0	3	33	0	78	7	2	4	7	.364	0	0	3.49

HOW MUCH HE PITCHED								WHAT HE GAVE UP												THE RESULTS					
Year Team	Lg Org	G	GS	CG	GF	IP	BFP	H	R	ER	HR	SH	SF	HB	TBB	IBB	SO	WP	Bk	W	L	Pct.	ShO	Sv	ERA
1996 Pawtucket	AAA Bos	27	9	1	7	82.1	357	78	55	44	14	0	2	4	27	2	78	3	0	5	6	.455	1	1	4.81
1993 Montreal	NL	3	1	0	1	6	28	8	2	2	0	0	0	0	2	0	7	0	1	0	0	.000	0	0	3.00
1994 Montreal	NL	1	0	0	0	2	11	4	5	5	1	0	0	1	0	0	2	0	0	0	0	.000	0	0	22.50
1995 Boston	AL	3	1	0	0	4.2	29	12	9	9	1	1	2	0	4	1	2	0	0	0	1	.000	0	0	17.36
6 Min. YEARS		137	89	6	15	631.1	2684	583	280	230	38	18	17	17	254	7	585	25	3	36	32	.529	4	1	3.28
3 Maj. YEARS		7	2	0	1	12.2	68	24	16	16	2	1	2	1	6	1	11	0	1	0	1	.000	0	0	11.37

Mendy Lopez

Bats: Right **Throws:** Right **Pos:** 3B **Ht:** 6'2" **Wt:** 165 **Born:** 10/15/74 **Age:** 22

BATTING																	BASERUNNING				PERCENTAGES		
Year Team	Lg Org	G	AB	H	2B	3B	HR	TB	R	RBI	TBB	IBB	SO	HBP	SH	SF	SB	CS	SB%	GDP	Avg	OBP	SLG
1994 Royals	R KC	59	235	85	19	3	5	125	56	50	22	0	27	3	2	5	19	2	.90	5	.362	.415	.532
1995 Wilmington	A+ KC	130	428	116	29	3	2	157	42	36	28	0	73	5	7	2	18	10	.64	12	.271	.322	.367
1996 Wichita	AA KC	93	327	92	20	5	6	140	47	32	26	1	67	4	2	1	14	4	.78	6	.281	.341	.428
3 Min. YEARS		282	990	293	68	11	13	422	145	118	76	1	167	12	11	8	51	16	.76	23	.296	.351	.426

Pedro Lopez

Bats: Right **Throws:** Right **Pos:** C **Ht:** 6'0" **Wt:** 160 **Born:** 3/29/69 **Age:** 28

BATTING																	BASERUNNING				PERCENTAGES		
Year Team	Lg Org	G	AB	H	2B	3B	HR	TB	R	RBI	TBB	IBB	SO	HBP	SH	SF	SB	CS	SB%	GDP	Avg	OBP	SLG
1988 Padres	R SD	42	156	44	4	6	1	63	18	22	10	0	24	0	0	0	9	4	.69	2	.282	.325	.404
1989 Waterloo	A SD	97	319	61	13	1	2	82	32	26	25	1	61	4	6	1	4	4	.50	12	.191	.258	.257
1990 Charlstn-SC	A SD	32	101	20	2	0	0	22	9	5	7	0	18	4	0	2	0	1	.00	2	.198	.272	.218
1991 Waterloo	A SD	102	342	97	13	1	8	136	49	57	47	5	66	2	2	4	3	3	.50	4	.284	.370	.398
1992 Wichita	AA SD	96	319	78	8	4	6	112	35	48	13	0	68	7	2	6	4	3	.57	7	.245	.284	.351
1993 Rancho Cuca	A+ SD	37	103	26	10	0	1	39	25	9	24	1	19	2	0	0	0	1	.00	3	.252	.403	.379
Wichita	AA SD	50	142	29	7	0	4	48	12	14	22	2	24	1	1	0	3	0	1.00	2	.204	.315	.338
1994 Wichita	AA SD	42	131	33	7	0	1	43	15	12	15	0	16	3	1	2	0	2	.00	2	.252	.338	.328
Rancho Cuca	A+ SD	7	20	5	2	0	0	7	1	1	1	0	2	0	0	0	0	0	.00	1	.250	.286	.350
Las Vegas	AAA SD	17	47	10	2	0	1	15	3	4	1	0	7	0	1	1	0	0	.00	1	.213	.224	.319
1995 El Paso	AA Mil	84	218	68	15	2	4	99	32	28	18	1	45	4	3	0	0	3	.00	8	.312	.375	.454
New Orleans	AAA Mil	3	8	0	0	0	0	0	0	0	0	0	3	0	0	0	0	0	.00	0	.000	.000	.000
1996 El Paso	AA Mil	46	144	44	10	1	2	62	22	20	17	1	24	0	3	2	2	2	.50	2	.306	.374	.431
New Orleans	AAA Mil	34	87	19	4	0	0	23	7	3	13	1	22	0	0	0	0	0	.00	5	.218	.320	.264
9 Min. YEARS		689	2137	534	97	15	30	751	260	249	213	12	399	27	19	18	25	23	.52	51	.250	.323	.351

Rene Lopez

Bats: Right **Throws:** Right **Pos:** C **Ht:** 5'11" **Wt:** 195 **Born:** 12/10/71 **Age:** 25

BATTING																	BASERUNNING				PERCENTAGES		
Year Team	Lg Org	G	AB	H	2B	3B	HR	TB	R	RBI	TBB	IBB	SO	HBP	SH	SF	SB	CS	SB%	GDP	Avg	OBP	SLG
1993 Fort Wayne	A Min	92	340	85	12	1	3	108	26	44	45	0	57	2	1	5	0	1	.00	12	.250	.337	.318
1994 Fort Myers	A+ Min	109	383	101	12	1	7	136	48	48	46	1	66	2	0	7	3	3	.50	12	.264	.340	.355
1995 New Britain	AA Min	82	264	65	8	0	3	82	22	26	27	0	48	0	5	2	0	0	.00	5	.246	.314	.311
1996 New Britain	AA Min	61	180	42	9	0	3	60	23	16	21	1	28	0	0	2	0	3	.00	2	.233	.310	.333
Salt Lake	AAA Min	22	58	14	4	0	0	18	5	14	5	0	10	0	2	3	1	0	1.00	2	.241	.288	.310
4 Min. YEARS		366	1225	307	45	2	16	404	124	148	144	2	209	4	8	19	4	7	.36	33	.251	.327	.330

Roberto Lopez

Bats: Both **Throws:** Right **Pos:** 2B **Ht:** 5'9" **Wt:** 150 **Born:** 11/15/71 **Age:** 25

BATTING																	BASERUNNING				PERCENTAGES		
Year Team	Lg Org	G	AB	H	2B	3B	HR	TB	R	RBI	TBB	IBB	SO	HBP	SH	SF	SB	CS	SB%	GDP	Avg	OBP	SLG
1994 Stockton	A+ Mil	5	16	2	1	0	0	3	2	1	3	0	1	0	0	0	1	1	.50	0	.125	.263	.188
1995 El Paso	AA Mil	114	417	130	22	8	1	171	80	44	77	2	63	4	6	5	9	4	.69	4	.312	.419	.410
1996 New Orleans	AAA Mil	129	438	102	20	3	7	149	50	39	62	4	67	4	8	3	8	6	.57	4	.233	.331	.340
3 Min. YEARS		248	871	234	43	11	8	323	132	84	142	6	131	8	14	8	18	11	.62	8	.269	.373	.371

Andrew Lorraine

Pitches: Left **Bats:** Left **Pos:** P **Ht:** 6' 3" **Wt:** 195 **Born:** 8/11/72 **Age:** 24

HOW MUCH HE PITCHED								WHAT HE GAVE UP												THE RESULTS					
Year Team	Lg Org	G	GS	CG	GF	IP	BFP	H	R	ER	HR	SH	SF	HB	TBB	IBB	SO	WP	Bk	W	L	Pct.	ShO	Sv	ERA
1993 Boise	A- Cal	6	6	3	0	42	159	33	6	6	3	0	0	2	6	0	39	0	0	4	1	.800	1	0	1.29
1994 Vancouver	AAA Cal	22	22	4	0	142	599	156	63	54	13	2	4	11	34	1	90	1	1	12	4	.750	2	0	3.42
1995 Nashville	AAA ChA	7	7	0	0	39	184	51	29	26	4	1	3	1	12	0	26	2	0	4	1	.800	0	0	6.00
Vancouver	AAA Cal	25	25	4	0	136.2	604	156	78	69	11	5	6	4	42	0	77	6	0	10	7	.588	1	0	4.54
1996 Edmonton	AAA Oak	30	25	0	0	141	640	181	95	89	19	4	5	4	46	2	73	5	1	8	10	.444	0	0	5.68
1994 California	AL	4	3	0	0	18.2	96	30	23	22	7	2	1	0	11	0	10	0	0	0	2	.000	0	0	10.61
1995 Chicago	AL	5	0	0	2	8	30	3	3	3	0	0	0	1	2	0	5	0	0	0	0	.000	0	0	3.38
4 Min. YEARS		90	85	11	0	500.2	2186	577	271	244	50	12	18	22	140	3	305	14	2	38	23	.623	4	0	4.39
2 Maj. YEARS		9	3	0	2	26.2	126	33	26	25	7	2	1	1	13	0	15	0	0	0	2	.000	0	0	8.44

Billy Lott

Bats: Right **Throws:** Right **Pos:** OF **Ht:** 6'4" **Wt:** 210 **Born:** 8/16/70 **Age:** 26

			BATTING															BASERUNNING				PERCENTAGES		
Year	Team	Lg	Org	G	AB	H	2B	3B	HR	TB	R	RBI	TBB	IBB	SO	HBP	SH	SF	SB	CS	SB%	GDP	Avg	OBP	SLG
1989	Dodgers	R	LA	46	150	29	2	4	0	39	18	9	10	0	48	1	1	0	5	1	.83	0	.193	.248	.260
1990	Bakersfield	A+	LA	38	133	27	1	1	2	36	11	14	6	0	46	1	1	1	3	2	.60	3	.203	.241	.271
	Yakima	A-	LA	65	240	66	13	2	4	95	37	38	10	0	62	3	0	4	4	0	1.00	1	.275	.307	.396
1991	Bakersfield	A+	LA	92	314	70	10	1	5	97	40	35	25	0	90	3	3	6	11	4	.73	8	.223	.282	.309
1992	Vero Beach	A+	LA	126	435	107	17	4	3	141	42	35	22	3	107	3	2	5	11	5	.69	18	.246	.284	.324
1993	San Antonio	AA	LA	114	418	106	17	2	15	172	49	49	23	3	111	1	1	2	5	11	.31	8	.254	.293	.411
1994	San Antonio	AA	LA	122	448	131	25	4	12	200	61	62	31	2	100	4	2	3	20	10	.67	7	.292	.342	.446
1995	Albuquerque	AAA	LA	41	146	46	7	2	5	72	23	26	13	2	48	0	1	0	1	2	.33	5	.315	.371	.493
1996	Albuquerque	AAA	LA	114	418	111	20	1	19	190	67	66	46	1	124	5	0	0	6	7	.46	6	.266	.345	.455
8 Min. YEARS				758	2702	693	112	21	65	1042	348	334	186	11	736	21	11	21	66	42	.61	56	.256	.307	.386

Kevin Lovingier

Pitches: Left **Bats:** Left **Pos:** P **Ht:** 6'1" **Wt:** 190 **Born:** 8/29/71 **Age:** 25

			HOW MUCH HE PITCHED						WHAT HE GAVE UP													THE RESULTS					
Year	Team	Lg	Org	G	GS	CG	GF	IP	BFP	H	R	ER	HR	SH	SF	HB	TBB	IBB	SO	WP	Bk	W	L	Pct.	ShO	Sv	ERA
1994	New Jersey	A-	StL	35	0	0	5	52.1	211	36	13	9	3	3	0	2	19	1	71	3	0	1	0	1.000	0	1	1.55
1995	St. Pete	A+	StL	22	0	0	6	21.2	82	9	4	4	0	1	1	2	10	1	14	1	0	1	0	1.000	0	0	1.66
	Savannah	A	StL	60	0	0	24	68.2	277	44	18	11	1	4	2	3	31	6	68	4	0	7	3	.700	0	1	1.44
1996	Arkansas	AA	StL	60	0	0	19	63.2	295	60	30	29	4	6	2	1	48	6	73	3	0	2	3	.400	0	1	4.10
3 Min. YEARS				177	0	0	54	206.1	865	149	65	53	8	14	5	8	108	14	226	11	0	11	6	.647	0	3	2.31

Derek Lowe

Pitches: Right **Bats:** Right **Pos:** P **Ht:** 6'6" **Wt:** 170 **Born:** 6/1/73 **Age:** 24

			HOW MUCH HE PITCHED						WHAT HE GAVE UP													THE RESULTS					
Year	Team	Lg	Org	G	GS	CG	GF	IP	BFP	H	R	ER	HR	SH	SF	HB	TBB	IBB	SO	WP	Bk	W	L	Pct.	ShO	Sv	ERA
1991	Mariners	R	Sea	12	12	0	0	71	295	58	26	19	2	1	4	2	21	0	60	4	6	5	3	.625	0	0	2.41
1992	Bellingham	A-	Sea	14	13	2	1	85.2	349	69	34	23	2	3	1	4	22	0	66	5	4	7	3	.700	1	0	2.42
1993	Riverside	A+	Sea	27	26	3	1	154	687	189	104	90	9	2	2	2	60	0	80	12	9	12	9	.571	2	0	5.26
1994	Jacksonvlle	AA	Sea	26	26	2	0	151.1	676	177	92	83	7	6	3	9	50	1	75	11	7	7	10	.412	0	0	4.94
1995	Mariners	R	Sea	2	2	0	0	9.2	35	5	1	1	0	0	0	0	2	0	11	0	0	1	0	1.000	0	0	0.93
	Port City	AA	Sea	12	12	1	0	63	279	75	42	37	8	3	2	3	24	1	41	2	0	2	6	.250	0	0	5.29
1996	Port City	AA	Sea	10	10	0	0	65	258	56	27	22	7	0	2	1	17	0	33	0	0	5	3	.625	0	0	3.05
	Tacoma	AAA	Sea	17	16	1	0	105	463	118	64	53	7	4	5	3	37	1	54	1	2	6	9	.400	1	0	4.54
6 Min. YEARS				120	117	9	2	704.2	3042	747	390	328	42	19	19	24	233	3	420	35	28	45	43	.511	4	0	4.19

Sean Lowe

Pitches: Right **Bats:** Right **Pos:** P **Ht:** 6'2" **Wt:** 200 **Born:** 3/29/71 **Age:** 26

			HOW MUCH HE PITCHED						WHAT HE GAVE UP													THE RESULTS					
Year	Team	Lg	Org	G	GS	CG	GF	IP	BFP	H	R	ER	HR	SH	SF	HB	TBB	IBB	SO	WP	Bk	W	L	Pct.	ShO	Sv	ERA
1992	Hamilton	A-	StL	5	5	0	0	28	109	14	8	5	0	0	0	1	14	0	22	1	1	2	0	1.000	0	0	1.61
1993	St. Pete	A+	StL	25	25	0	0	132.2	594	152	80	63	6	2	5	6	62	1	87	4	5	6	11	.353	0	0	4.27
1994	St. Pete	A+	StL	21	21	0	0	114	488	119	51	44	6	3	2	5	37	0	92	3	0	5	6	.455	0	0	3.47
	Arkansas	AA	StL	3	3	0	0	19.1	76	13	3	3	0	2	0	0	8	0	11	0	0	2	1	.667	0	0	1.40
1995	Arkansas	AA	StL	24	24	0	0	129	578	143	84	70	2	5	4	5	64	0	77	9	0	9	8	.529	0	0	4.88
1996	Arkansas	AA	StL	6	6	0	0	33	150	32	24	22	2	1	1	2	15	1	25	1	0	2	3	.400	0	0	6.00
	Louisville	AAA	StL	25	18	0	1	115	515	127	72	60	7	4	6	7	51	7	76	6	0	8	9	.471	0	0	4.70
5 Min. YEARS				109	102	0	1	571	2510	600	322	267	23	17	18	26	251	9	390	24	6	34	38	.472	0	0	4.21

Terrell Lowery

Bats: Right **Throws:** Right **Pos:** OF **Ht:** 6'3" **Wt:** 175 **Born:** 10/25/70 **Age:** 26

			BATTING															BASERUNNING				PERCENTAGES		
Year	Team	Lg	Org	G	AB	H	2B	3B	HR	TB	R	RBI	TBB	IBB	SO	HBP	SH	SF	SB	CS	SB%	GDP	Avg	OBP	SLG
1991	Butte	R+	Tex	54	214	64	10	7	3	97	38	33	29	0	44	1	0	2	23	12	.66	2	.299	.382	.453
1993	Charlotte	A+	Tex	65	257	77	7	9	3	111	46	36	46	2	47	2	1	1	14	15	.48	2	.300	.408	.432
	Tulsa	AA	Tex	66	258	62	5	1	3	78	29	14	28	1	50	1	1	1	10	12	.45	5	.240	.316	.302
1994	Tulsa	AA	Tex	129	496	142	34	8	8	216	89	54	59	0	113	5	5	5	33	15	.69	7	.286	.365	.435
1995	Rangers	R	Tex	10	34	9	3	1	3	23	10	7	6	0	7	0	0	0	1	0	1.00	1	.265	.375	.676
	Charlotte	A+	Tex	11	35	9	2	2	0	15	4	4	6	0	6	1	0	0	1	0	1.00	2	.257	.381	.429
1996	Binghamton	AA	NYN	62	211	58	13	4	7	100	34	32	44	2	44	2	2	3	5	6	.45	4	.275	.400	.474
	Norfolk	AAA	NYN	62	193	45	7	2	4	68	25	21	22	0	44	1	3	2	6	3	.67	1	.233	.312	.352
5 Min. YEARS				459	1698	466	81	34	31	708	275	201	240	5	355	13	12	14	93	63	.60	24	.274	.366	.417

Lou Lucca

Bats: Right **Throws:** Right **Pos:** 3B **Ht:** 5'11" **Wt:** 210 **Born:** 10/13/70 **Age:** 26

			BATTING															BASERUNNING				PERCENTAGES		
Year	Team	Lg	Org	G	AB	H	2B	3B	HR	TB	R	RBI	TBB	IBB	SO	HBP	SH	SF	SB	CS	SB%	GDP	Avg	OBP	SLG
1992	Erie	A-	Fla	76	263	74	16	1	13	131	51	44	33	0	40	5	0	2	6	3	.67	8	.281	.370	.498
1993	Kane County	A	Fla	127	419	116	25	2	6	163	52	53	60	0	58	9	2	7	4	10	.29	9	.277	.374	.389

							BATTING										BASERUNNING				PERCENTAGES		
Year	Team	Lg	Org	G	AB	H	2B	3B	HR	TB	R	RBI	TBB	IBB	SO	HBP	SH	SF	SB	CS	SB%	GDP	Avg	OBP	SLG
1994	Brevard Cty	A+	Fla	130	441	125	29	1	8	180	62	76	72	2	73	4	0	6	3	7	.30	18	.283	.384	.408
1995	Portland	AA	Fla	112	388	107	28	1	9	164	57	64	59	5	77	5	0	2	4	4	.50	18	.276	.377	.423
1996	Charlotte	AAA	Fla	87	273	71	14	1	7	108	26	35	11	0	62	4	0	3	0	3	.00	11	.260	.296	.396
5 Min. YEARS				532	1784	493	112	6	43	746	248	272	235	7	310	27	2	20	17	27	.39	64	.276	.365	.418

Roger Luce

Bats: Right **Throws:** Right **Pos:** C **Ht:** 6'4" **Wt:** 215 **Born:** 5/7/69 **Age:** 28

							BATTING												BASERUNNING				PERCENTAGES		
Year	Team	Lg	Org	G	AB	H	2B	3B	HR	TB	R	RBI	TBB	IBB	SO	HBP	SH	SF	SB	CS	SB%	GDP	Avg	OBP	SLG
1991	Gastonia	A	Tex	33	107	28	9	2	2	47	17	16	7	0	31	3	1	3	2	2	.50	1	.262	.317	.439
1992	Charlotte	A+	Tex	91	303	70	9	0	1	82	18	20	19	1	77	3	1	2	3	4	.43	3	.231	.281	.271
1993	Tulsa	AA	Tex	101	321	62	14	2	8	104	35	29	17	0	107	4	0	1	2	1	.67	5	.193	.242	.324
1994	Tulsa	AA	Tex	59	191	54	11	2	6	87	27	22	16	0	56	0	1	0	2	2	.50	2	.283	.338	.455
	Okla. City	AAA	Tex	49	169	40	9	1	1	54	20	14	4	0	40	0	1	0	0	0	.00	1	.237	.254	.320
1995	Okla. City	AAA	Tex	1	3	0	0	0	0	0	0	0	0	0	2	0	0	0	0	0	.00	0	.000	.000	.000
	Jackson	AA	Hou	18	52	11	2	1	1	18	4	4	3	0	12	0	0	0	0	0	.00	3	.212	.255	.346
1996	Jackson	AA	Hou	69	243	62	11	4	8	105	29	36	10	0	52	0	1	2	0	0	.00	12	.255	.282	.432
	Tucson	AAA	Hou	20	50	15	2	1	2	25	8	8	2	0	17	0	0	0	0	0	.00	0	.300	.327	.500
6 Min. YEARS				441	1439	342	67	13	29	522	158	149	78	1	394	10	5	8	9	9	.50	27	.238	.280	.363

Larry Luebbers

Pitches: Right **Bats:** Right **Pos:** P **Ht:** 6' 6" **Wt:** 205 **Born:** 10/11/69 **Age:** 27

					HOW MUCH HE PITCHED						WHAT HE GAVE UP												THE RESULTS				
Year	Team	Lg	Org	G	GS	CG	GF	IP	BFP	H	R	ER	HR	SH	SF	HB	TBB	IBB	SO	WP	Bk	W	L	Pct.	ShO	Sv	ERA
1990	Billings	R+	Cin	13	13	1	0	72.1	319	74	46	36	3	2	3	6	31	0	48	7	1	5	4	.556	1	0	4.48
1991	Cedar Rapds	A	Cin	28	28	3	0	184.2	781	177	85	64	8	12	6	10	64	5	98	11	4	8	10	.444	0	0	3.12
1992	Cedar Rapds	A	Cin	14	14	1	0	82.1	355	71	33	24	2	4	3	8	33	0	56	1	1	7	0	1.000	0	0	2.62
	Chattanooga	AA	Cin	14	14	1	0	87.1	368	86	34	22	5	2	1	4	34	1	56	5	2	6	5	.545	0	0	2.27
1993	Indianapols	AAA	Cin	15	15	0	0	84.1	380	81	45	39	7	6	2	6	47	5	51	1	0	4	7	.364	0	0	4.16
1994	Iowa	AAA	ChN	27	26	0	0	138.2	630	149	100	93	22	4	7	5	87	3	90	7	4	10	12	.455	0	0	6.04
1995	Chattanooga	AA	Cin	28	21	0	4	118	514	112	71	61	7	6	6	7	59	1	87	1	0	10	6	.625	0	0	4.65
1996	Chattanooga	AA	Cin	11	11	0	0	69.1	292	64	32	28	6	3	1	3	26	0	38	5	0	3	5	.375	0	0	3.63
	Indianapols	AAA	Cin	14	11	0	0	71.1	301	76	44	31	8	1	2	1	23	2	35	1	0	5	4	.556	0	0	3.91
1993	Cincinnati	NL		14	14	0	0	77.1	332	74	49	39	7	4	5	1	38	3	38	4	0	2	5	.286	0	0	4.54
7 Min. YEARS				164	153	6	4	908.1	3940	890	490	398	68	40	31	50	404	17	559	39	12	58	53	.523	1	0	3.94

Keith Luuloa

Bats: Right **Throws:** Right **Pos:** 2B **Ht:** 6'1" **Wt:** 185 **Born:** 12/24/74 **Age:** 22

							BATTING												BASERUNNING				PERCENTAGES		
Year	Team	Lg	Org	G	AB	H	2B	3B	HR	TB	R	RBI	TBB	IBB	SO	HBP	SH	SF	SB	CS	SB%	GDP	Avg	OBP	SLG
1994	Angels	R	Cal	28	97	29	4	1	1	38	14	10	8	0	14	4	1	3	3	4	.43	0	.299	.366	.392
1995	Lk Elsinore	A+	Cal	102	380	100	22	7	5	151	50	53	24	0	47	6	7	1	1	5	.17	9	.263	.316	.397
1996	Midland	AA	Cal	134	531	138	24	2	7	187	80	44	47	0	54	6	8	3	4	6	.40	14	.260	.325	.352
3 Min. YEARS				264	1008	267	50	10	13	376	144	107	79	0	115	16	16	7	8	15	.35	23	.265	.326	.373

Ryan Luzinski

Bats: Right **Throws:** Right **Pos:** C **Ht:** 6'0" **Wt:** 215 **Born:** 8/22/73 **Age:** 23

							BATTING												BASERUNNING				PERCENTAGES		
Year	Team	Lg	Org	G	AB	H	2B	3B	HR	TB	R	RBI	TBB	IBB	SO	HBP	SH	SF	SB	CS	SB%	GDP	Avg	OBP	SLG
1992	Great Falls	R+	LA	61	227	57	14	4	4	91	26	29	22	2	47	2	0	1	2	1	.67	1	.251	.321	.401
1993	Bakersfield	A+	LA	48	147	41	10	1	3	62	18	9	13	0	24	5	0	0	2	2	.50	3	.279	.358	.422
	Yakima	A-	LA	69	237	61	10	3	4	89	32	46	41	4	44	4	3	3	6	1	.86	2	.257	.372	.376
1994	Vero Beach	A+	LA	112	379	99	18	3	11	156	48	61	33	1	91	5	1	5	2	1	.67	11	.261	.325	.412
1995	San Antonio	AA	LA	44	144	33	5	0	1	41	18	9	13	1	32	3	2	1	1	1	.50	6	.229	.304	.285
	Vero Beach	A+	LA	38	134	45	12	0	5	72	15	23	9	3	21	0	0	1	1	0	1.00	4	.336	.375	.537
1996	Albuquerque	AAA	LA	9	14	2	0	0	0	2	0	1	0	0	6	0	0	0	0	0	.00	0	.143	.143	.143
	San Antonio	AA	LA	32	103	30	6	0	0	36	12	10	11	0	19	1	1	0	2	0	1.00	6	.291	.365	.350
	San Bernrdo	A+	LA	30	118	41	10	0	5	66	24	21	11	0	33	0	2	1	6	1	.86	2	.347	.400	.559
5 Min. YEARS				443	1503	409	85	11	33	615	193	209	153	11	317	20	9	12	22	7	.76	35	.272	.345	.409

Kevin Maas

Bats: Left **Throws:** Left **Pos:** DH **Ht:** 6' 3" **Wt:** 209 **Born:** 1/20/65 **Age:** 32

				BATTING															BASERUNNING				PERCENTAGES		
Year	Team	Lg	Org	G	AB	H	2B	3B	HR	TB	R	RBI	TBB	IBB	SO	HBP	SH	SF	SB	CS	SB%	GDP	Avg	OBP	SLG
1986	Oneonta	A-	NYA	28	101	36	10	0	0	46	14	18	7	1	9	0	0	1	5	1	.83	1	.356	.394	.455
1987	Ft. Laud	A+	NYA	116	439	122	28	4	11	191	77	73	53	4	108	2	0	8	14	4	.78	5	.278	.353	.435
1988	Pr. William	A+	NYA	29	108	32	7	0	12	75	24	35	17	1	28	4	0	4	3	1	.75	0	.296	.398	.694
	Albany-Colo	AA	NYA	109	372	98	14	3	16	166	66	55	64	4	103	4	3	2	5	1	.83	5	.263	.376	.446
1989	Columbus	AAA	NYA	83	291	93	23	2	6	138	42	45	40	0	73	1	0	4	2	3	.40	3	.320	.399	.474
1990	Columbus	AAA	NYA	57	194	55	15	2	13	113	37	38	34	1	45	0	0	0	2	2	.50	5	.284	.390	.582
1993	Columbus	AAA	NYA	28	104	29	6	0	4	47	14	18	19	2	22	1	0	1	0	1	.00	1	.279	.392	.452
1994	Wichita	AA	SD	4	15	8	3	0	3	20	4	8	3	0	0	0	0	0	0	0	.00	0	.533	.611	1.333
	Las Vegas	AAA	SD	29	90	22	6	2	4	44	15	12	9	0	25	1	0	1	1	0	1.00	1	.244	.317	.489
	Indianapols	AAA	Cin	78	283	82	18	2	19	161	55	45	29	0	49	2	1	3	2	3	.40	4	.290	.356	.569
1995	Yankees	R	NYA	2	9	4	0	0	1	7	1	3	0	0	0	0	0	0	0	0	.00	0	.444	.444	.778
	Columbus	AAA	NYA	44	161	45	7	2	9	83	28	33	23	0	40	2	0	2	0	0	.00	1	.280	.372	.516
1996	New Orleans	AAA	Mil	36	117	30	8	0	8	62	18	22	14	2	18	1	0	1	0	0	.00	2	.256	.338	.530
1990	New York	AL		79	254	64	9	0	21	136	42	41	43	10	76	3	0	0	1	2	.33	2	.252	.367	.535
1991	New York	AL		148	500	110	14	1	23	195	69	63	83	3	128	4	0	5	5	1	.83	4	.220	.333	.390
1992	New York	AL		98	286	71	12	0	11	116	35	35	25	4	63	0	0	4	3	1	.75	1	.248	.305	.406
1993	New York	AL		59	151	31	4	0	9	62	20	25	24	2	32	1	0	1	1	1	.50	2	.205	.316	.411
1995	Minnesota	AL		22	57	11	4	0	1	18	5	5	7	2	11	0	0	0	0	0	.00	4	.193	.281	.316
9	Min. YEARS			643	2284	656	145	17	106	1153	395	405	312	15	520	18	4	27	34	16	.68	28	.287	.373	.505
5	Maj. YEARS			406	1248	287	43	1	65	527	171	169	182	21	310	8	0	10	10	5	.67	13	.230	.329	.422

Chris Macca

Pitches: Right **Bats:** Right **Pos:** P **Ht:** 6'2" **Wt:** 185 **Born:** 11/14/74 **Age:** 22

				HOW MUCH HE PITCHED						WHAT HE GAVE UP												THE RESULTS					
Year	Team	Lg	Org	G	GS	CG	GF	IP	BFP	H	R	ER	HR	SH	SF	HB	TBB	IBB	SO	WP	Bk	W	L	Pct.	ShO	Sv	ERA
1995	Portland	A-	Col	24	0	0	16	35.2	152	25	15	13	1	2	2	6	17	1	41	6	0	3	2	.600	0	5	3.28
1996	Asheville	A	Col	26	0	0	25	33.2	132	18	5	4	2	1	0	3	11	1	46	2	1	1	1	.500	0	15	1.07
	New Haven	AA	Col	28	0	0	28	33.2	135	18	6	5	0	2	1	2	18	2	33	2	0	3	1	.750	0	15	1.34
2	Min. YEARS			78	0	0	69	103	419	61	26	22	3	5	3	11	46	4	120	10	1	7	4	.636	0	35	1.92

Fausto Macey

Pitches: Right **Bats:** Right **Pos:** P **Ht:** 6'4" **Wt:** 185 **Born:** 10/9/75 **Age:** 21

				HOW MUCH HE PITCHED						WHAT HE GAVE UP												THE RESULTS					
Year	Team	Lg	Org	G	GS	CG	GF	IP	BFP	H	R	ER	HR	SH	SF	HB	TBB	IBB	SO	WP	Bk	W	L	Pct.	ShO	Sv	ERA
1994	Giants	R	SF	9	9	0	0	50	194	37	14	12	0	2	2	0	8	0	26	1	0	2	2	.500	0	0	2.16
	Everett	A-	SF	5	5	0	0	27.2	120	30	12	11	1	1	0	0	8	0	22	1	2	2	1	.667	0	0	3.58
1995	San Jose	A+	SF	28	25	1	0	171	709	167	84	74	17	7	5	6	50	1	94	6	4	8	9	.471	0	0	3.89
1996	Shreveport	AA	SF	27	26	1	0	157	673	165	86	75	22	4	5	8	47	0	62	7	2	10	7	.588	0	0	4.30
3	Min. YEARS			69	65	2	0	405.2	1696	399	196	172	40	14	12	14	113	1	204	15	8	22	19	.537	0	0	3.82

Quinn Mack

Bats: Left **Throws:** Left **Pos:** OF **Ht:** 5'10" **Wt:** 185 **Born:** 9/11/65 **Age:** 31

				BATTING															BASERUNNING				PERCENTAGES		
Year	Team	Lg	Org	G	AB	H	2B	3B	HR	TB	R	RBI	TBB	IBB	SO	HBP	SH	SF	SB	CS	SB%	GDP	Avg	OBP	SLG
1987	Burlington	A	Mon	59	164	44	10	1	2	62	15	15	11	1	22	2	0	0	0	3	.00	7	.268	.322	.378
1988	W. Palm Bch	A+	Mon	100	349	97	10	5	2	123	51	25	21	1	42	2	3	4	10	5	.67	8	.278	.319	.352
1989	Jacksonvlle	AA	Mon	122	378	97	19	3	6	140	46	40	27	2	55	1	4	4	5	7	.42	12	.257	.305	.370
1990	Indianapols	AAA	Mon	121	392	108	25	2	7	158	55	53	25	5	46	5	2	1	11	6	.65	20	.276	.326	.403
1991	Indianapols	AAA	Mon	120	416	113	19	8	5	163	35	49	12	0	42	3	1	3	4	6	.40	13	.272	.295	.392
1992	Indianapols	AAA	Mon	103	301	85	19	0	4	116	33	36	20	2	44	1	2	2	5	4	.56	10	.282	.327	.385
1993	Ottawa	AAA	Mon	8	21	2	0	0	0	2	1	0	1	0	3	0	1	0	0	0	.00	1	.095	.136	.095
	Calgary	AAA	Sea	84	325	100	25	1	6	145	48	39	17	2	41	0	1	2	9	6	.60	12	.308	.340	.446
1994	Calgary	AAA	Sea	114	404	117	30	1	5	164	63	51	31	0	50	1	1	1	10	7	.59	19	.290	.341	.406
1995	Tacoma	AAA	Sea	70	204	54	11	0	1	68	30	17	24	5	21	1	1	0	9	2	.82	6	.265	.345	.333
	Memphis	AA	SD	20	63	15	1	0	2	22	6	6	8	1	8	2	1	0	2	1	.67	1	.238	.342	.349
1996	Portland	AA	Fla	36	111	24	5	0	3	38	12	19	7	0	20	0	3	0	3	3	.50	4	.216	.263	.342
1994	Seattle	AL		5	21	5	3	0	0	8	1	2	1	0	3	0	0	0	2	0	1.00	0	.238	.273	.381
10	Min. YEARS			957	3128	856	174	21	43	1201	395	350	204	19	394	18	20	17	68	50	.58	113	.274	.320	.384

Katsuhiro Maeda

Pitches: Right **Bats:** Right **Pos:** P **Ht:** 6'2" **Wt:** 215 **Born:** 6/23/71 **Age:** 26

				HOW MUCH HE PITCHED						WHAT HE GAVE UP												THE RESULTS					
Year	Team	Lg	Org	G	GS	CG	GF	IP	BFP	H	R	ER	HR	SH	SF	HB	TBB	IBB	SO	WP	Bk	W	L	Pct.	ShO	Sv	ERA
1996	Yankees	R	NYA	2	2	1	0	9	35	4	3	3	1	0	1	1	2	0	7	0	0	1	1	.500	1	0	3.00
	Tampa	A+	NYA	2	2	0	0	10.2	50	11	5	5	0	1	0	2	6	0	8	0	0	0	0	.000	0	0	4.22
	Norwich	AA	NYA	9	9	1	0	53.1	221	49	25	24	4	1	2	1	21	0	30	4	0	3	2	.600	1	0	4.05
1	Min. YEARS			13	13	2	0	73	306	64	33	32	5	2	3	4	29	0	45	4	0	4	3	.571	2	0	3.95

Bobby Magallanes

Bats: Right **Throws:** Right **Pos:** 2B **Ht:** 6'0" **Wt:** 175 **Born:** 8/18/69 **Age:** 27

				BATTING															BASERUNNING				PERCENTAGES		
Year	Team	Lg	Org	G	AB	H	2B	3B	HR	TB	R	RBI	TBB	IBB	SO	HBP	SH	SF	SB	CS	SB%	GDP	Avg	OBP	SLG
1990	San Bernrdo	A+	Sea	57	200	37	4	0	3	50	27	21	24	1	53	4	1	1	1	3	.25	2	.185	.284	.250
	Bellingham	A-	Sea	46	157	30	3	0	1	36	14	12	18	1	31	1	1	0	1	0	1.00	2	.191	.278	.229
1991	San Bernrdo	A+	Sea	83	271	61	13	0	7	95	40	31	30	0	64	2	0	3	7	6	.54	6	.225	.304	.351
	Peninsula	A+	Sea	41	150	30	4	0	4	46	11	16	14	0	30	1	1	1	1	1	.50	5	.200	.271	.307
1992	Peninsula	A+	Sea	41	108	20	3	0	1	26	7	10	5	0	17	1	1	2	1	2	.33	0	.185	.224	.241
1995	Pueblo	IND	—	40	152	42	5	2	4	63	30	22	11	0	23	4	1	1	6	0	1.00	2	.276	.339	.414
	Rio Grande	IND	—	39	121	33	5	0	7	59	17	21	9	0	20	1	2	0	1	1	.50	2	.273	.328	.488
1996	Jackson	AA	Hou	12	41	11	2	0	2	19	7	4	2	0	8	2	0	0	0	0	.00	2	.268	.333	.463
	5 Min. YEARS			359	1200	264	39	2	29	394	153	137	113	2	246	16	7	8	18	13	.58	21	.220	.294	.328

Ricky Magdaleno

Bats: Right **Throws:** Right **Pos:** SS **Ht:** 6'1" **Wt:** 170 **Born:** 7/6/74 **Age:** 22

				BATTING															BASERUNNING				PERCENTAGES		
Year	Team	Lg	Org	G	AB	H	2B	3B	HR	TB	R	RBI	TBB	IBB	SO	HBP	SH	SF	SB	CS	SB%	GDP	Avg	OBP	SLG
1993	Charlstn-WV	A	Cin	131	447	107	15	4	3	139	49	25	37	0	103	1	6	1	8	8	.50	15	.239	.298	.311
1994	Winston-Sal	A+	Cin	127	437	114	22	2	13	179	52	49	49	1	80	0	2	4	7	9	.44	9	.261	.333	.410
1995	Chattanooga	AA	Cin	11	40	7	2	0	1	12	2	2	4	0	13	0	0	0	0	0	.00	3	.175	.250	.300
	Winston-Sal	A+	Cin	91	309	69	13	1	7	105	30	40	15	0	69	2	3	3	3	1	.75	4	.223	.261	.340
	Indianapols	AAA	Cin	4	8	1	0	0	1	4	1	1	0	0	3	0	1	0	0	0	.00	0	.125	.125	.500
1996	Chattanooga	AA	Cin	132	424	94	21	1	17	168	60	63	64	4	135	1	5	4	2	7	.22	8	.222	.323	.396
	4 Min. YEARS			496	1665	392	73	8	42	607	194	180	169	5	403	4	17	12	20	25	.44	39	.235	.305	.365

John Mahalik

Bats: Right **Throws:** Right **Pos:** 2B **Ht:** 6'2" **Wt:** 190 **Born:** 7/28/71 **Age:** 25

				BATTING															BASERUNNING				PERCENTAGES		
Year	Team	Lg	Org	G	AB	H	2B	3B	HR	TB	R	RBI	TBB	IBB	SO	HBP	SH	SF	SB	CS	SB%	GDP	Avg	OBP	SLG
1993	Butte	R+	—	74	258	70	15	0	1	88	25	27	21	0	51	0	1	1	8	0	1.00	8	.271	.325	.341
1994	Burlington	A	Mon	9	30	5	0	0	0	5	1	3	1	0	5	0	1	0	0	1	.00	0	.167	.194	.167
	W. Palm Bch	A+	Mon	63	161	43	9	2	0	56	30	12	29	0	20	4	4	2	4	4	.50	4	.267	.388	.348
1995	Binghamton	AA	NYN	67	187	42	6	1	5	65	19	19	19	1	34	1	5	1	1	1	.50	6	.225	.298	.348
1996	Norfolk	AAA	NYN	8	17	4	0	0	0	4	1	0	0	0	1	0	1	0	0	0	.00	0	.235	.235	.235
	Binghamton	AA	NYN	78	216	52	11	2	3	76	37	22	27	0	35	2	6	3	6	2	.75	3	.241	.327	.352
	4 Min. YEARS			299	869	216	41	5	9	294	113	83	97	1	146	7	18	7	19	8	.70	21	.249	.327	.338

Ron Mahay

Bats: Left **Throws:** Left **Pos:** P **Ht:** 6' 2" **Wt:** 189 **Born:** 6/28/71 **Age:** 26

				HOW MUCH HE PITCHED						WHAT HE GAVE UP												THE RESULTS					
Year	Team	Lg	Org	G	GS	CG	GF	IP	BFP	H	R	ER	HR	SH	SF	HB	TBB	IBB	SO	WP	Bk	W	L	Pct.	ShO	Sv	ERA
1996	Sarasota	A+	Bos	31	4	0	13	70.2	295	61	33	30	5	1	0	0	35	0	68	4	1	2	2	.500	0	2	3.82
	Trenton	AA	Bos	1	1	0	0	3.2	29	12	13	12	1	0	0	0	6	0	0	1	0	0	1	.000	0	0	29.45
	1 Min. YEARS			32	5	0	13	74.1	324	73	46	42	6	1	0	0	41	0	68	5	1	2	3	.400	0	2	5.09

Dalton Maine

Pitches: Right **Bats:** Right **Pos:** P **Ht:** 6'3" **Wt:** 185 **Born:** 3/22/72 **Age:** 25

				HOW MUCH HE PITCHED						WHAT HE GAVE UP												THE RESULTS					
Year	Team	Lg	Org	G	GS	CG	GF	IP	BFP	H	R	ER	HR	SH	SF	HB	TBB	IBB	SO	WP	Bk	W	L	Pct.	ShO	Sv	ERA
1995	Bluefield	R+	Bal	1	0	0	1	4	18	7	5	5	2	0	0	1	0	0	2	0	0	0	1	.000	0	0	11.25
	Orioles	R	Bal	18	0	0	6	30.1	122	24	7	7	0	0	1	0	9	1	32	1	0	1	0	1.000	0	2	2.08
	Frederick	A+	Bal	38	0	0	17	56.1	238	51	22	21	4	0	2	3	20	1	55	6	0	2	2	.500	0	2	3.36
1996	Bakersfield	A+	Bal	23	2	0	18	47.1	204	42	25	17	4	2	0	1	14	0	58	5	2	2	3	.400	0	6	3.23
	Bowie	AA	Bal	11	0	0	5	21.1	98	24	14	12	3	2	0	2	11	0	18	0	2	0	1	.000	0	0	5.06
	High Desert	A+	Bal	10	0	0	6	12	45	8	2	2	1	0	2	0	2	0	9	1	0	1	0	1.000	0	2	1.50
	2 Min. YEARS			101	2	0	53	171.1	725	156	75	64	14	4	5	7	56	2	174	13	4	6	7	.462	0	12	3.36

Scott Makarewicz

Bats: Right **Throws:** Right **Pos:** C **Ht:** 6'0" **Wt:** 200 **Born:** 3/1/67 **Age:** 30

				BATTING															BASERUNNING				PERCENTAGES		
Year	Team	Lg	Org	G	AB	H	2B	3B	HR	TB	R	RBI	TBB	IBB	SO	HBP	SH	SF	SB	CS	SB%	GDP	Avg	OBP	SLG
1989	Auburn	A-	Hou	61	216	52	17	0	4	81	22	24	14	0	43	4	5	1	2	0	1.00	1	.241	.298	.375
1990	Osceola	A+	Hou	94	343	95	12	2	4	123	35	49	21	0	63	4	8	3	0	1	.00	11	.277	.323	.359
	Columbus	AA	Hou	28	85	20	1	0	2	27	5	11	10	2	14	1	0	2	0	1	.00	3	.235	.316	.318
1991	Jackson	AA	Hou	76	229	53	9	0	2	68	23	30	18	5	36	8	0	3	1	4	.20	7	.231	.306	.297
1992	Jackson	AA	Hou	105	345	99	15	0	7	135	39	39	23	3	62	6	3	5	2	2	.50	6	.287	.338	.391
1993	Jackson	AA	Hou	92	285	70	14	1	7	107	31	35	17	2	51	8	1	3	1	1	.50	7	.246	.304	.375
1994	Tucson	AAA	Hou	63	171	49	10	1	3	70	24	32	13	0	28	4	6	1	0	0	.00	5	.287	.349	.409
1995	Tucson	AAA	Hou	62	192	51	9	0	5	75	21	31	10	3	23	2	2	2	1	0	1.00	9	.266	.306	.391
1996	Jacksonvlle	AA	Det	83	258	81	16	1	14	141	42	49	18	2	46	7	3	3	4	3	.57	9	.314	.371	.547
	8 Min. YEARS			664	2124	570	103	5	48	827	242	300	144	17	366	44	28	23	11	12	.48	58	.268	.325	.389

Marty Malloy

Bats: Left **Throws:** Right **Pos:** 2B **Ht:** 5'10" **Wt:** 160 **Born:** 7/6/72 **Age:** 24

				BATTING															BASERUNNING				PERCENTAGES		
Year	Team	Lg	Org	G	AB	H	2B	3B	HR	TB	R	RBI	TBB	IBB	SO	HBP	SH	SF	SB	CS	SB%	GDP	Avg	OBP	SLG
1992	Idaho Falls	R+	Atl	62	251	79	18	1	2	105	45	28	11	0	43	2	0	1	8	4	.67	2	.315	.347	.418
1993	Macon	A	Atl	109	376	110	19	3	2	141	55	36	39	3	70	2	3	3	24	8	.75	4	.293	.360	.375
1994	Durham	A+	Atl	118	428	113	22	1	6	155	53	35	52	2	69	2	2	3	18	12	.60	9	.264	.344	.362
1995	Greenville	AA	Atl	124	461	128	20	3	10	184	73	59	39	1	58	0	7	8	11	12	.48	6	.278	.329	.399
1996	Richmond	AAA	Atl	18	64	13	2	1	0	17	7	8	5	1	7	0	2	1	3	0	1.00	1	.203	.257	.266
	Greenville	AA	Atl	111	429	134	27	2	4	177	82	36	54	6	50	4	6	2	11	10	.52	11	.312	.393	.413
5 Min. YEARS				542	2009	577	108	11	24	779	315	202	200	13	297	10	20	18	75	46	.62	33	.287	.352	.388

Sean Maloney

Pitches: Right **Bats:** Right **Pos:** P **Ht:** 6'7" **Wt:** 210 **Born:** 5/25/71 **Age:** 26

				HOW MUCH HE PITCHED						WHAT HE GAVE UP												THE RESULTS					
Year	Team	Lg	Org	G	GS	CG	GF	IP	BFP	H	R	ER	HR	SH	SF	HB	TBB	IBB	SO	WP	Bk	W	L	Pct.	ShO	Sv	ERA
1993	Helena	R+	Mil	17	3	1	10	47.2	209	55	31	23	2	3	2	2	11	1	35	3	0	2	2	.500	0	0	4.34
1994	Beloit	A	Mil	51	0	0	41	59	272	73	42	36	3	2	5	4	10	5	53	6	1	2	6	.250	0	22	5.49
1995	El Paso	AA	Mil	43	0	0	27	64.2	292	69	41	30	4	4	4	3	28	9	54	5	0	7	5	.583	0	15	4.18
1996	El Paso	AA	Mil	51	0	0	49	56.2	230	49	11	9	1	2	1	1	12	1	57	6	1	3	2	.600	0	38	1.43
4 Min. YEARS				162	3	1	127	228	1003	246	125	98	10	11	12	10	61	16	199	20	2	14	15	.483	0	75	3.87

Tony Manahan

Bats: Right **Throws:** Right **Pos:** SS **Ht:** 6'0" **Wt:** 190 **Born:** 12/15/68 **Age:** 28

				BATTING															BASERUNNING				PERCENTAGES		
Year	Team	Lg	Org	G	AB	H	2B	3B	HR	TB	R	RBI	TBB	IBB	SO	HBP	SH	SF	SB	CS	SB%	GDP	Avg	OBP	SLG
1990	San Bernrdo	A+	Sea	51	198	63	10	2	7	98	46	30	24	0	34	2	1	3	8	1	.89	4	.318	.392	.495
1991	Jacksonvlle	AA	Sea	113	410	104	23	2	7	152	67	45	54	0	81	6	2	3	11	5	.69	8	.254	.347	.371
1992	Jacksonvlle	AA	Sea	134	505	130	24	6	8	190	70	49	39	1	76	2	3	3	24	11	.69	12	.257	.311	.376
1993	Calgary	AAA	Sea	117	451	136	31	4	3	184	70	62	38	0	48	2	3	3	19	4	.83	12	.302	.356	.408
1994	Calgary	AAA	Sea	78	295	84	21	1	4	119	48	36	24	0	22	3	1	2	7	2	.78	5	.285	.343	.403
1995	Scranton-WB	AAA	Phi	90	299	86	11	1	3	108	36	32	28	4	39	4	2	0	6	1	.86	7	.288	.356	.361
1996	Scranton-WB	AAA	Phi	17	38	4	2	0	0	6	3	0	2	0	9	0	1	0	0	0	.00	1	.105	.150	.158
7 Min. YEARS				600	2196	607	122	16	32	857	340	254	209	5	309	19	13	14	75	24	.76	49	.276	.342	.390

Dwight Maness

Bats: Right **Throws:** Right **Pos:** OF **Ht:** 6'3" **Wt:** 180 **Born:** 4/3/74 **Age:** 23

				BATTING															BASERUNNING				PERCENTAGES		
Year	Team	Lg	Org	G	AB	H	2B	3B	HR	TB	R	RBI	TBB	IBB	SO	HBP	SH	SF	SB	CS	SB%	GDP	Avg	OBP	SLG
1992	Dodgers	R	LA	44	139	35	6	3	0	47	24	12	14	0	36	8	3	3	18	9	.67	1	.252	.348	.338
1993	Vero Beach	A+	LA	118	409	106	21	4	6	153	57	42	32	0	105	15	8	7	22	13	.63	3	.259	.330	.374
1994	San Antonio	AA	LA	57	215	47	5	5	5	77	32	20	25	0	54	6	2	0	15	16	.48	1	.219	.317	.358
	Bakersfield	A+	LA	74	248	62	13	1	3	86	38	26	29	3	67	11	5	5	21	9	.70	1	.250	.348	.347
1995	San Antonio	AA	LA	57	179	40	2	3	5	63	29	24	20	0	44	5	5	2	4	6	.40	3	.223	.316	.352
	Vero Beach	A+	LA	43	143	33	3	0	3	45	16	23	11	0	29	6	2	5	13	5	.72	2	.231	.303	.315
	St. Lucie	A+	NYN	14	44	9	4	0	0	13	4	5	7	0	6	0	1	0	1	2	.33	0	.205	.314	.295
1996	Binghamton	AA	NYN	130	399	97	14	7	6	143	65	47	52	2	80	8	7	5	25	8	.76	2	.243	.338	.358
5 Min. YEARS				537	1776	429	68	23	28	627	265	199	190	5	421	59	33	27	119	68	.64	13	.242	.330	.353

David Manning

Pitches: Right **Bats:** Right **Pos:** P **Ht:** 6'3" **Wt:** 205 **Born:** 8/14/71 **Age:** 25

				HOW MUCH HE PITCHED						WHAT HE GAVE UP												THE RESULTS					
Year	Team	Lg	Org	G	GS	CG	GF	IP	BFP	H	R	ER	HR	SH	SF	HB	TBB	IBB	SO	WP	Bk	W	L	Pct.	ShO	Sv	ERA
1992	Butte	R+	Tex	8	7	0	0	25.1	143	50	41	31	4	1	0	3	15	0	13	6	5	0	4	.000	0	0	11.01
	Rangers	R	Tex	5	3	0	0	16.1	75	22	13	11	0	1	0	1	4	0	9	1	0	1	1	.500	0	0	6.06
1993	Charlstn-SC	A	Tex	37	10	0	8	116	495	112	54	39	3	5	5	7	39	4	83	11	3	6	7	.462	0	2	3.03
1994	Charlotte	A+	Tex	20	20	0	0	97	438	119	69	60	5	4	3	6	39	0	46	8	3	4	11	.267	0	0	5.57
1995	Charlotte	A+	Tex	26	20	0	2	128.2	545	127	56	50	7	3	3	3	46	0	66	0	5	9	5	.643	0	0	3.50
1996	Okla. City	AAA	Tex	1	1	0	0	5	21	6	3	3	0	0	1	0	2	0	1	0	0	0	0	.000	0	0	5.40
	Tulsa	AA	Tex	39	5	0	13	91	394	89	36	33	5	3	5	2	45	6	48	5	0	6	5	.545	0	3	3.26
5 Min. YEARS				136	66	0	23	479.1	2111	525	272	227	24	17	17	22	190	10	266	31	16	26	33	.441	0	5	4.26

Derek Manning

Pitches: Left **Bats:** Left **Pos:** P **Ht:** 6'3" **Wt:** 220 **Born:** 7/21/70 **Age:** 26

				HOW MUCH HE PITCHED						WHAT HE GAVE UP												THE RESULTS					
Year	Team	Lg	Org	G	GS	CG	GF	IP	BFP	H	R	ER	HR	SH	SF	HB	TBB	IBB	SO	WP	Bk	W	L	Pct.	ShO	Sv	ERA
1993	Sou. Oregon	A-	Oak	15	13	2	0	79.1	322	71	35	32	5	2	3	3	21	2	63	3	4	5	4	.556	2	0	3.63
1994	W. Michigan	A	Oak	29	23	2	4	154	617	120	52	39	4	7	1	3	42	0	118	3	3	11	7	.611	1	2	2.28
1995	Huntsville	AA	Oak	5	5	0	0	28	114	26	14	14	4	1	0	0	7	0	22	0	0	1	2	.333	0	0	4.50
	Modesto	A+	Oak	30	17	0	4	139	581	138	57	44	11	7	4	1	32	0	124	3	1	11	3	.786	0	3	2.85
1996	Huntsville	AA	Oak	18	12	0	1	72	324	96	59	54	10	2	3	1	22	1	51	2	4	0	4	.000	0	1	6.75
4 Min. YEARS				97	70	4	9	472.1	1958	451	217	183	34	19	11	8	124	3	378	11	12	28	20	.583	3	6	3.49

Marc Marini

Bats: Left **Throws:** Left **Pos:** OF-DH **Ht:** 6'1" **Wt:** 185 **Born:** 3/17/70 **Age:** 27

			BATTING															BASERUNNING				PERCENTAGES		
Year	Team	Lg Org	G	AB	H	2B	3B	HR	TB	R	RBI	TBB	IBB	SO	HBP	SH	SF	SB	CS	SB%	GDP	Avg	OBP	SLG
1992	Columbus	A Cle	132	488	150	30	5	8	214	78	70	86	5	63	4	1	9	7	3	.70	10	.307	.409	.439
1993	Kinston	A+ Cle	124	440	132	34	4	5	189	65	53	63	4	70	3	6	9	7	6	.54	9	.300	.384	.430
1994	Canton-Akrn	AA Cle	91	331	91	21	2	17	167	58	65	50	3	62	0	2	3	2	4	.33	9	.275	.367	.505
1995	Canton-Akrn	AA Cle	83	310	95	28	1	3	134	41	56	30	7	51	0	0	8	3	3	.50	9	.306	.359	.432
	Buffalo	AAA Cle	32	85	23	5	0	3	37	12	15	7	0	14	0	0	1	0	0	.00	3	.271	.323	.435
1996	Columbus	AAA NYA	46	135	36	11	0	2	53	23	23	10	1	23	2	1	3	1	0	1.00	4	.267	.320	.393
	5 Min. YEARS		508	1789	527	129	12	38	794	277	282	246	20	283	9	10	33	20	16	.56	44	.295	.377	.444

Elieser Marrero

Bats: Right **Throws:** Right **Pos:** C **Ht:** 6'1" **Wt:** 180 **Born:** 11/17/73 **Age:** 23

			BATTING															BASERUNNING				PERCENTAGES		
Year	Team	Lg Org	G	AB	H	2B	3B	HR	TB	R	RBI	TBB	IBB	SO	HBP	SH	SF	SB	CS	SB%	GDP	Avg	OBP	SLG
1993	Johnson Cty	R+ StL	18	61	22	8	0	2	36	10	14	12	0	9	1	0	1	1	2	.33	0	.361	.467	.590
1994	Savannah	A StL	116	421	110	16	3	21	195	71	79	39	3	92	5	2	5	5	4	.56	6	.261	.328	.463
1995	St. Pete	A+ StL	107	383	81	16	1	10	129	43	55	23	2	55	1	0	7	9	4	.69	10	.211	.254	.337
1996	Arkansas	AA StL	116	374	101	17	3	19	181	65	65	32	1	55	6	0	2	9	6	.60	7	.270	.336	.484
	4 Min. YEARS		357	1239	314	57	7	52	541	189	213	106	6	211	13	2	15	24	16	.60	23	.253	.315	.437

Tom Marsh

Bats: Right **Throws:** Right **Pos:** OF **Ht:** 6' 2" **Wt:** 190 **Born:** 12/27/65 **Age:** 31

			BATTING															BASERUNNING				PERCENTAGES		
Year	Team	Lg Org	G	AB	H	2B	3B	HR	TB	R	RBI	TBB	IBB	SO	HBP	SH	SF	SB	CS	SB%	GDP	Avg	OBP	SLG
1988	Batavia	A- Phi	62	216	55	14	1	8	95	35	27	18	0	54	3	1	2	6	4	.60	2	.255	.318	.440
1989	Spartanburg	A Phi	79	288	73	18	1	10	123	42	42	29	2	66	3	2	5	8	5	.62	2	.253	.323	.427
	Clearwater	A+ Phi	43	141	24	2	1	1	31	12	10	7	0	30	2	4	0	5	2	.71	3	.170	.220	.220
1990	Spartanburg	A Phi	24	75	21	2	1	4	37	14	15	8	1	21	3	0	0	5	2	.71	0	.280	.372	.493
	Reading	AA Phi	41	132	34	6	1	1	45	13	10	8	0	27	3	4	1	5	0	1.00	3	.258	.313	.341
1991	Reading	AA Phi	67	236	62	12	5	7	105	27	35	11	0	47	1	3	3	8	4	.67	7	.263	.295	.445
1992	Scranton-WB	AAA Phi	45	158	38	7	2	8	73	26	25	10	0	30	2	1	0	5	4	.56	5	.241	.294	.462
1993	Scranton-WB	AAA Phi	78	315	90	16	8	12	158	45	57	14	2	47	4	1	3	10	4	.71	12	.286	.321	.502
1994	Scranton-WB	AAA Phi	114	448	120	31	5	9	188	52	59	13	2	58	4	1	6	5	6	.45	7	.268	.291	.420
1995	Scranton-WB	AAA Phi	78	296	91	22	5	10	153	46	47	13	1	39	4	0	2	9	3	.75	10	.307	.343	.517
1996	Buffalo	AAA Cle	112	395	93	16	1	10	141	45	49	16	0	58	4	2	2	9	5	.64	14	.235	.271	.357
1992	Philadelphia	NL	42	125	25	3	2	2	38	7	16	2	0	23	1	2	2	0	1	.00	2	.200	.215	.304
1994	Philadelphia	NL	8	18	5	1	1	0	8	3	3	1	0	1	0	1	0	0	0	.00	0	.278	.316	.444
1995	Philadelphia	NL	43	109	32	3	1	3	46	13	15	4	0	25	0	0	1	0	1	.00	1	.294	.316	.422
	9 Min. YEARS		743	2700	701	146	31	80	1149	357	376	147	8	477	33	19	24	75	39	.66	65	.260	.303	.426
	3 Maj. YEARS		93	252	62	7	4	5	92	23	34	7	0	49	1	3	3	0	2	.00	3	.246	.266	.365

Randy Marshall

Pitches: Left **Bats:** Left **Pos:** P **Ht:** 6'3" **Wt:** 170 **Born:** 10/12/66 **Age:** 30

			HOW MUCH HE PITCHED						WHAT HE GAVE UP												THE RESULTS					
Year	Team	Lg Org	G	GS	CG	GF	IP	BFP	H	R	ER	HR	SH	SF	HB	TBB	IBB	SO	WP	Bk	W	L	Pct.	ShO	Sv	ERA
1989	Niagara Fal	A- Det	6	0	0	2	12.2	57	18	11	11	3	1	0	0	3	0	14	0	2	0	2	.000	0	0	7.82
	Fayettevlle	A Det	34	3	0	7	64.1	276	62	32	23	3	2	1	0	21	3	61	3	0	5	3	.625	0	0	3.22
1990	Fayettevlle	A Det	14	14	5	0	101.2	377	64	17	15	3	2	1	0	9	1	81	0	0	13	0	1.000	3	0	1.33
	Lakeland	A+ Det	13	13	2	0	72	293	71	29	24	3	2	3	1	14	1	40	3	0	7	2	.778	2	0	3.00
1991	London	AA Det	27	27	4	0	159	672	186	92	79	13	4	5	2	27	0	105	4	2	8	10	.444	1	0	4.47
	Toledo	AAA Det	1	1	0	0	5	22	5	6	5	1	0	1	0	2	0	2	0	0	1	0	1.000	0	0	9.00
1992	Tidewater	AAA NYN	26	25	3	0	151.2	641	170	75	68	15	8	6	3	31	0	87	0	0	7	13	.350	1	0	4.04
1993	Norfolk	AAA NYN	4	1	0	1	7.1	47	19	18	16	2	0	0	0	4	1	3	1	0	0	2	.000	0	0	19.64
	Binghamton	AA NYN	7	7	0	0	35	173	61	39	33	3	1	2	0	8	0	21	1	0	0	3	.000	0	0	8.49
	Colo. Sprng	AAA Col	11	1	0	5	21	101	35	20	9	2	0	1	0	6	0	12	2	1	1	0	1.000	0	1	3.86
1994	Colo. Sprng	AAA Col	50	0	0	12	40.2	177	48	25	24	7	2	0	0	14	2	27	5	0	4	0	1.000	0	2	5.31
1995	Toledo	AAA Det	20	17	2	0	109.1	445	99	38	28	7	4	3	2	29	3	67	2	0	7	3	.700	1	0	2.30
1996	Toledo	AAA Det	29	11	0	8	95.1	400	97	49	44	7	3	5	3	25	2	60	0	0	3	5	.375	0	0	4.15
	8 Min. YEARS		242	120	16	35	875	3681	935	451	379	69	29	28	11	193	13	580	21	5	56	43	.566	8	3	3.90

Chandler Martin

Pitches: Right **Bats:** Right **Pos:** P **Ht:** 6'1" **Wt:** 180 **Born:** 10/23/73 **Age:** 23

			HOW MUCH HE PITCHED						WHAT HE GAVE UP												THE RESULTS					
Year	Team	Lg Org	G	GS	CG	GF	IP	BFP	H	R	ER	HR	SH	SF	HB	TBB	IBB	SO	WP	Bk	W	L	Pct.	ShO	Sv	ERA
1995	Portland	A- Col	7	7	0	0	38	153	20	10	7	0	2	0	2	21	0	34	3	3	4	1	.800	0	0	1.66
	Asheville	A Col	15	15	0	0	87.1	369	68	33	28	0	4	0	5	48	0	66	9	4	8	4	.667	0	0	2.89
1996	New Haven	AA Col	1	1	0	0	5	22	6	4	4	2	0	1	1	3	0	4	0	0	1	0	1.000	0	0	7.20
	Asheville	A Col	14	14	0	0	86	347	65	26	21	2	1	0	3	31	0	73	11	0	9	0	1.000	0	0	2.20
	Salem	A+ Col	13	13	1	0	69	333	80	56	45	5	0	2	5	53	1	59	12	0	2	8	.200	1	0	5.87
	2 Min. YEARS		50	50	1	0	285.1	1224	239	129	105	9	7	3	16	156	1	236	35	7	24	13	.649	1	0	3.31

Chris Martin

Bats: Right **Throws:** Right **Pos:** SS **Ht:** 6'1" **Wt:** 170 **Born:** 1/25/68 **Age:** 29

				BATTING															BASERUNNING				PERCENTAGES		
Year	Team	Lg	Org	G	AB	H	2B	3B	HR	TB	R	RBI	TBB	IBB	SO	HBP	SH	SF	SB	CS	SB%	GDP	Avg	OBP	SLG
1990	W. Palm Bch	A+	Mon	59	222	62	17	1	3	90	31	31	27	6	37	1	1	2	7	5	.58	4	.279	.357	.405
1991	Harrisburg	AA	Mon	87	294	66	10	0	6	94	30	36	22	0	61	4	2	5	1	4	.20	8	.224	.283	.320
1992	Harrisburg	AA	Mon	125	383	87	22	1	5	126	39	31	49	1	67	2	1	3	8	6	.57	15	.227	.316	.329
1993	Harrisburg	AA	Mon	116	395	116	23	1	7	162	68	54	40	2	48	6	7	3	16	6	.73	13	.294	.365	.410
1994	Ottawa	AAA	Mon	113	374	89	24	0	3	122	44	40	35	0	46	2	7	5	5	4	.56	17	.238	.303	.326
1995	Ottawa	AAA	Mon	126	412	106	19	1	3	136	55	40	46	1	59	4	8	3	30	5	.86	12	.257	.335	.330
1996	Ottawa	AAA	Mon	122	451	119	30	1	8	175	68	54	33	0	54	7	6	5	25	12	.68	16	.264	.321	.388
7 Min. YEARS				748	2531	645	145	5	35	905	335	286	252	10	372	26	32	26	92	42	.69	85	.255	.326	.358

Jerry Martin

Pitches: Right **Bats:** Right **Pos:** P **Ht:** 6'3" **Wt:** 175 **Born:** 3/15/72 **Age:** 25

				HOW MUCH HE PITCHED						WHAT HE GAVE UP												THE RESULTS					
Year	Team	Lg	Org	G	GS	CG	GF	IP	BFP	H	R	ER	HR	SH	SF	HB	TBB	IBB	SO	WP	Bk	W	L	Pct.	ShO	Sv	ERA
1992	Rangers	R	Tex	9	6	0	1	38.1	148	31	12	11	0	0	2	3	8	0	26	1	2	3	0	1.000	0	1	2.58
	Charlotte	A+	Tex	5	2	1	1	16.2	65	12	6	6	3	1	0	1	4	0	12	0	1	1	1	.500	0	1	3.24
1993	Charlstn-SC	A	Tex	28	28	1	0	161.2	680	157	83	75	18	1	4	4	61	2	109	7	7	8	10	.444	1	0	4.18
1994	Charlotte	A+	Tex	28	27	1	0	164.2	665	133	52	38	6	2	4	4	68	0	80	8	7	13	6	.684	1	0	2.08
1995	Tulsa	AA	Tex	22	17	0	1	88.2	405	100	55	51	12	4	3	2	51	1	46	7	0	3	7	.300	0	0	5.18
1996	Tulsa	AA	Tex	36	6	0	13	85.2	385	98	56	47	11	0	5	1	42	2	49	0	1	5	4	.556	0	5	4.94
5 Min. YEARS				128	86	3	16	555.2	2348	531	264	228	50	8	18	15	234	5	322	23	18	33	28	.541	2	7	3.69

Jim Martin

Bats: Left **Throws:** Right **Pos:** OF **Ht:** 6'1" **Wt:** 195 **Born:** 12/10/70 **Age:** 26

				BATTING															BASERUNNING				PERCENTAGES		
Year	Team	Lg	Org	G	AB	H	2B	3B	HR	TB	R	RBI	TBB	IBB	SO	HBP	SH	SF	SB	CS	SB%	GDP	Avg	OBP	SLG
1992	Great Falls	R+	LA	56	204	63	5	7	5	97	37	30	28	2	52	7	0	3	8	2	.80	0	.309	.405	.475
1993	Bakersfield	A+	LA	118	441	114	17	3	12	173	60	50	45	2	131	13	0	4	27	12	.69	3	.259	.342	.392
1994	Bakersfield	A+	LA	93	360	96	15	8	12	163	50	58	36	3	90	7	0	2	37	16	.70	3	.267	.343	.453
	San Antonio	AA	LA	29	101	22	8	0	1	33	7	10	8	0	23	0	0	0	3	5	.38	1	.218	.275	.327
1995	San Antonio	AA	LA	95	327	77	20	3	4	115	43	36	36	2	83	5	0	4	18	10	.64	4	.235	.317	.352
	Albuquerque	AAA	LA	25	75	19	3	1	1	27	8	7	8	0	20	0	0	0	3	3	.50	3	.253	.325	.360
1996	San Antonio	AA	LA	38	114	24	6	1	1	35	9	8	9	1	42	3	0	2	2	2	.50	2	.211	.281	.307
	San Bernrdo	A+	LA	50	152	37	1	1	6	58	26	23	16	1	53	1	3	2	9	4	.69	1	.243	.316	.382
5 Min. YEARS				504	1774	452	75	24	42	701	240	222	186	11	494	36	3	17	107	54	.66	17	.255	.335	.395

Tom Martin

Pitches: Left **Bats:** Left **Pos:** P **Ht:** 6'1" **Wt:** 185 **Born:** 5/21/70 **Age:** 27

				HOW MUCH HE PITCHED						WHAT HE GAVE UP												THE RESULTS					
Year	Team	Lg	Org	G	GS	CG	GF	IP	BFP	H	R	ER	HR	SH	SF	HB	TBB	IBB	SO	WP	Bk	W	L	Pct.	ShO	Sv	ERA
1989	Bluefield	R+	Bal	8	8	0	0	39	176	36	28	20	3	1	1	0	25	0	31	2	1	3	3	.500	0	0	4.62
	Erie	A-	Bal	7	7	0	0	40.2	190	42	39	30	2	0	2	1	25	0	44	11	2	0	5	.000	0	0	6.64
1990	Wausau	A	Bal	9	9	0	0	40	183	31	25	11	1	3	0	5	27	0	45	4	0	2	3	.400	0	0	2.48
1991	Kane County	A	Bal	38	10	0	19	99	442	92	50	40	4	6	4	3	56	3	106	13	0	4	10	.286	0	6	3.64
1992	High Desert	A+	SD	11	0	0	8	16.1	85	23	19	17	4	0	0	0	16	0	10	2	0	0	2	.000	0	0	9.37
	Waterloo	A	SD	39	2	0	11	55	248	62	38	26	3	5	1	4	22	4	57	5	0	2	6	.250	0	3	4.25
1993	Rancho Cuca	A+	SD	47	1	0	16	59.1	290	72	41	37	4	1	7	7	39	2	53	9	0	1	4	.200	0	0	5.61
1994	Greenville	AA	Atl	36	6	0	9	74	324	82	40	38	6	7	1	4	27	3	51	3	0	5	6	.455	0	0	4.62
1995	Richmond	AAA	Atl	7	0	0	2	9	45	10	9	9	4	0	0	0	10	2	3	0	0	0	0	.000	0	0	9.00
1996	Tucson	AAA	Hou	5	0	0	3	6	25	6	0	0	0	0	0	0	2	2	1	0	0	0	0	.000	0	0	0.00
	Jackson	AA	Hou	57	0	0	18	75	338	71	35	27	8	5	3	4	42	4	58	4	0	6	2	.750	0	3	3.24
8 Min. YEARS				264	43	0	86	513.1	2346	527	324	255	39	28	19	28	291	20	459	53	3	23	41	.359	0	12	4.47

Ryan Martindale

Bats: Right **Throws:** Right **Pos:** C **Ht:** 6'3" **Wt:** 215 **Born:** 12/2/68 **Age:** 28

				BATTING															BASERUNNING				PERCENTAGES		
Year	Team	Lg	Org	G	AB	H	2B	3B	HR	TB	R	RBI	TBB	IBB	SO	HBP	SH	SF	SB	CS	SB%	GDP	Avg	OBP	SLG
1991	Watertown	A-	Cle	67	243	56	7	0	4	75	34	25	20	3	51	7	1	1	7	4	.64	7	.230	.306	.309
1992	Kinston	A+	Cle	99	331	75	8	1	5	100	38	40	25	1	74	12	1	2	8	2	.80	7	.227	.303	.302
1993	Canton-Akrn	AA	Cle	105	310	68	18	1	10	118	44	39	23	0	71	9	4	3	1	3	.25	4	.219	.290	.381
1994	Canton-Akrn	AA	Cle	86	276	81	14	3	6	119	41	41	26	1	54	7	2	2	3	2	.60	6	.293	.367	.431
1995	Buffalo	AAA	Cle	11	31	5	1	0	0	6	4	0	0	0	9	0	0	0	1	0	1.00	1	.161	.161	.194
	Canton-Akrn	AA	Cle	2	8	3	0	0	0	3	2	1	1	0	0	0	0	0	0	1	.00	1	.375	.444	.375
1996	Columbus	AAA	NYA	7	19	5	2	1	0	9	3	3	3	0	5	0	0	0	0	0	.00	0	.263	.364	.474
6 Min. YEARS				377	1218	293	50	6	25	430	166	149	98	5	264	35	8	8	20	12	.63	26	.241	.313	.353

Domingo Martinez

Bats: Right **Throws:** Right **Pos:** 1B **Ht:** 6' 2" **Wt:** 215 **Born:** 8/4/67 **Age:** 29

				BATTING															BASERUNNING				PERCENTAGES		
Year	Team	Lg	Org	G	AB	H	2B	3B	HR	TB	R	RBI	TBB	IBB	SO	HBP	SH	SF	SB	CS	SB%	GDP	Avg	OBP	SLG
1985	Blue Jays	R	Tor	58	219	65	10	2	4	91	36	19	12	0	42	2	0	0	3	4	.43	3	.297	.339	.416

Year Team	Lg Org	G	AB	H	2B	3B	HR	TB	R	RBI	TBB	IBB	SO	HBP	SH	SF	SB	CS	SB%	GDP	Avg	OBP	SLG
		BATTING															BASERUNNING				PERCENTAGES		
1986 Ventura	A+ Tor	129	455	113	19	6	9	171	51	57	36	2	127	4	3	3	9	9	.50	15	.248	.307	.376
1987 Dunedin	A+ Tor	118	435	112	32	2	8	172	53	65	41	2	88	3	0	2	8	3	.73	9	.257	.324	.395
1988 Knoxville	AA Tor	143	516	136	25	2	13	204	54	70	40	3	88	5	0	7	2	7	.22	13	.264	.319	.395
1989 Knoxville	AA Tor	120	415	102	19	2	10	155	56	53	42	3	82	9	1	5	2	2	.50	7	.246	.325	.373
1990 Knoxville	AA Tor	128	463	119	20	3	17	196	52	67	51	1	81	5	1	2	2	3	.40	24	.257	.336	.423
1991 Syracuse	AAA Tor	126	467	146	16	2	17	217	61	83	41	0	107	6	5	6	6	4	.60	10	.313	.371	.465
1992 Syracuse	AAA Tor	116	438	120	22	0	21	205	55	62	33	5	95	8	0	4	6	0	1.00	11	.274	.333	.468
1993 Syracuse	AAA Tor	127	465	127	24	2	24	227	50	79	31	6	115	10	0	4	4	5	.44	11	.273	.329	.488
1994 Nashville	AAA ChA	131	471	127	22	2	22	219	57	81	38	2	102	5	1	8	2	1	.67	12	.270	.326	.465
1995 Louisville	AAA StL	64	222	58	15	0	9	100	26	31	15	2	49	4	0	4	0	0	.00	7	.261	.314	.450
1996 Rochester	AAA Bal	29	116	42	7	0	7	70	18	38	10	0	17	0	0	3	0	1	.00	5	.362	.403	.603
1992 Toronto	AL	7	8	5	0	0	1	8	2	3	0	0	1	0	0	0	0	0	.00	0	.625	.625	1.000
1993 Toronto	AL	8	14	4	0	0	1	7	2	3	1	0	7	0	0	0	0	0	.00	0	.286	.333	.500
12 Min. YEARS		1289	4682	1267	231	23	161	2027	569	705	390	26	993	61	11	48	44	39	.53	127	.271	.332	.433
2 Maj. YEARS		15	22	9	0	0	2	15	4	6	1	0	8	0	0	0	0	0	.00	0	.409	.435	.682

Felix Martinez

Bats: Both **Throws:** Right **Pos:** SS **Ht:** 6'0" **Wt:** 168 **Born:** 5/18/74 **Age:** 23

Year Team	Lg Org	G	AB	H	2B	3B	HR	TB	R	RBI	TBB	IBB	SO	HBP	SH	SF	SB	CS	SB%	GDP	Avg	OBP	SLG
		BATTING															BASERUNNING				PERCENTAGES		
1993 Royals	R KC	57	165	42	5	1	0	49	23	12	17	0	26	3	1	0	22	5	.81	2	.255	.335	.297
1994 Wilmington	A+ KC	117	400	107	16	4	2	137	65	43	30	0	91	3	12	2	19	8	.70	10	.268	.322	.343
1995 Wichita	AA KC	127	426	112	15	3	3	142	53	30	31	0	71	6	4	1	44	20	.69	5	.263	.321	.333
1996 Omaha	AAA KC	118	395	93	13	3	5	127	54	35	44	0	79	5	10	0	18	10	.64	11	.235	.320	.322
4 Min. YEARS		419	1386	354	49	11	10	455	195	120	122	0	267	17	27	3	103	43	.71	28	.255	.323	.328

Greg Martinez

Bats: Both **Throws:** Right **Pos:** OF **Ht:** 5'10" **Wt:** 168 **Born:** 1/27/72 **Age:** 25

Year Team	Lg Org	G	AB	H	2B	3B	HR	TB	R	RBI	TBB	IBB	SO	HBP	SH	SF	SB	CS	SB%	GDP	Avg	OBP	SLG
		BATTING															BASERUNNING				PERCENTAGES		
1993 Brewers	R Mil	5	19	12	0	0	0	12	6	3	4	0	0	1	0	0	7	1	.88	0	.632	.708	.632
Helena	R+ Mil	52	183	53	4	2	0	61	45	19	30	0	26	6	3	5	30	6	.83	0	.290	.397	.333
1994 Beloit	A Mil	81	224	62	8	1	0	72	39	20	25	1	32	3	6	1	27	11	.71	4	.277	.356	.321
1995 Stockton	A+ Mil	114	410	113	8	2	0	125	80	43	69	1	64	2	10	1	55	9	.86	7	.276	.382	.305
1996 Stockton	A+ Mil	73	286	82	5	1	0	89	51	26	29	0	34	0	8	2	30	9	.77	3	.287	.350	.311
El Paso	AA Mil	41	166	52	2	2	1	61	27	21	13	0	19	3	6	1	14	4	.78	4	.313	.372	.367
4 Min. YEARS		366	1288	374	27	8	1	420	248	132	170	2	175	15	33	10	163	40	.80	18	.290	.377	.326

Jesus Martinez

Pitches: Left **Bats:** Left **Pos:** P **Ht:** 6' 2" **Wt:** 145 **Born:** 3/13/74 **Age:** 23

Year Team	Lg Org	G	GS	CG	GF	IP	BFP	H	R	ER	HR	SH	SF	HB	TBB	IBB	SO	WP	Bk	W	L	Pct.	ShO	Sv	ERA
		HOW MUCH HE PITCHED						WHAT HE GAVE UP												THE RESULTS					
1992 Great Falls	R+ LA	6	6	0	0	18.1	112	36	30	27	4	0	0	2	21	0	23	9	0	0	3	.000	0	0	13.25
Dodgers	R LA	7	7	1	0	41	174	38	19	15	1	2	0	1	11	0	39	5	0	1	4	.200	0	0	3.29
1993 Bakersfield	A+ LA	30	21	0	2	145.2	653	144	95	67	12	5	11	5	75	0	108	6	5	4	13	.235	0	0	4.14
1994 San Antonio	AA LA	1	1	0	0	4	14	3	2	2	0	0	0	0	2	0	3	0	0	0	1	.000	0	0	4.50
Vero Beach	A+ LA	18	18	1	0	87.2	386	91	65	61	7	2	3	6	43	0	69	3	0	7	9	.438	1	0	6.26
1995 Albuquerque	AAA LA	2	0	0	1	4	20	4	2	2	0	1	1	1	4	2	5	0	0	1	1	.500	0	0	4.50
San Antonio	AA LA	26	24	1	1	143.2	623	133	66	57	6	8	5	8	75	2	88	16	4	7	10	.412	0	0	3.57
1996 San Antonio	AA LA	27	27	0	0	161.2	706	157	90	79	7	5	7	5	92	0	124	20	0	10	13	.435	0	0	4.40
5 Min. YEARS		117	104	3	4	606	2688	606	369	310	37	23	27	28	323	4	459	59	9	30	54	.357	1	0	4.60

Johnny Martinez

Pitches: Right **Bats:** Right **Pos:** P **Ht:** 6'3" **Wt:** 168 **Born:** 11/25/72 **Age:** 24

Year Team	Lg Org	G	GS	CG	GF	IP	BFP	H	R	ER	HR	SH	SF	HB	TBB	IBB	SO	WP	Bk	W	L	Pct.	ShO	Sv	ERA
		HOW MUCH HE PITCHED						WHAT HE GAVE UP												THE RESULTS					
1993 Burlington	R+ Cle	11	10	1	0	73	290	63	21	18	3	2	0	1	25	2	54	3	4	6	1	.857	0	0	2.22
1994 Burlington	R+ Cle	11	11	1	0	70	305	73	45	31	4	2	1	3	16	1	72	8	3	2	6	.250	0	0	3.99
Kinston	A+ Cle	2	2	0	0	8	34	10	7	7	1	0	1	1	4	0	3	0	0	0	2	.000	0	0	7.88
1995 Kinston	A+ Cle	6	0	0	5	11	44	9	2	2	0	0	0	1	4	0	13	1	0	3	0	1.000	0	2	1.64
Columbus	A Cle	22	2	0	7	65	254	46	17	13	0	2	1	5	18	0	56	4	0	9	1	.900	0	2	1.80
1996 Canton-Akrn	AA Cle	5	0	0	2	8.1	39	9	6	5	1	0	0	2	4	0	3	0	0	0	1	.000	0	0	5.40
4 Min. YEARS		57	25	2	14	235.1	966	210	98	76	9	6	3	13	71	3	201	16	7	20	11	.645	0	4	2.91

Ramiro Martinez

Pitches: Left **Bats:** Left **Pos:** P **Ht:** 6'2" **Wt:** 185 **Born:** 1/28/72 **Age:** 25

Year Team	Lg Org	G	GS	CG	GF	IP	BFP	H	R	ER	HR	SH	SF	HB	TBB	IBB	SO	WP	Bk	W	L	Pct.	ShO	Sv	ERA
		HOW MUCH HE PITCHED						WHAT HE GAVE UP												THE RESULTS					
1992 Rangers	R Tex	10	10	1	0	45.2	184	28	15	6	0	0	1	4	22	0	52	3	1	4	1	.800	1	0	1.18
1993 Charlstn-SC	A Tex	27	27	2	0	124.2	588	129	91	81	10	2	3	10	90	4	129	11	0	6	10	.375	2	0	5.86
1994 Tulsa	AA Tex	23	23	2	0	139.1	589	126	79	70	21	1	3	4	69	0	107	2	1	6	10	.375	0	0	4.52
1995 Tulsa	AA Tex	13	5	0	0	47	220	53	29	27	5	0	3	1	34	2	37	3	0	0	5	.000	0	0	5.17

Year	Team	Lg	Org	HOW MUCH HE PITCHED G	GS	CG	GF	IP	BFP	WHAT HE GAVE UP H	R	ER	HR	SH	SF	HB	TBB	IBB	SO	WP	Bk	THE RESULTS W	L	Pct.	ShO	Sv	ERA
	Charlotte	A+	Tex	27	11	0	6	93.1	412	98	50	48	8	3	6	1	49	2	67	6	0	2	7	.222	0	2	4.63
1996	Tulsa	AA	Tex	11	0	0	3	13.2	65	23	13	13	2	0	0	0	5	0	7	0	0	0	2	.000	0	0	8.56
	Harrisburg	AA	Mon	8	5	0	3	24	109	23	13	12	2	3	0	2	15	0	10	2	0	0	4	.000	0	0	4.50
	W. Palm Bch	A+	Mon	9	7	0	1	42.1	185	47	20	16	1	1	3	1	14	0	44	2	0	1	0	1.000	0	0	3.40
5 Min. YEARS				128	88	5	13	530	2352	527	310	273	49	10	19	23	298	8	453	29	2	19	39	.328	3	2	4.64

Ramon Martinez

Bats: Right **Throws:** Right **Pos:** 2B **Ht:** 6'1" **Wt:** 170 **Born:** 10/10/72 **Age:** 24

Year	Team	Lg	Org	BATTING G	AB	H	2B	3B	HR	TB	R	RBI	TBB	IBB	SO	HBP	SH	SF	BASERUNNING SB	CS	SB%	GDP	PERCENTAGES Avg	OBP	SLG
1993	Royals	R	KC	37	97	23	5	0	0	28	16	9	8	0	6	2	2	2	3	0	1.00	5	.237	.303	.289
	Wilmington	A+	KC	24	75	19	4	0	0	23	8	6	11	0	9	1	3	1	1	4	.20	2	.253	.352	.307
1994	Rockford	A	KC	6	18	5	0	0	0	5	3	3	4	0	2	0	1	0	1	0	1.00	1	.278	.409	.278
	Wilmington	A+	KC	90	325	87	13	2	2	110	40	35	35	0	25	4	20	5	6	3	.67	14	.268	.341	.338
1995	Wichita	AA	KC	103	393	108	20	2	3	141	58	51	42	1	50	4	18	9	11	8	.58	11	.275	.344	.359
1996	Omaha	AAA	KC	85	320	81	12	3	6	117	35	41	21	1	34	3	13	0	3	2	.60	6	.253	.305	.366
	Wichita	AA	KC	26	93	32	4	1	1	41	16	8	7	0	8	0	7	0	4	1	.80	4	.344	.390	.441
4 Min. YEARS				371	1321	355	58	8	12	465	176	153	128	2	134	14	64	17	29	18	.62	43	.269	.336	.352

Ray Martinez

Bats: Right **Throws:** Right **Pos:** SS-2B **Ht:** 6'0" **Wt:** 165 **Born:** 10/1/68 **Age:** 28

Year	Team	Lg	Org	BATTING G	AB	H	2B	3B	HR	TB	R	RBI	TBB	IBB	SO	HBP	SH	SF	BASERUNNING SB	CS	SB%	GDP	PERCENTAGES Avg	OBP	SLG
1987	Salem	A-	Cal	44	106	20	1	0	0	21	8	13	10	0	23	0	1	1	1	0	1.00	0	.189	.256	.198
1988	Bend	A-	Cal	61	226	52	9	2	2	71	28	19	25	0	51	4	1	0	2	7	.22	5	.230	.318	.314
1989	Palm Spring	A+	Cal	103	317	61	8	1	0	71	40	20	43	0	76	5	0	4	4	4	.50	11	.192	.295	.224
1990	Quad City	A	Cal	105	306	68	10	0	9	105	47	40	58	1	82	9	4	6	4	6	.40	5	.222	.356	.343
1991	Quad City	A	Cal	6	21	5	1	0	0	6	3	0	4	0	5	0	0	0	0	0	.00	2	.238	.360	.286
	Palm Spring	A+	Cal	106	371	100	13	5	2	129	58	41	66	3	64	6	7	0	10	7	.59	3	.270	.388	.348
1992	Midland	AA	Cal	30	111	25	4	3	3	44	16	14	6	0	31	2	0	0	1	0	1.00	3	.225	.277	.396
	Edmonton	AAA	Cal	88	285	86	20	2	3	119	42	35	27	0	50	6	2	4	6	5	.55	9	.302	.370	.418
1993	Vancouver	AAA	Cal	114	357	90	24	2	3	127	54	35	35	0	64	7	4	4	5	6	.45	4	.252	.328	.356
1995	Ottawa	AAA	Mon	39	108	27	6	0	0	33	17	9	6	0	17	0	3	1	3	0	1.00	3	.250	.287	.306
	Harrisburg	AA	Mon	48	152	36	6	0	1	45	18	13	20	2	24	1	0	0	3	2	.60	6	.237	.329	.296
1996	Vancouver	AAA	Cal	24	87	22	5	2	0	31	8	10	1	0	13	2	3	3	1	0	1.00	4	.253	.269	.356
9 Min. YEARS				768	2447	592	107	17	23	802	339	249	301	6	500	42	25	23	40	37	.52	55	.242	.332	.328

Eric Martins

Bats: Right **Throws:** Right **Pos:** 3B-2B **Ht:** 5'9" **Wt:** 170 **Born:** 11/19/72 **Age:** 24

Year	Team	Lg	Org	BATTING G	AB	H	2B	3B	HR	TB	R	RBI	TBB	IBB	SO	HBP	SH	SF	BASERUNNING SB	CS	SB%	GDP	PERCENTAGES Avg	OBP	SLG
1994	Sou. Oregon	A-	Oak	56	236	78	16	3	4	112	47	34	23	1	36	5	2	0	17	10	.63	4	.331	.402	.475
	W. Michigan	A	Oak	18	71	22	4	1	0	28	11	7	5	0	12	0	1	2	1	2	.33	2	.310	.346	.394
1995	Modesto	A+	Oak	106	407	118	17	5	1	148	71	54	62	0	74	4	18	4	7	8	.47	8	.290	.386	.364
1996	Huntsville	AA	Oak	111	388	99	23	2	1	129	61	34	47	0	77	5	8	1	7	7	.50	6	.255	.342	.332
3 Min. YEARS				291	1102	317	60	11	6	417	190	129	137	1	199	14	29	7	32	27	.54	20	.288	.371	.378

Tim Marx

Bats: Right **Throws:** Right **Pos:** C **Ht:** 6'2" **Wt:** 190 **Born:** 11/27/68 **Age:** 28

Year	Team	Lg	Org	BATTING G	AB	H	2B	3B	HR	TB	R	RBI	TBB	IBB	SO	HBP	SH	SF	BASERUNNING SB	CS	SB%	GDP	PERCENTAGES Avg	OBP	SLG
1992	Augusta	A	Pit	44	138	30	7	0	0	37	20	9	23	0	16	1	3	0	0	1	.00	4	.217	.333	.268
1993	Salem	A+	Pit	13	43	10	0	0	0	10	2	5	7	0	9	0	1	1	1	1	.50	2	.233	.333	.233
	Augusta	A	Pit	53	162	45	8	0	3	62	28	21	34	0	18	2	2	2	3	4	.43	3	.278	.405	.383
	Buffalo	AAA	Pit	4	14	2	1	0	0	3	0	0	2	0	4	0	0	0	0	0	.00	1	.143	.250	.214
1994	Carolina	AA	Pit	77	239	71	11	2	7	107	32	42	20	1	29	1	2	5	1	3	.25	4	.297	.347	.448
1995	Calgary	AAA	Pit	61	185	55	11	1	1	71	27	12	19	2	16	0	1	3	2	3	.40	6	.297	.357	.384
1996	Calgary	AAA	Pit	95	296	96	20	1	1	121	50	37	29	1	50	2	3	6	6	2	.75	8	.324	.381	.409
5 Min. YEARS				347	1077	309	58	4	12	411	159	126	134	4	142	6	12	17	13	14	.48	28	.287	.364	.382

Justin Mashore

Bats: Right **Throws:** Right **Pos:** OF **Ht:** 5'9" **Wt:** 190 **Born:** 2/14/72 **Age:** 25

Year	Team	Lg	Org	BATTING G	AB	H	2B	3B	HR	TB	R	RBI	TBB	IBB	SO	HBP	SH	SF	BASERUNNING SB	CS	SB%	GDP	PERCENTAGES Avg	OBP	SLG
1991	Bristol	R+	Det	58	177	36	3	0	3	48	29	11	28	1	65	0	2	0	17	6	.74	1	.203	.312	.271
1992	Fayettevlle	A	Det	120	401	96	18	3	4	132	54	43	36	2	117	3	9	1	31	8	.79	3	.239	.306	.329
1993	Lakeland	A+	Det	118	442	113	11	4	3	141	64	30	37	4	92	6	16	5	26	13	.67	9	.256	.318	.319
1994	Trenton	AA	Det	131	450	100	13	5	7	144	63	45	36	0	120	3	8	3	31	7	.82	9	.222	.283	.320
1995	Toledo	AAA	Det	72	223	49	4	3	4	71	32	21	14	1	62	3	9	2	12	9	.57	1	.220	.273	.318
	Jacksonvlle	AA	Det	40	148	36	8	2	4	60	26	15	6	0	41	3	3	0	5	1	.83	2	.243	.287	.405
1996	Jacksonvlle	AA	Det	120	453	129	27	8	7	193	67	50	33	1	97	4	7	2	17	13	.57	10	.285	.337	.426
6 Min. YEARS				659	2294	559	84	25	32	789	335	215	190	9	594	22	54	13	139	57	.71	35	.244	.306	.344

John Massarelli

Bats: Right **Throws:** Right **Pos:** OF **Ht:** 6'2" **Wt:** 200 **Born:** 1/23/66 **Age:** 31

				BATTING														BASERUNNING				PERCENTAGES		
Year	Team	Lg	Org	G	AB	H	2B	3B	HR	TB	R	RBI	TBB	IBB	SO	HBP	SH	SF	SB	CS	SB%	GDP	Avg	OBP	SLG
1987	Auburn	A-	Hou	23	56	9	1	2	0	14	7	3	7	0	10	0	0	1	3	0	1.00	2	.161	.250	.250
	Asheville	A	Hou	6	17	6	0	0	0	6	6	1	2	0	1	0	0	0	3	0	1.00	0	.353	.421	.353
1988	Auburn	A-	Hou	59	179	54	8	1	0	64	29	26	32	0	31	3	1	4	25	5	.83	1	.302	.408	.358
1989	Asheville	A	Hou	90	246	61	13	2	3	87	43	21	35	0	42	3	2	2	25	6	.81	2	.248	.346	.354
1990	Osceola	A+	Hou	120	396	117	8	3	2	137	55	50	41	4	73	2	5	7	54	6	.90	9	.295	.359	.346
1991	Osceola	A+	Hou	51	194	60	9	0	1	72	27	22	16	2	34	4	2	2	18	8	.69	4	.309	.370	.371
	Jackson	AA	Hou	12	38	8	2	0	0	10	3	0	1	0	2	0	0	0	4	0	1.00	0	.211	.231	.263
	Tucson	AAA	Hou	46	127	34	7	1	0	43	19	16	15	1	18	0	1	1	10	2	.83	3	.268	.343	.339
1992	Jackson	AA	Hou	27	98	27	4	1	1	36	15	10	5	0	20	0	1	0	10	2	.83	2	.276	.311	.367
	Tucson	AAA	Hou	50	143	34	4	0	0	38	21	6	14	1	27	1	1	0	14	3	.82	2	.238	.310	.266
1993	Tucson	AAA	Hou	114	423	119	28	4	2	161	66	42	46	4	61	2	5	2	37	13	.74	14	.281	.353	.381
1994	Edmonton	AAA	Fla	120	414	108	18	10	4	158	67	36	34	1	72	0	0	3	39	7	.85	4	.261	.315	.382
1995	Charlotte	AAA	Fla	65	254	62	7	2	2	79	37	8	26	0	55	2	1	1	14	10	.58	2	.244	.318	.311
	Buffalo	AAA	Cle	3	1	0	0	0	0	0	0	0	1	0	0	0	0	0	0	0	.00	0	.000	.500	.000
	Canton-Akrn	AA	Cle	55	178	50	10	2	2	70	17	22	16	0	28	0	1	3	17	6	.74	1	.281	.335	.393
1996	Rancho Cuca	A+	SD	26	108	32	9	3	0	47	24	17	15	1	14	2	0	0	6	1	.86	3	.296	.392	.435
	Memphis	AA	SD	65	205	54	16	3	2	82	26	15	13	0	32	0	2	1	9	4	.69	1	.263	.306	.400
10 Min. YEARS				932	3077	835	144	34	19	1104	462	295	319	14	520	19	22	27	288	73	.80	50	.271	.341	.359

Dan Masteller

Bats: Left **Throws:** Left **Pos:** 1B **Ht:** 6' 0" **Wt:** 190 **Born:** 3/17/68 **Age:** 29

				BATTING														BASERUNNING				PERCENTAGES		
Year	Team	Lg	Org	G	AB	H	2B	3B	HR	TB	R	RBI	TBB	IBB	SO	HBP	SH	SF	SB	CS	SB%	GDP	Avg	OBP	SLG
1989	Elizabethtn	R+	Min	9	38	13	0	0	2	19	8	9	6	0	2	0	0	0	2	2	.50	0	.342	.432	.500
	Visalia	A+	Min	53	181	46	5	1	3	62	24	16	18	2	36	1	0	1	0	0	.00	2	.254	.323	.343
1990	Visalia	A+	Min	135	473	133	20	5	4	175	71	73	81	0	76	9	4	3	2	5	.29	15	.281	.394	.370
1991	Orlando	AA	Min	124	370	91	14	5	5	130	44	35	43	6	43	3	3	2	6	4	.60	5	.246	.328	.351
1992	Orlando	AA	Min	116	365	96	24	4	8	152	42	42	23	1	36	4	3	1	2	4	.33	7	.263	.313	.416
1993	Nashville	AA	Min	36	121	33	3	0	3	45	19	16	11	0	19	1	2	0	2	1	.67	0	.273	.338	.372
	Portland	AAA	Min	61	211	68	13	4	7	110	35	47	24	3	25	1	1	7	3	4	.43	2	.322	.383	.521
1994	Salt Lake	AAA	Min	98	338	102	26	3	8	158	53	58	21	1	27	1	2	4	4	1	.80	9	.302	.341	.467
1995	Salt Lake	AAA	Min	48	152	46	10	7	4	82	25	18	15	3	17	3	1	3	4	1	.80	3	.303	.370	.539
1996	Massachusts	IND	—	32	118	49	15	0	5	79	34	37	29	7	7	1	0	4	7	0	1.00	3	.415	.520	.669
	Harrisburg	AA	Mon	44	128	42	11	0	2	59	21	21	18	3	11	0	1	1	0	0	.00	3	.328	.408	.461
1995	Minnesota	AL		71	198	47	12	0	3	68	21	21	18	0	19	1	1	1	1	2	.33	7	.237	.303	.343
8 Min. YEARS				756	2495	719	141	29	51	1071	376	372	289	26	299	24	17	26	32	22	.59	49	.288	.364	.429

Francisco Matos

Bats: Right **Throws:** Right **Pos:** 2B **Ht:** 6' 1" **Wt:** 160 **Born:** 7/23/69 **Age:** 27

				BATTING														BASERUNNING				PERCENTAGES		
Year	Team	Lg	Org	G	AB	H	2B	3B	HR	TB	R	RBI	TBB	IBB	SO	HBP	SH	SF	SB	CS	SB%	GDP	Avg	OBP	SLG
1989	Modesto	A+	Oak	65	200	41	5	1	1	51	14	23	12	0	41	0	0	1	6	5	.55	5	.205	.249	.255
1990	Modesto	A+	Oak	83	321	88	12	1	1	105	46	20	15	0	65	5	7	2	26	5	.84	2	.274	.315	.327
	Huntsville	AA	Oak	45	180	41	3	3	0	50	18	12	9	1	18	1	2	1	7	4	.64	3	.228	.267	.278
1991	Huntsville	AA	Oak	55	191	37	1	2	0	42	18	19	17	1	28	2	5	0	12	2	.86	8	.194	.267	.220
	Modesto	A+	Oak	50	189	53	4	0	1	60	32	22	30	1	24	1	4	1	19	8	.70	5	.280	.380	.317
1992	Huntsville	AA	Oak	44	150	33	5	1	1	43	11	14	11	0	27	2	1	1	4	4	.50	4	.220	.280	.287
1993	Huntsville	AA	Oak	123	461	127	12	3	1	148	69	32	22	1	54	4	4	3	16	6	.73	6	.275	.312	.321
1994	Tacoma	AAA	Oak	86	336	103	10	1	0	115	40	30	14	0	32	0	4	3	16	9	.64	13	.307	.331	.342
1995	Calgary	AAA	Pit	100	341	110	11	6	3	142	36	40	5	0	25	2	3	1	9	2	.82	11	.323	.335	.416
1996	Ottawa	AAA	Mon	100	307	73	15	3	2	100	30	23	16	0	35	3	3	2	4	5	.44	14	.238	.280	.326
1994	Oakland	AL		14	28	7	1	0	0	8	1	2	1	0	2	0	0	1	1	0	1.00	1	.250	.267	.286
8 Min. YEARS				751	2676	706	78	21	10	856	314	235	151	4	349	20	33	15	119	50	.70	71	.264	.306	.320

Jeff Matranga

Pitches: Right **Bats:** Right **Pos:** P **Ht:** 6'2" **Wt:** 170 **Born:** 12/14/70 **Age:** 26

				HOW MUCH HE PITCHED						WHAT HE GAVE UP													THE RESULTS					
Year	Team	Lg	Org	G	GS	CG	GF	IP	BFP	H	R	ER	HR	SH	SF	HB	TBB	IBB	SO	WP	Bk	W	L	Pct.	ShO	Sv	ERA
1992	Johnson Cty	R+	StL	19	1	0	12	36.1	158	34	17	12	1	0	1	3	13	1	47	3	0	3	0	1.000	0	2	2.97
1993	St. Pete	A+	StL	5	3	0	1	28.1	113	23	10	7	1	0	0	0	6	0	21	3	0	2	0	1.000	0	0	2.22
	Savannah	A	StL	15	15	3	0	103	387	74	24	17	8	1	0	4	13	0	90	4	0	11	3	.786	2	0	1.49
1994	St. Pete	A+	StL	63	0	0	26	87.1	367	76	30	23	4	5	2	3	30	7	76	1	1	8	5	.615	0	3	2.37
1995	Arkansas	AA	StL	7	0	0	4	8	27	1	0	0	0	0	0	0	3	0	4	0	0	0	0	.000	0	0	0.00
	St. Pete	A+	StL	60	0	0	21	73.2	299	50	27	20	2	3	3	9	23	3	75	2	0	3	4	.429	0	3	2.44
1996	Arkansas	AA	StL	62	0	0	31	79.2	327	56	22	19	6	5	2	8	30	3	82	0	0	6	5	.545	0	4	2.15
5 Min. YEARS				231	19	3	95	416.1	1678	314	130	98	22	14	8	27	118	14	395	13	1	33	17	.660	2	12	2.12

Mike Matthews

Pitches: Left **Bats:** Left **Pos:** P **Ht:** 6'3" **Wt:** 180 **Born:** 10/24/73 **Age:** 23

				HOW MUCH HE PITCHED						WHAT HE GAVE UP												THE RESULTS					
Year	Team	Lg	Org	G	GS	CG	GF	IP	BFP	H	R	ER	HR	SH	SF	HB	TBB	IBB	SO	WP	Bk	W	L	Pct.	ShO	Sv	ERA
1992	Burlington	R+	Cle	10	10	0	0	62.1	245	33	13	7	1	2	1	3	27	0	55	3	1	7	0	1.000	0	0	1.01
	Watertown	A-	Cle	2	2	0	0	11	47	10	4	4	0	0	1	0	8	0	5	1	0	1	0	1.000	0	0	3.27
1994	Columbus	A	Cle	23	23	0	0	119.2	502	120	53	41	8	3	3	7	44	1	99	7	3	6	8	.429	0	0	3.08
1995	Canton-Akrn	AA	Cle	15	15	1	0	74.1	345	82	62	49	6	2	8	2	43	1	37	8	1	5	8	.385	0	0	5.93
1996	Canton-Akrn	AA	Cle	27	27	3	0	162.1	713	178	96	84	13	6	7	5	74	3	112	6	1	9	11	.450	0	0	4.66
4 Min. YEARS				77	77	4	0	429.2	1852	423	228	185	28	13	20	17	196	5	308	25	6	28	27	.509	0	0	3.88

Rob Mattson

Pitches: Right **Bats:** Left **Pos:** P **Ht:** 6'1" **Wt:** 190 **Born:** 11/18/66 **Age:** 30

				HOW MUCH HE PITCHED						WHAT HE GAVE UP												THE RESULTS					
Year	Team	Lg	Org	G	GS	CG	GF	IP	BFP	H	R	ER	HR	SH	SF	HB	TBB	IBB	SO	WP	Bk	W	L	Pct.	ShO	Sv	ERA
1991	Macon	A	Atl	23	7	3	4	76.2	312	61	29	24	1	1	4	4	17	1	51	5	1	5	2	.714	1	0	2.82
	Durham	A+	Atl	9	8	2	1	45.2	190	48	23	22	2	2	1	0	9	1	32	3	2	1	4	.200	0	1	4.34
1992	Beloit	A	Mil	8	1	0	2	17.1	76	15	8	8	1	1	1	0	7	1	16	0	2	1	0	1.000	0	0	4.15
1995	Memphis	AA	SD	30	28	11	1	201.2	862	199	109	92	20	7	15	20	73	2	139	4	4	12	13	.480	3	0	4.11
1996	Memphis	AA	SD	27	27	3	0	164.1	708	172	87	79	19	2	4	7	54	2	88	5	2	13	8	.619	1	0	4.33
4 Min. YEARS				97	71	19	8	505.2	2148	495	256	225	43	13	25	31	160	7	326	17	11	32	27	.542	5	1	4.00

Jeff Matulevich

Pitches: Right **Bats:** Right **Pos:** P **Ht:** 6'3" **Wt:** 200 **Born:** 4/15/70 **Age:** 27

				HOW MUCH HE PITCHED						WHAT HE GAVE UP												THE RESULTS					
Year	Team	Lg	Org	G	GS	CG	GF	IP	BFP	H	R	ER	HR	SH	SF	HB	TBB	IBB	SO	WP	Bk	W	L	Pct.	ShO	Sv	ERA
1992	Johnson Cty	R+	StL	13	13	0	0	71.1	326	77	41	30	2	2	1	2	31	2	46	7	0	3	4	.429	0	0	3.79
1993	Savannah	A	StL	34	1	0	13	50.2	231	61	31	27	4	1	1	1	14	1	42	0	0	4	4	.500	0	0	4.80
1994	Madison	A	StL	47	0	0	46	50.2	217	40	24	16	2	3	1	5	21	1	40	6	0	3	4	.429	0	30	2.84
1995	St. Pete	A+	StL	51	0	0	48	58.2	253	50	20	18	3	2	1	0	30	3	61	4	0	1	5	.167	0	30	2.76
1996	Arkansas	AA	StL	41	0	0	16	59.1	254	48	33	24	5	2	3	1	29	4	51	6	0	4	3	.571	0	1	3.64
5 Min. YEARS				186	14	0	123	290.2	1281	276	149	115	16	10	7	9	125	11	240	23	0	15	20	.429	0	61	3.56

Mike Maurer

Pitches: Right **Bats:** Right **Pos:** P **Ht:** 6'2" **Wt:** 185 **Born:** 7/4/72 **Age:** 24

				HOW MUCH HE PITCHED						WHAT HE GAVE UP												THE RESULTS					
Year	Team	Lg	Org	G	GS	CG	GF	IP	BFP	H	R	ER	HR	SH	SF	HB	TBB	IBB	SO	WP	Bk	W	L	Pct.	ShO	Sv	ERA
1994	Sou. Oregon	A-	Oak	17	8	0	5	63.1	285	68	42	25	2	4	4	5	20	1	67	7	3	2	6	.250	0	3	3.55
1995	Huntsville	AA	Oak	17	0	0	14	20.2	100	34	18	15	0	2	1	0	5	2	19	2	0	0	2	.000	0	6	6.53
	Modesto	A+	Oak	56	0	0	51	61	257	61	27	23	3	4	3	2	14	2	63	4	0	2	4	.333	0	24	3.39
1996	Huntsville	AA	Oak	52	0	0	41	64.2	298	67	31	27	3	3	2	3	35	9	46	5	0	4	6	.400	0	8	3.76
3 Min. YEARS				142	8	0	111	209.2	940	230	118	90	8	13	10	10	74	14	195	18	3	8	18	.308	0	41	3.86

Ron Maurer

Bats: Right **Throws:** Right **Pos:** SS-3B **Ht:** 6'1" **Wt:** 185 **Born:** 6/10/68 **Age:** 29

				BATTING															BASERUNNING				PERCENTAGES		
Year	Team	Lg	Org	G	AB	H	2B	3B	HR	TB	R	RBI	TBB	IBB	SO	HBP	SH	SF	SB	CS	SB%	GDP	Avg	OBP	SLG
1990	Great Falls	R+	LA	62	238	64	8	0	6	90	43	43	27	0	38	6	5	4	5	2	.71	4	.269	.353	.378
1991	Bakersfield	A+	LA	129	442	128	21	5	7	180	59	53	63	3	68	7	13	3	8	8	.50	15	.290	.384	.407
1992	San Antonio	AA	LA	82	224	61	13	0	0	74	29	14	15	3	32	5	4	0	4	3	.57	6	.272	.332	.330
1993	San Antonio	AA	LA	11	37	7	1	0	1	11	6	4	7	0	12	0	1	0	0	1	.00	0	.189	.318	.297
	Albuquerque	AAA	LA	58	116	34	7	0	3	50	19	14	11	1	17	0	4	0	1	1	.50	6	.293	.354	.431
1994	Albuquerque	AAA	LA	55	125	35	8	1	2	51	20	16	4	0	15	3	1	1	1	0	1.00	4	.280	.316	.408
1995	Albuquerque	AAA	LA	84	185	48	14	2	5	81	29	25	19	2	34	3	1	1	1	2	.33	1	.259	.337	.438
1996	San Antonio	AA	LA	6	19	5	0	0	0	5	3	0	3	0	7	0	0	0	0	0	.00	0	.263	.364	.263
	Albuquerque	AAA	LA	80	222	61	14	1	5	92	32	30	30	2	50	3	4	3	2	4	.33	5	.275	.364	.414
7 Min. YEARS				567	1608	443	86	9	29	634	240	199	179	11	273	27	33	12	22	21	.51	41	.275	.355	.394

Tim Mauser

Pitches: Right **Bats:** Right **Pos:** P **Ht:** 6' 0" **Wt:** 195 **Born:** 10/4/66 **Age:** 30

				HOW MUCH HE PITCHED						WHAT HE GAVE UP												THE RESULTS					
Year	Team	Lg	Org	G	GS	CG	GF	IP	BFP	H	R	ER	HR	SH	SF	HB	TBB	IBB	SO	WP	Bk	W	L	Pct.	ShO	Sv	ERA
1988	Spartanburg	A	Phi	4	3	0	0	23	88	15	6	5	0	2	2	0	5	0	18	1	0	2	1	.667	0	0	1.96
	Reading	AA	Phi	5	5	0	0	28.1	120	27	14	11	4	2	0	2	6	0	17	0	0	2	3	.400	0	0	3.49
1989	Clearwater	A+	Phi	16	16	5	0	107	457	105	40	32	4	2	0	5	40	0	73	2	1	6	7	.462	0	0	2.69
	Reading	AA	Phi	11	11	4	0	72	302	62	36	29	5	0	2	1	33	0	54	3	1	7	4	.636	2	0	3.63
1990	Reading	AA	Phi	8	8	1	0	46.1	194	35	20	17	2	0	2	3	15	0	40	4	0	3	4	.429	0	0	3.30
	Scranton-WB	AAA	Phi	16	16	4	0	98.1	396	75	48	40	10	1	3	3	34	1	54	4	0	5	7	.417	1	0	3.66
1991	Scranton-WB	AAA	Phi	26	18	1	3	128.1	544	119	66	53	11	4	4	2	55	3	75	3	0	6	11	.353	0	1	3.72
1992	Scranton-WB	AAA	Phi	45	5	0	15	100	427	87	37	33	6	6	6	0	45	4	75	4	0	8	6	.571	0	4	2.97
1993	Scranton-WB	AAA	Phi	19	0	0	19	20.2	79	10	2	2	1	1	0	0	5	0	25	4	0	2	0	1.000	0	10	0.87
1995	Las Vegas	AAA	SD	35	0	0	15	50.2	233	63	39	27	6	4	13	1	20	2	32	1	0	3	4	.429	0	0	4.80
1996	Okla. City	AAA	Tex	8	0	0	4	8.1	37	8	3	2	1	0	0	0	2	0	11	0	0	1	1	.500	0	0	2.16
1991	Philadelphia	NL		3	0	0	1	10.2	53	18	10	9	3	1	0	0	3	0	6	0	0	0	0	.000	0	0	7.59

			HOW MUCH HE PITCHED						WHAT HE GAVE UP												THE RESULTS					
Year	Team	Lg Org	G	GS	CG	GF	IP	BFP	H	R	ER	HR	SH	SF	HB	TBB	IBB	SO	WP	Bk	W	L	Pct.	ShO	Sv	ERA
1993	Philadelphia	NL	8	0	0	1	16.1	71	15	9	9	1	0	0	1	7	0	14	1	0	0	0	.000	0	0	4.96
	San Diego	NL	28	0	0	15	37.2	164	36	19	15	5	1	1	0	17	5	32	1	0	0	1	.000	0	0	3.58
1994	San Diego	NL	35	0	0	12	49	211	50	21	19	3	2	3	1	19	3	32	5	1	2	4	.333	0	2	3.49
1995	San Diego	NL	5	0	0	1	5.2	30	4	6	6	0	0	0	0	9	0	9	0	0	0	1	.000	0	0	9.53
8	Min. YEARS		193	82	15	56	683	2877	606	311	251	50	22	32	17	260	10	474	26	2	45	48	.484	3	15	3.31
4	Maj. YEARS		79	0	0	30	119.1	529	123	65	58	12	4	4	2	55	8	93	7	1	2	6	.250	0	2	4.37

Jason Maxwell

Bats: Right **Throws:** Right **Pos:** SS **Ht:** 6'0" **Wt:** 175 **Born:** 3/21/72 **Age:** 25

			BATTING														BASERUNNING				PERCENTAGES		
Year	Team	Lg Org	G	AB	H	2B	3B	HR	TB	R	RBI	TBB	IBB	SO	HBP	SH	SF	SB	CS	SB%	GDP	Avg	OBP	SLG
1993	Huntington	R+ ChN	61	179	52	7	2	7	84	50	38	35	0	39	4	2	1	6	5	.55	0	.291	.416	.469
1994	Daytona	A+ ChN	116	368	85	18	2	10	137	71	32	55	0	96	8	6	2	7	7	.50	6	.231	.342	.372
1995	Daytona	A+ ChN	117	388	102	13	3	10	151	66	58	63	1	68	6	1	8	12	7	.63	6	.263	.368	.389
1996	Orlando	AA ChN	126	433	115	20	1	9	164	64	45	56	3	77	6	4	3	19	4	.83	5	.266	.355	.379
4	Min. YEARS		420	1368	354	58	8	36	536	251	173	209	4	280	24	13	14	44	23	.66	17	.259	.363	.392

Craig Mayes

Bats: Left **Throws:** Right **Pos:** C **Ht:** 5'10" **Wt:** 195 **Born:** 5/8/70 **Age:** 27

			BATTING														BASERUNNING				PERCENTAGES		
Year	Team	Lg Org	G	AB	H	2B	3B	HR	TB	R	RBI	TBB	IBB	SO	HBP	SH	SF	SB	CS	SB%	GDP	Avg	OBP	SLG
1992	Everett	A- SF	38	110	38	3	0	0	41	17	10	10	1	13	0	0	0	3	3	.50	5	.345	.400	.373
1993	Clinton	A SF	75	226	67	12	1	3	90	25	37	10	0	52	0	3	3	1	0	1.00	8	.296	.322	.398
1994	Clinton	A SF	49	155	32	5	1	1	42	13	14	11	1	33	0	2	1	0	2	.00	4	.206	.257	.271
	San Bernrdo	A+ —	50	191	48	5	0	2	59	20	21	17	1	35	1	0	0	2	2	.50	3	.251	.316	.309
1995	Shreveport	AA SF	3	9	2	1	0	0	3	0	3	0	0	2	0	0	0	0	0	.00	0	.222	.222	.333
	San Jose	A+ SF	90	318	80	17	4	0	105	34	39	27	1	50	0	1	2	3	1	.75	7	.252	.308	.330
1996	Shreveport	AA SF	10	40	16	2	0	0	18	5	3	5	1	2	0	0	0	0	1	.00	0	.400	.467	.450
	Ohio Valley	IND —	4	6	1	0	0	0	1	0	0	1	0	0	0	0	0	1	0	1.00	0	.167	.286	.167
	San Jose	A+ SF	114	472	155	26	4	3	198	56	68	29	2	43	0	2	4	6	8	.43	5	.328	.364	.419
5	Min. YEARS		433	1527	439	71	10	9	557	170	195	110	7	230	1	8	10	16	17	.48	32	.287	.334	.365

Charles McBride

Bats: Right **Throws:** Right **Pos:** OF **Ht:** 5'10" **Wt:** 170 **Born:** 8/12/73 **Age:** 23

			BATTING														BASERUNNING				PERCENTAGES		
Year	Team	Lg Org	G	AB	H	2B	3B	HR	TB	R	RBI	TBB	IBB	SO	HBP	SH	SF	SB	CS	SB%	GDP	Avg	OBP	SLG
1993	Idaho Falls	R+ Atl	49	142	41	6	4	2	61	25	20	13	0	27	3	0	1	8	3	.73	4	.289	.358	.430
1994	Macon	A Atl	81	296	100	21	6	13	172	60	54	29	0	80	0	4	3	17	4	.81	5	.338	.393	.581
1995	Durham	A+ Atl	102	360	85	15	1	13	141	60	59	54	1	109	5	1	2	11	4	.73	5	.236	.342	.392
1996	Durham	A+ Atl	14	49	12	4	0	2	22	7	6	5	0	14	0	0	0	1	0	1.00	3	.245	.315	.449
	Greenville	AA Atl	85	291	78	17	5	4	117	38	50	27	1	75	3	0	3	4	3	.57	3	.268	.333	.402
4	Min. YEARS		331	1138	316	63	16	34	513	190	189	128	2	305	11	5	9	41	14	.75	20	.278	.354	.451

Rod McCall

Bats: Left **Throws:** Right **Pos:** DH **Ht:** 6'7" **Wt:** 220 **Born:** 11/4/71 **Age:** 25

			BATTING														BASERUNNING				PERCENTAGES		
Year	Team	Lg Org	G	AB	H	2B	3B	HR	TB	R	RBI	TBB	IBB	SO	HBP	SH	SF	SB	CS	SB%	GDP	Avg	OBP	SLG
1990	Indians	R Cle	10	36	10	2	0	0	12	5	6	5	1	10	0	0	0	0	0	.00	0	.278	.366	.333
	Burlington	R+ Cle	31	92	15	5	0	1	23	8	11	10	0	43	2	0	2	0	1	.00	1	.163	.255	.250
1991	Columbus	A Cle	103	323	70	14	1	5	101	34	35	61	3	128	3	0	1	2	2	.50	5	.217	.345	.313
1992	Columbus	A Cle	116	404	97	15	0	20	172	55	80	68	4	121	4	0	6	1	1	.50	9	.240	.351	.426
1993	Kinston	A+ Cle	71	245	51	13	0	9	91	32	33	32	2	85	3	0	4	3	1	.75	3	.208	.303	.371
1994	Kinston	A+ Cle	58	205	44	14	0	11	91	32	27	26	1	75	7	1	0	1	1	.50	2	.215	.324	.444
	High Desert	A+ Cle	48	183	51	14	0	17	116	40	43	20	0	63	5	0	1	2	1	.67	4	.279	.364	.634
	Canton-Akrn	AA Cle	20	66	13	4	0	3	26	8	9	2	0	27	2	1	1	0	0	.00	1	.197	.239	.394
1995	Bakersfield	A+ Cle	96	345	114	19	1	20	195	61	70	40	7	90	8	2	4	2	5	.29	6	.330	.408	.565
	Canton-Akrn	AA Cle	26	95	26	5	0	9	58	16	18	12	3	21	1	0	0	1	1	.50	3	.274	.361	.611
1996	Canton-Akrn	AA Cle	120	440	132	29	2	27	246	80	85	52	4	118	6	0	0	2	0	1.00	4	.300	.382	.559
7	Min. YEARS		699	2434	623	134	4	122	1131	371	417	328	25	781	41	4	19	14	13	.52	38	.256	.352	.465

Scott McClain

Bats: Right **Throws:** Right **Pos:** 3B **Ht:** 6'3" **Wt:** 209 **Born:** 5/19/72 **Age:** 25

			BATTING														BASERUNNING				PERCENTAGES		
Year	Team	Lg Org	G	AB	H	2B	3B	HR	TB	R	RBI	TBB	IBB	SO	HBP	SH	SF	SB	CS	SB%	GDP	Avg	OBP	SLG
1990	Bluefield	R+ Bal	40	107	21	2	0	4	35	20	15	22	0	35	2	0	4	2	3	.40	1	.196	.333	.327
1991	Kane County	A Bal	25	81	18	0	0	0	18	9	4	17	0	25	0	1	0	1	1	.50	4	.222	.357	.222
	Bluefield	R+ Bal	41	149	39	5	0	0	44	16	24	14	0	39	3	0	1	5	3	.63	3	.262	.335	.295
1992	Kane County	A Bal	96	316	84	12	2	3	109	43	30	48	1	62	6	6	1	7	4	.64	5	.266	.372	.345
1993	Frederick	A+ Bal	133	427	111	22	2	9	164	65	54	70	0	88	6	3	2	10	6	.63	8	.260	.370	.384
1994	Bowie	AA Bal	133	427	103	29	1	11	167	71	58	72	2	89	1	2	7	6	3	.67	14	.241	.347	.301
1995	Rochester	AAA Bal	61	199	50	9	1	8	85	32	22	23	0	34	1	1	2	0	1	.00	5	.251	.329	.427
	Bowie	AA Bal	70	259	72	14	1	13	127	41	61	25	1	44	3	0	4	2	1	.67	13	.278	.344	.490

Year	Team	Lg	Org	G	AB	H	2B	3B	HR	TB	R	RBI	TBB	IBB	SO	HBP	SH	SF	SB	CS	SB%	GDP	Avg	OBP	SLG
	BATTING																		BASERUNNING				PERCENTAGES		
1996	Rochester	AAA	Bal	131	463	130	23	4	17	212	76	69	61	1	109	1	0	7	8	6	.57	6	.281	.361	.458
7 Min. YEARS				730	2428	628	116	11	65	961	373	337	352	5	525	23	13	28	41	28	.59	59	.259	.354	.396

Jason McCommon

Pitches: Right **Bats:** Right **Pos:** P **Ht:** 6'0" **Wt:** 190 **Born:** 8/9/71 **Age:** 25

Year	Team	Lg	Org	G	GS	CG	GF	IP	BFP	H	R	ER	HR	SH	SF	HB	TBB	IBB	SO	WP	Bk	W	L	Pct.	ShO	Sv	ERA
	HOW MUCH HE PITCHED									WHAT HE GAVE UP												THE RESULTS					
1994	Vermont	A-	Mon	24	3	0	13	48	196	47	20	19	0	1	3	0	15	2	47	7	1	3	4	.429	0	4	3.56
1995	W. Palm Bch	A+	Mon	26	26	3	0	156	650	153	75	65	13	7	6	10	38	0	94	6	7	7	11	.389	1	0	3.75
1996	Harrisburg	AA	Mon	30	24	1	2	153	663	169	88	67	13	2	8	7	44	1	92	5	0	10	10	.500	0	1	3.94
3 Min. YEARS				80	53	4	15	357	1509	369	183	151	26	10	17	17	97	3	233	18	8	20	25	.444	1	5	3.81

Chad McConnell

Bats: Right **Throws:** Right **Pos:** OF **Ht:** 6'1" **Wt:** 180 **Born:** 10/13/70 **Age:** 26

Year	Team	Lg	Org	G	AB	H	2B	3B	HR	TB	R	RBI	TBB	IBB	SO	HBP	SH	SF	SB	CS	SB%	GDP	Avg	OBP	SLG
	BATTING																		BASERUNNING				PERCENTAGES		
1993	Clearwater	A+	Phi	90	300	72	17	3	6	113	43	37	51	2	98	4	0	2	9	5	.64	6	.240	.356	.377
1994	Clearwater	A+	Phi	29	101	32	3	3	4	53	19	19	16	0	28	0	0	0	2	1	.67	4	.317	.410	.525
	Reading	AA	Phi	88	267	62	9	3	6	95	30	41	24	1	86	6	2	2	7	5	.58	6	.232	.308	.356
1995	Reading	AA	Phi	94	319	88	12	1	11	135	46	52	27	1	59	10	1	2	8	3	.73	8	.276	.349	.423
1996	Reading	AA	Phi	116	385	95	18	1	12	151	70	50	40	0	119	19	3	2	6	5	.55	8	.247	.345	.392
4 Min. YEARS				417	1372	349	59	11	39	547	208	199	158	4	390	39	6	8	32	19	.63	32	.254	.346	.399

Andy McCormack

Pitches: Left **Bats:** Right **Pos:** P **Ht:** 6'1" **Wt:** 205 **Born:** 2/4/74 **Age:** 23

Year	Team	Lg	Org	G	GS	CG	GF	IP	BFP	H	R	ER	HR	SH	SF	HB	TBB	IBB	SO	WP	Bk	W	L	Pct.	ShO	Sv	ERA
	HOW MUCH HE PITCHED									WHAT HE GAVE UP												THE RESULTS					
1993	White Sox	R	ChA	1	1	0	0	6	21	1	0	0	0	1	0	0	0	0	7	0	0	0	0	.000	0	0	0.00
	Hickory	A	ChA	14	14	1	0	83.1	355	89	47	43	5	2	1	3	26	0	67	3	4	4	7	.364	0	0	4.64
1994	South Bend	A	ChA	27	26	4	1	188	797	209	86	74	15	8	5	6	51	1	115	6	3	9	11	.450	1	0	3.54
1995	White Sox	R	ChA	1	1	0	0	6	21	4	1	1	1	0	0	0	0	0	4	0	0	1	0	1.000	0	0	1.50
	South Bend	A	ChA	7	5	0	2	29.1	126	30	15	13	4	2	1	1	11	0	14	1	0	2	2	.500	0	0	3.99
1996	Kinston	A+	Cle	5	0	0	3	10.1	35	4	0	0	0	0	0	0	2	0	8	0	0	0	0	.000	0	1	0.00
	Canton-Akrn	AA	Cle	1	0	0	0	0.1	2	0	1	1	0	1	0	0	1	0	0	0	0	0	1	.000	0	0	27.00
4 Min. YEARS				56	47	5	6	323.1	1357	337	150	132	25	14	7	10	91	1	215	10	7	16	21	.432	1	1	3.67

Trey McCoy

Bats: Right **Throws:** Right **Pos:** DH **Ht:** 6'3" **Wt:** 215 **Born:** 10/12/66 **Age:** 30

Year	Team	Lg	Org	G	AB	H	2B	3B	HR	TB	R	RBI	TBB	IBB	SO	HBP	SH	SF	SB	CS	SB%	GDP	Avg	OBP	SLG
	BATTING																		BASERUNNING				PERCENTAGES		
1990	Charlotte	A+	Tex	45	160	37	11	0	3	57	19	18	23	0	35	1	0	0	0	0	.00	0	.231	.332	.356
	Gastonia	A	Tex	24	80	27	6	0	4	45	13	11	12	1	12	0	0	2	1	1	.50	0	.338	.415	.563
1991	Tulsa	AA	Tex	44	137	33	7	0	10	70	21	32	33	4	26	2	0	2	0	0	.00	6	.241	.391	.511
1992	Tulsa	AA	Tex	15	52	10	0	0	2	16	5	6	8	0	15	0	0	0	0	1	.00	0	.192	.300	.308
	Gastonia	A	Tex	32	99	35	6	0	8	65	17	30	23	0	19	7	0	2	3	0	1.00	0	.354	.496	.657
1993	Tulsa	AA	Tex	125	420	123	27	3	29	243	72	95	65	4	79	19	0	2	3	2	.60	9	.293	.409	.579
	Okla. City	AAA	Tex	8	28	7	1	1	3	19	6	11	5	0	5	1	0	0	0	0	.00	0	.250	.382	.679
1994	Okla. City	AAA	Tex	101	353	108	29	1	15	184	54	67	41	1	65	10	0	5	1	0	1.00	9	.306	.389	.521
1995	Okla. City	AAA	Tex	9	29	9	1	0	0	10	4	2	7	1	7	0	0	0	0	0	.00	1	.310	.444	.345
	Norfolk	AAA	NYN	25	67	14	5	0	3	28	6	7	5	0	11	2	0	0	0	0	.00	2	.209	.284	.418
1996	Norfolk	AAA	NYN	25	47	9	1	0	1	13	2	7	8	0	5	2	0	1	0	0	.00	2	.191	.328	.277
7 Min. YEARS				453	1472	412	94	5	78	750	219	286	230	11	279	44	0	14	8	4	.67	29	.280	.390	.510

Jim McCready

Pitches: Right **Bats:** Right **Pos:** P **Ht:** 6'1" **Wt:** 187 **Born:** 11/25/69 **Age:** 27

Year	Team	Lg	Org	G	GS	CG	GF	IP	BFP	H	R	ER	HR	SH	SF	HB	TBB	IBB	SO	WP	Bk	W	L	Pct.	ShO	Sv	ERA
	HOW MUCH HE PITCHED									WHAT HE GAVE UP												THE RESULTS					
1991	Mets	R	NYN	16	6	2	8	77.2	328	69	36	28	1	0	2	4	18	1	59	5	4	6	4	.600	0	1	3.24
1992	Columbia	A	NYN	35	9	1	17	87.1	362	85	35	24	3	3	0	5	23	0	54	4	0	5	3	.625	1	5	2.47
1993	St. Lucie	A+	NYN	40	0	0	30	61.1	250	51	18	12	0	8	2	2	22	6	40	2	0	6	4	.600	0	16	1.76
	Binghamton	AA	NYN	14	0	0	4	18.1	73	18	7	7	0	2	0	0	4	1	12	0	0	1	1	.500	0	0	3.44
1994	Binghamton	AA	NYN	63	0	0	26	83.2	359	78	35	30	4	6	5	9	28	3	52	7	0	6	6	.500	0	7	3.23
1995	Norfolk	AAA	NYN	28	0	0	8	40.1	175	41	14	9	0	5	1	0	20	1	21	1	0	0	1	.000	0	0	2.01
	Binghamton	AA	NYN	60	0	0	24	79.1	353	83	35	23	4	8	3	2	34	2	38	6	0	1	2	.333	0	4	2.61
1996	Mets	R	NYN	5	1	0	0	8	34	4	3	1	0	2	0	2	2	0	8	0	0	1	1	.500	0	0	1.13
	St. Lucie	A+	NYN	10	0	0	3	16.1	65	18	8	7	1	1	0	0	2	0	12	2	0	1	2	.333	0	0	3.86
	Binghamton	AA	NYN	1	0	0	0	1	3	0	0	0	0	0	0	0	0	0	0	0	0	0	0	.000	0	0	0.00
	Norfolk	AAA	NYN	6	0	0	2	8.2	36	11	4	4	3	0	0	0	0	0	1	0	0	0	0	.000	0	0	4.15
6 Min. YEARS				278	16	3	122	482	2038	458	195	145	16	35	13	24	153	14	297	27	4	27	24	.529	1	33	2.71

Ray McDavid

Bats: Left **Throws:** Right **Pos:** OF **Ht:** 6' 2" **Wt:** 200 **Born:** 7/20/71 **Age:** 25

			BATTING															BASERUNNING				PERCENTAGES		
Year Team	Lg	Org	G	AB	H	2B	3B	HR	TB	R	RBI	TBB	IBB	SO	HBP	SH	SF	SB	CS	SB%	GDP	Avg	OBP	SLG
1990 Padres	R	SD	13	41	6	0	2	0	10	4	1	6	1	5	0	1	0	3	2	.60	1	.146	.255	.244
1991 Charlstn-SC	A	SD	127	425	105	16	9	10	169	93	45	106	1	119	8	0	0	60	14	.81	3	.247	.406	.398
1992 High Desert	A+	SD	123	428	118	22	5	24	222	94	94	94	1	126	7	3	6	43	9	.83	3	.276	.409	.519
1993 Wichita	AA	SD	126	441	119	18	5	11	180	65	55	70	6	104	6	0	8	33	17	.66	6	.270	.371	.408
1994 Las Vegas	AAA	SD	128	476	129	24	6	13	204	85	62	67	4	110	8	1	1	24	15	.62	9	.271	.370	.429
1995 Padres	R	SD	9	28	13	2	1	1	20	13	6	8	0	7	0	0	0	3	1	.75	0	.464	.583	.714
Las Vegas	AAA	SD	52	166	45	8	1	5	70	28	27	30	0	35	4	0	1	7	1	.88	2	.271	.393	.422
1996 Ottawa	AAA	Mon	18	58	9	1	0	0	10	7	2	9	1	11	0	1	0	6	2	.75	0	.155	.269	.172
Expos	R	Mon	3	9	3	0	1	0	5	1	0	2	0	3	0	0	0	1	0	1.00	0	.333	.455	.556
W. Palm Bch	A+	Mon	4	16	6	2	0	1	11	2	3	3	2	1	1	0	0	1	0	1.00	0	.375	.500	.688
1994 San Diego	NL		9	28	7	1	0	0	8	2	2	1	0	8	0	0	0	1	0	1.00	0	.250	.276	.286
1995 San Diego	NL		11	17	3	0	0	0	3	2	0	2	0	6	0	0	0	1	1	.50	1	.176	.263	.176
7 Min. YEARS			603	2088	553	93	30	65	901	392	295	395	16	521	34	6	16	181	61	.75	24	.265	.388	.432
2 Maj. YEARS			20	45	10	1	0	0	11	4	2	3	0	14	0	0	0	2	1	.67	1	.222	.271	.244

Allen McDill

Pitches: Left **Bats:** Left **Pos:** P **Ht:** 6'1" **Wt:** 160 **Born:** 8/23/71 **Age:** 25

			HOW MUCH HE PITCHED						WHAT HE GAVE UP												THE RESULTS					
Year Team	Lg	Org	G	GS	CG	GF	IP	BFP	H	R	ER	HR	SH	SF	HB	TBB	IBB	SO	WP	Bk	W	L	Pct.	ShO	Sv	ERA
1992 Kingsport	R+	NYN	1	0	0	0	0.1	3	0	0	0	0	0	0	0	2	0	0	0	0	0	0	.000	0	0	0.00
Mets	R	NYN	10	9	0	0	53.1	216	36	23	16	3	0	0	4	15	0	60	3	0	3	4	.429	0	0	2.70
1993 Kingsport	R+	NYN	9	9	0	0	53.1	224	52	19	13	1	1	2	0	14	0	42	2	2	5	2	.714	0	0	2.19
Pittsfield	A-	NYN	5	5	0	0	28.1	132	31	22	17	0	2	2	1	15	0	24	3	0	2	3	.400	0	0	5.40
1994 Columbia	A	NYN	19	19	1	0	111.2	461	101	52	44	11	5	2	4	38	2	102	9	0	9	6	.600	0	0	3.55
1995 St. Lucie	A+	NYN	7	7	1	0	49.1	190	36	11	9	2	1	0	1	13	0	28	3	0	4	2	.667	1	0	1.64
Wichita	AA	KC	12	1	0	5	21.1	85	16	7	5	2	0	0	1	5	0	20	1	0	1	0	1.000	0	1	2.11
Binghamton	AA	NYN	31	20	2	5	143.2	599	121	60	51	9	2	4	5	56	2	92	7	1	8	7	.533	1	1	3.19
1996 Omaha	AAA	KC	2	0	0	0	0.1	5	3	2	2	0	0	0	0	1	0	1	2	0	0	1	.000	0	0	54.00
Wichita	AA	KC	54	0	0	30	65	288	79	43	40	10	2	4	4	21	3	62	7	0	1	5	.167	0	11	5.54
5 Min. YEARS			150	70	4	40	526.2	2203	475	239	197	38	13	14	20	180	7	431	37	3	33	30	.524	2	13	3.37

Jason McDonald

Bats: Both **Throws:** Right **Pos:** 2B **Ht:** 5'8" **Wt:** 175 **Born:** 3/20/72 **Age:** 25

			BATTING															BASERUNNING				PERCENTAGES		
Year Team	Lg	Org	G	AB	H	2B	3B	HR	TB	R	RBI	TBB	IBB	SO	HBP	SH	SF	SB	CS	SB%	GDP	Avg	OBP	SLG
1993 Sou. Oregon	A-	Oak	35	112	33	5	2	0	42	26	8	31	2	17	0	2	0	22	4	.85	0	.295	.448	.375
1994 W. Michigan	A	Oak	116	404	96	11	9	2	131	67	31	81	1	87	4	9	1	52	23	.69	5	.238	.369	.324
1995 Modesto	A+	Oak	133	493	129	25	7	6	186	109	50	110	0	84	6	8	2	70	20	.78	6	.262	.401	.377
1996 Edmonton	AAA	Oak	137	479	114	7	5	8	155	71	46	63	0	82	15	10	6	33	13	.72	8	.238	.341	.324
4 Min. YEARS			421	1488	372	48	23	16	514	273	135	285	3	270	25	29	9	177	60	.75	19	.250	.377	.345

Joe McEwing

Bats: Right **Throws:** Right **Pos:** OF **Ht:** 5'10" **Wt:** 170 **Born:** 10/19/72 **Age:** 24

			BATTING															BASERUNNING				PERCENTAGES		
Year Team	Lg	Org	G	AB	H	2B	3B	HR	TB	R	RBI	TBB	IBB	SO	HBP	SH	SF	SB	CS	SB%	GDP	Avg	OBP	SLG
1992 Cardinals	R	StL	55	211	71	4	2	0	79	55	13	24	0	18	5	1	1	23	7	.77	1	.336	.415	.374
1993 Savannah	A	StL	138	511	127	35	1	0	164	94	43	89	0	73	4	15	4	22	9	.71	7	.249	.362	.321
1994 Madison	A	StL	90	346	112	24	2	4	152	58	47	32	4	53	1	5	3	18	15	.55	5	.324	.380	.439
St. Pete	A+	StL	50	197	49	7	0	1	59	22	20	19	0	32	1	4	3	8	4	.67	3	.249	.314	.299
1995 St. Pete	A+	StL	75	281	64	13	0	1	80	33	23	25	3	49	1	6	4	2	3	.40	5	.228	.289	.285
Arkansas	AA	StL	42	121	30	4	0	2	40	16	12	9	2	13	1	6	0	3	2	.60	4	.248	.305	.331
1996 Arkansas	AA	StL	106	216	45	7	3	2	64	27	14	13	0	32	0	5	1	2	4	.33	8	.208	.252	.296
5 Min. YEARS			556	1883	498	94	8	10	638	305	172	211	9	270	13	42	16	78	44	.64	34	.264	.340	.339

Jason McFarlin

Bats: Left **Throws:** Left **Pos:** OF **Ht:** 6'0" **Wt:** 175 **Born:** 6/28/70 **Age:** 27

			BATTING															BASERUNNING				PERCENTAGES		
Year Team	Lg	Org	G	AB	H	2B	3B	HR	TB	R	RBI	TBB	IBB	SO	HBP	SH	SF	SB	CS	SB%	GDP	Avg	OBP	SLG
1989 Everett	A-	SF	37	131	34	4	3	0	44	17	12	5	1	25	1	2	2	7	3	.70	3	.260	.288	.336
1990 Clinton	A	SF	129	476	108	9	5	0	127	68	31	47	2	79	9	7	1	72	19	.79	7	.227	.308	.267
1991 San Jose	A+	SF	103	407	95	10	5	2	121	65	33	47	2	72	14	10	2	46	20	.70	6	.233	.332	.297
1992 San Jose	A+	SF	70	276	84	7	3	1	100	61	24	27	1	43	9	5	1	32	11	.74	4	.304	.383	.362
Shreveport	AA	SF	28	106	22	3	3	1	34	13	3	5	0	20	4	2	0	10	1	.91	0	.208	.270	.321
1993 Shreveport	AA	SF	21	59	11	2	1	0	15	12	1	4	0	12	2	1	0	4	1	.80	0	.186	.262	.254
San Jose	A+	SF	97	395	123	20	4	7	172	71	53	29	0	67	3	7	4	49	10	.83	5	.311	.360	.435
1994 Shreveport	AA	SF	106	306	87	11	4	5	121	37	29	17	5	31	6	2	4	21	8	.72	6	.284	.330	.395
1995 Shreveport	AA	SF	93	252	85	13	2	6	120	39	37	25	7	26	10	4	2	8	7	.53	8	.337	.415	.476
1996 Tulsa	AA	Tex	2	11	3	1	0	0	4	1	2	0	0	1	0	0	0	0	1	.00	0	.273	.273	.364
Okla. City	AAA	Tex	3	12	2	1	0	0	3	0	1	1	0	2	0	0	0	0	0	.00	1	.167	.231	.250
Greenville	AA	Atl	79	244	56	14	0	4	82	40	21	29	1	60	3	2	2	6	2	.75	6	.230	.317	.336
8 Min. YEARS			768	2675	710	95	30	26	943	424	247	236	19	438	61	42	18	255	83	.75	46	.265	.337	.353

Tom McGraw

Pitches: Left **Bats:** Left **Pos:** P **Ht:** 6'2" **Wt:** 195 **Born:** 12/8/67 **Age:** 29

		HOW MUCH HE PITCHED						WHAT HE GAVE UP												THE RESULTS					
Year Team	Lg Org	G	GS	CG	GF	IP	BFP	H	R	ER	HR	SH	SF	HB	TBB	IBB	SO	WP	Bk	W	L	Pct.	ShO	Sv	ERA
1990 Beloit	A Mil	12	12	1	0	70	299	49	33	15	1	1	2	2	34	0	61	4	4	7	3	.700	1	0	1.93
1991 El Paso	AA Mil	9	7	0	2	35.2	163	43	28	23	1	2	1	1	21	0	28	0	0	1	1	.500	0	1	5.80
Stockton	A+ Mil	11	7	0	1	47	183	35	15	12	2	2	1	2	13	0	39	3	1	3	0	1.000	0	0	2.30
1992 Stockton	A+ Mil	15	15	1	0	97.1	414	97	44	29	1	4	3	2	31	5	70	5	0	6	4	.600	0	0	2.68
El Paso	AA Mil	11	10	1	1	69.1	299	75	24	21	2	2	0	0	26	1	53	2	0	6	0	1.000	0	0	2.73
1993 High Desert	A+ Fla	6	6	1	0	38	153	38	17	15	3	1	2	1	7	0	31	1	0	2	3	.400	0	0	3.55
Edmonton	AAA Fla	5	2	0	1	9.2	45	12	7	6	1	0	1	0	4	0	8	1	0	2	0	1.000	0	0	5.59
1994 Portland	AA Fla	37	7	0	11	74	327	81	44	38	9	3	1	5	35	3	56	6	0	3	5	.375	0	2	4.62
1995 Portland	AA Fla	51	0	0	11	74.2	322	69	21	15	2	7	3	4	31	3	60	4	0	5	0	1.000	0	2	1.81
1996 Trenton	AA Bos	30	0	0	12	34	149	34	15	12	1	3	0	0	19	7	32	1	0	3	4	.429	0	1	3.18
7 Min. YEARS		187	66	4	39	549.2	2354	533	248	186	23	25	14	17	221	19	438	27	5	38	20	.655	1	6	3.05

Terry McGriff

Bats: Right **Throws:** Right **Pos:** C **Ht:** 6' 2" **Wt:** 195 **Born:** 9/23/63 **Age:** 33

		BATTING														BASERUNNING				PERCENTAGES		
Year Team	Lg Org	G	AB	H	2B	3B	HR	TB	R	RBI	TBB	IBB	SO	HBP	SH	SF	SB	CS	SB%	GDP	Avg	OBP	SLG
1984 Tampa	A+ Cin	110	345	96	19	0	7	136	48	41	48	4	62	2	0	5	5	4	.56	13	.278	.365	.394
1985 Vermont	AA Cin	110	363	92	10	4	13	149	52	60	54	2	81	3	0	1	1	0	1.00	6	.253	.354	.410
1986 Denver	AAA Cin	108	340	99	22	1	9	150	54	54	41	4	71	2	2	6	0	0	.00	11	.291	.365	.441
1987 Nashville	AAA Cin	67	228	62	11	3	10	109	36	33	25	5	47	0	0	5	0	0	.00	10	.272	.337	.478
1988 Nashville	AAA Cin	35	97	21	3	1	1	29	8	12	10	2	15	0	0	1	0	0	.00	4	.216	.287	.299
1989 Nashville	AAA Cin	102	335	94	24	1	5	135	42	28	29	3	68	1	1	0	1	1	.50	12	.281	.340	.403
1990 Nashville	AAA Cin	94	325	91	17	0	9	135	44	54	38	1	46	2	2	6	2	2	.50	8	.280	.353	.415
1991 Tucson	AAA Hou	51	146	42	15	1	0	59	18	24	16	0	20	3	0	2	0	1	.00	5	.288	.365	.404
1992 Syracuse	AAA Tor	21	56	14	2	0	2	22	4	7	9	0	11	0	0	1	1	0	1.00	2	.250	.348	.393
1993 Edmonton	AAA Fla	105	339	117	29	2	7	171	62	55	49	2	29	1	0	3	2	1	.67	10	.345	.426	.504
1995 Toledo	AAA Det	58	188	51	8	0	4	71	14	23	20	0	29	0	0	0	0	0	.00	9	.271	.341	.378
1996 Syracuse	AAA Tor	27	59	11	1	0	1	15	7	6	8	0	9	1	1	1	0	0	.00	0	.186	.290	.254
1987 Cincinnati	NL	34	89	20	3	0	2	29	6	11	8	0	17	0	0	0	0	0	.00	3	.225	.289	.326
1988 Cincinnati	NL	35	96	19	3	0	1	25	9	4	12	0	31	0	0	1	1	0	1.00	3	.198	.284	.260
1989 Cincinnati	NL	6	11	3	0	0	0	3	1	2	2	1	3	0	0	0	0	0	.00	0	.273	.385	.273
1990 Cincinnati	NL	2	4	0	0	0	0	0	0	0	0	0	1	0	0	0	0	0	.00	0	.000	.000	.000
Houston	NL	4	5	0	0	0	0	0	0	0	0	0	0	0	0	0	0	0	.00	0	.000	.000	.000
1993 Florida	NL	3	7	0	0	0	0	0	0	0	1	0	2	0	0	0	0	0	.00	0	.000	.125	.000
1994 St. Louis	NL	42	114	25	6	0	0	31	10	13	13	1	11	2	1	1	0	0	.00	8	.219	.308	.272
12 Min. YEARS		888	2821	790	161	13	68	1181	389	397	347	23	488	15	6	31	12	9	.57	90	.280	.358	.419
6 Maj. YEARS		126	326	67	12	0	3	88	26	30	36	2	65	2	1	2	1	0	1.00	14	.206	.287	.270

Ryan McGuire

Bats: Left **Throws:** Left **Pos:** 1B **Ht:** 6'1" **Wt:** 195 **Born:** 11/23/71 **Age:** 25

		BATTING														BASERUNNING				PERCENTAGES		
Year Team	Lg Org	G	AB	H	2B	3B	HR	TB	R	RBI	TBB	IBB	SO	HBP	SH	SF	SB	CS	SB%	GDP	Avg	OBP	SLG
1993 Ft. Laud	A+ Bos	58	213	69	12	2	4	97	23	38	27	3	34	2	1	3	2	4	.33	11	.324	.400	.455
1994 Lynchburg	A+ Bos	137	489	133	29	0	10	192	70	73	79	2	77	2	4	7	10	9	.53	19	.272	.371	.393
1995 Trenton	AA Bos	109	414	138	29	1	7	190	59	59	58	5	51	0	4	1	11	8	.58	10	.333	.414	.459
1996 Ottawa	AAA Mon	134	451	116	21	2	12	177	62	60	59	4	80	2	1	3	11	4	.73	12	.257	.344	.392
4 Min. YEARS		438	1567	456	91	5	33	656	214	230	223	14	242	6	10	14	34	25	.58	52	.291	.378	.419

Sean McKamie

Bats: Right **Throws:** Right **Pos:** SS **Ht:** 6'2" **Wt:** 160 **Born:** 9/27/69 **Age:** 27

		BATTING														BASERUNNING				PERCENTAGES		
Year Team	Lg Org	G	AB	H	2B	3B	HR	TB	R	RBI	TBB	IBB	SO	HBP	SH	SF	SB	CS	SB%	GDP	Avg	OBP	SLG
1989 Dodgers	R LA	42	133	42	3	0	0	45	20	15	23	0	22	2	4	2	13	2	.87	0	.316	.419	.338
1991 Vero Beach	A+ LA	66	198	52	8	0	1	63	25	13	8	0	35	6	5	1	12	3	.80	2	.263	.310	.318
1992 Vero Beach	A+ LA	43	118	27	0	1	0	29	14	11	6	0	21	0	3	1	11	5	.69	3	.229	.264	.246
1993 Bakersfield	A+ LA	21	67	22	4	0	2	32	15	12	7	0	6	2	1	0	4	3	.57	1	.328	.408	.478
1994 Minneapolis	IND —	69	267	81	13	4	2	108	44	28	31	3	35	2	1	0	21	7	.75	5	.303	.380	.404
1996 El Paso	AA Mil	1	0	0	0	0	0	0	0	0	0	0	0	0	0	0	0	0	.00	0	.000	.000	.000
Sou Minny	IND —	68	287	102	18	3	8	150	61	58	27	1	28	3	1	3	14	3	.82	3	.355	.413	.523
6 Min. YEARS		310	1070	326	46	8	13	427	179	137	102	4	147	15	15	7	75	23	.77	14	.305	.371	.399

Scott McKenzie

Pitches: Right **Bats:** Right **Pos:** P **Ht:** 6'0" **Wt:** 185 **Born:** 9/30/70 **Age:** 26

		HOW MUCH HE PITCHED						WHAT HE GAVE UP												THE RESULTS					
Year Team	Lg Org	G	GS	CG	GF	IP	BFP	H	R	ER	HR	SH	SF	HB	TBB	IBB	SO	WP	Bk	W	L	Pct.	ShO	Sv	ERA
1993 Billings	R+ Cin	14	1	0	5	30	130	27	16	12	2	2	3	1	14	0	37	6	4	1	2	.333	0	0	3.60
1994 Charlstn-WV	A Cin	17	17	5	0	105.2	434	105	50	43	6	3	4	5	20	0	65	2	0	8	5	.615	1	0	3.66
1995 Winston-Sal	A+ Cin	49	0	0	41	72	294	42	27	22	7	5	0	5	30	2	55	7	0	3	4	.429	0	20	2.75
1996 Chattanooga	AA Cin	27	0	0	7	47.2	214	51	25	18	7	0	2	0	23	3	28	4	0	2	4	.333	0	0	3.40
4 Min. YEARS		107	18	5	53	255.1	1072	225	118	95	22	10	9	11	87	5	185	19	4	14	15	.483	1	20	3.35

Buck McNabb

Bats: Left **Throws:** Right **Pos:** OF **Ht:** 6'0" **Wt:** 180 **Born:** 1/17/73 **Age:** 24

		BATTING															BASERUNNING				PERCENTAGES		
Year Team	Lg Org	G	AB	H	2B	3B	HR	TB	R	RBI	TBB	IBB	SO	HBP	SH	SF	SB	CS	SB%	GDP	Avg	OBP	SLG
1991 Astros	R Hou	48	174	51	3	3	0	60	34	9	12	0	33	4	3	2	23	8	.74	0	.293	.349	.345
1992 Burlington	A Hou	123	456	118	12	3	1	139	82	34	60	0	80	10	3	2	56	19	.75	4	.259	.356	.305
1993 Osceola	A+ Hou	125	487	139	15	7	1	171	69	35	52	2	66	6	4	1	28	15	.65	8	.285	.361	.351
1994 Jackson	AA Hou	125	454	124	25	7	0	163	67	27	26	0	63	1	4	2	15	17	.47	10	.273	.313	.359
1995 Jackson	AA Hou	15	50	13	1	0	0	14	4	3	5	0	11	0	0	0	1	0	1.00	1	.260	.327	.280
Canton-Akrn	AA Cle	19	48	8	0	0	0	8	3	1	6	0	14	1	2	0	0	1	.00	0	.167	.273	.167
Bakersfield	A+ Cle	63	237	71	8	1	0	81	34	27	38	1	38	0	4	2	11	1	.92	5	.300	.394	.342
1996 Kissimmee	A+ Hou	7	26	9	1	0	0	10	4	3	3	1	5	0	0	0	3	0	1.00	0	.346	.414	.385
Jackson	AA Hou	88	279	84	15	5	0	109	38	26	41	1	37	2	1	2	10	6	.63	3	.301	.392	.391
6 Min. YEARS		613	2211	617	80	26	2	755	335	165	243	5	347	24	21	11	147	67	.69	31	.279	.355	.341

Fred McNair

Bats: Right **Throws:** Right **Pos:** 1B **Ht:** 6'4" **Wt:** 215 **Born:** 1/31/70 **Age:** 27

		BATTING															BASERUNNING				PERCENTAGES		
Year Team	Lg Org	G	AB	H	2B	3B	HR	TB	R	RBI	TBB	IBB	SO	HBP	SH	SF	SB	CS	SB%	GDP	Avg	OBP	SLG
1989 Mariners	R Sea	36	142	40	6	2	4	62	24	18	7	0	38	2	0	2	4	2	.67	2	.282	.320	.437
1990 Bellingham	A- Sea	50	176	36	8	0	3	53	16	17	15	1	55	3	1	0	7	3	.70	3	.205	.278	.301
1992 Bellingham	A- Sea	69	255	84	9	2	8	121	41	54	21	4	69	4	0	0	13	10	.57	9	.329	.389	.475
1993 Riverside	A+ Sea	112	400	108	21	1	14	173	70	65	41	2	91	5	1	4	6	7	.46	11	.270	.342	.433
1994 Jacksonvlle	AA Sea	57	200	44	11	0	4	67	17	21	12	1	47	1	0	1	3	1	.75	5	.220	.266	.335
Appleton	A Sea	60	222	67	15	3	9	115	34	49	11	0	48	2	0	3	7	0	1.00	6	.302	.336	.518
1995 Scranton-WB	AAA Phi	9	25	6	1	0	0	7	1	2	3	0	6	0	0	1	0	0	.00	1	.240	.310	.280
Reading	AA Phi	108	395	107	24	1	23	202	64	68	38	1	86	3	1	0	3	2	.60	12	.271	.339	.511
1996 Scranton-WB	AAA Phi	14	25	4	0	0	0	4	3	3	8	0	12	0	1	0	0	0	.00	0	.160	.364	.160
Norwich	AA NYA	69	246	68	10	1	7	101	31	43	11	0	53	0	1	3	2	0	1.00	7	.276	.304	.411
7 Min. YEARS		584	2086	564	105	10	72	905	301	340	167	9	505	20	5	14	45	25	.64	56	.270	.328	.434

Jeff McNeely

Bats: Right **Throws:** Right **Pos:** OF **Ht:** 6' 2" **Wt:** 200 **Born:** 10/18/69 **Age:** 27

		BATTING															BASERUNNING				PERCENTAGES		
Year Team	Lg Org	G	AB	H	2B	3B	HR	TB	R	RBI	TBB	IBB	SO	HBP	SH	SF	SB	CS	SB%	GDP	Avg	OBP	SLG
1989 Red Sox	R Bos	9	32	13	1	1	0	16	10	4	7	0	3	0	0	1	5	1	.83	1	.406	.500	.500
Elmira	A- Bos	61	208	52	7	0	2	65	20	21	26	0	54	4	1	0	16	8	.67	4	.250	.345	.313
1990 Winter Havn	A+ Bos	16	62	10	0	0	0	10	4	3	3	0	19	0	0	0	7	1	.88	1	.161	.200	.161
Elmira	A- Bos	73	246	77	4	5	6	109	41	37	40	5	60	3	8	2	39	10	.80	7	.313	.412	.443
1991 Lynchburg	A+ Bos	106	382	123	16	5	4	161	58	38	74	3	74	4	4	1	38	21	.64	5	.322	.436	.421
1992 New Britain	AA Bos	85	261	57	8	4	2	79	30	11	26	0	78	2	4	0	10	5	.67	10	.218	.294	.303
1993 Pawtucket	AAA Bos	129	498	130	14	3	2	156	65	35	43	1	102	3	10	2	40	7	.85	4	.261	.322	.313
1994 Pawtucket	AAA Bos	117	458	106	15	5	4	143	60	34	49	0	100	9	5	3	13	17	.43	6	.231	.316	.312
1995 Louisville	AAA StL	109	271	64	6	1	0	72	31	19	23	0	53	0	0	1	5	8	.38	8	.236	.295	.266
1996 Louisville	AAA StL	3	8	1	0	0	0	1	0	1	0	0	2	0	0	0	0	0	.00	0	.125	.125	.125
Midland	AA Cal	36	125	30	8	1	0	40	11	18	19	0	27	0	0	2	2	1	.67	7	.240	.336	.320
1993 Boston	AL	21	37	11	1	1	0	14	10	1	7	0	9	0	0	0	6	0	1.00	0	.297	.409	.378
8 Min. YEARS		744	2551	663	79	25	20	852	330	221	310	9	572	25	32	12	175	79	.69	53	.260	.344	.334

Brian Meadows

Pitches: Right **Bats:** Right **Pos:** P **Ht:** 6'4" **Wt:** 210 **Born:** 11/21/75 **Age:** 21

		HOW MUCH HE PITCHED						WHAT HE GAVE UP												THE RESULTS					
Year Team	Lg Org	G	GS	CG	GF	IP	BFP	H	R	ER	HR	SH	SF	HB	TBB	IBB	SO	WP	Bk	W	L	Pct.	ShO	Sv	ERA
1994 Marlins	R Fla	8	7	0	0	37	151	34	9	8	1	0	0	1	6	0	33	0	0	3	0	1.000	0	0	1.95
1995 Kane County	A Fla	26	26	1	0	147	646	163	90	69	11	8	4	12	41	0	103	3	2	9	9	.500	1	0	4.22
1996 Brevard Cty	A+ Fla	24	23	3	1	146	600	129	73	58	13	3	4	10	25	1	69	4	1	8	7	.533	1	0	3.58
Portland	AA Fla	4	4	1	0	27	108	26	15	13	1	3	1	1	4	0	13	0	0	0	1	.000	0	0	4.33
3 Min. YEARS		62	60	5	1	357	1505	352	187	148	26	14	9	24	76	1	218	7	3	20	17	.541	2	0	3.73

Rafael Medina

Pitches: Right **Bats:** Right **Pos:** P **Ht:** 6'3" **Wt:** 194 **Born:** 2/15/75 **Age:** 22

		HOW MUCH HE PITCHED						WHAT HE GAVE UP												THE RESULTS					
Year Team	Lg Org	G	GS	CG	GF	IP	BFP	H	R	ER	HR	SH	SF	HB	TBB	IBB	SO	WP	Bk	W	L	Pct.	ShO	Sv	ERA
1993 Yankees	R NYA	5	5	0	0	27.1	107	16	6	2	0	1	1	1	12	0	21	1	1	2	0	1.000	0	0	0.66
1994 Oneonta	A- NYA	14	14	1	0	73.1	319	67	54	38	7	2	5	1	35	0	59	7	3	3	7	.300	0	0	4.66
1995 Tampa	A+ NYA	6	6	0	0	30.1	131	29	12	8	0	0	0	1	12	0	25	0	2	2	2	.500	0	0	2.37
Greensboro	A NYA	25	25	1	0	129	549	115	60	52	8	0	5	7	50	0	133	6	5	6	6	.500	0	0	3.63
1996 Norwich	AA NYA	19	19	1	0	103	446	78	48	35	7	5	1	6	55	2	112	11	4	5	8	.385	0	0	3.06
4 Min. YEARS		69	69	3	0	363	1552	305	180	135	22	8	12	16	164	2	350	25	15	18	23	.439	0	0	3.35

Tony Medrano

Bats: Right **Throws:** Right **Pos:** SS **Ht:** 5'11" **Wt:** 155 **Born:** 12/8/74 **Age:** 22

BATTING																			BASERUNNING				PERCENTAGES		
Year	Team	Lg	Org	G	AB	H	2B	3B	HR	TB	R	RBI	TBB	IBB	SO	HBP	SH	SF	SB	CS	SB%	GDP	Avg	OBP	SLG
1993	Blue Jays	R	Tor	39	158	42	9	0	0	51	20	9	10	0	9	3	0	0	6	2	.75	1	.266	.322	.323
1994	Blue Jays	R	Tor	6	22	8	4	0	1	15	2	5	1	0	0	0	0	0	0	0	.00	2	.364	.391	.682
	Dunedin	A+	Tor	60	199	47	6	4	4	73	20	21	12	0	26	3	3	1	3	3	.50	4	.236	.288	.367
1995	Wichita	AA	KC	1	5	0	0	0	0	0	0	0	0	0	3	0	0	0	0	0	.00	0	.000	.000	.000
	Wilmington	A+	KC	123	460	131	20	6	3	172	69	43	34	2	42	5	15	4	11	6	.65	10	.285	.338	.374
1996	Wichita	AA	KC	125	474	130	26	1	8	182	59	55	18	0	36	2	7	2	10	8	.56	8	.274	.302	.384
4	Min. YEARS			354	1318	358	65	11	16	493	170	133	75	2	116	13	25	7	30	19	.61	25	.272	.316	.374

Mike Meggers

Bats: Right **Throws:** Right **Pos:** OF **Ht:** 6'2" **Wt:** 200 **Born:** 7/6/70 **Age:** 26

BATTING																			BASERUNNING				PERCENTAGES		
Year	Team	Lg	Org	G	AB	H	2B	3B	HR	TB	R	RBI	TBB	IBB	SO	HBP	SH	SF	SB	CS	SB%	GDP	Avg	OBP	SLG
1992	Billings	R+	Cin	73	257	69	16	3	12	127	47	48	48	1	72	3	1	2	10	7	.59	4	.268	.387	.494
1993	Charlstn-WV	A	Cin	116	388	80	14	2	12	134	43	49	33	1	118	3	2	5	3	5	.38	2	.206	.270	.345
1994	Winston-Sal	A+	Cin	114	418	95	25	2	25	199	62	80	31	0	139	1	0	7	6	2	.75	8	.227	.278	.476
1995	Winston-Sal	A+	Cin	76	272	67	18	1	20	147	45	54	32	5	69	1	0	4	7	3	.70	5	.246	.324	.540
1996	Chattanooga	AA	Cin	38	111	22	6	0	5	43	13	18	16	0	33	1	0	2	1	2	.33	1	.198	.300	.387
	Madison	IND	—	57	215	64	15	1	14	123	40	39	25	0	70	1	2	1	0	0	.00	4	.298	.372	.572
5	Min. YEARS			474	1661	397	94	9	88	773	250	288	185	7	501	10	5	21	27	19	.59	24	.239	.315	.465

Roberto Mejia

Bats: Right **Throws:** Right **Pos:** 2B **Ht:** 5'11" **Wt:** 165 **Born:** 4/14/72 **Age:** 25

BATTING																			BASERUNNING				PERCENTAGES		
Year	Team	Lg	Org	G	AB	H	2B	3B	HR	TB	R	RBI	TBB	IBB	SO	HBP	SH	SF	SB	CS	SB%	GDP	Avg	OBP	SLG
1991	Great Falls	R+	LA	23	84	22	6	2	2	38	17	14	7	0	22	1	0	1	3	1	.75	0	.262	.323	.452
1992	Vero Beach	A+	LA	96	330	82	17	1	12	137	42	40	37	4	60	2	0	5	14	10	.58	6	.248	.324	.415
1993	Colo. Sprng	AAA	Col	77	291	87	15	2	14	148	51	48	18	0	56	1	0	3	12	5	.71	6	.299	.339	.509
1994	Colo. Sprng	AAA	Col	73	283	80	24	2	6	126	54	37	21	2	49	4	4	2	7	4	.64	5	.283	.339	.445
1995	Colo. Sprng	AAA	Col	38	143	42	10	2	2	62	18	14	7	2	29	1	2	0	0	2	.00	6	.294	.331	.434
1996	Indianapols	AAA	Cin	101	374	109	24	9	13	190	55	58	29	1	79	1	1	5	13	5	.72	7	.291	.340	.508
	Pawtucket	AAA	Bos	21	74	19	4	0	0	23	9	4	5	0	18	1	0	1	4	1	.80	3	.257	.309	.311
1993	Colorado	NL		65	229	53	14	5	5	92	31	20	13	1	63	1	4	1	4	1	.80	2	.231	.275	.402
1994	Colorado	NL		38	116	28	8	1	4	50	11	14	15	2	33	0	0	1	3	1	.75	1	.241	.326	.431
1995	Colorado	NL		23	52	8	1	0	1	12	5	4	0	0	17	1	0	1	0	1	.00	1	.154	.167	.231
6	Min. YEARS			429	1579	441	100	18	49	724	246	215	124	9	313	11	7	17	53	28	.65	33	.279	.333	.459
3	Maj. YEARS			126	397	89	23	6	10	154	47	38	28	3	113	2	4	3	7	3	.70	4	.224	.277	.388

Dan Melendez

Bats: Left **Throws:** Left **Pos:** 1B-DH **Ht:** 6'4" **Wt:** 195 **Born:** 1/4/71 **Age:** 26

BATTING																			BASERUNNING				PERCENTAGES		
Year	Team	Lg	Org	G	AB	H	2B	3B	HR	TB	R	RBI	TBB	IBB	SO	HBP	SH	SF	SB	CS	SB%	GDP	Avg	OBP	SLG
1992	Bakersfield	A+	LA	39	146	39	11	2	0	54	18	11	22	5	18	0	0	1	1	0	1.00	1	.267	.361	.370
1993	San Antonio	AA	LA	47	158	38	11	0	7	70	25	30	11	0	29	1	0	5	0	0	.00	2	.241	.286	.443
1995	San Antonio	AA	LA	128	464	121	28	1	7	172	46	59	51	5	66	1	0	6	0	3	.00	11	.261	.331	.371
1996	Albuquerque	AAA	LA	31	46	7	2	0	0	9	5	2	8	0	14	0	0	1	0	0	.00	0	.152	.273	.196
	San Antonio	AA	LA	67	189	45	10	0	1	58	19	29	20	4	31	3	0	3	0	0	.00	3	.238	.316	.307
4	Min. YEARS			312	1003	250	62	3	15	363	113	131	112	14	158	5	0	16	1	3	.25	17	.249	.323	.362

Jose Melendez

Pitches: Right **Bats:** Right **Pos:** P **Ht:** 6' 2" **Wt:** 190 **Born:** 9/2/65 **Age:** 31

HOW MUCH HE PITCHED										WHAT HE GAVE UP												THE RESULTS					
Year	Team	Lg	Org	G	GS	CG	GF	IP	BFP	H	R	ER	HR	SH	SF	HB	TBB	IBB	SO	WP	Bk	W	L	Pct.	ShO	Sv	ERA
1984	Watertown	A-	Pit	15	15	3	0	91	372	61	37	28	6	1	2	6	40	0	68	4	2	5	7	.417	1	0	2.77
1985	Pr. William	A+	Pit	9	8	1	1	44.1	180	25	17	12	2	0	3	0	26	0	41	2	0	3	2	.600	0	1	2.44
1986	Pr. William	A+	Pit	28	27	6	0	186.1	768	141	75	54	9	7	5	2	81	1	146	6	5	13	10	.565	1	0	2.61
1987	Harrisburg	AA	Pit	6	6	0	0	18.1	91	28	24	22	4	1	0	0	11	0	13	0	1	1	3	.250	0	0	10.80
	Salem	A+	Pit	20	20	1	0	116.1	493	96	62	59	17	0	5	8	56	0	86	4	0	9	6	.600	1	0	4.56
1988	Salem	A+	Pit	8	8	2	0	53.2	233	55	26	24	10	0	0	1	19	0	50	2	1	4	2	.667	1	0	4.02
	Harrisburg	AA	Pit	22	4	2	6	71.1	274	46	20	18	2	2	3	1	19	1	38	3	4	5	3	.625	2	1	2.27
1989	Williamsprt	AA	Sea	11	11	0	0	73.1	295	54	23	20	7	1	2	2	22	1	56	0	6	3	4	.429	0	0	2.45
	Calgary	AAA	Sea	17	2	0	4	40.2	184	42	27	26	6	2	3	3	19	2	24	1	0	1	2	.333	0	0	5.75
1990	Calgary	AAA	Sea	45	10	1	14	124.2	525	119	61	54	11	2	5	6	44	2	95	2	1	11	4	.733	0	2	3.90
1991	Las Vegas	AAA	SD	9	8	1	1	58.2	238	54	27	26	8	1	4	3	11	0	45	0	0	7	0	1.000	0	0	3.99
1993	Pawtucket	AAA	Bos	19	0	0	10	35	156	37	24	21	7	2	2	2	7	0	31	2	0	2	3	.400	0	2	5.40
1994	Pawtucket	AAA	Bos	28	5	1	10	73.2	314	74	42	40	13	0	5	2	25	2	65	2	0	1	5	.167	0	4	4.89
1995	Scranton-WB	AAA	Phi	2	0	0	0	3	19	6	4	2	0	1	1	1	2	0	1	0	0	0	0	.000	0	0	6.00
	Omaha	AAA	KC	23	1	0	8	38	182	50	25	21	8	2	1	5	16	2	31	0	0	3	4	.429	0	0	4.97
1996	Columbus	AAA	NYA	8	1	0	2	9.2	43	9	10	7	4	0	0	1	2	0	7	0	0	1	0	1.000	0	0	6.52
1990	Seattle	AL		3	0	0	1	5.1	28	8	8	7	2	0	0	1	3	0	7	1	0	0	0	.000	0	0	11.81
1991	San Diego	NL		31	9	0	10	93.2	381	77	35	34	11	2	6	1	24	3	60	3	2	8	5	.615	0	3	3.27
1992	San Diego	NL		56	3	0	18	89.1	363	82	32	29	9	7	4	3	20	7	82	1	1	6	7	.462	0	0	2.92

		HOW MUCH HE PITCHED						WHAT HE GAVE UP												THE RESULTS					
Year Team	Lg Org	G	GS	CG	GF	IP	BFP	H	R	ER	HR	SH	SF	HB	TBB	IBB	SO	WP	Bk	W	L	Pct.	ShO	Sv	ERA
1993 Boston	AL	9	0	0	5	16	63	10	4	4	2	0	2	0	5	3	14	0	0	2	1	.667	0	0	2.25
1994 Boston	AL	10	0	0	3	16.1	76	20	11	11	3	4	0	2	8	2	9	0	0	0	1	.000	0	0	6.06
12 Min. YEARS		270	126	18	56	1038	4367	897	504	434	114	22	41	43	400	11	797	28	20	69	55	.556	6	10	3.76
5 Maj. YEARS		109	12	0	37	220.2	911	197	90	85	27	13	12	7	60	15	172	5	3	16	14	.533	0	3	3.47

Adam Melhuse

Bats: Both **Throws:** Right **Pos:** C **Ht:** 6'2" **Wt:** 185 **Born:** 3/27/72 **Age:** 25

		BATTING																BASERUNNING				PERCENTAGES		
Year Team	Lg Org	G	AB	H	2B	3B	HR	TB	R	RBI	TBB	IBB	SO	HBP	SH	SF		SB	CS	SB%	GDP	Avg	OBP	SLG
1993 St. Cathrns	A- Tor	73	266	68	14	2	5	101	40	32	45	4	61	0	2	3		4	0	1.00	4	.256	.360	.380
1994 Hagerstown	A Tor	118	422	109	16	3	11	164	61	58	53	3	77	1	1	6		6	8	.43	13	.258	.338	.389
1995 Dunedin	A+ Tor	123	428	92	20	0	4	124	43	41	61	1	87	1	1	4		6	1	.86	7	.215	.312	.290
1996 Dunedin	A+ Tor	97	315	78	23	2	13	144	50	51	69	2	68	3	0	4		3	1	.75	5	.248	.384	.457
Knoxville	AA Tor	32	94	20	3	0	1	26	13	6	14	1	29	0	1	1		0	1	.00	3	.213	.312	.277
4 Min. YEARS		443	1525	367	76	7	34	559	207	188	242	11	322	5	5	18		19	11	.63	32	.241	.343	.367

Mitch Meluskey

Bats: Both **Throws:** Right **Pos:** C **Ht:** 5'11" **Wt:** 185 **Born:** 9/18/73 **Age:** 23

		BATTING																BASERUNNING				PERCENTAGES		
Year Team	Lg Org	G	AB	H	2B	3B	HR	TB	R	RBI	TBB	IBB	SO	HBP	SH	SF		SB	CS	SB%	GDP	Avg	OBP	SLG
1992 Burlington	R+ Cle	43	126	29	7	0	3	45	23	16	29	0	36	0	0	2		3	0	1.00	0	.230	.369	.357
1993 Columbus	A Cle	101	342	84	18	3	3	117	36	47	35	4	69	4	4	7		1	1	.50	5	.246	.317	.342
1994 Kinston	A+ Cle	100	319	77	16	1	3	104	36	41	49	0	62	2	2	4		3	4	.43	4	.241	.342	.326
1995 Kinston	A+ Cle	8	29	7	5	0	0	12	5	2	2	0	9	0	0	0		0	0	.00	1	.241	.290	.414
Kissimmee	A+ Hou	78	261	56	18	1	3	85	23	31	27	2	33	1	2	4		3	0	1.00	12	.215	.287	.326
1996 Kissimmee	A+ Hou	74	231	77	19	0	1	99	29	31	29	5	26	1	1	5		1	1	.50	9	.333	.402	.429
Jackson	AA Hou	38	134	42	11	0	0	53	18	21	18	0	24	1	1	1		0	0	.00	6	.313	.396	.396
5 Min. YEARS		442	1442	372	94	5	13	515	170	189	189	11	259	9	10	23		11	6	.65	37	.258	.343	.357

Reynol Mendoza

Pitches: Right **Bats:** Right **Pos:** P **Ht:** 6'0" **Wt:** 215 **Born:** 10/27/70 **Age:** 26

		HOW MUCH HE PITCHED						WHAT HE GAVE UP												THE RESULTS					
Year Team	Lg Org	G	GS	CG	GF	IP	BFP	H	R	ER	HR	SH	SF	HB	TBB	IBB	SO	WP	Bk	W	L	Pct.	ShO	Sv	ERA
1992 Erie	A- Fla	15	15	1	0	69.2	310	70	46	36	5	2	3	8	25	0	59	6	1	3	6	.333	1	0	4.65
1993 Kane County	A Fla	26	23	3	3	163.2	647	129	59	52	5	6	0	9	45	3	153	13	3	12	5	.706	0	2	2.86
1994 Marlins	R Fla	2	1	0	0	4.1	16	1	0	0	0	0	0	0	2	0	6	0	0	0	0	.000	0	0	0.00
Brevard Cty	A+ Fla	10	9	1	0	37	183	47	33	26	2	3	1	2	26	0	26	4	2	1	3	.250	0	0	6.32
1995 Portland	AA Fla	27	27	1	0	168	715	163	73	64	6	10	4	9	69	3	120	15	0	9	10	.474	1	0	3.43
1996 Portland	AA Fla	10	10	2	0	63	255	60	27	24	7	0	0	3	14	0	41	5	0	4	2	.667	2	0	3.43
Charlotte	AAA Fla	15	14	2	1	91	413	112	67	57	18	6	2	4	33	0	41	8	0	7	4	.636	0	0	5.64
5 Min. YEARS		105	99	10	4	596.2	2539	582	305	259	43	27	10	35	214	6	446	51	6	36	30	.545	4	2	3.91

Frankie Menechino

Bats: Right **Throws:** Right **Pos:** 2B **Ht:** 5'9" **Wt:** 175 **Born:** 1/7/71 **Age:** 26

		BATTING																BASERUNNING				PERCENTAGES		
Year Team	Lg Org	G	AB	H	2B	3B	HR	TB	R	RBI	TBB	IBB	SO	HBP	SH	SF		SB	CS	SB%	GDP	Avg	OBP	SLG
1993 White Sox	R ChA	17	45	11	4	1	1	20	10	9	12	0	4	4	0	0		3	1	.75	1	.244	.443	.444
Hickory	A ChA	50	178	50	6	3	4	74	35	19	33	0	28	4	1	1		11	2	.85	4	.281	.403	.416
1994 South Bend	A ChA	106	379	113	21	5	5	159	77	48	78	1	70	9	3	2		15	8	.65	8	.298	.427	.420
1995 Pr. William	A+ ChA	137	476	124	31	3	6	179	65	58	96	2	75	11	3	8		6	2	.75	17	.261	.391	.376
1996 Birmingham	AA ChA	125	415	121	25	3	12	188	77	62	64	0	84	8	3	6		7	9	.44	5	.292	.391	.453
4 Min. YEARS		435	1493	419	87	15	28	620	264	196	283	3	261	36	10	17		42	22	.66	35	.281	.403	.415

Mark Merchant

Bats: Both **Throws:** Right **Pos:** DH **Ht:** 6'2" **Wt:** 185 **Born:** 1/23/69 **Age:** 28

		BATTING																BASERUNNING				PERCENTAGES		
Year Team	Lg Org	G	AB	H	2B	3B	HR	TB	R	RBI	TBB	IBB	SO	HBP	SH	SF		SB	CS	SB%	GDP	Avg	OBP	SLG
1987 Pirates	R Pit	50	185	49	5	1	3	65	32	17	30	4	29	1	0	0		33	13	.72	0	.265	.370	.351
1988 Augusta	A Pit	60	211	51	6	0	2	63	36	19	41	2	38	2	0	2		14	3	.82	5	.242	.367	.299
1989 Augusta	A Pit	15	59	19	6	1	0	27	11	8	7	1	13	0	0	1		3	1	.75	1	.322	.388	.458
San Bernrdo	A+ Sea	119	429	90	15	2	11	142	65	46	61	1	101	2	0	4		17	6	.74	12	.210	.308	.331
1990 Williamsprt	AA Sea	44	156	28	5	0	0	33	16	10	14	2	36	1	0	2		7	2	.78	8	.179	.249	.212
San Bernrdo	A+ Sea	29	102	32	3	0	4	47	22	19	20	0	34	0	0	0		8	2	.80	1	.314	.426	.461
1991 Peninsula	A+ Sea	78	270	68	8	1	6	96	31	34	51	6	70	0	0	0		11	4	.73	7	.252	.371	.356
Jacksonvlle	AA Sea	51	156	44	10	0	5	69	22	17	21	4	37	1	0	1		3	4	.43	2	.282	.369	.442
1992 Jacksonvlle	AA Sea	109	381	93	9	1	13	143	42	47	37	2	91	2	1	6		3	2	.60	11	.244	.310	.375
1993 Indianapols	AAA Cin	3	6	1	1	0	0	2	2	0	2	0	3	0	1	0		0	0	.00	0	.167	.375	.333
Chattanooga	AA Cin	109	336	101	16	0	17	168	56	61	50	2	79	3	0	3		3	5	.38	9	.301	.393	.500
1994 Chattanooga	AA Cin	106	329	102	14	2	5	135	31	56	39	8	46	0	1	5		1	2	.33	10	.310	.378	.410
1995 Chattanooga	AA Cin	25	53	11	0	0	1	14	4	6	7	1	15	0	0	0		0	0	.00	4	.200	.300	.204
Sioux City	IND —	61	217	69	14	0	11	116	41	41	36	2	40	1	0	1		1	1	.50	2	.318	.416	.535
1996 Nashville	AAA ChA	42	131	28	6	0	4	46	21	15	17	1	29	2	1	1		1	1	.50	6	.214	.311	.351

Year Team	Lg Org	BATTING G	AB	H	2B	3B	HR	TB	R	RBI	TBB	IBB	SO	HBP	SH	SF	BASERUNNING SB	CS	SB%	GDP	PERCENTAGES Avg	OBP	SLG
Omaha	AAA KC	38	118	33	7	0	4	52	18	21	22	0	26	0	1	0	1	0	1.00	6	.280	.393	.441
10 Min. YEARS		939	3139	819	125	8	86	1218	450	417	455	36	687	15	5	26	106	46	.70	84	.261	.355	.388

Lou Merloni

Bats: Right **Throws:** Right **Pos:** 3B **Ht:** 5'10" **Wt:** 188 **Born:** 4/6/71 **Age:** 26

Year Team	Lg Org	BATTING G	AB	H	2B	3B	HR	TB	R	RBI	TBB	IBB	SO	HBP	SH	SF	BASERUNNING SB	CS	SB%	GDP	PERCENTAGES Avg	OBP	SLG
1993 Red Sox	R Bos	4	14	5	1	0	0	6	4	1	1	0	1	1	0	0	1	1	.50	0	.357	.438	.429
Ft. Laud	A+ Bos	44	156	38	1	1	2	47	14	21	13	1	26	1	0	4	1	1	.50	6	.244	.299	.301
1994 Sarasota	A+ Bos	113	419	120	16	2	1	143	59	63	36	4	57	7	7	10	5	2	.71	11	.286	.345	.341
1995 Trenton	AA Bos	93	318	88	16	1	1	109	42	30	39	3	50	11	11	2	7	7	.50	1	.277	.373	.343
1996 Trenton	AA Bos	28	95	22	6	1	3	39	11	16	9	1	18	5	1	0	0	2	.00	2	.232	.330	.411
Red Sox	R Bos	1	4	1	0	0	0	1	1	1	0	0	0	0	0	1	0	0	.00	0	.250	.200	.250
Pawtucket	AAA Bos	38	115	29	6	0	1	38	19	12	10	0	20	3	4	0	0	1	.00	1	.252	.328	.330
4 Min. YEARS		321	1121	303	46	5	8	383	150	144	108	9	172	28	23	17	14	14	.50	21	.270	.345	.342

Ethan Merrill

Pitches: Left **Bats:** Left **Pos:** P **Ht:** 6'3" **Wt:** 200 **Born:** 4/21/72 **Age:** 25

Year Team	Lg Org	HOW MUCH HE PITCHED G	GS	CG	GF	IP	BFP	WHAT HE GAVE UP H	R	ER	HR	SH	SF	HB	TBB	IBB	SO	WP	Bk	THE RESULTS W	L	Pct.	ShO	Sv	ERA
1994 Utica	A- Bos	13	4	0	2	44.2	176	36	16	7	0	0	1	2	11	0	35	2	5	2	3	.400	0	1	1.41
1995 Sarasota	A+ Bos	27	25	1	2	150	672	155	86	63	11	3	5	11	67	2	78	7	0	11	7	.611	1	0	3.78
1996 Sarasota	A+ Bos	14	14	0	0	87.2	383	96	50	42	1	3	4	5	26	2	54	5	0	5	6	.455	0	0	4.31
Trenton	AA Bos	13	10	1	0	60	279	71	55	47	12	1	1	3	26	0	42	5	0	3	6	.333	0	0	7.05
3 Min. YEARS		67	53	2	4	342.1	1510	358	207	159	24	7	11	21	130	4	209	19	5	21	22	.488	1	1	4.18

Matt Merullo

Bats: Left **Throws:** Right **Pos:** DH **Ht:** 6' 2" **Wt:** 200 **Born:** 8/4/65 **Age:** 31

Year Team	Lg Org	BATTING G	AB	H	2B	3B	HR	TB	R	RBI	TBB	IBB	SO	HBP	SH	SF	BASERUNNING SB	CS	SB%	GDP	PERCENTAGES Avg	OBP	SLG
1986 Peninsula	A+ ChA	64	208	63	12	2	3	88	21	35	19	3	16	1	0	3	1	0	1.00	5	.303	.359	.423
1987 Daytona Bch	A+ ChA	70	250	65	11	6	4	100	26	47	20	1	18	0	0	6	1	1	.50	6	.260	.308	.400
Birmingham	AA ChA	48	167	46	7	0	2	59	13	17	6	0	20	0	0	0	1	0	1.00	5	.275	.301	.353
1988 Birmingham	AA ChA	125	449	117	26	0	6	161	58	60	40	3	60	3	1	3	3	2	.60	9	.261	.323	.359
1989 Vancouver	AAA ChA	3	9	2	1	0	0	3	0	2	2	0	1	0	1	0	0	0	.00	1	.222	.364	.333
Birmingham	AA ChA	33	119	35	6	0	3	50	19	23	16	2	15	0	2	3	0	1	.00	3	.294	.370	.420
1990 Birmingham	AA ChA	102	378	110	26	1	8	162	57	50	34	6	49	3	3	2	2	4	.33	6	.291	.353	.429
1991 Birmingham	AA ChA	8	28	6	0	0	2	12	5	3	2	0	4	0	0	0	0	0	.00	1	.214	.267	.429
1992 Vancouver	AAA ChA	14	45	8	1	1	1	14	2	4	1	0	2	0	0	0	0	0	.00	3	.178	.196	.311
1993 Nashville	AAA ChA	103	352	117	30	1	12	185	50	65	28	6	47	3	1	2	0	2	.00	12	.332	.384	.526
1994 Charlotte	AAA Cle	112	417	125	20	6	12	193	52	75	25	4	47	4	2	7	2	0	1.00	15	.300	.340	.463
1996 Iowa	AAA ChN	30	89	21	8	0	1	32	8	10	8	0	15	1	0	1	1	0	1.00	1	.236	.303	.360
Lk Elsinore	A+ Cal	9	36	8	2	0	1	13	8	6	5	0	7	0	0	1	0	0	.00	1	.222	.310	.361
1989 Chicago	AL	31	81	18	1	0	1	22	5	8	6	0	14	0	2	1	0	1	.00	2	.222	.273	.272
1991 Chicago	AL	80	140	32	1	0	5	48	8	21	9	1	18	0	1	4	0	0	.00	1	.229	.268	.343
1992 Chicago	AL	24	50	9	1	1	0	12	3	3	1	0	8	1	0	1	0	0	.00	0	.180	.208	.240
1993 Chicago	AL	8	20	1	0	0	0	1	1	0	0	0	1	0	1	0	0	0	.00	1	.050	.050	.050
1994 Cleveland	AL	4	10	1	0	0	0	1	1	0	2	0	1	0	1	0	0	0	.00	0	.100	.250	.100
1995 Minnesota	AL	76	195	55	14	1	1	74	19	27	14	0	27	3	1	3	0	1	.00	5	.282	.335	.379
10 Min. YEARS		721	2547	723	150	17	55	1072	319	397	206	25	301	15	10	28	11	10	.52	68	.284	.338	.421
6 Maj. YEARS		223	496	116	17	2	7	158	37	59	32	1	69	4	6	9	0	2	.00	9	.234	.281	.319

Nelson Metheney

Pitches: Right **Bats:** Right **Pos:** P **Ht:** 6'3" **Wt:** 205 **Born:** 6/14/71 **Age:** 26

Year Team	Lg Org	HOW MUCH HE PITCHED G	GS	CG	GF	IP	BFP	WHAT HE GAVE UP H	R	ER	HR	SH	SF	HB	TBB	IBB	SO	WP	Bk	THE RESULTS W	L	Pct.	ShO	Sv	ERA
1993 Batavia	A- Phi	7	7	0	0	27.1	111	24	10	9	2	0	0	0	7	0	16	0	1	3	0	1.000	0	0	2.96
1994 Clearwater	A+ Phi	12	11	0	0	63.1	275	77	42	35	6	2	0	1	18	1	28	1	2	3	5	.375	0	0	4.97
Spartanburg	A Phi	8	8	2	0	50.1	202	43	17	14	2	2	1	0	12	0	30	3	0	3	4	.429	0	0	2.50
1995 Clearwater	A+ Phi	59	0	0	11	72	310	65	32	24	2	7	4	0	25	3	38	3	2	5	5	.500	0	1	3.00
1996 Clearwater	A+ Phi	21	0	0	5	34	134	29	4	3	0	2	0	1	6	4	19	0	0	1	0	1.000	0	1	0.79
Reading	AA Phi	26	0	0	5	38.2	180	50	30	24	8	0	1	1	19	3	17	2	0	0	2	.000	0	0	5.59
4 Min. YEARS		133	26	2	21	285.2	1212	288	135	109	20	13	6	3	87	11	148	9	5	15	16	.484	0	2	3.43

David Meyer

Pitches: Left **Bats:** Left **Pos:** P **Ht:** 6'5" **Wt:** 215 **Born:** 12/15/71 **Age:** 25

Year Team	Lg Org	HOW MUCH HE PITCHED G	GS	CG	GF	IP	BFP	WHAT HE GAVE UP H	R	ER	HR	SH	SF	HB	TBB	IBB	SO	WP	Bk	THE RESULTS W	L	Pct.	ShO	Sv	ERA
1994 Oneonta	A- NYA	9	9	2	0	49.2	206	45	30	16	1	3	0	0	17	0	30	7	0	3	4	.429	0	0	2.90
Greensboro	A NYA	5	5	0	0	32.2	127	25	9	7	0	1	1	3	14	0	25	0	0	4	1	.800	0	0	1.93
Tampa	A+ NYA	1	1	0	0	3	17	7	5	5	2	0	0	0	2	0	4	1	0	0	1	.000	0	0	15.00
1995 Tampa	A+ NYA	12	11	0	0	58	281	84	49	42	3	2	3	4	29	0	29	6	4	3	4	.429	0	0	6.52

			HOW MUCH HE PITCHED						WHAT HE GAVE UP												THE RESULTS					
Year Team	Lg	Org	G	GS	CG	GF	IP	BFP	H	R	ER	HR	SH	SF	HB	TBB	IBB	SO	WP	Bk	W	L	Pct.	ShO	Sv	ERA
Greensboro	A	NYA	26	25	1	0	145	658	188	101	89	8	5	5	7	57	0	83	11	5	11	8	.579	1	0	5.52
1996 Greensboro	A	NYA	6	0	0	3	18.2	66	9	0	0	0	1	0	1	1	1	24	0	0	1	0	1.000	0	0	0.00
Tampa	A+	NYA	11	6	0	0	38.1	177	46	16	9	2	2	2	1	17	1	18	1	0	3	2	.600	0	0	2.11
Norwich	AA	NYA	19	0	0	9	21	95	20	12	11	1	0	1	1	11	1	13	3	1	0	0	.000	0	1	4.71
3 Min. YEARS			89	57	3	12	366.1	1627	424	222	179	17	14	12	17	148	3	226	29	10	25	20	.556	1	1	4.40

Chris Michalak

Pitches: Left **Bats:** Left **Pos:** P **Ht:** 6'2" **Wt:** 195 **Born:** 1/4/71 **Age:** 26

			HOW MUCH HE PITCHED						WHAT HE GAVE UP												THE RESULTS					
Year Team	Lg	Org	G	GS	CG	GF	IP	BFP	H	R	ER	HR	SH	SF	HB	TBB	IBB	SO	WP	Bk	W	L	Pct.	ShO	Sv	ERA
1993 Sou. Oregon	A-	Oak	16	15	0	0	79	346	77	41	25	2	2	5	6	36	0	57	4	3	7	3	.700	0	0	2.85
1994 W. Michigan	A	Oak	15	10	0	2	67	291	66	32	29	3	4	2	8	28	0	38	2	3	5	3	.625	0	0	3.90
Modesto	A+	Oak	17	10	1	3	77.1	310	67	28	25	13	2	3	3	20	1	46	4	3	5	3	.625	0	2	2.91
1995 Huntsville	AA	Oak	7	0	0	4	5.2	32	10	7	7	1	1	0	1	5	0	4	2	0	1	1	.500	0	1	11.12
Modesto	A+	Oak	51	0	0	20	71	298	66	33	26	4	5	3	5	32	1	53	4	1	4	3	.571	0	3	3.30
1996 Modesto	A+	Oak	21	0	0	13	38.2	173	37	21	13	4	0	2	2	17	0	39	0	2	2	2	.500	0	4	3.03
Huntsville	AA	Oak	21	0	0	4	23.1	123	32	29	20	2	1	1	1	26	4	15	4	0	4	0	1.000	0	0	7.71
4 Min. YEARS			148	35	1	46	362	1573	355	191	145	29	15	16	26	164	6	252	20	12	28	15	.651	0	10	3.60

Kevin Millar

Bats: Right **Throws:** Right **Pos:** 1B **Ht:** 6'1" **Wt:** 195 **Born:** 9/24/71 **Age:** 25

			BATTING															BASERUNNING				PERCENTAGES		
Year Team	Lg	Org	G	AB	H	2B	3B	HR	TB	R	RBI	TBB	IBB	SO	HBP	SH	SF	SB	CS	SB%	GDP	Avg	OBP	SLG
1994 Kane County	A	Fla	135	477	144	35	2	19	240	75	93	74	2	88	13	0	6	3	3	.50	12	.302	.405	.503
1995 Brevard Cty	A+	Fla	129	459	132	32	2	13	207	53	68	70	2	66	12	0	10	4	4	.50	8	.288	.388	.451
1996 Portland	AA	Fla	130	472	150	32	0	18	236	69	86	37	4	53	9	0	5	6	5	.55	13	.318	.375	.500
3 Min. YEARS			394	1408	426	99	4	50	683	197	247	181	8	207	34	0	21	13	12	.52	33	.303	.390	.485

Jose Millares

Bats: Right **Throws:** Right **Pos:** 2B **Ht:** 5'11" **Wt:** 190 **Born:** 3/24/68 **Age:** 29

			BATTING															BASERUNNING				PERCENTAGES		
Year Team	Lg	Org	G	AB	H	2B	3B	HR	TB	R	RBI	TBB	IBB	SO	HBP	SH	SF	SB	CS	SB%	GDP	Avg	OBP	SLG
1990 Bluefield	R+	Bal	48	176	49	12	0	3	70	25	25	10	1	27	0	0	1	6	5	.55	1	.278	.316	.398
1991 Kane County	A	Bal	114	425	115	28	2	5	162	57	71	20	4	71	11	2	6	3	4	.43	6	.271	.316	.381
1992 Frederick	A+	Bal	129	452	98	21	1	10	151	48	68	25	2	79	9	3	10	8	5	.62	6	.217	.266	.334
1993 Bowie	AA	Bal	30	50	14	1	2	0	19	6	5	1	0	9	7	2	0	1	1	.50	2	.280	.379	.380
Frederick	A+	Bal	85	299	75	11	0	9	113	38	36	23	0	44	12	2	2	4	4	.50	10	.251	.327	.378
1994 Bowie	AA	Bal	89	231	52	13	1	3	76	24	39	13	1	39	3	0	6	4	2	.67	10	.225	.269	.329
1995 Bowie	AA	Bal	120	411	102	30	3	4	150	50	50	20	0	62	19	2	6	7	6	.54	14	.248	.309	.365
1996 Bowie	AA	Bal	25	70	13	3	0	0	16	3	1	4	0	6	3	2	0	1	1	.50	0	.186	.260	.229
7 Min. YEARS			640	2114	518	119	9	34	757	251	295	116	8	337	64	13	31	34	28	.55	49	.245	.300	.358

Damian Miller

Bats: Right **Throws:** Right **Pos:** C **Ht:** 6'2" **Wt:** 190 **Born:** 10/13/69 **Age:** 27

			BATTING															BASERUNNING				PERCENTAGES		
Year Team	Lg	Org	G	AB	H	2B	3B	HR	TB	R	RBI	TBB	IBB	SO	HBP	SH	SF	SB	CS	SB%	GDP	Avg	OBP	SLG
1990 Elizabethtn	R+	Min	14	45	10	1	0	1	14	7	6	9	0	3	0	0	0	1	0	1.00	2	.222	.352	.311
1991 Kenosha	A	Min	80	267	62	11	1	3	84	28	34	24	1	53	2	2	3	3	2	.60	4	.232	.297	.315
1992 Kenosha	A	Min	115	377	110	27	2	5	156	53	56	53	1	66	7	2	4	6	1	.86	13	.292	.385	.414
1993 Fort Myers	A+	Min	87	325	69	12	1	1	86	31	26	31	0	44	0	1	0	6	3	.67	5	.212	.281	.265
Nashville	AA	Min	4	13	3	0	0	0	3	0	0	2	0	4	0	0	0	0	0	.00	0	.231	.333	.231
1994 Nashville	AA	Min	103	328	88	10	0	8	122	36	35	35	2	51	1	2	5	4	6	.40	11	.268	.336	.372
1995 Salt Lake	AAA	Min	83	295	84	23	1	3	118	39	41	15	1	39	3	5	2	2	4	.33	11	.285	.324	.400
1996 Salt Lake	AAA	Min	104	385	110	27	1	7	160	54	55	25	2	58	6	2	4	1	4	.20	13	.286	.336	.416
7 Min. YEARS			590	2035	536	111	6	28	743	248	253	194	7	318	19	14	18	23	20	.53	59	.263	.331	.365

Roger Miller

Bats: Right **Throws:** Right **Pos:** C **Ht:** 6'0" **Wt:** 190 **Born:** 4/4/67 **Age:** 30

			BATTING															BASERUNNING				PERCENTAGES		
Year Team	Lg	Org	G	AB	H	2B	3B	HR	TB	R	RBI	TBB	IBB	SO	HBP	SH	SF	SB	CS	SB%	GDP	Avg	OBP	SLG
1989 Pocatello	R+	SF	57	199	66	8	3	6	98	39	38	19	1	14	4	2	4	8	5	.62	7	.332	.394	.492
1990 Clinton	A	SF	111	319	82	11	1	3	104	31	41	28	3	30	1	8	3	1	3	.25	2	.257	.316	.326
San Jose	A+	SF	3	7	4	0	0	0	4	1	2	1	0	0	0	0	0	0	0	.00	1	.571	.625	.571
1991 San Jose	A+	SF	108	369	101	10	1	9	140	59	59	52	5	38	6	9	3	4	0	1.00	10	.274	.370	.379
1993 Clinton	A	SF	10	26	5	0	0	1	8	1	4	2	0	3	0	1	1	0	0	.00	1	.192	.241	.308
Shreveport	AA	SF	61	194	48	10	0	2	64	19	12	14	1	24	3	3	0	0	2	.00	6	.247	.308	.330
1994 San Jose	A+	SF	48	165	33	8	0	2	47	19	15	19	0	20	4	1	2	0	0	.00	4	.200	.295	.285
1995 Shreveport	AA	SF	19	62	17	6	0	2	29	11	10	6	0	1	2	2	1	0	0	.00	1	.274	.352	.468
Phoenix	AAA	SF	43	137	29	4	1	1	38	14	10	9	0	15	0	4	0	0	0	.00	3	.212	.260	.277
1996 Colo. Sprng	AAA	Col	1	2	0	0	0	0	0	0	0	0	0	0	0	0	0	0	0	.00	0	.000	.000	.000
New Haven	AA	Col	85	256	62	8	1	3	81	23	29	26	0	32	2	6	3	0	1	.00	11	.242	.314	.316
7 Min. YEARS			546	1736	447	65	7	29	613	217	220	176	10	177	22	36	17	13	11	.54	46	.257	.331	.353

Joe Millette

Bats: Right **Throws:** Right **Pos:** 3B **Ht:** 6' 1" **Wt:** 175 **Born:** 8/12/66 **Age:** 30

			BATTING															BASERUNNING				PERCENTAGES		
Year	Team	Lg Org	G	AB	H	2B	3B	HR	TB	R	RBI	TBB	IBB	SO	HBP	SH	SF	SB	CS	SB%	GDP	Avg	OBP	SLG
1989	Batavia	A- Phi	11	42	10	3	0	0	13	4	4	4	0	6	0	0	0	3	0	1.00	0	.238	.304	.310
	Spartanburg	A Phi	60	209	50	4	3	0	60	27	18	28	0	36	7	3	3	4	2	.67	5	.239	.344	.287
1990	Clearwater	A+ Phi	108	295	54	5	0	0	59	31	18	29	0	53	7	7	6	4	4	.50	5	.183	.267	.200
1991	Clearwater	A+ Phi	18	55	14	2	0	0	16	6	6	7	0	6	1	3	2	1	2	.33	1	.255	.338	.291
	Reading	AA Phi	115	353	87	9	4	3	113	52	28	36	2	54	7	10	3	6	6	.50	5	.246	.326	.320
1992	Scranton-WB	AAA Phi	78	256	68	11	1	1	84	24	23	15	0	30	6	7	0	3	2	.60	8	.266	.321	.328
1993	Scranton-WB	AAA Phi	107	343	77	15	2	1	99	27	24	19	2	56	5	7	1	5	4	.56	9	.224	.274	.289
1994	Edmonton	AAA Fla	118	406	107	22	3	4	147	41	38	13	3	73	6	6	2	5	5	.50	15	.264	.295	.362
1995	Charlotte	AAA Fla	74	193	36	6	0	4	54	22	20	10	0	36	4	1	4	1	1	.50	4	.187	.237	.280
1996	Calgary	AAA Pit	53	108	23	8	0	0	31	7	7	9	0	19	2	1	0	0	2	.00	8	.213	.286	.287
1992	Philadelphia	NL	33	78	16	0	0	0	16	5	2	5	2	10	2	2	0	1	0	1.00	8	.205	.271	.205
1993	Philadelphia	NL	10	10	2	0	0	0	2	3	2	1	0	2	0	3	0	0	0	.00	1	.200	.273	.200
8	Min. YEARS		742	2260	526	85	13	13	676	241	186	170	7	369	45	45	21	32	28	.53	60	.233	.297	.299
2	Maj. YEARS		43	88	18	0	0	0	18	8	4	6	2	12	2	5	0	1	0	1.00	9	.205	.271	.205

Doug Million

Pitches: Left **Bats:** Left **Pos:** P **Ht:** 6'4" **Wt:** 175 **Born:** 10/13/75 **Age:** 21

			HOW MUCH HE PITCHED					WHAT HE GAVE UP												THE RESULTS					
Year	Team	Lg Org	G	GS	CG	GF	IP	BFP	H	R	ER	HR	SH	SF	HB	TBB	IBB	SO	WP	Bk	W	L	Pct.	ShO	Sv	ERA
1994	Rockies	R Col	3	3	0	0	12	46	8	3	2	0	0	0	0	3	0	19	2	0	1	0	1.000	0	0	1.50
	Bend	A- Col	10	10	0	0	57.2	246	50	23	15	4	1	0	4	21	0	75	4	0	5	3	.625	0	0	2.34
1995	Salem	A+ Col	24	23	0	0	111	513	111	71	57	6	6	1	9	79	4	85	9	4	5	7	.417	0	0	4.62
1996	Salem	A+ Col	17	16	1	0	106.2	443	84	37	30	1	2	0	2	60	1	99	8	1	7	5	.583	1	0	2.53
	New Haven	AA Col	10	10	0	0	54.1	247	54	23	19	2	1	1	1	40	1	40	8	2	3	3	.500	0	0	3.15
3	Min. YEARS		64	62	1	0	341.2	1495	307	157	123	13	10	2	16	203	6	318	31	7	21	18	.538	1	0	3.24

Mark Mimbs

Pitches: Left **Bats:** Left **Pos:** P **Ht:** 6'2" **Wt:** 180 **Born:** 2/13/69 **Age:** 28

			HOW MUCH HE PITCHED					WHAT HE GAVE UP												THE RESULTS					
Year	Team	Lg Org	G	GS	CG	GF	IP	BFP	H	R	ER	HR	SH	SF	HB	TBB	IBB	SO	WP	Bk	W	L	Pct.	ShO	Sv	ERA
1990	Great Falls	R+ LA	14	14	0	0	78	325	69	32	28	3	0	0	1	29	0	94	4	3	7	4	.636	0	0	3.23
1991	Bakersfield	A+ LA	27	25	0	1	170	687	134	49	42	2	3	2	3	59	2	164	4	2	12	6	.667	0	0	2.22
1992	Albuquerque	AAA LA	12	7	0	0	48.2	217	58	34	33	4	1	1	0	19	1	32	4	0	0	4	.000	0	0	6.10
	San Antonio	AA LA	13	13	0	0	82.1	340	78	43	33	3	5	2	2	22	4	55	3	0	1	5	.167	0	0	3.61
1993	Albuquerque	AAA LA	19	1	0	3	18.2	90	20	21	21	0	2	2	0	16	1	12	2	1	0	1	.000	0	1	10.13
	San Antonio	AA LA	49	0	0	23	67.2	272	49	21	12	0	6	4	2	18	7	77	2	0	3	3	.500	0	10	1.60
1994	Bakersfield	A+ LA	1	0	0	0	1.2	7	3	0	0	0	0	0	0	0	0	0	0	0	0	0	.000	0	0	0.00
	Albuquerque	AAA LA	6	0	0	3	6.2	28	8	3	3	1	0	0	0	0	0	9	1	0	1	0	1.000	0	0	4.05
1995	Albuquerque	AAA LA	23	16	1	2	106	433	105	40	35	7	3	3	1	22	0	96	7	1	6	5	.545	0	0	2.97
1996	Albuquerque	AAA LA	34	23	1	1	151	656	165	93	77	14	4	2	3	43	2	136	7	1	8	8	.500	1	0	4.59
7	Min. YEARS		198	99	2	33	730.2	3055	689	336	284	34	24	16	12	228	17	675	34	8	38	36	.514	1	11	3.50

Steve Mintz

Pitches: Right **Bats:** Left **Pos:** P **Ht:** 5'11" **Wt:** 195 **Born:** 11/28/68 **Age:** 28

			HOW MUCH HE PITCHED					WHAT HE GAVE UP												THE RESULTS					
Year	Team	Lg Org	G	GS	CG	GF	IP	BFP	H	R	ER	HR	SH	SF	HB	TBB	IBB	SO	WP	Bk	W	L	Pct.	ShO	Sv	ERA
1990	Yakima	A- LA	20	0	0	12	26	113	21	9	7	1	3	1	1	16	1	38	2	1	2	3	.400	0	3	2.42
1991	Bakersfield	A+ LA	28	11	0	6	92	419	85	56	44	2	5	4	4	58	1	101	9	1	6	6	.500	0	3	4.30
1992	Vero Beach	A+ LA	43	2	0	21	77.2	323	66	29	27	7	5	3	3	30	2	66	7	3	3	6	.333	0	6	3.13
1993	New Britain	AA Bos	43	1	0	20	69.1	287	52	22	16	3	5	1	2	30	5	51	7	0	2	4	.333	0	7	2.08
1994	Phoenix	AAA SF	24	0	0	13	36	161	40	24	22	8	1	3	1	13	3	27	3	0	0	1	.000	0	3	5.50
	Shreveport	AA SF	30	0	0	12	65.1	261	45	29	16	5	2	1	2	22	1	42	8	0	10	2	.833	0	0	2.20
1995	Phoenix	AAA SF	31	0	0	19	49	205	42	16	13	4	3	0	2	21	4	36	4	0	5	2	.714	0	7	2.39
1996	Phoenix	AAA SF	59	0	0	45	57	256	63	39	34	6	1	3	2	25	3	35	5	2	3	5	.375	0	27	5.37
1995	San Francisco	NL	14	0	0	3	19.1	96	26	16	16	4	2	1	2	12	3	7	0	0	1	2	.333	0	0	7.45
7	Min. YEARS		278	14	0	148	472.1	2025	414	224	179	36	25	16	17	215	20	396	45	7	31	29	.517	0	56	3.41

Mike Misuraca

Pitches: Right **Bats:** Right **Pos:** P **Ht:** 6'0" **Wt:** 188 **Born:** 8/21/68 **Age:** 28

			HOW MUCH HE PITCHED					WHAT HE GAVE UP												THE RESULTS					
Year	Team	Lg Org	G	GS	CG	GF	IP	BFP	H	R	ER	HR	SH	SF	HB	TBB	IBB	SO	WP	Bk	W	L	Pct.	ShO	Sv	ERA
1989	Kenosha	A Min	9	9	0	0	46	204	47	32	27	9	3	0	5	15	0	30	1	4	1	5	.167	0	0	5.28
	Elizabethtn	R+ Min	13	13	9	0	103	424	92	34	29	3	4	4	5	33	0	89	8	6	10	3	.769	2	0	2.53
1990	Kenosha	A Min	26	26	1	0	167.1	718	164	81	62	6	5	4	12	57	1	116	6	8	9	9	.500	0	0	3.33
1991	Visalia	A+ Min	21	19	2	0	116	512	131	65	55	12	3	5	8	39	1	82	13	0	7	9	.438	1	0	4.27
1992	Miracle	A+ Min	28	28	3	0	157	687	163	84	63	7	7	4	9	63	1	107	4	0	7	14	.333	1	0	3.61
1993	Nashville	AA Min	25	17	2	2	113	483	103	57	48	9	6	1	5	40	0	80	7	1	6	6	.500	1	0	3.82
1994	Nashville	AA Min	17	17	0	0	106.2	450	115	56	43	10	1	2	5	22	0	80	4	0	8	4	.667	0	0	3.63
	Salt Lake	AAA Min	10	10	1	0	65.2	295	88	43	38	5	2	2	4	13	0	51	6	0	3	5	.375	0	0	5.21
1995	Salt Lake	AAA Min	31	19	1	2	143.1	628	174	93	85	15	0	6	8	36	1	67	7	0	9	6	.600	0	0	5.34
1996	Salt Lake	AAA Min	18	2	0	4	37.1	173	50	33	26	4	1	3	0	16	2	25	3	1	1	2	.333	0	1	6.27

		HOW MUCH HE PITCHED						WHAT HE GAVE UP												THE RESULTS					
Year Team	Lg Org	G	GS	CG	GF	IP	BFP	H	R	ER	HR	SH	SF	HB	TBB	IBB	SO	WP	Bk	W	L	Pct.	ShO	Sv	ERA
New Orleans	AAA Mil	23	12	0	5	80.2	358	93	42	37	11	4	0	3	31	3	57	5	1	2	7	.222	0	2	4.13
8 Min. YEARS		221	172	19	13	1136	4932	1220	620	513	91	36	31	64	365	9	784	64	21	63	70	.474	5	3	4.06

Donovan Mitchell

Bats: Left **Throws:** Right **Pos:** 2B-OF **Ht:** 5'9" **Wt:** 175 **Born:** 11/27/69 **Age:** 27

		BATTING															BASERUNNING				PERCENTAGES		
Year Team	Lg Org	G	AB	H	2B	3B	HR	TB	R	RBI	TBB	IBB	SO	HBP	SH	SF	SB	CS	SB%	GDP	Avg	OBP	SLG
1992 Auburn	A- Hou	70	292	85	8	3	1	102	44	18	13	0	32	1	3	0	25	8	.76	4	.291	.324	.349
1993 Asheville	A Hou	113	453	132	20	3	3	167	67	45	33	1	52	1	2	1	28	18	.61	5	.291	.340	.369
1994 Osceola	A+ Hou	119	455	109	14	4	0	131	47	36	34	1	56	2	5	3	20	13	.61	7	.240	.294	.288
1995 Quad City	A Hou	111	383	126	23	1	4	163	72	42	29	0	38	2	5	3	21	15	.58	10	.329	.376	.426
1996 Jackson	AA Hou	120	408	103	22	2	3	138	57	32	33	2	51	3	4	2	11	4	.73	8	.252	.312	.338
5 Min. YEARS		533	1991	555	87	13	11	701	287	173	142	4	229	9	19	9	105	58	.64	34	.279	.328	.352

Tony Mitchell

Bats: Both **Throws:** Right **Pos:** OF **Ht:** 6'4" **Wt:** 225 **Born:** 10/14/70 **Age:** 26

		BATTING															BASERUNNING				PERCENTAGES		
Year Team	Lg Org	G	AB	H	2B	3B	HR	TB	R	RBI	TBB	IBB	SO	HBP	SH	SF	SB	CS	SB%	GDP	Avg	OBP	SLG
1989 Pirates	R Pit	13	40	11	0	0	0	11	4	1	4	0	10	0	0	1	1	0	1.00	3	.275	.333	.275
1990 Pirates	R Pit	44	102	30	4	2	3	47	18	13	8	0	21	1	0	0	3	4	.43	3	.294	.351	.461
1991 Welland	A- Pit	59	211	57	9	0	10	96	30	38	17	0	62	1	1	1	7	2	.78	4	.270	.326	.455
1992 Augusta	A Pit	66	219	65	8	3	13	118	34	47	29	1	60	0	0	1	6	3	.67	3	.297	.378	.539
Columbus	A Cle	55	202	59	8	2	10	101	36	36	22	3	54	0	0	0	1	6	.14	5	.292	.362	.500
1993 Kinston	A+ Cle	96	318	78	16	2	8	122	43	44	33	2	88	3	2	5	5	4	.56	8	.245	.318	.384
1994 Canton-Akrn	AA Cle	130	494	130	24	0	25	229	70	89	41	0	114	5	0	5	6	1	.86	13	.263	.323	.464
1995 Jackson	AA Hou	96	331	88	17	2	19	166	45	61	35	1	82	1	0	3	1	2	.33	10	.266	.335	.502
1996 Jacksonvile	AA Det	51	173	54	13	0	11	100	30	41	21	2	45	2	1	2	1	0	1.00	4	.312	.389	.578
Toledo	AAA Det	82	288	80	10	4	12	134	45	43	41	1	89	1	0	2	3	2	.60	8	.278	.367	.465
8 Min. YEARS		692	2378	652	109	15	111	1124	355	413	251	10	625	14	4	20	34	24	.59	61	.274	.344	.473

Greg Mix

Pitches: Right **Bats:** Right **Pos:** P **Ht:** 6'4" **Wt:** 210 **Born:** 8/21/71 **Age:** 25

		HOW MUCH HE PITCHED						WHAT HE GAVE UP												THE RESULTS					
Year Team	Lg Org	G	GS	CG	GF	IP	BFP	H	R	ER	HR	SH	SF	HB	TBB	IBB	SO	WP	Bk	W	L	Pct.	ShO	Sv	ERA
1993 Elmira	A- Fla	17	1	0	8	45.1	205	51	26	21	4	0	1	4	17	0	38	4	0	3	3	.500	0	2	4.17
1994 Brevard Cty	A+ Fla	44	0	0	22	78	314	65	29	27	2	4	4	2	20	2	51	1	0	6	2	.750	0	4	3.12
1995 Brevard Cty	A+ Fla	5	4	1	0	29.2	119	27	13	13	1	0	0	3	10	0	17	1	1	3	1	.750	0	0	3.94
Portland	AA Fla	29	17	1	1	122	520	125	64	61	10	2	4	7	35	5	73	4	1	9	5	.643	0	0	4.50
1996 Charlotte	AAA Fla	4	4	0	0	18.1	87	27	15	14	4	2	0	2	7	1	9	1	0	1	3	.250	0	0	6.87
Portland	AA Fla	25	5	0	8	65.2	296	80	40	33	8	4	5	5	19	5	57	6	2	3	0	1.000	0	1	4.52
4 Min. YEARS		124	31	2	39	359	1541	375	187	169	29	12	14	23	108	13	245	17	4	25	14	.641	0	7	4.24

Douga Mlicki

Pitches: Right **Bats:** Right **Pos:** P **Ht:** 6'3" **Wt:** 175 **Born:** 4/23/71 **Age:** 26

		HOW MUCH HE PITCHED						WHAT HE GAVE UP												THE RESULTS					
Year Team	Lg Org	G	GS	CG	GF	IP	BFP	H	R	ER	HR	SH	SF	HB	TBB	IBB	SO	WP	Bk	W	L	Pct.	ShO	Sv	ERA
1992 Auburn	A- Hou	14	13	0	0	81.1	330	50	35	27	4	1	3	6	30	0	83	9	2	1	6	.143	0	0	2.99
1993 Osceola	A+ Hou	26	23	0	0	158.2	668	158	81	69	16	6	5	2	65	1	111	9	0	11	10	.524	0	0	3.91
1994 Jackson	AA Hou	23	23	1	0	138.2	575	107	62	52	20	5	2	8	54	5	130	13	3	13	7	.650	0	0	3.38
1995 Tucson	AAA Hou	6	6	0	0	34	155	44	27	21	3	2	1	2	6	0	22	1	0	1	2	.333	0	0	5.56
Jackson	AA Hou	22	22	2	0	130.2	545	117	68	51	9	3	3	6	39	0	94	6	0	9	5	.643	0	0	3.51
1996 Tucson	AAA Hou	26	26	0	0	137.1	624	171	89	72	9	4	9	4	41	2	98	12	0	5	11	.313	0	0	4.72
5 Min. YEARS		117	113	3	0	680.2	2897	647	362	292	61	21	23	28	235	8	538	50	5	40	41	.494	0	0	3.86

Tony Moeder

Bats: Right **Throws:** Right **Pos:** OF-1B **Ht:** 6'2" **Wt:** 205 **Born:** 7/14/71 **Age:** 25

		BATTING															BASERUNNING				PERCENTAGES		
Year Team	Lg Org	G	AB	H	2B	3B	HR	TB	R	RBI	TBB	IBB	SO	HBP	SH	SF	SB	CS	SB%	GDP	Avg	OBP	SLG
1994 Cedar Rapds	A Cal	117	410	110	20	0	18	184	64	64	45	1	89	8	2	2	7	4	.64	10	.268	.351	.449
1995 Lk Elsinore	A+ Cal	68	252	60	18	1	6	98	39	26	27	2	61	3	0	1	2	3	.40	7	.238	.318	.389
Cedar Rapds	A Cal	48	168	45	11	1	15	103	32	47	19	0	36	4	0	3	2	2	.50	2	.268	.351	.613
1996 Midland	AA Cal	23	85	19	3	1	5	39	19	7	12	0	30	1	0	0	0	0	.00	3	.224	.327	.459
Lk Elsinore	A+ Cal	94	339	104	21	2	14	171	57	66	38	1	92	3	0	3	3	3	.50	9	.307	.379	.504
3 Min. YEARS		350	1254	338	73	5	58	595	211	210	141	4	308	19	2	9	14	12	.54	31	.270	.350	.474

Jason Moler

Bats: Right **Throws:** Right **Pos:** 3B **Ht:** 6'1" **Wt:** 195 **Born:** 10/29/69 **Age:** 27

		BATTING															BASERUNNING				PERCENTAGES		
Year Team	Lg Org	G	AB	H	2B	3B	HR	TB	R	RBI	TBB	IBB	SO	HBP	SH	SF	SB	CS	SB%	GDP	Avg	OBP	SLG
1993 Clearwater	A+ Phi	97	350	101	17	2	15	167	59	64	46	3	40	3	0	4	5	7	.42	10	.289	.372	.477
Reading	AA Phi	38	138	39	11	0	2	56	15	19	12	0	31	2	0	1	1	1	.50	4	.283	.346	.406
1994 Scranton-WB	AAA Phi	44	144	35	9	1	2	52	16	16	18	1	26	1	2	2	2	2	.50	5	.243	.327	.361

			BATTING														BASERUNNING				PERCENTAGES		
Year Team	Lg	Org	G	AB	H	2B	3B	HR	TB	R	RBI	TBB	IBB	SO	HBP	SH	SF	SB	CS	SB%	GDP	Avg	OBP	SLG
Reading	AA	Phi	78	285	81	13	3	4	112	37	37	29	1	21	2	0	1	7	6	.54	8	.284	.353	.393
1995 Reading	AA	Phi	22	83	22	3	0	2	31	17	14	12	2	13	0	0	1	2	2	.50	1	.265	.354	.373
1996 Reading	AA	Phi	109	374	92	22	0	18	168	59	59	54	3	50	4	1	5	4	5	.44	7	.246	.343	.449
4 Min. YEARS			388	1374	370	75	6	43	586	203	209	171	10	181	12	3	14	21	23	.48	35	.269	.352	.426

Ben Molina

Bats: Right **Throws:** Right **Pos:** C **Ht:** 5'11" **Wt:** 190 **Born:** 7/20/74 **Age:** 22

			BATTING														BASERUNNING				PERCENTAGES		
Year Team	Lg	Org	G	AB	H	2B	3B	HR	TB	R	RBI	TBB	IBB	SO	HBP	SH	SF	SB	CS	SB%	GDP	Avg	OBP	SLG
1993 Angels	R	Cal	27	80	21	6	2	0	31	9	10	10	0	4	1	0	1	0	2	.00	1	.263	.348	.388
1994 Cedar Rapds	A	Cal	48	171	48	8	0	3	65	14	16	8	0	12	3	1	0	1	2	.33	3	.281	.324	.380
1995 Vancouver	AAA	Cal	1	2	0	0	0	0	0	0	0	0	0	1	0	0	0	0	0	.00	0	.000	.000	.000
Cedar Rapds	A	Cal	39	133	39	9	0	4	60	15	17	15	0	11	1	1	1	1	1	.50	4	.293	.367	.451
Lk Elsinore	A+	Cal	27	96	37	7	2	2	54	21	12	8	1	7	4	3	1	0	0	.00	2	.385	.450	.563
1996 Midland	AA	Cal	108	365	100	21	2	8	149	45	54	25	1	25	6	4	5	0	1	.00	16	.274	.327	.408
4 Min. YEARS			250	847	245	51	6	17	359	104	109	66	2	60	15	9	8	2	6	.25	26	.289	.348	.424

Wonder Monds

Bats: Right **Throws:** Right **Pos:** OF **Ht:** 6'3" **Wt:** 190 **Born:** 1/11/73 **Age:** 24

			BATTING														BASERUNNING				PERCENTAGES		
Year Team	Lg	Org	G	AB	H	2B	3B	HR	TB	R	RBI	TBB	IBB	SO	HBP	SH	SF	SB	CS	SB%	GDP	Avg	OBP	SLG
1993 Idaho Falls	R+	Atl	60	214	64	13	8	4	105	47	35	25	1	43	2	2	0	16	4	.80	4	.299	.378	.491
1994 Durham	A+	Atl	18	53	11	2	0	2	19	7	10	2	1	11	0	0	1	5	0	1.00	3	.208	.232	.358
Macon	A	Atl	104	365	106	23	12	10	183	70	41	22	0	82	9	8	2	42	9	.82	6	.290	.344	.501
1995 Braves	R	Atl	4	15	2	0	0	0	2	1	1	1	0	8	0	0	0	2	1	.67	0	.133	.188	.133
Durham	A+	Atl	81	297	83	17	0	6	118	44	33	17	1	63	1	1	1	28	7	.80	7	.279	.320	.397
1996 Braves	R	Atl	3	5	2	0	0	2	8	3	3	2	0	1	0	0	1	0	0	.00	0	.400	.500	1.600
Greenville	AA	Atl	32	110	33	9	1	2	50	17	14	9	0	17	0	0	1	7	3	.70	2	.300	.350	.455
4 Min. YEARS			302	1059	301	64	21	26	485	189	137	78	3	225	12	11	6	100	24	.81	22	.284	.339	.458

Ivan Montane

Pitches: Right **Bats:** Right **Pos:** P **Ht:** 6'2" **Wt:** 195 **Born:** 6/3/73 **Age:** 24

			HOW MUCH HE PITCHED						WHAT HE GAVE UP												THE RESULTS					
Year Team	Lg	Org	G	GS	CG	GF	IP	BFP	H	R	ER	HR	SH	SF	HB	TBB	IBB	SO	WP	Bk	W	L	Pct.	ShO	Sv	ERA
1992 Mariners	R	Sea	13	11	0	1	46	224	44	39	29	0	0	0	3	41	0	48	18	4	1	3	.250	0	0	5.67
1993 Bellingham	A-	Sea	15	15	1	0	73.1	305	55	36	32	7	2	1	3	37	0	53	9	3	5	4	.556	0	0	3.93
1994 Appleton	A	Sea	29	26	1	0	159	680	132	79	68	13	4	6	12	82	0	155	19	2	8	9	.471	1	0	3.85
1995 Riverside	A+	Sea	24	16	0	6	92.2	442	101	67	58	3	3	6	10	71	0	79	19	0	5	5	.500	0	0	5.63
1996 Lancaster	A+	Sea	11	11	0	0	59.1	273	57	37	24	2	5	3	2	43	0	54	9	0	2	2	.500	0	0	3.64
Port City	AA	Sea	18	18	0	0	100.1	461	96	67	57	6	1	2	9	75	0	81	16	2	3	8	.273	0	0	5.11
5 Min. YEARS			110	97	2	7	530.2	2385	485	325	268	31	15	18	39	349	0	470	90	11	24	31	.436	1	0	4.55

Norm Montoya

Pitches: Left **Bats:** Left **Pos:** P **Ht:** 6'1" **Wt:** 190 **Born:** 9/24/70 **Age:** 26

			HOW MUCH HE PITCHED						WHAT HE GAVE UP												THE RESULTS					
Year Team	Lg	Org	G	GS	CG	GF	IP	BFP	H	R	ER	HR	SH	SF	HB	TBB	IBB	SO	WP	Bk	W	L	Pct.	ShO	Sv	ERA
1990 Angels	R	Cal	10	6	1	2	47	199	49	20	11	1	1	0	1	7	0	28	0	0	3	3	.500	0	1	2.11
Quad City	A	Cal	4	4	1	0	28.2	117	30	12	10	0	1	1	0	6	0	13	0	1	3	1	.750	0	0	3.14
1991 Quad City	A	Cal	8	8	0	0	40.1	186	55	27	23	2	1	1	0	12	0	22	4	1	4	1	.800	0	0	5.13
Palm Spring	A+	Cal	17	17	1	0	105	455	117	64	48	10	3	2	2	26	4	45	3	1	4	7	.364	0	0	4.11
1992 Palm Spring	A+	Cal	14	6	2	6	43.2	194	42	21	18	3	4	2	1	19	1	46	2	1	2	3	.400	0	0	3.71
1993 Palm Spring	A+	Cal	28	4	0	8	63.2	286	83	38	34	0	3	4	3	21	5	35	6	0	1	3	.250	0	0	4.81
1994 Stockton	A+	Mil	11	0	0	3	16.1	65	12	6	4	1	2	0	1	3	0	15	0	0	0	1	.000	0	1	2.20
El Paso	AA	Mil	9	0	0	4	12.1	48	10	5	4	0	1	0	0	4	2	8	0	0	1	1	.500	0	1	2.92
1995 El Paso	AA	Mil	51	0	0	9	76.1	331	88	36	29	3	5	2	2	18	5	43	4	0	2	5	.286	0	2	3.42
1996 New Orleans	AAA	Mil	11	0	0	6	12.2	63	23	16	12	3	0	0	0	5	1	8	0	0	0	0	.000	0	2	8.53
El Paso	AA	Mil	24	17	1	4	125.1	545	153	74	65	6	3	2	2	28	2	73	4	1	9	8	.529	0	1	4.67
7 Min. YEARS			187	62	6	42	571.1	2489	662	319	258	29	24	14	12	149	20	336	23	5	29	33	.468	0	8	4.06

Wilmer Montoya

Pitches: Right **Bats:** Right **Pos:** P **Ht:** 5'10" **Wt:** 165 **Born:** 3/15/74 **Age:** 23

			HOW MUCH HE PITCHED						WHAT HE GAVE UP												THE RESULTS					
Year Team	Lg	Org	G	GS	CG	GF	IP	BFP	H	R	ER	HR	SH	SF	HB	TBB	IBB	SO	WP	Bk	W	L	Pct.	ShO	Sv	ERA
1994 Watertown	A-	Cle	11	11	1	0	49	199	39	18	14	2	2	0	2	23	0	50	3	1	3	2	.600	0	0	2.57
1995 Kinston	A+	Cle	1	0	0	0	3.1	15	4	2	2	0	1	0	0	1	0	2	0	0	1	0	1.000	0	0	5.40
Columbus	A	Cle	52	0	0	41	84	352	69	35	30	4	2	0	2	37	1	93	6	2	4	3	.571	0	31	3.21
1996 Kinston	A+	Cle	11	0	0	10	15	64	10	5	2	0	1	1	1	6	0	12	1	0	1	2	.333	0	2	1.20
Canton-Akrn	AA	Cle	43	0	0	38	50.2	225	41	24	19	2	4	3	8	28	3	42	2	3	2	5	.286	0	23	3.38
3 Min. YEARS			118	11	1	89	202	855	163	84	67	8	10	4	13	95	4	199	12	6	11	12	.478	0	56	2.99

Charlie Montoyo

Bats: Right **Throws:** Right **Pos:** 1B **Ht:** 5'11" **Wt:** 170 **Born:** 10/17/65 **Age:** 31

		BATTING															BASERUNNING				PERCENTAGES		
Year Team	Lg Org	G	AB	H	2B	3B	HR	TB	R	RBI	TBB	IBB	SO	HBP	SH	SF	SB	CS	SB%	GDP	Avg	OBP	SLG
1987 Helena	R+ Mil	13	45	13	1	2	0	18	12	2	12	0	3	0	0	1	2	1	.67	0	.289	.431	.400
Beloit	A Mil	55	188	50	9	2	5	78	46	19	52	0	22	4	1	1	8	0	1.00	4	.266	.433	.415
1988 Stockton	A+ Mil	132	450	115	14	1	3	140	103	61	156	0	93	5	6	2	16	6	.73	7	.256	.450	.311
1989 Stockton	A+ Mil	129	448	111	22	2	0	137	69	48	102	3	40	11	6	4	13	9	.59	7	.248	.396	.306
1990 El Paso	AA Mil	94	322	93	13	3	3	121	71	44	72	1	43	8	1	2	9	0	1.00	9	.289	.428	.376
1991 Denver	AAA Mil	120	394	94	13	1	12	145	68	45	69	0	51	5	6	4	15	4	.79	6	.239	.356	.368
1992 Denver	AAA Mil	84	259	84	7	4	2	105	40	34	47	0	36	1	2	1	3	5	.38	10	.324	.429	.405
1993 Ottawa	AAA Mon	99	319	89	18	2	1	114	43	43	71	0	37	4	6	5	0	9	.00	11	.279	.411	.357
1994 Scranton-WB	AAA Phi	114	387	109	28	0	9	164	64	47	74	4	61	5	10	1	3	3	.50	10	.282	.403	.424
1995 Scranton-WB	AAA Phi	92	288	70	13	1	3	94	32	34	50	1	45	1	5	3	2	3	.40	4	.243	.354	.326
1996 Ottawa	AAA Mon	22	57	20	5	1	0	27	10	5	7	0	6	0	2	0	0	0	.00	1	.351	.422	.474
Harrisburg	AA Mon	74	183	41	3	1	0	46	21	18	32	0	23	2	2	1	1	0	1.00	6	.224	.344	.251
1993 Montreal	NL	4	5	2	1	0	0	3	1	3	0	0	0	0	0	0	0	0	.00	0	.400	.400	.600
10 Min. YEARS		1028	3340	889	146	20	38	1189	579	400	744	9	460	46	47	25	72	40	.64	75	.266	.404	.356

Jose Monzon

Bats: Right **Throws:** Right **Pos:** C **Ht:** 6'1" **Wt:** 178 **Born:** 11/8/68 **Age:** 28

		BATTING															BASERUNNING				PERCENTAGES		
Year Team	Lg Org	G	AB	H	2B	3B	HR	TB	R	RBI	TBB	IBB	SO	HBP	SH	SF	SB	CS	SB%	GDP	Avg	OBP	SLG
1987 Bristol	R+ Det	7	12	3	1	0	0	4	3	1	0	0	1	0	0	0	0	0	.00	1	.250	.250	.333
Lakeland	A+ Det	4	5	0	0	0	0	0	0	0	0	0	4	0	2	0	0	0	.00	0	.000	.000	.000
Fayettevlle	A Det	11	19	1	0	0	0	1	1	0	2	0	5	0	0	0	0	0	.00	0	.053	.143	.053
1989 Dunedin	A+ Tor	16	48	12	2	1	0	16	4	7	5	0	11	0	0	0	0	0	.00	1	.250	.321	.333
Myrtle Bch	A Tor	50	165	39	7	0	1	49	18	10	19	0	31	0	0	0	3	2	.60	7	.236	.315	.297
1990 Dunedin	A+ Tor	30	76	23	5	1	0	30	11	7	10	0	18	1	1	0	1	0	1.00	0	.303	.391	.395
Knoxville	AA Tor	1	3	1	0	0	0	1	1	0	0	0	0	0	0	0	0	0	.00	0	.333	.333	.333
1991 Dunedin	A+ Tor	46	144	31	6	0	3	46	14	17	17	0	31	0	6	2	2	0	1.00	4	.215	.294	.319
Knoxville	AA Tor	44	116	31	5	0	0	36	12	11	13	1	23	0	1	1	1	1	.50	5	.267	.338	.310
1992 Knoxville	AA Tor	65	178	41	9	1	0	52	17	10	12	0	42	2	3	1	3	2	.60	3	.230	.285	.292
Syracuse	AAA Tor	9	18	1	0	0	0	1	3	1	2	0	1	0	0	0	0	0	.00	1	.056	.150	.056
1993 Syracuse	AAA Tor	71	197	47	7	0	3	63	14	21	11	0	37	0	4	0	0	1	.00	9	.239	.279	.320
1994 Midland	AA Cal	83	283	71	18	3	4	107	41	35	24	0	52	2	3	0	1	1	.50	7	.251	.314	.378
1995 Vancouver	AAA Cal	13	23	5	1	0	1	9	5	5	3	0	2	0	0	0	0	0	.00	1	.217	.308	.391
Midland	AA Cal	57	180	52	11	1	1	68	29	19	22	0	36	2	3	2	0	0	.00	6	.289	.369	.378
1996 Midland	AA Cal	43	140	39	4	0	3	52	15	22	9	1	22	0	0	2	1	0	1.00	6	.279	.318	.371
9 Min. YEARS		550	1607	397	76	7	16	535	188	166	149	2	316	7	23	8	12	7	.63	51	.247	.312	.333

Eric Moody

Pitches: Right **Bats:** Right **Pos:** P **Ht:** 6'6" **Wt:** 185 **Born:** 1/6/71 **Age:** 26

		HOW MUCH HE PITCHED						WHAT HE GAVE UP												THE RESULTS					
Year Team	Lg Org	G	GS	CG	GF	IP	BFP	H	R	ER	HR	SH	SF	HB	TBB	IBB	SO	WP	Bk	W	L	Pct.	ShO	Sv	ERA
1993 Erie	A- Tex	17	7	0	4	54	229	54	30	23	3	0	1	2	13	1	33	3	1	3	3	.500	0	0	3.83
1994 Hudson Vall	A- Tex	15	12	1	1	89	355	82	32	28	2	2	3	2	18	1	68	3	4	7	3	.700	0	0	2.83
1995 Charlotte	A+ Tex	13	13	2	0	88.1	353	84	30	27	2	3	1	5	13	0	57	0	0	5	5	.500	2	0	2.75
1996 Tulsa	AA Tex	44	5	0	29	95.2	395	92	40	38	4	1	3	1	23	2	80	4	0	8	4	.667	0	16	3.57
4 Min. YEARS		89	37	3	34	327	1332	312	132	116	11	6	8	10	67	4	238	10	5	23	15	.605	2	16	3.19

Bobby Moore

Bats: Right **Throws:** Right **Pos:** OF **Ht:** 5' 9" **Wt:** 165 **Born:** 10/27/65 **Age:** 31

		BATTING															BASERUNNING				PERCENTAGES		
Year Team	Lg Org	G	AB	H	2B	3B	HR	TB	R	RBI	TBB	IBB	SO	HBP	SH	SF	SB	CS	SB%	GDP	Avg	OBP	SLG
1987 Eugene	A- KC	57	235	88	13	4	1	112	40	25	14	2	22	1	2	1	23	1	.96	5	.374	.410	.477
1988 Baseball Cy	A+ KC	60	224	52	4	2	0	60	25	10	17	0	20	2	4	0	12	7	.63	4	.232	.292	.268
1989 Baseball Cy	A+ KC	131	483	131	21	5	0	162	85	42	51	1	35	6	6	3	34	19	.64	6	.271	.346	.335
1990 Memphis	AA KC	112	422	128	20	6	2	166	93	36	56	0	32	2	8	4	27	7	.79	5	.303	.384	.393
1991 Omaha	AAA KC	130	494	120	13	3	0	139	65	34	37	0	41	3	13	2	35	15	.70	10	.243	.299	.281
1992 Richmond	AAA Atl	92	316	79	13	3	0	98	41	25	21	0	26	0	6	3	14	6	.70	6	.250	.294	.310
1993 Richmond	AAA Atl	1	3	2	0	0	0	2	2	0	1	0	0	0	0	0	1	0	1.00	0	.667	.750	.667
1994 Memphis	AA KC	27	97	23	2	1	2	33	10	7	8	0	15	1	2	1	1	2	.33	3	.237	.299	.340
Richmond	AAA Atl	60	216	79	6	3	5	106	37	18	18	1	16	0	1	2	10	6	.63	4	.366	.411	.491
1995 Richmond	AAA Atl	108	329	85	18	2	3	116	45	27	27	1	27	4	3	2	9	7	.56	6	.258	.320	.353
1996 Richmond	AAA Atl	67	200	54	10	0	3	73	29	14	15	0	11	0	1	1	9	2	.82	3	.270	.319	.365
1991 Kansas City	AL	18	14	5	1	0	0	6	3	0	1	0	2	0	0	0	3	2	.60	0	.357	.400	.429
10 Min. YEARS		845	3019	841	120	29	16	1067	472	238	265	5	245	19	46	19	175	72	.71	52	.279	.339	.353

Joel Moore

Pitches: Right **Bats:** Left **Pos:** P **Ht:** 6'3" **Wt:** 200 **Born:** 8/13/72 **Age:** 24

		HOW MUCH HE PITCHED						WHAT HE GAVE UP												THE RESULTS					
Year Team	Lg Org	G	GS	CG	GF	IP	BFP	H	R	ER	HR	SH	SF	HB	TBB	IBB	SO	WP	Bk	W	L	Pct.	ShO	Sv	ERA
1993 Bend	A- Col	15	15	0	0	89.2	365	75	35	32	2	1	2	2	31	1	79	5	0	4	7	.364	0	0	3.21
1994 Central Val	A+ Col	25	24	0	0	133	607	149	78	67	8	6	1	8	64	1	89	12	1	11	8	.579	0	0	4.53

Year	Team	Lg	Org	G	GS	CG	GF	IP	BFP	H	R	ER	HR	SH	SF	HB	TBB	IBB	SO	WP	Bk	W	L	Pct.	ShO	Sv	ERA
				HOW MUCH HE PITCHED						WHAT HE GAVE UP												THE RESULTS					
1995	New Haven	AA	Col	27	26	1	0	157.1	682	156	69	56	8	6	6	8	67	2	102	5	1	14	6	.700	1	0	3.20
1996	Rockies	R	Col	4	4	0	0	18	70	13	2	2	0	1	0	1	0	0	19	0	1	1	0	1.000	0	0	1.00
	New Haven	AA	Col	6	6	0	0	31.1	134	35	18	16	4	2	1	3	5	0	15	1	0	0	5	.000	0	0	4.60
4	Min. YEARS			77	75	1	0	429.1	1858	428	202	173	22	16	10	22	167	4	304	23	3	30	26	.536	1	0	3.63

Mike Moore

Bats: Right **Throws:** Right **Pos:** OF **Ht:** 6'4" **Wt:** 200 **Born:** 3/7/71 **Age:** 26

Year	Team	Lg	Org	G	AB	H	2B	3B	HR	TB	R	RBI	TBB	IBB	SO	HBP	SH	SF	SB	CS	SB%	GDP	Avg	OBP	SLG
				BATTING															BASERUNNING				PERCENTAGES		
1992	Yakima	A-	LA	18	58	12	1	0	2	19	12	6	9	1	25	0	0	0	3	2	.60	1	.207	.313	.328
1993	Bakersfield	A+	LA	100	403	116	25	1	13	182	61	58	29	0	103	3	0	4	23	10	.70	6	.288	.337	.452
1994	San Antonio	AA	LA	72	254	57	12	1	5	86	32	32	22	0	75	6	0	1	11	7	.61	2	.224	.300	.339
	Bakersfield	A+	LA	21	81	24	5	0	2	35	17	8	13	1	21	0	0	0	2	0	1.00	3	.296	.394	.432
1995	Vero Beach	A+	LA	7	22	6	1	0	0	7	3	1	6	0	8	0	0	0	0	1	.00	1	.273	.429	.318
1996	San Antonio	AA	LA	64	200	48	10	4	2	72	21	21	17	0	64	2	0	1	8	4	.67	4	.240	.305	.360
5	Min. YEARS			282	1018	263	54	6	24	401	146	126	96	2	296	11	0	6	47	24	.66	17	.258	.327	.394

Tim Moore

Pitches: Right **Bats:** Right **Pos:** P **Ht:** 6'4" **Wt:** 190 **Born:** 9/4/70 **Age:** 26

Year	Team	Lg	Org	G	GS	CG	GF	IP	BFP	H	R	ER	HR	SH	SF	HB	TBB	IBB	SO	WP	Bk	W	L	Pct.	ShO	Sv	ERA
				HOW MUCH HE PITCHED						WHAT HE GAVE UP												THE RESULTS					
1992	Utica	A-	ChA	14	13	0	0	84.2	360	82	46	30	7	3	2	3	21	0	66	8	1	6	5	.545	0	0	3.19
1993	South Bend	A	ChA	26	26	4	0	165.1	692	156	89	83	21	6	7	12	52	0	108	8	1	11	9	.550	0	0	4.52
1994	Pr. William	A+	ChA	27	0	0	13	66	279	59	24	19	4	6	1	2	24	0	77	3	1	2	2	.500	0	5	2.59
	Birmingham	AA	ChA	8	0	0	5	12.2	55	16	12	8	2	0	1	1	3	1	10	1	0	0	0	.000	0	0	5.68
1995	Birmingham	AA	ChA	29	19	0	3	120	521	118	58	49	10	7	6	4	40	1	78	6	2	7	5	.583	0	0	3.68
1996	Birmingham	AA	ChA	9	6	0	2	26.1	127	43	31	25	6	0	1	1	6	1	23	0	0	1	4	.200	0	0	8.54
5	Min. YEARS			113	64	4	23	475	2034	474	260	214	50	22	18	23	146	3	362	26	5	27	25	.519	0	5	4.05

Trey Moore

Pitches: Left **Bats:** Left **Pos:** P **Ht:** 6'1" **Wt:** 200 **Born:** 10/2/72 **Age:** 24

Year	Team	Lg	Org	G	GS	CG	GF	IP	BFP	H	R	ER	HR	SH	SF	HB	TBB	IBB	SO	WP	Bk	W	L	Pct.	ShO	Sv	ERA
				HOW MUCH HE PITCHED						WHAT HE GAVE UP												THE RESULTS					
1994	Bellingham	A-	Sea	11	10	1	0	61.2	247	48	18	18	4	0	2	2	24	0	73	4	0	5	2	.714	0	0	2.63
1995	Riverside	A+	Sea	24	24	0	0	148.1	605	122	65	51	6	2	5	2	58	1	134	6	1	14	6	.700	0	0	3.09
1996	Port City	AA	Sea	11	11	0	0	53.2	265	73	54	46	6	2	5	0	33	0	42	4	1	1	6	.143	0	0	7.71
	Lancaster	A+	Sea	15	15	2	0	94.1	413	106	57	43	10	2	0	7	31	0	77	7	0	7	5	.583	0	0	4.10
3	Min. YEARS			61	60	3	0	358	1530	349	194	158	26	6	12	11	146	1	326	21	2	27	19	.587	0	0	3.97

Vince Moore

Bats: Left **Throws:** Left **Pos:** OF **Ht:** 6'1" **Wt:** 177 **Born:** 9/22/71 **Age:** 25

Year	Team	Lg	Org	G	AB	H	2B	3B	HR	TB	R	RBI	TBB	IBB	SO	HBP	SH	SF	SB	CS	SB%	GDP	Avg	OBP	SLG
				BATTING															BASERUNNING				PERCENTAGES		
1991	Braves	R	Atl	30	110	44	4	6	2	66	28	22	13	0	20	0	0	1	7	2	.78	1	.400	.460	.600
	Macon	A	Atl	35	120	24	5	1	0	31	17	12	7	0	24	0	0	0	6	0	1.00	2	.200	.244	.258
1992	Macon	A	Atl	123	436	99	15	5	6	142	52	48	48	2	118	1	4	3	25	11	.69	10	.227	.303	.326
1993	Durham	A+	Atl	87	319	93	14	1	14	151	53	64	29	2	93	6	1	2	21	8	.72	5	.292	.360	.473
1994	Wichita	AA	SD	48	132	20	5	0	2	31	15	9	16	1	46	1	0	1	4	2	.67	4	.152	.247	.235
	Rancho Cuca	A+	SD	6	23	5	1	0	1	9	5	2	3	0	9	0	0	0	0	0	.00	0	.217	.308	.391
1995	Rancho Cuca	A+	SD	84	299	68	11	1	15	126	50	57	35	0	102	2	0	1	10	5	.67	5	.227	.312	.421
1996	Memphis	AA	SD	44	141	29	11	2	1	47	24	11	20	0	47	0	0	1	7	4	.64	1	.206	.302	.333
	Rancho Cuca	A+	SD	63	219	63	13	2	8	104	49	38	42	1	78	4	0	0	12	1	.92	4	.288	.411	.475
6	Min. YEARS			520	1799	445	79	18	49	707	293	263	213	6	537	14	5	9	92	33	.74	32	.247	.330	.393

Melvin Mora

Bats: Right **Throws:** Right **Pos:** OF **Ht:** 5'10" **Wt:** 160 **Born:** 2/2/72 **Age:** 25

Year	Team	Lg	Org	G	AB	H	2B	3B	HR	TB	R	RBI	TBB	IBB	SO	HBP	SH	SF	SB	CS	SB%	GDP	Avg	OBP	SLG
				BATTING															BASERUNNING				PERCENTAGES		
1992	Astros	R	Hou	49	144	32	3	0	0	35	28	8	18	0	16	5	0	1	16	3	.84	2	.222	.327	.243
1993	Asheville	A	Hou	108	365	104	22	2	2	136	66	31	36	0	46	9	5	8	20	13	.61	7	.285	.356	.373
1994	Osceola	A+	Hou	118	425	120	29	4	8	181	57	46	37	1	60	10	3	3	24	16	.60	8	.282	.352	.426
1995	Jackson	AA	Hou	123	467	139	32	0	3	180	63	45	32	1	57	9	7	7	22	11	.67	11	.298	.350	.385
	Tucson	AAA	Hou	2	5	3	0	1	0	5	3	1	2	1	0	0	0	0	1	0	1.00	0	.600	.714	1.000
1996	Tucson	AAA	Hou	62	228	64	11	2	3	88	35	26	17	1	27	1	3	4	3	5	.38	7	.281	.328	.386
	Jackson	AA	Hou	70	255	73	6	1	5	96	36	23	14	1	23	6	1	2	4	7	.36	4	.286	.336	.376
5	Min. YEARS			532	1889	535	103	10	21	721	288	180	156	5	229	40	19	25	90	55	.62	39	.283	.346	.382

Willie Morales

Bats: Right **Throws:** Right **Pos:** C **Ht:** 5'10" **Wt:** 182 **Born:** 9/7/72 **Age:** 24

Year	Team	Lg	Org	G	AB	H	2B	3B	HR	TB	R	RBI	TBB	IBB	SO	HBP	SH	SF	SB	CS	SB%	GDP	Avg	OBP	SLG
				BATTING															BASERUNNING				PERCENTAGES		
1993	Sou. Oregon	A-	Oak	60	208	56	16	0	1	75	34	27	19	2	36	4	1	4	0	3	.00	2	.269	.336	.361

BATTING																		BASERUNNING				PERCENTAGES		
Year Team	Lg Org	G	AB	H	2B	3B	HR	TB	R	RBI	TBB	IBB	SO	HBP	SH	SF	SB	CS	SB%	GDP	Avg	OBP	SLG
1994 W. Michigan	A Oak	111	380	101	26	0	13	166	47	51	36	4	64	3	3	2	3	5	.38	12	.266	.333	.437
1995 Modesto	A+ Oak	109	419	116	32	0	4	160	49	60	28	1	75	7	2	4	1	4	.20	13	.277	.330	.382
1996 Huntsville	AA Oak	108	377	110	24	0	18	188	54	73	38	2	67	7	4	6	0	2	.00	11	.292	.362	.499
4 Min. YEARS		388	1384	383	98	0	36	589	184	211	121	9	242	21	10	16	4	14	.22	38	.277	.340	.426

Bats: Right **Throws:** Right **Pos:** SS

Kevin Morgan

Ht: 6'1" **Wt:** 170 **Born:** 3/3/70 **Age:** 27

BATTING																		BASERUNNING				PERCENTAGES		
Year Team	Lg Org	G	AB	H	2B	3B	HR	TB	R	RBI	TBB	IBB	SO	HBP	SH	SF	SB	CS	SB%	GDP	Avg	OBP	SLG
1991 Niagara Fal	A- Det	70	252	60	13	0	0	73	23	26	21	0	49	3	4	4	8	6	.57	2	.238	.300	.290
1992 Fayettevlle	A Det	123	466	106	19	2	0	129	55	37	49	2	61	6	6	4	15	19	.44	10	.227	.307	.277
1993 Lakeland	A+ Det	112	417	99	12	2	2	121	45	34	32	2	84	2	3	4	9	6	.60	9	.237	.292	.290
1994 St. Lucie	A+ NYN	132	448	122	8	3	1	139	63	47	37	0	62	7	9	3	7	7	.50	5	.272	.335	.310
1995 Binghamton	AA NYN	114	430	119	21	1	4	154	63	51	44	4	52	5	7	2	9	9	.50	2	.277	.349	.358
Norfolk	AAA NYN	19	62	20	1	0	0	21	10	8	4	0	8	1	0	0	1	3	.25	1	.323	.373	.339
1996 Norfolk	AAA NYN	29	82	11	3	0	0	14	7	3	9	0	14	2	4	1	3	1	.75	0	.134	.234	.171
Binghamton	AA NYN	107	409	103	11	2	6	136	61	35	53	2	59	3	10	3	13	4	.76	15	.252	.340	.333
6 Min. YEARS		706	2566	640	88	10	13	787	327	241	249	10	389	29	43	21	65	55	.54	44	.249	.320	.307

Bats: Both **Throws:** Right **Pos:** SS

Cesar Morillo

Ht: 5'11" **Wt:** 180 **Born:** 7/21/73 **Age:** 23

BATTING																		BASERUNNING				PERCENTAGES		
Year Team	Lg Org	G	AB	H	2B	3B	HR	TB	R	RBI	TBB	IBB	SO	HBP	SH	SF	SB	CS	SB%	GDP	Avg	OBP	SLG
1990 Royals	R KC	55	185	50	6	2	1	63	21	17	22	0	45	2	3	0	7	4	.64	4	.270	.354	.341
1991 Baseball Cy	A+ KC	62	226	39	8	0	0	47	11	13	13	0	68	2	7	2	6	5	.55	4	.173	.222	.208
Appleton	A KC	63	236	59	9	3	1	77	35	17	38	0	54	1	1	1	9	8	.53	2	.250	.355	.326
1992 Baseball Cy	A+ KC	35	102	17	5	1	0	24	8	7	10	0	23	1	3	1	1	0	1.00	7	.167	.246	.235
Eugene	A- KC	51	180	44	9	1	1	58	28	17	21	0	40	1	3	0	6	4	.60	1	.244	.327	.322
1993 Rockford	A KC	101	327	85	13	3	3	113	47	36	30	3	65	3	5	2	4	1	.80	4	.260	.326	.346
1994 Wilmington	A+ KC	16	55	9	1	0	0	10	3	4	5	1	17	1	0	1	1	0	1.00	1	.164	.242	.182
Rockford	A KC	70	242	68	11	2	2	89	23	25	15	2	35	2	1	2	4	3	.57	6	.281	.326	.368
1995 Bakersfield	A+ KC	108	371	113	25	1	1	143	41	37	31	2	71	4	5	1	4	12	.25	6	.305	.364	.385
1996 Wichita	AA KC	45	119	28	3	1	2	39	8	7	7	0	18	0	5	0	3	0	1.00	3	.235	.278	.328
7 Min. YEARS		606	2043	512	90	14	11	663	225	180	192	8	436	17	33	10	45	37	.55	38	.251	.319	.325

Pitches: Right **Bats:** Right **Pos:** P

Geno Morones

Ht: 5'11" **Wt:** 197 **Born:** 3/26/71 **Age:** 26

		HOW MUCH HE PITCHED						WHAT HE GAVE UP												THE RESULTS					
Year Team	Lg Org	G	GS	CG	GF	IP	BFP	H	R	ER	HR	SH	SF	HB	TBB	IBB	SO	WP	Bk	W	L	Pct.	ShO	Sv	ERA
1991 Huntington	R+ ChN	22	0	0	16	35.1	166	37	18	17	2	2	1	3	24	1	36	7	0	2	3	.400	0	3	4.33
1992 Geneva	A- ChN	11	0	0	8	12.1	55	8	5	1	0	0	2	0	10	1	7	1	0	1	0	1.000	0	3	0.73
1993 Peoria	A ChN	13	0	0	8	18.1	82	12	8	5	0	0	1	3	7	1	21	1	1	0	2	.000	0	0	2.45
Daytona	A+ ChN	13	6	1	1	51	206	44	10	10	0	2	1	3	16	2	27	3	0	5	1	.833	1	0	1.76
Orlando	AA ChN	4	4	1	0	24	108	29	14	13	2	0	2	2	9	0	14	1	0	2	2	.500	0	0	4.88
1994 Daytona	A+ ChN	16	16	2	0	99.2	399	87	37	30	3	1	1	2	28	0	69	3	0	5	3	.625	2	0	2.71
1995 Wichita	AA KC	17	16	0	0	79	353	85	49	36	5	4	6	3	39	0	32	3	0	3	6	.333	0	0	4.10
1996 Wilmington	A+ KC	19	14	0	1	96	393	86	40	33	8	2	1	4	27	0	60	3	1	6	3	.667	0	0	3.09
Wichita	AA KC	13	4	1	4	37.2	178	50	32	29	6	3	1	1	19	0	24	5	1	1	5	.167	0	0	6.93
6 Min. YEARS		128	60	5	38	453.1	1940	438	213	174	26	14	16	21	179	5	290	27	3	25	25	.500	3	6	3.45

Bats: Left **Throws:** Right **Pos:** 1B

Bobby Morris

Ht: 6'0" **Wt:** 180 **Born:** 11/22/72 **Age:** 24

BATTING																		BASERUNNING				PERCENTAGES		
Year Team	Lg Org	G	AB	H	2B	3B	HR	TB	R	RBI	TBB	IBB	SO	HBP	SH	SF	SB	CS	SB%	GDP	Avg	OBP	SLG
1993 Huntington	R+ ChN	50	170	49	8	3	1	66	29	24	24	0	29	1	2	3	6	7	.46	2	.288	.374	.388
1994 Peoria	A ChN	101	362	128	33	1	7	184	61	64	53	4	63	7	10	2	7	7	.50	10	.354	.443	.508
1995 Daytona	A+ ChN	95	344	106	18	2	2	134	44	55	38	6	46	8	2	5	22	8	.73	5	.308	.385	.390
1996 Orlando	AA ChN	131	465	122	29	3	8	181	72	62	65	4	73	6	0	8	12	14	.46	12	.262	.355	.389
4 Min. YEARS		377	1341	405	88	9	18	565	206	205	180	14	211	22	14	18	47	36	.57	29	.302	.389	.421

Pitches: Right **Bats:** Right **Pos:** P

Matt Morris

Ht: 6'5" **Wt:** 210 **Born:** 8/9/74 **Age:** 22

		HOW MUCH HE PITCHED						WHAT HE GAVE UP												THE RESULTS					
Year Team	Lg Org	G	GS	CG	GF	IP	BFP	H	R	ER	HR	SH	SF	HB	TBB	IBB	SO	WP	Bk	W	L	Pct.	ShO	Sv	ERA
1995 New Jersey	A- StL	2	2	0	0	11	45	12	3	2	1	0	0	0	3	0	13	0	3	2	0	1.000	0	0	1.64
St. Pete	A+ StL	8	8	1	0	45	179	34	19	11	2	2	0	0	14	0	44	0	5	5	2	.714	1	0	2.20
1996 Arkansas	AA StL	27	27	4	0	167	711	178	79	72	14	8	4	2	48	1	120	9	0	12	12	.500	4	0	3.88
Louisville	AAA StL	1	1	0	0	8	32	8	3	3	0	0	0	0	1	0	9	0	0	0	1	.000	0	0	3.38
2 Min. YEARS		38	38	5	0	231	967	232	104	88	17	10	4	2	66	1	186	9	8	19	15	.559	5	0	3.43

Nick Morrow

Bats: Right **Throws:** Right **Pos:** OF **Ht:** 5'11" **Wt:** 180 **Born:** 4/17/72 **Age:** 25

		BATTING															BASERUNNING				PERCENTAGES		
Year Team	Lg Org	G	AB	H	2B	3B	HR	TB	R	RBI	TBB	IBB	SO	HBP	SH	SF	SB	CS	SB%	GDP	Avg	OBP	SLG
1994 Billings	R+ Cin	66	246	82	16	4	14	148	60	56	33	1	46	2	0	1	6	2	.75	1	.333	.415	.602
1995 Charlstn-WV	A Cin	139	467	117	28	8	9	188	67	54	77	2	123	2	2	1	41	17	.71	5	.251	.358	.403
1996 Winston-Sal	A+ Cin	123	422	109	19	3	18	188	78	54	59	1	93	5	3	3	28	6	.82	6	.258	.354	.445
Chattanooga	AA Cin	1	1	1	0	0	0	1	1	0	0	0	0	0	0	0	0	0	.00	0	1.000	1.000	1.000
3 Min. YEARS		329	1136	309	63	15	41	525	206	164	169	4	262	9	5	5	75	25	.75	12	.272	.369	.462

Paul Morse

Pitches: Right **Bats:** Right **Pos:** P **Ht:** 6'2" **Wt:** 185 **Born:** 2/27/73 **Age:** 24

		HOW MUCH HE PITCHED						WHAT HE GAVE UP												THE RESULTS					
Year Team	Lg Org	G	GS	CG	GF	IP	BFP	H	R	ER	HR	SH	SF	HB	TBB	IBB	SO	WP	Bk	W	L	Pct.	ShO	Sv	ERA
1994 Elizabethtn	R+ Min	7	0	0	5	7.1	35	8	7	6	2	0	1	2	3	0	8	0	0	0	0	.000	0	0	7.36
Fort Wayne	A Min	16	0	0	11	20.1	97	27	15	13	2	1	0	2	10	0	17	0	0	0	3	.000	0	3	5.75
1995 Fort Myers	A+ Min	35	0	0	29	61.1	247	57	30	26	3	1	4	3	12	0	56	4	1	3	1	.750	0	15	3.82
1996 Fort Myers	A+ Min	13	0	0	12	14	50	8	4	4	1	0	0	0	5	0	10	0	0	1	0	1.000	0	9	2.57
New Britain	AA Min	35	1	0	23	55.2	249	55	36	33	5	4	4	1	26	2	48	4	1	6	4	.600	0	4	5.34
3 Min. YEARS		106	1	0	80	158.2	678	155	92	82	13	6	9	8	56	2	139	8	2	10	8	.556	0	31	4.65

Joe Morvay

Pitches: Right **Bats:** Left **Pos:** P **Ht:** 6'4" **Wt:** 210 **Born:** 2/8/71 **Age:** 26

		HOW MUCH HE PITCHED						WHAT HE GAVE UP												THE RESULTS					
Year Team	Lg Org	G	GS	CG	GF	IP	BFP	H	R	ER	HR	SH	SF	HB	TBB	IBB	SO	WP	Bk	W	L	Pct.	ShO	Sv	ERA
1993 Erie	A- Tex	18	2	0	8	38.1	160	32	18	12	0	1	2	2	14	1	42	1	0	2	3	.400	0	2	2.82
1994 Charlstn-SC	A Tex	37	1	0	11	71	303	50	27	22	4	4	1	9	30	1	85	4	0	2	4	.333	0	0	2.79
1995 Tulsa	AA Tex	37	0	0	28	65.2	305	82	45	38	4	6	1	4	28	6	30	4	0	5	8	.385	0	8	5.21
1996 Tulsa	AA Tex	24	1	0	11	46	213	55	32	32	3	5	2	4	20	2	27	2	0	2	2	.500	0	2	6.26
4 Min. YEARS		116	4	0	58	221	981	219	122	104	11	16	6	19	92	10	184	11	0	11	17	.393	0	12	4.24

Damian Moss

Pitches: Left **Bats:** Right **Pos:** P **Ht:** 6'0" **Wt:** 187 **Born:** 11/24/76 **Age:** 20

		HOW MUCH HE PITCHED						WHAT HE GAVE UP												THE RESULTS					
Year Team	Lg Org	G	GS	CG	GF	IP	BFP	H	R	ER	HR	SH	SF	HB	TBB	IBB	SO	WP	Bk	W	L	Pct.	ShO	Sv	ERA
1994 Danville	R+ Atl	12	12	1	0	60.1	265	30	28	24	1	1	0	14	55	0	77	12	3	2	5	.286	1	0	3.58
1995 Macon	A Atl	27	27	0	0	149.1	653	134	73	59	13	0	2	12	70	0	177	14	5	9	10	.474	0	0	3.56
1996 Durham	A+ Atl	14	14	0	0	84	333	52	25	21	9	3	3	2	40	0	89	7	2	9	1	.900	0	0	2.25
Greenville	AA Atl	11	10	0	0	58	262	57	41	32	5	0	3	3	35	0	48	12	0	2	5	.286	0	0	4.97
3 Min. YEARS		64	63	1	0	351.2	1513	273	167	136	28	4	8	31	200	0	391	45	10	22	21	.512	1	0	3.48

Gary Mota

Bats: Right **Throws:** Right **Pos:** OF **Ht:** 6'0" **Wt:** 195 **Born:** 10/6/70 **Age:** 26

		BATTING															BASERUNNING				PERCENTAGES		
Year Team	Lg Org	G	AB	H	2B	3B	HR	TB	R	RBI	TBB	IBB	SO	HBP	SH	SF	SB	CS	SB%	GDP	Avg	OBP	SLG
1990 Auburn	A- Hou	69	248	64	12	4	3	93	39	19	26	2	74	2	3	2	12	1	.92	5	.258	.331	.375
1991 Osceola	A+ Hou	22	71	14	2	2	0	20	10	3	8	0	19	0	0	0	4	1	.80	0	.197	.278	.282
1992 Asheville	A Hou	137	484	141	21	5	23	241	92	89	58	5	131	3	0	6	22	10	.69	13	.291	.367	.498
1993 Jackson	AA Hou	27	90	13	2	0	3	24	7	8	2	0	25	0	2	1	1	1	.50	2	.144	.161	.267
1994 Jackson	AA Hou	108	314	75	13	4	10	126	46	54	57	2	80	3	0	4	12	7	.63	5	.239	.357	.401
1995 Reading	AA Phi	33	110	25	4	2	1	36	13	9	8	2	23	0	1	0	0	2	.00	2	.227	.280	.327
1996 Jackson	AA Hou	12	25	6	0	0	0	6	3	0	4	0	2	0	0	0	0	0	.00	3	.240	.345	.240
Kissimmee	A+ Hou	45	152	50	8	3	2	70	17	20	5	0	31	1	3	0	0	3	.00	2	.329	.354	.461
7 Min. YEARS		453	1494	388	62	20	42	616	227	202	168	11	385	9	9	13	51	25	.67	32	.260	.336	.412

Jose Mota

Bats: Both **Throws:** Right **Pos:** 3B **Ht:** 5' 9" **Wt:** 155 **Born:** 3/16/65 **Age:** 32

		BATTING															BASERUNNING				PERCENTAGES		
Year Team	Lg Org	G	AB	H	2B	3B	HR	TB	R	RBI	TBB	IBB	SO	HBP	SH	SF	SB	CS	SB%	GDP	Avg	OBP	SLG
1985 Buffalo	AAA ChA	6	18	5	0	0	0	5	3	1	2	0	0	0	0	0	0	0	.00	1	.278	.350	.278
Niagara Fal	A- ChA	65	254	77	9	2	0	90	35	27	28	3	29	2	5	2	8	5	.62	1	.303	.374	.354
1986 Tulsa	AA Tex	41	158	51	7	3	1	67	26	11	22	0	13	0	3	1	14	8	.64	0	.323	.403	.424
Okla. City	AAA Tex	71	255	71	9	1	0	82	38	20	24	1	43	3	5	0	7	5	.58	7	.278	.348	.322
1987 Tulsa	AA Tex	21	71	15	2	0	0	17	11	4	13	0	12	0	0	1	2	2	.50	0	.211	.329	.239
San Antonio	AA LA	54	190	50	4	3	0	60	23	11	21	1	34	2	5	0	3	4	.43	3	.263	.343	.316
1988 Albuquerque	AAA LA	6	15	5	0	0	0	5	4	1	3	0	3	0	1	0	1	0	1.00	1	.333	.444	.333
San Antonio	AA LA	82	214	56	11	1	1	72	32	18	27	1	35	0	3	1	10	4	.71	7	.262	.343	.336
1989 Huntsville	AA Oak	27	81	11	1	0	0	12	15	6	30	0	15	1	5	1	3	2	.60	0	.136	.372	.148
Wichita	AA SD	41	109	35	5	1	1	45	17	9	17	0	21	0	4	0	3	2	.60	1	.321	.413	.413
1990 Las Vegas	AAA SD	92	247	74	4	4	4	98	44	21	42	2	35	3	3	1	2	1	.67	0	.300	.406	.397
1991 Las Vegas	AAA SD	107	377	109	10	2	1	126	56	37	54	2	48	2	6	3	15	10	.60	10	.289	.378	.334
1992 Omaha	AAA KC	131	469	108	11	0	3	128	45	28	41	1	56	2	7	1	21	8	.72	3	.230	.294	.273
1993 Omaha	AAA KC	105	330	93	11	2	3	117	46	35	34	0	34	2	3	5	27	10	.73	4	.282	.348	.355
1994 Omaha	AAA KC	100	358	92	13	6	0	117	60	32	47	1	41	1	6	3	25	11	.69	3	.257	.342	.327

		BATTING															BASERUNNING				PERCENTAGES		
Year Team	Lg Org	G	AB	H	2B	3B	HR	TB	R	RBI	TBB	IBB	SO	HBP	SH	SF	SB	CS	SB%	GDP	Avg	OBP	SLG
1995 Omaha	AAA KC	27	87	28	4	0	0	32	6	10	6	0	9	1	4	2	1	2	.33	3	.322	.365	.368
1996 Omaha	AAA KC	72	229	56	5	2	3	74	24	20	17	1	28	0	1	1	7	6	.54	1	.245	.296	.323
1991 San Diego	NL	17	36	8	0	0	0	8	4	2	2	0	7	1	2	0	0	0	.00	0	.222	.282	.222
1995 Kansas City	AL	2	2	0	0	0	0	0	0	0	0	0	0	0	0	0	0	0	.00	0	.000	.000	.000
12 Min. YEARS		1048	3462	936	106	27	17	1147	485	291	428	13	456	19	61	22	149	80	.65	45	.270	.352	.331
2 Maj. YEARS		19	38	8	0	0	0	8	4	2	2	0	7	1	2	0	0	0	.00	0	.211	.268	.211

Scott Moten

Pitches: Right **Bats:** Right **Pos:** P **Ht:** 6'1" **Wt:** 198 **Born:** 4/12/72 **Age:** 25

		HOW MUCH HE PITCHED						WHAT HE GAVE UP												THE RESULTS					
Year Team	Lg Org	G	GS	CG	GF	IP	BFP	H	R	ER	HR	SH	SF	HB	TBB	IBB	SO	WP	Bk	W	L	Pct.	ShO	Sv	ERA
1992 Elizabethtn	R+ Min	13	12	1	0	78.2	334	60	31	21	1	1	1	6	32	0	71	2	2	8	1	.889	1	0	2.40
1993 Fort Wayne	A Min	30	22	0	4	140.2	627	152	99	79	8	6	3	11	63	2	141	7	2	7	11	.389	0	1	5.05
1994 Fort Myers	A+ Min	44	1	0	17	96	404	87	32	23	1	4	0	2	38	3	68	2	0	8	4	.667	0	7	2.16
Nashville	AA Min	3	0	0	0	4.2	23	5	4	2	0	0	0	1	2	0	4	1	0	0	1	.000	0	0	3.86
1995 New Britain	AA Min	40	1	0	18	75.1	323	65	40	33	8	6	3	0	36	2	43	5	0	8	5	.615	0	3	3.94
1996 Iowa	AAA ChN	21	1	0	9	42	199	55	47	43	9	4	4	4	18	1	18	8	0	1	2	.333	0	0	9.21
Orlando	AA ChN	18	7	1	5	54.1	252	59	40	34	8	2	5	2	31	3	35	3	0	2	6	.250	0	1	5.63
5 Min. YEARS		169	44	2	53	491.2	2162	483	293	235	35	23	16	26	220	11	380	28	4	34	30	.531	1	12	4.30

Jeff Motuzas

Bats: Right **Throws:** Right **Pos:** C **Ht:** 6'2" **Wt:** 205 **Born:** 10/1/71 **Age:** 25

		BATTING															BASERUNNING				PERCENTAGES		
Year Team	Lg Org	G	AB	H	2B	3B	HR	TB	R	RBI	TBB	IBB	SO	HBP	SH	SF	SB	CS	SB%	GDP	Avg	OBP	SLG
1990 Yankees	R NYA	29	82	12	0	0	1	15	9	9	15	0	34	3	0	1	0	3	.00	1	.146	.297	.183
1991 Yankees	R NYA	39	145	28	8	1	1	41	17	17	13	0	44	4	2	1	5	1	.83	2	.193	.276	.283
Oneonta	A- NYA	3	7	2	0	0	0	2	1	0	0	0	2	1	0	0	0	0	.00	0	.286	.375	.286
1992 Pr. William	A+ NYA	63	203	36	13	0	5	64	21	20	14	0	74	3	5	2	1	1	.50	6	.177	.239	.315
1993 Pr. William	A+ NYA	16	53	11	4	1	0	17	5	3	1	0	20	0	0	1	0	1	.00	2	.208	.218	.321
San Bernrdo	A+ NYA	52	154	24	7	0	2	37	16	13	13	1	45	2	1	3	2	3	.40	4	.156	.227	.240
1994 San Bernrdo	A+ NYA	69	244	50	9	1	8	85	25	26	14	0	91	4	1	1	3	2	.60	10	.205	.259	.348
Albany-Colo	AA NYA	13	44	5	0	0	0	5	3	1	3	0	14	0	1	0	0	1	.00	0	.114	.170	.114
1995 Tampa	A+ NYA	28	69	11	0	0	1	14	6	8	4	0	24	2	1	0	1	0	1.00	0	.159	.227	.203
1996 Tampa	A+ NYA	2	3	0	0	0	0	0	0	0	0	0	3	0	0	0	0	0	.00	0	.000	.000	.000
Norwich	AA NYA	5	9	3	0	0	0	3	1	2	0	0	4	0	0	0	0	0	.00	0	.333	.333	.333
Columbus	AAA NYA	5	12	3	0	1	0	5	1	1	0	0	7	0	0	0	0	0	.00	0	.250	.250	.417
7 Min. YEARS		324	1025	185	41	4	18	288	105	100	77	1	362	19	11	9	12	12	.50	25	.180	.249	.281

Greg Mullins

Pitches: Left **Bats:** Left **Pos:** P **Ht:** 5'10" **Wt:** 160 **Born:** 12/13/71 **Age:** 25

		HOW MUCH HE PITCHED						WHAT HE GAVE UP												THE RESULTS					
Year Team	Lg Org	G	GS	CG	GF	IP	BFP	H	R	ER	HR	SH	SF	HB	TBB	IBB	SO	WP	Bk	W	L	Pct.	ShO	Sv	ERA
1995 Helena	R+ Mil	4	4	0	0	23	98	22	7	7	0	0	0	2	6	0	14	0	2	4	0	1.000	0	0	2.74
Beloit	A Mil	19	8	0	6	59.1	249	48	23	23	2	0	1	7	20	0	62	2	5	7	1	.875	0	2	3.49
1996 El Paso	AA Mil	23	1	0	6	28	130	30	25	22	7	3	0	1	17	2	28	0	1	1	5	.167	0	2	7.07
Stockton	A+ Mil	10	0	0	3	11.1	51	13	5	5	0	0	0	1	4	0	12	0	0	0	0	.000	0	1	3.97
2 Min. YEARS		56	13	0	15	121.2	528	113	60	57	9	3	1	11	47	2	116	2	8	12	6	.667	0	5	4.22

Bob Mummau

Bats: Right **Throws:** Right **Pos:** 3B **Ht:** 5'11" **Wt:** 180 **Born:** 8/21/71 **Age:** 25

		BATTING															BASERUNNING				PERCENTAGES		
Year Team	Lg Org	G	AB	H	2B	3B	HR	TB	R	RBI	TBB	IBB	SO	HBP	SH	SF	SB	CS	SB%	GDP	Avg	OBP	SLG
1993 St. Cathrns	A- Tor	75	257	62	9	3	3	86	35	21	23	1	44	5	2	0	7	12	.37	3	.241	.316	.335
1994 Dunedin	A+ Tor	21	50	11	1	0	0	12	5	6	4	0	15	0	1	0	0	2	.00	0	.220	.278	.240
Hagerstown	A Tor	46	169	50	10	2	1	67	20	24	10	0	32	2	0	3	2	2	.50	4	.296	.337	.396
1995 Hagerstown	A Tor	107	366	94	17	3	5	132	63	42	42	1	74	14	6	3	6	1	.86	7	.257	.353	.361
1996 Dunedin	A+ Tor	36	106	22	3	0	0	25	10	10	12	0	22	0	7	0	2	4	.33	2	.208	.288	.236
Syracuse	AAA Tor	4	3	0	0	0	0	0	1	0	0	0	1	0	0	0	0	0	.00	0	.000	.000	.000
Knoxville	AA Tor	47	154	43	11	0	2	60	23	22	15	1	25	3	3	2	1	4	.20	6	.279	.351	.390
4 Min. YEARS		336	1105	282	51	8	11	382	157	125	106	3	213	24	19	8	18	25	.42	22	.255	.331	.346

Omer Munoz

Bats: Right **Throws:** Right **Pos:** 2B **Ht:** 5'9" **Wt:** 156 **Born:** 3/3/66 **Age:** 31

		BATTING															BASERUNNING				PERCENTAGES		
Year Team	Lg Org	G	AB	H	2B	3B	HR	TB	R	RBI	TBB	IBB	SO	HBP	SH	SF	SB	CS	SB%	GDP	Avg	OBP	SLG
1985 Clinton	A SF	47	121	25	4	0	0	29	9	11	7	0	7	0	4	0	3	2	.60	4	.207	.250	.240
1987 W. Palm Bch	A+ Mon	5	7	0	0	0	0	0	0	0	1	0	1	0	0	0	0	1	.00	0	.000	.125	.000
Burlington	A Mon	52	195	47	8	2	0	59	22	16	7	0	13	3	6	0	5	3	.63	4	.241	.278	.303
1988 W. Palm Bch	A+ Mon	103	369	95	15	1	0	112	36	27	14	0	28	1	8	2	8	6	.57	3	.257	.285	.304
1989 W. Palm Bch	A+ Mon	68	246	67	2	0	0	69	22	27	5	0	17	1	8	0	8	5	.62	12	.272	.290	.280
1990 Jacksonvlle	AA Mon	70	197	50	5	0	1	58	19	18	5	0	18	2	1	1	3	0	1.00	1	.254	.278	.294
1991 Harrisburg	AA Mon	63	214	66	7	1	1	78	27	21	3	0	17	0	11	1	1	0	1.00	4	.308	.317	.364

Year	Team	Lg	Org	G	AB	H	2B	3B	HR	TB	R	RBI	TBB	IBB	SO	HBP	SH	SF	SB	CS	SB%	GDP	Avg	OBP	SLG
	BATTING																		BASERUNNING				PERCENTAGES		
	Indianapols	AAA	Mon	26	92	26	2	0	0	28	7	12	3	1	14	3	6	0	0	0	.00	2	.283	.327	.304
1992	Indianapols	AAA	Mon	116	375	94	12	1	1	111	33	30	10	0	32	4	9	4	7	2	.78	15	.251	.275	.296
1993	Buffalo	AAA	Pit	40	129	28	4	1	2	40	7	16	3	2	11	1	2	1	0	0	.00	2	.217	.239	.310
1994	Carolina	AA	Pit	79	287	90	15	1	5	122	30	38	12	2	29	2	3	3	2	4	.33	7	.314	.342	.425
1995	Carolina	AA	Pit	67	234	62	10	1	2	80	29	25	5	0	23	3	5	2	2	0	1.00	7	.265	.287	.342
1996	Lynchburg	A+	Pit	3	10	3	0	0	0	3	0	1	0	0	1	0	1	0	0	0	.00	0	.300	.300	.300
	Carolina	AA	Pit	1	1	1	0	0	0	1	0	0	0	0	0	0	0	0	0	0	.00	0	1.000	1.000	1.000
11	Min. YEARS			740	2477	654	84	8	12	790	241	242	75	5	211	20	64	14	39	23	.63	61	.264	.290	.319

Oscar Munoz

Pitches: Right **Bats:** Right **Pos:** P **Ht:** 6' 3" **Wt:** 220 **Born:** 9/25/69 **Age:** 27

Year	Team	Lg	Org	G	GS	CG	GF	IP	BFP	H	R	ER	HR	SH	SF	HB	TBB	IBB	SO	WP	Bk	W	L	Pct.	ShO	Sv	ERA
	HOW MUCH HE PITCHED									WHAT HE GAVE UP												THE RESULTS					
1990	Watertown	A-	Cle	2	2	0	0	10.2	43	8	2	2	1	0	0	0	3	0	9	1	1	1	1	.500	0	0	1.69
	Kinston	A+	Cle	9	9	2	0	64	248	43	18	17	6	1	1	1	18	0	55	3	0	7	0	1.000	1	0	2.39
1991	Kinston	A+	Cle	14	14	2	0	93.2	375	60	23	15	2	4	0	5	36	0	111	6	0	6	3	.667	1	0	1.44
	Canton-Akrn	AA	Cle	15	15	2	0	85	378	88	54	54	5	1	2	0	51	1	71	1	1	3	8	.273	1	0	5.72
1992	Orlando	AA	Min	14	12	1	1	67.2	306	73	44	38	10	1	1	4	32	1	74	6	0	3	5	.375	0	0	5.05
1993	Nashville	AA	Min	20	20	1	0	131.2	567	123	56	45	10	1	4	4	51	0	139	12	0	11	4	.733	0	0	3.08
	Portland	AAA	Min	5	5	0	0	31.1	138	29	18	15	2	2	1	0	17	1	29	6	0	2	2	.500	0	0	4.31
1994	Nashville	AA	Min	3	3	2	0	22	86	16	1	1	0	0	0	1	5	0	21	1	0	3	0	1.000	1	0	0.41
	Salt Lake	AAA	Min	26	26	1	0	139.1	662	180	113	91	20	6	5	3	68	1	100	8	0	9	8	.529	0	0	5.88
1995	Salt Lake	AAA	Min	19	19	1	0	112.2	486	121	67	62	9	0	7	3	35	1	74	7	0	8	6	.571	1	0	4.95
1996	Orioles	R	Bal	2	0	0	1	3	9	0	0	0	0	0	0	0	0	0	1	0	0	0	0	.000	0	1	0.00
	Rochester	AAA	Bal	21	17	1	2	112.2	465	100	60	53	17	2	6	2	37	1	85	7	1	6	7	.462	0	0	4.23
1995	Minnesota	AL		10	3	0	4	35.1	164	40	28	22	6	0	1	1	17	0	25	0	0	2	1	.667	0	0	5.60
7	Min. YEARS			150	142	13	4	873.2	3763	841	456	393	82	18	27	23	353	6	769	58	3	59	44	.573	5	1	4.05

Jeff Murphy

Bats: Both **Throws:** Right **Pos:** C **Ht:** 6'2" **Wt:** 210 **Born:** 12/27/70 **Age:** 26

Year	Team	Lg	Org	G	AB	H	2B	3B	HR	TB	R	RBI	TBB	IBB	SO	HBP	SH	SF	SB	CS	SB%	GDP	Avg	OBP	SLG
	BATTING																		BASERUNNING				PERCENTAGES		
1992	Hamilton	A-	StL	57	201	53	14	1	6	87	27	27	21	3	53	3	0	0	1	2	.33	8	.264	.342	.433
1993	Savannah	A	StL	98	345	78	21	1	7	122	40	47	49	1	105	5	3	4	2	1	.67	9	.226	.328	.354
1994	St. Pete	A+	StL	49	139	27	5	0	0	32	11	8	22	1	37	3	1	2	2	0	1.00	4	.194	.313	.230
1995	St. Pete	A+	StL	50	122	22	3	1	2	33	9	14	19	0	36	2	0	0	0	0	.00	5	.180	.301	.270
1996	Arkansas	AA	StL	2	7	4	1	0	0	5	3	1	0	0	2	0	0	0	0	0	.00	0	.571	.571	.714
5	Min. YEARS			256	814	184	44	3	15	279	90	97	111	5	233	13	4	6	5	3	.63	26	.226	.326	.343

Mike Murphy

Bats: Right **Throws:** Right **Pos:** OF **Ht:** 6'2" **Wt:** 185 **Born:** 1/23/72 **Age:** 25

Year	Team	Lg	Org	G	AB	H	2B	3B	HR	TB	R	RBI	TBB	IBB	SO	HBP	SH	SF	SB	CS	SB%	GDP	Avg	OBP	SLG
	BATTING																		BASERUNNING				PERCENTAGES		
1990	Martinsvlle	R+	Phi	9	31	3	0	0	0	3	4	1	7	0	17	0	0	0	1	2	.33	1	.097	.263	.097
1991	Martinsvlle	R+	Phi	44	156	34	3	0	0	37	15	7	11	1	40	1	2	0	9	2	.82	5	.218	.274	.237
1992	Batavia	A-	Phi	63	228	58	6	2	2	74	32	27	21	0	48	4	3	0	15	8	.65	6	.254	.328	.325
1993	Spartanburg	A	Phi	133	509	147	29	6	3	197	70	60	35	1	91	9	9	2	33	14	.70	15	.289	.344	.387
1994	Dunedin	A+	Tor	125	469	129	11	4	1	151	57	34	55	3	106	9	4	3	31	10	.76	9	.275	.360	.322
1995	Canton-Akrn	AA	Cle	10	23	1	0	0	0	1	3	0	4	0	3	0	0	0	0	1	.00	0	.043	.185	.043
	Kinston	A+	Cle	67	177	41	6	0	1	50	26	15	15	1	30	3	1	1	13	4	.76	2	.232	.301	.282
1996	Charlotte	A+	Tex	87	358	119	20	7	7	174	73	52	32	1	94	3	3	0	22	9	.71	5	.332	.392	.486
	Tulsa	AA	Tex	34	121	28	7	2	4	51	22	16	21	0	29	3	1	1	1	0	1.00	2	.231	.356	.421
7	Min. YEARS			572	2072	560	82	21	18	738	302	212	201	7	458	32	23	7	125	50	.71	45	.270	.343	.356

Calvin Murray

Bats: Right **Throws:** Right **Pos:** OF **Ht:** 5'11" **Wt:** 185 **Born:** 7/30/71 **Age:** 25

Year	Team	Lg	Org	G	AB	H	2B	3B	HR	TB	R	RBI	TBB	IBB	SO	HBP	SH	SF	SB	CS	SB%	GDP	Avg	OBP	SLG
	BATTING																		BASERUNNING				PERCENTAGES		
1993	Shreveport	AA	SF	37	138	26	6	0	0	32	15	6	14	0	29	2	3	1	12	6	.67	0	.188	.271	.232
	San Jose	A+	SF	85	345	97	24	1	9	150	61	42	40	0	63	4	2	0	42	10	.81	4	.281	.362	.435
	Phoenix	AAA	SF	5	19	6	1	1	0	9	4	0	2	0	5	0	0	0	1	1	.50	0	.316	.381	.474
1994	Shreveport	AA	SF	129	480	111	19	5	2	146	67	35	47	0	81	5	8	4	33	13	.72	4	.231	.304	.304
1995	Phoenix	AAA	SF	13	50	9	1	0	4	22	8	10	4	0	6	0	1	1	2	2	.50	2	.180	.236	.440
	Shreveport	AA	SF	110	441	104	17	3	2	133	77	29	59	2	70	3	5	1	26	10	.72	5	.236	.329	.302
1996	Shreveport	AA	SF	50	169	44	7	0	7	72	32	24	25	0	33	1	3	4	6	5	.55	5	.260	.352	.426
	Phoenix	AAA	SF	83	311	76	16	6	3	113	50	28	43	0	60	3	5	1	12	6	.67	1	.244	.341	.363
4	Min. YEARS			512	1953	473	91	16	27	677	314	174	234	2	347	18	27	12	134	53	.72	21	.242	.327	.347

Heath Murray

Pitches: Left **Bats:** Left **Pos:** P **Ht:** 6'4" **Wt:** 205 **Born:** 4/19/73 **Age:** 24

		HOW MUCH HE PITCHED						WHAT HE GAVE UP												THE RESULTS					
Year Team	Lg Org	G	GS	CG	GF	IP	BFP	H	R	ER	HR	SH	SF	HB	TBB	IBB	SO	WP	Bk	W	L	Pct.	ShO	Sv	ERA
1994 Spokane	A- SD	15	15	2	0	99.1	408	101	46	32	6	6	2	5	18	0	78	4	3	5	6	.455	1	0	2.90
1995 Rancho Cuca	A+ SD	14	14	4	0	92.1	381	80	37	32	5	3	2	4	38	1	81	6	3	9	4	.692	2	0	3.12
Memphis	AA SD	28	28	4	0	169.2	744	163	73	61	6	6	5	8	80	2	152	13	4	14	8	.636	2	0	3.24
1996 Memphis	AA SD	27	27	1	0	174	728	154	83	62	13	4	3	6	60	2	156	7	3	13	9	.591	1	0	3.21
3 Min. YEARS		84	84	11	0	535.1	2261	498	239	187	30	19	12	23	196	5	467	30	13	41	27	.603	6	0	3.14

Matt Murray

Pitches: Right **Bats:** Left **Pos:** P **Ht:** 6' 6" **Wt:** 235 **Born:** 9/26/70 **Age:** 26

		HOW MUCH HE PITCHED						WHAT HE GAVE UP												THE RESULTS					
Year Team	Lg Org	G	GS	CG	GF	IP	BFP	H	R	ER	HR	SH	SF	HB	TBB	IBB	SO	WP	Bk	W	L	Pct.	ShO	Sv	ERA
1988 Pulaski	R+ Atl	13	8	0	3	54	234	48	32	25	4	4	1	1	26	0	76	5	2	2	4	.333	0	1	4.17
1989 Braves	R Atl	2	2	0	0	7	27	3	0	0	0	0	0	1	0	0	10	0	0	1	0	1.000	0	0	0.00
Sumter	A Atl	12	12	0	0	72.2	295	62	37	35	10	2	2	1	22	0	69	4	1	3	5	.375	0	0	4.33
1990 Burlington	A Atl	26	26	6	0	163	671	139	72	59	9	4	2	3	60	0	134	10	1	11	7	.611	3	0	3.26
1991 Durham	A+ Atl	2	2	0	0	7	26	5	1	1	0	0	0	0	0	0	7	0	0	1	0	1.000	0	0	1.29
1993 Macon	A Atl	15	15	3	0	83.2	338	70	24	17	3	2	0	3	27	0	77	0	1	7	3	.700	0	0	1.83
1994 Durham	A+ Atl	15	15	1	0	97.1	398	93	43	41	20	0	1	7	22	3	76	6	0	6	7	.462	0	0	3.79
Greenville	AA Atl	12	12	0	0	67.1	312	89	43	38	7	1	2	2	31	0	48	3	0	3	4	.429	0	0	5.08
1995 Greenville	AA Atl	5	5	0	0	29.1	111	20	5	5	0	1	0	1	8	0	25	2	0	4	0	1.000	0	0	1.53
Richmond	AAA Atl	24	24	0	0	152.1	612	128	46	43	6	2	4	4	42	1	103	11	1	14	3	.824	0	0	2.54
1996 Scranton-WB	AAA Phi	13	13	0	0	56.1	280	63	52	48	13	2	3	3	49	0	34	6	0	1	8	.111	0	0	7.67
Richmond	AAA Atl	5	2	0	1	12	59	12	8	8	0	0	0	2	14	0	9	1	0	1	2	.333	0	0	6.00
1995 Atlanta	NL	4	1	0	1	10.2	46	10	8	8	3	1	0	1	5	0	3	0	0	0	2	.000	0	0	6.75
Boston	AL	2	1	0	0	3.1	24	11	10	7	1	0	0	0	3	0	1	0	0	0	1	.000	0	0	18.90
8 Min. YEARS		144	136	10	4	802	3363	732	363	320	72	18	15	28	301	4	668	48	6	54	43	.557	3	1	3.59

Jim Musselwhite

Pitches: Right **Bats:** Right **Pos:** P **Ht:** 6'1" **Wt:** 190 **Born:** 10/25/71 **Age:** 25

		HOW MUCH HE PITCHED						WHAT HE GAVE UP												THE RESULTS					
Year Team	Lg Org	G	GS	CG	GF	IP	BFP	H	R	ER	HR	SH	SF	HB	TBB	IBB	SO	WP	Bk	W	L	Pct.	ShO	Sv	ERA
1993 Oneonta	A- NYA	5	4	0	0	20	84	15	7	5	0	1	1	0	8	0	18	1	0	1	1	.500	0	0	2.25
Greensboro	A NYA	11	10	0	1	67.2	285	60	29	21	4	3	2	2	24	0	60	4	2	5	3	.625	0	0	2.79
1994 Tampa	A+ NYA	17	17	3	0	107.2	429	87	50	41	8	0	3	3	23	0	106	4	0	9	6	.600	2	0	3.43
Albany-Colo	AA NYA	5	5	1	0	29.2	116	28	4	4	0	0	0	2	5	0	31	2	0	2	1	.667	1	0	1.21
1995 Norwich	AA NYA	24	24	1	0	131.2	566	136	75	67	11	5	6	6	34	3	96	8	1	5	9	.357	0	0	4.58
1996 Greensboro	A NYA	4	4	0	0	20	91	26	9	7	1	0	1	4	3	0	15	1	0	2	1	.667	0	0	3.15
Tampa	A+ NYA	3	3	0	0	15	77	24	16	13	2	0	0	2	5	0	5	0	0	0	2	.000	0	0	7.80
Norwich	AA NYA	5	5	1	0	36	144	28	9	9	4	1	2	0	10	0	25	1	0	2	1	.667	0	0	2.25
4 Min. YEARS		74	72	6	1	427.2	1792	404	199	167	30	10	15	19	112	3	356	21	3	26	24	.520	3	0	3.51

Jeff Mutis

Pitches: Left **Bats:** Left **Pos:** P **Ht:** 6' 2" **Wt:** 195 **Born:** 12/20/66 **Age:** 30

		HOW MUCH HE PITCHED						WHAT HE GAVE UP												THE RESULTS					
Year Team	Lg Org	G	GS	CG	GF	IP	BFP	H	R	ER	HR	SH	SF	HB	TBB	IBB	SO	WP	Bk	W	L	Pct.	ShO	Sv	ERA
1988 Burlington	R+ Cle	3	3	0	0	22	79	8	1	1	0	0	0	0	6	0	20	1	2	3	0	1.000	0	0	0.41
Kinston	A+ Cle	1	1	0	0	5.2	24	6	1	1	0	1	0	0	3	0	2	1	0	1	0	1.000	0	0	1.59
1989 Kinston	A+ Cle	16	15	5	1	99.2	406	87	42	29	6	1	4	2	20	0	68	3	2	7	3	.700	2	0	2.62
1990 Canton-Akrn	AA Cle	26	26	7	0	165	702	178	73	58	6	3	2	3	44	2	94	5	1	11	10	.524	3	0	3.16
1991 Canton-Akrn	AA Cle	25	24	7	0	169.2	682	138	42	34	0	8	4	6	51	2	89	3	1	11	5	.688	4	0	1.80
1992 Colo. Sprng	AAA Cle	25	24	4	0	145.1	652	177	99	82	8	6	8	5	57	1	77	8	4	9	9	.500	0	0	5.08
1993 Charlotte	AAA Cle	12	11	3	0	75.2	315	64	27	22	1	1	2	3	25	3	59	1	1	6	0	1.000	0	0	2.62
1994 Edmonton	AAA Fla	13	4	0	5	26.2	127	36	26	25	1	0	2	0	13	0	18	1	1	0	3	.000	0	0	8.44
1995 Charlotte	AAA Fla	27	0	0	5	36.1	153	31	18	15	2	2	4	1	14	2	21	1	0	0	1	.000	0	2	3.72
1996 Louisville	AAA StL	32	0	0	12	38.1	174	44	26	25	4	1	1	3	19	2	21	0	0	2	3	.400	0	1	5.87
1991 Cleveland	AL	3	3	0	0	12.1	68	23	16	16	1	2	1	0	7	1	6	1	0	0	3	.000	0	0	11.68
1992 Cleveland	AL	3	2	0	0	11.1	64	24	14	12	4	0	2	0	6	0	8	2	0	0	2	.000	0	0	9.53
1993 Cleveland	AL	17	13	1	1	81	364	93	56	52	14	0	2	7	33	2	29	1	0	3	6	.333	1	0	5.78
1994 Florida	NL	35	0	0	7	38.1	177	51	25	23	6	5	2	1	15	3	30	0	1	1	0	1.000	0	0	5.40
9 Min. YEARS		180	108	26	23	784.1	3314	769	355	292	28	23	27	23	252	12	469	24	12	50	34	.595	9	3	3.35
4 Maj. YEARS		58	18	1	8	143	673	191	111	103	25	7	7	8	61	6	73	4	1	4	11	.267	1	0	6.48

John Myrow

Bats: Right **Throws:** Right **Pos:** OF **Ht:** 6'0" **Wt:** 177 **Born:** 2/11/72 **Age:** 25

		BATTING															BASERUNNING				PERCENTAGES		
Year Team	Lg Org	G	AB	H	2B	3B	HR	TB	R	RBI	TBB	IBB	SO	HBP	SH	SF	SB	CS	SB%	GDP	Avg	OBP	SLG
1993 Bend	A- Col	70	260	52	11	0	4	75	27	24	16	0	62	4	8	3	12	5	.71	3	.200	.254	.288
1994 Central Val	A+ Col	128	521	143	26	2	8	197	81	73	27	1	85	7	3	9	26	5	.84	16	.274	.314	.378
1995 New Haven	AA Col	96	353	87	18	1	3	116	52	50	25	2	67	8	3	3	16	5	.76	13	.246	.308	.329
1996 New Haven	AA Col	122	406	102	11	3	4	131	46	36	30	3	61	2	6	2	11	3	.79	14	.251	.305	.323
4 Min. YEARS		416	1540	384	66	6	19	519	206	183	98	6	275	21	20	17	65	18	.78	46	.249	.300	.337

Tyrone Narcisse

Pitches: Right **Bats:** Right **Pos:** P **Ht:** 6'5" **Wt:** 205 **Born:** 2/4/72 **Age:** 25

				HOW MUCH HE PITCHED						WHAT HE GAVE UP												THE RESULTS					
Year	Team	Lg	Org	G	GS	CG	GF	IP	BFP	H	R	ER	HR	SH	SF	HB	TBB	IBB	SO	WP	Bk	W	L	Pct.	ShO	Sv	ERA
1990	Padres	R	SD	7	1	0	3	10.2	52	13	11	6	0	0	0	2	6	0	6	3	2	0	0	.000	0	0	5.06
1991	Padres	R	SD	11	10	0	0	37.1	193	43	41	31	1	1	1	4	37	0	23	5	3	2	3	.400	0	0	7.47
1992	Astros	R	Hou	11	6	0	2	34.2	158	31	25	19	0	1	3	2	24	0	32	5	1	3	2	.600	0	0	4.93
1993	Asheville	A	Hou	29	29	2	0	160.1	702	173	95	78	11	4	8	12	66	0	114	9	5	6	12	.333	0	0	4.38
1994	Osceola	A+	Hou	26	26	2	0	146	633	153	91	79	7	5	5	11	57	2	86	9	4	7	11	.389	0	0	4.87
1995	Jackson	AA	Hou	27	27	2	0	163.2	686	140	76	59	8	11	7	10	60	5	93	8	0	5	14	.263	0	0	3.24
1996	Jackson	AA	Hou	27	26	0	0	126.2	572	151	92	78	15	9	4	6	55	2	88	9	1	7	12	.368	0	0	5.54
7 Min. YEARS				138	125	6	5	679.1	2996	704	431	350	42	31	28	47	305	9	442	48	16	30	54	.357	0	0	4.64

Mike Neal

Bats: Right **Throws:** Right **Pos:** 2B **Ht:** 6'1" **Wt:** 180 **Born:** 11/5/71 **Age:** 25

				BATTING															BASERUNNING				PERCENTAGES		
Year	Team	Lg	Org	G	AB	H	2B	3B	HR	TB	R	RBI	TBB	IBB	SO	HBP	SH	SF	SB	CS	SB%	GDP	Avg	OBP	SLG
1993	Watertown	A-	Cle	67	234	68	15	3	4	101	47	43	55	4	45	6	1	3	7	1	.88	2	.291	.433	.432
1994	Kinston	A+	Cle	101	378	99	21	1	5	137	51	38	40	1	94	3	3	1	8	12	.40	6	.262	.336	.362
1995	Canton-Akrn	AA	Cle	134	419	112	24	2	5	155	64	46	71	3	79	9	4	8	5	6	.45	7	.267	.379	.370
1996	Canton-Akrn	AA	Cle	94	254	57	9	3	4	84	42	32	39	0	53	5	2	6	2	3	.40	3	.224	.332	.331
4 Min. YEARS				396	1285	336	69	9	18	477	204	159	205	8	271	23	10	18	22	22	.50	18	.261	.368	.371

Chris Neier

Pitches: Right **Bats:** Right **Pos:** P **Ht:** 6'4" **Wt:** 205 **Born:** 11/19/71 **Age:** 25

				HOW MUCH HE PITCHED						WHAT HE GAVE UP												THE RESULTS					
Year	Team	Lg	Org	G	GS	CG	GF	IP	BFP	H	R	ER	HR	SH	SF	HB	TBB	IBB	SO	WP	Bk	W	L	Pct.	ShO	Sv	ERA
1992	Rockies/Cub	R	Col	14	6	1	2	56.1	235	53	23	14	0	2	0	3	7	0	49	2	2	5	1	.833	0	0	2.24
1993	Bend	A-	Col	15	15	0	0	77	347	90	55	41	6	5	2	3	32	2	58	3	1	3	5	.375	0	0	4.79
1994	Asheville	A	Col	31	0	0	9	56.1	247	61	28	23	4	1	5	3	19	1	49	1	0	2	2	.500	0	1	3.67
	Central Val	A+	Col	19	0	0	10	27.2	113	28	10	9	1	0	1	0	4	1	23	4	0	1	0	1.000	0	4	2.93
1995	New Haven	AA	Col	38	18	1	5	123.1	550	164	62	57	10	4	3	1	47	5	74	2	1	10	4	.714	0	0	4.16
1996	New Haven	AA	Col	55	0	0	20	81.1	388	99	63	45	9	7	1	2	44	9	54	9	3	1	7	.125	0	2	4.98
5 Min. YEARS				172	39	2	46	422	1880	495	241	189	30	19	12	12	153	18	307	21	7	22	19	.537	0	7	4.03

Mike Neill

Bats: Left **Throws:** Left **Pos:** OF **Ht:** 6'2" **Wt:** 189 **Born:** 4/27/70 **Age:** 27

				BATTING															BASERUNNING				PERCENTAGES		
Year	Team	Lg	Org	G	AB	H	2B	3B	HR	TB	R	RBI	TBB	IBB	SO	HBP	SH	SF	SB	CS	SB%	GDP	Avg	OBP	SLG
1991	Sou. Oregon	A-	Oak	63	240	84	14	0	5	113	42	42	35	3	54	0	4	1	9	3	.75	1	.350	.431	.471
1992	Reno	A+	Oak	130	473	159	26	7	5	214	101	76	81	2	96	5	6	2	23	11	.68	15	.336	.437	.452
	Huntsville	AA	Oak	5	16	5	0	0	0	5	4	2	2	0	7	0	1	1	1	0	1.00	0	.313	.368	.313
1993	Huntsville	AA	Oak	54	179	44	8	0	1	55	30	15	34	0	45	1	0	1	3	4	.43	4	.246	.367	.307
	Modesto	A+	Oak	17	62	12	3	0	0	15	4	4	12	0	12	0	1	0	0	1	.00	0	.194	.324	.242
1994	Tacoma	AAA	Oak	7	22	5	1	0	0	6	1	2	3	0	7	0	0	0	0	0	.00	2	.227	.320	.273
	Modesto	A+	Oak	47	165	48	4	1	2	60	22	18	26	1	50	1	2	1	1	1	.50	4	.291	.389	.364
1995	Modesto	A+	Oak	71	257	71	17	1	6	108	39	36	34	2	65	2	5	1	4	4	.50	6	.276	.364	.420
	Huntsville	AA	Oak	33	107	32	6	1	2	46	11	16	12	1	29	0	0	1	1	0	1.00	1	.299	.367	.430
1996	Edmonton	AAA	Oak	6	20	3	1	0	1	7	4	4	2	0	3	0	1	0	0	0	.00	0	.150	.227	.350
	Modesto	A+	Oak	114	442	150	20	6	19	239	101	78	68	4	123	4	2	2	28	7	.80	3	.339	.430	.541
6 Min. YEARS				547	1983	613	100	16	41	868	359	293	309	13	491	13	22	10	70	31	.69	36	.309	.404	.438

Tom Nevers

Bats: Right **Throws:** Right **Pos:** SS **Ht:** 6'1" **Wt:** 175 **Born:** 9/13/71 **Age:** 25

				BATTING															BASERUNNING				PERCENTAGES		
Year	Team	Lg	Org	G	AB	H	2B	3B	HR	TB	R	RBI	TBB	IBB	SO	HBP	SH	SF	SB	CS	SB%	GDP	Avg	OBP	SLG
1990	Astros	R	Hou	50	185	44	10	5	2	70	23	32	27	0	38	3	0	3	13	3	.81	3	.238	.339	.378
1991	Asheville	A	Hou	129	441	111	26	2	16	189	59	71	53	0	124	3	2	5	10	12	.45	11	.252	.333	.429
1992	Osceola	A+	Hou	125	455	114	24	6	8	174	49	55	22	1	124	3	2	1	6	2	.75	10	.251	.289	.382
1993	Jackson	AA	Hou	55	184	50	8	2	1	65	21	10	16	2	36	2	1	1	7	2	.78	5	.272	.335	.353
1994	Jackson	AA	Hou	125	449	120	25	2	8	173	54	62	31	2	101	4	1	7	10	5	.67	8	.267	.316	.385
1995	Jackson	AA	Hou	83	298	72	7	3	8	109	36	35	24	2	58	2	0	2	5	2	.71	10	.242	.301	.366
	Stockton	A+	Mil	4	14	4	0	0	0	4	2	3	0	0	6	2	0	0	1	0	1.00	0	.286	.375	.286
	El Paso	AA	Mil	35	118	30	5	0	1	38	19	12	11	0	21	3	0	0	2	1	.67	6	.254	.333	.322
1996	New Britain	AA	Min	127	459	121	27	7	7	183	65	44	46	1	87	3	2	3	3	10	.23	18	.264	.333	.399
7 Min. YEARS				733	2603	666	132	27	51	1005	328	324	230	8	595	25	8	22	57	37	.61	71	.256	.320	.386

Brett Newell

Bats: Right **Throws:** Right **Pos:** SS **Ht:** 6'0" **Wt:** 180 **Born:** 10/25/72 **Age:** 24

				BATTING															BASERUNNING				PERCENTAGES		
Year	Team	Lg	Org	G	AB	H	2B	3B	HR	TB	R	RBI	TBB	IBB	SO	HBP	SH	SF	SB	CS	SB%	GDP	Avg	OBP	SLG
1994	Danville	R+	Atl	66	228	60	9	0	0	69	35	20	39	0	53	13	3	1	5	5	.50	7	.263	.399	.303
1995	Macon	A	Atl	76	285	73	9	1	0	84	39	29	24	0	72	7	5	1	5	1	.83	5	.256	.328	.295
	Durham	A+	Atl	33	79	17	1	0	0	18	10	3	4	0	20	1	2	1	0	1	.00	2	.215	.259	.228

Year	Team	Lg	Org	G	AB	H	2B	3B	HR	TB	R	RBI	TBB	IBB	SO	HBP	SH	SF	SB	CS	SB%	GDP	Avg	OBP	SLG
	BATTING																		**BASERUNNING**				**PERCENTAGES**		
1996	Greenville	AA	Atl	103	297	65	5	0	1	73	23	21	19	0	98	2	7	1	0	6	.00	4	.219	.270	.246
3 Min. YEARS				278	889	215	24	1	1	244	107	73	86	0	243	23	17	4	10	13	.43	18	.242	.323	.274

Geronimo Newton

Pitches: Left **Bats:** Left **Pos:** P **Ht:** 6'0" **Wt:** 150 **Born:** 12/31/73 **Age:** 23

Year	Team	Lg	Org	G	GS	CG	GF	IP	BFP	H	R	ER	HR	SH	SF	HB	TBB	IBB	SO	WP	Bk	W	L	Pct.	ShO	Sv	ERA
	HOW MUCH HE PITCHED									**WHAT HE GAVE UP**												**THE RESULTS**					
1993	Mariners	R	Sea	21	1	0	12	40.1	182	31	27	10	0	6	1	1	23	2	39	7	0	1	4	.200	0	1	2.23
1994	Riverside	A+	Sea	2	1	0	0	8	32	5	4	4	2	0	0	0	3	0	4	0	1	0	0	.000	0	0	4.50
	Bellingham	A-	Sea	21	8	0	4	60	255	43	19	14	1	2	2	2	36	3	43	8	3	3	4	.429	0	0	2.10
1995	Riverside	A+	Sea	46	0	0	11	71.1	307	74	35	25	1	3	3	4	24	3	42	2	4	4	4	.500	0	2	3.15
1996	Port City	AA	Sea	33	1	0	9	45.2	195	45	16	14	6	2	1	1	22	4	25	0	1	4	1	.800	0	0	2.76
4 Min. YEARS				123	11	0	36	225.1	971	198	101	67	10	13	7	8	108	12	153	17	9	12	13	.480	0	3	2.68

Darrell Nicholas

Bats: Right **Throws:** Right **Pos:** OF **Ht:** 6'0" **Wt:** 180 **Born:** 5/26/72 **Age:** 25

Year	Team	Lg	Org	G	AB	H	2B	3B	HR	TB	R	RBI	TBB	IBB	SO	HBP	SH	SF	SB	CS	SB%	GDP	Avg	OBP	SLG
	BATTING																		**BASERUNNING**				**PERCENTAGES**		
1994	Helena	R+	Mil	15	61	23	3	2	0	30	18	13	10	0	10	1	0	0	11	3	.79	0	.377	.472	.492
	Beloit	A	Mil	59	221	63	8	3	1	80	33	35	22	1	54	1	2	4	17	4	.81	4	.285	.347	.362
1995	El Paso	AA	Mil	15	39	8	0	1	0	10	4	2	0	0	11	0	1	0	4	0	1.00	0	.205	.205	.256
	Stockton	A+	Mil	87	350	112	16	3	5	149	54	39	23	1	75	1	11	1	26	8	.76	6	.320	.363	.426
1996	El Paso	AA	Mil	70	237	65	12	4	2	91	46	24	27	2	57	1	4	1	7	9	.44	6	.274	.350	.384
3 Min. YEARS				246	908	271	39	13	8	360	155	113	82	4	207	4	18	6	65	24	.73	16	.298	.357	.396

Rod Nichols

Pitches: Right **Bats:** Right **Pos:** P **Ht:** 6' 2" **Wt:** 190 **Born:** 12/29/64 **Age:** 32

Year	Team	Lg	Org	G	GS	CG	GF	IP	BFP	H	R	ER	HR	SH	SF	HB	TBB	IBB	SO	WP	Bk	W	L	Pct.	ShO	Sv	ERA
	HOW MUCH HE PITCHED									**WHAT HE GAVE UP**												**THE RESULTS**					
1985	Batavia	A-	Cle	13	13	3	0	84	361	74	40	28	10	0	2	3	33	0	93	6	0	5	5	.500	0	0	3.00
1986	Waterloo	A	Cle	20	20	3	0	115.1	493	128	56	52	8	3	4	13	21	1	83	3	1	8	5	.615	1	0	4.06
1987	Kinston	A+	Cle	9	8	1	1	56	231	53	27	25	3	0	2	1	14	0	61	4	0	4	2	.667	1	0	4.02
	Williamsprt	AA	Cle	16	16	1	0	100	441	107	53	41	9	2	3	9	33	0	60	5	1	4	3	.571	0	0	3.69
1988	Kinston	A+	Cle	4	4	0	0	24	109	26	13	12	1	0	2	0	15	0	19	2	0	3	1	.750	0	0	4.50
	Colo. Sprng	AAA	Cle	10	9	2	1	58.2	256	69	41	37	8	1	2	3	17	2	43	3	2	2	6	.250	0	0	5.68
1989	Colo. Sprng	AAA	Cle	10	10	2	0	65.1	274	57	28	26	2	1	3	1	30	0	41	1	2	8	1	.889	1	0	3.58
1990	Colo. Sprng	AAA	Cle	22	22	4	0	133.1	602	160	84	76	12	0	4	11	48	3	74	3	2	12	9	.571	2	0	5.13
1992	Colo. Sprng	AAA	Cle	9	9	1	0	54	233	65	39	34	6	0	4	1	16	1	35	4	1	3	3	.500	0	0	5.67
1993	Albuquerque	AAA	LA	21	21	3	0	127.2	552	132	68	61	16	6	3	3	50	3	79	9	3	8	5	.615	1	0	4.30
1994	Omaha	AAA	KC	33	22	3	3	142	634	163	102	89	21	9	4	9	52	2	92	7	0	5	10	.333	1	1	5.64
1995	Richmond	AAA	Atl	41	3	0	37	57	232	54	16	16	5	0	1	2	6	1	57	1	0	1	2	.333	0	25	2.53
1996	Richmond	AAA	Atl	57	0	0	51	72.1	294	54	20	16	5	3	2	2	20	1	64	3	1	3	3	.500	0	20	1.99
1988	Cleveland	AL		11	10	3	1	69.1	297	73	41	39	5	2	2	2	23	1	31	2	3	1	7	.125	0	0	5.06
1989	Cleveland	AL		15	11	0	2	71.2	315	81	42	35	9	3	2	2	24	0	42	0	0	4	6	.400	0	0	4.40
1990	Cleveland	AL		4	2	0	0	16	79	24	14	14	5	1	0	2	6	0	3	0	0	0	3	.000	0	0	7.88
1991	Cleveland	AL		31	16	3	4	137.1	578	145	63	54	6	6	4	6	30	3	76	3	0	2	11	.154	1	1	3.54
1992	Cleveland	AL		30	9	0	5	105.1	456	114	58	53	13	1	5	2	31	1	56	3	0	4	3	.571	0	0	4.53
1993	Los Angeles	NL		4	0	0	2	6.1	28	9	5	4	1	1	0	0	2	2	3	0	0	0	1	.000	0	0	5.68
1995	Atlanta	NL		5	0	0	0	6.2	38	14	11	4	3	0	0	0	5	1	3	0	0	0	0	.000	0	0	5.40
11 Min. YEARS				265	157	23	93	1089.2	4712	1142	587	513	106	25	36	58	355	14	801	51	13	66	55	.545	7	46	4.24
7 Maj. YEARS				100	48	6	14	412.2	1791	460	234	203	42	14	13	14	121	8	214	8	3	11	31	.262	1	1	4.43

Chris Nichting

Pitches: Right **Bats:** Right **Pos:** P **Ht:** 6' 1" **Wt:** 205 **Born:** 5/13/66 **Age:** 31

Year	Team	Lg	Org	G	GS	CG	GF	IP	BFP	H	R	ER	HR	SH	SF	HB	TBB	IBB	SO	WP	Bk	W	L	Pct.	ShO	Sv	ERA
	HOW MUCH HE PITCHED									**WHAT HE GAVE UP**												**THE RESULTS**					
1988	Vero Beach	A+	LA	21	19	5	2	138	545	90	40	32	7	0	2	2	51	0	151	7	0	11	4	.733	1	1	2.09
1989	San Antonio	AA	LA	26	26	2	0	154	698	160	96	86	13	9	6	6	101	6	136	14	4	4	14	.222	0	0	5.03
1992	Albuquerque	AAA	LA	10	9	0	0	42	205	64	42	37	2	2	0	0	23	1	25	5	1	1	3	.250	0	0	7.93
	San Antonio	AA	LA	13	13	0	0	78.2	309	58	25	22	3	4	0	1	37	0	81	4	0	4	5	.444	0	0	2.52
1993	Vero Beach	A+	LA	4	4	0	0	17.1	75	18	9	8	2	0	0	0	6	0	18	1	0	0	1	.000	0	0	4.15
1994	Albuquerque	AAA	LA	10	7	0	1	41.1	209	61	39	34	5	0	0	3	28	1	25	6	0	2	2	.500	0	0	7.40
	San Antonio	AA	LA	21	8	0	8	65.2	277	47	21	12	1	4	1	2	34	1	74	7	1	3	4	.429	0	1	1.64
1995	Okla. City	AAA	Tex	23	7	3	8	67.2	275	58	19	16	4	4	2	2	19	0	72	2	0	5	5	.500	2	1	2.13
1996	Okla. City	AAA	Tex	4	1	0	1	9	37	9	1	1	0	0	0	0	3	0	7	0	0	1	0	1.000	0	0	1.00
1995	Texas	AL		13	0	0	3	24.1	122	36	19	19	1	1	2	1	13	1	6	3	0	0	0	.000	0	0	7.03
7 Min. YEARS				132	94	10	20	613.2	2630	565	292	248	37	23	11	16	302	9	589	46	6	31	38	.449	3	3	3.64

Jim Nix

Pitches: Right **Bats:** Right **Pos:** P **Ht:** 5'11" **Wt:** 175 **Born:** 9/6/70 **Age:** 26

				HOW MUCH HE PITCHED						WHAT HE GAVE UP												THE RESULTS					
Year	Team	Lg	Org	G	GS	CG	GF	IP	BFP	H	R	ER	HR	SH	SF	HB	TBB	IBB	SO	WP	Bk	W	L	Pct.	ShO	Sv	ERA
1992	Princeton	R+	Cin	27	0	0	24	34.2	142	27	16	11	3	3	0	0	13	2	44	4	1	0	4	.000	0	13	2.86
	Charlstn-WV	A	Cin	2	0	0	1	3.1	15	3	0	0	0	0	0	1	1	1	5	0	0	0	0	.000	0	0	0.00
1993	Charlstn-WV	A	Cin	26	5	1	18	60.2	237	28	19	15	1	2	1	5	24	3	75	5	1	7	2	.778	0	5	2.23
	Winston-Sal	A+	Cin	11	4	0	3	35.1	153	37	24	14	8	0	1	0	15	0	33	2	0	3	3	.500	0	0	3.57
1994	Winston-Sal	A+	Cin	29	28	1	1	169	753	168	103	86	23	6	9	9	87	1	139	10	2	11	10	.524	0	0	4.58
1995	Chattanooga	AA	Cin	40	5	0	14	84.1	360	84	43	30	8	6	4	2	30	1	71	7	1	3	5	.375	0	2	3.20
1996	Chattanooga	AA	Cin	62	0	0	25	89	378	80	43	33	5	4	1	2	46	2	93	5	0	7	2	.778	0	11	3.34
5 Min. YEARS				197	42	2	86	476.1	2038	427	248	189	48	21	16	19	216	10	460	33	5	31	26	.544	0	31	3.57

Scott Norman

Pitches: Right **Bats:** Right **Pos:** P **Ht:** 6'0" **Wt:** 195 **Born:** 9/1/72 **Age:** 24

				HOW MUCH HE PITCHED						WHAT HE GAVE UP												THE RESULTS					
Year	Team	Lg	Org	G	GS	CG	GF	IP	BFP	H	R	ER	HR	SH	SF	HB	TBB	IBB	SO	WP	Bk	W	L	Pct.	ShO	Sv	ERA
1993	Bristol	R+	Det	13	13	1	0	77	355	100	54	45	7	1	1	6	18	0	43	9	5	3	6	.333	0	0	5.26
1994	Fayettevlle	A	Det	25	25	4	0	165	672	148	63	51	9	3	4	4	41	0	95	12	0	14	7	.667	2	0	2.78
	Lakeland	A+	Det	3	3	1	0	18.1	77	19	7	6	2	0	1	1	5	0	9	2	0	0	2	.000	1	0	2.95
1995	Jacksonvlle	AA	Det	4	4	2	0	29	122	31	12	8	4	1	0	1	6	0	9	1	0	1	3	.250	0	0	2.48
	Lakeland	A+	Det	26	25	5	0	157.1	693	172	98	66	8	3	9	7	44	1	72	5	2	8	10	.444	0	0	3.78
1996	Jacksonvlle	AA	Det	27	14	0	5	97	437	122	58	52	8	4	1	4	37	4	30	5	1	6	5	.545	0	0	4.82
4 Min. YEARS				98	84	13	5	543.2	2356	592	292	228	38	12	16	23	151	5	258	34	8	32	33	.492	3	0	3.77

Joe Norris

Pitches: Right **Bats:** Right **Pos:** P **Ht:** 6'4" **Wt:** 215 **Born:** 11/29/70 **Age:** 26

				HOW MUCH HE PITCHED						WHAT HE GAVE UP												THE RESULTS					
Year	Team	Lg	Org	G	GS	CG	GF	IP	BFP	H	R	ER	HR	SH	SF	HB	TBB	IBB	SO	WP	Bk	W	L	Pct.	ShO	Sv	ERA
1990	Jamestown	A-	Mon	13	13	1	0	62.1	290	63	48	36	2	1	2	4	43	0	72	9	5	3	7	.300	0	0	5.20
1991	Sumter	A	Mon	8	8	0	0	35	161	41	25	20	2	0	1	3	17	0	42	6	2	1	3	.250	0	0	5.14
1992	Rockford	A	Mon	27	27	1	0	163	723	160	88	68	5	11	5	10	79	2	143	21	3	5	15	.250	0	0	3.75
1993	W. Palm Bch	A+	Mon	26	13	0	4	81	336	62	27	24	3	2	4	9	29	0	63	6	0	7	4	.636	0	0	2.67
1994	Nashville	AA	Min	36	13	0	8	111	474	106	58	52	6	4	7	7	45	2	83	10	3	6	8	.429	0	1	4.22
1995	New Britain	AA	Min	46	0	0	20	82.2	364	79	42	33	4	11	3	2	36	5	81	4	0	5	6	.455	0	5	3.59
1996	Salt Lake	AAA	Min	21	0	0	5	37.1	174	48	27	24	3	3	1	0	17	0	38	4	0	1	1	.500	0	2	5.79
7 Min. YEARS				177	74	2	37	572.1	2522	559	315	257	25	32	23	35	266	9	522	60	13	28	44	.389	0	8	4.04

Kevin Northrup

Bats: Right **Throws:** Right **Pos:** OF **Ht:** 6'1" **Wt:** 190 **Born:** 1/27/70 **Age:** 27

				BATTING															BASERUNNING				PERCENTAGES		
Year	Team	Lg	Org	G	AB	H	2B	3B	HR	TB	R	RBI	TBB	IBB	SO	HBP	SH	SF	SB	CS	SB%	GDP	Avg	OBP	SLG
1992	Jamestown	A-	Mon	18	72	21	4	1	4	39	14	15	8	0	17	3	0	0	8	1	.89	1	.292	.386	.542
1993	W. Palm Bch	A+	Mon	131	459	136	29	0	6	183	65	63	70	7	76	3	4	5	10	7	.59	9	.296	.389	.399
1994	Harrisburg	AA	Mon	92	341	113	21	0	11	167	53	55	34	2	38	4	2	3	6	3	.67	14	.331	.395	.490
	Ottawa	AAA	Mon	33	102	29	7	1	3	47	19	16	16	0	16	1	0	0	2	0	1.00	4	.284	.387	.461
1995	St. Lucie	A+	NYN	17	64	19	1	1	0	22	7	12	4	0	6	0	0	2	2	1	.67	2	.297	.329	.344
	Harrisburg	AA	Mon	40	152	47	14	0	1	64	23	27	10	1	16	0	0	1	0	1	.00	3	.309	.350	.421
	Edmonton	AAA	Oak	17	44	8	2	0	0	10	4	1	5	1	8	0	1	0	0	0	.00	0	.182	.265	.227
1996	Columbus	AAA	NYA	56	168	48	13	1	4	75	22	20	12	0	25	0	0	1	4	2	.67	7	.286	.331	.446
	Norwich	AA	NYA	63	235	57	10	2	7	92	36	37	26	2	36	1	3	2	3	1	.75	14	.243	.318	.391
5 Min. YEARS				467	1637	478	101	6	36	699	243	246	185	13	238	12	10	14	35	16	.69	54	.292	.365	.427

Chris Norton

Bats: Right **Throws:** Right **Pos:** 1B **Ht:** 6'2" **Wt:** 215 **Born:** 9/21/70 **Age:** 26

				BATTING															BASERUNNING				PERCENTAGES		
Year	Team	Lg	Org	G	AB	H	2B	3B	HR	TB	R	RBI	TBB	IBB	SO	HBP	SH	SF	SB	CS	SB%	GDP	Avg	OBP	SLG
1992	Watertown	A-	Cle	1	4	0	0	0	0	0	1	0	0	0	2	0	0	0	0	0	.00	0	.000	.000	.000
	Burlington	R+	Cle	4	12	3	0	0	0	3	2	2	1	0	4	0	0	1	0	0	.00	0	.250	.286	.250
	Jamestown	A-	Mon	60	207	42	4	1	4	60	15	27	15	0	64	2	0	2	3	0	1.00	3	.203	.261	.290
1993	Cardinals	R	StL	27	83	19	5	3	0	30	10	11	11	1	23	1	0	0	0	0	.00	2	.229	.326	.361
1994	Savannah	A	StL	126	439	116	11	2	26	209	75	82	73	4	144	4	3	2	6	4	.60	11	.264	.373	.476
1995	Arkansas	AA	StL	10	25	6	2	0	0	8	6	6	11	2	5	0	0	1	0	0	.00	0	.240	.459	.320
	Lubbock	IND	—	97	327	95	16	3	21	180	61	61	75	7	87	1	0	2	6	2	.75	5	.291	.422	.550
1996	Lubbock	IND	—	51	187	71	13	1	15	131	39	54	27	3	27	4	0	2	6	0	1.00	7	.380	.464	.701
	Norwich	AA	NYA	47	172	48	12	1	7	83	24	28	15	0	43	1	0	0	3	2	.60	3	.279	.340	.483
5 Min. YEARS				423	1456	400	63	11	73	704	233	271	228	17	399	13	3	10	24	8	.75	31	.275	.376	.484

Rafael Novoa

Pitches: Left **Bats:** Left **Pos:** P **Ht:** 6' 1" **Wt:** 190 **Born:** 10/26/67 **Age:** 29

				HOW MUCH HE PITCHED						WHAT HE GAVE UP												THE RESULTS					
Year	Team	Lg	Org	G	GS	CG	GF	IP	BFP	H	R	ER	HR	SH	SF	HB	TBB	IBB	SO	WP	Bk	W	L	Pct.	ShO	Sv	ERA
1989	Everett	A-	SF	3	3	0	0	15	73	20	11	8	2	0	0	1	8	0	20	3	1	0	1	.000	0	0	4.80
	Clinton	A	SF	13	10	0	0	63.2	267	58	20	18	1	9	1	4	18	1	61	1	6	5	4	.556	0	0	2.54

			HOW MUCH HE PITCHED						WHAT HE GAVE UP												THE RESULTS					
Year	Team	Lg Org	G	GS	CG	GF	IP	BFP	H	R	ER	HR	SH	SF	HB	TBB	IBB	SO	WP	Bk	W	L	Pct.	ShO	Sv	ERA
1990	Clinton	A SF	15	14	3	0	97.2	397	73	32	26	6	2	3	4	30	0	113	2	2	9	2	.818	1	0	2.40
	Shreveport	AA SF	11	10	2	1	71.2	297	60	21	21	3	1	2	3	25	0	66	1	0	5	4	.556	1	0	2.64
1991	Phoenix	AAA SF	17	17	0	0	93.2	450	135	83	62	16	5	6	5	37	3	46	3	1	6	6	.500	0	0	5.96
1992	El Paso	AA Mil	22	21	6	1	146.1	617	143	63	53	6	4	3	9	48	3	124	8	1	10	7	.588	0	0	3.26
1993	New Orleans	AAA Mil	20	18	2	0	113	471	105	55	43	20	1	3	5	38	3	74	4	1	10	5	.667	1	0	3.42
1994	Iowa	AAA ChN	27	23	1	0	137.1	621	151	90	80	12	7	4	8	67	3	54	7	1	6	10	.375	0	0	5.24
1995	Nashville	AAA ChA	3	3	0	0	10	58	17	13	12	0	0	1	2	9	0	3	0	0	0	1	.000	0	0	10.80
	Binghamton	AA NYN	7	3	0	2	18	92	23	15	14	0	1	1	2	14	0	9	0	0	0	2	.000	0	0	7.00
1996	Lk Elsinore	A+ Cal	16	0	0	5	26.2	118	29	14	13	6	2	1	0	12	1	31	2	0	2	2	.500	0	1	4.39
	Midland	AA Cal	19	0	0	8	24.1	113	28	20	18	0	1	3	1	12	2	16	5	0	0	1	.000	0	2	6.66
	Vancouver	AAA Cal	13	0	0	6	12.2	63	19	10	10	3	0	0	2	5	0	10	0	1	1	1	.500	0	1	7.11
1990	San Francisco	NL	7	2	0	2	18.2	88	21	14	14	3	0	1	0	13	1	14	0	0	0	1	.000	0	1	6.75
1993	Milwaukee	AL	15	7	2	0	56	249	58	32	28	7	4	2	4	22	2	17	1	0	0	3	.000	0	0	4.50
8 Min. YEARS			186	122	14	23	830	3637	861	447	378	75	33	28	46	323	16	627	36	14	54	46	.540	3	4	4.10
2 Maj. YEARS			22	9	2	2	74.2	337	79	46	42	10	4	3	4	35	3	31	1	0	0	4	.000	0	1	5.06

Clemente Nunez

Pitches: Right **Bats:** Right **Pos:** P **Ht:** 5'11" **Wt:** 181 **Born:** 2/10/75 **Age:** 22

			HOW MUCH HE PITCHED						WHAT HE GAVE UP												THE RESULTS					
Year	Team	Lg Org	G	GS	CG	GF	IP	BFP	H	R	ER	HR	SH	SF	HB	TBB	IBB	SO	WP	Bk	W	L	Pct.	ShO	Sv	ERA
1992	Marlins	R Fla	12	12	3	0	71.1	292	55	24	22	2	4	1	2	25	0	26	3	3	5	5	.500	2	0	2.78
1993	Elmira	A- Fla	14	9	0	3	63.1	272	66	31	28	4	2	2	5	17	0	34	7	1	4	3	.571	0	0	3.98
1994	Brevard Cty	A+ Fla	19	16	2	1	98.2	407	86	45	34	8	5	2	1	24	0	66	3	1	6	5	.545	1	0	3.10
1995	Brevard Cty	A+ Fla	19	19	4	0	123.1	490	99	48	34	3	2	2	5	22	1	79	3	5	12	6	.667	2	0	2.48
1996	Portland	AA Fla	32	10	0	2	97	441	119	74	59	18	6	4	9	31	4	52	7	1	2	7	.222	0	0	5.47
5 Min. YEARS			96	66	9	6	453.2	1902	425	222	177	35	19	11	22	119	5	257	23	11	29	26	.527	5	0	3.51

Ramon Nunez

Bats: Right **Throws:** Right **Pos:** 1B **Ht:** 6'0" **Wt:** 150 **Born:** 9/22/72 **Age:** 24

			BATTING															BASERUNNING				PERCENTAGES		
Year	Team	Lg Org	G	AB	H	2B	3B	HR	TB	R	RBI	TBB	IBB	SO	HBP	SH	SF	SB	CS	SB%	GDP	Avg	OBP	SLG
1992	Pulaski	R+ Atl	59	218	55	9	2	5	83	28	32	14	1	57	3	0	1	8	3	.73	7	.252	.305	.381
1993	Macon	A Atl	115	377	108	18	5	7	157	57	40	37	2	73	4	6	2	6	5	.55	6	.286	.355	.416
1994	Durham	A+ Atl	124	453	125	23	0	17	199	59	62	38	1	98	2	0	4	4	9	.31	9	.276	.332	.439
1995	Durham	A+ Atl	17	54	20	4	0	5	39	13	15	8	0	9	0	1	1	0	0	.00	4	.370	.444	.722
	Greenville	AA Atl	81	241	63	15	2	9	109	34	34	15	0	63	3	0	3	1	1	.50	8	.261	.309	.452
1996	Greenville	AA Atl	58	169	34	6	0	4	52	15	26	9	1	43	1	1	2	1	2	.33	2	.201	.243	.308
	Durham	A+ Atl	65	243	75	18	1	10	125	30	55	12	1	45	1	1	7	2	2	.50	6	.309	.335	.514
5 Min. YEARS			519	1755	480	93	10	57	764	236	264	133	6	388	14	9	20	22	22	.50	42	.274	.326	.435

Ryan Nye

Pitches: Right **Bats:** Right **Pos:** P **Ht:** 6'2" **Wt:** 195 **Born:** 6/24/73 **Age:** 24

			HOW MUCH HE PITCHED						WHAT HE GAVE UP												THE RESULTS					
Year	Team	Lg Org	G	GS	CG	GF	IP	BFP	H	R	ER	HR	SH	SF	HB	TBB	IBB	SO	WP	Bk	W	L	Pct.	ShO	Sv	ERA
1994	Batavia	A- Phi	13	12	1	0	71.2	301	64	27	21	3	1	0	6	15	0	71	2	1	7	2	.778	0	0	2.64
1995	Clearwater	A+ Phi	27	27	5	0	167	681	164	71	63	8	5	5	6	33	1	116	4	3	12	7	.632	1	0	3.40
1996	Reading	AA Phi	14	14	0	0	86.2	365	76	41	37	9	1	3	6	30	1	90	3	1	8	2	.800	0	0	3.84
	Scranton-WB	AAA Phi	14	14	0	0	80.2	362	97	52	45	10	0	2	3	30	0	51	1	1	5	2	.714	0	0	5.02
3 Min. YEARS			68	67	6	0	406	1709	401	191	166	30	7	10	21	108	2	328	10	6	32	13	.711	1	0	3.68

John O'Donoghue

Pitches: Left **Bats:** Left **Pos:** P **Ht:** 6' 6" **Wt:** 210 **Born:** 5/26/69 **Age:** 28

			HOW MUCH HE PITCHED						WHAT HE GAVE UP												THE RESULTS					
Year	Team	Lg Org	G	GS	CG	GF	IP	BFP	H	R	ER	HR	SH	SF	HB	TBB	IBB	SO	WP	Bk	W	L	Pct.	ShO	Sv	ERA
1990	Bluefield	R+ Bal	10	6	2	3	49.1	200	49	13	11	2	2	0	1	10	0	67	2	1	4	2	.667	2	0	2.01
	Frederick	A+ Bal	1	1	0	0	4	18	5	2	2	0	0	0	0	0	0	3	0	0	0	1	.000	0	0	4.50
1991	Frederick	A+ Bal	22	21	2	1	133.2	567	131	55	43	6	0	2	2	50	2	128	8	1	7	8	.467	1	0	2.90
1992	Hagerstown	AA Bal	17	16	2	1	112.1	459	78	37	28	6	4	2	4	40	0	87	7	4	7	4	.636	0	0	2.24
	Rochester	AAA Bal	13	10	3	1	69.2	282	60	31	25	5	4	0	0	19	1	47	5	0	5	4	.556	1	0	3.23
1993	Rochester	AAA Bal	22	20	2	1	127.2	543	122	60	55	11	8	3	3	41	0	111	3	0	7	4	.636	1	0	3.88
1994	Rochester	AAA Bal	38	12	0	9	105.1	508	142	76	67	13	5	5	5	55	6	78	6	2	4	7	.364	0	1	5.72
1995	Albuquerque	AAA LA	25	18	1	3	92	394	97	58	39	10	1	1	0	25	0	59	3	0	5	6	.455	1	0	3.82
1996	Bowie	AA Bal	7	7	0	0	37	162	42	21	18	6	4	2	2	16	0	26	0	0	1	3	.250	0	0	4.38
	Tulsa	AA Tex	27	9	0	4	79.2	355	89	47	37	9	3	3	6	23	1	46	2	0	2	4	.333	0	0	4.18
1993	Baltimore	AL	11	1	0	3	19.2	90	22	12	10	4	0	0	1	10	1	16	0	0	0	1	.000	0	0	4.58
7 Min. YEARS			182	120	12	23	810.2	3488	815	400	325	68	31	18	23	279	10	652	36	8	42	43	.494	6	1	3.61

Doug O'Neill

Bats: Right **Throws:** Right **Pos:** OF **Ht:** 5'10" **Wt:** 200 **Born:** 6/29/70 **Age:** 27

			BATTING															BASERUNNING				PERCENTAGES		
Year	Team	Lg Org	G	AB	H	2B	3B	HR	TB	R	RBI	TBB	IBB	SO	HBP	SH	SF	SB	CS	SB%	GDP	Avg	OBP	SLG
1991	Jamestown	A- Mon	33	119	28	4	0	2	38	19	11	14	0	29	2	0	0	17	4	.81	2	.235	.326	.319

Year	Team	Lg	Org	G	AB	H	2B	3B	HR	TB	R	RBI	TBB	IBB	SO	HBP	SH	SF	SB	CS	SB%	GDP	Avg	OBP	SLG
1992	Expos	R	Mon	3	10	2	0	0	0	2	0	0	2	0	3	0	0	0	1	1	.50	0	.200	.333	.200
	Albany	A	Mon	11	36	9	3	0	0	12	3	3	6	0	13	0	0	0	1	1	.50	1	.250	.357	.333
1993	Burlington	A	Mon	67	203	43	6	3	3	64	26	20	33	1	69	2	2	1	3	1	.75	2	.212	.326	.315
1994	Ogden	R+	—	70	259	72	21	4	10	131	55	53	45	0	101	0	3	2	10	6	.63	2	.278	.382	.506
1995	St. Paul	IND	—	84	356	111	20	2	17	186	75	58	38	0	68	2	4	5	24	9	.73	7	.312	.377	.522
1996	Portland	AA	Fla	72	241	62	10	2	7	97	39	26	26	1	64	2	2	2	8	4	.67	3	.257	.332	.402
	Tulsa	AA	Tex	20	75	23	3	0	5	41	8	15	11	0	19	1	1	0	1	2	.33	2	.307	.402	.547
6	Min. YEARS			360	1299	350	67	11	44	571	225	186	175	2	366	9	12	10	65	28	.70	19	.269	.358	.440

Bobby O'Toole

Bats: Right **Throws:** Right **Pos:** C **Ht:** 6'0" **Wt:** 195 **Born:** 5/19/74 **Age:** 23

Year	Team	Lg	Org	G	AB	H	2B	3B	HR	TB	R	RBI	TBB	IBB	SO	HBP	SH	SF	SB	CS	SB%	GDP	Avg	OBP	SLG
1996	Bowie	AA	Bal	6	10	0	0	0	0	0	0	0	0	0	5	0	0	0	0	0	.00	0	.000	.000	.000
	Bluefield	R+	Bal	8	19	5	1	0	1	9	2	4	4	0	7	1	0	0	2	0	1.00	0	.263	.417	.474
	High Desert	A+	Bal	16	35	6	1	0	0	7	8	3	8	0	10	2	0	0	0	0	.00	3	.171	.356	.200
	Frederick	A+	Bal	3	7	1	0	0	0	1	0	0	0	0	2	0	0	0	0	0	.00	0	.143	.143	.143
1	Min. YEARS			33	71	12	2	0	1	17	10	7	12	0	24	3	0	0	2	0	1.00	3	.169	.314	.239

Jamie Ogden

Bats: Left **Throws:** Left **Pos:** 1B-OF **Ht:** 6'5" **Wt:** 215 **Born:** 1/19/72 **Age:** 25

Year	Team	Lg	Org	G	AB	H	2B	3B	HR	TB	R	RBI	TBB	IBB	SO	HBP	SH	SF	SB	CS	SB%	GDP	Avg	OBP	SLG
1990	Twins	R	Min	28	101	20	1	2	0	25	11	5	7	0	41	0	0	0	2	0	1.00	2	.198	.250	.248
1991	Twins	R	Min	37	122	39	9	7	2	68	22	25	11	0	30	0	0	4	7	4	.64	0	.320	.365	.557
1992	Kenosha	A	Min	108	372	91	14	3	3	120	36	51	52	1	108	2	0	4	9	2	.82	9	.245	.337	.323
1993	Fort Myers	A+	Min	118	396	96	22	4	8	150	37	46	34	1	89	6	4	1	7	1	.88	11	.242	.311	.379
1994	Fort Myers	A+	Min	69	251	66	12	0	7	99	32	22	16	0	52	2	1	1	12	8	.60	6	.263	.311	.394
1995	New Britain	AA	Min	117	384	109	22	1	13	172	54	61	48	5	90	1	0	5	6	5	.55	10	.284	.361	.448
1996	Salt Lake	AAA	Min	123	448	118	22	2	18	198	80	74	45	6	105	2	2	2	17	2	.89	9	.263	.332	.442
7	Min. YEARS			600	2074	539	102	19	51	832	272	284	213	13	515	13	7	17	60	22	.73	47	.260	.330	.401

Kevin Ohme

Pitches: Left **Bats:** Left **Pos:** P **Ht:** 6'1" **Wt:** 175 **Born:** 4/13/71 **Age:** 26

Year	Team	Lg	Org	G	GS	CG	GF	IP	BFP	H	R	ER	HR	SH	SF	HB	TBB	IBB	SO	WP	Bk	W	L	Pct.	ShO	Sv	ERA
1993	Fort Wayne	A	Min	15	4	0	6	46.1	184	38	19	13	1	2	2	1	15	1	45	4	1	3	2	.600	0	0	2.53
1994	Fort Wayne	A	Min	2	2	0	0	7	29	7	2	2	0	0	0	1	0	0	8	0	0	0	1	.000	0	0	2.57
1995	New Britain	AA	Min	35	11	0	7	101.1	427	89	51	39	5	7	7	3	45	1	52	7	0	3	4	.429	0	0	3.46
1996	New Britain	AA	Min	51	0	0	22	81	363	83	49	39	7	6	4	6	33	5	42	5	2	5	6	.455	0	3	4.33
4	Min. YEARS			103	17	0	35	235.2	1003	217	121	93	13	15	13	11	93	7	147	16	3	11	13	.458	0	3	3.55

Kirt Ojala

Pitches: Left **Bats:** Left **Pos:** P **Ht:** 6'2" **Wt:** 200 **Born:** 12/24/68 **Age:** 28

Year	Team	Lg	Org	G	GS	CG	GF	IP	BFP	H	R	ER	HR	SH	SF	HB	TBB	IBB	SO	WP	Bk	W	L	Pct.	ShO	Sv	ERA
1990	Oneonta	A-	NYA	14	14	1	0	79	353	75	28	19	2	5	2	3	43	0	87	1	2	7	2	.778	0	0	2.16
1991	Pr. William	A+	NYA	25	23	1	0	156.2	636	120	52	44	5	3	4	4	61	1	112	3	1	8	7	.533	0	0	2.53
1992	Albany-Colo	AA	NYA	24	23	2	0	151.2	642	130	71	61	10	3	7	0	80	0	116	10	0	12	8	.600	1	0	3.62
1993	Albany-Colo	AA	NYA	1	1	0	0	6.1	26	5	0	0	0	0	0	0	2	0	6	2	0	1	0	1.000	0	0	0.00
	Columbus	AAA	NYA	31	20	0	3	126	575	145	85	77	13	4	5	3	71	2	83	13	1	8	9	.471	0	0	5.50
1994	Columbus	AAA	NYA	25	23	1	0	148	638	157	78	63	12	2	2	4	46	1	81	10	1	11	7	.611	1	0	3.83
1995	Columbus	AAA	NYA	32	20	0	5	145.2	619	138	74	64	15	6	2	3	54	3	107	7	1	8	7	.533	0	1	3.95
1996	Indianapolis	AAA	Cin	22	21	3	0	133.2	569	143	67	56	15	2	6	6	31	0	92	3	0	7	7	.500	0	0	3.77
7	Min. YEARS			174	145	8	8	947	4058	913	455	384	72	25	28	23	388	7	684	49	6	62	47	.569	2	1	3.65

Jose Oliva

Bats: Right **Throws:** Right **Pos:** DH **Ht:** 6' 3" **Wt:** 215 **Born:** 3/3/71 **Age:** 26

Year	Team	Lg	Org	G	AB	H	2B	3B	HR	TB	R	RBI	TBB	IBB	SO	HBP	SH	SF	SB	CS	SB%	GDP	Avg	OBP	SLG
1988	Rangers	R	Tex	27	70	15	3	0	1	21	5	11	3	1	14	0	0	1	0	0	.00	1	.214	.243	.300
1989	Butte	R+	Tex	41	114	24	2	3	4	44	18	13	14	1	41	1	0	2	4	3	.57	0	.211	.298	.386
1990	Gastonia	A	Tex	119	383	80	24	1	10	136	44	52	26	0	104	4	3	8	9	3	.75	5	.209	.261	.355
1991	Rangers	R	Tex	3	11	1	1	0	0	2	0	1	2	0	3	0	0	1	0	0	.00	0	.091	.214	.182
	Charlotte	A+	Tex	108	384	92	17	4	14	159	55	59	44	3	107	5	1	6	9	9	.50	15	.240	.321	.414
1992	Tulsa	AA	Tex	124	445	120	28	6	16	208	57	75	40	3	135	2	2	7	4	0	1.00	7	.270	.328	.467
1993	Richmond	AAA	Atl	125	412	97	20	6	21	192	63	65	35	2	134	4	0	1	1	5	.17	10	.235	.301	.466
1994	Richmond	AAA	Atl	99	371	94	17	0	24	183	52	64	25	3	92	2	0	3	2	2	.50	7	.253	.302	.493
1996	Louisville	AAA	StL	118	413	100	13	0	31	206	53	86	34	5	101	1	0	1	3	3	.50	11	.242	.301	.499
1994	Atlanta	NL		19	59	17	5	0	6	40	9	11	7	0	10	0	0	0	0	1	.00	2	.288	.364	.678
1995	Atlanta	NL		48	109	17	4	0	5	36	7	12	7	0	22	0	0	0	0	0	.00	2	.156	.207	.330
	St. Louis	NL		22	74	9	1	0	2	16	8	8	5	0	24	2	0	1	0	0	.00	3	.122	.195	.216

Year Team	Lg Org	G	AB	H	2B	3B	HR	TB	R	RBI	TBB	IBB	SO	HBP	SH	SF	SB	CS	SB%	GDP	Avg	OBP	SLG
		BATTING															**BASERUNNING**				**PERCENTAGES**		
8 Min. YEARS		764	2603	623	125	20	121	1151	347	426	223	18	731	19	6	30	32	25	.56	56	.239	.301	.442
2 Maj. YEARS		89	242	43	10	0	13	92	24	31	19	0	56	2	0	1	0	1	.00	7	.178	.242	.380

Jose Olmeda

Bats: Both **Throws:** Right **Pos:** 3B **Ht:** 5'9" **Wt:** 155 **Born:** 6/20/68 **Age:** 29

Year Team	Lg Org	G	AB	H	2B	3B	HR	TB	R	RBI	TBB	IBB	SO	HBP	SH	SF	SB	CS	SB%	GDP	Avg	OBP	SLG
		BATTING															**BASERUNNING**				**PERCENTAGES**		
1989 Idaho Falls	R+ Atl	61	230	57	5	6	1	77	36	27	31	0	40	0	0	1	9	4	.69	7	.248	.336	.335
1990 Sumter	A Atl	103	367	93	14	6	7	140	60	40	55	2	49	2	4	4	17	9	.65	3	.253	.350	.381
Burlington	A Atl	27	112	29	3	0	0	32	6	7	8	0	17	0	0	1	1	1	.50	1	.259	.306	.286
Greenville	AA Atl	2	8	1	0	0	0	1	1	0	1	0	3	0	0	0	0	0	.00	0	.125	.222	.125
1991 Macon	A Atl	81	305	84	16	8	3	125	66	30	38	0	38	1	2	1	34	7	.83	3	.275	.357	.410
Greenville	AA Atl	50	173	35	10	1	3	56	18	16	15	0	36	2	5	2	9	2	.82	2	.202	.271	.324
1992 Durham	A+ Atl	24	89	23	6	1	2	37	17	9	14	0	14	0	1	0	7	4	.64	0	.258	.359	.416
Greenville	AA Atl	106	341	84	22	4	2	120	54	33	38	3	50	0	1	6	12	6	.67	4	.246	.317	.352
1993 Greenville	AA Atl	122	451	126	33	2	9	190	61	51	29	2	63	0	5	9	15	7	.68	8	.279	.317	.421
1994 Richmond	AAA Atl	109	387	89	19	6	4	132	49	39	30	6	74	1	8	1	17	4	.81	12	.230	.286	.341
1995 Richmond	AAA Atl	80	241	61	11	3	1	81	22	24	16	2	41	1	3	2	2	1	.67	5	.253	.300	.336
Greenville	AA Atl	31	108	27	5	1	4	46	16	10	7	0	18	0	0	0	1	0	1.00	4	.250	.296	.426
1996 Charlotte	AAA Fla	115	375	120	26	1	9	175	52	49	21	0	58	1	4	3	7	6	.54	7	.320	.355	.467
8 Min. YEARS		911	3187	829	170	39	45	1212	458	335	303	15	501	8	33	30	131	51	.72	56	.260	.323	.380

Steve Olsen

Pitches: Right **Bats:** Right **Pos:** P **Ht:** 6'4" **Wt:** 225 **Born:** 11/2/69 **Age:** 27

Year Team	Lg Org	G	GS	CG	GF	IP	BFP	H	R	ER	HR	SH	SF	HB	TBB	IBB	SO	WP	Bk	W	L	Pct.	ShO	Sv	ERA
		HOW MUCH HE PITCHED						**WHAT HE GAVE UP**												**THE RESULTS**					
1991 Utica	A- ChA	2	2	0	0	14	51	3	3	1	0	0	0	0	4	0	20	1	0	1	0	1.000	0	0	0.64
South Bend	A ChA	13	13	0	0	81.2	352	80	44	33	4	2	4	3	28	1	76	3	3	5	2	.714	0	0	3.64
1992 Sarasota	A+ ChA	13	13	3	0	88	363	68	22	19	4	2	1	3	32	0	85	3	2	11	1	.917	1	0	1.94
Birmingham	AA ChA	12	12	1	0	77.1	320	68	28	26	5	0	2	0	29	1	46	2	0	6	4	.600	0	0	3.03
1993 Birmingham	AA ChA	25	25	1	0	142	618	156	87	75	22	1	5	7	52	2	92	4	0	10	9	.526	1	0	4.75
1994 Birmingham	AA ChA	16	16	1	0	102.2	432	100	47	42	8	2	2	3	28	1	69	9	0	5	7	.417	0	0	3.68
Nashville	AAA ChA	11	11	2	0	71.1	289	69	30	26	4	2	1	0	18	0	58	0	1	7	2	.778	0	0	3.28
1995 Birmingham	AA ChA	14	14	2	0	85.1	357	84	44	33	4	3	7	1	21	2	56	1	0	8	3	.727	1	0	3.48
Nashville	AAA ChA	28	28	2	0	162.1	686	169	88	74	14	6	12	1	37	2	101	5	0	9	10	.474	1	0	4.10
1996 Wichita	AA KC	15	3	0	3	55.1	213	40	18	17	9	1	2	0	14	0	39	3	0	6	0	1.000	0	1	2.77
Omaha	AAA KC	24	4	1	6	65.2	283	70	39	37	7	2	1	4	23	4	41	6	0	7	4	.636	1	0	5.07
6 Min. YEARS		173	141	13	9	945.2	3964	907	450	383	81	21	37	22	286	13	683	37	6	75	42	.641	5	1	3.65

Magglio Ordonez

Bats: Right **Throws:** Right **Pos:** OF **Ht:** 5'11" **Wt:** 155 **Born:** 1/28/74 **Age:** 23

Year Team	Lg Org	G	AB	H	2B	3B	HR	TB	R	RBI	TBB	IBB	SO	HBP	SH	SF	SB	CS	SB%	GDP	Avg	OBP	SLG
		BATTING															**BASERUNNING**				**PERCENTAGES**		
1992 White Sox	R ChA	38	111	20	10	2	1	37	17	14	13	0	26	2	0	1	6	4	.60	2	.180	.276	.333
1993 Hickory	A ChA	84	273	59	14	4	3	90	32	20	26	0	66	0	2	0	5	5	.50	6	.216	.284	.330
1994 Hickory	A ChA	132	490	144	24	5	11	211	86	69	45	1	57	1	7	3	16	7	.70	11	.294	.353	.431
1995 Pr. William	A+ ChA	131	487	116	24	2	12	180	61	65	41	0	71	3	0	4	11	5	.69	16	.238	.299	.370
1996 Birmingham	AA ChA	130	479	126	41	0	18	221	66	67	39	1	74	9	1	0	9	10	.47	16	.263	.330	.461
5 Min. YEARS		515	1840	465	113	13	45	739	262	235	164	2	294	15	10	8	47	31	.60	51	.253	.318	.402

Rafael Orellano

Pitches: Left **Bats:** Left **Pos:** P **Ht:** 6'2" **Wt:** 160 **Born:** 4/28/73 **Age:** 24

Year Team	Lg Org	G	GS	CG	GF	IP	BFP	H	R	ER	HR	SH	SF	HB	TBB	IBB	SO	WP	Bk	W	L	Pct.	ShO	Sv	ERA
		HOW MUCH HE PITCHED						**WHAT HE GAVE UP**												**THE RESULTS**					
1993 Utica	A- Bos	11	0	0	7	18.2	84	22	15	12	4	2	1	1	7	0	13	1	0	1	2	.333	0	2	5.79
1994 Red Sox	R Bos	4	3	0	0	13.1	50	6	3	3	0	0	0	0	4	0	10	1	2	1	0	1.000	0	0	2.03
Sarasota	A+ Bos	16	16	2	0	97.1	375	68	28	26	5	1	0	4	25	0	103	2	3	11	3	.786	1	0	2.40
1995 Trenton	AA Bos	27	27	2	0	186.2	772	146	68	64	18	4	1	11	72	0	160	9	4	11	7	.611	0	0	3.09
1996 Pawtucket	AAA Bos	22	20	0	0	99.1	476	124	94	87	20	2	9	6	62	0	66	10	1	4	11	.267	0	0	7.88
4 Min. YEARS		80	66	4	7	415.1	1757	366	208	192	47	9	11	22	170	0	352	23	10	28	23	.549	1	2	4.16

Kevin Orie

Bats: Right **Throws:** Right **Pos:** 3B **Ht:** 6'4" **Wt:** 215 **Born:** 9/1/72 **Age:** 24

Year Team	Lg Org	G	AB	H	2B	3B	HR	TB	R	RBI	TBB	IBB	SO	HBP	SH	SF	SB	CS	SB%	GDP	Avg	OBP	SLG
		BATTING															**BASERUNNING**				**PERCENTAGES**		
1993 Peoria	A ChN	65	238	64	17	1	7	104	28	45	21	1	51	10	2	2	3	5	.38	7	.269	.351	.437
1994 Daytona	A+ ChN	6	17	7	3	1	1	15	4	5	8	1	4	1	0	0	0	1	.00	0	.412	.615	.882
1995 Daytona	A+ ChN	119	409	100	17	4	9	152	54	51	42	2	71	15	0	6	5	4	.56	11	.244	.333	.372
1996 Orlando	AA ChN	82	296	93	25	0	8	142	42	58	48	3	52	0	0	6	2	0	1.00	7	.314	.403	.480
Iowa	AAA ChN	14	48	10	1	0	2	17	5	6	6	1	10	0	0	0	0	0	.00	1	.208	.296	.354
4 Min. YEARS		286	1008	274	63	6	27	430	133	165	125	8	188	26	2	14	10	10	.50	26	.272	.362	.427

Hector Ortega

Bats: Right **Throws:** Right **Pos:** 3B **Ht:** 6'3" **Wt:** 183 **Born:** 8/31/72 **Age:** 24

			BATTING															BASERUNNING				PERCENTAGES		
Year	Team	Lg	Org	G	AB	H	2B	3B	HR	TB	R	RBI	TBB	IBB	SO	HBP	SH	SF	SB	CS	SB%	GDP	Avg	OBP	SLG
1989	Expos	R	Mon	5	13	1	0	0	0	1	3	0	3	0	5	0	0	0	1	1	.50	0	.077	.250	.077
1990	Gate City	R+	Mon	65	244	69	6	5	1	88	34	17	22	0	60	1	0	2	20	6	.77	2	.283	.342	.361
1991	Sumter	A	Mon	112	365	97	19	2	2	126	43	36	28	0	78	2	2	3	13	4	.76	5	.266	.319	.345
1992	Rockford	A	Mon	125	405	100	17	3	1	126	50	44	38	1	93	5	3	5	28	10	.74	6	.247	.316	.311
1995	Stockton	A+	Mil	137	539	162	27	4	8	221	81	76	39	0	109	10	6	7	26	13	.67	8	.301	.355	.410
1996	New Orleans	AAA	Mil	5	18	10	0	1	0	12	2	2	0	0	2	0	0	0	0	0	.00	1	.556	.556	.667
	El Paso	AA	Mil	99	351	85	12	4	7	126	52	53	27	1	74	5	3	4	11	6	.65	12	.242	.302	.359
6 Min. YEARS				548	1935	524	81	19	19	700	265	228	157	2	421	23	14	21	99	40	.71	34	.271	.330	.362

Bo Ortiz

Bats: Right **Throws:** Right **Pos:** OF **Ht:** 5'11" **Wt:** 170 **Born:** 4/4/70 **Age:** 27

			BATTING															BASERUNNING				PERCENTAGES		
Year	Team	Lg	Org	G	AB	H	2B	3B	HR	TB	R	RBI	TBB	IBB	SO	HBP	SH	SF	SB	CS	SB%	GDP	Avg	OBP	SLG
1991	Bluefield	R+	Bal	12	53	16	2	1	1	23	4	7	2	0	6	0	0	1	1	0	1.00	2	.302	.321	.434
	Kane County	A	Bal	57	215	58	8	1	0	68	34	27	17	1	38	2	4	2	2	2	.50	4	.270	.326	.316
1992	Frederick	A+	Bal	54	182	50	11	3	0	67	26	19	18	0	40	3	2	1	7	3	.70	4	.275	.348	.368
1993	Frederick	A+	Bal	104	351	99	18	7	10	161	72	60	44	0	65	7	6	1	12	11	.52	7	.282	.372	.459
	Bowie	AA	Bal	8	30	6	0	1	0	8	1	3	1	0	5	1	2	0	0	0	.00	0	.200	.250	.267
1994	Bowie	AA	Bal	85	320	99	21	3	10	156	58	54	28	2	47	4	1	0	13	4	.76	10	.309	.372	.488
	Midland	AA	Cal	22	80	14	4	0	0	18	9	6	6	0	11	1	0	0	3	1	.75	2	.175	.241	.225
1995	Midland	AA	Cal	96	360	99	10	3	8	139	48	56	17	2	40	2	4	5	12	11	.52	6	.275	.307	.386
1996	Midland	AA	Cal	127	507	150	32	5	11	225	73	64	32	0	80	2	4	4	12	7	.63	9	.296	.338	.444
6 Min. YEARS				565	2098	591	106	24	40	865	325	296	165	5	332	22	23	14	62	39	.61	44	.282	.338	.412

Hector Ortiz

Bats: Right **Throws:** Right **Pos:** C **Ht:** 6'0" **Wt:** 178 **Born:** 10/14/69 **Age:** 27

			BATTING															BASERUNNING				PERCENTAGES		
Year	Team	Lg	Org	G	AB	H	2B	3B	HR	TB	R	RBI	TBB	IBB	SO	HBP	SH	SF	SB	CS	SB%	GDP	Avg	OBP	SLG
1988	Salem	A-	LA	32	77	11	1	0	0	12	5	4	5	0	16	1	1	0	0	2	.00	5	.143	.205	.156
1989	Vero Beach	A+	LA	42	85	12	0	1	0	14	5	4	6	0	15	2	4	0	0	0	.00	1	.141	.215	.165
	Salem	A-	LA	44	140	32	3	1	0	37	13	12	4	0	24	1	2	0	2	1	.67	6	.229	.255	.264
1990	Yakima	A-	LA	52	173	47	3	1	0	52	16	12	5	0	15	1	1	0	1	1	.50	6	.272	.296	.301
1991	Vero Beach	A+	LA	42	123	28	2	0	0	30	3	8	5	0	8	3	0	0	0	0	.00	2	.228	.275	.244
1992	Bakersfield	A+	LA	63	206	58	8	1	1	71	19	31	21	0	16	5	3	2	2	3	.40	8	.282	.359	.345
	San Antonio	AA	LA	26	59	12	1	0	0	13	1	5	11	0	13	1	1	0	0	0	.00	2	.203	.338	.220
1993	San Antonio	AA	LA	49	131	28	5	0	1	36	6	6	9	2	17	0	3	0	0	2	.00	3	.214	.264	.275
	Albuquerque	AAA	LA	18	44	8	1	1	0	11	0	3	0	0	6	1	2	0	0	0	.00	1	.182	.200	.250
1994	Albuquerque	AAA	LA	34	93	28	1	1	0	31	7	10	3	0	12	0	0	1	0	0	.00	7	.301	.320	.333
	San Antonio	AA	LA	24	75	9	0	0	0	9	4	4	2	0	7	1	0	2	0	0	.00	4	.120	.150	.120
1995	Orlando	AA	ChN	96	299	70	12	0	0	82	13	18	20	0	39	1	1	4	0	5	.00	10	.234	.281	.274
1996	Orlando	AA	ChN	78	216	47	8	0	0	55	16	15	26	2	23	0	1	3	1	2	.33	12	.218	.298	.255
	Iowa	AAA	ChN	27	79	19	2	0	0	21	6	3	3	1	16	0	0	1	0	0	.00	5	.241	.265	.266
9 Min. YEARS				627	1800	409	47	6	2	474	114	135	120	5	227	17	19	13	6	16	.27	72	.227	.280	.263

Nicky Ortiz

Bats: Right **Throws:** Right **Pos:** 2B **Ht:** 6'0" **Wt:** 165 **Born:** 7/9/73 **Age:** 23

			BATTING															BASERUNNING				PERCENTAGES		
Year	Team	Lg	Org	G	AB	H	2B	3B	HR	TB	R	RBI	TBB	IBB	SO	HBP	SH	SF	SB	CS	SB%	GDP	Avg	OBP	SLG
1991	Red Sox	R	Bos	35	100	26	3	1	0	31	16	13	22	0	24	4	1	0	1	2	.33	1	.260	.413	.310
1992	Red Sox	R	Bos	50	163	43	9	3	0	58	25	15	28	0	36	0	2	1	3	2	.60	4	.264	.370	.356
	Elmira	A-	Bos	9	28	5	3	0	0	8	2	1	5	0	13	0	0	0	0	0	.00	0	.179	.303	.286
1993	Ft. Laud	A+	Bos	36	112	23	9	1	1	37	9	14	9	0	39	0	4	0	2	1	.67	4	.205	.264	.330
	Utica	A-	Bos	63	197	53	14	1	2	75	31	26	19	0	56	6	1	2	4	1	.80	3	.269	.348	.381
1994	Sarasota	A+	Bos	81	283	76	18	3	2	106	34	40	21	1	57	3	6	3	7	2	.78	11	.269	.323	.375
1995	Sarasota	A+	Bos	91	304	75	20	1	5	112	38	38	27	0	68	4	1	1	6	4	.60	3	.247	.315	.368
1996	Michigan	A	Bos	73	242	73	14	4	2	101	37	25	20	1	44	5	1	1	1	1	.50	4	.302	.366	.417
	Trenton	AA	Bos	38	130	29	4	0	3	42	20	13	13	2	28	0	1	0	2	2	.50	3	.223	.294	.323
6 Min. YEARS				476	1559	403	94	14	15	570	212	185	164	4	365	22	17	8	26	15	.63	33	.258	.336	.366

Russ Ortiz

Pitches: Right **Bats:** Right **Pos:** P **Ht:** 6'1" **Wt:** 190 **Born:** 6/5/74 **Age:** 23

			HOW MUCH HE PITCHED						WHAT HE GAVE UP												THE RESULTS					
Year	Team	Lg	Org	G	GS	CG	GF	IP	BFP	H	R	ER	HR	SH	SF	HB	TBB	IBB	SO	WP	Bk	W	L	Pct.	ShO	Sv	ERA
1995	San Jose	A+	SF	5	0	0	5	6	24	4	1	1	0	0	1	0	2	0	7	0	0	0	1	.000	0	0	1.50
	Bellingham	A-	SF	30	0	0	25	40.1	155	23	5	3	1	0	2	0	15	0	62	2	1	2	1	.667	0	11	0.67
1996	San Jose	A+	SF	34	0	0	31	36.2	145	16	2	1	0	0	0	2	20	0	63	0	0	0	0	.000	0	23	0.25
	Shreveport	AA	SF	26	0	0	20	26.2	123	22	14	12	0	0	0	2	21	3	29	1	0	1	2	.333	0	13	4.05
2 Min. YEARS				95	0	0	81	109.2	447	65	22	17	1	0	3	4	58	3	161	3	1	3	4	.429	0	47	1.40

John Orton

Bats: Right **Throws:** Right **Pos:** DH-C **Ht:** 6' 1" **Wt:** 192 **Born:** 12/8/65 **Age:** 31

				BATTING															BASERUNNING				PERCENTAGES		
Year	Team	Lg	Org	G	AB	H	2B	3B	HR	TB	R	RBI	TBB	IBB	SO	HBP	SH	SF	SB	CS	SB%	GDP	Avg	OBP	SLG
1987	Salem	A-	Cal	51	176	46	8	1	8	80	31	36	32	1	61	7	1	2	6	2	.75	5	.261	.392	.455
	Midland	AA	Cal	5	13	2	1	0	0	3	1	0	2	0	3	1	0	0	0	0	.00	0	.154	.313	.231
1988	Palm Spring	A+	Cal	68	230	46	6	1	1	57	42	28	45	0	79	10	2	0	5	2	.71	4	.200	.354	.248
1989	Midland	AA	Cal	99	344	80	20	6	10	142	51	53	37	1	102	7	6	7	2	1	.67	5	.233	.314	.413
1990	Edmonton	AAA	Cal	50	174	42	8	0	6	68	29	26	19	1	63	0	1	1	4	2	.67	7	.241	.314	.391
1991	Edmonton	AAA	Cal	76	245	55	14	1	5	86	39	32	31	1	66	5	4	2	5	0	1.00	4	.224	.322	.351
1992	Edmonton	AAA	Cal	49	149	38	9	3	3	62	28	25	28	0	32	3	4	2	3	5	.38	3	.255	.379	.416
1993	Palm Spring	A+	Cal	2	7	0	0	0	0	0	0	0	1	0	1	0	0	0	0	0	.00	0	.000	.125	.000
1994	Richmond	AAA	Atl	36	81	10	3	0	1	16	3	2	5	0	30	0	0	1	0	0	.00	3	.123	.172	.198
1995	Richmond	AAA	Atl	17	50	9	3	0	1	15	6	6	3	0	22	1	1	1	2	2	.50	1	.180	.236	.300
	Norfolk	AAA	NYN	56	170	49	8	0	3	66	20	20	14	0	45	3	0	0	1	3	.25	4	.288	.353	.388
1996	Vancouver	AAA	Cal	6	18	1	0	0	0	1	0	0	2	0	5	0	0	0	0	0	.00	0	.056	.150	.056
1989	California	AL		16	39	7	1	0	0	8	4	4	2	0	17	0	1	0	0	0	.00	0	.179	.220	.205
1990	California	AL		31	84	16	5	0	1	24	8	6	5	0	31	1	2	0	0	1	.00	2	.190	.244	.286
1991	California	AL		29	69	14	4	0	0	18	7	3	10	0	17	1	4	0	0	1	.00	2	.203	.313	.261
1992	California	AL		43	114	25	3	0	2	34	11	12	7	0	32	2	2	0	1	1	.50	1	.219	.276	.298
1993	California	AL		37	95	18	5	0	1	26	5	4	7	0	24	1	2	0	1	2	.33	1	.189	.252	.274
10	Min. YEARS			515	1657	378	80	12	38	596	250	228	219	4	509	37	19	16	28	17	.62	36	.228	.329	.360
5	Maj. YEARS			156	401	80	18	0	4	110	35	29	31	0	121	5	11	0	2	5	.29	6	.200	.265	.274

Willis Otanez

Bats: Right **Throws:** Right **Pos:** 3B **Ht:** 5'11" **Wt:** 150 **Born:** 4/19/73 **Age:** 24

				BATTING															BASERUNNING				PERCENTAGES		
Year	Team	Lg	Org	G	AB	H	2B	3B	HR	TB	R	RBI	TBB	IBB	SO	HBP	SH	SF	SB	CS	SB%	GDP	Avg	OBP	SLG
1991	Great Falls	R+	LA	58	222	64	9	2	6	95	38	39	19	0	34	2	1	4	3	3	.50	7	.288	.344	.428
1992	Vero Beach	A+	LA	117	390	86	18	0	3	113	27	27	24	0	60	4	5	3	2	4	.33	10	.221	.271	.290
1993	Bakersfield	A+	LA	95	325	85	11	2	10	130	34	39	29	1	63	2	4	2	1	4	.20	9	.262	.324	.400
1994	Vero Beach	A+	LA	131	476	132	27	1	19	218	77	72	53	2	98	4	0	7	4	2	.67	10	.277	.350	.458
1995	Vero Beach	A+	LA	92	354	92	24	0	10	146	39	53	28	3	59	2	0	5	1	1	.50	15	.260	.314	.412
	San Antonio	AA	LA	27	100	24	4	1	1	33	8	7	6	0	25	0	0	2	0	1	.00	3	.240	.278	.330
1996	Bowie	AA	Bal	138	506	134	27	2	24	237	60	75	45	2	97	1	2	5	3	7	.30	17	.265	.323	.468
6	Min. YEARS			658	2373	617	120	8	73	972	283	312	204	8	436	15	12	28	14	22	.39	71	.260	.319	.410

Spike Owen

Bats: Both **Throws:** Right **Pos:** SS **Ht:** 5'10" **Wt:** 170 **Born:** 4/19/61 **Age:** 36

				BATTING															BASERUNNING				PERCENTAGES		
Year	Team	Lg	Org	G	AB	H	2B	3B	HR	TB	R	RBI	TBB	IBB	SO	HBP	SH	SF	SB	CS	SB%	GDP	Avg	OBP	SLG
1982	Lynn	AA	Sea	78	241	64	9	2	1	80	32	27	44	-	33	1	7	0	18	8	.69	-	.266	.381	.332
1983	Salt Lake	AAA	Sea	72	256	68	8	9	1	97	58	32	57	-	23	0	4	2	22	7	.76	-	.266	.397	.379
1995	Lk Elsinore	A+	Cal	3	10	2	1	0	0	3	1	0	2	0	2	0	0	0	0	0	.00	0	.200	.333	.300
1996	Okla. City	AAA	Tex	2	4	0	0	0	0	0	0	0	0	0	0	0	0	0	0	0	.00	0	.000	.000	.000
1983	Seattle	AL		80	306	60	11	3	2	83	36	21	24	0	44	2	5	3	10	6	.63	2	.196	.257	.271
1984	Seattle	AL		152	530	130	18	8	3	173	67	43	46	0	63	3	9	2	16	8	.67	5	.245	.308	.326
1985	Seattle	AL		118	352	91	10	6	6	131	41	37	34	0	27	0	5	2	11	5	.69	5	.259	.322	.372
1986	Seattle	AL		112	402	99	22	6	0	133	46	35	34	1	42	1	7	2	1	3	.25	11	.246	.305	.331
	Boston	AL		42	126	23	2	1	1	30	21	10	17	0	9	1	2	1	3	1	.75	2	.183	.283	.238
1987	Boston	AL		132	437	113	17	7	2	150	50	48	53	2	43	1	9	4	11	8	.58	9	.259	.337	.343
1988	Boston	AL		89	257	64	14	1	5	95	40	18	27	0	27	2	7	1	0	1	.00	7	.249	.324	.370
1989	Montreal	NL		142	437	102	17	4	6	145	52	41	76	25	44	3	3	3	3	2	.60	11	.233	.349	.332
1990	Montreal	NL		149	453	106	24	5	5	155	55	35	70	12	60	0	5	5	8	6	.57	6	.234	.333	.342
1991	Montreal	NL		139	424	108	22	8	3	155	39	26	42	11	61	1	4	4	2	6	.25	11	.255	.321	.366
1992	Montreal	NL		122	386	104	16	3	7	147	52	40	50	3	30	0	4	6	9	4	.69	10	.269	.348	.381
1993	New York	AL		103	334	78	16	2	2	104	41	20	29	2	30	0	3	1	3	2	.60	6	.234	.294	.311
1994	California	AL		82	268	83	17	2	3	113	30	37	49	0	17	1	3	0	2	8	.20	4	.310	.418	.422
1995	California	AL		82	218	50	9	3	1	68	17	28	18	1	22	0	1	0	3	2	.60	7	.229	.288	.312
4	Min. YEARS			155	511	134	18	11	2	180	91	59	103	0	58	1	11	2	40	15	.73	0	.262	.386	.352
13	Maj. YEARS			1544	4930	1211	215	59	46	1682	587	439	569	57	519	15	67	34	82	62	.57	96	.246	.324	.341

Billy Owens

Bats: Both **Throws:** Right **Pos:** 1B **Ht:** 6'1" **Wt:** 210 **Born:** 4/12/71 **Age:** 26

				BATTING															BASERUNNING				PERCENTAGES		
Year	Team	Lg	Org	G	AB	H	2B	3B	HR	TB	R	RBI	TBB	IBB	SO	HBP	SH	SF	SB	CS	SB%	GDP	Avg	OBP	SLG
1992	Kane County	A	Bal	73	283	72	16	0	2	94	23	33	26	1	63	0	2	4	4	3	.57	2	.254	.313	.332
1993	Albany	A	Bal	120	458	136	23	2	11	196	64	66	49	6	70	2	1	5	3	5	.38	8	.297	.364	.428
	Frederick	A+	Bal	17	60	21	4	0	0	25	8	8	3	0	8	0	0	1	0	0	.00	2	.350	.375	.417
1994	Bowie	AA	Bal	43	145	33	7	1	4	54	13	19	10	1	37	0	0	1	1	0	1.00	3	.228	.276	.372
	Frederick	A+	Bal	86	324	74	16	0	13	129	50	52	44	5	73	1	0	1	1	1	.50	3	.228	.322	.398
1995	Rochester	AAA	Bal	9	28	4	0	0	0	4	2	1	1	0	6	0	0	0	0	0	.00	0	.143	.172	.143
	Bowie	AA	Bal	122	453	122	27	0	17	200	57	91	43	6	87	1	0	8	2	1	.67	13	.269	.329	.442
1996	Orioles	R	Bal	6	18	3	0	0	0	3	0	3	0	0	4	0	0	1	0	0	.00	1	.167	.158	.167
	Rochester	AAA	Bal	61	201	51	14	0	5	80	19	30	10	0	35	1	0	2	2	2	.50	6	.254	.290	.398
5	Min. YEARS			537	1970	516	107	3	52	785	236	303	186	19	383	5	3	23	13	12	.52	38	.262	.324	.398

Scotty Pace

Pitches: Left **Bats:** Left **Pos:** P **Ht:** 6'4" **Wt:** 210 **Born:** 9/16/71 **Age:** 25

				HOW MUCH HE PITCHED						WHAT HE GAVE UP												THE RESULTS					
Year	Team	Lg	Org	G	GS	CG	GF	IP	BFP	H	R	ER	HR	SH	SF	HB	TBB	IBB	SO	WP	Bk	W	L	Pct.	ShO	Sv	ERA
1994	Elmira	A-	Fla	13	12	2	0	70.2	307	73	35	32	3	3	0	1	27	2	50	7	0	3	7	.300	0	0	4.08
1995	Hagerstown	A	Tor	11	6	2	2	57.2	211	32	8	7	2	1	0	2	12	0	57	4	0	4	2	.667	1	1	1.09
	Knoxville	AA	Tor	29	24	3	2	160	673	149	74	59	10	7	6	6	60	3	128	11	0	10	10	.500	2	1	3.32
1996	Dunedin	A+	Tor	19	0	0	12	30.1	123	24	7	6	0	2	0	3	13	1	20	3	0	0	0	.000	0	6	1.78
	Syracuse	AAA	Tor	20	5	1	11	51.2	227	53	37	29	4	0	1	2	27	0	35	4	0	3	3	.500	0	0	5.05
	Knoxville	AA	Tor	4	1	0	0	12	49	8	4	4	2	0	1	0	6	0	5	1	0	2	0	1.000	0	0	3.00
3 Min. YEARS				96	48	8	27	382.1	1590	339	165	137	21	13	8	14	145	6	295	30	0	22	22	.500	3	8	3.22

Scott Pagano

Bats: Both **Throws:** Right **Pos:** OF **Ht:** 5'11" **Wt:** 175 **Born:** 4/26/71 **Age:** 26

				BATTING															BASERUNNING				PERCENTAGES		
Year	Team	Lg	Org	G	AB	H	2B	3B	HR	TB	R	RBI	TBB	IBB	SO	HBP	SH	SF	SB	CS	SB%	GDP	Avg	OBP	SLG
1992	Niagara Fal	A-	Det	67	193	47	9	2	1	63	17	22	14	1	27	4	3	2	6	10	.38	7	.244	.305	.326
1993	Niagara Fal	A-	Det	5	6	1	0	0	1	4	1	3	1	0	0	0	0	0	1	0	1.00	1	.167	.286	.667
1994	Ohio Valley	IND	—	58	232	89	19	1	7	131	62	31	32	2	29	2	1	1	53	17	.76	4	.384	.461	.565
1995	Durham	A+	Atl	110	354	94	12	1	1	111	47	26	38	5	75	5	7	1	41	21	.66	8	.266	.344	.314
1996	Binghamton	AA	NYN	126	464	120	15	3	1	144	63	46	43	3	55	7	9	2	26	16	.62	11	.259	.329	.310
5 Min. YEARS				366	1249	351	55	7	11	453	190	128	128	11	186	18	20	6	127	64	.66	31	.281	.355	.363

Javier Pages

Bats: Right **Throws:** Right **Pos:** C **Ht:** 6'0" **Wt:** 190 **Born:** 7/27/71 **Age:** 25

				BATTING															BASERUNNING				PERCENTAGES		
Year	Team	Lg	Org	G	AB	H	2B	3B	HR	TB	R	RBI	TBB	IBB	SO	HBP	SH	SF	SB	CS	SB%	GDP	Avg	OBP	SLG
1990	Expos	R	Mon	34	104	23	8	0	2	37	14	17	11	0	27	2	0	4	0	3	.00	1	.221	.298	.356
1991	Expos	R	Mon	42	140	34	4	1	0	40	16	15	19	0	39	3	1	0	1	1	.50	1	.243	.346	.286
1992	Albany	A	Mon	70	246	47	5	0	4	64	24	24	20	0	87	3	1	1	2	1	.67	3	.191	.259	.260
1993	Burlington	A	Mon	96	295	77	20	0	7	118	35	47	44	0	74	3	7	4	2	2	.50	1	.261	.358	.400
1994	W. Palm Bch	A+	Mon	19	57	17	5	0	2	28	10	9	11	0	18	1	0	1	0	0	.00	0	.298	.414	.491
	High Desert	A+	Mon	34	101	19	0	0	3	28	8	14	11	1	32	2	0	1	0	0	.00	4	.188	.278	.277
1995	Rio Grande	IND	—	13	29	5	1	0	1	9	2	5	7	0	9	3	0	1	0	0	.00	0	.172	.375	.310
1996	St. Pete	A+	StL	39	106	24	7	1	3	42	14	8	22	1	29	1	2	0	1	1	.50	3	.226	.364	.396
	Arkansas	AA	StL	26	46	12	2	0	1	17	3	7	3	0	11	0	0	0	0	0	.00	0	.261	.306	.370
7 Min. YEARS				373	1124	258	52	2	23	383	126	146	148	2	326	18	11	12	6	8	.43	13	.230	.326	.341

Erik Pappas

Bats: Right **Throws:** Right **Pos:** C **Ht:** 6' 0" **Wt:** 190 **Born:** 4/25/66 **Age:** 31

				BATTING															BASERUNNING				PERCENTAGES		
Year	Team	Lg	Org	G	AB	H	2B	3B	HR	TB	R	RBI	TBB	IBB	SO	HBP	SH	SF	SB	CS	SB%	GDP	Avg	OBP	SLG
1984	Salem	A-	Cal	56	177	43	3	3	1	55	24	15	31	0	26	3	3	1	10	5	.67	1	.243	.363	.311
1985	Quad City	A	Cal	100	317	76	8	4	2	98	53	29	61	1	56	3	3	1	16	6	.73	3	.240	.366	.309
1986	Palm Spring	A+	Cal	74	248	61	16	2	5	96	40	38	56	1	58	1	1	4	9	5	.64	7	.246	.382	.387
1987	Palm Spring	A+	Cal	119	395	96	20	3	3	131	50	64	66	0	77	0	3	7	16	6	.73	8	.243	.346	.332
1988	Midland	AA	Cal	83	275	76	17	2	4	109	40	38	29	0	53	2	4	4	16	3	.84	6	.276	.345	.396
1989	Charlotte	AA	ChN	119	354	106	31	1	16	187	69	49	66	1	50	8	4	2	7	8	.47	8	.299	.419	.528
1990	Iowa	AAA	ChN	131	405	101	19	2	16	172	56	55	65	1	84	8	6	3	6	5	.55	13	.249	.362	.425
1991	Iowa	AAA	ChN	88	284	78	19	1	7	120	41	48	45	4	47	4	4	3	5	3	.63	12	.275	.378	.423
1992	Omaha	AAA	KC	45	138	30	8	1	1	43	18	11	25	1	23	0	1	2	4	1	.80	3	.217	.333	.312
	Vancouver	AAA	ChA	37	98	27	4	0	4	43	17	17	14	0	17	2	1	2	4	0	1.00	3	.276	.371	.439
1993	Louisville	AAA	StL	21	71	24	6	1	4	44	19	13	11	0	12	0	0	0	0	2	.00	1	.338	.427	.620
1994	Louisville	AAA	StL	64	206	41	7	2	7	73	33	30	29	0	44	5	0	3	2	3	.40	5	.199	.309	.354
1995	Charlotte	AAA	Fla	122	389	86	28	3	10	150	48	52	61	0	78	6	1	4	10	7	.59	11	.221	.333	.386
1996	Okla. City	AAA	Tex	107	330	68	15	0	5	98	38	36	63	3	69	1	3	7	3	8	.27	7	.206	.329	.297
1991	Chicago	NL		7	17	3	0	0	0	3	1	2	1	0	5	0	0	0	0	0	.00	0	.176	.222	.176
1993	St. Louis	NL		82	228	63	12	0	1	78	25	28	35	2	35	0	0	3	1	3	.25	7	.276	.368	.342
1994	St. Louis	NL		15	44	4	1	0	0	5	8	5	10	0	13	1	0	3	0	0	.00	1	.091	.259	.114
13 Min. YEARS				1166	3687	913	201	25	85	1419	546	495	622	12	694	43	34	43	108	62	.64	88	.248	.359	.385
3 Maj. YEARS				104	289	70	13	0	1	86	34	35	46	2	53	1	0	6	1	3	.25	8	.242	.342	.298

Manny Patel

Bats: Left **Throws:** Right **Pos:** 2B **Ht:** 5'10" **Wt:** 165 **Born:** 4/22/72 **Age:** 25

				BATTING															BASERUNNING				PERCENTAGES		
Year	Team	Lg	Org	G	AB	H	2B	3B	HR	TB	R	RBI	TBB	IBB	SO	HBP	SH	SF	SB	CS	SB%	GDP	Avg	OBP	SLG
1993	Bellingham	A-	Sea	66	227	53	8	0	3	70	41	38	54	3	43	7	2	4	12	9	.57	1	.233	.390	.308
1994	Appleton	A	Sea	95	315	79	9	4	1	99	48	28	27	1	42	9	5	1	5	9	.36	6	.251	.327	.314
1995	Riverside	A+	Sea	83	274	78	8	6	0	98	45	32	33	0	30	5	1	1	9	4	.69	5	.285	.371	.358
1996	Port City	AA	Sea	126	369	81	9	1	1	95	48	32	56	1	51	4	4	4	12	6	.67	5	.220	.326	.257
4 Min. YEARS				370	1185	291	34	11	5	362	182	130	170	5	166	25	12	10	38	28	.58	17	.246	.350	.305

Bronswell Patrick

Pitches: Right **Bats:** Right **Pos:** P **Ht:** 6'1" **Wt:** 205 **Born:** 9/16/70 **Age:** 26

			HOW MUCH HE PITCHED						WHAT HE GAVE UP												THE RESULTS					
Year	Team	Lg Org	G	GS	CG	GF	IP	BFP	H	R	ER	HR	SH	SF	HB	TBB	IBB	SO	WP	Bk	W	L	Pct.	ShO	Sv	ERA
1988	Athletics	R Oak	14	13	2	0	96.1	390	99	37	32	7	1	2	2	16	1	64	1	2	8	3	.727	0	0	2.99
1989	Madison	A Oak	12	10	0	1	54.1	238	62	29	22	3	2	0	0	14	0	32	3	2	2	5	.286	0	0	3.64
1990	Modesto	A+ Oak	14	14	0	0	74.2	340	92	58	43	10	3	1	4	32	0	37	5	1	3	7	.300	0	0	5.18
	Madison	A Oak	13	12	3	0	80	337	88	44	32	6	5	4	1	19	0	40	3	0	3	7	.300	0	0	3.60
1991	Modesto	A+ Oak	28	26	3	1	169.2	716	158	77	61	9	4	4	1	60	4	95	7	0	12	12	.500	1	0	3.24
1992	Huntsville	AA Oak	29	29	3	0	179.1	758	187	84	75	20	1	3	4	46	0	98	3	0	13	7	.650	0	0	3.76
1993	Tacoma	AAA Oak	35	13	1	12	104.2	496	156	87	82	12	3	12	4	42	3	56	3	0	3	8	.273	0	1	7.05
1994	Huntsville	AA Oak	7	3	0	1	27.2	120	31	11	9	2	1	0	2	10	0	16	1	1	2	0	1.000	0	1	2.93
	Tacoma	AAA Oak	30	0	0	9	47.1	208	50	31	25	5	3	1	0	20	2	38	2	0	1	1	.500	0	2	4.75
1995	Tucson	AAA Hou	43	4	0	10	81.2	352	91	42	38	3	2	3	1	21	1	62	4	0	5	1	.833	0	1	4.19
1996	Tucson	AAA Hou	33	15	0	2	118	521	137	59	46	7	1	14	0	33	4	82	1	0	7	3	.700	0	1	3.51
9	Min. YEARS		258	139	12	36	1033.2	4476	1151	559	465	84	26	44	19	313	15	620	33	6	59	54	.522	1	6	4.05

Ken Patterson

Pitches: Left **Bats:** Left **Pos:** P **Ht:** 6' 4" **Wt:** 222 **Born:** 7/8/64 **Age:** 32

			HOW MUCH HE PITCHED						WHAT HE GAVE UP												THE RESULTS					
Year	Team	Lg Org	G	GS	CG	GF	IP	BFP	H	R	ER	HR	SH	SF	HB	TBB	IBB	SO	WP	Bk	W	L	Pct.	ShO	Sv	ERA
1985	Oneonta	A- NYA	6	6	0	0	22.1	103	23	14	12	0	1	0	2	14	0	21	1	0	2	2	.500	0	0	4.84
1986	Ft. Laud	A+ NYA	5	5	0	0	18.2	100	30	20	16	2	0	0	3	16	0	13	2	0	0	2	.000	0	0	7.71
	Oneonta	A- NYA	15	15	5	0	100.1	399	67	25	15	2	1	1	4	45	0	102	7	1	9	3	.750	4	0	1.35
1987	Ft. Laud	A+ NYA	9	9	0	0	42.2	202	46	34	30	0	1	2	2	31	0	36	5	1	1	3	.250	0	0	6.33
	Albany-Colo	AA NYA	24	8	1	14	63.2	272	59	31	28	2	3	3	2	31	1	47	4	0	3	6	.333	0	5	3.96
	Hawaii	AAA ChA	3	0	0	3	3.1	14	1	0	0	0	0	0	0	3	0	5	0	0	0	0	.000	0	2	0.00
1988	Vancouver	AAA ChA	55	4	1	23	86.1	349	64	37	31	4	5	4	2	36	7	89	7	2	6	5	.545	0	13	3.23
1989	Vancouver	AAA ChA	2	2	0	0	9	35	6	2	1	0	1	1	1	1	0	17	2	0	0	1	.000	0	0	1.00
1992	Peoria	A ChN	2	0	0	1	3	16	5	4	4	0	0	0	0	2	0	5	0	0	0	0	.000	0	0	12.00
	Iowa	AAA ChN	1	0	0	0	1.2	11	4	4	4	2	1	0	1	1	0	1	0	0	0	1	.000	0	0	21.60
1994	Vancouver	AAA Cal	3	0	0	1	5.2	30	5	7	6	0	0	1	0	6	0	5	0	0	0	0	.000	0	0	9.53
1995	Lk Elsinore	A+ Cal	6	0	0	2	9.2	35	7	0	0	0	0	0	0	1	0	9	1	0	0	0	.000	0	1	0.00
	Angels	R Cal	1	1	0	0	3	10	0	0	0	0	0	0	0	1	0	3	0	0	0	0	.000	0	0	0.00
	Vancouver	AAA Cal	15	1	0	5	23.2	91	19	1	1	0	0	0	0	6	1	16	2	0	0	0	.000	0	2	0.38
1996	Tyler	IND —	20	1	0	15	25.1	105	22	7	6	0	1	1	0	5	0	28	3	0	1	1	.500	0	6	2.13
	Omaha	AAA KC	16	0	0	2	20	79	16	5	4	2	1	0	0	4	0	13	1	0	0	1	.000	0	1	1.80
1988	Chicago	AL	9	2	0	3	20.2	92	25	11	11	2	0	0	0	7	0	8	1	1	0	2	.000	0	1	4.79
1989	Chicago	AL	50	1	0	18	65.2	284	64	37	33	11	1	4	2	28	3	43	3	1	6	1	.857	0	0	4.52
1990	Chicago	AL	43	0	0	15	66.1	283	58	27	25	6	2	5	2	34	1	40	2	0	2	1	.667	0	2	3.39
1991	Chicago	AL	43	0	0	13	63.2	265	48	22	20	5	3	2	1	35	1	32	2	0	3	0	1.000	0	1	2.83
1992	Chicago	NL	32	1	0	4	41.2	191	41	25	18	7	6	4	1	27	6	23	3	1	2	3	.400	0	0	3.89
1993	California	AL	46	0	0	9	59	255	54	30	30	7	2	1	0	35	5	36	2	0	1	1	.500	0	1	4.58
1994	California	AL	1	0	0	0	0.2	2	0	0	0	0	0	0	0	0	0	1	0	0	0	0	.000	0	0	0.00
9	Min. YEARS		183	52	7	66	438.1	1851	374	191	158	14	15	13	17	203	9	410	35	4	22	25	.468	4	30	3.24
7	Maj. YEARS		224	4	0	62	317.2	1372	290	152	137	38	14	16	6	166	16	183	13	3	14	8	.636	0	5	3.88

Greg Patton

Bats: Right **Throws:** Right **Pos:** 3B **Ht:** 6'4" **Wt:** 190 **Born:** 3/8/72 **Age:** 25

			BATTING														BASERUNNING				PERCENTAGES		
Year	Team	Lg Org	G	AB	H	2B	3B	HR	TB	R	RBI	TBB	IBB	SO	HBP	SH	SF	SB	CS	SB%	GDP	Avg	OBP	SLG
1993	Red Sox	R Bos	4	16	9	2	0	0	11	6	5	2	0	2	0	0	0	0	2	.00	0	.563	.611	.688
	Utica	A- Bos	54	169	38	8	1	3	57	22	24	23	1	45	4	3	1	0	2	.00	0	.225	.330	.337
1994	Lynchburg	A+ Bos	63	216	48	8	3	6	80	30	21	27	0	49	1	1	1	0	1	.00	5	.222	.310	.370
1995	Sarasota	A+ Bos	8	23	5	0	0	0	5	1	0	2	0	8	0	0	0	0	0	.00	0	.217	.280	.217
	Michigan	A Bos	69	226	56	13	0	9	96	34	27	31	2	58	2	2	2	4	3	.57	2	.248	.341	.425
1996	Trenton	AA Bos	6	16	3	1	0	0	4	3	1	4	0	4	0	0	0	0	1	.00	0	.188	.350	.250
	Sarasota	A+ Bos	80	275	67	16	2	3	96	31	24	35	1	64	4	1	2	2	3	.40	5	.244	.335	.349
4	Min. YEARS		284	941	226	48	6	21	349	127	102	124	4	230	11	7	6	6	12	.33	12	.240	.334	.371

Jeff Patzke

Bats: Both **Throws:** Right **Pos:** 2B **Ht:** 6'0" **Wt:** 170 **Born:** 11/19/73 **Age:** 23

			BATTING														BASERUNNING				PERCENTAGES		
Year	Team	Lg Org	G	AB	H	2B	3B	HR	TB	R	RBI	TBB	IBB	SO	HBP	SH	SF	SB	CS	SB%	GDP	Avg	OBP	SLG
1992	Blue Jays	R Tor	6	21	2	0	0	0	2	3	1	3	0	2	0	0	0	0	1	.00	0	.095	.208	.095
	Medicne Hat	R+ Tor	59	193	42	4	0	2	52	19	17	17	0	42	0	3	0	3	1	.75	4	.218	.281	.269
1993	Medicne Hat	R+ Tor	71	273	80	11	2	1	98	45	22	34	1	31	2	3	1	5	7	.42	5	.293	.374	.359
1994	Hagerstown	A Tor	80	271	55	10	1	4	79	43	22	36	1	57	3	2	3	7	3	.70	4	.203	.300	.292
1995	Dunedin	A+ Tor	129	470	124	32	6	11	201	68	75	85	8	81	2	1	2	5	3	.63	10	.264	.377	.428
1996	Knoxville	AA Tor	124	429	130	31	4	4	181	70	66	80	6	103	6	0	2	6	5	.55	2	.303	.418	.422
5	Min. YEARS		469	1657	433	88	13	22	613	248	203	255	16	316	13	9	8	26	20	.57	25	.261	.363	.370

Andy Paul

Pitches: Right **Bats:** Right **Pos:** P **Ht:** 6'4" **Wt:** 195 **Born:** 9/4/71 **Age:** 25

HOW MUCH HE PITCHED									WHAT HE GAVE UP												THE RESULTS					
Year Team	Lg Org	G	GS	CG	GF	IP	BFP	H	R	ER	HR	SH	SF	HB	TBB	IBB	SO	WP	Bk	W	L	Pct.	ShO	Sv	ERA
1992 Helena	R+ Mil	13	4	0	3	32.1	158	45	31	26	3	0	0	2	21	0	41	7	3	3	0	1.000	0	1	7.24
1993 Brewers	R Mil	5	5	2	0	36	141	18	7	5	0	0	0	1	9	0	55	3	0	4	1	.800	2	0	1.25
Beloit	A Mil	8	8	1	0	54.2	238	53	22	18	1	2	1	1	30	0	52	5	0	1	3	.250	0	0	2.96
1994 Stockton	A+ Mil	16	7	0	4	49	223	56	30	21	4	2	4	1	19	1	38	7	2	3	4	.429	0	1	3.86
1995 Stockton	A+ Mil	38	13	0	11	106.1	473	116	59	48	7	5	1	8	42	4	87	6	3	7	5	.583	0	1	4.06
1996 El Paso	AA Mil	38	7	0	16	95.1	426	105	60	50	4	5	1	1	43	2	72	8	2	5	6	.455	0	3	4.72
5 Min. YEARS		118	44	3	34	373.2	1659	393	209	168	19	14	7	14	164	7	345	36	10	23	19	.548	2	6	4.05

Carl Pavano

Pitches: Right **Bats:** Right **Pos:** P **Ht:** 6'5" **Wt:** 225 **Born:** 1/8/76 **Age:** 21

HOW MUCH HE PITCHED									WHAT HE GAVE UP												THE RESULTS					
Year Team	Lg Org	G	GS	CG	GF	IP	BFP	H	R	ER	HR	SH	SF	HB	TBB	IBB	SO	WP	Bk	W	L	Pct.	ShO	Sv	ERA
1994 Red Sox	R Bos	9	7	0	0	44	176	31	14	9	1	0	1	1	7	0	47	4	1	4	3	.571	0	0	1.84
1995 Michigan	A Bos	22	22	1	0	141.1	591	118	63	54	7	6	7	6	52	0	138	9	0	6	6	.500	0	0	3.44
1996 Trenton	AA Bos	27	26	6	1	185	741	154	66	54	16	5	7	11	47	2	146	7	1	16	5	.762	2	0	2.63
3 Min. YEARS		58	55	7	1	370.1	1508	303	143	117	24	11	15	18	106	2	331	20	2	26	14	.650	2	0	2.84

Jay Payton

Bats: Right **Throws:** Right **Pos:** DH **Ht:** 5'10" **Wt:** 190 **Born:** 11/22/72 **Age:** 24

BATTING																BASERUNNING				PERCENTAGES		
Year Team	Lg Org	G	AB	H	2B	3B	HR	TB	R	RBI	TBB	IBB	SO	HBP	SH	SF	SB	CS	SB%	GDP	Avg	OBP	SLG
1994 Pittsfield	A- NYN	58	219	80	16	2	3	109	47	37	23	2	18	9	0	4	10	2	.83	1	.365	.439	.498
Binghamton	AA NYN	8	25	7	1	0	0	8	3	1	2	0	3	1	0	0	1	1	.50	1	.280	.357	.320
1995 Binghamton	AA NYN	85	357	123	20	3	14	191	59	54	29	2	32	2	0	2	16	7	.70	11	.345	.395	.535
Norfolk	AAA NYN	50	196	47	11	4	4	78	33	30	11	0	22	2	4	2	11	3	.79	5	.240	.284	.398
1996 Mets	R NYN	3	13	5	1	0	1	9	3	2	0	0	1	0	0	0	1	0	1.00	0	.385	.385	.692
Binghamton	AA NYN	4	10	2	0	0	0	2	0	2	2	1	2	0	0	2	0	1	.00	0	.200	.286	.200
St. Lucie	A+ NYN	9	26	8	2	0	0	10	4	1	4	1	5	0	0	0	2	1	.67	1	.308	.400	.385
Norfolk	AAA NYN	55	153	47	6	3	6	77	30	26	11	1	25	3	0	1	10	1	.91	3	.307	.363	.503
3 Min. YEARS		272	999	319	57	12	28	484	179	153	82	7	108	17	4	11	51	16	.76	22	.319	.377	.484

Eddie Pearson

Bats: Both **Throws:** Right **Pos:** 1B **Ht:** 6'3" **Wt:** 225 **Born:** 1/31/74 **Age:** 23

BATTING																BASERUNNING				PERCENTAGES		
Year Team	Lg Org	G	AB	H	2B	3B	HR	TB	R	RBI	TBB	IBB	SO	HBP	SH	SF	SB	CS	SB%	GDP	Avg	OBP	SLG
1992 White Sox	R ChA	28	102	24	5	0	0	29	10	12	9	1	17	2	0	1	1	3	.25	3	.235	.307	.284
1993 Hickory	A ChA	87	343	83	15	3	4	116	37	40	20	0	59	1	5	1	5	1	.83	8	.242	.285	.338
South Bend	A ChA	48	190	62	16	0	1	81	23	26	13	2	29	1	0	3	0	1	.00	1	.326	.367	.426
1994 Pr. William	A+ ChA	130	502	139	28	3	12	209	58	80	45	1	80	3	0	3	0	0	.00	11	.277	.338	.416
1995 White Sox	R ChA	6	20	6	2	0	1	11	7	6	3	0	2	0	0	0	0	0	.00	0	.300	.391	.550
Birmingham	AA ChA	50	201	45	13	0	2	64	20	25	7	0	36	1	0	2	1	0	1.00	9	.224	.251	.318
1996 Birmingham	AA ChA	85	323	72	20	0	8	116	38	40	31	3	57	2	0	3	2	2	.50	6	.223	.292	.359
5 Min. YEARS		434	1681	431	99	6	28	626	193	229	128	7	280	10	5	13	9	7	.56	38	.256	.311	.372

Aldo Pecorilli

Bats: Right **Throws:** Right **Pos:** 1B **Ht:** 5'11" **Wt:** 185 **Born:** 9/12/70 **Age:** 26

BATTING																BASERUNNING				PERCENTAGES		
Year Team	Lg Org	G	AB	H	2B	3B	HR	TB	R	RBI	TBB	IBB	SO	HBP	SH	SF	SB	CS	SB%	GDP	Avg	OBP	SLG
1992 Johnson Cty	R+ StL	54	201	65	14	2	6	101	36	41	25	1	21	2	0	2	6	2	.75	4	.323	.400	.502
1993 Savannah	A StL	141	515	157	30	7	14	243	75	93	81	7	86	6	0	8	16	11	.59	5	.305	.400	.472
1994 St. Pete	A+ StL	135	508	141	26	3	18	227	76	78	56	4	69	4	1	3	13	9	.59	7	.278	.352	.447
1995 Greenville	AA Atl	70	265	102	17	2	7	144	51	42	22	2	39	6	1	4	2	8	.20	4	.385	.438	.543
Richmond	AAA Atl	49	127	33	3	0	6	54	16	17	19	2	20	2	2	0	0	0	.00	5	.260	.365	.425
1996 Richmond	AAA Atl	122	403	117	27	0	15	189	61	62	31	1	87	3	1	3	5	6	.45	8	.290	.343	.469
5 Min. YEARS		571	2019	615	117	14	66	958	315	333	234	17	322	23	5	20	42	36	.54	33	.305	.380	.474

Rod Pedraza

Pitches: Right **Bats:** Right **Pos:** P **Ht:** 6'2" **Wt:** 210 **Born:** 12/28/69 **Age:** 27

HOW MUCH HE PITCHED									WHAT HE GAVE UP												THE RESULTS					
Year Team	Lg Org	G	GS	CG	GF	IP	BFP	H	R	ER	HR	SH	SF	HB	TBB	IBB	SO	WP	Bk	W	L	Pct.	ShO	Sv	ERA
1991 Jamestown	A- Mon	7	7	1	0	44	182	41	16	10	3	0	1	1	6	0	30	2	1	3	1	.750	1	0	2.05
Sumter	A Mon	8	8	1	0	49	212	61	29	24	3	0	3	1	10	0	22	5	1	2	2	.500	0	0	4.41
1992 Albany	A Mon	27	26	2	0	176.2	742	187	90	64	7	4	8	9	30	0	106	10	5	13	8	.619	0	0	3.26
1993 San Bernrdo	A+ Mon	24	23	2	0	141.2	601	145	74	50	7	4	7	3	33	1	95	9	0	9	7	.563	1	0	3.18
1994 Colo. Sprng	AAA Col	7	7	0	0	33	175	60	37	34	2	0	3	2	13	0	20	3	0	1	3	.250	0	0	9.27
New Haven	AA Col	22	20	4	0	127.2	528	129	59	46	2	5	3	3	23	2	58	0	1	13	3	.813	2	0	3.24
1996 New Haven	AA Col	19	18	3	0	122	488	115	49	40	10	2	4	2	21	3	74	1	1	7	3	.700	2	0	2.95
Colo. Sprng	AAA Col	6	5	0	0	28	125	39	26	26	3	1	0	2	4	0	13	0	0	1	1	.500	0	0	8.36
5 Min. YEARS		120	114	13	0	722	3053	777	380	294	37	16	29	23	140	6	418	30	9	49	28	.636	6	0	3.66

Julio Peguero

Bats: Both **Throws:** Right **Pos:** OF **Ht:** 6' 0" **Wt:** 160 **Born:** 9/7/68 **Age:** 28

				BATTING															BASERUNNING				PERCENTAGES		
Year	Team	Lg	Org	G	AB	H	2B	3B	HR	TB	R	RBI	TBB	IBB	SO	HBP	SH	SF	SB	CS	SB%	GDP	Avg	OBP	SLG
1987	Macon	A	Pit	132	520	148	11	6	4	183	88	53	56	3	76	1	1	4	23	9	.72	5	.285	.353	.352
1988	Salem	A+	Pit	128	517	135	17	5	5	177	89	50	64	3	81	5	2	1	43	11	.80	11	.261	.348	.342
1989	Harrisburg	AA	Pit	76	284	70	14	1	2	92	34	21	29	0	39	2	1	0	14	12	.54	5	.246	.321	.324
1990	Harrisburg	AA	Pit	104	411	116	14	9	1	151	40	26	29	1	53	0	0	2	8	12	.40	17	.282	.328	.367
	Reading	AA	Phi	3	12	1	0	0	0	1	0	2	2	0	1	0	0	0	0	0	.00	0	.083	.214	.083
1991	Scranton-WB	AAA	Phi	133	506	138	20	9	2	182	71	39	40	3	71	1	5	2	21	14	.60	12	.273	.326	.360
1992	Scranton-WB	AAA	Phi	74	289	74	14	2	1	95	41	21	24	2	56	2	2	2	14	15	.48	5	.256	.315	.329
	Albuquerque	AAA	LA	30	76	20	4	0	1	27	13	8	13	0	13	2	2	1	1	1	.50	1	.263	.380	.355
1993	Canton-Akrn	AA	Cle	65	177	40	6	5	0	56	19	14	17	1	32	1	4	1	4	1	.80	4	.226	.296	.316
1994	Riverside	A+	Sea	28	99	38	2	1	2	48	16	23	11	0	17	1	4	1	3	4	.43	2	.384	.446	.485
1995	Port City	AA	Sea	71	256	81	15	1	3	107	42	18	16	1	34	1	4	1	12	8	.60	3	.316	.358	.418
	Tacoma	AAA	Sea	11	25	5	0	1	0	7	2	1	1	0	7	0	0	0	0	0	.00	0	.200	.231	.280
1996	Tacoma	AAA	Sea	100	328	92	15	1	1	112	41	21	20	1	47	1	11	5	7	7	.50	10	.280	.319	.341
1992	Philadelphia	NL		14	9	2	0	0	0	2	3	0	3	0	3	0	1	0	0	0	.00	0	.222	.417	.222
10 Min. YEARS				955	3500	958	132	41	22	1238	496	297	322	15	527	17	36	20	150	94	.61	75	.274	.336	.354

Steve Pegues

Bats: Right **Throws:** Right **Pos:** OF **Ht:** 6' 2" **Wt:** 190 **Born:** 5/21/68 **Age:** 29

				BATTING															BASERUNNING				PERCENTAGES		
Year	Team	Lg	Org	G	AB	H	2B	3B	HR	TB	R	RBI	TBB	IBB	SO	HBP	SH	SF	SB	CS	SB%	GDP	Avg	OBP	SLG
1987	Bristol	R+	Det	59	236	67	6	5	2	89	36	23	16	0	43	0	0	2	22	7	.76	8	.284	.327	.377
1988	Fayettevlle	A	Det	118	437	112	17	5	6	157	50	46	21	3	90	3	2	4	21	11	.66	6	.256	.292	.359
1989	Fayettevlle	A	Det	70	269	83	11	6	1	109	35	38	15	2	52	2	1	3	16	10	.62	5	.309	.346	.405
	Lakeland	A+	Det	55	193	49	7	2	0	60	24	15	7	0	19	2	0	1	12	4	.75	5	.254	.286	.311
1990	London	AA	Det	126	483	131	22	5	8	187	48	63	12	1	58	3	3	4	17	8	.68	17	.271	.291	.387
1991	London	AA	Det	56	216	65	3	2	6	90	24	26	8	0	24	6	0	2	4	7	.36	6	.301	.341	.417
	Toledo	AAA	Det	68	222	50	13	3	4	81	21	23	3	0	31	3	1	0	8	5	.62	7	.225	.246	.365
1992	Las Vegas	AAA	SD	123	376	99	21	4	9	155	51	56	7	1	64	6	3	9	12	3	.80	8	.263	.281	.412
1993	Las Vegas	AAA	SD	68	270	95	20	5	9	152	52	50	7	0	43	1	0	3	12	6	.67	8	.352	.367	.563
1994	Indianapols	AAA	Cin	63	245	71	16	11	6	127	36	29	6	0	44	3	1	2	10	3	.77	9	.290	.313	.518
1996	Richmond	AAA	Atl	52	167	57	10	1	7	90	31	30	6	0	43	4	0	1	0	0	.00	4	.341	.376	.539
1994	Cincinnati	NL		11	10	3	0	0	0	3	1	0	1	0	3	0	0	0	0	0	.00	0	.300	.364	.300
	Pittsburgh	NL		7	26	10	2	0	0	12	1	2	1	0	2	0	0	0	1	0	1.00	3	.385	.407	.462
1995	Pittsburgh	NL		82	171	42	8	0	6	68	17	16	4	0	36	1	0	3	1	2	.33	3	.246	.263	.398
9 Min. YEARS				858	3114	879	146	49	58	1297	408	399	108	7	511	33	11	31	134	64	.68	83	.282	.310	.417
2 Maj. YEARS				100	207	55	10	0	6	83	19	18	6	0	41	1	0	3	2	2	.50	6	.266	.286	.401

William Pennyfeather

Bats: Right **Throws:** Right **Pos:** OF **Ht:** 6' 2" **Wt:** 215 **Born:** 5/25/68 **Age:** 29

				BATTING															BASERUNNING				PERCENTAGES		
Year	Team	Lg	Org	G	AB	H	2B	3B	HR	TB	R	RBI	TBB	IBB	SO	HBP	SH	SF	SB	CS	SB%	GDP	Avg	OBP	SLG
1988	Pirates	R	Pit	17	74	18	2	1	1	25	6	7	2	0	18	0	0	1	3	3	.50	0	.243	.260	.338
	Princeton	R+	Pit	16	57	19	2	0	1	24	11	5	6	0	15	0	0	0	7	2	.78	0	.333	.397	.421
1989	Welland	A-	Pit	75	289	55	10	1	3	76	34	26	12	1	75	2	1	6	18	5	.78	6	.190	.223	.263
1990	Augusta	A	Pit	122	465	122	14	4	4	156	69	48	23	0	85	3	3	3	21	10	.68	7	.262	.300	.335
1991	Salem	A+	Pit	81	319	85	17	3	8	132	35	46	8	0	52	1	1	2	11	8	.58	9	.266	.285	.414
	Carolina	AA	Pit	42	149	41	5	0	0	46	13	9	7	0	17	1	1	1	3	2	.60	8	.275	.310	.309
1992	Carolina	AA	Pit	51	199	67	13	1	6	100	28	25	9	1	34	0	0	3	7	6	.54	5	.337	.360	.503
	Buffalo	AAA	Pit	55	160	38	6	2	1	51	19	12	2	0	24	3	2	0	3	2	.60	4	.238	.261	.319
1993	Buffalo	AAA	Pit	112	457	114	18	3	14	180	54	41	18	2	92	0	8	1	10	12	.45	3	.249	.277	.394
1994	Buffalo	AAA	Pit	10	36	9	2	0	0	11	2	3	3	0	9	0	1	0	0	0	.00	1	.250	.308	.306
	Indianapols	AAA	Cin	93	361	98	25	3	7	150	52	45	23	1	58	1	4	5	14	4	.78	5	.271	.313	.416
1995	Princeton	R+	Cin	1	3	0	0	0	0	0	0	0	0	0	1	0	0	0	0	0	.00	0	.000	.000	.000
1996	Vancouver	AAA	Cal	108	413	117	36	3	5	174	56	63	19	0	71	1	5	2	19	10	.66	7	.283	.315	.421
1992	Pittsburgh	NL		15	9	2	0	0	0	2	2	0	0	0	0	0	1	0	0	0	.00	1	.222	.222	.222
1993	Pittsburgh	NL		21	34	7	1	0	0	8	4	2	0	0	6	0	0	0	0	1	.00	1	.206	.206	.235
1994	Pittsburgh	NL		4	3	0	0	0	0	0	0	0	0	0	0	0	0	0	0	0	.00	0	.000	.000	.000
9 Min. YEARS				783	2982	783	150	21	50	1125	379	330	132	5	551	12	26	24	116	64	.64	55	.263	.294	.377
3 Maj. YEARS				40	46	9	1	0	0	10	6	2	0	0	6	0	1	0	0	1	.00	2	.196	.196	.217

Melido Perez

Pitches: Right **Bats:** Right **Pos:** P **Ht:** 6' 4" **Wt:** 210 **Born:** 2/15/66 **Age:** 31

				HOW MUCH HE PITCHED						WHAT HE GAVE UP												THE RESULTS					
Year	Team	Lg	Org	G	GS	CG	GF	IP	BFP	H	R	ER	HR	SH	SF	HB	TBB	IBB	SO	WP	Bk	W	L	Pct.	ShO	Sv	ERA
1984	Charleston	A	KC	16	15	0	0	89	387	99	52	43	9	2	2	2	19	0	55	4	1	5	7	.417	0	0	4.35
1985	Eugene	A-	KC	17	15	2	1	101	0	116	65	61	13	0	0	1	35	2	88	4	2	6	7	.462	0	0	5.44
1986	Burlington	A	KC	28	23	13	5	170.1	712	148	83	70	15	5	10	3	49	3	153	8	1	10	12	.455	1	0	3.70
1987	Fort Myers	A+	KC	8	8	5	0	64.1	247	51	20	17	3	3	1	0	7	0	51	3	0	4	3	.571	1	0	2.38
	Memphis	AA	KC	20	20	5	0	133.2	538	125	60	51	13	1	1	0	20	1	126	4	0	8	5	.615	2	0	3.43
1995	Norwich	AA	NYA	2	2	0	0	9	35	7	0	0	0	0	0	0	3	0	9	0	1	1	0	1.000	0	0	0.00
1996	Yankees	R	NYA	2	2	0	0	11	46	9	4	2	0	0	1	0	3	0	7	1	0	1	0	1.000	0	0	1.64
	Norwich	AA	NYA	1	1	0	0	8	27	4	0	0	0	0	0	0	1	0	7	0	0	1	0	1.000	0	0	0.00

Year	Team	Lg	Org	G	GS	CG	GF	IP	BFP	H	R	ER	HR	SH	SF	HB	TBB	IBB	SO	WP	Bk	W	L	Pct.	ShO	Sv	ERA
				HOW MUCH HE PITCHED						WHAT HE GAVE UP												THE RESULTS					
1987	Kansas City	AL		3	3	0	0	10.1	53	18	12	9	2	0	0	0	5	0	5	0	0	1	1	.500	0	0	7.84
1988	Chicago	AL		32	32	3	0	197	836	186	105	83	26	5	8	2	72	0	138	13	3	12	10	.545	1	0	3.79
1989	Chicago	AL		31	31	2	0	183.1	810	187	106	102	23	5	4	3	90	3	141	12	5	11	14	.440	0	0	5.01
1990	Chicago	AL		35	35	3	0	197	833	177	111	101	14	4	6	2	86	1	161	8	4	13	14	.481	3	0	4.61
1991	Chicago	AL		49	8	0	16	135.2	553	111	49	47	15	4	1	1	52	0	128	11	1	8	7	.533	0	1	3.12
1992	New York	AL		33	33	10	0	247.2	1013	212	94	79	16	6	8	5	93	5	218	13	0	13	16	.448	1	0	2.87
1993	New York	AL		25	25	0	0	163	718	173	103	94	22	4	2	1	64	5	148	3	1	6	14	.300	0	0	5.19
1994	New York	AL		22	22	1	0	151.1	632	134	74	69	16	5	3	3	58	5	109	7	1	9	4	.692	0	0	4.10
1995	New York	AL		13	12	1	1	69.1	304	70	46	43	10	1	3	1	31	2	44	4	0	5	5	.500	0	0	5.58
6 Min. YEARS				94	86	25	6	586.1	1992	559	284	244	53	11	15	6	137	6	496	24	5	36	34	.514	4	0	3.75
9 Maj. YEARS				243	201	20	17	1354.2	5752	1268	700	627	144	34	35	18	551	21	1092	71	15	78	85	.479	5	1	4.17

Richard Perez

Bats: Right **Throws:** Right **Pos:** 3B **Ht:** 6'2" **Wt:** 175 **Born:** 1/30/73 **Age:** 24

Year	Team	Lg	Org	G	AB	H	2B	3B	HR	TB	R	RBI	TBB	IBB	SO	HBP	SH	SF	SB	CS	SB%	GDP	Avg	OBP	SLG
				BATTING															BASERUNNING				PERCENTAGES		
1991	Huntington	R+	ChN	48	166	30	4	0	0	34	19	8	19	0	29	7	4	1	5	2	.71	5	.181	.290	.205
1992	Huntington	R+	ChN	51	190	55	7	3	0	68	33	22	17	0	25	4	4	3	5	3	.63	3	.289	.355	.358
1993	Peoria	A	ChN	109	370	90	12	1	0	104	59	34	31	0	64	8	29	5	5	8	.38	3	.243	.312	.281
1994	Daytona	A+	ChN	99	325	77	9	1	0	88	45	21	22	0	54	5	10	0	8	5	.62	14	.237	.295	.271
1995	Daytona	A+	ChN	85	255	56	8	0	0	64	31	26	28	0	41	1	4	1	4	2	.67	5	.220	.298	.251
1996	Orlando	AA	ChN	10	18	3	0	0	0	3	0	1	1	0	3	0	0	1	0	0	.00	1	.167	.200	.167
	Rockford	A	ChN	33	83	21	6	0	3	36	12	13	10	0	17	2	5	1	2	0	1.00	3	.253	.344	.434
	Daytona	A+	ChN	52	184	42	7	1	0	51	20	8	12	0	24	3	3	0	4	3	.57	6	.228	.286	.277
6 Min. YEARS				487	1591	374	53	6	3	448	219	133	140	0	257	30	59	12	33	23	.59	40	.235	.307	.282

Matt Perisho

Pitches: Left **Bats:** Left **Pos:** P **Ht:** 6'0" **Wt:** 190 **Born:** 6/8/75 **Age:** 22

Year	Team	Lg	Org	G	GS	CG	GF	IP	BFP	H	R	ER	HR	SH	SF	HB	TBB	IBB	SO	WP	Bk	W	L	Pct.	ShO	Sv	ERA
				HOW MUCH HE PITCHED						WHAT HE GAVE UP												THE RESULTS					
1993	Angels	R	Cal	11	11	1	0	64	266	58	32	26	1	1	3	2	23	0	65	2	2	7	3	.700	1	0	3.66
1994	Cedar Rapds	A	Cal	27	27	0	0	147.2	689	165	90	71	11	7	7	4	88	0	107	8	3	12	9	.571	0	0	4.33
1995	Lk Elsinore	A+	Cal	24	22	0	0	115.1	541	137	91	81	10	0	8	6	60	0	68	7	0	8	9	.471	0	0	6.32
1996	Lk Elsinore	A+	Cal	21	18	1	1	128.2	565	131	72	60	9	8	7	7	58	0	97	5	4	7	5	.583	1	0	4.20
	Midland	AA	Cal	8	8	0	0	53.1	222	48	22	19	4	4	1	2	20	0	50	1	0	3	2	.600	0	0	3.21
4 Min. YEARS				91	86	2	1	509	2283	539	307	257	35	20	26	21	249	0	387	23	9	37	28	.569	2	0	4.54

Greg Perschke

Pitches: Right **Bats:** Right **Pos:** P **Ht:** 6'3" **Wt:** 180 **Born:** 8/3/67 **Age:** 29

Year	Team	Lg	Org	G	GS	CG	GF	IP	BFP	H	R	ER	HR	SH	SF	HB	TBB	IBB	SO	WP	Bk	W	L	Pct.	ShO	Sv	ERA
				HOW MUCH HE PITCHED						WHAT HE GAVE UP												THE RESULTS					
1989	Utica	A-	ChA	14	0	0	14	17	61	5	3	3	0	0	0	1	4	0	20	0	3	0	0	.000	0	9	1.59
	South Bend	A	ChA	13	0	0	8	20.1	80	19	10	7	0	0	1	1	2	0	16	2	1	0	2	.000	0	1	3.10
1990	Sarasota	A+	ChA	42	10	2	23	111.1	450	83	32	15	3	3	4	4	29	3	107	5	8	7	3	.700	0	9	1.21
	Birmingham	AA	ChA	4	4	1	0	27.2	110	20	9	8	3	0	1	3	6	0	18	1	0	3	1	.750	0	0	2.60
1991	Vancouver	AAA	ChA	27	27	3	0	176	759	170	104	91	18	7	10	7	62	0	98	8	3	7	12	.368	0	0	4.65
1992	Vancouver	AAA	ChA	29	28	1	0	165	692	159	83	69	13	1	7	7	44	0	82	4	2	12	7	.632	1	0	3.76
1993	Albuquerque	AAA	LA	33	13	0	5	104.2	475	146	76	74	12	3	6	2	24	3	63	6	2	7	4	.636	0	0	6.36
1994	Orlando	AA	ChN	25	0	0	14	41	158	28	9	7	2	3	0	1	10	4	26	0	1	4	3	.571	0	3	1.54
	Iowa	AAA	ChN	21	2	0	9	53	228	51	37	32	7	3	2	8	14	2	33	3	0	1	1	.500	0	1	5.43
1995	Canton-Akrn	AA	Cle	3	0	0	1	5.1	21	4	2	2	1	0	0	0	2	0	4	1	0	1	0	1.000	0	0	3.38
	Buffalo	AAA	Cle	6	3	0	1	21	86	17	12	12	3	0	1	0	8	0	15	1	0	2	1	.667	0	0	5.14
1996	Birmingham	AA	ChA	9	0	0	6	12	52	12	6	3	0	0	0	0	3	0	12	1	2	2	1	.667	0	0	2.25
8 Min. YEARS				226	87	7	81	754.1	3172	714	383	323	62	20	32	34	208	12	494	32	22	46	35	.568	1	23	3.85

Chris Petersen

Bats: Right **Throws:** Right **Pos:** SS **Ht:** 5'10" **Wt:** 160 **Born:** 11/6/70 **Age:** 26

Year	Team	Lg	Org	G	AB	H	2B	3B	HR	TB	R	RBI	TBB	IBB	SO	HBP	SH	SF	SB	CS	SB%	GDP	Avg	OBP	SLG
				BATTING															BASERUNNING				PERCENTAGES		
1992	Geneva	A-	ChN	71	244	55	8	0	1	66	36	23	32	0	69	4	9	2	11	7	.61	4	.225	.323	.270
1993	Daytona	A+	ChN	130	473	101	10	0	0	111	66	28	58	0	105	9	17	1	19	11	.63	10	.214	.311	.235
1994	Orlando	AA	ChN	117	376	85	12	3	1	106	34	26	37	0	89	2	16	1	8	11	.42	7	.226	.298	.282
1995	Orlando	AA	ChN	125	382	81	10	3	4	109	48	36	45	3	97	4	5	3	7	3	.70	14	.212	.300	.285
1996	Orlando	AA	ChN	47	152	45	3	4	2	62	21	12	18	0	31	5	0	1	3	5	.38	5	.296	.386	.408
	Iowa	AAA	ChN	63	194	48	6	3	2	66	12	23	12	1	46	1	2	1	1	2	.33	4	.247	.293	.340
5 Min. YEARS				553	1821	415	49	13	10	520	217	148	202	4	437	25	49	9	49	39	.56	44	.228	.312	.286

Charles Peterson

Bats: Right **Throws:** Right **Pos:** OF **Ht:** 6'3" **Wt:** 200 **Born:** 5/8/74 **Age:** 23

Year	Team	Lg	Org	G	AB	H	2B	3B	HR	TB	R	RBI	TBB	IBB	SO	HBP	SH	SF	SB	CS	SB%	GDP	Avg	OBP	SLG
				BATTING															BASERUNNING				PERCENTAGES		
1993	Pirates	R	Pit	49	188	57	11	3	1	77	28	23	22	0	22	0	0	1	8	6	.57	4	.303	.374	.410

BATTING																	BASERUNNING				PERCENTAGES		
Year Team	Lg Org	G	AB	H	2B	3B	HR	TB	R	RBI	TBB	IBB	SO	HBP	SH	SF	SB	CS	SB%	GDP	Avg	OBP	SLG
1994 Augusta	A Pit	108	415	106	14	6	4	144	55	40	35	2	78	3	0	2	27	18	.60	7	.255	.316	.347
1995 Lynchburg	A+ Pit	107	391	107	9	4	7	145	61	51	43	1	73	2	6	5	31	17	.65	11	.274	.345	.371
Carolina	AA Pit	20	70	23	3	1	0	28	13	7	9	1	15	2	0	1	2	1	.67	1	.329	.415	.400
1996 Carolina	AA Pit	125	462	127	24	2	7	176	71	63	50	5	104	0	3	1	33	10	.77	18	.275	.345	.381
4 Min. YEARS		409	1526	420	61	16	19	570	228	184	159	9	292	7	9	10	101	52	.66	41	.275	.344	.374

Mark Peterson

Pitches: Left **Bats:** Left **Pos:** P **Ht:** 5'11" **Wt:** 195 **Born:** 11/27/70 **Age:** 26

HOW MUCH HE PITCHED								WHAT HE GAVE UP												THE RESULTS					
Year Team	Lg Org	G	GS	CG	GF	IP	BFP	H	R	ER	HR	SH	SF	HB	TBB	IBB	SO	WP	Bk	W	L	Pct.	ShO	Sv	ERA
1992 Everett	A- SF	20	5	0	7	53	226	58	23	19	5	2	0	1	17	1	47	0	4	3	2	.600	0	2	3.23
1993 San Jose	A+ SF	37	7	1	19	81.1	349	95	36	31	5	3	3	2	15	0	45	3	0	4	1	.800	1	0	3.43
1994 San Jose	A+ SF	9	4	0	2	36	139	36	16	16	4	2	2	0	6	1	27	1	0	3	3	.500	0	0	4.00
Shreveport	AA SF	28	3	1	11	55.2	223	56	24	21	1	2	2	1	6	1	31	0	0	3	2	.600	0	1	3.40
1995 Shreveport	AA SF	37	0	0	14	64	248	51	15	9	2	2	5	4	6	2	38	0	0	4	3	.571	0	2	1.27
1996 Shreveport	AA SF	41	0	0	16	56	235	58	23	20	5	1	2	4	8	2	32	0	0	5	3	.625	0	2	3.21
5 Min. YEARS		172	19	2	69	346	1420	354	137	116	22	12	14	12	58	7	220	4	4	22	14	.611	1	7	3.02

Nate Peterson

Bats: Left **Throws:** Right **Pos:** OF **Ht:** 6'2" **Wt:** 185 **Born:** 7/12/71 **Age:** 25

BATTING																	BASERUNNING				PERCENTAGES		
Year Team	Lg Org	G	AB	H	2B	3B	HR	TB	R	RBI	TBB	IBB	SO	HBP	SH	SF	SB	CS	SB%	GDP	Avg	OBP	SLG
1993 Auburn	A- Hou	69	277	72	17	1	2	97	35	29	17	0	34	5	1	0	5	2	.71	14	.260	.314	.350
1994 Quad City	A Hou	68	215	59	11	2	4	86	27	21	14	3	29	2	0	1	1	3	.25	7	.274	.323	.400
1995 Kissimmee	A+ Hou	76	257	72	17	0	4	101	34	22	21	2	42	4	0	1	3	1	.75	5	.280	.343	.393
1996 Jackson	AA Hou	114	324	90	19	0	2	115	36	34	27	1	49	6	1	4	1	1	.50	5	.278	.341	.355
4 Min. YEARS		327	1073	293	64	3	12	399	132	106	79	6	154	17	2	6	10	7	.59	31	.273	.331	.372

Jose Pett

Pitches: Right **Bats:** Right **Pos:** P **Ht:** 6'6" **Wt:** 190 **Born:** 1/8/76 **Age:** 21

HOW MUCH HE PITCHED								WHAT HE GAVE UP												THE RESULTS					
Year Team	Lg Org	G	GS	CG	GF	IP	BFP	H	R	ER	HR	SH	SF	HB	TBB	IBB	SO	WP	Bk	W	L	Pct.	ShO	Sv	ERA
1993 Blue Jays	R Tor	4	4	0	0	10	43	10	4	4	0	0	0	0	3	0	7	0	0	1	1	.500	0	0	3.60
1994 Dunedin	A+ Tor	15	15	1	0	90.2	389	103	47	38	1	5	5	3	20	0	49	3	3	4	8	.333	0	0	3.77
1995 Knoxville	AA Tor	26	25	1	0	141.2	602	132	87	67	16	4	4	4	48	0	89	8	0	8	9	.471	1	0	4.26
1996 Knoxville	AA Tor	7	7	1	0	44	169	37	20	20	4	1	0	0	10	0	38	1	1	4	2	.667	1	0	4.09
Syracuse	AAA Tor	20	18	1	0	109.2	503	134	81	71	10	4	4	10	42	1	50	6	1	2	9	.182	0	0	5.83
4 Min. YEARS		72	69	4	0	396	1706	416	239	200	31	14	13	17	123	1	233	18	5	19	29	.396	2	0	4.55

Tom Phelps

Pitches: Left **Bats:** Left **Pos:** P **Ht:** 6'3" **Wt:** 192 **Born:** 3/4/74 **Age:** 23

HOW MUCH HE PITCHED								WHAT HE GAVE UP												THE RESULTS					
Year Team	Lg Org	G	GS	CG	GF	IP	BFP	H	R	ER	HR	SH	SF	HB	TBB	IBB	SO	WP	Bk	W	L	Pct.	ShO	Sv	ERA
1993 Burlington	A Mon	8	8	0	0	41	173	36	18	17	4	1	1	1	13	0	33	2	0	2	4	.333	0	0	3.73
Jamestown	A- Mon	16	15	1	0	92.1	416	102	62	47	4	4	3	5	37	1	74	7	1	3	8	.273	0	0	4.58
1994 Burlington	A Mon	23	23	1	0	118.1	534	143	91	73	9	7	7	5	48	1	82	7	0	8	8	.500	1	0	5.55
1995 W. Palm Bch	A+ Mon	2	2	0	0	5	33	10	10	9	0	0	0	0	11	0	5	2	0	0	2	.000	0	0	16.20
Albany	A Mon	26	26	1	0	140.1	630	152	86	59	6	0	4	5	56	0	124	7	1	10	11	.476	0	0	3.78
1996 W. Palm Bch	A+ Mon	18	18	1	0	112	468	105	42	36	5	4	1	2	35	0	71	8	0	10	2	.833	1	0	2.89
Harrisburg	AA Mon	8	8	2	0	47.1	195	43	16	13	3	2	0	1	19	2	23	0	0	2	2	.500	2	0	2.47
4 Min. YEARS		101	100	6	0	556.1	2449	591	325	254	31	18	16	19	219	4	412	33	2	35	37	.486	4	0	4.11

Gary Phillips

Bats: Right **Throws:** Right **Pos:** 3B **Ht:** 5'11" **Wt:** 165 **Born:** 9/25/71 **Age:** 25

BATTING																	BASERUNNING				PERCENTAGES		
Year Team	Lg Org	G	AB	H	2B	3B	HR	TB	R	RBI	TBB	IBB	SO	HBP	SH	SF	SB	CS	SB%	GDP	Avg	OBP	SLG
1992 Giants	R SF	29	109	41	14	0	0	55	14	21	9	0	22	0	0	2	2	2	.50	2	.376	.417	.505
1993 Everett	A- SF	54	180	43	8	0	7	72	24	31	25	1	45	2	1	0	4	4	.50	1	.239	.338	.400
1994 Clinton	A SF	124	438	109	23	4	9	167	62	50	40	3	98	6	5	4	4	7	.36	6	.249	.318	.381
1995 San Jose	A+ SF	106	363	96	17	8	1	132	51	32	26	0	68	9	6	2	3	1	.75	6	.264	.328	.364
1996 Shreveport	AA SF	111	337	83	18	4	2	115	37	43	22	0	71	6	3	5	1	6	.14	12	.246	.300	.341
5 Min. YEARS		424	1427	372	80	16	19	541	188	177	122	4	304	23	15	13	14	20	.41	27	.261	.326	.379

Randy Phillips

Pitches: Right **Bats:** Right **Pos:** P **Ht:** 6'3" **Wt:** 210 **Born:** 3/18/71 **Age:** 26

HOW MUCH HE PITCHED								WHAT HE GAVE UP												THE RESULTS					
Year Team	Lg Org	G	GS	CG	GF	IP	BFP	H	R	ER	HR	SH	SF	HB	TBB	IBB	SO	WP	Bk	W	L	Pct.	ShO	Sv	ERA
1992 Medicne Hat	R+ Tor	15	13	1	0	91	390	88	48	34	9	1	2	9	25	0	69	4	3	2	4	.333	0	0	3.36
1993 Dunedin	A+ Tor	17	17	0	0	110.1	453	99	51	47	12	4	2	5	30	3	87	5	6	7	6	.538	0	0	3.83
Knoxville	AA Tor	5	5	0	0	25	120	32	20	17	3	2	0	2	12	0	12	3	2	2	2	.500	0	0	6.12
1994 Knoxville	AA Tor	8	8	0	0	48	192	37	16	13	4	1	2	1	12	0	31	2	2	3	2	.600	0	0	2.44
Syracuse	AAA Tor	22	19	0	1	108.2	493	126	81	73	16	1	4	7	45	1	81	4	2	6	9	.400	0	0	6.05

			HOW MUCH HE PITCHED						WHAT HE GAVE UP												THE RESULTS					
Year	Team	Lg	Org	G	GS	CG	GF	IP	BFP	H	R	ER	HR	SH	SF	HB	TBB	IBB	SO	WP	Bk	W	L	Pct.	ShO	Sv	ERA
1995	Phoenix	AAA	SF	25	24	2	0	132	574	155	83	75	11	4	6	4	40	2	66	8	2	4	13	.235	1	0	5.11
1996	Shreveport	AA	SF	35	2	0	9	69.2	308	77	34	25	5	5	2	3	21	5	31	4	1	1	4	.200	0	4	3.23
	5 Min. YEARS			127	88	3	10	584.2	2530	614	333	284	60	18	18	31	185	11	377	30	18	25	40	.385	1	4	4.37

Tony Phillips

Pitches: Right **Bats:** Right **Pos:** P **Ht:** 6'4" **Wt:** 195 **Born:** 6/9/69 **Age:** 28

			HOW MUCH HE PITCHED						WHAT HE GAVE UP												THE RESULTS					
Year	Team	Lg	Org	G	GS	CG	GF	IP	BFP	H	R	ER	HR	SH	SF	HB	TBB	IBB	SO	WP	Bk	W	L	Pct.	ShO	Sv	ERA
1992	San Bernrdo	A+	Sea	37	0	0	29	51	227	44	23	18	1	4	4	2	28	2	40	3	3	4	3	.571	0	12	3.18
1993	Riverside	A+	Sea	25	0	0	23	30	118	22	8	6	1	2	2	2	4	1	19	0	1	3	1	.750	0	15	1.80
	Jacksonvlle	AA	Sea	26	0	0	21	30.1	125	34	6	6	1	1	0	0	5	1	23	1	1	1	3	.250	0	5	1.78
1994	Jacksonvlle	AA	Sea	5	0	0	4	5.2	22	3	2	1	1	0	0	0	3	0	3	0	0	0	0	.000	0	1	1.59
	Calgary	AAA	Sea	55	1	0	29	98	438	132	66	61	11	2	5	2	23	5	51	2	4	6	3	.667	0	6	5.60
1995	Tacoma	AAA	Sea	47	1	0	19	87.1	370	98	44	40	6	3	7	6	14	7	44	0	2	3	2	.600	0	1	4.12
1996	Tacoma	AAA	Sea	21	3	0	9	52	233	70	40	37	10	1	4	3	9	1	24	0	1	1	3	.250	0	1	6.40
	New Orleans	AAA	Mil	20	6	0	4	52.1	214	51	25	17	6	0	3	4	7	0	32	2	0	2	1	.667	0	0	2.92
	5 Min. YEARS			236	11	0	138	406.2	1747	454	214	186	37	13	25	19	93	17	236	8	12	20	16	.556	0	41	4.12

Steve Phoenix

Pitches: Right **Bats:** Right **Pos:** P **Ht:** 6' 2" **Wt:** 185 **Born:** 1/31/68 **Age:** 29

			HOW MUCH HE PITCHED						WHAT HE GAVE UP												THE RESULTS					
Year	Team	Lg	Org	G	GS	CG	GF	IP	BFP	H	R	ER	HR	SH	SF	HB	TBB	IBB	SO	WP	Bk	W	L	Pct.	ShO	Sv	ERA
1990	Athletics	R	Oak	6	6	0	0	31	128	25	14	5	0	1	0	1	4	0	31	0	2	3	1	.750	0	0	1.45
	Modesto	A+	Oak	6	6	0	0	37.1	164	43	21	19	2	0	1	2	10	0	23	3	0	4	1	.800	0	0	4.58
1991	Huntsville	AA	Oak	2	0	0	1	3	18	7	3	2	1	0	0	0	1	0	3	0	0	0	0	.000	0	0	6.00
	Madison	A	Oak	7	2	0	3	21.1	96	26	8	7	0	2	0	0	10	0	19	0	0	3	0	1.000	0	2	2.95
	Modesto	A+	Oak	27	3	1	10	84.1	372	87	44	35	13	3	1	5	33	4	65	3	0	5	2	.714	1	2	3.74
1992	Huntsville	AA	Oak	32	24	0	1	174	722	179	68	54	8	4	5	7	36	1	124	5	1	11	5	.688	0	0	2.79
1993	Tacoma	AAA	Oak	11	5	0	1	31	159	42	27	24	4	1	0	0	27	2	21	2	0	0	2	.000	0	0	6.97
	Huntsville	AA	Oak	11	0	0	7	19.1	73	13	5	3	0	0	1	0	5	2	15	0	0	2	2	.500	0	1	1.40
1994	Tacoma	AAA	Oak	20	0	0	17	22	83	16	5	3	0	2	0	1	4	1	16	2	0	0	2	.000	0	9	1.23
	Huntsville	AA	Oak	38	0	0	33	48.2	202	42	9	7	1	3	2	1	16	1	40	0	0	6	2	.750	0	20	1.29
1995	Edmonton	AAA	Oak	40	0	0	25	64	280	66	36	32	6	5	3	1	28	4	28	5	0	4	3	.571	0	5	4.50
1996	Calgary	AAA	Pit	10	1	0	3	16	68	16	8	3	3	0	3	1	5	1	9	0	0	1	1	.500	0	0	1.69
	Carolina	AA	Pit	20	0	0	15	21.2	102	31	12	12	3	0	2	1	6	2	16	4	0	2	2	.500	0	5	4.98
1994	Oakland	AL		2	0	0	0	4.1	19	4	3	3	0	0	0	0	2	0	3	0	0	0	0	.000	0	0	6.23
1995	Oakland	AL		1	0	0	0	1.2	11	3	6	6	1	1	0	0	3	0	3	0	0	0	0	.000	0	0	32.40
	7 Min. YEARS			230	47	1	116	573.2	2467	593	260	206	41	21	18	20	185	18	410	24	3	41	23	.641	1	44	3.23
	2 Maj. YEARS			3	0	0	0	6	30	7	9	9	1	1	0	0	5	0	6	0	0	0	0	.000	0	0	13.50

Sandy Pichardo

Bats: Both **Throws:** Right **Pos:** 2B **Ht:** 5'11" **Wt:** 173 **Born:** 11/26/74 **Age:** 22

			BATTING														BASERUNNING				PERCENTAGES		
Year	Team	Lg	Org	G	AB	H	2B	3B	HR	TB	R	RBI	TBB	IBB	SO	HBP	SH	SF	SB	CS	SB%	GDP	Avg	OBP	SLG
1992	Mets	R	NYN	44	142	42	7	3	0	55	26	12	26	0	31	2	2	0	14	5	.74	0	.296	.412	.387
1993	Kingsport	R+	NYN	51	192	58	6	2	1	71	25	15	22	1	25	3	4	0	12	10	.55	1	.302	.382	.370
1994	Columbia	A	NYN	118	420	108	6	7	2	134	48	30	36	0	99	6	9	2	34	28	.55	3	.257	.323	.319
1995	St. Lucie	A+	NYN	125	478	131	10	6	0	153	55	27	28	3	64	3	12	1	29	17	.63	6	.274	.318	.320
1996	Tampa	A+	NYA	84	294	74	7	7	2	101	40	33	21	0	49	3	8	2	4	6	.40	6	.252	.306	.344
	Norwich	AA	NYA	6	17	6	1	0	1	10	3	3	1	0	5	0	1	0	1	0	1.00	0	.353	.389	.588
	5 Min. YEARS			428	1543	419	37	25	6	524	197	120	134	4	273	17	36	5	94	66	.59	16	.272	.335	.340

Ricky Pickett

Pitches: Left **Bats:** Left **Pos:** P **Ht:** 6'0" **Wt:** 185 **Born:** 1/19/70 **Age:** 27

			HOW MUCH HE PITCHED						WHAT HE GAVE UP												THE RESULTS					
Year	Team	Lg	Org	G	GS	CG	GF	IP	BFP	H	R	ER	HR	SH	SF	HB	TBB	IBB	SO	WP	Bk	W	L	Pct.	ShO	Sv	ERA
1992	Billings	R+	Cin	20	4	0	4	53.2	225	35	21	14	2	1	2	5	28	0	41	3	1	1	2	.333	0	2	2.35
1993	Charlstn-WV	A	Cin	44	1	0	5	43.2	227	42	40	33	1	1	1	5	48	0	65	6	3	1	2	.333	0	0	6.80
1994	Charlstn-WV	A	Cin	28	0	0	19	27.1	121	14	8	6	1	0	1	2	20	0	48	4	0	1	1	.500	0	13	1.98
	Winston-Sal	A+	Cin	21	0	0	17	24	112	16	11	10	0	1	1	2	23	1	33	2	0	2	1	.667	0	4	3.75
1995	Shreveport	AA	SF	14	0	0	9	21	82	9	5	4	1	0	1	0	9	0	23	2	0	2	0	1.000	0	3	1.71
	Chattanooga	AA	Cin	54	0	0	28	67.2	285	31	25	21	4	2	1	0	53	3	92	3	0	6	5	.545	0	12	2.79
1996	Phoenix	AAA	SF	8	0	0	2	8.1	43	12	8	8	1	0	0	1	5	0	7	1	0	0	3	.000	0	0	8.64
	Shreveport	AA	SF	29	0	0	12	48.2	214	35	21	15	4	3	2	3	35	3	51	2	0	4	1	.800	0	2	2.77
	5 Min. YEARS			218	5	0	96	294.1	1309	194	139	111	14	8	9	18	221	7	360	23	4	17	15	.531	0	36	3.39

Jeff Pierce

Pitches: Right **Bats:** Right **Pos:** P **Ht:** 6' 1" **Wt:** 185 **Born:** 6/7/69 **Age:** 28

			HOW MUCH HE PITCHED						WHAT HE GAVE UP												THE RESULTS					
Year	Team	Lg	Org	G	GS	CG	GF	IP	BFP	H	R	ER	HR	SH	SF	HB	TBB	IBB	SO	WP	Bk	W	L	Pct.	ShO	Sv	ERA
1992	South Bend	A	ChA	52	0	0	46	69.2	281	46	22	16	1	5	4	6	18	0	88	8	0	3	5	.375	0	30	2.07
	Sarasota	A+	ChA	1	0	0	1	0.2	3	0	0	0	0	0	0	1	0	0	1	0	0	0	0	.000	0	0	0.00

Year	Team	Lg	Org	G	GS	CG	GF	IP	BFP	H	R	ER	HR	SH	SF	HB	TBB	IBB	SO	WP	Bk	W	L	Pct.	ShO	Sv	ERA
				HOW MUCH HE PITCHED						WHAT HE GAVE UP												THE RESULTS					
1993	Birmingham	AA	ChA	33	0	0	26	48.2	188	34	16	14	3	4	2	3	7	0	45	1	1	3	4	.429	0	18	2.59
	Chattanooga	AA	Cin	13	0	0	8	20.2	87	17	6	6	1	0	1	0	9	1	22	2	0	0	0	.000	0	4	2.61
1994	New Britain	AA	Bos	29	0	0	25	39.1	163	31	13	10	3	1	0	2	12	3	54	4	0	1	2	.333	0	10	2.29
	Pawtucket	AAA	Bos	32	0	0	14	60.1	249	53	27	23	4	1	0	0	21	1	57	2	1	6	1	.857	0	2	3.43
1995	Pawtucket	AAA	Bos	23	3	0	8	41.1	172	34	21	19	5	2	2	2	16	1	43	2	1	4	2	.667	0	0	4.14
1996	Red Sox	R	Bos	5	4	0	1	11.1	44	12	1	1	0	0	0	1	1	0	10	0	1	0	0	.000	0	1	0.79
	Trenton	AA	Bos	4	0	0	1	9	38	6	1	1	0	0	0	1	4	1	5	1	0	0	0	.000	0	0	1.00
	Pawtucket	AAA	Bos	12	3	0	2	31	136	37	18	17	6	2	1	0	8	0	22	2	0	2	1	.667	0	0	4.94
1995	Boston	AL		12	0	0	2	15	72	16	12	11	0	1	1	0	14	4	12	0	0	0	3	.000	0	0	6.60
5 Min. YEARS				204	10	0	132	332	1361	270	125	107	23	15	10	16	96	7	347	22	4	19	15	.559	0	65	2.90

Jason Pierson

Pitches: Left **Bats:** Right **Pos:** P **Ht:** 6'0" **Wt:** 190 **Born:** 1/6/71 **Age:** 26

Year	Team	Lg	Org	G	GS	CG	GF	IP	BFP	H	R	ER	HR	SH	SF	HB	TBB	IBB	SO	WP	Bk	W	L	Pct.	ShO	Sv	ERA
				HOW MUCH HE PITCHED						WHAT HE GAVE UP												THE RESULTS					
1992	Utica	A-	ChA	15	15	1	0	87	358	90	34	23	5	0	3	1	18	2	62	2	4	8	2	.800	1	0	2.38
1993	South Bend	A	ChA	26	25	2	0	147.1	637	160	92	77	16	4	5	5	43	1	107	8	2	13	9	.591	0	0	4.70
1994	Pr. William	A+	ChA	28	28	3	0	189.1	785	183	85	70	22	10	3	6	48	0	117	11	2	14	8	.636	1	0	3.33
1995	Birmingham	AA	ChA	4	4	0	0	23.1	102	29	22	21	6	0	1	2	6	0	15	0	1	0	2	.000	0	0	8.10
	Pr. William	A+	ChA	25	16	0	5	115	484	120	70	66	15	1	5	4	28	0	84	1	1	5	6	.455	0	0	5.17
1996	Binghamton	AA	NYN	34	5	0	12	53.1	227	56	21	20	6	2	1	2	15	2	42	0	0	5	3	.625	0	1	3.38
5 Min. YEARS				132	93	6	17	615.1	2593	638	324	277	70	17	18	20	158	5	427	22	10	45	30	.600	2	1	4.05

Kevin Pincavitch

Pitches: Right **Bats:** Right **Pos:** P **Ht:** 5'11" **Wt:** 170 **Born:** 7/5/70 **Age:** 26

Year	Team	Lg	Org	G	GS	CG	GF	IP	BFP	H	R	ER	HR	SH	SF	HB	TBB	IBB	SO	WP	Bk	W	L	Pct.	ShO	Sv	ERA
				HOW MUCH HE PITCHED						WHAT HE GAVE UP												THE RESULTS					
1992	Great Falls	R+	LA	26	0	0	9	50.2	219	36	16	11	1	1	0	4	26	1	65	4	0	2	2	.500	0	1	1.95
1993	Vero Beach	A+	LA	6	0	0	0	9.2	52	11	10	5	0	0	0	0	10	1	3	1	1	0	0	.000	0	0	4.66
	Yakima	A-	LA	9	9	0	0	57	234	40	22	12	2	1	1	5	29	1	43	7	3	3	4	.429	0	0	1.89
	Bakersfield	A+	LA	6	5	0	0	31.2	141	27	11	7	2	2	0	1	25	2	32	6	0	1	2	.333	0	0	1.99
1994	San Antonio	AA	LA	4	2	0	0	10.1	54	12	15	11	1	1	0	0	12	0	7	2	0	0	2	.000	0	0	9.58
	Bakersfield	A+	LA	27	16	1	4	111.2	469	94	53	43	9	3	3	3	48	0	113	13	1	7	4	.636	0	1	3.47
1995	San Bernrdo	A+	LA	3	0	0	0	10	46	8	5	3	1	1	0	0	6	1	10	0	0	2	0	1.000	0	0	2.70
	Vero Beach	A+	LA	35	13	2	5	134.2	550	91	42	26	8	6	1	5	54	1	113	12	1	12	7	.632	1	2	1.74
1996	San Antonio	AA	LA	11	0	0	8	16	82	26	14	10	1	0	1	2	10	0	11	3	1	0	0	.000	0	0	5.63
	San Bernrdo	A+	LA	20	17	0	2	101.1	479	95	66	55	10	3	3	16	75	1	79	23	4	8	8	.500	0	0	4.88
5 Min. YEARS				147	62	3	28	533	2326	440	254	183	35	18	9	36	295	8	476	71	11	35	29	.547	1	4	3.09

Marc Pisciotta

Pitches: Right **Bats:** Right **Pos:** P **Ht:** 6'5" **Wt:** 240 **Born:** 8/7/70 **Age:** 26

Year	Team	Lg	Org	G	GS	CG	GF	IP	BFP	H	R	ER	HR	SH	SF	HB	TBB	IBB	SO	WP	Bk	W	L	Pct.	ShO	Sv	ERA
				HOW MUCH HE PITCHED						WHAT HE GAVE UP												THE RESULTS					
1991	Welland	A-	Pit	24	0	0	21	34	143	16	4	1	0	2	1	3	20	1	47	7	1	1	1	.500	0	8	0.26
1992	Augusta	A	Pit	20	12	1	5	79.1	372	91	51	40	4	5	1	10	43	2	54	12	2	4	5	.444	0	1	4.54
1993	Augusta	A	Pit	34	0	0	28	43.2	188	31	18	13	0	5	0	5	17	1	49	5	0	5	2	.714	0	12	2.68
	Salem	A+	Pit	20	0	0	18	18.1	88	23	13	6	0	1	1	0	13	0	13	2	0	0	0	.000	0	12	2.95
1994	Carolina	AA	Pit	26	0	0	17	25.2	127	32	21	16	2	6	2	3	15	2	21	1	1	3	4	.429	0	5	5.61
	Salem	A+	Pit	31	0	0	30	29.1	134	24	14	5	1	2	1	3	13	1	23	4	0	1	4	.200	0	19	1.53
1995	Carolina	AA	Pit	56	0	0	27	69.1	313	60	37	32	2	7	3	6	45	8	57	4	0	6	4	.600	0	9	4.15
1996	Calgary	AAA	Pit	57	0	0	27	65.2	308	71	38	30	3	1	2	2	46	8	46	7	0	2	7	.222	0	1	4.11
6 Min. YEARS				268	12	1	173	365.1	1673	348	196	143	12	29	11	32	212	23	310	42	4	22	27	.449	0	67	3.52

Scott Pisciotta

Pitches: Right **Bats:** Right **Pos:** P **Ht:** 6'7" **Wt:** 225 **Born:** 6/8/73 **Age:** 24

Year	Team	Lg	Org	G	GS	CG	GF	IP	BFP	H	R	ER	HR	SH	SF	HB	TBB	IBB	SO	WP	Bk	W	L	Pct.	ShO	Sv	ERA
				HOW MUCH HE PITCHED						WHAT HE GAVE UP												THE RESULTS					
1992	Jamestown	A-	Mon	14	14	4	0	85.2	352	61	39	27	1	2	2	5	35	2	77	9	3	6	3	.667	4	0	2.84
1993	Burlington	A	Mon	24	24	1	0	135.1	613	129	85	61	7	8	2	9	79	1	112	16	2	9	12	.429	0	0	4.06
1994	W. Palm Bch	A+	Mon	4	4	0	0	21	93	20	12	11	1	0	2	2	14	1	11	8	0	0	3	.000	0	0	4.71
	Burlington	A	Mon	40	4	0	15	73.2	325	69	46	36	6	1	1	5	39	2	64	10	0	2	4	.333	0	0	4.40
1995	W. Palm Bch	A+	Mon	53	0	0	29	60.2	271	55	26	17	1	1	4	0	36	2	38	11	0	5	4	.556	0	2	2.52
1996	Harrisburg	AA	Mon	27	0	0	5	36	165	35	22	22	4	3	0	3	27	2	18	3	1	2	1	.667	0	1	5.50
5 Min. YEARS				162	46	5	49	412.1	1819	369	230	174	20	15	11	24	230	10	320	57	6	24	27	.471	4	3	3.80

Jim Pittsley

Pitches: Right **Bats:** Right **Pos:** P **Ht:** 6' 7" **Wt:** 215 **Born:** 4/3/74 **Age:** 23

Year	Team	Lg	Org	G	GS	CG	GF	IP	BFP	H	R	ER	HR	SH	SF	HB	TBB	IBB	SO	WP	Bk	W	L	Pct.	ShO	Sv	ERA
				HOW MUCH HE PITCHED						WHAT HE GAVE UP												THE RESULTS					
1992	Royals	R	KC	9	9	0	0	43.1	175	27	16	16	0	0	2	5	15	0	47	2	2	4	1	.800	0	0	3.32
	Baseball Cy	A+	KC	1	1	0	0	3	11	2	0	0	0	0	0	0	1	0	4	0	0	0	0	.000	0	0	0.00
1993	Rockford	A	KC	15	15	2	0	80.1	344	76	43	38	3	2	4	5	32	0	87	5	3	5	5	.500	1	0	4.26

			HOW MUCH HE PITCHED						WHAT HE GAVE UP												THE RESULTS					
Year Team	Lg	Org	G	GS	CG	GF	IP	BFP	H	R	ER	HR	SH	SF	HB	TBB	IBB	SO	WP	Bk	W	L	Pct.	ShO	Sv	ERA
1994 Wilmington	A+	KC	27	27	1	0	161.2	673	154	73	57	15	3	9	4	42	0	171	2	1	11	5	.688	1	0	3.17
1995 Omaha	AAA	KC	8	8	0	0	47.2	189	38	20	17	5	0	0	2	16	0	39	0	2	4	1	.800	0	0	3.21
1996 Wilmington	A+	KC	2	2	0	0	9	42	13	12	11	4	0	0	0	5	1	10	0	0	0	1	.000	0	0	11.00
Wichita	AA	KC	3	3	0	0	22	78	9	1	1	0	0	1	0	5	0	7	0	0	3	0	1.000	0	0	0.41
Omaha	AAA	KC	13	13	0	0	70.1	312	74	34	31	8	3	2	1	39	0	53	0	0	7	1	.875	0	0	3.97
1995 Kansas City	AL		1	1	0	0	3.1	17	7	5	5	3	0	0	0	1	0	0	0	0	0	0	.000	0	0	13.50
5 Min. YEARS			78	78	3	0	437.1	1824	393	199	171	35	8	18	17	155	1	418	9	8	34	14	.708	2	0	3.52

Mike Place

Pitches: Right **Bats:** Right **Pos:** P **Ht:** 6'4" **Wt:** 190 **Born:** 8/13/70 **Age:** 26

			HOW MUCH HE PITCHED						WHAT HE GAVE UP												THE RESULTS					
Year Team	Lg	Org	G	GS	CG	GF	IP	BFP	H	R	ER	HR	SH	SF	HB	TBB	IBB	SO	WP	Bk	W	L	Pct.	ShO	Sv	ERA
1990 Pulaski	R+	Atl	22	1	0	15	48.1	205	42	20	14	2	2	2	3	17	3	38	1	2	4	3	.571	0	3	2.61
1991 Idaho Falls	R+	Atl	5	5	0	0	24.1	107	28	16	12	2	0	0	1	10	0	9	0	0	2	1	.667	0	0	4.44
Pulaski	R+	Atl	12	4	0	3	44.2	193	45	22	20	1	0	1	3	15	1	35	10	5	1	2	.333	0	1	4.03
1992 Macon	A	Atl	32	8	1	5	92	400	105	59	40	5	3	3	3	35	2	54	12	5	2	7	.222	0	0	3.91
1993 Macon	A	Atl	31	9	1	11	99.2	407	91	44	26	3	7	2	0	23	0	74	3	3	6	5	.545	0	2	2.35
Durham	A+	Atl	5	5	0	0	31.2	134	30	15	11	3	1	1	0	9	3	26	1	1	1	2	.333	0	0	3.13
1994 Durham	A+	Atl	10	3	0	2	22.2	109	39	21	18	6	1	1	0	4	1	12	0	1	0	3	.000	0	0	7.15
Macon	A	Atl	4	4	0	0	23.2	93	15	5	5	2	1	0	1	7	0	19	1	0	3	0	1.000	0	0	1.90
1995 Durham	A+	Atl	7	0	0	1	7.2	36	11	11	9	0	0	0	0	6	0	2	0	0	2	1	.667	0	0	10.57
South Bend	A	ChA	35	2	0	14	62.1	271	67	41	33	3	4	4	4	25	2	36	7	0	6	6	.500	0	3	4.76
1996 Pr. William	A+	ChA	23	0	0	20	39	161	30	17	10	1	4	3	3	7	0	31	1	0	6	2	.750	0	7	2.31
Birmingham	AA	ChA	22	0	0	9	33	154	43	26	26	9	1	0	1	18	2	20	2	0	2	3	.400	0	1	7.09
7 Min. YEARS			208	41	2	80	529	2270	546	297	224	37	24	17	19	176	14	356	38	17	35	35	.500	0	17	3.81

Erik Plantenberg

Pitches: Left **Bats:** Right **Pos:** P **Ht:** 6' 1" **Wt:** 180 **Born:** 10/30/68 **Age:** 28

			HOW MUCH HE PITCHED						WHAT HE GAVE UP												THE RESULTS					
Year Team	Lg	Org	G	GS	CG	GF	IP	BFP	H	R	ER	HR	SH	SF	HB	TBB	IBB	SO	WP	Bk	W	L	Pct.	ShO	Sv	ERA
1990 Elmira	A-	Bos	16	5	0	4	40.1	186	44	26	18	2	6	1	0	19	0	36	4	1	2	3	.400	0	1	4.02
1991 Lynchburg	A+	Bos	20	20	0	0	103	461	116	59	43	3	4	2	4	51	1	73	8	0	11	5	.688	0	0	3.76
1992 Lynchburg	A+	Bos	21	12	0	4	81.2	384	112	69	47	7	2	4	5	36	0	62	6	0	2	3	.400	0	0	5.18
1993 Jacksonvlle	AA	Sea	34	0	0	13	44.2	182	38	11	10	0	1	0	0	14	1	49	1	0	2	1	.667	0	1	2.01
1994 Jacksonvlle	AA	Sea	14	0	0	7	20.1	85	19	6	3	0	1	1	0	8	2	23	0	0	0	1	.000	0	4	1.33
Calgary	AAA	Sea	19	19	1	0	101.2	480	122	82	66	10	2	3	2	62	1	69	14	0	6	7	.462	1	0	5.84
1995 Las Vegas	AAA	SD	2	0	0	0	0.1	5	3	3	3	0	0	0	1	0	0	1	0	0	0	0	.000	0	0	81.00
Memphis	AA	SD	22	0	0	9	22	85	22	7	7	2	1	0	2	2	1	17	1	0	2	0	1.000	0	2	2.86
1996 Canton-Akrn	AA	Cle	19	0	0	9	21	84	21	7	7	3	1	0	0	2	1	26	2	0	0	0	.000	0	0	3.00
Buffalo	AAA	Cle	17	1	0	7	33.2	148	35	16	14	2	0	1	0	14	0	29	0	0	2	2	.500	0	1	3.74
1993 Seattle	AL		20	0	0	4	9.2	53	11	7	7	0	1	0	1	12	1	3	1	0	0	0	.000	0	1	6.52
1994 Seattle	AL		6	0	0	2	7	31	4	0	0	0	0	0	1	7	0	1	0	0	0	0	.000	0	0	0.00
7 Min. YEARS			184	57	1	53	468.2	2100	532	286	218	29	18	12	14	208	7	385	36	1	27	22	.551	1	9	4.19
2 Maj. YEARS			26	0	0	6	16.2	84	15	7	7	0	1	0	2	19	1	4	1	0	0	0	.000	0	1	3.78

Allen Plaster

Pitches: Right **Bats:** Right **Pos:** P **Ht:** 6'3" **Wt:** 210 **Born:** 8/13/70 **Age:** 26

			HOW MUCH HE PITCHED						WHAT HE GAVE UP												THE RESULTS					
Year Team	Lg	Org	G	GS	CG	GF	IP	BFP	H	R	ER	HR	SH	SF	HB	TBB	IBB	SO	WP	Bk	W	L	Pct.	ShO	Sv	ERA
1991 Bluefield	R+	Bal	10	9	1	0	51.2	213	39	24	14	3	1	2	2	23	0	53	5	4	4	1	.800	1	0	2.44
Frederick	A+	Bal	4	2	0	1	9	50	13	14	11	2	1	0	0	8	0	10	0	0	0	3	.000	0	0	11.00
1992 Frederick	A+	Bal	27	26	3	0	150.1	640	113	70	48	6	5	6	6	75	1	129	8	4	9	12	.429	1	0	2.87
1993 Modesto	A+	Oak	21	18	0	0	95.2	422	89	55	50	11	0	2	3	61	1	89	3	0	4	4	.500	0	0	4.70
1994 Modesto	A+	Oak	45	0	0	30	51.1	214	27	21	11	3	2	1	1	31	2	71	5	0	6	2	.750	0	13	1.93
1995 Huntsville	AA	Oak	43	0	0	14	68	290	63	26	24	4	4	2	0	26	0	47	7	0	1	0	1.000	0	2	3.18
1996 Bowie	AA	Bal	1	0	0	0	2	12	5	3	3	0	0	0	0	1	0	3	1	0	0	0	.000	0	0	13.50
6 Min. YEARS			151	55	4	45	428	1841	349	213	161	29	13	13	12	225	4	402	29	8	24	22	.522	2	15	3.39

Kinnis Pledger

Bats: Left **Throws:** Right **Pos:** OF **Ht:** 6'4" **Wt:** 215 **Born:** 7/17/68 **Age:** 28

			BATTING														BASERUNNING				PERCENTAGES		
Year Team	Lg	Org	G	AB	H	2B	3B	HR	TB	R	RBI	TBB	IBB	SO	HBP	SH	SF	SB	CS	SB%	GDP	Avg	OBP	SLG
1987 White Sox	R	ChA	37	127	32	6	3	1	47	18	13	13	3	46	0	0	1	20	0	1.00	1	.252	.319	.370
1988 South Bend	A	ChA	107	371	75	13	4	3	105	42	34	39	2	106	0	4	3	18	10	.64	2	.202	.276	.283
1989 South Bend	A	ChA	89	293	78	13	5	3	110	49	39	56	3	79	0	4	4	26	14	.65	0	.266	.380	.375
1990 Sarasota	A+	ChA	131	460	114	18	4	3	149	72	40	94	3	134	8	6	3	26	14	.65	10	.248	.382	.324
Vancouver	AAA	ChA	1	1	0	0	0	0	0	0	0	0	0	0	0	0	0	0	0	.00	0	.000	.000	.000
1991 Birmingham	AA	ChA	117	363	79	16	8	9	138	53	51	60	3	104	4	4	1	15	10	.60	2	.218	.334	.380
1992 Sarasota	A+	ChA	59	217	70	11	2	7	106	42	38	28	4	47	3	0	1	13	9	.59	6	.323	.406	.488
Birmingham	AA	ChA	60	191	34	5	2	1	46	18	14	19	3	65	0	5	3	2	4	.33	5	.178	.249	.241
1993 Birmingham	AA	ChA	125	393	95	10	6	14	159	70	56	74	0	120	3	5	4	19	6	.76	9	.242	.363	.405
1994 Daytona	A+	ChN	11	37	8	1	1	1	14	5	3	10	0	12	0	0	0	0	0	.00	2	.216	.383	.378
Orlando	AA	ChN	23	70	19	3	1	2	30	4	8	7	1	17	1	0	0	3	1	.75	4	.271	.346	.429

Year	Team	Lg	Org	G	AB	H	2B	3B	HR	TB	R	RBI	TBB	IBB	SO	HBP	SH	SF	SB	CS	SB%	GDP	Avg	OBP	SLG
				BATTING															BASERUNNING				PERCENTAGES		
	Iowa	AAA	ChN	69	230	65	17	3	8	112	47	34	24	1	54	1	6	3	2	5	.29	2	.283	.349	.487
1995	Iowa	AAA	ChN	9	24	2	0	0	0	2	1	0	2	0	12	0	0	0	0	0	.00	1	.083	.154	.083
	Mobile	IND	—	85	299	80	17	3	21	166	57	61	53	4	76	2	2	3	14	7	.67	2	.268	.378	.555
1996	Norwich	AA	NYA	131	445	118	27	6	19	214	80	67	65	7	123	2	1	0	20	5	.80	4	.265	.361	.481
10 Min. YEARS				1054	3521	869	157	48	92	1398	558	458	544	34	995	24	37	26	178	85	.68	50	.247	.349	.397

Charles Poe

Bats: Right **Throws:** Right **Pos:** OF **Ht:** 6'0" **Wt:** 185 **Born:** 11/9/71 **Age:** 25

Year	Team	Lg	Org	G	AB	H	2B	3B	HR	TB	R	RBI	TBB	IBB	SO	HBP	SH	SF	SB	CS	SB%	GDP	Avg	OBP	SLG
				BATTING															BASERUNNING				PERCENTAGES		
1990	White Sox	R	ChA	46	147	26	3	2	0	33	13	16	16	0	38	4	0	4	10	5	.67	2	.177	.269	.224
1991	South Bend	A	ChA	117	418	89	29	6	5	145	57	59	38	1	136	2	4	5	20	5	.80	5	.213	.279	.347
1992	South Bend	A	ChA	67	228	41	9	3	3	65	26	26	23	0	64	2	2	3	4	1	.80	9	.180	.258	.285
	Utica	A-	ChA	47	164	49	8	1	5	74	27	29	18	0	39	2	0	2	10	2	.83	3	.299	.371	.451
1993	White Sox	R	ChA	3	13	4	3	0	1	10	2	2	1	0	3	0	0	0	0	1	.00	0	.308	.357	.769
	Sarasota	A+	ChA	95	313	78	16	6	11	139	45	47	33	0	91	4	2	0	5	8	.38	6	.249	.329	.444
1994	Pr. William	A+	ChA	130	469	126	21	3	14	195	72	83	51	2	103	5	2	2	14	2	.88	9	.269	.345	.416
1995	Birmingham	AA	ChA	120	427	121	28	2	13	192	75	60	51	4	79	10	7	5	19	4	.83	7	.283	.369	.450
1996	Huntsville	AA	Oak	122	416	110	18	3	12	170	74	68	46	2	99	8	4	2	5	4	.56	14	.264	.347	.409
	Edmonton	AAA	Oak	3	15	3	0	0	0	3	2	0	1	1	5	0	1	0	0	0	.00	0	.200	.250	.200
7 Min. YEARS				750	2610	647	135	26	64	1026	393	390	278	10	657	37	22	23	87	32	.73	55	.248	.326	.393

Kevin Polcovich

Bats: Right **Throws:** Right **Pos:** SS-2B **Ht:** 5'9" **Wt:** 165 **Born:** 6/28/70 **Age:** 27

Year	Team	Lg	Org	G	AB	H	2B	3B	HR	TB	R	RBI	TBB	IBB	SO	HBP	SH	SF	SB	CS	SB%	GDP	Avg	OBP	SLG
				BATTING															BASERUNNING				PERCENTAGES		
1992	Carolina	AA	Pit	13	35	6	0	0	0	6	1	1	4	0	4	2	0	0	0	2	.00	1	.171	.293	.171
	Augusta	A	Pit	46	153	40	6	2	0	50	24	10	18	0	30	8	3	0	7	7	.50	1	.261	.369	.327
1993	Augusta	A	Pit	14	48	13	2	0	0	15	9	4	7	0	8	0	2	1	2	1	.67	1	.271	.357	.313
	Carolina	AA	Pit	4	11	3	0	0	0	3	1	1	1	0	1	0	2	0	0	0	.00	1	.273	.333	.273
	Salem	A+	Pit	94	282	72	10	3	1	91	44	25	49	0	42	12	6	3	13	6	.68	7	.255	.384	.323
1994	Carolina	AA	Pit	125	406	95	14	2	2	119	46	33	38	4	70	11	10	8	9	4	.69	6	.234	.311	.293
1995	Carolina	AA	Pit	64	221	70	8	0	3	87	27	18	14	1	29	5	3	1	10	5	.67	3	.317	.369	.394
	Calgary	AAA	Pit	62	213	60	8	1	3	79	31	27	11	0	32	8	2	3	5	6	.45	7	.282	.336	.371
1996	Calgary	AAA	Pit	104	336	92	21	3	1	122	53	46	18	3	49	14	5	2	7	6	.54	9	.274	.335	.363
5 Min. YEARS				526	1705	451	69	11	10	572	236	165	160	8	265	60	33	18	53	37	.59	36	.265	.345	.335

Wil Polidor

Bats: Both **Throws:** Right **Pos:** 2B-3B **Ht:** 6'1" **Wt:** 158 **Born:** 9/23/73 **Age:** 23

Year	Team	Lg	Org	G	AB	H	2B	3B	HR	TB	R	RBI	TBB	IBB	SO	HBP	SH	SF	SB	CS	SB%	GDP	Avg	OBP	SLG
				BATTING															BASERUNNING				PERCENTAGES		
1991	White Sox	R	ChA	54	217	45	2	0	0	47	19	18	6	2	17	0	1	2	9	2	.82	6	.207	.227	.217
1992	White Sox	R	ChA	27	78	22	2	0	0	24	3	4	2	0	8	0	0	0	1	3	.25	3	.282	.300	.308
	Utica	A-	ChA	16	42	14	1	0	0	15	5	5	1	0	6	0	2	0	2	1	.67	1	.333	.349	.357
1993	Hickory	A	ChA	15	43	10	0	0	0	10	4	3	2	0	7	1	1	0	0	1	.00	0	.233	.283	.233
	South Bend	A	ChA	42	120	34	2	4	0	44	14	9	1	0	15	0	2	0	0	1	.00	6	.283	.289	.367
1994	South Bend	A	ChA	97	355	101	14	2	3	128	43	36	10	0	40	3	4	2	1	2	.33	9	.285	.308	.361
1995	Pr. William	A+	ChA	95	346	86	14	4	0	108	34	24	9	0	33	0	5	2	2	6	.25	18	.249	.266	.312
1996	Birmingham	AA	ChA	25	81	19	3	0	0	22	7	6	2	0	13	0	1	0	0	0	.00	1	.235	.253	.272
	Pr. William	A+	ChA	72	276	64	7	3	2	83	26	26	15	0	34	0	5	4	2	4	.33	13	.232	.268	.301
6 Min. YEARS				443	1558	395	45	13	5	481	155	131	48	2	173	4	21	10	17	20	.46	57	.254	.276	.309

Matt Pontbriant

Pitches: Left **Bats:** Left **Pos:** P **Ht:** 6'4" **Wt:** 200 **Born:** 5/20/72 **Age:** 25

Year	Team	Lg	Org	G	GS	CG	GF	IP	BFP	H	R	ER	HR	SH	SF	HB	TBB	IBB	SO	WP	Bk	W	L	Pct.	ShO	Sv	ERA
				HOW MUCH HE PITCHED						WHAT HE GAVE UP												THE RESULTS					
1991	Pirates	R	Pit	14	8	1	4	53	236	62	27	21	1	4	2	1	14	0	41	5	1	2	5	.286	0	2	3.57
1992	Augusta	A	Pit	6	5	0	0	30.1	137	36	22	19	1	1	3	1	16	0	15	6	0	1	2	.333	0	0	5.64
	Welland	A-	Pit	4	2	0	0	11.2	47	4	4	4	0	0	1	0	9	0	4	0	1	0	1	.000	0	0	3.09
1993	Augusta	A	Pit	3	3	0	0	11	58	13	13	4	0	1	0	2	6	0	12	1	1	0	2	.000	0	0	3.27
1994	Augusta	A	Pit	21	21	2	0	126.1	551	134	65	43	7	3	4	5	41	0	76	8	0	3	8	.273	0	0	3.06
1995	Lynchburg	A+	Pit	27	17	1	4	108.2	476	137	67	61	16	5	2	1	28	3	60	2	1	7	7	.500	1	0	5.05
1996	Carolina	AA	Pit	45	0	0	12	56	261	73	40	37	5	3	2	2	25	1	36	3	0	2	2	.500	0	0	5.95
6 Min. YEARS				120	56	4	20	397	1766	459	238	189	30	17	14	12	139	4	244	25	4	15	27	.357	1	2	4.28

Matt Pool

Pitches: Right **Bats:** Both **Pos:** P **Ht:** 6'6" **Wt:** 190 **Born:** 7/8/73 **Age:** 23

Year	Team	Lg	Org	G	GS	CG	GF	IP	BFP	H	R	ER	HR	SH	SF	HB	TBB	IBB	SO	WP	Bk	W	L	Pct.	ShO	Sv	ERA
				HOW MUCH HE PITCHED						WHAT HE GAVE UP												THE RESULTS					
1994	Bend	A-	Col	6	6	0	0	30.2	132	28	13	11	1	1	0	2	14	0	28	0	1	1	1	.500	0	0	3.23
	Asheville	A	Col	9	8	0	1	58	236	51	21	18	4	0	1	1	18	0	40	4	1	4	3	.571	0	1	2.79
1995	Salem	A+	Col	28	28	2	0	165	705	191	90	88	18	5	2	6	50	5	95	16	1	9	9	.500	0	0	4.80

Year	Team	Lg	Org	HOW MUCH HE PITCHED G	GS	CG	GF	IP	BFP	WHAT HE GAVE UP H	R	ER	HR	SH	SF	HB	TBB	IBB	SO	WP	Bk	THE RESULTS W	L	Pct.	ShO	Sv	ERA
1996	Salem	A+	Col	27	21	0	3	135.2	591	158	80	70	8	6	2	6	41	3	93	10	0	5	6	.455	0	0	4.64
	New Haven	AA	Col	4	0	0	3	6.2	30	9	2	2	0	1	0	2	1	0	7	1	0	0	1	.000	0	0	2.70
3 Min. YEARS				74	63	2	7	396	1694	437	206	189	31	13	5	17	124	8	263	31	3	19	20	.487	0	1	4.30

Scott Pose

Bats: Left **Throws:** Right **Pos:** OF **Ht:** 5'11" **Wt:** 165 **Born:** 2/11/67 **Age:** 30

Year	Team	Lg	Org	BATTING G	AB	H	2B	3B	HR	TB	R	RBI	TBB	IBB	SO	HBP	SH	SF	BASERUNNING SB	CS	SB%	GDP	PERCENTAGES Avg	OBP	SLG
1989	Billings	R+	Cin	60	210	74	7	2	0	85	52	25	54	3	31	1	1	1	26	3	.90	2	.352	.485	.405
1990	Charlstn-WV	A	Cin	135	480	143	13	5	0	166	106	46	114	8	56	7	5	6	49	21	.70	5	.298	.436	.346
1991	Nashville	AAA	Cin	15	52	10	0	0	0	10	7	3	2	0	9	2	2	0	3	1	.75	0	.192	.250	.192
	Chattanooga	AA	Cin	117	402	110	8	5	1	131	61	31	69	3	50	2	7	3	17	13	.57	7	.274	.380	.326
1992	Chattanooga	AA	Cin	136	526	180	22	8	2	224	87	45	63	5	66	4	4	3	21	27	.44	8	.342	.414	.426
1993	Edmonton	AAA	Fla	109	398	113	8	6	0	133	61	27	42	3	36	1	5	1	19	9	.68	8	.284	.353	.334
1994	New Orleans	AAA	Mil	124	429	121	13	7	0	148	60	52	47	2	52	2	9	4	20	8	.71	7	.282	.353	.345
1995	Albuquerque	AAA	LA	7	16	3	1	0	0	4	5	1	2	0	0	0	0	0	2	0	1.00	0	.188	.278	.250
	Salt Lake	AAA	Min	77	219	66	10	1	0	78	46	20	31	2	28	1	3	3	15	4	.79	2	.301	.386	.356
1996	Syracuse	AAA	Tor	113	419	114	11	6	0	137	71	39	58	0	71	3	9	4	30	16	.65	3	.272	.362	.327
1993	Florida	NL		15	41	8	2	0	0	10	0	3	2	0	4	0	0	0	0	2	.00	0	.195	.233	.244
8 Min. YEARS				893	3151	934	93	40	3	1116	556	289	482	26	399	23	45	25	202	102	.66	42	.296	.391	.354

Lou Pote

Pitches: Right **Bats:** Right **Pos:** P **Ht:** 6'3" **Wt:** 190 **Born:** 8/27/71 **Age:** 25

Year	Team	Lg	Org	HOW MUCH HE PITCHED G	GS	CG	GF	IP	BFP	WHAT HE GAVE UP H	R	ER	HR	SH	SF	HB	TBB	IBB	SO	WP	Bk	THE RESULTS W	L	Pct.	ShO	Sv	ERA
1991	Giants	R	SF	8	8	0	0	42.1	184	38	23	12	0	0	1	0	18	0	41	5	0	2	3	.400	0	0	2.55
	Everett	A-	SF	5	4	0	0	28.2	117	24	8	8	2	0	1	2	7	0	26	2	0	2	0	1.000	0	0	2.51
1992	Shreveport	AA	SF	20	3	0	9	37.2	146	20	7	4	1	3	1	1	15	2	26	3	0	4	2	.667	0	0	0.96
	San Jose	A+	SF	4	3	0	1	9.2	46	11	5	5	0	1	1	0	7	0	8	3	0	0	1	.000	0	0	4.66
1993	Shreveport	AA	SF	19	19	0	0	108.1	458	111	53	49	10	1	3	0	45	1	81	3	1	8	7	.533	0	0	4.07
1994	Giants	R	SF	4	4	0	0	19.2	73	9	0	0	0	1	0	0	6	0	30	0	0	1	0	1.000	0	0	0.00
	Shreveport	AA	SF	5	5	0	0	28.2	122	31	11	9	2	2	2	0	7	0	15	1	1	2	2	.500	0	0	2.83
1995	Harrisburg	AA	Mon	9	4	0	2	28.1	123	32	17	17	3	0	2	1	7	0	24	1	0	0	1	.000	0	0	5.40
	Shreveport	AA	SF	37	4	0	13	79	349	85	58	47	11	4	3	1	33	1	54	5	0	2	3	.400	0	3	5.35
1996	Harrisburg	AA	Mon	25	18	0	3	104.2	467	114	66	59	15	3	2	2	48	2	61	8	0	1	7	.125	0	1	5.07
6 Min. YEARS				136	72	0	28	487	2085	475	248	210	44	15	16	7	193	6	366	31	2	22	26	.458	0	4	3.88

Chop Pough

Bats: Right **Throws:** Right **Pos:** 3B **Ht:** 6'0" **Wt:** 173 **Born:** 12/25/69 **Age:** 27

Year	Team	Lg	Org	BATTING G	AB	H	2B	3B	HR	TB	R	RBI	TBB	IBB	SO	HBP	SH	SF	BASERUNNING SB	CS	SB%	GDP	PERCENTAGES Avg	OBP	SLG
1988	Indians	R	Cle	52	173	45	11	0	3	65	28	21	24	1	52	1	2	0	1	3	.25	3	.260	.354	.376
1989	Burlington	R+	Cle	67	225	58	15	1	8	99	39	37	36	0	64	3	0	2	9	5	.64	1	.258	.365	.440
1990	Reno	A+	Cle	16	53	8	0	1	0	10	1	2	6	1	18	0	0	0	0	1	.00	1	.151	.237	.189
	Watertown	A-	Cle	76	285	72	15	1	9	116	47	49	40	0	71	2	0	4	21	4	.84	7	.253	.344	.407
1991	Kinston	A+	Cle	11	30	5	1	0	0	6	2	2	1	0	9	1	0	0	1	0	1.00	1	.167	.219	.200
	Columbus	A	Cle	115	414	127	35	3	11	201	76	73	62	2	63	8	2	9	11	6	.65	6	.307	.400	.486
	Colo. Sprng	AAA	Cle	2	2	0	0	0	0	0	0	0	0	0	0	0	0	0	0	0	.00	0	.000	.000	.000
1992	Kinston	A+	Cle	114	411	93	23	1	11	151	59	58	50	1	98	6	4	5	12	3	.80	13	.226	.316	.367
1993	Kinston	A+	Cle	120	418	113	18	1	13	172	66	57	59	2	95	5	1	4	8	3	.73	8	.270	.364	.411
1994	Canton-Akrn	AA	Cle	105	379	113	24	3	20	203	69	66	43	3	86	5	0	6	3	2	.60	9	.298	.372	.536
	Charlotte	AAA	Cle	16	42	9	4	0	0	13	1	4	6	0	13	0	0	1	0	0	.00	0	.214	.306	.310
1995	Trenton	AA	Bos	97	363	101	23	5	21	197	68	69	50	8	101	7	0	4	11	5	.69	1	.278	.373	.543
	Pawtucket	AAA	Bos	30	99	23	8	1	5	48	12	23	7	1	27	1	0	1	0	0	.00	2	.232	.287	.485
1996	Pawtucket	AAA	Bos	74	242	57	17	2	12	114	43	40	32	0	68	1	0	1	2	2	.50	7	.236	.326	.471
	Jacksonvlle	AA	Det	2	4	2	0	0	0	2	1	0	0	0	2	1	0	0	0	0	.00	0	.500	.600	.500
9 Min. YEARS				897	3140	826	194	19	113	1397	512	501	416	19	767	41	9	37	79	34	.70	59	.263	.353	.445

Dante Powell

Bats: Right **Throws:** Right **Pos:** OF **Ht:** 6'2" **Wt:** 185 **Born:** 8/25/73 **Age:** 23

Year	Team	Lg	Org	BATTING G	AB	H	2B	3B	HR	TB	R	RBI	TBB	IBB	SO	HBP	SH	SF	BASERUNNING SB	CS	SB%	GDP	PERCENTAGES Avg	OBP	SLG
1994	Everett	A-	SF	41	165	51	15	1	5	83	31	25	19	1	47	4	0	2	27	1	.96	1	.309	.389	.503
	San Jose	A+	SF	1	4	2	0	1	0	4	0	0	0	0	1	0	0	0	0	0	.00	0	.500	.500	1.000
1995	San Jose	A+	SF	135	505	125	23	8	10	194	74	70	46	2	131	3	1	4	43	12	.78	8	.248	.312	.384
1996	Shreveport	AA	SF	135	508	142	27	2	21	236	92	78	72	4	92	3	1	2	43	23	.65	6	.280	.371	.465
	Phoenix	AAA	SF	2	8	2	0	1	0	4	0	0	2	0	3	0	0	0	0	1	.00	0	.250	.400	.500
3 Min. YEARS				314	1190	322	65	13	36	521	197	173	139	7	274	10	2	8	113	37	.75	15	.271	.350	.438

Dennis Powell

Pitches: Left **Bats:** Right **Pos:** P **Ht:** 6' 3" **Wt:** 200 **Born:** 8/13/63 **Age:** 33

		HOW MUCH HE PITCHED						WHAT HE GAVE UP												THE RESULTS					
Year Team	Lg Org	G	GS	CG	GF	IP	BFP	H	R	ER	HR	SH	SF	HB	TBB	IBB	SO	WP	Bk	W	L	Pct.	ShO	Sv	ERA
1984 Vero Beach	A+ LA	4	4	0	0	26	106	19	7	4	0	2	1	1	12	1	14	3	0	1	1	.500	0	0	1.38
San Antonio	AA LA	24	24	5	0	168	721	153	81	63	8	3	4	2	87	0	82	3	2	9	8	.529	2	0	3.38
1985 Albuquerque	AAA LA	18	17	3	1	111.2	0	106	40	34	5	0	0	1	48	0	55	6	2	9	0	1.000	0	0	2.74
1986 Albuquerque	AAA LA	7	7	0	0	41.2	176	45	23	19	3	0	1	0	15	0	27	1	0	3	3	.500	0	0	4.10
1987 Calgary	AAA Sea	20	20	2	0	117.1	538	145	80	64	12	4	3	2	48	1	65	3	1	4	8	.333	1	0	4.91
1988 Calgary	AAA Sea	21	18	2	1	108	481	116	57	50	9	6	2	1	49	1	81	6	3	6	4	.600	1	1	4.17
1989 Calgary	AAA Sea	18	0	0	14	25.1	109	21	10	6	0	0	2	1	12	0	15	0	0	3	2	.600	0	6	2.13
1990 Denver	AAA Mil	11	11	2	0	62.1	263	63	34	25	6	2	2	0	21	0	46	3	1	4	4	.500	0	0	3.61
1991 Calgary	AAA Sea	27	26	5	1	173.2	761	200	90	80	20	7	6	6	59	0	96	12	1	9	8	.529	1	0	4.15
1993 Calgary	AAA Sea	12	4	0	2	40	164	37	16	16	3	1	0	1	19	1	30	0	0	3	2	.600	0	1	3.60
1994 Nashville	AAA ChA	25	0	0	6	22	107	26	13	11	2	3	2	2	16	5	27	3	1	1	3	.250	0	1	4.50
1996 Rochester	AAA Bal	5	0	0	2	6.2	24	4	1	1	0	0	0	0	1	0	4	1	0	0	0	.000	0	1	1.35
1985 Los Angeles	NL	16	2	0	6	29.1	133	30	19	17	7	4	1	1	13	3	19	3	0	1	1	.500	0	1	5.22
1986 Los Angeles	NL	27	6	0	5	65.1	272	65	32	31	5	5	2	1	25	7	31	7	2	2	7	.222	0	0	4.27
1987 Seattle	AL	16	3	0	1	34.1	147	32	13	12	3	2	2	0	15	0	17	0	0	1	3	.250	0	0	3.15
1988 Seattle	AL	12	2	0	1	18.2	95	29	20	18	2	0	2	2	11	2	15	0	0	1	3	.250	0	0	8.68
1989 Seattle	AL	43	1	0	9	45	201	49	25	25	6	3	3	2	21	0	27	1	0	2	2	.500	0	2	5.00
1990 Seattle	AL	2	0	0	1	3	17	5	3	3	0	0	0	1	2	0	0	0	0	0	0	.000	0	0	9.00
Milwaukee	AL	9	7	0	1	39.1	197	59	37	30	0	2	2	1	19	0	23	2	0	0	4	.000	0	0	6.86
1992 Seattle	AL	49	0	0	11	57	243	49	30	29	5	5	0	3	29	2	35	2	0	4	2	.667	0	0	4.58
1993 Seattle	AL	33	2	0	7	47.2	197	42	22	22	7	5	2	1	24	2	32	2	0	0	0	.000	0	0	4.15
11 Min. YEARS		192	131	19	27	902.2	3450	935	452	373	68	28	23	17	387	9	542	41	11	52	43	.547	5	10	3.72
8 Maj. YEARS		207	23	0	42	339.2	1502	360	201	187	35	26	14	12	159	16	199	17	2	11	22	.333	0	3	4.95

John Powell

Pitches: Right **Bats:** Right **Pos:** P **Ht:** 5'10" **Wt:** 180 **Born:** 4/7/71 **Age:** 26

		HOW MUCH HE PITCHED						WHAT HE GAVE UP												THE RESULTS					
Year Team	Lg Org	G	GS	CG	GF	IP	BFP	H	R	ER	HR	SH	SF	HB	TBB	IBB	SO	WP	Bk	W	L	Pct.	ShO	Sv	ERA
1994 Charlotte	A+ Tex	17	12	2	0	81.1	327	61	38	32	4	6	0	4	28	1	85	2	4	2	8	.200	0	0	3.54
1995 Tulsa	AA Tex	7	7	0	0	39.1	174	45	21	17	9	0	1	2	16	0	27	1	1	1	4	.200	0	0	3.89
Charlotte	A+ Tex	26	9	0	9	87.1	375	89	39	33	11	2	3	5	29	1	74	2	2	5	5	.500	0	2	3.40
1996 Tulsa	AA Tex	39	10	0	16	114	486	121	71	62	18	3	5	11	31	0	79	4	0	3	8	.273	0	4	4.89
3 Min. YEARS		89	38	2	25	322	1362	316	169	144	42	11	9	22	104	2	265	9	7	11	25	.306	0	6	4.02

Ross Powell

Pitches: Left **Bats:** Left **Pos:** P **Ht:** 6' 0" **Wt:** 180 **Born:** 1/24/68 **Age:** 29

		HOW MUCH HE PITCHED						WHAT HE GAVE UP												THE RESULTS					
Year Team	Lg Org	G	GS	CG	GF	IP	BFP	H	R	ER	HR	SH	SF	HB	TBB	IBB	SO	WP	Bk	W	L	Pct.	ShO	Sv	ERA
1989 Cedar Rapds	A Cin	13	13	1	0	76.1	319	68	37	30	4	1	1	1	23	0	58	4	3	7	4	.636	1	0	3.54
1990 Chattanooga	AA Cin	29	27	6	1	185	783	172	89	73	10	11	8	6	57	5	132	11	2	8	14	.364	1	0	3.55
Nashville	AAA Cin	3	0	0	1	2.2	9	1	1	1	0	2	0	0	0	0	4	0	0	0	0	.000	0	0	3.38
1991 Nashville	AAA Cin	24	24	1	0	129.2	568	125	74	63	10	5	2	2	63	1	82	3	0	8	8	.500	0	0	4.37
1992 Chattanooga	AA Cin	14	5	0	2	57.1	224	43	9	8	2	3	2	0	17	1	56	3	1	4	1	.800	0	1	1.26
Nashville	AAA Cin	25	12	0	4	93.1	403	89	37	35	5	4	2	3	42	1	84	2	1	4	8	.333	0	0	3.38
1993 Indianapols	AAA Cin	28	27	4	1	179.2	764	159	89	82	27	1	2	5	71	1	133	13	2	10	10	.500	0	0	4.11
1994 Indianapols	AAA Cin	4	1	0	0	9.2	57	16	10	7	1	2	0	0	11	0	11	1	0	1	1	.500	0	0	6.52
Tucson	AAA Hou	16	10	0	1	67.2	302	81	47	45	8	3	0	0	27	1	45	5	0	4	2	.667	0	1	5.99
1995 Tucson	AAA Hou	13	4	0	5	38	169	37	16	13	3	5	0	1	15	0	34	1	0	3	3	.500	0	1	3.08
1996 Louisville	AAA StL	5	0	0	4	8.1	35	8	2	2	0	1	0	0	2	0	10	1	1	0	0	.000	0	0	2.16
Indianapols	AAA Cin	12	11	0	0	59.2	272	74	41	40	9	2	3	0	26	0	51	1	2	6	3	.667	0	0	6.03
1993 Cincinnati	NL	9	1	0	1	16.1	66	13	8	8	1	2	0	0	6	0	17	0	0	0	3	.000	0	0	4.41
1994 Houston	NL	12	0	0	1	7.1	32	6	1	1	0	1	0	1	5	0	5	0	0	0	0	.000	0	0	1.23
1995 Houston	NL	15	0	0	1	9	55	16	12	11	1	1	1	0	11	4	8	1	0	0	0	.000	0	0	11.00
Pittsburgh	NL	12	3	0	5	20.2	93	20	14	12	5	2	0	2	10	0	12	3	0	0	2	.000	0	0	5.23
8 Min. YEARS		186	134	12	19	907.1	3905	873	452	399	79	40	20	18	354	10	700	45	12	55	54	.505	2	3	3.96
3 Maj. YEARS		48	4	0	8	53.1	246	55	35	32	7	6	1	3	32	4	42	4	0	0	5	.000	0	0	5.40

Yohel Pozo

Bats: Right **Throws:** Right **Pos:** C **Ht:** 6'1" **Wt:** 187 **Born:** 10/17/73 **Age:** 23

		BATTING															BASERUNNING				PERCENTAGES		
Year Team	Lg Org	G	AB	H	2B	3B	HR	TB	R	RBI	TBB	IBB	SO	HBP	SH	SF	SB	CS	SB%	GDP	Avg	OBP	SLG
1992 Rockies/Cub	R Col	36	100	22	1	0	0	23	10	6	1	0	26	1	0	1	1	1	.50	1	.220	.233	.230
1993 Central Val	A+ Col	1	3	1	0	0	0	1	1	0	0	0	1	0	0	0	0	0	.00	0	.333	.333	.333
Rockies	R Col	21	74	21	4	0	1	28	5	17	4	0	13	0	0	3	1	1	.50	3	.284	.309	.378
1994 Bend	A- Col	45	137	26	9	0	0	35	13	13	6	0	20	1	4	1	0	0	.00	7	.190	.228	.255
1995 Asheville	A Col	40	139	30	3	0	1	36	7	15	4	0	32	0	1	1	0	3	.00	7	.216	.236	.259
Salem	A+ Col	43	135	23	4	0	0	27	7	3	2	0	21	1	4	0	0	1	.00	4	.170	.188	.200
1996 Asheville	A Col	27	85	12	1	0	0	13	5	4	5	0	20	1	0	1	0	1	.00	3	.141	.196	.153
Colo. Sprng	AAA Col	20	47	13	2	0	1	18	8	5	2	0	8	1	1	1	0	0	.00	5	.277	.314	.383
5 Min. YEARS		233	720	148	24	0	3	181	56	63	24	0	141	5	10	8	2	7	.22	30	.200	.204	.251

Jose Prado

Pitches: Right **Bats:** Right **Pos:** P **Ht:** 6'2" **Wt:** 195 **Born:** 5/9/72 **Age:** 25

			HOW MUCH HE PITCHED						WHAT HE GAVE UP												THE RESULTS					
Year	Team	Lg Org	G	GS	CG	GF	IP	BFP	H	R	ER	HR	SH	SF	HB	TBB	IBB	SO	WP	Bk	W	L	Pct.	ShO	Sv	ERA
1993	Vero Beach	A+ LA	12	9	0	0	55.2	233	45	31	27	2	1	3	1	29	3	31	1	4	3	4	.429	0	0	4.37
1994	Bakersfield	A+ LA	28	28	0	0	163.1	684	159	75	64	8	3	3	5	56	0	143	11	5	15	9	.625	0	0	3.53
1995	San Antonio	AA LA	28	22	0	3	144.2	621	126	70	56	9	7	9	7	64	0	93	13	2	7	11	.389	0	1	3.48
1996	San Antonio	AA LA	18	1	0	5	32.1	149	32	21	18	3	3	1	0	24	0	20	6	0	2	1	.667	0	1	5.01
4 Min. YEARS			86	60	0	8	396	1687	362	197	165	22	14	16	13	173	3	287	31	11	27	25	.519	0	2	3.75

Richard Pratt

Pitches: Left **Bats:** Left **Pos:** P **Ht:** 6'3" **Wt:** 201 **Born:** 5/7/71 **Age:** 26

			HOW MUCH HE PITCHED						WHAT HE GAVE UP												THE RESULTS					
Year	Team	Lg Org	G	GS	CG	GF	IP	BFP	H	R	ER	HR	SH	SF	HB	TBB	IBB	SO	WP	Bk	W	L	Pct.	ShO	Sv	ERA
1993	White Sox	R ChA	3	0	0	1	10	40	10	3	3	0	2	1	0	2	0	10	0	0	0	1	.000	0	0	2.70
	Hickory	A ChA	13	4	0	6	44	193	36	23	18	3	1	1	7	24	1	29	1	1	1	4	.200	0	2	3.68
1994	Hickory	A ChA	29	23	3	3	165	661	138	51	37	9	5	4	3	29	0	153	1	1	11	6	.647	1	0	2.02
1995	Pr. William	A+ ChA	25	25	2	0	152	619	139	66	53	12	2	5	4	42	0	120	10	2	5	11	.313	1	0	3.14
1996	Birmingham	AA ChA	27	27	5	0	177.1	732	180	87	76	24	3	7	6	40	2	122	5	1	13	9	.591	2	0	3.86
4 Min. YEARS			97	79	10	10	548.1	2245	503	230	187	48	13	18	20	137	3	434	17	5	30	31	.492	4	2	3.07

Tom Price

Pitches: Left **Bats:** Left **Pos:** P **Ht:** 6'0" **Wt:** 190 **Born:** 3/19/72 **Age:** 25

			HOW MUCH HE PITCHED						WHAT HE GAVE UP												THE RESULTS					
Year	Team	Lg Org	G	GS	CG	GF	IP	BFP	H	R	ER	HR	SH	SF	HB	TBB	IBB	SO	WP	Bk	W	L	Pct.	ShO	Sv	ERA
1994	Great Falls	R+ LA	19	0	0	10	38	164	40	20	13	3	2	5	2	9	2	22	5	0	3	4	.429	0	0	3.08
1995	San Bernrdo	A+ LA	42	13	2	9	151.2	605	145	49	37	5	5	1	3	14	4	82	5	0	10	5	.667	0	3	2.20
1996	San Antonio	AA LA	7	5	0	0	25	125	50	30	26	5	1	1	0	3	0	11	2	0	0	4	.000	0	0	9.36
	San Bernrdo	A+ LA	15	11	1	1	82	344	94	42	35	8	5	1	3	5	0	60	1	0	5	3	.625	0	0	3.84
3 Min. YEARS			83	29	3	20	296.2	1238	329	141	111	21	13	8	8	31	6	175	13	0	18	16	.529	0	3	3.37

Chris Prieto

Bats: Left **Throws:** Left **Pos:** OF **Ht:** 5'10" **Wt:** 170 **Born:** 8/24/72 **Age:** 24

			BATTING														BASERUNNING				PERCENTAGES		
Year	Team	Lg Org	G	AB	H	2B	3B	HR	TB	R	RBI	TBB	IBB	SO	HBP	SH	SF	SB	CS	SB%	GDP	Avg	OBP	SLG
1993	Spokane	A- SD	73	280	81	17	5	1	111	64	28	47	0	30	5	0	3	36	3	.92	4	.289	.397	.396
1994	Rancho Cuca	A+ SD	102	353	87	10	3	1	106	64	29	52	1	49	5	6	4	29	11	.73	3	.246	.348	.300
1995	Rancho Cuca	A+ SD	114	366	100	12	6	2	130	80	35	64	2	55	5	8	5	39	14	.74	10	.273	.384	.355
1996	Rancho Cuca	A+ SD	55	217	52	11	2	2	73	36	23	39	1	36	0	1	0	23	8	.74	2	.240	.355	.336
	Las Vegas	AAA SD	5	7	0	0	0	0	0	1	0	0	0	0	0	0	0	0	0	.00	0	.000	.000	.000
	Memphis	AA SD	7	12	4	0	1	0	6	1	0	1	0	2	0	0	0	2	0	1.00	0	.333	.385	.500
4 Min. YEARS			356	1235	324	50	17	6	426	246	115	203	4	172	15	15	12	129	36	.78	19	.262	.370	.345

Alan Probst

Bats: Right **Throws:** Right **Pos:** C **Ht:** 6'4" **Wt:** 205 **Born:** 10/24/70 **Age:** 26

			BATTING														BASERUNNING				PERCENTAGES		
Year	Team	Lg Org	G	AB	H	2B	3B	HR	TB	R	RBI	TBB	IBB	SO	HBP	SH	SF	SB	CS	SB%	GDP	Avg	OBP	SLG
1992	Auburn	A- Hou	66	224	53	14	1	5	84	24	34	23	1	48	3	1	2	1	0	1.00	5	.237	.313	.375
1993	Asheville	A Hou	40	124	32	4	0	5	51	14	21	12	0	34	0	0	1	0	2	.00	5	.258	.321	.411
	Quad City	A Hou	49	176	48	9	2	3	70	18	28	16	1	48	3	0	3	2	0	1.00	1	.273	.338	.398
1994	Quad City	A Hou	113	375	87	14	1	9	130	50	41	37	3	98	2	3	3	2	5	.29	8	.232	.302	.347
1995	Quad City	A Hou	51	151	39	12	1	7	74	23	27	13	0	28	1	1	1	2	0	1.00	3	.258	.319	.490
	Jackson	AA Hou	28	89	21	5	0	1	29	11	8	7	0	25	1	0	2	0	0	.00	3	.236	.293	.326
1996	Tucson	AAA Hou	2	7	2	1	0	0	3	0	1	1	0	3	0	0	0	0	0	.00	0	.286	.375	.429
	Jackson	AA Hou	63	180	44	9	1	7	76	20	33	16	1	43	2	2	2	1	0	1.00	1	.244	.310	.422
5 Min. YEARS			412	1326	326	68	6	37	517	160	193	125	6	327	12	7	14	8	7	.53	26	.246	.313	.390

Carlos Pulido

Pitches: Left **Bats:** Left **Pos:** P **Ht:** 6' 0" **Wt:** 200 **Born:** 8/5/71 **Age:** 25

			HOW MUCH HE PITCHED						WHAT HE GAVE UP												THE RESULTS					
Year	Team	Lg Org	G	GS	CG	GF	IP	BFP	H	R	ER	HR	SH	SF	HB	TBB	IBB	SO	WP	Bk	W	L	Pct.	ShO	Sv	ERA
1989	Twins	R Min	22	0	0	11	36	143	22	9	9	0	0	2	3	14	0	46	6	3	3	0	1.000	0	2	2.25
1990	Kenosha	A Min	56	0	0	29	61.2	270	55	21	16	2	2	1	4	36	3	70	3	4	5	5	.500	0	6	2.34
1991	Visalia	A+ Min	57	0	0	32	80.2	334	77	34	18	2	5	2	0	23	2	102	3	1	1	5	.167	0	17	2.01
	Portland	AAA Min	2	0	0	2	1.2	10	4	3	3	1	0	0	0	1	0	2	0	0	0	0	.000	0	0	16.20
1992	Orlando	AA Min	52	5	0	20	100.1	432	99	52	49	7	1	6	3	37	0	87	4	1	6	2	.750	0	1	4.40
1993	Portland	AAA Min	33	22	1	5	146	625	169	74	68	8	3	4	2	45	1	79	8	1	10	6	.625	0	0	4.19
1995	Salt Lake	AAA Min	43	3	0	9	71.1	321	87	42	37	10	1	0	2	20	4	38	0	1	8	1	.889	0	3	4.67
1996	Iowa	AAA ChN	28	17	0	3	101.2	461	133	64	60	17	6	3	3	36	3	48	5	1	2	8	.200	0	0	5.31
	Orlando	AA ChN	6	0	0	1	9.2	50	17	9	8	0	0	0	0	3	0	12	3	0	2	2	.500	0	0	7.45
1994	Minnesota	AL	19	14	0	1	84.1	366	87	57	56	17	2	4	1	40	1	32	3	2	3	7	.300	0	0	5.98
7 Min. YEARS			299	47	1	112	609	2646	663	308	268	47	18	18	17	215	13	484	32	12	37	29	.561	0	29	3.96

Shawn Purdy

Pitches: Right **Bats:** Right **Pos:** P **Ht:** 6'0" **Wt:** 205 **Born:** 7/30/68 **Age:** 28

		HOW MUCH HE PITCHED						WHAT HE GAVE UP												THE RESULTS					
Year Team	Lg Org	G	GS	CG	GF	IP	BFP	H	R	ER	HR	SH	SF	HB	TBB	IBB	SO	WP	Bk	W	L	Pct.	ShO	Sv	ERA
1991 Boise	A- Cal	15	15	1	0	95.2	394	87	37	32	3	3	2	4	27	2	78	6	0	8	4	.667	0	0	3.01
1992 Palm Spring	A+ Cal	26	26	7	0	168	740	203	90	77	7	2	7	5	51	3	113	5	3	13	8	.619	0	0	4.13
1993 Angels	R Cal	2	2	0	0	13	49	7	3	3	0	0	0	1	1	0	11	0	0	1	0	1.000	0	0	2.08
Boise	A- Cal	1	1	0	0	6	25	2	2	0	0	0	1	0	5	2	1	0	0	1	0	1.000	0	0	0.00
Palm Spring	A+ Cal	5	3	0	2	27	120	30	12	11	2	1	0	3	5	2	17	1	0	1	1	.500	0	1	3.67
Midland	AA Cal	5	5	1	0	32	136	38	19	18	2	1	2	1	9	0	18	2	0	2	2	.500	0	0	5.06
1994 Midland	AA Cal	10	5	0	1	36	170	48	39	35	2	2	2	2	15	1	19	6	1	1	6	.143	0	0	8.75
Lk Elsinore	A+ Cal	25	11	1	6	117.2	493	113	63	49	8	7	3	10	30	0	76	5	2	7	5	.583	0	0	3.75
1995 Shreveport	AA SF	52	1	0	40	62.1	260	61	31	26	7	1	3	1	18	2	33	3	0	6	3	.667	0	21	3.75
1996 Shreveport	AA SF	54	0	0	37	52.1	218	46	23	18	3	4	1	1	16	4	23	4	0	5	4	.556	0	16	3.10
6 Min. YEARS		195	69	10	86	610	2605	635	319	269	34	21	21	28	177	16	389	32	6	45	33	.577	0	38	3.97

Dave Pyc

Pitches: Left **Bats:** Left **Pos:** P **Ht:** 6'3" **Wt:** 235 **Born:** 2/11/71 **Age:** 26

		HOW MUCH HE PITCHED						WHAT HE GAVE UP												THE RESULTS					
Year Team	Lg Org	G	GS	CG	GF	IP	BFP	H	R	ER	HR	SH	SF	HB	TBB	IBB	SO	WP	Bk	W	L	Pct.	ShO	Sv	ERA
1992 Great Falls	R+ LA	25	0	0	19	34.2	155	32	15	11	0	3	1	1	16	5	34	1	0	2	3	.400	0	9	2.86
1993 Vero Beach	A+ LA	23	15	1	2	113.1	469	97	41	30	1	6	3	1	47	2	78	5	4	7	8	.467	0	0	2.38
1994 San Antonio	AA LA	25	25	0	0	154.2	656	165	77	64	2	9	4	3	47	5	120	3	0	4	11	.267	0	0	3.72
1995 Albuquerque	AAA LA	1	1	0	0	7	31	7	5	3	1	0	1	0	2	1	3	0	0	0	1	.000	0	0	3.86
San Antonio	AA LA	27	27	1	0	164	707	177	77	62	7	6	5	3	51	2	81	3	1	12	7	.632	0	0	3.40
1996 Albuquerque	AAA LA	13	4	0	2	35.1	179	53	39	36	4	1	1	5	19	3	27	2	0	2	3	.400	0	0	9.17
San Antonio	AA LA	14	14	1	0	96.2	415	106	45	32	5	10	1	2	24	0	62	4	0	7	5	.583	1	0	2.98
5 Min. YEARS		128	86	3	23	605.2	2612	637	299	238	20	35	16	15	206	18	405	18	5	34	38	.472	1	9	3.54

Eddie Pye

Bats: Right **Throws:** Right **Pos:** 2B **Ht:** 5'10" **Wt:** 183 **Born:** 2/13/67 **Age:** 30

		BATTING															BASERUNNING				PERCENTAGES		
Year Team	Lg Org	G	AB	H	2B	3B	HR	TB	R	RBI	TBB	IBB	SO	HBP	SH	SF	SB	CS	SB%	GDP	Avg	OBP	SLG
1988 Great Falls	R+ LA	61	237	71	8	4	2	93	50	30	29	0	26	4	2	1	19	9	.68	6	.300	.384	.392
1989 Bakersfield	A+ LA	129	488	126	21	2	8	175	59	47	41	1	87	6	3	0	19	9	.68	6	.258	.323	.359
1990 San Antonio	AA LA	119	455	113	18	7	2	151	67	44	45	1	68	6	3	5	19	6	.76	7	.248	.321	.332
1991 Albuquerque	AAA LA	12	30	13	1	0	1	17	4	8	4	0	4	0	1	0	1	2	.33	0	.433	.500	.567
1992 Albuquerque	AAA LA	72	222	67	11	2	1	85	30	25	13	0	41	2	5	2	6	4	.60	4	.302	.343	.383
1993 Albuquerque	AAA LA	101	365	120	21	7	7	176	53	66	32	0	43	7	4	3	5	9	.36	13	.329	.391	.482
1994 Albuquerque	AAA LA	100	361	121	19	6	2	158	79	42	48	2	43	7	2	4	11	6	.65	5	.335	.419	.438
1995 Albuquerque	AAA LA	84	302	89	20	1	3	120	49	32	30	2	36	1	2	2	11	2	.85	7	.295	.358	.397
1996 Tucson	AAA Hou	92	275	71	15	6	2	104	39	25	29	2	41	1	2	3	5	3	.63	8	.258	.328	.378
1994 Los Angeles	NL	7	10	1	0	0	0	1	2	0	1	0	4	0	1	0	0	0	.00	0	.100	.182	.100
1995 Los Angeles	NL	7	8	0	0	0	0	0	0	0	0	0	4	0	0	0	0	0	.00	0	.000	.000	.000
9 Min. YEARS		770	2735	791	134	35	28	1079	430	319	271	8	389	34	24	20	96	50	.66	56	.289	.358	.395
2 Maj. YEARS		14	18	1	0	0	0	1	2	0	1	0	8	0	1	0	0	0	.00	0	.056	.105	.056

Keifer Rackley

Bats: Left **Throws:** Right **Pos:** OF **Ht:** 6'1" **Wt:** 200 **Born:** 2/27/71 **Age:** 26

		BATTING															BASERUNNING				PERCENTAGES		
Year Team	Lg Org	G	AB	H	2B	3B	HR	TB	R	RBI	TBB	IBB	SO	HBP	SH	SF	SB	CS	SB%	GDP	Avg	OBP	SLG
1993 Bellingham	A- Sea	33	114	28	4	0	2	38	21	15	12	1	16	0	1	2	3	1	.75	3	.246	.313	.333
1994 Riverside	A+ Sea	64	236	71	14	1	10	117	43	43	25	1	46	5	1	3	6	1	.86	6	.301	.375	.496
1995 Port City	AA Sea	114	430	110	17	2	6	149	55	40	39	2	96	4	6	5	8	4	.67	11	.256	.320	.347
1996 Port City	AA Sea	6	19	3	1	0	0	4	0	1	1	0	5	0	0	0	0	0	.00	0	.158	.200	.211
Wilmington	A+ KC	95	290	81	13	2	10	128	47	47	46	2	55	7	0	3	4	2	.67	5	.279	.387	.441
4 Min. YEARS		312	1089	293	49	5	28	436	166	146	123	6	218	16	8	13	21	8	.72	25	.269	.348	.400

Ryan Radmanovich

Bats: Left **Throws:** Right **Pos:** OF **Ht:** 6'2" **Wt:** 185 **Born:** 8/9/71 **Age:** 25

		BATTING															BASERUNNING				PERCENTAGES		
Year Team	Lg Org	G	AB	H	2B	3B	HR	TB	R	RBI	TBB	IBB	SO	HBP	SH	SF	SB	CS	SB%	GDP	Avg	OBP	SLG
1993 Fort Wayne	A Min	62	204	59	7	5	8	100	36	38	30	2	60	7	2	2	8	2	.80	4	.289	.395	.490
1994 Fort Myers	A+ Min	26	85	16	4	0	2	26	11	9	7	0	19	2	0	0	3	1	.75	0	.188	.266	.306
Fort Wayne	A Min	101	383	105	20	6	19	194	64	69	45	3	98	3	1	1	19	14	.58	7	.274	.354	.507
1995 Fort Myers	A+ Min	12	41	13	2	0	0	15	3	5	2	0	8	1	0	0	0	0	.00	0	.317	.364	.366
1996 New Britain	AA Min	125	453	127	31	2	25	237	77	86	49	6	122	3	3	2	4	11	.27	12	.280	.353	.523
4 Min. YEARS		326	1166	320	64	13	54	572	191	207	133	11	307	16	6	5	34	28	.55	23	.274	.355	.491

Brady Raggio

Pitches: Right **Bats:** Right **Pos:** P **Ht:** 6'4" **Wt:** 210 **Born:** 9/17/72 **Age:** 24

		HOW MUCH HE PITCHED						WHAT HE GAVE UP												THE RESULTS					
Year Team	Lg Org	G	GS	CG	GF	IP	BFP	H	R	ER	HR	SH	SF	HB	TBB	IBB	SO	WP	Bk	W	L	Pct.	ShO	Sv	ERA
1992 Cardinals	R StL	14	6	3	4	48.1	207	51	26	19	1	2	2	3	7	1	48	5	0	4	3	.571	0	1	3.54

Year	Team	Lg	Org	G	GS	CG	GF	IP	BFP	H	R	ER	HR	SH	SF	HB	TBB	IBB	SO	WP	Bk	W	L	Pct.	ShO	Sv	ERA
				HOW MUCH HE PITCHED						WHAT HE GAVE UP												THE RESULTS					
1994	New Jersey	A-	StL	4	4	0	0	27	115	28	7	5	0	0	1	0	4	0	20	1	0	3	0	1.000	0	0	1.67
	Madison	A	StL	11	11	1	0	67.1	277	63	31	24	8	3	2	3	14	1	66	3	0	4	3	.571	0	0	3.21
1995	Peoria	A	StL	8	8	3	0	48.2	181	42	13	10	1	1	1	0	2	0	34	0	0	3	0	1.000	2	0	1.85
	St. Pete	A+	StL	28	11	3	4	96	376	85	37	30	3	4	2	1	15	2	69	2	1	5	3	.625	2	0	2.81
1996	Arkansas	AA	StL	26	24	4	0	162.1	667	160	68	58	17	8	2	3	40	2	123	3	2	9	10	.474	1	0	3.22
4 Min. YEARS				91	64	14	8	449.2	1823	429	182	146	30	18	10	10	82	6	360	14	3	28	19	.596	5	1	2.92

Steve Rain

Pitches: Right **Bats:** Right **Pos:** P **Ht:** 6'6" **Wt:** 225 **Born:** 6/2/75 **Age:** 22

Year	Team	Lg	Org	G	GS	CG	GF	IP	BFP	H	R	ER	HR	SH	SF	HB	TBB	IBB	SO	WP	Bk	W	L	Pct.	ShO	Sv	ERA
				HOW MUCH HE PITCHED						WHAT HE GAVE UP												THE RESULTS					
1993	Cubs	R	ChN	10	6	0	3	37	162	37	20	16	0	1	1	2	17	0	29	5	1	1	3	.250	0	0	3.89
1994	Huntington	R+	ChN	14	10	1	1	68	272	55	26	20	2	2	2	2	19	0	55	4	4	3	3	.500	1	0	2.65
1995	Rockford	A	ChN	53	0	0	51	59.1	234	38	12	8	0	3	2	2	23	3	66	8	0	5	2	.714	0	23	1.21
1996	Orlando	AA	ChN	35	0	0	29	38.2	163	32	15	11	4	0	0	3	12	1	48	2	1	1	0	1.000	0	10	2.56
	Iowa	AAA	ChN	26	0	0	26	26	103	17	9	9	3	3	3	0	8	3	23	1	0	2	1	.667	0	10	3.12
4 Min. YEARS				138	16	1	110	229	934	179	82	64	9	9	8	9	79	7	221	20	6	12	9	.571	1	43	2.52

Matt Raleigh

Bats: Right **Throws:** Right **Pos:** DH-1B **Ht:** 5'11" **Wt:** 205 **Born:** 7/18/70 **Age:** 26

Year	Team	Lg	Org	G	AB	H	2B	3B	HR	TB	R	RBI	TBB	IBB	SO	HBP	SH	SF	SB	CS	SB%	GDP	Avg	OBP	SLG
				BATTING															BASERUNNING				PERCENTAGES		
1992	Jamestown	A-	Mon	77	261	57	14	2	11	108	41	44	45	2	101	0	0	2	14	2	.88	3	.218	.331	.414
1993	Jamestown	A-	Mon	77	263	62	17	0	15	124	51	42	39	0	99	1	0	4	5	2	.71	3	.236	.332	.471
1994	Burlington	A	Mon	114	398	109	18	2	34	233	78	83	75	3	138	5	0	3	6	2	.75	8	.274	.393	.585
1995	W. Palm Bch	A+	Mon	66	179	37	11	0	2	54	29	18	54	1	64	6	1	3	4	2	.67	4	.207	.401	.302
1996	Frederick	A+	Bal	21	57	13	0	1	1	18	8	8	12	0	22	2	0	2	3	0	1.00	0	.228	.370	.316
	High Desert	A+	Bal	27	84	24	6	0	7	51	17	13	14	0	33	0	0	1	2	0	1.00	2	.286	.384	.607
	Bowie	AA	Bal	4	8	2	1	0	0	3	0	2	1	0	3	0	0	0	0	0	.00	0	.250	.333	.375
5 Min. YEARS				386	1250	304	67	5	70	591	224	210	240	6	460	14	1	15	34	8	.81	20	.243	.367	.473

Kris Ralston

Pitches: Right **Bats:** Right **Pos:** P **Ht:** 6' 2" **Wt:** 200 **Born:** 8/8/71 **Age:** 25

Year	Team	Lg	Org	G	GS	CG	GF	IP	BFP	H	R	ER	HR	SH	SF	HB	TBB	IBB	SO	WP	Bk	W	L	Pct.	ShO	Sv	ERA
				HOW MUCH HE PITCHED						WHAT HE GAVE UP												THE RESULTS					
1993	Eugene	A-	KC	15	15	1	0	82	325	52	29	25	5	2	1	3	36	3	75	1	1	7	3	.700	0	0	2.74
1994	Wilmington	A+	KC	20	18	2	0	109.1	448	84	36	29	11	2	2	5	38	0	102	4	2	10	4	.714	1	0	2.39
1995	Wichita	AA	KC	18	16	0	0	93.2	389	85	40	37	10	3	2	7	28	0	84	6	0	9	4	.692	0	0	3.56
1996	Omaha	AAA	KC	1	0	0	0	3	12	3	1	1	0	0	0	0	0	0	1	0	0	0	0	.000	0	0	3.00
4 Min. YEARS				54	49	3	0	288	1174	224	106	92	26	7	5	15	102	3	262	11	3	26	11	.703	1	0	2.88

Alex Ramirez

Bats: Right **Throws:** Right **Pos:** OF **Ht:** 5'11" **Wt:** 176 **Born:** 10/3/74 **Age:** 22

Year	Team	Lg	Org	G	AB	H	2B	3B	HR	TB	R	RBI	TBB	IBB	SO	HBP	SH	SF	SB	CS	SB%	GDP	Avg	OBP	SLG
				BATTING															BASERUNNING				PERCENTAGES		
1993	Burlington	R+	Cle	64	252	68	14	4	13	129	44	58	13	1	52	4	0	3	12	8	.60	4	.270	.313	.512
	Kinston	A+	Cle	3	12	2	0	0	0	2	0	1	0	0	5	0	0	0	0	1	.00	0	.167	.167	.167
1994	Columbus	A	Cle	125	458	115	23	3	18	198	64	57	26	0	100	4	0	4	7	5	.58	11	.251	.295	.432
1995	Bakersfield	A+	Cle	98	406	131	25	2	10	190	56	52	18	1	76	3	0	1	13	9	.59	9	.323	.355	.468
	Canton-Akrn	AA	Cle	33	133	33	3	4	1	47	15	11	5	1	24	0	1	1	3	5	.38	5	.248	.273	.353
1996	Canton-Akrn	AA	Cle	131	513	169	28	12	14	263	79	85	16	1	74	3	1	1	18	10	.64	8	.329	.353	.513
4 Min. YEARS				454	1774	518	93	25	56	829	258	264	78	4	331	14	2	10	53	38	.58	37	.292	.325	.467

Angel Ramirez

Bats: Right **Throws:** Right **Pos:** OF **Ht:** 5'10" **Wt:** 166 **Born:** 1/24/73 **Age:** 24

Year	Team	Lg	Org	G	AB	H	2B	3B	HR	TB	R	RBI	TBB	IBB	SO	HBP	SH	SF	SB	CS	SB%	GDP	Avg	OBP	SLG
				BATTING															BASERUNNING				PERCENTAGES		
1993	Medicne Hat	R+	Tor	62	227	80	8	5	4	110	40	30	8	0	43	4	1	1	15	9	.63	3	.352	.383	.485
	St. Cathrns	A-	Tor	6	22	6	1	0	0	7	2	2	0	0	7	0	0	0	0	2	.00	1	.273	.273	.318
1994	Hagerstown	A	Tor	117	454	127	17	14	9	199	71	51	21	2	103	7	4	3	21	14	.60	3	.280	.320	.438
1995	Dunedin	A+	Tor	131	541	149	19	5	8	202	78	52	21	0	99	5	0	2	17	12	.59	12	.275	.308	.373
1996	Knoxville	AA	Tor	102	392	110	25	7	5	164	64	51	15	1	69	6	1	4	16	6	.73	9	.281	.314	.418
4 Min. YEARS				418	1636	472	70	31	26	682	255	186	65	3	321	22	6	10	69	43	.62	28	.289	.323	.417

Hector Ramirez

Pitches: Right **Bats:** Right **Pos:** P **Ht:** 6'3" **Wt:** 218 **Born:** 12/15/71 **Age:** 25

Year	Team	Lg	Org	G	GS	CG	GF	IP	BFP	H	R	ER	HR	SH	SF	HB	TBB	IBB	SO	WP	Bk	W	L	Pct.	ShO	Sv	ERA
				HOW MUCH HE PITCHED						WHAT HE GAVE UP												THE RESULTS					
1989	Mets	R	NYN	15	5	0	8	42	189	35	29	21	0	0	3	3	24	0	14	8	2	0	5	.000	0	0	4.50
1990	Mets	R	NYN	11	8	1	1	50.2	226	54	34	23	2	1	1	4	21	1	43	2	2	3	5	.375	0	0	4.09
1991	Kingsport	R+	NYN	14	13	1	0	85	364	83	39	24	5	0	5	4	28	2	64	9	0	8	2	.800	0	0	2.54
1992	Columbia	A	NYN	17	17	1	0	94.2	404	93	50	38	5	3	3	3	33	1	53	4	3	5	4	.556	0	0	3.61

Year	Team	Lg	Org	G	GS	CG	GF	IP	BFP	H	R	ER	HR	SH	SF	HB	TBB	IBB	SO	WP	Bk	W	L	Pct.	ShO	Sv	ERA
				HOW MUCH HE PITCHED						WHAT HE GAVE UP												THE RESULTS					
1993	Mets	R	NYN	1	1	0	0	7	26	5	1	0	0	0	0	0	1	0	6	0	0	1	0	1.000	0	0	0.00
	Capital City	A	NYN	14	14	0	0	64	294	86	51	38	2	3	4	2	23	0	42	7	0	4	6	.400	0	0	5.34
1994	St. Lucie	A+	NYN	27	27	6	0	194	802	202	86	74	10	10	6	5	50	2	110	6	8	11	12	.478	1	0	3.43
1995	Binghamton	AA	NYN	20	20	2	0	123.1	534	127	69	63	12	2	2	3	48	2	63	3	5	4	12	.250	0	0	4.60
1996	Norfolk	AAA	NYN	3	1	0	1	10.2	49	13	7	4	1	1	1	0	3	0	8	1	0	1	0	1.000	0	0	3.38
	Binghamton	AA	NYN	38	0	0	17	56	245	51	34	32	3	5	3	6	23	5	49	4	2	1	5	.167	0	6	5.14
8 Min. YEARS				160	106	11	27	727.1	3133	749	400	317	40	25	28	30	254	13	452	44	22	38	51	.427	1	6	3.92

Hiram Ramirez

Bats: Right **Throws:** Right **Pos:** DH **Ht:** 6'2" **Wt:** 200 **Born:** 9/10/72 **Age:** 24

Year	Team	Lg	Org	G	AB	H	2B	3B	HR	TB	R	RBI	TBB	IBB	SO	HBP	SH	SF	SB	CS	SB%	GDP	Avg	OBP	SLG
				BATTING															BASERUNNING				PERCENTAGES		
1991	Giants	R	SF	26	49	8	1	0	0	9	5	4	8	0	17	1	0	0	0	2	.00	1	.163	.293	.184
1992	Giants	R	SF	42	143	39	4	3	3	58	23	21	16	1	36	1	0	0	2	0	1.00	4	.273	.350	.406
1993	Giants	R	SF	54	201	59	14	1	3	84	31	34	26	3	40	1	2	2	3	2	.60	7	.294	.374	.418
1994	Clinton	A	SF	55	180	58	12	0	7	91	30	23	18	1	47	2	1	0	0	1	.00	4	.322	.390	.506
1995	Sarasota	A+	Bos	40	140	26	2	0	2	34	13	12	3	0	29	0	2	1	3	2	.60	2	.186	.201	.243
1996	Burlington	A	SF	101	327	80	17	0	11	130	42	55	52	1	94	3	2	3	2	1	.67	13	.245	.351	.398
	Shreveport	AA	SF	1	3	3	1	0	0	4	2	4	0	0	0	0	0	0	0	0	.00	0	1.000	1.000	1.333
6 Min. YEARS				319	1043	273	51	4	26	410	146	153	123	6	263	8	7	6	10	8	.56	31	.262	.342	.393

Roberto Ramirez

Bats: Right **Throws:** Right **Pos:** OF **Ht:** 6'2" **Wt:** 180 **Born:** 3/18/70 **Age:** 27

Year	Team	Lg	Org	G	AB	H	2B	3B	HR	TB	R	RBI	TBB	IBB	SO	HBP	SH	SF	SB	CS	SB%	GDP	Avg	OBP	SLG
				BATTING															BASERUNNING				PERCENTAGES		
1991	Clinton	A	SF	17	55	10	0	1	0	12	4	5	2	0	18	0	0	2	0	1	.00	1	.182	.203	.218
	Everett	A-	SF	53	153	35	10	2	1	52	20	10	19	0	51	0	0	0	7	7	.50	5	.229	.314	.340
1992	Sou. Oregon	A-	Oak	5	22	10	3	1	2	21	8	4	1	0	4	0	0	0	0	0	.00	0	.455	.478	.955
	Reno	A+	Oak	55	190	65	13	3	7	105	31	29	15	2	45	2	2	2	3	5	.38	5	.342	.392	.553
1993	Madison	A	Oak	14	55	17	4	0	1	24	9	7	3	0	10	1	0	1	2	2	.50	2	.309	.350	.436
	Modesto	A+	Oak	41	140	36	8	0	3	53	17	14	17	0	36	1	0	2	2	5	.29	3	.257	.338	.379
1994	Riverside	A+	Sea	117	430	129	28	7	14	213	70	79	25	0	88	4	1	4	8	4	.67	9	.300	.341	.495
1995	Port City	AA	Sea	129	490	136	24	6	17	223	67	82	35	4	98	6	3	6	11	10	.52	14	.278	.330	.455
1996	Port City	AA	Sea	52	182	41	12	1	3	64	19	19	15	1	37	0	2	0	1	1	.50	6	.225	.284	.352
	Lubbock	IND	—	46	180	55	14	1	11	104	35	45	18	1	29	0	0	2	1	0	1.00	2	.306	.365	.578
6 Min. YEARS				529	1897	534	116	22	59	871	280	294	150	8	416	14	8	19	35	35	.50	47	.281	.336	.459

Edgar Ramos

Pitches: Right **Bats:** Right **Pos:** P **Ht:** 6'4" **Wt:** 170 **Born:** 3/6/75 **Age:** 22

Year	Team	Lg	Org	G	GS	CG	GF	IP	BFP	H	R	ER	HR	SH	SF	HB	TBB	IBB	SO	WP	Bk	W	L	Pct.	ShO	Sv	ERA
				HOW MUCH HE PITCHED						WHAT HE GAVE UP												THE RESULTS					
1993	Astros	R	Hou	14	12	0	1	75	297	59	23	18	0	0	2	3	13	0	70	4	2	5	2	.714	0	0	2.16
1994	Quad City	A	Hou	22	16	1	4	98.2	429	110	59	49	3	2	1	3	30	1	92	6	0	2	8	.200	0	1	4.47
1995	Quad City	A	Hou	2	2	0	0	4.2	27	5	9	8	0	0	0	1	7	0	5	1	0	0	1	.000	0	0	15.43
	Kissimmee	A+	Hou	4	4	0	0	22	80	11	4	1	1	0	0	0	1	0	16	0	0	4	0	1.000	0	0	0.41
	Astros	R	Hou	11	11	0	0	41.1	169	30	19	12	1	1	0	3	13	0	37	2	0	4	2	.667	0	0	2.61
1996	Kissimmee	A+	Hou	11	11	1	0	77.2	298	51	17	13	4	3	1	6	15	0	81	4	0	9	0	1.000	0	0	1.51
	Jackson	AA	Hou	12	12	1	0	66.1	293	63	41	36	2	3	1	11	29	0	52	7	0	4	5	.444	1	0	4.88
4 Min. YEARS				76	68	3	5	385.2	1593	329	172	137	11	9	5	27	108	1	353	24	2	28	18	.609	1	1	3.20

John Ramos

Bats: Right **Throws:** Right **Pos:** 1B **Ht:** 6' 0" **Wt:** 190 **Born:** 8/6/65 **Age:** 31

Year	Team	Lg	Org	G	AB	H	2B	3B	HR	TB	R	RBI	TBB	IBB	SO	HBP	SH	SF	SB	CS	SB%	GDP	Avg	OBP	SLG
				BATTING															BASERUNNING				PERCENTAGES		
1986	Ft. Laud	A+	NYA	54	184	49	10	1	2	67	25	28	26	0	23	1	4	2	8	3	.73	5	.266	.357	.364
	Oneonta	A-	NYA	3	8	4	2	1	0	8	3	1	2	0	1	0	0	0	0	0	.00	0	.500	.600	1.000
1987	Pr. William	A+	NYA	76	235	51	6	1	2	65	26	27	28	3	30	2	3	3	8	5	.62	10	.217	.302	.277
1988	Pr. William	A+	NYA	109	391	119	18	2	8	165	47	57	49	1	34	7	2	5	8	2	.80	7	.304	.387	.422
	Albany-Colo	AA	NYA	21	72	16	1	3	1	26	11	13	12	0	9	1	0	2	2	1	.67	1	.222	.333	.361
1989	Albany-Colo	AA	NYA	105	359	98	21	0	9	146	55	60	40	2	65	7	2	2	7	5	.58	14	.273	.355	.407
1990	Columbus	AAA	NYA	2	6	0	0	0	0	0	0	1	0	0	0	0	0	0	0	0	.00	0	.000	.000	.000
	Albany-Colo	AA	NYA	84	287	90	20	1	4	124	38	45	36	0	39	3	0	5	1	0	1.00	10	.314	.390	.432
1991	Columbus	AAA	NYA	104	377	116	18	3	10	170	52	63	56	3	54	3	1	9	1	5	.17	15	.308	.393	.451
1992	Columbus	AAA	NYA	18	64	11	4	1	1	20	5	12	8	0	14	0	0	1	1	0	1.00	1	.172	.260	.313
1993	Columbus	AAA	NYA	49	158	41	7	0	1	51	17	18	19	1	32	0	0	2	1	2	.33	6	.259	.335	.323
1994	Las Vegas	AAA	SD	114	312	102	25	1	10	159	51	46	40	1	41	1	2	3	0	0	.00	9	.327	.402	.510
1995	Syracuse	AAA	Tor	116	413	104	24	1	20	190	59	75	38	1	83	6	1	5	2	2	.50	11	.252	.320	.460
1996	Syracuse	AAA	Tor	89	317	77	16	0	8	117	38	42	41	1	51	0	0	7	1	1	.50	9	.243	.323	.369
1991	New York	AL		10	26	8	1	0	0	9	4	3	1	0	3	0	0	2	0	0	.00	1	.308	.310	.346
11 Min. YEARS				944	3183	878	172	15	76	1300	427	488	395	13	476	31	15	46	40	26	.61	98	.276	.357	.411

Ken Ramos

Bats: Left **Throws:** Left **Pos:** OF **Ht:** 6'1" **Wt:** 185 **Born:** 6/8/67 **Age:** 30

				BATTING															BASERUNNING				PERCENTAGES		
Year	Team	Lg	Org	G	AB	H	2B	3B	HR	TB	R	RBI	TBB	IBB	SO	HBP	SH	SF	SB	CS	SB%	GDP	Avg	OBP	SLG
1989	Indians	R	Cle	54	193	60	7	2	1	74	41	14	39	1	18	3	3	2	17	7	.71	4	.311	.430	.383
	Kinston	A+	Cle	8	21	3	0	0	0	3	6	0	5	0	2	0	1	0	2	0	1.00	0	.143	.308	.143
1990	Kinston	A+	Cle	96	339	117	16	6	0	145	71	31	48	4	34	1	5	2	18	14	.56	4	.345	.426	.428
	Canton-Akrn	AA	Cle	19	73	24	2	2	0	30	12	11	8	0	10	0	0	1	2	1	.67	1	.329	.390	.411
1991	Canton-Akrn	AA	Cle	74	257	62	6	3	2	80	41	13	28	0	22	1	4	1	8	4	.67	3	.241	.317	.311
1992	Canton-Akrn	AA	Cle	125	442	150	23	5	5	198	93	42	82	6	37	0	5	1	14	11	.56	8	.339	.442	.448
1993	Charlotte	AAA	Cle	132	480	140	16	11	3	187	77	41	47	4	41	0	7	3	12	8	.60	10	.292	.353	.390
1994	Tucson	AAA	Hou	121	393	118	19	7	1	154	81	32	74	5	27	0	3	5	22	12	.65	8	.300	.407	.392
1995	Tucson	AAA	Hou	112	327	103	24	8	3	152	57	47	51	3	27	3	4	5	14	5	.74	3	.315	.407	.465
1996	Tucson	AAA	Hou	104	385	104	22	3	4	144	54	34	41	2	41	0	3	4	6	9	.40	3	.270	.337	.374
8 Min. YEARS				845	2910	881	135	47	19	1167	533	265	423	25	259	8	35	24	115	71	.62	44	.303	.390	.401

Fernando Ramsey

Bats: Right **Throws:** Right **Pos:** OF **Ht:** 6' 1" **Wt:** 175 **Born:** 12/20/65 **Age:** 31

				BATTING															BASERUNNING				PERCENTAGES		
Year	Team	Lg	Org	G	AB	H	2B	3B	HR	TB	R	RBI	TBB	IBB	SO	HBP	SH	SF	SB	CS	SB%	GDP	Avg	OBP	SLG
1987	Geneva	A-	ChN	39	56	9	1	0	0	10	9	3	5	1	10	0	2	0	2	0	1.00	0	.161	.230	.179
1988	Charlstn-WV	A	ChN	121	381	92	5	1	0	99	36	15	14	1	68	4	6	0	15	7	.68	4	.241	.276	.260
1989	Peoria	A	ChN	131	410	100	7	5	0	117	56	34	25	0	70	10	11	3	16	10	.62	6	.244	.301	.285
1990	Winston-Sal	A+	ChN	124	428	109	12	4	5	144	52	48	19	0	50	3	9	2	43	7	.86	4	.255	.290	.336
1991	Charlotte	AA	ChN	139	547	151	18	6	6	199	78	49	36	0	90	3	7	2	37	17	.69	8	.276	.323	.364
1992	Iowa	AAA	ChN	133	480	129	9	5	1	151	62	38	23	0	78	2	11	0	39	12	.76	14	.269	.305	.315
1993	Iowa	AAA	ChN	134	545	147	30	7	5	206	76	42	25	2	72	2	9	0	13	13	.50	7	.270	.304	.378
1994	Norfolk	AAA	NYN	19	49	5	0	1	0	7	5	1	3	0	8	0	0	0	1	2	.33	0	.102	.154	.143
	Indianapols	AAA	Cin	14	51	18	4	0	0	22	9	4	0	0	7	0	0	0	3	1	.75	1	.353	.353	.431
1995	Nashville	AAA	ChA	98	406	126	19	3	5	166	61	45	13	2	47	3	4	2	26	8	.76	9	.310	.335	.409
1996	Nashville	AAA	ChA	110	395	86	3	0	7	110	42	24	10	0	57	3	6	0	12	10	.55	9	.218	.243	.278
1992	Chicago	NL		18	25	3	0	0	0	3	0	2	0	0	6	0	0	0	0	0	.00	0	.120	.120	.120
10 Min. YEARS				1062	3748	972	108	32	29	1231	486	303	173	6	557	30	65	9	207	87	.70	62	.259	.297	.328

Paul Rappoli

Bats: Left **Throws:** Right **Pos:** OF **Ht:** 6'1" **Wt:** 195 **Born:** 10/4/71 **Age:** 25

				BATTING															BASERUNNING				PERCENTAGES		
Year	Team	Lg	Org	G	AB	H	2B	3B	HR	TB	R	RBI	TBB	IBB	SO	HBP	SH	SF	SB	CS	SB%	GDP	Avg	OBP	SLG
1990	Red Sox	R	Bos	53	161	46	4	0	1	53	31	22	35	0	16	8	1	3	4	4	.50	4	.286	.430	.329
1991	Winter Havn	A+	Bos	4	5	0	0	0	0	0	2	0	0	0	1	0	0	0	0	0	.00	0	.000	.000	.000
	Elmira	A-	Bos	69	209	55	15	1	3	81	37	19	34	0	38	6	2	2	11	3	.79	0	.263	.378	.388
1992	Lynchburg	A+	Bos	111	344	92	17	2	6	131	47	42	48	1	66	6	4	3	11	13	.46	8	.267	.364	.381
1993	New Britain	AA	Bos	115	356	76	16	5	3	111	49	26	64	4	77	6	6	2	6	8	.43	5	.213	.341	.312
1994	Sarasota	A+	Bos	20	72	25	7	1	1	37	14	12	6	0	15	2	0	0	1	2	.33	2	.347	.413	.514
	New Britain	AA	Bos	109	355	99	14	6	4	137	52	40	50	1	56	7	3	0	18	10	.64	3	.279	.379	.386
1996	Trenton	AA	Bos	69	193	41	8	0	3	58	16	22	27	1	54	3	4	4	4	5	.44	4	.212	.313	.301
6 Min. YEARS				550	1695	434	81	15	21	608	248	183	264	7	323	38	20	14	55	45	.55	26	.256	.366	.359

Gary Rath

Pitches: Left **Bats:** Left **Pos:** P **Ht:** 6'2" **Wt:** 185 **Born:** 1/10/73 **Age:** 24

				HOW MUCH HE PITCHED						WHAT HE GAVE UP												THE RESULTS					
Year	Team	Lg	Org	G	GS	CG	GF	IP	BFP	H	R	ER	HR	SH	SF	HB	TBB	IBB	SO	WP	Bk	W	L	Pct.	ShO	Sv	ERA
1994	Vero Beach	A+	LA	13	11	0	0	62.2	261	55	26	19	3	3	3	2	23	0	50	4	0	5	6	.455	0	0	2.73
1995	Albuquerque	AAA	LA	8	8	0	0	39	178	46	31	22	4	1	1	2	20	0	23	2	0	3	5	.375	0	0	5.08
	San Antonio	AA	LA	26	26	3	0	156	661	142	73	58	10	4	3	6	68	0	104	6	2	16	8	.667	1	0	3.35
1996	Albuquerque	AAA	LA	30	30	1	0	180.1	784	177	97	84	13	9	4	3	89	8	125	8	0	10	11	.476	1	0	4.19
3 Min. YEARS				77	75	4	0	438	1884	420	227	183	30	17	11	13	200	8	302	20	2	34	30	.531	2	0	3.76

Darryl Ratliff

Bats: Right **Throws:** Right **Pos:** OF **Ht:** 6'1" **Wt:** 180 **Born:** 10/15/69 **Age:** 27

				BATTING															BASERUNNING				PERCENTAGES		
Year	Team	Lg	Org	G	AB	H	2B	3B	HR	TB	R	RBI	TBB	IBB	SO	HBP	SH	SF	SB	CS	SB%	GDP	Avg	OBP	SLG
1989	Princeton	R+	Pit	66	208	51	2	0	0	53	28	21	24	1	31	0	0	1	10	3	.77	2	.245	.322	.255
1990	Augusta	A	Pit	122	417	123	11	6	1	149	70	55	67	2	62	0	1	0	24	7	.77	12	.295	.393	.357
1991	Salem	A+	Pit	88	352	103	8	4	2	125	60	23	27	0	43	0	2	1	35	9	.80	6	.293	.342	.355
	Carolina	AA	Pit	24	93	20	3	0	0	23	10	9	6	0	16	0	1	0	7	3	.70	1	.215	.263	.247
1992	Carolina	AA	Pit	124	413	99	13	3	0	118	45	26	41	0	50	0	5	4	25	11	.69	7	.240	.306	.286
1993	Carolina	AA	Pit	121	454	129	15	4	0	152	59	47	35	0	58	2	14	5	29	13	.69	9	.284	.335	.335
1994	Salem	A+	Pit	36	138	44	9	2	1	60	25	19	12	0	18	0	1	0	5	5	.50	1	.319	.373	.435
	Carolina	AA	Pit	78	253	70	7	2	0	81	38	29	23	1	34	1	1	5	11	4	.73	8	.277	.333	.320
1995	Carolina	AA	Pit	16	63	18	4	0	1	25	10	5	8	1	10	0	2	0	2	1	.67	1	.286	.366	.397
	Calgary	AAA	Pit	95	286	98	11	1	0	111	41	37	18	2	30	2	4	0	9	6	.60	7	.343	.386	.388
1996	Carolina	AA	Pit	82	270	74	11	0	0	85	39	36	25	0	50	0	4	2	13	8	.62	7	.274	.333	.315
	Calgary	AAA	Pit	38	131	44	3	0	0	47	19	12	11	1	19	0	1	2	4	1	.80	5	.336	.382	.359
8 Min. YEARS				890	3078	873	97	22	5	1029	444	319	297	8	421	5	36	20	174	71	.71	66	.284	.346	.334

Jon Ratliff

Pitches: Right **Bats:** Right **Pos:** P — **Ht:** 6'5" **Wt:** 200 **Born:** 12/22/71 **Age:** 25

			HOW MUCH HE PITCHED						WHAT HE GAVE UP												THE RESULTS					
Year	Team	Lg Org	G	GS	CG	GF	IP	BFP	H	R	ER	HR	SH	SF	HB	TBB	IBB	SO	WP	Bk	W	L	Pct.	ShO	Sv	ERA
1993	Geneva	A- ChN	3	3	0	0	14	65	12	8	5	0	0	0	2	8	0	7	0	0	1	1	.500	0	0	3.21
	Daytona	A+ ChN	8	8	0	0	41	194	50	29	18	0	2	3	5	23	0	15	3	1	2	4	.333	0	0	3.95
1994	Daytona	A+ ChN	8	8	1	0	54	227	64	23	21	5	2	1	4	5	0	17	4	0	3	2	.600	0	0	3.50
	Iowa	AAA ChN	5	4	0	0	28.1	131	39	19	17	7	1	1	2	7	0	10	3	0	1	3	.250	0	0	5.40
	Orlando	AA ChN	12	12	1	0	62.1	292	78	44	39	4	4	5	8	26	1	19	5	0	1	9	.100	0	0	5.63
1995	Orlando	AA ChN	26	25	1	1	140	599	143	67	54	9	2	8	10	42	1	94	13	0	10	5	.667	1	0	3.47
1996	Iowa	AAA ChN	32	13	0	5	93.2	419	107	63	55	10	3	6	6	31	2	59	3	0	4	8	.333	0	1	5.28
4 Min. YEARS			94	73	3	6	433.1	1927	493	253	209	35	14	24	37	142	4	221	31	1	22	32	.407	1	1	4.34

Luis Raven

Bats: Right **Throws:** Right **Pos:** 3B — **Ht:** 6'4" **Wt:** 230 **Born:** 11/19/68 **Age:** 28

			BATTING															BASERUNNING				PERCENTAGES		
Year	Team	Lg Org	G	AB	H	2B	3B	HR	TB	R	RBI	TBB	IBB	SO	HBP	SH	SF	SB	CS	SB%	GDP	Avg	OBP	SLG
1989	Angels	R Cal	43	145	30	6	2	1	43	15	20	8	0	43	1	0	3	3	0	1.00	3	.207	.248	.297
1991	Boise	A- Cal	38	84	23	2	0	2	31	13	13	9	0	19	1	0	0	1	1	.50	6	.274	.351	.369
1992	Palm Spring	A+ Cal	107	378	109	16	2	9	156	59	55	24	2	81	2	0	4	18	7	.72	5	.288	.331	.413
1993	Midland	AA Cal	43	167	43	12	1	2	63	21	30	5	1	45	1	1	0	4	2	.67	4	.257	.283	.377
	Palm Spring	A+ Cal	85	343	95	20	2	7	140	38	52	22	0	84	3	1	2	15	11	.58	6	.277	.324	.408
1994	Midland	AA Cal	47	191	58	8	5	18	130	41	57	5	2	51	3	0	3	4	1	.80	9	.304	.327	.681
	Vancouver	AAA Cal	85	328	100	13	4	13	160	66	59	22	1	88	2	0	8	7	0	1.00	6	.305	.344	.488
1995	Lk Elsinore	A+ Cal	6	24	10	2	1	2	20	5	6	5	0	7	1	0	0	1	0	1.00	0	.417	.533	.833
	Vancouver	AAA Cal	37	135	33	11	1	5	61	18	26	15	0	35	0	1	1	3	1	.75	6	.244	.318	.452
	Midland	AA Cal	21	86	23	2	1	5	42	9	15	4	0	30	1	0	1	1	1	.50	2	.267	.304	.488
1996	Canton-Akrn	AA Cle	74	268	81	17	0	21	161	57	64	38	6	73	1	0	2	0	0	.00	6	.302	.388	.601
7 Min. YEARS			586	2149	605	109	19	85	1007	342	397	157	12	556	16	3	24	57	24	.70	53	.282	.332	.469

Kevin Rawitzer

Pitches: Left **Bats:** Left **Pos:** P — **Ht:** 5'10" **Wt:** 185 **Born:** 2/28/71 **Age:** 26

			HOW MUCH HE PITCHED						WHAT HE GAVE UP												THE RESULTS					
Year	Team	Lg Org	G	GS	CG	GF	IP	BFP	H	R	ER	HR	SH	SF	HB	TBB	IBB	SO	WP	Bk	W	L	Pct.	ShO	Sv	ERA
1993	Eugene	A- KC	6	4	0	0	18	69	13	1	1	0	0	0	1	5	0	20	0	0	1	0	1.000	0	0	0.50
	Rockford	A KC	5	5	0	0	30	126	23	7	5	0	0	0	1	11	0	34	0	0	3	0	1.000	0	0	1.50
1994	Rockford	A KC	15	15	0	0	76.1	329	80	27	21	5	0	4	3	27	1	75	6	1	5	2	.714	0	0	2.48
	Wilmington	A+ KC	7	1	0	2	17.2	79	18	10	9	0	1	0	0	11	0	13	1	0	0	1	.000	0	1	4.58
1995	Wilmington	A+ KC	15	1	0	7	27	111	21	8	7	0	1	0	3	8	1	22	1	0	2	0	1.000	0	3	2.33
	Wichita	AA KC	43	4	0	14	75	320	69	38	35	4	1	2	4	27	1	64	2	0	8	4	.667	0	4	4.20
1996	Wichita	AA KC	42	0	0	17	68.1	314	77	52	36	8	2	2	5	39	1	48	3	0	0	6	.000	0	3	4.74
4 Min. YEARS			133	30	0	40	312.1	1348	301	143	114	17	5	8	17	128	4	276	13	1	19	13	.594	0	11	3.28

Ken Ray

Pitches: Right **Bats:** Right **Pos:** P — **Ht:** 6'2" **Wt:** 160 **Born:** 11/27/74 **Age:** 22

			HOW MUCH HE PITCHED						WHAT HE GAVE UP												THE RESULTS					
Year	Team	Lg Org	G	GS	CG	GF	IP	BFP	H	R	ER	HR	SH	SF	HB	TBB	IBB	SO	WP	Bk	W	L	Pct.	ShO	Sv	ERA
1993	Royals	R KC	13	7	0	3	47.1	204	44	21	12	1	1	3	0	17	0	45	6	0	2	3	.400	0	0	2.28
1994	Rockford	A KC	27	18	0	6	128.2	516	94	34	26	5	4	1	0	56	2	128	18	2	10	4	.714	0	3	1.82
1995	Wilmington	A+ KC	13	13	1	0	77	320	74	32	23	3	3	3	1	22	2	63	17	2	6	4	.600	0	0	2.69
	Wichita	AA KC	27	27	1	0	152.1	662	157	87	73	10	4	3	2	68	2	116	25	3	10	9	.526	0	0	4.31
1996	Wichita	AA KC	22	22	1	0	120.2	553	151	94	82	17	5	6	1	57	1	79	15	1	4	12	.250	0	0	6.12
4 Min. YEARS			102	87	3	9	526	2255	520	268	216	36	17	16	4	220	7	431	81	8	32	32	.500	0	3	3.70

Randy Ready

Bats: Right **Throws:** Right **Pos:** DH — **Ht:** 5'11" **Wt:** 180 **Born:** 1/8/60 **Age:** 37

			BATTING															BASERUNNING				PERCENTAGES		
Year	Team	Lg Org	G	AB	H	2B	3B	HR	TB	R	RBI	TBB	IBB	SO	HBP	SH	SF	SB	CS	SB%	GDP	Avg	OBP	SLG
1984	Vancouver	AAA Mil	43	151	49	7	4	3	73	48	18	43	2	21	5	2	0	10	4	.71	4	.325	.487	.483
1985	Vancouver	AAA Mil	52	190	62	12	3	4	92	33	29	30	2	14	0	0	2	14	3	.82	3	.326	.414	.484
1986	Las Vegas	AAA SD	10	38	14	4	0	1	21	5	8	6	0	2	0	0	0	1	1	.50	0	.368	.455	.553
1993	Rochester	AAA Bal	84	305	88	17	3	9	138	48	46	50	2	37	1	1	3	4	0	1.00	7	.289	.387	.452
1994	Ottawa	AAA Mon	39	127	26	3	2	2	39	16	16	22	0	14	1	0	2	1	0	1.00	3	.205	.322	.307
1996	Las Vegas	AAA SD	35	105	34	7	0	3	50	19	11	23	0	13	1	0	2	0	1	.00	2	.324	.443	.476
1983	Milwaukee	AL	12	37	15	3	2	1	25	8	6	6	1	3	0	0	0	0	1	.00	0	.405	.488	.676
1984	Milwaukee	AL	37	123	23	6	1	3	40	13	13	14	0	18	0	3	0	0	0	.00	2	.187	.270	.325
1985	Milwaukee	AL	48	181	48	9	5	1	70	29	21	14	0	23	1	2	2	0	0	.00	6	.265	.318	.387
1986	Milwaukee	AL	23	79	15	4	0	1	22	8	4	9	0	9	0	1	0	2	0	1.00	3	.190	.273	.278
	San Diego	NL	1	3	0	0	0	0	0	0	0	0	0	1	0	0	0	0	0	.00	0	.000	.000	.000
1987	San Diego	NL	124	350	108	26	6	12	182	69	54	67	2	44	3	2	1	7	3	.70	7	.309	.423	.520
1988	San Diego	NL	114	331	88	16	2	7	129	43	39	39	1	38	3	4	3	6	2	.75	3	.266	.346	.390
1989	San Diego	NL	28	67	17	2	1	0	21	4	5	11	0	6	0	1	1	0	0	.00	2	.254	.354	.313
	Philadelphia	NL	72	187	50	11	1	8	87	33	21	31	0	31	2	0	3	4	3	.57	2	.267	.372	.465
1990	Philadelphia	NL	101	217	53	9	1	1	67	26	26	29	0	35	1	3	3	3	2	.60	3	.244	.332	.309
1991	Philadelphia	NL	76	205	51	10	1	1	66	32	20	47	3	25	1	1	4	2	1	.67	5	.249	.385	.322

Year	Team	Lg Org	G	AB	H	2B	3B	HR	TB	R	RBI	TBB	IBB	SO	HBP	SH	SF	SB	CS	SB%	GDP	Avg	OBP	SLG
1992	Oakland	AL	61	125	25	2	0	3	36	17	17	25	1	23	0	2	2	1	0	1.00	1	.200	.329	.288
1993	Montreal	NL	40	134	34	8	1	1	47	22	10	23	0	8	1	1	0	2	1	.67	4	.254	.367	.351
1994	Philadelphia	NL	17	42	16	1	0	1	20	5	3	8	0	6	0	0	0	0	1	.00	1	.381	.480	.476
1995	Philadelphia	NL	23	29	4	0	0	0	4	3	0	3	0	6	0	1	0	0	1	.00	2	.138	.219	.138
6 Min. YEARS			263	916	273	50	12	22	413	169	128	174	6	101	8	3	9	30	9	.77	19	.298	.411	.451
13 Maj. YEARS			777	2110	547	107	21	40	816	312	239	326	8	276	12	21	19	27	15	.64	41	.259	.359	.387

Mark Redman

Pitches: Left **Bats:** Left **Pos:** P **Ht:** 6'5" **Wt:** 220 **Born:** 1/5/74 **Age:** 23

Year	Team	Lg Org	G	GS	CG	GF	IP	BFP	H	R	ER	HR	SH	SF	HB	TBB	IBB	SO	WP	Bk	W	L	Pct.	ShO	Sv	ERA
1995	Fort Myers	A+ Min	8	5	0	0	32.2	134	28	13	10	4	1	2	1	13	0	26	2	0	2	1	.667	0	0	2.76
1996	Fort Myers	A+ Min	13	13	1	0	82.2	335	63	24	17	1	6	3	5	34	0	75	4	1	3	4	.429	0	0	1.85
	New Britain	AA Min	16	16	3	0	106.1	467	101	51	45	5	1	6	8	50	1	96	4	1	7	7	.500	0	0	3.81
	Salt Lake	AAA Min	1	1	0	0	4	21	7	4	4	1	0	0	1	2	0	4	0	0	0	0	.000	0	0	9.00
2 Min. YEARS			38	35	4	0	225.2	957	199	92	76	11	8	11	15	99	1	201	10	2	12	12	.500	0	0	3.03

Mike Redmond

Bats: Right **Throws:** Right **Pos:** C **Ht:** 6'0" **Wt:** 190 **Born:** 5/5/71 **Age:** 26

Year	Team	Lg Org	G	AB	H	2B	3B	HR	TB	R	RBI	TBB	IBB	SO	HBP	SH	SF	SB	CS	SB%	GDP	Avg	OBP	SLG
1993	Kane County	A Fla	43	100	20	2	0	0	22	10	10	6	0	17	4	2	0	2	0	1.00	1	.200	.273	.220
1994	Kane County	A Fla	92	306	83	10	0	1	96	39	24	26	0	31	9	6	2	3	4	.43	10	.271	.344	.314
	Brevard Cty	A+ Fla	12	42	11	4	0	0	15	4	2	3	0	4	1	0	0	0	0	.00	1	.262	.326	.357
1995	Portland	AA Fla	105	333	85	11	1	3	107	37	39	22	2	27	3	4	3	2	2	.50	9	.255	.305	.321
1996	Portland	AA Fla	120	394	113	22	0	4	147	43	44	26	2	45	5	5	5	3	4	.43	12	.287	.335	.373
4 Min. YEARS			372	1175	312	49	1	8	387	133	119	83	4	124	22	17	10	10	10	.50	33	.266	.323	.329

Brandon Reed

Pitches: Right **Bats:** Right **Pos:** P **Ht:** 6'4" **Wt:** 185 **Born:** 12/18/74 **Age:** 22

Year	Team	Lg Org	G	GS	CG	GF	IP	BFP	H	R	ER	HR	SH	SF	HB	TBB	IBB	SO	WP	Bk	W	L	Pct.	ShO	Sv	ERA
1994	Bristol	R+ Det	13	13	0	0	78	337	82	41	31	3	1	3	9	10	0	68	4	0	3	5	.375	0	0	3.58
1995	Fayettevlle	A Det	55	0	0	53	64.2	252	40	11	7	1	1	0	3	18	1	78	8	0	3	0	1.000	0	41	0.97
1996	Tigers	R Det	1	1	0	0	2	6	0	0	0	0	0	0	1	0	0	2	0	0	0	0	.000	0	0	0.00
	Jacksonvlle	AA Det	7	3	0	1	26	94	18	6	6	1	0	1	1	3	0	18	0	0	1	0	1.000	0	1	2.08
3 Min. YEARS			76	17	0	54	170.2	689	140	58	44	5	2	4	14	31	1	166	12	0	7	5	.583	0	42	2.32

Chris Reed

Pitches: Right **Bats:** Right **Pos:** P **Ht:** 6'3" **Wt:** 206 **Born:** 8/25/73 **Age:** 23

Year	Team	Lg Org	G	GS	CG	GF	IP	BFP	H	R	ER	HR	SH	SF	HB	TBB	IBB	SO	WP	Bk	W	L	Pct.	ShO	Sv	ERA
1991	Princeton	R+ Cin	13	13	0	0	63	290	68	53	34	5	0	3	7	30	2	51	10	6	3	6	.333	0	0	4.86
1992	Billings	R+ Cin	10	10	0	0	48	221	46	30	27	2	2	4	3	32	0	39	5	1	6	3	.667	0	0	5.06
1993	Charlstn-WV	A Cin	21	21	0	0	112.1	498	99	63	51	1	8	6	10	58	0	84	6	3	7	9	.438	0	0	4.09
1994	Charlstn-WV	A Cin	26	25	1	1	145.2	650	156	90	78	12	3	3	11	72	2	99	9	1	11	7	.611	0	0	4.82
1995	Winston-Sal	A+ Cin	24	24	3	0	149	613	116	63	55	11	3	1	4	68	1	104	3	1	10	7	.588	1	0	3.32
1996	Chattanooga	AA Cin	28	27	2	1	176	752	157	89	80	15	5	9	9	91	1	135	17	0	13	10	.565	0	1	4.09
6 Min. YEARS			122	120	6	2	694	3024	642	388	325	46	21	26	44	351	6	512	50	12	50	42	.543	1	1	4.21

Rick Reed

Pitches: Right **Bats:** Right **Pos:** P **Ht:** 6' 1" **Wt:** 195 **Born:** 8/16/65 **Age:** 31

Year	Team	Lg Org	G	GS	CG	GF	IP	BFP	H	R	ER	HR	SH	SF	HB	TBB	IBB	SO	WP	Bk	W	L	Pct.	ShO	Sv	ERA
1986	Pirates	R Pit	8	3	0	1	24	96	20	12	10	0	1	3	0	6	0	15	0	1	0	2	.000	0	0	3.75
	Macon	A Pit	1	1	0	0	6.1	26	5	3	2	0	1	0	0	2	0	1	0	0	0	0	.000	0	0	2.84
1987	Macon	A Pit	46	0	0	20	93.2	388	80	38	26	6	3	4	9	29	3	92	4	0	8	4	.667	0	7	2.50
1988	Salem	A+ Pit	15	8	4	2	72.1	294	56	28	22	6	0	1	5	17	1	73	3	1	6	2	.750	1	0	2.74
	Harrisburg	AA Pit	2	2	0	0	16	60	11	2	2	0	0	0	0	2	0	17	0	0	1	0	1.000	0	0	1.13
	Buffalo	AAA Pit	10	9	3	0	77	301	62	15	14	0	6	1	1	12	2	50	1	1	5	2	.714	2	0	1.64
1989	Buffalo	AAA Pit	20	20	3	0	125.2	522	130	58	52	9	6	3	1	28	0	75	3	0	9	8	.529	0	0	3.72
1990	Buffalo	AAA Pit	15	15	2	0	91	369	82	37	35	4	6	0	6	21	0	63	1	0	7	4	.636	2	0	3.46
1991	Buffalo	AAA Pit	25	25	5	0	167.2	660	151	45	40	3	9	6	2	26	3	102	2	1	14	4	.778	2	0	2.15
1992	Omaha	AAA KC	11	10	3	1	62	259	67	33	30	8	2	2	4	12	0	35	0	0	5	4	.556	0	1	4.35
1993	Omaha	AAA KC	19	19	3	0	128.1	502	116	48	44	19	1	5	2	14	1	58	1	0	11	4	.733	2	0	3.09
	Okla. City	AAA Tex	5	5	1	0	34.1	144	43	20	16	2	1	1	1	2	0	21	2	0	1	3	.250	0	0	4.19
1994	Okla. City	AAA Tex	2	2	0	0	11.2	45	10	5	5	0	0	0	0	0	0	8	0	0	1	1	.500	0	0	3.86
	Indianapols	AAA Cin	23	23	3	0	152	635	172	85	78	20	3	4	5	19	0	87	2	2	10	6	.625	1	0	4.62
1995	Indianapols	AAA Cin	22	21	3	0	135	551	127	60	50	16	4	2	2	26	2	92	0	0	11	4	.733	1	0	3.33
1996	Norfolk	AAA NYN	28	28	1	0	182	726	164	72	64	13	6	8	4	33	2	128	5	2	8	10	.444	0	0	3.16
1988	Pittsburgh	NL	2	2	0	0	12	47	10	4	4	1	2	0	0	2	0	6	0	0	1	0	1.000	0	0	3.00
1989	Pittsburgh	NL	15	7	0	2	54.2	232	62	35	34	5	2	3	2	11	3	34	0	3	1	4	.200	0	0	5.60

		HOW MUCH HE PITCHED						WHAT HE GAVE UP												THE RESULTS					
Year Team	Lg Org	G	GS	CG	GF	IP	BFP	H	R	ER	HR	SH	SF	HB	TBB	IBB	SO	WP	Bk	W	L	Pct.	ShO	Sv	ERA
1990 Pittsburgh	NL	13	8	1	2	53.2	238	62	32	26	6	2	1	1	12	6	27	0	0	2	3	.400	1	1	4.36
1991 Pittsburgh	NL	1	1	0	0	4.1	21	8	6	5	1	0	0	0	1	0	2	0	0	0	0	.000	0	0	10.38
1992 Kansas City	AL	19	18	1	0	100.1	419	105	47	41	10	2	5	5	20	3	49	0	0	3	7	.300	1	0	3.68
1993 Kansas City	AL	1	0	0	0	3.2	18	6	4	4	0	0	0	1	1	0	3	0	0	0	0	.000	0	0	9.82
Texas	AL	2	0	0	0	4	18	6	1	1	1	0	0	1	1	0	2	0	0	1	0	1.000	0	0	2.25
1994 Texas	AL	4	3	0	0	16.2	75	17	13	11	3	0	0	1	7	0	12	0	0	1	1	.500	0	0	5.94
1995 Cincinnati	NL	4	3	0	1	17	70	18	12	11	5	1	0	0	3	0	10	0	0	0	0	.000	0	0	5.82
11 Min. YEARS		252	191	31	24	1379	5578	1296	561	490	106	49	40	42	249	14	917	24	8	97	58	.626	11	8	3.20
8 Maj. YEARS		61	42	2	5	266.1	1138	294	154	137	32	9	9	11	58	12	145	0	3	9	15	.375	2	1	4.63

Pokey Reese

Bats: Right **Throws:** Right **Pos:** SS **Ht:** 6'0" **Wt:** 160 **Born:** 6/10/73 **Age:** 24

		BATTING														BASERUNNING				PERCENTAGES		
Year Team	Lg Org	G	AB	H	2B	3B	HR	TB	R	RBI	TBB	IBB	SO	HBP	SH	SF	SB	CS	SB%	GDP	Avg	OBP	SLG
1991 Princeton	R+ Cin	62	231	55	8	3	3	78	30	27	23	0	44	0	0	2	10	8	.56	4	.238	.305	.338
1992 Charlstn-WV	A Cin	106	380	102	19	3	6	145	50	53	24	0	75	5	4	7	19	8	.70	2	.268	.315	.382
1993 Chattanooga	AA Cin	102	345	73	17	4	3	107	35	37	23	1	77	1	3	7	8	5	.62	2	.212	.258	.310
1994 Chattanooga	AA Cin	134	484	130	23	4	12	197	77	49	43	1	75	7	6	1	21	4	.84	6	.269	.336	.407
1995 Indianapols	AAA Cin	89	343	82	21	1	10	135	51	46	36	0	81	4	1	3	8	5	.62	3	.239	.316	.394
1996 Indianapols	AAA Cin	79	280	65	16	0	1	84	26	23	21	0	46	5	4	3	5	2	.71	10	.232	.294	.300
6 Min. YEARS		572	2063	507	104	15	35	746	269	235	170	2	398	22	18	23	71	32	.69	27	.246	.307	.362

Derek Reid

Bats: Right **Throws:** Right **Pos:** OF **Ht:** 6'3" **Wt:** 195 **Born:** 2/4/70 **Age:** 27

		BATTING														BASERUNNING				PERCENTAGES		
Year Team	Lg Org	G	AB	H	2B	3B	HR	TB	R	RBI	TBB	IBB	SO	HBP	SH	SF	SB	CS	SB%	GDP	Avg	OBP	SLG
1990 Everett	A- SF	62	215	62	15	1	5	94	35	40	20	2	49	3	4	3	21	3	.88	3	.288	.353	.437
1991 San Jose	A+ SF	121	454	122	23	6	4	169	72	65	37	2	91	1	6	10	27	9	.75	7	.269	.319	.372
1992 Shreveport	AA SF	2	6	1	1	0	0	2	1	0	0	0	1	0	1	0	0	0	.00	0	.167	.167	.333
1993 Clinton	A SF	15	57	17	2	0	0	19	5	7	1	0	6	0	1	0	3	2	.60	1	.298	.310	.333
San Jose	A+ SF	29	80	15	1	1	0	18	9	8	6	0	16	1	0	0	5	2	.71	1	.188	.253	.225
1994 San Bernrdo	A+ SF	59	238	70	18	1	6	108	34	38	21	2	60	1	2	2	15	1	.94	7	.294	.351	.454
Shreveport	AA SF	51	137	30	4	0	4	46	11	9	4	2	36	1	3	0	5	2	.71	6	.219	.246	.336
1995 Shreveport	AA SF	8	14	2	0	1	0	4	2	1	0	0	4	0	0	0	0	0	.00	0	.143	.143	.286
Burlington	A SF	95	354	101	15	4	13	163	74	55	31	0	55	4	3	1	22	4	.85	7	.285	.349	.460
1996 San Jose	A+ SF	88	350	120	15	4	14	185	71	58	35	1	68	3	3	3	23	2	.92	4	.343	.404	.529
Shreveport	AA SF	30	118	29	4	0	4	45	16	18	11	1	18	3	0	3	2	2	.50	3	.246	.319	.381
7 Min. YEARS		560	2023	569	98	18	50	853	330	299	166	10	404	17	23	22	123	27	.82	39	.281	.338	.422

Kevin Reimer

Bats: Left **Throws:** Right **Pos:** OF-DH **Ht:** 6' 2" **Wt:** 230 **Born:** 6/28/64 **Age:** 33

		BATTING														BASERUNNING				PERCENTAGES		
Year Team	Lg Org	G	AB	H	2B	3B	HR	TB	R	RBI	TBB	IBB	SO	HBP	SH	SF	SB	CS	SB%	GDP	Avg	OBP	SLG
1985 Burlington	A Tex	80	292	67	12	0	8	103	25	33	22	0	43	8	0	1	0	4	.00	10	.229	.300	.353
1986 Salem	A+ Tex	133	453	111	21	2	16	184	57	76	61	6	71	7	2	2	4	5	.44	15	.245	.342	.406
1987 Charlotte	A+ Tex	74	271	66	13	7	6	111	36	34	29	2	48	2	0	2	2	1	.67	6	.244	.319	.410
1988 Tulsa	AA Tex	133	486	147	30	11	21	262	74	76	38	9	95	5	0	5	4	4	.50	9	.302	.356	.539
1989 Okla. City	AAA Tex	133	514	137	37	7	10	218	59	73	33	3	91	2	1	4	4	1	.80	13	.267	.311	.424
1990 Okla. City	AAA Tex	51	198	56	18	2	4	90	24	33	18	3	25	0	0	1	2	0	1.00	7	.283	.341	.455
1996 Salt Lake	AAA Min	54	193	55	9	0	10	94	29	33	11	3	31	5	0	3	4	1	.80	4	.285	.335	.487
Tacoma	AAA Sea	24	93	26	3	0	3	38	9	11	3	0	12	3	0	1	0	0	.00	3	.280	.320	.409
1988 Texas	AL	12	25	3	0	0	1	6	2	2	0	0	6	0	0	1	0	0	.00	0	.120	.115	.240
1989 Texas	AL	3	5	0	0	0	0	0	0	0	0	0	1	0	0	0	0	0	.00	1	.000	.000	.000
1990 Texas	AL	64	100	26	9	1	2	43	5	15	10	0	22	1	0	0	0	1	.00	3	.260	.333	.430
1991 Texas	AL	136	394	106	22	0	20	188	46	69	33	6	93	7	0	6	0	3	.00	10	.269	.332	.477
1992 Texas	AL	148	494	132	32	2	16	216	56	58	42	5	103	10	0	1	2	4	.33	10	.267	.336	.437
1993 Milwaukee	AL	125	437	109	22	1	13	172	53	60	30	4	72	5	1	4	5	4	.56	12	.249	.303	.394
7 Min. YEARS		682	2500	665	143	29	78	1100	313	369	215	26	416	32	3	19	20	16	.56	67	.266	.330	.440
6 Maj. YEARS		488	1455	376	85	4	52	625	162	204	115	15	297	23	1	12	7	12	.37	36	.258	.320	.430

Mike Rendina

Bats: Left **Throws:** Left **Pos:** 1B **Ht:** 6'4" **Wt:** 215 **Born:** 9/28/70 **Age:** 26

		BATTING														BASERUNNING				PERCENTAGES		
Year Team	Lg Org	G	AB	H	2B	3B	HR	TB	R	RBI	TBB	IBB	SO	HBP	SH	SF	SB	CS	SB%	GDP	Avg	OBP	SLG
1988 Bristol	R+ Det	39	75	15	3	0	3	27	12	16	9	0	18	0	0	2	0	1	.00	3	.200	.279	.360
1989 Fayettevlle	A Det	28	86	10	4	0	0	14	9	5	11	1	19	0	3	0	0	0	.00	4	.116	.216	.163
Bristol	R+ Det	62	224	61	13	0	11	107	34	34	28	3	36	1	0	0	5	3	.63	4	.272	.356	.478
1990 Fayettevlle	A Det	137	475	121	23	3	11	183	59	77	76	7	90	3	0	4	4	4	.50	13	.255	.358	.385
1991 Lakeland	A+ Det	115	359	77	7	2	4	100	36	41	54	5	61	4	2	3	2	2	.50	11	.214	.321	.279
1992 Lakeland	A+ Det	121	397	106	23	1	9	158	48	69	46	5	59	2	1	7	2	0	1.00	9	.267	.341	.398
1993 London	AA Det	135	475	134	30	1	10	196	59	77	55	1	96	0	0	3	8	4	.67	0	.202	.355	.413
1994 Trenton	AA Det	116	387	88	15	0	11	136	46	46	29	2	77	2	0	2	2	1	.67	5	.227	.283	.351
1995 Jacksonvlle	AA Det	31	98	22	5	0	3	36	12	16	7	2	20	0	0	0	0	0	.00	3	.224	.276	.367

			BATTING																BASERUNNING				PERCENTAGES		
Year	Team	Lg Org	G	AB	H	2B	3B	HR	TB	R	RBI	TBB	IBB	SO	HBP	SH	SF	SB	CS	SB%	GDP	Avg	OBP	SLG
1996	Harrisburg	AA Mon	16	42	6	2	0	0	8	4	0	3	0	11	0	1	0	0	0	.00	1	.143	.200	.190
	Reno	IND —	63	235	69	17	1	10	118	34	39	15	2	35	1	0	0	4	0	1.00	5	.294	.339	.502
9	Min. YEARS		863	2853	709	142	8	72	1083	353	420	333	28	522	13	7	21	27	15	.64	64	.249	.328	.380

Steve Renko

Pitches: Right **Bats:** Right **Pos:** P **Ht:** 6'3" **Wt:** 205 **Born:** 8/1/67 **Age:** 29

			HOW MUCH HE PITCHED						WHAT HE GAVE UP												THE RESULTS					
Year	Team	Lg Org	G	GS	CG	GF	IP	BFP	H	R	ER	HR	SH	SF	HB	TBB	IBB	SO	WP	Bk	W	L	Pct.	ShO	Sv	ERA
1990	Expos	R Mon	2	0	0	1	5	23	7	1	1	0	0	0	0	1	0	5	0	2	1	0	1.000	0	0	1.80
	Gate City	R+ Mon	11	10	2	0	59.2	263	56	32	26	4	2	0	2	23	1	68	6	1	3	4	.429	0	0	3.92
1991	W. Palm Bch	A+ Mon	4	3	0	0	9	44	14	8	8	2	0	0	1	5	0	4	0	0	0	1	.000	0	0	8.00
	Rockford	A Mon	16	16	1	0	99	431	95	43	35	3	3	3	4	34	0	102	16	1	4	5	.444	0	0	3.18
1992	Winter Havn	A+ Bos	10	10	1	0	61.1	264	65	33	27	7	1	1	2	16	0	56	2	0	3	5	.375	0	0	3.96
	Lynchburg	A+ Bos	6	6	0	0	34.1	153	39	18	15	6	2	4	0	14	0	23	6	0	1	1	.500	0	0	3.93
1993	Hagerstown	A Tor	23	1	0	12	42.1	170	35	20	16	2	5	1	1	11	1	45	5	0	4	2	.667	0	5	3.40
	Knoxville	AA Tor	12	5	0	1	34.2	149	38	21	14	1	6	2	1	8	0	30	7	0	1	3	.250	0	0	3.63
1994	Wichita	AA SD	42	0	0	16	78.2	375	90	56	44	4	7	5	1	49	8	59	10	1	3	8	.273	0	2	5.03
1995	Vancouver	AAA Cal	10	9	0	0	51.1	226	53	29	24	2	0	3	0	18	0	22	5	0	2	5	.286	0	0	4.21
	Midland	AA Cal	32	18	0	4	128	578	153	80	65	5	2	8	0	46	2	66	10	0	5	10	.333	0	1	4.57
1996	Salinas	IND —	14	11	0	0	72	306	75	36	30	6	3	1	2	22	0	44	4	0	4	3	.571	0	0	3.75
	Iowa	AAA ChN	3	3	1	0	21	82	16	6	6	1	0	1	0	5	0	11	1	0	2	0	1.000	0	0	2.57
7	Min. YEARS		185	92	5	34	696.1	3064	736	383	311	43	31	29	14	252	12	535	72	5	33	47	.413	0	8	4.02

Dave Renteria

Bats: Right **Throws:** Right **Pos:** SS **Ht:** 6'0" **Wt:** 175 **Born:** 12/1/72 **Age:** 24

			BATTING																BASERUNNING				PERCENTAGES		
Year	Team	Lg Org	G	AB	H	2B	3B	HR	TB	R	RBI	TBB	IBB	SO	HBP	SH	SF	SB	CS	SB%	GDP	Avg	OBP	SLG
1992	Yankees	R NYA	20	61	14	1	0	0	15	6	7	6	0	14	0	0	0	0	0	.00	1	.230	.299	.246
1993	Oneonta	A- NYA	43	129	30	7	0	0	37	19	16	14	0	25	0	3	1	1	3	.25	3	.233	.306	.287
1994	San Bernrdo	A+ NYA	23	72	10	0	0	0	10	11	6	18	1	24	1	1	1	0	1	.00	1	.139	.315	.139
	Greensboro	A NYA	38	101	23	3	0	1	29	12	11	12	0	16	0	1	1	1	2	.33	6	.228	.307	.287
	Tampa	A+ NYA	3	8	0	0	0	0	0	3	0	1	0	0	0	0	0	0	0	.00	0	.000	.111	.000
	Columbus	AAA NYA	2	1	0	0	0	0	0	0	0	0	0	0	0	0	0	0	0	.00	0	.000	.000	.000
	Albany-Colo	AA NYA	3	11	1	0	1	0	3	1	0	0	0	6	1	0	0	0	0	.00	1	.091	.167	.273
1995	Norwich	AA NYA	15	38	4	0	0	0	4	4	0	3	0	13	0	1	0	1	0	1.00	0	.105	.171	.105
	Tampa	A+ NYA	33	69	15	3	1	1	23	6	4	4	0	16	1	2	2	1	1	.50	1	.217	.263	.333
1996	W. Palm Bch	A+ Mon	31	107	20	2	1	0	24	10	5	9	0	20	0	2	0	2	3	.40	3	.187	.250	.224
	Harrisburg	AA Mon	24	72	17	6	0	0	23	7	4	5	0	13	1	2	0	0	0	.00	1	.236	.295	.319
5	Min. YEARS		235	669	134	22	3	2	168	79	53	72	1	147	4	12	5	6	10	.38	17	.200	.280	.251

Greg Resz

Pitches: Right **Bats:** Left **Pos:** P **Ht:** 6'5" **Wt:** 215 **Born:** 12/25/71 **Age:** 25

			HOW MUCH HE PITCHED						WHAT HE GAVE UP												THE RESULTS					
Year	Team	Lg Org	G	GS	CG	GF	IP	BFP	H	R	ER	HR	SH	SF	HB	TBB	IBB	SO	WP	Bk	W	L	Pct.	ShO	Sv	ERA
1993	Oneonta	A- NYA	24	0	0	18	26.1	117	18	14	11	2	1	1	4	16	1	16	4	0	3	0	1.000	0	9	3.76
1994	Greensboro	A NYA	7	0	0	7	7.2	32	6	3	3	0	0	0	0	2	0	14	1	0	0	0	.000	0	2	3.52
	Tampa	A+ NYA	18	0	0	18	18.2	79	21	8	3	0	0	1	1	4	0	20	0	0	0	2	.000	0	6	1.45
1995	Tampa	A+ NYA	12	0	0	3	13.1	61	10	9	5	0	0	0	1	9	2	16	3	0	0	1	.000	0	1	3.38
1996	Norwich	AA NYA	19	2	0	9	39	172	38	17	11	1	1	0	1	18	1	37	3	0	1	1	.500	0	2	2.54
	Tampa	A+ NYA	20	0	0	9	25	108	20	11	7	0	1	2	0	12	1	31	2	0	0	1	.000	0	4	2.52
4	Min. YEARS		100	2	0	64	130	569	113	62	40	3	3	4	7	61	5	134	13	0	4	5	.444	0	24	2.77

Todd Revenig

Pitches: Right **Bats:** Right **Pos:** P **Ht:** 6' 1" **Wt:** 185 **Born:** 6/28/69 **Age:** 28

			HOW MUCH HE PITCHED						WHAT HE GAVE UP												THE RESULTS					
Year	Team	Lg Org	G	GS	CG	GF	IP	BFP	H	R	ER	HR	SH	SF	HB	TBB	IBB	SO	WP	Bk	W	L	Pct.	ShO	Sv	ERA
1990	Sou. Oregon	A- Oak	24	0	0	14	44.2	176	33	13	4	2	4	1	0	9	2	46	1	2	3	2	.600	0	6	0.81
1991	Madison	A Oak	26	0	0	22	28.2	109	13	6	3	1	3	0	0	10	2	27	1	1	1	0	1.000	0	13	0.94
	Huntsville	AA Oak	12	0	0	6	18.1	68	11	3	2	1	0	1	2	4	0	10	0	0	1	2	.333	0	0	0.98
1992	Huntsville	AA Oak	53	0	0	48	63.2	233	33	14	12	8	2	2	0	11	0	49	1	0	1	1	.500	0	33	1.70
1994	Athletics	R Oak	4	4	0	0	7.2	33	7	4	3	1	1	0	0	2	0	6	0	0	0	0	.000	0	0	3.52
1995	Edmonton	AAA Oak	45	0	0	30	54.1	230	53	32	26	5	3	3	2	15	1	28	2	0	4	5	.444	0	10	4.31
1996	Rochester	AAA Bal	3	0	0	0	6	25	8	5	5	2	0	0	0	0	0	4	0	0	2	0	1.000	0	0	7.50
	Bowie	AA Bal	38	0	0	29	61.2	238	42	18	18	6	0	2	2	18	0	39	2	0	3	4	.429	0	7	2.63
1992	Oakland	AL	2	0	0	2	2	7	2	0	0	0	0	0	0	0	0	1	0	0	0	0	.000	0	0	0.00
6	Min. YEARS		205	4	0	149	285	1112	200	95	73	26	13	9	6	69	5	209	7	3	15	14	.517	0	69	2.31

Gil Reyes

Bats: Right **Throws:** Right **Pos:** C **Ht:** 6' 2" **Wt:** 212 **Born:** 12/10/63 **Age:** 33

			BATTING																BASERUNNING				PERCENTAGES		
Year	Team	Lg Org	G	AB	H	2B	3B	HR	TB	R	RBI	TBB	IBB	SO	HBP	SH	SF	SB	CS	SB%	GDP	Avg	OBP	SLG
1984	San Antonio	AA LA	120	433	131	16	2	10	181	55	78	29	2	50	2	2	5	1	4	.20	17	.303	.345	.418

Year Team	Lg Org	G	AB	H	2B	3B	HR	TB	R	RBI	TBB	IBB	SO	HBP	SH	SF	SB	CS	SB%	GDP	Avg	OBP	SLG
		BATTING															BASERUNNING				PERCENTAGES		
1985 Albuquerque	AAA LA	111	366	97	20	0	6	135	35	54	15	1	74	3	2	8	0	0	.00	6	.265	.293	.369
1986 Albuquerque	AAA LA	104	306	70	13	1	7	106	36	36	23	2	54	2	3	2	1	1	.50	5	.229	.285	.346
1987 Albuquerque	AAA LA	89	265	72	18	2	5	109	42	46	30	0	57	6	1	2	0	1	.00	7	.272	.356	.411
1988 Albuquerque	AAA LA	98	318	93	14	0	12	143	40	66	27	0	63	5	1	3	2	1	.67	7	.292	.354	.450
1989 Indianapols	AAA Mon	106	314	71	8	0	9	106	35	35	30	4	69	3	2	1	0	2	.00	11	.226	.299	.338
1990 Indianapols	AAA Mon	89	309	72	14	1	9	115	22	45	24	2	79	2	0	6	2	2	.50	10	.233	.287	.372
1993 Colo. Sprng	AAA Col	73	174	41	6	2	9	78	22	29	22	1	36	1	5	1	1	1	.50	5	.236	.323	.448
1996 Ottawa	AAA Mon	17	44	8	3	0	3	20	5	5	8	0	12	1	0	0	0	0	.00	0	.182	.321	.455
1983 Los Angeles	NL	19	31	5	2	0	0	7	1	0	0	0	5	1	0	0	0	0	.00	3	.161	.188	.226
1984 Los Angeles	NL	4	5	0	0	0	0	0	0	0	0	0	3	0	0	0	0	0	.00	0	.000	.000	.000
1985 Los Angeles	NL	6	1	0	0	0	0	0	0	0	1	0	1	1	0	0	0	0	.00	0	.000	.667	.000
1987 Los Angeles	NL	1	0	0	0	0	0	0	0	0	0	0	0	0	0	0	0	0	.00	0	.000	.000	.000
1988 Los Angeles	NL	5	9	1	0	0	0	1	1	0	0	0	3	0	0	0	0	0	.00	0	.111	.111	.111
1989 Montreal	NL	4	5	1	0	0	0	1	0	1	0	0	1	0	0	0	0	0	.00	0	.200	.200	.200
1991 Montreal	NL	83	207	45	9	0	0	54	11	13	19	2	51	1	1	1	2	4	.33	3	.217	.285	.261
9 Min. YEARS		807	2529	655	112	8	70	993	292	394	208	12	494	25	16	28	7	12	.37	68	.259	.318	.393
7 Maj. YEARS		122	258	52	11	0	0	63	13	14	20	2	64	3	1	1	2	4	.33	6	.202	.266	.244

Chance Reynolds

Bats: Both **Throws:** Right **Pos:** C **Ht:** 5'10" **Wt:** 185 **Born:** 9/16/71 **Age:** 25

Year Team	Lg Org	G	AB	H	2B	3B	HR	TB	R	RBI	TBB	IBB	SO	HBP	SH	SF	SB	CS	SB%	GDP	Avg	OBP	SLG
		BATTING															BASERUNNING				PERCENTAGES		
1993 Everett	A- SF	12	26	6	0	0	0	6	3	1	2	0	10	2	0	0	0	0	.00	0	.231	.333	.231
Giants	R SF	7	20	4	2	0	0	6	1	4	5	0	2	0	0	0	0	0	.00	0	.200	.360	.300
1994 Erie	IND —	42	142	41	9	1	3	61	19	16	12	0	22	4	2	3	2	0	1.00	3	.289	.354	.430
1995 Augusta	A Pit	24	65	14	2	0	1	19	8	6	12	1	11	4	0	0	0	2	.00	1	.215	.370	.292
Lynchburg	A+ Pit	5	15	3	0	0	0	3	0	2	3	0	2	2	0	0	0	1	.00	1	.200	.400	.200
Erie	A- Pit	37	120	29	2	0	0	31	17	18	14	0	18	3	1	4	0	2	.00	5	.242	.326	.258
1996 Carolina	AA Pit	4	6	1	0	0	0	1	0	1	0	0	2	0	0	0	0	0	.00	0	.167	.167	.167
Stockton	A+ Mil	20	67	11	2	0	0	13	3	7	8	0	10	4	0	0	1	2	.33	4	.164	.291	.194
4 Min. YEARS		151	461	109	17	1	4	140	51	55	56	1	77	19	3	7	3	7	.30	14	.236	.339	.304

Kendall Rhine

Pitches: Right **Bats:** Right **Pos:** P **Ht:** 6'7" **Wt:** 215 **Born:** 11/27/70 **Age:** 26

Year Team	Lg Org	G	GS	CG	GF	IP	BFP	H	R	ER	HR	SH	SF	HB	TBB	IBB	SO	WP	Bk	W	L	Pct.	ShO	Sv	ERA
		HOW MUCH HE PITCHED						WHAT HE GAVE UP												THE RESULTS					
1992 Auburn	A- Hou	8	8	0	0	31	153	34	21	17	2	1	3	2	31	0	21	8	2	0	3	.000	0	0	4.94
1993 Auburn	A- Hou	16	10	0	2	47.2	257	61	62	52	2	1	3	10	48	1	36	21	0	0	2	.000	0	0	9.82
1994 Auburn	A- Hou	8	0	0	2	19.2	92	18	14	11	1	1	0	3	11	0	15	6	1	0	1	.000	0	0	5.03
1995 Hagerstown	A Tor	42	0	0	36	55.1	230	41	20	16	2	4	0	3	28	1	49	8	0	3	3	.500	0	13	2.60
1996 Dunedin	A+ Tor	20	0	0	11	23	104	20	11	10	1	0	0	3	11	2	25	2	0	1	0	1.000	0	3	3.91
Knoxville	AA Tor	11	0	0	6	12.1	62	12	8	8	1	0	1	3	11	1	9	3	0	0	0	.000	0	2	5.84
5 Min. YEARS		105	18	0	57	189	898	186	136	114	9	7	7	24	140	5	155	48	3	4	9	.308	0	18	5.43

Joey Rhodes

Pitches: Right **Bats:** Right **Pos:** P **Ht:** 6'4" **Wt:** 190 **Born:** 1/8/75 **Age:** 22

Year Team	Lg Org	G	GS	CG	GF	IP	BFP	H	R	ER	HR	SH	SF	HB	TBB	IBB	SO	WP	Bk	W	L	Pct.	ShO	Sv	ERA
		HOW MUCH HE PITCHED						WHAT HE GAVE UP												THE RESULTS					
1994 Orioles	R Bal	8	1	0	5	14.2	69	19	14	13	1	0	3	0	9	0	10	4	0	2	1	.667	0	0	7.98
1995 Frederick	A+ Bal	2	1	0	1	6	28	8	3	3	0	1	0	0	2	0	2	1	0	0	1	.000	0	0	4.50
Orioles	R Bal	15	12	0	1	77	339	80	39	27	0	4	1	2	30	1	45	3	0	4	3	.571	0	0	3.16
1996 High Desert	A+ Bal	25	21	0	1	123.1	564	133	85	70	13	4	10	2	66	1	81	11	2	5	9	.357	0	0	5.11
Bowie	AA Bal	4	1	0	1	12	46	6	2	2	0	0	0	1	5	0	9	1	0	2	1	.667	0	0	1.50
3 Min. YEARS		54	36	0	9	233	1046	246	143	115	14	9	14	5	112	2	147	20	2	13	15	.464	0	0	4.44

Chuck Ricci

Pitches: Right **Bats:** Right **Pos:** P **Ht:** 6' 2" **Wt:** 180 **Born:** 11/20/68 **Age:** 28

Year Team	Lg Org	G	GS	CG	GF	IP	BFP	H	R	ER	HR	SH	SF	HB	TBB	IBB	SO	WP	Bk	W	L	Pct.	ShO	Sv	ERA
		HOW MUCH HE PITCHED						WHAT HE GAVE UP												THE RESULTS					
1987 Bluefield	R+ Bal	13	12	1	0	62.1	288	74	52	45	11	1	0	2	38	1	40	3	0	5	5	.500	0	0	6.50
1988 Bluefield	R+ Bal	14	14	1	0	73	355	92	61	54	7	1	3	2	48	0	73	6	0	4	6	.400	0	0	6.66
1989 Waterloo	A Bal	29	25	9	1	181.1	760	160	89	60	11	11	5	12	59	5	89	14	1	10	12	.455	0	0	2.98
1990 Frederick	A+ Bal	26	18	2	5	122.1	539	126	79	60	8	6	3	6	47	3	94	8	0	7	12	.368	1	0	4.41
1991 Frederick	A+ Bal	30	29	2	0	173.2	752	147	91	60	12	3	10	3	84	2	144	15	1	12	14	.462	0	0	3.11
1992 Frederick	A+ Bal	1	0	0	0	2.1	11	2	1	0	0	0	0	0	1	0	2	0	0	0	0	.000	0	0	0.00
Hagerstown	AA Bal	20	6	0	4	57.2	275	58	40	37	4	3	4	3	47	1	58	8	2	1	4	.200	0	0	5.77
1993 Rochester	AAA Bal	4	0	0	3	8	36	11	5	5	1	0	0	0	3	0	6	0	0	0	0	.000	0	0	5.63
Bowie	AA Bal	34	1	0	16	81.2	334	72	35	29	7	5	2	3	20	0	83	8	0	7	4	.636	0	5	3.20
1994 Reading	AA Phi	14	0	0	2	19	71	10	1	0	0	0	0	2	4	2	23	0	0	1	0	1.000	0	0	0.00
Scranton-WB	AAA Phi	44	1	0	17	64.2	274	60	30	29	7	2	3	5	22	5	72	4	0	4	3	.571	0	6	4.04
1995 Scranton-WB	AAA Phi	68	0	0	48	65	269	48	22	18	6	4	1	4	24	5	66	1	0	4	3	.571	0	25	2.49
1996 Pawtucket	AAA Bos	60	0	0	43	80.2	326	56	30	27	12	2	3	1	32	2	79	9	0	8	4	.667	0	13	3.01
1995 Philadelphia	NL	7	0	0	3	10	40	9	2	2	0	1	2	1	3	0	9	0	0	1	0	1.000	0	0	1.80

HOW MUCH HE PITCHED								WHAT HE GAVE UP												THE RESULTS					
Year Team	Lg Org	G	GS	CG	GF	IP	BFP	H	R	ER	HR	SH	SF	HB	TBB	IBB	SO	WP	Bk	W	L	Pct.	ShO	Sv	ERA
10 Min. YEARS		357	106	15	139	991.2	4290	916	536	424	86	38	34	43	429	26	829	76	4	63	67	.485	1	49	3.85

Lance Rice

Bats: Both **Throws:** Right **Pos:** C **Ht:** 6'1" **Wt:** 195 **Born:** 10/19/66 **Age:** 30

BATTING																	BASERUNNING				PERCENTAGES		
Year Team	Lg Org	G	AB	H	2B	3B	HR	TB	R	RBI	TBB	IBB	SO	HBP	SH	SF	SB	CS	SB%	GDP	Avg	OBP	SLG
1988 Great Falls	R+ LA	47	159	45	8	2	0	57	31	27	31	0	29	1	2	2	4	2	.67	2	.283	.399	.358
1989 Bakersfield	A+ LA	126	406	90	15	1	5	122	41	53	53	2	83	3	1	5	1	4	.20	9	.222	.313	.300
1990 San Antonio	AA LA	79	245	59	11	2	0	74	25	35	24	3	46	1	3	4	3	1	.75	6	.241	.307	.302
1991 San Antonio	AA LA	78	215	43	8	0	3	60	23	28	31	2	30	1	2	3	2	1	.67	7	.200	.300	.279
Albuquerque	AAA LA	1	3	1	1	0	0	2	0	1	0	0	0	0	0	0	0	0	.00	0	.333	.333	.667
1992 San Antonio	AA LA	75	194	45	9	0	2	60	17	18	17	3	34	1	6	2	0	1	.00	2	.232	.294	.309
1993 Harrisburg	AA Mon	46	136	32	10	0	1	45	12	20	16	0	22	0	2	2	0	1	.00	3	.235	.312	.331
1994 Harrisburg	AA Mon	13	30	9	1	0	0	10	8	2	7	0	4	0	0	0	0	0	.00	2	.300	.432	.333
1995 Toledo	AAA Det	15	41	11	1	0	1	15	2	6	4	0	6	0	1	0	0	3	.00	0	.268	.333	.366
Jacksonvlle	AA Det	65	154	19	1	1	3	31	8	11	11	0	23	0	2	0	0	0	.00	5	.123	.182	.201
1996 Bowie	AA Bal	55	164	35	4	0	2	45	8	17	13	1	19	0	3	2	0	0	.00	4	.213	.268	.274
9 Min. YEARS		600	1747	389	69	6	17	521	175	218	207	11	296	7	22	20	10	13	.43	40	.223	.304	.298

Brian Richardson

Bats: Right **Throws:** Right **Pos:** 3B **Ht:** 6'2" **Wt:** 190 **Born:** 8/31/75 **Age:** 21

BATTING																	BASERUNNING				PERCENTAGES		
Year Team	Lg Org	G	AB	H	2B	3B	HR	TB	R	RBI	TBB	IBB	SO	HBP	SH	SF	SB	CS	SB%	GDP	Avg	OBP	SLG
1992 Dodgers	R LA	37	122	26	6	2	0	36	8	15	11	0	27	0	0	2	3	0	1.00	2	.213	.274	.295
1993 Great Falls	R+ LA	54	178	40	11	0	0	51	16	13	14	1	47	3	1	2	1	2	.33	7	.225	.289	.287
1994 Vero Beach	A+ LA	19	52	12	0	1	0	14	3	3	4	0	15	0	0	2	3	0	1.00	2	.231	.276	.269
Yakima	A- LA	70	266	62	15	0	5	92	35	44	35	1	82	1	0	0	12	4	.75	3	.233	.325	.346
1995 San Bernrdo	A+ LA	127	462	131	18	1	12	187	68	58	35	2	122	7	6	3	17	16	.52	11	.284	.341	.405
1996 San Antonio	AA LA	19	62	20	1	1	0	23	10	7	2	0	10	2	0	0	0	2	.00	0	.323	.364	.371
Albuquerque	AAA LA	105	355	87	17	2	9	135	52	43	32	6	89	3	4	4	4	1	.80	5	.245	.310	.380
5 Min. YEARS		431	1497	378	68	7	26	538	192	183	133	10	392	16	11	13	40	25	.62	30	.253	.318	.359

Raymond Ricken

Pitches: Right **Bats:** Right **Pos:** P **Ht:** 6'5" **Wt:** 225 **Born:** 8/11/73 **Age:** 23

HOW MUCH HE PITCHED								WHAT HE GAVE UP												THE RESULTS					
Year Team	Lg Org	G	GS	CG	GF	IP	BFP	H	R	ER	HR	SH	SF	HB	TBB	IBB	SO	WP	Bk	W	L	Pct.	ShO	Sv	ERA
1994 Oneonta	A- NYA	10	10	0	0	50.1	206	45	25	20	1	1	1	2	17	1	55	6	3	2	3	.400	0	0	3.58
Greensboro	A NYA	5	5	0	0	25	109	27	13	13	1	0	1	0	12	0	19	3	0	1	2	.333	0	0	4.68
1995 Greensboro	A NYA	10	10	0	0	64.2	245	42	20	16	2	1	1	0	16	1	77	3	0	3	2	.600	0	0	2.23
Norwich	AA NYA	8	8	1	0	53	217	44	21	16	2	2	0	1	24	2	43	3	0	4	2	.667	1	0	2.72
Tampa	A+ NYA	29	29	2	0	193	753	133	66	50	7	5	2	2	67	3	178	7	2	10	8	.556	1	0	2.33
1996 Norwich	AA NYA	8	8	1	0	46.1	201	42	26	23	7	1	3	1	20	0	42	5	0	5	2	.714	1	0	4.47
Columbus	AAA NYA	20	11	1	2	68	301	62	44	36	4	1	3	3	37	2	58	8	0	4	5	.444	0	1	4.76
3 Min. YEARS		90	81	5	2	500.1	2032	395	215	174	24	11	11	9	193	9	472	35	5	29	24	.547	3	1	3.13

Brad Rigby

Pitches: Right **Bats:** Right **Pos:** P **Ht:** 6'6" **Wt:** 194 **Born:** 5/14/73 **Age:** 24

HOW MUCH HE PITCHED								WHAT HE GAVE UP												THE RESULTS					
Year Team	Lg Org	G	GS	CG	GF	IP	BFP	H	R	ER	HR	SH	SF	HB	TBB	IBB	SO	WP	Bk	W	L	Pct.	ShO	Sv	ERA
1994 Modesto	A+ Oak	11	1	0	3	23.2	101	20	10	10	0	1	1	2	10	1	28	1	0	2	1	.667	0	2	3.80
1995 Modesto	A+ Oak	31	23	0	4	154.2	653	135	79	66	5	2	7	12	48	0	145	8	2	11	4	.733	0	2	3.84
1996 Huntsville	AA Oak	26	26	3	0	159.1	682	161	89	70	13	3	3	7	59	8	127	13	2	9	12	.429	0	0	3.95
3 Min. YEARS		68	50	3	7	337.2	1436	316	178	146	18	6	11	21	117	9	300	22	4	22	17	.564	0	4	3.89

Adam Riggs

Bats: Right **Throws:** Right **Pos:** 2B **Ht:** 6'0" **Wt:** 190 **Born:** 10/4/72 **Age:** 24

BATTING																	BASERUNNING				PERCENTAGES		
Year Team	Lg Org	G	AB	H	2B	3B	HR	TB	R	RBI	TBB	IBB	SO	HBP	SH	SF	SB	CS	SB%	GDP	Avg	OBP	SLG
1994 Great Falls	R+ LA	62	234	73	20	3	5	114	55	44	31	1	38	4	2	2	19	8	.70	2	.312	.399	.487
Yakima	A- LA	4	7	2	1	0	0	3	1	0	0	0	1	0	0	0	0	0	.00	0	.286	.286	.429
1995 San Bernrdo	A+ LA	134	542	196	39	5	24	317	111	106	59	1	93	10	7	4	31	10	.76	9	.362	.431	.585
1996 San Antonio	AA LA	134	506	143	31	6	14	228	68	66	37	1	82	9	5	5	16	6	.73	13	.283	.339	.451
3 Min. YEARS		334	1289	414	91	14	43	662	235	216	127	3	214	23	14	11	66	24	.73	24	.321	.389	.514

Kevin Riggs

Bats: Left **Throws:** Right **Pos:** 2B **Ht:** 5'11" **Wt:** 190 **Born:** 2/3/69 **Age:** 28

BATTING																	BASERUNNING				PERCENTAGES		
Year Team	Lg Org	G	AB	H	2B	3B	HR	TB	R	RBI	TBB	IBB	SO	HBP	SH	SF	SB	CS	SB%	GDP	Avg	OBP	SLG
1990 Billings	R+ Cin	57	192	61	9	2	1	77	49	21	50	2	27	2	0	0	16	3	.84	5	.318	.463	.401
Charlstn-WV	A Cin	2	4	1	0	0	0	1	0	1	0	0	1	0	0	0	0	1	.00	0	.250	.250	.250
1991 Cedar Rapds	A Cin	118	406	109	21	2	2	140	72	43	91	2	50	3	2	6	23	8	.74	11	.268	.401	.345
Charlstn-WV	A Cin	1	2	1	0	0	0	1	0	0	1	0	0	0	0	0	0	0	.00	0	.500	.667	.500

Year	Team	Lg	Org	G	AB	H	2B	3B	HR	TB	R	RBI	TBB	IBB	SO	HBP	SH	SF	SB	CS	SB%	GDP	Avg	OBP	SLG
	BATTING																		BASERUNNING				PERCENTAGES		
1992	Cedar Rapds	A	Cin	126	457	132	24	4	2	170	87	44	97	3	63	5	4	5	23	15	.61	10	.289	.415	.372
1993	Stockton	A+	Mil	108	377	131	18	3	3	164	84	45	101	3	46	1	1	4	12	15	.44	8	.347	.482	.435
1994	El Paso	AA	Mil	66	230	68	10	2	1	85	38	22	46	1	39	1	0	0	3	7	.30	2	.296	.415	.370
1995	Norwich	AA	NYA	57	179	59	16	1	4	89	38	36	51	3	28	4	0	4	5	5	.50	4	.330	.479	.497
1996	Norwich	AA	NYA	118	403	117	24	1	2	149	75	37	81	4	66	6	2	5	9	9	.50	7	.290	.412	.370
	7 Min. YEARS			653	2250	679	122	15	15	876	443	249	518	18	320	22	9	24	91	63	.59	47	.302	.433	.389

Marquis Riley

Bats: Right **Throws:** Right **Pos:** OF **Ht:** 5'10" **Wt:** 170 **Born:** 12/27/70 **Age:** 26

Year	Team	Lg	Org	G	AB	H	2B	3B	HR	TB	R	RBI	TBB	IBB	SO	HBP	SH	SF	SB	CS	SB%	GDP	Avg	OBP	SLG
	BATTING																		BASERUNNING				PERCENTAGES		
1992	Boise	A-	Cal	52	201	48	12	1	0	62	47	12	37	0	29	2	2	0	7	4	.64	3	.239	.363	.308
1993	Palm Spring	A+	Cal	130	508	134	10	2	1	151	93	42	90	1	117	0	5	2	69	25	.73	3	.264	.373	.297
1994	Midland	AA	Cal	93	374	107	12	4	1	130	68	29	35	3	57	6	7	4	32	5	.86	10	.286	.353	.348
	Vancouver	AAA	Cal	4	14	3	0	0	0	3	3	1	3	0	3	0	0	0	1	0	1.00	1	.214	.353	.214
1995	Vancouver	AAA	Cal	120	477	125	6	6	0	143	70	43	49	3	69	1	2	4	29	10	.74	11	.262	.330	.300
1996	Vancouver	AAA	Cal	12	47	11	2	0	0	13	8	0	3	0	12	0	0	0	3	0	1.00	2	.234	.280	.277
	Charlotte	AAA	Fla	92	300	68	10	0	0	78	43	13	26	1	31	1	4	2	16	5	.76	8	.227	.289	.260
	5 Min. YEARS			503	1921	496	52	13	2	580	332	140	243	8	318	10	20	12	157	49	.76	38	.258	.343	.302

Armando Rios

Bats: Left **Throws:** Left **Pos:** OF **Ht:** 5'9" **Wt:** 178 **Born:** 9/13/71 **Age:** 25

Year	Team	Lg	Org	G	AB	H	2B	3B	HR	TB	R	RBI	TBB	IBB	SO	HBP	SH	SF	SB	CS	SB%	GDP	Avg	OBP	SLG
	BATTING																		BASERUNNING				PERCENTAGES		
1994	Clinton	A	SF	119	407	120	23	4	8	175	67	60	59	2	69	4	1	7	16	12	.57	7	.295	.384	.430
1995	San Jose	A+	SF	128	488	143	34	3	8	207	76	75	74	3	75	1	4	7	51	10	.84	8	.293	.382	.424
1996	Shreveport	AA	SF	92	329	93	22	2	12	155	62	49	44	3	42	1	3	4	9	9	.50	2	.283	.365	.471
	3 Min. YEARS			339	1224	356	79	9	28	537	205	184	177	8	186	6	8	18	76	31	.71	17	.291	.378	.439

Danny Rios

Pitches: Right **Bats:** Right **Pos:** P **Ht:** 6'2" **Wt:** 208 **Born:** 11/11/72 **Age:** 24

Year	Team	Lg	Org	G	GS	CG	GF	IP	BFP	H	R	ER	HR	SH	SF	HB	TBB	IBB	SO	WP	Bk	W	L	Pct.	ShO	Sv	ERA
	HOW MUCH HE PITCHED									WHAT HE GAVE UP												THE RESULTS					
1993	Yankees	R	NYA	24	0	0	17	38.1	170	34	18	15	0	2	1	5	16	0	29	9	3	2	1	.667	0	6	3.52
1994	Greensboro	A	NYA	37	0	0	34	41.1	164	32	4	4	1	2	0	3	13	1	36	3	0	3	2	.600	0	17	0.87
	Tampa	A+	NYA	9	0	0	8	10.1	41	6	2	0	0	0	1	1	4	0	11	0	0	0	0	.000	0	2	0.00
1995	Tampa	A+	NYA	57	0	0	52	67.1	296	67	24	15	1	5	2	8	20	4	72	2	0	0	4	.000	0	24	2.00
1996	Norwich	AA	NYA	38	0	0	29	43	183	34	14	10	0	2	0	3	21	1	38	3	2	3	1	.750	0	17	2.09
	Columbus	AAA	NYA	24	0	0	6	27.2	111	22	7	6	1	0	2	4	6	0	22	1	0	4	1	.800	0	0	1.95
	4 Min. YEARS			189	0	0	146	228	965	195	69	50	3	11	6	24	80	6	208	18	5	12	9	.571	0	66	1.97

Eduardo Rios

Bats: Right **Throws:** Right **Pos:** 3B **Ht:** 5'10" **Wt:** 160 **Born:** 10/13/72 **Age:** 24

Year	Team	Lg	Org	G	AB	H	2B	3B	HR	TB	R	RBI	TBB	IBB	SO	HBP	SH	SF	SB	CS	SB%	GDP	Avg	OBP	SLG
	BATTING																		BASERUNNING				PERCENTAGES		
1993	Great Falls	R+	LA	26	107	29	4	3	2	45	18	12	10	1	11	1	0	1	2	4	.33	1	.271	.336	.421
	Bakersfield	A+	LA	29	113	32	4	0	7	57	19	17	8	0	17	2	2	0	2	3	.40	1	.283	.341	.504
1994	Vero Beach	A+	LA	133	529	139	28	8	13	222	70	79	24	1	85	8	2	6	2	5	.29	15	.263	.302	.420
1995	San Antonio	AA	LA	98	365	104	22	4	5	149	43	53	20	2	47	1	1	5	2	4	.33	8	.285	.320	.408
1996	Albuquerque	AAA	LA	15	29	2	0	0	0	2	3	1	3	1	6	1	0	1	1	0	1.00	1	.069	.176	.069
	San Antonio	AA	LA	75	242	67	11	2	5	97	29	37	20	0	32	0	0	1	2	2	.50	7	.277	.331	.401
	4 Min. YEARS			376	1385	373	69	17	32	572	182	199	85	5	198	13	5	14	11	18	.38	33	.269	.315	.413

Brad Ripplemeyer

Bats: Right **Throws:** Right **Pos:** 3B **Ht:** 6'2" **Wt:** 190 **Born:** 2/6/70 **Age:** 27

Year	Team	Lg	Org	G	AB	H	2B	3B	HR	TB	R	RBI	TBB	IBB	SO	HBP	SH	SF	SB	CS	SB%	GDP	Avg	OBP	SLG
	BATTING																		BASERUNNING				PERCENTAGES		
1991	Idaho Falls	R+	Atl	37	120	43	12	2	5	74	28	22	24	1	29	3	2	0	1	2	.33	4	.358	.476	.617
1992	Durham	A+	Atl	115	392	89	16	1	19	164	38	48	25	1	134	4	6	6	2	5	.29	2	.227	.276	.418
1993	Greenville	AA	Atl	95	277	53	14	0	4	79	25	27	31	4	74	6	3	3	0	2	.00	8	.191	.284	.285
1994	Durham	A+	Atl	62	200	44	10	1	3	65	23	14	28	0	59	3	1	0	1	2	.33	6	.220	.325	.325
1995	Greenville	AA	Atl	53	165	30	8	0	2	44	8	16	11	0	54	0	5	2	1	0	1.00	5	.182	.230	.267
1996	Greenville	AA	Atl	7	15	1	0	0	0	1	2	1	1	0	6	0	0	0	0	0	.00	1	.067	.125	.067
	6 Min. YEARS			369	1169	260	60	4	33	427	124	128	120	6	356	16	17	11	5	11	.31	26	.222	.301	.365

Todd Ritchie

Pitches: Right **Bats:** Right **Pos:** P **Ht:** 6'3" **Wt:** 185 **Born:** 11/7/71 **Age:** 25

Year	Team	Lg	Org	G	GS	CG	GF	IP	BFP	H	R	ER	HR	SH	SF	HB	TBB	IBB	SO	WP	Bk	W	L	Pct.	ShO	Sv	ERA
	HOW MUCH HE PITCHED									WHAT HE GAVE UP												THE RESULTS					
1990	Elizabethtn	R+	Min	11	11	1	0	65	261	45	22	14	5	2	2	6	24	0	49	2	3	5	2	.714	0	0	1.94
1991	Kenosha	A	Min	21	21	0	0	116.2	498	113	53	46	3	4	1	7	50	0	101	10	1	7	6	.538	0	0	3.55
1992	Visalia	A+	Min	28	28	3	0	172.2	763	193	113	97	13	6	6	7	65	2	129	16	1	11	9	.550	1	0	5.06

Year	Team	Lg	Org	G	GS	CG	GF	IP	BFP	H	R	ER	HR	SH	SF	HB	TBB	IBB	SO	WP	Bk	W	L	Pct.	ShO	Sv	ERA
				HOW MUCH HE PITCHED						WHAT HE GAVE UP												THE RESULTS					
1993	Nashville	AA	Min	12	10	0	0	46.2	194	46	21	19	2	1	1	0	15	0	41	5	1	3	2	.600	0	0	3.66
1994	Nashville	AA	Min	4	4	0	0	17	74	24	10	8	1	1	0	0	7	0	9	2	0	0	2	.000	0	0	4.24
1995	New Britain	AA	Min	24	21	0	0	113	515	135	78	72	12	4	5	6	54	0	60	8	0	4	9	.308	0	0	5.73
1996	New Britain	AA	Min	29	10	0	14	82.2	376	101	55	50	6	3	4	5	30	1	53	4	0	3	7	.300	0	4	5.44
	Salt Lake	AAA	Min	16	0	0	4	24.2	113	27	15	15	5	2	1	1	11	0	19	4	0	0	4	.000	0	0	5.47
7 Min. YEARS				145	105	4	18	638.1	2794	684	367	321	47	23	20	32	256	3	461	51	6	33	41	.446	1	4	4.53

Ben Rivera

Pitches: Right **Bats:** Right **Pos:** P **Ht:** 6' 6" **Wt:** 250 **Born:** 1/11/68 **Age:** 29

Year	Team	Lg	Org	G	GS	CG	GF	IP	BFP	H	R	ER	HR	SH	SF	HB	TBB	IBB	SO	WP	Bk	W	L	Pct.	ShO	Sv	ERA
				HOW MUCH HE PITCHED						WHAT HE GAVE UP												THE RESULTS					
1987	Braves	R	Atl	16	5	0	2	49.2	220	55	26	18	0	1	2	2	19	1	29	2	2	1	5	.167	0	0	3.26
1988	Sumter	A	Atl	27	27	3	0	173.1	724	167	77	61	12	2	5	7	52	0	99	6	7	9	11	.450	2	0	3.17
1989	Durham	A+	Atl	23	22	1	0	102.1	462	113	55	51	6	4	3	5	51	1	58	10	3	5	7	.417	0	0	4.49
1990	Greenville	AA	Atl	13	13	0	0	52	243	68	40	38	6	2	1	3	26	0	32	10	0	1	4	.200	0	0	6.58
	Durham	A+	Atl	16	13	1	3	75	327	69	41	30	7	2	3	5	33	1	64	4	2	5	3	.625	1	1	3.60
1991	Greenville	AA	Atl	26	26	3	0	158.2	683	155	76	63	13	2	1	3	75	4	116	8	4	11	8	.579	2	0	3.57
1992	Scranton-WB	AAA	Phi	2	2	1	0	12	41	4	0	0	0	0	0	1	2	0	10	0	1	2	0	1.000	1	0	0.00
1994	Clearwater	A+	Phi	4	4	0	0	16	60	11	4	4	2	0	0	0	4	0	9	1	0	1	2	.333	0	0	2.25
	Scranton-WB	AAA	Phi	3	3	0	0	15	65	15	7	7	0	1	1	1	5	0	13	1	0	1	1	.500	0	0	4.20
1996	Ottawa	AAA	Mon	31	15	0	2	100.1	458	112	74	72	7	2	2	8	47	2	87	8	1	4	9	.308	0	1	6.46
1992	Atlanta	NL		8	0	0	3	15.1	78	21	8	8	1	0	1	2	13	2	11	0	0	0	1	.000	0	0	4.70
	Philadelphia	NL		20	14	4	4	102	409	78	32	32	8	5	1	2	32	2	66	5	0	7	3	.700	1	0	2.82
1993	Philadelphia	NL		30	28	1	1	163	742	175	99	91	16	5	5	6	85	4	123	13	0	13	9	.591	1	0	5.02
1994	Philadelphia	NL		9	7	0	1	38	176	40	29	29	7	6	1	1	22	0	19	3	0	3	4	.429	0	0	6.87
8 Min. YEARS				161	130	9	7	754.1	3283	769	400	344	53	16	18	35	314	9	517	50	20	40	50	.444	6	2	4.10
3 Maj. YEARS				67	49	5	9	318.1	1405	314	168	160	32	16	8	11	152	8	219	21	0	23	17	.575	2	0	4.52

Luis Rivera

Bats: Right **Throws:** Right **Pos:** SS **Ht:** 5'10" **Wt:** 175 **Born:** 1/3/64 **Age:** 33

Year	Team	Lg	Org	G	AB	H	2B	3B	HR	TB	R	RBI	TBB	IBB	SO	HBP	SH	SF	SB	CS	SB%	GDP	Avg	OBP	SLG
				BATTING															BASERUNNING				PERCENTAGES		
1984	W. Palm Bch	A+	Mon	124	439	100	23	0	6	141	54	43	50	5	79	5	0	3	14	2	.88	16	.228	.312	.321
1985	Jacksonvlle	AA	Mon	138	538	129	20	2	16	201	74	72	44	1	69	7	3	6	18	15	.55	7	.240	.303	.374
1986	Indianapols	AAA	Mon	108	407	100	17	5	7	148	60	43	29	0	68	4	1	6	18	8	.69	12	.246	.298	.364
1987	Indianapols	AAA	Mon	108	433	135	26	3	8	191	73	53	32	2	73	2	3	3	24	11	.69	4	.312	.360	.441
1989	Pawtucket	AAA	Bos	43	175	44	9	0	1	56	22	13	11	0	23	1	4	0	5	3	.63	3	.251	.299	.320
1995	Okla. City	AAA	Tex	19	58	8	4	0	1	15	3	3	1	0	6	1	0	0	0	0	.00	1	.138	.167	.259
1996	Norfolk	AAA	NYN	114	356	80	23	3	6	127	34	39	31	1	58	3	8	3	1	3	.25	10	.225	.290	.357
1986	Montreal	NL		55	166	34	11	1	0	47	20	13	17	0	33	2	1	1	1	1	.50	1	.205	.285	.283
1987	Montreal	NL		18	32	5	2	0	0	7	0	1	1	0	8	0	0	0	0	0	.00	0	.156	.182	.219
1988	Montreal	NL		123	371	83	17	3	4	118	35	30	24	4	69	1	3	3	3	4	.43	9	.224	.271	.318
1989	Boston	AL		93	323	83	17	1	5	117	35	29	20	1	60	1	4	1	2	3	.40	7	.257	.301	.362
1990	Boston	AL		118	346	78	20	0	7	119	38	45	25	0	58	1	12	1	4	3	.57	10	.225	.279	.344
1991	Boston	AL		129	414	107	22	3	8	159	64	40	35	0	86	3	12	4	4	4	.50	10	.258	.318	.384
1992	Boston	AL		102	288	62	11	1	0	75	17	29	26	0	56	3	5	0	4	3	.57	5	.215	.287	.260
1993	Boston	AL		62	130	27	8	1	1	40	13	7	11	0	36	1	2	1	1	2	.33	2	.208	.273	.308
1994	New York	NL		32	43	12	2	1	3	25	11	5	4	0	14	2	0	0	0	1	.00	1	.279	.367	.581
7 Min. YEARS				654	2406	596	122	13	45	879	320	266	198	9	376	23	19	21	80	42	.66	53	.248	.309	.365
9 Maj. YEARS				732	2113	491	110	11	28	707	233	199	163	5	420	14	39	11	19	21	.48	45	.232	.290	.335

Roberto Rivera

Pitches: Left **Bats:** Left **Pos:** P **Ht:** 6' 0" **Wt:** 200 **Born:** 1/1/69 **Age:** 28

Year	Team	Lg	Org	G	GS	CG	GF	IP	BFP	H	R	ER	HR	SH	SF	HB	TBB	IBB	SO	WP	Bk	W	L	Pct.	ShO	Sv	ERA
				HOW MUCH HE PITCHED						WHAT HE GAVE UP												THE RESULTS					
1988	Indians	R	Cle	14	12	1	1	69.1	295	64	32	25	2	2	4	3	21	1	38	2	4	6	5	.545	1	0	3.25
1989	Burlington	R+	Cle	18	2	1	8	51.1	214	44	24	20	4	4	2	1	16	3	42	0	2	3	4	.429	0	2	3.51
1990	Watertown	A-	Cle	14	13	2	0	85	345	85	43	34	9	2	1	1	10	0	63	2	0	4	4	.500	1	0	3.60
1991	Columbus	A	Cle	30	1	0	17	49	207	48	15	9	1	2	0	2	12	3	36	2	2	7	1	.875	0	3	1.65
	Kinston	A+	Cle	10	0	0	5	10.1	46	10	6	5	1	1	1	0	2	0	9	0	0	1	0	1.000	0	0	4.35
1992	Kinston	A+	Cle	24	8	4	5	88.2	353	83	35	32	7	3	3	3	11	3	56	4	0	3	5	.375	1	1	3.25
1993	Canton-Akrn	AA	Cle	8	0	0	4	14.1	68	22	8	8	0	0	0	2	3	0	6	0	2	0	1	.000	0	0	5.02
	Kinston	A+	Cle	19	1	0	9	35	150	44	26	24	4	1	2	1	4	0	32	0	0	2	3	.400	0	0	6.17
1994	Peoria	A	ChN	14	0	0	6	19.1	90	27	6	5	1	2	0	3	3	1	13	2	0	3	1	.750	0	0	2.33
	Orlando	AA	ChN	34	0	0	19	45.2	192	45	14	14	1	2	0	2	11	0	31	2	0	3	2	.600	0	4	2.76
1995	Orlando	AA	ChN	49	0	0	14	68	257	50	18	18	4	0	4	0	11	3	34	3	1	6	2	.750	0	6	2.38
1996	Orlando	AA	ChN	9	0	0	4	17	81	20	13	12	2	2	0	2	8	5	14	1	0	1	2	.333	0	1	6.35
	Iowa	AAA	ChN	35	0	0	13	33.1	130	26	10	10	3	3	0	0	8	1	18	0	0	1	0	1.000	0	2	2.70
1995	Chicago	NL		7	0	0	2	5	23	8	3	3	1	0	0	0	2	0	2	0	0	0	0	.000	0	0	5.40
9 Min. YEARS				278	37	8	105	586.1	2428	568	250	216	39	24	17	20	120	20	392	18	11	40	30	.571	3	19	3.32

Todd Rizzo

Pitches: Left **Bats:** Right **Pos:** P **Ht:** 6'3" **Wt:** 220 **Born:** 5/24/71 **Age:** 26

		HOW MUCH HE PITCHED						WHAT HE GAVE UP												THE RESULTS					
Year Team	Lg Org	G	GS	CG	GF	IP	BFP	H	R	ER	HR	SH	SF	HB	TBB	IBB	SO	WP	Bk	W	L	Pct.	ShO	Sv	ERA
1992 Yakima	A- LA	15	0	0	8	26	121	21	13	13	3	0	1	2	24	0	26	6	0	2	0	1.000	0	0	4.50
Dodgers	R LA	3	1	0	1	7	31	4	4	3	0	0	0	1	8	0	7	0	0	0	1	.000	0	0	3.86
1995 Pr. William	A+ ChA	36	0	0	10	68	307	68	30	21	2	2	1	3	39	8	59	13	0	3	5	.375	0	1	2.78
1996 Birmingham	AA ChA	46	0	0	19	68.2	300	61	28	21	0	3	2	1	40	7	48	7	0	4	4	.500	0	10	2.75
3 Min. YEARS		100	1	0	38	169.2	759	154	75	58	5	5	4	7	111	15	140	26	0	9	10	.474	0	11	3.08

Petie Roach

Pitches: Left **Bats:** Left **Pos:** P **Ht:** 6'2" **Wt:** 180 **Born:** 9/19/70 **Age:** 26

		HOW MUCH HE PITCHED						WHAT HE GAVE UP												THE RESULTS					
Year Team	Lg Org	G	GS	CG	GF	IP	BFP	H	R	ER	HR	SH	SF	HB	TBB	IBB	SO	WP	Bk	W	L	Pct.	ShO	Sv	ERA
1994 Yakima	A- LA	8	4	0	2	40	147	24	5	3	0	0	0	1	6	0	32	0	1	3	1	.750	0	0	0.68
Vero Beach	A+ LA	7	6	0	0	36.2	157	41	20	18	0	0	1	1	12	0	19	1	1	2	3	.400	0	0	4.42
1995 San Bernrdo	A+ LA	30	0	0	14	33	143	28	16	11	2	2	2	2	14	1	38	5	0	1	2	.333	0	8	3.00
1996 Vero Beach	A+ LA	17	10	0	2	69	273	56	30	28	6	1	1	1	17	1	52	3	2	3	4	.429	0	0	3.65
San Antonio	AA LA	13	13	1	0	75.1	336	81	41	32	5	3	3	5	34	0	40	5	4	6	3	.667	0	0	3.82
3 Min. YEARS		75	33	1	18	254	1056	230	112	92	13	6	7	10	83	2	181	14	8	15	13	.536	0	8	3.26

Jason Robbins

Pitches: Right **Bats:** Right **Pos:** P **Ht:** 6'3" **Wt:** 195 **Born:** 12/20/72 **Age:** 24

		HOW MUCH HE PITCHED						WHAT HE GAVE UP												THE RESULTS					
Year Team	Lg Org	G	GS	CG	GF	IP	BFP	H	R	ER	HR	SH	SF	HB	TBB	IBB	SO	WP	Bk	W	L	Pct.	ShO	Sv	ERA
1993 Princeton	R+ Cin	17	5	0	4	44	203	50	41	32	3	1	1	2	20	1	34	3	2	1	5	.167	0	1	6.55
1994 Billings	R+ Cin	14	14	4	0	85.2	364	63	39	30	2	2	0	9	35	2	76	4	0	11	1	.917	1	0	3.15
1995 Winston-Sal	A+ Cin	23	23	3	0	141	571	113	62	48	16	0	5	7	42	1	106	5	1	9	6	.600	1	0	3.06
1996 Chattanooga	AA Cin	25	12	0	8	76.1	342	81	46	40	9	1	3	3	43	1	72	12	0	5	3	.625	0	1	4.72
4 Min. YEARS		79	54	7	12	347	1480	307	188	150	30	4	9	21	140	5	288	24	3	26	15	.634	2	2	3.89

J.P. Roberge

Bats: Right **Throws:** Right **Pos:** OF-3B **Ht:** 6'0" **Wt:** 180 **Born:** 9/12/72 **Age:** 24

		BATTING														BASERUNNING				PERCENTAGES		
Year Team	Lg Org	G	AB	H	2B	3B	HR	TB	R	RBI	TBB	IBB	SO	HBP	SH	SF	SB	CS	SB%	GDP	Avg	OBP	SLG
1994 Great Falls	R+ LA	63	256	82	17	1	1	104	55	42	20	0	22	5	2	5	24	4	.86	7	.320	.374	.406
Yakima	A- LA	4	8	3	1	0	0	4	1	0	0	0	3	1	0	0	0	1	.00	0	.375	.444	.500
1995 Vero Beach	A+ LA	3	9	0	0	0	0	0	1	0	0	0	2	0	0	0	0	0	.00	0	.000	.000	.000
San Bernrdo	A+ LA	116	450	129	22	1	17	204	92	59	34	0	62	8	2	3	31	8	.79	9	.287	.345	.453
1996 San Bernrdo	A+ LA	12	44	16	3	1	1	24	8	6	3	0	9	2	0	1	1	2	.33	0	.364	.420	.545
San Antonio	AA LA	62	232	68	14	2	6	104	28	27	14	1	39	2	2	2	9	3	.75	5	.293	.336	.448
Albuquerque	AAA LA	53	156	50	6	1	4	70	17	17	14	1	28	1	3	0	3	0	1.00	1	.321	.380	.449
3 Min. YEARS		313	1155	348	63	6	29	510	202	151	85	2	165	19	9	11	68	18	.79	22	.301	.356	.442

Sid Roberson

Pitches: Left **Bats:** Left **Pos:** P **Ht:** 5' 9" **Wt:** 170 **Born:** 9/7/71 **Age:** 25

		HOW MUCH HE PITCHED						WHAT HE GAVE UP												THE RESULTS					
Year Team	Lg Org	G	GS	CG	GF	IP	BFP	H	R	ER	HR	SH	SF	HB	TBB	IBB	SO	WP	Bk	W	L	Pct.	ShO	Sv	ERA
1992 Helena	R+ Mil	9	8	1	1	65	276	68	32	25	8	3	1	2	18	0	65	4	1	4	4	.500	0	0	3.46
1993 Stockton	A+ Mil	24	23	6	0	166	684	157	68	48	8	7	3	12	34	0	87	6	4	12	8	.600	1	0	2.60
1994 El Paso	AA Mil	25	25	8	0	181.1	771	190	70	57	7	5	7	17	48	3	119	4	1	15	8	.652	1	0	2.83
1995 New Orleans	AAA Mil	4	3	0	0	13	69	20	11	11	1	0	2	1	10	0	8	0	0	0	2	.000	0	0	7.62
1996 New Orleans	AAA Mil	2	2	0	0	11	48	10	6	6	2	0	1	0	9	0	3	1	0	0	1	.000	0	0	4.91
1995 Milwaukee	AL	26	13	0	8	84.1	379	102	55	54	16	0	2	8	37	3	40	3	0	6	4	.600	0	0	5.76
5 Min. YEARS		64	61	15	1	436.1	1848	445	187	147	26	15	14	32	119	3	282	15	6	31	23	.574	1	0	3.03

Brett Roberts

Pitches: Right **Bats:** Right **Pos:** P **Ht:** 6'7" **Wt:** 225 **Born:** 3/24/70 **Age:** 27

		HOW MUCH HE PITCHED						WHAT HE GAVE UP												THE RESULTS					
Year Team	Lg Org	G	GS	CG	GF	IP	BFP	H	R	ER	HR	SH	SF	HB	TBB	IBB	SO	WP	Bk	W	L	Pct.	ShO	Sv	ERA
1991 Elizabethtn	R+ Min	6	6	1	0	28	112	21	8	7	0	0	0	0	10	0	27	2	4	3	0	1.000	0	0	2.25
1992 Kenosha	A Min	7	6	0	1	22.2	105	23	18	14	4	1	0	0	15	0	23	1	0	1	1	.500	0	0	5.56
1993 Fort Myers	A+ Min	28	28	3	0	173.2	772	184	93	84	5	5	5	4	86	5	108	10	2	9	16	.360	0	0	4.35
1994 Fort Myers	A+ Min	21	21	1	0	116.2	520	123	71	56	5	4	8	3	47	3	75	8	0	6	7	.462	0	0	4.32
Nashville	AA Min	5	5	0	0	20	102	30	18	15	1	0	1	1	12	1	11	0	0	2	1	.667	0	0	6.75
1995 New Britain	AA Min	28	28	5	0	174	729	162	72	66	9	4	5	5	50	0	135	6	0	11	9	.550	1	0	3.41
1996 Salt Lake	AAA Min	31	30	2	1	168.1	772	211	115	101	28	2	5	9	71	0	86	7	0	9	7	.563	1	0	5.40
6 Min. YEARS		126	124	12	2	703.1	3112	754	395	343	52	16	24	22	291	9	465	34	6	41	41	.500	2	0	4.39

Chris Roberts

Pitches: Left **Bats:** Right **Pos:** P **Ht:** 5'10" **Wt:** 185 **Born:** 6/25/71 **Age:** 26

		HOW MUCH HE PITCHED						WHAT HE GAVE UP												THE RESULTS					
Year Team	Lg Org	G	GS	CG	GF	IP	BFP	H	R	ER	HR	SH	SF	HB	TBB	IBB	SO	WP	Bk	W	L	Pct.	ShO	Sv	ERA
1993 St. Lucie	A+ NYN	25	25	3	0	173.1	703	162	64	53	3	2	4	7	36	0	111	2	1	13	5	.722	2	0	2.75
1994 Binghamton	AA NYN	27	27	2	0	175.1	751	164	77	64	11	8	5	6	77	1	128	12	1	13	8	.619	2	0	3.29
1995 Norfolk	AAA NYN	25	25	2	0	150	676	197	99	92	24	6	4	8	58	0	88	5	0	7	13	.350	0	0	5.52
1996 Mets	R NYN	3	3	0	0	13	48	11	2	2	0	0	0	1	0	0	12	1	0	0	0	.000	0	0	1.38
St. Lucie	A+ NYN	1	1	0	0	6	21	1	0	0	0	0	0	0	3	0	2	0	0	1	0	1.000	0	0	0.00
Binghamton	AA NYN	9	9	1	0	46	225	55	40	37	6	6	2	1	37	0	30	1	0	2	7	.222	0	0	7.24
4 Min. YEARS		90	90	8	0	563.2	2424	590	282	248	44	22	15	23	211	1	371	21	2	36	33	.522	4	0	3.96

David Roberts

Bats: Left **Throws:** Left **Pos:** OF **Ht:** 5'10" **Wt:** 172 **Born:** 5/31/72 **Age:** 25

		BATTING														BASERUNNING				PERCENTAGES		
Year Team	Lg Org	G	AB	H	2B	3B	HR	TB	R	RBI	TBB	IBB	SO	HBP	SH	SF	SB	CS	SB%	GDP	Avg	OBP	SLG
1994 Jamestown	A- Det	54	178	52	7	2	0	63	33	12	29	4	27	1	3	1	12	8	.60	0	.292	.392	.354
1995 Lakeland	A+ Det	92	357	108	10	5	3	137	67	30	39	2	43	1	2	2	30	8	.79	7	.303	.371	.384
1996 Visalia	A+ Det	126	482	131	24	7	5	184	112	37	98	0	105	1	3	7	65	21	.76	6	.272	.391	.382
Jacksonvlle	AA Det	3	9	2	0	0	0	2	0	0	1	0	0	0	0	0	0	1	.00	0	.222	.300	.222
3 Min. YEARS		275	1026	293	41	14	8	386	212	79	167	6	175	3	8	10	107	38	.74	13	.286	.384	.376

Lonell Roberts

Bats: Both **Throws:** Right **Pos:** OF **Ht:** 6'0" **Wt:** 172 **Born:** 6/7/71 **Age:** 26

		BATTING														BASERUNNING				PERCENTAGES		
Year Team	Lg Org	G	AB	H	2B	3B	HR	TB	R	RBI	TBB	IBB	SO	HBP	SH	SF	SB	CS	SB%	GDP	Avg	OBP	SLG
1989 Medicne Hat	R+ Tor	29	78	11	1	0	0	12	2	6	7	0	27	1	1	0	3	3	.50	1	.141	.221	.154
1990 Medicne Hat	R+ Tor	38	118	25	2	0	0	27	14	8	5	0	29	0	0	0	8	1	.89	3	.212	.244	.229
1991 Myrtle Bch	A Tor	110	388	86	7	2	2	103	39	27	27	1	84	2	10	2	35	14	.71	0	.222	.274	.265
1992 St. Cathrns	A- Tor	62	244	50	3	1	0	55	37	11	19	1	75	3	4	0	33	13	.72	0	.205	.271	.225
Knoxville	AA Tor	5	14	0	0	0	0	0	1	0	1	0	4	0	0	0	1	0	1.00	0	.000	.067	.000
1993 Hagerstown	A Tor	131	501	120	21	4	3	158	78	46	53	1	103	4	2	3	54	15	.78	8	.240	.316	.315
1994 Dunedin	A+ Tor	118	490	132	18	3	3	165	74	31	32	3	104	3	2	4	61	12	.84	4	.269	.316	.337
1995 Knoxville	AA Tor	116	454	107	12	3	1	128	66	29	27	1	97	3	4	4	57	18	.76	7	.236	.281	.282
1996 Knoxville	AA Tor	58	237	69	1	0	1	73	35	12	32	1	39	0	3	0	24	14	.63	1	.291	.375	.308
8 Min. YEARS		667	2524	600	65	13	10	721	346	170	203	8	562	16	26	13	276	90	.75	24	.238	.297	.286

Jason Robertson

Bats: Left **Throws:** Left **Pos:** OF **Ht:** 6'2" **Wt:** 200 **Born:** 3/24/71 **Age:** 26

		BATTING														BASERUNNING				PERCENTAGES		
Year Team	Lg Org	G	AB	H	2B	3B	HR	TB	R	RBI	TBB	IBB	SO	HBP	SH	SF	SB	CS	SB%	GDP	Avg	OBP	SLG
1989 Yankees	R NYA	58	214	61	12	5	0	83	27	31	28	0	28	0	0	4	4	4	.50	2	.285	.362	.388
1990 Greensboro	A NYA	133	496	125	22	5	6	175	71	44	67	2	110	2	4	1	21	13	.62	8	.252	.343	.353
1991 Pr. William	A+ NYA	131	515	136	21	6	3	178	67	54	53	2	138	2	1	4	32	9	.78	8	.264	.333	.346
1992 Pr. William	A+ NYA	68	254	61	6	4	5	90	34	34	31	0	55	1	1	3	14	6	.70	7	.240	.322	.354
Albany-Colo	AA NYA	55	204	44	12	1	3	67	18	33	10	0	44	2	2	2	9	3	.75	5	.216	.257	.328
1993 Albany-Colo	AA NYA	130	483	110	29	4	6	165	65	41	43	3	126	4	3	2	35	12	.74	7	.228	.295	.342
1994 Albany-Colo	AA NYA	124	432	94	10	7	11	151	54	53	50	3	120	3	5	4	20	10	.67	6	.218	.301	.350
1995 Norwich	AA NYA	117	456	126	29	10	6	193	60	54	41	3	106	1	4	5	19	12	.61	5	.276	.334	.423
1996 Charlotte	AAA Fla	11	25	1	0	0	1	4	2	2	2	0	12	0	0	0	0	1	.00	0	.040	.111	.160
Portland	AA Fla	99	338	92	17	3	12	151	65	48	31	2	91	2	0	4	12	6	.67	3	.272	.333	.447
8 Min. YEARS		926	3417	850	158	45	53	1257	463	394	356	15	830	17	20	29	166	76	.69	51	.249	.320	.368

Nilson Robledo

Bats: Right **Throws:** Right **Pos:** C **Ht:** 6'1" **Wt:** 165 **Born:** 11/3/68 **Age:** 28

		BATTING														BASERUNNING				PERCENTAGES		
Year Team	Lg Org	G	AB	H	2B	3B	HR	TB	R	RBI	TBB	IBB	SO	HBP	SH	SF	SB	CS	SB%	GDP	Avg	OBP	SLG
1990 White Sox	R ChA	35	105	20	3	0	4	35	10	11	5	0	34	1	1	1	4	3	.57	1	.190	.232	.333
1991 South Bend	A ChA	40	142	41	7	1	5	65	15	20	9	0	42	0	1	1	3	2	.60	2	.289	.329	.458
White Sox	R ChA	6	20	4	0	0	0	4	2	2	1	0	6	0	0	0	1	0	1.00	0	.200	.238	.200
1992 White Sox	R ChA	10	31	4	1	0	0	5	0	3	0	0	7	0	0	0	1	0	1.00	2	.129	.129	.161
South Bend	A ChA	32	117	34	11	2	2	55	14	14	7	0	38	0	2	1	0	1	.00	0	.291	.328	.470
1993 Sarasota	A+ ChA	74	259	67	18	1	7	108	35	34	13	2	63	2	3	5	0	1	.00	6	.259	.294	.417
1994 South Bend	A ChA	103	373	106	25	4	9	166	63	69	39	0	97	3	2	5	0	1	.00	8	.284	.352	.445
1995 South Bend	A ChA	135	537	153	24	3	20	243	71	108	30	4	100	3	1	16	0	2	.00	8	.285	.317	.453
1996 Pr. William	A+ ChA	80	313	81	16	0	8	121	37	46	21	0	55	2	0	2	0	0	.00	2	.259	.308	.387
Birmingham	AA ChA	7	26	6	1	0	1	10	3	6	3	0	2	0	0	1	0	0	.00	3	.231	.300	.385
Nashville	AAA ChA	9	10	1	0	0	0	1	0	0	1	0	7	1	0	0	0	0	.00	0	.100	.250	.100
7 Min. YEARS		531	1933	517	106	11	56	813	250	313	129	6	451	12	10	32	9	10	.47	32	.267	.312	.421

Raul Rodarte

Bats: Right **Throws:** Right **Pos:** OF — **Ht:** 5'11" **Wt:** 190 **Born:** 4/9/70 **Age:** 27

				BATTING													BASERUNNING				PERCENTAGES		
Year Team	Lg	Org	G	AB	H	2B	3B	HR	TB	R	RBI	TBB	IBB	SO	HBP	SH	SF	SB	CS	SB%	GDP	Avg	OBP	SLG
1991 Peninsula	A+	Sea	65	216	48	4	1	0	54	19	14	32	0	56	0	1	2	5	1	.83	5	.222	.320	.250
1992 Peninsula	A+	Sea	94	290	72	8	6	2	98	37	22	35	2	37	1	3	2	15	10	.60	7	.248	.329	.338
1993 Riverside	A+	Sea	106	402	116	19	1	5	152	79	48	51	0	66	0	6	2	13	14	.48	7	.289	.367	.378
1994 Jacksonvlle	AA	Sea	34	91	22	3	1	3	36	13	13	8	1	15	1	3	0	2	2	.50	2	.242	.310	.396
Riverside	A+	Sea	39	156	50	6	4	4	76	29	37	15	1	31	2	1	1	5	2	.71	3	.321	.385	.487
1995 Lynchburg	A+	Pit	104	346	99	18	2	12	157	57	48	35	2	49	4	2	1	19	13	.59	8	.286	.358	.454
Carolina	AA	Pit	16	54	20	5	1	0	27	8	11	10	3	14	0	2	0	2	2	.50	2	.370	.469	.500
1996 Carolina	AA	Pit	20	43	9	1	0	0	10	6	6	12	0	12	1	1	0	2	1	.67	1	.209	.393	.233
Greenville	AA	Atl	48	176	58	11	0	6	87	33	28	16	2	23	0	1	3	0	3	.00	6	.330	.379	.494
Richmond	AAA	Atl	61	219	74	12	2	9	117	30	46	19	1	43	1	0	4	4	2	.67	6	.338	.387	.534
6 Min. YEARS			587	1993	568	87	18	41	814	311	273	233	12	346	10	20	15	67	50	.57	47	.285	.360	.408

Boi Rodriguez

Bats: Left **Throws:** Right **Pos:** DH — **Ht:** 6'0" **Wt:** 180 **Born:** 4/14/66 **Age:** 31

				BATTING													BASERUNNING				PERCENTAGES		
Year Team	Lg	Org	G	AB	H	2B	3B	HR	TB	R	RBI	TBB	IBB	SO	HBP	SH	SF	SB	CS	SB%	GDP	Avg	OBP	SLG
1987 Jamestown	A-	Mon	77	274	77	9	5	15	141	51	65	37	5	58	3	0	7	14	8	.64	2	.281	.364	.515
1988 W. Palm Bch	A+	Mon	121	425	103	22	8	8	165	56	54	59	2	61	2	0	3	6	5	.55	6	.242	.335	.388
1989 Jacksonvlle	AA	Mon	130	388	96	19	6	9	154	53	50	53	3	58	2	1	5	6	3	.67	3	.247	.337	.397
1990 Jacksonvlle	AA	Mon	105	367	104	22	5	9	163	50	58	45	0	80	2	7	7	2	0	1.00	8	.283	.359	.444
1991 Greenville	AA	Atl	29	92	26	10	1	1	41	14	14	15	3	16	0	2	3	0	1	.00	2	.283	.373	.446
Richmond	AAA	Atl	105	392	110	25	1	8	161	50	49	34	5	100	2	2	5	1	3	.25	4	.281	.337	.411
1992 Richmond	AAA	Atl	93	278	77	8	3	16	139	40	40	32	5	61	1	0	0	0	0	.00	4	.277	.354	.500
1993 Richmond	AAA	Atl	88	236	63	13	1	10	108	34	22	26	3	55	1	0	0	4	1	.80	5	.267	.342	.458
1995 Calgary	AAA	Pit	11	39	10	2	0	2	18	10	10	3	1	5	0	0	0	1	0	1.00	0	.256	.310	.462
1996 Wichita	AA	KC	16	32	2	1	0	0	3	0	1	4	0	15	0	0	0	0	0	.00	0	.063	.167	.094
9 Min. YEARS			775	2523	668	131	30	78	1093	358	363	308	27	509	13	12	30	34	21	.62	34	.265	.344	.433

Felix Rodriguez

Pitches: Right **Bats:** Right **Pos:** P — **Ht:** 6' 1" **Wt:** 180 **Born:** 12/5/72 **Age:** 24

			HOW MUCH HE PITCHED						WHAT HE GAVE UP												THE RESULTS					
Year Team	Lg	Org	G	GS	CG	GF	IP	BFP	H	R	ER	HR	SH	SF	HB	TBB	IBB	SO	WP	Bk	W	L	Pct.	ShO	Sv	ERA
1993 Vero Beach	A+	LA	32	20	2	7	132	570	109	71	55	15	6	3	6	71	1	80	9	6	8	8	.500	1	0	3.75
1994 San Antonio	AA	LA	26	26	0	0	136.1	588	106	70	61	8	6	7	4	88	3	126	4	5	6	8	.429	0	0	4.03
1995 Albuquerque	AAA	LA	14	11	0	0	51	224	52	29	24	5	4	1	0	26	0	46	0	1	3	2	.600	0	0	4.24
1996 Albuquerque	AAA	LA	27	19	0	1	107.1	476	111	70	66	17	7	4	9	60	1	65	5	4	3	9	.250	0	0	5.53
1995 Los Angeles	NL		11	0	0	5	10.2	45	11	3	3	2	0	0	0	5	0	5	0	0	1	1	.500	0	0	2.53
4 Min. YEARS			99	76	2	8	426.2	1858	378	240	206	45	23	15	19	245	5	317	18	16	20	27	.426	1	0	4.35

Frank Rodriguez

Pitches: Right **Bats:** Right **Pos:** P — **Ht:** 5'9" **Wt:** 160 **Born:** 1/6/73 **Age:** 24

			HOW MUCH HE PITCHED						WHAT HE GAVE UP												THE RESULTS					
Year Team	Lg	Org	G	GS	CG	GF	IP	BFP	H	R	ER	HR	SH	SF	HB	TBB	IBB	SO	WP	Bk	W	L	Pct.	ShO	Sv	ERA
1992 Brewers	R	Mil	9	7	0	0	49	193	35	9	6	1	0	1	1	14	0	37	1	0	3	1	.750	0	0	1.10
Helena	R+	Mil	6	1	0	2	10.2	46	14	6	3	1	0	0	1	3	0	3	3	0	1	1	.500	0	0	2.53
1993 Helena	R+	Mil	18	1	0	9	41	176	31	19	11	0	2	0	1	17	3	63	8	1	2	1	.667	0	5	2.41
1994 Stockton	A+	Mil	26	24	3	0	151	627	139	67	57	6	6	9	13	52	1	124	6	0	10	9	.526	1	0	3.40
1995 El Paso	AA	Mil	28	27	1	1	142.2	650	157	90	79	9	9	9	5	80	2	129	16	1	9	8	.529	0	0	4.98
1996 New Orleans	AAA	Mil	13	1	0	7	18.2	87	24	15	14	1	1	1	0	11	3	16	0	0	0	2	.000	0	0	6.75
El Paso	AA	Mil	16	7	0	3	34.1	169	45	32	26	1	0	2	2	24	0	39	1	0	3	4	.429	0	0	6.82
5 Min. YEARS			116	68	4	22	447.1	1948	445	238	196	19	18	22	23	201	9	411	35	2	28	26	.519	1	5	3.94

Maximo Rodriguez

Bats: Right **Throws:** Right **Pos:** C — **Ht:** 6'0" **Wt:** 170 **Born:** 11/18/73 **Age:** 23

				BATTING													BASERUNNING				PERCENTAGES		
Year Team	Lg	Org	G	AB	H	2B	3B	HR	TB	R	RBI	TBB	IBB	SO	HBP	SH	SF	SB	CS	SB%	GDP	Avg	OBP	SLG
1993 Marlins	R	Fla	48	187	61	8	5	0	79	30	29	10	1	26	1	0	2	3	2	.60	5	.326	.360	.422
1994 Brevard Cty	A+	Fla	12	40	5	1	0	2	12	4	12	1	0	16	1	0	0	0	0	.00	1	.125	.167	.300
Marlins	R	Fla	5	21	4	1	0	0	5	3	2	1	0	4	1	0	0	0	0	.00	1	.190	.261	.238
Elmira	A-	Fla	51	170	40	9	1	2	57	20	19	8	0	42	1	1	0	3	1	.75	4	.235	.274	.335
1995 Kane County	A	Fla	72	236	45	7	1	5	69	18	30	18	0	65	2	1	2	0	1	.00	7	.191	.252	.292
1996 Brevard Cty	A+	Fla	84	273	62	16	0	3	87	19	39	18	2	62	3	2	4	3	3	.50	17	.227	.279	.319
Portland	AA	Fla	6	17	3	0	0	0	3	1	1	1	0	6	0	0	0	0	1	.00	1	.176	.222	.176
4 Min. YEARS			278	944	220	42	7	12	312	95	132	57	3	221	9	4	8	9	8	.53	36	.233	.281	.331

Rich Rodriguez

Pitches: Left **Bats:** Left **Pos:** P — **Ht:** 6' 0" **Wt:** 200 **Born:** 3/1/63 **Age:** 34

			HOW MUCH HE PITCHED						WHAT HE GAVE UP												THE RESULTS					
Year Team	Lg	Org	G	GS	CG	GF	IP	BFP	H	R	ER	HR	SH	SF	HB	TBB	IBB	SO	WP	Bk	W	L	Pct.	ShO	Sv	ERA
1984 Little Fall	A-	NYN	25	1	0	6	35.1	171	28	21	11	0	4	2	1	36	7	27	3	0	2	1	.667	0	0	2.80

Year Team	Lg Org	G	GS	CG	GF	IP	BFP	H	R	ER	HR	SH	SF	HB	TBB	IBB	SO	WP	Bk	W	L	Pct.	ShO	Sv	ERA
		HOW MUCH HE PITCHED						WHAT HE GAVE UP												THE RESULTS					
1985 Columbia	A NYN	49	3	0	19	80.1	365	89	41	36	4	6	1	1	36	2	71	7	1	6	3	.667	0	6	4.03
1986 Jackson	AA NYN	13	5	1	2	33	161	51	35	33	5	2	2	0	15	2	15	2	0	3	4	.429	0	0	9.00
Lynchburg	A+ NYN	36	0	0	16	45.1	184	37	20	18	2	1	1	1	19	0	38	4	1	2	1	.667	0	3	3.57
1987 Lynchburg	A+ NYN	69	0	0	30	68	291	69	23	21	3	1	2	0	26	6	59	8	0	3	1	.750	0	5	2.78
1988 Jackson	AA NYN	47	1	0	25	78.1	335	66	35	25	3	9	4	1	42	6	68	6	5	2	7	.222	0	6	2.87
1989 Wichita	AA SD	54	0	0	38	74.1	319	74	30	30	3	3	1	2	37	11	40	4	1	8	3	.727	0	8	3.63
1990 Las Vegas	AAA SD	27	2	0	13	59	243	50	24	23	5	1	3	1	22	1	46	3	1	3	4	.429	0	8	3.51
1996 Omaha	AAA KC	47	0	0	22	70	304	75	40	31	11	1	1	3	20	1	68	2	0	2	3	.400	0	3	3.99
1990 San Diego	NL	32	0	0	15	47.2	201	52	17	15	2	2	1	1	16	4	22	1	1	1	1	.500	0	1	2.83
1991 San Diego	NL	64	1	0	19	80	335	66	31	29	8	7	2	0	44	8	40	4	1	3	1	.750	0	0	3.26
1992 San Diego	NL	61	1	0	15	91	369	77	28	24	4	2	2	0	29	4	64	1	1	6	3	.667	0	0	2.37
1993 San Diego	NL	34	0	0	10	30	133	34	15	11	2	2	0	1	9	3	22	1	0	2	3	.400	0	2	3.30
Florida	NL	36	0	0	11	46	198	39	23	21	8	3	0	1	24	5	21	2	0	0	1	.000	0	1	4.11
1994 St. Louis	NL	56	0	0	15	60.1	260	62	30	27	6	2	1	1	26	4	43	4	0	3	5	.375	0	0	4.03
1995 St. Louis	NL	1	0	0	0	1.2	4	0	0	0	0	0	0	0	0	0	0	0	0	0	0	.000	0	0	0.00
8 Min. YEARS		367	12	1	171	543.2	2373	539	269	228	36	28	17	10	253	36	432	39	9	31	27	.534	0	39	3.77
6 Maj. YEARS		284	2	0	85	356.2	1500	330	144	127	30	18	6	4	148	28	212	13	3	15	14	.517	0	4	3.20

Steve Rodriguez

Bats: Right **Throws:** Right **Pos:** 2B **Ht:** 5' 8" **Wt:** 170 **Born:** 11/29/70 **Age:** 26

Year Team	Lg Org	G	AB	H	2B	3B	HR	TB	R	RBI	TBB	IBB	SO	HBP	SH	SF	SB	CS	SB%	GDP	Avg	OBP	SLG
		BATTING															BASERUNNING				PERCENTAGES		
1992 Winter Havn	A+ Bos	26	87	15	0	0	1	18	13	5	9	0	17	2	3	0	4	1	.80	3	.172	.265	.207
1993 Lynchburg	A+ Bos	120	493	135	26	3	3	176	78	42	31	0	69	4	8	3	20	13	.61	15	.274	.320	.357
1994 New Britain	AA Bos	38	159	45	5	2	0	54	25	14	9	0	14	1	3	1	8	4	.67	3	.283	.324	.340
Pawtucket	AAA Bos	62	233	70	11	0	1	84	28	21	14	0	30	1	3	2	11	3	.79	6	.300	.340	.361
1995 Pawtucket	AAA Bos	82	324	78	16	3	1	103	39	24	25	1	34	4	2	3	12	10	.55	7	.241	.301	.318
1996 Toledo	AAA Det	96	333	95	18	2	4	129	49	30	23	0	43	2	7	2	18	3	.86	8	.285	.333	.387
1995 Boston	AL	6	8	1	0	0	0	1	1	0	1	0	1	0	0	0	1	0	1.00	0	.125	.222	.125
Detroit	AL	12	31	6	1	0	0	7	4	0	5	0	9	0	1	0	1	2	.33	1	.194	.306	.226
5 Min. YEARS		424	1629	438	76	10	10	564	232	136	111	1	207	14	26	11	73	34	.68	42	.269	.319	.346

Cecil Rodriques

Bats: Right **Throws:** Right **Pos:** OF **Ht:** 6'0" **Wt:** 175 **Born:** 9/3/71 **Age:** 25

Year Team	Lg Org	G	AB	H	2B	3B	HR	TB	R	RBI	TBB	IBB	SO	HBP	SH	SF	SB	CS	SB%	GDP	Avg	OBP	SLG
		BATTING															BASERUNNING				PERCENTAGES		
1991 Brewers	R Mil	29	111	26	3	0	0	29	19	7	25	0	19	1	0	1	11	5	.69	2	.234	.377	.261
1992 Helena	R+ Mil	72	279	85	17	6	12	150	63	49	30	2	62	4	1	3	23	7	.77	1	.305	.377	.538
1993 Beloit	A Mil	104	349	83	21	4	8	136	50	49	43	1	94	2	3	3	18	12	.60	4	.238	.322	.390
1994 Beloit	A Mil	38	116	33	5	0	3	47	16	24	13	1	29	0	3	2	10	3	.77	1	.284	.351	.405
Stockton	A+ Mil	56	205	54	12	3	3	81	29	19	25	1	48	2	6	0	14	3	.82	1	.263	.349	.395
1995 Stockton	A+ Mil	45	173	46	6	3	4	70	21	20	13	0	31	0	1	3	4	8	.33	4	.266	.312	.405
El Paso	AA Mil	72	244	65	9	7	2	94	36	24	15	0	51	1	0	4	5	2	.71	2	.266	.307	.385
1996 El Paso	AA Mil	119	389	110	23	6	5	160	63	50	32	0	92	2	5	5	5	8	.38	3	.283	.336	.411
6 Min. YEARS		535	1866	502	96	29	37	767	297	242	196	5	426	12	19	21	90	48	.65	18	.269	.339	.411

Bryan Rogers

Pitches: Right **Bats:** Right **Pos:** P **Ht:** 5'11" **Wt:** 170 **Born:** 10/30/67 **Age:** 29

Year Team	Lg Org	G	GS	CG	GF	IP	BFP	H	R	ER	HR	SH	SF	HB	TBB	IBB	SO	WP	Bk	W	L	Pct.	ShO	Sv	ERA
		HOW MUCH HE PITCHED						WHAT HE GAVE UP												THE RESULTS					
1988 Kingsport	R+ NYN	15	2	0	5	31.1	135	30	23	22	1	0	0	1	14	1	35	1	4	2	3	.400	0	0	6.32
1989 Columbia	A NYN	14	4	0	6	43.1	181	36	16	15	1	5	0	2	14	0	36	0	1	3	2	.600	0	3	3.12
1990 St. Lucie	A+ NYN	29	19	5	6	148.2	599	127	66	51	3	2	8	4	26	0	96	7	1	9	8	.529	0	4	3.09
1991 Williamsprt	AA NYN	41	0	0	32	61	267	73	33	32	5	5	2	1	18	1	33	1	0	6	8	.429	0	15	4.72
1992 Binghamton	AA NYN	22	0	0	10	35.1	152	37	21	17	4	2	1	1	7	0	20	0	0	3	2	.600	0	1	4.33
St. Lucie	A+ NYN	17	0	0	6	30.2	123	24	12	10	1	3	1	2	7	2	17	1	0	2	4	.333	0	2	2.93
1993 Binghamton	AA NYN	62	0	0	40	84.2	347	80	29	22	4	5	4	0	25	2	42	4	0	5	4	.556	0	8	2.34
1994 Norfolk	AAA NYN	20	0	0	4	30	133	35	19	18	4	1	2	1	10	2	8	0	0	2	2	.500	0	0	5.40
Binghamton	AA NYN	41	0	0	21	60	236	49	17	11	1	3	0	1	14	5	46	2	0	5	1	.833	0	11	1.65
1995 Norfolk	AAA NYN	56	0	0	34	77.1	303	58	22	19	4	4	3	0	22	1	50	8	0	8	3	.727	0	10	2.21
1996 St. Lucie	A+ NYN	9	0	0	4	11.2	50	12	2	2	0	0	0	0	4	0	11	0	1	2	0	1.000	0	0	1.54
Norfolk	AAA NYN	20	0	0	9	24	103	20	11	9	2	2	0	0	11	2	23	2	0	0	2	.000	0	0	3.38
9 Min. YEARS		346	25	5	177	638	2629	581	271	228	30	32	21	13	172	16	417	26	7	47	39	.547	0	54	3.22

Jimmy Rogers

Pitches: Right **Bats:** Right **Pos:** P **Ht:** 6' 2" **Wt:** 200 **Born:** 1/3/67 **Age:** 30

Year Team	Lg Org	G	GS	CG	GF	IP	BFP	H	R	ER	HR	SH	SF	HB	TBB	IBB	SO	WP	Bk	W	L	Pct.	ShO	Sv	ERA
		HOW MUCH HE PITCHED						WHAT HE GAVE UP												THE RESULTS					
1987 St. Cathrns	A- Tor	13	12	0	0	56.1	241	46	33	21	4	2	0	4	24	0	60	5	0	2	4	.333	0	0	3.36
1988 Myrtle Bch	A Tor	33	32	2	0	188.1	803	145	84	70	10	1	6	5	95	1	198	15	6	18	4	.818	0	0	3.35
1989 Knoxville	AA Tor	32	30	1	0	158	718	136	89	80	12	4	3	5	132	1	120	14	3	12	10	.545	0	0	4.56
1990 Knoxville	AA Tor	31	30	2	0	173.1	789	179	98	86	8	6	12	6	104	1	113	12	4	9	12	.429	1	0	4.47
1991 Knoxville	AA Tor	28	27	4	0	168.1	706	139	70	62	7	4	3	6	90	0	122	11	1	7	11	.389	3	0	3.31

Year Team	Lg Org	G	GS	CG	GF	IP	BFP	H	R	ER	HR	SH	SF	HB	TBB	IBB	SO	WP	Bk	W	L	Pct.	ShO	Sv	ERA
		HOW MUCH HE PITCHED						WHAT HE GAVE UP												THE RESULTS					
1993 Knoxville	AA Tor	19	19	0	0	100.1	431	107	54	45	9	3	2	2	33	1	80	5	0	7	7	.500	0	0	4.04
1994 Syracuse	AAA Tor	31	10	0	5	94	404	82	51	48	7	0	5	0	49	1	69	4	0	5	4	.556	0	0	4.60
1995 Syracuse	AAA Tor	38	0	0	9	73.2	308	65	26	25	4	3	3	3	31	2	82	6	0	3	4	.429	0	1	3.05
1996 Syracuse	AAA Tor	8	3	0	0	22.1	102	28	16	15	4	2	0	1	7	0	15	1	0	1	3	.250	0	0	6.04
1995 Toronto	AL	19	0	0	9	23.2	110	21	15	15	4	3	1	0	18	4	13	0	0	2	4	.333	0	0	5.70
9 Min. YEARS		233	163	9	14	1034.2	4502	927	521	452	65	25	34	32	565	7	859	73	14	64	59	.520	4	1	3.93

Dan Rohrmeier

Bats: Right **Throws:** Right **Pos:** DH-OF **Ht:** 6'0" **Wt:** 185 **Born:** 9/27/65 **Age:** 31

Year Team	Lg Org	G	AB	H	2B	3B	HR	TB	R	RBI	TBB	IBB	SO	HBP	SH	SF	SB	CS	SB%	GDP	Avg	OBP	SLG
		BATTING															BASERUNNING				PERCENTAGES		
1987 Peninsula	A+ ChA	68	243	80	13	2	5	112	43	34	29	0	37	2	2	3	2	3	.40	3	.329	.401	.461
1988 Tampa	A+ ChA	114	421	109	28	8	5	168	53	50	27	2	58	1	1	5	11	7	.61	4	.259	.302	.399
1989 Sarasota	A+ ChA	25	74	16	2	0	1	21	11	4	12	0	15	0	1	1	1	0	1.00	2	.216	.322	.284
Charlotte	A+ Tex	18	65	20	3	1	1	28	9	11	7	0	8	1	0	1	0	1	.00	1	.308	.378	.431
Tulsa	AA Tex	57	210	67	3	4	5	93	24	27	11	0	20	1	4	0	5	8	.38	5	.319	.356	.443
1990 Tulsa	AA Tex	119	453	138	24	7	10	206	76	62	37	0	51	0	1	4	13	11	.54	14	.305	.354	.455
1991 Tulsa	AA Tex	121	418	122	20	2	5	161	67	62	60	1	57	4	4	7	3	2	.60	14	.292	.380	.385
1992 Memphis	AA KC	123	433	140	33	2	6	195	54	69	26	2	46	4	0	4	3	7	.30	11	.323	.364	.450
Omaha	AAA KC	8	29	7	1	0	1	11	4	5	3	0	4	0	0	0	0	1	.00	0	.241	.313	.379
1993 Omaha	AAA KC	118	432	107	23	3	17	187	51	70	23	0	59	3	1	7	2	1	.67	10	.248	.286	.433
1994 Memphis	AA KC	112	436	118	34	0	18	206	64	72	31	3	80	6	0	3	2	2	.50	15	.271	.326	.472
Chattanooga	AA Cin	17	66	22	7	0	0	29	9	10	5	0	5	0	0	1	0	1	.00	5	.333	.375	.439
1995 Indianapols	AAA Cin	10	34	6	3	1	0	11	5	3	0	0	4	0	0	0	0	0	.00	1	.176	.176	.324
Chattanooga	AA Cin	118	426	139	31	0	17	221	77	76	41	5	63	7	1	7	0	1	.00	9	.326	.389	.519
1996 Memphis	AA SD	134	471	162	29	2	28	279	98	95	77	10	76	2	0	4	2	5	.29	12	.344	.435	.592
10 Min. YEARS		1162	4211	1253	254	32	119	1928	645	650	389	23	583	31	15	47	44	50	.47	106	.298	.358	.458

Euclides Rojas

Pitches: Right **Bats:** Right **Pos:** P **Ht:** 6'0" **Wt:** 190 **Born:** 8/25/67 **Age:** 29

Year Team	Lg Org	G	GS	CG	GF	IP	BFP	H	R	ER	HR	SH	SF	HB	TBB	IBB	SO	WP	Bk	W	L	Pct.	ShO	Sv	ERA
		HOW MUCH HE PITCHED						WHAT HE GAVE UP												THE RESULTS					
1996 Charlotte	AAA Fla	6	0	0	3	9	42	12	6	6	2	0	0	1	3	0	8	2	0	0	0	.000	0	0	6.00

Mike Romano

Pitches: Right **Bats:** Both **Pos:** P **Ht:** 6'2" **Wt:** 195 **Born:** 3/3/72 **Age:** 25

Year Team	Lg Org	G	GS	CG	GF	IP	BFP	H	R	ER	HR	SH	SF	HB	TBB	IBB	SO	WP	Bk	W	L	Pct.	ShO	Sv	ERA
		HOW MUCH HE PITCHED						WHAT HE GAVE UP												THE RESULTS					
1993 Medicne Hat	R+ Tor	9	8	0	0	41	175	34	20	12	1	0	0	7	11	0	28	3	0	4	1	.800	0	0	2.63
1994 Hagerstown	A Tor	18	18	2	0	108.1	453	91	47	37	10	2	3	9	40	0	90	5	2	10	2	.833	0	0	3.07
1995 Dunedin	A+ Tor	28	26	1	1	150.1	654	141	79	69	15	4	3	11	75	0	102	5	3	11	7	.611	1	0	4.13
1996 Knoxville	AA Tor	34	21	0	5	130	600	148	98	72	17	5	8	5	72	1	92	5	2	9	9	.500	0	1	4.98
4 Min. YEARS		89	73	3	6	429.2	1882	414	244	190	43	11	14	32	198	1	312	18	7	34	19	.642	1	1	3.98

Scott Romano

Bats: Right **Throws:** Right **Pos:** 3B **Ht:** 6'1" **Wt:** 185 **Born:** 8/3/71 **Age:** 25

Year Team	Lg Org	G	AB	H	2B	3B	HR	TB	R	RBI	TBB	IBB	SO	HBP	SH	SF	SB	CS	SB%	GDP	Avg	OBP	SLG
		BATTING															BASERUNNING				PERCENTAGES		
1989 Yankees	R NYA	51	195	42	9	1	2	59	28	24	22	0	38	2	3	2	4	2	.67	2	.215	.299	.303
1990 Greensboro	A NYA	58	189	38	8	0	0	46	17	11	23	0	43	3	4	0	12	5	.71	2	.201	.298	.243
Oneonta	A- NYA	57	178	43	8	2	1	58	30	19	30	1	38	6	2	2	18	2	.90	3	.242	.366	.326
1991 Greensboro	A NYA	92	307	67	13	2	1	87	35	30	45	1	70	7	3	1	14	10	.58	5	.218	.331	.283
1992 Ft. Laud	A+ NYA	106	358	86	17	2	3	116	30	24	27	0	62	3	4	1	11	6	.65	12	.240	.298	.324
1993 Greensboro	A NYA	121	418	118	33	4	7	180	75	62	63	0	69	9	2	3	14	7	.67	10	.282	.385	.431
1994 Tampa	A+ NYA	120	419	127	35	3	20	228	88	87	59	2	55	15	1	6	5	3	.63	3	.303	.403	.544
1995 Norwich	AA NYA	100	353	87	15	1	7	125	43	51	48	1	57	7	4	2	7	2	.78	13	.246	.346	.354
1996 Trenton	AA Bos	1	6	1	1	0	0	2	0	0	1	0	2	0	0	0	0	0	.00	0	.167	.286	.333
Norwich	AA NYA	30	107	31	3	0	3	43	14	8	10	0	24	2	1	0	2	0	1.00	2	.290	.361	.402
Columbus	AAA NYA	18	40	6	2	0	0	8	5	4	5	0	6	0	1	0	1	0	1.00	1	.150	.244	.200
8 Min. YEARS		754	2570	646	144	15	44	952	365	320	333	5	464	54	25	17	88	37	.70	53	.251	.347	.370

Mandy Romero

Bats: Both **Throws:** Right **Pos:** C **Ht:** 5'11" **Wt:** 196 **Born:** 10/19/67 **Age:** 29

Year Team	Lg Org	G	AB	H	2B	3B	HR	TB	R	RBI	TBB	IBB	SO	HBP	SH	SF	SB	CS	SB%	GDP	Avg	OBP	SLG
		BATTING															BASERUNNING				PERCENTAGES		
1988 Princeton	R+ Pit	30	71	22	6	0	2	34	7	11	13	0	15	1	0	0	1	0	1.00	0	.310	.424	.479
1989 Augusta	A Pit	121	388	87	26	3	4	131	58	55	67	4	74	6	3	6	8	5	.62	10	.224	.343	.338
1990 Salem	A+ Pit	124	460	134	31	3	17	222	62	90	55	3	68	5	2	4	0	2	.00	10	.291	.370	.483
1991 Carolina	AA Pit	98	323	70	12	0	3	91	28	31	45	4	53	1	2	2	1	2	.33	9	.217	.313	.282
1992 Carolina	AA Pit	80	269	58	16	0	3	83	28	27	29	0	30	1	1	2	0	3	.00	10	.216	.292	.309
1993 Buffalo	AAA Pit	42	136	31	6	1	2	45	11	14	6	1	12	0	1	1	1	0	1.00	5	.228	.259	.331
1994 Buffalo	AAA Pit	7	23	3	0	0	0	3	3	1	2	0	1	0	1	0	0	0	.00	2	.130	.200	.130

BATTING																			BASERUNNING				PERCENTAGES		
Year Team	Lg	Org	G	AB	H	2B	3B	HR	TB	R	RBI	TBB	IBB	SO	HBP	SH	SF		SB	CS	SB%	GDP	Avg	OBP	SLG
1995 Wichita	AA	KC	121	440	133	32	1	21	230	73	82	69	10	60	5	0	1		1	3	.25	15	.302	.402	.523
1996 Memphis	AA	SD	88	297	80	15	0	10	125	40	46	41	2	52	1	1	2		3	1	.75	15	.269	.358	.421
9 Min. YEARS			711	2407	618	144	8	62	964	310	357	327	24	374	20	11	18		15	16	.48	76	.257	.348	.400

Wilfredo Romero

Bats: Right **Throws:** Right **Pos:** OF **Ht:** 5'11" **Wt:** 158 **Born:** 8/5/74 **Age:** 22

BATTING																		BASERUNNING				PERCENTAGES		
Year Team	Lg	Org	G	AB	H	2B	3B	HR	TB	R	RBI	TBB	IBB	SO	HBP	SH	SF	SB	CS	SB%	GDP	Avg	OBP	SLG
1993 Great Falls	R+	LA	15	58	16	5	0	0	21	12	9	2	0	9	0	0	0	2	1	.67	2	.276	.300	.362
Yakima	A-	LA	13	51	13	0	0	0	13	8	1	1	0	12	2	0	1	3	0	1.00	1	.255	.291	.255
Bakersfield	A+	LA	20	77	27	5	0	1	35	8	12	5	0	16	0	0	0	4	2	.67	2	.351	.390	.455
1994 Vero Beach	A+	LA	38	126	29	6	0	2	41	15	13	9	0	19	1	2	0	0	2	.00	2	.230	.287	.325
Bakersfield	A+	LA	70	260	71	19	1	7	113	36	36	19	0	53	3	1	0	15	5	.75	3	.273	.330	.435
1995 San Antonio	AA	LA	105	376	100	20	1	7	143	46	44	40	1	69	5	0	6	10	12	.45	7	.266	.340	.380
1996 San Antonio	AA	LA	122	444	131	36	6	6	197	66	48	34	2	52	3	2	8	21	15	.58	11	.295	.344	.444
Albuquerque	AAA	LA	4	13	5	0	0	1	8	1	3	1	0	1	0	0	0	1	0	1.00	0	.385	.429	.615
4 Min. YEARS			387	1405	392	91	8	24	571	192	166	111	3	231	14	5	15	56	37	.60	28	.279	.335	.406

Marc Ronan

Bats: Left **Throws:** Right **Pos:** C **Ht:** 6' 2" **Wt:** 190 **Born:** 9/19/69 **Age:** 27

BATTING																		BASERUNNING				PERCENTAGES		
Year Team	Lg	Org	G	AB	H	2B	3B	HR	TB	R	RBI	TBB	IBB	SO	HBP	SH	SF	SB	CS	SB%	GDP	Avg	OBP	SLG
1990 Hamilton	A-	StL	56	167	38	6	0	1	47	14	15	15	0	37	1	0	3	1	2	.33	3	.228	.290	.281
1991 Savannah	A	StL	108	343	81	10	1	0	93	41	45	37	1	54	4	3	1	11	2	.85	13	.236	.317	.271
1992 Springfield	A	StL	110	376	81	19	2	6	122	45	48	23	2	58	1	0	4	4	5	.44	11	.215	.260	.324
1993 St. Pete	A+	StL	25	87	27	5	0	0	32	13	6	6	0	10	0	3	2	0	0	.00	1	.310	.347	.368
Arkansas	AA	StL	96	281	60	16	1	7	99	33	34	26	2	47	2	3	3	1	3	.25	4	.214	.282	.352
1994 Louisville	AAA	StL	84	269	64	11	2	2	85	32	21	12	2	43	2	2	2	3	1	.75	9	.238	.274	.316
1995 Louisville	AAA	StL	78	225	48	8	0	0	56	15	8	14	2	42	0	2	0	4	3	.57	10	.213	.259	.249
1996 Charlotte	AAA	Fla	79	220	67	10	0	4	89	23	20	16	2	37	2	0	2	3	4	.43	4	.305	.354	.405
1993 St. Louis	NL		6	12	1	0	0	0	1	0	0	0	0	5	0	0	0	0	0	.00	0	.083	.083	.083
7 Min. YEARS			636	1968	466	85	6	20	623	216	197	149	11	328	12	13	17	27	20	.57	55	.237	.292	.317

Chad Roper

Bats: Right **Throws:** Right **Pos:** 3B **Ht:** 6'1" **Wt:** 212 **Born:** 3/29/74 **Age:** 23

BATTING																		BASERUNNING				PERCENTAGES		
Year Team	Lg	Org	G	AB	H	2B	3B	HR	TB	R	RBI	TBB	IBB	SO	HBP	SH	SF	SB	CS	SB%	GDP	Avg	OBP	SLG
1992 Twins	R	Min	20	76	25	5	3	1	39	16	11	5	1	16	1	0	1	1	0	1.00	2	.329	.373	.513
Elizabethtn	R+	Min	39	147	42	4	1	1	51	20	25	12	0	29	1	0	2	0	1	.00	3	.286	.340	.347
1993 Fort Myers	A+	Min	125	452	112	17	3	9	162	46	65	43	2	96	6	4	5	1	2	.33	10	.248	.318	.358
1994 Fort Myers	A+	Min	92	337	81	17	0	4	110	32	44	32	3	76	4	0	7	7	8	.47	8	.240	.308	.326
1995 New Britain	AA	Min	120	443	100	22	3	11	161	41	61	27	3	86	3	1	4	2	3	.40	9	.226	.273	.363
1996 New Britain	AA	Min	128	466	117	18	2	10	169	59	48	42	4	73	3	1	2	4	7	.36	12	.251	.316	.363
5 Min. YEARS			524	1921	477	83	12	36	692	214	254	161	13	376	18	6	21	15	21	.42	44	.248	.309	.360

John Roper

Pitches: Right **Bats:** Right **Pos:** P **Ht:** 6' 0" **Wt:** 175 **Born:** 11/21/71 **Age:** 25

HOW MUCH HE PITCHED									WHAT HE GAVE UP												THE RESULTS					
Year Team	Lg	Org	G	GS	CG	GF	IP	BFP	H	R	ER	HR	SH	SF	HB	TBB	IBB	SO	WP	Bk	W	L	Pct.	ShO	Sv	ERA
1990 Reds	R	Cin	13	13	0	0	74	281	41	10	8	1	0	0	3	31	0	76	2	0	7	2	.778	0	0	0.97
1991 Charlstn-WV	A	Cin	27	27	5	0	186.2	741	133	59	48	5	1	5	4	67	0	189	8	1	14	9	.609	3	0	2.31
1992 Chattanooga	AA	Cin	20	20	1	0	120.2	513	115	57	55	11	5	6	4	37	2	99	15	5	10	9	.526	1	0	4.10
1993 Indianapolis	AAA	Cin	12	12	0	0	54.2	248	56	33	27	12	0	0	3	30	1	42	2	2	3	5	.375	0	0	4.45
1994 Indianapolis	AAA	Cin	8	8	1	0	58	228	48	17	14	0	0	2	2	10	0	33	4	1	7	0	1.000	0	0	2.17
1995 Chattanooga	AA	Cin	3	3	0	0	9	33	5	1	1	0	0	0	0	1	0	6	0	0	0	0	.000	0	0	1.00
Phoenix	AAA	SF	1	1	0	0	3	14	5	3	3	0	0	1	0	0	0	2	0	0	0	1	.000	0	0	9.00
Indianapolis	AAA	Cin	12	12	0	0	53.2	233	57	30	27	9	0	1	1	17	1	31	4	0	2	6	.250	0	0	4.53
1996 Chattanooga	AA	Cin	3	3	0	0	12	62	19	18	13	2	1	0	2	7	2	6	1	0	0	2	.000	0	0	9.75
1993 Cincinnati	NL		16	15	0	0	80	360	92	51	50	10	5	3	4	36	3	54	5	1	2	5	.286	0	0	5.63
1994 Cincinnati	NL		16	15	0	0	92	390	90	49	46	16	0	3	4	30	0	51	4	1	6	2	.750	0	0	4.50
1995 Cincinnati	NL		2	2	0	0	7	37	13	9	8	3	1	0	0	4	0	6	0	1	0	0	.000	0	0	10.29
San Francisco	NL		1	0	0	0	1	7	2	3	3	0	0	1	0	2	0	0	0	0	0	0	.000	0	0	27.00
7 Min. YEARS			99	99	7	0	571.2	2353	479	228	196	40	7	15	19	200	6	484	36	9	43	34	.558	4	0	3.09
3 Maj. YEARS			35	32	0	0	180	794	197	112	107	29	6	7	8	72	3	111	9	3	8	7	.533	0	0	5.35

Rafael Roque

Pitches: Left **Bats:** Left **Pos:** P **Ht:** 6'2" **Wt:** 152 **Born:** 1/1/72 **Age:** 25

HOW MUCH HE PITCHED									WHAT HE GAVE UP												THE RESULTS					
Year Team	Lg	Org	G	GS	CG	GF	IP	BFP	H	R	ER	HR	SH	SF	HB	TBB	IBB	SO	WP	Bk	W	L	Pct.	ShO	Sv	ERA
1992 Mets	R	NYN	20	0	0	18	33.2	149	28	13	8	0	4	0	1	16	2	33	3	1	3	1	.750	0	8	2.14
1993 Kingsport	R+	NYN	14	7	0	4	45.1	222	58	44	31	9	3	2	7	26	0	36	8	1	1	3	.250	0	0	6.15
1994 St. Lucie	A+	NYN	2	0	0	2	3	15	2	1	0	0	1	1	1	3	1	2	0	0	0	0	.000	0	0	0.00

Year	Team	Lg	Org	HOW MUCH HE PITCHED						WHAT HE GAVE UP												THE RESULTS					
				G	GS	CG	GF	IP	BFP	H	R	ER	HR	SH	SF	HB	TBB	IBB	SO	WP	Bk	W	L	Pct.	ShO	Sv	ERA
	Columbia	A	NYN	15	15	1	0	86.1	353	73	26	23	6	1	3	4	30	1	74	7	1	6	3	.667	0	0	2.40
1995	St. Lucie	A+	NYN	24	24	2	0	136.2	582	114	65	54	7	2	4	4	72	1	81	11	4	6	9	.400	1	0	3.56
1996	Binghamton	AA	NYN	13	13	0	0	60.2	291	71	57	49	8	2	1	2	39	0	46	4	0	0	4	.000	0	0	7.27
	St. Lucie	A+	NYN	14	12	1	1	76.1	311	57	22	18	2	5	0	3	39	0	59	8	0	6	4	.600	0	0	2.12
5 Min. YEARS				102	71	4	25	442	1923	403	228	183	32	18	11	22	225	5	331	41	7	22	24	.478	1	8	3.73

Mel Rosario

Bats: Both **Throws:** Right **Pos:** C **Ht:** 6'0" **Wt:** 191 **Born:** 5/25/73 **Age:** 24

Year	Team	Lg	Org	BATTING															BASERUNNING				PERCENTAGES		
				G	AB	H	2B	3B	HR	TB	R	RBI	TBB	IBB	SO	HBP	SH	SF	SB	CS	SB%	GDP	Avg	OBP	SLG
1992	Spokane	A-	SD	66	237	54	13	1	10	99	38	40	20	2	62	4	0	4	5	3	.63	6	.228	.294	.418
1993	Waterloo	A	SD	32	105	22	6	2	5	47	15	15	7	1	37	2	0	0	5	2	.71	0	.210	.272	.448
	Spokane	A-	SD	41	140	32	5	0	4	49	17	19	8	2	36	0	0	0	2	1	.67	1	.229	.270	.350
1995	South Bend	A	ChA	118	450	123	30	6	15	210	58	57	30	7	109	4	1	3	1	8	.11	0	.273	.322	.467
1996	Rancho Cuca	A+	SD	10	33	9	3	0	3	21	7	10	3	0	8	0	0	0	1	0	1.00	0	.273	.333	.636
	High Desert	A+	Bal	42	163	52	9	1	10	93	35	34	21	0	45	9	0	0	4	0	1.00	3	.319	.425	.571
	Bowie	AA	Bal	47	162	34	10	0	2	50	14	17	6	1	43	5	1	2	3	2	.60	4	.210	.257	.309
	Rochester	AAA	Bal	3	2	0	0	0	0	0	0	0	0	0	1	0	0	0	0	0	.00	0	.000	.000	.000
4 Min. YEARS				359	1292	326	76	10	49	569	184	192	95	13	341	24	2	9	21	16	.57	14	.252	.313	.440

Brian Rose

Pitches: Right **Bats:** Right **Pos:** P **Ht:** 6'2" **Wt:** 190 **Born:** 2/13/76 **Age:** 21

Year	Team	Lg	Org	HOW MUCH HE PITCHED						WHAT HE GAVE UP												THE RESULTS					
				G	GS	CG	GF	IP	BFP	H	R	ER	HR	SH	SF	HB	TBB	IBB	SO	WP	Bk	W	L	Pct.	ShO	Sv	ERA
1995	Michigan	A	Bos	21	20	2	0	136	561	127	63	52	5	3	1	9	31	0	105	4	0	8	5	.615	0	0	3.44
1996	Trenton	AA	Bos	27	27	4	0	163.2	687	157	82	73	21	6	4	13	45	3	115	1	1	12	7	.632	2	0	4.01
2 Min. YEARS				48	47	6	0	299.2	1248	284	145	125	26	9	5	22	76	3	220	5	1	20	12	.625	2	0	3.75

Pete Rose

Bats: Left **Throws:** Right **Pos:** 3B **Ht:** 6'1" **Wt:** 180 **Born:** 11/16/69 **Age:** 27

Year	Team	Lg	Org	BATTING															BASERUNNING				PERCENTAGES		
				G	AB	H	2B	3B	HR	TB	R	RBI	TBB	IBB	SO	HBP	SH	SF	SB	CS	SB%	GDP	Avg	OBP	SLG
1989	Frederick	A+	Bal	24	67	12	3	0	0	15	3	7	0	0	15	1	0	0	1	1	.50	1	.179	.191	.224
	Erie	A-	Bal	58	228	63	13	5	2	92	30	26	12	1	34	1	2	0	1	2	.33	3	.276	.315	.404
1990	Frederick	A+	Bal	97	323	75	14	2	1	96	32	41	26	0	33	1	7	5	0	3	.00	6	.232	.287	.297
1991	Sarasota	A+	ChA	99	323	70	12	2	0	86	31	35	36	3	35	2	8	3	5	6	.45	3	.217	.297	.266
1992	Columbus	A	Cle	131	510	129	24	6	9	192	67	54	48	2	53	6	8	3	4	3	.57	9	.253	.323	.376
1993	Kinston	A+	Cle	74	284	62	10	1	7	95	33	30	25	0	34	2	6	1	1	3	.25	5	.218	.285	.335
1994	Hickory	A	ChA	32	114	25	4	1	0	31	14	12	13	2	18	2	3	2	0	0	.00	3	.219	.305	.272
	White Sox	R	ChA	2	4	2	0	0	0	2	1	1	0	0	0	0	0	0	0	0	.00	0	.500	.500	.500
	Pr. William	A+	ChA	45	146	41	3	1	4	58	18	22	18	0	15	0	2	3	0	1	.00	2	.281	.353	.397
1995	Birmingham	AA	ChA	5	13	5	1	0	0	6	1	2	3	0	3	0	0	0	0	0	.00	0	.385	.500	.462
	South Bend	A	ChA	116	423	117	24	6	4	165	56	65	54	0	45	5	2	7	2	0	1.00	6	.277	.360	.390
1996	Birmingham	AA	ChA	108	399	97	13	1	3	121	40	44	32	1	54	2	5	3	1	3	.25	9	.243	.300	.303
8 Min. YEARS				791	2834	698	121	25	30	959	326	339	267	9	339	22	43	27	15	22	.41	47	.246	.313	.338

Scott Rose

Pitches: Right **Bats:** Right **Pos:** P **Ht:** 6'3" **Wt:** 200 **Born:** 5/12/70 **Age:** 27

Year	Team	Lg	Org	HOW MUCH HE PITCHED						WHAT HE GAVE UP												THE RESULTS					
				G	GS	CG	GF	IP	BFP	H	R	ER	HR	SH	SF	HB	TBB	IBB	SO	WP	Bk	W	L	Pct.	ShO	Sv	ERA
1990	Athletics	R	Oak	9	1	0	4	18.1	69	12	5	3	0	0	0	0	3	0	21	1	0	0	0	.000	0	2	1.47
	Modesto	A+	Oak	6	0	0	3	14	61	14	5	2	0	0	0	0	6	1	10	2	0	0	0	.000	0	1	1.29
1991	Modesto	A+	Oak	13	13	0	0	67.2	306	66	45	33	7	3	3	2	38	1	31	7	1	3	3	.500	0	0	4.39
1992	Madison	A	Oak	8	8	1	0	36	154	35	22	17	2	1	2	2	10	0	15	3	1	2	2	.500	0	0	4.25
	Reno	A+	Oak	20	9	0	2	64	314	97	73	60	11	2	2	2	37	3	29	4	0	2	4	.333	0	0	8.44
1993	San Bernrdo	A+	Oak	28	25	1	0	173.1	765	184	110	82	16	6	8	10	63	6	73	10	0	9	10	.474	1	0	4.26
1994	Huntsville	AA	Oak	41	0	0	25	73	328	87	44	38	2	9	4	2	24	8	43	9	0	6	10	.375	0	3	4.68
1995	Edmonton	AAA	Oak	5	1	0	2	10	45	13	7	7	0	1	0	0	7	0	0	0	0	0	2	.000	0	0	6.30
	Huntsville	AA	Oak	43	6	0	25	90	361	83	31	30	2	6	3	2	30	5	35	6	0	4	8	.333	0	13	3.00
1996	Edmonton	AAA	Oak	50	0	0	41	55.2	239	57	21	18	2	4	2	1	16	4	20	4	0	4	4	.500	0	10	2.91
7 Min. YEARS				223	63	2	102	602	2642	648	363	290	42	32	24	21	234	28	277	46	2	30	43	.411	1	29	4.34

John Rosengren

Pitches: Left **Bats:** Left **Pos:** P **Ht:** 6'4" **Wt:** 190 **Born:** 8/10/72 **Age:** 24

Year	Team	Lg	Org	HOW MUCH HE PITCHED						WHAT HE GAVE UP												THE RESULTS					
				G	GS	CG	GF	IP	BFP	H	R	ER	HR	SH	SF	HB	TBB	IBB	SO	WP	Bk	W	L	Pct.	ShO	Sv	ERA
1992	Bristol	R+	Det	14	3	0	3	23	113	16	21	20	2	0	5	0	30	0	28	6	2	0	3	.000	0	0	7.83
1993	Niagara Fal	A-	Det	15	15	0	0	82	333	52	32	22	3	1	4	6	38	0	91	6	1	7	3	.700	0	0	2.41
1994	Lakeland	A+	Det	22	22	4	0	135.2	569	113	51	38	4	2	4	7	56	0	101	3	2	9	6	.600	3	0	2.52
	Trenton	AA	Det	3	3	0	0	17.1	79	21	15	14	2	1	1	0	11	0	7	0	1	0	2	.000	0	0	7.27
1995	Lakeland	A+	Det	13	8	0	1	56.1	253	46	33	25	6	2	2	7	36	0	35	2	0	3	3	.500	0	0	3.99
	Jacksonvlle	AA	Det	27	21	0	1	124	561	119	72	59	13	4	4	12	76	0	94	14	2	5	10	.333	0	0	4.28

		HOW MUCH HE PITCHED						WHAT HE GAVE UP												THE RESULTS					
Year Team	Lg Org	G	GS	CG	GF	IP	BFP	H	R	ER	HR	SH	SF	HB	TBB	IBB	SO	WP	Bk	W	L	Pct.	ShO	Sv	ERA
1996 Jacksonvlle	AA Det	60	0	0	15	55.1	249	48	36	28	9	2	1	3	37	3	47	4	0	5	1	.833	0	1	4.55
5 Min. YEARS		154	72	4	20	493.2	2157	415	260	206	39	12	21	35	284	3	403	35	8	29	28	.509	3	1	3.76

Johnny Roskos

Bats: Right **Throws:** Right **Pos:** 1B **Ht:** 5'11" **Wt:** 198 **Born:** 11/19/74 **Age:** 22

		BATTING														BASERUNNING				PERCENTAGES		
Year Team	Lg Org	G	AB	H	2B	3B	HR	TB	R	RBI	TBB	IBB	SO	HBP	SH	SF	SB	CS	SB%	GDP	Avg	OBP	SLG
1993 Marlins	R Fla	11	40	7	1	0	1	11	6	3	5	0	11	1	0	0	1	1	.50	0	.175	.283	.275
1994 Elmira	A- Fla	39	136	38	7	0	4	57	11	23	27	0	37	0	0	2	0	1	.00	0	.279	.394	.419
1995 Kane County	A Fla	114	418	124	36	3	12	202	74	88	42	1	86	6	0	6	2	0	1.00	6	.297	.364	.483
1996 Portland	AA Fla	121	396	109	26	3	9	168	53	58	67	4	102	5	0	2	3	4	.43	5	.275	.385	.424
4 Min. YEARS		285	990	278	70	6	26	438	144	172	141	5	236	12	0	10	6	6	.50	11	.281	.374	.442

Tony Ross

Bats: Right **Throws:** Right **Pos:** OF **Ht:** 5'11" **Wt:** 175 **Born:** 5/11/75 **Age:** 22

		BATTING														BASERUNNING				PERCENTAGES		
Year Team	Lg Org	G	AB	H	2B	3B	HR	TB	R	RBI	TBB	IBB	SO	HBP	SH	SF	SB	CS	SB%	GDP	Avg	OBP	SLG
1992 Astros	R Hou	3	10	2	0	0	0	2	0	1	1	0	3	0	0	0	2	1	.67	0	.200	.273	.200
1993 Astros	R Hou	37	133	42	4	2	1	53	29	9	8	0	19	2	0	0	11	1	.92	0	.316	.364	.398
Osceola	A+ Hou	9	25	4	0	0	0	4	3	1	1	0	9	1	0	0	0	0	.00	0	.160	.222	.160
1994 Auburn	A- Hou	45	135	39	3	5	0	52	24	14	23	0	21	0	2	0	14	6	.70	1	.289	.392	.385
1995 Quad City	A Hou	107	339	87	11	4	3	115	46	41	31	0	57	3	2	3	21	5	.81	4	.257	.322	.339
1996 Kissimmee	A+ Hou	57	193	43	8	2	1	58	22	17	15	0	42	0	4	2	10	2	.83	2	.223	.276	.301
Jackson	AA Hou	34	80	14	0	1	0	16	13	3	7	0	11	3	4	0	2	1	.67	0	.175	.267	.200
5 Min. YEARS		292	915	231	26	14	5	300	137	86	86	0	162	9	12	5	60	16	.79	7	.252	.321	.328

Joe Rosselli

Pitches: Left **Bats:** Right **Pos:** P **Ht:** 6' 1" **Wt:** 185 **Born:** 5/28/72 **Age:** 25

		HOW MUCH HE PITCHED						WHAT HE GAVE UP												THE RESULTS					
Year Team	Lg Org	G	GS	CG	GF	IP	BFP	H	R	ER	HR	SH	SF	HB	TBB	IBB	SO	WP	Bk	W	L	Pct.	ShO	Sv	ERA
1990 Everett	A- SF	15	15	0	0	78.1	340	87	47	41	10	0	2	0	29	0	90	4	0	4	4	.500	0	0	4.71
1991 Clinton	A SF	22	22	2	0	153.2	640	144	70	53	5	4	8	1	49	0	127	11	4	8	7	.533	0	0	3.10
1992 San Jose	A+ SF	22	22	4	0	149.2	614	145	50	40	7	2	2	2	46	1	111	2	4	11	4	.733	0	0	2.41
1993 Shreveport	AA SF	4	4	0	0	23	96	22	9	8	1	0	0	0	7	0	19	1	0	0	1	.000	0	0	3.13
1994 Shreveport	AA SF	14	14	2	0	90.2	350	67	24	19	2	6	2	0	17	0	54	1	0	7	2	.778	2	0	1.89
Phoenix	AAA SF	13	13	0	0	74.2	322	96	46	41	10	6	1	1	15	0	35	1	1	1	8	.111	0	0	4.94
1995 Phoenix	AAA SF	13	13	1	0	79.1	332	94	47	44	8	2	4	0	12	0	34	2	0	4	3	.571	0	0	4.99
1996 Vancouver	AAA Cal	47	0	0	18	58.2	253	53	22	19	3	5	2	0	26	3	37	4	0	2	3	.400	0	3	2.91
1995 San Francisco	NL	9	5	0	0	30	140	39	29	29	5	2	4	0	20	2	7	0	1	2	1	.667	0	0	8.70
7 Min. YEARS		150	103	9	18	708	2947	708	315	265	46	25	21	4	201	4	507	26	9	37	32	.536	2	3	3.37

Mike Rossiter

Pitches: Right **Bats:** Right **Pos:** P **Ht:** 6'6" **Wt:** 217 **Born:** 6/20/73 **Age:** 24

		HOW MUCH HE PITCHED						WHAT HE GAVE UP												THE RESULTS					
Year Team	Lg Org	G	GS	CG	GF	IP	BFP	H	R	ER	HR	SH	SF	HB	TBB	IBB	SO	WP	Bk	W	L	Pct.	ShO	Sv	ERA
1991 Athletics	R Oak	10	9	0	0	38.1	179	43	24	17	3	1	0	2	22	0	35	6	0	3	4	.429	0	0	3.99
1992 Madison	A Oak	27	27	2	0	154.2	651	135	83	68	17	2	5	4	68	1	135	4	3	8	14	.364	0	0	3.96
1993 Modesto	A+ Oak	20	17	2	0	112	491	120	62	54	14	4	1	1	45	0	96	5	0	8	6	.571	0	0	4.34
1994 Athletics	R Oak	2	0	0	0	3.2	20	8	6	2	0	1	0	0	0	0	3	1	0	0	1	.000	0	0	4.91
1995 Modesto	A+ Oak	18	7	0	3	68.2	290	68	33	32	5	2	2	2	19	0	70	1	1	7	2	.778	0	0	4.19
1996 Huntsville	AA Oak	27	25	2	1	145	636	167	92	78	15	2	10	7	44	4	116	5	0	8	9	.471	1	0	4.84
6 Min. YEARS		104	85	6	4	522.1	2267	541	300	251	54	12	18	16	198	5	455	22	4	34	36	.486	1	0	4.32

Rico Rossy

Bats: Right **Throws:** Right **Pos:** SS **Ht:** 5'10" **Wt:** 175 **Born:** 2/16/64 **Age:** 33

		BATTING														BASERUNNING				PERCENTAGES		
Year Team	Lg Org	G	AB	H	2B	3B	HR	TB	R	RBI	TBB	IBB	SO	HBP	SH	SF	SB	CS	SB%	GDP	Avg	OBP	SLG
1985 Newark	A- Bal	73	246	53	14	2	3	80	38	25	32	1	22	1	3	1	17	7	.71	13	.215	.307	.325
1986 Miami	A+ Bal	38	134	34	7	1	1	46	26	9	24	0	8	1	6	1	10	6	.63	4	.254	.369	.343
Charlotte	AA Bal	77	232	68	16	2	3	97	40	25	26	0	19	2	8	1	13	5	.72	2	.293	.368	.418
1987 Charlotte	AA Bal	127	471	135	22	3	4	175	69	50	43	0	38	3	3	1	20	9	.69	20	.287	.349	.372
1988 Buffalo	AAA Pit	68	187	46	4	0	1	53	12	20	13	0	17	0	0	1	1	5	.17	4	.246	.294	.283
1989 Harrisburg	AA Pit	78	238	60	16	1	2	84	20	25	27	0	19	3	0	2	2	4	.33	5	.252	.333	.353
Buffalo	AAA Pit	38	109	21	5	0	0	26	11	10	18	1	11	1	1	2	4	0	1.00	4	.193	.308	.239
1990 Buffalo	AAA Pit	8	17	3	0	1	0	5	3	2	4	0	2	0	1	1	1	0	1.00	0	.176	.318	.294
Greenville	AA Atl	5	21	4	1	0	0	5	4	0	1	0	2	0	0	0	0	2	.00	1	.190	.227	.238
Richmond	AAA Atl	107	380	88	13	0	4	113	58	32	69	1	43	3	7	2	11	6	.65	12	.232	.352	.297
1991 Richmond	AAA Atl	139	482	124	25	1	2	157	58	48	67	1	46	5	13	3	4	8	.33	12	.257	.352	.326
1992 Omaha	AAA KC	48	174	55	10	1	4	79	29	17	34	0	14	0	2	3	3	5	.38	5	.316	.422	.454
1993 Omaha	AAA KC	37	131	39	10	1	5	66	25	21	20	1	19	3	0	1	3	2	.60	1	.298	.400	.504
1994 Omaha	AAA KC	120	412	97	23	0	11	153	49	63	61	1	60	5	5	4	9	10	.47	14	.235	.338	.371
1995 Las Vegas	AAA SD	98	316	95	11	2	1	113	44	45	55	2	36	2	2	6	3	7	.30	13	.301	.401	.358

Year Team	Lg Org	G	AB	H	2B	3B	HR	TB	R	RBI	TBB	IBB	SO	HBP	SH	SF	SB	CS	SB%	GDP	Avg	OBP	SLG
		BATTING															BASERUNNING				PERCENTAGES		
1996 Las Vegas	AAA SD	130	413	104	21	2	4	141	56	35	70	7	63	6	9	5	6	6	.50	11	.252	.364	.341
1991 Atlanta	NL	5	1	0	0	0	0	0	0	0	0	0	1	0	0	0	0	0	.00	0	.000	.000	.000
1992 Kansas City	AL	59	149	32	8	1	1	45	21	12	20	1	20	1	7	1	0	3	.00	6	.215	.310	.302
1993 Kansas City	AL	46	86	19	4	0	2	29	10	12	9	0	11	1	1	0	0	0	.00	0	.221	.302	.337
12 Min. YEARS		1191	3963	1026	198	17	45	1393	542	427	564	15	419	35	60	34	107	82	.57	121	.259	.354	.352
3 Maj. YEARS		110	236	51	12	1	3	74	31	24	29	1	32	2	8	1	0	3	.00	6	.216	.306	.314

Rich Rowland

Bats: Right **Throws:** Right **Pos:** C **Ht:** 6' 1" **Wt:** 215 **Born:** 2/25/64 **Age:** 33

Year Team	Lg Org	G	AB	H	2B	3B	HR	TB	R	RBI	TBB	IBB	SO	HBP	SH	SF	SB	CS	SB%	GDP	Avg	OBP	SLG
		BATTING															BASERUNNING				PERCENTAGES		
1988 Bristol	R+ Det	56	186	51	10	1	4	75	29	41	27	1	39	1	0	3	1	2	.33	2	.274	.364	.403
1989 Fayettevlle	A Det	108	375	102	17	1	9	148	43	59	54	2	98	3	3	3	4	1	.80	8	.272	.366	.395
1990 London	AA Det	47	161	46	10	0	8	80	22	30	20	3	33	3	0	1	1	1	.50	7	.286	.373	.497
Toledo	AAA Det	62	192	50	12	0	7	83	28	22	15	0	33	1	3	2	2	3	.40	3	.260	.314	.432
1991 Toledo	AAA Det	109	383	104	25	0	13	168	56	68	60	3	77	3	0	1	4	2	.67	8	.272	.374	.439
1992 Toledo	AAA Det	136	473	111	19	1	25	207	75	82	56	6	112	3	0	4	9	3	.75	20	.235	.317	.438
1993 Toledo	AAA Det	96	325	87	24	2	21	178	58	59	51	3	72	3	0	3	1	6	.14	11	.268	.369	.548
1995 Pawtucket	AAA Bos	34	124	32	7	0	8	63	20	24	7	1	24	1	0	1	0	1	.00	2	.258	.301	.508
1996 Syracuse	AAA Tor	96	288	65	24	2	8	117	43	45	50	3	79	4	2	4	1	1	.50	9	.226	.344	.406
1990 Detroit	AL	7	19	3	1	0	0	4	3	0	2	1	4	0	0	0	0	0	.00	1	.158	.238	.211
1991 Detroit	AL	4	4	1	0	0	0	1	0	1	1	0	2	0	0	1	0	0	.00	0	.250	.333	.250
1992 Detroit	AL	6	14	3	0	0	0	3	2	0	3	0	3	0	0	0	0	0	.00	1	.214	.353	.214
1993 Detroit	AL	21	46	10	3	0	0	13	2	4	5	0	16	0	1	0	0	0	.00	1	.217	.294	.283
1994 Boston	AL	46	118	27	3	0	9	57	14	20	11	0	35	0	0	0	0	0	.00	2	.229	.295	.483
1995 Boston	AL	14	29	5	1	0	0	6	1	1	0	0	11	0	0	0	0	0	.00	0	.172	.172	.207
8 Min. YEARS		744	2507	648	148	7	103	1119	374	430	340	22	567	22	8	22	23	20	.53	70	.258	.349	.446
6 Maj. YEARS		98	230	49	8	0	9	84	22	26	22	1	71	0	1	1	0	0	.00	5	.213	.281	.365

Aaron Royster

Bats: Right **Throws:** Right **Pos:** OF **Ht:** 6'1" **Wt:** 220 **Born:** 11/30/72 **Age:** 24

Year Team	Lg Org	G	AB	H	2B	3B	HR	TB	R	RBI	TBB	IBB	SO	HBP	SH	SF	SB	CS	SB%	GDP	Avg	OBP	SLG
		BATTING															BASERUNNING				PERCENTAGES		
1994 Martinsvlle	R+ Phi	54	168	46	11	2	7	82	31	39	28	1	47	2	0	1	7	4	.64	2	.274	.382	.488
1995 Piedmont	A Phi	126	489	129	23	3	8	182	73	58	39	1	106	7	0	4	22	9	.71	16	.264	.325	.372
1996 Clearwater	A+ Phi	72	289	81	10	2	11	128	35	60	23	1	56	3	3	2	4	3	.57	7	.280	.338	.443
Reading	AA Phi	65	230	59	11	0	4	82	42	20	30	2	56	5	3	1	4	5	.44	3	.257	.353	.357
3 Min. YEARS		317	1176	315	55	7	30	474	181	177	120	5	265	17	6	8	37	21	.64	28	.268	.342	.403

Tim Rumer

Pitches: Left **Bats:** Left **Pos:** P **Ht:** 6'3" **Wt:** 205 **Born:** 8/8/69 **Age:** 27

Year Team	Lg Org	G	GS	CG	GF	IP	BFP	H	R	ER	HR	SH	SF	HB	TBB	IBB	SO	WP	Bk	W	L	Pct.	ShO	Sv	ERA
		HOW MUCH HE PITCHED						WHAT HE GAVE UP												THE RESULTS					
1990 Yankees	R NYA	12	12	2	0	74	291	34	23	14	1	1	0	3	20	0	88	4	3	6	3	.667	0	0	1.70
1991 Ft. Laud	A+ NYA	24	23	3	0	149.1	623	125	59	48	6	9	3	5	49	2	112	7	1	10	7	.588	2	0	2.89
1992 Pr. William	A+ NYA	23	23	1	0	128	538	122	61	51	8	6	5	5	34	2	105	0	1	10	7	.588	0	0	3.59
Columbus	AAA NYA	1	1	0	0	1	3	0	0	0	0	0	0	0	0	0	1	0	0	0	0	.000	0	0	0.00
1994 Albany-Colo	AA NYA	25	25	2	0	150.2	639	127	61	52	10	2	4	9	75	0	130	7	0	8	10	.444	1	0	3.11
1995 Columbus	AAA NYA	28	25	0	1	141.1	654	156	98	82	13	7	5	16	76	1	110	5	1	10	8	.556	0	0	5.22
1996 Yankees	R NYA	2	1	0	0	8	29	1	0	0	0	0	0	0	2	0	15	0	0	0	0	.000	0	0	0.00
Norwich	AA NYA	8	7	0	0	40	165	32	12	10	3	2	0	0	18	0	44	1	0	3	1	.750	0	0	2.25
Columbus	AAA NYA	12	8	0	1	49.2	204	39	20	15	3	1	1	2	14	0	35	5	0	3	1	.750	0	0	2.72
6 Min. YEARS		135	125	8	2	742	3146	636	334	272	44	28	18	40	288	5	640	29	6	50	37	.575	3	0	3.30

Toby Rumfield

Bats: Right **Throws:** Right **Pos:** 1B **Ht:** 6'3" **Wt:** 190 **Born:** 9/4/72 **Age:** 24

Year Team	Lg Org	G	AB	H	2B	3B	HR	TB	R	RBI	TBB	IBB	SO	HBP	SH	SF	SB	CS	SB%	GDP	Avg	OBP	SLG
		BATTING															BASERUNNING				PERCENTAGES		
1991 Princeton	R+ Cin	59	226	62	13	3	3	90	22	30	9	0	43	5	2	3	1	7	.13	6	.274	.313	.398
1992 Billings	R+ Cin	66	253	68	15	3	4	101	34	50	7	0	34	4	0	4	5	2	.71	4	.269	.295	.399
1993 Charlstn-WV	A Cin	97	333	75	20	1	5	112	36	50	26	1	74	3	0	4	6	4	.60	7	.225	.284	.336
1994 Winston-Sal	A+ Cin	123	462	115	11	4	29	221	79	88	48	1	107	2	0	7	2	3	.40	9	.249	.318	.478
1995 Chattanooga	AA Cin	92	273	72	12	1	8	110	32	53	26	2	47	3	3	5	0	3	.00	14	.264	.329	.403
1996 Chattanooga	AA Cin	113	364	102	25	1	9	156	49	53	37	1	51	6	3	6	2	1	.67	12	.280	.351	.429
6 Min. YEARS		550	1911	494	96	13	58	790	252	324	153	5	356	23	8	29	16	20	.44	52	.259	.317	.413

Brian Rupp

Bats: Right **Throws:** Right **Pos:** 1B **Ht:** 6'5" **Wt:** 185 **Born:** 9/20/71 **Age:** 25

Year Team	Lg Org	G	AB	H	2B	3B	HR	TB	R	RBI	TBB	IBB	SO	HBP	SH	SF	SB	CS	SB%	GDP	Avg	OBP	SLG
		BATTING															BASERUNNING				PERCENTAGES		
1992 Cardinals	R StL	56	207	80	20	1	0	102	34	40	21	5	16	1	0	7	10	7	.59	3	.386	.432	.493
1993 Savannah	A StL	122	472	151	31	7	4	208	80	81	48	2	70	3	1	5	3	2	.60	11	.320	.383	.441

BATTING																			BASERUNNING				PERCENTAGES		
Year	Team	Lg	Org	G	AB	H	2B	3B	HR	TB	R	RBI	TBB	IBB	SO	HBP	SH	SF	SB	CS	SB%	GDP	Avg	OBP	SLG
1994	St. Pete	A+	StL	129	438	115	19	4	2	148	40	34	61	1	77	0	5	0	9	3	.75	20	.263	.353	.338
1995	St. Pete	A+	StL	90	325	90	12	2	0	106	30	23	27	1	43	1	4	0	0	0	.00	14	.277	.334	.326
	Arkansas	AA	StL	23	77	25	3	0	0	28	10	6	6	0	12	0	1	0	0	1	.00	3	.325	.373	.364
1996	Arkansas	AA	StL	114	353	107	17	2	4	140	46	41	33	4	44	0	5	4	5	6	.45	14	.303	.359	.397
5 Min. YEARS				534	1872	568	102	16	10	732	240	225	196	13	262	5	16	16	27	19	.59	65	.303	.368	.391

Chad Rupp

Bats: Right **Throws:** Right **Pos:** 1B **Ht:** 6'2" **Wt:** 215 **Born:** 9/30/71 **Age:** 25

BATTING																			BASERUNNING				PERCENTAGES		
Year	Team	Lg	Org	G	AB	H	2B	3B	HR	TB	R	RBI	TBB	IBB	SO	HBP	SH	SF	SB	CS	SB%	GDP	Avg	OBP	SLG
1993	Elizabethtn	R+	Min	67	228	56	14	1	10	102	54	36	44	2	79	9	1	4	0	1	.00	2	.246	.382	.447
1994	Fort Wayne	A	Min	85	257	63	20	0	15	128	46	50	50	0	79	4	0	7	2	0	1.00	0	.245	.368	.498
1995	Fort Myers	A+	Min	107	376	100	23	1	12	161	44	52	38	1	77	2	0	3	14	3	.82	10	.266	.334	.428
1996	New Britain	AA	Min	77	278	70	14	0	18	138	38	48	13	0	56	4	3	5	3	2	.60	8	.252	.290	.496
4 Min. YEARS				336	1139	289	71	2	55	529	182	186	145	3	291	19	4	19	19	6	.76	20	.254	.343	.464

Glendon Rusch

Pitches: Left **Bats:** Left **Pos:** P **Ht:** 6'2" **Wt:** 170 **Born:** 11/7/74 **Age:** 22

HOW MUCH HE PITCHED										WHAT HE GAVE UP												THE RESULTS					
Year	Team	Lg	Org	G	GS	CG	GF	IP	BFP	H	R	ER	HR	SH	SF	HB	TBB	IBB	SO	WP	Bk	W	L	Pct.	ShO	Sv	ERA
1993	Royals	R	KC	11	10	0	0	62	234	43	14	11	0	3	1	1	11	0	48	2	1	4	2	.667	0	0	1.60
	Rockford	A	KC	2	2	0	0	8	40	10	6	3	0	0	1	0	7	0	8	1	0	0	1	.000	0	0	3.38
1994	Rockford	A	KC	28	17	1	5	114	485	111	61	59	5	6	5	6	34	2	122	7	1	8	5	.615	1	1	4.66
1995	Wilmington	A+	KC	26	26	1	0	165.2	629	110	41	32	5	4	3	4	34	3	147	3	1	14	6	.700	1	0	1.74
1996	Omaha	AAA	KC	28	28	1	0	169.2	723	177	88	75	15	7	8	6	40	3	117	3	0	11	9	.550	0	0	3.98
4 Min. YEARS				95	83	3	5	519.1	2111	451	210	180	25	20	18	17	126	8	442	16	3	37	23	.617	2	1	3.12

Lee Russell

Pitches: Right **Bats:** Right **Pos:** P **Ht:** 6'2" **Wt:** 175 **Born:** 8/20/70 **Age:** 26

HOW MUCH HE PITCHED										WHAT HE GAVE UP												THE RESULTS					
Year	Team	Lg	Org	G	GS	CG	GF	IP	BFP	H	R	ER	HR	SH	SF	HB	TBB	IBB	SO	WP	Bk	W	L	Pct.	ShO	Sv	ERA
1990	Mariners	R	Sea	19	5	0	3	55	251	50	33	19	1	0	3	6	27	1	51	1	1	5	1	.833	0	0	3.11
1991	Bellingham	A-	Sea	15	15	0	0	95.1	414	85	48	31	6	3	1	1	43	1	77	13	0	6	7	.462	0	0	2.93
1992	Peninsula	A+	Sea	27	26	2	1	157.1	665	132	76	55	4	6	3	8	59	4	130	5	1	7	10	.412	1	0	3.15
1993	Jacksonvlle	AA	Sea	17	17	0	0	89.2	400	115	67	55	14	2	2	2	32	1	52	5	0	4	9	.308	0	0	5.52
1994	Jacksonvlle	AA	Sea	36	3	0	19	71.2	314	82	44	36	8	3	2	0	25	5	39	5	0	1	9	.100	0	3	4.52
1995	Port City	AA	Sea	39	0	0	13	72.1	329	68	32	26	7	4	3	1	43	3	54	9	0	4	3	.571	0	1	3.24
1996	Port City	AA	Sea	42	9	1	12	118.1	526	127	70	57	8	8	4	2	50	1	89	3	0	7	7	.500	0	2	4.34
7 Min. YEARS				195	75	3	48	659.2	2899	659	370	279	48	26	18	20	279	16	492	41	2	34	46	.425	1	6	3.81

Paul Russo

Bats: Right **Throws:** Right **Pos:** 3B **Ht:** 5'11" **Wt:** 215 **Born:** 8/26/69 **Age:** 27

BATTING																			BASERUNNING				PERCENTAGES		
Year	Team	Lg	Org	G	AB	H	2B	3B	HR	TB	R	RBI	TBB	IBB	SO	HBP	SH	SF	SB	CS	SB%	GDP	Avg	OBP	SLG
1990	Elizabethtn	R+	Min	62	221	74	9	3	22	155	58	67	38	5	56	1	0	2	4	1	.80	3	.335	.431	.701
1991	Kenosha	A	Min	125	421	114	20	3	20	200	60	100	64	4	105	7	0	10	4	1	.80	5	.271	.369	.475
1992	Orlando	AA	Min	126	420	107	13	2	22	190	63	74	48	0	122	1	2	5	0	0	.00	17	.255	.329	.452
1993	Portland	AAA	Min	83	288	81	24	2	10	139	43	47	29	0	69	0	0	6	0	1	.00	10	.281	.341	.483
1994	Salt Lake	AAA	Min	35	115	34	7	0	3	50	18	17	12	0	28	2	0	3	0	3	.00	4	.296	.364	.435
	Nashville	AA	Min	82	299	68	14	3	10	118	43	40	31	1	77	3	3	0	1	0	1.00	11	.227	.306	.395
1995	Memphis	AA	SD	45	122	38	9	1	6	67	19	18	22	1	33	1	0	0	1	0	1.00	3	.311	.421	.549
	Las Vegas	AAA	SD	44	148	44	10	0	4	66	17	19	9	2	31	0	1	2	0	1	.00	4	.297	.333	.446
1996	Las Vegas	AAA	SD	80	226	57	15	2	4	88	16	33	23	1	53	1	0	2	2	1	.67	7	.252	.321	.389
7 Min. YEARS				682	2260	617	121	16	101	1073	337	415	276	14	574	16	6	30	12	8	.60	64	.273	.352	.475

Jay Ryan

Pitches: Right **Bats:** Both **Pos:** P **Ht:** 6'2" **Wt:** 180 **Born:** 1/23/76 **Age:** 21

HOW MUCH HE PITCHED										WHAT HE GAVE UP												THE RESULTS					
Year	Team	Lg	Org	G	GS	CG	GF	IP	BFP	H	R	ER	HR	SH	SF	HB	TBB	IBB	SO	WP	Bk	W	L	Pct.	ShO	Sv	ERA
1994	Cubs	R	ChN	7	7	0	0	33	143	32	19	15	2	1	1	2	4	0	30	5	0	1	2	.333	0	0	4.09
	Huntington	R+	ChN	4	4	1	0	26	93	7	1	1	0	1	0	1	8	0	32	0	0	2	0	1.000	1	0	0.35
	Orlando	AA	ChN	2	2	0	0	11	45	6	3	3	1	0	0	1	6	0	12	0	0	2	0	1.000	0	0	2.45
1995	Daytona	A+	ChN	26	26	0	0	134.2	579	128	61	52	10	3	2	9	54	0	98	13	1	11	5	.688	0	0	3.48
1996	Orlando	AA	ChN	7	7	0	0	34.2	169	39	30	22	6	1	0	4	24	0	25	2	0	2	5	.286	0	0	5.71
	Daytona	A+	ChN	17	10	0	3	67	298	72	42	39	8	5	2	4	33	0	49	1	0	1	8	.111	0	1	5.24
3 Min. YEARS				63	56	1	3	306.1	1327	284	156	132	27	11	5	21	129	0	246	21	1	19	20	.487	1	1	3.88

Kevin Ryan

Pitches: Right **Bats:** Right **Pos:** P **Ht:** 6'1" **Wt:** 187 **Born:** 9/23/70 **Age:** 26

HOW MUCH HE PITCHED										WHAT HE GAVE UP												THE RESULTS					
Year	Team	Lg	Org	G	GS	CG	GF	IP	BFP	H	R	ER	HR	SH	SF	HB	TBB	IBB	SO	WP	Bk	W	L	Pct.	ShO	Sv	ERA
1991	Bluefield	R+	Bal	14	11	0	3	76.1	315	71	26	22	3	0	3	1	24	0	71	6	4	5	4	.556	0	1	2.59

Year	Team	Lg	Org	HOW MUCH HE PITCHED						WHAT HE GAVE UP												THE RESULTS					
Year	Team	Lg	Org	G	GS	CG	GF	IP	BFP	H	R	ER	HR	SH	SF	HB	TBB	IBB	SO	WP	Bk	W	L	Pct.	ShO	Sv	ERA
	Kane County	A	Bal	1	1	0	0	9.1	35	6	1	1	0	1	0	1	2	0	8	0	0	0	0	.000	0	0	0.96
1992	Frederick	A+	Bal	27	25	2	1	148.2	666	175	88	78	11	3	4	2	63	1	103	16	3	7	12	.368	0	0	4.72
1993	Bowie	AA	Bal	16	15	2	1	88.1	401	106	67	52	8	2	4	1	34	0	40	5	2	3	10	.231	0	0	5.30
	Frederick	A+	Bal	15	2	0	4	33.1	136	28	11	9	3	1	0	2	9	0	23	3	0	0	3	.000	0	1	2.43
1994	Bowie	AA	Bal	41	4	0	14	81	351	86	40	33	8	7	2	2	30	2	37	9	0	8	2	.800	0	1	3.67
1995	Rochester	AAA	Bal	6	2	0	0	17.1	83	27	20	18	3	0	1	1	4	0	7	1	0	0	3	.000	0	0	9.35
	Bowie	AA	Bal	45	3	0	14	80.1	350	94	51	42	8	2	3	2	19	2	38	2	0	4	6	.400	0	5	4.71
1996	Orioles	R	Bal	2	0	0	0	3.1	12	2	1	0	0	0	0	0	0	0	2	0	0	1	0	1.000	0	0	0.00
	Bowie	AA	Bal	2	1	0	0	3	17	7	4	3	0	0	0	1	1	0	2	0	0	0	1	.000	0	0	9.00
6 Min. YEARS				169	64	4	37	541	2366	602	309	258	44	16	17	13	186	5	331	42	9	28	41	.406	0	8	4.29

Matt Ryan

Pitches: Right **Bats:** Right **Pos:** P **Ht:** 6'5" **Wt:** 190 **Born:** 3/20/72 **Age:** 25

Year	Team	Lg	Org	HOW MUCH HE PITCHED						WHAT HE GAVE UP												THE RESULTS					
Year	Team	Lg	Org	G	GS	CG	GF	IP	BFP	H	R	ER	HR	SH	SF	HB	TBB	IBB	SO	WP	Bk	W	L	Pct.	ShO	Sv	ERA
1993	Pirates	R	Pit	9	0	0	5	19.1	81	17	8	5	0	1	0	1	9	0	20	0	0	1	1	.500	0	2	2.33
	Welland	A-	Pit	16	0	0	12	17.1	84	11	10	3	0	0	1	1	12	1	25	5	0	0	1	.000	0	5	1.56
1994	Augusta	A	Pit	34	0	0	31	41	174	33	14	6	0	1	0	4	7	1	49	0	0	2	1	.667	0	13	1.32
	Salem	A+	Pit	25	0	0	16	28.1	120	27	12	6	0	3	0	2	8	1	13	2	0	2	2	.500	0	7	1.91
1995	Calgary	AAA	Pit	5	0	0	4	4.2	20	5	1	1	0	0	0	1	1	1	2	0	0	0	0	.000	0	1	1.93
	Carolina	AA	Pit	49	0	0	42	50.2	208	38	11	9	0	4	0	3	20	3	25	3	0	2	1	.667	0	27	1.60
1996	Calgary	AAA	Pit	51	0	0	44	52.2	259	70	39	31	4	3	1	6	28	8	35	6	0	2	6	.250	0	20	5.30
4 Min. YEARS				189	0	0	154	214	946	201	95	61	4	12	2	18	85	15	169	16	0	9	12	.429	0	75	2.57

Kevin Rychel

Pitches: Right **Bats:** Right **Pos:** P **Ht:** 5'9" **Wt:** 176 **Born:** 9/24/71 **Age:** 25

Year	Team	Lg	Org	HOW MUCH HE PITCHED						WHAT HE GAVE UP												THE RESULTS					
Year	Team	Lg	Org	G	GS	CG	GF	IP	BFP	H	R	ER	HR	SH	SF	HB	TBB	IBB	SO	WP	Bk	W	L	Pct.	ShO	Sv	ERA
1989	Pirates	R	Pit	13	13	0	0	67	296	52	40	23	0	3	2	9	31	0	79	6	4	1	6	.143	0	0	3.09
1990	Augusta	A	Pit	27	23	0	0	129	615	127	79	59	3	5	4	8	87	0	105	26	6	10	4	.714	0	0	4.12
1991	Salem	A+	Pit	11	11	0	0	49.1	230	48	44	33	7	1	4	3	27	0	34	10	3	1	7	.125	0	0	6.02
	Augusta	A	Pit	8	6	1	1	32.1	151	30	24	20	1	0	2	7	24	0	26	11	0	1	3	.250	1	0	5.57
1992	Augusta	A	Pit	13	0	0	8	16	74	12	12	8	0	2	0	0	12	1	16	0	0	1	3	.250	0	2	4.50
	Salem	A+	Pit	37	0	0	25	39.1	182	37	22	17	4	3	2	4	27	3	35	9	0	2	3	.400	0	7	3.89
1993	Salem	A+	Pit	53	2	0	11	73	333	68	41	32	3	1	2	10	44	2	86	27	0	5	4	.556	0	0	3.95
1994	Carolina	AA	Pit	36	3	0	11	74.2	331	69	45	39	5	2	3	8	42	0	52	12	0	5	3	.625	0	1	4.70
1995	Calgary	AAA	Pit	10	0	0	3	8.2	45	14	11	10	3	0	0	0	6	0	4	1	0	0	1	.000	0	0	10.38
	Carolina	AA	Pit	50	0	0	17	60	255	49	32	29	4	1	1	6	30	4	64	9	0	3	3	.500	0	1	4.35
1996	Calgary	AAA	Pit	11	0	0	1	11	56	15	11	10	2	0	0	1	8	1	5	2	0	2	0	1.000	0	0	8.18
	Carolina	AA	Pit	26	0	0	8	36.1	156	32	21	18	2	1	3	6	11	3	21	7	0	1	1	.500	0	1	4.46
8 Min. YEARS				295	58	1	85	596.2	2724	553	382	298	34	19	23	62	349	14	527	120	13	32	38	.457	1	12	4.49

Aldren Sadler

Pitches: Right **Bats:** Right **Pos:** P **Ht:** 6'6" **Wt:** 180 **Born:** 2/10/72 **Age:** 25

Year	Team	Lg	Org	HOW MUCH HE PITCHED						WHAT HE GAVE UP												THE RESULTS					
Year	Team	Lg	Org	G	GS	CG	GF	IP	BFP	H	R	ER	HR	SH	SF	HB	TBB	IBB	SO	WP	Bk	W	L	Pct.	ShO	Sv	ERA
1992	Brewers	R	Mil	7	5	0	0	30	127	32	12	7	0	1	0	0	6	0	33	3	1	2	2	.500	0	0	2.10
	Helena	R+	Mil	4	3	0	1	23	96	19	10	7	1	0	2	3	7	0	19	3	0	1	1	.500	0	0	2.74
1993	Beloit	A	Mil	20	20	1	0	116	510	126	67	53	9	5	6	9	47	1	87	10	0	6	6	.500	0	0	4.11
1994	Beloit	A	Mil	16	16	5	0	99	428	96	48	39	9	3	3	3	51	1	79	13	0	7	4	.636	1	0	3.55
1995	Stockton	A+	Mil	37	14	1	10	114	501	113	62	56	9	3	2	8	59	0	82	6	2	4	9	.308	1	2	4.42
1996	Stockton	A+	Mil	18	0	0	17	20	79	12	7	6	3	1	0	0	7	0	19	1	0	1	2	.333	0	7	2.70
	El Paso	AA	Mil	26	0	0	10	42	207	39	28	22	3	2	1	3	40	2	31	4	0	3	3	.500	0	1	4.71
5 Min. YEARS				128	58	7	38	444	1948	437	234	190	34	15	14	26	217	4	350	40	3	24	27	.471	2	10	3.85

Donnie Sadler

Bats: Right **Throws:** Right **Pos:** SS **Ht:** 5'7" **Wt:** 160 **Born:** 6/17/75 **Age:** 22

Year	Team	Lg	Org	BATTING														BASERUNNING				PERCENTAGES		
Year	Team	Lg	Org	G	AB	H	2B	3B	HR	TB	R	RBI	TBB	IBB	SO	HBP	SH	SF	SB	CS	SB%	GDP	Avg	OBP	SLG
1994	Red Sox	R	Bos	53	206	56	8	6	1	79	52	16	23	0	27	3	1	3	32	8	.80	1	.272	.349	.383
1995	Michigan	A	Bos	118	438	124	25	8	9	192	103	55	79	0	85	6	3	3	41	13	.76	5	.283	.397	.438
1996	Trenton	AA	Bos	115	454	121	20	8	6	175	68	46	38	3	75	6	6	3	34	8	.81	6	.267	.329	.385
3 Min. YEARS				286	1098	301	53	22	16	446	223	117	140	3	187	15	10	9	107	29	.79	12	.274	.361	.406

Olmedo Saenz

Bats: Right **Throws:** Right **Pos:** 3B **Ht:** 6' 0" **Wt:** 185 **Born:** 10/8/70 **Age:** 26

Year	Team	Lg	Org	BATTING														BASERUNNING				PERCENTAGES		
Year	Team	Lg	Org	G	AB	H	2B	3B	HR	TB	R	RBI	TBB	IBB	SO	HBP	SH	SF	SB	CS	SB%	GDP	Avg	OBP	SLG
1991	Sarasota	A+	ChA	5	19	2	0	1	0	4	1	2	2	0	0	0	0	0	0	1	.00	1	.105	.190	.211
	South Bend	A	ChA	56	192	47	10	1	2	65	23	22	21	0	48	5	1	2	5	3	.63	3	.245	.332	.339
1992	South Bend	A	ChA	132	493	121	26	4	7	176	66	59	36	4	52	11	2	3	16	13	.55	16	.245	.309	.357
1993	South Bend	A	ChA	13	50	18	4	1	0	24	3	7	7	0	7	0	0	0	1	1	.50	1	.360	.439	.480

BATTING																	BASERUNNING				PERCENTAGES		
Year Team	Lg Org	G	AB	H	2B	3B	HR	TB	R	RBI	TBB	IBB	SO	HBP	SH	SF	SB	CS	SB%	GDP	Avg	OBP	SLG
Sarasota	A+ ChA	33	121	31	9	4	0	48	13	27	9	0	18	2	1	1	3	1	.75	1	.256	.316	.397
Birmingham	AA ChA	49	173	60	17	2	6	99	30	29	20	2	21	5	0	1	2	1	.67	7	.347	.427	.572
1994 Nashville	AAA ChA	107	383	100	27	2	12	167	48	59	30	0	57	9	2	5	3	2	.60	5	.261	.326	.436
1995 Nashville	AAA ChA	111	415	126	26	1	13	193	60	74	45	1	60	12	3	3	0	2	.00	11	.304	.385	.465
1996 Nashville	AAA ChA	134	476	124	29	1	18	209	86	63	53	1	80	13	2	1	4	2	.67	5	.261	.350	.439
1994 Chicago	AL	5	14	2	0	1	0	4	2	0	0	0	5	0	1	0	0	0	.00	1	.143	.143	.286
6 Min. YEARS		640	2322	629	148	17	58	985	330	342	223	8	343	57	11	16	34	26	.57	50	.271	.347	.424

Jon Saffer

Bats: Left **Throws:** Right **Pos:** OF **Ht:** 6'2" **Wt:** 200 **Born:** 7/6/73 **Age:** 23

BATTING																	BASERUNNING				PERCENTAGES		
Year Team	Lg Org	G	AB	H	2B	3B	HR	TB	R	RBI	TBB	IBB	SO	HBP	SH	SF	SB	CS	SB%	GDP	Avg	OBP	SLG
1992 Expos	R Mon	36	139	38	2	0	0	40	18	11	11	0	23	1	2	1	7	5	.58	2	.273	.329	.288
1993 W. Palm Bch	A+ Mon	7	24	5	0	0	0	5	3	2	2	0	5	1	1	0	1	3	.25	0	.208	.296	.208
Jamestown	A- Mon	61	225	58	17	5	0	85	31	18	31	1	46	2	3	1	11	5	.69	4	.258	.351	.378
1994 Vermont	A- Mon	70	263	83	18	5	3	120	44	43	33	1	47	1	1	1	14	3	.82	9	.316	.393	.456
1995 W. Palm Bch	A+ Mon	92	324	103	10	6	4	137	60	35	53	1	49	2	4	1	18	9	.67	7	.318	.416	.423
Harrisburg	AA Mon	20	76	18	4	0	0	22	9	4	6	0	14	0	0	0	2	1	.67	2	.237	.293	.289
1996 Harrisburg	AA Mon	134	487	146	26	4	10	210	96	52	78	1	77	6	5	3	8	16	.33	8	.300	.401	.431
5 Min. YEARS		420	1538	451	77	20	17	619	261	165	214	4	261	13	16	7	61	42	.59	32	.293	.383	.402

Marc Sagmoen

Bats: Left **Throws:** Left **Pos:** OF **Ht:** 5'11" **Wt:** 180 **Born:** 4/6/71 **Age:** 26

BATTING																	BASERUNNING				PERCENTAGES		
Year Team	Lg Org	G	AB	H	2B	3B	HR	TB	R	RBI	TBB	IBB	SO	HBP	SH	SF	SB	CS	SB%	GDP	Avg	OBP	SLG
1993 Erie	A- Tex	6	23	7	1	1	0	10	6	2	3	0	7	1	0	1	0	0	.00	0	.304	.393	.435
Charlstn-SC	A Tex	63	234	69	13	4	6	108	44	34	23	0	39	3	3	3	16	4	.80	2	.295	.361	.462
1994 Charlotte	A+ Tex	122	475	139	25	10	3	193	74	47	37	2	56	3	1	3	15	10	.60	15	.293	.346	.406
1995 Okla. City	AAA Tex	56	188	42	11	3	3	68	20	25	16	0	31	2	1	4	5	2	.71	2	.223	.286	.362
Tulsa	AA Tex	63	242	56	8	5	6	92	36	22	23	0	23	4	1	2	5	4	.56	2	.231	.306	.380
1996 Tulsa	AA Tex	96	387	109	21	6	10	172	58	62	33	4	58	2	0	7	5	8	.38	7	.282	.336	.444
Okla. City	AAA Tex	32	116	34	6	0	5	55	16	16	4	0	20	1	0	1	1	0	1.00	0	.293	.320	.474
4 Min. YEARS		438	1665	456	85	29	33	698	254	208	139	6	234	16	6	21	47	28	.63	28	.274	.332	.419

Mike Saipe

Pitches: Right **Bats:** Right **Pos:** P **Ht:** 6'1" **Wt:** 190 **Born:** 9/10/73 **Age:** 23

HOW MUCH HE PITCHED								WHAT HE GAVE UP												THE RESULTS					
Year Team	Lg Org	G	GS	CG	GF	IP	BFP	H	R	ER	HR	SH	SF	HB	TBB	IBB	SO	WP	Bk	W	L	Pct.	ShO	Sv	ERA
1994 Bend	A- Col	16	16	0	0	84.1	363	73	52	39	7	3	4	7	34	0	74	6	2	3	7	.300	0	0	4.16
1995 Salem	A+ Col	21	9	0	7	85.1	347	68	35	33	7	1	1	2	32	4	90	9	1	4	5	.444	0	3	3.48
1996 New Haven	AA Col	32	19	1	5	138	562	114	53	47	12	4	3	4	42	6	126	4	4	10	7	.588	1	3	3.07
3 Min. YEARS		69	44	1	12	307.2	1272	255	140	119	26	8	8	13	108	10	290	19	7	17	19	.472	1	6	3.48

Luis Salazar

Pitches: Right **Bats:** Right **Pos:** P **Ht:** 5'11" **Wt:** 170 **Born:** 7/7/70 **Age:** 26

HOW MUCH HE PITCHED								WHAT HE GAVE UP												THE RESULTS					
Year Team	Lg Org	G	GS	CG	GF	IP	BFP	H	R	ER	HR	SH	SF	HB	TBB	IBB	SO	WP	Bk	W	L	Pct.	ShO	Sv	ERA
1990 Bristol	R+ Det	7	0	0	4	9.1	43	7	4	2	1	0	0	1	9	0	7	1	0	0	0	.000	0	1	1.93
1995 Stockton	A+ Mil	52	0	0	26	89.1	350	66	28	23	6	5	3	7	18	5	71	0	1	6	2	.750	0	10	2.32
1996 El Paso	AA Mil	3	0	0	2	5.1	32	14	8	7	2	1	0	2	1	0	2	0	0	1	0	1.000	0	0	11.81
Stockton	A+ Mil	44	0	0	27	56.2	227	46	23	22	9	2	5	2	16	1	34	3	0	3	2	.600	0	6	3.49
3 Min. YEARS		106	0	0	59	160.2	652	133	63	54	18	8	8	12	44	6	114	4	1	10	4	.714	0	17	3.02

Michael Salazar

Pitches: Left **Bats:** Left **Pos:** P **Ht:** 6'4" **Wt:** 200 **Born:** 4/16/71 **Age:** 26

HOW MUCH HE PITCHED								WHAT HE GAVE UP												THE RESULTS					
Year Team	Lg Org	G	GS	CG	GF	IP	BFP	H	R	ER	HR	SH	SF	HB	TBB	IBB	SO	WP	Bk	W	L	Pct.	ShO	Sv	ERA
1993 Niagara Fal	A- Det	15	15	0	0	82.1	354	80	36	29	1	3	4	2	24	0	68	4	3	3	4	.429	0	0	3.17
1994 Fayettevlle	A Det	35	11	0	9	105.2	441	97	47	36	6	1	3	4	36	1	103	4	2	3	5	.375	0	1	3.07
1995 Lakeland	A+ Det	42	3	0	18	87.1	371	86	37	31	4	4	1	6	21	1	52	2	1	7	3	.700	0	5	3.19
1996 Lakeland	A+ Det	19	1	0	4	36	143	31	16	10	1	1	1	1	6	1	24	0	0	1	1	.500	0	0	2.50
Jacksonvlle	AA Det	16	4	0	2	29.1	137	34	25	14	3	1	1	0	14	1	19	4	0	2	5	.286	0	0	4.30
Visalia	A+ Det	6	4	0	1	25	116	31	19	15	1	1	2	3	11	0	14	1	0	0	2	.000	0	0	5.40
4 Min. YEARS		133	38	0	34	365.2	1562	359	180	135	16	11	12	16	112	4	280	15	6	16	20	.444	0	6	3.32

Benj Sampson

Pitches: Left **Bats:** Left **Pos:** P **Ht:** 6'0" **Wt:** 185 **Born:** 4/27/75 **Age:** 22

HOW MUCH HE PITCHED								WHAT HE GAVE UP												THE RESULTS					
Year Team	Lg Org	G	GS	CG	GF	IP	BFP	H	R	ER	HR	SH	SF	HB	TBB	IBB	SO	WP	Bk	W	L	Pct.	ShO	Sv	ERA
1993 Elizabethtn	R+ Min	11	6	0	2	42.1	171	33	12	9	1	2	0	1	15	1	34	5	0	4	1	.800	0	1	1.91
1994 Fort Wayne	A Min	25	25	0	0	139.2	617	149	72	59	10	7	5	5	60	0	111	5	4	6	9	.400	0	0	3.80
1995 Fort Myers	A+ Min	28	27	3	1	160	664	148	71	62	11	8	8	4	52	0	95	5	0	11	9	.550	2	0	3.49

Year	Team	Lg	Org	HOW MUCH HE PITCHED G	GS	CG	GF	IP	BFP	WHAT HE GAVE UP H	R	ER	HR	SH	SF	HB	TBB	IBB	SO	WP	Bk	THE RESULTS W	L	Pct.	ShO	Sv	ERA
1996	Fort Myers	A+	Min	11	11	2	0	70	282	55	28	27	5	1	2	1	26	0	65	1	0	7	1	.875	0	0	3.47
	New Britain	AA	Min	16	16	1	0	75.1	353	108	54	48	8	0	2	2	25	0	51	2	1	5	7	.417	0	0	5.73
4 Min. YEARS				91	85	6	3	487.1	2087	493	237	205	35	18	17	13	178	1	356	18	5	33	27	.550	2	1	3.79

Scott Samuels

Bats: Left **Throws:** Right **Pos:** OF **Ht:** 5'11" **Wt:** 190 **Born:** 5/19/71 **Age:** 26

Year	Team	Lg	Org	BATTING G	AB	H	2B	3B	HR	TB	R	RBI	TBB	IBB	SO	HBP	SH	SF	BASERUNNING SB	CS	SB%	GDP	PERCENTAGES Avg	OBP	SLG
1992	Erie	A-	Fla	43	128	26	7	1	0	35	17	14	19	0	39	2	0	0	7	3	.70	2	.203	.315	.273
1993	High Desert	A+	Fla	76	219	65	10	4	6	101	43	40	45	0	55	1	0	1	12	4	.75	7	.297	.417	.461
1994	Brevard Cty	A+	Fla	89	281	65	11	0	3	85	35	25	46	1	70	4	1	1	11	5	.69	7	.231	.346	.302
1995	Orlando	AA	ChN	5	21	6	1	0	1	10	3	4	3	0	4	0	0	0	2	0	1.00	0	.286	.375	.476
	Daytona	A+	ChN	112	388	127	29	12	2	186	92	42	69	7	63	8	3	4	38	14	.73	8	.327	.435	.479
1996	Orlando	AA	ChN	106	342	89	19	5	2	124	62	33	62	2	81	0	3	1	21	10	.68	3	.260	.373	.363
5 Min. YEARS				431	1379	378	77	22	14	541	252	158	244	10	312	15	7	7	91	36	.72	27	.274	.387	.392

Victor Sanchez

Bats: Right **Throws:** Right **Pos:** 1B **Ht:** 5'11" **Wt:** 175 **Born:** 12/20/71 **Age:** 25

Year	Team	Lg	Org	BATTING G	AB	H	2B	3B	HR	TB	R	RBI	TBB	IBB	SO	HBP	SH	SF	BASERUNNING SB	CS	SB%	GDP	PERCENTAGES Avg	OBP	SLG
1994	Auburn	A-	Hou	58	219	63	15	0	3	87	33	35	13	1	40	4	0	1	0	1	.00	7	.288	.338	.397
1995	Quad City	A	Hou	13	34	8	0	0	0	8	3	1	6	0	10	0	0	0	1	0	1.00	2	.235	.350	.235
	Kissimmee	A+	Hou	78	272	73	11	0	7	105	34	38	23	1	69	8	1	4	6	3	.67	6	.268	.339	.386
1996	Jackson	AA	Hou	86	210	46	9	0	13	94	30	34	15	0	58	4	0	0	4	1	.80	7	.219	.284	.448
3 Min. YEARS				235	735	190	35	0	23	294	100	108	57	2	177	16	1	5	11	5	.69	22	.259	.323	.400

Yuri Sanchez

Bats: Left **Throws:** Right **Pos:** SS **Ht:** 6'1" **Wt:** 165 **Born:** 11/11/73 **Age:** 23

Year	Team	Lg	Org	BATTING G	AB	H	2B	3B	HR	TB	R	RBI	TBB	IBB	SO	HBP	SH	SF	BASERUNNING SB	CS	SB%	GDP	PERCENTAGES Avg	OBP	SLG
1992	Bristol	R+	Det	36	102	18	2	2	0	24	11	5	21	0	41	0	1	0	5	3	.63	1	.176	.317	.235
1993	Fayettevlle	A	Det	111	340	69	7	6	0	88	53	30	73	0	125	2	7	3	20	9	.69	3	.203	.344	.259
1994	Lakeland	A+	Det	89	254	59	5	5	1	77	41	19	39	0	75	4	5	1	21	8	.72	6	.232	.342	.303
	Trenton	AA	Det	28	78	16	2	2	0	22	7	2	11	0	25	0	2	0	4	1	.80	0	.205	.303	.282
1995	Jacksonvlle	AA	Det	121	342	73	8	7	6	113	52	26	38	0	116	1	15	0	15	6	.71	3	.213	.294	.330
1996	Visalia	A+	Det	18	59	14	1	0	3	24	9	6	7	0	19	0	3	0	1	1	.50	0	.237	.318	.407
	Winston-Sal	A+	Cin	100	353	76	15	3	5	112	48	39	43	0	103	0	10	3	9	6	.60	10	.215	.298	.317
	Indianapols	AAA	Cin	1	4	0	0	0	0	0	0	0	0	0	2	0	0	0	0	0	.00	0	.000	.000	.000
5 Min. YEARS				504	1532	325	40	25	15	460	221	127	232	0	506	7	43	7	75	34	.69	23	.212	.317	.300

Anthony Sanders

Bats: Right **Throws:** Right **Pos:** OF **Ht:** 6'2" **Wt:** 180 **Born:** 3/2/74 **Age:** 23

Year	Team	Lg	Org	BATTING G	AB	H	2B	3B	HR	TB	R	RBI	TBB	IBB	SO	HBP	SH	SF	BASERUNNING SB	CS	SB%	GDP	PERCENTAGES Avg	OBP	SLG
1993	Medicne Hat	R+	Tor	63	225	59	9	3	4	86	44	33	20	0	49	2	3	1	6	5	.55	2	.262	.327	.382
1994	St. Cathrns	A-	Tor	74	258	66	17	3	6	107	36	45	27	0	53	1	4	2	8	7	.53	2	.256	.326	.415
1995	Hagerstown	A	Tor	133	512	119	28	1	8	173	72	48	52	0	103	5	9	5	26	14	.65	8	.232	.307	.338
1996	Dunedin	A+	Tor	102	417	108	25	0	17	184	75	50	34	0	93	6	0	0	16	12	.57	5	.259	.324	.441
	Knoxville	AA	Tor	38	133	36	8	0	1	47	16	18	7	0	33	2	1	0	1	3	.25	0	.271	.317	.353
4 Min. YEARS				410	1545	388	87	7	36	597	243	194	140	0	331	16	17	8	57	41	.58	17	.251	.318	.386

Tracy Sanders

Bats: Left **Throws:** Right **Pos:** DH **Ht:** 6'0" **Wt:** 206 **Born:** 7/26/69 **Age:** 27

Year	Team	Lg	Org	BATTING G	AB	H	2B	3B	HR	TB	R	RBI	TBB	IBB	SO	HBP	SH	SF	BASERUNNING SB	CS	SB%	GDP	PERCENTAGES Avg	OBP	SLG
1990	Burlington	R+	Cle	51	178	50	12	1	10	94	38	34	33	0	36	2	0	1	10	3	.77	2	.281	.397	.528
	Kinston	A+	Cle	10	32	14	3	3	0	23	6	9	7	0	6	0	0	0	1	1	.50	0	.438	.538	.719
1991	Kinston	A+	Cle	118	421	112	20	8	18	202	80	63	83	4	95	6	2	2	8	5	.62	9	.266	.393	.480
1992	Canton-Akrn	AA	Cle	114	381	92	11	3	21	172	66	87	77	3	113	3	4	3	3	6	.33	8	.241	.371	.451
1993	Canton-Akrn	AA	Cle	42	136	29	6	2	5	54	20	20	31	1	30	1	0	1	4	1	.80	1	.213	.361	.397
	Wichita	AA	SD	77	266	86	13	4	13	146	44	47	34	1	67	2	0	1	6	5	.55	2	.323	.403	.549
1994	Binghamton	AA	NYN	101	275	66	20	4	8	118	44	37	60	1	88	3	0	5	8	6	.57	1	.240	.376	.429
1995	Binghamton	AA	NYN	10	32	9	3	0	2	18	6	8	5	0	11	0	0	0	1	0	1.00	0	.281	.378	.563
	Norfolk	AAA	NYN	64	110	25	6	0	4	43	21	14	34	0	34	4	0	0	3	1	.75	2	.227	.426	.391
1996	Tulsa	AA	Tex	52	168	39	10	0	7	70	31	20	33	2	49	2	0	0	2	1	.67	3	.232	.365	.417
	Tri-City	IND	—	35	123	30	6	0	9	63	25	24	29	1	38	2	0	0	5	3	.63	0	.244	.396	.512
7 Min. YEARS				674	2122	552	110	25	97	1003	381	363	426	13	567	25	6	13	51	32	.61	28	.260	.388	.473

Chance Sanford

Bats: Left **Throws:** Right **Pos:** 2B **Ht:** 5'10" **Wt:** 165 **Born:** 6/2/72 **Age:** 25

		BATTING															BASERUNNING				PERCENTAGES		
Year Team	Lg Org	G	AB	H	2B	3B	HR	TB	R	RBI	TBB	IBB	SO	HBP	SH	SF	SB	CS	SB%	GDP	Avg	OBP	SLG
1992 Welland	A- Pit	59	214	61	11	3	5	93	36	21	35	4	39	0	0	3	13	4	.76	2	.285	.381	.435
Augusta	A Pit	14	46	5	1	0	0	6	3	2	3	0	10	1	0	0	0	2	.00	0	.109	.180	.130
1993 Salem	A+ Pit	115	428	109	21	5	10	170	54	37	33	0	80	1	3	2	11	10	.52	0	.255	.308	.397
1994 Salem	A+ Pit	127	474	130	32	6	19	231	81	78	56	0	95	2	1	4	12	6	.67	7	.274	.351	.487
1995 Carolina	AA Pit	16	36	10	3	1	3	24	6	10	5	1	7	1	0	0	3	1	.75	0	.278	.381	.667
Pirates	R Pit	6	19	4	0	0	1	7	2	1	2	0	2	0	0	0	0	0	.00	0	.211	.286	.368
Lynchburg	A+ Pit	16	66	22	4	0	3	35	8	14	7	0	13	0	0	1	1	0	1.00	1	.333	.392	.530
1996 Carolina	AA Pit	131	470	115	16	13	4	169	62	56	72	2	108	0	2	7	11	11	.50	9	.245	.341	.360
5 Min. YEARS		484	1753	456	88	28	45	735	252	219	213	7	354	5	6	17	51	34	.60	19	.260	.339	.419

Mo Sanford

Pitches: Right **Bats:** Right **Pos:** P **Ht:** 6' 6" **Wt:** 233 **Born:** 12/24/66 **Age:** 30

		HOW MUCH HE PITCHED						WHAT HE GAVE UP												THE RESULTS					
Year Team	Lg Org	G	GS	CG	GF	IP	BFP	H	R	ER	HR	SH	SF	HB	TBB	IBB	SO	WP	Bk	W	L	Pct.	ShO	Sv	ERA
1988 Reds	R Cin	14	11	0	1	53	217	34	24	19	6	0	1	0	25	1	64	3	4	3	4	.429	0	1	3.23
1989 Greensboro	A Cin	25	25	3	0	153.2	629	112	52	48	8	4	2	2	64	0	160	6	3	12	6	.667	1	0	2.81
1990 Cedar Rapds	A Cin	25	25	2	0	157.2	628	112	50	48	15	3	2	4	55	1	180	8	1	13	4	.765	1	0	2.74
1991 Chattanooga	AA Cin	16	16	1	0	95.1	395	69	37	29	7	4	3	1	55	2	124	1	0	7	4	.636	1	0	2.74
Nashville	AAA Cin	5	5	2	0	33.2	140	19	7	6	0	0	0	1	22	0	38	3	0	3	0	1.000	2	0	1.60
1992 Chattanooga	AA Cin	4	4	1	0	26.2	101	13	5	4	2	0	0	2	6	0	28	1	0	4	0	1.000	1	0	1.35
Nashville	AAA Cin	25	25	0	0	122	549	128	81	77	22	6	5	3	65	1	129	2	0	8	8	.500	0	0	5.68
1993 Colo. Sprng	AAA Col	20	17	0	1	105	456	103	64	61	8	3	6	4	57	2	104	7	1	3	6	.333	0	0	5.23
1994 Salt Lake	AAA Min	37	11	0	9	125.2	553	121	74	68	21	1	9	8	52	0	141	5	1	7	5	.583	0	4	4.87
1995 Salt Lake	AAA Min	4	0	0	0	5.2	27	6	4	4	1	0	0	0	4	0	8	0	0	0	1	.000	0	0	6.35
1996 Okla. City	AAA Tex	30	24	0	0	143	627	155	77	63	18	3	4	3	49	2	130	2	2	6	10	.375	0	0	3.97
1991 Cincinnati	NL	5	5	0	0	28	118	19	14	12	3	0	0	1	15	1	31	4	0	1	2	.333	0	0	3.86
1993 Colorado	NL	11	6	0	1	35.2	166	37	25	21	4	4	2	0	27	0	36	2	1	1	2	.333	0	0	5.30
1995 Minnesota	AL	11	0	0	6	18.2	89	16	11	11	7	0	0	2	16	0	17	1	0	0	0	.000	0	0	5.30
9 Min. YEARS		205	163	9	11	1021.1	4322	872	475	427	108	24	32	28	454	9	1106	38	12	66	48	.579	6	5	3.76
3 Maj. YEARS		27	11	0	7	82.1	373	72	50	44	14	4	2	3	58	1	84	7	1	2	4	.333	0	0	4.81

Julio Santana

Pitches: Right **Bats:** Right **Pos:** P **Ht:** 6'0" **Wt:** 175 **Born:** 1/20/73 **Age:** 24

		HOW MUCH HE PITCHED						WHAT HE GAVE UP												THE RESULTS					
Year Team	Lg Org	G	GS	CG	GF	IP	BFP	H	R	ER	HR	SH	SF	HB	TBB	IBB	SO	WP	Bk	W	L	Pct.	ShO	Sv	ERA
1993 Rangers	R Tex	26	0	0	12	39	153	31	9	6	0	0	0	1	7	0	50	1	0	4	1	.800	0	7	1.38
1994 Charlstn-SC	A Tex	16	16	0	0	91.1	383	65	38	25	3	0	4	7	44	0	103	7	1	6	7	.462	0	0	2.46
Tulsa	AA Tex	11	11	2	0	71.1	290	50	26	23	1	1	2	2	41	0	45	2	0	7	2	.778	0	0	2.90
1995 Okla. City	AAA Tex	2	2	0	0	3	25	9	14	13	3	0	0	0	7	0	6	1	1	0	2	.000	0	0	39.00
Charlotte	A+ Tex	5	5	1	0	31.1	136	32	16	13	1	1	1	0	16	0	27	7	2	0	3	.000	0	0	3.73
Tulsa	AA Tex	22	22	4	0	137.1	599	132	70	63	12	3	5	0	75	2	104	16	4	6	9	.400	0	0	4.13
1996 Okla. City	AAA Tex	29	29	4	0	185.2	787	171	102	83	12	5	9	5	66	1	113	12	1	11	12	.478	1	0	4.02
4 Min. YEARS		111	85	11	12	559	2373	490	275	226	32	10	21	15	256	3	448	46	9	34	36	.486	1	7	3.64

Ruben Santana

Bats: Right **Throws:** Right **Pos:** OF **Ht:** 6'2" **Wt:** 175 **Born:** 3/7/70 **Age:** 27

		BATTING															BASERUNNING				PERCENTAGES		
Year Team	Lg Org	G	AB	H	2B	3B	HR	TB	R	RBI	TBB	IBB	SO	HBP	SH	SF	SB	CS	SB%	GDP	Avg	OBP	SLG
1990 Peninsula	A+ Sea	26	80	17	1	0	0	18	3	5	1	0	22	1	0	0	6	1	.86	1	.213	.232	.225
Bellingham	A- Sea	47	155	39	3	2	4	58	22	13	18	2	39	6	0	1	10	9	.53	1	.252	.350	.374
1991 San Bernrdo	A+ Sea	108	394	119	16	4	3	152	55	43	26	4	74	6	9	5	34	12	.74	4	.302	.350	.386
Jacksonvlle	AA Sea	5	15	3	0	0	1	6	2	3	1	0	3	0	0	0	0	0	.00	0	.200	.250	.400
1992 Peninsula	A+ Sea	113	401	118	19	4	8	169	54	61	21	0	54	9	6	1	17	16	.52	8	.294	.343	.421
1993 Jacksonvlle	AA Sea	128	499	150	21	2	21	238	79	84	38	7	101	9	3	5	13	8	.62	2	.301	.358	.477
1994 Jacksonvlle	AA Sea	131	501	148	25	4	7	202	62	68	28	1	62	11	3	4	10	7	.59	9	.295	.344	.403
1995 Chattanooga	AA Cin	142	556	163	23	10	11	239	89	79	50	5	77	8	6	5	2	5	.29	17	.293	.357	.430
1996 Chattanooga	AA Cin	98	343	106	21	2	8	155	47	56	26	1	39	5	0	4	5	3	.63	7	.309	.362	.452
Indianapolis	AAA Cin	6	17	2	1	0	0	3	4	2	3	0	3	0	0	0	0	0	.00	1	.118	.250	.176
7 Min. YEARS		804	2961	865	130	28	63	1240	417	414	212	20	474	55	27	25	97	61	.61	50	.292	.348	.419

Henry Santos

Pitches: Left **Bats:** Left **Pos:** P **Ht:** 6'1" **Wt:** 175 **Born:** 1/17/73 **Age:** 24

		HOW MUCH HE PITCHED						WHAT HE GAVE UP												THE RESULTS					
Year Team	Lg Org	G	GS	CG	GF	IP	BFP	H	R	ER	HR	SH	SF	HB	TBB	IBB	SO	WP	Bk	W	L	Pct.	ShO	Sv	ERA
1992 Bristol	R+ Det	12	0	0	7	15	74	17	18	11	3	0	1	0	12	0	16	4	0	0	1	.000	0	0	6.60
1993 Niagara Fal	A- Det	7	7	0	0	42.1	172	29	15	11	3	1	0	2	17	0	50	0	0	2	1	.667	0	0	2.34
Fayettevlle	A Det	8	8	0	0	44	199	43	25	23	3	1	1	3	30	0	29	6	1	3	2	.600	0	0	4.70
1994 Fayettevlle	A Det	15	15	0	0	82.2	356	76	44	36	11	1	1	3	42	0	57	3	0	4	8	.333	0	0	3.92
Lakeland	A+ Det	11	11	0	0	52.2	276	88	52	45	11	6	1	4	34	0	35	5	2	1	6	.143	0	0	7.69
1995 Toledo	AAA Det	1	0	0	0	2.2	13	3	2	2	1	0	0	0	2	0	4	0	0	0	1	.000	0	0	6.75
Lakeland	A+ Det	36	10	0	7	100.1	447	114	61	48	4	5	4	6	42	0	84	10	0	5	7	.417	0	0	4.31

		HOW MUCH HE PITCHED						WHAT HE GAVE UP												THE RESULTS					
Year Team	Lg Org	G	GS	CG	GF	IP	BFP	H	R	ER	HR	SH	SF	HB	TBB	IBB	SO	WP	Bk	W	L	Pct.	ShO	Sv	ERA
1996 El Paso	AA Mil	35	12	0	11	100.1	468	126	76	68	11	3	7	2	50	0	74	13	1	7	7	.500	0	0	6.10
5 Min. YEARS		125	63	0	25	440	2005	496	293	244	47	17	15	20	229	0	349	41	4	22	33	.400	0	0	4.99

Steve Santucci

Bats: Right **Throws:** Right **Pos:** OF **Ht:** 6'0" **Wt:** 190 **Born:** 12/16/71 **Age:** 25

		BATTING															BASERUNNING				PERCENTAGES		
Year Team	Lg Org	G	AB	H	2B	3B	HR	TB	R	RBI	TBB	IBB	SO	HBP	SH	SF	SB	CS	SB%	GDP	Avg	OBP	SLG
1993 Glens Falls	A- StL	68	209	53	5	1	5	75	21	23	27	0	58	2	2	0	9	7	.56	6	.254	.345	.359
1994 Madison	A StL	37	95	16	2	0	0	18	12	7	9	0	26	0	3	1	2	1	.67	2	.168	.238	.189
New Jersey	A- StL	70	261	75	9	5	1	97	31	37	33	0	39	2	3	2	13	5	.72	9	.287	.369	.372
1995 St. Pete	A+ StL	106	292	69	5	3	4	92	25	25	27	0	60	0	2	3	9	3	.75	8	.236	.298	.315
1996 St. Pete	A+ StL	111	349	80	10	2	6	112	38	29	27	0	66	1	6	4	3	5	.38	8	.229	.283	.321
Arkansas	AA StL	11	20	3	0	0	0	3	2	0	0	0	5	0	0	0	0	1	.00	0	.150	.150	.150
4 Min. YEARS		403	1226	296	31	11	16	397	129	121	123	0	254	5	16	10	36	22	.62	33	.241	.311	.324

Scott Sauerbeck

Pitches: Left **Bats:** Right **Pos:** P **Ht:** 6'3" **Wt:** 190 **Born:** 11/9/71 **Age:** 25

		HOW MUCH HE PITCHED						WHAT HE GAVE UP												THE RESULTS					
Year Team	Lg Org	G	GS	CG	GF	IP	BFP	H	R	ER	HR	SH	SF	HB	TBB	IBB	SO	WP	Bk	W	L	Pct.	ShO	Sv	ERA
1994 Pittsfield	A- NYN	21	0	0	9	48.1	200	39	16	11	0	3	1	1	19	2	39	4	0	3	1	.750	0	1	2.05
1995 Columbia	A NYN	19	0	0	13	33	139	28	14	12	2	2	0	1	14	1	33	3	1	5	4	.556	0	2	3.27
St. Lucie	A+ NYN	39	1	0	17	59.2	255	54	24	18	2	2	2	1	28	2	58	5	3	5	5	.500	0	2	2.72
1996 St. Lucie	A+ NYN	17	16	2	0	99.1	406	101	37	25	1	3	0	1	27	0	62	4	1	6	6	.500	2	0	2.27
Binghamton	AA NYN	8	8	2	0	46.2	191	48	24	18	4	1	2	1	12	0	30	0	0	3	3	.500	0	0	3.47
3 Min. YEARS		104	25	4	39	287	1191	270	115	84	9	11	5	5	100	5	222	16	5	22	19	.537	2	5	2.63

Chris Saunders

Bats: Right **Throws:** Right **Pos:** 3B **Ht:** 6'2" **Wt:** 200 **Born:** 7/19/70 **Age:** 26

		BATTING															BASERUNNING				PERCENTAGES		
Year Team	Lg Org	G	AB	H	2B	3B	HR	TB	R	RBI	TBB	IBB	SO	HBP	SH	SF	SB	CS	SB%	GDP	Avg	OBP	SLG
1992 Pittsfield	A- NYN	72	254	64	11	2	2	85	34	32	34	0	50	1	1	5	5	2	.71	5	.252	.337	.335
1993 St. Lucie	A+ NYN	123	456	115	14	4	4	149	45	64	40	4	89	1	1	4	6	7	.46	10	.252	.311	.327
1994 Binghamton	AA NYN	132	499	134	29	0	10	193	68	70	43	0	96	4	2	7	6	6	.50	12	.269	.327	.387
1995 Norfolk	AAA NYN	16	56	13	3	1	3	27	9	7	9	0	15	0	0	0	1	1	.50	1	.232	.338	.482
Binghamton	AA NYN	122	441	114	22	5	8	170	58	66	45	1	98	5	5	7	3	6	.33	7	.259	.329	.385
1996 Binghamton	AA NYN	141	510	152	27	3	17	236	82	105	73	3	88	8	2	11	5	4	.56	11	.298	.387	.463
5 Min. YEARS		606	2216	592	106	15	44	860	296	344	244	8	436	19	11	34	26	26	.50	46	.267	.340	.388

Doug Saunders

Bats: Right **Throws:** Right **Pos:** 3B **Ht:** 6' 0" **Wt:** 172 **Born:** 12/13/69 **Age:** 27

		BATTING															BASERUNNING				PERCENTAGES		
Year Team	Lg Org	G	AB	H	2B	3B	HR	TB	R	RBI	TBB	IBB	SO	HBP	SH	SF	SB	CS	SB%	GDP	Avg	OBP	SLG
1988 Mets	R NYN	16	64	16	4	1	0	22	8	10	9	0	14	0	2	0	2	3	.40	0	.250	.342	.344
Little Fall	A- NYN	29	100	30	6	1	0	38	10	11	6	0	15	0	1	0	1	4	.20	2	.300	.340	.380
1989 Columbia	A NYN	115	377	99	18	4	4	137	53	38	35	2	78	3	4	3	5	5	.50	5	.263	.328	.363
1990 St. Lucie	A+ NYN	115	408	92	8	4	1	111	52	43	43	0	96	2	7	2	24	10	.71	7	.225	.301	.272
1991 St. Lucie	A+ NYN	70	230	54	9	2	2	73	19	18	25	0	43	4	5	0	5	6	.45	6	.235	.320	.317
1992 Binghamton	AA NYN	130	435	108	16	2	5	143	45	38	52	0	68	1	5	4	8	12	.40	9	.248	.327	.329
1993 Norfolk	AAA NYN	105	356	88	12	6	2	118	37	24	44	1	63	3	7	1	6	5	.55	13	.247	.334	.331
1994 Binghamton	AA NYN	96	338	96	19	4	8	147	48	45	43	2	63	0	6	4	3	4	.43	6	.284	.361	.435
1995 Edmonton	AAA Oak	5	16	3	2	1	0	7	2	4	0	0	2	0	0	0	0	0	.00	0	.188	.188	.438
Tacoma	AAA Sea	50	135	38	5	2	5	62	19	24	7	0	30	1	1	2	0	0	.00	3	.281	.317	.459
Port City	AA Sea	28	114	30	9	1	4	53	13	16	10	1	28	2	0	2	2	0	1.00	4	.263	.328	.465
1996 Tacoma	AAA Sea	40	131	33	6	0	3	48	16	13	19	0	22	0	3	0	1	0	1.00	1	.252	.347	.366
1993 New York	NL	28	67	14	2	0	0	16	8	0	3	0	4	0	3	0	0	0	.00	2	.209	.243	.239
9 Min. YEARS		799	2704	687	114	28	34	959	322	284	293	6	522	16	41	18	57	49	.54	56	.254	.329	.355

Tony Saunders

Pitches: Left **Bats:** Left **Pos:** P **Ht:** 6'1" **Wt:** 189 **Born:** 4/29/74 **Age:** 23

		HOW MUCH HE PITCHED						WHAT HE GAVE UP												THE RESULTS					
Year Team	Lg Org	G	GS	CG	GF	IP	BFP	H	R	ER	HR	SH	SF	HB	TBB	IBB	SO	WP	Bk	W	L	Pct.	ShO	Sv	ERA
1992 Marlins	R Fla	24	0	0	16	45.2	180	29	10	6	0	2	3	1	13	2	37	4	0	4	1	.800	0	7	1.18
1993 Kane County	A Fla	23	10	2	1	83.1	344	72	23	21	3	6	0	2	32	3	87	2	1	6	1	.857	0	1	2.27
1994 Brevard Cty	A+ Fla	10	10	1	0	60	237	54	24	21	4	2	1	2	9	0	46	2	0	5	5	.500	0	0	3.15
1995 Brevard Cty	A+ Fla	13	13	0	0	71	275	60	29	24	6	1	4	7	15	0	54	3	0	6	5	.545	0	0	3.04
1996 Portland	AA Fla	26	26	2	0	167.2	669	121	51	49	10	8	4	0	62	3	156	8	1	13	4	.765	0	0	2.63
5 Min. YEARS		96	59	5	17	427.2	1705	336	137	121	23	19	12	12	131	8	380	19	2	34	16	.680	0	8	2.55

Warren Sawkiw

Bats: Both **Throws:** Right **Pos:** 2B **Ht:** 5'11" **Wt:** 180 **Born:** 1/19/68 **Age:** 29

		BATTING															BASERUNNING				PERCENTAGES		
Year Team	Lg Org	G	AB	H	2B	3B	HR	TB	R	RBI	TBB	IBB	SO	HBP	SH	SF	SB	CS	SB%	GDP	Avg	OBP	SLG
1990 Niagara Fal	A- Det	7	20	8	1	1	0	11	7	4	15	2	3	0	0	0	2	0	1.00	0	.400	.657	.550
Fayettevlle	A Det	59	210	54	6	0	1	63	31	18	30	1	35	1	2	4	4	1	.80	6	.257	.347	.300
1991 Lakeland	A+ Det	112	420	114	20	7	2	154	58	42	42	2	87	3	3	3	2	9	.18	8	.271	.340	.367
1992 Lakeland	A+ Det	118	423	103	18	4	2	135	56	47	39	1	62	3	0	7	6	7	.46	13	.243	.307	.319
1993 Rochester	IND —	70	272	89	21	2	9	141	42	45	31	2	53	1	0	2	14	2	.88	6	.327	.395	.518
1994 Winnipeg	IND —	20	76	19	3	0	1	25	7	10	9	0	13	0	0	2	3	1	.75	0	.250	.322	.329
Thunder Bay	IND —	48	183	63	11	0	3	83	25	27	22	1	32	0	3	2	2	6	.25	2	.344	.411	.454
1995 Syracuse	AAA Tor	11	42	8	1	0	0	9	3	0	5	0	8	0	0	0	2	0	1.00	1	.190	.277	.214
Knoxville	AA Tor	44	121	30	4	1	1	39	11	11	13	0	36	0	3	1	2	2	.50	2	.248	.319	.322
1996 Grand Forks	IND —	33	138	48	5	3	9	86	26	39	15	1	19	0	0	2	3	4	.43	1	.348	.406	.623
Birmingham	AA ChA	20	56	13	2	0	0	15	7	5	11	1	17	1	0	0	2	3	.40	0	.232	.368	.268
7 Min. YEARS		542	1961	549	92	18	28	761	273	248	232	11	365	9	11	23	42	35	.55	39	.280	.355	.388

Jon Sbrocco

Bats: Left **Throws:** Right **Pos:** 2B **Ht:** 5'10" **Wt:** 165 **Born:** 1/5/71 **Age:** 26

		BATTING															BASERUNNING				PERCENTAGES		
Year Team	Lg Org	G	AB	H	2B	3B	HR	TB	R	RBI	TBB	IBB	SO	HBP	SH	SF	SB	CS	SB%	GDP	Avg	OBP	SLG
1993 Everett	A- SF	2	3	1	0	0	0	1	0	0	0	0	0	1	0	0	0	0	.00	0	.333	.500	.333
Clinton	A SF	56	179	48	6	2	0	58	28	17	29	0	31	4	5	0	8	6	.57	2	.268	.382	.324
1994 Clinton	A SF	64	214	53	8	0	0	61	48	22	42	1	27	6	7	1	6	3	.67	3	.248	.384	.285
1995 San Jose	A+ SF	120	425	128	14	5	2	158	66	46	55	3	43	10	17	1	12	10	.55	5	.301	.393	.372
1996 San Jose	A+ SF	95	358	111	12	5	2	139	76	48	67	1	36	8	8	3	29	11	.73	6	.310	.427	.388
Shreveport	AA SF	23	81	20	2	1	1	27	16	5	11	0	10	2	2	1	5	0	1.00	2	.247	.347	.333
4 Min. YEARS		360	1260	361	42	13	5	444	234	138	204	5	147	31	39	6	60	30	.67	18	.287	.397	.352

Will Scalzitti

Bats: Right **Throws:** Right **Pos:** DH **Ht:** 6'0" **Wt:** 190 **Born:** 8/29/72 **Age:** 24

		BATTING															BASERUNNING				PERCENTAGES		
Year Team	Lg Org	G	AB	H	2B	3B	HR	TB	R	RBI	TBB	IBB	SO	HBP	SH	SF	SB	CS	SB%	GDP	Avg	OBP	SLG
1992 Bend	A- Col	62	230	66	16	0	7	103	35	40	20	0	40	1	2	1	0	2	.00	9	.287	.345	.448
1993 Central Val	A+ Col	75	248	60	10	0	2	76	25	17	17	1	40	1	3	1	0	1	.00	6	.242	.292	.306
1994 Colo. Sprng	AAA Col	1	1	0	0	0	0	0	0	0	0	0	1	0	0	0	0	0	.00	0	.000	.000	.000
Central Val	A+ Col	81	297	75	13	0	9	115	27	37	16	0	56	4	2	1	0	3	.00	8	.253	.299	.387
New Haven	AA Col	10	30	7	0	0	1	10	2	6	0	0	4	0	0	0	0	0	.00	0	.233	.233	.333
1995 New Haven	AA Col	39	123	23	6	0	1	32	9	14	10	0	17	1	1	2	0	0	.00	0	.187	.250	.260
Salem	A+ Col	11	35	7	1	0	0	8	4	0	4	1	5	1	1	0	0	1	.00	1	.200	.300	.229
1996 New Haven	AA Col	7	26	6	2	0	0	8	1	1	0	0	3	0	1	0	0	0	.00	2	.231	.231	.308
Salem	A+ Col	81	270	53	14	0	6	85	24	23	16	2	33	1	0	0	0	2	.00	5	.196	.244	.315
5 Min. YEARS		367	1260	297	62	0	26	437	127	138	83	4	199	9	10	5	0	9	.00	31	.236	.287	.347

Curt Schmidt

Pitches: Right **Bats:** Right **Pos:** P **Ht:** 6' 5" **Wt:** 200 **Born:** 3/16/70 **Age:** 27

		HOW MUCH HE PITCHED						WHAT HE GAVE UP												THE RESULTS					
Year Team	Lg Org	G	GS	CG	GF	IP	BFP	H	R	ER	HR	SH	SF	HB	TBB	IBB	SO	WP	Bk	W	L	Pct.	ShO	Sv	ERA
1992 Jamestown	A- Mon	29	1	1	19	63.1	261	42	21	19	1	3	0	5	29	2	61	6	1	3	4	.429	1	2	2.70
W. Palm Bch	A+ Mon	3	0	0	2	5	18	3	0	0	0	0	0	0	1	0	3	0	0	0	0	.000	0	0	0.00
1993 Expos	R Mon	1	1	0	0	5	16	1	0	0	0	0	0	0	0	0	7	0	0	1	0	1.000	0	0	0.00
W. Palm Bch	A+ Mon	44	2	0	22	65.1	285	63	32	23	3	5	1	0	25	3	51	1	1	4	6	.400	0	5	3.17
1994 Harrisburg	AA Mon	53	0	0	26	71.2	291	51	19	15	4	6	4	0	29	1	75	4	0	6	2	.750	0	5	1.88
1995 Ottawa	AAA Mon	43	0	0	38	52.2	206	40	14	13	1	0	1	4	18	0	38	2	0	5	0	1.000	0	15	2.22
1996 Ottawa	AAA Mon	54	0	0	31	70.1	283	60	27	19	2	5	6	1	22	3	45	1	0	1	5	.167	0	13	2.43
1995 Montreal	NL	11	0	0	0	10.1	54	15	8	8	1	1	0	2	9	0	7	0	0	0	0	.000	0	0	6.97
5 Min. YEARS		227	4	1	138	333.1	1360	260	113	89	11	19	12	10	124	9	280	14	2	20	17	.541	1	40	2.40

Tom Schmidt

Bats: Right **Throws:** Right **Pos:** 3B **Ht:** 6'3" **Wt:** 200 **Born:** 2/12/73 **Age:** 24

		BATTING															BASERUNNING				PERCENTAGES		
Year Team	Lg Org	G	AB	H	2B	3B	HR	TB	R	RBI	TBB	IBB	SO	HBP	SH	SF	SB	CS	SB%	GDP	Avg	OBP	SLG
1992 Bend	A- Col	68	249	64	13	1	7	100	39	27	24	1	78	4	0	1	17	3	.85	5	.257	.331	.402
1993 Central Val	A+ Col	126	478	117	15	1	19	191	61	62	40	2	107	4	1	5	5	3	.63	15	.245	.306	.400
1994 Central Val	A+ Col	99	334	81	8	1	9	118	36	50	52	2	100	8	2	2	3	4	.43	3	.243	.356	.353
1995 New Haven	AA Col	115	423	92	25	3	6	141	55	49	24	2	99	5	1	5	2	1	.67	13	.217	.265	.333
1996 Jacksonvlle	AA Det	115	385	85	24	2	11	146	45	45	31	1	91	2	2	2	4	1	.80	12	.221	.281	.379
5 Min. YEARS		523	1869	439	85	8	52	696	236	233	171	8	475	23	6	15	31	12	.72	48	.235	.305	.372

Todd Schmitt

Pitches: Right **Bats:** Right **Pos:** P **Ht:** 6'2" **Wt:** 170 **Born:** 2/12/70 **Age:** 27

		HOW MUCH HE PITCHED						WHAT HE GAVE UP												THE RESULTS					
Year Team	Lg Org	G	GS	CG	GF	IP	BFP	H	R	ER	HR	SH	SF	HB	TBB	IBB	SO	WP	Bk	W	L	Pct.	ShO	Sv	ERA
1992 Spokane	A- SD	29	0	0	29	38	162	23	7	5	1	3	0	2	23	5	48	3	0	6	1	.857	0	15	1.18

Year	Team	Lg	Org	HOW MUCH HE PITCHED						WHAT HE GAVE UP												THE RESULTS					
				G	GS	CG	GF	IP	BFP	H	R	ER	HR	SH	SF	HB	TBB	IBB	SO	WP	Bk	W	L	Pct.	ShO	Sv	ERA
1993	Waterloo	A	SD	51	0	0	47	58.2	254	41	15	13	0	1	1	6	33	5	76	5	2	1	4	.200	0	25	1.99
1994	Rancho Cuca	A+	SD	53	0	0	50	50.2	215	43	15	11	2	5	1	2	24	1	45	2	1	2	4	.333	0	29	1.95
1995	Las Vegas	AAA	SD	12	0	0	8	12.2	61	16	11	11	0	0	1	2	9	0	6	2	0	0	2	.000	0	2	7.82
	Memphis	AA	SD	38	0	0	32	40.1	169	34	15	15	2	0	2	3	20	2	33	2	0	0	2	.000	0	20	3.35
1996	Rancho Cuca	A+	SD	7	0	0	7	6.2	33	6	6	5	1	1	1	4	3	0	8	1	1	0	1	.000	0	4	6.75
	Las Vegas	AAA	SD	4	0	0	1	4	22	2	2	2	1	0	1	1	6	0	6	0	1	0	0	.000	0	0	4.50
	Memphis	AA	SD	38	0	0	25	39.1	181	39	26	15	1	3	0	1	21	1	47	4	4	4	4	.500	0	11	3.43
5 Min. YEARS				232	0	0	199	250.1	1097	204	97	77	8	13	7	21	139	14	269	19	9	13	18	.419	0	106	2.77

Dan Schneider

Bats: Right **Throws:** Right **Pos:** C **Ht:** 6'2" **Wt:** 195 **Born:** 4/18/72 **Age:** 25

Year	Team	Lg	Org	BATTING															BASERUNNING				PERCENTAGES		
				G	AB	H	2B	3B	HR	TB	R	RBI	TBB	IBB	SO	HBP	SH	SF	SB	CS	SB%	GDP	Avg	OBP	SLG
1994	Everett	A-	SF	40	136	32	6	2	1	45	17	18	9	0	34	1	0	1	2	0	1.00	6	.235	.286	.331
1995	Burlington	A	SF	51	141	30	4	0	2	40	13	12	10	0	27	3	3	0	1	1	.50	6	.213	.279	.284
	San Jose	A+	SF	13	36	6	1	0	0	7	3	2	1	0	7	0	1	0	0	0	.00	1	.167	.189	.194
1996	Shreveport	AA	SF	7	21	5	1	0	2	12	3	6	0	0	11	2	0	0	0	0	.00	0	.238	.304	.571
3 Min. YEARS				111	334	73	12	2	5	104	36	38	20	0	79	6	4	1	3	1	.75	13	.219	.274	.311

Steve Schrenk

Pitches: Right **Bats:** Right **Pos:** P **Ht:** 6'3" **Wt:** 185 **Born:** 11/20/68 **Age:** 28

Year	Team	Lg	Org	HOW MUCH HE PITCHED						WHAT HE GAVE UP												THE RESULTS					
				G	GS	CG	GF	IP	BFP	H	R	ER	HR	SH	SF	HB	TBB	IBB	SO	WP	Bk	W	L	Pct.	ShO	Sv	ERA
1987	White Sox	R	ChA	8	6	1	0	28.1	115	23	10	3	0	3	0	2	12	0	19	2	1	1	2	.333	1	0	0.95
1988	South Bend	A	ChA	21	18	1	1	90	417	95	63	50	4	0	3	13	37	0	58	7	2	3	7	.300	0	0	5.00
1989	South Bend	A	ChA	16	16	1	0	79	353	71	44	38	6	2	0	8	44	1	49	9	0	5	2	.714	1	0	4.33
1990	South Bend	A	ChA	20	14	2	2	103.2	419	79	44	34	7	3	3	11	25	0	92	7	1	7	6	.538	1	0	2.95
1991	White Sox	R	ChA	11	7	0	2	37	144	30	20	12	0	1	0	5	6	0	39	1	0	1	3	.250	0	0	2.92
1992	Sarasota	A+	ChA	25	22	4	2	154	621	130	48	35	1	4	6	7	40	2	113	7	6	15	2	.882	2	1	2.05
	Birmingham	AA	ChA	2	2	0	0	12.1	59	13	5	5	0	0	1	1	11	0	9	1	0	1	1	.500	0	0	3.65
1993	Birmingham	AA	ChA	8	8	2	0	61.2	224	31	11	8	2	1	1	1	7	0	51	3	0	5	1	.833	1	0	1.17
	Nashville	AAA	ChA	21	20	0	0	122.1	526	117	61	53	11	5	2	3	47	3	78	6	3	6	8	.429	0	0	3.90
1994	Nashville	AAA	ChA	29	28	2	0	178.2	769	175	82	69	15	10	4	6	69	3	134	14	1	14	6	.700	1	0	3.48
1995	White Sox	R	ChA	2	2	0	0	7	27	5	2	0	0	0	0	0	0	0	6	0	0	0	1	.000	0	0	0.00
1996	Nashville	AAA	ChA	16	15	1	1	95.2	395	93	54	47	12	3	1	3	29	2	58	3	0	4	10	.286	0	0	4.42
10 Min. YEARS				179	158	14	8	969.2	4069	862	444	354	58	32	21	60	327	11	706	60	14	62	49	.559	7	1	3.29

Lance Schuermann

Pitches: Left **Bats:** Left **Pos:** P **Ht:** 6'2" **Wt:** 200 **Born:** 2/7/70 **Age:** 27

Year	Team	Lg	Org	HOW MUCH HE PITCHED						WHAT HE GAVE UP												THE RESULTS					
				G	GS	CG	GF	IP	BFP	H	R	ER	HR	SH	SF	HB	TBB	IBB	SO	WP	Bk	W	L	Pct.	ShO	Sv	ERA
1991	Butte	R+	Tex	30	0	0	16	43.2	203	45	29	22	0	2	2	1	34	2	46	6	7	4	4	.500	0	4	4.53
1992	Miracle	A+	Tex	51	5	0	17	86.1	390	87	51	45	1	5	9	2	56	1	68	7	2	4	7	.364	0	2	4.69
1993	Charlotte	A+	Tex	46	0	0	24	65.1	256	40	20	15	1	3	5	1	28	2	59	2	0	1	4	.200	0	16	2.07
1994	Tulsa	AA	Tex	27	27	3	0	175.2	743	182	87	80	21	9	7	7	49	2	124	3	2	10	11	.476	0	0	4.10
1995	Okla. City	AAA	Tex	33	13	0	6	88.2	398	101	51	46	12	1	4	2	40	0	44	8	0	4	7	.364	0	0	4.67
1996	Bowie	AA	Bal	6	0	0	4	5.2	28	7	5	2	2	0	0	0	2	0	6	0	0	0	0	.000	0	0	3.18
	Abilene	IND	—	24	14	4	5	109.1	486	121	45	42	8	5	2	6	38	0	69	6	0	12	0	1.000	0	1	3.46
6 Min. YEARS				217	59	7	72	574.2	2504	583	288	252	45	25	29	19	247	7	416	32	11	35	33	.515	0	23	3.95

Erik Schullstrom

Pitches: Right **Bats:** Right **Pos:** P **Ht:** 6' 5" **Wt:** 235 **Born:** 3/25/69 **Age:** 28

Year	Team	Lg	Org	HOW MUCH HE PITCHED						WHAT HE GAVE UP												THE RESULTS					
				G	GS	CG	GF	IP	BFP	H	R	ER	HR	SH	SF	HB	TBB	IBB	SO	WP	Bk	W	L	Pct.	ShO	Sv	ERA
1990	Wausau	A	Bal	5	5	0	0	19.1	82	20	12	10	3	0	1	0	7	0	21	0	2	0	2	.000	0	0	4.66
	Frederick	A+	Bal	2	2	0	0	13	54	9	5	5	0	1	2	1	6	0	8	0	0	2	0	1.000	0	0	3.46
1991	Frederick	A+	Bal	19	17	1	0	86	361	70	32	29	5	4	1	1	45	1	73	4	2	5	6	.455	1	0	3.03
	Hagerstown	AA	Bal	2	2	0	0	13	54	11	5	4	0	1	0	1	3	0	9	1	0	1	0	1.000	0	0	2.77
1992	Hagerstown	AA	Bal	23	22	2	0	127	556	120	66	51	7	6	2	3	63	0	128	7	3	5	9	.357	0	0	3.61
	Las Vegas	AAA	SD	1	1	0	0	5	20	3	0	0	0	0	0	0	3	0	4	0	0	1	0	1.000	0	0	0.00
1993	Bowie	AA	Bal	24	14	2	4	109.2	480	119	63	52	6	6	3	3	45	0	97	7	0	5	10	.333	0	1	4.27
	Nashville	AA	Min	4	3	0	0	13	61	16	7	7	1	0	1	0	6	0	11	1	0	1	0	1.000	0	0	4.85
1994	Nashville	AA	Min	26	0	0	17	41	164	36	14	12	2	4	1	1	6	0	43	2	0	1	2	.333	0	8	2.63
	Salt Lake	AAA	Min	8	0	0	7	11.1	47	12	5	5	0	0	0	0	3	2	8	0	0	0	1	.000	0	2	3.97
1995	Salt Lake	AAA	Min	10	0	0	7	9.2	43	12	5	5	1	0	0	0	4	0	8	0	0	2	0	1.000	0	2	4.66
1996	Trenton	AA	Bos	19	0	0	8	28.1	124	23	11	8	1	2	4	4	13	2	22	3	0	3	0	1.000	0	1	2.54
	Pawtucket	AAA	Bos	15	10	0	1	55.2	246	57	37	31	9	2	2	2	28	1	62	3	0	1	4	.200	0	0	5.01
1994	Minnesota	AL		9	0	0	5	13	57	13	7	4	0	1	0	1	5	0	13	0	0	0	0	.000	0	1	2.77
1995	Minnesota	AL		37	0	0	16	47	225	66	36	36	8	2	1	1	22	1	21	5	0	0	0	.000	0	0	6.89
7 Min. YEARS				158	76	5	44	532	2292	508	262	219	35	26	17	16	232	6	494	28	7	27	34	.443	1	14	3.70
2 Maj. YEARS				46	0	0	21	60	282	79	43	40	8	3	1	2	27	1	34	5	0	0	0	.000	0	1	6.00

Jeff Schwarz

Pitches: Right **Bats:** Right **Pos:** P **Ht:** 6' 5" **Wt:** 190 **Born:** 5/20/64 **Age:** 33

		HOW MUCH HE PITCHED						WHAT HE GAVE UP												THE RESULTS					
Year Team	Lg Org	G	GS	CG	GF	IP	BFP	H	R	ER	HR	SH	SF	HB	TBB	IBB	SO	WP	Bk	W	L	Pct.	ShO	Sv	ERA
1984 Quad City	A ChN	27	24	2	1	130	606	106	88	73	11	11	3	11	111	2	123	17	0	4	14	.222	0	0	5.05
1985 Peoria	A ChN	27	19	6	3	143.1	605	99	60	51	4	3	7	9	79	2	140	9	0	7	9	.438	2	0	3.20
1986 Winston-Sal	A+ ChN	4	2	0	1	12	57	10	10	10	3	0	0	1	12	0	11	3	2	0	1	.000	0	0	7.50
1987 Peoria	A ChN	20	13	2	1	92.1	418	79	59	47	7	6	6	8	59	1	91	9	1	5	7	.417	2	0	4.58
1988 Winston-Sal	A+ ChN	24	24	2	0	151.1	689	133	93	76	10	3	8	6	110	1	153	12	4	7	12	.368	2	0	4.52
Pittsfield	AA ChN	3	3	0	0	14.1	72	19	9	9	1	0	0	0	11	0	5	1	3	0	1	.000	0	0	5.65
1989 Hagerstown	AA Bal	17	9	0	5	69	311	66	45	30	3	4	4	4	41	0	78	7	5	0	6	.000	0	1	3.91
Rochester	AAA Bal	9	0	0	4	12.1	62	5	9	8	0	2	0	1	16	0	12	2	0	0	2	.000	0	2	5.84
1990 Rochester	AAA Bal	5	1	0	0	12.2	60	10	10	10	1	0	3	0	19	0	4	4	0	0	0	.000	0	0	7.11
Stockton	A+ Mil	19	8	0	3	56.1	265	59	36	30	1	2	0	9	36	0	59	5	1	3	3	.500	0	2	4.79
1991 El Paso	AA Mil	27	24	3	1	141.2	650	139	91	77	11	7	8	8	97	1	134	18	3	11	8	.579	1	0	4.89
1992 Birmingham	AA ChA	21	0	0	16	38.2	147	16	5	5	1	0	0	4	9	2	53	2	0	2	1	.667	0	6	1.16
Vancouver	AAA ChA	23	0	0	17	36	162	26	18	12	0	1	1	0	31	4	42	5	0	1	3	.250	0	3	3.00
1993 Nashville	AAA ChA	7	0	0	2	11	43	1	3	3	0	0	2	0	12	1	8	0	1	0	0	.000	0	0	2.45
1994 Nashville	AAA ChA	14	0	0	6	16.1	89	18	22	21	3	0	0	4	20	0	21	3	0	0	1	.000	0	0	11.57
1996 Richmond	AAA Atl	2	0	0	1	1.1	12	4	4	4	0	0	0	0	4	0	1	0	0	0	1	.000	0	0	27.00
1993 Chicago	AL	41	0	0	10	51	218	35	21	21	1	0	3	3	38	2	41	5	1	2	2	.500	0	0	3.71
1994 Chicago	AL	9	0	0	5	11.1	60	9	10	8	0	0	0	0	16	0	14	2	0	0	0	.000	0	0	6.35
California	AL	4	0	0	0	6.2	28	5	3	3	0	1	1	0	6	0	4	1	0	0	0	.000	0	0	4.05
12 Min. YEARS		249	127	15	61	938.2	4248	790	562	466	56	39	42	65	667	14	935	97	20	40	69	.367	7	14	4.47
2 Maj. YEARS		54	0	0	15	69	306	49	34	32	1	1	4	3	60	2	59	8	1	2	2	.500	0	0	4.17

Matt Schwenke

Bats: Right **Throws:** Right **Pos:** C **Ht:** 6'2" **Wt:** 210 **Born:** 8/12/72 **Age:** 24

		BATTING															BASERUNNING				PERCENTAGES		
Year Team	Lg Org	G	AB	H	2B	3B	HR	TB	R	RBI	TBB	IBB	SO	HBP	SH	SF	SB	CS	SB%	GDP	Avg	OBP	SLG
1993 Bakersfield	A+ LA	13	41	9	0	0	0	9	2	4	3	0	12	0	0	0	0	0	.00	0	.220	.273	.220
Great Falls	R+ LA	29	79	18	4	0	0	22	6	4	10	0	21	0	2	0	0	0	.00	2	.228	.315	.278
1994 Bakersfield	A+ LA	42	131	22	3	0	1	28	7	14	6	0	41	3	2	0	0	0	.00	3	.168	.221	.214
1995 Clinton	A SD	36	100	19	5	1	1	29	3	8	2	0	34	1	2	1	0	0	.00	3	.190	.212	.290
Rancho Cuca	A+ SD	22	56	10	2	0	0	12	7	7	2	0	20	0	1	1	0	0	.00	0	.179	.203	.214
Memphis	AA SD	23	62	15	3	0	0	18	7	4	3	0	16	1	1	1	0	0	.00	0	.242	.284	.290
1996 Clinton	A SD	28	86	13	3	0	0	16	4	2	6	0	28	3	0	0	0	1	.00	3	.151	.232	.186
Rancho Cuca	A+ SD	10	29	6	0	0	1	9	2	2	2	0	13	1	2	0	0	0	.00	1	.207	.281	.310
Las Vegas	AAA SD	11	16	4	0	0	0	4	0	2	0	0	7	1	0	0	0	0	.00	0	.250	.294	.250
4 Min. YEARS		214	600	116	20	1	3	147	38	47	34	0	192	10	10	3	0	1	.00	12	.193	.247	.245

Darryl Scott

Pitches: Right **Bats:** Right **Pos:** P **Ht:** 6' 1" **Wt:** 185 **Born:** 8/6/68 **Age:** 28

		HOW MUCH HE PITCHED						WHAT HE GAVE UP												THE RESULTS					
Year Team	Lg Org	G	GS	CG	GF	IP	BFP	H	R	ER	HR	SH	SF	HB	TBB	IBB	SO	WP	Bk	W	L	Pct.	ShO	Sv	ERA
1990 Boise	A- Cal	27	0	0	11	53.2	221	40	11	8	3	0	1	0	19	1	57	5	0	2	1	.667	0	5	1.34
1991 Quad City	A Cal	47	0	0	36	75.1	285	35	18	13	2	2	0	1	26	4	123	9	1	4	3	.571	0	19	1.55
1992 Midland	AA Cal	27	0	0	22	29.2	126	20	9	6	0	2	2	2	14	1	35	4	0	1	1	.500	0	9	1.82
Edmonton	AAA Cal	31	0	0	17	36.1	164	41	21	21	1	0	3	0	21	1	48	4	2	0	2	.000	0	6	5.20
1993 Vancouver	AAA Cal	46	0	0	33	51.2	206	35	12	12	4	2	1	1	19	2	57	3	0	7	1	.875	0	15	2.09
1995 Colo. Sprng	AAA Col	59	1	0	27	95.2	429	113	63	50	7	4	7	3	41	7	77	7	0	4	10	.286	0	4	4.70
1996 Buffalo	AAA Cle	50	1	0	30	81	323	61	29	26	11	4	2	0	24	4	73	2	0	3	5	.375	0	9	2.89
1993 California	AL	16	0	0	2	20	90	19	13	13	1	0	2	1	11	1	13	2	0	1	2	.333	0	0	5.85
6 Min. YEARS		287	2	0	176	423.1	1754	345	163	136	28	14	16	7	164	20	470	34	3	21	23	.477	0	67	2.89

Gary Scott

Bats: Right **Throws:** Right **Pos:** 3B **Ht:** 6' 0" **Wt:** 175 **Born:** 8/22/68 **Age:** 28

		BATTING															BASERUNNING				PERCENTAGES		
Year Team	Lg Org	G	AB	H	2B	3B	HR	TB	R	RBI	TBB	IBB	SO	HBP	SH	SF	SB	CS	SB%	GDP	Avg	OBP	SLG
1989 Geneva	A- ChN	48	175	49	10	1	10	91	33	42	22	2	23	9	0	2	4	1	.80	2	.280	.385	.520
1990 Winston-Sal	A+ ChN	102	380	112	22	0	12	170	63	70	29	4	66	14	5	6	17	3	.85	7	.295	.361	.447
Charlotte	AA ChN	35	143	44	9	0	4	65	21	17	7	1	17	0	0	3	3	4	.43	3	.308	.333	.455
1991 Iowa	AAA ChN	63	231	48	10	2	3	71	21	34	20	2	45	6	3	2	0	6	.00	11	.208	.286	.307
1992 Iowa	AAA ChN	95	354	93	26	0	10	149	48	48	37	1	48	6	4	5	3	1	.75	8	.263	.338	.421
1993 Indianapols	AAA Cin	77	284	60	12	1	3	83	39	18	21	0	33	4	2	2	2	1	.67	7	.211	.273	.292
Portland	AAA Min	54	189	55	8	4	1	74	26	28	27	0	33	7	1	6	3	1	.75	8	.291	.389	.392
1994 Phoenix	AAA SF	121	426	122	24	3	9	179	55	58	35	3	61	10	1	4	4	7	.36	14	.286	.352	.420
1995 Phoenix	AAA SF	68	219	58	16	2	5	93	33	26	26	5	39	7	0	1	2	2	.50	3	.265	.360	.425
Richmond	AAA Atl	27	86	13	1	0	0	14	7	2	10	0	13	1	0	1	0	1	.00	0	.151	.245	.163
1996 Las Vegas	AAA SD	65	217	59	16	2	2	85	24	27	31	1	47	0	0	1	0	2	.00	6	.272	.361	.392
1991 Chicago	NL	31	79	13	3	0	1	19	8	5	13	4	14	3	1	0	0	1	.00	2	.165	.305	.241
1992 Chicago	NL	36	96	15	2	0	2	23	8	11	5	1	14	0	1	0	0	1	.00	3	.156	.198	.240
8 Min. YEARS		755	2704	713	154	15	59	1074	370	370	265	19	425	64	16	33	38	29	.57	69	.264	.340	.397
2 Maj. YEARS		67	175	28	5	0	3	42	16	16	18	5	28	3	2	0	0	2	.00	5	.160	.250	.240

Scot Sealy

Bats: Right **Throws:** Right **Pos:** C **Ht:** 6'2" **Wt:** 200 **Born:** 2/10/71 **Age:** 26

		BATTING															BASERUNNING				PERCENTAGES		
Year Team	Lg Org	G	AB	H	2B	3B	HR	TB	R	RBI	TBB	IBB	SO	HBP	SH	SF	SB	CS	SB%	GDP	Avg	OBP	SLG
1992 Gastonia	A Tex	56	175	42	8	0	3	59	16	16	14	0	46	0	0	2	1	2	.33	4	.240	.293	.337
1993 Charlstn-SC	A Tex	2	7	1	0	0	0	1	0	0	0	0	4	0	0	0	0	0	.00	0	.143	.143	.143
1995 Tacoma	AAA Sea	4	10	3	0	0	0	3	1	0	0	0	0	0	0	0	0	0	.00	0	.300	.300	.300
Riverside	A+ Sea	58	206	50	5	0	2	61	23	30	16	0	36	1	1	1	2	2	.50	4	.243	.299	.296
1996 Lancaster	A+ Sea	75	254	69	22	3	9	124	47	49	41	0	63	8	2	1	3	2	.60	7	.272	.388	.488
Port City	AA Sea	18	59	5	1	0	0	6	2	1	8	0	24	0	1	1	0	2	.00	1	.085	.191	.102
4 Min. YEARS		213	711	170	36	3	14	254	89	96	79	0	173	9	4	5	6	8	.43	16	.239	.321	.357

Rudy Seanez

Pitches: Right **Bats:** Right **Pos:** P **Ht:** 5'10" **Wt:** 190 **Born:** 10/20/68 **Age:** 28

		HOW MUCH HE PITCHED						WHAT HE GAVE UP												THE RESULTS					
Year Team	Lg Org	G	GS	CG	GF	IP	BFP	H	R	ER	HR	SH	SF	HB	TBB	IBB	SO	WP	Bk	W	L	Pct.	ShO	Sv	ERA
1986 Burlington	R+ Cle	13	12	1	1	76	318	59	37	27	5	1	3	3	32	0	56	6	0	5	2	.714	1	0	3.20
1987 Waterloo	A Cle	10	10	0	0	34.2	159	35	29	26	6	0	2	1	23	0	23	2	2	0	4	.000	0	0	6.75
1988 Waterloo	A Cle	22	22	1	0	113.1	505	98	69	59	10	2	2	6	68	0	93	14	2	6	6	.500	1	0	4.69
1989 Kinston	A+ Cle	25	25	1	0	113	539	94	66	52	0	1	1	5	111	1	149	13	1	8	10	.444	0	0	4.14
Colo. Sprng	AAA Cle	1	0	0	1	1	4	1	0	0	0	0	0	0	0	0	0	0	0	0	0	.000	0	0	0.00
1990 Canton-Akrn	AA Cle	15	0	0	11	16.2	68	9	4	4	0	2	0	1	12	0	27	0	0	1	0	1.000	0	5	2.16
Colo. Sprng	AAA Cle	12	0	0	10	12	59	15	10	9	2	0	1	0	10	0	7	3	0	1	4	.200	0	1	6.75
1991 Canton-Akrn	AA Cle	25	0	0	18	38.1	161	17	12	11	2	0	1	1	30	1	73	1	0	4	2	.667	0	7	2.58
Colo. Sprng	AAA Cle	16	0	0	11	17.1	86	17	14	14	2	0	1	1	22	0	19	5	0	0	0	.000	0	0	7.27
1993 Central Val	A+ Col	5	1	0	1	8.1	46	9	9	9	0	0	1	0	11	0	7	1	0	0	2	.000	0	0	9.72
Colo. Sprng	AAA Col	3	0	0	3	3	13	3	3	3	1	0	0	0	1	0	5	0	0	0	0	.000	0	0	9.00
Las Vegas	AAA SD	14	0	0	8	19.2	90	24	15	14	2	0	1	0	11	0	14	7	1	0	1	.000	0	0	6.41
1994 Albuquerque	AAA LA	20	0	0	16	22	105	28	14	13	3	0	1	0	13	1	26	8	0	2	1	.667	0	9	5.32
1995 San Bernrdo	A+ LA	4	0	0	2	6	23	2	0	0	0	0	0	0	3	0	5	0	0	2	0	1.000	0	1	0.00
1996 Albuquerque	AAA LA	21	0	0	13	19.1	98	27	18	14	0	1	2	1	11	1	20	3	0	0	2	.000	0	6	6.52
1989 Cleveland	AL	5	0	0	2	5	20	1	2	2	0	0	2	0	4	1	7	1	1	0	0	.000	0	0	3.60
1990 Cleveland	AL	24	0	0	12	27.1	127	22	17	17	2	0	1	1	25	1	24	5	0	2	1	.667	0	0	5.60
1991 Cleveland	AL	5	0	0	0	5	33	10	12	9	2	0	0	0	7	0	7	2	0	0	0	.000	0	0	16.20
1993 San Diego	NL	3	0	0	3	3.1	20	8	6	5	1	1	0	0	2	0	1	0	0	0	0	.000	0	0	13.50
1994 Los Angeles	NL	17	0	0	6	23.2	104	24	7	7	2	4	2	1	9	1	18	3	0	1	1	.500	0	0	2.66
1995 Los Angeles	NL	37	0	0	12	34.2	159	39	27	26	5	3	0	1	18	3	29	0	0	1	3	.250	0	3	6.75
10 Min. YEARS		206	70	3	95	500.2	2274	438	300	255	33	7	16	19	358	4	524	63	6	29	34	.460	2	29	4.58
6 Maj. YEARS		91	0	0	35	99	463	104	71	66	12	8	5	3	65	6	86	11	1	4	5	.444	0	3	6.00

Kyle Sebach

Pitches: Right **Bats:** Right **Pos:** P **Ht:** 6'4" **Wt:** 195 **Born:** 9/6/71 **Age:** 25

		HOW MUCH HE PITCHED						WHAT HE GAVE UP												THE RESULTS					
Year Team	Lg Org	G	GS	CG	GF	IP	BFP	H	R	ER	HR	SH	SF	HB	TBB	IBB	SO	WP	Bk	W	L	Pct.	ShO	Sv	ERA
1991 Angels	R Cal	13	11	1	1	64.2	296	62	49	45	4	2	3	7	39	1	58	7	2	3	5	.375	0	0	6.26
1992 Quad City	A Cal	13	13	0	0	61.1	274	52	31	27	5	0	0	8	40	0	50	8	1	3	4	.429	0	0	3.96
Boise	A- Cal	13	8	0	3	40.2	215	50	42	34	0	0	6	8	34	0	41	9	1	1	5	.167	0	1	7.52
1993 Cedar Rapds	A Cal	26	26	4	0	154	678	138	73	52	7	4	7	14	70	1	138	10	2	6	9	.400	0	0	3.04
1994 Lk Elsinore	A+ Cal	10	10	3	0	73	306	67	35	28	5	2	2	4	24	1	39	5	0	3	4	.429	0	0	3.45
Midland	AA Cal	16	16	4	0	112.2	494	129	69	58	11	2	4	9	40	0	85	3	0	5	5	.500	2	0	4.63
1995 Midland	AA Cal	5	5	0	0	18.1	93	31	24	21	1	2	2	3	12	0	7	3	0	1	2	.333	0	0	10.31
Lk Elsinore	A+ Cal	19	18	0	0	94.2	433	122	64	60	11	3	3	7	41	0	67	9	0	8	4	.667	0	0	5.70
1996 Midland	AA Cal	4	4	0	0	21.1	109	31	20	18	2	0	1	3	15	2	11	2	0	2	0	1.000	0	0	7.59
Lk Elsinore	A+ Cal	26	13	0	5	109.2	477	124	73	68	15	1	7	4	31	0	105	2	0	8	4	.667	0	0	5.58
6 Min. YEARS		145	124	12	9	750.1	3375	806	480	411	61	16	35	67	346	5	601	58	6	40	42	.488	2	1	4.93

Reed Secrist

Bats: Left **Throws:** Right **Pos:** 3B **Ht:** 6'1" **Wt:** 205 **Born:** 5/7/70 **Age:** 27

		BATTING															BASERUNNING				PERCENTAGES		
Year Team	Lg Org	G	AB	H	2B	3B	HR	TB	R	RBI	TBB	IBB	SO	HBP	SH	SF	SB	CS	SB%	GDP	Avg	OBP	SLG
1992 Welland	A- Pit	42	117	25	6	0	1	34	16	13	19	0	36	2	2	1	4	3	.57	2	.214	.331	.291
1993 Augusta	A Pit	90	266	71	16	3	6	111	38	47	27	1	43	1	2	4	4	1	.80	10	.267	.332	.417
1994 Salem	A+ Pit	80	221	54	12	0	10	96	29	35	22	0	58	1	2	1	2	2	.50	4	.244	.314	.434
1995 Lynchburg	A+ Pit	112	380	107	18	3	19	188	60	75	54	7	88	3	1	4	3	4	.43	6	.282	.372	.495
1996 Calgary	AAA Pit	128	420	129	30	0	17	210	68	66	52	11	105	4	3	5	2	4	.33	8	.307	.385	.500
5 Min. YEARS		452	1404	386	82	6	53	639	211	236	174	19	330	11	10	15	15	14	.52	30	.275	.356	.455

Tate Seefried

Bats: Left **Throws:** Right **Pos:** 1B **Ht:** 6'4" **Wt:** 180 **Born:** 4/22/72 **Age:** 25

		BATTING															BASERUNNING				PERCENTAGES		
Year Team	Lg Org	G	AB	H	2B	3B	HR	TB	R	RBI	TBB	IBB	SO	HBP	SH	SF	SB	CS	SB%	GDP	Avg	OBP	SLG
1990 Yankees	R NYA	52	170	20	3	0	0	31	15	20	22	0	53	2	0	1	2	1	.67	6	.157	.256	.174
1991 Oneonta	A- NYA	73	264	65	19	0	7	105	40	51	32	0	66	2	0	7	12	3	.80	6	.246	.325	.398
1992 Greensboro	A NYA	141	532	129	23	5	20	222	73	90	51	0	166	2	1	3	8	8	.50	12	.242	.310	.417
1993 Pr. William	A+ NYA	125	464	123	25	4	21	219	63	89	50	4	150	2	3	6	8	8	.50	8	.265	.335	.472

BATTING																			BASERUNNING				PERCENTAGES		
Year	Team	Lg	Org	G	AB	H	2B	3B	HR	TB	R	RBI	TBB	IBB	SO	HBP	SH	SF	SB	CS	SB%	GDP	Avg	OBP	SLG
1994	Albany-Colo	AA	NYA	118	444	100	14	2	27	199	63	83	48	4	149	5	1	2	1	5	.17	12	.225	.307	.448
1995	Columbus	AAA	NYA	29	110	18	6	0	1	27	7	12	1	0	34	0	0	2	0	0	.00	2	.164	.168	.245
	Norwich	AA	NYA	77	274	62	18	1	5	97	34	33	31	4	86	4	1	4	0	1	.00	6	.226	.310	.354
1996	Norwich	AA	NYA	115	361	75	17	0	14	134	52	47	47	3	128	1	2	1	2	3	.40	9	.208	.300	.371
7 Min. YEARS				730	2627	600	125	12	95	1034	347	425	282	15	832	18	8	26	33	29	.53	61	.228	.305	.394

Chris Seelbach

Pitches: Right **Bats:** Right **Pos:** P **Ht:** 6' 4" **Wt:** 180 **Born:** 12/18/72 **Age:** 24

HOW MUCH HE PITCHED										WHAT HE GAVE UP												THE RESULTS					
Year	Team	Lg	Org	G	GS	CG	GF	IP	BFP	H	R	ER	HR	SH	SF	HB	TBB	IBB	SO	WP	Bk	W	L	Pct.	ShO	Sv	ERA
1991	Braves	R	Atl	4	4	0	0	15	65	13	7	7	3	1	0	0	6	0	19	3	1	0	1	.000	0	0	4.20
1992	Macon	A	Atl	27	27	1	0	157.1	662	134	65	58	11	3	5	9	68	0	144	5	1	9	11	.450	0	0	3.32
1993	Durham	A+	Atl	25	25	0	0	131.1	590	133	85	72	15	4	4	7	74	1	112	10	0	9	9	.500	0	0	4.93
1994	Greenville	AA	Atl	15	15	2	0	92.2	363	64	26	24	3	5	3	4	38	2	79	5	0	4	6	.400	0	0	2.33
	Richmond	AAA	Atl	12	11	0	0	61.1	273	68	37	33	6	2	3	0	36	2	35	3	0	3	5	.375	0	0	4.84
1995	Greenville	AA	Atl	9	9	1	0	60.1	249	38	15	11	2	5	3	4	30	0	65	3	1	6	0	1.000	1	0	1.64
	Richmond	AAA	Atl	23	23	2	0	133.2	563	102	54	49	9	5	6	6	69	0	130	6	1	10	6	.625	1	0	3.30
1996	Charlotte	AAA	Fla	25	25	1	0	138.1	650	167	123	113	26	2	5	5	76	3	98	9	1	6	13	.316	0	0	7.35
6 Min. YEARS				140	139	7	0	790	3415	719	412	367	75	27	29	35	397	8	682	44	5	47	51	.480	2	0	4.18

Brad Seitzer

Bats: Right **Throws:** Right **Pos:** 3B **Ht:** 6'2" **Wt:** 195 **Born:** 2/2/70 **Age:** 27

BATTING																			BASERUNNING				PERCENTAGES		
Year	Team	Lg	Org	G	AB	H	2B	3B	HR	TB	R	RBI	TBB	IBB	SO	HBP	SH	SF	SB	CS	SB%	GDP	Avg	OBP	SLG
1991	Bluefield	R+	Bal	12	45	13	2	0	3	24	5	5	5	0	10	0	0	0	1	1	.50	1	.289	.360	.533
	Kane County	A	Bal	58	197	55	11	1	2	74	34	28	36	3	36	1	1	1	1	0	1.00	3	.279	.391	.376
1992	Frederick	A+	Bal	129	459	114	21	3	14	183	59	61	38	2	111	7	4	3	2	4	.33	9	.248	.314	.399
1993	Frederick	A+	Bal	130	439	111	24	3	10	171	44	68	58	1	95	5	3	9	3	3	.50	6	.253	.341	.390
1994	Beloit	A	Mil	102	343	86	13	0	11	132	45	53	58	1	78	3	6	4	2	2	.50	7	.251	.360	.385
1995	Stockton	A+	Mil	127	428	132	28	3	6	184	66	56	72	2	68	3	2	2	7	4	.64	10	.308	.410	.430
1996	El Paso	AA	Mil	115	433	138	31	1	17	222	78	87	51	0	67	7	2	5	6	4	.60	9	.319	.395	.513
6 Min. YEARS				673	2344	649	130	11	63	990	331	358	318	9	465	26	18	24	22	18	.55	45	.277	.366	.422

Shawn Senior

Pitches: Left **Bats:** Left **Pos:** P **Ht:** 6'1" **Wt:** 195 **Born:** 3/17/72 **Age:** 25

HOW MUCH HE PITCHED										WHAT HE GAVE UP												THE RESULTS					
Year	Team	Lg	Org	G	GS	CG	GF	IP	BFP	H	R	ER	HR	SH	SF	HB	TBB	IBB	SO	WP	Bk	W	L	Pct.	ShO	Sv	ERA
1993	Red Sox	R	Bos	3	2	0	0	14	60	10	7	3	0	1	0	1	6	0	17	0	0	3	0	1.000	0	0	1.93
	Utica	A-	Bos	13	13	1	0	76.1	340	84	40	33	2	3	2	3	34	0	77	8	2	7	2	.778	0	0	3.89
1994	Lynchburg	A+	Bos	13	13	0	0	76.1	338	73	45	30	6	3	2	2	34	1	62	5	1	4	4	.500	0	0	3.54
	Sarasota	A+	Bos	14	13	0	0	83.1	360	82	33	28	6	2	0	2	47	0	58	8	2	8	3	.727	0	0	3.02
1995	Pawtucket	AAA	Bos	1	1	0	0	6	29	9	4	4	0	1	0	0	2	0	1	0	0	0	1	.000	0	0	6.00
	Trenton	AA	Bos	28	28	0	0	157.1	702	163	95	80	15	6	11	9	70	2	91	10	4	11	8	.579	0	0	4.58
1996	Trenton	AA	Bos	16	13	1	0	82	372	89	53	43	13	6	3	6	42	2	49	1	0	5	6	.455	0	0	4.72
4 Min. YEARS				88	83	2	0	495.1	2201	510	277	221	42	22	18	23	235	5	355	32	9	38	24	.613	0	0	4.02

Richie Sexson

Bats: Right **Throws:** Right **Pos:** 1B **Ht:** 6'6" **Wt:** 206 **Born:** 12/29/74 **Age:** 22

BATTING																			BASERUNNING				PERCENTAGES		
Year	Team	Lg	Org	G	AB	H	2B	3B	HR	TB	R	RBI	TBB	IBB	SO	HBP	SH	SF	SB	CS	SB%	GDP	Avg	OBP	SLG
1993	Burlington	R+	Cle	40	97	18	3	0	1	24	11	5	18	2	21	1	2	1	1	1	.50	1	.186	.316	.247
1994	Columbus	A	Cle	130	488	133	25	2	14	204	88	77	37	2	87	14	0	5	7	3	.70	5	.273	.338	.418
1995	Kinston	A+	Cle	131	494	151	34	0	22	251	80	85	43	5	115	10	0	7	4	6	.40	8	.306	.368	.508
1996	Canton-Akrn	AA	Cle	133	518	143	33	3	16	230	85	76	39	5	118	6	0	5	2	1	.67	13	.276	.331	.444
4 Min. YEARS				434	1597	445	95	5	53	709	264	243	137	14	341	31	2	18	14	11	.56	27	.279	.344	.444

Chris Sexton

Bats: Right **Throws:** Right **Pos:** SS **Ht:** 5'11" **Wt:** 180 **Born:** 8/3/71 **Age:** 25

BATTING																			BASERUNNING				PERCENTAGES		
Year	Team	Lg	Org	G	AB	H	2B	3B	HR	TB	R	RBI	TBB	IBB	SO	HBP	SH	SF	SB	CS	SB%	GDP	Avg	OBP	SLG
1993	Billings	R+	Cin	72	273	91	14	4	4	125	63	46	35	1	27	1	0	8	13	4	.76	6	.333	.401	.458
1994	Charlstn-WV	A	Cin	133	467	140	21	4	5	184	82	59	91	3	67	2	6	6	18	11	.62	9	.300	.412	.394
1995	Winston-Sal	A+	Cin	4	15	6	0	0	1	9	3	5	4	0	0	0	0	0	0	0	.00	0	.400	.526	.600
	Salem	A+	Col	123	461	123	16	6	4	163	81	32	93	2	55	1	12	1	14	11	.56	11	.267	.390	.354
	New Haven	AA	Col	1	3	0	0	0	0	0	0	0	0	0	0	0	0	0	0	0	.00	0	.000	.000	.000
1996	New Haven	AA	Col	127	444	96	12	2	0	112	50	28	71	2	68	1	7	3	8	5	.62	10	.216	.324	.252
4 Min. YEARS				460	1663	456	63	16	14	593	279	170	294	8	217	5	25	18	53	31	.63	36	.274	.381	.357

Jeff Sexton

Pitches: Right **Bats:** Right **Pos:** P **Ht:** 6'2" **Wt:** 190 **Born:** 10/4/71 **Age:** 25

			HOW MUCH HE PITCHED						WHAT HE GAVE UP												THE RESULTS					
Year	Team	Lg Org	G	GS	CG	GF	IP	BFP	H	R	ER	HR	SH	SF	HB	TBB	IBB	SO	WP	Bk	W	L	Pct.	ShO	Sv	ERA
1993	Watertown	A- Cle	17	1	1	9	33.2	145	35	15	10	1	1	0	1	10	3	30	3	0	1	1	.500	1	2	2.67
1994	Watertown	A- Cle	10	0	0	5	23	95	19	3	1	0	1	0	0	7	2	16	3	1	1	0	1.000	0	3	0.39
	Columbus	A Cle	14	2	0	6	30	121	17	13	12	2	1	0	3	9	2	35	1	0	1	0	1.000	0	1	3.60
1995	Kinston	A+ Cle	8	8	2	0	57	226	52	17	16	3	0	0	2	7	0	41	6	1	5	1	.833	1	0	2.53
	Columbus	A Cle	22	21	4	0	139.1	544	118	44	36	5	1	1	5	23	0	112	7	1	11	3	.786	3	0	2.33
1996	Canton-Akrn	AA Cle	9	9	0	0	49.1	210	45	29	28	6	2	0	2	23	1	34	1	0	2	4	.333	0	0	5.11
4 Min. YEARS			80	41	7	20	332.1	1341	286	121	103	17	6	1	13	79	8	268	21	3	21	9	.700	5	6	2.79

Mike Sharperson

Bats: Right **Throws:** Right **Pos:** 3B **Ht:** 6' 3" **Wt:** 205 **Born:** 10/4/61 **Age:** 35

			BATTING														BASERUNNING				PERCENTAGES		
Year	Team	Lg Org	G	AB	H	2B	3B	HR	TB	R	RBI	TBB	IBB	SO	HBP	SH	SF	SB	CS	SB%	GDP	Avg	OBP	SLG
1984	Knoxville	AA Tor	140	542	165	25	7	4	216	86	48	48	2	66	1	4	1	20	13	.61	10	.304	.361	.399
1985	Syracuse	AAA Tor	134	536	155	19	7	1	191	86	59	71	1	75	2	3	4	14	15	.48	5	.289	.372	.356
1986	Syracuse	AAA Tor	133	519	150	18	9	4	198	86	45	69	1	67	7	4	1	17	13	.57	15	.289	.379	.382
1987	Syracuse	AAA Tor	88	338	101	21	5	5	147	67	26	40	0	41	1	2	1	14	10	.58	5	.299	.374	.435
1988	Albuquerque	AAA LA	56	210	67	10	2	0	81	55	30	31	0	25	1	1	1	19	6	.76	7	.319	.407	.386
1989	Albuquerque	AAA LA	98	359	111	15	7	3	149	81	48	66	2	46	2	4	3	17	12	.59	9	.309	.416	.415
1994	Pawtucket	AAA Bos	37	131	39	10	0	0	49	16	13	21	1	17	0	0	2	5	3	.63	3	.298	.390	.374
	Iowa	AAA ChN	31	90	25	3	2	5	47	16	16	9	0	14	2	0	3	3	2	.60	1	.278	.346	.522
1995	Richmond	AAA Atl	87	298	95	16	1	3	122	42	47	35	3	34	2	1	7	7	2	.78	6	.319	.386	.409
1996	Las Vegas	AAA SD	32	112	34	8	0	1	45	17	21	20	1	11	1	0	0	1	0	1.00	6	.304	.414	.402
1987	Toronto	AL	32	96	20	4	1	0	26	4	9	7	0	15	1	1	0	2	1	.67	2	.208	.269	.271
	Los Angeles	NL	10	33	9	2	0	0	11	7	1	4	1	5	0	0	0	0	0	.00	1	.273	.351	.333
1988	Los Angeles	NL	46	59	16	1	0	0	17	8	4	1	0	12	1	2	1	0	1	.00	1	.271	.290	.288
1989	Los Angeles	NL	27	28	7	3	0	0	10	2	5	4	1	7	0	1	1	0	1	.00	1	.250	.333	.357
1990	Los Angeles	NL	129	357	106	14	2	3	133	42	36	46	6	39	1	8	3	15	6	.71	5	.297	.376	.373
1991	Los Angeles	NL	105	216	60	11	2	2	81	24	20	25	0	24	1	10	0	1	3	.25	2	.278	.355	.375
1992	Los Angeles	NL	128	317	95	21	0	3	125	48	36	47	1	33	0	5	3	2	2	.50	9	.300	.387	.394
1993	Los Angeles	NL	73	90	23	4	0	2	33	13	10	5	0	17	1	0	1	2	0	1.00	2	.256	.299	.367
1995	Atlanta	NL	7	7	1	1	0	0	2	1	2	0	0	2	0	0	0	0	0	.00	0	.143	.143	.286
9 Min. YEARS			836	3135	942	145	40	26	1245	552	353	410	11	396	19	19	23	117	76	.61	67	.300	.382	.397
8 Maj. YEARS			557	1203	337	61	5	10	438	149	123	139	9	154	5	27	9	22	14	.61	23	.280	.355	.364

Jon Shave

Bats: Right **Throws:** Right **Pos:** 2B **Ht:** 6' 0" **Wt:** 180 **Born:** 11/4/67 **Age:** 29

			BATTING														BASERUNNING				PERCENTAGES		
Year	Team	Lg Org	G	AB	H	2B	3B	HR	TB	R	RBI	TBB	IBB	SO	HBP	SH	SF	SB	CS	SB%	GDP	Avg	OBP	SLG
1990	Butte	R+ Tex	64	250	88	9	3	2	109	41	42	25	0	27	3	2	4	21	7	.75	8	.352	.411	.436
1991	Gastonia	A Tex	55	213	62	11	0	2	79	29	24	20	0	26	1	3	0	11	9	.55	3	.291	.355	.371
	Charlotte	A+ Tex	56	189	43	4	1	1	52	17	20	18	1	30	5	2	4	7	7	.50	3	.228	.306	.275
1992	Tulsa	AA Tex	118	453	130	23	5	2	169	57	36	37	1	59	4	7	5	6	7	.46	10	.287	.343	.373
1993	Okla. City	AAA Tex	100	399	105	17	3	4	140	58	41	20	0	60	2	9	1	4	3	.57	12	.263	.301	.351
1994	Okla. City	AAA Tex	95	332	73	15	2	1	95	29	31	14	1	61	5	12	5	6	2	.75	6	.220	.258	.286
1995	Okla. City	AAA Tex	32	83	17	1	0	0	18	10	5	7	0	28	1	1	0	1	0	1.00	1	.205	.275	.217
1996	Okla. City	AAA Tex	116	414	110	20	2	7	155	54	41	41	0	97	10	4	4	8	6	.57	7	.266	.343	.374
1993	Texas	AL	17	47	15	2	0	0	17	3	7	0	0	8	0	3	2	1	3	.25	0	.319	.306	.362
7 Min. YEARS			636	2333	628	100	16	19	817	295	240	182	3	388	31	40	23	64	41	.61	50	.269	.327	.350

Curtis Shaw

Pitches: Left **Bats:** Left **Pos:** P **Ht:** 6'2" **Wt:** 190 **Born:** 8/16/69 **Age:** 27

			HOW MUCH HE PITCHED						WHAT HE GAVE UP												THE RESULTS					
Year	Team	Lg Org	G	GS	CG	GF	IP	BFP	H	R	ER	HR	SH	SF	HB	TBB	IBB	SO	WP	Bk	W	L	Pct.	ShO	Sv	ERA
1990	Sou. Oregon	A- Oak	17	9	0	3	66.1	274	54	28	26	4	1	0	3	30	0	74	5	1	4	6	.400	0	0	3.53
1991	Madison	A Oak	20	20	1	0	100.1	457	82	45	29	1	1	1	6	79	1	87	11	0	7	5	.583	0	0	2.60
1992	Modesto	A+ Oak	27	27	2	0	177.1	749	146	71	60	5	7	7	6	98	0	154	12	1	13	4	.765	0	0	3.05
1993	Huntsville	AA Oak	28	28	2	0	151.2	676	141	98	83	8	2	3	14	89	2	132	19	4	6	16	.273	1	0	4.93
1994	Huntsville	AA Oak	7	7	0	0	42	181	39	22	21	1	4	1	1	20	0	33	3	0	2	1	.667	0	0	4.50
	Tacoma	AAA Oak	32	8	0	7	82	396	98	69	63	10	5	6	7	61	0	46	11	2	2	6	.250	0	0	6.91
1995	Edmonton	AAA Oak	42	3	0	11	98.1	454	91	60	51	4	5	6	6	88	8	52	17	1	6	5	.545	0	2	4.67
1996	Edmonton	AAA Oak	1	1	0	0	3	17	6	6	6	0	1	0	0	2	0	1	2	1	0	0	.000	0	0	18.00
	Modesto	A+ Oak	39	10	0	11	107.1	481	101	63	45	5	8	2	10	63	0	89	9	2	10	5	.667	0	1	3.77
7 Min. YEARS			213	113	5	32	828.1	3685	758	462	384	38	34	26	53	530	11	668	89	12	50	48	.510	1	3	4.17

John Shea

Pitches: Left **Bats:** Right **Pos:** P **Ht:** 6'6" **Wt:** 210 **Born:** 6/23/66 **Age:** 31

			HOW MUCH HE PITCHED						WHAT HE GAVE UP												THE RESULTS					
Year	Team	Lg Org	G	GS	CG	GF	IP	BFP	H	R	ER	HR	SH	SF	HB	TBB	IBB	SO	WP	Bk	W	L	Pct.	ShO	Sv	ERA
1986	St. Cathrns	A- Tor	14	2	0	5	49	218	44	24	20	2	1	0	0	29	0	59	3	0	3	1	.750	0	0	3.67
1987	Myrtle Bch	A Tor	26	23	1	1	140	604	147	67	54	13	3	3	5	42	1	92	2	3	11	5	.688	1	0	3.47
1988	Knoxville	AA Tor	13	0	0	5	18.1	92	23	14	11	1	2	2	1	12	0	14	3	2	1	3	.250	0	1	5.40

		HOW MUCH HE PITCHED						WHAT HE GAVE UP												THE RESULTS					
Year Team	Lg Org	G	GS	CG	GF	IP	BFP	H	R	ER	HR	SH	SF	HB	TBB	IBB	SO	WP	Bk	W	L	Pct.	ShO	Sv	ERA
Dunedin	A+ Tor	24	18	1	2	122.2	498	115	43	30	4	8	1	1	25	0	83	5	15	4	6	.400	0	1	2.20
1989 Knoxville	AA Tor	31	29	3	1	190.1	803	183	79	57	14	6	2	6	57	1	96	4	6	9	12	.429	1	0	2.70
1990 Syracuse	AAA Tor	40	0	0	26	81.2	363	83	45	33	9	3	1	4	40	4	58	5	2	8	5	.615	0	3	3.64
1991 Syracuse	AAA Tor	35	24	3	5	172	767	198	104	87	15	4	11	8	78	2	76	4	3	12	10	.545	0	2	4.55
1992 Syracuse	AAA Tor	25	21	1	2	118	546	151	92	81	8	3	6	5	49	1	50	8	1	8	8	.500	1	0	6.18
1993 New Britain	AA Bos	48	0	0	12	56.2	241	48	27	23	2	3	1	2	22	3	62	5	1	4	2	.667	0	1	3.65
Pawtucket	AAA Bos	12	3	0	1	36	170	51	31	28	6	1	2	0	19	0	20	1	0	2	2	.500	0	0	7.00
1994 El Paso	AA Mil	40	0	0	9	53.1	233	52	17	14	0	0	2	1	25	4	50	5	0	5	2	.714	0	3	2.36
1995 Rochester	AAA Bal	38	0	0	19	39.2	172	38	16	13	8	1	1	1	17	2	37	2	0	0	1	.000	0	4	2.95
1996 Tulsa	AA Tex	9	0	0	1	9.2	56	23	15	15	2	0	1	0	5	1	4	3	1	0	1	.000	0	0	13.97
11 Min. YEARS		355	120	9	89	1087.1	4763	1156	574	466	84	35	33	34	420	19	701	50	34	67	58	.536	3	15	3.86

Chris Sheff

Bats: Right **Throws:** Right **Pos:** OF **Ht:** 6'3" **Wt:** 210 **Born:** 2/4/71 **Age:** 26

		BATTING															BASERUNNING				PERCENTAGES		
Year Team	Lg Org	G	AB	H	2B	3B	HR	TB	R	RBI	TBB	IBB	SO	HBP	SH	SF	SB	CS	SB%	GDP	Avg	OBP	SLG
1992 Erie	A- Fla	57	193	46	8	2	3	67	29	16	32	1	47	1	1	1	15	2	.88	8	.238	.348	.347
1993 Kane County	A Fla	129	456	124	22	5	5	171	79	50	58	2	100	2	3	5	33	10	.77	11	.272	.353	.375
1994 Brevard Cty	A+ Fla	32	118	44	8	3	1	61	21	19	17	0	23	0	0	1	7	2	.78	2	.373	.449	.517
Portland	AA Fla	106	395	101	19	1	5	137	50	30	31	0	76	0	3	2	18	4	.82	13	.256	.308	.347
1995 Portland	AA Fla	131	471	130	25	7	12	205	85	91	72	6	84	5	1	8	23	6	.79	10	.276	.372	.435
1996 Portland	AA Fla	27	105	31	12	2	2	53	16	17	13	3	23	0	0	0	3	2	.60	3	.295	.373	.505
Charlotte	AAA Fla	92	284	75	15	1	12	128	41	49	21	1	55	0	0	1	7	1	.88	10	.264	.314	.451
5 Min. YEARS		574	2022	551	109	21	40	822	321	272	244	13	408	8	8	18	106	27	.80	57	.273	.350	.407

Scott Sheldon

Bats: Right **Throws:** Right **Pos:** SS **Ht:** 6'3" **Wt:** 185 **Born:** 11/28/68 **Age:** 28

		BATTING															BASERUNNING				PERCENTAGES		
Year Team	Lg Org	G	AB	H	2B	3B	HR	TB	R	RBI	TBB	IBB	SO	HBP	SH	SF	SB	CS	SB%	GDP	Avg	OBP	SLG
1991 Sou. Oregon	A- Oak	65	229	58	10	3	0	74	34	24	23	0	44	2	3	1	9	5	.64	5	.253	.325	.323
1992 Madison	A Oak	74	279	76	16	0	6	110	41	24	32	1	78	1	3	4	5	4	.56	2	.272	.345	.394
1993 Madison	A Oak	131	428	91	22	1	8	139	67	67	49	3	121	8	3	8	8	7	.53	8	.213	.300	.325
1994 Huntsville	AA Oak	91	268	62	10	1	0	74	31	28	28	1	69	7	7	3	7	1	.88	4	.231	.317	.276
1995 Edmonton	AAA Oak	45	128	33	7	1	4	54	21	12	15	0	15	2	4	1	4	2	.67	0	.258	.342	.422
Huntsville	AA Oak	66	235	51	10	2	4	77	25	15	23	0	60	1	3	1	5	0	1.00	7	.217	.288	.328
1996 Edmonton	AAA Oak	98	350	105	27	3	10	168	61	60	43	3	83	4	3	4	5	3	.63	8	.300	.379	.480
6 Min. YEARS		570	1917	476	102	11	32	696	280	230	213	8	470	25	26	22	43	22	.66	34	.248	.328	.363

Don Sheppard

Bats: Right **Throws:** Right **Pos:** OF **Ht:** 6'2" **Wt:** 180 **Born:** 5/2/71 **Age:** 26

		BATTING															BASERUNNING				PERCENTAGES		
Year Team	Lg Org	G	AB	H	2B	3B	HR	TB	R	RBI	TBB	IBB	SO	HBP	SH	SF	SB	CS	SB%	GDP	Avg	OBP	SLG
1989 White Sox	R ChA	26	82	15	4	0	0	19	11	4	7	0	28	0	1	0	4	4	.50	1	.183	.247	.232
1990 White Sox	R ChA	46	151	27	6	1	0	35	15	6	12	0	39	0	1	0	12	5	.71	2	.179	.239	.232
1991 South Bend	A ChA	83	178	37	5	2	1	49	24	11	21	0	57	1	1	1	7	2	.78	2	.208	.294	.275
1992 Salinas	A+ ChA	114	377	96	17	4	2	127	50	43	40	0	101	0	7	3	27	14	.66	10	.255	.324	.337
1993 Dunedin	A+ Tor	39	116	36	4	2	0	44	12	10	17	1	26	0	2	0	6	4	.60	2	.310	.398	.379
Knoxville	AA Tor	72	249	70	11	1	2	89	32	27	14	0	70	1	2	2	5	5	.50	3	.281	.320	.357
1994 Syracuse	AAA Tor	26	57	7	0	0	0	7	5	2	12	0	28	0	1	2	4	2	.67	0	.123	.268	.123
Knoxville	AA Tor	39	82	14	3	1	0	19	7	3	12	0	29	0	3	0	2	3	.40	0	.171	.277	.232
1995 Salinas	IND —	88	316	83	12	7	5	124	44	47	32	0	89	1	7	2	13	8	.62	1	.263	.330	.392
1996 Wichita	AA KC	45	97	21	2	0	3	32	12	12	9	1	24	0	1	1	3	4	.43	0	.216	.280	.330
8 Min. YEARS		578	1705	406	64	18	13	545	212	165	176	2	491	3	26	11	83	51	.62	21	.238	.309	.320

Greg Shockey

Bats: Left **Throws:** Left **Pos:** OF **Ht:** 6'1" **Wt:** 190 **Born:** 4/11/70 **Age:** 27

		BATTING															BASERUNNING				PERCENTAGES		
Year Team	Lg Org	G	AB	H	2B	3B	HR	TB	R	RBI	TBB	IBB	SO	HBP	SH	SF	SB	CS	SB%	GDP	Avg	OBP	SLG
1992 Bellingham	A- Sea	62	232	67	11	1	2	86	31	36	27	3	34	1	1	2	3	3	.50	6	.289	.363	.371
1993 Riverside	A+ Sea	95	354	110	10	0	6	138	61	63	50	6	50	4	1	4	2	2	.50	13	.311	.398	.390
Fort Myers	A+ Min	16	54	14	3	0	0	17	8	5	12	2	7	0	0	1	4	2	.67	1	.259	.388	.315
1994 Duluth-Sup.	IND —	60	209	63	11	0	4	86	19	23	23	0	41	4	0	1	2	2	.50	3	.301	.380	.411
1995 Lk Elsinore	A+ Cal	114	441	144	32	3	20	242	85	88	42	2	88	6	0	2	2	2	.50	6	.327	.391	.549
1996 Midland	AA Cal	98	325	103	26	6	7	162	58	49	47	1	56	3	0	2	2	2	.50	5	.317	.406	.498
5 Min. YEARS		445	1615	501	93	10	39	731	262	264	201	14	276	18	2	12	15	13	.54	34	.310	.390	.453

Scott Shores

Bats: Right **Throws:** Right **Pos:** OF **Ht:** 6'1" **Wt:** 190 **Born:** 2/4/72 **Age:** 25

		BATTING															BASERUNNING				PERCENTAGES		
Year Team	Lg Org	G	AB	H	2B	3B	HR	TB	R	RBI	TBB	IBB	SO	HBP	SH	SF	SB	CS	SB%	GDP	Avg	OBP	SLG
1994 Batavia	A- Phi	72	264	66	10	5	6	104	46	32	27	0	54	4	3	2	19	7	.73	3	.250	.327	.394
1995 Clearwater	A+ Phi	133	460	117	23	5	7	171	74	52	55	1	127	10	3	2	30	16	.65	11	.254	.345	.372

BATTING																	BASERUNNING				PERCENTAGES		
Year Team	Lg Org	G	AB	H	2B	3B	HR	TB	R	RBI	TBB	IBB	SO	HBP	SH	SF	SB	CS	SB%	GDP	Avg	OBP	SLG
1996 Reading	AA Phi	120	398	91	19	8	11	159	52	51	46	2	133	6	3	4	19	10	.66	3	.229	.315	.399
3 Min. YEARS		325	1122	274	52	18	24	434	172	135	128	3	314	20	9	8	68	33	.67	17	.244	.330	.387

Brian Shouse

Pitches: Left **Bats:** Left **Pos:** P **Ht:** 5'11" **Wt:** 175 **Born:** 9/26/68 **Age:** 28

HOW MUCH HE PITCHED								WHAT HE GAVE UP												THE RESULTS					
Year Team	Lg Org	G	GS	CG	GF	IP	BFP	H	R	ER	HR	SH	SF	HB	TBB	IBB	SO	WP	Bk	W	L	Pct.	ShO	Sv	ERA
1990 Welland	A- Pit	17	1	0	7	39.2	177	50	27	23	2	3	2	3	7	0	39	1	2	4	3	.571	0	2	5.22
1991 Augusta	A Pit	26	0	0	25	31	124	22	13	11	1	1	1	3	9	1	32	5	0	2	3	.400	0	8	3.19
Salem	A+ Pit	17	0	0	9	33.2	147	35	12	11	2	2	0	0	15	2	25	1	0	2	1	.667	0	3	2.94
1992 Carolina	AA Pit	59	0	0	33	77.1	323	71	31	21	3	8	2	2	28	4	79	4	1	5	6	.455	0	4	2.44
1993 Buffalo	AAA Pit	48	0	0	14	51.2	218	54	24	22	7	0	3	2	17	2	25	1	0	1	0	1.000	0	2	3.83
1994 Buffalo	AAA Pit	43	0	0	20	52	212	44	22	21	6	4	2	1	15	4	31	0	0	3	4	.429	0	0	3.63
1995 Calgary	AAA Pit	8	8	1	0	39.1	185	62	35	27	2	1	1	1	7	0	17	3	0	4	4	.500	0	0	6.18
Carolina	AA Pit	29	28	1	0	154	665	188	99	84	16	6	4	5	26	2	93	4	1	11	10	.524	0	0	4.91
1996 Calgary	AAA Pit	12	1	0	2	12.2	65	22	15	15	4	0	1	0	4	1	12	1	0	1	0	1.000	0	0	10.66
Rochester	AAA Bal	32	0	0	10	50	217	53	27	25	6	2	2	1	16	1	45	5	0	1	2	.333	0	2	4.50
1993 Pittsburgh	NL	6	0	0	1	4	22	7	4	4	1	0	1	0	2	0	3	1	0	0	0	.000	0	0	9.00
7 Min. YEARS		291	38	2	120	541.1	2333	601	305	260	49	27	18	18	144	17	398	25	4	34	33	.507	0	21	4.32

Mark Sievert

Pitches: Right **Bats:** Left **Pos:** P **Ht:** 6'4" **Wt:** 180 **Born:** 2/16/73 **Age:** 24

HOW MUCH HE PITCHED								WHAT HE GAVE UP												THE RESULTS					
Year Team	Lg Org	G	GS	CG	GF	IP	BFP	H	R	ER	HR	SH	SF	HB	TBB	IBB	SO	WP	Bk	W	L	Pct.	ShO	Sv	ERA
1993 Medicne Hat	R+ Tor	15	15	0	0	63	280	63	40	35	2	2	2	3	30	0	52	12	0	6	3	.667	0	0	5.00
1994 St. Cathrns	A- Tor	14	14	1	0	81.2	319	59	30	28	4	1	3	1	28	0	82	4	0	7	4	.636	1	0	3.09
1995 Hagerstown	A Tor	27	27	3	0	160.2	644	126	59	52	14	5	1	2	46	0	140	2	0	12	6	.667	0	0	2.91
1996 Knoxville	AA Tor	17	17	0	0	101.1	415	79	32	29	6	2	0	3	51	0	75	3	0	9	2	.818	0	0	2.58
Syracuse	AAA Tor	10	10	1	0	54.2	256	62	40	36	6	4	1	1	33	0	46	4	0	2	5	.286	0	0	5.93
4 Min. YEARS		83	83	5	0	461.1	1914	389	201	180	32	14	7	10	188	0	395	25	0	36	20	.643	1	0	3.51

Luis Silva

Pitches: Right **Bats:** Right **Pos:** P **Ht:** 6'2" **Wt:** 185 **Born:** 4/18/75 **Age:** 22

HOW MUCH HE PITCHED								WHAT HE GAVE UP												THE RESULTS					
Year Team	Lg Org	G	GS	CG	GF	IP	BFP	H	R	ER	HR	SH	SF	HB	TBB	IBB	SO	WP	Bk	W	L	Pct.	ShO	Sv	ERA
1994 Athletics	R Oak	14	8	1	3	72.2	299	61	26	23	5	0	0	2	16	1	88	5	1	5	3	.625	0	0	2.85
1995 W. Michigan	A Oak	10	1	0	1	21.1	102	31	16	16	2	1	1	2	7	0	24	2	3	1	0	1.000	0	0	6.75
Sou. Oregon	A- Oak	29	15	0	4	99.1	439	110	59	49	10	4	4	9	27	0	100	7	3	5	3	.625	0	1	4.44
1996 Modesto	A+ Oak	1	0	0	0	1	4	0	0	0	0	0	0	0	1	0	1	0	0	0	0	.000	0	0	0.00
Athletics	R Oak	5	0	0	1	9	35	9	5	5	0	0	0	0	0	0	10	0	0	1	0	1.000	0	0	5.00
Sou. Oregon	A- Oak	5	4	0	0	18	89	25	22	19	3	1	0	1	10	0	18	2	0	1	3	.250	0	0	9.50
Huntsville	AA Oak	1	0	0	0	2.2	14	5	4	4	1	0	1	0	2	0	2	0	1	0	0	.000	0	0	13.50
3 Min. YEARS		65	28	1	9	224	982	241	132	116	21	6	6	14	63	1	243	16	8	13	9	.591	0	1	4.66

Theodore Silva

Pitches: Right **Bats:** Right **Pos:** P **Ht:** 6'0" **Wt:** 170 **Born:** 8/4/74 **Age:** 22

HOW MUCH HE PITCHED								WHAT HE GAVE UP												THE RESULTS					
Year Team	Lg Org	G	GS	CG	GF	IP	BFP	H	R	ER	HR	SH	SF	HB	TBB	IBB	SO	WP	Bk	W	L	Pct.	ShO	Sv	ERA
1995 Charlstn-SC	A Tex	11	11	0	0	66.2	276	59	26	25	4	1	3	7	12	2	66	5	2	5	4	.556	0	0	3.38
1996 Charlotte	A+ Tex	16	16	4	0	113.1	463	98	39	36	9	1	2	3	27	1	95	3	1	10	2	.833	0	0	2.86
Tulsa	AA Tex	11	11	2	0	75.1	314	72	27	25	5	4	2	2	16	0	27	0	0	7	2	.778	1	0	2.99
2 Min. YEARS		38	38	6	0	255.1	1053	229	92	86	18	6	7	12	55	3	188	8	3	22	8	.733	1	0	3.03

Scott Simmons

Pitches: Left **Bats:** Right **Pos:** P **Ht:** 6'2" **Wt:** 200 **Born:** 8/15/69 **Age:** 27

HOW MUCH HE PITCHED								WHAT HE GAVE UP												THE RESULTS					
Year Team	Lg Org	G	GS	CG	GF	IP	BFP	H	R	ER	HR	SH	SF	HB	TBB	IBB	SO	WP	Bk	W	L	Pct.	ShO	Sv	ERA
1991 Hamilton	A- StL	15	14	0	0	90.1	376	82	34	26	4	0	2	1	25	0	78	1	2	6	4	.600	0	0	2.59
1992 Springfield	A StL	27	27	2	0	170.1	699	160	63	53	10	9	3	2	39	0	116	10	2	15	7	.682	1	0	2.80
1993 St. Pete	A+ StL	13	12	1	1	78.2	326	70	38	30	1	4	4	0	31	0	54	6	1	4	5	.444	0	0	3.43
Arkansas	AA StL	13	10	0	0	76.2	306	68	26	23	1	2	2	0	18	3	35	4	0	6	3	.667	0	0	2.70
1994 Arkansas	AA StL	26	26	2	0	162.1	663	148	63	49	4	10	4	3	39	1	115	4	1	7	11	.389	1	0	2.72
1995 Louisville	AAA StL	2	2	0	0	9	40	11	9	8	3	0	0	1	1	0	2	0	0	0	2	.000	0	0	8.00
Arkansas	AA StL	24	24	1	0	148	609	156	75	61	12	5	6	2	29	1	75	5	0	11	11	.500	1	0	3.71
1996 Louisville	AAA StL	30	8	0	10	99.2	416	98	51	46	17	1	1	0	35	5	58	4	1	5	6	.455	0	1	4.15
Port City	AA Sea	11	0	0	3	19	79	19	8	8	1	1	0	0	6	1	12	3	0	1	1	.500	0	0	3.79
6 Min. YEARS		161	123	6	14	854	3514	812	367	304	53	32	22	9	223	11	545	37	7	55	50	.524	3	1	3.20

Randall Simon

Bats: Left **Throws:** Left **Pos:** 1B **Ht:** 6'0" **Wt:** 180 **Born:** 5/26/75 **Age:** 22

				BATTING															BASERUNNING				PERCENTAGES		
Year	Team	Lg	Org	G	AB	H	2B	3B	HR	TB	R	RBI	TBB	IBB	SO	HBP	SH	SF	SB	CS	SB%	GDP	Avg	OBP	SLG
1993	Danville	R+	Atl	61	232	59	17	1	3	87	28	31	10	2	34	2	0	2	1	1	.50	4	.254	.289	.375
1994	Macon	A	Atl	106	358	105	23	1	10	160	45	54	6	2	56	1	1	2	7	6	.54	7	.293	.305	.447
1995	Durham	A+	Atl	122	420	111	18	1	18	185	56	79	36	14	63	5	0	5	6	5	.55	15	.264	.326	.440
1996	Greenville	AA	Atl	134	498	139	26	2	18	223	74	77	37	7	61	4	0	4	4	9	.31	13	.279	.331	.448
4 Min. YEARS				423	1508	414	84	5	49	655	203	241	89	25	214	12	1	13	18	21	.46	39	.275	.318	.434

Doug Simons

Pitches: Left **Bats:** Left **Pos:** P **Ht:** 6' 0" **Wt:** 170 **Born:** 9/15/66 **Age:** 30

				HOW MUCH HE PITCHED						WHAT HE GAVE UP												THE RESULTS					
Year	Team	Lg	Org	G	GS	CG	GF	IP	BFP	H	R	ER	HR	SH	SF	HB	TBB	IBB	SO	WP	Bk	W	L	Pct.	ShO	Sv	ERA
1988	Visalia	A+	Min	17	16	5	1	107.1	467	100	59	47	10	4	3	5	46	0	123	6	1	6	5	.545	2	0	3.94
1989	Visalia	A+	Min	14	14	1	0	90.2	372	77	33	15	4	1	4	5	33	1	79	4	1	6	2	.750	0	0	1.49
	Orlando	AA	Min	14	14	3	0	87.1	374	83	39	37	7	2	2	2	37	0	58	1	2	7	3	.700	0	0	3.81
1990	Orlando	AA	Min	29	28	5	0	188	765	160	76	53	13	9	4	6	43	2	109	7	1	15	12	.556	0	0	2.54
1992	Indianapols	AAA	Mon	32	14	2	6	120	481	114	45	41	7	2	6	2	25	1	66	3	0	11	4	.733	1	0	3.08
1993	Ottawa	AAA	Mon	34	13	1	6	115.2	487	134	67	61	13	2	1	2	16	2	75	3	0	7	7	.500	0	0	4.75
1994	Omaha	AAA	KC	17	17	0	0	96.1	405	97	56	49	20	3	0	5	26	0	43	3	1	5	8	.385	0	0	4.58
1995	Mobile	IND	—	8	7	2	0	49	199	55	20	16	2	4	1	0	3	0	30	0	0	4	2	.667	0	0	2.94
1996	Jackson	AA	Hou	20	19	1	0	126.2	520	132	53	49	11	7	2	3	30	0	75	5	0	8	7	.533	1	0	3.48
	Tucson	AAA	Hou	8	6	0	1	41.2	187	53	25	25	1	2	2	1	15	2	27	2	0	3	4	.429	0	0	5.40
1991	New York	NL		42	1	0	11	60.2	258	55	40	35	5	9	4	2	19	5	38	3	0	2	3	.400	0	1	5.19
1992	Montreal	NL		7	0	0	2	5.1	35	15	14	14	3	1	1	1	2	0	6	1	0	0	0	.000	0	0	23.63
8 Min. YEARS				193	148	20	14	1022.2	4257	1005	473	393	88	36	25	31	274	8	685	34	6	72	54	.571	4	0	3.46
2 Maj. YEARS				49	1	0	13	66	293	70	54	49	8	10	5	3	21	5	44	4	0	2	3	.400	0	1	6.68

Mitch Simons

Bats: Right **Throws:** Right **Pos:** SS **Ht:** 5'9" **Wt:** 170 **Born:** 12/13/68 **Age:** 28

				BATTING															BASERUNNING				PERCENTAGES		
Year	Team	Lg	Org	G	AB	H	2B	3B	HR	TB	R	RBI	TBB	IBB	SO	HBP	SH	SF	SB	CS	SB%	GDP	Avg	OBP	SLG
1991	Jamestown	A-	Mon	41	153	47	12	0	1	62	38	16	39	1	20	0	2	2	23	5	.82	1	.307	.443	.405
	W. Palm Bch	A+	Mon	15	50	9	2	1	0	13	3	4	5	0	8	0	0	0	1	0	1.00	0	.180	.255	.260
1992	Albany	A	Mon	130	481	136	26	5	1	175	57	61	60	0	47	7	2	10	34	12	.74	6	.283	.364	.364
1993	W. Palm Bch	A+	Mon	45	156	40	4	1	1	49	24	13	19	0	9	3	1	2	14	8	.64	3	.256	.344	.314
	Harrisburg	AA	Mon	29	77	18	1	1	0	21	5	5	7	0	14	0	2	1	2	0	1.00	1	.234	.294	.273
1994	Nashville	AA	Min	102	391	124	26	0	3	159	46	48	39	0	38	6	3	5	30	9	.77	6	.317	.383	.407
1995	Salt Lake	AAA	Min	130	480	156	34	4	3	207	87	46	47	2	45	10	4	2	32	16	.67	9	.325	.395	.431
1996	Salt Lake	AAA	Min	129	512	135	27	8	5	193	76	59	43	3	59	8	3	4	35	11	.76	7	.264	.328	.377
6 Min. YEARS				621	2300	665	132	20	14	879	336	252	259	6	240	34	17	26	171	61	.74	33	.289	.366	.382

Benji Simonton

Bats: Right **Throws:** Right **Pos:** 1B **Ht:** 6'1" **Wt:** 225 **Born:** 5/12/72 **Age:** 25

				BATTING															BASERUNNING				PERCENTAGES		
Year	Team	Lg	Org	G	AB	H	2B	3B	HR	TB	R	RBI	TBB	IBB	SO	HBP	SH	SF	SB	CS	SB%	GDP	Avg	OBP	SLG
1992	Everett	A-	SF	68	225	55	10	0	6	83	37	34	39	0	78	3	2	3	9	4	.69	1	.244	.359	.369
1993	Clinton	A	SF	100	310	79	18	4	12	141	52	49	40	2	112	6	0	2	8	7	.53	3	.255	.349	.455
1994	Clinton	A	SF	67	237	64	16	4	14	130	47	57	52	3	73	5	1	0	10	3	.77	7	.270	.412	.549
	San Jose	A+	SF	68	259	77	20	0	14	139	41	51	32	0	86	5	1	1	0	2	.00	5	.297	.384	.537
1995	San Jose	A+	SF	61	225	65	9	6	8	110	38	37	40	2	78	10	0	4	7	0	1.00	5	.289	.412	.489
	Shreveport	AA	SF	38	108	33	9	3	4	60	18	30	11	0	32	2	1	1	3	1	.75	1	.306	.377	.556
1996	Shreveport	AA	SF	137	469	117	25	1	23	213	86	76	101	4	144	6	1	0	6	4	.60	12	.249	.389	.454
	Phoenix	AAA	SF	1	4	3	0	0	1	6	1	2	1	0	0	0	0	0	0	0	.00	0	.750	.800	1.500
5 Min. YEARS				540	1837	493	107	18	82	882	320	336	316	11	603	37	6	11	43	21	.67	34	.268	.384	.480

Christopher Singleton

Bats: Left **Throws:** Left **Pos:** OF **Ht:** 6'2" **Wt:** 195 **Born:** 8/15/72 **Age:** 24

				BATTING															BASERUNNING				PERCENTAGES		
Year	Team	Lg	Org	G	AB	H	2B	3B	HR	TB	R	RBI	TBB	IBB	SO	HBP	SH	SF	SB	CS	SB%	GDP	Avg	OBP	SLG
1993	Everett	A-	SF	58	219	58	14	4	3	89	39	18	18	0	46	1	5	1	14	3	.82	3	.265	.322	.406
1994	San Jose	A+	SF	113	425	106	17	5	2	139	51	49	27	0	62	3	5	3	19	6	.76	9	.249	.297	.327
1995	San Jose	A+	SF	94	405	112	13	5	2	141	55	31	17	1	49	5	5	1	33	13	.72	5	.277	.313	.348
1996	Shreveport	AA	SF	129	500	149	31	9	5	213	68	72	24	2	58	6	3	8	27	12	.69	12	.298	.333	.426
	Phoenix	AAA	SF	9	32	4	0	0	0	4	3	0	1	0	2	0	1	0	0	0	.00	0	.125	.152	.125
4 Min. YEARS				403	1581	429	75	23	12	586	216	170	87	3	217	15	19	13	93	34	.73	29	.271	.313	.371

Steve Sisco

Bats: Right **Throws:** Right **Pos:** OF **Ht:** 5'9" **Wt:** 180 **Born:** 12/2/69 **Age:** 27

				BATTING															BASERUNNING				PERCENTAGES		
Year	Team	Lg	Org	G	AB	H	2B	3B	HR	TB	R	RBI	TBB	IBB	SO	HBP	SH	SF	SB	CS	SB%	GDP	Avg	OBP	SLG
1992	Eugene	A-	KC	67	261	86	7	1	0	95	41	30	26	0	32	4	2	2	22	12	.65	7	.330	.396	.364
	Appleton	A	KC	1	4	1	0	0	0	1	1	0	0	0	1	0	0	0	0	0	.00	0	.250	.250	.250

		BATTING															BASERUNNING				PERCENTAGES		
Year Team	Lg Org	G	AB	H	2B	3B	HR	TB	R	RBI	TBB	IBB	SO	HBP	SH	SF	SB	CS	SB%	GDP	Avg	OBP	SLG
1993 Rockford	A KC	124	460	132	22	4	2	168	62	57	42	2	65	2	4	5	25	10	.71	14	.287	.346	.365
1994 Wilmington	A+ KC	76	270	74	11	4	3	102	41	32	37	0	39	2	6	4	5	6	.45	2	.274	.361	.378
1995 Omaha	AAA KC	7	24	5	1	0	0	6	4	0	2	0	8	0	1	0	0	0	.00	0	.208	.269	.250
Wichita	AA KC	54	209	63	12	1	3	86	29	23	15	0	31	1	1	1	3	1	.75	5	.301	.350	.411
1996 Wichita	AA KC	122	462	137	24	1	13	202	80	74	40	0	69	3	5	5	4	2	.67	14	.297	.353	.437
5 Min. YEARS		451	1690	498	77	11	21	660	258	216	162	2	245	12	19	17	59	31	.66	42	.295	.357	.391

Matt Skrmetta

Pitches: Right **Bats:** Both **Pos:** P **Ht:** 6'3" **Wt:** 220 **Born:** 11/6/72 **Age:** 24

		HOW MUCH HE PITCHED						WHAT HE GAVE UP												THE RESULTS					
Year Team	Lg Org	G	GS	CG	GF	IP	BFP	H	R	ER	HR	SH	SF	HB	TBB	IBB	SO	WP	Bk	W	L	Pct.	ShO	Sv	ERA
1993 Bristol	R+ Det	8	5	0	1	35	158	30	23	19	1	0	3	3	22	1	29	6	3	2	3	.400	0	0	4.89
1994 Jamestown	A- Det	17	15	1	1	93.2	389	74	42	33	4	2	3	7	37	0	56	2	3	5	3	.625	0	0	3.17
1995 Fayettevlle	A Det	44	2	0	15	89.2	371	66	36	27	9	6	1	3	35	2	105	2	0	9	4	.692	0	2	2.71
1996 Jacksonvlle	AA Det	4	0	0	1	6	27	4	3	3	0	0	1	0	5	1	7	1	0	0	0	.000	0	0	4.50
Lakeland	A+ Det	40	0	0	20	52.2	223	44	23	21	5	2	0	2	19	1	52	2	1	5	5	.500	0	5	3.59
4 Min. YEARS		113	22	1	38	277	1168	218	127	103	19	10	8	15	118	5	249	13	7	21	15	.583	0	7	3.35

Joe Slusarski

Pitches: Right **Bats:** Right **Pos:** P **Ht:** 6' 4" **Wt:** 195 **Born:** 12/19/66 **Age:** 30

		HOW MUCH HE PITCHED						WHAT HE GAVE UP												THE RESULTS					
Year Team	Lg Org	G	GS	CG	GF	IP	BFP	H	R	ER	HR	SH	SF	HB	TBB	IBB	SO	WP	Bk	W	L	Pct.	ShO	Sv	ERA
1989 Modesto	A+ Oak	27	27	4	0	184	753	155	78	65	15	5	3	8	50	0	160	13	1	13	10	.565	1	0	3.18
1990 Huntsville	AA Oak	17	17	2	0	108.2	471	114	65	54	9	2	9	3	35	0	75	5	0	6	8	.429	0	0	4.47
Tacoma	AAA Oak	9	9	0	0	55.2	241	54	24	21	3	1	3	2	22	0	37	1	1	4	2	.667	0	0	3.40
1991 Tacoma	AAA Oak	7	7	0	0	46.1	182	42	20	14	4	0	0	0	10	0	25	0	2	4	2	.667	0	0	2.72
1992 Tacoma	AAA Oak	11	10	0	0	57.1	249	67	30	24	6	0	5	1	18	1	26	1	0	2	4	.333	0	0	3.77
1993 Tacoma	AAA Oak	24	21	1	0	113.1	501	133	67	60	6	3	7	1	40	1	61	2	0	7	5	.583	1	0	4.76
1994 Tacoma	AAA Oak	7	7	0	0	37.1	167	45	28	25	6	0	3	3	11	0	24	1	0	2	3	.400	0	0	6.03
Reading	AA Phi	5	4	0	0	23.1	97	25	15	12	2	2	0	0	5	0	17	0	1	1	2	.333	0	0	4.63
Scranton-WB	AAA Phi	10	4	0	3	38	172	50	36	33	8	1	2	3	10	0	29	2	0	2	3	.400	0	0	7.82
1995 Buffalo	AAA Cle	4	2	0	0	15.2	67	18	12	11	2	0	1	1	4	0	9	0	0	1	1	.500	0	0	6.32
New Orleans	AAA Mil	37	2	0	23	64	255	55	22	17	6	1	2	1	15	2	39	0	0	2	2	.500	0	11	2.39
1996 New Orleans	AAA Mil	40	0	0	19	60	280	70	38	33	4	6	3	3	24	5	36	1	0	2	4	.333	0	1	4.95
1991 Oakland	AL	20	19	1	0	109.1	486	121	69	64	14	0	3	4	52	1	60	4	0	5	7	.417	0	0	5.27
1992 Oakland	AL	15	14	0	1	76	338	85	52	46	15	1	5	6	27	0	38	0	1	5	5	.500	0	0	5.45
1993 Oakland	AL	2	1	0	0	8.2	43	9	5	5	1	2	0	0	11	3	1	0	0	0	0	.000	0	0	5.19
1995 Milwaukee	AL	12	0	0	6	15	73	21	11	9	3	1	1	2	6	1	6	0	0	1	1	.500	0	0	5.40
8 Min. YEARS		198	110	7	45	803.2	3435	828	435	369	71	21	38	26	244	9	538	26	5	46	46	.500	2	12	4.13
4 Maj. YEARS		49	34	1	7	209	940	236	137	124	33	4	9	12	96	5	105	4	1	11	13	.458	0	0	5.34

Bobby Smith

Bats: Right **Throws:** Right **Pos:** 3B **Ht:** 6'3" **Wt:** 190 **Born:** 4/10/74 **Age:** 23

		BATTING															BASERUNNING				PERCENTAGES		
Year Team	Lg Org	G	AB	H	2B	3B	HR	TB	R	RBI	TBB	IBB	SO	HBP	SH	SF	SB	CS	SB%	GDP	Avg	OBP	SLG
1992 Braves	R Atl	57	217	51	9	1	3	71	31	28	17	1	55	3	0	2	5	6	.45	5	.235	.297	.327
1993 Macon	A Atl	108	384	94	16	7	4	136	53	38	23	1	81	5	8	0	12	8	.60	1	.245	.296	.354
1994 Durham	A+ Atl	127	478	127	27	2	12	194	49	71	41	1	112	4	1	0	18	7	.72	19	.266	.329	.406
1995 Greenville	AA Atl	127	444	116	27	3	14	191	75	58	40	2	109	7	4	1	12	6	.67	12	.261	.331	.430
1996 Richmond	AAA Atl	124	445	114	27	0	8	165	49	58	32	0	114	4	2	3	15	9	.63	12	.256	.310	.371
5 Min. YEARS		543	1968	502	106	13	41	757	257	253	153	5	471	23	15	6	62	36	.63	49	.255	.315	.385

Brian Smith

Pitches: Right **Bats:** Right **Pos:** P **Ht:** 5'11" **Wt:** 185 **Born:** 7/19/72 **Age:** 24

		HOW MUCH HE PITCHED						WHAT HE GAVE UP												THE RESULTS					
Year Team	Lg Org	G	GS	CG	GF	IP	BFP	H	R	ER	HR	SH	SF	HB	TBB	IBB	SO	WP	Bk	W	L	Pct.	ShO	Sv	ERA
1994 Medicne Hat	R+ Tor	20	5	0	11	64	268	58	36	24	3	2	4	5	20	0	53	6	3	5	4	.556	0	4	3.38
1995 Hagerstown	A Tor	47	0	0	36	104	402	77	18	10	1	5	0	5	16	1	101	2	2	9	1	.900	0	21	0.87
1996 Knoxville	AA Tor	54	0	0	43	75.2	333	76	42	32	7	6	3	4	31	6	58	4	0	3	5	.375	0	16	3.81
3 Min. YEARS		121	5	0	90	243.2	1003	211	96	66	11	13	7	14	67	7	212	12	5	17	10	.630	0	41	2.44

Bubba Smith

Bats: Right **Throws:** Right **Pos:** 1B **Ht:** 6' 2" **Wt:** 225 **Born:** 12/18/69 **Age:** 27

		BATTING															BASERUNNING				PERCENTAGES		
Year Team	Lg Org	G	AB	H	2B	3B	HR	TB	R	RBI	TBB	IBB	SO	HBP	SH	SF	SB	CS	SB%	GDP	Avg	OBP	SLG
1991 Bellingham	A- Sea	66	253	66	14	2	10	114	28	43	13	1	47	2	0	2	0	2	.00	9	.261	.300	.451
1992 Peninsula	A+ Sea	137	482	126	22	1	32	246	70	93	65	7	138	5	0	5	4	10	.29	13	.261	.352	.510
1993 Jacksonvlle	AA Sea	37	137	30	8	0	6	56	12	21	7	0	52	2	0	1	0	3	.00	1	.219	.265	.409
Riverside	A+ Sea	5	19	8	3	0	0	11	5	3	7	0	3	0	0	0	0	0	.00	1	.421	.577	.579
Winston-Sal	A+ Cin	92	342	103	16	0	27	200	55	81	35	1	109	7	0	4	2	0	1.00	8	.301	.374	.585
1994 Chattanooga	AA Cin	4	9	0	0	0	0	0	0	0	0	0	7	0	0	0	0	0	.00	0	.000	.000	.000
Charlstn-WV	A Cin	100	354	83	26	1	15	156	38	59	20	1	113	5	1	2	1	2	.33	9	.234	.283	.441

			BATTING															BASERUNNING				PERCENTAGES		
Year Team	Lg	Org	G	AB	H	2B	3B	HR	TB	R	RBI	TBB	IBB	SO	HBP	SH	SF	SB	CS	SB%	GDP	Avg	OBP	SLG
1995 Fort Myers	A+	Min	60	176	58	15	0	13	112	27	51	16	4	38	0	0	3	1	2	.33	8	.330	.379	.636
New Britain	AA	Min	42	148	36	11	0	6	65	20	21	6	1	41	0	0	1	0	0	.00	5	.243	.271	.439
1996 Tulsa	AA	Tex	134	513	150	28	0	32	274	82	94	48	5	121	5	0	3	0	1	.00	10	.292	.357	.534
6 Min. YEARS			677	2433	660	143	4	141	1234	337	466	217	20	669	26	1	21	8	20	.29	64	.271	.335	.507

Chuck Smith

Pitches: Right **Bats:** Right **Pos:** P **Ht:** 6'1" **Wt:** 175 **Born:** 10/21/69 **Age:** 27

			HOW MUCH HE PITCHED						WHAT HE GAVE UP												THE RESULTS					
Year Team	Lg	Org	G	GS	CG	GF	IP	BFP	H	R	ER	HR	SH	SF	HB	TBB	IBB	SO	WP	Bk	W	L	Pct.	ShO	Sv	ERA
1991 Astros	R	Hou	15	7	1	2	59.1	272	56	36	23	2	3	0	7	37	0	64	7	5	4	3	.571	0	0	3.49
1992 Asheville	A	Hou	28	20	1	3	132	596	128	93	76	14	5	4	4	78	1	117	4	7	9	9	.500	0	1	5.18
1993 Quad City	A	Hou	22	17	2	3	110.2	488	109	73	57	16	3	2	6	52	0	103	7	4	7	5	.583	0	0	4.64
1994 Jackson	AA	Hou	2	0	0	0	6	30	6	6	3	0	2	0	0	5	0	7	0	1	0	0	.000	0	0	4.50
Osceola	A+	Hou	35	2	0	11	84.2	376	73	41	35	2	2	2	2	49	3	60	7	3	4	4	.500	0	0	3.72
1995 South Bend	A	ChA	26	25	4	1	167	688	128	70	50	8	7	2	13	61	0	145	21	11	10	10	.500	2	0	2.69
1996 Pr. William	A+	ChA	20	20	2	0	123.1	545	125	65	55	7	3	2	10	49	1	99	13	1	6	6	.500	1	0	4.01
Birmingham	AA	ChA	7	3	0	2	30.2	124	25	11	9	1	0	0	1	15	2	30	0	1	2	1	.667	0	1	2.64
Nashville	AAA	ChA	1	0	0	0	0.2	5	2	2	2	0	0	0	0	1	0	1	0	0	0	0	.000	0	0	27.00
6 Min. YEARS			156	94	10	22	714.1	3124	652	397	310	50	25	12	43	347	7	626	59	33	42	38	.525	3	2	3.91

Danny Smith

Pitches: Left **Bats:** Left **Pos:** P **Ht:** 6' 5" **Wt:** 205 **Born:** 4/20/69 **Age:** 28

			HOW MUCH HE PITCHED						WHAT HE GAVE UP												THE RESULTS					
Year Team	Lg	Org	G	GS	CG	GF	IP	BFP	H	R	ER	HR	SH	SF	HB	TBB	IBB	SO	WP	Bk	W	L	Pct.	ShO	Sv	ERA
1990 Butte	R+	Tex	5	5	0	0	24.2	102	23	10	10	3	2	0	2	6	0	27	3	1	2	0	1.000	0	0	3.65
Tulsa	AA	Tex	7	7	0	0	38.1	151	27	16	16	2	0	3	0	16	0	32	0	0	3	2	.600	0	0	3.76
1991 Okla. City	AAA	Tex	28	27	3	1	151.2	713	195	114	93	10	6	8	4	75	1	85	5	5	4	17	.190	0	0	5.52
1992 Tulsa	AA	Tex	24	23	4	0	146.1	571	110	48	41	4	9	3	6	34	0	122	3	3	11	7	.611	3	0	2.52
1993 Charlotte	A+	Tex	1	1	0	0	7	24	3	0	0	0	0	0	0	0	0	5	1	0	1	0	1.000	0	0	0.00
Okla. City	AAA	Tex	3	3	0	0	15.1	66	16	11	8	2	1	1	1	5	0	12	0	0	1	2	.333	0	0	4.70
1994 Charlotte	A+	Tex	2	0	0	0	3.2	13	2	0	0	0	1	1	0	2	0	3	0	0	0	0	.000	0	0	0.00
Okla. City	AAA	Tex	10	2	0	3	25.1	110	27	9	8	2	0	2	2	9	0	15	0	0	2	1	.667	0	2	2.84
1996 Okla. City	AAA	Tex	5	5	0	0	15	78	27	19	15	4	0	1	1	7	0	12	1	0	0	2	.000	0	0	9.00
Charlotte	A+	Tex	5	5	0	0	23	92	21	7	7	1	0	0	0	8	0	16	1	1	0	1	.000	0	0	2.74
Tulsa	AA	Tex	9	9	0	0	50.1	227	53	27	24	6	3	3	1	21	0	29	0	0	2	3	.400	0	0	4.29
1992 Texas	AL		4	2	0	1	14.1	67	18	8	8	1	2	1	0	8	1	5	0	0	0	3	.000	0	0	5.02
1994 Texas	AL		13	0	0	2	14.2	76	18	11	7	2	0	0	0	12	0	9	2	0	1	2	.333	0	0	4.30
6 Min. YEARS			99	87	7	4	500.2	2147	504	261	222	34	22	22	17	183	1	358	14	10	26	35	.426	3	2	3.99
2 Maj. YEARS			17	2	0	3	29	143	36	19	15	3	2	1	0	20	1	14	2	0	1	5	.167	0	0	4.66

Demond Smith

Bats: Both **Throws:** Right **Pos:** OF **Ht:** 5'11" **Wt:** 170 **Born:** 11/6/72 **Age:** 24

			BATTING															BASERUNNING				PERCENTAGES		
Year Team	Lg	Org	G	AB	H	2B	3B	HR	TB	R	RBI	TBB	IBB	SO	HBP	SH	SF	SB	CS	SB%	GDP	Avg	OBP	SLG
1990 Mets	R	NYN	46	153	40	9	2	1	56	19	7	20	0	34	0	1	2	16	10	.62	2	.261	.343	.366
1991 Kingsport	R+	NYN	35	116	29	3	4	1	43	28	12	12	0	25	6	0	1	16	7	.70	0	.250	.348	.371
1992 Pittsfield	A-	NYN	66	233	58	10	4	1	79	39	24	23	0	42	7	1	3	21	15	.58	0	.249	.331	.339
1993 Capital Cty	A	NYN	1	2	0	0	0	0	0	0	0	1	0	0	0	0	0	2	0	1.00	0	.000	.333	.000
1994 Lk Elsinore	A+	Cal	12	26	3	0	1	0	5	1	1	4	0	8	0	1	0	0	4	.00	1	.115	.233	.192
Boise	A-	Cal	71	279	78	9	7	5	116	60	45	43	2	57	2	7	4	26	9	.74	0	.280	.375	.416
1995 Cedar Rapds	A	Cal	79	317	108	25	7	7	168	64	41	32	2	61	6	5	1	37	12	.76	3	.341	.410	.530
Lk Elsinore	A+	Cal	34	148	52	8	2	7	85	32	26	11	0	36	2	0	1	14	3	.82	1	.351	.401	.574
W. Michigan	A	Oak	8	32	10	1	1	2	19	6	3	2	1	8	1	1	0	3	2	.60	0	.313	.371	.594
1996 Huntsville	AA	Oak	123	447	116	17	14	9	188	75	62	55	1	89	11	8	5	30	15	.67	6	.260	.351	.421
Edmonton	AAA	Oak	2	3	1	0	0	0	1	0	0	0	0	2	0	0	0	0	0	.00	0	.333	.333	.333
7 Min. YEARS			477	1756	495	82	42	33	760	324	221	203	6	362	35	24	17	165	77	.68	13	.282	.364	.433

Ira Smith

Bats: Right **Throws:** Right **Pos:** OF **Ht:** 5'11" **Wt:** 185 **Born:** 8/4/67 **Age:** 29

			BATTING															BASERUNNING				PERCENTAGES		
Year Team	Lg	Org	G	AB	H	2B	3B	HR	TB	R	RBI	TBB	IBB	SO	HBP	SH	SF	SB	CS	SB%	GDP	Avg	OBP	SLG
1990 Great Falls	R+	LA	50	142	37	7	3	1	53	31	28	25	0	32	3	2	3	8	6	.57	3	.261	.376	.373
1991 Vero Beach	A+	LA	52	176	57	5	3	1	71	27	24	18	0	30	2	0	0	15	3	.83	7	.324	.393	.403
1992 Bakersfield	A+	LA	118	413	119	17	4	7	165	79	45	48	3	56	6	8	6	26	14	.65	12	.288	.366	.400
San Antonio	AA	LA	6	11	4	0	1	0	6	3	1	1	0	2	0	0	0	0	0	.00	0	.364	.417	.545
1993 Rancho Cuca	A+	SD	92	347	120	30	6	7	183	71	47	55	1	41	5	2	3	32	16	.67	7	.346	.439	.527
Wichita	AA	SD	13	39	9	0	1	0	11	7	4	4	0	9	0	1	0	0	2	.00	2	.231	.302	.282
1994 Wichita	AA	SD	107	358	115	17	6	7	165	58	41	53	2	59	3	3	6	6	12	.33	5	.321	.407	.461
1995 Memphis	AA	SD	64	238	72	13	3	5	106	40	36	23	0	32	2	0	3	11	4	.73	6	.303	.365	.445
Las Vegas	AAA	SD	59	209	68	19	5	3	106	39	22	13	0	25	2	4	1	5	4	.56	3	.325	.369	.507
1996 Las Vegas	AAA	SD	72	252	61	16	1	5	94	37	25	20	0	27	1	5	1	3	3	.50	9	.242	.299	.373
7 Min. YEARS			633	2185	662	124	33	36	960	392	273	260	6	313	24	25	23	106	64	.62	54	.303	.380	.439

Mike Smith

Bats: Right **Throws:** Right **Pos:** 2B **Ht:** 6'0" **Wt:** 180 **Born:** 12/1/69 **Age:** 27

		BATTING															BASERUNNING				PERCENTAGES		
Year Team	Lg Org	G	AB	H	2B	3B	HR	TB	R	RBI	TBB	IBB	SO	HBP	SH	SF	SB	CS	SB%	GDP	Avg	OBP	SLG
1992 Gastonia	A Tex	81	302	61	15	3	4	94	30	23	37	0	48	1	2	4	3	11	.21	7	.202	.288	.311
1993 Charlotte	A+ Tex	86	327	77	16	4	3	110	33	43	37	0	55	3	3	3	3	6	.33	7	.235	.316	.336
1994 High Desert	A+ Tex	132	512	149	23	6	21	247	96	94	73	2	89	5	4	5	28	15	.65	13	.291	.382	.482
1995 Tulsa	AA Tex	132	499	128	22	3	16	204	65	64	60	1	72	2	5	5	11	6	.65	13	.257	.336	.409
1996 Okla. City	AAA Tex	81	200	45	12	0	6	75	22	20	22	0	53	4	3	1	4	2	.67	5	.225	.313	.375
5 Min. YEARS		512	1840	460	88	16	50	730	246	244	229	3	317	15	17	18	49	40	.55	45	.250	.335	.397

Pete Smith

Pitches: Right **Bats:** Right **Pos:** P **Ht:** 6' 2" **Wt:** 200 **Born:** 2/27/66 **Age:** 31

		HOW MUCH HE PITCHED						WHAT HE GAVE UP												THE RESULTS					
Year Team	Lg Org	G	GS	CG	GF	IP	BFP	H	R	ER	HR	SH	SF	HB	TBB	IBB	SO	WP	Bk	W	L	Pct.	ShO	Sv	ERA
1984 Phillies	R Phi	8	8	0	0	37	155	28	11	6	0	3	1	0	16	0	35	2	0	1	2	.333	0	0	1.46
1985 Clearwater	A+ Phi	26	25	4	0	153	663	135	68	56	2	1	7	2	80	1	86	3	6	12	10	.545	1	0	3.29
1986 Greenville	AA Atl	24	19	0	1	104.2	499	117	88	68	11	7	8	4	78	0	64	4	2	1	8	.111	0	0	5.85
1987 Greenville	AA Atl	29	25	5	2	177.1	744	162	76	66	10	1	4	3	67	0	119	11	2	9	9	.500	1	1	3.35
1990 Greenville	AA Atl	2	2	0	0	3.1	12	1	0	0	0	0	0	0	0	0	2	0	0	0	0	.000	0	0	0.00
1991 Macon	A Atl	3	3	0	0	9.2	45	15	11	9	1	0	0	0	2	0	14	2	0	0	0	.000	0	0	8.38
Richmond	AAA Atl	10	10	1	0	51	239	66	44	41	10	1	5	0	24	0	41	2	1	3	3	.500	0	0	7.24
1992 Richmond	AAA Atl	15	15	4	0	109.1	415	75	27	26	6	2	1	4	24	0	93	1	0	7	4	.636	1	0	2.14
1995 Charlotte	AAA Fla	10	8	0	1	49	206	51	21	21	5	1	2	1	17	0	20	2	2	2	1	.667	0	0	3.86
1996 Las Vegas	AAA SD	26	26	2	0	169	723	192	106	93	17	5	10	3	42	8	95	5	2	11	9	.550	1	0	4.95
1987 Atlanta	NL	6	6	0	0	31.2	143	39	21	17	3	0	2	0	14	0	11	3	1	1	2	.333	0	0	4.83
1988 Atlanta	NL	32	32	5	0	195.1	837	183	89	80	15	12	4	1	88	3	124	5	7	7	15	.318	3	0	3.69
1989 Atlanta	NL	28	27	1	0	142	613	144	83	75	13	4	5	0	57	2	115	3	7	5	14	.263	0	0	4.75
1990 Atlanta	NL	13	13	3	0	77	327	77	45	41	11	4	3	0	24	2	56	2	1	5	6	.455	0	0	4.79
1991 Atlanta	NL	14	10	0	2	48	211	48	33	27	5	2	4	0	22	3	29	1	4	1	3	.250	0	0	5.06
1992 Atlanta	NL	12	11	2	0	79	323	63	19	18	3	4	1	0	28	2	43	2	1	7	0	1.000	1	0	2.05
1993 Atlanta	NL	20	14	0	2	90.2	390	92	45	44	15	6	5	2	36	3	53	1	1	4	8	.333	0	0	4.37
1994 New York	NL	21	21	1	0	131.1	565	145	83	81	25	5	7	2	42	4	62	3	1	4	10	.286	0	0	5.55
1995 Cincinnati	NL	11	2	0	3	24.1	106	30	19	18	8	1	3	1	7	1	14	1	0	1	2	.333	0	0	6.66
9 Min. YEARS		153	141	16	4	863.1	3701	842	452	386	62	21	38	17	350	9	569	32	15	46	46	.500	4	1	4.02
9 Maj. YEARS		157	136	12	7	819.1	3515	821	437	401	98	38	34	6	318	20	507	21	23	35	60	.368	4	0	4.40

Ryan Smith

Pitches: Right **Bats:** Right **Pos:** P **Ht:** 6'2" **Wt:** 190 **Born:** 11/11/71 **Age:** 25

		HOW MUCH HE PITCHED						WHAT HE GAVE UP												THE RESULTS					
Year Team	Lg Org	G	GS	CG	GF	IP	BFP	H	R	ER	HR	SH	SF	HB	TBB	IBB	SO	WP	Bk	W	L	Pct.	ShO	Sv	ERA
1991 Mariners	R Sea	13	13	2	0	75	350	87	59	38	3	4	1	11	42	0	51	10	0	4	6	.400	0	0	4.56
1992 Bellingham	A- Sea	9	9	0	0	49	215	48	26	18	2	0	3	5	19	0	34	5	0	4	3	.571	0	0	3.31
1994 Appleton	A Sea	21	21	5	0	144.1	589	129	54	45	10	4	5	12	28	0	82	7	0	10	6	.625	1	0	2.81
1995 Riverside	A+ Sea	23	23	2	0	141.2	609	142	68	49	7	7	5	10	50	1	108	5	3	10	7	.588	1	0	3.11
1996 Port City	AA Sea	50	0	0	22	97.2	420	92	42	34	5	10	4	9	37	5	65	6	3	6	9	.400	0	2	3.13
5 Min. YEARS		116	66	9	22	507.2	2183	498	249	184	27	25	18	47	176	6	340	33	6	34	31	.523	2	2	3.26

Sloan Smith

Bats: Both **Throws:** Right **Pos:** OF **Ht:** 6'4" **Wt:** 215 **Born:** 11/29/72 **Age:** 24

		BATTING															BASERUNNING				PERCENTAGES		
Year Team	Lg Org	G	AB	H	2B	3B	HR	TB	R	RBI	TBB	IBB	SO	HBP	SH	SF	SB	CS	SB%	GDP	Avg	OBP	SLG
1993 Oneonta	A- NYA	34	116	23	5	1	1	33	14	10	15	0	33	6	3	1	3	2	.60	1	.198	.319	.284
1994 Oneonta	A- NYA	38	138	34	5	5	0	49	24	16	25	0	41	2	1	0	2	1	.67	1	.246	.370	.355
Greensboro	A NYA	79	269	51	4	3	5	76	35	26	42	2	98	2	3	3	13	5	.72	4	.190	.301	.283
Albany-Colo	AA NYA	7	23	4	2	1	0	8	4	5	3	0	6	0	0	0	0	0	.00	1	.174	.269	.348
1995 Tampa	A+ NYA	124	412	107	23	1	13	171	61	64	74	3	136	4	1	3	6	8	.43	8	.260	.375	.415
1996 Norwich	AA NYA	60	202	44	10	2	2	64	27	20	30	2	96	0	3	0	4	1	.80	0	.218	.319	.317
Tampa	A+ NYA	61	194	43	10	1	4	67	25	21	46	2	60	0	1	2	5	6	.45	6	.222	.368	.345
4 Min. YEARS		403	1354	306	59	14	25	468	190	162	235	9	470	14	12	9	33	23	.59	21	.226	.344	.346

Toby Smith

Pitches: Right **Bats:** Right **Pos:** P **Ht:** 6'6" **Wt:** 225 **Born:** 11/16/71 **Age:** 25

		HOW MUCH HE PITCHED						WHAT HE GAVE UP												THE RESULTS					
Year Team	Lg Org	G	GS	CG	GF	IP	BFP	H	R	ER	HR	SH	SF	HB	TBB	IBB	SO	WP	Bk	W	L	Pct.	ShO	Sv	ERA
1993 Eugene	A- KC	14	0	0	8	23	90	14	8	6	1	2	0	1	7	0	31	0	1	1	1	.500	0	4	2.35
1994 Rockford	A KC	29	16	0	12	121	489	104	50	44	8	3	3	4	31	1	91	14	2	11	9	.550	0	4	3.27
1995 Wilmington	A+ KC	30	7	0	13	79	320	67	32	27	9	2	1	3	20	2	65	6	2	5	7	.417	0	4	3.08
1996 Wichita	AA KC	42	0	0	30	52.1	221	46	25	24	7	4	2	2	19	4	44	7	0	4	2	.667	0	8	4.13
4 Min. YEARS		115	23	0	63	275.1	1120	231	115	101	25	11	6	10	77	7	231	27	5	21	19	.525	0	20	3.30

Travis Smith

Pitches: Right **Bats:** Right **Pos:** P **Ht:** 5'10" **Wt:** 170 **Born:** 11/7/72 **Age:** 24

				HOW MUCH HE PITCHED						WHAT HE GAVE UP												THE RESULTS					
Year	Team	Lg	Org	G	GS	CG	GF	IP	BFP	H	R	ER	HR	SH	SF	HB	TBB	IBB	SO	WP	Bk	W	L	Pct.	ShO	Sv	ERA
1995	Helena	R+	Mil	20	7	0	11	56	224	41	16	15	4	0	0	7	19	0	63	4	2	4	2	.667	0	5	2.41
1996	Stockton	A+	Mil	14	6	0	3	58.2	241	56	17	12	4	1	0	4	21	0	48	2	4	6	1	.857	0	1	1.84
	El Paso	AA	Mil	17	17	3	0	107.2	478	119	56	50	6	4	5	6	39	0	68	2	0	7	4	.636	1	0	4.18
2 Min. YEARS				51	30	3	14	222.1	943	216	89	77	14	5	5	17	79	0	179	8	6	17	7	.708	1	6	3.12

John Snyder

Pitches: Right **Bats:** Right **Pos:** P **Ht:** 6'3" **Wt:** 185 **Born:** 8/16/74 **Age:** 22

				HOW MUCH HE PITCHED						WHAT HE GAVE UP												THE RESULTS					
Year	Team	Lg	Org	G	GS	CG	GF	IP	BFP	H	R	ER	HR	SH	SF	HB	TBB	IBB	SO	WP	Bk	W	L	Pct.	ShO	Sv	ERA
1992	Angels	R	Cal	15	0	0	7	44	195	40	27	16	0	2	5	3	16	1	38	1	4	2	4	.333	0	3	3.27
1993	Cedar Rapds	A	Cal	21	16	1	0	99	467	126	88	65	13	7	5	8	39	1	79	6	4	5	6	.455	1	0	5.91
1994	Lk Elsinore	A+	Cal	26	26	2	0	159	698	181	101	79	16	5	5	6	56	0	108	11	2	10	11	.476	0	0	4.47
1995	Birmingham	AA	ChA	5	4	0	0	20.1	87	24	16	15	6	0	1	2	6	0	13	1	0	1	0	1.000	0	0	6.64
	Midland	AA	Cal	26	25	4	0	153.2	678	182	109	100	18	3	7	12	54	1	94	8	3	9	9	.500	0	0	5.86
1996	White Sox	R	ChA	4	4	0	0	16.1	58	5	3	3	1	1	0	0	4	0	23	0	0	1	0	1.000	0	0	1.65
	Birmingham	AA	ChA	9	9	0	0	54	236	59	35	29	10	2	2	1	16	1	58	4	3	3	5	.375	0	0	4.83
5 Min. YEARS				106	84	7	7	546.1	2419	617	379	307	64	20	25	32	191	4	413	31	16	31	35	.470	1	3	5.06

Jeff Sobkoviak

Pitches: Right **Bats:** Right **Pos:** P **Ht:** 6'7" **Wt:** 220 **Born:** 8/22/71 **Age:** 25

				HOW MUCH HE PITCHED						WHAT HE GAVE UP												THE RESULTS					
Year	Team	Lg	Org	G	GS	CG	GF	IP	BFP	H	R	ER	HR	SH	SF	HB	TBB	IBB	SO	WP	Bk	W	L	Pct.	ShO	Sv	ERA
1992	Rockies/Cub	R	Col	16	6	1	3	53	238	58	37	27	0	1	2	3	21	1	35	3	2	1	6	.143	0	0	4.58
1993	Bend	A-	Col	15	15	1	0	77	345	90	50	38	4	2	3	6	38	1	34	4	1	4	6	.400	0	0	4.44
1994	Asheville	A	Col	17	0	0	9	32.1	149	31	14	10	5	3	0	4	16	3	24	2	0	2	2	.500	0	3	2.78
	Central Val	A+	Col	34	0	0	5	59.1	268	66	36	30	7	3	2	2	22	1	51	2	0	4	0	1.000	0	0	4.55
1995	Salem	A+	Col	40	5	0	10	86.1	371	96	52	46	13	3	4	5	37	5	44	7	0	5	3	.625	0	2	4.80
1996	New Haven	AA	Col	4	0	0	1	6.2	32	7	5	4	0	0	0	0	5	1	4	2	0	0	1	.000	0	0	5.40
	Salem	A+	Col	46	1	0	26	77.1	331	67	31	27	7	7	1	6	26	6	52	0	1	6	6	.500	0	9	3.14
5 Min. YEARS				172	27	2	54	392	1734	415	225	182	36	19	12	26	165	18	244	20	4	22	24	.478	0	14	4.18

Steve Soliz

Bats: Right **Throws:** Right **Pos:** C **Ht:** 5'10" **Wt:** 180 **Born:** 1/27/71 **Age:** 26

				BATTING															BASERUNNING				PERCENTAGES		
Year	Team	Lg	Org	G	AB	H	2B	3B	HR	TB	R	RBI	TBB	IBB	SO	HBP	SH	SF	SB	CS	SB%	GDP	Avg	OBP	SLG
1993	Watertown	A-	Cle	56	209	62	12	0	0	74	30	35	15	0	41	1	2	3	2	0	1.00	3	.297	.342	.354
1994	Kinston	A+	Cle	51	163	43	7	1	3	61	26	19	16	0	32	1	2	1	3	0	1.00	0	.264	.331	.374
	Canton-Akrn	AA	Cle	18	54	10	1	0	0	11	4	0	2	0	9	1	1	0	0	0	.00	4	.185	.228	.204
1995	Bakersfield	A+	LA	44	159	39	5	0	1	47	9	11	15	0	34	2	0	0	2	1	.67	6	.245	.318	.296
	Canton-Akrn	AA	Cle	32	81	14	3	0	2	23	9	7	13	0	16	0	1	1	0	0	.00	3	.173	.284	.284
1996	Canton-Akrn	AA	Cle	46	143	37	4	2	2	51	18	15	11	0	28	2	0	2	1	2	.33	1	.259	.316	.357
4 Min. YEARS				247	809	205	32	3	8	267	96	87	72	0	160	7	6	7	8	3	.73	17	.253	.317	.330

Don Sparks

Bats: Right **Throws:** Right **Pos:** 3B **Ht:** 6'2" **Wt:** 185 **Born:** 6/19/66 **Age:** 31

				BATTING															BASERUNNING				PERCENTAGES		
Year	Team	Lg	Org	G	AB	H	2B	3B	HR	TB	R	RBI	TBB	IBB	SO	HBP	SH	SF	SB	CS	SB%	GDP	Avg	OBP	SLG
1988	Pr. William	A+	NYA	70	267	66	14	0	3	89	22	28	8	0	51	4	1	1	1	0	1.00	8	.247	.279	.333
1989	Pr. William	A+	NYA	115	449	126	32	1	6	178	52	65	24	2	85	2	0	4	1	2	.33	20	.281	.317	.396
1990	Columbus	AAA	NYA	16	51	6	3	0	0	9	3	2	2	0	10	1	0	0	0	0	.00	3	.118	.167	.176
	Albany-Colo	AA	NYA	112	418	110	20	5	4	152	48	52	33	2	70	4	0	5	3	4	.43	14	.263	.320	.364
1991	Columbus	AAA	NYA	52	152	39	6	2	0	49	11	25	12	0	27	4	3	2	0	0	.00	7	.257	.324	.322
1992	Albany-Colo	AA	NYA	134	505	158	31	2	14	235	64	72	30	2	71	2	0	8	2	2	.50	14	.313	.349	.465
1993	Columbus	AAA	NYA	128	475	135	33	7	11	215	63	72	29	0	83	4	1	6	0	3	.00	14	.284	.327	.453
1994	Columbus	AAA	NYA	139	515	140	21	6	7	194	60	63	42	3	76	4	2	8	2	7	.22	17	.272	.327	.377
1995	Columbus	AAA	NYA	137	545	170	26	10	7	237	67	90	29	3	75	1	1	9	2	0	1.00	17	.312	.342	.435
1996	Buffalo	AAA	Cle	137	511	151	32	5	8	217	69	68	54	4	72	2	1	12	2	2	.50	14	.295	.358	.425
9 Min. YEARS				1040	3888	1101	218	38	60	1575	459	537	263	16	620	28	9	55	13	20	.39	128	.283	.329	.405

Jeff Sparks

Pitches: Right **Bats:** Right **Pos:** P **Ht:** 6'3" **Wt:** 210 **Born:** 4/4/72 **Age:** 25

				HOW MUCH HE PITCHED						WHAT HE GAVE UP												THE RESULTS					
Year	Team	Lg	Org	G	GS	CG	GF	IP	BFP	H	R	ER	HR	SH	SF	HB	TBB	IBB	SO	WP	Bk	W	L	Pct.	ShO	Sv	ERA
1995	Princeton	R+	Cin	16	2	0	7	39	172	32	19	14	2	0	1	0	27	2	49	2	1	2	0	1.000	0	2	3.23
1996	Chattanooga	AA	Cin	3	0	0	0	2	10	5	1	1	1	0	0	0	1	0	2	0	0	0	0	.000	0	0	4.50
	Charlstn-WV	A	Cin	46	3	0	14	89.1	394	79	51	47	4	4	4	9	46	6	94	10	1	2	7	.222	0	0	4.74
2 Min. YEARS				65	5	0	21	130.1	576	116	71	62	7	4	5	9	74	8	145	12	2	4	7	.364	0	2	4.28

Vernon Spearman

Bats: Left **Throws:** Left **Pos:** OF **Ht:** 5'10" **Wt:** 160 **Born:** 12/17/69 **Age:** 27

		BATTING																BASERUNNING				PERCENTAGES		
Year	Team	Lg Org	G	AB	H	2B	3B	HR	TB	R	RBI	TBB	IBB	SO	HBP	SH	SF	SB	CS	SB%	GDP	Avg	OBP	SLG
1991	Yakima	A- LA	71	248	72	8	0	0	80	63	17	50	0	37	4	7	1	56	9	.86	1	.290	.416	.323
1992	Vero Beach	A+ LA	73	276	84	13	1	0	99	50	16	26	1	25	1	3	1	33	14	.70	5	.304	.365	.359
	San Antonio	AA LA	48	185	52	3	3	0	61	24	11	15	0	16	1	6	1	18	9	.67	2	.281	.337	.330
1993	San Antonio	AA LA	56	162	42	4	2	0	50	22	13	11	0	21	1	5	0	13	4	.76	3	.259	.310	.309
	Albuquerque	AAA LA	62	185	47	6	5	0	63	31	15	17	0	28	0	4	0	11	4	.73	4	.254	.317	.341
1994	San Antonio	AA LA	105	331	88	14	3	0	108	43	24	39	0	39	2	15	0	21	15	.58	2	.266	.347	.326
1995	Albuquerque	AAA LA	22	29	5	0	1	0	7	7	2	11	0	4	0	0	0	2	2	.50	2	.172	.400	.241
	San Bernrdo	A+ LA	93	365	105	15	7	3	143	78	36	56	1	50	0	8	4	43	12	.78	5	.288	.379	.392
1996	San Antonio	AA LA	123	471	121	15	9	1	157	66	30	35	0	38	5	7	3	26	17	.60	10	.257	.313	.333
6 Min. YEARS			653	2252	616	78	31	4	768	384	164	260	2	258	14	55	10	223	86	.72	34	.274	.351	.341

Justin Speier

Pitches: Right **Bats:** Right **Pos:** P **Ht:** 6'4" **Wt:** 195 **Born:** 11/6/73 **Age:** 23

		HOW MUCH HE PITCHED						WHAT HE GAVE UP												THE RESULTS					
Year	Team	Lg Org	G	GS	CG	GF	IP	BFP	H	R	ER	HR	SH	SF	HB	TBB	IBB	SO	WP	Bk	W	L	Pct.	ShO	Sv	ERA
1995	Williamsprt	A- ChN	30	0	0	22	36.1	142	27	6	6	1	2	2	1	4	0	39	0	0	2	1	.667	0	12	1.49
1996	Daytona	A+ ChN	33	0	0	29	38.1	168	32	19	16	3	3	2	2	19	3	34	5	0	2	4	.333	0	13	3.76
	Orlando	AA ChN	24	0	0	19	26.1	110	23	7	6	2	1	1	2	5	1	14	0	0	4	1	.800	0	6	2.05
2 Min. YEARS			87	0	0	70	101	420	82	32	28	6	6	5	5	28	4	87	5	0	8	6	.571	0	31	2.50

Shane Spencer

Bats: Right **Throws:** Right **Pos:** OF **Ht:** 5'11" **Wt:** 182 **Born:** 2/20/72 **Age:** 25

		BATTING																BASERUNNING				PERCENTAGES		
Year	Team	Lg Org	G	AB	H	2B	3B	HR	TB	R	RBI	TBB	IBB	SO	HBP	SH	SF	SB	CS	SB%	GDP	Avg	OBP	SLG
1990	Yankees	R NYA	42	147	27	4	0	0	31	20	7	20	0	23	1	0	1	11	2	.85	3	.184	.284	.211
1991	Yankees	R NYA	41	160	49	7	0	0	56	25	30	14	0	19	2	0	4	8	2	.80	6	.306	.361	.350
	Oneonta	A- NYA	18	53	13	2	1	0	17	10	3	10	0	9	1	3	0	2	2	.50	1	.245	.375	.321
1992	Greensboro	A NYA	83	258	74	10	2	3	97	43	27	33	0	37	3	1	2	8	2	.80	12	.287	.372	.376
1993	Greensboro	A NYA	122	431	116	35	2	12	191	89	80	52	0	62	3	0	8	14	2	.88	8	.269	.346	.443
1994	Tampa	A+ NYA	90	334	97	22	3	8	149	44	53	30	0	53	1	1	1	5	3	.63	8	.290	.350	.446
1995	Tampa	A+ NYA	134	500	150	31	3	16	235	87	88	61	2	60	7	2	3	14	8	.64	7	.300	.382	.470
1996	Norwich	AA NYA	126	450	114	19	0	29	220	70	89	68	2	99	4	1	5	4	2	.67	6	.253	.353	.489
	Columbus	AAA NYA	9	31	11	4	0	3	24	7	6	5	0	5	1	0	0	0	1	.00	0	.355	.459	.774
7 Min. YEARS			665	2364	651	134	11	71	1020	395	383	293	4	367	23	8	24	66	24	.73	51	.275	.358	.431

Robby Stanifer

Pitches: Right **Bats:** Right **Pos:** P **Ht:** 6'2" **Wt:** 195 **Born:** 3/10/72 **Age:** 25

		HOW MUCH HE PITCHED						WHAT HE GAVE UP												THE RESULTS					
Year	Team	Lg Org	G	GS	CG	GF	IP	BFP	H	R	ER	HR	SH	SF	HB	TBB	IBB	SO	WP	Bk	W	L	Pct.	ShO	Sv	ERA
1994	Elmira	A- Fla	9	8	1	0	49	211	54	17	14	2	0	1	2	12	1	38	2	3	2	1	.667	0	0	2.57
	Brevard Cty	A+ Fla	5	5	0	0	24.1	115	32	20	17	2	1	1	3	10	0	12	2	1	1	2	.333	0	0	6.29
1995	Brevard Cty	A+ Fla	18	13	0	0	82.2	360	97	47	38	4	4	5	7	15	0	45	2	0	3	6	.333	0	0	4.14
1996	Brevard Cty	A+ Fla	22	0	0	4	49	206	54	17	13	3	0	1	1	9	0	32	1	0	4	2	.667	0	0	2.39
	Portland	AA Fla	18	0	0	10	34.1	137	27	15	6	3	1	2	1	9	0	33	2	0	3	1	.750	0	2	1.57
3 Min. YEARS			72	26	1	14	239.1	1029	264	116	88	14	6	10	14	55	1	160	9	4	13	12	.520	0	2	3.31

Lonny Stare

Bats: Right **Throws:** Right **Pos:** OF **Ht:** 5'11" **Wt:** 185 **Born:** 5/20/71 **Age:** 26

		BATTING																BASERUNNING				PERCENTAGES		
Year	Team	Lg Org	G	AB	H	2B	3B	HR	TB	R	RBI	TBB	IBB	SO	HBP	SH	SF	SB	CS	SB%	GDP	Avg	OBP	SLG
1994	Clinton	A SF	38	76	22	3	2	0	29	12	5	4	0	14	1	1	0	2	3	.40	0	.289	.333	.382
1995	Bakersfield	A+ LA	104	372	101	21	2	9	153	54	59	33	1	65	7	8	2	14	10	.58	9	.272	.341	.411
1996	San Antonio	AA LA	32	67	15	2	0	0	17	7	4	11	0	11	1	2	0	2	2	.50	3	.224	.342	.254
3 Min. YEARS			174	515	138	26	4	9	199	73	68	48	1	90	9	11	2	18	15	.55	12	.268	.340	.386

T.J. Staton

Bats: Left **Throws:** Left **Pos:** OF **Ht:** 6'3" **Wt:** 200 **Born:** 2/17/75 **Age:** 22

		BATTING																BASERUNNING				PERCENTAGES		
Year	Team	Lg Org	G	AB	H	2B	3B	HR	TB	R	RBI	TBB	IBB	SO	HBP	SH	SF	SB	CS	SB%	GDP	Avg	OBP	SLG
1993	Pirates	R Pit	32	115	41	9	2	1	57	23	18	8	0	14	0	0	0	10	2	.83	0	.357	.398	.496
1994	Welland	A- Pit	12	45	8	3	0	0	11	4	4	0	0	7	0	0	0	5	0	1.00	1	.178	.178	.244
	Pirates	R Pit	11	39	10	3	0	1	16	3	5	1	0	8	1	0	0	0	0	.00	0	.256	.293	.410
	Augusta	A Pit	37	125	27	6	1	0	35	9	5	10	0	38	0	1	1	6	1	.86	5	.216	.272	.280
1995	Augusta	A Pit	112	391	114	21	5	5	160	43	53	27	5	97	2	0	1	27	13	.68	6	.292	.340	.409
1996	Carolina	AA Pit	112	386	119	24	3	15	194	72	57	58	1	99	6	0	4	17	7	.71	4	.308	.403	.503
4 Min. YEARS			316	1101	319	66	11	22	473	154	142	104	6	263	9	1	6	65	23	.74	16	.290	.354	.430

David Steed

Bats: Right **Throws:** Right **Pos:** C **Ht:** 6'1" **Wt:** 205 **Born:** 2/25/73 **Age:** 24

				BATTING															BASERUNNING				PERCENTAGES		
Year	Team	Lg	Org	G	AB	H	2B	3B	HR	TB	R	RBI	TBB	IBB	SO	HBP	SH	SF	SB	CS	SB%	GDP	Avg	OBP	SLG
1994	Yakima	A-	LA	48	147	37	5	2	5	61	21	24	28	0	43	5	1	0	1	2	.33	4	.252	.389	.415
1995	Vero Beach	A+	LA	59	195	49	16	0	0	65	11	24	18	0	53	3	1	1	0	0	.00	5	.251	.323	.333
	San Antonio	AA	LA	40	123	31	10	1	3	52	13	16	11	0	32	1	0	2	0	1	.00	2	.252	.314	.423
1996	San Bernrdo	A+	LA	28	87	26	6	0	1	35	11	13	14	0	19	1	0	1	2	3	.40	1	.299	.398	.402
	Vero Beach	A+	LA	23	73	21	3	0	1	27	6	10	6	0	15	0	1	0	1	0	1.00	1	.288	.342	.370
	San Antonio	AA	LA	7	17	2	1	0	0	3	0	2	1	0	6	0	0	0	0	0	.00	1	.118	.167	.176
3 Min. YEARS				205	642	166	41	3	10	243	62	89	78	0	168	10	3	4	4	6	.40	14	.259	.346	.379

Rick Steed

Pitches: Right **Bats:** Right **Pos:** P **Ht:** 6'2" **Wt:** 185 **Born:** 9/8/70 **Age:** 26

				HOW MUCH HE PITCHED						WHAT HE GAVE UP												THE RESULTS					
Year	Team	Lg	Org	G	GS	CG	GF	IP	BFP	H	R	ER	HR	SH	SF	HB	TBB	IBB	SO	WP	Bk	W	L	Pct.	ShO	Sv	ERA
1989	Medicne Hat	R+	Tor	7	6	0	0	16	73	14	10	6	1	0	0	1	11	0	11	2	3	0	2	.000	0	0	3.38
1990	St. Cathrns	A-	Tor	14	14	0	0	73.1	311	58	32	25	4	2	1	2	39	2	72	10	1	3	6	.333	0	0	3.07
1991	Myrtle Bch	A	Tor	28	27	4	0	172	745	161	96	77	11	7	5	5	62	0	122	15	2	12	13	.480	0	0	4.03
1992	Dunedin	A+	Tor	20	19	2	1	104	451	106	56	44	4	3	5	9	40	0	57	11	1	6	6	.500	0	1	3.81
1993	Dunedin	A+	Tor	22	20	2	0	111	502	120	81	62	10	2	4	3	62	1	66	9	1	4	9	.308	1	0	5.03
1994	Dunedin	A+	Tor	30	0	0	17	44	195	33	14	13	1	2	1	1	30	1	55	10	1	3	1	.750	0	6	2.66
1995	Knoxville	AA	Tor	27	0	0	23	31.2	136	23	15	13	1	3	2	2	16	2	29	4	0	2	4	.333	0	9	3.69
	Syracuse	AAA	Tor	58	0	0	38	87.1	375	74	44	36	3	5	4	2	39	3	63	5	1	6	7	.462	0	10	3.71
1996	Greenville	AA	Atl	33	9	0	7	101	449	100	51	44	4	5	4	11	44	2	70	11	1	6	9	.400	0	0	3.92
8 Min. YEARS				239	95	8	86	740.1	3237	689	399	320	39	29	26	36	343	11	545	77	11	42	57	.424	1	26	3.89

Kennie Steenstra

Pitches: Right **Bats:** Right **Pos:** P **Ht:** 6'5" **Wt:** 220 **Born:** 10/13/70 **Age:** 26

				HOW MUCH HE PITCHED						WHAT HE GAVE UP												THE RESULTS					
Year	Team	Lg	Org	G	GS	CG	GF	IP	BFP	H	R	ER	HR	SH	SF	HB	TBB	IBB	SO	WP	Bk	W	L	Pct.	ShO	Sv	ERA
1992	Geneva	A-	ChN	3	3	1	0	20	76	11	4	2	0	0	0	0	3	0	12	0	1	3	0	1.000	0	0	0.90
	Peoria	A	ChN	12	12	4	0	89.2	364	79	29	21	5	2	1	3	21	1	68	4	3	6	3	.667	2	0	2.11
1993	Daytona	A+	ChN	13	13	1	0	81.1	317	64	26	23	2	3	2	8	12	1	57	2	1	5	3	.625	1	0	2.55
	Iowa	AAA	ChN	1	1	0	0	6.2	32	9	5	5	2	0	0	0	4	0	6	0	0	1	0	1.000	0	0	6.75
	Orlando	AA	ChN	14	14	2	0	100.1	427	103	47	40	4	4	2	9	25	0	60	5	2	8	3	.727	2	0	3.59
1994	Iowa	AAA	ChN	3	3	0	0	13	68	24	21	19	2	0	2	2	4	0	10	0	0	1	2	.333	0	0	13.15
	Orlando	AA	ChN	23	23	2	0	158.1	654	146	55	46	12	9	3	9	39	4	83	4	1	9	7	.563	1	0	2.61
1995	Iowa	AAA	ChN	29	26	6	1	171.1	722	174	85	74	15	6	6	8	48	3	96	6	0	9	12	.429	2	0	3.89
1996	Iowa	AAA	ChN	26	26	1	0	158	686	170	96	88	24	5	9	9	47	4	101	2	0	8	12	.400	0	0	5.01
5 Min. YEARS				124	121	17	1	798.2	3346	780	368	318	66	29	25	48	203	13	493	23	8	50	42	.543	8	0	3.58

Mike Stefanski

Bats: Right **Throws:** Right **Pos:** C **Ht:** 6' 2" **Wt:** 202 **Born:** 9/12/69 **Age:** 27

				BATTING															BASERUNNING				PERCENTAGES		
Year	Team	Lg	Org	G	AB	H	2B	3B	HR	TB	R	RBI	TBB	IBB	SO	HBP	SH	SF	SB	CS	SB%	GDP	Avg	OBP	SLG
1991	Brewers	R	Mil	56	206	76	5	5	0	91	43	43	22	0	22	5	0	6	3	2	.60	4	.369	.431	.442
1992	Beloit	A	Mil	116	385	105	12	0	4	129	66	45	55	1	81	4	3	3	9	4	.69	11	.273	.367	.335
1993	Stockton	A+	Mil	97	345	111	22	2	10	167	58	57	49	2	45	5	1	2	6	1	.86	15	.322	.411	.484
1994	El Paso	AA	Mil	95	312	82	7	6	8	125	59	56	32	0	80	0	2	5	4	3	.57	5	.263	.327	.401
1995	El Paso	AA	Mil	6	27	11	3	0	1	17	5	6	0	0	3	0	0	0	1	0	1.00	0	.407	.407	.630
	New Orleans	AAA	Mil	78	228	56	10	2	2	76	30	24	14	0	28	1	5	5	2	0	1.00	8	.246	.286	.333
1996	Louisville	AAA	StL	53	126	26	7	1	2	41	11	9	11	1	11	1	1	2	1	2	.33	4	.206	.271	.325
6 Min. YEARS				501	1629	467	66	16	27	646	272	240	183	4	270	16	12	23	26	12	.68	47	.287	.360	.397

Rod Steph

Pitches: Right **Bats:** Right **Pos:** P **Ht:** 5'11" **Wt:** 185 **Born:** 8/27/69 **Age:** 27

				HOW MUCH HE PITCHED						WHAT HE GAVE UP												THE RESULTS					
Year	Team	Lg	Org	G	GS	CG	GF	IP	BFP	H	R	ER	HR	SH	SF	HB	TBB	IBB	SO	WP	Bk	W	L	Pct.	ShO	Sv	ERA
1991	Princeton	R+	Cin	7	7	1	0	46.1	186	37	19	16	1	0	1	4	11	0	52	4	3	2	3	.400	1	0	3.11
	Cedar Rapds	A	Cin	8	7	3	0	56.2	229	46	19	16	5	2	0	4	15	1	46	3	4	4	3	.571	2	0	2.54
1992	Cedar Rapds	A	Cin	27	27	1	0	154.1	668	157	86	74	18	3	4	6	54	0	136	11	2	12	9	.571	1	0	4.32
1993	Winston-Sal	A+	Cin	28	28	4	0	167.2	717	166	101	73	21	6	3	8	57	0	130	14	0	7	11	.389	2	0	3.92
1994	Thunder Bay	IND	—	13	13	3	0	88.1	354	68	30	24	5	3	1	4	17	0	76	5	0	8	1	.889	2	0	2.45
	Canton-Akrn	AA	Cle	3	3	1	0	20	89	27	13	12	2	1	0	0	4	0	6	1	0	1	2	.333	0	0	5.40
1995	Canton-Akrn	AA	Cle	32	20	1	5	137	595	150	74	58	6	7	2	9	33	1	82	5	0	8	10	.444	0	0	3.81
1996	Greenville	AA	Atl	2	0	0	0	3.1	10	1	0	0	0	0	0	0	0	0	3	1	0	0	0	.000	0	0	0.00
	Richmond	AAA	Atl	38	0	0	16	79.2	324	75	34	34	6	0	2	3	17	2	41	5	0	2	3	.400	0	1	3.84
6 Min. YEARS				158	105	14	21	753.1	3172	727	376	307	64	22	13	38	208	4	572	49	9	44	42	.512	8	1	3.67

Brian Stephenson

Pitches: Right **Bats:** Right **Pos:** P **Ht:** 6'3" **Wt:** 205 **Born:** 7/17/73 **Age:** 23

			HOW MUCH HE PITCHED						WHAT HE GAVE UP												THE RESULTS					
Year Team	Lg	Org	G	GS	CG	GF	IP	BFP	H	R	ER	HR	SH	SF	HB	TBB	IBB	SO	WP	Bk	W	L	Pct.	ShO	Sv	ERA
1994 Williamsprt	A-	ChN	5	5	0	0	19	80	17	9	9	2	0	2	4	4	0	13	1	1	0	2	.000	0	0	4.26
Peoria	A	ChN	6	6	2	0	42.1	180	41	18	15	3	3	0	6	6	1	29	1	0	3	1	.750	0	0	3.19
1995 Daytona	A+	ChN	26	26	0	0	150	640	145	79	66	7	6	3	7	58	2	109	14	2	10	9	.526	0	0	3.96
1996 Orlando	AA	ChN	32	20	0	3	128.2	574	130	82	67	13	4	9	5	61	3	106	10	1	5	13	.278	0	1	4.69
3 Min. YEARS			69	57	2	3	340	1474	333	188	157	25	13	14	22	129	6	257	26	4	18	25	.419	0	1	4.16

Andy Stewart

Bats: Right **Throws:** Right **Pos:** C **Ht:** 5'11" **Wt:** 205 **Born:** 12/5/70 **Age:** 26

			BATTING														BASERUNNING				PERCENTAGES		
Year Team	Lg	Org	G	AB	H	2B	3B	HR	TB	R	RBI	TBB	IBB	SO	HBP	SH	SF	SB	CS	SB%	GDP	Avg	OBP	SLG
1990 Royals	R	KC	21	52	10	4	0	0	14	5	1	9	1	13	3	3	0	3	0	1.00	0	.192	.344	.269
1991 Baseball Cy	A+	KC	78	276	64	16	1	3	91	30	36	7	1	59	4	4	2	6	4	.60	6	.232	.260	.330
1992 Baseball Cy	A+	KC	94	283	73	13	1	4	100	31	38	21	1	45	2	4	1	3	8	.27	4	.258	.313	.353
1993 Wilmington	A+	KC	110	361	100	20	3	8	150	54	42	26	0	88	8	0	1	7	1	.88	6	.277	.338	.416
1994 Wilmington	A+	KC	94	360	114	24	3	17	195	53	66	30	4	56	13	2	4	0	2	.00	11	.317	.386	.542
Memphis	AA	KC	20	72	17	1	0	0	18	10	5	3	1	5	4	1	1	0	0	.00	3	.236	.300	.250
1995 Wichita	AA	KC	60	216	56	18	0	3	83	28	32	11	0	31	4	0	2	1	2	.33	9	.259	.305	.384
Omaha	AAA	KC	44	156	47	11	0	3	67	24	21	12	1	18	8	0	0	0	1	.00	4	.301	.381	.429
1996 Omaha	AAA	KC	50	181	39	10	2	2	59	23	13	15	0	25	5	0	1	0	2	.00	9	.215	.292	.326
Wichita	AA	KC	58	202	61	17	3	3	93	29	32	14	1	25	4	2	2	3	2	.60	9	.302	.356	.460
7 Min. YEARS			629	2159	581	134	13	43	870	287	286	148	10	365	55	16	14	23	22	.51	61	.269	.330	.403

Chaad Stewart

Pitches: Left **Bats:** Left **Pos:** P **Ht:** 6'4" **Wt:** 212 **Born:** 10/8/74 **Age:** 22

			HOW MUCH HE PITCHED						WHAT HE GAVE UP												THE RESULTS					
Year Team	Lg	Org	G	GS	CG	GF	IP	BFP	H	R	ER	HR	SH	SF	HB	TBB	IBB	SO	WP	Bk	W	L	Pct.	ShO	Sv	ERA
1994 Orioles	R	Bal	1	1	0	0	3	15	6	5	5	0	0	1	0	0	0	3	0	2	0	0	.000	0	0	15.00
Bluefield	R+	Bal	14	3	0	7	43.1	171	34	11	8	0	2	1	2	10	0	43	4	3	3	1	.750	0	2	1.66
1995 Frederick	A+	Bal	26	26	1	0	150.2	635	126	71	61	8	5	1	10	66	1	140	12	4	8	8	.500	1	0	3.64
1996 Greenville	AA	Atl	24	13	0	2	71.1	348	89	55	48	4	6	3	0	48	2	74	12	2	3	5	.375	0	0	6.06
3 Min. YEARS			65	43	1	9	268.1	1169	255	142	122	12	13	6	12	124	3	260	28	11	14	14	.500	1	2	4.09

Phil Stidham

Pitches: Right **Bats:** Right **Pos:** P **Ht:** 6' 0" **Wt:** 180 **Born:** 11/18/68 **Age:** 28

			HOW MUCH HE PITCHED						WHAT HE GAVE UP												THE RESULTS					
Year Team	Lg	Org	G	GS	CG	GF	IP	BFP	H	R	ER	HR	SH	SF	HB	TBB	IBB	SO	WP	Bk	W	L	Pct.	ShO	Sv	ERA
1991 Fayettevlle	A	Det	28	0	0	26	33.2	139	25	10	6	0	1	2	0	16	0	20	3	3	0	1	.000	0	8	1.60
1992 Lakeland	A+	Det	45	0	0	27	53.2	252	61	28	22	3	2	1	3	28	2	47	4	1	2	7	.222	0	6	3.69
1993 Lakeland	A+	Det	25	0	0	23	29.2	119	22	6	5	2	2	0	2	9	1	24	0	0	2	1	.667	0	9	1.52
London	AA	Det	33	0	0	8	34	164	40	18	9	3	1	0	2	19	3	39	1	0	2	2	.500	0	2	2.38
1994 Trenton	AA	Det	6	0	0	6	6	22	4	0	0	0	0	0	0	0	0	6	2	0	0	0	.000	0	3	0.00
Toledo	AAA	Det	49	0	0	16	69	278	48	25	24	3	4	2	1	31	3	57	1	0	3	3	.500	0	3	3.13
1995 Binghamton	AA	NYN	7	0	0	4	9.2	47	9	6	5	0	1	0	0	9	0	7	0	0	0	0	.000	0	0	4.66
Norfolk	AAA	NYN	41	6	0	16	79.2	352	65	39	30	4	3	6	5	45	1	63	5	0	6	2	.750	0	1	3.39
1996 New Britain	AA	Min	12	0	0	4	13.2	61	11	5	4	1	2	1	2	8	1	16	4	0	1	0	1.000	0	1	2.63
Salt Lake	AAA	Min	33	7	0	8	78.1	366	100	63	59	8	3	2	4	40	1	54	10	1	10	5	.667	0	0	6.78
1994 Detroit	AL		5	0	0	0	4.1	26	12	12	12	3	0	1	0	4	1	4	0	0	0	0	.000	0	0	24.92
6 Min. YEARS			279	13	0	138	407.1	1800	385	200	164	24	19	14	19	205	12	333	30	5	26	21	.553	0	33	3.62

Darond Stovall

Bats: Both **Throws:** Left **Pos:** OF **Ht:** 6'1" **Wt:** 185 **Born:** 1/3/73 **Age:** 24

			BATTING														BASERUNNING				PERCENTAGES		
Year Team	Lg	Org	G	AB	H	2B	3B	HR	TB	R	RBI	TBB	IBB	SO	HBP	SH	SF	SB	CS	SB%	GDP	Avg	OBP	SLG
1991 Johnson Cty	R+	StL	48	134	19	2	2	0	25	16	5	23	1	63	0	0	0	8	3	.73	1	.142	.268	.187
1992 Savannah	A	StL	135	450	92	13	7	7	140	51	40	63	0	138	0	1	1	20	14	.59	13	.204	.302	.311
1993 Springfield	A	StL	135	460	118	19	4	20	205	73	81	53	2	143	0	2	1	18	12	.60	5	.257	.333	.446
1994 St. Pete	A+	StL	134	507	113	20	6	15	190	68	69	62	4	154	0	2	5	24	8	.75	10	.223	.305	.375
1995 W. Palm Bch	A+	Mon	121	461	107	22	2	4	145	52	51	44	2	117	0	2	3	18	12	.60	4	.232	.297	.315
1996 Expos	R	Mon	9	34	15	3	2	0	22	5	7	3	0	6	0	0	0	3	0	1.00	0	.441	.486	.647
W. Palm Bch	A+	Mon	8	31	14	4	0	1	21	8	8	6	0	7	0	0	0	2	2	.50	1	.452	.541	.677
Harrisburg	AA	Mon	74	272	60	7	1	10	99	38	36	32	1	86	2	4	0	10	5	.67	5	.221	.307	.364
6 Min. YEARS			664	2349	538	90	24	57	847	311	297	286	10	714	2	11	10	103	56	.65	39	.229	.312	.361

Don Strange

Pitches: Right **Bats:** Right **Pos:** P **Ht:** 6'0" **Wt:** 195 **Born:** 5/26/67 **Age:** 30

			HOW MUCH HE PITCHED						WHAT HE GAVE UP												THE RESULTS					
Year Team	Lg	Org	G	GS	CG	GF	IP	BFP	H	R	ER	HR	SH	SF	HB	TBB	IBB	SO	WP	Bk	W	L	Pct.	ShO	Sv	ERA
1989 Pulaski	R+	Atl	27	0	0	20	33	136	27	9	9	1	0	1	0	6	2	30	4	1	3	0	1.000	0	5	2.45
1990 Sumter	A	Atl	46	0	0	41	54.1	208	34	6	4	0	1	3	3	12	3	53	2	0	4	1	.800	0	24	0.66
1991 Durham	A+	Atl	38	0	0	32	40.1	172	39	13	8	1	2	2	1	8	1	51	7	0	0	0	.000	0	19	1.79

HOW MUCH HE PITCHED										WHAT HE GAVE UP												THE RESULTS					
Year	Team	Lg	Org	G	GS	CG	GF	IP	BFP	H	R	ER	HR	SH	SF	HB	TBB	IBB	SO	WP	Bk	W	L	Pct.	ShO	Sv	ERA
	Greenville	AA	Atl	4	0	0	1	4.2	23	9	7	7	1	0	0	0	2	0	8	1	0	1	0	1.000	0	1	13.50
1992	Greenville	AA	Atl	48	0	0	41	60	234	43	19	16	3	0	1	1	19	3	58	3	0	5	3	.625	0	18	2.40
1993	Greenville	AA	Atl	27	0	0	24	24.2	109	27	11	10	3	0	2	0	9	1	27	2	0	1	1	.500	0	18	3.65
	Richmond	AAA	Atl	34	0	0	19	46.1	200	45	24	20	1	2	1	0	19	6	34	4	0	1	2	.333	0	1	3.88
1994	Richmond	AAA	Atl	12	1	0	8	20.1	100	31	15	15	2	1	4	1	7	4	18	2	0	2	1	.667	0	0	6.64
	Memphis	AA	KC	14	0	0	11	21	80	11	4	4	3	1	0	1	6	1	18	0	0	0	0	.000	0	6	1.71
1995	Omaha	AAA	KC	9	0	0	3	15.2	75	24	13	13	2	0	1	0	6	0	11	0	0	0	0	.000	0	1	7.47
	Wichita	AA	KC	33	0	0	20	51.2	211	52	20	19	4	0	2	0	13	0	47	5	0	0	1	.000	0	9	3.31
1996	Bowie	AA	Bal	12	0	0	9	14.2	58	11	4	4	0	2	0	0	5	0	10	2	0	2	1	.667	0	3	2.45
8 Min. YEARS				304	1	0	229	386.2	1606	353	145	129	21	9	17	7	112	21	374	32	1	19	10	.655	0	105	3.00

Chad Strickland

Bats: Right **Throws:** Right **Pos:** C **Ht:** 6'1" **Wt:** 185 **Born:** 3/16/72 **Age:** 25

BATTING																			BASERUNNING				PERCENTAGES		
Year	Team	Lg	Org	G	AB	H	2B	3B	HR	TB	R	RBI	TBB	IBB	SO	HBP	SH	SF	SB	CS	SB%	GDP	Avg	OBP	SLG
1990	Royals	R	KC	50	163	36	7	0	0	43	14	12	11	0	24	0	2	4	6	2	.75	5	.221	.264	.264
1991	Appleton	A	KC	28	81	14	4	0	1	21	5	5	2	0	12	0	1	1	2	1	.67	0	.173	.190	.259
	Eugene	A-	KC	34	118	19	7	0	1	29	13	11	13	0	16	2	2	2	1	1	.50	1	.161	.252	.246
1992	Appleton	A	KC	112	396	101	16	1	2	125	29	49	12	0	37	1	0	5	2	5	.29	6	.255	.275	.316
1993	Wilmington	A+	KC	122	409	102	16	6	2	136	51	46	23	0	46	3	7	9	4	3	.57	7	.249	.288	.333
1994	Memphis	AA	KC	114	379	82	14	2	6	118	37	47	17	1	40	3	5	3	1	3	.25	8	.216	.254	.311
1995	Omaha	AAA	KC	8	22	6	2	0	0	8	3	5	1	0	4	0	0	1	0	0	.00	1	.273	.292	.364
	Wichita	AA	KC	51	183	41	7	0	1	51	16	21	5	0	22	0	2	1	0	0	.00	9	.224	.243	.279
1996	Wilmington	A+	KC	11	33	2	1	0	0	3	2	0	3	0	5	0	2	0	1	0	1.00	1	.061	.139	.091
	Wichita	AA	KC	77	239	54	15	2	5	88	35	34	16	0	23	2	3	4	1	1	.50	10	.226	.276	.368
7 Min. YEARS				607	2023	457	89	11	18	622	205	230	103	1	229	11	24	30	18	16	.53	48	.226	.263	.307

Scott Stricklin

Bats: Left **Throws:** Right **Pos:** C **Ht:** 5'11" **Wt:** 180 **Born:** 2/17/72 **Age:** 25

BATTING																			BASERUNNING				PERCENTAGES		
Year	Team	Lg	Org	G	AB	H	2B	3B	HR	TB	R	RBI	TBB	IBB	SO	HBP	SH	SF	SB	CS	SB%	GDP	Avg	OBP	SLG
1993	Elizabethtn	R+	Min	38	125	28	2	0	1	33	18	15	16	0	17	0	4	1	1	0	1.00	3	.224	.310	.264
	Fort Wayne	A	Min	9	31	2	0	0	0	2	1	0	4	0	7	0	0	0	0	0	.00	0	.065	.171	.065
1994	Salt Lake	AAA	Min	2	2	0	0	0	0	0	0	0	0	0	0	0	0	0	0	0	.00	0	.000	.000	.000
	Fort Wayne	A	Min	65	182	55	12	0	2	73	18	19	30	3	38	0	2	1	1	3	.25	2	.302	.399	.401
	Nashville	AA	Min	16	38	9	4	0	0	13	4	1	7	0	11	0	0	0	0	1	.00	0	.237	.356	.342
1995	Fort Myers	A+	Min	65	166	31	1	0	0	32	20	8	41	2	25	0	5	0	4	4	.50	3	.187	.348	.193
1996	Greenville	AA	Atl	45	131	19	4	0	0	23	14	11	16	1	29	1	3	1	1	1	.50	0	.145	.242	.176
4 Min. YEARS				240	675	144	23	0	3	176	75	54	114	6	127	1	14	3	7	9	.44	8	.213	.327	.261

Mark Strittmatter

Bats: Right **Throws:** Right **Pos:** C **Ht:** 6'1" **Wt:** 200 **Born:** 4/4/69 **Age:** 28

BATTING																			BASERUNNING				PERCENTAGES		
Year	Team	Lg	Org	G	AB	H	2B	3B	HR	TB	R	RBI	TBB	IBB	SO	HBP	SH	SF	SB	CS	SB%	GDP	Avg	OBP	SLG
1992	Bend	A-	Col	35	101	26	6	0	2	38	17	13	12	0	28	3	0	0	0	4	.00	2	.257	.353	.376
1993	Central Val	A+	Col	59	179	47	8	0	2	61	21	15	31	0	29	2	2	3	3	0	1.00	8	.263	.372	.341
	Colo. Sprng	AAA	Col	5	10	2	1	0	0	3	1	2	0	0	2	1	0	0	0	0	.00	2	.200	.273	.300
1994	New Haven	AA	Col	73	215	49	8	0	2	63	20	26	33	1	39	9	3	4	1	2	.33	7	.228	.349	.293
1995	Colo. Sprng	AAA	Col	5	17	5	2	0	0	7	1	3	0	0	3	0	0	0	0	0	.00	0	.294	.294	.412
	New Haven	AA	Col	90	288	70	12	1	7	105	44	42	47	1	51	6	1	2	1	0	1.00	5	.243	.359	.365
1996	Colo. Sprng	AAA	Col	58	159	37	8	1	2	53	21	18	17	3	30	7	1	0	2	1	.67	5	.233	.333	.333
5 Min. YEARS				325	969	236	45	2	15	330	125	119	140	5	182	28	7	9	7	7	.50	29	.244	.353	.341

Everett Stull

Pitches: Right **Bats:** Right **Pos:** P **Ht:** 6'3" **Wt:** 195 **Born:** 8/24/71 **Age:** 25

HOW MUCH HE PITCHED										WHAT HE GAVE UP												THE RESULTS					
Year	Team	Lg	Org	G	GS	CG	GF	IP	BFP	H	R	ER	HR	SH	SF	HB	TBB	IBB	SO	WP	Bk	W	L	Pct.	ShO	Sv	ERA
1992	Jamestown	A-	Mon	14	14	0	0	63.1	303	52	49	38	2	2	3	3	61	0	64	18	4	3	5	.375	0	0	5.40
1993	Burlington	A	Mon	15	15	1	0	82.1	366	68	44	35	8	2	1	3	59	0	85	11	4	4	9	.308	0	0	3.83
1994	W. Palm Bch	A+	Mon	27	26	3	0	147	627	116	60	54	3	7	3	12	78	0	165	15	6	10	10	.500	1	0	3.31
1995	Harrisburg	AA	Mon	24	24	0	0	126.2	569	114	88	78	12	5	5	9	79	2	132	7	1	3	12	.200	0	0	5.54
1996	Harrisburg	AA	Mon	14	14	0	0	80	345	64	31	28	8	3	2	2	52	1	81	6	0	6	3	.667	0	0	3.15
	Ottawa	AAA	Mon	13	13	1	0	69.2	331	87	57	49	7	3	3	3	39	1	69	5	0	2	6	.250	0	0	6.33
5 Min. YEARS				107	106	5	0	569	2541	501	329	282	40	22	17	32	368	4	596	62	15	28	45	.384	1	0	4.46

Jack Sturdivant

Bats: Left **Throws:** Left **Pos:** OF **Ht:** 5'10" **Wt:** 150 **Born:** 10/29/73 **Age:** 23

BATTING																			BASERUNNING				PERCENTAGES		
Year	Team	Lg	Org	G	AB	H	2B	3B	HR	TB	R	RBI	TBB	IBB	SO	HBP	SH	SF	SB	CS	SB%	GDP	Avg	OBP	SLG
1992	Mariners	R	Sea	42	141	44	6	1	0	52	27	14	12	3	14	1	0	3	7	5	.58	0	.312	.363	.369
1993	Bellingham	A-	Sea	64	238	61	8	3	4	87	34	32	22	1	28	2	2	0	8	5	.62	4	.256	.324	.366
1994	Appleton	A	Sea	113	413	104	12	7	2	136	50	36	33	1	43	4	4	0	20	17	.54	7	.252	.313	.329

Year	Team	Lg	Org	G	AB	H	2B	3B	HR	TB	R	RBI	TBB	IBB	SO	HBP	SH	SF	SB	CS	SB%	GDP	Avg	OBP	SLG
				BATTING															BASERUNNING				PERCENTAGES		
1995	Riverside	A+	Sea	99	347	95	13	5	1	121	60	34	39	1	41	1	2	4	31	13	.70	3	.274	.345	.349
1996	Lancaster	A+	Sea	68	292	83	19	6	0	114	54	31	32	1	35	3	0	1	23	9	.72	3	.284	.360	.390
	Port City	AA	Sea	63	243	69	11	4	2	94	34	23	26	1	33	0	0	2	13	7	.65	2	.284	.351	.387
5 Min. YEARS				449	1674	456	69	26	9	604	259	170	164	8	194	11	8	10	102	56	.65	19	.272	.339	.361

John Sutherland

Pitches: Right **Bats:** Right **Pos:** P **Ht:** 6'2" **Wt:** 185 **Born:** 10/11/68 **Age:** 28

Year	Team	Lg	Org	G	GS	CG	GF	IP	BFP	H	R	ER	HR	SH	SF	HB	TBB	IBB	SO	WP	Bk	W	L	Pct.	ShO	Sv	ERA
				HOW MUCH HE PITCHED						WHAT HE GAVE UP												THE RESULTS					
1991	Yankees	R	NYA	4	1	0	0	7.2	31	5	6	5	0	0	1	0	3	0	5	0	1	0	2	.000	0	0	5.87
1992	Oneonta	A-	NYA	4	1	0	1	15.2	61	10	2	2	1	1	0	0	2	0	16	0	0	3	0	1.000	0	0	1.15
	Greensboro	A	NYA	14	3	0	1	34	144	29	17	15	2	2	0	1	12	0	27	3	0	3	2	.600	0	0	3.97
1993	San Bernrdo	A+	NYA	43	1	0	24	70.1	314	73	46	39	7	2	0	0	37	2	59	5	0	3	7	.300	0	4	4.99
1994	Albany-Colo	AA	NYA	31	4	0	11	63.2	276	62	35	27	6	1	1	2	25	2	49	1	0	6	4	.600	0	1	3.82
1995	Columbus	AAA	NYA	3	0	0	2	3	14	5	3	3	0	0	0	0	0	0	2	0	0	0	0	.000	0	0	9.00
	Norwich	AA	NYA	16	0	0	8	16	65	17	8	7	3	0	1	1	3	0	14	0	0	1	0	1.000	0	2	3.94
1996	Norwich	AA	NYA	26	0	0	6	42.2	187	37	15	13	3	2	1	3	19	3	31	3	0	3	2	.600	0	1	2.74
6 Min. YEARS				141	10	0	53	253	1092	238	132	111	22	8	4	7	101	7	203	12	1	19	17	.528	0	8	3.95

Larry Sutton

Bats: Left **Throws:** Left **Pos:** 1B **Ht:** 5'11" **Wt:** 175 **Born:** 5/14/70 **Age:** 27

Year	Team	Lg	Org	G	AB	H	2B	3B	HR	TB	R	RBI	TBB	IBB	SO	HBP	SH	SF	SB	CS	SB%	GDP	Avg	OBP	SLG
				BATTING															BASERUNNING				PERCENTAGES		
1992	Eugene	A-	KC	70	238	74	17	3	15	142	45	58	48	5	33	5	0	2	3	6	.33	3	.311	.433	.597
	Appleton	A	KC	1	2	0	0	0	0	0	1	0	2	0	1	0	0	0	0	1	.00	0	.000	.500	.000
1993	Rockford	A	KC	113	361	97	24	1	7	144	67	50	95	5	65	8	0	8	3	5	.38	3	.269	.424	.399
1994	Wilmington	A+	KC	129	480	147	33	1	26	260	91	94	81	10	71	6	1	9	2	1	.67	7	.306	.406	.542
1995	Wichita	AA	KC	53	197	53	11	1	5	81	31	32	26	0	33	2	0	2	1	1	.50	3	.269	.357	.411
1996	Wichita	AA	KC	125	463	137	22	2	22	229	84	84	77	3	66	8	0	6	4	1	.80	11	.296	.401	.495
5 Min. YEARS				491	1741	508	107	8	75	856	319	318	329	23	269	29	1	27	13	15	.46	27	.292	.407	.492

Russ Swan

Pitches: Left **Bats:** Left **Pos:** P **Ht:** 6' 4" **Wt:** 210 **Born:** 1/3/64 **Age:** 33

Year	Team	Lg	Org	G	GS	CG	GF	IP	BFP	H	R	ER	HR	SH	SF	HB	TBB	IBB	SO	WP	Bk	W	L	Pct.	ShO	Sv	ERA
				HOW MUCH HE PITCHED						WHAT HE GAVE UP												THE RESULTS					
1986	Everett	A-	SF	7	7	2	0	46	0	30	17	11	2	0	0	1	22	0	45	1	1	5	0	1.000	0	0	2.15
	Clinton	A	SF	7	7	2	0	43.2	179	36	18	15	2	0	2	1	8	0	37	1	1	3	3	.500	1	0	3.09
1987	Fresno	A+	SF	12	12	0	0	64	274	54	40	27	5	4	0	1	29	0	59	4	0	6	3	.667	0	0	3.80
1988	San Jose	A+	SF	11	11	2	0	76.2	301	53	28	19	2	7	0	1	26	0	62	2	0	7	0	1.000	1	0	2.23
1989	Shreveport	AA	SF	11	11	0	0	75.1	304	62	25	22	2	1	1	1	22	1	56	3	2	2	3	.400	0	0	2.63
	Phoenix	AAA	SF	14	13	1	0	83	348	75	37	31	8	5	2	3	29	0	49	2	3	4	3	.571	0	0	3.36
1990	Phoenix	AAA	SF	6	6	0	0	33.2	153	41	17	13	1	1	1	2	15	0	21	1	1	2	4	.333	0	0	3.48
	Calgary	AAA	Sea	5	5	0	0	23	105	28	18	15	0	1	0	0	12	0	14	3	0	1	2	.333	0	0	5.87
1993	Calgary	AAA	Sea	9	0	0	3	10.2	51	14	11	10	1	0	0	0	8	0	7	0	0	2	1	.667	0	0	8.44
1994	Charlotte	AAA	Cle	21	2	0	1	39.1	186	53	34	31	4	4	1	1	18	2	13	5	0	1	3	.250	0	0	7.09
1995	Amarillo	IND	—	7	0	0	4	6.2	37	10	7	5	1	2	0	0	6	2	4	2	0	1	2	.333	0	1	6.75
	Edmonton	AAA	Oak	24	0	0	16	25.1	122	33	16	14	3	3	1	0	17	6	14	6	0	4	5	.444	0	5	4.97
1996	Las Vegas	AAA	SD	25	20	1	0	125.2	565	148	80	71	17	4	0	6	47	6	71	10	1	5	6	.455	0	0	5.08
1989	San Francisco	NL		2	2	0	0	6.2	34	11	10	8	4	2	0	0	4	0	2	0	0	0	2	.000	0	0	10.80
1990	San Francisco	NL		2	1	0	0	2.1	18	6	4	1	0	0	0	0	4	0	1	1	0	0	1	.000	0	0	3.86
	Seattle	AL		11	8	0	0	47	195	42	22	19	3	2	3	0	18	2	15	0	1	2	3	.400	0	0	3.64
1991	Seattle	AL		63	0	0	11	78.2	336	81	35	30	8	6	1	0	28	7	33	8	0	6	2	.750	0	2	3.43
1992	Seattle	AL		55	9	1	26	104.1	457	104	60	55	8	7	5	3	45	7	45	6	0	3	10	.231	0	9	4.74
1993	Seattle	AL		23	0	0	6	19.2	100	25	20	20	2	1	0	2	18	1	10	0	0	3	3	.500	0	0	9.15
1994	Cleveland	AL		12	0	0	2	8	43	13	11	10	1	2	0	0	7	1	2	0	0	0	1	.000	0	0	11.25
9 Min. YEARS				159	94	8	24	653	2625	637	348	284	48	32	8	17	259	17	452	40	9	43	35	.551	2	6	3.91
6 Maj. YEARS				168	20	1	45	266.2	1183	282	162	143	26	20	9	5	124	18	108	15	1	14	22	.389	0	11	4.83

Pedro Swann

Bats: Left **Throws:** Right **Pos:** OF **Ht:** 6'0" **Wt:** 195 **Born:** 10/27/70 **Age:** 26

Year	Team	Lg	Org	G	AB	H	2B	3B	HR	TB	R	RBI	TBB	IBB	SO	HBP	SH	SF	SB	CS	SB%	GDP	Avg	OBP	SLG
				BATTING															BASERUNNING				PERCENTAGES		
1991	Idaho Falls	R+	Atl	55	174	48	6	1	3	65	35	28	33	0	45	2	1	2	8	5	.62	4	.276	.393	.374
1992	Pulaski	R+	Atl	59	203	61	18	1	5	96	36	34	32	3	33	7	0	1	13	6	.68	6	.300	.412	.473
1993	Durham	A+	Atl	61	182	63	8	2	6	93	27	27	19	0	38	1	0	0	6	12	.33	2	.346	.411	.511
	Greenville	AA	Atl	44	157	48	9	2	3	70	19	21	9	0	23	1	1	0	2	2	.50	5	.306	.347	.446
1994	Greenville	AA	Atl	126	428	121	25	2	10	180	55	49	46	2	85	4	0	2	16	9	.64	14	.283	.356	.421
1995	Richmond	AAA	Atl	15	38	8	1	0	0	9	2	3	1	0	2	1	0	0	0	2	.00	0	.211	.250	.237
	Greenville	AA	Atl	102	339	110	24	2	11	171	57	64	45	2	63	3	0	3	14	11	.56	8	.324	.405	.504
1996	Greenville	AA	Atl	35	129	40	5	0	3	54	15	20	18	2	23	3	1	1	4	4	.50	3	.310	.404	.419
	Richmond	AAA	Atl	93	296	74	11	4	4	105	42	35	22	2	56	4	2	3	7	7	.50	5	.250	.308	.355
6 Min. YEARS				590	1946	573	107	14	45	843	288	281	225	11	368	26	5	12	70	58	.55	47	.294	.373	.433

Jon Sweet

Bats: Left **Throws:** Right **Pos:** C **Ht:** 6'0" **Wt:** 183 **Born:** 11/10/71 **Age:** 25

			BATTING															BASERUNNING				PERCENTAGES		
Year	Team	Lg Org	G	AB	H	2B	3B	HR	TB	R	RBI	TBB	IBB	SO	HBP	SH	SF	SB	CS	SB%	GDP	Avg	OBP	SLG
1994	Welland	A- Pit	51	154	39	8	0	0	47	17	17	17	1	20	5	1	1	0	3	.00	3	.253	.345	.305
1995	Augusta	A Pit	87	267	76	9	1	1	90	28	22	18	2	31	5	2	2	5	4	.56	6	.285	.339	.337
1996	Lynchburg	A+ Pit	72	212	58	10	0	0	68	16	35	17	1	26	2	5	3	2	4	.33	0	.274	.329	.321
	Carolina	AA Pit	20	40	4	2	0	0	6	2	1	0	0	3	0	2	0	0	0	.00	5	.100	.100	.150
3 Min. YEARS			230	673	177	29	1	1	211	63	75	52	4	80	12	10	6	7	11	.39	14	.263	.324	.314

Paul Swingle

Pitches: Right **Bats:** Right **Pos:** P **Ht:** 6' 0" **Wt:** 185 **Born:** 12/21/66 **Age:** 30

			HOW MUCH HE PITCHED					WHAT HE GAVE UP												THE RESULTS					
Year	Team	Lg Org	G	GS	CG	GF	IP	BFP	H	R	ER	HR	SH	SF	HB	TBB	IBB	SO	WP	Bk	W	L	Pct.	ShO	Sv	ERA
1989	Bend	A- Cal	9	0	0	2	18.1	81	7	9	6	0	1	0	0	19	0	26	5	1	1	0	1.000	0	0	2.95
1990	Boise	A- Cal	14	0	0	12	13.2	51	5	1	1	0	1	0	0	3	1	24	0	0	0	1	.000	0	5	0.66
1991	Palm Spring	A+ Cal	43	0	0	28	57	268	51	37	28	2	3	3	1	41	8	63	11	0	5	4	.556	0	10	4.42
1992	Midland	AA Cal	25	25	2	0	149.2	648	158	88	78	14	3	6	6	51	1	104	8	2	8	10	.444	0	0	4.69
1993	Vancouver	AAA Cal	37	4	0	11	67.2	318	85	61	52	4	2	4	1	32	1	61	3	1	2	9	.182	0	1	6.92
1995	New Orleans	AAA Mil	35	0	0	9	43.1	185	42	25	22	7	1	0	1	15	2	41	5	0	1	4	.200	0	0	4.57
1996	Angels	R Cal	1	1	0	0	0.2	11	6	9	0	0	0	0	0	1	0	1	0	0	0	1	.000	0	0	0.00
	Vancouver	AAA Cal	15	0	0	6	24	104	20	10	8	1	1	0	1	11	0	24	1	0	2	2	.500	0	1	3.00
1993	California	AL	9	0	0	2	9.2	49	15	9	9	2	0	1	0	6	0	6	0	0	0	1	.000	0	0	8.38
7 Min. YEARS			179	30	2	68	374.1	1666	374	240	195	28	12	13	10	173	13	344	33	4	19	31	.380	0	17	4.69

Jeff Tackett

Bats: Right **Throws:** Right **Pos:** C **Ht:** 6' 2" **Wt:** 206 **Born:** 12/1/65 **Age:** 31

			BATTING															BASERUNNING				PERCENTAGES		
Year	Team	Lg Org	G	AB	H	2B	3B	HR	TB	R	RBI	TBB	IBB	SO	HBP	SH	SF	SB	CS	SB%	GDP	Avg	OBP	SLG
1984	Bluefield	R+ Bal	34	98	16	2	0	0	18	9	12	23	0	28	0	0	2	1	1	.50	1	.163	.317	.184
1985	Daytona Bch	A+ Bal	40	103	20	5	2	0	29	8	10	13	0	16	1	0	1	1	3	.25	6	.194	.288	.282
	Newark	A- Bal	62	187	39	6	0	0	45	21	22	22	0	33	2	3	1	2	2	.50	4	.209	.297	.241
1986	Hagerstown	A+ Bal	83	246	70	15	1	0	87	53	21	36	0	36	5	0	1	16	5	.76	2	.285	.385	.354
1987	Charlotte	AA Bal	61	205	46	6	1	0	54	18	13	12	0	34	2	1	1	5	5	.50	2	.224	.273	.263
1988	Charlotte	AA Bal	81	272	56	9	0	0	65	24	18	42	0	46	2	0	1	6	4	.60	7	.206	.315	.239
1989	Rochester	AAA Bal	67	199	36	3	1	2	47	13	17	19	0	45	1	2	2	3	1	.75	3	.181	.253	.236
1990	Rochester	AAA Bal	108	306	73	8	3	4	99	37	33	47	0	50	7	3	0	4	8	.33	3	.239	.353	.324
1991	Rochester	AAA Bal	126	433	102	18	2	6	142	64	50	54	0	60	2	4	3	3	3	.50	15	.236	.321	.328
1993	Rochester	AAA Bal	8	25	8	2	0	0	10	1	2	3	0	8	2	0	1	0	0	.00	0	.320	.419	.400
1995	Toledo	AAA Det	96	301	81	15	0	6	114	32	30	35	0	46	7	5	1	2	1	.67	6	.269	.358	.379
1996	Toledo	AAA Det	89	283	67	10	3	7	104	41	49	36	1	54	6	2	4	4	2	.67	7	.237	.331	.367
1991	Baltimore	AL	6	8	1	0	0	0	1	1	0	2	0	2	0	1	0	0	0	.00	0	.125	.300	.125
1992	Baltimore	AL	65	179	43	8	1	5	68	21	24	17	1	28	2	6	4	0	0	.00	11	.240	.307	.380
1993	Baltimore	AL	39	87	15	3	0	0	18	8	9	13	0	28	0	2	1	0	0	.00	5	.172	.277	.207
1994	Baltimore	AL	26	53	12	3	1	2	23	5	9	5	0	13	2	0	0	0	0	.00	4	.226	.317	.434
11 Min. YEARS			855	2658	614	99	13	25	814	321	277	342	1	456	37	20	18	47	35	.57	56	.231	.325	.306
4 Maj. YEARS			136	327	71	14	2	7	110	35	42	37	1	71	4	9	5	0	0	.00	20	.217	.300	.336

Todd Takayoshi

Bats: Left **Throws:** Right **Pos:** DH **Ht:** 6'1" **Wt:** 190 **Born:** 10/4/70 **Age:** 26

			BATTING															BASERUNNING				PERCENTAGES		
Year	Team	Lg Org	G	AB	H	2B	3B	HR	TB	R	RBI	TBB	IBB	SO	HBP	SH	SF	SB	CS	SB%	GDP	Avg	OBP	SLG
1993	Pocatello	R+ Cle	69	243	87	9	1	5	113	38	40	50	0	25	2	0	3	3	1	.75	4	.358	.466	.465
1994	Lk Elsinore	A+ Cal	7	18	3	0	0	0	3	2	1	3	1	1	0	0	0	1	1	.50	1	.167	.286	.167
	Cedar Rapds	A Cal	95	302	93	16	1	8	135	42	46	44	7	43	2	1	2	2	2	.50	8	.308	.397	.447
1995	Midland	AA Cal	7	18	5	0	1	0	7	2	0	1	0	4	0	1	0	1	0	1.00	0	.278	.316	.389
	Lk Elsinore	A+ Cal	60	157	38	6	1	3	55	19	30	42	1	30	0	2	0	1	1	.50	5	.242	.402	.350
1996	Vancouver	AAA Cal	3	7	2	0	0	0	2	1	2	0	0	0	0	0	0	0	0	.00	0	.286	.286	.286
	Lk Elsinore	A+ Cal	99	310	96	18	0	11	147	58	61	74	5	50	3	0	2	0	1	.00	13	.310	.445	.474
4 Min. YEARS			340	1055	324	49	4	27	462	162	180	214	14	153	7	4	7	8	6	.57	31	.307	.425	.438

Scott Talanoa

Bats: Right **Throws:** Right **Pos:** 1B **Ht:** 6'5" **Wt:** 240 **Born:** 11/12/69 **Age:** 27

			BATTING															BASERUNNING				PERCENTAGES		
Year	Team	Lg Org	G	AB	H	2B	3B	HR	TB	R	RBI	TBB	IBB	SO	HBP	SH	SF	SB	CS	SB%	GDP	Avg	OBP	SLG
1991	Helena	R+ Mil	37	127	37	10	0	6	65	24	29	29	2	32	3	0	2	1	2	.33	4	.291	.429	.512
1992	Beloit	A Mil	106	357	82	18	0	13	139	57	56	49	1	109	2	3	2	7	4	.64	3	.230	.324	.389
1993	Beloit	A Mil	87	258	74	12	0	25	161	55	66	71	6	86	8	0	4	5	3	.63	3	.287	.449	.624
1994	El Paso	AA Mil	127	429	111	20	1	28	217	89	88	77	6	138	9	0	4	1	2	.33	11	.259	.380	.506
1995	New Orleans	AAA Mil	31	98	14	4	0	1	21	9	3	6	0	26	2	0	1	0	0	.00	5	.143	.206	.214
	El Paso	AA Mil	2	9	2	2	0	0	4	0	1	1	0	0	0	0	0	0	0	.00	1	.222	.300	.444
1996	New Orleans	AAA Mil	32	80	15	1	0	2	22	9	11	8	0	26	2	0	0	2	0	1.00	5	.188	.278	.275
	Harrisburg	AA Mon	50	138	29	5	0	11	67	20	23	31	3	50	1	0	0	0	0	.00	4	.210	.359	.486
6 Min. YEARS			472	1496	364	72	1	86	696	263	277	272	18	467	27	3	13	16	11	.59	36	.243	.367	.465

Jeff Tam

Pitches: Right **Bats:** Right **Pos:** P — **Ht:** 6'1" **Wt:** 185 **Born:** 8/19/70 **Age:** 26

				HOW MUCH HE PITCHED						WHAT HE GAVE UP												THE RESULTS					
Year	Team	Lg	Org	G	GS	CG	GF	IP	BFP	H	R	ER	HR	SH	SF	HB	TBB	IBB	SO	WP	Bk	W	L	Pct.	ShO	Sv	ERA
1993	Pittsfield	A-	NYN	21	1	0	13	40.1	180	50	21	15	0	0	1	1	7	0	31	1	3	3	3	.500	0	0	3.35
1994	Columbia	A	NYN	26	0	0	26	28	115	23	14	4	0	1	0	2	6	0	22	0	2	1	1	.500	0	18	1.29
	St. Lucie	A+	NYN	24	0	0	22	26.2	99	13	0	0	0	0	0	3	6	1	15	1	2	0	0	.000	0	16	0.00
	Binghamton	AA	NYN	4	0	0	1	6.2	35	9	6	6	0	1	0	1	5	0	7	0	0	0	0	.000	0	0	8.10
1995	Mets	R	NYN	2	1	0	0	3	13	2	1	1	0	1	0	1	1	0	2	1	0	0	0	.000	0	0	3.00
	Binghamton	AA	NYN	16	1	0	7	21	96	22	12	10	1	3	1	5	5	2	11	4	0	0	2	.000	0	3	4.29
1996	Binghamton	AA	NYN	49	0	0	18	62.2	241	51	19	17	6	2	1	2	16	3	48	2	4	6	2	.750	0	2	2.44
4 Min. YEARS				142	3	0	87	188.1	779	170	73	53	7	8	3	15	46	6	136	9	11	10	8	.556	0	39	2.53

Fernando Tatis

Bats: Both **Throws:** Right **Pos:** 3B — **Ht:** 6'1" **Wt:** 175 **Born:** 1/1/75 **Age:** 22

				BATTING															BASERUNNING				PERCENTAGES		
Year	Team	Lg	Org	G	AB	H	2B	3B	HR	TB	R	RBI	TBB	IBB	SO	HBP	SH	SF	SB	CS	SB%	GDP	Avg	OBP	SLG
1994	Rangers	R	Tex	60	212	70	10	2	6	102	34	32	25	4	33	3	0	2	20	4	.83	4	.330	.405	.481
1995	Charlstn-SC	A	Tex	131	499	151	43	4	15	247	74	84	45	4	94	7	1	4	22	19	.54	5	.303	.366	.495
1996	Charlotte	A+	Tex	85	325	93	25	0	12	154	46	53	30	4	48	6	1	4	9	3	.75	9	.286	.353	.474
	Okla. City	AAA	Tex	2	4	2	1	0	0	3	0	0	0	0	1	0	0	0	0	0	.00	0	.500	.500	.750
3 Min. YEARS				278	1040	316	79	6	33	506	154	169	100	12	176	16	2	10	51	26	.66	18	.304	.370	.487

Andy Taulbee

Pitches: Right **Bats:** Right **Pos:** P — **Ht:** 6'4" **Wt:** 210 **Born:** 10/5/72 **Age:** 24

				HOW MUCH HE PITCHED						WHAT HE GAVE UP												THE RESULTS					
Year	Team	Lg	Org	G	GS	CG	GF	IP	BFP	H	R	ER	HR	SH	SF	HB	TBB	IBB	SO	WP	Bk	W	L	Pct.	ShO	Sv	ERA
1994	San Jose	A+	SF	13	13	0	0	71	300	66	28	21	5	5	1	6	20	0	51	0	5	4	3	.571	0	0	2.66
1995	San Jose	A+	SF	10	9	1	0	62.2	251	50	27	21	7	4	0	4	22	0	33	2	0	3	2	.600	1	0	3.02
	Shreveport	AA	SF	24	23	2	0	149.1	639	157	74	59	12	10	3	7	49	2	71	5	1	7	7	.500	2	0	3.56
1996	Shreveport	AA	SF	27	24	0	3	138.2	617	169	87	77	10	5	4	6	47	2	55	2	1	6	10	.375	0	1	5.00
3 Min. YEARS				74	69	3	3	421.2	1807	442	216	178	34	24	8	23	138	4	210	9	7	20	22	.476	3	1	3.80

Jamie Taylor

Bats: Left **Throws:** Right **Pos:** 3B — **Ht:** 6'2" **Wt:** 220 **Born:** 10/10/70 **Age:** 26

				BATTING															BASERUNNING				PERCENTAGES		
Year	Team	Lg	Org	G	AB	H	2B	3B	HR	TB	R	RBI	TBB	IBB	SO	HBP	SH	SF	SB	CS	SB%	GDP	Avg	OBP	SLG
1992	Watertown	A-	Cle	60	208	61	13	1	1	79	25	35	30	1	36	1	0	3	4	0	1.00	2	.293	.380	.380
1993	Columbus	A	Cle	111	402	91	21	0	8	136	46	46	36	2	115	0	2	4	4	2	.67	2	.226	.287	.338
1994	Kinston	A+	Cle	76	217	51	14	0	5	80	30	19	29	0	63	2	2	1	3	4	.43	2	.235	.329	.369
1995	Canton-Akrn	AA	Cle	4	11	0	0	0	0	0	0	0	0	0	4	1	1	0	0	0	.00	0	.000	.083	.000
	Duluth-Sup.	IND	—	75	285	84	18	1	4	116	36	28	31	1	50	1	2	2	1	2	.33	9	.295	.364	.407
1996	New Haven	AA	Col	124	362	88	20	1	8	134	46	37	45	6	74	3	3	5	1	2	.33	12	.243	.328	.370
5 Min. YEARS				450	1485	375	86	3	26	545	183	165	171	10	342	8	10	15	13	10	.57	27	.253	.330	.367

Scott M. Taylor

Pitches: Right **Bats:** Right **Pos:** P — **Ht:** 6' 3" **Wt:** 200 **Born:** 10/3/66 **Age:** 30

				HOW MUCH HE PITCHED						WHAT HE GAVE UP												THE RESULTS					
Year	Team	Lg	Org	G	GS	CG	GF	IP	BFP	H	R	ER	HR	SH	SF	HB	TBB	IBB	SO	WP	Bk	W	L	Pct.	ShO	Sv	ERA
1989	Wausau	A	Sea	16	16	6	0	106.1	445	92	49	38	5	3	2	6	37	1	65	8	3	9	7	.563	2	0	3.22
	Williamsprt	AA	Sea	10	7	1	1	40.2	185	49	26	26	6	1	5	1	20	1	22	2	0	1	4	.200	0	0	5.75
1990	San Bernrdo	A+	Sea	34	21	1	3	126.1	596	148	100	76	17	0	3	7	69	0	86	10	1	8	8	.500	0	1	5.41
1991	Durham	A+	Atl	24	16	2	5	111.1	452	94	32	27	3	6	2	2	33	3	78	10	0	10	3	.769	0	3	2.18
	Greenville	AA	Atl	8	7	1	0	43	191	49	25	20	4	1	1	2	16	2	26	6	0	3	4	.429	1	0	4.19
1992	Greenville	AA	Atl	22	4	0	6	39	172	44	31	29	6	0	3	3	18	0	20	3	0	1	1	.500	0	1	6.69
	El Paso	AA	Mil	11	9	0	0	54.1	224	45	21	21	5	3	1	0	19	1	37	2	1	4	2	.667	0	0	3.48
1993	El Paso	AA	Mil	17	16	1	1	104.1	434	105	53	44	4	2	2	11	31	2	76	0	0	6	6	.500	0	0	3.80
	New Orleans	AAA	Mil	12	8	1	3	62.1	244	48	17	16	3	5	1	2	21	1	47	1	1	5	1	.833	0	0	2.31
1994	New Orleans	AAA	Mil	28	27	4	0	165.2	720	177	88	79	12	4	5	12	59	2	106	3	0	14	9	.609	1	0	4.29
1995	New Orleans	AAA	Mil	2	2	0	0	11.1	47	10	3	3	0	0	0	1	3	0	9	0	0	1	0	1.000	0	0	2.38
	Okla. City	AAA	Tex	24	21	1	0	129.1	557	132	62	51	12	4	2	7	41	0	74	5	0	8	8	.500	1	0	3.55
1996	Carolina	AA	Pit	29	25	0	1	158	692	170	94	81	16	4	5	6	62	4	100	10	1	11	7	.611	0	0	4.61
1995	Texas	AL		3	3	0	0	15.1	71	25	16	16	6	0	0	0	5	0	10	0	0	1	2	.333	0	0	9.39
8 Min. YEARS				237	179	18	20	1152	4959	1163	601	511	93	33	32	60	429	17	746	60	7	81	60	.574	5	5	3.99

Tommy Taylor

Pitches: Right **Bats:** Right **Pos:** P — **Ht:** 6'1" **Wt:** 180 **Born:** 7/16/70 **Age:** 26

				HOW MUCH HE PITCHED						WHAT HE GAVE UP												THE RESULTS					
Year	Team	Lg	Org	G	GS	CG	GF	IP	BFP	H	R	ER	HR	SH	SF	HB	TBB	IBB	SO	WP	Bk	W	L	Pct.	ShO	Sv	ERA
1989	Bluefield	R+	Bal	11	10	0	0	41.2	208	56	42	30	4	1	3	0	29	1	36	1	0	1	3	.250	0	0	6.48
1990	Wausau	A	Bal	23	20	1	1	111	498	103	74	65	11	3	1	5	62	0	78	8	3	3	11	.214	1	0	5.27
1991	Kane County	A	Bal	26	14	1	2	96.1	443	110	70	56	1	5	2	1	54	6	59	9	2	4	11	.267	0	0	5.23
1992	Hagerstown	AA	Bal	1	0	0	0	0.2	4	1	1	1	0	0	1	0	1	0	0	0	0	0	0	.000	0	0	13.50
	Frederick	A+	Bal	27	14	1	3	118.1	518	116	63	55	9	3	4	7	48	3	84	6	1	4	8	.333	1	0	4.18

Year	Team	Lg	Org	HOW MUCH HE PITCHED: G	GS	CG	GF	IP	BFP	WHAT HE GAVE UP: H	R	ER	HR	SH	SF	HB	TBB	IBB	SO	WP	Bk	THE RESULTS: W	L	Pct.	ShO	Sv	ERA
1993	Bowie	AA	Bal	40	4	0	19	89.2	407	90	65	56	9	7	6	2	47	1	69	5	1	4	7	.364	0	4	5.62
1994	Frederick	A+	Bal	32	0	0	16	43.1	207	54	29	21	5	2	1	2	18	1	48	3	0	4	1	.800	0	2	4.36
	Kinston	A+	Cle	35	3	0	16	57.2	268	63	34	26	6	3	1	2	26	1	61	6	0	4	1	.800	0	2	4.06
1995	Canton-Akrn	AA	Cle	5	0	0	3	9.2	41	9	4	4	2	1	1	0	6	0	3	0	0	1	1	.500	0	0	3.72
	Amarillo	IND	—	12	4	0	5	35	160	40	24	18	3	3	4	0	18	1	16	1	0	1	4	.200	0	0	4.63
1996	Regina	IND	—	16	0	0	13	21.1	84	11	6	6	0	0	0	2	5	0	26	2	0	4	1	.800	0	3	2.53
	El Paso	AA	Mil	14	0	0	5	17.1	79	24	9	9	0	0	0	0	6	0	20	2	0	2	1	.667	0	0	4.67
8 Min. YEARS				242	69	3	83	642	2917	677	421	347	50	28	24	21	320	14	500	43	7	32	49	.395	2	11	4.86

Bats: Right **Throws:** Right **Pos:** C

Fausto Tejero

Ht: 6'2" **Wt:** 205 **Born:** 10/26/68 **Age:** 28

Year	Team	Lg	Org	BATTING: G	AB	H	2B	3B	HR	TB	R	RBI	TBB	IBB	SO	HBP	SH	SF	BASERUNNING: SB	CS	SB%	GDP	PERCENTAGES: Avg	OBP	SLG
1990	Boise	A-	Cal	39	74	16	2	0	0	18	14	7	23	1	23	2	3	3	1	0	1.00	0	.216	.402	.243
1991	Quad City	A	Cal	83	244	42	7	0	1	52	16	18	14	0	52	4	3	1	0	1	.00	5	.172	.228	.213
1992	Edmonton	AAA	Cal	8	17	4	1	0	0	5	0	0	4	0	2	1	2	0	0	2	.00	0	.235	.409	.294
	Midland	AA	Cal	84	266	50	11	0	2	67	21	30	11	0	63	4	5	3	1	2	.33	6	.188	.229	.252
1993	Palm Spring	A+	Cal	7	20	6	2	0	0	8	2	1	2	0	1	0	1	0	0	1	.00	0	.300	.364	.400
	Vancouver	AAA	Cal	20	59	9	0	0	0	9	2	2	4	1	12	1	2	1	1	1	.50	0	.153	.215	.153
	Midland	AA	Cal	26	69	9	1	1	1	15	3	7	8	0	17	2	1	1	0	0	.00	3	.130	.238	.217
1994	Midland	AA	Cal	50	150	32	3	0	5	50	17	24	15	0	31	1	1	2	2	2	.50	6	.213	.286	.333
	Vancouver	AAA	Cal	16	45	9	2	0	0	11	6	6	4	0	9	0	2	1	1	1	.50	1	.200	.260	.244
1995	Lk Elsinore	A+	Cal	8	21	5	1	0	0	6	5	3	5	0	6	0	0	1	1	0	1.00	1	.238	.370	.286
	Vancouver	AAA	Cal	37	96	25	3	0	0	28	10	8	10	1	22	0	1	0	2	0	1.00	0	.260	.330	.292
	Midland	AA	Cal	16	53	12	3	0	1	18	7	11	1	0	13	1	0	1	0	1	.00	1	.226	.250	.340
1996	Vancouver	AAA	Cal	54	155	31	4	1	1	40	21	12	22	0	41	1	6	0	0	1	.00	6	.200	.303	.258
7 Min. YEARS				448	1269	250	40	2	11	327	124	129	123	3	292	17	27	14	9	12	.43	29	.197	.274	.258

Pitches: Right **Bats:** Right **Pos:** P

Anthony Telford

Ht: 6' 0" **Wt:** 184 **Born:** 3/6/66 **Age:** 31

Year	Team	Lg	Org	HOW MUCH HE PITCHED: G	GS	CG	GF	IP	BFP	WHAT HE GAVE UP: H	R	ER	HR	SH	SF	HB	TBB	IBB	SO	WP	Bk	THE RESULTS: W	L	Pct.	ShO	Sv	ERA
1987	Newark	A-	Bal	6	2	0	3	17.2	72	16	2	2	0	0	0	0	3	0	27	0	0	1	0	1.000	0	0	1.02
	Hagerstown	A+	Bal	2	2	0	0	11.1	46	9	2	2	0	0	0	1	5	0	10	0	0	1	0	1.000	0	0	1.59
	Rochester	AAA	Bal	1	0	0	0	2	9	0	0	0	0	0	0	0	3	0	3	1	0	0	0	.000	0	0	0.00
1988	Hagerstown	A+	Bal	1	1	0	0	7	24	3	0	0	0	0	0	0	0	0	10	0	0	1	0	1.000	0	0	0.00
1989	Frederick	A+	Bal	9	5	0	2	25.2	116	25	15	12	1	1	2	2	12	0	19	2	0	2	1	.667	0	1	4.21
1990	Frederick	A+	Bal	8	8	1	0	53.2	207	35	15	10	1	0	0	4	11	1	49	4	0	4	2	.667	0	0	1.68
	Hagerstown	AA	Bal	14	13	3	1	96	384	80	26	21	3	5	3	3	25	1	73	4	0	10	2	.833	1	0	1.97
1991	Rochester	AAA	Bal	27	25	3	0	157.1	666	166	82	69	18	5	3	4	48	2	115	7	1	12	9	.571	0	0	3.95
1992	Rochester	AAA	Bal	27	26	3	1	181	766	183	89	84	15	4	4	6	64	0	129	9	2	12	7	.632	0	0	4.18
1993	Rochester	AAA	Bal	38	6	0	12	90.2	397	98	51	43	10	2	4	3	33	3	66	6	0	7	7	.500	0	2	4.27
1994	Richmond	AAA	Atl	38	20	3	0	142.2	607	148	82	67	17	4	4	4	41	2	111	1	0	10	6	.625	1	0	4.23
1995	Edmonton	AAA	Oak	8	6	0	0	36.1	173	47	32	29	5	2	2	2	16	0	17	2	0	3	2	.600	0	0	7.18
	Canton-Akrn	AA	Cle	2	2	0	0	11	42	6	2	1	0	0	0	0	4	1	4	0	0	2	0	1.000	0	0	0.82
	Buffalo	AAA	Cle	26	10	0	4	86.1	376	88	49	45	6	3	6	4	30	4	45	3	0	9	3	.750	0	0	4.69
1996	Ottawa	AAA	Mon	30	15	1	0	118.1	506	128	62	54	12	6	1	5	34	1	69	4	0	7	2	.778	1	0	4.11
1990	Baltimore	AL		8	8	0	0	36.1	168	43	22	20	4	0	2	1	19	0	20	1	0	3	3	.500	0	0	4.95
1991	Baltimore	AL		9	1	0	4	26.2	109	27	12	12	3	0	1	0	6	1	24	1	0	0	0	.000	0	0	4.05
1993	Baltimore	AL		3	0	0	2	7.1	34	11	8	8	3	0	0	1	1	0	6	1	0	0	0	.000	0	0	9.82
10 Min. YEARS				237	141	14	23	1037	4391	1032	509	439	88	32	29	38	329	15	747	43	3	81	41	.664	3	3	3.81
3 Maj. YEARS				20	9	0	6	70.1	311	81	42	40	10	0	3	2	26	1	50	3	0	3	3	.500	0	0	5.12

Pitches: Right **Bats:** Right **Pos:** P

Jim Telgheder

Ht: 6'3" **Wt:** 210 **Born:** 3/22/71 **Age:** 26

Year	Team	Lg	Org	HOW MUCH HE PITCHED: G	GS	CG	GF	IP	BFP	WHAT HE GAVE UP: H	R	ER	HR	SH	SF	HB	TBB	IBB	SO	WP	Bk	THE RESULTS: W	L	Pct.	ShO	Sv	ERA
1993	Red Sox	R	Bos	7	1	0	3	18.2	77	16	11	7	2	1	1	1	2	0	17	2	1	1	2	.333	0	1	3.38
	Utica	A-	Bos	2	0	0	1	2	9	0	1	0	0	0	0	1	1	0	0	0	0	0	0	.000	0	0	0.00
1994	Sarasota	A+	Bos	33	10	0	9	84	345	85	52	46	7	7	3	2	17	1	43	1	2	5	5	.500	0	6	4.93
1995	Michigan	A	Bos	22	1	0	18	35	142	29	8	7	0	2	2	1	8	2	39	3	0	5	1	.833	0	4	1.80
	Sarasota	A+	Bos	44	1	0	23	60	264	59	28	25	3	4	2	3	23	4	63	7	1	5	4	.556	0	4	3.75
1996	Wilmington	A+	KC	31	2	0	9	74.1	294	60	24	20	8	3	1	2	14	2	50	5	0	8	3	.727	0	2	2.42
	Wichita	AA	KC	13	0	0	6	21	92	23	9	8	2	0	0	1	6	1	11	1	0	0	2	.000	0	0	3.43
4 Min. YEARS				152	15	0	69	295	1223	272	133	113	22	17	9	11	71	10	223	19	4	24	17	.585	0	17	3.45

Bats: Right **Throws:** Right **Pos:** OF

Jose Texidor

Ht: 6'0" **Wt:** 150 **Born:** 12/14/71 **Age:** 25

Year	Team	Lg	Org	BATTING: G	AB	H	2B	3B	HR	TB	R	RBI	TBB	IBB	SO	HBP	SH	SF	BASERUNNING: SB	CS	SB%	GDP	PERCENTAGES: Avg	OBP	SLG
1989	Rangers	R	Tex	8	11	0	0	0	0	0	0	0	2	0	2	0	0	0	0	1	.00	0	.000	.154	.000
1990	Rangers	R	Tex	50	168	39	5	3	1	53	29	20	20	1	24	1	0	1	3	3	.50	2	.232	.316	.315
1991	Charlotte	A+	Tex	13	39	11	1	1	0	14	8	3	2	0	6	1	1	0	1	1	.50	2	.282	.333	.359

Year Team	Lg Org	G	AB	H	2B	3B	HR	TB	R	RBI	TBB	IBB	SO	HBP	SH	SF	SB	CS	SB%	GDP	Avg	OBP	SLG
		BATTING															BASERUNNING				PERCENTAGES		
Butte	R+ Tex	37	130	49	6	1	3	66	26	23	9	1	23	0	1	0	5	2	.71	4	.377	.417	.508
1992 Gastonia	A Tex	118	410	115	23	2	3	151	45	32	24	0	65	1	4	0	6	13	.32	5	.280	.322	.368
1993 Charlotte	A+ Tex	19	72	23	4	0	0	27	14	4	5	1	11	0	0	0	2	0	1.00	1	.319	.364	.375
1994 Charlotte	A+ Tex	131	501	129	24	5	5	178	69	68	48	0	80	3	1	4	3	11	.21	6	.257	.324	.355
1995 Tulsa	AA Tex	129	494	133	33	1	5	183	55	64	31	3	61	3	2	2	1	1	.50	19	.269	.315	.370
1996 Tulsa	AA Tex	85	301	77	15	0	11	125	34	37	18	1	44	0	3	3	2	1	.67	8	.256	.295	.415
8 Min. YEARS		590	2126	576	111	13	28	797	280	251	159	7	316	9	12	10	23	33	.41	47	.271	.323	.375

Bobby Thigpen

Pitches: Right **Bats:** Right **Pos:** P **Ht:** 6' 3" **Wt:** 220 **Born:** 7/17/63 **Age:** 33

Year Team	Lg Org	G	GS	CG	GF	IP	BFP	H	R	ER	HR	SH	SF	HB	TBB	IBB	SO	WP	Bk	W	L	Pct.	ShO	Sv	ERA
		HOW MUCH HE PITCHED						WHAT HE GAVE UP												THE RESULTS					
1985 Niagara Fal	A- ChA	28	1	0	25	52.1	211	30	12	10	0	1	1	1	19	2	74	2	0	2	3	.400	0	9	1.72
Appleton	A ChA	1	0	0	0	2.2	11	1	0	0	0	0	0	0	1	1	4	0	0	1	0	1.000	0	0	0.00
1986 Birmingham	AA ChA	25	25	5	0	159.2	707	182	97	83	12	3	7	11	54	1	90	4	2	8	11	.421	0	0	4.68
1987 Hawaii	AAA ChA	9	9	2	0	52.2	234	72	38	36	5	1	1	1	14	1	17	0	1	2	3	.400	1	0	6.15
1996 Nashville	AAA ChA	4	0	0	0	6.1	27	8	5	5	2	0	0	0	2	0	6	1	0	0	1	.000	0	0	7.11
1986 Chicago	AL	20	0	0	14	35.2	142	26	7	7	1	1	1	1	12	0	20	0	0	2	0	1.000	0	7	1.77
1987 Chicago	AL	51	0	0	37	89	369	86	30	27	10	6	0	3	24	5	52	0	0	7	5	.583	0	16	2.73
1988 Chicago	AL	68	0	0	59	90	398	96	38	33	6	4	5	4	33	3	62	6	2	5	8	.385	0	34	3.30
1989 Chicago	AL	61	0	0	56	79	336	62	34	33	10	5	5	1	40	3	47	2	1	2	6	.250	0	34	3.76
1990 Chicago	AL	77	0	0	73	88.2	347	60	20	18	5	4	3	1	32	3	70	2	0	4	6	.400	0	57	1.83
1991 Chicago	AL	67	0	0	58	69.2	309	63	32	27	10	7	3	4	38	8	47	2	0	7	5	.583	0	30	3.49
1992 Chicago	AL	55	0	0	40	55	253	58	29	29	4	2	4	3	33	5	45	0	0	1	3	.250	0	22	4.75
1993 Chicago	AL	25	0	0	11	34.2	166	51	25	22	5	0	3	5	12	0	19	0	0	0	0	.000	0	1	5.71
Philadelphia	NL	17	0	0	5	19.1	88	23	13	13	2	2	1	1	9	1	10	0	1	3	1	.750	0	0	6.05
1994 Seattle	AL	7	0	0	3	7.2	40	12	9	8	3	1	0	0	5	0	4	0	0	0	2	.000	0	0	9.39
4 Min. YEARS		67	35	7	25	273.2	1190	293	152	134	19	5	9	13	90	5	191	7	3	13	18	.419	1	9	4.41
9 Maj. YEARS		448	0	0	356	568.2	2448	537	237	217	56	32	25	23	238	28	376	12	4	31	36	.463	0	201	3.43

Brian Thomas

Bats: Left **Throws:** Right **Pos:** OF **Ht:** 6'0" **Wt:** 185 **Born:** 5/6/71 **Age:** 26

Year Team	Lg Org	G	AB	H	2B	3B	HR	TB	R	RBI	TBB	IBB	SO	HBP	SH	SF	SB	CS	SB%	GDP	Avg	OBP	SLG
		BATTING															BASERUNNING				PERCENTAGES		
1993 Charlotte	A+ Tex	34	135	39	3	2	2	52	25	11	18	1	29	0	3	3	4	1	.80	0	.289	.365	.385
1994 Charlotte	A+ Tex	124	450	127	26	9	5	186	60	61	55	4	122	5	5	8	23	9	.72	6	.282	.361	.413
1995 Tulsa	AA Tex	131	458	123	24	9	4	177	61	35	50	6	87	2	5	5	8	4	.67	8	.269	.340	.386
1996 Tulsa	AA Tex	3	9	2	0	0	0	2	0	0	0	0	5	2	0	0	0	1	.00	0	.222	.364	.222
Okla. City	AAA Tex	88	247	65	14	4	7	108	30	36	31	3	63	3	4	2	1	0	1.00	2	.263	.350	.437
4 Min. YEARS		380	1299	356	67	24	18	525	176	143	154	14	306	12	17	18	36	15	.71	16	.274	.352	.404

Greg Thomas

Bats: Left **Throws:** Left **Pos:** OF **Ht:** 6'3" **Wt:** 200 **Born:** 7/19/72 **Age:** 24

Year Team	Lg Org	G	AB	H	2B	3B	HR	TB	R	RBI	TBB	IBB	SO	HBP	SH	SF	SB	CS	SB%	GDP	Avg	OBP	SLG
		BATTING															BASERUNNING				PERCENTAGES		
1993 Watertown	A- Cle	73	277	85	20	5	9	142	48	63	27	3	47	2	0	1	3	4	.43	3	.307	.371	.513
1994 Kinston	A+ Cle	103	351	67	14	2	15	130	46	42	26	3	97	5	2	2	5	2	.71	4	.191	.255	.370
1995 Kinston	A+ Cle	102	329	72	21	0	11	126	32	43	25	4	98	3	1	7	0	2	.00	2	.219	.275	.383
1996 Canton-Akrn	AA Cle	97	301	84	14	4	13	145	44	55	26	4	56	1	1	2	2	1	.67	8	.279	.336	.482
4 Min. YEARS		375	1258	308	69	11	48	543	170	203	104	14	298	11	4	12	10	9	.53	17	.245	.305	.432

Keith Thomas

Bats: Both **Throws:** Right **Pos:** OF **Ht:** 6'1" **Wt:** 180 **Born:** 9/12/68 **Age:** 28

Year Team	Lg Org	G	AB	H	2B	3B	HR	TB	R	RBI	TBB	IBB	SO	HBP	SH	SF	SB	CS	SB%	GDP	Avg	OBP	SLG
		BATTING															BASERUNNING				PERCENTAGES		
1986 Reds	R Cin	42	145	31	1	2	2	42	24	13	23	0	57	3	2	1	18	6	.75	1	.214	.331	.290
1987 Billings	R+ Cin	45	142	36	6	2	4	58	22	24	7	1	45	0	1	0	11	4	.73	1	.254	.289	.408
1988 Greensboro	A Cin	108	438	105	12	4	4	137	63	26	17	0	122	2	4	0	30	6	.83	2	.240	.271	.313
1989 Modesto	A+ Oak	93	330	70	5	2	6	97	36	29	24	1	102	2	3	0	19	10	.66	5	.212	.270	.294
1990 Modesto	A+ Oak	62	215	48	7	0	4	67	24	21	14	0	65	1	1	2	16	10	.62	4	.223	.272	.312
Madison	A Oak	44	142	30	3	1	3	44	21	20	10	0	43	0	1	2	12	1	.92	3	.211	.260	.310
1991 Madison	A Oak	13	44	9	1	0	0	10	4	4	3	0	11	0	1	0	3	1	.75	1	.205	.255	.227
Appleton	A KC	74	232	62	10	4	7	101	32	28	12	0	60	2	3	2	21	5	.81	1	.267	.306	.435
1992 Salem	A+ Pit	104	372	103	24	8	16	191	54	51	18	2	90	5	1	6	30	7	.81	12	.277	.314	.513
Carolina	AA Pit	22	78	23	2	4	4	45	13	15	7	0	23	0	0	0	9	1	.90	2	.295	.353	.577
1993 Salem	A+ Pit	25	94	25	8	0	4	45	17	11	7	0	30	2	1	0	8	1	.89	1	.266	.330	.479
Carolina	AA Pit	94	336	80	9	2	15	138	40	52	22	0	110	2	1	4	12	8	.60	2	.238	.286	.411
1994 Wichita	AA SD	109	307	73	13	4	7	115	38	33	32	1	82	5	1	1	46	10	.82	7	.238	.319	.375
1995 Memphis	AA SD	109	356	90	13	4	10	141	66	33	20	0	85	1	1	0	43	11	.80	6	.253	.294	.396
1996 Chattanooga	AA Cin	9	21	2	1	0	0	3	3	3	0	0	8	0	0	0	0	0	.00	0	.095	.095	.143
Clarksville	IND —	21	83	22	6	1	5	45	16	16	7	0	22	0	0	1	5	0	1.00	2	.265	.319	.542
11 Min. YEARS		974	3335	809	121	38	91	1279	473	379	223	5	955	25	21	19	283	81	.78	50	.243	.293	.384

Royal Thomas

Pitches: Right **Bats:** Right **Pos:** P **Ht:** 6'2" **Wt:** 187 **Born:** 9/3/69 **Age:** 27

			HOW MUCH HE PITCHED						WHAT HE GAVE UP												THE RESULTS					
Year	Team	Lg Org	G	GS	CG	GF	IP	BFP	H	R	ER	HR	SH	SF	HB	TBB	IBB	SO	WP	Bk	W	L	Pct.	ShO	Sv	ERA
1987	Utica	A- Phi	19	6	0	7	76	308	67	23	16	1	2	2	0	18	3	62	3	1	6	0	1.000	0	2	1.89
1988	Clearwater	A+ Phi	9	2	0	4	19	95	24	21	19	0	3	2	3	14	2	6	3	2	0	4	.000	0	2	9.00
	Spartanburg	A Phi	22	22	7	0	145.2	611	134	74	49	7	6	3	7	47	0	67	7	1	6	13	.316	2	0	3.03
1989	Clearwater	A+ Phi	27	21	11	0	154	630	141	70	57	7	6	6	1	39	1	49	1	0	11	9	.550	3	0	3.33
1990	Riverside	A+ SD	27	27	1	0	166	740	209	103	87	11	4	6	4	49	3	93	10	0	9	13	.409	0	0	4.72
1991	High Desert	A+ SD	27	27	4	0	155	699	178	108	81	15	4	6	5	61	2	99	9	1	8	13	.381	0	0	4.70
1992	Wichita	AA SD	41	14	0	6	125.1	573	151	104	88	12	5	5	6	51	3	91	8	1	7	7	.500	0	2	6.32
1993	San Antonio	AA LA	47	6	0	16	109.2	475	116	58	48	11	6	6	3	44	5	52	4	0	4	6	.400	0	2	3.94
1994	Greenville	AA Atl	46	0	0	18	85.1	367	90	38	30	4	5	2	1	28	3	48	2	1	6	4	.600	0	2	3.16
1995	Richmond	AAA Atl	39	8	1	12	88	389	103	43	34	6	3	2	2	24	2	39	1	0	7	7	.500	1	0	3.48
1996	Greenville	AA Atl	2	0	0	1	2	12	2	2	2	0	1	1	0	4	0	0	0	0	0	0	.000	0	0	9.00
	Orlando	AA ChN	8	8	0	0	43.1	196	55	37	30	3	0	1	2	14	0	20	5	0	3	2	.600	0	0	6.23
10 Min. YEARS			314	141	24	64	1169.1	5095	1270	681	541	77	45	42	34	393	24	626	53	7	67	78	.462	6	10	4.16

Bliiy Thompson

Bats: Right **Throws:** Right **Pos:** C-OF **Ht:** 5'11" **Wt:** 185 **Born:** 11/5/70 **Age:** 26

			BATTING															BASERUNNING				PERCENTAGES		
Year	Team	Lg Org	G	AB	H	2B	3B	HR	TB	R	RBI	TBB	IBB	SO	HBP	SH	SF	SB	CS	SB%	GDP	Avg	OBP	SLG
1993	Fayettevlle	A Det	42	142	39	6	1	1	50	14	19	20	1	28	2	0	2	2	2	.50	2	.275	.367	.352
1994	Lakeland	A+ Det	82	274	58	17	0	7	96	28	28	24	0	61	4	1	2	4	3	.57	8	.212	.283	.350
1995	Lakeland	A+ Det	73	223	54	13	1	5	84	26	28	15	0	45	1	1	3	4	0	1.00	2	.242	.289	.377
1996	Jacksonvlle	AA Det	41	112	26	5	0	3	40	9	10	7	1	31	3	1	0	1	2	.33	0	.232	.295	.357
4 Min. YEARS			238	751	177	41	2	16	270	77	85	66	2	165	10	3	7	11	7	.61	12	.236	.303	.360

Fletcher Thompson

Bats: Left **Throws:** Right **Pos:** 3B **Ht:** 5'11" **Wt:** 180 **Born:** 9/14/68 **Age:** 28

			BATTING															BASERUNNING				PERCENTAGES		
Year	Team	Lg Org	G	AB	H	2B	3B	HR	TB	R	RBI	TBB	IBB	SO	HBP	SH	SF	SB	CS	SB%	GDP	Avg	OBP	SLG
1990	Auburn	A- Hou	59	199	56	8	3	0	70	35	21	37	3	45	6	5	2	19	9	.68	2	.281	.406	.352
1991	Burlington	A Hou	116	428	116	15	3	5	152	85	33	104	0	116	5	5	2	34	16	.68	2	.271	.417	.355
1993	Jackson	AA Hou	98	316	93	15	2	4	124	64	29	55	2	83	1	7	1	23	12	.66	6	.294	.399	.392
1994	Jackson	AA Hou	121	388	102	14	2	4	132	69	31	58	2	106	10	4	0	28	13	.68	5	.263	.373	.340
1995	El Paso	AA Mil	11	26	5	0	0	0	5	3	3	1	0	9	0	0	0	0	0	.00	1	.192	.222	.192
	Alexandria	IND —	99	353	121	28	2	15	198	106	66	97	5	101	4	1	3	47	6	.89	4	.343	.486	.561
1996	High Desert	A+ Bal	25	72	21	4	1	0	27	10	8	10	0	6	0	1	0	3	2	.60	2	.292	.378	.375
	Bowie	AA Bal	59	172	44	4	1	1	53	30	19	32	1	52	0	0	0	8	4	.67	3	.256	.373	.308
6 Min. YEARS			588	1954	558	88	14	29	761	402	210	394	13	518	26	23	8	162	62	.72	25	.286	.411	.389

John Thomson

Pitches: Right **Bats:** Right **Pos:** P **Ht:** 6'3" **Wt:** 170 **Born:** 10/1/73 **Age:** 23

			HOW MUCH HE PITCHED						WHAT HE GAVE UP												THE RESULTS					
Year	Team	Lg Org	G	GS	CG	GF	IP	BFP	H	R	ER	HR	SH	SF	HB	TBB	IBB	SO	WP	Bk	W	L	Pct.	ShO	Sv	ERA
1993	Rockies	R Col	11	11	0	0	50.2	228	43	40	26	0	0	2	3	31	0	36	14	1	3	5	.375	0	0	4.62
1994	Asheville	A Col	19	15	1	1	88.1	361	70	34	28	3	2	1	5	33	1	79	1	0	6	6	.500	1	0	2.85
	Central Val	A+ Col	9	8	0	0	49.1	201	43	20	18	0	0	2	1	18	1	41	3	1	3	1	.750	0	0	3.28
1995	New Haven	AA Col	26	24	0	0	131.1	572	132	69	61	8	2	7	2	56	0	82	3	2	7	8	.467	0	0	4.18
1996	New Haven	AA Col	16	16	1	0	97.2	389	82	35	31	8	2	2	1	27	1	86	2	1	9	4	.692	0	0	2.86
	Colo. Sprng	AAA Col	11	11	0	0	69.2	305	76	45	39	6	3	1	4	26	2	62	4	1	4	7	.364	0	0	5.04
4 Min. YEARS			92	85	2	1	487	2056	446	243	203	25	9	15	16	191	5	386	27	6	32	31	.508	1	0	3.75

Paul Thornton

Pitches: Right **Bats:** Right **Pos:** P **Ht:** 6'2" **Wt:** 210 **Born:** 6/21/70 **Age:** 27

			HOW MUCH HE PITCHED						WHAT HE GAVE UP												THE RESULTS					
Year	Team	Lg Org	G	GS	CG	GF	IP	BFP	H	R	ER	HR	SH	SF	HB	TBB	IBB	SO	WP	Bk	W	L	Pct.	ShO	Sv	ERA
1993	Elmira	A- Fla	16	7	1	7	63.2	270	51	29	16	2	1	1	1	27	0	59	1	4	3	5	.375	0	2	2.26
1994	Kane County	A Fla	27	27	2	0	164.2	696	150	81	65	12	2	5	15	51	2	118	9	1	7	14	.333	2	0	3.55
1995	Brevard Cty	A+ Fla	42	1	0	27	71.2	311	66	34	26	5	5	1	8	27	2	56	3	0	4	5	.444	0	4	3.27
1996	Brevard Cty	A+ Fla	1	0	0	0	2.2	12	4	0	0	0	0	0	0	0	0	2	0	0	0	0	.000	0	0	0.00
	Portland	AA Fla	52	0	0	28	77.2	357	74	45	36	6	7	2	8	44	5	64	7	0	3	6	.333	0	4	4.17
4 Min. YEARS			138	35	3	62	380.1	1646	345	189	143	25	15	9	32	149	9	299	20	5	17	30	.362	2	10	3.38

Paul Thoutsis

Bats: Left **Throws:** Right **Pos:** 1B **Ht:** 6'1" **Wt:** 185 **Born:** 10/23/65 **Age:** 31

			BATTING															BASERUNNING				PERCENTAGES		
Year	Team	Lg Org	G	AB	H	2B	3B	HR	TB	R	RBI	TBB	IBB	SO	HBP	SH	SF	SB	CS	SB%	GDP	Avg	OBP	SLG
1984	Winston-Sal	A+ Bos	90	299	67	9	2	2	86	32	26	32	3	55	4	2	2	1	1	.50	6	.224	.306	.288
1985	Winter Havn	A+ Bos	75	209	48	6	0	1	57	18	18	18	1	44	3	1	0	0	3	.00	2	.230	.300	.273
1986	Greensboro	A Bos	106	364	105	16	3	15	172	83	77	77	3	57	6	1	11	0	0	.00	4	.288	.410	.473
1987	Winter Havn	A+ Bos	105	336	83	14	2	7	122	47	41	35	3	50	7	2	2	2	1	.67	6	.247	.329	.363
	New Britain	AA Bos	1	4	0	0	0	0	0	0	0	0	0	0	0	0	0	0	0	.00	0	.000	.000	.000

			BATTING															BASERUNNING				PERCENTAGES		
Year	Team	Lg Org	G	AB	H	2B	3B	HR	TB	R	RBI	TBB	IBB	SO	HBP	SH	SF	SB	CS	SB%	GDP	Avg	OBP	SLG
1988	Springfield	A StL	28	92	25	3	0	0	28	5	12	8	2	10	0	0	2	0	0	.00	4	.272	.324	.304
	Arkansas	AA StL	7	9	3	0	0	0	3	0	2	0	0	0	0	0	1	0	0	.00	0	.333	.300	.333
	St. Pete	A+ StL	30	91	25	4	0	0	29	14	8	14	3	7	0	0	1	0	1	.00	1	.275	.368	.319
1989	St. Pete	A+ StL	74	243	70	10	3	2	92	21	21	22	2	17	5	0	3	0	1	.00	6	.288	.355	.379
1990	Arkansas	AA StL	101	266	75	14	5	5	114	25	37	12	2	37	1	0	3	0	2	.00	3	.282	.312	.429
1992	New Britain	AA Bos	108	327	79	21	3	4	118	31	47	24	2	46	4	1	4	0	5	.00	8	.242	.298	.361
1993	New Britain	AA Bos	64	213	62	12	2	0	78	17	21	27	1	24	0	1	2	0	2	.00	4	.291	.368	.366
	Pawtucket	AAA Bos	60	216	69	10	1	4	93	30	27	24	1	28	2	1	0	1	1	.50	9	.319	.393	.431
1994	Pawtucket	AAA Bos	94	304	68	10	1	10	110	28	40	37	4	56	1	2	6	3	0	1.00	6	.224	.305	.362
1995	Columbus	AAA NYA	52	130	28	4	1	0	34	10	15	4	0	16	1	1	1	1	0	1.00	4	.215	.243	.262
1996	Harrisburg	AA Mon	5	20	4	3	0	0	7	1	3	2	0	6	0	0	1	0	0	.00	0	.200	.261	.350
12 Min. YEARS			1000	3123	811	136	23	50	1143	362	395	336	27	453	34	12	39	8	17	.32	63	.260	.334	.366

Gary Thurman

Bats: Right **Throws:** Right **Pos:** OF **Ht:** 5'10" **Wt:** 180 **Born:** 11/12/64 **Age:** 32

			BATTING															BASERUNNING				PERCENTAGES		
Year	Team	Lg Org	G	AB	H	2B	3B	HR	TB	R	RBI	TBB	IBB	SO	HBP	SH	SF	SB	CS	SB%	GDP	Avg	OBP	SLG
1984	Charleston	A KC	129	478	109	6	8	6	149	71	51	81	1	127	8	1	3	44	17	.72	6	.228	.347	.312
1985	Fort Myers	A+ KC	134	453	137	9	9	0	164	68	45	68	1	93	4	3	4	70	18	.80	7	.302	.395	.362
1986	Memphis	AA KC	131	525	164	24	12	7	233	88	62	57	0	81	0	4	3	53	18	.75	5	.312	.378	.444
	Omaha	AAA KC	3	2	1	0	0	0	1	1	0	2	0	0	0	0	0	2	0	1.00	0	.500	.750	.500
1987	Omaha	AAA KC	115	450	132	14	9	8	188	88	39	48	0	84	3	5	3	58	7	.89	4	.293	.363	.418
1988	Omaha	AAA KC	106	422	106	12	6	3	139	77	40	38	2	80	4	8	3	35	12	.74	8	.251	.317	.329
1989	Omaha	AAA KC	17	64	14	3	2	0	21	5	3	7	0	18	0	0	0	5	4	.56	0	.219	.296	.328
1990	Omaha	AAA KC	98	381	126	14	8	0	156	65	26	31	1	68	4	6	2	39	15	.72	6	.331	.385	.409
1994	Nashville	AAA ChA	130	470	124	17	12	5	180	76	60	35	1	85	10	4	3	20	7	.74	6	.264	.326	.383
1995	Tacoma	AAA Sea	93	363	109	10	12	5	158	65	46	20	0	62	5	3	1	22	8	.73	2	.300	.344	.435
1996	Norfolk	AAA NYN	127	449	120	24	6	9	183	81	39	40	0	108	7	3	1	25	12	.68	4	.267	.336	.408
1987	Kansas City	AL	27	81	24	2	0	0	26	12	5	8	0	20	0	1	0	7	2	.78	1	.296	.360	.321
1988	Kansas City	AL	35	66	11	1	0	0	12	6	2	4	0	20	0	0	0	5	1	.83	0	.167	.214	.182
1989	Kansas City	AL	72	87	17	2	1	0	21	24	5	15	0	26	0	2	1	16	0	1.00	0	.195	.311	.241
1990	Kansas City	AL	23	60	14	3	0	0	17	5	3	2	0	12	0	1	0	1	1	.50	2	.233	.258	.283
1991	Kansas City	AL	80	184	51	9	0	2	66	24	13	11	0	42	1	3	1	15	5	.75	4	.277	.320	.359
1992	Kansas City	AL	88	200	49	6	3	0	61	25	20	9	0	34	1	6	0	9	6	.60	3	.245	.281	.305
1993	Detroit	AL	75	89	19	2	2	0	25	22	13	11	0	30	0	1	1	7	0	1.00	2	.213	.297	.281
1995	Seattle	AL	13	25	8	2	0	0	10	3	3	1	0	3	0	0	1	5	2	.71	0	.320	.333	.400
10 Min. YEARS			1083	4057	1142	133	84	43	1572	685	411	427	6	806	45	37	23	373	118	.76	48	.281	.355	.387
8 Maj. YEARS			413	792	193	27	6	2	238	121	64	61	0	187	2	14	4	65	17	.79	12	.244	.298	.301

Mike Thurman

Pitches: Right **Bats:** Right **Pos:** P **Ht:** 6'5" **Wt:** 190 **Born:** 7/22/73 **Age:** 23

			HOW MUCH HE PITCHED						WHAT HE GAVE UP													THE RESULTS					
Year	Team	Lg Org	G	GS	CG	GF	IP	BFP	H	R	ER	HR	SH	SF	HB	TBB	IBB	SO	WP	Bk	W	L	Pct.	ShO	Sv	ERA
1994	Vermont	A- Mon	2	2	0	0	6.2	28	6	4	4	1	0	0	0	2	0	3	0	0	0	1	.000	0	0	5.40
1995	Albany	A Mon	22	22	2	0	110.1	482	133	79	67	4	3	7	4	32	0	77	7	0	3	8	.273	0	0	5.47
1996	W. Palm Bch	A+ Mon	19	19	0	0	113.2	479	122	53	43	3	2	2	5	23	0	68	7	1	6	8	.429	0	0	3.40
	Harrisburg	AA Mon	4	4	1	0	24.2	101	25	14	14	6	1	1	3	5	0	14	0	0	3	1	.750	0	0	5.11
3 Min. YEARS			47	47	3	0	255.1	1090	286	150	128	14	6	10	12	62	0	162	14	1	12	18	.400	0	0	4.51

Jerrey Thurston

Bats: Right **Throws:** Right **Pos:** C **Ht:** 6'4" **Wt:** 200 **Born:** 4/17/72 **Age:** 25

			BATTING															BASERUNNING				PERCENTAGES		
Year	Team	Lg Org	G	AB	H	2B	3B	HR	TB	R	RBI	TBB	IBB	SO	HBP	SH	SF	SB	CS	SB%	GDP	Avg	OBP	SLG
1990	Padres	R SD	42	144	33	6	1	0	41	22	16	14	0	37	0	2	0	4	1	.80	1	.229	.297	.285
1991	Charlstn-SC	A SD	42	137	14	2	0	0	16	5	4	9	0	50	0	1	1	1	1	.50	3	.102	.156	.117
	Spokane	A- SD	60	201	43	9	0	1	55	26	20	20	1	61	2	2	2	2	2	.50	2	.214	.289	.274
1992	Waterloo	A SD	96	263	37	7	0	0	44	20	14	12	0	73	2	6	2	1	0	1.00	4	.141	.183	.167
1993	Wichita	AA SD	78	197	48	10	0	2	64	22	22	14	0	62	6	3	0	2	0	1.00	3	.244	.313	.325
1994	Wichita	AA SD	77	238	51	10	2	4	77	30	28	19	1	73	8	2	1	1	4	.20	8	.214	.293	.324
1995	Las Vegas	AAA SD	5	20	4	1	0	0	5	2	0	0	0	5	1	0	0	0	0	.00	0	.200	.238	.250
	Rancho Cuca	A+ SD	76	200	44	9	0	1	56	24	13	21	0	64	7	4	3	1	0	1.00	2	.220	.312	.280
1996	Orlando	AA ChN	67	177	37	6	1	3	54	16	23	14	0	57	0	3	0	0	0	.00	5	.209	.267	.305
7 Min. YEARS			543	1577	311	60	4	11	412	167	140	123	2	482	26	23	9	12	8	.60	28	.197	.265	.261

Dave Tokheim

Bats: Left **Throws:** Left **Pos:** OF **Ht:** 6'1" **Wt:** 185 **Born:** 5/25/69 **Age:** 28

			BATTING															BASERUNNING				PERCENTAGES		
Year	Team	Lg Org	G	AB	H	2B	3B	HR	TB	R	RBI	TBB	IBB	SO	HBP	SH	SF	SB	CS	SB%	GDP	Avg	OBP	SLG
1991	Batavia	A- Phi	40	158	51	12	3	2	75	28	21	9	0	20	1	2	1	6	2	.75	1	.323	.361	.475
1992	Clearwater	A+ Phi	106	396	93	12	6	4	129	40	41	30	4	40	5	2	2	10	12	.45	6	.235	.296	.326
1993	Clearwater	A+ Phi	41	155	51	8	2	0	63	27	11	14	4	17	2	1	1	7	5	.58	1	.329	.390	.406
	Reading	AA Phi	65	257	75	11	6	2	104	30	25	12	0	36	0	3	0	8	6	.57	3	.292	.323	.405
1994	Reading	AA Phi	126	438	132	17	6	13	200	56	47	27	2	70	4	1	3	12	10	.55	10	.301	.345	.457

Year Team	Lg Org	G	AB	H	2B	3B	HR	TB	R	RBI	TBB	IBB	SO	HBP	SH	SF	SB	CS	SB%	GDP	Avg	OBP	SLG
		BATTING															BASERUNNING				PERCENTAGES		
1995 Scranton-WB	AAA Phi	127	450	122	18	8	11	189	64	66	18	2	55	5	3	7	6	7	.46	11	.271	.302	.420
1996 Scranton-WB	AAA Phi	92	255	54	10	4	1	75	35	21	11	1	37	5	4	1	5	5	.50	3	.212	.257	.294
6 Min. YEARS		597	2109	578	88	35	33	835	280	232	121	13	275	22	16	15	54	47	.53	35	.274	.318	.396

Kevin Tolar

Pitches: Left **Bats:** Right **Pos:** P **Ht:** 6'3" **Wt:** 225 **Born:** 1/28/71 **Age:** 26

Year Team	Lg Org	G	GS	CG	GF	IP	BFP	H	R	ER	HR	SH	SF	HB	TBB	IBB	SO	WP	Bk	W	L	Pct.	ShO	Sv	ERA
		HOW MUCH HE PITCHED						WHAT HE GAVE UP												THE RESULTS					
1989 White Sox	R ChA	13	12	1	0	60	256	29	16	11	0	1	1	1	54	0	58	10	0	6	2	.750	0	0	1.65
1990 Utica	A- ChA	15	15	1	0	90.1	407	80	44	33	2	1	3	4	61	1	69	9	1	4	6	.400	0	0	3.29
1991 South Bend	A ChA	30	19	0	6	114.2	510	87	54	35	3	5	5	8	85	0	87	6	0	8	5	.615	0	1	2.75
1992 Salinas	A+ ChA	14	8	3	3	53.1	255	55	43	36	4	1	7	5	46	0	24	6	0	1	8	.111	0	0	6.08
South Bend	A ChA	18	10	0	6	81.1	339	59	34	26	5	7	4	2	41	0	81	5	1	6	5	.545	0	0	2.88
1993 Sarasota	A+ ChA	23	11	0	8	77.1	358	75	55	46	1	5	7	6	51	1	60	8	0	2	6	.250	0	1	5.35
1995 Carolina	AA Pit	12	0	0	3	12.1	59	16	5	5	0	0	2	0	7	0	9	2	0	1	0	1.000	0	0	3.65
Lynchburg	A+ Pit	30	0	0	7	31.2	136	29	12	11	1	0	3	1	13	0	28	5	0	3	0	1.000	0	0	3.13
1996 Canton-Akrn	AA Cle	50	0	0	15	44.2	201	42	19	13	1	4	2	3	26	2	39	5	0	1	3	.250	0	1	2.62
7 Min. YEARS		205	75	5	48	565.2	2521	472	282	216	17	24	34	30	384	4	455	56	2	32	35	.478	0	3	3.44

Brian Tollberg

Pitches: Right **Bats:** Right **Pos:** P **Ht:** 6'3" **Wt:** 195 **Born:** 9/16/72 **Age:** 24

Year Team	Lg Org	G	GS	CG	GF	IP	BFP	H	R	ER	HR	SH	SF	HB	TBB	IBB	SO	WP	Bk	W	L	Pct.	ShO	Sv	ERA
		HOW MUCH HE PITCHED						WHAT HE GAVE UP												THE RESULTS					
1994 Chillicothe	IND —	13	13	4	0	94.2	402	90	34	30	5	2	2	8	27	2	69	8	0	7	4	.636	0	0	2.85
1995 Beloit	A Mil	22	22	1	0	132	529	119	59	50	10	2	5	6	27	0	110	5	4	13	4	.765	1	0	3.41
1996 El Paso	AA Mil	26	26	0	0	154.1	663	183	90	84	15	2	3	10	23	0	109	4	1	7	5	.583	0	0	4.90
3 Min. YEARS		61	61	5	0	381	1594	392	183	164	30	6	10	24	77	2	288	17	5	27	13	.675	1	0	3.87

Brett Tomko

Pitches: Right **Bats:** Right **Pos:** P **Ht:** 6'4" **Wt:** 205 **Born:** 4/7/73 **Age:** 24

Year Team	Lg Org	G	GS	CG	GF	IP	BFP	H	R	ER	HR	SH	SF	HB	TBB	IBB	SO	WP	Bk	W	L	Pct.	ShO	Sv	ERA
		HOW MUCH HE PITCHED						WHAT HE GAVE UP												THE RESULTS					
1995 Charlstn-WV	A Cin	9	7	0	0	49	192	41	12	10	1	1	1	1	9	1	46	4	2	4	2	.667	0	0	1.84
1996 Chattanooga	AA Cin	27	27	0	0	157.2	647	131	73	68	20	3	4	5	54	4	164	6	5	11	7	.611	0	0	3.88
2 Min. YEARS		36	34	0	0	206.2	839	172	85	78	21	4	5	6	63	5	210	10	7	15	9	.625	0	0	3.40

Randy Tomlin

Pitches: Left **Bats:** Left **Pos:** P **Ht:** 5'10" **Wt:** 182 **Born:** 6/14/66 **Age:** 31

Year Team	Lg Org	G	GS	CG	GF	IP	BFP	H	R	ER	HR	SH	SF	HB	TBB	IBB	SO	WP	Bk	W	L	Pct.	ShO	Sv	ERA
		HOW MUCH HE PITCHED						WHAT HE GAVE UP												THE RESULTS					
1988 Watertown	A- Pit	15	15	5	0	103.1	407	75	31	25	4	3	3	6	25	1	87	4	2	7	5	.583	2	0	2.18
1989 Salem	A+ Pit	21	21	3	0	138.2	582	131	60	50	11	2	2	3	43	0	99	7	0	12	6	.667	2	0	3.25
Harrisburg	AA Pit	5	5	1	0	32	119	18	6	3	0	1	3	1	6	0	31	0	0	2	2	.500	0	0	0.84
1990 Buffalo	AAA Pit	3	1	0	1	8	33	12	3	3	1	0	1	0	1	0	3	0	0	0	0	.000	0	0	3.38
Harrisburg	AA Pit	19	18	4	1	126.1	521	101	43	32	3	2	4	6	34	6	92	2	1	9	6	.600	3	0	2.28
1993 Carolina	AA Pit	2	2	0	0	12	41	7	1	1	1	0	0	0	1	0	9	0	0	1	0	1.000	0	0	0.75
1994 Buffalo	AAA Pit	11	11	0	0	52.2	232	70	32	31	5	1	3	1	17	1	28	2	0	2	2	.500	0	0	5.30
1996 Pawtucket	AAA Bos	5	2	0	3	13	58	17	12	12	5	0	0	0	5	0	5	1	1	0	2	.000	0	1	8.31
Nashua	IND —	6	0	0	4	6.1	28	7	1	1	0	0	0	0	2	0	9	1	0	0	1	.000	0	0	1.42
1990 Pittsburgh	NL	12	12	2	0	77.2	297	62	24	22	5	2	2	1	12	1	42	1	3	4	4	.500	0	0	2.55
1991 Pittsburgh	NL	31	27	4	0	175	736	170	75	58	9	5	2	6	54	4	104	2	3	8	7	.533	2	0	2.98
1992 Pittsburgh	NL	35	33	1	0	208.2	866	226	85	79	11	13	5	5	42	4	90	7	2	14	9	.609	1	0	3.41
1993 Pittsburgh	NL	18	18	1	0	98.1	411	109	57	53	11	8	8	5	15	0	44	4	2	4	8	.333	0	0	4.85
1994 Pittsburgh	NL	10	4	0	1	20.2	89	23	9	9	1	0	0	0	10	0	17	0	0	0	3	.000	0	0	3.92
6 Min. YEARS		87	75	13	9	492.1	2021	438	189	158	30	9	16	17	134	8	363	17	4	33	24	.579	7	1	2.89
5 Maj. YEARS		106	94	8	1	580.1	2399	590	250	221	37	28	17	17	133	9	297	14	10	30	31	.492	3	0	3.43

Dilson Torres

Pitches: Right **Bats:** Right **Pos:** P **Ht:** 6' 3" **Wt:** 200 **Born:** 5/31/70 **Age:** 27

Year Team	Lg Org	G	GS	CG	GF	IP	BFP	H	R	ER	HR	SH	SF	HB	TBB	IBB	SO	WP	Bk	W	L	Pct.	ShO	Sv	ERA
		HOW MUCH HE PITCHED						WHAT HE GAVE UP												THE RESULTS					
1993 St. Cathrns	A- Tor	17	0	0	12	23	98	21	13	8	3	1	0	0	6	0	23	2	0	1	4	.200	0	3	3.13
1994 Wilmington	A+ KC	15	9	0	5	59.1	239	47	15	9	5	3	2	0	15	0	49	2	2	7	2	.778	0	2	1.37
Memphis	AA KC	10	9	0	0	59	229	47	15	12	3	2	1	5	10	0	47	1	0	6	0	1.000	0	0	1.83
1995 Omaha	AAA KC	5	5	1	0	27.1	113	28	11	8	2	2	1	1	7	0	12	1	1	3	1	.750	1	0	2.63
1996 Omaha	AAA KC	16	14	2	0	86	376	102	54	44	11	3	1	3	19	2	36	3	3	4	7	.364	1	0	4.60
Wichita	AA KC	9	8	0	1	55.2	234	62	27	24	6	1	2	3	13	2	27	0	1	5	3	.625	0	1	3.88
1995 Kansas City	AL	24	2	0	7	44.1	198	56	30	30	6	0	0	1	17	2	28	1	0	1	2	.333	0	0	6.09
4 Min. YEARS		72	45	3	18	310.1	1289	307	135	105	30	12	7	12	70	4	194	9	7	26	17	.605	2	6	3.05

Jaime Torres

Bats: Right **Throws:** Right **Pos:** C **Ht:** 6'0" **Wt:** 176 **Born:** 3/12/73 **Age:** 24

				BATTING															BASERUNNING				PERCENTAGES		
Year	Team	Lg	Org	G	AB	H	2B	3B	HR	TB	R	RBI	TBB	IBB	SO	HBP	SH	SF	SB	CS	SB%	GDP	Avg	OBP	SLG
1992	Yankees	R	NYA	33	121	42	8	2	2	60	21	23	6	0	12	3	0	2	0	0	.00	2	.347	.386	.496
	Ft. Laud	A+	NYA	3	12	4	3	0	0	7	1	1	1	0	4	0	0	0	0	0	.00	0	.333	.385	.583
1993	Oneonta	A-	NYA	28	104	27	6	0	1	36	13	8	9	0	9	1	0	0	2	0	1.00	4	.260	.325	.346
	Greensboro	A	NYA	25	92	26	5	0	1	34	9	12	7	0	7	2	1	1	1	0	1.00	2	.283	.343	.370
1994	Greensboro	A	NYA	89	322	87	22	1	6	129	27	63	13	0	39	8	0	8	4	4	.50	17	.270	.308	.401
1995	Tampa	A+	NYA	107	364	87	17	0	8	128	45	45	28	1	29	10	3	3	1	1	.50	14	.239	.309	.352
1996	Norwich	AA	NYA	100	334	84	19	2	6	125	42	40	21	2	28	4	7	2	1	3	.25	7	.251	.302	.374
	Columbus	AAA	NYA	12	37	10	3	0	1	16	5	7	2	0	4	0	1	0	1	0	1.00	1	.270	.308	.432
5 Min. YEARS				397	1386	367	83	5	25	535	163	199	87	3	132	28	12	16	10	8	.56	47	.265	.318	.386

Paul Torres

Bats: Right **Throws:** Right **Pos:** OF **Ht:** 6'3" **Wt:** 210 **Born:** 10/19/70 **Age:** 26

				BATTING															BASERUNNING				PERCENTAGES		
Year	Team	Lg	Org	G	AB	H	2B	3B	HR	TB	R	RBI	TBB	IBB	SO	HBP	SH	SF	SB	CS	SB%	GDP	Avg	OBP	SLG
1989	Wytheville	R+	ChN	54	191	45	9	1	7	77	34	38	32	0	55	6	0	2	2	4	.33	3	.236	.359	.403
1990	Peoria	A	ChN	36	123	30	4	1	5	51	18	18	13	0	33	2	1	0	1	1	.50	2	.244	.326	.415
	Geneva	A-	ChN	77	271	72	23	1	10	127	46	45	39	1	72	10	2	5	9	3	.75	3	.266	.372	.469
1991	Winston-Sal	A+	ChN	27	87	10	1	0	2	17	9	7	11	0	30	2	0	1	4	0	1.00	3	.115	.228	.195
	Peoria	A	ChN	99	352	75	24	2	13	142	60	50	48	2	91	9	3	0	6	2	.75	7	.213	.323	.403
1992	Winston-Sal	A+	ChN	134	458	109	15	6	14	178	55	78	60	2	114	5	2	7	4	4	.50	10	.238	.328	.389
1993	Daytona	A+	ChN	100	353	98	17	5	13	164	63	43	52	0	94	8	1	3	5	4	.56	5	.278	.380	.465
	Orlando	AA	ChN	19	55	14	4	0	3	27	10	10	7	0	18	0	0	0	3	0	1.00	1	.255	.339	.491
1994	Orlando	AA	ChN	61	160	38	2	1	10	72	21	26	31	1	41	2	1	2	2	6	.25	5	.238	.364	.450
	Daytona	A+	ChN	26	90	28	6	3	4	52	12	20	11	2	26	0	0	1	4	1	.80	1	.311	.382	.578
1995	Orlando	AA	ChN	63	228	68	14	1	10	114	38	45	29	4	40	1	0	2	0	3	.00	1	.298	.377	.500
	Arkansas	AA	StL	66	231	52	11	0	10	93	24	33	21	0	56	5	1	0	2	1	.67	9	.225	.304	.403
1996	Louisville	AAA	StL	1	2	1	0	0	0	1	0	0	0	0	1	0	0	0	0	0	.00	0	.500	.500	.500
	Arkansas	AA	StL	102	309	81	16	0	11	130	38	44	44	1	62	2	0	1	1	1	.50	3	.262	.357	.421
8 Min. YEARS				865	2910	721	146	21	112	1245	428	457	398	13	733	52	11	24	43	30	.59	53	.248	.346	.428

Tomas Torres

Bats: Right **Throws:** Right **Pos:** 3B **Ht:** 5'11" **Wt:** 165 **Born:** 9/29/74 **Age:** 22

				BATTING															BASERUNNING				PERCENTAGES		
Year	Team	Lg	Org	G	AB	H	2B	3B	HR	TB	R	RBI	TBB	IBB	SO	HBP	SH	SF	SB	CS	SB%	GDP	Avg	OBP	SLG
1996	Charlotte	AAA	Fla	5	4	1	0	0	0	1	0	1	0	0	0	0	0	0	0	0	.00	0	.250	.250	.250

Tony Torres

Bats: Right **Throws:** Right **Pos:** 2B **Ht:** 5'9" **Wt:** 165 **Born:** 6/1/70 **Age:** 27

				BATTING															BASERUNNING				PERCENTAGES		
Year	Team	Lg	Org	G	AB	H	2B	3B	HR	TB	R	RBI	TBB	IBB	SO	HBP	SH	SF	SB	CS	SB%	GDP	Avg	OBP	SLG
1992	Erie	A-	Fla	40	157	46	9	1	0	57	31	16	20	0	26	4	0	2	13	5	.72	1	.293	.383	.363
1993	High Desert	A+	Fla	89	287	66	9	3	1	84	45	25	24	0	69	2	5	3	14	8	.64	7	.230	.291	.293
1994	Brevard Cty	A+	Fla	98	368	93	14	7	4	133	58	39	39	1	67	2	3	3	17	6	.74	6	.253	.325	.361
1995	Portland	AA	Fla	58	81	24	3	2	0	31	15	4	11	0	23	1	8	0	9	0	1.00	1	.296	.387	.383
1996	Portland	AA	Fla	47	126	34	11	0	1	48	21	13	14	0	24	5	1	0	3	1	.75	2	.270	.366	.381
5 Min. YEARS				332	1019	263	46	13	6	353	170	97	108	1	209	14	17	8	56	20	.74	17	.258	.335	.346

Dave Toth

Bats: Right **Throws:** Right **Pos:** C **Ht:** 6'1" **Wt:** 195 **Born:** 12/8/69 **Age:** 27

				BATTING															BASERUNNING				PERCENTAGES		
Year	Team	Lg	Org	G	AB	H	2B	3B	HR	TB	R	RBI	TBB	IBB	SO	HBP	SH	SF	SB	CS	SB%	GDP	Avg	OBP	SLG
1990	Pulaski	R+	Atl	26	82	22	0	0	0	22	9	10	11	0	12	1	1	2	2	0	1.00	0	.268	.354	.268
1991	Idaho Falls	R+	Atl	47	160	34	3	0	4	49	27	22	18	1	21	4	1	2	1	0	1.00	6	.213	.304	.306
1992	Macon	A	Atl	87	310	80	15	2	3	108	32	41	21	0	44	4	0	2	3	3	.50	6	.258	.312	.348
1993	Macon	A	Atl	104	353	87	22	0	4	121	38	40	28	1	53	7	5	3	6	5	.55	11	.246	.312	.343
1994	Durham	A+	Atl	72	165	40	11	0	2	57	23	20	19	0	28	1	1	1	1	0	1.00	4	.242	.323	.345
1995	Richmond	AAA	Atl	7	13	3	0	0	0	3	1	1	1	0	2	0	0	0	0	1	.00	1	.231	.286	.231
	Durham	A+	Atl	85	257	63	6	0	6	87	20	26	25	1	42	6	0	1	3	3	.50	6	.245	.325	.339
1996	Greenville	AA	Atl	120	376	100	31	1	10	163	63	55	58	0	61	11	1	4	2	3	.40	4	.266	.376	.434
7 Min. YEARS				548	1716	429	88	3	29	610	213	215	181	3	263	34	9	15	18	15	.55	38	.250	.331	.355

Robert Toth

Pitches: Right **Bats:** Right **Pos:** P **Ht:** 6'2" **Wt:** 180 **Born:** 7/30/72 **Age:** 24

				HOW MUCH HE PITCHED						WHAT HE GAVE UP												THE RESULTS					
Year	Team	Lg	Org	G	GS	CG	GF	IP	BFP	H	R	ER	HR	SH	SF	HB	TBB	IBB	SO	WP	Bk	W	L	Pct.	ShO	Sv	ERA
1990	Royals	R	KC	7	7	0	0	38	148	34	8	7	1	0	0	2	4	0	22	3	0	2	2	.500	0	0	1.66
1991	Baseball Cy	A+	KC	13	10	0	0	63.2	263	53	24	20	1	5	1	2	23	2	42	0	0	2	3	.400	0	0	2.83
1992	Appleton	A	KC	23	22	2	1	127.1	515	111	58	48	9	6	5	5	34	0	100	3	0	7	6	.538	0	0	3.39
1993	Wilmington	A+	KC	25	24	0	1	151.2	609	129	57	49	13	5	2	3	40	1	129	7	1	8	7	.533	0	0	2.91
1994	Wilmington	A+	KC	11	7	3	1	59.1	234	52	14	12	3	2	0	2	9	0	36	0	0	6	1	.857	2	0	1.82

Year	Team	Lg	Org	G	GS	CG	GF	IP	BFP	H	R	ER	HR	SH	SF	HB	TBB	IBB	SO	WP	Bk	W	L	Pct.	ShO	Sv	ERA
	HOW MUCH HE PITCHED									**WHAT HE GAVE UP**												**THE RESULTS**					
	Memphis	AA	KC	20	12	0	4	88.2	372	89	46	41	13	3	1	7	24	0	61	14	0	5	8	.385	0	1	4.16
1995	Omaha	AAA	KC	8	8	1	0	47.1	205	53	25	19	7	3	2	2	8	0	31	0	0	1	2	.333	0	0	3.61
	Wichita	AA	KC	29	17	2	2	151	632	148	55	44	13	6	5	6	35	1	108	6	1	9	6	.600	0	0	2.62
1996	Omaha	AAA	KC	11	8	0	0	46	214	63	40	36	6	1	2	3	17	1	20	2	0	3	3	.500	0	0	7.04
	Wichita	AA	KC	19	13	2	5	104.2	433	100	48	44	5	5	5	2	24	0	51	3	0	4	6	.400	0	4	3.78
7	Min. YEARS			166	128	10	14	877.2	3625	832	375	320	71	36	23	34	218	5	600	38	2	47	44	.516	2	5	3.28

Bubba Trammell

Bats: Right **Throws:** Right **Pos:** OF **Ht:** 6'2" **Wt:** 205 **Born:** 11/6/71 **Age:** 25

				BATTING														**BASERUNNING**				**PERCENTAGES**		
Year	Team	Lg	Org	G	AB	H	2B	3B	HR	TB	R	RBI	TBB	IBB	SO	HBP	SH	SF	SB	CS	SB%	GDP	Avg	OBP	SLG
1994	Jamestown	A-	Det	65	235	70	18	6	5	115	37	41	23	0	32	4	0	4	9	7	.56	1	.298	.365	.489
1995	Lakeland	A+	Det	122	454	129	32	3	16	215	61	72	48	2	80	4	0	4	13	3	.81	9	.284	.355	.474
1996	Jacksonvlle	AA	Det	83	311	102	23	2	27	210	63	75	32	6	61	8	0	1	3	2	.60	11	.328	.403	.675
	Toledo	AAA	Det	51	180	53	14	1	6	87	32	24	22	1	44	0	0	1	5	1	.83	1	.294	.369	.483
3	Min. YEARS			321	1180	354	87	12	54	627	193	212	125	9	217	16	0	10	30	13	.70	22	.300	.372	.531

Gary Trammell

Bats: Left **Throws:** Right **Pos:** OF **Ht:** 6'0" **Wt:** 180 **Born:** 10/16/72 **Age:** 24

				BATTING														**BASERUNNING**				**PERCENTAGES**		
Year	Team	Lg	Org	G	AB	H	2B	3B	HR	TB	R	RBI	TBB	IBB	SO	HBP	SH	SF	SB	CS	SB%	GDP	Avg	OBP	SLG
1993	Astros	R	Hou	59	215	62	5	5	0	77	25	19	14	0	38	3	1	2	11	3	.79	2	.288	.338	.358
1994	Auburn	A-	Hou	70	272	82	10	4	3	109	44	47	22	0	23	0	2	6	15	7	.68	3	.301	.347	.401
1995	Quad City	A	Hou	102	336	100	12	3	2	124	44	33	32	0	62	1	5	3	14	8	.64	4	.298	.358	.369
1996	Kissimmee	A+	Hou	118	402	116	16	8	0	148	48	39	20	0	52	0	3	4	11	3	.79	5	.289	.319	.368
	Tucson	AAA	Hou	3	10	4	0	0	1	7	3	2	2	0	2	0	0	0	0	0	.00	1	.400	.500	.700
4	Min. YEARS			352	1235	364	43	20	6	465	164	140	90	0	177	4	11	15	51	21	.71	15	.295	.341	.377

Mark Tranbarger

Pitches: Left **Bats:** Left **Pos:** P **Ht:** 6'2" **Wt:** 205 **Born:** 9/17/69 **Age:** 27

	HOW MUCH HE PITCHED									**WHAT HE GAVE UP**												**THE RESULTS**					
Year	Team	Lg	Org	G	GS	CG	GF	IP	BFP	H	R	ER	HR	SH	SF	HB	TBB	IBB	SO	WP	Bk	W	L	Pct.	ShO	Sv	ERA
1991	Johnson Cty	R+	StL	4	0	0	0	8	37	11	7	2	0	0	0	2	0	0	6	1	1	1	0	1.000	0	0	2.25
	Cardinals	R	StL	23	0	0	4	29.1	115	22	5	4	0	1	2	0	4	0	37	3	1	3	0	1.000	0	0	1.23
1992	Springfield	A	StL	42	0	0	17	49.2	220	47	27	20	4	1	3	3	24	0	38	2	1	1	0	1.000	0	2	3.62
1993	Savannah	A	StL	56	1	0	11	66	276	56	25	23	3	3	2	3	29	0	50	2	0	5	2	.714	0	1	3.14
1994	Chattanooga	AA	Cin	12	0	0	6	10	46	12	6	6	0	0	1	1	4	0	9	1	0	0	1	.000	0	1	5.40
	Winston-Sal	A+	Cin	37	1	0	24	39.2	174	36	18	15	3	1	0	3	19	3	31	3	0	4	3	.571	0	12	3.40
1995	Chattanooga	AA	Cin	48	0	0	12	55.1	236	50	15	12	4	2	4	2	20	1	46	2	0	3	1	.750	0	0	1.95
1996	Bowie	AA	Bal	40	2	0	17	55	263	67	37	33	5	5	2	3	35	1	45	2	1	3	3	.500	0	3	5.40
6	Min. YEARS			262	4	0	91	313	1367	301	140	115	19	13	14	17	135	5	262	16	4	20	10	.667	0	19	3.31

Jody Treadwell

Pitches: Right **Bats:** Right **Pos:** P **Ht:** 6'0" **Wt:** 190 **Born:** 12/14/68 **Age:** 28

	HOW MUCH HE PITCHED									**WHAT HE GAVE UP**												**THE RESULTS**					
Year	Team	Lg	Org	G	GS	CG	GF	IP	BFP	H	R	ER	HR	SH	SF	HB	TBB	IBB	SO	WP	Bk	W	L	Pct.	ShO	Sv	ERA
1990	Vero Beach	A+	LA	16	8	2	5	80.1	316	59	17	16	2	3	1	1	22	6	80	2	3	9	1	.900	1	1	1.79
1991	San Antonio	AA	LA	10	10	1	0	61	271	73	41	32	7	2	1	4	22	1	43	0	2	3	3	.500	0	0	4.72
	Bakersfield	A+	LA	17	14	0	0	91.1	392	92	46	38	8	2	0	4	34	2	84	7	1	5	4	.556	0	0	3.74
1992	San Antonio	AA	LA	29	4	2	4	76	331	74	40	35	3	2	3	4	40	4	68	6	2	3	5	.375	1	1	4.14
1993	Albuquerque	AAA	LA	39	10	0	6	105.1	481	119	58	55	7	3	2	7	52	7	102	11	2	5	4	.556	0	0	4.70
1994	Albuquerque	AAA	LA	33	24	0	4	158.2	676	151	78	75	11	5	2	10	59	3	114	7	1	10	6	.625	0	2	4.25
1995	Albuquerque	AAA	LA	30	15	1	4	125	510	121	61	55	15	2	5	2	32	4	79	9	1	7	5	.583	1	1	3.96
1996	Albuquerque	AAA	LA	5	3	0	0	18.1	93	30	18	16	4	0	3	0	10	1	16	0	0	1	1	.500	0	0	7.85
7	Min. YEARS			179	88	6	23	716	3070	719	359	322	57	19	17	32	271	28	586	42	12	43	29	.597	3	5	4.05

Chad Tredaway

Bats: Both **Throws:** Right **Pos:** 2B **Ht:** 6'0" **Wt:** 180 **Born:** 6/18/72 **Age:** 25

				BATTING														**BASERUNNING**				**PERCENTAGES**		
Year	Team	Lg	Org	G	AB	H	2B	3B	HR	TB	R	RBI	TBB	IBB	SO	HBP	SH	SF	SB	CS	SB%	GDP	Avg	OBP	SLG
1992	Geneva	A-	ChN	73	270	81	19	2	5	119	39	31	24	1	24	3	3	5	6	4	.60	3	.300	.358	.441
1993	Daytona	A+	ChN	66	242	62	12	0	0	74	32	21	27	2	25	0	3	4	4	3	.57	1	.256	.326	.306
1994	Orlando	AA	ChN	45	146	28	3	0	1	34	13	15	10	0	20	1	1	3	2	0	1.00	3	.192	.244	.233
	Daytona	A+	ChN	77	284	69	14	3	5	104	26	28	23	0	39	1	4	1	1	5	.17	6	.243	.301	.366
1995	Memphis	AA	SD	10	30	8	1	0	0	9	5	4	3	1	5	0	0	0	1	0	1.00	0	.267	.333	.300
	Rancho Cuca	A+	SD	109	408	113	17	2	6	152	53	57	29	3	43	3	1	8	4	2	.67	10	.277	.324	.373
1996	Rancho Cuca	A+	SD	21	84	21	3	0	2	30	13	13	7	0	7	0	0	3	1	0	1.00	1	.250	.298	.357
	Las Vegas	AAA	SD	76	196	44	10	2	5	73	26	19	17	2	25	1	5	1	4	1	.80	4	.224	.288	.372
5	Min. YEARS			477	1660	426	79	9	24	595	207	188	140	9	188	9	17	25	23	15	.61	28	.257	.314	.358

Chris Tremie

Bats: Right **Throws:** Right **Pos:** C **Ht:** 6' 0" **Wt:** 200 **Born:** 10/17/69 **Age:** 27

				BATTING															BASERUNNING				PERCENTAGES		
Year	Team	Lg	Org	G	AB	H	2B	3B	HR	TB	R	RBI	TBB	IBB	SO	HBP	SH	SF	SB	CS	SB%	GDP	Avg	OBP	SLG
1992	Utica	A-	ChA	6	16	1	0	0	0	1	1	0	0	0	5	0	0	0	0	0	.00	0	.063	.063	.063
1993	White Sox	R	ChA	2	4	0	0	0	0	0	0	0	0	0	0	0	0	0	0	0	.00	0	.000	.000	.000
	Sarasota	A+	ChA	14	37	6	1	0	0	7	2	5	2	0	4	3	0	0	0	0	.00	1	.162	.262	.189
	Hickory	A	ChA	49	155	29	6	1	1	40	7	17	9	0	26	4	1	0	0	0	.00	5	.187	.250	.258
1994	Birmingham	AA	ChA	92	302	68	13	0	2	87	32	29	17	0	44	6	3	2	4	1	.80	3	.225	.278	.288
1995	Nashville	AAA	ChA	67	190	38	4	0	2	48	13	16	13	0	37	2	4	0	0	0	.00	6	.200	.259	.253
1996	Nashville	AAA	ChA	70	215	47	10	1	0	59	17	26	18	0	48	2	6	3	2	0	1.00	4	.219	.282	.274
1995	Chicago	AL		10	24	4	0	0	0	4	0	0	1	0	2	0	1	0	0	0	.00	0	.167	.200	.167
	5 Min. YEARS			300	919	189	34	2	5	242	72	93	59	0	164	17	14	5	6	1	.86	19	.206	.265	.263

Hector Trinidad

Pitches: Right **Bats:** Right **Pos:** P **Ht:** 6'2" **Wt:** 190 **Born:** 9/8/73 **Age:** 23

				HOW MUCH HE PITCHED						WHAT HE GAVE UP													THE RESULTS					
Year	Team	Lg	Org	G	GS	CG	GF	IP	BFP	H	R	ER	HR	SH	SF	HB	TBB	IBB	SO	WP	Bk	W	L	Pct.	ShO	Sv	ERA
1991	Huntington	R+	ChN	12	10	2	1	69	286	64	28	22	4	0	1	3	11	0	61	3	0	6	3	.667	0	0	2.87
1992	Geneva	A-	ChN	15	15	2	0	93.2	377	78	33	25	6	5	0	4	13	2	70	1	0	8	6	.571	0	0	2.40
1993	Peoria	A	ChN	22	22	4	0	153	622	142	56	42	6	5	7	4	29	1	118	7	1	7	6	.538	0	0	2.47
	Orlando	AA	ChN	4	4	1	0	24.2	108	34	19	18	5	1	0	1	7	0	13	2	0	1	3	.250	0	0	6.57
1994	Daytona	A+	ChN	28	27	4	1	175.2	726	171	72	63	8	7	3	7	40	0	142	3	1	11	9	.550	1	0	3.23
1995	New Britain	AA	Min	23	22	0	1	121	516	137	67	62	6	1	10	7	22	0	92	6	2	4	11	.267	0	0	4.61
1996	New Britain	AA	Min	25	24	1	0	138.1	583	137	75	59	6	4	1	7	31	0	93	7	0	6	6	.500	1	0	3.84
	6 Min. YEARS			129	124	14	3	775.1	3218	763	350	291	41	23	22	33	153	3	589	29	4	43	44	.494	2	0	3.38

Jason Troilo

Bats: Right **Throws:** Right **Pos:** C **Ht:** 6'1" **Wt:** 195 **Born:** 9/7/72 **Age:** 24

				BATTING															BASERUNNING				PERCENTAGES		
Year	Team	Lg	Org	G	AB	H	2B	3B	HR	TB	R	RBI	TBB	IBB	SO	HBP	SH	SF	SB	CS	SB%	GDP	Avg	OBP	SLG
1994	Oneonta	A-	NYA	7	15	2	1	0	0	3	0	1	4	0	3	0	1	0	0	0	.00	0	.133	.316	.200
	Greensboro	A	NYA	22	58	11	3	0	0	14	5	6	5	0	16	1	0	0	0	0	.00	3	.190	.266	.241
1995	Tampa	A+	NYA	1	2	0	0	0	0	0	0	0	0	0	2	1	0	0	0	0	.00	0	.000	.333	.000
	Greensboro	A	NYA	19	59	17	4	0	3	30	6	9	3	0	19	0	3	1	0	1	.00	0	.288	.317	.508
1996	Tampa	A+	NYA	11	25	5	1	0	1	9	2	5	1	0	7	1	0	0	0	0	.00	1	.200	.259	.360
	Greensboro	A	NYA	67	199	38	10	0	3	57	19	17	9	0	62	4	5	1	2	1	.67	3	.191	.239	.286
	Norwich	AA	NYA	3	8	4	0	0	2	10	3	2	0	0	1	0	0	0	0	0	.00	0	.500	.500	1.250
	3 Min. YEARS			130	366	77	19	0	9	123	35	40	22	0	110	7	9	2	2	2	.50	7	.210	.267	.336

Keith Troutman

Pitches: Right **Bats:** Right **Pos:** P **Ht:** 6'1" **Wt:** 200 **Born:** 5/29/73 **Age:** 24

				HOW MUCH HE PITCHED						WHAT HE GAVE UP													THE RESULTS					
Year	Team	Lg	Org	G	GS	CG	GF	IP	BFP	H	R	ER	HR	SH	SF	HB	TBB	IBB	SO	WP	Bk	W	L	Pct.	ShO	Sv	ERA
1992	Yakima	A-	LA	26	0	0	19	37.1	163	33	19	14	2	2	2	1	15	3	43	2	2	4	1	.800	0	3	3.38
1993	Great Falls	R+	LA	27	0	0	23	42	166	26	12	8	2	1	3	2	12	1	48	2	0	1	1	.500	0	16	1.71
1994	Vero Beach	A+	LA	43	0	0	10	78.1	328	69	39	34	6	3	2	1	35	5	66	5	1	3	2	.600	0	0	3.91
1995	San Antonio	AA	LA	38	0	0	22	65.2	268	64	24	23	3	1	3	1	18	1	50	3	0	1	2	.333	0	2	3.15
1996	Scranton-WB	AAA	Phi	8	0	0	4	14	65	19	9	8	1	1	0	1	5	1	9	1	0	1	1	.500	0	0	5.14
	Reading	AA	Phi	52	1	0	13	73.1	323	62	36	27	7	3	2	3	40	3	73	3	1	6	3	.667	0	1	3.31
	5 Min. YEARS			194	1	0	91	310.2	1313	273	139	114	21	11	12	9	125	14	289	16	4	16	10	.615	0	22	3.30

Scooter Tucker

Bats: Right **Throws:** Right **Pos:** C **Ht:** 6' 2" **Wt:** 205 **Born:** 11/18/66 **Age:** 30

				BATTING															BASERUNNING				PERCENTAGES		
Year	Team	Lg	Org	G	AB	H	2B	3B	HR	TB	R	RBI	TBB	IBB	SO	HBP	SH	SF	SB	CS	SB%	GDP	Avg	OBP	SLG
1988	Everett	A-	SF	45	153	40	5	0	3	54	24	23	30	0	34	3	0	3	0	0	.00	8	.261	.386	.353
1989	Clinton	A	SF	126	426	105	20	2	3	138	44	43	58	2	80	9	3	4	6	5	.55	11	.246	.346	.324
1990	San Jose	A+	SF	123	439	123	28	2	5	170	59	71	71	4	69	13	2	6	9	3	.75	14	.280	.391	.387
1991	Shreveport	AA	SF	110	352	100	29	1	4	143	49	49	48	1	58	5	6	2	3	4	.43	8	.284	.376	.406
1992	Tucson	AAA	Hou	83	288	87	15	1	1	107	36	29	28	1	35	3	1	2	5	1	.83	12	.302	.368	.372
1993	Tucson	AAA	Hou	98	318	87	20	2	1	114	54	37	47	8	37	2	2	2	1	5	.17	7	.274	.369	.358
1994	Tucson	AAA	Hou	113	408	131	38	1	14	213	64	80	48	2	56	6	2	5	3	2	.60	9	.321	.396	.522
1995	Richmond	AAA	Atl	22	66	11	3	1	0	16	5	6	8	0	16	1	0	1	0	0	.00	2	.167	.263	.242
1996	Omaha	AAA	KC	24	74	12	2	0	1	17	5	4	2	0	12	2	2	3	0	0	.00	3	.162	.198	.230
1992	Houston	NL		20	50	6	1	0	0	7	5	3	3	0	13	2	1	0	1	1	.50	2	.120	.200	.140
1993	Houston	NL		9	26	5	1	0	0	6	1	3	2	0	3	0	0	0	0	0	.00	0	.192	.250	.231
1995	Houston	NL		5	7	2	0	0	1	5	1	1	0	0	0	0	0	0	0	0	.00	0	.286	.286	.714
	Cleveland	AL		17	20	0	0	0	0	0	2	0	5	0	4	1	1	0	0	0	.00	0	.000	.231	.000
	9 Min. YEARS			744	2524	696	160	10	32	972	340	342	340	18	397	44	18	28	27	20	.57	74	.276	.368	.385
	3 Maj. YEARS			51	103	13	2	0	1	18	9	7	10	0	20	3	2	0	1	1	.50	2	.126	.224	.175

Brian Turang

Bats: Right **Throws:** Right **Pos:** 3B **Ht:** 5'10" **Wt:** 170 **Born:** 6/14/67 **Age:** 30

BATTING																	BASERUNNING				PERCENTAGES		
Year Team	Lg Org	G	AB	H	2B	3B	HR	TB	R	RBI	TBB	IBB	SO	HBP	SH	SF	SB	CS	SB%	GDP	Avg	OBP	SLG
1989 Bellingham	A- Sea	60	207	59	10	3	4	87	42	11	33	0	50	12	2	0	9	6	.60	1	.285	.413	.420
1990 San Bernrdo	A+ Sea	132	487	144	25	5	12	215	86	67	69	0	98	7	6	4	25	16	.61	8	.296	.388	.441
Calgary	AAA Sea	3	9	2	0	0	0	2	1	1	2	0	4	0	0	0	0	0	.00	0	.222	.364	.222
1991 Jacksonvlle	AA Sea	41	130	28	6	2	0	38	14	7	13	1	33	2	2	0	5	2	.71	1	.215	.297	.292
San Bernrdo	A+ Sea	34	100	18	2	1	0	22	9	4	15	0	31	3	1	0	6	6	.50	1	.180	.305	.220
1992 Jacksonvlle	AA Sea	129	483	121	21	3	14	190	67	63	44	1	61	12	2	3	19	9	.68	12	.251	.327	.393
1993 Calgary	AAA Sea	110	423	137	20	11	8	203	84	54	40	2	48	3	5	4	24	8	.75	7	.324	.383	.480
1994 Jacksonvlle	AA Sea	3	13	4	1	0	0	5	1	1	0	0	3	0	0	0	0	0	.00	0	.308	.308	.385
Calgary	AAA Sea	65	277	95	16	5	5	136	51	40	17	0	37	0	4	3	5	4	.56	7	.343	.377	.491
1995 Tacoma	AAA Sea	59	196	47	4	1	1	56	22	18	13	0	35	0	3	3	7	4	.64	7	.240	.283	.286
1996 Syracuse	AAA Tor	37	93	16	2	1	1	23	13	8	9	0	14	1	3	0	3	0	1.00	3	.172	.252	.247
1993 Seattle	AL	40	140	35	11	1	0	48	22	7	17	0	20	2	1	0	6	2	.75	3	.250	.340	.343
1994 Seattle	AL	38	112	21	5	1	1	31	9	8	7	0	25	1	3	0	3	1	.75	0	.188	.242	.277
8 Min. YEARS		673	2418	671	107	32	45	977	390	274	255	4	414	40	28	17	103	55	.65	47	.278	.354	.404
2 Maj. YEARS		78	252	56	16	2	1	79	31	15	24	0	45	3	4	0	9	3	.75	3	.222	.297	.313

Brian Turner

Bats: Left **Throws:** Left **Pos:** 1B **Ht:** 6'2" **Wt:** 210 **Born:** 6/9/71 **Age:** 26

BATTING																	BASERUNNING				PERCENTAGES		
Year Team	Lg Org	G	AB	H	2B	3B	HR	TB	R	RBI	TBB	IBB	SO	HBP	SH	SF	SB	CS	SB%	GDP	Avg	OBP	SLG
1989 Yankees	R NYA	50	188	39	7	3	1	55	29	28	20	0	30	2	2	3	5	2	.71	4	.207	.286	.293
1990 Greensboro	A NYA	37	118	24	5	1	0	31	14	5	16	0	29	0	1	0	3	2	.60	1	.203	.299	.263
Oneonta	A- NYA	69	227	56	13	1	0	71	28	24	36	1	49	2	1	1	7	4	.64	1	.247	.353	.313
1991 Greensboro	A NYA	123	424	113	17	2	8	158	58	63	59	1	93	2	2	4	10	11	.48	4	.267	.356	.373
1992 Ft. Laud	A+ NYA	127	454	107	16	1	7	146	39	54	46	2	103	0	5	5	3	8	.27	13	.236	.303	.322
1993 San Bernrdo	A+ NYA	109	406	132	23	3	21	224	69	68	49	4	75	2	2	3	4	2	.67	3	.325	.398	.552
1994 Albany-Colo	AA NYA	2	4	2	0	0	0	2	1	1	1	1	0	0	0	0	1	0	1.00	0	.500	.600	.500
Tampa	A+ NYA	118	420	101	24	3	10	161	63	64	63	3	84	4	1	4	2	1	.67	7	.240	.342	.383
1995 Norwich	AA NYA	86	311	92	21	3	4	131	39	43	25	2	72	1	2	4	3	2	.60	5	.296	.346	.421
1996 St. Lucie	A+ NYN	33	99	20	3	0	2	29	15	15	11	0	27	1	0	1	1	0	1.00	1	.202	.286	.293
Binghamton	AA NYN	32	84	17	5	2	2	32	8	12	9	2	18	3	1	2	1	1	.50	1	.202	.296	.381
New Britain	AA Min	48	157	38	8	0	6	64	19	18	13	0	35	1	4	4	5	2	.71	5	.242	.297	.408
8 Min. YEARS		834	2892	741	142	19	61	1104	382	395	348	16	615	18	21	31	45	35	.56	45	.256	.337	.382

Rich Turrentine

Pitches: Right **Bats:** Right **Pos:** P **Ht:** 6'0" **Wt:** 175 **Born:** 5/21/71 **Age:** 26

HOW MUCH HE PITCHED							WHAT HE GAVE UP												THE RESULTS					
Year Team	Lg Org	G	GS	CG	GF	IP	BFP	H	R	ER	HR	SH	SF	HB	TBB	IBB	SO	WP	Bk	W	L	Pct.	ShO	Sv	ERA
1992 Yankees	R NYA	2	0	0	2	2	6	0	0	0	0	0	0	0	0	0	6	0	0	0	0	.000	0	1	0.00
Oneonta	A- NYA	1	0	0	0	0	2	1	2	2	0	0	0	0	1	0	0	0	0	0	0	.000	0	0	0.00
1994 Yankees	R NYA	6	0	0	1	8.2	40	10	8	7	1	1	0	1	4	0	11	2	0	0	0	.000	0	0	7.27
Tampa	A+ NYA	10	0	0	2	14.2	70	14	10	10	0	0	1	2	13	0	10	3	0	1	0	1.000	0	0	6.14
1995 St. Lucie	A+ NYN	4	4	0	0	19.1	92	17	14	13	3	1	0	2	17	0	14	3	0	0	3	.000	0	0	6.05
Columbia	A NYN	30	18	0	8	123.1	529	87	52	42	6	7	4	8	77	1	125	19	1	4	7	.364	0	2	3.06
1996 St. Lucie	A+ NYN	45	0	0	40	51.1	232	31	18	13	0	4	1	2	45	1	63	9	0	4	4	.500	0	21	2.28
Binghamton	AA NYN	8	0	0	7	9.1	43	12	3	3	0	0	1	0	5	0	10	0	0	1	1	.500	0	3	2.89
4 Min. YEARS		106	22	0	60	228.2	1014	172	107	90	10	13	7	15	162	2	239	36	1	10	15	.400	0	27	3.54

Greg Twiggs

Pitches: Left **Bats:** Right **Pos:** P **Ht:** 5'10" **Wt:** 155 **Born:** 10/15/71 **Age:** 25

HOW MUCH HE PITCHED							WHAT HE GAVE UP												THE RESULTS					
Year Team	Lg Org	G	GS	CG	GF	IP	BFP	H	R	ER	HR	SH	SF	HB	TBB	IBB	SO	WP	Bk	W	L	Pct.	ShO	Sv	ERA
1993 Geneva	A- ChN	14	14	2	0	79.2	340	65	39	28	4	6	3	1	37	2	67	6	0	5	6	.455	1	0	3.16
1994 Daytona	A+ ChN	45	0	0	14	70.1	316	70	48	34	4	4	3	3	33	2	45	3	1	3	4	.429	0	2	4.35
1995 Daytona	A+ ChN	18	13	1	1	89.1	355	64	30	14	3	1	1	5	28	0	80	4	0	8	3	.727	0	0	1.41
1996 Orlando	AA ChN	44	0	0	15	54.2	243	53	27	24	2	3	4	0	33	5	40	2	0	4	2	.667	0	1	3.95
4 Min. YEARS		121	27	3	30	294	1254	252	144	100	13	14	11	9	131	9	232	15	1	20	15	.571	1	3	3.06

Brad Tyler

Bats: Left **Throws:** Right **Pos:** 2B **Ht:** 6'2" **Wt:** 175 **Born:** 3/3/69 **Age:** 28

BATTING																	BASERUNNING				PERCENTAGES		
Year Team	Lg Org	G	AB	H	2B	3B	HR	TB	R	RBI	TBB	IBB	SO	HBP	SH	SF	SB	CS	SB%	GDP	Avg	OBP	SLG
1990 Wausau	A Bal	56	187	44	4	3	2	60	31	24	44	2	45	2	1	2	11	4	.73	2	.235	.383	.321
1991 Kane County	A Bal	60	199	54	10	3	3	79	35	29	44	1	25	1	1	2	5	3	.63	0	.271	.402	.397
Frederick	A+ Bal	56	187	48	6	0	4	66	26	26	33	3	33	2	1	1	3	2	.60	0	.257	.372	.353
1992 Frederick	A+ Bal	54	185	47	11	2	3	71	34	22	43	2	34	2	1	4	9	3	.75	2	.254	.393	.384
Hagerstown	AA Bal	83	256	57	9	1	2	74	41	21	34	2	45	2	1	0	23	5	.82	5	.223	.318	.289
1993 Bowie	AA Bal	129	437	103	23	17	10	190	85	44	84	2	89	1	1	3	24	11	.69	2	.236	.358	.435
1994 Rochester	AAA Bal	101	314	82	15	8	7	134	38	43	38	2	69	2	1	0	7	4	.64	4	.261	.345	.427
1995 Rochester	AAA Bal	114	361	93	17	3	17	167	60	52	71	4	63	4	0	5	10	5	.67	3	.258	.381	.463
1996 Rochester	AAA Bal	118	382	103	18	10	13	180	68	52	67	2	95	5	1	3	19	7	.73	2	.270	.383	.471

Year	Team	Lg	Org	G	AB	H	2B	3B	HR	TB	R	RBI	TBB	IBB	SO	HBP	SH	SF	SB	CS	SB%	GDP	Avg	OBP	SLG
				BATTING															BASERUNNING				PERCENTAGES		
7 Min. YEARS				771	2508	631	113	47	61	1021	418	313	458	20	498	21	8	20	111	44	.72	20	.252	.369	.407

Chris Unrat

Bats: Left **Throws:** Right **Pos:** C **Ht:** 6'1" **Wt:** 205 **Born:** 3/28/71 **Age:** 26

Year	Team	Lg	Org	G	AB	H	2B	3B	HR	TB	R	RBI	TBB	IBB	SO	HBP	SH	SF	SB	CS	SB%	GDP	Avg	OBP	SLG
				BATTING															BASERUNNING				PERCENTAGES		
1993	Rangers	R	Tex	12	31	8	2	0	0	10	3	5	4	1	4	1	0	2	1	0	1.00	2	.258	.342	.323
	Erie	A-	Tex	36	124	36	8	1	8	70	25	22	11	0	27	0	0	0	1	1	.50	3	.290	.348	.565
1994	Charlstn-SC	A	Tex	64	192	41	10	0	7	72	28	24	29	1	73	3	0	1	1	3	.25	3	.214	.324	.375
1995	Charlotte	A+	Tex	66	172	43	8	1	1	56	22	17	23	1	38	0	4	2	1	2	.33	6	.250	.335	.326
1996	Charlotte	A+	Tex	41	135	37	8	0	2	51	18	11	27	1	28	0	0	0	2	3	.40	4	.274	.395	.378
	Tulsa	AA	Tex	20	55	10	2	0	1	15	6	7	16	0	13	0	0	0	0	0	.00	2	.182	.366	.273
4 Min. YEARS				239	709	175	38	2	19	274	102	86	110	4	183	4	4	5	6	9	.40	20	.247	.349	.386

Sal Urso

Pitches: Left **Bats:** Right **Pos:** P **Ht:** 5'11" **Wt:** 175 **Born:** 1/19/72 **Age:** 25

Year	Team	Lg	Org	G	GS	CG	GF	IP	BFP	H	R	ER	HR	SH	SF	HB	TBB	IBB	SO	WP	Bk	W	L	Pct.	ShO	Sv	ERA
				HOW MUCH HE PITCHED						WHAT HE GAVE UP												THE RESULTS					
1990	Mariners	R	Sea	20	0	0	6	50.2	219	38	25	13	3	2	6	5	23	1	63	5	0	3	2	.600	0	1	2.31
1991	Peninsula	A+	Sea	46	0	0	29	61.2	290	74	36	21	1	3	4	5	30	7	44	6	0	0	3	.000	0	8	3.06
1992	San Bernrdo	A+	Sea	37	0	0	21	51.1	239	66	34	29	2	2	5	1	32	0	40	4	1	0	1	.000	0	1	5.08
1993	Appleton	A	Sea	36	1	0	18	53.2	226	57	24	20	2	4	2	1	24	1	50	7	1	4	4	.500	0	2	3.35
1994	Riverside	A+	Sea	30	1	0	12	34.2	156	44	27	23	4	1	2	3	14	0	26	3	0	1	2	.333	0	0	5.97
1995	Port City	AA	Sea	51	0	0	8	45.2	185	41	13	11	0	0	0	0	21	0	44	7	1	2	0	1.000	0	1	2.17
1996	Tacoma	AAA	Sea	46	0	0	19	72.2	302	69	22	19	5	4	1	1	32	1	45	2	6	6	2	.750	0	3	2.35
7 Min. YEARS				266	2	0	113	370.1	1617	389	181	136	17	16	20	16	176	10	312	34	9	16	14	.533	0	16	3.31

Carlos Valdez

Pitches: Right **Bats:** Right **Pos:** P **Ht:** 5'11" **Wt:** 175 **Born:** 12/26/71 **Age:** 25

Year	Team	Lg	Org	G	GS	CG	GF	IP	BFP	H	R	ER	HR	SH	SF	HB	TBB	IBB	SO	WP	Bk	W	L	Pct.	ShO	Sv	ERA
				HOW MUCH HE PITCHED						WHAT HE GAVE UP												THE RESULTS					
1991	Giants	R	SF	13	10	0	1	63.1	288	75	48	40	3	1	4	0	32	0	48	6	1	2	3	.400	0	0	5.68
1992	Everett	A-	SF	3	0	0	2	6.1	29	4	2	1	0	0	1	2	7	0	6	1	0	0	1	.000	0	0	1.42
	Giants	R	SF	6	0	0	3	14.2	56	7	2	0	0	1	0	0	5	0	14	1	0	3	1	.750	0	0	0.00
1993	Clinton	A	SF	35	2	0	14	90.1	389	74	47	40	6	7	3	2	44	1	85	8	0	4	7	.364	0	3	3.99
1994	San Jose	A+	SF	36	17	0	10	123.2	536	109	70	62	7	3	6	12	61	0	116	6	0	8	6	.571	0	0	4.51
1995	Phoenix	AAA	SF	18	0	0	12	29.1	131	29	10	9	2	2	0	0	13	2	30	3	0	1	0	1.000	0	2	2.76
	Shreveport	AA	SF	40	3	0	20	93.1	371	69	21	18	2	3	0	3	27	4	81	4	0	4	2	.667	0	7	1.74
1996	Phoenix	AAA	SF	44	0	0	17	59.2	276	63	38	33	4	4	2	4	34	5	38	6	1	4	3	.571	0	5	4.98
1995	San Francisco	NL		11	0	0	3	14.2	69	19	10	10	1	0	1	1	8	1	7	1	1	0	1	.000	0	0	6.14
6 Min. YEARS				195	32	0	79	480.2	2076	430	238	203	24	21	16	23	223	12	418	35	2	26	23	.531	0	17	3.80

Mario Valdez

Bats: Left **Throws:** Right **Pos:** 1B **Ht:** 6'2" **Wt:** 190 **Born:** 11/19/74 **Age:** 22

Year	Team	Lg	Org	G	AB	H	2B	3B	HR	TB	R	RBI	TBB	IBB	SO	HBP	SH	SF	SB	CS	SB%	GDP	Avg	OBP	SLG
				BATTING															BASERUNNING				PERCENTAGES		
1994	White Sox	R	ChA	53	157	37	11	2	2	58	20	25	30	0	28	2	0	1	0	6	.00	3	.236	.363	.369
1995	Hickory	A	ChA	130	441	120	30	5	11	193	65	56	67	2	107	5	0	3	9	7	.56	5	.272	.372	.438
1996	South Bend	A	ChA	61	202	76	19	0	10	125	46	43	36	2	42	6	0	2	2	4	.33	3	.376	.480	.619
	Birmingham	AA	ChA	51	168	46	10	2	3	69	22	28	32	2	34	5	0	3	0	0	.00	3	.274	.399	.411
3 Min. YEARS				295	968	279	70	9	26	445	153	152	165	6	211	18	0	9	11	17	.39	14	.288	.398	.460

Trovin Valdez

Bats: Both **Throws:** Right **Pos:** OF **Ht:** 5'10" **Wt:** 163 **Born:** 11/18/73 **Age:** 23

Year	Team	Lg	Org	G	AB	H	2B	3B	HR	TB	R	RBI	TBB	IBB	SO	HBP	SH	SF	SB	CS	SB%	GDP	Avg	OBP	SLG
				BATTING															BASERUNNING				PERCENTAGES		
1993	Orioles	R	Bal	39	151	32	2	2	0	38	16	6	9	0	23	0	2	0	21	5	.81	1	.212	.256	.252
1994	Albany	A	Bal	20	65	17	0	2	0	21	10	4	1	0	17	2	0	1	9	1	.90	1	.262	.290	.323
	Bluefield	R+	Bal	55	184	53	7	3	3	75	43	18	11	1	26	5	5	5	20	6	.77	1	.288	.337	.408
1995	Bowie	AA	Bal	2	0	0	0	0	0	0	0	0	0	0	0	0	0	0	0	0	.00	0	.000	.000	.000
	Frederick	A+	Bal	112	375	92	12	4	0	112	51	13	18	0	77	5	6	1	34	21	.62	2	.245	.288	.299
1996	Winston-Sal	A+	Cin	90	343	87	11	3	3	113	49	30	22	1	62	2	6	1	26	14	.65	3	.254	.302	.329
	Indianapols	AAA	Cin	1	1	0	0	0	0	0	0	0	0	0	0	0	0	0	0	0	.00	0	.000	.000	.000
4 Min. YEARS				319	1119	281	32	14	6	359	169	71	61	2	205	14	19	8	110	47	.70	8	.251	.296	.321

Jose Valentin

Bats: Both **Throws:** Right **Pos:** C **Ht:** 5'10" **Wt:** 191 **Born:** 9/19/75 **Age:** 21

Year	Team	Lg	Org	G	AB	H	2B	3B	HR	TB	R	RBI	TBB	IBB	SO	HBP	SH	SF	SB	CS	SB%	GDP	Avg	OBP	SLG
				BATTING															BASERUNNING				PERCENTAGES		
1993	Twins	R	Min	32	103	27	6	1	1	38	18	19	14	0	19	1	0	4	0	2	.00	1	.262	.344	.369
	Elizabethtn	R+	Min	9	24	5	1	0	0	6	3	3	4	0	2	1	0	0	0	0	.00	0	.208	.345	.250
1994	Elizabethtn	R+	Min	54	210	44	5	0	9	76	23	27	15	0	44	2	0	5	0	1	.00	9	.210	.263	.362

				BATTING															BASERUNNING				PERCENTAGES		
Year	Team	Lg	Org	G	AB	H	2B	3B	HR	TB	R	RBI	TBB	IBB	SO	HBP	SH	SF	SB	CS	SB%	GDP	Avg	OBP	SLG
1995	Fort Wayne	A	Min	112	383	123	26	5	19	216	59	65	47	7	75	2	1	0	0	5	.00	7	.321	.398	.564
1996	Fort Myers	A+	Min	87	338	89	26	1	7	138	34	54	32	4	65	4	0	5	1	0	1.00	5	.263	.330	.408
	New Britain	AA	Min	48	165	39	8	0	3	56	22	14	16	1	35	1	3	0	0	3	.00	2	.236	.308	.339
4 Min. YEARS				342	1223	327	72	7	39	530	159	182	128	12	240	11	4	14	1	11	.08	24	.267	.339	.433

Ramon Valette

Bats: Right **Throws:** Right **Pos:** SS **Ht:** 6'1" **Wt:** 160 **Born:** 1/20/72 **Age:** 25

				BATTING															BASERUNNING				PERCENTAGES		
Year	Team	Lg	Org	G	AB	H	2B	3B	HR	TB	R	RBI	TBB	IBB	SO	HBP	SH	SF	SB	CS	SB%	GDP	Avg	OBP	SLG
1990	Twins	R	Min	34	109	28	2	0	0	30	12	10	2	0	20	1	2	0	3	1	.75	3	.257	.277	.275
1991	Elizabethtn	R+	Min	25	74	11	2	0	0	13	7	1	6	0	24	0	0	1	1	0	1.00	5	.149	.210	.176
1992	Elizabethtn	R+	Min	44	140	28	6	0	0	34	21	11	15	0	34	1	1	3	6	0	1.00	3	.200	.277	.243
1993	Fort Wayne	A	Min	112	382	91	20	0	6	129	46	38	23	0	89	4	2	4	12	7	.63	11	.238	.286	.338
1994	Fort Myers	A+	Min	122	404	97	21	1	4	132	50	49	22	0	80	5	3	1	19	7	.73	9	.240	.287	.327
1995	New Britain	AA	Min	111	346	74	11	2	4	101	40	32	21	0	52	1	1	2	19	2	.90	14	.214	.259	.292
1996	New Britain	AA	Min	23	71	17	2	2	1	26	7	6	0	0	11	3	0	0	6	0	1.00	2	.239	.270	.366
	Tri-City	IND	—	16	41	6	4	0	0	10	5	2	2	0	7	2	2	1	0	0	.00	1	.146	.217	.244
	Daytona	A+	ChN	14	31	6	2	1	0	10	5	2	3	0	5	0	2	1	1	0	1.00	0	.194	.257	.323
7 Min. YEARS				501	1598	358	70	6	15	485	193	151	94	0	322	17	13	13	67	17	.80	48	.224	.272	.304

Kerry Valrie

Bats: Right **Throws:** Right **Pos:** OF **Ht:** 5'10" **Wt:** 195 **Born:** 10/31/68 **Age:** 28

				BATTING															BASERUNNING				PERCENTAGES		
Year	Team	Lg	Org	G	AB	H	2B	3B	HR	TB	R	RBI	TBB	IBB	SO	HBP	SH	SF	SB	CS	SB%	GDP	Avg	OBP	SLG
1990	Utica	A-	ChA	42	149	28	4	1	0	34	14	10	8	1	46	1	1	0	12	6	.67	4	.188	.234	.228
1991	South Bend	A	ChA	87	331	71	11	2	6	104	47	29	23	1	78	3	3	0	32	6	.84	3	.215	.272	.314
1992	South Bend	A	ChA	79	314	81	12	2	5	112	34	37	16	0	53	1	0	4	22	15	.59	6	.258	.293	.357
	Sarasota	A+	ChA	51	174	41	9	0	1	53	13	23	14	0	42	1	0	2	13	1	.93	2	.236	.293	.305
1993	Sarasota	A+	ChA	115	386	82	14	2	12	136	47	52	17	1	81	4	2	7	19	7	.73	3	.212	.249	.352
1994	Birmingham	AA	ChA	119	423	121	27	3	3	163	59	58	34	4	75	4	2	4	29	10	.74	3	.286	.342	.385
1995	Nashville	AAA	ChA	138	544	136	30	3	7	193	75	55	40	0	107	3	2	4	22	15	.59	15	.250	.303	.355
1996	Nashville	AAA	ChA	138	498	136	32	5	13	217	59	66	28	0	94	3	1	6	10	9	.53	12	.273	.312	.436
7 Min. YEARS				769	2819	696	139	18	47	1012	348	330	180	7	576	20	11	27	159	69	.70	48	.247	.294	.359

Doug Vanderweele

Pitches: Right **Bats:** Right **Pos:** P **Ht:** 6'3" **Wt:** 200 **Born:** 3/18/70 **Age:** 27

				HOW MUCH HE PITCHED						WHAT HE GAVE UP												THE RESULTS					
Year	Team	Lg	Org	G	GS	CG	GF	IP	BFP	H	R	ER	HR	SH	SF	HB	TBB	IBB	SO	WP	Bk	W	L	Pct.	ShO	Sv	ERA
1991	Everett	A-	SF	15	15	0	0	87	371	73	42	19	1	1	3	8	35	1	65	12	7	6	4	.600	0	0	1.97
1992	Clinton	A	SF	9	9	0	0	51	228	61	33	28	5	2	2	2	24	1	39	7	3	3	3	.500	0	0	4.94
	San Jose	A+	SF	16	15	1	0	87.1	387	77	49	36	7	3	2	8	50	1	51	4	2	6	4	.600	0	0	3.71
	Phoenix	AAA	SF	1	0	0	0	1.2	8	3	2	2	0	0	0	0	0	0	0	1	0	0	0	.000	0	0	10.80
1993	Shreveport	AA	SF	1	0	0	0	2	7	0	0	0	0	0	0	0	0	0	3	0	0	0	0	.000	0	0	0.00
	San Jose	A+	SF	25	24	3	1	171	728	188	78	74	17	12	5	3	55	3	106	8	2	10	6	.625	0	0	3.89
1994	San Jose	A+	SF	8	8	0	0	51.2	215	46	21	16	3	4	1	5	10	0	33	0	0	3	3	.500	0	0	2.79
	Shreveport	AA	SF	21	21	1	0	125.1	533	146	62	53	7	7	3	3	32	2	55	4	0	6	9	.400	0	0	3.81
1995	Phoenix	AAA	SF	11	4	1	1	38.1	178	57	29	26	9	2	3	1	11	3	20	1	1	2	4	.333	0	0	6.10
	Shreveport	AA	SF	24	13	1	1	102.2	431	118	47	44	12	3	3	3	24	3	42	4	1	7	6	.538	0	0	3.86
1996	Phoenix	AAA	SF	41	3	0	6	89	397	101	55	53	13	4	5	2	35	4	42	4	0	4	2	.667	0	0	5.36
6 Min. YEARS				172	112	7	9	807	3483	870	418	351	74	38	27	35	276	18	456	45	16	47	41	.534	0	0	3.91

Jason Varitek

Bats: Both **Throws:** Right **Pos:** C **Ht:** 6'2" **Wt:** 210 **Born:** 4/11/72 **Age:** 25

				BATTING															BASERUNNING				PERCENTAGES		
Year	Team	Lg	Org	G	AB	H	2B	3B	HR	TB	R	RBI	TBB	IBB	SO	HBP	SH	SF	SB	CS	SB%	GDP	Avg	OBP	SLG
1995	Port City	AA	Sea	104	352	79	14	2	10	127	42	44	61	4	126	2	3	3	0	1	.00	8	.224	.340	.361
1996	Port City	AA	Sea	134	503	132	34	1	12	204	63	67	66	7	93	4	0	4	7	6	.54	14	.262	.350	.406
2 Min. YEARS				238	855	211	48	3	22	331	105	111	127	11	219	6	3	7	7	7	.50	22	.247	.346	.387

Jay Vaught

Pitches: Right **Bats:** Left **Pos:** P **Ht:** 6'1" **Wt:** 185 **Born:** 12/21/71 **Age:** 25

				HOW MUCH HE PITCHED						WHAT HE GAVE UP												THE RESULTS					
Year	Team	Lg	Org	G	GS	CG	GF	IP	BFP	H	R	ER	HR	SH	SF	HB	TBB	IBB	SO	WP	Bk	W	L	Pct.	ShO	Sv	ERA
1994	Watertown	A-	Cle	14	13	2	0	82.1	340	73	38	30	5	3	5	3	16	1	50	3	6	7	4	.636	0	0	3.28
1995	Kinston	A+	Cle	27	26	4	0	171	717	184	80	64	19	8	5	15	28	3	82	6	1	8	12	.400	1	0	3.37
1996	Canton-Akrn	AA	Cle	51	0	0	26	94.1	415	101	58	50	10	5	2	4	35	9	78	6	1	5	4	.556	0	3	4.77
3 Min. YEARS				92	39	6	26	347.2	1472	358	176	144	34	16	12	22	79	13	210	15	8	20	20	.500	1	3	3.73

Archie Vazquez

Pitches: Right **Bats:** Right **Pos:** P **Ht:** 6'4" **Wt:** 233 **Born:** 4/4/72 **Age:** 25

		HOW MUCH HE PITCHED						WHAT HE GAVE UP												THE RESULTS					
Year Team	Lg Org	G	GS	CG	GF	IP	BFP	H	R	ER	HR	SH	SF	HB	TBB	IBB	SO	WP	Bk	W	L	Pct.	ShO	Sv	ERA
1991 Spokane	A- SD	1	0	0	0	1.1	9	2	2	2	0	0	0	0	3	0	0	1	0	0	0	.000	0	0	13.50
Padres	R SD	17	1	0	6	40	182	39	20	11	2	1	1	2	25	1	31	3	0	1	1	.500	0	1	2.48
1992 Spokane	A- SD	15	1	0	5	36.2	179	38	39	28	4	1	2	5	30	0	41	9	0	0	2	.000	0	0	6.87
1994 Hickory	A ChA	50	0	0	48	67	264	37	14	9	5	3	1	1	22	0	78	6	0	7	3	.700	0	28	1.21
1995 Pr. William	A+ ChA	47	0	0	45	57.2	261	53	26	23	5	9	1	1	30	4	70	8	0	3	4	.429	0	20	3.59
1996 Birmingham	AA ChA	31	1	0	9	65.1	313	68	53	48	11	4	9	6	48	3	51	4	0	0	6	.000	0	1	6.61
5 Min. YEARS		161	3	0	113	268	1208	237	154	121	27	18	14	15	158	8	271	31	0	11	16	.407	0	50	4.06

Ramon Vazquez

Bats: Left **Throws:** Right **Pos:** SS **Ht:** 5'11" **Wt:** 170 **Born:** 8/21/76 **Age:** 20

		BATTING															BASERUNNING				PERCENTAGES		
Year Team	Lg Org	G	AB	H	2B	3B	HR	TB	R	RBI	TBB	IBB	SO	HBP	SH	SF	SB	CS	SB%	GDP	Avg	OBP	SLG
1995 Mariners	R Sea	39	141	29	3	1	0	34	20	11	19	0	27	2	0	0	4	3	.57	2	.206	.309	.241
1996 Everett	A- Sea	33	126	35	5	2	1	47	25	18	26	0	26	1	2	5	7	2	.78	3	.278	.392	.373
Tacoma	AAA Sea	18	49	11	2	1	0	15	7	4	4	0	12	1	0	0	0	0	.00	2	.224	.296	.306
Wisconsin	A Sea	3	10	3	1	0	0	4	1	1	2	0	2	0	0	0	0	0	.00	1	.300	.417	.400
2 Min. YEARS		93	326	78	11	4	1	100	53	34	51	0	67	4	2	5	11	5	.69	8	.239	.345	.307

Jorge Velandia

Bats: Right **Throws:** Right **Pos:** SS **Ht:** 5'9" **Wt:** 160 **Born:** 1/12/75 **Age:** 22

		BATTING															BASERUNNING				PERCENTAGES		
Year Team	Lg Org	G	AB	H	2B	3B	HR	TB	R	RBI	TBB	IBB	SO	HBP	SH	SF	SB	CS	SB%	GDP	Avg	OBP	SLG
1992 Bristol	R+ Det	45	119	24	6	1	0	32	20	9	15	0	16	0	3	0	3	2	.60	1	.202	.291	.269
1993 Fayettevlle	A Det	37	106	17	4	0	0	21	15	11	13	0	21	3	0	2	5	0	1.00	3	.160	.266	.198
Niagara Fal	A- Det	72	212	41	11	0	1	55	30	22	19	0	48	0	3	2	22	4	.85	2	.193	.258	.259
1994 Lakeland	A+ Det	22	60	14	4	0	0	18	8	3	6	0	14	0	3	1	0	2	.00	0	.233	.299	.300
Springfield	A SD	98	290	71	14	0	4	97	42	36	21	0	46	4	6	3	5	6	.45	8	.245	.302	.334
1995 Memphis	AA SD	63	186	38	10	2	4	64	23	17	14	2	37	1	1	1	0	2	.00	4	.204	.262	.344
Las Vegas	AAA SD	66	206	54	12	3	0	72	25	25	13	1	37	2	7	2	0	0	.00	5	.262	.309	.350
1996 Memphis	AA SD	122	392	94	19	0	9	140	42	48	31	3	65	3	5	8	3	7	.30	10	.240	.295	.357
5 Min. YEARS		525	1571	353	80	6	18	499	205	171	132	6	284	13	28	19	38	23	.62	33	.225	.287	.318

Andy Velazquez

Bats: Right **Throws:** Right **Pos:** OF **Ht:** 6'0" **Wt:** 170 **Born:** 12/15/75 **Age:** 21

		BATTING															BASERUNNING				PERCENTAGES		
Year Team	Lg Org	G	AB	H	2B	3B	HR	TB	R	RBI	TBB	IBB	SO	HBP	SH	SF	SB	CS	SB%	GDP	Avg	OBP	SLG
1993 Rockies	R Col	39	147	36	4	2	2	50	20	20	16	0	35	0	2	2	7	5	.58	2	.245	.315	.340
1994 Asheville	A Col	119	447	106	22	3	11	167	50	39	23	0	120	3	3	2	9	9	.50	14	.237	.278	.374
1995 Salem	A+ Col	131	497	149	25	6	13	225	74	69	40	4	102	4	3	7	7	10	.41	17	.300	.352	.453
1996 New Haven	AA Col	132	486	141	29	4	19	235	72	62	53	5	114	4	0	0	6	2	.75	7	.290	.365	.484
4 Min. YEARS		421	1577	432	80	15	45	677	216	190	132	9	371	11	8	11	29	26	.53	40	.274	.332	.429

Jose Velez

Bats: Both **Throws:** Left **Pos:** OF **Ht:** 6'1" **Wt:** 160 **Born:** 3/6/73 **Age:** 24

		BATTING															BASERUNNING				PERCENTAGES		
Year Team	Lg Org	G	AB	H	2B	3B	HR	TB	R	RBI	TBB	IBB	SO	HBP	SH	SF	SB	CS	SB%	GDP	Avg	OBP	SLG
1990 Cardinals	R StL	46	183	58	7	6	0	77	26	29	8	0	12	2	1	2	5	3	.63	1	.317	.349	.421
1991 Springfield	A StL	116	410	99	10	3	0	115	46	35	15	2	50	1	3	3	10	5	.67	8	.241	.268	.280
1992 Savannah	A StL	93	316	86	12	1	0	100	32	25	18	0	56	2	4	2	8	5	.62	2	.272	.314	.316
1993 St. Pete	A+ StL	81	178	42	3	2	0	49	12	15	6	1	32	0	3	0	0	1	.00	2	.236	.261	.275
1994 St. Pete	A+ StL	100	279	73	8	0	2	87	30	22	15	2	18	3	4	3	6	3	.67	8	.262	.303	.312
1995 Arkansas	AA StL	107	287	85	13	1	7	121	37	41	13	1	36	2	2	2	5	4	.56	8	.296	.329	.422
1996 Arkansas	AA StL	86	264	72	11	2	2	93	36	32	14	0	29	1	3	2	8	4	.67	10	.273	.310	.352
7 Min. YEARS		629	1917	515	64	15	11	642	219	199	89	6	233	11	20	14	42	25	.63	39	.269	.303	.335

Wilfredo Ventura

Bats: Right **Throws:** Right **Pos:** C-DH **Ht:** 5'10" **Wt:** 190 **Born:** 10/11/76 **Age:** 20

		BATTING															BASERUNNING				PERCENTAGES		
Year Team	Lg Org	G	AB	H	2B	3B	HR	TB	R	RBI	TBB	IBB	SO	HBP	SH	SF	SB	CS	SB%	GDP	Avg	OBP	SLG
1995 Athletics	R Oak	34	104	29	3	1	3	43	19	20	20	0	32	3	1	1	7	3	.70	0	.279	.406	.413
1996 Edmonton	AAA Oak	2	4	1	0	0	0	1	1	0	0	0	1	0	0	0	0	0	.00	0	.250	.250	.250
Athletics	R Oak	8	25	4	1	0	0	5	5	2	6	0	8	0	0	1	1	0	1.00	0	.160	.313	.200
Modesto	A+ Oak	32	100	26	3	1	4	43	15	23	8	0	37	1	1	2	1	0	1.00	2	.260	.315	.430
2 Min. YEARS		76	233	60	7	2	7	92	40	45	34	0	78	4	2	4	9	3	.75	2	.258	.356	.395

Jake Viano

Pitches: Right **Bats:** Right **Pos:** P **Ht:** 5'10" **Wt:** 170 **Born:** 9/4/73 **Age:** 23

			HOW MUCH HE PITCHED						WHAT HE GAVE UP												THE RESULTS					
Year Team	Lg	Org	G	GS	CG	GF	IP	BFP	H	R	ER	HR	SH	SF	HB	TBB	IBB	SO	WP	Bk	W	L	Pct.	ShO	Sv	ERA
1993 Rockies	R	Col	22	1	0	8	33	136	24	15	12	1	0	1	3	6	0	32	6	0	2	2	.500	0	1	3.27
1994 Asheville	A	Col	41	0	0	35	53.1	219	36	11	8	3	4	0	2	24	4	58	9	0	4	1	.800	0	23	1.35
New Haven	AA	Col	8	0	0	5	11.1	51	7	7	3	0	0	1	0	8	0	14	1	0	0	3	.000	0	0	2.38
1995 New Haven	AA	Col	57	0	0	49	72	304	51	31	27	5	7	3	2	38	1	85	2	0	3	6	.333	0	19	3.38
1996 Colo. Sprng	AAA	Col	7	3	0	1	20.2	104	33	25	25	7	1	0	1	13	0	12	0	0	0	2	.000	0	0	10.89
New Haven	AA	Col	23	5	0	11	44.2	196	39	28	24	6	1	0	2	24	2	32	2	0	4	3	.571	0	0	4.84
4 Min. YEARS			158	9	0	109	235	1010	190	117	99	22	13	5	10	113	7	233	20	0	13	17	.433	0	43	3.79

Jose Vidro

Bats: Both **Throws:** Right **Pos:** 3B **Ht:** 5'11" **Wt:** 175 **Born:** 8/27/74 **Age:** 22

			BATTING														BASERUNNING				PERCENTAGES		
Year Team	Lg	Org	G	AB	H	2B	3B	HR	TB	R	RBI	TBB	IBB	SO	HBP	SH	SF	SB	CS	SB%	GDP	Avg	OBP	SLG
1992 Expos	R	Mon	54	200	66	6	2	4	88	29	31	16	1	31	0	1	2	10	1	.91	5	.330	.376	.440
1993 Burlington	A	Mon	76	287	69	19	0	2	94	39	34	28	3	54	5	4	2	3	2	.60	7	.240	.317	.328
1994 W. Palm Bch	A+	Mon	125	465	124	30	2	4	170	57	49	51	4	56	5	3	3	8	2	.80	5	.267	.344	.366
1995 Harrisburg	AA	Mon	64	246	64	16	2	4	96	33	38	20	2	37	1	4	3	3	7	.30	5	.260	.315	.390
W. Palm Bch	A+	Mon	44	163	53	15	2	3	81	20	24	8	0	21	2	2	2	0	1	.00	5	.325	.360	.497
1996 Harrisburg	AA	Mon	126	452	117	25	3	18	202	57	82	29	3	71	2	9	10	3	1	.75	6	.259	.300	.447
5 Min. YEARS			489	1813	493	111	11	35	731	235	258	152	13	270	15	23	22	27	14	.66	33	.272	.330	.403

Joey Vierra

Pitches: Left **Bats:** Left **Pos:** P **Ht:** 5'7" **Wt:** 170 **Born:** 1/31/66 **Age:** 31

			HOW MUCH HE PITCHED						WHAT HE GAVE UP												THE RESULTS					
Year Team	Lg	Org	G	GS	CG	GF	IP	BFP	H	R	ER	HR	SH	SF	HB	TBB	IBB	SO	WP	Bk	W	L	Pct.	ShO	Sv	ERA
1987 Reds	R	Cin	14	0	0	11	21	78	11	4	2	0	1	1	0	5	0	29	0	0	1	2	.333	0	8	0.86
Tampa	A+	Cin	9	0	0	6	8	40	14	11	9	3	1	0	1	3	0	7	0	0	1	1	.500	0	1	10.13
1988 Greensboro	A	Cin	34	0	0	24	41.1	162	30	13	11	0	3	0	1	8	2	42	6	3	2	1	.667	0	7	2.40
1989 Cedar Rapds	A	Cin	47	0	0	28	74.1	293	43	22	14	4	1	1	4	20	3	81	3	1	5	3	.625	0	7	1.70
1990 Nashville	AAA	Cin	49	0	0	17	57.2	246	55	25	21	6	7	4	0	25	2	37	1	0	3	3	.500	0	1	3.28
1991 Nashville	AAA	Cin	62	2	0	15	95.2	412	81	60	46	8	4	1	6	43	2	84	5	2	5	4	.556	0	2	4.33
1992 Chattanooga	AA	Cin	1	1	0	0	6	23	5	0	0	0	1	0	0	0	0	3	0	0	1	0	1.000	0	0	0.00
Nashville	AAA	Cin	52	3	0	19	81.2	336	65	29	27	6	2	2	2	28	2	62	6	1	4	1	.800	0	0	2.98
1993 San Antonio	AA	LA	9	0	0	4	11.2	53	14	7	7	1	3	0	1	4	1	6	1	0	1	0	1.000	0	1	5.40
Albuquerque	AAA	LA	29	0	0	15	33	155	38	22	18	3	4	0	2	18	6	24	4	1	0	4	.000	0	1	4.91
1994 Birmingham	AA	ChA	27	6	1	7	66.2	271	60	23	22	1	5	2	3	19	1	63	4	2	4	2	.667	1	1	2.97
Nashville	AAA	ChA	19	0	0	10	21.1	96	25	11	9	2	0	2	1	11	1	18	2	0	0	0	.000	0	3	3.80
1995 Nashville	AAA	ChA	56	1	0	22	58.1	237	47	28	27	6	1	5	1	19	4	57	4	0	2	2	.500	0	4	4.17
1996 Okla. City	AAA	Tex	4	0	0	2	4.2	23	7	7	5	2	0	1	0	2	1	4	0	0	0	1	.000	0	0	9.64
10 Min. YEARS			412	13	1	180	581.1	2425	495	262	218	42	33	19	22	205	25	517	36	10	29	24	.547	1	36	3.38

Mike Villano

Pitches: Right **Bats:** Right **Pos:** P **Ht:** 6'0" **Wt:** 200 **Born:** 8/10/71 **Age:** 25

			HOW MUCH HE PITCHED						WHAT HE GAVE UP												THE RESULTS					
Year Team	Lg	Org	G	GS	CG	GF	IP	BFP	H	R	ER	HR	SH	SF	HB	TBB	IBB	SO	WP	Bk	W	L	Pct.	ShO	Sv	ERA
1995 Burlington	A	SF	16	0	0	7	25.1	120	20	12	8	1	2	1	4	21	0	29	5	0	3	1	.750	0	1	2.84
San Jose	A+	SF	37	0	0	23	58	257	47	19	14	3	2	2	7	32	0	71	8	0	3	2	.600	0	2	2.17
1996 San Jose	A+	SF	39	2	0	21	88	341	48	12	7	2	1	1	0	33	4	133	7	1	7	1	.875	0	8	0.72
Shreveport	AA	SF	2	2	0	0	12	47	6	4	4	0	0	0	0	8	0	7	0	0	2	0	1.000	0	0	3.00
2 Min. YEARS			94	4	0	51	183.1	765	121	47	33	6	5	4	11	94	4	240	20	1	15	4	.789	0	11	1.62

Julio Vinas

Bats: Right **Throws:** Right **Pos:** C **Ht:** 6'0" **Wt:** 200 **Born:** 2/14/73 **Age:** 24

			BATTING														BASERUNNING				PERCENTAGES		
Year Team	Lg	Org	G	AB	H	2B	3B	HR	TB	R	RBI	TBB	IBB	SO	HBP	SH	SF	SB	CS	SB%	GDP	Avg	OBP	SLG
1991 White Sox	R	ChA	50	187	42	9	0	3	60	21	29	19	0	40	2	0	2	2	3	.40	5	.225	.300	.321
1992 South Bend	A	ChA	33	94	16	3	0	0	19	7	10	9	0	17	1	0	2	1	3	.25	1	.170	.245	.202
Utica	A-	ChA	47	151	37	6	4	0	51	22	24	11	0	29	2	1	5	1	2	.33	2	.245	.296	.338
1993 South Bend	A	ChA	55	188	60	15	1	9	104	24	37	12	1	29	1	2	2	1	1	.50	2	.319	.360	.553
Sarasota	A+	ChA	18	65	16	2	1	1	23	5	7	5	0	13	0	0	0	0	0	.00	2	.246	.300	.354
1994 South Bend	A	ChA	121	466	118	31	1	9	178	68	75	43	4	75	4	6	6	0	2	.00	9	.253	.318	.382
1995 Birmingham	AA	ChA	102	372	100	16	2	6	138	47	61	37	1	80	5	0	7	3	3	.50	6	.269	.337	.371
1996 Nashville	AAA	ChA	104	338	80	18	2	11	135	48	52	36	2	63	2	0	4	1	4	.20	8	.237	.311	.399
6 Min. YEARS			530	1861	469	100	11	39	708	242	295	172	8	346	17	9	28	9	18	.33	35	.252	.317	.380

Mark Voisard

Pitches: Right **Bats:** Right **Pos:** P **Ht:** 6'5" **Wt:** 210 **Born:** 11/4/69 **Age:** 27

			HOW MUCH HE PITCHED						WHAT HE GAVE UP												THE RESULTS					
Year Team	Lg	Org	G	GS	CG	GF	IP	BFP	H	R	ER	HR	SH	SF	HB	TBB	IBB	SO	WP	Bk	W	L	Pct.	ShO	Sv	ERA
1992 Bend	A-	Col	26	1	0	5	53	233	51	28	26	5	2	2	3	29	2	65	4	0	5	2	.714	0	2	4.42
1993 Central Val	A+	Col	21	14	0	1	82.1	365	72	58	56	6	0	2	1	53	0	61	6	0	3	6	.333	0	0	6.12

		HOW MUCH HE PITCHED						WHAT HE GAVE UP												THE RESULTS					
Year Team	Lg Org	G	GS	CG	GF	IP	BFP	H	R	ER	HR	SH	SF	HB	TBB	IBB	SO	WP	Bk	W	L	Pct.	ShO	Sv	ERA
1994 Central Val	A+ Col	18	4	0	4	46.2	197	29	18	9	2	3	0	3	22	2	38	3	2	3	2	.600	0	2	1.74
New Haven	AA Col	30	1	0	27	43.1	174	34	9	8	1	2	2	0	17	5	36	3	1	3	2	.600	0	15	1.66
1995 Salem	A+ Col	6	0	0	2	7.1	33	8	6	6	4	0	1	1	4	0	5	0	0	0	0	.000	0	0	7.36
New Haven	AA Col	33	0	0	12	38	165	39	18	17	5	0	2	3	18	0	27	4	0	2	0	1.000	0	2	4.03
1996 New Haven	AA Col	8	0	0	3	8.2	43	10	9	9	1	1	0	1	5	1	7	0	1	0	2	.000	0	0	9.35
Minot	IND —	11	5	0	4	40.1	172	38	21	10	1	1	1	4	10	1	28	2	0	4	3	.571	0	1	2.23
5 Min. YEARS		153	25	0	58	319.2	1382	281	167	141	25	9	10	16	158	11	267	22	4	20	17	.541	0	22	3.97

Scott Vollmer

Bats: Right **Throws:** Right **Pos:** C **Ht:** 6'1" **Wt:** 175 **Born:** 2/9/71 **Age:** 26

		BATTING															BASERUNNING				PERCENTAGES		
Year Team	Lg Org	G	AB	H	2B	3B	HR	TB	R	RBI	TBB	IBB	SO	HBP	SH	SF	SB	CS	SB%	GDP	Avg	OBP	SLG
1993 White Sox	R ChA	43	132	36	9	0	0	45	19	11	17	0	11	2	1	2	3	4	.43	4	.273	.359	.341
1994 Hickory	A ChA	110	420	115	24	4	7	168	52	81	39	2	63	4	4	6	0	1	.00	17	.274	.337	.400
1995 Birmingham	AA ChA	81	258	61	5	0	6	84	35	39	42	1	39	1	4	4	0	1	.00	5	.236	.341	.326
1996 Birmingham	AA ChA	98	361	94	21	0	4	127	41	31	32	0	60	4	1	1	0	0	.00	8	.260	.327	.352
4 Min. YEARS		332	1171	306	59	4	17	424	147	162	130	3	173	11	10	13	3	6	.33	34	.261	.337	.362

Bret Wagner

Pitches: Left **Bats:** Left **Pos:** P **Ht:** 6'0" **Wt:** 190 **Born:** 4/17/73 **Age:** 24

		HOW MUCH HE PITCHED						WHAT HE GAVE UP												THE RESULTS					
Year Team	Lg Org	G	GS	CG	GF	IP	BFP	H	R	ER	HR	SH	SF	HB	TBB	IBB	SO	WP	Bk	W	L	Pct.	ShO	Sv	ERA
1994 New Jersey	A- StL	3	3	0	0	12.1	53	10	9	7	0	0	0	0	4	0	10	3	0	0	1	.000	0	0	5.11
Savannah	A StL	7	7	0	0	44	161	27	8	6	2	0	1	0	6	0	43	3	1	4	1	.800	0	0	1.23
1995 Arkansas	AA StL	6	6	0	0	36.2	161	34	14	13	1	1	1	0	18	0	31	3	0	1	2	.333	0	0	3.19
St. Pete	A+ StL	23	23	1	0	130	534	111	50	35	4	4	3	2	46	0	90	7	0	6	6	.500	0	0	2.42
1996 Huntsville	AA Oak	27	27	0	0	134	597	125	77	63	6	5	5	7	77	3	98	19	2	8	8	.500	0	0	4.23
3 Min. YEARS		66	66	1	0	357	1506	307	158	124	13	10	10	9	151	3	272	35	3	19	18	.514	0	0	3.13

Don Wakamatsu

Bats: Right **Throws:** Right **Pos:** C **Ht:** 6' 2" **Wt:** 210 **Born:** 2/22/63 **Age:** 34

		BATTING															BASERUNNING				PERCENTAGES		
Year Team	Lg Org	G	AB	H	2B	3B	HR	TB	R	RBI	TBB	IBB	SO	HBP	SH	SF	SB	CS	SB%	GDP	Avg	OBP	SLG
1985 Billings	R+ Cin	58	196	49	7	0	0	56	20	24	25	2	36	0	5	2	1	0	1.00	7	.250	.332	.286
1986 Tampa	A+ Cin	112	361	100	18	2	1	125	41	66	53	2	66	5	0	8	6	1	.86	11	.277	.370	.346
1987 Cedar Rapds	A Cin	103	365	79	13	1	7	115	33	41	30	1	71	3	2	3	3	3	.50	9	.216	.279	.315
1988 Chattanooga	AA Cin	79	235	56	9	1	1	70	22	26	37	0	41	0	1	2	0	1	.00	5	.238	.339	.298
1989 Birmingham	AA ChA	92	287	73	15	0	2	94	45	45	32	0	54	7	5	5	7	6	.54	4	.254	.338	.328
1990 Vancouver	AAA ChA	62	187	49	10	0	0	59	20	13	13	1	35	7	1	1	2	2	.50	2	.262	.332	.316
1991 Vancouver	AAA ChA	55	172	34	8	0	4	54	20	19	12	0	39	1	4	2	0	0	.00	3	.198	.251	.314
1992 Albuquerque	AAA LA	60	167	54	10	0	2	70	22	15	15	0	23	4	1	0	0	1	.00	5	.323	.392	.419
1993 Albuquerque	AAA LA	54	181	61	11	1	7	95	30	31	15	2	31	4	0	4	0	1	.00	3	.337	.392	.525
1994 Okla. City	AAA Tex	1	2	0	0	0	0	0	0	0	0	0	1	0	0	0	0	0	.00	0	.000	.000	.000
1995 Tacoma	AAA Sea	9	32	5	1	0	0	6	3	6	2	0	8	1	0	0	0	0	.00	4	.156	.229	.188
Canton-Akrn	AA Cle	51	143	38	10	0	4	60	16	23	17	2	21	6	3	2	0	0	.00	7	.266	.363	.420
1996 New Orleans	AAA Mil	1	0	0	0	0	0	0	0	0	0	0	0	0	0	0	0	0	.00	0	.000	.000	.000
Tacoma	AAA Sea	1	3	0	0	0	0	0	0	0	0	0	0	0	0	0	0	0	.00	0	.000	.000	.000
Port City	AA Sea	24	70	22	4	0	2	32	10	9	4	0	11	4	0	0	1	0	1.00	2	.314	.385	.457
1991 Chicago	AL	18	31	7	0	0	0	7	2	0	1	0	6	0	0	0	0	0	.00	0	.226	.250	.226
12 Min. YEARS		762	2401	620	116	5	30	836	282	318	255	10	437	42	22	29	20	15	.57	62	.258	.336	.348

Jamie Walker

Pitches: Left **Bats:** Left **Pos:** P **Ht:** 6'2" **Wt:** 190 **Born:** 7/1/71 **Age:** 26

		HOW MUCH HE PITCHED						WHAT HE GAVE UP												THE RESULTS					
Year Team	Lg Org	G	GS	CG	GF	IP	BFP	H	R	ER	HR	SH	SF	HB	TBB	IBB	SO	WP	Bk	W	L	Pct.	ShO	Sv	ERA
1992 Auburn	A- Hou	15	14	0	0	83.1	341	75	35	29	4	4	1	6	21	0	67	4	1	4	6	.400	0	0	3.13
1993 Quad City	A Hou	25	24	1	1	131.2	585	140	92	75	12	10	5	6	48	1	121	12	0	3	11	.214	1	0	5.13
1994 Quad City	A Hou	32	18	0	4	125	569	133	80	58	10	14	3	16	42	2	104	5	1	8	10	.444	0	1	4.18
1995 Jackson	AA Hou	50	0	0	19	58	250	59	29	29	6	3	2	2	24	5	38	4	1	4	2	.667	0	2	4.50
1996 Jackson	AA Hou	45	7	0	13	101	424	94	34	28	7	3	1	8	35	2	79	2	0	5	1	.833	0	2	2.50
5 Min. YEARS		167	63	1	37	499	2169	501	270	219	39	34	12	38	170	10	409	27	3	24	30	.444	1	5	3.95

Steve Walker

Bats: Both **Throws:** Right **Pos:** OF **Ht:** 6'1" **Wt:** 180 **Born:** 2/11/72 **Age:** 25

		BATTING															BASERUNNING				PERCENTAGES		
Year Team	Lg Org	G	AB	H	2B	3B	HR	TB	R	RBI	TBB	IBB	SO	HBP	SH	SF	SB	CS	SB%	GDP	Avg	OBP	SLG
1991 Huntington	R+ ChN	58	187	37	2	4	1	50	19	15	6	0	64	4	3	3	11	1	.92	1	.198	.235	.267
1992 Huntington	R+ ChN	52	161	35	3	0	5	53	35	27	16	0	47	4	4	2	16	6	.73	1	.217	.301	.329
1993 Peoria	A ChN	128	466	116	27	2	7	168	60	58	21	4	123	7	8	5	15	6	.71	9	.249	.289	.361
1994 Daytona	A+ ChN	20	61	12	3	0	1	18	5	9	3	0	25	1	0	0	4	1	.80	1	.197	.246	.295
Peoria	A ChN	90	266	57	13	5	2	86	38	22	20	3	83	3	6	0	15	5	.75	5	.214	.277	.323
1995 Rockford	A ChN	103	415	120	24	7	3	167	78	44	37	3	104	10	0	0	40	16	.71	1	.289	.361	.402

Year Team	Lg Org	G	AB	H	2B	3B	HR	TB	R	RBI	TBB	IBB	SO	HBP	SH	SF	SB	CS	SB%	GDP	Avg	OBP	SLG
BATTING																	BASERUNNING				PERCENTAGES		
1996 Daytona	A+ ChN	58	225	71	17	2	9	119	39	39	17	3	53	7	1	2	21	4	.84	4	.316	.378	.529
Orlando	AA ChN	54	224	57	7	4	4	84	31	21	18	2	65	1	1	1	6	9	.40	1	.254	.311	.375
6 Min. YEARS		563	2005	505	96	24	32	745	305	235	138	15	564	37	23	13	128	48	.73	23	.252	.310	.372

Wade Walker

Pitches: Right **Bats:** Right **Pos:** P **Ht:** 6'1" **Wt:** 190 **Born:** 9/18/71 **Age:** 25

Year Team	Lg Org	G	GS	CG	GF	IP	BFP	H	R	ER	HR	SH	SF	HB	TBB	IBB	SO	WP	Bk	W	L	Pct.	ShO	Sv	ERA
HOW MUCH HE PITCHED								WHAT HE GAVE UP												THE RESULTS					
1993 Geneva	A- ChN	13	13	1	0	83.2	356	76	38	29	2	4	4	4	36	1	47	15	2	5	2	.714	0	0	3.12
1994 Peoria	A ChN	28	28	4	0	178.1	789	192	108	79	11	6	9	8	72	0	117	17	4	14	12	.538	1	0	3.99
1995 Daytona	A+ ChN	25	24	2	0	135	541	113	50	38	5	3	2	2	36	0	117	8	1	8	6	.571	1	0	2.53
1996 Orlando	AA ChN	29	29	2	0	187.2	833	205	112	92	20	9	4	13	76	2	117	11	1	8	14	.364	0	0	4.41
4 Min. YEARS		95	94	9	0	584.2	2519	586	308	238	38	22	19	27	220	3	398	51	8	35	34	.507	2	0	3.66

Kent Wallace

Pitches: Right **Bats:** Left **Pos:** P **Ht:** 6'3" **Wt:** 192 **Born:** 8/22/70 **Age:** 26

Year Team	Lg Org	G	GS	CG	GF	IP	BFP	H	R	ER	HR	SH	SF	HB	TBB	IBB	SO	WP	Bk	W	L	Pct.	ShO	Sv	ERA
HOW MUCH HE PITCHED								WHAT HE GAVE UP												THE RESULTS					
1992 Oneonta	A- NYA	14	14	1	0	81.1	336	76	32	23	2	1	3	0	11	0	55	3	0	8	4	.667	1	0	2.55
1993 Greensboro	A NYA	13	10	2	2	66	277	63	31	22	2	0	2	2	12	0	49	3	2	4	2	.667	1	2	3.00
1994 Tampa	A+ NYA	39	0	0	17	77.2	310	60	23	18	2	2	3	3	22	4	61	2	0	6	3	.667	0	7	2.09
1995 Columbus	AAA NYA	9	9	0	0	50.2	200	44	19	17	8	0	0	0	11	0	31	3	0	4	1	.800	0	0	3.02
Norwich	AA NYA	27	25	0	1	145.1	595	137	60	54	17	2	2	1	35	0	103	5	1	11	7	.611	0	0	3.34
1996 Yankees	R NYA	1	1	0	0	5	18	3	1	1	0	0	0	0	0	0	5	0	0	1	0	1.000	0	0	1.80
Norwich	AA NYA	1	1	0	0	6	28	10	4	4	2	0	1	0	0	0	1	0	0	0	0	.000	0	0	6.00
Columbus	AAA NYA	13	12	2	0	67.1	284	69	37	35	15	1	1	2	15	0	34	1	0	4	2	.667	0	0	4.68
5 Min. YEARS		117	72	5	20	499.1	2048	462	207	174	48	6	12	8	106	4	339	17	3	38	19	.667	2	9	3.14

Dan Walters

Bats: Right **Throws:** Right **Pos:** C **Ht:** 6' 4" **Wt:** 230 **Born:** 8/15/66 **Age:** 30

Year Team	Lg Org	G	AB	H	2B	3B	HR	TB	R	RBI	TBB	IBB	SO	HBP	SH	SF	SB	CS	SB%	GDP	Avg	OBP	SLG
BATTING																	BASERUNNING				PERCENTAGES		
1985 Asheville	A Hou	15	28	1	0	0	0	1	1	1	1	0	11	0	1	0	0	0	.00	1	.036	.069	.036
Auburn	A- Hou	44	144	30	6	0	0	36	15	10	8	0	23	1	0	3	1	0	1.00	6	.208	.250	.250
1986 Asheville	A Hou	101	366	96	21	1	8	143	42	46	14	0	59	1	1	2	1	1	.50	12	.262	.290	.391
1987 Osceola	A+ Hou	99	338	84	8	0	1	95	23	30	33	2	42	0	5	5	2	4	.33	15	.249	.311	.281
1988 Tucson	AAA Hou	2	7	0	0	0	0	0	0	0	0	0	2	0	0	0	0	0	.00	0	.000	.000	.000
Columbus	AA Hou	98	305	71	10	1	7	104	31	28	26	0	42	3	3	4	1	0	1.00	11	.233	.296	.341
1989 Wichita	AA SD	89	300	82	15	0	6	115	30	45	25	2	31	3	3	2	0	2	.00	5	.273	.333	.383
1990 Wichita	AA SD	58	199	59	12	0	7	92	25	40	21	2	21	1	0	2	0	0	.00	8	.296	.363	.462
Las Vegas	AAA SD	53	184	47	9	0	3	65	19	26	13	0	24	0	0	3	0	0	.00	10	.255	.300	.353
1991 Las Vegas	AAA SD	96	293	93	22	0	4	127	39	44	22	5	35	0	0	0	0	0	.00	12	.317	.365	.433
1992 Las Vegas	AAA SD	35	127	50	9	0	2	65	16	25	10	1	12	2	1	2	0	0	.00	5	.394	.440	.512
1993 Las Vegas	AAA SD	66	223	64	14	0	5	93	26	39	14	0	26	1	0	1	1	2	.33	13	.287	.331	.417
1995 Colo. Sprng	AAA Col	52	155	44	9	2	3	66	15	23	7	1	20	1	1	1	0	0	.00	6	.284	.317	.426
1996 Edmonton	AAA Oak	25	64	16	5	0	1	24	5	8	4	0	7	0	1	0	0	0	.00	5	.250	.294	.375
1992 San Diego	NL	57	179	45	11	1	4	70	14	22	10	0	28	2	1	2	1	0	1.00	3	.251	.295	.391
1993 San Diego	NL	27	94	19	3	0	1	25	6	10	7	2	13	0	0	1	0	0	.00	2	.202	.255	.266
11 Min. YEARS		833	2733	737	140	4	47	1026	287	365	198	13	355	13	16	25	6	9	.40	109	.270	.319	.375
2 Maj. YEARS		84	273	64	14	1	5	95	20	32	17	2	41	2	1	3	1	0	1.00	5	.234	.281	.348

Bryan Ward

Pitches: Left **Bats:** Left **Pos:** P **Ht:** 6'2" **Wt:** 210 **Born:** 1/28/72 **Age:** 25

Year Team	Lg Org	G	GS	CG	GF	IP	BFP	H	R	ER	HR	SH	SF	HB	TBB	IBB	SO	WP	Bk	W	L	Pct.	ShO	Sv	ERA
HOW MUCH HE PITCHED								WHAT HE GAVE UP												THE RESULTS					
1993 Elmira	A- Fla	14	11	0	2	61.1	291	82	41	34	6	2	4	4	26	2	63	5	5	2	5	.286	0	0	4.99
1994 Kane County	A Fla	47	0	0	40	55.2	235	46	27	21	4	3	4	2	21	2	62	2	0	3	4	.429	0	11	3.40
1995 Brevard Cty	A+ Fla	11	11	0	0	72	296	68	27	23	5	4	0	2	17	0	65	1	1	5	1	.833	0	0	2.88
Portland	AA Fla	31	22	1	5	144	617	138	69	59	14	5	1	4	48	3	136	8	4	12	4	.750	1	2	3.69
1996 Portland	AA Fla	28	25	2	0	146.2	633	170	97	80	23	9	6	7	32	3	124	0	2	9	9	.500	0	0	4.91
4 Min. YEARS		131	69	3	47	479.2	2072	504	261	217	52	23	15	19	144	10	450	16	12	31	23	.574	1	13	4.07

Daryle Ward

Bats: Left **Throws:** Left **Pos:** 1B **Ht:** 6'2" **Wt:** 230 **Born:** 6/27/75 **Age:** 22

Year Team	Lg Org	G	AB	H	2B	3B	HR	TB	R	RBI	TBB	IBB	SO	HBP	SH	SF	SB	CS	SB%	GDP	Avg	OBP	SLG
BATTING																	BASERUNNING				PERCENTAGES		
1994 Bristol	R+ Det	48	161	43	6	0	5	64	17	30	19	4	33	0	1	1	5	1	.83	3	.267	.343	.398
1995 Fayettevlle	A Det	137	524	149	32	0	14	223	75	106	46	11	111	5	0	7	1	2	.33	13	.284	.344	.426
1996 Toledo	AAA Det	6	23	4	0	0	0	4	1	1	0	0	3	0	0	0	0	0	.00	2	.174	.174	.174
Lakeland	A+ Det	128	464	135	29	4	10	202	65	68	57	6	77	6	0	4	1	1	.50	9	.291	.373	.435
3 Min. YEARS		319	1172	331	67	4	29	493	158	205	122	21	224	11	1	12	7	4	.64	27	.282	.352	.421

Duane Ward

Pitches: Right **Bats:** Right **Pos:** P **Ht:** 6' 4" **Wt:** 225 **Born:** 5/28/64 **Age:** 33

			HOW MUCH HE PITCHED						WHAT HE GAVE UP												THE RESULTS					
Year Team	Lg	Org	G	GS	CG	GF	IP	BFP	H	R	ER	HR	SH	SF	HB	TBB	IBB	SO	WP	Bk	W	L	Pct.	ShO	Sv	ERA
1984 Greenville	AA	Atl	21	20	4	0	104.2	471	108	71	58	9	4	6	2	57	0	54	8	1	4	9	.308	0	0	4.99
1985 Greenville	AA	Atl	28	24	3	1	150	671	141	83	70	4	3	5	4	105	1	100	9	0	11	10	.524	0	0	4.20
Richmond	AAA	Atl	5	1	0	3	5.1	30	8	9	7	1	0	0	1	8	0	3	0	0	0	1	.000	0	0	11.81
1986 Richmond	AAA	Atl	6	6	0	0	34.2	158	34	13	13	0	3	0	1	23	0	17	0	0	1	1	.500	0	0	3.38
Syracuse	AAA	Tor	14	14	3	0	83	359	91	43	39	9	2	1	2	29	0	50	4	1	6	4	.600	0	0	4.23
1987 Syracuse	AAA	Tor	46	3	0	29	76.1	319	59	35	33	7	2	2	2	42	1	67	7	1	2	2	.500	0	14	3.89
1994 Dunedin	A+	Tor	3	1	0	0	4	16	4	2	2	0	0	0	0	0	0	4	0	0	1	0	1.000	0	0	4.50
1995 Dunedin	A+	Tor	3	2	0	0	4.1	19	4	3	3	1	1	0	2	1	0	4	0	1	0	1	.000	0	0	6.23
Syracuse	AAA	Tor	9	2	0	1	10.1	52	18	13	13	1	2	0	2	3	1	8	0	1	1	2	.333	0	0	11.32
1996 Daytona	A+	ChN	6	0	0	0	5.2	25	5	4	4	2	2	0	0	4	0	3	1	0	0	1	.000	0	0	6.35
Orlando	AA	ChN	2	0	0	1	1.1	10	4	4	4	0	1	0	0	2	0	0	0	1	0	1	.000	0	0	27.00
1986 Atlanta	NL		10	0	0	6	16	73	22	13	13	2	2	0	0	8	0	8	0	1	0	1	.000	0	0	7.31
Toronto	AL		2	1	0	1	2	15	3	4	3	0	0	0	1	4	0	1	1	0	0	1	.000	0	0	13.50
1987 Toronto	AL		12	1	0	4	11.2	57	14	9	9	0	1	1	0	12	2	10	0	0	1	0	1.000	0	0	6.94
1988 Toronto	AL		64	0	0	32	111.2	487	101	46	41	5	4	5	5	60	8	91	10	3	9	3	.750	0	15	3.30
1989 Toronto	AL		66	0	0	39	114.2	494	94	55	48	4	12	11	5	58	11	122	13	0	4	10	.286	0	15	3.77
1990 Toronto	AL		73	0	0	39	127.2	508	101	51	49	9	6	2	1	42	10	112	5	0	2	8	.200	0	11	3.45
1991 Toronto	AL		81	0	0	46	107.1	428	80	36	33	3	3	4	2	33	3	132	6	0	7	6	.538	0	23	2.77
1992 Toronto	AL		79	0	0	35	101.1	414	76	27	22	5	3	4	1	39	3	103	7	0	7	4	.636	0	12	1.95
1993 Toronto	AL		71	0	0	70	71.2	282	49	17	17	4	0	2	1	25	2	97	7	0	2	3	.400	0	45	2.13
1995 Toronto	AL		4	0	0	0	2.2	25	11	10	8	0	0	0	1	5	0	3	2	0	0	1	.000	0	0	27.00
7 Min. YEARS			143	73	10	35	479.2	2130	476	280	246	34	20	14	16	274	3	310	29	6	26	32	.448	0	14	4.62
9 Maj. YEARS			462	2	0	272	666.2	2783	551	268	243	32	31	29	17	286	39	679	51	4	32	37	.464	0	121	3.28

Mike Warner

Bats: Left **Throws:** Left **Pos:** OF **Ht:** 5'10" **Wt:** 170 **Born:** 5/9/71 **Age:** 26

			BATTING														BASERUNNING				PERCENTAGES		
Year Team	Lg	Org	G	AB	H	2B	3B	HR	TB	R	RBI	TBB	IBB	SO	HBP	SH	SF	SB	CS	SB%	GDP	Avg	OBP	SLG
1992 Idaho Falls	R+	Atl	10	33	9	3	0	1	15	4	6	3	0	5	0	0	0	1	0	1.00	0	.273	.333	.455
Macon	A	Atl	50	180	50	7	2	1	64	40	8	34	0	28	0	3	0	21	4	.84	2	.278	.393	.356
1993 Durham	A+	Atl	77	263	84	18	4	5	125	55	32	50	3	45	2	3	3	29	12	.71	4	.319	.428	.475
Greenville	AA	Atl	5	20	7	0	2	0	11	4	3	2	0	4	0	0	0	2	1	.67	0	.350	.409	.550
1994 Durham	A+	Atl	88	321	103	23	8	13	181	80	44	51	1	50	2	1	1	24	10	.71	3	.321	.416	.564
Greenville	AA	Atl	16	55	18	5	0	1	26	13	3	9	0	5	1	0	0	3	0	1.00	0	.327	.431	.473
1995 Richmond	AAA	Atl	28	97	20	4	1	2	32	10	8	10	0	21	1	2	0	0	3	.00	0	.206	.287	.330
Greenville	AA	Atl	53	173	41	12	0	0	53	31	7	47	0	36	1	2	2	12	4	.75	1	.237	.399	.306
1996 Durham	A+	Atl	3	9	1	1	0	0	2	1	2	2	0	2	1	0	0	1	0	1.00	0	.111	.333	.222
Richmond	AAA	Atl	7	29	6	1	0	0	7	4	1	1	0	8	0	0	0	1	2	.33	0	.207	.233	.241
Greenville	AA	Atl	64	205	53	19	2	6	94	39	33	47	0	45	4	3	0	10	7	.59	4	.259	.406	.459
5 Min. YEARS			401	1385	392	93	19	29	610	281	147	256	4	249	12	14	6	104	43	.71	14	.283	.398	.440

Ron Warner

Bats: Right **Throws:** Right **Pos:** 3B **Ht:** 6'3" **Wt:** 185 **Born:** 12/2/68 **Age:** 28

			BATTING														BASERUNNING				PERCENTAGES		
Year Team	Lg	Org	G	AB	H	2B	3B	HR	TB	R	RBI	TBB	IBB	SO	HBP	SH	SF	SB	CS	SB%	GDP	Avg	OBP	SLG
1991 Hamilton	A-	StL	71	219	66	11	3	1	86	31	20	28	0	43	3	4	1	9	2	.82	4	.301	.386	.393
1992 Savannah	A	StL	85	242	53	8	1	0	63	30	12	29	2	63	1	5	2	2	3	.40	5	.219	.303	.260
1993 St. Pete	A+	StL	103	311	90	8	3	4	116	42	37	31	2	39	5	7	4	5	1	.83	9	.289	.359	.373
1994 Arkansas	AA	StL	95	233	56	14	1	4	84	28	25	39	5	57	1	2	0	1	1	.50	4	.240	.352	.361
1995 Arkansas	AA	StL	47	98	24	3	0	0	27	9	8	16	1	15	1	3	2	0	0	.00	3	.245	.350	.276
1996 Arkansas	AA	StL	84	233	70	22	4	6	118	36	39	38	1	25	1	2	2	5	1	.83	4	.300	.398	.506
6 Min. YEARS			485	1336	359	66	12	15	494	176	141	181	11	242	12	23	11	22	8	.73	29	.269	.358	.370

Brian Warren

Pitches: Right **Bats:** Right **Pos:** P **Ht:** 6'1" **Wt:** 165 **Born:** 4/26/67 **Age:** 30

			HOW MUCH HE PITCHED						WHAT HE GAVE UP												THE RESULTS					
Year Team	Lg	Org	G	GS	CG	GF	IP	BFP	H	R	ER	HR	SH	SF	HB	TBB	IBB	SO	WP	Bk	W	L	Pct.	ShO	Sv	ERA
1990 Bristol	R+	Det	1	1	0	0	4	17	4	1	1	0	0	0	0	2	0	0	0	1	0	0	.000	0	0	2.25
Niagara Fal	A-	Det	12	10	1	2	62.1	258	53	26	15	3	0	2	4	15	0	62	2	0	2	6	.250	0	0	2.17
1991 Fayettevlle	A	Det	10	1	0	0	25.2	99	18	6	6	0	0	0	2	5	0	28	3	2	3	1	.750	0	0	2.10
Lakeland	A+	Det	17	16	4	0	103.1	406	86	34	29	3	6	1	1	15	1	75	6	3	8	2	.800	2	0	2.53
1992 London	AA	Det	25	25	3	0	147.1	606	146	66	54	10	1	0	5	32	1	83	7	0	7	9	.438	2	0	3.30
1993 London	AA	Det	22	1	0	13	29.1	125	36	19	19	6	0	1	0	9	0	21	1	0	3	3	.500	0	5	5.83
Toledo	AAA	Det	24	1	0	11	36.2	160	40	17	14	3	0	1	2	11	2	26	3	0	2	2	.500	0	0	3.44
1994 Indianapols	AAA	Cin	55	0	0	14	80.1	329	82	33	28	4	4	4	3	16	4	56	3	0	5	2	.714	0	1	3.14
1995 Indianapols	AAA	Cin	41	0	0	9	56	234	56	18	10	2	1	1	5	9	2	35	2	1	2	1	.667	0	2	1.61
1996 Indianapols	AAA	Cin	50	0	0	17	64.2	277	68	30	28	7	2	4	2	25	3	40	4	0	2	3	.400	0	0	3.90
7 Min. YEARS			257	55	8	66	609.2	2511	589	250	204	38	14	14	24	139	13	426	31	7	34	29	.540	4	8	3.01

Jarrod Washburn

Pitches: Left **Bats:** Left **Pos:** P **Ht:** 6'1" **Wt:** 185 **Born:** 8/13/74 **Age:** 22

		HOW MUCH HE PITCHED						WHAT HE GAVE UP												THE RESULTS					
Year Team	Lg Org	G	GS	CG	GF	IP	BFP	H	R	ER	HR	SH	SF	HB	TBB	IBB	SO	WP	Bk	W	L	Pct.	ShO	Sv	ERA
1995 Cedar Rapds	A Cal	3	3	0	0	18.1	79	17	7	7	1	2	1	3	7	0	20	1	0	0	1	.000	0	0	3.44
Boise	A- Cal	11	11	0	0	64.1	264	52	24	24	2	2	2	5	21	0	74	2	0	3	3	.500	0	0	3.36
1996 Lk Elsinore	A+ Cal	14	14	3	0	92.2	384	79	38	34	5	2	2	2	33	0	93	8	0	6	3	.667	0	0	3.30
Vancouver	AAA Cal	2	2	0	0	8.1	48	12	16	10	1	0	0	0	12	0	5	1	0	0	2	.000	0	0	10.80
Midland	AA Cal	13	13	1	0	88	361	77	44	43	11	1	2	5	25	0	58	1	1	5	6	.455	0	0	4.40
2 Min. YEARS		43	43	4	0	271.2	1136	237	129	118	20	7	7	15	98	0	250	13	1	14	15	.483	0	0	3.91

B.J. Waszgis

Bats: Right **Throws:** Right **Pos:** C **Ht:** 6'2" **Wt:** 210 **Born:** 8/24/70 **Age:** 26

		BATTING															BASERUNNING				PERCENTAGES		
Year Team	Lg Org	G	AB	H	2B	3B	HR	TB	R	RBI	TBB	IBB	SO	HBP	SH	SF	SB	CS	SB%	GDP	Avg	OBP	SLG
1991 Bluefield	R+ Bal	12	35	8	1	0	3	18	8	8	5	0	11	1	0	0	3	0	1.00	1	.229	.341	.514
1992 Kane County	A Bal	111	340	73	18	1	11	126	39	47	54	2	94	4	3	2	3	2	.60	8	.215	.328	.371
1993 Frederick	A+ Bal	31	109	27	4	0	3	40	12	9	9	0	30	2	0	1	1	1	.50	2	.248	.314	.367
Albany	A Bal	86	300	92	25	3	8	147	45	52	27	0	55	6	0	5	4	0	1.00	8	.307	.370	.490
1994 Frederick	A+ Bal	122	426	120	16	3	21	205	76	100	65	2	94	5	3	4	6	1	.86	3	.282	.380	.481
1995 Bowie	AA Bal	130	438	111	22	0	10	163	53	50	70	1	91	9	1	3	2	4	.33	5	.253	.365	.372
1996 Rochester	AAA Bal	96	304	81	16	0	11	130	37	48	41	0	87	4	1	1	2	3	.40	7	.266	.360	.428
6 Min. YEARS		588	1952	512	102	7	67	829	270	314	271	5	462	31	8	16	21	11	.66	34	.262	.359	.425

Pat Watkins

Bats: Right **Throws:** Right **Pos:** OF **Ht:** 6'2" **Wt:** 185 **Born:** 9/2/72 **Age:** 24

		BATTING															BASERUNNING				PERCENTAGES		
Year Team	Lg Org	G	AB	H	2B	3B	HR	TB	R	RBI	TBB	IBB	SO	HBP	SH	SF	SB	CS	SB%	GDP	Avg	OBP	SLG
1993 Billings	R+ Cin	66	235	63	10	3	6	97	46	30	22	0	44	2	1	1	15	4	.79	4	.268	.335	.413
1994 Winston-Sal	A+ Cin	132	524	152	24	5	27	267	107	83	62	3	84	7	1	6	31	13	.70	8	.290	.369	.510
1995 Winston-Sal	A+ Cin	27	107	22	3	1	4	39	14	13	10	0	24	0	1	2	1	0	1.00	5	.206	.269	.364
Chattanooga	AA Cin	105	358	104	26	2	12	170	57	57	33	4	53	3	0	4	5	5	.50	7	.291	.352	.475
1996 Chattanooga	AA Cin	127	492	136	31	2	8	195	63	59	30	0	64	7	2	4	15	11	.58	17	.276	.325	.396
4 Min. YEARS		457	1716	477	94	13	57	768	287	242	157	7	269	19	5	17	67	33	.67	41	.278	.342	.448

Scott Watkins

Pitches: Left **Bats:** Left **Pos:** P **Ht:** 6' 3" **Wt:** 180 **Born:** 5/15/70 **Age:** 27

		HOW MUCH HE PITCHED						WHAT HE GAVE UP												THE RESULTS					
Year Team	Lg Org	G	GS	CG	GF	IP	BFP	H	R	ER	HR	SH	SF	HB	TBB	IBB	SO	WP	Bk	W	L	Pct.	ShO	Sv	ERA
1992 Kenosha	A Min	27	0	0	11	46.1	196	43	21	19	4	2	1	3	14	0	58	1	0	2	5	.286	0	1	3.69
1993 Fort Wayne	A Min	15	0	0	8	30.1	124	26	13	11	0	1	2	1	9	0	31	0	1	2	0	1.000	0	1	3.26
Fort Myers	A+ Min	20	0	0	10	27.2	125	27	14	9	0	2	0	0	12	0	41	2	1	2	2	.500	0	3	2.93
Nashville	AA Min	13	0	0	3	16.2	75	19	15	11	2	0	1	1	7	0	17	2	1	0	1	.000	0	0	5.94
1994 Nashville	AA Min	11	0	0	8	13.2	60	13	9	7	1	1	2	0	4	0	11	1	0	1	0	1.000	0	3	4.61
Salt Lake	AAA Min	46	0	0	26	57.1	269	73	46	43	10	4	5	1	28	5	47	1	1	2	6	.250	0	3	6.75
1995 Salt Lake	AAA Min	45	0	0	33	54.2	217	45	18	17	4	1	3	1	13	1	57	1	0	4	2	.667	0	20	2.80
1996 Salt Lake	AAA Min	47	0	0	29	50.1	244	60	46	43	6	5	3	2	34	5	43	3	1	4	6	.400	0	1	7.69
1995 Minnesota	AL	27	0	0	7	21.2	94	22	14	13	2	1	3	0	11	1	11	0	0	0	0	.000	0	0	5.40
5 Min. YEARS		224	0	0	128	297	1310	306	182	160	27	16	17	9	121	11	305	11	5	17	22	.436	0	32	4.85

Brandon Watts

Pitches: Left **Bats:** Left **Pos:** P **Ht:** 6'3" **Wt:** 190 **Born:** 9/13/72 **Age:** 24

		HOW MUCH HE PITCHED						WHAT HE GAVE UP												THE RESULTS					
Year Team	Lg Org	G	GS	CG	GF	IP	BFP	H	R	ER	HR	SH	SF	HB	TBB	IBB	SO	WP	Bk	W	L	Pct.	ShO	Sv	ERA
1991 Dodgers	R LA	12	5	0	4	33	148	28	20	17	1	2	0	2	25	0	30	5	1	1	3	.250	0	1	4.64
1992 Great Falls	R+ LA	13	0	0	6	17.2	80	12	11	10	0	0	0	1	14	0	15	1	0	1	1	.500	0	1	5.09
Dodgers	R LA	4	4	1	0	24	95	15	9	8	1	0	1	0	8	0	19	3	0	2	1	.667	1	0	3.00
1993 Vero Beach	A+ LA	8	0	0	1	17.2	81	14	11	8	0	0	1	1	16	0	12	2	0	0	1	.000	0	0	4.08
Yakima	A- LA	2	2	0	0	9	41	8	8	8	3	0	0	0	7	0	12	1	0	0	2	.000	0	0	8.00
1995 Vero Beach	A+ LA	13	8	0	1	49	215	46	29	22	5	0	2	1	22	0	42	4	1	5	3	.625	0	0	4.04
1996 San Antonio	AA LA	22	22	2	0	126	561	136	69	63	21	8	4	2	70	0	79	4	2	6	10	.375	1	0	4.50
5 Min. YEARS		74	41	3	12	276.1	1221	259	157	136	31	10	8	7	162	0	209	20	4	15	21	.417	2	2	4.43

Jim Wawruck

Bats: Left **Throws:** Left **Pos:** OF **Ht:** 5'11" **Wt:** 185 **Born:** 4/23/70 **Age:** 27

		BATTING															BASERUNNING				PERCENTAGES		
Year Team	Lg Org	G	AB	H	2B	3B	HR	TB	R	RBI	TBB	IBB	SO	HBP	SH	SF	SB	CS	SB%	GDP	Avg	OBP	SLG
1991 Orioles	R Bal	14	45	17	1	1	0	20	6	6	6	0	4	0	0	0	2	2	.50	0	.378	.451	.444
Frederick	A+ Bal	22	83	23	3	0	0	26	15	7	7	0	14	1	1	0	10	0	1.00	2	.277	.341	.313
1992 Frederick	A+ Bal	102	350	108	18	4	8	158	61	46	47	2	69	2	1	5	11	8	.58	9	.309	.389	.451
1993 Bowie	AA Bal	128	475	141	21	5	4	184	59	44	43	3	66	1	5	2	28	11	.72	7	.297	.355	.387
1994 Rochester	AAA Bal	114	440	132	20	7	9	193	63	53	32	1	77	4	1	2	17	2	.89	6	.300	.351	.439
1995 Bowie	AA Bal	56	212	59	7	1	6	86	29	30	20	2	31	3	1	3	7	3	.70	7	.278	.345	.406
Rochester	AAA Bal	39	149	45	12	3	1	66	21	23	13	0	23	2	1	2	5	4	.56	3	.302	.361	.443

		BATTING															BASERUNNING				PERCENTAGES		
Year Team	Lg Org	G	AB	H	2B	3B	HR	TB	R	RBI	TBB	IBB	SO	HBP	SH	SF	SB	CS	SB%	GDP	Avg	OBP	SLG
1996 Rochester	AAA Bal	59	204	58	14	6	0	84	31	15	14	1	29	1	4	1	4	2	.67	2	.284	.332	.412
6 Min. YEARS		534	1958	583	96	27	28	817	285	224	182	9	313	14	14	15	84	32	.72	36	.298	.359	.417

Eric Weaver

Pitches: Right **Bats:** Right **Pos:** P **Ht:** 6'5" **Wt:** 230 **Born:** 8/4/73 **Age:** 23

		HOW MUCH HE PITCHED						WHAT HE GAVE UP												THE RESULTS					
Year Team	Lg Org	G	GS	CG	GF	IP	BFP	H	R	ER	HR	SH	SF	HB	TBB	IBB	SO	WP	Bk	W	L	Pct.	ShO	Sv	ERA
1992 Vero Beach	A+ LA	19	18	1	0	89.2	394	73	52	41	7	5	6	1	57	0	73	17	2	4	11	.267	0	0	4.12
1993 Bakersfield	A+ LA	28	27	0	0	157.2	703	135	89	75	10	2	9	2	118	2	110	16	0	6	11	.353	0	0	4.28
1994 Vero Beach	A+ LA	7	7	0	0	24	109	28	20	18	3	0	0	1	9	1	22	1	0	1	3	.250	0	0	6.75
1995 San Antonio	AA LA	27	26	1	1	141.2	635	147	83	64	10	9	7	7	72	1	105	8	2	8	11	.421	0	0	4.07
1996 San Antonio	AA LA	18	18	1	0	122.2	509	106	51	45	6	7	2	3	44	0	69	2	1	10	5	.667	1	0	3.30
Albuquerque	AAA LA	13	8	0	0	46.2	225	63	39	28	5	2	1	3	22	0	38	3	0	1	4	.200	0	0	5.40
5 Min. YEARS		112	104	3	1	582.1	2575	552	334	271	41	25	25	17	322	4	417	47	5	30	45	.400	1	0	4.19

Terry Weaver

Bats: Right **Throws:** Right **Pos:** 2B **Ht:** 6'0" **Wt:** 175 **Born:** 10/8/72 **Age:** 24

		BATTING															BASERUNNING				PERCENTAGES		
Year Team	Lg Org	G	AB	H	2B	3B	HR	TB	R	RBI	TBB	IBB	SO	HBP	SH	SF	SB	CS	SB%	GDP	Avg	OBP	SLG
1995 Bellingham	A- SF	37	116	29	2	0	3	40	24	13	9	1	30	1	0	0	2	1	.67	0	.250	.310	.345
1996 Burlington	A SF	72	216	45	13	2	1	65	25	20	29	0	49	0	4	3	2	4	.33	6	.208	.298	.301
San Jose	A+ SF	6	14	3	0	0	0	3	1	0	1	0	1	0	0	0	0	0	.00	0	.214	.267	.214
Shreveport	AA SF	5	8	1	0	0	0	1	1	1	1	0	1	0	0	0	0	0	.00	0	.125	.222	.125
2 Min. YEARS		120	354	78	15	2	4	109	51	34	40	1	81	1	4	3	4	5	.44	6	.220	.299	.308

Doug Webb

Pitches: Right **Bats:** Right **Pos:** P **Ht:** 6'3" **Wt:** 205 **Born:** 8/25/73 **Age:** 23

		HOW MUCH HE PITCHED						WHAT HE GAVE UP												THE RESULTS					
Year Team	Lg Org	G	GS	CG	GF	IP	BFP	H	R	ER	HR	SH	SF	HB	TBB	IBB	SO	WP	Bk	W	L	Pct.	ShO	Sv	ERA
1994 Brewers	R Mil	1	0	0	1	1	3	0	0	0	0	0	0	0	0	0	1	0	0	0	0	.000	0	0	0.00
Stockton	A+ Mil	29	0	0	12	35	179	38	33	21	2	1	4	2	27	0	34	5	4	0	2	.000	0	0	5.40
1995 El Paso	AA Mil	18	0	0	16	18.1	77	11	9	9	3	1	1	0	13	1	11	2	0	2	1	.667	0	8	4.42
Stockton	A+ Mil	50	0	0	47	55.1	217	28	16	16	6	2	1	1	21	1	45	2	0	2	1	.667	0	30	2.60
1996 El Paso	AA Mil	10	0	0	3	8	38	4	6	6	0	0	0	0	10	0	3	1	0	1	0	1.000	0	0	6.75
3 Min. YEARS		108	0	0	79	117.2	514	81	64	52	11	4	6	3	71	2	94	10	4	5	4	.556	0	38	3.98

Neil Weber

Pitches: Left **Bats:** Left **Pos:** P **Ht:** 6'5" **Wt:** 205 **Born:** 12/6/72 **Age:** 24

		HOW MUCH HE PITCHED						WHAT HE GAVE UP												THE RESULTS					
Year Team	Lg Org	G	GS	CG	GF	IP	BFP	H	R	ER	HR	SH	SF	HB	TBB	IBB	SO	WP	Bk	W	L	Pct.	ShO	Sv	ERA
1993 Jamestown	A- Mon	16	16	2	0	94.1	398	84	46	29	3	0	4	4	36	0	80	3	3	6	5	.545	1	0	2.77
1994 W. Palm Bch	A+ Mon	25	24	1	0	135	566	113	58	48	8	4	4	4	62	0	134	7	5	9	7	.563	0	0	3.20
1995 Harrisburg	AA Mon	28	28	0	0	152.2	696	157	98	85	16	11	7	8	90	1	119	7	1	6	11	.353	0	0	5.01
1996 Harrisburg	AA Mon	18	18	1	0	107	440	90	37	36	8	3	3	5	44	0	74	5	0	7	4	.636	0	0	3.03
4 Min. YEARS		87	86	4	0	489	2100	444	239	198	35	18	18	21	232	1	407	22	9	28	27	.509	1	0	3.64

Weston Weber

Pitches: Right **Bats:** Right **Pos:** P **Ht:** 6'0" **Wt:** 175 **Born:** 1/5/64 **Age:** 33

		HOW MUCH HE PITCHED						WHAT HE GAVE UP												THE RESULTS					
Year Team	Lg Org	G	GS	CG	GF	IP	BFP	H	R	ER	HR	SH	SF	HB	TBB	IBB	SO	WP	Bk	W	L	Pct.	ShO	Sv	ERA
1986 Medford	A- Oak	13	13	0	0	68	0	64	42	26	4	0	0	4	28	0	69	5	1	5	5	.500	0	0	3.44
1987 Madison	A Oak	9	8	0	0	46.2	203	44	21	18	4	0	2	1	27	0	38	2	1	4	1	.800	0	0	3.47
1988 Modesto	A+ Oak	17	17	1	0	98	440	91	59	44	7	4	5	2	54	0	81	14	1	6	7	.462	0	0	4.04
1989 Huntsville	AA Oak	15	2	0	4	34	161	34	25	20	2	1	3	1	29	0	17	0	3	3	2	.600	0	0	5.29
Modesto	A+ Oak	11	11	1	0	69	293	60	32	25	1	3	2	3	34	1	49	4	1	3	6	.333	0	0	3.26
Tacoma	AAA Oak	6	0	0	2	11	48	8	9	9	1	0	0	1	7	0	6	0	1	0	0	.000	0	0	7.36
1990 Tacoma	AAA Oak	35	2	0	9	63	291	64	44	35	4	2	4	4	43	2	35	3	0	5	2	.714	0	1	5.00
Portland	AAA Min	4	1	0	1	10	52	15	10	9	0	0	1	1	5	0	7	0	0	0	0	.000	0	0	8.10
1991 Huntsville	AA Oak	34	0	0	17	54	240	57	23	13	1	1	2	4	18	1	26	4	1	2	3	.400	0	3	2.17
Tacoma	AAA Oak	15	0	0	11	31.2	129	28	14	7	0	1	1	2	7	0	15	1	1	2	0	1.000	0	1	1.99
1992 Tacoma	AAA Oak	52	0	0	23	94	421	95	45	43	6	9	3	8	53	9	51	10	0	4	5	.444	0	2	4.12
1993 Jacksonvlle	AA Sea	17	0	0	8	26.2	109	25	6	5	1	0	1	1	7	1	12	2	0	2	1	.667	0	1	1.69
1994 Calgary	AAA Sea	32	24	2	1	158.2	734	216	118	105	24	0	5	4	53	4	108	3	2	12	8	.600	0	0	5.96
1995 Las Vegas	AAA SD	29	21	2	3	150.1	663	170	92	78	16	5	6	4	50	10	86	6	3	6	11	.353	0	0	4.67
Tacoma	AAA Sea	29	21	2	3	150.1	663	170	92	78	16	5	6	4	50	10	86	6	3	6	11	.353	0	0	4.67
1996 Las Vegas	AAA SD	7	0	0	3	10	47	12	7	7	1	0	0	0	8	2	4	0	0	2	1	.667	0	0	6.30
11 Min. YEARS		325	120	8	85	1075.1	4494	1153	639	522	88	31	41	44	473	40	690	60	18	62	63	.496	0	8	4.37

Eric Wedge

Bats: Right **Throws:** Right **Pos:** DH **Ht:** 6' 3" **Wt:** 230 **Born:** 1/27/68 **Age:** 29

				BATTING															BASERUNNING				PERCENTAGES		
Year	Team	Lg	Org	G	AB	H	2B	3B	HR	TB	R	RBI	TBB	IBB	SO	HBP	SH	SF	SB	CS	SB%	GDP	Avg	OBP	SLG
1989	Elmira	A-	Bos	41	145	34	6	2	7	65	20	22	15	0	21	0	0	0	1	1	.50	3	.234	.306	.448
	New Britain	AA	Bos	14	40	8	2	0	0	10	3	2	5	0	10	0	2	0	0	0	.00	1	.200	.289	.250
1990	New Britain	AA	Bos	103	339	77	13	1	5	107	36	48	51	2	54	1	0	5	1	3	.25	14	.227	.326	.316
1991	New Britain	AA	Bos	2	8	2	0	0	0	2	0	2	0	0	2	0	0	1	0	0	.00	0	.250	.222	.250
	Winter Havn	A+	Bos	8	21	5	0	0	1	8	2	1	3	0	7	0	1	0	1	0	1.00	1	.238	.333	.381
	Pawtucket	AAA	Bos	53	163	38	14	1	5	69	24	18	25	0	26	1	2	5	1	2	.33	3	.233	.330	.423
1992	Pawtucket	AAA	Bos	65	211	63	9	0	11	105	28	40	32	3	40	1	0	3	0	0	.00	6	.299	.389	.498
1993	Central Val	A+	Col	6	23	7	0	0	3	16	6	11	2	1	6	0	0	0	0	0	.00	1	.304	.360	.696
	Colo. Sprng	AAA	Col	38	90	24	6	0	3	39	17	13	16	1	22	2	0	0	0	0	.00	4	.267	.389	.433
1994	Pawtucket	AAA	Bos	77	255	73	14	0	19	144	44	59	51	5	48	2	0	2	0	1	.00	6	.286	.406	.565
1995	Pawtucket	AAA	Bos	108	376	88	17	1	20	167	52	68	63	4	96	2	0	3	1	3	.25	9	.234	.345	.444
1996	Toledo	AAA	Det	96	332	78	25	0	15	148	61	57	43	0	81	0	1	4	2	2	.50	5	.235	.319	.446
1991	Boston	AL		1	1	1	0	0	0	1	0	0	0	0	0	0	0	0	0	0	.00	0	1.000	1.000	1.000
1992	Boston	AL		27	68	17	2	0	5	34	11	11	13	0	18	0	0	0	0	0	.00	0	.250	.370	.500
1993	Colorado	NL		9	11	2	0	0	0	2	2	1	0	0	4	0	0	0	0	0	.00	0	.182	.182	.182
1994	Boston	AL		2	6	0	0	0	0	0	0	0	1	0	3	0	0	0	0	0	.00	0	.000	.143	.000
8 Min. YEARS				611	2003	497	106	5	89	880	293	341	306	16	413	9	6	23	7	12	.37	53	.248	.347	.439
4 Maj. YEARS				39	86	20	2	0	5	37	13	12	14	0	25	0	0	0	0	0	.00	0	.233	.340	.430

Wes Weger

Bats: Right **Throws:** Right **Pos:** 2B-3B **Ht:** 6'0" **Wt:** 170 **Born:** 10/3/70 **Age:** 26

				BATTING															BASERUNNING				PERCENTAGES		
Year	Team	Lg	Org	G	AB	H	2B	3B	HR	TB	R	RBI	TBB	IBB	SO	HBP	SH	SF	SB	CS	SB%	GDP	Avg	OBP	SLG
1992	Helena	R+	Mil	36	133	57	9	1	5	83	36	31	22	0	9	0	2	5	7	2	.78	1	.429	.494	.624
	Stockton	A+	Mil	32	120	31	7	2	1	45	26	18	20	0	17	3	0	0	3	3	.50	2	.258	.378	.375
1993	El Paso	AA	Mil	123	471	137	24	5	5	186	69	53	31	4	44	4	7	2	9	9	.50	6	.291	.339	.395
1995	El Paso	AA	Mil	45	160	41	9	2	0	54	22	19	10	1	14	0	1	1	1	1	.50	9	.256	.298	.338
	New Orleans	AAA	Mil	64	234	67	16	0	2	89	28	24	10	0	31	1	1	1	0	2	.00	5	.286	.317	.380
1996	New Orleans	AAA	Mil	64	210	44	11	0	4	67	23	23	18	0	33	1	1	0	0	0	.00	10	.210	.275	.319
4 Min. YEARS				364	1328	377	76	10	17	524	204	168	111	5	148	9	12	9	20	17	.54	33	.284	.341	.395

Chris Weinke

Bats: Left **Throws:** Right **Pos:** DH-1B **Ht:** 6'3" **Wt:** 205 **Born:** 7/31/72 **Age:** 24

				BATTING															BASERUNNING				PERCENTAGES		
Year	Team	Lg	Org	G	AB	H	2B	3B	HR	TB	R	RBI	TBB	IBB	SO	HBP	SH	SF	SB	CS	SB%	GDP	Avg	OBP	SLG
1991	St. Cathrns	A-	Tor	75	271	65	9	1	3	85	31	41	41	1	61	0	3	4	12	9	.57	1	.240	.335	.314
1992	Myrtle Bch	A	Tor	135	458	110	16	2	13	169	61	63	70	7	89	6	4	5	4	9	.31	6	.240	.345	.369
1993	Dunedin	A+	Tor	128	476	135	16	2	17	206	68	98	66	8	78	2	1	4	8	6	.57	7	.284	.370	.433
1994	Knoxville	AA	Tor	139	526	133	23	2	8	184	61	87	45	6	121	0	4	5	12	4	.75	10	.253	.309	.350
1995	Syracuse	AAA	Tor	113	341	77	12	2	10	123	42	41	44	2	74	1	0	2	4	3	.57	10	.226	.314	.361
1996	Knoxville	AA	Tor	75	265	70	18	2	15	137	48	55	52	4	74	0	0	4	2	2	.50	3	.264	.380	.517
	Syracuse	AAA	Tor	51	161	30	8	1	3	49	21	18	19	2	49	1	0	1	0	1	.00	6	.186	.275	.304
6 Min. YEARS				716	2498	620	102	12	69	953	332	403	337	30	546	10	12	25	42	34	.55	43	.248	.337	.382

Mike Welch

Pitches: Right **Bats:** Left **Pos:** P **Ht:** 6'2" **Wt:** 195 **Born:** 8/25/72 **Age:** 24

				HOW MUCH HE PITCHED						WHAT HE GAVE UP												THE RESULTS					
Year	Team	Lg	Org	G	GS	CG	GF	IP	BFP	H	R	ER	HR	SH	SF	HB	TBB	IBB	SO	WP	Bk	W	L	Pct.	ShO	Sv	ERA
1993	Pittsfield	A-	NYN	17	0	0	14	31	126	23	9	5	0	2	4	0	6	1	34	3	1	3	1	.750	0	9	1.45
1994	Columbia	A	NYN	24	24	5	0	159.2	667	151	81	64	14	7	5	11	33	0	127	5	0	7	11	.389	2	0	3.61
1995	Binghamton	AA	NYN	1	0	0	1	1	3	0	0	0	0	0	0	0	0	0	2	0	0	0	0	.000	0	0	0.00
	St. Lucie	A+	NYN	45	6	0	34	71	325	96	50	42	7	4	3	6	18	4	53	4	0	4	4	.500	0	15	5.32
1996	Binghamton	AA	NYN	46	0	0	37	51	216	55	29	26	4	3	1	3	10	0	53	0	0	4	2	.667	0	27	4.59
	Norfolk	AAA	NYN	10	0	0	5	8.2	36	8	4	4	0	0	0	0	2	0	6	0	0	0	1	.000	0	2	4.15
4 Min. YEARS				143	30	5	91	322.1	1373	333	173	141	25	16	13	20	69	5	275	12	1	18	19	.486	2	53	3.94

Forry Wells

Bats: Left **Throws:** Right **Pos:** OF **Ht:** 6'4" **Wt:** 205 **Born:** 3/21/71 **Age:** 26

				BATTING															BASERUNNING				PERCENTAGES		
Year	Team	Lg	Org	G	AB	H	2B	3B	HR	TB	R	RBI	TBB	IBB	SO	HBP	SH	SF	SB	CS	SB%	GDP	Avg	OBP	SLG
1994	Bend	A-	Col	37	117	30	8	0	1	41	19	13	23	2	29	4	0	0	9	1	.90	2	.256	.396	.350
1995	Salem	A+	Col	119	402	102	23	4	18	187	60	67	56	6	105	7	3	1	6	3	.67	2	.254	.354	.465
	New Haven	AA	Col	4	14	3	0	0	0	3	3	1	1	1	2	1	0	0	0	0	.00	1	.214	.313	.214
1996	New Haven	AA	Col	108	304	70	19	1	7	112	44	43	46	4	73	4	2	2	1	2	.33	4	.230	.337	.368
3 Min. YEARS				268	837	205	50	5	26	343	126	124	126	13	209	16	5	3	16	6	.73	9	.245	.353	.410

Bill Wertz

Pitches: Right **Bats:** Right **Pos:** P **Ht:** 6' 6" **Wt:** 220 **Born:** 1/15/67 **Age:** 30

		HOW MUCH HE PITCHED						WHAT HE GAVE UP												THE RESULTS					
Year Team	Lg Org	G	GS	CG	GF	IP	BFP	H	R	ER	HR	SH	SF	HB	TBB	IBB	SO	WP	Bk	W	L	Pct.	ShO	Sv	ERA
1989 Indians	R Cle	12	11	1	0	66	282	57	23	23	0	1	4	4	36	0	56	11	0	4	3	.571	1	0	3.14
1990 Reno	A+ Cle	17	9	0	1	61.1	295	61	58	45	6	3	4	5	52	0	52	12	0	1	3	.250	0	0	6.60
Watertown	A- Cle	14	14	2	0	100.2	431	81	39	32	3	2	3	4	48	0	92	6	0	10	2	.833	0	0	2.86
1991 Columbus	A Cle	49	0	0	31	91	391	81	41	30	6	6	4	6	32	3	95	5	0	6	8	.429	0	9	2.97
1992 Canton-Akrn	AA Cle	57	0	0	24	97.1	382	75	16	13	1	3	2	3	30	6	69	3	0	8	4	.667	0	8	1.20
1993 Charlotte	AAA Cle	28	1	0	9	50.2	207	42	18	11	4	3	0	1	14	4	47	1	0	7	2	.778	0	0	1.95
1994 Charlotte	AAA Cle	44	2	0	8	66	278	53	30	23	5	2	2	1	34	3	60	5	0	4	3	.571	0	1	3.14
1995 Pawtucket	AAA Bos	29	6	0	12	63.2	298	74	47	41	11	4	4	1	31	1	55	7	0	4	5	.444	0	2	5.80
1996 Buffalo	AAA Cle	17	1	0	11	28.2	133	32	16	15	3	1	1	2	19	1	22	0	0	1	2	.333	0	0	4.71
Tacoma	AAA Sea	16	2	0	8	32.1	162	46	21	18	2	0	0	1	23	2	25	3	0	0	3	.000	0	0	5.01
Port City	AA Sea	6	5	1	1	28	120	28	10	8	1	1	1	0	9	0	26	1	0	2	2	.500	0	0	2.57
1993 Cleveland	AL	34	0	0	7	59.2	262	54	28	24	5	1	1	1	32	2	53	0	0	2	3	.400	0	0	3.62
1994 Cleveland	AL	1	0	0	0	4.1	23	9	5	5	0	0	0	0	1	0	1	0	0	0	0	.000	0	0	10.38
8 Min. YEARS		289	51	4	105	685.2	2979	630	319	259	42	26	25	28	328	20	599	54	0	47	37	.560	1	20	3.40
2 Maj. YEARS		35	0	0	7	64	285	63	33	29	5	1	1	1	33	2	54	0	0	2	3	.400	0	0	4.08

Destry Westbrook

Pitches: Right **Bats:** Right **Pos:** P **Ht:** 6'1" **Wt:** 195 **Born:** 12/13/70 **Age:** 26

		HOW MUCH HE PITCHED						WHAT HE GAVE UP												THE RESULTS					
Year Team	Lg Org	G	GS	CG	GF	IP	BFP	H	R	ER	HR	SH	SF	HB	TBB	IBB	SO	WP	Bk	W	L	Pct.	ShO	Sv	ERA
1992 Auburn	A- Hou	12	2	0	5	17	105	29	33	29	5	0	2	4	19	0	19	6	2	0	3	.000	0	0	15.35
1993 Quad City	A Hou	27	0	0	14	36.1	158	29	11	10	3	0	2	0	23	1	41	0	0	3	1	.750	0	2	2.48
1994 Quad City	A Hou	27	0	0	12	46.1	205	48	25	23	3	2	2	2	23	1	50	3	0	0	2	.000	0	1	4.47
1995 Tucson	AAA Hou	5	0	0	2	12.1	60	20	10	10	2	0	0	0	7	0	8	2	0	0	0	.000	0	0	7.30
Mobile	IND —	8	1	0	1	13	66	13	13	10	1	0	1	0	13	2	11	1	0	0	1	.000	0	0	6.92
Kissimmee	A+ Hou	23	1	0	5	45	232	67	47	42	5	1	1	0	33	3	41	5	0	0	2	.000	0	1	8.40
1996 Clearwater	A+ Phi	34	0	0	12	43.1	180	35	12	10	3	0	1	1	11	2	35	2	0	3	3	.500	0	0	2.08
Reading	AA Phi	25	0	0	11	34	156	40	19	15	4	3	0	0	14	4	15	1	0	4	3	.571	0	0	3.97
5 Min. YEARS		161	4	0	62	247.1	1162	281	170	149	26	6	9	7	143	13	220	20	2	10	15	.400	0	4	5.42

Mickey Weston

Pitches: Right **Bats:** Right **Pos:** P **Ht:** 6' 1" **Wt:** 180 **Born:** 3/26/61 **Age:** 36

		HOW MUCH HE PITCHED						WHAT HE GAVE UP												THE RESULTS					
Year Team	Lg Org	G	GS	CG	GF	IP	BFP	H	R	ER	HR	SH	SF	HB	TBB	IBB	SO	WP	Bk	W	L	Pct.	ShO	Sv	ERA
1984 Columbia	A NYN	32	2	0	20	63.2	272	58	27	13	2	6	1	2	27	6	40	5	0	6	5	.545	0	2	1.84
1985 Lynchburg	A+ NYN	49	3	1	24	100.1	407	81	29	24	4	3	2	0	22	2	62	4	1	6	5	.545	1	10	2.15
1986 Jackson	AA NYN	34	4	0	7	70.2	308	73	40	34	9	3	2	4	27	3	36	3	0	4	4	.500	0	2	4.33
1987 Jackson	AA NYN	58	1	0	21	82	346	96	39	31	4	0	1	1	18	5	50	6	1	8	4	.667	0	3	3.40
1988 Jackson	AA NYN	30	14	1	4	125.1	507	127	50	31	3	8	5	0	20	4	61	4	0	8	5	.615	0	0	2.23
Tidewater	AAA NYN	4	4	2	0	29.2	115	21	6	5	0	3	0	1	5	1	16	1	0	2	1	.667	1	0	1.52
1989 Rochester	AAA Bal	23	14	2	7	112	445	103	30	26	6	2	2	1	19	0	51	1	0	8	3	.727	1	4	2.09
1990 Rochester	AAA Bal	29	12	2	13	109.1	432	93	36	24	3	1	2	0	22	0	58	3	0	11	1	.917	0	6	1.98
1991 Syracuse	AAA Tor	27	25	3	1	166	710	193	85	69	7	4	5	3	36	1	60	10	0	12	6	.667	0	0	3.74
1992 Scranton-WB	AAA Phi	26	24	2	1	170.2	683	165	65	59	12	5	5	3	29	2	79	4	1	10	6	.625	1	1	3.11
1993 Norfolk	AAA NYN	21	20	3	1	127.1	542	149	77	60	10	3	2	2	18	2	41	4	0	10	9	.526	0	0	4.24
1994 New Haven	AA Col	9	0	0	9	12	48	10	2	1	1	0	0	0	2	1	11	2	0	2	1	.667	0	2	0.75
Colo. Sprng	AAA Col	37	0	0	14	53.1	252	80	40	37	7	2	2	0	17	0	30	2	0	5	5	.500	0	1	6.24
1995 Toledo	AAA Det	28	27	2	0	180	734	170	68	58	14	2	5	7	41	1	69	4	0	11	7	.611	1	0	2.90
1996 Charlotte	AAA Fla	31	14	0	5	104.1	472	131	73	67	11	7	3	3	39	2	47	1	1	5	9	.357	0	1	5.78
1989 Baltimore	AL	7	0	0	2	13	55	18	8	8	1	0	0	1	2	0	7	0	0	1	0	1.000	0	1	5.54
1990 Baltimore	AL	9	2	0	4	21	94	28	20	18	6	1	0	0	6	1	9	1	0	0	1	.000	0	0	7.71
1991 Toronto	AL	2	0	0	2	2	8	1	0	0	0	0	0	0	1	1	1	0	0	0	0	.000	0	0	0.00
1992 Philadelphia	NL	1	1	0	0	3.2	19	7	5	5	1	0	0	1	1	0	0	0	0	0	1	.000	0	0	12.27
1993 New York	NL	4	0	0	0	5.2	30	11	5	5	0	0	0	1	1	0	2	0	0	0	0	.000	0	0	7.94
13 Min. YEARS		438	164	18	127	1506.2	6273	1550	667	539	93	49	37	27	342	30	711	54	4	108	71	.603	5	32	3.22
5 Maj. YEARS		23	3	0	8	45.1	206	65	38	36	8	1	0	3	11	2	19	1	0	1	2	.333	0	1	7.15

Matt Whisenant

Pitches: Left **Bats:** Both **Pos:** P **Ht:** 6'3" **Wt:** 215 **Born:** 6/8/71 **Age:** 26

		HOW MUCH HE PITCHED						WHAT HE GAVE UP												THE RESULTS					
Year Team	Lg Org	G	GS	CG	GF	IP	BFP	H	R	ER	HR	SH	SF	HB	TBB	IBB	SO	WP	Bk	W	L	Pct.	ShO	Sv	ERA
1990 Princeton	R+ Phi	9	2	0	2	15	85	16	27	19	3	0	1	3	20	0	25	7	0	0	0	.000	0	0	11.40
1991 Batavia	A- Phi	11	10	0	1	47.2	208	31	19	13	2	1	1	0	42	0	55	4	2	2	1	.667	0	0	2.45
1992 Spartanburg	A Phi	27	27	2	0	150.2	652	117	69	54	9	5	6	10	85	0	151	10	6	11	7	.611	0	0	3.23
1993 Kane County	A Fla	15	15	0	0	71	331	68	45	37	3	8	2	3	56	0	74	8	3	2	6	.250	0	0	4.69
1994 Brevard Cty	A+ Fla	28	26	5	0	160	679	125	71	60	7	6	7	9	82	2	103	18	1	6	9	.400	1	0	3.38
1995 Portland	AA Fla	23	22	2	0	128.2	544	106	57	50	8	7	4	9	65	3	107	8	0	10	6	.625	0	0	3.50
1996 Charlotte	AAA Fla	28	22	1	1	121	590	149	107	93	15	8	2	3	101	3	97	30	0	8	10	.444	0	0	6.92
7 Min. YEARS		141	124	10	4	694	3089	612	395	326	47	35	23	37	451	8	612	85	12	39	39	.500	1	0	4.23

Steve Whitaker

Pitches: Left **Bats:** Left **Pos:** P **Ht:** 6'6" **Wt:** 225 **Born:** 4/15/70 **Age:** 27

				HOW MUCH HE PITCHED						WHAT HE GAVE UP												THE RESULTS					
Year	Team	Lg	Org	G	GS	CG	GF	IP	BFP	H	R	ER	HR	SH	SF	HB	TBB	IBB	SO	WP	Bk	W	L	Pct.	ShO	Sv	ERA
1991	San Jose	A+	SF	6	6	0	0	29.1	129	25	15	11	2	0	3	1	25	0	21	3	1	2	1	.667	0	0	3.38
1992	San Jose	A+	SF	26	26	3	0	148.1	648	157	80	69	7	6	5	6	86	2	83	10	0	8	9	.471	0	0	4.19
1993	San Jose	A+	SF	22	21	1	1	127.1	582	106	70	54	9	2	6	5	114	0	94	7	0	8	10	.444	0	0	3.82
	Shreveport	AA	SF	4	1	0	2	8.1	38	5	1	1	0	1	0	0	7	0	12	0	0	1	0	1.000	0	0	1.08
1994	Shreveport	AA	SF	27	26	1	0	154.2	648	140	69	58	13	7	6	5	68	0	108	3	0	11	8	.579	1	0	3.38
1995	San Jose	A+	SF	2	0	0	1	6	26	7	3	3	0	0	0	0	2	0	2	0	0	0	0	.000	0	1	4.50
	Shreveport	AA	SF	4	3	0	0	16.1	70	17	8	7	0	1	0	0	10	0	10	1	0	2	0	1.000	0	0	3.86
	Phoenix	AAA	SF	22	13	0	4	76.1	357	96	58	52	2	7	4	0	48	2	42	4	1	2	5	.286	0	1	6.13
1996	El Paso	AA	Mil	25	24	2	0	145.1	672	157	92	74	9	7	5	5	87	3	85	7	1	11	7	.611	0	0	4.58
6 Min. YEARS				138	120	7	8	712	3170	710	396	329	42	31	29	22	447	7	457	35	3	45	40	.529	1	2	4.16

Billy White

Bats: Right **Throws:** Right **Pos:** 2B **Ht:** 6'0" **Wt:** 185 **Born:** 7/3/68 **Age:** 28

				BATTING															BASERUNNING				PERCENTAGES		
Year	Team	Lg	Org	G	AB	H	2B	3B	HR	TB	R	RBI	TBB	IBB	SO	HBP	SH	SF	SB	CS	SB%	GDP	Avg	OBP	SLG
1989	Geneva	A-	ChN	68	254	82	19	1	3	112	44	29	43	0	36	3	2	1	16	5	.76	9	.323	.425	.441
1990	Winston-Sal	A+	ChN	134	505	136	15	2	5	170	85	54	70	3	108	9	9	3	25	8	.76	13	.269	.366	.337
1991	Charlotte	AA	ChN	123	396	106	16	3	3	137	52	50	66	2	72	4	4	5	13	9	.59	9	.268	.374	.346
1992	Charlotte	AA	ChN	121	403	102	12	0	4	126	57	33	46	0	90	3	6	4	10	8	.56	9	.253	.331	.313
1993	Daytona	A+	ChN	38	125	42	9	2	3	64	19	22	16	0	23	5	4	1	2	0	1.00	1	.336	.429	.512
	Orlando	AA	ChN	40	120	29	11	1	2	48	14	14	15	1	28	0	2	2	1	2	.33	2	.242	.321	.400
1994	New Haven	AA	Col	82	236	58	13	0	1	74	31	22	37	0	48	2	4	1	0	3	.00	11	.246	.351	.314
1995	New Haven	AA	Col	58	181	42	9	1	3	62	25	34	27	0	44	0	0	0	2	2	.50	3	.232	.332	.343
1996	Colo. Sprng	AAA	Col	103	284	69	11	2	3	93	24	26	32	1	80	1	4	1	2	2	.50	7	.243	.321	.327
8 Min. YEARS				767	2504	666	115	12	27	886	351	284	352	7	529	27	35	18	71	39	.65	64	.266	.360	.354

Donnie White

Bats: Right **Throws:** Right **Pos:** OF **Ht:** 5'10" **Wt:** 180 **Born:** 3/13/72 **Age:** 25

				BATTING															BASERUNNING				PERCENTAGES		
Year	Team	Lg	Org	G	AB	H	2B	3B	HR	TB	R	RBI	TBB	IBB	SO	HBP	SH	SF	SB	CS	SB%	GDP	Avg	OBP	SLG
1991	Mets	R	NYN	54	196	47	10	2	0	61	32	13	24	0	37	3	0	3	30	7	.81	0	.240	.327	.311
1992	Kingsport	R+	NYN	55	221	67	10	1	4	91	37	27	21	0	38	3	2	4	25	9	.74	1	.303	.365	.412
1993	Capital Cty	A	NYN	114	441	134	18	6	3	173	86	41	54	0	75	5	5	1	43	14	.75	4	.304	.385	.392
1994	St. Lucie	A+	NYN	118	463	132	17	9	5	182	73	44	38	2	97	5	9	4	31	9	.78	7	.285	.343	.393
1995	Binghamton	AA	NYN	94	314	74	17	2	3	104	48	20	40	0	56	2	6	3	25	6	.81	10	.236	.323	.331
1996	Binghamton	AA	NYN	82	219	42	6	1	6	68	29	22	26	0	61	3	1	1	5	4	.56	5	.192	.285	.311
6 Min. YEARS				517	1854	496	78	21	21	679	305	167	203	2	364	21	27	16	159	49	.76	27	.268	.344	.366

Gabe White

Pitches: Left **Bats:** Left **Pos:** P **Ht:** 6' 2" **Wt:** 200 **Born:** 11/20/71 **Age:** 25

				HOW MUCH HE PITCHED						WHAT HE GAVE UP												THE RESULTS					
Year	Team	Lg	Org	G	GS	CG	GF	IP	BFP	H	R	ER	HR	SH	SF	HB	TBB	IBB	SO	WP	Bk	W	L	Pct.	ShO	Sv	ERA
1990	Expos	R	Mon	11	11	1	0	57.1	233	50	21	20	3	1	1	3	12	0	42	5	1	4	2	.667	0	0	3.14
1991	Sumter	A	Mon	24	24	5	0	149	626	129	73	54	7	7	6	5	53	0	138	8	0	6	9	.400	0	0	3.26
1992	Rockford	A	Mon	27	27	7	0	187	774	148	73	59	10	9	4	11	61	0	176	9	9	14	8	.636	0	0	2.84
1993	Harrisburg	AA	Mon	16	16	2	0	100	394	80	30	24	4	1	1	2	28	0	80	5	2	7	2	.778	1	0	2.16
	Ottawa	AAA	Mon	6	6	1	0	40.1	165	38	15	14	3	0	1	1	6	0	28	2	0	2	1	.667	1	0	3.12
1994	W. Palm Bch	A+	Mon	1	1	0	0	6	20	2	2	1	0	0	0	0	1	0	4	1	0	1	0	1.000	0	0	1.50
	Ottawa	AAA	Mon	14	14	0	0	73	320	77	49	41	11	2	3	2	28	2	63	2	0	8	3	.727	0	0	5.05
1995	Ottawa	AAA	Mon	12	12	0	0	62.1	264	58	31	27	10	1	4	4	17	0	37	2	1	2	3	.400	0	0	3.90
1996	Indianapols	AAA	Cin	11	11	0	0	68.1	273	69	25	21	6	2	2	1	9	3	51	1	0	6	3	.667	0	0	2.77
1994	Montreal	NL		7	5	0	2	23.2	106	24	16	16	4	1	1	1	11	0	17	0	0	1	1	.500	0	1	6.08
1995	Montreal	NL		19	1	0	8	25.2	115	26	21	20	7	2	3	1	9	0	25	0	0	1	2	.333	0	0	7.01
7 Min. YEARS				122	122	16	0	743.1	3069	651	319	261	54	23	22	29	215	5	619	35	13	50	31	.617	2	0	3.16
2 Maj. YEARS				26	6	0	10	49.1	221	50	37	36	11	3	4	2	20	0	42	0	0	2	3	.400	0	1	6.57

Jimmy White

Bats: Left **Throws:** Right **Pos:** OF **Ht:** 6'1" **Wt:** 170 **Born:** 12/1/72 **Age:** 24

				BATTING															BASERUNNING				PERCENTAGES		
Year	Team	Lg	Org	G	AB	H	2B	3B	HR	TB	R	RBI	TBB	IBB	SO	HBP	SH	SF	SB	CS	SB%	GDP	Avg	OBP	SLG
1990	Astros	R	Hou	52	180	44	6	4	0	58	32	18	29	1	51	1	0	2	11	8	.58	2	.244	.349	.322
1991	Asheville	A	Hou	128	437	112	22	2	8	162	66	43	43	2	133	5	0	2	12	15	.44	8	.256	.329	.371
1992	Burlington	A	Hou	102	370	106	20	7	1	143	39	47	38	0	84	2	1	6	17	13	.57	7	.286	.351	.386
	Asheville	A	Hou	24	83	28	6	1	2	42	12	14	7	1	15	0	0	0	5	0	1.00	0	.337	.389	.506
1993	Osceola	A+	Hou	125	447	123	9	12	7	177	80	37	54	1	120	5	0	3	24	17	.59	1	.275	.358	.396
1994	Osceola	A+	Hou	48	174	55	14	6	5	96	37	21	21	1	43	3	0	0	9	3	.75	2	.316	.399	.552
	Jackson	AA	Hou	64	211	62	7	7	8	107	30	26	12	0	68	0	1	3	1	5	.17	7	.294	.327	.507
1995	Kissimmee	A+	Hou	16	55	10	3	1	0	15	6	3	9	0	9	1	1	0	4	0	1.00	2	.182	.308	.273
	Jackson	AA	Hou	2	1	0	0	0	0	0	1	0	1	0	0	0	0	0	0	0	.00	0	.000	.500	.000
	Charlstn-WV	A	Cin	20	65	11	3	1	1	19	7	8	6	0	27	1	1	1	1	1	.50	0	.169	.247	.292
	Winston-Sal	A+	Cin	31	111	29	5	1	7	57	15	18	4	0	33	2	1	1	1	1	.50	1	.261	.297	.514

Year Team	Lg Org	BATTING G	AB	H	2B	3B	HR	TB	R	RBI	TBB	IBB	SO	HBP	SH	SF	BASERUNNING SB	CS	SB%	GDP	PERCENTAGES Avg	OBP	SLG
1996 Chattanooga	AA Cin	15	38	5	1	1	0	8	5	2	4	0	12	0	0	0	0	0	.00	0	.132	.214	.211
7 Min. YEARS		627	2172	585	96	43	39	884	330	237	228	6	595	20	5	18	85	63	.57	30	.269	.342	.407

Rick White

Pitches: Right **Bats:** Right **Pos:** P **Ht:** 6' 4" **Wt:** 215 **Born:** 12/23/68 **Age:** 28

Year Team	Lg Org	HOW MUCH HE PITCHED G	GS	CG	GF	IP	BFP	WHAT HE GAVE UP H	R	ER	HR	SH	SF	HB	TBB	IBB	SO	WP	Bk	THE RESULTS W	L	Pct.	ShO	Sv	ERA
1990 Pirates	R Pit	7	6	0	0	35.2	142	26	11	2	0	1	1	2	4	0	27	2	2	3	1	.750	0	0	0.50
Welland	A- Pit	9	5	1	1	38.2	165	38	19	14	2	0	2	2	14	2	43	4	0	1	4	.200	0	0	3.26
1991 Augusta	A Pit	34	0	0	18	63	280	68	26	21	2	0	3	1	18	2	52	4	3	4	4	.500	0	6	3.00
Salem	A+ Pit	13	5	1	4	46.1	189	41	27	24	2	3	1	0	9	3	36	2	0	2	3	.400	0	1	4.66
1992 Salem	A+ Pit	18	18	5	0	120.2	490	116	58	51	15	2	4	5	24	1	70	5	0	7	9	.438	0	0	3.80
Carolina	AA Pit	10	10	1	0	57.2	247	59	32	27	8	2	1	3	18	1	45	6	0	1	7	.125	0	0	4.21
1993 Carolina	AA Pit	12	12	1	0	69.1	275	59	29	27	5	2	2	4	12	0	52	4	1	4	3	.571	0	0	3.50
Buffalo	AAA Pit	7	3	0	1	28	117	25	13	11	1	2	0	1	8	0	16	1	0	0	3	.000	0	0	3.54
1995 Calgary	AAA Pit	14	11	1	1	79.1	338	97	40	37	13	0	4	3	10	0	56	2	0	6	4	.600	0	0	4.20
1996 Pirates	R Pit	3	3	0	0	12	43	8	4	3	0	0	1	0	3	0	8	0	0	0	0	.000	0	0	2.25
Carolina	AA Pit	2	1	0	0	6.1	30	9	8	8	2	0	0	1	1	0	7	0	1	0	1	.000	0	0	11.37
1994 Pittsburgh	NL	43	5	0	23	75.1	317	79	35	32	9	7	5	6	17	3	38	2	2	4	5	.444	0	6	3.82
1995 Pittsburgh	NL	15	9	0	2	55	247	66	33	29	3	3	3	2	18	0	29	2	0	2	3	.400	0	0	4.75
6 Min. YEARS		129	74	10	25	557	2316	546	267	225	50	12	19	22	121	9	412	30	7	28	39	.418	0	7	3.64
2 Maj. YEARS		58	14	0	25	130.1	564	145	68	61	12	10	8	8	35	3	67	4	2	6	8	.429	0	6	4.21

Sean Whiteside

Pitches: Left **Bats:** Left **Pos:** P **Ht:** 6' 4" **Wt:** 190 **Born:** 4/19/71 **Age:** 26

Year Team	Lg Org	HOW MUCH HE PITCHED G	GS	CG	GF	IP	BFP	WHAT HE GAVE UP H	R	ER	HR	SH	SF	HB	TBB	IBB	SO	WP	Bk	THE RESULTS W	L	Pct.	ShO	Sv	ERA
1992 Niagara Fal	A- Det	15	11	0	0	69.2	289	54	26	19	2	1	2	0	24	0	72	7	5	8	4	.667	0	0	2.45
1993 Fayettevlle	A Det	24	16	0	4	100.2	443	113	68	52	8	0	5	3	41	0	85	18	0	3	5	.375	0	0	4.65
1994 Lakeland	A+ Det	13	0	0	6	31.1	126	21	6	4	0	1	0	0	12	0	39	4	0	0	2	.000	0	2	1.15
Trenton	AA Det	25	0	0	16	36.2	155	26	13	10	2	2	2	1	15	2	31	4	1	2	2	.500	0	5	2.45
1995 Jacksonvlle	AA Det	27	1	0	4	33.1	148	34	17	14	4	2	3	0	20	4	17	4	0	2	0	1.000	0	0	3.78
1996 Jacksonvlle	AA Det	8	0	0	3	12.1	54	11	9	8	2	0	0	0	9	0	9	3	0	1	0	1.000	0	0	5.84
Lakeland	A+ Det	19	18	0	0	102.2	432	104	51	44	6	3	3	0	32	0	63	6	0	4	10	.286	0	0	3.86
1995 Detroit	AL	2	0	0	0	3.2	22	7	6	6	1	0	2	0	4	1	2	1	0	0	0	.000	0	0	14.73
5 Min. YEARS		131	46	0	33	386.2	1647	363	190	151	24	9	15	4	153	6	316	46	6	20	23	.465	0	7	3.51

Darrell Whitmore

Bats: Left **Throws:** Right **Pos:** OF **Ht:** 6' 1" **Wt:** 210 **Born:** 11/18/68 **Age:** 28

Year Team	Lg Org	BATTING G	AB	H	2B	3B	HR	TB	R	RBI	TBB	IBB	SO	HBP	SH	SF	BASERUNNING SB	CS	SB%	GDP	PERCENTAGES Avg	OBP	SLG
1990 Burlington	R+ Cle	30	112	27	3	2	0	34	18	13	9	0	30	2	0	1	9	5	.64	0	.241	.306	.304
1991 Watertown	A- Cle	6	19	7	2	1	0	11	2	3	3	0	2	0	0	0	0	0	.00	0	.368	.455	.579
1992 Kinston	A+ Cle	121	443	124	22	2	10	180	71	52	56	5	92	5	0	5	17	9	.65	8	.280	.363	.406
1993 Edmonton	AAA Fla	73	273	97	24	2	9	152	52	62	22	0	53	0	0	3	11	8	.58	12	.355	.399	.557
1994 Edmonton	AAA Fla	115	421	119	24	5	20	213	72	61	41	3	76	2	0	3	14	3	.82	12	.283	.347	.506
1996 Charlotte	AAA Fla	55	204	62	13	0	11	108	27	36	7	2	43	1	0	2	2	5	.29	2	.304	.327	.529
1993 Florida	NL	76	250	51	8	2	4	75	24	19	10	0	72	5	2	0	4	2	.67	8	.204	.249	.300
1994 Florida	NL	9	22	5	1	0	0	6	1	0	3	0	5	0	0	0	0	1	.00	0	.227	.320	.273
1995 Florida	NL	27	58	11	2	0	1	16	6	2	5	0	15	0	1	1	0	0	.00	1	.190	.250	.276
6 Min. YEARS		400	1472	436	88	12	50	698	242	227	138	10	296	10	0	14	53	30	.64	34	.296	.357	.474
3 Maj. YEARS		112	330	67	11	2	5	97	31	21	18	0	92	5	3	1	4	3	.57	9	.203	.254	.294

Casey Whitten

Pitches: Left **Bats:** Left **Pos:** P **Ht:** 6'0" **Wt:** 175 **Born:** 5/23/72 **Age:** 25

Year Team	Lg Org	HOW MUCH HE PITCHED G	GS	CG	GF	IP	BFP	WHAT HE GAVE UP H	R	ER	HR	SH	SF	HB	TBB	IBB	SO	WP	Bk	THE RESULTS W	L	Pct.	ShO	Sv	ERA
1993 Watertown	A- Cle	14	14	0	0	81.2	331	75	28	22	8	0	4	3	18	0	81	5	0	6	3	.667	0	0	2.42
1994 Kinston	A+ Cle	27	27	0	0	153.1	634	127	78	73	21	4	5	4	64	0	148	9	0	9	10	.474	0	0	4.28
1995 Canton-Akrn	AA Cle	20	20	2	0	114.1	469	100	49	42	10	1	2	3	38	0	91	5	2	9	8	.529	1	0	3.31
1996 Canton-Akrn	AA Cle	8	8	0	0	37.2	150	23	8	7	2	0	0	2	13	0	44	3	0	3	1	.750	0	0	1.67
Buffalo	AAA Cle	12	10	0	1	43.2	209	54	47	39	8	0	3	1	24	0	35	3	0	3	4	.429	0	0	8.04
4 Min. YEARS		81	79	2	1	430.2	1793	379	210	183	49	5	14	13	157	0	399	25	2	30	26	.536	1	0	3.82

Scott Wiegandt

Pitches: Left **Bats:** Left **Pos:** P **Ht:** 5'11" **Wt:** 180 **Born:** 12/9/67 **Age:** 29

Year Team	Lg Org	HOW MUCH HE PITCHED G	GS	CG	GF	IP	BFP	WHAT HE GAVE UP H	R	ER	HR	SH	SF	HB	TBB	IBB	SO	WP	Bk	THE RESULTS W	L	Pct.	ShO	Sv	ERA
1989 Martinsvlle	R+ Phi	9	9	0	0	45.2	187	44	22	13	4	2	0	1	15	0	47	0	0	2	5	.286	0	0	2.56
1990 Spartanburg	A Phi	10	0	0	8	18.1	66	12	2	2	0	0	0	0	2	0	17	0	0	2	0	1.000	0	2	0.08
Clearwater	A+ Phi	33	4	0	16	75.2	316	70	33	22	4	4	3	3	37	2	52	6	3	4	8	.333	0	4	2.62
1991 Clearwater	A+ Phi	11	0	0	5	10.1	47	14	7	4	0	0	0	0	3	0	11	2	0	0	1	.000	0	1	3.48

Year Team	Lg Org	G	GS	CG	GF	IP	BFP	H	R	ER	HR	SH	SF	HB	TBB	IBB	SO	WP	Bk	W	L	Pct.	ShO	Sv	ERA
		HOW MUCH HE PITCHED						WHAT HE GAVE UP												THE RESULTS					
Reading	AA Phi	48	0	0	5	81	341	66	26	24	4	3	2	1	40	2	50	5	1	2	3	.400	0	1	2.67
1992 Scranton-WB	AAA Phi	1	0	0	1	1	4	0	0	0	0	0	0	0	1	0	2	0	0	0	0	.000	0	0	0.00
Reading	AA Phi	56	0	0	12	81.2	354	66	31	27	3	5	1	1	48	5	65	8	1	6	3	.667	0	2	2.98
1993 Reading	AA Phi	56	0	0	16	73.1	326	75	41	29	3	7	2	0	44	7	60	5	1	6	2	.750	0	0	3.56
1994 Scranton-WB	AAA Phi	6	0	0	1	4.2	30	11	8	7	0	1	1	1	3	0	3	0	0	0	0	.000	0	0	13.50
Reading	AA Phi	52	0	0	16	52.1	219	49	23	18	4	2	3	2	19	1	35	1	1	2	4	.333	0	0	3.10
1995 Scranton-WB	AAA Phi	47	0	0	15	54.1	234	55	19	18	0	1	0	2	27	8	41	5	2	1	3	.250	0	2	2.98
1996 Scranton-WB	AAA Phi	46	0	0	13	63	276	63	21	19	3	4	3	2	33	7	46	1	0	5	6	.455	0	2	2.71
8 Min. YEARS		375	13	0	108	561.1	2400	525	233	183	25	29	15	13	272	32	429	33	9	30	35	.462	0	14	2.93

Greg Williams

Pitches: Left **Bats:** Left **Pos:** P **Ht:** 6'1" **Wt:** 195 **Born:** 4/30/72 **Age:** 25

Year Team	Lg Org	G	GS	CG	GF	IP	BFP	H	R	ER	HR	SH	SF	HB	TBB	IBB	SO	WP	Bk	W	L	Pct.	ShO	Sv	ERA
		HOW MUCH HE PITCHED						WHAT HE GAVE UP												THE RESULTS					
1993 Watertown	A- Cle	1	0	0	1	0	4	1	1	0	0	0	0	0	2	1	0	0	0	0	1	.000	0	0	0.00
Burlington	R+ Cle	11	4	0	2	41	188	31	30	20	2	1	2	3	29	2	48	6	2	3	1	.750	0	2	4.39
Kinston	A+ Cle	2	1	0	0	3	15	6	3	3	1	0	0	0	1	0	2	1	0	0	1	.000	0	0	9.00
1994 Columbus	A Cle	37	0	0	12	73.1	312	49	32	28	2	1	4	5	52	0	84	8	1	6	1	.857	0	1	3.44
1995 Canton-Akrn	AA Cle	24	0	0	7	27.2	115	15	14	13	2	2	1	0	21	3	17	0	0	0	0	.000	0	0	4.23
Kinston	A+ Cle	54	0	0	15	49.2	203	30	23	19	3	3	1	2	29	3	35	5	0	2	1	.667	0	3	3.44
1996 Fargo-Mh	IND —	7	0	0	1	6.1	43	17	18	12	0	0	1	0	8	1	3	1	1	0	1	.000	0	0	17.05
Orlando	AA ChN	12	2	0	3	19	89	21	12	9	0	1	1	1	13	1	11	3	0	0	0	.000	0	0	4.26
4 Min. YEARS		148	7	0	41	220	969	170	133	104	10	8	10	11	155	11	200	24	4	11	6	.647	0	6	4.25

Harold Williams

Bats: Left **Throws:** Left **Pos:** DH-1B **Ht:** 6'4" **Wt:** 200 **Born:** 2/14/71 **Age:** 26

Year Team	Lg Org	G	AB	H	2B	3B	HR	TB	R	RBI	TBB	IBB	SO	HBP	SH	SF	SB	CS	SB%	GDP	Avg	OBP	SLG
		BATTING															BASERUNNING				PERCENTAGES		
1993 White Sox	R ChA	52	186	52	6	4	1	69	18	21	17	0	40	2	1	2	4	5	.44	6	.280	.343	.371
1994 Hickory	A ChA	137	535	162	27	3	24	267	99	104	53	6	103	11	1	3	1	1	.50	12	.303	.375	.499
1995 Pr. William	A+ ChA	129	472	133	30	1	14	207	56	72	48	11	98	11	1	2	4	2	.67	16	.282	.360	.439
1996 Birmingham	AA ChA	14	46	13	4	0	0	17	3	4	4	1	12	2	0	0	1	1	.50	1	.283	.365	.370
Orlando	AA ChN	80	255	67	6	0	10	103	33	36	27	4	55	1	1	1	1	2	.33	9	.263	.335	.404
4 Min. YEARS		412	1494	427	73	8	49	663	209	237	149	22	308	27	4	8	11	11	.50	44	.286	.359	.444

Jeff Williams

Pitches: Right **Bats:** Right **Pos:** P **Ht:** 6'4" **Wt:** 230 **Born:** 4/16/69 **Age:** 28

Year Team	Lg Org	G	GS	CG	GF	IP	BFP	H	R	ER	HR	SH	SF	HB	TBB	IBB	SO	WP	Bk	W	L	Pct.	ShO	Sv	ERA
		HOW MUCH HE PITCHED						WHAT HE GAVE UP												THE RESULTS					
1990 Bluefield	R+ Bal	9	0	0	9	11.1	48	7	3	2	0	0	0	1	5	0	14	1	0	2	0	1.000	0	0	1.59
Frederick	A+ Bal	16	0	0	13	25	115	23	17	13	2	0	2	2	17	0	31	1	0	2	1	.667	0	1	4.68
1991 Frederick	A+ Bal	12	0	0	11	16.2	68	17	6	5	1	1	1	0	6	0	20	0	0	1	2	.333	0	6	2.70
Hagerstown	AA Bal	39	0	0	29	55.1	247	52	23	16	1	2	3	0	32	1	42	6	0	3	5	.375	0	17	2.60
1992 Hagerstown	AA Bal	36	15	3	16	123	579	148	91	66	9	5	6	6	70	0	82	15	1	8	10	.444	0	6	4.83
1993 Rochester	AAA Bal	33	5	0	11	86	389	95	59	55	10	2	7	4	47	3	59	8	1	2	5	.286	0	1	5.76
1994 Albuquerque	AAA LA	3	0	0	0	4.1	21	7	4	4	0	0	0	0	3	0	4	0	0	0	1	.000	0	0	8.31
Calgary	AAA Sea	43	1	0	16	74	349	95	57	47	4	1	4	2	46	3	34	11	0	3	4	.429	0	0	5.72
1995 Tacoma	AAA Sea	8	3	0	4	23	109	31	21	21	1	0	3	2	12	0	8	0	0	0	3	.000	0	0	8.22
1996 Rochester	AAA Bal	8	0	0	5	8	42	11	7	1	0	0	0	1	4	0	4	2	0	1	1	.500	0	0	1.13
7 Min. YEARS		207	24	3	114	426.2	1967	486	288	230	28	11	26	18	242	7	298	44	2	22	32	.407	0	31	4.85

Juan Williams

Bats: Left **Throws:** Right **Pos:** OF **Ht:** 6'0" **Wt:** 180 **Born:** 10/9/72 **Age:** 24

Year Team	Lg Org	G	AB	H	2B	3B	HR	TB	R	RBI	TBB	IBB	SO	HBP	SH	SF	SB	CS	SB%	GDP	Avg	OBP	SLG
		BATTING															BASERUNNING				PERCENTAGES		
1990 Pulaski	R+ Atl	58	198	54	6	1	0	62	18	22	11	1	45	2	1	0	9	7	.56	6	.273	.318	.313
1991 Macon	A Atl	106	347	81	13	2	1	101	44	32	39	1	100	3	6	2	12	11	.52	5	.233	.315	.291
1992 Macon	A Atl	67	232	54	12	2	2	76	24	14	25	1	77	0	0	0	16	6	.73	2	.233	.307	.328
Pulaski	R+ Atl	47	169	47	6	4	6	79	26	31	13	1	46	0	1	1	9	3	.75	2	.278	.328	.467
1993 Durham	A+ Atl	124	403	93	16	2	11	146	49	44	36	4	120	1	6	1	11	12	.48	9	.231	.295	.362
1994 Durham	A+ Atl	122	394	86	14	0	19	157	55	57	54	1	131	1	0	4	7	10	.41	2	.218	.311	.398
1995 Greenville	AA Atl	62	192	60	14	2	15	123	40	39	19	3	44	0	0	3	4	3	.57	5	.313	.369	.641
Richmond	AAA Atl	45	129	34	5	0	5	54	18	11	17	0	38	0	0	1	1	3	.25	5	.264	.347	.419
1996 Richmond	AAA Atl	119	357	97	22	2	15	168	55	52	51	5	127	0	3	2	5	4	.56	10	.272	.361	.471
7 Min. YEARS		750	2421	606	108	15	74	966	329	302	265	17	728	7	17	14	74	59	.56	46	.250	.324	.399

Mitch Williams

Pitches: Left **Bats:** Left **Pos:** P **Ht:** 6' 4" **Wt:** 205 **Born:** 11/17/64 **Age:** 32

Year Team	Lg Org	G	GS	CG	GF	IP	BFP	H	R	ER	HR	SH	SF	HB	TBB	IBB	SO	WP	Bk	W	L	Pct.	ShO	Sv	ERA
		HOW MUCH HE PITCHED						WHAT HE GAVE UP												THE RESULTS					
1984 Reno	A+ SD	26	26	3	0	164	0	163	113	91	11	0	0	9	127	1	165	19	3	9	8	.529	1	0	4.99
1985 Salem	A+ Tex	22	21	1	1	99	471	57	64	60	6	2	2	6	117	0	138	12	1	6	9	.400	0	0	5.45

Year	Team	Lg	Org	G	GS	CG	GF	IP	BFP	H	R	ER	HR	SH	SF	HB	TBB	IBB	SO	WP	Bk	W	L	Pct.	ShO	Sv	ERA
	HOW MUCH HE PITCHED									**WHAT HE GAVE UP**												**THE RESULTS**					
	Tulsa	AA	Tex	6	6	0	0	33	165	17	24	17	1	2	1	2	48	0	37	3	1	2	2	.500	0	0	4.64
1996	Clearwater	A+	Phi	6	0	0	1	8	37	10	3	2	0	0	1	1	1	0	6	0	0	0	0	.000	0	0	2.25
	Scranton-WB	AAA	Phi	9	0	0	2	15	79	25	20	17	3	0	0	0	11	1	15	0	1	2	2	.500	0	0	10.20
1986	Texas	AL		80	0	0	38	98	435	69	39	39	8	1	3	11	79	8	90	5	5	8	6	.571	0	8	3.58
1987	Texas	AL		85	1	0	32	108.2	469	63	47	39	9	4	3	7	94	7	129	4	2	8	6	.571	0	6	3.23
1988	Texas	AL		67	0	0	51	68	296	48	38	35	4	3	4	6	47	3	61	5	6	2	7	.222	0	18	4.63
1989	Chicago	NL		76	0	0	61	81.2	365	71	27	24	6	2	5	8	52	4	67	6	4	4	4	.500	0	36	2.64
1990	Chicago	NL		59	2	0	39	66.1	310	60	38	29	4	5	3	1	50	6	55	4	2	1	8	.111	0	16	3.93
1991	Philadelphia	NL		69	0	0	60	88.1	386	56	24	23	4	4	4	8	62	5	84	4	1	12	5	.706	0	30	2.34
1992	Philadelphia	NL		66	0	0	56	81	368	69	39	34	4	8	3	6	64	2	74	5	3	5	8	.385	0	29	3.78
1993	Philadelphia	NL		65	0	0	57	62	281	56	30	23	3	4	2	2	44	1	60	6	0	3	7	.300	0	43	3.34
1994	Houston	NL		25	0	0	18	20	106	21	17	17	4	2	1	1	24	2	21	1	0	1	4	.200	0	6	7.65
1995	California	AL		20	0	0	3	10.2	65	13	10	8	1	0	1	2	21	0	9	2	1	1	2	.333	0	0	6.75
3	Min. YEARS			69	53	4	4	319	752	272	224	187	21	4	4	18	304	2	361	34	6	19	21	.475	1	0	5.28
10	Maj. YEARS			612	3	0	415	684.2	3081	526	309	271	47	33	29	52	537	38	650	42	24	45	57	.441	0	192	3.56

Reggie Williams

Bats: Both **Throws:** Right **Pos:** OF **Ht:** 6' 1" **Wt:** 189 **Born:** 5/5/66 **Age:** 31

Year	Team	Lg	Org	G	AB	H	2B	3B	HR	TB	R	RBI	TBB	IBB	SO	HBP	SH	SF	SB	CS	SB%	GDP	Avg	OBP	SLG
	BATTING																		**BASERUNNING**				**PERCENTAGES**		
1988	Everett	A-	SF	60	223	56	8	1	3	75	52	29	47	0	43	3	0	2	36	10	.78	5	.251	.385	.336
1989	Clinton	A	SF	68	236	46	9	2	3	68	38	18	29	0	66	3	5	1	14	9	.61	1	.195	.290	.288
	Boise	A-	—	42	153	41	5	1	3	57	33	14	24	0	29	2	0	1	18	5	.78	2	.268	.372	.373
1990	Quad City	A	Cal	58	189	46	11	2	3	70	50	12	39	0	60	4	2	1	24	6	.80	2	.243	.382	.370
1991	Palm Spring	A+	Cal	14	44	13	1	0	1	17	10	2	21	0	15	1	1	0	6	5	.55	0	.295	.530	.386
	Midland	AA	Cal	83	319	99	12	3	1	120	77	30	62	2	67	0	5	3	21	9	.70	3	.310	.419	.376
1992	Edmonton	AAA	Cal	139	519	141	26	9	3	194	96	64	88	1	110	3	7	8	44	14	.76	9	.272	.375	.374
1993	Vancouver	AAA	Cal	130	481	132	17	6	2	167	92	53	88	2	99	5	9	6	50	17	.75	7	.274	.388	.347
1994	Albuquerque	AAA	LA	104	288	90	15	8	4	133	55	42	33	1	62	0	1	2	21	10	.68	6	.313	.381	.462
1995	Albuquerque	AAA	LA	66	234	73	15	5	6	116	44	29	30	0	46	1	1	3	6	4	.60	3	.312	.388	.496
1996	Albuquerque	AAA	LA	92	352	101	25	2	6	148	60	42	37	5	72	1	5	1	17	7	.71	6	.287	.355	.420
1992	California	AL		14	26	6	1	1	0	9	5	2	1	0	10	0	0	0	0	2	.00	0	.231	.259	.346
1995	Los Angeles	NL		15	11	1	0	0	0	1	2	1	2	0	3	0	0	0	0	0	.00	0	.091	.231	.091
9	Min. YEARS			856	3038	838	144	39	35	1165	607	335	498	11	669	23	36	28	257	96	.73	44	.276	.379	.383
2	Maj. YEARS			29	37	7	1	1	0	10	7	3	3	0	13	0	0	0	0	2	.00	0	.189	.250	.270

Slim Williams

Pitches: Left **Bats:** Left **Pos:** P **Ht:** 6'7" **Wt:** 232 **Born:** 5/18/65 **Age:** 32

Year	Team	Lg	Org	G	GS	CG	GF	IP	BFP	H	R	ER	HR	SH	SF	HB	TBB	IBB	SO	WP	Bk	W	L	Pct.	ShO	Sv	ERA
	HOW MUCH HE PITCHED									**WHAT HE GAVE UP**												**THE RESULTS**					
1984	Great Falls	R+	LA	8	0	0	3	11	0	10	14	11	0	0	0	0	16	0	9	1	0	0	1	.000	0	0	9.00
	Dodgers	R	LA	2	0	0	0	3	20	4	4	0	0	0	0	0	4	0	1	0	0	0	0	.000	0	0	0.00
1985	Dodgers	R	LA	13	13	1	0	66.2	306	54	35	28	1	3	2	2	55	0	59	5	4	4	4	.500	1	0	3.78
1986	Vero Beach	A+	LA	30	6	0	16	60	285	47	35	29	1	6	3	1	66	2	40	8	4	1	1	.500	0	0	4.35
1987	Visalia	A+	Min	13	13	2	0	85	373	66	38	21	5	6	1	5	62	2	81	10	0	7	4	.636	0	0	2.22
1988	Visalia	A+	Min	37	0	0	28	51	221	41	23	21	2	4	2	2	33	0	55	5	3	3	4	.429	0	12	3.71
1989	Orlando	AA	Min	43	0	0	39	53.1	240	50	23	18	3	1	1	0	35	1	62	1	2	6	4	.600	0	14	3.04
	Portland	AAA	Min	16	0	0	8	23.2	112	24	15	11	0	0	1	0	18	0	22	2	1	3	2	.600	0	3	4.18
1990	Portland	AAA	Min	51	3	0	27	84	388	73	64	47	4	3	6	3	74	2	62	7	1	4	6	.400	0	3	5.04
1991	Phoenix	AAA	SF	30	28	3	1	160	748	192	120	106	17	3	5	1	93	0	69	12	5	7	9	.438	0	0	5.96
1993	Orlando	AA	ChN	15	14	0	0	90.2	377	84	29	25	4	5	0	2	38	1	65	2	2	5	5	.500	0	0	2.48
	Iowa	AAA	ChN	17	13	0	1	78	329	74	32	30	5	5	2	1	37	0	49	3	2	5	3	.625	0	0	3.46
1994	Harrisburg	AA	Mon	1	1	0	0	4	18	3	1	0	0	0	0	0	2	0	5	0	0	0	0	.000	0	0	0.00
	Ottawa	AAA	Mon	27	11	1	3	99.1	448	105	60	50	5	2	3	1	53	1	57	7	0	9	2	.818	1	1	4.53
1995	Rochester	AAA	Bal	32	16	0	6	119	522	110	55	46	3	1	5	2	65	0	100	12	4	12	6	.667	0	2	3.48
	Norfolk	AAA	NYN	32	16	0	6	119	522	110	55	46	3	1	5	2	65	0	100	12	4	12	6	.667	0	2	3.48
1996	Buffalo	AAA	Cle	35	13	0	2	113.2	496	116	60	51	13	3	3	1	45	0	96	9	0	12	3	.800	0	0	4.04
12	Min. YEARS			402	147	7	140	1221.1	5405	1163	663	540	66	43	39	23	761	9	932	96	32	90	60	.600	2	37	3.98

Todd Williams

Pitches: Right **Bats:** Right **Pos:** P **Ht:** 6' 3" **Wt:** 185 **Born:** 2/13/71 **Age:** 26

Year	Team	Lg	Org	G	GS	CG	GF	IP	BFP	H	R	ER	HR	SH	SF	HB	TBB	IBB	SO	WP	Bk	W	L	Pct.	ShO	Sv	ERA
	HOW MUCH HE PITCHED									**WHAT HE GAVE UP**												**THE RESULTS**					
1991	Great Falls	R+	LA	28	0	0	14	53	232	50	26	16	1	0	0	1	24	1	59	4	1	5	2	.714	0	8	2.72
1992	Bakersfield	A+	LA	13	0	0	13	15.2	64	11	4	4	1	1	0	0	7	1	11	0	0	0	0	.000	0	9	2.30
	San Antonio	AA	LA	39	0	0	34	44	196	47	17	16	0	4	1	1	23	6	35	3	0	7	4	.636	0	13	3.27
1993	Albuquerque	AAA	LA	65	0	0	50	70.1	321	87	44	39	2	0	1	1	31	6	56	6	0	5	5	.500	0	21	4.99
1994	Albuquerque	AAA	LA	59	0	0	36	72.1	299	78	29	25	5	1	3	6	17	3	30	6	1	4	2	.667	0	13	3.11
1995	Albuquerque	AAA	LA	25	0	0	5	45.1	203	59	21	17	4	1	1	1	15	4	23	1	2	4	1	.800	0	0	3.38
1996	Edmonton	AAA	Oak	35	10	0	7	91.2	427	125	71	56	4	2	5	3	37	3	33	3	0	5	3	.625	0	0	5.50
1995	Los Angeles	NL		16	0	0	5	19.1	83	19	11	11	3	3	1	0	7	2	8	0	0	2	2	.500	0	0	5.12
6	Min. YEARS			264	10	0	159	392.1	1742	457	212	173	17	9	11	13	154	24	247	23	4	30	17	.638	0	64	3.97

Antone Williamson

Bats: Left **Throws:** Right **Pos:** 1B-DH **Ht:** 6'1" **Wt:** 195 **Born:** 7/18/73 **Age:** 23

			BATTING															BASERUNNING				PERCENTAGES		
Year	Team	Lg Org	G	AB	H	2B	3B	HR	TB	R	RBI	TBB	IBB	SO	HBP	SH	SF	SB	CS	SB%	GDP	Avg	OBP	SLG
1994	Helena	R+ Mil	6	26	11	2	1	0	15	5	4	2	0	4	0	0	0	0	0	.00	1	.423	.464	.577
	Stockton	A+ Mil	23	85	19	4	0	3	32	6	13	7	0	19	0	1	3	0	1	.00	1	.224	.274	.376
	El Paso	AA Mil	14	48	12	3	0	1	18	8	9	7	0	8	0	0	1	0	0	.00	1	.250	.339	.375
1995	El Paso	AA Mil	104	392	121	30	6	7	184	62	90	47	3	57	3	0	4	3	1	.75	10	.309	.383	.469
1996	New Orleans	AAA Mil	55	199	52	10	1	5	79	23	23	19	1	40	1	0	2	1	0	1.00	9	.261	.326	.397
3 Min. YEARS			202	750	215	49	8	16	328	104	139	82	4	128	4	1	10	4	2	.67	22	.287	.356	.437

Brandon Wilson

Bats: Right **Throws:** Right **Pos:** SS **Ht:** 6'1" **Wt:** 175 **Born:** 2/26/69 **Age:** 28

			BATTING															BASERUNNING				PERCENTAGES		
Year	Team	Lg Org	G	AB	H	2B	3B	HR	TB	R	RBI	TBB	IBB	SO	HBP	SH	SF	SB	CS	SB%	GDP	Avg	OBP	SLG
1990	White Sox	R ChA	11	41	11	1	0	0	12	4	5	4	0	5	0	1	1	3	1	.75	1	.268	.326	.293
	Utica	A- ChA	53	165	41	2	0	0	43	31	14	28	0	45	0	3	2	14	5	.74	1	.248	.354	.261
1991	South Bend	A ChA	125	463	145	18	6	2	181	75	49	61	2	70	2	7	4	41	11	.79	3	.313	.392	.391
	Birmingham	AA ChA	2	10	4	1	0	0	5	3	2	0	0	2	0	0	0	0	0	.00	0	.400	.400	.500
1992	Sarasota	A+ ChA	103	399	118	22	6	4	164	68	54	45	2	64	4	5	2	30	16	.65	4	.296	.371	.411
	Birmingham	AA ChA	27	107	29	4	0	0	33	10	4	4	0	16	0	0	0	5	0	1.00	1	.271	.297	.308
1993	Birmingham	AA ChA	137	500	135	19	5	2	170	76	48	52	0	77	3	4	3	43	10	.81	7	.270	.341	.340
1994	Nashville	AAA ChA	114	370	83	16	3	5	120	42	26	30	0	67	3	10	2	13	5	.72	4	.224	.286	.324
1995	Nashville	AAA ChA	27	85	25	5	0	1	33	8	10	4	0	11	0	1	0	3	1	.75	3	.294	.326	.388
	Indianapolis	AAA Cin	4	12	2	0	0	0	2	3	0	2	0	1	0	0	0	0	0	.00	0	.167	.286	.167
	Chattanooga	AA Cin	75	308	101	29	1	9	159	56	50	28	0	52	3	2	2	12	6	.67	7	.328	.387	.516
1996	Indianapolis	AAA Cin	95	305	71	7	3	4	96	48	31	39	0	53	0	1	2	10	6	.63	8	.233	.318	.315
7 Min. YEARS			773	2765	765	124	24	27	1018	424	293	297	4	463	15	34	18	174	61	.74	39	.277	.348	.368

Craig Wilson

Bats: Right **Throws:** Right **Pos:** SS **Ht:** 6'1" **Wt:** 190 **Born:** 9/3/70 **Age:** 26

			BATTING															BASERUNNING				PERCENTAGES		
Year	Team	Lg Org	G	AB	H	2B	3B	HR	TB	R	RBI	TBB	IBB	SO	HBP	SH	SF	SB	CS	SB%	GDP	Avg	OBP	SLG
1993	South Bend	A ChA	132	455	118	27	2	5	164	56	59	49	2	50	8	7	6	4	4	.50	16	.259	.338	.360
1994	Pr. William	A+ ChA	131	496	131	36	4	4	187	70	66	58	2	44	6	5	6	1	2	.33	16	.264	.345	.377
1995	Birmingham	AA ChA	132	471	136	19	1	4	169	56	46	43	0	44	5	10	2	2	2	.50	21	.289	.353	.359
1996	Nashville	AAA ChA	44	123	22	4	1	1	31	13	6	10	0	15	0	5	1	0	0	.00	6	.179	.239	.252
	Birmingham	AA ChA	58	202	57	9	0	3	75	36	26	40	1	28	1	6	4	1	1	.50	7	.282	.397	.371
4 Min. YEARS			497	1747	464	95	8	17	626	231	203	200	5	181	20	33	19	8	9	.47	66	.266	.344	.358

Enrique Wilson

Bats: Both **Throws:** Right **Pos:** SS **Ht:** 5'11" **Wt:** 160 **Born:** 7/27/75 **Age:** 21

			BATTING															BASERUNNING				PERCENTAGES		
Year	Team	Lg Org	G	AB	H	2B	3B	HR	TB	R	RBI	TBB	IBB	SO	HBP	SH	SF	SB	CS	SB%	GDP	Avg	OBP	SLG
1992	Twins	R Min	13	44	15	1	0	0	16	12	8	4	0	4	4	0	1	3	0	1.00	0	.341	.434	.364
1993	Elizabethtn	R+ Min	58	197	57	8	4	13	112	42	50	14	1	18	6	0	2	5	4	.56	1	.289	.352	.569
1994	Columbus	A Cle	133	512	143	28	12	10	225	82	72	44	5	34	6	0	4	21	13	.62	7	.279	.341	.439
1995	Kinston	A+ Cle	117	464	124	24	7	6	180	55	52	25	2	38	2	4	10	18	19	.49	10	.267	.301	.388
1996	Canton-Akrn	AA Cle	117	484	147	17	5	5	189	70	50	31	2	46	4	0	7	23	16	.59	9	.304	.346	.390
	Buffalo	AAA Cle	3	8	4	1	0	0	5	1	0	1	0	1	0	0	0	0	2	.00	1	.500	.556	.625
5 Min. YEARS			441	1709	490	79	28	34	727	262	232	119	10	141	22	4	24	70	54	.56	28	.287	.337	.425

Gary Wilson

Pitches: Right **Bats:** Right **Pos:** P **Ht:** 6' 3" **Wt:** 190 **Born:** 1/1/70 **Age:** 27

			HOW MUCH HE PITCHED						WHAT HE GAVE UP												THE RESULTS					
Year	Team	Lg Org	G	GS	CG	GF	IP	BFP	H	R	ER	HR	SH	SF	HB	TBB	IBB	SO	WP	Bk	W	L	Pct.	ShO	Sv	ERA
1992	Welland	A- Pit	13	4	0	5	42.1	170	27	9	5	0	1	0	1	13	1	40	1	0	3	2	.600	0	0	1.06
	Augusta	A Pit	7	7	0	0	41.2	177	43	22	17	2	3	3	3	7	0	27	1	1	2	3	.400	0	0	3.67
1993	Salem	A+ Pit	15	15	0	0	78.1	356	102	58	50	15	1	1	2	25	0	54	3	0	5	5	.500	0	0	5.74
	Augusta	A Pit	20	6	0	4	51	229	66	35	31	4	1	1	3	11	0	42	3	1	3	7	.300	0	0	5.47
1994	Salem	A+ Pit	6	6	1	0	35	147	41	12	9	2	0	0	0	4	0	26	3	0	3	1	.750	1	0	2.31
	Carolina	AA Pit	22	22	7	0	161.2	654	144	55	46	11	8	5	10	37	0	97	2	0	8	5	.615	2	0	2.56
1995	Carolina	AA Pit	1	1	0	0	4.2	16	0	0	0	0	0	0	0	3	0	5	0	0	0	0	.000	0	0	0.00
	Calgary	AAA Pit	7	5	0	0	21	91	19	16	10	1	1	2	0	12	0	17	2	1	1	2	.333	0	0	4.29
1996	Calgary	AAA Pit	27	27	1	0	161.1	725	209	105	91	18	6	6	9	44	1	88	2	1	6	9	.400	0	0	5.08
1995	Pittsburgh	NL	10	0	0	1	14.1	61	13	8	8	2	0	0	2	5	0	8	1	0	0	1	.000	0	0	5.02
5 Min. YEARS			118	93	9	9	597	2565	651	312	259	53	21	18	28	156	2	396	17	4	31	34	.477	3	0	3.90

Pookie Wilson

Bats: Left **Throws:** Left **Pos:** OF **Ht:** 5'10" **Wt:** 180 **Born:** 10/24/70 **Age:** 26

			BATTING															BASERUNNING				PERCENTAGES		
Year	Team	Lg Org	G	AB	H	2B	3B	HR	TB	R	RBI	TBB	IBB	SO	HBP	SH	SF	SB	CS	SB%	GDP	Avg	OBP	SLG
1992	Salt Lake	R+ —	66	241	80	5	2	0	89	57	20	26	0	24	4	2	2	24	12	.67	5	.332	.403	.369
1993	Kane County	A Fla	129	469	117	8	2	0	129	74	27	52	0	55	9	10	2	34	15	.69	6	.249	.335	.275

					BATTING													BASERUNNING				PERCENTAGES		
Year	Team	Lg	Org	G	AB	H	2B	3B	HR	TB	R	RBI	TBB	IBB	SO	HBP	SH	SF	SB	CS	SB%	GDP	Avg	OBP	SLG
1994	Brevard Cty	A+	Fla	125	483	129	12	4	1	152	81	29	50	1	49	3	8	3	26	14	.65	4	.267	.338	.315
1995	Portland	AA	Fla	107	348	95	13	5	3	127	51	44	18	2	51	11	5	4	9	4	.69	9	.273	.325	.365
1996	Portland	AA	Fla	113	375	96	16	5	6	140	46	35	33	3	49	8	9	4	7	10	.41	4	.256	.326	.373
5 Min. YEARS				540	1916	517	54	18	10	637	309	155	179	6	228	35	34	15	100	55	.65	28	.270	.341	.332

Tom Wilson

Bats: Right **Throws:** Right **Pos:** C **Ht:** 6'3" **Wt:** 185 **Born:** 12/19/70 **Age:** 26

					BATTING													BASERUNNING				PERCENTAGES		
Year	Team	Lg	Org	G	AB	H	2B	3B	HR	TB	R	RBI	TBB	IBB	SO	HBP	SH	SF	SB	CS	SB%	GDP	Avg	OBP	SLG
1991	Oneonta	A-	NYA	70	243	59	12	2	4	87	38	42	34	2	71	3	0	5	4	4	.50	6	.243	.337	.358
1992	Greensboro	A	NYA	117	395	83	22	0	6	123	50	48	68	0	128	3	1	8	2	1	.67	8	.210	.325	.311
1993	Greensboro	A	NYA	120	394	98	20	1	10	150	55	63	91	0	112	4	3	8	2	5	.29	5	.249	.388	.381
1994	Albany-Colo	AA	NYA	123	408	100	20	1	7	143	54	42	58	2	100	6	4	4	4	6	.40	6	.245	.345	.350
1995	Columbus	AAA	NYA	22	62	16	3	1	0	21	11	9	9	0	10	0	2	0	0	0	.00	0	.258	.352	.339
	Tampa	A+	NYA	17	48	8	0	0	0	8	3	2	11	0	13	0	1	1	1	0	1.00	0	.167	.317	.167
	Norwich	AA	NYA	28	84	12	4	0	0	16	6	4	17	0	22	0	0	0	0	0	.00	3	.143	.287	.190
1996	Columbus	AAA	NYA	1	1	0	0	0	0	0	0	0	1	0	0	0	0	0	0	0	.00	0	.000	.500	.000
	Buffalo	AAA	Cle	72	208	56	14	2	9	101	28	30	35	0	66	6	1	0	0	1	.00	4	.269	.390	.486
6 Min. YEARS				570	1843	432	95	7	36	649	245	240	324	4	522	22	12	26	13	17	.43	32	.234	.351	.352

Judd Wilstead

Pitches: Right **Bats:** Left **Pos:** P **Ht:** 6'4" **Wt:** 205 **Born:** 3/14/73 **Age:** 24

				HOW MUCH HE PITCHED						WHAT HE GAVE UP												THE RESULTS					
Year	Team	Lg	Org	G	GS	CG	GF	IP	BFP	H	R	ER	HR	SH	SF	HB	TBB	IBB	SO	WP	Bk	W	L	Pct.	ShO	Sv	ERA
1991	Brewers	R	Mil	1	1	0	0	1.1	7	0	1	1	0	0	0	0	3	0	3	2	0	0	0	.000	0	0	6.75
1993	Helena	R+	Mil	11	10	0	0	42.1	214	55	46	40	5	2	2	3	36	0	17	6	4	1	5	.167	0	0	8.50
1994	Beloit	A	Mil	26	9	0	10	75	344	82	48	38	5	6	1	7	36	2	46	2	1	5	6	.455	0	0	4.56
1995	Stockton	A+	Mil	31	21	0	1	139.2	653	165	94	79	15	10	5	14	71	1	72	12	3	8	9	.471	0	0	5.09
1996	El Paso	AA	Mil	7	0	0	3	17	79	19	18	16	1	1	3	2	7	0	11	1	0	0	1	.000	0	0	8.47
5 Min. YEARS				76	41	0	14	275.1	1297	321	207	174	26	19	11	26	153	3	149	23	8	14	21	.400	0	0	5.69

Chris Wimmer

Bats: Right **Throws:** Right **Pos:** OF **Ht:** 5'11" **Wt:** 170 **Born:** 9/25/70 **Age:** 26

					BATTING													BASERUNNING				PERCENTAGES		
Year	Team	Lg	Org	G	AB	H	2B	3B	HR	TB	R	RBI	TBB	IBB	SO	HBP	SH	SF	SB	CS	SB%	GDP	Avg	OBP	SLG
1993	San Jose	A+	SF	123	493	130	21	4	3	168	76	53	42	1	72	8	7	6	49	12	.80	6	.264	.328	.341
1994	Shreveport	AA	SF	126	462	131	21	3	4	170	63	49	25	2	56	8	5	4	21	13	.62	7	.284	.329	.368
1995	Phoenix	AAA	SF	132	449	118	23	4	2	155	55	44	31	1	49	13	5	5	13	7	.65	10	.263	.325	.345
1996	Louisville	AAA	StL	112	345	86	11	2	2	107	40	23	16	0	41	6	3	2	11	3	.79	11	.249	.293	.310
4 Min. YEARS				493	1749	465	76	13	11	600	234	169	114	4	218	35	20	17	94	35	.73	34	.266	.321	.343

Dax Winslett

Pitches: Right **Bats:** Right **Pos:** P **Ht:** 6'1" **Wt:** 200 **Born:** 1/1/72 **Age:** 25

				HOW MUCH HE PITCHED						WHAT HE GAVE UP												THE RESULTS					
Year	Team	Lg	Org	G	GS	CG	GF	IP	BFP	H	R	ER	HR	SH	SF	HB	TBB	IBB	SO	WP	Bk	W	L	Pct.	ShO	Sv	ERA
1993	Yakima	A-	LA	8	4	0	3	32.2	157	46	23	20	2	1	1	6	10	0	25	2	3	0	2	.000	0	1	5.51
1994	Bakersfield	A+	LA	27	27	0	0	159.1	686	163	89	79	13	10	4	6	57	0	111	12	1	10	11	.476	0	0	4.46
1995	Daytona	A+	ChN	26	25	0	0	152	627	148	59	47	11	4	2	2	39	0	111	13	2	12	6	.667	0	0	2.78
	Vero Beach	A+	LA	26	25	0	0	152	627	148	59	47	11	4	2	2	39	0	111	13	2	12	6	.667	0	0	2.78
1996	Orlando	AA	ChN	4	4	0	0	20.2	97	31	19	18	4	1	1	1	7	0	13	2	0	1	3	.250	0	0	7.84
	Daytona	A+	ChN	2	1	0	0	6	34	10	10	9	1	0	1	1	5	1	3	0	0	0	1	.000	0	0	13.50
4 Min. YEARS				93	86	0	3	522.2	2228	546	259	220	42	20	11	18	157	1	374	42	8	35	29	.547	0	1	3.79

Shannon Withem

Pitches: Right **Bats:** Right **Pos:** P **Ht:** 6'3" **Wt:** 185 **Born:** 9/21/72 **Age:** 24

				HOW MUCH HE PITCHED						WHAT HE GAVE UP												THE RESULTS					
Year	Team	Lg	Org	G	GS	CG	GF	IP	BFP	H	R	ER	HR	SH	SF	HB	TBB	IBB	SO	WP	Bk	W	L	Pct.	ShO	Sv	ERA
1990	Bristol	R+	Det	14	13	0	1	62	288	70	43	37	4	0	0	5	35	1	48	12	2	3	9	.250	0	0	5.37
1991	Fayettevlle	A	Det	11	11	0	0	47.2	241	71	53	45	2	2	0	0	30	0	19	8	0	2	6	.250	0	0	8.50
	Niagara Fal	A-	Det	8	3	0	2	27	115	26	12	10	0	0	2	2	11	0	17	2	0	1	2	.333	0	0	3.33
1992	Fayettevlle	A	Det	22	2	0	8	38	173	40	23	20	3	2	2	4	20	0	34	9	2	1	3	.250	0	2	4.74
1993	Lakeland	A+	Det	16	16	2	0	113	462	108	47	43	5	1	5	5	24	0	62	3	0	10	2	.833	1	0	3.42
1994	Trenton	AA	Det	25	25	5	0	178	735	190	80	68	10	4	4	4	37	0	135	5	2	7	12	.368	1	0	3.44
1995	Jacksonvlle	AA	Det	19	18	0	1	108	481	142	77	69	17	5	1	5	24	1	80	4	0	5	8	.385	0	0	5.75
1996	St. Lucie	A+	NYN	2	2	0	0	14	53	8	2	2	0	0	0	1	1	0	13	1	0	1	0	1.000	0	0	1.29
	Binghamton	AA	NYN	12	12	1	0	86	355	86	32	31	8	3	0	3	17	0	59	2	0	6	3	.667	1	0	3.24
	Norfolk	AAA	NYN	8	8	0	0	42.2	188	56	25	22	6	2	1	0	6	0	30	2	0	3	3	.500	0	0	4.64
7 Min. YEARS				137	110	8	12	716.1	3091	797	394	347	55	19	15	29	205	2	497	48	6	39	48	.448	3	2	4.36

Trey Witte

Pitches: Right **Bats:** Right **Pos:** P **Ht:** 6'1" **Wt:** 190 **Born:** 1/15/70 **Age:** 27

			HOW MUCH HE PITCHED						WHAT HE GAVE UP												THE RESULTS					
Year	Team	Lg Org	G	GS	CG	GF	IP	BFP	H	R	ER	HR	SH	SF	HB	TBB	IBB	SO	WP	Bk	W	L	Pct.	ShO	Sv	ERA
1991	Bellingham	A- Sea	27	0	0	22	45	189	27	12	11	0	1	1	0	31	1	44	5	0	2	2	.500	0	8	2.20
1992	San Bernrdo	A+ Sea	21	0	0	10	36.2	183	58	36	27	3	3	2	2	11	0	27	3	1	1	1	.500	0	1	6.63
1993	Appleton	A Sea	28	14	1	3	101	425	111	57	48	8	4	8	9	22	0	62	3	0	3	9	.250	0	0	4.28
1994	Riverside	A+ Sea	25	0	0	4	54.1	235	57	29	26	2	1	2	5	15	2	45	3	0	4	3	.571	0	0	4.31
1995	Port City	AA Sea	48	0	0	34	62.1	250	48	17	12	0	6	3	5	14	0	39	0	1	3	2	.600	0	11	1.73
1996	Tacoma	AAA Sea	35	0	0	20	46	191	47	12	11	2	3	3	1	13	2	22	1	0	2	2	.500	0	7	2.15
6 Min. YEARS			184	14	1	93	345.1	1473	348	163	135	15	18	19	22	106	5	239	15	2	15	19	.441	0	27	3.52

Joel Wolfe

Bats: Right **Throws:** Right **Pos:** 1B **Ht:** 6'3" **Wt:** 205 **Born:** 6/18/70 **Age:** 27

			BATTING														BASERUNNING				PERCENTAGES		
Year	Team	Lg Org	G	AB	H	2B	3B	HR	TB	R	RBI	TBB	IBB	SO	HBP	SH	SF	SB	CS	SB%	GDP	Avg	OBP	SLG
1991	Sou. Oregon	A- Oak	59	251	76	17	3	2	105	49	34	25	0	28	3	0	0	19	5	.79	8	.303	.373	.418
1992	Reno	A+ Oak	122	463	118	18	5	1	149	80	44	59	1	72	0	4	2	19	13	.59	15	.255	.338	.322
1993	Modesto	A+ Oak	87	300	105	29	1	6	154	54	56	51	0	42	6	0	6	18	14	.56	5	.350	.446	.513
	Huntsville	AA Oak	36	134	40	6	0	3	55	20	18	13	1	24	0	1	0	6	3	.67	5	.299	.361	.410
1994	Huntsville	AA Oak	121	436	120	26	3	5	167	65	57	61	2	79	4	6	7	26	10	.72	13	.275	.364	.383
1995	Edmonton	AAA Oak	11	39	8	3	0	0	11	4	4	2	0	7	0	1	1	0	2	.00	1	.205	.238	.282
	Huntsville	AA Oak	108	399	102	15	2	12	157	58	41	54	4	75	5	6	2	23	12	.66	5	.256	.350	.393
1996	Arkansas	AA StL	72	200	43	11	2	4	70	29	26	28	1	36	3	2	1	11	7	.61	5	.215	.319	.350
6 Min. YEARS			616	2222	612	125	16	33	868	359	280	293	9	363	21	20	19	122	66	.65	57	.275	.362	.391

Mike Wolff

Bats: Right **Throws:** Right **Pos:** OF **Ht:** 6'1" **Wt:** 195 **Born:** 12/19/70 **Age:** 26

			BATTING														BASERUNNING				PERCENTAGES		
Year	Team	Lg Org	G	AB	H	2B	3B	HR	TB	R	RBI	TBB	IBB	SO	HBP	SH	SF	SB	CS	SB%	GDP	Avg	OBP	SLG
1992	Boise	A- Cal	68	244	66	12	1	11	113	49	39	32	1	60	6	1	2	5	5	.50	0	.270	.366	.463
1993	Cedar Rapds	A Cal	120	407	100	18	5	17	179	63	72	74	1	104	2	5	5	8	8	.50	4	.246	.361	.440
1994	Midland	AA Cal	113	397	115	30	1	13	186	64	58	54	3	91	6	5	6	10	9	.53	4	.290	.378	.469
1995	Midland	AA Cal	127	445	135	28	3	14	211	76	70	65	3	83	3	4	7	10	9	.53	10	.303	.390	.474
1996	Lk Elsinore	A+ Cal	12	42	12	3	0	2	21	12	7	9	0	10	0	0	0	3	0	1.00	1	.286	.412	.500
	Vancouver	AAA Cal	71	256	64	15	3	10	115	46	38	34	2	69	4	3	6	6	4	.60	3	.250	.340	.449
5 Min. YEARS			511	1791	492	106	13	67	825	310	284	268	10	417	21	18	26	42	35	.55	22	.275	.371	.461

Jason Wood

Bats: Right **Throws:** Right **Pos:** 3B **Ht:** 6'1" **Wt:** 170 **Born:** 12/16/69 **Age:** 27

			BATTING														BASERUNNING				PERCENTAGES		
Year	Team	Lg Org	G	AB	H	2B	3B	HR	TB	R	RBI	TBB	IBB	SO	HBP	SH	SF	SB	CS	SB%	GDP	Avg	OBP	SLG
1991	Sou. Oregon	A- Oak	44	142	44	3	4	3	64	30	23	28	0	30	2	2	3	5	2	.71	0	.310	.423	.451
1992	Modesto	A+ Oak	128	454	105	28	3	6	157	66	49	40	1	106	4	3	5	5	4	.56	15	.231	.296	.346
1993	Huntsville	AA Oak	103	370	85	21	2	3	119	44	36	33	0	97	2	9	3	2	4	.33	7	.230	.294	.322
1994	Huntsville	AA Oak	134	468	128	29	2	6	179	54	84	46	1	83	6	5	15	3	6	.33	9	.274	.336	.382
1995	Edmonton	AAA Oak	127	421	99	20	5	2	135	49	50	29	3	72	3	6	12	1	4	.20	12	.235	.282	.321
1996	Huntsville	AA Oak	133	491	128	21	1	20	211	77	84	72	2	87	5	2	11	2	5	.29	14	.261	.354	.430
	Edmonton	AAA Oak	3	12	0	0	0	0	0	0	0	5	0	6	0	0	0	0	1	.00	0	.000	.294	.000
6 Min. YEARS			672	2358	589	122	17	40	865	320	326	253	7	481	22	27	49	18	26	.41	57	.250	.322	.367

Dickie Woodridge

Bats: Left **Throws:** Right **Pos:** 2B **Ht:** 5'9" **Wt:** 170 **Born:** 1/24/71 **Age:** 26

			BATTING														BASERUNNING				PERCENTAGES		
Year	Team	Lg Org	G	AB	H	2B	3B	HR	TB	R	RBI	TBB	IBB	SO	HBP	SH	SF	SB	CS	SB%	GDP	Avg	OBP	SLG
1993	Spokane	A- SD	70	250	66	13	5	1	92	42	34	49	1	21	4	2	2	16	5	.76	4	.264	.390	.368
1994	Springfield	A SD	96	261	65	9	0	2	80	33	33	34	0	30	2	6	3	14	9	.61	3	.249	.337	.307
1995	Rancho Cuca	A+ SD	116	358	101	9	3	3	125	67	58	71	1	40	2	2	5	9	4	.69	5	.282	.399	.349
1996	Rancho Cuca	A+ SD	36	141	42	4	3	2	58	32	23	24	1	14	5	0	1	1	0	1.00	3	.298	.415	.411
	Memphis	AA SD	34	65	10	0	0	0	10	10	11	16	1	6	0	1	2	1	0	1.00	1	.154	.313	.154
4 Min. YEARS			352	1075	284	35	11	8	365	184	159	194	4	111	13	11	13	41	18	.69	16	.264	.379	.340

Brian Woods

Pitches: Right **Bats:** Left **Pos:** P **Ht:** 6'6" **Wt:** 212 **Born:** 6/7/71 **Age:** 26

			HOW MUCH HE PITCHED						WHAT HE GAVE UP												THE RESULTS					
Year	Team	Lg Org	G	GS	CG	GF	IP	BFP	H	R	ER	HR	SH	SF	HB	TBB	IBB	SO	WP	Bk	W	L	Pct.	ShO	Sv	ERA
1993	White Sox	R ChA	2	2	0	0	8	32	4	3	2	0	0	0	1	6	0	6	2	0	0	0	.000	0	0	2.25
	Hickory	A ChA	10	10	0	0	61	250	49	20	17	3	0	1	3	31	0	53	2	1	2	5	.286	0	0	2.51
	South Bend	A ChA	2	1	0	1	7	31	7	5	3	0	0	1	0	3	0	4	2	0	0	1	.000	0	0	3.86
1994	South Bend	A ChA	20	18	2	2	115.1	499	108	65	50	9	5	3	5	49	0	107	10	4	4	12	.250	0	0	3.90
1995	Mohawk Vall	IND —	14	13	0	0	81.1	338	75	35	33	5	2	1	3	23	0	69	1	1	7	2	.778	0	0	3.65
	Pr. William	A+ ChA	41	40	3	0	220.2	970	230	124	113	19	7	5	17	76	1	171	13	4	16	17	.485	0	0	4.61
1996	Birmingham	AA ChA	53	0	0	26	67	301	59	32	28	11	4	0	7	38	2	46	1	0	5	5	.500	0	5	3.76
4 Min. YEARS			142	84	5	29	560.1	2421	532	284	246	47	18	11	36	226	3	456	31	10	34	42	.447	0	5	3.95

Ken Woods

Bats: Right **Throws:** Right **Pos:** 3B **Ht:** 5'9" **Wt:** 173 **Born:** 8/2/70 **Age:** 26

		BATTING															BASERUNNING				PERCENTAGES		
Year Team	Lg Org	G	AB	H	2B	3B	HR	TB	R	RBI	TBB	IBB	SO	HBP	SH	SF	SB	CS	SB%	GDP	Avg	OBP	SLG
1992 Everett	A- SF	64	257	65	9	1	0	76	50	31	35	1	46	7	1	0	20	17	.54	2	.253	.358	.296
1993 Clinton	A SF	108	320	90	10	1	4	114	56	44	41	1	55	4	7	2	30	5	.86	13	.281	.368	.356
1994 San Jose	A+ SF	90	336	100	18	3	6	142	58	49	45	0	43	4	3	3	15	7	.68	9	.298	.384	.423
1995 Shreveport	AA SF	89	209	53	11	0	3	73	30	23	23	2	29	1	2	1	4	5	.44	4	.254	.329	.349
1996 Shreveport	AA SF	83	287	80	17	1	1	102	36	29	29	0	35	4	4	6	14	10	.58	11	.279	.347	.355
Phoenix	AAA SF	56	208	58	12	1	2	78	32	13	19	0	29	1	0	3	3	4	.43	6	.279	.338	.375
5 Min. YEARS		490	1617	446	77	7	16	585	262	189	192	4	237	21	17	15	86	48	.64	45	.276	.357	.362

Tyrone Woods

Bats: Right **Throws:** Right **Pos:** DH **Ht:** 6'1" **Wt:** 190 **Born:** 8/19/69 **Age:** 27

		BATTING															BASERUNNING				PERCENTAGES		
Year Team	Lg Org	G	AB	H	2B	3B	HR	TB	R	RBI	TBB	IBB	SO	HBP	SH	SF	SB	CS	SB%	GDP	Avg	OBP	SLG
1988 Expos	R Mon	43	149	18	2	0	2	26	12	12	7	0	47	0	0	2	2	4	.33	3	.121	.158	.174
1989 Jamestown	A- Mon	63	209	55	6	4	9	96	23	29	20	1	59	2	0	3	8	9	.47	5	.263	.329	.459
1990 Rockford	A Mon	123	455	110	27	5	8	171	50	46	45	1	121	1	0	3	5	7	.42	13	.242	.310	.376
1991 W. Palm Bch	A+ Mon	96	295	65	15	3	5	101	34	31	28	0	85	3	0	3	4	4	.50	5	.220	.292	.342
1992 Rockford	A Mon	101	374	109	22	3	12	173	54	47	34	4	83	1	0	6	15	6	.71	6	.291	.347	.463
W. Palm Bch	A+ Mon	15	56	16	1	2	1	24	7	7	6	0	15	1	0	1	2	1	.67	1	.286	.359	.429
Harrisburg	AA Mon	4	4	0	0	0	0	0	0	0	0	0	3	0	0	0	0	0	.00	0	.000	.000	.000
1993 Harrisburg	AA Mon	106	318	80	15	1	16	145	51	59	35	0	77	2	2	1	4	1	.80	8	.252	.329	.456
1994 Ottawa	AAA Mon	88	294	66	12	0	6	96	34	30	26	4	76	2	0	3	2	1	.67	8	.224	.289	.327
Harrisburg	AA Mon	38	133	42	16	2	5	77	23	28	13	2	29	1	0	2	2	1	.67	3	.316	.376	.579
1995 Rochester	AAA Bal	70	238	62	17	1	8	105	30	31	24	1	68	1	0	2	2	3	.40	6	.261	.328	.441
1996 Trenton	AA Bos	99	356	111	16	2	25	206	75	71	56	3	66	0	0	2	5	4	.56	6	.312	.403	.579
9 Min. YEARS		846	2881	734	149	23	97	1220	393	391	294	16	729	14	2	28	51	41	.55	64	.255	.324	.423

Tracy Woodson

Bats: Right **Throws:** Right **Pos:** 3B **Ht:** 6' 3" **Wt:** 216 **Born:** 10/5/62 **Age:** 34

		BATTING															BASERUNNING				PERCENTAGES		
Year Team	Lg Org	G	AB	H	2B	3B	HR	TB	R	RBI	TBB	IBB	SO	HBP	SH	SF	SB	CS	SB%	GDP	Avg	OBP	SLG
1984 Vero Beach	A+ LA	76	256	56	9	0	4	77	29	36	27	2	41	6	0	4	7	4	.64	5	.219	.304	.301
1985 Vero Beach	A+ LA	138	504	126	30	4	9	191	55	62	50	6	78	9	5	8	10	5	.67	12	.250	.324	.379
1986 San Antonio	AA LA	131	495	133	27	3	18	220	65	90	33	7	59	5	1	1	4	1	.80	11	.269	.320	.444
1987 Albuquerque	AAA LA	67	259	75	13	2	5	107	37	44	17	0	22	2	0	4	1	1	.50	12	.290	.333	.413
1988 Albuquerque	AAA LA	85	313	100	21	1	17	174	46	73	39	4	48	2	1	4	1	3	.25	8	.319	.394	.556
1989 Albuquerque	AAA LA	89	325	95	21	0	14	158	49	59	32	2	40	4	0	3	2	1	.67	7	.292	.360	.486
1990 Vancouver	AAA ChA	131	480	128	22	5	17	211	70	81	50	2	70	6	0	5	6	4	.60	18	.267	.340	.440
1991 Richmond	AAA Atl	120	441	122	20	3	6	166	43	56	28	0	43	2	3	8	1	4	.20	18	.277	.317	.376
1992 Louisville	AAA StL	109	412	122	23	2	12	185	62	59	24	2	46	2	5	4	4	3	.57	12	.296	.335	.449
1994 Rochester	AAA Bal	75	279	66	15	1	5	98	26	36	16	0	32	0	0	1	2	0	1.00	11	.237	.277	.351
Louisville	AAA StL	43	158	55	16	1	7	94	29	26	11	2	12	0	0	0	0	1	.00	4	.348	.391	.595
1995 Louisville	AAA StL	118	431	113	35	0	18	202	62	76	27	5	43	5	0	6	12	4	.75	18	.262	.309	.469
1996 Iowa	AAA ChN	10	38	7	3	0	2	16	2	8	2	0	4	0	0	1	0	0	.00	1	.184	.220	.421
Columbus	AAA NYA	114	420	121	34	3	21	224	53	81	16	2	52	3	0	11	4	0	1.00	5	.288	.311	.533
1987 Los Angeles	NL	53	136	31	8	1	1	44	14	11	9	2	21	2	0	1	1	1	.50	2	.228	.284	.324
1988 Los Angeles	NL	65	173	43	4	1	3	58	15	15	7	1	32	1	0	2	1	2	.33	4	.249	.279	.335
1989 Los Angeles	NL	4	6	0	0	0	0	0	0	0	0	0	1	0	0	0	0	0	.00	2	.000	.000	.000
1992 St. Louis	NL	31	114	35	8	0	1	46	9	22	3	0	10	1	1	0	0	0	.00	1	.307	.331	.404
1993 St. Louis	NL	62	77	16	2	0	0	18	4	2	1	0	14	0	0	1	0	0	.00	1	.208	.215	.234
12 Min. YEARS		1306	4811	1319	289	25	155	2123	628	787	372	34	590	46	15	60	54	31	.64	142	.274	.328	.441
5 Maj. YEARS		215	506	125	22	2	5	166	42	50	20	3	78	4	1	4	2	3	.40	10	.247	.279	.328

Robert Worley

Pitches: Right **Bats:** Right **Pos:** P **Ht:** 6'3" **Wt:** 185 **Born:** 2/15/71 **Age:** 26

		HOW MUCH HE PITCHED						WHAT HE GAVE UP												THE RESULTS					
Year Team	Lg Org	G	GS	CG	GF	IP	BFP	H	R	ER	HR	SH	SF	HB	TBB	IBB	SO	WP	Bk	W	L	Pct.	ShO	Sv	ERA
1992 Bellingham	A- Sea	18	0	0	6	28.2	136	31	23	19	2	3	1	3	17	1	20	3	1	1	5	.167	0	1	5.97
1993 Appleton	A Sea	45	0	0	41	53	229	48	23	13	1	2	1	2	23	4	37	4	0	3	3	.500	0	22	2.21
1994 Riverside	A+ Sea	40	0	0	35	48.1	218	47	29	23	3	3	0	1	32	2	37	3	1	2	2	.500	0	8	4.28
1995 Riverside	A+ Sea	11	11	0	0	61	275	64	44	36	4	2	2	3	30	0	44	8	2	6	4	.600	0	0	5.31
Port City	AA Sea	33	16	0	6	118	538	124	86	65	9	5	4	7	60	1	70	16	2	7	11	.389	0	0	4.96
1996 Lancaster	A+ Sea	4	4	0	0	26.1	100	20	2	1	0	1	1	0	5	0	17	3	0	3	0	1.000	0	0	0.34
Port City	AA Sea	35	1	0	13	66.1	298	66	40	29	3	2	4	4	39	6	40	9	0	2	5	.286	0	0	3.93
5 Min. YEARS		186	32	0	101	401.2	1794	400	247	186	22	18	13	20	206	14	265	46	6	24	30	.444	0	31	4.17

Steve Worrell

Pitches: Left **Bats:** Left **Pos:** P **Ht:** 6'2" **Wt:** 190 **Born:** 11/25/69 **Age:** 27

		HOW MUCH HE PITCHED						WHAT HE GAVE UP												THE RESULTS					
Year Team	Lg Org	G	GS	CG	GF	IP	BFP	H	R	ER	HR	SH	SF	HB	TBB	IBB	SO	WP	Bk	W	L	Pct.	ShO	Sv	ERA
1992 White Sox	R ChA	2	0	0	2	3	10	1	0	0	0	0	0	0	0	0	5	0	0	0	0	.000	0	2	0.00
Utica	A- ChA	4	0	0	2	10	45	11	5	4	0	0	1	1	2	0	10	3	0	1	0	1.000	0	1	3.60

				HOW MUCH HE PITCHED						WHAT HE GAVE UP												THE RESULTS					
Year	Team	Lg	Org	G	GS	CG	GF	IP	BFP	H	R	ER	HR	SH	SF	HB	TBB	IBB	SO	WP	Bk	W	L	Pct.	ShO	Sv	ERA
	South Bend	A	ChA	14	0	0	5	22.1	91	17	2	0	0	1	0	0	7	0	21	0	0	1	1	.500	0	2	0.00
1993	South Bend	A	ChA	36	0	0	24	59	231	37	12	11	0	7	0	2	23	3	57	2	0	4	2	.667	0	10	1.68
1994	Pr. William	A+	ChA	26	0	0	20	48	199	37	23	19	6	1	1	3	19	1	47	2	1	4	2	.667	0	3	3.56
	Birmingham	AA	ChA	7	0	0	1	10.1	35	2	0	0	0	0	0	0	5	0	6	0	0	1	0	1.000	0	0	0.00
1995	Birmingham	AA	ChA	4	0	0	2	4.1	21	5	5	4	2	0	0	0	2	0	2	2	0	0	1	.000	0	0	8.31
	Pr. William	A+	ChA	33	0	0	20	51.2	201	37	15	12	5	3	1	1	9	2	54	3	0	3	2	.600	0	3	2.09
1996	Birmingham	AA	ChA	35	0	0	16	51	200	28	14	12	4	1	0	0	21	0	55	0	0	5	1	.833	0	3	2.12
	Nashville	AAA	ChA	11	2	0	7	20	84	19	8	7	2	0	0	0	5	1	11	2	0	1	1	.500	0	0	3.15
5 Min. YEARS				172	2	0	99	279.2	1117	194	84	69	19	13	3	7	93	7	268	14	1	20	10	.667	0	24	2.22

Ron Wright

Bats: Right **Throws:** Right **Pos:** 1B **Ht:** 6'0" **Wt:** 215 **Born:** 1/21/76 **Age:** 21

				BATTING															BASERUNNING				PERCENTAGES		
Year	Team	Lg	Org	G	AB	H	2B	3B	HR	TB	R	RBI	TBB	IBB	SO	HBP	SH	SF	SB	CS	SB%	GDP	Avg	OBP	SLG
1994	Braves	R	Atl	45	169	29	9	0	1	41	10	16	10	0	21	0	0	0	1	0	1.00	3	.172	.218	.243
1995	Macon	A	Atl	135	527	143	23	1	32	264	93	104	62	1	118	2	0	3	2	0	1.00	11	.271	.348	.501
1996	Durham	A+	Atl	66	240	66	15	2	20	145	47	62	37	2	71	0	0	7	1	0	1.00	5	.275	.363	.604
	Greenville	AA	Atl	63	232	59	11	1	16	120	39	52	38	5	73	2	0	3	1	0	1.00	2	.254	.360	.517
	Carolina	AA	Pit	4	14	2	0	0	0	2	1	0	2	0	7	0	0	0	0	1	.00	0	.143	.250	.143
3 Min. YEARS				313	1182	299	58	4	69	572	190	234	149	8	290	4	0	13	5	1	.83	21	.253	.335	.484

Rick Wrona

Bats: Right **Throws:** Right **Pos:** C **Ht:** 6' 1" **Wt:** 195 **Born:** 12/10/63 **Age:** 33

				BATTING															BASERUNNING				PERCENTAGES		
Year	Team	Lg	Org	G	AB	H	2B	3B	HR	TB	R	RBI	TBB	IBB	SO	HBP	SH	SF	SB	CS	SB%	GDP	Avg	OBP	SLG
1985	Peoria	A	ChN	6	16	4	1	0	0	5	2	2	2	0	5	0	0	0	0	0	.00	2	.250	.333	.313
	Winston-Sal	A+	ChN	20	49	11	4	0	0	15	4	2	3	0	15	0	0	0	0	1	.00	0	.224	.269	.306
1986	Winston-Sal	A+	ChN	91	267	68	15	0	4	95	43	32	25	1	37	5	8	0	5	2	.71	9	.255	.330	.356
1987	Pittsfield	AA	ChN	70	218	48	10	3	1	67	22	25	7	3	32	1	2	3	5	1	.83	4	.220	.245	.307
1988	Pittsfield	AA	ChN	5	6	0	0	0	0	0	0	1	1	1	2	0	1	1	0	0	.00	0	.000	.125	.000
	Iowa	AAA	ChN	83	193	51	9	0	2	66	28	23	17	1	34	0	0	0	0	0	.00	6	.264	.324	.342
1989	Iowa	AAA	ChN	60	189	41	8	3	2	61	15	13	7	2	40	1	0	0	1	1	.50	4	.217	.249	.323
1990	Iowa	AAA	ChN	58	146	33	4	0	2	43	16	15	10	1	35	1	3	0	0	2	.00	7	.226	.280	.295
1992	Nashville	AAA	Cin	40	118	29	8	2	2	47	16	10	5	0	21	1	1	0	1	1	.50	2	.246	.282	.398
1993	Nashville	AAA	ChA	73	184	39	13	0	3	61	24	22	11	0	35	2	4	3	0	1	.00	1	.212	.260	.332
1994	Indianapols	AAA	Cin	6	21	6	0	0	0	6	2	0	0	0	6	2	0	0	0	0	.00	1	.286	.348	.286
	New Orleans	AAA	Mil	53	158	39	8	3	1	56	20	21	7	0	33	2	2	1	2	1	.67	8	.247	.286	.354
1995	Buffalo	AAA	Cle	31	93	21	6	0	0	27	9	10	3	0	19	2	2	1	0	1	.00	7	.226	.263	.290
	Louisville	AAA	StL	16	31	7	1	1	1	13	1	2	2	0	6	0	0	1	0	0	.00	1	.226	.265	.419
1996	Scranton-WB	AAA	Phi	61	175	40	8	0	5	63	10	20	7	0	41	3	4	2	1	1	.50	4	.229	.267	.360
1988	Chicago	NL		4	6	0	0	0	0	0	0	0	0	0	1	0	0	0	0	0	.00	0	.000	.000	.000
1989	Chicago	NL		38	92	26	2	1	2	36	11	14	2	1	21	1	0	2	0	0	.00	1	.283	.299	.391
1990	Chicago	NL		16	29	5	0	0	0	5	3	0	2	1	11	0	1	0	1	0	1.00	0	.172	.226	.172
1992	Cincinnati	NL		11	23	4	0	0	0	4	0	0	0	0	3	0	0	0	0	0	.00	2	.174	.174	.174
1993	Chicago	AL		4	8	1	0	0	0	1	0	1	0	0	4	0	0	0	0	0	.00	0	.125	.125	.125
1994	Milwaukee	AL		6	10	5	4	0	1	12	2	3	1	0	1	0	1	0	0	0	.00	0	.500	.545	1.200
11 Min. YEARS				673	1864	437	95	12	23	625	212	198	107	9	361	20	27	12	15	12	.56	56	.234	.282	.335
6 Maj. YEARS				79	168	41	6	1	3	58	16	18	5	2	41	1	2	2	1	0	1.00	3	.244	.267	.345

Julian Yan

Bats: Right **Throws:** Right **Pos:** 1B-DH **Ht:** 6'4" **Wt:** 190 **Born:** 7/24/65 **Age:** 31

				BATTING															BASERUNNING				PERCENTAGES		
Year	Team	Lg	Org	G	AB	H	2B	3B	HR	TB	R	RBI	TBB	IBB	SO	HBP	SH	SF	SB	CS	SB%	GDP	Avg	OBP	SLG
1986	St. Cathrns	A-	Tor	73	282	77	7	2	15	133	40	49	25	1	72	2	0	1	2	1	.67	5	.273	.335	.472
1987	Myrtle Bch	A	Tor	132	481	111	21	2	17	187	67	71	41	1	129	8	0	5	3	3	.50	7	.231	.299	.389
1988	Dunedin	A+	Tor	136	498	124	21	5	16	203	55	75	37	3	115	14	0	5	0	1	.00	12	.249	.316	.408
1989	Dunedin	A+	Tor	133	460	115	21	5	24	218	68	72	47	5	130	10	1	4	2	4	.33	7	.250	.330	.474
1990	Knoxville	AA	Tor	113	389	95	18	3	15	164	55	48	25	1	108	6	0	4	2	1	.67	7	.244	.297	.422
1991	Knoxville	AA	Tor	103	351	98	16	3	16	168	45	61	22	0	108	5	3	2	2	4	.33	9	.279	.329	.479
1992	Knoxville	AA	Tor	111	392	106	23	4	16	185	51	49	28	6	93	6	0	5	1	5	.17	12	.270	.325	.472
1993	Syracuse	AAA	Tor	91	278	74	9	5	7	114	30	36	14	0	91	1	1	3	3	2	.60	6	.266	.301	.410
1994	Syracuse	AAA	Tor	34	81	21	4	2	2	35	13	11	9	0	17	0	0	0	2	1	.67	4	.259	.333	.432
1995	Ottawa	AAA	Mon	114	372	104	22	3	22	198	49	79	15	2	90	2	2	1	5	1	.83	10	.280	.310	.532
1996	Ottawa	AAA	Mon	48	136	25	3	1	4	42	17	21	10	1	40	2	0	1	0	0	.00	4	.184	.248	.309
11 Min. YEARS				1088	3720	950	165	35	154	1647	490	572	273	20	993	56	7	31	22	23	.49	83	.255	.313	.443

Bruce Yard

Bats: Left **Throws:** Right **Pos:** SS **Ht:** 6'0" **Wt:** 175 **Born:** 10/17/71 **Age:** 25

				BATTING															BASERUNNING				PERCENTAGES		
Year	Team	Lg	Org	G	AB	H	2B	3B	HR	TB	R	RBI	TBB	IBB	SO	HBP	SH	SF	SB	CS	SB%	GDP	Avg	OBP	SLG
1993	Yakima	A-	LA	44	129	29	5	1	0	36	18	12	22	1	12	0	2	0	0	1	.00	9	.225	.338	.279
1994	Bakersfield	A+	LA	27	81	18	2	0	1	23	7	7	10	1	8	0	2	0	2	1	.67	5	.222	.308	.284
	Vero Beach	A+	LA	43	135	35	7	0	1	45	13	10	14	0	12	1	2	2	0	1	.00	2	.259	.329	.333

Year	Team	Lg	Org	BATTING G	AB	H	2B	3B	HR	TB	R	RBI	TBB	IBB	SO	HBP	SH	SF	BASERUNNING SB	CS	SB%	GDP	PERCENTAGES Avg	OBP	SLG
1995	Bakersfield	A+	LA	59	191	44	8	1	1	57	19	17	27	0	22	1	7	2	2	5	.29	10	.230	.326	.298
	San Antonio	AA	LA	16	39	14	3	0	0	17	7	4	5	0	6	0	0	0	0	1	.00	0	.359	.432	.436
1996	Vero Beach	A+	LA	59	192	51	7	2	1	65	24	15	18	1	19	0	6	4	2	2	.50	7	.266	.322	.339
	San Antonio	AA	LA	48	153	48	15	1	1	68	25	13	7	2	11	2	5	3	0	0	.00	5	.314	.345	.444
4 Min. YEARS				296	920	239	47	5	5	311	113	78	103	5	90	4	24	11	6	11	.35	38	.260	.333	.338

Eric Yelding

Bats: Right **Throws:** Right **Pos:** 2B **Ht:** 5'11" **Wt:** 165 **Born:** 2/22/65 **Age:** 32

Year	Team	Lg	Org	BATTING G	AB	H	2B	3B	HR	TB	R	RBI	TBB	IBB	SO	HBP	SH	SF	BASERUNNING SB	CS	SB%	GDP	PERCENTAGES Avg	OBP	SLG
1984	Medicne Hat	R+	Tor	67	304	94	14	6	4	132	61	29	26	0	46	0	0	2	31	11	.74	3	.309	.361	.434
1985	Kinston	A+	Tor	135	526	137	14	4	2	165	59	31	33	0	70	4	5	3	62	26	.70	4	.260	.307	.314
1986	Ventura	A+	Tor	131	560	157	14	7	4	197	83	40	33	3	84	0	6	2	41	18	.69	6	.280	.319	.352
1987	Knoxville	AA	Tor	39	150	30	6	1	0	38	23	7	12	0	25	1	1	1	10	5	.67	4	.200	.262	.253
	Myrtle Bch	A	Tor	88	357	109	12	2	1	128	53	31	18	0	30	4	1	4	73	13	.85	5	.305	.342	.359
1988	Syracuse	AAA	Tor	138	556	139	15	2	1	161	69	38	36	3	102	0	2	0	59	23	.72	4	.250	.296	.290
1991	Tucson	AAA	Hou	11	43	17	3	0	0	20	6	3	4	0	4	2	0	0	4	2	.67	0	.395	.469	.465
1992	Tucson	AAA	Hou	57	218	63	8	5	0	81	30	23	13	0	50	0	2	1	17	9	.65	6	.289	.328	.372
	Vancouver	AAA	ChA	36	120	26	3	0	0	29	17	6	13	0	17	0	4	2	15	2	.88	2	.217	.289	.242
1994	Iowa	AAA	ChN	29	73	18	2	0	0	20	10	6	3	0	17	0	0	0	4	2	.67	2	.247	.276	.274
1995	Buffalo	AAA	Cle	29	81	28	7	0	1	38	13	9	6	0	12	0	0	1	3	1	.75	0	.346	.386	.469
	Canton-Akrn	AA	Cle	10	37	13	1	0	0	14	5	7	1	0	6	1	0	1	3	0	1.00	0	.351	.375	.378
	Abilene	IND	—	48	188	46	4	0	3	59	35	22	14	0	25	0	2	3	8	5	.62	4	.245	.293	.314
1996	Altoona	IND	—	32	123	26	7	1	0	35	15	15	11	0	16	0	0	2	9	1	.90	0	.211	.272	.285
	Sioux Falls	IND	—	16	68	22	2	0	2	30	16	6	4	0	12	0	1	0	1	2	.33	0	.324	.361	.441
	Tacoma	AAA	Sea	19	60	16	2	1	0	20	5	5	5	0	12	0	1	1	3	4	.43	0	.267	.318	.333
1989	Houston	NL		70	90	21	2	0	0	23	19	9	7	0	19	1	2	2	11	5	.69	2	.233	.290	.256
1990	Houston	NL		142	511	130	9	5	1	152	69	28	39	1	87	0	4	5	64	25	.72	11	.254	.305	.297
1991	Houston	NL		78	276	67	11	1	1	83	19	20	13	3	46	0	3	1	11	9	.55	4	.243	.276	.301
1992	Houston	NL		9	8	2	0	0	0	2	1	0	0	0	3	0	0	0	0	0	.00	0	.250	.250	.250
1993	Chicago	NL		69	108	22	5	1	1	32	14	10	11	2	22	0	4	0	3	2	.60	3	.204	.277	.296
10 Min. YEARS				885	3464	941	114	29	18	1167	500	278	232	6	528	12	25	23	343	124	.73	40	.272	.318	.337
5 Maj. YEARS				368	993	242	27	7	3	292	122	67	70	6	177	1	13	8	89	41	.68	20	.244	.292	.294

Tsuyoshi Yoda

Pitches: Right **Bats:** Right **Pos:** P **Ht:** NA **Wt:** NA **Born:** 12/4/65 **Age:** 31

Year	Team	Lg	Org	HOW MUCH HE PITCHED G	GS	CG	GF	IP	BFP	WHAT HE GAVE UP H	R	ER	HR	SH	SF	HB	TBB	IBB	SO	WP	Bk	THE RESULTS W	L	Pct.	ShO	Sv	ERA
1996	Memphis	AA	SD	9	0	0	5	7.2	40	9	11	10	0	0	0	1	8	0	3	6	1	0	0	.000	0	0	11.74

Eddie Zambrano

Bats: Right **Throws:** Right **Pos:** OF **Ht:** 6' 3" **Wt:** 200 **Born:** 2/1/66 **Age:** 31

Year	Team	Lg	Org	BATTING G	AB	H	2B	3B	HR	TB	R	RBI	TBB	IBB	SO	HBP	SH	SF	BASERUNNING SB	CS	SB%	GDP	PERCENTAGES Avg	OBP	SLG
1990	Kinston	A+	Cle	63	204	50	7	2	3	70	26	30	29	1	36	1	1	2	1	3	.25	6	.245	.339	.343
1991	Carolina	AA	Pit	83	269	68	17	3	3	100	28	39	22	0	57	4	2	7	4	2	.67	4	.253	.311	.372
	Buffalo	AAA	Pit	48	144	49	8	5	3	76	19	35	17	1	25	2	2	4	1	1	.50	1	.340	.407	.528
1992	Buffalo	AAA	Pit	126	394	112	22	4	16	190	47	79	51	2	75	4	3	5	3	2	.60	7	.284	.368	.482
1993	Iowa	AAA	ChN	133	469	142	29	2	32	271	95	115	54	11	93	6	2	7	10	7	.59	10	.303	.377	.578
1995	Trenton	AA	Bos	19	68	10	1	0	1	14	5	7	6	1	25	1	0	1	0	0	.00	1	.147	.224	.206
1996	Pawtucket	AAA	Bos	3	9	1	0	0	0	1	0	1	0	0	4	0	0	0	0	0	.00	1	.111	.111	.111
1993	Chicago	NL		8	17	5	0	0	0	5	1	2	1	0	3	0	0	0	0	0	.00	1	.294	.333	.294
1994	Chicago	NL		67	116	30	7	0	6	55	17	18	16	0	29	1	0	0	2	1	.67	3	.259	.353	.474
6 Min. YEARS				475	1557	432	84	16	58	722	220	306	179	16	315	18	10	26	19	15	.56	30	.277	.353	.464
2 Maj. YEARS				75	133	35	7	0	6	60	18	20	17	0	32	1	0	0	2	1	.67	4	.263	.351	.451

Dave Zancanaro

Pitches: Left **Bats:** Both **Pos:** P **Ht:** 6'1" **Wt:** 170 **Born:** 1/8/69 **Age:** 28

Year	Team	Lg	Org	HOW MUCH HE PITCHED G	GS	CG	GF	IP	BFP	WHAT HE GAVE UP H	R	ER	HR	SH	SF	HB	TBB	IBB	SO	WP	Bk	THE RESULTS W	L	Pct.	ShO	Sv	ERA
1990	Sou. Oregon	A-	Oak	10	8	0	0	44.1	188	44	22	19	2	1	0	1	13	0	42	3	4	3	0	1.000	0	0	3.86
	Modesto	A+	Oak	4	2	0	0	13	64	13	9	9	1	0	0	0	14	0	7	0	0	1	2	.333	0	0	6.23
1991	Huntsville	AA	Oak	29	28	0	1	165	727	151	87	62	7	3	4	6	92	0	104	8	4	5	10	.333	0	0	3.38
1992	Tacoma	AAA	Oak	23	19	0	0	105.2	486	108	61	50	3	5	7	2	75	0	47	7	2	2	11	.154	0	0	4.26
1995	W. Michigan	A	Oak	16	16	0	0	32.2	132	19	8	8	1	2	0	3	15	0	42	1	2	0	2	.000	0	0	2.20
1996	Modesto	A+	Oak	20	3	0	6	77.1	331	61	38	29	9	4	2	3	37	0	66	5	1	7	3	.700	0	3	3.38
	Huntsville	AA	Oak	10	10	0	0	43.1	206	54	32	27	4	0	1	2	26	1	36	3	0	3	3	.500	0	0	5.61
5 Min. YEARS				112	86	0	7	481.1	2134	450	257	204	27	15	14	17	272	1	344	27	13	21	31	.404	0	3	3.81

Mark Zappelli

Pitches: Right **Bats:** Right **Pos:** P **Ht:** 6'0" **Wt:** 185 **Born:** 7/21/66 **Age:** 30

		HOW MUCH HE PITCHED						WHAT HE GAVE UP												THE RESULTS					
Year Team	Lg Org	G	GS	CG	GF	IP	BFP	H	R	ER	HR	SH	SF	HB	TBB	IBB	SO	WP	Bk	W	L	Pct.	ShO	Sv	ERA
1989 Quad City	A Cal	48	0	0	41	68	266	44	15	14	2	4	0	3	21	2	71	1	3	5	3	.625	0	22	1.85
1990 Palm Spring	A+ Cal	21	0	0	19	22	86	17	7	6	0	1	1	0	9	1	25	4	0	0	1	.000	0	6	2.45
Midland	AA Cal	35	0	0	22	45	212	57	28	22	1	5	1	4	14	3	35	4	1	3	4	.429	0	6	4.40
1991 Midland	AA Cal	32	0	0	29	32.2	141	26	15	9	1	1	2	1	13	0	31	1	0	2	2	.500	0	11	2.48
Edmonton	AAA Cal	17	0	0	5	24.1	115	24	16	12	1	3	3	1	19	3	16	0	0	2	1	.667	0	0	4.44
1992 Midland	AA Cal	27	14	0	4	98.2	414	104	41	35	10	4	2	5	19	1	59	2	0	7	1	.875	0	1	3.19
Edmonton	AAA Cal	10	10	0	0	61.2	272	73	30	25	3	1	1	5	28	1	51	2	0	5	3	.625	0	0	3.65
1993 Vancouver	AAA Cal	17	0	0	7	25.1	116	31	12	11	2	4	0	2	5	1	13	2	0	0	1	.000	0	1	3.91
1995 Tri-City	IND —	7	4	1	1	34.1	136	32	14	10	0	1	1	2	5	0	22	0	1	3	2	.600	1	0	2.62
1996 Pr. William	A+ ChA	4	3	1	1	24.2	107	28	16	16	3	1	2	0	8	0	9	0	1	0	2	.000	0	0	5.84
Nashville	AAA ChA	9	0	0	6	13.1	54	11	3	1	0	0	0	0	2	0	9	1	0	0	0	.000	0	1	0.68
7 Min. YEARS		227	31	2	135	450	1919	447	197	161	23	25	13	23	143	12	341	17	6	27	20	.574	1	48	3.22

Chad Zerbe

Pitches: Left **Bats:** Left **Pos:** P **Ht:** 6'0" **Wt:** 180 **Born:** 4/27/72 **Age:** 25

		HOW MUCH HE PITCHED						WHAT HE GAVE UP												THE RESULTS					
Year Team	Lg Org	G	GS	CG	GF	IP	BFP	H	R	ER	HR	SH	SF	HB	TBB	IBB	SO	WP	Bk	W	L	Pct.	ShO	Sv	ERA
1991 Dodgers	R LA	16	1	0	4	32.2	145	31	19	8	1	0	3	1	15	0	23	6	3	0	2	.000	0	0	2.20
1992 Great Falls	R+ LA	15	15	1	0	92.1	378	75	27	22	2	1	1	5	26	0	70	5	0	8	3	.727	1	0	2.14
1993 Bakersfield	A+ LA	14	12	1	1	67	326	83	60	44	2	1	2	2	47	0	41	2	2	0	10	.000	0	0	5.91
Vero Beach	A+ LA	10	0	0	1	12.1	64	12	10	9	0	0	2	2	13	1	11	3	1	1	0	1.000	0	0	6.57
1994 Vero Beach	A+ LA	18	18	1	0	98.1	412	88	50	37	6	0	4	2	32	0	68	6	0	5	5	.500	0	0	3.39
1995 San Bernrdo	A+ LA	28	27	1	0	163.1	718	168	103	83	15	10	5	3	64	0	94	4	0	11	7	.611	0	0	4.57
1996 San Antonio	AA LA	17	11	1	1	86	384	98	52	43	9	5	2	2	37	0	38	4	0	4	6	.400	0	1	4.50
6 Min. YEARS		118	84	5	7	552	2427	555	321	246	35	17	19	17	234	1	345	30	6	29	33	.468	1	1	4.01

Mike Zimmerman

Pitches: Right **Bats:** Right **Pos:** P **Ht:** 6'0" **Wt:** 180 **Born:** 2/6/69 **Age:** 28

		HOW MUCH HE PITCHED						WHAT HE GAVE UP												THE RESULTS					
Year Team	Lg Org	G	GS	CG	GF	IP	BFP	H	R	ER	HR	SH	SF	HB	TBB	IBB	SO	WP	Bk	W	L	Pct.	ShO	Sv	ERA
1990 Welland	A- Pit	9	0	0	7	13.1	58	8	4	1	0	1	0	1	9	0	22	1	1	2	0	1.000	0	2	0.68
Salem	A+ Pit	19	0	0	13	25.2	122	28	19	17	1	1	1	5	16	3	24	3	2	1	1	.500	0	8	5.96
1991 Salem	A+ Pit	49	1	0	44	70	344	51	47	34	1	2	1	14	72	2	63	20	0	4	2	.667	0	9	4.37
1992 Carolina	AA Pit	27	27	1	0	153	673	141	82	65	10	8	7	7	75	2	107	13	4	4	15	.211	0	0	3.82
1993 Carolina	AA Pit	33	0	0	23	45	198	40	26	18	2	1	1	4	21	2	30	2	1	2	3	.400	0	9	3.60
Buffalo	AAA Pit	33	0	0	8	46.1	199	45	23	21	5	4	2	0	28	3	32	2	0	3	1	.750	0	1	4.08
1994 Carolina	AA Pit	16	0	0	15	16.1	72	13	6	5	1	1	0	1	8	0	9	2	0	2	2	.500	0	9	2.76
Buffalo	AAA Pit	19	0	0	4	23.1	99	25	10	9	0	2	0	2	13	1	14	3	0	0	1	.000	0	0	3.47
Edmonton	AAA Fla	9	7	0	1	38.2	179	33	19	15	0	1	3	5	29	0	23	7	1	5	1	.833	0	1	3.49
1995 Charlotte	AAA Fla	31	7	0	9	69.2	319	84	46	41	6	3	3	4	41	0	30	10	0	2	2	.500	0	0	5.30
1996 Tacoma	AAA Sea	13	0	0	6	17.2	92	23	19	18	1	0	2	4	13	0	13	2	0	1	1	.500	0	0	9.17
Port City	AA Sea	14	8	0	2	48	231	56	40	37	3	2	2	7	33	0	25	2	0	4	4	.500	0	0	6.94
7 Min. YEARS		272	50	1	132	567	2586	547	341	281	30	26	22	54	358	13	392	67	9	30	33	.476	0	39	4.46

Alan Zinter

Bats: Both **Throws:** Right **Pos:** 1B **Ht:** 6'2" **Wt:** 190 **Born:** 5/19/68 **Age:** 29

		BATTING															BASERUNNING				PERCENTAGES		
Year Team	Lg Org	G	AB	H	2B	3B	HR	TB	R	RBI	TBB	IBB	SO	HBP	SH	SF	SB	CS	SB%	GDP	Avg	OBP	SLG
1989 Pittsfield	A- NYN	12	41	15	2	1	2	25	11	12	12	0	4	0	0	1	0	1	.00	0	.366	.500	.610
St. Lucie	A+ NYN	48	159	38	10	0	3	57	17	32	18	2	31	1	1	5	0	1	.00	5	.239	.311	.358
1990 St. Lucie	A+ NYN	98	333	97	19	6	7	149	63	63	54	1	70	1	0	6	8	1	.89	10	.291	.386	.447
Jackson	AA NYN	6	20	4	1	0	0	5	2	1	3	0	11	0	0	0	1	0	1.00	1	.200	.304	.250
1991 Williamsprt	AA NYN	124	422	93	13	6	9	145	44	54	59	1	106	3	2	2	3	3	.50	10	.220	.319	.344
1992 Binghamton	AA NYN	128	431	96	13	5	16	167	63	50	70	5	117	4	0	0	0	0	.00	7	.223	.337	.387
1993 Binghamton	AA NYN	134	432	113	24	4	24	217	68	87	90	7	105	1	0	5	1	0	1.00	4	.262	.386	.502
1994 Toledo	AAA Det	134	471	112	29	5	21	214	66	58	69	4	185	7	0	0	13	5	.72	3	.238	.344	.454
1995 Toledo	AAA Det	101	334	74	15	4	13	136	42	48	36	1	102	2	2	5	4	1	.80	5	.222	.297	.407
1996 Pawtucket	AAA Bos	108	357	96	19	5	26	203	78	69	58	2	123	4	0	5	5	1	.83	3	.269	.373	.569
8 Min. YEARS		893	3000	738	145	36	121	1318	454	474	469	23	854	23	5	29	35	13	.73	48	.246	.349	.439

Mike Zolecki

Pitches: Right **Bats:** Right **Pos:** P **Ht:** 6'2" **Wt:** 185 **Born:** 12/6/71 **Age:** 25

		HOW MUCH HE PITCHED						WHAT HE GAVE UP												THE RESULTS					
Year Team	Lg Org	G	GS	CG	GF	IP	BFP	H	R	ER	HR	SH	SF	HB	TBB	IBB	SO	WP	Bk	W	L	Pct.	ShO	Sv	ERA
1993 Bend	A- Col	14	8	1	3	55	247	47	35	27	7	0	3	2	30	1	78	5	1	4	3	.571	0	1	4.42
1994 Central Val	A+ Col	10	8	0	0	35.2	150	27	14	11	0	1	1	1	23	1	30	1	0	0	1	.000	0	0	2.78
1995 Salem	A+ Col	9	0	0	1	15	73	22	15	12	2	0	1	0	7	0	12	4	0	0	1	.000	0	0	7.20
Asheville	A Col	9	9	0	0	42.2	187	34	20	18	3	1	0	3	29	0	33	6	1	3	2	.600	0	0	3.80
New Haven	AA Col	27	16	0	2	113	489	112	60	50	7	2	2	4	56	1	77	10	3	6	7	.462	0	0	3.98
1996 New Haven	AA Col	47	10	0	10	91.2	421	82	60	55	13	1	4	5	68	6	84	8	0	2	8	.200	0	2	5.40
4 Min. YEARS		116	51	1	16	353	1567	324	204	173	32	5	11	15	213	9	314	34	5	15	22	.405	0	3	4.41

Eddie Zosky

Bats: Right **Throws:** Right **Pos:** SS — **Ht:** 6' 0" **Wt:** 180 **Born:** 2/10/68 **Age:** 29

		BATTING															BASERUNNING				PERCENTAGES		
Year Team	Lg Org	G	AB	H	2B	3B	HR	TB	R	RBI	TBB	IBB	SO	HBP	SH	SF	SB	CS	SB%	GDP	Avg	OBP	SLG
1989 Knoxville	AA Tor	56	208	46	5	3	2	63	21	14	10	0	32	0	2	1	1	1	.50	4	.221	.256	.303
1990 Knoxville	AA Tor	115	450	122	20	7	3	165	53	45	26	1	73	5	6	3	3	13	.19	7	.271	.316	.367
1991 Syracuse	AAA Tor	119	511	135	18	4	6	179	69	39	35	1	82	5	7	5	9	4	.69	11	.264	.315	.350
1992 Syracuse	AAA Tor	96	342	79	11	6	4	114	31	38	19	0	53	1	7	4	3	4	.43	10	.231	.270	.333
1993 Hagerstown	A Tor	5	20	2	0	0	0	2	2	1	2	0	1	0	0	1	0	0	.00	1	.100	.174	.100
Syracuse	AAA Tor	28	93	20	5	0	0	25	9	8	1	0	20	4	2	3	0	1	.00	1	.215	.248	.269
1994 Syracuse	AAA Tor	85	284	75	15	3	7	117	41	37	9	0	46	2	6	5	3	1	.75	8	.264	.287	.412
1995 Charlotte	AAA Fla	92	312	77	15	2	3	105	27	42	7	0	48	1	5	1	2	3	.40	8	.247	.265	.337
1996 Orioles	R Bal	1	3	1	1	0	0	2	1	0	1	0	0	0	0	0	0	0	.00	0	.333	.500	.667
Rochester	AAA Bal	95	340	87	22	4	3	126	42	34	21	1	40	2	3	6	5	2	.71	8	.256	.298	.371
1991 Toronto	AL	18	27	4	1	1	0	7	2	2	0	0	8	0	1	0	0	0	.00	1	.148	.148	.259
1992 Toronto	AL	8	7	2	0	1	0	4	1	1	0	0	2	0	0	1	0	0	.00	0	.286	.250	.571
1995 Florida	NL	6	5	1	0	0	0	1	0	0	0	0	0	0	0	0	0	0	.00	0	.200	.200	.200
8 Min. YEARS		692	2563	644	112	29	28	898	296	258	131	3	395	20	38	29	26	29	.47	58	.251	.290	.350
3 Maj. YEARS		32	39	7	1	2	0	12	3	3	0	0	10	0	1	1	0	0	.00	1	.179	.175	.308

Bob Zupcic

Bats: Right **Throws:** Right **Pos:** OF — **Ht:** 6' 4" **Wt:** 220 **Born:** 8/18/66 **Age:** 30

		BATTING															BASERUNNING				PERCENTAGES		
Year Team	Lg Org	G	AB	H	2B	3B	HR	TB	R	RBI	TBB	IBB	SO	HBP	SH	SF	SB	CS	SB%	GDP	Avg	OBP	SLG
1987 Elmira	A- Bos	66	238	72	12	2	7	109	39	37	17	0	35	2	3	2	5	4	.56	5	.303	.351	.458
1988 Lynchburg	A+ Bos	135	482	143	33	5	13	225	69	97	60	4	64	8	7	8	10	6	.63	6	.297	.378	.467
1989 Pawtucket	AAA Bos	27	94	24	7	1	1	36	8	11	3	0	15	0	0	2	1	3	.25	2	.255	.273	.383
New Britain	AA Bos	94	346	75	12	2	2	97	37	28	19	0	55	1	7	2	15	1	.94	7	.217	.258	.280
1990 New Britain	AA Bos	132	461	98	26	1	2	132	45	41	36	2	63	6	6	7	10	8	.56	7	.213	.275	.286
1991 Pawtucket	AAA Bos	129	429	103	27	1	18	186	70	70	55	2	58	1	12	8	10	6	.63	5	.240	.323	.434
1992 Pawtucket	AAA Bos	9	25	8	1	0	2	15	3	5	8	0	6	0	0	1	0	1	.00	0	.320	.471	.600
1994 Pawtucket	AAA Bos	9	25	7	0	0	0	7	7	3	4	1	4	0	0	0	0	1	.00	0	.280	.379	.280
Nashville	AAA ChA	5	18	6	1	0	1	10	3	3	3	0	4	0	0	0	1	1	.50	1	.333	.429	.556
1995 Nashville	AAA ChA	13	41	10	2	0	2	18	9	5	13	1	6	0	0	1	1	0	1.00	2	.244	.418	.439
Duluth-Sup.	IND —	9	35	11	3	0	1	17	4	5	5	2	3	0	0	0	1	1	.50	0	.314	.400	.486
Charlotte	AAA Fla	72	254	75	12	0	11	120	34	47	24	0	35	0	1	4	2	2	.50	3	.295	.351	.472
1996 Scranton-WB	AAA Phi	44	119	28	5	0	2	39	12	16	13	1	20	0	0	2	1	0	1.00	0	.235	.306	.328
Omaha	AAA KC	4	7	1	0	0	0	1	1	1	1	0	0	0	0	0	0	0	.00	1	.143	.250	.143
1991 Boston	AL	18	25	4	0	0	1	7	3	3	1	0	6	0	1	0	0	0	.00	0	.160	.192	.280
1992 Boston	AL	124	392	108	19	1	3	138	46	43	25	1	60	4	7	4	2	2	.50	6	.276	.322	.352
1993 Boston	AL	141	286	69	24	2	2	103	40	26	27	2	54	2	8	3	5	2	.71	7	.241	.308	.360
1994 Boston	AL	4	4	0	0	0	0	0	0	0	0	0	1	0	0	0	0	1	.00	0	.000	.000	.000
Chicago	AL	32	88	18	4	1	1	27	10	8	4	0	16	0	4	1	0	0	.00	2	.205	.237	.307
9 Min. YEARS		748	2574	661	141	12	62	1012	341	369	261	13	368	18	36	37	57	34	.63	39	.257	.325	.393
4 Maj. YEARS		319	795	199	47	4	7	275	99	80	57	3	137	6	20	8	7	5	.58	15	.250	.303	.346

1996 Single-A & Rookie League Stats

This is where it all starts. In the vast ocean that is Single-A and Rookie League baseball, the true prospects fight to distinguish themselves from the minor league lifers. Some of them will surface in the majors as early as next season; others won't see the light of day until years from now. This may be your first encounter with many of these names. If you check back in a couple of years, many of them will look much more familiar.

As we noted in the introduction to the career register, some leagues are given a "+" or "-" designation to better identify the caliber of play within a classification. "Org" is the major league organization for the minor league team in question.

Note: Players from independent leagues are not included in this section.

1996 Batting — Single-A and Rookie Leagues

BATTING																				BASERUNNING				PERCENTAGES		
Player	Team	Org	Lg	A	G	AB	H	2B	3B	HR	TB	R	RBI	TBB	IBB	SO	HBP	SH	SF	SB	CS	SB%	GDP	Avg	OBP	SLG
Thoen,E.J.	Boise	Cal	A-	21	18	60	12	1	0	2	19	6	4	4	0	17	1	1	0	0	0	.00	2	.200	.262	.317
Abbott,Charles	Boise	Cal	A-	22	70	268	53	9	2	0	66	41	20	24	0	59	5	4	4	11	5	.69	8	.198	.272	.246
Abell,Tony	Johnson Cty	StL	R+	22	45	131	35	6	1	1	46	38	9	22	0	43	7	1	1	10	6	.63	2	.267	.398	.351
	New Jersey	StL	A-	22	7	25	3	0	0	0	3	4	1	4	0	11	0	0	0	1	0	1.00	1	.120	.241	.120
Abernathy,Matt	Clinton	SD	A	23	60	211	42	6	1	5	65	23	36	11	0	53	6	2	2	0	1	.00	4	.199	.257	.308
Abreu,Dennis	Cubs	ChN	R	19	56	192	60	5	0	0	65	32	15	21	0	20	2	7	1	35	9	.80	6	.313	.384	.339
Abreu,Miguel	Marlins	Fla	R	NA	22	59	13	1	0	0	14	4	1	4	0	13	1	0	0	3	0	1.00	2	.220	.281	.237
Abreu,Nelson	Cubs	ChN	R	20	44	136	30	2	3	1	41	15	11	19	0	31	0	6	0	15	4	.79	5	.221	.316	.301
Acevedo,Luis	Rangers	Tex	R	19	53	174	34	8	2	0	46	17	19	25	0	31	2	1	2	7	1	.88	3	.195	.300	.264
Acosta,Ed	Delmarva	Mon	A	25	32	68	13	0	1	0	15	11	5	3	0	20	0	2	0	0	0	.00	2	.191	.225	.221
Adams,Jason	Quad City	Hou	A	24	74	226	60	14	0	2	80	35	27	29	2	36	0	2	4	6	6	.50	6	.265	.344	.354
Adams,Tommy	Charlotte	Tex	A+	27	53	183	47	8	0	2	61	28	21	26	1	39	3	0	1	8	3	.73	2	.257	.357	.333
Adolfo,Carlos	Delmarva	Mon	A	21	132	492	134	20	8	10	200	82	71	47	3	106	1	2	6	18	6	.75	11	.272	.333	.407
Afenir,Tom	Watertown	Cle	A-	25	3	9	2	0	0	0	2	0	1	0	0	3	0	0	1	0	0	.00	0	.222	.200	.222
	Burlington	Cle	R+	25	26	96	23	5	0	1	31	4	7	0	0	22	0	1	0	1	1	.50	3	.240	.240	.323
Agnoly,Earl	Kane County	Fla	A	21	63	203	50	8	2	1	65	19	20	14	0	40	7	1	0	2	4	.33	5	.246	.317	.320
Ahrendt,Jay	Orioles	Bal	R	23	25	66	21	4	0	1	28	9	11	14	0	15	2	0	4	0	2	.00	0	.318	.430	.424
	Bluefield	Bal	R+	23	3	4	2	0	0	0	2	1	2	1	0	1	0	0	0	0	0	.00	0	.500	.600	.500
Ahumada,Alejand.	Red Sox	Bos	R	18	37	122	34	6	0	0	40	14	15	3	0	32	3	1	0	1	5	.17	0	.279	.313	.328
Airoso,Kurt	Jamestown	Det	A-	22	27	78	22	5	2	2	37	12	12	10	0	31	2	0	2	3	1	.75	1	.282	.370	.474
Akins,Carlos	High Desert	Bal	A+	22	11	24	5	1	0	0	6	4	2	6	0	8	1	0	0	1	0	1.00	0	.208	.387	.250
	Bluefield	Bal	R+	22	18	57	17	4	0	0	21	19	14	15	0	11	4	0	1	15	0	1.00	0	.298	.468	.368
	Frederick	Bal	A+	22	42	145	42	7	1	5	66	36	14	34	0	31	2	0	1	9	5	.64	3	.290	.429	.455
Alaimo,Jason	Marlins	Fla	R	21	47	173	47	11	0	0	58	20	24	15	0	43	7	0	2	2	1	.67	5	.272	.350	.335
	Brevard Cty	Fla	A+	21	6	21	5	0	0	0	5	1	0	1	0	4	0	0	0	0	0	.00	2	.238	.273	.238
Alamo,Efrain	Asheville	Col	A	20	67	250	55	13	0	6	86	34	18	23	0	68	2	2	0	8	10	.44	2	.220	.291	.344
Alayon,Elvis	Lowell	Bos	A-	22	63	213	59	3	1	4	76	28	20	11	3	37	4	1	2	10	3	.77	4	.277	.322	.357
Albaral,Randy	Medicne Hat	Tor	R+	20	60	228	59	4	1	0	65	50	19	27	0	39	3	5	1	33	6	.85	0	.259	.344	.285
Albert,Chernan	Hickory	ChA	A	21	49	179	42	7	3	2	61	31	10	14	0	51	2	0	2	18	6	.75	2	.235	.294	.341
	Bristol	ChA	R+	21	55	204	47	4	2	5	70	23	22	9	0	51	2	1	2	16	8	.67	3	.230	.267	.343
Alexander,Chad	Quad City	Hou	A	23	118	435	115	25	4	13	187	68	69	57	4	108	2	0	3	16	11	.59	11	.264	.350	.430
Alfano,Jeff	Ogden	Mil	R+	20	45	159	45	9	0	4	66	29	29	12	0	30	4	2	2	2	2	.50	2	.283	.345	.415
Allen,Dustin	Clinton	SD	A	24	77	243	65	10	3	10	111	46	46	67	1	59	4	0	3	4	7	.36	7	.267	.429	.457
	Rancho Cuca	SD	A+	24	55	208	62	15	1	10	109	41	45	38	1	65	2	0	3	3	2	.60	3	.298	.406	.524
Allen,John	Fort Wayne	Min	A	22	7	21	9	0	0	0	9	2	2	3	1	2	0	0	1	1	1	.50	0	.429	.480	.429
Allen,Marlon	Winston-Sal	Cin	A+	24	121	426	101	19	1	17	173	57	82	32	2	133	5	1	12	8	2	.80	3	.237	.291	.406
Alley,William	Bluefield	Bal	R+	20	24	67	13	4	0	0	17	7	4	15	0	16	1	0	1	0	2	.00	2	.194	.345	.254
Alleyne,Roberto	Astros	Hou	R	20	48	151	50	9	0	7	80	32	27	20	2	32	2	0	3	4	4	.50	4	.331	.409	.530
Allison,Brad	Lethbridge	Ari	R+	23	25	43	9	0	0	1	12	7	6	9	0	16	1	0	1	0	1	.00	1	.209	.352	.279
Allison,Cody	Burlington	Cle	R+	22	27	96	25	2	0	1	30	10	14	12	1	17	1	0	2	1	0	1.00	2	.260	.342	.313
Almanzar,Richard	Lakeland	Det	A+	21	124	471	144	22	2	1	173	81	36	49	0	49	8	12	3	53	19	.74	5	.306	.379	.367
Almond,Greg	Peoria	StL	A	26	90	273	63	14	0	2	83	28	41	26	0	75	0	5	5	2	0	1.00	8	.231	.293	.304
Almonte,Wady	Orioles	Bal	R	22	1	3	1	0	0	0	1	2	1	1	0	0	0	0	0	1	0	1.00	0	.333	.500	.333
	Frederick	Bal	A+	22	85	287	82	12	2	12	134	45	44	21	2	59	6	4	1	1	5	.17	12	.286	.346	.467
Alvarado,Basilio	Delmarva	Mon	A	22	6	13	4	0	0	0	4	1	1	0	0	2	1	0	0	0	0	.00	0	.308	.357	.308
	Vermont	Mon	A-	22	49	171	40	8	1	1	53	16	22	3	0	37	4	1	1	0	3	.00	4	.234	.263	.310
Alvarez,Julio	Tigers	Det	R	18	28	92	24	2	0	0	26	13	10	11	0	22	0	1	1	5	1	.83	0	.261	.337	.283
Alvarez,Rafael	Fort Myers	Min	A+	20	6	22	3	0	0	0	3	1	1	1	0	7	0	0	1	0	1	.00	0	.136	.167	.136
	Fort Wayne	Min	A	20	119	473	143	30	7	4	199	61	58	43	5	55	3	2	1	11	9	.55	5	.302	.363	.421
Amado,Jose	Wisconsin	Sea	A	22	61	232	67	13	0	5	95	43	36	20	1	20	8	2	3	6	5	.55	5	.289	.361	.409
	Lansing	KC	A	22	57	212	74	18	1	5	109	39	47	17	2	17	8	1	2	8	4	.67	6	.349	.414	.514
Amerson,Gordie	Clinton	SD	A	20	116	394	80	14	4	9	129	47	48	60	4	113	3	0	3	9	5	.64	6	.203	.311	.327
Amezcua,Adan	Kissimmee	Hou	A+	23	88	264	75	16	1	0	93	24	29	25	0	42	3	8	3	0	1	.00	2	.284	.349	.352
Ammirato,Zak	Utica	Fla	A-	23	74	262	58	13	2	6	93	26	36	39	4	80	3	1	5	3	2	.60	3	.221	.324	.355
Andersen,Ryan	Williamsprt	ChN	A-	23	25	75	20	2	0	0	22	6	8	5	0	11	3	1	1	2	2	.50	2	.267	.333	.293
Anderson,Chris.	Hudson Vall	TB	A-	22	52	156	23	4	1	5	44	17	18	15	0	70	4	0	1	2	0	1.00	1	.147	.239	.282
Anderson,Blake	Portland	Col	A-	23	39	134	31	5	2	3	49	24	16	26	2	27	1	0	1	1	1	.50	3	.231	.358	.366
Anderson,Frank	South Bend	ChA	A	21	68	213	33	5	3	4	56	8	19	10	0	89	2	3	2	1	2	.33	3	.155	.198	.263
Anderson,Milt	Columbus	Cle	A	24	81	251	58	12	2	5	89	46	27	42	1	53	3	2	1	29	10	.74	2	.231	.347	.355
Andreopoulos,Alex	Stockton	Mil	A+	24	87	291	88	17	2	5	124	52	41	40	2	33	5	2	4	10	3	.77	5	.302	.391	.426
Antczak,Chuck	Hickory	ChA	A	23	9	13	2	0	0	0	2	0	1	3	0	2	0	1	0	0	0	.00	0	.154	.313	.154
	South Bend	ChA	A	23	16	31	3	2	0	0	5	3	1	1	0	9	2	1	0	0	0	.00	1	.097	.176	.161
	Bristol	ChA	R+	23	7	23	7	0	0	0	7	2	0	2	0	5	0	0	0	0	0	.00	0	.304	.360	.304
	Pr. William	ChA	A+	23	5	11	1	0	0	0	1	2	0	1	0	2	1	0	0	0	0	.00	0	.091	.231	.091
Anthony,Brian	Portland	Col	A-	23	30	107	15	5	0	1	23	6	5	10	0	30	0	0	0	1	0	1.00	3	.140	.214	.215
Antigua,Nilson	Erie	Pit	A-	21	57	187	51	9	0	4	72	24	26	9	0	26	0	7	2	5	3	.63	7	.273	.303	.385
Antrim,Patrick	Oneonta	NYA	A-	23	14	49	11	0	0	0	11	4	2	5	0	14	0	1	0	3	3	.50	0	.224	.296	.224
	Greensboro	NYA	A	23	15	12	1	0	0	0	1	2	0	1	0	7	0	1	0	1	1	.50	0	.083	.154	.083
Antunez,Francisco	Angels	Cal	R	24	5	14	3	0	0	1	6	2	1	1	0	6	2	0	0	0	0	.00	0	.214	.353	.429
Arano,Eloy	Visalia	Det	A+	23	43	140	32	6	0	0	38	19	16	17	0	30	0	1	0	4	2	.67	5	.229	.312	.271
	Lakeland	Det	A+	23	46	155	37	4	1	0	43	16	7	8	0	23	1	1	1	0	1	.00	2	.239	.279	.277
Ardoin,Danny	Modesto	Oak	A+	22	91	317	83	13	3	6	120	55	34	47	0	81	9	3	2	5	7	.42	9	.262	.371	.379
Arenas,Pedro	Utica	Fla	A-	23	66	182	35	5	0	0	40	25	12	31	0	61	0	4	2	1	3	.25	4	.192	.307	.220
Arias,David	Wisconsin	Sea	A	21	130	487	156	34	2	18	248	89	93	52	8	108	5	2	4	3	4	.43	5	.320	.389	.509
Arias,Jeison	Devil Rays	TB	R	18	19	66	17	4	1	0	23	7	4	3	0	31	0	3	0	3	1	.75	1	.258	.290	.348
Arias,Rogelio	Portland	Col	A-	21	44	168	40	3	1	1	48	15	15	5	0	24	2	4	2	1	1	.50	4	.238	.266	.286
	Asheville	Col	A	21	27	84	14	0	0	0	14	7	5	3	0	12	2	0	0	1	3	.25	2	.167	.213	.167

1996 Batting — Single-A and Rookie Leagues

BATTING																				BASERUNNING				PERCENTAGES		
Player	Team	Org	Lg	A	G	AB	H	2B	3B	HR	TB	R	RBI	TBB	IBB	SO	HBP	SH	SF	SB	CS	SB%	GDP	Avg	OBP	SLG
Arnold,John	Danville	Atl	R+	22	7	26	6	1	0	0	7	3	1	1	0	8	0	0	0	0	0	.00	0	.231	.259	.269
	Eugene	Atl	A-	22	31	78	20	5	0	5	40	16	19	14	2	25	0	1	0	1	0	1.00	2	.256	.370	.513
Arrendondo,Hern.	Butte	TB	R+	19	67	252	90	21	7	4	137	59	49	24	0	31	9	1	2	8	3	.73	6	.357	.429	.544
Arrollado,Courtney	Spokane	KC	A-	22	22	47	10	1	0	0	11	2	2	1	0	13	0	0	1	2	0	1.00	2	.213	.224	.234
	Lansing	KC	A	22	17	39	10	1	0	0	11	5	6	7	0	13	0	0	0	2	1	.67	1	.256	.370	.282
Arvelo,Thomas	Columbia	NYN	A	23	72	218	44	3	0	0	47	35	14	17	0	42	4	9	2	8	8	.50	2	.202	.270	.216
Asche,Mike	Lynchburg	Pit	A+	25	129	498	147	25	6	7	205	79	54	38	1	92	2	8	7	26	5	.84	11	.295	.343	.412
Asencio,Fernando	Vero Beach	LA	A+	23	115	402	107	12	6	2	137	56	49	29	2	68	2	3	0	15	6	.71	11	.266	.319	.341
Ashby,Chris	Tampa	NYA	A+	22	100	325	80	28	0	6	126	55	46	71	1	78	5	1	1	16	4	.80	5	.246	.388	.388
Augustine,Andy	Lancaster	Sea	A+	24	41	115	32	5	1	0	39	16	12	22	0	40	3	1	1	2	0	1.00	4	.278	.404	.339
Auterson,Jeffrey	Great Falls	LA	R+	19	51	165	34	4	1	4	52	22	12	20	0	72	5	0	1	6	8	.43	2	.206	.309	.315
Avalos,Gilbert	Daytona	ChN	A+	24	90	285	72	12	0	0	84	38	25	20	0	49	7	3	2	23	8	.74	5	.253	.315	.295
Avery,Mark	Pr. William	ChA	A+	26	75	270	64	16	2	9	111	33	31	32	0	66	3	1	2	0	0	.00	11	.237	.322	.411
Aybar,Ramon	Tigers	Det	R	21	43	154	44	7	1	0	53	30	16	19	0	38	3	1	0	32	3	.91	1	.286	.375	.344
Aylor,Brian	Oneonta	NYA	A-	23	8	25	11	3	3	0	20	9	5	2	1	5	2	0	1	3	1	.75	1	.440	.500	.800
Ayotte,Scott	Oneonta	NYA	A-	23	27	89	18	5	1	0	25	9	8	8	0	32	0	0	2	2	1	.67	0	.202	.263	.281
Ayuso,Julio	Twins	Min	R	20	33	98	21	3	0	3	33	15	11	15	0	29	3	0	0	1	2	.33	1	.214	.336	.337
Babin,Brady	Brevard Cty	Fla	A+	21	2	5	1	0	0	0	1	0	0	0	0	2	0	0	0	0	0	.00	0	.200	.200	.200
Backowski,Lance	Savannah	LA	A	22	30	49	6	0	0	0	6	7	0	7	0	19	1	1	0	0	2	.00	1	.122	.246	.122
	San Bernrdo	LA	A+	22	1	0	0	0	0	0	0	0	0	0	0	0	0	0	0	0	0	.00	0	.000	.000	.000
Bady,Edward	W. Palm Bch	Mon	A+	24	128	484	136	9	3	1	154	62	34	42	0	93	10	12	3	42	17	.71	2	.281	.349	.318
Baeza,Art	Burlington	SF	A	23	17	43	4	1	0	1	8	4	5	5	0	7	1	2	0	0	0	.00	2	.093	.204	.186
	Bellingham	SF	A-	23	25	86	17	2	0	2	25	11	9	10	0	24	4	3	1	2	0	1.00	4	.198	.307	.291
Bagley,Lorenzo	Medicne Hat	Tor	R+	21	67	235	68	16	1	13	125	61	46	45	0	57	1	0	1	14	5	.74	4	.289	.404	.532
Bagley,Sean	Expos	Mon	R	21	42	118	29	7	0	0	36	27	12	11	0	29	0	3	0	9	2	.82	1	.246	.310	.305
Bain,Tyler	Butte	TB	R+	22	61	233	72	11	5	3	102	45	29	31	2	33	0	0	3	13	6	.68	3	.309	.386	.438
Bair,Rod	Portland	Col	A-	22	56	221	48	11	2	4	75	34	33	17	2	29	7	5	4	9	4	.69	2	.217	.289	.339
Baker,Derek	Charlstn-SC	Tex	A	21	46	160	39	8	1	5	64	21	31	19	0	37	3	0	3	1	1	.50	0	.244	.330	.400
Baker,Jason	San Bernrdo	LA	A+	23	19	29	3	0	0	0	3	2	1	0	0	10	0	0	0	0	0	.00	1	.103	.103	.103
Balfe,Ryan	Lakeland	Det	A+	21	92	347	97	21	1	11	153	48	66	24	2	66	5	0	3	3	0	1.00	13	.280	.332	.441
Baltzell,Beau	Lethbridge	Ari	R+	23	19	37	5	2	0	0	7	1	5	4	0	9	1	0	0	0	0	.00	1	.135	.238	.189
Barajas,Rodrigo	Visalia	Ari	A+	21	27	74	12	3	0	0	15	6	8	7	0	21	1	0	0	0	0	.00	3	.162	.244	.203
	Lethbridge	Ari	R+	21	51	175	59	9	3	10	104	47	50	12	0	24	2	0	4	2	1	.67	6	.337	.378	.594
Barker,Kevin	Ogden	Mil	R+	21	71	281	89	19	4	9	143	61	56	46	4	54	3	0	5	0	2	.00	4	.317	.412	.509
Barkett,Andy	Charlotte	Tex	A+	22	115	392	112	22	3	6	158	57	54	57	2	59	5	0	4	3	1	.75	6	.286	.380	.403
Barlok,Todd	Vero Beach	LA	A+	25	116	384	99	19	4	4	138	63	47	55	3	94	8	1	2	7	6	.54	7	.258	.361	.359
Barlow,Ethan	Vermont	Mon	A-	23	42	116	29	1	0	0	30	18	8	14	0	20	3	2	0	8	5	.62	3	.250	.346	.259
Barner,Doug	Devil Rays	TB	R	22	1	5	1	0	0	0	1	1	0	0	0	1	0	0	0	0	0	.00	0	.200	.200	.200
	Butte	TB	R+	22	6	18	2	0	0	0	2	1	0	4	0	6	0	0	0	0	1	.00	1	.111	.273	.111
	Hudson Vall	TB	A-	22	46	147	32	7	0	2	45	21	17	30	2	42	4	0	1	3	3	.50	2	.218	.363	.306
Barnes,John	Red Sox	Bos	R	21	30	101	28	4	0	1	35	9	17	5	0	17	6	0	5	4	0	1.00	3	.277	.333	.347
Barnes,Kelvin	Rockford	ChN	A	22	125	429	101	19	8	11	169	59	63	42	2	100	6	1	4	23	3	.88	16	.235	.310	.394
Barnes,Larry	Cedar Rapds	Cal	A	22	131	489	155	36	5	27	282	84	112	58	5	101	6	1	6	9	6	.60	8	.317	.392	.577
Barr,Tucker	Auburn	Hou	A-	22	44	165	36	12	0	4	60	16	22	5	0	39	1	0	2	1	1	.50	2	.218	.243	.364
Barrera,Rafael	Rangers	Tex	R	20	40	136	40	4	2	1	51	20	13	10	0	24	3	4	3	13	2	.87	1	.294	.349	.375
Barrett,Michael	Delmarva	Mon	A	20	129	474	113	29	4	4	162	57	62	18	0	42	9	2	5	5	11	.31	9	.238	.277	.342
Barrientos,Edgar	Red Sox	Bos	R	18	23	41	5	0	0	0	5	6	1	6	0	14	1	1	0	0	0	.00	0	.122	.250	.122
Barthelemy,Edy	Mariners	Sea	R	21	38	111	24	5	3	1	38	18	14	19	1	30	1	1	1	3	4	.43	2	.216	.333	.342
Barthol,Blake	Salem	Col	A+	24	109	375	107	17	2	13	167	58	67	36	0	48	12	6	1	12	5	.71	5	.285	.366	.445
Bass,Jayson	Fayettevlle	Det	A	23	104	295	68	12	3	11	119	44	43	54	3	118	2	3	2	19	10	.66	2	.231	.351	.403
Bass,Jayson	Danville	Atl	R+	21	57	207	50	11	6	2	79	41	23	34	0	32	6	1	5	22	5	.81	1	.242	.357	.382
	Macon	Atl	A	21	5	22	8	0	0	1	11	2	1	0	0	5	1	0	0	3	1	.75	0	.364	.391	.500
Baston,Stanley	Medicne Hat	Tor	R+	20	68	271	76	14	1	5	107	45	45	36	0	58	2	2	1	10	3	.77	5	.280	.368	.395
Bates,Fletcher	Columbia	NYN	A	23	132	491	127	21	13	15	219	84	72	64	4	162	3	4	3	16	6	.73	3	.259	.346	.446
Batts,Rodney	Batavia	Phi	A-	23	41	153	22	5	1	0	29	20	15	12	0	36	2	2	2	7	2	.78	0	.144	.213	.190
Baugh,Darren	Hickory	ChA	A	21	68	267	76	5	2	2	91	46	24	27	0	48	7	3	4	17	5	.77	3	.285	.361	.341
Baugh,Gavin	Brevard Cty	Fla	A+	23	19	33	4	1	0	0	5	5	1	2	0	17	0	0	0	1	2	.33	0	.121	.171	.152
	Bakersfield	—	A+	23	6	20	3	1	0	0	4	3	0	3	0	9	0	1	0	0	0	.00	1	.150	.261	.200
Baughman,Justin	Cedar Rapds	Cal	A	22	127	464	115	17	8	5	163	78	48	45	2	78	6	15	1	50	17	.75	13	.248	.322	.351
Bautista,Francisco	Royals	KC	R	21	29	89	26	3	0	0	29	11	8	8	0	24	1	0	0	3	3	.50	0	.292	.357	.326
Bautista,Jorge	Marlins	Fla	R	20	47	151	40	4	1	7	67	23	24	26	1	28	5	0	1	4	2	.67	2	.265	.388	.444
Bautista,Juan	DiamondbackAri		R	18	49	140	28	3	1	0	33	14	14	11	0	51	3	0	2	5	2	.71	2	.200	.269	.236
Bazzani,Matt	Red Sox	Bos	R	23	11	25	10	5	0	1	18	7	3	3	0	4	2	0	0	0	0	.00	1	.400	.500	.720
	Sarasota	Bos	A+	23	12	37	10	1	1	1	16	5	4	2	0	6	2	0	0	0	0	.00	0	.270	.341	.432
	Bakersfield	Bos	A+	23	20	69	14	3	0	2	23	5	8	7	0	21	1	0	1	0	0	.00	3	.203	.282	.333
Bearden,Doug	Hickory	ChA	A	21	49	169	37	7	0	1	47	12	11	3	0	35	0	2	0	0	3	.00	2	.219	.233	.278
	Bristol	ChA	R+	21	40	127	20	1	0	1	24	6	6	7	0	29	0	3	0	2	1	.67	5	.157	.201	.189
Beaumont,Hamil	Oneonta	NYA	A-	22	1	3	0	0	0	0	0	0	0	0	0	1	1	0	0	0	0	.00	0	.000	.250	.000
Becker,Brian	Devil Rays	TB	R	22	52	199	54	12	0	2	72	31	27	13	0	28	3	0	4	3	1	.75	3	.271	.320	.362
Beeney,Ryan	Tampa	NYA	A+	24	13	39	8	1	0	0	9	7	4	7	0	12	1	0	0	0	0	.00	0	.205	.340	.231
	Oneonta	NYA	A-	24	2	4	2	0	0	0	2	1	0	0	0	0	0	0	0	0	0	.00	0	.500	.500	.500
Bellenger,Butch	Augusta	Pit	A	23	8	26	5	2	0	0	7	5	1	2	0	6	0	1	0	1	0	1.00	0	.192	.250	.269
	Erie	Pit	A-	23	52	193	46	8	0	3	63	21	15	9	0	33	1	2	2	9	4	.69	5	.238	.273	.326
Bello,Jilberto	Orioles	Bal	R	20	40	134	21	5	1	0	28	10	9	11	0	48	1	1	2	8	4	.67	2	.157	.223	.209
Beltran,Carlos	Lansing	KC	A	20	11	42	6	2	0	0	8	3	0	1	0	11	0	0	0	1	0	1.00	0	.143	.163	.190
	Spokane	KC	A-	20	59	215	58	8	3	7	93	29	29	31	0	65	0	3	2	10	2	.83	4	.270	.359	.433
Beltre,Adrian	Savannah	LA	A	19	68	244	75	14	3	16	143	48	59	35	2	46	7	0	2	4	3	.57	7	.307	.406	.586

1996 Batting — Single-A and Rookie Leagues

BATTING																				BASERUNNING				PERCENTAGES		
Player	Team	Org	Lg	A	G	AB	H	2B	3B	HR	TB	R	RBI	TBB	IBB	SO	HBP	SH	SF	SB	CS	SB%	GDP	Avg	OBP	SLG
	San Bernrdo	LA	A+	19	63	238	62	13	1	10	107	40	40	19	0	44	5	1	5	3	4	.43	3	.261	.322	.450
Benes,Richard	Royals	KC	R	19	29	68	10	2	0	0	12	6	2	3	0	16	1	4	0	1	2	.33	2	.147	.194	.176
Benjamin,Aljereau	Pirates	Pit	R	19	45	172	39	5	4	3	61	23	25	12	0	35	1	1	2	1	3	.25	7	.227	.278	.355
Bennett,Ryan	Pittsfield	NYN	A-	22	27	79	19	2	1	0	23	11	14	13	1	21	0	0	2	0	0	.00	1	.241	.340	.291
Bentley,Kevin	Bakersfield	ChN	A+	24	22	84	23	3	1	5	43	19	21	9	0	30	3	0	2	7	1	.88	2	.274	.357	.512
	Daytona	ChN	A+	24	78	254	69	9	2	5	97	32	30	19	1	79	2	0	1	9	3	.75	9	.272	.326	.382
Berger,Brandon	Spokane	KC	A-	22	71	283	87	12	1	13	140	46	58	31	0	64	2	1	3	17	5	.77	7	.307	.376	.495
Bergeron,Peter	Yakima	LA	A-	19	61	232	59	5	3	5	85	36	21	28	0	59	0	3	0	13	9	.59	2	.254	.335	.366
Besford,Timothy	Expos	Mon	R	20	10	12	1	0	0	0	1	1	0	1	0	5	0	0	0	0	0	.00	0	.083	.154	.083
Betances,Junior	Stockton	Mil	A+	24	125	458	116	9	7	1	142	69	41	51	0	61	6	4	6	14	11	.56	9	.253	.332	.310
Betancourt,Rafael	Michigan	Bos	A	22	62	168	28	1	2	3	42	14	14	12	0	39	2	3	2	5	2	.71	7	.167	.228	.250
Betts,Darrell	New Jersey	StL	A-	24	21	59	6	1	0	0	7	6	3	8	0	18	1	0	0	1	0	1.00	1	.102	.221	.119
Bierek,Kurt	Tampa	NYA	A+	24	88	320	97	14	2	11	148	48	55	41	3	40	6	0	3	6	3	.67	5	.303	.389	.463
Biermann,Steve	St. Pete	StL	A+	25	52	81	10	3	0	0	13	13	4	8	0	23	0	1	3	0	0	.00	1	.123	.196	.160
Bigler,Jeff	Augusta	Pit	A	27	40	121	32	10	0	0	42	16	14	29	1	24	3	3	3	0	2	.00	1	.264	.410	.347
Bilderback,Ty	Lk Elsinore	Cal	A+	23	42	150	40	10	0	3	59	21	22	17	1	38	4	0	1	4	2	.67	1	.267	.355	.393
Bishop,Tim	Kingsport	NYN	R+	23	61	237	77	6	4	4	103	47	29	20	1	42	1	1	1	23	10	.70	1	.325	.378	.435
	Pittsfield	NYN	A-	23	3	6	0	0	0	0	0	1	1	0	0	1	0	0	0	0	0	.00	0	.000	.000	.000
Black,Brandon	Columbia	NYN	A	22	25	63	12	6	1	0	20	3	12	8	2	16	1	0	1	0	3	.00	0	.190	.288	.317
	Kingsport	NYN	R+	22	62	219	56	4	1	3	71	39	31	32	0	38	1	1	2	1	1	.50	0	.256	.350	.324
Blake,William	Hagerstown	Tor	A	23	48	172	43	13	1	2	64	29	18	11	1	40	7	0	2	5	3	.63	3	.250	.318	.372
Blakeney,Mo	W. Palm Bch	Mon	A+	24	7	17	3	0	1	0	5	1	2	0	0	0	0	2	0	0	0	.00	0	.176	.176	.294
	Delmarva	Mon	A	24	41	110	28	7	0	1	38	13	11	7	0	20	0	1	1	3	5	.38	2	.255	.297	.345
Blanco,Octavio	Devil Rays	TB	R	18	11	20	6	0	0	0	6	0	2	0	0	5	0	0	0	0	0	.00	1	.300	.300	.300
Blandford,Paul	Vermont	Mon	A-	23	64	231	57	11	7	1	85	39	39	34	0	37	2	4	5	11	9	.55	2	.247	.342	.368
Blessing,Chad	Williamsprt	ChN	A-	21	38	105	25	3	0	1	31	15	12	14	0	25	3	2	0	5	2	.71	1	.238	.344	.295
Blosser,Doug	Lansing	KC	A	20	36	117	24	5	0	5	44	14	18	15	0	38	1	0	4	2	0	1.00	0	.205	.292	.376
	Spokane	KC	A-	20	16	47	12	4	1	3	27	10	8	6	1	14	1	0	0	0	0	.00	0	.255	.352	.574
	Royals	KC	R	20	12	37	8	2	0	0	10	4	4	4	1	10	1	0	0	0	0	.00	1	.216	.310	.270
Bly,Derrick	Cubs	ChN	R	22	53	195	55	11	2	13	109	37	32	21	1	54	5	0	1	8	3	.73	0	.282	.365	.559
	Rockford	ChN	A	22	4	7	2	0	0	1	5	1	4	2	0	5	1	0	1	0	0	.00	0	.286	.455	.714
Bocachica,Hiram	Expos	Mon	R	21	9	32	8	3	0	0	11	11	2	5	1	3	1	0	0	2	1	.67	0	.250	.368	.344
	W. Palm Bch	Mon	A+	21	71	267	90	17	5	2	123	50	26	34	0	47	6	3	3	21	3	.88	6	.337	.419	.461
Bogle,Bryan	High Desert	Bal	A+	24	126	495	157	32	6	22	267	86	92	36	0	142	5	2	8	14	9	.61	7	.317	.364	.539
Bokemeier,Mathew	Charlotte	Tex	A+	24	131	503	138	31	4	2	183	74	62	28	6	81	3	3	7	18	2	.90	15	.274	.312	.364
Bolivar,Cesar	Twins	Min	R	18	41	155	53	7	1	1	65	30	18	8	0	32	2	0	3	26	6	.81	2	.342	.375	.419
Bonds,Bobby	San Jose	SF	A+	27	110	420	104	16	5	11	163	65	51	43	0	126	2	1	3	21	5	.81	15	.248	.318	.388
Borel,Jamie	Lakeland	Det	A+	25	31	44	10	1	0	0	11	10	1	7	0	8	0	0	0	1	2	.33	0	.227	.333	.250
Borges,Alexander	Braves	Atl	R	22	5	13	5	0	0	0	5	1	1	4	0	1	0	0	0	1	0	1.00	0	.385	.529	.385
	Danville	Atl	R+	22	5	13	2	0	0	0	2	1	2	2	0	4	1	0	0	1	0	1.00	0	.154	.313	.154
Borrego,Ramon	Twins	Min	R	19	19	70	25	5	1	0	32	16	4	9	0	4	0	0	0	7	3	.70	1	.357	.430	.457
	Fort Myers	Min	A+	19	16	56	11	2	1	0	15	10	5	4	0	13	2	1	0	1	4	.20	1	.196	.274	.268
Boryczewski,Marty	Lakeland	Det	A+	23	13	16	3	1	0	0	4	1	2	4	0	7	1	0	0	0	0	.00	0	.188	.381	.250
Boughton,Michael	Lethbridge	Ari	R+	22	62	224	64	7	2	1	78	32	29	16	1	50	2	3	4	4	6	.40	2	.286	.333	.348
Boulo,Tyler	Idaho Falls	SD	R+	23	35	127	33	8	1	3	52	15	33	15	0	24	6	0	3	1	0	1.00	4	.260	.358	.409
Boulware,Ben	Pr. William	ChA	A+	25	117	443	112	18	1	5	147	41	52	28	0	51	2	4	2	16	6	.73	9	.253	.299	.332
Bovender,Brent	Quad City	Hou	A	24	76	269	70	18	2	8	116	41	36	31	0	61	4	1	0	4	7	.36	6	.260	.345	.431
Bowers,Ray	Quad City	Hou	A	23	64	226	58	23	0	4	93	35	20	33	2	59	1	1	2	6	10	.38	5	.257	.351	.412
	Kissimmee	Hou	A+	23	40	122	30	2	1	5	49	19	14	16	1	32	4	0	1	5	2	.71	0	.246	.350	.402
Bowles,John	Sarasota	Bos	A+	22	33	93	17	3	0	1	23	17	8	13	0	18	0	2	1	2	2	.50	1	.183	.280	.247
Bowness,Brian	South Bend	ChA	A	23	65	203	41	4	1	0	47	19	18	18	1	36	1	0	1	1	2	.33	8	.202	.269	.232
Boyd,Quincy	Columbia	NYN	A	26	2	6	0	0	0	0	0	0	0	1	0	3	0	0	0	0	0	.00	0	.000	.143	.000
Boyette,Tony	Princeton	Cin	R+	21	5	15	4	0	0	0	4	0	2	2	0	3	0	0	0	0	0	.00	0	.267	.353	.267
Bracho,Darwin	Princeton	Cin	R+	22	14	53	13	1	0	0	14	5	5	2	0	13	0	0	0	0	0	.00	0	.245	.273	.264
Braddy,Junior	Sarasota	Bos	A+	25	98	345	83	20	5	7	134	37	36	26	1	97	3	2	2	7	2	.78	5	.241	.298	.388
Bradley,Milton	Expos	Mon	R	19	31	109	27	7	1	1	39	18	12	13	0	14	1	1	2	7	4	.64	2	.248	.328	.358
Brambilla,Michael	Royals	KC	R	21	49	166	45	13	1	5	75	21	25	9	0	32	5	0	1	0	0	.00	3	.271	.326	.452
Bramlett,Jeff	Great Falls	LA	R+	21	56	222	58	14	6	7	105	42	41	17	0	62	2	0	0	12	3	.80	1	.261	.320	.473
Branyan,Russ	Columbus	Cle	A	21	130	482	129	20	4	40	277	102	106	62	5	166	5	0	3	7	4	.64	4	.268	.355	.575
Braughler,Matt	Utica	Fla	A-	24	42	125	27	4	0	1	34	15	5	11	1	33	0	0	0	0	0	.00	2	.216	.279	.272
Bravo,Danny	W. Palm Bch	Mon	A+	20	48	137	27	2	2	0	33	15	12	14	0	30	1	3	0	3	4	.43	0	.197	.276	.241
	Delmarva	Mon	A	20	18	61	14	6	1	0	22	10	7	2	0	14	1	2	1	1	0	1.00	1	.230	.262	.361
Brignac,Junior	Braves	Atl	R	19	53	191	37	7	0	0	44	15	8	9	0	60	4	1	1	3	7	.30	2	.194	.244	.230
Brinkley,Josh	W. Palm Bch	Mon	A+	23	87	268	70	11	2	5	100	34	27	26	0	44	14	5	3	1	2	.33	6	.261	.354	.373
Briones,Chris	Charlstn-SC	Tex	A	24	26	79	15	4	1	0	21	10	10	2	0	39	1	0	1	0	1	.00	2	.190	.217	.266
Brissey,Jason	Visalia	Ari	A+	24	83	234	53	15	3	7	95	32	34	18	0	80	3	2	5	2	4	.33	4	.226	.285	.406
Brito,Bobby	Red Sox	Bos	R	19	33	115	29	10	0	0	39	10	14	5	0	21	0	0	1	5	0	1.00	2	.252	.281	.339
Brito,Domingo	Piedmont	Phi	A	21	43	102	12	3	0	0	15	5	9	14	0	36	0	3	0	1	0	1.00	2	.118	.224	.147
Britt,Bryan	New Jersey	StL	A-	22	69	268	64	12	1	7	99	28	42	19	2	86	2	1	1	3	5	.38	4	.239	.293	.369
Bronson,Benjamin	Royals	KC	R	24	27	94	29	8	1	0	39	19	8	16	0	16	1	3	1	9	3	.75	1	.309	.411	.415
Brooks,Ali	Pirates	Pit	R	21	31	97	18	0	1	0	20	8	9	5	0	10	0	3	0	8	5	.62	2	.186	.225	.206
Brooks,Anthony	Danville	Atl	R+	20	2	8	2	1	0	0	3	0	1	0	0	3	0	0	0	0	0	.00	1	.250	.250	.375
	Braves	Atl	R	20	43	164	36	8	1	0	46	15	10	11	0	33	5	7	1	2	9	.18	0	.220	.287	.280
Brooks,Eddie	Lynchburg	Pit	A+	24	85	270	72	23	1	4	109	41	28	15	1	73	4	4	3	4	2	.67	7	.267	.312	.404
Brooks,Rayme	Wilmington	KC	A+	27	111	363	91	24	2	15	164	54	66	45	0	80	0	2	7	4	3	.57	10	.251	.328	.452
Brosam,Eric	Twins	Min	R	19	21	55	10	2	1	0	14	6	8	7	0	11	3	1	1	1	0	1.00	0	.182	.303	.255
Brown,Armann	Fort Myers	Min	A+	24	112	403	100	14	8	3	139	75	27	65	0	75	5	7	3	36	15	.71	5	.248	.357	.345

1996 Batting — Single-A and Rookie Leagues

BATTING																				BASERUNNING				PERCENTAGES		
Player	Team	Org	Lg	A	G	AB	H	2B	3B	HR	TB	R	RBI	TBB	IBB	SO	HBP	SH	SF	SB	CS	SB%	GDP	Avg	OBP	SLG
Brown,Dermal	Royals	KC	R	19	7	20	1	1	0	0	2	1	1	0	0	6	1	0	0	0	2	.00	0	.050	.095	.100
Brown,Emil	Athletics	Oak	R	22	4	15	4	3	0	0	7	5	2	3	0	2	1	0	0	1	1	.50	0	.267	.421	.467
	Modesto	Oak	A+	22	57	211	64	10	1	10	106	50	47	32	1	51	6	0	2	13	5	.72	5	.303	.406	.502
Brown,Eric	Yakima	LA	A-	20	53	171	40	9	0	7	70	19	21	16	1	68	2	0	2	5	2	.71	4	.234	.304	.409
Brown,Gavin	Eugene	Atl	A-	22	58	206	54	6	1	6	80	31	34	22	0	33	2	0	3	0	2	.00	5	.262	.335	.388
Brown,Jerome	Elizabethtn	Min	R+	21	50	165	44	10	2	4	70	32	25	21	1	58	1	0	1	4	1	.80	5	.267	.351	.424
Brown,Nate	W. Palm Bch	Mon	A+	26	95	285	61	12	1	3	84	39	25	30	2	68	4	0	3	12	4	.75	7	.214	.295	.295
Brown,Richard	Yankees	NYA	R	20	47	164	47	8	3	0	61	33	23	23	1	32	1	1	3	2	1	.67	2	.287	.372	.372
Brown,Roosevelt	Macon	Atl	A	21	113	413	115	27	0	19	199	61	64	33	4	60	3	0	3	21	11	.66	9	.278	.334	.482
	Kane County	Fla	A	21	11	40	6	2	0	0	8	1	3	1	0	10	1	0	0	0	1	.00	0	.150	.190	.200
Brown,Vick	Tampa	NYA	A+	24	35	89	18	3	0	0	21	17	7	14	0	22	2	2	0	2	0	1.00	3	.202	.324	.236
	Greensboro	NYA	A	24	25	91	29	6	0	1	38	8	9	11	0	23	1	0	0	9	2	.82	0	.319	.398	.418
Bruce,Maurice	Kingsport	NYN	R+	NA	11	38	7	0	1	0	9	5	4	0	0	7	1	0	1	2	1	.67	1	.184	.200	.237
	Mets	NYN	R	NA	30	120	33	5	3	0	44	16	7	3	0	15	0	3	1	6	1	.86	1	.275	.290	.367
Brumbaugh,Cliff	Charlstn-SC	Tex	A	23	132	458	111	23	7	6	166	70	45	72	2	103	1	1	2	20	7	.74	5	.242	.345	.362
Brunson,Matt	Brevard Cty	Fla	A+	22	127	396	81	13	1	0	96	51	29	66	0	89	4	7	3	28	11	.72	6	.205	.322	.242
Bryant,Chris	Frederick	Bal	A+	24	3	8	0	0	0	0	0	0	0	0	0	4	1	0	0	0	0	.00	0	.000	.111	.000
	High Desert	Bal	A+	24	68	234	70	10	2	5	99	53	41	32	0	55	4	4	2	3	2	.60	6	.299	.390	.423
Bryant,Clint	Asheville	Col	A	23	68	228	56	9	2	5	84	33	30	36	1	45	6	2	4	10	10	.50	0	.246	.358	.368
Bucci,Carmen	Clinton	SD	A	24	28	65	11	1	0	0	12	9	5	8	0	22	1	1	0	3	0	1.00	2	.169	.270	.185
	Rancho Cuca	SD	A+	24	9	16	0	0	0	0	0	1	1	0	0	5	0	1	0	0	0	.00	0	.000	.000	.000
Buchanan,Brian	Tampa	NYA	A+	23	131	526	137	22	4	10	197	65	58	37	6	108	10	1	1	23	8	.74	14	.260	.321	.375
Buchman,Thomas	Elizabethtn	Min	R+	22	6	17	6	3	0	1	12	3	3	4	0	4	1	0	0	0	0	.00	1	.353	.500	.706
Buckles,Matt	Martinsvlle	Phi	R+	20	34	109	28	5	2	3	46	13	21	7	0	24	1	0	1	4	0	1.00	0	.257	.305	.422
Buczkowski,Matt	Piedmont	Phi	A	23	5	23	5	1	0	0	6	2	1	0	0	8	1	0	0	0	0	.00	0	.217	.250	.261
	Martinsvlle	Phi	R+	23	50	158	48	12	1	3	71	25	23	27	0	52	4	1	2	2	3	.40	3	.304	.414	.449
Budzinski,Mark	Columbus	Cle	A	23	74	260	68	12	4	3	97	42	38	59	4	68	4	2	1	12	3	.80	5	.262	.404	.373
Buhner,Shawn	Lancaster	Sea	A+	24	69	239	50	19	1	3	80	28	25	20	0	55	9	1	1	0	0	.00	10	.209	.294	.335
Buirley,Matthew	Vermont	Mon	A-	21	35	115	20	4	0	1	27	10	8	9	0	46	1	1	0	1	2	.33	4	.174	.240	.235
Bulheller,Greg	White Sox	ChA	R	23	9	20	2	1	0	0	3	0	1	0	0	4	0	0	0	0	0	.00	0	.100	.100	.150
Bunkley,Antuan	Fort Wayne	Min	A	21	58	172	40	11	1	1	56	19	12	16	1	39	7	1	0	1	0	1.00	6	.233	.323	.326
Burke,Stoney	Lynchburg	Pit	A+	26	37	92	19	4	0	0	23	10	9	7	0	24	0	1	1	0	0	.00	3	.207	.260	.250
Burns,Kevin	Auburn	Hou	A-	21	71	269	71	19	3	11	129	27	55	15	1	77	4	0	5	2	1	.67	1	.264	.307	.480
Burns,Patrick	Mets	NYN	R	19	44	147	34	9	0	0	43	17	15	19	1	32	2	1	2	1	3	.25	2	.231	.324	.293
Burns,Xavier	Erie	Pit	A-	22	14	38	6	1	0	0	7	6	2	3	0	12	2	0	0	2	1	.67	1	.158	.256	.184
	Pirates	Pit	R	22	22	73	12	1	1	0	15	17	3	11	0	24	1	0	1	6	0	1.00	1	.164	.279	.205
Burress,Andy	Billings	Cin	R+	19	27	107	34	5	2	5	58	23	25	7	0	16	1	0	1	4	1	.80	3	.318	.362	.542
Burrows,Mike	Everett	Sea	A-	21	43	147	31	9	2	3	53	18	19	21	0	41	1	0	1	5	3	.63	2	.211	.312	.361
Bustos,Saul	Daytona	ChN	A+	24	100	298	56	7	2	5	82	35	29	22	1	76	2	4	2	5	4	.56	7	.188	.247	.275
Butkus,Benjamin	Orioles	Bal	R	21	20	41	6	0	1	0	8	1	3	1	0	13	0	0	0	0	1	.00	1	.146	.167	.195
Butler,Allen	Oneonta	NYA	A-	22	72	249	54	7	2	1	68	32	24	32	4	66	3	4	1	0	1	.00	6	.217	.312	.273
Butler,Garrett	Oneonta	NYA	A-	21	69	207	58	3	1	0	63	36	16	30	0	46	1	7	1	29	7	.81	2	.280	.372	.304
Butler,Brent	Johnson Cty	StL	R+	19	62	248	85	21	1	8	132	45	50	25	1	29	2	1	2	8	1	.89	11	.343	.404	.532
Butler,Rich	Dunedin	Tor	A+	24	10	28	2	0	0	0	2	1	0	5	0	9	0	0	0	4	1	.80	1	.071	.212	.071
Buxbaum,Danny	Lk Elsinore	Cal	A+	24	74	298	87	17	2	14	150	53	60	31	2	41	2	0	2	1	0	1.00	8	.292	.360	.503
Byers,Macgregor	Athletics	Oak	R	22	21	77	25	9	1	1	39	15	13	18	0	20	0	0	1	2	0	1.00	0	.325	.448	.506
	Sou. Oregon	Oak	A-	22	34	126	38	9	1	1	52	28	20	23	1	32	4	0	2	5	2	.71	2	.302	.419	.413
Byers,Scott	Boise	Cal	A-	23	66	257	72	19	1	6	111	31	39	27	1	21	1	0	2	0	0	.00	4	.280	.348	.432
Byington,Jimmie	Wilmington	KC	A+	23	105	297	88	20	2	1	115	46	32	19	0	44	5	6	5	12	8	.60	4	.296	.344	.387
Byrd,Brandon	Astros	Hou	R	19	37	124	24	11	1	1	40	7	20	12	0	41	2	1	2	0	2	.00	0	.194	.271	.323
Byrd,Isaac	Johnson Cty	StL	R+	22	24	94	26	6	1	2	40	16	15	8	0	19	4	0	1	5	2	.71	1	.277	.355	.426
Cabrera,Alex	Bakersfield	ChN	A+	25	89	345	97	18	1	15	162	45	53	14	0	80	11	0	4	0	1	.00	13	.281	.326	.470
Cabrera,Orlando	Delmarva	Mon	A	23	134	512	129	28	4	14	207	86	65	54	4	63	5	5	4	51	18	.74	4	.252	.327	.404
Cady,Todd	Brevard Cty	Fla	A+	24	101	340	73	10	1	7	106	34	34	38	3	83	4	2	1	3	6	.33	9	.215	.300	.312
Cafaro,Gio	Helena	Mil	R+	23	49	157	55	7	2	0	66	34	22	20	0	36	1	2	3	15	8	.65	2	.350	.420	.420
Calderon,Ricardo	Burlington	SF	A	21	19	63	9	0	0	2	15	8	4	6	0	16	0	0	0	0	0	.00	1	.143	.217	.238
	Bellingham	SF	A-	21	43	108	24	5	1	3	40	10	11	11	0	42	1	0	2	3	2	.60	2	.222	.295	.370
Camacaro,Pedro	Rangers	Tex	R	19	36	121	23	5	1	0	30	8	13	7	0	29	3	1	1	6	1	.86	2	.190	.250	.248
Cameron,Ken	New Jersey	StL	A-	24	53	190	55	10	6	0	77	43	20	34	2	37	6	0	1	8	4	.67	4	.289	.411	.405
Camfield,Eric	Tampa	NYA	A+	24	13	41	9	1	0	0	10	4	0	2	0	7	0	0	0	0	1	.00	1	.220	.256	.244
	Greensboro	NYA	A	24	76	238	42	2	2	0	48	19	24	18	0	63	3	1	5	13	5	.72	2	.176	.239	.202
Camilli,Jason	Delmarva	Mon	A	21	119	426	95	13	2	3	121	53	36	63	1	89	5	9	2	26	17	.60	4	.223	.329	.284
Camilo,Jose	Kane County	Fla	A	20	30	96	17	0	2	5	36	10	14	10	0	26	1	2	0	7	0	1.00	0	.177	.262	.375
	Brevard Cty	Fla	A+	20	12	44	8	0	1	2	16	6	4	3	0	11	0	1	1	2	0	1.00	0	.182	.229	.364
Campbell,Richard	Billings	Cin	R+	22	70	259	96	15	7	0	125	69	30	45	2	29	8	5	3	24	6	.80	1	.371	.473	.483
Campillo,Rob	Stockton	Mil	A+	25	46	145	35	4	1	0	41	11	18	15	0	27	1	4	2	2	3	.40	6	.241	.313	.283
Campusano,Carlos	Beloit	Mil	A	21	108	337	83	17	4	1	111	33	20	10	0	63	5	5	1	4	3	.57	7	.246	.278	.329
Cancel,David	South Bend	ChA	A	23	96	315	79	7	2	2	96	30	29	13	2	37	0	7	5	12	8	.60	7	.251	.276	.305
Cancel,Robby	Beloit	Mil	A	21	72	218	48	3	1	1	56	26	29	14	0	31	1	5	1	13	5	.72	7	.220	.269	.257
Candelaria,Vidal	Yankees	NYA	R	19	25	68	19	3	0	0	22	8	11	6	0	11	0	0	2	0	0	.00	0	.279	.329	.324
Canetto,John	Augusta	Pit	A	24	8	14	5	1	0	0	6	1	3	1	0	4	0	0	0	1	0	1.00	0	.357	.400	.429
Capallen,Rene	Fayettevlle	Det	A	19	72	250	65	10	0	1	78	26	31	12	1	47	7	4	2	1	1	.50	2	.260	.310	.312
Cardona,Javier	Fayettevlle	Det	A	21	97	348	98	21	0	4	131	42	28	28	1	53	2	3	3	1	5	.17	9	.282	.336	.376
Cardona,Luis	Red Sox	Bos	R	19	29	75	10	2	0	1	15	5	5	0	0	18	2	0	1	1	1	.50	1	.133	.154	.200
Carey,Orlando	Yankees	NYA	R	21	57	213	53	4	3	0	63	32	20	14	0	47	6	2	3	5	3	.63	3	.249	.309	.296
Carmona,Antonio	White Sox	ChA	R	20	47	154	36	5	1	0	43	15	15	7	0	26	3	0	2	4	2	.67	1	.234	.277	.279
Carmona,Cesarin	Clinton	SD	A	20	104	315	62	7	2	2	79	38	21	44	0	104	1	6	1	8	6	.57	6	.197	.296	.251

1996 Batting — Single-A and Rookie Leagues

BATTING																				BASERUNNING				PERCENTAGES		
Player	Team	Org	Lg	A	G	AB	H	2B	3B	HR	TB	R	RBI	TBB	IBB	SO	HBP	SH	SF	SB	CS	SB%	GDP	Avg	OBP	SLG
Carney,Bartt	Orioles	Bal	R	23	6	12	3	0	0	0	3	4	1	5	0	1	0	0	0	1	0	1.00	0	.250	.471	.250
	High Desert	Bal	A+	23	47	116	29	3	3	1	41	31	11	15	0	26	4	2	0	6	4	.60	1	.250	.356	.353
Carone,Rick	Pr. William	ChA	A+	26	7	27	3	1	0	1	7	1	3	3	0	7	0	1	0	0	1	.00	1	.111	.200	.259
Carpentier,Mike	San Bernrdo	LA	A+	22	15	42	9	1	1	0	12	5	7	4	0	4	0	2	0	2	3	.40	3	.214	.283	.286
	Vero Beach	LA	A+	22	64	208	47	9	0	4	68	28	23	19	1	34	1	2	1	3	4	.43	3	.226	.293	.327
Carrasquel,Domin.	Beloit	Mil	A	25	73	190	32	6	0	0	38	16	10	21	0	14	0	3	0	1	1	.50	1	.168	.251	.200
Carrion,Jorge	Rangers	Tex	R	20	19	55	17	2	0	0	19	13	8	3	0	6	0	0	1	9	1	.90	2	.309	.339	.345
	Charlstn-SC	Tex	A	20	10	38	11	0	1	0	13	7	6	3	0	10	0	1	1	0	2	.00	0	.289	.333	.342
Carroll,Doug	Bakersfield	Sea	A+	23	58	215	64	17	2	7	106	35	39	27	1	53	3	1	3	3	2	.60	3	.298	.379	.493
	Lancaster	Sea	A+	23	32	111	29	4	0	5	48	20	14	12	1	30	3	0	0	0	0	.00	2	.261	.349	.432
	Wisconsin	Sea	A	23	22	68	14	2	0	1	19	12	7	8	0	10	0	0	1	1	1	.50	5	.206	.286	.279
Carroll,Jamey	Vermont	Mon	A-	22	54	203	56	6	1	0	64	40	17	29	0	25	0	3	2	16	11	.59	1	.276	.363	.315
Carter,Cale	Lk Elsinore	Cal	A+	23	38	113	33	9	0	1	45	12	15	14	1	21	0	2	0	4	4	.50	3	.292	.370	.398
Carter,Quincy	Cubs	ChN	R	19	55	181	39	6	1	3	56	31	37	35	0	36	3	2	5	18	6	.75	5	.215	.344	.309
	Daytona	ChN	A+	19	1	0	0	0	0	0	0	1	0	0	0	0	0	0	0	0	0	.00	0	.000	.000	.000
Caruso,Michael	Bellingham	SF	A-	20	73	312	91	13	1	2	112	48	24	16	2	23	2	3	6	24	10	.71	2	.292	.324	.359
Carver,Steve	Clearwater	Phi	A+	24	117	436	121	32	0	17	204	59	79	52	7	89	1	0	4	1	1	.50	12	.278	.353	.468
Casey,Sean	Kinston	Cle	A+	22	92	344	114	31	3	12	187	62	57	36	3	47	6	0	2	1	1	.50	5	.331	.402	.544
Casimiro,Carlos	Bluefield	Bal	R+	20	62	239	66	16	0	10	112	51	33	20	1	52	2	2	2	22	9	.71	3	.276	.335	.469
Castaldo,Eric	Danville	Atl	R+	22	26	83	19	3	0	1	25	11	12	13	0	27	3	0	0	2	3	.40	3	.229	.354	.301
Castro,Dennis	Brevard Cty	Fla	A+	24	67	225	58	11	2	3	82	15	27	16	0	56	3	1	3	0	4	.00	5	.258	.312	.364
Castro,Jose	Modesto	Oak	A+	22	95	363	82	16	1	8	124	58	48	42	0	124	3	8	3	25	12	.68	4	.226	.309	.342
Castro,Jose	Everett	Sea	A-	21	1	4	1	0	0	0	1	0	0	0	0	1	0	0	0	0	0	.00	0	.250	.250	.250
	Wisconsin	Sea	A	21	37	111	24	3	0	0	27	12	10	9	0	22	1	2	1	2	5	.29	4	.216	.279	.243
Castro,Juan	Rockies	Col	R	22	22	77	19	3	2	0	26	10	6	2	0	10	1	0	0	3	1	.75	1	.247	.275	.338
Castro,Nelson	Boise	Cal	A-	21	1	1	0	0	0	0	0	0	0	0	0	0	0	0	0	0	0	.00	0	.000	.000	.000
	Angels	Cal	R	21	53	186	38	4	3	3	57	31	14	32	0	42	2	1	0	25	8	.76	3	.204	.327	.306
Castro,Ramon	Quad City	Hou	A	21	96	314	78	15	0	7	114	38	43	31	1	61	2	0	3	2	0	1.00	12	.248	.317	.363
Catlett,David	Rockford	ChN	A	23	78	224	52	18	1	1	75	31	30	23	0	73	5	2	0	5	3	.63	6	.232	.317	.335
Cawhorn,Gerad	Kinston	Cle	A+	25	53	174	41	14	1	2	63	29	23	22	0	35	3	6	1	2	1	.67	3	.236	.330	.362
Cedeno,Eduardo	Wilmington	KC	A+	24	78	163	34	7	0	1	44	28	18	14	0	65	3	2	2	11	5	.69	2	.209	.280	.270
Cedeno,Jesus	Jamestown	Det	A-	21	74	236	66	16	2	9	113	43	39	31	0	57	10	6	3	7	6	.54	4	.280	.382	.479
Cepeda,Jose	Lansing	KC	A	22	135	558	161	29	3	3	205	87	81	38	0	44	11	9	8	10	3	.77	8	.289	.341	.367
Cepeda,Malcolm	Burlington	SF	A	24	82	209	33	9	1	0	44	20	15	41	1	73	7	3	1	1	2	.33	3	.158	.314	.211
Cesar,Dionys	Modesto	Oak	A+	20	22	60	12	2	0	0	14	5	4	7	0	19	0	6	0	1	3	.25	0	.200	.284	.233
	Sou. Oregon	Oak	A-	20	52	203	55	7	4	1	73	37	12	19	0	46	4	7	1	18	6	.75	3	.271	.344	.360
Cespedes,Angel	Portland	Col	A-	19	27	80	15	1	1	1	21	8	3	10	0	28	0	1	1	1	1	.50	0	.188	.275	.263
Cey,Dan	Fort Wayne	Min	A	21	27	85	22	4	0	0	26	8	6	8	0	11	0	0	0	2	1	.67	2	.259	.323	.306
Chaidez,Juan	Red Sox	Bos	R	20	22	47	6	0	1	0	8	1	0	2	0	16	1	0	0	0	1	.00	1	.128	.180	.170
Chamblee,James	Michigan	Bos	A	22	100	303	66	15	2	1	88	31	39	16	0	75	7	4	4	2	2	.50	1	.218	.270	.290
Champion,Jeffrey	Braves	Atl	R	21	29	88	15	1	2	0	20	6	2	8	0	23	1	1	0	2	2	.50	0	.170	.247	.227
	Danville	Atl	R+	21	4	11	3	0	0	0	3	2	1	0	0	3	0	0	0	0	0	.00	0	.273	.273	.273
Chancey,Bailey	Kingsport	NYN	R+	22	59	197	53	6	3	0	65	44	25	42	1	35	7	5	3	30	5	.86	2	.269	.410	.330
Chancey,Rob	Kingsport	NYN	R+	24	6	19	5	0	0	1	8	4	3	2	0	5	0	0	0	1	0	1.00	0	.263	.333	.421
Chapman,David	Diamondback	Ari	R	19	37	118	14	2	2	0	20	12	12	10	1	28	0	0	1	0	1	.00	4	.119	.186	.169
Chapman,Scott	Astros	Hou	R	19	45	142	37	8	1	2	53	17	19	18	1	25	0	1	2	3	1	.75	3	.261	.340	.373
Charles,Curtis	Bluefield	Bal	R+	21	60	182	37	7	1	6	64	36	17	32	1	76	4	0	1	31	6	.84	4	.203	.333	.352
Charles,Steve	St. Cathrns	Tor	A-	22	68	200	41	7	2	1	55	22	15	18	0	48	3	3	1	5	2	.71	3	.205	.279	.275
Charvel,Ali	Angels	Cal	R	20	11	41	16	4	1	0	22	7	2	0	0	9	0	0	0	1	0	1.00	0	.390	.390	.537
Chatman,Karl	Vermont	Mon	A-	22	72	260	69	11	3	1	89	47	38	27	1	52	4	0	5	16	6	.73	5	.265	.338	.342
Chavera,Arnoldo	Quad City	Hou	A	23	77	184	45	16	1	3	72	22	34	19	0	46	1	0	1	0	1	.00	4	.245	.317	.391
Chavez,Eric	Frederick	Bal	A+	26	122	416	116	29	1	18	201	60	64	72	5	101	3	2	5	5	3	.63	10	.279	.385	.483
Chavez,Steven	Idaho Falls	SD	R+	21	69	277	90	19	2	7	134	55	50	49	0	52	4	0	8	5	3	.63	4	.325	.423	.484
Chevalier,Virgil	Michigan	Bos	A	23	126	483	120	31	3	8	181	61	62	33	1	69	1	1	5	11	4	.73	11	.248	.295	.375
Christensen,Mckay	White Sox	ChA	R	21	35	133	35	7	5	1	55	17	16	10	0	23	3	0	1	10	3	.77	1	.263	.327	.414
	Hickory	ChA	A	21	6	11	0	0	0	0	0	0	0	1	0	4	0	0	0	0	0	.00	0	.000	.083	.000
Christenson,Ryan	Sou. Oregon	Oak	A-	23	36	136	39	11	0	5	65	31	21	19	1	21	1	1	1	8	6	.57	3	.287	.376	.478
	W. Michigan	Oak	A	23	33	122	38	2	2	2	50	21	18	13	0	22	4	1	3	2	4	.33	2	.311	.387	.410
Ciminiello,Michael	Jamestown	Det	A-	23	10	18	2	0	0	0	2	1	1	0	0	2	0	0	0	0	0	.00	1	.111	.111	.111
Clapp,Stubby	Johnson Cty	StL	R+	24	29	94	21	3	2	1	31	25	15	26	0	15	1	1	1	9	2	.82	2	.223	.393	.330
Clark,John	Princeton	Cin	R+	23	58	196	49	5	2	0	58	30	17	38	0	41	3	1	2	7	2	.78	7	.250	.377	.296
Clark,John	Portland	Col	A-	20	58	211	43	8	3	2	63	17	19	12	0	62	4	2	1	0	2	.00	4	.204	.259	.299
Clark,Kevin	Michigan	Bos	A	24	126	474	131	32	3	10	199	53	56	30	2	94	12	1	4	4	5	.44	11	.276	.333	.420
Clark,Kirby	Batavia	Phi	A-	23	51	183	48	11	1	3	70	25	24	16	1	39	4	0	0	1	1	.50	3	.262	.335	.383
Claudio,Patricio	Kinston	Cle	A+	25	100	361	105	15	2	1	127	67	38	47	2	74	6	2	3	36	14	.72	2	.291	.379	.352
Claybrook,Steve	Charlstn-WV	Cin	A	24	123	439	115	18	3	4	151	62	40	69	2	144	1	3	0	37	11	.77	0	.262	.363	.344
Clifford,Jim	Lancaster	Sea	A+	27	112	389	100	19	6	20	191	78	85	53	2	92	15	0	7	4	4	.50	3	.257	.362	.491
Clifford,John	Asheville	Col	A	23	94	317	68	14	1	1	87	29	27	25	0	69	9	5	1	19	8	.70	3	.215	.290	.274
Clifton,Rodney	Athletics	Oak	R	20	42	164	34	4	1	2	46	27	11	13	0	34	2	1	1	10	2	.83	1	.207	.272	.280
Cline,Pat	Daytona	ChN	A+	22	124	434	121	30	2	17	206	75	76	54	2	79	12	0	2	10	2	.83	6	.279	.373	.475
Coats,Nathan	Watertown	Cle	A-	23	31	102	27	5	1	0	34	13	7	8	0	20	6	4	0	1	1	.50	2	.265	.353	.333
Coburn,Todd	Piedmont	Phi	A	25	46	155	30	9	0	1	42	15	16	15	0	34	0	3	0	2	1	.67	2	.194	.265	.271
Cochran,Edwin	White Sox	ChA	R	19	53	144	25	5	1	0	32	20	12	11	0	45	8	2	1	6	1	.86	2	.174	.268	.222
Coe,Ryan	Quad City	Hou	A	24	77	246	72	10	1	14	126	38	47	18	0	56	10	3	2	0	0	.00	6	.293	.362	.512
Coffee,Gary	Lansing	KC	A	22	105	393	91	17	2	11	145	52	59	53	2	141	5	0	3	6	1	.86	11	.232	.328	.369
Coffie,Evanon	Orioles	Bal	R	20	56	193	42	8	4	0	58	29	20	23	1	26	2	0	0	6	2	.75	4	.218	.307	.301
Cole,Ala	Utica	Fla	A-	21	67	202	43	15	1	2	66	21	27	24	1	78	8	4	3	7	2	.78	5	.213	.316	.327

1996 Batting — Single-A and Rookie Leagues

BATTING																				BASERUNNING				PERCENTAGES		
Player	Team	Org	Lg	A	G	AB	H	2B	3B	HR	TB	R	RBI	TBB	IBB	SO	HBP	SH	SF	SB	CS	SB%	GDP	Avg	OBP	SLG
Cole,Eric	Auburn	Hou	A-	21	46	151	26	4	0	1	33	9	10	6	0	46	3	1	4	3	1	.75	7	.172	.213	.219
Coleman,Michael	Sarasota	Bos	A+	21	110	407	100	20	5	1	133	54	36	38	1	86	8	7	3	24	5	.83	10	.246	.320	.327
Collier,Marc	Angels	Cal	R	19	30	87	18	6	0	0	24	9	7	7	0	22	1	2	1	4	2	.67	1	.207	.271	.276
Colon,Ariel	Mets	NYN	R	19	23	65	7	1	0	0	8	8	5	7	0	23	2	1	1	1	1	.50	2	.108	.213	.123
Colon,Jose	Williamsprt	ChN	A-	21	36	125	27	5	1	0	34	13	15	11	0	31	1	2	1	3	3	.50	2	.216	.283	.272
	Rockford	ChN	A	21	8	12	3	0	0	0	3	1	1	3	0	5	0	0	0	0	2	.00	0	.250	.400	.250
Colson,Julian	Braves	Atl	R	20	15	41	11	4	0	1	18	5	2	2	0	13	2	2	0	0	0	.00	0	.268	.333	.439
Concepcion,David	Princeton	Cin	R+	22	4	16	4	1	0	0	5	2	0	2	0	3	0	1	0	2	0	1.00	0	.250	.333	.313
	Charlstn-WV	Cin	A	22	40	116	23	3	1	0	28	9	11	10	0	31	1	0	0	3	1	.75	2	.198	.268	.241
Connell,Jerry	Cubs	ChN	R	19	19	64	23	3	0	2	32	7	12	7	0	13	1	0	2	4	1	.80	3	.359	.419	.500
	Williamsprt	ChN	A-	19	2	6	0	0	0	0	0	0	0	0	0	0	0	0	0	0	0	.00	0	.000	.000	.000
Conner,Decomba	Winston-Sal	Cin	A+	23	129	512	144	18	5	20	232	77	64	43	1	117	2	5	4	33	11	.75	6	.281	.337	.453
Connolly,Sean	Bristol	ChA	R+	23	39	116	18	4	0	1	25	10	13	10	0	44	1	2	2	2	2	.50	3	.155	.225	.216
Conroy,Danny	Idaho Falls	SD	R+	24	23	54	15	3	1	1	23	11	5	6	0	8	1	0	0	5	3	.63	4	.278	.361	.426
Conti,Stanley	Lethbridge	Ari	R+	22	63	226	83	15	1	4	112	63	49	30	0	29	6	0	3	30	7	.81	3	.367	.449	.496
Contreras,Efrain	St. Pete	StL	A+	24	31	79	12	4	1	1	21	6	12	10	1	20	2	0	1	0	0	.00	0	.152	.261	.266
Conway,Scott	Marlins	Fla	R	18	30	101	24	6	0	2	36	7	15	7	0	23	5	0	3	3	1	.75	1	.238	.310	.356
Cook,Jason	Lancaster	Sea	A+	25	124	450	130	22	4	5	175	95	58	89	0	68	16	4	4	5	2	.71	6	.289	.420	.389
Cook,John	Auburn	Hou	A-	24	10	35	3	0	0	0	3	0	1	0	0	7	0	0	0	1	0	1.00	1	.086	.086	.086
Cooley,Shannon	Batavia	Phi	A-	23	62	229	63	9	3	2	84	30	23	17	2	40	1	2	0	6	6	.50	3	.275	.328	.367
Cooney,Kyle	San Bernrdo	LA	A+	24	107	406	111	20	0	14	173	57	67	28	1	78	14	0	5	9	8	.53	8	.273	.338	.426
Copeland,Brandon	Mets	NYN	R	20	46	135	32	9	2	3	54	31	17	36	0	32	7	0	0	4	0	1.00	0	.237	.421	.400
Coquillette,Trace	Expos	Mon	R	23	7	25	4	1	0	0	5	4	0	4	0	6	0	0	0	1	0	1.00	0	.160	.276	.200
	W. Palm Bch	Mon	A+	23	72	266	67	17	4	1	95	39	27	27	1	72	8	0	3	9	7	.56	5	.252	.336	.357
Cora,Alex	Vero Beach	LA	A+	21	61	214	55	5	4	0	68	26	26	12	0	36	3	4	0	5	5	.50	1	.257	.306	.318
Cordero,Edward	Durham	Atl	A+	22	68	177	35	6	1	0	43	27	12	15	1	59	2	4	1	1	3	.25	1	.198	.267	.243
Cordero,Pablo	Burlington	SF	A	24	33	79	7	3	0	0	10	5	4	6	0	17	1	1	1	2	0	1.00	2	.089	.161	.127
Cornelius,Jon	Piedmont	Phi	A	23	123	454	106	16	2	12	162	41	51	33	1	132	8	5	1	6	5	.55	9	.233	.296	.357
Corujo,Rey	San Jose	SF	A+	25	57	188	51	12	1	4	77	26	28	19	0	43	2	0	3	1	0	1.00	4	.271	.340	.410
Costello,Brian	Clearwater	Phi	A+	22	81	282	58	13	2	2	81	28	31	17	0	84	4	4	4	6	4	.60	3	.206	.257	.287
Coston,Sean	Vero Beach	LA	A+	25	10	22	5	1	0	0	6	4	0	1	0	9	1	0	0	0	0	.00	0	.227	.292	.273
Cox,Chuck	Clearwater	Phi	A+	24	4	10	1	1	0	0	2	0	2	1	0	4	0	1	1	0	0	.00	1	.100	.167	.200
	Piedmont	Phi	A	24	27	89	18	5	0	1	26	8	5	6	1	26	2	2	0	1	1	.50	2	.202	.268	.292
Crane,Todd	Piedmont	Phi	A	23	9	23	5	0	0	0	5	4	1	6	1	6	0	0	0	0	1	.00	0	.217	.379	.217
	Batavia	Phi	A-	23	35	134	32	9	2	3	54	21	18	11	0	31	2	1	1	3	4	.43	2	.239	.304	.403
Cranford,Joseph	Elizabethtn	Min	R+	22	32	121	34	6	3	4	58	20	18	13	0	28	0	0	0	2	1	.67	4	.281	.351	.479
	Fort Myers	Min	A+	22	30	105	23	3	1	0	28	9	17	7	0	21	0	2	1	3	1	.75	0	.219	.265	.267
Crawford,Marty	Batavia	Phi	A-	23	63	219	59	8	1	2	75	26	30	18	1	22	2	3	1	5	2	.71	4	.269	.329	.342
Crede,Bradley	Batavia	Phi	A-	22	75	280	77	15	1	8	118	44	51	30	1	85	3	1	3	0	5	.00	6	.275	.348	.421
Crede,Joseph	White Sox	ChA	R	19	56	221	66	17	1	4	97	30	32	9	0	41	2	1	4	1	1	.50	8	.299	.326	.439
Crespo,Jesse	Braves	Atl	R	19	44	129	28	4	0	0	32	11	9	8	0	28	3	5	1	4	0	1.00	3	.217	.277	.248
Cripps,Bobby	Great Falls	LA	R+	20	49	139	43	4	3	2	59	23	28	9	0	19	2	1	5	6	5	.55	5	.309	.348	.424
Cromer,David	Modesto	Oak	A+	26	124	505	166	40	10	30	316	100	130	32	4	67	6	3	4	20	7	.74	5	.329	.373	.626
Cronin,Shane	Padres	SD	R	21	53	205	67	13	0	9	107	40	54	12	0	32	3	0	4	4	1	.80	6	.327	.366	.522
Cross,Adam	Eugene	Atl	A-	23	55	196	50	12	0	3	71	34	24	27	1	41	4	1	2	9	5	.64	0	.255	.354	.362
Cruz,Alain	Yankees	NYA	R	21	45	165	42	13	2	3	68	33	26	16	1	46	1	0	1	3	0	1.00	4	.255	.322	.412
Cruz,Andres	Twins	Min	R	20	28	78	17	4	1	1	26	14	9	16	0	13	3	2	2	1	0	1.00	4	.218	.364	.333
Cruz,Cirilo	Everett	Sea	A-	22	44	163	44	6	0	0	50	12	21	8	0	34	2	0	1	1	5	.17	3	.270	.310	.307
Cruz,Deivi	Burlington	SF	A	22	127	517	152	27	2	9	210	72	64	35	3	49	4	4	3	12	5	.71	20	.294	.342	.406
Cuevas,Eduardo	Rancho Cuca	SD	A+	23	7	23	8	0	0	0	8	3	5	2	0	4	0	0	1	0	0	.00	1	.348	.385	.348
	Clinton	SD	A	23	88	312	86	15	5	1	114	33	34	22	0	47	2	4	3	19	5	.79	7	.276	.324	.365
Cueves,Trent	Savannah	LA	A	20	15	46	7	1	0	0	8	2	6	0	0	14	0	0	2	0	0	.00	0	.152	.146	.174
	Great Falls	LA	R+	20	51	155	40	12	1	3	63	24	20	11	0	30	1	1	3	2	5	.29	2	.258	.306	.406
Culp,Brian	Salem	Col	A+	26	36	121	24	4	0	1	31	8	15	16	0	14	1	0	2	3	1	.75	2	.198	.293	.256
Cunningham,Earl	Asheville	Col	A	27	35	133	34	11	0	9	72	19	30	7	2	42	9	0	1	5	1	.83	0	.256	.333	.541
	Salem	Col	A+	27	29	87	15	1	0	1	19	9	6	9	0	24	2	1	1	3	0	1.00	0	.172	.263	.218
Curl,John	Dunedin	Tor	A+	24	125	447	110	20	2	18	188	52	62	44	1	133	1	2	5	7	4	.64	6	.246	.312	.421
Curtis,Matt	Boise	Cal	A-	22	75	305	93	29	3	12	164	57	62	37	0	47	8	0	4	2	1	.67	7	.305	.390	.538
Curtis,Randy	Rancho Cuca	SD	A+	26	104	359	96	14	5	5	135	63	52	76	2	94	4	4	8	22	6	.79	2	.267	.394	.376
D'Amico,Jeffrey	Athletics	Oak	R	22	8	0	0	0	0	0	0	0	0	0	0	0	0	0	0	0	0	.00	0	.000	.000	.000
	Modesto	Oak	A+	22	47	172	46	7	1	4	67	28	21	19	0	31	4	1	1	3	1	.75	3	.267	.352	.390
D'Aquila,Tom	Frederick	Bal	A+	24	45	130	19	3	0	1	25	21	11	25	1	55	3	1	2	9	4	.69	3	.146	.294	.192
	High Desert	Bal	A+	24	6	16	1	0	1	0	3	2	1	1	0	7	0	0	0	0	0	.00	0	.063	.118	.188
Daedelow,Craig	Bakersfield	Bal	A+	21	86	298	70	17	1	1	92	37	28	31	0	60	4	4	2	10	4	.71	6	.235	.313	.309
	Frederick	Bal	A+	21	26	72	15	4	0	0	19	13	8	6	1	9	1	2	0	2	0	1.00	0	.208	.278	.264
Dallimore,Brian	Auburn	Hou	A-	23	74	290	77	17	3	5	115	50	30	18	0	38	10	0	4	7	5	.58	5	.266	.326	.397
Dalton,Jed	Cedar Rapds	Cal	A	24	79	304	85	16	1	12	139	52	47	23	0	38	12	0	2	20	8	.71	10	.280	.352	.457
	Lk Elsinore	Cal	A+	24	38	121	31	4	2	1	42	19	15	11	0	19	2	2	1	6	3	.67	3	.256	.326	.347
Daly,Bob	Columbia	NYN	A	24	44	140	42	7	1	2	57	20	17	18	2	19	0	1	0	1	2	.33	1	.300	.380	.407
	St. Lucie	NYN	A+	24	53	183	50	8	0	2	64	18	24	12	0	22	0	0	2	1	3	.25	9	.273	.315	.350
Danapilis,Eric	Visalia	Det	A+	26	105	377	97	29	1	10	158	58	64	66	0	122	8	0	1	2	1	.67	6	.257	.378	.419
Daniels,Deion	Twins	Min	R	21	4	9	1	0	0	0	1	0	0	0	0	4	1	0	0	0	0	.00	2	.111	.200	.111
Daniels,Ronney	Expos	Mon	R	20	46	159	33	6	4	3	56	29	28	18	0	44	2	0	2	9	2	.82	2	.208	.293	.352
Darcuiel,Faruq	Wisconsin	Sea	A	24	74	213	45	6	3	0	57	28	30	18	1	46	10	4	2	6	4	.60	5	.211	.300	.268
Darden,Tony	Brevard Cty	Fla	A+	23	108	390	94	21	4	1	126	37	43	28	1	55	7	4	8	6	11	.35	7	.241	.298	.323
Darnell,Bryce	Visalia	Ari	A+	24	7	13	1	0	0	0	1	1	1	0	0	2	0	0	1	0	0	.00	0	.077	.071	.077
Darr,Mike	Lakeland	Det	A+	21	85	311	77	14	7	0	105	26	38	28	0	64	0	0	3	7	3	.70	7	.248	.307	.338

1996 Batting — Single-A and Rookie Leagues

BATTING																				BASERUNNING				PERCENTAGES		
Player	Team	Org	Lg	A	G	AB	H	2B	3B	HR	TB	R	RBI	TBB	IBB	SO	HBP	SH	SF	SB	CS	SB%	GDP	Avg	OBP	SLG
Darula,Robert	Ogden	Mil	R+	22	45	106	29	4	0	4	45	19	23	17	0	22	2	0	1	2	0	1.00	2	.274	.381	.425
Dasher,Melvin	Royals	KC	R	20	17	52	14	3	1	1	22	10	6	5	0	14	1	0	0	1	0	1.00	2	.269	.345	.423
Daugherty,Keith	Macon	Atl	A	23	106	327	76	17	2	10	127	38	39	26	1	89	6	0	0	5	3	.63	6	.232	.301	.388
Dauphin,Phil	Lk Elsinore	Cal	A+	28	67	245	56	13	1	8	95	43	38	36	1	52	4	1	5	8	3	.73	2	.229	.331	.388
Davanon,Jeff	W. Michigan	Oak	A	23	89	289	70	13	4	2	97	43	33	49	2	66	1	2	1	5	7	.42	6	.242	.353	.336
Davidson,Cleatus	Fort Wayne	Min	A	20	59	203	36	8	3	0	50	20	30	23	0	45	0	1	2	2	3	.40	4	.177	.259	.246
	Elizabethtn	Min	R+	20	65	248	71	10	6	6	111	53	31	39	2	45	2	3	1	17	6	.74	5	.286	.386	.448
Davila,Angel	Kingsport	NYN	R+	22	2	0	0	0	0	0	0	1	0	2	0	0	0	0	0	0	0	.00	0	.000	1.000	.000
	Mets	NYN	R	22	9	28	5	0	0	0	5	3	2	1	0	8	0	0	0	0	1	.00	1	.179	.207	.179
Davila,Victor	Dunedin	Tor	A+	24	122	398	107	26	2	8	161	54	72	33	3	76	8	2	2	1	3	.25	15	.269	.336	.405
Davis,Eddie	San Bernrdo	LA	A+	24	136	546	140	34	2	29	265	107	89	62	1	150	8	3	4	31	23	.57	8	.256	.339	.485
Davis,Monty	Athletics	Oak	R	19	52	206	59	9	4	1	79	40	20	21	1	27	11	0	0	7	8	.47	4	.286	.382	.383
Davis,James	Charlstn-WV	Cin	A	24	84	313	90	14	1	3	115	42	38	32	0	57	1	1	3	8	3	.73	6	.288	.352	.367
Davis,Josh	Clinton	SD	A	21	9	18	1	0	0	0	1	0	0	0	0	5	0	0	0	0	0	.00	0	.056	.056	.056
	Idaho Falls	SD	R+	21	32	101	19	2	0	2	27	12	13	21	0	39	0	2	2	5	0	1.00	1	.188	.323	.267
Davis,Ben	Rancho Cuca	SD	A+	20	98	353	71	10	1	6	101	35	41	31	0	89	0	4	2	1	1	.50	8	.201	.264	.286
Davis,Reginald	Lethbridge	Ari	R+	22	31	89	28	7	1	1	40	18	18	13	1	19	1	1	0	0	2	.00	3	.315	.408	.449
Davis,Torrance	Expos	Mon	R	21	27	55	14	1	0	0	15	13	7	4	0	7	1	2	0	1	4	.20	0	.255	.317	.273
Davison,Ashanti	Orioles	Bal	R	18	31	76	20	2	0	0	22	13	4	11	0	14	5	0	0	9	2	.82	1	.263	.391	.289
De La Espada,Mig.	Astros	Hou	R	20	42	123	26	8	0	2	40	14	9	7	0	40	3	1	1	1	2	.33	1	.211	.269	.325
De La Rosa,Elvis	Visalia	Det	A+	22	69	204	45	10	1	6	75	33	27	24	0	76	5	3	1	2	2	.50	1	.221	.316	.368
De La Rosa,Miguel	Charlstn-SC	Tex	A	20	26	61	11	0	1	0	13	5	1	8	0	39	1	0	0	1	3	.25	0	.180	.286	.213
	Rangers	Tex	R	20	16	43	6	1	0	0	7	4	1	4	0	20	0	2	0	1	0	1.00	0	.140	.213	.163
Dean,Chris	Wisconsin	Sea	A	23	53	210	57	8	2	4	81	32	32	18	1	46	4	1	1	11	7	.61	5	.271	.339	.386
	Lancaster	Sea	A+	23	48	174	48	10	1	5	75	30	22	16	0	31	3	1	1	7	1	.88	3	.276	.345	.431
Decelle,Michael	Butte	TB	R+	22	69	258	75	18	7	8	131	54	51	45	1	68	9	2	3	6	2	.75	6	.291	.410	.508
Decinces,Tim	Bluefield	Bal	R+	23	39	128	38	8	0	7	67	24	32	24	0	28	2	0	5	3	1	.75	5	.297	.403	.523
Deck,Billy	Johnson Cty	StL	R+	20	52	182	52	14	0	5	81	40	33	38	1	59	10	0	3	5	2	.71	4	.286	.429	.445
Dedonatis,Donald	Jamestown	Det	A-	22	42	141	42	4	0	0	46	21	17	17	0	15	1	1	0	9	4	.69	2	.298	.377	.326
Dejesus,Eddie	Angels	Cal	R	20	48	178	47	11	3	1	67	27	25	7	0	35	4	1	2	12	3	.80	4	.264	.304	.376
DeJesus,Malvin	Visalia	Det	A+	25	124	485	117	24	4	6	167	66	51	63	0	107	6	7	3	34	13	.72	4	.241	.334	.344
De La Cruz,Carlos	Fayettevlle	Det	A	21	98	318	72	21	4	5	116	34	39	21	1	100	4	3	2	18	8	.69	4	.226	.281	.365
De La Cruz,Wilfred.	Yankees	NYA	R	21	16	43	7	0	0	0	7	3	6	4	0	9	2	1	2	1	0	1.00	0	.163	.255	.163
	Oneonta	NYA	A-	21	4	15	6	1	0	0	7	3	0	1	0	2	0	0	0	0	0	.00	0	.400	.438	.467
Delaney,Donnie	Wilmington	KC	A+	23	124	386	105	17	4	4	142	45	38	21	0	63	3	4	3	18	7	.72	6	.272	.312	.368
De La Rosa,Tomas	Expos	Mon	R	19	53	184	46	7	1	0	55	34	21	22	0	25	2	4	1	8	5	.62	2	.250	.335	.299
	Vermont	Mon	A-	19	3	8	2	0	0	0	2	1	1	0	0	3	0	0	0	0	0	.00	1	.250	.250	.250
Delgado,Ariel	Angels	Cal	R	20	47	166	38	6	1	1	49	21	11	20	1	38	1	2	0	15	2	.88	2	.229	.316	.295
Delgado,Daniel	Pirates	Pit	R	20	37	96	28	2	1	0	32	16	11	8	0	14	0	1	1	3	3	.50	4	.292	.343	.333
Delgado,Jose	Macon	Atl	A	22	102	345	101	16	0	0	117	43	50	27	2	56	5	3	2	23	11	.68	5	.293	.351	.339
Delosantos,Eddy	Devil Rays	TB	R	19	50	196	48	6	1	0	56	18	20	13	0	58	3	2	0	11	3	.79	4	.245	.302	.286
	Butte	TB	R+	19	16	59	16	0	0	0	16	15	12	6	0	17	0	2	2	1	1	.50	1	.271	.328	.271
Deman,Lou	New Jersey	StL	A-	24	8	21	3	2	0	0	5	2	3	2	0	6	0	0	0	0	0	.00	1	.143	.217	.238
Denbow,Don	Burlington	SF	A	24	92	302	84	17	2	21	168	64	62	81	12	123	8	1	2	19	5	.79	5	.278	.440	.556
	San Jose	SF	A+	24	26	97	36	8	3	6	68	19	19	17	1	30	1	0	1	1	1	.50	2	.371	.466	.701
Denman,Demond	Princeton	Cin	R+	22	55	203	45	12	1	3	68	21	27	11	0	70	6	0	2	0	2	.00	7	.222	.279	.335
Denning,Wes	Delmarva	Mon	A	24	115	349	77	17	8	4	122	60	37	43	2	63	7	3	2	31	10	.76	1	.221	.317	.350
Dennis,Les	Greensboro	NYA	A	24	33	75	19	3	0	1	25	15	9	11	0	27	1	2	0	1	2	.33	2	.253	.356	.333
	Oneonta	NYA	A-	24	72	276	67	3	2	0	74	36	43	33	1	76	1	5	6	20	9	.69	2	.243	.320	.268
Dent,Darrell	Bluefield	Bal	R+	20	59	193	43	6	2	0	53	40	14	28	1	49	0	1	4	30	9	.77	2	.223	.316	.275
Depastino,Joe	Sarasota	Bos	A+	23	97	344	90	16	2	6	128	35	44	29	1	71	3	0	4	2	3	.40	7	.262	.321	.372
Derosa,Mark	Eugene	Atl	A-	22	70	255	66	13	1	2	87	43	28	38	1	48	5	0	2	3	4	.43	10	.259	.363	.341
Derosso,Tony	Sarasota	Bos	A+	21	116	416	107	19	5	14	178	64	60	31	2	84	8	2	5	15	2	.88	10	.257	.317	.428
Deshazer,Jeremy	Astros	Hou	R	20	52	170	40	5	4	0	53	20	12	9	1	49	1	4	1	5	5	.50	2	.235	.276	.312
Diaz,Alain	Utica	Fla	A-	22	46	141	30	6	1	1	41	14	11	16	0	25	2	2	1	1	1	.50	5	.213	.300	.291
Diaz,Cesar	St. Lucie	NYN	A+	22	74	247	59	15	1	7	97	29	34	18	1	72	3	0	3	9	2	.82	12	.239	.295	.393
Diaz,Diogenes	Pirates	Pit	R	NA	26	90	21	7	2	2	38	7	9	5	0	22	0	0	0	0	0	.00	4	.233	.274	.422
Didion,Kristopher	Spokane	KC	A-	21	61	201	44	7	4	6	77	30	32	26	0	60	3	0	6	7	2	.78	8	.219	.309	.383
Dilone,Juan	Modesto	Oak	A+	24	111	404	107	17	1	14	168	78	66	45	0	138	6	8	5	31	10	.76	11	.265	.343	.416
Dishington,Nate	Peoria	StL	A	22	75	208	47	12	3	3	74	22	30	25	0	73	7	0	4	1	1	.50	6	.226	.324	.356
Donati,John	Columbus	Cle	A	24	40	145	41	6	1	6	67	23	28	10	0	27	4	0	3	1	0	1.00	5	.283	.340	.462
Downs,Brian	Hickory	ChA	A	22	84	279	58	10	0	3	77	23	28	15	0	78	4	3	2	0	1	.00	6	.208	.257	.276
Dransfeldt,Kelly	Hudson Vall	Tex	A-	22	75	284	67	17	1	7	107	42	29	27	1	76	4	1	3	13	4	.76	2	.236	.308	.377
Drent,Brian	South Bend	ChA	A	23	93	291	55	17	1	2	80	37	23	44	1	107	1	6	2	12	6	.67	5	.189	.296	.275
Dresch,Michael	Billings	Cin	R+	23	34	115	28	6	1	2	42	15	17	13	2	26	0	0	1	3	3	.50	1	.243	.318	.365
Drizos,Justin	Asheville	Col	A	23	127	438	116	29	2	18	203	64	76	70	7	126	6	0	2	7	3	.70	11	.265	.372	.463
Dukart,Derek	Tampa	NYA	A+	25	59	194	61	17	0	2	84	19	27	8	0	28	2	5	3	1	2	.33	9	.314	.343	.433
Dunham,Traylon	Padres	SD	R	19	32	77	21	1	0	0	22	13	9	13	0	23	4	0	1	2	2	.50	1	.273	.400	.286
Dunlop,Steve	Visalia	—	A+	22	23	71	16	3	0	0	19	12	3	5	0	20	3	1	0	2	1	.67	2	.225	.304	.268
Dunn,Nathan	Clinton	SD	A	22	50	166	42	11	2	0	57	20	23	29	0	44	1	0	2	10	1	.91	7	.253	.364	.343
Durick,Chad	Mets	NYN	R	20	43	133	29	6	0	0	35	14	12	8	0	27	1	1	3	6	2	.75	0	.218	.262	.263
Durkac,Bo	Visalia	Ari	A+	24	126	453	135	29	2	4	180	67	81	79	0	84	2	0	16	6	3	.67	14	.298	.393	.397
Durrington,Trent	Boise	Cal	A-	21	40	154	43	7	2	0	54	38	14	31	1	32	13	0	0	24	5	.83	4	.279	.439	.351
	Cedar Rapds	Cal	A	21	25	76	19	1	0	0	20	12	4	33	0	20	2	2	1	15	2	.88	2	.250	.482	.263
Duverge,Salvadore	Asheville	Col	A	21	103	349	69	12	1	3	92	38	31	32	3	84	15	0	3	8	12	.40	2	.198	.291	.264
Eaddy,Keith	High Desert	Bal	A+	26	12	25	2	0	0	0	2	1	0	0	0	7	1	0	0	2	1	.67	0	.080	.115	.080
	Rancho Cuca	SD	A+	26	40	104	23	5	1	3	39	13	10	18	0	41	1	1	0	1	3	.25	1	.221	.341	.375

1996 Batting — Single-A and Rookie Leagues

BATTING																				BASERUNNING				PERCENTAGES		
Player	Team	Org	Lg	A	G	AB	H	2B	3B	HR	TB	R	RBI	TBB	IBB	SO	HBP	SH	SF	SB	CS	SB%	GDP	Avg	OBP	SLG
Eady,Gerald	Mariners	Sea	R	21	46	176	39	9	4	1	59	24	26	21	0	53	2	1	0	7	2	.78	2	.222	.312	.335
Eaglin,Mike	Durham	Atl	A+	24	131	466	118	25	2	11	180	84	54	50	0	88	18	4	4	23	12	.66	1	.253	.346	.386
Ebbert,Chad	Clinton	SD	A	23	27	77	14	1	1	0	17	5	6	2	0	13	2	1	0	0	0	.00	3	.182	.222	.221
	Idaho Falls	SD	R+	23	27	102	28	5	0	0	33	10	12	3	0	23	2	0	0	0	0	.00	2	.275	.308	.324
Ebling,Jamie	Butte	TB	R+	23	50	194	54	10	3	3	79	49	32	38	0	62	1	4	1	6	4	.60	4	.278	.397	.407
Eddie,Steve	Winston-Sal	Cin	A+	26	137	497	135	23	2	9	189	56	64	45	3	78	4	6	4	14	9	.61	14	.272	.335	.380
Edmondson,Tracy	Columbia	NYN	A	22	93	273	52	12	0	2	70	43	21	55	0	64	7	6	3	5	5	.50	6	.190	.337	.256
Edwards,Aaron	Erie	Pit	A-	23	12	47	8	0	0	0	8	4	3	2	0	6	0	0	1	2	0	1.00	1	.170	.200	.170
	Augusta	Pit	A	23	40	126	30	4	2	1	41	22	11	11	0	28	3	3	1	7	5	.58	3	.238	.312	.325
Edwards,Joseph	Martinsvlle	Phi	R+	23	54	198	52	10	5	1	75	30	26	21	0	35	3	1	1	7	3	.70	9	.263	.341	.379
Edwards,Donald	Burlington	Cle	R+	20	58	206	58	13	1	1	76	31	17	37	0	26	3	3	3	5	4	.56	4	.282	.394	.369
Elam,Brett	Asheville	Col	A	24	122	412	100	12	2	5	131	49	37	49	0	100	4	5	5	5	5	.50	4	.243	.326	.318
Elliott,Dave	Beloit	Mil	A	23	112	365	98	12	3	12	152	65	58	62	4	80	7	0	4	17	10	.63	10	.268	.381	.416
Elliott,Dawan	Pirates	Pit	R	20	24	90	27	7	1	0	36	9	18	8	0	12	1	0	0	5	2	.71	3	.300	.364	.400
	Erie	Pit	A-	20	39	115	17	5	0	2	28	17	6	16	0	42	1	2	0	3	3	.50	2	.148	.258	.243
Elliott,Zach	Piedmont	Phi	A	23	135	470	107	23	0	4	142	57	41	67	2	90	15	10	7	20	11	.65	11	.228	.338	.302
Ellis,John	Hudson Vall	Tex	A-	21	64	221	54	13	2	1	74	22	23	5	0	45	2	3	3	2	1	.67	5	.244	.264	.335
Ellis,Kevin	Daytona	ChN	A+	25	128	481	131	23	2	16	206	69	89	25	1	64	7	0	5	5	4	.56	15	.272	.315	.428
Ellison,Tony	Rockford	ChN	A	22	31	94	16	3	0	2	25	7	7	3	0	30	2	0	0	0	2	.00	1	.170	.212	.266
	Williamsprt	ChN	A-	22	63	229	65	10	1	7	98	33	35	20	1	51	4	1	1	4	0	1.00	2	.284	.350	.428
Ellison,Skeeter	Danville	Atl	R+	21	58	190	50	7	5	8	91	29	34	40	1	71	0	2	1	8	6	.57	3	.263	.390	.479
	Eugene	Atl	A-	21	7	20	7	3	1	1	15	4	6	3	0	6	1	0	1	0	1	.00	1	.350	.440	.750
Emmons,Scott	Greensboro	NYA	A	23	15	46	11	1	0	1	15	7	9	2	0	6	1	1	1	0	1	.00	0	.239	.280	.326
	Tampa	NYA	A+	23	36	98	20	2	1	1	27	6	10	10	1	26	2	3	0	0	1	.00	1	.204	.291	.276
Encarnacion,Juan	Lakeland	Det	A+	21	131	499	120	31	2	15	200	54	58	24	2	104	12	0	3	11	5	.69	10	.240	.290	.401
Encarnacion,Mario	W. Michigan	Oak	A	19	118	401	92	14	3	7	133	55	43	49	0	131	5	4	0	23	8	.74	12	.229	.321	.332
Engle,Beau	Mets	NYN	R	22	2	2	0	0	0	0	0	1	0	1	0	2	0	0	0	0	0	.00	0	.000	.333	.000
	Columbia	NYN	A	22	3	2	0	0	0	0	0	0	0	0	0	0	0	0	0	0	0	.00	0	.000	.000	.000
Engleka,Matt	Fayettevlle	Det	A	24	93	262	60	18	0	1	81	28	25	48	0	36	12	7	1	6	6	.50	7	.229	.372	.309
Ephan,Larry	Charlotte	Tex	A+	26	9	31	7	2	0	0	9	3	8	8	1	6	0	0	0	0	0	.00	2	.226	.385	.290
Erickson,Corey	Columbia	NYN	A	20	58	209	46	14	0	1	63	16	17	19	0	57	3	3	4	5	3	.63	2	.220	.289	.301
	Pittsfield	NYN	A-	20	73	258	68	19	1	11	122	49	49	43	2	71	4	0	4	6	3	.67	3	.264	.372	.473
Erwin,Mat	Brevard Cty	Fla	A+	24	60	212	59	13	1	1	77	24	31	22	4	30	5	0	1	0	2	.00	3	.278	.358	.363
Escalona,Felix	Astros	Hou	R	NA	28	75	11	2	0	1	16	8	9	8	0	31	4	1	1	1	2	.33	0	.147	.261	.213
Escamilla,Roman	Spokane	KC	A-	23	46	152	33	7	0	2	46	11	21	12	0	22	0	1	0	1	0	1.00	1	.217	.274	.303
Escandon,Emiliano	Lansing	KC	A	22	107	372	101	18	5	4	141	50	52	46	3	47	3	6	2	8	5	.62	3	.272	.355	.379
Escobar,Alexander	Mets	NYN	R	NA	24	75	27	4	0	0	31	15	10	4	0	9	3	0	1	7	1	.88	0	.360	.410	.413
Espada,Angel	Eugene	Atl	A-	22	24	98	24	4	0	0	28	15	5	3	0	11	1	0	1	13	5	.72	2	.245	.272	.286
Espada,Josue	Sou. Oregon	Oak	A-	21	15	54	12	1	0	1	16	7	5	5	0	10	1	1	0	0	0	.00	1	.222	.300	.296
	W. Michigan	Oak	A	21	23	74	20	2	0	0	22	9	4	13	0	11	2	0	0	3	1	.75	2	.270	.393	.297
Espinal,Juan	Bakersfield	SD	A+	22	137	522	143	38	0	26	259	81	98	74	2	126	6	1	6	1	4	.20	11	.274	.367	.496
Evans,Brad	Johnson Cty	StL	R+	20	13	32	8	0	0	0	8	6	4	2	0	8	0	0	0	0	1	.00	1	.250	.294	.250
Evans,Jason	Pr. William	ChA	A+	26	95	329	87	24	2	4	127	41	41	58	1	80	2	2	3	4	3	.57	7	.264	.375	.386
Evans,Lee	Pirates	Pit	R	19	32	111	31	5	2	3	49	27	20	18	1	26	3	1	0	3	0	1.00	2	.279	.394	.441
Evans,Mick	Wilmington	KC	A+	24	98	278	53	9	1	10	94	36	40	56	2	78	4	1	1	1	2	.33	1	.191	.333	.338
Evans,Pat	Columbus	Cle	A	24	6	16	2	0	0	0	2	0	0	2	0	5	0	0	0	0	0	.00	0	.125	.222	.125
	Kinston	Cle	A+	24	21	27	7	3	1	0	12	5	6	4	0	12	0	1	0	0	1	.00	0	.259	.355	.444
Evans,Stan	Clearwater	Phi	A+	26	80	241	58	5	2	2	73	42	23	33	1	36	2	9	3	12	5	.71	8	.241	.333	.303
Facione,Chris	Visalia	Det	A+	26	78	310	80	16	6	7	129	50	38	22	0	60	3	1	1	9	11	.45	7	.258	.313	.416
Faggett,Ethan	Sarasota	Bos	A+	22	110	408	112	12	8	4	152	48	35	35	0	118	6	7	1	24	10	.71	9	.275	.340	.373
Failla,Paul	Lk Elsinore	Cal	A+	24	91	285	59	11	4	1	81	39	32	50	0	66	0	7	3	13	8	.62	7	.207	.322	.284
Faircloth,Kevin	Vero Beach	LA	A+	24	4	9	3	0	0	1	6	4	3	2	0	1	1	0	0	0	0	.00	0	.333	.500	.667
	San Bernrdo	LA	A+	24	56	171	51	6	3	4	75	30	23	20	0	30	4	5	0	9	8	.53	1	.298	.385	.439
Falciglia,Tony	New Jersey	StL	A-	24	15	41	7	2	0	1	12	3	6	2	0	13	1	0	0	0	0	.00	1	.171	.227	.293
	St. Pete	StL	A+	24	16	43	10	3	0	0	13	5	4	1	0	16	1	1	0	0	2	.00	0	.233	.267	.302
Falcon,Edwin	Great Falls	LA	R+	18	20	53	17	3	0	1	23	6	8	12	0	8	1	0	0	2	0	1.00	0	.321	.455	.434
Fantauzzi,John	Salem	Col	A+	25	62	95	27	10	0	0	37	10	11	17	1	25	3	2	0	2	0	1.00	3	.284	.409	.389
Farley,Cordell	Johnson Cty	StL	R+	24	15	63	18	4	3	0	28	17	9	4	0	20	1	0	0	2	2	.50	1	.286	.338	.444
	Peoria	StL	A	24	29	82	19	1	1	0	22	10	7	4	0	23	0	0	0	1	4	.20	3	.232	.267	.268
	St. Pete	StL	A+	24	5	4	0	0	0	0	0	1	0	1	0	1	1	0	0	0	0	.00	0	.000	.333	.000
Farner,Matt	Hagerstown	Tor	A	22	11	26	4	1	0	0	5	10	3	8	0	11	0	2	0	0	0	.00	0	.154	.353	.192
Farraenz,Jesus	Auburn	Hou	A-	24	42	129	29	4	4	2	47	13	11	10	0	34	0	1	1	2	2	.50	0	.225	.279	.364
Farris,Mark	Augusta	Pit	A	22	78	299	65	10	0	2	81	31	30	31	1	66	2	1	2	6	5	.55	5	.217	.293	.271
Faurot,Adam	Ogden	Mil	R+	22	67	238	56	9	0	2	71	41	18	26	0	35	11	6	1	18	10	.64	8	.235	.337	.298
Fauske,Joshua	Hickory	ChA	A	23	115	412	100	20	0	9	147	43	62	51	1	132	8	2	4	1	1	.50	5	.243	.335	.357
Febles,Carlos	Lansing	KC	A	21	102	363	107	23	5	5	155	84	43	66	0	64	11	7	4	30	14	.68	8	.295	.414	.427
Fefee,Theo	Angels	Cal	R	23	13	49	14	2	3	1	25	14	8	6	0	9	0	0	1	4	0	1.00	0	.286	.357	.510
	Boise	Cal	A-	23	41	156	47	3	3	3	65	23	25	7	1	44	0	2	3	1	2	.33	3	.301	.325	.417
Fehrenbach,Todd	Princeton	Cin	R+	21	19	59	9	3	0	1	15	8	5	2	0	34	0	0	0	0	0	.00	0	.153	.180	.254
Felix,Pedro	Burlington	SF	A	20	93	321	85	12	2	5	116	36	36	18	0	65	1	0	3	5	2	.71	11	.265	.303	.361
Feliz,Edgar	Pirates	Pit	R	19	1	1	0	0	0	0	0	0	0	0	0	0	0	0	0	0	0	.00	0	.000	.000	.000
Felston,Anthony	Twins	Min	R	22	2	4	2	0	0	0	2	2	0	2	0	0	0	0	0	0	0	.00	0	.500	.667	.500
	Fort Wayne	Min	A	22	62	201	63	4	1	0	69	53	18	43	0	36	4	2	1	22	4	.85	2	.313	.442	.343
Fennell,Jason	White Sox	ChA	R	19	56	197	47	8	0	2	61	24	19	27	0	39	1	3	0	4	0	1.00	2	.239	.333	.310
Fenton,Cary	Charlotte	Tex	A+	24	87	290	79	9	1	0	90	47	22	31	0	49	6	7	2	21	11	.66	5	.272	.353	.310
Ferguson,Dwight	Red Sox	Bos	R	20	36	68	22	2	1	2	32	23	11	15	0	22	3	1	1	10	5	.67	1	.324	.460	.471
	Michigan	Bos	A	20	10	36	4	0	0	0	4	2	0	4	0	14	0	0	0	0	1	.00	0	.111	.200	.111

1996 Batting — Single-A and Rookie Leagues

BATTING																				BASERUNNING				PERCENTAGES		
Player	Team	Org	Lg	A	G	AB	H	2B	3B	HR	TB	R	RBI	TBB	IBB	SO	HBP	SH	SF	SB	CS	SB%	GDP	Avg	OBP	SLG
Ferguson,Ryan	Martinsvlle	Phi	R+	22	44	154	37	9	1	6	66	19	20	11	0	52	2	0	1	3	1	.75	2	.240	.298	.429
Fernandez,Antonio	Rancho Cuca	SD	A+	24	121	471	145	27	0	9	199	77	73	43	1	96	10	1	5	2	2	.50	17	.308	.374	.423
Fernandez,Jose	Delmarva	Mon	A	22	126	421	115	23	6	12	186	72	70	50	5	76	7	0	3	23	13	.64	5	.273	.358	.442
Fernandez,Ramon	Helena	Mil	R+	19	3	6	0	0	0	0	0	0	0	0	0	3	0	0	0	0	0	.00	0	.000	.000	.000
	Ogden	Mil	R+	19	38	64	5	2	0	0	7	7	3	7	0	28	0	0	0	0	2	.00	4	.078	.169	.109
Ferrand,Thomas	Martinsvlle	Phi	R+	23	48	158	27	6	3	0	39	20	14	18	0	74	7	1	1	6	4	.60	2	.171	.283	.247
Ferrer,Eduardo	Boise	Cal	A-	23	54	183	48	8	2	1	63	31	19	32	1	21	0	3	1	4	4	.50	7	.262	.370	.344
Feuerstein,Dave	Asheville	Col	A	23	130	514	147	27	7	1	191	69	69	42	0	68	5	5	5	21	10	.68	7	.286	.343	.372
Fick,Robert	Jamestown	Det	A-	23	43	133	33	6	0	1	42	18	14	12	1	25	0	0	2	3	1	.75	4	.248	.306	.316
Figueroa,Francisco	Orioles	Bal	R	20	43	150	51	8	1	0	61	22	23	8	0	25	3	0	2	3	0	1.00	7	.340	.380	.407
Figueroa,Jose	Athletics	Oak	R	19	49	157	24	8	0	1	35	18	17	23	0	38	5	0	2	8	1	.89	3	.153	.278	.223
Figueroa,Luis	Lancaster	Sea	A+	20	9	31	12	4	1	0	18	5	6	2	0	6	0	0	0	0	1	.00	0	.387	.424	.581
	Everett	Sea	A-	20	4	13	6	1	1	0	9	4	3	2	0	1	0	0	0	0	0	.00	1	.462	.533	.692
	Wisconsin	Sea	A	20	36	137	40	9	0	2	55	18	19	6	0	14	3	1	2	1	1	.50	6	.292	.331	.401
Filardi,Wladimir	Royals	KC	R	19	21	39	7	2	0	1	12	3	5	2	0	15	1	0	1	0	1	.00	0	.179	.233	.308
Filchner,Duane	W. Michigan	Oak	A	24	133	477	126	24	3	7	177	66	82	73	5	82	3	1	10	2	0	1.00	5	.264	.359	.371
Fink,Marc	Helena	Mil	R+	20	37	107	38	8	0	9	73	18	28	26	2	27	0	0	1	0	0	.00	4	.355	.478	.682
Finnerty,Keith	New Jersey	StL	A-	23	55	172	36	7	1	2	51	21	16	17	0	31	1	2	3	7	0	1.00	4	.209	.280	.297
Finnieston,Adam	Lansing	KC	A	24	60	193	35	3	3	2	50	19	13	13	1	61	0	0	1	4	1	.80	3	.181	.232	.259
Fisher,Anthony	Charlstn-SC	Tex	A	22	30	111	26	4	0	3	39	10	13	3	0	45	2	0	1	4	3	.57	1	.234	.265	.351
	Rangers	Tex	R	22	9	29	7	1	1	0	10	2	6	2	0	8	3	0	0	2	1	.67	0	.241	.353	.345
Flanigan,Steven	Augusta	Pit	A	25	49	144	30	6	0	0	36	14	17	5	0	29	3	1	1	2	1	.67	6	.208	.248	.250
Flores,Eric	Yakima	LA	A-	20	38	100	19	4	0	0	23	7	8	12	0	42	3	1	1	0	0	.00	1	.190	.293	.230
Flores,Oswaldo	Red Sox	Bos	R	19	37	120	36	7	2	0	47	22	9	8	0	28	3	1	0	14	3	.82	2	.300	.359	.392
Font,Franklin	Cubs	ChN	R	19	59	239	72	5	4	0	85	43	18	17	0	36	4	2	2	31	9	.78	0	.301	.355	.356
Foote,Derek	Macon	Atl	A	22	107	330	78	10	1	17	141	29	45	30	5	141	1	0	1	3	1	.75	7	.236	.301	.427
Forchic,Derek	Utica	Fla	A-	23	27	87	25	5	1	2	38	12	10	5	0	20	1	0	3	0	0	.00	0	.287	.323	.437
Fortin,Blaine	St. Cathrns	Tor	A-	19	29	82	18	2	0	3	29	14	10	6	1	7	0	1	0	0	1	.00	1	.220	.273	.354
Fortin,Troy	Fort Myers	Min	A+	22	104	358	89	11	2	7	125	40	52	29	0	29	4	6	4	1	1	.50	10	.249	.309	.349
Foster,Jeff	W. Palm Bch	Mon	A+	25	3	13	2	0	0	0	2	0	1	0	0	6	1	0	0	1	0	1.00	0	.154	.214	.154
Foster,Quincy	Utica	Fla	A-	22	73	240	53	7	1	1	65	34	22	30	0	71	4	3	4	24	6	.80	3	.221	.313	.271
Foulks,Brian	Great Falls	LA	R+	23	35	121	38	7	1	1	50	14	9	1	0	24	3	0	1	4	2	.67	2	.314	.333	.413
Fowler,Maleke	Bluefield	Bal	R+	21	26	86	32	5	0	0	37	23	8	14	1	16	1	0	1	17	3	.85	1	.372	.461	.430
	Frederick	Bal	A+	21	5	11	2	0	0	0	2	3	1	3	0	2	0	0	0	1	1	.50	0	.182	.357	.182
Francia,David	Batavia	Phi	A-	22	69	280	81	14	5	4	117	45	29	8	0	25	6	2	2	16	6	.73	1	.289	.321	.418
Franco,Raul	Marlins	Fla	R	21	59	238	66	14	2	0	84	39	15	13	0	29	3	9	1	15	7	.68	6	.277	.322	.353
Fraraccio,Dan	Pr. William	ChA	A+	26	44	149	41	9	0	0	50	16	20	12	0	20	1	2	0	1	0	1.00	5	.275	.333	.336
Fraser,Joe	Fort Wayne	Min	A	22	101	331	74	17	1	6	111	42	43	26	2	60	8	8	2	7	2	.78	7	.224	.294	.335
Freel,Ryan	Dunedin	Tor	A+	21	104	381	97	23	3	4	138	64	41	33	0	76	5	14	2	19	15	.56	4	.255	.321	.362
Freeman,Ricky	Daytona	ChN	A+	25	127	477	145	36	6	13	232	70	64	36	2	72	10	0	2	10	8	.56	9	.304	.364	.486
Freeman,Terrance	Sou. Oregon	Oak	A-	22	56	167	39	5	1	0	46	26	18	23	0	29	5	4	0	21	7	.75	5	.234	.344	.275
Freire,Alejandro	Kissimmee	Hou	A+	22	115	384	98	24	1	12	160	40	42	24	1	66	7	1	2	11	7	.61	11	.255	.309	.417
Freitas,Joseph	New Jersey	StL	A-	23	45	163	56	10	3	4	84	29	37	25	0	35	0	0	6	0	1	.00	4	.344	.418	.515
French,Anton	Durham	Atl	A+	21	52	210	52	10	2	5	81	25	22	13	0	42	0	2	0	23	3	.88	0	.248	.291	.386
	Lakeland	Det	A+	21	61	253	70	10	6	0	92	36	14	12	0	38	2	0	1	24	10	.71	2	.277	.313	.364
Frias,Ovidio	Erie	Pit	A-	20	12	46	13	1	0	0	14	5	3	1	0	7	0	2	0	0	0	.00	0	.283	.298	.304
	Augusta	Pit	A	20	54	177	47	8	0	0	55	18	22	25	0	17	1	2	3	6	8	.43	5	.266	.354	.311
Friedrich,Steve	South Bend	ChA	A	24	133	545	144	25	6	3	190	51	46	20	3	114	7	6	4	18	11	.62	11	.264	.297	.349
Frost,Robert	Kingsport	NYN	R+	24	6	18	5	2	0	0	7	1	3	0	0	3	0	0	0	0	0	.00	1	.278	.278	.389
Fuentes,Javier	Lowell	Bos	A-	22	46	157	45	6	1	2	59	21	21	21	0	23	2	0	0	2	1	.67	4	.287	.378	.376
Fuller,Brian	Fayettevlle	Det	A	24	76	239	60	12	3	10	108	48	30	32	1	50	10	5	1	2	2	.50	5	.251	.362	.452
Funaro,Joe	Kane County	Fla	A	24	89	291	90	20	2	7	135	57	43	40	2	42	7	5	4	5	3	.63	5	.309	.401	.464
Gabriel,Denio	Frederick	Bal	A+	21	40	133	24	1	1	0	27	12	5	11	0	29	1	1	1	6	9	.40	1	.180	.247	.203
Gainey,Bryon	Columbia	NYN	A	21	122	446	97	23	0	14	162	53	62	41	3	169	5	0	3	5	2	.71	13	.217	.289	.363
Galarza,Joel	San Jose	SF	A+	23	81	291	84	17	0	8	125	39	50	25	1	60	9	0	3	10	3	.77	9	.289	.360	.430
Gallagher,Shawn	Charlstn-SC	Tex	A	20	88	303	68	11	4	7	108	29	32	18	0	104	6	3	2	6	1	.86	6	.224	.280	.356
	Hudson Vall	Tex	A-	20	44	176	48	10	2	4	74	15	29	7	0	48	2	0	1	8	5	.62	5	.273	.306	.420
Galloway,Paul	Bellingham	SF	A-	23	47	177	49	11	2	5	79	22	24	15	3	35	4	1	1	1	1	.50	3	.277	.345	.446
Gama,Rick	Rancho Cuca	SD	A+	24	108	417	113	28	2	7	166	59	50	37	1	57	4	5	4	13	5	.72	10	.271	.333	.398
Gambill,Chad	Salem	Col	A+	21	115	406	120	22	2	7	167	61	41	33	2	83	3	6	1	6	6	.50	4	.296	.352	.411
Gann,Jamie	Lethbridge	Ari	R+	22	49	129	37	10	1	2	55	19	22	10	0	42	2	0	1	3	3	.50	4	.287	.345	.426
Garcia,Amaury	Kane County	Fla	A	22	105	391	103	19	7	6	154	65	36	62	2	83	5	7	2	37	19	.66	8	.263	.370	.394
Garcia,Apostol	Fayettevlle	Det	A	20	74	242	47	7	1	2	62	33	17	21	0	77	3	4	2	12	3	.80	4	.194	.265	.256
Garcia,Carlos	Fort Wayne	Min	A	21	40	128	27	2	0	1	32	18	9	20	0	24	2	0	1	14	5	.74	5	.211	.325	.250
	Fort Myers	Min	A+	21	26	90	13	2	0	1	18	10	8	6	0	26	0	0	1	9	2	.82	0	.144	.196	.200
Garcia,Freddy	Lynchburg	Pit	A+	24	129	474	145	39	3	21	253	79	86	44	2	86	1	0	12	4	2	.67	10	.306	.358	.534
Garcia,Jaime	Delmarva	Mon	A	25	62	182	43	14	1	5	74	27	19	22	0	51	5	3	1	1	4	.20	3	.236	.333	.407
Garcia,Jesse	High Desert	Bal	A+	23	137	459	122	21	5	10	183	94	66	57	0	81	8	20	4	25	7	.78	7	.266	.354	.399
Garcia,Juan	Diamondback	Ari	R	18	36	110	28	3	3	3	46	25	14	24	0	26	3	2	1	16	6	.73	0	.255	.399	.418
Garcia,Luis	Hickory	ChA	A	21	76	289	79	18	3	3	112	31	38	14	2	41	2	1	0	9	6	.60	8	.273	.311	.388
	South Bend	ChA	A	21	55	211	48	9	1	1	62	23	16	9	2	29	1	0	1	3	4	.43	5	.227	.261	.294
Garcia,Ozzie	Peoria	StL	A	23	120	359	85	14	1	0	101	70	38	46	0	68	14	14	4	20	13	.61	6	.237	.343	.281
Garcia,Sandro	Padres	SD	R	19	53	189	55	6	4	1	72	29	17	8	0	27	2	3	2	11	6	.65	3	.291	.323	.381
Gargiulo,Jimmy	Johnson Cty	StL	R+	21	46	175	45	11	0	3	65	24	21	9	0	28	2	1	0	1	0	1.00	2	.257	.301	.371
Gargiulo,Mike	Frederick	Bal	A+	22	51	161	32	9	0	2	47	14	16	15	2	35	4	1	1	2	1	.67	5	.199	.282	.292
Garland,Tim	San Jose	SF	A+	28	132	550	171	18	7	5	218	96	61	54	1	77	10	5	6	51	18	.74	6	.311	.379	.396
Garrett,Jason	Utica	Fla	A-	24	68	243	67	8	4	4	95	34	35	25	0	53	5	0	4	1	2	.33	5	.276	.350	.391

1996 Batting — Single-A and Rookie Leagues

BATTING																				BASERUNNING				PERCENTAGES		
Player	Team	Org	Lg	A	G	AB	H	2B	3B	HR	TB	R	RBI	TBB	IBB	SO	HBP	SH	SF	SB	CS	SB%	GDP	Avg	OBP	SLG
Garrett,William	Billings	Cin	R+	23	41	136	25	6	0	2	37	14	17	9	0	41	6	3	0	0	1	.00	2	.184	.265	.272
Gazarek,Marty	Daytona	ChN	A+	24	129	472	131	31	4	11	203	68	77	28	0	52	12	0	5	15	13	.54	10	.278	.331	.430
Germosen,Julio	Pirates	Pit	R	20	35	123	30	4	2	1	41	20	11	8	0	24	1	0	0	2	1	.67	1	.244	.295	.333
Geronimo,Cesar	Angels	Cal	R	NA	33	121	34	9	1	0	45	9	16	8	0	11	2	1	0	3	1	.75	3	.281	.336	.372
Giambi,Jeremy	Spokane	KC	A-	22	67	231	63	17	0	6	98	58	39	61	2	32	8	0	0	22	5	.81	5	.273	.440	.424
Giardi,Rocco	Greensboro	NYA	A	24	20	63	14	5	0	3	28	11	5	10	0	13	1	0	0	0	1	.00	4	.222	.338	.444
	Tampa	NYA	A+	24	5	13	2	0	0	0	2	3	1	4	0	3	0	0	1	0	0	.00	2	.154	.333	.154
	W. Palm Bch	Mon	A+	24	48	150	38	6	1	5	61	19	19	27	1	33	5	0	1	2	1	.67	3	.253	.383	.407
Gibbs,Kevin	Vero Beach	LA	A+	23	118	423	114	9	11	0	145	69	33	65	0	80	4	6	4	60	19	.76	6	.270	.369	.343
Gibralter,David	Sarasota	Bos	A+	22	120	452	129	34	3	12	205	47	70	30	3	101	9	0	4	8	7	.53	9	.285	.339	.454
Gil,Geronimo	Savannah	LA	A	NA	79	276	67	13	1	7	103	29	38	8	3	69	5	1	3	0	2	.00	4	.243	.274	.373
Giles,Tim	Medicne Hat	Tor	R+	21	68	258	69	17	0	10	116	36	45	19	2	52	0	0	3	5	0	1.00	7	.267	.314	.450
Gillespie,Eric	Boise	Cal	A-	22	61	192	53	11	5	3	83	28	38	25	1	50	1	1	3	0	1	.00	4	.276	.357	.432
Glass,Chip	Kinston	Cle	A+	26	134	479	128	18	9	5	179	64	52	40	2	67	4	5	1	11	6	.65	8	.267	.328	.374
Glasser,Scott	Diamondback	Ari	R	21	41	128	38	0	4	0	46	25	10	14	0	16	1	1	0	13	2	.87	6	.297	.371	.359
	Lethbridge	Ari	R+	21	9	27	8	1	1	0	11	7	3	5	0	7	1	0	0	0	0	.00	1	.296	.424	.407
Glassey,Joshua	Yakima	LA	A-	20	50	137	30	5	0	0	35	11	20	26	1	44	0	0	0	0	0	.00	3	.219	.344	.255
Glavine,Mike	Columbus	Cle	A	24	38	119	33	5	0	6	56	17	16	28	2	33	1	0	1	0	0	.00	2	.277	.416	.471
Glendenning,Mich.	Bellingham	SF	A-	20	73	265	69	19	4	12	132	54	48	39	0	80	1	1	2	4	6	.40	6	.260	.355	.498
Glover,Jason	Ogden	Mil	R+	23	58	194	56	10	4	8	98	42	35	32	0	52	3	6	4	8	4	.67	4	.289	.391	.505
Glozier,Larry	Utica	Fla	A-	23	2	3	0	0	0	0	0	0	0	1	0	2	0	0	0	0	0	.00	0	.000	.250	.000
	Brevard Cty	Fla	A+	23	5	13	2	0	0	0	2	0	0	1	0	3	0	0	0	1	0	1.00	0	.154	.214	.154
	Kane County	Fla	A	23	26	79	17	3	1	0	22	13	4	18	0	17	3	3	1	1	3	.25	4	.215	.376	.278
Gomez,Paul	St. Lucie	NYN	A+	24	7	24	9	2	0	2	17	3	7	2	0	5	1	0	0	0	0	.00	0	.375	.444	.708
	Columbia	NYN	A	24	11	20	3	0	0	0	3	2	2	4	0	6	0	0	0	0	0	.00	0	.150	.292	.150
Gomez,Ramon	Hickory	ChA	A	21	116	418	104	8	3	1	121	73	30	44	0	99	2	11	2	57	19	.75	5	.249	.322	.289
Gomez,Rudolfo	Yankees	NYA	R	22	16	58	16	6	0	0	22	12	10	9	2	7	4	0	1	0	1	.00	1	.276	.403	.379
	Tampa	NYA	A+	22	40	130	38	9	1	1	52	15	24	26	0	12	0	4	3	4	1	.80	8	.292	.403	.400
Gonzalez,Ender	White Sox	ChA	R	19	51	166	46	6	3	0	58	22	14	12	0	31	2	7	2	4	6	.40	3	.277	.330	.349
Gonzalez,Freddy	Vermont	Mon	A-	22	14	43	9	2	1	0	13	7	6	7	0	12	0	0	0	2	0	1.00	2	.209	.320	.302
Gonzalez,Manuel	San Bernrdo	LA	A+	21	43	168	51	7	3	0	64	29	21	12	0	32	0	2	0	10	8	.56	2	.304	.350	.381
	Savannah	LA	A	21	65	231	53	10	2	1	70	30	19	20	0	52	1	1	2	15	8	.65	3	.229	.291	.303
Gonzalez,Mauricio	Bakersfield	—	A+	25	97	418	116	29	1	4	159	48	48	13	1	63	2	9	2	2	5	.29	15	.278	.301	.380
	Columbus	Cle	A	25	25	95	23	4	0	1	30	13	7	1	0	18	1	0	2	0	1	.00	0	.242	.253	.316
Gonzalez,Milciades	Devil Rays	TB	R	18	17	44	3	0	0	0	3	7	2	5	0	13	0	0	0	2	0	1.00	0	.068	.163	.068
Gonzalez,Richard	Columbus	Cle	A	22	75	247	58	11	0	1	72	19	12	17	0	42	0	3	1	0	0	.00	4	.235	.283	.291
Gonzalez,Santos	Padres	SD	R	20	38	131	38	5	3	1	52	27	17	5	0	20	1	0	2	10	2	.83	2	.290	.317	.397
Gonzalez,Wikle.	Augusta	Pit	A	23	118	419	106	21	3	4	145	52	62	58	1	41	7	2	5	4	6	.40	14	.253	.350	.346
Goodell,Steve	Brevard Cty	Fla	A+	22	1	4	1	0	0	0	1	0	0	0	0	0	0	0	0	0	0	.00	0	.250	.250	.250
	Kane County	Fla	A	22	86	282	79	17	2	9	127	34	39	30	2	68	13	2	5	1	1	.50	8	.280	.370	.450
Goodhart,Steve	Charlstn-WV	Cin	A	24	115	380	82	16	3	0	104	61	26	94	1	95	7	5	2	16	12	.57	4	.216	.379	.274
Goodman,Herb	Princeton	Cin	R+	22	39	121	27	4	0	1	34	15	12	11	0	39	0	1	0	5	8	.38	1	.223	.288	.281
Goodwin,Joseph	Charlstn-SC	Tex	A	23	80	252	65	13	1	0	80	25	31	32	1	34	5	3	3	3	5	.38	4	.258	.349	.317
Goodwin,Keith	Michigan	Bos	A	22	66	238	65	18	0	1	86	40	28	25	0	52	2	6	3	11	6	.65	0	.273	.343	.361
Gordon,Adrian	Fort Wayne	Min	A	23	110	343	102	15	7	1	134	58	47	47	1	90	5	3	9	9	9	.50	5	.297	.381	.391
Gordon,Buck	Williamsprt	ChN	A-	22	32	94	21	6	0	0	27	13	7	6	0	35	0	0	0	1	3	.25	0	.223	.270	.287
Gordon,Gary	Rockies	Col	R	20	47	179	52	5	0	0	57	35	10	33	0	54	4	0	0	23	6	.79	0	.291	.412	.318
	Salem	Col	A+	20	10	35	13	3	0	0	16	5	1	3	0	6	0	0	0	2	1	.67	0	.371	.421	.457
Gordon,Herman	Dunedin	Tor	A+	22	20	30	4	1	1	0	7	4	2	3	0	11	0	0	0	1	0	1.00	1	.133	.212	.233
	Hagerstown	Tor	A	22	41	114	18	3	2	1	28	7	11	5	0	40	3	2	1	3	5	.38	2	.158	.211	.246
	St. Cathrns	Tor	A-	22	13	40	6	2	0	1	11	5	9	3	0	9	1	0	2	1	0	1.00	0	.150	.217	.275
Gorecki,Ryan	Charlotte	Tex	A+	23	82	288	83	5	0	0	88	26	28	20	0	6	0	10	1	1	3	.25	8	.288	.333	.306
Goris,Braulio	Athletics	Oak	R	20	49	172	42	10	3	2	64	24	34	31	0	52	3	0	3	5	2	.71	0	.244	.364	.372
Graves,Bryan	Cedar Rapds	Cal	A	22	83	228	51	5	2	4	72	27	27	46	0	59	5	1	3	4	2	.67	3	.224	.362	.316
Green,Chad	Ogden	Mil	R+	22	21	81	29	4	1	3	44	22	8	15	0	23	1	1	2	12	3	.80	0	.358	.455	.543
Greene,Eric	Bakersfield	—	A+	25	2	9	2	0	0	0	2	1	0	0	0	3	0	0	0	0	0	.00	0	.222	.222	.222
Greer,Ryan	Bakersfield	—	A+	26	2	5	0	0	0	0	0	0	0	0	0	3	0	0	0	0	0	.00	0	.000	.000	.000
Griggs,Rodrickus	Billings	Cin	R+	23	49	151	41	3	0	0	44	24	20	19	0	29	4	0	3	6	1	.86	2	.272	.362	.291
Groseclose,David	Asheville	Col	A	24	84	250	61	9	0	0	70	40	31	43	0	55	10	5	3	13	12	.52	2	.244	.373	.280
Gross,Rafael	San Bernrdo	LA	A+	22	112	362	85	18	2	6	125	58	43	18	0	68	2	5	2	31	14	.69	5	.235	.273	.345
Grubbs,Christopher	Cubs	ChN	R	21	30	80	12	2	1	0	16	11	3	8	0	27	12	0	1	5	3	.63	3	.150	.317	.200
Gruber,Nick	Red Sox	Bos	R	20	5	6	1	0	0	0	1	0	1	1	0	1	0	0	0	0	0	.00	0	.167	.286	.167
Guerrero,Francisco	Devil Rays	TB	R	17	11	23	1	0	0	0	1	1	1	5	0	10	0	0	0	0	1	.00	1	.043	.214	.043
Guerrero,Hamlet	Mets	NYN	R	22	34	127	33	8	2	2	51	16	14	9	0	12	0	1	1	0	2	.00	1	.260	.307	.402
	Kingsport	NYN	R+	22	6	16	4	0	1	0	6	0	2	3	0	3	0	0	0	0	0	.00	0	.250	.368	.375
Guerrero,Rafael	St. Lucie	NYN	A+	22	83	260	64	12	0	2	82	32	26	20	0	37	1	0	2	4	0	1.00	9	.246	.300	.315
Guerrero,Sergio	Helena	Mil	R+	22	57	217	69	13	0	2	88	48	40	25	0	14	6	2	4	6	3	.67	6	.318	.397	.406
Guerrero,Wascar	Mariners	Sea	R	21	31	111	26	6	1	1	37	9	10	4	0	37	2	0	0	0	0	.00	3	.234	.274	.333
Guillen,Carlos	Quad City	Hou	A	21	29	112	37	7	1	3	55	23	17	16	2	25	0	0	3	13	6	.68	1	.330	.405	.491
Guillen,Jose	Lynchburg	Pit	A+	21	136	528	170	30	0	21	263	78	94	20	1	73	13	1	8	24	13	.65	16	.322	.357	.498
Gulseth,Mark	Burlington	SF	A	25	125	423	111	35	4	5	169	61	41	89	3	95	1	4	3	4	2	.67	11	.262	.390	.400
Gunderson,Shane	Fort Myers	Min	A+	23	117	410	103	20	5	5	148	61	50	63	2	85	14	6	2	12	8	.60	5	.251	.368	.361
Gunner,Chie	Devil Rays	TB	R	18	44	131	23	2	0	0	25	8	8	10	0	45	1	3	0	2	1	.67	2	.176	.239	.191
Guthrie,David	Billings	Cin	R+	23	48	181	41	6	3	4	65	45	28	26	0	48	7	3	2	10	1	.91	4	.227	.343	.359
Guzman,Cristian	Yankees	NYA	R	19	42	170	50	8	2	1	65	37	21	10	0	31	3	2	2	7	6	.54	2	.294	.341	.382
Guzman,Edwards	San Jose	SF	A+	20	106	367	99	19	5	1	131	41	40	39	4	60	5	6	5	3	5	.38	6	.270	.344	.357
Haas,Chris	Peoria	StL	A	20	124	421	101	19	1	11	155	56	65	64	3	169	7	1	3	3	2	.60	4	.240	.347	.368

1996 Batting — Single-A and Rookie Leagues

BATTING																				BASERUNNING				PERCENTAGES		
Player	Team	Org	Lg	A	G	AB	H	2B	3B	HR	TB	R	RBI	TBB	IBB	SO	HBP	SH	SF	SB	CS	SB%	GDP	Avg	OBP	SLG
Haas,Matthew	W. Palm Bch	Mon	A+	25	77	207	55	7	1	1	67	22	26	22	1	27	3	0	3	4	2	.67	2	.266	.340	.324
Hacker,Steve	Eugene	Atl	A-	22	75	292	73	15	1	21	153	45	61	26	3	64	6	0	6	0	0	.00	2	.250	.318	.524
Hacopian,Derek	W. Palm Bch	Mon	A+	27	43	157	42	12	0	2	60	23	22	13	1	11	3	0	3	0	3	.00	2	.268	.330	.382
Hagy,Gary	Kinston	Cle	A+	28	74	174	38	10	1	5	65	30	22	40	2	50	3	5	5	4	3	.57	1	.218	.365	.374
Hairston,John	Greensboro	NYA	A	29	59	194	42	5	1	5	64	19	19	19	0	81	5	1	1	4	2	.67	3	.216	.301	.330
Hall,Andy	Peoria	StL	A	23	128	446	134	29	5	4	185	80	68	75	1	90	15	10	5	21	7	.75	6	.300	.414	.415
Hall,Douglas	Williamsprt	ChN	A-	22	67	227	60	5	3	2	77	35	19	20	0	58	1	5	4	12	11	.52	3	.264	.321	.339
Hall,Noah	Expos	Mon	R	20	41	134	32	5	3	1	46	24	18	19	2	22	5	1	2	6	2	.75	2	.239	.350	.343
Hall,Ron	Salem	Col	A+	21	14	53	8	2	0	0	10	7	2	4	0	8	1	0	0	1	1	.50	2	.151	.224	.189
Hall,Ryan	St. Pete	StL	A+	25	66	174	37	10	0	0	47	7	11	19	2	37	0	1	1	0	0	.00	2	.213	.289	.270
Hallead,John	Asheville	Col	A	21	38	136	22	4	1	0	28	17	9	17	1	39	3	0	0	5	4	.56	0	.162	.269	.206
	Portland	Col	A-	21	52	181	44	9	0	1	56	22	21	15	1	42	0	3	3	6	1	.86	1	.243	.296	.309
Hallmark,Patrick	Lansing	KC	A	23	118	453	127	23	5	1	163	68	53	34	2	80	3	6	1	33	9	.79	3	.280	.334	.360
Halloran,Matthew	Padres	SD	R	19	39	134	35	7	4	0	50	22	15	10	0	22	2	0	0	2	1	.67	3	.261	.322	.373
Haltiwanger,Garr.	Pittsfield	NYN	A-	22	60	203	52	9	2	9	92	36	37	24	3	55	4	1	2	9	4	.69	3	.256	.343	.453
Ham,Kevin	Cedar Rapds	Cal	A	22	100	326	70	14	0	10	114	38	35	29	0	102	6	5	3	4	4	.50	7	.215	.288	.350
Hamilton,Joe	Red Sox	Bos	R	22	1	4	1	0	0	0	1	1	0	0	0	1	0	0	0	0	0	.00	0	.250	.250	.250
	Michigan	Bos	A	22	108	389	102	20	2	13	165	54	58	45	1	117	2	0	1	3	5	.38	10	.262	.341	.424
Hamlin,Mark	Portland	Col	A-	23	54	202	55	8	2	4	79	22	26	16	0	53	3	2	0	5	3	.63	3	.272	.335	.391
	Salem	Col	A+	23	9	28	4	0	0	1	7	1	2	4	0	3	1	0	0	0	0	.00	2	.143	.273	.250
Hampton,Michael	Charlstn-WV	Cin	A	25	134	475	103	22	4	13	172	69	68	61	0	120	13	3	6	22	6	.79	6	.217	.319	.362
Hampton,Robby	St. Cathrns	Tor	A-	21	34	130	34	6	3	4	58	17	17	9	1	48	1	0	1	5	1	.83	2	.262	.312	.446
	Hagerstown	Tor	A	21	19	69	14	3	1	1	22	9	8	4	0	28	0	1	0	1	0	1.00	0	.203	.247	.319
Hardy,Brett	Diamondback	Ari	R	23	4	3	0	0	0	0	0	0	0	2	0	3	0	0	0	0	0	.00	0	.000	.400	.000
	Lethbridge	Ari	R+	23	30	90	33	3	0	1	39	28	15	22	1	14	0	0	2	2	0	1.00	0	.367	.482	.433
Hardy,Bryan	Burlington	Cle	R+	20	52	186	29	10	0	6	57	16	25	9	1	84	4	0	1	0	0	.00	0	.156	.210	.306
Harmer,Frank	Bakersfield	Bal	A+	22	28	67	12	2	0	0	14	6	4	8	0	16	0	2	1	0	1	.00	3	.179	.263	.209
	High Desert	Bal	A+	22	36	95	23	5	0	3	37	20	16	22	0	25	0	2	0	1	0	1.00	2	.242	.385	.389
Harmon,Brian	Savannah	LA	A	21	85	230	50	11	0	10	91	36	37	50	1	56	2	0	2	0	3	.00	1	.217	.359	.396
Harp,Scott	Spokane	KC	A-	23	55	178	49	10	1	2	67	31	16	21	0	28	4	5	1	6	1	.86	7	.275	.363	.376
Harris,Mike	Utica	Fla	A-	23	38	92	26	8	0	1	37	9	8	11	0	23	3	0	1	0	0	.00	3	.283	.374	.402
Harris,Rodger	Johnson Cty	StL	R+	21	44	168	62	12	2	5	93	38	30	10	0	28	1	2	3	16	6	.73	3	.369	.401	.554
Harrison,Adonis	Lancaster	Sea	A+	20	16	40	14	4	0	0	18	7	5	8	0	13	0	0	0	4	1	.80	0	.350	.458	.450
	Wisconsin	Sea	A	20	54	196	52	15	2	1	74	29	24	19	0	36	1	1	0	5	3	.63	3	.265	.333	.378
Harrison,Kenny	Lynchburg	Pit	A+	25	18	50	6	3	0	0	9	2	3	4	0	8	0	0	0	0	1	.00	2	.120	.185	.180
Harriss,Robin	Kinston	Cle	A+	25	89	262	57	7	1	5	81	25	32	16	1	57	5	12	3	1	2	.33	8	.218	.273	.309
Hartman,Ron	Lethbridge	Ari	R+	22	66	258	84	23	0	16	155	69	72	36	0	42	6	0	8	5	2	.71	6	.326	.409	.601
Harvey,Aaron	Brevard Cty	Fla	A+	24	99	360	94	18	3	5	133	37	40	21	6	55	1	4	2	13	8	.62	3	.261	.302	.369
Hawkins,Kraig	Tampa	NYA	A+	25	75	268	80	2	5	1	95	41	21	35	0	41	2	9	1	13	6	.68	2	.299	.382	.354
Hayes,Chris	Hagerstown	Tor	A	23	88	315	78	15	4	5	116	48	51	32	2	59	9	0	4	7	6	.54	6	.248	.331	.368
	Dunedin	Tor	A+	23	32	106	25	6	0	1	34	14	12	11	0	21	5	4	1	1	2	.33	6	.236	.333	.321
Hayes,Darren	South Bend	ChA	A	24	9	28	2	0	0	1	5	5	5	4	0	14	4	0	2	1	1	.50	0	.071	.263	.179
	Pr. William	ChA	A+	24	66	189	40	8	2	1	55	28	19	29	0	64	10	8	0	5	2	.71	1	.212	.346	.291
Hayes,Heath	Columbus	Cle	A	25	104	348	81	14	0	22	161	51	57	36	0	106	6	0	5	2	1	.67	2	.233	.311	.463
Hayman,David	Lethbridge	Ari	R+	22	63	233	73	8	4	17	140	68	59	43	1	78	6	0	9	4	0	1.00	2	.313	.419	.601
Hazelton,Justin	Tigers	Det	R	18	47	141	18	3	0	1	24	15	12	21	0	45	1	1	2	1	2	.33	5	.128	.242	.170
Heintz,Chris	Bristol	ChA	R+	22	8	29	10	7	0	2	23	7	8	4	0	2	0	0	0	1	1	.50	0	.345	.424	.793
	South Bend	ChA	A	22	64	230	61	12	1	1	78	25	22	23	1	46	3	1	1	1	1	.50	3	.265	.339	.339
Hemphill,Bret	Lk Elsinore	Cal	A+	25	108	399	105	21	3	17	183	64	64	52	1	93	4	6	1	4	3	.57	7	.263	.353	.459
Hemphill,James	Helena	Mil	R+	23	51	128	40	8	1	2	56	26	18	21	0	31	1	0	1	4	2	.67	2	.313	.411	.438
Henderson,Juan	Lk Elsinore	Cal	A+	23	50	147	29	7	2	0	40	24	17	31	0	47	4	5	1	13	8	.62	2	.197	.350	.272
	Cedar Rapds	Cal	A	23	23	0	0	0	0	0	0	0	0	0	0	0	0	0	0	0	1	.00	0	.000	.000	.000
Hendricks,Ryan	High Desert	Bal	A+	24	14	29	7	2	0	0	9	3	4	5	0	11	1	2	0	1	0	1.00	1	.241	.371	.310
	Bakersfield	Bal	A+	24	30	94	15	1	0	3	25	13	8	12	0	31	1	0	1	1	0	1.00	1	.160	.259	.266
Herdman,Eli	Fort Wayne	Min	A	21	7	21	4	0	0	1	7	2	8	7	1	7	0	0	2	0	1	.00	1	.190	.367	.333
	Elizabethtn	Min	R+	21	62	198	48	12	1	8	86	31	37	48	1	70	1	0	5	1	2	.33	3	.242	.385	.434
Heredia,Rafael	Cubs	ChN	R	21	23	76	17	4	1	1	26	12	8	9	0	21	4	0	0	11	1	.92	4	.224	.337	.342
Herider,Jeremy	Visalia	Ari	A+	25	49	145	34	6	0	1	43	22	14	33	1	36	1	0	0	2	6	.25	3	.234	.380	.297
	Bakersfield	Ari	A+	25	29	107	21	4	0	0	25	18	12	26	0	32	1	1	0	1	1	.50	2	.196	.358	.234
Hermansen,Chad	Augusta	Pit	A	19	62	226	57	11	3	14	116	41	41	38	5	65	8	0	1	11	3	.79	1	.252	.377	.513
	Lynchburg	Pit	A+	19	66	251	69	11	3	10	116	40	46	29	1	56	3	0	4	5	1	.83	8	.275	.352	.462
Hernaiz,Juan	Savannah	LA	A	22	132	492	137	19	8	14	214	68	73	21	3	96	8	3	3	42	15	.74	5	.278	.317	.435
Hernandez,Alex.	Erie	Pit	A-	20	61	225	65	13	4	4	98	38	30	20	1	47	0	1	2	7	8	.47	1	.289	.344	.436
Hernandez,Carlos	Quad City	Hou	A	21	112	456	123	15	7	5	167	67	49	27	0	71	4	9	5	41	14	.75	6	.270	.313	.366
Hernandez,Jesus	Burlington	Cle	R+	20	19	66	15	2	0	2	23	15	6	13	0	8	0	1	0	5	0	1.00	1	.227	.354	.348
Hernandez,Rafael	Expos	Mon	R	21	36	97	20	2	1	0	24	13	11	10	0	29	0	1	1	6	3	.67	0	.206	.278	.247
Hernandez,Ramon	W. Michigan	Oak	A	21	123	447	114	26	2	12	180	62	68	69	1	62	4	1	7	2	3	.40	22	.255	.355	.403
Hernandez,Victor	Athletics	Oak	R	20	46	144	34	5	1	5	56	27	22	20	0	29	4	5	0	11	2	.85	3	.236	.345	.389
Herrera,Jesus	Princeton	Cin	R+	20	25	68	15	6	0	0	21	8	7	2	0	17	3	1	1	0	0	.00	0	.221	.270	.309
Herrera,Pedro	Royals	KC	R	18	31	99	25	4	0	0	29	8	10	3	0	21	0	2	0	1	2	.33	2	.253	.275	.293
Herrick,Jason	Lk Elsinore	Cal	A+	23	58	210	67	13	2	6	102	35	30	25	2	52	0	2	2	5	4	.56	5	.319	.388	.486
Hessman,Michael	Braves	Atl	R	19	53	190	41	10	1	1	56	13	15	12	1	41	4	4	0	1	1	.50	0	.216	.277	.295
Hill,Jason	Astros	Hou	R	22	42	140	40	13	2	4	69	22	31	13	0	21	3	0	4	7	5	.58	3	.286	.350	.493
Hill,Jeremy	Royals	KC	R	19	31	90	16	6	0	0	22	4	4	12	0	17	2	1	1	0	0	.00	3	.178	.286	.244
Hillenbrand,Shea	Lowell	Bos	A-	21	72	279	88	18	2	2	116	33	38	18	1	32	8	0	2	4	3	.57	6	.315	.371	.416
Hills,Rich	Clinton	SD	A	23	124	433	108	34	0	7	163	42	58	50	2	69	12	0	3	4	4	.50	11	.249	.341	.376
Hine,Steven	Lowell	Bos	A-	23	27	73	20	2	0	0	22	5	3	10	0	6	0	0	0	0	0	.00	0	.274	.361	.301

1996 Batting — Single-A and Rookie Leagues

BATTING																				BASERUNNING				PERCENTAGES		
Player	Team	Org	Lg	A	G	AB	H	2B	3B	HR	TB	R	RBI	TBB	IBB	SO	HBP	SH	SF	SB	CS	SB%	GDP	Avg	OBP	SLG
Hines,Pooh	Eugene	Atl	A-	22	21	88	31	5	5	2	52	20	8	7	0	18	0	3	1	3	4	.43	1	.352	.396	.591
Hobbie,Matt	Boise	Cal	A-	22	51	127	32	6	1	2	46	26	22	20	1	24	0	0	1	5	1	.83	2	.252	.351	.362
Hodge,Roy	Frederick	Bal	A+	26	4	12	0	0	0	0	0	2	0	3	0	5	1	0	0	1	0	1.00	0	.000	.250	.000
	High Desert	Bal	A+	26	112	393	110	21	2	8	159	71	54	47	0	58	2	8	4	9	7	.56	8	.280	.357	.405
Hodges,Randy	Macon	Atl	A	23	101	278	67	12	1	2	87	36	28	18	1	42	4	3	0	10	10	.50	4	.241	.297	.313
Hogan,Todd	Johnson Cty	StL	R+	21	47	183	63	7	3	0	76	38	32	20	0	41	6	1	2	18	6	.75	5	.344	.422	.415
	St. Pete	StL	A+	21	2	6	2	0	0	0	2	1	0	0	0	3	0	0	0	0	0	.00	0	.333	.333	.333
Hollins,Darontaye	Hickory	ChA	A	22	37	132	22	2	0	0	24	10	6	10	0	41	1	1	1	3	3	.50	2	.167	.229	.182
	Bristol	ChA	R+	22	16	58	10	2	0	0	12	8	6	6	0	20	0	0	1	5	2	.71	2	.172	.246	.207
Hooper,Daren	Orioles	Bal	R	20	33	104	26	4	0	3	39	22	12	16	0	30	2	0	1	1	0	1.00	4	.250	.358	.375
Horn,Marv	White Sox	ChA	R	22	9	28	7	0	0	0	7	4	2	6	0	3	1	0	0	1	0	1.00	1	.250	.400	.250
	Bristol	ChA	R+	22	20	55	5	1	0	3	15	6	9	9	0	28	1	0	2	0	0	.00	1	.091	.224	.273
Horner,Jim	Everett	Sea	A-	23	18	60	9	2	0	2	17	6	5	10	1	16	1	0	0	0	0	.00	1	.150	.282	.283
Houser,Jeremy	Salem	Col	A+	22	117	436	104	12	3	1	125	59	48	68	1	47	1	5	3	13	9	.59	12	.239	.341	.287
Hucks,Brian	Princeton	Cin	R+	24	34	122	36	4	1	6	60	25	25	23	0	21	1	1	3	2	1	.67	1	.295	.403	.492
	Billings	Cin	R+	24	20	59	19	6	0	2	31	10	12	12	0	14	3	1	0	0	0	.00	0	.322	.459	.525
Hudde,Alejandro	Rockies	Col	R	22	26	93	20	3	2	0	27	9	8	2	0	25	2	3	1	4	0	1.00	0	.215	.245	.290
Hudson,Robert	DiamondbackAri		R	19	35	112	31	5	4	0	44	12	20	8	0	33	1	0	1	2	0	1.00	3	.277	.328	.393
Huelsmann,Mike	Watertown	Cle	A-	22	41	130	34	5	1	0	41	21	21	17	0	14	2	3	0	14	4	.78	0	.262	.356	.315
Huff,B.J.	Pittsfield	NYN	A-	21	42	138	27	4	2	2	41	19	14	7	0	36	1	1	1	3	1	.75	2	.196	.238	.297
Huff,Larry	Clearwater	Phi	A+	25	128	483	132	17	5	0	159	73	37	60	1	65	6	10	4	37	11	.77	4	.273	.358	.329
Huffman,Ryan	Oneonta	NYA	A-	23	23	61	12	4	1	0	18	8	6	6	0	24	6	0	0	0	0	.00	0	.197	.329	.295
Hugo,Sean	High Desert	Bal	A+	24	18	39	6	1	0	2	13	3	5	4	0	11	1	1	0	0	2	.00	1	.154	.250	.333
Huls,Steve	Fort Wayne	Min	A	22	60	201	43	3	1	1	51	21	11	12	1	53	1	6	2	2	2	.50	3	.214	.259	.254
Hundt,Bo	Erie	Pit	A-	22	20	55	9	0	1	1	14	8	4	4	0	11	1	1	0	1	0	1.00	0	.164	.233	.255
	Pirates	Pit	R	22	20	69	17	2	0	1	22	12	9	5	0	9	4	0	2	0	0	.00	3	.246	.325	.319
Hunter,Andy	Rancho CucaSD		A+	20	4	9	2	0	0	0	2	2	0	0	0	2	1	0	0	0	0	.00	0	.222	.300	.222
	Idaho Falls	SD	R+	20	32	102	25	3	0	0	28	13	9	21	0	30	0	0	0	3	3	.50	3	.245	.374	.275
Hunter,Scott	St. Lucie	NYN	A+	21	127	475	122	19	1	2	149	71	38	38	4	68	8	3	3	49	12	.80	6	.257	.321	.314
Hutchins,Norm	Cedar Rapds	Cal	A	21	126	466	105	13	16	2	156	59	52	28	0	110	6	8	2	22	8	.73	5	.225	.277	.335
Hutchison,Bernard	Portland	Col	A-	23	51	192	50	6	0	0	56	29	13	16	0	34	3	2	1	20	3	.87	3	.260	.325	.292
Hyers,James	Auburn	Hou	A-	21	63	231	59	13	1	1	77	50	20	36	2	50	2	3	0	14	4	.78	3	.255	.361	.333
Iapoce,Anthony	Beloit	Mil	A	23	77	266	78	6	3	1	93	62	11	43	0	53	7	3	0	23	13	.64	4	.293	.405	.350
Ibarra,Jesus	San Jose	SF	A+	24	126	498	141	38	0	17	230	74	95	63	3	108	3	0	2	5	1	.83	12	.283	.366	.462
Illig,Brett	Great Falls	LA	R+	19	44	119	27	3	0	1	33	15	11	6	0	36	0	1	1	4	2	.67	4	.227	.262	.277
Inglin,Jeff	Bristol	ChA	R+	21	50	193	56	10	0	8	90	27	24	11	0	25	9	0	0	9	6	.60	8	.290	.357	.466
	Hickory	ChA	A	21	22	83	30	6	2	2	46	12	15	4	0	11	1	0	1	2	1	.67	3	.361	.393	.554
Ingram,Darron	Charlstn-WV	Cin	A	21	15	48	9	3	0	1	15	5	6	8	1	19	0	0	1	0	0	.00	0	.188	.298	.313
	Billings	Cin	R+	21	65	251	74	13	0	17	138	49	56	34	2	88	2	0	1	7	3	.70	1	.295	.382	.550
Inzunza,Miguel	Peoria	StL	A	24	26	61	12	1	0	0	13	10	8	11	0	8	0	3	2	0	0	.00	2	.197	.311	.213
	Fayettevlle	Det	A	24	68	232	58	12	0	0	70	24	31	27	0	19	7	8	2	2	3	.40	4	.250	.343	.302
Irvis,Damon	Elizabethtn	Min	R+	21	56	172	29	5	1	0	36	30	15	26	0	62	3	2	2	8	3	.73	1	.169	.286	.209
Isom,Johnny	Frederick	Bal	A+	23	124	486	141	27	3	18	228	69	104	40	4	87	7	0	6	8	6	.57	15	.290	.349	.469
Izquierdo,Sergio	South Bend	ChA	A	24	2	2	0	0	0	0	0	0	0	0	0	1	0	0	0	0	0	.00	0	.000	.000	.000
Jackson,Jeff	Daytona	ChN	A+	25	16	53	13	2	1	0	17	5	4	8	0	18	0	0	1	7	1	.88	1	.245	.339	.321
Jackson,Quantaa	Marlins	Fla	R	19	26	77	11	3	0	0	14	5	6	8	0	30	3	2	1	2	0	1.00	2	.143	.247	.182
Jackson,Rod	Idaho Falls	SD	R+	22	54	250	71	3	5	1	87	56	21	12	1	32	5	1	2	25	6	.81	4	.284	.327	.348
Jackson,Ryan	Marlins	Fla	R	25	7	25	9	0	0	0	9	5	5	1	0	3	1	0	0	2	0	1.00	0	.360	.407	.360
	Brevard Cty	Fla	A+	25	6	26	8	2	0	1	13	4	4	1	0	7	0	0	0	1	0	1.00	0	.308	.333	.500
Jackson,Wade	Boise	Cal	A-	23	43	117	33	5	2	2	48	17	25	17	0	25	2	0	3	5	1	.83	3	.282	.374	.410
Jackson,William	Burlington	Cle	R+	23	35	103	13	1	0	1	17	15	3	9	0	38	4	0	0	6	2	.75	0	.126	.224	.165
Jacobo,Roberto	Padres	SD	R	21	40	111	24	4	2	0	32	18	12	12	0	27	0	1	1	6	2	.75	1	.216	.290	.288
Jacobus,Brian	Padres	SD	R	21	50	193	51	8	7	0	73	29	24	9	0	33	0	0	2	2	3	.40	7	.264	.294	.378
Jaime,Angel	St. Lucie	NYN	A+	24	98	288	74	10	1	3	95	38	21	34	0	47	6	6	3	12	6	.67	5	.257	.344	.330
James,Kenny	Expos	Mon	R	20	44	165	35	5	2	0	44	24	12	15	1	33	3	2	0	4	3	.57	0	.212	.290	.267
Jamison,Nicholas	Tigers	Det	R	18	31	95	10	1	1	0	13	11	9	12	0	18	1	0	0	1	2	.33	1	.105	.213	.137
Janke,Jared	Piedmont	Phi	A	23	104	388	85	21	0	6	124	36	46	24	1	70	4	3	3	2	2	.50	8	.219	.270	.320
Jaramillo,Francisco	Charlstn-SC	Tex	A	22	45	131	25	5	0	1	33	14	7	10	0	41	7	1	0	2	0	1.00	4	.191	.284	.252
Jaroncyk,Ryan	Kingsport	NYN	R+	20	57	221	52	5	5	1	70	35	21	27	0	59	6	3	3	4	2	.67	3	.235	.331	.317
Jasco,Elinton	Rockford	ChN	A	22	120	464	136	11	7	1	164	95	43	62	1	97	5	12	2	48	14	.77	1	.293	.381	.353
Jefferies,Daryl	Williamsprt	ChN	A-	23	34	101	26	2	1	0	30	12	11	10	0	18	3	0	1	12	2	.86	1	.257	.339	.297
Jefferson,Dave	Rockford	ChN	A	22	93	301	70	8	2	1	85	35	40	37	0	53	4	1	2	15	6	.71	6	.233	.323	.282
Jenkins,Benjamin	Martinsvlle	Phi	R+	23	41	140	29	6	0	1	38	10	14	12	0	35	0	0	0	4	3	.57	0	.207	.270	.271
Jenkins,Corey	Lowell	Bos	A-	20	65	228	51	7	2	8	86	37	29	28	0	81	1	0	1	5	0	1.00	8	.224	.310	.377
Jenkins,Daniel	Billings	Cin	R+	22	55	126	28	7	2	0	39	21	14	16	0	39	2	2	2	0	3	.00	6	.222	.315	.310
Jenkins,Demetrish	Winston-Sal	Cin	A+	24	108	380	102	20	2	9	153	58	59	54	1	96	1	3	3	15	7	.68	11	.268	.358	.403
Jenkins,Peter	Ogden	Mil	R+	22	14	25	5	0	0	1	8	4	3	6	0	8	0	0	0	0	0	.00	0	.200	.355	.320
	Helena	Mil	R+	22	7	21	3	2	0	0	5	3	2	5	0	5	1	0	0	0	0	.00	3	.143	.333	.238
Jensen,Jake	Pirates	Pit	R	20	31	96	18	4	2	1	29	14	13	10	0	22	3	1	0	2	3	.40	2	.188	.284	.302
Jimenez,D'Angelo	Greensboro	NYA	A	19	138	537	131	25	5	6	184	68	48	56	2	113	3	4	3	15	17	.47	7	.244	.317	.343
Jimenez,Felipe	Cubs	ChN	R	20	49	171	42	4	0	0	46	18	10	5	0	44	1	4	0	20	9	.69	3	.246	.271	.269
Jimenez,Miguel	Mariners	Sea	R	21	44	158	42	9	0	4	63	22	18	6	0	44	2	0	2	6	2	.75	3	.266	.298	.399
Jimenez,Ruben	New Jersey	StL	A-	21	64	236	54	5	4	0	67	53	12	41	0	51	8	8	1	20	3	.87	2	.229	.360	.284
Johnson,Adam	Eugene	Atl	A-	21	76	318	100	22	9	7	161	58	56	19	3	32	4	1	2	4	1	.80	4	.314	.359	.506
Johnson,A.J.	Charlstn-WV	Cin	A	24	9	26	6	1	0	1	10	3	5	6	0	9	1	0	0	1	2	.33	0	.231	.394	.385
Johnson,Tony	Mets	NYN	R	19	48	164	40	6	2	7	71	18	27	24	0	42	0	1	2	5	3	.63	3	.244	.337	.433
Johnson,Carlisle	Twins	Min	R	20	26	76	12	1	0	0	13	8	6	12	0	29	1	3	1	0	0	.00	1	.158	.278	.171

1996 Batting — Single-A and Rookie Leagues

BATTING																				BASERUNNING				PERCENTAGES		
Player	Team	Org	Lg	A	G	AB	H	2B	3B	HR	TB	R	RBI	TBB	IBB	SO	HBP	SH	SF	SB	CS	SB%	GDP	Avg	OBP	SLG
Johnson,Todd	Bakersfield	Cle	A+	26	110	369	88	23	0	2	117	45	31	32	0	90	5	1	0	1	1	.50	6	.238	.308	.317
Johnson,Damon	Hagerstown	Tor	A	21	43	126	23	6	1	1	34	17	11	11	0	42	2	0	1	3	3	.50	4	.183	.257	.270
	St. Cathrns	Tor	A-	21	19	58	14	6	0	0	20	12	3	3	0	17	1	1	0	0	1	.00	0	.241	.290	.345
Johnson,Douglas	Devil Rays	TB	R	19	28	108	25	3	1	1	33	12	9	7	1	41	2	0	2	0	2	.00	0	.231	.286	.306
Johnson,Heath	Fort Wayne	Min	A	20	8	25	4	1	0	0	5	4	1	6	0	9	1	0	0	0	0	.00	0	.160	.344	.200
	Elizabethtn	Min	R+	20	48	149	36	9	0	7	66	24	32	30	0	60	2	0	0	2	0	1.00	0	.242	.376	.443
Johnson,Jace	Sou. Oregon	Oak	A-	22	36	114	26	9	0	1	38	13	8	14	0	29	0	2	1	3	1	.75	0	.228	.310	.333
Johnson,Jay	Clinton	SD	A	24	118	428	108	12	3	0	126	67	26	53	1	67	2	11	2	44	15	.75	8	.252	.336	.294
Johnson,J.J.	Charlstn-SC	Tex	A	21	116	391	85	18	4	1	114	40	38	43	1	115	6	2	1	11	7	.61	5	.217	.304	.292
Johnson,J.J.	Martinsvlle	Phi	R+	26	55	213	58	5	2	0	67	29	13	14	0	27	2	0	1	20	7	.74	2	.272	.322	.315
Johnson,Jeffrey	South Bend	ChA	A	24	102	345	62	13	0	2	81	27	39	22	1	49	0	10	4	10	7	.59	3	.180	.226	.235
Johnson,Duan	Everett	Sea	A-	21	51	202	53	7	2	1	67	32	19	7	0	26	1	1	1	3	3	.50	8	.262	.289	.332
Johnson,Ledowick	Helena	Mil	R+	24	59	208	71	8	3	7	106	70	33	58	1	43	3	0	3	19	6	.76	3	.341	.485	.510
Johnson,Mark	South Bend	ChA	A	21	67	214	55	14	3	2	81	29	27	39	2	25	1	4	4	3	3	.50	8	.257	.368	.379
	Pr. William	ChA	A+	21	18	58	14	3	0	0	17	9	3	13	0	6	1	0	0	0	0	.00	0	.241	.389	.293
Johnson,Nick	Yankees	NYA	R	1	47	157	45	11	1	2	64	31	33	30	0	35	9	0	3	0	0	.00	5	.287	.422	.408
Johnson,Patrick	Boise	Cal	A-	22	27	75	15	0	0	0	15	2	4	8	0	12	1	0	0	0	0	.00	3	.200	.286	.200
Johnson,Ric	Quad City	Hou	A	23	95	318	75	9	3	3	99	36	39	16	0	47	8	4	6	10	4	.71	12	.236	.284	.311
Johnson,Rontrez	Red Sox	Bos	R	20	28	85	25	6	0	0	31	20	9	17	0	11	0	1	0	6	2	.75	2	.294	.412	.365
	Lowell	Bos	A-	20	35	135	30	4	0	4	46	27	12	21	1	30	0	0	2	7	3	.70	2	.222	.323	.341
Johnson,Thomas	Mets	NYN	R	21	32	115	30	5	1	1	40	19	9	6	1	26	3	3	1	5	2	.71	1	.261	.312	.348
Johnson,T.J.	Fort Wayne	Min	A	23	57	183	60	18	2	3	91	32	18	32	0	49	11	1	1	5	5	.50	4	.328	.454	.497
Jones,Ben	Fort Myers	Min	A+	23	56	162	34	1	0	0	35	22	8	17	0	26	0	4	1	17	3	.85	4	.210	.283	.216
Jones,Ivory	Fort Myers	Min	A+	24	48	144	34	7	1	0	43	20	10	21	0	32	1	3	1	9	7	.56	2	.236	.335	.299
Jones,Jack	San Bernrdo	LA	A+	22	10	29	7	3	0	1	13	5	6	6	0	8	1	0	0	1	1	.50	1	.241	.389	.448
Jones,Jacque	Fort Myers	Min	A+	NA	1	3	2	1	0	0	3	0	1	0	0	0	0	0	0	0	1	.00	0	.667	.667	1.000
Jones,Jaime	Kane County	Fla	A	20	62	237	59	17	1	8	102	29	45	19	0	74	0	0	5	7	2	.78	6	.249	.299	.430
Jones,Jay	Utica	Fla	A-	22	37	116	33	6	0	0	39	9	9	6	0	17	0	2	1	0	1	.00	5	.284	.317	.336
Jones,Pookie	Salem	Col	A+	25	102	335	94	18	1	6	132	45	40	29	0	76	1	7	4	16	6	.73	12	.281	.336	.394
Jones,Timothy	Sou. Oregon	Oak	A-	19	62	173	35	8	0	6	61	25	18	27	0	69	2	2	2	7	5	.58	2	.202	.314	.353
Jordan,Yustin	Pirates	Pit	R	18	27	85	21	1	0	1	25	10	5	10	0	23	2	1	0	1	0	1.00	3	.247	.340	.294
Jorgensen,Timothy	Kinston	Cle	A+	24	119	412	89	24	0	17	164	56	64	41	2	103	6	1	3	1	2	.33	7	.216	.294	.398
Joseph,Terry	Rockford	ChN	A	23	128	449	137	23	6	9	199	98	94	69	0	88	25	2	9	28	15	.65	7	.305	.418	.443
Juarez,Raul	Fort Wayne	Min	A	21	54	170	38	6	0	2	50	24	21	20	1	51	3	1	1	1	2	.33	4	.224	.314	.294
	Twins	Min	R	21	11	0	0	0	0	0	0	0	0	0	0	0	0	0	0	0	0	.00	0	.000	.000	.000
Jumonville,Joe	St. Pete	StL	A+	26	41	101	16	3	1	0	21	10	7	8	1	22	1	0	0	0	0	.00	5	.158	.227	.208
Kane,Kevin	Oneonta	NYA	A-	23	4	4	1	0	0	0	1	1	0	0	0	1	0	0	0	0	0	.00	0	.250	.250	.250
Kane,Ryan	Cedar Rapds	Cal	A	23	125	485	125	29	2	14	200	56	75	40	3	120	4	1	8	5	5	.50	9	.258	.315	.412
Kapler,Gabriel	Fayettevlle	Det	A	21	138	524	157	45	0	26	280	81	99	62	6	73	7	3	5	14	4	.78	6	.300	.378	.534
Kastelic,Matthew	Butte	TB	R+	23	40	158	56	8	1	2	72	26	26	6	0	16	3	0	1	6	0	1.00	4	.354	.387	.456
Katz,Jason	Danville	Atl	R+	23	45	139	33	8	1	1	46	20	17	22	0	38	5	0	4	7	5	.58	3	.237	.353	.331
	Eugene	Atl	A-	23	7	28	5	1	0	0	6	3	2	4	0	11	0	0	0	0	0	.00	0	.179	.281	.214
Keaveney,Jeffrey	Lowell	Bos	A-	21	49	169	42	13	1	4	69	15	20	10	1	65	9	0	1	1	1	.50	1	.249	.323	.408
Keck,Brian	Portland	Col	A-	23	43	156	41	1	2	0	46	29	20	22	0	23	1	3	1	7	2	.78	1	.263	.356	.295
Keech,Erik	Greensboro	NYA	A	22	16	35	8	2	0	0	10	4	2	3	0	4	0	0	0	0	0	.00	2	.229	.289	.286
Kehoe,John	Hagerstown	Tor	A	24	117	383	104	24	2	6	150	66	47	73	0	92	5	3	5	16	9	.64	2	.272	.391	.392
Keller,Jeremy	Billings	Cin	R+	23	59	237	57	12	0	7	90	39	39	24	0	52	2	0	3	0	2	.00	3	.241	.312	.380
Kelley,Erskine	Lynchburg	Pit	A+	26	111	344	97	22	5	5	144	61	43	25	2	93	4	2	3	13	8	.62	8	.282	.335	.419
Kenna,David	Bellingham	SF	A-	19	56	180	39	9	3	1	57	11	25	20	1	78	2	0	2	2	0	1.00	1	.217	.299	.317
Kennedy,Brad	New Jersey	StL	A-	23	64	199	42	10	4	4	72	24	24	30	0	48	0	0	3	8	0	1.00	2	.211	.310	.362
Kennedy,Brian	Twins	Min	R	19	37	110	24	2	1	0	28	8	16	13	0	30	2	2	3	3	4	.43	0	.218	.305	.255
Kennedy,Gus	Durham	Atl	A+	23	116	348	73	11	2	19	145	52	50	58	2	124	3	0	2	6	6	.50	3	.210	.326	.417
Kennedy,Jed	Piedmont	Phi	A	19	27	107	23	5	1	0	30	12	14	3	0	24	0	0	0	1	2	.33	4	.215	.236	.280
Kent,Robbie	Idaho Falls	SD	R+	23	47	181	56	14	0	2	76	40	25	21	0	28	4	1	1	4	1	.80	5	.309	.391	.420
Kent,Troy	Watertown	Cle	A-	23	72	263	66	20	2	3	99	34	32	33	2	54	4	2	2	1	5	.17	5	.251	.341	.376
Kerr,Jim	Butte	TB	R+	22	32	98	15	3	0	2	24	9	6	10	0	32	0	1	2	3	1	.75	1	.153	.227	.245
Key,Jeffrey	Clearwater	Phi	A+	22	101	348	85	15	4	3	117	53	34	16	1	82	10	3	1	15	3	.83	5	.244	.296	.336
Kiefer,Dax	Williamsprt	ChN	A-	23	64	229	52	7	3	3	74	36	20	27	0	50	3	4	2	12	2	.86	2	.227	.314	.323
Kieffer,Brian	Sou. Oregon	Oak	A-	23	2	2	0	0	0	0	0	0	0	3	1	2	0	0	0	0	0	.00	0	.000	.600	.000
Kimm,Tyson	Piedmont	Phi	A	24	35	106	21	4	0	0	25	11	6	9	0	23	4	1	0	1	0	1.00	3	.198	.286	.236
Kinard,Kirk	Lethbridge	Ari	R+	23	5	13	0	0	0	0	0	0	0	0	0	7	0	0	0	0	0	.00	2	.000	.000	.000
	Bakersfield	Ari	A+	23	37	116	23	3	2	0	30	16	5	13	1	44	3	5	0	3	1	.75	4	.198	.295	.259
King,Bradford	Williamsprt	ChN	A-	22	23	70	12	2	1	0	16	7	8	4	0	20	4	0	1	0	1	.00	0	.171	.253	.229
King,Brion	Orioles	Bal	R	20	9	26	3	1	0	0	4	5	1	2	0	5	0	0	0	2	0	1.00	1	.115	.179	.154
	Dunedin	Tor	A+	20	7	14	1	0	0	0	1	1	1	0	0	5	1	1	0	0	0	.00	2	.071	.133	.071
King,Cesar	Charlstn-SC	Tex	A	19	84	276	69	10	1	7	102	35	28	21	0	58	1	0	2	8	5	.62	5	.250	.303	.370
King,Michael	Butte	TB	R+	23	50	192	60	13	3	1	82	35	27	12	0	27	2	4	1	7	3	.70	7	.313	.357	.427
King,William	Yakima	LA	A-	19	24	39	6	0	0	0	6	4	1	7	0	16	0	0	0	0	0	.00	0	.154	.283	.154
Kingsbury,Willy	Red Sox	Bos	R	23	28	93	31	9	0	2	46	7	22	10	0	18	1	1	0	3	0	1.00	3	.333	.404	.495
	Lowell	Bos	A-	23	19	63	10	1	0	1	14	3	5	2	0	28	0	0	2	0	1	.00	2	.159	.179	.222
Kinkade,Mike	Beloit	Mil	A	24	135	499	151	33	4	15	237	105	100	47	7	69	32	3	6	23	12	.66	10	.303	.394	.475
Kinnie,Donald	Cubs	ChN	R	23	11	39	12	3	1	1	20	6	7	2	0	6	1	0	2	3	1	.75	1	.308	.341	.513
	Rockford	ChN	A	23	31	65	15	4	0	0	19	12	3	3	0	20	0	0	0	7	0	1.00	3	.231	.265	.292
Kirby,Douglas	Billings	Cin	R+	22	57	182	43	10	1	3	64	29	20	39	1	48	0	0	2	4	1	.80	2	.236	.368	.352
Kirby,Scott	Helena	Mil	R+	19	47	145	29	4	0	4	45	26	21	19	0	42	4	1	2	0	3	.00	4	.200	.306	.310
Kirgan,Chris	High Desert	Bal	A+	24	136	529	157	23	1	35	287	96	131	54	3	162	5	1	2	2	3	.40	9	.297	.366	.543
Kirkpatrick,Brian	Rockies	Col	R	20	11	32	5	1	0	0	6	2	2	1	0	7	1	2	1	0	1	.00	0	.156	.200	.188

1996 Batting — Single-A and Rookie Leagues

BATTING																				BASERUNNING				PERCENTAGES		
Player	Team	Org	Lg	A	G	AB	H	2B	3B	HR	TB	R	RBI	TBB	IBB	SO	HBP	SH	SF	SB	CS	SB%	GDP	Avg	OBP	SLG
Kirkpatrick,Michael	Orioles	Bal	R	19	17	31	7	0	0	0	7	3	2	0	0	5	3	0	0	2	3	.40	1	.226	.294	.226
Klassen,Danny	Stockton	Mil	A+	21	118	432	116	22	4	2	152	58	46	34	0	77	10	5	2	14	8	.64	12	.269	.335	.352
Klee,Charles	Hickory	ChA	A	20	38	109	22	2	1	0	26	7	7	5	0	31	0	0	0	2	2	.50	4	.202	.237	.239
	Bristol	ChA	R+	20	48	184	38	6	0	4	56	22	17	7	1	38	0	1	2	2	2	.50	4	.207	.233	.304
	South Bend	ChA	A	20	18	55	13	0	0	2	19	8	4	7	0	13	0	1	1	2	2	.50	2	.236	.317	.345
Kleiner,Stacy	New Jersey	StL	A-	22	56	177	52	10	2	2	72	24	23	9	0	32	1	2	0	2	1	.67	5	.294	.332	.407
Kleinz,Larry	Utica	Fla	A-	23	73	256	62	14	1	0	78	21	34	20	0	44	13	2	3	1	0	1.00	6	.242	.325	.305
Klimek,Joshua	Helena	Mil	R+	23	67	253	75	17	0	6	110	56	51	42	5	39	0	0	3	5	1	.83	4	.296	.393	.435
Kliner,Joshua	Lethbridge	Ari	R+	24	12	28	7	1	0	0	8	6	2	3	0	3	1	1	0	1	0	1.00	1	.250	.344	.286
	Bakersfield	Ari	A+	24	43	156	48	6	1	5	71	37	33	37	1	25	8	0	1	0	3	.00	1	.308	.460	.455
Knauss,Tom	Fort Myers	Min	A+	23	36	117	22	1	0	5	38	11	12	12	0	28	1	0	0	2	1	.67	1	.188	.269	.325
	Fort Wayne	Min	A	23	56	207	62	18	2	7	105	30	39	25	3	46	2	1	4	1	0	1.00	8	.300	.374	.507
Knight,Marcus	Angels	Cal	R	18	54	203	59	16	5	3	94	36	30	28	0	50	3	0	1	10	7	.59	2	.291	.383	.463
Knupfer,Jason	Batavia	Phi	A-	22	66	218	61	5	1	1	71	32	24	25	0	43	4	3	2	5	5	.50	4	.280	.361	.326
Koehler,Jason	St. Cathrns	Tor	A-	22	47	135	31	6	0	4	49	21	18	19	0	40	1	0	0	2	1	.67	2	.230	.329	.363
Kofler,Eric	Oneonta	NYA	A-	21	46	176	40	8	0	3	57	18	22	10	2	33	1	1	3	3	1	.75	2	.227	.268	.324
Kokinda,Stephen	Everett	Sea	A-	22	16	48	7	2	0	0	9	7	8	8	0	16	1	0	0	0	0	.00	0	.146	.281	.188
Kominek,Toby	Stockton	Mil	A+	24	100	358	106	17	7	7	158	76	47	49	1	97	8	4	3	10	7	.59	7	.296	.390	.441
Konrady,Dennis	Watertown	Cle	A-	22	60	183	46	10	1	1	61	23	30	42	0	32	1	5	3	2	5	.29	1	.251	.389	.333
Koonce,Gray	Fayettevlle	Det	A	22	133	487	116	22	3	8	168	61	59	58	2	97	5	2	4	7	7	.50	9	.238	.323	.345
Kopacz,Derek	Fayettevlle	Det	A	22	49	186	43	11	3	3	69	25	14	14	0	49	0	2	1	2	2	.50	2	.231	.284	.371
	Jamestown	Det	A-	22	68	242	57	17	4	7	103	34	40	21	2	74	5	1	5	2	5	.29	5	.236	.304	.426
Kopriva,Dan	Pr. William	ChA	A+	27	91	337	85	21	1	8	132	53	39	59	2	44	4	0	3	0	0	.00	12	.252	.367	.392
Koskie,Corey	Fort Myers	Min	A+	24	95	338	88	19	4	9	142	43	55	40	0	76	1	1	3	1	1	.50	4	.260	.338	.420
Kotsay,Mark	Kane County	Fla	A	21	17	60	17	5	0	2	28	16	8	16	0	8	1	0	1	3	0	1.00	3	.283	.436	.467
Kratochvil,Tim	Lowell	Bos	A-	23	44	158	48	11	0	3	68	20	19	8	0	31	1	1	1	1	1	.50	3	.304	.339	.430
Kritscher,Ryan	Johnson Cty	StL	R+	23	46	168	52	19	0	5	86	34	33	16	0	18	8	0	3	3	4	.43	0	.310	.390	.512
Kuilan,Robles	Kane County	Fla	A	21	94	308	62	12	1	6	94	28	30	22	0	52	3	3	2	1	3	.25	7	.201	.260	.305
Kushma,Glenn	Kingsport	NYN	R+	23	45	129	37	7	1	2	52	20	20	16	0	27	4	2	2	2	1	.67	1	.287	.377	.403
Lackey,Steve	Fayettevlle	Det	A	22	82	310	67	13	0	4	92	38	43	28	0	58	3	5	5	24	6	.80	4	.216	.283	.297
	Visalia	Det	A+	22	46	184	49	11	1	4	74	27	29	16	0	44	1	2	2	7	1	.88	7	.266	.325	.402
Lakovic,Greg	Fort Wayne	Min	A	22	36	94	24	3	0	0	27	12	11	16	0	22	4	4	0	2	2	.50	3	.255	.386	.287
Lamb,David	High Desert	Bal	A+	22	116	460	118	24	3	3	157	63	55	50	1	68	10	5	2	5	6	.45	19	.257	.341	.341
Landaeta,Luis	Rockies	Col	R	20	44	176	49	9	1	0	60	27	20	5	0	22	4	1	4	7	2	.78	5	.278	.307	.341
Landaker,Dave	Kissimmee	Hou	A+	23	41	108	21	2	0	0	23	10	7	15	0	23	1	2	0	1	3	.25	1	.194	.298	.213
Landrum,Tito	San Bernrdo	LA	A+	26	51	157	42	7	0	3	58	29	20	21	0	38	2	0	1	8	4	.67	2	.268	.359	.369
	Vero Beach	LA	A+	26	44	122	29	5	0	2	40	12	14	10	1	33	1	2	2	2	0	1.00	0	.238	.296	.328
Landry,Jacques	Lakeland	Det	A+	23	11	35	3	1	0	0	4	2	2	3	0	15	0	0	1	0	0	.00	0	.086	.154	.114
	Fayettevlle	Det	A	23	31	101	19	4	0	1	26	10	3	5	0	36	1	0	0	1	0	1.00	2	.188	.234	.257
Landry,Lonny	Lakeland	Det	A+	24	75	292	69	9	7	3	101	35	21	24	1	72	8	2	0	19	3	.86	4	.236	.312	.346
	Visalia	Det	A+	24	51	191	41	7	2	2	58	23	10	9	0	54	3	4	0	10	2	.83	0	.215	.261	.304
Landstad,Rob	Burlington	Cle	R+	24	53	167	49	10	3	7	86	31	27	40	2	34	2	0	0	9	3	.75	0	.293	.435	.515
	Watertown	Cle	A-	24	6	20	6	2	1	0	10	3	3	2	1	6	0	0	0	0	0	.00	0	.300	.364	.500
Langaigne,Selwyn	Medicne Hat	Tor	R+	21	32	100	26	4	1	2	38	19	11	17	0	20	1	2	0	8	2	.80	4	.260	.373	.380
	Hagerstown	Tor	A	21	4	14	2	0	0	0	2	1	1	1	0	5	0	0	0	2	0	1.00	0	.143	.200	.143
	Dunedin	Tor	A+	21	31	117	26	2	3	0	34	16	4	9	0	30	2	4	0	1	3	.25	5	.222	.289	.291
Lantigua,Eddie	Daytona	ChN	A+	23	43	143	28	1	0	5	44	10	14	3	1	31	1	0	0	3	1	.75	3	.196	.218	.308
Lanza,Mike	Lancaster	Sea	A+	23	109	380	100	12	6	3	133	53	42	18	0	73	3	4	4	3	4	.43	7	.263	.299	.350
Lara,Edward	W. Michigan	Oak	A	21	87	259	56	7	1	0	65	29	16	25	0	39	5	5	2	16	6	.73	9	.216	.296	.251
Lariviere,Jason	Peoria	StL	A	23	64	225	56	13	1	1	74	33	36	25	0	31	0	2	3	6	5	.55	5	.249	.320	.329
	St. Pete	StL	A+	23	41	140	42	6	0	3	57	27	18	18	1	19	0	4	1	1	1	.50	1	.300	.377	.407
Larkin,Garrett	Erie	Pit	A-	22	19	53	11	2	0	0	13	6	4	7	0	8	0	0	0	0	1	.00	1	.208	.300	.245
	Pirates	Pit	R	22	17	69	26	4	2	0	34	7	6	2	0	5	0	0	0	1	1	.50	1	.377	.394	.493
Larkin,Stephen	Winston-Sal	Cin	A+	23	39	117	21	2	0	3	32	13	6	14	2	25	0	1	1	6	1	.86	6	.179	.265	.274
	Charlstn-WV	Cin	A	23	58	203	55	7	2	5	81	30	33	35	1	40	4	1	1	5	4	.56	2	.271	.387	.399
Larue,Jason	Charlstn-WV	Cin	A	23	37	123	26	8	0	2	40	17	14	11	0	28	2	1	0	3	0	1.00	2	.211	.287	.325
Larue,Shaun	Charlstn-WV	Cin	A	25	4	0	0	0	0	0	0	0	0	0	0	0	0	0	0	0	0	.00	0	.000	.000	.000
Lawrence,Chip	Bluefield	Bal	R+	22	15	34	7	0	0	1	10	6	4	4	0	4	2	0	0	0	0	.00	1	.206	.325	.294
	Frederick	Bal	A+	22	43	132	31	1	1	0	34	9	14	8	0	13	1	4	0	6	3	.67	3	.235	.284	.258
Lawrence,Joseph	St. Cathrns	Tor	A-	20	27	92	20	7	2	0	31	22	11	14	1	16	2	1	3	1	1	.50	1	.217	.324	.337
Lawrence,Mike	Angels	Cal	R	21	38	117	21	2	0	0	23	9	12	11	0	28	0	3	1	1	3	.25	2	.179	.248	.197
Layne,Jason	Spokane	KC	A-	24	41	126	36	9	3	5	66	24	27	17	1	34	5	0	0	0	0	.00	0	.286	.392	.524
	Lansing	KC	A	24	25	91	23	4	0	1	30	11	16	13	0	23	0	0	0	1	0	1.00	1	.253	.346	.330
Leach,Nicholas	Great Falls	LA	R+	19	58	199	50	8	1	9	87	42	25	36	2	33	3	0	0	2	4	.33	3	.251	.374	.437
Lebron,Juan	Royals	KC	R	20	58	215	62	9	2	3	84	19	30	6	0	34	2	0	0	1	2	.33	9	.288	.314	.391
LeBron,Ruben	Michigan	Bos	A	21	38	107	19	5	0	0	24	17	6	7	0	18	2	1	0	3	0	1.00	3	.178	.241	.224
	Lowell	Bos	A-	21	46	159	35	5	1	0	42	24	7	7	0	31	4	2	0	11	3	.79	3	.220	.271	.264
Lecronier,Jason	High Desert	Bal	A+	24	52	135	32	3	1	4	49	20	25	6	0	37	1	2	2	1	0	1.00	5	.237	.271	.363
	Frederick	Bal	A+	24	29	92	21	3	0	4	36	13	12	10	4	29	1	2	0	0	0	.00	0	.228	.311	.391
Lee,Carlos	Hickory	ChA	A	21	119	480	150	23	6	8	209	65	70	23	5	50	0	0	11	18	13	.58	15	.313	.337	.435
Lee,Jason	Johnson Cty	StL	R+	20	36	114	35	10	3	2	57	21	21	20	1	25	1	1	0	1	2	.33	1	.307	.415	.500
Legree,Keith	Fort Myers	Min	A+	25	58	198	54	8	2	5	81	39	37	42	2	52	5	0	2	2	2	.50	2	.273	.409	.409
Leidens,Enrique	Expos	Mon	R	NA	27	77	17	1	0	1	21	8	6	8	0	14	1	2	0	6	2	.75	0	.221	.302	.273
Lemonis,Chris	Visalia	Det	A+	23	126	482	134	27	3	14	209	69	82	35	1	99	6	2	4	12	5	.71	12	.278	.332	.434
Leon,Jose	Johnson Cty	StL	R+	20	59	222	55	9	3	10	100	29	36	17	0	92	2	2	1	5	3	.63	1	.248	.306	.450
	New Jersey	StL	A-	20	7	28	8	3	1	1	16	4	3	0	0	7	2	0	0	0	0	.00	0	.286	.333	.571
Leon,Donny	Yankees	NYA	R	21	53	191	69	14	4	6	109	30	46	9	2	30	4	1	4	1	2	.33	2	.361	.394	.571

1996 Batting — Single-A and Rookie Leagues

BATTING																				BASERUNNING				PERCENTAGES		
Player	Team	Org	Lg	A	G	AB	H	2B	3B	HR	TB	R	RBI	TBB	IBB	SO	HBP	SH	SF	SB	CS	SB%	GDP	Avg	OBP	SLG
Levias,Andres	Pr. William	ChA	A+	23	15	40	4	1	0	0	5	3	1	4	0	15	0	1	1	0	1	.00	2	.100	.178	.125
Lewis,Tyrone	San Bernrdo	LA	A+	23	67	217	57	14	2	5	90	30	30	14	0	51	1	4	1	6	2	.75	4	.263	.309	.415
Lewis,Andreaus	Bakersfield	Cle	A+	23	62	205	50	13	0	3	72	40	16	22	0	78	9	1	0	9	2	.82	7	.244	.343	.351
	Columbus	Cle	A	23	23	64	5	2	0	0	7	6	1	7	0	31	4	0	0	2	0	1.00	1	.078	.213	.109
Lewis,Dwayne	Charlstn-WV	Cin	A	24	22	61	11	0	2	0	15	12	8	17	0	13	1	1	1	5	2	.71	0	.180	.363	.246
Lewis,Jeremy	Rockford	ChN	A	24	105	365	90	23	4	5	136	50	61	46	1	85	1	1	2	13	3	.81	9	.247	.331	.373
Lewis,Keith	Williamsprt	ChN	A-	22	60	188	36	4	2	0	44	25	13	17	0	46	4	4	1	10	3	.77	3	.191	.271	.234
Lewis,Marc	Macon	Atl	A	22	66	241	76	14	3	5	111	36	28	21	1	31	1	1	6	25	8	.76	6	.315	.364	.461
	Durham	Atl	A+	22	68	262	78	12	2	6	112	43	26	24	2	37	2	3	1	25	9	.74	5	.298	.360	.427
Leyba,Jhonathan	Diamondback	Ari	R	18	24	31	8	1	0	0	9	2	0	6	0	11	1	0	0	0	0	.00	0	.258	.395	.290
Liefer,Jeffrey	South Bend	ChA	A	22	74	277	90	14	0	15	149	60	58	30	3	62	5	0	4	6	5	.55	3	.325	.396	.538
	Pr. William	ChA	A+	22	37	147	33	6	0	1	42	17	13	11	2	27	0	0	1	0	0	.00	6	.224	.277	.286
Light,Tal	Asheville	Col	A	23	52	205	67	15	0	12	118	34	51	21	0	58	1	0	2	8	4	.67	3	.327	.389	.576
	Salem	Col	A+	23	64	234	55	10	0	13	104	29	36	19	0	59	5	0	1	3	1	.75	6	.235	.305	.444
Lignitz,Jeremiah	Tigers	Det	R	20	46	153	27	2	2	1	36	9	13	18	0	53	3	0	1	2	1	.67	1	.176	.274	.235
Ligons,Merrell	Royals	KC	R	20	48	130	24	4	1	0	30	18	5	15	0	24	6	1	0	2	1	.67	3	.185	.298	.231
Lina,Estivinson	Rangers	Tex	R	20	50	146	38	7	2	5	64	25	34	17	1	43	4	2	1	4	4	.50	4	.260	.351	.438
Linares,Sendry	Astros	Hou	R	21	23	58	12	6	0	0	18	5	6	3	0	10	4	3	0	1	0	1.00	2	.207	.292	.310
	Kissimmee	Hou	A+	21	2	4	1	0	0	0	1	0	0	0	0	0	0	0	0	0	0	.00	0	.250	.250	.250
Linder,Brian	Everett	Sea	A-	23	64	248	51	8	1	2	67	27	27	42	0	67	2	2	0	6	1	.86	9	.206	.325	.270
Lindsey,John	Portland	Col	A-	20	57	208	53	11	1	2	72	32	22	26	0	63	4	0	0	1	1	.50	3	.255	.349	.346
Lindsey,Rod	Clinton	SD	A	21	23	87	14	2	0	0	16	11	4	11	0	30	3	0	1	12	8	.60	2	.161	.275	.184
	Idaho Falls	SD	R+	21	48	185	56	4	6	5	87	45	17	23	0	53	2	0	0	16	3	.84	1	.303	.386	.470
Lindstrom,David	Jamestown	Det	A-	22	52	165	41	10	0	5	66	19	13	10	0	29	2	5	0	1	0	1.00	3	.248	.299	.400
Liniak,Cole	Michigan	Bos	A	20	121	437	115	26	2	3	154	65	46	59	1	59	10	3	8	7	6	.54	12	.263	.358	.352
Lisanti,Robert	Williamsprt	ChN	A-	24	43	119	23	7	0	0	30	10	15	13	0	27	1	3	0	0	3	.00	2	.193	.278	.252
Livingston,Clyde	Martinsvlle	Phi	R+	24	5	16	2	0	0	0	2	1	2	1	0	5	0	0	0	0	0	.00	1	.125	.176	.125
Livingston,Doug	Portland	Col	A-	23	57	224	67	18	4	5	108	36	34	23	1	45	3	6	2	6	0	1.00	4	.299	.369	.482
Llanos,Alexis	Angels	Cal	R	20	51	203	57	9	3	1	75	31	26	14	0	48	2	4	0	10	5	.67	4	.281	.333	.369
Llanos,Francisco	Expos	Mon	R	20	26	72	12	5	0	0	17	5	10	7	0	22	3	2	0	0	1	.00	2	.167	.268	.236
Llibre,Brian	Rangers	Tex	R	19	33	108	33	5	0	8	62	18	24	2	0	29	1	0	2	3	1	.75	0	.306	.319	.574
Lobaton,Jose	Tampa	NYA	A+	23	113	375	87	16	5	5	128	39	37	34	1	74	8	11	4	11	7	.61	6	.232	.306	.341
Locurto,Gary	Red Sox	Bos	R	19	36	137	43	8	0	4	63	25	22	18	0	44	2	0	0	5	4	.56	2	.314	.401	.460
Loduca,Paul	Vero Beach	LA	A+	25	124	439	134	22	0	3	165	54	66	70	2	38	2	0	4	8	2	.80	14	.305	.400	.376
Lofton,James	Winston-Sal	Cin	A+	23	82	277	62	9	0	3	80	27	33	27	1	55	1	5	2	14	8	.64	7	.224	.293	.289
Lomasney,Steve	Lowell	Bos	A-	19	59	173	24	10	0	4	46	26	21	42	0	63	2	0	0	2	0	1.00	2	.139	.313	.266
Lombard,George	Macon	Atl	A	21	116	444	109	16	8	15	186	76	51	36	0	122	7	8	2	24	17	.59	4	.245	.311	.419
Long,Garrett	Erie	Pit	A-	20	20	70	20	2	1	0	24	5	7	9	0	17	1	1	1	1	2	.33	3	.286	.370	.343
Long,Terrence	Columbia	NYN	A	21	123	473	136	26	9	12	216	66	78	36	3	120	5	1	4	32	7	.82	9	.288	.342	.457
Longmire,Marcel	Cubs	ChN	R	19	34	115	22	2	1	2	32	11	7	8	0	35	4	0	1	6	4	.60	0	.191	.266	.278
Longueira,Tony	Lansing	KC	A	22	45	153	29	2	1	1	36	14	15	14	0	23	2	5	1	4	3	.57	6	.190	.265	.235
Lopes,Omar	Bristol	ChA	R+	20	55	171	37	8	1	1	50	19	14	27	0	30	2	4	1	6	4	.60	3	.216	.328	.292
Lopez,Henry	Twins	Min	R	19	34	122	31	5	6	5	63	24	26	15	1	25	1	0	0	9	2	.82	1	.254	.341	.516
Lopez,Jose	St. Lucie	NYN	A+	21	121	419	122	17	5	11	182	63	60	39	2	103	9	1	2	18	10	.64	7	.291	.362	.434
Lopez,Luis	St. Cathrns	Tor	A-	23	74	260	74	17	2	7	116	36	40	27	1	31	7	4	3	2	3	.40	4	.285	.364	.446
Lopez,Luis	Bellingham	SF	A-	19	1	2	0	0	0	0	0	0	0	0	0	2	0	0	0	0	0	.00	0	.000	.000	.000
Lopez,Rafael	Kingsport	NYN	R+	20	65	250	79	22	4	7	130	53	58	31	1	25	4	0	2	0	1	.00	4	.316	.397	.520
	Pittsfield	NYN	A-	20	5	14	6	0	1	0	8	2	3	1	0	1	0	0	0	0	0	.00	0	.429	.467	.571
Lopez,Mickey	Beloit	Mil	A	23	61	236	64	10	2	0	78	35	14	28	0	36	1	10	0	12	8	.60	8	.271	.351	.331
	Stockton	Mil	A+	23	64	217	61	10	1	0	73	30	25	23	0	36	4	9	1	6	4	.60	0	.281	.359	.336
Lopiccolo,Jamie	Beloit	Mil	A	24	96	304	80	19	2	4	115	44	57	39	0	48	8	2	9	4	6	.40	8	.263	.353	.378
Lorenzana,Luis	Pirates	Pit	R	18	18	53	8	1	0	0	9	4	5	12	0	8	1	1	1	0	1	.00	1	.151	.313	.170
	Erie	Pit	A-	18	44	128	25	8	1	0	35	19	12	16	0	26	3	4	3	1	4	.20	4	.195	.293	.273
Lorenzo,Juan	Twins	Min	R	19	37	134	34	5	0	3	48	23	15	2	0	20	2	2	0	4	1	.80	1	.254	.275	.358
Lowell,Mike	Greensboro	NYA	A	23	113	433	122	33	0	8	179	58	64	46	0	43	4	2	2	10	3	.77	7	.282	.355	.413
	Tampa	NYA	A+	23	24	78	22	5	0	0	27	8	11	3	0	13	0	1	3	1	1	.50	2	.282	.298	.346
Lowry,Curt	Clinton	SD	A	24	32	70	13	2	1	1	20	9	7	8	0	21	1	0	0	0	1	.00	0	.186	.278	.286
Loyd,Brian	Clinton	SD	A	23	10	37	11	2	0	0	13	3	2	0	0	6	2	0	0	0	0	.00	0	.297	.333	.351
Luderer,Brian	Athletics	Oak	R	18	6	13	4	0	0	0	4	1	2	0	0	1	0	1	0	0	0	.00	0	.308	.308	.308
Lugo,Jesus	St. Pete	StL	A+	22	19	64	13	2	0	0	15	5	3	1	0	7	0	0	0	1	2	.33	1	.203	.215	.234
	Johnson City	StL	R+	22	3	0	0	0	0	0	0	0	0	0	0	0	0	0	0	0	0	.00	0	.000	.000	.000
Lugo,Julio	Quad City	Hou	A	21	101	393	116	18	2	10	168	60	50	32	0	75	3	4	4	24	11	.69	7	.295	.350	.427
Lunar,Fernando	Macon	Atl	A	20	104	343	63	9	0	7	93	33	33	20	0	65	12	3	2	3	2	.60	11	.184	.252	.271
Lutz,Manuel	Hickory	ChA	A	21	44	143	34	2	0	1	39	10	12	9	2	46	3	1	3	0	1	.00	3	.238	.291	.273
	Bristol	ChA	R+	21	55	202	51	12	1	6	83	26	23	17	3	53	2	2	1	5	1	.83	3	.252	.315	.411
MacAlutas,Jon	Ogden	Mil	R+	22	54	178	61	10	0	3	80	41	24	18	0	21	7	0	3	8	2	.80	4	.343	.417	.449
Macias,Jose	Delmarva	Mon	A	23	116	369	91	13	4	1	115	64	33	56	1	48	6	7	2	38	15	.72	2	.247	.353	.312
MacKay,Jack	Vermont	Mon	A-	23	46	172	42	4	0	1	49	29	12	25	2	29	2	1	1	9	7	.56	1	.244	.345	.285
MacKowiak,Robert	Pirates	Pit	R	21	27	86	23	6	1	0	31	8	14	13	1	11	1	0	1	3	1	.75	3	.267	.366	.360
Macon,Leland	Charlotte	Tex	A+	24	99	338	84	12	3	2	108	45	31	39	2	74	13	3	4	9	12	.43	7	.249	.345	.320
Madsen,Dave	Modesto	Oak	A+	25	52	174	42	7	0	4	61	25	19	31	0	31	4	3	1	2	0	1.00	5	.241	.367	.351
Maduro,Remy	Marlins	Fla	R	20	24	84	19	2	0	0	21	8	14	15	0	9	2	0	1	2	0	1.00	5	.226	.353	.250
Magee,Danny	Durham	Atl	A+	22	95	344	103	19	3	12	164	59	40	20	0	70	14	4	1	17	5	.77	6	.299	.361	.477
Mahoney,Mike	Durham	Atl	A+	24	101	363	94	24	2	9	149	52	46	23	0	64	7	4	4	4	3	.57	8	.259	.312	.410
Mahoney,Ricardo	Rockies	Col	R	18	23	82	21	5	0	0	26	12	12	8	0	20	2	0	1	1	1	.50	4	.256	.333	.317
Majcherek,Matt.	Hudson Vall	Tex	A-	22	40	80	15	4	1	0	21	16	9	20	0	24	1	0	1	5	1	.83	2	.188	.353	.263
Majeski,Brian	Vero Beach	LA	A+	25	69	205	51	9	1	0	62	30	14	29	0	56	3	5	1	16	7	.70	1	.249	.349	.302

1996 Batting — Single-A and Rookie Leagues

								BATTING												BASERUNNING				PERCENTAGES		
Player	Team	Org	Lg	A	G	AB	H	2B	3B	HR	TB	R	RBI	TBB	IBB	SO	HBP	SH	SF	SB	CS	SB%	GDP	Avg	OBP	SLG
Malave,Jaime	Savannah	LA	A	22	6	16	4	0	0	0	4	2	5	0	0	3	1	0	1	0	0	.00	0	.250	.278	.250
	Yakima	LA	A-	22	40	108	22	6	0	5	43	14	16	6	0	33	0	1	0	0	0	.00	2	.204	.246	.398
Maldonado,Carlos	Mariners	Sea	R	18	29	100	22	0	0	2	28	10	18	6	0	10	1	1	4	0	1	.00	7	.220	.261	.280
Maleski,Tom	Rockford	ChN	A	19	6	8	1	0	0	0	1	1	1	2	0	3	0	0	0	0	0	.00	0	.125	.300	.125
Maloney,Jeffrey	Medicne Hat	Tor	R+	20	65	222	44	9	2	4	69	36	27	39	1	85	5	2	3	11	6	.65	2	.198	.327	.311
	St. Cathrns	Tor	A-	20	1	4	1	0	0	0	1	0	1	0	0	2	0	0	0	0	0	.00	0	.250	.250	.250
Manning,Brian	Bellingham	SF	A-	22	35	138	41	6	2	3	60	26	22	13	0	27	6	0	1	0	3	.00	2	.297	.380	.435
	Burlington	SF	A	22	33	111	33	4	2	3	50	16	22	22	1	18	4	0	1	2	1	.67	2	.297	.428	.450
Manning,Nate	Williamsprt	ChN	A-	23	62	240	76	14	1	4	104	28	32	14	2	62	2	0	2	4	0	1.00	3	.317	.357	.433
Mansavage,Jay	Auburn	Hou	A-	21	49	148	25	7	2	1	39	17	17	18	0	33	3	1	1	5	2	.71	1	.169	.271	.264
Manwarren,Marc	Kissimmee	Hou	A+	24	74	158	30	7	0	1	40	16	10	15	1	58	5	3	0	17	2	.89	1	.190	.281	.253
Mapp,Eric	Billings	Cin	R+	19	56	175	46	10	6	3	77	21	34	13	1	41	3	0	1	1	3	.25	5	.263	.323	.440
Marcinczyk,Ed.	Sou. Oregon	Oak	A-	23	63	216	48	13	2	7	86	29	38	22	0	57	5	5	4	3	3	.50	3	.222	.304	.398
Marine,Del	Visalia	Det	A+	25	105	378	97	20	1	16	167	58	69	47	1	121	10	0	7	8	2	.80	6	.257	.348	.442
Marn,Kevin	Billings	Cin	R+	23	66	271	75	11	1	1	91	48	38	24	0	49	3	1	4	19	3	.86	5	.277	.338	.336
Marnell,Dean	Portland	Col	A-	21	38	131	39	7	0	0	46	20	23	9	0	12	1	2	1	0	1	.00	4	.298	.345	.351
Marquez,Jesus	Lancaster	Sea	A+	24	126	490	147	31	10	20	258	84	106	45	1	78	9	4	9	19	8	.70	5	.300	.363	.527
Marshall,Monte	Great Falls	LA	R+	23	52	181	48	7	1	0	57	36	22	19	0	34	3	0	4	10	7	.59	3	.265	.338	.315
	Yakima	LA	A-	23	17	68	13	1	1	0	16	9	7	7	0	14	2	2	0	0	1	.00	1	.191	.286	.235
Marsters,Brandon	Batavia	Phi	A-	22	42	151	35	8	2	1	50	15	13	8	0	46	1	0	0	1	0	1.00	1	.232	.275	.331
Martin,Jeff	Bakersfield	Bos	A+	26	5	22	4	0	0	0	4	2	1	0	0	10	0	0	0	0	0	.00	0	.182	.182	.182
Martin,Lincoln	Frederick	Bal	A+	25	114	421	112	17	7	2	149	77	31	50	2	66	8	7	2	22	7	.76	9	.266	.353	.354
Martin,Mike	Clinton	SD	A	24	77	206	36	7	0	1	46	16	23	29	2	33	3	2	3	1	0	1.00	3	.175	.282	.223
Martinez,Alejandro	Princeton	Cin	R+	18	38	108	23	3	0	0	26	17	13	14	0	33	3	0	1	2	1	.67	1	.213	.317	.241
Martinez,David	Ogden	Mil	R+	21	35	103	34	6	1	0	42	25	13	26	0	30	0	5	1	0	3	.00	2	.330	.462	.408
Martinez,Eddy	Frederick	Bal	A+	19	74	244	54	4	0	2	64	21	25	21	0	48	2	1	1	13	8	.62	5	.221	.287	.262
	Bluefield	Bal	R+	19	37	122	27	3	0	1	33	18	15	13	0	29	2	3	0	15	5	.75	1	.221	.307	.270
Martinez,Hipolito	Athletics	Oak	R	20	48	185	49	8	3	5	78	29	34	19	0	39	4	0	2	9	0	1.00	3	.265	.343	.422
Martinez,Jorge	DiamondbackAri		R	19	20	31	5	0	0	1	8	6	4	6	0	12	0	0	0	0	0	.00	0	.161	.297	.258
Martinez,Leonardo	Butte	TB	R+	22	39	128	30	1	1	0	33	13	16	5	0	24	0	2	0	5	2	.71	3	.234	.263	.258
Martinez,Obed	Idaho Falls	SD	R+	21	28	110	27	4	1	0	33	14	10	10	0	27	1	0	0	1	2	.33	2	.245	.314	.300
Martinez,Rafael	Vero Beach	LA	A+	21	115	351	70	8	3	5	99	38	45	40	2	103	5	6	2	1	5	.17	9	.199	.289	.282
Martinez,Ramon	Lynchburg	Pit	A+	27	91	306	94	10	5	1	117	58	30	24	0	53	2	9	0	12	5	.71	4	.307	.361	.382
Martinez,Roger	Pittsfield	NYN	A-	24	41	126	31	4	1	2	43	14	14	22	0	40	2	0	0	1	5	.17	1	.246	.367	.341
Martinez,Tony	Visalia	StL	A+	24	31	83	16	6	0	0	22	7	11	7	0	20	1	0	3	0	0	.00	5	.193	.255	.265
Martinez,Victor	Mariners	Sea	R	18	16	61	21	1	4	0	30	10	10	9	0	17	2	2	0	4	0	1.00	2	.344	.444	.492
Marval,Raul	Burlington	SF	A	21	44	159	32	10	0	0	42	13	9	6	0	12	3	4	2	3	1	.75	7	.201	.241	.264
	San Jose	SF	A+	21	39	137	32	6	0	0	38	19	19	9	0	13	1	4	1	0	0	.00	3	.234	.284	.277
Mason,Lamont	Charlstn-WV	Cin	A	24	68	190	41	2	1	1	48	24	16	28	1	48	2	3	1	11	6	.65	0	.216	.321	.253
Mata,Manuel	Martinsvlle	Phi	R+	20	16	41	5	0	0	0	5	3	1	3	0	17	0	0	0	0	0	.00	1	.122	.182	.122
Mateo,Henry	Expos	Mon	R	20	14	44	11	3	0	0	14	8	3	5	0	11	3	2	0	5	1	.83	0	.250	.365	.318
Mateo,Jose	Savannah	LA	A	20	111	308	50	3	1	2	61	33	16	34	0	89	8	9	0	15	5	.75	2	.162	.263	.198
Mateo,Amaury	Charlstn-SC	Tex	A	19	134	496	129	30	8	8	199	65	58	26	1	78	12	2	7	30	9	.77	8	.260	.309	.401
Mateo,Victor	Yankees	NYA	R	20	32	127	40	1	3	0	47	25	15	9	0	29	2	1	1	0	2	.00	1	.315	.367	.370
Mathews,Byron	W. Palm Bch	Mon	A+	26	10	19	5	0	0	0	5	4	0	4	0	5	1	0	0	0	0	.00	0	.263	.417	.263
Mathis,Joe	Wisconsin	Sea	A	22	126	473	135	19	8	5	185	79	47	36	0	75	4	3	2	19	6	.76	4	.285	.340	.391
Matos,Luis	Orioles	Bal	R	18	43	130	38	2	0	0	40	21	13	15	0	18	2	4	0	12	7	.63	3	.292	.374	.308
Matos,Pascual	Durham	Atl	A+	22	67	219	49	9	3	6	82	24	28	7	0	70	3	0	1	6	0	1.00	2	.224	.257	.374
Matos,Wellington	Yankees	NYA	R	20	35	97	24	5	0	0	29	13	14	11	0	29	2	0	0	0	0	.00	4	.247	.336	.299
Matthews,Gary	Rancho CucaSD		A+	22	123	435	118	21	11	7	182	65	54	60	1	102	6	4	2	7	8	.47	11	.271	.366	.418
Matvey,Mike	St. Pete	StL	A+	25	127	407	104	10	3	1	123	51	40	47	2	90	4	2	5	3	6	.33	8	.256	.335	.302
Maxwell,Pat	Modesto	Oak	A+	27	4	11	5	1	0	0	6	1	0	1	1	1	1	1	0	0	0	.00	0	.455	.538	.545
Maxwell,Vernon	Padres	SD	R	20	55	194	49	6	4	0	63	41	17	31	0	45	8	0	2	15	4	.79	2	.253	.374	.325
May,Freddie	Augusta	Pit	A	21	123	390	79	8	6	5	114	58	43	72	3	119	4	4	3	22	18	.55	5	.203	.330	.292
May,Scott	Erie	Pit	A-	24	25	40	10	2	0	0	12	5	0	7	0	11	0	0	0	0	0	.00	1	.250	.362	.300
Mayber,Chan	Salem	Col	A+	24	97	264	55	5	0	1	63	38	20	27	0	50	5	11	3	22	9	.71	2	.208	.291	.239
Maynard,Scott	Mariners	Sea	R	19	47	164	46	7	1	1	58	20	17	15	0	53	1	1	0	1	3	.25	3	.280	.344	.354
Mazurek,Brian	New Jersey	StL	A-	23	69	274	85	18	1	2	111	31	48	16	0	39	2	5	3	0	2	.00	8	.310	.349	.405
Mc Neal,Aaron	Astros	Hou	R	19	55	200	50	10	2	2	70	22	31	13	1	52	4	0	2	0	2	.00	5	.250	.306	.350
McAffee,Joshua	DiamondbackAri		R	19	39	102	15	5	0	0	20	13	7	18	0	39	6	0	2	1	1	.50	1	.147	.305	.196
McAninch,John	Cedar Rapds	Cal	A	23	86	298	74	16	1	10	122	43	42	21	1	81	6	0	4	0	2	.00	3	.248	.307	.409
McAulay,John	Charlstn-SC	Tex	A	24	5	12	2	0	0	0	2	2	1	7	0	1	1	0	0	1	1	.50	0	.167	.500	.167
	Charlotte	Tex	A+	24	49	122	24	7	0	2	37	15	11	23	0	38	4	4	1	0	0	.00	2	.197	.340	.303
McCain,Marcus	Butte	TB	R+	23	55	256	97	9	4	1	117	66	27	16	1	21	6	0	5	34	10	.77	5	.379	.420	.457
McCalmont,Jim	Fort Myers	Min	A+	25	30	89	18	3	0	0	21	8	6	4	0	15	1	2	0	1	0	1.00	2	.202	.245	.236
McCarthy,Kevin	Kingsport	NYN	R+	20	64	235	68	14	1	6	102	46	43	28	1	41	2	0	4	10	1	.91	2	.289	.364	.434
McCartney,Som.	Kane County	Fla	A	24	51	160	48	14	0	5	77	21	19	14	0	50	4	1	1	1	1	.50	3	.300	.369	.481
McCarty,Matt	San Bernrdo	LA	A+	21	38	110	26	2	2	6	50	30	19	14	1	35	4	1	1	5	2	.71	1	.236	.341	.455
	Great Falls	LA	R+	21	58	208	59	7	10	3	95	40	32	24	0	56	5	0	0	16	2	.89	3	.284	.371	.457
McCladdie,Tony	Devil Rays	TB	R	21	50	166	49	7	4	0	64	21	21	9	0	27	4	1	2	14	1	.93	2	.295	.343	.386
McClendon,Trav	Peoria	StL	A	24	60	155	30	8	0	0	38	23	23	17	1	27	4	4	1	1	4	.20	5	.194	.288	.245
McClure,Brian	Idaho Falls	SD	R+	23	72	308	99	18	6	6	147	62	45	38	0	63	3	0	4	10	2	.83	6	.321	.397	.477
McClure,Craig	Hickory	ChA	A	21	59	212	43	8	3	2	63	21	19	20	2	62	3	2	1	6	2	.75	3	.203	.280	.297
	Bristol	ChA	R+	21	66	253	65	13	1	2	86	30	23	20	1	48	4	0	2	7	3	.70	11	.257	.319	.340
McCollough,Adam	Frederick	Bal	A+	23	4	10	0	0	0	0	0	0	0	0	0	4	0	0	0	0	0	.00	0	.000	.000	.000
	Bluefield	Bal	R+	23	31	93	28	7	1	4	49	16	23	5	0	20	0	0	1	2	0	1.00	1	.301	.333	.527
McCormick,An.	Dunedin	Tor	A+	24	55	126	27	3	1	0	32	15	7	20	1	36	3	3	1	4	0	1.00	4	.214	.333	.254

1996 Batting — Single-A and Rookie Leagues

BATTING																				BASERUNNING				PERCENTAGES		
Player	Team	Org	Lg	A	G	AB	H	2B	3B	HR	TB	R	RBI	TBB	IBB	SO	HBP	SH	SF	SB	CS	SB%	GDP	Avg	OBP	SLG
	Hagerstown	Tor	A	24	33	102	18	2	0	0	20	11	5	20	0	39	1	1	0	3	1	.75	4	.176	.317	.196
McCormick,Cody	Greensboro	NYA	A	22	65	173	34	9	0	6	61	16	20	12	0	46	3	2	2	0	1	.00	2	.197	.258	.353
McDermott,Mich.	White Sox	ChA	R	24	44	144	36	11	0	2	53	17	18	11	0	38	8	3	0	1	2	.33	3	.250	.337	.368
McDonald,Ashanti	Rockford	ChN	A	24	76	202	47	6	2	0	57	19	17	21	2	40	3	4	1	6	2	.75	5	.233	.313	.282
McDonald,Donzell	Oneonta	NYA	A-	22	74	282	78	8	10	2	112	57	30	43	0	62	2	3	2	54	4	.93	1	.277	.374	.397
McDonald,John	Watertown	Cle	A-	22	75	278	75	11	0	2	92	48	26	32	0	49	5	11	1	11	1	.92	3	.270	.354	.331
McDonald,Keith	St. Pete	StL	A+	24	114	410	111	25	0	2	142	30	52	34	1	65	5	1	5	1	3	.25	18	.271	.330	.346
McDougall,Matt	Mariners	Sea	R	20	28	79	16	3	2	1	26	18	2	10	0	22	3	1	0	9	2	.82	0	.203	.315	.329
McGehee,Mike	Butte	TB	R+	21	28	71	18	1	1	0	21	12	8	13	0	20	1	0	1	0	0	.00	2	.254	.372	.296
McGonigle,Bill	Stockton	Mil	A+	25	74	227	61	12	0	1	76	29	25	18	0	27	1	4	6	2	4	.33	8	.269	.317	.335
McGuire,Matthew	Bellingham	SF	A-	21	7	15	2	0	0	0	2	1	0	1	0	4	0	1	0	1	0	1.00	0	.133	.188	.133
	San Jose	SF	A+	21	4	6	2	1	0	0	3	1	0	0	0	1	0	0	0	0	0	.00	0	.333	.333	.500
McHenry,Joe	Elizabethtn	Min	R+	21	51	159	26	5	2	0	35	24	9	29	0	58	1	1	0	6	1	.86	0	.164	.296	.220
McHugh,Ryan	Peoria	StL	A	23	76	237	60	17	4	6	103	46	40	33	1	46	0	1	1	7	4	.64	10	.253	.343	.435
McKay,Cody	Sou. Oregon	Oak	A-	23	69	254	68	13	0	3	90	33	30	25	0	42	6	1	3	0	5	.00	7	.268	.344	.354
McKenzie,Carlton	Pirates	Pit	R	21	36	114	35	2	2	0	41	14	12	8	0	13	0	0	0	5	5	.50	2	.307	.352	.360
McKinley,Michael	Lowell	Bos	A-	22	30	64	12	4	0	0	16	10	6	9	0	22	0	0	1	1	4	.20	1	.188	.284	.250
McKinney,Antonio	Tigers	Det	R	19	44	147	31	4	2	1	42	27	13	15	0	44	6	0	1	8	0	1.00	2	.211	.308	.286
McKinnis,Leroy	Rancho Cuca	SD	A+	24	87	328	88	20	2	4	124	49	39	38	0	74	3	0	1	2	3	.40	6	.268	.349	.378
McKinnon,Sandy	Pr. William	ChA	A+	23	113	410	108	28	5	8	170	56	60	23	0	68	2	9	2	20	10	.67	4	.263	.304	.415
McLamb,Brian	Tampa	NYA	A+	24	85	266	56	13	0	2	75	31	25	23	1	62	4	4	3	7	5	.58	5	.211	.280	.282
McMullen,Jon	Clearwater	Phi	A+	23	31	119	21	4	0	2	31	10	8	12	0	26	1	0	0	0	0	.00	7	.176	.258	.261
McNally,Sean	Wilmington	KC	A+	24	126	428	118	27	1	8	171	49	63	57	2	83	5	1	8	3	3	.50	8	.276	.361	.400
McNally,Shawn	Peoria	StL	A	24	123	431	120	19	5	7	170	59	75	57	3	60	4	2	11	9	8	.53	7	.278	.360	.394
McNeal,Pepe	Johnson Cty	StL	R+	21	24	90	27	6	1	1	38	22	11	11	0	23	3	0	2	0	0	.00	3	.300	.387	.422
	New Jersey	StL	A-	21	19	54	15	2	1	1	22	4	4	3	0	14	0	0	0	0	0	.00	3	.278	.316	.407
McSparin,Paul	Augusta	Pit	A	23	6	14	1	1	0	0	2	1	1	0	0	6	0	0	0	0	0	.00	1	.071	.071	.143
Meadows,Mike	Mets	NYN	R	18	8	30	6	0	0	0	6	1	3	1	0	9	0	0	0	0	0	.00	1	.200	.226	.200
Mealing,Allen	Beloit	Mil	A	23	88	274	71	15	4	6	112	41	24	20	0	66	1	0	0	13	12	.52	5	.259	.312	.409
Medina,Robert	Medicne Hat	Tor	R+	21	40	112	29	8	0	5	52	18	19	14	0	39	0	2	2	1	4	.20	2	.259	.336	.464
Medrano,Steve	Royals	KC	R	19	46	154	42	10	0	1	55	24	11	19	2	21	2	3	0	3	1	.75	4	.273	.360	.357
Medrano,Teodoro	Wisconsin	Sea	A	21	63	172	35	9	1	4	58	20	22	15	1	58	3	2	2	3	3	.50	1	.203	.276	.337
Meier,Rob	Yankees	NYA	R	18	3	3	1	1	0	0	2	0	0	0	0	1	0	0	0	0	0	.00	0	.333	.333	.667
Mejia,Juan	Martinsvlle	Phi	R+	21	25	72	13	4	0	0	17	9	5	6	0	19	0	1	1	4	0	1.00	0	.181	.241	.236
Mejia,Marlon	Auburn	Hou	A-	22	34	107	22	3	2	1	32	11	8	0	0	20	1	2	0	1	0	1.00	5	.206	.213	.299
Melito,Mark	Lansing	KC	A	25	59	201	51	12	1	1	68	29	18	27	0	28	5	1	0	8	3	.73	5	.254	.356	.338
Melo,Juan	Rancho Cuca	SD	A+	21	128	503	153	27	6	8	216	75	75	22	0	102	10	0	1	6	8	.43	10	.304	.345	.429
Mendez,Carlos	Wilmington	KC	A+	23	109	406	119	25	3	4	162	40	59	22	4	39	3	3	7	3	1	.75	6	.293	.329	.399
Mendez,Sergio	Augusta	Pit	A	23	46	172	40	9	0	7	70	23	26	9	2	31	5	0	0	3	3	.50	4	.233	.290	.407
	Lynchburg	Pit	A+	23	39	137	38	9	1	4	61	19	17	6	0	24	1	0	1	0	1	.00	2	.277	.310	.445
Mendoza,Angel	Red Sox	Bos	R	18	49	160	43	13	2	2	66	17	13	9	0	42	3	1	1	3	4	.43	2	.269	.318	.413
Mendoza,Carlos	Columbia	NYN	A	22	85	300	101	10	2	0	115	61	37	57	1	46	8	11	2	31	13	.70	2	.337	.452	.383
Mensik,Todd	Sou. Oregon	Oak	A-	22	59	192	46	8	0	0	54	21	14	19	2	39	2	0	4	2	0	1.00	6	.240	.309	.281
Meran,Jorge	Tigers	Det	R	22	51	168	53	13	3	2	78	25	32	13	0	42	5	1	2	7	2	.78	3	.315	.378	.464
Mercado,Julio	Rangers	Tex	R	20	42	107	23	4	1	3	38	18	7	10	0	24	4	2	1	10	4	.71	0	.215	.303	.355
Mercedes,Guiller.	Kinston	Cle	A+	23	117	382	94	12	1	0	108	45	27	30	1	41	5	14	1	3	3	.50	13	.246	.309	.283
Mercedes,Matia	Tigers	Det	R	21	16	50	10	6	0	0	16	9	6	7	0	10	1	1	0	2	1	.67	1	.200	.310	.320
Messner,Jake	Burlington	Cle	R+	20	47	164	41	7	1	3	59	20	20	11	0	41	1	0	2	6	3	.67	0	.250	.298	.360
Metcalfe,Mike	Vero Beach	LA	A+	24	2	5	0	0	0	0	0	0	0	0	0	0	0	0	0	0	0	.00	0	.000	.000	.000
Metzger,Erik	Lowell	Bos	A-	22	9	26	3	1	0	2	10	2	3	4	0	6	2	0	0	0	1	.00	0	.115	.281	.385
	Red Sox	Bos	R	22	19	56	13	3	0	0	16	4	5	4	0	14	0	0	1	0	0	.00	1	.232	.279	.286
	Sarasota	Bos	A+	22	1	3	1	0	0	0	1	0	0	0	0	2	0	0	0	0	0	.00	0	.333	.333	.333
Meyer,Matthew	Yakima	LA	A-	23	66	235	71	14	6	4	109	40	28	27	1	73	5	1	1	6	0	1.00	1	.302	.384	.464
Meyer,Bobby	Yakima	LA	A-	22	33	80	17	5	0	1	25	12	7	12	0	25	0	1	1	2	0	1.00	3	.213	.312	.313
	Great Falls	LA	R+	22	14	53	20	2	3	0	28	12	4	10	0	16	0	1	0	7	4	.64	0	.377	.476	.528
Meyer,Travis	Savannah	LA	A	23	68	185	54	8	2	3	75	23	20	22	1	42	3	2	0	0	0	.00	4	.292	.376	.405
	Vero Beach	LA	A+	23	12	33	8	1	0	3	18	6	8	3	0	6	0	0	0	0	0	.00	2	.242	.306	.545
Meyers,Chad	Williamsprt	ChN	A-	21	67	230	56	9	2	2	75	46	26	33	0	39	5	2	1	27	6	.82	2	.243	.349	.326
Michael,Jeff	High Desert	Bal	A+	25	3	7	2	0	0	0	2	2	0	2	0	1	0	0	0	0	1	.00	0	.286	.444	.286
Micucci,Mike	Daytona	ChN	A+	24	39	82	15	0	0	0	15	6	3	5	0	16	1	1	0	0	3	.00	3	.183	.239	.183
Mientkiewicz,Doug	Fort Myers	Min	A+	23	133	492	143	36	4	5	202	69	79	66	3	47	3	1	6	12	2	.86	10	.291	.374	.411
Mikesell,Steve	San Bernrdo	LA	A+	23	6	15	1	0	1	0	3	2	1	2	0	6	1	0	1	0	0	.00	2	.067	.211	.200
Miles,Aaron	Astros	Hou	R	20	55	214	63	3	2	0	70	48	15	20	0	18	1	5	0	14	7	.67	3	.294	.357	.327
Millan,Adam	Clearwater	Phi	A+	25	101	348	94	21	1	11	150	55	55	52	2	52	3	0	6	1	2	.33	15	.270	.364	.431
Miller,David	Kinston	Cle	A+	23	129	488	124	23	1	7	170	71	54	38	4	94	0	2	5	14	7	.67	7	.254	.305	.348
Miller,Logan	Dunedin	Tor	A+	23	10	23	4	0	0	0	4	2	1	3	0	8	0	0	0	0	0	.00	0	.174	.269	.174
Miller,Ryan	St. Lucie	NYN	A+	24	86	310	79	8	3	2	99	32	23	22	1	51	3	13	1	8	5	.62	5	.255	.310	.319
Minici,Jason	Columbus	Cle	A	23	98	334	71	18	2	4	105	37	23	31	1	84	2	2	0	9	4	.69	8	.213	.283	.314
Minor,Damon	Bellingham	SF	A-	23	75	269	65	11	1	12	114	44	55	47	4	86	5	1	1	0	2	.00	5	.242	.363	.424
Minor,Ryan	Bluefield	Bal	R+	23	25	87	22	6	0	4	40	14	9	7	0	32	3	0	0	1	0	1.00	0	.253	.330	.460
Miranda,Alex	W. Michigan	Oak	A	25	123	414	92	18	2	5	129	57	48	86	1	84	5	4	4	3	0	1.00	15	.222	.360	.312
Miranda,Tony	Spokane	KC	A-	24	21	53	9	3	0	2	18	11	8	9	0	13	2	1	1	2	1	.67	1	.170	.308	.340
	Lansing	KC	A	24	39	136	39	6	1	2	53	28	23	17	1	24	3	2	1	3	0	1.00	9	.287	.376	.390
Miskolczi,Levi	Bellingham	SF	A-	22	57	187	40	6	0	0	46	19	17	3	0	36	1	1	2	4	2	.67	3	.214	.228	.246
Mitchell,Andres	Rockies	Col	R	21	51	175	31	1	1	0	34	23	13	23	0	54	3	1	3	17	7	.71	2	.177	.279	.194
Mitchell,Derek	Jamestown	Det	A-	22	56	184	45	10	2	2	65	25	25	18	0	38	2	7	2	7	4	.64	1	.245	.316	.353
Miyake,Chris	Augusta	Pit	A	23	101	367	88	12	0	2	106	40	33	22	0	55	2	6	2	10	10	.50	7	.240	.285	.289

1996 Batting — Single-A and Rookie Leagues

BATTING																				BASERUNNING				PERCENTAGES		
Player	Team	Org	Lg	A	G	AB	H	2B	3B	HR	TB	R	RBI	TBB	IBB	SO	HBP	SH	SF	SB	CS	SB%	GDP	Avg	OBP	SLG
Moeller,Chad	Elizabethtn	Min	R+	22	17	59	21	4	0	4	37	17	13	18	0	9	2	0	0	1	2	.33	3	.356	.519	.627
Molina,Jose	Rockford	ChN	A	22	96	305	69	10	1	2	87	35	27	36	0	71	3	7	4	2	4	.33	8	.226	.310	.285
Molina,Luis	Lancaster	Sea	A+	23	37	122	31	4	0	0	35	13	10	14	0	24	2	2	2	3	2	.60	2	.254	.336	.287
Monahan,Shane	Lancaster	Sea	A+	22	132	585	164	31	12	14	261	107	97	30	2	124	4	3	8	19	5	.79	8	.280	.316	.446
Monroe,Craig	Charlstn-SC	Tex	A	20	49	153	23	11	1	0	36	11	9	18	0	48	3	0	0	2	2	.50	3	.150	.253	.235
	Hudson Vall	Tex	A-	20	67	268	74	16	6	5	117	53	29	23	0	63	2	0	2	21	7	.75	4	.276	.336	.437
Montas,Ricardo	Lansing	KC	A	20	8	24	7	0	0	0	7	1	0	2	0	4	0	0	0	0	0	.00	0	.292	.346	.292
	Royals	KC	R	20	50	182	48	6	1	2	62	25	22	20	2	31	3	2	1	5	1	.83	7	.264	.345	.341
Montgomery,Andre	Princeton	Cin	R+	20	41	133	38	6	3	4	62	24	18	20	0	29	1	1	1	5	2	.71	2	.286	.381	.466
Montilla,Julio	Wilmington	KC	A+	24	49	150	39	10	0	0	49	22	12	9	0	18	2	2	0	3	1	.75	3	.260	.311	.327
Moon,Bradley	Medicne Hat	Tor	R+	19	34	51	9	1	0	0	10	5	1	2	0	15	0	0	1	0	1	.00	2	.176	.204	.196
Moore,Donnie	Ogden	Mil	R+	21	50	85	23	0	3	1	32	16	13	7	0	30	1	2	1	5	1	.83	0	.271	.330	.376
Moore,Jason	Lethbridge	Ari	R+	21	47	151	37	6	0	8	67	34	35	27	0	61	6	0	2	1	3	.25	2	.245	.376	.444
Moore,Kenderick	Spokane	KC	A-	24	52	204	53	6	1	2	67	37	25	23	0	29	3	5	2	19	3	.86	4	.260	.341	.328
Moore,Mark	Modesto	Oak	A+	26	31	95	17	6	0	4	35	13	24	17	0	37	1	0	2	0	0	.00	2	.179	.304	.368
Moore,Tris	Jamestown	Det	A-	23	13	48	13	2	0	1	18	9	13	5	0	10	1	0	1	2	3	.40	0	.271	.345	.375
	Tigers	Det	R	23	16	54	14	1	0	2	21	9	12	8	0	12	3	1	1	2	0	1.00	1	.259	.379	.389
	Lakeland	Det	A+	23	11	33	5	2	0	0	7	6	4	7	0	11	0	3	0	2	0	1.00	1	.152	.300	.212
Moore,Brandon	Pr. William	ChA	A+	24	125	439	106	13	2	1	126	56	41	82	1	70	3	2	3	9	11	.45	14	.241	.362	.287
Morales,Domingo	Orioles	Bal	R	20	19	70	27	5	3	0	38	9	15	2	0	4	0	0	0	6	2	.75	3	.386	.403	.543
Morales,Francisco	St. Pete	StL	A+	24	21	67	14	5	1	1	24	6	6	5	0	25	2	0	1	0	0	.00	1	.209	.280	.358
	W. Palm Bch	Mon	A+	24	75	259	71	20	2	3	104	32	42	19	0	79	5	3	1	3	1	.75	5	.274	.335	.402
Morales,Erick	Columbia	NYN	A	23	45	121	28	3	0	0	31	10	14	7	0	22	2	1	0	0	3	.00	0	.231	.285	.256
Morales,Alex	San Jose	SF	A+	23	17	54	9	2	0	1	14	9	5	13	1	17	0	1	0	5	2	.71	0	.167	.328	.259
	Burlington	SF	A	23	41	138	31	6	1	6	57	26	17	27	0	37	4	4	0	15	2	.88	0	.225	.367	.413
Morales,Steven	Marlins	Fla	R	26	28	81	13	2	0	1	18	7	7	5	0	13	2	2	0	0	0	.00	1	.160	.227	.222
Moreno,Jose	Mariners	Sea	R	19	49	176	49	4	2	0	57	34	18	18	0	33	6	3	0	12	5	.71	2	.278	.365	.324
Moreno,Juan	Mets	NYN	R	21	16	53	14	4	1	0	20	7	7	4	0	11	1	0	0	2	0	1.00	2	.264	.328	.377
Morenz,Shea	Greensboro	NYA	A	23	91	338	84	14	4	2	112	40	48	38	4	92	12	2	3	13	3	.81	2	.249	.343	.331
Morgan,Dave	Dunedin	Tor	A+	25	39	88	23	3	1	4	40	13	15	18	0	24	3	0	0	0	1	.00	3	.261	.404	.455
Morgan,Scott	Columbus	Cle	A	23	87	305	95	25	1	22	188	62	80	46	0	70	11	0	4	9	5	.64	5	.311	.415	.616
Morgan,Todd	Orioles	Bal	R	19	18	29	5	0	0	0	5	2	0	4	0	7	1	0	0	1	1	.50	0	.172	.294	.172
Moriarty,Mike	Fort Myers	Min	A+	23	133	428	107	18	2	3	138	76	39	59	0	67	8	5	4	14	15	.48	2	.250	.349	.322
Morimoto,Ken	Vero Beach	LA	A+	22	6	11	0	0	0	0	0	1	0	1	0	4	0	0	0	0	0	.00	0	.000	.083	.000
	San Bernrdo	LA	A+	22	24	92	23	3	0	0	26	13	8	12	0	28	1	5	1	14	3	.82	0	.250	.340	.283
	Great Falls	LA	R+	22	32	123	35	3	1	1	43	40	12	19	0	26	1	3	2	27	4	.87	1	.285	.379	.350
Morreale,John	Stockton	Mil	A+	25	50	148	35	7	0	2	48	19	19	16	0	33	4	4	1	3	3	.50	4	.236	.325	.324
Morris,Greg	Lk Elsinore	Cal	A+	25	62	234	59	20	1	2	87	26	31	23	0	50	0	0	1	1	3	.25	9	.252	.318	.372
Morrison,Greg	Savannah	LA	A	21	94	299	76	11	4	4	107	32	39	19	1	65	1	0	2	4	7	.36	0	.254	.299	.358
Morrison,Ryan	Pittsfield	NYN	A-	22	39	86	13	3	0	0	16	11	6	11	1	26	2	0	2	4	2	.67	2	.151	.257	.186
Morrison,Scott	Yakima	LA	A-	24	60	184	38	11	1	1	54	22	26	32	0	42	7	0	2	2	1	.67	2	.207	.342	.293
Moss,Rick	Twins	Min	R	21	28	107	37	8	2	0	49	18	23	7	1	7	3	0	1	2	2	.50	2	.346	.398	.458
	Elizabethtn	Min	R+	21	32	116	41	10	0	5	66	21	18	14	0	17	0	0	0	3	1	.75	3	.353	.423	.569
Mota,Alfonso	Cedar Rapds	Cal	A	23	35	63	14	3	0	2	23	7	4	12	0	15	1	0	0	1	2	.33	2	.222	.355	.365
Mota,Antonio	Yakima	LA	A-	19	60	225	62	11	3	3	88	29	29	13	0	37	1	3	1	13	7	.65	0	.276	.317	.391
Mota,Cristian	Columbus	Cle	A	21	32	122	26	4	0	3	39	17	10	10	1	31	2	2	2	1	2	.33	3	.213	.279	.320
	Burlington	Cle	R+	21	63	251	67	14	1	3	92	36	34	19	0	56	2	1	1	13	6	.68	8	.267	.322	.367
Mota,Guillermo	St. Lucie	NYN	A+	23	102	304	71	10	3	1	90	34	21	34	0	90	1	7	2	8	8	.50	6	.234	.311	.296
Motley,Mel	Watertown	Cle	A-	23	61	199	49	8	2	1	64	24	27	24	0	55	3	0	3	5	5	.50	8	.246	.332	.322
Moultrie,Pat	Bakersfield	Tor	A+	24	48	158	33	4	0	3	46	19	15	29	0	37	0	9	3	15	5	.75	0	.209	.326	.291
	Hagerstown	Tor	A	24	39	129	35	5	1	1	45	25	12	12	1	24	1	1	0	10	1	.91	1	.271	.338	.349
Mouton,Aaron	Diamondback	Ari	R	20	1	4	1	1	0	0	2	0	0	1	0	0	0	0	0	0	0	.00	1	.250	.400	.500
Moyle,Mike	Kinston	Cle	A+	25	60	197	53	12	1	7	88	37	34	30	1	32	4	1	1	3	2	.60	3	.269	.375	.447
Mucker,Kelcey	Fort Myers	Min	A+	22	100	331	79	9	3	2	100	34	32	36	4	66	2	1	1	5	2	.71	11	.239	.316	.302
Mueller,Bret	Peoria	StL	A	24	12	33	7	3	0	0	10	5	3	3	0	9	0	0	0	1	1	.50	3	.212	.278	.303
Mulvehill,Chase	Mets	NYN	R	19	22	65	11	1	3	0	18	9	3	3	0	11	0	1	0	1	1	.50	2	.169	.206	.277
Munoz,Juan	Peoria	StL	A	23	31	111	38	9	0	0	47	19	19	14	0	14	1	0	3	4	1	.80	2	.342	.411	.423
	St. Pete	StL	A+	23	90	330	80	12	3	1	101	41	46	38	0	35	1	3	3	6	5	.55	8	.242	.320	.306
Munson,Michael	Yankees	NYA	R	21	19	40	12	2	0	1	17	6	4	2	0	9	0	0	0	0	0	.00	0	.300	.333	.425
Murphy,Nathan	Boise	Cal	A-	22	67	266	76	18	1	7	117	58	41	41	1	63	1	0	1	12	4	.75	4	.286	.382	.440
Murphy,Quinn	Burlington	Cle	R+	21	18	59	9	1	0	0	10	7	3	6	0	30	1	0	0	2	1	.67	0	.153	.242	.169
Murray,Doug	Lansing	KC	A	22	18	35	5	0	0	0	5	2	4	1	0	11	2	0	0	0	0	.00	0	.143	.211	.143
Myers,Aaron	Portland	Col	A-	21	72	290	80	24	3	5	125	52	46	25	2	48	6	1	5	1	2	.33	9	.276	.340	.431
Myers,Adrian	Hudson Vall	Tex	A-	22	54	142	24	5	4	1	40	22	15	17	0	44	8	0	2	19	2	.90	2	.169	.290	.282
Naples,Brandon	St. Lucie	NYN	A+	24	3	8	0	0	0	0	0	0	0	0	0	0	0	0	0	0	0	.00	0	.000	.000	.000
	Pittsfield	NYN	A-	24	71	263	80	7	4	0	95	44	29	28	0	45	2	0	1	13	5	.72	8	.304	.374	.361
Neal,Robert	Boise	Cal	A-	24	47	173	50	13	1	5	80	36	35	20	0	40	5	0	2	3	1	.75	3	.289	.375	.462
Neikirk,Derick	Tigers	Det	R	22	18	38	8	0	0	0	8	4	1	5	0	7	3	1	0	0	0	.00	4	.211	.348	.211
	Visalia	Det	A+	22	9	27	4	0	0	0	4	3	2	2	0	9	0	0	0	0	0	.00	1	.148	.207	.148
Nelson,Brian	Everett	Sea	A-	21	30	98	18	5	0	1	26	11	11	19	0	32	5	0	0	0	0	.00	1	.184	.344	.265
Nelson,Bryant	Kissimmee	Hou	A+	23	89	345	87	21	6	3	129	38	52	19	3	27	1	1	4	8	2	.80	13	.252	.290	.374
Nelson,Kevin	Twins	Min	R	20	34	122	29	4	0	1	36	8	11	7	1	27	2	1	2	0	0	.00	4	.238	.286	.295
Neubart,Garrett	Asheville	Col	A	23	71	282	79	11	3	0	96	60	22	31	0	45	3	1	3	34	5	.87	2	.280	.354	.340
	Salem	Col	A+	23	24	85	31	2	2	0	37	16	6	12	0	13	4	1	0	8	6	.57	0	.365	.465	.435
Newhan,David	Modesto	Oak	A+	23	117	455	137	27	3	25	245	96	75	62	1	106	2	6	2	17	8	.68	8	.301	.386	.538
Newstrom,Doug	High Desert	Bal	A+	25	122	403	126	30	3	11	195	84	75	72	0	62	0	2	6	15	8	.65	9	.313	.412	.484
Newton,Kimani	Yakima	LA	A-	18	33	45	7	1	0	0	8	8	3	6	0	13	2	0	1	1	2	.33	1	.156	.278	.178

1996 Batting — Single-A and Rookie Leagues

BATTING																				BASERUNNING				PERCENTAGES		
Player	Team	Org	Lg	A	G	AB	H	2B	3B	HR	TB	R	RBI	TBB	IBB	SO	HBP	SH	SF	SB	CS	SB%	GDP	Avg	OBP	SLG
Nichols,Kevin	Martinsvlle	Phi	R+	24	42	158	40	8	0	4	60	21	26	6	0	23	1	0	3	1	1	.50	6	.253	.280	.380
	Piedmont	Phi	A	24	22	72	16	6	0	0	22	5	5	3	1	18	1	1	0	0	1	.00	0	.222	.263	.306
Nicley,Dru	Astros	Hou	R	19	25	66	7	0	0	0	7	4	3	7	0	20	4	0	0	2	0	1.00	3	.106	.234	.106
Niethammer,Marc	Hudson Vall	TB	A-	23	67	212	44	8	1	8	78	21	27	21	1	80	9	1	2	2	5	.29	2	.208	.303	.368
Nieves,Jose	Rockford	ChN	A	22	113	396	96	20	4	5	139	55	57	33	1	59	5	4	3	17	9	.65	8	.242	.307	.351
Nieves,Wilbert	Padres	SD	R	19	43	113	39	5	0	2	50	23	22	13	0	19	0	2	0	3	4	.43	1	.345	.413	.442
Nolte,Bruce	Columbia	NYN	A	23	6	17	1	0	0	0	1	0	1	0	0	2	0	0	1	0	0	.00	0	.059	.056	.059
	Pittsfield	NYN	A-	23	31	91	29	2	1	0	33	16	10	6	0	23	0	1	1	1	0	1.00	1	.319	.357	.363
Noriega,Kevin	Beloit	Mil	A	23	115	414	111	22	2	4	149	55	59	39	0	69	2	0	6	5	5	.50	10	.268	.330	.360
Norris,Dax	Eugene	Atl	A-	23	60	232	67	17	0	7	105	31	37	18	0	32	3	3	1	2	0	1.00	4	.289	.346	.453
Northeimer,Jamie	Clearwater	Phi	A+	24	101	327	83	21	0	10	134	52	42	60	1	69	16	4	4	0	2	.00	7	.254	.391	.410
Nova,Fernando	White Sox	ChA	R	21	58	203	61	12	1	1	78	24	22	18	1	48	7	0	1	9	6	.60	3	.300	.376	.384
Nova,Geraldo	Red Sox	Bos	R	19	33	84	16	3	2	0	23	15	10	17	0	32	2	1	1	3	2	.60	1	.190	.337	.274
Nova,Felix	Williamsprt	ChN	A-	22	60	203	47	7	3	4	72	27	38	25	2	62	2	1	1	5	2	.71	7	.232	.320	.355
Nova,Kelvin	Athletics	Oak	R	20	47	164	44	12	3	0	62	37	18	21	0	43	1	2	2	14	3	.82	1	.268	.351	.378
Nova,Pasqual	Idaho Falls	SD	R+	22	15	58	11	2	3	0	19	2	10	4	0	32	2	0	1	0	0	.00	2	.190	.262	.328
Nunez,Abraham	St. Cathrns	Tor	A-	21	75	297	83	6	4	3	106	43	26	31	0	43	4	8	2	37	14	.73	2	.279	.353	.357
Nunez,Isaias	Peoria	StL	A	23	107	267	60	12	1	1	77	33	26	26	4	52	1	3	2	2	4	.33	3	.225	.294	.288
Nunez,Jose	DiamondbackAri		R	21	4	17	3	0	0	0	3	1	2	1	0	2	0	0	0	1	0	1.00	0	.176	.222	.176
	Lethbridge	Ari	R+	21	40	122	38	5	2	3	56	43	24	24	0	25	7	0	0	5	0	1.00	3	.311	.451	.459
Nunez,Jose	Mets	NYN	R	18	41	120	28	3	1	0	33	11	15	16	0	28	0	1	0	4	9	.31	2	.233	.324	.275
Nunez,Juan	Charlstn-SC	Tex	A	20	88	326	86	7	4	1	104	55	18	36	0	77	5	2	0	53	13	.80	1	.264	.346	.319
Nunez,Sergio	Wilmington	KC	A+	22	105	402	109	23	6	3	153	60	40	38	0	54	4	6	2	44	11	.80	2	.271	.339	.381
O'Connor,Rich	Piedmont	Phi	A	23	23	55	11	1	0	0	12	11	0	11	0	13	0	2	0	1	0	1.00	1	.200	.333	.218
	Clearwater	Phi	A+	23	12	25	6	1	0	0	7	3	2	3	0	5	0	2	1	0	0	.00	0	.240	.310	.280
O'Hearn,Brandon	Princeton	Cin	R+	22	65	235	65	17	2	13	125	33	52	29	2	88	1	0	3	2	0	1.00	4	.277	.354	.532
O'Neal,Troy	Beloit	Mil	A	25	74	206	50	4	0	0	54	18	20	16	0	28	6	4	2	1	2	.33	8	.243	.313	.262
Oliva,Osvaldo	Bellingham	SF	A-	23	3	4	0	0	0	0	0	0	0	1	0	2	0	0	0	0	0	.00	0	.000	.200	.000
Olivares,Teuris	Yankees	NYA	R	18	9	20	6	1	0	0	7	3	4	1	0	2	0	1	0	0	0	.00	0	.300	.333	.350
Oliver,John	Princeton	Cin	R+	19	41	143	29	5	0	2	40	20	13	11	0	31	4	0	1	3	1	.75	6	.203	.277	.280
Oliveros,Leonardo	Batavia	Phi	A-	21	42	121	30	7	0	0	37	12	18	11	1	22	1	1	1	1	1	.50	1	.248	.313	.306
Oliveros,Ricardo	Expos	Mon	R	22	1	0	0	0	0	0	0	0	0	0	0	0	0	0	0	0	0	.00	0	.000	.000	.000
	Delmarva	Mon	A	22	4	4	1	1	0	0	2	0	0	0	0	2	0	0	0	0	0	.00	0	.250	.250	.500
Olmeda,Jose	Red Sox	Bos	R	19	15	55	16	4	0	2	26	8	5	3	0	13	0	0	1	1	1	.50	1	.291	.322	.473
	Lowell	Bos	A-	19	27	89	20	2	0	2	28	6	10	12	0	27	0	2	0	1	2	.33	1	.225	.317	.315
Olsen,D.C.	Delmarva	Mon	A	25	91	291	62	13	1	5	92	26	42	24	1	60	3	2	8	3	2	.60	3	.213	.273	.316
Olson,Dan	White Sox	ChA	R	22	3	11	4	3	0	0	7	4	5	4	0	4	0	0	0	0	0	.00	0	.364	.533	.636
	Hickory	ChA	A	22	57	193	48	8	2	2	66	25	19	31	3	65	0	0	0	2	3	.40	1	.249	.353	.342
Ordaz,Luis	St. Pete	StL	A+	21	126	423	115	13	3	3	143	46	49	30	0	53	1	7	6	10	5	.67	10	.272	.317	.338
Orndorff,Dave	Twins	Min	R	19	8	22	2	1	0	0	3	4	1	6	0	10	1	0	0	0	0	.00	0	.091	.310	.136
	Elizabethtn	Min	R+	19	13	47	15	2	1	2	25	8	6	1	0	10	0	0	0	4	1	.80	0	.319	.333	.532
Oropeza,William	Expos	Mon	R	21	5	18	3	0	0	0	3	2	0	1	0	5	0	1	0	0	0	.00	1	.167	.211	.167
	Vermont	Mon	A-	21	37	128	38	9	1	1	52	13	26	3	0	20	0	2	2	1	1	.50	1	.297	.308	.406
Ortega,Randy	Modesto	Oak	A+	24	23	65	16	2	1	1	23	8	5	9	1	11	1	1	0	1	2	.33	1	.246	.347	.354
	W. Michigan	Oak	A	24	49	139	35	4	0	2	45	15	21	25	0	34	1	0	3	0	1	.00	3	.252	.363	.324
Ortiz,Asbel	Charlstn-SC	Tex	A	21	88	310	67	11	3	1	87	23	32	13	0	94	4	1	3	1	3	.25	2	.216	.255	.281
Ortiz,Jose	Athletics	Oak	R	20	52	200	66	12	8	4	106	43	25	20	2	34	1	1	1	16	5	.76	1	.330	.392	.530
	Modesto	Oak	A+	20	1	4	1	0	0	0	1	0	0	0	0	1	0	0	0	0	0	.00	0	.250	.250	.250
Ortiz,Pedro	Orioles	Bal	R	20	43	126	31	8	0	3	48	16	6	4	0	33	1	0	1	5	0	1.00	1	.246	.273	.381
Osborne,Mark	DiamondbackAri		R	19	31	105	28	6	3	1	43	15	16	9	0	24	3	0	1	0	0	.00	2	.267	.339	.410
Osilka,Garret	Helena	Mil	R+	19	53	165	35	2	1	2	45	34	19	25	0	33	4	5	0	6	6	.50	1	.212	.330	.273
Otero,Oscar	Braves	Atl	R	20	54	191	47	9	2	1	63	15	24	8	1	18	3	1	1	4	5	.44	2	.246	.286	.330
Ottavinia,Paul	Expos	Mon	R	24	3	10	4	0	0	0	4	1	1	2	0	1	0	0	0	0	0	.00	0	.400	.500	.400
	W. Palm Bch	Mon	A+	24	45	141	30	2	1	1	37	15	10	12	0	20	0	3	1	2	1	.67	2	.213	.273	.262
Ovalles,Homy	Expos	Mon	R	20	47	158	40	7	4	0	55	18	29	7	1	24	0	5	6	4	6	.40	0	.253	.275	.348
Owen,Andy	Vero Beach	LA	A+	23	101	342	93	21	2	3	127	35	54	34	3	63	1	4	2	5	5	.50	8	.272	.338	.371
Owen,Tom	Brevard Cty	Fla	A+	24	49	124	26	2	1	1	33	14	9	27	0	22	5	1	0	2	2	.50	4	.210	.372	.266
Owens-bragg,Luke	Hudson Vall	TB	A-	23	67	214	39	7	2	0	50	22	13	36	3	53	2	3	2	12	8	.60	1	.182	.303	.234
Oyola,Carlos	Burlington	SF	A	19	7	25	4	2	0	0	6	1	3	0	0	5	0	1	0	0	0	.00	1	.160	.160	.240
Ozorio,Yudith	St. Pete	StL	A+	22	136	505	122	11	10	1	156	67	42	57	1	110	1	8	2	30	8	.79	5	.242	.319	.309
Ozuna,Pedro	Yankees	NYA	R	21	34	108	33	3	1	0	38	24	20	11	0	17	1	0	1	3	1	.75	2	.306	.372	.352
Ozuna,Rafael	Vero Beach	LA	A+	22	33	113	25	1	1	0	28	16	9	14	0	21	0	3	1	3	2	.60	5	.221	.305	.248
	Savannah	LA	A	22	87	307	75	12	5	5	112	41	27	28	2	69	2	7	2	9	3	.75	4	.244	.310	.365
Pacheco,Domingo	Mariners	Sea	R	18	8	16	4	1	0	0	5	0	1	0	0	6	0	0	1	0	0	.00	0	.250	.235	.313
Pachot,John	Expos	Mon	R	22	8	30	9	1	1	0	12	3	3	1	0	0	1	1	0	0	0	.00	0	.300	.344	.400
	W. Palm Bch	Mon	A+	22	44	163	31	9	0	0	40	8	19	2	0	19	0	1	0	0	1	.00	1	.190	.200	.245
Paciorek,Pete	Idaho Falls	SD	R+	21	72	283	84	15	2	15	148	56	69	36	1	64	4	0	6	6	1	.86	6	.297	.377	.523
Padilla,Roy	Michigan	Bos	A	21	103	386	108	20	6	2	146	58	40	34	2	56	2	1	2	21	8	.72	5	.280	.340	.378
	Sarasota	Bos	A+	21	8	27	8	2	0	0	10	2	2	2	1	3	0	0	0	4	0	1.00	1	.296	.345	.370
Paez,Israel	Fort Wayne	Min	A	20	128	451	120	22	5	5	167	86	50	51	2	76	5	4	3	11	8	.58	18	.266	.345	.370
Panaro,Carmen	DiamondbackAri		R	21	28	33	8	2	0	0	10	6	4	7	1	8	1	0	0	0	1	.00	3	.242	.390	.303
Parent,Gerald	Beloit	Mil	A	23	40	95	20	6	1	0	28	12	12	18	0	19	0	1	0	2	3	.40	1	.211	.336	.295
	Ogden	Mil	R+	23	62	218	84	18	0	6	120	42	42	37	0	34	1	1	3	5	1	.83	3	.385	.471	.550
Parker,Allan	Lk Elsinore	Cal	A+	25	51	134	26	3	0	1	32	13	10	10	0	29	1	2	0	1	2	.33	0	.194	.255	.239
Parmenter,Ross	Ogden	Mil	R+	22	45	141	43	9	0	2	58	21	18	21	0	31	3	0	1	0	3	.00	5	.305	.404	.411
Parra,Alejandro	White Sox	ChA	R	19	39	86	10	0	0	0	10	12	3	21	0	28	2	2	0	2	2	.50	3	.116	.303	.116
Parra,Jose	Charlstn-SC	Tex	A	20	36	87	13	1	0	0	14	2	6	7	0	43	1	1	1	5	3	.63	0	.149	.219	.161

1996 Batting — Single-A and Rookie Leagues

BATTING																				BASERUNNING				PERCENTAGES		
Player	Team	Org	Lg	A	G	AB	H	2B	3B	HR	TB	R	RBI	TBB	IBB	SO	HBP	SH	SF	SB	CS	SB%	GDP	Avg	OBP	SLG
	Rangers	Tex	R	20	15	31	8	0	0	1	11	4	3	3	0	8	1	1	0	4	1	.80	0	.258	.343	.355
	Charlotte	Tex	A+	20	3	6	2	0	0	0	2	1	1	1	0	3	0	0	0	0	0	.00	0	.333	.429	.333
Parsons,Jason	Princeton	Cin	R+	24	23	91	37	9	0	5	61	22	17	5	1	9	1	0	1	0	2	.00	2	.407	.439	.670
	Charlstn-WV	Cin	A	24	48	162	46	11	0	3	66	18	24	15	0	25	3	1	2	3	1	.75	2	.284	.352	.407
	Winston-Sal	Cin	A+	24	14	46	16	3	0	0	19	4	7	2	0	5	1	0	0	0	2	.00	0	.348	.388	.413
Parsons,Jeff	Columbia	NYN	A	23	51	147	27	3	2	0	34	13	9	22	0	43	1	5	0	7	4	.64	3	.184	.294	.231
	Pittsfield	NYN	A-	23	72	274	66	5	1	1	76	46	14	39	1	60	1	3	1	20	7	.74	2	.241	.337	.277
Pascual,Edison	Pirates	Pit	R	20	43	149	41	15	1	3	67	28	20	13	0	35	1	0	0	7	2	.78	3	.275	.337	.450
Pass,Patrick	Marlins	Fla	R	19	29	90	22	4	0	0	26	14	8	15	2	27	2	0	0	5	2	.71	0	.244	.364	.289
Patellis,Anthony	Charlstn-WV	Cin	A	23	61	227	41	9	1	3	61	23	27	13	2	72	4	1	2	4	3	.57	6	.181	.236	.269
	Billings	Cin	R+	23	44	172	49	9	5	8	92	35	32	22	3	45	3	0	1	3	2	.60	2	.285	.374	.535
Patterson,Jarrod	St. Lucie	NYN	A+	23	17	61	11	2	0	1	16	6	6	3	0	19	1	0	1	1	0	1.00	0	.180	.227	.262
	Columbia	NYN	A	23	70	213	49	9	1	3	69	26	37	33	3	65	2	0	4	1	1	.50	3	.230	.333	.324
Patton,Cory	Kingsport	NYN	R+	21	24	31	4	0	0	0	4	13	1	12	0	10	3	1	0	4	0	1.00	1	.129	.413	.129
Paul,Josh	White Sox	ChA	R	22	1	0	0	0	0	0	0	0	0	1	0	0	0	0	0	0	0	.00	0	.000	1.000	.000
	Hickory	ChA	A	22	59	226	74	16	0	8	114	41	37	21	3	53	1	3	1	13	4	.76	2	.327	.386	.504
Paulino,Arturo	W. Michigan	Oak	A	22	87	231	51	7	1	2	66	27	19	24	0	46	2	5	1	9	10	.47	8	.221	.298	.286
Paxton,Chris	Bakersfield	Bal	A+	20	85	270	67	14	0	11	114	30	39	35	0	90	3	2	2	0	0	.00	6	.248	.339	.422
Payano,Alexi	Cubs	ChN	R	20	28	83	21	5	1	0	28	15	10	4	0	12	5	0	1	3	1	.75	1	.253	.323	.337
Paz,Richard	High Desert	Bal	A+	19	7	17	3	1	0	0	4	2	0	1	0	4	0	2	0	0	0	.00	1	.176	.222	.235
	Bluefield	Bal	R+	19	50	170	50	7	0	1	60	42	21	42	0	24	3	1	4	9	4	.69	1	.294	.434	.353
Peck,Tom	Hagerstown	Tor	A	22	19	48	16	2	0	0	18	7	7	10	0	11	0	0	2	1	1	.50	1	.333	.433	.375
Pedrosa,Alex	Orioles	Bal	R	22	3	13	4	1	0	0	5	0	0	0	0	1	0	0	0	1	0	1.00	0	.308	.308	.385
	Bluefield	Bal	R+	22	34	77	19	9	0	0	28	12	8	15	0	13	0	0	1	2	0	1.00	2	.247	.366	.364
Peeples,Michael	Hagerstown	Tor	A	20	74	268	63	15	1	3	89	30	31	37	0	55	3	4	3	15	5	.75	5	.235	.331	.332
Pellow,Kit	Spokane	KC	A-	23	71	279	80	18	2	18	156	48	66	20	0	52	8	1	7	8	3	.73	5	.287	.344	.559
Pena,Adelis	Erie	Pit	A-	20	66	252	71	11	1	1	87	31	26	15	0	41	0	4	2	7	4	.64	7	.282	.320	.345
Pena,Alex	Augusta	Pit	A	19	52	167	27	4	2	0	35	9	12	7	0	51	0	1	1	2	1	.67	5	.162	.194	.210
	Erie	Pit	A-	19	74	281	75	10	3	4	103	31	33	14	0	52	2	0	1	10	4	.71	5	.267	.305	.367
Pena,Angel	Savannah	LA	A	22	36	127	26	4	0	6	48	13	16	7	1	37	0	1	0	1	1	.50	1	.205	.246	.378
Pena,Elvis	Salem	Col	A+	20	102	341	76	9	4	0	93	48	28	61	2	70	3	13	1	30	16	.65	12	.223	.345	.273
Pena,Frank	Elizabethtn	Min	R+	20	35	84	14	1	0	0	15	12	9	18	0	29	0	0	1	0	0	.00	5	.167	.311	.179
Pena,Jose	Rangers	Tex	R	20	30	98	28	6	4	0	42	19	11	9	0	16	0	0	2	13	0	1.00	1	.286	.339	.429
Penalver,Juan	Mets	NYN	R	21	15	52	18	3	0	0	21	9	7	11	0	10	1	0	0	2	0	1.00	0	.346	.469	.404
	Kingsport	NYN	R+	21	36	107	32	5	1	2	45	24	17	21	0	20	1	3	0	0	2	.00	3	.299	.419	.421
Pendergrass,Tyro.	Danville	Atl	R+	20	54	220	68	8	7	3	99	50	23	24	0	39	4	2	2	40	6	.87	4	.309	.384	.450
	Macon	Atl	A	20	12	45	12	1	1	1	18	8	3	4	0	12	1	0	0	5	3	.63	0	.267	.340	.400
Peniche,Fray	Tigers	Det	R	20	40	119	23	6	2	0	33	17	5	12	0	39	2	0	0	2	3	.40	2	.193	.278	.277
Peoples,Danny	Watertown	Cle	A-	22	35	117	28	7	0	3	44	20	26	28	2	36	2	0	1	3	1	.75	2	.239	.392	.376
Perez,Alejandro	Red Sox	Bos	R	18	15	43	10	3	1	0	15	6	3	1	0	10	1	0	0	1	0	1.00	1	.233	.267	.349
Perez,Edwin	Burlington	Cle	R+	22	51	176	41	4	0	9	72	22	31	15	0	48	3	0	0	5	4	.56	2	.233	.304	.409
Perez,Jersen	Mets	NYN	R	21	40	151	42	5	3	0	53	24	12	17	1	18	1	0	0	7	2	.78	2	.278	.355	.351
	Kingsport	NYN	R+	21	6	17	3	0	0	0	3	4	3	5	0	6	0	0	2	0	0	.00	2	.176	.333	.176
	Pittsfield	NYN	A-	21	1	3	1	0	0	0	1	1	0	1	0	1	0	0	0	0	0	.00	0	.333	.500	.333
Perez,Jesse	Orioles	Bal	R	18	36	104	18	3	0	0	21	9	10	7	0	33	1	4	2	2	3	.40	0	.173	.228	.202
Perez,Jhonny	Kissimmee	Hou	A+	20	90	322	87	20	2	12	147	54	49	26	1	70	2	3	0	16	16	.50	3	.270	.329	.457
Perez,Mickey	Bakersfield	—	A+	25	6	17	3	0	0	0	3	1	0	3	0	8	0	1	0	0	0	.00	0	.176	.300	.176
Perez,Richard	Orioles	Bal	R	NA	41	138	35	5	2	3	53	25	18	12	0	34	1	4	1	10	5	.67	3	.254	.316	.384
Perez,Santiago	Lakeland	Det	A+	21	122	418	105	18	2	1	130	33	27	16	1	88	3	7	2	6	5	.55	9	.251	.282	.311
Perini,Michael	Red Sox	Bos	R	19	34	94	16	1	1	0	19	8	7	13	0	27	0	0	1	3	2	.60	1	.170	.269	.202
Pernell,Brandon	Padres	SD	R	20	53	174	58	9	10	1	90	38	33	18	0	30	0	1	2	14	4	.78	1	.333	.392	.517
Perry,Chan	Kinston	Cle	A+	24	96	358	104	27	1	10	163	44	62	36	3	33	2	3	3	2	3	.40	9	.291	.356	.455
Person,Wilt	Macon	Atl	A	23	40	122	19	0	0	0	19	9	7	4	0	23	1	1	0	2	3	.40	3	.156	.189	.156
Peterman,Thomas	Elizabethtn	Min	R+	22	3	10	3	0	0	1	6	5	4	5	0	1	0	0	0	0	0	.00	0	.300	.533	.600
	Fort Wayne	Min	A	22	58	176	45	11	0	3	65	17	28	10	3	30	2	0	3	0	1	.00	1	.256	.298	.369
Peters,Tony	Beloit	Mil	A	22	71	179	46	13	3	2	71	20	23	18	0	47	0	1	1	5	1	.83	3	.257	.323	.397
Petersen,Mike	Rockies	Col	R	20	52	205	66	12	2	1	85	26	25	11	0	25	1	0	2	3	2	.60	2	.322	.356	.415
Petke,Jonathan	Watertown	Cle	A-	24	63	224	55	10	0	1	68	35	26	44	1	36	3	1	4	8	4	.67	4	.246	.371	.304
Petrick,Ben	Asheville	Col	A	20	122	446	105	24	2	14	175	74	52	75	1	98	5	2	3	19	9	.68	5	.235	.350	.392
Pettiford,Torrey	Piedmont	Phi	A	24	74	259	54	6	2	0	64	26	19	18	0	49	3	9	2	13	3	.81	5	.208	.266	.247
Phair,Kelly	Ogden	Mil	R+	24	41	163	48	12	1	2	68	41	24	27	0	36	9	1	1	17	4	.81	3	.294	.420	.417
	Beloit	Mil	A	24	30	99	21	5	0	0	26	16	12	13	0	18	2	1	2	3	1	.75	3	.212	.310	.263
Phelps,Joshua	Medicne Hat	Tor	R+	19	59	191	46	3	0	5	64	28	29	27	0	65	6	2	1	5	3	.63	5	.241	.351	.335
Phillips,Blaine	Oneonta	NYA	A-	24	46	144	30	2	0	0	32	12	12	11	0	49	1	2	1	0	2	.00	3	.208	.268	.222
Pickering,Calvin	Bluefield	Bal	R+	20	60	200	65	14	1	18	135	45	66	28	4	64	2	0	1	8	2	.80	4	.325	.411	.675
Pickett,Eric	Eugene	Atl	A-	21	61	214	48	7	4	6	81	32	25	25	3	77	1	0	0	1	4	.20	2	.224	.308	.379
Pico,Brandon	Daytona	ChN	A+	23	19	67	13	0	1	1	18	10	8	5	0	9	0	1	0	1	0	1.00	0	.194	.250	.269
	Rockford	ChN	A	23	12	35	11	0	1	0	13	3	7	3	0	3	0	0	1	0	0	.00	0	.314	.359	.371
Pierce,Kirk	Piedmont	Phi	A	24	67	198	50	12	0	2	68	22	28	22	0	43	12	1	2	0	1	.00	6	.253	.359	.343
Pierzynski,A.J.	Fort Wayne	Min	A	20	114	431	118	30	3	7	175	48	70	22	1	53	2	0	6	0	4	.00	10	.274	.308	.406
Pimentel,Jose	Savannah	LA	A	22	123	461	128	21	4	7	178	66	54	28	1	100	10	5	4	50	19	.72	9	.278	.330	.386
Pimentel,Marino	Marlins	Fla	R	NA	15	40	5	1	0	0	6	4	1	1	0	17	1	0	0	0	3	.00	0	.125	.167	.150
Piniella,Juan	Rangers	Tex	R	19	55	223	53	6	2	0	63	38	18	15	0	54	5	4	2	19	5	.79	1	.238	.298	.283
Pinson,Brian	Mariners	Sea	R	19	10	22	9	0	0	0	9	2	1	0	0	6	0	0	0	0	1	.00	0	.409	.409	.409
Pinto,Rene	Greensboro	NYA	A	19	52	165	34	9	1	1	48	13	14	5	0	41	2	2	0	2	1	.67	5	.206	.238	.291
	Oneonta	NYA	A-	19	53	199	41	1	2	2	52	15	20	13	0	54	3	3	3	1	1	.50	4	.206	.261	.261
Pitts,Rick	Lansing	KC	A	21	13	48	10	1	0	0	11	7	2	5	0	14	0	0	0	2	1	.67	1	.208	.283	.229

1996 Batting — Single-A and Rookie Leagues

BATTING																				BASERUNNING				PERCENTAGES		
Player	Team	Org	Lg	A	G	AB	H	2B	3B	HR	TB	R	RBI	TBB	IBB	SO	HBP	SH	SF	SB	CS	SB%	GDP	Avg	OBP	SLG
	Spokane	KC	A-	21	55	135	26	2	0	2	34	23	11	18	0	37	3	2	1	14	1	.93	0	.193	.299	.252
Podsednik,Scott	Brevard Cty	Fla	A+	21	108	383	100	9	2	0	113	39	30	45	0	65	3	7	0	20	10	.67	8	.261	.343	.295
Pointer,Corey	Macon	Atl	A	21	8	25	6	1	0	1	10	4	2	0	0	9	1	0	0	2	1	.67	0	.240	.269	.400
	Eugene	Atl	A-	21	65	233	57	12	3	14	117	46	39	35	4	88	5	0	5	10	2	.83	3	.245	.349	.502
	Erie	Pit	A-	21	5	21	4	1	0	0	5	1	2	0	0	9	1	0	0	0	0	.00	1	.190	.227	.238
Polanco,Enohel	Columbia	NYN	A	21	92	299	65	12	1	1	82	34	24	18	0	78	5	9	1	6	3	.67	5	.217	.272	.274
Polanco,Juan	Modesto	Oak	A+	22	8	28	6	2	0	1	11	4	2	3	0	7	0	0	0	1	2	.33	1	.214	.290	.393
	Sou. Oregon	Oak	A-	22	56	208	45	7	2	4	68	22	24	15	0	57	2	1	2	13	3	.81	0	.216	.273	.327
Polanco,Placido	St. Pete	StL	A+	21	137	540	157	29	5	0	196	65	51	24	1	34	5	6	7	4	4	.50	31	.291	.323	.363
Pollock,Elton	Augusta	Pit	A	24	132	452	106	13	5	5	144	65	47	68	0	100	5	5	3	29	11	.73	4	.235	.339	.319
Polonia,Isreal	Marlins	Fla	R	NA	49	168	53	6	2	4	75	22	31	10	2	50	2	2	3	6	6	.50	6	.315	.355	.446
Pomierski,Joe	Hudson Vall	TB	A-	23	74	285	74	25	3	8	129	45	54	35	1	91	4	0	6	2	4	.33	6	.260	.342	.453
Pond,Simon	Vermont	Mon	A-	20	69	253	76	16	1	3	103	37	40	26	2	26	3	1	3	9	3	.75	7	.300	.368	.407
Poor,Jeff	Burlington	SF	A	23	104	359	87	17	0	1	107	27	40	49	1	54	2	2	2	1	0	1.00	14	.242	.335	.298
Porter,Bo	Daytona	ChN	A+	24	20	63	11	4	1	0	17	9	6	6	0	24	0	0	2	5	1	.83	0	.175	.239	.270
	Rockford	ChN	A	24	105	378	91	22	3	7	140	83	44	72	1	107	1	3	4	30	14	.68	7	.241	.360	.370
Post,Dave	Expos	Mon	R	23	8	25	2	0	0	1	5	3	1	4	1	6	0	1	0	1	0	1.00	0	.080	.207	.200
	W. Palm Bch	Mon	A+	23	79	258	72	15	6	5	114	42	35	37	1	32	5	5	4	8	4	.67	6	.279	.375	.442
Powers,John	Clinton	SD	A	23	64	237	61	8	4	1	80	29	21	34	0	38	4	3	3	1	4	.20	5	.257	.356	.338
Prada,Nelson	Twins	Min	R	21	41	144	35	11	1	2	54	16	16	6	0	30	3	2	1	1	1	.50	6	.243	.286	.375
Pratt,Wes	Kissimmee	Hou	A+	24	48	142	25	6	0	2	37	18	15	9	0	33	2	4	1	2	1	.67	3	.176	.234	.261
	Auburn	Hou	A-	24	70	246	77	22	1	5	116	43	35	39	2	37	2	0	1	11	3	.79	8	.313	.410	.472
Preciado,Victor	Yankees	NYA	R	20	45	164	41	7	2	0	52	15	22	11	0	27	1	2	1	1	2	.33	1	.250	.299	.317
Pressley,Kasey	Cubs	ChN	R	20	35	124	17	1	0	1	21	9	13	13	0	49	0	0	1	1	1	.50	3	.137	.217	.169
Presto,Nicholas	Princeton	Cin	R+	22	12	42	11	2	1	0	15	12	1	6	0	4	0	0	0	1	2	.33	1	.262	.354	.357
	Billings	Cin	R+	22	4	16	2	0	0	0	2	2	1	2	0	6	0	0	1	0	1	.00	0	.125	.211	.125
Price,Leonard	Billings	Cin	R+	20	49	131	25	3	0	0	28	18	16	24	0	32	0	3	2	2	2	.50	2	.191	.312	.214
Prieto,Alejandro	Wilmington	KC	A+	21	119	447	127	19	6	1	161	65	40	31	0	66	3	8	5	26	15	.63	7	.284	.331	.360
Proctor,Jerry	DiamondbackAri		R	19	45	163	33	5	4	0	46	14	9	8	0	60	6	0	1	2	0	1.00	4	.202	.264	.282
Prodanov,Peter	Red Sox	Bos	R	23	9	25	3	1	0	0	4	5	1	2	0	3	0	0	0	0	0	.00	1	.120	.185	.160
	Michigan	Bos	A	23	44	147	34	7	1	3	52	21	14	18	1	23	0	0	2	2	1	.67	3	.231	.311	.354
Prokopec,Luke	Savannah	LA	A	19	82	245	53	12	1	4	79	34	29	27	2	78	4	0	4	0	5	.00	5	.216	.300	.322
Prospero,Teo	Bellingham	SF	A-	20	26	76	16	1	1	3	28	7	8	2	0	28	1	0	2	0	3	.00	0	.211	.235	.368
	Burlington	SF	A	20	10	24	4	0	0	0	4	0	2	2	0	9	1	1	0	0	0	.00	0	.167	.259	.167
Pryor,Pete	White Sox	ChA	R	23	3	9	1	0	0	0	1	0	0	0	0	2	0	0	0	0	0	.00	0	.111	.111	.111
	Hickory	ChA	A	23	59	205	63	18	1	6	101	37	37	36	4	43	5	0	1	3	2	.60	7	.307	.421	.493
Pugh,David	Braves	Atl	R	19	30	89	23	4	0	1	30	8	12	7	0	23	0	1	1	1	0	1.00	0	.258	.309	.337
	Danville	Atl	R+	19	6	21	3	0	0	0	3	0	1	0	0	3	0	1	1	0	0	.00	2	.143	.136	.143
Pullen,Shane	Piedmont	Phi	A	24	46	171	46	9	1	2	63	15	28	16	3	30	2	1	3	1	2	.33	3	.269	.333	.368
	Clearwater	Phi	A+	24	23	75	20	2	0	0	22	11	8	8	0	20	0	2	2	1	0	1.00	0	.267	.329	.293
Quatraro,Matthew	Butte	TB	R+	23	59	244	84	16	4	1	111	53	59	25	0	29	8	0	3	3	1	.75	4	.344	.418	.455
Quesada,Travis	Boise	Cal	A-	NA	10	20	2	0	1	0	4	3	0	7	0	7	0	0	0	0	1	.00	0	.100	.333	.200
Quinn,Mark	Lansing	KC	A	23	113	437	132	23	3	9	188	63	71	43	2	54	5	0	6	14	8	.64	12	.302	.367	.430
Quintero,Christian	Yankees	NYA	R	21	21	68	18	4	0	1	25	13	8	4	0	13	3	1	1	1	0	1.00	1	.265	.329	.368
Radcliff,Vic	Royals	KC	R	20	48	165	51	11	2	3	75	24	20	15	0	34	10	2	1	1	1	.50	1	.309	.398	.455
Raifstanger,John	Michigan	Bos	A	24	111	345	100	17	1	5	134	55	41	62	1	48	1	6	2	5	4	.56	3	.290	.398	.388
Ramirez,Joel	Wisconsin	Sea	A	23	110	364	87	14	0	1	104	53	52	30	0	45	10	4	1	5	7	.42	10	.239	.314	.286
Ramirez,Aramis	Erie	Pit	A-	19	61	223	68	14	4	9	117	37	42	31	1	41	7	0	2	0	0	.00	7	.305	.403	.525
	Augusta	Pit	A	19	6	20	4	1	0	1	8	3	2	1	0	7	2	0	0	0	2	.00	0	.200	.304	.400
Ramirez,Daniel	Columbia	NYN	A	23	47	143	33	5	0	1	41	20	13	11	0	30	1	6	0	6	4	.60	2	.231	.290	.287
	Pittsfield	NYN	A-	23	70	260	73	5	5	1	91	28	22	14	0	45	4	4	2	24	9	.73	3	.281	.325	.350
Ramirez,Oscar	Rangers	Tex	R	20	56	195	38	12	2	2	60	21	23	16	0	59	5	4	0	3	3	.50	1	.195	.273	.308
Ramirez,Edgar	Devil Rays	TB	R	17	38	114	18	0	0	0	18	12	8	10	0	29	0	2	0	3	2	.60	2	.158	.226	.158
Ramirez,Francisco	Jamestown	Det	A-	21	19	37	2	1	0	0	3	5	3	2	0	17	1	0	0	1	0	1.00	0	.054	.125	.081
Ramirez,Juan	Royals	KC	R	19	34	91	21	4	0	1	28	10	8	4	0	22	1	0	0	0	0	.00	2	.231	.271	.308
Ramirez,Julio	Brevard Cty	Fla	A+	19	17	61	15	0	1	0	17	11	2	4	0	18	0	0	1	2	3	.40	1	.246	.288	.279
	Marlins	Fla	R	19	42	171	49	5	3	0	60	33	15	14	0	34	3	1	0	25	8	.76	0	.287	.351	.351
Ramirez,Luis	Orioles	Bal	R	18	41	131	21	4	3	0	31	13	12	7	0	47	1	2	0	1	2	.33	4	.160	.209	.237
Ramirez,Omar	Kinston	Cle	A+	26	2	5	2	0	0	1	5	1	3	1	0	0	0	0	0	0	0	.00	1	.400	.500	1.000
Ramos,Isandel	Braves	Atl	R	NA	49	149	33	4	0	0	37	9	12	21	0	31	1	3	1	0	1	.00	1	.221	.320	.248
Ramos,Kelly	Mets	NYN	R	20	20	59	11	0	1	0	13	3	7	3	0	10	0	1	0	0	2	.00	2	.186	.226	.220
Ramos,Noel	Orioles	Bal	R	20	18	46	10	3	0	2	19	4	6	4	0	17	3	0	0	0	0	.00	0	.217	.321	.413
Rand,Ian	Bellingham	SF	A-	20	53	149	32	3	1	1	40	23	8	8	0	48	2	2	0	5	1	.83	2	.215	.264	.268
Randolph,Ed	Wisconsin	Sea	A	22	70	196	35	9	1	1	49	23	13	23	2	43	1	3	1	3	0	1.00	7	.179	.267	.250
Rascon,Rene	Kane County	Fla	A	23	56	188	32	6	0	4	50	23	20	17	1	61	1	1	3	0	1	.00	7	.170	.239	.266
	Brevard Cty	Fla	A+	23	10	31	8	1	0	1	12	3	5	6	0	10	0	1	0	0	2	.00	1	.258	.378	.387
Rathmell,Lance	Michigan	Bos	A	23	20	54	7	2	1	1	14	5	5	3	0	9	0	0	1	0	0	.00	0	.130	.172	.259
Rauer,Troy	W. Michigan	Oak	A	24	13	22	1	0	0	0	1	3	1	3	0	13	0	0	0	0	0	.00	0	.045	.160	.045
	Sou. Oregon	Oak	A-	24	62	215	44	10	0	8	78	29	24	21	0	85	3	2	0	7	1	.88	3	.205	.285	.363
Raymondi,Mike	Hudson Vall	TB	A-	21	16	25	1	0	0	0	1	1	1	4	0	10	3	0	0	0	0	.00	0	.040	.250	.040
Raynor,Mark	Clearwater	Phi	A+	24	18	55	11	1	1	0	14	8	4	17	0	9	0	1	2	2	1	.67	1	.200	.378	.255
	Piedmont	Phi	A	24	111	428	130	21	2	4	167	73	62	50	0	67	3	5	6	16	10	.62	7	.304	.376	.390
Redman,Julian	Pirates	Pit	R	20	26	104	31	4	1	1	40	20	16	12	1	12	0	0	1	15	3	.83	0	.298	.368	.385
	Erie	Pit	A-	20	43	170	50	4	6	2	72	31	21	17	0	30	0	2	3	7	3	.70	2	.294	.353	.424
Reeder,James	Auburn	Hou	A-	22	69	241	68	8	4	0	84	24	25	23	2	32	4	1	4	6	1	.86	5	.282	.349	.349
Reese,Mat	Lk Elsinore	Cal	A+	26	2	2	1	0	0	0	1	0	2	0	0	0	0	0	0	0	0	.00	0	.500	.500	.500
	Cedar Rapds	Cal	A	26	9	14	1	0	0	0	1	0	0	0	0	5	0	0	0	0	0	.00	0	.071	.071	.071

1996 Batting — Single-A and Rookie Leagues

BATTING																				BASERUNNING				PERCENTAGES		
Player	Team	Org	Lg	A	G	AB	H	2B	3B	HR	TB	R	RBI	TBB	IBB	SO	HBP	SH	SF	SB	CS	SB%	GDP	Avg	OBP	SLG
Reeves,Glenn	Brevard Cty	Fla	A+	23	123	478	143	29	4	6	198	72	41	63	0	82	5	4	4	8	5	.62	6	.299	.384	.414
Regan,Jason	Everett	Sea	A-	21	40	124	26	11	0	3	46	17	22	25	0	47	4	2	2	3	3	.50	1	.210	.355	.371
Rennhack,Mike	Stockton	Mil	A+	22	121	456	146	32	4	17	237	67	103	53	1	66	4	2	7	8	10	.44	11	.320	.390	.520
Restovich,George	Jamestown	Det	A-	23	48	151	27	5	0	6	50	25	22	30	2	55	1	0	2	1	1	.50	1	.179	.315	.331
Rexrode,Jackie	Diamondback	Ari	R	18	48	140	46	2	0	1	51	28	17	44	0	27	0	0	4	8	5	.62	1	.329	.479	.364
Reyes,Deurys	Tigers	Det	R	17	5	7	1	0	1	0	3	3	0	2	0	3	0	0	0	0	0	.00	0	.143	.333	.429
Reyes,Freddy	Elizabethtn	Min	R+	21	65	252	81	20	1	8	127	46	55	19	0	49	9	0	2	0	1	.00	3	.321	.387	.504
Reynoso,Benjamin	Idaho Falls	SD	R+	22	72	284	98	26	0	4	136	45	50	26	0	42	6	0	4	20	7	.74	6	.345	.406	.479
Reynoso,Ismael	Marlins	Fla	R	19	30	97	15	4	0	0	19	8	9	3	0	22	2	0	0	3	2	.60	2	.155	.196	.196
	Brevard Cty	Fla	A+	19	11	35	4	0	0	0	4	5	1	1	0	11	0	1	0	2	1	.67	2	.114	.139	.114
Rhea,Chip	Lethbridge	Ari	R+	23	43	139	35	5	2	3	53	25	22	15	0	47	1	0	1	1	2	.33	4	.252	.327	.381
Ribaudo,Mike	Bluefield	Bal	R+	22	7	22	2	0	0	0	2	1	1	2	0	7	0	2	0	0	0	.00	0	.091	.167	.091
Rice,Charles	Augusta	Pit	A	21	56	185	33	5	1	3	49	22	13	18	1	57	7	0	0	4	2	.67	2	.178	.276	.265
	Erie	Pit	A-	21	56	187	47	12	1	4	73	24	19	23	0	39	10	0	4	6	4	.60	4	.251	.357	.390
Richard,Chris	St. Pete	StL	A+	23	129	460	130	28	6	14	212	65	82	57	6	50	9	0	5	7	3	.70	11	.283	.369	.461
Richards,Rowan	Hudson Vall	Tex	A-	23	30	113	31	6	0	5	52	18	18	16	0	33	5	0	2	4	1	.80	4	.274	.382	.460
	Charlotte	Tex	A+	23	34	118	20	3	1	1	28	10	10	5	0	33	2	1	2	2	1	.67	1	.169	.213	.237
Richardson,Scott	San Bernrdo	LA	A+	26	128	458	140	30	0	13	209	80	69	46	0	71	4	4	4	31	14	.69	9	.306	.371	.456
Richey,Mikal	Great Falls	LA	R+	18	34	65	7	1	0	0	8	8	0	8	0	25	0	1	0	4	1	.80	0	.108	.205	.123
Riley,William	Great Falls	LA	R+	20	44	145	44	8	1	3	63	23	26	14	0	30	5	0	0	6	6	.50	3	.303	.384	.434
Rios,Brian	Jamestown	Det	A-	22	36	102	31	6	2	1	44	19	17	19	0	15	0	0	1	4	1	.80	3	.304	.410	.431
Ritter,Ryan	Beloit	Mil	A	23	99	347	83	12	6	7	128	43	42	24	0	103	3	5	2	20	6	.77	4	.239	.293	.369
Rivas,Luis	Twins	Min	R	17	53	201	52	12	1	1	69	29	13	18	0	37	0	1	0	35	10	.78	2	.259	.320	.343
Rivera,Carlos	Pirates	Pit	R	19	48	183	52	8	3	3	75	24	26	15	1	22	1	0	2	1	1	.50	8	.284	.338	.410
Rivera,Juan	Rangers	Tex	R	20	26	78	22	5	1	2	35	14	7	6	0	30	0	1	0	6	0	1.00	3	.282	.333	.449
Rivera,Luis	Expos	Mon	R	19	22	48	3	1	0	0	4	2	2	5	0	12	1	1	0	0	1	.00	0	.063	.167	.083
Rivera,Micky	Peoria	StL	A	23	72	210	47	10	1	1	62	26	22	14	0	33	3	6	2	2	3	.40	3	.224	.279	.295
Rivera,Roberto	Orioles	Bal	R	20	4	8	5	1	1	0	8	7	2	3	0	1	0	0	1	3	0	1.00	0	.625	.667	1.000
	Bluefield	Bal	R+	20	46	158	34	8	0	5	57	20	26	10	0	54	0	0	0	14	4	.78	3	.215	.262	.361
Rivera,Santiago	Daytona	ChN	A+	24	10	20	3	1	1	0	6	3	1	4	0	5	0	0	0	0	0	.00	2	.150	.292	.300
Rivera,Wilfredo	Michigan	Bos	A	23	65	149	37	9	2	2	56	17	18	7	0	32	1	1	2	1	0	1.00	5	.248	.283	.376
Rivero,Eddie	Batavia	Phi	A-	23	13	55	14	1	2	1	22	7	6	2	0	14	0	1	0	1	2	.33	1	.255	.281	.400
	Piedmont	Phi	A	23	52	196	53	10	4	4	83	27	34	19	4	37	2	1	4	5	3	.63	3	.270	.335	.423
Rivers,Jonathan	Dunedin	Tor	A+	22	97	333	83	14	3	6	121	46	43	38	3	67	1	1	1	8	9	.47	10	.249	.327	.363
Roberts,John	Rancho Cuca	SD	A+	23	23	73	12	4	1	2	24	11	6	11	1	27	1	0	0	4	1	.80	0	.164	.282	.329
	W. Palm Bch	Mon	A+	23	28	67	9	1	2	2	20	7	8	7	0	26	1	0	1	1	0	1.00	0	.134	.224	.299
Roberts,Ryan	Peoria	StL	A	23	9	20	4	0	0	0	4	0	0	1	0	4	1	1	0	1	0	1.00	0	.200	.273	.200
	New Jersey	StL	A-	23	50	190	43	8	3	0	57	28	18	18	0	49	1	4	2	1	2	.33	3	.226	.294	.300
Robertson,Dean	Orioles	Bal	R	21	53	179	54	11	2	2	75	32	25	28	0	17	1	2	0	16	8	.67	6	.302	.399	.419
Robertson,Geoff.	Astros	Hou	R	20	38	81	11	1	0	0	12	8	2	15	0	38	1	1	0	7	4	.64	2	.136	.278	.148
Robertson,Ryan	Kane County	Fla	A	24	55	160	37	8	0	3	54	21	16	37	1	31	1	2	3	0	1	.00	3	.231	.373	.338
Robinson,Tony	Lynchburg	Pit	A+	21	31	93	16	3	0	0	19	13	7	17	0	17	2	3	0	5	3	.63	2	.172	.313	.204
Robinson,David	Piedmont	Phi	A	24	50	149	37	8	2	3	58	22	13	12	0	34	2	0	0	5	3	.63	3	.248	.313	.389
Robinson,Hassan	Quad City	Hou	A	24	106	373	101	11	2	1	119	53	38	14	2	35	3	5	3	15	6	.71	4	.271	.300	.319
Robinson,Kerry	Peoria	StL	A	23	123	440	158	17	14	2	209	98	47	51	5	51	3	4	8	50	26	.66	2	.359	.422	.475
Robles,Juan	Lansing	KC	A	25	27	67	18	4	0	1	25	11	5	6	0	10	1	1	0	2	0	1.00	1	.269	.338	.373
	Spokane	KC	A-	25	53	178	49	6	1	2	63	27	20	17	1	37	1	0	4	4	1	.80	4	.275	.335	.354
Robles,Oscar	Kissimmee	Hou	A+	21	125	427	115	13	2	0	132	57	29	74	3	37	6	8	2	10	8	.56	13	.269	.383	.309
Rocha,Juan	Lansing	KC	A	23	131	459	123	22	8	14	203	79	83	68	2	116	5	5	9	15	9	.63	8	.268	.362	.442
Roche,Marlon	Quad City	Hou	A	22	85	275	75	5	4	4	100	34	25	26	1	60	2	2	0	5	12	.29	7	.273	.340	.364
Rockow,Jeremy	Pirates	Pit	R	19	33	108	24	4	1	1	33	13	8	9	0	37	2	0	1	0	3	.00	3	.222	.292	.306
Rodriguez,Adam	Lakeland	Det	A+	26	57	160	38	7	1	3	56	18	25	20	0	37	1	1	6	0	0	.00	7	.238	.316	.350
Rodriguez,Aurelio	Burlington	Cle	R+	23	18	76	10	3	1	0	15	12	3	4	0	10	0	1	0	2	3	.40	1	.132	.175	.197
Rodriguez,Chris	Rockies	Col	R	21	31	98	17	4	0	0	21	13	6	11	0	16	3	0	0	1	1	.50	5	.173	.277	.214
Rodriguez,Chris	Watertown	Cle	A-	23	2	5	0	0	0	0	0	0	0	0	0	1	0	0	0	0	0	.00	0	.000	.000	.000
	Burlington	Cle	R+	23	19	49	3	0	0	0	3	5	1	8	0	20	0	1	0	0	0	.00	1	.061	.193	.061
Rodriguez,Diogen.	Diamondback	Ari	R	18	32	106	23	7	1	0	32	8	11	7	0	40	1	0	1	2	0	1.00	1	.217	.270	.302
Rodriguez,Guiller.	Bellingham	SF	A-	19	3	4	0	0	0	0	0	1	0	0	0	1	0	0	0	0	0	.00	0	.000	.000	.000
Rodriguez,John	Padres	SD	R	21	43	120	27	2	1	0	31	11	11	4	0	24	1	4	0	1	1	.50	4	.225	.256	.258
Rodriguez,Juan	Cedar Rapds	Cal	A	22	8	25	6	0	1	0	8	3	3	1	0	6	0	0	0	2	1	.67	1	.240	.269	.320
	Boise	Cal	A-	22	52	192	57	9	0	2	72	24	28	12	3	52	0	1	4	3	3	.50	5	.297	.332	.375
Rodriguez,Liubie.	Hickory	ChA	A	20	122	430	107	18	0	0	125	57	30	60	2	77	9	8	2	15	14	.52	3	.249	.351	.291
Rodriguez,Luis	Hagerstown	Tor	A	23	79	256	53	8	1	1	66	19	25	24	0	58	1	5	1	6	4	.60	3	.207	.277	.258
Rodriguez,Mark	Kingsport	NYN	R+	23	8	24	6	0	0	0	6	3	3	0	0	5	1	0	0	0	0	.00	2	.250	.280	.250
Rodriguez,Miguel	Diamondback	Ari	R	19	23	56	13	2	3	2	27	9	7	4	1	18	2	0	1	1	0	1.00	0	.232	.302	.482
Rodriguez,Miguel	Ogden	Mil	R+	22	69	274	78	18	2	17	151	66	65	21	0	44	5	0	2	22	5	.81	6	.285	.344	.551
Rodriguez,Mike	St. Cathrns	Tor	A-	22	46	145	39	2	1	0	43	14	12	7	3	14	1	0	2	4	4	.50	4	.269	.303	.297
Rodriguez,Noel	Quad City	Hou	A	23	39	144	39	10	0	4	61	26	19	14	0	18	1	0	0	1	0	1.00	1	.271	.340	.424
	Kissimmee	Hou	A+	23	82	291	73	16	1	5	106	24	38	26	1	31	3	2	1	0	1	.00	9	.251	.318	.364
Rodriguez,Sammy	Pittsfield	NYN	A-	21	32	93	18	3	0	1	24	8	10	11	0	25	1	0	1	1	0	1.00	3	.194	.283	.258
Rodriguez,Victor	Brevard Cty	Fla	A+	20	114	438	120	14	4	0	142	54	26	32	0	42	2	8	3	20	7	.74	13	.274	.324	.324
Rodriquez,Gary	Watertown	Cle	A-	20	67	247	58	7	0	0	65	45	17	44	1	70	5	8	1	20	7	.74	1	.235	.360	.263
Rogue,Francisco	Helena	Mil	R+	21	30	109	25	3	0	0	28	14	8	8	0	19	2	1	2	1	0	1.00	2	.229	.289	.257
Rojas,Christian	Charlstn-WV	Cin	A	22	129	468	102	27	3	12	171	71	70	46	2	147	5	1	9	6	9	.40	8	.218	.290	.365
Rojas,Mo	Red Sox	Bos	R	20	39	114	26	4	1	3	41	21	9	9	0	17	3	2	0	3	1	.75	0	.228	.302	.360
	Sarasota	Bos	A+	20	2	5	0	0	0	0	0	0	0	0	0	2	0	0	0	0	0	.00	0	.000	.000	.000
Rolison,Nate	Kane County	Fla	A	20	131	474	115	28	1	14	187	63	75	66	9	170	8	1	0	3	3	.50	9	.243	.345	.395

1996 Batting — Single-A and Rookie Leagues

BATTING																				BASERUNNING				PERCENTAGES		
Player	Team	Org	Lg	A	G	AB	H	2B	3B	HR	TB	R	RBI	TBB	IBB	SO	HBP	SH	SF	SB	CS	SB%	GDP	Avg	OBP	SLG
Rollins,James	Martinsvlle	Phi	R+	18	49	172	41	3	1	1	49	22	16	28	1	20	2	1	0	11	5	.69	2	.238	.351	.285
Rolls,Damian	Yakima	LA	A-	19	66	257	68	11	1	4	93	31	27	7	0	46	3	2	1	8	3	.73	5	.265	.291	.362
Roman,Felipe	Red Sox	Bos	R	20	47	162	44	7	1	1	56	15	17	7	0	35	1	0	0	2	5	.29	3	.272	.306	.346
Romero,Marty	Hickory	ChA	A	20	5	18	2	0	0	0	2	2	1	1	0	4	0	0	0	0	0	.00	1	.111	.158	.111
	Bristol	ChA	R+	20	36	111	25	8	0	1	36	10	10	11	0	34	2	0	2	2	1	.67	3	.225	.302	.324
Rondon,Alexander	W. Michigan	Oak	A	22	19	47	10	1	1	0	13	3	7	4	0	15	1	1	2	1	0	1.00	2	.213	.278	.277
	Sou. Oregon	Oak	A-	22	49	174	37	10	0	5	62	15	20	14	2	43	1	2	1	0	1	.00	2	.213	.274	.356
Roneberg,Brett	Marlins	Fla	R	18	49	172	36	8	0	1	47	23	15	10	0	39	4	2	1	0	0	.00	3	.209	.267	.273
Roney,Chad	Savannah	LA	A	22	24	41	14	2	0	0	16	3	4	5	0	6	0	1	0	0	0	.00	1	.341	.413	.390
Rosado,Luis	Greensboro	NYA	A	21	7	12	3	0	0	0	3	2	0	1	0	6	1	0	0	0	0	.00	0	.250	.357	.250
Rosario,Carlos	Rockies	Col	R	20	50	199	57	7	5	2	80	27	34	12	0	42	1	0	3	9	7	.56	5	.286	.326	.402
Rose,Carlos	Mariners	Sea	R	21	40	132	17	1	1	2	26	12	13	11	2	56	2	0	0	0	0	.00	2	.129	.207	.197
Rose,Mike	Kissimmee	Hou	A+	20	2	1	0	0	0	0	0	0	0	0	0	1	0	0	0	0	0	.00	0	.000	.000	.000
	Auburn	Hou	A-	20	61	180	45	5	1	2	58	20	11	30	0	41	1	4	0	9	3	.75	5	.250	.360	.322
Ross,Jason	Danville	Atl	R+	23	43	149	40	8	1	3	59	26	20	11	0	42	4	0	0	6	3	.67	2	.268	.335	.396
	Macon	Atl	A	23	5	19	3	0	0	1	6	2	3	2	0	7	0	0	0	1	0	1.00	0	.158	.238	.316
Rottman,Paul	Diamondback	Ari	R	19	17	43	6	2	0	0	8	3	2	4	0	13	0	0	0	1	1	.50	1	.140	.213	.186
Rowson,James	Everett	Sea	A-	20	53	181	40	9	2	4	65	30	24	26	2	68	3	0	1	4	2	.67	1	.221	.327	.359
Rudolph,Jeremi	Medicne Hat	Tor	R+	NA	12	28	7	1	0	0	8	4	3	4	0	13	0	0	0	1	1	.50	0	.250	.344	.286
Ruiz,Cesar	Fayettevlle	Det	A	22	10	31	3	1	0	0	4	0	1	2	0	9	1	0	0	1	0	1.00	0	.097	.176	.129
Ruotsinoja,Jacob	Padres	SD	R	20	52	172	50	14	3	6	88	37	40	40	3	38	2	0	4	2	2	.50	3	.291	.422	.512
Russin,Tom	Frederick	Bal	A+	23	19	65	13	4	0	0	17	2	6	1	0	16	0	0	0	2	2	.50	1	.200	.212	.262
	High Desert	Bal	A+	23	6	6	0	0	0	0	0	0	0	0	0	2	0	0	0	0	0	.00	0	.000	.000	.000
	Bluefield	Bal	R+	23	57	190	49	15	1	8	90	32	40	17	1	38	2	0	2	1	2	.33	5	.258	.322	.474
Russoniello,Mich.	Angels	Cal	R	20	13	25	2	0	0	0	2	1	1	1	0	10	0	0	0	0	1	.00	1	.080	.115	.080
Rust,Brian	Macon	Atl	A	22	7	9	1	0	0	0	1	2	2	2	0	2	0	0	0	0	0	.00	0	.111	.273	.111
	Eugene	Atl	A-	22	71	275	79	24	3	10	139	52	43	20	2	74	3	0	0	4	2	.67	4	.287	.342	.505
Rutherford,Daryl	Idaho Falls	SD	R+	21	46	175	53	9	1	2	70	29	23	20	1	30	3	0	2	4	5	.44	3	.303	.380	.400
Ryan,Mike	Twins	Min	R	19	43	157	31	8	2	0	43	12	13	13	1	20	1	1	2	3	0	1.00	3	.197	.260	.274
Ryan,Robert	Lethbridge	Ari	R+	24	59	211	64	8	1	4	86	55	37	43	1	33	2	5	3	23	6	.79	2	.303	.421	.408
Ryder,Derek	Cedar Rapds	Cal	A	24	62	153	36	5	2	0	45	11	11	21	0	31	2	6	1	0	2	.00	5	.235	.333	.294
Sachse,Matt	Everett	Sea	A-	21	67	237	56	9	1	5	82	24	27	14	2	94	2	1	2	4	2	.67	6	.236	.282	.346
Saffer,Jeff	Greensboro	NYA	A	22	45	154	42	10	3	3	67	17	16	7	1	60	5	1	0	0	0	.00	3	.273	.325	.435
	Oneonta	NYA	A-	22	53	197	49	4	1	4	67	18	27	22	1	62	4	0	5	2	1	.67	1	.249	.329	.340
Saitta,Richard	Yakima	LA	A-	21	44	165	41	5	0	1	49	17	17	11	0	34	2	2	1	7	5	.58	5	.248	.302	.297
Salazar,Juan	Cubs	ChN	R	19	52	186	55	16	1	6	91	32	31	22	2	40	5	1	1	12	2	.86	3	.296	.383	.489
Salga,Andres	Rockies	Col	R	19	30	100	17	5	0	0	22	13	5	2	0	32	0	0	2	0	1	.00	1	.170	.183	.220
Salinas,Hector	Butte	TB	R+	22	67	279	84	15	4	8	131	44	52	19	0	43	3	0	5	4	3	.57	10	.301	.346	.470
Salzano,Jerry	Lakeland	Det	A+	22	123	426	113	28	4	6	167	52	60	38	0	66	9	2	4	6	7	.46	10	.265	.335	.392
Samboy,Nelson	Kissimmee	Hou	A+	20	105	372	94	20	2	0	118	43	21	20	1	61	1	3	1	17	7	.71	7	.253	.292	.317
Samuel,Quiva	Greensboro	NYA	A	23	126	477	121	19	0	19	197	50	86	37	2	165	3	0	6	0	2	.00	10	.254	.308	.413
Sanchez,Alexis	Devil Rays	TB	R	20	56	227	64	7	6	1	86	36	22	10	0	35	6	1	1	20	12	.63	2	.282	.328	.379
Sanchez,Marcos	Clinton	SD	A	22	42	123	25	6	1	3	42	14	13	15	2	49	0	0	0	2	0	1.00	4	.203	.290	.341
Sanchez,Omar	Dunedin	Tor	A+	26	45	126	29	1	4	0	38	17	12	14	1	36	1	5	1	3	3	.50	3	.230	.310	.302
	Hagerstown	Tor	A	26	80	294	80	13	4	5	116	59	25	56	2	56	7	3	1	20	8	.71	1	.272	.399	.395
Sanchez,Orlando	Sarasota	Bos	A+	18	5	15	5	2	0	0	7	2	4	1	0	3	0	2	0	0	0	.00	0	.333	.375	.467
	Red Sox	Bos	R	18	16	56	15	1	1	0	18	8	3	6	0	9	0	2	0	2	0	1.00	4	.268	.339	.321
	Lowell	Bos	A-	18	33	115	21	2	0	0	23	15	5	10	0	29	3	0	0	3	0	1.00	4	.183	.266	.200
Sandberg,Jared	Devil Rays	TB	R	19	22	77	13	2	1	0	17	6	7	9	0	26	0	3	0	1	0	1.00	1	.169	.256	.221
Sanderson,David	Columbia	NYN	A	24	33	61	13	3	2	0	20	13	3	12	1	12	1	0	0	1	2	.33	0	.213	.351	.328
	St. Lucie	NYN	A+	24	50	163	39	2	3	1	50	17	13	22	1	42	1	3	0	8	3	.73	2	.239	.333	.307
Sandoval,Jhensy	Diamondback	Ari	R	18	38	149	43	11	0	2	60	22	26	7	0	41	1	0	2	1	1	.50	5	.289	.321	.403
Sankey,Brian	Yakima	LA	A-	23	72	255	75	19	2	11	131	40	52	34	2	53	2	0	3	2	0	1.00	1	.294	.378	.514
Santana,Pedro	Astros	Hou	R	20	56	207	56	6	5	1	75	40	20	21	1	44	4	2	0	33	4	.89	3	.271	.349	.362
Santo,Jose	Charlstn-SC	Tex	A	19	37	136	27	4	2	4	47	15	13	13	0	48	1	2	0	3	3	.50	2	.199	.273	.346
	Rangers	Tex	R	19	54	197	49	10	7	7	94	42	33	26	0	61	6	0	5	11	3	.79	2	.249	.346	.477
Sapp,Damian	Michigan	Bos	A	21	90	335	108	21	4	18	191	55	52	38	1	88	4	0	3	3	2	.60	5	.322	.395	.570
Sasser,Rob	Macon	Atl	A	22	135	465	122	35	3	8	187	64	64	65	4	108	5	3	6	38	8	.83	4	.262	.355	.402
Saturria,Luis	Johnson Cty	StL	R+	20	57	227	58	7	1	5	82	43	40	24	0	61	7	1	0	12	1	.92	11	.256	.345	.361
Saucedo,Roberto	Cedar Rapds	Cal	A	21	3	3	0	0	0	0	0	0	0	0	0	1	0	0	0	0	0	.00	0	.000	.000	.000
	Boise	Cal	A-	21	1	2	1	0	0	0	1	2	1	3	0	0	0	0	0	0	0	.00	0	.500	.800	.500
	Angels	Cal	R	21	18	64	18	5	0	1	26	5	13	8	1	11	2	0	0	1	1	.50	0	.281	.378	.406
Saylor,Jamie	Kissimmee	Hou	A+	22	59	181	37	3	3	1	49	17	6	10	0	43	0	3	2	8	6	.57	3	.204	.244	.271
	Quad City	Hou	A	22	23	58	7	1	0	0	8	8	5	3	0	13	2	2	2	4	2	.67	0	.121	.185	.138
Schaaf,Bob	Vero Beach	LA	A+	24	61	186	41	8	1	0	51	23	11	12	1	47	0	3	0	4	2	.67	3	.220	.268	.274
Schafer,Brett	Lansing	KC	A	23	15	47	12	2	1	0	16	5	3	7	0	7	1	0	1	3	2	.60	3	.255	.357	.340
Scharrer,Jim	Danville	Atl	R+	20	62	242	55	17	2	3	85	31	32	22	0	74	1	1	5	3	4	.43	3	.227	.289	.351
Schaub,Greg	Helena	Mil	R+	20	63	245	65	13	6	9	117	39	50	19	0	38	3	3	1	4	3	.57	9	.265	.325	.478
Schlicher,Blair	Martinsvlle	Phi	R+	19	54	187	42	7	0	4	61	23	16	23	1	63	1	0	0	1	1	.50	2	.225	.313	.326
Schmidt,Dave	New Jersey	StL	A-	23	57	189	48	9	2	1	64	17	23	16	0	55	0	3	2	1	1	.50	2	.254	.309	.339
Schneider,Brian	Expos	Mon	R	20	52	164	44	5	2	0	53	26	23	24	3	15	3	2	0	2	3	.40	3	.268	.372	.323
	Delmarva	Mon	A	20	5	9	3	0	0	0	3	0	1	1	0	1	1	0	0	0	0	.00	1	.333	.455	.333
Schofield,Andy	New Jersey	StL	A-	23	11	27	5	0	1	0	7	1	1	4	0	8	0	0	0	0	1	.00	1	.185	.290	.259
Schramm,Kevin	Rangers	Tex	R	22	23	88	29	8	1	3	48	16	16	4	0	22	1	0	0	2	2	.50	1	.330	.366	.545
Schreiber,Stanley	Augusta	Pit	A	21	112	367	83	10	5	1	106	59	31	52	1	96	8	8	1	20	9	.69	8	.226	.334	.289
Schreimann,Eric	Piedmont	Phi	A	22	91	298	75	13	1	7	111	44	33	29	2	66	26	4	2	3	1	.75	1	.252	.366	.372
Schroeder,Johnny	Fort Wayne	Min	A	21	111	425	112	20	2	14	178	54	58	18	3	119	12	0	5	3	5	.38	3	.264	.309	.419

1996 Batting — Single-A and Rookie Leagues

BATTING																				BASERUNNING				PERCENTAGES		
Player	Team	Org	Lg	A	G	AB	H	2B	3B	HR	TB	R	RBI	TBB	IBB	SO	HBP	SH	SF	SB	CS	SB%	GDP	Avg	OBP	SLG
Schwab,Chris	Delmarva	Mon	A	22	119	428	96	30	3	9	159	52	64	45	6	135	1	0	6	3	4	.43	9	.224	.296	.371
Schwartzbauer,Br.	Rockies	Col	R	20	43	154	53	9	2	1	69	20	18	19	0	30	2	2	1	3	3	.50	3	.344	.420	.448
Scott,Thomas	Charlstn-WV	Cin	A	24	123	429	95	27	6	11	167	54	52	66	0	156	3	5	4	19	7	.73	2	.221	.327	.389
Scutaro,Marcos	Columbus	Cle	A	21	85	315	79	12	3	10	127	66	45	38	0	86	4	4	5	6	3	.67	6	.251	.334	.403
Seabol,Scott	Oneonta	NYA	A-	22	43	142	30	9	1	3	50	16	10	15	0	30	6	2	0	2	3	.40	1	.211	.313	.352
Sears,Jayson	Angels	Cal	R	21	4	14	3	0	1	0	5	4	2	3	0	4	0	0	1	1	0	1.00	1	.214	.333	.357
Sees,Eric	Spokane	KC	A-	22	59	168	34	7	1	0	43	25	8	21	0	36	5	5	2	8	5	.62	5	.202	.306	.256
Seguignol,Fernan.	Delmarva	Mon	A	22	118	410	98	14	5	8	146	59	55	48	4	126	6	0	1	12	13	.48	5	.239	.327	.356
Seguro,Winston	Rangers	Tex	R	18	24	53	9	0	0	0	9	7	3	3	0	9	1	1	1	1	0	1.00	0	.170	.224	.170
Seidel,Ryan	Rockford	ChN	A	24	47	105	20	3	0	0	23	14	10	6	1	25	1	3	0	6	3	.67	1	.190	.241	.219
	Daytona	ChN	A+	24	9	17	2	1	0	0	3	0	1	3	0	5	1	0	0	0	0	.00	0	.118	.286	.176
Sell,Chip	San Bernrdo	LA	A+	26	95	321	90	12	0	1	105	47	23	27	2	68	5	3	1	13	5	.72	6	.280	.345	.327
Sencion,Pablo	Medicne Hat	Tor	R+	21	68	229	55	15	0	4	82	44	29	40	0	52	2	1	5	5	6	.45	3	.240	.351	.358
Serafin,Ricardo	Martinsvlle	Phi	R+	20	34	98	18	2	1	0	22	11	6	10	0	28	1	1	0	11	4	.73	1	.184	.266	.224
Serrano,Danny	Boise	Cal	A-	22	8	7	1	0	0	0	1	3	1	2	0	0	2	0	0	0	0	.00	1	.143	.455	.143
	Angels	Cal	R	22	19	63	16	6	0	1	25	12	6	7	0	11	4	0	0	2	2	.50	0	.254	.365	.397
Severence,Lawren.	Devil Rays	TB	R	21	9	23	4	0	0	0	4	0	2	4	0	1	0	0	0	0	0	.00	1	.174	.296	.174
Shanahan,Jason	Brevard Cty	Fla	A+	23	102	371	76	19	2	2	105	39	32	36	1	63	8	0	4	2	1	.67	4	.205	.286	.283
Sharp,Scott	Winston-Sal	Cin	A+	24	34	95	22	8	0	0	30	14	8	13	0	39	2	6	0	3	1	.75	2	.232	.336	.316
Sharpe,Grant	Burlington	Cle	R+	19	26	82	20	6	1	4	40	14	17	18	0	26	1	0	2	1	1	.50	2	.244	.379	.488
Shatley,Andy	Hagerstown	Tor	A	21	60	191	39	3	0	3	51	24	24	28	0	65	3	2	1	2	1	.67	4	.204	.314	.267
	St. Cathrns	Tor	A-	21	76	256	72	17	2	5	108	34	36	21	1	64	6	2	2	4	3	.57	3	.281	.347	.422
Sheffer,Chad	Wisconsin	Sea	A	23	101	315	62	11	0	4	85	60	35	63	0	79	6	2	2	13	10	.57	0	.197	.339	.270
Sheffield,Tony	Bakersfield	Bos	A+	23	49	171	40	8	1	3	59	14	13	13	3	72	0	4	0	8	5	.62	4	.234	.288	.345
	Michigan	Bos	A	23	48	133	31	10	1	5	58	20	31	12	0	38	1	0	5	3	2	.60	4	.233	.291	.436
Shelton,Barry	Hickory	ChA	A	23	47	161	34	9	0	3	52	15	13	12	0	52	6	1	1	1	2	.33	2	.211	.289	.323
	Bristol	ChA	R+	23	45	154	38	8	0	2	52	19	13	8	1	50	4	2	0	2	2	.50	2	.247	.301	.338
Sheppard,Gregory	South Bend	ChA	A	22	54	142	38	5	1	0	45	17	9	11	1	40	1	4	0	5	2	.71	3	.268	.325	.317
Shipman,Nate	Tigers	Det	R	20	35	113	23	6	1	1	34	16	12	7	0	37	7	0	1	7	2	.78	1	.204	.289	.301
Shipp,Skip	Erie	Pit	A-	21	55	189	48	7	0	3	64	19	26	16	1	50	1	0	1	3	2	.60	7	.254	.314	.339
Shirley,Al	Wilmington	KC	A+	23	116	340	78	13	2	17	146	54	47	57	3	149	9	0	1	8	7	.53	1	.229	.354	.429
Short,Rick	Frederick	Bal	A+	24	126	474	148	33	0	3	190	68	54	29	2	44	5	5	4	12	7	.63	14	.312	.355	.401
Shotwell,Robert	Elizabethtn	Min	R+	22	25	76	18	1	0	0	19	8	3	5	0	13	0	0	0	0	1	.00	2	.237	.284	.250
Shumpert,Derek	Greensboro	NYA	A	21	141	522	132	20	10	3	181	76	45	57	0	144	14	4	4	28	18	.61	6	.253	.340	.347
Shy,Jason	Danville	Atl	R+	23	11	37	9	1	0	1	13	5	3	1	0	8	0	0	0	1	1	.50	0	.243	.263	.351
Silva,Carlos	Twins	Min	R	18	24	53	10	2	0	0	12	4	6	8	0	16	2	0	1	2	3	.40	2	.189	.313	.226
Sime,Rafael	Utica	Fla	A-	20	67	216	52	9	5	3	80	26	31	28	1	62	0	0	3	10	4	.71	1	.241	.324	.370
Simmons,Brian	South Bend	ChA	A	23	92	356	106	29	6	17	198	73	58	48	2	69	2	1	4	14	9	.61	3	.298	.380	.556
	Pr. William	ChA	A+	23	33	131	26	4	3	4	48	17	14	9	1	39	0	1	0	2	0	1.00	3	.198	.250	.366
Simonton,Cy-Leon	Everett	Sea	A-	20	40	136	29	1	0	1	33	18	8	19	1	37	0	0	0	3	3	.50	1	.213	.310	.243
Simpson,Jeramie	St. Lucie	NYN	A+	22	59	222	48	7	5	0	65	25	19	17	1	55	4	1	0	21	11	.66	2	.216	.284	.293
	Columbia	NYN	A	22	58	204	53	2	5	1	68	31	25	21	0	45	8	12	2	11	9	.55	1	.260	.349	.333
Siponmaa,Ryan	Burlington	Cle	R+	22	6	13	2	0	0	0	2	3	0	5	0	7	1	0	0	1	0	1.00	1	.154	.421	.154
Skeels,David	Everett	Sea	A-	24	25	77	22	3	0	1	28	8	8	3	0	13	1	0	0	2	1	.67	3	.286	.321	.364
Skeens,Jeremy	Princeton	Cin	R+	19	54	188	51	3	7	1	71	34	12	25	1	49	2	3	2	19	2	.90	1	.271	.359	.378
Skett,William	St. Cathrns	Tor	A-	23	75	272	75	13	1	15	135	47	52	33	0	73	10	5	4	13	3	.81	2	.276	.370	.496
Slemmer,Dave	Sou. Oregon	Oak	A-	24	35	139	38	5	0	10	73	17	29	15	0	30	1	1	1	6	2	.75	2	.273	.346	.525
	Modesto	Oak	A+	24	26	85	25	9	0	3	43	17	13	11	0	15	1	1	1	2	2	.50	4	.294	.378	.506
Smella,Steven	Charlstn-SC	Tex	A	23	44	127	20	3	0	3	32	19	12	16	0	44	3	2	0	5	1	.83	1	.157	.267	.252
Smith,Brian	Mariners	Sea	R	20	54	223	66	15	6	3	102	39	16	21	0	46	1	1	0	13	11	.54	2	.296	.359	.457
Smith,Chris	Lk Elsinore	Cal	A+	23	63	241	64	12	2	10	110	38	45	24	0	35	3	0	3	1	1	.50	9	.266	.336	.456
Smith,David	Bakersfield	Bos	A+	25	35	117	28	9	1	3	48	25	18	20	1	36	4	2	2	1	0	1.00	0	.239	.364	.410
	Red Sox	Bos	R	25	3	9	3	1	0	0	4	0	1	1	0	1	0	0	0	0	1	.00	1	.333	.400	.444
	Sarasota	Bos	A+	25	45	124	31	3	1	3	45	24	12	23	0	27	2	2	0	6	3	.67	2	.250	.376	.363
Smith,Jeff	Fort Wayne	Min	A	23	63	208	49	6	0	2	61	20	26	22	0	32	0	1	2	2	1	.67	4	.236	.306	.293
Smith,Marcus	Twins	Min	R	21	33	102	19	2	3	0	27	11	12	9	0	29	1	2	1	7	2	.78	1	.186	.257	.265
Smith,Matt	Wilmington	KC	A+	21	125	451	112	17	2	5	148	48	59	42	5	110	5	1	7	3	4	.43	6	.248	.315	.328
Smith,Nestor	Yankees	NYA	R	19	14	25	6	0	0	0	6	5	0	4	0	9	1	0	0	1	1	.50	0	.240	.367	.240
Smith,Rick	Beloit	Mil	A	25	114	372	91	27	1	7	141	41	57	39	2	81	6	2	4	4	5	.44	9	.245	.323	.379
Smith,Rod	Greensboro	NYA	A	21	132	481	102	15	8	4	145	71	32	64	0	128	7	10	0	57	13	.81	5	.212	.313	.301
Smith,Scott	Lancaster	Sea	A+	25	61	252	75	19	0	10	124	52	52	16	0	74	5	0	3	9	2	.82	5	.298	.348	.492
	Wisconsin	Sea	A	25	67	241	80	11	4	10	129	43	49	24	1	74	8	2	2	11	7	.61	1	.332	.407	.535
Smith,Sean	Durham	Atl	A+	23	87	278	63	9	1	8	98	18	34	32	0	59	2	2	1	3	1	.75	3	.227	.310	.353
Snelling,Allen	St. Cathrns	Tor	A-	24	39	104	15	1	0	0	16	10	5	6	0	23	2	1	0	2	0	1.00	0	.144	.205	.154
Snow,Casey	Great Falls	LA	R+	22	43	130	35	6	0	2	47	19	23	13	0	33	5	0	3	1	4	.20	0	.269	.351	.362
Snusz,Chris	Batavia	Phi	A-	24	13	31	5	0	0	0	5	6	0	6	0	4	0	1	0	0	0	.00	0	.161	.297	.161
	Piedmont	Phi	A	24	4	11	1	0	0	0	1	2	0	2	0	1	0	0	0	0	1	.00	0	.091	.231	.091
Snyder,Jared	Daytona	ChN	A+	27	12	29	6	0	0	0	6	5	4	2	0	6	0	0	0	0	0	.00	3	.207	.258	.207
Solano,Angel	White Sox	ChA	R	21	9	34	10	0	0	0	10	6	3	3	0	4	0	0	0	1	2	.33	0	.294	.351	.294
	Bristol	ChA	R+	21	37	134	29	2	0	0	31	10	5	6	0	11	1	2	1	6	4	.60	1	.216	.254	.231
Solano,Fausto	Hagerstown	Tor	A	23	134	514	132	32	5	3	183	89	36	89	2	72	7	3	4	35	25	.58	8	.257	.371	.356
Solano,Manuel	Princeton	Cin	R+	19	57	209	45	11	3	5	77	41	23	18	0	40	2	0	0	7	2	.78	7	.215	.284	.368
Sollman,Scott	Jamestown	Det	A-	22	67	253	71	5	5	0	86	49	19	34	1	47	7	6	2	35	14	.71	2	.281	.378	.340
Sorg,Jay	Charlstn-WV	Cin	A	24	72	275	68	7	0	1	78	30	27	27	0	70	5	2	1	3	6	.33	4	.247	.325	.284
Soriano,Carlos	Columbia	NYN	A	22	52	177	42	4	0	1	49	22	17	17	1	34	1	1	2	5	2	.71	4	.237	.305	.277
Soriano,Fred	Modesto	Oak	A+	22	33	126	33	3	0	2	42	21	19	14	0	33	0	4	4	14	3	.82	1	.262	.326	.333
Soriano,Jose	W. Michigan	Oak	A	23	126	434	107	20	3	4	145	57	44	31	1	86	5	2	4	20	11	.65	15	.247	.302	.334

1996 Batting — Single-A and Rookie Leagues

BATTING																				BASERUNNING				PERCENTAGES		
Player	Team	Org	Lg	A	G	AB	H	2B	3B	HR	TB	R	RBI	TBB	IBB	SO	HBP	SH	SF	SB	CS	SB%	GDP	Avg	OBP	SLG
Sorrow,Michael	Bellingham	SF	A-	23	2	3	1	0	0	0	1	1	0	1	0	0	1	0	0	0	0	.00	0	.333	.600	.333
	Burlington	SF	A	23	61	224	54	7	1	0	63	30	13	42	0	33	5	1	1	0	1	.00	5	.241	.371	.281
Sosa,Franklin	Fayetteville	Det	A	21	34	90	16	3	0	0	19	6	4	8	0	17	0	3	0	1	3	.25	1	.178	.245	.211
Sosa,Juan	Savannah	LA	A	21	112	370	94	21	2	7	140	58	38	30	2	64	1	4	1	14	12	.54	9	.254	.311	.378
Sosa,Nicolas	Athletics	Oak	R	19	46	168	35	9	1	1	49	23	27	21	1	52	3	0	2	2	1	.67	2	.208	.304	.292
Sotelo,Danilo	Savannah	LA	A	22	10	38	8	2	2	0	14	5	3	5	0	6	0	0	0	2	0	1.00	1	.211	.302	.368
	Vero Beach	LA	A+	22	72	239	57	14	4	4	91	39	32	28	0	56	3	7	4	3	2	.60	4	.238	.321	.381
Soto,Luis	Padres	SD	R	22	28	69	14	2	0	2	22	9	10	8	0	19	3	0	2	0	0	.00	0	.203	.305	.319
Sowards,Ryan	Vero Beach	LA	A+	23	7	15	3	1	0	0	4	0	2	3	0	5	0	0	0	0	0	.00	0	.200	.333	.267
	San Bernrdo	LA	A+	23	5	2	0	0	0	0	0	0	0	2	0	1	0	0	0	0	0	.00	0	.000	.500	.000
Spencer,Jeffrey	Danville	Atl	R+	20	64	241	57	21	3	9	111	40	41	31	2	61	2	0	3	6	3	.67	2	.237	.325	.461
Spivey,Ernest	Diamondback	Ari	R	22	20	69	23	0	0	0	23	13	3	12	0	16	4	1	1	11	2	.85	0	.333	.453	.333
	Lethbridge	Ari	R+	22	31	107	36	3	4	2	53	30	25	23	0	24	3	1	2	8	3	.73	2	.336	.459	.495
Springfield,Bo	Augusta	Pit	A	21	59	180	47	4	2	0	55	29	17	29	0	47	0	2	1	6	4	.60	1	.261	.362	.306
Stafford,Kimani	Royals	KC	R	21	21	39	2	0	0	0	2	5	3	8	0	16	0	2	0	1	1	.50	1	.051	.213	.051
Stanton,Rob	Watertown	Cle	A-	22	44	146	27	5	0	3	41	19	20	15	1	49	3	0	1	0	0	.00	5	.185	.273	.281
Stanton,Thomas	Mets	NYN	R	21	43	152	33	6	1	4	53	19	19	14	2	36	7	1	0	0	3	.00	3	.217	.312	.349
	Columbia	NYN	A	21	1	3	2	0	0	0	2	1	0	1	0	1	0	0	0	0	0	.00	0	.667	.750	.667
Starkey,Nathan	Angels	Cal	R	20	42	138	34	9	1	1	48	15	22	14	0	39	3	0	0	3	2	.60	4	.246	.329	.348
Stearns,Randy	Yakima	LA	A-	22	57	183	47	8	3	0	61	29	10	17	2	60	0	1	1	17	6	.74	2	.257	.318	.333
Steinmann,Scott	Everett	Sea	A-	23	30	100	14	4	1	0	20	13	4	15	1	33	1	0	0	0	0	.00	0	.140	.259	.200
	Lancaster	Sea	A+	23	5	10	2	0	0	0	2	2	0	0	0	4	0	0	0	0	0	.00	0	.200	.200	.200
Stenson,Dernell	Red Sox	Bos	R	19	32	97	21	3	1	2	32	16	15	16	0	26	7	0	3	4	3	.57	0	.216	.358	.330
Stephens,Jesus	Devil Rays	TB	R	19	33	76	17	1	0	0	18	12	10	11	1	26	0	0	0	3	2	.60	1	.224	.322	.237
Stephens,Joel	Bluefield	Bal	R+	21	41	101	25	5	0	0	30	14	9	15	0	17	4	0	1	8	3	.73	1	.248	.364	.297
Stevens,Clay	Hickory	ChA	A	21	35	113	24	4	1	2	36	6	14	7	0	47	0	0	1	0	1	.00	1	.212	.256	.319
	Bristol	ChA	R+	21	48	149	32	3	2	5	54	19	23	24	0	69	4	0	3	5	4	.56	2	.215	.333	.362
Stevenson,Chad	Tigers	Det	R	21	46	158	46	18	0	0	64	13	16	9	0	47	4	0	0	1	0	1.00	3	.291	.345	.405
Stewart,Adrian	Padres	SD	R	20	22	50	5	0	0	1	8	4	7	13	0	20	1	0	0	1	1	.50	0	.100	.297	.160
Stewart,Courtney	Cubs	ChN	R	21	21	78	20	3	0	0	23	6	5	4	0	28	0	1	0	4	1	.80	4	.256	.293	.295
Stewart,Keith	Everett	Sea	A-	23	32	90	13	1	0	2	20	13	6	8	0	47	0	3	1	3	2	.60	0	.144	.212	.222
Stewart,Paxton	St. Cathrns	Tor	A-	23	65	206	57	13	0	1	73	21	8	12	0	40	1	1	0	3	2	.60	3	.277	.320	.354
Stone,Craig	Hagerstown	Tor	A	21	56	200	62	17	0	10	109	36	35	20	1	59	6	2	3	3	4	.43	2	.310	.384	.545
	Dunedin	Tor	A+	21	61	228	60	25	0	4	97	26	22	20	3	55	3	0	2	0	0	.00	3	.263	.328	.425
Stoner,Michael	Lethbridge	Ari	R+	24	24	78	25	1	2	1	33	13	13	12	0	13	2	1	2	1	0	1.00	1	.321	.415	.423
	Bakersfield	Ari	A+	24	36	147	43	6	1	6	69	25	22	8	0	18	0	0	1	1	1	.50	4	.293	.327	.469
Stowers,Chris	Vermont	Mon	A-	22	72	282	90	21	9	7	150	58	44	21	6	37	2	0	0	16	5	.76	4	.319	.370	.532
Strange,Mike	Dunedin	Tor	A+	23	51	154	49	4	2	0	57	25	13	26	0	42	0	5	0	5	5	.50	3	.318	.417	.370
Strangfeld,Aaron	Danville	Atl	R+	19	31	106	25	5	0	2	36	15	15	17	0	19	1	0	1	1	0	1.00	2	.236	.344	.340
Strasser,John	South Bend	ChA	A	22	2	8	1	0	0	0	1	0	0	0	0	4	0	0	0	0	0	.00	0	.125	.125	.125
	Hickory	ChA	A	22	41	101	15	3	0	1	21	10	8	11	0	24	8	3	0	2	5	.29	3	.149	.283	.208
	Pr. William	ChA	A+	22	18	55	11	0	0	1	14	7	2	8	0	18	1	2	0	0	0	.00	1	.200	.313	.255
Stratton,Robert	Mets	NYN	R	19	17	59	15	2	0	2	23	5	9	2	0	22	0	1	0	3	2	.60	0	.254	.279	.390
Stromsborg,Ryan	Medicne Hat	Tor	R+	22	55	216	67	10	3	8	107	34	38	16	0	42	5	5	3	8	2	.80	4	.310	.367	.495
Stuart,Rich	Boise	Cal	A-	20	22	93	29	6	1	8	61	36	24	12	2	15	0	0	2	8	2	.80	1	.312	.383	.656
	Cedar Rapds	Cal	A	20	39	133	38	5	1	2	51	19	15	11	0	33	2	0	0	5	1	.83	2	.286	.349	.383
Stuckenschneide,E.	Savannah	LA	A	25	140	470	130	28	6	16	218	111	63	111	5	96	12	2	4	50	18	.74	4	.277	.424	.464
Stumberger,Darren	Columbus	Cle	A	24	129	471	146	30	3	22	248	77	89	53	2	72	7	1	4	0	1	.00	13	.310	.385	.527
Suero,Ignacio	Helena	Mil	R+	23	55	210	71	11	1	12	120	46	63	23	3	29	6	1	5	3	4	.43	0	.338	.410	.571
Suplee,Ray	High Desert	Bal	A+	26	112	352	105	16	2	6	143	54	56	32	0	72	12	0	4	3	3	.50	7	.298	.373	.406
Suriel,Miguel	Devil Rays	TB	R	20	49	181	44	4	2	1	55	21	25	8	0	25	0	0	1	5	2	.71	5	.243	.274	.304
Sutton,Joe	White Sox	ChA	R	22	40	113	25	7	1	1	37	10	11	15	0	33	1	0	0	1	0	1.00	3	.221	.318	.327
Swafford,Derek	Lynchburg	Pit	A+	22	117	433	112	18	4	2	144	77	48	48	0	107	8	12	1	35	18	.66	2	.259	.343	.333
Swaino,Shannon	Vermont	Mon	A-	22	50	155	44	10	1	0	56	20	21	23	3	31	0	0	0	0	2	.00	3	.284	.376	.361
Sweeney,Kevin	Lethbridge	Ari	R+	23	63	203	86	19	1	14	149	72	72	60	3	36	3	0	4	3	0	1.00	5	.424	.552	.734
Swinton,Jermaine	Stockton	Mil	A+	24	40	164	46	9	0	10	85	30	35	13	0	72	1	0	1	0	0	.00	4	.280	.335	.518
Taft,Brett	Spokane	KC	A-	23	42	126	24	5	0	2	35	21	15	12	0	27	1	6	1	2	1	.67	2	.190	.264	.278
Tagliaferri,Jeff	Jamestown	Det	A-	21	72	252	62	12	3	9	107	42	36	42	1	61	1	0	0	2	2	.50	5	.246	.356	.425
Tamargo,John	Pittsfield	NYN	A-	22	55	184	41	5	3	0	52	26	19	35	0	34	2	1	3	5	3	.63	5	.223	.348	.283
Tanaka,Shuta	Tigers	Det	R	20	44	116	19	7	1	0	28	16	11	18	0	21	2	3	1	5	1	.83	2	.164	.285	.241
Tanner,Paul	Johnson Cty	StL	R+	22	41	139	37	4	2	1	48	29	12	14	0	37	0	0	0	1	1	.50	2	.266	.333	.345
	St. Pete	StL	A+	22	1	2	0	0	0	0	0	0	0	0	0	2	0	0	0	0	0	.00	0	.000	.000	.000
Tardiff,Jeremy	Red Sox	Bos	R	20	4	5	1	0	0	0	1	0	0	1	0	1	0	0	0	0	0	.00	0	.200	.333	.200
Taveras,Franklyn	Burlington	Cle	R+	21	46	161	38	4	0	3	51	18	15	6	0	50	0	2	1	6	3	.67	4	.236	.262	.317
Taveras,Jose	Royals	KC	R	20	13	47	9	2	0	0	11	3	4	1	0	7	0	0	1	0	2	.00	0	.191	.204	.234
Taylor,Adam	Watertown	Cle	A-	23	49	147	27	5	0	7	53	25	27	36	1	57	3	0	0	1	0	1.00	2	.184	.355	.361
Taylor,Avery	Orioles	Bal	R	21	9	25	4	0	0	0	4	0	2	0	0	8	0	0	0	2	1	.67	1	.160	.160	.160
Taylor,Gregory	Batavia	Phi	A-	23	19	53	13	0	3	0	19	5	5	3	0	9	1	0	1	1	0	1.00	1	.245	.293	.358
Taylor,Jerry	Kinston	Cle	A+	24	64	146	38	9	1	1	52	19	19	48	2	37	3	4	0	1	1	.50	2	.260	.452	.356
Taylor,Reggie	Piedmont	Phi	A	20	128	499	131	20	6	0	163	68	31	29	0	136	3	2	3	36	17	.68	10	.263	.305	.327
Teasley,Ken	Bakersfield	—	A+	24	21	57	9	1	0	0	10	4	2	4	0	19	1	1	0	0	0	.00	2	.158	.226	.175
Tebbs,Nate	Sarasota	Bos	A+	24	116	420	105	11	2	1	123	44	34	24	1	68	3	10	1	17	4	.81	7	.250	.295	.293
Teeters,Brian	Wilmington	KC	A+	24	61	172	37	9	3	2	58	41	17	33	1	50	4	1	1	19	3	.86	5	.215	.352	.337
Tegland,Ron	Athletics	Oak	R	23	27	85	24	6	0	3	39	10	18	4	0	25	7	0	1	6	0	1.00	0	.282	.361	.459
Tejada,Miguel	Modesto	Oak	A+	21	114	458	128	12	5	20	210	97	72	51	3	93	4	1	7	27	16	.63	9	.279	.352	.459
Terhune,Michael	Danville	Atl	R+	21	56	214	60	9	5	2	85	32	27	23	0	26	2	2	7	6	3	.67	6	.280	.346	.397
Terrell,James	White Sox	ChA	R	19	56	220	49	7	0	2	62	21	9	13	0	45	0	0	0	3	3	.50	6	.223	.266	.282

1996 Batting — Single-A and Rookie Leagues

BATTING																				BASERUNNING				PERCENTAGES		
Player	Team	Org	Lg	A	G	AB	H	2B	3B	HR	TB	R	RBI	TBB	IBB	SO	HBP	SH	SF	SB	CS	SB%	GDP	Avg	OBP	SLG
Terry,Tony	Princeton	Cin	R+	21	55	174	37	5	0	3	51	14	21	13	0	59	7	2	2	5	4	.56	1	.213	.291	.293
Tessmar,Tim	Kingsport	NYN	R+	23	65	247	70	10	1	5	97	36	46	26	1	32	2	2	2	3	2	.60	5	.283	.354	.393
Thieleke,Craig	Elizabethtn	Min	R+	22	43	146	43	4	1	0	49	18	16	27	0	26	1	1	1	4	3	.57	4	.295	.406	.336
Thielen,D.J.	San Jose	SF	A+	25	6	22	6	1	0	1	10	4	4	3	0	8	0	1	0	0	1	.00	1	.273	.360	.455
Thobe,Steve	Lynchburg	Pit	A+	25	109	359	82	15	0	11	130	49	42	29	0	93	6	0	0	4	4	.50	13	.228	.297	.362
Thomas,Allen	White Sox	ChA	R	23	7	24	5	1	2	0	10	4	2	1	0	8	0	0	0	0	0	.00	0	.208	.240	.417
	Hickory	ChA	A	23	36	100	25	6	0	1	34	19	20	11	0	31	1	0	2	3	0	1.00	1	.250	.325	.340
Thomas,Juan	Pr. William	ChA	A+	25	134	495	148	28	6	20	248	88	71	54	3	129	5	0	2	9	3	.75	15	.299	.372	.501
Thomas,Rod	Winston-Sal	Cin	A+	23	3	7	0	0	0	0	0	0	0	0	0	4	0	0	0	0	0	.00	2	.000	.000	.000
	Charlstn-WV	Cin	A	23	81	257	53	9	1	4	76	34	24	41	0	92	6	0	0	6	5	.55	2	.206	.329	.296
Thompson,Andrew	Dunedin	Tor	A+	21	129	425	120	26	5	11	189	64	50	60	1	108	1	1	3	16	4	.80	5	.282	.370	.445
Thompson,Bruce	Burlington	SF	A	24	116	366	72	6	0	1	81	47	20	61	1	107	1	11	1	17	11	.61	7	.197	.312	.221
Thompson,James	Martinsvlle	Phi	R+	22	39	124	29	3	0	1	35	15	8	12	0	18	4	0	1	5	1	.83	4	.234	.319	.282
Thompson,Andre	Lowell	Bos	A-	22	35	107	18	4	1	2	30	12	8	7	0	35	1	0	0	1	0	1.00	0	.168	.226	.280
Thompson,Dan	Helena	Mil	R+	23	50	145	49	6	1	6	75	29	30	9	1	28	3	0	1	3	2	.60	1	.338	.386	.517
Thompson,Karl	Wisconsin	Sea	A	23	119	439	128	36	1	9	193	76	66	35	1	79	6	6	5	1	2	.33	9	.292	.348	.440
Thornhill,Chad	Columbus	Cle	A	24	52	160	29	1	2	2	40	34	18	30	0	32	0	1	3	1	2	.33	1	.181	.306	.250
Thorpe,Angres	Braves	Atl	R	20	12	41	11	1	0	0	12	9	1	4	0	7	1	1	0	5	2	.71	0	.268	.348	.293
	Danville	Atl	R+	20	43	148	34	1	2	0	39	23	11	33	0	25	4	0	0	18	6	.75	2	.230	.384	.264
Tijerina,Tony	St. Lucie	NYN	A+	27	19	42	3	0	1	0	5	1	3	5	1	7	1	0	0	1	0	1.00	0	.071	.188	.119
Tiller,Brad	Watertown	Cle	A-	21	55	202	47	5	3	3	67	26	24	10	0	50	3	2	3	7	5	.58	6	.233	.275	.332
Tillero,Ingmar	Royals	KC	R	19	40	127	29	4	0	1	36	12	12	10	0	18	0	2	0	1	0	1.00	2	.228	.285	.283
Tingley,Ron	Lk Elsinore	Cal	A+	38	13	39	12	1	1	1	18	6	10	9	0	6	1	0	2	0	0	.00	1	.308	.431	.462
Tinoco,Luis	Wisconsin	Sea	A	22	120	431	135	31	5	12	212	71	71	53	1	85	18	1	6	4	9	.31	14	.313	.406	.492
Tippin,Greg	Michigan	Bos	A	24	93	229	62	12	1	7	97	29	31	16	0	62	4	3	5	1	0	1.00	2	.271	.323	.424
Tolbert,Ernest	Mariners	Sea	R	21	52	179	38	6	1	2	52	22	15	11	0	46	1	1	1	9	4	.69	3	.212	.260	.291
Tolentino,Juan	Angels	Cal	R	21	49	170	48	9	6	2	75	30	14	11	0	33	1	0	0	21	2	.91	4	.282	.330	.441
Topaum,Tom	Bellingham	SF	A-	20	38	129	35	9	0	4	56	15	18	4	0	34	1	1	3	0	0	.00	4	.271	.292	.434
Topham,Ryan	South Bend	ChA	A	23	114	392	91	17	7	5	137	50	39	53	0	106	3	5	3	18	9	.67	4	.232	.326	.349
Topping,Dan	Burlington	SF	A	21	45	131	30	4	0	4	46	16	22	19	0	24	0	1	0	0	1	.00	3	.229	.327	.351
Torrealba,Steve	Danville	Atl	R+	19	2	5	1	0	0	0	1	1	0	0	0	2	0	0	0	0	1	.00	1	.200	.200	.200
	Braves	Atl	R	19	52	146	25	2	0	0	27	9	7	16	0	19	2	5	0	1	2	.33	3	.171	.262	.185
Torrealba,Yoruit	San Jose	SF	A+	18	2	5	0	0	0	0	0	0	0	1	0	1	0	0	0	0	0	.00	0	.000	.167	.000
	Burlington	SF	A	18	1	4	0	0	0	0	0	0	0	0	0	1	0	0	0	0	0	.00	1	.000	.000	.000
	Bellingham	SF	A-	18	48	150	40	4	0	1	47	23	10	9	0	27	0	4	2	4	1	.80	7	.267	.304	.313
Torres,Gabriel	Twins	Min	R	19	22	66	23	4	1	1	32	9	5	7	0	10	1	0	0	1	3	.25	3	.348	.419	.485
Torres,Jose	Diamondback	Ari	R	19	29	54	17	1	3	0	24	13	5	4	0	18	3	0	1	5	3	.63	1	.315	.387	.444
Torres,Wolfrando	Rockies	Col	R	NA	49	187	43	5	1	0	50	29	22	22	0	46	4	3	1	4	2	.67	4	.230	.322	.267
Torti,Michael	Batavia	Phi	A-	22	59	216	54	14	4	5	91	35	44	27	0	55	5	1	2	7	0	1.00	3	.250	.344	.421
Totman,Jason	Clinton	SD	A	24	39	121	26	7	2	0	37	15	11	22	0	17	5	1	0	2	1	.67	1	.215	.358	.306
Towle,Justin	Winston-Sal	Cin	A+	23	116	351	90	19	1	16	159	60	47	93	3	96	4	2	1	17	3	.85	12	.256	.416	.453
Towner,Kyle	Bakersfield	Sea	A+	24	90	349	80	12	1	4	106	65	17	55	0	80	4	4	2	53	13	.80	4	.229	.339	.304
Townsend,Chad	San Bernrdo	LA	A+	25	116	421	124	18	1	22	210	63	72	50	1	100	3	0	2	3	2	.60	7	.295	.372	.499
Tracy,Andrew	Vermont	Mon	A-	23	57	175	47	11	1	4	72	26	24	32	2	37	2	1	2	1	1	.50	8	.269	.384	.411
Treanor,Matt	Lansing	KC	A	21	119	384	100	18	2	6	140	56	33	35	1	63	13	6	1	5	3	.63	9	.260	.342	.365
Trippy,Joe	Macon	Atl	A	23	128	439	119	22	8	4	169	78	42	55	7	48	8	4	4	47	20	.70	6	.271	.360	.385
	Durham	Atl	A+	23	5	20	5	0	0	1	8	3	3	2	0	3	0	0	0	1	2	.33	2	.250	.318	.400
Truby,Chris	Quad City	Hou	A	23	109	362	91	15	3	8	136	45	37	28	1	74	2	6	5	6	10	.38	8	.251	.305	.376
Tucci,Peter	St. Cathrns	Tor	A-	21	54	205	52	8	7	7	95	28	33	23	1	58	1	2	3	5	3	.63	1	.254	.328	.463
Tucker,Jon	Great Falls	LA	R+	20	48	174	60	12	1	12	110	39	54	15	1	30	2	0	3	13	5	.72	0	.345	.397	.632
	Savannah	LA	A	20	14	47	15	2	1	1	22	8	12	6	0	7	1	1	1	1	0	1.00	2	.319	.400	.468
Turlais,John	Rockford	ChN	A	23	11	26	4	1	0	0	5	2	2	4	0	9	0	0	1	0	0	.00	1	.154	.258	.192
Twist,Jeff	Bakersfield	—	A+	24	7	26	3	0	0	0	3	0	1	1	0	8	0	0	0	0	0	.00	1	.115	.148	.115
Twombley,Dennis	Oneonta	NYA	A-	22	6	19	4	1	0	1	8	2	3	4	0	5	0	0	0	0	0	.00	0	.211	.348	.421
	Tampa	NYA	A+	22	28	76	21	4	0	1	28	7	8	12	0	18	1	0	0	0	0	.00	7	.276	.382	.368
Tyler,Joshua	Stockton	Mil	A+	23	75	273	88	14	2	2	112	42	33	25	0	35	11	7	2	4	8	.33	6	.322	.399	.410
Ubaldo,Nelson	Astros	Hou	R	23	5	17	1	1	0	0	2	0	2	1	0	7	0	0	0	0	0	.00	0	.059	.111	.118
Ugueto,Hector	New Jersey	StL	A-	23	52	170	42	4	0	0	46	22	11	9	1	40	3	3	1	4	2	.67	2	.247	.295	.271
Umbria,Jose	Medicne Hat	Tor	R+	19	36	122	23	3	0	0	26	9	10	7	0	23	1	2	0	1	2	.33	1	.189	.238	.213
	Dunedin	Tor	A+	19	6	16	3	0	0	0	3	1	2	1	0	3	0	0	0	0	0	.00	0	.188	.235	.188
Underwood,Devin	Sarasota	Bos	A+	23	27	67	18	3	0	1	24	12	13	8	0	9	1	1	0	0	0	.00	1	.269	.355	.358
Urso,Joe	Lk Elsinore	Cal	A+	26	125	474	138	47	2	9	216	106	66	75	0	57	8	12	8	6	2	.75	17	.291	.391	.456
Ussery,Brian	Boise	Cal	A-	23	39	115	30	5	0	0	35	15	12	18	1	31	0	0	0	1	0	1.00	3	.261	.361	.304
Utting,Andrew	Frederick	Bal	A+	19	1	3	1	0	0	0	1	0	1	0	0	1	0	0	0	0	0	.00	0	.333	.333	.333
	Orioles	Bal	R	19	36	114	30	7	2	1	44	10	19	17	1	16	2	2	0	4	0	1.00	0	.263	.368	.386
Utting,Ben	Macon	Atl	A	21	119	330	75	12	2	0	91	36	19	22	0	68	5	11	2	16	5	.76	7	.227	.284	.276
Valencia,Victor	Oneonta	NYA	A-	20	72	261	51	8	0	3	68	30	25	21	0	86	0	3	3	3	0	1.00	4	.195	.253	.261
Valenti,Jon	W. Michigan	Oak	A	23	125	462	120	19	4	11	180	46	57	33	0	91	5	1	3	5	3	.63	12	.260	.314	.390
Valenzuela,Mario	White Sox	ChA	R	20	21	73	19	3	2	1	29	6	8	4	0	20	1	0	1	0	0	.00	2	.260	.304	.397
Valera,Ramon	Mariners	Sea	R	21	4	18	8	1	0	0	9	2	3	1	0	1	0	0	0	4	1	.80	0	.444	.474	.500
	Everett	Sea	A-	21	50	166	38	3	3	0	47	28	12	35	0	48	2	3	0	11	2	.85	2	.229	.369	.283
Valera,Willy	Columbus	Cle	A	21	116	393	84	16	2	4	116	47	34	19	0	88	3	2	3	11	7	.61	9	.214	.254	.295
Valera,Yojanny	Columbia	NYN	A	20	108	372	79	18	0	6	115	38	38	17	3	78	13	1	7	2	4	.33	9	.212	.267	.309
Vallone,Gar	Cedar Rapds	Cal	A	24	66	151	34	4	0	1	41	21	14	30	0	55	3	2	1	2	5	.29	2	.225	.362	.272
Van Burkleo,Ty	Lk Elsinore	Cal	A+	33	61	202	63	14	3	14	125	44	50	58	6	42	2	0	2	4	1	.80	5	.312	.466	.619
Vandergriend,Jon	Cedar Rapds	Cal	A	25	122	434	114	32	2	19	207	72	64	51	3	142	13	0	3	10	5	.67	2	.263	.355	.477
Vaniten,Robert	Martinsvlle	Phi	R+	20	33	113	27	4	0	1	34	9	9	4	0	21	2	0	2	0	1	.00	3	.239	.273	.301

1996 Batting — Single-A and Rookie Leagues

BATTING																				BASERUNNING				PERCENTAGES		
Player	Team	Org	Lg	A	G	AB	H	2B	3B	HR	TB	R	RBI	TBB	IBB	SO	HBP	SH	SF	SB	CS	SB%	GDP	Avg	OBP	SLG
Vanrossum,Chris	Bellingham	SF	A-	23	23	42	6	0	0	0	6	3	4	3	0	12	2	0	2	5	1	.83	0	.143	.224	.143
	San Jose	SF	A+	23	11	31	8	2	0	0	10	7	4	6	0	10	1	0	0	1	2	.33	0	.258	.395	.323
Vasquez,Danny	Charlotte	Tex	A+	23	77	256	51	14	2	6	87	30	30	7	0	62	4	1	0	3	5	.38	6	.199	.232	.340
Vasquez,Jose	Athletics	Oak	R	19	45	142	31	5	2	1	43	18	19	16	0	42	3	0	0	7	4	.64	5	.218	.311	.303
Vazquez,Manny	Hudson Vall	TB	A-	22	73	258	62	5	4	1	78	41	21	24	1	41	4	2	2	27	7	.79	6	.240	.313	.302
Vecchioni,Jerry	Danville	Atl	R+	20	12	38	4	0	1	0	6	3	2	6	0	11	1	0	0	0	0	.00	0	.105	.244	.158
	Eugene	Atl	A-	20	26	51	7	2	0	1	12	7	4	8	0	21	0	2	2	0	0	.00	0	.137	.246	.235
Velazquez,Jose	Greensboro	NYA	A	21	116	415	102	17	2	6	141	55	43	36	3	75	2	2	6	4	2	.67	8	.246	.305	.340
Venghaus,Jeff	Utica	Fla	A-	22	75	258	59	12	2	1	78	53	24	60	1	70	4	3	4	16	12	.57	2	.229	.377	.302
Ventura,Jose	Angels	Cal	R	19	32	59	10	2	1	0	14	13	5	13	0	26	0	1	0	11	1	.92	1	.169	.319	.237
Veras,Wilton	Lowell	Bos	A-	19	67	250	60	15	0	0	75	22	19	13	0	29	0	1	2	2	1	.67	9	.240	.275	.300
Verrall,Jared	Butte	TB	R+	23	57	206	63	17	4	9	115	51	46	15	0	78	11	1	5	1	1	.50	3	.306	.376	.558
Vessel,Andrew	Charlotte	Tex	A+	22	126	484	111	25	6	3	157	63	67	45	0	94	7	2	11	1	6	.14	14	.229	.298	.324
Vickers,Randy	Wisconsin	Sea	A	21	51	181	45	12	0	7	78	27	31	12	0	63	4	2	3	1	4	.20	5	.249	.305	.431
	Columbia	NYN	A	21	4	16	3	0	0	0	3	1	0	0	0	5	0	0	0	0	0	.00	0	.188	.188	.188
	Pittsfield	NYN	A-	21	35	133	32	5	1	11	72	22	30	4	0	52	3	0	0	1	1	.50	0	.241	.279	.541
Vidal,Carlos	Portland	Col	A-	22	32	106	24	8	1	1	37	16	11	18	2	20	0	0	2	0	1	.00	3	.226	.333	.349
Vieira,Scott	Rockford	ChN	A	23	134	442	143	30	4	8	205	81	81	84	7	89	26	2	9	9	8	.53	6	.324	.451	.464
Viera,Rob	Pirates	Pit	R	24	10	26	8	0	0	0	8	3	1	2	0	3	0	0	0	0	0	.00	1	.308	.357	.308
Vilchez,Jose	Elizabethtn	Min	R+	21	45	134	29	5	0	1	37	20	16	15	0	27	0	2	1	8	2	.80	2	.216	.293	.276
Villalobos,Carlos	Lancaster	Sea	A+	22	111	415	121	21	5	5	167	69	63	50	0	89	4	2	3	9	4	.69	9	.292	.371	.402
Vilorio,Leonel	Twins	Min	R	19	10	32	5	0	1	0	7	5	1	3	0	6	0	0	0	0	1	.00	0	.156	.229	.219
Vinas,Alexander	Diamondback	Ari	R	19	18	55	12	2	0	0	14	5	7	4	0	20	0	0	0	2	0	1.00	3	.218	.271	.255
Voita,Sam	Devil Rays	TB	R	23	22	58	15	1	0	1	19	8	6	10	0	14	1	0	1	1	0	1.00	1	.259	.371	.328
	Butte	TB	R+	23	5	5	3	0	0	0	3	1	2	3	1	0	1	0	0	0	0	.00	0	.600	.778	.600
Vopata,Nate	Charlstn-SC	Tex	A	24	129	506	127	19	9	8	188	70	55	38	3	105	2	0	3	13	10	.57	2	.251	.304	.372
Waggoner,Jay	Lakeland	Det	A+	24	64	195	46	7	0	0	53	17	21	11	0	44	2	0	2	1	2	.33	11	.236	.281	.272
Wakeland,Chris.	Jamestown	Det	A-	23	70	220	68	14	5	10	122	38	49	43	0	83	4	1	3	8	3	.73	1	.309	.426	.555
Walkanoff,A.J.	Vero Beach	LA	A+	23	29	85	24	5	2	3	42	15	19	11	0	15	0	0	0	0	0	.00	1	.282	.365	.494
Walker,Corey	Braves	Atl	R	23	3	8	3	2	0	0	5	2	0	0	0	1	0	0	0	0	0	.00	0	.375	.375	.625
	Danville	Atl	R+	23	30	91	18	3	1	2	29	15	19	12	0	30	7	0	0	2	2	.50	1	.198	.336	.319
Walker,Dane	W. Michigan	Oak	A	27	127	477	132	25	3	7	184	97	47	112	2	75	3	3	3	14	10	.58	11	.277	.415	.386
Walker,Joe	Pr. William	ChA	A+	25	54	161	32	9	0	5	56	22	14	18	0	65	1	1	1	0	0	.00	0	.199	.282	.348
Walker,Morgan	Augusta	Pit	A	22	68	253	76	15	1	8	117	28	50	18	1	57	2	0	2	5	1	.83	7	.300	.349	.462
Walker,Shon	Lynchburg	Pit	A+	23	97	323	98	19	3	14	165	61	70	49	6	99	2	0	4	3	4	.43	7	.303	.394	.511
Walther,Chris	Ogden	Mil	R+	20	63	239	84	16	4	6	126	47	54	14	0	21	1	3	2	3	2	.60	7	.351	.387	.527
Ward,Christopher	Princeton	Cin	R+	22	8	24	4	1	0	1	8	3	6	2	0	8	3	0	0	0	0	.00	0	.167	.310	.333
	Charlstn-WV	Cin	A	22	34	109	15	5	0	0	20	5	7	4	0	44	3	2	0	0	0	.00	1	.138	.190	.183
Ward,Gregory	Braves	Atl	R	19	3	5	0	0	0	0	0	0	0	1	0	3	0	0	0	0	0	.00	0	.000	.167	.000
Ware,Jeremy	Expos	Mon	R	21	15	44	16	3	3	0	25	10	17	9	0	4	0	2	0	6	1	.86	0	.364	.472	.568
	Vermont	Mon	A-	21	32	94	18	2	0	0	20	12	6	15	0	25	0	1	0	5	3	.63	1	.191	.303	.213
Warner,Bryan	Kinston	Cle	A+	22	43	111	25	2	0	1	30	9	12	8	0	23	0	1	1	2	1	.67	1	.225	.275	.270
	Columbus	Cle	A	22	81	328	87	14	0	4	113	38	34	19	1	44	1	0	5	7	4	.64	8	.265	.303	.345
Warner,Randy	St. Lucie	NYN	A+	23	109	386	107	20	3	8	157	43	69	23	1	65	6	0	6	5	1	.83	6	.277	.323	.407
Washam,Jason	Helena	Mil	R+	22	60	226	74	10	1	8	110	56	51	38	1	39	15	2	1	3	4	.43	4	.327	.454	.487
Washington,Cory	Marlins	Fla	R	19	41	134	32	2	0	1	37	25	11	17	0	25	4	2	2	10	2	.83	2	.239	.338	.276
Wathan,Dusty	Lancaster	Sea	A+	23	74	246	64	10	1	8	100	41	40	26	0	65	6	3	1	1	1	.50	5	.260	.344	.407
Watkins,Sean	Rancho Cuca	SD	A+	22	97	363	99	21	4	6	146	57	51	56	0	104	7	0	5	0	2	.00	11	.273	.376	.402
	Clinton	SD	A	22	16	55	11	3	0	1	17	7	6	9	0	17	0	0	0	0	0	.00	2	.200	.313	.309
Watson,Jon	Burlington	SF	A	23	81	318	83	15	2	0	102	46	25	31	0	38	10	4	3	23	5	.82	7	.261	.343	.321
Watson,Kevin	Burlington	SF	A	24	32	78	9	1	1	5	27	8	11	10	0	34	0	2	0	0	0	.00	3	.115	.216	.346
Watts,Josh	Bakersfield	Sea	A+	22	34	134	42	6	1	6	68	24	23	12	1	36	0	0	0	2	2	.50	2	.313	.370	.507
	Lancaster	Sea	A+	22	21	71	15	1	1	1	21	6	11	9	0	17	0	0	1	2	1	.67	1	.211	.296	.296
Weaver,Scott	Fayettevlle	Det	A	23	115	430	101	20	0	2	127	68	43	60	0	59	5	4	2	28	20	.58	9	.235	.334	.295
Weber,James	Devil Rays	TB	R	20	37	81	20	2	0	0	22	8	11	11	0	24	0	4	0	1	0	1.00	3	.247	.337	.272
Weekley,Jason	Great Falls	LA	R+	23	64	238	87	12	5	7	130	35	43	18	0	63	1	0	1	18	12	.60	1	.366	.411	.546
	Savannah	LA	A	23	1	4	0	0	0	0	0	0	0	1	1	0	0	0	0	0	0	.00	0	.000	.200	.000
Wesemann,Jason	Batavia	Phi	A-	23	49	156	34	9	0	1	46	21	11	8	0	30	3	4	2	3	1	.75	1	.218	.266	.295
Wesson,Barry	Auburn	Hou	A-	20	55	176	28	7	0	0	35	11	12	12	1	46	1	1	3	5	3	.63	5	.159	.214	.199
Wetmore,Mike	Helena	Mil	R+	22	50	202	56	10	3	1	75	44	23	24	3	38	0	2	4	11	6	.65	3	.277	.348	.371
Whatley,Gabe	Daytona	ChN	A+	25	56	186	42	14	1	2	64	24	25	26	1	27	1	0	2	9	1	.90	2	.226	.321	.344
	Durham	Atl	A+	25	49	160	53	11	0	3	73	29	26	32	1	23	1	2	0	7	6	.54	2	.331	.446	.456
Wheeler,Ryan	Oneonta	NYA	A-	23	24	65	20	3	1	0	25	12	5	1	0	11	1	0	0	4	0	1.00	1	.308	.328	.385
Wheeler,Michael	Astros	Hou	R	19	39	129	34	9	1	0	45	16	18	4	0	40	1	1	1	7	1	.88	3	.264	.289	.349
Whipple,Boomer	Augusta	Pit	A	24	128	444	105	23	0	2	134	75	45	72	2	58	12	9	3	8	7	.53	18	.236	.356	.302
Whitaker,Chad	Columbus	Cle	A	20	66	234	55	10	1	12	103	32	29	25	1	80	1	0	1	2	2	.50	4	.235	.310	.440
White,Derrick	W. Michigan	Oak	A	27	73	263	69	17	0	10	116	49	43	44	2	63	6	0	4	12	3	.80	7	.262	.375	.441
	Modesto	Oak	A+	27	54	197	58	15	1	7	96	45	39	29	1	41	4	0	3	8	3	.73	1	.294	.391	.487
White,Eric	Kinston	Cle	A+	24	114	422	101	26	1	4	141	50	52	32	1	65	6	7	4	3	4	.43	10	.239	.300	.334
White,Walt	Kane County	Fla	A	25	95	308	54	15	3	1	78	26	24	35	0	90	4	5	1	1	4	.20	3	.175	.267	.253
Whitley,Matt	Asheville	Col	A	25	104	368	94	12	1	0	108	40	33	44	0	38	5	7	2	10	14	.42	6	.255	.341	.293
Whitlock,Brian	Watertown	Cle	A-	22	47	152	33	5	2	3	51	23	14	23	0	49	3	2	1	2	0	1.00	5	.217	.330	.336
Whitlock,Michael	Hagerstown	Tor	A	20	131	424	107	22	1	20	191	72	91	108	8	132	11	0	6	1	4	.20	7	.252	.412	.450
Whitner,Keith	Tigers	Det	R	21	43	124	25	2	0	1	30	13	8	15	0	40	12	1	1	8	2	.80	1	.202	.342	.242
Whittaker,Jay	Pr. William	ChA	A+	23	83	303	78	12	3	10	126	50	42	24	0	70	6	0	2	13	4	.76	7	.257	.322	.416
Wilcox,Chris	Tampa	NYA	A+	23	119	470	133	32	5	11	208	72	76	40	1	71	3	4	6	14	10	.58	14	.283	.339	.443
Wilder,Paul	Devil Rays	TB	R	19	53	184	38	10	2	3	61	31	20	37	0	66	4	1	0	7	5	.58	2	.207	.351	.332

1996 Batting — Single-A and Rookie Leagues

BATTING																				BASERUNNING				PERCENTAGES		
Player	Team	Org	Lg	A	G	AB	H	2B	3B	HR	TB	R	RBI	TBB	IBB	SO	HBP	SH	SF	SB	CS	SB%	GDP	Avg	OBP	SLG
Wilders,Paul	New Jersey	StL	A-	23	10	27	5	1	0	0	6	1	0	7	0	9	0	0	0	0	1	.00	1	.185	.353	.222
	Peoria	StL	A	23	25	61	14	4	0	1	21	10	9	12	0	13	1	1	1	0	0	.00	3	.230	.360	.344
Wilhelm,Brent	South Bend	ChA	A	24	107	380	92	21	2	4	129	55	38	57	4	55	6	3	4	8	8	.50	8	.242	.347	.339
Wilkes,Brian	Marlins	Fla	R	22	16	34	5	0	0	0	5	4	1	9	0	7	2	0	0	1	0	1.00	2	.147	.356	.147
	Brevard Cty	Fla	A+	22	4	11	4	0	0	0	4	4	2	2	0	3	0	0	0	0	1	.00	0	.364	.462	.364
Williams,Bryan	Dunedin	Tor	A+	23	6	17	0	0	0	0	0	0	0	0	0	9	0	0	0	0	0	.00	0	.000	.000	.000
Williams,Ricky	Piedmont	Phi	A	20	84	266	50	4	3	3	69	30	20	18	1	87	2	2	0	17	8	.68	2	.188	.245	.259
Williams,Glenn	Macon	Atl	A	19	51	181	35	7	3	3	57	14	18	18	2	47	2	1	2	4	2	.67	3	.193	.271	.315
Williams,Drew	Stockton	Mil	A+	25	112	433	132	28	3	24	238	78	85	64	4	86	4	0	6	8	8	.50	12	.305	.394	.550
Williams,Jewell	Burlington	Cle	R+	20	64	236	56	10	1	7	89	44	35	25	1	83	5	0	2	16	4	.80	2	.237	.321	.377
Williams,Marc	Mariners	Sea	R	20	11	39	6	0	0	0	6	5	2	9	0	6	1	0	1	3	0	1.00	0	.154	.320	.154
Williams,Patrick	Mariners	Sea	R	19	38	140	35	4	1	6	59	18	26	12	1	46	5	0	1	1	1	.50	1	.250	.329	.421
Willis,Symmion	Medicne Hat	Tor	R+	24	40	144	39	4	0	1	46	21	17	18	0	43	0	0	2	11	3	.79	1	.271	.348	.319
Wilson,Steve	Yakima	LA	A-	23	42	113	20	5	0	1	28	9	8	5	0	44	7	0	1	3	0	1.00	1	.177	.254	.248
Wilson,Craig	Hagerstown	Tor	A	20	131	495	129	27	5	11	199	66	70	32	1	120	10	0	4	17	11	.61	12	.261	.316	.402
Wilson,Heath	Braves	Atl	R	18	3	6	1	0	0	0	1	1	0	0	0	2	0	0	0	0	0	.00	0	.167	.167	.167
Wilson,Keith	DiamondbackAri		R	23	42	143	38	14	0	1	55	19	20	12	0	21	2	0	0	1	1	.50	5	.266	.331	.385
Wilson,Brian	Charlstn-WV	Cin	A	24	101	303	62	11	0	1	76	31	25	42	1	89	2	8	5	10	8	.56	3	.205	.301	.251
Wilson,Preston	St. Lucie	NYN	A+	22	23	85	15	3	0	1	21	6	7	8	0	21	2	0	0	1	1	.50	3	.176	.263	.247
Wilson,Todd	San Jose	SF	A+	25	90	318	97	18	1	5	132	50	40	18	0	47	3	4	1	3	2	.60	10	.305	.347	.415
Wilson,Vance	St. Lucie	NYN	A+	24	93	311	76	14	2	6	112	29	44	31	2	41	6	0	4	2	4	.33	7	.244	.321	.360
Wingate,Ervan	San Bernrdo	LA	A+	23	115	383	124	16	0	12	176	60	55	32	1	75	6	4	6	7	9	.44	7	.324	.379	.460
Winn,Randy	Kane County	Fla	A	23	130	514	139	16	3	0	161	90	35	47	0	115	8	11	1	30	18	.63	3	.270	.340	.313
Witt,Kevin	Dunedin	Tor	A+	21	124	446	121	18	6	13	190	63	70	39	3	96	6	2	5	9	4	.69	9	.271	.335	.426
Wolff,Mike	Frederick	Bal	A+	24	105	352	89	21	0	7	131	44	50	16	5	32	1	2	3	6	3	.67	12	.253	.285	.372
Wong,Jerrod	Braves	Atl	R	23	13	45	13	6	0	0	19	7	4	1	0	7	2	0	0	0	1	.00	0	.289	.333	.422
	Eugene	Atl	A-	23	28	84	22	2	0	1	27	10	8	4	0	26	1	1	1	1	0	1.00	4	.262	.300	.321
Wood,Tony	Durham	Atl	A+	24	60	118	17	1	0	0	18	11	5	5	0	38	0	1	0	5	4	.56	3	.144	.179	.153
Woodward,Chris	Hagerstown	Tor	A	21	123	424	95	24	2	1	126	41	48	43	1	70	5	7	5	11	3	.79	3	.224	.300	.297
Woolf,Jay	Peoria	StL	A	20	108	362	93	12	8	1	124	68	27	57	1	87	2	3	1	28	12	.70	3	.257	.360	.343
Worthy,Tommy	Martinsvlle	Phi	R+	20	31	76	23	3	0	0	26	9	7	6	0	13	1	1	0	4	2	.67	2	.303	.361	.342
Wright,Terry	Winston-Sal	Cin	A+	26	9	29	7	0	0	0	7	4	3	3	0	4	0	0	0	0	1	.00	0	.241	.313	.241
	Durham	Atl	A+	26	49	131	25	4	1	0	31	11	8	9	0	14	0	0	0	4	4	.50	2	.191	.243	.237
Wulfert,Mark	Clinton	SD	A	24	127	450	113	24	6	16	197	66	65	69	3	111	1	0	1	26	9	.74	10	.251	.351	.438
Yedo,Carlos	Tampa	NYA	A+	23	131	463	105	21	1	11	161	58	55	64	1	131	2	0	4	1	0	1.00	15	.227	.321	.348
Yoder,P.J.	Pittsfield	NYN	A-	22	63	182	44	9	3	2	65	26	27	39	2	52	1	2	3	5	6	.45	4	.242	.373	.357
Young,Kevin	Lk Elsinore	Cal	A+	25	114	462	134	17	3	2	163	78	39	50	0	58	4	7	4	24	14	.63	8	.290	.362	.353
Young,Randel	Auburn	Hou	A-	24	40	131	30	2	0	0	32	17	4	9	0	22	5	4	0	13	6	.68	1	.229	.303	.244
Zachmann,Robert	Everett	Sea	A-	23	74	285	83	13	1	19	155	49	64	30	3	87	1	0	2	4	0	1.00	3	.291	.358	.544
Zamora,Junior	Kingsport	NYN	R+	21	60	227	55	13	0	7	89	37	41	11	0	59	7	0	3	2	1	.67	3	.242	.294	.392
	Columbia	NYN	A	21	1	4	0	0	0	0	0	0	0	0	0	3	0	0	0	0	0	.00	0	.000	.000	.000
Zapata,Alexis	Tigers	Det	R	20	51	189	63	13	5	6	104	34	41	12	2	35	3	0	4	8	4	.67	2	.333	.375	.550
	Jamestown	Det	A-	20	15	53	15	1	2	2	26	8	7	3	2	19	0	0	0	0	0	.00	0	.283	.321	.491
Zapp,A.J.	Braves	Atl	R	19	47	161	24	9	0	0	33	9	5	15	0	58	1	1	1	0	0	.00	0	.149	.225	.205
Zaun,Brian	Savannah	LA	A	23	52	147	30	5	0	0	35	14	11	7	1	41	6	0	0	1	0	1.00	3	.204	.269	.238
Zepeda,Jesse	Jamestown	Det	A-	23	54	178	37	3	2	0	44	23	17	21	0	31	1	7	0	6	3	.67	5	.208	.295	.247
Zorrilla,Julio	St. Lucie	NYN	A+	22	110	403	100	7	1	0	109	43	27	25	0	72	0	3	1	24	17	.59	10	.248	.291	.270
Zuleta,Julio	Williamsprt	ChN	A-	22	62	221	57	12	2	1	76	35	29	19	2	36	8	0	2	7	4	.64	8	.258	.336	.344
Zuniga,Jose	Bellingham	SF	A-	22	69	264	79	11	1	2	98	36	35	34	2	47	0	4	2	0	5	.00	2	.299	.377	.371
Zweifel,Kent	Rockies	Col	R	20	40	148	34	5	4	2	53	13	19	13	1	54	1	2	2	1	1	.50	3	.230	.293	.358
	Portland	Col	A-	20	4	17	8	3	1	0	13	5	4	0	0	4	0	0	0	0	0	.00	0	.471	.471	.765
Zwisler,Josh	Beloit	Mil	A	22	8	27	2	0	0	0	2	3	1	5	0	9	0	0	0	0	0	.00	1	.074	.219	.074
Zydowsky,John	Braves	Atl	R	19	52	174	33	3	0	1	39	15	12	10	0	38	2	3	1	3	3	.50	1	.190	.241	.224
Zywica,Michael	Rangers	Tex	R	21	33	110	30	7	1	3	48	18	22	14	1	24	8	0	0	3	0	1.00	1	.273	.394	.436
	Charlstn-SC	Tex	A	21	20	67	9	1	1	2	18	5	4	7	0	13	1	0	0	3	1	.75	2	.134	.227	.269

1996 Pitching — Single-A and Rookie Leagues

HOW MUCH HE PITCHED											WHAT HE GAVE UP												THE RESULTS					
Player	Team	Org	Lg	A	G	GS	CG	GF	IP	BFP	H	R	ER	HR	SH	SF	HB	TBB	IBB	SO	WP	Bk	W	L	Pct.	ShO	Sv	ERA
Abbott,Todd	W. Michigan	Oak	A	23	32	13	0	4	131	560	135	66	58	8	2	7	5	41	1	104	4	1	11	7	.611	0	1	3.98
Abreu,Jose	Bellingham	SF	A-	22	8	0	0	3	15	73	15	8	7	0	1	1	1	14	0	14	2	0	1	0	1.000	0	0	4.20
Abreu,Oscar	Athletics	Oak	R	21	17	6	0	4	50	229	47	43	36	4	0	0	0	37	0	62	15	1	5	3	.625	0	1	6.48
Abreu,Winston	Macon	Atl	A	20	12	12	0	0	60	247	51	29	20	4	1	0	1	25	1	60	3	1	4	3	.571	0	0	3.00
Achilles,Matthew	Orioles	Bal	R	20	5	5	0	0	20	84	16	6	5	2	1	2	2	10	0	12	2	0	0	1	.000	0	0	2.25
	Bluefield	Bal	R+	20	13	0	0	6	23.2	113	20	16	10	0	1	0	2	19	1	22	1	0	3	2	.600	0	0	3.80
Adachi,Tomojiro	Tigers	Det	R	22	5	0	0	0	9.2	55	15	15	9	1	0	0	0	7	1	7	2	0	0	1	.000	0	0	8.38
Adair,Scott	Idaho Falls	SD	R+	21	23	3	0	5	46.2	232	73	42	40	9	2	2	5	21	0	29	2	0	2	3	.400	0	1	7.71
Adam,Justin	Lansing	KC	A	22	46	0	0	18	80	371	84	59	46	7	4	2	3	58	0	61	14	0	3	7	.300	0	1	5.18
Adge,Jason	Columbus	Cle	A	25	16	0	0	10	23.2	118	37	23	18	2	2	1	0	11	3	21	2	0	0	4	.000	0	0	6.85
Adkins,Tim	Dunedin	Tor	A+	23	39	11	0	14	103.1	475	88	68	45	4	3	1	8	73	1	91	2	2	7	9	.438	0	2	3.92
Agosto,Stevenson	Cedar Rapds	Cal	A	21	28	28	1	0	156.2	680	143	91	77	12	7	6	7	86	2	121	8	7	8	10	.444	0	0	4.42
Aguiar,Douglas	Martinsvlle	Phi	R+	20	15	2	0	4	35.2	170	40	32	26	3	1	0	3	20	0	42	11	0	1	2	.333	0	1	6.56
Aguilar,Alonzo	Spokane	KC	A-	22	15	0	0	9	20	93	20	14	9	1	1	1	1	11	0	22	5	0	2	2	.500	0	1	4.05
Aguilar,Carlo	Oneonta	NYA	A-	21	23	0	0	7	49.2	221	44	29	20	0	2	2	4	27	0	43	6	1	0	4	.000	0	0	3.62
Ahyat,Paul	Erie	Pit	A-	23	26	0	0	4	27.2	114	24	15	10	1	1	0	0	6	0	34	0	0	1	1	.500	0	1	3.25
Alarcon,James	Padres	SD	R	20	14	0	0	2	19	102	25	20	13	1	0	2	2	17	0	14	2	2	0	0	.000	0	0	6.16
Albrecht,Daniel	Utica	Fla	A-	23	13	0	0	4	21.1	113	25	19	18	2	0	1	0	25	0	19	3	0	0	0	.000	0	0	7.59
Alejo,Nigel	Brevard Cty	Fla	A+	22	37	0	0	26	39.1	183	47	23	20	1	5	0	3	13	3	35	3	0	1	6	.143	0	11	4.58
Allen,Brandon	Batavia	Phi	A-	22	13	11	0	1	64	268	69	36	25	2	2	1	4	10	0	39	2	1	2	6	.250	0	0	3.52
Allen,Craig	Great Falls	LA	R+	24	13	12	0	1	61	268	52	38	26	1	1	2	7	31	0	46	7	0	4	2	.667	0	0	3.84
	Savannah	LA	A	24	1	1	0	0	3.2	18	4	4	1	2	0	0	0	3	0	2	1	0	0	0	.000	0	0	2.45
Allen,Rodney	Eugene	Atl	A-	23	22	1	0	12	43.2	190	47	21	17	1	1	0	2	13	1	39	5	0	1	0	1.000	0	6	3.50
Almanza,Armando	Peoria	StL	A	24	52	1	0	18	62	271	50	27	19	2	3	2	2	32	5	67	8	2	8	6	.571	0	0	2.76
Altman,Heath	Brevard Cty	Fla	A+	26	16	0	0	7	23.1	137	31	38	31	2	0	6	9	27	2	7	7	0	0	1	.000	0	0	11.96
Altman,Elbert	Princeton	Cin	R+	18	18	1	0	8	41.2	178	34	24	19	5	1	5	2	15	0	36	4	3	2	0	1.000	0	3	4.10
Alvarado,David	Pirates	Pit	R	19	1	0	0	0	4	14	0	1	0	0	0	0	0	1	0	8	0	0	0	0	.000	0	0	0.00
Alvarado,Carlos	Pirates	Pit	R	19	11	1	0	4	27.1	125	32	20	15	1	1	1	2	10	0	31	2	2	1	1	.500	0	0	4.94
Alvarez,Juan	Cedar Rapds	Cal	A	23	40	0	0	14	53	238	50	25	20	0	3	1	7	30	1	53	4	0	1	2	.333	0	3	3.40
Alvino,Royel	Cubs	ChN	R	21	13	1	0	10	18.1	82	10	10	9	1	0	3	2	17	1	23	0	0	2	2	.500	0	3	4.42
Alvord,Aaron	Tigers	Det	R	20	16	0	0	6	42.2	193	60	28	23	0	1	3	2	6	0	21	2	0	4	3	.571	0	2	4.85
Ames,Skip	Rockford	ChN	A	22	22	0	0	17	19.2	104	25	16	13	1	2	1	2	17	0	18	2	0	3	3	.500	0	9	5.95
Anderson,Dallas	Lethbridge	Ari	R+	23	16	0	0	6	17.1	87	15	10	8	1	0	1	3	20	0	15	6	0	1	0	1.000	0	0	4.15
Anderson,Eric	Wilmington	KC	A+	22	27	26	1	0	158.1	665	161	81	65	19	4	4	6	44	1	69	6	0	12	5	.706	1	0	3.69
Andrade,Jancy	Orioles	Bal	R	19	18	3	0	11	37	150	30	13	11	0	2	2	2	13	0	30	2	0	3	2	.600	0	5	2.68
Andrews,Clayton	Medicne Hat	Tor	R+	19	8	4	0	1	25.2	120	37	23	21	4	0	3	1	10	0	14	1	0	2	4	.333	0	0	7.36
Angerhofer,Chad	Billings	Cin	R+	21	13	13	0	0	62.1	317	93	71	56	7	4	4	4	33	0	48	12	1	1	7	.125	0	0	8.09
Antonini,Adrian	Piedmont	Phi	A	24	2	2	0	0	8	37	12	6	6	1	0	0	2	4	0	10	1	0	0	1	.000	0	0	6.75
Aquino,Julio	Hudson Vall	TB	A-	24	22	0	0	10	45	183	36	16	13	2	2	1	2	7	0	46	5	0	3	1	.750	0	3	2.60
Aracena,Juan	Burlington	Cle	R+	20	13	5	0	3	42.2	197	61	38	26	4	0	0	1	7	0	28	5	3	3	4	.429	0	0	5.48
Arffa,Steve	Bakersfield	NYN	A+	24	15	11	1	0	72.2	338	98	61	55	18	2	4	5	22	0	71	3	0	5	6	.455	0	0	6.81
	St. Lucie	NYN	A+	24	11	4	0	5	32.2	132	29	14	12	2	0	2	1	8	1	18	0	1	1	2	.333	0	1	3.31
Arias,Jose	Martinsvlle	Phi	R+	23	5	0	0	1	10.2	63	21	21	13	1	0	0	0	10	0	6	3	0	0	0	.000	0	0	10.97
Arias,Jose	Devil Rays	TB	R	NA	10	0	0	3	19	94	22	8	5	0	0	0	2	9	2	20	1	0	0	1	.000	0	1	2.37
Arias,Rafael	Red Sox	Bos	R	20	13	5	0	4	49.1	228	68	39	27	2	6	1	1	8	2	20	4	4	1	6	.143	0	0	4.93
Arias,Wagner	Beloit	Mil	A	22	21	5	0	6	69	276	52	26	21	2	2	3	3	24	1	58	8	3	3	4	.429	0	2	2.74
Armas,Tony	Oneonta	NYA	A-	19	3	3	0	0	15.2	73	14	12	10	1	0	1	0	11	0	14	4	0	1	1	.500	0	0	5.74
	Yankees	NYA	R	19	8	7	0	1	45.2	191	41	18	16	1	0	2	2	13	0	45	4	2	4	1	.800	0	1	3.15
Armenta,Alfredo	Braves	Atl	R	18	14	2	0	9	42.2	187	38	23	20	1	1	1	1	20	1	39	3	1	2	4	.333	0	1	4.22
Arnold,Jay	Ogden	Mil	R+	20	6	3	0	0	17	79	12	12	7	0	0	0	4	12	0	7	7	1	1	0	1.000	0	0	3.71
	Helena	Mil	R+	20	1	1	0	0	0.2	8	3	4	4	1	0	1	0	3	0	1	0	0	0	1	.000	0	0	54.00
Arroyo,Bronson	Augusta	Pit	A	20	26	26	0	0	135.2	562	123	64	53	11	9	1	7	36	0	107	10	0	8	6	.571	0	0	3.52
Arroyo,Luis	St. Lucie	NYN	A+	23	22	0	0	4	42	170	36	17	14	1	0	3	1	15	1	28	3	0	1	0	1.000	0	2	3.00
Ashley,Antonio	Angels	Cal	R	20	17	0	0	10	25.2	120	32	17	15	0	0	2	0	7	0	21	3	0	3	0	1.000	0	1	5.26
Atchley,Justin	Charlstn-WV	Cin	A	23	17	16	0	1	91	392	98	42	35	7	4	2	1	23	0	78	0	1	3	3	.500	0	1	3.46
	Winston-Sal	Cin	A+	23	12	12	0	0	69	290	74	48	39	13	3	3	2	16	0	50	2	0	3	3	.500	0	0	5.09
Atkins,Dannon	Columbus	Cle	A	23	28	28	2	0	169.2	712	156	85	74	19	5	3	6	64	0	129	10	1	11	10	.524	2	0	3.93
Atwater,Joe	St. Lucie	NYN	A+	22	19	16	1	0	86.1	365	79	47	42	3	3	2	3	39	0	66	2	1	2	6	.250	1	0	4.38
Austin,Kevie	Red Sox	Bos	R	23	16	0	0	8	22.2	110	24	17	8	0	4	2	2	13	0	26	5	3	3	4	.429	0	1	3.18
	Lowell	Bos	A-	23	8	0	0	3	15.1	68	14	11	10	3	0	1	0	10	0	15	0	0	2	0	1.000	0	0	5.87
Avila,Jose	Erie	Pit	A-	22	14	14	0	0	78	337	75	37	35	4	1	4	5	33	0	74	2	4	4	3	.571	0	0	4.04
Avrard,Corey	Peoria	StL	A	20	21	21	2	0	110.1	489	105	73	52	6	6	2	8	58	0	103	5	0	5	9	.357	0	0	4.24
Ayala,Julio	Everett	Sea	A-	22	12	6	0	2	44	185	43	20	17	2	2	1	4	10	0	28	2	2	1	3	.250	0	0	3.48
Ayers,Michael	Augusta	Pit	A	23	27	0	0	7	30.1	134	33	21	14	1	2	2	0	8	0	31	4	0	3	0	1.000	0	0	4.15
Babineaux,Darrin	San Bernrdo	LA	A+	22	5	5	0	0	17	97	34	27	27	3	0	0	0	14	0	16	3	0	1	3	.250	0	0	14.29
	Savannah	LA	A	22	13	12	1	0	71	307	70	45	38	6	1	3	1	30	1	48	6	2	5	5	.500	0	0	4.82
	Vero Beach	LA	A+	22	10	10	1	0	63	267	56	30	23	6	2	0	2	23	0	41	8	2	1	7	.125	0	0	3.29
Bacsik,Mike	Burlington	Cle	R+	19	13	13	1	0	69.2	276	49	23	17	3	0	2	1	14	0	61	3	1	4	2	.667	0	0	2.20
Baez,Benito	W. Michigan	Oak	A	20	32	20	0	4	129.2	557	123	60	50	6	5	6	2	52	1	92	4	1	8	4	.667	0	4	3.47
Bailey,Ben	Charlstn-WV	Cin	A	22	11	11	0	0	63	268	58	33	27	2	3	1	4	25	2	66	2	3	3	7	.300	0	0	3.86
	Winston-Sal	Cin	A+	22	16	15	2	0	101	409	91	34	32	10	1	1	4	32	0	78	3	0	7	4	.636	0	0	2.85
Bailey,Phillip	San Jose	SF	A+	23	35	6	0	9	73.2	308	76	30	25	4	4	2	7	22	1	53	6	0	9	2	.818	0	0	3.05
Bair,Denny	Daytona	ChN	A+	22	29	28	2	1	174.1	737	167	82	71	8	3	5	13	42	2	127	7	0	9	8	.529	1	0	3.67
Baird,Brandon	Spokane	KC	A-	23	5	1	0	2	11.1	52	10	8	6	1	0	0	1	8	0	13	2	0	1	1	.500	0	0	4.76
Baker,Jason	Delmarva	Mon	A	22	27	27	2	0	160.1	688	127	70	50	6	3	3	16	77	0	147	22	0	9	7	.563	0	0	2.81
Bale,John	St. Cathrns	Tor	A-	23	8	8	0	0	33.1	148	39	21	18	2	0	1	0	11	0	35	4	2	3	2	.600	0	0	4.86
Bales,Joseph	Hickory	ChA	A	22	15	2	0	6	32.1	166	45	35	30	5	0	0	0	29	0	24	2	0	1	1	.500	0	0	8.35

1996 Pitching — Single-A and Rookie Leagues

	HOW MUCH HE PITCHED										WHAT HE GAVE UP												THE RESULTS					
Player	Team	Org	Lg	A	G	GS	CG	GF	IP	BFP	H	R	ER	HR	SH	SF	HB	TBB	IBB	SO	WP	Bk	W	L	Pct.	ShO	Sv	ERA
	Bristol	ChA	R+	22	13	12	1	0	71.2	325	74	49	41	8	2	5	5	39	1	55	13	1	1	10	.091	0	0	5.15
Ballew,Preston	Kingsport	NYN	R+	20	5	5	0	0	20.1	87	22	9	7	2	0	1	0	2	0	15	2	0	2	1	.667	0	0	3.10
Barbao,Joe	Piedmont	Phi	A	25	17	0	0	4	34	137	30	7	4	1	0	0	1	8	0	32	4	1	2	0	1.000	0	0	1.06
	Clearwater	Phi	A+	25	28	0	0	10	40.1	170	49	19	15	0	2	2	1	5	2	14	0	0	4	2	.667	0	1	3.35
Barboza,Carlos	Rockies	Col	R	19	18	0	0	5	30	144	34	18	10	0	1	0	2	12	0	18	4	2	1	2	.333	0	1	3.00
Barcelo,Lorenzo	Burlington	SF	A	19	26	26	1	0	152.2	633	138	70	60	19	5	5	5	46	0	139	5	5	12	10	.545	0	0	3.54
Barfield,Rodney	Johnson Cty	StL	R+	22	10	10	0	0	40.1	205	53	36	33	2	1	0	1	29	0	27	0	1	2	2	.500	0	0	7.36
Barker,Richie	Daytona	ChN	A+	24	17	0	0	7	27	135	34	23	17	0	2	1	2	18	0	14	10	0	4	0	1.000	0	0	5.67
	Rockford	ChN	A	24	19	0	0	9	33	156	42	24	19	2	1	4	0	15	0	23	3	0	1	1	.500	0	1	5.18
Barksdale,Joe	Sarasota	Bos	A+	23	19	11	0	4	64.2	320	88	62	56	9	0	1	8	41	1	37	3	1	2	7	.222	0	0	7.79
	Michigan	Bos	A	23	8	8	0	0	44	210	42	30	26	3	2	1	7	33	0	16	9	0	2	5	.286	0	0	5.32
Barksdale,Shane	Astros	Hou	R	20	12	0	0	3	18	77	14	6	6	0	2	2	2	8	0	16	2	0	0	2	.000	0	1	3.00
Barnes,Keith	Salem	Col	A+	22	4	0	0	1	8	34	10	3	3	0	0	0	0	2	0	9	1	0	1	0	1.000	0	0	3.38
	Asheville	Col	A	22	17	16	1	0	97.1	408	83	43	32	4	3	2	8	31	1	76	3	0	4	5	.444	0	0	2.96
Barnes,Larry	Beloit	Mil	A	20	9	9	0	0	33.1	163	30	30	26	1	0	3	3	34	1	34	12	1	0	5	.000	0	0	7.02
	Ogden	Mil	R+	20	11	10	0	0	50.1	236	45	45	29	4	1	3	5	31	0	54	15	2	4	4	.500	0	0	5.19
Baron,Jim	Rancho Cuca	SD	A+	23	54	0	0	17	87	383	87	44	29	9	2	3	1	35	0	85	7	2	6	3	.667	0	1	3.00
Barry,Chad	White Sox	ChA	R	23	10	0	0	4	12.1	66	17	15	14	0	1	0	4	9	0	15	2	1	0	1	.000	0	0	10.22
Bartels,Todd	Fort Wayne	Min	A	23	11	10	0	0	52.2	220	51	29	24	5	0	2	2	11	0	34	0	1	2	3	.400	0	0	4.10
Batchelder,Billy	Sou. Oregon	Oak	A-	24	6	0	0	1	10.1	64	19	17	10	3	0	1	0	12	0	10	1	0	0	0	.000	0	0	8.71
Bates,Norm	Bakersfield	Bal	A+	22	4	0	0	2	5	32	13	8	7	0	2	0	1	4	0	1	1	0	1	1	.500	0	0	12.60
Bauder,Michael	Elizabethtn	Min	R+	22	18	2	0	7	36	156	31	22	18	5	1	0	2	13	0	41	8	1	1	1	.500	0	2	4.50
Bauer,Charles	Charlstn-SC	Tex	A	24	28	12	2	8	103.1	449	108	55	44	2	2	1	9	38	1	71	7	1	2	7	.222	0	4	3.83
Bauer,Chris	Jamestown	Det	A-	23	11	11	0	0	57.1	250	65	31	26	2	3	4	1	15	0	35	6	3	3	4	.429	0	0	4.08
Bauldree,Joey	Danville	Atl	R+	20	23	0	0	10	44.2	195	32	14	7	0	1	3	5	18	2	52	3	0	3	2	.600	0	5	1.41
	Eugene	Atl	A-	20	3	1	0	0	7	37	10	8	7	0	0	1	1	4	0	5	2	0	0	0	.000	0	0	9.00
Beach,Scott	Pirates	Pit	R	23	7	0	0	7	7.2	42	16	9	9	0	1	0	3	3	0	4	0	0	2	1	.667	0	0	10.57
	Erie	Pit	A-	23	17	0	0	5	22	98	16	7	4	0	2	0	3	14	0	25	2	0	0	1	.000	0	0	1.64
Beagle,Chad	Utica	Fla	A-	26	1	0	0	0	0.1	5	3	3	3	0	0	0	0	2	0	0	0	0	0	1	.000	0	0	81.00
Beale,Charles	Lowell	Bos	A-	23	28	0	0	26	29	112	16	7	4	1	2	0	1	7	0	33	2	1	0	0	.000	0	16	1.24
Beasley,Raymond	Danville	Atl	R+	21	27	0	0	21	36.2	145	28	8	7	0	1	1	1	10	0	47	1	1	1	2	.333	0	12	1.72
	Eugene	Atl	A-	21	3	0	0	0	4	19	4	2	0	0	0	0	0	2	0	7	0	0	0	0	.000	0	0	0.00
Beck,Chris	Lancaster	Sea	A+	25	23	11	0	4	86.2	381	90	45	34	7	3	4	2	43	3	57	5	1	6	5	.545	0	1	3.53
Beck,Greg	Stockton	Mil	A+	24	28	28	0	0	152.1	695	197	119	104	18	8	7	12	53	1	96	7	0	9	11	.450	0	0	6.14
Becker,Tom	Greensboro	NYA	A	22	40	14	1	9	127	558	116	69	52	7	2	6	3	75	4	97	10	2	6	9	.400	0	0	3.69
Beebe,Joey	Pittsfield	NYN	A-	22	14	14	2	0	99	398	94	39	34	3	6	4	4	17	0	74	1	0	6	5	.545	1	0	3.09
Beirne,Kevin	South Bend	ChA	A	23	26	25	1	0	145.1	627	153	85	67	5	5	5	9	60	0	110	12	3	4	11	.267	0	0	4.15
Bell,Matthew	Diamondback	Ari	R	19	18	0	0	5	32.2	148	36	27	17	1	0	1	1	11	0	24	2	2	1	4	.200	0	0	4.68
Bell,Mike	W. Palm Bch	Mon	A+	24	13	0	0	5	15.1	82	27	19	15	1	2	0	1	11	1	11	1	0	0	1	.000	0	0	8.80
	Delmarva	Mon	A	24	40	0	0	15	59.2	232	39	13	9	1	6	0	3	18	0	59	1	1	6	1	.857	0	5	1.36
Bell,Rob	Eugene	Atl	A-	20	16	16	0	0	81	356	89	49	46	5	5	3	3	29	1	74	2	0	5	6	.455	0	0	5.11
Benes,Adam	Peoria	StL	A	24	43	0	0	15	65	278	58	31	27	4	2	0	2	28	0	64	2	1	2	2	.500	0	0	3.74
Benesh,Edward	Butte	TB	R+	22	17	0	0	7	38.1	198	55	37	34	1	1	1	7	20	1	31	6	0	3	0	1.000	0	1	7.98
Bennett,Jason	Columbus	Cle	A	22	40	0	0	17	69.2	289	51	31	27	2	3	2	7	25	3	51	8	1	3	4	.429	0	1	3.49
Bennett,Thomas	Athletics	Oak	R	21	4	4	0	0	13	50	2	2	2	0	0	0	1	11	0	12	1	1	0	0	.000	0	0	1.38
	W. Michigan	Oak	A	21	6	5	0	0	20.2	96	17	11	9	1	0	1	2	18	0	17	0	0	0	1	.000	0	0	3.92
Benny,Pete	Beloit	Mil	A	21	26	26	2	0	156.2	674	136	80	66	11	4	2	6	87	2	150	11	1	7	10	.412	0	0	3.79
Benzing,Skipp	Red Sox	Bos	R	20	12	9	0	0	52	232	55	31	25	3	0	0	7	16	0	51	6	0	2	2	.500	0	0	4.33
Bermudez,Manuel	Burlington	SF	A	20	26	26	1	0	135.1	589	119	73	66	13	2	4	7	73	0	95	7	1	10	9	.526	1	0	4.39
Bernal,Manuel	Lansing	KC	A	23	34	6	0	7	95	417	123	55	48	7	6	2	3	16	0	41	2	1	2	4	.333	0	2	4.55
Bernhard,David	Auburn	Hou	A-	22	24	2	0	8	49	223	56	31	26	4	4	3	7	23	2	27	6	3	3	2	.600	0	1	4.78
Berninger,D.J.	Beloit	Mil	A	24	41	0	0	22	61.2	278	69	48	37	7	3	4	2	28	1	39	5	1	2	3	.400	0	5	5.40
Berroa,Oliver	Red Sox	Bos	R	19	17	0	0	8	31.2	149	21	28	18	4	0	1	8	23	1	28	10	1	1	2	.333	0	1	5.12
Berry,Jason	Hudson Vall	TB	A-	23	28	0	0	21	37.2	180	41	28	23	4	5	2	1	20	3	48	4	2	4	7	.364	0	4	5.50
Bettencourt,Justin	Fayettevlle	Det	A	23	26	26	2	0	153	646	127	78	55	8	4	4	13	58	0	148	11	1	7	11	.389	0	0	3.24
Bevel,Bobby	Asheville	Col	A	23	41	0	0	10	68	286	61	25	24	4	3	1	2	30	2	60	6	0	4	2	.667	0	0	3.18
Bice,Justin	Lethbridge	Ari	R+	22	17	6	0	0	43.2	201	54	34	25	7	1	2	1	18	0	49	3	0	2	3	.400	0	0	5.15
Bido,Jose	Diamondback	Ari	R	18	11	11	0	0	50.1	214	51	30	27	1	0	0	3	22	1	24	3	3	2	3	.400	0	0	4.83
Biehle,Mike	Oneonta	NYA	A-	23	20	0	0	12	36.1	171	37	22	16	1	4	1	2	18	2	42	2	2	2	3	.400	0	0	3.96
Bierbrodt,Nicholas	Diamondback	Ari	R	19	8	8	0	0	38	147	25	9	7	1	0	0	0	13	0	46	2	0	1	1	.500	0	0	1.66
	Lethbridge	Ari	R+	19	3	3	0	0	18	72	12	4	1	0	0	1	1	5	0	23	1	0	2	0	1.000	0	0	0.50
Bigham,Dave	Frederick	Bal	A+	26	29	9	0	7	68.2	307	82	52	43	13	6	4	5	14	1	56	5	0	4	6	.400	0	2	5.64
Billingsley,Brent	Utica	Fla	A-	22	15	15	0	0	89.2	373	83	46	40	6	0	4	3	28	0	82	5	1	4	5	.444	0	0	4.01
Birrell,Simon	Danville	Atl	R+	19	5	0	0	2	5	32	5	6	4	0	1	0	1	8	0	2	3	0	0	2	.000	0	0	7.20
	Braves	Atl	R	19	10	10	0	0	56.1	239	50	18	15	0	1	1	7	22	1	32	4	0	0	4	.000	0	0	2.40
Birsner,Roark	Rockford	ChN	A	21	5	0	0	4	4.1	24	6	6	6	1	0	0	0	5	0	4	0	0	0	0	.000	0	0	12.46
	Williamsprt	ChN	A-	21	31	0	0	8	51	238	53	33	31	3	1	0	5	27	2	58	7	0	2	4	.333	0	1	5.47
Bishop,Joshua	Beloit	Mil	A	22	29	29	4	0	170	737	177	84	73	14	8	8	7	62	3	111	11	1	12	9	.571	0	0	3.86
Bishop,Terry	Martinsvlle	Phi	R+	22	13	11	0	0	51.1	266	82	55	49	7	2	2	2	33	0	48	9	0	1	8	.111	0	0	8.59
Blackmore,John	Astros	Hou	R	19	16	1	0	5	26	121	22	15	10	0	1	0	3	17	0	17	2	3	1	0	1.000	0	0	3.46
Blanco,Alberto	Quad City	Hou	A	21	11	11	0	0	46.2	198	42	25	18	3	0	2	3	15	0	58	3	0	2	2	.500	0	0	3.47
Blanco,Edgar	Twins	Min	R	19	12	0	0	3	20.2	89	16	10	10	2	0	0	2	13	0	19	4	1	1	1	.500	0	0	4.35
Blanco,Pablo	Marlins	Fla	R	NA	11	10	1	0	58	256	52	39	32	3	4	3	2	35	1	37	8	0	3	5	.375	1	0	4.97
Blanco,Roger	Everett	Sea	A-	20	11	11	0	0	49.2	241	62	46	34	6	1	0	6	28	0	35	6	0	1	7	.125	0	0	6.16
	Eugene	Atl	A-	20	5	3	0	1	15.1	73	17	13	11	0	0	1	0	12	0	12	1	0	2	1	.667	0	0	6.46
Bland,Nate	Savannah	LA	A	22	5	5	0	0	27.2	115	24	8	5	0	0	1	1	10	0	24	2	0	1	0	1.000	0	0	1.63
	Vero Beach	LA	A+	22	17	17	0	0	96	414	99	42	33	3	4	2	4	35	0	69	5	0	10	4	.714	0	0	3.09

1996 Pitching — Single-A and Rookie Leagues

HOW MUCH HE PITCHED											WHAT HE GAVE UP												THE RESULTS					
Player	Team	Org	Lg	A	G	GS	CG	GF	IP	BFP	H	R	ER	HR	SH	SF	HB	TBB	IBB	SO	WP	Bk	W	L	Pct.	ShO	Sv	ERA
Blank,John	Elizabethtn	Min	R+	23	16	0	0	9	22	106	31	22	20	1	0	1	3	9	0	36	5	0	1	1	.500	0	0	8.18
Blasingim,Joseph	Bellingham	SF	A-	24	4	4	0	0	23	92	16	5	2	0	0	0	3	5	0	23	1	0	1	1	.500	0	0	0.78
	Burlington	SF	A	24	27	4	0	4	66.2	285	54	39	36	11	6	2	1	35	0	60	4	1	1	4	.200	0	0	4.86
Bleazard,David	Medicne Hat	Tor	R+	23	20	0	0	19	23.2	115	29	16	12	0	0	1	2	14	0	31	1	0	0	0	.000	0	10	4.56
Blevins,Jeremy	Boise	Cal	A-	19	14	13	0	0	58.2	283	54	49	43	4	1	6	5	58	2	39	13	1	2	3	.400	0	0	6.60
Blood,Darin	San Jose	SF	A+	22	27	25	2	0	170	717	140	59	50	4	5	2	10	71	0	193	26	2	17	6	.739	2	0	2.65
Blumenstock,Brad	Sou. Oregon	Oak	A-	22	23	1	0	5	34.2	190	48	49	38	7	1	3	5	34	1	20	5	5	3	1	.750	0	0	9.87
Blyleven,Todd	Augusta	Pit	A	24	12	0	0	4	29	126	32	15	12	2	0	0	2	10	0	27	1	0	1	2	.333	0	2	3.72
	Lynchburg	Pit	A+	24	23	3	0	4	56	224	49	18	13	4	2	1	0	14	1	33	5	0	2	1	.667	0	1	2.09
Blythe,Billy	Macon	Atl	A	21	26	26	0	0	122.2	597	128	98	73	6	4	7	12	107	0	85	19	0	4	12	.250	0	0	5.36
Boggs,Robert	Fort Wayne	Min	A	22	28	27	1	1	150	660	153	81	67	8	6	7	13	64	0	134	4	0	9	12	.429	1	0	4.02
Bohannon,Jason	Kingsport	NYN	R+	23	19	1	0	4	26	129	34	23	20	2	3	1	2	16	0	26	7	0	2	1	.667	0	0	6.92
Bohman,John	Great Falls	LA	R+	21	12	0	0	3	18.1	105	24	28	25	4	0	1	6	15	0	5	4	0	1	0	1.000	0	0	12.27
Boker,John	Ogden	Mil	R+	22	15	6	0	2	49.2	226	53	29	24	5	0	1	3	24	0	41	7	0	5	1	.833	0	0	4.35
Bond,Jason	Everett	Sea	A-	22	20	0	0	4	43.1	165	24	10	9	3	1	0	1	12	0	52	4	1	2	0	1.000	0	4	1.87
Bonilla,Denys	Wisconsin	Sea	A	23	45	0	0	14	70	292	56	21	17	1	1	1	0	25	2	62	4	0	6	1	.857	0	4	2.19
Bonilla,Miguel	Pirates	Pit	R	23	3	0	0	3	3	15	6	3	3	0	0	1	0	1	0	2	0	0	0	0	.000	0	0	9.00
Booker,Chris	Daytona	ChN	A+	20	1	1	0	0	2.1	11	1	1	0	0	0	0	0	3	0	2	1	0	0	0	.000	0	0	0.00
	Williamsprt	ChN	A-	20	14	14	0	0	61	292	57	51	36	2	0	6	3	51	1	52	7	2	4	6	.400	0	0	5.31
Boring,Richard	Royals	KC	R	21	15	0	0	7	27.2	116	21	10	6	1	0	1	3	5	0	10	2	0	1	1	.500	0	4	1.95
	Lansing	KC	A	21	3	0	0	3	3	14	4	1	1	0	0	1	0	2	0	2	0	0	0	0	.000	0	0	3.00
Borkowski,Dave	Fayettevlle	Det	A	20	27	27	5	0	178.1	739	158	85	66	7	4	5	15	54	0	117	12	3	10	10	.500	0	0	3.33
Borkowski,Rob	Mets	NYN	R	20	12	7	1	1	43	190	44	24	22	3	0	0	4	17	0	33	6	0	3	3	.500	0	0	4.60
Bourbakis,Mike	Great Falls	LA	R+	20	17	5	0	5	41.1	218	47	45	41	2	1	2	4	39	0	36	7	0	4	2	.667	0	0	8.93
Bowen,Mitch	Brevard Cty	Fla	A+	24	29	0	0	13	54	244	66	33	28	3	1	0	4	14	2	29	1	0	0	2	.000	0	2	4.67
Bowers,Cedrick	Devil Rays	TB	R	19	13	13	0	0	60.1	268	50	39	36	2	0	2	3	39	0	85	5	5	3	5	.375	0	0	5.37
Bowie,Micah	Durham	Atl	A+	22	14	13	0	0	66.1	283	55	29	27	4	6	3	7	33	0	65	2	0	3	6	.333	0	0	3.66
Bowles,Brian	Medicne Hat	Tor	R+	20	24	0	0	7	39.2	193	53	35	28	5	1	3	5	21	1	29	9	0	2	2	.500	0	1	6.35
Box,Shawn	Daytona	ChN	A+	24	14	9	0	0	52.2	218	50	28	25	4	3	0	1	12	0	32	2	0	6	2	.750	0	0	4.27
Boyd,Jason	Clearwater	Phi	A+	24	26	26	2	0	161.2	674	160	75	70	12	3	6	3	49	1	120	7	1	11	8	.579	0	0	3.90
Brabant,Dan	Kinston	Cle	A+	24	26	1	0	11	60	257	52	34	29	8	0	1	4	29	0	50	3	0	1	1	.500	0	2	4.35
Bracho,Alejandro	Tampa	NYA	A+	21	2	0	0	1	1.2	9	2	1	1	0	0	0	0	2	0	0	0	0	0	0	.000	0	0	5.40
	Greensboro	NYA	A	21	34	5	0	9	92.1	395	95	47	39	7	4	1	4	34	4	70	10	2	4	4	.500	0	1	3.80
	Oneonta	NYA	A-	21	4	1	0	2	10	49	8	8	8	0	1	0	1	13	0	11	3	0	0	2	.000	0	1	7.20
Bradford,Chad	Hickory	ChA	A	22	28	0	0	27	30	121	21	7	3	1	2	1	3	7	1	27	0	0	0	2	.000	0	18	0.90
Bradford,Josh	St. Cathrns	Tor	A-	23	18	7	0	3	53.2	232	49	27	20	1	1	3	4	17	0	63	8	2	5	4	.556	0	1	3.35
Brammer,John	Watertown	Cle	A-	22	17	0	0	5	38	173	27	22	15	0	0	3	3	28	1	49	8	5	5	0	1.000	0	1	3.55
Brand,Scott	Oneonta	NYA	A-	21	9	1	0	1	24.1	114	20	17	10	0	0	2	4	19	1	22	2	0	1	2	.333	0	0	3.70
Braswell,Ronald	Auburn	Hou	A-	22	15	14	0	1	73	325	70	40	35	2	1	2	11	29	2	77	9	1	4	8	.333	0	0	4.32
Bravo,Franklin	Pirates	Pit	R	NA	11	11	2	0	62	260	62	23	16	1	2	1	3	10	0	36	1	1	5	3	.625	1	0	2.32
Bray,Chris	Bakersfield	Bal	A+	22	17	0	0	8	22	134	28	34	31	1	1	2	6	38	0	15	5	1	0	2	.000	0	1	12.68
	Bluefield	Bal	R+	22	7	0	0	3	10	50	9	13	11	0	0	0	2	12	0	9	3	0	0	0	.000	0	1	9.90
Brea,Lesli	Mariners	Sea	R	18	7	0	0	3	10.2	47	7	10	6	1	0	1	0	6	0	12	1	1	1	0	1.000	0	0	5.06
Brester,Jason	Burlington	SF	A	20	27	27	0	0	157	659	139	78	69	14	4	7	3	64	0	143	13	1	10	9	.526	0	0	3.96
Brewer,Ryan	Spokane	KC	A-	23	17	2	0	11	43	182	41	20	16	4	4	2	1	16	0	39	3	0	3	2	.600	0	5	3.35
Briggs,Anthony	Durham	Atl	A+	23	31	18	1	3	124.2	548	131	84	61	10	7	9	3	60	1	76	9	1	9	10	.474	0	0	4.40
Brittan,Corey	Pittsfield	NYN	A-	22	14	14	2	0	98	390	74	30	25	2	5	1	4	20	0	84	5	2	8	3	.727	0	0	2.30
Brixey,Dusty	Wilmington	KC	A+	23	34	12	1	8	115	490	109	58	44	4	7	6	8	41	3	38	4	0	10	5	.667	0	1	3.44
Brookens,Casey	Williamsprt	ChN	A-	23	25	1	0	8	51.1	219	50	20	19	1	1	1	0	20	2	42	4	0	3	1	.750	0	2	3.33
Brooks,Antone	Macon	Atl	A	23	43	0	0	26	80.1	334	57	24	20	5	2	2	5	36	4	101	8	0	9	4	.692	0	10	2.24
	Durham	Atl	A+	23	2	0	0	1	3	10	1	0	0	0	0	0	0	0	0	6	0	0	0	0	.000	0	0	0.00
Brooks,Wyatt	Erie	Pit	A-	23	15	0	0	2	23.1	96	20	5	4	1	4	1	2	7	1	24	1	1	1	0	1.000	0	1	1.54
Broome,Curtis	Pr. William	ChA	A+	25	27	2	0	12	56	271	68	41	34	6	4	1	8	38	3	33	1	2	3	3	.500	0	0	5.46
Brown,Alvin	San Bernrdo	LA	A+	26	42	2	0	16	68.2	306	43	40	29	2	5	2	2	62	0	84	17	1	2	4	.333	0	2	3.80
Brown,Darold	Daytona	ChN	A+	23	35	0	0	11	52.2	221	42	20	16	3	7	2	3	20	4	43	2	0	4	4	.500	0	4	2.73
Brown,Derek	Orioles	Bal	R	20	9	8	1	1	55	219	50	19	19	1	1	2	0	11	0	37	5	3	6	1	.857	1	1	3.11
	Frederick	Bal	A+	20	1	1	0	0	4	18	6	4	4	0	0	0	0	3	0	0	0	0	0	1	.000	0	0	9.00
	Bluefield	Bal	R+	20	2	2	0	0	5.1	29	12	10	10	5	0	0	0	2	0	3	0	0	0	1	.000	0	0	16.88
Brown,Michael	Lynchburg	Pit	A+	25	34	11	0	6	69.1	356	91	66	54	6	2	4	8	52	1	62	8	2	1	5	.167	0	0	7.01
Brown,Michael	Devil Rays	TB	R	20	3	1	0	0	4.2	31	7	9	6	0	0	1	1	8	0	2	1	2	0	0	.000	0	0	11.57
Brown,Trent	Devil Rays	TB	R	21	15	3	0	5	45.1	188	37	18	11	2	3	0	3	14	3	53	0	0	3	2	.600	0	1	2.18
	Butte	TB	R+	21	3	0	0	0	4.1	24	9	6	6	1	0	0	0	2	0	4	0	0	0	0	.000	0	0	12.46
Browning,Thomas	Jamestown	Det	A-	24	5	1	0	2	6.2	38	13	7	6	0	0	0	0	6	1	5	0	0	0	1	.000	0	0	8.10
Brueggemann,D.	Portland	Col	A-	21	8	2	0	0	22.2	96	21	15	11	2	0	0	1	8	0	12	0	0	1	1	.500	0	0	4.37
	Rockies	Col	R	21	3	3	0	0	22.1	91	22	10	9	1	1	1	1	3	0	11	0	0	1	2	.333	0	0	3.63
Bruner,Clay	Fayettevlle	Det	A	20	27	26	0	1	156.2	669	124	64	45	6	3	2	4	77	0	152	13	0	14	5	.737	0	0	2.59
Bryant,Chris	Rockford	ChN	A	21	43	4	0	11	71.2	341	87	54	45	6	5	2	4	37	2	51	6	1	4	7	.364	0	1	5.65
Brzozoski,Marc	Portland	Col	A-	23	18	0	0	13	25.2	115	27	15	13	2	1	2	3	10	0	22	4	0	1	3	.250	0	4	4.56
Buchanan,Brian	Yankees	NYA	R	20	12	11	1	1	59.2	254	47	26	20	0	2	2	1	29	0	45	5	2	4	1	.800	1	0	3.02
Buckles,Brandall	Charlotte	Tex	A+	24	21	3	0	5	55	228	55	25	22	3	5	1	2	13	1	43	2	1	1	4	.200	0	0	3.60
Buckley,Matthew	Billings	Cin	R+	23	24	0	0	5	45	213	55	36	25	4	1	7	2	22	1	37	5	0	1	2	.333	0	0	5.00
Buckman,Thomas	Hickory	ChA	A	23	16	0	0	13	28	126	36	16	8	3	0	2	1	7	0	15	2	2	0	3	.000	0	1	2.57
	Bristol	ChA	R+	23	17	7	1	5	51.2	245	62	39	28	5	1	0	9	21	1	51	9	2	1	6	.143	0	0	4.88
Bullock,Brian	White Sox	ChA	R	20	1	0	0	0	1	4	0	0	0	0	0	0	0	2	0	0	0	0	0	0	.000	0	0	0.00
Bullock,Craig	St. Lucie	NYN	A+	25	7	0	0	5	5.2	30	8	6	5	0	1	0	0	5	1	4	1	0	0	2	.000	0	0	7.94
Bullock,Derek	Augusta	Pit	A	24	14	8	2	0	60.2	252	55	18	14	1	4	1	3	16	0	52	3	1	2	4	.333	1	0	2.08
Burchart,Kyle	Medicne Hat	Tor	R+	20	15	15	0	0	72.1	359	75	69	53	8	4	5	0	67	0	33	8	2	4	7	.364	0	0	6.59

1996 Pitching — Single-A and Rookie Leagues

HOW MUCH HE PITCHED											WHAT HE GAVE UP												THE RESULTS					
Player	Team	Org	Lg	A	G	GS	CG	GF	IP	BFP	H	R	ER	HR	SH	SF	HB	TBB	IBB	SO	WP	Bk	W	L	Pct.	ShO	Sv	ERA
Burger,Rob	Piedmont	Phi	A	21	27	26	2	1	160	673	129	74	60	9	5	8	9	61	0	171	7	6	10	12	.455	2	0	3.38
Burgus,Travis	Kane County	Fla	A	24	30	7	1	11	96.1	404	80	29	19	1	4	3	5	39	1	111	9	1	5	4	.556	0	4	1.78
Burke,Ethan	Kingsport	NYN	R+	21	9	0	0	5	10	59	25	20	19	3	0	1	1	6	0	5	0	0	0	3	.000	0	0	17.10
Burnett,A.J.	Kingsport	NYN	R+	20	12	12	0	0	58	245	31	26	25	0	1	2	7	54	0	68	16	3	4	0	1.000	0	0	3.88
Burnside,Adrian	Great Falls	LA	R+	20	14	5	0	1	41	204	44	35	31	3	0	2	6	38	0	33	6	0	1	3	.250	0	0	6.80
Burt,Chris	Stockton	Mil	A+	24	1	0	0	0	0.1	5	3	2	2	0	0	0	0	1	0	0	0	0	0	0	.000	0	0	54.00
Burton,Jaime	Spokane	KC	A-	22	11	0	0	5	13.1	67	11	11	8	2	0	1	3	13	0	12	4	0	0	1	.000	0	0	5.40
Bush,Craig	Bakersfield	Bos	A+	23	41	0	0	28	72.1	332	84	44	40	8	4	2	3	36	0	80	5	0	4	6	.400	0	8	4.98
	Michigan	Bos	A	23	4	0	0	0	8	36	11	3	3	0	0	0	0	2	0	7	1	0	1	1	.500	0	0	3.38
Bussa,Todd	Rancho Cuca	SD	A+	24	16	0	0	5	16.2	93	27	20	18	3	1	0	1	16	1	19	0	0	0	1	.000	0	0	9.72
	Clinton	SD	A	24	32	0	0	31	34.2	140	22	7	5	0	1	0	3	7	0	50	1	0	1	0	1.000	0	18	1.30
Buteaux,Shane	South Bend	ChA	A	25	25	0	0	11	39	178	37	20	13	0	1	3	2	15	0	33	4	1	3	4	.429	0	2	3.00
	Pr. William	ChA	A+	25	23	0	0	17	40.1	171	34	18	15	3	7	1	3	22	1	29	2	0	2	3	.400	0	2	3.35
Caddell,Carl	Princeton	Cin	R+	21	9	9	0	0	31	163	33	31	23	5	1	2	4	32	0	33	4	1	2	5	.286	0	0	6.68
Cafaro,Robert	Devil Rays	TB	R	21	2	0	0	0	3	9	0	0	0	0	0	0	0	0	0	3	0	0	0	0	.000	0	0	0.00
Cafferty,Jason	Batavia	Phi	A-	23	14	6	0	2	40.2	183	44	30	29	4	2	0	5	14	0	35	4	1	3	4	.429	0	0	6.42
Cain,Travis	Hudson Vall	TB	A-	21	15	15	0	0	76.1	337	67	50	39	2	0	5	3	44	0	87	12	0	2	5	.286	0	0	4.60
Caldwell,David	Kinston	Cle	A+	22	23	23	0	0	139	582	142	66	51	11	4	3	1	37	0	80	1	2	13	9	.591	0	0	3.30
Calero,Enrique	Spokane	KC	A-	22	17	11	0	3	75	318	77	34	21	5	0	6	3	18	0	61	2	2	4	2	.667	0	1	2.52
Callahan,Damon	Charlstn-WV	Cin	A	21	27	19	0	4	102.2	458	112	66	60	5	3	3	5	39	0	85	11	2	5	8	.385	0	1	5.26
Callaway,Michael	Butte	TB	R+	22	16	11	0	1	63	274	70	37	26	5	0	3	3	25	0	57	7	0	6	2	.750	0	0	3.71
Calmus,Lance	Watertown	Cle	A-	24	11	11	0	0	46.1	212	53	40	33	8	2	0	0	18	1	51	2	0	1	3	.250	0	0	6.41
Calvert,Klae	Red Sox	Bos	R	20	20	3	0	11	35.2	169	41	29	21	5	2	2	2	17	1	34	3	0	1	4	.200	0	3	5.30
Cames,Aaron	Utica	Fla	A-	21	18	9	1	3	73.2	301	60	28	23	2	3	5	2	18	2	77	5	4	6	2	.750	0	0	2.81
Camp,Jared	Beloit	Mil	A	22	11	11	0	0	53	251	56	42	32	4	3	9	2	39	0	47	10	1	3	5	.375	0	0	5.43
	Watertown	Cle	A-	22	15	15	1	0	95.2	380	68	29	18	2	1	1	7	30	0	99	6	0	10	2	.833	1	0	1.69
Campbell,Tedde	Erie	Pit	A-	24	27	0	0	15	32.1	140	24	17	12	2	2	1	6	16	0	30	3	0	3	4	.429	0	4	3.34
Campbell,Tim	Clinton	SD	A	24	42	0	0	21	63.1	260	44	27	22	4	5	1	4	18	3	67	6	0	0	3	.000	0	3	3.13
Cana,Nelson	Stockton	Mil	A+	22	29	0	0	13	52.2	239	47	30	26	4	7	2	1	36	2	36	2	2	4	4	.500	0	2	4.44
	Beloit	Mil	A	22	21	0	0	12	35	157	34	15	11	2	1	1	0	21	6	38	2	2	3	0	1.000	0	4	2.83
Canciobello,Ant.	Braves	Atl	R	20	15	0	0	12	35.1	151	30	10	9	1	3	1	0	16	0	30	7	0	1	1	.500	0	3	2.29
Cannon,Jonathan	Williamsprt	ChN	A-	22	14	13	0	1	83.1	329	61	31	28	6	0	0	3	26	0	66	2	5	6	4	.600	0	0	3.02
Cannon,Kevan	Michigan	Bos	A	22	37	0	0	17	73	308	70	24	21	0	5	3	4	21	4	72	5	1	2	6	.250	0	5	2.59
	Sarasota	Bos	A+	22	2	0	0	1	1	5	1	0	0	0	0	0	1	0	0	3	0	0	0	0	.000	0	0	0.00
Cantu,Alvin	Royals	KC	R	20	9	9	0	0	48.2	205	54	24	20	4	0	0	0	12	0	42	0	0	4	2	.667	0	0	3.70
Carcamo,Kevin	Royals	KC	R	NA	9	0	0	5	24.2	95	15	9	7	3	2	0	2	5	0	22	0	0	2	0	1.000	0	2	2.55
	Spokane	KC	A-	NA	10	0	0	3	21.1	101	31	19	15	3	0	0	4	7	0	13	1	0	0	0	.000	0	0	6.33
Cardona,Steve	White Sox	ChA	R	23	15	0	0	8	24	108	28	10	7	0	2	1	2	9	0	31	1	2	1	1	.500	0	0	2.63
	Bristol	ChA	R+	23	6	0	0	2	5	27	7	3	3	0	0	0	0	4	0	7	2	0	0	1	.000	0	0	5.40
Carl,Todd	Daytona	ChN	A+	24	5	0	0	3	8.2	49	19	11	7	0	3	1	0	6	0	2	1	0	0	1	.000	0	0	7.27
Carlson,Garret	Bristol	ChA	R+	23	16	0	0	7	24.1	149	43	48	33	4	0	1	3	29	0	20	10	0	0	0	.000	0	0	12.21
Carlyle,Earl	Princeton	Cin	R+	19	10	9	1	1	46.1	204	47	33	24	4	2	1	1	16	0	42	8	0	2	4	.333	0	0	4.66
Carmody,Brian	Clinton	SD	A	22	13	13	1	0	76.2	325	79	42	30	4	5	4	1	22	1	46	4	4	7	4	.636	0	0	3.52
Carr,Tim	Mets	NYN	R	19	16	2	0	10	39.2	174	34	20	17	2	6	1	4	13	1	34	3	1	0	3	.000	0	6	3.86
Carter,Lance	Wilmington	KC	A+	22	16	12	0	3	65.1	292	81	50	46	8	1	0	2	17	2	49	3	0	3	6	.333	0	0	6.34
Caruthers,Clay	Winston-Sal	Cin	A+	24	28	28	2	0	169	745	179	93	82	20	3	7	13	60	1	105	11	2	10	10	.500	0	0	4.37
Carvelli,Mike	Brevard Cty	Fla	A+	24	47	0	0	23	71.1	297	69	20	18	2	4	2	5	16	0	46	2	0	4	3	.571	0	1	2.27
Case,Christopher	Macon	Atl	A	22	23	4	0	9	53	240	52	35	24	2	0	3	2	25	3	36	7	2	2	4	.333	0	0	4.08
Casey,Shaw	Marlins	Fla	R	22	15	0	0	9	28.1	128	22	12	11	1	2	1	4	18	2	25	4	2	2	3	.400	0	2	3.49
Castillo,Alberto	Bellingham	SF	A-	21	9	7	0	1	24	102	20	5	5	2	0	0	3	12	0	18	2	1	3	0	1.000	0	0	1.88
Castillo,Carlos	South Bend	ChA	A	22	20	19	5	1	133.1	557	131	74	60	12	3	9	5	29	0	128	9	6	9	9	.500	0	0	4.05
	Pr. William	ChA	A+	22	6	6	4	0	43.1	180	45	22	19	0	3	5	2	4	1	30	1	1	2	4	.333	0	0	3.95
Castro,Tony	Kane County	Fla	A	25	39	0	0	16	66.1	287	55	38	26	2	4	3	1	31	0	63	7	3	6	7	.462	0	7	3.53
Castro,Nelson	San Bernrdo	LA	A+	25	12	0	0	6	20	92	25	14	14	3	0	1	0	9	4	22	3	1	2	4	.333	0	1	6.30
Ceasar,Donald	Braves	Atl	R	18	10	3	0	3	24.1	106	25	12	12	1	3	0	0	15	0	17	2	1	0	1	.000	0	0	4.44
Celta,Nicolas	Astros	Hou	R	19	17	0	0	6	26.2	124	30	19	10	0	2	2	3	8	1	30	6	2	2	2	.500	0	0	3.38
Censale,Silvio	Clearwater	Phi	A+	25	24	22	1	1	126.1	546	118	65	55	5	3	6	7	54	1	100	4	3	8	9	.471	1	0	3.92
Centeno,Jose	Delmarva	Mon	A	24	11	0	0	2	23.2	95	20	7	6	1	1	0	2	4	0	22	0	0	1	0	1.000	0	0	2.28
	W. Palm Bch	Mon	A+	24	37	0	0	13	60	261	64	30	26	4	2	3	1	19	2	47	1	0	4	4	.500	0	4	3.90
Cervantes,Peter	Great Falls	LA	R+	22	9	8	1	1	51.1	220	52	29	17	0	0	2	4	11	0	40	4	1	3	4	.429	0	0	2.98
Chacon,Shawn	Rockies	Col	R	19	11	11	1	0	56.1	241	46	17	10	1	0	2	4	15	0	64	3	2	1	2	.333	0	0	1.60
	Portland	Col	A-	19	4	4	0	0	19.2	92	24	18	15	2	0	0	1	9	0	17	5	0	0	2	.000	0	0	6.86
Chambers,Scott	Vero Beach	LA	A+	21	10	0	0	3	12	50	7	6	3	1	1	0	0	5	0	20	1	0	0	0	.000	0	0	2.25
Chaney,Michael	Erie	Pit	A-	22	10	5	0	2	29	125	27	20	17	1	2	3	1	14	1	21	1	3	1	1	.500	0	0	5.28
Chantres,Carlos	Hickory	ChA	A	21	18	18	0	0	119.2	497	108	63	50	10	6	3	1	38	0	93	8	5	6	7	.462	0	0	3.76
	South Bend	ChA	A	21	10	9	1	0	65	274	61	31	26	3	1	2	2	19	0	41	3	1	4	5	.444	0	0	3.60
Chapman,Walker	Fort Wayne	Min	A	21	19	18	1	0	97	436	107	61	51	3	1	4	4	41	0	61	6	1	6	8	.429	0	0	4.73
Chapman,Jake	Spokane	KC	A-	23	19	7	0	3	68.1	274	44	19	18	2	2	2	6	20	1	71	3	1	7	1	.875	0	1	2.37
Charbonneau,Marc	Savannah	LA	A	21	25	9	0	6	80.1	353	84	52	42	6	2	3	3	31	2	82	6	2	4	6	.400	0	0	4.71
Chavarria,David	Charlotte	Tex	A+	24	38	4	0	22	81.2	364	76	46	28	4	3	8	0	43	0	76	14	1	1	6	.143	0	7	3.09
Chavez,Mark	Lethbridge	Ari	R+	24	24	0	0	14	30	134	35	20	12	3	2	2	2	4	1	26	3	0	1	2	.333	0	4	3.60
Chen,Bruce	Eugene	Atl	A-	20	11	8	0	0	35.2	151	23	13	9	1	1	0	3	14	0	55	2	1	4	1	.800	0	0	2.27
Christianson,Rob.	Mariners	Sea	R	21	14	9	0	3	64.2	271	63	30	27	2	1	2	4	13	0	36	2	3	5	1	.833	0	2	3.76
Christman,Scott	White Sox	ChA	R	25	4	4	0	0	12	57	13	8	5	0	0	1	2	4	0	13	1	0	1	1	.500	0	0	3.75
	Pr. William	ChA	A+	25	1	1	0	0	5	21	4	0	0	0	0	0	0	3	0	4	0	0	1	0	1.000	0	0	0.00
Christman,Tim	Portland	Col	A-	22	21	0	0	7	40	176	30	23	19	6	1	3	1	23	0	56	2	1	1	2	.333	0	2	4.28
Christmas,Mo	Macon	Atl	A	23	39	1	0	14	83.1	364	89	45	38	9	2	7	4	21	3	62	4	1	5	4	.556	0	1	4.10

1996 Pitching — Single-A and Rookie Leagues

HOW MUCH HE PITCHED											WHAT HE GAVE UP												THE RESULTS					
Player	Team	Org	Lg	A	G	GS	CG	GF	IP	BFP	H	R	ER	HR	SH	SF	HB	TBB	IBB	SO	WP	Bk	W	L	Pct.	ShO	Sv	ERA
Cintron,Jose	Cedar Rapds	Cal	A	21	28	28	1	0	178.2	754	192	88	77	15	5	7	7	41	2	127	6	3	10	8	.556	0	0	3.88
Civit,Xavier	Delmarva	Mon	A	24	34	0	0	14	51.1	226	42	31	21	4	2	4	3	20	0	57	4	0	3	4	.429	0	0	3.68
Clark,Bryan	New Jersey	StL	A-	24	32	0	0	14	44	188	42	21	14	3	2	3	0	15	3	29	3	0	3	5	.375	0	1	2.86
Clark,Chris	Clinton	SD	A	22	24	11	0	7	82	385	96	58	46	5	4	3	7	51	1	74	9	1	3	8	.273	0	1	5.05
Clark,Greg	Twins	Min	R	19	13	12	0	0	66.1	302	84	42	25	4	4	1	5	19	0	37	3	1	6	4	.600	0	0	3.39
Classen,Ender	Pirates	Pit	R	19	7	0	0	3	7.2	37	12	5	4	0	0	0	1	3	0	6	1	1	1	1	.500	0	1	4.70
Clement,Matt	Clinton	SD	A	22	16	16	1	0	96.1	410	66	31	30	3	1	3	9	52	0	109	15	0	8	3	.727	1	0	2.80
	Rancho Cuca	SD	A+	22	11	11	0	0	56.1	261	61	40	35	8	5	3	9	26	0	75	5	1	4	5	.444	0	0	5.59
Clifford,Eric	Everett	Sea	A-	22	2	0	0	1	3	15	4	2	2	0	1	0	1	1	0	4	1	0	0	0	.000	0	0	6.00
	Lancaster	Sea	A+	22	11	0	0	5	24	99	21	14	14	2	0	4	4	5	0	11	4	0	0	0	.000	0	1	5.25
Cloud,Antonia	Billings	Cin	R+	21	12	11	0	0	53.2	268	69	53	38	8	3	2	5	34	1	44	8	0	0	5	.000	0	0	6.37
Cloude,Ken	Lancaster	Sea	A+	22	28	28	1	0	168.1	727	167	94	79	15	4	6	8	60	0	161	6	1	15	4	.789	0	0	4.22
Cobb,Trevor	Fort Myers	Min	A+	23	31	14	1	5	126.1	520	101	44	37	1	4	6	5	43	0	98	12	1	7	3	.700	1	0	2.64
Coble,Jason	Yankees	NYA	R	19	9	9	0	0	32.2	137	23	11	9	0	0	0	2	20	0	40	1	1	1	1	.500	0	0	2.48
Cochran,Andrew	Macon	Atl	A	22	13	0	0	6	23.2	106	19	16	13	1	1	3	3	14	0	17	4	2	0	3	.000	0	0	4.94
	Eugene	Atl	A-	22	15	7	0	1	58.1	262	54	33	23	4	0	1	7	26	0	51	6	2	6	0	1.000	0	0	3.55
Cochrane,Chris	Modesto	Oak	A+	24	21	10	0	2	74.1	314	74	38	33	6	3	1	1	21	2	68	2	2	5	4	.556	0	0	4.00
Codd,Timothy	Charlstn-SC	Tex	A	23	3	0	0	1	6.2	29	6	3	3	1	0	0	0	3	0	10	2	0	0	0	.000	0	0	4.05
Coe,Keith	Cedar Rapds	Cal	A	23	6	0	0	3	6.2	43	9	10	8	0	2	2	2	9	3	5	0	0	0	1	.000	0	0	10.80
Coggin,Dave	Piedmont	Phi	A	20	28	28	3	0	169.1	699	156	87	81	12	3	3	7	46	1	129	12	1	9	12	.429	3	0	4.31
Cole,Jason	Delmarva	Mon	A	24	10	0	0	2	17.2	65	11	4	2	1	1	0	0	1	0	20	1	0	1	2	.333	0	1	1.02
	W. Palm Bch	Mon	A+	24	39	0	0	24	62.1	256	57	25	16	2	3	1	2	20	0	40	1	0	6	1	.857	0	3	2.31
Coleman,Billy	Oneonta	NYA	A-	28	3	0	0	0	3.2	23	4	6	6	1	0	0	3	6	0	4	1	0	1	0	1.000	0	0	14.73
	Greensboro	NYA	A	28	4	0	0	1	7.1	32	5	4	4	0	0	0	2	3	0	9	2	0	0	0	.000	0	0	4.91
Collett,Andy	Wisconsin	Sea	A	23	22	0	0	8	37	169	32	18	15	2	2	2	5	23	1	31	6	1	2	2	.500	0	0	3.65
Collie,Timothy	Augusta	Pit	A	23	24	0	0	20	29.2	124	28	11	7	1	4	1	0	4	1	20	0	0	4	2	.667	0	12	2.12
	Lynchburg	Pit	A+	23	24	0	0	17	25	110	26	10	10	2	3	0	1	10	4	14	1	0	4	1	.800	0	1	3.60
Collins,E.J.	Beloit	Mil	A	20	38	3	0	16	67	315	79	44	35	1	4	1	7	37	4	50	7	0	6	5	.545	0	3	4.70
Colmenares,Luis	Salem	Col	A+	22	32	0	0	25	32.2	156	28	21	19	4	5	2	2	22	1	45	6	3	4	5	.444	0	12	5.23
	Asheville	Col	A	22	12	12	1	0	65	282	58	36	32	6	0	4	2	25	1	56	5	7	2	6	.250	0	0	4.43
Comer,Scott	Mets	NYN	R	20	13	8	0	3	50	200	40	16	12	1	1	0	1	3	0	40	1	3	2	2	.500	0	0	2.16
Connell,Brian	Cubs	ChN	R	19	7	5	0	0	13.2	70	12	18	16	0	0	0	3	15	0	11	9	0	2	1	.667	0	0	10.54
Connelly,Steve	Modesto	Oak	A+	23	52	0	0	42	64.2	283	58	33	27	5	1	1	5	32	1	65	5	2	4	7	.364	0	14	3.76
Contreras,Orlando	Rockies	Col	R	20	16	0	0	2	29.2	133	28	21	15	1	1	0	1	15	0	26	5	0	3	4	.429	0	1	4.55
Conway,Keith	St. Pete	StL	A+	24	59	0	0	21	69.1	294	63	18	16	1	4	1	1	25	1	67	3	1	7	3	.700	0	2	2.08
Cook,Derrick	Rangers	Tex	R	21	6	5	1	0	23	100	25	14	12	1	0	1	2	11	0	13	1	0	2	1	.667	1	0	4.70
Cook,Jake	Sarasota	Bos	A+	22	20	13	1	3	85.1	406	100	67	51	3	2	5	3	44	3	49	7	2	2	9	.182	0	1	5.38
Cook,O.J.	Pirates	Pit	R	20	11	6	0	1	50.2	211	43	23	20	4	1	1	2	19	0	36	4	1	5	2	.714	0	0	3.55
Cook,Rodney	Charlotte	Tex	A+	26	39	0	0	25	79.2	332	78	30	26	2	5	1	2	26	2	48	2	0	6	4	.600	0	8	2.94
Cooper,Brian	Lk Elsinore	Cal	A+	22	26	23	1	0	162.1	702	177	100	76	17	5	8	10	39	0	155	4	1	7	9	.438	1	0	4.21
Cooper,Chadwick	Kingsport	NYN	R+	22	5	2	0	0	12.2	66	21	20	18	3	0	0	1	8	0	9	1	1	1	1	.500	0	0	12.79
Cope,Craig	Mets	NYN	R	21	1	0	0	0	2	8	0	0	0	0	0	0	0	2	0	3	0	0	0	0	.000	0	0	0.00
Corba,Lisandro	Macon	Atl	A	21	2	0	0	0	5	21	3	1	1	0	1	0	0	5	0	1	0	1	0	0	.000	0	0	1.80
Cordero,Francisco	Fayettevlle	Det	A	19	2	1	0	0	7	27	2	2	2	0	0	0	0	6	0	7	0	0	0	0	.000	0	0	2.57
	Jamestown	Det	A-	19	2	2	0	0	11	39	5	1	1	0	0	0	0	2	0	10	0	0	0	0	.000	0	0	0.82
Corey,Bryan	Fayettevlle	Det	A	23	60	0	0	53	82	315	50	19	11	2	4	6	2	17	3	101	6	2	6	4	.600	0	34	1.21
Coriolan,Roberto	Yankees	NYA	R	20	12	0	0	2	29.1	130	27	18	14	0	1	2	1	16	0	26	3	0	2	1	.667	0	1	4.30
Corn,Chris	Tampa	NYA	A+	25	26	25	2	0	170.1	686	145	67	55	10	5	3	9	38	0	109	6	0	12	4	.750	1	0	2.91
Cornett,Brad	Dunedin	Tor	A+	28	4	0	0	2	7.1	41	15	7	7	1	0	0	1	3	0	5	1	1	0	1	.000	0	0	8.59
Coronado,Osvaldo	Columbia	NYN	A	23	32	16	0	9	111.1	479	120	68	56	12	5	1	1	28	1	96	6	1	8	10	.444	0	1	4.53
Corral,Ruben	Hagerstown	Tor	A	21	14	4	0	3	42.1	196	52	32	26	3	4	0	3	21	1	36	0	0	1	5	.167	0	1	5.53
Correa,Elvis	Great Falls	LA	R+	18	16	1	0	5	27	137	41	32	30	6	2	2	2	11	0	25	2	5	1	0	1.000	0	1	10.00
Cortes,David	Eugene	Atl	A-	23	15	0	0	11	24.2	95	13	2	2	0	1	0	0	6	0	33	0	0	2	1	.667	0	4	0.73
Cosman,Jeff	Mets	NYN	R	26	2	1	0	1	6	28	4	0	0	0	0	0	0	3	0	10	0	0	0	0	.000	0	1	0.00
	St. Lucie	NYN	A+	26	3	2	0	0	7.1	35	11	7	7	2	0	0	0	2	0	5	0	0	0	1	.000	0	0	8.59
Costello,T.J.	Sou. Oregon	Oak	A-	23	9	0	0	8	12	58	15	8	8	2	0	0	0	11	0	9	0	0	0	0	.000	0	0	6.00
Cotton,Joseph	Batavia	Phi	A-	22	9	9	0	0	46.1	196	43	23	22	2	3	1	1	19	0	37	4	0	2	4	.333	0	0	4.27
Cowsill,Brendon	Boise	Cal	A-	22	16	0	0	9	23	100	19	5	4	1	1	2	5	9	2	26	0	0	1	0	1.000	0	6	1.57
Cox,Rob	Mets	NYN	R	21	5	0	0	3	9	42	11	4	2	0	0	1	0	4	0	8	0	2	0	0	.000	0	1	2.00
	St. Lucie	NYN	A+	21	4	0	0	3	5.1	23	4	4	4	1	0	0	0	3	0	6	0	0	1	0	1.000	0	0	6.75
Crabtree,Robbie	Bellingham	SF	A-	24	28	0	0	13	52	206	38	18	16	8	2	1	0	14	1	72	3	0	3	3	.500	0	4	2.77
Crafton,Kevin	New Jersey	StL	A-	23	23	0	0	10	33	132	28	8	8	1	3	1	1	6	2	43	2	0	2	3	.400	0	2	2.18
Crane,John	Batavia	Phi	A-	22	21	0	0	8	35	157	38	20	15	0	2	1	1	17	0	31	5	3	1	0	1.000	0	0	3.86
Crane,Randy	Cubs	ChN	R	21	15	0	0	6	29	127	17	11	6	0	1	2	4	16	0	35	0	1	0	3	.000	0	1	1.86
Crawford,Chris	Astros	Hou	R	22	1	0	0	0	2	10	3	2	2	0	0	0	0	1	0	3	0	0	0	0	.000	0	0	9.00
	Auburn	Hou	A-	22	12	9	0	0	59	252	51	28	27	1	0	4	5	29	0	36	9	2	2	4	.333	0	0	4.12
Crawford,James	Williamsprt	ChN	A-	22	21	0	0	6	27	142	40	35	29	4	2	0	2	20	1	31	3	1	0	3	.000	0	1	9.67
Crawford,Paxton	Michigan	Bos	A	19	22	22	1	0	128.1	548	120	62	51	5	2	5	8	42	1	105	8	1	6	11	.353	0	0	3.58
Cremer,Richard	Yankees	NYA	R	20	2	1	0	0	4.2	23	3	7	6	0	0	0	0	8	0	4	3	0	0	1	.000	0	0	11.57
Cressend,Jack	Lowell	Bos	A-	22	9	8	0	1	45.2	189	37	15	12	0	2	2	4	17	1	57	6	1	3	2	.600	0	0	2.36
Crews,Jason	Lethbridge	Ari	R+	23	25	1	0	19	39.2	164	30	12	11	2	2	3	0	15	1	37	3	0	1	1	.500	0	5	2.50
Crills,Brad	High Desert	Bal	A+	25	14	14	1	0	77	332	79	45	40	10	2	2	5	26	3	45	3	1	2	4	.333	0	0	4.68
Crossan,Clay	Lethbridge	Ari	R+	23	19	4	0	2	40	186	55	29	21	1	0	2	1	18	0	27	4	1	4	1	.800	0	0	4.72
Crowell,Jim	Columbus	Cle	A	23	28	28	3	0	165.1	710	163	89	76	16	9	5	9	69	0	104	12	0	7	10	.412	0	0	4.14
Crowther,John	Hagerstown	Tor	A	23	41	0	0	25	67	304	59	33	24	2	2	1	7	43	3	61	14	2	2	3	.400	0	10	3.22
Cruz,Charlie	Durham	Atl	A+	23	8	0	0	1	18.2	82	15	12	12	2	0	0	3	7	0	12	0	0	1	1	.500	0	0	5.79
	Macon	Atl	A	23	35	0	0	18	77.1	338	70	40	32	8	5	1	5	34	3	89	4	1	5	4	.556	0	4	3.72

1996 Pitching — Single-A and Rookie Leagues

HOW MUCH HE PITCHED											WHAT HE GAVE UP												THE RESULTS					
Player	Team	Org	Lg	A	G	GS	CG	GF	IP	BFP	H	R	ER	HR	SH	SF	HB	TBB	IBB	SO	WP	Bk	W	L	Pct.	ShO	Sv	ERA
Cruz,Charlie	Orioles	Bal	R	20	9	0	0	4	14	69	19	10	7	0	0	1	5	6	0	7	3	1	1	0	1.000	0	0	4.50
Culmo,Kevin	Yakima	LA	A-	22	17	5	0	5	63.1	262	47	18	16	2	1	2	1	22	0	60	5	0	4	2	.667	0	2	2.27
Cushman,Scooter	Charlstn-WV	Cin	A	25	55	0	0	39	73	308	70	29	17	2	4	2	6	13	3	57	0	0	3	5	.375	0	15	2.10
Cutchins,Todd	Pittsfield	NYN	A-	21	6	3	0	1	25.1	108	24	15	13	0	2	1	2	10	0	29	0	0	2	1	.667	0	0	4.62
D'Alessandro,Marc	Asheville	Col	A	21	28	28	1	0	158.1	694	182	92	62	12	6	7	8	56	1	118	8	0	7	13	.350	0	0	3.52
Daigle,Tim	High Desert	Bal	A+	25	4	0	0	2	3.2	19	7	4	4	1	0	0	0	1	0	2	1	0	1	0	1.000	0	0	9.82
Dale,Carl	Modesto	Oak	A+	24	26	24	0	0	128.1	565	124	79	61	11	2	5	5	72	0	102	12	0	8	2	.800	0	0	4.28
Dalton,Brian	Stockton	Mil	A+	25	6	0	0	2	10.1	51	12	9	8	1	1	0	0	10	0	9	3	0	0	1	.000	0	0	6.97
	Fayettevlle	Det	A	25	7	0	0	2	9	36	5	2	1	0	0	0	0	5	0	7	1	0	0	0	.000	0	0	1.00
	Visalia	Det	A+	25	13	0	0	4	26.2	121	26	16	16	6	0	1	1	19	0	19	3	1	1	1	.500	0	0	5.40
Daniels,David	Augusta	Pit	A	23	11	0	0	7	12.1	58	21	8	7	0	1	0	0	3	1	14	0	1	0	1	.000	0	3	5.11
	Erie	Pit	A-	23	31	0	0	19	36.1	150	33	12	11	3	3	1	4	5	3	45	0	0	1	3	.250	0	7	2.72
Daniels,John	Lancaster	Sea	A+	23	43	0	0	23	95.1	412	91	51	35	9	3	2	8	30	1	100	3	0	3	5	.375	0	8	3.30
Darley,Ned	High Desert	Bal	A+	26	30	1	0	12	42.1	196	44	34	30	4	2	3	3	29	2	34	8	0	2	1	.667	0	1	6.38
Darrell,Tom	Boise	Cal	A-	20	15	15	1	0	101	433	114	56	39	11	2	2	4	13	2	76	2	0	8	1	.889	1	0	3.48
Darwin,David	Fayettevlle	Det	A	23	17	9	0	0	59	234	54	22	21	2	0	1	2	12	1	49	5	3	5	2	.714	0	0	3.20
DaSilva,Fernando	W. Palm Bch	Mon	A+	25	40	0	0	10	66.2	275	58	23	19	4	3	2	3	20	3	45	2	0	4	2	.667	0	0	2.57
Davenport,Joe	St. Cathrns	Tor	A-	21	20	8	0	3	66.2	295	71	44	38	5	4	3	5	23	0	43	8	0	2	4	.333	0	0	5.13
Davey,Tom	Hagerstown	Tor	A	23	26	26	2	0	155.2	675	132	76	67	7	5	5	15	91	0	98	15	1	10	9	.526	1	0	3.87
Davis,Douglas	Rangers	Tex	R	21	8	7	0	0	42.2	174	28	13	9	0	1	2	0	26	1	49	2	2	3	1	.750	0	0	1.90
Davis,Jason	Piedmont	Phi	A	22	19	0	0	10	24.2	100	16	6	5	1	0	2	4	5	1	22	1	1	6	1	.857	0	2	1.82
Davis,John	Savannah	LA	A	23	38	10	2	8	111.2	461	72	39	34	7	4	1	10	58	3	123	16	2	9	5	.643	0	1	2.74
Davis,Lance	Charlstn-WV	Cin	A	20	4	0	0	2	3.2	17	4	1	1	1	0	0	0	2	0	5	0	0	1	0	1.000	0	0	2.45
	Billings	Cin	R+	20	16	5	0	1	45.2	232	59	41	34	5	1	2	1	33	0	43	5	2	2	3	.400	0	0	6.70
	Princeton	Cin	R+	20	2	2	1	0	15	55	6	4	2	0	0	0	0	3	0	19	0	0	2	0	1.000	1	0	1.20
Davis,Kane	Lynchburg	Pit	A+	22	26	26	3	0	157.1	684	160	84	75	12	12	3	10	56	0	116	11	2	11	9	.550	1	0	4.29
Davis,Keith	Rancho Cuca	SD	A+	24	28	28	0	0	153.1	719	180	119	98	14	3	6	18	78	0	123	18	2	6	15	.286	0	0	5.75
Davis,Michael	Kingsport	NYN	R+	21	11	0	0	7	17.2	80	15	13	8	0	0	2	0	7	0	15	3	6	1	0	1.000	0	1	4.08
Dawsey,Jason	Beloit	Mil	A	23	31	14	1	4	101.1	411	71	21	17	4	4	0	1	42	0	119	2	1	6	4	.600	1	2	1.51
Day,Stephen	Yankees	NYA	R	19	7	5	0	1	33.2	139	41	26	21	3	0	0	4	3	0	23	0	0	5	2	.714	0	0	5.61
Deakman,Josh	Lk Elsinore	Cal	A+	23	27	25	2	0	163	734	188	109	91	16	3	5	13	56	1	115	14	3	8	10	.444	0	0	5.02
Deckard,Edward	Devil Rays	TB	R	19	9	0	0	1	22.1	98	23	10	7	0	2	2	4	11	1	15	3	0	1	1	.500	0	0	2.82
Dejesus,Tony	Mariners	Sea	R	19	12	11	0	0	57	252	54	29	23	1	0	2	2	28	0	61	7	0	2	5	.286	0	0	3.63
De La Cruz,Fernan.	Lk Elsinore	Cal	A+	22	5	0	0	3	7.1	40	8	12	7	2	0	0	1	10	0	3	2	1	0	0	.000	0	0	8.59
	Cedar Rapds	Cal	A	22	6	6	0	0	27	139	35	25	24	1	1	3	7	21	0	18	4	3	0	5	.000	0	0	8.00
	Boise	Cal	A-	22	15	15	0	0	85.2	400	85	55	47	5	0	1	13	51	3	61	6	2	6	3	.667	0	0	4.94
De La Rosa,Raul	White Sox	ChA	R	21	18	1	0	8	26	131	43	31	20	1	2	2	2	9	2	16	1	0	0	2	.000	0	1	6.92
Deleon,Jose	Johnson Cty	StL	R+	20	27	0	0	26	34	138	28	8	8	2	0	1	1	10	1	32	0	0	3	1	.750	0	15	2.12
Deleon,Julio	Devil Rays	TB	R	NA	7	0	0	2	15.1	63	18	9	8	1	0	0	0	4	0	6	0	1	0	0	.000	0	0	4.70
Delgado,Ernesto	Hagerstown	Tor	A	21	35	2	0	16	85.1	386	89	50	34	2	5	3	7	45	1	70	12	2	4	7	.364	0	2	3.59
Dellamano,An.	Hudson Vall	Tex	A-	22	18	10	0	2	65.2	311	83	54	45	5	1	1	4	33	2	61	13	2	4	7	.364	0	1	6.17
Dellaratta,Peter	Sou. Oregon	Oak	A-	23	22	0	0	6	41.1	194	45	34	33	10	2	2	4	24	4	41	3	1	0	5	.000	0	2	7.19
De Los Santos,Luis	Greensboro	NYA	A	19	7	6	0	0	31.2	141	39	17	17	4	0	1	0	11	0	21	0	0	4	1	.800	0	0	4.83
	Oneonta	NYA	A-	19	10	10	3	0	58	240	44	28	24	3	0	3	3	21	0	62	2	1	4	4	.500	2	0	3.72
De Los Santos,Val.	Beloit	Mil	A	21	33	23	5	10	164.2	715	164	83	65	11	8	5	3	59	4	137	8	3	10	8	.556	1	4	3.55
Demorejon,Pedro	Hickory	ChA	A	22	17	1	0	6	42.2	193	45	26	21	5	1	1	5	22	0	34	4	3	1	2	.333	0	0	4.43
	Bristol	ChA	R+	22	18	1	0	6	37.1	183	49	33	29	7	1	3	3	22	1	39	4	3	1	2	.333	0	1	6.99
Dempster,Ryan	Charlstn-SC	Tex	A	20	23	23	2	0	144.1	603	120	71	53	13	6	9	6	58	1	141	17	5	7	11	.389	0	0	3.30
	Kane County	Fla	A	20	4	4	1	0	26.1	109	18	10	8	0	1	0	1	18	0	16	2	0	2	1	.667	1	0	2.73
Depaula,Sean	Burlington	Cle	R+	23	23	0	0	11	35.1	151	31	16	15	3	2	2	2	13	0	42	4	3	4	2	.667	0	1	3.82
	Watertown	Cle	A-	23	1	0	0	0	2	6	0	0	0	0	0	0	0	0	0	5	0	0	0	0	.000	0	0	0.00
Derenches,Albert	Mariners	Sea	R	20	20	3	1	10	60.1	256	57	31	21	2	2	1	4	19	3	73	3	0	3	3	.500	1	3	3.13
Desabrias,Mark	Idaho Falls	SD	R+	21	27	0	0	7	45.2	220	65	35	34	2	1	1	2	22	1	43	5	1	1	0	1.000	0	0	6.70
Deschenes,Marc	Columbus	Cle	A	24	16	16	0	0	76.2	343	70	38	29	9	1	3	1	41	0	67	6	0	5	2	.714	0	0	3.40
Deskins,Casey	San Bernrdo	LA	A+	25	12	7	0	3	43	198	61	38	29	5	3	1	0	12	0	26	2	0	3	3	.500	0	0	6.07
	Yakima	LA	A-	25	15	9	0	2	62.1	279	69	40	33	6	4	2	2	20	1	43	0	0	4	5	.444	0	0	4.76
Desrosiers,Erik	Pr. William	ChA	A+	22	7	7	1	0	40	174	47	29	25	7	3	1	1	9	0	25	0	0	1	4	.200	0	0	5.63
	South Bend	ChA	A	22	14	12	0	2	68.2	293	68	41	36	8	1	0	2	19	0	39	1	1	3	5	.375	0	1	4.72
Dewitt,Chris	Columbia	NYN	A	23	13	0	0	5	30.2	125	22	9	8	0	1	0	0	11	2	31	2	1	3	0	1.000	0	1	2.35
	Rockford	ChN	A	23	15	13	0	0	81	357	88	48	36	3	3	4	6	21	1	45	4	3	6	4	.600	0	0	4.00
Dewitt,Matt	Johnson Cty	StL	R+	19	14	14	0	0	79.2	353	96	53	48	17	1	0	3	26	0	58	7	0	5	5	.500	0	0	5.42
Dewitt,Scott	Kane County	Fla	A	22	27	27	1	0	148.2	667	151	96	78	8	5	4	19	59	0	119	2	2	10	11	.476	1	0	4.72
Diaz,Jairo	Rockford	ChN	A	21	25	11	0	6	88.1	363	80	33	31	6	2	2	6	26	0	84	1	5	6	3	.667	0	0	3.16
	Daytona	ChN	A+	21	8	3	0	1	26.1	126	31	14	9	1	0	2	1	14	1	18	5	0	1	1	.500	0	0	3.08
Dietrich,Jason	Asheville	Col	A	24	7	0	0	3	12.1	48	7	2	2	1	0	0	0	6	0	21	1	0	1	0	1.000	0	1	1.46
Dillinger,John	Lynchburg	Pit	A+	23	33	15	2	0	132.1	554	101	65	55	11	3	3	4	58	0	113	11	1	10	5	.667	0	0	3.74
Dingman,Craig	Oneonta	NYA	A-	23	20	0	0	15	35.1	137	17	11	8	0	1	1	1	9	0	52	0	1	0	2	.000	0	9	2.04
Dinyar,Eric	Lakeland	Det	A+	23	58	0	0	56	65.2	278	42	19	13	0	5	3	12	35	2	55	4	0	3	3	.500	0	27	1.78
Dixon,Jim	Pr. William	ChA	A+	24	38	2	0	27	73.1	320	71	46	39	6	5	3	4	31	8	56	8	0	5	7	.417	0	4	4.79
Dixon,Tim	W. Palm Bch	Mon	A+	25	37	16	0	8	124	528	126	55	40	10	8	5	6	35	3	87	7	0	5	11	.313	0	2	2.90
Dollar,Toby	Great Falls	LA	R+	22	14	7	0	3	49.1	249	72	54	46	2	0	4	5	24	1	42	9	0	1	6	.143	0	0	8.39
Donastorg,Raul	Tigers	Det	R	19	20	0	0	17	25	108	24	13	11	1	0	1	1	9	0	17	4	0	1	2	.333	0	4	3.96
Done,Johnny	Lethbridge	Ari	R+	21	22	0	0	9	37	159	41	16	8	1	4	2	1	8	1	30	2	0	2	1	.667	0	1	1.95
Donnelly,Robert	Peoria	StL	A	23	46	0	0	16	60.1	246	45	27	23	3	1	1	2	24	1	76	3	0	2	2	.500	0	0	3.43
Donovan,Scot	Kinston	Cle	A+	24	28	0	0	12	53	236	60	39	31	6	4	3	1	25	1	36	3	0	2	2	.500	0	0	5.26
Dooley,Chris	Johnson Cty	StL	R+	24	13	0	0	2	25.2	118	26	14	12	2	0	0	0	14	1	28	2	2	1	1	.500	0	1	4.21
Dose,Gary	Elizabethtn	Min	R+	23	17	0	0	10	21.2	106	22	13	10	1	0	0	2	19	0	24	5	0	1	0	1.000	0	0	4.15

1996 Pitching — Single-A and Rookie Leagues

HOW MUCH HE PITCHED											WHAT HE GAVE UP												THE RESULTS					
Player	Team	Org	Lg	A	G	GS	CG	GF	IP	BFP	H	R	ER	HR	SH	SF	HB	TBB	IBB	SO	WP	Bk	W	L	Pct.	ShO	Sv	ERA
Dotel,Octavio	Columbia	NYN	A	23	22	19	0	3	115.1	480	89	49	46	7	1	4	7	49	0	142	12	4	11	3	.786	0	0	3.59
Douglas,Reggie	Rockies	Col	R	20	12	0	0	5	14	87	23	28	20	0	0	1	2	19	0	12	6	3	0	0	.000	0	0	12.86
Dowhower,Deron	Fort Myers	Min	A+	25	39	2	0	9	75.1	329	63	37	31	5	3	2	5	45	0	83	17	0	2	4	.333	0	1	3.70
Draeger,Mark	Charlstn-SC	Tex	A	24	19	0	0	8	30	140	26	23	15	1	0	2	4	18	0	24	7	0	1	1	.500	0	0	4.50
	Hudson Vall	Tex	A-	24	17	0	0	3	32.1	166	44	35	22	1	1	2	2	17	1	28	7	1	1	2	.333	0	0	6.12
Druckrey,Chris.	Portland	Col	A-	22	6	0	0	2	17	90	29	20	15	3	1	1	0	12	0	19	5	1	0	1	.000	0	0	7.94
Drumheller,Al	Tampa	NYA	A+	25	36	0	0	7	51.1	215	34	15	13	2	4	0	0	33	2	57	2	0	9	3	.750	0	1	2.28
Drysdale,Brooks	Stockton	Mil	A+	26	35	0	0	5	59.2	266	61	35	34	10	2	2	4	28	1	61	3	0	6	1	.857	0	0	5.13
Duchscherer,Justin	Red Sox	Bos	R	19	13	8	0	2	54.2	232	52	26	19	0	3	3	3	14	0	45	4	6	0	2	.000	0	1	3.13
Duffy,John	Lowell	Bos	A-	23	29	0	0	10	41.1	207	56	32	26	3	4	3	3	27	4	32	3	2	3	4	.429	0	0	5.66
Duffy,Ryan	Visalia	Ari	A+	24	15	0	0	1	15.1	60	6	3	2	0	1	0	2	6	0	9	1	0	0	0	.000	0	0	1.17
	Lethbridge	Ari	R+	24	25	0	0	9	30.2	132	24	11	9	0	1	1	2	20	0	30	5	3	6	2	.750	0	1	2.64
Duncan,Courtney	Williamsprt	ChN	A-	22	15	15	1	0	90.1	360	58	28	22	6	3	0	5	34	0	91	8	0	11	1	.917	0	0	2.19
Duncan,Geoff	Utica	Fla	A-	22	24	1	0	8	40.1	191	46	23	17	3	0	1	4	19	5	52	5	3	2	5	.286	0	2	3.79
Duncan,Sean	South Bend	ChA	A	24	43	0	0	16	56	238	43	29	21	3	10	1	2	23	0	54	5	0	2	5	.286	0	3	3.38
	Pr. William	ChA	A+	24	6	0	0	6	15.2	75	17	11	10	3	1	0	0	9	1	13	2	0	0	0	.000	0	1	5.74
Dunn,Cordell	Augusta	Pit	A	21	3	3	0	0	10.2	57	14	15	15	1	1	0	2	9	0	7	0	0	0	3	.000	0	0	12.66
	Pirates	Pit	R	21	7	6	0	0	28	136	32	24	17	1	1	2	0	14	0	24	5	0	0	5	.000	0	0	5.46
Durbin,Chad	Royals	KC	R	19	11	8	1	1	44.1	187	34	22	21	3	0	1	1	25	0	43	6	3	3	2	.600	1	0	4.26
Durkovic,Peter	Fayettevlle	Det	A	23	53	0	0	19	52.2	237	54	35	27	3	4	3	5	16	1	67	6	2	3	3	.500	0	3	4.61
Durocher,Jayson	W. Palm Bch	Mon	A+	22	23	23	1	0	129.1	557	118	65	48	5	4	3	7	44	0	101	15	3	7	6	.538	1	0	3.34
Duvall,Mike	Kane County	Fla	A	22	41	0	0	28	48	210	43	20	11	0	2	0	0	21	2	46	3	0	4	1	.800	0	8	2.06
Dyess,Todd	Frederick	Bal	A+	24	20	17	0	1	96	411	99	63	56	7	1	2	4	39	2	90	15	2	4	7	.364	0	0	5.25
Dykhoff,Radhames	Frederick	Bal	A+	22	33	0	0	15	62	290	77	45	39	7	4	4	1	22	2	75	0	0	2	6	.250	0	3	5.66
Eaddy,Brad	Vero Beach	LA	A+	27	12	0	0	5	10.2	44	9	8	7	1	2	0	1	4	1	8	2	1	0	1	.000	0	0	5.91
Eason,Michael	Utica	Fla	A-	23	9	0	0	5	14.2	71	21	12	11	2	1	1	2	7	2	9	3	0	0	1	.000	0	1	6.75
Ebert,Derrin	Durham	Atl	A+	20	27	27	2	0	166.1	711	189	102	74	13	8	9	4	37	1	99	5	0	12	9	.571	0	0	4.00
Eby,Mike	Fayettevlle	Det	A	25	27	0	0	9	50.2	206	27	11	6	0	5	0	2	30	3	58	2	1	3	1	.750	0	4	1.07
	Lakeland	Det	A+	25	17	0	0	5	29	135	28	16	14	0	1	2	2	24	1	27	3	0	0	0	.000	0	0	4.34
Edwards,Jon	Watertown	Cle	A-	24	23	0	0	17	34.1	141	26	12	12	2	2	0	2	14	2	37	2	0	1	3	.250	0	4	3.15
Edwards,Wayne	Bakersfield	—	A+	33	3	2	0	1	18.1	108	38	30	22	4	1	0	1	13	0	13	2	0	0	2	.000	0	0	10.80
Ehler,Dan	Brevard Cty	Fla	A+	22	28	23	1	0	150	658	176	88	79	10	5	4	10	41	2	88	9	0	5	16	.238	0	0	4.74
Eibey,Scott	High Desert	Bal	A+	23	11	0	0	1	11.2	65	17	16	11	0	0	1	0	10	2	7	2	0	1	0	1.000	0	0	8.49
	Bluefield	Bal	R+	23	24	0	0	10	45	187	30	19	14	3	0	3	3	17	0	59	4	1	5	1	.833	0	2	2.80
Einerston,Darrell	Greensboro	NYA	A	24	48	0	0	26	70	306	69	29	21	1	4	2	2	19	3	48	4	1	3	9	.250	0	8	2.70
Elarton,Scott	Kissimmee	Hou	A+	21	27	27	3	0	172.1	715	154	67	56	13	7	6	8	54	0	130	5	0	12	7	.632	1	0	2.92
Ellison,Jason	Yankees	NYA	R	21	21	3	0	17	36	151	24	8	5	0	1	0	3	15	0	42	2	1	3	2	.600	0	7	1.25
	Oneonta	NYA	A-	21	1	0	0	1	1	5	2	1	1	0	0	0	0	0	0	2	0	0	0	0	.000	0	0	9.00
Elmore,George	Erie	Pit	A-	23	19	0	0	6	32	155	38	22	17	1	1	4	3	21	0	17	9	0	1	0	1.000	0	0	4.78
Emiliano,Jamie	Asheville	Col	A	22	6	0	0	4	5.2	25	7	6	6	1	0	0	0	2	0	7	1	1	1	1	.500	0	1	9.53
Enard,Tony	Kane County	Fla	A	22	3	0	0	1	2.2	16	1	2	2	0	0	1	2	4	0	1	4	0	0	0	.000	0	0	6.75
	Marlins	Fla	R	22	2	0	0	0	6.2	23	3	0	0	0	0	0	0	3	0	5	1	0	0	0	.000	0	0	0.00
	Brevard Cty	Fla	A+	22	2	0	0	0	4.2	19	2	3	3	1	0	1	0	4	0	6	0	0	0	1	.000	0	0	5.79
Enders,Trevor	Butte	TB	R+	22	19	0	0	6	27.2	132	34	22	15	1	2	2	2	13	1	24	2	0	0	1	.000	0	1	4.88
Erdos,Todd	Rancho Cuca	SD	A+	23	55	0	0	41	67.1	305	63	33	28	2	7	2	6	37	3	82	6	0	3	3	.500	0	17	3.74
Ervin,Kent	Idaho Falls	SD	R+	23	22	4	0	5	54	254	72	52	39	7	2	2	4	18	0	35	6	2	2	5	.286	0	0	6.50
Escalante,Piter	Diamondback	Ari	R	19	15	0	0	8	24.2	110	35	17	17	2	0	0	0	5	0	24	3	1	0	1	.000	0	0	6.20
Escamilla,Jaime	Charlotte	Tex	A+	25	37	0	0	18	61.2	272	68	31	28	4	2	3	3	28	3	39	2	0	3	3	.500	0	1	4.09
Espina,Rendy	Twins	Min	R	19	7	1	0	2	11.2	54	18	12	12	0	0	0	1	8	0	10	1	1	0	2	.000	0	0	9.26
Estrada,Horacio	Beloit	Mil	A	21	17	0	0	9	29.1	113	21	8	4	2	2	0	0	11	1	34	5	1	2	1	.667	0	1	1.23
	Stockton	Mil	A+	21	29	0	0	11	51	214	43	29	26	7	1	1	2	21	2	62	3	0	1	3	.250	0	3	4.59
Estrella,Leoncio	Kingsport	NYN	R+	22	15	7	1	3	58	248	54	32	25	3	4	1	1	24	0	52	6	2	6	3	.667	0	0	3.88
Estrella,Luis	Bellingham	SF	A-	22	23	0	0	6	55.1	213	35	13	11	3	1	0	0	22	1	52	6	0	4	0	1.000	0	1	1.79
Etler,Todd	Winston-Sal	Cin	A+	23	33	1	0	16	77.1	321	72	30	30	7	3	2	5	17	0	59	2	0	4	5	.444	0	2	3.49
Evans,Mike	Kane County	Fla	A	28	2	0	0	0	1.2	12	3	2	2	0	0	0	0	4	0	1	3	0	0	0	.000	0	0	10.80
Evans,Mike	Marlins	Fla	R	21	19	0	0	13	35.1	143	24	8	5	0	2	0	1	13	3	40	5	1	0	1	.000	0	3	1.27
Fajardo,Alexis	Yankees	NYA	R	20	2	0	0	1	4.1	19	2	0	0	0	0	0	0	4	0	8	0	0	0	0	.000	0	0	0.00
Falkenborg,Brian	Orioles	Bal	R	19	8	6	0	1	28	116	21	13	8	1	0	0	1	8	0	36	2	1	0	3	.000	0	0	2.57
	High Desert	Bal	A+	19	1	0	0	0	1	3	1	0	0	0	0	0	0	0	0	1	0	0	0	0	.000	0	0	0.00
Farfan,David	Cedar Rapds	Cal	A	23	5	0	0	4	7.2	37	8	9	2	0	0	1	1	6	0	6	2	0	0	1	.000	0	1	2.35
Farley,Joe	Bristol	ChA	R+	22	10	10	3	0	64.2	277	73	34	25	5	1	2	2	11	0	54	3	2	3	6	.333	1	0	3.48
	Hickory	ChA	A	22	4	4	0	0	25.2	104	21	6	6	2	0	0	1	5	0	15	1	0	3	0	1.000	0	0	2.10
Farnsworth,Jeff	Everett	Sea	A-	21	10	7	0	1	39.1	158	33	19	18	4	0	1	0	13	0	42	6	5	3	3	.500	0	0	4.12
Farnsworth,Kyle	Rockford	ChN	A	21	20	20	1	0	112	495	122	62	46	7	2	4	9	35	0	82	8	1	9	6	.600	0	0	3.70
Farrell,James	Michigan	Bos	A	23	7	7	2	0	44	185	39	15	12	2	1	0	1	17	1	32	1	0	6	1	.857	0	0	2.45
	Sarasota	Bos	A+	23	21	21	3	0	133.1	539	116	58	52	11	4	5	4	34	0	92	9	0	9	8	.529	1	0	3.51
Farrow,Jason	Augusta	Pit	A	23	46	0	0	14	77.1	331	61	26	18	3	4	2	8	34	2	81	7	2	5	3	.625	0	3	2.09
Faulk,Eric	Athletics	Oak	R	20	6	4	0	0	18	80	18	8	7	0	2	0	2	6	0	19	1	0	0	1	.000	0	0	3.50
Faulkner,Neal	Daytona	ChN	A+	22	11	0	0	5	12.2	61	17	11	11	0	0	1	1	5	0	10	1	0	1	1	.500	0	2	7.82
Feliciano,Pedro	Great Falls	LA	R+	20	22	1	0	10	41	206	50	36	26	1	0	5	3	26	2	39	4	3	2	3	.400	0	3	5.71
Felix,Miguel	White Sox	ChA	R	20	12	12	1	0	73.1	317	73	39	27	2	0	3	5	19	0	64	2	3	3	6	.333	0	0	3.31
Feliz,Bienvenido	Watertown	Cle	A-	20	13	11	2	1	71.2	297	59	37	31	7	0	1	1	26	1	56	4	6	5	6	.455	1	0	3.89
Feliz,Jose	Cubs	ChN	R	20	11	7	0	2	61	246	46	20	15	0	1	2	4	18	0	57	8	1	4	1	.800	0	0	2.21
Fennell,Barry	Cubs	ChN	R	20	10	7	0	2	42.2	179	37	19	14	0	4	0	2	12	0	42	2	0	0	4	.000	0	1	2.95
Fenus,Justin	Martinsvlle	Phi	R+	22	14	8	0	3	44.2	212	46	33	30	5	1	2	3	29	0	26	9	4	2	7	.222	0	0	6.04
Ferrell,Dan	Utica	Fla	A-	22	14	13	1	1	70.2	298	74	40	37	6	0	2	0	17	0	61	4	2	2	5	.286	1	1	4.71
Ferullo,Matt	Mets	NYN	R	24	2	2	0	0	11	45	11	6	6	0	0	0	2	2	0	13	0	2	1	0	1.000	0	0	4.91

1996 Pitching — Single-A and Rookie Leagues

HOW MUCH HE PITCHED											WHAT HE GAVE UP												THE RESULTS					
Player	Team	Org	Lg	A	G	GS	CG	GF	IP	BFP	H	R	ER	HR	SH	SF	HB	TBB	IBB	SO	WP	Bk	W	L	Pct.	ShO	Sv	ERA
	Kingsport	NYN	R+	24	1	1	0	0	6.1	27	9	5	5	1	0	0	0	1	0	7	0	0	0	0	.000	0	0	7.11
	Pittsfield	NYN	A-	24	11	4	0	5	32.2	146	38	20	17	1	2	0	2	9	1	22	2	2	4	1	.800	0	2	4.68
Festa,Christopher	Sarasota	Bos	A+	NA	6	2	0	2	20	109	37	24	19	2	2	1	1	11	0	12	2	0	0	2	.000	0	0	8.55
	Lowell	Bos	A-	NA	20	9	1	3	72.1	341	94	53	41	6	3	2	5	20	1	43	8	4	2	5	.286	0	0	5.10
Fieldbinder,Mick	Helena	Mil	R+	23	2	2	0	0	10	40	8	4	4	1	0	0	0	1	0	12	1	0	2	0	1.000	0	0	3.60
	Beloit	Mil	A	23	12	12	1	0	77	312	74	33	29	2	1	2	1	18	2	66	5	1	9	2	.818	0	0	3.39
Figueroa,Julio	Vermont	Mon	A-	23	14	14	1	0	79	334	78	37	29	6	1	2	4	32	0	59	3	2	5	3	.625	0	0	3.30
Figueroa,Nelson	Columbia	NYN	A	23	26	25	8	1	185.1	723	119	55	42	10	3	2	2	58	1	200	9	2	14	7	.667	4	0	2.04
Filbeck,Ryan	Brevard Cty	Fla	A+	24	9	0	0	6	10.2	54	16	13	10	1	0	0	0	5	1	9	1	0	1	1	.500	0	0	8.44
	South Bend	ChA	A	24	19	2	0	12	34.2	142	27	16	14	2	2	2	4	11	0	20	0	0	1	4	.200	0	3	3.63
Finol,Ricardo	Pirates	Pit	R	23	6	0	0	2	10	53	19	10	10	1	0	0	0	5	0	9	2	1	1	0	1.000	0	0	9.00
Fisher,Louis	Bluefield	Bal	R+	20	14	13	1	0	71.2	318	58	43	35	2	0	1	2	48	0	52	15	1	3	4	.429	1	0	4.40
Fisher,Ryan	Augusta	Pit	A	23	14	0	0	4	20.2	95	23	14	7	3	0	1	2	9	1	16	2	2	3	1	.750	0	0	3.05
Fitterer,Scott	Dunedin	Tor	A+	23	20	0	0	13	26	126	43	21	18	0	0	1	1	8	1	15	3	0	2	3	.400	0	5	6.23
	Hagerstown	Tor	A	23	2	0	0	1	3	14	5	3	3	0	0	0	0	0	0	4	0	0	1	0	1.000	0	0	9.00
Fitzgerald,Brian	Everett	Sea	A-	22	21	1	0	8	39	181	56	36	28	2	1	1	0	8	0	31	1	2	1	2	.333	0	1	6.46
Flach,Jason	Eugene	Atl	A-	23	27	0	0	14	59.2	238	45	18	15	2	3	1	1	17	1	68	2	0	4	1	.800	0	11	2.26
Fleetwood,Tony	Watertown	Cle	A-	25	12	0	0	5	18	83	22	13	10	1	0	1	1	6	0	19	0	1	0	0	.000	0	1	5.00
Fleming,Emar	Rangers	Tex	R	20	12	12	0	0	69.2	286	70	33	29	3	1	2	5	13	0	52	1	1	4	4	.500	0	0	3.75
Fleming,John	Diamondback	Ari	R	19	10	5	0	0	31.1	137	33	17	14	4	1	1	1	17	0	29	7	0	1	4	.200	0	0	4.02
Flores,Pedro	Great Falls	LA	R+	20	18	3	0	1	46.2	215	44	37	30	2	4	2	2	28	1	24	10	1	4	2	.667	0	0	5.79
Flury,Pat	Wilmington	KC	A+	24	45	0	0	19	84.1	339	66	22	18	2	2	1	0	29	4	67	9	0	7	2	.778	0	5	1.92
Foderaro,Kevin	Peoria	StL	A	24	32	3	0	5	56.2	245	54	25	25	3	3	2	1	26	1	41	5	1	1	0	1.000	0	0	3.97
Fonceca,Chad	Billings	Cin	R+	21	22	0	0	4	37	190	58	50	42	5	2	1	4	18	3	36	4	2	1	4	.200	0	1	10.22
Fontenot,Joseph	San Jose	SF	A+	20	26	23	0	1	144	642	137	87	71	7	10	6	11	74	0	124	13	1	9	4	.692	0	0	4.44
Foran,John	Fayettevlle	Det	A	23	35	17	0	6	111	485	107	57	51	6	1	4	3	53	0	82	8	0	4	7	.364	0	0	4.14
Forbes,Cameron	Orioles	Bal	R	20	13	13	0	0	76.2	326	73	48	37	5	6	5	3	22	0	71	3	2	4	5	.444	0	0	4.34
Ford,Ben	Greensboro	NYA	A	21	43	0	0	16	82.1	359	75	48	39	3	4	1	11	33	6	84	9	0	2	6	.250	0	2	4.26
Ford,Brian	Piedmont	Phi	A	24	37	0	0	16	56	258	73	33	29	5	3	3	3	18	3	40	3	2	1	4	.200	0	1	4.66
Ford,Jason	Portland	Col	A-	23	13	0	0	5	18.2	93	22	21	21	4	0	0	1	14	0	29	4	0	0	2	.000	0	1	10.13
Ford,Jack	Pr. William	ChA	A+	25	36	0	0	15	75.1	332	78	40	35	9	2	2	4	29	2	59	4	0	3	4	.429	0	1	4.18
Forster,Pete	Elizabethtn	Min	R+	22	4	4	0	0	23	104	23	19	18	5	0	0	2	12	0	20	0	0	2	2	.500	0	0	7.04
Forti,Gene	White Sox	ChA	R	19	12	8	0	1	56.2	238	50	28	23	3	2	0	4	20	0	44	5	0	4	2	.667	0	1	3.65
Fortune,Peter	Expos	Mon	R	22	13	13	0	0	73.1	292	52	23	16	1	4	4	3	21	0	66	2	0	6	0	1.000	0	0	1.96
	Vermont	Mon	A-	22	2	0	0	1	2.1	12	3	2	1	0	0	1	0	2	0	2	0	1	0	1	.000	0	0	3.86
Foster,Kris	San Bernrdo	LA	A+	22	30	8	0	9	81.2	355	66	46	35	5	3	4	3	54	3	78	10	4	3	5	.375	0	2	3.86
Fowler,Ben	Danville	Atl	R+	20	4	0	0	0	5.2	32	8	13	9	3	0	0	0	5	0	2	3	0	0	0	.000	0	0	14.29
	Braves	Atl	R	20	8	6	0	1	29.2	131	27	21	11	0	3	2	0	11	0	22	2	1	1	4	.200	0	0	3.34
Fowler,Jered	Devil Rays	TB	R	24	4	0	0	3	7.2	43	8	7	4	0	1	0	2	8	2	10	2	1	0	0	.000	0	2	4.70
	Hudson Vall	TB	A-	24	2	0	0	1	4	15	2	2	1	1	0	0	0	0	0	1	0	0	0	0	.000	0	0	2.25
	Butte	TB	R+	24	9	0	0	3	10.1	58	17	13	8	1	0	1	3	8	0	4	4	0	1	2	.333	0	0	6.97
Frace,Ryan	Batavia	Phi	A-	25	25	1	0	11	53.2	221	49	19	16	5	3	1	2	14	0	57	6	0	4	1	.800	0	0	2.68
France,Aaron	Lynchburg	Pit	A+	23	13	13	0	0	60.1	286	79	53	43	6	1	0	3	32	1	40	8	3	0	8	.000	0	0	6.41
	Augusta	Pit	A	23	5	5	0	0	25	105	23	9	7	2	2	0	1	7	0	24	0	1	2	1	.667	0	0	2.52
Franklin,Wayne	Yakima	LA	A-	23	20	0	0	5	25	115	32	10	7	2	0	0	0	12	3	22	3	1	1	0	1.000	0	1	2.52
Franko,Kris	W. Palm Bch	Mon	A+	26	9	0	0	6	12	46	10	6	5	1	0	0	0	4	0	3	1	0	2	1	.667	0	0	3.75
Fraser,Joe	Expos	Mon	R	19	11	10	0	0	49.2	197	35	14	10	1	4	0	0	18	0	45	5	0	4	0	1.000	0	0	1.81
Frazier,Harold	Oneonta	NYA	A-	23	5	0	0	1	6.2	24	2	2	2	0	0	0	0	2	0	7	0	0	2	1	.667	0	0	2.70
	Greensboro	NYA	A	23	2	0	0	0	0.2	6	3	3	2	0	0	0	0	1	0	0	0	0	0	0	.000	0	0	27.00
Frias,Miguel	Diamondback	Ari	R	19	19	0	0	10	30.2	137	28	18	8	1	2	3	2	17	0	30	3	0	1	1	.500	0	2	2.35
Fuentes,Brian	Everett	Sea	A-	21	13	2	0	3	26.2	114	23	14	13	2	0	1	0	13	0	26	5	0	0	1	.000	0	0	4.39
Fulcher,John	Ogden	Mil	R+	22	13	10	0	1	58	261	67	45	35	4	1	1	3	15	0	65	8	4	2	3	.400	0	0	5.43
Fuller,Duane	Auburn	Hou	A-	22	11	2	0	1	17.2	92	17	18	17	1	1	0	5	21	0	16	4	0	1	0	1.000	0	0	8.66
Fuller,Stephen	Auburn	Hou	A-	22	18	9	0	4	70	324	80	52	44	4	5	3	8	38	0	45	9	1	2	6	.250	0	0	5.66
Fultz,Aaron	San Jose	SF	A+	23	36	12	0	11	104.2	460	101	52	46	7	9	3	8	54	2	103	13	0	9	5	.643	0	1	3.96
Fussell,Chris	Frederick	Bal	A+	21	15	14	1	0	86.1	369	71	36	27	8	1	1	5	44	0	94	5	0	5	2	.714	1	0	2.81
Gaerte,Travis	Pirates	Pit	R	20	14	0	0	8	30	122	17	9	8	0	1	0	3	18	0	24	5	2	1	0	1.000	0	5	2.40
Gagne,Eric	Savannah	LA	A	21	23	21	1	0	115.1	474	94	48	42	11	3	2	1	43	1	131	7	5	7	6	.538	1	0	3.28
Galban,Juan	Braves	Atl	R	23	5	1	0	3	6	42	14	14	9	0	0	2	1	9	0	3	0	4	0	2	.000	0	0	13.50
Gallagher,Bryan	Athletics	Oak	R	20	16	1	0	2	30.1	141	37	24	11	1	1	1	1	10	0	27	2	2	2	1	.667	0	0	3.26
Gallagher,Keith	New Jersey	StL	A-	23	12	12	0	0	52.1	244	64	51	42	1	1	2	1	28	0	28	6	0	1	7	.125	0	0	7.22
Gandarillas,Gus	Twins	Min	R	25	3	1	0	2	9	43	10	3	1	1	1	0	0	3	0	14	1	0	0	0	.000	0	2	1.00
	Fort Myers	Min	A+	25	4	0	0	3	6	35	9	7	6	0	0	0	1	8	0	3	1	0	0	0	.000	0	1	9.00
Garagozzo,Keith	Brevard Cty	Fla	A+	27	2	2	0	0	5	25	9	6	6	2	0	0	1	4	0	1	0	0	0	1	.000	0	0	10.80
Garber,Joel	South Bend	ChA	A	23	14	7	0	4	47.2	224	60	40	27	6	3	5	2	15	0	27	1	6	0	5	.000	0	0	5.10
	Hickory	ChA	A	23	17	1	0	4	51.1	228	60	26	23	2	2	1	4	16	0	46	2	5	1	1	.500	0	2	4.03
Garcia,Ariel	South Bend	ChA	A	21	26	26	0	0	151.1	659	159	96	77	11	5	6	7	48	0	76	5	3	6	10	.375	0	0	4.58
Garcia,Bryan	Athletics	Oak	R	19	18	3	0	8	51	219	58	36	31	4	0	5	5	11	1	39	0	1	4	2	.667	0	1	5.47
Garcia,Eddy	Charlstn-WV	Cin	A	21	30	11	1	3	107	456	91	48	36	3	2	5	3	58	1	74	14	3	7	6	.538	0	1	3.03
Garcia,Freddy	Quad City	Hou	A	20	13	13	0	0	60.2	265	57	27	21	3	1	1	4	27	0	50	5	5	5	4	.556	0	0	3.12
Garcia,Gabriel	Astros	Hou	R	20	13	5	0	2	36.1	154	30	12	10	3	0	0	3	10	0	50	2	3	3	4	.429	0	1	2.48
	Kissimmee	Hou	A+	20	3	0	0	3	8.2	37	6	2	0	0	1	0	1	3	1	4	0	0	0	1	.000	0	0	0.00
Garcia,Jose	Helena	Mil	R+	19	2	0	0	0	1.2	9	1	3	3	0	0	0	0	3	0	2	1	0	0	0	.000	0	0	16.20
Garcia,Jose	Macon	Atl	A	22	32	19	0	3	122.1	527	108	64	57	10	2	6	1	58	1	109	3	4	8	8	.500	0	0	4.19
Garcia,Miguel	Great Falls	LA	R+	22	22	5	0	11	40	190	53	27	23	5	0	1	0	17	4	29	3	0	3	5	.375	0	3	5.18
Garcia,Ricky	Kane County	Fla	A	23	32	1	0	9	57.1	273	63	48	40	3	3	4	7	41	1	47	6	0	0	4	.000	0	0	6.28
Gardner,Scott	Stockton	Mil	A+	25	27	21	3	0	144	608	127	77	66	11	4	0	7	52	0	148	19	2	10	8	.556	1	0	4.13

1996 Pitching — Single-A and Rookie Leagues

HOW MUCH HE PITCHED											WHAT HE GAVE UP												THE RESULTS					
Player	Team	Org	Lg	A	G	GS	CG	GF	IP	BFP	H	R	ER	HR	SH	SF	HB	TBB	IBB	SO	WP	Bk	W	L	Pct.	ShO	Sv	ERA
Garey,Daniel	Mariners	Sea	R	19	12	11	0	0	53	250	65	37	30	2	2	1	5	18	0	38	7	1	3	5	.375	0	0	5.09
Garff,Jeff	Elizabethtn	Min	R+	21	12	12	2	0	72.2	304	71	44	37	11	1	1	4	13	0	38	7	0	6	5	.545	1	0	4.58
Garmon,Adam	Mets	NYN	R	19	12	2	0	3	25.1	113	18	7	7	0	1	0	1	19	0	31	5	0	2	1	.667	0	1	2.49
Garrett,Hal	Clinton	SD	A	22	25	3	0	11	49.2	229	45	28	25	4	2	2	5	31	2	60	3	0	2	3	.400	0	1	4.53
	Rancho Cuca	SD	A+	22	24	1	0	3	51	214	41	12	11	3	1	2	3	20	0	56	6	0	4	1	.800	0	0	1.94
Garrett,Joshua	Red Sox	Bos	R	19	7	5	0	0	27	108	22	8	5	0	2	0	5	5	0	17	0	0	1	1	.500	0	0	1.67
Garrett,Neil	Salem	Col	A+	22	1	1	0	0	7	29	8	4	4	1	1	0	0	2	0	8	1	0	0	1	.000	0	0	5.14
	Asheville	Col	A	22	22	22	1	0	135.1	566	131	61	54	13	4	2	8	37	3	120	7	2	12	4	.750	0	0	3.59
Garsky,Brian	Vermont	Mon	A-	21	25	0	0	10	28.1	129	25	13	10	1	2	2	1	15	1	34	2	0	5	1	.833	0	1	3.18
Garza,Alberto	Burlington	Cle	R+	20	9	9	0	0	39.2	169	34	24	24	5	1	2	1	15	0	34	2	0	2	4	.333	0	0	5.45
Garza,Chris	Elizabethtn	Min	R+	21	22	0	0	12	36.1	145	26	8	8	3	1	1	2	12	0	44	3	3	4	0	1.000	0	5	1.98
Gaskill,Derek	St. Cathrns	Tor	A-	23	19	6	1	6	58.2	258	61	37	31	7	2	6	9	18	1	51	6	0	4	4	.500	0	1	4.76
Gaspar,Cade	Rancho Cuca	SD	A+	23	24	19	0	2	112.1	502	121	69	63	13	3	3	8	50	0	106	11	2	7	4	.636	0	0	5.05
Geis,John	Johnson Cty	StL	R+	23	5	1	0	0	10	41	8	5	5	2	1	0	0	4	1	12	3	0	1	0	1.000	0	0	4.50
Genke,Todd	Salem	Col	A+	26	41	1	0	13	86.2	372	88	41	34	7	8	3	3	28	1	55	5	0	8	7	.533	0	3	3.53
Getz,Rodney	Kane County	Fla	A	21	25	25	1	0	120.1	546	146	79	67	8	4	3	6	41	0	85	9	4	3	14	.176	0	0	5.01
Gholar,Antonio	Twins	Min	R	23	15	7	0	4	52.1	213	30	18	10	0	0	0	4	30	0	50	5	1	1	2	.333	0	2	1.72
Giard,Ken	Macon	Atl	A	24	5	0	0	4	5.2	20	3	1	1	0	0	0	0	1	0	9	0	0	1	0	1.000	0	1	1.59
	Durham	Atl	A+	24	42	0	0	15	68	310	69	44	39	9	4	2	1	43	3	93	5	0	3	5	.375	0	1	5.16
Gillian,Charles	Fort Wayne	Min	A	23	20	0	0	19	22.2	91	24	9	8	3	0	1	2	5	1	14	1	0	0	0	.000	0	5	3.18
Gillispie,Ryan	Pirates	Pit	R	20	1	0	0	0	3	14	4	1	0	0	0	0	0	0	0	5	0	0	0	0	.000	0	0	0.00
Giron,Roberto	Princeton	Cin	R+	21	22	1	0	19	40.2	168	34	18	14	1	2	1	4	11	1	44	1	1	1	3	.250	0	7	3.10
Gissell,Christopher	Cubs	ChN	R	19	11	10	0	0	61.1	246	54	23	16	1	0	1	4	8	0	64	1	3	4	2	.667	0	0	2.35
Giuliano,Joe	Eugene	Atl	A-	21	26	1	0	11	66	298	61	39	26	1	3	3	3	26	4	58	5	0	4	5	.444	0	3	3.55
Glauber,Keith	Peoria	StL	A	25	54	0	0	36	64	276	54	31	22	2	2	5	1	26	2	80	2	1	3	3	.500	0	14	3.09
Glaze,Randy	Sou. Oregon	Oak	A-	23	19	1	0	12	28.1	138	23	22	20	4	0	1	3	23	0	26	2	4	1	2	.333	0	3	6.35
Glick,David	Ogden	Mil	R+	21	24	0	0	4	34.1	165	31	15	13	3	2	1	4	21	3	41	3	0	3	1	.750	0	0	3.41
Glover,Gary	Medicne Hat	Tor	R+	20	15	15	2	0	83.2	410	119	94	72	14	2	4	6	29	1	54	8	1	3	12	.200	0	0	7.75
Glynn,Ryan	Charlstn-SC	Tex	A	22	19	19	2	0	121	526	118	70	61	10	6	6	8	59	2	72	12	0	8	7	.533	1	0	4.54
Gnirk,Mark	Helena	Mil	R+	22	10	2	0	5	23.2	100	26	12	9	3	2	1	3	4	0	26	3	0	1	0	1.000	0	1	3.42
Goedde,Roger	Pirates	Pit	R	21	12	3	0	2	28.2	149	45	41	29	2	4	2	4	11	0	23	2	1	0	2	.000	0	0	9.10
Goldsmith,Gary	Visalia	Det	A+	25	28	27	0	0	170	752	188	108	94	23	4	10	7	76	1	120	2	1	10	11	.476	0	0	4.98
Gomez,Dennys	Bakersfield	SF	A+	26	10	0	0	3	23	97	22	11	9	2	0	0	1	12	0	11	2	1	3	1	.750	0	0	3.52
	San Jose	SF	A+	26	22	0	0	10	28.1	142	30	28	22	0	0	3	8	16	0	27	5	0	1	0	1.000	0	0	6.99
Gomez,Javier	Visalia	Ari	A+	23	22	0	0	4	36.2	163	32	17	15	3	1	1	4	18	1	40	1	1	1	3	.250	0	0	3.68
	Lethbridge	Ari	R+	23	19	0	0	4	42	187	41	25	21	4	1	0	3	17	2	35	5	0	3	2	.600	0	1	4.50
Gomez,Miguel	Dunedin	Tor	A+	23	33	0	0	14	50.2	218	45	27	19	5	4	3	3	17	1	35	7	1	5	4	.556	0	5	3.38
Gonzalez,Dicky	Mets	NYN	R	18	11	8	2	1	47.1	195	50	19	14	1	2	0	2	3	0	51	1	0	4	2	.667	1	0	2.66
	Kingsport	NYN	R+	18	1	1	0	0	5	20	4	2	1	0	1	0	0	0	0	7	1	0	1	0	1.000	0	0	1.80
Gonzalez,Edwin	Royals	KC	R	19	12	8	1	2	57.2	253	60	32	24	5	4	2	7	14	0	39	5	2	5	3	.625	0	1	3.75
Gonzalez,Francis.	Padres	SD	R	19	25	4	0	5	50	222	65	33	24	5	0	2	1	6	0	32	0	0	6	2	.750	0	2	4.32
Gonzalez,Genero.	Fayettevlle	Det	A	21	17	0	0	6	32.1	145	27	17	11	2	1	1	0	23	1	32	4	2	5	3	.625	0	0	3.06
	Lakeland	Det	A+	21	1	0	0	1	2	12	3	5	1	2	0	1	0	2	0	1	0	0	0	0	.000	0	0	4.50
	Tigers	Det	R	21	4	4	0	0	19	85	17	9	7	1	0	1	1	9	0	19	3	0	2	1	.667	0	0	3.32
	Jamestown	Det	A-	21	6	0	0	1	10	49	16	8	6	3	0	0	1	4	0	10	0	0	0	0	.000	0	0	5.40
Gonzalez,Jose	Mariners	Sea	R	20	2	2	0	0	10	38	5	2	1	0	0	0	0	3	0	10	0	0	2	0	1.000	0	0	0.90
Gonzalez,Juan	Brevard Cty	Fla	A+	22	23	17	0	2	86.1	385	102	57	51	6	5	3	7	27	0	48	12	1	1	9	.100	0	0	5.32
Gonzalez,Lariel	Asheville	Col	A	21	35	0	0	24	45	208	37	21	18	2	0	0	1	37	0	53	4	2	1	1	.500	0	4	3.60
Gonzalez,Luis	Erie	Pit	A-	23	21	1	0	8	25.1	113	32	19	16	2	0	1	0	6	0	19	1	1	1	4	.200	0	0	5.68
Gooch,Arnie	St. Lucie	NYN	A+	20	26	26	2	0	167.2	680	131	74	48	7	6	4	4	51	3	141	11	0	12	12	.500	0	0	2.58
Gooda,David	Beloit	Mil	A	20	4	4	0	0	14.2	81	24	21	17	1	0	1	2	11	0	6	0	3	1	3	.250	0	0	10.43
Gordon,Andrew	New Jersey	StL	A-	23	25	5	0	0	49	222	67	33	23	3	2	4	1	9	0	46	9	3	0	0	.000	0	0	4.22
Gordon,Mike	Dunedin	Tor	A+	24	24	24	0	0	133.1	588	127	70	51	7	2	5	7	64	1	102	15	1	3	12	.200	0	0	3.44
Gorrell,Chris	Athletics	Oak	R	21	12	2	0	3	36.2	149	36	18	16	1	1	1	3	8	0	32	2	3	1	2	.333	0	1	3.93
Gourdin,Tom	Fort Myers	Min	A+	24	52	1	0	32	63.1	277	64	37	30	6	6	1	3	29	3	44	7	1	4	6	.400	0	16	4.26
Goure,Sam	Medicne Hat	Tor	R+	19	18	4	0	3	48	242	70	48	32	4	0	2	1	19	0	43	9	0	1	4	.200	0	0	6.00
Gourlay,Matthew	Medicne Hat	Tor	R+	NA	16	13	0	1	66.1	327	95	71	62	17	0	7	1	39	1	35	8	4	2	6	.250	0	0	8.41
Graham,Rich	Sarasota	Bos	A+	27	11	0	0	4	22.2	99	23	13	9	1	0	0	2	7	1	21	1	1	2	0	1.000	0	0	3.57
Granata,Chris	Kinston	Cle	A+	25	35	6	1	6	95.1	417	105	51	46	5	2	4	6	43	4	57	9	0	7	6	.538	1	0	4.34
Granger,Greg	Lakeland	Det	A+	24	5	0	0	1	6.1	29	7	1	1	0	1	0	0	3	0	4	0	0	1	0	1.000	0	0	1.42
	Visalia	Det	A+	24	4	4	0	0	20.1	95	24	12	11	1	0	0	3	10	0	13	3	0	2	0	1.000	0	0	4.87
	Columbus	Cle	A	24	20	12	0	3	84.1	364	90	42	31	5	3	2	3	28	2	67	6	0	8	4	.667	0	2	3.31
Graterol,Beiker	St. Cathrns	Tor	A-	22	14	13	1	0	84	330	59	24	14	6	3	3	4	21	0	66	2	1	9	1	.900	1	0	1.50
Gray,Jason	Hickory	ChA	A	20	13	13	1	0	68.2	300	67	45	35	12	1	2	5	28	0	61	7	1	3	8	.273	1	0	4.59
Green,Blake	Bakersfield	—	A+	45	1	1	0	0	1.2	12	0	4	3	0	0	0	0	8	0	1	2	0	0	1	.000	0	0	16.20
Green,Jason	Auburn	Hou	A-	23	2	2	0	0	6	22	4	1	0	0	0	0	0	1	0	2	0	0	0	0	.000	0	0	0.00
	Daytona	ChN	A+	23	5	4	0	1	14	82	13	17	17	0	0	1	0	29	0	13	8	0	0	3	.000	0	0	10.93
Greene,Danny	Boise	Cal	A-	24	9	0	0	7	11.2	54	12	6	5	2	3	0	0	8	4	12	0	0	0	3	.000	0	1	3.86
Greene,Brian	Daytona	ChN	A+	23	26	1	0	10	55.2	244	51	26	19	5	2	2	10	18	3	37	6	2	5	2	.714	0	1	3.07
Gregg,Kevin	Athletics	Oak	R	19	11	9	0	0	40.2	169	30	14	14	1	1	1	2	21	0	48	11	0	3	3	.500	0	0	3.10
Grenert,Geoff	Cedar Rapds	Cal	A	26	14	12	1	1	67.1	304	73	52	44	10	0	3	6	30	0	57	6	0	3	7	.300	0	0	5.88
Gresko,Michael	Pirates	Pit	R	20	5	0	0	1	6	31	3	8	2	1	1	0	1	5	0	7	2	0	0	1	.000	0	0	3.00
Grieve,Tim	Royals	KC	R	25	2	0	0	0	3	11	1	1	0	0	0	0	0	1	0	2	0	0	0	1	.000	0	0	0.00
	Lansing	KC	A	25	3	0	0	3	3	15	0	1	1	0	1	0	0	6	1	5	1	0	0	1	.000	0	0	3.00
	Wilmington	KC	A+	25	22	0	0	13	34.1	143	28	9	5	1	2	1	0	13	3	30	1	0	4	1	.800	0	4	1.31
Grife,Rich	Columbus	Cle	A	25	36	0	0	17	58	249	56	29	25	1	2	2	5	20	5	42	5	2	2	4	.333	0	3	3.88
Griffiths,Everard	Butte	TB	R+	23	7	0	0	1	12.1	72	18	17	11	0	1	1	1	15	2	12	4	1	0	2	.000	0	0	8.03

1996 Pitching — Single-A and Rookie Leagues

HOW MUCH HE PITCHED											WHAT HE GAVE UP												THE RESULTS					
Player	Team	Org	Lg	A	G	GS	CG	GF	IP	BFP	H	R	ER	HR	SH	SF	HB	TBB	IBB	SO	WP	Bk	W	L	Pct.	ShO	Sv	ERA
	Hudson Vall	TB	A-	23	11	4	0	4	32.1	137	26	12	11	2	0	0	2	13	0	39	6	0	1	1	.500	0	0	3.06
Grote,Jason	Burlington	SF	A	22	28	26	1	0	139.2	604	146	80	68	18	3	5	0	55	0	103	11	3	11	9	.550	1	0	4.38
Gryboski,Kevin	Wisconsin	Sea	A	23	32	21	3	5	138.2	630	146	90	73	7	9	6	12	62	2	100	12	0	10	5	.667	0	1	4.74
Gulin,Lindsay	Columbia	NYN	A	20	19	19	1	0	112.1	470	88	40	33	6	0	2	6	57	0	134	5	6	7	7	.500	0	0	2.64
Gunderson,Mike	Quad City	Hou	A	24	34	7	0	11	80.1	380	80	60	46	7	5	3	5	64	0	59	6	0	4	4	.500	0	3	5.15
Gunther,Kevin	W. Michigan	Oak	A	24	43	0	0	21	95.2	398	83	37	31	6	7	2	1	25	4	90	3	0	5	5	.500	0	6	2.92
Gutierrez,Alfredo	Ogden	Mil	R+	21	19	0	0	18	21.1	97	18	12	10	2	1	0	1	11	2	28	3	0	0	3	.000	0	9	4.22
Gutierrez,Javier	Everett	Sea	A-	22	7	7	0	0	34	158	43	25	21	6	0	1	2	12	0	35	2	0	4	1	.800	0	0	5.56
Guzman,Domingo	Clinton	SD	A	22	6	5	0	1	20.2	112	32	33	29	2	0	1	2	19	0	18	5	0	0	5	.000	0	0	12.63
	Idaho Falls	SD	R+	22	15	10	1	1	65.1	278	52	41	30	7	2	1	7	29	0	75	13	0	4	2	.667	1	0	4.13
Guzman,Jonathan	Helena	Mil	R+	19	20	5	0	3	49.2	243	64	48	41	5	2	6	3	32	0	40	3	1	2	3	.400	0	0	7.43
Guzman,Toribio	Johnson Cty	StL	R+	20	23	0	0	4	31	148	39	19	13	0	0	0	2	18	1	24	1	1	2	2	.500	0	0	3.77
Hacen,Abraham	High Desert	Bal	A+	26	3	0	0	0	3.1	29	12	13	12	4	0	0	0	7	0	2	1	1	0	0	.000	0	0	32.40
	Bluefield	Bal	R+	26	15	12	2	2	63.1	280	54	29	24	4	0	3	5	36	0	69	9	2	8	3	.727	0	0	3.41
Hackett,Jason	High Desert	Bal	A+	22	5	0	0	0	7.2	43	9	4	4	0	0	0	0	15	0	4	1	0	0	0	.000	0	0	4.70
	Bluefield	Bal	R+	22	19	5	0	4	46	215	47	33	28	6	0	1	2	28	0	56	6	1	1	1	.500	0	1	5.48
Hackman,Luther	Salem	Col	A+	22	21	21	1	0	110.1	484	93	60	52	2	4	7	5	69	1	83	6	2	5	7	.417	0	0	4.24
Hafer,Jeffrey	Kingsport	NYN	R+	22	24	0	0	14	33.2	137	29	9	8	1	1	0	1	8	1	43	7	0	0	2	.000	0	6	2.14
Haigler,Phillip	Fort Wayne	Min	A	23	15	13	0	0	68.1	305	80	42	40	3	1	3	6	25	0	35	1	3	4	3	.571	0	0	5.27
Hale,Chad	Sarasota	Bos	A+	25	42	0	0	19	60.2	260	56	33	21	2	2	5	1	17	1	37	2	3	3	0	1.000	0	7	3.12
Hale,Mark	Butte	TB	R+	21	21	0	0	19	38.2	162	32	17	14	2	3	1	1	10	3	56	7	1	2	2	.500	0	7	3.26
Hall,Billy	Kissimmee	Hou	A+	23	2	0	0	0	3	12	2	0	0	0	0	0	0	0	0	1	0	0	0	0	.000	0	0	0.00
Hall,Yates	St. Pete	StL	A+	24	26	17	0	6	89.1	411	93	62	54	6	5	4	4	58	0	58	10	2	1	10	.091	0	1	5.44
Halladay,Roy	Dunedin	Tor	A+	20	27	27	2	0	164.2	688	158	75	50	7	5	1	6	46	0	109	1	2	15	7	.682	2	0	2.73
Halley,Allen	Pr. William	ChA	A+	25	24	24	4	0	137.1	568	123	69	54	16	3	1	7	49	2	131	7	4	7	12	.368	0	0	3.54
	Hagerstown	Tor	A	25	2	0	0	1	4	15	0	0	0	0	0	0	0	4	0	6	1	0	1	0	1.000	0	0	0.00
Hamilton,Jimmy	Burlington	Cle	R+	21	10	10	0	0	45	193	45	22	20	7	1	2	3	16	0	50	8	0	1	3	.250	0	0	4.00
Hamilton,Paul	Piedmont	Phi	A	25	6	2	0	2	13.1	66	16	15	14	1	0	1	2	9	0	12	1	0	2	1	.667	0	0	9.45
Hammack,Brandon	Rockford	ChN	A	24	30	0	0	28	31.2	140	22	13	8	0	2	0	1	19	1	45	1	0	2	3	.400	0	13	2.27
	Daytona	ChN	A+	24	27	0	0	25	31.1	132	27	10	8	1	4	2	0	10	0	36	0	0	2	1	.667	0	16	2.30
Hammerschmidt,A.	Rancho Cuca	SD	A+	25	35	6	0	6	82.1	366	102	59	48	6	3	3	5	20	1	59	3	3	6	4	.600	0	2	5.25
Hammons,Matt	Rockford	ChN	A	20	5	5	0	0	25	105	24	19	17	3	1	0	3	8	1	22	3	0	1	3	.250	0	0	6.12
Hamulack,Timothy	Astros	Hou	R	20	22	0	0	9	27	115	23	9	7	1	0	0	2	13	1	24	1	0	4	1	.800	0	2	2.33
Handy,Russell	W. Palm Bch	Mon	A+	22	14	5	0	3	31.2	168	43	40	32	3	1	1	7	28	0	12	5	0	2	4	.333	0	0	9.09
	Delmarva	Mon	A	22	24	0	0	15	38	187	40	38	23	2	1	4	3	36	0	28	10	0	2	3	.400	0	4	5.45
Hannah,Michael	Yakima	LA	A-	22	18	0	0	3	23.2	119	25	26	15	1	1	2	2	22	0	13	3	0	1	1	.500	0	1	5.70
Hanson,Kris	Kinston	Cle	A+	26	9	8	0	0	47	204	46	31	28	6	1	0	4	16	0	26	1	1	2	5	.286	0	0	5.36
Harden,Nathan	Braves	Atl	R	19	14	2	0	6	39	170	32	29	20	2	1	1	3	15	0	30	5	1	2	2	.500	0	0	4.62
Hardwick,Bubba	Helena	Mil	R+	25	3	3	0	0	5	28	8	5	5	1	0	1	0	6	0	4	0	0	0	1	.000	0	0	9.00
Harper,David	Visalia	Det	A+	22	12	0	0	3	8.2	52	15	19	19	3	1	0	2	10	0	5	0	1	0	0	.000	0	0	19.73
Harriger,Mark	Boise	Cal	A-	22	7	0	0	1	4.1	26	9	5	4	1	1	0	0	3	0	3	1	1	0	0	.000	0	0	8.31
Harris,D.J.	Dunedin	Tor	A+	26	35	0	0	19	43.1	203	49	30	25	3	3	3	4	19	1	31	3	0	4	3	.571	0	6	5.19
Harris,Bryan	Lk Elsinore	Cal	A+	25	20	2	0	7	37	164	29	20	18	3	3	3	2	26	1	31	5	4	0	7	.000	0	0	4.38
Harris,Jeff	Fort Wayne	Min	A	22	42	0	0	15	89.2	387	90	35	31	4	3	8	4	33	1	85	10	1	8	3	.727	0	3	3.11
Harris,Joshua	Billings	Cin	R+	19	20	2	0	6	41.1	189	58	33	29	5	0	2	0	21	1	30	3	1	1	1	.500	0	0	6.31
Hart,Len	Williamsprt	ChN	A-	23	28	0	0	13	31.1	129	15	6	5	0	2	0	0	24	1	26	1	0	2	3	.400	0	2	1.44
Hartgrove,Lyle	Sarasota	Bos	A+	25	15	0	0	6	19.1	86	30	12	10	2	0	1	0	3	1	7	1	2	2	0	1.000	0	0	4.66
Hartshorn,Ty	Hagerstown	Tor	A	22	26	26	1	0	147	648	153	86	75	15	5	6	9	64	1	109	22	1	5	11	.313	0	0	4.59
Hartvigson,Chad	San Jose	SF	A+	26	36	10	0	7	103	427	94	46	37	10	1	4	1	30	0	114	4	0	4	7	.364	0	2	3.23
Harvey,Terry	Kinston	Cle	A+	24	12	12	0	0	69.2	293	80	38	31	5	4	2	3	16	0	34	2	1	2	4	.333	0	0	4.00
Hasselhoff,Derek	South Bend	ChA	A	23	35	0	0	29	47.2	205	46	19	17	4	4	1	2	17	0	39	5	0	6	3	.667	0	10	3.21
	Pr. William	ChA	A+	23	5	0	0	4	10.1	49	14	7	6	1	0	0	0	6	2	9	0	0	0	1	.000	0	1	5.23
Hause,Brendan	Modesto	Oak	A+	22	1	0	0	0	2	12	4	3	3	1	0	0	1	1	0	2	1	0	0	0	.000	0	0	13.50
Hausmann,Isaac	Charlstn-SC	Tex	A	21	1	1	1	0	6	22	3	2	2	0	1	0	0	1	0	8	1	0	0	1	.000	0	0	3.00
	Rangers	Tex	R	21	12	11	2	1	81	343	85	38	26	5	3	3	1	14	1	48	1	1	7	3	.700	1	0	2.89
Havens,Jeff	Augusta	Pit	A	24	34	1	0	11	44.1	201	51	22	18	2	0	0	3	12	1	43	3	1	1	3	.250	0	2	3.65
Hawkins,Alsharik	Ogden	Mil	R+	19	9	5	0	1	33.2	144	31	16	12	1	0	0	0	13	0	23	1	3	3	3	.500	0	0	3.21
Haynes,Heath	Lk Elsinore	Cal	A+	28	31	0	0	11	38.1	142	29	9	7	1	1	0	3	2	0	44	1	1	5	1	.833	0	2	1.64
Haynie,Jason	Erie	Pit	A-	23	16	12	1	2	80.1	345	86	36	29	2	5	4	3	22	2	74	4	3	3	4	.429	0	0	3.25
Hearns,Shane	Mariners	Sea	R	21	9	0	0	5	15.1	64	10	7	5	0	0	0	1	6	0	12	3	1	1	1	.500	0	2	2.93
Hedley,Brian	Helena	Mil	R+	22	14	0	0	6	24.1	123	38	29	28	4	0	4	1	15	0	19	2	1	1	2	.333	0	1	10.36
Heffernan,Greg	New Jersey	StL	A-	22	18	0	0	4	23.2	110	24	16	9	2	2	2	1	13	0	22	1	2	0	1	.000	0	0	3.42
Heineman,Rick	Bristol	ChA	R+	23	23	0	0	14	36	168	37	25	18	3	0	1	1	22	1	34	5	3	2	1	.667	0	4	4.50
Heiserman,Rick	St. Pete	StL	A+	24	26	26	1	0	155.1	663	168	68	56	8	6	3	9	41	0	104	4	0	10	8	.556	1	0	3.24
Henderson,Kenny	Rancho Cuca	SD	A+	24	5	5	0	0	17.1	81	19	14	11	1	1	3	2	10	0	14	0	1	1	1	.500	0	0	5.71
	Clinton	SD	A	24	7	7	0	0	27	116	30	13	7	0	1	1	2	5	0	26	5	0	0	3	.000	0	0	2.33
Hendrikx,Brandon	Yankees	NYA	R	21	7	0	0	4	9.1	43	9	10	4	1	0	1	0	3	0	10	0	0	0	1	.000	0	1	3.86
	Oneonta	NYA	A-	21	17	0	0	10	27	109	17	6	4	3	1	1	2	15	0	23	2	0	3	2	.600	0	1	1.33
Henriquez,Joban.	Rangers	Tex	R	20	13	6	0	2	41.2	178	42	22	19	3	1	1	1	19	2	29	7	2	2	3	.400	0	0	4.10
Henriquez,Oscar	Kissimmee	Hou	A+	23	37	0	0	33	34	162	28	18	15	0	1	1	3	29	2	40	4	0	0	4	.000	0	15	3.97
Herbert,Russell	Pr. William	ChA	A+	25	25	25	1	0	144	609	129	73	54	12	8	11	6	62	3	148	3	2	6	10	.375	0	0	3.38
Herbison,Brett	Kingsport	NYN	R+	20	13	12	0	0	76.2	297	43	18	11	4	0	1	3	31	0	86	6	0	6	2	.750	0	0	1.29
	Pittsfield	NYN	A-	20	1	1	0	0	2	15	4	6	5	0	0	0	0	4	0	1	1	0	0	1	.000	0	0	22.50
Heredia,Maximo	Orioles	Bal	R	20	17	0	0	7	34.1	143	22	15	11	1	1	0	4	12	0	25	2	0	3	1	.750	0	4	2.88
Hermanson,Mike	Lk Elsinore	Cal	A+	25	29	0	0	11	35	166	40	25	16	6	0	1	2	22	0	30	3	0	0	3	.000	0	0	4.11
	Cedar Rapds	Cal	A	25	4	3	0	0	15.2	66	15	11	10	2	0	0	1	9	0	12	3	0	0	0	.000	0	0	5.74
Hernandez,Elvin	Augusta	Pit	A	19	27	27	2	0	157.2	624	140	60	55	13	0	2	5	16	2	171	7	0	17	5	.773	1	0	3.14

1996 Pitching — Single-A and Rookie Leagues

HOW MUCH HE PITCHED											WHAT HE GAVE UP												THE RESULTS					
Player	Team	Org	Lg	A	G	GS	CG	GF	IP	BFP	H	R	ER	HR	SH	SF	HB	TBB	IBB	SO	WP	Bk	W	L	Pct.	ShO	Sv	ERA
Hernandez,Francis	Frederick	Bal	A+	20	37	0	0	30	45.1	197	44	26	23	6	5	1	1	21	7	39	2	0	4	3	.571	0	12	4.57
Hernandez,Jeremy	Visalia	Ari	A+	30	24	15	0	3	102.2	471	133	89	68	15	3	2	3	30	0	88	8	2	2	9	.182	0	0	5.96
Hernandez,Santos	Burlington	SF	A	24	61	0	0	58	66.2	249	39	15	14	4	3	1	2	13	0	79	7	1	3	3	.500	0	35	1.89
Herrera,Desmond	Billings	Cin	R+	23	30	0	0	10	34.2	185	61	38	34	8	1	4	2	11	0	32	5	0	2	2	.500	0	2	8.83
Herrera,Ivan	Bellingham	SF	A-	20	6	0	0	3	5.2	34	10	11	8	0	0	0	1	4	0	0	1	0	0	1	.000	0	0	12.71
Herring,Jonathan	Medicne Hat	Tor	R+	NA	20	0	0	6	20	122	30	35	31	7	1	1	5	27	0	14	8	0	0	0	.000	0	0	13.95
Higuchi,Roberto	Medicne Hat	Tor	R+	NA	15	0	0	8	22.1	135	37	39	32	5	0	1	5	23	1	17	9	2	0	0	.000	0	0	12.90
Hill,Chris	Quad City	Hou	A	22	18	5	0	4	49	212	48	39	34	7	3	1	8	15	0	39	1	2	3	5	.375	0	0	6.24
Hill,Jason	Cedar Rapds	Cal	A	25	18	6	0	2	43.2	197	38	19	15	2	3	1	5	31	1	26	4	0	2	2	.500	0	1	3.09
	Lk Elsinore	Cal	A+	25	32	0	0	8	39.2	167	39	16	11	4	1	0	2	14	0	28	0	2	4	3	.571	0	0	2.50
Hill,Ty	Stockton	Mil	A+	25	5	5	0	0	19.2	87	18	14	11	1	0	0	0	9	1	11	0	4	0	2	.000	0	0	5.03
Hilton,Willy	Sou. Oregon	Oak	A-	24	26	2	0	8	61.2	291	71	44	40	4	4	0	6	27	1	38	6	3	2	1	.667	0	2	5.84
Hinchliffe,Brett	Lancaster	Sea	A+	22	27	26	0	0	163.1	731	179	105	77	19	6	5	9	64	1	146	10	1	11	10	.524	0	0	4.24
Hinchy,Brian	Rockies	Col	R	21	14	0	0	11	15	64	15	8	5	0	0	0	0	5	0	7	3	0	1	1	.500	0	4	3.00
	Portland	Col	A-	21	9	0	0	6	11	58	13	16	9	1	1	1	1	9	1	5	0	1	0	3	.000	0	0	7.36
Hinojosa,Joel	Devil Rays	TB	R	23	1	0	0	0	1.1	10	3	5	3	0	0	1	0	2	0	1	1	0	0	0	.000	0	0	20.25
	Butte	TB	R+	23	27	0	0	14	42.2	203	49	31	25	5	3	2	7	25	2	32	8	2	3	4	.429	0	1	5.27
Hite,Kevin	Padres	SD	R	22	13	12	2	0	77	326	86	44	31	1	3	0	1	15	0	65	4	2	5	5	.500	1	0	3.62
Hloden,George	Pirates	Pit	R	21	7	6	0	0	27	117	29	12	8	0	1	4	2	7	0	15	1	1	3	2	.600	0	0	2.67
Hodges,Reid	Bristol	ChA	R+	22	16	3	0	4	29.2	155	38	41	37	5	0	3	3	25	0	24	5	0	0	2	.000	0	0	11.22
Hodges,Kevin	Lansing	KC	A	24	9	9	0	0	48.1	208	47	32	25	3	2	1	6	19	0	23	3	1	1	2	.333	0	0	4.66
	Wilmington	KC	A+	24	8	8	0	0	38.2	172	45	30	23	2	0	3	1	18	0	15	5	1	2	4	.333	0	0	5.35
Hoff,Steve	Padres	SD	R	20	16	13	0	1	85.1	356	66	37	27	2	0	1	9	36	0	104	6	0	8	2	.800	0	0	2.85
Hogge,Shawn	Johnson Cty	StL	R+	19	12	0	0	1	9.2	68	14	17	12	1	0	1	4	21	0	6	6	0	0	1	.000	0	0	11.17
Hohenstein,And.	Pirates	Pit	R	19	7	5	0	1	26.1	125	36	20	9	1	0	1	2	12	0	18	1	0	2	0	1.000	0	0	3.08
Holden,Jason	Modesto	Oak	A+	23	1	0	0	0	2	12	5	3	3	1	0	0	2	0	0	1	0	0	0	0	.000	0	0	13.50
	Sou. Oregon	Oak	A-	23	9	8	0	0	32.2	156	39	27	21	2	0	0	2	14	0	21	2	1	3	5	.375	0	0	5.79
Holobinko,Mike	Williamsprt	ChN	A-	20	4	2	0	0	17.1	69	11	4	3	0	0	1	0	7	0	9	2	1	1	0	1.000	0	0	1.56
	Cubs	ChN	R	20	11	0	0	8	17.1	67	10	1	1	0	0	0	0	7	0	22	2	0	2	0	1.000	0	3	0.52
Hommel,Brian	Stockton	Mil	A+	24	4	0	0	1	5	21	2	1	0	0	1	0	0	4	0	4	0	0	0	0	.000	0	0	0.00
Hook,Jeff	Ogden	Mil	R+	22	3	0	0	1	5.1	32	7	5	5	0	1	0	1	8	0	3	0	0	0	0	.000	0	0	8.44
Hooten,David	Elizabethtn	Min	R+	22	6	0	0	5	8.1	37	6	4	4	0	0	2	1	5	0	15	0	2	1	0	1.000	0	1	4.32
	Fort Wayne	Min	A	22	21	0	0	14	37.1	155	30	11	10	0	2	4	2	13	1	39	3	1	4	1	.800	0	2	2.41
Horgan,Joe	Burlington	Cle	R+	20	23	0	0	18	34.1	157	37	25	16	1	0	0	4	9	0	48	4	0	1	2	.333	0	7	4.19
Horn,Keith	Columbus	Cle	A	23	25	12	0	5	89.2	374	80	48	39	7	1	3	4	24	2	78	3	0	5	5	.500	0	1	3.91
Horne,Jeffrey	Princeton	Cin	R+	22	10	8	3	0	46.2	204	42	30	18	2	0	3	1	21	0	45	7	0	3	3	.500	1	0	3.47
	Charlstn-WV	Cin	A	22	3	3	0	0	12	66	18	16	12	2	1	1	0	8	0	8	0	1	0	2	.000	0	0	9.00
Horton,Aaron	Hudson Vall	TB	A-	22	9	7	0	0	25.1	154	55	46	35	2	1	2	3	15	0	15	7	2	0	3	.000	0	0	12.43
Horton,Eric	Hagerstown	Tor	A	26	13	1	0	4	22	98	21	14	12	0	0	0	2	13	0	17	2	2	1	2	.333	0	1	4.91
	Medicne Hat	Tor	R+	26	5	0	0	3	13	66	19	15	12	1	0	1	1	9	1	11	5	0	0	1	.000	0	0	8.31
Hoshiba,Takahisa	Visalia	—	A+	NA	21	16	0	2	126	552	151	77	62	22	4	2	2	39	1	108	8	0	8	6	.571	0	1	4.43
Housely,Adam	Beloit	Mil	A	25	34	0	0	18	69.1	315	74	33	23	5	7	2	9	28	5	49	1	4	2	4	.333	0	4	2.99
Howard,Jamie	Macon	Atl	A	23	8	6	0	0	26.1	135	37	26	23	4	3	3	4	16	1	11	1	0	0	4	.000	0	0	7.86
Howatt,Jeffrey	Columbia	NYN	A	23	37	0	0	26	61	278	49	23	20	5	2	0	2	19	1	61	4	2	4	4	.500	0	7	2.61
Howerton,Roy	Butte	TB	R+	23	15	13	0	0	61	291	72	47	30	3	0	1	4	42	0	47	13	0	3	1	.750	0	0	4.43
Hritz,Derrick	Bakersfield	Cle	A+	24	31	7	0	14	81.1	386	100	68	53	10	6	4	0	50	1	60	5	1	4	6	.400	0	2	5.86
	Columbus	Cle	A	24	5	0	0	2	7	36	17	9	9	1	0	1	0	0	0	2	0	0	0	0	.000	0	0	11.57
Huber,Jeff	Stockton	Mil	A+	26	18	0	0	13	19.2	84	24	9	4	0	0	2	1	3	0	12	0	0	1	1	.500	0	6	1.83
Huber,John	Astros	Hou	R	19	10	6	0	0	35.2	161	33	20	16	1	0	0	3	23	0	37	9	2	1	2	.333	0	0	4.04
Hueda,Alejandro	St. Cathrns	Tor	A-	21	12	5	0	1	31	151	41	33	30	5	0	1	2	16	0	17	2	1	0	3	.000	0	0	8.71
Hueston,Stephen	Spokane	KC	A-	23	13	13	0	0	64.1	272	54	27	22	8	3	2	5	31	0	60	5	2	3	2	.600	0	0	3.08
Hughes,Michael	Boise	Cal	A-	20	13	0	0	4	16.2	79	16	12	9	1	0	1	1	13	1	20	1	0	0	0	.000	0	1	4.86
Humphreys,Kevin	Boise	Cal	A-	NA	19	0	0	9	45.1	190	32	17	10	4	1	4	4	15	3	34	6	0	3	2	.600	0	0	1.99
Humphry,Trevor	Clearwater	Phi	A+	25	16	0	0	1	33.2	134	21	8	7	0	1	1	1	17	0	12	1	0	2	0	1.000	0	0	1.87
Hunt,Jon	Hickory	ChA	A	23	25	25	3	0	143	628	136	85	60	3	2	5	11	70	1	80	13	0	7	10	.412	0	0	3.78
Huntsman,Brandon	High Desert	Bal	A+	21	13	2	0	2	27.1	142	36	29	29	6	2	1	3	27	1	25	1	0	1	3	.250	0	0	9.55
	Bluefield	Bal	R+	21	14	13	0	0	68.1	297	54	37	31	4	0	2	6	38	0	79	9	0	5	4	.556	0	0	4.08
Huntsman,Scott	Stockton	Mil	A+	24	43	0	0	29	48.1	213	37	21	15	3	0	3	2	27	0	56	2	0	4	3	.571	0	12	2.79
Hurtado,Omar	Princeton	Cin	R+	18	15	0	0	7	26.1	124	24	22	18	2	1	1	3	17	0	19	3	2	1	2	.333	0	0	6.15
Hurtado,Victor	Kane County	Fla	A	20	27	27	5	0	176	748	167	79	64	10	5	4	19	56	0	126	14	2	15	7	.682	0	0	3.27
Hutzler,Jeff	Burlington	SF	A	24	25	25	2	0	139.1	580	133	71	59	7	2	7	5	33	0	79	11	1	8	7	.533	0	0	3.81
Iddon,Brent	Wisconsin	Sea	A	21	50	0	0	22	97	409	82	32	30	4	6	4	6	41	3	114	3	0	11	4	.733	0	11	2.78
Iglesias,Mario	Bristol	ChA	R+	23	3	0	0	1	8.1	29	6	2	2	1	0	1	0	1	0	2	1	0	0	0	.000	0	1	2.16
	Hickory	ChA	A	23	10	5	0	2	34.2	155	45	19	19	4	0	0	6	6	0	31	1	1	2	3	.400	0	1	4.93
Iglesias,Mike	Vero Beach	LA	A+	24	31	16	0	14	104	463	112	68	59	9	1	4	5	37	1	101	6	1	5	8	.385	0	7	5.11
Ingerick,Rhett	Oneonta	NYA	A-	22	11	0	0	7	20	97	26	16	13	0	0	0	0	11	0	21	3	0	1	1	.500	0	0	5.85
Ireland,Eric	Astros	Hou	R	NA	12	11	0	1	53.2	235	54	33	28	1	3	1	3	23	1	43	13	1	3	4	.429	0	0	4.70
Irvine,Kirk	Bristol	ChA	R+	22	11	5	1	2	40.2	180	49	30	22	5	2	0	4	10	2	39	4	2	0	4	.000	0	0	4.87
Ishee,Gabe	Ogden	Mil	R+	22	15	14	1	0	85.2	388	94	55	45	9	4	3	6	42	0	83	13	4	6	4	.600	0	0	4.73
Ishimaru,Taisuke	Great Falls	LA	R+	19	9	2	0	3	21	101	22	13	12	1	1	3	1	14	1	11	1	0	0	1	.000	0	1	5.14
Ito,Makoto	Visalia	—	A+	NA	34	0	0	8	32	139	34	16	14	1	3	0	0	12	2	26	1	0	0	1	.000	0	0	3.94
Izquierdo,Hansel	Marlins	Fla	R	20	12	0	0	10	13.1	52	7	4	4	0	0	0	3	5	0	17	3	1	0	1	.000	0	3	2.70
Jacobs,Jake	Twins	Min	R	19	6	6	0	0	26.2	119	31	22	17	4	2	0	1	7	0	29	2	1	1	2	.333	0	0	5.74
Jacobs,Dwayne	Macon	Atl	A	20	26	15	0	4	82	409	85	82	62	2	2	5	11	76	2	76	18	4	2	7	.222	0	0	6.80
Jacobs,Mike	Macon	Atl	A	24	11	2	0	2	25.2	130	31	26	15	2	0	2	4	19	1	21	5	0	0	2	.000	0	0	5.26
Jacobs,Russell	Wisconsin	Sea	A	22	24	10	0	4	68.1	313	67	48	40	2	2	3	2	53	0	63	13	2	4	4	.500	0	2	5.27
Jacobson,Brian	Great Falls	LA	R+	22	29	0	0	15	38	182	56	37	23	3	1	1	1	13	0	31	3	0	4	2	.667	0	7	5.45

1996 Pitching — Single-A and Rookie Leagues

HOW MUCH HE PITCHED											WHAT HE GAVE UP												THE RESULTS					
Player	Team	Org	Lg	A	G	GS	CG	GF	IP	BFP	H	R	ER	HR	SH	SF	HB	TBB	IBB	SO	WP	Bk	W	L	Pct.	ShO	Sv	ERA
Jacobson,K.J.	Fayettevlle	Det	A	26	6	0	0	3	8.2	39	7	3	3	1	0	0	3	3	0	8	1	0	0	1	.000	0	0	3.12
	Lakeland	Det	A+	26	26	3	0	12	56.1	257	53	30	23	0	3	5	4	36	0	44	12	2	0	4	.000	0	1	3.67
James,Delvin	Devil Rays	TB	R	19	11	11	1	0	47.2	236	64	52	47	0	1	3	11	21	0	40	11	2	2	8	.200	0	0	8.87
Jarvis,Jason	Dunedin	Tor	A+	23	36	13	2	8	112.1	485	117	66	61	5	4	3	10	40	1	65	6	0	7	3	.700	1	1	4.89
Jelsovsky,Craig	Kingsport	NYN	R+	21	13	1	0	4	24.1	101	18	9	7	1	0	0	3	10	1	20	1	1	4	1	.800	0	2	2.59
Jensen,Ryan	Bellingham	SF	A-	21	13	11	0	0	47	208	35	30	26	4	1	0	1	38	0	31	7	0	2	4	.333	0	0	4.98
Jimenez,Jhonny	Everett	Sea	A-	21	24	0	0	16	31.1	138	34	20	16	3	4	2	1	12	1	26	3	2	1	3	.250	0	5	4.60
Jimenez,Jose	Peoria	StL	A	23	28	27	3	0	172.1	720	158	75	56	6	5	6	9	53	0	129	8	1	12	9	.571	1	0	2.92
Jimenez,Ricardo	Orioles	Bal	R	19	12	12	0	0	62.2	267	46	22	14	1	1	1	4	34	0	44	1	0	5	3	.625	0	0	2.01
Johannsen,Jeff	Utica	Fla	A-	24	14	14	0	0	79	324	68	40	38	9	2	2	6	22	0	73	2	3	4	5	.444	0	0	4.33
Johnson,Carl	Visalia	Det	A+	26	15	5	0	3	22	137	35	44	38	5	1	2	3	35	0	16	11	1	3	5	.375	0	0	15.55
Johnson,Gregory	Boise	Cal	A-	23	8	0	0	5	9.2	47	17	11	11	2	0	1	0	2	1	6	0	0	0	0	.000	0	0	10.24
Johnson,Jason	Lynchburg	Pit	A+	23	15	5	0	1	44.1	204	56	37	32	6	5	1	1	12	0	27	0	0	1	4	.200	0	0	6.50
	Augusta	Pit	A	23	14	14	1	0	84	359	82	40	29	2	5	3	6	25	0	83	5	2	4	4	.500	1	0	3.11
Johnson,Jeremiah	Orioles	Bal	R	19	4	0	0	1	6	23	4	0	0	0	0	0	0	1	0	10	0	0	0	0	.000	0	0	0.00
Johnson,Mike	Hagerstown	Tor	A	21	29	23	5	1	162.2	671	157	74	57	6	5	5	8	39	0	155	12	1	11	8	.579	3	0	3.15
Jones,Scott	Michigan	Bos	A	24	48	0	0	42	44.2	219	32	33	27	3	3	3	5	45	2	41	14	1	0	3	.000	0	18	5.44
Jones,Michael	Eugene	Atl	A-	24	13	2	0	2	40.2	186	40	24	18	3	2	1	3	17	0	41	1	0	5	4	.556	0	0	3.98
	Durham	Atl	A+	24	7	3	0	2	20.2	94	21	14	11	2	0	2	1	14	0	16	0	0	0	2	.000	0	0	4.79
Jones,Travis	Padres	SD	R	19	14	9	0	0	42	216	52	38	29	6	1	3	3	37	0	29	5	3	0	2	.000	0	0	6.21
Jordan,Jason	Visalia	Det	A+	24	30	20	1	2	144.2	650	175	89	78	14	5	6	6	54	2	110	17	0	6	10	.375	0	0	4.85
Judd,Mike	Greensboro	NYA	A	22	29	0	0	26	28.1	119	22	14	12	2	2	0	2	8	3	36	2	1	2	2	.500	0	10	3.81
	Savannah	LA	A	22	15	8	1	7	55.1	220	40	21	15	2	2	0	2	15	0	62	9	0	4	2	.667	0	3	2.44
Kahlon,Harbrinder	Macon	Atl	A	24	14	0	0	12	23	100	21	10	9	1	2	1	0	10	8	25	1	1	2	1	.667	0	4	3.52
Kammerer,James	Asheville	Col	A	23	9	8	0	1	43	181	36	18	15	0	0	0	1	18	1	44	1	0	4	2	.667	0	0	3.14
Karsay,Steve	Modesto	Oak	A+	25	14	14	0	0	34	141	35	16	10	2	0	0	3	1	0	31	3	1	0	1	.000	0	0	2.65
Kast,Nick	Peoria	StL	A	24	5	0	0	2	4.2	28	6	11	9	0	0	0	2	8	0	8	0	0	0	1	.000	0	0	17.36
Kauffman,George	Royals	KC	R	22	1	0	0	0	0.2	3	1	0	0	0	0	0	0	0	0	1	0	0	0	0	.000	0	0	0.00
Kauflin,Dave	Jamestown	Det	A-	21	22	7	0	3	64	266	55	25	22	5	0	3	3	26	0	56	10	0	6	2	.750	0	0	3.09
Kaufman,John	Butte	TB	R+	22	13	12	0	0	46.1	214	53	36	24	2	3	3	0	24	0	55	7	2	2	3	.400	0	0	4.66
Kawabata,Kyle	Batavia	Phi	A-	23	25	0	0	25	28	115	21	7	6	2	2	0	1	7	1	24	2	0	1	2	.333	0	20	1.93
Kawahara,Orin	Mariners	Sea	R	19	18	10	0	5	71.1	318	64	42	33	4	3	3	6	40	0	87	2	1	5	5	.500	0	1	4.16
Kaye,Justin	Mariners	Sea	R	21	20	0	0	12	32.1	156	34	23	13	4	0	1	5	19	1	36	7	2	1	0	1.000	0	3	3.62
Kaysner,Brent	Lansing	KC	A	23	38	0	0	19	44.1	234	38	34	25	3	1	0	13	57	0	39	14	1	2	3	.400	0	0	5.08
Kazmirski,Robert	W. Michigan	Oak	A	25	51	0	0	48	53.2	234	45	19	16	2	6	1	1	28	5	37	3	1	3	5	.375	0	28	2.68
Keathley,Davan	Medicne Hat	Tor	R+	19	15	2	0	4	39.2	207	56	46	38	7	0	2	2	29	0	36	3	2	3	2	.600	0	0	8.62
Keehn,Drew	Asheville	Col	A	22	26	1	0	14	55	266	61	51	37	7	0	2	5	42	2	35	4	3	3	2	.600	0	0	6.05
Keith,Jeff	Burlington	SF	A	25	35	0	0	19	52.1	239	45	32	22	5	5	2	5	40	0	41	2	2	1	2	.333	0	1	3.78
Keller,Kristopher	Tigers	Det	R	19	8	6	0	0	34	143	23	12	9	0	1	2	0	21	0	23	7	1	1	1	.500	0	0	2.38
Kelley,Jason	Cubs	ChN	R	21	8	7	0	1	25.2	115	18	22	17	3	0	1	7	16	0	29	7	2	2	3	.400	0	0	5.96
Kelly,Jeff	Augusta	Pit	A	22	14	14	0	0	84	360	76	39	31	4	0	3	15	27	0	68	4	0	6	3	.667	0	0	3.32
	Lynchburg	Pit	A+	22	13	13	0	0	75	335	77	45	30	7	0	0	10	24	0	57	6	1	4	5	.444	0	0	3.60
Kelly,John	St. Lucie	NYN	A+	24	1	0	0	0	3	13	3	1	1	1	0	0	1	0	0	6	0	0	0	0	.000	0	0	3.00
	Lynchburg	Pit	A+	24	7	0	0	4	7.1	35	11	4	3	0	0	0	0	5	0	3	2	0	0	0	.000	0	0	3.68
Kempton,Ryan	Diamondback	Ari	R	20	14	0	0	6	26	111	29	14	9	1	5	2	0	7	1	14	0	1	0	3	.000	0	1	3.12
Kenady,Jake	San Bernrdo	LA	A+	23	45	0	0	12	70.1	375	83	65	50	6	4	2	9	68	2	81	10	1	2	3	.400	0	0	6.40
Kendall,Philip	Helena	Mil	R+	19	2	0	0	0	1.1	13	3	4	3	0	0	0	0	5	0	3	1	0	0	0	.000	0	0	20.25
Kennedy,Ryan	Rockies	Col	R	21	18	3	0	9	32.1	161	40	27	20	0	0	1	4	18	0	41	8	0	0	4	.000	0	3	5.57
Kennison,Kyle	Everett	Sea	A-	24	12	2	0	5	19.2	95	25	18	18	3	0	2	3	11	0	25	4	1	1	2	.333	0	0	8.24
Keppen,Jeffrey	San Bernrdo	LA	A+	23	24	1	0	7	55.2	274	56	44	36	3	0	1	5	46	0	45	11	0	3	1	.750	0	0	5.82
	Savannah	LA	A	23	12	0	0	4	20	100	13	10	5	0	0	0	5	20	3	26	3	0	0	1	.000	0	0	2.25
Kern,Brian	Athletics	Oak	R	23	10	4	0	4	26.1	114	23	11	6	0	1	1	0	5	0	27	4	1	0	0	.000	0	3	2.05
Kershner,Jason	Piedmont	Phi	A	20	28	28	2	0	168	703	154	81	70	12	5	4	3	59	0	156	12	1	11	9	.550	1	0	3.75
Kertis,John	Rangers	Tex	R	22	4	2	0	1	12	55	11	8	3	0	2	0	1	6	0	12	2	0	0	1	.000	0	0	2.25
Kessel,Kyle	Pittsfield	NYN	A-	21	13	13	0	0	79.2	332	80	44	42	6	0	1	4	19	0	67	4	2	2	6	.250	0	0	4.74
Key,Bubba	Lansing	KC	A	20	42	0	0	22	61.2	285	51	45	37	4	4	1	13	46	4	60	14	3	1	5	.167	0	5	5.40
Kimbrell,Michael	Butte	TB	R+	23	23	0	0	5	49	221	35	30	21	4	1	2	1	37	0	65	10	1	7	1	.875	0	2	3.86
King,Raymond	Macon	Atl	A	23	18	10	1	2	70.2	286	63	34	22	4	0	0	0	20	0	63	2	1	3	5	.375	0	0	2.80
	Durham	Atl	A+	23	14	14	2	0	82.2	364	104	54	41	3	4	4	3	15	2	52	2	1	3	6	.333	0	0	4.46
King,Bill	Modesto	Oak	A+	24	29	27	0	1	163	716	193	102	86	11	3	8	8	40	0	100	8	2	16	4	.800	0	1	4.75
Kinney,Matt	Lowell	Bos	A-	20	15	15	0	0	87.1	387	68	51	26	0	3	3	9	44	2	72	13	1	3	9	.250	0	0	2.68
Kirkreit,Daron	Kinston	Cle	A+	24	6	6	0	0	32.2	125	23	7	7	3	0	1	2	10	0	19	3	0	2	0	1.000	0	0	1.93
Kjos,Ryan	Sou. Oregon	Oak	A-	24	24	1	0	6	48.1	217	41	33	20	6	1	3	3	26	3	64	5	0	0	3	.000	0	0	3.72
Knickerbocker,T.	Athletics	Oak	R	21	8	0	0	1	20.1	100	21	21	16	0	0	2	1	16	0	19	5	2	0	2	.000	0	0	7.08
	Sou. Oregon	Oak	A-	21	12	1	0	5	21	102	22	11	11	2	0	0	2	17	0	11	4	0	1	1	.500	0	1	4.71
Knight,Brandon	Hudson Vall	Tex	A-	21	9	9	0	0	53	236	59	29	26	1	2	1	1	21	0	52	2	1	2	2	.500	0	0	4.42
	Charlotte	Tex	A+	21	19	17	2	0	102	463	118	65	58	9	4	7	2	45	0	74	6	0	4	10	.286	0	0	5.12
Knighton,Toure	Bakersfield	Tex	A+	21	25	24	1	0	150	705	197	134	109	18	5	7	4	67	1	108	18	1	5	15	.250	0	0	6.54
	Charlotte	Tex	A+	21	5	2	0	2	22.1	88	15	11	7	3	0	1	0	11	0	11	2	0	0	2	.000	0	0	2.82
Knoll,Brian	Burlington	SF	A	23	52	0	0	16	79	342	76	43	32	5	6	2	4	34	2	56	4	0	3	8	.273	0	1	3.65
Knoll,Randy	Piedmont	Phi	A	20	22	22	3	0	151	592	111	48	35	7	4	5	6	31	0	144	20	2	10	7	.588	3	0	2.09
	Clearwater	Phi	A+	20	4	4	0	0	20.2	79	17	8	7	2	0	1	0	2	0	19	0	0	1	0	1.000	0	0	3.05
Knotts,Gary	Marlins	Fla	R	20	12	9	1	2	57.1	227	35	16	13	0	2	2	6	17	0	46	5	0	4	2	.667	1	0	2.04
Koehler,P.K.	Eugene	Atl	A-	23	17	11	0	2	74.1	320	74	38	30	6	0	4	0	23	0	54	5	2	4	2	.667	0	0	3.63
Koeman,Matthew	Burlington	Cle	R+	23	13	3	0	2	38.2	165	33	18	16	4	0	0	2	10	0	49	2	1	5	2	.714	0	1	3.72
Kofler,Edward	Devil Rays	TB	R	19	10	10	0	0	41	189	49	30	24	2	0	4	4	11	0	36	2	2	1	4	.200	0	0	5.27
Kolb,Brandon	Clinton	SD	A	23	27	27	3	0	181.1	776	170	84	69	7	6	7	8	76	1	138	19	0	16	9	.640	0	0	3.42

1996 Pitching — Single-A and Rookie Leagues

HOW MUCH HE PITCHED											WHAT HE GAVE UP												THE RESULTS					
Player	Team	Org	Lg	A	G	GS	CG	GF	IP	BFP	H	R	ER	HR	SH	SF	HB	TBB	IBB	SO	WP	Bk	W	L	Pct.	ShO	Sv	ERA
Kosek,Kory	Clearwater	Phi	A+	24	42	4	0	9	74	339	84	43	31	5	5	2	6	32	4	50	1	0	3	4	.429	0	1	3.77
Kown,John	Peoria	StL	A	24	26	11	0	5	78.2	329	80	32	27	2	1	3	0	19	0	46	1	1	9	4	.692	0	0	3.09
Krall,Eric	Oneonta	NYA	A-	23	15	6	0	6	44.2	203	43	27	12	2	3	2	1	25	1	29	1	2	0	5	.000	0	0	2.42
Kramer,Matthew	Yakima	LA	A-	21	12	5	0	2	38	164	36	13	11	3	0	2	0	21	0	31	7	7	2	0	1.000	0	0	2.61
Kraus,Timothy	South Bend	ChA	A	24	35	5	0	13	81	355	82	42	24	4	4	2	2	31	0	48	1	0	3	4	.429	0	0	2.67
Kruse,Kelly	South Bend	ChA	A	25	26	0	0	11	35	163	36	21	19	2	2	2	6	20	0	16	1	1	1	2	.333	0	2	4.89
Kubenka,Jeffrey	Yakima	LA	A-	22	28	0	0	24	32.1	127	20	11	9	2	0	0	0	10	1	61	4	1	5	1	.833	0	14	2.51
Kurtz,Danny	Wisconsin	Sea	A	23	38	4	0	18	53.1	289	51	51	48	1	1	1	11	74	3	37	15	1	2	5	.286	0	0	8.10
Kyzar,Cory	Royals	KC	R	19	7	2	0	1	16.1	83	21	16	15	2	1	2	4	10	0	19	1	0	0	2	.000	0	1	8.27
Lachapelle,Yan	St. Cathrns	Tor	A-	21	3	0	0	1	4	12	0	0	0	0	0	0	0	0	0	8	0	0	0	0	.000	0	0	0.00
Lagattuta,Rico	Sou. Oregon	Oak	A-	23	28	0	0	14	54.1	230	49	23	17	4	2	1	1	23	2	31	1	0	3	3	.500	0	3	2.82
Lagrandeur,Yan	Danville	Atl	R+	20	19	2	0	2	37.1	168	39	19	17	3	0	2	2	19	1	34	9	0	3	1	.750	0	0	4.10
Lail,J.	Greensboro	NYA	A	22	11	0	0	1	23	100	19	16	12	2	0	0	2	11	1	24	4	0	1	0	1.000	0	0	4.70
	Tampa	NYA	A+	22	31	0	0	8	35.1	152	37	11	10	0	1	0	1	14	2	21	2	0	4	0	1.000	0	1	2.55
Lake,Kevin	Burlington	SF	A	24	43	4	0	11	97	421	107	57	48	11	5	4	5	38	2	85	11	1	3	7	.300	0	0	4.45
Lakman,Jason	Hickory	ChA	A	20	13	13	0	0	63.2	302	66	55	48	7	0	1	4	43	0	43	7	3	0	6	.000	0	0	6.79
	Bristol	ChA	R+	20	13	13	1	0	66.2	312	70	48	42	5	0	3	6	38	0	64	13	1	4	4	.500	0	0	5.67
Lapka,Rick	Charlstn-WV	Cin	A	25	29	18	0	5	98	441	101	67	52	6	4	6	2	55	2	63	13	1	4	10	.286	0	0	4.78
Lara,Nelson	Marlins	Fla	R	18	7	0	0	1	9.2	54	6	11	6	0	2	1	3	12	2	3	4	1	1	2	.333	0	0	5.59
Lara,Yovanny	Vermont	Mon	A-	21	15	15	2	0	92.1	392	95	54	48	5	3	3	4	27	0	63	7	1	6	3	.667	0	0	4.68
Larocca,Todd	Orioles	Bal	R	24	4	0	0	1	5.2	30	8	8	8	0	1	0	4	2	0	9	3	0	1	0	1.000	0	0	12.71
Larock,Scott	Salem	Col	A+	24	39	1	0	13	81.1	341	72	38	33	4	2	3	0	31	3	57	2	1	3	2	.600	0	1	3.65
Larosa,Thomas	Fort Wayne	Min	A	22	15	13	2	0	89.1	367	77	46	35	7	1	2	4	33	0	90	7	2	7	3	.700	0	0	3.53
Larreal,Guillermo	Bellingham	SF	A-	NA	22	0	0	9	50	205	46	15	8	4	0	2	0	10	1	48	0	0	3	2	.600	0	1	1.44
Lawrence,Clint	St. Cathrns	Tor	A-	20	9	8	2	0	57.2	230	53	18	16	1	1	2	1	11	0	25	5	0	4	1	.800	1	0	2.50
	Hagerstown	Tor	A	20	6	6	0	0	36.1	144	26	12	8	2	1	2	0	10	0	27	1	0	3	1	.750	0	0	1.98
Lawrence,Rich	Princeton	Cin	R+	22	1	0	0	0	1	6	3	1	0	0	0	1	0	0	0	2	0	0	0	0	.000	0	0	0.00
Laxton,Brett	Sou. Oregon	Oak	A-	23	13	8	0	1	32.2	162	39	34	28	4	1	1	3	26	1	38	5	3	0	5	.000	0	0	7.71
Leach,James	Angels	Cal	R	19	5	0	0	1	3.2	22	3	5	4	0	0	2	0	5	0	3	0	0	0	0	.000	0	0	9.82
Leach,Jumaane	Clinton	SD	A	24	10	0	0	3	12.2	61	17	8	7	1	0	0	1	6	0	3	5	2	1	1	.500	0	0	4.97
Leaman,Jeff	Clearwater	Phi	A+	24	3	0	0	0	5	26	8	4	2	0	0	0	0	2	0	3	1	0	1	0	1.000	0	0	3.60
	Piedmont	Phi	A	24	19	1	0	9	37.2	162	46	23	22	2	1	1	0	10	0	21	3	1	0	2	.000	0	0	5.26
Leblanc,Eric	Princeton	Cin	R+	23	9	6	0	3	45.2	198	39	29	23	0	0	1	2	16	0	51	2	1	4	1	.800	0	1	4.53
	Charlstn-WV	Cin	A	23	6	5	0	0	29	129	33	18	16	2	0	2	0	13	0	28	0	0	1	2	.333	0	0	4.97
Ledeit,Rich	Ogden	Mil	R+	24	11	1	0	2	20.2	93	24	12	9	2	1	0	1	9	0	16	4	0	0	1	.000	0	0	3.92
Lee,Corey	Hudson Vall	TB	A-	22	9	9	0	0	54.2	226	42	24	20	1	2	3	1	21	1	59	1	2	1	4	.200	0	0	3.29
Lee,David	Portland	Col	A-	24	17	0	0	16	23	96	13	3	2	0	1	0	3	16	3	24	1	0	5	1	.833	0	7	0.78
	Salem	Col	A+	24	8	0	0	5	12	56	14	6	3	1	0	0	2	6	0	10	2	0	0	2	.000	0	1	2.25
Lee,Jeremy	Hagerstown	Tor	A	22	19	12	0	3	91.2	385	86	38	30	1	3	1	12	24	0	77	6	1	7	2	.778	0	1	2.95
	Dunedin	Tor	A+	22	10	10	0	0	50.2	235	69	38	28	2	2	1	6	19	2	27	0	1	2	4	.333	0	0	4.97
Lee,Winston	Braves	Atl	R	20	13	3	0	2	39	152	32	12	12	2	2	0	4	3	0	36	4	2	1	2	.333	0	1	2.77
Leese,Brandon	Bellingham	SF	A-	21	16	15	0	0	80.1	341	59	39	29	6	0	2	5	37	0	90	8	0	5	6	.455	0	0	3.25
Lehman,Toby	High Desert	Bal	A+	25	6	5	0	0	23.2	112	24	19	17	1	1	1	1	22	0	18	3	0	1	2	.333	0	0	6.46
Lemke,Steve	Modesto	Oak	A+	27	12	6	0	1	44.1	209	65	34	28	2	2	2	3	17	0	29	2	0	4	5	.444	0	0	5.68
Leon,Scott	Hudson Vall	TB	A-	22	15	15	1	0	88	378	82	54	46	4	2	4	4	36	2	73	9	6	3	5	.375	0	0	4.70
Leshay,Maney	Helena	Mil	R+	24	4	4	0	0	18	86	17	14	7	3	0	1	0	12	0	11	3	1	2	0	1.000	0	0	3.50
Leslie,Sean	Delmarva	Mon	A	23	18	4	1	7	37.2	147	25	13	11	3	1	1	0	9	0	23	5	1	1	2	.333	1	0	2.63
	Vermont	Mon	A-	23	17	7	0	5	54.2	232	52	28	25	3	1	2	2	14	0	46	3	0	2	4	.333	0	0	4.12
Levan,Matt	Marlins	Fla	R	2	9	6	0	2	26.1	108	24	14	10	1	0	0	0	11	0	26	0	3	1	3	.250	0	0	3.42
Levrault,Allen	Helena	Mil	R+	19	18	11	0	2	71	302	70	43	42	9	0	0	8	22	0	68	4	3	4	3	.571	0	1	5.32
Lewis,Ron	Utica	Fla	A-	23	20	0	0	8	36.1	159	36	17	16	3	1	0	2	15	2	42	6	1	2	2	.500	0	2	3.96
Leyva,Edgar	Angels	Cal	R	19	14	13	1	0	82.1	359	79	53	36	7	1	3	9	27	0	74	3	3	4	7	.364	1	0	3.94
Leyva,Julian	Athletics	Oak	R	19	1	0	0	0	2	8	1	0	0	0	0	0	0	1	0	2	0	0	0	0	.000	0	0	0.00
Licciardi,Ron	Daytona	ChN	A+	21	2	1	0	1	8	31	3	2	1	0	0	1	1	2	0	3	0	2	1	0	1.000	0	0	1.13
	Williamsprt	ChN	A-	21	15	15	0	0	76	338	78	51	38	4	0	4	2	38	0	53	5	7	3	5	.375	0	0	4.50
Ligtenberg,Kerry	Durham	Atl	A+	26	49	0	0	42	59.2	255	58	20	16	3	3	2	3	16	3	76	4	1	7	4	.636	0	20	2.41
Lilly,Theodore	Yakima	LA	A-	21	13	8	0	1	53.2	200	25	9	5	0	0	0	1	14	1	75	0	2	4	0	1.000	0	0	0.84
Linares,Rich	San Bernrdo	LA	A+	24	60	0	0	52	61.2	266	59	30	23	2	2	1	6	19	0	59	2	1	4	3	.571	0	33	3.36
Lincoln,Mike	Fort Myers	Min	A+	22	12	11	0	0	59.2	263	64	31	27	5	2	4	3	25	0	24	4	1	5	2	.714	0	0	4.07
Lindemann,Jeffrey	Braves	Atl	R	19	4	2	0	2	16	65	12	4	2	0	0	0	3	3	0	12	0	0	2	1	.667	0	0	1.13
Lineweaver,Aaron	Spokane	KC	A-	23	21	5	0	5	49	227	62	43	41	6	1	3	2	23	0	34	3	4	3	4	.429	0	1	7.53
Link,Bryan	Charlotte	Tex	A+	24	15	10	1	1	74.2	318	79	41	34	8	3	2	1	18	0	62	2	1	5	4	.556	0	0	4.10
Lisio,Joe	Columbia	NYN	A	23	40	0	0	37	44.1	186	40	16	10	0	3	2	1	15	1	42	3	2	2	5	.286	0	18	2.03
Lloyd,John	Cedar Rapds	Cal	A	23	27	17	1	3	99.2	445	98	62	44	13	1	4	6	58	1	63	11	3	8	7	.533	1	1	3.97
Lock,Dan	Kissimmee	Hou	A+	24	27	27	1	0	147.2	672	166	109	78	3	9	8	7	62	0	72	8	1	5	18	.217	0	0	4.75
Logan,Chris	Rancho Cuca	SD	A+	26	53	0	0	26	71.2	322	80	44	39	4	3	3	4	36	1	56	9	0	5	2	.714	0	6	4.90
Logan,Marcus	St. Pete	StL	A+	25	30	19	0	2	133	556	125	49	43	9	4	3	6	49	1	99	7	2	7	7	.500	0	0	2.91
Loiz,Niuman	Quad City	Hou	A	23	28	14	1	7	115	508	121	75	63	8	0	5	5	53	0	75	11	1	8	6	.571	0	1	4.93
Loonam,Rick	Twins	Min	R	21	22	1	0	15	46	186	46	16	9	1	1	0	3	8	0	35	1	1	5	3	.625	0	4	1.76
Lopez,Johann	Kissimmee	Hou	A+	22	19	19	2	0	98.1	434	114	50	41	5	0	5	1	35	1	70	9	3	3	10	.231	1	0	3.75
Lopez,Jose	White Sox	ChA	R	21	16	1	0	6	23.2	96	21	12	11	1	1	2	0	6	1	9	1	0	0	3	.000	0	0	4.18
Lopez,Jose	Angels	Cal	R	20	6	4	0	1	30.2	141	30	24	23	0	0	3	2	18	1	27	5	0	1	2	.333	0	0	6.75
Lopez,Orlando	Rockford	ChN	A	24	1	0	0	0	1.2	12	6	5	2	0	0	0	0	0	0	1	1	0	0	0	.000	0	0	10.80
Lopez,Rodrigo	Idaho Falls	SD	R+	21	15	14	0	1	71	314	76	52	45	3	4	3	4	34	0	72	8	4	4	4	.500	0	1	5.70
Lorenzo,Martin	Helena	Mil	R+	NA	23	1	0	8	40.1	191	45	29	25	9	0	3	4	22	0	31	2	0	0	1	.000	0	1	5.58
Lott,Brian	Winston-Sal	Cin	A+	25	26	26	2	0	147.1	659	169	99	71	19	1	5	3	49	0	85	8	1	8	11	.421	0	0	4.34
Loudermilk,Darren	Burlington	Cle	R+	22	16	0	0	7	32.2	143	35	23	17	1	0	1	2	8	0	29	6	0	1	0	1.000	0	0	4.68

1996 Pitching — Single-A and Rookie Leagues

HOW MUCH HE PITCHED											WHAT HE GAVE UP												THE RESULTS					
Player	Team	Org	Lg	A	G	GS	CG	GF	IP	BFP	H	R	ER	HR	SH	SF	HB	TBB	IBB	SO	WP	Bk	W	L	Pct.	ShO	Sv	ERA
	Columbus	Cle	A	22	3	0	0	0	6	26	5	2	2	0	1	0	0	4	2	8	2	0	0	0	.000	0	0	3.00
Love,Jeffrey	New Jersey	StL	A-	23	17	5	0	2	39	187	47	35	28	4	2	1	1	19	2	29	0	4	2	2	.500	0	0	6.46
Lovinger,Eric	Yakima	LA	A-	24	4	0	0	3	5	24	4	3	1	0	0	0	0	2	0	3	1	1	0	1	.000	0	0	1.80
Lovingood,Jeromie	Mets	NYN	R	19	10	8	1	1	46	184	28	11	5	1	2	1	3	18	0	32	4	0	4	3	.571	0	0	0.98
	Kingsport	NYN	R+	19	1	1	0	0	4	16	3	3	3	0	0	1	0	1	0	2	0	0	0	1	.000	0	0	6.75
Lowe,Benny	Hagerstown	Tor	A	23	46	1	0	34	65.2	289	40	24	17	2	2	1	7	52	0	89	2	0	2	3	.400	0	9	2.33
Luce,Robert	Everett	Sea	A-	22	23	0	0	16	41	187	45	26	20	6	3	1	1	16	1	47	6	1	3	4	.429	0	7	4.39
Lugo,Marcelino	Marlins	Fla	R	21	8	0	0	8	24.1	86	9	5	5	1	1	1	1	7	1	13	0	1	5	0	1.000	0	0	1.85
Lukasiewicz,Mark	Dunedin	Tor	A+	24	23	0	0	5	31.1	144	28	20	16	1	1	1	4	22	1	31	1	0	2	1	.667	0	1	4.60
	Bakersfield	Tor	A+	24	7	0	0	3	12.2	66	17	14	13	2	1	0	1	11	0	9	1	0	0	2	.000	0	0	9.24
	Hagerstown	Tor	A	24	9	1	0	4	15.2	63	8	5	4	0	0	0	1	7	0	20	1	0	2	0	1.000	0	0	2.30
Lundquist,David	White Sox	ChA	R	24	3	3	0	0	13.2	49	8	4	4	1	0	0	0	2	0	16	0	0	1	1	.500	0	0	2.63
	Pr. William	ChA	A+	24	5	5	0	0	27	125	31	17	17	2	1	0	1	14	1	23	2	1	0	2	.000	0	0	5.67
Lynch,Jim	Quad City	Hou	A	21	31	1	0	15	60.2	276	51	28	27	3	1	0	4	50	0	51	7	1	1	1	.500	0	1	4.01
Lynch,Ryan	Elizabethtn	Min	R+	22	11	9	0	0	45	197	43	19	17	2	1	1	3	22	0	35	2	0	3	2	.600	0	0	3.40
Lyons,Michael	Kingsport	NYN	R+	22	25	0	0	15	38	157	27	14	8	1	1	0	3	14	1	52	1	1	3	2	.600	0	5	1.89
MacRae,Scott	Charlstn-WV	Cin	A	22	29	20	1	2	123.2	530	118	61	46	3	4	3	7	53	0	82	8	0	8	7	.533	0	0	3.35
Madison,Scott	Butte	TB	R+	22	2	2	0	0	7.2	40	17	11	10	1	0	0	2	3	0	5	1	0	0	1	.000	0	0	11.74
	Devil Rays	TB	R	22	1	0	0	0	1	6	3	3	3	0	0	1	0	0	0	0	0	0	0	0	.000	0	0	27.00
Maestas,Mickey	Yakima	LA	A-	21	14	6	0	1	30.1	149	44	34	31	7	0	2	1	17	0	25	8	0	0	6	.000	0	0	9.20
Magre,Pete	Winston-Sal	Cin	A+	26	37	0	0	14	59.1	255	44	22	17	5	1	1	3	32	2	33	4	0	2	2	.500	0	1	2.58
Mahaffey,Alan	Fort Wayne	Min	A	23	30	19	2	1	126.1	545	139	84	68	13	8	6	3	35	1	75	4	7	7	10	.412	0	0	4.84
Mahan,Dallas	Mariners	Sea	R	19	2	0	0	0	4.2	21	4	4	4	0	0	0	1	5	0	2	0	0	0	0	.000	0	0	7.71
Mahlberg,John	Portland	Col	A-	20	17	10	0	2	56.1	263	67	43	34	5	1	4	9	15	0	47	3	0	2	7	.222	0	1	5.43
Maldonado,Este.	Auburn	Hou	A-	21	6	6	0	0	15.2	76	20	14	9	1	1	1	1	9	0	9	0	2	0	1	.000	0	0	5.17
Malenfant,David	Jamestown	Det	A-	22	2	0	0	0	3	12	1	1	0	0	1	0	1	2	0	0	0	1	0	0	.000	0	0	0.00
	Fayettevlle	Det	A	22	23	1	0	9	30.1	147	29	26	18	2	1	1	2	25	1	34	7	2	0	3	.000	0	2	5.34
Malko,Bryan	Elizabethtn	Min	R+	20	12	12	1	0	66.2	288	73	36	34	5	1	3	4	27	0	54	5	0	5	3	.625	0	0	4.59
Mallard,Randi	Princeton	Cin	R+	21	13	11	1	1	66	302	66	42	27	2	0	3	4	38	0	72	16	1	2	7	.222	0	0	3.68
Mallory,Andrew	Cubs	ChN	R	20	12	7	0	0	53.2	234	49	31	23	2	2	0	8	22	0	33	4	0	0	3	.000	0	0	3.86
Malloy,William	Bellingham	SF	A-	22	15	7	0	3	34	155	34	27	22	0	2	3	3	15	0	41	7	4	2	3	.400	0	0	5.82
Manias,James	Butte	TB	R+	22	16	13	0	1	72	336	98	64	42	8	2	5	3	22	0	55	5	1	5	4	.556	0	0	5.25
Manley,Kevin	Mets	NYN	R	21	10	1	0	1	14	95	23	32	27	0	2	2	2	30	0	13	12	2	0	1	.000	0	1	17.36
Mann,Jim	St. Cathrns	Tor	A-	22	26	0	0	23	27.1	117	22	12	11	3	2	2	3	10	1	37	0	1	2	1	.667	0	17	3.62
Manning,Len	Clearwater	Phi	A+	25	20	18	1	1	102.1	448	94	51	42	6	5	1	4	63	1	77	10	1	3	7	.300	0	0	3.69
Marenghi,Matt	High Desert	Bal	A+	24	33	23	1	3	170.2	750	205	119	111	27	3	4	6	54	1	114	9	4	9	7	.563	0	1	5.85
Margaritis,John	Angels	Cal	R	20	7	0	0	3	12.1	61	19	10	9	0	1	0	1	3	0	11	0	0	0	1	.000	0	0	6.57
Marine,Justin	Billings	Cin	R+	22	21	0	0	9	33	178	46	32	27	3	0	5	3	20	0	22	6	0	0	1	.000	0	0	7.36
Marino,Dominic	Padres	SD	R	19	20	0	0	10	27.2	131	28	20	20	3	0	4	2	17	1	27	1	0	1	1	.500	0	1	6.51
Markey,Barry	Rockford	ChN	A	20	15	13	2	0	97	403	97	43	34	8	4	3	7	16	0	39	3	0	6	2	.750	1	0	3.15
Marquardt,Scott	Mets	NYN	R	24	4	1	0	1	10	39	5	3	3	1	0	0	3	1	0	8	0	2	0	0	.000	0	0	2.70
	St. Lucie	NYN	A+	24	1	0	0	1	1	5	1	0	0	0	0	0	0	1	1	1	0	0	0	0	.000	0	0	0.00
Marquez,Robert	W. Palm Bch	Mon	A+	24	11	0	0	7	11	54	14	10	9	0	0	0	4	5	0	8	0	0	1	1	.500	0	6	7.36
	Delmarva	Mon	A	24	29	0	0	14	46.2	210	44	23	19	4	2	5	3	22	0	49	5	0	1	2	.333	0	1	3.66
Marquis,Jason	Danville	Atl	R+	18	7	4	0	0	23.1	113	30	18	12	0	0	0	1	7	0	24	2	0	1	1	.500	0	0	4.63
Marrero,Kenny	Lakeland	Det	A+	27	34	0	0	13	66.2	282	60	26	17	1	0	2	1	25	1	82	6	0	0	3	.000	0	0	2.30
Marshall,Lee	Twins	Min	R	20	12	12	3	0	70	283	59	31	18	0	1	1	2	18	2	39	2	1	4	4	.500	1	0	2.31
Marshall,Gary	Rockford	ChN	A	23	50	0	0	18	46	192	39	20	17	3	2	6	0	19	3	35	1	0	4	1	.800	0	2	3.33
Marte,Damaso	Wisconsin	Sea	A	23	26	26	2	0	142.1	626	134	82	71	8	1	3	6	75	5	115	4	3	8	6	.571	1	0	4.49
Martin,Trey	Expos	Mon	R	20	13	8	1	5	51.1	226	50	36	31	5	1	2	5	14	0	35	6	1	6	0	1.000	0	2	5.44
Martin,Adam	Expos	Mon	R	19	8	1	0	2	15	59	13	4	4	1	0	1	0	2	0	6	1	1	2	0	1.000	0	0	2.40
Martin,Jeff	San Jose	SF	A+	24	42	0	0	17	60.1	268	52	36	31	4	4	3	4	29	3	54	6	1	2	4	.333	0	3	4.62
Martin,Jeff	Wilmington	KC	A+	23	5	5	0	0	20.1	87	24	11	11	3	1	0	0	5	0	12	0	0	0	1	.000	0	0	4.87
Martineau,Brian	Charlstn-SC	Tex	A	22	2	0	0	2	1.2	6	1	0	0	0	0	0	0	0	0	1	0	0	0	0	.000	0	1	0.00
Martinez,Cesar	Sarasota	Bos	A+	24	35	0	0	16	68.2	325	82	40	36	1	2	3	6	40	2	50	7	0	3	4	.429	0	1	4.72
Martinez,Javier	Cubs	ChN	R	20	3	3	0	0	15	62	11	4	1	0	0	0	1	6	0	15	1	0	2	1	.667	0	0	0.60
	Rockford	ChN	A	20	10	10	3	0	59	250	49	26	22	5	2	2	1	30	0	53	9	0	4	3	.571	0	0	3.36
Martinez,Jose	Charlstn-SC	Tex	A	22	11	1	0	3	21	105	34	24	23	7	0	1	2	7	1	17	6	2	1	2	.333	0	0	9.86
	Hudson Vall	Tex	A-	22	16	5	0	4	54.2	233	56	35	23	3	3	2	0	11	0	38	6	3	2	3	.400	0	0	3.79
Martinez,Dennis	Watertown	Cle	A-	23	12	6	0	2	44.1	177	30	14	12	1	1	1	0	20	1	37	4	1	4	2	.667	0	0	2.44
Martinez,Oscar	Yankees	NYA	R	18	7	0	0	3	9.2	58	22	19	16	2	0	0	3	4	0	3	5	0	0	0	.000	0	0	14.90
Martinez,Romulo	Tigers	Det	R	20	12	12	0	0	62.2	261	67	28	19	1	3	1	2	9	0	51	4	3	1	6	.143	0	0	2.73
Martinez,Uriel	Clinton	SD	A	22	1	0	0	0	2	12	3	4	3	0	0	1	0	3	0	1	2	0	0	1	.000	0	0	13.50
Martinez,William	Watertown	Cle	A-	19	14	14	1	0	90	358	79	25	24	5	2	0	0	21	2	92	6	0	6	5	.545	1	0	2.40
Martino,Wilfredo	Rockies	Col	R	19	17	0	0	6	24.2	115	26	21	12	0	3	2	2	8	0	29	3	0	1	3	.250	0	4	4.38
Masaoka,Onan	Savannah	LA	A	19	13	13	0	0	65	283	55	35	31	7	1	0	6	35	0	80	3	2	2	5	.286	0	0	4.29
Maskivish,Joe	Lynchburg	Pit	A+	25	12	0	0	10	10.2	56	17	9	8	1	1	0	2	5	0	10	2	1	1	2	.333	0	4	6.75
	Augusta	Pit	A	25	50	0	0	40	50	217	46	18	12	0	0	1	4	14	0	58	4	0	1	4	.200	0	18	2.16
Matcuk,Steve	Portland	Col	A-	21	10	10	0	0	56.2	238	52	31	27	11	1	2	4	15	0	49	1	1	5	3	.625	0	0	4.29
Mathews,Del	Durham	Atl	A+	22	42	2	0	26	65	292	74	39	32	9	1	3	6	26	0	46	6	0	4	3	.571	0	5	4.43
Mathis,Sammie	Columbus	Cle	A	24	31	4	1	10	85.1	359	84	43	38	6	6	2	3	31	1	67	7	3	8	3	.727	0	2	4.01
Matos,Luis	Lansing	KC	A	22	8	0	0	2	17	81	23	13	12	2	1	0	0	9	0	10	7	4	1	1	.500	0	0	6.35
Mattes,Troy	Delmarva	Mon	A	21	27	27	5	0	173.1	714	142	77	55	14	6	4	14	50	0	151	17	1	10	9	.526	3	0	2.86
Mattox,Gene	Princeton	Cin	R+	22	3	0	0	1	4	18	1	1	0	0	0	0	0	4	0	3	1	0	0	0	.000	0	0	0.00
	Charlstn-WV	Cin	A	22	22	0	0	10	27.1	137	35	22	20	1	1	0	1	18	1	15	1	1	1	2	.333	0	1	6.59
Mattson,Craig	Lynchburg	Pit	A+	23	6	0	0	2	7	36	10	6	6	3	0	1	0	5	0	4	0	0	0	0	.000	0	0	7.71
	Pirates	Pit	R	23	1	0	0	0	1	3	0	0	0	0	0	0	0	0	0	0	0	0	0	0	.000	0	0	0.00

1996 Pitching — Single-A and Rookie Leagues

HOW MUCH HE PITCHED											WHAT HE GAVE UP												THE RESULTS					
Player	Team	Org	Lg	A	G	GS	CG	GF	IP	BFP	H	R	ER	HR	SH	SF	HB	TBB	IBB	SO	WP	Bk	W	L	Pct.	ShO	Sv	ERA
	Augusta	Pit	A	23	18	0	0	8	25.1	105	19	6	5	2	3	1	1	7	0	18	0	2	1	2	.333	0	0	1.78
Matz,Brian	Vermont	Mon	A-	22	14	9	0	3	55.1	224	41	20	16	3	1	0	2	18	0	53	2	0	5	3	.625	0	0	2.60
Mayer,Aaron	Boise	Cal	A-	22	5	0	0	2	9	39	6	2	1	0	0	0	3	3	1	11	3	0	2	0	1.000	0	0	1.00
	Cedar Rapds	Cal	A	22	18	5	0	8	48	210	53	28	22	2	2	4	3	20	2	31	7	0	1	4	.200	0	4	4.13
Mayo,Blake	Yakima	LA	A-	24	20	6	0	8	67.1	256	44	15	9	1	0	1	0	12	0	68	5	1	5	2	.714	0	1	1.20
Mays,Jarrod	Watertown	Cle	A-	22	12	12	0	0	59.1	257	62	29	22	1	0	4	2	18	1	56	5	3	5	2	.714	0	0	3.34
Mays,Joseph	Everett	Sea	A-	21	13	10	0	0	64.1	271	55	33	22	3	3	2	2	22	0	56	9	1	4	4	.500	0	0	3.08
McBride,Jason	Yankees	NYA	R	21	23	0	0	13	31	137	35	15	14	3	0	0	2	8	0	27	3	0	3	4	.429	0	2	4.06
McBride,Chris	St. Cathrns	Tor	A-	23	6	6	1	0	43	169	37	14	12	2	0	0	4	7	0	28	2	0	3	1	.750	0	0	2.51
	Hagerstown	Tor	A	23	8	8	3	0	58.2	222	42	13	11	4	0	2	4	9	0	34	0	0	5	2	.714	2	0	1.69
McBride,Rodney	Fort Wayne	Min	A	22	16	10	0	3	45.2	235	69	47	41	5	1	2	3	24	0	44	2	0	0	5	.000	0	0	8.08
	Elizabethtn	Min	R+	22	12	12	1	0	74	309	60	29	20	4	4	0	5	28	0	83	8	1	3	2	.600	1	0	2.43
McCall,Travis	Diamondback	Ari	R	19	16	0	0	3	37.2	167	45	21	17	2	1	2	5	11	1	38	1	0	3	2	.600	0	0	4.06
McCarter,Jason	Astros	Hou	R	20	21	0	0	20	22.1	94	13	6	3	0	0	0	3	14	0	26	6	1	0	1	.000	0	8	1.21
McClaskey,Tim	Marlins	Fla	R	21	12	12	2	0	73	288	58	28	21	3	5	3	2	13	0	63	2	0	4	3	.571	2	0	2.59
McClellan,Sean	Medicne Hat	Tor	R+	24	12	8	0	2	51.2	228	52	38	35	5	0	0	4	19	0	61	2	2	3	3	.500	0	1	6.10
McClinton,Patrick	Salem	Col	A+	25	39	0	0	20	64.2	278	58	28	15	2	3	6	3	21	1	47	2	2	3	1	.750	0	1	2.09
McCreery,Rick	Devil Rays	TB	R	21	11	0	0	11	15.1	63	12	5	2	0	1	0	0	4	1	16	1	1	0	2	.000	0	5	1.17
	Butte	TB	R+	21	8	0	0	6	16	68	14	5	3	0	3	1	2	7	0	12	0	0	0	1	.000	0	1	1.69
McCutcheon,Mike	Diamondback	Ari	R	19	14	0	0	11	18.1	70	9	3	1	0	1	0	2	7	0	18	1	0	0	1	.000	0	2	0.49
McDade,Neal	Erie	Pit	A-	21	13	13	3	0	76.2	319	76	33	29	3	3	4	6	21	0	67	5	2	7	3	.700	0	0	3.40
	Lynchburg	Pit	A+	21	1	1	0	0	5	23	6	6	5	1	1	0	1	1	0	2	0	0	0	1	.000	0	0	9.00
McDaniel,Denton	Royals	KC	R	20	7	5	0	1	19.1	84	15	11	8	0	2	0	3	10	0	25	2	1	1	1	.500	0	0	3.72
McDermott,Ryan	Burlington	Cle	R+	19	13	13	0	0	54.2	256	55	38	28	2	0	2	1	40	0	38	9	1	2	8	.200	0	0	4.61
McDonald,Matt	San Bernrdo	LA	A+	23	4	0	0	1	9	53	14	14	12	3	0	1	0	12	0	11	1	0	0	0	.000	0	0	12.00
	Savannah	LA	A	23	28	13	0	7	83.2	365	66	56	44	6	4	4	3	50	0	85	6	1	5	6	.455	0	3	4.73
McDougal,Mike	New Jersey	StL	A-	22	14	0	0	4	20.1	87	20	17	16	4	1	1	1	4	0	25	1	0	1	1	.500	0	0	7.08
McEntire,Ethan	Columbia	NYN	A	21	27	27	1	0	174	689	123	51	43	10	2	0	4	61	0	190	6	0	9	6	.600	1	0	2.22
McFarlane,Joe	Tigers	Det	R	20	15	2	0	5	36.2	158	32	21	16	2	2	1	6	14	0	34	2	0	2	0	1.000	0	2	3.93
McFerrin,Chris	Kissimmee	Hou	A+	21	4	0	0	1	2.2	19	7	7	3	0	0	0	2	3	0	2	1	0	0	0	.000	0	0	10.13
	Auburn	Hou	A-	21	33	0	0	32	42	175	23	16	8	2	1	0	5	24	1	45	3	0	4	2	.667	0	20	1.71
McGlinchy,Kevin	Danville	Atl	R+	20	13	13	0	0	72	283	52	21	9	2	1	2	2	11	0	77	4	4	3	2	.600	0	0	1.13
	Eugene	Atl	A-	20	2	2	0	0	6.2	31	7	5	4	2	1	0	0	1	0	5	0	0	0	0	.000	0	0	5.40
McGuire,Brandon	Angels	Cal	R	19	4	0	0	0	4.1	34	8	16	15	0	0	0	2	6	0	3	4	0	0	0	.000	0	0	31.15
McHugh,Mike	Charlstn-SC	Tex	A	24	43	0	0	17	54.1	276	47	43	37	4	0	1	11	55	3	52	10	1	2	5	.286	0	1	6.13
McKenzie,Jason	Fort Wayne	Min	A	23	17	0	0	2	38.1	165	38	24	22	2	2	1	0	14	1	29	2	1	1	1	.500	0	0	5.17
McKnight,Tony	Astros	Hou	R	20	8	5	0	0	21.2	108	28	21	15	1	0	2	3	7	0	15	3	0	2	1	.667	0	0	6.23
McLaughlin,Denis	Michigan	Bos	A	24	39	0	0	22	59	280	59	47	41	6	2	0	3	43	5	45	9	2	2	4	.333	0	0	6.25
McMullen,Mike	Burlington	SF	A	23	38	0	0	7	56.1	241	47	22	18	3	4	2	5	28	0	33	5	0	0	2	.000	0	0	2.88
McNatt,Joshua	Orioles	Bal	R	19	12	8	0	2	53.2	206	36	15	13	1	1	2	0	12	0	42	1	0	3	2	.600	0	0	2.18
	Bluefield	Bal	R+	19	2	1	0	0	6.1	33	10	6	6	1	0	0	0	6	0	7	1	0	0	1	.000	0	0	8.53
McNeely,Mitch	Vero Beach	LA	A+	23	23	1	1	11	47.2	188	32	13	11	0	1	3	2	12	2	34	0	0	1	1	.500	0	2	2.08
McNeese,John	Daytona	ChN	A+	25	9	0	0	2	14	66	18	8	8	0	0	2	1	7	0	10	3	0	1	1	.500	0	0	5.14
McNeill,Kevin	St. Pete	StL	A+	26	45	0	0	8	61	256	56	28	20	1	8	1	5	18	0	44	3	0	4	2	.667	0	0	2.95
McNichol,Brian	Daytona	ChN	A+	23	8	7	0	0	34.2	162	39	24	18	4	0	1	0	14	0	22	1	0	1	2	.333	0	0	4.67
	Cubs	ChN	R	23	1	1	0	0	3.1	16	4	2	0	0	0	0	0	0	0	2	0	0	0	0	.000	0	0	0.00
Meady,Todd	Royals	KC	R	20	11	10	1	0	58.1	254	58	31	22	2	3	4	6	16	0	47	5	3	2	5	.286	1	0	3.39
Mear,Richard	Johnson Cty	StL	R+	21	10	6	0	1	30.1	160	35	31	28	1	0	1	2	37	0	26	5	0	2	2	.500	0	0	8.31
Mears,Chris	Mariners	Sea	R	19	6	5	0	0	25	103	23	11	10	0	1	0	1	5	0	27	1	0	1	2	.333	0	0	3.60
Meche,Gilbert	Mariners	Sea	R	18	2	0	0	0	3	13	4	2	2	0	0	0	0	1	0	4	0	0	0	1	.000	0	0	6.00
Medina,Carlos	Marlins	Fla	R	NA	4	1	0	1	9.2	48	16	7	4	0	1	0	2	1	0	9	3	0	0	1	.000	0	0	3.72
Medina,Tomas	Astros	Hou	R	22	8	0	0	8	13	60	13	7	6	0	1	0	5	6	0	10	1	0	1	1	.500	0	2	4.15
	Kissimmee	Hou	A+	22	9	0	0	4	12	65	16	11	10	0	0	1	6	9	0	7	8	0	1	0	1.000	0	0	7.50
Meiners,Doug	Dunedin	Tor	A+	23	17	3	0	6	38.2	165	37	21	14	2	0	2	4	8	1	16	0	0	1	1	.500	0	0	3.26
Mejia,Francisco	Piedmont	Phi	A	22	2	0	0	2	3	15	3	2	2	0	0	0	0	3	0	8	0	0	0	0	.000	0	0	6.00
Mejia,Javier	Martinsvlle	Phi	R+	18	29	0	0	27	35.1	158	29	15	11	1	3	3	2	15	3	50	4	0	2	2	.500	0	12	2.80
Melendez,David	Fayettevlle	Det	A	21	27	21	1	2	130.2	549	114	56	38	7	4	2	16	40	1	121	8	8	11	4	.733	0	0	2.62
Mendes,Jaime	Piedmont	Phi	A	24	37	0	0	13	70	297	78	28	25	4	2	0	2	13	5	64	2	1	3	2	.600	0	3	3.21
Mendez,Manuel	St. Pete	StL	A+	23	59	0	0	9	69	290	61	25	22	3	3	2	5	36	2	53	0	4	4	3	.571	0	0	2.87
Mendoza,Geroni.	White Sox	ChA	R	19	12	7	0	0	38.2	202	55	49	42	2	3	3	3	26	0	29	6	1	1	8	.111	0	0	9.78
Mensink,Brian	Batavia	Phi	A-	23	8	8	1	0	50.1	211	48	22	21	4	1	0	3	16	0	35	5	0	3	1	.750	1	0	3.75
	Piedmont	Phi	A	23	6	6	0	0	37.2	155	32	15	14	2	0	0	1	13	0	27	4	0	2	1	.667	0	0	3.35
Mercado,Hector	Kissimmee	Hou	A+	23	56	0	0	18	80	353	78	43	37	4	3	1	4	48	1	68	6	0	3	5	.375	0	3	4.16
Mercedes,Alexis	Athletics	Oak	R	20	10	5	0	2	31	148	42	28	24	3	1	2	2	14	0	19	2	0	2	2	.500	0	1	6.97
Mercedes,Carlos	Bluefield	Bal	R+	21	14	0	0	8	24.1	112	24	24	14	5	1	2	2	9	0	18	3	1	1	2	.333	0	1	5.18
	Orioles	Bal	R	21	5	1	0	4	8.1	41	15	7	5	1	0	1	0	2	1	6	0	1	1	2	.333	0	1	5.40
Merrell,Philip	Billings	Cin	R+	19	14	13	1	1	69	339	83	63	54	11	1	4	5	48	0	54	11	2	4	7	.364	0	1	7.04
Merrick,Brett	Columbus	Cle	A	23	44	0	0	14	54.1	224	36	21	17	2	5	5	3	24	3	51	5	0	6	2	.750	0	1	2.82
Mesa,Rafael	Kinston	Cle	A+	23	45	1	0	34	81.1	330	58	26	21	4	5	1	8	28	3	56	1	1	8	3	.727	0	15	2.32
Meyers,Ryan	St. Cathrns	Tor	A-	23	7	1	0	1	12	43	6	2	2	0	1	1	0	5	0	9	0	0	3	0	1.000	0	0	1.50
Milburn,Robert	Eugene	Atl	A-	23	24	0	0	16	42.1	176	28	17	14	1	2	3	1	21	4	33	4	1	3	1	.750	0	7	2.98
Miles,Chad	Brevard Cty	Fla	A+	24	27	7	0	12	70.2	328	90	57	43	8	4	4	3	31	3	37	7	1	1	5	.167	0	0	5.48
Militello,Sam	Greensboro	NYA	A	27	3	3	0	0	6.1	35	1	7	6	0	0	2	1	15	0	5	7	0	0	2	.000	0	0	8.53
Miller,Brian	Batavia	Phi	A-	24	17	10	1	2	82.2	332	70	22	19	4	3	0	0	25	0	43	3	1	8	3	.727	1	0	2.07
Miller,David	Brevard Cty	Fla	A+	23	26	11	0	5	85	374	94	51	45	12	2	4	9	26	0	40	1	1	4	5	.444	0	0	4.76
Miller,Matt	Jamestown	Det	A-	22	6	6	0	0	25.1	115	33	16	13	0	1	0	3	13	0	21	6	2	1	3	.250	0	0	4.62
Miller,Shawn	Ogden	Mil	R+	23	17	0	0	5	41	182	41	14	11	2	1	1	3	15	0	43	1	0	3	1	.750	0	3	2.41

1996 Pitching — Single-A and Rookie Leagues

HOW MUCH HE PITCHED											WHAT HE GAVE UP												THE RESULTS					
Player	Team	Org	Lg	A	G	GS	CG	GF	IP	BFP	H	R	ER	HR	SH	SF	HB	TBB	IBB	SO	WP	Bk	W	L	Pct.	ShO	Sv	ERA
Miller,Wade	Astros	Hou	R	20	11	10	0	0	57	233	49	26	24	1	2	5	4	12	0	53	5	0	3	4	.429	0	0	3.79
	Auburn	Hou	A-	20	2	2	0	0	9	41	8	9	5	0	0	0	0	4	0	11	0	1	1	1	.500	0	0	5.00
Millwood,Kevin	Durham	Atl	A+	22	33	20	1	3	149.1	638	138	77	71	17	9	6	8	58	0	139	8	3	6	9	.400	0	1	4.28
Minter,Matt	Watertown	Cle	A-	24	21	3	0	5	36	151	29	14	10	2	1	0	0	13	0	38	2	0	2	1	.667	0	3	2.50
Mirando,Walter	Brevard Cty	Fla	A+	22	2	2	0	0	6.1	31	8	7	7	0	0	0	1	6	0	1	1	1	0	1	.000	0	0	9.95
Mitchell,Chris.	Jamestown	Det	A-	22	25	7	0	7	56.2	249	54	33	25	6	3	3	4	30	0	43	3	1	1	5	.167	0	1	3.97
Mitchell,Courtney	Batavia	Phi	A-	24	24	0	0	8	43	183	38	14	9	0	3	2	1	17	1	49	2	0	0	1	.000	0	0	1.88
Mitchell,Ken	Vero Beach	LA	A+	23	39	6	0	12	80.2	365	75	61	49	9	5	3	9	51	1	58	12	4	3	8	.273	0	1	5.47
Mitchell,Dean	Yakima	LA	A-	23	15	5	0	3	52.1	233	53	25	20	4	1	5	0	25	1	61	3	1	2	2	.500	0	2	3.44
Mitchell,Scott	Delmarva	Mon	A	24	33	5	1	10	76.2	320	69	29	20	7	3	1	5	24	1	76	3	3	5	6	.455	0	1	2.35
Mittauer,Casey	Tampa	NYA	A+	24	21	0	0	11	31.1	126	28	10	7	0	4	1	1	5	1	23	2	0	1	1	.500	0	4	2.01
Mlodik,Kevin	W. Michigan	Oak	A	22	31	22	0	6	136.1	581	118	53	42	3	4	6	5	53	1	135	5	5	8	6	.571	0	1	2.77
Mojica,Gonzalo	Burlington	Cle	R+	20	14	1	0	6	26.1	136	28	25	25	5	0	1	2	28	0	35	3	0	1	0	1.000	0	0	8.54
Molina,Gabe	Bluefield	Bal	R+	22	23	0	0	19	30	131	29	12	12	1	1	0	2	13	1	33	5	3	4	0	1.000	0	7	3.60
Molta,Salvatore	Martinsvlle	Phi	R+	19	12	12	0	0	43.1	223	45	46	40	3	0	2	11	39	0	37	3	2	1	9	.100	0	0	8.31
Montanez,Jorge	Red Sox	Bos	R	20	10	0	0	4	13.1	62	15	12	3	0	0	0	2	5	0	7	2	0	0	0	.000	0	0	2.03
Montelongo,Jo.	Daytona	ChN	A+	23	19	14	1	1	101.2	432	84	53	35	5	4	0	5	36	2	77	10	0	6	6	.500	0	0	3.10
Montemayor,Humb.	Red Sox	Bos	R	19	10	2	0	4	32.1	139	30	14	10	0	3	1	0	11	0	19	2	2	4	3	.571	0	0	2.78
	Lowell	Bos	A-	19	5	5	0	0	24.2	109	30	20	17	1	2	4	1	6	0	19	2	0	1	2	.333	0	0	6.20
Montero,Francisco	Martinsvlle	Phi	R+	21	21	0	0	10	39	200	58	38	28	5	0	1	7	18	1	28	4	0	0	2	.000	0	0	6.46
Montgomery,Greg	New Jersey	StL	A-	22	11	0	0	5	14.2	60	9	5	2	0	1	1	1	4	0	22	2	0	0	1	.000	0	1	1.23
	Peoria	StL	A	22	14	0	0	3	19.2	79	11	6	6	0	2	2	1	9	0	22	1	0	0	0	.000	0	0	2.75
Montgomery,Joe	Charlstn-WV	Cin	A	24	14	0	0	2	24	113	23	17	12	2	1	0	0	19	1	16	0	0	0	1	.000	0	0	4.50
Montgomery,Steve	High Desert	Bal	A+	23	44	3	0	17	71.2	331	85	54	42	8	0	2	8	34	3	79	7	1	5	6	.455	0	2	5.27
Moody,Ritch	Rangers	Tex	R	26	3	0	0	1	6	19	2	1	0	0	0	0	0	0	0	9	1	0	0	0	.000	0	0	0.00
	Charlotte	Tex	A+	26	18	1	0	11	33.1	156	34	17	15	1	1	2	2	22	0	25	3	0	1	1	.500	0	1	4.05
Moore,Jody	Utica	Fla	A-	23	11	0	0	6	16.2	85	22	15	7	0	1	1	1	10	0	14	4	0	0	5	.000	0	1	3.78
Moore,Bobby	Charlstn-SC	Tex	A	24	25	25	2	0	142	599	128	82	64	11	8	5	9	45	0	125	6	4	11	11	.500	1	0	4.06
Moraga,David	W. Palm Bch	Mon	A+	21	29	20	1	1	125.2	560	138	74	64	6	4	7	4	50	0	96	12	0	7	10	.412	0	0	4.58
Moreno,Claudio	San Bernrdo	LA	A+	23	6	6	0	0	25.1	132	41	28	22	1	3	1	1	9	0	27	1	0	1	2	.333	0	0	7.82
Moreno,Juan	W. Michigan	Oak	A	22	38	11	0	5	107	475	98	60	52	6	6	6	2	69	5	97	6	2	4	6	.400	0	0	4.37
Moreno,Julio	Frederick	Bal	A+	21	28	26	0	1	162	682	167	80	63	14	8	0	9	38	0	147	9	3	9	10	.474	0	0	3.50
Moreno,Orber	Royals	KC	R	20	12	7	0	5	46.1	187	37	15	7	2	2	0	1	10	0	50	1	2	5	1	.833	0	1	1.36
Moreno,Willy	Yankees	NYA	R	20	11	0	0	5	16	83	27	24	17	1	1	0	6	8	0	8	1	0	0	1	.000	0	0	9.56
Morgan,Eric	Mariners	Sea	R	24	3	0	0	1	5.1	24	6	3	0	0	0	0	0	3	0	4	0	0	2	0	1.000	0	0	0.00
	Everett	Sea	A-	24	4	4	0	0	15.1	74	20	14	8	2	0	0	2	12	0	11	4	0	0	1	.000	0	0	4.70
	Lancaster	Sea	A+	24	10	0	0	3	12.2	64	13	7	6	2	1	1	3	12	0	5	0	0	0	1	.000	0	1	4.26
Morgan,Steven	Lowell	Bos	A-	22	13	1	0	3	22.2	119	25	18	12	3	2	1	3	20	2	19	4	1	1	1	.500	0	0	4.76
	Michigan	Bos	A	22	5	1	0	0	15.1	72	16	13	10	1	1	0	2	12	0	3	0	1	0	1	.000	0	0	5.87
Morillo,Donald	Charlotte	Tex	A+	23	32	0	0	17	51	234	51	33	27	2	1	7	2	40	2	34	6	0	2	3	.400	0	2	4.76
	Charlstn-SC	Tex	A	23	2	0	0	0	1	6	0	1	1	0	0	0	0	3	0	0	4	0	0	0	.000	0	0	9.00
Morris,Alexander	Marlins	Fla	R	20	14	2	0	4	37.1	141	20	11	5	0	2	1	3	8	1	36	4	1	2	0	1.000	0	2	1.21
Morris,Chad	Vermont	Mon	A-	24	20	0	0	6	31.2	124	20	13	13	4	1	0	2	10	0	44	1	0	2	1	.667	0	0	3.69
Morrison,Chris	W. Michigan	Oak	A	25	40	0	0	20	58.1	262	64	38	28	7	5	4	1	20	4	51	1	2	5	5	.500	0	1	4.32
Morseman,Bob	Frederick	Bal	A+	23	29	0	0	18	48.2	234	56	36	33	4	3	2	1	31	1	50	4	0	3	0	1.000	0	3	6.10
Mosley,Tim	Rockford	ChN	A	22	37	0	0	5	57.1	282	74	47	32	1	1	3	6	32	1	36	6	4	3	4	.429	0	1	5.02
	Daytona	ChN	A+	22	6	0	0	3	8.2	47	16	15	11	1	1	0	0	6	2	7	2	0	0	3	.000	0	0	11.42
Mosquea,Alberto	Martinsvlle	Phi	R+	21	14	0	0	6	27.2	139	25	28	17	3	0	1	5	22	0	18	6	0	2	1	.667	0	0	5.53
Mota,Daniel	Oneonta	NYA	A-	21	10	0	0	8	10	42	10	5	5	0	0	0	0	2	0	11	0	1	0	1	.000	0	7	4.50
Mota,Henry	Charlstn-SC	Tex	A	19	32	10	2	11	97	384	71	39	30	8	3	4	2	28	2	68	6	4	7	5	.583	1	2	2.78
Mott,Tom	Fort Myers	Min	A+	23	14	14	0	0	74.2	328	80	43	40	5	3	0	3	37	0	48	10	0	7	5	.583	0	0	4.82
Mounce,Tony	Kissimmee	Hou	A+	22	25	25	4	0	155.2	675	139	65	39	7	6	3	10	68	1	102	7	0	9	9	.500	2	0	2.25
Moylan,Peter	Twins	Min	R	18	13	0	0	4	28.2	128	34	16	13	3	1	2	3	9	0	16	4	0	1	1	.500	0	1	4.08
Mudd,Scott	Charlstn-SC	Tex	A	24	28	27	5	0	182	775	196	94	71	12	6	5	4	49	1	115	14	3	12	9	.571	0	0	3.51
Mull,Blaine	Lansing	KC	A	20	28	28	1	0	174.2	734	186	91	63	9	7	5	9	40	0	114	6	0	15	8	.652	0	0	3.25
Mullen,Scott	Spokane	KC	A-	22	15	15	0	0	80.1	352	78	45	35	6	1	2	8	29	0	78	1	0	5	6	.455	0	0	3.92
Mundine,John	Twins	Min	R	19	14	0	0	9	27.2	124	31	19	16	2	1	2	0	13	0	21	5	1	2	1	.667	0	1	5.20
Munro,Peter	Sarasota	Bos	A+	22	27	25	2	1	155	667	153	76	62	4	3	2	7	62	1	115	7	1	11	6	.647	2	1	3.60
Murphy,Chris	Winston-Sal	Cin	A+	25	29	19	1	3	123.2	550	164	87	70	19	2	5	1	36	1	80	10	0	8	11	.421	1	1	5.09
Murphy,Sean	Salem	Col	A+	24	3	0	0	2	6.1	29	9	5	4	0	0	1	0	1	0	4	0	1	0	1	.000	0	1	5.68
	Asheville	Col	A	24	35	6	0	6	83	347	58	35	25	3	5	2	7	43	2	80	7	2	9	4	.692	0	2	2.71
Murray,Dan	St. Lucie	NYN	A+	23	33	13	0	5	101.2	465	114	60	48	2	3	3	8	53	3	56	11	0	7	5	.583	0	0	4.25
Musgrave,Brian	Lowell	Bos	A-	23	2	0	0	2	5	23	4	1	0	0	0	0	1	2	0	7	0	0	0	0	.000	0	0	0.00
Myers,Jason	San Jose	SF	A+	23	33	16	1	10	119.2	529	140	74	65	10	3	2	3	38	1	82	7	0	8	7	.533	1	1	4.89
Najera,Noe	Kinston	Cle	A+	26	24	24	1	0	140	576	124	52	42	12	0	3	0	62	1	131	9	0	12	2	.857	0	0	2.70
Nakashima,Tony	Vero Beach	LA	A+	19	2	0	0	1	3	14	4	1	0	0	0	0	0	0	0	2	0	0	0	0	.000	0	1	0.00
	Savannah	LA	A	19	27	0	0	8	36.2	150	20	11	10	2	2	0	0	19	1	39	0	0	3	2	.600	0	2	2.45
Nall,John	Cubs	ChN	R	23	10	1	0	4	24.1	104	25	12	7	0	1	0	1	4	0	11	1	1	2	0	1.000	0	1	2.59
	Williamsprt	ChN	A-	23	9	0	0	5	13.1	60	13	11	9	1	1	1	1	3	0	9	1	0	0	0	.000	0	0	6.08
Naranjo,Ivan	Royals	KC	R	19	15	0	0	10	28.2	126	33	16	14	0	1	1	6	9	0	18	2	1	1	0	1.000	0	1	4.40
Nartker,Steve	Visalia	Min	A+	25	3	3	0	0	12	64	22	10	9	3	0	0	0	7	0	11	4	2	1	1	.500	0	0	6.75
Nash,Damond	Padres	SD	R	21	22	4	0	7	59	258	45	30	20	0	2	1	2	36	0	78	7	1	5	3	.625	0	5	3.05
Neal,Billy	Vero Beach	LA	A+	25	51	0	0	12	110.2	455	94	37	28	4	4	3	5	39	4	75	6	2	16	6	.727	0	1	2.28
Neal,Blaine	Marlins	Fla	R	19	7	5	0	1	29.1	126	32	18	15	1	0	0	3	6	0	15	3	3	1	1	.500	0	1	4.60
Needham,Kevin	Billings	Cin	R+	22	26	0	0	11	36	166	44	23	23	0	1	0	4	18	0	37	3	1	1	2	.333	0	2	5.75
Needle,Chad	St. Cathrns	Tor	A-	18	20	0	0	5	26.1	129	24	22	15	5	0	1	0	28	1	26	6	0	0	1	.000	0	0	5.13
Negrette,Richard	Burlington	Cle	R+	21	14	13	0	0	59.1	283	57	50	34	3	1	3	5	36	0	52	12	0	2	6	.250	0	0	5.16

1996 Pitching — Single-A and Rookie Leagues

HOW MUCH HE PITCHED											WHAT HE GAVE UP												THE RESULTS					
Player	Team	Org	Lg	A	G	GS	CG	GF	IP	BFP	H	R	ER	HR	SH	SF	HB	TBB	IBB	SO	WP	Bk	W	L	Pct.	ShO	Sv	ERA
	Kinston	Cle	A+	21	1	1	0	0	2.1	20	9	7	6	0	0	0	0	4	0	0	0	0	0	1	.000	0	0	23.14
Nelson,Chris	W. Michigan	Oak	A	24	16	9	0	3	70.2	275	53	19	19	3	3	1	1	20	0	79	4	8	3	1	.750	0	1	2.42
	Modesto	Oak	A+	24	14	13	0	0	63.1	292	86	50	38	7	1	3	4	17	0	62	6	1	3	5	.375	0	0	5.40
Nelson,Joseph	Eugene	Atl	A-	22	14	13	0	0	70	309	69	43	34	5	3	1	5	29	1	67	6	0	5	3	.625	0	0	4.37
Nelson,Ron	Charlstn-SC	Tex	A	23	20	1	0	10	29	125	29	17	15	2	1	0	0	18	2	22	7	0	0	2	.000	0	0	4.66
Newman,Eric	Clinton	SD	A	24	34	14	0	6	113.1	501	101	71	54	9	3	7	7	67	0	108	13	1	5	7	.417	0	1	4.29
Nichols,Jamie	Hickory	ChA	A	21	20	1	0	11	50	224	52	30	15	4	3	1	4	18	0	45	5	0	0	4	.000	0	1	2.70
	Bristol	ChA	R+	21	12	4	0	6	41.2	168	31	21	19	5	1	3	0	17	0	36	3	0	4	3	.571	0	1	4.10
Nicholson,John	Rockies	Col	R	19	11	11	1	0	65.2	255	42	16	12	1	1	1	5	14	0	65	2	1	3	5	.375	1	0	1.64
	Portland	Col	A-	19	3	3	0	0	15	68	12	8	7	0	2	1	1	10	0	11	0	2	0	1	.000	0	0	4.20
Niedermaier,Brad	Fort Wayne	Min	A	24	32	3	0	14	69.1	295	64	39	25	3	3	4	0	29	2	72	11	0	6	4	.600	0	2	3.25
Niemeier,Todd	Lancaster	Sea	A+	24	41	0	0	12	40.2	194	42	30	21	2	3	0	2	30	2	30	3	1	0	2	.000	0	0	4.65
Nieto,Tony	Winston-Sal	Cin	A+	24	37	0	0	16	56	259	66	37	32	4	3	5	6	22	2	30	6	0	3	2	.600	0	4	5.14
Noe,Matt	Mariners	Sea	R	20	11	5	0	3	35.2	169	34	25	14	1	0	0	1	26	0	18	5	2	2	2	.500	0	0	3.53
Noel,Todd	Cubs	ChN	R	18	3	0	0	1	4	19	4	4	3	0	0	0	0	2	0	4	0	0	0	0	.000	0	0	6.75
Noffke,Andy	Michigan	Bos	A	24	28	7	0	6	74	347	74	51	40	2	1	5	7	57	1	34	7	4	5	3	.625	0	3	4.86
Nogowski,Brandon	Everett	Sea	A-	21	19	0	0	10	26.1	128	27	18	13	1	0	2	2	25	0	31	7	0	0	0	.000	0	1	4.44
Noriega,Raymundo	Sou. Oregon	Oak	A-	23	17	14	0	0	61	263	61	28	24	3	2	0	2	22	0	50	4	0	4	4	.500	0	0	3.54
Norris,Ben	Diamondback	Ari	R	19	8	7	0	0	31.1	133	33	21	16	3	3	0	4	4	0	37	2	0	2	2	.500	0	0	4.60
	Lethbridge	Ari	R+	19	3	3	0	0	11.1	54	14	9	8	0	0	2	0	5	0	12	2	1	0	0	.000	0	0	6.35
Norris,Mckenzie	Helena	Mil	R+	21	18	6	0	7	39.1	196	43	31	23	2	0	1	2	33	0	36	6	2	3	2	.600	0	4	5.26
Norris,Stephen	Johnson Cty	StL	R+	21	16	10	0	2	50.2	252	68	49	39	4	0	2	4	36	0	36	8	2	4	3	.571	0	0	6.93
Norton,Phillip	Cubs	ChN	R	21	1	0	0	1	3	10	1	0	0	0	0	0	0	0	0	6	0	1	0	0	.000	0	0	0.00
	Williamsprt	ChN	A-	21	15	13	2	1	85	364	68	33	24	1	3	2	3	33	2	77	7	3	7	4	.636	1	0	2.54
Nunez,Maximo	Hickory	ChA	A	24	31	24	3	3	152.1	660	173	93	79	12	3	9	7	45	0	105	5	3	5	16	.238	1	0	4.67
Nunez,Vladimir	Visalia	Ari	A+	22	12	10	0	0	53	233	64	45	32	10	1	3	3	17	0	37	3	2	1	6	.143	0	0	5.43
	Lethbridge	Ari	R+	22	14	13	0	0	85	342	78	25	21	4	1	1	9	10	0	93	6	0	10	0	1.000	0	0	2.22
Nussbeck,Mark	New Jersey	StL	A-	23	16	14	0	1	79.2	325	72	31	26	4	2	2	4	16	0	74	3	3	6	3	.667	0	0	2.94
Nyari,Pete	Piedmont	Phi	A	25	45	0	0	38	52.1	223	40	27	21	3	2	1	2	21	2	67	7	2	2	3	.400	0	18	3.61
Nye,Richie	Twins	Min	R	22	1	1	0	0	5	19	4	1	1	0	0	0	0	1	0	4	0	0	0	0	.000	0	0	1.80
	Elizabethtn	Min	R+	22	15	1	0	2	24.2	122	34	25	20	3	1	2	7	6	0	24	1	0	1	2	.333	0	0	7.30
O'Connor,Brian	Augusta	Pit	A	20	19	0	0	5	35.1	147	33	13	12	2	3	1	1	8	0	37	6	0	0	1	.000	0	1	3.06
	Erie	Pit	A-	20	15	15	0	0	67.2	329	75	60	44	4	3	2	3	47	0	60	10	1	4	10	.286	0	0	5.85
O'Flynn,Gardner	Charlotte	Tex	A+	25	28	17	1	7	109.1	483	130	71	56	9	9	2	6	31	0	37	6	4	8	9	.471	0	0	4.61
O'Leary,Kevin	Ogden	Mil	R+	23	2	2	0	0	8	34	7	5	5	0	0	1	0	3	0	6	1	0	1	0	1.000	0	0	5.63
O'Malley,Paul	Quad City	Hou	A	24	26	26	1	0	178	753	173	80	66	10	7	9	11	51	0	111	15	2	11	9	.550	0	0	3.34
O'Quinn,Jimmy	Cedar Rapds	Cal	A	23	41	0	0	9	55.2	271	52	40	35	5	4	2	6	41	3	58	18	0	2	4	.333	0	0	5.66
O'Reilly,John	Ogden	Mil	R+	22	13	12	0	0	63.2	285	66	34	28	3	1	2	3	27	0	82	7	1	7	1	.875	0	0	3.96
O'Shaughnessy,J.	Yakima	LA	A-	22	13	11	0	1	55.2	231	26	24	20	2	2	2	3	36	0	85	8	1	4	3	.571	0	1	3.23
Oakley,Matt	Jamestown	Det	A-	23	24	1	0	6	48.2	218	30	18	12	3	4	2	4	34	0	54	5	0	4	2	.667	0	1	2.22
Ochsenfeld,Chris	Savannah	LA	A	20	26	18	0	3	109.2	487	118	66	51	7	4	5	8	52	0	79	17	3	6	7	.462	0	1	4.19
Odell,Jacob	Sou. Oregon	Oak	A-	23	13	10	0	0	48.2	205	41	25	18	2	1	3	1	16	1	46	2	1	2	3	.400	0	0	3.33
	Modesto	Oak	A+	23	1	1	0	0	5	22	6	4	3	1	0	0	1	0	0	4	0	1	1	0	1.000	0	0	5.40
Ojeda,Erick	Columbia	NYN	A	21	35	0	0	20	58.2	247	55	31	26	8	4	1	2	14	2	51	2	1	3	5	.375	0	4	3.99
Oldham,Bob	Bakersfield	Cle	A+	23	41	17	0	6	143	774	224	187	154	25	3	9	9	105	0	107	19	0	2	10	.167	0	0	9.69
Oleksik,George	Lethbridge	Ari	R+	23	14	14	0	0	67	311	82	53	49	9	3	5	7	36	1	30	2	1	6	1	.857	0	0	6.58
Olivier,Rich	Greensboro	NYA	A	22	9	9	0	0	46.2	216	51	28	22	2	1	0	2	23	0	44	8	0	3	2	.600	0	0	4.24
	Yankees	NYA	R	22	4	0	0	3	8.2	31	4	0	0	0	0	0	0	1	0	7	0	0	1	0	1.000	0	1	0.00
Olsen,Jo	South Bend	ChA	A	22	9	9	0	0	56.2	220	39	16	11	3	2	1	2	13	0	55	3	0	4	1	.800	0	0	1.75
	Hickory	ChA	A	22	4	4	1	0	26.1	101	19	5	4	1	0	0	0	6	0	32	0	0	2	1	.667	0	0	1.37
	Pr. William	ChA	A+	22	12	12	0	0	79	343	74	39	34	5	0	2	5	31	1	55	3	0	6	4	.600	0	0	3.87
Olson,Phil	St. Lucie	NYN	A+	23	15	7	0	2	50	220	63	26	24	5	1	3	4	18	0	27	5	0	1	5	.167	0	1	4.32
	Columbia	NYN	A	23	16	13	1	0	92	368	55	34	26	7	4	1	10	32	0	63	6	0	7	6	.538	1	0	2.54
Olszewski,Eric	Durham	Atl	A+	22	32	0	0	15	52.2	212	34	12	11	3	2	2	4	21	0	69	5	0	2	2	.500	0	4	1.88
Olszewski,Timothy	High Desert	Bal	A+	23	49	0	0	16	64	307	78	53	47	5	3	5	3	41	5	38	2	3	6	3	.667	0	0	6.61
Onley,Shawn	Danville	Atl	R+	22	13	12	0	0	64	269	53	31	27	8	1	1	3	23	0	59	4	0	3	2	.600	0	0	3.80
Onofrei,Tim	Johnson Cty	StL	R+	22	12	7	0	2	42.1	192	45	24	22	3	1	2	3	22	1	28	8	0	1	2	.333	0	0	4.68
Ontiveros,Steve	Lk Elsinore	Cal	A+	36	2	2	0	0	8	35	12	3	2	0	0	0	0	0	0	8	1	0	1	1	.500	0	0	2.25
Opipari,Mario	Twins	Min	R	22	4	0	0	3	6	23	2	0	0	0	0	0	0	3	0	6	0	0	0	0	.000	0	1	0.00
	Elizabethtn	Min	R+	22	19	1	0	16	32.1	135	26	10	7	2	0	0	1	9	0	36	2	0	3	1	.750	0	6	1.95
Oropesa,Eddie	San Bernrdo	LA	A+	25	33	19	0	2	156.1	669	133	74	58	8	1	3	6	77	1	133	8	4	11	6	.647	0	1	3.34
Oropeza,Igor	Kinston	Cle	A+	24	8	4	0	2	26	120	23	13	11	3	0	0	4	18	0	20	4	1	1	2	.333	0	0	3.81
	Bakersfield	Cle	A+	24	23	21	4	1	137.2	641	160	113	104	30	3	7	9	92	0	94	15	1	1	14	.067	0	0	6.80
Orta,Juan	Expos	Mon	R	19	20	0	0	9	32	122	21	10	9	0	3	0	3	11	0	15	3	1	3	0	1.000	0	1	2.53
Ortega,Pablo	Devil Rays	TB	R	NA	13	13	1	0	82.1	330	61	24	18	1	2	0	3	12	0	86	7	4	4	6	.400	0	0	1.97
Ortiz,Ramon	Angels	Cal	R	21	16	8	2	5	68	285	55	28	16	5	0	1	2	27	0	78	5	2	5	4	.556	2	1	2.12
	Boise	Cal	A-	21	3	3	0	0	19.2	89	21	10	8	3	2	0	1	6	0	18	0	1	1	1	.500	0	0	3.66
Ortiz,Edickson	Diamondback	Ari	R	20	7	0	0	5	15	66	13	10	6	1	1	1	1	7	0	15	0	0	2	2	.500	0	0	3.60
Ortiz,Jose	Angels	Cal	R	19	14	0	0	9	24.2	124	23	17	17	1	1	1	5	21	2	32	6	1	2	1	.667	0	2	6.20
Ortiz,Rosario	Jamestown	Det	A-	22	6	0	0	0	8	31	3	0	0	0	0	0	1	6	0	6	0	0	2	0	1.000	0	0	0.00
Osting,Jimmy	Eugene	Atl	A-	20	5	5	0	0	24.1	99	14	11	7	1	0	0	0	13	0	35	1	0	2	1	.667	0	0	2.59
Ovalle,Bonnelly	Rangers	Tex	R	18	18	0	0	12	44.1	180	36	17	11	2	2	2	1	13	1	38	2	0	2	1	.667	0	7	2.23
Pacheco,Delvis	Danville	Atl	R+	19	13	12	0	0	64.2	271	56	28	19	1	1	1	2	21	0	60	5	0	8	1	.889	0	0	2.64
Pack,Steve	Columbia	NYN	A	23	6	0	0	2	7.1	29	8	2	2	0	0	0	0	2	0	8	0	1	0	0	.000	0	0	2.45
	St. Lucie	NYN	A+	23	23	0	0	7	34.2	151	41	20	14	3	1	4	0	10	1	16	2	0	0	0	.000	0	0	3.63
Padilla,Charly	Angels	Cal	R	18	9	0	0	3	10	46	12	10	10	2	1	1	0	4	0	7	2	0	1	0	1.000	0	0	9.00
Pageler,Michael	Bellingham	SF	A-	21	30	0	0	25	34.1	137	22	9	6	2	2	2	0	10	0	55	2	1	2	0	1.000	0	12	1.57

1996 Pitching — Single-A and Rookie Leagues

HOW MUCH HE PITCHED											WHAT HE GAVE UP												THE RESULTS					
Player	Team	Org	Lg	A	G	GS	CG	GF	IP	BFP	H	R	ER	HR	SH	SF	HB	TBB	IBB	SO	WP	Bk	W	L	Pct.	ShO	Sv	ERA
Pailthorpe,Rob	Kane County	Fla	A	24	43	0	0	18	72.1	321	76	36	28	2	3	2	3	30	3	74	7	2	4	5	.444	0	2	3.48
Palki,Jeromy	Mariners	Sea	R	21	18	0	0	12	47.1	194	31	14	13	3	1	1	2	17	0	56	2	0	1	1	.500	0	6	2.47
Palmer,Brett	Columbus	Cle	A	22	5	3	0	2	13	65	19	12	9	2	0	1	0	10	0	14	0	1	0	2	.000	0	0	6.23
	Bakersfield	Cle	A+	22	12	11	2	0	60.2	317	91	63	50	8	3	3	4	45	0	37	5	1	2	6	.250	0	0	7.42
	Watertown	Cle	A-	22	2	2	0	0	10.2	45	6	3	3	2	0	0	0	6	0	12	0	0	1	1	.500	0	0	2.53
Paluk,Brian	Yakima	LA	A-	21	20	5	0	5	45	185	36	24	17	1	3	2	1	17	1	37	4	1	4	1	.800	0	0	3.40
Paluk,Jeff	San Bernrdo	LA	A+	24	50	0	0	21	69.1	318	79	47	39	11	5	3	2	31	1	70	5	2	4	3	.571	0	5	5.06
Paraqueima,Jesus	Yankees	NYA	R	19	11	9	0	0	49.1	209	43	24	11	4	1	0	3	15	0	49	7	4	3	2	.600	0	0	2.01
Paredes,Bladimir	DiamondbackAri		R	19	17	0	0	5	27.1	126	18	15	12	0	0	1	2	27	0	20	3	0	1	1	.500	0	0	3.95
Paredes,Carlos	Lansing	KC	A	21	23	23	0	0	118.2	549	138	75	64	2	5	1	7	69	0	72	15	3	7	8	.467	0	0	4.85
Paredes,Roberto	Helena	Mil	R+	23	25	0	0	16	30.1	131	23	13	9	1	3	2	1	16	0	41	6	0	3	1	.750	0	6	2.67
Parisi,Mike	Brevard Cty	Fla	A+	24	21	19	1	0	119.1	515	117	59	55	9	2	4	10	39	1	65	1	0	6	8	.429	0	0	4.15
Parker,Christian	Vermont	Mon	A-	21	14	14	2	0	80	322	63	26	22	1	2	1	4	22	0	61	8	3	7	1	.875	1	0	2.47
Parks,Wes	Marlins	Fla	R	19	6	2	0	2	25	94	10	1	0	0	1	0	0	8	0	19	0	0	2	1	.667	0	0	0.00
Paronto,Chad	Frederick	Bal	A+	21	8	1	0	2	15	63	11	9	8	0	2	0	0	8	0	6	2	0	0	1	.000	0	0	4.80
	Bluefield	Bal	R+	21	9	2	0	1	21.1	82	16	4	4	0	0	0	0	5	0	24	0	1	1	1	.500	0	1	1.69
Parotte,Frisco	Greensboro	NYA	A	21	24	0	0	5	53	237	35	24	15	2	1	4	5	35	2	41	6	2	0	0	.000	0	0	2.55
Parra,Julio	Savannah	LA	A	22	12	0	0	5	15.2	59	8	4	4	2	0	0	1	6	0	19	0	0	1	1	.500	0	2	2.30
	Vero Beach	LA	A+	22	12	0	0	7	21.1	79	12	3	3	1	0	0	0	5	0	17	0	1	0	0	.000	0	1	1.27
Parrish,John	Orioles	Bal	R	19	11	0	0	6	19.1	83	13	5	4	0	0	0	0	11	0	33	2	0	2	0	1.000	0	2	1.86
	Bluefield	Bal	R+	19	8	0	0	5	13.1	60	11	6	4	0	1	2	0	9	1	18	2	0	2	1	.667	0	1	2.70
Pascarella,Joshua	Astros	Hou	R	20	15	4	0	1	37.2	176	35	29	20	1	0	3	1	24	0	43	9	0	1	0	1.000	0	0	4.78
Pasqualicchio,Mich.	Stockton	Mil	A+	22	18	17	0	0	71.1	307	67	35	28	3	1	0	2	36	0	69	2	4	3	3	.500	0	0	3.53
Passini,Brian	Helena	Mil	R+	22	15	14	1	0	77.2	343	91	37	30	5	0	2	6	27	0	71	7	3	7	2	.778	0	0	3.48
Patino,Leonardo	Boise	Cal	A-	23	30	0	0	14	56	228	37	15	10	7	4	0	2	21	2	71	3	1	6	5	.545	0	6	1.61
Patterson,Casey	Pittsfield	NYN	A-	24	17	0	0	12	23.2	111	30	14	14	2	2	0	2	10	0	20	4	0	1	3	.250	0	0	5.32
Paugh,Richard	Lynchburg	Pit	A+	25	45	0	0	17	52	230	48	33	22	1	4	0	2	20	0	41	6	0	1	4	.200	0	4	3.81
Paulino,Jose	Athletics	Oak	R	20	6	6	0	0	29.1	119	32	13	12	0	0	0	2	0	0	31	1	0	4	0	1.000	0	0	3.68
	Sou. Oregon	Oak	A-	20	10	8	0	0	40.2	175	43	20	14	3	0	2	2	9	0	21	3	3	4	1	.800	0	0	3.10
Pauls,Matt	Rangers	Tex	R	22	1	0	0	0	1	6	0	1	0	0	0	0	1	1	0	0	1	0	1	0	1.000	0	0	0.00
Pavicich,Paul	Fort Myers	Min	A+	24	29	0	0	8	42.2	190	49	30	24	4	1	2	0	13	0	29	3	0	2	3	.400	0	0	5.06
Pavlovich,Tony	Beloit	Mil	A	22	28	0	0	15	33.2	141	26	12	12	1	4	0	0	15	1	31	2	0	2	3	.400	0	4	3.21
Payne,William	Mets	NYN	R	19	11	0	0	6	18	78	17	14	10	1	3	0	0	8	2	17	1	0	2	1	.667	0	2	5.00
Pearce,Jeffrey	Lancaster	Sea	A+	27	21	0	0	4	21.2	102	13	7	5	0	0	0	5	23	1	17	4	2	0	0	.000	0	0	2.08
Pearsall,J.J.	Savannah	LA	A	23	45	2	0	13	87.2	394	76	48	32	6	3	2	7	46	3	88	8	3	6	5	.545	0	3	3.29
Peguero,Americo	Bluefield	Bal	R+	20	9	9	0	0	51	217	38	24	16	6	0	1	8	22	0	54	12	0	4	2	.667	0	0	2.82
Pelton,Brad	Burlington	Cle	R+	22	15	0	0	9	25.2	104	19	11	8	1	1	0	0	9	0	21	3	0	0	3	.000	0	3	2.81
Pena,Alex	Frederick	Bal	A+	24	2	0	0	1	2	10	3	3	3	0	0	0	0	1	0	1	0	0	0	1	.000	0	0	13.50
	Visalia	Bal	A+	24	44	2	0	14	70.2	334	94	53	45	8	3	6	1	31	3	30	4	0	1	3	.250	0	0	5.73
Pena,Jesus	Erie	Pit	A-	22	21	3	0	5	35.2	164	32	24	19	3	2	0	2	24	1	34	2	0	2	5	.286	0	0	4.79
Pena,Juan	Michigan	Bos	A	20	26	26	4	1	187.2	743	149	70	62	16	9	5	10	34	2	156	10	2	12	10	.545	0	0	2.97
Penny,Brad	DiamondbackAri		R	19	11	8	0	1	49.2	201	36	18	13	1	0	1	3	14	0	52	3	2	2	2	.500	0	0	2.36
Penny,Tony	Royals	KC	R	21	14	0	0	10	24.1	101	22	8	7	2	0	1	1	4	0	20	1	1	3	1	.750	0	2	2.59
Perez,Elvis	White Sox	ChA	R	19	14	0	0	2	14.2	83	27	26	19	4	1	0	1	12	0	9	6	0	0	0	.000	0	0	11.66
Perez,J.P.	Ogden	Mil	R+	21	19	0	0	12	21	94	19	12	6	0	1	0	1	11	1	16	1	0	2	1	.667	0	3	2.57
Perez,Juan	Modesto	Oak	A+	24	38	8	0	15	98.2	445	120	68	55	12	5	3	2	34	0	89	5	1	2	4	.333	0	4	5.02
Perez,Julio	Kinston	Cle	A+	23	24	0	0	13	43.2	186	44	22	15	3	3	1	3	17	3	21	3	0	1	2	.333	0	3	3.09
Perez,Odaliz	Eugene	Atl	A-	19	10	6	0	0	23.2	110	26	16	10	2	2	0	0	11	0	38	3	0	2	1	.667	0	0	3.80
Perez,Pablo	Twins	Min	R	23	12	10	2	0	59.2	246	54	23	20	4	0	3	0	17	0	43	3	0	5	4	.556	0	0	3.02
Perkins,Dan	Fort Myers	Min	A+	22	39	13	3	10	136.2	557	125	52	45	5	4	6	11	37	1	111	9	1	13	7	.650	1	2	2.96
Perpetuo,Nelson	Bakersfield	Tex	A+	26	8	7	0	0	40.2	203	35	31	26	0	3	3	7	38	0	45	4	0	0	5	.000	0	0	5.75
Persails,Mark	Jamestown	Det	A-	21	13	13	0	0	63.2	275	53	35	30	6	1	0	6	29	0	37	6	0	1	4	.200	0	0	4.24
Perusek,Bill	Fayettevlle	Det	A	23	39	1	0	8	45.1	249	51	38	33	3	3	0	9	51	1	50	9	0	0	0	.000	0	1	6.55
Peters,Tim	Fort Wayne	Min	A	24	13	0	0	4	20.2	75	13	5	3	1	1	1	1	4	0	10	0	0	2	0	1.000	0	0	1.31
	Fort Myers	Min	A+	24	28	0	0	16	28	120	31	11	11	2	1	2	2	5	2	23	2	0	0	3	.000	0	1	3.54
Peterson,Dean	Red Sox	Bos	R	24	2	2	0	0	6	25	4	0	0	0	0	0	0	0	0	7	0	0	0	0	.000	0	0	0.00
	Sarasota	Bos	A+	24	26	3	0	11	62	252	45	30	21	5	3	1	2	21	1	58	0	2	7	2	.778	0	3	3.05
Peterson,Jay	Rockford	ChN	A	21	15	15	2	0	94	406	82	50	36	8	0	2	4	39	0	87	4	0	4	7	.364	1	0	3.45
	Daytona	ChN	A+	21	8	7	0	0	27.2	134	35	29	20	3	0	3	1	21	0	15	4	0	0	2	.000	0	0	6.51
Petroff,Dan	Cedar Rapds	Cal	A	23	9	9	2	0	49.2	227	44	34	21	3	2	3	4	34	0	29	5	1	2	3	.400	0	0	3.81
Phillips,Ben	Oneonta	NYA	A-	21	14	14	0	0	78.2	337	58	40	26	1	2	5	2	41	0	56	4	6	3	4	.429	0	0	2.97
Phillips,Jason	Augusta	Pit	A	23	14	14	1	0	89.2	366	79	35	24	3	2	3	6	29	1	75	9	1	5	4	.556	1	0	2.41
	Lynchburg	Pit	A+	23	13	13	1	0	73.2	343	82	47	37	3	2	2	5	35	0	63	6	1	5	6	.455	1	0	4.52
Phillips,Jon	Princeton	Cin	R+	22	23	0	0	13	42	192	40	25	20	5	2	1	1	28	2	53	7	0	3	4	.429	0	2	4.29
Phillips,Marc	Wilmington	KC	A+	25	31	0	0	14	49.2	219	59	33	29	4	3	3	2	19	0	19	4	0	2	0	1.000	0	0	5.26
Phipps,Jeff	Orioles	Bal	R	22	17	0	0	5	27.1	120	30	20	18	3	2	2	5	12	0	23	5	0	3	1	.750	0	0	5.93
Pickford,Kevin	Lynchburg	Pit	A+	22	28	28	4	0	172.1	749	195	99	78	15	7	6	11	25	0	100	4	1	11	11	.500	1	0	4.07
Pinales,Aquiles	Macon	Atl	A	22	18	0	0	6	28.1	135	26	23	18	3	0	1	1	21	0	22	4	2	3	1	.750	0	0	5.72
	Eugene	Atl	A-	22	3	0	0	3	5.1	20	4	3	2	1	1	0	0	2	0	4	0	0	0	0	.000	0	1	3.38
Pineda,Luis	Rangers	Tex	R	19	11	11	1	0	71.2	306	67	31	28	6	3	1	3	25	0	66	10	5	6	3	.667	0	0	3.52
Pitt,Jye	Cubs	ChN	R	19	12	0	0	3	29.1	116	21	8	6	0	2	0	3	9	0	38	3	3	1	2	.333	0	0	1.84
Pivaral,Hugo	Vero Beach	LA	A+	20	7	6	0	0	26.1	122	34	15	13	1	1	0	1	8	0	16	10	0	1	1	.500	0	0	4.44
Plooy,Eric	Boise	Cal	A-	22	20	0	0	6	35	156	39	23	18	2	2	1	1	15	0	31	3	0	1	1	.500	0	0	4.63
Podjan,Jimmy	Ogden	Mil	R+	22	16	0	0	5	23	104	19	15	12	2	1	0	3	16	1	16	3	0	0	1	.000	0	3	4.70
	Helena	Mil	R+	22	4	0	0	2	6.2	32	11	5	4	0	0	0	0	3	0	5	1	0	1	1	.500	0	0	5.40
Pohl,Jeff	Bellingham	SF	A-	21	17	0	0	3	32	146	33	17	14	1	2	0	0	19	1	19	2	0	3	5	.375	0	0	3.94
Polanco,Elvis	Cubs	ChN	R	19	14	7	1	5	55.2	234	55	28	16	1	1	0	4	18	0	37	5	3	6	3	.667	0	2	2.59

1996 Pitching — Single-A and Rookie Leagues

HOW MUCH HE PITCHED											WHAT HE GAVE UP												THE RESULTS					
Player	Team	Org	Lg	A	G	GS	CG	GF	IP	BFP	H	R	ER	HR	SH	SF	HB	TBB	IBB	SO	WP	Bk	W	L	Pct.	ShO	Sv	ERA
Politte,Cliff	Peoria	StL	A	23	25	25	0	0	149.2	603	108	50	43	8	3	2	7	47	0	151	5	1	14	6	.700	0	0	2.59
Pollock,Jason	New Jersey	StL	A-	22	18	10	0	1	57	265	59	37	31	4	4	1	5	36	0	61	4	0	3	7	.300	0	0	4.89
Ponson,Sidney	Frederick	Bal	A+	20	18	16	3	2	107	443	98	56	41	6	3	4	5	28	0	110	6	3	7	6	.538	0	0	3.45
Pontes,Dan	St. Pete	StL	A+	26	27	22	1	2	120.1	495	120	56	51	8	3	5	3	34	0	73	3	1	7	8	.467	0	0	3.81
Portillo,Alex	Pr. William	ChA	A+	22	25	0	0	11	49.1	211	55	35	29	6	1	0	1	16	2	30	1	1	1	1	.500	0	2	5.29
	South Bend	ChA	A	22	7	0	0	7	9.1	39	9	4	3	0	0	0	0	1	0	9	1	0	0	0	.000	0	0	2.89
Portillo,Ramon	Martinsvlle	Phi	R+	19	21	0	0	7	45	215	52	34	30	5	0	5	6	29	0	34	2	1	4	2	.667	0	1	6.00
Poupart,Melvin	Columbia	NYN	A	22	5	1	0	1	9.2	39	8	3	3	0	0	0	1	3	0	13	0	0	1	0	1.000	0	0	2.79
	Pittsfield	NYN	A-	22	23	0	0	20	28.2	127	25	12	10	2	2	5	5	14	1	30	4	0	2	2	.500	0	7	3.14
Powell,Jeremy	Delmarva	Mon	A	21	27	27	1	0	157.2	665	127	68	53	9	1	6	15	66	0	109	11	4	12	9	.571	0	0	3.03
Powell,Brian	Lakeland	Det	A+	23	29	27	5	2	174.1	746	195	106	95	12	9	2	7	47	0	84	1	2	8	13	.381	0	0	4.90
Powley,Greg	Expos	Mon	R	21	12	5	0	0	39.2	162	32	15	15	0	0	2	3	9	0	32	0	3	1	3	.250	0	0	3.40
Prater,Andrew	Pirates	Pit	R	19	12	12	1	0	68	288	63	24	24	3	2	1	9	11	0	53	2	0	4	5	.444	0	0	3.18
Precinal,Huilberto	Padres	SD	R	19	2	0	0	0	2	7	1	0	0	0	0	1	0	0	0	2	0	0	0	0	.000	0	0	0.00
Prempas,Lyle	Helena	Mil	R+	22	21	2	0	7	42.2	222	51	47	43	3	2	1	3	46	0	52	9	1	2	1	.667	0	2	9.07
Presley,Kirk	Pittsfield	NYN	A-	22	5	5	0	0	18	80	19	9	6	0	0	0	0	10	0	14	4	0	1	0	1.000	0	0	3.00
Press,Gregg	Brevard Cty	Fla	A+	25	28	23	0	1	150.1	604	134	62	46	9	6	1	4	37	4	90	10	0	9	9	.500	0	0	2.75
Prestash,J.D.	Astros	Hou	R	21	4	0	0	0	5.2	27	9	4	1	0	0	0	0	0	0	5	1	0	0	0	.000	0	0	1.59
Price,Jamie	W. Michigan	Oak	A	25	20	16	0	1	89.1	360	80	22	17	1	0	2	1	19	1	88	2	1	6	1	.857	0	0	1.71
Priest,Eddie	Winston-Sal	Cin	A+	23	4	4	0	0	12.1	48	5	2	1	1	0	0	0	6	0	9	1	0	1	0	1.000	0	0	0.73
Prihoda,Steve	Wilmington	KC	A+	24	47	0	0	40	79.1	313	50	17	13	1	6	1	3	22	4	89	3	0	6	6	.500	0	25	1.47
Puffer,Brandon	Angels	Cal	R	21	1	1	0	0	5	23	7	2	2	0	0	0	0	1	0	3	1	0	0	1	.000	0	0	3.60
	Boise	Cal	A-	21	16	0	0	8	30.1	129	27	19	15	3	1	3	1	11	0	22	3	0	2	0	1.000	0	1	4.45
Pujals,Denis	Butte	TB	R+	24	15	15	0	0	87.1	392	110	65	49	9	1	0	5	19	0	82	6	3	2	7	.222	0	0	5.05
Pumphrey,Kenny	Pittsfield	NYN	A-	20	14	14	1	0	87	373	68	41	31	1	1	2	4	41	0	61	10	2	7	2	.778	1	0	3.21
Putt,Eric	Diamondback	Ari	R	19	12	8	0	1	45	203	45	37	23	1	2	1	3	22	0	29	7	1	3	3	.500	0	0	4.60
Pyrtle,Joe	Mets	NYN	R	23	4	0	0	0	7	27	3	1	1	0	0	0	0	3	0	9	1	1	0	0	.000	0	0	1.29
	Kingsport	NYN	R+	23	3	0	0	0	6	23	4	0	0	0	0	0	0	1	0	4	1	0	0	0	.000	0	0	0.00
	Pittsfield	NYN	A-	23	8	0	0	5	15.2	68	18	8	6	1	0	1	0	4	0	17	1	0	0	0	.000	0	0	3.45
Queen,Mike	Mets	NYN	R	19	11	3	0	3	33.2	147	33	15	13	1	1	0	0	15	0	28	4	0	3	3	.500	0	0	3.48
Quevedo,Ruben	Braves	Atl	R	NA	10	10	0	0	55	221	50	19	14	1	4	1	1	9	0	49	3	2	2	6	.250	0	0	2.29
Quezada,Edward	Vermont	Mon	A-	22	14	14	2	0	92.2	378	82	32	24	3	3	1	7	20	0	79	7	0	6	5	.545	0	0	2.33
Quigley,Donald	Spokane	KC	A-	22	19	0	0	6	27.1	142	41	24	19	0	1	2	4	18	1	18	1	0	0	1	.000	0	1	6.26
Quintal,Craig	Jamestown	Det	A-	22	15	15	0	0	86.1	374	93	51	33	5	2	5	5	23	0	49	5	4	4	8	.333	0	0	3.44
Quintana,Urbano	Martinsvlle	Phi	R+	22	15	12	0	1	77	320	71	44	35	8	3	5	5	22	1	43	3	2	3	5	.375	0	0	4.09
Quirk,John	Pr. William	ChA	A+	26	18	3	0	10	42	206	52	34	29	3	0	4	2	28	1	22	4	0	1	2	.333	0	0	6.21
	South Bend	ChA	A	26	5	0	0	3	6.1	33	8	3	3	0	0	1	0	7	0	1	1	0	0	0	.000	0	0	4.26
Radlosky,Rob	Fort Myers	Min	A+	23	28	16	1	5	104	467	116	70	63	11	2	3	9	46	0	80	10	0	4	6	.400	1	1	5.45
Raines,Ken	Charlotte	Tex	A+	24	23	0	0	13	30.1	144	44	20	19	4	0	1	0	14	1	23	0	0	0	4	.000	0	2	5.64
	Hudson Vall	Tex	A-	24	38	0	0	23	67	273	51	19	8	1	5	0	1	21	3	64	2	1	6	2	.750	0	5	1.07
Rajotte,Jason	Modesto	Oak	A+	24	47	0	0	29	75	295	50	24	21	4	1	0	2	28	2	57	1	0	3	6	.333	0	7	2.52
Rakers,Jason	Columbus	Cle	A	24	14	14	1	0	77.1	319	84	37	31	5	1	1	3	17	0	64	8	1	5	4	.556	1	0	3.61
Rama,Shelby	Clearwater	Phi	A+	25	34	7	0	5	83.1	356	88	41	27	4	4	4	1	25	1	38	2	0	7	3	.700	0	0	2.92
Ramirez,Felix	Red Sox	Bos	R	22	1	0	0	1	1	6	1	2	1	0	0	0	0	2	0	1	0	0	0	0	.000	0	0	9.00
	Sarasota	Bos	A+	22	5	0	0	3	11	49	10	8	4	0	0	0	1	8	0	7	1	0	1	0	1.000	0	0	3.27
Ramirez,Jose	Fayettevlle	Det	A	21	15	1	0	5	26	126	35	15	12	2	1	0	1	14	1	30	3	0	1	1	.500	0	0	4.15
	Tigers	Det	R	21	13	11	0	2	59.2	280	69	49	26	0	4	1	3	23	0	47	7	5	2	7	.222	0	0	3.92
Ramsay,Robert	Red Sox	Bos	R	23	2	0	0	1	3.2	19	5	2	2	0	0	0	1	3	0	5	0	0	0	1	.000	0	0	4.91
	Sarasota	Bos	A+	23	12	7	0	0	34	165	42	23	23	1	1	1	1	27	0	32	2	2	2	2	.500	0	0	6.09
Randall,Scott	Asheville	Col	A	21	24	24	1	0	154.1	615	121	53	47	11	5	1	7	50	3	136	4	0	14	4	.778	1	0	2.74
Randolph,Stephen	Greensboro	NYA	A	23	32	17	0	7	100.1	451	64	46	42	8	4	5	5	96	1	111	13	3	4	7	.364	0	0	3.77
Rangel,Julio	Oneonta	NYA	A-	21	15	14	0	1	85	355	64	35	28	2	3	4	5	36	0	79	4	1	7	2	.778	0	0	2.96
Rath,Fred	Fort Wayne	Min	A	24	32	0	0	29	41.2	163	26	12	7	1	0	2	0	10	0	63	3	0	1	2	.333	0	14	1.51
	Fort Myers	Min	A+	24	22	0	0	16	29	123	25	10	9	1	1	0	2	10	0	29	3	0	2	5	.286	0	4	2.79
Rayment,Justin	Oneonta	NYA	A-	23	1	1	0	0	2	12	3	4	4	0	0	1	0	3	0	0	0	0	0	1	.000	0	0	18.00
Reames,Jim	New Jersey	StL	A-	22	31	0	0	20	43.1	187	42	20	16	4	3	1	2	18	0	48	2	2	2	2	.500	0	10	3.32
Reames,Britt	Peoria	StL	A	23	25	25	2	0	161	620	97	43	34	5	3	2	4	41	0	167	7	0	15	7	.682	1	0	1.90
Rector,Bobby	San Jose	SF	A+	22	28	26	1	1	165.1	694	161	77	66	14	4	5	8	43	0	145	4	0	12	8	.600	0	0	3.59
Reed,Aaron	Tigers	Det	R	19	18	0	0	15	27	136	34	25	18	3	0	0	1	17	1	26	8	0	0	1	.000	0	0	6.00
Reed,Brian	St. Pete	StL	A+	25	58	0	0	27	68	295	55	26	23	2	2	6	7	35	2	76	5	1	5	4	.556	0	3	3.04
Reed,Daniel	Bakersfield	Bal	A+	22	20	7	0	3	68.1	316	83	52	38	4	3	2	0	36	1	48	1	1	2	4	.333	0	0	5.00
	High Desert	Bal	A+	22	17	6	0	1	51	225	53	28	27	7	2	0	2	22	0	43	1	0	4	0	1.000	0	0	4.76
Reed,Jason	Savannah	LA	A	24	5	0	0	2	11.1	54	14	10	9	2	0	1	0	7	0	8	0	0	0	0	.000	0	0	7.15
Reed,Steve	Johnson Cty	StL	R+	21	31	0	0	15	40	170	39	21	18	4	1	2	3	12	1	38	0	0	5	1	.833	0	4	4.05
Reeder,Galen	Braves	Atl	R	21	16	0	0	11	32	140	38	20	16	2	2	0	1	11	1	26	2	1	1	2	.333	0	1	4.50
Reich,Steve	High Desert	Bal	A+	26	2	2	0	0	6.2	37	14	11	8	0	2	0	0	3	0	0	1	0	0	2	.000	0	0	10.80
Reichow,Bob	Burlington	Cle	R+	23	21	0	0	4	43.2	193	51	23	22	1	1	0	3	10	0	41	3	0	2	2	.500	0	1	4.53
Reid,Rayon	Augusta	Pit	A	23	3	0	0	0	3.2	20	4	5	1	0	0	2	1	4	0	3	0	0	0	0	.000	0	0	2.45
Reilly,Sean	Twins	Min	R	20	12	1	0	5	21.1	98	23	15	13	0	0	1	2	11	0	25	5	2	0	1	.000	0	1	5.48
Reimers,Tom	White Sox	ChA	R	22	1	0	0	1	3	14	3	0	0	0	0	0	0	1	0	1	0	1	0	0	.000	0	1	0.00
	Hickory	ChA	A	22	14	12	0	0	56	259	66	43	40	6	0	2	6	25	0	55	7	2	2	2	.500	0	0	6.43
Reinfelder,Dave	Jamestown	Det	A-	23	28	0	0	8	57.1	233	46	24	18	4	1	0	5	14	0	52	0	0	2	2	.500	0	2	2.83
Reith,Brian	Yankees	NYA	R	19	10	4	0	1	32.2	143	31	16	15	1	2	2	1	16	0	21	3	0	2	3	.400	0	0	4.13
Reitsma,Chris.	Red Sox	Bos	R	19	7	6	0	0	26.2	109	24	7	4	0	1	0	2	1	0	32	3	0	3	1	.750	0	0	1.35
Remington,Jake	Clinton	SD	A	21	27	7	1	7	85	381	98	60	49	3	4	2	4	25	3	59	8	0	6	7	.462	0	0	5.19
Reyes,Dennis	San Bernrdo	LA	A+	20	29	28	0	0	166	731	166	106	77	11	4	2	6	77	0	176	9	3	11	12	.478	0	0	4.17
Reyes,Jose	Augusta	Pit	A	24	23	8	0	2	67	307	79	51	46	8	2	4	4	30	3	57	6	1	5	4	.556	0	0	6.18

1996 Pitching — Single-A and Rookie Leagues

HOW MUCH HE PITCHED											WHAT HE GAVE UP												THE RESULTS					
Player	Team	Org	Lg	A	G	GS	CG	GF	IP	BFP	H	R	ER	HR	SH	SF	HB	TBB	IBB	SO	WP	Bk	W	L	Pct.	ShO	Sv	ERA
Rhodriguez,Rory	W. Palm Bch	Mon	A+	26	35	2	0	10	68	293	57	33	31	2	2	2	4	37	1	48	10	0	5	2	.714	0	0	4.10
Ricabal,Dan	Vero Beach	LA	A+	24	13	1	0	8	30	119	14	7	4	1	3	0	0	17	4	36	0	1	0	2	.000	0	1	1.20
	Savannah	LA	A	24	40	0	0	37	55.1	225	32	19	14	4	4	1	5	17	2	78	2	1	2	4	.333	0	24	2.28
Richardson,Brad.	Ogden	Mil	R+	21	19	0	0	8	22.2	128	28	37	27	2	1	3	0	28	0	25	8	0	1	1	.500	0	1	10.72
Richardson,Kasey	Fort Wayne	Min	A	20	30	13	1	7	111.2	481	113	56	43	5	5	5	5	39	1	81	12	2	6	8	.429	0	1	3.47
	Fort Myers	Min	A+	20	3	3	0	0	15.2	69	18	11	11	2	0	1	0	8	0	12	2	0	1	0	1.000	0	0	6.32
Ricketts,Chad	Rockford	ChN	A	22	37	9	0	17	87.2	389	89	60	49	8	5	2	7	29	2	70	5	1	3	8	.273	0	4	5.03
Riedling,John	Charlstn-WV	Cin	A	21	26	26	0	0	140	615	135	85	62	2	10	6	10	66	6	90	6	1	6	10	.375	0	0	3.99
Riegert,Tim	Johnson Cty	StL	R+	23	26	0	0	5	38.2	163	41	19	18	3	1	2	3	16	2	40	1	2	3	0	1.000	0	0	4.19
Rigdon,Paul	Watertown	Cle	A-	21	22	0	0	21	39.2	174	41	24	18	4	1	0	2	10	0	46	1	1	2	2	.500	0	6	4.08
Riggan,Jerrod	Boise	Cal	A-	23	15	15	1	0	89.1	395	90	62	46	10	3	6	5	38	5	80	6	0	3	5	.375	0	0	4.63
Rijo,Jose	Auburn	Hou	A-	21	33	0	0	15	53.1	241	65	29	21	0	2	3	6	16	1	39	8	1	1	3	.250	0	3	3.54
Riley,Michael	Bellingham	SF	A-	22	17	3	0	2	36.2	181	38	26	17	3	1	1	2	29	0	38	5	2	1	3	.250	0	0	4.17
Ritter,Jason	Lansing	KC	A	22	13	0	0	8	17	95	35	24	18	4	0	0	0	10	0	8	0	1	0	0	.000	0	0	9.53
Rivera,Alvin	Rockies	Col	R	18	11	7	0	2	49.1	208	48	22	18	0	0	3	4	12	0	44	3	2	4	2	.667	0	1	3.28
Rivera,Luis	Braves	Atl	R	NA	8	6	0	0	24.1	97	18	9	7	0	0	0	1	7	1	26	5	0	1	1	.500	0	0	2.59
Rivera,Marcos	Expos	Mon	R	20	17	1	0	10	33	140	33	9	8	0	3	0	1	7	0	16	2	1	4	2	.667	0	3	2.18
Rivera,Rafael	Everett	Sea	A-	21	24	0	0	3	49.1	203	47	19	12	1	1	0	0	10	0	61	2	0	4	1	.800	0	0	2.19
Rivette,Scott	W. Michigan	Oak	A	23	32	29	0	1	153.1	667	145	80	60	7	2	3	12	51	0	142	9	2	8	9	.471	0	1	3.52
Robbins,Mike	Lansing	KC	A	23	25	15	0	3	116.1	497	122	56	44	5	7	5	6	37	1	76	6	1	9	6	.600	0	0	3.40
Robbins,Jacob	Greensboro	NYA	A	21	18	12	0	2	74	349	80	59	53	5	4	5	7	49	0	50	10	4	1	8	.111	0	0	6.45
	Oneonta	NYA	A-	21	11	11	0	0	66	298	64	42	33	3	5	1	2	35	1	47	6	1	3	4	.429	0	0	4.50
Roberts,Grant	Kingsport	NYN	R+	19	13	13	2	0	68.2	285	43	18	16	3	1	0	7	37	1	92	4	0	9	1	.900	2	0	2.10
Roberts,Mark	Hickory	ChA	A	21	13	13	0	0	72	298	70	42	39	12	3	2	3	19	0	62	4	3	4	6	.400	0	0	4.88
Roberts,Randolph	Princeton	Cin	R+	23	12	4	1	2	50.2	213	33	20	15	0	0	1	2	29	0	49	15	1	3	2	.600	0	0	2.66
	Charlstn-WV	Cin	A	23	5	1	0	2	10	65	20	18	10	0	0	1	0	14	0	7	4	1	0	2	.000	0	0	9.00
Roberts,Willis	Lakeland	Det	A+	22	23	22	2	0	149.1	636	133	60	48	5	8	9	9	69	0	105	13	3	9	7	.563	0	0	2.89
Robertson,Douglas	Sou. Oregon	Oak	A-	22	23	4	0	7	52.1	242	69	44	35	5	3	2	1	17	6	48	2	0	2	3	.400	0	3	6.02
Robertson,Jerome	Astros	Hou	R	20	13	13	1	0	78.1	304	51	20	15	2	3	0	4	15	0	98	6	2	5	3	.625	1	0	1.72
	Kissimmee	Hou	A+	20	1	1	0	0	7	27	4	4	2	0	0	0	0	1	0	2	0	0	0	0	.000	0	0	2.57
Robinson,Marty	Greensboro	NYA	A	20	10	10	1	0	48.2	232	60	43	31	1	2	1	3	30	1	38	5	3	1	8	.111	0	0	5.73
	Oneonta	NYA	A-	20	15	15	1	0	80.2	370	83	49	35	3	3	5	2	43	0	50	9	5	3	6	.333	0	0	3.90
Rocker,John	Macon	Atl	A	22	20	19	2	1	106.1	453	85	60	46	7	1	4	6	63	1	107	12	3	5	3	.625	2	0	3.89
	Durham	Atl	A+	22	9	9	0	0	58.1	245	63	24	22	4	0	0	1	25	0	43	4	0	4	3	.571	0	0	3.39
Rodgers,Bobby	Lowell	Bos	A-	22	14	14	2	0	90	363	60	33	19	3	2	2	3	31	0	108	9	2	7	4	.636	1	0	1.90
Rodgers,Marcus	White Sox	ChA	R	20	10	6	1	1	37.2	166	44	17	14	1	1	1	2	16	0	29	4	1	1	3	.250	0	0	3.35
Rodrigues,Larry	Visalia	Ari	A+	22	13	10	0	0	56.2	265	72	49	33	8	2	1	3	19	1	37	5	0	2	5	.286	0	0	5.24
	Lethbridge	Ari	R+	22	10	10	1	0	54	231	56	31	23	1	2	2	6	9	0	46	3	1	7	1	.875	0	0	3.83
Rodriguez,Chad	Spokane	KC	A-	23	15	0	0	13	20.2	95	22	16	12	2	1	2	0	8	1	24	1	0	0	2	.000	0	3	5.23
Rodriguez,Hector	Boise	Cal	A-	22	20	0	0	6	24.1	109	27	13	10	2	2	3	1	11	0	25	2	0	1	1	.500	0	0	3.70
Rodriguez,Humber.	Rockies	Col	R	19	17	0	0	10	21.1	113	30	23	16	2	0	0	3	12	0	18	5	3	1	2	.333	0	0	6.75
Rodriguez,Jorge	Yankees	NYA	R	20	1	0	0	1	0.2	5	3	1	1	0	0	0	0	0	0	0	0	0	0	0	.000	0	0	13.50
Rodriguez,Jose	Devil Rays	TB	R	19	11	2	0	5	26.2	117	28	17	15	1	2	1	2	7	0	19	5	3	3	1	.750	0	0	5.06
Rodriguez,Luis	Bellingham	SF	A-	21	1	0	0	0	0	1	1	0	0	0	0	0	0	0	0	0	0	0	0	0	.000	0	0	0.00
Rodriguez,Victor	St. Cathrns	Tor	A-	23	21	8	0	7	64	296	50	55	42	2	3	2	6	54	2	54	8	0	2	7	.222	0	2	5.91
Roeder,Jason	Royals	KC	R	23	3	0	0	2	4	21	6	4	4	1	0	0	0	3	0	3	0	0	0	1	.000	0	0	9.00
Roettgen,Mark	Peoria	StL	A	20	6	6	0	0	26.1	127	27	22	15	5	1	2	1	24	0	18	6	1	2	1	.667	0	0	5.13
Rogers,Jason	Frederick	Bal	A+	24	31	18	1	1	115	540	136	87	70	8	8	3	4	62	0	87	5	2	7	8	.467	0	0	5.48
Rojas,Renney	Angels	Cal	R	18	10	1	1	4	27.2	111	23	14	11	1	1	1	3	8	0	28	2	0	2	0	1.000	0	1	3.58
Rolocut,Brian	Vero Beach	LA	A+	23	33	6	0	12	65.1	320	69	50	40	6	3	1	6	53	1	52	9	0	1	7	.125	0	0	5.51
Romboli,Curtis	Michigan	Bos	A	24	41	2	0	11	79	351	78	43	37	4	2	3	2	45	3	75	12	2	3	5	.375	0	0	4.22
Romero,John	Angels	Cal	R	21	14	11	0	1	67	295	63	43	30	1	1	1	7	27	0	53	9	2	2	3	.400	0	1	4.03
Romine,Jason	Portland	Col	A-	22	16	5	0	6	59.1	246	48	18	18	6	1	2	2	20	0	53	4	0	4	1	.800	0	2	2.73
Romo,Gregory	Tigers	Det	R	22	8	1	0	7	23	93	19	7	4	0	0	1	2	4	0	29	1	0	1	0	1.000	0	1	1.57
	Jamestown	Det	A-	22	6	6	1	0	38.1	155	35	17	10	3	0	1	1	6	0	39	3	0	4	2	.667	0	0	2.35
Root,Derek	Quad City	Hou	A	22	40	2	0	22	63	272	55	25	21	1	4	4	4	26	4	47	6	0	5	3	.625	0	7	3.00
Roque,Jorge	New Jersey	StL	A-	22	13	0	0	7	16.2	90	15	15	13	1	1	2	2	23	0	18	7	0	1	2	.333	0	2	7.02
Rosa,Cristy	Portland	Col	A-	19	3	3	0	0	9.1	47	14	10	7	2	0	0	1	3	0	5	1	0	0	1	.000	0	0	6.75
	Rockies	Col	R	19	6	3	0	1	17	74	22	11	11	0	0	0	4	4	0	12	0	0	1	0	1.000	0	0	5.82
Rosado,Juan	Vermont	Mon	A-	22	12	0	0	6	19	84	20	9	7	0	1	2	0	9	0	19	2	2	1	0	1.000	0	0	3.32
Rosario,Juan	Devil Rays	TB	R	21	3	0	0	1	3	16	0	3	0	0	0	1	1	3	0	3	2	1	0	0	.000	0	0	0.00
Rosario,Ruben	Johnson Cty	StL	R+	22	13	13	1	0	71.1	296	53	30	26	3	1	3	1	37	0	72	7	4	7	3	.700	1	0	3.28
Rose,Brian	Salem	Col	A+	24	5	0	0	3	7.1	32	10	7	5	0	0	0	0	2	0	2	1	1	0	0	.000	0	0	6.14
	Asheville	Col	A	24	38	1	0	14	68.1	273	53	30	27	4	6	5	3	16	2	73	4	1	4	5	.444	0	3	3.56
Rose,Ted	Princeton	Cin	R+	23	11	11	1	0	59.1	262	70	44	41	9	2	3	3	21	0	53	9	2	3	5	.375	1	0	6.22
Rosenbohm,Jim	Pittsfield	NYN	A-	23	20	0	0	7	26.2	134	22	10	10	0	1	2	5	26	0	37	4	1	1	1	.500	0	1	3.38
Roup,Randy	Royals	KC	R	20	8	0	0	4	8.2	49	15	13	12	1	0	1	0	7	0	8	3	0	0	0	.000	0	0	12.46
Ruch,Rob	Visalia	Min	A+	24	37	5	0	14	96	424	94	57	44	5	3	4	2	47	0	75	19	2	2	7	.222	0	3	4.13
Ruhl,Nathan	Devil Rays	TB	R	20	16	0	0	7	27	109	18	9	7	0	3	1	1	11	1	25	4	0	2	2	.500	0	0	2.33
Ruiz,Rafael	Hickory	ChA	A	22	34	0	0	9	51	228	58	32	19	4	1	2	0	13	0	52	0	0	1	2	.333	0	0	3.35
Runion,Tony	Kinston	Cle	A+	25	6	1	0	2	14	71	16	10	9	0	1	0	3	14	0	11	3	0	1	1	.500	0	0	5.79
	Bakersfield	Cle	A+	25	7	6	1	0	35.2	197	61	56	45	5	2	2	3	27	0	20	9	0	0	6	.000	0	0	11.36
Runion,Jeff	Rangers	Tex	R	22	7	2	0	1	19	79	14	8	5	0	1	1	0	12	0	19	0	1	1	0	1.000	0	0	2.37
	Charlstn-SC	Tex	A	22	5	1	0	2	12	52	13	5	5	0	0	1	0	5	0	9	0	0	0	1	.000	0	1	3.75
Runyan,Paul	Charlstn-WV	Cin	A	25	29	7	0	7	80	339	81	47	34	3	3	3	8	19	1	41	9	0	7	5	.583	0	2	3.83
	Winston-Sal	Cin	A+	25	6	5	0	0	37.1	151	38	11	10	2	0	0	1	8	0	11	2	0	3	1	.750	0	0	2.41
Runyan,Sean	Quad City	Hou	A	23	29	17	0	3	132.1	551	128	61	57	10	1	5	14	30	0	104	4	1	9	4	.692	0	0	3.88

1996 Pitching — Single-A and Rookie Leagues

HOW MUCH HE PITCHED											WHAT HE GAVE UP												THE RESULTS					
Player	Team	Org	Lg	A	G	GS	CG	GF	IP	BFP	H	R	ER	HR	SH	SF	HB	TBB	IBB	SO	WP	Bk	W	L	Pct.	ShO	Sv	ERA
Rushing,Will	Fort Myers	Min	A+	24	28	25	2	1	165	699	157	72	64	10	8	3	9	74	0	111	5	2	13	6	.684	1	1	3.49
Sabel,Eric	Lethbridge	Ari	R+	22	20	3	0	5	42	184	43	23	13	3	1	1	3	7	0	41	4	0	1	4	.200	0	1	2.79
Sadler,Carl	Expos	Mon	R	20	17	3	0	6	37	170	41	24	16	2	2	0	2	12	0	24	3	3	2	2	.500	0	1	3.89
Saier,Matt	Wilmington	KC	A+	24	26	26	0	0	134	585	136	74	60	9	4	0	6	52	2	129	9	2	9	9	.500	0	0	4.03
Sak,Jim	Rancho Cuca	SD	A+	23	4	4	0	0	15.2	78	21	13	11	2	1	0	2	12	0	14	0	0	0	3	.000	0	0	6.32
	Clinton	SD	A	23	21	7	0	6	65.2	291	46	31	26	2	4	2	4	45	1	72	4	0	3	4	.429	0	0	3.56
Salvevold,Gregory	Devil Rays	TB	R	21	15	0	0	9	30.2	129	26	17	13	0	1	3	5	13	0	22	3	1	1	1	.500	0	2	3.82
Salyers,Jeremy	Expos	Mon	R	21	11	9	2	1	57	246	47	36	27	4	3	1	8	26	0	30	1	0	1	4	.200	0	1	4.26
Samboy,Juan	Lethbridge	Ari	R+	22	17	3	0	3	27	119	26	15	13	1	0	1	1	17	0	19	4	0	1	1	.500	0	0	4.33
Sanchez,Bienveni.	Expos	Mon	R	21	6	0	0	1	10.1	54	20	12	7	0	1	0	3	2	0	5	0	1	1	2	.333	0	0	6.10
Sanchez,Jesus	St. Lucie	NYN	A+	22	16	16	2	0	92	344	53	22	20	6	3	1	1	24	0	81	4	2	9	3	.750	1	0	1.96
Sanchez,Martin	Macon	Atl	A	20	31	13	0	6	106.2	483	109	60	47	8	3	4	9	53	1	92	13	0	5	5	.500	0	1	3.97
Sanchez,Mike	San Bernrdo	LA	A+	21	11	0	0	2	23	124	23	30	21	2	2	3	2	28	1	29	6	1	0	0	.000	0	0	8.22
	Great Falls	LA	R+	21	9	0	0	5	9.1	46	8	11	10	1	0	1	0	10	0	7	11	1	0	0	.000	0	1	9.64
Sanders,Frankie	Columbus	Cle	A	21	22	22	0	0	121.1	508	103	52	34	8	3	2	6	37	1	109	13	4	9	3	.750	0	0	2.52
Sanders,Allen	Spokane	KC	A-	22	13	5	0	2	43.2	183	49	25	22	3	1	4	3	9	0	19	1	0	5	2	.714	0	0	4.53
	Lansing	KC	A	22	5	5	0	0	31.1	130	38	18	15	3	2	0	3	2	0	5	0	0	3	0	1.000	0	0	4.31
Sanders,Craig	Lansing	KC	A	24	8	0	0	0	15	71	10	13	8	0	1	1	3	17	0	15	3	1	2	1	.667	0	0	4.80
	Spokane	KC	A-	24	6	0	0	1	11.1	64	14	16	13	3	0	2	2	15	0	5	4	0	0	1	.000	0	1	10.32
Saneaux,Francisco	Frederick	Bal	A+	23	2	1	0	0	2.2	23	9	11	11	3	0	0	1	6	0	3	0	0	0	0	.000	0	0	37.13
	High Desert	Bal	A+	23	20	19	0	0	102	474	98	71	63	13	4	0	7	91	4	101	17	2	4	5	.444	0	0	5.56
Santamaria,Juan	Tigers	Det	R	20	12	12	0	0	55.2	254	52	47	33	4	0	2	10	25	0	43	12	1	2	7	.222	0	0	5.34
Santamaria,Bill	Columbia	NYN	A	21	31	0	0	16	50.1	215	43	22	20	6	5	2	0	26	1	28	2	0	2	0	1.000	0	1	3.58
Santana,Humberto	Mets	NYN	R	20	10	9	0	0	52.2	207	45	16	13	0	0	3	3	7	0	40	2	5	4	3	.571	0	0	2.22
Santana,Marino	Lancaster	Sea	A+	25	28	28	1	0	157.1	688	164	105	88	26	5	8	8	57	0	167	18	6	8	15	.348	0	0	5.03
Santana,Orlando	Orioles	Bal	R	18	16	0	0	5	25.2	106	24	12	9	2	0	1	1	6	0	19	2	2	1	1	.500	0	2	3.16
Santana,Pedro	Red Sox	Bos	R	19	13	8	0	2	71.1	289	59	24	15	4	5	1	2	12	1	33	2	3	5	3	.625	0	0	1.89
Santiago,Derek	Utica	Fla	A-	21	12	10	0	1	54.2	245	57	30	27	4	1	0	3	28	0	41	8	1	2	2	.500	0	0	4.45
Santiago,Jose	Lansing	KC	A	22	54	0	0	46	77	331	78	34	22	4	7	1	5	21	3	55	3	1	7	6	.538	0	19	2.57
Santiago,Sandi	Tampa	NYA	A+	27	9	1	0	3	12.1	60	18	9	7	1	2	0	0	4	0	11	1	0	0	1	.000	0	1	5.11
Santoro,Gary	Kane County	Fla	A	24	31	0	0	29	32.2	137	30	13	10	0	2	5	2	12	2	35	2	0	1	2	.333	0	9	2.76
Santos,Juan	Orioles	Bal	R	21	6	0	0	3	9.1	41	9	4	4	1	1	0	0	2	0	4	1	1	0	0	.000	0	2	3.86
Santos,Juan	Bluefield	Bal	R+	21	16	0	0	5	24.2	117	32	19	17	1	0	2	1	11	1	20	1	2	0	1	.000	0	0	6.20
Santos,Rafael	Erie	Pit	A-	21	18	4	0	3	54.2	238	55	31	23	5	2	0	3	19	0	32	4	0	1	2	.333	0	0	3.79
Santos,Victor	Tigers	Det	R	20	9	9	0	0	50	199	44	12	11	1	3	1	7	13	0	39	3	0	3	2	.600	0	0	1.98
	Lakeland	Det	A+	20	5	4	0	0	28.1	114	19	11	7	2	2	1	4	9	0	25	2	0	2	2	.500	0	0	2.22
Satterfield,Jeremy	Medicne Hat	Tor	R+	21	14	0	0	3	32.1	164	39	31	22	5	0	3	5	27	1	25	9	0	0	3	.000	0	0	6.12
Sauget,Richard	Hickory	ChA	A	23	25	0	0	13	47.1	202	48	24	21	5	6	1	2	9	1	39	2	3	2	1	.667	0	1	3.99
Sauritch,Chris	High Desert	Bal	A+	25	35	0	0	11	52.1	244	52	33	33	10	2	6	4	33	2	41	6	3	4	1	.800	0	0	5.68
Sauve,Jeff	Michigan	Bos	A	24	36	0	0	17	61.2	258	51	34	28	4	4	0	2	26	4	55	3	0	0	3	.000	0	0	4.09
Sawyer,Zack	Salem	Col	A+	24	4	0	0	4	2	13	6	3	3	1	0	0	0	1	0	2	1	0	0	1	.000	0	1	13.50
Schaffner,Eric	Greensboro	NYA	A	22	27	12	0	4	91.1	427	97	65	51	4	2	4	3	62	2	62	15	4	3	7	.300	0	0	5.03
Scheer,Greg	Wisconsin	Sea	A	25	35	0	0	14	54.1	258	60	43	41	3	2	1	4	33	1	55	2	0	3	1	.750	0	0	6.79
Scheffer,Aaron	Wisconsin	Sea	A	21	45	1	0	28	67.2	292	55	35	28	5	2	2	3	34	4	89	16	5	8	1	.889	0	14	3.72
Scheffler,Craig	Vero Beach	LA	A+	25	32	1	0	16	41.1	197	50	33	30	1	2	4	3	27	1	23	5	1	0	0	.000	0	1	6.53
Schlomann,Brett	Tampa	NYA	A+	22	26	26	1	0	145.2	628	152	81	69	13	3	4	8	49	2	103	10	1	11	8	.579	1	0	4.26
Schlutt,Jason	Padres	SD	R	25	3	0	0	1	5	22	6	3	2	1	0	0	0	0	0	7	0	0	0	1	.000	0	0	3.60
	Rancho Cuca	SD	A+	25	7	0	0	3	8	34	10	5	5	2	0	1	0	2	0	6	4	0	0	0	.000	0	0	5.63
Schmack,Brian	Hickory	ChA	A	23	43	0	0	25	62.1	264	61	24	16	4	9	0	4	16	5	56	3	1	6	4	.600	0	5	2.31
Schmidt,Don	Portland	Col	A-	22	19	5	0	7	59	251	53	31	22	6	0	3	3	20	0	51	1	1	2	2	.500	0	0	3.36
Schmitt,Jo Jo	Durham	Atl	A+	26	42	0	0	14	73.2	347	80	47	36	5	3	2	4	45	3	65	5	1	3	1	.750	0	0	4.40
Schnautz,Bradley	Yankees	NYA	R	21	10	1	0	1	22.2	101	28	13	13	2	0	0	0	5	0	31	0	1	2	0	1.000	0	0	5.16
Schoeneweis,Scott	Lk Elsinore	Cal	A+	23	14	12	0	1	93.2	387	86	47	41	6	3	2	2	27	0	83	2	1	8	3	.727	0	0	3.94
Schorzman,Steven	Bristol	ChA	R+	22	14	13	1	1	69	310	73	43	35	5	1	3	6	31	0	50	5	0	0	9	.000	0	0	4.57
Schramm,Carl	San Jose	SF	A+	27	39	0	0	10	70.1	303	64	31	27	5	8	0	5	25	1	66	4	1	7	3	.700	0	1	3.45
Schroeder,Chad	Jamestown	Det	A-	23	31	0	0	26	38.2	153	29	15	6	1	1	3	0	6	0	41	0	0	5	0	1.000	0	6	1.40
Schroeder,Rodney	Idaho Falls	SD	R+	22	20	9	0	5	58.1	265	71	39	30	3	0	2	6	29	0	58	6	0	5	5	.500	0	0	4.63
Schroeffel,Scott	Portland	Col	A-	23	16	6	0	7	59.2	235	36	15	11	1	2	2	4	17	0	61	4	1	1	1	.500	0	1	1.66
	Asheville	Col	A	23	2	2	0	0	11.2	52	10	7	5	0	0	3	1	6	1	15	4	0	1	0	1.000	0	0	3.86
Schurman,Ryan	Danville	Atl	R+	20	21	1	0	7	45.1	203	45	30	25	5	2	4	6	18	1	49	5	0	2	4	.333	0	1	4.96
Scutero,Brian	Cedar Rapds	Cal	A	23	53	0	0	21	88	366	74	38	31	9	3	3	3	43	6	52	5	0	10	5	.667	0	3	3.17
Seabury,Jaron	Medicne Hat	Tor	R+	21	5	0	0	5	6	27	4	4	3	1	0	0	0	5	0	5	1	0	0	0	.000	0	3	4.50
	St. Cathrns	Tor	A-	21	19	0	0	6	30.1	135	29	16	11	1	2	1	0	10	1	24	5	2	3	1	.750	0	1	3.26
Seaver,Mark	Bluefield	Bal	R+	22	3	2	0	0	15	55	4	2	2	1	0	0	1	5	0	18	0	0	1	0	1.000	0	0	1.20
	High Desert	Bal	A+	22	4	4	0	0	23.2	99	19	12	9	1	1	0	1	10	0	16	6	1	2	1	.667	0	0	3.42
Seberino,Ronni	Devil Rays	TB	R	18	18	6	0	8	52	215	50	22	20	2	2	2	2	15	0	49	10	1	4	2	.667	0	1	3.46
Sebring,Jeff	Portland	Col	A-	22	16	12	0	3	76	337	78	38	32	6	2	5	7	28	1	49	3	0	5	5	.500	0	0	3.79
Secoda,Jason	South Bend	ChA	A	22	32	22	0	6	133.2	605	132	84	59	9	2	3	3	75	0	94	18	1	6	12	.333	0	1	3.97
Seebode,Michael	Tigers	Det	R	19	12	2	0	5	36	159	34	22	15	1	3	2	2	11	0	25	5	2	4	2	.667	0	0	3.75
Seip,Rod	Rangers	Tex	R	23	1	0	0	0	1	4	1	0	0	0	0	0	0	1	0	0	0	0	0	0	.000	0	0	0.00
Sekany,Jason	Red Sox	Bos	R	21	5	2	0	2	11.2	50	14	3	3	1	0	0	1	3	0	16	2	0	0	0	.000	0	1	2.31
Sellers,Justin	Padres	SD	R	20	26	0	0	23	32	139	31	14	8	0	0	3	2	14	0	36	2	1	1	0	1.000	0	6	2.25
Sellner,Aaron	Bakersfield	Bal	A+	23	16	0	0	8	25.2	135	33	32	22	5	0	3	1	20	0	26	5	0	0	2	.000	0	0	7.71
	High Desert	Bal	A+	23	4	0	0	0	8.1	40	11	9	7	1	2	0	1	5	0	5	3	1	0	1	.000	0	0	7.56
Serrano,Liosbany	Braves	Atl	R	21	12	2	0	4	27	136	29	27	22	1	2	4	8	22	0	7	4	7	1	2	.333	0	0	7.33
Settle,Brian	Pirates	Pit	R	19	7	0	0	3	11.1	56	5	10	10	0	1	0	6	14	0	13	2	0	0	1	.000	0	0	7.94
Severino,Edy	Medicne Hat	Tor	R+	21	16	11	0	3	57	289	76	68	50	6	1	6	0	41	0	34	7	1	2	6	.250	0	1	7.89

1996 Pitching — Single-A and Rookie Leagues

HOW MUCH HE PITCHED											WHAT HE GAVE UP												THE RESULTS					
Player	Team	Org	Lg	A	G	GS	CG	GF	IP	BFP	H	R	ER	HR	SH	SF	HB	TBB	IBB	SO	WP	Bk	W	L	Pct.	ShO	Sv	ERA
Shadburne,Adam	Batavia	Phi	A-	23	20	0	0	11	34	143	34	16	12	3	1	2	3	8	2	37	0	2	2	0	1.000	0	0	3.18
Shaffer,Trevor	Williamsprt	ChN	A-	23	25	0	0	19	32	134	25	6	6	0	3	3	1	16	1	29	0	2	2	0	1.000	0	8	1.69
Shannon,Bob	Royals	KC	R	19	2	0	0	2	2	7	2	0	0	0	0	0	0	0	0	0	0	0	0	0	.000	0	0	0.00
Shaver,Tony	Kissimmee	Hou	A+	25	42	0	0	24	64	275	57	24	17	3	6	1	1	23	1	35	2	0	4	4	.500	0	4	2.39
Shearn,Thomas	Astros	Hou	R	19	17	3	0	3	41.2	162	34	13	8	2	1	2	2	10	0	43	3	1	5	2	.714	0	0	1.73
Shelby,Anthony	Greensboro	NYA	A	23	16	0	0	6	26	105	16	5	4	0	1	1	2	10	2	25	1	0	2	1	.667	0	1	1.38
	Tampa	NYA	A+	23	24	0	0	8	30	124	26	12	6	1	1	1	1	7	1	18	1	0	2	2	.500	0	1	1.80
Shepard,David	Billings	Cin	R+	23	15	14	1	1	80.2	376	109	69	53	10	1	4	11	21	2	80	6	1	6	7	.462	1	0	5.91
Shepherd,Al	Frederick	Bal	A+	23	41	6	0	19	96.2	445	112	67	60	13	3	4	2	47	2	104	5	0	6	5	.545	0	10	5.59
Sheredy,Kevin	New Jersey	StL	A-	22	8	5	0	0	23	100	21	15	11	2	2	1	1	13	0	13	1	0	0	1	.000	0	0	4.30
Shiell,Jason	Danville	Atl	R+	20	12	12	0	0	59.1	231	44	14	13	1	0	1	1	19	0	57	3	0	3	1	.750	0	0	1.97
Shockley,Keith	Martinsvlle	Phi	R+	20	14	6	1	3	45	212	62	44	40	8	1	4	1	10	0	29	1	7	2	2	.500	0	0	8.00
Shoemaker,Steph.	Salem	Col	A+	24	25	13	0	5	86.1	371	63	49	45	6	1	5	4	63	0	105	1	1	2	7	.222	0	1	4.69
Short,Barry	St. Lucie	NYN	A+	23	58	0	0	24	88.1	350	70	28	23	5	4	1	1	18	1	70	1	0	6	2	.750	0	10	2.34
Shourds,Anthony	Rangers	Tex	R	20	20	0	0	9	35	148	27	12	9	0	0	1	5	12	0	28	1	0	3	2	.600	0	0	2.31
Shumaker,Anthony	Piedmont	Phi	A	24	20	0	0	13	32.2	120	16	7	5	2	0	0	0	10	1	51	3	0	3	0	1.000	0	4	1.38
	Clearwater	Phi	A+	24	31	0	0	13	29.1	137	42	18	18	1	3	0	0	12	5	25	1	0	5	3	.625	0	3	5.52
Shumate,Jacob	Macon	Atl	A	21	1	1	0	0	3	16	5	5	4	0	0	1	0	2	0	2	1	0	0	0	.000	0	0	12.00
Siciliano,Jess	Erie	Pit	A-	20	4	0	0	0	5.1	28	7	5	4	0	1	0	1	4	0	4	1	0	0	0	.000	0	0	6.75
	Pirates	Pit	R	20	3	0	0	1	5	24	4	3	2	0	0	0	2	2	0	1	0	0	0	0	.000	0	0	3.60
Sick,Dave	Cedar Rapds	Cal	A	25	26	0	0	21	27	124	27	10	6	1	2	1	6	13	4	19	5	0	1	2	.333	0	6	2.00
	Lk Elsinore	Cal	A+	25	16	0	0	3	22.2	112	25	19	18	2	0	1	5	14	1	17	1	0	1	0	1.000	0	1	7.15
Siegel,Justin	Hudson Vall	Tex	A-	21	5	0	0	1	6.1	30	8	5	4	1	1	0	0	5	1	8	0	2	0	1	.000	0	0	5.68
Sikes,Jason	Piedmont	Phi	A	21	17	17	0	0	77.2	359	87	60	44	4	5	6	5	41	0	47	8	2	4	6	.400	0	0	5.10
Sikes,Ken	San Bernrdo	LA	A+	24	17	17	0	0	91.2	410	89	58	49	12	2	6	4	56	0	65	2	2	6	3	.667	0	0	4.81
Sikorski,Brian	Quad City	Hou	A	22	26	25	1	0	166.2	704	140	79	58	12	4	7	10	70	2	150	7	9	11	8	.579	0	0	3.13
Siler,Jeff	Lakeland	Det	A+	26	37	0	0	7	58	237	52	20	17	3	4	1	1	18	0	45	0	1	6	3	.667	0	1	2.64
Silva,Carlos	Martinsvlle	Phi	R+	18	7	1	0	1	18	78	20	11	8	1	4	1	1	5	0	16	0	0	0	0	.000	0	0	4.00
Silva,Juan	Red Sox	Bos	R	19	14	0	0	9	25.2	112	34	16	15	2	1	2	1	12	0	31	3	3	0	3	.000	0	2	5.26
Simmons,Carlos	Charlstn-SC	Tex	A	23	33	1	0	17	56.2	264	56	43	32	9	2	3	6	33	1	34	5	1	3	7	.300	0	4	5.08
Simmons,Mike	White Sox	ChA	R	23	17	1	0	6	41	180	46	22	16	2	2	0	2	12	0	32	5	0	2	2	.500	0	1	3.51
Simon,Benjamin	Yakima	LA	A-	22	15	10	0	1	66.1	275	59	34	27	5	3	5	3	21	2	62	0	1	2	6	.250	0	1	3.66
Simontacchi,Jason	Spokane	KC	A-	23	14	6	0	3	47	214	59	37	27	8	3	3	3	15	0	43	1	0	2	5	.286	0	2	5.17
Sims,Ken	Orioles	Bal	R	21	11	2	0	6	16.1	79	22	12	9	2	0	0	0	8	0	20	4	0	0	2	.000	0	2	4.96
Sinclair,Steve	Dunedin	Tor	A+	25	3	0	0	1	2.2	12	4	2	1	1	0	0	0	0	0	1	0	0	0	1	.000	0	0	3.38
Skuse,Nick	Lk Elsinore	Cal	A+	25	6	6	0	0	32	155	36	27	23	1	5	3	0	22	0	18	7	2	0	3	.000	0	0	6.47
	Cedar Rapds	Cal	A	25	18	16	0	1	94.2	415	77	47	43	10	2	0	5	58	2	50	7	4	5	6	.455	0	0	4.09
Slamka,John	Rockies	Col	R	23	1	0	0	0	1	6	0	0	0	0	0	0	0	2	0	3	0	0	0	0	.000	0	0	0.00
Smart,Jon	Delmarva	Mon	A	23	25	25	3	0	156.2	655	155	75	59	14	2	7	10	31	0	109	8	0	9	8	.529	2	0	3.39
Smatana,Steve	Lowell	Bos	A-	24	19	0	0	9	31	116	22	5	5	1	2	1	0	3	0	33	1	0	5	0	1.000	0	2	1.45
Smith,Andy	W. Michigan	Oak	A	22	37	13	0	9	116	527	112	71	59	8	3	4	7	68	5	94	8	1	10	7	.588	0	1	4.58
Smith,Hut	High Desert	Bal	A+	24	10	7	1	0	50.1	216	59	34	30	7	1	1	3	16	0	34	6	3	3	4	.429	0	0	5.36
Smith,Cam	Lakeland	Det	A+	23	22	21	0	1	113.2	500	93	64	58	10	1	5	7	71	0	114	8	0	5	8	.385	0	0	4.59
Smith,Dan	Charlotte	Tex	A+	21	18	18	1	0	87	403	100	61	49	6	5	5	4	38	0	55	3	0	3	7	.300	0	0	5.07
Smith,Eric	Quad City	Hou	A	23	26	7	0	5	75.1	320	66	32	26	4	3	2	3	26	1	59	6	0	6	3	.667	0	1	3.11
Smith,Josh	Padres	SD	R	19	10	0	0	5	21	77	12	3	1	0	0	0	0	3	0	22	2	0	2	1	.667	0	2	0.43
	Idaho Falls	SD	R+	19	17	0	0	6	14.2	61	11	9	8	0	1	1	1	11	0	11	3	0	2	1	.667	0	1	4.91
Smith,Keilan	Hagerstown	Tor	A	23	19	1	0	13	29	129	32	19	12	1	2	0	1	8	1	21	5	1	2	3	.400	0	2	3.72
	Dunedin	Tor	A+	23	23	1	0	9	44.2	205	50	32	25	3	3	4	2	22	4	37	5	0	0	3	.000	0	2	5.04
Smith,Ryan	Rangers	Tex	R	22	14	0	0	3	25	116	18	15	13	1	0	0	2	24	0	24	13	2	2	0	1.000	0	0	4.68
Smith,Stephen	Billings	Cin	R+	24	24	0	0	22	31.2	146	39	20	15	1	0	4	3	16	1	23	3	3	2	2	.500	0	3	4.26
Smith,Roy	Wisconsin	Sea	A	21	27	27	0	0	146	679	164	113	83	9	6	4	8	73	3	99	11	2	6	13	.316	0	0	5.12
Snead,George	Braves	Atl	R	23	3	0	0	2	7	34	7	6	3	1	1	0	1	4	1	5	0	0	0	1	.000	0	0	3.86
	Danville	Atl	R+	23	10	0	0	5	18	87	26	17	15	2	0	2	2	8	0	9	0	0	2	1	.667	0	0	7.50
	Macon	Atl	A	23	3	0	0	2	7.1	37	13	10	9	2	0	0	0	0	0	3	0	0	0	1	.000	0	0	11.05
Snyder,Matt	High Desert	Bal	A+	22	58	0	0	49	72	317	60	34	30	6	5	2	1	38	2	93	9	1	6	2	.750	0	20	3.75
Sobik,Trad	Lakeland	Det	A+	21	13	13	2	0	81.1	362	79	51	40	5	8	2	6	48	1	49	3	0	4	6	.400	0	0	4.43
Soden,Chad	Wisconsin	Sea	A	23	19	1	0	4	28.2	126	26	10	5	2	0	0	0	10	1	21	1	0	3	0	1.000	0	0	1.57
	Lancaster	Sea	A+	23	9	0	0	4	11	59	17	14	13	1	1	0	0	9	1	8	1	0	0	1	.000	0	0	10.64
Solomon,Dave	Winston-Sal	Cin	A+	25	38	0	0	16	53.1	240	56	32	27	4	1	5	3	27	2	28	3	0	3	2	.600	0	0	4.56
Soriano,Jacobo	Angels	Cal	R	22	15	0	0	12	19.2	88	17	13	11	0	2	3	3	12	1	22	1	1	1	3	.250	0	5	5.03
Sorzano,Ronnie	Expos	Mon	R	21	15	5	0	6	45	183	39	16	13	0	3	1	2	8	0	27	1	1	3	2	.600	0	3	2.60
Soto,Seferino	Great Falls	LA	R+	21	15	11	0	3	55.2	261	56	45	38	4	1	2	6	35	0	51	10	5	2	4	.333	0	1	6.14
South,Carl	Savannah	LA	A	22	33	10	0	7	96	422	85	58	44	8	4	4	3	42	4	84	12	0	6	5	.545	0	0	4.13
	Augusta	Pit	A	22	1	1	0	0	6	25	5	2	2	0	0	0	0	2	0	9	0	0	0	1	.000	0	0	3.00
Southall,Pete	Visalia	Ari	A+	NA	32	0	0	26	54	273	83	64	55	7	3	3	7	27	0	26	7	0	1	1	.500	0	0	9.17
Spade,Matt	Lynchburg	Pit	A+	24	53	0	0	17	80.1	353	88	38	27	7	6	3	1	27	6	71	10	1	6	4	.600	0	2	3.02
Sparks,Eric	Expos	Mon	R	23	14	1	0	6	29.1	119	25	10	9	1	0	0	3	5	0	16	6	1	4	0	1.000	0	3	2.76
Spear,Russell	Clinton	SD	A	19	11	10	0	0	51.2	257	60	43	35	3	1	4	4	42	0	44	8	1	4	3	.571	0	0	6.10
	Jamestown	Det	A-	19	8	7	0	0	34.2	158	39	24	20	5	1	2	2	15	0	28	4	0	2	1	.667	0	0	5.19
Spence,Cam	Tampa	NYA	A+	22	8	8	0	0	40.1	181	51	31	26	3	0	2	3	12	0	20	2	1	2	4	.333	0	0	5.80
	Greensboro	NYA	A	22	19	19	0	0	114.2	492	108	66	49	8	5	3	4	38	1	89	7	0	6	6	.500	0	0	3.85
Spiegel,Mike	Burlington	Cle	R+	21	14	0	0	6	21.2	97	19	12	9	0	1	0	2	12	0	14	1	0	1	0	1.000	0	0	3.74
Spiers,Corey	Elizabethtn	Min	R+	22	17	8	0	2	59.1	289	69	45	22	3	0	3	2	26	0	67	9	1	6	5	.545	0	0	3.34
	Fort Wayne	Min	A	22	2	1	0	1	4	23	6	3	3	0	0	0	0	5	0	2	0	0	0	1	.000	0	0	6.75
Spinelli,Michael	Michigan	Boo	A	20	11	11	0	0	60	275	58	43	35	1	3	1	4	39	1	41	9	0	3	4	.429	0	0	5.25
	Red Sox	Bos	R	20	1	0	0	0	4	15	4	1	1	0	0	0	0	0	0	2	1	1	1	0	1.000	0	0	2.25

1996 Pitching — Single-A and Rookie Leagues

HOW MUCH HE PITCHED											WHAT HE GAVE UP												THE RESULTS					
Player	Team	Org	Lg	A	G	GS	CG	GF	IP	BFP	H	R	ER	HR	SH	SF	HB	TBB	IBB	SO	WP	Bk	W	L	Pct.	ShO	Sv	ERA
Splawn,Matthew	Pittsfield	NYN	A-	24	22	0	0	15	36.1	145	26	5	4	0	1	0	0	10	1	44	0	4	4	1	.800	0	8	0.99
Splittorff,Jamie	Fort Wayne	Min	A	23	8	6	0	1	27.2	124	28	14	13	2	0	1	1	12	0	21	3	0	2	1	.667	0	0	4.23
Spykstra,Dave	Savannah	LA	A	23	28	14	2	5	100.2	440	83	47	37	8	2	0	6	44	0	104	19	0	6	4	.600	0	0	3.31
St. Pierre,Bobby	Tampa	NYA	A+	23	29	22	0	3	140	579	133	69	50	8	5	3	6	38	1	107	7	2	12	6	.667	0	1	3.21
Stachler,Eric	Kissimmee	Hou	A+	24	30	0	0	11	56.1	257	50	35	24	3	1	4	3	39	2	41	3	0	4	3	.571	0	0	3.83
Stadelhofer,Mike	Utica	Fla	A-	23	4	0	0	0	9.2	51	15	12	10	2	1	0	2	5	0	9	3	0	0	0	.000	0	0	9.31
Stading,Kris	Expos	Mon	R	20	11	1	0	4	17.2	71	11	4	4	0	0	0	1	9	0	17	1	0	2	1	.667	0	0	2.04
Stallings,Ben	Red Sox	Bos	R	20	11	6	0	1	42.1	198	45	33	23	3	2	3	3	22	2	36	5	2	1	4	.200	0	0	4.89
Stanley,Brandon	White Sox	ChA	R	23	1	0	0	1	2	8	0	0	0	0	0	0	0	2	0	3	0	0	0	0	.000	0	0	0.00
	Bristol	ChA	R+	23	17	0	0	10	20.1	103	23	21	12	2	1	0	1	19	2	13	9	0	1	3	.250	0	1	5.31
Stark,Dennis	Everett	Sea	A-	22	12	4	0	4	30.1	133	25	19	15	2	3	1	1	17	0	49	5	1	1	3	.250	0	0	4.45
Stechschulte,Gene	New Jersey	StL	A-	23	20	1	0	6	33	159	41	17	12	0	2	1	2	16	2	27	4	0	1	2	.333	0	0	3.27
Steele,Brandon	Angels	Cal	R	18	7	4	0	1	26.2	121	31	18	13	0	0	0	3	13	0	19	3	1	1	3	.250	0	1	4.39
Stein,Ethan	Spokane	KC	A-	22	9	8	0	0	38.1	174	48	27	27	5	1	1	3	12	0	20	2	1	0	3	.000	0	0	6.34
Stein,Blake	St. Pete	StL	A+	23	28	27	2	1	172	667	122	48	41	4	3	4	5	54	0	159	4	0	16	5	.762	1	1	2.15
Steinert,Rob	Bakersfield	—	A+	25	4	1	0	1	3	27	4	9	9	0	0	1	0	14	0	5	5	0	0	1	.000	0	0	27.00
	Beloit	Mil	A	25	3	0	0	2	2	12	2	1	1	0	0	0	0	4	0	1	1	0	0	0	.000	0	0	4.50
Steinke,Brock	Kissimmee	Hou	A+	22	16	8	0	2	46.1	227	62	39	33	2	0	4	6	31	0	22	6	1	4	3	.571	0	1	6.41
	Quad City	Hou	A	22	24	3	0	9	48.2	235	53	38	33	3	1	3	4	36	4	55	5	0	2	4	.333	0	2	6.10
Stentz,Brent	Fayettevlle	Det	A	21	45	8	0	7	98	413	91	51	38	4	4	1	6	27	1	92	5	2	7	8	.467	0	2	3.49
Stephens,Jason	Boise	Cal	A-	21	3	0	0	2	3.1	16	4	3	3	1	0	0	0	1	0	5	0	0	2	0	1.000	0	1	8.10
	Cedar Rapds	Cal	A	21	21	0	0	20	26	118	27	12	10	1	1	2	3	14	2	19	2	0	2	3	.400	0	6	3.46
Stephens,Shannon	Kane County	Fla	A	23	17	17	1	0	106.1	432	92	41	34	8	6	1	7	25	0	85	7	1	8	3	.727	1	0	2.88
	Brevard Cty	Fla	A+	23	4	4	0	0	24.1	114	33	22	17	2	0	2	0	9	0	12	0	0	0	4	.000	0	0	6.29
Stepka,Tom	Portland	Col	A-	21	12	12	0	0	68	291	74	42	28	8	1	0	2	10	0	48	2	1	5	4	.556	0	0	3.71
	Asheville	Col	A	21	2	2	1	0	16	56	6	2	1	1	0	0	0	1	0	16	0	0	2	0	1.000	1	0	0.56
Stevens,Kris	Martinsvlle	Phi	R+	19	10	10	0	0	47	194	54	23	19	2	3	1	1	10	0	41	2	1	1	4	.200	0	0	3.64
	Batavia	Phi	A-	19	3	3	0	0	13.1	61	16	12	12	2	1	0	0	6	0	11	0	0	1	1	.500	0	0	8.10
Stevenson,Jason	Daytona	ChN	A+	22	27	17	2	5	122	519	136	56	48	7	6	5	5	22	2	86	8	1	8	5	.615	1	0	3.54
Stevenson,Rodney	Vermont	Mon	A-	23	22	0	0	5	31.2	133	24	11	10	1	1	0	1	13	0	46	2	2	5	2	.714	0	1	2.84
Stewart,Paul	Ogden	Mil	R+	18	12	9	0	1	43.2	211	47	49	38	11	0	4	4	26	0	39	6	1	1	4	.200	0	0	7.83
Stewart,Stan	Tampa	NYA	A+	24	14	0	0	3	26.2	117	29	14	8	1	1	2	1	5	0	23	1	1	0	0	.000	0	0	2.70
	Yankees	NYA	R	24	1	0	0	1	2.1	10	2	1	1	0	1	0	0	1	0	4	0	2	0	0	.000	0	0	3.86
	Greensboro	NYA	A	24	10	10	1	0	57	260	64	43	39	5	2	6	6	26	2	51	5	0	3	3	.500	1	0	6.16
Stinson,Kevin	White Sox	ChA	R	21	24	0	0	18	35.1	159	39	16	9	0	0	1	3	11	0	34	5	1	1	5	.167	0	6	2.29
Stockstill,Jason	Boise	Cal	A-	20	2	2	0	0	8	42	12	11	11	2	0	0	0	10	0	7	1	0	0	0	.000	0	0	12.38
	Angels	Cal	R	20	13	13	0	0	73.1	329	74	45	34	5	0	2	2	34	0	61	8	0	2	6	.250	0	0	4.17
Stone,Ricky	Savannah	LA	A	22	5	5	0	0	31.2	130	34	15	14	2	2	1	0	9	0	31	5	0	2	1	.667	0	0	3.98
	Vero Beach	LA	A+	22	21	21	1	0	112.2	488	115	58	48	9	4	3	3	46	0	74	10	0	8	6	.571	0	0	3.83
Stoops,Jim	Burlington	SF	A	25	46	0	0	18	60.2	262	43	24	17	2	4	1	6	40	4	69	6	1	3	3	.500	0	5	2.52
Stover,C.D.	Yakima	LA	A-	21	15	4	0	4	32.1	151	36	23	20	1	3	0	2	16	0	25	4	0	1	4	.200	0	1	5.57
Stubbs,Jerald	W. Palm Bch	Mon	A+	25	7	0	0	0	9	46	11	7	6	0	0	0	3	5	0	3	0	0	1	0	1.000	0	0	6.00
Stumpf,Brian	Clearwater	Phi	A+	25	56	0	0	50	59	260	54	25	22	3	5	2	0	32	3	48	2	0	1	6	.143	0	26	3.36
Stutz,Shawn	Butte	TB	R+	22	19	6	0	4	48.2	256	63	60	46	8	1	1	4	40	0	46	9	1	2	3	.400	0	0	8.51
Styles,Bobby	Rangers	Tex	R	20	23	0	0	23	34	144	27	12	6	1	3	1	2	9	3	20	2	1	2	3	.400	0	13	1.59
Suggs,Willie	Mets	NYN	R	18	10	3	0	1	29.1	131	28	15	14	1	0	1	1	17	0	22	5	3	3	2	.600	0	0	4.30
Sullivan,Brendan	Idaho Falls	SD	R+	22	33	0	0	15	43	190	41	25	25	6	1	0	1	27	0	41	1	0	2	1	.667	0	5	5.23
Sumter,Kevin	Cedar Rapds	Cal	A	24	3	0	0	0	2.2	14	4	2	2	0	0	0	1	1	0	4	0	0	0	0	.000	0	0	6.75
Swan,Tyrone	Clearwater	Phi	A+	28	10	6	0	1	40.2	170	38	21	16	1	2	1	3	12	0	22	1	0	3	2	.600	0	0	3.54
Symmonds,Maika	Lowell	Bos	A-	24	5	0	0	1	10.1	60	11	12	12	1	1	2	4	15	0	10	3	1	1	0	1.000	0	0	10.45
	Michigan	Bos	A	24	5	0	0	3	8.1	46	12	11	11	1	0	0	1	10	0	4	3	0	0	0	.000	0	0	11.88
	Bakersfield	Bos	A+	24	7	2	1	2	24.1	127	34	32	24	1	0	4	0	21	0	3	3	0	0	2	.000	0	0	8.88
Szimanski,Tom	Lancaster	Sea	A+	24	35	0	0	21	42.2	194	55	24	20	3	1	1	4	12	1	46	2	2	2	2	.500	0	9	4.22
Szymborski,Tom	Idaho Falls	SD	R+	22	16	14	0	2	80	348	80	39	35	6	1	4	6	30	0	65	11	5	7	3	.700	0	1	3.94
Taczy,Craig	Yakima	LA	A-	20	16	0	0	7	21.2	110	27	22	18	1	1	1	0	16	0	14	3	0	1	1	.500	0	1	7.48
Takahashi,Kurt	Bellingham	SF	A-	23	16	6	0	2	54	230	45	25	24	7	1	0	3	20	0	55	4	0	1	2	.333	0	1	4.00
Tank,Travis	Helena	Mil	R+	22	29	0	0	7	64.1	291	65	38	23	5	3	7	1	30	2	74	8	1	7	3	.700	0	3	3.22
Tanksley,Scott	Fort Wayne	Min	A	23	16	0	0	6	28.2	124	24	16	10	0	3	0	0	8	0	25	1	0	2	1	.667	0	0	3.14
Tatar,Jason	Twins	Min	R	22	2	0	0	0	5	16	2	1	1	0	1	0	0	1	0	7	0	0	0	0	.000	0	0	1.80
	Fort Myers	Min	A+	22	4	0	0	3	3.2	21	6	4	4	0	0	0	0	4	0	4	2	0	0	0	.000	0	0	9.82
Tatis,Ramon	St. Lucie	NYN	A+	24	46	1	0	20	74.1	325	71	35	28	4	7	2	2	38	8	46	14	1	4	2	.667	0	6	3.39
Taylor,Aaron	Braves	Atl	R	19	13	9	0	3	52.1	259	68	54	45	0	7	2	6	28	0	33	14	2	0	9	.000	0	0	7.74
Taylor,Brien	Greensboro	NYA	A	25	9	9	0	0	16.1	113	21	40	34	3	2	3	3	43	0	11	17	1	0	5	.000	0	0	18.73
Taylor,Mark	Watertown	Cle	A-	22	12	0	0	3	20.1	90	18	9	8	0	1	2	0	16	1	17	1	0	1	0	1.000	0	0	3.54
Tebbetts,Scott	Piedmont	Phi	A	24	5	0	0	1	5.1	28	8	9	8	2	1	0	2	2	0	2	0	0	0	2	.000	0	0	13.50
Tejera,Michael	Marlins	Fla	R	20	2	0	0	0	5	21	6	2	2	0	0	0	0	0	0	2	0	0	1	0	1.000	0	0	3.60
Tellez,Eloy	White Sox	ChA	R	21	11	11	2	0	70.1	291	57	30	23	4	2	1	7	27	0	34	3	5	3	4	.429	0	0	2.94
Temple,Jason	Lynchburg	Pit	A+	22	21	0	0	16	22.2	115	24	14	12	0	1	0	3	19	1	18	1	0	2	2	.500	0	3	4.76
Tessmer,Jay	Tampa	NYA	A+	24	68	0	0	63	97.1	381	68	18	16	2	6	0	6	19	3	104	1	0	12	4	.750	0	35	1.48
Theodile,Robert	Pr. William	ChA	A+	24	25	22	1	1	132	571	133	73	63	5	6	5	7	56	3	91	8	1	7	9	.438	1	1	4.30
Thobe,J.J.	Columbus	Cle	A	26	2	2	0	0	7	36	11	6	6	0	1	1	0	6	1	4	0	0	0	2	.000	0	0	7.71
Thomas,Bradley	Great Falls	LA	R+	19	11	5	0	3	35.2	163	48	27	25	2	1	1	0	11	0	28	5	4	3	2	.600	0	0	6.31
Thomas,Carlos	Rancho Cuca	SD	A+	26	9	0	0	2	8.2	50	13	12	11	1	0	0	0	10	1	10	1	0	1	1	.500	0	0	11.42
Thomas,Evan	Batavia	Phi	A-	23	13	13	0	0	81	321	60	29	25	3	1	3	5	23	0	75	6	0	10	2	.833	0	0	2.78
Thomas,Ryan	Idaho Falls	SD	R+	24	30	4	0	16	62.1	281	55	44	36	5	4	1	5	32	2	44	16	0	4	3	.571	0	4	5.20
Thompson,Chris.	Lowell	Bos	A-	24	25	0	0	12	47	214	43	34	23	2	1	4	5	20	1	51	8	1	2	5	.286	0	0	4.40
Thompson,Frank	Great Falls	LA	R+	24	14	7	0	1	47	225	60	50	45	8	0	2	1	25	0	39	4	1	0	3	.000	0	0	8.62

1996 Pitching — Single-A and Rookie Leagues

HOW MUCH HE PITCHED											WHAT HE GAVE UP												THE RESULTS					
Player	Team	Org	Lg	A	G	GS	CG	GF	IP	BFP	H	R	ER	HR	SH	SF	HB	TBB	IBB	SO	WP	Bk	W	L	Pct.	ShO	Sv	ERA
Thompson,John	Lancaster	Sea	A+	24	50	0	0	41	61.2	287	72	50	42	12	3	4	5	29	1	53	6	1	3	8	.273	0	14	6.13
Thompson,Josef	Padres	SD	R	24	13	12	0	0	74.2	319	67	33	22	3	1	2	2	22	0	50	1	2	8	2	.800	0	0	2.65
Thompson,Travis	Portland	Col	A-	22	9	0	0	2	16.2	73	21	11	11	0	2	0	0	6	0	8	1	1	0	2	.000	0	0	5.94
	Rockies	Col	R	22	9	3	0	3	30	128	34	12	11	1	1	0	0	5	0	25	0	1	4	1	.800	0	0	3.30
Thorn,Todd	Lansing	KC	A	20	27	27	2	0	170.2	695	161	70	59	13	6	4	5	34	0	107	8	0	11	5	.688	0	0	3.11
Thurman,Corey	Royals	KC	R	18	11	11	0	0	47.1	221	53	32	32	2	0	2	3	28	0	52	8	1	1	6	.143	0	0	6.08
Thurmond,Travis	Cedar Rapds	Cal	A	23	4	4	1	0	29	120	20	6	5	1	0	0	1	14	0	29	2	0	2	0	1.000	0	0	1.55
	Lk Elsinore	Cal	A+	23	6	5	0	0	36.2	159	36	18	16	4	0	2	2	17	0	39	2	1	2	2	.500	0	0	3.93
Tickell,Brian	Quad City	Hou	A	22	7	0	0	3	8.1	45	17	10	9	0	0	0	1	5	0	4	2	0	0	2	.000	0	0	9.72
Tijerina,Tano	Beloit	Mil	A	23	5	0	0	2	12.2	75	31	17	16	1	0	1	1	8	0	4	0	1	0	1	.000	0	0	11.37
	Helena	Mil	R+	23	19	8	0	4	57.2	290	93	65	56	11	1	3	2	27	0	33	3	0	3	6	.333	0	1	8.74
Tillmon,Darrell	Michigan	Bos	A	24	7	7	0	0	38	170	38	25	22	4	0	1	2	17	1	27	2	0	4	3	.571	0	0	5.21
	Sarasota	Bos	A+	24	18	18	1	0	112.1	450	104	41	40	4	3	3	2	28	0	59	3	0	7	6	.538	1	0	3.20
Tilton,Ira	Batavia	Phi	A-	22	14	14	0	0	69	302	66	47	42	1	3	9	9	26	0	40	3	1	5	6	.455	0	0	5.48
Tober,David	Martinsvlle	Phi	R+	23	9	1	0	1	15.2	66	12	6	4	1	0	0	1	6	0	15	7	0	1	0	1.000	0	0	2.30
	Batavia	Phi	A-	23	4	0	0	4	6	34	8	6	4	0	0	1	1	5	1	8	0	0	0	2	.000	0	0	6.00
Tobias,Daniel	Pirates	Pit	R	21	5	0	0	3	5.2	29	4	6	1	0	1	0	2	4	0	4	0	0	0	1	.000	0	0	1.59
Torrealba,Aquiles	Angels	Cal	R	18	5	0	0	2	5.1	25	9	5	5	0	0	1	1	1	0	0	0	0	0	0	.000	0	0	8.44
Torres,Eric	Mets	NYN	R	20	20	0	0	19	24.1	117	34	24	20	1	2	1	2	9	2	20	3	2	0	4	.000	0	5	7.40
Torres,Luis	Clinton	SD	A	21	35	1	0	16	67.1	306	76	46	38	9	2	4	5	26	1	65	5	3	2	2	.500	0	1	5.08
Torres,Michael	Royals	KC	R	19	18	0	0	7	33.1	159	47	35	24	2	1	5	5	6	0	26	6	1	2	3	.400	0	2	6.48
Torres,Jackson	Savannah	LA	A	22	42	0	0	20	61	270	52	39	29	5	3	0	9	29	0	32	4	2	3	4	.429	0	3	4.28
Towers,Joshua	Bluefield	Bal	R+	20	14	9	0	1	55	234	63	35	32	9	0	1	1	5	0	61	4	1	4	1	.800	0	0	5.24
Townsend,Dave	Utica	Fla	A-	22	14	14	2	0	77.2	320	69	38	31	4	1	1	4	18	0	51	4	3	3	6	.333	0	0	3.59
Trawick,Tim	Lancaster	Sea	A+	25	16	0	0	4	31	139	43	26	22	4	0	2	2	9	0	20	3	1	0	2	.000	0	0	6.39
	Wisconsin	Sea	A	25	15	13	1	1	79.2	347	87	42	38	4	4	2	1	28	3	51	4	2	5	5	.500	0	0	4.29
Treend,Patrick	Brevard Cty	Fla	A+	25	1	0	0	0	1	3	0	0	0	0	0	0	0	0	0	1	0	0	1	0	1.000	0	0	0.00
	Kane County	Fla	A	25	27	0	0	9	48.2	220	46	32	24	2	2	4	3	23	1	40	3	2	0	2	.000	0	0	4.44
Tribe,Byron	Williamsprt	ChN	A-	22	15	0	0	10	21.2	97	16	10	6	2	1	0	2	13	2	33	2	1	2	1	.667	0	4	2.49
	Rockford	ChN	A	22	9	1	0	4	14.2	64	10	4	4	0	0	0	2	12	1	22	2	0	0	0	.000	0	0	2.45
Trimarco,Mike	Frederick	Bal	A+	25	43	0	0	21	78.1	351	96	52	43	10	2	5	1	23	0	47	6	0	5	3	.625	0	3	4.94
Trumpour,Andy	Columbia	NYN	A	23	26	18	4	3	133.2	527	91	47	34	8	2	2	10	37	0	105	7	0	10	4	.714	2	1	2.29
Trunk,Todd	Yankees	NYA	R	23	1	0	0	0	0.2	3	0	0	0	0	0	0	0	1	0	1	1	0	0	0	.000	0	0	0.00
	Oneonta	NYA	A-	23	1	0	0	1	1	9	5	4	4	0	0	0	0	1	0	1	0	0	0	0	.000	0	0	36.00
Tucker,Ben	San Jose	SF	A+	23	13	13	0	0	67.2	301	71	54	47	8	3	3	1	36	0	30	6	4	1	4	.200	0	0	6.25
Tucker,Julien	Kissimmee	Hou	A+	24	32	16	0	6	116	525	131	79	55	8	4	6	12	41	1	55	9	1	4	8	.333	0	1	4.27
Tull,Billy	Mets	NYN	R	21	1	0	0	0	2	10	3	0	0	0	0	0	0	1	0	2	0	0	0	0	.000	0	0	0.00
	Kingsport	NYN	R+	21	20	0	0	11	32.2	118	18	3	3	0	0	1	0	8	0	40	3	0	1	0	1.000	0	6	0.83
Turley,Jason	Auburn	Hou	A-	22	19	0	0	7	43.2	217	39	35	27	4	2	2	5	36	2	31	7	0	3	0	1.000	0	0	5.56
Tuttle,Dave	Visalia	Det	A+	27	55	0	0	52	70.1	308	71	39	29	3	3	1	3	33	5	56	1	0	7	9	.438	0	21	3.71
Tuttle,John	Johnson Cty	StL	R+	19	21	0	0	7	34	152	33	22	16	4	2	1	0	13	3	25	0	1	2	2	.500	0	0	4.24
Tweedlie,Brad	Winston-Sal	Cin	A+	25	33	0	0	30	29.2	144	35	23	22	6	1	2	1	22	0	22	6	0	1	5	.167	0	11	6.67
	Sarasota	Bos	A+	25	11	0	0	11	11.1	45	6	1	1	0	0	0	1	3	1	9	0	0	2	0	1.000	0	7	0.79
Tyrrell,Jim	Sarasota	Bos	A+	24	8	0	0	3	13.2	60	11	9	8	1	0	0	1	8	1	14	1	0	1	2	.333	0	0	5.27
	Red Sox	Bos	R	24	1	0	0	0	0.2	9	5	6	6	0	0	0	0	2	0	1	0	0	0	0	.000	0	0	81.00
Urbina,Dan	San Bernrdo	LA	A+	22	3	3	0	0	10.2	55	11	8	7	0	0	1	3	9	0	13	1	0	0	0	.000	0	0	5.91
Vail,Keith	Devil Rays	TB	R	21	5	0	0	2	8.1	48	12	13	11	0	1	1	1	7	1	4	2	1	0	0	.000	0	0	11.88
Valle,Yoiset	Yankees	NYA	R	19	7	1	0	1	17.2	73	20	9	5	0	3	0	1	1	0	15	2	0	3	0	1.000	0	0	2.55
Vallis,Jamie	Twins	Min	R	20	12	8	0	0	38.1	161	37	18	15	0	1	1	2	15	0	25	10	2	1	3	.250	0	0	3.52
Van De Weg,Ryan	Rancho Cuca	SD	A+	23	26	26	0	0	146.1	636	164	78	66	15	1	2	10	52	1	129	8	0	9	6	.600	0	0	4.06
Van Winkle,Judd	Tigers	Det	R	21	8	0	0	3	22	103	37	17	17	3	0	1	0	4	0	22	2	0	3	1	.750	0	1	6.95
Vandemark,John	Clearwater	Phi	A+	25	27	0	0	5	26.1	114	21	10	7	0	2	0	1	14	0	27	3	0	0	2	.000	0	3	2.39
Vanderbush,Matt	Fort Wayne	Min	A	23	35	3	0	12	66	314	92	47	39	2	1	3	0	35	1	55	5	0	2	1	.667	0	1	5.32
Vanhof,Dave	Wisconsin	Sea	A	23	27	19	0	3	93.2	477	104	89	82	10	1	2	3	105	3	58	20	3	1	10	.091	0	0	7.88
Vanwormer,Marc	Diamondback	Ari	R	19	10	9	0	0	31	152	42	33	25	1	0	1	3	13	0	25	5	0	1	5	.167	0	0	7.26
Vardijan,Dan	Kane County	Fla	A	20	25	25	2	0	145	603	128	71	54	5	5	2	16	55	4	92	13	0	7	7	.500	1	0	3.35
Vavrek,Mike	Salem	Col	A+	23	26	25	2	0	149.2	658	167	92	81	15	6	8	5	59	0	103	10	0	10	8	.556	1	0	4.87
Vazquez,Javier	Delmarva	Mon	A	21	27	27	1	0	164.1	668	138	64	49	12	1	1	7	57	0	173	12	2	14	3	.824	0	0	2.68
Velez,Jeffrey	Williamsprt	ChN	A-	22	1	1	0	0	2	14	4	4	3	0	0	0	0	4	0	1	0	0	0	0	.000	0	0	13.50
Venafro,Michael	Charlstn-SC	Tex	A	23	50	0	0	42	59	258	57	27	23	0	4	2	3	21	3	62	13	0	1	3	.250	0	19	3.51
Veniard,Jay	Hagerstown	Tor	A	22	8	8	1	0	44.2	187	35	28	20	5	0	2	1	24	0	43	2	1	3	3	.500	0	0	4.03
	Dunedin	Tor	A+	22	14	14	0	0	64.2	270	63	37	29	7	0	2	5	19	0	40	4	1	4	5	.444	0	0	4.04
Verdin,Cesar	Greensboro	NYA	A	20	14	10	1	1	67	286	56	34	18	5	4	2	7	24	0	71	1	2	5	2	.714	0	0	2.42
Vergara,Luis	Braves	Atl	R	NA	4	3	0	0	16	75	21	14	11	0	2	0	1	4	1	10	4	0	0	2	.000	0	0	6.19
Vermillion,Grant	Lk Elsinore	Cal	A+	25	18	0	0	8	19.2	91	29	18	17	4	0	3	0	7	0	9	2	0	2	1	.667	0	0	7.78
	Cedar Rapds	Cal	A	25	38	1	0	12	61	270	59	34	32	4	1	2	2	32	2	54	1	0	3	2	.600	0	2	4.72
Verplancke,Joseph	Lethbridge	Ari	R+	22	12	12	0	0	48	209	44	22	16	4	0	1	4	25	0	63	4	0	3	3	.500	0	0	3.00
Vicentino,Andy	Princeton	Cin	R+	21	11	6	0	3	45.2	216	52	38	33	6	1	4	1	25	0	47	6	1	0	4	.000	0	0	6.50
Victery,Joe	Everett	Sea	A-	22	13	8	0	2	51.2	218	43	22	18	4	2	1	2	15	0	45	4	3	5	4	.556	0	1	3.14
Viegas,Randy	Erie	Pit	A-	21	2	0	0	1	3.2	19	4	3	3	0	0	1	0	4	0	3	2	0	0	0	.000	0	0	7.36
	Augusta	Pit	A	21	13	0	0	5	18.2	88	16	14	13	0	0	0	3	14	1	15	4	1	0	0	.000	0	0	6.27
Villafuerte,Brandon	Pittsfield	NYN	A-	21	18	7	1	4	62.2	267	53	21	21	5	2	3	6	27	0	59	4	0	8	3	.727	0	1	3.02
Villar,Maximo	Erie	Pit	A-	20	9	9	0	0	28.2	142	46	27	23	3	0	3	7	9	0	10	1	0	0	5	.000	0	0	7.22
Villarreal,Modesto	Lansing	KC	A	21	15	5	0	2	42	191	54	37	29	6	2	3	4	12	0	29	2	0	0	5	.000	0	0	6.21
	Spokane	KC	A-	21	19	3	0	10	47	209	57	33	30	6	1	1	4	11	0	35	5	0	2	4	.333	0	3	5.74
Villegas,Ismael	Rockford	ChN	A	20	10	10	1	0	47.1	223	63	40	27	5	1	2	3	25	0	30	3	1	2	5	.286	0	0	5.13
	Williamsprt	ChN	A-	20	2	2	0	0	7	31	7	3	2	0	0	0	0	4	0	5	1	0	0	0	.000	0	0	2.57

1996 Pitching — Single-A and Rookie Leagues

HOW MUCH HE PITCHED											WHAT HE GAVE UP												THE RESULTS					
Player	Team	Org	Lg	A	G	GS	CG	GF	IP	BFP	H	R	ER	HR	SH	SF	HB	TBB	IBB	SO	WP	Bk	W	L	Pct.	ShO	Sv	ERA
	Danville	Atl	R+	20	1	0	0	0	3	11	2	1	1	0	0	0	0	1	0	4	1	0	0	0	.000	0	0	3.00
	Macon	Atl	A	20	12	12	2	0	72	313	80	46	40	8	2	4	1	19	1	60	6	0	3	7	.300	1	0	5.00
Vining,Kenneth	Bellingham	SF	A-	22	12	11	0	0	60.1	238	45	16	14	4	1	0	1	23	0	69	5	0	4	2	.667	0	0	2.09
Virchis,Adam	Hickory	ChA	A	23	26	3	0	13	82.2	348	82	38	30	10	7	5	6	25	5	42	3	3	8	6	.571	0	0	3.27
Vizcaino,Ed	Cubs	ChN	R	20	14	4	0	5	44.1	169	34	8	8	3	0	0	4	8	0	24	2	0	5	0	1.000	0	2	1.62
Vizcaino,Luis	Athletics	Oak	R	20	15	10	0	4	59.2	264	58	36	27	1	1	1	2	24	1	52	6	3	6	3	.667	0	1	4.07
Vogt,Robert	Pirates	Pit	R	18	13	5	0	4	42.2	182	36	23	14	2	1	0	0	19	0	46	4	0	2	3	.400	0	0	2.95
Volkert,Rusty	Hagerstown	Tor	A	22	38	0	0	21	63.1	260	53	28	20	3	2	3	3	19	0	44	6	1	1	3	.250	0	2	2.84
Volkman,Keith	Boise	Cal	A-	21	16	13	0	1	68.1	327	74	66	50	0	6	2	7	46	3	38	7	0	5	8	.385	0	0	6.59
Vota,Michael	South Bend	ChA	A	24	34	0	0	13	65	299	79	41	33	6	1	1	5	23	0	35	2	0	2	2	.500	0	0	4.57
Wagner,Joe	Stockton	Mil	A+	25	28	28	0	0	167.1	745	171	102	89	16	6	3	12	86	0	103	7	0	12	6	.667	0	0	4.79
Wagner,Ken	Watertown	Cle	A-	22	21	1	0	12	45	188	32	12	11	1	3	1	2	20	1	47	3	0	2	3	.400	0	5	2.20
Wagner,Matt	Peoria	StL	A	22	16	12	0	1	64.1	295	80	47	42	4	2	1	6	26	0	38	2	3	4	2	.667	0	0	5.88
Walker,Kevin	Idaho Falls	SD	R+	20	1	1	0	0	6	24	4	3	2	1	0	0	0	2	0	4	1	0	1	0	1.000	0	0	3.00
	Clinton	SD	A	20	13	13	0	0	76	339	80	46	40	9	1	6	9	33	0	43	1	0	4	6	.400	0	0	4.74
Wallace,B.J.	Clearwater	Phi	A+	26	15	12	0	0	63.1	299	71	47	41	3	1	3	8	41	0	37	3	0	3	4	.429	0	0	5.83
Wallace,Flint	Sou. Oregon	Oak	A-	22	17	14	0	1	70.1	301	86	34	33	3	0	6	5	15	0	45	2	0	2	6	.250	0	0	4.22
Wallace,Jeff	Lansing	KC	A	21	30	21	0	2	122.1	560	140	79	72	10	8	3	7	66	0	84	12	7	4	9	.308	0	0	5.30
Walls,Doug	Salem	Col	A+	23	5	3	0	1	14	70	17	12	11	3	0	0	0	10	0	17	3	0	0	0	.000	0	1	7.07
Walsh,Matt	Modesto	Oak	A+	24	38	0	0	10	69.2	293	54	38	27	5	1	1	6	31	1	68	7	1	3	1	.750	0	4	3.49
Walter,Mike	Quad City	Hou	A	22	52	0	0	48	61.2	261	37	20	14	3	2	1	7	34	1	85	7	1	3	6	.333	0	21	2.04
Walters,Brett	Rancho Cuca	SD	A+	22	24	24	0	0	135.1	575	150	73	65	16	10	6	7	39	0	89	1	0	9	9	.500	0	0	4.32
Walton,Tim	Martinsvlle	Phi	R+	24	4	4	1	0	20.2	101	27	19	12	3	0	2	0	8	0	20	4	1	0	3	.000	0	0	5.23
	Piedmont	Phi	A	24	8	5	0	1	37.2	149	28	7	5	0	0	1	2	14	1	19	3	0	2	1	.667	0	0	1.19
Ward,Brandon	Cubs	ChN	R	21	16	0	0	11	25.2	105	16	9	8	0	1	1	2	10	0	32	3	0	2	1	.667	0	2	2.81
Ward,Jon	New Jersey	StL	A-	22	9	9	0	0	35.2	178	56	35	23	1	0	3	2	21	1	29	2	0	1	6	.143	0	0	5.80
Warrecker,Teddy	Kinston	Cle	A+	24	27	26	1	0	131.1	616	137	105	88	12	3	7	11	88	0	88	14	1	9	11	.450	1	0	6.03
Warren,Deshawn	Ogden	Mil	R+	23	3	0	0	1	2.2	14	2	3	2	0	0	0	0	3	0	7	1	0	1	0	1.000	0	0	6.75
Watson,Mark	Helena	Mil	R+	23	13	13	0	0	60.1	262	59	43	32	2	1	2	1	28	0	68	7	0	5	2	.714	0	0	4.77
Weber,Lenny	Kinston	Cle	A+	24	36	0	0	25	59	250	44	12	12	0	6	1	1	36	5	49	2	0	2	4	.333	0	6	1.83
Weglarz,John	Frederick	Bal	A+	26	2	0	0	1	2.1	10	3	2	2	0	0	0	0	1	0	2	0	0	0	0	.000	0	0	7.71
Wegmann,Tom	Orioles	Bal	R	28	4	1	0	0	8.2	34	4	2	0	0	0	0	1	2	0	12	0	0	0	0	.000	0	0	0.00
	Frederick	Bal	A+	28	3	3	0	0	15	64	13	9	3	0	0	0	0	5	0	16	0	0	1	1	.500	0	0	1.80
Weibl,Clint	Johnson Cty	StL	R+	22	7	7	0	0	44	172	27	12	10	1	0	0	1	12	0	51	0	0	4	1	.800	0	0	2.05
	Peoria	StL	A	22	5	5	0	0	29.2	122	27	16	16	2	0	1	2	7	0	21	0	0	1	2	.333	0	0	4.85
Weidert,Chris	Expos	Mon	R	23	2	1	0	1	5	17	2	1	1	1	0	0	0	0	0	2	0	0	0	0	.000	0	0	1.80
	W. Palm Bch	Mon	A+	23	20	20	1	0	106	462	106	54	40	4	3	3	7	37	1	64	4	1	3	8	.273	0	0	3.40
Weinberg,Todd	W. Michigan	Oak	A	25	43	0	0	16	57.1	253	48	25	22	4	2	1	3	31	4	64	3	0	6	4	.600	0	1	3.45
Welch,Robb	Lowell	Bos	A-	21	14	14	1	0	81.1	371	85	50	46	7	2	1	7	37	0	63	9	0	2	7	.222	1	0	5.09
Welch,Travis	Peoria	StL	A	23	34	0	0	28	40.1	173	31	17	14	4	2	1	4	17	1	34	2	2	1	3	.250	0	17	3.12
Wells,Matt	Bellingham	SF	A-	22	12	11	0	0	44.2	220	57	38	35	9	1	2	2	30	0	41	0	0	2	4	.333	0	0	7.05
Wesolowski,David	Marlins	Fla	R	19	2	2	0	0	9	43	11	8	6	0	2	0	0	2	0	4	2	0	0	0	.000	0	0	6.00
West,Adam	New Jersey	StL	A-	23	15	14	0	0	87.2	370	82	41	36	3	5	3	5	29	0	94	5	0	5	4	.556	0	0	3.70
Westbrook,Jake	Rockies	Col	R	19	11	11	0	0	62.2	271	66	33	20	0	3	1	8	14	0	57	4	0	4	2	.667	0	0	2.87
	Portland	Col	A-	19	4	4	0	0	24.2	99	22	8	7	1	0	0	1	5	0	19	2	0	1	1	.500	0	0	2.55
Westover,Richard	Expos	Mon	R	1	1	0	0	0	1	4	0	0	0	0	0	0	0	0	0	1	0	0	0	0	.000	0	0	0.00
	Vermont	Mon	A-	1	18	1	0	5	33.2	131	24	10	9	1	0	0	1	8	0	23	6	0	3	2	.600	0	0	2.41
Weymouth,Marty	Everett	Sea	A-	19	10	10	0	0	41	185	46	28	22	3	0	2	0	16	0	35	9	0	2	3	.400	0	0	4.83
Whitaker,Ryan	Modesto	Oak	A+	25	37	9	0	8	113.2	520	142	83	63	8	7	3	9	39	2	87	10	1	6	8	.429	0	0	4.99
White,Darell	Rancho Cuca	SD	A+	25	38	0	0	17	54	258	76	48	39	1	4	4	0	25	0	43	6	0	1	1	.500	0	0	6.50
White,Gary	High Desert	Bal	A+	24	16	8	0	1	51	232	62	36	33	10	0	3	1	26	0	34	3	2	4	2	.667	0	0	5.82
Whiteman,Greg	Lakeland	Det	A+	24	27	27	1	0	150.1	640	134	66	62	5	4	6	7	89	0	122	8	2	11	10	.524	0	0	3.71
Whitley,Kyle	Butte	TB	R+	23	10	0	0	4	11	57	17	15	11	1	0	0	1	7	0	14	2	3	1	1	.500	0	1	9.00
Whitson,Eric	Hudson Vall	TB	A-	24	19	2	0	3	44	174	31	17	14	4	1	3	0	16	0	34	10	1	3	0	1.000	0	0	2.86
Widerski,Jonathan	Marlins	Fla	R	20	12	10	0	0	67	275	59	26	19	3	1	1	1	22	0	55	6	3	8	2	.800	0	0	2.55
Wiley,Chad	Rangers	Tex	R	25	1	0	0	1	2	9	3	1	1	0	0	0	0	0	0	2	0	0	0	1	.000	0	0	4.50
	Charlotte	Tex	A+	25	5	5	0	0	26.2	101	19	7	6	0	1	1	1	4	0	14	0	0	2	1	.667	0	0	2.03
Williams,Matt	Lynchburg	Pit	A+	26	23	0	0	5	41.1	189	40	27	24	9	0	1	2	28	1	45	3	1	0	0	.000	0	0	5.23
Wilmot,Toby	Auburn	Hou	A-	23	13	0	0	3	22.2	113	23	11	9	0	0	2	1	17	1	19	5	3	2	2	.500	0	0	3.57
Wimberly,Larry	Sarasota	Bos	A+	21	6	6	0	0	30	142	38	26	23	2	1	2	2	16	1	16	1	0	2	4	.333	0	0	6.90
	Michigan	Bos	A	21	14	14	2	0	66.1	272	58	27	21	5	1	3	4	24	1	41	1	2	3	4	.429	1	0	2.85
Winchester,Scott	Columbus	Cle	A	24	52	0	0	47	61.1	254	50	27	22	8	5	2	5	16	4	60	4	0	7	3	.700	0	26	3.23
Windham,Mike	St. Pete	StL	A+	25	25	25	1	0	143.2	610	153	59	50	4	4	4	6	57	1	87	7	0	7	10	.412	0	0	3.13
Winkelsas,Joseph	Danville	Atl	R+	23	8	0	0	6	11.1	54	11	10	9	0	0	0	4	4	0	9	2	0	1	1	.500	0	2	7.15
Winkleman,Greg.	Athletics	Oak	R	23	25	0	0	20	36.2	152	31	11	7	0	1	1	0	15	1	32	1	1	1	1	.500	0	6	1.72
Wise,Will	Danville	Atl	R+	21	21	0	0	12	33.2	174	40	39	26	1	6	1	2	26	0	25	12	0	2	6	.250	0	1	6.95
Witte,Dominic	Idaho Falls	SD	R+	23	21	0	0	8	29.1	137	39	23	20	4	1	1	1	5	1	19	3	1	0	2	.000	0	0	6.14
Wolff,Bryan	Wilmington	KC	A+	25	42	0	0	28	62.1	280	49	35	25	2	3	1	3	38	1	56	6	0	1	2	.333	0	4	3.61
Wolger,Michael	Bakersfield	—	A+	24	1	0	0	0	1.1	13	4	7	6	1	0	1	1	4	0	1	0	0	0	0	.000	0	0	40.50
Wood,Kerry	Daytona	ChN	A+	20	22	22	0	0	114.1	495	72	51	37	6	5	4	14	70	0	136	10	7	10	2	.833	0	0	2.91
Woodard,Steven	Stockton	Mil	A+	22	28	28	3	0	181.1	762	201	89	81	14	4	6	3	33	1	142	7	2	12	9	.571	0	0	4.02
Woodring,Jason	Delmarva	Mon	A	23	46	0	0	33	58.2	237	42	17	12	2	3	0	7	17	1	43	5	0	8	3	.727	0	12	1.84
Woodrow,Jim	Bellingham	SF	A-	24	17	0	0	5	25	116	26	16	11	4	2	0	0	14	0	25	3	0	2	0	1.000	0	0	3.96
Wooten,Gregory	Wisconsin	Sea	A	23	13	13	3	0	83.2	336	58	27	23	3	1	2	5	29	0	68	4	1	7	1	.875	1	0	2.47
	Lancaster	Sea	A+	23	14	14	1	0	97	408	101	47	41	7	1	2	3	25	1	71	9	0	8	4	.667	0	0	3.80
Workman,Widd	Idaho Falls	SD	R+	23	14	13	0	0	55.2	271	77	48	42	3	2	9	5	31	0	42	6	2	4	5	.444	0	0	6.79
Wright,Jaret	Kinston	Cle	A+	21	19	19	0	0	101	413	65	32	28	1	6	3	7	55	0	109	7	1	7	4	.636	0	0	2.50

1996 Pitching — Single-A and Rookie Leagues

HOW MUCH HE PITCHED											WHAT HE GAVE UP												THE RESULTS					
Player	Team	Org	Lg	A	G	GS	CG	GF	IP	BFP	H	R	ER	HR	SH	SF	HB	TBB	IBB	SO	WP	Bk	W	L	Pct.	ShO	Sv	ERA
Wright,Jason	Pirates	Pit	R	21	13	0	0	11	20.1	79	13	3	3	1	0	0	1	6	0	25	2	0	0	1	.000	0	7	1.33
Wright,Scott	Charlstn-WV	Cin	A	24	28	1	1	8	66.2	270	54	24	20	1	0	1	4	20	4	53	4	0	5	4	.556	0	1	2.70
	Winston-Sal	Cin	A+	24	1	1	0	0	4.2	20	7	4	4	2	0	0	0	3	0	2	0	0	0	0	.000	0	0	7.71
Wyatt,Ben	Danville	Atl	R+	20	10	10	0	0	53	225	50	27	26	2	2	5	1	19	0	31	3	0	5	3	.625	0	0	4.42
Wyckoff,Travis	Utica	Fla	A-	23	24	0	0	10	36.2	166	39	21	12	1	3	0	2	14	2	16	4	0	2	5	.286	0	1	2.95
Yanez,Luis	Auburn	Hou	A-	19	15	15	2	0	99	416	85	38	27	4	2	2	3	31	2	73	3	1	5	5	.500	0	0	2.45
Yeager,Gary	Piedmont	Phi	A	23	40	1	0	18	80.2	330	73	26	24	2	8	1	3	19	3	66	3	1	5	2	.714	0	6	2.68
Yennaco,Jay	Michigan	Bos	A	21	28	28	4	0	169.2	763	195	112	87	13	2	7	6	68	0	117	20	1	10	10	.500	1	0	4.61
Yeskie,Nate	Elizabethtn	Min	R+	22	7	6	0	0	32.2	141	38	27	19	3	0	0	0	8	0	28	2	0	3	3	.500	0	0	5.23
Yocum,David	Vero Beach	LA	A+	23	7	7	0	0	14.2	69	22	11	10	1	0	0	1	7	0	8	0	0	0	2	.000	0	0	6.14
Yoder,Jeff	Rockford	ChN	A	21	25	24	2	0	154.1	640	139	70	59	10	2	4	10	48	1	124	12	5	12	5	.706	0	0	3.44
Young,Ryan	Augusta	Pit	A	24	21	18	1	0	96	438	117	66	61	8	6	6	10	32	1	48	11	2	3	12	.200	0	0	5.72
Young,Danny	Augusta	Pit	A	25	22	1	0	6	33.2	171	36	33	22	1	2	3	3	29	2	36	12	2	0	4	.000	0	2	5.88
Young,Joe	Hagerstown	Tor	A	22	21	21	3	0	122	527	101	64	52	7	4	4	11	63	0	157	9	0	9	9	.500	1	0	3.84
	Dunedin	Tor	A+	22	6	6	0	0	33.2	145	30	24	22	3	2	1	2	17	1	36	3	0	1	3	.250	0	0	5.88
Young,Tim	Vermont	Mon	A-	23	27	0	0	26	29.1	106	14	1	1	1	2	1	2	4	0	46	0	1	1	0	1.000	0	18	0.31
Yount,Andy	Lowell	Bos	A-	20	8	8	0	0	34.1	181	38	30	24	0	1	3	9	38	0	30	15	0	1	2	.333	0	0	6.29
Zaleski,Kevin	Utica	Fla	A-	23	26	0	0	26	25.1	120	30	16	11	0	1	1	2	8	3	21	2	1	2	3	.400	0	7	3.91
Zamarripa,Mark	Jamestown	Det	A-	22	29	0	0	22	48.2	187	25	13	11	4	3	0	2	14	0	61	4	0	4	2	.667	0	4	2.03
Zambrano,Victor	Devil Rays	TB	R	22	1	0	0	0	3.1	16	4	4	3	0	0	0	0	0	0	6	0	0	0	0	.000	0	0	8.10
Zapata,Juan	Ogden	Mil	R+	21	20	0	0	10	35.2	158	43	26	24	7	1	0	1	11	1	32	10	0	2	1	.667	0	0	6.06
Zavershnik,Mike	St. Cathrns	Tor	A-	21	25	1	0	14	38.2	190	45	32	27	3	0	0	1	24	0	25	2	2	4	2	.667	0	2	6.28
Zubiri,Jon	Kinston	Cle	A+	22	3	3	0	0	14	65	14	8	5	0	0	0	1	9	0	11	3	0	1	1	.500	0	0	3.21
Zwemke,Bryan	Billings	Cin	R+	23	14	14	0	0	63.2	331	101	74	53	5	1	2	13	28	0	35	19	3	2	6	.250	0	0	7.49
Zwirchitz,Andy	Kingsport	NYN	R+	21	12	11	1	0	75.1	305	51	22	13	4	2	0	7	19	2	76	1	2	8	1	.889	0	0	1.55

Team Stats

American Association Batting - AAA

BATTING																	BASERUNNING				PERCENTAGES		
Team	Org	G	AB	H	2B	3B	HR	TB	R	RBI	TBB	IBB	SO	HBP	SH	SF	SB	CS	SB%	GDP	Avg	OBP	SLG
Buffalo	Cle	144	4870	1330	245	32	163	2128	723	676	456	43	885	62	33	48	65	41	.61	99	.273	.340	.437
Omaha	KC	144	4740	1263	258	28	148	2021	712	663	497	34	887	73	63	34	106	57	.65	107	.266	.343	.426
Indianapolis	Cin	144	4806	1263	258	39	131	1992	689	634	460	31	988	30	30	40	131	49	.73	103	.263	.329	.414
Oklahoma City	Tex	144	4821	1282	271	20	139	2010	658	620	516	33	952	45	33	56	77	64	.55	111	.266	.339	.417
Nashville	ChA	144	4708	1194	237	28	124	1859	624	583	368	23	772	44	45	27	78	48	.62	105	.254	.312	.395
New Orleans	Mil	142	4750	1160	217	28	142	1859	606	552	465	23	999	53	26	38	79	44	.64	117	.244	.316	.391
Iowa	ChN	142	4771	1250	226	25	121	1889	593	554	362	19	820	26	43	36	64	35	.65	111	.262	.315	.396
Louisville	StL	144	4708	1178	215	37	145	1902	583	545	387	31	912	36	39	25	100	60	.63	113	.250	.311	.404
Total		574	38174	9920	1927	237	1113	15660	5188	4827	3511	237	7215	369	312	304	700	398	.64	866	.260	.326	.410

American Association Pitching - AAA

		HOW MUCH THEY PITCHED						WHAT THEY GAVE UP												THE RESULTS					
Team	Org	G	GS	CG	GF	IP	BFP	H	R	ER	HR	SH	SF	HB	TBB	IBB	SO	WP	Bk	W	L	Pct.	ShO	Sv	ERA
Indianapolis	Cin	144	144	6	138	1245	5233	1171	578	489	130	37	32	40	394	24	942	53	4	78	66	.542	13	39	3.53
Nashville	ChA	144	144	13	131	1234.2	5255	1167	590	517	129	36	38	38	472	33	880	55	3	77	67	.535	12	40	3.77
Oklahoma City	Tex	144	144	11	133	1250.1	5313	1249	595	500	97	35	33	48	381	18	943	57	11	74	70	.514	10	25	3.60
Buffalo	Cle	144	144	11	133	1252.2	5342	1198	632	552	126	35	38	50	454	12	935	54	8	84	60	.583	9	40	3.97
Omaha	KC	144	144	5	139	1245	5367	1299	668	582	164	31	33	48	412	19	912	54	10	79	65	.549	10	42	4.21
Iowa	ChN	142	142	8	134	1232.1	5281	1261	676	611	170	48	46	39	405	36	837	55	6	64	78	.451	7	36	4.46
New Orleans	Mil	142	142	8	134	1253	5487	1278	708	598	159	50	44	51	526	45	871	59	7	58	84	.408	11	32	4.30
Louisville	StL	144	144	8	136	1234	5398	1297	741	652	138	40	40	55	467	50	895	64	8	60	84	.417	5	36	4.76
Total		574	574	70	504	9947	42676	9920	5188	4501	1113	312	304	369	3511	237	7215	451	57	574	574	.500	77	290	4.07

International League Batting - AAA

BATTING																	BASERUNNING				PERCENTAGES		
Team	Org	G	AB	H	2B	3B	HR	TB	R	RBI	TBB	IBB	SO	HBP	SH	SF	SB	CS	SB%	GDP	Avg	OBP	SLG
Pawtucket	Bos	142	4782	1350	301	36	209	2350	840	790	497	13	932	60	28	40	84	49	.63	116	.282	.355	.491
Columbus	NYA	142	4665	1268	298	46	151	2111	766	713	483	18	858	51	25	52	100	49	.67	98	.272	.343	.453
Rochester	Bal	141	4641	1304	258	56	131	2067	727	676	488	11	855	33	17	54	117	55	.68	86	.281	.350	.445
Charlotte	Fla	142	4656	1320	271	15	165	2116	722	681	391	17	832	35	35	35	99	59	.63	117	.284	.341	.454
Toledo	Det	142	4675	1195	221	39	165	1989	716	670	490	12	1086	43	28	38	130	62	.68	95	.256	.329	.425
Syracuse	Tor	142	4624	1215	236	47	106	1863	694	620	532	19	815	49	40	48	167	74	.69	90	.263	.342	.403
Norfolk	NYN	141	4645	1238	258	42	110	1910	643	605	437	27	900	56	69	43	109	63	.63	77	.267	.334	.411
Scranton-WB	Phi	142	4692	1210	240	49	101	1851	640	583	450	14	819	43	43	41	92	49	.65	118	.258	.326	.395
Ottawa	Mon	142	4618	1240	241	34	102	1855	606	565	404	29	798	48	69	36	160	64	.71	103	.269	.331	.402
Richmond	Atl	142	4604	1215	253	20	100	1808	593	543	360	22	966	34	50	32	92	68	.58	94	.264	.320	.393
Total		709	46602	12555	2577	384	1340	19920	6947	6446	4532	182	8861	452	404	419	1150	592	.66	994	.269	.337	.427

International League Pitching - AAA

HOW MUCH THEY PITCHED								WHAT THEY GAVE UP													THE RESULTS					
Team	Org	G	GS	CG	GF	IP	BFP	H	R	ER	HR	SH	SF	HB	TBB	IBB	SO	WP	Bk	W	L	Pct.	ShO	Sv	ERA
Norfolk	NYN	141	141	9	132	1221	5071	1122	545	476	120	43	43	40	356	20	921	47	9	82	59	.582	12	46	3.51
Columbus	NYA	142	142	14	128	1210.1	5175	1176	628	540	113	34	35	69	420	10	912	70	4	85	57	.599	6	38	4.02
Richmond	Atl	142	142	14	128	1195.2	5136	1190	640	554	102	50	52	33	432	17	826	65	3	62	79	.440	7	34	4.17
Rochester	Bal	141	141	7	134	1178.2	5143	1248	684	599	145	37	49	42	458	10	888	66	10	72	69	.511	3	33	4.57
Pawtucket	Bos	142	142	16	126	1215.1	5250	1255	704	622	169	21	37	40	417	12	944	75	6	78	64	.549	9	31	4.61
Syracuse	Tor	142	142	10	132	1205.2	5265	1265	709	622	122	42	56	45	470	21	890	62	8	67	75	.472	4	28	4.64
Scranton-WB	Phi	142	142	6	136	1218.2	5365	1271	712	633	145	48	43	40	509	37	860	62	10	70	72	.493	4	36	4.67
Ottawa	Mon	142	142	10	132	1200.2	5326	1327	751	680	138	40	33	56	476	20	862	60	2	60	82	.423	10	36	5.10
Toledo	Det	142	142	9	133	1213.2	5309	1317	761	668	130	38	24	41	457	17	920	75	9	70	72	.493	4	34	4.95
Charlotte	Fla	142	142	7	135	1181	5378	1384	813	720	156	51	47	46	537	18	838	93	9	62	79	.440	3	41	5.49
Total		709	709	102	607	12040.2	52418	12555	6947	6114	1340	404	419	452	4532	182	8861	675	70	708	708	.500	62	357	4.57

Pacific Coast League Batting - AAA

BATTING																	BASERUNNING				PERCENTAGES		
Team	Org	G	AB	H	2B	3B	HR	TB	R	RBI	TBB	IBB	SO	HBP	SH	SF	SB	CS	SB%	GDP	Avg	OBP	SLG
Salt Lake	Min	144	5085	1490	319	49	151	2360	855	797	530	48	892	70	29	61	141	71	.67	107	.293	.364	.464
Edmonton	Oak	142	4728	1306	245	45	147	2082	785	729	582	24	968	56	42	46	123	59	.68	108	.276	.359	.440
Calgary	Pit	143	4871	1412	288	40	96	2068	764	695	390	46	844	60	65	47	119	56	.68	111	.290	.347	.425
Tucson	Hou	144	4894	1381	250	62	122	2121	742	689	491	40	912	27	32	45	103	75	.58	103	.282	.348	.433
Colorado Springs	Col	142	4863	1370	264	35	117	2055	719	665	519	34	879	38	37	39	81	65	.55	129	.282	.353	.423
Albuquerque	LA	143	4940	1372	237	46	113	2040	712	646	474	46	1076	36	61	34	104	72	.59	98	.278	.343	.413
Phoenix	SF	144	4984	1371	273	58	77	1991	700	632	477	38	900	49	41	47	77	58	.57	114	.275	.341	.399
Vancouver	Cal	138	4732	1304	285	35	66	1857	677	617	488	30	775	47	51	53	89	51	.64	102	.276	.346	.392
Tacoma	Sea	142	4852	1341	245	33	143	2081	665	612	412	16	789	39	39	48	72	63	.53	122	.276	.335	.429
Las Vegas	SD	140	4669	1232	272	24	126	1930	654	597	531	51	949	39	57	33	74	59	.56	117	.264	.342	.413
Total		711	48618	13579	2678	427	1158	20585	7273	6679	4894	373	8984	461	454	453	983	629	.61	1111	.279	.348	.423

Pacific Coast League Pitching - AAA

HOW MUCH THEY PITCHED								WHAT THEY GAVE UP													THE RESULTS					
Team	Org	G	GS	CG	GF	IP	BFP	H	R	ER	HR	SH	SF	HB	TBB	IBB	SO	WP	Bk	W	L	Pct.	ShO	Sv	ERA
Edmonton	Oak	142	142	6	136	1226.1	5279	1259	628	549	100	31	34	36	406	44	840	60	6	84	58	.592	9	28	4.03
Vancouver	Cal	138	138	25	113	1215.1	5253	1175	639	554	105	55	38	55	530	17	840	66	14	68	70	.493	5	29	4.10
Calgary	Pit	143	143	4	139	1240	5492	1398	691	594	114	51	50	50	461	57	788	55	4	74	68	.521	6	31	4.31
Tacoma	Sea	142	142	10	132	1254.1	5506	1344	699	608	115	39	42	56	485	21	978	62	18	69	73	.486	8	28	4.36
Las Vegas	SD	140	140	11	129	1221.1	5333	1328	711	627	126	44	50	39	441	55	897	66	8	73	67	.521	7	35	4.62
Tucson	Hou	144	144	7	137	1247.1	5533	1400	732	581	70	54	55	39	439	38	987	74	5	70	74	.486	7	28	4.19
Phoenix	SF	144	144	5	139	1276.2	5586	1354	734	662	121	51	43	54	513	24	818	77	10	69	75	.479	10	40	4.67
Salt Lake	Min	144	144	13	131	1285	5707	1501	798	727	140	42	49	41	486	24	946	83	8	78	66	.542	5	31	5.09
Albuquerque	LA	143	143	5	138	1262	5675	1409	799	675	116	49	40	47	598	66	981	60	13	67	76	.469	6	30	4.81
Colorado Springs	Col	142	142	3	139	1225.2	5526	1411	842	759	151	38	52	44	535	27	909	59	8	58	83	.411	6	31	5.57
Total		711	711	89	622	12454	54890	13579	7273	6336	1158	454	453	461	4894	373	8984	662	94	710	710	.500	69	311	4.58

Eastern League Batting - AA

BATTING																	BASERUNNING				PERCENTAGES		
Team	Org	G	AB	H	2B	3B	HR	TB	R	RBI	TBB	IBB	SO	HBP	SH	SF	SB	CS	SB%	GDP	Avg	OBP	SLG
Canton-Akron	Cle	142	4913	1377	248	46	142	2143	768	709	431	27	896	71	11	41	105	54	.66	91	.280	.344	.436
Trenton	Bos	142	4677	1259	228	33	150	2003	751	689	567	44	924	51	49	37	134	92	.59	76	.269	.352	.428
Portland	Fla	141	4726	1301	260	38	106	1955	694	643	476	35	907	61	52	38	153	101	.60	93	.275	.347	.414
Reading	Phi	141	4686	1179	226	39	132	1879	684	603	554	27	1056	88	58	36	130	83	.61	84	.252	.339	.401
Norwich	NYA	141	4619	1193	235	21	126	1848	675	619	521	29	1016	40	51	32	82	49	.63	101	.258	.337	.400
Binghamton	NYN	142	4582	1160	204	27	103	1727	662	597	572	38	867	52	75	47	109	66	.62	97	.253	.340	.377
Harrisburg	Mon	142	4580	1195	233	29	110	1816	620	580	515	38	881	37	73	37	72	67	.52	104	.261	.338	.397
New Britain	Min	142	4605	1174	227	26	137	1864	617	563	446	26	950	40	35	37	71	88	.45	102	.255	.324	.405
Bowie	Bal	142	4730	1193	227	24	114	1810	582	527	417	21	968	59	38	33	86	77	.53	93	.252	.319	.383
New Haven	Col	141	4502	1084	193	24	77	1556	510	457	465	36	893	40	70	31	41	48	.46	115	.241	.315	.346
Total		708	46620	12115	2281	307	1197	18601	6563	5987	4964	321	9358	539	512	369	983	725	.58	956	.260	.336	.399

Eastern League Pitching - AA

		HOW MUCH THEY PITCHED						WHAT THEY GAVE UP													THE RESULTS					
Team	Org	G	GS	CG	GF	IP	BFP	H	R	ER	HR	SH	SF	HB	TBB	IBB	SO	WP	Bk	W	L	Pct.	ShO	Sv	ERA
Harrisburg	Mon	142	142	6	136	1219	5250	1169	592	498	117	48	30	58	529	23	813	51	7	74	68	.521	10	44	3.68
Portland	Fla	141	141	12	129	1232.2	5210	1206	609	509	132	58	34	46	387	37	986	57	8	83	58	.589	7	45	3.72
New Haven	Col	141	141	7	134	1199.2	5153	1151	609	512	107	50	33	41	496	52	1016	61	18	66	75	.468	14	37	3.84
Binghamton	NYN	142	142	17	125	1224.2	5223	1268	626	551	123	63	32	40	412	30	851	44	14	76	66	.535	8	40	4.05
Norwich	NYA	141	141	11	130	1208.2	5268	1154	633	488	92	52	36	51	523	36	979	79	12	71	70	.504	11	33	3.63
Trenton	Bos	142	142	15	127	1231.2	5303	1170	644	563	135	49	45	67	494	44	896	63	7	86	56	.606	8	39	4.11
Canton-Akron	Cle	142	142	8	134	1228	5330	1190	663	566	101	55	35	47	530	33	1020	63	13	71	71	.500	4	33	4.15
Reading	Phi	141	141	6	135	1236	5461	1221	717	600	140	43	37	65	576	35	1026	86	12	66	75	.468	8	26	4.37
New Britain	Min	142	142	13	129	1207.1	5397	1278	726	619	104	47	46	73	513	22	886	83	12	61	81	.430	7	24	4.61
Bowie	Bal	142	142	8	134	1234.1	5417	1308	744	646	146	47	41	51	503	9	885	66	22	54	88	.380	8	25	4.71
Total		708	708	103	605	12222	53012	12115	6563	5552	1197	512	369	539	4963	321	9358	653	125	708	708	.500	85	346	4.09

Southern League Batting - AA

BATTING																	BASERUNNING				PERCENTAGES		
Team	Org	G	AB	H	2B	3B	HR	TB	R	RBI	TBB	IBB	SO	HBP	SH	SF	SB	CS	SB%	GDP	Avg	OBP	SLG
Huntsville	Oak	140	4646	1219	229	31	120	1870	748	673	584	28	993	72	58	47	98	51	.66	106	.262	.351	.402
Jacksonville	Det	138	4617	1227	238	35	200	2135	725	686	451	36	1081	79	30	31	103	71	.59	97	.266	.339	.462
Memphis	SD	139	4563	1208	245	35	136	1931	714	648	550	38	981	32	41	54	107	79	.58	105	.265	.344	.423
Knoxville	Tor	140	4685	1264	263	41	113	1948	708	635	620	28	1028	61	27	38	103	73	.59	84	.270	.360	.416
Chattanooga	Cin	140	4700	1284	270	32	104	1930	687	625	469	36	897	51	37	36	139	75	.65	101	.273	.343	.411
Birmingham	ChA	139	4676	1242	260	26	120	1914	670	624	502	27	896	57	35	38	93	66	.58	99	.266	.342	.409
Greenville	Atl	140	4625	1210	250	25	106	1828	667	611	461	33	958	50	56	33	84	69	.55	99	.262	.333	.395
Orlando	ChN	139	4593	1158	223	34	84	1701	643	574	557	30	912	40	36	43	116	74	.61	106	.252	.335	.370
Carolina	Pit	139	4550	1178	220	40	69	1685	617	546	540	39	968	44	43	39	175	86	.67	98	.259	.341	.370
Port City	Sea	140	4717	1189	234	34	48	1635	591	510	551	32	833	59	44	32	142	71	.67	115	.252	.336	.347
Total		697	46372	12179	2432	333	1100	18577	6770	6132	5285	327	9547	545	407	391	1160	715	.62	1010	.263	.342	.401

Southern League Pitching - AA

		HOW MUCH THEY PITCHED						WHAT THEY GAVE UP													THE RESULTS					
Team	Org	G	GS	CG	GF	IP	BFP	H	R	ER	HR	SH	SF	HB	TBB	IBB	SO	WP	Bk	W	L	Pct.	ShO	Sv	ERA
Memphis	SD	139	139	8	131	1219	5256	1125	599	500	109	35	34	50	510	22	1106	79	15	81	58	.583	11	40	3.69
Birmingham	ChA	139	139	9	130	1222.1	5253	1190	624	535	121	36	42	53	493	32	1017	49	9	74	65	.532	7	40	3.94
Chattanooga	Cin	140	140	7	133	1218.1	5213	1153	637	542	111	30	42	52	520	24	1013	85	9	81	59	.579	11	51	4.00
Carolina	Pit	139	139	1	138	1208.2	5237	1226	641	561	106	39	32	63	456	44	969	66	13	70	69	.504	10	35	4.18
Knoxville	Tor	140	140	2	138	1214.2	5323	1223	673	570	100	39	31	46	582	30	1013	88	17	75	65	.536	12	40	4.22
Jacksonville	Det	138	138	6	132	1198.1	5259	1219	683	541	98	42	33	49	550	33	859	86	10	75	63	.543	10	37	4.06
Orlando	ChN	139	139	6	133	1199.1	5323	1259	699	582	121	46	46	60	503	35	910	69	6	61	78	.439	5	27	4.37
Port City	Sea	140	140	5	135	1239	5434	1221	702	598	105	49	42	58	591	22	869	81	12	56	84	.400	5	31	4.34
Huntsville	Oak	140	140	8	132	1208.1	5346	1257	743	615	106	36	39	57	526	59	950	92	16	66	74	.471	9	22	4.58
Greenville	Atl	140	140	2	138	1192.1	5376	1306	769	681	123	55	50	57	554	26	841	103	7	58	82	.414	1	35	5.14
Total		697	697	54	643	12120.1	53020	12179	6770	5725	1100	407	391	545	5285	327	9547	798	114	697	697	.500	81	358	4.25

Texas League Batting - AA

		BATTING															BASERUNNING				PERCENTAGES		
Team	Org	G	AB	H	2B	3B	HR	TB	R	RBI	TBB	IBB	SO	HBP	SH	SF	SB	CS	SB%	GDP	Avg	OBP	SLG
El Paso	Mil	139	4664	1356	265	68	117	2108	809	716	504	13	871	50	61	55	129	80	.62	108	.291	.362	.452
Wichita	KC	140	4797	1331	279	32	124	2046	713	648	423	9	669	49	44	38	124	66	.65	122	.277	.340	.427
Tulsa	Tex	139	4745	1274	271	36	156	2085	699	641	478	21	1006	54	34	33	64	57	.53	98	.268	.340	.439
Shreveport	SF	139	4622	1219	235	33	123	1889	692	634	553	21	889	52	56	43	143	89	.62	97	.264	.346	.409
Midland	Cal	140	4711	1254	274	42	97	1903	670	594	462	12	824	39	38	37	67	62	.52	115	.266	.334	.404
Jackson	Hou	140	4753	1319	229	30	108	1932	647	587	406	20	697	56	55	31	60	45	.57	143	.278	.339	.406
San Antonio	LA	139	4645	1267	244	43	93	1876	616	554	376	24	773	48	50	46	112	72	.61	110	.273	.331	.404
Arkansas	StL	140	4495	1154	214	34	96	1724	610	561	487	19	724	38	51	34	106	70	.60	111	.257	.332	.384
Total		558	37432	10174	2011	318	914	15563	5456	4935	3689	139	6453	386	389	317	805	541	.60	904	.272	.341	.416

Texas League Pitching - AA

		HOW MUCH THEY PITCHED						WHAT THEY GAVE UP												THE RESULTS					
Team	Org	G	GS	CG	GF	IP	BFP	H	R	ER	HR	SH	SF	HB	TBB	IBB	SO	WP	Bk	W	L	Pct.	ShO	Sv	ERA
Arkansas	StL	140	140	10	130	1187.1	5132	1180	597	501	108	55	32	25	470	26	888	57	5	67	73	.479	8	28	3.80
San Antonio	LA	139	139	6	133	1205.1	5252	1229	625	518	82	60	40	34	534	2	764	88	10	69	70	.496	5	37	3.87
Jackson	Hou	140	140	5	135	1220	5308	1199	631	513	100	52	35	76	513	15	894	70	3	70	70	.500	10	36	3.78
Shreveport	SF	139	139	5	134	1211	5160	1211	635	540	129	51	32	51	395	30	675	43	10	73	66	.525	6	43	4.01
Tulsa	Tex	139	139	12	127	1224	5302	1306	677	596	126	36	49	57	403	18	721	38	5	75	64	.540	8	42	4.38
Wichita	KC	140	140	9	131	1225.1	5329	1344	737	636	154	47	49	38	432	17	785	86	3	70	70	.500	10	34	4.67
El Paso	Mil	139	139	9	130	1201.2	5362	1353	746	633	92	41	41	46	465	16	872	61	9	76	63	.547	2	47	4.74
Midland	Cal	140	140	11	129	1206.2	5377	1352	808	679	123	47	39	59	477	15	854	89	8	58	82	.414	2	28	5.06
Total		558	558	67	491	9681.1	42222	10174	5456	4616	914	389	317	386	3689	139	6453	532	53	558	558	.500	51	295	4.29

California League Batting - A+

		BATTING															BASERUNNING				PERCENTAGES		
Team	Org	G	AB	H	2B	3B	HR	TB	R	RBI	TBB	IBB	SO	HBP	SH	SF	SB	CS	SB%	GDP	Avg	OBP	SLG
Modesto	Oak	140	4858	1386	242	41	187	2271	952	832	650	18	1192	63	50	46	219	102	.68	86	.285	.374	.467
High Desert	Bal	140	4957	1446	274	38	146	2234	924	842	617	7	1034	76	58	40	119	66	.64	107	.292	.376	.451
Lancaster	Sea	140	4900	1362	275	59	115	2100	852	775	544	8	1019	93	27	53	120	48	.71	84	.278	.358	.429
San Bernardino	LA	140	4853	1349	243	22	152	2092	807	711	456	9	1074	71	48	41	208	128	.62	76	.278	.346	.431
Lake Elsinore	Cal	140	4846	1327	286	33	125	2054	805	736	681	22	930	52	50	43	113	68	.62	118	.274	.366	.424
Rancho Cucamonga	SD	140	4827	1327	269	47	96	1978	779	699	599	13	1096	65	23	44	124	61	.67	110	.275	.360	.410
San Jose	SF	140	4950	1433	241	45	82	2010	771	679	518	16	902	58	49	41	185	71	.72	99	.289	.361	.406
Stockton	Mil	140	4759	1359	225	42	102	1974	767	689	536	9	894	84	56	52	147	91	.62	103	.286	.364	.415
Visalia	C-O	140	4786	1216	254	34	106	1856	738	655	598	5	1249	56	29	54	179	79	.69	93	.254	.340	.388
Bakersfield	C-O	140	4821	1205	256	15	114	1833	682	595	517	11	1256	76	51	35	127	55	.70	105	.250	.330	.380
Total		700	48557	13410	2565	376	1225	20402	8077	7213	5716	118	10646	694	441	449	1541	769	.67	981	.276	.358	.420

California League Pitching - A+

		HOW MUCH THEY PITCHED						WHAT THEY GAVE UP												THE RESULTS					
Team	Org	G	GS	CG	GF	IP	BFP	H	R	ER	HR	SH	SF	HB	TBB	IBB	SO	WP	Bk	W	L	Pct.	ShO	Sv	ERA
San Jose	SF	140	140	4	136	1262.1	5393	1154	594	497	76	53	34	68	494	12	1236	101	10	89	51	.636	16	40	3.54
Stockton	Mil	140	140	6	134	1228	5345	1244	686	582	113	42	33	60	497	9	995	69	18	79	61	.564	4	39	4.27
Lake Elsinore	Cal	140	140	7	133	1250	5445	1292	717	590	111	42	54	64	469	5	1111	72	21	75	65	.536	5	28	4.25
Lancaster	Sea	140	140	5	135	1241	5488	1301	747	585	124	40	45	74	504	13	1070	96	16	71	69	.507	3	36	4.24
Modesto	Oak	140	140	0	140	1251	5507	1318	749	585	100	38	35	70	487	8	1048	89	17	82	58	.586	6	39	4.21
Rancho Cucamonga	SD	140	140	1	139	1229	5525	1381	775	655	119	47	46	87	513	8	1112	98	13	69	71	.493	4	30	4.80
San Bernardino	LA	140	140	1	139	1248.1	5739	1282	864	699	109	42	40	74	738	14	1165	131	27	70	70	.500	3	45	5.04
High Desert	Bal	140	140	3	137	1244.2	5709	1372	881	766	153	44	49	63	702	28	965	138	28	76	64	.543	3	29	5.54
Visalia	C-O	140	140	2	138	1241.2	5697	1467	926	755	148	44	55	68	566	17	936	116	15	50	90	.357	1	26	5.47
Bakersfield	C-O	140	140	11	129	1238.1	6034	1599	1138	931	172	49	58	66	746	4	1008	129	10	39	101	.279	1	20	6.77
Total		700	700	40	660	12434.1	55882	13410	8077	6645	1225	441	449	694	5716	118	10646	1039	175	700	700	.500	46	332	4.81

Carolina League Batting - A+

BATTING																	BASERUNNING				PERCENTAGES		
Team	Org	G	AB	H	2B	3B	HR	TB	R	RBI	TBB	IBB	SO	HBP	SH	SF	SB	CS	SB%	GDP	Avg	OBP	SLG
Lynchburg	Pit	139	4673	1323	253	34	105	1959	730	649	405	17	965	55	47	48	155	80	.66	97	.283	.344	.419
Durham	Atl	139	4701	1232	245	30	152	1993	702	637	425	14	1007	69	35	33	168	74	.69	71	.262	.330	.424
Frederick	Bal	139	4568	1184	226	25	93	1739	648	574	495	34	819	63	36	37	150	81	.65	112	.259	.337	.381
Winston-Salem	Cin	139	4494	1131	192	24	121	1734	641	580	524	16	1070	39	57	39	219	88	.71	90	.252	.332	.386
Wilmington	KC	140	4609	1195	234	34	81	1740	637	579	493	19	960	57	39	52	160	72	.69	67	.259	.335	.378
Kinston	Cle	138	4529	1166	245	24	82	1705	635	584	490	25	812	54	65	35	86	51	.63	84	.257	.335	.376
Prince William	ChA	138	4583	1138	224	30	88	1686	603	538	504	10	930	44	39	28	81	45	.64	113	.248	.327	.368
Salem	Col	138	4539	1164	216	18	89	1683	585	527	477	19	835	61	68	28	155	89	.64	98	.256	.333	.371
Total		555	36696	9533	1835	219	811	14239	5181	4668	3813	154	7398	442	386	300	1174	580	.67	732	.260	.334	.388

Carolina League Pitching - A+

HOW MUCH THEY PITCHED								WHAT THEY GAVE UP												THE RESULTS					
Team	Org	G	GS	CG	GF	IP	BFP	H	R	ER	HR	SH	SF	HB	TBB	IBB	SO	WP	Bk	W	L	Pct.	ShO	Sv	ERA
Kinston	Cle	138	138	3	135	1188.2	5074	1095	566	470	81	44	32	62	534	19	869	75	9	76	62	.551	14	37	3.56
Wilmington	KC	140	140	5	135	1221	5134	1158	595	479	95	47	26	44	395	26	835	64	6	80	60	.571	8	41	3.53
Durham	Atl	139	139	6	133	1216.2	5235	1178	630	517	99	54	52	53	499	13	1054	72	11	73	66	.525	12	36	3.82
Winston-Salem	Cin	139	139	11	128	1203	5196	1255	643	538	143	30	46	51	423	9	746	70	7	74	65	.532	7	27	4.02
Salem	Col	138	138	7	131	1205.1	5253	1167	656	549	75	53	44	49	558	19	969	84	13	62	76	.449	9	33	4.10
Prince William	ChA	138	138	14	124	1193	5189	1194	668	550	101	52	45	68	479	32	923	61	14	58	80	.420	9	19	4.15
Lynchburg	Pit	139	139	11	128	1192.2	5303	1249	704	556	99	55	25	69	459	21	896	87	15	65	74	.468	7	20	4.20
Frederick	Bal	139	139	6	133	1200	5264	1237	719	588	118	51	30	46	466	15	1104	75	11	67	72	.482	9	37	4.41
Total		555	555	63	492	9620.1	41648	9533	5181	4247	811	386	300	442	3813	154	7396	588	86	555	555	.500	75	250	3.97

Florida State League Batting - A+

BATTING																	BASERUNNING				PERCENTAGES		
Team	Org	G	AB	H	2B	3B	HR	TB	R	RBI	TBB	IBB	SO	HBP	SH	SF	SB	CS	SB%	GDP	Avg	OBP	SLG
Charlotte	Tex	139	4713	1246	253	32	65	1758	678	595	456	22	890	69	41	42	110	73	.60	108	.264	.335	.373
Daytona	ChN	137	4510	1205	234	36	92	1787	660	585	404	15	795	81	19	33	181	76	.70	91	.267	.336	.396
Fort Myers	Min	138	4538	1134	202	42	61	1603	641	565	570	15	834	58	45	46	148	77	.66	66	.250	.338	.353
Dunedin	Tor	137	4500	1135	229	35	102	1740	629	552	506	19	1056	49	52	27	102	78	.57	94	.252	.333	.387
Clearwater	Phi	137	4534	1141	207	31	74	1632	628	558	508	17	902	83	60	43	152	49	.76	101	.252	.335	.360
Vero Beach	LA	131	4280	1092	171	41	52	1501	598	514	490	19	859	36	53	28	139	67	.67	86	.255	.335	.351
West Palm Beach	Mon	135	4450	1156	214	34	49	1585	587	508	428	11	815	89	47	45	142	83	.63	76	.260	.334	.356
Tampa	NYA	134	4407	1131	212	32	74	1629	587	542	526	19	892	56	54	37	110	62	.64	114	.257	.341	.370
Lakeland	Det	138	4651	1200	234	42	63	1707	579	518	379	12	920	66	28	37	144	61	.70	98	.258	.320	.367
Sarasota	Bos	136	4476	1171	215	42	64	1662	566	512	439	12	915	64	52	33	159	64	.71	88	.262	.334	.371
St. Petersburg	StL	139	4508	1138	185	37	37	1508	533	480	436	19	745	38	45	44	82	54	.60	116	.252	.321	.335
Brevard County	Fla	139	4611	1134	192	36	40	1518	520	449	467	18	896	58	45	36	128	86	.60	99	.246	.321	.329
St. Lucie	NYN	133	4356	1083	161	31	51	1459	517	461	378	16	863	54	37	31	177	84	.68	91	.249	.314	.335
Kissimmee	Hou	135	4348	1105	206	33	52	1533	500	441	376	18	746	40	52	31	121	65	.65	93	.254	.317	.353
Total		954	62882	16071	2915	504	876	22622	8223	7280	6363	232	12128	841	630	513	1895	979	.66	1321	.256	.330	.360

Florida State League Pitching - A+

HOW MUCH THEY PITCHED								WHAT THEY GAVE UP												THE RESULTS					
Team	Org	G	GS	CG	GF	IP	BFP	H	R	ER	HR	SH	SF	HB	TBB	IBB	SO	WP	Bk	W	L	Pct.	ShO	Sv	ERA
St. Petersburg	StL	139	139	5	134	1200.1	5031	1111	474	406	47	49	36	59	451	13	892	51	11	75	63	.543	13	44	3.04
St. Lucie	NYN	133	133	9	124	1156	4834	1045	505	404	53	43	28	37	431	22	852	82	8	71	62	.534	12	41	3.15
Tampa	NYA	134	134	4	130	1180.2	4942	1123	522	413	63	43	26	51	337	18	912	48	8	84	50	.627	8	49	3.15
Fort Myers	Min	138	138	10	128	1213	5119	1115	541	472	66	47	37	66	478	6	966	98	7	79	58	.577	10	37	3.50
Vero Beach	LA	131	131	4	127	1124.1	4829	1046	554	446	67	41	29	54	469	17	894	86	18	65	66	.496	9	27	3.57
Clearwater	Phi	137	137	7	130	1207.2	5169	1152	569	469	54	43	36	47	478	25	838	57	10	75	62	.547	8	37	3.50
West Palm Beach	Mon	135	135	4	131	1176.2	5081	1170	581	464	52	46	34	60	420	12	841	94	7	68	67	.504	9	35	3.55
Lakeland	Det	138	138	10	128	1201	5146	1103	581	486	60	53	43	64	543	7	911	72	11	61	77	.442	14	34	3.64
Kissimmee	Hou	135	135	11	124	1150.2	5044	1125	603	453	56	45	41	74	491	12	793	75	7	60	75	.444	9	30	3.54
Charlotte	Tex	139	139	14	125	1228.1	5292	1256	636	537	82	48	52	38	442	10	844	64	13	63	76	.453	9	21	3.93
Daytona	ChN	137	137	6	131	1162.1	5124	1146	648	518	72	56	43	69	488	24	912	101	14	71	66	.518	7	38	4.01
Dunedin	Tor	137	137	6	131	1187.1	5190	1166	654	490	63	35	32	78	489	21	924	76	11	67	70	.489	11	35	3.71
Brevard County	Fla	139	139	5	134	1212.2	5256	1277	669	558	86	46	38	87	364	26	715	66	5	47	92	.338	5	23	4.14
Sarasota	Bos	136	136	8	128	1180	5196	1236	686	576	55	35	38	57	482	19	834	65	18	67	69	.493	10	35	4.39
Total		954	954	103	851	16581	71253	16071	8223	6692	876	630	513	841	6363	232	12128	1035	148	953	953	.500	134	486	3.63

Midwest League Batting - A

BATTING																	BASERUNNING				PERCENTAGES		
Team	Org	G	AB	H	2B	3B	HR	TB	R	RBI	TBB	IBB	SO	HBP	SH	SF	SB	CS	SB%	GDP	Avg	OBP	SLG
Wisconsin	Sea	135	4561	1228	250	29	84	1788	731	649	466	17	925	92	39	39	95	79	.55	91	.269	.346	.392
Lansing	KC	139	4824	1285	233	41	71	1813	727	645	528	16	893	79	49	44	161	67	.71	98	.266	.346	.376
Peoria	StL	136	4402	1148	214	45	40	1572	696	584	561	19	933	63	60	56	159	95	.63	81	.261	.349	.357
Rockford	ChN	135	4392	1126	207	43	56	1587	694	605	561	16	979	90	47	44	211	88	.71	88	.256	.349	.361
Cedar Rapids	Cal	135	4491	1146	218	41	111	1779	645	587	477	14	1049	77	44	38	153	77	.67	78	.255	.334	.396
West Michigan	Oak	138	4559	1133	199	29	71	1603	639	551	653	14	920	52	30	47	117	67	.64	131	.249	.346	.352
Michigan	Bos	138	4693	1216	261	35	84	1799	638	567	443	11	945	56	32	50	83	50	.62	87	.259	.327	.383
Beloit	Mil	136	4434	1131	210	36	60	1593	637	549	456	13	835	81	45	38	150	93	.62	99	.255	.333	.359
Fort Wayne	Min	136	4553	1197	229	35	58	1670	632	566	470	25	911	72	36	46	96	65	.60	95	.263	.338	.367
Quad City	Hou	131	4391	1162	212	30	89	1701	629	555	394	15	845	45	39	43	153	100	.60	96	.265	.329	.387
Kane County	Fla	133	4280	1026	215	26	92	1569	580	518	496	17	1137	69	46	35	101	67	.60	86	.240	.326	.367
Burlington	SF	138	4480	1055	207	20	78	1536	572	501	641	23	972	58	52	29	108	44	.71	124	.235	.337	.343
South Bend	ChA	136	4450	1090	213	34	71	1584	566	494	445	25	947	45	52	44	117	84	.58	80	.245	.317	.356
Clinton	SD	134	4240	974	180	35	60	1404	529	472	583	15	964	57	31	27	153	69	.69	92	.230	.329	.331
Total		950	62750	15917	3048	479	1025	22998	8915	7843	7174	240	13255	936	602	580	1857	1045	.64	1326	.254	.336	.367

Midwest League Pitching - A

		HOW MUCH THEY PITCHED						WHAT THEY GAVE UP												THE RESULTS					
Team	Org	G	GS	CG	GF	IP	BFP	H	R	ER	HR	SH	SF	HB	TBB	IBB	SO	WP	Bk	W	L	Pct.	ShO	Sv	ERA
Peoria	StL	136	136	7	129	1165	4901	991	533	428	56	36	32	52	445	10	1065	57	14	79	57	.581	13	31	3.31
West Michigan	Oak	138	138	0	138	1219	5245	1121	561	463	62	45	44	43	495	31	1090	52	24	77	61	.558	9	45	3.42
Kane County	Fla	133	133	12	121	1148.2	4985	1099	596	466	49	46	36	91	459	14	941	91	17	65	68	.489	7	30	3.65
Quad City	Hou	131	131	3	128	1147.1	4983	1068	599	493	74	32	43	83	502	12	948	85	22	70	61	.534	5	36	3.87
Burlington	SF	138	138	5	133	1202.2	5104	1086	604	509	112	49	42	48	499	8	982	86	17	65	73	.471	9	42	3.81
Beloit	Mil	136	136	13	123	1178.2	5145	1147	610	491	70	52	42	47	538	31	1000	93	27	69	67	.507	11	29	3.75
Clinton	SD	134	134	6	128	1143.2	5061	1095	643	522	66	40	49	78	536	13	1013	116	13	64	70	.478	7	34	4.11
Cedar Rapids	Cal	135	135	7	128	1172	5188	1123	657	538	94	40	47	87	610	33	855	103	22	63	72	.467	4	29	4.13
Fort Wayne	Min	136	136	7	129	1187	5165	1224	661	540	67	38	56	50	440	9	969	75	19	69	67	.507	8	28	4.09
Rockford	ChN	135	135	11	124	1149	5071	1170	663	513	78	35	42	75	457	13	886	80	21	70	65	.519	4	31	4.02
South Bend	ChA	136	136	7	129	1176.2	5119	1174	665	512	78	46	45	56	426	0	825	72	23	54	82	.397	2	22	3.92
Michigan	Bos	138	138	13	125	1211	5315	1147	675	560	75	40	38	71	573	26	901	121	18	60	78	.435	4	26	4.16
Wisconsin	Sea	135	135	9	126	1172.2	5302	1135	709	601	62	39	34	66	673	31	974	120	21	77	58	.570	4	33	4.61
Lansing	KC	139	139	3	136	1239.1	5490	1336	739	591	82	64	30	89	521	9	806	110	24	68	71	.489	6	27	4.29
Total		950	950	103	847	16512.2	72074	15916	8915	7227	1025	602	580	936	7174	240	13255	1261	282	950	950	.500	93	443	3.94

Northwest League Batting - A-

BATTING																	BASERUNNING				PERCENTAGES		
Team	Org	G	AB	H	2B	3B	HR	TB	R	RBI	TBB	IBB	SO	HBP	SH	SF	SB	CS	SB%	GDP	Avg	OBP	SLG
Boise	Cal	76	2764	747	149	25	53	1105	477	414	347	13	561	40	12	30	79	31	.72	64	.270	.356	.400
Eugene	Atl	76	2669	710	150	28	86	1174	447	399	273	19	607	36	12	27	51	30	.63	44	.266	.339	.440
Spokane	KC	76	2623	667	122	18	72	1041	433	385	326	5	563	46	30	31	122	30	.80	55	.254	.343	.397
Southern Oregon	Oak	76	2587	631	136	11	63	978	374	326	295	9	644	38	29	22	101	45	.69	40	.244	.328	.378
Portland	Col	76	2628	653	128	23	30	917	367	311	250	10	544	35	31	24	59	23	.72	47	.248	.319	.349
Bellingham	SF	75	2560	646	110	17	51	943	355	318	237	12	636	33	22	29	55	37	.60	43	.252	.320	.368
Everett	Sea	75	2519	581	100	16	45	848	344	311	319	10	738	28	14	16	56	29	.66	45	.231	.322	.337
Yakima	LA	76	2597	635	120	20	43	924	337	301	266	7	703	36	17	16	79	36	.69	34	.245	.321	.356
Total		303	20947	5270	1015	158	443	7930	3134	2765	2313	85	4996	292	167	195	602	261	.70	372	.252	.332	.379

Northwest League Pitching - A-

		HOW MUCH THEY PITCHED						WHAT THEY GAVE UP												THE RESULTS					
Team	Org	G	GS	CG	GF	IP	BFP	H	R	ER	HR	SH	SF	HB	TBB	IBB	SO	WP	Bk	W	L	Pct.	ShO	Sv	ERA
Bellingham	SF	75	75	0	75	673.1	2898	575	318	255	57	17	14	25	316	4	691	58	8	39	36	.520	5	19	3.41
Yakima	LA	76	76	0	76	677.1	2893	588	333	260	38	19	26	16	283	10	689	58	17	40	36	.526	6	25	3.45
Eugene	Atl	76	76	0	76	686.2	2999	634	365	280	36	25	19	29	272	12	682	46	6	49	27	.645	4	33	3.67
Portland	Col	76	76	0	76	678.1	2964	656	386	309	66	17	26	45	250	5	585	43	10	33	43	.434	4	18	4.10
Everett	Sea	75	75	0	75	657.1	2877	658	390	306	53	22	18	28	254	2	657	80	19	33	42	.440	4	19	4.19
Spokane	KC	76	76	0	76	681.1	3019	718	418	341	64	20	34	53	264	3	567	44	10	37	39	.487	2	19	4.50
Boise	Cal	76	76	2	74	699.1	3142	695	440	344	61	29	32	53	334	29	585	57	6	43	33	.566	2	16	4.43
Southern Oregon	Oak	76	76	0	76	677.2	3126	746	484	398	68	18	26	43	340	20	540	50	22	29	47	.382	2	14	5.29
Total		303	303	2	301	5431.1	23918	5270	3134	2493	443	167	195	292	2313	85	4996	436	98	303	303	.500	29	163	4.13

New York-Penn League Batting - A-

BATTING																	BASERUNNING				PERCENTAGES		
Team	Org	G	AB	H	2B	3B	HR	TB	R	RBI	TBB	IBB	SO	HBP	SH	SF	SB	CS	SB%	GDP	Avg	OBP	SLG
Jamestown	Det	76	2491	634	117	29	55	974	391	344	318	9	609	38	34	23	91	48	.65	38	.255	.345	.391
Vermont	Mon	74	2406	637	116	26	20	865	373	312	268	16	437	23	17	21	95	58	.62	47	.265	.341	.360
Pittsfield	NYN	75	2401	600	82	26	40	854	360	299	301	10	593	27	13	23	93	46	.67	38	.250	.337	.356
Watertown	Cle	75	2424	580	105	13	27	792	359	301	358	9	581	43	38	21	75	38	.66	44	.239	.345	.327
Hudson Valley	2Tm	76	2581	588	127	27	47	910	356	303	280	9	720	54	10	28	120	48	.71	42	.228	.313	.353
Batavia	Phi	75	2516	635	116	26	32	899	348	313	207	6	510	35	22	17	57	35	.62	34	.252	.316	.357
St. Catharines	Tor	76	2493	634	113	24	51	948	347	296	232	9	535	41	29	23	84	39	.68	28	.254	.325	.380
New Jersey	StL	75	2541	634	114	30	26	886	347	300	269	6	604	28	28	24	56	23	.71	50	.250	.325	.349
Williamsport	ChN	76	2482	606	96	20	24	814	342	289	238	7	582	44	25	18	104	44	.70	38	.244	.319	.328
Erie	Pit	76	2530	647	111	22	37	913	334	283	220	3	510	31	26	24	66	43	.61	59	.256	.320	.361
Oneonta	NYA	76	2471	584	70	25	19	761	319	258	257	9	661	32	31	28	126	34	.79	28	.236	.313	.308
Auburn	Hou	76	2499	596	123	21	33	860	308	261	221	8	522	37	18	25	80	32	.71	49	.238	.307	.344
Lowell	Bos	74	2458	586	108	9	38	826	306	246	233	6	575	37	7	14	51	24	.68	48	.238	.312	.336
Utica	Fla	76	2426	570	112	18	22	784	299	264	308	8	641	43	21	34	64	33	.66	44	.235	.328	.323
Total		528	34719	8531	1510	316	471	12086	4789	4069	3710	115	8080	513	319	323	1162	545	.68	587	.246	.325	.348

New York-Penn League Pitching - A-

		HOW MUCH THEY PITCHED						WHAT THEY GAVE UP												THE RESULTS					
Team	Org	G	GS	CG	GF	IP	BFP	H	R	ER	HR	SH	SF	HB	TBB	IBB	SO	WP	Bk	W	L	Pct.	ShO	Sv	ERA
Vermont	Mon	74	74	7	67	630	2601	541	256	215	29	18	15	30	194	1	575	43	12	48	26	.649	7	20	3.07
Pittsfield	NYN	75	75	6	69	635.1	2694	575	274	238	23	24	20	38	221	3	559	44	13	46	29	.613	8	19	3.37
Watertown	Cle	75	75	4	71	651.1	2732	552	283	225	36	14	14	20	246	11	661	44	17	45	30	.600	13	20	3.11
Batavia	Phi	75	75	2	73	650	2738	606	304	258	32	27	22	36	207	5	523	42	9	42	33	.560	8	20	3.57
Jamestown	Det	76	76	1	75	658.1	2802	595	319	239	47	21	23	39	245	1	547	52	11	39	36	.520	2	14	3.27
Williamsport	ChN	76	76	3	73	654.2	2836	560	326	261	30	17	18	27	322	12	585	50	23	43	32	.573	4	18	3.59
Utica	Fla	76	76	4	72	646.2	2822	648	360	301	44	15	19	33	236	16	567	58	19	29	47	.382	2	15	4.19
St. Catharines	Tor	76	76	5	71	651	2813	599	361	290	43	19	26	40	262	6	542	61	11	44	32	.579	7	24	4.01
Oneonta	NYA	76	76	4	72	655.2	2889	565	364	269	20	25	29	32	338	5	576	49	21	31	45	.408	7	18	3.69
Auburn	Hou	76	76	2	74	661	2944	639	371	295	30	21	23	60	317	13	519	64	15	37	39	.487	4	24	4.02
Lowell	Bos	74	74	4	70	637.1	2860	603	372	277	31	27	29	55	297	11	592	83	14	33	41	.446	3	18	3.91
Erie	Pit	76	76	4	72	658.2	2912	670	373	300	35	32	29	49	272	8	573	48	15	30	46	.395	2	13	4.10
New Jersey	StL	75	75	0	75	653.2	2914	692	399	309	37	33	30	30	270	10	608	52	14	28	47	.373	3	16	4.25
Hudson Valley	2Tm	76	76	1	75	688	3045	686	427	330	34	26	26	24	283	13	653	84	23	32	44	.421	2	13	4.32
Total		528	528	47	481	9131.2	39602	8531	4789	3807	471	319	323	513	3710	115	8080	774	217	527	527	.500	72	252	3.75

South Atlantic League Batting - A

		BATTING															BASERUNNING				PERCENTAGES		
Team	Org	G	AB	H	2B	3B	HR	TB	R	RBI	TBB	IBB	SO	HBP	SH	SF	SB	CS	SB%	GDP	Avg	OBP	SLG
Columbus	Cle	142	4689	1170	216	25	167	1937	729	654	535	18	1136	59	19	44	99	49	.67	82	.250	.331	.413
Delmarva	Mon	142	4621	1116	228	48	76	1668	673	579	483	27	918	58	38	42	215	118	.65	62	.242	.318	.361
Savannah	LA	141	4699	1162	202	42	103	1757	671	574	479	26	1070	73	38	33	212	106	.67	66	.247	.324	.374
Hagerstown	Tor	141	4564	1115	235	31	74	1634	666	559	624	19	1078	81	36	43	161	94	.63	68	.244	.343	.358
Fayetteville	Det	139	4596	1123	238	19	80	1639	612	530	510	17	963	76	59	33	163	91	.64	75	.244	.328	.357
Asheville	Col	136	4498	1099	203	22	74	1568	612	525	523	15	968	86	34	35	173	111	.61	42	.244	.332	.349
Augusta	Pit	141	4563	1066	178	30	55	1469	612	521	568	18	964	74	48	32	147	98	.60	97	.234	.326	.322
Charleston-WV	Cin	142	4605	1043	200	28	65	1494	600	521	625	11	1299	64	38	38	162	86	.65	50	.226	.325	.324
Hickory	ChA	140	4743	1191	200	27	57	1616	596	512	433	24	1127	63	42	39	172	94	.65	82	.251	.320	.341
Columbia	NYN	139	4421	1057	182	37	59	1490	593	514	479	23	1122	70	72	40	142	81	.64	65	.239	.321	.337
Macon	Atl	140	4596	1131	208	32	97	1694	589	518	393	28	982	65	39	32	235	107	.69	80	.246	.312	.369
Greensboro	NYA	142	4758	1136	209	37	74	1641	586	521	449	12	1229	75	41	36	160	75	.68	71	.239	.312	.345
Piedmont	Phi	138	4548	1070	197	25	49	1464	540	463	408	17	1038	90	55	33	131	73	.64	83	.235	.309	.322
Charleston-SC	Tex	141	4480	1028	183	49	57	1480	533	450	412	8	1176	66	21	30	172	81	.68	53	.229	.302	.330
Total		982	64381	15507	2879	452	1087	22551	8612	7441	6921	263	15070	1000	580	510	2344	1264	.65	976	.241	.322	.350

South Atlantic League Pitching - A

		HOW MUCH THEY PITCHED						WHAT THEY GAVE UP												THE RESULTS					
Team	Org	G	GS	CG	GF	IP	BFP	H	R	ER	HR	SH	SF	HB	TBB	IBB	SO	WP	Bk	W	L	Pct.	ShO	Sv	ERA
Columbia	NYN	139	139	16	123	1201	4886	916	451	370	79	32	17	46	416	9	1168	64	20	82	57	.590	18	33	2.77
Asheville	Col	136	136	6	130	1214	5079	1039	526	423	76	40	29	60	461	25	1131	74	19	84	52	.618	11	41	3.14
Delmarva	Mon	142	142	14	128	1243	5189	1031	534	393	82	35	36	88	441	2	1101	107	12	83	59	.585	17	38	2.85
Piedmont	Phi	138	138	10	128	1219	5103	1108	561	474	70	39	36	54	387	17	1088	94	21	72	66	.522	12	34	3.50
Fayetteville	Det	139	139	8	131	1235.2	5280	1067	582	439	55	39	30	83	511	14	1162	101	26	76	63	.547	7	46	3.20
Hagerstown	Tor	141	141	15	126	1220	5232	1095	602	475	60	40	35	92	540	7	1072	113	13	70	71	.496	13	28	3.50
Augusta	Pit	141	141	7	134	1232.2	5291	1197	605	485	70	50	37	87	386	16	1106	98	19	71	70	.504	10	43	3.54
Columbus	Cle	142	142	7	135	1218.2	5188	1142	610	503	96	50	38	59	449	27	982	95	14	79	63	.556	4	37	3.71
Savannah	LA	141	141	7	134	1241.1	5336	1046	637	502	93	41	29	71	567	20	1229	126	23	72	69	.511	9	42	3.64
Charleston-SC	Tex	141	141	20	121	1193	5133	1093	649	515	85	45	40	70	501	19	958	139	25	63	78	.447	11	32	3.89
Charleston-WV	Cin	142	142	3	139	1224.1	5339	1194	674	533	50	45	43	65	518	29	954	92	17	58	84	.408	8	34	3.92
Hickory	ChA	140	140	8	132	1244.2	5422	1282	714	566	112	46	38	73	447	13	962	77	35	55	85	.393	5	29	4.09
Greensboro	NYA	142	142	4	138	1246	5548	1150	725	577	72	47	48	82	667	35	1080	141	25	56	86	.394	5	30	4.17
Macon	Atl	140	140	5	135	1208.1	5384	1147	742	579	87	31	54	70	630	30	1077	117	23	61	79	.436	9	29	4.31
Total		982	982	130	852	17141.2	73410	15507	8612	6834	1087	580	510	1000	6921	263	15070	1438	292	982	982	.500	139	496	3.59

Appalachian League Batting - R+

BATTING																	BASERUNNING				PERCENTAGES		
Team	Org	G	AB	H	2B	3B	HR	TB	R	RBI	TBB	IBB	SO	HBP	SH	SF	SB	CS	SB%	GDP	Avg	OBP	SLG
Johnson City	StL	68	2330	679	139	23	49	1011	465	371	266	3	546	55	11	19	96	39	.71	50	.291	.375	.434
Bluefield	Bal	68	2229	581	125	6	66	916	423	350	311	9	558	33	9	25	180	50	.78	36	.261	.356	.411
Kingsport	NYN	67	2240	613	94	23	38	867	412	350	279	5	418	40	18	25	82	27	.75	31	.274	.361	.387
Elizabethton	Min	67	2153	559	107	18	51	855	372	310	332	4	566	23	9	14	60	25	.71	41	.260	.362	.397
Danville	Atl	66	2189	539	104	34	37	822	348	285	292	3	526	41	9	29	123	48	.72	36	.246	.342	.376
Princeton	Cin	68	2200	542	98	20	45	815	334	276	236	4	591	37	11	19	60	29	.67	41	.246	.327	.370
Burlington	Cle	67	2187	499	92	9	48	753	303	258	237	5	600	28	10	14	79	35	.69	31	.228	.310	.344
Martinsville	Phi	67	2187	519	87	16	25	713	269	227	209	2	526	31	7	14	83	36	.70	40	.237	.311	.326
Bristol	ChA	68	2163	488	89	7	41	714	244	216	178	6	537	32	17	19	70	41	.63	51	.226	.292	.330
Total		303	19878	5019	935	156	400	7466	3170	2643	2340	41	4868	320	101	178	833	330	.72	357	.252	.338	.376

Appalachian League Pitching - R+

HOW MUCH THEY PITCHED								WHAT THEY GAVE UP												THE RESULTS					
Team	Org	G	GS	CG	GF	IP	BFP	H	R	ER	HR	SH	SF	HB	TBB	IBB	SO	WP	Bk	W	L	Pct.	ShO	Sv	ERA
Kingsport	NYN	67	67	4	63	573.1	2400	451	246	197	28	14	11	36	247	6	619	60	16	48	19	.716	12	20	3.09
Danville	Atl	66	66	0	66	578	2498	522	296	226	28	16	23	33	218	4	541	61	5	37	29	.561	5	21	3.52
Elizabethton	Min	67	67	4	63	554.2	2439	553	323	254	48	10	14	38	209	0	545	57	8	40	27	.597	4	14	4.12
Bluefield	Bal	68	68	3	65	574.2	2535	514	335	273	48	4	18	37	286	4	602	75	13	42	26	.618	6	14	4.28
Burlington	Cle	67	67	1	66	569.1	2520	554	348	277	40	8	15	29	227	0	542	65	9	29	38	.433	3	13	4.38
Johnson City	StL	68	68	1	67	585	2638	606	360	308	49	9	15	28	307	11	505	48	13	42	26	.618	2	20	4.74
Princeton	Cin	68	68	8	60	565	2524	532	370	285	42	12	27	28	279	3	572	85	13	28	40	.412	4	13	4.54
Bristol	ChA	68	68	8	60	569.2	2643	637	437	346	60	10	25	43	291	8	489	86	14	17	51	.250	2	8	5.47
Martinsville	Phi	67	67	2	65	557	2626	650	455	368	57	18	30	48	276	5	453	68	18	20	47	.299	2	14	5.95
Total		303	303	31	272	5126.2	22823	5019	3170	2534	400	101	178	320	2340	41	4868	605	109	303	303	.500	40	137	4.45

Arizona League Batting - R

BATTING																	BASERUNNING				PERCENTAGES		
Team	Org	G	AB	H	2B	3B	HR	TB	R	RBI	TBB	IBB	SO	HBP	SH	SF	SB	CS	SB%	GDP	Avg	OBP	SLG
Padres	SD	56	1939	538	83	38	23	766	345	289	196	3	379	28	11	22	73	34	.68	34	.277	.349	.395
Athletics	Oak	56	1917	479	101	27	26	712	322	264	236	4	446	45	10	16	99	29	.77	23	.250	.343	.371
Angels	Cal	56	1909	477	100	29	16	683	276	215	191	2	436	27	15	7	124	40	.76	32	.250	.326	.358
Mariners	Sea	56	1905	468	72	26	24	664	265	210	173	4	512	30	12	11	72	37	.66	32	.246	.317	.349
Diamondbacks	Ari	56	1912	461	74	28	11	624	265	210	223	3	527	38	4	19	72	26	.73	43	.241	.329	.326
Rockies	Col	56	1905	484	74	20	6	616	259	200	164	1	437	29	14	21	76	35	.68	35	.254	.319	.323
Total		168	11487	2907	504	168	106	4065	1732	1388	1183	17	2737	197	66	96	516	201	.72	199	.253	.331	.354

Arizona League Pitching - R

HOW MUCH THEY PITCHED								WHAT THEY GAVE UP												THE RESULTS					
Team	Org	G	GS	CG	GF	IP	BFP	H	R	ER	HR	SH	SF	HB	TBB	IBB	SO	WP	Bk	W	L	Pct.	ShO	Sv	ERA
Rockies	Col	56	56	2	54	489.1	2161	489	269	191	7	12	12	41	158	0	451	46	15	26	30	.464	6	14	3.51
Mariners	Sea	56	56	1	55	497	2183	462	271	203	20	10	12	32	211	4	478	40	11	29	27	.518	5	17	3.68
Padres	SD	56	56	2	54	498.2	2192	488	276	198	22	8	19	24	203	1	471	30	11	36	20	.643	2	16	3.57
Athletics	Oak	56	56	0	56	493.1	2172	498	293	236	15	12	18	30	195	4	468	54	16	33	23	.589	2	15	4.31
Diamondbacks	Ari	56	56	0	56	490	2131	479	294	211	20	16	14	30	201	4	426	42	10	20	36	.357	1	5	3.88
Angels	Cal	56	56	4	52	487	2195	491	329	251	22	8	21	40	215	4	443	52	10	24	32	.429	5	12	4.64
Total		168	168	9	159	2955.1	13034	2907	1732	1290	106	66	96	197	1183	17	2737	264	73	168	168	.500	21	79	3.93

Gulf Coast League Batting - R

		BATTING															BASERUNNING				PERCENTAGES		
Team	Org	G	AB	H	2B	3B	HR	TB	R	RBI	TBB	IBB	SO	HBP	SH	SF	SB	CS	SB%	GDP	Avg	OBP	SLG
Yankees	NYA	58	1948	560	101	21	17	754	345	298	190	6	387	43	12	25	32	20	.62	30	.287	.359	.387
Rangers	Tex	60	1992	487	91	27	35	737	304	261	176	2	497	47	23	21	117	29	.80	22	.244	.318	.370
Expos	Mon	59	1884	443	76	25	11	602	299	239	206	11	353	27	33	14	82	42	.66	17	.235	.317	.320
Cubs	ChN	60	1969	498	72	16	30	692	285	219	196	3	455	47	24	18	178	55	.76	42	.253	.332	.351
Pirates	Pit	60	1995	510	82	27	20	706	284	241	186	4	367	22	9	12	63	34	.65	54	.256	.324	.354
Red Sox	Bos	60	2035	516	105	15	22	717	279	228	184	1	481	42	12	18	71	40	.64	36	.254	.326	.352
Orioles	Bal	60	1978	490	84	20	15	659	271	221	198	3	423	31	19	16	96	43	.69	43	.248	.323	.333
Tigers	Det	60	1918	439	91	19	15	613	264	217	204	2	513	56	11	15	91	24	.79	30	.229	.319	.320
Astros	Hou	59	1898	462	92	18	20	650	263	224	171	6	469	34	20	17	85	39	.69	34	.243	.315	.342
Twins	Min	60	1917	473	86	22	18	657	262	214	183	4	389	32	17	18	103	40	.72	36	.247	.320	.343
Marlins	Fla	59	1944	476	76	8	16	616	257	208	175	5	421	49	20	15	84	34	.71	40	.245	.321	.317
Mets	NYN	59	1865	453	78	20	20	631	249	202	189	5	384	28	16	12	55	35	.61	25	.243	.320	.338
Devil Rays	TB	59	1979	460	61	18	9	584	240	205	175	2	505	24	20	11	76	33	.70	32	.232	.301	.295
White Sox	ChA	60	1980	484	93	17	14	653	236	192	173	1	442	39	18	12	47	28	.63	38	.244	.316	.330
Royals	KC	60	1904	469	94	9	18	635	227	188	160	5	378	38	22	7	29	22	.57	43	.246	.316	.334
Braves	Atl	59	1883	398	75	6	7	506	155	129	143	3	419	31	36	9	27	33	.45	15	.211	.277	.269
Total		476	31089	7618	1357	288	287	10412	4220	3486	2909	63	6883	590	312	240	1236	551	.69	537	.245	.319	.335

Gulf Coast League Pitching - R

		HOW MUCH THEY PITCHED						WHAT THEY GAVE UP												THE RESULTS					
Team	Org	G	GS	CG	GF	IP	BFP	H	R	ER	HR	SH	SF	HB	TBB	IBB	SO	WP	Bk	W	L	Pct.	ShO	Sv	ERA
Marlins	Fla	59	59	4	55	516.2	2122	396	210	158	13	25	13	31	181	10	416	50	16	34	25	.576	10	11	2.75
Expos	Mon	59	59	3	56	507.2	2111	431	221	177	16	25	11	35	150	0	343	31	16	41	18	.695	7	16	3.14
Cubs	ChN	60	60	1	59	527.1	2201	424	230	166	11	13	10	49	188	1	485	48	15	34	26	.567	3	15	2.83
Rangers	Tex	60	60	4	56	527.1	2223	467	232	175	24	17	15	24	196	8	431	47	15	37	23	.617	4	20	2.99
Mets	NYN	59	59	4	55	495	2127	449	236	192	13	22	11	31	178	5	439	50	23	29	30	.492	5	18	3.49
Orioles	Bal	60	60	1	59	525	2202	456	238	187	21	17	19	32	175	1	451	39	11	36	24	.600	6	20	3.21
Astros	Hou	59	59	1	58	505.1	2178	447	247	184	13	15	17	43	191	3	515	70	15	31	28	.525	5	14	3.28
Yankees	NYA	58	58	2	56	484.2	2089	452	256	194	19	12	11	31	178	0	453	41	13	37	21	.638	9	13	3.60
Twins	Min	60	60	5	55	506	2159	493	258	190	21	14	12	27	183	2	389	48	12	30	30	.500	2	12	3.38
Royals	KC	60	60	3	57	495.1	2162	495	279	223	30	16	20	42	165	0	427	42	15	30	29	.508	4	14	4.05
Pirates	Pit	60	60	3	57	511.2	2256	511	291	214	18	19	15	45	184	0	418	36	10	28	31	.475	4	14	3.76
Braves	Atl	59	59	0	59	505	2221	494	293	229	12	33	15	38	204	9	379	59	23	14	45	.237	1	6	4.08
Devil Rays	TB	59	59	2	57	517.1	2278	495	304	243	11	19	23	45	199	11	501	60	25	24	35	.407	0	12	4.23
Tigers	Det	60	60	0	60	505	2233	527	305	218	18	17	17	38	172	2	405	62	12	26	34	.433	2	10	3.89
Red Sox	Bos	60	60	0	60	527	2332	546	308	216	25	30	16	41	173	8	423	52	26	24	36	.400	3	10	3.69
White Sox	ChA	60	60	4	56	510.2	2263	535	312	238	22	18	15	38	192	3	408	42	15	20	40	.333	3	10	4.19
Total		476	476	37	439	8167	35157	7618	4220	3204	287	312	240	590	2909	63	6883	777	262	475	475	.500	68	215	3.53

Pioneer League Batting - R+

BATTING																	BASERUNNING				PERCENTAGES		
Team	Org	G	AB	H	2B	3B	HR	TB	R	RBI	TBB	IBB	SO	HBP	SH	SF	SB	CS	SB%	GDP	Avg	OBP	SLG
Lethbridge	Ari	72	2583	811	133	25	88	1258	637	558	407	8	579	53	12	46	93	36	.72	51	.314	.411	.487
Helena	Mil	72	2544	755	122	19	68	1119	543	459	362	16	464	49	19	31	80	48	.63	48	.297	.390	.440
Butte	TB	72	2651	819	143	44	42	1176	533	442	272	5	507	54	17	34	97	38	.72	60	.309	.380	.444
Ogden	Mil	72	2551	770	146	20	68	1160	525	428	332	4	499	51	27	29	102	44	.70	54	.302	.389	.455
Idaho Falls	SD	72	2597	765	135	28	48	1100	465	392	305	3	547	43	4	33	105	36	.74	53	.295	.374	.424
Billings	Cin	72	2569	683	122	28	54	1023	462	399	329	11	603	44	18	27	83	33	.72	39	.266	.356	.398
Great Falls	LA	72	2490	702	113	35	56	1053	440	370	252	3	597	39	8	24	140	74	.65	30	.282	.354	.423
Medicine Hat	Tor	72	2412	617	109	9	57	915	410	339	311	3	605	26	23	23	113	44	.72	40	.256	.344	.379
Total		288	20397	5922	1023	208	481	8804	4015	3387	2570	53	4401	359	128	247	813	353	.70	375	.290	.375	.432

Pioneer League Pitching - R+

HOW MUCH THEY PITCHED								WHAT THEY GAVE UP												THE RESULTS					
Team	Org	G	GS	CG	GF	IP	BFP	H	R	ER	HR	SH	SF	HB	TBB	IBB	SO	WP	Bk	W	L	Pct.	ShO	Sv	ERA
Lethbridge	Ari	72	72	1	71	632.2	2772	650	339	259	41	18	27	44	234	6	576	57	7	50	22	.694	5	13	3.68
Ogden	Mil	72	72	1	71	637.1	2931	654	441	342	57	17	20	43	326	8	627	99	16	42	30	.583	1	19	4.83
Idaho Falls	SD	72	72	1	71	633.1	2881	718	452	386	56	21	27	47	291	4	538	82	15	38	34	.528	1	13	5.49
Helena	Mil	72	72	1	71	631	2940	727	479	396	66	14	36	35	338	2	602	67	13	43	29	.597	1	20	5.65
Butte	TB	72	72	0	72	638.1	3013	767	516	376	52	21	24	46	323	9	602	93	15	37	35	.514	1	16	5.30
Great Falls	LA	72	72	1	71	623.2	2990	729	544	448	45	12	33	48	348	9	486	90	21	33	39	.458	0	17	6.46
Billings	Cin	72	72	2	70	633.2	3130	875	603	477	72	16	41	57	323	9	521	90	16	23	49	.319	1	9	6.77
Medicine Hat	Tor	72	72	2	70	609	3049	803	641	509	92	9	39	39	387	6	449	90	14	22	50	.306	3	16	7.52
Total		288	288	9	279	5039	23706	5923	4015	3193	481	128	247	359	2570	53	4401	668	117	288	288	.500	13	123	5.70

1996 Leader Boards

This is where to find the high minors' best and brightest. The leader boards cover everyone in Double-A and Triple-A. Batters need 383 plate appearances to qualify, and pitchers must throw at least 112 innings. If a player split time between Double-A and Triple-A, we present his combined totals.

League Abbreviations

AMAS - American Association	PCL - Pacific Coast League
EAST - Eastern League	SOU - Southern League
INT - International League	TEX - Texas League

Triple-A/Double-A Batting Leaders

Batting Average

Player, Team	Lg	Org	Avg
Vladimir Guerrero, Harrisburg	**EAST**	**Mon**	**.360**
Billy McMillon, Charlotte	INT	Fla	.352
Brian Raabe, Salt Lake	PCL	Min	.351
Brent Brede, Salt Lake	PCL	Min	.348
Dan Rohrmeier, Memphis	SOU	SD	.344
Wilton Guerrero, Albuquerque	PCL	LA	.344
Todd Dunn, El Paso	TEX	Mil	.340
Todd Walker, Salt Lake	PCL	Min	.339
Desi Wilson, Phoenix	PCL	SF	.339
Pedro Castellano, Colorado Springs	PCL	Col	.337
Adam Hyzdu, Trenton	EAST	Bos	.337
Angel Echevarria, Colorado Springs	PCL	Col	.337
Todd Helton, Colorado Springs	PCL	Col	.336
Dmitri Young, Louisville	AMAS	StL	.333
Jermaine Allensworth, Calgary	PCL	Pit	.330

On-Base Percentage

Player, Team	Lg	Org	OBP
Tom Evans, Knoxville	**SOU**	**Tor**	**.452**
Brent Brede, Salt Lake	PCL	Min	.446
Vladimir Guerrero, Harrisburg	EAST	Mon	.438
Dan Rohrmeier, Memphis	SOU	SD	.435
Todd Helton, Colorado Springs	PCL	Col	.427
Adam Hyzdu, Trenton	EAST	Bos	.424
Jeff Patzke, Knoxville	SOU	Tor	.418
Billy McMillon, Charlotte	INT	Fla	.418
Scott Rolen, Scranton/Wilkes-Barre	INT	Phi	.416
Doug Mirabelli, Shreveport	TEX	SF	.414
Todd Dunn, El Paso	TEX	Mil	.412
Lauro Felix, El Paso	TEX	Mil	.412
Kevin Riggs, Norwich	EAST	NYA	.412
Ray Brown, Chattanooga	SOU	Cin	.412
Luis Castillo, Portland	EAST	Fla	.411

Slugging Percentage

Player, Team	Lg	Org	Slg
Lee Stevens, Oklahoma City	**AMAS**	**Tex**	**.643**
Adam Hyzdu, Trenton	EAST	Bos	.618
Vladimir Guerrero, Harrisburg	EAST	Mon	.612
Bubba Trammell, Toledo	INT	Det	.605
Billy McMillon, Charlotte	INT	Fla	.602
Mike Cameron, Birmingham	SOU	ChA	.600
Kelly Stinnett, New Orleans	AMAS	Mil	.599
Todd Walker, Salt Lake	PCL	Min	.599
Dale Sveum, Calgary	PCL	Pit	.595
Todd Dunn, El Paso	TEX	Mil	.593
Dan Rohrmeier, Memphis	SOU	SD	.592
Jon Nunnally, Omaha	AMAS	KC	.583
Rudy Pemberton, Pawtucket	INT	Bos	.580
Tyrone Woods, Trenton	EAST	Bos	.579
Jerry Brooks, Charlotte	INT	Fla	.577

Home Runs

Player, Team	Lg	Org	HR
Phil Hiatt, Toledo	**INT**	**Det**	**42**
Jerry Brooks, Charlotte	INT	Fla	34
Derrek Lee, Memphis	SOU	SD	34
Bubba Trammell, Toledo	INT	Det	33
Lee Stevens, Oklahoma City	AMAS	Tex	32
Shane Spencer, Columbus	INT	NYA	32
Bubba Smith, Tulsa	TEX	Tex	32
Jose Oliva, Louisville	AMAS	StL	31
Chris Hatcher, Tucson	PCL	Hou	31
Nigel Wilson, Buffalo	AMAS	Cle	30
Paul Konerko, Albuquerque	PCL	LA	30
Rudy Pemberton, Pawtucket	INT	Bos	29
Ricky Ledee, Columbus	INT	NYA	29
Several tied at			28

Runs Batted In

Player, Team	Lg	Org	RBI
Phil Hiatt, Toledo	**INT**	**Det**	**119**
Todd Walker, Salt Lake	PCL	Min	111
Jerry Brooks, Charlotte	INT	Fla	107
Chris Saunders, Binghamton	EAST	NYN	105
Derrek Lee, Memphis	SOU	SD	104
Rudy Pemberton, Pawtucket	INT	Bos	103
Ricky Ledee, Columbus	INT	NYA	101
Bubba Trammell, Toledo	INT	Det	99
Ryan Jones, Knoxville	SOU	Tor	97
Chris Hatcher, Tucson	PCL	Hou	97
Ivan Cruz, Columbus	INT	NYA	96
Several tied at			95

Stolen Bases

Player, Team	Lg	Org	SB
Luis Castillo, Portland	**EAST**	**Fla**	**51**
Essex Burton, Reading	EAST	Phi	45
Dante Powell, Phoenix	PCL	SF	43
Jeremy Carr, Wichita	TEX	KC	41
Curtis Goodwin, Indianapolis	AMAS	Cin	40
Mike Cameron, Birmingham	SOU	ChA	39
Kerwin Moore, Edmonton	PCL	Oak	38
Rod Myers, Omaha	AMAS	KC	37
Tony Womack, Calgary	PCL	Pit	37
Rick Holifield, Trenton	EAST	Bos	36
Shannon Stewart, Syracuse	INT	Tor	35
Mitch Simons, Salt Lake	PCL	Min	35
Donnie Sadler, Trenton	EAST	Bos	34
Billy Hall, Chattanooga	SOU	Cin	34
Several tied at			33

Triple-A/Double-A Batting Leaders

Catchers Batting Average

Player, Team	Lg	Org	Avg
Chris Widger, Tacoma	**PCL**	**Sea**	**.304**
Walt McKeel, Trenton	EAST	Bos	.302
Mike Sweeney, Omaha	AMAS	KC	.301
Doug Mirabelli, Shreveport	TEX	SF	.295
Paul Bako, Chattanooga	SOU	Cin	.294
Phil Nevin, Jacksonville	SOU	Det	.294
Willie Morales, Huntsville	SOU	Oak	.292
Sean Mulligan, Las Vegas	PCL	SD	.288
Kelly Stinnett, New Orleans	AMAS	Mil	.287
Mike Redmond, Portland	EAST	Fla	.287
Damian Miller, Salt Lake	PCL	Min	.286
Einar Diaz, Canton-Akron	EAST	Cle	.281
Brook Fordyce, Indianapolis	AMAS	Cin	.275
Ben Molina, Midland	TEX	Cal	.274
Jorge Posada, Columbus	INT	NYA	.271

First Basemen Batting Average

Player, Team	Lg	Org	Avg
Desi Wilson, Phoenix	**PCL**	**SF**	**.339**
Todd Helton, Colorado Springs	PCL	Col	.336
Dmitri Young, Louisville	AMAS	StL	.333
Ray Brown, Chattanooga	SOU	Cin	.327
Jeff Ball, Tucson	PCL	Hou	.324
Kevin Millar, Portland	EAST	Fla	.318
Luis Ortiz, Oklahoma City	AMAS	Tex	.317
Jon Zuber, Scranton/Wilkes-Barre	INT	Phi	.311
Paul Konerko, Albuquerque	PCL	LA	.304
Brian Rupp, Arkansas	TEX	StL	.303
Jason M Thompson, Las Vegas	PCL	SD	.300
Larry Sutton, Wichita	TEX	KC	.296
Chris Pritchett, Vancouver	PCL	Cal	.295
Webster Garrison, Edmonton	PCL	Oak	.294
Several tied at			.292

Second Basemen Batting Average

Player, Team	Lg	Org	Avg
Brian Raabe, Salt Lake	**PCL**	**Min**	**.351**
Wilton Guerrero, Albuquerque	PCL	LA	.344
Kary Bridges, Tucson	PCL	Hou	.322
Dave Hajek, Tucson	PCL	Hou	.317
Luis Castillo, Portland	EAST	Fla	.317
Casey Candaele, Buffalo	AMAS	Cle	.311
Jeff Patzke, Knoxville	SOU	Tor	.303
Frank Catalanotto, Jacksonville	SOU	Det	.298
Marty Malloy, Greenville	SOU	Atl	.298
Billy Hall, Chattanooga	SOU	Cin	.295
Frankie Menechino, Birmingham	SOU	ChA	.292
Kevin Riggs, Norwich	EAST	NYA	.290
Jeff Berblinger, Arkansas	TEX	StL	.288
Several tied at			.287

Third Basemen Batting Average

Player, Team	Lg	Org	Avg
Todd Walker, Salt Lake	**PCL**	**Min**	**.339**
Pedro Castellano, Colorado Springs	PCL	Col	.337
Phil Clark, Pawtucket	INT	Bos	.325
Scott Rolen, Scranton/Wilkes-Barre	INT	Phi	.324
Matt Franco, Norfolk	INT	NYN	.323
Jose Olmeda, Charlotte	INT	Fla	.320
Brad Seitzer, El Paso	TEX	Mil	.319
Enrique Wilson, Buffalo	AMAS	Cle	.307
Reed Secrist, Calgary	PCL	Pit	.307
Bill Mueller, Phoenix	PCL	SF	.302
Ruben Santana, Indianapolis	AMAS	Cin	.300
Dale Sveum, Calgary	PCL	Pit	.300
Kevin Orie, Iowa	AMAS	ChN	.299
Chris Saunders, Binghamton	EAST	NYN	.298
Don Sparks, Buffalo	AMAS	Cle	.295

Shortstops Batting Average

Player, Team	Lg	Org	Avg
Neifi Perez, Colorado Springs	**PCL**	**Col**	**.316**
Russ Johnson, Jackson	TEX	Hou	.310
Aaron Ledesma, Vancouver	PCL	Cal	.305
Dave Berg, Portland	EAST	Fla	.302
Clay Bellinger, Rochester	INT	Bal	.301
Scott Sheldon, Edmonton	PCL	Oak	.300
Tony Womack, Calgary	PCL	Pit	.298
Hanley Frias, Tulsa	TEX	Tex	.287
Greg Norton, Nashville	AMAS	ChA	.284
Eddy Diaz, Tacoma	PCL	Sea	.280
Lou Collier, Carolina	SOU	Pit	.280
Chris Clapinski, Charlotte	INT	Fla	.280
Tilson Brito, Syracuse	INT	Tor	.278
Brandon Cromer, Knoxville	SOU	Tor	.277
Several tied at			.274

Outfielders Batting Average

Player, Team	Lg	Org	Avg
Vladimir Guerrero, Harrisburg	**EAST**	**Mon**	**.360**
Billy McMillon, Charlotte	INT	Fla	.352
Brent Brede, Salt Lake	PCL	Min	.348
Todd Dunn, El Paso	TEX	Mil	.340
Adam Hyzdu, Trenton	EAST	Bos	.337
Angel Echevarria, Colorado Springs	PCL	Col	.337
Jermaine Allensworth, Calgary	PCL	Pit	.330
Alex Ramirez, Canton-Akron	EAST	Cle	.329
Jeff Abbott, Nashville	AMAS	ChA	.325
Jalal Leach, Ottawa	INT	Mon	.325
Raul Rodarte, Richmond	INT	Atl	.322
Steve Bieser, Ottawa	INT	Mon	.322
Brent Bowers, Rochester	INT	Bal	.318
Bubba Trammell, Toledo	INT	Det	.316
Several tied at			.315

Triple-A/Double-A Batting Leaders

Hits

Player, Team	Lg	Org	H
Todd Walker, Salt Lake	**PCL**	**Min**	**187**
Neifi Perez, Colorado Springs	PCL	Col	180
Alex Ramirez, Canton-Akron	EAST	Cle	169
Brian Raabe, Salt Lake	PCL	Min	169
Brent Brede, Salt Lake	PCL	Min	168
Matt Franco, Norfolk	INT	NYN	164
Dan Rohrmeier, Memphis	SOU	SD	162
Dave Hajek, Tucson	PCL	Hou	161
Luis Ortiz, Oklahoma City	AMAS	Tex	159
Aaron Boone, Chattanooga	SOU	Cin	158
Bubba Trammell, Toledo	INT	Det	155
Kary Bridges, Tucson	PCL	Hou	154
Russ Johnson, Jackson	TEX	Hou	154
Several tied at			153

Doubles

Player, Team	Lg	Org	2B
Aaron Boone, Chattanooga	**SOU**	**Cin**	**44**
Magglio Ordonez, Birmingham	SOU	ChA	41
Todd Walker, Salt Lake	PCL	Min	41
Matt Franco, Norfolk	INT	NYN	40
Chris Pritchett, Vancouver	PCL	Cal	39
Brian Raabe, Salt Lake	PCL	Min	39
Scott Rolen, Scranton/Wilkes-Barre	INT	Phi	39
Derrek Lee, Memphis	SOU	SD	39
Brent Brede, Salt Lake	PCL	Min	38
Tom Quinlan, Salt Lake	PCL	Min	38
Lee Stevens, Oklahoma City	AMAS	Tex	37
Bubba Trammell, Toledo	INT	Det	37
Tracy Woodson, Columbus	INT	NYA	37
Several tied at			36

Triples

Player, Team	Lg	Org	3B
Bob Abreu, Tucson	**PCL**	**Hou**	**16**
Demond Smith, Edmonton	PCL	Oak	14
Chance Sanford, Carolina	SOU	Pit	13
Mike Cameron, Birmingham	SOU	ChA	12
Alex Ramirez, Canton-Akron	EAST	Cle	12
Hanley Frias, Tulsa	TEX	Tex	12
Wilton Guerrero, Albuquerque	PCL	LA	12
Neifi Perez, Colorado Springs	PCL	Col	12
Kerwin Moore, Edmonton	PCL	Oak	11
Karim Garcia, Albuquerque	PCL	LA	11
Tony Womack, Calgary	PCL	Pit	11
Brad Tyler, Rochester	INT	Bal	10
Joe Hall, Rochester	INT	Bal	10
Several tied at			9

Extra Base Hits

Player, Team	Lg	Org	XBH
Todd Walker, Salt Lake	**PCL**	**Min**	**78**
Derrek Lee, Memphis	SOU	SD	75
Mike Cameron, Birmingham	SOU	ChA	74
Bubba Trammell, Toledo	INT	Det	73
Phil Hiatt, Toledo	INT	Det	72
Lee Stevens, Oklahoma City	AMAS	Tex	71
Ricky Ledee, Columbus	INT	NYA	69
Aaron Boone, Chattanooga	SOU	Cin	68
Chris Hatcher, Tucson	PCL	Hou	66
Jerry Brooks, Charlotte	INT	Fla	65
Jonas Hamlin, El Paso	TEX	Mil	64
Rudy Pemberton, Pawtucket	INT	Bos	63
Tracy Woodson, Columbus	INT	NYA	63
Brian Raabe, Salt Lake	PCL	Min	61
Several tied at			60

Plate Appearances per Strikeout

Player, Team	Lg	Org	PA/K
Brian Raabe, Salt Lake	**PCL**	**Min**	**28.37**
Kary Bridges, Tucson	PCL	Hou	24.23
Einar Diaz, Canton-Akron	EAST	Cle	19.00
Ben Molina, Midland	TEX	Cal	16.20
Dave Hajek, Tucson	PCL	Hou	14.97
Luis Ortiz, Oklahoma City	AMAS	Tex	14.81
Tony Medrano, Wichita	TEX	KC	13.97
Kevin Long, Wichita	TEX	KC	13.89
Vernon Spearman, San Antonio	TEX	LA	13.71
Edgar Caceres, New Orleans	AMAS	Mil	13.41
Jaime Torres, Columbus	INT	NYA	12.75
Neifi Perez, Colorado Springs	PCL	Col	12.65
Phil Clark, Pawtucket	INT	Bos	12.47
Bill Mueller, Phoenix	PCL	SF	12.20
Casey Candaele, Buffalo	AMAS	Cle	12.17

Switch-Hitters Batting Average

Player, Team	Lg	Org	Avg
Dmitri Young, Louisville	**AMAS**	**StL**	**.333**
Steve Bieser, Ottawa	INT	Mon	.322
Jose Olmeda, Charlotte	INT	Fla	.320
Luis Castillo, Portland	EAST	Fla	.317
Neifi Perez, Colorado Springs	PCL	Col	.316
Casey Candaele, Buffalo	AMAS	Cle	.311
Enrique Wilson, Buffalo	AMAS	Cle	.307
Eddie Christian, Midland	TEX	Cal	.305
Jeff Patzke, Knoxville	SOU	Tor	.303
Bill Mueller, Phoenix	PCL	SF	.302
Dale Sveum, Calgary	PCL	Pit	.300
Dwayne Hosey, Pawtucket	INT	Bos	.297
Billy Hall, Chattanooga	SOU	Cin	.295
Tony Mitchell, Toledo	INT	Det	.291
Terry Jones, Colorado Springs	PCL	Col	.288

Triple-A/Double-A Pitching Leaders

Earned Run Average

Player, Team	Lg	Org	ERA
Chris Peters, Calgary	**PCL**	**Pit**	**2.26**
Shane Dennis, Memphis	SOU	SD	2.27
Curt Lyons, Chattanooga	SOU	Cin	2.41
Barry Johnson, Nashville	AMAS	ChA	2.53
Carl Pavano, Trenton	EAST	Bos	2.63
Tony Saunders, Portland	EAST	Fla	2.63
Matt Herges, Albuquerque	PCL	LA	2.68
Bob Milacki, Tacoma	PCL	Sea	2.74
Keith Foulke, Shreveport	TEX	SF	2.76
Joe Crawford, Norfolk	INT	NYN	2.77
Mike Oquist, Las Vegas	PCL	SD	2.89
Rick Helling, Oklahoma City	AMAS	Tex	2.96
Brian Bevil, Omaha	AMAS	KC	3.01
Brian Givens, New Orleans	AMAS	Mil	3.02
Mike Fyhrie, Norfolk	INT	NYN	3.04

Wins

Player, Team	Lg	Org	W
Carl Pavano, Trenton	**EAST**	**Bos**	**16**
Brian Bevil, Omaha	**AMAS**	**KC**	**16**
Brian Moehler, Jacksonville	SOU	Det	15
Mike Fyhrie, Norfolk	INT	NYN	15
Cory Lidle, Binghamton	EAST	NYN	14
Travis Buckley, Indianapolis	AMAS	Cin	14
Jonathan Johnson, Tulsa	TEX	Tex	14
Several tied at			13

Saves

Player, Team	Lg	Org	Sv
Sean Maloney, El Paso	**TEX**	**Mil**	**38**
Domingo Jean, Chattanooga	SOU	Cin	31
Rick Greene, Jacksonville	SOU	Det	30
Bill Hurst, Portland	EAST	Fla	30
Mike Welch, Norfolk	INT	NYN	29
Richard Batchelor, Louisville	AMAS	StL	28
Steve Mintz, Phoenix	PCL	SF	27
Stacy Jones, Nashville	AMAS	ChA	26
Paul Crow, Port City	SOU	Sea	26
Dave Pavlas, Columbus	INT	NYA	26
Derek Wallace, Norfolk	INT	NYN	26
Jaime Bluma, Omaha	AMAS	KC	25
David Wainhouse, Carolina	SOU	Pit	25
Wayne Gomes, Reading	EAST	Phi	24
Several tied at			23

Games Pitched

Player, Team	Lg	Org	GP
Wayne Gomes, Reading	**EAST**	**Phi**	**67**
Matt Arrandale, Louisville	AMAS	StL	63
Tom Martin, Jackson	TEX	Hou	62
Danny Rios, Columbus	INT	NYA	62
Jim Nix, Chattanooga	SOU	Cin	62
Ricky Trlicek, Norfolk	INT	NYN	62
Jeff Matranga, Arkansas	TEX	StL	62
Frank Lankford, Norwich	EAST	NYA	61
Steve Rain, Iowa	AMAS	ChN	61
Rich Sauveur, Nashville	AMAS	ChA	61
Several tied at			60

Complete Games

Player, Team	Lg	Org	CG
Jason Dickson, Vancouver	**PCL**	**Cal**	**10**
Jeff Suppan, Pawtucket	INT	Bos	7
Jonathan Johnson, Tulsa	TEX	Tex	7
Carl Pavano, Trenton	EAST	Bos	6
Cory Lidle, Binghamton	EAST	NYN	6
Dennis Springer, Vancouver	PCL	Cal	6
Nate Minchey, Pawtucket	INT	Bos	6
Scott Klingenbeck, Salt Lake	PCL	Min	5
Richard Pratt, Birmingham	SOU	ChA	5
Bob Milacki, Tacoma	PCL	Sea	5
Joe Roa, Buffalo	AMAS	Cle	5
Brad Woodall, Richmond	INT	Atl	5
Several tied at			4

Shutouts

Player, Team	Lg	Org	ShO
Matt Morris, Louisville	**AMAS**	**StL**	**4**
Calvin Maduro, Rochester	INT	Bal	3
Several tied at			2

Triple-A/Double-A Pitching Leaders

Strikeouts

Player, Team	Lg	Org	K
Curt Lyons, Chattanooga	**SOU**	**Cin**	**176**
Brett Tomko, Chattanooga	SOU	Cin	164
Brad Kaufman, Memphis	SOU	SD	163
Fernando Hernandez, Memphis	SOU	SD	161
Rick Helling, Oklahoma City	AMAS	Tex	157
Heath Murray, Memphis	SOU	SD	156
Tony Saunders, Portland	EAST	Fla	156
Tom Fordham, Nashville	AMAS	ChA	155
Mark Brownson, New Haven	EAST	Col	155
Chris Carpenter, Knoxville	SOU	Tor	150
Everett Stull, Ottawa	INT	Mon	150
Travis Driskill, Canton-Akron	EAST	Cle	148
John Thomson, Colorado Springs	PCL	Col	148
Brian Bevil, Omaha	AMAS	KC	147
Several tied at			146

Strikeouts per 9 IP — Starters

Player, Team	Lg	Org	K/9
Curt Lyons, Chattanooga	**SOU**	**Cin**	**11.18**
Rick Helling, Oklahoma City	AMAS	Tex	10.09
Fernando Hernandez, Memphis	SOU	SD	9.83
Brett Tomko, Chattanooga	SOU	Cin	9.36
Brian Bevil, Omaha	AMAS	KC	9.23
Everett Stull, Ottawa	INT	Mon	9.02
Matt Beech, Scranton/Wilkes-Barre	INT	Phi	8.86
Livan Hernandez, Portland	EAST	Fla	8.85
Jeff Suppan, Pawtucket	INT	Bos	8.79
Tony Saunders, Portland	EAST	Fla	8.37
Brad Kaufman, Memphis	SOU	SD	8.23
Mo Sanford, Oklahoma City	AMAS	Tex	8.18
Mark Mimbs, Albuquerque	PCL	LA	8.11
Salomon Torres, Tacoma	PCL	Sea	8.11
Heath Murray, Memphis	SOU	SD	8.07

Strikeouts per 9 IP — Relievers

Player, Team	Lg	Org	K/9
Wayne Gomes, Reading	**EAST**	**Phi**	**11.05**
Mariano De Los Santos, Carolina	SOU	Pit	10.72
Ken Robinson, Syracuse	INT	Tor	10.39
Kevin Lovingier, Arkansas	TEX	StL	10.32
Carlos Almanzar, Knoxville	SOU	Tor	9.98
Andy Croghan, Norwich	EAST	NYA	9.95
Mike Grzanich, Jackson	TEX	Hou	9.95
Steve Rain, Iowa	AMAS	ChN	9.88
Dan Hubbs, Albuquerque	PCL	LA	9.75
Jason Hart, Orlando	SOU	ChN	9.62
Mark Lee, Richmond	INT	Atl	9.54
Jim Nix, Chattanooga	SOU	Cin	9.40
Richard Batchelor, Louisville	AMAS	StL	9.38
Vic Darensbourg, Charlotte	INT	Fla	9.38
Scott Fredrickson, Colorado Springs	PCL	Col	9.33

Innings Pitched

Player, Team	Lg	Org	IP
Geoff Edsell, Vancouver	**PCL**	**Cal**	**193.0**
Cory Lidle, Binghamton	EAST	NYN	190.1
Wade Walker, Orlando	SOU	ChN	187.2
Chris Holt, Tucson	PCL	Hou	186.1
Jason Dickson, Vancouver	PCL	Cal	185.2
Julio Santana, Oklahoma City	AMAS	Tex	185.2
Carl Pavano, Trenton	EAST	Bos	185.0
Jonathan Johnson, Tulsa	TEX	Tex	183.1
Rich Loiselle, Calgary	PCL	Pit	182.2
Keith Foulke, Shreveport	TEX	SF	182.2
Ryan Franklin, Port City	SOU	Sea	182.0
Rick Reed, Norfolk	INT	NYN	182.0
Gary Rath, Albuquerque	PCL	LA	180.1
Jared Fernandez, Trenton	EAST	Bos	179.0
Brad Kaufman, Memphis	SOU	SD	178.1

Opponent Batting Average — Starters

Player, Team	Lg	Org	OAvg
Tony Saunders, Portland	**EAST**	**Fla**	**.203**
Matt Beech, Scranton/Wilkes-Barre	INT	Phi	.209
Bob Milacki, Tacoma	PCL	Sea	.216
Curt Lyons, Chattanooga	SOU	Cin	.220
Brian Bevil, Omaha	AMAS	KC	.221
Tom Fordham, Nashville	AMAS	ChA	.223
Keith Foulke, Shreveport	TEX	SF	.225
Brett Tomko, Chattanooga	SOU	Cin	.226
Carl Pavano, Trenton	EAST	Bos	.230
Mike Gardiner, Norfolk	INT	NYN	.231
Jeff Suppan, Pawtucket	INT	Bos	.233
Fernando Hernandez, Memphis	SOU	SD	.233
Matt Drews, Jacksonville	SOU	Det	.234
Heath Murray, Memphis	SOU	SD	.235
Mike Fyhrie, Norfolk	INT	NYN	.236

Opponent Batting Average — Relievers

Player, Team	Lg	Org	OAvg
Derek Wallace, Norfolk	**INT**	**NYN**	**.180**
Chuck Ricci, Pawtucket	INT	Bos	.194
Ricky Trlicek, Norfolk	INT	NYN	.194
Jeff Matranga, Arkansas	TEX	StL	.198
Rod Nichols, Richmond	INT	Atl	.202
Kerry Lacy, Pawtucket	INT	Bos	.207
Steve Rain, Iowa	AMAS	ChN	.207
Darryl Scott, Buffalo	AMAS	Cle	.208
Danny Rios, Columbus	INT	NYA	.218
Dave Pavlas, Columbus	INT	NYA	.219
Jason Hart, Orlando	SOU	ChN	.219
Ken Robinson, Syracuse	INT	Tor	.220
Ken Edenfield, Columbus	INT	NYA	.221
Wayne Gomes, Reading	EAST	Phi	.222
Felix Heredia, Portland	EAST	Fla	.223

1996 Park Data

After watching the Rockies for four years, by now, everyone seems to be pretty well convinced that a ballpark can have a huge impact on the statistics of the players who perform there. But Colorado isn't the only park that makes a difference; remember, there's also a Triple-A franchise in Colorado Springs. How does that park shape its players' stats? The following pages should help you to get a better idea.

In any given season, a pitcher's park can masquerade as a hitter's park, or vice-versa. For that reason, we decided to use four years' worth of data for the Double-A and Triple-A parks, whenever possible. If a new park was built during the last four years, or the dimensions of an existing park were altered, our data goes all the way back through to the first full year that the park existed in its current configuration. A single asterisk beside the data means that the park changed before the 1996 season, so we used the 1996 data only. Two asterisks means we used 1995-1996 data, and three asterisks means we used data from 1994 through 1996. For Single-A and Rookie league parks, we list splits for 1996 only.

What is a park index? It's a way of expressing the characteristics of a park in numerical terms, with 100 being neutral. A home-run index of 105 means that 5% more home runs were hit during the team's home games than during its road games. If 5% *fewer* homers were hit during the home games, the index would be 95. Pretty simple stuff, if you think about it. But just keep one thing in mind: if a guy played in a park with a home-run index of 140, don't go lopping off 40% his home runs. Remember, the guy also played half of his games *on the road.* Discounting his homers by about 20% would be much more realistic.

American Association — AAA

Buffalo* — Cleveland Indians — Surface: Grass

	G	Avg	AB	R	H	2B	3B	HR	SO
Home	72	.259	4755	663	1230	217	16	143	857
Road	72	.266	4879	692	1298	266	36	146	963
Index	—	97	97	96	95	84	46	100	91

Indianapolis* — Cincinnati Reds — Surface: Grass

	G	Avg	AB	R	H	2B	3B	HR	SO
Home	72	.256	4763	616	1219	239	31	123	964
Road	72	.255	4773	651	1215	242	28	138	966
Index	—	101	100	95	100	99	111	89	100

Iowa — Chicago Cubs — Surface: Grass

	G	Avg	AB	R	H	2B	3B	HR	SO
Home	288	.264	19162	2609	5066	1096	105	555	3525
Road	284	.270	18980	2591	5122	1007	122	489	3285
Index	—	98	100	99	98	108	85	112	106

Louisville — St. Louis Cardinals — Surface: Turf

	G	Avg	AB	R	H	2B	3B	HR	SO
Home	287	.261	19271	2686	5038	1007	175	575	3727
Road	287	.265	18944	2579	5019	1071	137	453	3352
Index	—	99	102	104	100	92	126	125	109

Nashville — Chicago White Sox — Surface: Grass

	G	Avg	AB	R	H	2B	3B	HR	SO
Home	286	.260	19326	2602	5023	966	123	507	3619
Road	289	.260	19196	2532	4992	997	127	505	3482
Index	—	100	102	104	102	96	96	100	103

New Orleans — Milwaukee Brewers — Surface: Grass

	G	Avg	AB	R	H	2B	3B	HR	SO
Home	285	.262	18714	2533	4912	1000	136	481	3506
Road	287	.264	19046	2654	5037	970	143	467	3315
Index	—	99	99	96	98	105	97	105	108

Oklahoma City — Texas Rangers — Surface: Grass

	G	Avg	AB	R	H	2B	3B	HR	SO
Home	287	.276	19276	2749	5312	1097	180	367	3437
Road	288	.264	19215	2679	5080	1000	124	534	3629
Index	—	104	101	103	105	109	145	69	94

Omaha — Kansas City Royals — Surface: Grass

	G	Avg	AB	R	H	2B	3B	HR	SO
Home	289	.277	19105	2905	5283	967	121	681	3085
Road	287	.267	19178	2682	5116	979	142	515	3555
Index	—	104	99	108	103	99	86	133	87

International League — AAA

Charlotte — Florida Marlins — Surface: Grass

	G	Avg	AB	R	H	2B	3B	HR	SO
Home	284	.277	19230	2921	5323	923	99	687	3250
Road	281	.269	18637	2741	5012	952	136	467	3283
Index	—	103	102	105	105	94	71	143	96

Columbus — New York Yankees — Surface: Turf

	G	Avg	AB	R	H	2B	3B	HR	SO
Home	286	.264	18973	2809	5018	1056	206	463	3609
Road	279	.264	18391	2605	4864	933	124	480	3471
Index	—	100	101	105	101	110	161	93	101

Norfolk — New York Mets — Surface: Grass

	G	Avg	AB	R	H	2B	3B	HR	SO
Home	281	.249	18442	2145	4586	837	141	287	3321
Road	285	.263	19142	2540	5033	922	170	467	3455
Index	—	95	98	86	92	94	86	64	100

Ottawa — Montreal Expos — Surface: Grass

	G	Avg	AB	R	H	2B	3B	HR	SO
Home	284	.260	18855	2480	4900	1019	130	322	3306
Road	284	.268	18611	2696	4989	928	138	500	3450
Index	—	97	101	92	98	108	93	64	95

Pawtucket — Boston Red Sox — Surface: Grass

	G	Avg	AB	R	H	2B	3B	HR	SO
Home	284	.269	19373	2934	5202	1002	57	783	3712
Road	284	.260	18988	2574	4939	968	183	441	3607
Index	—	103	102	114	105	101	31	174	101

Richmond — Atlanta Braves — Surface: Grass

	G	Avg	AB	R	H	2B	3B	HR	SO
Home	283	.261	18759	2325	4901	838	122	331	3504
Road	283	.261	19008	2580	4963	976	142	488	3716
Index	—	100	99	90	99	87	87	69	96

Rochester — Baltimore Orioles — Surface: Grass

	G	Avg	AB	R	H	2B	3B	HR	SO
Home	282	.274	18866	2819	5166	1073	173	525	3740
Road	283	.262	18924	2660	4963	915	132	527	3443
Index	—	104	100	106	104	118	131	100	109

Scranton-WB — Philadelphia Phillies — Surface: Turf

	G	Avg	AB	R	H	2B	3B	HR	SO
Home	283	.261	18852	2634	4915	1073	220	369	3280
Road	285	.261	18967	2569	4946	996	118	462	3432
Index	—	100	100	103	100	108	188	80	96

Syracuse — Toronto Blue Jays — Surface: Grass

	G	Avg	AB	R	H	2B	3B	HR	SO
Home	282	.264	18616	2669	4916	916	185	464	3575
Road	285	.266	18969	2735	5053	1010	163	494	3486
Index	—	99	99	99	98	92	116	96	104

Toledo — Detroit Tigers — Surface: Grass

	G	Avg	AB	R	H	2B	3B	HR	SO
Home	284	.261	18758	2604	4896	857	147	556	3745
Road	284	.265	19087	2640	5061	994	174	461	3699
Index	—	98	98	99	97	88	86	123	103

Pacific Coast League — AAA

Albuquerque — Los Angeles Dodgers — Surface: Grass

	G	Avg	AB	R	H	2B	3B	HR	SO
Home	286	.300	20106	3460	6029	1053	189	511	3660
Road	283	.279	19295	2806	5388	1045	184	454	3504
Index	—	107	103	122	111	97	99	108	100

Calgary — Pittsburgh Pirates — Surface: Grass

	G	Avg	AB	R	H	2B	3B	HR	SO
Home	281	.302	19329	3302	5841	1305	123	558	2918
Road	286	.294	19848	3215	5842	1119	215	466	3437
Index	—	103	99	105	102	120	59	123	87

Colorado Springs — Colorado Rockies — Surface: Grass

	G	Avg	AB	R	H	2B	3B	HR	SO
Home	281	.305	19349	3512	5906	1205	212	597	3338
Road	284	.282	19071	2933	5374	1082	183	428	3575
Index	—	108	103	121	111	110	114	137	92

Edmonton** — Oakland Athletics — Surface: Mixed

	G	Avg	AB	R	H	2B	3B	HR	SO
Home	143	.274	9462	1449	2591	548	80	213	1569
Road	143	.279	9671	1513	2698	546	93	229	1753
Index	—	98	98	96	96	103	88	95	91

Las Vegas — San Diego Padres — Surface: Grass

	G	Avg	AB	R	H	2B	3B	HR	SO
Home	288	.288	20076	3250	5783	1134	183	555	3818
Road	283	.278	18835	2799	5241	1036	179	421	3425
Index	—	104	105	114	108	103	96	124	105

Phoenix — San Francisco Giants — Surface: Grass

	G	Avg	AB	R	H	2B	3B	HR	SO
Home	288	.283	20099	2931	5686	1053	261	406	3627
Road	286	.283	19375	2930	5482	1117	178	428	3218
Index	—	100	103	99	103	91	141	91	109

Salt Lake*** — Minnesota Twins — Surface: Grass

	G	Avg	AB	R	H	2B	3B	HR	SO
Home	216	.299	15218	2557	4550	890	142	442	2439
Road	216	.297	14989	2475	4456	920	145	363	2529
Index	—	101	102	103	102	95	96	120	95

Tacoma — Seattle Mariners — Surface: Grass

	G	Avg	AB	R	H	2B	3B	HR	SO
Home	286	.263	18969	2503	4986	1013	106	405	3549
Road	285	.296	19934	3220	5900	1099	205	502	3227
Index	—	89	95	77	84	97	54	85	116

Tucson — Houston Astros — Surface: Grass

	G	Avg	AB	R	H	2B	3B	HR	SO
Home	290	.297	20089	3165	5962	1178	315	267	3473
Road	284	.281	19517	3019	5493	1081	174	467	3594
Index	—	105	101	103	106	106	176	56	94

Vancouver — California Angels — Surface: Grass

	G	Avg	AB	R	H	2B	3B	HR	SO
Home	277	.255	17943	2232	4580	827	101	255	3248
Road	284	.297	19587	3365	5814	1234	192	486	3307
Index	—	86	94	68	81	73	57	57	107

Eastern League — AA

Binghamton — New York Mets — Surface: Grass

	G	Avg	AB	R	H	2B	3B	HR	SO
Home	283	.267	18780	2663	5006	935	163	416	3449
Road	282	.256	18786	2440	4801	922	116	378	3409
Index	—	104	100	109	104	101	141	110	101

Bowie** — Baltimore Orioles — Surface: Grass

	G	Avg	AB	R	H	2B	3B	HR	SO
Home	142	.261	9439	1344	2459	469	36	248	1773
Road	142	.260	9466	1326	2460	488	64	229	1810
Index	—	100	100	101	100	96	56	109	98

Canton-Akron — Cleveland Indians — Surface: Grass

	G	Avg	AB	R	H	2B	3B	HR	SO
Home	281	.267	18530	2603	4949	878	131	357	3302
Road	283	.258	18754	2729	4845	901	137	487	3811
Index	—	103	100	96	103	99	97	74	88

Harrisburg — Montreal Expos — Surface: Grass

	G	Avg	AB	R	H	2B	3B	HR	SO
Home	278	.254	18192	2556	4628	791	124	501	3793
Road	282	.255	18601	2591	4746	925	142	398	3842
Index	—	100	99	100	99	87	89	129	101

New Britain* — Minnesota Twins — Surface: Grass

	G	Avg	AB	R	H	2B	3B	HR	SO
Home	71	.257	4587	594	1181	252	35	94	887
Road	71	.268	4736	749	1271	240	39	147	949
Index	—	96	97	79	93	108	93	66	97

New Haven*** — Colorado Rockies — Surface: Grass

	G	Avg	AB	R	H	2B	3B	HR	SO
Home	214	.246	14041	1816	3452	657	87	222	2975
Road	209	.256	13620	1809	3481	635	90	309	2728
Index	—	96	101	98	97	100	94	70	106

Norwich* — New York Yankees — Surface: Grass

	G	Avg	AB	R	H	2B	3B	HR	SO
Home	70	.245	4617	607	1133	207	23	84	1017
Road	71	.264	4603	701	1214	255	24	134	978
Index	—	93	102	88	95	81	96	62	104

Portland*** — Florida Marlins — Surface: Grass

	G	Avg	AB	R	H	2B	3B	HR	SO
Home	214	.264	14496	2125	3824	737	110	393	2944
Road	210	.259	13871	1833	3593	628	88	254	2625
Index	—	102	103	114	104	112	120	148	107

Reading — Philadelphia Phillies — Surface: Grass

	G	Avg	AB	R	H	2B	3B	HR	SO
Home	283	.260	19003	2821	4946	903	151	567	3779
Road	280	.254	18388	2404	4662	844	115	339	3628
Index	—	103	102	116	105	104	127	162	101

Trenton*** — Boston Red Sox — Surface: Grass

	G	Avg	AB	R	H	2B	3B	HR	SO
Home	208	.251	13773	1826	3453	672	93	274	2588
Road	216	.258	14178	1993	3663	688	83	380	2790
Index	—	97	101	95	98	101	115	74	95

Southern League — AA

Birmingham — Chicago White Sox — Surface: Grass

	G	Avg	AB	R	H	2B	3B	HR	SO
Home	283	.250	18536	2359	4631	866	102	257	3614
Road	281	.262	18622	2615	4883	901	134	457	3674
Index	—	95	99	90	94	97	76	56	99

Carolina — Pittsburgh Pirates — Surface: Grass

	G	Avg	AB	R	H	2B	3B	HR	SO
Home	282	.265	18945	2586	5011	1045	157	331	3747
Road	282	.257	19206	2474	4935	869	129	376	3485
Index	—	103	99	105	102	122	123	89	109

Chattanooga — Cincinnati Reds — Surface: Grass

	G	Avg	AB	R	H	2B	3B	HR	SO
Home	284	.263	18691	2548	4907	934	118	361	3718
Road	280	.258	18693	2533	4828	967	115	435	3793
Index	—	102	99	99	100	97	103	83	98

Greenville — Atlanta Braves — Surface: Grass

	G	Avg	AB	R	H	2B	3B	HR	SO
Home	281	.268	18624	2683	4993	949	125	465	3570
Road	279	.257	18410	2459	4739	924	131	372	3579
Index	—	104	100	108	105	102	94	124	99

Huntsville — Oakland Athletics — Surface: Grass

	G	Avg	AB	R	H	2B	3B	HR	SO
Home	284	.255	18716	2571	4773	883	121	409	3824
Road	279	.262	18315	2703	4801	946	103	380	3650
Index	—	97	100	93	98	91	115	105	103

Jacksonville — Detroit Tigers — Surface: Grass

	G	Avg	AB	R	H	2B	3B	HR	SO
Home	277	.253	18611	2565	4703	947	66	590	3550
Road	283	.268	18636	2642	4999	952	145	428	3590
Index	—	94	102	99	96	100	46	138	99

Knoxville — Toronto Blue Jays — Surface: Grass

	G	Avg	AB	R	H	2B	3B	HR	SO
Home	283	.279	18998	2881	5304	1037	206	364	3650
Road	283	.250	18132	2379	4530	817	124	360	3856
Index	—	112	105	121	117	121	159	97	90

Memphis — San Diego Padres — Surface: Mixed

	G	Avg	AB	R	H	2B	3B	HR	SO
Home	276	.254	18224	2493	4632	877	106	483	3773
Road	282	.262	18897	2607	4951	969	145	382	3756
Index	—	97	99	98	96	94	76	131	104

Orlando — Chicago Cubs — Surface: Grass

	G	Avg	AB	R	H	2B	3B	HR	SO
Home	280	.263	18434	2416	4855	812	148	400	3233
Road	281	.259	18640	2515	4824	966	116	398	3550
Index	—	102	99	96	101	85	129	102	92

Port City** — Seattle Mariners — Surface: Grass

	G	Avg	AB	R	H	2B	3B	HR	SO
Home	141	.243	9446	1192	2294	437	55	155	1889
Road	141	.264	9520	1322	2511	479	55	180	1750
Index	—	92	99	90	91	92	101	87	109

Texas League — AA

Arkansas — St. Louis Cardinals — Surface: Grass

	G	Avg	AB	R	H	2B	3B	HR	SO
Home	270	.256	17184	2283	4400	908	122	382	3238
Road	276	.252	18144	2282	4570	888	141	366	3589
Index	—	102	97	102	98	108	91	110	95

El Paso — Milwaukee Brewers — Surface: Grass

	G	Avg	AB	R	H	2B	3B	HR	SO
Home	275	.294	18689	3170	5488	1168	326	276	3446
Road	271	.272	18555	2708	5055	933	160	423	3465
Index	—	108	99	115	107	124	202	65	99

Jackson — Houston Astros — Surface: Grass

	G	Avg	AB	R	H	2B	3B	HR	SO
Home	273	.255	17680	2245	4501	736	89	378	3553
Road	272	.265	18008	2463	4770	929	128	371	3289
Index	—	96	98	91	94	81	71	104	110

Midland — California Angels — Surface: Grass

	G	Avg	AB	R	H	2B	3B	HR	SO
Home	272	.296	18877	3286	5596	1233	190	480	3410
Road	276	.266	18434	2587	4912	889	180	370	3335
Index	—	111	104	129	116	135	103	127	100

San Antonio*** — Los Angeles Dodgers — Surface: Grass

	G	Avg	AB	R	H	2B	3B	HR	SO
Home	207	.252	13790	1525	3475	632	112	154	2587
Road	204	.274	13453	2006	3692	724	127	310	2431
Index	—	92	101	75	93	85	86	48	104

Shreveport — San Francisco Giants — Surface: Grass

	G	Avg	AB	R	H	2B	3B	HR	SO
Home	273	.248	17809	2136	4411	810	130	283	3116
Road	273	.273	18332	2563	5001	962	121	413	3159
Index	—	91	97	83	88	87	111	71	102

Tulsa — Texas Rangers — Surface: Grass

	G	Avg	AB	R	H	2B	3B	HR	SO
Home	275	.263	18398	2478	4846	908	105	524	3524
Road	270	.265	17713	2454	4696	935	141	396	3215
Index	—	99	102	99	101	93	72	127	106

Wichita — Kansas City Royals — Surface: Mixed

	G	Avg	AB	R	H	2B	3B	HR	SO
Home	273	.275	18715	2755	5139	895	123	531	3186
Road	275	.270	18348	2630	4945	963	194	331	3579
Index	—	102	103	106	105	91	62	157	87

California League — A+

Bakersfield* — Co-Op

	G	Avg	AB	R	H	2B	3B	HR	SO
Home	70	.281	5016	894	1410	321	8	156	1164
Road	70	.283	4918	926	1394	278	43	130	1100
Index	—	99	102	97	101	113	18	118	104

High Desert* — Baltimore Orioles

	G	Avg	AB	R	H	2B	3B	HR	SO
Home	70	.300	4995	1019	1498	282	56	192	992
Road	70	.274	4811	786	1320	252	30	107	1007
Index	—	109	104	130	113	108	180	173	95

Lake Elsinore* — California Angels

	G	Avg	AB	R	H	2B	3B	HR	SO
Home	70	.274	4799	736	1314	279	35	82	954
Road	70	.269	4859	786	1305	245	35	154	1087
Index	—	102	99	94	101	115	101	54	89

Lancaster* — Seattle Mariners

	G	Avg	AB	R	H	2B	3B	HR	SO
Home	70	.286	4992	887	1428	267	49	146	1004
Road	70	.261	4732	712	1235	228	40	93	1085
Index	—	110	105	125	116	111	116	149	88

Modesto* — Oakland Athletics

	G	Avg	AB	R	H	2B	3B	HR	SO
Home	70	.271	4792	817	1300	263	31	159	1170
Road	70	.284	4939	884	1404	244	43	128	1070
Index	—	95	97	92	93	111	74	128	113

Rancho Cucamonga* — San Diego Padres

	G	Avg	AB	R	H	2B	3B	HR	SO
Home	70	.286	4860	787	1390	250	53	108	1063
Road	70	.275	4799	767	1318	269	41	107	1145
Index	—	104	101	103	105	92	128	100	92

San Bernardino* — Los Angeles Dodgers

	G	Avg	AB	R	H	2B	3B	HR	SO
Home	70	.268	4860	843	1301	244	24	135	1196
Road	70	.275	4837	828	1330	262	35	126	1043
Index	—	97	100	102	98	93	68	107	114

San Jose* — San Francisco Giants

	G	Avg	AB	R	H	2B	3B	HR	SO
Home	70	.250	4698	560	1173	203	41	43	1090
Road	70	.283	4994	805	1414	261	38	115	1048
Index	—	88	94	70	83	83	115	40	111

Stockton* — Milwaukee Brewers

	G	Avg	AB	R	H	2B	3B	HR	SO
Home	70	.263	4617	659	1213	186	35	82	881
Road	70	.286	4855	794	1390	251	39	133	1008
Index	—	92	95	83	87	78	94	65	92

Visalia* — Co-Op

	G	Avg	AB	R	H	2B	3B	HR	SO
Home	70	.281	4928	875	1383	270	44	122	1132
Road	70	.270	4813	789	1300	275	32	132	1053
Index	—	104	102	111	106	96	134	90	105

Carolina League — A+

Durham* — Atlanta Braves

	G	Avg	AB	R	H	2B	3B	HR	SO
Home	70	.269	4700	723	1265	248	27	151	1008
Road	69	.250	4578	609	1145	230	29	100	1053
Index	—	108	101	117	109	105	91	147	93

Frederick* — Baltimore Orioles

	G	Avg	AB	R	H	2B	3B	HR	SO
Home	70	.272	4634	715	1259	251	27	115	998
Road	69	.252	4604	652	1162	219	29	96	925
Index	—	108	99	108	107	114	93	119	107

Kinston* — Cleveland Indians

	G	Avg	AB	R	H	2B	3B	HR	SO
Home	69	.244	4436	542	1081	201	15	81	858
Road	69	.263	4494	659	1180	254	24	82	823
Index	—	93	99	82	92	80	63	100	106

Lynchburg* — Pittsburgh Pirates

	G	Avg	AB	R	H	2B	3B	HR	SO
Home	68	.269	4624	688	1243	246	26	98	892
Road	71	.280	4744	746	1329	243	33	106	969
Index	—	96	102	96	98	104	81	95	94

Prince William* — Chicago White Sox

	G	Avg	AB	R	H	2B	3B	HR	SO
Home	68	.257	4504	621	1158	233	36	84	876
Road	70	.254	4623	650	1174	222	29	105	977
Index	—	101	100	98	102	108	127	82	92

Salem* — Colorado Rockies

	G	Avg	AB	R	H	2B	3B	HR	SO
Home	71	.258	4590	619	1184	264	27	60	871
Road	67	.255	4492	622	1147	205	19	104	935
Index	—	101	96	94	97	126	139	56	91

Wilmington* — Kansas City Royals

	G	Avg	AB	R	H	2B	3B	HR	SO
Home	70	.251	4594	607	1151	228	38	64	919
Road	70	.259	4636	625	1202	231	33	112	876
Index	—	97	99	97	96	100	116	58	106

Winston-Salem* — Cincinnati Reds

	G	Avg	AB	R	H	2B	3B	HR	SO
Home	69	.258	4614	666	1192	164	23	158	976
Road	70	.264	4525	618	1194	231	23	106	840
Index	—	98	103	109	101	70	98	146	114

Florida State League — A+

Brevard County* — Florida Marlins

	G	Avg	AB	R	H	2B	3B	HR	SO
Home	69	.253	4636	580	1174	214	28	60	856
Road	70	.263	4695	609	1237	211	41	66	755
Index	—	96	100	97	96	103	69	92	115

Charlotte* — Florida Marlins

	G	Avg	AB	R	H	2B	3B	HR	SO
Home	71	.260	4822	636	1252	246	42	82	927
Road	68	.272	4599	678	1250	238	45	65	807
Index	—	96	100	90	96	99	89	120	110

Clearwater* — Philadelphia Phillies

	G	Avg	AB	R	H	2B	3B	HR	SO
Home	67	.251	4455	596	1116	221	30	55	808
Road	70	.253	4644	601	1177	215	42	73	932
Index	—	99	100	104	99	107	74	79	90

Daytona* — Chicago Cubs

	G	Avg	AB	R	H	2B	3B	HR	SO
Home	68	.272	4496	733	1225	208	37	98	889
Road	69	.251	4480	575	1126	229	34	66	818
Index	—	108	102	129	110	91	108	148	108

Dunedin* — Toronto Blue Jays

	G	Avg	AB	R	H	2B	3B	HR	SO
Home	68	.252	4545	663	1146	243	31	91	978
Road	69	.256	4509	620	1155	232	38	74	1002
Index	—	98	102	109	101	104	81	122	97

Fort Myers* — Minnesota Twins

	G	Avg	AB	R	H	2B	3B	HR	SO
Home	66	.250	4254	551	1063	185	30	59	857
Road	72	.248	4775	631	1186	205	52	68	943
Index	—	101	97	95	98	101	65	97	102

Kissimmee* — Houston Astros

	G	Avg	AB	R	H	2B	3B	HR	SO
Home	70	.251	4522	541	1136	191	38	37	799
Road	65	.259	4217	562	1094	202	31	71	740
Index	—	97	100	89	96	88	114	49	101

Lakeland* — Detroit Tigers

	G	Avg	AB	R	H	2B	3B	HR	SO
Home	66	.261	4362	587	1140	221	54	58	799
Road	72	.246	4731	573	1163	222	31	65	1032
Index	—	106	101	112	107	108	189	97	84

St. Lucie* — New York Mets

	G	Avg	AB	R	H	2B	3B	HR	SO
Home	67	.249	4362	539	1087	176	28	49	832
Road	66	.243	4287	483	1041	171	38	55	883
Index	—	103	100	110	103	101	72	88	93

St. Petersburg* — St. Louis Cardinals

	G	Avg	AB	R	H	2B	3B	HR	SO
Home	72	.244	4476	446	1090	176	43	23	837
Road	67	.260	4465	561	1159	192	33	61	800
Index	—	94	93	74	88	91	130	38	104

Sarasota* — **Boston Red Sox**

	G	Avg	AB	R	H	2B	3B	HR	SO
Home	71	.277	4778	684	1324	268	45	66	905
Road	65	.253	4280	568	1083	210	35	53	844
Index	—	110	102	110	112	114	115	112	96

Tampa* — **New York Yankees**

	G	Avg	AB	R	H	2B	3B	HR	SO
Home	66	.249	4413	519	1101	182	23	69	884
Road	68	.257	4478	590	1153	217	32	68	920
Index	—	97	102	91	98	85	73	103	98

Vero Beach* — **Los Angeles Dodgers**

	G	Avg	AB	R	H	2B	3B	HR	SO
Home	64	.253	4216	576	1065	181	31	84	883
Road	67	.250	4299	576	1073	167	25	35	870
Index	—	101	103	105	104	111	126	245	103

West Palm Beach* — **Montreal Expos**

	G	Avg	AB	R	H	2B	3B	HR	SO
Home	69	.253	4545	572	1152	203	44	45	874
Road	66	.265	4423	596	1174	204	27	56	782
Index	—	95	98	92	94	97	159	78	109

Midwest League — A

Beloit* — **Milwaukee Brewers**

	G	Avg	AB	R	H	2B	3B	HR	SO
Home	68	.258	4471	612	1155	203	22	68	904
Road	68	.254	4424	635	1123	214	39	62	931
Index	—	102	101	96	103	94	56	109	96

Burlington* — **San Francisco Giants**

	G	Avg	AB	R	H	2B	3B	HR	SO
Home	70	.243	4484	640	1091	193	15	127	986
Road	68	.235	4461	536	1050	220	19	63	968
Index	—	103	98	116	101	87	79	201	101

Cedar Rapids* — **California Angels**

	G	Avg	AB	R	H	2B	3B	HR	SO
Home	68	.266	4581	705	1220	242	35	126	996
Road	67	.243	4311	597	1049	193	41	79	908
Index	—	109	105	116	115	118	80	150	103

Clinton* — **San Diego Padres**

	G	Avg	AB	R	H	2B	3B	HR	SO
Home	64	.237	4127	547	978	185	41	54	952
Road	70	.244	4470	625	1091	212	28	72	1025
Index	—	97	101	96	98	95	159	81	101

Fort Wayne* — **Minnesota Twins**

	G	Avg	AB	R	H	2B	3B	HR	SO
Home	70	.267	4788	644	1279	238	31	70	992
Road	66	.263	4342	649	1142	218	47	55	888
Index	—	102	104	94	106	99	60	115	101

Kane County* — **Florida Marlins**

	G	Avg	AB	R	H	2B	3B	HR	SO
Home	70	.248	4576	632	1135	225	35	72	1105
Road	63	.244	4056	544	990	185	24	69	973
Index	—	102	102	105	103	108	129	92	101

Lansing* — **Kansas City Royals**

	G	Avg	AB	R	H	2B	3B	HR	SO
Home	70	.282	4830	809	1363	268	50	86	800
Road	69	.263	4780	657	1258	221	40	67	899
Index	—	107	100	121	107	120	124	127	88

Michigan* — **Boston Red Sox**

	G	Avg	AB	R	H	2B	3B	HR	SO
Home	70	.245	4657	588	1143	216	25	73	947
Road	68	.264	4627	725	1220	248	40	86	899
Index	—	93	98	79	91	87	62	84	105

Peoria* — **St. Louis Cardinals**

	G	Avg	AB	R	H	2B	3B	HR	SO
Home	68	.245	4362	617	1070	205	46	46	1017
Road	68	.244	4375	612	1069	202	31	50	981
Index	—	100	100	101	100	102	149	92	104

Quad City* — **Houston Astros**

	G	Avg	AB	R	H	2B	3B	HR	SO
Home	61	.246	3958	555	973	180	22	66	810
Road	70	.264	4754	673	1257	216	44	97	983
Index	—	93	96	95	89	100	60	82	99

Rockford* — **Chicago Cubs**

	G	Avg	AB	R	H	2B	3B	HR	SO
Home	66	.262	4361	667	1141	211	53	59	884
Road	69	.257	4493	690	1155	229	34	75	981
Index	—	102	101	101	103	95	161	81	93

South Bend* — **Chicago White Sox**

	G	Avg	AB	R	H	2B	3B	HR	SO
Home	68	.248	4529	594	1121	230	35	63	903
Road	68	.256	4465	637	1144	218	21	86	869
Index	—	97	101	93	98	104	164	72	102

West Michigan* — **Oakland Athletics**

	G	Avg	AB	R	H	2B	3B	HR	SO
Home	70	.237	4599	586	1090	189	26	48	996
Road	68	.255	4572	614	1164	209	35	85	1014
Index	—	93	98	93	91	90	74	56	98

Wisconsin* — **Seattle Mariners**

	G	Avg	AB	R	H	2B	3B	HR	SO
Home	67	.262	4427	719	1158	263	43	67	963
Road	68	.261	4620	721	1205	263	36	79	936
Index	—	100	97	101	98	104	125	89	107

South Atlantic League — A

Asheville* — **Colorado Rockies**

	G	Avg	AB	R	H	2B	3B	HR	SO
Home	65	.253	4389	619	1112	209	14	94	982
Road	71	.223	4597	519	1026	160	26	56	1117
Index	—	114	104	130	118	137	56	176	92

Augusta* — **Pittsburgh Pirates**

	G	Avg	AB	R	H	2B	3B	HR	SO
Home	70	.240	4557	565	1093	191	35	42	1063
Road	71	.247	4735	652	1170	228	37	83	1007
Index	—	97	98	88	95	87	98	53	110

Charleston-SC* — **Texas Rangers**

	G	Avg	AB	R	H	2B	3B	HR	SO
Home	71	.231	4626	560	1067	212	63	59	1095
Road	70	.243	4330	622	1054	160	36	83	1039
Index	—	95	105	89	100	124	164	67	99

Charleston-WV* — **Cincinnati Reds**

	G	Avg	AB	R	H	2B	3B	HR	SO
Home	71	.235	4633	623	1089	223	41	24	1145
Road	71	.247	4640	651	1148	233	31	91	1108
Index	—	95	100	96	95	96	132	26	103

Columbia* — **New York Mets**

	G	Avg	AB	R	H	2B	3B	HR	SO
Home	70	.228	4430	548	1012	205	30	62	1190
Road	69	.220	4365	496	961	159	34	76	1100
Index	—	104	100	109	104	127	87	80	107

Columbus* — **New York Yankees**

	G	Avg	AB	R	H	2B	3B	HR	SO
Home	72	.252	4654	711	1175	208	20	168	963
Road	70	.246	4626	628	1137	201	39	95	1155
Index	—	103	98	110	100	103	51	176	83

Delmarva* — **Montreal Expos**

	G	Avg	AB	R	H	2B	3B	HR	SO
Home	71	.220	4492	589	988	197	35	80	985
Road	71	.246	4717	618	1159	214	34	78	1034
Index	—	90	95	95	85	97	108	108	100

Fayetteville* — **Detroit Tigers**

	G	Avg	AB	R	H	2B	3B	HR	SO
Home	71	.237	4598	561	1090	196	23	55	1063
Road	68	.238	4614	633	1100	232	25	80	1062
Index	—	99	95	85	95	85	92	69	100

Greensboro* — **New York Yankees**

	G	Avg	AB	R	H	2B	3B	HR	SO
Home	70	.236	4658	625	1101	207	35	84	1178
Road	72	.247	4799	686	1185	224	34	62	1131
Index	—	96	100	94	96	95	106	140	107

Hagerstown* — **Toronto Blue Jays**

	G	Avg	AB	R	H	2B	3B	HR	SO
Home	70	.254	4503	666	1146	243	24	70	1045
Road	71	.232	4585	602	1064	216	28	64	1105
Index	—	110	100	112	109	115	87	111	96

Hickory* — **Chicago White Sox**

	G	Avg	AB	R	H	2B	3B	HR	SO
Home	70	.260	4834	652	1259	195	29	107	1036
Road	70	.257	4725	658	1214	226	33	62	1053
Index	—	**101**	**102**	**99**	**104**	**84**	**86**	**169**	**96**

Macon* — **Atlanta Braves**

	G	Avg	AB	R	H	2B	3B	HR	SO
Home	71	.253	4788	742	1210	217	29	89	1052
Road	69	.242	4406	589	1068	206	33	95	1007
Index	—	**104**	**106**	**122**	**110**	**97**	**81**	**86**	**96**

Piedmont* — **Philadelphia Phillies**

	G	Avg	AB	R	H	2B	3B	HR	SO
Home	69	.231	4517	512	1044	211	32	45	1093
Road	69	.246	4617	589	1134	224	28	74	1033
Index	—	**94**	**98**	**87**	**92**	**96**	**117**	**62**	**108**

Savannah* — **Los Angeles Dodgers**

	G	Avg	AB	R	H	2B	3B	HR	SO
Home	71	.238	4702	639	1121	165	42	108	1180
Road	70	.235	4625	669	1087	196	34	88	1119
Index	—	**101**	**100**	**94**	**102**	**83**	**122**	**121**	**104**

New York - Penn League — A-

Auburn* — **Houston Astros**

	G	Avg	AB	R	H	2B	3B	HR	SO
Home	37	.255	2520	363	642	126	12	25	494
Road	39	.237	2500	316	593	95	18	38	547
Index	—	**107**	**106**	**121**	**114**	**132**	**66**	**65**	**90**

Batavia* — **Philadelphia Phillies**

	G	Avg	AB	R	H	2B	3B	HR	SO
Home	37	.250	2401	322	601	121	32	25	494
Road	38	.250	2560	330	640	103	22	39	539
Index	—	**100**	**96**	**100**	**96**	**125**	**155**	**68**	**98**

Erie* — **Pittsburgh Pirates**

	G	Avg	AB	R	H	2B	3B	HR	SO
Home	39	.266	2681	397	712	143	21	46	532
Road	37	.255	2377	310	605	106	20	26	551
Index	—	**104**	**107**	**121**	**112**	**120**	**93**	**157**	**86**

Hudson Valley* — **Rangers/Devil Rays**

	G	Avg	AB	R	H	2B	3B	HR	SO
Home	38	.240	2626	374	631	125	27	39	688
Road	38	.244	2640	409	643	136	34	42	685
Index	—	**99**	**99**	**91**	**98**	**92**	**80**	**93**	**101**

Jamestown* — **Detroit Tigers**

	G	Avg	AB	R	H	2B	3B	HR	SO
Home	37	.253	2400	347	608	100	30	60	578
Road	39	.242	2564	363	621	107	16	42	578
Index	—	**105**	**99**	**101**	**103**	**100**	**200**	**153**	**107**

Lowell* — **Boston Red Sox**

	G	Avg	AB	R	H	2B	3B	HR	SO
Home	37	.247	2494	363	615	126	14	37	596
Road	37	.238	2416	315	574	85	21	32	571
Index	—	**104**	**103**	**115**	**107**	**144**	**65**	**112**	**101**

New Jersey* — **St. Louis Cardinals**

	G	Avg	AB	R	H	2B	3B	HR	SO
Home	39	.261	2667	390	697	106	45	33	632
Road	36	.260	2421	356	629	119	25	30	580
Index	—	**101**	**102**	**101**	**102**	**81**	**163**	**100**	**99**

Oneonta* — **New York Yankees**

	G	Avg	AB	R	H	2B	3B	HR	SO
Home	38	.229	2408	317	552	79	31	15	580
Road	38	.236	2528	366	597	99	26	24	657
Index	—	**97**	**95**	**87**	**92**	**84**	**125**	**66**	**93**

Pittsfield* — **New York Mets**

	G	Avg	AB	R	H	2B	3B	HR	SO
Home	37	.235	2293	291	540	94	22	24	560
Road	38	.254	2498	343	635	108	22	39	592
Index	—	**93**	**94**	**87**	**87**	**95**	**109**	**67**	**103**

St. Catharines* — **Toronto Blue Jays**

	G	Avg	AB	R	H	2B	3B	HR	SO
Home	38	.245	2491	358	611	94	12	54	554
Road	38	.252	2464	350	622	127	25	40	523
Index	—	**97**	**101**	**102**	**98**	**73**	**47**	**134**	**105**

Utica* — **Florida Marlins**

	G	Avg	AB	R	H	2B	3B	HR	SO
Home	38	.252	2476	342	624	124	21	32	619
Road	38	.241	2469	317	594	106	17	34	589
Index	—	**105**	**100**	**108**	**105**	**117**	**123**	**94**	**105**

Vermont* — **Montreal Expos**

	G	Avg	AB	R	H	2B	3B	HR	SO
Home	38	.258	2453	341	633	101	19	24	524
Road	36	.237	2296	288	545	91	28	25	488
Index	—	**109**	**101**	**112**	**110**	**104**	**64**	**90**	**101**

Watertown* — **Cleveland Indians**

	G	Avg	AB	R	H	2B	3B	HR	SO
Home	36	.220	2325	288	511	82	15	34	626
Road	39	.245	2537	354	621	117	18	29	616
Index	—	**90**	**99**	**88**	**89**	**76**	**91**	**128**	**111**

Williamsport* — **Chicago Cubs**

	G	Avg	AB	R	H	2B	3B	HR	SO
Home	39	.223	2484	296	554	89	15	23	603
Road	37	.250	2449	372	612	111	24	31	564
Index	—	**89**	**96**	**75**	**86**	**79**	**62**	**73**	**105**

Northwest League — A-

Bellingham* — **San Francisco Giants**

	G	Avg	AB	R	H	2B	3B	HR	SO
Home	37	.229	2493	293	571	94	8	57	643
Road	38	.251	2592	380	650	107	23	51	684
Index	—	**91**	**99**	**79**	**90**	**91**	**36**	**116**	**98**

Boise* — **California Angels**

	G	Avg	AB	R	H	2B	3B	HR	SO
Home	38	.281	2752	497	772	132	25	65	512
Road	38	.248	2706	420	670	153	16	49	634
Index	—	**113**	**102**	**118**	**115**	**85**	**154**	**130**	**79**

Eugene* — **Atlanta Braves**

	G	Avg	AB	R	H	2B	3B	HR	SO
Home	38	.253	2663	422	673	135	32	64	665
Road	38	.252	2659	390	671	135	25	58	624
Index	—	**100**	**100**	**108**	**100**	**100**	**128**	**110**	**106**

Everett* — **Seattle Mariners**

	G	Avg	AB	R	H	2B	3B	HR	SO
Home	38	.239	2578	394	615	126	12	52	794
Road	37	.250	2496	340	624	118	18	46	601
Index	—	**95**	**101**	**113**	**96**	**103**	**65**	**109**	**128**

Portland* — **Florida Marlins**

	G	Avg	AB	R	H	2B	3B	HR	SO
Home	38	.240	2587	337	620	110	29	41	586
Road	38	.258	2667	416	689	138	21	55	543
Index	—	**93**	**97**	**81**	**90**	**82**	**142**	**77**	**111**

Southern Oregon* — **Oakland Athletics**

	G	Avg	AB	R	H	2B	3B	HR	SO
Home	38	.278	2709	444	753	160	16	70	590
Road	38	.242	2576	414	624	128	19	61	594
Index	—	**115**	**105**	**107**	**121**	**119**	**80**	**109**	**94**

Spokane* — **Kansas City Royals**

	G	Avg	AB	R	H	2B	3B	HR	SO
Home	38	.261	2615	438	682	140	17	64	544
Road	38	.265	2655	413	703	122	20	72	586
Index	—	**98**	**98**	**106**	**97**	**117**	**86**	**90**	**94**

Yakima* — **Los Angeles Dodgers**

	G	Avg	AB	R	H	2B	3B	HR	SO
Home	38	.229	2550	309	584	118	19	30	662
Road	38	.246	2596	361	639	114	16	51	730
Index	—	**93**	**98**	**86**	**91**	**105**	**121**	**60**	**92**

1996 Triple-A Lefty-Righty Stats

The following section includes batting splits for all hitters with 200 or more Triple-A at-bats in 1996, and pitching splits for all hurlers with 200 or more Triple-A batters faced.

Batters' splits now include home runs and RBI vs. left- and righthanders, while pitchers' splits include home runs allowed and strikeouts vs. lefties and righties.

AAA Batting vs. Left-Handed and Right-Handed Pitchers

			vs Left					vs Right				
Player	Team	Org	AB	H	HR	RBI	Avg	AB	H	HR	RBI	Avg
Abbott,Jeff	Nashville	ChA	115	38	6	16	.330	325	105	8	44	.323
Abreu,Bob	Tucson	Hou	113	20	0	8	.177	371	117	13	60	.315
Adriana,Sharnol	Syracuse	Tor	75	25	4	14	.333	217	57	6	23	.263
Agbayani,Benny	Norfolk	NYN	94	26	1	12	.277	237	66	6	44	.278
Allensworth,J.	Calgary	Pit	83	28	3	9	.337	269	88	5	34	.327
Amaro,Ruben	Syracuse	Tor	47	9	0	1	.191	183	53	2	23	.290
Arias,George	Vancouver	Cal	67	29	4	16	.433	176	53	5	39	.301
Aude,Rich	Calgary	Pit	87	25	3	17	.287	307	90	14	64	.293
Ayrault,Joe	Richmond	Atl	92	22	3	13	.239	222	50	2	21	.225
Baez,Kevin	Toledo	Det	81	24	2	10	.296	221	50	9	34	.226
Ball,Jeff	Tucson	Hou	107	27	5	17	.252	322	112	14	56	.348
Banks,Brian	New Orleans	Mil	104	27	4	11	.260	383	105	12	53	.274
Barberie,Bret	Iowa	ChN	42	9	0	1	.214	168	40	5	23	.238
Barker,Tim	Columbus	NYA	120	43	1	18	.358	282	64	1	27	.227
Barron,Tony	Ottawa	Mon	98	35	2	7	.357	296	91	12	52	.307
Batista,Tony	Edmonton	Oak	65	18	1	6	.277	140	48	7	34	.343
Battle,Allen	Edmonton	Oak	59	17	1	7	.288	165	51	2	26	.309
Battle,Howard	Scranton-WB	Phi	101	23	1	14	.228	290	66	7	30	.228
Beamon,Trey	Calgary	Pit	88	24	0	9	.273	290	85	5	43	.293
Belk,Tim	Indianapolis	Cin	114	37	7	20	.325	322	88	8	43	.273
Bell,Juan	Pawtucket	Bos	68	22	0	8	.324	142	30	5	15	.211
Bellinger,Clay	Rochester	Bal	140	44	1	27	.314	319	94	14	51	.295
Benbow,Lou	Richmond	Atl	83	22	1	8	.265	167	36	0	15	.216
Benitez,Yamil	Ottawa	Mon	106	28	7	22	.264	333	94	16	59	.282
Bennett,Gary	Scranton-WB	Phi	81	24	5	13	.296	205	47	3	24	.229
Berg,David	Portland	Fla	111	40	2	14	.360	303	85	7	59	.281
Bieser,Steve	Ottawa	Mon	96	28	0	2	.292	286	95	1	30	.332
Bonnici,James	Tacoma	Sea	119	41	6	21	.345	378	104	20	53	.275
Bowers,Brent	Rochester	Bal	51	14	1	5	.275	155	53	3	14	.342
Bradshaw,Terry	Louisville	StL	94	29	4	12	.309	295	89	8	32	.302
Brady,Doug	Nashville	ChA	107	22	0	8	.206	320	81	6	34	.253
Brede,Brent	Salt Lake	Min	122	39	0	21	.320	361	129	11	65	.357
Brito,Tilson	Syracuse	Tor	97	28	2	21	.289	303	83	8	33	.274
Brooks,Jerry	Charlotte	Fla	167	50	12	39	.299	299	84	22	68	.281
Brown,Brant	Iowa	ChN	104	24	2	10	.231	238	80	8	33	.336
Brown,Jarvis	Rochester	Bal	71	16	0	4	.225	133	27	4	15	.203
Brumley,Mike	Tucson	Hou	51	9	0	3	.176	227	56	4	25	.247
Bruno,Julio	Las Vegas	SD	87	22	2	12	.253	210	59	0	18	.281
Bryant,Scott	Tacoma	Sea	62	18	0	4	.290	152	39	2	15	.257
Buccheri,Jim	Ottawa	Mon	53	16	0	5	.302	153	37	1	7	.242
Burton,Darren	Omaha	KC	119	34	5	15	.286	344	91	10	52	.265
Butler,Robert	Scranton-WB	Phi	81	22	1	11	.272	217	54	3	23	.249
Caceres,Edgar	New Orleans	Mil	118	33	2	5	.280	279	74	2	24	.265
Cairo,Miguel	Syracuse	Tor	118	38	0	12	.322	347	91	3	36	.262
Candaele,Casey	Buffalo	Cle	112	33	1	7	.295	280	89	5	30	.318
Canizaro,Jay	Phoenix	SF	77	19	1	13	.247	286	76	6	51	.266
Cappuccio,C.	Nashville	ChA	87	23	1	10	.264	320	88	9	51	.275
Carpenter,Bubba	Columbus	NYA	128	23	0	11	.180	338	91	7	37	.269
Carter,Mike	Iowa	ChN	135	39	0	6	.289	249	63	2	12	.253
Carvajal,Jovino	Vancouver	Cal	64	17	0	9	.266	208	48	4	22	.231
Castellano,Pedro	Col. Springs	Col	84	34	1	10	.405	278	88	12	49	.317
Castillo,Alberto	Norfolk	NYN	88	22	6	18	.250	253	49	5	21	.194
Castillo,Luis	Portland	Fla	130	43	1	14	.331	290	90	0	21	.310
Christopherson,E.	Tucson	Hou	67	17	1	7	.254	156	47	5	29	.301
Clapinski,Chris	Charlotte	Fla	127	31	2	7	.244	235	72	8	32	.306
Clark,Jerald	Calgary	Pit	75	25	2	15	.333	173	41	6	30	.237
Clark,Phil	Pawtucket	Bos	114	46	5	25	.404	255	74	7	44	.290
Cockrell,Alan	Col. Springs	Col	72	26	1	16	.361	285	81	13	44	.284
Colbert,Craig	Las Vegas	SD	51	15	1	5	.294	149	35	4	14	.235
Cole,Alex	Pawtucket	Bos	60	14	0	8	.233	244	76	4	31	.311
Cookson,Brent	Rochester	Bal	109	33	9	25	.303	259	66	16	46	.255
Costo,Tim	Buffalo	Cle	111	28	5	12	.252	141	26	3	16	.184
Crespo,Felipe	Syracuse	Tor	94	30	3	18	.319	261	70	5	40	.268
Cromer,Tripp	Louisville	StL	84	20	0	5	.238	160	35	4	20	.219
Cruz,Fausto	Toledo	Det	94	25	0	8	.266	290	71	12	51	.245
Cruz,Ivan	Columbus	NYA	129	22	3	14	.171	317	93	25	82	.293
Cruz,Jacob	Phoenix	SF	104	25	0	15	.240	331	99	7	60	.299
Cummings,Midre	Calgary	Pit	79	22	0	13	.278	289	90	8	42	.311
Dalesandro,Mark	Columbus	NYA	86	28	0	11	.326	169	44	2	27	.260
Dascenzo,Doug	Las Vegas	SD	76	25	0	4	.329	244	66	0	16	.270
Deer,Rob	Las Vegas	SD	73	19	5	16	.260	186	39	15	31	.210
Demetral,Chris	Albequerque	LA	16	2	0	0	.125	193	53	4	26	.275
Devarez,Cesar	Rochester	Bal	58	18	1	8	.310	165	46	3	19	.279
Diaz,Eddy	Tacoma	Sea	103	27	2	12	.262	319	91	11	46	.285
Diaz,Lino	Omaha	KC	67	14	1	7	.209	199	58	2	21	.291

			vs Left					vs Right				
Player	Team	Org	AB	H	HR	RBI	Avg	AB	H	HR	RBI	Avg
Diaz,Mario	Scranton-WB	Phi	68	17	1	12	.250	173	49	4	21	.283
Difelice,Mike	Louisville	StL	68	20	1	4	.294	178	50	8	29	.281
Diggs,Tony	Louisville	StL	87	17	1	5	.195	221	46	6	18	.208
Dodson,Bo	Pawtucket	Bos	56	18	1	7	.321	220	77	10	36	.350
Doster,David	Scranton-WB	Phi	76	21	0	9	.276	246	62	7	39	.252
Dunn,Steve	Buffalo	Cle	51	10	1	7	.196	249	77	11	41	.309
Dunwoody,Todd	Portland	Fla	160	47	5	32	.294	392	106	19	61	.270
Echevarria,Angel	Col. Springs	Col	106	35	4	20	.330	309	105	12	54	.340
Encarnacion,A.	Calgary	Pit	65	25	1	6	.385	198	59	3	25	.298
Erstad,Darin	Vancouver	Cal	114	32	3	19	.281	237	75	3	22	.316
Espinosa,Ramon	Calgary	Pit	70	23	0	10	.329	175	46	0	15	.263
Faneyte,Rikkert	Oklahoma City	Tex	101	30	3	14	.297	263	56	8	30	.213
Faries,Paul	New Orleans	Mil	132	38	3	9	.288	265	60	0	22	.226
Felder,Ken	New Orleans	Mil	113	25	6	8	.221	317	68	11	37	.215
Florez,Tim	Phoenix	SF	87	24	1	7	.276	279	82	3	32	.294
Forbes,P.J.	Vancouver	Cal	118	28	0	11	.237	291	84	0	35	.289
Fordyce,Brook	Indianapolis	Cin	99	26	5	16	.263	275	77	11	48	.280
Franco,Matt	Norfolk	NYN	155	48	3	27	.310	353	116	4	54	.329
Franklin,Micah	Louisville	StL	73	17	3	15	.233	216	50	12	38	.231
Frazier,Lou	Oklahoma City	Tex	65	17	2	9	.262	143	34	1	7	.238
Gainer,Jay	Col. Springs	Col	50	6	1	6	.120	283	72	13	43	.254
Garcia,Karim	Albequerque	LA	75	21	1	9	.280	252	76	12	49	.302
Garcia,Omar	Richmond	Atl	109	28	3	10	.257	202	54	1	25	.267
Garrison,Webster	Edmonton	Oak	75	25	4	15	.333	219	64	6	34	.292
Gibralter,Steve	Indianapolis	Cin	127	34	5	17	.268	320	80	6	37	.250
Gil,Benji	Oklahoma City	Tex	79	21	2	9	.266	213	44	4	19	.207
Gilbert,Shawn	Norfolk	NYN	134	36	2	16	.269	359	90	7	34	.251
Giles,Brian	Buffalo	Cle	96	27	7	18	.281	222	73	13	46	.329
Giovanola,Ed	Richmond	Atl	62	21	2	9	.339	148	41	1	7	.277
Glanville,Doug	Iowa	ChN	85	32	1	11	.376	288	83	2	23	.288
Goff,Jerry	Tucson	Hou	46	15	1	12	.326	229	50	8	40	.218
Goodwin,Curtis	Indianapolis	Cin	85	18	0	5	.212	252	70	2	25	.278
Graffanino,Tony	Richmond	Atl	116	29	0	14	.250	237	71	7	19	.300
Grebeck,Brian	Vancouver	Cal	70	19	1	12	.271	167	36	0	15	.216
Greene,Todd	Vancouver	Cal	62	26	1	13	.419	161	42	4	20	.261
Gregg,Tommy	Charlotte	Fla	138	35	3	20	.254	267	81	19	60	.303
Grotewold,Jeff	Omaha	KC	89	16	2	15	.180	249	78	8	36	.313
Guerrero,Wilton	Albequerque	LA	112	40	1	14	.357	313	106	1	24	.339
Gulan,Mike	Louisville	StL	114	28	5	13	.246	305	79	12	42	.259
Hajek,Dave	Tucson	Hou	111	34	1	10	.306	397	127	3	54	.320
Hall,Joe	Rochester	Bal	130	43	7	31	.331	349	95	12	64	.272
Halter,Shane	Omaha	KC	75	20	0	7	.267	224	57	3	26	.254
Haney,Todd	Iowa	ChN	67	13	0	6	.194	173	46	2	13	.266
Hardtke,Jason	Norfolk	NYN	70	20	2	6	.286	187	57	7	29	.305
Hastings,Lionel	Portland	Fla	115	38	3	25	.330	178	30	3	19	.169
Hatcher,Chris	Tucson	Hou	72	20	2	8	.278	276	85	16	53	.308
Hatteberg,Scott	Pawtucket	Bos	54	11	2	5	.204	233	66	10	44	.283
Hazlett,Steve	Salt Lake	Min	95	19	2	10	.200	206	42	8	31	.204
Helfand,Eric	Buffalo	Cle	50	12	0	6	.240	208	42	5	16	.202
Hernandez,Carl.	Albequerque	LA	55	15	3	8	.273	178	41	2	22	.230
Hiatt,Phil	Toledo	Det	139	38	11	30	.273	416	107	31	89	.257
Holbert,Aaron	Louisville	StL	113	28	1	8	.248	323	87	3	24	.269
Horne,Tyrone	Edmonton	Oak	56	8	1	4	.143	148	39	3	12	.264
Hosey,Dwayne	Pawtucket	Bos	88	30	4	14	.341	279	79	10	39	.283
Howard,Matt	Columbus	NYA	64	23	1	5	.359	138	47	1	11	.341
Howitt,Dann	Louisville	StL	52	17	1	8	.327	245	62	7	32	.253
Hubbard,Mike	Iowa	ChN	80	23	2	12	.287	152	45	5	21	.296
Huckaby,Ken	Albequerque	LA	82	25	2	16	.305	204	54	1	25	.265
Huff,Michael	Syracuse	Tor	75	19	3	12	.253	173	53	5	30	.306
Hyers,Tim	Toledo	Det	123	31	0	17	.252	314	82	7	42	.261
Ibanez,Raul	Tacoma	Sea	97	30	3	13	.309	308	85	8	34	.276
Ingram,Riccardo	Las Vegas	SD	91	22	0	8	.242	318	80	8	43	.252
Jackson,Damian	Buffalo	Cle	142	39	3	15	.275	310	77	9	34	.248
Jennings,Robin	Iowa	ChN	102	30	5	15	.294	229	64	13	41	.279
Jensen,Marcus	Phoenix	SF	93	20	0	10	.215	312	87	5	43	.279
Jones,Dax	Phoenix	SF	71	20	2	12	.282	227	72	4	29	.317
Jones,Terry	Col. Springs	Col	128	34	0	8	.266	369	109	0	25	.295
Jose,Felix	Syracuse	Tor	87	19	3	8	.218	272	72	15	58	.265
Kellner,Frank	Tucson	Hou	57	17	0	10	.298	197	52	1	21	.264
Kelly,Mike	Indianapolis	Cin	58	9	2	5	.155	234	52	6	25	.222
Kennedy,David	Col. Springs	Col	94	22	6	22	.234	239	63	5	28	.264
Kieschnick,Br.	Iowa	ChN	145	37	6	21	.255	296	77	12	43	.260
Koslofski,Kevin	New Orleans	Mil	49	11	1	4	.224	189	44	3	21	.233
Landry,Todd	New Orleans	Mil	94	21	2	9	.223	297	73	3	35	.246
Latham,Chris	Salt Lake	Min	103	33	2	16	.320	273	70	7	34	.256

AAA Batting vs. Left-Handed and Right-Handed Pitchers

			vs Left					vs Right				
Player	Team	Org	AB	H	HR	RBI	Avg	AB	H	HR	RBI	Avg
Lawton,Matt	Salt Lake	Min	49	18	2	11	.367	163	45	5	22	.276
Ledee,Ricky	Columbus	NYA	104	23	4	14	.221	254	78	17	50	.307
Ledesma,Aaron	Vancouver	Cal	132	44	0	16	.333	308	90	1	35	.292
Lee,Derek	Oklahoma City	Tex	130	34	6	23	.262	279	89	7	39	.319
Lennon,Patrick	Edmonton	Oak	54	22	6	17	.407	197	60	6	25	.305
Lesher,Brian	Edmonton	Oak	117	28	5	14	.239	297	91	13	61	.306
Lewis,T.R.	Pawtucket	Bos	107	36	2	16	.336	167	50	12	36	.299
Lopez,Roberto	New Orleans	Mil	103	21	3	13	.204	335	81	4	26	.242
Lott,Billy	Albequerque	LA	99	27	6	17	.273	318	84	13	49	.264
Lucca,Lou	Charlotte	Fla	94	27	4	18	.287	179	44	3	17	.246
Lukachyk,Rob	Ottawa	Mon	53	14	2	15	.264	193	51	7	24	.264
Luke,Matt	Columbus	NYA	85	27	9	33	.318	179	47	10	37	.263
Marrero,Oreste	Albequerque	LA	86	23	5	20	.267	355	102	8	56	.287
Marsh,Tom	Buffalo	Cle	123	35	2	13	.285	272	58	8	36	.213
Martin,Chris	Ottawa	Mon	110	29	3	8	.264	341	90	5	46	.264
Martinez,Felix	Omaha	KC	97	20	1	3	.206	298	73	4	32	.245
Martinez,Manny	Tacoma	Sea	71	19	1	6	.268	206	68	3	18	.330
Martinez,Pablo	Richmond	Atl	78	19	0	5	.244	185	52	1	13	.281
Martinez,Ramon	Omaha	KC	76	21	1	5	.276	244	60	5	36	.246
Marx,Tim	Calgary	Pit	76	27	0	12	.355	220	69	1	25	.314
Matos,Francisco	Ottawa	Mon	93	22	1	9	.237	214	51	1	14	.238
Maurer,Ron	Albequerque	LA	71	23	2	10	.324	151	38	3	20	.252
McClain,Scott	Rochester	Bal	133	30	3	14	.226	330	100	14	55	.303
McDonald,Jason	Edmonton	Oak	133	26	1	8	.195	346	88	7	38	.254
McGuire,Ryan	Ottawa	Mon	112	24	4	9	.214	339	92	8	51	.271
McIntosh,Tim	Columbus	NYA	70	19	2	10	.271	136	38	8	18	.279
McMillon,Billy	Charlotte	Fla	131	47	4	25	.359	216	75	13	45	.347
Mejia,Roberto	Indianapolis	Cin	101	27	2	18	.267	273	82	11	40	.300
Mercedes,Henry	Omaha	KC	53	14	0	4	.264	170	34	8	31	.200
Merchant,Mark	Omaha	KC	62	15	1	4	.242	187	46	7	32	.246
Millar,Kevin	Portland	Fla	129	55	9	28	.426	343	95	9	58	.277
Miller,Damian	Salt Lake	Min	92	31	2	16	.337	293	79	5	39	.270
Milliard,Ralph	Charlotte	Fla	104	32	4	12	.308	146	37	2	14	.253
Mitchell,Keith	Indianapolis	Cin	84	36	8	22	.429	273	71	8	44	.260
Mitchell,Tony	Toledo	Det	77	21	6	16	.273	211	59	6	27	.280
Molina,Izzy	Edmonton	Oak	89	26	1	8	.292	253	64	11	48	.253
Montgomery,Ray	Tucson	Hou	78	20	3	15	.256	281	90	19	60	.320
Moore,Bobby	Richmond	Atl	86	32	1	6	.372	114	22	2	8	.193
Moore,Kerwin	Edmonton	Oak	120	21	1	5	.175	332	83	1	27	.250
Mora,Melvin	Tucson	Hou	47	16	0	6	.340	181	48	3	20	.265
Morman,Russ	Charlotte	Fla	102	31	5	22	.304	187	65	13	55	.348
Mota,Jose	Omaha	KC	44	6	1	1	.136	185	50	2	19	.270
Mottola,Chad	Indianapolis	Cin	111	26	2	12	.234	251	69	7	35	.275
Mueller,Bill	Phoenix	SF	106	35	1	9	.330	334	98	3	27	.293
Mulligan,Sean	Las Vegas	SD	83	28	8	18	.337	275	75	11	57	.273
Munoz,Jose	Nashville	ChA	75	23	0	9	.307	220	46	6	25	.209
Murray,Calvin	Phoenix	SF	75	17	1	10	.227	236	59	2	18	.250
Myers,Rod	Omaha	KC	114	30	3	12	.263	297	90	13	42	.303
Nunnally,Jon	Omaha	KC	85	25	6	18	.294	260	72	19	59	.277
O'Neill,Doug	Portland	Fla	73	15	1	7	.205	168	47	6	18	.280
Ochoa,Alex	Norfolk	NYN	70	26	6	17	.371	163	53	2	22	.325
Ogden,Jamie	Salt Lake	Min	115	30	4	20	.261	333	88	14	54	.264
Oliva,Jose	Louisville	StL	109	25	5	18	.229	304	75	26	68	.247
Olmeda,Jose	Charlotte	Fla	126	43	5	19	.341	249	77	4	30	.309
Ortiz,Luis	Oklahoma City	Tex	144	46	3	21	.319	357	113	11	52	.317
Owens,Billy	Rochester	Bal	57	14	3	8	.246	144	37	2	22	.257
Palmeiro,Orlando	Vancouver	Cal	71	24	0	11	.338	174	51	0	22	.293
Pappas,Erik	Oklahoma City	Tex	109	26	2	16	.239	221	42	3	20	.190
Pecorilli,Aldo	Richmond	Atl	137	41	7	23	.299	266	76	8	39	.286
Peguero,Julio	Tacoma	Sea	73	22	0	7	.301	255	70	1	14	.275
Peltier,Dan	Phoenix	SF	84	23	0	14	.274	183	53	0	13	.290
Pemberton,Rudy	Pawtucket	Bos	100	27	6	16	.270	296	102	21	76	.345
Penn,Shannon	Toledo	Det	90	30	2	10	.333	266	72	4	32	.271
Pennyfeather,W.	Vancouver	Cal	125	36	2	16	.288	288	81	3	47	.281
Perez,Eduardo	Indianapolis	Cin	108	29	6	18	.269	343	103	15	66	.300
Perez,Neifi	Col. Springs	Col	141	40	3	17	.284	429	140	4	55	.326
Petagine,Roberto	Norfolk	NYN	93	29	3	18	.312	221	71	9	47	.321
Phillips,J.R.	Scranton-WB	Phi	72	21	5	14	.292	128	36	8	28	.281
Pirkl,Greg	Tacoma	Sea	78	22	5	15	.282	270	83	16	60	.307
Polcovich,Kevin	Calgary	Pit	71	23	0	8	.324	265	69	1	38	.260
Posada,Jorge	Columbus	NYA	129	35	3	18	.271	225	61	8	44	.271
Pose,Scott	Syracuse	Tor	99	21	0	10	.212	320	93	0	29	.291
Pough,Pork Chop	Pawtucket	Bos	85	19	5	10	.224	157	38	7	30	.242
Pozo,Arquimedez	Tacoma	Sea	85	16	3	14	.188	280	86	12	50	.307
Pritchett,Chris	Vancouver	Cal	155	43	3	20	.277	330	100	13	53	.303

			vs Left					vs Right				
Player	Team	Org	AB	H	HR	RBI	Avg	AB	H	HR	RBI	Avg
Pulliam,Harvey	Col. Springs	Col	60	16	1	13	.267	223	62	9	45	.278
Pye,Eddie	Tucson	Hou	79	15	1	7	.190	196	56	1	18	.286
Quinlan,Tom	Salt Lake	Min	116	40	3	19	.345	375	99	12	62	.264
Raabe,Brian	Salt Lake	Min	118	37	3	11	.314	364	132	15	58	.363
Ramos,John	Syracuse	Tor	101	26	4	17	.257	216	51	4	25	.236
Ramos,Ken	Tucson	Hou	105	23	1	9	.219	280	81	3	25	.289
Ramsey,F.	Nashville	ChA	120	19	1	5	.158	275	67	6	19	.244
Redmond,Mike	Portland	Fla	102	39	1	19	.382	292	74	3	25	.253
Reese,Pokey	Indianapolis	Cin	67	19	0	8	.284	213	46	1	15	.216
Reimer,Kevin	Tacoma	Sea	58	14	2	8	.241	228	67	11	36	.294
Relaford,Desi	Tacoma	Sea	75	12	1	8	.160	242	53	3	24	.219
Richardson,Brian	Albequerque	LA	86	29	4	19	.337	269	58	5	24	.216
Riley,Marquis	Charlotte	Fla	122	25	0	4	.205	178	43	0	9	.242
Rivera,Luis	Norfolk	NYN	104	31	3	16	.298	252	49	3	23	.194
Rivera,Ruben	Columbus	NYA	98	17	2	11	.173	264	68	8	35	.258
Roberson,Kevin	Norfolk	NYN	63	16	1	8	.254	152	41	6	25	.270
Robertson,Jason	Portland	Fla	87	20	0	9	.230	251	72	12	39	.287
Robertson,Mike	Nashville	ChA	112	26	4	19	.232	338	90	17	55	.266
Rodarte,Raul	Richmond	Atl	80	28	3	14	.350	139	46	6	32	.331
Rodriguez,Steve	Toledo	Det	85	29	2	11	.341	248	66	2	19	.266
Rodriguez,Tony	Pawtucket	Bos	65	17	1	6	.262	200	48	2	22	.240
Ronan,Marc	Charlotte	Fla	66	20	1	2	.303	154	47	3	18	.305
Roskos,John	Portland	Fla	109	30	4	16	.275	287	79	5	42	.275
Rossy,Rico	Las Vegas	SD	90	24	0	7	.267	323	80	4	28	.248
Rowland,Rich	Syracuse	Tor	74	18	3	13	.243	214	47	5	32	.220
Russo,Paul	Las Vegas	SD	58	15	1	7	.259	168	42	3	26	.250
Saenz,Olmedo	Nashville	ChA	122	26	3	10	.213	354	98	15	53	.277
Schall,Gene	Scranton-WB	Phi	102	26	3	10	.255	269	81	14	57	.301
Schu,Rick	Ottawa	Mon	98	35	4	22	.357	297	72	8	32	.242
Scott,Gary	Las Vegas	SD	49	11	0	5	.224	168	48	2	22	.286
Secrist,Reed	Calgary	Pit	83	26	3	18	.313	337	103	14	48	.306
Selby,Bill	Pawtucket	Bos	73	17	2	14	.233	187	49	9	33	.262
Shave,Jon	Oklahoma City	Tex	124	32	2	10	.258	290	78	5	31	.269
Sheets,Andy	Tacoma	Sea	59	23	5	13	.390	173	60	0	20	.347
Sheff,Chris	Charlotte	Fla	114	27	6	18	.237	170	48	6	31	.282
Sheldon,Scott	Edmonton	Oak	112	35	4	21	.313	238	70	6	39	.294
Shumpert,Terry	Iowa	ChN	65	13	2	6	.200	181	55	3	26	.304
Simons,Mitch	Salt Lake	Min	120	27	0	13	.225	392	108	5	46	.276
Singleton,Duane	Toledo	Det	74	15	2	7	.203	220	50	6	23	.227
Smith,Alex	Oklahoma City	Tex	82	22	2	8	.268	118	23	4	12	.195
Smith,Ira	Las Vegas	SD	55	12	0	0	.218	197	49	5	25	.249
Smith,Robert	Richmond	Atl	137	35	2	18	.255	308	79	6	40	.256
Sparks,Don	Buffalo	Cle	156	41	3	21	.263	355	110	5	47	.310
Spiezio,Scott	Edmonton	Oak	143	35	6	24	.245	380	102	14	67	.268
Stevens,Lee	Oklahoma City	Tex	159	53	17	50	.333	272	87	15	44	.320
Steverson,Todd	Las Vegas	SD	75	14	1	8	.187	226	58	11	42	.257
Stewart,Shannon	Syracuse	Tor	100	32	3	13	.320	320	93	3	29	.291
Stinnett,Kelly	New Orleans	Mil	77	24	10	27	.312	257	72	17	43	.280
Stynes,Chris	Omaha	KC	67	24	1	5	.358	217	77	9	35	.355
Sveum,Dale	Calgary	Pit	85	25	4	18	.294	258	78	19	66	.302
Swann,Pedro	Richmond	Atl	66	13	1	7	.197	230	61	3	28	.265
Tackett,Jeff	Toledo	Det	77	21	4	14	.273	206	46	3	35	.223
Tatum,Jimmy	Las Vegas	SD	62	17	3	15	.274	171	63	9	41	.368
Thomas,Brian	Oklahoma City	Tex	43	14	0	5	.326	204	51	7	31	.250
Thompson,Jason	Las Vegas	SD	86	22	2	13	.256	301	94	19	44	.312
Thompson,Ryan	Buffalo	Cle	168	43	11	30	.256	372	97	10	53	.261
Thurman,Gary	Norfolk	NYN	124	31	1	6	.250	325	89	8	33	.274
Timmons,Ozzie	Iowa	ChN	66	19	8	16	.288	147	34	9	24	.231
Tokheim,David	Scranton-WB	Phi	47	9	0	3	.191	208	45	1	18	.216
Tremie,Chris	Nashville	ChA	65	12	0	5	.185	150	35	0	21	.233
Turner,Chris	Vancouver	Cal	103	27	1	13	.262	287	73	1	34	.254
Tyler,Brad	Rochester	Bal	99	26	4	20	.263	283	77	9	32	.272
Unroe,Tim	New Orleans	Mil	97	25	6	14	.258	307	84	19	53	.274
Valdes,Pedro	Iowa	ChN	122	38	4	19	.311	275	79	11	41	.287
Valrie,Kerry	Nashville	ChA	136	42	4	18	.309	362	94	9	48	.260
Vinas,Julio	Nashville	ChA	99	21	1	5	.212	239	59	10	47	.247
Voigt,Jack	Oklahoma City	Tex	138	43	8	25	.312	307	89	13	55	.290
Walker,Todd	Salt Lake	Min	146	35	5	24	.240	405	152	23	87	.375
Waszgis,B.J.	Rochester	Bal	82	27	3	19	.329	222	54	8	29	.243
Wawruck,Jim	Rochester	Bal	48	14	0	3	.292	156	44	0	12	.282
Wedge,Eric	Toledo	Det	99	30	4	20	.303	233	48	11	37	.206
Weger,Wes	New Orleans	Mil	65	14	2	8	.215	145	30	2	15	.207
White,Billy	Col. Springs	Col	82	23	1	10	.280	202	46	2	16	.228
Whitmore,Darrell	Charlotte	Fla	74	23	4	14	.311	130	39	7	22	.300
Widger,Chris	Tacoma	Sea	85	22	3	13	.259	267	85	10	35	.318

AAA Batting vs. Left-Handed and Right-Handed Pitchers

			vs Left					vs Right				
Player	Team	Org	AB	H	HR	RBI	Avg	AB	H	HR	RBI	Avg
Williams,Juan	Richmond	Atl	76	13	1	7	.171	281	84	14	45	.299
Williams,Keith	Phoenix	SF	108	30	3	13	.278	290	79	10	50	.272
Williams,Reggie	Albequerque	LA	97	25	1	11	.258	255	76	5	31	.298
Wilson,Brandon	Indianapolis	Cin	88	21	1	5	.239	217	50	3	26	.230
Wilson,Desi	Phoenix	SF	77	21	0	3	.273	330	117	5	56	.355
Wilson,Nigel	Buffalo	Cle	154	41	10	30	.266	328	103	20	65	.314
Wilson,Pookie	Portland	Fla	117	28	1	9	.239	258	68	5	26	.264
Wilson,Tom	Buffalo	Cle	102	28	7	15	.275	106	28	2	15	.264
Wimmer,Chris	Louisville	StL	112	23	0	10	.205	233	63	2	13	.270
Wolff,Mike	Vancouver	Cal	66	12	5	13	.182	190	52	5	25	.274
Womack,Tony	Calgary	Pit	124	32	0	10	.258	382	120	1	37	.314
Woods,Ken	Phoenix	SF	55	20	0	5	.364	153	38	2	8	.248
Woodson,Tracy	Columbus	NYA	131	43	9	30	.328	289	78	12	51	.270
Young,Dmitri	Louisville	StL	143	50	5	31	.350	316	103	10	33	.326
Zinter,Alan	Pawtucket	Bos	75	19	3	15	.253	282	77	23	54	.273
Zosky,Eddie	Rochester	Bal	107	31	1	14	.290	233	56	2	20	.240
Zuber,Jon	Scranton-WB	Phi	108	31	1	16	.287	304	97	3	43	.319

AAA Pitching vs. Left-Handed and Right-Handed Batters

			vs Left					vs Right				
Player	Team	Org	AB	H	HR	SO	Avg	AB	H	HR	SO	Avg
Acevedo,Juan	Norfolk	NYN	171	59	6	39	.345	230	57	9	44	.248
Adams,Willie	Edmonton	Oak	188	41	4	42	.218	231	54	8	38	.234
Adamson,Joel	Charlotte	Fla	94	21	3	30	.223	293	87	12	54	.297
Alberro,Jose	Oklahoma City	Tex	271	65	8	50	.240	378	89	4	90	.235
Alfonseca,Ant.	Charlotte	Fla	112	35	4	21	.313	179	51	2	30	.285
Alvarez,Tavo	Ottawa	Mon	183	58	6	37	.317	272	70	6	49	.257
Anderson,Brian	Buffalo	Cle	84	27	3	11	.321	411	98	11	74	.238
Arrandale,Matt	Louisville	StL	110	36	3	12	.327	202	47	3	26	.233
Aucoin,Derek	Ottawa	Mon	109	31	3	30	.284	178	43	3	39	.242
Bakkum,Scott	Scranton-WB	Phi	136	41	3	19	.301	259	78	13	31	.301
Baptist,Travis	Syracuse	Tor	134	37	1	20	.276	434	150	14	57	.346
Barcelo,Marc	Salt Lake	Min	95	32	4	14	.337	145	50	4	20	.345
Barnes,Brian	Toledo	Det	53	12	2	12	.226	286	73	6	58	.255
Batchelor,Richard	Louisville	StL	73	20	2	19	.274	146	39	3	38	.267
Batista,Miguel	Charlotte	Fla	124	35	3	28	.282	183	58	1	28	.317
Baxter,Bob	Ottawa	Mon	91	19	1	21	.209	241	85	7	39	.353
Bell,Eric	Tucson	Hou	83	36	2	11	.434	452	141	5	47	.312
Beltran,Rigo	Louisville	StL	119	28	7	29	.235	394	104	10	103	.264
Bertotti,Mike	Nashville	ChA	64	16	1	18	.250	248	64	9	55	.258
Berumen,Andres	Las Vegas	SD	102	27	1	25	.265	169	46	3	34	.272
Bevil,Brian	Omaha	KC	108	32	4	21	.296	157	30	6	52	.191
Blomdahl,Ben	Toledo	Det	76	24	5	12	.316	174	53	4	22	.305
Bluma,Jaime	Omaha	KC	85	24	4	11	.282	143	33	3	29	.231
Boehringer,Brian	Columbus	NYA	212	74	7	39	.349	378	81	6	93	.214
Boever,Joe	Calgary	Pit	109	32	0	20	.294	208	46	1	46	.221
Bohanon,Brian	Syracuse	Tor	62	12	0	12	.194	156	44	4	26	.282
Bolton,Tom	Calgary	Pit	92	27	2	26	.293	365	94	5	66	.258
Boucher,Denis	Ottawa	Mon	50	21	4	2	.420	210	69	13	22	.329
Bourgeois,Steve	Phoenix	SF	151	43	2	23	.285	230	69	4	42	.300
Brandow,Derek	Syracuse	Tor	184	57	9	43	.310	286	61	5	60	.213
Brewington,Jamie	Phoenix	SF	172	55	6	22	.320	268	75	8	53	.280
Briscoe,John	Edmonton	Oak	80	20	2	23	.250	147	49	4	39	.333
Brock,Chris	Richmond	Atl	253	65	9	40	.257	321	72	11	72	.224
Brow,Scott	Syracuse	Tor	131	35	1	26	.267	171	49	5	26	.287
Browne,Byron	New Orleans	Mil	147	32	2	32	.218	254	72	16	48	.283
Brunson,William	Albequerque	LA	37	7	2	13	.189	174	46	5	34	.264
Bruske,Jim	Albequerque	LA	80	22	2	15	.275	159	41	1	36	.258
Buckley,Travis	Indianapolis	Cin	207	56	12	20	.271	270	70	11	38	.259
Bunch,Mel	Omaha	KC	226	71	9	34	.314	366	110	23	60	.301
Burke,John	Col. Springs	Col	105	43	2	19	.410	152	32	1	35	.211
Burlingame,Ben	Iowa	ChN	149	37	5	21	.248	234	67	8	45	.286
Busby,Mike	Louisville	StL	129	36	5	29	.279	160	53	6	24	.331
Bustillos,Albert	Col. Springs	Col	232	73	12	38	.315	340	94	14	57	.276
Cadaret,Greg	Buffalo	Cle	52	12	0	17	.231	186	47	3	27	.253
Campbell,Mike	Iowa	ChN	124	27	1	32	.218	225	48	7	55	.213
Carlson,Dan	Phoenix	SF	214	59	10	41	.276	331	76	8	82	.230
Carter,Andy	Phoenix	SF	79	24	1	18	.304	247	74	4	32	.300
Chergey,Dan	Charlotte	Fla	111	27	3	17	.243	187	59	13	26	.316
Chouinard,Bobby	Edmonton	Oak	133	24	2	25	.180	183	46	5	20	.251
Coppinger,Rocky	Rochester	Bal	101	32	2	24	.317	172	33	4	57	.192
Cornelius,Reid	Buffalo	Cle	127	36	2	22	.283	235	65	4	40	.277
Crawford,Carlos	Scranton-WB	Phi	269	70	7	41	.260	349	99	8	48	.284
Crawford,Joe	Norfolk	NYN	72	19	3	15	.264	303	79	7	53	.261
Cumberland,Chr.	Columbus	NYA	46	15	0	7	.326	194	71	9	28	.366
Cummings,John	Albequerque	LA	76	25	0	11	.329	226	66	5	38	.292
Cunnane,Will	Portland	Fla	219	60	5	34	.274	374	96	10	67	.257
Curtis,Chris	Oklahoma City	Tex	103	23	3	15	.223	198	68	3	23	.343
Czajkowski,Jim	Syracuse	Tor	120	28	1	29	.233	220	57	3	42	.259
Dabney,Fred	Iowa	ChN	60	20	2	8	.333	198	56	7	25	.283
Darensbourg,Vic	Charlotte	Fla	61	13	2	17	.213	180	48	5	49	.267
Darwin,Jeff	Nashville	ChA	85	14	3	11	.165	152	38	5	22	.250
Daspit,Jamie	Edmonton	Oak	133	37	4	16	.278	223	59	1	60	.265
Dedrick,Jim	Rochester	Bal	92	32	6	15	.348	176	56	8	22	.318
DeSilva,John	Pawtucket	Bos	148	46	3	28	.311	195	53	9	40	.272
Dettmer,John	Richmond	Atl	95	23	4	11	.242	138	46	4	15	.333
Dickson,Jason	Vancouver	Cal	215	63	4	32	.293	286	71	5	38	.248
Dishman,Glenn	Las Vegas	SD	131	30	1	27	.229	480	147	16	88	.306
Doherty,John	Pawtucket	Bos	87	40	1	5	.460	137	39	3	8	.285
Dougherty,Jim	Tucson	Hou	80	25	0	19	.313	157	40	0	34	.255
Dreifort,Darren	Albequerque	LA	116	36	3	20	.310	208	52	3	55	.250
Dreyer,Steve	Oklahoma City	Tex	178	46	3	42	.258	283	84	3	37	.297
Edens,Tom	Rochester	Bal	109	26	0	20	.239	158	47	9	16	.297
Edsell,Geoff	Vancouver	Cal	153	36	4	17	.235	227	57	3	31	.251
Eiland,Dave	Columbus	NYA	134	29	5	33	.216	205	48	4	40	.234
Elliott,Donnie	Scranton-WB	Phi	170	53	7	35	.312	219	52	5	58	.237

			vs Left					vs Right				
Player	Team	Org	AB	H	HR	SO	Avg	AB	H	HR	SO	Avg
Ellis,Robert	Nashville	ChA	104	39	4	13	.375	163	39	2	22	.239
Estes,Shawn	Phoenix	SF	66	15	1	18	.227	338	77	6	77	.228
Evans,Dave	Tucson	Hou	184	48	2	34	.261	257	72	6	46	.280
Eversgerd,Bryan	Oklahoma City	Tex	50	13	1	12	.260	195	44	2	48	.226
Falteisek,Steve	Ottawa	Mon	94	29	2	11	.309	147	46	8	15	.313
Farmer,Mike	Col. Springs	Col	46	15	1	5	.326	167	36	3	23	.216
Farrell,Mike	New Orleans	Mil	54	19	5	7	.352	204	53	2	32	.260
Flener,Huck	Syracuse	Tor	71	13	1	12	.183	247	60	2	50	.243
Fletcher,Paul	Edmonton	Oak	110	22	4	29	.200	193	44	4	47	.228
Florence,Don	Rochester	Bal	75	22	2	14	.293	274	89	9	39	.325
Fordham,Tom	Nashville	ChA	88	20	1	20	.227	422	97	14	98	.230
Fortugno,Tim	Indianapolis	Cin	64	19	2	18	.297	152	36	4	28	.237
Foster,Kevin	Iowa	ChN	196	47	9	34	.240	238	59	14	53	.248
Fox,Chad	Richmond	Atl	129	39	5	29	.302	220	52	4	58	.236
Frascatore,John	Louisville	StL	235	67	12	41	.285	394	113	10	54	.287
Fredrickson,Scott	Col. Springs	Col	79	27	4	15	.342	172	44	5	51	.256
Fyhrie,Mike	Norfolk	NYN	257	65	8	46	.253	379	85	8	57	.224
Gajkowski,Steve	Nashville	ChA	118	31	5	16	.263	299	82	6	31	.274
Gallaher,Kevin	Tucson	Hou	126	30	2	22	.238	207	58	3	59	.280
Ganote,Joe	New Orleans	Mil	131	38	5	20	.290	292	83	12	45	.284
Garcia,Jose	Albequerque	LA	110	32	3	7	.291	204	65	7	27	.319
Gardiner,Mike	Norfolk	NYN	234	46	5	50	.197	308	79	13	75	.256
Givens,Brian	New Orleans	Mil	77	17	4	16	.221	447	107	7	101	.239
Granger,Jeff	Omaha	KC	72	22	4	22	.306	207	43	6	46	.208
Graves,Dan	Buffalo	Cle	92	21	1	13	.228	182	36	0	33	.198
Greer,Ken	Calgary	Pit	103	32	4	13	.311	164	42	5	23	.256
Grott,Matt	Scranton-WB	Phi	96	33	2	18	.344	277	72	19	50	.260
Grundt,Ken	Pawtucket	Bos	68	15	1	16	.221	184	57	3	30	.310
Hancock,Ryan	Vancouver	Cal	122	27	4	25	.221	174	42	3	40	.241
Harikkala,Tim	Tacoma	Sea	276	86	6	50	.312	377	118	6	65	.313
Harkey,Mike	Albequerque	LA	185	62	3	29	.335	300	84	8	61	.280
Harriger,Denny	Las Vegas	SD	288	80	4	44	.278	354	103	8	58	.291
Harris,Doug	Portland	Fla	77	22	2	11	.286	145	36	5	20	.248
Harris,Pep	Vancouver	Cal	202	52	6	25	.257	258	83	6	36	.322
Hawblitzel,Ryan	Col. Springs	Col	174	49	4	27	.282	287	82	13	48	.286
Hawkins,Latroy	Salt Lake	Min	211	54	1	43	.256	314	84	10	56	.268
Helling,Rick	Oklahoma City	Tex	201	54	4	49	.269	320	70	6	108	.219
Henderson,Rod	Ottawa	Mon	193	49	5	42	.254	274	68	7	41	.248
Heredia,Felix	Portland	Fla	76	10	1	20	.132	139	38	2	22	.273
Heredia,Julian	Phoenix	SF	87	24	4	26	.276	173	47	8	33	.272
Hernandez,Livan	Portland	Fla	131	38	5	29	.290	209	43	9	66	.206
Hines,Rich	Columbus	NYA	66	20	2	10	.303	191	50	5	38	.262
Holman,Craig	Scranton-WB	Phi	103	37	4	17	.359	139	40	6	19	.288
Holt,Chris	Tucson	Hou	292	84	7	65	.288	436	125	4	72	.287
Hook,Chris	Phoenix	SF	178	57	7	30	.320	315	82	11	40	.260
Hope,John	Calgary	Pit	190	53	6	28	.279	298	94	5	43	.315
Hostetler,Mike	Richmond	Atl	236	68	2	34	.288	334	100	6	47	.299
Hubbs,Dan	Albequerque	LA	104	35	0	17	.337	199	54	4	65	.271
Huisman,Rick	Omaha	KC	66	18	3	15	.273	150	36	6	35	.240
Ilsley,Blaise	Scranton-WB	Phi	50	11	0	3	.220	200	62	11	28	.310
Janicki,Pete	Vancouver	Cal	162	44	7	33	.272	264	91	8	53	.345
Janzen,Marty	Syracuse	Tor	89	34	5	11	.382	137	40	7	23	.292
Johnson,Barry	Nashville	ChA	121	23	2	20	.190	264	70	9	48	.265
Johnstone,John	Tucson	Hou	78	22	0	27	.282	142	37	2	43	.261
Jones,Bobby	Col. Springs	Col	106	24	1	30	.226	230	64	7	48	.278
Kiefer,Mark	Omaha	KC	176	41	8	37	.233	274	68	14	62	.248
Klingenbeck,Sc.	Salt Lake	Min	242	60	1	51	.248	339	99	7	49	.292
Kramer,Tom	Col. Springs	Col	170	56	7	26	.329	279	73	9	53	.262
Lacy,Kerry	Oklahoma City	Tex	81	14	2	10	.173	134	34	0	21	.254
Lee,Mark	Richmond	Atl	77	23	2	27	.299	175	46	4	44	.263
Leftwich,Phil	Vancouver	Cal	169	39	4	39	.231	250	74	10	48	.296
Legault,Kevin	Salt Lake	Min	124	34	4	22	.274	199	66	6	35	.332
Levine,Alan	Nashville	ChA	54	14	2	11	.259	182	44	2	34	.242
Lewis,James	Buffalo	Cle	176	56	3	27	.318	288	78	7	44	.271
Lewis,Scott	Las Vegas	SD	259	78	12	44	.301	334	96	10	65	.287
Lima,Jose	Toledo	Det	132	43	7	38	.326	157	50	4	19	.318
Loaiza,Esteban	Calgary	Pit	119	27	2	23	.227	132	34	3	15	.258
Loiselle,Rich	Tucson	Hou	155	45	3	30	.290	190	47	1	42	.247
Lomon,Kevin	Richmond	Atl	238	64	5	41	.269	312	87	6	61	.279
Looney,Brian	Pawtucket	Bos	62	10	1	18	.161	262	68	13	60	.260
Lopez,Albie	Buffalo	Cle	173	46	5	40	.266	217	44	8	49	.203
Lorraine,Andrew	Edmonton	Oak	117	32	3	17	.274	464	149	16	56	.321
Lowe,Derek	Tacoma	Sea	180	53	2	31	.294	234	65	5	23	.278
Lowe,Sean	Louisville	StL	166	47	3	31	.283	281	80	4	45	.285
Ludwick,Eric	Louisville	StL	90	32	1	24	.356	134	23	3	49	.172

AAA Pitching vs. Left-Handed and Right-Handed Batters

			vs Left					vs Right				
Player	Team	Org	AB	H	HR	SO	Avg	AB	H	HR	SO	Avg
Luebbers,Larry	Indianapolis	Cin	105	31	4	12	.295	169	45	4	23	.266
Marshall,Randy	Toledo	Det	79	24	2	11	.304	285	73	5	49	.256
Martinez,Pedro	Norfolk	NYN	53	15	2	7	.283	155	30	2	30	.194
Maxcy,Brian	Louisville	StL	79	23	3	12	.291	154	40	2	40	.260
May,Darrell	Calgary	Pit	95	27	4	15	.284	419	119	13	60	.284
McCarthy,Greg	Tacoma	Sea	74	20	1	15	.270	181	38	1	75	.210
McCurry,Jeff	Toledo	Det	77	23	1	15	.299	160	43	1	41	.269
Meacham,Rusty	Omaha	KC	57	18	1	11	.316	151	38	5	28	.252
Mendoza,Ramiro	Columbus	NYA	115	32	0	18	.278	246	64	2	43	.260
Mendoza,Reynol	Charlotte	Fla	161	50	9	15	.311	207	62	9	26	.300
Mendoza,Reynol	Portland	Fla	84	18	0	10	.214	154	42	7	31	.273
Mercedes,Jose	New Orleans	Mil	175	64	9	18	.366	221	45	5	29	.204
Milacki,Bob	Tacoma	Sea	254	57	6	45	.224	352	74	6	72	.210
Miller,Kurt	Charlotte	Fla	102	34	3	11	.333	153	43	4	27	.281
Miller,Travis	Salt Lake	Min	116	27	0	25	.233	521	160	17	118	.307
Miller,Trever	Toledo	Det	140	38	4	33	.271	503	129	15	82	.256
Mimbs,Mark	Albequerque	LA	128	29	2	32	.227	476	136	12	104	.286
Minchey,Nate	Pawtucket	Bos	151	47	3	21	.311	218	42	5	40	.193
Mintz,Steve	Phoenix	SF	84	20	1	13	.238	141	43	5	22	.305
Misuraca,Mike	New Orleans	Mil	124	40	9	22	.323	196	53	2	35	.270
Mix,Greg	Portland	Fla	81	24	3	17	.296	182	56	5	40	.308
Mlicki,Doug	Tucson	Hou	228	68	2	44	.298	337	103	7	54	.306
Montgomery,S.	Edmonton	Oak	74	17	4	19	.230	141	34	3	21	.241
Moore,Marcus	Indianapolis	Cin	118	27	6	28	.229	207	45	2	42	.217
Munoz,Oscar	Rochester	Bal	169	43	8	44	.254	249	57	9	41	.229
Murray,Matt	Scranton-WB	Phi	101	31	4	11	.307	165	44	9	32	.267
Nichols,Rod	Richmond	Atl	101	17	0	29	.168	166	37	5	35	.223
Nied,David	Col. Springs	Col	123	49	9	25	.398	166	67	7	28	.404
Nitkowski,C.J.	Toledo	Det	93	22	1	23	.237	317	82	12	80	.259
Nunez,Clemente	Portland	Fla	139	39	5	20	.281	252	80	13	32	.317
Nye,Ryan	Scranton-WB	Phi	139	49	4	23	.353	188	48	6	28	.255
Ojala,Kirt	Indianapolis	Cin	109	35	5	27	.321	415	108	10	65	.260
Olsen,Steve	Omaha	KC	93	34	4	10	.366	160	36	3	31	.225
Oquist,Mike	Las Vegas	SD	232	61	4	47	.263	295	75	8	63	.254
Orellano,Rafael	Pawtucket	Bos	84	21	5	20	.250	313	103	15	46	.329
Paniagua,Jose	Ottawa	Mon	140	39	1	24	.279	180	33	6	37	.183
Patrick,Bronswell	Tucson	Hou	188	60	3	28	.319	285	77	4	54	.270
Patterson,Danny	Oklahoma City	Tex	115	31	2	22	.270	194	48	3	31	.247
Pavlas,Dave	Columbus	NYA	100	23	1	18	.230	192	41	4	47	.214
Pett,Jose	Syracuse	Tor	177	59	6	22	.333	266	75	4	28	.282
Phillips,Tony	New Orleans	Mil	69	22	3	16	.319	131	29	3	16	.221
Phillips,Tony	Tacoma	Sea	95	24	3	14	.253	121	46	7	10	.380
Pisciotta,Marc	Calgary	Pit	101	32	1	14	.317	152	38	2	31	.250
Pittsley,Jim	Omaha	KC	111	32	3	22	.288	156	42	5	31	.269
Powell,Ross	Louisville	StL	59	17	3	16	.288	214	65	6	45	.304
Pulido,Carlos	Iowa	ChN	70	26	4	10	.371	343	107	13	38	.312
Quirico,Rafael	Scranton-WB	Phi	51	11	1	13	.216	185	37	7	38	.200
Rath,Gary	Albequerque	LA	144	38	3	35	.264	535	139	10	90	.260
Ratliff,Jon	Iowa	ChN	137	38	4	22	.277	236	69	6	37	.292
Reed,Rick	Norfolk	NYN	258	56	7	55	.217	416	108	6	73	.260
Rekar,Bryan	Col. Springs	Col	193	58	5	27	.301	294	80	8	48	.272
Remlinger,Mike	Indianapolis	Cin	67	19	1	18	.284	249	45	3	79	.181
Ricci,Chuck	Pawtucket	Bos	90	20	5	17	.222	198	36	7	62	.182
Ricken,Ray	Columbus	NYA	108	33	3	19	.306	149	29	1	39	.195
Rivera,Ben	Ottawa	Mon	166	49	3	32	.295	233	63	4	55	.270
Roa,Joe	Buffalo	Cle	261	61	9	43	.234	365	100	10	39	.274
Roberts,Brett	Salt Lake	Min	287	86	9	40	.300	398	125	19	46	.314
Robinson,Ken	Syracuse	Tor	77	19	3	28	.247	153	33	11	50	.216
Rodriguez,Felix	Albequerque	LA	163	43	6	34	.264	233	68	11	31	.292
Rodriguez,Rich	Omaha	KC	71	24	1	25	.338	208	51	10	43	.245
Rosado,Jose	Omaha	KC	33	4	1	14	.121	322	76	15	68	.236
Rose,Scott	Edmonton	Oak	74	16	0	7	.216	142	41	2	13	.289
Rosselli,Joe	Vancouver	Cal	63	17	1	13	.270	157	36	2	24	.229
Ruebel,Matt	Calgary	Pit	73	16	1	16	.219	227	73	7	32	.322
Ruffcorn,Scott	Nashville	ChA	208	61	7	49	.293	365	81	11	80	.222
Rusch,Glendon	Omaha	KC	102	26	2	20	.255	560	151	13	97	.270
Ryan,Matt	Calgary	Pit	93	32	3	11	.344	132	39	1	25	.295
Sackinsky,Brian	Rochester	Bal	102	29	7	12	.284	152	46	5	26	.303
Sanford,Mo	Oklahoma City	Tex	228	61	11	48	.268	340	94	7	82	.276
Santana,Julio	Oklahoma City	Tex	268	67	5	38	.250	434	104	7	75	.240
Saunders,Tony	Portland	Fla	126	20	2	44	.159	469	101	8	112	.215
Sauveur,Rich	Nashville	ChA	87	15	1	33	.172	188	48	7	36	.255
Schmidt,Curt	Ottawa	Mon	81	23	2	7	.284	168	37	0	38	.220
Schrenk,Steve	Nashville	ChA	140	39	4	21	.279	218	54	8	37	.248
Schullstrom,Erik	Pawtucket	Bos	77	21	4	23	.273	135	36	5	39	.267
Schutz,Carl	Richmond	Atl	65	21	1	20	.323	218	65	3	32	.298
Scott,Darryl	Buffalo	Cle	93	17	2	32	.183	200	44	9	41	.220
Seelbach,Chris	Charlotte	Fla	228	70	13	40	.307	334	97	13	58	.290
Serafini,Dan	Salt Lake	Min	92	26	1	22	.283	425	138	19	87	.325
Shepherd,Keith	Rochester	Bal	164	43	4	44	.262	202	48	8	54	.238
Sievert,Mark	Syracuse	Tor	76	24	1	15	.316	141	38	5	31	.270
Simmons,Scott	Louisville	StL	95	19	6	22	.200	284	79	11	36	.278
Sirotka,Mike	Nashville	ChA	57	10	2	13	.175	296	80	8	45	.270
Slusarski,Joseph	New Orleans	Mil	78	21	2	14	.269	166	49	2	22	.295
Small,Aaron	Edmonton	Oak	184	49	4	37	.266	271	62	5	46	.229
Smith,Pete	Las Vegas	SD	287	71	3	39	.247	376	121	14	56	.322
Soderstrom,Steve	Phoenix	SF	252	66	3	26	.262	398	112	10	54	.281
Sodowsky,Clint	Toledo	Det	175	45	2	23	.257	282	83	6	36	.294
Sparks,Steve	New Orleans	Mil	95	29	2	13	.305	130	35	6	14	.269
Spradlin,Jerry	Indianapolis	Cin	161	48	5	32	.298	223	46	9	47	.206
Springer,Dennis	Vancouver	Cal	165	41	4	31	.248	228	48	5	47	.211
Steenstra,Kennie	Iowa	ChN	240	65	7	50	.271	376	105	17	51	.279
Steph,Rod	Richmond	Atl	113	25	3	19	.221	189	50	3	22	.265
Stephenson,G.	Rochester	Bal	179	52	8	33	.291	275	71	5	53	.258
Stidham,Phil	Salt Lake	Min	118	40	3	23	.339	199	60	5	31	.302
Stull,Everett	Ottawa	Mon	110	38	4	28	.345	173	49	3	41	.283
Sturtze,Tanyon	Iowa	ChN	74	29	5	11	.392	202	51	2	40	.252
Sullivan,Scott	Indianapolis	Cin	138	33	5	19	.239	270	62	5	58	.230
Suppan,Jeff	Pawtucket	Bos	232	57	6	63	.246	327	73	10	79	.223
Swan,Russ	Las Vegas	SD	106	32	1	13	.302	402	116	16	58	.289
Swartzbaugh,D.	Iowa	ChN	145	39	11	28	.269	301	67	11	75	.223
Telford,Anthony	Ottawa	Mon	167	38	2	30	.228	293	90	10	39	.307
Telgheder,Dave	Edmonton	Oak	175	44	2	26	.251	217	58	5	33	.267
Thobe,Tom	Richmond	Atl	86	23	2	15	.267	214	66	4	25	.308
Thompson,Justin	Toledo	Det	53	11	1	18	.208	255	63	1	51	.247
Thomson,John	Col. Springs	Col	116	34	3	35	.293	155	42	3	27	.271
Thornton,Paul	Portland	Fla	89	29	4	14	.326	207	45	2	50	.217
Torres,Dilson	Omaha	KC	160	48	3	18	.300	190	54	8	18	.284
Torres,Salomon	Tacoma	Sea	226	68	5	42	.301	312	82	11	79	.263
Trlicek,Rick	Norfolk	NYN	84	21	1	16	.250	184	31	0	38	.168
Urso,Sal	Tacoma	Sea	62	24	3	9	.387	202	45	2	36	.223
Valdes,Marc	Charlotte	Fla	90	31	7	11	.344	115	35	3	13	.304
Valdes,Marc	Portland	Fla	87	22	1	10	.253	158	38	4	39	.241
Valdez,Carlos	Phoenix	SF	84	23	1	10	.274	148	40	3	28	.270
Vanderweele,D.	Phoenix	SF	127	31	3	15	.244	224	70	10	27	.313
VanEgmond,Tim	Pawtucket	Bos	94	27	3	23	.287	139	39	6	23	.281
VanRyn,Ben	Louisville	StL	61	20	4	8	.328	195	49	5	34	.251
Wagner,Billy	Tucson	Hou	68	16	0	23	.235	208	46	2	63	.221
Wagner,Matt	Tacoma	Sea	153	42	4	36	.275	195	47	4	46	.241
Wall,Donne	Tucson	Hou	101	32	0	21	.317	113	35	2	15	.310
Wallace,Derek	Norfolk	NYN	77	16	1	22	.208	128	21	3	30	.164
Wallace,Kent	Columbus	NYA	97	25	5	9	.258	168	44	10	25	.262
Ward,Bryan	Portland	Fla	102	36	7	30	.353	477	134	16	94	.281
Ware,Jeff	Syracuse	Tor	96	25	3	18	.260	207	58	3	41	.280
Warren,Brian	Indianapolis	Cin	71	17	2	12	.239	173	51	5	28	.295
Watkins,Scott	Salt Lake	Min	51	12	0	13	.235	149	48	6	30	.322
Weston,Mickey	Charlotte	Fla	171	54	3	19	.316	249	77	8	28	.309
Whisenant,Matt	Charlotte	Fla	69	12	2	13	.174	406	137	13	84	.337
White,Gabe	Indianapolis	Cin	45	11	1	10	.244	214	58	5	41	.271
Whitehurst,Wally	Ottawa	Mon	164	44	3	40	.268	242	57	4	43	.236
Whiteside,Matt	Oklahoma City	Tex	148	48	5	17	.324	211	47	3	35	.223
Wiegandt,Scott	Scranton-WB	Phi	72	25	0	12	.347	162	38	3	34	.235
Williams,Jimmy	Buffalo	Cle	77	17	4	19	.221	367	99	9	77	.270
Williams,Shad	Vancouver	Cal	132	34	3	23	.258	155	39	5	34	.252
Williams,Todd	Edmonton	Oak	146	50	3	12	.342	234	75	1	21	.321
Wilson,Gary	Calgary	Pit	281	88	6	42	.313	379	121	12	46	.319
Wojciechowski,S.	Edmonton	Oak	57	16	1	10	.281	173	40	2	36	.231
Woodall,Brad	Richmond	Atl	80	23	0	20	.287	428	101	10	54	.236
Wright,Jamey	Col. Springs	Col	102	25	1	25	.245	119	28	2	15	.235
Yan,Esteban	Rochester	Bal	114	28	2	27	.246	165	47	4	34	.285

1996 Major League Equivalencies

Eleven years ago, when Bill James introduced the "Major League Equivalency," he underlined its importance by stating, "This is, I think, by far the most important research I have ever done." Considering all that he has done to help us to better understand the game of baseball, his estimation of the significance of the MLE certainly says something about its value. And more than a decade later, we would have to agree with his evaluation.

There simply is no better way to get a "read" on a young hitter in the high minors. What the MLE method does is to adjust for a number of illusions to give us a purer stat line, one that more accurately represents a player's ability. The first thing it factors in is the level of competition. The player will be facing tougher competition as he moves up the ladder, so that's taken into account. Next, the numbers are adjusted to account for the environment in which they were complied. A bandbox? Lop off some points. Pitcher's haven? Give the guy a little more credit. Finally, they're tailored to fit the particular major league park the player will likely play in. Don't come away thinking the Rockies' system is loaded with prospects; that's just Coors Field making its presence felt, as it undoubtedly will when these guys make the majors. In sum, what you get is a stat line that represents approximately *what the hitter would have done had he been in the majors last year.*

These are *not* projections. If a guy's MLE shows him hitting .300, that's no guarantee that he's going to hit .300 next year—no more than Ken Caminiti's .326 average guarantees that he'll bat that high again. In other words, don't give an MLE any more weight than you would to a single season of major league performance. That being said, we stand by our MLEs. If you check last year's book, it was one of the few places where you could see that Alex Rodriguez was capable of putting up superstar-quality numbers. We can't gaze into a crystal ball and tell you who will end up getting 500 at-bats, but we *can* give you an inside look into who the most talented young hitters are.

Major League Equivalencies for 1996 AAA/AA Batters

ATLANTA BRAVES		Age	Avg	G	AB	R	H	2B	3B	HR	RBI	BB	SO	SB	CS	OBP	SLG
Ayrault,Joe	C	25	.209	98	306	19	64	13	0	4	28	21	58	0	0	.260	.291
Benbow,Lou	3B	26	.213	91	244	17	52	7	0	0	19	13	66	2	3	.253	.242
Correa,Miguel	OF	25	.186	64	215	13	40	10	1	3	17	6	67	1	1	.208	.284
Garcia,Omar	1B	25	.242	93	302	30	73	13	0	3	29	7	32	2	3	.259	.315
Giovanola,Ed	SS	28	.275	62	204	24	56	13	0	2	13	30	34	1	5	.368	.368
Graffanino,Tony	2B	25	.260	96	342	48	89	26	1	6	27	28	74	7	6	.316	.395
Helms,Wesley	3B	21	.215	64	219	16	47	10	1	2	15	7	50	1	0	.239	.297
Jimenez,Manny	SS	25	.234	131	449	46	105	17	1	2	39	16	70	7	6	.260	.290
Malloy,Marty	2B	24	.258	129	466	61	120	22	1	3	30	35	59	8	9	.309	.328
Martinez,Pablo	SS	28	.249	86	289	28	72	11	3	0	22	10	64	10	6	.274	.308
McBride,Charles	OF	23	.225	85	275	26	62	13	2	2	34	15	78	2	2	.266	.309
McFarlin,Jason	OF	27	.189	84	254	27	48	11	0	3	15	16	65	3	1	.237	.268
Newell,Brett	SS	24	.183	103	284	15	52	4	0	0	14	10	102	0	5	.211	.197
Pecorilli,Aldo	1B	26	.269	122	391	51	105	24	0	13	52	25	89	3	5	.313	.430
Rodarte,Raul	OF	27	.286	129	416	51	119	18	1	11	61	31	80	3	3	.336	.413
Simon,Randall	1B	22	.241	134	473	50	114	21	1	13	52	21	64	2	8	.273	.372
Smith,Bobby	3B	23	.236	124	433	41	102	24	0	6	49	26	117	10	8	.279	.333
Swann,Pedro	OF	26	.241	128	410	45	99	13	2	5	42	28	81	7	9	.290	.320
Toth,Dave	C	27	.225	120	356	43	80	25	0	7	37	33	64	1	2	.290	.354
Warner,Mike	OF	26	.215	71	223	29	48	15	1	4	22	27	55	5	7	.300	.345
Williams,Juan	OF	24	.255	119	349	46	89	19	1	14	43	42	130	3	3	.335	.436

BALTIMORE ORIOLES		Age	Avg	G	AB	R	H	2B	3B	HR	RBI	BB	SO	SB	CS	OBP	SLG
Avila,Rolo	OF	23	.250	72	272	33	68	12	0	1	20	16	40	7	5	.292	.305
Bautista,Juan	SS	22	.218	129	432	31	94	16	2	2	29	16	110	11	12	.246	.278
Bellinger,Clay	SS	28	.283	125	448	61	127	31	2	14	70	29	95	6	4	.327	.455
Bowers,Brent	OF	26	.304	107	425	68	129	17	2	11	39	25	86	14	7	.342	.431
Clark,Howie	2B	23	.259	127	441	49	114	26	2	3	46	45	58	1	8	.327	.347
Clyburn,Danny	OF-DH	23	.237	95	358	45	85	12	3	17	49	13	95	3	3	.264	.430
Cookson,Brent	OF	27	.249	103	358	61	89	17	0	22	59	27	97	2	5	.301	.480
Curtis,Kevin	OF	24	.231	129	451	62	104	19	1	17	52	41	102	1	1	.295	.390
Davis,Tommy	1B	24	.246	137	513	67	126	29	1	13	48	31	122	3	8	.289	.382
Dellucci,David	OF	23	.276	66	246	24	68	12	0	1	29	21	60	1	7	.333	.337
Devarez,Cesar	C	27	.267	67	217	21	58	8	0	3	24	8	27	3	1	.293	.346
Gordon,Keith	OF	28	.242	115	401	47	97	14	1	8	42	24	114	9	14	.285	.342
Hall,Joe	OF	31	.271	131	468	86	127	23	6	18	85	60	73	11	9	.354	.462
McClain,Scott	3B	25	.265	131	453	68	120	21	2	16	62	54	115	6	6	.343	.426
Otanez,Willis	3B	24	.250	138	496	53	124	24	1	23	67	34	104	2	7	.298	.442
Tyler,Brad	2B	28	.256	118	375	61	96	16	6	12	46	60	100	14	7	.359	.427
Waszgis,B.J.	C	26	.252	96	298	33	75	14	0	10	43	36	92	1	3	.332	.399
Zosky,Eddie	SS	29	.238	95	332	37	79	20	2	2	30	18	42	3	2	.277	.328

BOSTON RED SOX		Age	Avg	G	AB	R	H	2B	3B	HR	RBI	BB	SO	SB	CS	OBP	SLG
Abad,Andy	1B-OF	24	.280	65	214	31	60	24	0	3	36	26	43	3	2	.358	.435
Allison,Chris	2B	25	.228	109	356	46	81	7	0	0	20	22	65	10	10	.272	.247
Bell,Juan	2B	29	.240	68	208	24	50	15	1	4	19	19	45	1	1	.304	.380
Brown,Randy	SS	27	.289	75	249	43	72	16	1	10	35	21	60	6	3	.344	.482
Carey,Todd	3B	25	.252	125	441	73	111	37	2	18	73	38	131	2	3	.311	.467
Clark,Phil	3B-DH	29	.318	97	365	49	116	38	1	10	59	14	33	2	5	.343	.510
Cole,Alex	OF	31	.287	82	300	49	86	14	6	3	33	43	49	7	6	.376	.403
Dodson,Bo	1B	26	.335	82	272	32	91	21	0	9	37	27	52	2	0	.395	.511
Hatteberg,Scott	C	27	.261	90	284	45	74	16	0	9	42	50	69	0	0	.371	.412

Major League Equivalencies for 1996 AAA/AA Batters

BOSTON RED SOX		Age	Avg	G	AB	R	H	2B	3B	HR	RBI	BB	SO	SB	CS	OBP	SLG
Holifield,Rick	OF	27	.251	118	403	68	101	23	3	9	35	42	116	25	9	.321	.390
Hosey,Dwayne	OF	30	.289	93	363	66	105	29	3	11	45	34	70	13	5	.350	.477
Hyzdu,Adam	OF	25	.335	109	373	66	125	26	2	23	75	44	80	0	7	.405	.601
Lewis,T.R.	OF	26	.306	79	271	47	83	24	0	11	45	29	52	1	1	.373	.517
McKeel,Walt	C	25	.300	128	463	80	139	21	0	14	73	47	55	1	3	.365	.436
Mejia,Roberto	2B	25	.286	122	448	59	128	30	7	12	58	31	100	11	4	.332	.464
Merloni,Lou	3B	26	.239	66	209	26	50	12	0	2	25	15	40	0	1	.290	.325
Nixon,Trot	OF	23	.249	123	437	51	109	12	3	9	59	39	69	5	8	.311	.352
Pemberton,Rudy	OF	27	.306	119	461	72	141	32	2	23	90	16	76	11	9	.329	.534
Pirkl,Greg	1B-DH	26	.298	88	346	46	103	24	1	18	69	12	60	0	0	.321	.529
Pozo,Arquimedez	3B	23	.271	106	399	55	108	14	4	13	60	37	48	2	2	.333	.424
Rodriguez,Tony	SS	26	.237	72	262	32	62	14	0	2	24	13	33	2	0	.273	.313
Sadler,Donnie	SS	22	.267	115	454	63	121	22	6	5	43	30	80	24	9	.312	.374
Selby,Bill	2B	27	.245	71	257	33	63	14	3	9	40	19	40	0	2	.297	.428
Woods,Tyrone	DH	27	.308	99	354	70	109	17	1	23	66	44	70	3	3	.384	.556
Zinter,Alan	1B	29	.259	108	352	67	91	22	3	21	59	50	129	3	0	.351	.517
CALIFORNIA ANGELS		Age	Avg	G	AB	R	H	2B	3B	HR	RBI	BB	SO	SB	CS	OBP	SLG
Alfonzo,Edgar	3B-SS	30	.245	83	298	29	73	18	0	3	32	16	49	0	2	.283	.336
Arias,George	3B	25	.318	59	236	44	75	21	0	8	49	17	40	1	1	.364	.508
Bryant,Ralph	DH	36	.186	60	210	26	39	13	0	7	20	12	81	0	1	.230	.348
Burke,Jamie	3B	25	.256	86	289	29	74	10	1	1	24	19	43	1	2	.302	.308
Carvajal,Jovino	OF	28	.229	118	420	42	96	9	1	5	44	18	67	16	14	.260	.290
Christian,Eddie	OF	25	.273	107	407	47	111	24	2	4	36	24	79	4	9	.313	.371
Diaz,Freddy	SS	24	.203	88	271	35	55	12	1	5	34	20	74	0	1	.258	.310
Erstad,Darin	OF	23	.287	85	342	56	98	19	3	5	36	39	56	8	6	.360	.404
Forbes,P.J.	2B	29	.254	117	398	52	101	21	1	0	41	37	47	2	3	.317	.312
Glenn,Leon	1B	27	.190	94	310	24	59	11	1	8	42	15	93	5	9	.228	.310
Grebeck,Brian	3B	29	.212	78	231	22	49	8	1	0	24	30	28	0	1	.303	.255
Greene,Todd	C	26	.286	60	217	24	62	16	0	4	29	14	38	0	2	.329	.415
Guiel,Aaron	3B	24	.239	129	422	57	101	24	3	8	38	37	77	7	7	.301	.367
Ledesma,Aaron	SS	26	.283	109	427	54	121	24	2	0	45	28	63	1	3	.327	.349
Luuloa,Keith	2B	22	.232	134	512	64	119	20	1	6	35	31	58	2	6	.276	.311
Molina,Ben	C	22	.245	108	351	36	86	17	1	6	43	16	27	0	1	.278	.350
Ortiz,Bo	OF	27	.265	127	486	58	129	26	2	9	51	21	87	8	7	.296	.383
Palmeiro,Orlando	OF	28	.286	62	238	36	68	11	2	0	29	26	20	5	3	.356	.349
Pennyfeather,Will.	OF	29	.264	108	402	50	106	32	1	4	56	16	76	14	10	.292	.378
Pritchett,Chris	1B	27	.277	130	473	70	131	34	0	15	65	63	102	3	4	.362	.444
Shockey,Greg	OF	27	.284	98	310	46	88	21	3	6	39	31	61	1	2	.349	.429
Turner,Chris	C	28	.239	113	381	45	91	16	0	1	42	54	91	0	3	.333	.289
Wolff,Mike	OF	26	.232	71	250	41	58	13	1	9	34	30	73	4	4	.314	.400
CHICAGO CUBS		Age	Avg	G	AB	R	H	2B	3B	HR	RBI	BB	SO	SB	CS	OBP	SLG
Barberie,Bret	3B	29	.218	68	206	23	45	7	0	4	21	28	24	2	2	.312	.311
Brown,Brant	1B	26	.292	94	336	43	98	23	2	9	39	17	68	4	6	.326	.452
Carter,Mike	OF	28	.250	113	376	37	94	12	0	1	16	9	44	3	6	.268	.290
Cholowsky,Dan	3B	26	.192	88	245	29	47	8	0	4	21	29	74	1	6	.277	.273
Dowler,Dee	OF	25	.257	113	342	50	88	13	4	5	40	34	44	18	7	.324	.363
Finn,John	2B	29	.224	86	237	26	53	10	0	0	27	21	36	1	6	.287	.266
Fryman,Troy	OF	25	.209	68	244	29	51	15	0	0	23	17	64	1	2	.261	.270
Glanville,Doug	OF	26	.291	90	364	48	106	21	2	2	31	10	36	12	10	.310	.376
Haney,Todd	2B	31	.230	66	235	18	54	12	0	1	17	17	25	2	1	.282	.294

Major League Equivalencies for 1996 AAA/AA Batters

CHICAGO CUBS		Age	Avg	G	AB	R	H	2B	3B	HR	RBI	BB	SO	SB	CS	OBP	SLG
Hubbard,Mike	C	26	.278	67	227	34	63	11	0	6	30	9	58	1	0	.305	.405
Hughes,Troy	OF	26	.253	123	438	64	111	23	2	16	80	36	92	2	4	.310	.425
Jennings,Robin	OF	25	.271	86	325	48	88	14	4	16	51	29	55	1	0	.331	.486
Kieschnick,Brooks	1B-OF	25	.247	117	434	42	107	18	0	16	58	33	113	0	1	.300	.399
Livsey,Shane	2B	23	.236	75	250	30	59	13	1	1	28	19	41	9	8	.290	.308
Maxwell,Jason	SS	25	.246	126	422	55	104	18	0	8	38	40	82	13	4	.312	.346
Morris,Bobby	1B	24	.244	131	454	61	111	26	2	6	53	47	78	8	14	.315	.350
Orie,Kevin	3B	24	.278	96	334	40	93	22	0	8	54	40	65	1	0	.356	.416
Ortiz,Hector	C	27	.205	105	288	18	59	8	0	0	14	21	40	0	2	.259	.233
Petersen,Chris	SS	26	.249	110	337	28	84	7	4	2	30	23	81	2	7	.297	.312
Samuels,Scott	OF	26	.243	106	334	53	81	17	3	1	28	45	86	15	5	.332	.320
Shumpert,Terry	2B	30	.261	72	241	41	63	12	3	4	29	21	46	10	3	.321	.386
Timmons,Ozzie	OF	26	.238	59	210	29	50	6	0	16	36	25	44	0	1	.319	.495
Valdes,Pedro	OF	24	.282	103	390	55	110	21	0	13	54	28	59	1	0	.330	.436
Walker,Steve	OF	25	.234	54	218	26	51	6	2	3	18	13	69	4	9	.277	.321
Williams,Harold	DH-1B	26	.246	94	293	30	72	8	0	8	33	21	70	0	3	.296	.355
CHICAGO WHITE SOX		Age	Avg	G	AB	R	H	2B	3B	HR	RBI	BB	SO	SB	CS	OBP	SLG
Abbott,Jeff	OF	24	.317	113	435	63	138	25	0	13	59	31	51	10	4	.363	.464
Brady,Doug	2B	27	.234	115	423	58	99	16	6	5	41	30	61	16	6	.285	.336
Cameron,Mike	OF	24	.287	123	464	111	133	31	9	25	71	55	122	29	11	.362	.554
Cappuccio,Carmine	OF	27	.260	120	400	54	104	20	2	9	60	24	49	0	3	.302	.388
Disarcina,Glenn	SS-3B	27	.299	81	264	30	79	17	2	5	43	9	67	3	1	.322	.436
Hurst,Jimmy	OF	25	.252	129	469	58	118	21	0	16	82	41	137	14	11	.312	.399
Larregui,Edgardo	OF	24	.234	82	278	35	65	12	0	0	17	16	41	0	3	.276	.277
Machado,Robert	C	24	.227	87	304	32	69	14	0	5	26	15	58	0	4	.263	.322
Menechino,Frankie	2B	26	.278	125	407	71	113	22	2	11	57	50	88	5	9	.357	.423
Munoz,Jose	DH	29	.226	78	292	29	66	15	0	5	33	19	37	6	1	.273	.329
Norton,Greg	SS	24	.269	119	442	64	119	24	3	12	65	41	98	4	8	.331	.419
Ordonez,Magglio	OF	23	.249	130	470	61	117	37	0	16	62	30	77	7	10	.294	.430
Pearson,Eddie	1B	23	.208	85	317	35	66	17	0	6	37	24	59	1	2	.264	.319
Ramsey,Fernando	OF	31	.214	110	393	41	84	2	0	6	23	9	58	10	10	.231	.265
Robertson,Mike	1B	26	.246	138	443	63	109	15	3	19	72	37	85	0	2	.304	.422
Rose,Pete	3B	27	.228	108	391	37	89	11	0	2	40	25	56	0	3	.274	.271
Saenz,Olmedo	3B	26	.253	134	471	84	119	27	0	17	62	51	82	3	2	.326	.418
Tremie,Chris	C	27	.211	70	213	16	45	9	0	0	25	17	49	1	0	.270	.254
Valrie,Kerry	OF	28	.266	138	493	58	131	30	4	12	65	27	96	8	9	.304	.416
Vinas,Julio	C	24	.230	104	335	47	77	16	1	10	51	35	64	0	4	.303	.373
Vollmer,Scott	C	26	.248	98	355	38	88	19	0	3	28	25	62	0	0	.297	.327
Wilson,Craig	SS	26	.231	102	320	45	74	11	0	2	29	40	44	0	1	.317	.284
CINCINNATI REDS		Age	Avg	G	AB	R	H	2B	3B	HR	RBI	BB	SO	SB	CS	OBP	SLG
Bako,Paul	C	25	.272	110	349	43	95	25	0	6	39	34	96	0	0	.337	.395
Belk,Tim	1B	27	.263	120	422	52	111	25	2	12	52	23	73	3	1	.301	.417
Boone,Aaron	3B	24	.263	136	529	70	139	41	4	13	77	27	79	15	5	.299	.429
Broach,Donald	OF	25	.234	110	337	47	79	9	1	4	30	28	52	14	5	.293	.303
Brown,Ray	1B	24	.302	115	351	55	106	24	3	11	42	37	64	1	0	.369	.481
Fordyce,Brook	C	27	.251	107	362	40	91	19	2	13	53	21	57	1	0	.292	.423
Garcia,Guillermo	C	25	.275	76	240	23	66	12	0	4	29	9	39	2	2	.301	.375
Gibralter,Steve	OF	24	.233	126	434	48	101	27	1	9	45	22	116	1	2	.270	.362
Goodwin,Curtis	OF	24	.241	91	328	47	79	18	2	1	25	46	68	30	11	.334	.317
Hall,Billy	2B	28	.268	117	444	65	119	23	1	1	35	42	73	25	9	.331	.331

Major League Equivalencies for 1996 AAA/AA Batters

CINCINNATI REDS		Age	Avg	G	AB	R	H	2B	3B	HR	RBI	BB	SO	SB	CS	OBP	SLG
Howitt,Dann	OF	33	.246	96	289	31	71	10	0	6	33	26	66	3	2	.308	.343
Kelly,Mike	OF	27	.189	88	285	35	54	9	0	6	25	26	81	9	1	.257	.284
Ladell,Cleveland	OF	26	.223	129	399	48	89	14	4	3	33	22	92	22	8	.264	.301
Magdaleno,Ricky	SS	22	.199	132	412	48	82	19	0	13	51	46	140	1	6	.279	.340
Mitchell,Keith	OF	27	.273	112	344	50	94	19	2	13	55	55	69	6	0	.373	.453
Mottola,Chad	OF	25	.239	103	351	37	84	22	2	7	39	18	94	6	5	.276	.373
Perez,Eduardo	3B	27	.268	122	436	70	117	27	3	17	70	44	70	8	0	.335	.461
Reese,Pokey	SS	24	.210	79	272	21	57	15	0	0	19	18	46	3	1	.259	.265
Rumfield,Toby	1B	24	.254	113	351	39	89	23	0	7	43	26	52	1	0	.305	.379
Santana,Ruben	OF	27	.270	104	345	41	93	19	1	6	46	20	43	3	2	.310	.383
Watkins,Pat	OF	24	.251	127	475	51	119	29	1	6	48	21	66	11	10	.282	.354
Wilson,Brandon	SS	28	.209	95	296	40	62	6	2	3	25	33	53	7	5	.289	.274
CLEVELAND INDIANS		Age	Avg	G	AB	R	H	2B	3B	HR	RBI	BB	SO	SB	CS	OBP	SLG
Aven,Bruce	OF	25	.287	134	478	85	137	30	2	20	71	32	108	16	7	.331	.483
Betts,Todd	3B	24	.236	77	233	31	55	12	0	0	23	29	54	0	1	.321	.288
Betzsold,Jim	OF	24	.224	84	263	31	59	10	3	2	31	22	78	3	1	.284	.308
Candaele,Casey	2B-OF	36	.297	94	384	60	114	22	1	5	34	24	36	2	5	.338	.398
Costo,Tim	1B	28	.202	83	248	22	50	11	0	7	25	17	61	0	2	.253	.331
Diaz,Einar	C	24	.266	104	387	42	103	25	1	2	31	9	23	2	2	.283	.351
Dunn,Steve	1B-DH	27	.276	92	294	32	81	19	0	10	44	27	76	1	1	.336	.442
Faries,Paul	2B	32	.235	121	391	41	92	13	1	1	27	34	49	7	3	.296	.281
Giles,Brian S.	OF	26	.299	83	311	59	93	16	4	18	58	38	30	0	0	.375	.550
Gutierrez,Rick	2B	27	.236	119	474	61	112	10	2	6	49	28	59	13	9	.279	.304
Helfand,Eric	C	28	.197	90	254	28	50	9	0	4	20	42	53	0	3	.311	.280
Jackson,Damian	SS	23	.243	133	444	70	108	14	0	10	45	44	81	19	7	.311	.342
Marsh,Tom	OF	31	.224	112	389	41	87	15	0	9	45	14	60	7	5	.251	.332
McCall,Rod	DH	25	.284	120	430	71	122	28	1	24	76	39	125	1	0	.343	.521
Neal,Mike	2B	25	.209	94	249	37	52	8	2	3	28	29	56	1	3	.291	.293
Ramirez,Alex	OF	22	.312	131	500	70	156	27	8	12	76	12	78	14	10	.328	.470
Raven,Luis	3B	28	.286	74	262	51	75	16	0	18	57	29	77	0	0	.357	.553
Sexson,Richie	1B	22	.262	133	508	76	133	32	2	14	68	29	125	1	1	.302	.415
Sparks,Don	3B	31	.281	137	501	63	141	31	3	7	62	49	74	1	2	.345	.397
Thomas,Greg	OF	24	.262	97	294	39	77	13	2	11	49	19	59	1	1	.307	.432
Thompson,Ryan	OF	29	.247	138	531	72	131	25	3	19	76	19	123	9	5	.273	.412
Wilson,Enrique	SS	21	.288	120	479	62	138	18	3	4	44	23	49	18	9	.321	.363
Wilson,Nigel	OF-DH	27	.285	128	473	80	135	22	4	27	87	45	121	3	4	.347	.520
Wilson,Tom	C	26	.254	73	205	25	52	13	1	8	27	32	68	0	1	.354	.444
COLORADO ROCKIES		Age	Avg	G	AB	R	H	2B	3B	HR	RBI	BB	SO	SB	CS	OBP	SLG
Castellano,Pedro	3B	27	.350	94	369	47	129	30	2	16	50	33	46	0	2	.403	.572
Cockrell,Alan	OF	34	.313	109	364	46	114	25	2	17	50	44	88	0	2	.387	.533
Echevarria,Angel	OF	26	.351	110	424	56	149	19	1	19	62	32	81	3	3	.397	.535
Gainer,Jay	1B	30	.234	108	333	43	78	16	0	14	41	30	71	4	2	.298	.408
Garcia,Vicente	2B	22	.242	87	306	34	74	11	1	4	19	25	44	0	2	.299	.324
Gibson,Derrick	OF	22	.295	122	474	62	140	24	4	23	67	28	128	2	12	.335	.508
Gonzalez,Pete	C	27	.196	78	209	17	41	8	0	5	19	26	39	0	3	.285	.306
Grunewald,Keith	2B	25	.255	111	365	29	93	16	3	5	30	23	98	1	1	.299	.356
Helton,Todd	1B	23	.359	114	404	60	145	32	3	11	66	56	50	1	5	.437	.535
Jones,Terry	OF	26	.292	128	500	63	146	7	4	0	28	31	78	19	7	.333	.322
Kennedy,Dave	1B	26	.266	117	338	39	90	27	0	13	42	30	82	0	2	.326	.462
Miller,Roger	C	30	.271	86	269	24	73	9	1	4	31	23	32	0	1	.329	.357

Major League Equivalencies for 1996 AAA/AA Batters

COLORADO ROCKIES		Age	Avg	G	AB	R	H	2B	3B	HR	RBI	BB	SO	SB	CS	OBP	SLG
Myrow,John	OF	25	.285	122	425	49	121	12	3	6	39	27	62	9	3	.327	.369
Perez,Neifi	SS	22	.324	133	577	65	187	31	14	9	61	17	47	12	13	.343	.473
Pulliam,Harvey	OF	29	.288	79	288	39	83	13	0	12	49	27	49	1	3	.349	.458
Sexton,Chris	SS	25	.243	127	460	54	112	14	2	0	30	65	69	6	5	.337	.283
Taylor,Jamie	3B	26	.267	124	374	49	100	23	1	10	40	41	76	0	2	.340	.414
Velazquez,Andy	OF	21	.331	132	516	78	171	33	4	30	67	48	117	5	2	.388	.585
Wells,Forry	OF	26	.255	108	314	47	80	22	1	9	46	42	75	0	2	.343	.417
White,Billy	2B	28	.251	103	287	20	72	11	1	3	22	27	80	1	2	.315	.328

DETROIT TIGERS		Age	Avg	G	AB	R	H	2B	3B	HR	RBI	BB	SO	SB	CS	OBP	SLG
Baez,Kevin	SS-2B	30	.235	98	298	33	70	11	2	11	42	23	56	2	0	.290	.396
Catalanotto,Frank	2B	23	.286	132	489	100	140	31	4	17	63	59	74	11	13	.363	.470
Cotton,John	OF	26	.208	113	384	45	80	12	3	17	55	21	138	14	5	.249	.388
Cruz,Fausto	SS	25	.240	107	379	47	91	17	1	12	57	32	85	9	9	.299	.385
Freeman,Sean	1B	25	.258	124	407	68	105	16	0	26	70	53	126	2	3	.343	.489
Garcia,Luis	SS	22	.233	131	514	64	120	20	3	9	43	9	97	12	11	.247	.337
Hansen,Terrel	OF	30	.247	109	377	47	93	16	1	26	62	15	123	4	1	.276	.501
Hiatt,Phil	3B	28	.255	142	550	96	140	25	2	43	115	48	190	14	5	.314	.542
Hyers,Tim	1B	25	.248	117	431	53	107	16	5	7	57	38	60	5	0	.309	.357
Makarewicz,Scott	C	30	.300	83	253	40	76	14	0	14	46	14	49	3	2	.337	.522
Mashore,Justin	OF	25	.272	120	445	63	121	25	6	7	47	26	104	13	12	.312	.402
Mitchell,Tony	OF	26	.280	133	454	71	127	20	3	25	80	56	144	2	1	.359	.502
Nevin,Phil	C	26	.283	98	339	73	96	16	0	24	65	48	89	4	1	.372	.543
Penn,Shannon	OF	27	.276	97	351	63	97	11	3	6	40	25	62	18	6	.324	.376
Pough,Chop	3B	27	.218	76	239	37	52	15	1	11	35	28	74	1	1	.300	.427
Rodriguez,Steve	2B	26	.274	96	328	47	90	17	1	4	29	22	45	15	2	.320	.369
Schmidt,Tom	3B	24	.211	115	380	42	80	22	1	11	42	25	98	3	0	.259	.361
Singleton,Duane	OF	24	.213	88	291	40	62	14	5	8	29	35	89	14	6	.298	.378
Tackett,Jeff	C	31	.226	89	279	39	63	9	2	7	47	35	57	3	1	.312	.348
Trammell,Bubba	OF	25	.304	134	483	91	147	34	1	33	94	46	111	6	1	.365	.584
Wedge,Eric	DH	29	.226	96	328	59	74	23	0	15	55	41	85	1	1	.312	.433

FLORIDA MARLINS		Age	Avg	G	AB	R	H	2B	3B	HR	RBI	BB	SO	SB	CS	OBP	SLG
Berg,Dave	SS	26	.272	109	397	49	108	23	3	6	56	27	64	11	6	.318	.390
Brooks,Jerry	OF	30	.249	136	442	51	110	23	1	23	76	22	81	3	4	.284	.462
Castillo,Luis	2B	21	.288	109	403	64	116	12	6	0	27	43	72	34	13	.357	.347
Clapinski,Chris	SS	25	.244	128	414	64	101	21	0	8	36	41	69	9	5	.312	.353
Dunwoody,Todd	OF	22	.246	138	529	68	130	25	4	16	72	29	159	16	6	.285	.399
Gregg,Tommy	1B	33	.245	119	383	49	94	19	0	14	57	35	65	6	0	.309	.405
Hastings,Lionel	3B	24	.205	97	283	23	58	10	0	4	34	9	53	3	1	.229	.283
Lucca,Lou	3B	26	.226	87	261	18	59	11	0	4	25	7	65	0	2	.246	.314
McMillon,Billy	OF	25	.306	97	324	51	99	26	1	10	50	25	79	3	2	.355	.485
Millar,Kevin	1B	25	.286	130	451	53	129	27	0	13	67	24	56	4	4	.322	.432
Milliard,Ralph	2B	23	.233	75	257	34	60	12	1	4	19	27	50	5	3	.306	.335
Morman,Russ	1B	35	.290	80	272	42	79	14	0	12	55	20	53	1	3	.339	.474
Olmeda,Jose	3B	29	.280	115	354	37	99	20	0	5	35	15	60	4	5	.309	.379
Redmond,Mike	C	26	.257	120	378	33	97	18	0	3	34	17	48	2	3	.289	.328
Riley,Marquis	OF	26	.195	104	333	36	65	9	0	0	9	20	44	12	4	.241	.222
Robertson,Jason	OF	26	.224	110	348	51	78	14	2	8	38	21	109	8	5	.268	.345
Ronan,Marc	C	27	.264	79	208	16	55	8	0	2	14	11	38	2	3	.301	.332
Roskos,Johnny	1B	22	.247	121	381	41	94	22	2	6	45	44	109	1	3	.325	.362
Sheff,Chris	OF	26	.237	119	371	41	88	22	1	9	48	23	81	6	1	.282	.375

Major League Equivalencies for 1996 AAA/AA Batters

FLORIDA MARLINS		Age	Avg	G	AB	R	H	2B	3B	HR	RBI	BB	SO	SB	CS	OBP	SLG
Wilson,Pookie	OF	26	.227	113	361	35	82	13	3	4	27	21	52	4	9	.270	.313
HOUSTON ASTROS		Age	Avg	G	AB	R	H	2B	3B	HR	RBI	BB	SO	SB	CS	OBP	SLG
Abreu,Bob	OF	23	.249	132	461	66	115	12	9	8	52	62	123	16	6	.338	.367
Ball,Jeff	1B	28	.284	116	405	49	115	26	1	13	56	25	92	7	8	.326	.449
Bridges,Kary	2B	25	.297	129	461	63	137	18	1	3	45	29	23	3	8	.339	.360
Brumley,Mike	SS	34	.202	88	267	30	54	9	3	2	21	29	91	6	3	.280	.281
Christopherson,Eric	C	28	.250	67	212	23	53	13	1	4	27	15	52	1	0	.300	.377
Colon,Dennis	1B	23	.260	127	420	43	109	21	0	9	51	15	55	0	3	.285	.374
Forkner,Tim	3B	24	.272	114	368	48	100	18	2	5	40	40	53	0	4	.343	.372
Goff,Jerry	C	33	.205	96	264	30	54	12	1	6	40	41	107	0	0	.311	.326
Groppuso,Mike	3B	27	.220	83	245	26	54	2	1	5	23	14	89	1	1	.263	.298
Hajek,Dave	2B	29	.279	121	481	62	134	26	3	2	49	18	40	6	6	.305	.358
Hatcher,Chris	OF	28	.269	136	480	65	129	26	2	22	79	16	140	8	9	.292	.469
Hidalgo,Richard	OF	21	.272	130	497	58	135	31	1	11	69	21	62	8	7	.301	.404
Johnson,Russ	SS	24	.286	132	479	76	137	22	3	12	65	41	56	6	4	.342	.420
Kellner,Frank	SS	30	.236	96	242	28	57	10	2	0	23	16	49	2	6	.283	.293
Luce,Roger	C	28	.237	89	283	31	67	11	2	7	38	8	77	0	0	.258	.364
McNabb,Buck	OF	24	.280	88	271	33	76	14	3	0	23	30	42	7	6	.352	.354
Mitchell,Donovan	2B-OF	27	.234	120	398	50	93	20	1	2	28	24	57	8	4	.277	.304
Montgomery,Ray	OF	27	.267	100	341	53	91	17	0	15	57	44	60	4	1	.351	.449
Mora,Melvin	OF	25	.254	132	464	58	118	14	1	6	40	22	56	5	12	.288	.328
Peterson,Nate	OF	25	.259	114	316	32	82	17	0	1	30	20	55	0	1	.304	.323
Pye,Eddie	2B	30	.224	92	263	30	59	13	3	1	19	21	45	3	3	.282	.308
Ramos,Ken	OF	30	.238	104	369	41	88	19	1	2	26	30	45	4	9	.296	.312
Sanchez,Victor	1B	25	.196	86	204	26	40	8	0	10	30	11	65	3	1	.237	.382
KANSAS CITY ROYALS		Age	Avg	G	AB	R	H	2B	3B	HR	RBI	BB	SO	SB	CS	OBP	SLG
Burton,Darren	OF	24	.246	129	448	60	110	25	4	10	54	46	79	5	7	.316	.386
Carr,Jeremy	OF	26	.228	129	434	50	99	19	1	4	29	29	65	27	10	.276	.304
Diaz,Lino	3B	26	.235	119	409	38	96	17	1	4	36	18	39	1	4	.267	.311
Grotewold,Jeff	DH	31	.252	98	326	50	82	17	0	7	41	46	83	0	3	.344	.368
Halter,Shane	OF	27	.235	109	328	36	77	21	0	2	28	25	55	5	2	.289	.317
Hansen,Jed	2B	24	.243	128	482	55	117	26	3	10	44	27	94	10	8	.283	.371
Long,Kevin	OF	30	.242	128	418	46	101	26	2	2	35	35	36	5	14	.300	.328
Long,Ryan	OF-DH	24	.247	122	421	47	104	25	0	13	58	10	72	4	5	.265	.399
Lopez,Mendy	3B	22	.249	93	313	35	78	17	3	4	23	16	68	9	4	.286	.361
Martinez,Felix	SS	23	.214	118	384	43	82	11	2	3	28	34	76	12	10	.278	.276
Martinez,Ramon	2B	24	.246	111	398	39	98	13	2	4	38	20	41	4	3	.282	.319
Medrano,Tony	SS	22	.241	125	453	44	109	22	0	5	41	11	36	6	8	.259	.322
Mercedes,Henry	C	27	.190	72	216	22	41	8	0	5	28	22	59	0	0	.265	.296
Merchant,Mark	DH	28	.220	80	241	32	53	11	0	5	29	31	52	0	1	.309	.328
Mota,Jose	3B	32	.221	72	222	19	49	4	1	2	16	13	26	5	6	.264	.275
Myers,Rod	OF	24	.265	112	396	54	105	24	0	12	43	39	105	26	10	.331	.417
Nunnally,Jon	OF	25	.253	103	332	61	84	18	3	19	62	37	99	7	9	.328	.497
Sisco,Steve	OF	27	.261	122	440	59	115	20	0	8	55	25	70	2	2	.301	.361
Stewart,Andy	C	26	.231	108	368	39	85	22	3	3	33	19	49	2	4	.269	.332
Strickland,Chad	C	25	.196	77	230	26	45	12	1	3	25	10	23	0	1	.229	.296
Stynes,Chris	OF-3B	24	.325	72	271	40	88	19	1	7	32	14	16	5	3	.358	.480
Sutton,Larry	1B	27	.261	125	441	62	115	18	1	15	62	48	67	2	1	.333	.408
Sweeney,Mike	C-DH	23	.263	91	319	44	84	23	0	11	50	24	41	1	2	.315	.439

Major League Equivalencies for 1996 AAA/AA Batters

LA DODGERS		Age	Avg	G	AB	R	H	2B	3B	HR	RBI	BB	SO	SB	CS	OBP	SLG
Battle,Howard	3B	25	.188	115	372	27	70	18	0	5	32	15	55	2	8	.220	.277
Blanco,Henry	C	25	.226	94	297	30	67	10	0	3	31	18	43	1	3	.270	.290
Dandridge,Brad	OF	25	.231	77	242	26	56	7	0	3	23	9	27	2	3	.259	.298
Garcia,Karim	OF	21	.232	119	426	52	99	16	4	11	56	24	110	4	5	.273	.366
Guerrero,Wilton	2B	22	.283	98	389	53	110	12	5	1	25	17	50	18	6	.313	.347
Hernandez,Carlos	C	30	.192	66	219	12	42	7	0	3	20	7	51	3	4	.217	.265
Huckaby,Ken	C	26	.222	103	266	25	59	11	0	1	27	11	36	0	0	.253	.274
Johnson,Keith	SS	26	.234	131	509	59	119	21	2	7	45	11	88	11	8	.250	.324
Konerko,Paul	1B	21	.259	137	455	62	118	17	0	21	68	47	93	0	4	.329	.435
Lott,Billy	OF	26	.215	114	391	45	84	14	0	11	44	30	130	4	7	.271	.335
Marrero,Oreste	1B	27	.231	121	411	33	95	20	0	8	51	24	124	1	6	.274	.338
Maurer,Ron	SS-3B	29	.222	86	225	23	50	10	0	3	20	21	59	1	4	.289	.307
Melendez,Dan	1B-DH	26	.187	98	225	17	42	8	0	0	23	18	47	0	0	.247	.222
Richardson,Brian	3B	21	.207	124	391	42	81	12	0	5	34	22	103	2	3	.249	.276
Riggs,Adam	2B	24	.241	134	478	53	115	24	2	10	51	24	87	11	6	.277	.362
Rios,Eduardo	3B	24	.214	90	257	24	55	8	0	3	29	15	40	1	2	.257	.280
Roberge,J.P.	OF-3B	24	.256	115	363	32	93	14	0	6	32	18	70	8	3	.291	.344
Romero,Wilfredo	OF	22	.252	126	429	51	108	28	2	4	39	22	56	15	5	.288	.354
Spearman,Vernon	OF	27	.222	123	450	51	100	11	4	0	23	23	40	18	7	.260	.264
Williams,Reggie	OF	31	.232	92	327	40	76	16	0	3	28	24	75	11	7	.285	.309
MILWAUKEE BREWERS		Age	Avg	G	AB	R	H	2B	3B	HR	RBI	BB	SO	SB	CS	OBP	SLG
Banks,Brian	OF	26	.270	137	486	71	131	29	6	14	64	67	106	15	7	.358	.440
Belliard,Ronnie	2B	22	.254	109	402	57	102	17	5	2	44	40	53	18	6	.321	.336
Caceres,Edgar	SS	33	.270	115	397	40	107	10	1	3	29	23	32	7	4	.310	.322
Dunn,Todd	OF	26	.309	98	343	56	106	21	3	14	61	30	88	9	3	.365	.510
Felder,Ken	OF	26	.213	122	428	55	91	20	0	16	45	28	132	1	3	.261	.371
Felix,Lauro	SS	27	.241	103	295	55	71	13	1	7	46	49	74	7	4	.349	.363
Hamlin,Jonas	1B	27	.256	131	496	63	127	31	5	15	73	24	106	6	6	.290	.429
Harris,Mike	OF	27	.249	116	401	53	100	15	3	6	38	25	60	3	2	.293	.347
Hughes,Bobby	C	26	.245	104	351	44	86	21	0	14	45	24	72	2	2	.293	.425
Koslofski,Kevin	OF	30	.231	75	238	39	55	8	2	3	25	31	65	4	1	.320	.319
Landry,Todd	1B	24	.238	113	390	41	93	19	1	4	44	32	62	12	3	.296	.323
Lopez,Pedro	C	28	.250	80	224	24	56	12	0	1	18	24	47	1	1	.323	.317
Lopez,Roberto	2B	25	.231	129	437	50	101	20	2	6	39	63	68	7	5	.328	.327
Nicholas,Darrell	OF	25	.249	70	229	35	57	10	2	1	18	18	59	5	8	.304	.323
Ortega,Hector	3B	24	.235	104	358	42	84	10	2	5	43	18	79	8	5	.271	.316
Perez,Danny	OF	26	.241	103	344	49	83	19	4	2	29	40	89	6	1	.320	.337
Rodriques,Cecil	OF	25	.256	119	375	49	96	20	4	3	39	21	96	3	7	.295	.355
Seitzer,Brad	3B	27	.289	115	415	61	120	27	0	12	68	34	70	4	3	.343	.441
Stinnett,Kelly	C	27	.283	95	332	63	94	21	0	25	70	31	85	2	2	.344	.572
Unroe,Tim	3B	26	.266	109	402	72	107	26	3	24	67	36	124	7	2	.326	.525
Weger,Wes	2B-3B	26	.206	64	209	23	43	11	0	3	23	18	33	0	0	.269	.301
MINNESOTA TWINS		Age	Avg	G	AB	R	H	2B	3B	HR	RBI	BB	SO	SB	CS	OBP	SLG
Brede,Brent	OF	25	.318	132	462	81	147	34	5	9	68	70	94	10	6	.408	.472
Caraballo,Gary	3B	25	.234	85	290	30	68	16	0	7	30	22	68	0	3	.288	.362
Ferguson,Jeff	2B	24	.278	89	281	44	78	16	1	5	19	30	73	4	4	.347	.395
Hazlett,Steve	OF	27	.184	101	294	35	54	12	2	8	32	26	91	5	2	.250	.320
Hunter,Torii	OF	21	.257	99	339	47	87	20	2	7	31	23	66	5	7	.304	.389
Johnson,J.J.	OF	23	.270	132	489	65	132	25	2	16	66	33	110	8	12	.316	.427
Latham,Chris	OF	24	.248	115	363	47	90	14	4	7	39	29	100	19	7	.304	.366

Major League Equivalencies for 1996 AAA/AA Batters

MINNESOTA TWINS		Age	Avg	G	AB	R	H	2B	3B	HR	RBI	BB	SO	SB	CS	OBP	SLG
Lawton,Matt	OF	25	.270	53	204	31	55	14	0	5	26	21	36	1	4	.338	.412
Lewis,Anthony	DH	26	.247	134	454	56	112	15	1	24	91	39	109	4	9	.306	.443
Lopez,Rene	C	25	.222	83	234	25	52	12	0	3	26	21	40	0	3	.286	.312
Miller,Damian	C	27	.261	104	372	43	97	24	0	5	43	20	62	0	4	.298	.366
Nevers,Tom	SS	25	.257	127	455	62	117	27	6	7	42	38	95	2	10	.314	.389
Ogden,Jamie	1B-OF	25	.238	123	433	63	103	20	1	15	59	36	113	12	2	.296	.393
Quinlan,Tom	3B	29	.259	121	475	64	123	34	0	12	64	30	130	3	8	.303	.406
Raabe,Brian	2B	29	.323	116	462	82	149	35	2	15	55	38	20	6	8	.374	.504
Radmanovich,Ryan	OF	25	.274	125	449	74	123	31	1	25	83	41	134	3	11	.335	.514
Roper,Chad	3B	23	.245	128	462	56	113	18	1	10	46	35	80	3	7	.298	.353
Rupp,Chad	1B	25	.246	77	276	36	68	14	0	18	46	10	61	2	2	.273	.493
Simons,Mitch	SS	28	.240	129	496	60	119	24	5	4	47	35	63	26	10	.290	.333
Turner,Brian	1B	26	.218	80	238	25	52	13	1	8	28	17	57	4	3	.271	.382
Walker,Todd	3B	24	.311	135	528	75	164	37	6	23	88	46	98	9	8	.366	.534
MONTREAL EXPOS		Age	Avg	G	AB	R	H	2B	3B	HR	RBI	BB	SO	SB	CS	OBP	SLG
Alcantara,Israel	3B	24	.185	62	211	20	39	4	0	5	15	9	66	0	0	.218	.275
Barron,Tony	OF	30	.283	123	441	54	125	29	1	12	55	20	97	6	3	.315	.435
Benitez,Yamil	OF	24	.247	114	421	43	104	18	1	16	63	22	125	8	3	.284	.409
Bieser,Steve	OF	29	.294	123	367	49	108	23	2	0	25	28	57	20	7	.344	.368
Blum,Geoff	2B	24	.218	120	385	37	84	22	1	0	33	42	54	4	6	.295	.281
Cabrera,Jolbert	SS	24	.218	107	344	32	75	17	1	2	23	16	67	7	4	.253	.291
Campos,Jesus	OF	23	.234	73	201	12	47	3	0	0	13	6	18	3	8	.256	.249
Guerrero,Vladimir	OF	21	.329	118	398	67	131	30	5	13	62	35	44	12	9	.383	.528
Henley,Bob	C	24	.206	103	281	26	58	11	0	2	21	49	83	0	1	.324	.267
Leach,Jalal	OF	28	.301	120	356	39	107	24	2	6	45	20	75	2	6	.338	.430
Lukachyk,Rob	OF	28	.255	97	326	46	83	19	2	9	49	18	75	9	1	.294	.408
Martin,Chris	SS	29	.237	122	435	53	103	28	0	5	42	26	56	18	6	.280	.336
Matos,Francisco	2B	27	.212	100	297	23	63	14	2	1	18	12	36	2	4	.243	.283
McGuire,Ryan	1B	25	.233	134	437	48	102	19	1	9	47	47	84	8	3	.308	.343
Montoyo,Charlie	1B	31	.225	96	231	23	52	6	0	0	17	27	30	0	0	.306	.251
Saffer,Jon	OF	23	.278	134	472	77	131	24	2	7	41	55	82	5	15	.353	.381
Schu,Rick	3B	35	.242	116	380	37	92	22	2	8	42	33	53	6	2	.303	.374
Stovall,Darond	OF	24	.197	74	264	30	52	7	0	7	29	23	92	7	4	.261	.303
Talanoa,Scott	1B	27	.175	82	211	23	37	4	0	8	26	27	80	1	0	.269	.308
Vidro,Jose	3B	22	.235	126	438	45	103	25	2	13	66	20	76	2	0	.269	.390
NEW YORK METS		Age	Avg	G	AB	R	H	2B	3B	HR	RBI	BB	SO	SB	CS	OBP	SLG
Agbayani,Benny	OF	25	.243	120	374	44	91	11	7	7	57	33	72	10	5	.305	.366
Azuaje,Jesus	2B	24	.212	86	241	29	51	13	0	1	21	30	35	3	6	.299	.278
Castillo,Alberto	C	27	.192	113	334	30	64	10	0	9	35	34	70	1	2	.266	.302
Daubach,Brian	1B	25	.262	139	474	72	124	21	0	18	67	55	124	4	10	.338	.420
Franco,Matt	3B	27	.305	133	495	67	151	35	1	6	73	32	57	3	2	.347	.416
Geisler,Phil	OF	27	.227	107	344	38	78	14	1	9	48	22	102	3	4	.273	.352
Gilbert,Shawn	3B-2B	32	.239	131	482	69	115	25	0	7	45	41	101	13	9	.298	.334
Greene,Charlie	C	26	.218	100	325	28	71	14	0	1	22	11	55	1	0	.244	.271
Hardtke,Jason	2B	25	.264	106	382	62	101	23	1	10	44	35	47	3	7	.326	.408
Horne,Tyrone	OF	26	.213	110	315	34	67	13	1	4	26	32	96	5	3	.285	.298
Lowery,Terrell	OF	26	.232	124	392	50	91	17	3	8	45	49	93	7	9	.317	.352
Mahalik,John	2B	25	.213	86	225	30	48	9	1	2	18	18	38	4	2	.272	.289
Maness,Dwight	OF	23	.218	130	386	53	84	11	5	4	38	35	85	17	7	.203	.303
Morgan,Kevin	SS	27	.210	136	477	56	100	11	1	4	30	44	77	10	5	.276	.262

Major League Equivalencies for 1996 AAA/AA Batters

NEW YORK METS		Age	Avg	G	AB	R	H	2B	3B	HR	RBI	BB	SO	SB	CS	OBP	SLG
Ochoa,Alex	OF	25	.319	67	226	40	72	10	3	6	35	28	23	3	11	.394	.469
Pagano,Scott	OF	26	.234	126	449	51	105	12	2	0	37	29	58	17	7	.280	.269
Petagine,Roberto	1B	26	.301	95	306	44	92	21	2	11	59	45	78	3	1	.390	.490
Rivera,Luis	SS	33	.207	114	348	30	72	20	2	5	35	27	60	0	3	.264	.319
Roberson,Kevin	OF	29	.248	70	210	23	52	11	2	6	30	12	68	0	1	.288	.405
Saunders,Chris	3B	26	.269	141	490	67	132	23	2	13	86	50	94	3	4	.337	.404
Thurman,Gary	OF	32	.249	127	438	73	109	21	4	7	35	35	113	19	8	.304	.363
White,Donnie	OF	25	.169	82	213	23	36	5	0	4	18	17	65	3	4	.230	.249
NEW YORK YANKEES		Age	Avg	G	AB	R	H	2B	3B	HR	RBI	BB	SO	SB	CS	OBP	SLG
Barker,Tim	2B-SS	29	.244	116	390	60	95	24	5	1	38	47	58	17	7	.325	.338
Carpenter,Bubba	OF	28	.228	132	456	47	104	20	1	6	41	40	82	7	7	.290	.316
Cruz,Ivan	1B	29	.243	130	437	72	106	23	0	25	82	40	101	1	4	.306	.467
Dalesandro,Mark	DH	29	.259	78	247	29	64	26	2	1	32	14	31	1	0	.299	.393
Donato,Dan	3B	24	.269	134	449	40	121	24	0	1	41	24	53	3	6	.307	.330
Knowles,Eric	SS	23	.225	126	386	48	87	21	0	5	36	23	96	6	6	.269	.319
Ledee,Ricky	OF	23	.288	135	483	90	139	29	3	26	86	48	123	5	5	.352	.522
Luke,Matt	OF	26	.264	74	258	39	68	12	1	17	60	14	53	0	1	.301	.516
McNair,Fred	1B	27	.243	83	263	28	64	9	0	5	39	13	67	1	0	.279	.335
Northrup,Kevin	OF	27	.238	119	391	49	93	20	1	8	49	28	62	4	3	.289	.355
Pledger,Kinnis	OF	28	.250	131	436	69	109	24	3	17	58	47	129	13	5	.323	.436
Posada,Jorge	C	25	.250	106	344	65	86	19	3	10	53	65	87	2	3	.369	.410
Riggs,Kevin	2B	28	.274	118	394	65	108	21	0	1	32	58	69	6	9	.367	.335
Rivera,Ruben	OF	23	.213	101	352	50	75	18	2	8	39	33	98	10	10	.281	.344
Seefried,Tate	1B	25	.194	115	355	45	69	15	0	13	40	34	134	1	3	.265	.346
Spencer,Shane	OF	25	.238	135	467	66	111	20	0	26	82	53	108	2	3	.315	.448
Torres,Jaime	C	24	.231	112	360	40	83	19	1	5	40	16	33	0	3	.263	.331
Woodson,Tracy	3B	34	.257	124	444	46	114	32	1	18	76	14	57	2	0	.279	.455
OAKLAND ATHLETICS		Age	Avg	G	AB	R	H	2B	3B	HR	RBI	BB	SO	SB	CS	OBP	SLG
Battle,Allen	OF	28	.278	62	216	44	60	11	2	2	27	30	38	6	3	.366	.375
Bellhorn,Mark	2B-SS	22	.230	131	456	74	105	22	3	8	62	52	132	13	2	.309	.344
Correia,Rod	SS	29	.198	109	369	39	73	10	0	2	33	22	50	8	3	.243	.241
Cox,Steven	1B	22	.259	104	370	52	96	19	0	9	53	37	69	1	2	.327	.384
Francisco,David	OF	25	.239	114	376	52	90	11	0	2	24	20	77	9	4	.278	.285
Garrison,Webster	2B	31	.270	127	456	71	123	27	1	13	68	49	84	1	2	.341	.419
Grieve,Ben	OF	21	.217	63	226	29	49	7	0	6	28	25	56	0	3	.295	.327
Gubanich,Creighton	C	25	.244	96	324	46	79	23	0	10	52	26	110	2	0	.300	.407
Lennon,Patrick	OF-DH	29	.299	68	241	31	72	14	1	9	35	23	86	2	3	.360	.477
Lesher,Brian	1B-OF	26	.263	109	400	47	105	26	1	14	63	29	113	4	5	.312	.438
Martins,Eric	3B-2B	24	.235	111	378	53	89	21	1	0	29	34	82	5	7	.299	.296
McDonald,Jason	2B	25	.215	137	465	59	100	6	3	6	38	51	86	24	9	.293	.280
Molina,Izzy	C	26	.239	98	331	37	79	11	2	9	47	20	57	1	5	.282	.366
Moore,Kerwin	OF	26	.207	119	439	75	91	11	7	1	26	77	120	28	10	.326	.271
Morales,Willie	C	24	.270	108	366	47	99	22	0	15	64	27	71	0	2	.321	.454
Poe,Charles	OF	25	.241	125	419	66	101	16	2	10	59	33	111	3	4	.296	.360
Sheldon,Scott	SS	28	.273	98	337	51	92	24	2	8	50	35	87	3	3	.341	.427
Smith,Demond	OF	24	.240	125	438	66	105	15	10	7	54	39	97	22	8	.302	.368
Spiezio,Scott	3B	24	.237	140	506	73	120	27	2	15	76	45	69	4	5	.299	.387
Wood,Jason	3B	27	.235	136	490	67	115	19	0	17	74	56	99	1	6	.313	.378
PHIL. PHILLIES		Age	Avg	G	AB	R	H	2B	3B	HR	RBI	BB	SO	SB	CS	OBP	SLG
Amaro,Ruben	OF	32	.240	68	221	26	53	9	1	1	18	17	42	9	3	.294	.303

Major League Equivalencies for 1996 AAA/AA Batters

PHIL. PHILLIES		Age	Avg	G	AB	R	H	2B	3B	HR	RBI	BB	SO	SB	CS	OBP	SLG
Anderson,Marlon	2B	23	.243	75	301	28	73	12	1	2	21	16	48	11	9	.281	.309
Bennett,Gary	C	25	.221	91	276	28	61	14	0	6	28	18	46	0	0	.269	.337
Burton,Essex	2B	28	.253	118	419	52	106	19	3	0	22	28	78	30	13	.300	.313
Butler,Rob	OF	27	.229	91	288	30	66	14	5	3	26	15	48	2	5	.267	.344
Dawkins,Walt	OF	24	.238	77	244	30	58	14	1	2	21	23	52	2	4	.303	.328
Diaz,Mario	2B	35	.242	62	231	21	56	7	0	3	25	8	15	0	2	.268	.312
Doster,David	2B	26	.232	88	311	28	72	18	0	5	37	20	57	5	3	.278	.338
Estalella,Bobby	C	22	.213	122	385	41	82	14	1	18	60	45	123	1	4	.295	.395
Fisher,David	3B	27	.208	83	226	19	47	8	0	2	20	12	35	3	4	.248	.270
Guiliano,Matthew	SS	25	.174	74	213	14	37	8	1	0	14	15	64	0	0	.228	.221
Held,Dan	1B	26	.207	140	492	57	102	15	3	19	69	38	160	2	8	.264	.366
Magee,Wendell	OF	24	.258	115	407	52	105	21	4	11	46	31	76	8	7	.311	.410
Martinez,Manny	OF	26	.259	83	328	46	85	13	0	2	20	20	61	11	10	.302	.317
McConnell,Chad	OF	26	.218	116	371	52	81	16	0	8	37	25	129	4	5	.268	.326
Moler,Jason	3B	27	.217	109	360	44	78	20	0	13	44	34	54	2	5	.284	.381
Relaford,Desi	2B-SS	23	.185	114	389	29	72	14	0	3	31	23	82	12	7	.231	.244
Rolen,Scott	3B	22	.292	106	380	50	111	36	1	7	45	42	63	7	8	.363	.447
Royster,Aaron	OF	24	.226	65	221	31	50	10	0	2	15	19	61	2	5	.288	.299
Schall,Gene	1B	27	.258	104	356	51	92	15	3	13	52	37	98	0	0	.328	.427
Shores,Scott	OF	25	.201	120	384	39	77	17	5	8	38	29	145	12	10	.257	.333
Tokheim,Dave	OF	28	.190	92	248	27	47	9	2	0	16	8	39	3	5	.215	.242
Zuber,Jon	1B-OF	27	.281	118	395	48	111	20	3	3	46	45	53	2	2	.355	.370
PITTSBURGH PIRATES		Age	Avg	G	AB	R	H	2B	3B	HR	RBI	BB	SO	SB	CS	OBP	SLG
Allensworth,J.	OF	25	.296	95	335	57	99	20	3	5	32	29	64	18	6	.352	.418
Aude,Rich	1B	25	.260	103	377	51	98	26	0	12	60	19	72	2	3	.295	.424
Beamon,Trey	OF	23	.257	111	362	46	93	13	1	3	39	41	66	11	2	.333	.323
Beasley,Tony	OF	30	.294	96	262	34	77	16	3	3	26	22	35	7	8	.349	.412
Bonifay,Ken	3B	26	.228	95	267	28	61	17	1	5	36	30	72	2	2	.306	.356
Boston,D.J.	1B	25	.253	119	395	49	100	21	2	9	50	47	89	3	2	.333	.385
Brown,Adrian	OF	23	.277	84	332	41	92	10	2	2	21	18	42	20	7	.314	.337
Clark,Jerald	OF	33	.235	75	238	24	56	18	0	5	33	9	45	0	0	.263	.374
Collier,Lou	SS	23	.263	119	433	66	114	19	2	2	42	35	78	21	8	.318	.330
Cranford,Jay	3B	26	.252	90	262	29	66	14	1	1	32	34	72	4	3	.338	.324
Cummings,Midre	OF	25	.273	97	352	45	96	21	1	5	41	15	62	4	3	.302	.381
Encarnacion,Angelo	C	24	.287	75	251	28	72	16	0	2	23	7	19	4	1	.306	.375
Espinosa,Ramon	OF	25	.248	78	234	27	58	7	5	0	18	4	29	1	2	.261	.321
Hanel,Marcus	C	25	.165	101	327	19	54	18	0	4	31	11	61	1	1	.192	.257
Marx,Tim	C	28	.291	95	282	37	82	18	0	0	27	21	52	4	1	.340	.355
Peterson,Charles	OF	23	.259	125	452	61	117	23	1	6	54	37	111	25	9	.315	.354
Polcovich,Kevin	SS-2B	27	.245	104	323	39	79	19	1	0	34	13	51	5	5	.274	.310
Ratliff,Darryl	OF	27	.271	120	388	47	105	12	0	0	40	26	72	11	7	.316	.302
Sanford,Chance	2B	25	.228	131	460	53	105	15	9	3	48	53	115	8	10	.308	.320
Secrist,Reed	3B	27	.274	128	401	51	110	27	0	12	49	39	110	1	3	.339	.431
Staton,T.J.	OF	22	.290	112	376	62	109	23	2	12	49	42	106	12	6	.361	.457
Sveum,Dale	3B	33	.268	101	328	46	88	26	1	17	63	24	74	1	0	.318	.509
Womack,Tony	SS	27	.267	131	484	56	129	17	7	0	35	23	82	26	10	.300	.331
Wright,Ron	1B	21	.219	67	237	30	52	10	0	12	40	26	85	0	0	.297	.414
SAN DIEGO PADRES		Age	Avg	G	AB	R	H	2B	3B	HR	RBI	BB	SO	SB	CS	OBP	SLG
Alvarez,Gabe	3B	23	.222	104	356	45	79	19	0	7	31	42	92	1	3	.304	.334
Barry,Jeff	3B-OF	28	.205	95	229	22	47	5	0	2	19	21	50	1	7	.272	.253

Major League Equivalencies for 1996 AAA/AA Batters

SAN DIEGO PADRES		Age	Avg	G	AB	R	H	2B	3B	HR	RBI	BB	SO	SB	CS	OBP	SLG
Briggs,Stoney	OF	25	.248	133	436	56	108	20	3	10	62	41	130	18	7	.312	.376
Bruno,Julio	2B	24	.231	107	364	35	84	19	0	1	29	15	53	4	7	.261	.291
Dascenzo,Doug	OF	33	.249	86	305	36	76	13	1	0	15	23	39	9	13	.302	.298
Deer,Rob	OF	36	.199	84	251	32	50	11	1	17	35	41	122	3	1	.312	.454
Ingram,Riccardo	OF	30	.221	124	394	40	87	17	0	6	38	36	66	4	6	.286	.310
Johnson,Earl	OF	25	.222	82	324	39	72	8	3	1	25	11	62	9	13	.248	.275
Killeen,Tim	C	26	.224	83	214	34	48	8	3	8	40	17	60	0	2	.281	.402
Larocca,Greg	2B	24	.245	128	428	51	105	18	3	5	33	33	61	3	9	.299	.336
Lee,Derrek	1B	21	.255	134	483	77	123	32	1	30	81	43	180	8	6	.316	.511
Mulligan,Sean	C	27	.257	102	343	41	88	19	1	16	56	22	70	0	2	.301	.458
Rohrmeier,Dan	DH-OF	31	.315	134	451	77	142	24	1	24	74	50	80	1	5	.383	.532
Romero,Mandy	C	29	.241	88	286	31	69	12	0	8	36	26	54	1	1	.304	.367
Rossy,Rico	SS	33	.222	130	397	42	88	17	1	3	26	52	65	3	6	.312	.292
Russo,Paul	3B	27	.221	80	217	12	48	12	1	3	24	17	55	1	1	.278	.327
Scott,Gary	3B	28	.237	65	207	18	49	13	1	1	20	23	48	0	2	.313	.324
Smith,Ira	OF	29	.211	72	242	28	51	13	0	4	18	14	28	2	3	.254	.314
Steverson,Todd	OF	25	.210	100	290	31	61	13	1	10	37	35	90	3	5	.295	.366
Tatum,Jimmy	OF	29	.292	83	284	37	83	17	0	14	53	22	67	3	0	.343	.500
Thompson,Jason M	1B	26	.262	111	367	60	96	22	0	16	43	38	96	4	5	.331	.452
Velandia,Jorge	SS	22	.216	122	380	33	82	15	0	8	37	20	68	2	7	.255	.318

SF GIANTS		Age	Avg	G	AB	R	H	2B	3B	HR	RBI	BB	SO	SB	CS	OBP	SLG
Canizaro,Jay	2B-SS	23	.234	102	350	41	82	18	1	5	52	38	81	10	4	.309	.334
Cruz,Jacob	OF	24	.254	121	417	49	106	22	2	5	61	51	81	3	9	.335	.353
DeLeon,Roberto	2B	26	.207	104	290	25	60	10	2	3	29	16	53	0	2	.248	.286
Duncan,Andres	SS	25	.222	110	288	37	64	10	2	1	17	20	64	6	3	.273	.281
Florez,Tim	2B	27	.256	131	414	41	106	26	1	4	38	33	70	1	5	.311	.353
Jensen,Marcus	C	24	.236	120	390	33	92	18	2	3	43	36	101	0	1	.300	.315
Jones,Dax	OF	26	.277	74	285	42	79	17	3	4	33	15	22	9	8	.313	.400
Kennedy,Darryl	C	28	.273	81	231	31	63	11	1	1	27	11	33	1	3	.306	.342
King,Brett	SS	24	.211	127	446	51	94	20	2	6	40	35	125	13	9	.268	.305
Mirabelli,Doug	C	26	.269	129	412	59	111	26	0	18	64	58	60	0	1	.360	.464
Mueller,Bill	3B	26	.271	106	421	59	114	11	3	3	29	36	42	1	5	.328	.333
Murray,Calvin	OF	25	.224	133	464	68	104	19	3	8	43	53	98	12	11	.304	.330
Peltier,Dan	1B	29	.254	70	256	32	65	6	1	0	22	23	41	0	2	.315	.285
Phillips,Gary	3B	25	.223	111	327	31	73	15	2	1	36	16	76	0	6	.259	.291
Powell,Dante	OF	23	.253	137	498	78	126	23	1	18	66	53	102	30	13	.325	.412
Rios,Armando	OF	25	.253	92	316	52	80	19	1	9	41	32	45	6	9	.322	.405
Simonton,Benji	1B	25	.229	138	458	73	105	22	0	19	65	73	155	4	4	.335	.402
Singleton,C	OF	24	.258	138	511	59	132	27	5	4	61	17	64	20	8	.282	.354
Williams,Keith	OF	25	.245	108	383	51	94	21	1	10	51	43	101	1	2	.322	.384
Wilson,Desi	1B	29	.305	113	387	46	118	22	4	3	48	14	84	11	4	.329	.406
Woods,Ken	3B	26	.252	139	477	56	120	25	0	1	34	36	67	12	14	.304	.310

SEATTLE MARINERS		Age	Avg	G	AB	R	H	2B	3B	HR	RBI	BB	SO	SB	CS	OBP	SLG
Barger,Mike	OF	26	.203	108	365	45	74	18	3	0	26	22	52	15	3	.248	.268
Bonnici,James	1B	25	.282	139	490	71	138	26	0	24	69	56	109	0	2	.355	.482
Bryant,Scott	OF	29	.258	70	252	23	65	13	2	1	20	16	54	0	2	.302	.337
Cruz,Jose	OF	23	.263	69	255	53	67	12	2	9	45	40	56	4	0	.363	.431
Diaz,Eddy	SS	25	.269	107	416	58	112	29	2	12	54	14	41	2	3	.293	.435
Friedman,Jason	DH	27	.172	65	204	15	35	11	2	2	14	7	32	0	0	.199	.275
Gipson,Charles	OF-SS	24	.262	119	404	54	106	13	2	1	30	35	69	21	7	.321	.312

Major League Equivalencies for 1996 AAA/AA Batters

SEATTLE MARINERS		Age	Avg	G	AB	R	H	2B	3B	HR	RBI	BB	SO	SB	CS	OBP	SLG
Griffey,Craig	OF	26	.218	120	394	43	86	15	5	2	35	40	98	16	5	.290	.297
Guevara,Giomar	SS	24	.264	119	413	60	109	20	1	2	41	47	116	17	6	.339	.332
Hickey,Mike	3B-2B	27	.252	75	246	35	62	15	2	1	23	51	58	7	5	.380	.341
Ibanez,Raul	OF	25	.291	130	477	67	139	28	2	12	56	47	68	7	7	.355	.434
Jorgensen,Randy	1B	25	.282	137	461	61	130	34	0	8	81	50	83	1	0	.352	.408
Ladjevich,Rick	3B	25	.279	115	412	44	115	24	0	7	48	30	64	0	3	.328	.388
Patel,Manny	2B	25	.217	126	368	48	80	9	0	1	32	48	56	9	5	.308	.250
Peguero,Julio	OF	28	.269	100	323	38	87	16	0	1	19	19	52	6	6	.310	.328
Reimer,Kevin	OF-DH	33	.265	78	279	31	74	11	0	11	36	11	46	3	0	.293	.423
Sheets,Andy	SS	25	.344	62	227	41	78	16	3	4	30	23	61	5	3	.404	.493
Sturdivant,Jack	OF	23	.281	63	242	34	68	11	3	2	23	22	36	10	6	.341	.376
Varitek,Jason	C	25	.262	134	503	63	132	38	0	13	67	58	106	5	5	.339	.416
Widger,Chris	C	26	.294	97	347	39	102	20	1	12	44	25	67	5	0	.341	.461
ST. LOUIS CARDINALS		**Age**	**Avg**	**G**	**AB**	**R**	**H**	**2B**	**3B**	**HR**	**RBI**	**BB**	**SO**	**SB**	**CS**	**OBP**	**SLG**
Berblinger,Jeff	2B	26	.263	134	483	63	127	29	4	8	42	35	70	16	6	.313	.389
Bradshaw,Terry	OF	28	.277	102	375	45	104	21	0	9	35	33	67	15	6	.336	.405
Cromer,Tripp	SS	29	.203	80	237	22	48	3	2	3	20	17	49	2	1	.256	.270
Dalton,Dee	3B	25	.215	113	335	30	72	15	1	4	33	25	65	2	4	.269	.301
Difelice,Mike	C	28	.257	79	237	20	61	12	0	7	26	16	45	0	3	.304	.397
Diggs,Tony	OF	30	.212	127	433	46	92	19	2	7	35	34	68	7	9	.270	.314
Fick,Chris	OF	27	.233	134	434	51	101	23	1	14	59	45	99	1	5	.305	.387
Franklin,Micah	OF	25	.214	139	454	58	97	26	1	16	58	51	136	3	5	.293	.381
Green,Bert	OF	23	.178	92	292	36	52	5	2	2	19	25	62	14	5	.243	.229
Gulan,Mike	3B	26	.232	123	406	38	94	25	2	13	44	20	124	5	2	.268	.399
Holbert,Aaron	2B-SS	24	.239	112	422	43	101	14	4	3	25	16	64	14	5	.267	.313
Johns,Keith	SS	25	.224	127	434	42	97	15	0	0	32	31	65	5	9	.275	.258
Marrero,Elieser	C	23	.246	116	362	52	89	15	2	15	52	21	58	6	6	.287	.423
McEwing,Joe	OF	24	.186	106	210	21	39	6	2	1	11	8	34	1	4	.216	.248
Oliva,Jose	DH	26	.219	118	401	42	88	12	0	24	69	27	106	2	3	.269	.429
Rupp,Brian	1B	25	.276	114	340	37	94	15	1	3	33	22	47	3	6	.320	.353
Torres,Paul	OF	26	.237	103	300	30	71	14	0	8	35	29	67	0	1	.304	.363
Velez,Jose	OF	24	.247	86	255	29	63	10	1	1	25	9	31	5	4	.273	.306
Warner,Ron	3B	28	.276	84	225	29	62	20	2	4	31	25	26	3	1	.348	.436
Wimmer,Chris	OF	26	.227	112	335	32	76	10	1	1	18	12	43	8	3	.254	.272
Young,Dmitri	1B	23	.306	122	441	73	135	29	5	11	51	27	70	11	5	.346	.469
TEXAS RANGERS		**Age**	**Avg**	**G**	**AB**	**R**	**H**	**2B**	**3B**	**HR**	**RBI**	**BB**	**SO**	**SB**	**CS**	**OBP**	**SLG**
Bell,Mike	3B	22	.246	128	471	54	116	27	2	12	51	31	80	2	0	.293	.389
Blair,Brian	OF	25	.229	113	371	41	85	25	2	2	25	33	92	4	7	.292	.323
Brown,Kevin L.	C	24	.242	128	447	67	108	24	0	20	75	54	160	0	2	.323	.430
Charles,Frank	C-DH	28	.216	76	255	24	55	11	1	4	20	10	59	1	2	.245	.314
Diaz,Edwin	2B	22	.245	121	486	61	119	29	5	12	56	18	130	5	8	.272	.399
Estrada,Osmani	3B	28	.243	77	210	24	51	8	0	1	25	19	40	2	0	.306	.295
Faneyte,Rikkert	OF	28	.226	93	359	50	81	14	0	9	41	32	68	11	8	.289	.340
Frazier,Lou	OF	32	.238	58	206	26	49	7	3	2	15	13	44	10	3	.283	.330
Frias,Hanley	SS	23	.271	134	494	63	134	20	11	1	35	22	78	6	8	.302	.362
Gil,Benji	SS	24	.212	84	288	30	61	14	0	5	26	20	94	3	5	.263	.313
Lee,Derek	OF	30	.285	129	428	58	122	29	1	13	59	52	74	4	8	.363	.449
Little,Mark	OF	24	.271	101	398	60	108	21	1	10	43	35	94	15	6	.330	.405
O'Neill,Doug	OF	27	.250	92	308	40	77	11	1	9	36	27	88	5	4	.310	.300
Ortiz,Luis	1B	27	.306	124	493	66	151	23	0	12	69	21	37	0	4	.335	.426

Major League Equivalencies for 1996 AAA/AA Batters

TEXAS RANGERS		Age	Avg	G	AB	R	H	2B	3B	HR	RBI	BB	SO	SB	CS	OBP	SLG
Pappas,Erik	C	31	.196	107	326	36	64	14	0	4	34	60	72	2	7	.321	.276
Sagmoen,Marc	OF	26	.268	128	492	65	132	23	5	14	69	27	83	3	7	.306	.421
Shave,Jon	2B	29	.255	116	408	51	104	18	1	6	39	39	101	6	5	.320	.348
Smith,Bubba	1B	27	.270	134	497	71	134	25	0	25	82	35	129	0	0	.318	.471
Stevens,Lee	DH	29	.317	117	426	80	135	34	1	32	89	55	94	2	0	.395	.627
Texidor,Jose	OF	25	.235	85	293	29	69	13	0	8	32	13	47	1	0	.268	.362
Thomas,Brian	OF	26	.250	91	252	28	63	13	3	7	34	29	71	0	0	.327	.409
Voigt,Jack	OF-3B	31	.284	127	437	73	124	24	0	18	76	73	108	3	4	.386	.462
TORONTO BLUE JAYS		**Age**	**Avg**	**G**	**AB**	**R**	**H**	**2B**	**3B**	**HR**	**RBI**	**BB**	**SO**	**SB**	**CS**	**OBP**	**SLG**
Adriana,Sharnol	3B	26	.258	90	283	39	73	11	3	9	30	19	77	13	6	.305	.413
Brito,Tilson	SS	25	.255	108	388	51	99	20	5	9	44	30	70	8	9	.309	.402
Cairo,Miguel	2B	23	.252	120	449	57	113	12	2	2	39	21	47	20	7	.285	.301
Cradle,Rickey	OF	24	.239	132	451	65	108	25	3	18	55	49	113	10	10	.314	.428
Crespo,Felipe	2B	24	.257	98	343	43	88	23	0	7	47	45	43	7	10	.343	.385
Cromer,Brandon	SS	23	.253	98	308	46	78	13	6	6	26	42	92	2	5	.343	.393
de la Cruz,Lorenzo	OF	25	.230	122	431	49	99	22	3	16	65	25	135	5	3	.272	.406
Evans,Tom	3B-DH	22	.261	120	383	72	100	25	0	15	53	80	124	2	0	.389	.444
Henry,Santiago	SS	24	.247	110	360	30	89	13	5	2	26	13	72	8	6	.273	.328
Huff,Michael	OF	33	.267	78	240	32	64	18	2	7	34	22	42	6	2	.328	.446
Jones,Ryan	1B	22	.250	134	492	57	123	24	2	18	80	42	97	1	1	.309	.417
Jose,Felix	DH	32	.232	99	349	40	81	15	1	15	52	28	80	2	0	.289	.410
Mosquera,Julio	C	25	.211	115	379	33	80	15	0	1	29	24	75	4	4	.258	.259
Patzke,Jeff	2B	23	.278	124	414	57	115	29	3	3	54	56	115	4	4	.364	.384
Pose,Scott	OF	30	.245	113	404	57	99	10	4	0	31	47	76	22	8	.324	.290
Ramirez,Angel	OF	24	.258	102	380	52	98	23	5	4	42	10	76	12	5	.277	.376
Ramos,John	1B	31	.221	89	308	30	68	14	0	7	34	33	55	0	0	.296	.334
Roberts,Lonell	OF	26	.263	58	228	28	60	0	0	0	9	22	43	17	6	.328	.263
Rowland,Rich	C	33	.206	96	281	35	58	22	1	7	36	40	85	0	0	.305	.367
Stewart,Shannon	OF	23	.273	112	406	62	111	23	5	5	34	44	65	26	9	.344	.392
Weinke,Chris	DH-1B	24	.213	126	414	56	88	23	1	15	59	51	133	1	1	.299	.382

Appendix

Minor League Team	Organization	League	Level
Albany	Expos	South Atlantic League	A
Albuquerque	Dodgers	Pacific Coast League	AAA
Angels (Mesa)	Angels	Arizona League	R
Arizona (Phoenix)	Diamondbacks	Arizona League	R
Arkansas	Cardinals	Texas League	AA
Asheville	Rockies	South Atlantic League	A
Astros (Kissimmee)	Astros	Gulf Coast League	R
Athletics (Scottsdale)	Athletics	Arizona League	R
Auburn	Astros	New York-Penn League	A-
Augusta	Pirates	South Atlantic League	A
Bakersfield	Co-Op	California League	A+
Batavia	Phillies	New York-Penn League	A-
Bellingham	Giants	Northwest League	A-
Beloit	Brewers	Midwest League	A
Billings	Reds	Pioneer League	R+
Binghamton	Mets	Eastern League	AA
Birmingham	White Sox	Southern League	AA
Bluefield	Orioles	Appalachian League	R+
Boise	Angels	Northwest League	A-
Bowie	Orioles	Eastern League	AA
Braves (W.Palm Beach)	Braves	Gulf Coast League	R
Brevard County	Marlins	Florida State League	A+
Bristol	White Sox	Appalachian League	R+
Buffalo	Indians	American Association	AAA
Burlington	Giants	Midwest League	A
Burlington	Indians	Appalachian League	R+
Butte	Devil Rays	Pioneer League	R+
Calgary	Pirates	Pacific Coast League	AAA
Canton-Akron	Indians	Eastern League	AA
Carolina	Pirates	Southern League	AA
Cedar Rapids	Angels	Midwest League	A
Charleston-SC	Rangers	South Atlantic League	A
Charleston-WV	Reds	South Atlantic League	A
Charlotte	Marlins	International League	AAA
Charlotte	Rangers	Florida State League	A+
Chattanooga	Reds	Southern League	AA
Clearwater	Phillies	Florida State League	A+
Clinton	Padres	Midwest League	A
Colorado Springs	Rockies	Pacific Coast League	AAA
Columbia	Mets	South Atlantic League	A
Columbus	Yankees	International League	AAA
Columbus	Indians	South Atlantic League	A
Cubs (Fort Myers)	Cubs	Gulf Coast League	R

Minor League Team	Organization	League	Level
Danville	Braves	Appalachian League	R+
Daytona	Cubs	Florida State League	A+
Delmarva	Expos	South Atlantic League	A
Devil Rays	Devil Rays	Gulf Coast League	R
Dunedin	Blue Jays	Florida State League	A+
Durham	Braves	Carolina League	A+
Edmonton	Athletics	Pacific Coast League	AAA
El Paso	Brewers	Texas League	AA
Elizabethton	Twins	Appalachian League	R+
Erie	Pirates	New York-Penn League	A-
Eugene	Braves	Northwest League	A-
Everett	Mariners	Northwest League	A-
Expos (W.Palm Beach)	Expos	Gulf Coast League	R
Fayetteville	Tigers	South Atlantic League	A
Frederick	Orioles	Carolina League	A+
Fort Myers	Twins	Florida State League	A+
Fort Wayne	Twins	Midwest League	A
Great Falls	Dodgers	Pioneer League	R+
Greensboro	Yankees	South Atlantic League	A
Greenville	Braves	Southern League	AA
Hagerstown	Blue Jays	South Atlantic League	A
Harrisburg	Expos	Eastern League	AA
Helena	Brewers	Pioneer League	R+
Hickory	White Sox	South Atlantic League	A
High Desert	Orioles	California League	A+
Hudson Valley	Rangers, Rays	New York-Penn League	A-
Huntsville	Athletics	Southern League	AA
Idaho Falls	Padres	Pioneer League	R+
Indianapolis	Reds	American Association	AAA
Iowa	Cubs	American Association	AAA
Jackson	Astros	Texas League	AA
Jacksonville	Tigers	Southern League	AA
Jamestown	Tigers	New York-Penn League	A-
Johnson City	Cardinals	Appalachian League	R+
Kane County	Marlins	Midwest League	A
Kingsport	Mets	Appalachian League	R+
Kinston	Indians	Carolina League	A+
Kissimmee	Astros	Florida State League	A+
Knoxville	Blue Jays	Southern League	AA
Lake Elsinore	Angels	California League	A+
Lakeland	Tigers	Florida State League	A+
Lancaster	Mariners	California League	A+
Lansing	Royals	Midwest League	A

Minor League Team	Organization	League	Level
Las Vegas	Padres	Pacific Coast League	AAA
Lethbridge	Diamondbacks	Pioneer League	R+
Louisville	Cardinals	American Association	AAA
Lowell	Red Sox	New York-Penn League	A-
Lynchburg	Pirates	Carolina League	A+
Macon	Braves	South Atlantic League	A
Mariners (Peoria)	Mariners	Arizona League	R
Marlins (Melbourne)	Marlins	Gulf Coast League	R
Martinsville	Phillies	Appalachian League	R+
Medicine Hat	Blue Jays	Pioneer League	R+
Memphis	Padres	Southern League	AA
Mets (St. Lucie)	Mets	Gulf Coast League	R
Michigan	Red Sox	Midwest League	A
Midland	Angels	Texas League	AA
Modesto	Athletics	California League	A+
Nashville	White Sox	American Association	AAA
New Britain	Twins	Eastern League	AA
New Haven	Rockies	Eastern League	AA
New Jersey	Cardinals	New York-Penn League	A-
New Orleans	Brewers	American Association	AAA
Norfolk	Mets	International League	AAA
Norwich	Yankees	Eastern League	AA
Ogden	Brewers	Pioneer League	R+
Oklahoma City	Rangers	American Association	AAA
Omaha	Royals	American Association	AAA
Oneonta	Yankees	New York-Penn League	A-
Orioles (Sarasota)	Orioles	Gulf Coast League	R
Orlando	Cubs	Southern League	AA
Ottawa	Expos	International League	AAA
Padres (Peoria)	Padres	Arizona League	R
Pawtucket	Red Sox	International League	AAA
Peoria	Cardinals	Midwest League	A
Phoenix	Giants	Pacific Coast League	AAA
Piedmont	Phillies	South Atlantic League	A
Pirates (Bradenton)	Pirates	Gulf Coast League	R
Pittsfield	Mets	New York-Penn League	A-
Port City	Mariners	Southern League	AA
Portland	Marlins	Eastern League	AA
Portland	Rockies	Northwest League	A-
Prince William	White Sox	Carolina League	A+
Princeton	Reds	Appalachian League	R+
Quad City	Astros	Midwest League	A
Rancho Cucamonga	Padres	California League	A+
Rangers (Pt. Charlotte)	Rangers	Gulf Coast League	R
Reading	Phillies	Eastern League	AA
Red Sox (Fort Myers)	Red Sox	Gulf Coast League	R

Minor League Team	Organization	League	Level
Richmond	Braves	International League	AAA
Rochester	Orioles	International League	AAA
Rockford	Cubs	Midwest League	A
Rockies (Chandler)	Rockies	Arizona League	R
Royals (Fort Myers)	Royals	Gulf Coast League	R
Salem	Rockies	Carolina League	A+
Salt Lake	Twins	Pacific Coast League	AAA
San Antonio	Dodgers	Texas League	AA
San Bernardino	Dodgers	California League	A+
San Jose	Giants	California League	A+
Sarasota	Red Sox	Florida State League	A+
Savannah	Dodgers	South Atlantic League	A
Scranton-WB	Phillies	International League	AAA
Shreveport	Giants	Texas League	AA
South Bend	White Sox	Midwest League	A
Southern Oregon	Athletics	Northwest League	A-
Spokane	Royals	Northwest League	A-
St. Catharines	Blue Jays	New York-Penn League	A-
St. Lucie	Mets	Florida State League	A+
St. Petersburg	Cardinals	Florida State League	A+
Stockton	Brewers	California League	A+
Syracuse	Blue Jays	International League	AAA
Tacoma	Mariners	Pacific Coast League	AAA
Tampa	Yankees	Florida State League	A+
Tigers (Lakeland)	Tigers	Gulf Coast League	R
Toledo	Tigers	International League	AAA
Tucson	Astros	Pacific Coast League	AAA
Trenton	Red Sox	Eastern League	AA
Tulsa	Rangers	Texas League	AA
Twins (Fort Myers)	Twins	Gulf Coast League	R
Utica	Marlins	New York-Penn League	A-
Vancouver	Angels	Pacific Coast League	AAA
Vermont	Expos	New York-Penn League	A-
Vero Beach	Dodgers	Florida State League	A+
Visalia	Co-Op	California League	A+
Watertown	Indians	New York-Penn League	A-
West Michigan	Athletics	Midwest League	A
West Palm Beach	Expos	Florida State League	A+
White Sox (Sarasota)	White Sox	Gulf Coast League	R
Wichita	Royals	Texas League	AA
Williamsport	Cubs	New York-Penn League	A-
Wilmington	Royals	Carolina League	A+
Winston-Salem	Reds	Carolina League	A+
Wisconsin Foxes	Mariners	Midwest League	A
Yakima	Dodgers	Northwest League	A-
Yankees (Tampa)	Yankees	Gulf Coast League	R

About STATS, Inc. & Howe Sportsdata

About STATS, Inc.

STATS, Inc. is the nation's leading independent sports information and statistical analysis company, providing detailed sports services for a wide array of clients.

As one of the fastest-growing sports companies—in 1994, we ranked 144th on the "Inc. 500" list of fastest-growing privately held firms—STATS provides the most up-to-the-minute sports information to professional teams, print and broadcast media, software developers and interactive service providers around the country. Some of our major clients are ESPN, the Associated Press, *The Sporting News*, Electronic Arts, Motorola, SONY and Topps. Much of the information we provide is available to the public via STATS On-Line. With a computer and a modem, you can follow action in the four major professional sports, as well as NCAA football and basketball. . . as it happens!

STATS Publishing, a division of STATS, Inc., produces 11 annual books, including the *Major League Handbook*, *The Scouting Notebook*, the *Pro Football Handbook*, the *Pro Basketball Handbook* and the *Hockey Handbook.* These publications deliver STATS' expertise to fans, scouts, general managers and media around the country.

In addition, STATS offers the most innovative—and fun—fantasy sports games around, from *Bill James Fantasy Baseball* and *Bill James Classic Baseball* to *STATS Fantasy Football* and *STATS Fantasy Hoops*.

Information technology has grown by leaps and bounds in the last decade, and STATS plays a leading role as both a vendor and supplier of the most up-to-date, in-depth sports information available. One of the best places to catch STATS is at our site on America Online (Keyword: STATS).

For more information on our products, or on joining our reporter network, write us at:

STATS, Inc.
8131 Monticello Ave.
Skokie, IL 60076-3300

. . . or call us at 1-800-63-STATS (1-800-637-8287). Outside the U.S., dial 1-847-676-3383.

About Howe Sportsdata

Howe Sportsdata International has been keeping statistics on professional baseball since 1910. Currently, Howe is the official statistician for all 17 U.S.-based National Association professional baseball leagues (though independent league stats are not contained in this book). Howe also compiles statistics for the Arizona Fall League, the Hawaiian Winter League and winter leagues located in Mexico, Puerto Rico, the Dominican Republic, Venezuela and Australia. In addition, Howe keeps the official statistics of the Continental Basketball Association, all professional minor hockey leagues and the National Professional Soccer League.

Originally based in Chicago, Howe Sportsdata International is now located in Boston, Massachusetts on the historic Fish Pier, maintaining 24-hour/seven-days-per-week operation during the baseball season. Howe also maintains a satellite office in San Mateo, California. Howe is responsible for maintaining statistics for more than 250 teams who collectively play more than 13,000 games per year.

Howe also provides statistical information to all 28 major-league teams and to major media outlets such as *USA Today, The Sporting News, Baseball America,* the *Associated Press* and *Sports Illustrated.* Howe also counts as its customers many leading newspapers, of which the following are a small representative sample: *The Los Angeles Times, The Detroit Free Press, The Miami Herald* and both the *Chicago Sun-Times* and the *Chicago Tribune*. For more information about Howe, write to:

Howe Sportsdata International
Boston Fish Pier, West Building #2, Suite 306
Boston, Massachusetts 02110

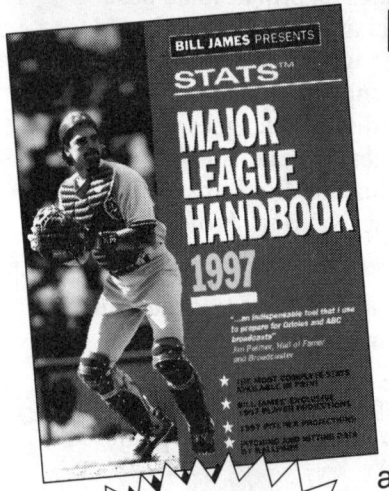

STATS INC.™

Meet the Winning Lineup...

Bill James Presents:

STATS Major League Handbook 1997

- Bill James' exclusive 1997 player projections
- Career data for every 1996 Major League Baseball player
- Leader boards, fielding stats and stadium data
- **Item #HB97, $19.95, Available NOW!**

Bill James Presents:

STATS Minor League Handbook 1997

- Year-by-year career statistical data for AA and AAA players
- Bill James' exclusive Major League Equivalencies
- Complete 1996 Single-A and rookie statistics
- **Item #MH97, $19.95, Available NOW!**

STATS Player Profiles 1997

- Exclusive 1996 breakdowns for pitchers and hitters, over 30 in all: lefty/righty, home/road, clutch situations, ahead/behind in the count, month-by-month, etc.
- Complete breakdowns by player for the last five seasons
- **Item #PP97, $19.95, Available NOW!**

STATS Scouting Notebook: 1997

- Extensive scouting reports on over 700 major league players
- Evaluations of nearly 200 minor league prospects
- **Item #SN97, $18.95, Available Early January, 1997!**

STATS Minor League Scouting Notebook 1997

- Evaluation of each organization's top prospects
- Essays, stat lines and grades for more than 400 prospects
- **Item #MN97, $18.95, Available Mid January, 1997!**

STATS, Inc. Order Form

Name____

Address____

City_____________________________________ State__________ Zip______________

Phone________________ Fax________________ Internet Address______________

Method of Payment (U.S. Funds Only):

❑ Check ❑ Money Order ❑ Visa ❑ MasterCard

Credit Card Information:

Cardholder Name____

Credit Card Number___________________________________ Exp. Date__________

Signature____

BOOKS (STATS publications now include free first class shipping)

Qty.	Product Name	Item Number	Price	Total
	STATS Major League Handbook 1997	**HB97**	**$19.95**	
	STATS Major League Handbook 1997 (Comb-bound)	**HC97**	**$21.95**	
	STATS Projections Update 1997	**PJUP**	**$9.95**	
	The Scouting Notebook: 1997	**SN97**	**$18.95**	
	The Scouting Notebook: 1997 (Comb-bound)	**SC97**	**$20.95**	
	STATS Minor League Scouting Notebook 1997	**MN97**	**$18.95**	
	STATS Minor League Handbook 1997	**MH97**	**$19.95**	
	STATS Minor League Handbook 1997 (Comb-bound)	**MC97**	**$21.95**	
	STATS Player Profiles 1997	**PP97**	**$19.95**	
	STATS Player Profiles 1997 (Comb-bound)	**PC97**	**$21.95**	
	STATS 1997 BVSP Match-Ups!	**BP97**	**$14.95**	
	STATS Baseball Scoreboard 1997	**SB97**	**$18.95**	
	Pro Football Revealed: The 100 Yard War (1996 Edition)	**PF96**	**$16.95**	
	STATS Pro Football Handbook 1996	**FH96**	**$17.95**	
	STATS Basketball Handbook 1996-97	**BH97**	**$17.95**	
	STATS Hockey Handbook 1996-97	**HH97**	**$17.95**	
	Prior Editions **(Please circle appropriate year)**			
	STATS Major League Handbook ‘90 ‘91 ‘92 ‘93 ‘94 ‘95 ‘96		$9.95	
	The Scouting Report/Notebook ‘94 ‘95 ‘96		$9.95	
	STATS Player Profiles ‘93 ‘94 ‘95 ‘96		$9.95	
	STATS Minor League Handbook ‘92 ‘93 ‘94 ‘95 ‘96		$9.95	
	STATS BVSP Match-Ups! ‘94 ‘95 ‘96		$3.95	
	STATS Baseball Scoreboard ‘92 ‘93 ‘94 ‘95 ‘96		$9.95	
	STATS Basketball Scoreboard/Handbook ‘93-’94 ‘94-’95 ‘95-’96		$9.95	
	Pro Football Revealed: The 100 Yard War ‘94 ’95		$9.95	
	STATS Pro Football Handbook ‘95		$9.95	
	STATS Minor League Scouting Notebook ‘95 ‘96		$9.95	

MULTIMEDIA PRODUCTS (Prices include shipping & handling charges)

Qty.	Product Name	Item Number	Price	Total
	Bill James Encyclopedia CD-Rom	BJCD	$49.95	
	Macmillan’s Baseball Encyclopedia CD-Rom	MACD	$44.95	
	Motorola SportsTrax for Baseball	BBTX	$199.00	
	STATS On-Line	STON	$30.00	

SEASON FINAL & YEAR-END REPORTS (Prices include shipping & handling charges)				
Qty.	Product Name	Circle Format	Price	Total
	Season Final Report	Paper 3 1/2" disk 5" disk Mac	$12.95	
	Lefty/Righty Report	Paper 3 1/2" disk 5" disk Mac	$19.95	
	Stolen Base Report	Paper 3 1/2" disk 5" disk Mac	$34.95	
	Defensive Games by Position	Paper 3 1/2" disk 5" disk Mac	$9.95	
	Catcher Report	Paper 3 1/2" disk 5" disk Mac	$49.95	
	Relief Pitching Report	Paper 3 1/2" disk 5" disk Mac	$49.95	
	Zone Ratings/Outfield Arms Report	Paper 3 1/2" disk 5" disk Mac	$99.95	
	End of Season STATpak	Paper 3 1/2" disk 5" disk	$9.95	
	Team(s):			
	STATpak Subscription	Paper 3 1/2" disk 5" disk	$29.95	
	Team(s):			

FANTASY GAMES & STATSfax (STATSfax prices reflect the monthly charge for service)				
Qty.	Product Name	Item Number	Price	Total
	Bill James Classic Baseball	BJCB	$129.00	
	How to Win the Classic Game	CGBK	$16.95	
	Classic Game STATSfax	CFX5	$20.00	
	STATS Fantasy Hoops	SFH	$85.00	
	STATS Fantasy Hoops STATSfax—5-Day	SFH5	$20.00	
	STATS Fantasy Hoops STATSfax—7-Day	SFH7	$25.00	
	STATS Fantasy Football	SFF	$69.00	
	STATS Fantasy Football STATSfax—3-Day	SFF3	$15.00	
	Bill James Fantasy Baseball	BJFB	$89.00	
	Fantasy Baseball STATSfax—5-Day	SFX5	$20.00	
	Fantasy Baseball STATSfax—7-Day	SFX7	$25.00	

1st Fantasy Team Name (ex. Colt 45's):____________________

What Fantasy Game is this team for?____________________

2nd Fantasy Team Name (ex. Colt 45's):____________________

What Fantasy Game is this team for?____________________

NOTE: $1.00/player is charged for all roster moves and transactions.

For Bill James Fantasy Baseball:

Would you like to play in a league drafted by Bill James? ❑ Yes ❑ No

For faster service, call:

1-800-63-STATS or 847-676-3383,

or fax this form to STATS:

847-676-0821

TOTALS		
	Price	Total
Product Total (excl. Fantasy Games)		
Canada—all orders—add:	$2.50/book	
Order 2 or more books—subtract:	$1.00/book	
(NOT to be combined with other specials)		
IL residents add 8.5% sales tax		
Subtotal		
Fantasy Games Total		
GRAND TOTAL		

All books now include free 1st class shipping!

Thanks for ordering from STATS, Inc.